The
Paston Letters

The Paston Letters

Edited by

James Gairdner

ALAN SUTTON
1986

ALAN SUTTON PUBLISHING
BRUNSWICK ROAD · GLOUCESTER

© Copyright in Reprint Alan Sutton Publishing Limited
© in Introduction Roger Virgoe, 1983

This Microprint ® edition first published 1983
Reprinted from the Library Edition of 1904

Reprinted 1986

British Library Cataloguing in Publication Data

The Paston letters.
    1. Paston (Family)   2. England — Biography
    I. Gairdner, James
    929'.20942   DA247.P3

    ISBN 0-86299-002-5 (case)
    ISBN 0-86299-306-7 (paper)

Printed in Great Britain
by Redwood Burn Limited, Trowbridge

INTRODUCTION

Roger Virgoe
University of East Anglia

For nearly three hundred years the Pastons were one of the leading gentry families of Norfolk — one of that group, constantly changing as families died out and estates were bought and sold, which dominated the administrative and social life of East Anglia and whose relations with one another, with the great magnates and with the Crown formed the stuff of regional politics. Until the late seventeenth century, when they became Earls of Yarmouth and briefly played an important role in national politics, they were on a par with a score or more of other Norfolk families. Their activities differed little from those of Heydons, Sheltons, Wyndhams, Cleres, Townshends, Wodehouses and others. Like them they held local offices such as sheriff and escheator, were on the commission of the peace and other commissions and were elected to parliaments; some were lawyers, some courtiers, some soldiers or sailors; all ran their estates or shared in some of its profits and went to law to maintain or increase their holdings. Most, though by no means all members of the family married within the Norfolk gentry and they acquired comparatively little land outside East Anglia, but their interests were not parochial and much time was spent in London and Westminster, Cambridge and elsewhere, and many travelled abroad to the wars and for other reasons.

Such patterns of life were shared to a greater or lesser extent by most of the leading gentry families of the period. What gives the Pastons significance is not the things they did but the records of those things which have come down to us, in particular the mass of private correspondence which survives — with large gaps — from the fifteenth to the late seventeenth century. And of this it is not the interesting letters of the seventeenth century which have brought them fame — for that period other collections survive — but those of the fifteenth century which, if not unique, far outstrip in size and significance all other groups of English letters from the pre-Reformation period.

These letters have fascinated readers since their first publication two centuries ago by the Norfolk antiquary, John Fenn; but it was the edition by

James Gairdner in the 1870s that made them a major source for the historian. Gairdner re-printed the volumes, with additions, several times and in 1904 produced a comprehensive standard edition which has been a necessary tool for the historian of late medieval England ever since, but is now difficult to find. During the last few years Professor Norman Davis has published from Oxford two volumes of a brand new edition working, as Gairdner, for reasons he explains in his introduction, could not, from the original manuscripts. This undoubtedly provides a more accurate text and re-dates a number of the letters but it suffers from the decision to group the letters by correspondent rather than chronologically. Thus Gairdner's edition remains for the historian and for the general reader more convenient and meaningful and its re-printing is to be welcomed.

Gairdner's introduction describes in some detail the provenance and chequered history of the Paston manuscripts. The Pastons were, of course, not alone among gentry families in preserving muniments such as wills, deeds, accounts and court-rolls which related to ownership and rights in land and other property. Private letters which might contain useful evidence on such matters might also be bundled and placed in the family's muniments chest — such as that described in letter 785 of the *Paston Letters* where 'a bundle of letters from my brother John' nestles cheek by jowl with bundles of wills and legal documents. But obviously informal letters seemed of less permanent value and nearly all the private correspondence of the fifteenth century has been destroyed over the years either deliberately or by the ravages of water, fire and pests.

Some groups of fifteenth-century letters, like the Stonor correspondence, survived because they formed part of papers seized by the Crown and were then preserved in the safer custody of the Tower of London. This was not the case with the Paston Letters. Why, then, did they survive when so many did not? It is possible that the Pastons did show rather greater than normal diligence in preserving their letters, and the family was certainly unusual, though far from unique, in maintaining continuity of ownership of their main estates at Paston and Oxnead for nearly three hundred years. And when the main branch of the family did come to an end Norfolk happened to contain a number of learned and assiduous antiquaries, avid for historical documents and with the initiative and contacts to search them out. Peter Le Neve, Norroy King of Arms, certainly obtained access to the Paston Collections before the death of the 2nd Earl of Yarmouth in 1732 and removed an unknown quantity of them, but much was still left when the historian of Norfolk, Francis Blomefield, searched the muniment room at Oxnead after the Earl's death. He, too, seems to have removed much material which, with Le Neve's collections, later came into the possession of the Thetford antiquary, Thomas Martin. Martin's enormous manuscript collections were dispersed after his death but most of the Paston papers, with other documents, were eventually purchased by John Fenn of Dereham, who published his first selection from the correspondence in two volumes in 1787 and two further volumes in 1789: a fifth was posthumously pubished in 1823. Fenn saw the documents not as a unified 'archive group' but as illustrations of fifteenth century life and language and he thus included a number of letters and papers which certainly did not derive from the Pastons but no doubt were also acquired by Fenn from Martin — some of these such as document 24, the instructions for the upbringing of King Henry VI, and documents 65, 78, 90 and 100 are among the most interesting in the collection.

Gairdner added to his edition a number of important letters and papers deriving from the muniments of Sir John Fastolf of Caister who left his estates to John Paston on his death in 1459: most of his papers eventually came to Magdalen College, Oxford. The bulk of the papers published by Gairdner, however, comprised the letters of the successive heads of the Paston family in the fifteenth century — William, his son John I, and John's sons, John II and John III — and their wives. The great majority derive from the period 1450 to 1480. For much of this time the head of the family was away from Norfolk and the consequent correspondence was preserved for its reference to the various business matters discussed. Drafts of out-letters were also retained for the same reason as were in-letters from the family's agents and friends. It is clear, even from internal evidence, that many letters have been lost and the 'Paston Letters' as they exist today are only a fragment of the total family correspondence even for the period from which most survives.

Inevitably business affairs loom large in the correspondence. The Pastons were a 'new' gentry family in the fifteenth century: in spite of their attempts to prove a long aristocratic pedigree their fortunes were founded by William Paston the judge (d. 1444) and much of their land came by purchase or from the controversial will of Sir John Fastolf. In the fifteenth century the state of the English land-law meant that most purchased land had some defects in its title and the Pastons were inevitably engaged in constant litigation to defend their new holdings — the letters are full of references to such business. Legal disputes in the fifteenth century were not decided purely on legal grounds. Verdicts were given by juries empanelled by sheriffs and their deputies. These, and judges too, could be influenced by friendship, bribes and threats, above all by pressure from men of influence — great lords, courtiers and senior royal officials. "Good lordship" was essential in this competitive world and for the Pastons this brought involvement in the faction struggles among the magnates of the region — the Dukes of Norfolk and Suffolk, the Earl of Oxford, Lord Scales and others — and thus inevitably at times, in national politics. The bulk of the surviving fifteenth-century Paston Letters coincides with the 'Wars of the Roses' and, particularly after the disputes over the Fastolf inheritance began in 1459, the Pastons could not avoid being drawn into these violent disputes among the lords, particularly as they were at odds with both the local dukes over parts of that inheritance. The letters, again, are full of references to the Pastons' lobbying of lords from the king downwards for support in their claims to property, and provide insights into the nature of East Anglian politics and the way in which local government and the law worked in practice which exist for no other region during this period.

Few gentry families could avoid going to law but the troubles of the Pastons and their intense involvement in magnate disputes may not have been typical. Many gentlemen avoided excessive commitment and were able to live fairly quiet lives, tending their estates and taking on the minimum of local government duties commensurate with their status. In spite of the great interest of the references to national and regional politics in the Paston Letters it is for the insights they provide into the social history of the period that their main attraction and importance lies. The English language was still a fairly crude instrument in the hands of these men and women and the letters are not and were not intended to be, very revealing of opinions, emotions and character (and it must not be forgotten that many, particularly those of the women, were written by secretaries and servants). But, although the personalities of the Pastons can only be perceived in outline, marked divergences of character among the members of the family are apparent. Particularly eloquent are the famous episodes of Agnes Paston's treatment of her daughter, Elizabeth (letters 93–4, 236–7, 242–3 etc.); the horrified reactions to the clandestine marriage of Margery Paston to one of the family's servants (letters 710, 713, 721 etc.); the courtship of John Paston III and Margery Brews (letters 894–8, 901–2 etc.) and the long-drawn out marriage negotiations of his brother, Sir John (letters 687, 704, 742, etc.). But many other letters throw light on the relationship of husbands and wives and parents and children and of the gentry with their social superiors and inferiors and with their neighbours. They illustrate, too, attitudes to the church and religion; relations between the provinces and London; attitudes to the law and government; social mobility; the position of women; housing and furnishing; literacy, culture and the state of the English language. All topics which have always fascinated the general reader and which in recent years have become increasingly the subject of scholarly study.

Again, some caution is necessary. Because this is almost a unique source it is tempting to generalise too strongly from its evidence. As has been pointed out the Pastons were not necessarily typical in their involvement in litigation and faction; nor were they necessarily typical in their family and social relationships. Indeed individuals within the family differed greatly in their attitudes and actions. The conventional 'arranged' marriage of John Paston I with the heiress, Margaret Mauteby, for instance, was quite different from the courtships of his sons. Equally Elizabeth Paston's troubles in finding a husband contrast sharply with those of her niece, Margery, who found her own. Again, the attitudes of John Paston I to estate and business affairs were very different from those of his son, the courtier Sir John. It is too easy to label the fifteenth century gentry as all ambitious, avaricious, unscrupulous and humourless on the evidence of the intense involvement in property acquisition and protection shown by the correspondence of Sir John Fastolf and John Paston I, and, to a lesser extent, of John's sons. The nature of surviving evidence, even of correspondence, is inevitably biassed towards that impression. For most other gentry families legal records almost alone survive and inevitably reinforce a view of the fifteenth-century gentleman as pure 'economic man'. Fortunately the Paston Letters, if carefully read, provide evidence leading to different conclusions. Many references to other things than property show that they did have a variety of interests and pre-occupations, could show affection and sympathy as well as severity in with some men and women of later ages we see those of the fifteenth-century through a glass darkly, but the Paston Correspondence, by the fortunate accident, perhaps, of the interest of four Norfolk antiquaries, survives to shed a little light on that obscurity in which most of their contemporaries lie for ever buried.

The
Paston Letters
Volume 1

PREFACE

PUBLIC attention was first drawn to the Paston Letters First in the year 1787, when there issued from the press publication of the two quarto volumes with a very lengthy title, setting Letters. forth that the contents were original letters written 'by various persons of rank and consequence' during the reigns of Henry VI., Edward IV., and Richard III. The materials were derived from autographs in the possession of the Editor, a Mr. Fenn, of East Dereham, in Norfolk, who was well enough known in society as a gentleman of literary and antiquarian tastes, but who had not at that time attained any great degree of celebrity. Horace Walpole had described him, thirteen years before, as 'a smatterer in antiquity, but a very good sort of man.' What the great literary magnate afterwards thought of him we are not informed, but we know that he took a lively interest in the Paston Letters the moment they were published. He appears, indeed, to have given some assistance in the progress of the work through the press. On its appearance he expressed himself with characteristic enthusiasm :—'The letters of Henry VI.'s reign, etc., are come out, and *to me* make all other letters not worth reading. I have gone through one volume, and cannot bear to be writing when I am so eager to be reading. . . . There are letters from *all* my acquaintance, Lord Rivers, Lord Hastings, the Earl of Warwick, whom I remember still better than Mrs. Straw-bridge, though she died within these fifty years. What antiquary would be answering a letter from a living countess, when he may read one from Eleanor Mowbray, Duchess of Norfolk ? '[1]

So wrote the great literary exquisite and virtuoso, the man

[1] *Walpole's Letters* (Cunningham's ed.), ix. 92.

VOL. I.—A   1

THE PASTON LETTERS

whose opinion in those days was life or death to a young author or a new publication. And in spite of all that was artificial and affected in his character,—in spite even of the affectation of pretending a snobbish interest in ancient duchesses—Walpole was one of the fittest men of that day to appreciate What was thought of them by some. such a publication. Miss Hannah More was less easily pleased, and she no doubt was the type of many other readers. The letters, she declared, were quite barbarous in style, with none of the elegance of their supposed contemporary Rowley. They might perhaps be of some use to correct history, but as letters and fine reading, nothing was to be said for them.[1] It was natural enough that an age which took this view of the matter should have preferred the forgeries of Chatterton to the most genuine productions of the fifteenth century. The style of the Paston Letters, even if it had been the most polished imaginable, of course could not have exhibited the polish of the eighteenth century, unless a Chatterton had had some hand in their composition.

General interest in the work. Yet the interest excited by the work was such that the editor had no reason to complain of its reception. The Paston Letters were soon in everybody's hands. The work, indeed, appeared under royal patronage, for Fenn had got leave beforehand to dedicate it to the King as 'the avowed patron' of antiquarian knowledge. This alone had doubtless some influence upon the sale ; but the novel character of the publication itself must have excited curiosity still more. A whole edition was disposed of in a week, and a second edition called for, which, after undergoing some little revision, with the assistance of Mr. George Steevens, the Shaksperian editor, was published the same year. Meanwhile, to gratify the curious, the original MS. letters were deposited for a time in the Library of the Society of Antiquaries ; but the King having expressed a wish to see them, Fenn sent them to Buckingham Palace, then called the Queen's Palace, requesting that, if they were thought worthy of a place in the Royal Collection, His Majesty would be pleased to accept them.

[1] Roberts's *Memoirs of Hannah More*, ii. 50.

PREFACE

They were accordingly, it would seem, added to the Royal Library ; and as an acknowledgment of the value of the gift, Fenn was summoned to Court, and received the honour of knighthood.

But the two volumes hitherto published by Fenn contained only a small selection out of a pretty considerable number of original letters of the same period in his possession. The reception these two volumes had met with now encouraged him to make a further selection, and he announced with his second edition that another series of the Letters was in preparation, which was to cover the same period as the first two volumes, and to include also the reign of Henry VII. Accordingly a third and fourth volume of the work were issued together in the year 1789, containing the new letters down to the middle of Edward IV.'s reign. A fifth and concluding volume, bringing the work down to the end of Henry VII.'s reign, was left ready for publication at Sir John Fenn's death in 1794, and was published by his nephew, Mr. Serjeant Frere, in 1823.

Of the original MSS. of these letters and their descent Fenn gives but a brief account in the preface to his first volume, which we will endeavour to supplement with additional facts to the best of our ability. The letters, it will be seen, The MSS. were for the most part written by or to particular members of the family of Paston in Norfolk. Here and there, it is true, are to be found among them State papers and other letters of great interest, which must have come to the hands of the family through some indirect channel ; but the great majority are letters distinctly addressed to persons of the name of Paston, and in the possession of the Pastons they remained for several generations. In the days of Charles II. the head of the family, Sir Robert Paston, was created Earl of Yarmouth ; but his son William, the second bearer of the title, having got into debt and encumbered his inheritance, finally died without male issue, so that his title became extinct. While living in reduced circumstances, he appears to have parted with a portion of his family papers, which were purchased by the great antiquary and collector, Peter Le Neve, Norroy King of Arms.

THE PASTON LETTERS

Le Neve was a Norfolk man, possessed of considerable estates at Witchingham and elsewhere in the county ; and he made it a special object to collect MSS. and records relating to Norfolk and Suffolk. Just before his death in 1729 he made a will,[1] by which he bequeathed his MSS. to the erudite Dr. Tanner, afterwards Bishop of St. Asaph's, and Thomas Martin of Palgrave ; but this bequest was subject to the condition that within a year after his death they should ' procure a good and safe repository in the Cathedral Church of Norwich, or in some other good and public building in the said city ' for their preservation, the object being to make them at all times accessible to those who wished to consult them. The condition, however, was not fulfilled, and the bequest would naturally have become null ; but ' honest Tom Martin of Palgrave ' (to give him the familiar name by which he himself desired to be known) married the widow of his friend, and thus became possessed of his MSS. by another title.

The Le Neve collection, however, contained only a portion of the Paston family papers. On the death, in 1732, of the Earl of Yarmouth, who outlived Le Neve by three years, some thirty or forty chests of valuable letters and documents still remained at the family seat at Oxnead. These treasures the Rev. Francis Blomefield was allowed to examine three years later with a view to his county history, for which purpose he boarded at Oxnead for a fortnight.[2] Of the results of a general survey of the papers he writes, on the 13th May 1735, to Major Weldon a number of interesting particulars, of which the following may be quoted as bearing upon the subject before us :—' There is another box full of the pardons, grants, and old deeds, freedoms, etc., belonging to the Paston family only, which I laid by themselves, for fear you should think them proper to be preserved with the family ; they don't relate to any estates. . . . There are innumerable letters of good consequence in history still lying among the loose papers, all which I laid up in a corner of the room on a heap which

[1] *See* Appendix after Introduction, No. I.
[2] *Cursory Notices of the Reverend Francis Blomefield.* By J. Wilton Rix, Esq.

4

PREFACE

contains several sacks full.'[1] But Blomefield afterwards became the owner of a considerable portion of these papers ; for he not only wrote his initials on several of them, and marked a good many others with a mark by which he was in the habit of distinguishing original documents that he had examined and noted, but he also made a present to a friend of one letter which must certainly have once been in the Paston family archives. He himself refers to his ownership of certain collections of documents in the Preface to his *History of Norfolk*, where he informs the reader that he has made distinct reference to the several authors and originals he had made use of in all cases, ' except ' (these are his words) ' where the originals are either in Mr. Le Neve's or my own collections, which at present I design to join to his, so that, being together, they may be consulted at all times.' Apparently honest Tom Martin was still intending to carry out Le Neve's design, and Blomefield purposed to aid it further by adding his own collections to the Le Neve MSS. But though Martin lived for nearly forty years after his marriage with Le Neve's widow, and always kept this design in view, he failed to carry it out. His necessities compelled him to part with some of his treasures, but these apparently were mainly books enriched with MS. notes, not original ancient MSS., and even as he grew old he did not altogether drop the project. He frequently formed resolutions that he would, *next year*, arrange what remained, and make a selection for public use. But at last, at the age of seventy-four, he suddenly died in his chair without having given effect to his purpose.

Neither did his friend Blomefield, who died nine years before him, in January 1762, succeed in giving effect to *his* good intention of uniting his collections with the Le Neve MSS. For he died deeply in debt, and by his will, made just before death, he directed all his personal property to be sold in payment of his liabilities. His executors, however, declined to act, and administration was granted to two principal creditors. Of the Paston MSS. which were owned by him, a few are now to be found in one of the volumes of the Douce Collection in the Bodleian Library at Oxford. These, it would seem, were

[1] *Norfolk Archæology,* ii. 210, 211.

5

THE PASTON LETTERS

first purchased by the noted antiquary John Ives,[1] who acquired a number of Le Neve's, Martin's, and Blomefield's MSS. ; and after his library was sold by auction in March 1777, they became part of the collections relating to the counties of Oxford and Cambridge, which Gough, in his *British Topography* (vol. ii. p. 5), informs us that he purchased at the sale of Mr. Ives' papers. To this same collection, probably, belonged also a few of the scattered documents relating to the Paston family which have been met with among the miscellaneous stores of the Bodleian Library, for a knowledge of which I was indebted to the late Mr. W. H. Turner of Oxford.

Martin's executors seem to have done what they could to preserve the integrity of his collections. A catalogue of his library was printed at Lynn in 1771, in the hope that some purchaser would be found to take the whole. Such a purchaser did present himself, but not in the interest of the public. A By Mr. certain Mr. John Worth, a chemist at Diss, bought both the Worth. library and the other collections, as a speculation, for £630. The printed books he immediately sold to a firm at Norwich, who disposed of them by auction ; the pictures and smaller curiosities he sold by auction at Diss, and certain portions of the MSS. were sent, at different times, to the London market. But before he had completed the sale of all the collections, Mr. Worth died suddenly in December 1774. That portion of the MSS. which contained the Paston Letters he had up to that time reserved. Mr. Fenn immediately purchased them of his executors, and they had been twelve years in his possession when he published his first two volumes of selections from them.

So much for the early history of the MSS. Their subsequent fate is not a little curious. On the 23rd May 1787, Fenn received his knighthood at St. James's, having then and there presented to the King three bound volumes of MSS. which were the originals of his first two printed volumes.[2] Yet,

[1] *See* Nichols's *Literary Anecdotes,* iii. 199.
[2] The following announcement appears in the *Morning Chronicle* of the 24th May 1787: ' Yesterday, John Fenn, Esq., attended the levee at St. James's, and had the honour of presenting to His Majesty (bound in three volumes) the original letters of which he had before presented a printed copy ; when His Majesty, as a mark of his gracious acceptance, was pleased to confer on him the honour of knighthood.'

6

PREFACE

strange to say, these MSS. were afterwards lost sight of so completely that for a whole century nobody could tell what had become of them. They were not in the Royal Library afterwards given up to the British Museum ; they were not to be found in any of the Royal Palaces. The late Prince Consort, just before his death, caused a careful search to be made for them, but it proved quite ineffectual. Their hiding-place remained unknown even when I first republished these Letters in the years 1872-75.

To this mystery succeeded another of the same kind. The originals of the other three volumes were not presented to the king ; but they, too, disappeared, and remained for a long time equally undiscoverable. Even Mr. Serjeant Frere, who edited the fifth volume from transcripts left by Sir John Fenn after his death, declared that he had not been able to find the originals of that volume any more than those of the others. Strange to say, however, the originals of that volume were in his house all the time, and were discovered by his son, Mr. Philip Frere, in the year 1865, just after an ingenious *littérateur* had made the complete disappearance of *all* the MSS. a ground for casting doubt on the authenticity of the published letters. It is certainly a misfortune for historical literature, or at all events was in those days, that the owners of ancient MSS. commonly took so little pains to ascertain what it was that they had got. Since then the proceedings of the Historical MSS. Commission, which have brought to light vast stores of unsuspected materials for history, have awakened much more interest in such matters.

Thus three distinct portions of MSS. that had been carefully edited had all been lost sight of and remained undiscoverable for a long series of years. The originals of the first two volumes presented to the King could not be found. The originals of volumes iii. and iv. could not be found. The originals of volume v. could not be found. These last, however, after a time, came to light, as we have seen, in 1865, having been discovered in the house of the late Mr. Philip Frere at Dungate, in Cambridgeshire ; and with them were found a large number of additional MSS., also belonging to the

7

THE PASTON LETTERS

Paston Collection, among which was the original of one of the letters of volume iii. separated from all its fellows, whose place of concealment remained still unknown.

This discovery, however, was important, and at once suggested to me the possibility of producing a new edition of the Letters arranged in true chronological order, and augmented by those hitherto unedited. It suggested, moreover, that more of the originals might even yet be discovered with a little further search, perhaps even in the same house. But a further search at Dungate, though it brought to light a vast quantity of papers of different ages, many of them very curious, did not lead to the discovery of any other than the single document above referred to belonging to any of the first four volumes. All that Mr. Philip Frere could find belonging to the Paston Collection he sold to the British Museum, and the rest he disposed of by auction.

The question then occurred : Since the originals of volumes iii. and iv. had not been found at Dungate, might they be in the possession of the head of the Frere family, the late Mr. George Frere of Roydon Hall, near Diss, in Norfolk? This was suggested to me as probable by Mr. Philip Frere, his cousin, and I wrote to him accordingly on the 3rd December 1867. I received an answer from him dated on the 6th, that he did not see how such MSS. should have found their way to Roydon, but if they turned up at any time he would let me know. Unluckily he seems to have dismissed the subject from his mind, and I received no answer to further inquiries repeated at various intervals. At last it appeared hopeless to wait longer and defer my edition of the Letters indefinitely on the chance of finding more originals anywhere. So the first volume of my edition went to press, and the second, and the third. But just after I had printed off two Appendices to vol. iii., a friend of Mr. George Frere's called upon me at the Record Office, and informed me that a number of original Paston letters had been discovered at Roydon, which he had conveyed up to London. After some further communication with Mr. Frere himself I was allowed to inspect them at his son's chambers in the Temple, when I found among them those

8

PREFACE

very originals of Fenn's third and fourth volumes which eight years before he could not believe were in his possession ! Every one of them, I think, was there with just two exceptions —the first a document which, as already mentioned, was found at Dungate ; the second a letter (No. 52 in this edition) now preserved at Holland House, the existence of which was made known to me before my second volume was issued by a recent book of the Princess Marie Liechtenstein.[1]

It was mortifying, I confess, not to have received earlier intelligence of a fact that I had suspected all along. But it was better to have learned it at the last moment than not till after my last volume was published. So, having made two Appendices already to that volume, the only thing to do was to add a third, in which the reader would find a brief note of the discovery, with copies of some of the unpublished letters, and as full an account of the others belonging to the same period as circumstances would permit. Altogether there were no less than ninety-five new original letters belonging to the period found at Roydon Hall, along with the originals of Fenn's third and fourth volumes.

In July 1888 these Roydon Hall MSS. were offered for sale at Christie's. They consisted then of 311 letters, mainly the originals of Fenn's third and fourth volumes, and of those described in my third Appendix. Of the former set there were only four letters wanting, viz. the two in volume iii. whose existence is accounted for elsewhere, and two in volume iv. 'which,' the sale catalogue observes, 'are noted by Fenn himself as being no longer in his possession.' As to the letters in my Appendix the catalogue goes on to say :—

'Of the ninety-five additional letters above mentioned (Gairdner, 992-1086) *four* are missing (Nos. 1016, 1029, 1077, 1085). On the other hand, on collating the present collection with the printed volumes, it was found to contain *four others* of which no record exists either in Fenn's or Mr. Gairdner's edition, and which consequently appear to have escaped the notice of the latter gentleman while examining the treasures at Roydon Hall.'

'The latter gentleman' begs leave to say here that he never

[1] *Holland House.* By Princess Marie Liechtenstein, vol. ii. p. 198.

9

THE PASTON LETTERS

was at Roydon Hall in his life, and was only allowed to examine such of the 'treasures' found there as were placed before him in the year 1875 in a certain chamber in the Temple. A well-known bookseller purchased the MSS. offered at Christie's for 500 guineas, and some years later (in 1896), sold them to the British Museum. They are thus, at length, available for general consultation. The number of missing originals, however, is not quite as given in Christie's sale catalogue. There are four, not two, lacking of volume iv. On the other hand, only two letters of the Appendix are wanting.[1]

About fifteen years after the discovery at Roydon there came another discovery elsewhere. On the 29th March 1890 it was announced in the *Athenæum* that the missing originals of Fenn's first and second volumes—that is to say, the MSS. presented to King George III.—had likewise come to light again. They were found at Orwell Park, in Suffolk, in 1889, after the death of the late Colonel Tomline, and they remain there in the possession of his cousin, Mr. E. G. Pretyman, M.P., now Secretary to the Admiralty, who kindly showed them to me at his house soon after their discovery. They have come to him among family papers and heirlooms of which, being only tenant for life, he is not free to dispose until some doubts can be removed as to their past history ; and I accordingly forbear from saying more on this point except that their place of deposit indicates that they may either have got mixed with the private papers and books of Pitt, of which a large number are in the Orwell library, or with those of his old tutor and secretary, Dr. George Pretyman, better known as Bishop Tomline. Dr. Pretyman had just been appointed Bishop of Lincoln when Fenn published his first two volumes, and it was many years afterwards that he assumed the name of Tomline. But whether these MSS. came to his hands or to Pitt's, or under what

[1] The missing letters of volume iv. are Nos. 24, 97, 99, and 105 (Nos. 551, 726, 735, and 758 of this edition). The last never formed part of Fenn's collection. I do not know of any other noted by him as 'no longer in his possession.' The letters missing of the Appendix are only Nos. 997 and 1019. Of the four said to be missing in Christie's catalogue, 1016 is not a document at all, the number having been accidentally skipped in the Inventory, and the other three are in the British Museum. No. 1077, however, is inaccurately described in the Appendix.

10

PREFACE

circumstances they were delivered to either, there is no evidence to show. Possibly the King's illness in 1788 prevented their being placed, or, it may be, replaced, in the Royal Library, where they were intended to remain.

The edition of these Letters published by Mr. Arber in 1872-75 was in three volumes. It was printed from stereotype plates, and has been reissued more than once by the Messrs. Constable with corrections, and latterly with an additional volume containing the Preface and Introduction by themselves, and a Supplement giving the full text of those newly-found letters of which the reader had to be content with a bare catalogue in 1875. My original aim to have a complete collection of all extant Paston Letters had been defeated ; and there seemed nothing for it but to let them remain even at the last in a general series, an Appendix and a Supplement. The present publishers, however, by arrangement with Messrs. Constable, were anxious to meet the wants of scholars who desired to possess the letters, now that the collection seems to be as complete as it is ever likely to be, in a single series, and in a more luxurious form than that in which they have hitherto appeared. I have accordingly rearranged the letters as desired—a task not altogether without its difficulties when nice chronological questions had to be weighed and the story of the Pastons in all its details had for so many years ceased to occupy a foremost place in my thoughts ; and I trust that the unity of the series will now give satisfaction. At the same time, the opportunity has not been lost of rectifying such errors as have been brought to my notice, which could not have been conveniently corrected in the stereotype editions.

Notwithstanding the recovery of the originals of the letters printed by Fenn, it has not been thought necessary to edit these anew from the MSS. Whether such a thing would be altogether practicable even now may perhaps be a question ; at all events it would have delayed the work unduly. Fenn's editing is, as I have shown in previous editions, fairly satisfactory on the whole, and it is not to be supposed that a comparison of all the printed letters with the original MSS. would lead to results of any very material consequence. A large number

11

THE PASTON LETTERS

have been compared already, and the comparison inspires the greatest confidence in his care and accuracy. His misreadings are really very few, his method of procedure having been such as to prevent their being either many or serious; while as to his suppressions I have found no reason to believe, from what examination I have been able to make, that any of them were of very material importance.

It was not editorial carelessness on Fenn's part which made a new edition desirable in 1872. It was, first of all, the advance of historical criticism since his day—or rather, perhaps, I should say, of the means of verifying many things by the publication of historical sources and the greater accessibility of historical records. And secondly, the discovery of such a large number of unprinted documents belonging to the Paston Collection made it possible to study that collection as a whole, and fill up the outlines of information which they contained on matters both public and private. On this subject I may be allowed simply to quote what I said in 1872 in the preface to the first volume :—

'The errors in Fenn's chronology are numerous, and so exceedingly misleading that, indispensable as these Letters now are to the historian, there is not a single historian who has made use of them but has misdated some event or other, owing to their inaccurate arrangement. Even writers who have been most on their guard in some places have suffered themselves to be misled in others. This is no reproach to the former Editor, whose work is indeed a perfect model of care and accuracy for the days in which he lived; but historical criticism has advanced since that time, and facilities abound which did not then exist for comparing one set of documents with another, and testing the accuracy of dates by public records. The completion of Blomefield's *History of Norfolk*, and the admirable index added to that work of late years by Mr. Chadwick, have also been of eminent service in verifying minute facts. Moreover, the comprehensive study of the whole correspondence, with the advantage of having a part already published to refer to, has enabled me in many cases to see the exact bearing of particular letters, which before seemed to have no certain place in the chronology, not only upon public events, but upon the private affairs of the Paston family. . . .

Accuracy of Fenn's text.

The care taken by Sir John Fenn to secure the accuracy of his text can be proved by many tests. It might, indeed, be inferred from

12

PREFACE

the elaborate plan of editing that he adopted, exhibiting in every case two transcripts of the same letter, the one to show the precise spelling and punctuation of the original, the other to facilitate the perusal by modern orthography. A work on which so much pains were bestowed, and which was illustrated besides by numerous facsimiles of the original handwritings, signatures, paper-marks, and seals of the letters, was not likely to have been executed in a slovenly manner, in so far as the text is concerned. But we are not left in this case to mere presumptive evidence. The originals of the fifth volume have been minutely examined by a committee of the Society of Antiquaries, and compared all through with the printed text, and the general result of this examination was that the errors are very few, and for the most part trivial. Now, if this was the case with regard to that volume, which it must be remembered was published after Fenn's death from transcripts prepared for the press, and had not the benefit of a final revision of the proof-sheets by the editor, we have surely every reason to suppose that the preceding volumes were at least not less accurate.

'At all events, any inaccuracies that may exist in them were certainly not the result of negligence. I have been favoured by Mr. Almack, of Melford, near Sudbury, in Suffolk, with the loan of several sheets of MS. notes bequeathed to him by the late Mr. Dalton, of Bury St. Edmunds, who transcribed a number of the original MSS. for Sir John Fenn. These papers contain a host of minute queries and criticisms, which were the result of a close examination of the first four volumes, undertaken at Fenn's request. Those on the first two volumes are dated on the 3rd and 7th of May 1788, more than a year after the book was published. But on vols. iii. and iv. there are two separate sets of observations, the first of which were made on the transcripts before they were sent to press, the other, like those on the two first volumes, on the published letters. From an examination of these criticisms, and also from the results of the examination of the fifth volume by the committee of the Society of Antiquaries,[1] I have been led to the opinion that the manner in which Sir John Fenn prepared his materials for the press was as follows :—Two copies were first made of every letter, the one in the exact spelling and punctuation of the original, the other in modern orthography. Both these copies were taken direct from the original, and possibly in the case of the first two volumes they were both made by Fenn himself. In vols. iii. and iv., however, it is stated that many of the transcripts were made by Mr. Dalton, while those of vol. v. were found to be almost all in his handwriting when that volume was sent to press in 1823.[2] But

Mode in which Fenn prepared the letters for publication.

[1] *Archæol.* vol. xli. p. 39.
[2] *See* Advertisement in the beginning of the volume, p. vii.

13

THE PASTON LETTERS

this statement probably refers only to the copies in the antique spelling. Those in modern spelling I believe to have been made for the most part, if not altogether, by Fenn himself. When completed, the two copies were placed side by side, and given to Mr. Dalton to take home with him. Mr. Dalton then made a close comparison of the two versions, and pointed out every instance in which he found the slightest disagreement between them, or where he thought an explanation might be usefully bracketed into the modern version. These comments in the case of vol. iii. are upwards of 400 in number, and extend over eighteen closely written pages quarto. It is clear that they one and all received the fullest consideration from Sir John Fenn before the work was published. Every one of the discrepancies pointed out between the two versions is rectified in the printed volume, and there cannot be a doubt that in every such case the original MS. was again referred to, to settle the disputed reading.

Examples.

'One or two illustrations of this may not be unacceptable to the reader. The following are among the observations made by Mr. Dalton on the transcripts of vol. iii. as prepared for press. In Letter viii. was a passage in which occurred the words, "that had of your father certain lands *one* seven years or eight years agone." Mr. Dalton's experience as a transcriber appears to have suggested to him that "one" was a very common misreading of the word "over" in ancient MSS., and he accordingly suggested that word as making better sense. His surmise turned out to be the true reading, and the passage stands corrected accordingly in the printed volume. In Letter xxiv. there was a discrepancy in the date between the transcript in ancient spelling and the modern version. In the latter it was "the 4th day of December," whereas the former gave it as the 3rd. On examination it appears that the *modern* version was found to be correct, a Roman "iiij." having been misread in the other as "iij." Thus we have very sufficient evidence that the modern copy could not have been taken from the ancient, but was made independently from the original MS. Another instance of the same thing occurs in the beginning of Letter xli., where the words "to my power" had been omitted in the literal transcript, but were found in the modern copy.

'Mr. Dalton's part in the work of transcription appears clearly in several of his observations. One of the transcripts is frequently referred to as "my copy"; and an observation made on Letter lxxxvi. shows pretty clearly that the copy so referred to was the literal one. At the bottom of that letter is the following brief postscript :—"Utinam iste mundus malignus transiret et concupiscentia ejus"; on which Mr. Dalton remarks as follows :—"I have added this on *your* copy as supposing it an oversight, and hope it is properly inserted." Thus it appears that Mr. Dalton's own transcript had the words which were

14

PREFACE

deficient in the other, and that, being tolerably certain they existed in the original, he transferred them to the copy made by Fenn. Now when it is considered that these words are written in the original MS. with peculiarly crabbed contractions, which had to be preserved in the literal version as exactly as they could be represented in type,[1] it will, I think, appear evident that Mr. Dalton could never have ventured to supply them in such a form without the original before him. It is clear, therefore, that his copy was the literal transcript, and that of Fenn the modern version.

'Again, in Letter xxxi. of the same volume, on the second last line of page 137, occur the words, "that he obey not the certiorari." On this passage occurs the following query—"The word for 'obey' seems unintelligible. Have I not erred from the original in my copy?" Another case will show how by this examination the errors of the original transcripts were eliminated. In Letter xxxiv., at the bottom of pp. 144-5, occurs the name of Will or William Staunton. It appears this name was first transcribed as "Robert Fraunton" in the right or modern version; on which Mr. Dalton remarks, "It is William in orig." (Mr. Dalton constantly speaks of the transcript in ancient spelling as the "original" in these notes, though it is clear he had not the real original before him at the time he made them). Strangely enough, Mr. Dalton does not suspect the surname as well as the Christian name, but it is clear that both were wrong, and that they were set right in consequence of this query directing the editor's attention once more to the original MS.'

To this I may add some further evidences of Fenn's editorial care and accuracy. When the second volume of my first edition was published in 1874, my attention was called, as already mentioned, to the existence at Holland House of the original of one of those letters[2] which I had reprinted from Fenn. It was one of the letters in Fenn's third volume, and only one[3] other letter in that volume had then turned up. I carefully compared both these papers with the documents as printed, and in both, as I remarked in the Preface to vol. ii., the exact spelling was given with the most scrupulous accuracy, so that there was scarcely the most trivial variation between the originals and the printed text. But a more careful

[1] The following is the exact form in which they stand in the literal or left-hand version :—'Utia'z iste mu'd maligu' t'nsir' & c'up'ia e.'
[2] No. 38 in that edition, No. 52 in this.
[3] It was Letter 1 in Fenn's third volume, No. 18 in my first edition, No. 24 in this.

15

THE PASTON LETTERS

estimate, alike of Fenn's merits and of his defects as an editor, became possible when, on the publication of the third volume of the same edition, I was able, as I have already shown, to announce at the last moment the result of a cursory inspection of the originals of his third and fourth volumes. And what I said at that time may be here transcribed :—

'The recovery of these long-lost originals, although, unfortunately, too late to be of the use it might have been in this edition, is important in two ways : first, as affording an additional means of testing Fenn's accuracy as an editor ; and secondly, as a means of testing the soundness of some occasional inferences which the present Editor was obliged to draw for himself in the absence of the originals. More than one instance occurs in this work in which it will be seen that I have ventured to eliminate from the text as spurious a heading printed by Fenn as if it were a part of the document which it precedes. Thus, in No. 19,[1] I pointed out that the title, in which Judge Paston is called "Sir William Paston, knight," could not possibly be contemporaneous ; and the document itself shows that this opinion was well founded. It bears, indeed, a modern endorsement in a handwriting of the last century much to the same effect as Sir John Fenn's heading ; but this, of course, is no authority at all. In the same way I showed that the title printed by Fenn, as a heading to No. 191,[2] was utterly erroneous, and could not possibly have existed in the original MS. This conclusion is also substantiated by the document, which, I may add, bears in the margin the heading "Copia," showing that it was a transcript. The document itself being an important State Paper, there were probably a number of copies made at the time ; but as no others have been preserved, it is only known to us as one of the Paston Letters.

'Another State Paper (No. 238),[3] of which a copy was likewise sent to John Paston, has a heading which Sir John Fenn very curiously misread. It is printed in this edition[4] as it stands in the first, *Vadatur J. P.*, meaning apparently "John Paston gives security, or stands pledged." But it turns out on examination that the reading of the original is *Tradatur J. P.* (Let this be delivered to John Paston).

'To return to No. 19, it will be seen that I was obliged to reprint from Fenn in the preliminary note a few words which he had found written on the back of the letter, of which it was difficult to make any perfect sense, but which seemed to imply that the bill was delivered to

[1] No. 25 in present edition.
[2] No. 230 in present edition.   [3] No. 282 in present edition.
[4] That is to say, in the edition published by Mr. Arber in 1875, when it was impossible to correct the text.

16

PREFACE

Parliament in the 13th year of Henry VI. I pointed out that there seemed to be some error in this, as no Parliament actually met in the 13th year of Henry VI. The original endorsement, however, is perfectly intelligible and consistent with facts, when once it has been accurately deciphered. The handwriting, indeed, is very crabbed, and for a considerable time I was puzzled ; but the words are as follows :— " Falsa billa Will'i Dallyng ad parliamentum tempore quo Henricus Grey fuit vicecomes, ante annum terciodecimum Regis Henrici vj[ti]." I find as a matter of fact that Henry Grey was sheriff (*vicecomes*) of Norfolk, first in the 8th and 9th, and again in the 12th and 13th year of Henry VI., and that Parliament sat in November and December of the 12th year (1433) ; so that the date of the document is one year earlier than that assigned to it.

'Again, I ventured to question on internal evidence the authorship of a letter (No. 910)[1] which Fenn had assigned to William Paston, the uncle of Sir John Paston. At the end is the signature "Wyll'm Paston," with a reference in Fenn to a facsimile engraved in a previous volume. But the evidence seemed to me very strong that the William Paston who wrote this letter was not Sir John's uncle, but his brother. The inspection of the original letter itself has proved to me that I was right. The signatures of the two Williams were not altogether unlike each other ; but the signature appended to this letter is unquestionably that of the younger man, not of his uncle ; while the facsimile, to which Fenn erroneously refers the reader, is that of the uncle's signature taken from a different letter.

'It may perhaps be conceived that if even these few errors could be detected in Fenn's work by one who had not yet an opportunity of consulting the original MSS., a large number of others would be discovered by a minute comparison of the printed volumes with the letters themselves. This suspicion, however, is scarcely borne out by the facts. I cannot profess to have made anything like an exhaustive examination, but so far as I have compared these MSS. with the printed text, I find no evidence of more than very occasional inaccuracy, and, generally speaking, in matters very immaterial. On the contrary, an inspection of these last recovered originals has greatly confirmed the opinion, which the originals previously discovered enabled me to form, of the scrupulous fidelity and care with which the letters were first edited. For the most part, not only the words, but the exact spelling of the MSS. is preserved, with merely the most trifling variations. Sir John, indeed, was not a trained archivist, and there are what may be called errors of system in his mode of reading, such as, for instance, the omission of contractions that may be held to represent a final *e*, or the rendering a final dash by *s* instead of *es*. In such things the plan

[1] No. 1033 in present edition.

VOL. I.—B   17

THE PASTON LETTERS

that he pursued was obvious. But it is manifest that in other respects he is very accurate indeed ; for he had made so careful a study of these MSS. that he was quite familiar with most of the ancient modes of handwriting, and, on the whole, very seldom mistook a reading.

'I may add, that this recent discovery enables me to vindicate his accuracy in one place, even where it seemed before to be very strangely at fault. At the end of Letter iii. of the fifth volume,[1] occurs in the original edition the following postscript :—" I warn you keep this letter close, and lose it not ; rather burn it." On comparing this letter with the original, the Committee of the Society of Antiquaries, some years ago, were amazed to find that there was no such postscript in the MS., and they were a good deal at a loss to account for its insertion. It now appears, however, that this letter was preserved in duplicate, for among the newly-recovered MSS. I discovered a second copy, being a corrected draft, in Margaret Paston's own hand, at the end of which occurs the P.S. in question.

'It must be acknowledged, however, that Fenn's mode of editing was not in all respects quite so satisfactory. Defects, of which no one could reasonably have complained in his own day, are now a serious drawback, especially where the original MSS. are no longer accessible. Occasionally, as we have seen, he inserts a heading of his own in the text of a document without any intimation that it is not in the original ; but this is so rare a matter that little need be said about it. A more serious fault is, that in vols. iii. and iv. he has published occasionally mere extracts from a letter as if it were the whole letter. In vols. i. and ii. he avowedly left out passages of little interest, and marked the places where they occurred with asterisks ; but in the two succeeding volumes he has not thought it necessary to be so particular, and he has made the omissions *sub silentio*. For this indeed no one can seriously blame him. The work itself, as he had planned it, was only a selection of letters from a correspondence, and a liberal use of asterisks would not have helped to make it more interesting to the public. Occasionally he even inverts the order of his extracts, printing a postscript, or part of a postscript, in the body of a letter, and placing at the end some passage that occurs in the letter itself, for no other reason apparently than that it might read better as a whole.

'Thus Letter 37 of this edition[2] (vol. iii., Letter vi., in Fenn) is only a brief extract, the original being a very long letter, though the subjects touched upon are not of very great interest. So also Letter 171 (Letter xxx. in Fenn's third volume)[3] is a set of extracts. Letter 182 (vol. iii., Letter xxxix., in Fenn)[4] is the same ; and the first part

[1] No. 787 of this edition.   [2] No. 51 of present edition.
[3] No. 205.   [4] No. 221.
18

PREFACE

of what is given as a postscript is not a postscript in the original, but actually comes before the first printed paragraph.

'In short, it was the aim of Sir John Fenn to reproduce with accuracy the spelling and the style of the MSS. he had before him ; but as for the substance, to give only so much as he thought would be really interesting. The letters themselves he regarded rather as specimens of epistolary art in the fifteenth century than as a substantial contribution to our knowledge of the times. To have given a complete transcript of every letter, or even a *résumé* in his own words of all that concerned lawsuits, leases, bailiffs' accounts, and a number of other matters of equally little interest, formed no part of his design ; but the task that he had really set himself he executed with admirable fidelity. He grudged no labour or expense in tracing facsimiles of the signatures, the seals, and the watermarks on the paper. All that could serve to illustrate the manners of the period, either in the contents of the letters, or in the handwritings, or the mode in which they were folded, he esteemed most valuable ; and for these things his edition will continue still to be much prized. But as it was clearly impossible in that day to think of printing the whole correspondence, and determining precisely the chronology by an exhaustive study of minutiæ, there seemed no good reason why he should not give two or three paragraphs from a letter without feeling bound to specify that they were merely extracts. Yet even these defects are not of frequent occurrence. The omissions are by no means numerous, and the matter they contain is generally unimportant in itself.'

I took advantage, however, at that time, of the recovery of so many of the missing originals to make a cursory examination for the further testing of Fenn's editorial accuracy. Two or three letters I compared carefully with the originals throughout, and in others I made special reference to passages where doubts were naturally suggested, either from the obscurity of the words or from any other cause as to the correctness of the reading. The results of this examination I gave in an Appendix at the end of the Introduction to the third volume in 1875, and such errors as I was then able to detect are corrected in the present edition.

Apart from such corrections, the letters are here reproduced as they are printed in previous editions, only in a better order. Fenn's text has been followed, where no corrections have been found, in all the letters printed by him except those of his fifth volume. The exact transcript given on the left-hand pages of

THE PASTON LETTERS

PREFACE

Fenn's edition has been strictly adhered to, except that the contractions have been extended ; and even in this process we have always been guided by the interpretation given by Fenn himself in his modern version on the right-hand pages. All the other letters in this publication are edited from the original MSS., with a very few exceptions in which these cannot be found. In some places, indeed, where the contents of a letter are of very little interest, it has been thought sufficient merely to give an abstract instead of a transcript, placing the abstract in what is believed to be its true place in the series chronologically. Abstracts are also given of documents that are too lengthy and formal to be printed, and, in one case, of a letter sold at a public sale, of which a transcript is not now procurable. In the same manner, wherever I have found the slightest note or reference, whether in Fenn's footnotes or in Blomefield's *Norfolk*—where a few such references may be met with—to any letter that appears originally to have belonged to the Paston correspondence, even though the original be now inaccessible, and our information about the contents the most scanty, the reader will find a notice of all that is known about the missing document in the present publication.

I wish it were in my power to make the present edition better still. But there have been always formidable obstacles to completeness during the thirty years and more since I first took up the business of editing the letters ; and though many of these obstacles have been removed, my energies are naturally not quite what they once were. The publishers, however, have thought it time for a more satisfactory edition, and I hope I have done my best. It remains to say a few words about the original MSS. and the places in which they now exist.

Of those at Orwell Park I have already spoken. They are contained in three half-bound volumes, and are the originals of the letters printed by Fenn in his first and second volumes.

In the British Museum are contained, first of all, four volumes of the 'Additional MSS.' numbered 27,443 to 27,446, consisting of the originals of volume V. of Fenn's edition which was published after his death, and a number of other letters first printed by me in the edition of 1872-75. The nine

20

volumes which follow these, viz. 'Additional MSS.,' 27,447-27,455, contain also Paston letters but of a later date, and papers relating to Sir John Fenn's publication. There is also a separate volume of 'Paston letters' in 'Additional MS.' 33,597 ; but these, too, are mostly of later date, only eight being of the fifteenth century. Further, there are the Roydon Hall MSS. (including with, I believe, only two exceptions the originals of Fenn's third and fourth volumes), which are contained in the volumes 'Additional,' 34,888-9. And finally there are two Paston letters (included in this edition) in 'Additional MS.' 35,251. These are all that are in the British Museum. Besides these there are, as above noticed, a few MSS. in a volume of the Douce Collection and the other stray MSS. in the Bodleian Library at Oxford above referred to. At Oxford, also, though not strictly belonging to the Paston family correspondence, are a number of valuable papers, some of which are included in this edition, having an important bearing on the fortunes of the family. These are among the muniments contained in the tower of Magdalene College. As the execution of Sir John Fastolf's will ultimately devolved upon Bishop Waynflete, who, instead of a college at Caister, made provision for a foundation of seven priests and seven poor scholars in Magdalene College, a number of papers relative to the disputes between the executors and the arrangement between the Bishop and John Paston's sons have been preserved among the documents of that college. My attention was first called to these many years ago by Mr. Macray, through whom I obtained copies, in the first place, of some entries from an old index of the deeds relating to Norfolk and Suffolk, which had already been referred to by Chandler in his Life of Bishop Waynflete. Afterwards Mr. Macray, who had for some time been engaged in a catalogue of the whole collection, was obliging enough to send me one or two abstracts of his own made from the original documents even before he was able to refer me to his report on the muniments of Magdalene College, printed in the Fourth Report of the Historical MSS. Commission. It will be seen that I have transcribed several interesting entries from this source.

21

THE PASTON LETTERS

PREFACE

Further, there are just a few Paston letters preserved in Pembroke College, Cambridge.

What remains to be said is only the confession of personal obligations, incurred mainly long ago in connection with this work. The lapse of years since my first edition of these letters was issued, in 1872, naturally reminds me of the loss of various friends who favoured and assisted it in various ways. Among these were the late Colonel Chester, Mr. H. C. Coote, Mr. Richard Almack of Melford, Mr. W. H. Turner of Oxford, Mr. J. H. Gurney, Mr. Fitch, and Mr. L'Estrange of Norwich. On the other hand, I am happy to reckon still among the living Dr. Jessopp, Mr. Aldis Wright, Miss Toulmin Smith, and Mr. J. C. C. Smith, now a retired official of the Probate Office at Somerset House, who all gave me kindly help so long ago. And I have further to declare my obligations to Mr. Walter Rye, a gentleman well known as the best living authority on Norfolk topography and families, for most friendly and useful assistance in the way of notes and suggestions towards later editions. I have also quite recently received help (confessed elsewhere) from the Rev. William Hudson of Eastbourne, and have further had my attention called to significant documents in the Public Record Office by some of my old friends and colleagues there.

But among the departed, there is one whom I have reserved for mention by himself, not so much for any particular assistance given me long ago in the preparation of this work as for the previous education in historical study which I feel that I received from intercourse with him. I had been years engaged in the public service, and always thought that the records of the realm ought to be better utilised than they were in those days for the purpose of historical research ; but how even Record clerks were to become well acquainted with them under the conditions then existing it was difficult to see. For each of us had his own little task assigned to him, and had really very little opportunity, if ever so willing, to go beyond it. Nor was there too much encouragement given under official regulations to anything like historical training ; for the Record Office, when

22

first constituted, was supposed to exist for the sake of litigants who wanted copies of documents, rather than for that of historical students who wanted to read them with other objects. Besides, people did not generally imagine then that past history could be rewritten, except by able and graphic pens which, perhaps, could put new life into old facts without a very large amount of additional research. The idea that the country contained vast stores of long-neglected letters capable of yielding up copious new information to supplement and to correct the old story of our national annals had hardly dawned upon anybody—least of all, perhaps, on humble officials bound to furnish office copies of 'fines' and 'recoveries' and antiquated legal processes. Even the State Papers, at that time, were kept apart from the Public Records, and could only be consulted by special permission from a Secretary of State. No clerk, either of the Record or State Paper Department, knew more than was contained within his own particular province. But by the wise policy of the late Lord Romilly these red-tape bands were ultimately broken ; and just at that time I had the rare privilege of being appointed to assist the late Reverend John S. Brewer in one of the great works which his Lordship set on foot to enable the British public to understand the value of its own MSS. It was to this association with Mr. Brewer that I feel I owe all my historical training, and I made some acknowledgment of that debt in 1872 when I dedicated to him my first edition of this work.

23

INTRODUCTION

The Paston Family

THE little village of Paston, in Norfolk, lies not far from the sea, where the land descends gently behind the elevated ground of Mundesley, and the line of the shore, proceeding eastward from Cromer, begins to tend a little more towards the south. It is about twenty miles north of Norwich. The country, though destitute of any marked features, is not uninteresting. Southwards, where it is low and flat, the ruins of Bromholm Priory attract attention. But, on the whole, it is an out-of-the-way district, unapproachable by sea, for the coast is dangerous, and offering few attractions to those who visit it by land. Indeed, till quite recently, no railways had come near it, and the means of access were not superabundant. Here, however, lived for several centuries a family which took its surname from the place, and whose private correspondence at one particular epoch sheds no inconsiderable light on the annals of their country.

Of the early history of this family our notices are scanty and uncertain. A Norman descent was claimed for them not only by the county historian Blomefield but by the laborious herald, Francis Sandford, author of a *Genealogical History of the Kings of England*, on the evidence of documents which have been since dispersed. Sandford's genealogy of the Paston family was drawn up in the year 1674, just after Sir Robert Paston had been raised to the peerage by the title of Viscount Yarmouth, before he was promoted to the higher dignity of earl. It still remains in MS.; but a pretty full account of it will be found in the fourth volume of *Norfolk Archæology*. The

25

THE PASTON LETTERS

story of the early ancestors, however, does not concern us here. At the time the family and their doings become best known to us, their social position was merely that of small gentry. One of these, however, was a justice of the Common Pleas in the reign of Henry VI., whose uprightness of conduct caused him to be commonly spoken of by the name of the Good Judge. He had a son, John, brought up to the law, who became executor to the old soldier and statesman, Sir John Fastolf. This John Paston had a considerable family, of whom the two eldest sons, strange to say, both bore the same Christian name as their father. They were also both of them soldiers, and each, in his time, attained the dignity of knighthood. But of them and their father, and their grandfather the judge, we shall have more to say presently. After them came Sir William Paston, a lawyer, one of whose daughters, Eleanor, married Thomas Manners, first Earl of Rutland. He had also two sons, of whom the first, Erasmus, died before him. The second, whose name was Clement, was perhaps the most illustrious of the whole line. Born at Paston Hall, in the immediate neighbourhood of the sea, he had an early love for ships, was admitted when young into the naval service of Henry VIII., and became a great commander. In an engagement with the French he captured their admiral, the Baron de St. Blankheare or Blankard, and kept him prisoner at Caister, near Yarmouth, till he had paid 7000 crowns for his ransom, besides giving up a number of valuables contained in his ship. Of this event Clement Paston preserved till his death a curious memorial among his household utensils, and we read in his will that he bequeathed to his nephew his ' standing bowl called the Baron St. Blankheare.' He served also by land as well as by sea, and was with the Protector Somerset in Scotland at the battle of Pinkie. In Mary's reign he is said to have been the person to whom the rebel Sir Thomas Wyat surrendered. In his later years he was more peacefully occupied in building a fine family seat at Oxnead. He lived till near the close of the reign of Elizabeth, having earned golden opinions from each of the sovereigns under whom he served. ' Henry VIII.,' we are told, ' called him his champion; the Duke of Somerset,

Clement Paston.

26

INTRODUCTION

Protector in King Edward's reign, called him his soldier; Queen Mary, her seaman; and Queen Elizabeth, her father.'[1]

Clement Paston died childless, and was succeeded by his nephew, another Sir William, whose name is well known in Norfolk as the founder of North Walsham School, and whose effigy in armour is visible in North Walsham Church, with a Latin epitaph recording acts of munificence on his part, not only to the grammar-school, but also to the cathedrals of Bath and Norwich, to Gonville and Caius College, Cambridge, and to the poor at Yarmouth.

From Sir William the line descended through Christopher Paston (who, on succeeding his father, was found to be an idiot, incapable of managing his affairs), Sir Edmund and Sir William Paston, Baronet, to Sir Robert Paston, who, in the reign of Charles II., was created, first Viscount and afterwards Earl of Yarmouth. He is described as a person of good learning, and a traveller who brought home a number of curiosities collected in foreign countries. Before he was raised to the peerage he sat in Parliament for Castle Rising. It was he who, in the year 1664, was bold enough to propose to the House of Commons the unprecedented grant of two and a half millions to the king for a war against the Dutch.[2] This act not unnaturally brought him into favour with the Court, and paved the way for his advancement. Another incident in his life is too remarkable to be passed over. On the 9th of August 1676 he was waylaid while travelling in the night-time by a band of ruffians, who shot five bullets into his coach, one of which entered his body. The wound, however, was not mortal, and he lived six years longer.

The Earl of Yarmouth.

His relations with the Court were not altogether of good omen for his family. We are told that he once entertained the king and queen, and the king's brother, James, Duke of York, with a number of the nobility, at his family seat at Oxnead. His son, William, who became second Earl of Yarmouth, married the Lady Charlotte Boyle, one of King Charles's natural daughters. This great alliance, and all the magnificence

[1] Blomefield's *History of Norfolk*, vi. 487, 488.
[2] Clarendon's *Life*, ii. 440.

27

THE PASTON LETTERS

it involved, was too much for his slender fortunes. Earl William was led into a profuse expenditure which involved him in pecuniary difficulties. He soon deeply encumbered his inheritance; the library and the curiosities collected by his accomplished father had to be sold. The magnificent seat at Oxnead was allowed to fall into ruin; and on the death of this second earl it was pulled down, and the materials turned into money to satisfy his creditors. The family line itself came to an end, for Earl William had survived all his male issue, and the title became extinct.

Thrifty ancestors. From this brief summary of the family history we must now turn to a more specific account of William Paston, the old judge in the days of Henry VI., and of his children. Of them, and of their more immediate ancestor Clement, we have a description drawn by an unfriendly hand some time after the judge's death; and as it is, notwithstanding its bias, our sole authority for some facts which should engage our attention at the outset, we cannot do better than quote the paper at length:—

'*A remembrance of the worshipful kin and ancestry of Paston, born in Paston in Gemyngham Soken.*

'First, There was one Clement Paston dwelling in Paston, and he was a good, plain husband (*i.e.* husbandman), and lived upon his land that he had in Paston, and kept thereon a plough all times in the year, and sometimes in barlysell two ploughs. The said Clement yede (*i.e.* went) at one plough both winter and summer, and he rode to mill on the bare horseback with his corn under him, and brought home meal again under him, and also drove his cart with divers corns to Wynterton to sell, as a good husband[man] ought to do. Also, he had in Paston a five score or a six score acres of land at the most, and much thereof bond land to Gemyngham Hall, with a little poor water-mill running by a little river there, as it appeareth there of old time. Other livelode nor manors had he none there, nor in none other place.

'And he wedded Geoffrey of Somerton (whose true surname is Goneld)'s sister, which was a bondwoman, to whom it is not unknown (to the prior of Bromholm and Bakton also, as it is said) if that men will inquire.

'And as for Geoffrey Somerton, he was bond also, to whom, etc., 28

INTRODUCTION

he was both a pardoner and an attorney; and then was a good world, for he gathered many pence and half-pence, and therewith he made a fair chapel at Somerton, as it appeareth, etc.

'Also, the said Clement had a son William, which that he set to school, and often he borrowed money to find him to school; and after that he yede (went) to court with the help of Geoffrey Somerton, his uncle, and learned the law, and there begat he much good; and then he was made a serjeant, and afterwards made a justice, and a right cunning man in the law. And he purchased much land in Paston, and also he purchased the moiety of the fifth part of the manor of Bakton, called either Latymer's, or Styward's, or Huntingfield, which moiety stretched into Paston; and so with it, and with another part of the said five parts he hath seignory in Paston, but no manor place; and thereby would John Paston, son to the said William, make himself a lordship there, to the Duke (qu. Duchy?) of Lancaster's great hurt.

'And the said John would and hath untruly increased him by one tenant, as where that the prior of Bromholm borrowed money of the said William for to pay withal his dismes, the said William would not lend it him unless the said prior would mortgage to the said William one John Albon, the said prior's bondsman, dwelling in Paston, which was a stiff churl and a thrifty man, and would not obey him unto the said William; and for that cause, and for evil will that the said William had unto him, he desired him of the prior. And now after the death of the said William, the said John Albon died; and now John Paston, son to the said William, by force of the mortgage sent for the son of the said John Albon to Norwich.'

The reader will probably be of opinion that several of the facts here recorded are by no means so discreditable to the Pastons as the writer certainly intended that they should appear. The object of the whole paper is to cast a stigma on the family in general, as a crafty, money-getting race who had risen above their natural rank and station. It is insinuated that they were originally mere *adscripti glebæ*; that Clement Paston was only a thrifty husbandman (note the original signification of the word, 'housebondman'), that he married a bondwoman, and transmitted to his son and grandson lands held by a servile tenure; and the writer further contends that they had no manorial rights in Paston, although William Paston, the justice, had purchased land in the neighbourhood, and his son John was endeavouring to 'make himself a lordship' there to the prejudice of the rights of the Duchy of Lancaster.

29

THE PASTON LETTERS

It is altogether a singular statement, very interesting in its bearing upon the obscure question of the origin of copyholds, and the gradual emancipation of villeins. Whether it be true or false is another question; if true, it appears to discredit entirely the supposed Norman ancestry of the Pastons; but the remarkable thing is that an imputation of this kind could have been preferred against a family who, whatever may have been their origin, had certainly long before obtained a recognised position in the county.

It would appear, however, from the accuser's own statement, that Clement Paston, the father of the justice, was an industrious peasant, who tilled his own land, and who set so high a value on a good education that he borrowed money to keep his son at school. With the help of his brother-in-law, he also sent the young man to London to learn the law, a profession which in that day, as in the present, was considered to afford an excellent education for a gentleman.[1] The good education was not thrown away. William Paston rose in the profession and became one of its ornaments. He improved his fortunes by marrying Agnes, daughter and heiress of Sir Edmund Berry of Harlingbury Hall, in Hertfordshire. Some years before his father's death, Richard Courtenay, Bishop of Norwich, appointed him his steward. In 1414 he was called in, along with two others, to mediate in a dispute which had for some time prevailed in the city of Norwich, as to the mode in which the mayors should be elected; and he had the good fortune with his coadjutors to adjust the matter satisfactorily.[2] In 1421 he was made a serjeant, and in 1429 a judge of the Common Pleas.[3] Before that time we find him acting as trustee for various properties, as of the Appleyard family in Dunston,[4] of Sir Richard Carbonel,[5] Sir Simon Felbrigg,[6] John

William Paston the justice.

[1] 'Here everything good and virtuous is to be learned; all vice is discouraged and banished. So that knights, barons, and the greatest nobility of the kingdom, often place their children in those Inns of Court; not so much to make the law their study, much less to live by the profession (having large patrimonies of their own), but to form their manners, and to preserve them from the contagion of vice.'—*Fortescue de Laudibus Legum Angliæ* (ed. Amos), 185.

[2] Blomefield's *Norfolk*, iii. 126. [3] Dugdale's *Origines*.
[4] Blomefield, v. 56. [5] *Ibid.* ii. 257, 285; vii. 217.
[6] *Ibid.* viii. 109.

30

INTRODUCTION

Berney,[1] Sir John Rothenhale,[2] Sir John Gyney of Dilham,[3] Lord Cobham,[4] and Ralph Lord Cromwell.[5] He was also executor to Sir William Calthorp.[6] The confidence reposed in him by so many different persons is a remarkable testimony to the esteem in which he was held. He was, moreover, appointed one of the king's council for the duchy of Lancaster, and on his elevation to the judicial bench the king gave him a salary of 110 marks (£73, 6s. 8d.), with two robes more than the ordinary allowance of the judges.

In addition to all this he is supposed to have been a knight, and is called Sir William Paston in Fenn's publication. But this dignity was never conferred upon him in his own day. There is, indeed, one paper printed by Fenn from the MSS. which were for a long time missing that speaks of him in the heading as 'Sir William Paston, Knight'; but the original MS. since recovered shows that the heading so printed is taken from an endorsement of a more modern date. This was, indeed, a confident surmise of mine at a time when the MS. was inaccessible; for it was clear that William Paston never could have been knighted. His name occurs over and over again on the patent rolls of Henry VI. He is named in at least one commission of the peace every year to his death, and in a good many other commissions besides, as justices invariably were. He is named also in many of the other papers of the same collection, simply as William Paston of Paston, Esquire; and even in the body of the petition so inaccurately headed, he is simply styled William Paston, one of the justices. Nor does there appear to be any other foundation for the error than that single endorsement. He left a name behind him of so great repute, that Fuller could not help giving him a place among his 'Worthies of England,' although, as he remarks, it did not fall strictly within the plan of his work to notice a lawyer who was neither a chief justice nor an author.

Not a knight.

Of his personal character we are entitled to form a favour- *His character.*

[1] Blomefield, x. 67. [2] *See* Letter 13.
[3] Blomefield, vi. 353. [4] *Ibid.* x. 176.
[5] *Ibid.* v. 27. [6] *Ibid.* vi. 517.

31

able estimate, not only from the honourable name conferred on him as a judge, but also from the evidences already alluded to of the general confidence felt in his integrity. True it is that among these papers we have a complaint against him for accepting fees and pensions when he was justice, from various persons in the counties of Norfolk and Suffolk ;[1] but this only proves, what we might have expected, that he had enemies and cavillers as well as friends. Of the justice of the charges in themselves we have no means of forming an independent judgment; but in days when all England, and not least so the county of Norfolk, was full of party spirit and contention, it was not likely that a man in the position of William Paston should escape imputations of partiality and one-sidedness. Before his elevation to the bench, he had already suffered for doing his duty to more than one client. Having defended the Prior of Norwich in an action brought against him by a certain Walter Aslak, touching the advowson of the church of Sprouston, the latter appears to have pursued him with unrelenting hatred. The county of Norfolk was at the time ringing with the news of an outrage committed by a band of unknown rioters at Wighton. On the last day of the year 1423, one John Grys of Wighton had been entertaining company, and was heated with 'wassail,' when he was suddenly

Outrage by William Aslak. attacked in his own house. He and his son and a servant were carried a mile from home and led to a pair of gallows, where it was intended to hang them ; but as ropes were not at once to be had, they were murdered in another fashion, and their bodies horribly mutilated before death.[2] For nearly three years the murderers went unpunished, while the country stood aghast at the crime. But while it was still recent, at a county court holden at Norwich, Aslak caused a number of bills, partly in rhyme, to be posted on the gates of Norwich priory, and of the Grey Friars, and some of the city gates, distinctly threatening William Paston with the fate of John

[1] No. 25.
[2] See No. 6. Compare J. Amundesham Annales, 16. In the latter Grys's Christian name is given as William, and the outrage is said to have taken place on Christmas Day instead of New Year's Eve.

Grys, and insinuating that even worse things were in store for him.

Against open threats like these William Paston of course appealed to the law ; but law in those days was but a feeble protector. Aslak had the powerful support of Sir Thomas Erpingham, by which he was enabled not only to evade the execution of sentence passed against him, but even to continue his persecution. He found means to deprive Paston of the favour of the Duke of Norfolk, got bills introduced in Parliament to his prejudice, and made it unsafe for him to stir abroad. The whole country appears to have been disorganised by faction ; quarrels at that very time were rife in the king's council-chamber itself, between Humphrey, Duke of Gloucester, the Protector, and Bishop Beaufort ; nor was anything so firmly established by authority but that hopes might be entertained of setting it aside by favour.

William Paston had two other enemies at this time. 'I pray the Holy Trinity,' he writes in one place, 'deliver me of my three adversaries, this cursed Bishop for Bromholm, Aslak for Sprouston, and Julian Herberd for Thornham.' The bishop whom he mentions with so much vehemence, claimed to be a kinsman of his own, and named himself John Paston, but William Paston denied the relationship, maintaining that his true name was John Wortes. He appears to have been John Wortes. in the first place a monk of Bromholm, the prior of which monastery having brought an action against him as an apostate from his order, engaged William Paston as his counsel in the prosecution. Wortes, however, escaped abroad, and brought the matter before the spiritual jurisdiction of the court of Rome, bringing actions against both the prior and William Paston, the latter of whom he got condemned in a penalty of £205. On this William Paston was advised by friends at Rome to come at once to an arrangement with him ; but he determined to contest the validity of the sentence, the result of which appears to have been that he was excommunicated. His adversary, meanwhile, found interest to get himself appointed and consecrated Bishop of Cork ; and though his name does not appear in the ordinary lists of bishops of

VOL. I.—C

that see, the Vatican archives show that he was provided to it on the 23rd May 1425.[1]

As for Julian Herberd, William Paston's third enemy, we have hitherto known nothing of her but the name. It appears, however, by some Chancery proceedings[2] recently discovered, that Julian Herberd was a widow who considered herself to have been wronged by Paston as regards her mother's inheritance, of which he had kept her from the full use for no less than forty years. Paston had, indeed, made her some pecuniary offers which she did not think sufficient, and she had attempted to pursue her rights against him at a Parliament at Westminster, when he caused her to be imprisoned in the King's Bench. There, as she grievously complains, she lay a year, suffering much and 'nigh dead from cold, hunger, and thirst.' The case was apparently one of parliamentary privilege, which she had violated by her attempted action, though she adds that he threatened to keep her in prison for life if she would not release to him her right, and give him a full acquittance. She also accuses him of having actually procured one from her by coercion, and of having by false suggestion to the Lord Chancellor caused her committal to the Fleet, where she was kept for a whole year, 'beaten, fettered, and stocked,' that no man might know where she was. At another time, also, she says he kept her three years in the pit within Norwich Castle on starvation diet. The accusation culminates in a charge which seems really inconceivable :—

'Item, the said Paston did bring her out of the Round House into your Palace and brought her afore your Chief Justice, and then the said Paston commanded certain persons to bring her to prison to your Bench, and bade at his peril certain persons to smite the brain out of her head for suing of her right ; and there being in grievous prison during half year and more, fettered and chained, suffering cold, hunger, thirst, in point of death, God and ye, gracious King, help her to her right.'

[1] Nos. 10, 11, 12. Maziere Brady in his book on the Episcopal Succession, vol. ii. p. 79, gives the following entry from the archives of the Vatican :—
'Die 10° kal. Junii 1425, provisum est ecclesiæ Corcagen. in Hibernia, vacanti per mortem Milis (Milonis), de persona Ven. Fratis Johannis Pasten, prioris conventualis Prioratus Bromholm, Ordinis Chuniacensis.'—Vatican.
Also on Sept. 14, 1425, 'Johannes Paston, Dei gratia electus Korkagen, solvit personaliter 120 florenos auri,' etc.—Obligazioni.
[2] Printed in Appendix to this introduction.

What we are to think of all this, not having Paston's reply, I cannot say.

Scanty and disconnected as are the notices we possess of William Paston, we must not pass by without comment his letter to the vicar of the abbot of Clugny, in behalf of Bromholm Priory.[1] It was not, indeed, the only occasion[2] on which we find that he exerted himself in behalf of this ancient monastery, within a mile of which, he tells us, he was born. Brom- Bromholm Priory. holm Priory was, in fact, about that distance from Paston Hall, as miles were reckoned then (though it is nearer two of our statute miles), and must have been regarded with special interest by the family. It was there that John Paston, the son of the judge, was sumptuously buried in the reign of Edward IV. It was a monastery of some celebrity. Though not, at least in its latter days, one of the most wealthy religious houses, for it fell among the smaller monasteries at the first parliamentary suppression of Henry VIII., its ruins still attest that it was by no means insignificant. Situated by the seashore, with a flat, unbroken country round about, they are conspicuous from a distance both by sea and land. Among the numerous monasteries of Norfolk, none but Walsingham was more visited by strangers, and many of the pilgrims to Walsingham turned aside on their way homeward to visit the Rood of Bromholm. For this was a very special treasure brought from Constantinople two hundred years before, and composed of a portion of the wood of the true Cross. Many were the miracles recorded to have been wrought in the monastery since that precious relic was set up ; the blind had received their sight, the lame had walked, and lepers had been cleansed ; even the dead had been restored to life. It was impossible that a native of Paston could be uninterested in a place so renowned throughout all England.

Yet about this time the priory must have been less prosperous than it had once been. Its government and constitution were in a transition state. It was one of the twenty-eight monasteries in England which belonged to the Cluniac order, and were originally subject to the visitation of the Abbot of

[1] No. 20.   [2] See No. 47, p. 56.

THE PASTON LETTERS

Clugny in France. Subjection to a foreign head did not tend at any time to make them popular in this country, and in the reign of Henry v. that connection was suddenly broken off. An act was passed suppressing at once all the alien priories, or religious houses that acknowledged foreign superiors. The priors of several of the Cluniac monasteries took out new foundation charters, and attached themselves to other orders. Those that continued signed deeds of surrender, and their monasteries were taken into the king's hands. About nine or ten years later, however, it would seem that a vicar of the Abbot of Clugny was allowed to visit England, and to him William Paston made an appeal to profess in due form a number of virtuous young men who had joined the priory in the interval.

Land purchased by Judge Paston. From the statement already quoted as to the history of the Paston family, it appears that William Paston purchased a good deal of land in Paston besides what had originally belonged to them. It was evidently his intention to make a family residence, and transmit to his sons a more absolute ownership in the land from which they derived their name. Much of his father's land in Paston had been copyhold belonging to the manor of Gimingham Hall; but William Paston bought 'a moiety of the fifth part' of the adjacent manor of Bacton, with free land extending into Paston. He thus established himself as undoubted lord of the greater part of the soil, and must have felt a pardonable pride in the improved position he thereby bequeathed to his descendants. At Paston he apparently contemplated building a manor house; for he made inquiry about getting stone from Yorkshire conveyed by sea to Mundesley, where there was then a small harbour [1] within two miles of Paston village. To carry out the improvements he proposed to make there and on other parts of his *Highways diverted.* property, he obtained licence from the king a year before his death to divert two public highways, the one at Paston and the other at Oxnead, a little from their course.[2] The alterations do not appear to have been of a nature that any one had a right to complain of. Full inquiry was made beforehand by

[1] No. 7.   [2] Patent 6th July, 21 Henry VI., p. 1, m. 10.

36

INTRODUCTION

an inquisition *ad quod damnum*[1] whether they would be to the prejudice of neighbours. At Paston the extent of roadway which he obtained leave to enclose was only thirty-two and a half perches in length by one perch in breadth. It ran on the south side of his mansion, and he agreed to make a new highway of the same dimensions on the north side. The vicar of Paston seems to have been the neighbour principally concerned in the course that the new thoroughfare was to take, and all particulars had been arranged with him a few months before William Paston died.

But it would seem upon the judge's death his great designs *John Paston has disputes with his neighbours.* were for some time interrupted. The family were looked upon by many as upstarts, and young John Paston, who was only four-and-twenty, though bred to the law like his father, could not expect to possess the same weight and influence with his neighbours. A claim was revived by the lord of Gimingham Hall to a rent of eight shillings from one of Paston's tenants, which had never been demanded so long as the judge was alive. The vicar of Paston pulled up the 'doles' which were set to mark the new highway, and various other disturbances were committed by the neighbours. It seems to have required all the energies not only of John Paston upon the spot, but also of his brother Edmund, who was in London at Clifford's Inn, to secure the rights of the family; insomuch that their mother, in writing to the latter of the opposition to which they had been exposed, expresses a fear lest she should make him weary of Paston.[2] And, indeed, if Edmund Paston was not weary of the dispute, his mother herself had cause to be; for it not only lasted years after this, but for some years after Edmund Paston was dead the stopping of the king's highway was a fruitful theme of remonstrance. When Agnes Paston built a wall it was thrown down before it was half completed; threats of heavy amercements were addressed to her in church, and the men of Paston spoke of showing their displeasure when they went in public procession on St. Mark's day.[3]

The Manor of Oxnead, which in later times became the *Oxnead.*

[1] *Inquis. a. q. d.* (arranged with *Inquisitions post-mortem*), 21 Henry VI., No. 53.
[2] Letter 62.   [3] Nos. 194, 195, 196.

37

THE PASTON LETTERS

principal seat of the family, was also among the possessions purchased by Judge Paston. He bought it of William Clopton of Long Melford, and settled it upon Agnes, his wife. But after his death her right to it was disputed. It had formerly belonged to a family of the name of Hauteyn, and there suddenly started up a claimant in the person of one John *John Hauteyn.* Hauteyn, whose right to hold property of any kind was supposed to have been entirely annulled by the fact of his having entered the Order of Carmelite Friars. It seems, however, he had succeeded in getting from the Pope a dispensation to renounce the Order on the plea that he had been forced into it against his will when he was under age, and being thus restored by the ecclesiastical power to the condition of a layman, he next appealed to the civil courts to get back his inheritance. This danger must have been seen by William Paston before his death, and a paper was drawn up (No. 46) to show that Hauteyn had been released from his vows on false pretences. Nevertheless he pursued his claim at law, and although he complained of the difficulty of getting counsel (owing, as he himself intimated, to the respect in which the bar held the memory of Judge Paston, and the fact that his son John was one of their own members), he seems to have had hopes of succeeding through the influence of the Duke of Suffolk. His suit, however, had not been brought to a successful determination at the date of Suffolk's fall. It was still going on in the succeeding summer; but as we hear no more of it after that, we may presume that the altered state of the political world induced him to abandon it. According to Blomefield, he and others of the Hauteyn family released their rights to Agnes Paston 'about 1449'; but this date is certainly at least a year too early.[1]

William Paston also purchased various other lands in the county of Norfolk.[2] Among others, he purchased from

[1] Nos. 63, 87, 93, 128; Blomefield, vi. 479.
[2] It would appear that he had also an estate at Therfield, in Hertfordshire, as shown by an inscription in the east window of the north aisle of the parish church, in which were portraits of himself and his wife underwritten with the words, *Orate pro animabus domini Willelmi Paston et Agnetis uxoris ejus, benefactorum hujus ecclesiæ* (Chauncey's *Hertfordshire*, 88).

38

INTRODUCTION

Thomas Chaucer, a son of the famous poet, the manor of Gresham,[1] of which we shall have something more to say a little later. We also find that in the fourth year of Henry VI. he obtained, in conjunction with one Thomas Poye, a grant of a market, fair and free-warren in his manor of Shipden which had belonged to his father Clement before him.[2]

The notices of John Paston begin when he was on the eve *John Paston's marriage.* of marrying, a few years before his father's death. The match was evidently one that was arranged by the parents, after the fashion of the times. The lady was of a good family—daughter and heiress of John Mauteby, Esq. of Mauteby in Norfolk. The friends on both sides must have been satisfied that the union was a good one; for it had the one great merit which was then considered everything—it was no disparagement to the fortunes or the rank of either family. Beyond this hard business view, indeed, might have been found better arguments to recommend it; but English men and women in those days did not read novels, and had no great notion of cultivating sentiment for its own sake. Agnes Paston writes to her husband to intimate 'the bringing home of the gentlewoman from Reedham,' according to the arrangement he had made about it. It was, in her words, 'the first acquaintance between John Paston and the said gentlewoman' (one would think Dame Agnes must have learned from her husband to express herself with something of the formality of a lawyer); and we are glad to find that the young lady's sense of propriety did not spoil her natural affability. 'She made him gentle cheer in gentle wise, and said he was verily your son; and so I hope there shall need no great treaty between them.' Finally the judge is requested by his wife to buy a gown for his future daughter-in-law, to which her mother would add a goodly fur. 'The gown,' says Dame Agnes, 'needeth for to

[1] Blomefield, viii. 127.
[2] *Patent Roll*, 4 Henry VI., p. 2, m. 13; Blomefield, viii. 102. A further notice relating to Judge Paston has been given me by Sir James Ramsay in the following memorandum :—'£432 for arrears of salary due to late William Paston, paid to his executor, John Paston, from *parva custuma* of the port of London. L.T.R. Enrolled Customs Account of Henry VI. (entry 8 Nov. 37 Hen. VI.—Mich. 38 Hen. VI.)' in Public Record Office. So the arrears of the judge's salary were only paid in 1458, fourteen years after his death.

39

THE PASTON LETTERS

INTRODUCTION

be had ; and of colour it would be a goodly blue, or else a bright sanguine.'[1]

Character of his wife.

'The gentlewoman' thus introduced to John Paston and the reader proved to the former a most devoted wife during about six-and-twenty years of married life. Her letters to her husband form no inconsiderable portion of the correspondence in these volumes, and it is impossible to peruse them without being convinced that the writer was a woman not only of great force of character, but of truly affectionate nature. It is true the ordinary style of these epistles is very different from that of wives addressing their husbands nowadays. There are no conventional expressions of tenderness—the conventionality of the age seems to have required not tenderness but humility on the part of women towards the head of a family ; the subjects of the letters, too, are for the most part matters of pure business ; yet the genuine womanly nature is seen bursting out whenever there is occasion to call it forth. Very early in the correspondence we meet with a letter of hers (No. 47) which in itself is pretty sufficient evidence that women, at least, were human in the fifteenth century. Her husband was at the time in London just beginning to recover from an illness which seems to have been occasioned by some injury he had met with. His mother had vowed to give an image of wax the weight of himself to Our Lady of Walsingham on his recovery, and Margaret to go on a pilgrimage thither, and also to St. Leonard's at Norwich. That she did not undertake a journey of a hundred miles to do more efficient service was certainly not owing to any want of will on her part. The difficulties of travelling in those days, and the care of a young child, sufficiently account for her remaining in Norfolk ; but apparently even these considerations would not have deterred her from the journey had she not been dissuaded from it by others. 'If I might have had my will,' she writes, 'I should have seen you ere this time. I would ye were at home, if it were for your ease (and your sore might be as well looked to here as it is there ye be), now liever than a gown, though it were

[1] No. 34.

40

of scarlet.' Could the sincerity of a woman's wishes be more artlessly expressed ?

Let not the reader suppose, however, that Margaret Paston's acknowledged love of a scarlet gown indicates anything like frivolity of character or inordinate love of display. We have little reason to believe from her correspondence that dress was a ruling passion. The chief aim discernible in all she writes —the chief motive that influenced everything she did—was simply the desire to give her husband satisfaction. And her will to do him service was, in general, only equalled by her ability. During term time, when John Paston was in London, she was his agent at home. It was she who negotiated with farmers, receiving overtures for leases and threats of lawsuits, and reported to her husband everything that might affect his interests, with the news of the country generally. Nor were threats always the worst thing she had to encounter on his account. For even domestic life, in those days, was not always exempt from violence ; and there were at least two occasions when Margaret had to endure, in her husband's absence, things that a woman ought to have been spared.

One of these occasions we proceed to notice. The manor of Gresham, which William Paston had purchased from the son of the poet Chaucer, had been in the days of Edward II. the property of one Edmund Bacon, who obtained from that king a licence to embattle the manor-house. It descended from him to his two daughters, Margaret and Margery. The former became the wife of Sir William de Kerdeston, and her rights were inherited by a daughter named Maud, who married Sir John Burghersh.[1] This moiety came to Thomas Chaucer by his marriage with Maud Burghersh, the daughter of the Maud just mentioned. The other became at first the property of Sir William Molynes, who married Bacon's second daughter Margery. But this Margery having survived her husband, made a settlement of it by will, according to which the reversion of it after the decease of one Philip Vache and

The Manor of Gresham.

[1] *Inquisitions post-mortem*, 27 Edw. III. No. 28, and 30 Edw. III., No. 42. Blomefield inaccurately makes Maud, whom Sir John Burghersh married, the daughter of Edmond Bacon instead of his granddaughter.—(*Hist. of Norf.* viii. 127.)

41

THE PASTON LETTERS

INTRODUCTION

of Elizabeth his wife, was to be sold ; and William, son of Robert Molynes, was to have the first option of purchase. This William Molynes at first declined to buy it, being apparently in want of funds ; but he afterwards got one Thomas Fauconer, a London merchant, to advance the purchase-money, on an agreement that his son should marry Fauconer's daughter. The marriage, however, never took effect ; the Molynes family lost all claim upon the manor, and the same Thomas Chaucer who acquired the other moiety by his wife, purchased this moiety also, and conveyed both to William Paston.[1]

The whole manor of Gresham thus descended to John Paston, as his father's heir. But a few years after his father's death he was troubled in the possession of it by Robert Hungerford, son of Lord Hungerford, who, having married Eleanor Molynes, a descendant of the Sir William Molynes above referred to, had been raised to the peerage as Lord Molynes, and laid claim to the whole inheritance of the Molynes family. He was still but a young man,[2] heir-apparent to another barony ; and, with the prospect of a great inheritance both from his father and from his mother, who was the daughter and sole heir of William Lord Botraux, he certainly had little occasion to covet lands that were not his own. Nevertheless he listened to the counsels of John Heydon of Baconsthorpe, a lawyer who had been sheriff and also recorder of Norwich, and whom the gentry of Norfolk looked upon with anything but goodwill, regarding him as the ready tool of every powerful oppressor. His chief patron, with whom his name was constantly coupled, was Sir Thomas Tuddenham ; and the two together, especially during the unpopular ministry of the Duke of Suffolk, exercised an ascendency in the county, of which we hear very numerous

Claimed by Lord Molynes.

[1] No. 16. Blomefield gives a somewhat different account, founded doubtless on documents to which I have not had access. He says that Margery, widow of Sir William Molynes, settled her portion of the manor on one Thomas de la Lynde, with the consent of her son Sir William Molynes, who resigned all claim to it.

[2] According to the inquisition taken on his father's death (*Inq. p. m.*, 37 Hen. VI., No. 17), he was over thirty in June 1459. If we are to understand that he was then only in his thirty-first year, he could not have been twenty when he first dispossessed John Paston of Gresham. But 'over thirty' may perhaps mean two or three years over.

42

complaints. Heydon persuaded Lord Molynes that he had a good claim to the manor of Gresham ; and Lord Molynes, without more ado, went in and took possession on the 17th of February 1448.[1]

To recover his rights against a powerful young nobleman connected with various wealthy and influential families required, as John Paston knew, the exercise of great discretion. Instead of resorting at once to an action at law, he made representations to Lord Molynes and his legal advisers to show how indefensible was the title they had set up for him. He secured some attention for his remonstrances by the intercession of Waynflete, bishop of Winchester.[2] Conferences took place between the counsel of both parties during the following summer, and the weakness of Lord Molynes' case was practically confessed by his solicitors, who in the end told Paston to apply to his lordship personally. Paston accordingly, at no small expense to himself, went and waited upon him at Salisbury and elsewhere, but was continually put off. At last, on the 6th of October, not, as I believe, the same year, but the year following, he succeeded in doing to Lord Molynes to some extent what Lord Molynes had already done to him. He took possession of 'a mansion within the said town,' and occupied it himself, having doubtless a sufficiency of servants to guard against any sudden surprise. After this fashion he maintained his rights for a period of over three months. The usual residence of Lord Molynes was in Wiltshire, and his agents probably did not like the responsibility of attempting to remove John Paston without express orders from their master. But on the 28th of January 1450, while John Paston was away in London on business, there came before the mansion at Gresham a company of a thousand persons, sent to recover possession for Lord Molynes. They were armed with cuirasses and brigandines, with guns, bows, and arrows, and with every kind of offensive and defensive armour. They had also mining instruments, long poles with hooks, called cromes, used for pulling down houses, ladders, pickaxes, and pans with fire burning in them.

[1] No. 102.   [2] No. 79.

43

THE PASTON LETTERS

INTRODUCTION

With these formidable implements they beset the house, at that time occupied only by Margaret Paston and twelve other persons; and having broken open the outer gates, they set to work undermining the very chamber in which Margaret was. Resistance under the circumstances was impossible. Margaret was forcibly carried out. The house was then thoroughly rifled of all that it contained—property estimated by John Paston at £200[1]—the doorposts were cut asunder, and the place was left little better than a ruin. Further, that there might be no mistake about the spirit in which the outrage was perpetrated, the rioters declared openly, that if they had found John Paston, or his friend John Damme, who had aided him with his counsel about these matters, neither of them should have escaped alive.[2]

John Paston drew up a petition for redress to Parliament, and another to the Lord Chancellor; but it was some months before his case could be attended to, for that year was one of confusion and disorder unparalleled. It was that year, in fact, which may be said to have witnessed the first outbreak of a long, intermittent civil war. History has not passed over in silence the troubles of 1450. The rebellion of Jack Cade, and the murder of two bishops in different parts of the country, were facts which no historian could treat as wholly insignificant. Many writers have even repeated the old slander, which there seems no good reason to believe, that Jack Cade's insurrection was promoted by the intrigues of the Duke of York; but no one appears to me to have realised the precise nature of the crisis that necessarily followed the removal of the Duke of Suffolk. And as we have now arrived at the point where the Paston Letters begin to have a most direct bearing on English history, we must endeavour in a few words of historical retrospect to make the matter as clear as possible.

Troubled times, A.D. 1450.

The Duke of Suffolk

Fall of the Duke of Suffolk. As to the causes of Suffolk's fall we are not left in ignorance. Not only do we possess the full text of the long

[1] A value probably equal to about £3000 of our money.   [2] Nos. 102, 135.

44

indictment drawn up against him this year in Parliament, but a number of political ballads and satires, in which he is continually spoken of by the name of Jack Napes, help us to realise the feeling with which he was generally regarded. Of his real merits as a statesman, it is hard to pronounce an opinion; for though, obviously enough, his whole policy was a failure, he himself seems to have been aware from the first that it was not likely to be popular. Two great difficulties he had to contend with, each sufficient to give serious anxiety to any minister whatever: the first being the utter weakness of the king's character; the second, the practical impossibility of maintaining the English conquests in France. To secure both himself and the nation against the uncertainties which might arise from the vacillating counsels of one who seems hardly ever to have been able to judge for himself in State affairs, he may have thought it politic to ally the king with a woman of stronger will than his own. At all events, if this was his intention, he certainly achieved it. The marriage of Henry with Margaret of Anjou was his work; and from Margaret he afterwards obtained a protection which he would certainly not have received from her well-intentioned but feeble-minded husband.

This marriage undoubtedly recommended itself to Henry *The king's* himself as a great means of promoting peace with France. *marriage.* The pious, humane, and Christian character of the king disposed him favourably towards all pacific counsels, and gave him a high opinion of the statesman whose policy most obviously had in view the termination of the disastrous war between France and England. King René, the father of Margaret of Anjou, was the brother of the French king's consort; so it was conceived that by his and Margaret's intercession a permanent peace might be obtained, honourable to both countries. For this end, Henry was willing to relinquish his barren title to the kingdom of France, if he could have been secured in the possession of those lands only, such as Guienne and Normandy, which he held irrespective of that title.[1] He was willing to relinquish even the duchies of

[1] Stevenson's *Wars of the English in France*, i. 132.

45

THE PASTON LETTERS

INTRODUCTION

Anjou and Maine, King René's patrimony, though the latter had long been in the possession of the English. It was of course out of the question that Henry should continue to keep the father of his bride by force out of his own lands. Suffolk therefore promised to give them up to the French king, for the use of René and his brother, Charles of Anjou; so that instead of the former giving his daughter a dower, England was called upon to part with some of her conquests. But how would the English nation reconcile itself to such a condition? Suffolk knew well he was treading in a dangerous path, and took every possible precaution to secure himself. He pleaded beforehand his own incompetency for the charge that was committed to him. He urged that his familiarity with the Duke of Orleans and other French prisoners lately detained in England brought him under suspicion at home, and rendered him a less fitting ambassador for arranging matters with France. Finally he obtained from the King and Council an instrument under the Great Seal, pardoning him beforehand any error of judgment he might possibly commit in conducting so critical a negotiation.[1]

His success, if judged by the immediate result, seemed to show that so much diffidence was unnecessary. The people at large rejoiced in the marriage of their king; the bride, if poor, was beautiful and attractive; the negotiator received the thanks of Parliament, and there was not a man in all the kingdom,—at least in all the legislature—durst wag his tongue in censure. The Duke of Gloucester, his chief rival and opponent in the senate, was the first to rise from his seat and recommend Suffolk, for his services, to the favour of the Crown.[2]

[1] Rymer, xi. 53.
[2] *Rolls of Parl.* v. 73. That Gloucester secretly disliked Suffolk's policy, and thought the peace with France too dearly bought, is more than probable. At the reception of the French ambassadors in 1445, we learn from their report that Henry looked exceedingly pleased, especially when his uncle the French king was mentioned. 'And on his left hand were my Lord of Gloucester, at whom he looked at the time, and then he turned round to the right to the chancellor, and the Earl of Suffolk, and the Cardinal of York, who were there, smiling to them, and it was very obvious that he made some signal. And it was afterwards mentioned by———(*blank in orig.*), that he pressed his Chancellor's hand and said to him in English, "I am very much rejoiced that some who are present should hear these words. They are not at their ease."'—Stevenson's *Wars of the English in France*, i. 110-11.

46

If he had really committed any mistakes, they were as yet unknown, or at all events uncriticised. Even the cession of Maine and Anjou at this time does not seem to have been spoken of.

Happy in the confidence of his sovereign, Suffolk was promoted to more distinguished honour. From an earl he was raised to the dignity of a marquis; from a marquisate, a few years later, to a dukedom. He had already supplanted older statesmen with far greater advantages of birth and pre-eminence of rank. The two great rivals, Humphrey, Duke of *Suffolk's* Gloucester, and Cardinal Beaufort, were both eclipsed, and *ascendency.* both died, within six weeks of each other, two years after the king's marriage, leaving Suffolk the only minister of mark. But his position was not improved by this undisputed ascendency. The death of Humphrey, Duke of Gloucester, *A.D. 1447.* aroused suspicions in the public mind that were perhaps due merely to time and circumstance. Duke Humphrey, with many defects in his character, had always been a popular favourite, and just before his death he had been arrested on a charge of treason. That he could not possibly have remained quiet under the new *régime* is a fact that we might presume as a matter of course, but there is no clear evidence that he was guilty of intrigue or conspiracy. The king, indeed, appears to have thought he was so, but his opinions were formed by those of Suffolk and the Queen; and both Suffolk and the Queen were such enemies of Duke Humphrey, that they were vehemently suspected of having procured his death.[1]

Complaints against the minister now began to be made more openly, and his conduct touching the surrender of Anjou and Maine was so generally censured, that he petitioned the king that a day might be appointed on which he should have an opportunity of clearing himself before the Council. On the 25th of May 1447 his wish was granted, and in the presence of a full Council, including the Duke of York, and others who might have been expected to be no very favourable

[1] An interesting and valuable account of the death of Duke Humphrey, from original sources, will be found in *The Hall of Lawford Hall*, pp. 104-13.

47

critics, he gave a detailed account of all that he had done. How far he made a really favourable impression upon his hearers we do not know; but in the end he was declared to have vindicated his integrity, and a proclamation was issued forbidding the circulation of such slanders against him in future, under penalty of the king's displeasure.[1]

The nature of the defence that he set up can only be a matter of speculation; but it may be observed that as yet no formal delivery of Anjou or Maine had really taken place at all. The former province, though it had been before this overrun and laid waste by the English, does not appear ever to have been permanently occupied by them. Delivery of Anjou would therefore have been an idle form; all that was required was that the English should forbear to invade it. But with Maine the case was different. It had been for a long time in the hands of the English, and pledges had certainly been given for its delivery by Suffolk and by Henry himself in December 1445.[2] As yet, however, nothing had been concluded by way of positive treaty. No definite peace had been made with France. Difficulties had always started up in the negotiations, and the ambassadors appointed on either side had been unable to do more than prolong from time to time the existing truce, leaving the matter in dispute to be adjusted at a personal interview between the two kings, for which express provision was made at the time of each new arrangement. But the personal interview never took place. In August 1445 it was arranged for the following summer. In January 1446 it was fixed to be before November. In February 1447 it was again to be in the summer following. In July it was settled to be before May 1448; but in October the time was again lengthened further.[3] There can be little doubt that these perpetual delays were due merely to hesitation on the part of England to carry out a policy to which she was already pledged. Charles, of course, could not allow them to go on for ever. In the treaty of July 1447, an express provision was for the first time

[1] Rymer, xi. 173.
[2] See Stevenson's Wars of the English in France, ii. [639] to [642].
[3] Rymer, xi. 97, 108, 151, 182, 189, etc.

48

inserted, that the town and castle of Le Mans, and other places within the county of Maine, should be delivered up to the French. It seems also to have been privately arranged that this should be done before the 1st of November; and that the further treaty made at Bourges on the 15th of October should not be published until the surrender was accomplished.[1] But the year 1447 had very nearly expired before even the first steps were taken to give effect to this arrangement. At length, on the 30th of December, an agreement was made by Matthew Gough, who had the keeping of Le Mans, that the place should be surrendered by the 15th of January, on receipt of letters patent from the King of France, for compensation to be made to grantees of the English crown.

Even this arrangement, however, was not adhered to. Matthew Gough still found reasons for refusing or delaying the surrender, although the English Government protested the sincerity of its intentions. But Charles now began to take the matter into his own hands. Count Dunois and others were *Siege of* sent to besiege the place, with a force raised suddenly out of *Le Mans, A.D. 1448.* various towns; for France had been carefully maturing, during those years of truce, a system of conscription which was now becoming serviceable. At the first rumour of these musters the English Government was alarmed, and Sir Thomas Hoo, Lord Hastings, Henry's Chancellor of France, wrote urgently to Pierre de Brézé, seneschal of Poitou, who had been the chief negotiator of the existing truce, deprecating the use of force against a town which it was the full intention of his Government to yield up honourably.[2] Such protests, however, availed nothing in the face of the obvious fact that the surrender had not taken place at the time agreed on. The French continued to muster forces. In great haste an embassy was despatched from England, consisting of Adam de Moleyns, Bishop of Chichester, and Sir Thomas Roos; but the conduct of the garrison itself rendered further negotiation nugatory. By no means could they be induced, even in obedience to

[1] Stevenson's Wars, ii. [714, 715].
[2] Stevenson's Wars, i. 198. See also a letter of the 18th Feb. 1448, of which an abstract is given in vol. ii. of the same work, p. 576.

49

their own king, to surrender the city peacefully. Dunois and his army accordingly drew nearer. Three sharp skirmishes took place before the siege could be formed; but at length the garrison were fully closed in. All that they could now do was to make a composition with the enemy; yet even this they would not have attempted of themselves. The efforts of the English envoys, however, secured for the besieged most favourable terms of surrender. Not only were they permitted to march out with bag and baggage, but a sum of money was delivered to each of the captains, by the French king's orders; with which, and a safe-conduct from Charles, they departed into Normandy.[1]

Its sur- It was on Friday, the 15th of March 1448, the day on *render.* which the truce between the two countries was to have expired, that the brave Matthew Gough, along with his colleague, Fulk Eton, formally delivered up to the French, not only the town and castle of Le Mans, but also the whole county of Maine except the lordship of Fresnay. Standing on the outer bridge, they made a public protest before their soldiers, and caused a notary to witness it by a formal document, that what they did was only in obedience to their own king's commands, and that the king himself, in giving up possession of the county of Maine, by no means parted with his sovereign rights therein; that he only gave up actual possession in order that King René and his brother, Charles of Anjou, might enjoy the fruits of their own lands, and in the hope that a firm peace might be established between England and France. Four days before this was done the truce had been prolonged for two years more.[2]

The reluctant cession of such a valuable province as Maine boded ill for the security of the neighbouring duchy of Normandy. The government of Normandy was at this time committed to Edmund Beaufort, Marquis of Dorset, who had just been created Duke of Somerset. His appointment to the post had been due rather to favour than to merit. The Duke of York was then Regent of France, and had given good proof

[1] Chron. de Mat. de Coussy (in Buchon's collection), p. 34.
[2] Rymer, xi. 199, 204. Stevenson's Wars, i. 207.

50

of his competence to take charge of the entire kingdom. But Somerset, who was head of the house of Beaufort, nearly allied in blood to the Crown, and who had come into possession of immense wealth by the death of his uncle, the Cardinal of Winchester, had the ambition of an Englishman to show his talent for governing. His influence with the king and Suffolk obtained for him the government of Normandy; and that he might exercise it undisturbed, York was recalled from France. The change was ill advised; for the times demanded the best of generalship, and the utmost political discretion. Somerset, though not without experience in war, had given no evidence of the possession of such qualities; and they had been notoriously wanting in his brother John, who was Duke of Somerset before him, when his ambition, too, had been gratified by a command in France. Duke John, we are told, absolutely refused to give any one his confidence as to what he was going to do at any period of the campaign. He used to say that if his shirt knew his plans he would burn it; and so, with a great deal of manoeuvring and mystery, he captured a small place in Brittany called La Guerche, made a vain attempt to reduce another fortress, and then returned to England.[1] It may have been owing to public discontent at the small result of his great preparations, that he was accused of treason on his return; when, unable to endure so great a reproach, he was believed to have put an end to his own life.[2]

With a full recollection of the indiscretions of his brother John, the King's Council must have hesitated to confide to Duke Edmund such an important trust as the government of Normandy. They must have hesitated all the more, as the appointment of Somerset involved the recall of the Duke of York. And we are told that their acts at the time betrayed symptoms of such irresolution; insomuch that one day a new governor of Normandy was proclaimed at Rouen, and the next his commission was revoked and another named in his stead.[3] But at last the influence of Somerset prevailed. He

[1] Basin, Histoire de Charles VII. etc. i. 150-1.
[2] Hist. Croylandensis Continuatio in Fulman's Scriptores, p. 519.
[3] Basin, i. 192.

51

THE PASTON LETTERS

was not, however, permitted to go abroad without warning of the dangers against which he had to provide. The veteran Sir John Fastolf drew up a paper for his guidance, pointing out that it was now peculiarly important to strengthen the fortifications on the new frontier, to protect the seaports, to preserve free communication with England, and (what was quite as politic a suggestion as any) to appoint a wise chancellor and a council for the impartial administration of justice, so as to protect the inhabitants from oppression.[1] From the comment made upon these suggestions, either by Fastolf himself or by his secretary William Worcester, it would seem that they were not acted upon; and to this cause he attributed the disasters which soon followed in quick succession, and brought upon the Duke of Somerset the indignation and contempt of a large number of his countrymen. These feelings, probably, were not altogether just. The duke had done good service before in France, and part of the blame of what occurred may perhaps be attributed to divided management—more especially to the unruly feelings of a number of the English soldiers.

The garrison which had been compelled against its will to give up Le Mans found it hard to obtain quarters in Normandy. It was doubtful whether they were not labouring under their own king's displeasure, and the captains of fortified towns were afraid to take them in. At last they took possession of Pontorson and St. James de Beuvron, two towns situated near the confines of Britanny which had been laid waste during the previous wars and had since been abandoned. They began to victual and fortify themselves in these positions, to the alarm of their neighbours, until the Duke of Britanny felt it necessary to complain to the Duke of Somerset, requesting that they might be dislodged. Somerset, in reply, promised to caution them not to do anything in violation of the truce, but declined to bid them evacuate their positions. Diplomatic intercourse went on between one side and the other, always in the most courteous terms, but every day it was becoming more apparent that all confidence was gone.

A.D. 1449. At last, in March 1449, the English justified the suspicions

[1] Stevenson's *Wars*, ii. [592].

52

INTRODUCTION

that had long been entertained of them. A detachment of about 600 men, under François de Surienne, popularly named L'Arragonois, a leader in the pay of England,[1] who had, not long before, been knighted by Henry, crossed the frontier southwards into Britanny, took by assault the town and castle of Fougères, and made dreadful havoc and slaughter among the unsuspecting inhabitants. The place was full of wealthy merchants, for it was the centre of a considerable woollen manufacture, and the booty found in it was estimated at no less than two millions of gold.[2] Such a prize in legitimate warfare would undoubtedly have been well worth the taking; but under the actual circumstances the deed was a glaring, perfidious violation of the truce. Somerset had been only a few days before protesting to the King of France that, even if all his towns were open and undefended, they would be perfectly secure from any assault by the English;[3] yet here was a town belonging to the Duke of Britanny, a vassal of the King of France who had been expressly included in the truce, assaulted and taken by fraud. Somerset disavowed the deed, but refused to make restitution. He professed to write to the king for instructions how to act; but he utterly destroyed his flimsy pretence of neutrality by writing to the King of France, desiring him not to give assistance to the Duke of Britanny.[4]

The truth is that the expedition had been fully authorised, not only by Somerset in Normandy, but by the king and the Duke of Suffolk in England. It was suggested to L'Arragonois when he was in England by Suffolk himself, who assured him that he would do the king a most excellent service by taking a place of so much consequence. He was further given to understand that he incurred no danger or responsibility; for even if he were besieged by the Duke of Britanny, ample succours would be despatched to relieve him. Unfortunately, during the next few months, the English had too much to do to keep their word, and L'Arragonois was compelled to sur-

Capture of Fougères.

[1] Stevenson's *Wars*, i. 473; ii. 573.
[2] Stevenson's *Reductio Normanniæ*, 406.
[3] *Ibid.* 402.   [4] *Ibid.* 406.

53

THE PASTON LETTERS

render the place again to the Duke of Britanny after a five weeks' siege. Feeling himself then absolved from every engagement to England, he next year sent back the Order of the Garter to Henry, declaring himself from that time a subject of his natural lord the King of Arragon, in whose country he proposed to spend the remainder of his days.[1]

Notwithstanding the richness of the booty won by the capture of Fougères, the English ought to have been aware that they would have a heavy price to pay for it. The alienation of a friend in the Duke of Britanny evidently did not grieve them, although that in itself should have been a matter of some concern; for the duke, though nearly related to the French king, had studied to keep himself neutral hitherto. To his and his father's pacific policy it was owing that the commerce of Britanny had prospered and Fougères itself become rich, while neighbouring districts were exposed to the ravages of war. But the resentment of the Duke of Britanny was not a cause of much apprehension. The effect of the outrage upon the French people was a much more serious matter, and this was felt immediately. The King of France, when he heard the news, was at Montils by Tours on the point of starting for Bourges. He immediately changed his purpose and turned back to Chinon that he might be nearer Britanny. A secret treaty was made between the king and the duke to aid each other on the recommencement of hostilities with the English. A plot was also laid to surprise the town of Pont-de-l'Arche on the Seine, just as Fougères had been surprised by the English. It was completely successful, and Pont-de-l'Arche was captured by stratagem early in the morning of the 16th of May, by a body of adventurers professedly in the service of Brittany. There could be no mistake about the significance of the retribution. To the Duke of Britanny the capture of Pont-de-l'Arche was of no value, except in the way of retaliation, for it was at a great distance from his borders; while to France it was a most important gain if used with a view to the recovery of Normandy. But France was quite as free to dis-

Pont-de-l'Arche taken by the French.

[1] Stevenson's *Wars*, i. 275, 278, etc.

54

INTRODUCTION

avow the deed as the English Government had been to disavow the taking of Fougères.

Charles had, in fact, gained, in a strategic point of view, quite as great an advantage as the English had gained in point of material wealth. But morally his advantage was greater still, for he showed himself perfectly open to treat for the redress of outrages on both sides, and was willing to put Pont-de-l'Arche again into the hands of the English if they would have restored Fougères. All conferences, however, were ineffectual, and the French followed up their advantage by taking Gerberoy and Conches. In the south they also won from the English two places in the neighbourhood of Bordeaux.[1] Still, Charles had not yet declared war, and these things were avowedly no more than the acts of desultory marauders. His ambassadors still demanded the restitution of Fougères, which possibly the English might now have been willing to accord if they could have had the French captures restored to them, but that in the surrender of the place they would have had to acknowledge Britanny as a feudal dependency of Charles.[2] Negotiations were accordingly broken off, and Charles having besides received particulars of a breach of the truce with Scotland in the preceding year, which even an English writer does not venture to defend,[3] at length made a formal declaration of hostilities.[4]

Never, it must be owned, did England incur the grave responsibilities of war with a greater degree of foolhardiness. Somerset himself seemed only now to have wakened up to the defenceless state of Normandy. He had just sent over Lord Hastings and the Abbot of Gloucester with a message to the

[1] *Reductio Normanniæ*, 251.   [2] *Ibid.* 503.
[3] 'Eodem anno [26 Hen. VI.], Rex visitans boreales partes Angliæ usque Donelmense monasterium, quasi omnes domini et alii plebei illius patriæ in magna multitudine quotidie ei in obviam ostendebant, quare, concilio habito, minus formidabant interrumpere trugas inter ipsum et Regem Scotiæ prius suis sigillis fidelitatis confirmatas; sed posterius hujus trugarum interruptio vertebatur Anglicis multo magis in dispendium quam honorem, quia recedente Rege Scoti magnam partem Northumbriæ bina vice absque repulsu destruxerunt, et juxta Carlele erant ex Anglicis capti et interfecti ad numerum duorum millium; et sic tandem Rex Angliæ cum ejus concilio pro saniori deliberatione cum damnis ad pacem inclinare reducitur.'—*Incerti Scriptoris Chronicum* (Ed. Giles), Hen. VI. p. 36.
[4] *Reductio Normanniæ*, 254.

55

THE PASTON LETTERS

English Parliament desiring immediate aid. The French, he said, were daily reinforcing their garrisons upon the frontier, and committing outrages against the truce. General musters were proclaimed throughout the kingdom, and every thirty men of the whole population were required to find a horseman fully equipped for war. Meanwhile, the English garrisons in Normandy were too feeble to resist attack. Not a single place was furnished with sufficient artillery, and the fortifications, almost everywhere, had fallen into such decay that even if filled with men and guns they could not possibly be defended. Besides this, the whole province was in such extreme poverty that it could no longer endure further imposts for the charges of its own defence.[1]

Progress of the French. No marvel, therefore, that the progress of the French arms was, from this time, uninterrupted. On the 19th July the town of Verneuil was taken by the aid of a miller who had been maltreated by some of the garrison; and, some time afterwards, the castle also surrendered. In August operations were carried on in several parts of the Duchy at once. Towns near the sea and towns near the French frontier were attacked at the same time; and Pont-Audemer, Lisieux, Mantes, Vernon, and other places were recovered from the English. Then followed in quick succession the capture of Essay, Fécamp, Harcourt, Chambrois, Roche-Guyon, and Coutances. In October, Rouen, the capital of the province, was invested. On the 19th the inhabitants with one accord rose in arms against the English, who found it necessary to retreat into the castle. In this stronghold Somerset himself was assailed by the King of France, and, after a vain attempt to secure better terms, agreed to surrender not only it but the fortresses of Arques, Caudebec, and several other places, leaving the gallant Talbot, Earl of Shrewsbury, as a hostage until they were delivered up. Meanwhile, the Duke of Britanny overran Lower Normandy and recovered his own Fougères after a siege of little more than a month. François L'Arragonois, finding no hope of succours, surrendered the place and afterwards went over to the French.

[1] *Rolls of Parl.* v. 147.

56

INTRODUCTION

In short, before the end of the year, the English had lost nearly everything in the North of France. The inhabitants everywhere conspired to betray towns and garrisons, and every man not English-born took part against the English. Even King René, Henry's father-in-law, assisted Charles at the siege of Rouen, and shared the honours of his triumphal entry. At the end of the year 1449 the English held nothing in Normandy except a few towns upon the sea-coast or a little way inland—the chief of these being Honfleur, Bayeux, Caen, and Cherbourg. The last-named fortress remained untaken till the 12th of August in the following year. When it surrendered, the whole of Normandy was finally lost.

The news of these reverses so rapidly following each other of course produced in England the most profound dissatisfaction. The Parliament to which Somerset had applied for aid had been removed after Whitsunday to Winchester on account of the insalubrity of the air in London and Westminster, and had been finally dissolved on the 16th of July. A new Parliament was then called for a winter session to provide for the defence of Normandy, when, in fact, it was too late.[1] By the *Unpopularity of Suffolk.* time it had assembled Rouen was already lost. The secret odium with which the policy of Suffolk had been viewed for years past could now no longer be restrained. It was difficult to persuade the many that the disgrace which had befallen the English arms was not due to treachery as much as to incompetence. The cession of Maine and Anjou was more loudly blamed than ever, and Suffolk was considered to have negotiated the king's marriage mainly with a view to his own advantage. It was remembered how he had once imprudently boasted that he possessed no less weight in the counsels of the King of France than in those of his own sovereign; it was again murmured that he had been the cause of Gloucester's death. And notwithstanding the protection of the Court, these feelings found expression in Parliament.

[1] *Rolls of Parl.* v. 143, 171. Even when the new Parliament met at Westminster on the 6th November it was obliged to adjourn to the City of London on account of the unhealthiness of the air. We must remember that Westminster was then little better than a flat muddy island, with a vast extent of marshy land and stagnant pools between Pimlico and the Thames.

57

THE PASTON LETTERS

A.D. 1450. At the beginning of the New Year, an incident occurred *Murder of the Bishop of Chichester.* which served still further to precipitate his ruin. Adam de Moleyns, Bishop of Chichester, keeper of the Privy Seal, who, as we have seen, had been sent over to France in the beginning of 1448, to arrange the peaceful cession of Le Mans, was at this time sent to Portsmouth to pay the wages of certain soldiers and sailors. He was a scholar as well as a statesman, and corresponded occasionally with the celebrated Æneas Sylvius, afterwards Pope Pius II.[1] But, like Suffolk, he was believed to make his own advantage out of public affairs. He had the reputation of being very covetous; the king's treasury was ill supplied with money, and he endeavoured to force the men to be satisfied with less than their due. On this they broke out into open mutiny, cried out that he was one of those who had sold Normandy, and thereupon put him to death.[2] This was on the 9th day of January 1450. During the altercation he let fall some words, probably in justification of his own conduct, which were considered to reflect most seriously upon that of the Duke of Suffolk,[3] and a cry arose for the duke's impeachment in Parliament.

It must certainly be acknowledged by any candid student of history that the state of the English Constitution in early times did not admit of true and impartial justice being done to an accused minister. So long as a man in Suffolk's position was upheld by the power of the Crown, it was to the last degree dangerous to say anything against him; but when the voice of complaint could no longer be restrained, the protection he had before received ceased to be of any use to him. It became then quite as dangerous to say anything in his favour as it had been formerly to accuse him. The Crown could not make common cause with one whose conduct was under suspicion; for the king could do no wrong, and the minister must be the scapegoat. The party, therefore, which would insist on any inquiry into the conduct of a minister, knew well that they must succeed in getting him condemned, or be branded as traitors

[1] *Æneæ Sylvii Epp.* 80, 186.
[2] According to his friend, Æneas Sylvius, the mode of death inflicted on him was decapitation. (*Opera,* 443.) [3] *Rolls of Parl.* v. 176.

58

INTRODUCTION

themselves. Such proceedings accordingly began inevitably with intrigue. Lord Cromwell was Suffolk's enemy at the council-table, and used his influence secretly with members of the House of Commons, to get them to bring forward an impeachment in that chamber. That he was a dangerous opponent Suffolk himself was very well aware. A little before Christmas, William Tailboys, one of the duke's principal supporters, had set a number of armed men in wait for him at the door of the Star Chamber, where the council met, and Lord Cromwell narrowly escaped being killed. The attempt, however, failed, and Tailboys was committed to the Tower; from which it would seem that he must soon afterwards have been released. Cromwell then brought an action against him in the Court of Exchequer to recover damages for the assault, and was awarded £3000; on which Tailboys was committed to the Sheriff of London's prison; and this was all the redress obtained by Cromwell till, by a special Act in the ensuing Parliament, Tailboys was removed from that place of confinement, and lodged in the Tower once more, for a period of twelve months. Owing to the king's protection he was not brought to trial.[1]

An evil day, nevertheless, had arrived for the Duke of Suffolk, which not all the influence of the king, nor the still greater influence of Margaret of Anjou, who owed to him her proud position as Henry's consort, was able to avert. On the 22nd of January the duke presented a petition to the king that he might be allowed to clear himself before Parliament of the imputations which had been cast on him in consequence of the dying words of Bishop Moleyns. He begged the king to remember how his father had died in the service of King Henry v. at Harfleur—how his elder brother had been with that king at Agincourt—how two other brothers had fallen in the king's own days at Jargeau, when he himself was taken prisoner and had to pay £20,000 for his ransom—how his

[1] W. Worc. *Rolls of Parl.* v. 200. I find by an entry in the *Controlment Roll,* 30 Hen. VI., that on St. Bartholomew's Day, 1451, William Tailboys and nineteen other persons belonging to South Kyme, in Lincolnshire, were outlawed at the suit of Elizabeth, widow of John Saunderson, for the murder of her husband.

59

THE PASTON LETTERS

fourth brother had been a hostage for him in the enemies' hands and died there. He also reminded the king that he had borne arms for four-and-thirty years, had been thirty years a Knight of the Garter, and had served in the wars abroad for seventeen years at a time, without ever coming home. Since then he had been fifteen years in England about the king's person, and he prayed God that if ever he died otherwise than in his bed, it might be in maintaining the quarrel that he had been at all times true to Henry.[1]

Four days after this a deputation from the Commons waited on the Lord Chancellor, desiring that as Suffolk had confessed the prevalence of injurious reports against him, he might be committed to custody. This request was laid by the Chancellor before the king and council on the following day, and the opinion of the judges being taken as to the legality of the proposed arrest, he was allowed to remain at liberty until a definite charge should be brought against him. Such a charge was accordingly declared two days later by the Speaker, who did not hesitate to tell the Lord Chancellor, in the name of the Commons, that Suffolk was believed to be in league with the French king to promote an invasion of England, and had fortified the castle of Wallingford with a view of assisting the invaders. The duke, on this, was committed to the Tower.

Suffolk impeached. On the 7th of February he was formally impeached by the Commons. A copy of the articles of impeachment will be found in the Paston Letters (No. 76). Nothing was said in them of the fortification of Wallingford Castle, but a number of specific charges were made, many of them authenticated by the exact day and place when the alleged treasonable acts were committed, tending to show that in his communications with the French he had been invariably opposed to the interests of his own country. It was alleged that he had been bribed to deliver Anjou and Maine, and that as long ago as the year 1440 he was influenced by corrupt motives to promote the liberation of the Duke of Orleans ; that he had disclosed the secrets of the English council-chamber to the French king's ambassadors ; that he had even given information by which France had

[1] *Rolls of Parl.* v. 176.

60

INTRODUCTION

profited in the war, and that he had rendered peace negotiations nugatory by letting the French know beforehand the instructions given to the English envoys. Further, in the midst of invasion and national disgrace, he had hoped to gratify his own ambition. The king, who was still childless, was to be deposed ; and the duke had actually hoped to make his own son king in his place. It seems that he had obtained some time before a grant of the wardship of Margaret Beaufort, daughter of the late Duke of Somerset, who was the nearest heir to the Crown in the Lancastrian line, and since his arrest he had caused her to be married to his own son, Lord John De la Pole.[1] Such was the foundation on which the worst charge rested.

A month passed before he was heard in his own defence. The Commons impeached, but it was for the Lords to try him. Meanwhile, another bill of indictment had been prepared by the malice of his enemies, in which all the failures of his policy were visited upon him as crimes, and attributed to the worst and most selfish motives. For his own private gain, he had caused the Crown to be prodigal of grants to other persons, till it was so impoverished that the wages of the household were unpaid, and the royal manors left to fall into decay. He had granted the earldom of Kendal, with large possessions both in England and in Guienne, to a Gascon, who ultimately sided with the French, but had happened to marry his niece. He had weakened the king's power in Guienne, alienated the Count of Armagnac, and caused a band of English to attack the king's German allies ; he had disposed of offices to unworthy persons without consulting the council, granted important possessions in Normandy to the French king's councillors, given to the French queen £13,000 of the revenues of England, appropriated and misapplied the king's treasure and the subsidies granted by Parliament for the keeping of the sea. These and some minor charges formed the contents of the second bill of indictment.[2]

[1] So it is stated in the impeachment. According to the inquisition on Suffolk's death, his son was born on the 27th September 1442, and was therefore at this time only in his eighth year.—Napier's *Historical Notices of Swyncombe and Ewelme*, 108.
[2] *Rolls of Parl.* v. 179-182.

61

THE PASTON LETTERS

He was brought from the Tower on the 9th day of March, and required to make answer before the Lords to the contents of both bills. He requested of the king that he might have copies, which were allowed him ; and that he might prepare his answer more at ease, he was removed for a few days to a *His defence.* tower within the king's palace at Westminster. On the 13th he was sent for to make his answer before the king and lords. Kneeling before the throne, he replied to each of the eight articles in the first bill separately. He denied their truth entirely, and offered to prove them false in whatever manner the king would direct. He declared it absurd to consider Margaret Beaufort as heir-presumptive to the Crown, and used other arguments to show the improbability of his designs on the succession. In all else he showed that the other lords of the council were quite as much committed as he ; and as to the delivery of Anjou and Maine, he laid the responsibility entirely upon the murdered Bishop of Chichester.[1]

Next day, the Chief Justice, by the king's command, asked the Lords what advice they would give the king in the matter. It was a Saturday, and the Lords deferred their answer till the following Monday ; but on the Monday nothing was done. On the Tuesday the king sent for all the Lords then in London to attend him in his own palace, where they met in an inner chamber. When they were assembled, Suffolk was sent for, and kneeling down, was addressed briefly by the Lord Chancellor. He was reminded that he had made answer to the first bill of the Commons without claiming the right of being tried by the peers ; and he was asked if he had anything further to say upon the subject. He replied that the accusations were too horrible to be further spoken of, and he hoped he had sufficiently answered all that touched the king's person, and the state of his kingdom. Nevertheless, he submitted himself entirely to the king, to do with him whatever he thought good.[2]

On this an answer was returned to him in the king's name by the Lord Chancellor. A miserably weak and evasive answer it was, showing clearly that the king desired to protect

[1] *Rolls of Parl.* v. 182.   [2] *Ibid.*

62

INTRODUCTION

his favourite, but had not the manliness to avow he thought him worthy of protection. The Lord Chancellor was commissioned to say, that as to the very serious charges contained in the first bill, the king regarded Suffolk as not having been proved either guilty or innocent ; but touching those contained in the second bill, which amounted only to misprisions, as Suffolk did not put himself upon his peerage, but submitted entirely to the king, the latter had determined, without consulting the Lords, and not in the way of judgment (for he was *He is not sitting in tribunal), but merely in virtue of the duke's own ordered to submission, to bid him absent himself from England for five leave years, from the first day of May ensuing.[1] England.*

It is clear upon the face of the matter, that although the king was made to take the sole responsibility of this decision, it was really a thing arranged, and not arranged without difficulty, between the friends of Suffolk and some of the leading members of the House of Lords. Immediately after it was pronounced, Viscount Beaumont, who was one of Suffolk's principal allies, made a protest on behalf of the Lords, that what the king had just done, he had done by his own authority, without their advice and counsel. He accordingly besought the king that their protest might be recorded in the rolls of Parliament, for their protection, so that the case might not henceforth be made a precedent in derogation of the privileges of the peerage.[2] Thus it was clearly hoped on all sides a great crisis had been averted. Suffolk was got rid of, but not condemned. A victim was given over to popular resentment, but the rights of the Peers for the future were to be maintained. And though the Crown lowered itself by an avowed dereliction of duty, it was not severely censured for preferring expediency to justice.

On the following night the duke left Westminster for Suffolk. The people of London were intensely excited, and about two thousand persons sallied out to St. Giles' hoping to intercept his departure, but they succeeded only in capturing his horse and some of his servants, whom they maltreated, as might have been expected. Even after this the excitement

[1] *Rolls of Parl.* v. 183.   [2] *Ibid.*

63

He embarks for Flanders.

was scarcely diminished. Seditious manifestoes were thrown about in public and secretly posted on church doors.[1] The duke had more than a month to prepare for leaving England, and seems to have spent the time in the county of Suffolk. On Thursday the 30th of April he embarked at Ipswich for Flanders ; but before going he assembled the gentlemen of the county, and, taking the sacrament, swore he was innocent of the sale of Normandy and of the other treasons imputed to him.[2] He also wrote an interesting letter of general admonitions for the use of his young son, at that time not eight years old, whom he was not to see again for at least five years, and too probably not at all. This letter, which is known to us only by a copy preserved in the Paston correspondence (No. 117), can hardly fail to awaken sympathy with the writer. As an evidence of unaffected piety to God and sincere loyalty to his king, it will probably outweigh with most readers all the aspersions cast by Parliament on the purity of his intentions.

Two ships and a little pinnace conveyed him from the Suffolk coast southwards till he stood off Dover, when he despatched the small vessel with letters to certain persons in Calais to ascertain how he should be received if he landed there. The pinnace was intercepted by some ships which seem to have been lying in wait for his passage ; and when it was ascertained where the duke actually was, they immediately bore down upon him. Foremost among the pursuers was a ship called the *Nicholas of the Tower*, the master of which, on nearing Suffolk's vessel, sent out a boat to ask who they were. Suffolk made answer in person, and said that he was going by the king's command to Calais ; on which they told him he must speak with their master. They accordingly conveyed him and two or three others in their boat to the *Nicholas*. When he came on board the master saluted him with the words, 'Welcome, traitor !' and sent to know if the shipmen meant to take part with the duke, which they at once disowned all intention of doing. The duke was then informed that he must die, but was allowed the whole of the next day and night to confess himself and prepare for the event.[3] On Monday

[1] Rymer, xi. 268. [2] W. Worc. 468, 469. [3] *English Chronicle*, ed. Davies, p. 69.

64

INTRODUCTION

Is murdered at sea.

the 2nd of May the rovers consummated their design. In sight of all his men Suffolk was drawn out of the *Nicholas* into a boat in which an axe and block were prepared. One of the crew, an Irish churl, then bade him lay down his head, telling him in cruel mockery that he should be fairly dealt with and die upon a sword. A rusty sword was brought out accordingly, and with nearly half a dozen strokes the fellow clumsily cut off his head. He was then stripped of his russet gown and velvet doublet. His body was brought to land and thrown upon the sands at Dover ; and his men were at the same time allowed to disembark.[1]

The source from which we learn most of these particulars is a letter of William Lomner to John Paston written when the news was fresh. The writer seems to have been quite overpowered by the tragic character of the event, and declares he had so blurred the writing with tears that he fears it would not be easy to decipher. Indications of genuine human feeling like this are so rare in letters of an early date that we are in danger of attributing to the men of those days a coldness and brutality which were by no means so universal as we are apt to suppose. The truth is that when men related facts they regarded their own feelings as an impertinence having nothing whatever to do with the matter in hand.[2] The art of letter-writing, besides, had not yet acquired the freedom of later days. It was used, in the main, for business purposes only. We shall meet, it is true, in this very correspondence, with one or two early specimens of jesting epistles ; but, on the whole, I suspect paper was too valuable a commodity and writing too great a labour to be wasted on things irrelevant.

But whatever feeling may have been excited by the news of Suffolk's murder in men like William Lomner, who possibly

[1] *Paston Letters*, Nos. 120, 121.
[2] Even the passage above referred to would probably be an illustration of this if the original letter were examined. As we have reprinted it from Fenn, it stands thus : 'Right worshipful Sir, I recommend me to you, and am right sorry of that I shall say, *and have so wesshe this little bill with sorrowful tears that uneathes ye shall read it.*' The words in italics would probably be found to be an interlineation in the original, for though they stand at the beginning of the letter, they were clearly written after it was penned, and the only reason why they were inserted was to excuse the illegibility of the writing.

VOL. I.—E

65

THE PASTON LETTERS

may have known the duke personally, we may well believe that the nation at large was neither afflicted nor very greatly shocked at the event. Even the prior of Croyland, the head of a great religious community in Lincolnshire, speaks of it as the just punishment of a traitor, and has not a word to say in reprobation.[1] Mocking dirges were composed and spread abroad, in which his partisans were represented as chanting his funeral service, and a blessing was invoked on the heads of his murderers. These were but the last of a host of satires in which the public indignation had for months past found a vent.[2] Suffolk had been represented on his imprisonment as a fox driven into his hole, who must on no account be let out again. He had been rhymed at as the Ape with his Clog who had tied Talbot our good dog, in allusion to the fact of Talbot, Earl of Shrewsbury, having been given up as a hostage to the French after the surrender of Rouen.[3] He had been reviled as an upstart who had usurped the place of better men, and who systematically thwarted and neutralised all that better men could do. If any one wept for the fall of such a man, it was not on public grounds.

As a specimen of these political satires we cannot resist the temptation to quote a short poem which must have been composed towards the close of the year 1449, after the surrender of Rouen and before Suffolk's fall. It is far less personal than the others, being not so much an invective against Suffolk as a wail over the loss of England's great men, and the decay of her fortunes. The leading statesmen and warriors of that and the former age are here spoken of by their badges, which the reader will find interpreted in the margin :—

'The Root [a] is dead, the Swan [b] is gone,
  The fiery Cresset [c] hath lost his light.
Therefore England may make great moan
  Were not the help of God Almight'.
The Castle [d] is won where care begun,
  The Portè-cullis [e] is laid adown ;
Yclosèd we have our Velvet Hat [f]
  That covered us from many stormes brown.

[a] The Regent Bedford.
[b] Humphrey, Duke of Glo'ster.
[c] The last Duke of Exeter.
[d] Rouen Castle.
[e] The Duke of Somerset.
[f] The Cardinal Beaufort.

[1] *Contin. of Croyland Chronicle*, p. 525.
[2] Wright's *Political Poems* (in Rolls series), ii. 232. [3] *Ibid.* 222, 224.

66

INTRODUCTION

The White Lion [g] is laid to sleep,
  Thorough the envy of th' Apè [h] Clog ;
And he is bounden that our door should keep ;
  That is Talbot, our good dog.
The Fisher [i] has lost his angle hook ;
  Get them again when it will be.
Our Millè-sail [k] will not about,
  It hath so long gone empty.
The Bear [l] is bound that was so wild,
  For he hath lost his Ragged Staff.
The Carte-nathe [m] is spoke-less
  For the counsel that he gaf.
The Lily [n] is both fair and green ;
  The Conduit [o] runneth not, I wean.
The Cornish Chough [p] oft with his train
  Hath made our Eagle [q] blind.
The White Hart [r] is put out of mind
  Because he will not to them consent ;
Therefore, the Commons saith, is both true and kind,
  Both in Sussex and in Kent.
The Water Bouge [s] and the Wine Botell
  With the Fetterlock's [t] chain bene fast.
The Wheat Ear [u] will them sustain
  As long as he may endure and last.
The Boar [w] is far into the West,
  That should us help with shield and spear.
The Falcon [x] fleeth and hath no rest
  Till he wit where to bigg his nest.'

[g] The Duke of Norfolk, who had gone on pilgrimage to Rome in 1447. (Dugdale.)
[h] The Duke of Suffolk.
[i] Lord Fauconberg who was taken prisoner by the French at the capture of Pont-de-l'Arche.
[k] Robert, Lord Willoughby.
[l] The Earl of Warwick.
[m] The Duke of Buckingham.
[n] Thomas Daniel. He and the two next are courtiers.
[o] John Norris.
[p] John Trevilian.
[q] The King.
[r] Earl of Arundel.
[s] Lord Bouchier.
[t] Prior of St. John's.
[u] The Duke of Exeter.
[w] The Earl of Devonshire.
[x] The Duke of York, who had been sent into Ireland to be out of the way.

Defeat of Sir T. Kiriel.

Almost concurrently with the news of Suffolk's murder came tidings, mentioned by William Lomner in the very same letter, of another disaster in France, more gloomy, if possible, than any that had occurred before. A force under Sir Thomas Kiriel had been sent to the aid of the Duke of Somerset in Normandy after the loss of Rouen. It disembarked at Cherbourg, and proceeding towards Caen, where the duke had now taken up his position, besieged and took Valognes. They were now in full communication with the garrisons of Caen and Bayeux, when they were suddenly attacked at the village of Fourmigni, and routed with great slaughter. Between three and four thousand Englishmen were left dead upon the field ; Kiriel himself was taken prisoner ; even the brave Matthew Gough (well known to Frenchmen of that day as Matago) found it needful to fall back with his company of

67

THE PASTON LETTERS

1500 men for the safeguard of Bayeux, which a month after-wards he was compelled after all to give up to the enemy.[1]

Meanwhile the Parliament, which had been prorogued over Easter, was ordered to meet again at Leicester instead of Westminster. The reason given for the change of place was still, as before, the unhealthiness of the air about Westminster; and doubtless it was a very true reason. It is possible, how-ever, that the political atmosphere of London was quite as oppressive to the Court as the physical atmosphere could be to the Parliament. During their sitting at Leicester a much needed subsidy was voted to the king, and an Act passed for the application of certain revenues to the expenses of the Royal Household in order to stop the exactions of purveyors. But they had hardly sat a month when the session was suddenly put an end to from a cause which we proceed to notice.

Rebellion of Jack Cade

The murder of the Duke of Suffolk had not made things better than they had been before. The ablest of the ministers, who had hitherto guided the king's counsels, was now removed, but his place was left for a time altogether unsupplied. The men of Suffolk's party, such as Lord Say, Viscount Beaumont, and Thomas Daniel, still remained about the king, and were nearly as unpopular as he had been. The offices formerly held by Suffolk were divided among them and their particular friends.[2] Even if the Court had desired to call in men of greater weight, they were not then at hand. The Duke of Somerset was in France, and the Duke of York in Ireland; so that some time must have elapsed before either of them could have taken part in public affairs at home. Meanwhile it was said that the resentment of the Court for Suffolk's

[1] Berry's narrative in Stevenson's *Expulsion of the English from Normandy*, 336. *Wars of the Engl.* ii. [360]. *Paston Letters*, No. 120.
[2] *See* No. 123. William Worcester says Lord Beauchamp was made treasurer, and Lord Cromwell the king's chamberlain. Lord Beauchamp's appointment is on the *Patent Rolls*. See *Calendarium Rot. Patent*, p. 294.

INTRODUCTION

murder would be visited upon the county of Kent; and the county of Kent was of opinion that it suffered abuses enough already. The exactions of the king's officers, both in the way of taxation and purveyance, were felt to be extortionate and capricious. The collectors of the revenue were appointed by the knights of the shire, and these, instead of being freely chosen by the people, were but the nominees of a few great men who compelled their tenants to vote according to their pleasure. There were, besides, grave cases of injustice in which people were accused of treason, and kept in prison without trial, on the information of persons about the Court who had influence to obtain grants of their lands from the Crown.

Hence arose Jack Cade's rebellion, a movement which we must not permit ourselves to look upon as a vulgar outbreak of the rabble. Whole districts of Kent, Surrey, and Sussex rose in arms, clamouring for redress of grievances; and it is certain that the insurgents met with a large amount of sym-pathy, even from those who did not actually take part with them.[1] As their leader, they selected a man who called him-self Mortimer, and who, besides some experience in war, was evidently possessed of no small talent for generalship. It afterwards turned out that his real name was Cade, that he was a native of Ireland, and that he had been living a year before in the household of Sir Thomas Dacre in Sussex, when he was obliged to abjure the kingdom for killing a woman who was with child. He then betook himself to France and served in the French war against England. What induced him to return does not appear, unless we may suppose, which is not unlikely, that some misdemeanour when in the service of France made the French soil fully as dangerous to him as the English. In England he seems to have assumed the name

Cade's Rebellion.

[1] The late Mr. Durrant Cooper, in an interesting paper read before a meeting of the Kent Archæological Society, examined the long list of names given on the *Patent Roll* of 28 Henry VI., and proved from them that the insurrection was by no means of a very plebeian or disorderly character. 'In several hundreds,' he says, 'the constables duly, and as if legally, summoned the men; and many parishes, particularly Marden, Penshurst, Hawkhurst, Northfleet, Boughton-Malherbe, Smarden, and Pluckley, furnished as many men as could be found in our day fit for arms.'

THE PASTON LETTERS

of Aylmer, and passed himself off as a physician. He married a squire's daughter, and dressed in scarlet; and when the rebellion broke out in Kent he called himself John Mortimer, a cousin of the Duke of York.

The first disturbances took place at Whitsuntide in the latter end of May. In the second week of June[1] a consider-able army from the counties of Kent, Surrey, and Sussex encamped upon Blackheath. The king, who, on receiving news of the rising, had dissolved the parliament then sitting at Leicester, arrived in London on Saturday the 13th, and took up his quarters at the priory of St. John's, near Smith-field. He had with him 20,000 men under arms, but for some reason or other did not set out against the rebels till the following Thursday, the 18th.[1] They, meanwhile, had with-drawn in the night-time,[2] and the king and his host occupied their position on Blackheath. The royal forces, however, pro-ceeded no further. Only a detachment, under Sir Humphrey Stafford and his brother William, was sent to pursue the insurgents. An encounter took place at Sevenoaks on the 18th,[3] in which both the Staffords were killed. Their defeat spread dismay and disaffection in the royal camp. The noble-men who had accompanied the king to Blackheath could no longer keep their men together, the latter protesting that unless justice were done on certain traitors who had misled the king, they would go over to the Captain of Kent. To satisfy them, Lord Say was arrested and sent to the Tower; but even with this concession the king did not dare presume upon their loyalty. He withdrew to Greenwich, and the whole of his army dispersed. The king himself returned to London by water, and made preparations during the next two or three days to remove to Kenilworth. The mayor and commons of the city went to him to beseech him to remain, offering to live

[1] These dates were given differently in previous issues of this Introduction. For a rectification of the chronology I am indebted to Kriehn's *English Rising in 1450*, pp. 125 and following.
[2] According to No. 119 of our collection this retreat would appear to have been on the 22nd June, but that date is certainly an error.
[3] The 18th June is given as the date of Sir Humphrey Stafford's death in *Inquis. post mortem*, 28 Henry VI. No. 7.

INTRODUCTION

and die with him, and pay half a year's cost of his household. But all was to no purpose. The king had not even the manli-ness of Richard II. at Smithfield, and he took his departure to Kenilworth.[1]

The city, thus deserted by its sovereign, knew not for a time what to do. A party within the Common Council itself ventured to open negotiations with the insurgents, and Alder-man Cooke passed to and fro under the safe-conduct of the Captain.[2] To many it may have seemed doubtful loyalty to support the government of Lord Say and his friends against an oppressed population. On the 1st day of July[3] the insur-gents entered Southwark. On the 2nd a Common Council was called by the Lord Mayor to provide means for resisting their entry into the city; but the majority voted for their free admission, and Alderman Robert Horne, who was the leading speaker against them, was committed to prison for his boldness. That same afternoon the so-called Mortimer and his followers passed over London Bridge into the city. The Captain, after passing the drawbridge, hewed the ropes asunder with his sword. His first proceedings were marked by order and discipline. He issued proclamations in the king's name against robbery and forced requisitions, but he rode through the different streets as if to place the capital under military govern-ment; and when he came to London Stone, he struck it with his sword, saying, 'Now is Mortimer lord of this city.' Finally, he gave instructions to the Lord Mayor about the order to be kept within his jurisdiction, and returned for the night to his quarters in Southwark. On the following morn-ing, Friday the 3rd, he again entered the city, when he caused Lord Say to be sent for from the Tower. That no resistance was made to this demand by Lord Scales, who had the keeping of the fortress, may seem strange. But there was a reason for it which most of the chroniclers do not tell us. The king had

The rebels enter London.

[1] W. Worc.—*Three Fifteenth Century Chronicles* (edited by me for the Camden Soc.), 67.—Chronicle in MS. Cott. Vitell. A. xvi.
[2] Holinshed, iii. 632.
[3] I leave this part of the story as it was originally written, though here, too, the chronology seems to require rectification, especially from sources since published, for which the reader may consult Kriehn's work, p. 129.

THE PASTON LETTERS

been obliged to listen to the grievances of his 'Commons' and to withdraw his protection from his favourites. He had granted a commission 'to certain lords and to the mayor and divers justices, to inquire of all persons that were traitors, extortioners, or oppressors of the king's people.'[1] Lord Say was accordingly formally arraigned at a regular sessions at the Guildhall. But when the unfortunate nobleman claimed the constitutional privilege of being tried by his peers, the pretence of law was finally laid aside. A company of the insurgents took him from the officers and hurried him off to the Standard in Cheap, where, before he was half shriven, his head was cut off and stuck upon a long pole. A son-in-law of his named Crowmer, who was then very unpopular as sheriff of Kent, met with a similar fate. He was beheaded in Cade's presence at Mile End. Barbarity now followed violence. The lifeless heads of Say and Crowmer were carried through the streets, and made to kiss each other. At the same time one Bailey was beheaded at Whitechapel on a charge of necromancy, the real cause of his death being, as it was reported, that he was an old acquaintance of Cade's who might have revealed something of his past history.

It may have been the expectation of inevitable exposure that induced Cade now to relax discipline, and set an example of spoliation himself. He entered and pillaged the house of Philip Malpas, an alderman known as a friend of the Court, and therefore unpopular in the city. Next day he dined at a house in the parish of St. Margaret Pattens, and then robbed his host. At each of these acts of robbery the rabble were sharers of the spoil. But, of course, such proceedings completely alienated all who had anything to lose, and the mayor and aldermen began to devise measures for expelling Cade and his followers from the city. For this end they negotiated with Lord Scales and Matthew Gough, who had then the keeping of the Tower.

For three days successively Cade had entered the city with his men, and retired in the evening to Southwark. But on Sunday, the 5th of July, he for some reason remained in South-

[1] MS. Vitellius A. xvi. fol. 107, quoted by Kriehn, p. 92.

72

INTRODUCTION

wark all day. In the evening the mayor and citizens, with a force under Matthew Gough, came and occupied London Bridge to prevent the Kentish men again entering the city. The Captain called his men to arms, and attacked the citizens **Battle on** with such impetuosity, that he drove them back from the **London** Southwark end of the bridge to the drawbridge in the centre. **Bridge** This the insurgents set on fire, after inflicting great losses on the citizens, many of whom were slain or drowned in defending it. Matthew Gough himself was among those who perished. Still, the fight was obstinately contested, the advantage being for the moment now with one party and now with the other. It continued all through the night till nine on the following morning ; when at last the Kentish men began to give way, and a truce was made for a certain number of hours.

A favourable opportunity now presented itself for mediation. Although the king had retired to Kenilworth, he had left behind him in London some leading members of his council, among whom were Cardinal Kemp, Archbishop of York,[1] then Lord Chancellor, and Waynflete, Bishop of Winchester. The former had taken refuge in the Tower, under the protection of Lord Scales ; and he called to him the latter, who lay concealed at Holywell.[2] A conference was arranged between them and the insurgents, and both the Cardinal and Bishop Waynflete[3] with some others crossed the river and met with Cade in St. Margaret's Church in Southwark. In the end matters were satisfactorily arranged, and the bishop produced two general pardons prepared by the Chancellor, the

[1] Inaccurately called Archbishop of Canterbury by Fabyan and others. He was not translated to Canterbury till 1452.

[2] Hall's *Chronicle*. Holy Well was a mineral spring to the north of London, much frequented before the Reformation, when it was stopped up as being considered a place of superstitious resort. A century afterwards it was discovered anew by a Mr. Sadler, from whom the locality is named to this day Sadler's Wells.

[3] Some doubt seems to be thrown on Hall's statement that both prelates crossed the river, as earlier writers say the Chancellor *sent* pardons under the Great Seal. William Worcester, moreover, makes no mention of the cardinal, but says that the Bishop of Winchester and others of the king's council spoke with the Captain of Kent. But the 'Short English Chronicle' in the *Three Fifteenth Century Chronicles*, edited by me for the Camden Society in 1880 (p. 68), does exactly the reverse, and omitting all reference to the Bishop of Winchester, says: 'And forthewithe went the Chaunseler to the Capteyne and sessed him and gave him a chartur and his men an other.'

73

THE PASTON LETTERS

first for the Captain himself, and the second for his followers. The offer was embraced with eagerness. The men were by this time disgusted with their leader, and alarmed at the result of their own acts. By thousands they accepted the amnesty and began to return homewards. But Cade, who knew that his pardon would avail him little when the history of his past life came to be investigated, wisely made friends to himself after the fashion of the Unjust Steward. He broke open the gaols of the King's Bench and Marshalsea, and formed a new company out of the liberated prisoners.[1] He then despatched to Rochester a barge laden with the goods he had taken from Malpas and others in London, and prepared to go thither himself by land. He and his new following appear to have been still in Southwark on the 8th of July, but to have passed through Dartford to Rochester on the 9th, where they continued still in arms against the king on the 10th and 11th.[2] An attempt they made upon the castle of Queenborough was resisted by Sir Roger Chamberlain, to whom a reward was given in the following year in acknowledgment of his services.[3] Meanwhile a proclamation was issued offering a reward of a thousand marks for Cade's apprehension, and ten marks for that of any of his followers ; 'for,' says a contemporary chronicler, 'it was openly known that his name was not Mortimer ; his name was John Cade ; and therefore his charter stood in no strength.'[4]

The feeble remains of the rebellion were already quarrelling about the booty Cade had conveyed out of London. Their leader now took horse and escaped in disguise towards the woody country about Lewes. He was pursued by Alexander Iden, a gentleman who had just been appointed sheriff of Kent **Capture** in place of the murdered Crowmer. Iden overtook him in a **and death** garden at Heathfield, and made him prisoner, not without a **of Cade.** scuffle, in which Cade was mortally wounded, so that on being conveyed to London he died on the way. It only remained

[1] Hall's *Chronicle*.
[2] See *Act of Attainder*, 29 Hen. VI. *Rolls of Parl.* vi. 224.
[3] Devon's *Issue Rolls*, 471. Davies' *English Chron.* 67.
[4] *Three Fifteenth Century Chronicles*, 68.

74

INTRODUCTION

to use his carcass as a terror to evil-doers. His head was cut off and placed upon London Bridge, with the face looking towards Kent. His body was drawn through the streets of London, then quartered, and the quarters sent to four different places very widely apart,—one of them to Blackheath, one to Norwich, one to Salisbury, and one to Gloucester.[1]

If the dispersion of traitors' limbs for exhibition in many places could have effectually repressed disloyalty, the whole realm ought now to have been at rest. The quarters of another Kentish rebel, who, under the name of Bluebeard, had raised disturbances in the preceding February, were at that moment undergoing public exhibition in London, Norwich, and the Cinque Ports. Those of two others were about this time despatched by the sheriffs of London to Chichester, Rochester, Portsmouth, Colchester, Stamford, Coventry, Newbury, and Winchester. The heads of all these wretches were set upon London Bridge, which in the course of this miserable year bore no less than twenty-three such horrid ornaments.[2]

But with all this, sedition was not put down, even in the **Further** county of Kent ; for I find by the evidence of authentic **disturb-** records that a new rising took place in August at Feversham, **ances.** under one William Parminter, who, undeterred by the fate of Cade, gathered about him 400 men, and called himself *the second* Captain of Kent. This affair is quite unnoticed by historians, and all I know of it is derived from a pardon to one of those engaged in it.[3] But even Parminter was not the last 'Captain of Kent' that made his appearance this year ; for the very same title was immediately afterwards assumed by one John Smyth, for whose capture a reward of £40 was ordered to be paid to the Duke of Somerset on the 3rd of October.[4] And the chroniclers, though they do not mention these disturbances, tell us that such things were general over

[1] W. Worc. Fabyan. Davies' *English Chronicle* (Camden Soc.), 67. Ellis' *Letters*, 2nd Series i. 115.
[2] Ellis, *ib.* MS. Vitell. A. xvi.
[3] *See* document in Appendix to this Introduction ; also Devon's *Issue Rolls*, p. 472. It would seem as if the entry there dated 5th August ought to have been 5th September, as Parminter does not seem to have been taken even on the last day of August.
[4] Nicolas's *Proceedings of the Privy Council*, vi. 101.

75

THE PASTON LETTERS

all the kingdom. In Wiltshire, at the time that Cade was at Blackheath, William Ayscough, Bishop of Salisbury, had one day said mass at Edington, when he was dragged from the altar by a band of his own tenants and murdered in his alb and stole at the top of a neighbouring hill. He was the second bishop who had been murdered that year by the populace. Another insurrection in the same county in August is mentioned in a letter of James Gresham's, the number of the insurgents being reported at nine or ten thousand men.[1] These instances may suffice as evidence of the widespread troubles of the time.

Sir John Fastolf.

Of the degree of private suffering and misery inflicted in particular cases by these commotions we have a lively picture in Letter 126. At the time when Cade and his followers were encamped upon Blackheath, Sir John Fastolf, a noted warrior of the time, of whom we shall have much to say hereafter, was residing at his house in Southwark. He was a man who had not succeeded in standing well with his contemporaries, and the fact may have contributed not a little to the sensitiveness of a naturally irascible character. In one engagement with the French[2] he was actually accused of cowardice, a charge which he seems afterwards satisfactorily to have disproved. For some years, however, he had given up soldiering and returned to his native country, where he served the king in a different manner as a member of his Privy Council. But in this capacity too he was unpopular. His advice should have been valuable at least in reference to the affairs of France; but it does not seem to have been taken. The warnings and counsels which he gave with reference to the maintenance of the English conquests in France he caused his secretary, William Worcester, to put in writing for his justification; but though his admonitions were neglected by those to whom they were addressed, popular rumour held him partly accountable for the loss of Normandy. Of this opinion some evidence was given in the course of Cade's insurrection.

As a member of the King's Council Fastolf thought it

[1] See No. 131. [2] The Battle of Patay.

76

INTRODUCTION

right to send a messenger to ascertain what were the demands of the insurgents. He therefore commanded one John Payn, who was in his service, to take a man with him and two of the best horses of his stable, and ride to Blackheath. When he arrived there, Cade ordered him to be taken prisoner. To save his master's horses from being stolen, Payn gave them to the attendant, who galloped away with them as fast as he could, while he himself was brought before the Captain. Cade then asked him what he had come for, and why he had caused his fellow to run away with the horses. He answered that he had come to join some brothers of his wife, and other companions who were among the insurgents. On this some one called out to the Captain that he was a man of Sir John Fastolf's, and that the two horses were Sir John's. The Captain raised a cry of 'Treason!' and sent him through the camp with a herald of the Duke of Exeter before him, in the duke's coat-of-arms. At four quarters of the field the herald proclaimed with an *Oyez* that Payn had been sent as a spy upon them by the greatest traitor in England or France, namely, by one Sir John Fastolf, who had diminished all the garrisons of Normandy, Le Mans, and Maine, and thereby caused the loss of all the king's inheritance beyond sea. It was added that Sir John had garrisoned his place with the old soldiers of Normandy, to oppose the Commons when they came to Southwark; and, as the emissary of such a traitor, Payn was informed that he should lose his head.

John Payn and the rebels.

He was brought to the Captain's tent, where an axe and block were produced. But fortunately he had friends among the host; and Robert Poynings, Cade's swordbearer and carver, who afterwards married John Paston's sister Elizabeth, declared plainly that there should die a hundred or two others if Payn were put to death. He was therefore allowed to live on taking an oath that he would go to Southwark and arm himself, and return to join the Commons. He accordingly carried to Fastolf a statement of their demands, advising him at the same time to put away his old soldiers and withdraw himself into the Tower. The old warrior felt that the advice was prudent; he left but two of his servants in the place, and

77

THE PASTON LETTERS

but for Payn the insurgents would have burned it to the ground. The faithful dependant, however, had to pay the full penalty of his master's unpopularity. He seems to have entertained the rioters for some time at his own cost. Afterwards the Captain took from him some valuable clothes and armour, and sent men to ransack his chamber of bonds, money, and other stores. The insurgents also robbed his house in Kent, and threatened to harm his wife and children. Finally, on the night of the battle on London Bridge, Cade thrust him into the thickest of the combat, where he continued six hours unable to extricate himself, and was dangerously wounded.

To have passed through all this was surely a severe enough trial; yet after that commotion he had further trouble to endure. He was impeached by the Bishop of Rochester, and thrown into the Marshalsea by command of the queen. He was also threatened to be hanged, drawn, and quartered, in order that he might accuse his master Fastolf of treason; but in the end his friends succeeded in procuring for him a charter of pardon. To earn this, however, as we find from the document itself, he had to appear before the king in person, during a progress which he made in Kent the year after the rebellion, and, amid a crowd of other supplicants whose bodies were stripped naked down to their legs, humbly to beg for mercy.[1]

The Dukes of York and Somerset

The Duke of York.

Cade's rebellion was attributed by the Court to the machinations of the Duke of York. The disturbances that had prevailed for some months previously seem to have been partly associated with his name. When Adam de Moleyns, Bishop of Chichester, was murdered in the beginning of the year, the malcontents talked of inviting York over from Ireland to redress the wrongs of the people. The

[1] See Appendix to Introduction.

78

INTRODUCTION

exclusion of York and other lords of royal blood from the king's councils was also made an express ground of complaint by the Kentish insurgents. The repetition of his name in the mouths of the disaffected was anything but grateful to the party then in power. It was construed as being in itself an evidence of his disloyalty. But the popular complaints as to his treatment were both just and reasonable, for it was a matter that concerned the public weal. The rank, wealth, and lineage of the Duke of York, his connection with the blood-royal, his large possessions, and finally his well-proved ability both as a general and an administrator—all marked him out as one who ought to have been invited to take a leading part in the government of the realm; but a faction about the king had taken care to keep him as much as possible at a distance from the Court. Moreover, it had maligned and aspersed him in his absence, so that it would have been positively insecure for himself to allow the charges to accumulate. A time had clearly come when it was no longer his duty to obey the orders of others. His enemies were becoming more and more unpopular every day, and the only hope of improving the administration of affairs depended upon his taking the initiative.

He accordingly determined to avail himself of the privilege due to his rank, and lay his requests at the foot of the throne. A little before Michaelmas he came over from Ireland, collected 4000 of his retainers upon the Welsh Marches, and with them proceeded to London. His coming, although unsolicited by the king and without leave asked, was nevertheless not altogether unexpected. Attempts were made to stop his landing at Beaumaris, and bodies of men lay in wait for him in various places to interrupt his progress. For this, however, he could not have been unprepared. He knew well the hatred entertained towards him at the Court, for he had experienced pretty much the same thing years before in going to Ireland, as now in coming from it. Although he was sent to that country in the king's service, and as the king's lieutenant, there were persons commissioned to apprehend him at several points in his journey thither; and now

Comes over from Ireland.

79

THE PASTON LETTERS

on his return similar efforts were made to prevent his advance to London. As regards himself they were altogether fruitless; but it is not improbable that they succeeded in deterring many of his followers from joining him. William Tresham, the Speaker of the last Parliament, having received a summons from the duke to meet him, was waylaid and murdered in Northamptonshire by a body of the retainers of Lord Grey of Ruthin. For two months the murderers went at large. The sheriff of the county durst not arrest them, and it was only on the meeting of Parliament that a special act was passed for their punishment.[1]

York, however, pursued his way, in spite of all opposition, to the royal presence, and great was the dismay of those then about the king. According to an act passed against him nine years later, his approach was not unaccompanied by violence. He and his followers, it is said, came in warlike array to Westminster Palace, and 'beat down the spears and walls' in the king's chamber. If so, we should infer that his access to the king was opposed even at the last moment. But the opposition was ineffectual, and the reception he met with from Henry himself did not indicate that the king at all resented his conduct.

It must have been on his first interview with Henry that he presented a petition and received a reply from him, which are printed in Holinshed as follows :—

Richard, Duke of York : his letter to King Henry[2]

Please it your Highness to conceive that since my departing out of this your realm by your commandment, and being in your service in your land of Ireland, I have been informed that divers language hath been said of me to your most excellent estate which should sound to my dishonour and reproach and charge of my person ; howbeit that I have been, and ever will be, your true liegeman and servant, and if there be any man that will or dare say the contrary or charge me

[1] Rolls of Parl. v. 211-12.
[2] The whole of this correspondence is attributed by Holinshed and Stow to the year 1452 ; but it appears to me clearly to belong to the year 1450, when the Duke had just returned from Ireland. See Chronicle of London, 136 ; though internal evidence alone will, I think, satisfy the careful student.

80

INTRODUCTION

otherwise, I beseech your rightwiseness to call him before your high presence, and I will declare me for my discharge as a true knight ought to do. And if I do not, as I doubt not but I shall, I beseech you to punish me as the poorest man of your land. And if he be found untrue in his suggestion and information, I beseech you of your highness that he be punished after his desert in example of all other.

Please it your Excellency to know that as well before my departing out of this your realm for to go into your land of Ireland in your full noble service, as since, certain persons have lain in wait for to hearken upon me, as Sir John Talbot, knight, at the castle of Holt, Sir Thomas Stanley, knight, in Cheshire, Pulford at Chester, Elton at Worcester, Brooke at Gloucester, and Richard, groom of your chamber, at Beaumaris ; which had in charge, as I am informed, to take me, and put me into your castle of Conway, and to strike off the head of Sir William Oldhall, knight, and to have put in prison Sir William Devereux, knight, and Sir Edmund Malso (Mulso), knight, withouten enlarging until the time that your Highness had appointed their deliverance.

Item, at such time as I was purposed for to have arrived at your haven of Beaumaris, for to have come to your noble presence to declare me your true man and subject, as my duty is, my landing was stopped and forebarred by Henry Norris, Thomas Norris, William Buckley, William Grust, and Bartholomew Bould, your officers in North Wales, that I should not land there, nor have victuals nor refreshing for me and my fellowship, as I have written to your Excellency here before ; so far forth, that Henry Norris, deputy to the chamberlain of North Wales, said unto me that he had in commandment that I should in no wise have landing, refreshing, nor lodging, for men nor horse, nor other thing that might turn to my worship or ease ; putting the blame upon Sir William Say, usher of your chamber, saying and affirming that I am against your intent and [held] as a traitor, as I am informed. And, moreover, certain letters were made and delivered unto Chester, Shrewsbury, and to other places, for to let mine entry into the same.

Item, above all wrongs and injuries above said, done unto me of malice without any cause, I being in your land of Ireland in your honourable service, certain commissions were made and directed unto divers persons, which for the execution of the same sat in certain places, and the juries impanelled and charged. Unto the which juries certain persons laboured instantly to have me indicted of treason, to the intent for to have undone me and mine issue, and corrupted my blood, as it is openly published. Beseeching your Majesty royal of your righteousness to examine these matters, and thereupon to do

81

THE PASTON LETTERS

such justice in this behalf as the cause requireth ; for mine intent is fully to pursue to your Highness for the conclusion of these matters.

The Answer of King Henry to the Duke of York

Cousin, we have seen the bill that ye took us late, and also understand the good humble obedience that ye in yourself show unto us, as well in word as in deed ; wherefore our intent is the more hastily to ease you of such things as were in your said bill. Howbeit that at our more leisure we might answer you to your said bill, yet we let you wit that, for the causes aforesaid, we will declare you now our intent in these matters. Sith it is that a long time among the people hath been upon you many strange language, and in especial anon after your [qu. their ?][1] disordinate and unlawful slaying of the bishop of Chichester,[2] divers and many of the untrue shipmen and other said, in their manner, words against our estate, making menace to our own person by your sayings, that ye should be fetched with many thousands, and ye should take upon you that which ye neither ought, nor, as we doubt not, ye will not attempt ; so far forth that it was said to our person by divers, and especially, we remember, of one Wasnes which had like words unto us. And also there were divers of such false people that went on and had like language in divers of our towns of our land, which by our subjects were taken and duly executed. Wherefore we sent to divers of our courts and places to hearken and to take heed if any such manner coming were, and if there had been, for to resist it ; but coming into our land our true subject as ye did, our intent was not that ye, nor less of estate of our subjects, nor none of your servants should not have been letted nor warned, but in goodly wise received ; howbeit that peradventure your sudden coming, without certain warning, caused our servants to do as they did, considering the causes abovesaid. And as to the indictment that ye spoke of, we think verily and hold for certain, that there was none such. And if ye may truly prove that any person was thereabouts, the matter shall be demeaned as the case shall require, so that he shall know it is to our great displeasure. Upon this, for the easing of your heart in all such matters, we declare, repute and admit you as our true and faithful subject, and as our faithful cousin.

[1] I have no doubt this is a misreading of the contracted form 'ye' which was intended for 'their.' To accuse York of the murder of the Bishop of Chichester, and apparently as a principal, not an accessory in that murder, when he was at the time in Ireland, would have been absurd. Besides, the tenor of the whole of this reply is to exculpate York of all charges.
[2] Misprinted 'Chester' in Holinshed.

82

INTRODUCTION

So far, York had gained his object. The charges against him were repudiated by the highest authority in the kingdom. But it was impossible that the matter could rest there. His own interests and those of the public alike compelled him to demand a full inquiry into the machinations of his adversaries, and when admitted to freer intercourse with Henry he was able to support this request by most inconvenient arguments. Town and country now listened with eagerness for news of a long looked-for crisis, while, as it seemed, the old régime was being quietly laid aside at Westminster. 'Sir, and it A change please,' writes one newsmonger, William Wayte, the clerk of of government. Justice Yelverton, 'Sir, and it please, I was in my lord of York's house, and I heard much thing more than my master writeth unto you of. I heard much thing in Fleet Street. But, sir, my lord was with the king, and he visaged so the matter that all the king's household was and is afraid right sore. And my said lord hath put a bill to the king and desired much thing which is much after the Commons' desire ; and all is upon justice, and to put all those that be indicted under arrest without surety or mainprise, and to be tried by law as law will ; insomuch that on Monday Sir William Oldhall was with the king at Westminster more than two hours, and had of the king good cheer.'[1]

Sir William Oldhall, a friend and companion-in-arms of the Duke of York in France, had been summoned to the king's councils more than once before.[2] But the last occasion was eleven years before this, at a time when it was doubtless felt to be necessary to obtain the sanction beforehand of all parties in the State to the proposed negotiations for peace at Calais. From that day till now we do not hear of him, and we may presume that he was not invited to Court. By the Duke of York's letter just quoted, it would seem that courtiers had planned to have him beheaded. But now the old exclusiveness was defeated. Men whose patriotism and generalship, it was believed, would have averted the loss of France, were at length allowed free access to their sovereign ; while

[1] See No. 142.
[2] Nicolas's Proceedings of the Privy Council, iv. 212, v. 108.

83

THE PASTON LETTERS

men who were believed to have culpably misdirected the king, and by their favouritism and partiality to have perverted the course of justice throughout the kingdom, stood in fear of a strict inquiry being made into their misdeeds. For such was the sole purport of the 'bill,' or petition presented by the Duke of York as mentioned by William Wayte, the exact text of which will be seen in No. 143. The king's answer to this is preserved in Holinshed as follows :—

The Answer of King Henry to the Duke of York

Cousin, as touching your bill last put up to us, we understand well that ye, of good heart, counsel and advertise us to the setting up of justice and to the speedy punishing of some persons indicted or noised, offering your service to be ready at commandment in the same ; sith it is, that for many causes moving us to have determined in our soul to stablish a sad and substantial Council, giving them more ample authority and power than ever we did before this, in the which we have appointed you to be one. But sith it is not accustomed, sure, nor expedient, to take a conclusion and conduct by advice or counsel of one person by himself, for the conservation (?) it is observed that the greatest and the best, the rich and the poor, in liberty, virtue and effect of their [1] voices be equal ; we have therefore determined within ourself to send for our Chancellor of England and for other Lords of our Council, yea and all other, together within short time, riply to common of these and other our great matters. In the which communication such conclusions, by the grace of God, shall be taken, as shall sound to His pleasure, the weal of us and our land, as well in these matters as in any other.

Politics in Norfolk.

The time was favourable to men like John Paston, who had been wronged by a powerful neighbour such as Lord Molynes, and had been hitherto denied redress. There seemed also a hope of destroying, once for all, the influence of Tuddenham and Heydon in the county of Norfolk. It was proposed that on the Duke of York visiting Norfolk, which he intended to do, the mayor and aldermen of Norwich should ride to meet him, and that complaints should be preferred against the party of Tuddenham and Heydon in the name of the whole city. 'And let that be done,' adds William Wayte,

[1] Misprinted 'your' in Holinshed.

84

INTRODUCTION

'in the most lamentable wise ; for, Sir, but if (i.e. unless) my Lord hear some foul tales of them, and some hideous noise and cry, by my faith they are else like to come to grace.' Owing to the influence of the Duke of York, a new Parliament was summoned to meet in November, and John Paston was urged by some friends to get himself returned as a member. But it was still more strongly recommended that the Earl of Oxford should meet the duke, apparently with the view of arranging the list of candidates—a responsibility which the earl, for his part, seems to have declined. The Duke of Norfolk met with the Duke of York at Bury St. Edmunds, and these two dukes settled that matter between them. The Earl of Oxford modestly contented himself with reporting their decision, and advising that their wishes should be carried into effect.[1]

The Parliament met on the 6th November, and Sir William Oldhall was chosen Speaker. About the same time a commission of *Oyer and Terminer* which had been issued as early as the first of August,[2] began its labours at Norwich, and the Earl of Oxford stayed away from Parliament to attend it. Mr. Justice Yelverton was sent down from Westminster to sit on that tribunal along with him. There seemed hope at last of redress being had for the wrongs and violence that had prevailed in the county of Norfolk ; but the course of justice was not yet an easy one. Great pressure had been put upon the king, even at the last moment, that Yelverton should be countermanded, and Lord Molynes had spoken of his own dispute with Paston in the king's presence in a manner that made the friends of the latter wish he had been then at Westminster to see after his own interests. The Lords of the Council, however, determined that Yelverton should keep

[1] Nos. 142, 145, 148, and 149. The influence of a powerful nobleman on the elections was evidently quite a matter of course. What use York made of it, or attempted to make of it, cannot so easily be determined. Of the two candidates proposed by him for the county of Norfolk, only one was returned, the name of Sir Miles Stapleton being substituted for that of Sir William Chamberlain (*see* vol. ii. p. 185 note 1). It appears from two of the above cited letters that Stapleton was a favourite candidate with the Pastons and their friends, and that he was urged to wait on the Duke of York on his coming to Norwich.
[2] *See* No. 119.

85

THE PASTON LETTERS

his day for going into Norfolk. When he arrived there, he had occasion to report that there were many persons ill-disposed towards Tuddenham and Heydon, but that it was most important they should be encouraged by a good sheriff and under-sheriff being appointed, else there would be a total miscarriage of justice. For the annual election of sheriffs had been delayed this year, apparently owing to the state of parties. Until the Duke of York arrived in London for the Parliament, his friends would not allow them to be nominated ; and the state of suspense and anxiety occasioned by this delay is clearly shown in the letters written during November.[1]

The truth is, the Duke of York had not yet succeeded in establishing the government upon anything like a firm or satisfactory basis. In times like our own there is little difficulty in determining the responsibility of ministers ; but in the rough judgment of the 'Commons' of those days an error in policy was nothing short of treason. Whoever took upon him to guide the king's counsels knew very well the danger of the task ; and York (if I understand his character aright) was anxious, until he was driven desperate, never to assume more authority than he was distinctly warranted in doing. He could not but remember that his father had suffered death for conspiring to depose Henry v., and that his own high birth and descent from Edward iii. caused his acts to be all the more jealously watched by those who sought to estrange him from his sovereign. He therefore made it by no means his aim to establish for himself a marked ascendency. He rather sought to show his moderation. I find, indeed, that at this particular period he not only removed two members of the Council, Lord Dudley and the Abbot of St. Peter's at Gloucester, but sent them prisoners to his own castle of Ludlow.[2] This, however, he could hardly have done without permission from the king, as it was the express object of his petition above referred to, that persons accused of misconducting themselves in high places should be committed for trial ; and judging from the terms of the king's answer, I should say that it must have been done by

[1] Nos. 151, 153, 154, 155, 156.
[2] Stow's *Chronicle*, p. 392.

86

INTRODUCTION

the authority of the new Council, which Henry therein declared it to be his intention to constitute.

This new Council was probably what we should call in these days a coalition ministry. York's great rival, the Duke of Somerset, had come over from Normandy a little before York himself came over from Ireland. On the 11th of September, while Cardinal Kemp, who was then Lord Chancellor, was sitting at Rochester on a commission of *Oyer and Terminer* to try the Kentish rebels,[1] he affixed the Great Seal to a patent appointing Somerset Constable of England.[2] In that capacity, as we have already seen, the duke arrested one of the new Kentish leaders that started up after Cade's rebellion had been quelled. There is no doubt that he stood high in the king's confidence, and that he was particularly acceptable to Queen Margaret. He was, nevertheless, one of the most unpopular men in England, on account of his surrender of Caen and total loss of Normandy in the preceding year ; and as the Parliament was now called, among other reasons, expressly to provide for the defence of the kingdom, and for speedy succours being sent to preserve the king's other dominions in France,[3] it was impossible that his conduct should not be inquired into. The short sitting of Parliament before Christmas was greatly occupied by controversy between York and Somerset.[4] On the 1st of December the latter was placed under arrest. His lodgings at the Black Friars were broken into and pillaged by the populace, and he himself was nearly killed, but was rescued from their violence by a barge of his brother-in-law the Earl of Devon. Next day the Dukes of York and Norfolk caused proclamation to be made through the city that no man should commit robbery on pain of death, and a man was actually beheaded in Cheap for disobeying this order. As a further demonstration against lawlessness, the king and his lords, on Thursday the 3rd December, rode through the city in armour, either side of the way being kept by a line of armed citizens throughout the route of the

The Duke of Somerset.

[1] *See* vol. ii. pp. 161-2.
[2] Rymer, xi. 276.
[3] *Rolls of Parl.* v. 210.
[4] W. Worc.

87

THE PASTON LETTERS

procession. It was the most brilliant display of the kind the Londoners of that day had ever seen.[1]

The Duke of Somerset did not long remain in prison. Very soon after Christmas the king made him captain of Calais, and gave him the entire control of the royal household.[2] The Court was evidently bent on the restoration of the old order of things, so far as it dared to do so. The chief obstacle to this undoubtedly was the Parliament, which was, on the whole, so favourable to the Duke of York, that one member, Young of Bristol, had even ventured to move that he should be declared heir to the crown.[3] Parliament, however, could be prorogued; and, as Young found shortly afterwards, its members could be committed to the Tower. The speech of the Lord Chancellor on the meeting of Parliament had declared that it was summoned for three important causes: first, to provide for the defence of the kingdom, and especially the safeguard of the sea; secondly, for the speedy relief of the king's subjects in the south of France, and aid against the French; thirdly, for pacifying the king's subjects at home, and punishing the disturbances which had lately been so frequent. But practically nothing was done about any of these matters before Christmas. An act was passed for the more speedy levying of a subsidy granted in the last Parliament, and also an act of attainder against the murderers of William Tresham. The Lord Chancellor then, in the king's name and in his presence, prorogued the Parliament till the 20th of January, declaring that the matters touching the defence of the kingdom were too great and difficult to be adequately discussed at that time. The same excuse, however, was again used for further prorogations until the 5th of May; and meanwhile fears began to be entertained in the country that all that had been done hitherto for a more impartial administration of justice was about to be upset.[4]

[1] MS. Cott. Vitell. A. xvi. Stow in his *Chronicle* dates this procession a day later.
[2] W. Worc.
[3] *The Chronicle of London* (p. 137) says that 'all the Commons' agreed to this proposition, and stood out for some time against the Lords on the subject.
[4] *Rolls of Parl.* v. 210-14.

88

INTRODUCTION

During the whole course of the succeeding year matters A.D. 1451. were in a very unsettled condition. At the very opening of the year we hear complaints that the sheriff, Jermyn, had not shown himself impartial, but was endeavouring to suppress complaints against certain persons at the coming sessions at Lynn. It was feared the king would pardon Tuddenham and Heydon the payment of their dues to the Exchequer for Suffolk; and if they did, payment of taxes would be generally refused, as Blake, the Bishop of Swaffham, having gone up to London, informed the Lord Chancellor himself. From London, too, men wrote in a manner that was anything but encouraging. The government was getting paralysed alike by debt and by indecision. 'As for tidings here,' writes John Bocking, 'I certify you all is nought, or will be nought. The king borroweth his expenses for Christmas. The King of Arragon, the Duke of Milan, the Duke of Austria, the Duke of Burgundy, would be assistant to us to make a conquest, and nothing is answered nor agreed in manner save abiding the great deliberation that at the last shall spill all together.' Chief-Justice Fortescue had been for a week expecting every night to be assaulted.[1] The only symptom of vigour at head-quarters was the despatch of a commission of *Oyer and Terminer* into Kent, for the trial of those who had raised disturbances during the preceding summer. As for the county of Norfolk, the only hope lay in a strong clamour being raised against oppressors. Sir John Fastolf showed himself anxious about the prosecution of certain indictments against Heydon, and his servant Bocking, and Wayte, the servant of Judge Yelverton, urged that strong representations should be made to Lord Scales against showing any favour to that unpopular lawyer.[2]

By and by it was seen what good reason the friends of Tudden-justice had for their apprehensions. It had been arranged that ham and Tuddenham and Heydon should be indicted at a sitting of the Heydon.

[1] In earlier issues of this Introduction was added: 'probably for no other reason than his high impartiality.' Mr. Plummer, I find, who knows him better, has not the same opinion of Fortescue's impartiality as a politician, but considers that he was in danger just because he was so strong a Lancastrian. *See* Introduction to *The Governance of England*, p. 50. [2] Nos. 167, 169-174.

89

THE PASTON LETTERS

commission of *Oyer and Terminer* at Norwich in the ensuing spring. Rumours, however, began to prevail in Norwich that they who had promoted this commission in the county of Norfolk—the Earl of Oxford and Justice Yelverton, as well as John Paston and John Damme—were to be indicted in Kent by way of revenge. John Damme had before this caused Heydon to be indicted of treason for taking down one of those hideous memorials of a savage justice—the quarter of a man exposed in public. The man was doubtless a political victim belonging to Heydon's own party; but Heydon was now looking to recover his influence, and he contrived to get the charge of treason retorted against Damme. Symptoms were observed in Norwich that the unpopular party were becoming bolder again. 'Heydon's men,' wrote James Gloys to John Paston, 'brought his own horse and his saddle through Aylesham on Monday, and they came in at the Bishop's Gates at Norwich, and came over Tombland and into the Abbey; and sithen they said they should go to London for Heydon. Item, some say that Heydon should be made a knight, and much other language there is which causeth men to be afeard, weening that he should have a rule again.'[1]

Full well might Sir John Fastolf and others apprehend that if Heydon or Tuddenham appeared in answer to the indict-ment, it would be with such a following at his back as would overawe the court. No appearance was put in for them at all at several of the sessions of *Oyer and Terminer*. One sitting was held at Norwich on the 2nd of March. Another was held just after Easter on the 29th of April, and Justice Prisot, not the most impartial of judges, was sent down to Norwich to hold it. Strong complaints were put in against Tuddenham and Heydon on the part of the city of Norwich, and also by the town of Swaffham, by Sir John Fastolf, Sir Harry Inglos, John Paston, and many others; but, as Fastolf's chaplain afterwards informed his master, 'the judges, by their wilful-ness, might not find in their heart to give not so much as a beck nor a twinkling of their eye toward, but took it to derision, God reform such partiality!' The one-sidedness of

[1] Nos. 179 and 180.

90

INTRODUCTION

Prisot, indeed, was such as to bring down upon him a rebuke from his colleague Yelverton. 'Ah, Sir Mayor and your brethren,' said the former, 'as to the process of *your* complaints we will put them in continuance, but in all other we will proceed.' Yelverton felt bound to protest against such unfairness. Yet even this was not the worst; for Prisot, Partial seeing that, with all he could do, the result of the proceedings justice. at Norwich would scarcely be satisfactory to Tuddenham and Heydon, took it upon him, apparently by his own authority, to remove them to Walsingham, where they had most supporters. And there, accordingly, another session was opened on Tuesday the 4th of May.[1]

It was, according to Sir Thomas Howys, 'the most partial place of all the shire.' All the friends and allies of Tuddenham and Heydon, knights and squires, and gentle-men who had always been devoted to their pleasure, received due warning to attend. A body of 400 horse also accom-panied the accused, and not one of the numerous com-plainants ventured to open his mouth except John Paston. Even he had received a friendly message only two days before that he had better consider well whether it was ad-visable to come himself, as there was 'great press of people and few friends'; and, moreover, the sheriff was 'not so whole' as he had been. What this expression meant re-quired but little explanation. As Sheriff of Norfolk, John Jermyn was willing to do Paston all the service in his power, but simple justice he did not dare to do.[2]

He had but too good an excuse for his timidity. Of John John Paston's complaint against Tuddenham and Heydon Paston we hear no more; we can easily imagine what became of and Lord it. But we know precisely what became of an action brought Molynes. by Paston at this sessions against his old adversary Lord Molynes, for his forcible expulsion from Gresham in the preceding year. John Paston, to be sure, was now peaceably reinstated in the possession of that manor;[3] but he had the boldness to conceive that undermining his wife's chamber, turning her forcibly out of doors, and then pillaging the

[1] Nos. 119, 185, 186, 192. [2] Nos. 189, 192. [3] No. 178.

91

THE PASTON LETTERS

whole mansion, were acts for which he might fairly expect redress against both Lord Molynes and his agents. He had accordingly procured two indictments to be framed, the first against his lordship, and the second against his men. But before the case came on at Walsingham, Sheriff Jermyn gave notice to Paston's friends that he had received a distinct injunction from the king to make up a panel to acquit Lord Molynes.[1] Royal letters of such a tenor do not seem to have been at all incompatible with the usages of Henry VI.'s reign. John Paston himself said the document was one that could be procured for six-and-eightpence.

There was no hope, therefore, of making Lord Molynes himself responsible for the attack on Gresham. The only question was whether the men who had done his bidding could not be made to suffer for it. After the acquittal of their master, John Osbern reports a remarkable conversation that he had with Sheriff Jermyn in which he did his best to induce him to accept a bribe in Paston's interest. The gift had been left with the under sheriff for his acceptance. Jermyn declined to take it until he had seen Paston himself, but Osbern was fully under the impression that he would be glad to have it. Osbern, however, appealed also to other arguments. 'I remembered him,' he tells Paston, 'of his promises made before to you at London, when he took his oath and charge, and that ye were with him when he took his oath and other divers times; and for those promises made by him to you at that time, and other times at the *Oyer and Terminer* at Lynn, ye proposed you by the trust that ye have in him to attempt and rear actions that should be to the avail of him and of his office.' The prospect of Paston being valuable to him as a litigant had its weight with the sheriff, and he promised to do him all the good in his power except in the action against Lord Molynes' men; for not only Lord Molynes himself but the Duke of Norfolk had written to him to show them favour, and if they were not acquitted he expected to incur both their displeasure and the king's. In vain did Osbern urge that Paston would

[1] No. 189.

92

INTRODUCTION

find sufficient surety to save the sheriff harmless. Jermyn said he could take no surety over £100, and Lord Molynes was a great lord who could do him more injury than that.[1]

The diplomacy on either side seems to have been conducted with considerable *finesse*. Jermyn declared that he had been offered twenty nobles at Walsingham in behalf of the Lord Molynes, but that he had never received a penny either from him or from any of Paston's adversaries. Osbern then offered if he would promise to be sincere towards Paston, that the latter would give him a sum in hand, as much as he could desire, or would place it in the hands of a middle man whom Jermyn could trust. In the end, however, he was obliged to be satisfied with Jermyn's assuring him that if he found it lay within his power to do anything for Paston, he would take his money with good will. The negotiator's impression was that he was fully pledged to get Lord Molynes' men acquitted, but that in all other actions he would be found favourable to Paston.[2]

About this time Parliament, which had now been pro- **Parliament.** rogued for nearly five months, met again at Westminster. The king's necessities were doubtless the all-sufficient cause why its meeting could no longer be dispensed with. The Crown was already in debt to the sum of £372,000, and was daily becoming more so. The expenses of the royal household amounted to £24,000 a year, while the yearly revenue out of which they should have been paid was only £5000. Nor was it by any means advisable to remedy the matter by imposing fresh taxation; for the people were so impoverished by the payment of subsidies, the exactions of the king's purveyors, and the general maladministration of justice, that the experiment could hardly have been made with safety. An act of resumption was the only expedient by which it seemed possible to meet the difficulty; and all grants of crown lands made to any persons since the first day of the reign were accordingly recalled by statute.[3] In return for this the Commons preferred a petition to the king that he would for ever remove from his presence and counsels a number

[1] No. 193.　　[2] *Ibid.*　　[3] *Rolls of Parl.* v. 217.

93

THE PASTON LETTERS

of persons to whom they alleged it was owing both that his possessions had been diminished, and that the laws had not been carried into execution. Foremost on the list was the Duke of Somerset; and with him were Alice, widow of the late Duke of Suffolk, William Booth, Bishop of Chester (that is to say, of Coventry and Lichfield),[1] Lord Dudley, Thomas Daniel, and twenty-five others. It was petitioned that they should never again be permitted to come within twelve miles of the royal presence, on pain of forfeiture of lands and goods. But the days had not yet come when a petition against ministers by the Commons was tantamount to their dismissal. The king indeed felt it best on this occasion to yield somewhat; but he yielded on no principle whatever. He declared in reply that he himself saw no cause for their removal; but he was content to dismiss the most of them for a year, during which period accusations brought against any of them might be inquired into. Those who were Peers of the realm, however, he refused to send away; and he insisted on retaining the services of one or two others who had been accustomed continually to wait upon him.[2]

Parliament seems shortly after this to have been dissolved, and no parliament met again till two years later. Of course the influence of Somerset increased when both Lords and Commons were dismissed into the country; and we perceive that by the end of the year Thomas Daniel, one of the old unpopular adherents of the Duke of Suffolk, who, nevertheless, had not always been acceptable to the Court, was expecting to recover favour by means of Somerset.[3] He is represented as having cultivated the Duke's friendship for a quarter of a year; so that we may conclude Somerset's ascendency was at this time unmistakable. With what degree of discretion he made use of it there is little evidence to show. One advantage that Daniel hoped to gain through his influence was the friendship of Tuddenham and Heydon, by whose means, and by the

[1] The modern see of Chester was separated from this diocese in the time of Henry VIII.
[2] *Rolls of Parl.* v. 216.
[3] No. 206. Daniel had been out of favour at one time during Suffolk's ascendency. *See* No. 75, p. 86.

94

INTRODUCTION

good offices of Lord Scales, he expected to be allowed to re-enter the manor of Bradeston, of which he had already dispossessed one Osbert Munford last year, but had subsequently been dispossessed himself. The value of a disputed title in any part of England probably depended very much upon who was supreme at Court.

But high as Somerset stood in the king's favour, the course of events did not tend to make him more acceptable to the people. The loss of Normandy, in the preceding year, was itself a thing not likely to be readily forgotten; but the misfortunes of the English arms did not end with the loss of Normandy. So great, indeed, was the despondency occasioned by that event that, in the opinion of French writers, Calais itself would not have been able to hold out if the French had immediately proceeded to attack it. But Charles was afraid he might have been deserted by the Duke of Burgundy, whose interests would hardly have been promoted by the French king strengthening himself in that quarter, and he declined to attempt it.[1] Relieved, however, of the necessity of maintaining a large force in Normandy, he found new occupation for his troops in completing the conquest of Guienne, of which a beginning had already been made by the capture of Cognac and of some places near Bayonne and the Pyrenees. In November 1450 the French laid siege to Bourg and Blaye on the Garonne, both of which places capitulated in the spring of the following year. They were the keys of the more important city of Bordeaux, which, now perceiving that there was no hope of succour from England, was obliged to follow their example. This was in June 1451. Two months afterwards Bayonne, too, **Loss of** was obliged to capitulate; and with it the whole of Gascony **Gascony** and Guienne was as completely lost to the English as **and** Normandy had been in the preceding year. Calais was now **Guienne.** all that remained to them of their conquests and possessions in France; nor were they without considerable apprehension that they might be expelled from Calais too.

These disasters, which were but the natural sequel to the

[1] Basin, i. 247-48.

95

loss of Normandy, only served to make more bitter the reflection how the government of that duchy had been taken out of the able hands of the Duke of York and given to the incompetent Somerset. The jealousy with which the latter regarded his rival was heightened by the consciousness of his own unpopularity. The Duke of York was living in seclusion at his castle of Ludlow, but Somerset seems to have regarded him with daily increasing apprehension. He was continually instilling into the king distrust of York's fidelity as a subject; until at last the latter thought it expedient to make a public declaration of his loyalty. He accordingly issued the following manifesto :—

Forasmuch as I, Richard Duke of York, am informed that the King, my sovereign lord, is my heavy lord, greatly displeased with me, and hath in me a distrust by sinister information of mine enemies, adversaries, and evil-willers, where[as] God knoweth, from whom nothing is hid, I am, and have been, and ever will be, his true liegeman, and so have I before this, divers times, as well by mouth as by writing, notified and declared to my said sovereign lord: And for that this notice so comen unto me of the displeasure of my said sovereign lord is to me so grievous, I have prayed the reverend father in God, the Bishop of Hereford,[1] and my cousin the Earl of Shrewsbury, to come hither and hear my declaration in this matter; wherein I have said to them that I am true liegeman to the King my sovereign lord, ever have been, and shall be to my dying day. And to the very proof that it is so, I offer myself to swear that on the blessed Sacrament, and receive it, the which I hope shall be my salvation at the day of doom. And so for my special comfort and consolation I have prayed the said lords to report and declare unto the King's highness my said offer ; and to the end and intent that I will be ready to do the same oath in presence of two or three lords, such as shall please the King's highness to send hither to accept it. In witness whereof I have signed this schedule with my sign manual, and set thereunto my signet of arms. Written in my castle of Ludlow, the 9th of January, the 30th year of the reign of my sovereign lord, King Henry the Sixth.[2]

He appears to have waited nearly a month to learn the effect of this remonstrance. Meanwhile reports came that the French were advancing to lay siege to Calais. At such a juncture it was peculiarly intolerable that the administration of

[1] Reginald Butler or Boulers, whose appointment to the see, dated 23rd December 1450, was no doubt due to the Duke of York's influence.
[2] Stow's *Chronicle*, p. 393.

96

affairs should still be intrusted to hands so notoriously incompetent as those of Somerset ; and York, as being the only man who could stir in such a matter with effect, now made up his mind to take active steps for Somerset's removal. Nothing, however, could be done for such an object without a considerable force of armed men to support him. York accordingly issued the following address to the burgesses of Shrewsbury :—

Right worshipful friends, I recommend me unto you ; and I suppose it is well known unto you, as well by experience as by common language said and reported throughout all Christendom, what laud, what worship, honour, and manhood, was ascribed of all nations unto the people of this realm whilst the kingdom's sovereign lord stood possessed of his lordship in the realm of France and duchy of Normandy ; and what derogation, loss of merchandize, lesion of honour, and villany, is said and reported generally unto the English nation for loss of the same ; namely (*i.e.* especially) unto the Duke of Somerset, when he had the commandance and charge thereof : the which loss hath caused and encouraged the King's enemies for to conquer and get Gascony and Guienne, and now daily they make their advance for to lay siege unto Calais, and to other places in the marches there, for to apply them to their obeisance, and so for to come into the land with great puissance, to the final destruction thereof, if they might prevail, and to put the land in their subjection, which God defend. And on the other part it is to be supposed it is not unknown to you how that, after my coming out of Ireland I, as the King's true liegeman and servant (and ever shall be to my life's end) and for my true acquittal, perceiving the inconvenience before rehearsed, advised his Royal Majesty of certain articles concerning the weal and safeguard, as well of his most royal person, as the tranquillity and conservation of all this his realm : the which advertisements, howbeit that it was thought that they were full necessary, were laid apart, and to be of none effect, through the envy, malice, and untruth of the said Duke of Somerset ; which for my truth, faith, and allegiance that I owe unto the King, and the good will and favour that I have to all the realm, laboreth continually about the King's highness for my undoing, and to corrupt my blood, and to disinherit me and my heirs, and such persons as be about me, without any desert or cause done or attempted, on my part or theirs, I make our Lord Judge. Wherefore, worshipful friends, to the intent that every man shall know my purpose and desire for to declare me such as I am, I signify unto you that, with the help and supportation of Almighty God, and of Our Lady, and of all the Company of Heaven, I, after long sufferance and delays, [though it is] not my will or intent

to displease my sovereign lord, seeing that the said Duke ever prevaileth and ruleth about the King's person, [and] that by this means the land is likely to be destroyed, am fully concluded to proceed in all haste against him with the help of my kinsmen and friends ; in such wise that it shall prove to promote ease, peace, tranquillity, and safeguard of all this land : and more, keeping me within the bounds of my liegeance, as it pertaineth to my duty, praying and exhorting you to fortify, enforce, and assist me, and to come to me with all diligence, wheresoever I shall be, or draw, with as many goodly and likely men as ye may, to execute the intent abovesaid. Written under my signet at my castle of Ludlow, the 3rd day of February.

Furthermore I pray you that such strait appointment and ordinance be made that the people which shall come in your fellowship, or be sent unto me by your agreement, be demeaned in such wise by the way, that they do no offence, nor robbery, nor oppression upon the people, in lesion of justice. Written as above, etc.

Your good friend,   R. YORK.[1]

To my right worshipful friends, the bailiffs, burgesses and commons of the good town of Shrewsbury.

Having thus collected a sufficient body of followers, the duke began his march to London. The Earl of Devonshire, Lord Cobham, and other noblemen also collected people and joined him.[2] The king and Somerset, however, being informed of his intentions, set out from the capital to meet him, issuing, at the same time, an imperative summons to Lord Cobham, and probably to the duke's other adherents, to repair immediately to the royal presence.[3] But the duke, who had no desire to engage the king's forces, turned aside and hoped to reach London unmolested. He sent a herald before him to desire liberty for himself and his allies to enter the city ; but strict injunctions to the contrary had been left by the king, and his request was refused. Disappointed in this quarter, it was natural that he should look for greater sympathy in Kent, where, doubtless, smouldered still the remains of past disaffection. He accordingly crossed the Thames at Kingston Bridge,

[1] Ellis's *Letters*, First Series, i. 11-13.
[2] *English Chronicle* (ed. Davies), 69.
[3] Nicolas's *Privy Council Proceedings*, vi. 116. According to Fabyan, the king and Somerset set out on the 16th of February. The summons to Lord Cobham, though dated Westminster, was issued on the 17th.

98

and proceeded with his host to Dartford. The king's army followed and pitched their camp upon Blackheath. And so, on the 1st of March 1452, there lay, within eight miles of each other, two formidable hosts, which any further movement must apparently bring into collision.

To judge from one contemporary account,[1] the duke's position must have been a strong one. He had a body of ordnance in the field, with no less than 3000 gunners. He himself had 8000 men in the centre of his position ; while the Earl of Devonshire lay to the south with another detachment of 6000, and Lord Cobham by the river-side commanded an equal force. Seven ships lay on the water filled with the baggage of the 'troops. But the strength of the king's army appears to have largely exceeded these numbers ; [2] and even if the duke had wished to provoke a conflict, it was evidently more prudent to remain simply on the defensive. He accordingly left the responsibility of further action to those of the king's party.

In this crisis the lords who were with the king took counsel together, and determined, if possible, to labour for a compromise.[3] An embassy was appointed to go to the Duke of York, and hear what he had to say. It consisted of the wise and good prelate Waynflete, Bishop of Winchester, and Bourchier, Bishop of Ely (afterwards Archbishop of Canterbury), the Earls of Salisbury and Warwick, Lord Beauchamp, Lord Sudeley, and some others. The answer made by York was, that no ill was intended against either the king or any of his Council ; that the duke and his followers were lovers of the commonweal ; but that it was their intention to remove from the king certain evil-disposed persons, through whose means the common people had been grievously oppressed. Of these the Duke of Somerset was declared to be the chief ; and, indeed, his unpopularity was such' that even those on the

[1] *Cottonian Roll*, ii. 23. *See* Appendix to this Introduction.
[2] *Rolls of Parl.* v. 346. The statement in the Act of Attainder passed against the Duke of York seven years afterwards, that he was 'of no power to withstand' the king on this occasion, is liable to suspicion, but it is confirmed by the testimony of Whethamstede, 348.
[3] 'The Lords, both spiritual and temporal, took the matter in hand.' *Three Fifteenth Century Chronicles* (Camden Soc.), 69. So also *Chronicle of London*, 137.

99

THE PASTON LETTERS

king's side would seem to have seconded the Duke of York's demand. After a consultation the king consented that Somerset should be committed to custody until he should make answer to such charges as York would bring against him.[1]

Nothing more seemed necessary to avert civil war. On a simple pledge given by the king that Somerset should be placed in confinement, and afterwards put on his trial, the Duke of York at once broke up his camp and ordered his men home. He then repaired himself to the king's tent to express his loyalty. But no sooner had he arrived there than he found *York is entrapped,* he was deceived. The king, in violation of his promise, kept the Duke of Somerset attending upon him as his chief adviser, and York was virtually a prisoner. He was sent on to London in advance of the king, in a kind of honourable custody, attended by two bishops, who conducted him to his own residence; but what to do with him when he got there was a difficulty. His enemies feared to send him to the Tower. There were 10,000 men yet remaining in the Welsh Marches, who, on such a rumour, would have come up to London; and it was not very long before they were reported to be all under arms, and actually on the march, with the duke's young son at their head—Edward, Earl of March, boy as he was, not yet quite ten years old.[2]

York had distinctly accused the Duke of Somerset as a traitor. He was now in Somerset's power, but the latter did not dare to retort the charge upon him. Yet if Somerset was not a traitor, the course pursued by York was utterly indefensible. He had actually taken up arms against the Crown, to remove by force the minister in whom the king had placed his confidence. But unfortunately Somerset knew too well that if he made this a ground of accusation against his rival, recrimination would be sure to follow, and he himself would incur a weight of public odium which might possibly lead to the same result as in the case of Suffolk. The wisest and most politic course for himself was not to impeach the Duke of York, but,

[1] Fabyan.
[2] Fabyan. *Three Fifteenth Century Chronicles*, 69, and the MS. Chronicle, Vitell. A. xvi.

100

INTRODUCTION

if possible, to shut his mouth and let him go free. No accusation, therefore, was drawn up. An oath of allegiance, *and combinding him over to keep the peace in time coming, was all pelled to that was required.* It was on the 1st of March that York had *swear allegiance.* repaired to the king's tent and found himself in his rival's power. On the 10th he was brought to St. Paul's, and there publicly made oath as follows :—

I, Richard, Duke of York, confess and beknow that I am and ought to be humble subject and liegeman to you, my sovereign Lord, King Henry the Sixth, and owe therefore to bear you faith and truth as to my sovereign lord, and shall do all the days unto my life's end; and shall not at any time will or assent, that anything be attempted or done against your noble person, but wheresoever I shall have knowledge of any such thing imagined or purposed I shall, with all the speed and diligence possible to me, make that your Highness shall have knowledge thereof, and even do all that shall be possible to me to the withstanding thereof, to the utterest of my life. I shall not in no wise any thing take upon me against your royal estate or the obeisance that is due thereto, nor suffer any other man to do, as far forth as it shall lie in my power to let it; and also I shall come at your commandment, whensoever I shall be called by the same, in humble and obeisant wise, but if [*i.e.* unless] I be letted by any sickness or impotency of my person or by such other causes as shall be thought reasonable to you, my sovereign lord. I shall never hereafter take upon me to gather any routs, or make any assembly of your people, without your commandment or licence, or in my lawful defence. In the interpretation of which my lawful defence, and declaration thereof, I shall report me at all times to your Highness, and, if the case require, unto my peers : nor anything attempt by way of faite against any of your subjects, of what estate, degree, or condition that they be. But whensoever I find myself wronged or aggrieved, I shall sue humbly for remedy to your Highness, and proceed after the course of your laws, and in none other wise, saving in mine own lawful defence in manner above said; and shall in all things abovesaid and other have me unto your Highness as an humble and true subject ought to have him to his Sovereign Lord.

All these things above said I promise truly to observe and keep, by the Holy Evangelists contained in this book that I lay my hand upon, and by the Holy Cross that I here touch, and by the blessed Sacrament of our Lord's body that I shall now with His mercy receive. And over this I agree me and will that if I any time hereafter, as with the grace of our Lord I never shall, anything attempt by way of fear or otherwise against your royal majesty and obeisance that I owe thereto,

101

THE PASTON LETTERS

or anything I take upon me otherwise than is above expressed, I from that time forth be unabled, [held and taken as an untrue and openly forsworn man, and unable][1] to all manner of worship, estate, and degree, be it such as I now occupy, or any other that might grow unto me in any wise.

And this I here have promised and sworn proceedeth of mine own desire and free voluntee and by no constraining or coercion. In witness of all the which things above written I, Richard, Duke of York above named, subscribe me with mine own hand and seal, with this mine own seal, &c.[2]

With this guarantee for his future loyalty, the duke was permitted to return into his own country.

Somerset might well be pleased that the matter should be settled thus; for if the charges York brought, or at least was prepared to have brought, against him were only one-half true (and some of them certainly were true altogether), his administration of the Duchy of Normandy was a mixture of indiscretion and dishonesty at which the nation had good right to be indignant. We have already seen how in concert with the Duke of Suffolk he had authorised a perfidious breach of the truce with France in the capture of Fougères. We have also seen how ill prepared he was for the consequences; how he discovered too late the weakness of all the garrisons; how the French king recovered town after town, and the English were finally expelled from Normandy in less than a year and *York's charges against Somerset.* a half after the unjustifiable outrage. But if any credit may be given to the further charges brought against him by the Duke of York,—charges which agree only too well with the character attributed to him by the most impartial authorities[3] —Somerset had himself to blame in great measure for the defenceless condition of the country committed to his pro-

[1] These words are not in the copy in the *Rolls of Parliament*, but they occur in that given in Holinshed's *Chronicle*.
[2] *Rolls of Parl.* v. 346.
[3] The character given of the Duke of Somerset by the contemporary historian Basin is on the whole favourable, and may be supposed to be impartial. He describes him as handsome in person, gentle and urbane in manner, and well inclined towards justice; but all these graces were marred by an insatiable avarice which would not let him rest content with the immense wealth he had inherited from Cardinal Beaufort; and by continually coveting the riches of others he brought ruin on himself. Basin, i. 193.

102

INTRODUCTION

tection. On his first going into Normandy he had jobbed the offices under his control. For the sake of private emolument he had removed a number of trusty and experienced captains, filling their places with creatures of his own, or men who had paid *douceurs* for their posts; and only on receipt of still greater bribes would he consent to restore any of those that had been put out. He had, however, actually reduced many garrisons, while he had taxed the inhabitants of the Duchy beyond all reason for the means of defence. His administration of justice, too, had been such as to excite the most vehement dissatisfaction, and had made the whole native population impatient of English government. He had, moreover, pocketed the compensation given by France to the dispossessed Englishmen of Anjou and Maine. Worse still, after all his maladministration and ill success, he had prevailed on the king to make him captain of Calais, which it seemed as if he was on the point of losing also in as careless and culpable a manner as he had already lost Normandy.

Here, however, is the full text of the accusation,[1] as prepared by York himself :—

Thies articles and pointes folowyng yeve, shewe and ministre I, Richard Duc of York, youre true liegman and servaunt unto youre highnesse, summarily purposyng and declaryng thaym ayeinst Edmond Duc of Somerset for the grete welfare and the comen availle and interesse of youre mageste Roiall and of this youre noble roialme, aswell to bryng to knawlege and understondyng the meanes and causes of the grete myscheves and inconvenientz which late befe[l] unto this youre said noble roiame, as in losse of youre lyvelode by yonde thee see and otherwyse in ponisshment of desviritours and excuse of innocencie, and also in puttyng aside and eschuyng of the grete and importable hurte and prejudice which ben like, withouten that purviaunce be had of remedie, to succede in shorte tyme. To the which articles and every of theym I, the seid Duc of York, desire of youre egall and indifferent rightewesnesse that the seid Edmond answere by his feith and trouth,

[1] Printed in this Introduction for the first time from the original in the Cottonian MS., Vesp. C. xiv. f. 40. The first paragraph of this document is quoted by Stowe in his *Chronicle*, p. 397, and the charges are referred by him to the thirty-third year of the king's reign, *i.e.* the latter part of A.D. 1454, which is certainly erroneous. The date which he intended, indeed, was the latter part of the year 1453, when the Duke of Somerset was arrested and sent to the Tower; but this date also is quite impossible.

103

THE PASTON LETTERS

the sacrement of his othe thereuppon made, duly and truly as lawe and conscience requireth ; I also desiryng, for the veraly examinacion and knowlech of trouth thereuppon to be had, and for the grete and singuler weel of this youre said Roiame, to be admytted to the prefe, and to yeve evidence in the said articles that folowyn in such as he woll denye, after the equite and consideracion of lawe in such case, and processe had, and also of good feith and conscience justice thereafter to be don and executid.

First, I article and declare that the seid Edmond Duc of Somersett hath be meane, consenter, occasioner, cause and mediatour, both by his inwarde knowlege and expresse consent, by counseill, and worchyng thurghe diverse subtyle weyes and meanes, as by violent presumpcion and otherwyse is knowen and understonde, and furthermore also by his inordinate negligence, lacchesse and wilfull rechelessnes and insaciate covetyse, of the losse and amission of youre Duchie of Normandie, rejoissed and possessed at this tyme, for the defence of his negligent kepyng and otherwyse before reherced, by youre enemyes. Which may clerly by (sic) understonde by the meanes and causes that folowen ; of the which and for such one he is openly called, reputed and had by the comen fame and voice. Of the which oon cause is that the seid Duc of Somersett, at his first comyng into Normandie, chaunged and putt out of theire occupacion and youre service, withoute skyll, cause or reason, all the true and feithfull officers, for the most partie, of all Normandie, and put in such as hym liked for his owne singuler availe and covetyse, as it apperith well, inasmoch as ther coude noon of theym that were so put out be restored agayn withoute grete giftes and rewardes, which was full unfittyng. And furthermore did put in prison many diverse and notable persones of youre seid Duchie, withoute cause, justice or any ordinarie processe made agayn theym or due examinacion, and by that meane did grete extorcions and rered unlawfully grete sommes undre colour of amendes and composicions, wherby the cuntre for such wrong and faute of justice grucched sore agayn hym and his governaunce and caused the people to arise in theire conseytes and to take grete displeasir ; and that was a grete occasion and cause of the losse of youre said Duchie of Normandie.

Item, the seid Edmond Duc of Somerset was cause and consenter voluntarie of the brekyng of the trues and pais for a tyme had betwene youre highnes and youre uncle of Fraunce, which was well understond at the taking of Fogiers in Britaigne by Sir Fraunceys Larragonneys thurgh his avise, consentement, and counseile ; and also duryng the said trues made more strong and fortified diverse places disopered by youre commaundement, as Morteyn and Seint Jakes de Beveron, ageyn the appointement of the seid trues ; uppon which youre uncle did sommon hym to make a-seeth [satisfaction] and for to

104

INTRODUCTION

disimpaire the seid fortifying and wrong don agayn the trues, and in asmoch as non aseeth by hym was don, nor [he] lefte not of his seid fortifyng, caused youre seid uncle to have, as he pretende, cause to breke the said trues on his partie ; which brekyng of trues was oon of the verray cause of losse of Normandie. And thus he brake the seide trues ayeinst his promysse and true feith made to youre highnes, which was to kepe and entretyn the said trues, and so did ayen the lawe in this behalve and youre statutes of the roiame.

Item, he put away and diminisshed diverse garnisons and other strong places of youre said Duchie of Normandie of soudiours and of men of werre which were accustumed to abide uppon the suerte and saufgarde of the same, howe he hit he had verrayly knowlege that youre ennmyes were full determi[ned] for to ley seges to put the same places in theire subjeccion, not paiyng duely nor contentyng such soudiours as abode uppon the defences of the same places ; he reryng at that tyme in youre said Duchie as grete tailles and aides as were in long tyme before duryng the werre ; and that caused the soudiours in diverse strong places for poverte, not havyng hors nor harneys, and also the nombre diminisshed, to be of non poiaire to make resistence, and that was a grete cause of the losse of Normandie. The losse of which caused the perdicion of Gascoigne and Guyen.

Item, the Duc of Somersett wold yeve noo counseile, aide ne helpe unto the capitanis of diverse stronge places and garnisons which at that tyme, constreyned by nede, desired of hym provision and relief for abillement of werre to resiste the malice of there enemyes daily makyng fressh feetes of werre uppon theym ; he gevyng theym noone aide nor help, but lete theym contynue in theire malice, howe be it that diverse places were lost before : and what tyme that the said places were beseged and sent for help and socour unto hym he wold graunte no maner of comforte, but suffred hem appoint and compounde with here enemyes as well as they myght for theire ease and suertee, makyng no maner of provision for the kepyng of the places which remayned ; insomuch that he made non ordinaunce nor provision for the toun, castell, and places of Rouen, neither of men, stuffe ne vitaile, the knowlage that he had of youre enemyes comyng thereunto notwithstondyng, yevyng licence unto the Archiebisshopp, chanons and burgeys of the same toun for to goo or sende to compounde with youre enemyes for the deliveraunce of the same, notwithstondyng that afore that tyme the enemyes which were entred in to the same toun were worshiply put oute and betyn of by the Erle of Shrowesbury and other notable persones, and withdrawen to Pontlarge and Loviers, and at that tyme, they beyng so withdrawen, licenced to appointe as it is aforeseid. Which was plainly ayeinst his promys, feith and liegeaunce that he of right oweth unto you, and ayeinst the tenure of the enden-

105

THE PASTON LETTERS

tures made betwix youre highnes and hym of the charge of that londe, the which licence, and it had not ben don, the seid toun had abiden undre youre obeisaunce, the losse of whiche was a verray ope . . . .[1] cause of the perdicion of Normandie.

Item, the said Duc of Somersett, for to colour his defautes and wilfull purp[o]s in the premisses, entred in to youre palaice of Rouen not vitailed nor fo[rnisshed][1] for defence, where he myght savely absentid hym, and yeldid up the said Palaice and Castell, and moreover other good tounes, castels and [fortresses],[1] as Caudebek, and other diverse, as Tancarville, Moustervillers, Arques, key of all Caulx, not beseged nor in perell of losse at that tyme, for the enlargisshyn[g] and deliveraunce of hym, his childre and goodes ; which myght not, nor hath not, be done nor seen by lawe, resoun or cronikel, or by cours or a . . . . . . any leftenant, all though that he had be prisoner : Witnesse the Duc of Orliaunce, the Duc of Burbon, the Duc of Alansum and other . . . . . . for whom was none delyvered, al though they had many strong places of theire owen. And furthermore fore the suertee of delyveraunce of . . . . . . tounes, castell and forteresses which were wel furnysshed for to have resisted youre enemyes, and to have biden within youre obeisaunce, delyvered in ostage the Erle of Shrowesbury, that tyme Marescal of Fraunce, and other notable persones which shuld have defended youre lande there ayens the malice of youre enemyes ; and in likewyse apointed to delyver Honflu, which was in noo gret perell, ne had be that it was retardyd by youre lettres and so by that fraudelent and inordinat meane all was lost and yoldon up, as hereafter by more evident declaracions it shalbe clerely [proved].[2]

Item, the said Duc of Somerset hath contrived and ymagined, helped or consented to the grete and importable losse of Cales to be undre the obeisaunce of the Duc of Burgoyn, as it apperith openly by diverse skilles, evidencez, and resons ; that is to sey, in asmuch as he desired and made laboures, or at the lest toke uppon hym, for to be capiten of the seid Town of Cales, knowyng and understondyng well the grete murmur and sclaunder which daily rennyth agayn hym for the losse and sale, as it is surmyttid, of Normandie, to the grete discoragyng of the soudiours of the said Toun ; where as the comen fame is that he will bylike sotill meanes contrive and ymagyn the losse and amission of youre said Toun of Cales, like as he hath afore causid the perdicion of youre Duchie of Normandie ; which apperith well, in asmoch as he hath desirid the terme of a monyth without more, that, in case that the said Toun were besegid and not rescuyd within the

INTRODUCTION

said monyth, that than he shuld stond discharged though it were delyvered to youre enemyes ; within which tyme it were impossible, or at the lest full unlikly, that never myght be assembled for the rescu therof, where as it may and hath be here-before kept ayens the force of youre enemyes moche lenger tyme in grete jupardy ; which is so grete an hevynesse and trouble to youre said soudiours, that by theire langage, demenyng and communicacion it may be understond that they will not be so herty nor feithfull to the welfare and defence of the said Toun as they shuld be in case they had a captayn more agreable unto theym. And also this premisse apperith well in asmoch as the comen voyce, langage, and fame is, and also grete prefe and evidence shalbe made theruppon, that the seid Duc of Somerset, in hope of mariage to be doon and had be twix the Duc son of Burgoyn[1] and one of his doughters, had made a promysse and behest to the said Duc of Burgoyne, or Duchesse by his meane, concent and massangers, of the delyverey of the Toun of Cales, to be done by such sotill meanes as shuld not be understond neither of youre highenes nor of youre subgettz.

Item, the said Duc of Somerset is cause of grete hurtte, robbery, manslauter and other myscheves daily done and contynued in this youre roialme, in asmoch as he resceyved and had at the delyverey of Anjoy and Mayn iij. xij. (72,000) frankes or there aboutes, which were graunted and ordeyned to the Englisshmen havyng theire [there] lyvelode for theire recompense and asyth for the lyverey up of theire seid lyvelode at the said delyveraunce, and wold not dispose the same money nor departe therfrom, bot kepith it still to his owne use and singuler availe, notwithstondyng that he was recompensid for his lyvelode in that cuntrey in youre Duchie of Normandie of a more value than the gift therof was worth, which causith the said Englisshmen to be here in grete povertee ; of which povertee no doute commyth grete myscheve daily within your said roiame. And also in so muche as many diverse soudiours of Normandye were not paied theire wages, where he rerid grete and notable sommes of youre Duchie of Normandie for ther agrement, which non paiement and poverte causith also daily grete inconvenientz within this your lande.

Item, that these forsaid articles and poyntz be just and true it may well appere by many grete presumpcions beside evident prefes that shalbe made thereuppon with open and notarie fame and voice of the people, and also inasmoch as the said Duc of Somerset hath be double and untrue in many and diverse pointes, and in especiall that he hath desirid a recompense of youre highnes for the counte of Mayn for the delyverance therof, where it was specified in youre lettres patentes of

THE PASTON LETTERS

your graunte therof to hym made that ye shuld be at your libertee to dispose it at your pleasere in case that ye for the mene of the pease wold do make a lyverey thereof unto youre uncle of Fraunce; and yit at the tyme of delyveraunce thereof he wold not agree therto unto tyme that he were recompensid, as it is aforesaid, in youre Duchie of Normandie to a more value than his said graunte drue to.

Item, thees forsaid articles, everyche of theym and every parte of theym, purposyth and ministre I, Richard, Duc of York, ayens the said Duc of Somersett joyntly and severally not atteigne to a more strate nor chargeable prefe than your lawe in such case and processe will require; desiryng of youre highnesse and rightuous justice that in asmoche as lawfully may ayenst hym be foundon or previd, that jugement in that partie be had and executid unto youre highnes for yours and youre roialmes prosperite and welfare, indende not elles bot the salvacion and indempnite of youre most roiale persone, and also alle youre feithfull subgettz, in which y reporte me to God and all the word [*world*].

I imagine this paper must have been really handed in by York to the lords of the king's Council. It is preserved among the MSS. in the Cottonian Library, a large number of which were undoubtedly at one time part of the public records of the realm. But in any case we can hardly doubt that Somerset understood quite sufficiently the grounds on which he was so generally hated; nor is it by any means improbable that the armed remonstrance of the Duke of York produced some real effect, if only for a time. This at least we know, that only four days after the oath taken by York at St. Paul's, *Defence of Calais.* active and energetic measures began to be taken for the defence of Calais. Historians, as Sir Harris Nicolas truly remarks, do not seem hitherto to have been aware of the imminent danger in which even Calais at this time stood of being lost, like the other English conquests, a full century before it was actually recovered by the French. Rumours that Calais would be besieged reached England in the beginning of May 1450, along with the news of the Duke of Suffolk's murder.[1] In August 1451 a reinforcement of 1150 men was sent thither in twelve vessels, under the Lords Beauchamp and Sudeley. In the February following, as we have seen, York wrote of the success of the French in Gascony having emboldened them to

[1] Letter 121.

108

INTRODUCTION

lay siege to Calais again. And now, on the 14th of March, when Charles was advancing towards the last English stronghold, with the most formidable army that had been seen for years, and when men had begun to fear that he would be able not only to gain possession of Calais with ease, but even to invade and ravage England, steps were at last taken for the immediate formation of a fleet.

A royal navy had undoubtedly existed for a long time before the days of Henry VI., but it never amounted in itself to a very formidable force, and in time of war recourse was always had to impressment on the large scale. But the neglect of the sea was during this reign the constant complaint of Englishmen. For want of an efficient fleet the mercantile interest continually suffered, the fisheries could not safely be visited, and even the dwellers at home were insecure. The fact was confessed by the greatest eulogists of Henry VI., who had not a thought of impugning his government. 'Our enemies,' says Capgrave in his *Illustrious Henries*,—'Our enemies laugh at us. They say, "Take off the ship from your precious money, and stamp a sheep upon it to signify your sheepish minds." We who used to be conquerors of all nations are now conquered by all. The men of old used to say that the sea was England's wall, and now our enemies have got upon the wall; what think you they will do to the defenceless inhabitants? Because this business has been neglected for so many years it now happens that ships are scanty, and sailors also few, and such as we have unskilled for want of exercise. May God take away our reproach and raise up a spirit of bravery in our nation!'[1]

There were already available for the king's service a certain number of ships in the Thames, and at Winchelsea and Sandwich. The chief of these vessels was called the *Grace Dieu*—a name which was perhaps traditional, for it was handed down to Tudor times when, with the king's own Christian name prefixed, it was always given to the largest of the fleet.[2] The

[1] *Capgrave de Illust. Henricis*, 135.
[2] The *Henry Grace Dieu* of Henry VIII.'s time is, however, better known by its popular epithet of the *Great Harry*.

109

THE PASTON LETTERS

Earl of Shrewsbury[1] was appointed to take the command of the whole army at sea, and efforts were made to augment the squadron with as large a force as possible. On the 14th of March 1452 a commission was given to Lord Clifford, which was doubtless one of a number given to various noblemen, to negotiate for this purpose with shipowners, knights, and gentlemen in the district where he commonly resided; and he was instructed to take the command of all such vessels as he could raise, and bring them into the Downs to join with Shrewsbury. The appeal to patriotism was not made in vain. Many shipowners came forward, offering not only to lend but to victual their own ships for the service. But full powers were also given to arrest ships, shipmasters, and mariners, to make up a sufficient number. To every man not furnished with victuals by the benevolence of others, twelve pence a week was offered on the king's behalf, with a customary share in any booty that he might help to capture at sea. Captains of ships were to have in addition a reward of ten marks, or £10, at the discretion of Lord Clifford. Altogether we may presume that the defensive measures taken at this time were sufficient, for we hear no more during the next few years of any attempt to lay siege to Calais.

Amnesty at Home—Disaster Abroad

General pardon. As to internal dissensions at home, it was quite in accordance with the weakness of the king's character to believe that he had now stilled the chief elements of danger. His piety suggested to him to complete the good work by a general political amnesty. The year 1450, as being the concluding year of a half-century, had been celebrated as a jubilee at Rome, during which a general indulgence and pardon were granted to all who visited the Imperial City. There was also,

[1] The Earl of Shrewsbury, as already mentioned, had been given up to the French in 1449 as a hostage for the delivery of certain towns in Normandy. It is said that he only recovered his liberty on taking oath never to bear arms again against the French, but that on visiting Rome in the year of Jubilee, 1450, he obtained an absolution from this engagement.—*Æneæ Sylvii Opera*, 441.

110

INTRODUCTION

according to precedent, a bull issued at the close of the year to extend these benefits still further. Taking his example from the great Spiritual Ruler, the king, on Good Friday, the 7th of April 1452, offered publicly a general pardon to all who had been guilty of acts of disloyalty to himself, and who would apply to his Chancery for letters patent.[1] The offer was, undoubtedly, both gracious and humane. It sprang from a genuine love of peace on the king's part, and probably went far to make the government of Somerset endurable for some months longer. Amid the confusion and troubles of the times, thousands must have felt that they needed the royal clemency to protect them against the severity of the laws. One hundred and forty-four persons, among whom was Thomas Young of Bristol—he who had proposed in Parliament that York should be proclaimed heir to the crown—obtained sealed pardons on that very Good Friday. Some two or three thousand others laid claim to the like indulgence, and had patents granted to them at a later date.[2] Only a very few persons were excepted on account of the enormity of their offences.

One part of his kingdom, however, Henry himself did not expect to pacify by such means only. The state of the county of Norfolk had been so represented to him that he felt it necessary to send thither the Duke of Norfolk. 'Great riots, extortions, horrible wrongs and hurts,' were the subject of complaint, and nothing but an impartial inquiry would give satisfaction. The duke on coming into the country issued a proclamation, urging all who had any complaints to make to lay them freely and fearlessly before him. But free and fearless evidence was not likely to be had without a strong

[1] Whethamstede, 317.
[2] The names are all entered on the *Pardon Roll* of 30 and 31 Henry VI. Among the hosts of less interesting names, we find that the Duke of York took out a pardon on the 3rd of June; the Duke of Norfolk and the young Duke of Suffolk on the 23rd of the same month; Thomas Percy, Lord Egremont, on the 1st; Thomas Courtenay, Earl of Devon, on the 20th, and Sir William Oldhall, who is called of Hunsdon, on the 26th. Ralph, Lord Cromwell, had one on the 22nd May, and Robert Wynnyngton of Dartmouth (the writer of Letter 90) on the 28th July. On the 12th July a joint pardon was given to Sir Henry Percy, Lord Ponynges, and Eleanor, his wife, kinswoman and heir of Sir Robert Ponynges. At later dates we have also pardons to Henry, Viscount Bourchier, and Sir John Talbot, son and heir of the Earl of Shrewsbury.

111

guarantee for the protection of witnesses. Already the news of the duke's coming had got wind, and some of the dependants of Lord Scales, who had been amongst the principal offenders, had given notice that any complaints against *them* would be redressed in another fashion after the duke's departure. In the absence of the duke Lord Scales had been always hitherto the natural ruler of the county, and it was under his protection that Sir Thomas Tuddenham, Sir Miles Stapleton, John Heydon, and others had dared to make themselves unpopular. Norfolk accordingly declared in the same proclamation that he intended henceforth to vindicate for himself so long as he lived the chief power and authority in the county which bore his name, subject only to that of the king himself. And to give still greater encouragement to the well-disposed, he announced that the king himself would shortly visit the county, before whom all who desired it should have their grievances redressed.[1]

Intended royal visit to Norfolk.

That the king actually visited Norfolk at this time I do not find from any other evidence. A letter written on St. George's Day says that he had been expected at Norwich or Claxton for ten days past. Encouraged by the duke's proclamation, several gentlemen of the county had drawn up a complaint against Charles Nowell, and were waiting to know in what manner they should present it. This Charles and a number of others appear to have been keeping the country east of Norwich at the time in continual alarm and confusion. They held their rendezvous at the house of one Robert Ledeham, from which they would issue out in bands of six, or twelve, or sometimes thirty or more, fully armed with bows and arrows, spears and bills, jacks and sallets.[2] No place was sacred from their outrages. On Mid-Lent Sunday they had attacked two servants of the Bishop of Norwich inside the church at Burlingham, and would have killed them behind the priest's back while they were kneeling at the mass. On the 6th of April they had endeavoured to break into the White Friars at Norwich on pretence of wishing to hear evensong; but having publicly declared in the town that they intended to get hold of

Complaint against Charles Nowell.

[1] No. 210. [2] Coats of mail and helmets.

certain citizens, either alive or dead, the doors were shut against them. Happily, before they accomplished their purpose the mayor and aldermen came to the spot. A multitude of people had meanwhile assembled in the streets, and the rioters, finding the odds considerably against them, quietly took their departure.[1]

John Paston had a complaint of his own to make against these wrongdoers. Charles Nowell himself, and five others, had attacked him at the door of Norwich Cathedral. He had with him at the time two servants, one of whom received a blow on the naked head with a sword; and he himself was seized and had his arms held behind him, while one of the company struck at him. But for a timely rescue his death would seem to have been certain. On the very day on which this occurred his wife's uncle, Philip Berney, was waylaid by some of the same fellowship, in the highway under Thorpe Wood. Berney was riding, accompanied by a single servant, when their two horses first were wounded by a discharge of arrows. They were then speedily overtaken by their assailants, who broke a bow over Philip Berney's head, and took him prisoner, declaring him to be a traitor. To give a further colour to their proceedings, they led him prisoner to the Bishop of Norwich, demanding surety of him to keep the peace, and, when they had obtained it, let him go. Philip Berney lived more than a year after the adventure, but he never recovered from the effects of this rough usage.[2]

John Paston assaulted at Norwich Cathedral.

Outrages like these, it must be remembered, were not the work of lawless brigands and recognised enemies of the whole community. They were merely the effect of party spirit. The men who did them were supported by noblemen and country gentlemen. One, by name Roger Church, probably the most daring, and at the same time the most subtle, of the gang, had got himself made bailiff of the hundred of Blofield.[3] Charles Nowell was a friend of Thomas Daniel, who, after being a year and a half out of favour, had recently recovered his influence in Norfolk through the medium of the Duke of

[1] Nos. 211, 217, 241.
[2] Nos. 212, 213, 227, 228, 241.
[3] Nos. 214, 241.

Somerset.[1] By this means he seems again to have obtained possession of the manor of Bradeston, the right to which he had disputed in 1450, apparently more by arms than by law, with Osbert Mountford, marshal of Calais. Charles Nowell was appointed by Daniel bailiff of the manor, with the slender but not insignificant salary of twopence a day; and he and his fellows, Roger Church, Robert Ledeham, John Ratcliff, and Robert Dalling, made it their chief business to maintain Daniel in possession.

To put an end to such a state of matters as this, the Duke of Norfolk's coming must have been truly welcome. But if any man expected that the power of duke or king could suddenly terminate the reign of anarchy, and initiate an era of plain impartial justice, he must have been a sanguine mortal. As one of the first effects of the duke's coming, some of the leading oppressors of the country were driven to a course of chicanery instead of violence. Roger Church got himself arrested by some of his own company, and was brought before the duke as a promoter of sedition. He was accused of having taken part in an unlawful assembly at Postwick, with the view of stirring up an insurrection. He confessed the fact, and offered to turn king's evidence on his accomplices. He then named a number of thrifty husbandmen, farmers, and gentlemen of the neighbourhood, alleging that about three hundred persons were implicated in the intended rising. The truth, as it presently turned out, and as Church himself afterwards confessed, was, that the movement had been got up by himself, at the instigation of Robert Ledeham, who promised to procure his pardon through the influence of Daniel. By solicitations addressed to various unsteady characters he had induced some to believe that an insurrection would be well supported. A little company of fifteen men accordingly met him under a wood at Postwick, and he told them he had discovered an excellent name for their captain, who should be called John Amend-All. But beyond this meeting and naming of the captain nothing seems ever to have come of the project.[2]

Roger Church.

[1] No. 206. [2] Nos. 214, 217, 218, 219, 241.

John Paston was certainly one of those mentioned by Church. The chief persons accused were the friends of Osbert Mountford, and Paston was one of them. But John Falgate, one of the deluded victims who had been present at the meeting at Postwick, being subjected to examination before the sheriff, exonerated Paston, and, while acknowledging his own share in the conspiracy, pronounced the tale told by Roger Church in his confession to be altogether an invention. We need not be surprised to hear that after this a petition from the county of Norfolk was sent up to the Lord Chancellor, praying that Church should not be allowed the benefit of the general pardon, offered upon Good Friday.[1] But Church persevered in his policy. He appears to have been a reckless kind of adventurer. He probably claimed the benefit of clergy, for we find him three months after his arrest in the hands of officers of the Bishop of Norwich. His goods also were seized for a debt that he owed the bishop. But in spite of the contradictions given by other witnesses, in July he adhered to what he had said in April, and instead of retracting his former accusations, said he meant to impeach some one else whom he could not at that time name,—a man who, he said, had more money in his purse than all of those whom he had accused before. The coolness with which he persisted in these statements gave an impression that he was even yet relying upon powerful friends to support him.[2]

The conclusion of the affair must be a matter of speculation, for we hear nothing more of it. The political history of England, too, is, at this point, almost a blank. We know from the Privy Council Proceedings that there was some difficulty in the spring of 1452 in preserving friendly relations with Scotland in consequence of some Border outrages perpetrated by the Earl of Douglas. And this is absolutely all the light we have on the domestic affairs of England for about a twelvemonth after the Duke of York's oath of allegiance at St. Paul's. I have found, however, by an examination of the

[1] The petition, I think, must have been effectual, for I did not find Church's name on the *Pardon Roll*, 30 and 31 Henry VI.
[2] Nos. 214, 216, 218.

THE PASTON LETTERS

INTRODUCTION

A royal progress.

dates of privy seals, that in July the king began a progress into the west of England, which is not altogether without significance. He reached Exeter on the 18th, and from thence proceeded by Wells, Gloucester, Monmouth, and Hereford to Ludlow, where he arrived on the 12th of August, and from which he returned homewards by Kenilworth and Woodstock, arriving at Eltham in the beginning of September. In October he made another circuit northwards by St. Albans to Stamford, Peterborough, and Cambridge. There can hardly be a doubt the object of these journeys was mainly to conciliate those who had declared their opposition to the Duke of Somerset, especially when we consider that the visit to Ludlow must have been nothing less than a visit to the Duke of York. York was now more than pardoned. He was honoured by his sovereign.

Financially, however, we may well suppose that the duke was not the better of the royal visit. Perhaps also the state of the country did not conduce to the prosperity of great landowners. At all events we find that at the end of the year York was glad to pledge some pieces of jewellery to Sir John Fastolf for a loan of £437, to be repaid next Mid-summer.[1] The transaction is in every way curious, as illustrating the sort of dealings in money matters which were at that time by no means uncommon among knights and noblemen. It is certainly highly characteristic of such a knight as Sir John Fastolf, who, quite unlike the Falstaff of the dramatist, instead of being always needy, was always seeking to increase the wealth that he had amassed by long years of thrift and frugality.

Sir John Fastolf.

We have had occasion to mention the historic Fastolf before; and it is time that we should now direct attention to the circumstances of his private life and his connection with the Paston family. John Paston, as the reader was already been informed, was ultimately his executor, and to this circumstance may safely be attributed the preservation of so many of his letters, most of which have certainly been handed down with the papers of the Paston family. Nevertheless, up

[1] No. 223.

116

to the time at which we have now arrived we do not find that he directly corresponded with any of them. We can see, however, that he had a high regard for John Paston's advice in business, and sometimes sent letters and documents of importance by him to his agent in Norfolk, Sir Thomas Howes.[1] He seems to have been related in blood to John Paston's wife,[2] and he acknowledges Paston himself as his cousin in his will. From the general tenor of most of his letters we should certainly no more suspect him of being the old soldier that he actually was than of being Shakespeare's fat, disorderly knight. Every sentence in them refers to lawsuits and title-deeds, extortions and injuries received from others, forged processes affecting property, writs of one kind or another to be issued against his adversaries, libels uttered against himself, and matters of the like description. Altogether the perusal is apt to give us an impression that Sir John would have made an acute and able, though perhaps not very highminded, solicitor. If ever his agent, Sir Thomas Howes, was, or seemed to be, a little remiss in regard to some particular interest, he was sure to hear of it, and yet woe to him if he did things on his own responsibility which turned out afterwards to be a failure.[3] Sir John was not the man to pass over lightly injuries done by inadvertence.

The familiarity shown by Fastolf with all the forms and processes of the law is probably due not so much to the peculiarity of his personal character as to the fact that a knowledge of legal technicalities was much more widely diffused in that day than it is in ours. Even in the days when Master Shallow first made himself ridiculous to a London audience by claiming to be justice of the peace and *coram*, *custalorum*, and *ratolorum*, there can hardly be a doubt that the knowledge of legal terms and processes was not a thing so entirely professional as it is now. But if we go back to an

[1] Nos. 153, 159, 162, 186, 188, 203.
[2] Note the passages in Margaret Paston's letter (No. 222):—'Yet I suppose Sir John, if he were spoken to, would be gladder to let his kinsmen have part than strangers.' And again:—'Assay him in my name of such places as ye suppose is most clear.'
[3] No. 202.

117

THE PASTON LETTERS

INTRODUCTION

earlier time, the Paston letters afford ample evidence that every man who had property to protect, if not every well-educated woman also, was perfectly well versed in the ordinary forms of legal processes. Sir John Fastolf had a great deal of property to take care of, and consequently had much more occasion to make use of legal phraseology than other people. Had it been otherwise we should hardly have had any letters of his at all; for the only use of writing to him, and probably to most other people in those days, was to communicate on matters of business.

There are also parts of his correspondence from which we might almost infer that Sir John was a merchant as well as a lawyer. His ships were continually passing between London and Yarmouth, carrying on the outward voyage building materials for his works at Caister, and bringing home malt or other produce from the county of Norfolk. In two of his letters we have references to his little ship *The Blythe*,[1] which, however, was only one of several; for, in the year 1443, he obtained a licence from the Crown to keep no less than six vessels in his service. These are described as of four different kinds : two being what were called 'playtes,' a third a 'cog-ship,' a fourth a 'farecoft,' and the two others 'balingers,' for the carriage of goods and building materials for the use of his household. These vessels were to be free from all liability to arrest for the service of the king.[2]

Building of Caister Castle.

The object of these building operations was the erection of a stately castle at Caister, not far from Yarmouth, the place of the old warrior's birth. As early as the reign of Henry v., it seems, he had obtained licence to fortify a dwelling there, 'so strong as himself could devise';[3] but his occupation in the French wars had suspended a design which must have been a special object with him all through life. The manor of Caister had come to him by natural descent from his paternal ancestry; but even during his mother's widowhood, when Sir John was a young man of about six-and-twenty, we find that

[1] Nos. 171, 173.   [2] Rymer, xi. 44.
[3] Dawson Turner's *Historical Sketch of Caister Castle*, p. 31. He does not state his authority.

118

she gave up her life tenure of it to vest it entirely in her son.[1] Since that day he had been abroad with Henry v. at Agincourt and at the siege of Rouen. He had afterwards served in France under the Regent Bedford,—had taken several strong castles and one illustrious prisoner,[2]—had held the government of conquered districts, and had fought, generally with success and glory, in almost every great battle of the period. Nor had he been free, even on his return to England, to go at once and spend the rest of his days on his paternal domains in Norfolk. His counsels were needed by his sovereign. His experience abroad must have qualified him to give important advice on many subjects of vital interest touching both France and England, and we have evidence that he was, at least occasionally, summoned to take part in the proceedings of the Privy Council. But now, when he was upwards of seventy years of age, the dream of his youth was going to be realised. Masons and bricklayers were busy at Caister,[3] building up for him a magnificent edifice, of which the ruins are at this day the most interesting feature in the neighbourhood. Sadly imperfect ruins indeed they are,—in some places even the foundations would seem to have disappeared, or else the plan of the building is not very intelligible; but a noble tower still rises to a height of ninety feet,—its top possessed by jackdaws,—and a large extent of mouldered walls, pierced with loopholes and surmounted by remains of battlements, enable the imagination to realise what Caister Castle must have been when it was finished over four hundred years ago. A detached fragment of these ruins, too, goes by the name of the Bargehouse; and there, beneath a low-browed arch still visible, tradition reports that Sir John Fastolf's barge or barges would issue out on their voyages or enter on their return home.

According to Dawson Turner, the foundations of Caister Castle must have enclosed a space of more than six acres of ground.[4] The inventory of the furniture contained in it at Fastolf's death[5] enumerates no less than six-and-twenty

[1] See 'Early Documents' in vol. ii. p. 4.   [2] The Duke of Alençon.
[3] Nos. 224, 225.   [4] *Historical Sketch*, p. 4.   [5] No. 389.

119

THE PASTON LETTERS

chambers, besides the public rooms, chapel, and offices. An edifice on such a scale must have been some time in building :—many years, we should suppose, passed away before it was completed. And we are not without evidence that such was actually the case ; for a chamber was set apart for the Lady Milicent, Fastolf's wife, who is believed to have died in 1446, and yet the works were still going on in 1453. In this latter year we find that John Paston was allowed to have some control of the building operations, and that chambers were to be built for him and his wife. Meanwhile it appears he had chosen an apartment in which to set up his coffers and his counting-board for the time. Possibly when he was able to visit Caister he may have acted as paymaster of the works.[1]

The great castle, however, was now not far from completion ; and before the end of the following year Sir John Fastolf had removed from London and taken up his residence at Caister, where, with the exception of one single visit to the capital, he seems to have spent all the remainder of his days.

We have said that very few notices are to be found of the internal affairs of England in the year 1452, subsequent to the Duke of York swearing allegiance at St. Paul's. But just about that time, or not very long after, the affairs of Guienne came once more to the serious consideration of the Council. It is true that Guienne and Gascony were now no Attempt longer English possessions. Bayonne, the last stronghold, to recover had been given up in the preceding August, and, the English Guienne. forces being now expelled, all hope of recovering the lost provinces might well have been abandoned, but that the inhabitants were desirous to put themselves once more under the protection of the King of England. The fact is that the Gascons, who had been three centuries under English rule, did not at all relish the change of masters. Under the crown of England they had enjoyed a liberty and freedom from taxation which were unknown in the dominions of Charles VII. ; and on the surrender of Bordeaux and Bayonne, the

[1] Nos. 224, 225.

120

INTRODUCTION

French king had expressly promised to exempt them from a number of impositions levied elsewhere. But for this promise, indeed, those cities would not so readily have come to terms.[1] Unfortunately, it was not very long before the ministers of Charles sought to evade its fulfilment. They represented to the people that for their own protection, and not for the benefit of the royal treasury, the imposition of a *taille* would enable the king to set a sufficient guard upon the country, and that the money would not in reality be taken from them, as it would all be spent within the province. The English, it was to be feared, would not remain patient under the loss, not only of the provinces themselves, but also of a very valuable commerce that they had hitherto maintained with the south of France ; for Gascony supplied England with wine, and was a large consumer of English wool. Hence there was every reason to fear that some attempt would be made by the enemy to recover the lands from which he had been expelled, and it was the interest of the inhabitants themselves to provide an adequate force to ward off invasion.[2]

With arguments like these the French king's officers went about among the people endeavouring to compel them to forego a liberty which had been secured to them under the Great Seal of France. In vain were deputations sent from Bordeaux and Gascony beseeching the king to be faithful to his promise. The petitioners were sent back with an answer urging the people to submit to exactions which were required for the defence of the country. The citizens of Bordeaux were greatly discontented, and an embassy, headed by the Sieur de l'Esparre, was sent over to the King of England to offer him the allegiance of the lost provinces once more, on his sending a sufficient fleet and army to their rescue. The proposal being laid before a meeting of the English Council, was of course most readily agreed to ; and it was arranged that a fleet, under the command of the Earl of Shrewsbury, should sail for the Garonne in October. On the 18th of that month the earl accordingly embarked with a body of 4000 or 5000 soldiers. The French army having withdrawn, he easily

[1] Basin, i. 251.   [2] *Ibid.* 257.

121

THE PASTON LETTERS

obtained possession of Bordeaux, and sent its captain, Oliver de Coëtivy, a prisoner into England. Other towns then readily opened their gates to the invaders, of which one of the principal was Castillon in Perigord ; and very soon, in spite of the opposition of their French governors, the greater part of the lost provinces had put themselves again under the protection of the English.[1]

The suddenness with which these things were done seems for a time to have disconcerted the French king. Winter was now coming on, and probably nothing effective could be done for some time, so Charles lay maturing his plans in silence. As he surveyed the position at leisure, he probably found that any further efforts of the invaders could be checked with tolerable facility. France still retained possession of the two little towns of Bourges and Blaye, which we have already mentioned as being the keys of Bordeaux, and also of various other strong places in which he had been careful to leave A.D. 1453. considerable garrisons. It was therefore the beginning of June in the following year before he took any active steps to expel the enemy from their conquests. He then marched southwards from Lusignan, near Poitiers, and laid siege to Chalais in Perigord, on the borders of Saintonge. In the space of five days it was taken by assault. Out of a garrison of 160 men no less than half were cut to pieces. The other half took refuge in a tower where they still held out for a time in the vain hope of succours, till at last they were compelled to surrender unconditionally. Of the prisoners taken, such as were of English birth were ransomed ; but as for those who were Gascons, as they had sworn fealty to Charles and departed from their allegiance, they were all beheaded. After this, one or two other ill-defended places fell into the hands of the French. On the 14th July siege was laid to Castillon on the Dordogne, a position which when won gave the French free navigation into the Gironde. The besieging army was furnished with the most perfect mechanism of war that the skill or science of that age could supply. It had a train of artillery, with no less than 700 gunners, under the

[1] Basin, i. 258-261. Leclerq (in Petitot's Collection), 37-38.

122

INTRODUCTION

conduct of two able engineers of Paris, the brothers Bureau. The place was thoroughly closed in, when Shrewsbury, hearing of the danger in which it stood, came with haste out of Bordeaux with a body of 800 or 1000 horse, followed shortly after by 4000 or 5000 foot.[1]

At daybreak on the 17th, the earl came suddenly upon the besiegers, and succeeded without difficulty in thoroughly defeating a body of archers, who had been posted at an abbey outside the town. This detachment being completely taken by surprise, was obliged to save itself by flight, and after a little skirmishing, in which some 80 or 100 men were slain on both sides, the greater number of the Frenchmen succeeded in gaining a park in which the main body of the besiegers had entrenched themselves. Further pursuit being now unnecessary, the English returned to the abbey, where they were able to refresh themselves with a quantity of victuals which the French had left behind them. 'And because the said skirmish,' writes the French chronicler De Coussy, 'had been begun and was done so early that as yet Talbot had not heard mass, his chaplain prepared himself to sing it there ; and for this purpose the altar and ornaments were got ready.' But this devout intention the earl presently abandoned ; for a cloud of dust was seen in the distance, and it was reported to him that even the main body of the French were rapidly retreating. Immediately the earl was again on horseback, and as he left the abbey he was heard to say, 'I will hear no mass to-day till I have overthrown the company of Frenchmen in the park before me.'[2]

Unfortunately, it turned out that the report of the retreat of the French was utterly unfounded. The cloud of dust had been raised by a body of horses which they had sent out of the camp to graze. The French army remained in its position, with artillery drawn up, ready to meet the earl on his advance. The English, nevertheless, came on with their usual shout, ' A Talbot ! A Talbot ! St. George !' and while their foremost men just succeeded for an instant in planting their standard on

[1] Basin, i. 261-4. Leclerq, 39-41. Matt. de Coussy, 121.
[2] Basin, i. 264-5. De Coussy, 122.

123

THE PASTON LETTERS

INTRODUCTION

the barrier of the French lines, they were mowed down behind by the formidable fire of the French artillery. Against this all valour was fruitless ; about 500 or 600 English lay dead in front ; and the French, opening the barrier of their park, rushed out and fought with their opponents hand to hand. For a while the conflict was still maintained, with great valour on both sides ; but the superior numbers of the French, and the advantage they had already gained by their artillery, left very little doubt about the issue. After about 4000 Englishmen had been slain in the hand-to-hand encounter, the remainder fled or were made prisoners. Some were able to withdraw into the town and join themselves to the besieged garrison ; others fled through the woods and across the river, in which a number of the fugitives were drowned. In the end the body of the veteran Talbot was found dead upon the field, covered with wounds upon the limbs, and a great gash across the face.[1]

Defeat and death of Talbot.

So fell the aged warrior, whose mere name had long been a terror to England's enemies. By the confession of a French historian, who hardly seems to feel it a disgrace to his countrymen, the archers, when they closed around him, distinctly refused to spare his life, so vindictively eager were they to despatch him with a multitude of wounds.[2] Yet it must be owned that in this action he courted his own death, and risked the destruction of a gallant army. For though he was led to the combat by a false report, he was certainly under no necessity of engaging the enemy when he had discovered his mistake, and he was strongly dissuaded from doing so by Thomas Everingham.[3] But his own natural impetuosity, inflamed probably still more by the unreasonable taunts of the men of Bordeaux, who, it seems, were dissatisfied that no earlier attempt had been made to resist the advance of the French king into Guienne,[4] induced him to stake everything on the issue of a most desperate and unequal conflict.

With him there also died upon the field his eldest son, Lord Lisle, his illegitimate son, Henry Talbot, Sir Edward Hull, and thirty other knights of England. About double

[1] De Coussy, 124.　　[2] Basin, i. 267-8.
[3] Ibid. 265.　　[4] De Coussy, 122.

124

that number were taken prisoners, the most notable of whom was John Paston's old persecutor, the Lord Moleyns.[1] Never had the English arms experienced such a disastrous overthrow.

The Gascons now gave up their cause as altogether hopeless. A fresh army had lately marched into their country, and was laying siege to several places at once towards the east of Bordeaux, so that it was manifest that city would soon be shut in by the royal forces. Castillon was no longer able to hold out. It surrendered on the second day after Talbot's death. About the same time Charles in person laid siege to Cadillac, one of the most important places in the neighbourhood, protected by a strong castle. The town was speedily carried by assault, and a few weeks later the castle was also taken. Other places in like manner came once more into the power of the French king. At Fronsac an English garrison capitulated and was allowed to leave the country, each soldier bearing in his hand a baton till he reached the seaside. Very soon Bordeaux was the only place that held out ; nor was the defence even of this last stronghold very long protracted. Its surrender was delayed for a time only in consequence of the severity of the conditions on which Charles at first insisted ; but a sickness which began to ravage his camp at length inclined him to clemency. On the 17th of October the city submitted to Charles, the inhabitants engaging to renew their oaths of allegiance, and the English having leave to return in their own ships to England. To secure himself against their future return, or any fresh rebellion of the citizens, Charles caused to be built and garrisoned, at the expense of the latter, two strong towers, which were still standing at the beginning of the last century. Thus was Gascony finally lost to the Crown of England.

We must now return to the domestic affairs of the kingdom. Matters had been hung up, as it were, in a state of unstable equilibrium ever since Good Friday 1452. The political amnesty, proceeding, as it did, from the king's own heart, and removing every stain of disloyalty from those who had laboured most to change his policy, helped, in all probability,

[1] J. Chartier, 265 ; Berry, 469.

125

THE PASTON LETTERS

INTRODUCTION

to keep up a precarious state of tranquillity much longer than it could otherwise have been preserved. The danger of Calais, too, had passed away for the time, although it was always recurring at intervals so long as Henry VI. was king. So that, perhaps, during the latter part of the year 1452, the country was in as quiet a state as could reasonably have been expected. At least, the absence of information to the contrary may be our warrant for so believing. But the new year had no sooner opened than evidences of disaffection began to be perceived. On the 2nd of January Robert Poynings—the same who had taken a leading part in Cade's rebellion, and had, it will be remembered, saved the life of one of Sir John Fastolf's servants from the violence of the insurgents—called together an assembly of people at Southwark, many of whom were outlaws. What his object was we have no distinct evidence to show. He had received the king's general pardon for the part he took in the movement under Cade ; but he had been obliged to enter into a recognisance of £2000, and find six sureties of £200 each, for his good behaviour ; so that he, of all men, had best cause to beware of laying himself open to any new suspicion of disloyalty. Yet it appears he not only did so by this meeting at Southwark, but that immediately afterwards he confederated with one Thomas Bigg of Lambeth, who had been one of Cade's petty captains, and having met with him and about thirty others at Westerham in Kent, tried to stir up a new rising in the former seat of rebellion. From Kent he further proceeded into Sussex, and sent letters to two persons who had been indicted of treason, urging them to come and meet him at Southwark on the last day of February ; 'at which time and place,' says the Parliament Roll, 'the same Robert Poynings gave them money, thanking them heartily of their good will and disposition that they were of unto him in time past, praying them to continue their good will, and to be ready and come to him at such time as he should give them warning.'[1] Altogether it would appear from the record of the charge itself that nothing very serious

A.D. 1453.

Robert Poynings.

[1] Rolls of Parl. v. 396.　See also the pardon granted to him five years later. Patent Roll, 36 Hen. VI. m. 12.

126

came of this display of disaffection on the part of Poynings ; but it must at least be noted as a symptom of the times.

Soon after this a Parliament was called. The Crown was Parliament. in need of money ; but Somerset did not dare to convoke the legislature at Westminster. It met in the refectory of the abbey of Reading on the 6th of March. In the absence of the Archbishop of Canterbury, Cardinal Kemp, who was Chancellor, the Bishop of Lincoln[1] opened the proceedings by a speech on behalf of the king, declaring the causes of their being summoned ; which were merely stated to be, in general terms, for the good government of the kingdom and for its outward defence. The necessity of sending reinforcements into Gascony was not mentioned, and apparently was not thought of ; for up to this time the success of Shrewsbury had been uninterrupted, and the French king had not yet begun his southward march. The Commons elected one Thomas Thorpe as their Speaker, and presented him to the king on the 8th. Within three weeks they voted a tenth and fifteenth, a subsidy of tonnage and poundage, a subsidy on wools, hides, and woolfells, and a capitation tax on aliens,—all these, except the tenth and fifteenth, to be levied for the term of the king's natural life. They also ordained that every county, city, and town should be charged to raise its quota towards the levying of a body of 20,000 archers within four months. For these important services they received the thanks of the king, communicated to them by the Chancellor, and were immediately prorogued over Easter, to sit at Westminster on the 25th of April.[2]

On their reassembling there, they proceeded to arrange the proportion of the number of archers which should be raised in each county, and the means by which they were to be levied. The Commons, however, were relieved of the charge of providing 7000 men of the number formerly agreed to, as 3000 were to be charged upon the Lords and 3000 more on Wales and the county palatine of Cheshire, while an additional thousand was

[1] Called William, Bishop of Lincoln, on the Rolls of Parliament, but his name was John Chedworth.
[2] Rolls of Parl. v. 227-31.

127

THE PASTON LETTERS

remitted by the king, probably as the just proportion to be levied out of his own household. For the remaining 13,000, the quota of each county was then determined. But soon afterwards it was found that the need of such a levy was not so urgent as had at first been supposed, and the actual raising of the men was respited for two years, provided that no emergency arose requiring earlier need of their services.[1]

The possibility of their being required in Gascony after the success of the Earl of Shrewsbury in the preceding year, seems no more to have occurred to the Government, than the thought of sending them to Constantinople, where possibly, had the fact been known, they might at this very time have done something to prevent that ancient city from falling into the hands of the Turks. For it was in this very year, and while these things occupied the attention of the English Parliament, that the long decaying Eastern Empire was finally extinguished by the fall of its metropolis.

After this, some new Acts were passed touching the pay of the garrison at Calais, and for the making of jetties and other much-needed repairs there. For these purposes large sums of money were required, and the mode in which they were to be provided gives us a remarkable insight into the state of the exchequer. To the Duke of Somerset, as Captain of Calais, there was owing a sum of £21,648, 10s., for the wages of himself and his suite since the date of his appointment; and on the duke's own petition, an Act was passed enabling him to be paid, not immediately, but after his predecessor, Humphrey, Duke of Buckingham, should have received all that was due to him in a like capacity.[2] The pay of the officers of Calais, it would thus appear, but that it seems to have been discharged by the Captain for the time being out of his own resources, must at this time have been more than two years in arrear. If such was the state of matters, we gain some light on the causes which induced Somerset, after his loss of Normandy, to add to his unpopularity by accepting a post of so much responsibility as the Captainship of Calais. He was one of the few men in England whose wealth was such that he could afford to

[1] Rolls of Parl. v. 231-3.   [2] Ibid. v. 233.

128

INTRODUCTION

wait for his money; and he was too responsible for the rotten government which had led to such financial results to give any other man a post in which he would certainly have found cause of dissatisfaction.

It was necessary, however, to provide ready money for the repairs and the wages of the garrison from this time, and it was accordingly enacted that a half of the fifteenth and tenth already voted should be immediately applied to the one object, and a certain proportion of the subsidy on wools to the other. At the same time a new vote of half a fifteenth and tenth additional was found necessary to meet the extraordinary expenditure, and was granted on the 2nd of July.[1]

This grant being announced by the Speaker to the king, who was then sitting in Parliament, Henry thanked the Commons with his own mouth, and then commissioned the chancellor, Cardinal Kemp, to prorogue the assembly; alleging as his reasons the consideration due to the zeal and attendance of the Commons, and the king's own intention of visiting different parts of his kingdom for the suppression of various malpractices. 'The king, also,' he added, 'understood that there were divers petitions exhibited in the present Parliament to which no answer had yet been returned, and which would require greater deliberation and leisure than could now conveniently be afforded, seeing that the autumn season was at hand, in which the Lords were at liberty to devote themselves to hunting and sport, and the Commons to the gathering in of their harvests.' As these weighty matters, whatever they were, required too much consideration to be disposed of before harvest-time, we might perhaps have expected an earlier day to be fixed for the reassembling of the legislature than that which was actually then announced. Perhaps, also, we might have expected that as the Parliament had returned to Westminster, it would have been ordered to meet there again when it renewed its sittings. But the king, or his counsellors, were of a different opinion; and the Parliament was ordered to meet again on the 12th of November at Reading.

Long before that day came, calamities of no ordinary kind

[1] Rolls of Parl. v. 234-6.

     129

THE PASTON LETTERS

had overtaken both king and nation. About the beginning of August,[1] news must have come to England of the defeat and death of the Earl of Shrewsbury; and Somerset at last was quickened into action when it was too late. Great preparations were made for sending an army into Guienne, when Guienne was already all but entirely lost. It is true the Government were aware of the danger in which Talbot stood for want of succours, at least as early as the 14th of July; even then they were endeavouring to raise money by way of loan, and to arrest ships and sailors. But it is evident that they had slept too long in false security, and when they were for the first time thoroughly awake to the danger, the disaster was so near at hand that it could not possibly have been averted.[2]

The King's Prostration

Whether it was in any degree owing to this national calamity,—in which case, the impression made by the event may well have been deepened by the knowledge that it was attributed to the remissness of Somerset,—or whether it was due entirely to physical or other causes quite unconnected with public affairs, in August the king fell ill at Clarendon, and began to exhibit symptoms of mental derangement.[3] Two months later an event occurred in which, under other circumstances, he could not but have felt a lively interest. After eight years of married life, the queen for the first time bore him a child. It was a son and received the name of Edward; but for a long time afterwards the father knew nothing of the event. So entirely were his mental faculties in abeyance, that it was found impossible to communicate to him the news. The affairs of his kingdom and those of his family were for the time equally beyond his comprehension.

The king falls ill.

[1] It appears not to have been known on the 4th of August. Stevenson's *Wars*, ii. 487-8.
[2] Nicolas's *Privy Council Proceedings*, vi. 151-4, 155-7. Stevenson's *Wars*, ii. 481-92.
[3] W. Worc. In an almanac of that time I find the following note, which dates the beginning of the king's illness on the 10th of August:—'In nocte S. Laurentii Rex infirmatur et continuavit usque ad Circumcisionem Anni 1455, in p. . . .' (?) (a word unintelligible at the end). MS. Reg. 13, C. 1.

130

INTRODUCTION

The failure of royalty to perform any of its functions, however weakly they might have been performed before, was a crisis that had not occurred till now. A heavier responsibility lay with Somerset and the Council, who could not expect that acts done by their own authority would meet with the same respect and recognition as those for which they had been able to plead the direct sanction of their sovereign. And now they had to deal with a factious world, in which feuds between powerful families had already begun to kindle a dangerous conflagration. In the month of August, probably of the year before this, Lord Thomas Nevill, a son of the Earl of Salisbury, married a niece of Lord Cromwell at Tattersall in Lincolnshire. After the wedding the earl returned into Yorkshire, when, having reached the neighbourhood of York, some disturbance arose between his retainers and those of Lord Egremont, son of the Earl of Northumberland.[1] As to the cause of the dispute we are left entirely ignorant; but it grew into a serious quarrel between the Nevills and the Percys. The chief maintainers of the feud were, on the one side, Sir John Nevill, a younger son of the Earl of Salisbury, and on the other Lord Egremont. Both parties were repeatedly summoned to lay their grievances before the Council; but the most peremptory letters and mandates had hitherto been ineffectual. Illegal gatherings of people on either side continued in spite of every prohibition; and the whole north of England seems to have been kept in continual disorder.[2]

The case was not likely to be improved when the source of all legal authority was paralysed. And yet so bad was the state of matters before, that the king's illness, instead of being an aggravation of the evil, positively brought with it some perceptible relief. The Council were no longer able to avoid calling in the aid of one whose capacity to rule was as indisputable as his birth and rank. A Great Council was summoned for the express purpose of promoting 'rest and union betwixt the lords of this land'; and according to the usage in such cases, every peer of the realm had notice to

[1] W. Worc.   [2] Nicolas's *Privy Council Proceedings*, vi. 140-2, 147-9, 154-5.

131

THE PASTON LETTERS

attend. Gladly, no doubt, would Somerset have omitted to send such notice to his rival; and it seems actually to have been the case that no summons was at first sent to the Duke of York. But afterwards the error was rectified, and York being duly summoned, came up to Westminster and took his seat at the Council-table[1] on the 21st of November. Before taking part in the proceedings, however, he addressed himself to the lords then assembled, declaring how he had come up in obedience to a writ of privy seal, and was ready to offer his best services to the king; but as a previous order had been issued, by what authority he could not say, to certain old councillors to forbear from attending the king's councils in future, he required that any such prohibition might be removed. This was unanimously agreed to, and the government of England was at once restored to a free and healthy condition.[2]

The Duke of Somerset was not present at this meeting of the Council. He doubtless saw too clearly the storm gathering against him. To his former responsibility for the loss of Normandy was now added further responsibility for the loss of Guienne. The accusations against him were accordingly renewed; but they were taken up this time, not by York but by the Duke of Norfolk. A set of articles of impeachment was drawn up by the latter, to which Somerset made some reply, and was answered again by Norfolk. The accuser then pressed the matter further, urging that the loss of Normandy and of Guienne should be made a subject of criminal inquiry according to the laws of France; and that other misdemeanours charged upon him should be investigated according to the modes of procedure in England. Finally, lest his petition should be refused by the Council, Norfolk desired that it might be exemplified under the king's Great Seal, protesting that he felt it necessary, for his own credit, that what he had done in the matter should be known as widely as possible.[3]

Norfolk accuses Somerset.

[1] Nicolas's *Privy Council Proceedings*, vi. 163-5.
[2] *Patent Roll*, 32 Hen. vi. m. 20. *See* Appendix to this Introduction.
[3] No. 230.

132

INTRODUCTION

In the end it was determined that the Duke of Somerset should be arrested and committed to the Tower. This resolution was carried into effect a little before Christmas, and the different lords retired during the festive season to their own country quarters. But all who had given their votes against Somerset knew well that they stood in considerable danger. The battle that he had lost would have to be fought over again with the queen, who now put in a claim to be intrusted with the entire government of the kingdom. Every man of Somerset's party got his retainers in readiness, and while other lords were out of town, the harbinger of the Duke of Somerset secured for his company all the lodgings that were to be got in Thames Street, Mark Lane, St. Katherine's, and the neighbourhood of the Tower. The Duke of Norfolk was warned by a faithful servant to beware of parties in ambush on his way to London. Everything clearly showed that the faction which had been dispossessed of power had sanguine hopes of reinstating themselves at an early opportunity.[1]

And this, it is probable, they might have done with the greatest possible ease, were it not that the king's loss of his faculties was so complete and absolute that it was impossible, by any means whatever, to obtain a semblance of acting upon his authority. About New Year's Day, when the new-born prince was conveyed to Windsor, the Duke of Buckingham took the child in his arms and presented him to the king, beseeching him to give him a father's blessing. Henry returned no answer. The duke remained some time with the child in the king's presence, but could not extract from him the slightest sign of intelligence. The queen then came in, and taking the infant in her arms, presented him to his father, with the same request that the duke had made before her. But all their efforts were in vain; the king continued dumb, and showed not the slightest perception of what they were doing, except that for one moment only he looked upon the babe, and then cast down his eyes again.[2]

There were no hopes, therefore, that the king himself would interfere in any way to protect his favourites in the

A.D. 1454.

The king and his child.

[1] No. 235.　　[2] *Ibid.*

133

THE PASTON LETTERS

Every man looks to himself.

Council. Every man felt it necessary to see to his own security. The Lord Chancellor himself, Cardinal Kemp, 'commanded all his servants to be ready, with bow and arrows, sword and buckler, crossbows, and all other habiliments of war, to await upon the safeguard of his person.' The Duke of Buckingham caused to be made '2000 bends with knots—to what intent,' said a cautious observer, 'men may construe as their wits will give them.' Further from the court, of course, the old disturbances were increased. 'The Duke of Exeter, in his own person, hath been at Tuxforth beside Doncaster, in the north country, and there the Lord Egremont met him, and the two be sworn together, and the duke is come home again.' The Earl of Wiltshire and Lord Bonvile made proclamations in Somersetshire, offering sixpence a day to every man that would serve them; and these two noblemen, along with the Lords Beaumont, Poynings, Clifford, and Egremont, were preparing to come up to London each with as strong a body of followers as he could possibly muster.[1]

The Duke of York and his friends on their side did the same; and it was high time they should, otherwise the machinations of Somerset would certainly have been their ruin. The latter had spies in every great household, who reported to him everything that could be construed to the disadvantage of his opponents. Among York's private enemies, moreover, was Thomas Thorpe, Speaker of the House of Commons, who was also a Baron of the Exchequer. In the former capacity his functions had been for some time suspended; for Parliament, which had been prorogued to the 12th November at Reading, only met on that day to be prorogued again to the 11th February, in consequence of the mortality which prevailed in the town. Meanwhile, in Michaelmas term, the Duke of York took an action of trespass against him in his own Court of Exchequer, and a jury had awarded damages to the amount of £1000. On this judgment was given that he should be committed to the Fleet till the damages were paid, and in the Fleet the Speaker accordingly remained till the next meeting

The Duke of York and Thorpe.

[1] No. 235.

134

INTRODUCTION

of Parliament.[1] In his confinement he was now busily employed in drawing up a bill of articles against the Duke of York, which doubtless, with the aid of a little favour at Court, would have been highly serviceable to the cause of Somerset.[2]

The legal proceedings of which Thorpe was a victim appear doubtless to have been connected with party politics. His son and heir, Roger Thorpe, at the beginning of the reign of Henry vii. procured an Act of Parliament in his favour, showing that both he and his father had suffered injustice in the cause of the House of Lancaster, and that the Duke of York's action of trespass against his father was owing to his having arrested, at the king's command, 'certain harness and other habiliments of war of the said duke's.'[3] No doubt this must have been the case, but was the king's command constitutional? Or was it, perhaps, only the command of Somerset given in the king's name? An agent had no right to obey an unconstitutional order.

About the 25th of January the Duke of York was expected in London, accompanied by a select body of men of his household retinue. With him came his son, the Earl of March, at this time not quite twelve years old; to whom, nevertheless, a separate household had already been assigned by his father, and consequently another company marched in the name of the Earl of March. These, however, were sent forward a little in advance. Along with the Duke of York there also came up, or was expected to come, his powerful friend the Earl of Warwick, who, besides the retinue by which he was attended, was to have a thousand men awaiting his arrival in London. Even these noblemen and their companies formed a most powerful confederacy. But there were two other great personages besides who travelled with them on the same road, whose sympathy and co-operation with York at this time no reader would have conjectured. The king's two half-brothers, the Earls of Richmond and Pembroke, were expected to reach London in the duke's company; and they, too, had wisely taken with them a good number of followers, for, notwith-

[1] *Rolls of Parl.* v. 238-9.　　[2] No. 235.　　[3] *Rolls of Parl.* vi. 295.

135

THE PASTON LETTERS

standing their relation to the Crown, it was thought not unlikely that they would be arrested on their arrival.[1]

In short, the continuance of the king's infirmity had now rendered it clear to every man that unless the Council were willing to comply with the Queen's demands, and yield up to her the uncontrolled management of public affairs, the government of the kingdom must be placed in the hands of the Duke of York. And yet some little time was necessarily allowed to pass before any special powers could be intrusted to him. Parliament was not to sit again till the 11th February, and Reading was still the place where it was appointed to assemble. The Earl of Worcester, who filled the office of Lord Treasurer, was commissioned to go down to Reading, and cause it to adjourn from the 11th to the 14th of the month, to meet that day at Westminster. Meanwhile a commission was granted to the Duke of York to act as the king's lieutenant on its reassembling [2]

Parliament and the Speaker.

On the 14th, accordingly, the Houses met in the royal palace of Westminster ; but the Commons were without a Speaker, and another of their members, by name Walter Rayle, was also undergoing imprisonment, from what cause does not appear. The Commons, therefore, before proceeding to business, demanded of the King and the Lords Spiritual and Temporal, that their ancient privileges should be respected, and their Speaker and the other member liberated. The case was taken into consideration by the Peers on the following day, when it was explained by the Duke of York's counsel that the Speaker had a few months before gone to the house of Robert Nevill, Bishop of Durham, and there taken away certain goods and chattels belonging to the duke against his will ; that for this he had been prosecuted in the Court of Exchequer, as it was a privilege of that court that its officers in such cases should not be sued before any other tribunal ; that a jury had found him guilty of trespass, and awarded to the duke damages of £1000 and £10 costs. Speaker Thorpe had accordingly been committed to the Fleet for the fine due to the king. The proceedings against him had not been taken

[1] No. 235.   [2] Rolls of Parl. v. 238-9.

INTRODUCTION

during the sitting of Parliament, and it was urged that if he should be released by privilege of Parliament a great wrong would be done to the duke. It was a delicate question of constitutional law, and the Lords desired to have the opinion of the judges. But the chief justices, after consultation with their brethren, answered, in the name of the whole body, that it was beyond their province to determine matters concerning the privilege of Parliament ; 'for this high court of Parliament,' they said, 'is so high and mighty in his nature that it may make law, and that that is law it may make no law ; and the determination and knowledge of the privilege belongeth to the Lords of the Parliament, and not to the Justices.' Nevertheless, as to the accustomed mode of procedure in the lower courts, the Judges remarked that in ordinary cases of arrest a prisoner was frequently liberated on a writ of *supersedeas* to enable him to attend the Parliament ; but no general writ of *supersedeas*, to surcease all processes, could be allowed ; 'for if there should be, it should seem that this high court of Parliament, that ministereth all justice and equity, should let the process of the common law, and so it should put the party complainant without remedy, for so much as actions at the common law be not determined in this high court of Parliament.'[1]

From this carefully considered reply it was clear to the Lords that they were at least nowise bound to interfere in behalf of the imprisoned Speaker, unless they considered the liberties of Parliament likely to be prejudiced by the circumstances of his particular case. It was accordingly decided that he should remain in prison, and that the Commons should be directed to choose another Speaker. This they did on the following day, and presented Sir Thomas Charleton to the Lord Chancellor as their new representative ; who being accepted by that functionary in the name of the king, both Houses at once proceeded to business.[2]

A month later the Commons came before the Duke of York, as the king's lieutenant, with two very urgent petitions. Defence of The first related to the defence of Calais and the safeguard of Calais.

[1] Rolls of Parl. v. 239-40.   [2] Ibid. 240.

THE PASTON LETTERS

the sea. Notwithstanding the very liberal grants which had already been voted by this Parliament, Calais was still in danger, and the sea was still very insufficiently protected ; insomuch that the Lord Chancellor had told the House of Commons £40,000 would be required to obviate very serious perils. The Commons were very naturally alarmed ; a modern House of Commons would have been indignant also. They had in the preceding year voted no less than £9300 for Calais, partly for repairs and partly for making jetties, besides all the sums voted for the pay of the garrison and the tonnage and poundage dues, which ought to have been applied to general purposes of defence. They therefore humbly petitioned to be excused from making any further grants ; 'for they cannot, may not, ne dare not make any mo grants, considered the great poverty and penury that be among the Commons of this land, for whom they be comen at this time ; and that this their excuse might be enacted in this high court of Parliament.' The money already voted was evidently conceived to be somewhere, and was considered to be quite sufficient to do the work required ; so the Commons were told in reply by my Lord Chancellor the Cardinal, 'that they should have good and comfortable answer, without any great delay or tarrying.'[1]

A council required.

The second petition was that 'a sad and wise Council' might be established, 'of the right discreet and wise lords and other of this land, to whom all people might have recourse for ministering justice, equity, and righteousness ; whereof they have no knowledge as yet.' The Duke of York was only the king's lieutenant in Parliament. With the assent of the Great Council he could prorogue or dissolve it and give the royal assent to any of its acts. But the business of the nation imperatively required that some smaller body of statesmen should be intrusted with more general powers. Even before the king's illness the constitution of some such body had been promised to the Parliament at Reading as a thing contemplated by the king himself ;[2] and it was now more necessary than ever. The only problem was how to confer upon it an authority that could not be disputed.

[1] Rolls of Parl. v. 240.   [2] Ibid. 241.

INTRODUCTION

But while the Lords are taking this point into consideration, we invite the reader's attention to a piece of private history.

A few years before the date at which we have now arrived, Thomas one Thomas Denyes, a trusted servant of the Earl of Oxford, Denyes. seems to have caused his master some little inconvenience by falling in love with a lady who resided in the neighbourhood of Norwich. We regret that we cannot inform the reader who she was. All that we know is that her Christian name was Agnes, which was at that time popularly corrupted into Anneys and frequently confounded with Anne, and that she was an acquaintance of John Paston's. With John Paston, accordingly, the earl thought it best to communicate, and in doing so earned for himself the heartfelt gratitude of Denyes by one of those small but truly gracious acts which reveal to us better than anything else the secret of the power of the English aristocracy. The lady seems not to have given her admirer any great encouragement in his suit. She had property of her own worth 500 marks, and could have had a husband in Norfolk with land of 100 marks value, which was more than Denyes could offer her. But the Earl of Oxford requested John Paston to intercede with her in behalf of her wooer, promising her that if the marriage took effect the Earl would show himself liberal to them both. He further offered, if it would be any satisfaction to her, to go himself into Norfolk and visit her.[1]

This intercession was effectual, and the lady became the wife of Thomas Denyes. It was a triumph of love and ambition to a poor dependant on a great earl. But with increase of wealth, as others have found in all ages, Denyes experienced an increase of anxieties and of business also. A suit in Chancery was commenced against him and his wife by a gentleman of the name of Ingham, who considered himself to have a claim on the lady's property for a considerable sum of money. Ingham's son Walter was active in procuring the *subpœna*. But Denyes, strong, as he believed, in a great lord's favour, conceived a plan by which he might either interrupt the

[1] Nos. 124, 240.

THE PASTON LETTERS

suit or revenge it on the person of Walter Ingham. On the 11th of January 1454—just about the time the queen and Buckingham were making those vain attempts to introduce his child to the notice of the unhappy king—when, consequently, it was still uncertain whether York or Somerset would have the rule, and when lawless persons all over the country must have felt that there was more than usual immunity for bad deeds to be hoped for,—Thomas Denyes wrote a letter in the name of the Earl of Oxford to Walter Ingham, requiring his presence at the earl's mansion at Wivenhoe, in Essex, on the 13th. This letter reached Ingham at Dunston, in Norfolk, and he at once set out in obedience to the summons. But as he was nearing his destination, on the 12th, he was waylaid by a party in ambush hired by Denyes, who beat him so severely upon the head, legs, and back that he was maimed for life, and compelled to go on crutches for the rest of his days. Ingham complained of the outrage to the Lord Chancellor, Cardinal Kemp, who sent a sergeant-at-arms to arrest Denyes at Lincoln's Inn ; but he at first refused to obey the arrest. Shortly afterwards, however, he was committed to the Fleet prison ; and Ingham, with the favour of the cardinal and the Earl of Oxford, who utterly repudiated the act of his dependant, presented a petition to Parliament that he should not be admitted to bail or mainprise until he had been tried for the outrage and all actions between him and Ingham had been fully discussed and settled.[1]

The Earl of Oxford seems to have been thoroughly incensed, and not without reason, against a servant who had so abused his trust. Cardinal Kemp, as chancellor, was not less righteously indignant ; and a bill was actually passed through the House of Peers in accordance with the prayer of Ingham's petition. Yet it is difficult to understand why the punishment of the wrong committed was not left to the operation of ordinary criminal law. The case, perhaps, affected too seriously the honour of a nobleman, and the discretion to be allowed to a retainer. But whatever may have been the cause, poor Denyes now becomes positively an

Walter Ingham waylaid.

[1] Nos. 238, 239.

140

INTRODUCTION

object for compassion—all the more so because his chief feeling in the matter was not a selfish one. Besides imprisoning Denyes himself in the Fleet, the cardinal and the Earl of Oxford threw his wife into the Counter, and afterwards sent her to Newgate, where she suffered the discomforts of a gaol apart from her husband, although she was then with child. 'Which standeth too nigh mine heart,' is the brief expression in which he conveys his feelings to John Paston, while apparently he was expecting to hear that his wife was either dead or prematurely delivered ; for the treatment she had met with brought on the pains of labour long before the right time had come. Denyes, however, made friends with the warden of the Fleet prison, who contrived in some manner to make interest for her with her gaoler, so that afterwards she was rather better treated, and at last admitted to bail.[1]

Denyes and his wife in prison.

Poor Denyes was in dread of still further evils arising out of the case when he wrote these facts to John Paston. The bill against him had already passed through the Lords, and he was in fear that it might pass through the Commons also, which we afterwards learn that it did not.[2] His adversary, moreover, was bent upon revenge ; 'for Ingham,' he said, 'lieth, beside that, to take away my wife's daughter out of Westminster,[3] to make an end of my wife if he can, and also to arrest my servants, that I dread that she nor I shall have no creature to attend us ne help us ; and such malice have I never heard of here before. And it is told me that beside that they will despoil, if any good they can find of mine in Norwich or Norfolk, and imprison my servants there.' All this he urgently implored Paston to prevent to the best of his ability. And it must be said that John Paston, although he considered himself little bound to Denyes, except in so far as he had promoted his marriage at the Earl of Oxford's solicitation, on this occasion stood his friend. He wrote a letter to the earl urgently interceding for the unhappy wife ; and though it

[1] No. 239. [2] No. 244.
[3] Apparently Agnes Denyes had taken sanctuary at Westminster before her imprisonment. The manner in which Denyes here speaks of her daughter gives us reason to believe that she was a widow before he married her.

141

THE PASTON LETTERS

seems probable the letter that he first wrote was not actually sent, we may fairly presume that he either devised a second to the same effect, or used his influence otherwise to the same end. Certain it is that he made some effort for which Denyes was beyond measure grateful.[1]

'The cardinal is dead and the king is relieved.' Such were the last words of a postscript which Denyes appended to his first melancholy letter, complaining of his own and his wife's imprisonment. A rumour apparently had been spread that the king's health was beginning to improve ; for which, as we shall see, there was very little foundation. But it was perfectly true that Cardinal Kemp, Archbishop of Canterbury and Chancellor of England, was dead. Little as we know, beyond a few broad facts of his career, whereby to judge his real character and aims, it is certain that he was an accomplished statesman. A follower originally of Cardinal Beaufort,—the man who of all others could serve two masters, Rome and England, with the least degree of repugnance, and of whom the best that can be said is, that he never scrupled to betray the former in what appeared to be the interest of the latter,—Kemp was, perhaps, as honest a specimen of the political churchman as an essentially bad system could produce. The clergy, however, were really needed as statesmen ; few laymen had the ability, learning, or education to enable them to do the essential work of the nation ; and Kemp was one who had gained for himself, by his own talents, the highest position to which a subject could aspire in England, not only in the realm but in the Church.

Death of Cardinal Kemp.

Thus, at a time when the functions of royalty itself were suspended, the chancellor, the official keeper of the king's conscience, was suddenly taken away ; and in him England also lost her primate, always one of the most important members of the Council. The formation of a governing Council was now more important than ever ; but the most pressing questions of all were the appointment of a new chancellor and of a new archbishop. Who was to take upon himself to nominate either the one or the other ? The queen's modest claim to be invested with the functions of her husband

[1] Nos. 240, 245.

142

INTRODUCTION

had not been listened to by the Lords ; but the powers as yet conferred upon the Duke of York were only to represent the king in Parliament.

It was upon the 19th of March that the Commons had pressed their petition for the establishment of a Council. Cardinal Kemp died on the 22nd. On the 23rd the Lords appointed twelve of their number as a deputation, headed by Waynflete, Bishop of Winchester, to ride to Windsor and endeavour, if possible, to lay the state of matters before the king. Their instructions were drawn up in six articles, but only two were to be communicated to the king if they found him unable to pay attention to what was said. These two were a mere assurance of anxiety to hear of his recovery, and that the Lords, under the presidency of the duke as his lieutenant, were using their best discretion in the affairs of the nation. If any response were made to these two articles, the deputation was then to tell him of the death of Cardinal Kemp, and ask to know his pleasure who should be the new archbishop and who should be appointed chancellor. They were to say that for the security of the Great Seals (there were at this time no less than three Great Seals used in the Chancery)[1] the Lords had caused them to be produced in Parliament, and after being seen by all the Lords they were enclosed in a coffer sealed by a number of the Peers present, and then laid up in the Treasury. Finally, they were to ask the king's mind touching the establishment of a Council, telling him how much it was desired by the Commons, and suggesting the names of certain Lords and persons whom it was thought desirable to appoint as Councillors. All these matters, however, were to be communicated only to the king in the strictest privacy.[2]

Deputation of Lords to the king.

The deputation returned two days after with a report of the total failure of their mission. They had waited on the king at Windsor just after he had dined, but could get from him no answer nor sign that he understood their message. The Bishop of Winchester then told the king that the Lords had not dined, and that after they had they would wait on him

The king's imbecility.

[1] Nicolas's *Privy Council Proceedings*, vol. vi. preface, pp. clxxviii.-ix.
[2] *Rolls of Parl.* 240-1.

143

THE PASTON LETTERS

again. After dinner accordingly they were again with him, and tried all they could to elicit an answer ; but the king was speechless. They then proposed that he should go into another room, and he was led between two men into his bedchamber. A third and last effort was then made to rouse him by every expedient that could be imagined ; and when all else failed, a question was put to him which involved no more than a simple yes or no. Was it his Highness's pleasure that they should wait on him any longer ? A long pause was allowed in the hope that any mere physical difficulty might be overcome. A faint nod, even a shake of the head, would have been regarded with some degree of satisfaction. But it was all in vain. 'They could have no answer, word ne sign ; and therefore with sorrowful hearts, came their way.'[1]

It was now clear that the highest constitutional authority resided for the time in the Lords Spiritual and Temporal. The reader, imbued with modern notions of the power and prestige of the House of Commons, may possibly think that their votes, too, should have been consulted in the formation of a Government. Such a view, however, would be radically erroneous. The influence which the House of Commons has in later times acquired—an influence so great that, at times unhappily, Acts are even passed by Peers against their own sense of right and justice, in deference to the will of the Lower Chamber—is a thing not directly recognised by the constitution, but only due to the control of the national purse-strings. Strictly speaking, the House of Commons is not a legislative body at all, but only an engine for voting supplies. The Peers of the realm, in Parliament or out of Parliament, are, according to the constitution, the sovereign's privileged advisers. A king may, no doubt, at any time call to him what other councillors he pleases, and the prerogative of the Lords may lie dormant for a very long period of time ; but the Peers of the realm have, individually or in a body, a right to tender their advice upon affairs of state, which belongs to no other class in the community.

On the 27th of March, therefore—two days after the

[1] Rolls of Parl. 241.

144

INTRODUCTION

report of the deputation that had seen the king at Windsor—the Lords took the first step towards the establishment of order and government, by electing Richard, Duke of York, as The Duke Protector and Defender of the realm. The title of Protector of York essentially implied an interim administrator during a period Protector. when the king, by legal or physical incapacity, was unable to exercise his regal functions in person. A Protector's tenure of power was therefore always limited by the clause *quamdiu Regi placeret*. It was terminable by the king himself the moment he found himself able to resume the actual duties of royalty. Even a protectorship like that of Humphrey, Duke of Gloucester, instituted in consequence of the king being an infant, was terminated before the royal child was eight years old by the act of his coronation. The crowned and anointed infant became a king indeed, and therefore no longer required the services of a Protector ; so from that day Duke Humphrey had ceased to wield any authority except that of an ordinary member of the Council. But, indeed, even during his protectorship, his powers were greatly circumscribed ; and it had been expressly decided by the Council that he was not competent to perform an act of state without the consent of a majority of the other Lords. Richard, therefore, knowing that his powers would be limited, was most anxious that his responsibility should be accurately defined, that no one might accuse him thereafter of having exceeded the just limits of his authority. He delivered in a paper containing certain articles, of which the first was as follows :—

'Howbeit that I am not sufficient of myself, of wisdom, cunning, nor ability, to take upon me that worthy name of Protector and Defender of this land, nor the charge thereto appertaining, whereunto it hath liked you, my Lords, to call, name, and desire me unworthy thereunto ;—under protestation, if I shall apply me to the performing of your said desire, and at your instance take upon me, with your supportation, the said name and charge, I desire and pray you that in this present Parliament and by authority thereof it be enacted, that of yourself and of your free and mere disposition, ye desire, name and call me to the said name and charge, and that of any presumption of myself, I take them not upon me, but only of the due and humble

THE PASTON LETTERS

obeisance that I owe to do unto the king, our most dread and Sovereign Lord, and to you the Peerage of this land, in whom by the occasion of the infirmity of our said Sovereign Lord, resteth the exercise of his authority, whose noble commandments I am as ready to perform and obey as any his liege man alive ; and at such time as it shall please our blessed Creator to restore his noble person to healthful disposition, it shall like you so to declare and notify to his good grace.'[1]

In reply to this, it was put on record that it was 'thought by the Lords that the said Duke desireth that of his great wisdom for his discharge.' And they, too, for their own justification, resolved that an Act should be made according to a precedent during the king's minority, setting forth that they themselves, from the sheer necessity of the case, had been compelled to take upon themselves the power of nominating a Protector. So jealous were the Lords of anything like an invasion of the royal prerogative !

Further, the duke required that the Lords would aid him cordially in the execution of his duties and to exactly define such powers and liberties as they meant him to exercise ; that they would arrange what salary he should receive ; and that all the Lords Spiritual and Temporal belonging to the King's Council would agree to act in the Councils of the Protector. These matters being at length satisfactorily adjusted, the duke was formally created Protector by patent on the 3rd of April. It was, however, at the same time provided by another patent that the office should devolve on the king's son as soon as he came of age.[2] After this, five Lords were appointed to have the keeping of the sea against the king's enemies, and in addition to the subsidies already voted by Parliament for that object, a loan, amounting in all to £1000, was levied upon the different seaports.[3] This was but light taxation, and was no doubt cheerfully submitted to. The good town of Bristol, we know, did more than it was asked ; for Sturmyn, the Mayor, fitted out a stately vessel expressly for the war.[4] Evidently there were zeal and patriotism in the

[1] Rolls of Parl. v. 242. [2] Ibid. 243.
[3] Rolls of Parl. 244-5. [4] No. 249.

146

INTRODUCTION

country whenever there was a government that could make good use of them.

And there was real need of that patriotism ; for the Calais French were again threatening Calais. They also made a again in descent in great force on the isles of Jersey and Guernsey, danger. but were defeated by the valour and loyalty of the inhabitants, who killed or took prisoners no less than five hundred of their assailants.[1] A Council was called to meet at Westminster on the 6th of May, to take measures for the defence of Calais,[2] the result of which and of further deliberations on the subject was seen in the appointment of the Duke of York as captain or governor of the town, castle, and marches. This office was granted to him by patent on the 18th of July,[3] but he only agreed to undertake it, as he had done the Protectorship, subject to certain express conditions to which he obtained the assent of the Lords in Parliament. Among these was one stipulation touching his remuneration, in which he affirms that he had served the king formerly at his own cost in the important offices he had filled in France and in Ireland, so that owing to non-payment of his salary, he had been obliged to sell part of his inheritance and pawn plate and jewels which were still unredeemed.[4] A very different sort of governor this from the avaricious Somerset !

Meanwhile other changes had been made in the administration. On the 2nd of April—the day before the duke's appointment as Protector—the Great Seal had been given to Richard Nevill, Earl of Salisbury, as chancellor ; and to prevent any renewal of disturbances in the North by the earl's Disturb-former opponent Lord Egremont, his father, the Earl of ances in Northumberland, was summoned before the Council. But the North. before the day came which was given him to make his appearance, news arrived that Lord Egremont had already been making large assemblies and issuing proclamations of rebellion, in concert with the Duke of Exeter. To restore tranquillity,

[1] No. 247.
[2] Nicolas's Privy Council Proceedings, vi. 174.
[3] Rymer, xi. 351. Carte's Gascon and French Rolls.
[4] Rolls of Parl. v. 252.

147

THE PASTON LETTERS

it was thought proper that the Duke of York should go down into Yorkshire, where he no sooner made his appearance than his presence seems to have put an end to all disturbances. The Duke of Exeter disappeared from the scene and was reported to have gone up secretly to London; but the adherents of Lord Egremont continued to give some trouble in Westmoreland. Thither the Duke of York accordingly received orders from the Council to proceed; but he probably found it unnecessary, for on the 8th of June it is stated that he intended remaining about York till after the 20th. Every appearance of disturbance seems to have been quelled with ease; and a number of the justices having been sent into Yorkshire for the punishment of past offences, the Protector was able to return to London in the beginning of July.[1]

It was at this time that the two eldest sons of the Duke of York, Edward, Earl of March, and Edmund, Earl of Rutland, who were of the ages of twelve and eleven respectively, addressed the following interesting letter to their father:[2]—

'To the ryght hiegh and myghty Prince, oure most worschipfull and gretely redoubted lorde and fader, the Duke of Yorke, Protector and Defensor of Englonde.

'Ryght hiegh and myghty Prince, oure most worschipfull and gretely redoubted lorde and Fader, in as lowely wyse as any sonnes con or may we recomaunde us un to youre good lordeschip. And plaese hit youre hieghnesse to witte that we have receyved youre worschipfull lettres yesturday by your servaunt William Cleton, beryng date at Yorke the xxix day of Maij, by the whiche William and by the relacion of John Milewatier we conceyve your worschipfull and victorious spede ageinest your enemyse, to ther grete shame, and to us the most comfortable tydinges that we desired to here. Where of we thonke Almyghty God of his yeftes, beseching Hym hertely to geve yowe that grace and cotidian fortune here aftur to knowe your enemyse and to have the victory of them. And yef hit plaese your hieghnesse to knowe of oure wilfare, at the makyng of this lettre we were in good helith of bodis, thonked be God; beseching your good and gracioue Faderhode of youre daily blessing. And where ye comaunde

---

[1] Nicolas's *Privy Council Proceedings*, vi, 178, 193-7. Nos. 247, 249.
[2] Printed from the original in MS. Cott., Vespasian F. xiii. fol. 35.

148

INTRODUCTION

us by your said lettres to attende specialy to oure lernyng in our yong age that schulde cause us to growe to honour and worschip in our olde age, Please hit youre hieghnesse to witte that we have attended owre lernyng sith we come heder, and schall here aftur; by the whiche we trust to God youre gracioue lordeschip and good Fadurhode schall be plaesid. Also we beseche your good lordeschip that hit may plaese yowe to sende us Harry Lovedeyne, grome of your kechyn, whos service is to us ryght agreable; and we will sende yow John Boyes to wayte on youre good Lordeschip. Ryght hiegh and myghty Prince, our most worschipfull and gretely redoubted lorde and Fader, We beseche Almyghty God yeve yowe as good lyfe and longe as youre owne Princely hert con best desire. Writen at your Castill of Lodelow the iij day of June.—Youre humble sonnes,

'E. MARCHE,
'E. RUTLOND.'

Soon after the duke had returned to London his presence was required at a Great Council summoned for the 18th of July, to consider the expediency of liberating on bail his great rival and personal enemy, the Duke of Somerset, The Duke who had been now seven months in prison. On this point of Somerset. York had only one piece of advice to offer, which was, that as he had been committed to custody upon suspicion of treason, the opinion of the judges should be taken before he was released from confinement. That he had remained so long without a trial was not unnatural, considering the nature of the times. It was a bold step indeed to try him at all, while there was a chance of the weak-minded king's recovery; but this step was certainly resolved on. The 28th of October was the day appointed for his trial; and the Duke of Norfolk, who, as we have seen, had been the first to move the capital charge against him, was ordered by that day to be ready to produce his proofs. Meanwhile the lords concurred that it was clearly inexpedient to let him go, especially as the number of lords assembled was not so great as it should have been on the occasion; and the opinion of the Duke of York was not only agreed to, but at his request was put on record.[1]

Six days later it was agreed at another meeting of the

---

[1] Nicolas's *Privy Council Proceedings*, vi. 207.

149

THE PASTON LETTERS

Council that the Duke of York should return into the North with the Duke of Exeter in his custody, whom he was to confine in the castle of Pomfret as a state prisoner.[1]

By these decisive steps the authority of the Duke of York was at length secured on something like a stable footing. During the remainder of his protectorate there could no longer be a doubt to whose hands power was committed; and England, at last, had the blessing of real government, able and vigorous, but at the same time moderate. The resolutions of the Council soon became known to the public. 'As for tidings,' wrote William Paston to his brother in Norfolk, 'my lord of York hath taken my lord of Exeter into his award. The Duke of Somerset is still in prison, in worse case than he was.' William Paston wrote in haste, but these were two matters of public importance to be mentioned before all private affairs whatever.[2] And yet the private affairs of which he wrote in the same letter will not be without interest to the readers of this Introduction. William Paston now Sir J. Fastolf goes to reside in Norfolk. reported to his brother that Sir John Fastolf was about to take his journey into Norfolk within a few days, and proposed to take up his residence at Caister. His going thither must have been regarded as an event not only in the neighbourhood of Yarmouth but even in the city of Norwich. At all events it was highly important to John Paston, whose advice the old knight valued in many matters. 'He saith,' wrote William Paston to his brother, 'ye are the heartiest kinsman and friend that he knoweth. He would have you at Mauteby[3] dwelling.' This must have been written in the latter part of July. Sir John did not actually go into Norfolk quite so soon as he intended; but he appears to have been there by the beginning of September.[4]

There in his completed castle of Caister he had at length taken up his abode, to spend the evening of his days in the place of his birth, and on the inheritance of his ancestors. There during the next five years he spent his time, counting

---

[1] Nicolas's *Privy Council Proceedings*, vi. 217, 218. [2] No. 254.
[2] The manor of Mauteby, which came to John Paston by his marriage, was only three miles distant from Caister. [4] No. 260.

150

INTRODUCTION

over the items of a number of unsettled claims he had against the crown,[1] and meditating also, it would seem, on another account he had with Heaven. For the latter the foundation of a college[2] or religious endowment, in which were to be maintained 'seven priests and seven poor folk' at Caister, might possibly liquidate his debts. But in his transactions with his fellowmen he was certainly for the most part a creditor, and by no means one of the most generous. Instances will be found in his letters in abundance showing with what vehemence (testy old soldier that he was!) he perpetually insisted on what was due to himself;—how he desired to know the names of those who would presume to resist his agent, Sir Thomas Howes—how they should be requited 'by Blackbeard or Whitebeard, that is to say, by God or the Devil';[3]—how he noted that Sir John Buck had fished his stanks and helped to break his dam;[4] how he had been informed that at a dinner at Norwich certain gentlemen had used scornful language about him, and desired to know who they were.[5] In this perpetual self-assertion he seems neither to have been over-indulgent towards adversaries nor even sufficiently considerate of friends and dependants. 'Cruel and vengeable he hath been ever,' says his own servant Henry Windsor, 'and for the most part without pity and mercy.'[6] So also on the part of his faithful secretary, William Worcester, we find a complaint of shabby treatment, apparently at this very time when the household was removed to Caister. To a letter in which John Paston had addressed him as 'Master Worcester,' the latter replied with a request that he would 'forget that name of mastership,' for his position was by no means so greatly improved as to entitle him to such respect. His salary was not increased by one farthing in certainty—only 'wages of household in common, *entaunt come nows plaira*' —which apparently means, assured to him only during his master's pleasure. When he complained to his master of this, all the satisfaction he obtained was that Sir John expressed a

---

[1] Nos. 309, 310. [2] Nos. 340, 350, 351, 385, 386, 387.
[3] No. 125. [4] Nos. 160, 161.
[5] No. 272. [6] No. 332.

151

THE PASTON LETTERS

wish he had been a priest, when he could have rewarded him with a living.[1]

There are, indeed, in more than one of Worcester's letters in this collection symptoms of ill-concealed chagrin and disappointment. Nor were such feelings unnatural in one who, probably out of regard for an ill-appreciated hero, had devoted the best energies of his life to the services of such a master William as Fastolf. A native of Bristol, the son of one William Worcester. Worcester, who lived in St. James's Bec in that town, he was descended by the mother's side from a wealthy family of Coventry, and often called himself, instead of Worcester, by his mother's maiden name of Botoner. Born in the year 1415, he had entered the university of Oxford in 1432, and been four years a student at Hart Hall, now Balliol College; after which he had gone into Fastolf's service. For many years he had been steward of Sir John's manor of Castle Combe in Wiltshire, and MSS. still exist in his handwriting relating to the holding of manorial courts there.[2] He had also been Fastolf's secretary in drawing up various statements regarding the wars in France in vindication of his master's policy.[3] He was a man of literary tastes, who had already presented some compositions to his patron.[4] Later in life he wrote a book of annals, which is an important historical authority for the period. It seems to have been about a year before his master's death that he set himself assiduously to learn French, under the tuition of a Lombard named Caroll Giles.[5] From this instructor he had purchased several books, and Henry Windsor suspected he had run himself into debt in consequence. He had fairly owned to Windsor 'he would be as glad and as fain of a good book of French or of poetry, as my master Fastolf would be to purchase a fair manor.'[6] But

[1] Nos. 258, 259.
[2] Add. MS. 28,208, B.M.   [3] Stevenson's *Wars*, ii. [519], *sq.*
[4] 'Stellæ versificatæ pro anno 1440 ad instantiam J. Fastolfe militis.' MS. Laud., B. 23 (according to the old pressmark).   [5] Letter 370.
[6] In previous editions it was here remarked:—'This French zeal appears to have excited the contempt of some of his acquaintances—among others of Friar Brackley, who nicknamed him Colinus Gallicus.' The discovery of additional letters, formerly published in a Supplement, but now incorporated with the series, seems to show that this was an error, or at all events very doubtful. It is clear from Letter 404 that

152

INTRODUCTION

he had a special object in view in which a knowledge of this language was important; for he had begun translating, at Fastolf's request, from a French version, Cicero's treatise *de Senectute*. This work appears to have been left on his hands at Sir John Fastolf's death, and on the 10th of August 1473 he presented it to his patron's old friend, Bishop Waynflete, at Esher. 'Sed nullum regardum recepi de episcopo' (but I received no reward from the bishop), is his melancholy comment on the occasion.[1] The work was ultimately printed by Caxton in 1481. Worcester was an assiduous collector of information on topics of every description, and a number of his commonplace books remain at this day. But like many men of letters after him, he found that industry of this sort may look in vain for any reward beyond the satisfaction of gratified curiosity.[2]

Along with the announcement that Sir John Fastolf was about to go into Norfolk, William Paston informed his brother that the old knight's stepson, Stephen Scrope, would reside at Caister along with him. Of this Stephen Scrope our Letters Stephen make not unfrequent mention; but the leading facts of his Scrope. history are obtained from other sources. He was the son of Sir Stephen Scrope, by his wife Lady Milicent, who married Fastolf after her husband's death. At the time of this second marriage of his mother, young Scrope was about ten or twelve years of age, and being heir to a considerable property, his stepfather had the management of his affairs during his minority. Bitterly did he complain in after years of the

a certain 'W. W.' and Colinus Gallicus were different persons (*see* vol. iii. p. 213, note 3), and the references to 'W. W.' at p. 230 as the knight's secretary and one of his executors remove any doubt that we might otherwise entertain that he was William Worcester. But a new difficulty arises from that identification, that Friar Brackley calls 'W. W.' an Irishman, which William Worcester was not; and the references at p. 220 of the same volume would imply that he was really an Irishman in nationality, and also a one-eyed man of dark visage. Such may have been Worcester's personal appearance; but why was he called an Irishman?

It is with some hesitation that I hazard a new conjecture as to the person nicknamed Colinus Gallicus; but on comparing the different passages where that nickname occurs, I am inclined to think it was meant for Judge Yelverton.

[1] Itin. 368.
[2] Tanner's *Bibliotheca*. *See* also a notice of William Worcester in *Retrospective Review*, Second Series, ii. 451-4.

153

THE PASTON LETTERS

manner in which Sir John had discharged the trust. According to the unfeeling, mercenary fashion in which such matters were then managed, Fastolf sold his wardship to Chief-Justice Gascoigne for 500 marks; 'through the which sale,' wrote Scrope at a later date, 'I took sickness that kept me a thirteen or fourteen years [en]suing; whereby I am disfigured in my person and shall be whilst I live.' Gascoigne held this wardship for three years, and by right of it intended to marry Scrope to one of his own daughters; but as the young lad's friends thought the match unequal to his fortune, Fastolf bought the wardship back again.[1] Stephen Scrope, however, when he grew up, was not more grateful for the redemption than for the original sale of his person. 'He bought me and sold me as a beast' (so he writes of Sir John Fastolf), 'against all right and law, to mine hurt more than 1000 marks.' In consequence of the stinginess of his stepfather he was obliged, on coming of age, to sell a manor which was part of his inheritance and take service with Humphrey, Duke of Gloucester in France; by whom, according to his own account, he had some hope of obtaining restitution of the lordship of the Isle of Man, which had belonged to his uncle the Earl of Wiltshire in the days of Richard II. But Sir John Fastolf got him to give up his engagement with the duke and serve with himself, which he did for several years, to the satisfaction of both parties. Afterwards, however, on some dispute arising, Scrope returned to England, when Sir John sent home word that he must pay for his meat and drink. To do this he was driven to contract a marriage which, by his own account, was not the most advantageous for himself; and his stepfather, instead of showing him any compassion, brought an action against him by which he was deprived of all the little property that his wife had brought him.[2]

Of this first wife of Stephen Scrope we know nothing,[3]

[1] No. 97.
[2] Scrope's *History of the Manor of Castle Combe*, pp. 264-283. The MSS. formerly at Castle Combe, to which Mr. Scrope refers in this work, have since been presented by him and Mr. Lowndes, the present lord of the manor, to the British Museum. One of them we have reprinted in No. 97.
[3] She is not unlikely to have been the lady mentioned in No. 97. 'Fauconer's

154

INTRODUCTION

except that she died and left him a daughter some years before we find any mention of him in the Paston correspondence. His necessities now compelled him to resort to the same evil system of bargaining in flesh and blood of which he had complained in his own case. 'For very need,' he writes, 'I was fain to sell a little daughter I have for much less than I should have done by possibility,'—a considerable point in his complaint being evidently the lowness of the price he got for his own child. It seems that he disposed of her wardship to a knight[1] whose name does not appear; but the terms of the contract became matter of interest some time afterwards to John Paston and his mother, when Scrope, who, besides being disfigured in person, was probably not far from fifty years of age, made an offer for the hand of Paston's sister Elizabeth, a girl of about twenty. The proposed match did not take effect; but it was for some time seriously entertained. Agnes Paston writes that she found the young lady herself 'never so willing to none as she is to him, if it be so that his land stand clear.'[2] The reader will perhaps think from this expression that the young lady had been pretty early taught the importance of considering worldly prospects; but there were other motives which not improbably helped to in̄uence her judgment. 'She was never in so great sorrow as she is now-a-days,' wrote Elizabeth Clere to John Paston, as a reason for concluding the matter at once with Scrope, if no more desirable suitor presented himself. Her mother would not allow her to see any visitor, and was suspicious even of her intercourse with the servants of her own house. 'And she hath since Easter the most part been beaten once in the week or twice, and sometimes twice in one day, and her head broken in two or three places.'[3] Such was the rough domestic discipline to which even girls in those days were occasionally subjected!

daughter of London, that Sir Reynold Cobham had wedded.' This I find need not have been, as I have stated in a footnote, the widow of Sir Reginald Cobham of Sterborough, who died in 1446; for there was an earlier Sir Reginald Cobham, whose widow Elizabeth was married to William Clifford as early as 1438. (*Inquisitions post mortem*, 16 Hen. VI. No. 31.) Thus there is the less difficulty in attributing Letter 97 to a much earlier date than that assigned to it by the endorsement.

[1] Letter 94.   [2] No. 93.   [3] No. 94.

155

THE PASTON LETTERS

Some years certainly elapsed after this before either Stephen Scrope found a wife or Elizabeth Paston a husband. The former ultimately married Joan, the daughter of Richard Bingham, judge of the King's Bench ; the latter was married to Robert Poynings, whom we have already had occasion to notice as an ally of Jack Cade in 1450, and a ringleader in other movements a few years later. This second marriage appears to have taken place about New Year's Day 1459 ;[1] before which time we find various other proposals for her hand besides that of Scrope.[2] Among these it may be noted that Edmund, Lord Grey of Hastings, wrote to her brother to say that he knew a gentleman with property worth 300 marks (£200) a year to whom she might be disposed of. No doubt, as in similar cases, this gentleman was a feudal ward, whose own opinion was the very last that was consulted as to the lady to whom he should be united. But it is time that we return to the current of public affairs.[3]

The Strife of Parties

The king's recovery. At Christmas, to the great joy of the nation, the king began to recover from his sad illness. He woke up, as it were, from a long sleep. So decidedly had he regained his faculties, that, first, on St. John's Day (27th December), he commanded his almoner to ride to Canterbury with an offering, and his secretary to present another at the shrine of St. Edward. On the following Monday, the 30th, the queen came to him and brought with her the infant prince, for whom nearly twelve months before she had in vain endeavoured to bespeak his notice. What occurred at that touching interview we

[1] See No. 374. [2] Nos. 236, 250, 252.
[3] We ought not to leave unnoticed one fact in the relations of Scrope and Fastolf which is much more creditable to both of them than the disputes above mentioned. In the year 1450, Scrope translated from the French and dedicated to Sir John, 'for his contemplation and solace,' a work entitled *Ditz de Philosophius* (Sayings of Philosophers), of which the original MS. is now in the Harleian Collection, No. 2266. That Fastolf was a real lover of literature, and encouraged literary tastes in those about him, there can be no question.

156

INTRODUCTION

know from a letter of Edmund Clere to John Paston, and it would be impossible to wish it recorded in other words. 'And then he asked what the Prince's name was, and the queen told him "Edward" ; and then he held up his hands and thanked God thereof. And he said he never knew till that time, nor wist what was said to him, nor wist not where he had been whilst he hath been sick, till now. And he asked who was godfathers, and the queen told him ; and he was well apaid. And she told him that the cardinal (Kemp) was dead ; and he said he knew never thereof till that time ; and he said one of the wisest lords in this land was dead.'[1]

On the 7th of January, Bishop Waynflete and the Prior of A.D. 1455. St. John's were admitted to speak with him, and finding his discourse as clear and coherent as they had ever known it, on coming out of the audience chamber they wept for joy.[2]

Joy was doubtless the prevailing sentiment among all ranks and classes of people ; but there was one to whom the news of the king's recovery must have afforded a delight and satisfaction beyond what any one else—unless it were Queen Margaret —could possibly derive from it. The Duke of Somerset had now lain in prison more than a year. The day appointed for his trial had passed away and nothing had been done. It certainly casts some suspicion upon the even-handed justice of the Duke of York, that his adversary was thus denied a hearing ; but the fault may have been due, after all, to weakness more than malice. In cases of treason, when once a trial was instituted against a leading nobleman, a conviction was, in those days, an absolutely invariable result ; but this made it a thing all the more dangerous to attempt when it was hopeless to expect the positive sanction of the king. The real cause, however, why Somerset was not brought to trial can only be a matter of conjecture. His continued confinement, however harsh, was, according to the practice of those days, legal ; nor was it till six weeks after the king's recovery that he was restored to liberty. A new day, meanwhile, and not a very early one, was fixed for the hearing of charges against him. On the morrow of All Souls—the 3rd of November following

[1] No. 270. [2] Ibid.

157

THE PASTON LETTERS

—he was to appear before the Council. This was determined on the 5th of February. Four lords undertook to give surety in their own proper persons that he would make his appearance on the day named ; and orders were immediately issued to release him from confinement.[1]

On the 4th day of March, he presented himself at a Council held before the king in his palace at Greenwich. The Duke of York was present, with ten bishops and twenty temporal peers, among whom were the Protector's friend, the Earl of Salisbury, Lord Chancellor, the Earl of Worcester, Treasurer of England, and the king's half-brother, the Earl of Pembroke. His accuser, the Duke of Norfolk, was absent, probably not without a reason. In presence of the assembled lords, Somerset then declared that he had been imprisoned without a cause and confined in the Tower of London one whole year and more than ten weeks over, and had only been liberated on bail on the 7th of February. So, as he declared there was no charge made against him for which he deserved to be confined, he besought the king that his sureties might be discharged ; offering, if any one would accuse him of anything contrary to his allegiance, that he would be ready at all times to answer according to law and like a true knight. His protestations of loyalty were at once Somerset released. accepted by the king, who thereupon declared that he knew the duke to be his true and faithful liegeman, and wished it to be understood that he so reputed him. After this, the mouths of all adversaries were of course sealed up. The duke's bail were discharged. His character was cleared from every insinuation of disloyalty ; and whatever questions might remain between him and the Duke of York were referred to the arbitration of eight other lords, whose judgment both parties were bound over in recognisances of 20,000 marks, that they would abide.[2]

The significance of all this could not be doubtful. The king's recovery had put an end to the Duke of York's power as Protector, and he was determined to be guided once more by the counsels of the queen and Somerset. On the 6th March,

[1] Rymer, xi. 361. [2] Ibid. 362, 363.

158

INTRODUCTION

York was deprived of the government of Calais which he had undertaken by indenture for seven years.[1] On the 7th, the Great Seal was taken from the Earl of Salisbury and given to Thomas Bourchier, Archbishop of Canterbury. These changes, or at least the former, promised little good to the country ; and in the beginning of May we not only find that Calais stood again in imminent danger of siege,[2] but that considerable fears were entertained of an invasion of England.[3] But to the Duke of York they gave cause for personal apprehension. Notwithstanding the specious appointment of a tribunal to settle the controversy between him and Somerset, it was utterly impossible for him to expect anything like an equitable adjustment. A Council was called at Westminster in the old exclusive spirit, neither York nor any of his friends being summoned to attend it. A Great Council was then arranged to meet at Leicester long before the day on which judgment was to be given by the arbitrators ; and it was feared both by York and his friends, the Earls of Salisbury and Warwick, that if they ventured to appear there they would find themselves entrapped. The ostensible ground of the calling of that council was to provide for the surety of the king's person ; from which it was fairly to be conjectured that a suspicion of treason was to be insinuated against persons who were too deservedly popular to be arrested in London with safety to the Government.[4]

York had by this time retired into the north, and uniting York and with Salisbury and Warwick, it was determined by all three his friends take arms. that the cause assigned for the calling of the Council justified them in seeking the king's presence with a strong body of followers. On the 20th May they arrived at Royston, and from thence addressed a letter to Archbishop Bourchier, as Chancellor, in which they not only repudiated all intention of disloyalty, but declared that, as the Council was summoned for the surety of the king's person, they had brought with them a

[1] Rymer, xi. 363. [2] Privy Council Proceedings, vi. 234-8.
[3] On the Patent Roll, 33. Hen. VI. p. 19 d., is a commission dated 5th May, for keeping watch on the coast of Kent against invasion.
[4] Rolls of Parl. v. 280-1.

159

THE PASTON LETTERS

company of armed followers expressly for his protection. If any real danger was to be apprehended they were come to do him service ; but if their own personal enemies were abusing their influence with the king to inspire him with causeless distrust, they were determined to remove unjust suspicions, and relied on their armed companies for protection to themselves. Meanwhile they requested the archbishop's intercession to explain to Henry the true motives of their conduct.[1]

Next day they marched on to Ware, and there penned an address to the king himself, of which copies seem to have been diffused, either at the time or very shortly afterwards, in justification of their proceedings. One of these came to the hands of John Paston, and the reader may consequently peruse the memorial for himself in Volume III.[2] In it, as will be seen, York and his friends again made most urgent protest of their good intent, and complained grievously of the unfair proceedings of their enemies in excluding them from the royal presence and poisoning the king's mind with doubts of their allegiance. They declared that they had no other intent in seeking the king's presence than to prove themselves his true liegemen by doing him all the service in their power ; and they referred him further to a copy of their letter to the archbishop, which they thought it well to forward along with their memorial, as they had not been informed that he had shown its contents to the king.

In point of fact, neither the letter to the archbishop nor the memorial to the king himself was allowed to come to Henry's hands. The archbishop, indeed, had done his duty, and on receipt of the letter to himself had sent it on, with all haste, to Kilburn, where his messenger overtook the king on his way northwards from London. But the man was not admitted into the royal presence ; for the Duke of Somerset and his friends were determined the Yorkists should not be heard, that their advance might wear as much as possible the aspect of a rebellion. York and his allies accordingly marched on from Ware to St. Albans, where they arrived at an early hour on the morning of the 22nd. Meanwhile the king, who had left

[1] *Rolls of Parl.* v. 280-1. [2] No. 282.

160

INTRODUCTION

London the day before, accompanied by the Dukes of Buckingham and Somerset, his half-brother, Jasper Tudor, Earl of Pembroke, the Earls of Northumberland, Devonshire, Stafford, Dorset, and Wiltshire, and a number of other lords, knights, and gentlemen, amounting in all to upwards of 2000, arrived at the very same place just before them, having rested at Watford the previous night. Anticipating the approach of the Duke of York, the king and his friends occupied the suburb of St. Peter's, which lay on that side of the town by which the duke must necessarily come. The duke accordingly, and the Earls of Salisbury and Warwick, drew up their forces in the Keyfield, outside the barriers of the town. From seven in the morning till near ten o'clock the two hosts remained facing each other without a blow being struck ; during which time the duke and the two earls, still endeavouring to obtain a peaceful interview with the king, petitioned to have an answer to their memorial of the preceding day. They were told in reply that it had not been received by the king, on which they made new and more urgent representations. At first, it would seem, they demanded access to the royal presence to declare and justify their true intentions ; but when this could not be obtained, they made a still more obnoxious request. They insisted that certain persons whom they would accuse of treason should be delivered into their hands, reminding the king, as respectfully as the fact could be alluded to, that past experience would not permit them to trust to a mere promise on his part that a traitor should be kept in confinement.[1]

For the answer made to this demand, and for the details of the battle which ensued, we may as well refer the reader to the very curious paper (No. 283) from which we have already derived most of the above particulars. We are not here writing the history of the times, and it may be sufficient for us to say that York and his friends were completely victorious. The action lasted only half an hour. The Duke of Somerset was slain, and with him the Earl of Northumberland, Lords Clifford and Clinton, with about 400 persons of inferior rank, *Battle of St. Albans.*

[1] No. 283. *Rolls of Parl.* v. 281-2.

161

THE PASTON LETTERS

as the numbers were at first reported. This, however, seems to have been an over-estimate.[1] The king himself was wounded by an arrow in the neck, and, after the engagement, was taken prisoner ; while the Earl of Wiltshire, and the Duke of York's old enemy, Thorpe, fled disgracefully. When all was over, the duke with the two earls came humbly and knelt before the king, beseeching his forgiveness for what they had done in his presence, and requesting him to acknowledge them as his true liegemen, seeing that they had never intended to do him personal injury. To this Henry at once agreed, and took them once more into favour.[2]

Thus again was effected 'a change of ministry'—by sharper and more violent means than had formerly been employed, but certainly by the only means which had now become at all practicable. The government of Somerset was distinctly unconstitutional. The deliberate and systematic exclusion from the king's councils of a leading peer of the realm—of one who, by mere hereditary right, quite apart from natural capacity and fitness, was entitled at any time to give his advice to royalty, was a crime that could not be justified. For conduct very similar the two Spencers had been banished by Parliament in the days of Edward II. ; and if it had been suffered now to remain unpunished, there would not have existed the smallest check upon arbitrary government and intolerable maladministration.

Such, we may be well assured, was the feeling of the city of London, which on the day following the battle received the victors in triumph with a general procession.[3] The Duke of York conducted the king to the Bishop of London's palace, and a council being assembled, writs were sent out for a Parliament to meet on the 9th of July following.[4] Meanwhile the duke was made Constable of England, and Lord Bourchier, Treasurer. The defence of Calais was committed to the Earl of Warwick.[5] There was, however, no entire and sweeping

[1] John Crane, writing from Lambeth on Whitsunday, three days after the battle, says, 'at most six score.' No. 285. Another authority says, '60 persons of gentlemen and other.' *English Chronicle*, ed. Davies, p. 72.
[2] Nos. 283, 284, 285. [3] No. 284. [4] No. 283. [5] No. 285.

162

INTRODUCTION

change made in the officers of state. The Great Seal was allowed to continue in the hands of Archbishop Bourchier.

It remained, however, for Parliament to ratify what had been done. However justifiable in a moral point of view, the conduct of York and his allies wore an aspect of violence towards the sovereign, which made it necessary that its legality should be investigated by the highest court in the realm. Inquiry was made both in Parliament and by the king's Council which of the lords about the king had been responsible for provoking the collision. Angry and unpleasant feelings, as might be expected, burst out in consequence. The Earl of Warwick accused Lord Cromwell to the king, and when the latter attempted to vindicate himself, swore that what he stated was untrue. So greatly was Lord Cromwell intimidated, that the Earl of Shrewsbury, at his request, took up his lodging at St. James's, beside the Mews, for his protection. The retainers of York, Warwick, and Salisbury went about fully armed, and kept their lords' barges on the river amply furnished with weapons. Proclamations, however, were presently issued against bearing arms. 'The Parliament, at last, laid the whole blame of the encounter upon the deceased Duke of Somerset, and the courtiers Thorpe and Joseph ; and by an Act which received the royal assent, it was declared that the Duke of York and his friends had acted the part of good and faithful subjects. 'To which bill,' said Henry Windsor in a letter to his friends Bocking and Worcester, 'many a man grudged full sore now it is past' ; but he requested them to burn a communication full of such uncomfortable matter to comment upon as the quarrels and heartburnings of lords.[1]

But with whatever grudge it may have been that Parliament condoned the acts of the Yorkists, it seems not to have been without some degree of pressure that the duke and his allies obtained a Parliament so much after their own minds. Here, for instance, we have the Duchess of Norfolk writing to John Paston, just before the election, that it was thought necessary ' that my lord have at this time in the Parliament such persons as long unto him and be of his menial servants (!)' ; on which *The Parliamentary elections.*

[1] No. 299.

163

account she requests his vote and influence in favour of John Howard and Sir Roger Chamberlain.[1] The application could scarcely have been agreeable to the person to whom it was addressed; for it seems that John Paston himself had on this occasion some thought of coming forward as a candidate for Norfolk. Exception was taken to John Howard, one of the duke's nominees (who, about eight-and-twenty years later, was created Duke of Norfolk himself, and was the ancestor of the present ducal family), on the ground that he possessed no lands within the county;[2] and at the nomination the names of Berney, Grey, and Paston were received with great favour.[3] John Jenney thought it 'an evil precedent for the shire that a strange man should be chosen, and no worship to my lord of York nor to my lord of Norfolk to write for him; for if the gentlemen of the shire will suffer such inconvenience, in good faith the shire shall not be called of such worship as it hath been.' So unpopular, in fact, was Howard's candidature that the Duke of Norfolk was half persuaded to give him up, declaring, that since his return was objected to he would write to the under-sheriff that the shire should have free election, provided they did not choose Sir Thomas Tuddenham or any of the old adherents of the Duke of Suffolk. And so, for a time it seemed as if free election would be allowed. The under-sheriff even ventured to write to John Paston that he meant to return his name and that of Master Grey; 'nevertheless,' he added significantly, 'I have a master.' Howard appeared to be savage with disappointment. He was 'as wode' (i.e. mad), wrote John Jenney, 'as a wild bullock.' But in the end it appeared he had no need to be exasperated, for when the poll came to be taken, he and the other nominee of the Duke of Norfolk were found to have gained the day.[4]

Besides the act of indemnity for the Duke of York and his partisans, and a new oath of allegiance being sworn to by the Lords, little was done at this meeting of the Parliament. On the 31st July it was prorogued, to meet again upon the 12th November. But in the interval another complication had arisen. The king, who seems to have suffered in health from

[1] No. 288.   [2] Nos. 294, 295.   [3] No. 291.   [4] No. 295.

164

the severe shock that he must have received by the battle of St. Albans,[1] had felt the necessity of retirement to recover his composure, and had withdrawn before the meeting of Parliament to Hertford; at which time the Duke of York, in order to be near him, took up his quarters at the Friars at Ware.[2] He was well, or at all events well enough to open Parliament in person on the 9th July; but shortly afterwards he retired to Hertford again, where according to the dates of his Privy Seals, I find that he remained during August and September. In the month of October following he was still there, and it was reported that he had fallen sick of his old infirmity;— The king which proved to be too true.[3]   *again ill.*

Altogether matters looked gloomy enough. Change of ministry by force of arms, whatever might be said for it, was not a thing to win the confidence either of king or people. There were prophecies bruited about that another battle would take place before St. Andrew's Day—the greatest that had been since the battle of Shrewsbury in the days of Henry IV. One Dr. Green ventured to predict it in detail. The scene of the conflict was to be between the Bishop of Salisbury's Inn and Westminster Bars, and three bishops and four temporal lords were to be among the slain. The Londoners were spared this excitement; but from the country there came news of a party outrage committed by the eldest son of the Earl of Devonshire, *Disturb-* on a dependant of the Lord Bonvile, and the West of England *ances in* seems to have been disturbed for some time afterwards.[4] From *the West.* a local MS. chronicle cited by Holinshed, it appears that a regular pitched battle took place between the two noblemen on Clist Heath, about two miles from Exeter, in which Lord Bonvile having gained the victory, entered triumphantly into the city. A modern historian of Exeter, however, seems to have read the MS. differently, and tells us that Lord Bonvile was driven into the city by defeat.[5] However this may be, the Earl of Devonshire did not allow the matter to rest. Accom-

[1] *See* Rymer, xi. 366.   [2] No. 287.   [3] No. 303.
[4] No. 303. *See* also a brief account of the same affair in W. Worcester's *Itinerary,* p. 114.
[5] Jenkins's *History of Exeter,* p. 78.

165

panied by a large body of retainers—no less, it is stated, than 800 horse and 4000 foot—he attacked the Dean and Canons of Exeter, made several of the latter prisoners, and robbed the cathedral.[1]

That one out of the number of those great lords who had been attached to the government of the queen and the Duke of Somerset should thus have abused his local influence, was pretty much what might have been expected at such a juncture. But the effect was only to strengthen the hands of York when Parliament met again in November. The situation was now once more what it had been in the beginning of the previous year. The day before Parliament met, the Duke of York obtained a commission to act as the king's lieutenant on its assembling.[2] The warrant for the issuing of this commission was signed by no less than thirty-nine Lords of the Council. The Houses then met under the presidency of the duke.[3] The Commons sent a deputation to the Upper House, to petition the Lords that they would 'be good means to the King's Highness' for the appointment of some person to undertake the defence of the realm and the repressing of disorders. But for some days this request remained unanswered. The appeal was renewed by the Commons a second time, and again a third time, with an intimation that no other business would be attended to till it was answered. On the *York* second occasion the Lords named the Duke of York Protector, *again* but he desired that they would excuse him, and elect some other. *Protector.* The Lords, however, declined to alter their choice, and the duke at last agreed to accept the office, on certain specific conditions which experience had taught him to make still more definite for his own protection than those on which he had before insisted. Among other things it was now agreed that the Protectorship should not again be terminated by the mere fact of the king's recovery; but that when the king should be in a position to

[1] *Rolls of Parl.* v. 285. It may be observed that the bishopric was at this time vacant, and the dean, whose name was John Hals, had received a papal provision to be the new bishop, but was forced to relinquish it in favour of George Nevill, son of the Earl of Salisbury, a young man of only three-and-twenty years of age. Godwin *de Præsulibus.* Le Neve's *Fasti.* Nicolas's *Privy Council Proceedings,* vi. 265.
[2] *Rolls of Parl.* v. 285.   [3] *Privy Council Proceedings,* vi. 262.

166

exercise his functions, the Protector should be discharged of his office in Parliament by the advice of the Lords Spiritual and Temporal.[1]

On the 19th of November, accordingly, York was formally appointed Protector for the second time. Three days afterwards, at Westminster, the king, whose infirmity on this occasion could scarcely have amounted to absolute loss of his faculties, committed the entire government of the kingdom to his Council, merely desiring that they would inform him of anything they might think fit to determine touching the honour and surety of his person.[2] The business of the nation was again placed on something like a stable and satisfactory footing; and Parliament, after sitting till the 13th December, was prorogued to the 14th January, in order that the Duke of York might go down into the west for the repressing of those disorders of which we have already spoken.[3]

Unluckily, things did not remain long in a condition so *A.D. 1456.* hopeful for the restoration of order. Early in the following year the king recovered his health, and notwithstanding the support of which he had been assured in Parliament, York knew that his authority as Protector would be taken from him. On the 9th of February, as we learn from a letter of John Bocking, it had been anticipated that he would have received his discharge in Parliament; but he was allowed to retain office for a fortnight longer. On that day he and Warwick thought fit to come to the Parliament with a company of 300 armed men, alleging that they stood in danger of being waylaid upon the road. The pretence does not seem to have been generally credited; and the practical result of this demonstration was simply to prevent any other lords from going to the Parliament at all.[4]

The real question, however, which had to be considered was the kind of government that should prevail when York was no more Protector. The queen was again making anxious efforts to get the management of affairs into her own hands; but the battle of St. Albans had deprived her of her great ally the Duke of Somerset, and there was no one now to fill his

[1] *Rolls of Parl.* v. 285-7.   [2] *Ibid.* v. 288-90.   [3] *Ibid.* 321.   [4] No. 322.

167

THE PASTON LETTERS

place. It is true he had left a son who was now Duke of Somerset in his stead, and quite as much attached to her interests. There were, moreover, the Duke of Buckingham and others who were by no means friendly to the Duke of York. But no man possessed anything like the degree of power, experience, and political ability to enable the king to dispense entirely with the services of his present Protector. The king himself, it was said, desired that he should be named his Chief Councillor and Lieutenant, and that powers should be conferred upon him by patent inferior only to those given him by the Parliament. But this was not thought a likely settlement, and no one really knew what was to be the new *régime*. The attention of the Lords was occupied with 'a great gleaming star' which had just made its appearance, and which really offered as much help to the solution of the enigma as any appearances purely mundane and political.[1]

Again discharged. At length on the 25th of February the Lords exonerated York from his duties as Protector; soon after which, if not on the same day, Parliament must have been dissolved.[2] An Act of Resumption, rendered necessary by the state of the revenue, was the principal fruit of its deliberations.[3] The finances of the kingdom were placed, if not in a sound, at least in a more hopeful condition than before; and Parliament and the Protector were both dismissed, without, apparently, the slightest provision being made for the future conduct of affairs. Government, in fact, seems almost to have fallen into abeyance. There is a most striking blank in the records of the Privy Council from the end of January 1456 to the end of November 1457. That some councils were held during this period we know from other evidences;[4] but with the exception of one single occasion, when it was necessary to

[1] No. 322. [2] *Rolls of Parl.* v. 321.
[3] *Ibid.* 300. A more sweeping bill for this purpose, which was rejected by the Lords, states that the revenue was so encumbered 'that the charge of every sheriff in substance exceedeth so far the receipt of the revenues thereof due and leviable to you (*i.e.* the king), that no person of goodwill dare take upon him to be sheriff in any shire, for the most party, in this land.' *Ibid.* 328. Additional illustrations of this fact will be found in Nicolas's *Privy Council Proceedings*, vi. 253-4, 272-3, and Preface lxxv-vi.
[4] Nos. 334, 345, 348.

168

INTRODUCTION

issue a commission for the trial of insurgents in Kent,[1] there is not a single record left to tell us what was done at them.

Yet the machine of state still moved, no one could tell exactly how. Acts were done in the king's name if not really and truly by the king, and by the sheer necessity of the case York appears to have had the ordering of all things. But his authority hung by a thread. His acts were without the slightest legal validity except in so far as they might be considered as having the sanction of the king; and in whatever way that sanction may or may not have been expressed, there was no security that it would not afterwards be withdrawn and disavowed.

The King of Scots. And so indeed it happened at this time in a matter that concerned deeply the honour of the whole country. The outbreak of civil war had provoked the interference of an enemy of whom Englishmen were always peculiarly intolerant. The Duke of Somerset slain at St. Albans was uncle to James II., the reigning king of Scotland, who is said to have resented his death on the ground of consanguinity. In less than six weeks after the battle, 'the King of Scots with the red face,' as he is called in a contemporary chronicle, laid siege to Berwick both by water and land. But the Bishop of Durham, the Earl of Northumberland, and other Lords of the Marches, took prompt measures for the relief of the town, and soon assembled such a force as to compel James not only to quit the siege but to leave all his ordnance and victuals behind him.[2] How matters stood between the two countries during the next ten months we have no precise information; but it is clear that England, although the injured party, could not have been anxious to turn the occasion into one of open rupture. Peace still continued to be preserved till, on the 10th of May 1456, James wrote to the King of England by Lyon herald, declaring that the truce of 1453 was injurious to his kingdom, and that unless more favourable conditions were conceded to him he would have recourse to arms.[3] A message more

[1] *Privy Council Proceedings*, vi. 287.
[2] *Three Fifteenth Century Chronicles*, 70 (edited by me, for the Camden Society): *Privy Council Proceedings*, vi. 248-9. [3] Lambeth MS. 211, f. 146 b.

169

THE PASTON LETTERS

calculated to fire the spirit of the English nation it would have been impossible for James to write; nevertheless, owing either to Henry's love of peace, or to his lack of advisers after his own mind, it was not till the 26th of July that any answer was returned to it. On that day the Duke of York obtained, or took, the liberty of replying in Henry's name. To the insolence of the King of Scots, he opposed all the haughtiness that might have been expected from the most warlike of Henry's ancestors. Insisting to the fullest extent on those claims of feudal superiority which England never had abandoned and Scotland never had acknowledged, he told James that his conduct was mere insolence and treason in a vassal against his lord; that it inspired not the slightest dread but only contempt on the part of England; and that measures would be speedily taken to punish his presumption.[1]

A month later the Duke of York addressed a letter to James in his own name, declaring that as he understood the Scotch king had entered England, he purposed to go and meet him. He at the same time reproached James with conduct unworthy of one who was 'called a mighty Prince and a courageous knight,' in making daily forays and suddenly retiring again.[2] The end of this expedition we do not know; but we know that not long afterwards Henry changed his policy. The letter written by the Duke of York in the king's name was regularly enrolled all the Scotch Roll among the records of Chancery; but to it was prefixed a note on the king's behalf, disclaiming responsibility for its tenor, and attributing to the duke the usurpation of authority, and the disturbance of all government since the time of Jack Cade's insurrection.[3]

The glimpses of light which we have on the political situation during this period are far from satisfactory. Repeated notice, however, is taken in these letters of a fact which seems significant of general distrust and mutual suspicion among the leading persons in the land. The king, queen, and lords were all separated and kept carefully at a distance from each other.

[1] Lambeth MS. 211, f. 147. Rymer, xi. 383.
[2] Lambeth MS. 211, f. 148. This letter is dated 24th August 1456.
[3] Rymer, xi. 383.

170

INTRODUCTION

Thus, while the king was at Sheen, the queen and her infant prince were staying at Tutbury, the Duke of York at Sandal, and the Earl of Warwick at Warwick.[1] Afterwards we find the queen removed to Chester, while the Duke of Buckingham was at Writtle, near Chelmsford in Essex. The only lord with the king at Sheen was his half-brother the Earl of Pembroke. His other brother, the Earl of Richmond, who died in the course of this year, was in Wales making war upon some chieftain of the country whose name seems rather ambiguous. 'My Lord [of] York,' it is said, 'is at Sendall still, and waiteth on the queen, and she on him.'[2] The state of matters was evidently such that it was apprehended serious outrages might break out; and reports were even spread abroad of a battle in which Lord Beaumont had been slain and the Earl of Warwick severely wounded.'[3]

The king and queen. The separation of the king and queen is especially remarkable. During May and June they were more than a hundred miles apart; and in the latter month the queen had increased the distance by removing from Tutbury in Staffordshire to Chester. It was then that she was said to be waiting on my Lord of York and he on her. The exact interpretation of the position must be partly matter of conjecture, but I take it to be as follows. The Duke of York, as we find stated only a few months later, was in very good favour with the king but not with the queen;[4] and we know from Fabyan that the latter was at this time doing all she could to put an end to his authority. It appears to me that by her influence the duke must have been ordered to withdraw from the Court, and that to prevent his again seeking access to the king's presence, she pursued him into the north. At Tutbury[5] she would block his way from Sandal up to London; and though for some reason or other she removed further off to Chester, she still kept an anxious watch upon the duke, and he did the same on her. Very probably her removal did give him the opportunity she dreaded of moving southwards; for he must have been

[1] Nos. 330, 331. [2] No. 334. [3] No. 331. [4] No. 348.
[5] Tutbury was one of the possessions given to her for her dower. *Rolls of Parl.* vi. 118.

171

with the king at Windsor on the 26th of July when he wrote in Henry's name that answer to the King of Scots of which we have already spoken.

However this may be, Margaret soon after had recourse to other means to effect her object. In consequence of the Duke of York's popularity in London, it was expedient to remove the king some distance from the capital.[1] He appears to have been staying at Windsor during July and the beginning of August. In the middle of the latter month he took his departure northwards. By the dates of his Privy Seals we find him to have been at Wycombe on the 18th, at Kenilworth on the 24th, and at Lichfield on the 29th. In September he moved about between Lichfield, Coventry, and Leicester; but by the beginning of October the Court seems to have settled itself at Coventry, where a council was assembled on the 7th.[2] To this council the Duke of York and his friends were regularly summoned, as well as the lords whom the queen intended to honour; but even before it met, changes had begun to be made in the principal officers of state. On the 5th, Viscount Bourchier, the brother of the Archbishop of Canterbury, was dismissed from his office of Lord Treasurer, and the Earl of Shrewsbury was appointed in his room. On the 11th, the archbishop himself was called upon to surrender the Great Seal, and Waynflete, Bishop of Winchester, was made Chancellor in his stead. Laurence Booth, afterwards Bishop of Durham, was made Lord Privy Seal.

The new appointments seem to have been on their own merits unexceptionable,—that of Waynflete more especially. Whether the superiority of the new men was such as to make it advisable to supersede the old is another question, on which we would not attempt to pronounce an opinion, either one way or other. One thing, however, we may believe on the evidence of James Gresham, whose letters frequently give us very interesting political intelligence: the changes created dissatisfaction in some of the queen's own friends, particularly in the Duke of Buckingham, who was half-brother to two of the discharged functionaries, the Archbishop of Canterbury and

[1] Fabyan. [2] No. 345.

172

Viscount Bourchier. Either from this cause or from a mere English love of fair-play, it would appear that Buckingham now supported the Duke of York, who, it is said, though at this time he had some interviews with the king and found Henry still as friendly as he could desire, would certainly have been troubled at his departure if Buckingham had not befriended him. About the Court there was a general atmosphere of suspicion and distrust. On the 11th October, the very day on which Waynflete was appointed Chancellor, an encounter took place between the Duke of Somerset's men and the watchmen of the city of Coventry, in which two or three of the citizens were killed. And probably it would have gone hard with the duke's retainers, had not Buckingham used his good offices here too as peacemaker; for the alarm-bell rang and the citizens rose in arms. But by the interposition of Buckingham the tumult was appeased.[1]

For about a twelvemonth from this time we find that the A.D. 1457. Court continued generally at Coventry,[2] occasionally moving about to Stafford, Coleshill, Chester, Shrewsbury, Kenilworth, Hereford, and Leicester.[3] The queen evidently feared all the while to bring her husband nearer London, lest he should fall once more under the power of the Duke of York. Meanwhile the want of a vigorous ruler became every day more apparent. Not only was Calais again in danger of siege,[4] but the coast of Kent was attacked by enemies, and within the kingdom a dangerous spirit of disaffection had shown itself in various places. On the Patent Rolls we meet with numerous commissions for keeping watch upon the coasts,[5] for arraying the country against invasion,[6] and for assembling the posse comitatus in various counties, against treasonable attempts to stir up the people.[7] During April the Court had removed to

[1] No. 348.
[2] Accounts of the pageants shown before Queen Margaret at Coventry are noticed as contained in the earliest Leet Book of the City. See Historical MSS. Commission Report I., 100.
[3] Privy Seals in Public Record Office. [4] No. 356.
[5] Patent Roll, 35 Hen. VI. p. 1 m. 16 d. (26 Nov.); m. 7 d. (19 May).
[6] Ibid. p. 2 m. 5 d. (29 Aug.).
[7] Ibid. (18 July).

173

Hereford,[1] apparently in consequence of some disturbances which had taken place in Wales under Sir William Herbert. Its sojourn upon the Welsh borders had an excellent effect, the burgesses and gentlemen about Hereford all declaring themselves ready to take the king's part unless a peace were made. On the 1st of May it was reported in London that Herbert had offered, on being granted his life and goods, to return to his allegiance and appear before the king and lords at Leicester; so we may conclude the insurrection did not last long after.[2]

But though the personal influence of the king was doubtless great and beneficial within his own immediate vicinity, it could do little for the good order and protection of the country generally. Distrust, exclusiveness, and a bankrupt exchequer were not likely to obtain for the king willing and hearty service. Notwithstanding the commissions issued to keep watch upon the coasts, the French managed to surprise and plunder Sandwich. On Sunday, the 28th August, a large force under the command of Pierre de Brézé, seneschal of Normandy, landed not far from the town, which they took and kept possession of during the entire day. A number of the inhabitants, on the first alarm, retreated on board some ships lying in the harbour, from whence they began presently to shoot at the enemy. But de Brézé having warned them that if they continued he would burn their ships, they found it prudent to leave off. Having killed the bailiffs and principal officers, the Frenchmen carried off a number of wealthy persons as prisoners, and returned to their ships in the evening, laden with valuable spoils from the town and neighbourhood.[3]

The disaster must have been keenly felt; but if Englishmen had known the whole truth, it would have been felt more keenly still. Our own old historians were not aware of the

The French attack Sandwich.

[1] No. 356. There are Privy Seals dated at Hereford between the 1st and the 23rd of April.
[2] No. 356. By the 4th of May the king had left Hereford and gone to Worcester, from which he proceeded to Winchcombe on the 10th and Kenilworth on the 13th. (Privy Seal dates.)
[3] English Chronicle (Davies), 74. Three Fifteenth Century Chronicles, 70, 71, 152-3. Contin. of Monstrelet, 70, 71.

174

fact, but an early French chronicler who lived at the time assures us that the attack had been purposely invited by Margaret of Anjou out of hatred to the Duke of York, in order to make a diversion, while the Scots should ravage England![1] It was well for her that the truth was not suspected.

Reconciliation and Civil War

At length, it would seem, the Court found it no longer possible to remain at a distance from the metropolis. In October the king had removed to Chertsey,[2] and soon after we find him presiding at a Great Council, which had been summoned to meet in his palace at Westminster in consequence of the urgent state of affairs. Though attended not only by the Duke of York, but by a large number of the principal lords on both sides, the meeting does not appear to have led to any very satisfactory results. All that we know of its proceedings is that some of them, at least, were of a stormy character,—one point on which all parties were agreed being the exclusion from the council chamber of Pecock, Bishop of Chichester, an ardent and honest-minded prelate, who, having laboured hard to reconcile the Lollards to the authority of the Church by arguments of common sense instead of persecution, was at this time stigmatised as a heretic and sedition-monger, and very soon after was deprived of his bishopric. It augured little good for that union of parties which was now felt to be necessary for the public weal, that the first act on which men generally could be got to agree was the persecution of sense and reason. There were other matters before the council on which they were unable to come to a conclusion, and they broke up on the 29th November, with a resolution to meet again on the 27th January; for which meeting summonses were at once sent out, notifying that on that day not one of the lords would be excused attendance.[3]

It was, indeed, particularly important that this meeting

Bishop Pecock.

[1] De Coussy, 209. [2] Privy Seal dates.
[3] Privy Council Proceedings, vi. 290-1.

175

should be a full one, and that every lord should be compelled to take his share of the responsibility for its decisions. The principal aim was expressly stated to be a general reconciliation and adjustment of private controversies [1]—an object to which it was impossible to offer direct opposition. But whether it was really distasteful to a number of the peers, or obstacles started up in individual cases, there were certainly several who had not arrived in town by the day appointed

A.D. 1458. for the meeting. The Earl of Salisbury's excuse, dated at Sheriff Hutton on the 24th of January,[2] does not refer to this, for it appears certainly to be of a different year. Fabyan says that he had already arrived in London on the 15th January. He made his appearance there at the head of 400 horse, with eighty knights and squires in his company. The Duke of York also came, though he arrived only on the 26th, 'with his own household only, to the number of 140 horse.' But the Duke of Somerset only arrived on the last day of the month with 200 horse; the Duke of Exeter delayed his coming till the first week of February; and the Earl of Warwick, who had to come from Calais, was detained by contrary winds. Thus, although the king had come up to Westminster by the time prefixed, a full Council could not be had for at least some days after; and even on the 14th of February there was one absentee, the Earl of Arundel, who had to be written to by letters of Privy Seal.[3]

A Great Council in London. But by the 14th Warwick had arrived in London with a body of 600 men, 'all apparelled in red jackets, with white ragged staves.'[4] The town was now full of the retinues of the different noblemen, and the mayor and sheriffs trembled for the peace of the city. A very special watch was instituted. 'The mayor,' says Fabyan, 'for so long as the king and the lords lay thus in the city, had daily in harness 5000 citizens, and rode daily about the city and suburbs of the same, to see that the king's peace were kept; and nightly he provided for 3000 men in harness to give attendance upon

[1] Privy Council Proceedings, vi. 293.
[2] No. 361.   [3] No. 364.   Privy Council Proceedings, vi. 293.
[4] Chronicle in MS. Cott., Vitell. A. xvi.

176

three aldermen, and they to keep the night-watch till 7 of the clock upon the morrow, till the day-watch were assembled.' If peace was to be the result of all this concourse, the settlement evidently could not bear to be protracted. The Duke of York and the Earls of Salisbury and Warwick had taken up their quarters within the city itself; but the young lords whose fathers had been slain at St. Albans—the Duke of Somerset, the Earl of Northumberland and his brother, Lord Egremont, and the Lord Clifford—were believed to be bent upon revenge, and the civic authorities refused them entrance within their bounds.[1] Thus the lords within the town and those without belonged to the two opposite parties respectively; and in consequence of their mutual jealousies, conferences had to be arranged between them in the morning at the Black Friars, and in the afternoon at the White Friars, in Fleet Street.[2] The king, for his part, having opened the proceedings with some very earnest exhortations addressed to both parties, withdrew himself and retired to Berkhampstead.[3] The Duke of Somerset and others went to and fro to consult with him during the deliberations. Meanwhile the necessity of some practical arrangement for government must have been felt more urgent every day. Sixty sail of Frenchmen were seen off the coast of Sussex; and though Lord Falconbridge was at Southampton in command of some vessels (probably on his own responsibility), there was a general feeling of insecurity among the merchants and among dwellers by the sea-coast. Botoner had heard privately from Calais that the French meditated a descent upon Norfolk at Cromer and Blakeney.[4] And the news shortly afterwards received from the district showed that his information was not far wrong.[5]

At last it was agreed on both sides that old animosities Terms of should be laid aside, and that some reparation should be made agreement. by the Yorkists to the sons and widows of the lords who had fallen on the king's side at St. Albans. The exact amount of this reparation was left to the award of Henry, who decided that it should consist of an endowment of £45 a year to the

[1] English Chronicle (ed. Davies), p. 77. Hall.   [2] Letter 366.
[3] Whethamstede, 417-18. Letter 365.   [4] Letter 365.   [5] Letter 366.

VOL. I.—M   177

Monastery of St. Albans, to be employed in masses for the slain, and of certain money payments, or assignments out of moneys due to them by the Crown, to be made by York, Warwick, and Salisbury, to Eleanor, Duchess Dowager of Somerset and to her son, Duke Henry, to Lord Clifford, and others, in lieu of all claims and actions which the latter parties might have against the former.[1] With what cordiality this arrangement was accepted on either side we do not presume to say. Historians universally speak of it as a hollow concord, unreal from the first. But it at least preserved the kingdom in something like peace for about a twelvemonth. It was celebrated by a great procession to St. Paul's on Lady Day, which must have been an imposing spectacle. The king marched in royal habit with the crown upon his head, York and the queen followed, arm in arm, and the principal rivals led the way, walking hand in hand.[2]

A sea fight. The keeping of the sea was now intrusted to the Earl of Warwick, and it was not long before he distinguished himself by an action which probably relieved the English coasts for some time from any immediate danger of being attacked by the enemy. On the morning of Trinity Sunday word was brought to him at Calais of a fleet of 28 Spaniards, of which 16 were described as 'great ships of forecastle.' Immediately he manned such vessels as he had in readiness, and went out to seek the enemy. The force at his command was only five ships of forecastle, three carvels, and four pinnaces; but with these he did not hesitate to come to an engagement. At four o'clock on Monday morning the battle began, and it continued till ten, when the English obtained a hard-won victory. 'As men say,' wrote one of the combatants, 'there was not so great a battle upon the sea this forty winter; and forsooth, we were well and truly beat.' Nevertheless, six of the enemy's ships were taken, and the rest were put to flight, not without very considerable slaughter on either side.[3]

[1] Whethamstede, 422 sq. Engl. Chron. (Davies), 77, 78.   [2] Hall.
[3] Letter 369. Compare Fabyan. Whethamstede, who writes with some confusion in this part of his narrative, speaks of a great naval victory won by Warwick on St. Alban's Day, the 22nd June 1459, over a fleet of Genoese and Spanish vessels, in which booty was taken to the value of £10,000, and upwards of a thousand

178

In the year following, the fire that had for some time A.D. 1459. smouldered, burst once more into a flame. About Candlemas, according to Fabyan—but an older authority says specifically on the 9th November preceding [1]—a fray occurred between one of the king's servants and one of the Earl of Warwick's, as the earl, who had been attending the Council at Westminster, was proceeding to his barge. The king's servant being wounded, the other made his escape; but a host of retainers attached to the royal household rushed out upon the earl and his attendants, and wounded several of them before they could embark. With hard rowing they got beyond the power of their assailants and made their way into the city; but the queen and her friends insisted on imputing the outrage to the earl himself, and demanded his arrest. The earl found it politic to retire to Warwick, and afterwards to his former post at Calais. On this the queen and her council turned their machinations against his father, the Earl of Salisbury, whom Lord Audley was commissioned to arrest and bring prisoner to London. Audley accordingly took with him a large body of men, and hearing that the earl was on his way from Middleham in Yorkshire, journeying either towards Salisbury or London, he hastened to intercept him. The earl, Civil war however, had received notice of what was intended, and renewed. having gathered about him a sufficient band of followers, defeated Lord Audley in a regular pitched battle at Bloreheath in Staffordshire, where he attempted to stop his way, on Sunday the 23rd of September.[2]

The old elements of confusion were now again let loose. Commissions to raise men were issued in the king's name, and the Duke of York and all his friends were denounced as

prisoners, for whom it was difficult to find room in all the prisons of Calais. It is not impossible that this may have been a different action, which took place on the very day, month, and year to which Whethamstede refers it; but the silence of other authorities about a second naval victory would lead us to suppose he is simply wrong in the matter of date. It must be observed that Whethamstede immediately goes on to speak of the Legate Coppini's arrival in England, which took place in June 1460, as having happened circa idem tempus, and as if it had been in the same month of June, only a few days earlier. This shows great inaccuracy.

[1] Engl. Chron. (Davies), 78.
[2] Fabyan, Engl. Chron. (Davies), 80. Parl. Rolls, v. 348.

179

THE PASTON LETTERS

a confederacy of traitors. They, for their parts, gathered together the men of the Marches in self-defence. At Ludlow, the duke was joined by the Earl of Salisbury, and also by the Earl of Warwick, who had come over again from Calais. On the other hand, the king himself entered into the strife in a way he had not done hitherto. He not only took the field in person against the rebellious lords, but exhibited a spirit in the endurance of fatigue and discomfort which seems to have commanded general admiration. Even at the time of Lord Audley's overthrow, it would appear that he was leading forward a reserve. For about a month he kept continually camping out, never resting at night, except on Sundays, in the same place he had occupied the night before, and sometimes, in spite of cold, rough weather, bivouacking for two nights successively on the bare field. After the battle of Bloreheath, he could only regard Salisbury as an overt enemy of his crown. At the same time he despatched heralds to the Duke of York and the Earl of Warwick, with proclamations of free and perfect pardon to themselves and all but a few of the leaders at Bloreheath, on condition of their submitting to him within six days.[1]

The king takes the field.

To Garter King of Arms, one of the messengers by whom these offers were conveyed, the confederate lords made answer, and also delivered a written reply to be conveyed to the king, declaring the perfect loyalty of their intentions, which they would have been glad to prove in the king's presence if it had been only possible for them to go to him with safety. They had already endeavoured to testify their unshaken fidelity to Henry by an indenture drawn up and signed by them in Worcester Cathedral. This instrument they had forwarded to the king by a deputation of churchmen, headed by the prior of that cathedral, and including among others Dr. William Lynwoode,[2] who administered to them the sacrament on the occasion. Again, after Garter left, they wrote from

[1] *Rolls of Parl.* vi. 348.
[2] Not, as Stow supposes, the author of the book on the Constitutions of the Church of England, but probably a nephew or other relation of his. The William Lynwoode who wrote upon the Church Constitutions was Bishop of St. David's, and died in 1446.

180

INTRODUCTION

Ludlow on the 10th of October, protesting that their actions had been misconstrued, and their tenants subjected to wrong and violence, while they themselves lay under unjust suspicion. Their enemies, they said, thirsted for the possession of their lands, and hoped to obtain them by their influence with the king. For their own part they had hitherto avoided a conflict, not from any fear of the power of their enemies, but only for dread of God and of his Highness, and they meant to persevere in this peaceful course, until driven by necessity to self-defence.[1]

These earnest, solemn, and repeated expressions of loyalty have scarcely, I think, received from historians the attention to which they are entitled.[2] Of their sincerity, of course, men may form different opinions ; but it is right to note that the confederate lords had done all that was in their power by three several and distinct protests to induce the king to think more favourably of their intentions. It is, moreover, to be observed that they remained at this time in an attitude strictly defensive. But the king and his forces still approaching, they drew themselves up in battle array at Ludford, in the immediate vicinity of the town of Ludlow. Here, as they were posted on Friday the 12th October, it would almost seem that the lords were not without apprehension of the defection of some of their followers. A report was spread through the camp that the king was suddenly deceased, witnesses were brought in who swore to the fact, and mass was said for the repose of his soul. But that very evening, Henry, at the head of his army, arrived within half a mile of their position. The state of the country, flooded by recent rains, had alone prevented him from coming upon them sooner. Before nightfall a few volleys of artillery were discharged against the royal army, and a regular engagement was expected next day. But, meanwhile, the royal proclamation of pardon seems to have had its effect. One Andrew Trollope, who had come over with the Earl of Warwick from

[1] *Engl. Chron.* (Davies), 81, 82.
[2] The Act of Attainder against the Yorkists most untruly says, 'they took no consideration' of Garter's message. See *Rolls of Parliament* above cited.

181

THE PASTON LETTERS

Calais, withdrew at dead of night and carried over a considerable body of men to the service of the king, to whom he communicated the secrets of the camp. The blow was absolutely fatal. The lords at once abandoned all thought of further resistance. Leaving their banners in the field, they withdrew at midnight. York and his second son, Edmund, Earl of Rutland, fled into Wales, from whence they sailed into Ireland. His eldest, Edward, Earl of March, accompanied by the two other earls, Warwick and Salisbury, and by Sir John Wenlock, made his way into Devonshire. There by the friendly aid of one John Dynham, afterwards Lord Dynham, and Lord High Treasurer to Henry VII., they bought a ship at Exmouth and sailed to Guernsey. At last, on Friday the 2nd of November, they landed at Calais, where they met with a most cordial reception from the inhabitants.

The Yorkists disperse.

Then followed in November the Parliament of Coventry, and the attainder of the Duke of York and all his party. The queen and her friends at last had it all their own way, at least in England. It was otherwise doubtless in Ireland, where the Duke of York remained for nearly a twelvemonth after his flight from Ludlow. It was otherwise too at Calais, where Warwick was all-powerful, and whither discontented Yorkists began to flock from England. It was otherwise, moreover, at sea, where the same Warwick still retained the command of the fleet, and could not be dispossessed, except on parchment. On parchment, however, he was presently superseded in both of his important offices. The Duke of Exeter was intrusted with the keeping of the sea, which even at the time of the great reconciliation of parties he had been displeased that Warwick was allowed to retain.[2] The young Duke of Somerset was appointed Captain of Calais, but was unable to take possession of his post. Accompanied by Lord Roos and Lord Audley, and fortified by the king's letters-patent, he crossed the sea, but was refused admittance into the town. Apparently he had put off too long before going

They are attainted.

[1] *Rolls of Parl.* vi. 348-9. Whethamstede, 459-62 ; Fabyan.
[2] W. Worc., 479.

182

INTRODUCTION

over,[1] and he found the three earls in possession of the place before him ; so that he was obliged to land at a place called Scales' Cliff and go to Guisnes.[2] But a worse humiliation still awaited him on landing ; for of the very sailors that had brought him over, a number conveyed their ships into Calais harbour, offered their services to the Earl of Warwick, and placed in his hands as prisoners certain persons who had taken part against him. They were shortly after beheaded in Calais.[3]

It would seem, in short, that ever since his great naval victory in 1458, Warwick was so highly popular with all the sailors of England, that it was quite as hopeless for the Duke of Exeter to contest his supremacy at sea as for Somerset to think of winning Calais out of his hands. Friends still came flocking over from England to join the three earls at Calais ; and though in London in the February following nine men were hanged, drawn, and beheaded for attempting to do so,[4] the cause of the Yorkists remained as popular as ever. In vain were letters written to foreign parts, ' that no relief be ministered to the traitor who kept Calais.'[5] In vain the Duke of Somerset at Guisnes endeavoured to contest his right to the government of that important town. All that Somerset could do was to waste his strength in fruitless skirmishes, until on St. George's Day he suffered such a severe defeat and loss of men at Newnham Bridge, that he was at length forced to abandon all idea of dispossessing the Earl of Warwick.[6]

A.D. 1460.

Not only were the three earls secure in their position at Calais, but there was every reason to believe that they had a large amount of sympathy in Kent, and would meet with a very cordial reception whenever they crossed the sea. To

[1] He received his appointment on the 9th October, three days before the dispersion of the Yorkists at Ludlow (Rymer, xi. 436), and, according to one authority (*Engl. Chron.*, ed. Davies, 84), he went over in the same month ; but as all agree that Warwick was there before him, it was more probably in the beginning of November.
[2] *Chronicle* in MS. Cott., Vitell. A. xvi.
[3] Fabyan.
[4] W. Worc., 478 ; *Three Fifteenth Century Chronicles*, 73. One of them was named Roger Nevile, a lawyer of the Temple, and probably a relation of the Earl of Warwick. [5] Speed. [6] W. Worc.

183

THE PASTON LETTERS

Lord Rivers at Sandwich.

avert the danger of any such attempt, and also, it would appear, with some design of reinforcing the Duke of Somerset at Guisnes, Lord Rivers and his son Sir Anthony Wydevile were sent to Sandwich about the beginning of the year, with a body of 400 men. Besides the command of the town, they were commissioned to take possession of certain ships which belonged to the Earl of Warwick, and lay quietly at anchor in the harbour.[1] But the issue of their exploit was such as to provoke universal ridicule. 'As to tidings here,' wrote Botoner from London to John Berney at Caister, 'I send some offhand, written to you and others, how the Lord Rivers, Sir Anthony his son and others *have won Calais* by a feeble assault at Sandwich made by John Denham, Esq., with the number of 800 men, on Tuesday between four and five o'clock in the morning.'[2]

The exact mode in which Rivers and his son 'won Calais' seems to have been described in a separate paper. The truth was that a small force under the command of John Denham (or Dynham) was despatched across the sea by Warwick, and landing at Sandwich during the night, contrived not only to seize the ships in the harbour, but even to surprise the earl and his son in their beds, and bring them over as prisoners to the other side of the Channel.[3] The victors did not fail to turn the incident to account by exhibiting as much contempt as possible for their unfortunate prisoners. 'My Lord Rivers,' writes William Paston, 'was brought to Calais, and before the lords with eight score torches, and there my lord of Salisbury rated him, calling him knave's son, that he should be so rude to call him and those other lords traitors; for they should be found the king's true liegemen when he should be found a traitor. And my Lord of Warwick rated him and said that his father was but a squire, and brought up with King Henry v., and since made himself by marriage, and also made a lord; and that it was not his part to have such language of lords, being of the king's blood. And my Lord of March rated him in like wise. And Sir Anthony was rated for his

[1] *Engl. Chron.* (Davies), 84, 85; *Three Fifteenth Century Chronicles*, 72.
[2] Letter 399.   [3] W. Worc. *Engl. Chron.* (Davies), 85.

184

INTRODUCTION

language of all the three lords in like wise.'[1] It must have been a curious reflection to the Earl of March when in after years, as King Edward IV., he married the daughter of this same Lord Rivers, that he had taken part in this vituperation of his future father-in-law !

By and by it became sufficiently evident that unless he was considerably reinforced, the Duke of Somerset could do no good at Guisnes. Instead of attempting to maintain a footing beside Calais, the queen's Government would have enough to do to keep the rebels out of England. The capture of Rivers had excited the most serious alarm, and the landing of Warwick himself upon the eastern coast was looked upon as not improbable.[2] A new force of 500 men was accordingly sent to Sandwich under the command of one Osbert Mountford or Mundeford,[3] an old officer of Calais. His instructions were to go from Sandwich to Guisnes, either in aid of the Duke of Somerset, as intimated in Worcester's *Annals*, or, according to another contemporary authority,[4] to bring him over to England. But while he waited for a wind to sail, John Dynham again crossed the sea, attacked the force under the command of Mundeford, and after a little skirmishing, in which he himself was wounded, succeeded in carrying him off to Calais, as he had before done Lord Rivers. Mundeford's treatment, however, was not so lenient as that of the more noble captive. On the 25th of June he was beheaded at the Tower of Rysebank, which stood near the town, on the opposite side of the harbour.[5]

Meanwhile the Earl of Warwick did not remain at Calais. He scoured the seas with his fleet and sailed into Ireland. Sir Baldwin Fulford, a knight of Devonshire, promised the king, on pain of losing his head, to destroy Warwick's fleet ;

[1] Letter 400.   [2] *See* Appendix to Introduction.
[3] The writer of Letter 378. He was a connection of the Paston family, having married Elizabeth, daughter of John Berney, Esq., another of whose daughters, Margaret, was the mother of Margaret Paston (Blomefield, ii. 182). He had been much engaged in the king's service in France, and had been treasurer of Normandy before it was lost—a fact which may account for his writing French in preference to English. *See* Stevenson's *Wars of the English in France*, index.
[4] *Engl. Chron.* (Davies), 85.
[5] W. Worc., 479; Fabyan; Stow, 406-7.

185

THE PASTON LETTERS

The Legate Coppini.

but having exhausted the sum of 1000 marks which was allowed him for his expenses, he returned home without having attained his object.[1] On the 16th of March, Warwick having met with the Duke of York in Ireland, the two noblemen entered the harbour of Waterford with a fleet of six-and-twenty ships well manned ; and on the following day, being St. Patrick's Day, they landed and were ceremoniously received by the mayor and burgesses.[2] Warwick seems to have remained in Ireland more than two months, concerting with the Duke of York plans for future action. About Whitsunday, which in this year fell on the 1st of June, his fleet was observed by the Duke of Exeter off the coast of Cornwall, on its return to Calais. Exeter's squadron was superior in strength, and an engagement might have been expected ; but the duke was not sure that he could trust his own sailors, and he allowed the earl to pass unmolested.

About this time there arrived at Calais a papal nuncio, by name Francesco Coppini, Bishop of Terni, returning from England to Rome. He had been sent by the new pope, Pius II., the ablest that had for a long time filled the pontifical chair, to urge Henry to send an ambassador to a congress at Mantua, in which measures were to be concerted for the union and defence of Christendom against the Turks. This was in the beginning of the preceding year,[4] and, as he himself states, he remained nearly a year and a half in England.[5] But the incapacity of the king, and the dissensions that prevailed among the lords, rendered his mission a total failure. Henry, indeed, who was never wanting in reverence for the Holy See, named a certain number of bishops and lords to go upon this mission, but they one and all refused. He accordingly sent two priests of little name, with an informal commission to excuse a greater embassy. England was thus discredited at the papal court, and the nuncio, finding his mission fruitless, at last crossed the sea to return home. At Calais, however,

[1] *English Chron.* (Davies), 85.   [2] Lambeth MS. 632, f. 255.
[3] *Chron.* (Davies), 85; W. Worc.
[4] His commission from the Pope is dated 7th January 1458[9]—Rymer, xi. 419.
[5] Brown's *Venetian Calendar*, i. p. 91.

186

INTRODUCTION

he was persuaded by Warwick to remain. The earl himself was about to return to England, and if the legate would come back in his company he might use the influence of his sacred office to heal the wounds of a divided kingdom.[1]

The nuncio had doubtless seen enough of the deplorable condition of England to be convinced that peace was impossible, so long as the lords most fit to govern were banished and proclaimed rebels by the queen and her favourites.[2] He was, moreover, furnished with powers, by which—the main object of his mission being the union of Christendom—he was authorised to make some efforts to compose the dissensions of England.[3] But he certainly overstrained them, and allowed himself to become a partisan. Flattered by the attentions shown him by Warwick, he acceded to his suggestion, and when, on the 26th of June,[4] the day after Mundeford was beheaded at Calais, the confederate lords crossed the Channel, the nuncio was in their company, bearing the standard of the Church. Archbishop Bourchier, too, met them at Sandwich, where they landed, with a great multitude of people ; and with his cross borne before him, the Primate of England conducted the three earls and their followers, who increased in number as they went along, until they reached the capital. After a very brief opposition on the part of some of the citizens, the city opened its gates to them. They entered London on the 2nd of July.[5]

The Earls of March, Warwick, and Salisbury.

Before they crossed the sea, the three earls had sent over a set of articles addressed to the archbishop and the commons of England in the name of themselves and the Duke of York, declaring how they had sued in vain to be admitted to the

[1] Gobellinus, 161.
[2] The Yorkists apparently were not sparing of insinuations against the queen. It had been rumoured, according to Fabyan, that the Prince of Wales was not really the king's son ; but the worst that was insinuated was that he was a changeling. But Warwick himself, according to Gobellinus, described the situation to the nuncio as follows :—'Rex noster stupidus est, et mente captus ; regitur, non regit ; apud uxorem et qui regis thalamum foedant, imperium est.'
[3] *See* the Pope's letter to him in Theiner, 423-4.
[4] 'The lords crossed the sea on Thursday,' writes Coppini from London on the 4th July.—Brown's *Venetian Calendar*, i. 90.
[5] *Engl. Chron.* (Davies), 94.

187

THE PASTON LETTERS

king's presence to set forth certain matters that concerned the common weal of all the land. Foremost among these was the oppression of the Church, a charge based, seemingly, on facts with which we are unacquainted, and which, if known, might shed a clearer light upon the conduct of the legate and Archbishop Bourchier. Secondly, they complained of the crying evil that the king had given away to favourites all the revenues of his crown, so that his household was supported by acts of rapine and extortion on the part of his purveyors. Thirdly, the laws were administered with great partiality, and justice was not to be obtained. Grievous taxes, moreover, were levied upon the commons, while the destroyers of the land were living upon the patrimony of the crown. And now a heavier charge than ever was imposed upon the inhabitants ; for the king, borrowing an idea from the new system of military service in France, had commanded every township to furnish at its own cost a certain number of men for the royal army ; 'which imposition and talliage,' wrote the lords in this manifesto, 'if it be continued to their heirs and successors, will be the heaviest charge and worst example that ever grew in England, and the foresaid subjects and the said heirs and successors in such bondage as their ancestors were never charged with.'[1]

Besides these evils, the infatuated policy into which the king had been led by his ill-advisers, threatened to lose Ireland and Calais to the crown, as France had been lost already ; for in the former country letters had been sent under the Privy Seal to the chieftains who had hitherto resisted the king's authority, actually encouraging them to attempt the conquest of the land, while in regard to Calais the king had been induced to write letters to his enemies not to show that town any favour, and thus had given them the greatest possible

[1] It appears by Letter 377 that privy seals were issued in 1459 addressed on the back to certain persons, requiring them to be with the king at Leicester on the 10th of May, each with a body of men sufficiently armed, and with provision for their own expenses for two months. One of these privy seals, signed by the king himself, was addressed specially to John Paston's eldest son, John, who at this time could not have been more than nineteen years of age. On its arrival, his mother consulted with neighbours whether it was indispensable to obey such an injunction, and on their opinion that it was, wrote to her husband for instructions.

INTRODUCTION

inducement to attempt its capture. Meanwhile the Earls of Shrewsbury and Wiltshire and Viscount Beaumont, who directed everything, kept the king himself, in some things, from the exercise of his own free will, and had caused him to assemble the Parliament of Coventry for the express purpose of ruining the Duke of York and his friends, whose domains they had everywhere pillaged and taken to their own use.[1]

It was impossible, in the nature of things, that evils such as these could be allowed to continue long, and the day of reckoning was now at hand. Of the great events that followed, it will be sufficient here to note the sequence in the briefest possible words. On the 10th July the king was taken prisoner at the battle of Northampton, and was brought to London by the confederate lords. The government, of course, came thus entirely into their hands. Young George Nevill, Bishop of Exeter, was made Chancellor of England, Lord Bourchier was appointed Lord Treasurer, and a Parliament was summoned to meet at Westminster for the purpose of reversing the attainders passed in the Parliament of Coventry. Of the elections for this Parliament we have some interesting notices in Letter 415, from which we may see how the new turn in affairs had affected the politics of the county of Norfolk. From the first it was feared that after the three earls had got the king into their hands, the old intriguers, Tuddenham and Heydon, would be busy to secure favour, or at all events indulgence, from the party now in the ascendant. But letters-missive were obtained from the three earls, directed to all mayors and other officers in Norfolk, commanding in the king's name that no one should do them injury, and intimating that the earls did not mean to show them any favour if any person proposed to sue them at law.[2] Heydon, however, did not choose to remain in Norfolk. He was presently heard of from Berkshire, for which county he had found interest to get himself returned in the new Parliament.

John Paston also was returned to this Parliament as one of the representatives of his own county of Norfolk. His

The battle of Northampton.

John Paston in Parliament.

[1] The articles will be found in Holinshed, iii. 652-3 ; and in Davies's *Chronicle*, 86-90. [2] No. 410.

THE PASTON LETTERS

sympathies were entirely with the new state of things. And his friend and correspondent, Friar Brackley, who felt with him that the wellbeing of the whole land depended entirely on the Earl of Warwick, sent him exhortations out of Scripture to encourage him in the performance of his political duties.[1] But what would be the effect of the coming over from Ireland of the Duke of York, who had by this time landed at Chester, and would now take the chief direction of affairs ?[2] Perhaps the chief fear was that he would be too indulgent to political antagonists. Moreover, the Dowager Duchess of Suffolk had contrived to marry her son to one of York's daughters, and it was apprehended her influence would be considerable. 'The Lady of Suffolk,' wrote Friar Brackley to Paston, 'hath sent up her son and his wife to my Lord of York to ask grace for a sheriff the next year, Stapleton, Boleyn, or Tyrell, *qui absit* ! God send you Poynings, W. Paston, W. Rokewood, or Arblaster. Ye have much to do, Jesus speed you ! Ye have many good prayers, what of the convent, city, and country.'[3]

Such was the state of hope, fear, and expectation which the new turn of affairs awakened in some, and particularly in the friends of John Paston. The next great move in the political game perhaps exceeded the anticipations even of Friar Brackley. Yet though the step was undoubtedly a bold one, never, perhaps, was a high course of action more strongly suggested by the results of past experience. After ten miserable years of fluctuating policy, the attainted Yorkists were now for the fourth time in possession of power ; but who could tell that they would not be a fourth time set aside and proclaimed as traitors ? For yet a fourth time since the fall of Suffolk, England might be subjected to the odious rule of favourites under a well-intentioned king, whose word was not to be relied on. To the commonweal the prospect was serious enough ; to the Duke of York and his friends it was absolute and hopeless ruin. But York had now determined what to do. On the 10th day of October, the third day of the Parliament, he came to Westminster with a body of 500 armed men, and took up quarters for himself within the royal palace. On the

York challenges the Crown.

[1] Letter 415. [2] Letter 419. [3] Letter 415.

INTRODUCTION

16th he entered the House of Lords, and having sat down in the king's throne, he delivered to the Lord Chancellor a writing in which he distinctly claimed that he, and not Henry, was by inheritance rightful king of England.[1]

The reader is of course aware of the fact on which this claim was based, namely, that York, through the female line, was descended from Lionel, Duke of Clarence, third son of Edward III., while King Henry, his father, and his grandfather had all derived their rights from John of Gaunt, who was Lionel's younger brother. Henry IV. indeed was an undoubted usurper ; but to set aside his family after they had been in possession of the throne for three generations must have seemed a very questionable proceeding. Very few of the lords at first appeared to regard it with favour. The greater number stayed away from the House.[2] But the duke's counsel insisting upon an answer, the House represented the matter to the king, desiring to know what he could allege in opposition to the claim of York. The king, however, left the lords to inquire into it themselves ; and as it was one of the gravest questions of law, the lords consulted the justices. But the justices declined the responsibility of advising in a matter of so high a nature. They were the king's justices, and could not be of counsel where the king himself was a party. The king's serjeants and attorney were then applied to, but were equally unwilling to commit themselves ; so that the lords themselves brought forward and discussed of their own accord a number of objections to the Duke of York's claim. At length it was declared as the opinion of the whole body of the peers that his title could not be defeated, but a compromise was suggested and mutually agreed to that the king should be allowed to retain his crown for life, the succession reverting to the duke and his heirs immediately after Henry's death.[3]

So the matter was settled by a great and solemn act of state. But even a parliamentary settlement, produced by a display of armed force, will scarcely command the respect that it ought

[1] W. Worc., 483 ; Fabyan ; *Rolls of Parl.* v. 375. [2] W. Worc., 484. [3] *Rolls of Parl.* v. 375-9.

THE PASTON LETTERS

to do if there is armed force to overthrow it. The king himself, it is true, appears to have been treated with respect, and with no more abridgment of personal liberty than was natural to the situation.[1] Nor could it be said that the peers were insensible of the responsibility they incurred in a grave constitutional crisis. But respect for constitutional safeguards had been severely shaken, and no securities now could bridle the spirit of faction : suspicion also of itself produced new dangers. The Duke of York, after all the willingness he had shown in Parliament to accept a compromise, seems to have been accused of violating the settlement as soon as it was made ; for on that very night on which it was arranged (31st October), we are told by a contemporary writer that 'the king removed unto London against his will to the bishop's palace, and the Duke of York came unto him that same night by torchlight and took upon him as king, and said in many places that "This is ours by right." '[2] Perhaps the facts looked worse than they were really ; for it had been agreed in Parliament, though not formally expressed in the Accord, that the duke should be once more Protector and have the actual government.[3] But it is not surprising that Margaret and her friends would recognise nothing of what had been done in Parliament. Since the battle of Northampton she had been separated from her husband. She fled with her son first into Cheshire, afterwards into Wales, to Harlech Castle, and then to Denbigh, which Jasper Tudor, Earl of Pembroke, had just won for the House of Lancaster.[4] Her flight had been attended with difficulties, especially near Malpas, where she was robbed by a servant of her own, who met her and put her in fear of the lives of herself and her child.[5] In Wales she was joined by the Duke of Exeter, who was with her in October.[6] From thence she sailed to Scotland, where the

[1] Though he was taken prisoner at the battle of Northampton, and had ever since been in the power of the victors, he does not appear to have been placed under any kind of restraint. In October, before the Parliament met, he was spending the time in hunting at Greenwich and Eltham.—No. 419.
[2] *Collections of a London Citizen,* 208 (Camden Society).
[3] *English Chronicle* (Davies), 106 ; Fabyan ; Hall, 249.
[4] *Privy Council Proceedings,* vi. 303.
[5] *Collections of a London Citizen,* 209.
[6] No. 419.

INTRODUCTION

enemies of the Duke of York were specially welcome. For James II., profiting, as might be expected, by the dissensions of England, a month after the battle of Northampton, had laid siege to Roxburgh, where he was killed by the bursting of a cannon. Margaret, with her son, arrived at Dumfries in January 1461, and met his widow, Mary of Gueldres, at Lincluden Abbey.[1] Meanwhile her adherents in the North of England held a council at York, and the Earl of Northumberland, with Lords Clifford, Dacres, and Nevill, ravaged the lands of the duke and of the Earl of Salisbury. The duke on this dissolved Parliament after obtaining from it powers to put down the rebellion,[2] and marched northwards with the Earl of Salisbury. A few days before Christmas they reached the duke's castle of Sandal, where they kept the festival, the enemy being not far off at Pomfret.[3] On the 30th December was fought the disastrous battle of Wakefield, when the Yorkists were defeated, the duke and the Earl of Salisbury being slain in the field, and the duke's son, the Earl of Rutland, ruthlessly murdered by Lord Clifford after the battle. {The battle of Wakefield.}

The story of poor young Rutland's butchery is graphically described by an historian of the succeeding age who, though perhaps with some inaccuracies of detail as to fact, is a witness to the strong impression left by this beginning of barbarities. The account of it given by Hall, the chronicler, is as follows :—

'While this battle was in fighting, a priest called Sir Robert Aspall, chaplain and schoolmaster to the young Earl of Rutland, second son to the above-named Duke of York, scarce of the age of twelve years [he was really in his eighteenth year], a fair gentleman and a maiden-like person, perceiving that flight was more safeguard than tarrying, both for him and his master, secretly conveyed the Earl out of the field by the Lord Clifford's band towards the town. But or he could enter into a house, he was by the said Lord Clifford espied, followed, and taken, and, by reason of his apparel, demanded what he was. The young gentleman, dismayed, had not a word to speak, but kneeled on his knees, imploring mercy and desiring grace, both with

[1] *Auchinleck Chronicle,* 21. *Exchequer Rolls of Scotland,* vii. 8, 39, 157.
[2] *Rolls of Parl.* v. 382.
[3] W. Worc., 484.

THE PASTON LETTERS

holding up his hands and making dolorous countenance, for his speech was gone for fear. "Save him," said his chaplain, "for he is a prince's son, and peradventure may do you good hereafter." With that word, the Lord Clifford marked him and said—"By God's blood, thy father slew mine ; and so will I do thee and all thy kin" ; and with that word stack the Earl to the heart with his dagger, and bade his chaplain bear the Earl's mother word what he had done and said.'

Another illustration which the chronicler goes on to give of Clifford's bloodthirsty spirit may be true in fact, but is certainly wrong as regards time. For he represents Queen Margaret as 'not far from the field' when the battle had been fought, and says that Clifford having caused the duke's head to be cut off and crowned in derision with a paper crown, presented the ghastly object to her upon a pole with the words :—'Madam, your war is done ; here is your king's ransom.' Margaret, as we have seen, was really in Scotland at the time, where she negotiated an alliance with the Scots, to whom she agreed to deliver up Berwick for aid to her husband's cause. But soon afterwards she came to York, where, at a council of war, she and her adherents determined to march on London. So it may have been a fact that Clifford presented to her the head of York upon a pole with the words recorded. But never was prophecy more unhappy ; for instead of the war being ended, or the king being ransomed, there cannot be a doubt these deeds of wickedness imparted a new ferocity to the strife and hastened on the termination of Henry's imbecile, unhappy reign. Within little more than two months after the battle of Wakefield the son of the murdered Duke of York was proclaimed king in London, by the title of Edward IV., and at the end of the third month the bloody victory of Towton almost destroyed, for a long time, the hopes of the House of Lancaster. From that day Henry led a wretched existence, now as an exile, now as a prisoner, for eleven unhappy years, saving only a few months' interval, during which he was made king again by the Earl of Warwick, without the reality of power, and finally fell a victim, as was generally believed, to political assassination. As for Margaret, she survived her husband, but she also survived her son, and the cause for

INTRODUCTION

which she had fought with so much pertinacity was lost to her for ever.

And now we must halt in our political survey. Henceforth, though public affairs must still require attention, we shall scarcely require to follow them with quite so great minuteness. We here take leave, for the most part, of matters, both public and private, contained in the Letters during the reign of Henry VI. But one event which affected greatly the domestic history of the Pastons in the succeeding reign, must be mentioned before we go further. It was not long after the commencement of those later troubles—more precisely, it was on the 5th November 1459, six weeks after the battle of Bloreheath, and little more than three after the dispersion of the Yorkists at Ludlow—that the aged Sir John Fastolf breathed his last, within the walls of that castle which it had been his pride to rear and to occupy in the place of his birth. {Death of Sir John Fastolf.} By his will, of which, as will be seen, no less than three different instruments were drawn up, he bequeathed to John Paston and his chaplain, Sir Thomas Howes, all his lands in the counties of Norfolk and Suffolk, for the purpose of founding that college or religious community at Caister, on the erection of which he had bestowed latterly so much thought. The manner in which this bequest affected the fortunes of the Paston family has now to be considered.

Fastolf's Lands

Under the feudal system, as is well known, on the death of any tenant *in capite* of the crown, his lands were seized in the king's name by an officer called the escheator, until it was ascertained by a jury of the county who was the next heir that should succeed to the property, and whether the king had any right of wardship by reason of his being under age. But when Sir John Fastolf died, he left no heir, nor was he, strictly speaking, at his death a tenant *in capite* of the crown. He had {A.D. 1459.} at different times handed over all his landed property to trustees, {The lands of Sir John Fastolf.} who were to hold it to his use so long as he lived, and to apply

THE PASTON LETTERS

it after his death to the purposes mentioned in his will. For the greater part of his lands in the counties of Norfolk, Suffolk, Essex, and Surrey, he had appointed one body of trustees as early as the year 1449, ten years before his death.[1] This body consisted of five bishops, including the two primates, three lords, two justices of the King's Bench, two knights, and ten other persons. But of these original trustees a good number were already dead, when, in the year 1457, a new trust was created, and the greater part of the Norfolk and Suffolk property was vested in the names of Thomas Bourchier, Archbishop of Canterbury, William Waynflete, Bishop of Winchester, William Yelverton, Justice of the King's Bench, John Paston, Esq., Henry Fylongley, Esq., Thomas Howes, clerk, and William Paston. In the preceding year he had already created these same persons, with the addition of William Jenney, his trustees for the manor of Titchwell, in Norfolk, and the same again, with Jenney, but without Bishop Waynflete, for the manor of Beighton. The trust-deed for the former manor was dated 1st April 34 Henry VI., and that for the latter 26th March 34 Henry VI.[2]

John and William Paston, trustees. Thus it appears that as early as the month of March 1456, about a year and a half after Sir John Fastolf had taken up his abode in Norfolk, John Paston and his brother William were already named by him as trustees for some of his property. From that time the influence of John Paston with the old knight continued to increase till, as it was evident that the latter drew near his end, it became a subject of jealousy and suspicion. Of course, these feelings were not diminished when it was found after Fastolf's death that, subject only to the obligation of founding his college at Caister, and paying 4000 marks to his other executors, he had in effect bequeathed to John Paston the whole of his lands in the counties of Norfolk and Suffolk. Yet it does not appear that in Fastolf's latter days John Paston was about him more than usual. He was just as frequently away in London as he had been in any

[1] The deed is dated 7 July 27 Hen. VI., and inrolled on the *Close Roll*, 29 Hen. VI. m., 39, *in dorso*.
[2] *Inquisition post mortem*, 38 and 39 Henry VI., No. 48.

196

INTRODUCTION

previous year.[1] But even when absent, he had a very staunch and hearty friend in Friar Brackley, who frequently visited the sick chamber, and took every opportunity to preserve and augment the high esteem that Fastolf entertained for him. At the last Brackley wrote to urge him to come down to Norfolk, as the patient evidently could not live much longer. 'It is high time; he draweth fast homeward, and is right low brought, and sore weakened and feebled.' Paston must bring with him a draft petition to the king about the foundation of the college at Caister, and an arrangement with the monks of St. Benet's, for the dying man's satisfaction. 'Every day this five days he saith, "God send me soon my good cousin Paston, for I hold him a faithful man, and ever one man." *Cui ego*: "That is sooth," &c. *Et ille*: "Show me not the meat, show me the man."'[?] Such is the curious report written by Dr. Brackley to Paston himself of the anxiety with which the old knight expected him shortly before his death.[2]

William Worcester. On the other hand, William Worcester, who had so long acted as Fastolf's private secretary, was perhaps a little jealous at the closer intimacy and greater influence of Paston with his master. At least, if this was not his feeling before Sir John Fastolf's death, he expressed it plainly shortly afterwards. It was, he considered, owing to himself that John Paston had stood so high in Fastolf's favour;[3] and it seemed scarcely reasonable that Paston should have the principal share in the administration of the property while he, who had been so long in Fastolf's service, so devoted to his interests, and yet so ill rewarded during his master's life, found no kind of provision made for him in the will. It was, indeed, perfectly true that Fastolf had named him one of his executors. But this executorship, as it turned out, was not a thing likely to yield him either profit or importance. For by the last will, made immediately before the testator's death, a body of ten executors was constituted, of whom two were to have the sole and absolute administration, the others having nothing whatever to do except when those two thought fit to ask for their

[1] *See* Nos. 376, 377, 379, 380, 383.
[2] No. 383.
[3] No. 401.

197

THE PASTON LETTERS

advice. The two acting executors were to be John Paston and Thomas Howes. William Worcester was one of the other eight.[1]

Yet, at first, he refrained from expressing dissatisfaction, and showed himself ready to co-operate with John Paston. Within a week after Fastolf's death, he accompanied William Paston up to London, and joined him in an interview with Bishop Waynflete, at that time Lord Chancellor, who was one of the other executors. In accordance with Bishop Waynflete's advice, he and William Paston proceeded to collect and sequester the goods of the deceased in different parts of London until the time that John Paston could have an interview with the bishop. They managed to have goods out of the Abbey of Bermondsey that no one knew about, except William Paston and Worcester themselves, and another man named Plomer. In short, William Worcester acted at this time as a most confidential and trusty friend to John Paston's interests, being either entirely ignorant how little provision was made for his own, or trusting to Paston's benevolence and sense of justice for that reward which was not expressly 'nominated in the bond.' And William Paston felt his claims so strongly that he could not help insinuating to his brother that he was bound in honour to make him a provision for life. 'I understand by him,' wrote William Paston, 'he will never have other master but his old master; and to my conceit it were pity but if he should stand in such case by my master he should never need service, considering how my master trusted him, and the long years that he hath been with him in and many shrewd journeys for his sake.'[2]

But very shortly afterwards the manner in which Worcester spoke of Paston revealed a bitter sense of disappointment and injustice. He asserted that Fastolf had actually granted him a portion of land to live upon, and that Sir Thomas Howes, Fastolf's confessor, who was his wife's uncle, had been present in the chapel at Caister when this gift was conceded. Worcester's wife had in fact asked Sir Thomas to choose the land. Nevertheless, when he came to demand of Paston that to which he considered he had a lawful claim, the latter was displeased

[1] No. 387.
[2] Nos. 391, 393.

198

INTRODUCTION

with him; nor did the two come to a good understanding again during Paston's life.[1]

It was but nine days after Sir John Fastolf's death, and three days after his first interview with the chancellor, Bishop Waynflete, that William Paston, in writing to his brother, expressed his intention of going to the bishop again for writs of *diem clausit extremum*. These writs were the ordinary authority under which the escheators of the different counties wherein the deceased had held lands would proceed to inquire what the manors were, and to whom they ought to descend. Claimants of Fastolf's property. That many pretenders would lay claim to the different portions of those rich domains, John Paston and his brother knew full well. The Duke of Exeter had already set up a claim to Fastolf's place in Southwark, on what grounds it is impossible to say. Others, who had no hope of proving title to any part of the property themselves, expected to win favour at court by offering to establish the rights of the crown in all the goods and chattels. William Paston accordingly endeavoured to secure the friendship of the Lord Treasurer, James, Earl of Wiltshire and Ormond; but though the earl gave him fair words, William Paston was advised to put no trust in him.[2] In point of fact, soon after Christmas, the earl entered Sir John's mansion in Southwark, and occupied it for a time as if it had been his own dwelling-house.[3]

The escheator of the counties of Norfolk and Suffolk was Richard Southwell, a friend of John Paston's, and if the writs of *diem clausit extremum* had been issued at once, the latter doubtless hoped that the rights of Fastolf's trustees would have been immediately acknowledged by two different juries, the one in Norfolk and the other in Suffolk. But the efforts

[1] No. 401. It appears by a document inrolled in the *Close Roll* of 39 Henry VI., m. 13, *in dorso*, that Worcester on the 28th August 1460 executed a deed making over all his goods and chattels (*bona mea et catalla mobilia et immobilia, viva et mortua, ubicumque et in quorumcumque manibus*), and all debts due to him from whatever persons, to Henry Everyngham, Esq., Hugh Fenne, gentleman, Henry Wyndesore, gentleman, Robert Toppes, jun., gentleman, and John Bokkyng, gentleman; which deed he acknowledged in Chancery on the 1st September following (*see* Appendix to this Introduction). Apparently the object of this was to give others an interest in vindicating what he supposed to be his rights. [2] No. 391.
[3] W. Worcester's *Annals*.

199

of William Paston were not crowned with such speedy success as he and his brother could have wished. Already, on the 10th November, writs of *diem clausit extremum* had issued without his applying for them, but they were only for the counties of Surrey and Essex, in which John Paston was not interested. Special commissions to the same effect for the counties of Wilts and Yorkshire were procured from the king A.D. 1460. at Coventry eighteen days later. But for Norfolk and Suffolk the writs were not issued till the 13th May in the following year.[1] The delay was most probably owing to representations on the part of Paston's enemies; and to the same cause we may attribute the fact that even after the writ was issued it was not acted on for five months longer, so that nearly a whole year had elapsed since Sir John Fastolf's death before the Norfolk and Suffolk inquisitions were held. But at length the opposition was overcome. 'A great day' was holden at Acle before the under-sheriff and the under-escheator, in presence of some of the most substantial gentlemen of Norfolk; 'and the matter,' wrote Margaret Paston to her husband, 'is well sped after your intent.'[2]

Already John Paston's increased importance in his native county had come to be acknowledged. He was at this time knight of the shire for Norfolk. His wife was living at Hellesdon, on the Fastolf estates, two miles out of Norwich; and the mayor and mayoress paid her the compliment of sending thither their dinners and inviting themselves out to dine with her. The mills at Hellesdon and the lands at Caister were let by his agents, and apparently, in spite of his opponents, whoever they may have been, he had succeeded in obtaining quiet possession of all Fastolf's lands in Norfolk.[3] Equally little resistance seems to have been made to his claims in the county of Suffolk, where an inquisition was taken at Bungay nine days after that which had been taken at Acle. In each county the jury limited themselves to declaring the names of the trustees in whose hands the property remained at Fastolf's death, and nothing was said about the will. A will,

[1] *Inquis. post mortem*, 38 and 39 Henry vi., No. 48.   [2] No. 423.
[3] *Ibid.*

200

in itself, could convey no title to lands, and the juries had nothing to do with it. But in both counties John Paston, either as executor or as one of the trustees, was allowed to assume at this time the entire control of the property.

But now came the renewal of civil war—the battle of Wakefield, soon avenged by the proclamation of Edward iv. as king, and the bloody victory of Towton. The kingdom A.D. 1461. was convulsed from end to end, and there was little chance for doubtful titles and disputed claims, except when supported by the strong arm of power. Long before the time at which we have now arrived, the Duke of Norfolk had set covetous eyes The Duke upon Sir John Fastolf's magnificent new castle of Caister, and of Norfolk. he had spread a report in the country that the owner had given it to him.[1] But it would seem that Sir John himself had never entertained such an idea, and if ever in conversation with the duke he had let fall something that might have encouraged the hope, he had taken special care before his death to show that it was unfounded. For the duke had visited Sir John in September before he died, and had proposed to purchase of him the reversion of the manor; but Sir John distinctly told him he had given it to Paston for the purpose of founding a college.[2] Indeed, it is perfectly clear that for years he had intended it to be turned into an abode of priests, and not made a residence for any such powerful nobleman. And this intention, which is apparent enough in several of the letters written during his lifetime, was expressed in the most unambiguous language in the document which John Paston declared to have been his last will.[3] Indeed, if we believe John Paston's testimony, interested though it no doubt may be, it was chiefly from a fear that his executors might sell the place, not, indeed, to the duke, of whom he seems at that time to have ceased to entertain any apprehension, but to the Viscount Beaumont, the Duke of Somerset, or the Earl of Warwick, that the old knight determined to make Paston his principal executor.[4] So, 'to avoid that no lord, nor great estate, should inhabit in time coming within the great mansion,' he made a covenant with Paston by which the

[1] No. 222 (in vol. ii.).   [2] No. 543.   [3] No. 385.   [4] No. 390.

201

latter was to have in fee-simple all his lands in the counties of Norfolk and Suffolk, subject only to the payment of a sum of 4000 marks and the duty of establishing in Caister Castle 'a college of seven religious men, monks, or secular priests, and seven poor folk, to pray for his soul and the souls of his wife, his father, and mother, and other that he was behold to, in perpetuity.' And if in endeavouring to carry out this object John Paston was interfered with by any one attempting to obtain possession of the place by force, he was enjoined to 'pull down the said mansion, and every stone and stick thereof, and do found three of the said seven priests or monks at St. Benet's, and one at Yarmouth, and one at Attleborough, and one at St. Olave's Church at Southwark.'[1]

Yet, notwithstanding all this, the Duke of Norfolk, within three months after the accession of Edward iv., and little more than a year and a half after Sir John Fastolf's death,[2] had certainly taken possession of the great mansion of Caister. The confusion of the time undoubtedly favoured the act, and redress might well have been a troublesome matter, as the Duke of Norfolk was a nobleman whom perhaps even the king would not care to displease. But Edward was a king who, with many faults, was most honourably anxious from the first to do justice even to the meanest of his subjects.[3] Paston repaired to the royal presence, and obtained letters from the king to the duke, which his servant, Richard Calle,

[1] No. 386.
[2] He had probably done so before by authority of Henry vi., for in the beginning of 1460 Friar Brackley writes: 'A man of my Lord Norfolk told me here he came from London, and there he had commonly voiced that the Duke of Norfolk should, by the king's commandment, keep his Easter at Caister for safeguard of the country against Warwick and other such of the king's enemies.'—Vol. iii. p. 212.
[3] Edward's reply to another suit preferred by John Paston this same year is an excellent example of this spirit of impartiality. John Paston's eldest son writes to his father as follows, touching an interview he had had with the Lord Treasurer, the Earl of Essex: 'And now of late I, remembering him of the same matter, inquired if he had moved the king's highness therein. And he answered me that he had felt and moved the king therein, rehearsing the king's answer therein: how that when he had moved the king in the said manor of Dedham, beseeching him to be your good lord therein, considering the service and true part that ye have done and ought to him, and in especial the right that ye have thereto, he said he would be your good lord therein, as he would to the poorest man in England. He would hold with you in your right; and as for favour, he will not be understood that he shall show favour more to one man than to another, not to one in England.'

202

conveyed to Framlingham. They were delivered to his lordship at the lodge of his demesne, but the messenger was not admitted to his presence. The duke, however, wrote an answer to the king, promising shortly to repair to Court, when he offered to prove that some of the statements in Paston's letters were erroneous, and that he himself was the person who had the best claim to the manor. It appears there was one other claimant besides, viz. Thomas Fastolf of Cowhaw; but he, not expecting to make his title good against Paston himself, and having need of a powerful friend in some other matters, gave up his claim to the duke, and brought documents to justify the latter in taking possession by the right derived from him.[1]

In the end, however, Paston's appeal to the king must have been successful. Caister was certainly restored to him, and in all probability it was restored within a month or two before the Duke of Norfolk's death, which occurred that same year, in the beginning of November.[2]

The Beginning of Edward IV.'s Reign

But notwithstanding the even-handed justice of the king, the times were wild and unsettled. The revolution by which Henry was deposed was not a thing calculated to bring sudden peace and quiet. On the Patent Rolls of this year we have innumerable evidences of the state of alarm, confusion, and Troubled tumult which prevailed continuously for at least a twelvemonth times. over the whole kingdom. Commissions of array,[3] commissions to put down insurrections,[4] and to punish outrages,[5] to arrest seditious persons,[6] to resist the king's enemies at sea,[7] or to

[1] Nos. 458, 465.
[2] This perhaps may be a reason for supposing Letter 630 to have been written in the year 1461, notwithstanding the difficulty mentioned in the preliminary note.
[3] *Patent Roll*, 1 Edward iv. p. 1, m. 18 d., dated March 16; and m. 19 d., dated May 10; p. 4, m. 22 d., February 24 and March 1 (1462); also p. 2, m. 12 d. (against the Scots), Nov. 13.
[4] *Ib.* p. 1, m. 27 d., March 28, and p. 3, m. 3 d., July 8.
[5] *Ib.* p. 2, m. 10 d., Aug. 17.
[6] *Ib.* p. 2, m. 12 d., Nov. 4; and p. 4, m. 22 d., Feb. 28 (1462).
[7] *Ib.* p. 3, m. 3 d., July 12.

203

THE PASTON LETTERS

prepare beacons on the coast to give warning of apprehended invasion,[1] are continually met with. Our Letters also tell the same tale. Margaret Paston writes at one time about 'Will. Lynys that was with Master Fastolf, and such other as he is with him,' who went about the country accusing men of being Scots, and only letting them go on payment of considerable bribes. 'He took last week the parson of Freton, and but for my cousin Jerningham the younger, there would have led him forth with him ; and he told them plainly, if they made any such doings there, unless they had the letter to show for them, they should have laid on[2] on their bodies.'[3] A still more flagrant instance of lawlessness had occurred just before, of which our old acquaintance Thomas Denys was the victim. He was at this time coroner of Norfolk. If not in Edward IV.'s service before he was king, he became a member of the royal household immediately afterwards, and accompanied the new king to York before his coronation. It appears that he had some complaints to make to the king of one Twyer, in Norfolk, and also of Sir John Howard, the sheriff of the county, a relation of the Duke of Norfolk, of whom we have already spoken,[4] and shall have more to say presently. But scarcely had he returned home when he was pulled out of his house by the parson of Snoring, a friend of Twyer's, who accused him of having procured indictments against Twyer and himself, and carried him off, we are not told whither.[5] All we know is that in the beginning of July Thomas Denys was murdered, and that there were various reports as to who had instigated the crime. William Lomner believed that some men of the Duke of Norfolk's council were implicated. Sir Miles Stapleton factiously endeavoured to lay the blame on John Berney of Witchingham. The parson of Snoring was put in the stocks, with four of his associates, but what further punishment they underwent does not appear. John Paston was entreated to use his influence to get them tried by a special commission.[6] The

Margin note: Thomas Denys.

[1] Ib. p. 3, m. 3 d. and 27 d., Aug. 6 and 12; also m. 8 d., Jan. 29.
[2] Such, I think, must be the meaning intended. The expression in the original is, 'they shuld aley (qu. should a' laid ?) on her bodyys.'
[3] No. 469.   [4] See p. 164.
[5] Nos. 455, 463.   [6] No. 472.

204

most precise account of the crime is found in the records of the King's Bench, which give us the date and place where it occurred. One Robert Grey of Warham, labourer, was indicted for having, along with others, attacked Denys on Thursday the 2nd July, and dragged him from his house at Gately to Egmere, not far from Walsingham, where they killed him on the Saturday following.

Elizabeth Poynings, too, John Paston's sister, has some experience of the bitterness of the times. She has by this time become a widow, having lost her husband at the second battle of St. Albans, and her lands are occupied by the Countess of Northumberland and Robert Fenys, in disregard of her rights.[1] In times of revolution and tumult the weak must go to the wall.

Besides these illustrations of the social condition of the times, our Letters still abound with information not to be found elsewhere as to the chief political events. Here we have the record of the battle of Towton, of those who fell, and of those who were wounded ;[2] after which we find Henry VI. shut up in Yorkshire, in a place the name of which is doubtful.[3] Then we hear of the beheading of the Earl of Wiltshire, and of his head being placed on London Bridge.[4] Then come matters relating to the coronation of Edward IV., which was delayed on account of the siege of Carlisle.[5] On this occasion, it seems, John Paston was to have received the honour of knighthood,[6] which he doubtless declined, having already compounded with Henry VI. not to be made a knight.[7] Two years later, however, his eldest son was made one, very probably as a substitute for himself, apparently just at the time when he attained the age of twenty-one.[8] To the father such an honour would evidently have been a burden rather than a satisfaction.

But on the whole John Paston stood well with his country-men, and the change of kings was an event from which he

Margin note: Political events.

[1] No. 461.   [2] No. 450.   [3] No. 451.
[4] Nos. 451, 452.   [5] No. 457.   [6] Nos. 457, 460.   [7] No. 373.
[8] Sir John Paston must have been born in 1442. At the inquisition taken in October 1466, after his father's death, he was found to be twenty-four years old and more.

205

THE PASTON LETTERS

had no reason to anticipate bad consequences to himself. Since the death of Sir John Fastolf he had become a man of much greater importance, and he had been returned to Parliament in the last year of Henry VI. as a supporter of the Duke of York. He was now, in the first year of Edward IV., returned to Parliament again. He was apparently in good favour with the king, and had been since the accession of Edward for a short time resident in his household.[1] The king also obtained from him the redelivery of the jewels pawned by his father, the Duke of York, to Sir John Fastolf,[2] in consideration of which he granted John Paston an assignment of 700 marks[3] on the fee-farm of the city of Norwich, and on the issues of the counties of Norfolk and Suffolk. But his election as knight of the shire for Norfolk did not pass altogether without question. Paston's wife's cousin, John Berney of Witchingham, whom Sir Miles Stapleton accused of being implicated in the murder of Denys, had taken a leading part in the proceedings, and Stapleton alleged that he was meditating further outrages. The people had appeared 'jacked and saletted' at the shire house, the under-sheriff was put in suspicion of Berney, and the sheriff, Sir John Howard, con-ceived it would be necessary to have a new election. To this neither Berney nor Paston very much objected. Berney was willing to give every assurance that he would do the under-sheriff no bodily hurt, but he considered his conduct that at the election had not been creditable, and he desired that he would either intimate to the people that the election should stand, or procure a new writ, and publicly announce the day on which another election should be holden. As for Paston, he was perfectly satisfied, provided that he were not put to further expense, as he believed it was the general desire of the people to ratify what they had done ; he only wished that it might be

Margin note: John Paston returned to Parliament.

[1] No. 459.
[2] No. 473. Compare No. 223. It is striking that, notwithstanding his large possessions in land, the Duke of York should have been unable for eight years to redeem these jewels.
[3] This was less than the sum (£487) for which the jewels were pledged, and yet it was the whole compensation granted both for the jewels and for a bond of 100 marks given by the Duke of York to Fastolf, which Paston also surrendered.

206

on a holiday, so as not to interfere with the people's work. The matter was discussed before the king himself, John Paston and the under-sheriff being present, each to answer for his part in the affair, and a writ was finally granted for a new election on St. Laurence's Day. But from what he had seen of the conduct of the under-sheriff, Paston seems to have been afraid the day might yet be changed, to his prejudice ; so, in a personal interview with that functionary, he got him to place the writ in his hands, and sent it down to his wife to keep until the new day of election came round, charging her to see that the under-sheriff had it again that day.[1]

His suspicions of unfair dealing were probably too well founded. At all events, the new election did not pass over peacefully any more than the previous one, perhaps not so much so. We do not, indeed, hear any more of John Berney and Sir Miles Stapleton ; but the sheriff, Sir John Howard, had a violent altercation with Paston himself in the shire house, and one of Howard's men struck Paston twice with a dagger, so that he would have been severely wounded but for the protection of a good doublet that he wore on the occasion.[2]

The occurrence was an awkward one. The feuds in the county of Norfolk had already occupied the king's attention once, and that which it was supposed would have been a settle-ment had proved no settlement at all. Perhaps Edward had been too lenient towards old offenders ; for Sir Miles Stapleton was but an ally of Sir Thomas Tuddenham and John Heydon, of whom we have heard so much in the days of Henry VI., and these two personages were almost as influential as ever. Some time before the king's coronation, they had received a royal pardon, on the strength of which, as we learn by a letter at that time, they intended going up to London with the Duchess of Suffolk to be present at the ceremony.[3] And very soon afterwards we have a renewal of the old com-plaints that 'the world was right wild, and had been sithence Heydon's safeguard was proclaimed at Walsingham.'[4] But

Margin note: John Paston and Sir John Howard.

[1] Nos. 466-8, 471, 475.   [2] Nos. 477, 478.
[3] No. 458.   [4] No. 465.

207

whoever was in fault, it was a serious thing for John Paston—who by this time hoped that he was in favour with the king, and had actually got his eldest son introduced into the king's household [1] — that royal influence itself could not still the angry feelings that had arisen about his election. The dispute must now once more come before the king, and his adversary, in consequence of his relation to the Duke of Norfolk, was doubtless a man of considerable influence. Paston himself, it is true, was in the position of the injured party, but he forbore to complain. The subject, however, was brought by others under the notice of the king, who commanded both Paston and Howard to appear before him, and was even incensed at the former for delaying to obey his summons. On the 11th of October the king said to one of John Paston's friends : ' We have sent two privy seals to Paston by two yeomen of our chamber, and he disobeyeth them ; but we will send him another to-morrow, and, by God's mercy, if he come not then, he shall die for it. We will make all other men beware by him how they shall disobey our writing. A servant of ours hath made a complaint of him. I cannot think that he hath informed us all truly. Yet not for that we will not suffer him to disobey our writing ; but sithence he disobeyeth our writing, we may believe the better his guiding is as we be informed.' [2]

These terrible words were reported to John Paston by his brother Clement, then in London, who urged him to come up from Norfolk in all possible haste, and to be sure that he had some very weighty excuse for having neglected the previous messages. But besides great despatch in coming, and a very weighty excuse, one thing more was very necessary to be attended to, and this further admonition was added : ' Also, if ye do well, come right strong ; for Howard's wife made her boast that if any of her husband's men might come to you, there should go no penny for your life, and Howard hath with the king a great fellowship.' [3]

It was clear this advice was not to be neglected. Paston seems to have been detained in Norfolk by a dispute he had

[1] No. 477, 478. [2] No. 484. [3] Ibid.

with his co-executors Judge Yelverton [1] and William Jenney, who refused to acknowledge his claims as chief administrator of Fastolf's will, and had entered on the possession of some of Sir John's manors in Suffolk, near the borders of Norfolk. [2] But his absence from London had done great mischief. Not only Howard, but the Dukes of Norfolk and Suffolk were endeavouring to put him out of the king's favour ; and it was said that Caister would be given to the king's brother, Richard, Duke of Gloucester. [3] Worst of all, however, was the fact that the king, who had evidently had a good opinion of Paston hitherto, was beginning to alter his tone so seriously. No time, therefore, was to be lost in going up to London, and no marvel though, when he got there, he was immediately committed to the Fleet. [4]

John Paston imprisoned.

John Paston's enemies, acting in several ways, had now done their worst. While the news of his dispute with Howard was reported to the king in the most unfavourable terms, Judge Yelverton (he had been made Sir William Yelverton at the coronation) [5] and William Jenney entered Sir John Fastolf's manor of Cotton in Suffolk, and distrained upon the tenants for rent. John Paston's faithful servant, Richard Calle, at first interrupted their proceedings, and when Jenney went to hold a court at Cotton, entered the place before he came, along with Paston's eldest son. By Calle's activity and watchfulness the court was holden in Paston's name, although it had been summoned in Jenney's ; and

Manor of Cotton.

[1] I have already indicated my belief that Judge Yelverton was the real person nicknamed Colinus Gallicus in Friar Brackley's letters. It is quite clear by No. 404 (one of the letters found after the text of Mr. Arber's edition had passed through the press) that Colinus Gallicus not only could not have been Worcester, but that he was a man of some social standing on familiar terms with the Earl of Wiltshire. This, and the fact that he was one of Fastolf's executors, seem to prove his identity. It is a satisfaction to find that, though Brackley did not love William Worcester, the bitter words in No. 383 were not levelled at him. Thus he wrote while Sir John Fastolf was on his deathbed : 'Colinus Gallicus says in Yarmouth and other places that he is an executor. He said also yesterday before several persons, if once he were in London, he wishes never to see Norfolk. He says also, whereas the executors think they will have keys, after the death others will have keys as well as they. He is a very deceitful man (*falsissimus*). . . . That same Gallicus intensely hates the rector (Howes), and would like to supplant him.'
[2] No. 481. [3] Nos. 482, 484.
[4] No. 488. [5] No. 457.

young John Paston next day, to requite the enemy for the trouble they had occasioned, took with him thirty men, and rode to Jenney's place, where he carried off thirty-six head of neat, and brought them into Norfolk. This was a bold exploit, for the enemy had threatened to drag him and Calle out of the place by violence ; but Calle still remained, and twelve men with him, and kept possession for five whole days, during which time he visited the farmers and tenants of the manor, and ascertained that they were all well disposed towards Paston, and would pay no money to any one else. But, unfortunately, just at this point came the summons to Paston which he did not dare to disobey ; and his opponents knew how to profit by his absence and imprisonment in London. Yelverton and Jenney did not re-enter the manor themselves ; but Jenney sold his interest in it to one Gilbert Debenham, who intended to give it to his son, Sir Gilbert, for a dwelling-house. Accordingly, by the encouragement of Jenney and Debenham, a body of unknown men took possession of the place, and garrisoned it against all comers as strongly as they could. They broke down the drawbridge over the moat, so that no one could enter the place except by means of a ladder. They melted lead, and damaged the property in various ways, while John Paston was a prisoner in the Fleet. At the same time Yelverton and Jenney took proceedings against Richard Calle. They succeeded in getting him imprisoned upon an indictment for felony in Norfolk ; and, fearing lest he should be acquitted upon that charge, they ' certified insurrections ' against him in the King's Bench, and sent the sheriff a writ to bring him up to London in the beginning of November. [1]

John Paston released from prison.

But before the day that Richard Calle was to appear in the King's Bench John Paston was delivered from the Fleet, and his adversary Howard was sent to prison in his place. The whole circumstances of the controversy had been laid before the king, and Paston was released after about a fortnight's imprisonment. The news that he had got into trouble had excited much sympathy in Norwich, for he was highly popular, and Howard's attempt to set aside his election met with very

[1] Nos. 485-487.

little approbation. Margaret Paston, especially, was sad and downcast at home, and though her husband had sent her comfortable messages and letters showing that his case was not so bad as it appeared to be, ' yet I could not be merry,' she wrote to him, ' till this day that the Mayor sent to me, and sent me word that he had knowledge for very truth that ye were delivered out of the Fleet.' [1]

The king was much interested in the dispute, and was laudably determined to insist upon justice and fair dealing. He appointed Sir Thomas Montgomery, one of the knights of his own household, in whom he had special confidence, sheriff of Norfolk for the ensuing year. And when Sir Thomas went down into Norfolk, he sent Sir William Yelverton along with him, who, though not very favourably disposed towards Paston, was still one of the justices, and bound to be impartial. Edward gave them both a very explicit message from his own mouth to declare to the people in the shire house, and Yelverton was made the spokesman. He said the king had been greatly displeased to hear that there had been ' a riotous fellowship ' in the county, but that he understood it was not owing to disaffection on the part of the people generally—that it had been stirred up only by two or three evil-disposed persons—that he and the sheriff were there by the king's command, ready to receive complaints from any man against any one whomsoever—and that if they could not prevail upon the wrongdoer to make restitution, the bills should be sent to the king ; moreover, that if any man was afraid to set forth his grievances, he should have full protection. At this point Yelverton asked the sheriff if he remembered anything more in the king's message, and requested him in that case to declare it himself. The sheriff said Sir William had set forth everything, except that the king had made special reference to two persons, Sir Thomas Tuddenham and Heydon. ' Ah, that is truth,' said Yelverton ; and he explained that any one who wished to complain of them should be protected also. The sheriff then added a few words for his part, in which he promised faithfully before all the people, ' and swore by great

Message from the king to the people of Norfolk.

[1] No. 488.

oaths,' that neither by fear nor by favour would he be restrained from communicating to the king the truth as he found it to be.[1]

A.D. 1462.
All this was reassuring; but yet it was remarked that John Paston did not come home again into Norfolk, and neither did his colleague in the representation of the county, John Berney of Witchingham. This alone caused Margaret Paston still to entertain apprehensions for her husband's safety, and her suspicions were shared by many, who feared that they and Paston alike were involved in some new charges of sedition. Busybodies, it was thought, had been insinuating to the king that a very rebellious spirit prevailed in Norfolk, and report said that the Dukes of Clarence and Suffolk would come down with certain judges commissioned to try such persons as were 'noised riotous.' The rumour scarcely tended to pacify discontent. If it were true, people said they might as well go up to the king in a body to complain of those who had done them wrong, and not wait quietly to be hanged at their own doors. The Duke of Suffolk and his mother were the maintainers of those who oppressed the country most, and nothing but severity could be expected from a commission of which the duke was a member, unless his influence were counteracted by that of more popular persons.[2] These misgivings, however, were happily soon after set at rest. The election of John Paston was confirmed, and no such dreaded commission appears to have been sent into Norfolk. 'The people of that country,' wrote Margaret Paston to her husband, 'be right glad that the day went with you on Monday as it did. You were never so welcome into Norfolk as ye shall be when ye come home, I trow.'[3] Paston, in fact, appears to have gained a complete triumph over his adversaries, and it was said that Howard was likely to lose his head.[4]

But the dispute with Yelverton and Jenney was still unsettled. Writs were sent down into Norfolk to attach John Paston's eldest son and Richard Calle upon indictments of trespass, and Debenham threatened to hold a court at Calcot in defiance of Paston's agents.[5] It is evident, too, that

[1] Nos. 497, 500.   [2] No. 504.   [3] No. 505.
[4] No. 510.   [5] No. 538.

he made good his word, and John Paston in consequence got his tenants to bring actions against him.[1] Cross pleas between the parties occupied the courts at Westminster for a year or more, during which time we find it suggested to John Paston that he would never get leave to live in peace, unless he could by some means obtain 'the good lordship' of the Duke of Suffolk.[2] Appeals to law and justice were all very well, and no one fought his battle in the courts with more unflinching energy than Paston; but unless he wished to be always fighting, the best way for him was to obtain the favour of the great.

It is a question, indeed, whether in this eternal turmoil of litigation at Westminster, and watch to keep out intruders in his Suffolk manors, John Paston had not to some extent neglected his duty to his children at home. Such, at least, was the world's opinion, and there were candid friends who did not hesitate to tell him so. His eldest son now attained *Sir John* the age of twenty-one, and received the dignity of knighthood *Paston.* —probably, as we have before suggested, as a substitute for A.D. 1463. himself. The young man had been summoned four years before to attend and do military service to King Henry VI.[3] He had since been for some little time a member of King Edward's household, travelling about with the court from place to place.[4] But he had scarcely seen the usual amount of service, and though now of full age, and known as Sir John Paston, knight, he was living again under his father's roof, wasting his time, as it was considered, in inglorious ease. 'At reverence of God, take heed,' wrote some one to his father, 'for I hear much talking thereof. . . . Some say that he and ye stand both out of the king's good grace, and some say that ye keep him at home for niggardship, and will nothing spend upon him; and so each man says his advice as it pleases him to talk. And I have inquired and said the most cause is in party for cause ye are so much out, that he is rather at home for the safeguard of the coasts.'[5]

The protection of the coast, especially about Yarmouth,

[1] No. 540.   [2] No. 544.   [3] No. 377.
[4] Nos. 477, 478, 511.   [5] No. 550.

might well be an object in which John Paston was specially concerned, for close to Yarmouth lay Caister Castle. And he had actually procured a commission for his son to be captain of a ship in the king's service, called the *Barge of Yarmouth.* But here again he was brought into collision with Gilbert Debenham, who had already procured a commission to the same effect for himself, and this field of usefulness seems to have been cut off.[1] Confinement at home, to superintend his father's servants, did not suit the young man's tastes. Once before he had displeased his father, probably by seeking too much liberty.[2] He now not only sought it, but took it without leave. Without signifying his intention to any one, he *He leaves* stole away from Caister, apparently with the view of joining *home.* himself again to the king's household. In passing by Lynn, he wrote a penitent letter to his mother, expressing his fear that he had done wrong, and given her uneasiness. And, in truth, she was by no means pleased; for hitherto in their little disagreements she had stood between him and his father, and now her own past efforts at conciliation caused his father to suspect that she had been privy to his escape. If on any occasion Margaret Paston ever deceived her husband, it must have been for the sake of shielding one of her sons; but we are not warranted in believing even this. The imputation in this instance was certainly untrue; but so great was the offence taken by the father, that she durst not even let him know that she had received a letter from her son since his departure. She, however, wrote to the runaway, and charged him, as he valued her blessing, to do all in his power to recover his father's goodwill. He must write to his offended parent again and again in the most humble terms he could think of, giving him all the news from court, and taking far more pains than he had done at home to avoid incurring expenses.[3]

John For his second son John's setting out in life, the father had *Paston the* made better provision than for his eldest. He had succeeded *youngest.* in getting him placed in the household of the new Duke of Norfolk, the last of the Mowbrays, who succeeded his father

[1] Nos. 521-3.   [2] Nos. 375, 377.   [3] No. 552.

towards the close of the year 1461, the first year of King Edward's reign. It was the preceding duke who had occupied Caister just before the coronation; but he died on the 6th November following, at the beginning of Edward's first Parliament, when his son and heir had just attained the age of seventeen.[1] John Paston the father evidently hoped to have the young duke for his friend, and so to maintain himself in undisturbed possession of the lands which he claimed under Sir John Fastolf's will. His son must have been as nearly as possible of the same age as the young nobleman, in whose service he was placed, and he was soon made familiar with the stir and bustle of life. At first he went down with the duke to his castle of Holt, in Wales, where he expected to keep his Christmas. The young duke, who was already married, being desired by the king to repair thither for the quiet of the country, had left his wife behind him, but after a while proposed to send for her to keep Christmas in Wales along with him. This intention, however, he was compelled to abandon. At that very time Queen Margaret had come out of France, and had won the castle of Bamborough : and though Warwick was sent *Bam-* to the north as the king's lieutenant, and the king himself was *borough* following with an army of his own, it was shortly afterwards *Castle* determined that the Duke of Norfolk also should repair into *taken by* Northumberland. The castles of Alnwick, Dunstanborough, *Margaret* and Bamborough were invested by the royal forces; but it was *of Anjou.* fully expected that the Scots would make a strong attempt to rescue *A.D. 1462.* them. The Earl of Warwick's headquarters were at Wark- *Oct.* worth, three miles out of Alnwick, but he rode daily to each of the three castles to superintend the siege operations at each. The Duke of Norfolk had the task assigned him to conduct the victuals and ordnance from Newcastle. The king himself lay at Durham; and young John Paston had an opportunity of making acquaintance with a number of influential persons, including the Lord Hastings and Lord Dacres, who had continual access to the presence of their sovereign. Altogether, John Paston the youngest had certainly begun the world well.[2]

[1] Fabyan. *Inquisition p. m.*, 1 Edward IV., No. 46.   [2] Nos. 532, 533.

THE PASTON LETTERS

Of the other children of John and Margaret Paston it is unnecessary to say anything at present. At the time of which we now treat there was hardly one of them far advanced beyond childhood; nor do they, in fact, occupy very much attention even in later years, although we shall meet with casual notices of one or two of them.

Troubles of John Paston

On the whole, though the conduct of one of them had not given him entire satisfaction, the two eldest sons of John Paston had probably both been of some service to their father in maintaining his influence at court. And this must have been a matter of no small consequence in the continued struggle that he was obliged to maintain with adversaries like Yelverton and Jenney. The dispute with them had now assumed another form. Sir William Yelverton, in conjunction with our old friend William Worcester, was contesting in the spiritual court of Canterbury the claim put forward by Paston to be the chief executor under Sir John Fastolf's will; while at the same time William Jenney, and one William Hogan, by Jenney's procurement, took actions for trespass against him in the Suffolk county court. Paston trusted to his influence with the king to deliver him from these vexatious suits. He neglected to put in an appearance at four several county courts, and allowed himself to be put in exigent, while he followed the king to Marlborough, and obtained from him a licence for the erection of the college at Caister provided for in Fastolf's will. Along with this the king covenanted to give him a free pardon when required for all offences against the peace, to save him harmless against Yelverton and Jenney; but undertook at the same time to cause inquiry to be made into the substance of their accusations, and if these proved to be unfounded, to compel them to make Paston compensation.[1]

Paston had partly trusted to the friendship of William Calthorpe, who was at this time Sheriff of Norfolk and Suffolk, to protect him against outlawry. His servant Richard Calle

margin: A.D. 1464. Litigation touching Fastolf's will.

[1] Nos. 568-9, 571-2.

216

INTRODUCTION

offered surety that Paston would save the sheriff harmless, either by making an appearance at a later date or by producing a *supersedeas*; and he requested that upon this assurance the sheriff would return that his master had appeared the first day. Calthorpe had every wish to do Paston a kindness; though he confessed that Jenney had been his good friend and legal adviser for two years past, Paston was still more his friend than Jenney, and he promised to do all that was required.[1] But this promise he failed to fulfil. Paston's non-appearance was proclaimed at four successive county courts at Ipswich; and a writ of exigent was granted against him. Paston obtained a *supersedeas* from the king at Fotheringay on the 3rd August; but in the end judgment was given against him in Suffolk on the 10th September, and he was proclaimed an outlaw. On the 3rd November following he was committed to the Fleet prison.[2]

This was his second experience of captivity since the death of Sir John Fastolf. We do not know that he ever suffered it before that time; but he was now paying the penalty of increased importance. His detention on this occasion does not seem to have been of long duration; but if we are right in the interpretation of a sarcastic anonymous letter[3] found among his correspondence, his fellow-prisoners threw out surmises when he left that the Fleet would see him yet a third time within its walls. At least, this may or may not have been the purport of what is certainly an ironical and ambiguous epistle addressed to him, we cannot tell by whom. If it was so, the prediction was verified before another twelvemonth had passed away.

How matters went during the winter we have very little indication, except that Paston's friend John Wykes, an officer of the king's household, writes to Margaret Paston on the 7th February from London, 'that my master your husband, my mistress your mother, my master Sir John, Mr. William, Mr.

margin: John Paston outlawed.
margin: A.D. 1465. Feb. 7.

[1] No. 572.
[2] No. 572. Itin. W. Worc., 366. Those who are interested in the subject may be referred to the Year Books of Mich. and Hil. 4 Edw. iv. for pleadings as to the validity of the outlawry and *supersedeas*. These, however, are purely technical and of no interest to the general reader. [3] No. 574.

217

THE PASTON LETTERS

Clement, and all their men, were in good health when this letter was written, thanked be Jesu; and also their matters be in a good way, for my Lord Chancellor is their singular good lord.' The crisis in the affairs of the family was certainly very serious, when old Agnes Paston, the judge's widow (for I have never found any other lady spoken of as Agnes Paston's 'mother'), took the trouble to go up to London to see them settled. It appears that there was a little family council on the occasion, and John Paston's two brothers, William and Clement, together with his son Sir John, were also present.[1] What kind of arrangement they all succeeded in making we have no means of ascertaining; but the next occasion of trouble to John Paston was not given by Yelverton and Jenney.

The first indications of it appear in a letter of Margaret Paston to her husband, written on the 8th April 1465, by which we find that the Duke of Suffolk had now set up a claim to Sir John Fastolf's manor of Drayton, about four miles north-west of Norwich. Margaret had also heard that he had bought up the rights of a person named Brytyeff or Bryghtylhed, who laid claim to the neighbouring manor of Hellesdon, a little nearer the city, and that he intended to take possession after Easter.[2] The claim appears to have been very ill founded, and the tenants, all but one or two, were favourable to Paston.[3] Nevertheless Philip Lipyate, the duke's bailiff, began taking distresses, and carried off the horses of one Dorlet as he was about to yoke them to his plough. But Margaret Paston, who had been staying at Caister, after waiting till her son Sir John could come to her, and leaving him to keep the castle, went over to Hellesdon to collect the rents for her husband, and put a stop, if possible, to the proceedings of the duke's officers. She soon began to feel that there was more need of a captain like her son Sir John at Hellesdon than at Caister. One single tenant named Piers Warin gave her servants a little trouble, and they took from him two mares as security for the rent. Warin made his complaint to Philip Lipyate and the duke's bailiff of Cossey,

margin: The Duke of Suffolk lays claim to Drayton.

[1] No. 576. [2] No. 578. [3] Nos. 579, 584.

218

INTRODUCTION

who came with a body of eightscore men in armour, and took away the plough-horses of the parson and another tenant, intimating that the beasts should not be restored unless their owners would appear and give answer to certain matters at Drayton on the Tuesday following. The duke's men further threatened that if Paston's servants ventured to take any further distresses in Drayton, even if it were but of the value of a hen, they would take the value of an ox in Hellesdon.[1]

John Paston, though not at this time in confinement, seems to have been unable to leave London. But it was impossible that he could underestimate the danger in which his property stood from the pretensions of such a formidable neighbour as the Duke of Suffolk. The letters written to him at this period by his wife are annotated all down the margin with very brief rough jottings in his own handwriting, for the most part only calling attention to the subjects touched upon in the letter, but occasionally indicating what he was about to say in his reply. He expressed, indeed, no great respect for the big threats of Suffolk's officers about taking the value of an ox for that of a hen, which he characterised in the margin by the simple monosyllable 'crack'; but he noted, in the brief words 'Periculum Heylesdon,' the fact that there was real cause for anxiety lest the duke, who had already occupied Drayton, should drive him out of Hellesdon as well.[2]

The Bishop of Norwich had been appealed to, as chief justice of the peace for the county, to use his influence with the Duke of Suffolk's officers, and especially with Philip Lipyate, who was a priest, and subject to his jurisdiction, to bring the dispute to a peaceful settlement. But John Paston probably trusted more to the fact that he had men of his own ready to repel force by force. The parishes of Hellesdon and Drayton are situated on the northern bank of the river Wensum, partly on a low ridge which slopes downward towards the stream. Opposite to Drayton, on the other side of the river, lay the Duke of Suffolk's mansion of Cossey,[3]

[1] Nos. 579, 581. [2] No. 581.
[3] Now commonly spelt Costessey, but pronounced, as it is usually spelt in the Paston Letters, Cossey.

219

from which, at any time that was thought advisable, an armed band could be sent along with a distraining officer to assert the duke's alleged rights over the tenants. It was really a case of two hostile camps keeping watch upon each other, and each of them ready to take advantage of the other's weakness. Not that either of them pretended to be above the law, but the duke and Paston each claimed to be lawful owner of the lordships of Hellesdon and Drayton, and, until any legal settlement could be come to, each was well aware of the importance of maintaining his claim by corresponding acts. If the duke could levy a distress, so could Paston. His officers made an inroad, undeterred by the menaces of the duke's men, into Drayton, took 77 neat, and brought them home to Hellesdon. The tenants followed, petitioning to have their cattle back again, but Margaret Paston told them they must first pay such duties as they owed to her husband, or find security to pay at such a day as she could agree to. An officer of the duke named Harleston was at Norwich, and told them that if they either paid or gave such surety they should be put out of their holdings. Harleston had a conference with Margaret Paston in the evening, but she refused to redeliver the distress on any other terms than those she had already intimated. This was on a Saturday evening. On Monday following a replevin was served upon her in the name of Harleston, who was under-steward of the duchy of Lancaster, on the ground that the cattle had been taken within the fee of the duchy. Margaret refused to deliver them until she had ascertained whether this was actually the case, and on inquiry she found that it was not so. The beasts were accordingly still detained in Hellesdon pin-fold, and Pynchemore, the officer who had brought the replevin, was obliged to return to his master. But in the afternoon he came again with a replevin under the seal of the sheriff of Norfolk, which it was impossible lawfully to disobey. So the beasts were at last taken out of the pin-fold and redelivered to the tenants.[1]

This sort of quasi-legal warfare continued for weeks and

[1] No. 583.

220

for months. At one time there would be a lull; but again it was reported that the duke's men were busier. The duke himself was coming to Cossey, and his servants boasted openly that he would have Drayton in peace and then Hellesdon.[1] And not very long after the duke did come to Norfolk, raising people on his way both in Norfolk and Suffolk,—for an attack, as every one knew, on Paston's stronghold at Hellesdon, which was now placed in the keeping of his son Sir John.[2]

On Monday the 8th July, Philip Lipyate and the bailiff of Cossey, with about 300 men, came before Hellesdon, but, finding Sir John Paston quite prepared for them, professed they had no intention of attempting to force an entry. For Sir John had a garrison of 60 men within the place, and such a quantity of guns and ordnance that the assailants would certainly have had the worst of it. Lipyate and the bailiff, however, informed Sir John that they had a warrant to attach John Daubeney, Wykes, Richard Calle, and some others. Sir John replied that they were not within, and if they had been he would not have delivered them. Afterwards it was mutually agreed that the Duke of Suffolk should dismiss his men and Sir John Paston should do the same. But this only transferred the scene of action to Norwich, where Richard Calle was attacked by twelve men in the streets and only rescued by the sheriff; nor did he escape without the pleasant assurance that if he were caught another time he would be put to death, so that he did not dare ride out without an escort. Daubeney and Wykes were in a similar state of apprehension, and to crown all, it was said that there was to be a special commission to inquire of riots, in which the Duke of Suffolk and Yelverton would be commissioners. If so, every man that had taken Paston's part was pretty sure of being hanged.[3]

Sir John Paston, however, acquired great credit for having withstood so numerous a force as Lipyate and the bailiff of Cossey had brought against him. It will be readily understood that his position must have been a strong one. He and

Attempt of the duke's men on Hellesdon.

[1] No. 585.   [2] No. 592.   [3] No. 593.

221

his mother were then living at a mansion in Hellesdon, which probably stood on comparatively low ground near the river.[1] But on the brow of the hill, nearer Drayton, stood a quadrangular fortress of which the ruins still exist, known at this day by the name of Drayton Lodge. This lodge lay within what was then called Hellesdon Warren, and commanded the entrance to the property. From its elevated position it must have been peculiarly difficult to attack. The country around was open heath, and the approach of an enemy could be descried distinctly in the distance. From the mansion below, where he had quartered his garrison of 60 men, he could doubtless bring up with ease at any time as many as seemed necessary for the defence of the lodge;[2] while from the battlements of the lodge a heavy fire could be opened on the advancing foe.[3]

Living within a house that was threatened with siege, Margaret Paston, at this juncture, seems to have taken an active part along with her son in the preparations for defence. Her husband in London writes to her as a commander-inchief might do to the governor of a besieged fort:—'In good faith ye acquit you right well and discreetly, and heartily to your worship and mine, and to the shame of your adversaries: and I am well content that ye avowed that ye kept possession at Drayton and so would do.' But the task imposed upon her had impaired her health; and John Paston, though for some potent reasons was not able even now to come to her aid, was anxious to give her every comfort and encouragement in his power. 'Take what may do your ease and spare not,' he says in the same letter; 'and in any wise take no thought nor too much labour for these matters, nor set it not so to

[1] At Hellesdon North Hall, the property of Mr. J. H. Gurney, old foundations have been recently discovered, which are in all probability those of John Paston's house. The place is about 400 yards from Hellesdon Church.
[2] One day in the beginning of May as many as sixty men were placed in the lodge itself, and kept there all day. At that time an attack was continually expected, but not more than sixteen or twenty persons could sleep in the building. *See* No. 581, at p. 139 (vol. iv.).
[3] 'The ruined Lodge at Drayton' is the subject of an interesting paper by the late Mr. Henry Harrod in the *Norfolk Archaeology*, vol. ii. p. 363. There are no remains of battlements now, but most probably they once existed.

222

your heart that ye fare the worse for it. And as for the matter, so they overcome you not with force or boasting, I shall have the manor surelier to me and mine than the duke shall have Cossey, doubt ye not.' In fact, if it were a question of law, John Paston's title seems to have been greatly superior to any that could possibly have been advanced by the duke: in proof of which he points out a few facts which he tells his wife she may if she think proper lay before the Bishop of Norwich. The manor of Drayton had belonged to a merchant of London called John Hellesdon, long before any of the De la Poles held land in Norfolk or Suffolk. It had descended to his daughter Alice, and John Paston was able to show his title to the property. On the other hand he traced the pedigree of the Duke of Suffolk from 'one William Poole of Hull, which was a worshipful man grown by fortune of the world,' and whose son Michael, the first Earl of Suffolk, had been so created by King Richard II. since Paston's father was born; and if any of their lineage held the manor of Drayton he would lose £100, if the duke would be bound in as much to prove the contrary. But the duke must not expect him to show his title to one who tried to oust him by violence. On this point John Paston was resolute. 'Let my lord of Norwich wit that it is not profitable, nor the common weal of gentlemen, that any gentleman should be compelled by an entry of a lord to show his evidence or title to his land, nor I will not begin that example ne thraldom, of gentlemen nor of other. It is good a lord take sad counsel ere he begin any such matter.'[1]

It might have been supposed that after the duke's attempt on Hellesdon, nothing but impediments of the most serious kind would have prevented John Paston from going down to Norfolk to take charge of his own interests and relieve his wife's anxiety. But it appears that he hardly expected to be able to leave London, and in the same letter from which we have just been quoting he desires that if he be not home within three weeks his wife will come to him. In that case she is, before leaving, to put everything under proper rule

[1] No. 595.

223

THE PASTON LETTERS

both at Caister and Hellesdon, 'if the war hold.' The state of matters between him and Suffolk was such as could only be spoken of as a state of war, even by plain matter-of-fact John Paston. And if the enemy offered peace his wife was to send him word.

What could have been the obstacle that prevented John Paston leaving London? It appears for one thing that he was at this time called upon to undergo an examination before the spiritual court of Canterbury, in defence of his claim to be Sir John Fastolf's executor. This alone was, perhaps, sufficient to detain him, for it was a thing on which his most important interests depended. But there is no doubt that additional obstacles were raised up for him expressly by the malice of his enemies; for it could not have been many weeks after his first examination that John Paston again found himself a prisoner in the Fleet, and within the walls of that prison his further depositions were taken.[1]

John Paston imprisoned a third time.

It was the malicious ingenuity of Judge Yelverton that had devised the means to inflict upon him this new incarceration. And the means employed were such as to make captivity doubly painful and humiliating. The king's clandestine marriage to Elizabeth Woodville had taken place in May of the preceding year. At Michaelmas it was openly avowed; and if it displeased, as no doubt it did, Warwick and the old nobility, even from the first, it informed a whole world of time-servers and place-hunters that there was a new avenue to fortune in securing the favour of the Woodvilles. Already Rivers had been created Lord Treasurer and advanced to the dignity of an earldom. Already marriages had been made for the queen's brothers and sisters, which were evidently provocative of envy, jealousy, and indignation.[2] The king's liberality towards his new relations was unbounded, and sycophants were not wanting to suggest to him how he might gratify their cupidity, sometimes at the expense of others than himself. Sir William Yelverton, accordingly, contrived to whisper in the royal ear that the king might fairly dispose of some fine property in Norfolk and Suffolk; for John

[1] No. 606. [2] W. Worc. *Annales*, 501, 506.

224

INTRODUCTION

Paston, who claimed to be the owner, was come of servile blood, and was really the king's bondman.[1]

The reader will remember the curious paper[2] in which it is set forth that the grandfather and father of John Paston had held lands in the village of Paston, by servile tenures, and that John Paston himself, without having any manor place, was endeavouring to 'make himself a lordship there,' to the prejudice of the duchy of Lancaster. There can be little doubt that this statement was drawn up in the year 1465 and that its author was Judge Yelverton. He had been at this time endeavouring to ingratiate himself with Anthony Woodville, Lord Scales, the queen's brother, and it was in the interest of that nobleman that he made this attempt to asperse the lineage of the Pastons. For Lord Scales had begun to cast covetous eyes on the magnificent castle at Caister; and if it were but satisfactorily shown that John Paston was disqualified from possessing it, no doubt the king, his brother-in-law, would be only too willing to grant it to himself. The case was already prejudiced; Caister and the lordship of Cotton as well were his by anticipation, and some time before Paston was committed to prison it was known that Lord Scales meant to ride down into Norfolk and oust him from his property.[3]

Lord Scales seeks to obtain Caister.

Although John Paston was thus unable to go home, as he wished to do, neither was Margaret Paston able for some time to go up and see him in London, as he had desired her. Wykes, who had promised to keep possession of the place at

[1] *Itin.* Will. de Worc., 323. [2] *See* pp. 28, 29.
[3] No. 598. It appears by the city records of Norwich, an extract from which, kindly communicated to me by the Rev. William Hudson, will be found in the Appendix to this Introduction, that Lord Scales arrived in the city 'a second time' towards the close of the year 1465—apparently just before Christmas day, for the date was within eighteen days of a document dated 10th January, 5 Edward IV.—for the express purpose of taking possession of all the goods and chattels of John Paston, whom the king had seized as his 'native.' This raised an awkward question about the privileges of the city, in which John Paston possessed a house. But the civic authorities found a way out of the difficulty, and agreed that Lord Scales should be allowed to enter by the act of John Paston's feoffees; for it was understood that certain aldermen and common council men were co-feoffees along with him, of the messuage which he held. Thus the city's liberty was theoretically preserved without offence to the higher powers.

225

THE PASTON LETTERS

Hellesdon in her absence, did not go down into Norfolk so soon as he had intended, but remained in London taking care of Paston's interests in another fashion in conferences with Nevill, Archbishop of York, at that time Lord Chancellor. Perhaps already the influence of Archbishop Nevill, like that of his brother the Earl of Warwick, had begun to decline, and Wykes was really wasting his labour in complaining to his lordship of the riotous attempt made by the Duke of Suffolk's men at Hellesdon. There was but one pretext on which the outrage could be justified,—a matter concerning the payment of 100 marks, but the money had been paid long ago. His lordship, however, durst swear the Duchess of Suffolk had no knowledge of it; and with that he left town, promising an answer when he came back next Tuesday.[1]

But Margaret Paston, though she could not yet come up to London, did not spend the time at home unprofitably. The judges had come down to Norwich on their circuit, when Margaret endeavoured to secure the advantage she had already gained in keeping possession at Drayton by getting a manor court held there in her husband's name. But to do this she required the services of one or more faithful dependants who did not mind incurring a little personal risk in the interest of John Paston. Not many, certainly, were disposed to undertake the task. John Paston had written to his wife to have a body of men to escort the officer that would keep the court for him. But upon consultation it was thought better to keep all the men they could in reserve, as the duke's officers had no less than 500 men ready to take advantage of the opportunity to force an entry into Hellesdon.

Attempt of Margaret Paston to hold a court at Drayton.

Thomas Bond and an attached and confidential priest named Sir James Gloys were adventurous enough to go to Drayton alone for the purpose of holding a court on Lammas Day. They found, as might have been expected, that officers of the Duke of Suffolk were there before them. Harleston, along with Philip Lipyate, the parson of Salle, and William Yelverton, a grandson of the judge, who was to sit as steward, were in the courtyard of the manor, prepared to hold the

[1] No. 598.

226

INTRODUCTION

court in the Duke of Suffolk's name. They were accompanied by about sixty persons or more, besides the tenants of Drayton, some having rusty poleaxes and bills to enforce respect for the duke's authority. In the face of this array, however, Bond and Gloys announced that they came to keep the court in the name of John Paston; on which the former was immediately delivered into the custody of William Ducket, a new bailiff of Drayton appointed by the duke, and was carried off to Cossey, his arms bound behind him with whipcord like a thief. But Margaret Paston spoke with the judges next morning before they went to the shirehouse, in presence of the bailiff of Cossey and the whole of the duke's council; and the judges calling the bailiff before them, gave him a severe reproof, and sent the sheriff to see what company had been mustered at Drayton. The sheriff rode first to Hellesdon, and expressed himself satisfied with the demeanour of Paston's men there. When he came to Drayton, the bands of Suffolk's retainers had disappeared. He demanded that Thomas Bond should be delivered to him, and was told that he had been sent to the Duke of Suffolk; but he was afterwards delivered to him at Norwich, with a request that he should not be set at liberty without a fine, as he had troubled the king's leet. The judges, however, on being informed of the real state of the case, commanded him to be set at liberty, and pronounced a very strong censure on the conduct of Suffolk's officers.[1]

As for the manors of Caister and Cotton, it does not appear that Lord Scales ever carried out his intention so far as the latter was concerned; nor had he taken possession even of the former some time after John Paston had been committed to the Fleet. That occurrence must have taken place about the middle of the month of August,[2] and towards the end of September we have evidence that Sir John Paston was in Caister Castle keeping possession for his father.[3] But the

[1] No. 599.
[2] On the 18th August Margaret Paston was still hoping that her husband would find it possible to come home himself, and save her the necessity of going up to London to see him. *See* No. 604. But we know that he was imprisoned before the 28th of the month. No. 606. [3] No. 610 (vol. iv. p. 192).

227

THE PASTON LETTERS

Paston family had been warned of the danger, and we may be well assured that they did not neglect the warning in either case. Indeed, the question how to make matters secure at Caister seems to have been the principal difficulty that caused Margaret to delay her journey up to London. As to Cotton, we shall see ere long that very effectual means were taken to secure possession there.

Margaret Paston visits her husband in prison. It would appear that when Margaret knew her husband was in prison she determined to delay no longer, but to visit him in London at all costs. Early in September she had already gone to him, and her son, John Paston the youngest, wrote to her from Norwich on the 14th, advising her, among other things, to visit the Rood of North-door (a cross beside St. Paul's Cathedral), and St. Saviour's at Bermondsey, during her stay in the capital. 'And let my sister Margery,' he suggests, 'go with you, to pray to them that she may have a good husband or she come home again.' It is difficult to tell whether this means devotion or sightseeing, jest or earnest. The young man had already seen a good deal of life, and was familiar with the principal attractions of the great city, to which in all probability his mother was as great a stranger as his young sister. Even the dame who had the care of his father's apartments in the prison was not unknown apparently to John Paston the youngest. 'And the Holy Trinity,' he writes, 'have you in keeping, and my fair Mistress of the Fleet.'

John Paston the father does not seem to have been very uncomfortable in prison. He made friends in the place of his confinement, and among other persons became acquainted with Henry, Lord Percy, son of the attainted Earl of Northumberland, who was afterwards restored by King Edward to his father's earldom. His spirits, indeed, if we may judge from his correspondence, were at this time particularly buoyant; for after his wife had taken leave of him to return homeward he wrote her a letter the latter half of which was composed of doggerel rhyme, jesting about having robbed her portmanteau, and referring her for redress to Richard Calle, whose ears he bade her nail to the post if he did not pay her the value. In none of his previous correspondence does he indulge in verse

228

INTRODUCTION

or betray anything of this rollicking humour. The only subject on which he even insinuates a complaint is the weather, which seems to have been unnaturally cold for September. He speaks of it satirically as 'this cold winter,' and wishes his wife to send him some worsted for doublets in which to protect himself from the severity of the season. But even in this we can tell that he is jesting, for he explains himself that he wishes to have a doublet entirely composed of the wool manufactured at Worsted, for the credit of his native county. And so far is he from wishing it for the sake of warmth, that he particularly desires to procure a fine quality of worsted 'almost like silk,' of which William Paston's tippet was composed.[1]

On her way back to Norwich, Margaret Paston entered *Margaret Paston enters Cotton.* the manor of Cotton and remained in it for three days. She had sent a message to her son John Paston the youngest at Hellesdon to come and meet her there,[2] and he came along with Wykes and twelve others, whom she had left at her departure to keep possession and collect the rents. It was within a week of Michaelmas Day, when rents fell due. As yet Lord Scales had made no attempt to seize upon this property. Sir Gilbert Debenham had occupied the manor for some years undisturbed, and he was doubtless considerably taken by surprise when he found that a lady on her way home from London had entered and taken possession in the name of John Paston. But when he heard that young John Paston was gathering money of the tenants, he raised a body of 300 men to expel the intruder. Young John Paston was expecting reinforcements to his little band from Caister or elsewhere, but they did not come; so that his position would have been a critical one had not some one been his friend in the household of the Duke of Norfolk. Sir Gilbert was the duke's

[1] No. 609.
[2] *See* No. 613. The heading of this letter is unfortunately wrong. Deceived by the facsimile to which Fenn refers as showing the character of the signature, I attributed the letter to Sir John Paston. But Margaret Paston expressly says it was John Paston the younger whom she left at Cotton (No. 610), and this letter must therefore have been written by him. Besides, the writer himself mentions that the dispute with Debenham was referred to the Duke of Norfolk to avoid the scandal of a quarrel *between two of his men.* It was not Sir John Paston, but his brother, that was in the Duke of Norfolk's service.

229

THE PASTON LETTERS

steward, and John Paston the youngest was still in the duke's service. A yeoman of his lordship's chamber represented to that nobleman that there was imminent risk of a quarrel between two of his men, which would be a great 'disworship' to his grace. The duke sent for the two immediately to attend upon him at Framlingham Castle, and proposed to them terms of compromise until the matter could be thoroughly investigated. He desired that neither party should muster men, that the court should be 'continued'— that is to say, adjourned—till he himself should have had an opportunity of speaking both with John Paston the father and on the other side with Yelverton and Jenney, who had conveyed to Debenham the title on which he founded his claim to the manor. Meanwhile he proposed that the place should be kept by some indifferent person to be chosen by both parties.

To these terms John Paston the youngest would not assent without consulting his mother, who had again come over from Norwich, or perhaps from Caister, to see how matters went. But after a conference, they sent an answer to the duke, declaring that they could not give up possession of the place, but out of their anxiety for peace, and to satisfy his lordship, they were willing to desist meanwhile from collecting rents, if the opposite party would engage not to distrain or keep courts there either. To this compromise Sir Gilbert said that he agreed, provided it met with the approval of Yelverton and Jenney; and the Duke of Norfolk, who was going up to London in anticipation of his birthday when he attained his majority, left all the sooner in the hope of bringing this matter to a favourable settlement.[1]

Thus far, at least, the entry into Cotton had been a distinct success. The compromise was greatly in favour of the Pastons, for an appeal to force would almost certainly have gone against them, and, though they engaged for the time to abstain from taking more money of the tenants, they had already succeeded in collecting almost all that they expected to receive for Michaelmas term.[2] So Margaret Paston on her return to Norfolk, and her son, when he was summoned to London

[1] Nos. 613, 614. [2] No. 613.

230

INTRODUCTION

shortly afterwards, to attend the duke on his coming of age,[1] may each have left Cotton with feelings akin to triumph. But scarcely had the former returned to Norwich when she discovered to her dismay that her clever manœuvre in Suffolk had left the family interests insufficiently protected elsewhere. The Duke of Suffolk had not only a great number of men at Cossey, but he had a powerful friend within the city of Norwich. Thomas Elys, the new mayor, was so flagrantly partial, that he had said at Drayton he would supply my lord of Suffolk with a hundred men whenever he should require them, and if any men of the city went to Paston he would lay them fast in prison.[2] Hellesdon, unfortunately, lay midway between Cossey and the city of Norwich, and as it was not now assize time there was practically no control over such magnates as the Duke of Suffolk and the mayor. So, on the morning of Tuesday the 15th of October, one Bottisforth, who was bailiff for the duke at Eye, came to Hellesdon, arrested four of John Paston's servants, and carried them off to Cossey without a warrant from any justice of the peace. His intention, he said, was to convey them to Eye prison along with as many more of Paston's adherents as he could lay his hands on. That same day the duke came to Norwich with a retinue of 500 men. He sent for the mayor and aldermen with the sheriffs, and desired them in the king's name to make inquiry of the constables in every ward of the city what men had taken part with Paston in recent gatherings. Any such persons he requested that they would arrest and punish, and send their names to him by eight o'clock on the following day. On this the mayor arrested one Robert Lovegold, brasier, and threatened him that he should be hanged, though he had only been with Margaret Paston at Lammas, when she was menaced by the companies of Harleston and the bailiff of Cossey.[3]

Attack on Hellesdon. Scarcely one of Paston's servants now durst openly show himself abroad, and, the duke having the city at his command, his followers made, that same Tuesday, a regular assault on the place at Hellesdon. The slender garrison knew that it was madness to resist, and no opposition was offered. The

[1] No. 614. [2] No. 581. [3] No. 616.

231

THE PASTON LETTERS

duke's men took possession, and set John Paston's own tenants to work, very much against their wills, to destroy the mansion and break down the walls of the lodge, while they themselves ransacked the church, turned out the parson, and spoiled the images. They also pillaged very completely every house in the village. As for John Paston's own place, they stripped it completely bare; and whatever there was of lead, brass, pewter, iron, doors, or gates, or other things that they could not conveniently carry off, they hacked and hewed them to pieces. The duke rode through Hellesdon to Drayton the following day, while his men were still busy completing the work of destruction by the demolition of the lodge. The wreck of the building, with the rents they made in its walls, is visible even now.[1]

This was carrying things with the high hand; but it did not improve the Duke of Suffolk's popularity at Norwich, and it created no small sympathy with Paston and his tenants. 'There cometh much people daily,' wrote Margaret Paston to her husband, 'to wonder thereupon, both of Norwich and of other places, and they speak shamefully thereof. The duke had been better than a thousand pound that it had never been done; and ye have the more good will of the people that it is so foully done.' Margaret was anxious that the effects of the outrage should be seen before winter came on by some one specially sent from the king to view and report upon the ruin. But no redress was obtained while her husband lived, and even some years after his death his sons petitioned for it in vain.

John Paston's Latter Days

The chagrin and mortification inflicted upon John Paston by an injury like this may not unlikely have contributed to shorten his days. The correspondence is scanty from the end of October 1465 till some time after his death, which occurred in London in May of the following year. We know nothing of the nature of the illness which carried him off; but three

[1] Nos. 616, 617.

INTRODUCTION

imprisonments in the course of five years, accompanied with a great deal of anxiety about his newly acquired property, the intrigues of lawyers and the enmity of great men, must have exercised a depressing influence even on the stoutest heart. He appears to have been released from prison some time before his death, and was so far well in February that he had A.D. 1466. a conference in Westminster Hall with William Jenney, who desired at last to come to some agreement with him. But the great lawsuit about Fastolf's will remained still undecided, and he left to his son Sir John an inheritance troubled by a disputed claim. He died on the 21st or 22nd May[1] 1466. His remains were carried down into Norfolk and buried with great magnificence in Bromholm Abbey.[2]

Of his character we see fewer indications than might have been expected in a correspondence extending over more than twenty years, and perhaps we are in danger of judging him too much from the negative point of view. A man of business habits and of little humour, but apparently of elastic spirits and thorough knowledge of the world, he was not easily conquered by any difficulties or overwhelmed by misfortunes. His early experience in that dispute with Lord Molynes about Gresham must have taught him, if he needed teaching, the crookedness of the times in which he lived, and the hopelessness of trusting to mere abstract right and justice for the protection of his own interests. But by unwearied energy, by constant watchfulness, by cultivating the friendship of Sir John Fastolf and the goodwill of the world in general, he succeeded in asserting for himself a position of some importance in his native county. That he was, at the same time, grasping and selfish to some extent, is no more than what we might be prepared to expect; and it would seem there were complaints to this effect even among the members of his own family.[3] As a parent he appears to have been somewhat unamiable and cold-hearted. Yet it is mainly to his self-seeking, businesslike character that we owe the preservation of

[1] No. 648. I do not know Fenn's authority for saying it was on the 26th May. Perhaps it is only a misprint.
[2] No. 637.   [3] Nos. 644, 645.

THE PASTON LETTERS

so valuable a correspondence. He knew well the importance of letters and of documents when rights came to be contested, and he was far more anxious about their security than about all the rest of his goods and chattels.[1]

Sir John Fastolf's will. Such being the nature of the man, and his personal history being as we have seen, what are we to say of the dark suspicion thrown upon his conduct in one important matter by his personal enemy Sir William Yelverton, and even by his quondam friend William Worcester? If their contention was true, the great addition made to the fortunes of the Paston family on the death of Sir John Fastolf was only due to a successful forgery. The will on which John Paston founded his claim to Caister, as well as to the manors of Drayton and Hellesdon, Cotton, Calcotes, and the whole of Fastolf's lands in the counties of Norfolk and Suffolk, was denounced by them as a fabrication and not the genuine will of Sir John Fastolf. And we must own that there are many things which seem to make the imputation credible. We have, unfortunately, only a portion of the depositions taken in the lawsuit, and these are entirely those of the adverse party, with the exception of two separate and individual testimonies given in Paston's favour.[2] We ought, therefore, undoubtedly to be on our guard against attaching undue weight to the many allegations of perjury and corruption against Paston's witnesses, as it is certainly quite conceivable that the interested testimony was on the other side, and it is truly shown in John Paston's own comments upon the evidence that the proofs given were insufficient. But, on the other hand, it is a very suspicious circumstance that a will drawn up by Fastolf on the 14th June before his death, was altered on the 3rd November so as to confer special powers in the administration to John Paston and Thomas Howes, and to give a large beneficiary interest to the former.[3] It is also singular that there should be three separate instruments of this latter date, each professing to be Fastolf's will.[4] And it by no means tends to allay suspicion when we find that two years after John Paston's death, and very shortly before his own, the parson Thomas Howes, a

[1] No. 649.   [2] Nos. 541, 543.   [3] No. 385.   [4] Nos. 385-387.

INTRODUCTION

Grey Friar, and partner with him in the principal charge of the administration of the alleged last will, made a declaration 'for the discharge of his conscience' that the document was a fabrication.[1]

This evidence might seem at first sight decisive and extremely damaging to the character of John Paston. But even here we must not be too precipitate in our conclusion. It is, for one thing, fairly open to remark that if this subsequent declaration of Sir Thomas Howes was an impeachment of Paston's honesty, it was no less so of his own; so that it becomes a question whether he was more honest at the time he was acting in concurrence with Paston or at the time of his professed repentance when he made this declaration. But on the whole we may admit that the latter alternative is more probable, and we frankly own it as our belief that Sir Thomas Howes, in his latter days, felt scruples of conscience with regard to the part he had taken in defending for his master Paston the validity of what, after all, he considered to be a questionable document. Yet what are we to say, in this case, to the testimony of another Grey Friar, our old friend Dr. Brackley, who had drawn up the final agreement between Fastolf and Paston relative to the college, got it engrossed on indented parchment, read it to Sir John, and saw him put his seal to it?[2] It was Brackley's dying testimony, when he was shriven by Friar Mowth, and informed that there were serious imputations on his conduct in reference to this matter, that as he would answer before God, in whose presence he was soon to appear, the will which John Paston produced in court was the genuine will of Sir John Fastolf. This testimony, too, he repeated unsolicited when, after seeming to rally for a day or two, he sank again, and saw himself once more in the presence of death.[3] Truly, if it seem hard to doubt the declaration of Sir Thomas Howes, it is harder still to cast suspicion on Brackley's dying evidence.

The true explanation of these discrepancies may, however, involve less serious charges against the character either of Paston, Brackley, or Howes than would at first sight appear

[1] No. 689.   [2] No. 606 (vol. iv. pp. 183-4).   [3] No. 666.

THE PASTON LETTERS

inevitable. The question was not really one about the authenticity of a document, but about the exact nature of a dying man's will. The document avowedly had not Fastolf's signature attached ; it seems that he was too ill to write. For some years before his death I do not find Fastolf's own signature attached to any of his letters. The point in dispute was whether it really represented Fastolf's latest intentions as to the disposal of his property. True, it bore Fastolf's seal of arms, which Yelverton and Worcester at first endeavoured to prove must have been affixed to it after his death. But Paston seems to have shown most successfully that this was impossible, as Fastolf's seal of arms was at his death contained in a purse sealed with his signet, and the signet itself was at that time taken off his finger, and sealed up in a chest under the seals of several of the executors.[1] Moreover, Paston's statements went to show that the terms of the will were settled in various conferences with Sir John during the months of September, October, and the beginning of November, and that corrections had been made in it by his express desire. With all this, however, it may have been a delicate question whether the latest corrections were truly in accordance with Fastolf's mind, and doubts may have been fairly entertained on the subject by Sir Thomas Howes ; especially when we consider that on the day the will was dated Fastolf was utterly unable to speak articulately, so that no one could hear him without putting his ear close to the mouth of the dying man.[2] With regard to John Paston's part in the matter, he was not present when Fastolf's seal was put to the document, so that the validity of that act rested entirely upon the testimony of others, particularly Dr. Brackley. And as to the charge of his 'fabricating' the will, it was never denied that he drew it up, or took a considerable part in doing so ; the only question is how far he did so in accordance with Sir John Fastolf's own instructions.

Some important matters of fact, indeed, were asserted by Paston in support of his case, and contested by the opposite

[1] No. 606 (vol. iv. p. 183).
[2] No. 565 (vol. iv. p. 104); No. 639 (vol. iv. p. 240).

236

INTRODUCTION

side. Among other things, it was contended that in the autumn of the year 1457, two years before his death, Sir John Fastolf had actually made estate to John Paston of the manor of Caister and other lands in Norfolk, and thereupon given him livery of seisin with a view to the foundation of the college :[1] also that the will made in 1459 was an imperfect document, in which no executors were named, and to which no seal was attached.[2] If these allegations were true, there was, after all, no great alteration in Sir John's intentions during the last two years of his life. On the other hand, Sir Thomas Howes, in his later declaration, asserts that only a year before Fastolf's death he had, at Paston's desire, urged Sir John to allow Paston to buy three of his manors and live in his college ; at which proposition the old knight started with indignation, and declared with a great oath, 'An I knew that Paston would buy any of my lands or my goods, he should never be my feoffee, nor mine executor.' But even Howes acknowledges that he was willing to allow Paston a lodging for term of his life within the manor of Caister.[3]

The whole controversy affords certainly an admirable illustration of the inconvenient state of the law before the passing of the Statute of Uses in the days of Henry VIII. The hearing of all causes touching the wills of dead men belonged to the spiritual courts of the Church, which did not own the king's jurisdiction. The king's courts, on the other hand, had cognisance of everything affecting real property. No lands or tenements could be bequeathed by will, because the courts of common law would not give effect to such an instrument. But legal ingenuity had found the means to enable wealthy persons to bequeath their lands as well as their goods to whomsoever they pleased. A man had only to execute a conveyance of his lands to a body of trustees, who thereupon became in law the owners, express provision being made at the same time that they were to hold it for his use so long as he lived, and after his death for the use of certain other persons named in his will, or for such purposes as might therein be

[1] Vol. iii. No. 386; vol. iv. Nos. 541, 606 (p. 183), 639 (p. 237).
[2] No. 606, p. 182 (vol. iv.).   [3] No. 689.

237

THE PASTON LETTERS

indicated. By this indirect means a title in lands was very effectually conveyed to a legatee without any abatement of the original owner's control over his own property so long as he lived. But the practice gave rise to a multitude of inconveniences. Private bargains, legal quibbles and subtleties, crafty influences brought to bear upon dying men, great uncertainty as to the destination of certain properties, were among its frequent results. At the very last moment, when the dying man, perhaps, was in imperfect possession of his faculties, mere words, or even a nod or sign, might affect the title to very large estates. And almost by the very nature of the case, wherever a trust was instituted like that of Sir John Fastolf, all the pettifogging devices of legal chicanery were necessarily brought into play, either to establish a title or to contest it.[1]

Sir John Paston

Sir John Paston now stepped into his father's place, as heir to Caister and to Fastolf's other possessions in Norfolk and Suffolk. But before he could vindicate his rights in any part of them it was necessary that he should wipe out that stain upon his pedigree which had been devised by calumny in bar of the claims made by his father. The case came before the king himself in council. An array of court rolls and other ancient records was produced by the family, to show that they had been lords of the soil in Paston from a very remote period. Some of their title-deeds went back as far as the reign of Henry III., and it was shown that their ancestors had given lands to religious houses in that reign. Indeed, so little truth was there in the imputation that John Paston the father was a bondman, that his ancestors, certainly by the mother's side if not by the father's also, had been the owners of bondmen. The evidences were considered satisfactory, and the family were declared by the king's council to be fully cleared of the imputation. The lands, of which Lord Scales had taken

[1] See the preamble to the Statute of Uses, 27 Henry VIII. c. 10.

238

INTRODUCTION

possession for about half a year,[1] were restored to Sir John Paston by a warrant under the king's signet, dated on the 26th July, little more than two months after the death of John Paston the father.[2]

After this Sir John Paston was much at court, and Lord Scales became his special friend. Even as early as the following April we find Sir John taking part in a tournament at Eltham, in which the king, Lord Scales, and himself were upon one side.[3] But the favour with which he was regarded at court both by the king and the Lord Scales appeared more evidently one year later, when the king's sister Margaret went over to the Low Countries to be married to Charles, Duke of Burgundy. This match had been more than a year in contemplation, and was highly popular in cementing the friendship of England and Burgundy in opposition to France. On the 1st May 1467 a curious bargain or wager was made by Sir John Paston as to the probability of its taking effect within two years.[4] But on the 18th April 1468 he received a summons from the king to be prepared to give his attendance on the princess by the 1st June following, and to accompany her into Flanders.[5] Not only he, but his brother John Paston the younger, crossed the sea in the Lady Margaret's train ; and we are indebted to the latter for an interesting account of the marriage and of the tournaments which followed in honour of it. Young John Paston was greatly struck with the splendour of the Burgundian court. He had never heard of anything like it, he said, except the court of King Arthur.[6] But his brother seems to have found another attraction abroad which fascinated him quite as much as all the pageants and the tournaments in honour of the Lady Margaret.

There lived, probably in the town of Calais, a certain Mrs. Anne Haute, a lady of English extraction and related to Lord Scales, whom Sir John Paston seems on this occasion to have met for the first time. Having been perhaps all her life

Tournament at Eltham.

A.D. 1468. Marriage of Margaret, sister of Edward IV., to Charles Duke of Burgundy.

Sir John Paston and Anne Haute.

[1] *Itin.* W. Worc., 323, where it is said that Lord Scales 'custodivit hospicium in Castre per spacium dimidii . . .' The blank must surely be supplied by the word *anni.*
[2] Nos. 641, 643.   [3] No. 665.   [4] No. 667.
[5] No. 683.   [6] No. 684.

239

THE PASTON LETTERS

abroad, she appears to have had an imperfect command of the English language; at least Sir John, in proposing to open a correspondence, wrote to her, 'Mistress Annes, I am proud that ye can read English.' For the rest we must not attempt to portray the lady, of whose appearance and qualities of mind or body we have no account whatever. But perhaps we may take it for granted that she was really beautiful; for though Sir John was a susceptible person, and had once been smitten before, his friend Daverse declared him to be the best chooser of a gentlewoman that he knew.[1] It is a pity that with this qualification his suit was not more successful. It went on for several years, but was in the end broken off, and Sir John Paston lived and died a bachelor.

A troubled inheritance.

But Sir John was heir to the troubles of a lawsuit, and his property was continually threatened by various claimants both at Hellesdon and at Caister. His mother writes to him on one occasion that Blickling of Hellesdon had come from London, 'and maketh his boast that within this fortnight at Hellesdon should be both new lords and new officers. And also this day Rysing of Fretton should have heard said in divers places, there as he was in Suffolk, that Fastolf of Cowhaw maketh all the strength that he may, and proposeth him to assault Caister and to enter there if he may, insomuch that it is said that he hath a five-score men ready, and sendeth daily espies to understand what fellowship keep the place.' For which reason Margaret Paston urges her son to send home either his brothers or Daubeney to command the garrison, for, as he well knew, she had been 'affrayed'[2] there before this time, and she could not 'well guide nor rule soldiers.'[3] Another time it is intimated to Sir John that the Duchess of Suffolk means to enter into Cotton suddenly at some time when few men should know what she is going to do.[4] And this intention she seems to have fully accomplished, for in the beginning of the year 1469 the Earl of Oxford sends Sir John a friendly warning that she means to

[1] No. 660.
[2] That is to say, menaced, if not attacked, an 'affray' being made upon her. It is curious to meet here our familiar word 'afraid' in its original form and signification.
[3] No. 671. [4] No. 690.

INTRODUCTION

hold a court there next Monday with a view to proving that the manor of Cotton Hemnales is holden of her by knight's service.[1] So that altogether Sir John Paston's inheritance was held by a very precarious tenure, and his mother, like a prudent woman, advises him 'not to be too hasty to be married till ye were more sure of your livelode.'[2]

The old dispute with the executors, however, was compromised in the court of audience: and the Archbishop of Canterbury, Bishop Waynflete, and Lord Beauchamp granted to Sir John full right in the manor of Caister, and a number of other lands both in Norfolk and Suffolk.[3] Sir John soon afterwards conveyed a portion of the Suffolk property called Hemnales in Cotton and the manor of Haynford to the Duke of Norfolk and others.[4] William Worcester became friends with John Paston's widow, imputed his old misunderstanding with her husband to the interference of others between them, and expressed himself well pleased that Caister was to be at her command. 'A rich jewel it is at need,' writes Worcester, 'for all the country in time of war; and my master Fastolf would rather he had never builded it than it should be in the governance of any sovereign that would oppress the country.' At the same time it seemed very doubtful whether Fastolf's intention of founding the college there could be carried out, and Worcester had some conferences with Sir John Paston about establishing it at Cambridge. Bishop Waynflete had already proposed doing so at Oxford; but Cambridge was nearer to the county of Norfolk, and by buying a few advowsons of wealthy parsonages an additional foundation might be established there at considerably less cost than by the purchase of manors. In this opinion Sir John Paston and William Worcester coincided, and the former promised to urge it upon Bishop Waynflete.[5]

Sir John Paston had now some reason to expect that with the settlement of this controversy he would have been left for life in peaceful possession of Caister. That which his father

[1] No. 696. [2] No. 704.
[3] No. 675. The deed, perhaps, was found to be irregular afterwards, for its general effect was confirmed about five months later by another instrument. No. 680.
[4] No. 677. [5] No. 681.

THE PASTON LETTERS

had not been able to attain was now apparently conceded to him: and even if Sir William Yelverton was still dissatisfied, the other executors had formally recognised his rights in the court of audience. But before many months had passed it appeared that Yelverton could still be troublesome, and he found an ally in one who had hitherto been his opponent.

Sir Thomas Howes unites with Yelverton,

Sir Thomas Howes was probably failing in health—for he seems to have died about the end of the year 1468[1]—when he made that declaration 'for the discharge of his conscience' to which we have already alluded. Scruples seem to have arisen in his mind as to the part he had taken with Sir John Paston's father in reference to the administration of Fastolf's will, and he now maintained that the will nuncupative which he himself had propounded along with John Paston in opposition to an earlier will propounded by Yelverton and Worcester, was a fabrication which did not truly express the mind of the deceased. We may observe, though the subject is exceedingly obscure, that of the three wills[2] printed in Volume III, each of which professes to be the will of Sir John Fastolf, the third, which is in Latin, is clearly a will nuncupative declaring the testator's mind in the third person, and defining the powers of the executors in regard to his goods and chattels.[3]

It was apparently this nuncupative will that Howes declared to be spurious. The validity of the others touching his lands depended upon the genuineness of a previous bargain made by Fastolf with John Paston, which was also disputed. But it was the nuncupative will that appointed ten executors and yet gave John Paston and Thomas Howes sole powers of administration, except in cases where those two thought fit to ask their assistance. This will seems to have been drawn up mainly by the instrumentality of one Master John Smyth, whom Howes

[1] See preliminary note to No. 703. [2] Nos. 385-7.
[3] The other two have relation to his lands, and are not inconsistent with each other; but the first is drawn up in the name of the testator himself, while the second speaks of him in the third person. The second is, in fact, a note of various instructions given by the testator in reference to his property on the 2nd and 3rd days of November before he died, and its contents may have been fully embodied in the first, when the will was regularly drawn up; but the first is printed from a draft which is probably imperfect.

INTRODUCTION

afterwards denounced as 'none wholesome counsellor.'[1] Howes now combined with Yelverton in declaring it to be spurious.

and they sell Caister to the Duke of Norfolk.

The result of this allegation was that Yelverton and Howes took it upon them, as executors of Sir John Fastolf, to recommend to Archbishop Bourchier that the Duke of Norfolk should be allowed to purchase the manor of Caister and certain other lands in Norfolk, and that the money received for it should be spent in charitable deeds for the good of Fastolf's soul. The transaction was not yet completed,[2] but the duke immediately proceeded to act upon it just as if it were. He did not, indeed, at once take possession of the place, but he warned the tenants of the manor to pay no money to Sir John, and his agents even spoke as if they had the king's authority. On the other hand, Sir John had the support of powerful men in the king's council—no less persons than the great Earl of Warwick and his brother, the Archbishop of York, who had lately been Lord Chancellor, and was hoping to be so again. The Earl of Warwick had spoken about the matter to the duke even in the king's chamber, and the archbishop had said, 'rather than the land should go so, he would come and dwell there himself.'

Archbishop Nevill.

'Ye would marvel,' adds the correspondent who communicates the news to Sir John Paston, 'ye would marvel what hearts my lord hath gotten and how this language put people in comfort.' It had its effect upon the Duke of Norfolk, who saw that he must not be too precipitate. He was urged on, it seems, by the duchess his wife, but he would go and speak to her and entreat her.[4]

On the other hand, Yelverton and Howes seem to have been pretty confident that my Lord of York would not be chancellor again unless their bargain with the duke was ratified. The Nevills were no longer regarded with favour at court. The coolness which had existed between the king and Warwick ever since the marriage with Elizabeth Woodville had last year come to an open rupture, and the Archbishop of York had

[1] No. 681. [2] Nos. 688-9.
[3] 'The bargain is not yet made,' says an anonymous writer on the 28th October. See No. 690. Nevertheless an ostensible title had been conveyed to the duke by a formal document on the 1st October. See No. 764.
[4] Nos. 688, 690.

THE PASTON LETTERS

been at the same time dismissed from the office of chancellor. Soon after the new year a reconciliation was effected through the medium of private friends, and the archbishop conducted his brother the Earl of Warwick to the king at Coventry.[1] But real confidence was not restored, and party spirit was anxious that it never should be. Nor could the public at large, perhaps, imagine the deep grounds of distrust that Warwick had already given to his sovereign.

Sir John Paston, nevertheless, was advised to put his trust chiefly in the friendship of the Nevills and in the probable reinstatement of the archbishop as Lord Chancellor. Another means, however, was not to be neglected. Sir Thomas Howes might be gammoned, or bullied, or got over in some way. He and Yelverton did not agree so well that it need be a very hard matter to separate them. Sir John's friends hoped to secure for him the good offices of the Bishop of Ely and a certain Master Tresham, who, it was thought, could put it nicely to Sir Thomas Howes half in jest and half in earnest, putting him 'in hope of the moon shine in the water,' and telling him that such efforts were made 'that either he should be a pope, or else in despair to be deprived *de omni beneficio ecclesiastico* for simony, lechery, perjury, and double variable peevishness, and for administering without authority.' Such were a few of the humours of the controversy.[2]

Sir John 'wages' men. A.D. 1469.

Better, however, than the friendship of the great, was the security to be derived from keeping Caister well guarded ; and Sir John Paston immediately set about ' waging ' men to add to the little garrison.[3] With this he seems to have been much occupied from November till January following, when by repeated letters from the king he was commanded to desist from making any assembly of the lieges, and to appear personally before the council at Westminster.[4] The matter, apparently, was hung up for a time without any decision being come to by the council. The friendship of Archbishop Nevill could have done little to recommend the cause of Sir John Paston to the king. On the other hand, if favour had any-thing to do with the result, his cause was warmly advocated by

[1] W. Worc., 512-13. [2] No. 690. [3] No. 691. [4] No. 698.

244

INTRODUCTION

Lord Scales, the king's own brother-in-law, on account of Sir John's intended marriage with his kinswoman, Anne Haute.[1] And it is certain that Judge Yelverton had conferences with Lord Scales in the hope of coming to some kind of under-standing. But King Edward, as we have already said, had a real desire to be impartial in the disputes and quarrels of his subjects ; and doubtless it was from a feeling of this that Sir John Paston and his mother rejoiced to hear that it was the king's intention to visit Norwich in the course of the ensuing summer. The rumour of this intention, it was believed, had a powerful influence in inducing the Duchess of Suffolk to remain at her family seat at Ewelme, in Oxfordshire, that she might be out of the way if sent for by the king, and plead age or sickness as her excuse.[2] The attempt made by her son to dispossess Sir John Paston at Hellesdon could best be judged on the spot. And in Norfolk, too, the king would learn what was thought of the Duke of Norfolk's claim to Caister.

So it was hoped that the king's presence in the county would tell most favourably on Sir John Paston's interests. And there was one circumstance in particular of which advan-tage might be taken. As Edward was to go from Norwich on pilgrimage to Walsingham, his way would of necessity lie through Hellesdon and Drayton. The lodge whose walls the Duke of Suffolk had caused to be broken down could hardly fail, from its conspicuous position, to meet his eye, and perhaps some friend in the king's suite could be got to call his attention to it and tell him the story of the outrage. This Thomas Wingfield engaged to do, and promised to get the king's own brother, the Duke of Gloucester, to join him in pointing out the ruin. Promises were also obtained from Earl Rivers, the queen's father, and from her brother Lord Scales and Sir John Woodville, that they would urge the king to command the Dukes of Norfolk and Suffolk to forbear claiming title to the lands of Sir John Fastolf. And by the time the king took his departure from Norwich the Pastons were encouraged to believe that steps had already been taken to end their con-troversy with one if not with both dukes. Unfortunately the

[1] Nos. 704, 706, 707. [2] No. 704.

245

THE PASTON LETTERS

belief, or at least the hope that it gave rise to, proved to be utterly unfounded.[1]

The ruined lodge is shown to the king.

The king rode through Hellesdon Warren on his way, as it had been expected that he would do. The ruined lodge was pointed out to him by William Paston, Sir John's uncle ; but his answer was altogether at variance with what the Woodvilles had led them to expect. The king said the building might have fallen by itself, and if it had been pulled down, as alleged, the Pastons might have put in bills at the session of *Oyer and Terminer* held by the judges when he was at Norwich. William Paston replied that his nephew had been induced to hope the king himself would have procured an amicable settle-ment with both the dukes, and therefore had forborne to vindicate his rights by law. But the king said he would neither treat nor speak for Sir John, but let the law take its course.[2]

Civil War—Public and Private

Possibly on the eve of his departure from Norwich, the king had heard news which took away all disposition he might once have entertained to hear personally complaints against such noblemen as the Dukes of Norfolk and Suffolk. It was just about the time of the insurrection of Robin of Redesdale in Yorkshire—a movement got up under fictitious names and really promoted by the discontented Earl of Warwick. From the day that Edward IV. had announced himself a married man, and disconcerted the subtle promoters of an alliance with France through the medium of the French king's sister-in-law, Bona of Savoy,[3] the Earl of Warwick had not only lost his old

Robin of Redes-dale's rebellion.

[1] No. 716. [2] *Ibid.*
[3] The story that the Earl of Warwick had gone to France to negotiate the marriage of Edward with Bona of Savoy, when Edward frustrated his diplomacy by marrying Elizabeth Woodville, is certainly not in accordance with facts. But the doubts of some modern historians that the project of such a match was ever entertained are quite set at rest by the evidence of two letters which have been recently printed in some of the publications of the Société de l'Histoire de France, to which attention is called by Mr. Kirk in his *History of Charles the Bold* (vol. i. p. 415 note, and ii. p. 15 note). It appears that although the earl had not actually gone to France, he was expected there just at the time the secret of the king's marriage was revealed. Nor can there be a reasonable doubt—indeed there is something like positive evidence to

246

INTRODUCTION

ascendency in the king's councils, but had seen his policy altogether thwarted and his own selfish interests continually set aside. He had been from the first in favour of an amicable compromise of the dispute with France, while the young king owed not a little of his popularity to the belief that he would maintain the old pretensions of England, and vindicate them if necessary upon the field of battle. Disappointed of one mode of promoting a French alliance, he had been disappointed still further in 1467, when the king, to humour his inclinations for a while, sent him over to France on embassy. The result was that he was magnificently entertained by Louis XI., captivated by the bland familiarity of the French monarch, and became for ever after his most ready and convenient tool. If he had anything to learn before in the arts of diplomacy and state-craft, he came back from France a most accomplished scholar. Edward, however, pursued a course of his own, treated the French ambassadors in England with rudeness, and cultivated instead a close alliance with Burgundy, the formidable rival and lately the enemy of Louis. He contracted his sister Margaret to the Duke of Burgundy's eldest son, Charles, Count of Charolois, who became duke himself in the following year, when the marriage was solemnised at Bruges with a splendour no court in Europe could have rivalled. To crown all, he announced in Parliament just before the marriage an intention to invade France in person.[1]

The Earl of Warwick dissembled. Charles of Burgundy was the man he hated most,[2] but he conducted the Princess Margaret to the coast on her way to Flanders. A number of personal wrongs and disappointments also rankled in his breast, and gave birth to sinister projects for gratifying a wounded ambition, and taking revenge upon an ungrateful king, who owed it in no small degree to himself that he was king at all. As yet Edward was without an heir-male. He had two

prove—that the first cause of the Earl of Warwick's alienation from the king arose out of this matter. I ought to add that the merit of placing before us for the first time a clear view of the consequences of Edward IV.'s marriage, in its bearing alike on the domestic history of England and on Edward's relations with France and Burgundy, is due to Mr. Kirk.
[1] W. Worc., 513-14. [2] *Contin. of Croyland Chronicle*, p. 551.

247

THE PASTON LETTERS

daughters;[1] but in the succession a brother might perhaps be preferred to a female. Warwick could marry his eldest daughter to George, Duke of Clarence, and encourage that vain prince in his expectation of the crown. The earl was governor of Calais. At midsummer in the year 1469 the Duke of Clarence stole across the sea without the leave of his brother, and landed in a territory where Warwick was like an independent king. There the wedding was celebrated by the Archbishop of York, the Earl of Warwick's brother. Soon after it was over, the duke, the earl, and the archbishop returned to England.

And now it was that the king, after leaving Norwich and visiting the famous shrine at Walsingham, found himself compelled to turn his steps northwards and face the insurrection that had been secretly stirred up by Warwick and his own brother. It appears by the Privy Seal dates that he had reached Lynn on the 26th June.[2] He passed on through Wisbeach with a company of two hundred horse to Crowland Abbey, where he stayed a night, and sailed from thence through the fenny country up the Nen to his father's castle of Fotheringay, one of his own favourite residences.[3] From thence, when a number of troops had flocked to his standard from all parts of the kingdom, he marched northwards to Nottingham; where, apparently, he learned, to his no little mortification, that his brother Clarence was in alliance with the Earl of Warwick and Archbishop Nevill, and that it was questionable whether they had not too good an understanding with the rebels in the North. That such was the actual fact we know to a certainty. The insurgents disseminated papers complaining that the kingdom was misgoverned, in consequence of the undue influence of the queen's relations and one or two other councillors, who had impoverished the crown by pro-

[1] The two eldest daughters of Edward IV. were born in the years 1465 and 1466; the third, Cecily, in the latter end of 1469. See Green's *Princesses*, vol. iii.; also an article by Sir Frederic Madden, in the *Gentleman's Magazine* for 1831 (vol. ci. pt. i., p. 24).
[2] He seems to have left Norwich on the 21st. There are Privy Seals dated on that day, some at Norwich and some at Walsingham.
[3] *Contin. Chron. Croyl.* p. 542.

248

INTRODUCTION

curing large grants of crown lands to themselves, and who had caused the king to tamper with the currency and impose inordinate taxes. Worst of all, they had estranged the true lords of the king's blood from his secret council, and thereby prevented any check being placed on their rapacity and misconduct.[1]

The Duke of Clarence, with Warwick and the archbishop, had no sooner landed from Calais, than copies of these manifestoes were laid before them, which they took it upon them to regard in the light of a petition calling upon the lords of England generally, and themselves in particular, to redress the evils of the state. They declared the petition just and reasonable, promised to lay it before the king, and by a proclamation under their signets, dated the 12th day of July, called upon all who loved the common weal to meet them at Canterbury on Sunday following, armed and arrayed to the best of their power.[2] Three days before the date of this proclamation, the king at Nottingham had addressed letters to the duke, earl, and archbishop separately, desiring credence for Sir Thomas Montgomery and Maurice Berkeley, and expressing a hope that the current rumour as to their intentions was erroneous.[3] A hope altogether vain. The king was surrounded with enemies, and no plan of action could be arranged among his friends. Herbert, Earl of Pembroke, whom he had summoned from Wales, met at Banbury with Humphrey, Lord Strafford of Southwick, lately created Earl of Devonshire,[4] who came out of Devonshire to do battle with the rebels. But the two leaders had a dispute about quarters; the Earl of Devonshire withdrew eight or ten miles back; and Sir William Conyers, the rebel captain, who had adopted the name Robin of Redesdale, came down upon the Earl of Pembroke and defeated him with great slaughter. The earl himself and his brother Sir Richard Herbert were taken prisoners, and were shortly afterwards put to death at Coventry, along with

Battle of Hedgecote, 26th July.

[1] See the petition printed by Halliwell in his notes to *Warkworth's Chronicle*, pp. 47-51.
[2] See the proclamation immediately preceding the above petition in the notes to *Warkworth's Chronicle*, pp. 46-7.
[3] No. 719.
[4] No. 714.

249

THE PASTON LETTERS

Lord Rivers and his son Sir John Woodville, who were about the same time captured in the Forest of Dean in Gloucestershire. They had parted with the king in alarm before he came to Nottingham, and fled for safety towards Wales; but their flight was to no purpose. Before their execution—apparently some time during the month of August—the king himself was taken prisoner near Coventry by the confederate lords, and led to Warwick Castle; from which place he was, soon after his committal, transferred to Middleham, another castle of the Earl of Warwick, in Yorkshire.[1]

The king taken prisoner.

He was shortly afterwards released, and arrived in London in the beginning of October. It was not easy to say what to do with such a prisoner, and Warwick thought it best to let him go. He had done enough for the present to show his power and wreak his revenge upon the Woodvilles; and Edward, even when he was set at liberty, saw clearly that prudence required him to forget the affront and not show himself in any way offended.[2]

But what kind of order could have prevailed throughout the kingdom at a time when the king was a captive in the hands of his own subjects? For the most part we know nothing of the facts, but perhaps we may judge to some extent from what took place in a small corner of the county of Norfolk. On Monday the 21st August,[3] the Duke of Norfolk began to lay a regular siege to Caister Castle. Sir John Paston was at the time in London, and his brother John kept the place as his lieutenant. At first the duke sent Sir John Heveningham, a

Siege of Caister, A.D. 1469, Aug.

[1] *Contin. Chron. Croyl.* pp. 542, 551. There are Privy Seals dated on the 2nd August at Coventry; on the 9th, 12th, and 13th at Warwick; and on the 25th and 28th at Middleham. [2] No. 736.
[3] At least William Worcester, in his *Itinerary*, p. 321, seems to indicate in very bad Latin that the siege began on the Monday before St. Bartholomew's Day, which in 1469 would be the 21st August. Yet a very bewildering sentence just before would imply that the siege began either on the Feast of the Assumption of the Virgin (15th August) or on St. Bartholomew's Day itself (24th August), and that it lasted five weeks and three days. But we know that the castle surrendered on the 26th September, so that if the duration of the siege was five weeks and three days it must have begun on the 19th August, a different date still. William Worcester's habit of continually jotting down memoranda in his commonplace books has been of very great service to the historian of this disordered epoch; but his memoranda reflect the character of the times in their confusion, inconsistency, and contradictions.

250

INTRODUCTION

kinsman of Sir John Fastolf, to demand peaceable entry, on the ground that he had bought the manor from Fastolf's executor Yelverton; but on being refused admittance, he surrounded the castle with a body of 3000 men.[1] Those within were not wholly unprepared. They had rather more than a month's supply of victuals and gunpowder, but they were only a handful of men. Sir John Heveningham, who was appointed by the duke one of the captains of the besieging force, had hitherto been friendly to the Paston family. He came and visited old Agnes Paston at Norwich, and Margaret Paston thought he might be induced to show a little favour to messengers coming from herself or her son Sir John. But this he steadily refused to do, and made a very suspicious suggestion for the settlement of the controversy, which he requested Margaret to write to her son Sir John in London. Could not the duke be allowed to enter peaceably on giving surety to Sir John to recompense all wrongs, if the law should afterwards declare the right to be in him? 'Be ye advised,' wrote Margaret, 'what answer ye will give.'[2]

Other proposals were shortly afterwards made on the duke's behalf, nearly the same in character but with somewhat greater show of fairness. The place, it was suggested, might be put in the keeping of indifferent parties, who would receive the profits for the benefit of whoever should prove to be the true claimant until the right could be determined, the duke and Paston both giving security not to disturb these occupants in the meanwhile. But who could be relied upon as indifferent, or what power existed in the kingdom to secure impartiality at a time when the king himself was a prisoner in the hands of his enemies? Margaret Paston could but forward these suggestions to her son, with a warning to lose no time in making up his mind about them. 'Send word how ye will be demeaned by as good advice as ye can get, and make no longer delay, for they must needs have hasty succour that be in the place; for they be sore hurt and have none help. And if they have hasty help, it shall be the greatest worship that ever ye had. And if they be not holpen it shall be to you a great disworship;

[1] *Itin. W. de Worc.*, 325. [2] No. 720.

251

THE PASTON LETTERS

and look never to have favour of your neighbours and friends but if this speed well.'[1]

Unfortunately the only relief which Sir John Paston had it easily in his power to obtain for the garrison was not in the shape of succours. Sir John was in London, and did not know for certain how long they had the power to hold out. But he addressed his complaints to the Duke of Clarence and Archbishop Nevill, who now ruled in the name of the captive king, and one Writtill, a servant of the former, was sent down to procure a suspension of hostilities, preparatory, if possible, to a settlement of the controversy. Terms were agreed upon by the lords in London which it was thought might be honourably offered to both parties. Apparently it was proposed that the Earl of Oxford, as a neutral person, should be allowed to keep the place until a final decision had been come to by a competent tribunal. But the Duke of Norfolk, after agreeing to the suspension of hostilities, which only diminished by so many days' allowance the scanty provisions of the garrison, utterly rejected the conditions which some of his own relations in the king's council had given it as their opinion that he ought not to refuse. On the other hand, Sir John Paston in London, fondly believing that the store of victuals within the place would last a much longer period, caught at an eager hope of obtaining a message from the king which would compel Norfolk to withdraw his forces, and in this idle expectation he was foolish enough to urge Writtill to get the truce prolonged a few days further. Shortly afterwards he received a letter from his mother which ought to have opened his eyes. Victuals, she informed him, were failing in the garrison; his brother and the little band within stood in great danger; Daubeney and Berney, two of their captains, were dead, and several others were wounded; the walls were severely battered, and the supply of gunpowder and arrows would very soon be exhausted. Since Writtill's attempt at negotiation the Duke of Norfolk had been more determined than ever to win the place, and with a view to a grand assault, whenever the truce should expire, he had sent for all his tenants to be there on Holy Rood day, the

[1] No. 720.

252

INTRODUCTION

14th September. If Sir John Paston had it in his power to relieve the garrison, let him do it at once. If not, let him obtain letters from the Duke of Clarence or the lords in London addressed to the Duke of Norfolk, to allow them to quit the place with their lives and goods.[1]

Sir John Paston still would not believe that the case was desperate. He had repeatedly declared that his desire to preserve the stronghold was exceeded only by his anxiety for the lives of his brother and those within. But what evidence was there to justify his mother's apprehensions? Daubeney and Berney had been alive the Saturday before, and since that day no one could have got leave to pass outside. Truce had been prolonged till Monday following, and he expected it to be renewed for another week. He had heard far worse tidings before than his mother told him now. As for means of relief to the besieged, the Duke of Clarence and Archbishop Nevill were no longer in London, but he was expecting an answer from the king in Yorkshire, which ought to arrive by Wednesday at farthest, and his mother might rest assured there could not possibly be any fear of victuals or gunpowder running short. When all else failed, a rescue he would certainly procure, if all the lands he held in England and all the friends he had would enable him to obtain it. But this was the very last remedy that could be thought of. It would not agree with the attempt to get the king or lords to interfere. It would besides cost fully a thousand crowns, and how to raise the money he was not sure. How much could his mother herself raise by mortgage, and what friends could she obtain to give their aid?[2]

Unluckily, while Sir John Paston was devising means how, Caister surrenders. after another week or fortnight's truce, effectual relief might at last be conveyed to the besieged, they were reduced to such extremities as to be compelled to capitulate. Owing to the representations that had been made in their behalf by Cardinal Bourchier and the Duke of Clarence, Norfolk allowed them to pass out in freedom, with bag and baggage, horses and harness, leaving only behind them their guns, crossbows and

[1] Nos. 722-6.   [2] No. 725.

253

THE PASTON LETTERS

'quarrels.'[1] Thus, after some weeks' suspense and the loss of one valuable soldier (Margaret Paston was misinformed about Berney being dead as well as Daubeney), the great castle in which Fastolf intended the Pastons to reside and to found a college, and which he was anxious that no great lord should occupy, fell into the hands of the most powerful nobleman of Eastern England.[2]

Sir John Paston had now lost the fairest gem of his inheritance—or, as he and his contemporaries called it, of his 'livelode.'[3] Hence it was become all the more important that he should see to the remainder. Just before the surrender of Caister, in answer to his appeal to see what money she could raise, his mother by a great effort obtained for him £10 on sureties, but it was all spent immediately in paying the discharged garrison and some other matters. Ways and means must be found to obtain money, for even his mother's rents did not come in as they ought to have done, and she expected to be reduced to borrowing, or breaking up her household. On consideration, he determined to part with the manor of East Beckham, and to ascertain what was likely to be realised by selling a quantity of wood at Sporle. The sale of East Beckham—with all Paston's lands both in East and West Beckham, Bodham, Sherringham, Beeston-near-the-Sea, Runton, Shipden, Felbrigg, Aylmerton, Sustead and Gresham, places which lie a few miles to the west and south of Cromer—was at length completed for the sum of 100 marks.[4]

It was unfortunate for Sir John Paston's interests that at such a time as this he happened to have a misunderstanding with his most faithful bailiff and general manager of his property, Richard Calle. The title-deeds of Beckham were in Calle's hands, but he at once gave up, when required, both these and every one of the documents in his possession relating

[1] Square pyramids of iron which were shot out of crossbows. The word is of French origin and was originally *quarreaux*.
[2] Nos. 730, 731.
[3] The modern confusion of this word with *livelihood*—a word which properly means a lively condition—is one of the things that would be unpardonable did not usage pardon everything in language.
[4] Nos. 733, 737, 738.

254

INTRODUCTION

to Paston's lands, and made a clear account of everything to John Paston the younger.[1] The coolness had arisen some months before the siege; the cause was a very old, old story. Richard Calle had presumed to fall in love with Sir John Richard Calle and Margery Paston. Paston's sister Margery. Margery Paston had not disdained to return his affection. She at once fell into disgrace with the whole family. Her eldest brother, Sir John, was in London when he heard of it, and it was insinuated to him that the matter was quite well known to his brother John and met with his approval. John the younger hastened to disavow the imputation. A little diplomacy had been used by Calle, who got a friend to inquire of him whether the engagement was a settled thing, intimating that if it were not he knew of a good marriage for the lady. But young John saw through the artifice, and gave the mediator an answer designed to set the question at rest for ever. 'I answered him,' writes young John himself to his brother, 'that an my father (whom God assoil) were alive, and had consented thereto, and my mother and ye both, he should never have my goodwill for to make my sister to sell candle and mustard in Framlingham.' If such a prospect did not disgust Margery herself, it was clear she must have a very strong will of her own.[2]

The anger of her relations was painful to bear in the extreme. For some time Margery found it difficult to avow that she had fairly plighted her troth to one who was deemed such an unequal match. For what was plighted troth in the eye of God but matrimony itself? And the Church acknowledged it as no less binding. Once that was avowed, the question was at an end, and no human hands could untie the knot. To interfere with it was deadly sin. Hence Richard Calle implored the woman of his love to emancipate both herself and him from an intolerable position by one act of boldness. 'I suppose, an ye tell them sadly the truth, they would not damn their souls for us.'[3] But it required much courage to take the step which when taken must be decisive. The avowal was at last made, and though the family would fain have suppressed it or got the poor girl to deny what she

[1] No. 737.   [2] No. 710.   [3] No. 713.

255

THE PASTON LETTERS

said, her lover appealed to the Bishop of Norwich to inquire into the matter, and free the point from any ambiguity. The bishop could not refuse. He sent for Margery Paston and for Richard Calle, and examined them both apart. He told the former that he was informed she loved one of whom her friends did not approve, reminded her of the great disadvantage and shame she would incur if she were not guided by their advice, and said he must inquire into the words that had passed between her and her lover, whether they amounted to matrimony or not. On this she told him what she had said to Calle, and added that if those words did not make it sure she would make it surer before she left the bishop's presence, for she thought herself in conscience bound to Calle, whatever the words were. Then Calle himself was examined, and his statements agreed with hers as to the nature of the pledges given and the time and place when it was done. The bishop then said that in case other impediments were found he would delay giving sentence till the Wednesday or Thursday after Michaelmas.[1]

When Margery Paston returned from her examination her mother's door was shut against her, and the bishop was forced to find a lodging for her until the day that he was to give sentence. Before that day came occurred the loss of Caister. The fortunes of the Paston family were diminished, and Sir John began to feel that he at least could ill afford to lose the services of one who had been such a faithful and attached dependant. In writing to his mother he expressed a wish merely that the marriage might be put off till Christmas. Calle, meanwhile, unmarried, was staying at Blackborough Nunnery near Lynn, where his bride had found a temporary asylum. He was still willing to give his services to Sir John Paston, and promised not to offer them to any other unless Sir John declined them. They appear to have been accepted, for we find Calle one or two years later still in the service of the family. But he never seems to have been recognised as one of its members.[2]

The siege of Caister was one of those strong and high-

[1] No. 721.　　　[2] Nos. 721, 736, 737.

256

INTRODUCTION

handed acts which could only have been possible when there was really no sovereign authority in the land to repress and punish violence. Acts of very much the same character had been seen before—the reader will not have forgotten the forcible ejection of John Paston's wife from Gresham. But they had been due more especially to the weak and incompetent rule of Henry VI., and not even then do we hear of a place being taken from one of the king's subjects after a five weeks' siege by a rival claimant. It was evident that the rebellion of Robin of Redesdale had destroyed King Edward's power. The king had been actually made a prisoner, and the ascendency of the Woodvilles had been abolished. The Duchess of Bedford, wife of the late Earl of Rivers, had even during the commotions been accused of witchcraft.[1] The Earl of Warwick enjoyed his revenge in the disorganisation of the whole kingdom. He had now made it almost impossible for Edward to recover his authority without getting rid of him ; nor did many months pass away before he stirred up another rebellion in Lincolnshire.[2] When that movement failed, he and Clarence escaped abroad ; but it was not many months before they reappeared in England and drove out the king. Henry VI. was proclaimed anew, and for the space of a short half-year Warwick the Kingmaker governed in the name of that sovereign in whose deposition ten years before he had been one of the principal agents.

Warwick the King-maker. A.D. 1470.

We have but a word or two to say as to matters affecting the family history of the Pastons during this brief interval. At the siege of Caister two men of the Duke of Norfolk's were killed by the fire of the garrison. The duke's council, not satisfied with having turned the Pastons out, now prompted the widows of these two men to sue an 'appeal'[3] against John Paston and those who acted with him. A true bill was also found against them for felony at the Norwich session of June 1470, in which Sir John Paston was included as an accessory ; but the indictment was held to be void by some of Paston's

Appeal of two widows.

[1] *Rolls of Parl.* vi. 232.　　　[2] *See* Nos. 742, 743.
[3] An appeal of murder was a criminal prosecution instituted by the nearest relation of the murdered person, and a pardon from the king could not be pleaded in bar of this process.

257

THE PASTON LETTERS

friends on the ground that two of the jury would not agree to it. This objection I presume must have been held sufficient to quash the proceedings in this form, of which we hear no more.[1] The 'appeal,' however, remained to be disposed of, as we shall see by and by.

Compromise touching Fastolf's will.

With respect to the title claimed by Sir John Paston in Caister and the performance of Fastolf's will, a compromise was arranged with Bishop Waynflete, who was now recognised as sole executor. It was agreed that as the whole of Fastolf's lands in Essex, Surrey, Norfolk, and Suffolk had been much wasted by the disputes between the executors, the manors should be divided between Sir John Paston and the bishop, the former promising to surrender the title-deeds of all except the manor of Caister. The project of a college in that place was given up, and a foundation of seven priests and seven poor scholars in Magdalen College, Oxford, was agreed to in its place.[2] Soon afterwards the Duke of Norfolk executed a release to the bishop of the manor of Caister and all the lands conveyed to him by Yelverton and Howes as executors of Sir John Fastolf, acknowledging that the bargain made with them was contrary to Fastolf's will, and receiving from the bishop the sum of 500 marks for the reconveyance. The duke accordingly sent notice to his servants and tenants to depart out of the manor as soon as they could conveniently remove such goods and furniture as he had placed in it.[3]

Thus by the mediation of Bishop Waynflete the long-standing disputes were nearly settled during the period of Henry VI.'s brief restoration. But, probably in consequence of the disturbed state of the country and the return of Edward IV., the duke's orders for the evacuation of Caister were not immediately obeyed, and, as we shall see hereafter, the place remained in Norfolk's possession for the space of three whole years.

Elizabeth Poynings remarries.

About this time, or rather, perhaps, two years later, Sir John Paston's aunt, Elizabeth Poynings, terminated her widowhood by marrying Sir George Browne of Betchworth Castle in Surrey. We have already seen how she was dispossessed of

[1] Nos. 740, 746, 747.　　　[2] Nos. 750, 755, 767.　　　[3] Nos. 763, 764.

258

INTRODUCTION

her lands soon after her first husband's death by the Countess of Northumberland. They were afterwards seized by the Crown as forfeited, and granted by patent to Edmund Grey, Earl of Kent, but without any title having been duly found for the king. The Earl of Kent after a time gave up possession of them to the Earl of Essex, but this did not make things pleasanter for Elizabeth Poynings ; while other of her lands were occupied by Sir Robert Fenys in violation, as she alleged, of her husband's will.[1] The date of her second marriage was probably about the end of the year 1471.[2]

These matters we are bound to mention as incidents in the history of the family. Of Elizabeth Paston, however, and her second husband we do not hear much henceforward ; in the Letters after this period the domestic interest centres chiefly round the two John Pastons, Sir John and his brother.

Changes and Counter-changes

Within the space of ten brief years Edward IV. had almost succeeded in convincing the world that he was no more capable of governing England than the rival whom he had deposed. Never did gambler throw away a fortune with more recklessness than Edward threw away the advantages which it had cost him and his friends so much hard fighting to secure. Just when he had reached the summit of his prosperity, he alienated the men to whom it was mainly due, and took no care to protect himself against the consequences of their concealed displeasure. The Earl of Warwick took him prisoner, then released him, then stirred up a new rebellion with impunity, and finally, returning to England once more, surprised and drove him out, notwithstanding the warnings of his brother-in-law, the Duke of Burgundy. Henry VI. was proclaimed anew, and the cause of the House of York seemed to be lost for ever.

Reckless government of Edward IV.

[1] Nos. 461, 627, 692, 693.
[2] On the 18th November 1471, Edmund Paston speaks of her as 'my Aunt Ponynges.' Before the 8th January 1472 she had married Sir George Browne. Nos. 789, 795.

259

THE PASTON LETTERS

It was not so, however, in fact. Adversity quickened Edward's energies in a manner almost miraculous, and in a few months he recovered his kingdom as suddenly as he had lost it. But it was not easy to believe, even after his most formidable enemy had been slain at Barnet, that a king who had shown himself so careless could maintain himself again upon the throne. Besides, men who desired a steady government had rested all their hopes in the restoration of Henry VI., and had found the new state of matters very promising, just before Edward reappeared. The king, it might have been hoped, would be governed this time by the Earl of Warwick, and not by Queen Margaret. The Pastons, *The Pastons favour Henry VI.* in particular, had very special reasons to rejoice in Henry's restoration. They had a powerful friend in the Earl of Oxford, whose influence with Henry and the Earl of Warwick stood very high. Owing partly, perhaps, to Oxford's intercession, the Duke of Norfolk had been obliged to quit his hold of Caister, and Sir John Paston had been reinstated in possession.[1] The Duke and Duchess of Norfolk sued to Oxford as humbly as the Pastons had been accustomed to sue to them, and the earl, from the very first, had been as careful of the interests of this family as if they had been his own. Even in the first days of the revolution—probably before Edward was yet driven out—he had sent a messenger to the Duchess of Norfolk from Colchester when John Paston was in London on a matter which concerned him alone. The family, indeed, seem at first to have built rather extravagant expectations upon the new turn of affairs, which John Paston felt it necessary to repress in writing to his mother. ' As for the offices that ye wrote to my brother for and to me, they be for no poor men, but I trust we shall speed of other offices meetly for us, for my master the Earl of Oxford biddeth me ask and have. I trow my brother Sir John shall have the constableship of Norwich Castle, with £20 of fee. All the lords be agreed to it.'[2]

Certainly, when they remembered the loss of Caister, which they had now regained—when they recalled his inability

[1] *See* preliminary note to Letter No. 879.   [2] No. 759.

INTRODUCTION

to protect them against armed aggression, and the disappointment of their expectations of redress against the Duke of Suffolk for the attack on the lodge at Hellesdon—the Pastons had little cause to pray for the return of Edward IV. They were completely committed to the cause of Henry ; and Sir John Paston and his brother fought, no doubt in the Earl of Oxford's company, against King Edward at Barnet. Both *Sir John Paston and his brother in the battle of Barnet. A.D. 1471.* the brothers came out of the battle alive, but John Paston was wounded with an arrow in the right arm, beneath the elbow.[1] His wound, however, was not of a very serious character, and in little more than a fortnight he was able to write a letter with his own hand.[2] A more serious consideration was, how far the family prospects were injured by the part they had taken against what seemed now to be the winning side. Perhaps they might be effectually befriended by their cousin Lomner, who seems to have adhered to Edward, and who had promised them his good offices, if required. But on the whole the Pastons did not look despondingly upon the situation, and rather advised their cousin Lomner not to commit himself too much to the other side, as times might change. ' I beseech you,' writes Sir John Paston to his mother, ' on my behalf to advise him to be well aware of his dealing or language as yet ; for the world, I ensure you, is right queasy, as ye shall know within this month. The people here feareth it sore. God hath showed Himself marvellously like Him that made all, and can undo again when Him list, and I can think that by all likelihood He shall show Himself as marvellous again, and that in short time.'[3]

In point of fact, Sir John Paston, when he wrote these words, had already heard of the landing of Queen Margaret and her son in the west, so that another conflict was certainly impending. His brother John, recovering from his wounds, but smarting severely in pocket from the cost of his surgery, looked forward to it with a sanguine hope that Edward would be defeated. ' With God's grace,' he writes, ' it shall not be long ere my wrongs and other men's shall be redressed, for

[1] No. 774.   [2] No. 776.   [3] No. 774.

THE PASTON LETTERS

the world was never so like to be ours as it is now. Wherefore I pray you let Lomner not be too busy yet.'[1] The issue, however, did not agree with his expectations. Four days *The battle of Tewkesbury.* later was fought the battle of Tewkesbury,[2] at which Margaret was defeated, and her son, though taken alive, put to death upon the field. Shortly afterwards she herself surrendered as a prisoner, while her chief captain, Somerset, was beheaded by the conqueror. The Lancastrian party was completely crushed ; and before three weeks were over, King Henry himself had ended his days—no doubt he was murdered—within the Tower. Edward, instead of being driven out again, was now seated on the throne more firmly than he had ever been before ; and the Paston brothers had to sue for the king's pardon for the part they had taken in opposing him.

Caister retaken by the Duke of Norfolk. Under these circumstances, it was only natural that the Duke of Norfolk, who had been forced to relinquish his claim to Caister under the government of Henry VI., should endeavour to reassert it against one who was in the eye of the law a rebel. On this occasion, however, the duke had recourse to stratagem, and one of his servants suddenly obtained possession of the place on Sunday, the 23rd June.[3] It is remarkable that we have no direct reference in the letters either to this event, or to the previous reinstatement of Sir John Paston during the restoration of Henry VI. ; but a statement in the itinerary of William Worcester and Sir John Paston's petition to the king in 1475[4] leave no doubt about the facts. After about six months of possession the Pastons were again driven out of Caister.[5]

The Pastons had need of friends, and offers of friendship

[1] No. 776.
[2] In connection with this battle, we have in No. 777 lists of the principal persons killed and beheaded after the fight, and of the knights made by King Edward upon the field. This document has never been published before.
[3] W. Worc. *Itin.*, 368.   [4] No. 879.
[5] Although the fact of this expulsion could not be gathered from the letters of this date, some allusion to it will be found in Letter 778, by which it seems that a horse of John Paston's had been left at Caister, which the family endeavoured to reclaim by pretending that it was his brother Edmund's. John Paston, however, seems to have preferred that the duke's men should keep the animal, in the hope that they would make other concessions of greater value.

INTRODUCTION

were made to them by Earl Rivers, formerly Lord Scales. *Earl Rivers offers his friendship.* The engagement of Sir John Paston to Rivers's kinswoman, Anne Haute,[1] still held ; and though there was some talk of breaking it off, the earl was willing to do what lay in his power in behalf both of Sir John and of his brother. The latter was not very grateful for his offer, considering, apparently, that the earl's influence with the king was not what it had been. ' Lord Scales,' he said, for so he continued to call him, ' may do least with the great master. But he would depart over the sea as hastily as he may ; and because he weeneth that I would go with him, as I had promised him ever, if he had kept forth his journey at that time, this is the cause that he will be my good lord, and help to get my pardon. The king is not best pleased with him, for that he desireth to depart ; insomuch that the king hath said of him that whenever he hath most to do, then the Lord Scales will soonest ask leave to depart, and weeneth that it is most because of cowardice.'[2]

Earl Rivers, in fact, was at this time meditating a voyage to Portugal, where he meant to go in an expedition against the Saracens, and he actually embarked on Christmas Eve following.[3] His friendship, perhaps, may have been unduly depreciated by the younger brother ; for within twelve days John Paston actually obtained the king's signature to a warrant for his pardon. This, it is true, may have been procured without his mediation ; but in any case the family were not in the position of persons for whom no one would intercede. They had still so much influence in the world that within three months after he had been a second time dispossessed of Caister, Sir John made a serious effort to

[1] A transcript of an old pedigree with which I was favoured by Mr. J. R. Scott during the publication of these letters long ago, confirmed my conjecture that Anne Haute was the daughter of William Haute, whose marriage with Joan, daughter of Sir Richard Woodville, is referred to in the *Excerpta Historica*, p. 249. She was, therefore, the niece of Richard, Earl Rivers, and cousin-german to Edward IV.'s queen. It appears also that she had a sister named Alice, who was married to Sir John Fogge of Ashford, Treasurer of the Household to Edward IV. This Sir John Fogge was the man whom Richard III., having previously regarded him as a deadly enemy, sent for out of sanctuary, and took publicly by the hand at his accession, in token that he had forgotten all old grudges.
[2] No. 778.   [3] Nos. 793, 795.

THE PASTON LETTERS

INTRODUCTION

Sir J. Paston petitions the Duke of Norfolk to give back Caister.

ascertain whether the Duke of Norfolk might not be induced to let him have it back again. This he did, as was only natural, through the medium of his brother John, whose former services in the duke's household gave him a claim to be heard in a matter touching the personal interests of the family. John Paston, however, wisely addressed himself, on this subject, rather to the duchess than to the duke; and though he received but a slender amount of encouragement, it was enough, for a few months, just to keep his hopes alive. 'I cannot yet,' he writes, 'make my peace with my lord of Norfolk by no means, yet every man telleth me that my lady sayeth passing well of me always notwithstanding.' This was written in the beginning of the year 1472, just seven months after Sir John's second expulsion from Caister. But the Pastons continued their suit for four years more, and only recovered possession of the place on the Duke of Norfolk's death, as we shall see hereafter.[1]

The Paston Brothers

Royal pardon to John Paston.

John Paston obtained a 'bill of pardon' signed by the king, on Wednesday the 17th July. This, however, was not in itself a pardon, but only a warrant to the Chancellor to give him one under the Great Seal. The pardon with the Great Seal attached he hoped to obtain from the Chancellor on the following Friday. Meanwhile he wrote home to his mother to let no one know of it but Lady Calthorpe, who, for some reason not explained, seems to have been a confidante in this particular matter.[2] Perhaps this was as well, for as a matter of fact the pardon was not sealed that Friday, nor for many a long week, and even for some months after. It seems to have been promised, but it did not come. At Norwich some one called John Paston traitor and sought to pick quarrels with him; and how far he could rely upon the protection of the law was a question not free from anxiety. His brother, Sir John, urged him to take steps to have the pardon made sure

[1] Nos. 781, 796, 802.   [2] No. 780.

without delay; but it was only passed at length upon the 7th of February following, nearly seven months after the king had signed the bill for it. His brother, Sir John, obtained one on the 21st December.[1]

But John Paston stood in another danger, from which even a royal pardon could not by law protect him. The 'appeal'[2] of the two widows still lay against him. The blood of their husbands cried for vengeance on the men who had defended Caister, and especially upon the captain of the garrison. Their appeal, however, was suspected to proceed from the instigation of others who would fain have encouraged them to keep it up longer than they cared to do themselves. Sir John Paston had information from some quarter which led him to believe that they had both found husbands again, and he recommended his brother to make inquiry, as in that case the appeals were abated. With regard to one of them, the intelligence turned out to be correct. A friend whom John Paston asked to go and converse with this woman, the widow of a fuller of South Walsham, reported that she was now married to one Tom Steward, dwelling in the parish of St. Giles in Norwich. She confessed to him that she never sued the appeal of her own accord, 'but that she was by subtle craft brought to the New Inn at Norwich. And there was Master Southwell; and he entreated her to be my lord's widow[3] by the space of an whole year next following; and thereto he made her to be bound in an obligation. And when that year was past he desired her to be my lord's widow another year. And then she said that she had liever lose that that she had done than to lose that and more; and therefore she said plainly that she would no more of that matter; and so she took her an husband, which is the said Tom Steward. And she saith that it was full sore against her will that ever the matter went so far forth, for she had never none avail thereof, but it was sued to her great labor and loss, for she had never of my lord's council but barely her costs to London.'[4]

The appeal of the widows.

[1] Nos. 780, 781, 795.   [2] See p. 257, note 3.
[3] The widow of a lord's vassal was called the lord's widow, and could only marry again by his leave.   [4] Nos. 782, 783.

THE PASTON LETTERS

INTRODUCTION

The other widow, however, had not married again as Sir John had imagined. With her the right of appeal still remained, and she was induced to exercise it. In this she seems to have been encouraged by the Duke of Norfolk, simply for the sake of giving trouble to Sir John Paston; for though it was his brother and the men with him who were the most direct cause of her husband's death, the appeal was not prosecuted against them, but against him only. In the following January the widow went up to London, and 100 shillings were given her to sue with. What came of the affair then we have no further record. Sir John Paston was warned of his danger both by his mother and by his brother; so perhaps he found the means to induce her to forbear proceeding further. An argument that has often enough stopped the course of justice would doubtless have been efficacious to put an end to such a purely vexatious prosecution. But it may be that the case was actually heard, and Sir John Paston acquitted.[1]

Great mortality.

In a social point of view the year of Edward IV.'s restoration was not one of gladness. The internal peace of the kingdom was secured by the two sharp battles of Barnet and Tewkesbury, and by the execution of the Bastard Falconbridge after his attempt on London, but the land was visited with pestilence and the mortality was severe. Hosts of pilgrims travelled through the country, eager to escape the prevailing infection or to return thanks for their recovery from illness. The king and queen went on pilgrimage to Canterbury; and never, it was said, had there been so many pilgrims at a time.[2] 'It is the most universal death that ever I wist in England,' says Sir John Paston; 'for by my truth I cannot hear by pilgrims that pass the country that any borough town in England is free from that sickness. God cease it when it pleaseth Him! Wherefore, for God's sake let my mother take heed to my young brethren, that they be in none place where that sickness is reigning, nor that they disport not with none other young people which resorteth where any sickness is; and if there be any of that sickness dead or infect in Norwich, for God's sake let her send them to some friends

[1] Nos. 796, 797.   [2] No. 782.

of hers into the country, and do ye the same by mine advice. Let my mother rather remove her household into the country.'[1]

The plague continued on till the beginning of winter. Margaret Paston does not seem to have removed into the country, but in writing to her son John in the beginning of November she notes the progress of the enemy. 'Your cousin Berney of Witchingham is passed to God, whom God assoyle! Veyl's wife, and London's wife, and Picard the baker of Tombland, be gone also. All this household and this parish is as ye left it, blessed be God! We live in fear, but we wot not whither to flee for to be better than we be here.'[2] In the same letter Margaret Paston speaks of other troubles. She had been obliged to borrow money for her son Sir John, and it was demanded. The fortunes of the family were at a low ebb, and she knew not what to do without selling her woods—a thing which would seriously impair the value of Sir John's succession to her estates, as there were so many wood sales then in Norfolk that no man was likely to give much more than within a hundred marks of their real value. She therefore urged Sir John in his own interest to consider what he could do to meet the difficulty. Already she had done much for him, and was not a little ashamed that it was known she had not reserved the means of paying the debts she had incurred for him. Sir John, however, returned for answer that he was utterly unable to make any shift for the money, and Margaret saw nothing for it but the humiliation of selling wood or land, or even furniture, to meet the emergency. 'It is a death to me to think upon it,' she wrote. She felt strongly that her son had not the art of managing with economy—that he spent double the money on his affairs that his father had done in matters of the same character, and, what grieved her even more, that duties which filial pride ought to have piously discharged long ago had been neglected owing to his extravagance. 'At the reverence of God,' she writes to his younger brother John, 'advise him yet to beware of his expenses and guiding, that it be no shame to us all. It is a

Money matters.

[1] No. 781.   [2] No. 787.

John Paston's gravestone.

shame and a thing that is much spoken of in this country that your father's gravestone is not made. For God's love, let it be remembered and purveyed in haste. There hath been much more spent in waste than should have made that.' Apparently direct remonstrances had failed to tell upon Sir John otherwise than to make him peevish and crusty. She therefore wrote to his younger brother instead. 'Me thinketh by your brother that he is weary to write to me, and therefore I will not accumber him with writing to him. Ye may tell him as I write to you.'[1]

Sir John Paston and Anne Haute.

Thriftless, extravagant, and irresolute, Sir John Paston was not the man to succeed, either in money matters or in anything else. No wonder, then, that his engagement with Anne Haute became unsatisfactory, apparently to both parties alike. The manner in which he speaks of it at this time is indeed ambiguous; but there can be no doubt that in the end both parties desired to be released, and were for a long time only restrained by the cost of a dispensation, which was necessary to dissolve even such a contract as theirs. It would not have been surprising, indeed, if on the restoration of Edward IV. Lord Rivers and the queen's relations had shown themselves unfavourable to a match between their kinswoman and one who had fought against the king at Barnet. But whether this was the case or not we have no positive evidence to show. Only we know that in the course of this year the issue of the matter was regarded as uncertain. In September Sir John Paston writes that he had almost spoken with Mrs. Anne Haute, but had not done so. 'Nevertheless,' he says, 'this next term I hope to take one way with her or other. She is agreed to speak with me and she hopeth to do me ease, as she saith.'[2]

A.D. 1471, Oct.

Six weeks later, in the end of October, the state of matters

---

[1] Nos. 787, 791. In justice to Sir John Paston it should be mentioned that he had been making inquiries two months before as to the dimensions of the space over his father's grave at Bromholm available for a monument.—See No. 782. More than five years, however, had elapsed since his father's death, and even two years after this the tomb was not attended to, as we find by repeated comments on the subject.—See Nos. 843 and 878. This last letter has been accidentally misplaced, and is really of the year 1472, as will be shown hereafter. [2] No. 781.

is reported, not by Sir John Paston but by his brother. 'As for Mrs. A. Haulte, the matter is moved by divers of the queen's council, and of fear by R. Haulte; but he would it should be first of our motion, and we would it should come of them first—our matter should be the better.'[1] In February [A.D. 1472, Feb.] following Sir John was admitted to another interview with the lady, but was unable to bring the matter to a decisive issue. 'I have spoken,' he says, 'with Mrs. Anne Haulte at a pretty leisure, and, blessed be God, we be as far forth as we were tofore, and so I hope we shall continue. And I promised her that at the next leisure that I could find thereto, that I would come again and see her, which will take a leisure, as I deem now. Since this observance is overdone, I purpose not to tempt God no more so.'[2]

A year later, in April 1473, he says that if he had had six days more leisure, he 'would have hoped to have been delivered of Mrs. Anne Haulte. Her friends, the queen, and Atcliff,' he writes, 'agreed to common and conclude with me, if I can find the mean to discharge her conscience, which I trust to God to do.'[3] But the discharge of her conscience required an application to the Court of Rome, and this involved a very unsentimental question of fees. 'I have answer again from Rome,' he writes in November following, 'that there is the well of grace and salve sufficient for such a sore, and that I may be dispensed with; nevertheless my proctor there asketh a thousand ducats, as he deemeth. But Master Lacy, another Rome runner here, which knoweth my said proctor there, as he saith, as well as Bernard knew his shield, sayeth that he meaneth but an hundred ducats, or two hundred ducats at the most; wherefore after this cometh more. He wrote to me also *quod Papa hoc facit hodiernis diebus multociens* (that the Pope does this nowadays very frequently).'[4]

Here we lose for a while nearly all further trace of the matter. Nothing more seems to have been done in it for a long time; for about fourteen months later we find Sir John Paston's mother still wishing he were 'delivered of Mrs.

---

[1] No. 784. [2] No. 798. [3] No. 831. [4] No. 842.

Anne Haulte,'[1] and this is all we hear about it until after an interval of two years more, when, in February 1477, Sir John reports that the matter between him and Mrs. Anne Haulte had been 'sore broken' to Cardinal Bourchier, the Lord Chamberlain (Hastings), and himself, and that he was 'in good hope.'[2] Finally, in August following, he expects that it 'shall, with God's grace, this term be at a perfect end.'[3] After this we hear nothing more of it. The pre-contract between Sir John and Anne Haulte seems therefore to have been at last annulled; and what is more remarkable, after it had been so, he was reported to be so influential at Court that another marriage was offered him 'right nigh of the Queen's blood.'[4] His mother, who writes to him on the subject in May 1478, had not been informed who the lady was, and neither can we tell the reader. We only know for certain that such a marriage never took effect.

John Paston's love affairs.

John Paston, too, had his love affairs as well as his brother, but was more fortunate in not being bound helplessly to one lady for a long series of years. In the summer of 1471, he seems to have been endeavouring to win the hand of a certain Lady Elizabeth Bourchier; but here he did not prosper, for she was married a few months later to Lord Thomas Howard—the nobleman who more than forty years after was created Duke of Norfolk by King Henry VIII. for his victory over the Scots at Flodden.[5] As to his further proceedings in

---

[1] No. 863. Some months before the time when he himself expressed that hope of being delivered from his engagement, I meet with a passage of rather doubtful meaning in a letter to Sir John Paston from his brother. There is a lady in the case, but the lady is not named. John Paston has delivered to her a ring which he had much difficulty in inducing her to take. But he promises that Sir John shall be her true knight, and she in return promises to be more at his commandment than any knight's in England, 'my lord' excepted. 'And that ye shall well understand' (so John Paston reports the message) 'if ye have aught to do wherein she may be an helper; for there was never knight did so much cost on her as ye have done.' (No. 817.) Is this anonymous lady Anne Haulte once more? Was the ring an engagement returned? And did they thus break off relations with each other, retaining mutual esteem? Let us hope this is the explanation, which indeed I should even think probable, but that the lady must have been at this time residing in the county of Norfolk, and I have no notice of Anne Haulte having been there at any time.
[2] No. 900. [3] No. 916. [4] No. 933. [5] Nos. 781, 800.

search of a wife, we shall have occasion to speak of them hereafter.

A.D. 1472. The Dukes of Clarence and Gloucester.

Property was at all times a matter of more importance than love to that selfish generation; it was plainly, avowedly regarded by every one as the principal point in marrying. In the royal family at this very time, the design of Richard, Duke of Gloucester, to marry the widow of Edward, Prince of Wales, awoke the jealousy of Clarence. For the lady was a younger sister of Clarence's own wife, and co-heir to her father, Warwick the Kingmaker; and since the death of that great earl at Barnet, Clarence seems to have pounced on the whole of his immense domains without the slightest regard even to the rights of his widow, who, indeed, was now in disgrace, and was living in sanctuary at Beaulieu. The idea of being compelled to share the property with his brother was a thing that had never occurred to him, and he could not endure the thought. He endeavoured to prevent the proposed marriage by concealing the lady in London.[1] Disputes arose between the two brothers in consequence, and though they went to Sheen together to pardon, it was truly suspected to be 'not all in charity.' The king endeavoured to act as mediator, and entreated Clarence to show a fair amount of consideration to his brother; but his efforts met with very little success. 'As it is said,' writes Sir John Paston, 'he answereth that he may well have my lady his sister-in-law, but they shall part no livelode,'—the elder sister was to have all the inheritance, and the younger sister nothing! No wonder the writer adds, 'So what will fall can I not say.'[2] What did fall, however, we know partly from the Paston Letters and partly from other sources. The Duke of Gloucester married the lady in spite of his brother's threats. The dispute about the property raged violently more than two years, and almost defied the king's efforts to keep his two brothers in subjection. In November 1473 we find it 'said for certain that the Duke of Clarence maketh him big in that he can, showing as he would but deal with the Duke of Gloucester; but the king intendeth, in eschewing all incon-

---

[1] *Contin. Chron. of Croyland*, 557. [2] No. 798.

THE PASTON LETTERS

venients, to be as big as they both, and to be a styffeler atween them. And some men think that under this there should be some other thing intended, and some treason conspired.' Sir John Paston again did not know what to make of it, and was driven to reiterate his former remark, 'So what shall fall can I not say.'[1] He only hoped the two brothers would yet be brought into agreement by the king's award.[2]

This hope was ultimately realised. Clarence at last consented with an ill will to let his sister-in-law have a share in her father's lands; and an arrangement was made by a special Act of Parliament for the division of the property.[3] To satisfy the rapacity of the royal brothers, the claims of the Countess of Warwick were deliberately set aside, and the Act expressly treated her as if she had been a dead woman. So the matter was finally settled in May 1474. Yet possibly the Countess's claims had some influence in hastening this settlement; for about a twelvemonth before she had been removed from her sanctuary at Beaulieu[4] and conveyed northwards by Sir James Tyrell. This, it appears, was not done avowedly by the king's command; nevertheless rumour said that it was by his assent, and also that it was contrary to the will of Clarence.[5]

Even so in the Paston family love affairs give place at this time to questions about property, in which their interests were very seriously at stake. Not only was there the great question between Sir John and the Duke of Norfolk about Caister, but there was also a minor question about the manor of Saxthorpe, the particulars of which are not very clear. On the 12th July 1471, Sir John Paston made a release of Saxthorpe and Titchwell and some other portions of the Fastolf estates, to David Husband and William Gyfford;[6] but this was probably only in the nature of a trust, for it appears that he did not intend A.D. 1472, to give up his interest in the property. In January following, ing, however, William Gurney entered into Saxthorpe and

---

[1] No. 841.   [2] No. 842.   [3] *Rolls of Parl.* vi. 100.
[4] 'Beweley Seyntwarye' in Fenn; but the reading is '*Beverley* sanctuary' in the right-hand version. Which is correct?   [5] No. 834.   [6] No. 779.

INTRODUCTION

endeavoured to hold a court there for the lord of the manor. But John Paston hearing of what was doing, went thither accompanied by one man only to protect his brother's interest, and charged the tenants, in the presence of Gurney himself and a number of his friends, to proceed no further. The protest was effective so far as to produce a momentary pause. But when it was seen that he had only one man with him, the proceedings were resumed; on which John Paston sat down by the steward and blotted his book with his finger as he wrote, and then called the tenants to witness that he had effectually interrupted the court in his brother's right.[1] Gurney, however, did not give up the game, but warned another court to be kept on Holy Rood day (May 3rd, the Invention of the Holy Cross), when he would have collected the half-year's rents from the tenants. The court was held, but before it was half over John Paston appeared again and persuaded him to stay proceedings once more, and to forbear gathering money until he and Sir John Paston should confer together in London. It seems to have required some tact and courtesy to get him to consent to this arrangement; for Henry Heydon, the son of the old ally of Sir Thomas Tuddenham, had raised a number of men-at-arms to give Gurney any assistance that might have been necessary, but the gentle demeanour of John Paston left him no pretext for calling in such aid.[2]

The real claimant of the manor against Sir John Paston was Waynflete, Bishop of Winchester, of whom, almost immediately after this, Henry Heydon bought both Saxthorpe and Titchwell. Sir John Paston, apparently, had been caught napping as usual, and knew nothing of the transaction. His mother wrote to him in dismay on the 5th June. Young Heydon had already taken possession. 'We beat the bushes,' said Margaret Paston, 'and have the loss and the disworship, and other men have the birds. My lord hath false counsel and simple that adviseth him thereto. And, as it is told me, Guton is like to go the same way in haste. And as for Hellesdon and Drayton, I trow it is there it shall be. What shall fall of the remnant God knoweth,—I trow as evil or worse.'[3]

Marginal notes: John Paston interrupts the Manor Court at Saxthorpe.

---

[1] No. 796.   [2] No. 801.   [3] No. 803.

THE PASTON LETTERS

John Paston in like manner writes on the same day that Heydon was sure of Saxthorpe, and Lady Boleyn of Guton.[1] Sir John Paston was letting the family property slip out of his fingers, while on the other hand he was running into debt, and in his straitened circumstances he was considering what he could sell. His mother had threatened if he parted with any of his lands to disinherit him of double the amount;[2] so he was looking out for a purchaser of his wood at Sporle, which he was proposing to cut down.[3] But by far the most serious matter of all was Caister; 'if we lose that,' said Margaret Paston, 'we lose the fairest flower of our garland.' To her, too, it would be peculiarly annoying, for she expected to have little comfort in her own family mansion at Mautby, if the Duke of Norfolk had possession of Caister only three miles off.[4] On this subject, however, Sir John Paston does not appear to have been remiss. It was the first thing that occupied his thoughts after he had secured his pardon. In the beginning of the year he had been with Archbishop Nevill, who, though he had been in disgrace and committed to the Tower just after the battle of Barnet, seems at this time again to have had some influence in the world, at his residence called the Moor. By the archbishop's means apparently he had received his pardon, and had spent a merrier Christmas in consequence; and he wrote to his mother that if he could have got any assurance of having Caister restored to him, he would have come away at once.[5] But it was not long before the archbishop again got into trouble. He was once more conducted to the Tower, and two days afterwards at midnight he was put on board a ship and conveyed out to sea.[6] Nothing more therefore was to be hoped for from the archbishop's friendship; but Sir John Paston did not cease to use what means lay in his power. His brother made incessant applications on his behalf to the Duchess of Norfolk, and to the duke's council at Framlingham. To be reinstated Sir John was willing to

Marginal note: Sir John Paston seeks to get Caister restored to him.

---

[1] No. 804.   [2] No. 802.
[3] Nos. 798, 804, 819, 820.—No. 819 is a little out of its place, the exact date of the letter being the 9th May.   [4] No. 803.
[5] No. 795.   [6] No. 800.

INTRODUCTION

make the duke a present of £40, an offer which the council acknowledged was 'more than reasonable.' If the matter were their own, they gave John Paston to understand, they could easily come to an understanding with him, but my lord was intractable. The duchess herself declined to interfere in the matter until my lord and the council were agreed, and the latter said that when they had mooted it to the duke 'he gave them such an answer that none of them all would tell it.' They suggested, however, that the duke might be swayed by more influential opinions, and that if Sir John could get my Lord Chamberlain Hastings, or some other nobleman of mark, to speak to the duke in his favour, there was great probability that he would attain his object.[1]

A favourable opportunity, however, presented itself shortly afterwards for urging a petition for justice on the duke himself. After ten years or more of married life the Duchess of Norfolk was at length with child. Duke and duchess received everywhere congratulations from their friends and dependants. Among the rest Sir John Paston offered his to my lady herself, in a vein of banter that seems slightly to have offended her, though not perhaps so much by its grossness, which was excessive, as by the undue familiarity exhibited in such a tone of address.[2] The Duke of Norfolk was going to be with his wife on the occasion of her lying-in, and John Paston, as an old servant of the family, went to give his attendance at Framlingham. It was resolved that the utmost should be made of the opportunity. John Paston drew up a petition in behalf of his brother to present to the duke, while Sir John Paston himself, then in London, obtained letters from the king to both the duke and duchess, and also to their council. The king seems to have been particularly interested in the case, and assured Sir John Paston that if his letters were ineffectual justice should be done in the matter without delay. The letters were despatched by a special messenger, 'a man of worship' in high favour with the king himself. With such powerful influence engaged on his behalf, most probably Sir John did not care to ask for letters from Lord Hastings, which his brother was

Marginal notes: The Duchess of Norfolk.

---

[1] No. 809.   [2] Nos. 812, 813.

THE PASTON LETTERS

even then expecting. But he suggested, if my lady's lying-in should be at Norwich instead of Framlingham, that his mother might obtain admittance to her chamber, and that her persuasions would be of considerable use.[1]

Birth of a daughter. The duchess was confined at Framlingham, and gave birth to a daughter, who received the name of Anne. Waynflete, Bishop of Winchester, came down to christen the child, and he, too, took an opportunity during his brief stay to say a word to my lady about Caister and the claim of Sir John Paston to restitution. But exhortations, royal letters, and all were thrown away upon the Duke of Norfolk. My lady promised secretly to another person to favour Sir John's suit, but the fact of her giving such a promise was not to be communicated to any one else. John Paston was made as uncomfortable as possible by the manner in which his representations were received. 'I let you plainly wit,' he wrote to his brother, 'I am not the man I was, for I was never so rough in my master's conceit as I am now, and that he told me himself before Richard Southwell, Tymperley, Sir W. Brandon, and twenty more; so that they that lowered now laugh upon me.'[2]

Sir John Paston seeks to enter Parliament. But although all arts were unsuccessful to bend the will of the Duke of Norfolk on this subject, Sir John Paston seems to have enjoyed the favour and approval of the duchess in offering himself as a candidate for the borough of Maldon in the Parliament of 1472. His friend James Arblaster wrote a letter to the bailiff of Maldon suggesting the great advantage it would be to the town to have for one of their two burgesses 'such a man of worship and of wit as were towards my said lady,' and advising all her tenants to vote for Sir John Paston, who not only had this great qualification, but also possessed the additional advantage of being in high favour with my Lord Chamberlain Hastings.[3] There was, however, some uncertainty as to the result, and his brother John suggested in writing to him that if he missed being elected for Maldon he might be for some other place. There were a dozen towns in

[1] Nos. 813, 814, 815, 817, 824. See also No. 878, which by a strange inadvertence has been put in the year 1475 instead of 1472. The preliminary note is correct except as to the year. [2] No. 823. [3] No. 808.

INTRODUCTION

England that ought to return members to Parliament which had chosen none, and by the influence of my Lord Chamberlain he might get returned for one of them.[1]

In point of fact, I find that Sir John Paston was not returned for Maldon to the Parliament of 1472; and whether he sat for any other borough I am not certain, though there is an expression in the correspondence a little later that might lead one to suppose so.[2] But that he went up to London we know by a letter dated on the 4th November;[3] and though he went to Calais, and even visited the court of the Duke and Duchess of Burgundy at Ghent early in the following year, when Parliament was no longer sitting, he had returned to London long before it had ended its second session in April 1473.[4] It is also clear that he took a strong interest in its proceedings; but this was only natural. That Parliament was summoned avowedly to provide for the safety of the kingdom. Although the Earl of Warwick was now dead, and Margaret of Anjou a prisoner at Wallingford,[5] and the line of Henry VI. extinct, it was still anticipated that the Earl of Oxford and Fear of others, supported by the power of France, would make a Invasion. descent upon the coast. Commissions of array were issued at various times for defence against apprehended invasion.[6] Information was therefore laid before Parliament of the danger in which the kingdom stood from a confederacy of the king's 'ancient and mortal enemies environing the same,' and a message was sent to the Commons to the effect that the king intended to equip an expedition in resistance of their malice.[7]

[1] No. 809.
[2] His name does not appear in any of the original returns preserved in the Record Office; but they are certainly very imperfect, and some of them are not very legible. The two burgesses returned for Maldon were William Pestell and William Albon. I find, however, that William Paston, probably Sir John's uncle, was returned for Newcastle-under-Lyne. [3] No. 812.
[4] He could scarcely have returned from Calais in time for the opening of that session on the 8th February, as he was at Calais on the 3rd, and says nothing about coming home at that date.—No. 826.
[5] No. 795.
[6] Patent, 7th March, 12 Edw. IV., p. 1, membs. 25 and 26 in dorso; and 10th May, p. 1, m. 13 in dorso.
[7] Even on the 1st June, four months before Parliament met, we find commissions issued to certain masters of ships to take sailors for the army going over sea.—Patent Roll, 12 Edw. IV., p. 1, m. 10 in dorso.

THE PASTON LETTERS

The result was that, in November 1472, the Commons agreed to a levy of 13,000 archers, and voted a tenth for their support, which was to be levied before Candlemas following.[1] An income and property tax was not a permanent institution of our ancestors, but when it came it pressed heavily; so that a demand of two shillings in the pound was not at all unprecedented. A higher tax had been imposed four years before, and also in 1453 by the Parliament of Reading. Still, a sudden demand of two shillings in the pound, to be levied within the next four months, was an uncomfortable thing to meet; and owing either to its unpopularity or the difficulty of arranging the machinery for its collection, it was not put in force within A.D. 1473. the time appointed. But in the following spring, when the Parliament had begun its second session, collectors were named throughout the country, and it was notified that some further demands were to be made upon the national pocket. On the 26th March, John Paston writes that his cousin John Blennerhasset had been appointed collector in Norfolk, and asks his brother Sir John in London to get him excused from serving in 'that thankless office,' as he had not a foot of ground in the county. At the same time the writer expresses the sentiments of himself and his neighbours in language quite sufficiently emphatic: 'I pray God send you the Holy Ghost among you in the Parliament House, and rather the Devil, we say, than ye should grant any more taxes.'[2] Unfortunately, before the Parliament ended its sittings, it granted a whole fifteenth and tenth additional.[3]

Family jars. At this time we find that there was some further unpleasant feeling within the Paston family circle. Margaret Paston had several times expressed her discontent with the thriftless extravagance of her eldest son, and even the second, John, did not stand continually in her good graces. A third brother, Edmund, was now just coming out in life, and as a preparation for it he too had to endure continual reproofs and remonstrances from his mother. Besides these, there were at home three other sons and one daughter, of whom we shall speak hereafter. The young generation apparently was a little too much for the lone widow;

[1] Rolls of Parl. vi. 4. [2] No. 829. [3] Rolls of Parl. vi. 39.

INTRODUCTION

and, finding her elder sons not very satisfactory advisers, she did what lone women are very apt to do under such circumstances—took counsel in matters of the affairs of this life of a confidential priest. In fact, she was a good and pious woman, to whom in her advancing years this world appeared more and more in its true character as a mere preparation for the next. She had now withdrawn from city life at Norwich, and was dwelling on her own family estate at Mautby. Bodily infirmities, perhaps—though we hear nothing explicitly said of them—made it somewhat less easy for her to move about; and she desired to obtain a licence from the Bishop of Norwich to have the sacrament in her own chapel.[1] She was also thinking, we know, of getting her fourth son Walter educated for the priesthood; and she wished her own spiritual adviser, Sir James Gloys,[2] to conduct him to Oxford, and see him put in the right way to pursue his studies creditably. She hoped, she said, to have more joy of him than of his elder brothers; and though she desired him to be a priest, she wished him not to take any orders that should be binding until he had reached the age of four-and-twenty. 'I will love him better,' she said, 'to be a good secular man than a lewd priest.'[3]

Sir James Gloys. But the influence of this spiritual adviser over their mother was by no means agreeable to the two eldest sons. John Paston speaks of him in a letter to his brother as 'the proud, peevish, and ill-disposed priest to us all,' and complains grievously of his interference in family affairs. 'Many quarrels,' he writes, 'are picked to get my brother Edmund and me out of her house. We go not to bed unchidden lightly; all that we do is ill done, and all that Sir James and Pecock doth is well done. Sir James and I be twain. We

[1] No. 821. She repeats the request more than two years later, and desires that if it cannot be obtained of the Bishop of Norwich, John Paston should endeavour to get it of the Archbishop of Canterbury, 'for that,' she says, 'is the most sure for all places.'—No. 866.
[2] We ought, perhaps, to have explained before that the prefix 'Sir' before a priest's name, as in Sir James Gloys and Sir Thomas Howes, was commonly used as equivalent to 'Reverend,' though strictly speaking it was applied to one who had taken no higher degree than bachelor.
[3] No. 825. Even so Erasmus says of More (Epp. lib. x. 30, col. 536). 'Maluit maritus esse castus quam sacerdos impurus.' The sentiment evidently was a very common one.

fell out before my mother with "Thou proud priest," and "Thou proud squire," my mother taking his part; so I have almost beshut the bolt as for my mother's house; yet summer shall be done or I get me any master.'[1] John Paston, in fact, was obliged to put up with it for some months longer, and though he afterwards reports that Sir James was always 'chopping at him,' and seeking to irritate him in his mother's presence, he had found out that it was not altogether the best policy to rail at him in return. So he learned to smile a little at the most severe speeches, and remark quietly, 'It is good hearing of these old tales.'[2] This mode of meeting the attack, if it did not soften Sir James's bitterness, may have made Margaret Paston less willing to take his part against her son. At all events we hear no more of these encounters. Sir James Gloys, however, died about twelve months later.[3]

Taxation, Private Affairs, and the French War

The impatience of taxation expressed by John Paston and others may perhaps be interpreted as showing that little was generally known, or at all events believed, of any such serious danger to the kingdom from outward enemies as had been represented to Parliament. Nevertheless, in March 1473, John Paston speaks of 'a few Frenchmen whirling on the coasts,' for fear of whom the fishermen did not venture to leave port without safe conducts.[4] A political prophet named Hogan also foretold that some attempt would shortly be made to invade the kingdom or to create trouble within it. But the French ships soon returned home, and Hogan's words were not greatly esteemed, though he was arrested and sent up to London for uttering them. He had, in fact, prophesied similar things before. Yet there was an impression in some quarters that he might be right on this occasion. He was committed to the Tower, and he desired leave to speak to the king, but Edward declined to give him any occasion for boasting that his warnings had been listened to. Ere long,

Hogan's prophecies.

[1] No. 805.   [2] No. 810.   [3] No. 842.   [4] No. 828.

280

however, his story was to some extent justified. News came that on Saturday, the 10th April, the Earl of Oxford had been at Dieppe with twelve ships, about to sail for Scotland. A man was examined in London, who gave information that large sums of money had been sent him from England, and that a hundred gentlemen in Norfolk and Suffolk had agreed to assist him if he should attempt a landing. On the 28th May he actually did land at St. Osith's, in Essex, but hearing that the Earl of Essex with the Lords Dynham and Durasse were coming to oppose him, he returned to his ships and sailed away. His attempt, however, saved Hogan his head, and gained him greater esteem as a prophet; for he had foretold 'that this trouble should begin in May, and that the king should northwards, and that the Scots should make us work and him battle.' People began everywhere to buy armour, expecting they knew not what.[1]

Sir John Paston, for his part, during his visit to the Burgundian court in the end of January,[2] had already ordered a complete suit of armour for himself, together with some horse armour, of Martin Rondelle, the armourer of the Bastard of Burgundy.[3] But the demand for armour increased as the year went on. The Earl of Oxford again suddenly appeared, *The Earl* this time on the coast of Cornwall, and took possession of *of Oxford* St. Michael's Mount on the last day of September. He was *at St.* besieged there by Sir Henry Bodrugan, but the place was so *Mount.* strong that, if properly victualled, twenty men could keep it against the world. The earl's men, however, parleyed with Sir Henry, who by some gross negligence allowed victuals to be conveyed into the Mount. The command of the besieging force was taken from him by the king and given to Richard Fortescue, sheriff of Cornwall.[4] At the same time the quarrel between the Dukes of Clarence and Gloucester contributed to make people uneasy. The world, as Sir John Paston phrased it, seemed 'queasy.' Every man about the king sent for his 'harness.' The king himself sent for the Great Seal, which

[1] Nos. 829, 830, 831, 833, 834.
[2] He was at Ghent on Thursday, 28th January.—No. 826.   [3] No. 838.
[4] Warkworth's *Chronicle*, 26-7.

281

was conveyed to him by Dr. Morton, Master of the Rolls. Some expected that he would make a new Chancellor, some that he would keep the Seal in his own hands as he had done during former commotions.[1]

The Earl of Oxford was fast shut up in the Mount. But during November he made a sally, took a gentleman prisoner, and dragged him within. Shortly afterwards, attempting to give more trouble to the besiegers, he was wounded in the face with an arrow.[2] But his gallant defence seems to have awakened sympathy in the West Country; for on the 10th December the king found it necessary to issue a proclamation against bearing arms in Devonshire.[3] However, after keeping possession of the place for four months and a half, he felt himself compelled to surrender, not by lack of victuals, but for want of reliance on his own men, to whom the king had offered pardons and rewards for deserting him. The earl himself was constrained to sue for pardon of his own life, and yielded himself a prisoner on the 15th February 1474.[4]

Projected royal expedition against France.

Meanwhile people were looking forward to a royal expedition against France. It was for this the 13,000 archers were to be raised, and it was agreed in Parliament that if the expedition did not take place before Michaelmas 1474, the money collected for the purpose should be repaid. As the time drew near, however, it was found impossible to carry out the project quite so soon. The tenth voted in November 1472 had been assessed by the commissioners before February 1473 over all the kingdom, except five northern shires and one or two separate hundreds and wapentakes. But the total amount of the assessment had only produced £31,410 : 14 : 1½, a sum which to the modern reader will appear inconceivably small as the proceeds of a ten per cent. income and property tax for nearly the whole of England. It was in fact not sufficient for the purpose intended; even such a tax, strange to say, could not maintain 13,000 archers; and the Commons, as we have already said, voted one-tenth and one-fifteenth additional. This impost, however, was not immediately levied. On the 26th

[1] No. 841.   [2] No. 843.   [3] *Close Roll*, 13 Edw. IV., m. 8.
[4] No. 846. Warkworth, 27.

282

March 1473 a truce was made at Brussels between England and Burgundy on the one side, and France on the other, till the 1st April 1474.[1] After it expired Edward announced to his Parliament that he intended as soon as possible to invade France in person; but as it was not likely that he could do so before Michaelmas following, the time at which the money was to be repaid to the taxpayers, in case of the expedition not taking place, was prolonged to St. John Baptist's Day (24th June) in 1476.[2]

The taxation pinched every one severely. 'The king *A.D. 1474.* goeth so near us in this country,' wrote Margaret Paston, *Effects of* 'both to poor and rich, that I wot not how we shall live but if *severe* the world amend.' The two taxes came so close upon each *taxation.* other that they had to be paid at one and the same time.[3] And to those who, like Sir John Paston, were in debt and trying to raise money for other purposes, the hardship was extreme. So many were selling corn and cattle that very little was to be realised in that way. Wheat was but 2s. 4d. a comb, and malt and oats but tenpence. During the year 1473 Sir John had applied in vain to his mother for a loan of £100 to redeem the manor of Sporle, which he had been obliged to mortgage. He had already been driven to sell a portion of the wood, and had thoughts of giving a seven years' lease of the manor to a neighbour of the name of Cocket, on receiving six years' rent in ready money.[4] But in 1474, having received £100 from the executors of Lyhart, Bishop of Norwich, in satisfaction of some old claim, his mother consented to lend another sum of like amount, which would enable him, with a very little further help from some other quarter, to meet the demands of Townsend the mortgagee.[5] In the end, however, a sum of £142 : 13 : 4 was advanced by his uncle William, and some other moneys by Margaret Paston, partly on the security of her own plate, and partly on that of Sir John Paston's lands in the hundred of Flegg.[6]

[1] No. 832. It is curious that we have no notice of this truce in Rymer.
[2] *Rolls of Parl.* vi. 113-14.
[3] No. 871. 'William Pecock shall send you a bill what he hath paid for you for two tasks (*taxes*) at this time.' Margaret Paston to Sir John, 23rd May 1475.
[4] Nos. 828, 831, 842, 865.   [5] No. 856.   [6] No. 865.

283

THE PASTON LETTERS

Arrange-
ment with
Bishop
Waynflete.
The
college at
Caister
abandoned.

About the same time Sir John came to an understanding with Bishop Waynflete about the lands of Sir John Fastolf; and the bishop having obtained a dispensation from the Pope enabling him to apply the endowments of Fastolf's intended college at Caister to the support of Magdalen College, Oxford, a division was made of the Norfolk lands between him and Paston. Sir John was allowed to enjoy Caister and the lands in Flegg, if he could recover them from the Duke of Norfolk, with the manor of Hellesdon, Tolthorpe, and certain tenements in Norwich and Earlham; but he gave up Drayton to the bishop. And so terminated one long-standing controversy.[1]

Anne
Paston
engaged to
William
Yelverton.

An event in the family now claims our notice, although the allusions to it are but slight, and the manner in which it is referred to is quite in keeping with that strange absence of domestic feeling which is so painfully characteristic of the times. Anne Paston, Sir John's sister, had come to a marriageable age; and her mother disposed of her hand to William Yelverton, a grandson of the judge, although she had an offer from one of the family of Bedingfield.[2] The engagement had lasted at least a year and a half, when Sir John Paston in London heard news that she had been exceedingly unwell; on which he quietly remarks that he had imagined she was already married. It seems scarcely possible to attribute this ignorance to any unusual detention of letters between Norwich and London; so that we are almost driven to conclude that his sister's marriage was an event of which Sir John did not expect to receive any very special intimation. The news even of her sickness, I suspect from the manner in which he refers to it, was conveyed to him not by letters from home, but by Yelverton, her intended husband, who had come up to London. Nor must it be supposed that Yelverton himself was deeply concerned about her state of health; for it was certainly not with a lover's anxiety that he communicated the intelligence to Sir John. In fact the marriage, so far from being a thing already accomplished, as Sir John supposed, was a matter that still remained uncertain. 'As for Yelverton,'

[1] Nos. 834, 859.　　　　[2] No. 804.

284

INTRODUCTION

writes Sir John himself, 'he said but late that he would have her if she had her money, and else not; wherefore me thinketh that they be not very sure.' Still the old song of 'Property, property,' like Tennyson's 'Northern Farmer.' And how very quietly this cold-hearted brother takes the news that the marriage which he thought already accomplished might very likely never take place at all! 'But among all other things,' he adds, 'I pray you beware that the old love of Pampyng renew not.' What, another sister ready to marry a servant of the family? If she could not have Yelverton, at least let her be preserved from that at all hazards.[1]

Married
to him.

Such was the state of matters in November 1473. And it seems by the course of events that Pampyng was not allowed to follow the example of Richard Calle. Anne Paston remained unmarried for about three and a half years longer, and the family, despairing of Yelverton, sought to match her somewhere else;[2] but between March and June of the year 1477, the marriage with Yelverton actually took place.[3] Of the married life of this couple we have in the Paston Letters no notices whatever; but one incident that occurred in it we learn from another source. Yelverton brought his bride home to his own house at Caister St. Edmund's, three miles from Norwich. Some time after their marriage this house was burned down by the carelessness of a servant girl while they were away at the marriage of a daughter of Sir William Calthorpe. The year of the occurrence is not stated, but must, I think, have been 1480, for it happened on a Tuesday night, the 18th of January, the eve of St. Wolstan's Day.[4] Now the 18th of January did not fall on a Tuesday during their married life in any earlier year, and

[1] Nos. 842, 843.　　　　[2] No. 885.
[3] Margaret Paston speaks of 'my son Yelverton' in June 1477.—No. 913. But Anne appears to have been unmarried at least as late as the 8th March 1477.—See No. 901.
[4] 'Memorandum, quod manerium. . . . Yelverton generosi in villa de Castre Sancti Edmundi, per iii. miliaria de civitate Norwici, in nocte diei Martis, 18 diei Januarii, videlicet in vigilia Sancti Wolstani, dum modo dictus Yelverton, cum filia Johannis Paston senioris, uxore dicti Yelverton, fuerunt ad nupcias filiæ Willelmi Calthorp militis, fuit per negligenciam parvæ puellæ in lectisternio leti (*qu.* lecti ?) per candelam igne consumptum.—W. Worc. *Itin.*, 269.

285

THE PASTON LETTERS

it did not so fall again till 1485, when William Worcester, in whose itinerary the event is recorded, was certainly dead.

John
Paston's
marriage
prospects.

John Paston, too, was seriously thinking of taking a wife; and, that he might not be disappointed in an object of so much importance, he had two strings to his bow. We must not, however, do him the injustice to suppose that he had absolutely no preference at all for one lady over another; for he writes his full mind upon the subject to his brother Sir John in London, whom he commissions to negotiate for him. If Harry Eberton the draper's wife were disposed to 'deal' with him, such was the 'fantasy' he had for Mistress Elizabeth Eberton, her daughter, that he requests his brother not to conclude 'in the other place,' even though old Eberton should not be disposed to give her so much dowry as he might have with the second lady. Nevertheless Sir John is also requested to ascertain 'how the matter at the Black Friars doth; and that ye will see and speak with the thing yourself, and with her father and mother or ye depart; and that it like you to desire John Lee's wife to send me a bill in all haste possible, how far forth the matter is, and whether it shall be necessary for me to come up to London hastily or not, or else to cast all at the cock.'[1] The reader, we trust, is fully impressed with the businesslike character of this diplomacy, and he ought certainly not to be less so with the appropriateness of the language employed. 'If Mrs. Eberton will *deal* with me,' and 'Speak with *the thing* yourself.' How truly does it indicate the fact that young ladies in those days were nothing but mere chattels!

It happened, however, that neither the 'thing' at the Black Friars, nor the lady for whom he had the somewhat greater 'fantasy,' was to be attained. Apparently the former was the daughter of one Stockton, and was married about four months later to a man of the name of Skerne. She herself confidentially told another woman just before her marriage that Master Paston had once come to the place where she was with twenty men, and endeavoured to take her away. As for Eberton's daughter, the matter quietly dropped, but before it

[1] No. 850.

286

INTRODUCTION

was quite broken off John Paston had engaged his brother's services as before in a new matter with the Lady Walgrave. Sir John Paston executed his commission here too with the utmost zeal to promote his brother's suit; but he received little comfort from the lady, and could not prevail upon her to accept John Paston's ring. Indeed she told him plainly she meant to abide by an answer she had already given to John Paston himself, and desired Sir John no more to intercede for him. Sir John, however, had secured possession of a small article belonging to her, a muskball, and told her he meant to send it to his brother, without creating in her any feeling of displeasure. Thus the lover was still left with some slight gleam of hope—if, at least, he cared to indulge it further; but it does not appear by the correspondence that he thought any more either of Lady Walgrave or of Elizabeth Eberton.[1]

John
Paston's
pilgrimage
to Com-
postella.

We have omitted to notice an incident characteristic of the times, which ought not to pass altogether unrecorded. The year before these love passages took place, John Paston took a voyage to Spain on pilgrimage to the shrine of St. James of Compostella. He sailed, or was about to sail, from Yarmouth early in July, for the letters only allude to the voyage when he was on the eve of departure, and he declared his purpose of coming home again by Calais, where his brother expected to see him within a month after he left.[2] It does not appear what prompted this pious expedition, unless it was the prevalence of sickness and epidemics in England. Margaret Paston's cousin, John Berney of Reedham, died in the beginning of that year;[3] and the letter, which first speaks of John Paston's intended pilgrimage, records also the deaths of the Earl of Wiltshire and the Lord Sudley, and mentions a false rumour of the death of Sir William Stanley.[4] The death of Sir James Gloys, Margaret Paston's priest, occurred about four months later; and the same letter in which that event is mentioned says also that Lady Bourchier (I presume John Paston's old flame, though she was now the wife of Thomas Howard) had been nearly dead, but had recovered.[5] It is

[1] Nos. 858, 860.　　　　[2] Nos. 833, 836.　　　　[3] No. 825.
[4] No. 833.　　　　[5] No. 842.

287

evident that the year was one of great mortality, though not perhaps quite so great as that of two years before.

Illness of Sir John Paston. During the autumn of the year following, Sir John Paston had an illness, which probably attacked him in London, and induced him to remove into Norfolk. After a little careful nursing by his mother, his appetite returned, and he felt himself so much stronger that he went back again to London to see to his pecuniary affairs, which required careful nursing as much as he had done himself. His brother Edmund, too, had been ill in London about the same time, but he found him 'well amended'; which was, perhaps, not altogether the case with himself, for during the winter he had a return of fever, with pain in the eyes and in one of his legs, particularly in the heel.[1] Sir John, however, was not the man to make much of a slight indisposition. About Christmas or the New Year he had gone over to Calais; and while his mother was solicitous about the state of his health, he said nothing about it, but wrote that he was going into Flanders, and hoped to get a sight of the siege of Neuss.[2] On receipt of his mother's letter, however, he wrote back that he was perfectly well again, except that the parts affected were still tender.[3]

Siege of Neuss. This siege of Neuss—a town on the Rhine near Düsseldorf—was an undertaking of Charles the Bold, Duke of Burgundy, on which the eyes of the whole world were riveted, and especially of Englishmen. A body of 3000 English took part in the operations.[4] But the work was arduous, and in the end proved ineffectual. Not only was the attempt a failure, but it caused the breakdown of other projects besides. The duke had hoped to be master of the place before the truce with France expired in June 1475, and afterwards to join with Edward in an invasion of that country, in which he was bound by treaty to co-operate. But month after month slipped away, and the Burgundian forces were still detained before Neuss, so that he was unable strictly to fulfil his engagement. His cunning enemy Louis saw his advantage in the circumstance, and contrived to cool Edward's ardour

[1] Nos. 856, 862, 863, 865.   [2] No. 861.
     No. 865.   [4] Comines, Book iv. ch. i.

for the war by arts peculiarly his own. He received with the greatest possible politeness the herald sent by Edward to defy him; asked him to a private conference; told him he was sure his master had not entered on the expedition on his own account, but only to satisfy the clamour of his own people and the Duke of Burgundy. He remarked that the duke, who had not even then returned from Neuss, had lost the flower of his army in the siege, and had occasioned the waste of so much time that the summer was already far spent. He then suggested that the herald might lay these and other considerations before his master to induce him to listen to a peace; and he dismissed him with a handsome present.[1]

The herald did what was expected of him, and the result Edward IV. and Louis XI. told in two ways. Edward's vanity was flattered and his cupidity was excited. The King of France, it seemed, stood in awe of him, and did not wish to fight. He was willing to pay handsomely for peace. How much easier, after all, to accept a large yearly tribute in recognition of his sovereignty over France than to vindicate it by conquering the country! Arguments, too, were not wanting in the shape of private pensions offered by Louis to the Lords of the English Council. Not, of course, that English noblemen regarded these gratuities as bribes—Lord Hastings, at least, stood upon his dignity and refused to give a receipt for money which was but a free-will offering on the one part, and involved no obligation on the other.[2] Still the money was very acceptable, and there was no doubt a great deal of weight in the arguments addressed by Louis to the herald. Indeed, any one worthy to be called a statesman knew quite well that the idea of conquering France was altogether chimerical.

This was true; but it would scarcely have been pleasant news to the nation at large, which had been taxed and taxed again for the sake of that same chimerical idea, to have been informed of what was going on in the king's council-chamber. For not only had a tenth been voted one year, and a tenth and fifteenth another, but the wealthy had been solicited to make still further contributions in a form till now unheard of

[1] Comines, Book iv. ch. v.   [2] Ibid. ch. viii.

Benevolences. —contributions called 'benevolences,' because they were supposed, by a cruel irony, to be offered and given with good will.[1] For the nation was quite sufficiently aware—there were many then alive who could testify it from past experience—that it was a difficult and costly business to make any conquests in France; and everybody had been pricked and goaded to furnish what he could towards the equipment of the expedition out of his own resources.

Peace with France. Sir John Paston's brothers, John[2] and Edmund,[3] and probably another named Clement, of whom we have very little notice in the correspondence, went over in the king's great army to Calais. Sir John himself had been in Calais for some time before, and his mother commended his younger brothers to his care, urging him to give them the benefit of his advice and experience for their safety, as some of them were but young soldiers.[4] Margaret Paston need not have been so anxious if she had been in the secrets of the Cabinet. No blood was drawn in that campaign. The army had crossed the sea in the end of June, and peace was already made in the end of August. Nominally, indeed, it was but a seven years' truce, but it was intended to be lasting. For a payment of 75,000 crowns in ready money, a pension of 50,000 crowns a year, and an undertaking that the Dauphin should hereafter marry Edward's eldest daughter, and that Louis should give her a dowry of 60,000 livres a year, the king consented to withdraw his forces and trouble France no longer with his claims.[5]

Was it a triumph or a humiliation? an easy victory of Edward over Louis, or of Louis over Edward? The thing

[1] Contin. Chron. Croyl. p. 558. The king, as is well known, went about soliciting contributions personally. During the year 1474, as appears by his Privy Seal dates, he visited Leicester, Nottingham, Derby, Coventry, Guildford, Farnham, Kenilworth, Worcester, Gloucester, Bristol, and Cirencester, in different excursions, returning to London in November; after which he again set out, going this time into Suffolk. He was at Bury on the 5th and 7th December, and at West Thorpe, on the northern confines of the county, on the 8th. From this it appears (though the Privy Seal dates do not show it) that he must have gone on to Norwich. After which we find him at Coventry on the 26th, so that he probably spent his Christmas there. That he visited Norwich about that time, and solicited benevolences there, is evident from Letter 863.
[2] Nos. 868, 876.   [3] No. 873.   [4] No. 871.   [5] Rymer, xii. 14-21.

might be, and was, looked at from different points of view. The English considered that they had forced France to pay tribute; the French king chuckled at having made Edward his pensioner. Louis, doubtless, had the best of the bargain, for he had managed to sow division between England and Burgundy, and to ward off a very serious danger from France. But common-place, dull-witted Englishmen saw the thing in a different light, and Sir John Paston gave thanks to God when he reported that the king's 'voyage' was finished and his host returned to Calais.[1]

Sir John, however, was the worse of his abode in Sir John Paston ill again. Calais air.[2] He had felt himself strong and vigorous when upon the march, but on the return of the army to Calais he was again taken ill in eight days. We may, perhaps, suspect that it was another outbreak of his old disease, and that he never allowed himself sufficient rest to make a perfect recovery. But it may be that from the general neglect of proper sanitary arrangements, pestilence was still rife both in Calais and in England. Six weeks later his brother John at Norwich was also much troubled with sickness.[3]

Sir John Paston and Caister

When Sir John Paston returned to England, the first thing William Paston. that he had to consider was how to meet a debt to his uncle William which was due at Michaelmas.[4] William Paston is a member of the family of whom we totally lose sight for many years after the very beginning of Edward's reign; but his pecuniary relations with his nephew about this time cause him again to be spoken of and to take part in the correspondence.[5] He was, doubtless, a rich man, although we find him pledging some of his plate to Elizabeth Clere of Ormesby.[6] He was one of the trustees of Elizabeth, Countess of Oxford, the mother of the banished earl.[7] He had married, probably since the decease of his brother the eldest John Paston, the Lady Anne Beaufort, third daughter of Edmund, Duke of Somerset,

[1] No. 875.   [2] Ibid.   [3] No. 877.   [4] No. 875.
[5] Nos. 854, 855, 856.   [6] No. 851.   [7] No. 845.

THE PASTON LETTERS

a lady of a wealthy family ; and he occupied the great mansion called Warwick's Inn, near Newgate, which had been the town-house of the mighty Kingmaker. His mother, Agnes Paston, lived there along with him.[1] Of his family we may mention here that the first child he had by the Lady Anne was a daughter named Mary, born, as we know from an old register, on St. Wolstan's Day, the 19th January 1470. The second, more than four years later, was also a daughter, and having been born on Tuesday the 19th July 1474, the eve of St. Margaret's Day,[2] was christened Margaret next day at St. Sepulchre's Church, having for her godfather the Duke of Buckingham, and for her godmothers, Margaret, Duchess of Somerset,[3] and Anne, Countess of Beaumont.[4] Neither of these two daughters, however, survived him. The second, Margaret, died four months after her birth, at a time when her father was absent from London, and was buried before he came home.[5] In the end, the lands of William Paston descended to two other daughters, for he had no sons.

Money matters. At this time Sir John had only borrowed of his uncle £4, a sum not quite so inconsiderable in those days as it is now, but still a mere trifle for a man of landed property, being perhaps equivalent to £50 or £60 at the present day. He repaid the money about November 1474, and his uncle, being perhaps agreeably surprised, inquired how he was going to redeem a mortgage of 400 marks held by one Townsend on the manor of Sporle. William Paston was already aware that Sir John had received a windfall of £100 from the executors

---

[1] No. 856.
[2] Our authority is very particular as to the time, and gives not only the day but the hour : 'Inter horam post nonam et horam ante horam secundam, viz., fere dimidiam horam ante horam secundam, luna curren., et erat clara dies.'
[3] Mother of the Lady Margaret Beaufort, Countess of Richmond, who was the mother of King Henry VII.
[4] So according to Sandford's Genealogy of the Paston family in Mr. Worship's communication to the *Norfolk Archæology*. But who was Anne, Countess of Beaumont ? I find no Earl Beaumont in the peerage, but there was a William, Viscount Beaumont, who succeeded his father in that title in 1459. According to Dugdale, he had two wives, the first of whom was named Elizabeth, and the second Joan. His mother, who may have been living at this time, was also named Elizabeth, but I can find no Anne.
[5] No. 857.

INTRODUCTION

of Walter Lyhart, Bishop of Norwich, who died two years before, and that some one else had offered to advance another £100, which left only 100 marks still to be raised. He was afraid his nephew had been compelled to offer an exorbitant rate of interest for the loan. Sir John, however, being pressed with his questions, told him that his mother had agreed to stand surety for the sum he had borrowed ; on which William Paston, to save him from the usurers, offered to advance the remaining 100 marks himself, and with this view placed, apparently unsolicited, 500 marks' worth of his own plate in pawn. Sir John thought the plate was in safer custody than it would have been at Warwick's Inn, where, in his uncle's absence, it remained in the keeping of his aged grandmother ; but he was anxious, if possible, not to lay himself under this kind of obligation to his uncle.[1]

The manor of Sporle was redeemed, but apparently not without his uncle William's assistance. Some other land was mortgaged to his uncle instead ; but the transaction was no sooner completed than Sir John declared he felt as much anxiety about the land in his uncle's hand as he had before about that which was in Townsend's. His mother, too, was not a little afraid, both for the land and for her own securities. She suspected William Paston was only too anxious to gain some advantage over them. She was jealous also of the influence he exercised over his aged mother, who had recently recovered from an illness, and she wished the old lady were again in Norfolk instead of living with her son in London.[2]

Sir John remained in debt to his uncle for at least a year,[3] and whether he repaid him at the end of that time I cannot tell ; but certainly, if out of debt to his uncle, he was two or three years later in debt to other men. In 1477 he was unable to meet promptly the claims of one named Cocket, and was labouring once more to redeem the manor of Sporle, which he had been obliged to mortgage to Townsend a second time. His mother, annoyed by his importunity for assistance, told him flatly she did not mean to pay his debts, and said she

---

[1] No. 856.   [2] Nos. 857, 862, 863.   [3] No. 875.

THE PASTON LETTERS

grieved to think what he was likely to do with her lands after her decease, seeing that he had wasted so shamefully what had been left him by his father.[1]

Sir John Paston's claim to Caister. But, however careless about his other property, Sir John, as we have already remarked, always showed himself particularly anxious for the recovery of Caister. During the whole of the year 1475, when he was abroad at Calais and with the army, he makes frequent reference to the matter in his letters. His brother John and his uncle William had undertaken to urge his suit in his absence to my lord and lady of Norfolk ; but he would have come home and brought it before the king in Parliament, had not the French king at that time come to the confines of Picardy, and made the Council of Calais anxious to retain the services of every available soldier on that side of the sea.[2] He was impatient at the non-fulfilment of a promise by Bishop Waynflete—'the slow Bishop of Winchester,' as he called him—to entreat the duke and duchess in his favour.[3] But he was consoled by news which reached him before he came home, that the king himself had spoken to the Duke of Norfolk on the subject, and that, though the matter was delayed till next term, the king had commanded the duke to take good advice on the subject and be sure of the validity of his title, for justice would certainly be done without favour to either party.[4] This report, however, was rather too highly coloured. The Duchess of Norfolk denied its accuracy to John Paston. The king, she said, had only asked the duke at his departure from Calais how he would deal with Caister, and my lord made him no answer. The king then asked Sir William Brandon, one of the duke's principal councillors, what my lord meant to do about it. Brandon had already received the king's commands to speak to the duke on the subject, and he said that he had done so ; but that my lord's answer was 'that the king should as soon have his life as that place.' The king then inquired of the duke if he had actually said so, and the duke said yes. On this the king simply turned his back without another word, although, as my lady informed

---

[1] Nos. 916, 917.   [2] No. 864.
[3] No. 873.   [4] Nos. 875, 876.

INTRODUCTION

John Paston, if he had spoken one word more, the duke would have made no refusal. John Paston, however, informed her ladyship that he would no longer be retained in the duke's service.[1]

His petition to the king. Sir John drew up a petition to the king upon the subject. He showed that the duke had been originally led to lay claim to Caister by the malice of Sir William Yelverton, William Jenney, and Thomas Howes, who were enfeoffed of that and other lands to his use ; that upon their suggestion the duke had entered the manor by force, and also taken from him 600 sheep and 30 neat, besides one hundred pounds' worth of furniture ; that he had done damage to the place itself which 200 marks would not suffice to repair, and that he had collected the revenues of the lands for three years to the value of £140. By the mediation of the Bishop of Winchester, the duke had afterwards restored him to possession of the manor on payment of 500 marks, and released to him his estate and interest therein by a deed under the seals of himself and his co-feoffees, and of the Bishop of Winchester. Sir John, however, had remained in possession only half a year, during which time he had laid out 100 marks in repairs, and £40 for the 'outrents' due for the three years preceding, when the duke again forcibly entered the manor, and had kept possession from that time for the space of four years and more, refusing to hear any remonstrances on the subject, or to allow Sir John to come to his presence. Moreover, when Sir John had applied to any of my lord's council, requesting them to bring the matter before his lordship, they told him that they had mentioned his request, but that he was always so exceedingly displeased with them that they did not dare to urge it. Thus Sir John had lost all his cost and trouble for four years, and thrown away 500 marks to no purpose.[2]

A.D. 1476, 16th Jan. Death of the Duke of Norfolk. This petition was probably never presented to the king. It must have been drawn up in the end of the year 1475, and in the middle of January 1476 the Duke of Norfolk suddenly died.[3] The event seems to have occurred at his seat at Framlingham, and Sir John Paston, who writes to notify it to his

---

[1] No. 877.   [2] No. 879.   [3] No. 881.

THE PASTON LETTERS

brother, must have been there at the time,[1] intending perhaps to have made one last effort with the duke's council or himself, before applying for justice to the king. But matters now stood on a different footing, and Sir John, after making his intention known to the duke's council, sent a messenger named Whetley to Caister to assert his rights there. Considering all that had passed, the act could not reasonably have been wondered at; but his brother John intimated to him a few days later that it was resented by some of the late duke's servants, as showing great want of respect for their master.[2] This imputation Sir John repudiated, pointing out most truly that no wise man could have blamed him, even if he had anticipated the duke's decease, and entered Caister an hour before it took place. Indeed, considering the justice of his claim, no one could be sorry to see Sir John in possession, who was a real friend to the duke, and loved the weal of his soul.[3]

It is curious to see the notions entertained in that day of the respect due to a duke, even from those whom he had very seriously wronged. However, Sir John Paston was not backward in yielding all that was conventionally due; and in the very letter in which he intimated the duke's death to his brother, he says he had promised his council the loan of some cloth of gold for the funeral. The article was one which it was difficult to procure in the country, and he proposed to lend them some that he had bought for his father's tomb.[4] His mother afterwards authorised him to sell it to them, if he could get a sufficient price for it.[5]

[1] Sir John's letter is distinctly dated Wednesday the 17th January, 15 Edward IV. (1476), and he says the event took place 'this night about midnight.' It is scarcely probable, however, that he wrote within an hour of the occurrence, as he mentions having spoken after it with the duke's council about furnishing cloth of gold for the funeral. I suppose therefore that the death took place on the night between the 16th and the 17th, and that Sir John wrote on the following morning. The date given in the *Inquisition post mortem* (17 Edw. IV., No. 58) is strange to say, erroneous; for it was found in twelve different counties that the duke died on *Tuesday after Epiphany*, in the fifteenth year of Edward IV., which would have been the 9th January instead of the 16th. These inquisitions, however, were not taken till more than a year and a half after the event, and it is clear the date they give is wrong by a week; but they may, nevertheless, be taken as additional evidence that the duke died on a Tuesday and not on a Wednesday.

[2] No. 883.   [3] No. 884.   [4] No. 881.   [5] No. 882.

296

INTRODUCTION

Sir John, however, after a brief visit to Norwich, hastened up to London. Now was the time that application must be made to the king; for it would be found by the inquisition that the Duke of Norfolk had actually died seised of the manor of Caister, and, unless efficient protest were made, the title would be confirmed to his widow.[1] Sir John's chief fear seems to have been that writs of *diem clausit extremum* would be issued before he had an opportunity of urging reasons for delay; in which case the inquisition would speedily be taken, and all that he could do would be to set forth his claim to the escheator before whom it was held. But he soon found that he need not be over anxious on this account. The duchess herself was anxious that the writs should not be issued too precipitately, and John Paston told his brother that he 'need not deal over largely with the escheators.'[2] The duchess, on the other hand, was suspicious of Sir John, and was warned to be upon her guard lest he should attempt to retake Caister by the strong hand. A favourable opportunity might have been found for such an attempt at that time, as the moat was frozen and could have been crossed with ease. John Paston, however, assured the duchess that his brother intended to make no entry without her knowledge and assent. The matter at last was brought before the king's council, and was decided in Sir John Paston's favour in May following, all the lords, judges, and serjeants pronouncing his title good. Privy seals were then Recovery made out for the duchess's officers to give up possession, and of Caister. seven years after the siege of Caister, Sir John was once more the acknowledged master of the place.[3]

The whole story of the duke's claim to Caister and of his injustice towards Sir John was finally recorded in the inquisition, which was taken, after an unusual delay, in October of the year following. It was shown that Yelverton, Jenney, and Howes, acting without the assent and against the will of the other trustees of Sir John Fastolf's lands, but in their names, had made a charter granting to the duke and to Thomas Hoo, Sir Richard Southwell, William Brandon, Ralph Asheton, John Tymperley, and James Hobert, the manors of Caister in Flegg,

[1] No. 882.   [2] No. 885.   [3] Nos. 891, 892.

297

THE PASTON LETTERS

by Great Yarmouth, called Redham Hall, Vaux, and Bosouns. This charter, which was not sealed, was shown to the jury, and it appeared that the said Yelverton, Jenney, and Howes had thereby demised what had belonged to them, that is to say, three out of eight parts of the same manors, to the said duke and the others. Afterwards the same duke and his co-feoffees, by the mediation of the Bishop of Winchester, seeing that the said demise and enfeoffment was against conscience, and in consideration of 500 marks paid by the bishop at the charge of Sir John Paston, enfeoffed John, Bishop of Hereford, John, Bishop of Coventry and Lichfield, and nine others, to the use of Sir John Paston. These again, by another deed, gave up their trust to Sir John Paston, and to Guy Fairfax and Richard Pigot, serjeants-at-law, John Paston, Esquire, and Roger Townsend, whom they enfeoffed to the use of Sir John Paston and his heirs for ever. Then the other trustees of Sir John Fastolf enfeoffed the same Sir John Paston, Fairfax, and the others in the same way; so that these last became seised to Sir John's use of the whole property—not merely of the three-eighths originally demised by Yelverton, Jenney, and Howes, but also of the remaining five-eighths—until they were violently disseised by the duke, who enfeoffed thereof Thomas, Archbishop of Canterbury, William, Bishop of Winchester, Henry, Earl of Essex, Richard Southwell, James Hobert, Richard Darby, clerk, and John York. After this the duke died; but while he lived, Sir John Paston had continually laid claim to the manors in his own name and in that of the said Guy Fairfax and others, sometimes entering the same, and sometimes going as near as he could with safety to himself. Finally, he entered after the duke's death, and had been seised for a long time when the inquisition was taken. The duke, therefore, it was found, did not die seised of the manors. It was further found that these manors were holden of the Abbey of St. Benet's, Hulme.[1]

[1] *Inquisition post mortem*, 17 Edw. IV., No. 58.

298

INTRODUCTION

Death of Charles the Bold

The allusions to public affairs contained in the letters about this time are of some interest. News came from Rome that a great embassy, consisting of Earl Rivers, Lord Ormond, Lord Scrope, and other lords of England, had been honourably received by the pope, but after their departure had been robbed of their plate and jewels at twelve miles' distance from Rome. On this they returned to the city to seek a remedy for the property they had lost was worth fully a thousand marks. In the same letter mention is made of the conquest of Lorraine Defeat by the Duke of Burgundy, and his disastrous expedition into of the Switzerland immediately after. By the first of these events Burgundy the prospects of Margaret of Anjou were seriously impaired, by the and the French king paid less attention to her interests. In Swiss. the second, the victorious career of Charles the Bold had been already checked by the first great defeat at Grandson. His vanguard had been broken, his artillery captured by the Swiss, his whole army repulsed, and booty of enormous value left in the hands of the enemy. 'And so,' as Sir John Paston reports the matter, 'the rich saletts, helmets, garters, nowches gilt, and all is gone, with tents, pavilions, and all; and so men deem his pride is abated. Men told him that they were froward karls, but he would not believe it. And yet men say that he will to them again. God speed them both!'[1]

This expectation, as we know, was verified, and the result His death. was that the defeat of Charles at Grandson was followed by A.D. 1477, another still more decisive defeat at Morat. Yet Charles, 5th Jan. undaunted, only transferred the scene of action to Lorraine, where he met with his final defeat and death at Nancy. The event made a mighty change. The duchy which he had nearly succeeded in erecting into an independent kingdom, and which, though nominally in feudal subjection to France, had been in his day a first-rate European power, now fell to a female. The greatness of Burgundy had already departed, and the days of its feudal independence were numbered. To England the state of matters was one of deep concern, for, should France

[1] No. 889.

299

THE PASTON LETTERS

turn hostile again, the keeping of Calais might not be so easy, unless the young Duchess Mary could succeed in organising a strong government in the Low Countries. A Great Council was accordingly convoked by the king, and met on the 18th of February. The world, as Sir John Paston wrote, seemed to be 'all quavering.' Disturbance was sure to break out somewhere, so that 'young men would be cherished.' A great comfort this, in Sir John's opinion, and he desires his brother John to 'take heart' accordingly.[1]

Conclusion of the Family History

John Paston and Margery Brews.

His brother John, however, found occupation of a more peaceful character. About this very time he had met with a lady named Margery Brews, daughter of Sir Thomas Brews, and had clearly determined in his own mind that she would be a desirable wife for him. In the spring of the year 1476, he had heard that a certain Mrs. Fitzwalter had a sister to marry, and thought his brother Sir John might negotiate a match for him in that quarter;[2] but the affair fell through, apparently because his brother refused to stand surety that he would make her a jointure of 50 marks a year.[3] Not many months, however, passed away, when he and Dame Elizabeth Brews were in correspondence about his proposed marriage with her daughter. He had promised the mother not to speak his mind to the young lady herself till he had come to an agreement with her parents; but Margery, I suppose, had read his purpose without an explicit declaration, or had forced it out of him. At all events she was no coy heroine of the modern type, but had a very decided mind upon the subject, and gave her mother no peace with her solicitations to bring the matter to effect.[4]

A.D. 1477, Feb.

Her mother, for her part, was not unwilling, and believing that pecuniary matters might be easily arranged with her husband, wrote to John Paston in February, reminding him that Friday was Valentine's Day, when every bird chose him a mate. She also invited him to visit her on Thursday night,

[1] No. 900. [2] No. 890. [3] No. 892. [4] Nos. 894, 895, 896.

300

INTRODUCTION

and stay till Monday, when she hoped he would have an opportunity of speaking to her husband. In fact, she showed herself quite eager for the match, and alluding apparently to some difficulty made by her husband to terms that had been already offered, said it was but a simple oak that was cut down at the first stroke.[1] Thus encouraged, John Paston persevered in his suit, and Margery wrote him very warm and ardent letters, calling him her well-beloved valentine, and vowing that she would accept him with half the 'livelode' he actually possessed.[2] The question, however, was how much the father could afford to give along with his daughter, and what Margaret Paston and Sir John could do that they might have a reasonable settlement. Sir John Paston's answer was very discouraging. He felt himself in no condition to help his brother, and after pointing out the difficulty of acting on some of his suggestions, he added in a surly fashion: 'This matter is driven thus far forth without my counsel; I pray you make an end without my counsel. If it be well, I would be glad; if it be otherwise, it is pity. I pray you trouble me no more.'[3]

Margaret Paston, however, showed a mother's heart in the affair, and consented to entail upon the young people her manor of Sparham, if Sir John would consent to ratify the gift, and forgo his prospective interest in the succession. Even to this Sir John would not quite consent. He wished well to his brother, owned that it would be a pity the match should be broken off, and did not wonder at what his mother had done; but he saw reasons why he could not 'with his honesty' confirm it. He did not, however, mean to raise any objection. 'The Pope,' he said, 'will suffer a thing to be used, but he will not license, nor grant it to be used nor done, and so I.' He would be as kind a brother as could be, and if Sir Thomas Brews was afraid he might hereafter disturb John Paston and his wife in the possession of the manor, he was quite ready to give a bond that he would attempt no such thing. The manor was not his, and he professed he did not covet it.[4]

[1] No. 896. [2] Nos. 897, 898.
[3] Nos. 902, 909. [4] Nos. 910, 911.

301

THE PASTON LETTERS

Sir John seems really to have desired his brother's happiness, though from his own bad management he knew not how to help him.[1] Hitherto he had been the mediator of all such schemes for him, probably because the younger brother believed his prospects to be mainly dependent upon the head of the house; and I am sorry to say he had been employed in the like duty even after John Paston had begun to carve for himself. For it is clear that after receiving those warm letters from Margery Brews, in which she called him her valentine, and was willing to share his lot if it were with half his actual means, he had commissioned his brother once more to make inquiries about a certain Mistress Barly. Sir John's report, however, was unfavourable. It was 'but a bare thing.' Her income was insignificant, and she herself was insignificant in person; for he had taken the pains to see her on his brother's account. She was said to be eighteen years of age, though she looked but thirteen; but if she was the mere girl that she looked, she might be a woman one day.[2]

Perhaps, after all, like Captain Absolute, John Paston had more of a mind of his own in the matter than might be inferred from his giving so many commissions to another to negotiate a wife for him. At all events, if he had not made up his mind before, he seems really to have made it up now, and he steered his way between difficulties on the one side and on the other with a good deal of curious diplomacy, for which we may refer the reader to the letters themselves.[3] In the end, though Sir John seems to have been in vain urged by his mother to show himself more liberal,[4] all other obstacles were removed, and during the autumn of the year 1477 the marriage took effect.[5]

Before Christmas in that same year, it had become apparent that children would soon follow of their union;[6] and after the New Year John Paston took Margery to her father's house to be with her friends a short time, while yet she could go about with ease.[7] Their eldest child was born in the following summer, and received the name of Christopher.[8] Other

[1] No. 913. [2] No. 903. [3] Nos. 901, 904, 905, 913, 915.
[4] No. 916. [5] No. 923. [6] Ibid.
[7] No. 925. [8] No. 936.

302

INTRODUCTION

children followed very soon,[1] and by the time they had been seven years married, John and Margery Paston had two lads old enough to be sent on messages,[2] besides, in all probability, one or more daughters. It was, however, their second son, William,[3] that continued their line, and became the ancestor of the future Earls of Yarmouth.

The Duke of Suffolk again gives trouble.

In the spring of 1478 Sir John Paston was again involved in a dispute with a powerful nobleman. The Duke of Suffolk revived his old claim to Hellesdon and Drayton, and ventured to sell the woods to Richard Ferror, the Mayor of Norwich, who thereupon began to cut them down. Sir John brought the matter into Chancery, and hastened up to London. Ferror professed great regret, and said he had no idea but that the manor was in peaceable possession of the duke, adding that if Sir John had sent him the slightest warning, he would have refrained from making such a bargain. This, however, was a mere pretence; for, as Sir John remarked to his brother, he must certainly have spoken about the matter beforehand with some well-informed men in Norwich, who would have set him right.[4] At all events Ferror went on with what he had begun, and nearly the whole of Drayton wood was felled by Corpus Christi Day, the 20th day of May. Whetley, a servant of Sir John Paston, who had been sent down from London on the business, writes on that day to his master that the duke had made a formal entry into Hellesdon on Wednesday in Whitsun week. He dined at the manor-house, 'drew a stew, and took plenty of fish.' I suppose from what follows that he also held a court as lord of the manor. 'At his being there that day,' writes Whetley, 'there was never no man that played Herod in Corpus Christi play better and more agreeable to his pageant than he did. But ye shall understand that it was afternoon, and the weather hot, and he so feeble for sickness that his legs would not bear him, but there was two men had great pain to keep him on his feet. And there ye were judged.

[1] No. 982. [2] No. 999.
[3] He was a lawyer of some eminence, received the honour of knighthood from Henry VIII., and was Sheriff of Norfolk in 1517-18. He died in 1554. It was his grandson, another Sir William, whose name is so well known in Norfolk as the founder of the North Walsham Grammar School. [4] Nos. 929, 930.

303

THE PASTON LETTERS

Some said "Slay"; some said "Put him in prison." And forth come my lord, and he would meet you with a spear, and have none other 'mends for the trouble ye have put him to but your heart's blood, and that will he get with his own hands; for and ye have Hellesdon and Drayton, ye shall have his life with it.'[1]

It appears, however, that the Duke of Suffolk was not in high favour with the king, and it was considered at this time that Sir John Paston's influence at court was very high. Although the affair with Anne Haute had been broken off, it was expected that he would marry some one nearly related to the queen's family; and Margaret Paston thought it a strong argument for the match, if her son could find it in his heart to love the lady, that it would probably set at rest the question of his title to Hellesdon and Drayton.[2] This ambitious hope was not destined to be gratified. We know not even who the lady was that is thus referred to; and as to the dispute with the Duke of Suffolk, it remained unsettled at least a year and a half—in fact, as long as Sir John Paston lived.[3]

The manor of Oxnead. Two or three months after the beginning of this dispute, William Paston the uncle accompanied the Duke of Buckingham into Norfolk on pilgrimage to the shrine of Our Lady at Walsingham. At his coming he brought a report that there was likely also to be trouble in the manor of Oxnead, which belonged to his mother Agnes, the widow of the judge. The nature of this trouble is not stated; but apparently it was either occasioned, like the other, by a claim of the Duke of Suffolk, or it was feared the duke might attempt to profit by it. 'Wherefore I pray you,' writes Sir John Paston to his brother, 'take heed lest that the Duke of Suffolk's council play therewith now at the vacation of the benefice, as they did with the benefice of Drayton, which by the help of Mr. John Salett and Donne, his men, there was a quest made by the said Donne that found that the Duke of Suffolk was very patron, which was false; yet they did it for an evidence.' Whether the duke's council attempted the same policy on this occasion, we cannot say; but by some means or other the Paston family

[1] No. 932.   [2] No. 933.   [3] No. 956.

INTRODUCTION

were hindered from exercising their right of presentation, so that they very nearly lost it. A rector named Thomas, presented to the living by Agnes Paston three years before, died in March 1478. On the 5th August following, Agnes Paston made out letters of presentation in favour of Dr. Richard Lincoln, but for some reason or other this presentation did not pass; and eight days later she presented a certain Sir William Holle, who we are told ran away. Her rights, however, were contested; and after the benefice had remained more than a year vacant, some insisted that it had lapsed to the bishop by the patron not having exercised her rights within six months. She had, however, as a matter of fact, delivered Sir William Holle his presentation within that period; and though he did not avail himself of it, she was, after a good deal of trouble, allowed to present again.[1]

Walter Paston. In the spring of 1478 Margaret Paston had a serious illness, and, thinking that it would carry her off, she made her will. She lived, however, six years longer, and the will she had made was superseded by another dated on the 4th of February 1482.[2] For in the interval considerable changes took place in the family, which we shall mention presently. At this time she had five, if not six, sons and two daughters, but the daughters were both of them married; and, as we have already intimated, she was particularly anxious about her son Walter, who was now at Oxford being educated for the priesthood.[3] He had not yet taken orders, when his mother, finding some benefice vacant, of which she expected to have the disposal,[4] thought of conferring it upon him, and took advice upon the matter of Dr. Pykenham, Judge of the Court of Arches. She was told, however, that her intention was quite against the canon law for three reasons: first, because her son had not received the tonsure, which was popularly called Benet; secondly, he had not attained the lawful age of four-and-twenty; and thirdly, he would require to

[1] Nos. 934, 935, 936, 937, 943.   [2] Nos. 912, 978.   [3] No. 931.
[4] Oxnead, which was certainly vacant at the date which I have supposed to be that of Margaret Paston's application to Dr. Pykenham, was in her mother-in-law Agnes Paston's gift; but it is not at all unlikely that this was the living in question, as she may reasonably have expected to be able to prevail upon the old lady to give it to her grandson.

THE PASTON LETTERS

take priest's orders within a twelvemonth after presentation to the benefice, unless he had a dispensation from the Pope, which Dr. Pykenham felt sure he could never obtain.[1] His progress at Oxford, however, seems to have given satisfaction to his tutor, Edmund Alyard, who reports on the 4th March 1479 that he might take a bachelor's degree in art when he pleased, and afterwards proceed to the faculty of law.[2] This course he intended to pursue; and he took his degree at Midsummer accordingly,[3] then returned home to Norwich for the vacation. His career, however, was arrested by sudden illness, and he died in August. He left a will, hastily drawn up before his death, by which it appears that he was possessed of the manor of Cressingham, which he bequeathed to his brother John Paston, with a proviso that if ever he came to inherit the lands of his father it should go to his other brother Edmund. He also possessed a flock of sheep at Mautby, which he desired might be divided between his sister Anne Yelverton and his sister-in-law Margery, John Paston's wife.[4]

Clement. Of Margaret Paston's other sons one named Clement is mentioned in Fenn's pedigree of the family; but he is nowhere spoken of in the correspondence. I presume that Fenn was not without authority for inserting his name in the family tree, and I have surmised that he was one of the 'young soldiers,' about whom Margaret Paston was solicitous, who went over to Calais in 1475. He may perhaps have died soon after. The absence of his name, especially in his mother's will, is at least strong presumptive evidence that he was not alive in 1482. Edmund Paston, another brother, was probably of about the same age as Walter, perhaps a year or two older; and the youngest of the family was William, who in the beginning of the year 1479 was learning to make Latin verses at Eton.[5] He must have been at this time barely nineteen years of age;[6] but he had precociously fallen in love with a certain Margaret Alborow. He writes to his brother John

[1] No. 941.   [2] No. 949.   [3] Nos. 945, 946.   [4] No. 950.
[5] No. 942. See a previous letter of his, No. 939, and also a notice of his schooling as early as August 1477, when Margaret Paston writes to Sir John to pay for his board and school-hire, gowns, and other necessaries (No. 917).
[6] No. 842.

INTRODUCTION

Paston how he first became acquainted with her at the marriage of her elder sister,—that she was not more than eighteen or nineteen (which was just about his own age); that she was to have a portion in money and plate whenever she was married, but he was afraid no 'livelode' or lands till after her mother's decease. His brother John, however, could find out that by inquiry.[1] As might have been expected, this calf-love came to nothing. I do not know if William Paston ever married at all. At a more advanced age his brother Edmund writes to him offering to visit on his behalf a widow, who had just 'fallen' at Worsted, whose deceased husband had been worth £1000, and had left her 100 marks in money, with plate of the same value, and £10 a year in land.[2]

For Edmund Paston himself the same kind of office had been performed in 1478 by his brother John, who, having heard while in London of 'a goodly young woman to marry,' spoke with some of her friends, and got their consent to her marrying his brother. She was a mercer's daughter, and was to have a portion of £200 in ready money, and 20 marks a year in land after the decease of a stepmother, who was close upon fifty. This match, however, did not take effect, and about three years later Edmund Paston married Catherine, the widow of William Clippesby.[3]

Death of Agnes Paston; The year 1479 was, like several of the years preceding, one of great mortality, and it was marked by several deaths in the Paston family. The grave had not yet closed over Walter Paston, when news came to Norwich of the death of his grandmother, old Agnes Paston, the widow of the judge. At the same time John Paston's wife, Margery, gave birth, in her husband's absence, to a child that died immediately after it was born.[4] This perhaps was a mere accidental coincidence. Two months later Sir John Paston found it necessary to go up to London on business, partly, it would seem, about his dispute with the Duke of Suffolk, and partly, perhaps, to keep

[1] No. 942.   [2] No. 974.
[3] No. 975. There is an oversight in the preliminary note to this letter. The date is certainly 1481, and no later, as Margaret Paston in her will makes bequests not only to Edmund and his wife Catherine, but to their son Robert, who must therefore have been born before February 1482.   [4] No. 952.

THE PASTON LETTERS

watch on the proceedings of his uncle William with regard to the lands of his grandmother; for it appears that his uncle, who immediately on his mother's death laid claim to the manor of Marlingford,[1] had been making certain applications to the escheator on the subject, which were naturally viewed with jealousy. On his arrival in town, Sir John found his chamber ill ventilated, and his 'stuff not so clean' as he had expected. He felt uneasy for fear of the prevailing sickness, and some disappointments in money matters added sensibly to his discomfort.[2] He fell ill, and died in November. John Paston was on the point of riding up to London to have brought down his body with that of his grandmother, who had been kept unburied nearly three months, to lay them both in Bromholm Priory, beside his father. But he was met by a messenger, who told him that his brother had already been buried at the White Friars, in London.[3]

and of Sir John Paston.

We cannot close the record of Sir John Paston's life without a certain feeling of regret. The very defects of his character give an interest to it which we do not feel in that of his father or of his brother John. He is a careless soldier, who loves adventure, has some influence at court, mortgages his lands, wastes his property, and is always in difficulties. Unsuccessful in love himself, he yet does a good deal of wooing and courting disinterestedly in behalf of a younger brother. He receives sprightly letters from his friends, with touches of broad humour occasionally, which are not worse than might be expected of the unrestrained freedom of the age.[4] He patronises literature too, and a transcriber copies books for him.[5] With his death the domestic interest of the Paston Letters almost comes to an end, and the quantity of the correspondence very greatly diminishes. The love-making, the tittle-tattle, and a good deal of the humour disappear, and the few desultory letters that remain relate, for the most part, either to politics or to business.

The title to Marlingford and Oxnead.

As soon as the news of his death arrived in Norfolk, John Paston wrote to his mother, desiring that his brother Edmund would ride to Marlingford, Oxnead, Paston, Cromer, and

[1] No. 953.   [2] No. 956.   [3] No. 962.   [4] Nos. 906-908.   [5] No. 695.

308

INTRODUCTION

Caister, to intimate his right of succession to the tenants of these different manors, and to warn those of Marlingford and Oxnead to pay no rents to the servants or officers of his uncle William.[1] These two manors, the reader will remember, belonged to Agnes Paston; and her son William, with whom she lived, had doubtless watched the old lady's failing health, and made preparations even before her actual decease to vindicate his claim to them as soon as the event occurred.[2] The manors, however, having been entailed under Judge Paston's will, properly descended to Sir John Paston, and after his death to his brother John. In accordance, therefore, with his brother's instructions, Edmund Paston rode to Marlingford on Sunday before St. Andrew's Day, 'and before all the tenants examined one James, keeper there for William Paston, where he was the week next before St. Andrew; and there he said that he was not at Marlingford from the Monday unto the Thursday at even, and so there was no man there but your brother's man at the time of his decease' (we are quoting a letter of William Lomnour to John Paston). 'So by that your brother died seised. And your brother Edmund bade your man keep possession to your behoof, and warned the tenants to pay no man till ye had spoken to them.' In the afternoon Edmund went on to Oxnead, where a servant named Piers kept possession for Sir John Paston, and he found that William Paston's agent was not there at the time, but had ordered another man to be there in his place. Whether that amounted to a continuance of the possession of William Paston, was a point to be considered.[3]

As usual in such cases, farmers and tenants had everywhere a bad time of it until uncle and nephew were agreed. John Paston's men threatened those of his uncle William at Har-wellbury, while, on the other hand, his uncle William's men molested those of John Paston at Marlingford.[4] During the interval between Agnes Paston's death and that of Sir John, the tenants at Cromer had been uncertain who was to be their lord, and at Paston there was a similar perplexity.[5] Sir John's

[1] No. 962.   [2] No. 940.   [3] No. 963.
[4] Nos. 970, 982, 983.   [5] No. 957.

309

THE PASTON LETTERS

bailiff ordered the Paston tenants to pay no rents to Mr. William Paston; but one Henry Warns wrote to Mr. William of the occurrence, and ordered them to pay none to any one else. After Sir John's death Warns still continued to be troublesome, making tenants afraid to harrow or sow lest they should lose their labour, pretending that John Paston had given him power over everything he had himself in the place.[1] Things went on in this unpleasant fashion for a period of at least five years.[2]

Death of Margaret Paston.

Margaret Paston survived her son Sir John five years, and died in 1484, in the reign of Richard III.[3] In her very interesting will, made two years before her decease, a number of bequests of a religious and charitable kind show how strongly she felt the claims of the poor, the sick, and the needy, as well as those of hospitals, friars, anchoresses, and parish churches. From the bequests she makes to her own family, it appears that not only John Paston, her eldest surviving son, but his brother Edmund also, was by that time married, and had children. To Edmund she gives 'a standing piece white covered, with a garlick head upon the knop,' 'a gilt piece covered, with a unicorn,' a feather bed and a 'transom,' and some tapestry. To his wife Catherine she leaves a purple girdle 'harnessed with silver and gilt,' and some other articles; and to their son Robert, who must have been quite an infant, all her swans marked with 'Daubeney's mark,' to remain with him and his heirs for ever. Various other articles are left to her daughter Anne, wife of William Yelverton, to her son William, to John and Margery Paston, and to their son William and to their daughter Elizabeth (apparently Christopher Paston, the eldest child, was by this time dead), and also to Constance, a natural daughter of Sir John Paston. She also left £20 to John Calle, son of her daughter Margery, when he should come to be twenty years of age, and if he died before that, it was to be divided between his brothers William

[1] Nos. 852 and 853, which by inadvertence I have assigned to the year 1474. They are undoubtedly of the year 1479, the former being written just before Sir John Paston's death, and the latter after it.   [2] No. 998.
[3] The exact date is given as the 4th November 1484 in a calendar prefixed to an old MS. missal in the possession of the late Mr. C. W. Reynell.

310

INTRODUCTION

and Richard when they grew up. To Margery Calle herself and her husband Richard she left nothing.[1]

Times of Richard III. and Henry VII.

The personal interest of the correspondence is not altogether exhausted, although, as we have already remarked, it is very greatly diminished after the death of Sir John Paston. But the political interest of the remaining letters is so great, that they are almost more indispensable to the historian than the preceding ones. The brief and troubled reign of Richard III. receives illustration from two letters of the Duke of Norfolk to John Paston. The first was written in anticipation of Buckingham's rebellion, requiring him to make ready and come to London immediately with 'six tall fellows in harness,' as the Kentish men were up in the Weald, and meant to come and rob the city.[2] Again, on the Earl of Richmond's invasion, the duke desires Paston to meet him at Bury with a company, to be raised at the duke's expense.[3] There is also a copy of King Richard's proclamation against Henry Tudor,[4] of which, however, the text is preserved in other MSS.

Richard III.

The troubles of the reign of Henry VII. at first were scarcely less in magnitude than those of the tyrant whom he overthrew. But somehow or other the new king had the art of discovering who was to be trusted and who was not. John Paston was soon found out to be a man deserving of confidence. Very early, indeed, in Henry's reign, he must have acquired some influence at court. Two months had not elapsed after the battle of Bosworth when we find him Sheriff of Norfolk. The Duke of Suffolk writes to him to issue proclamations in the king's name against certain rebels who were in confederacy with the Scots.[5] The Countess of Surrey writes to him to intercede with my Lord Fitzwalter and the Earl of Oxford in behalf of her imprisoned husband.[6] Lady Fitzhugh, a daughter of the great Kingmaker, calls him her

Henry VII.

John Paston Sheriff of Norfolk.

[1] No. 978.   [2] No. 994.   [3] No. 1002.
[4] No. 1001.   [5] No. 1006.   [6] No. 1004.

311

THE PASTON LETTERS

son, and requests his favour for her daughter Anne, wife of the fugitive Yorkist rebel Francis, Viscount Lovel, whose pardon she was making importunate suit to obtain.[1] The king himself writes to him,[2] and the Earl of Oxford addresses letters to him as his 'right well beloved councillor.'[3] The earl, of course, was his old friend, and we may presume it was through his influence that Paston was recommended to the king's favour.

Lambert Simnel's rebellion. So much honour, trust, and confidence had already been bestowed on him when the rebellion of Lambert Simnel broke out in the second year of Henry's reign. Of that commotion we have some interesting illustrations, by which it is clear that the gentry of Norfolk were at first doubtful of the success of the king's cause, and that many were indisposed to obey his summons to battle. Sir William Boleyn and Sir Harry Heydon had gone as far as Thetford on their way towards Kent, when they received advice which induced them to return. Sir Edmund Bedingfield wrote to John Paston, he believed that they would not go if the king wanted them. But there were similar rumours about John Paston himself, and it was even said that he meditated mischief. It is true he had actually waited on the king, in the train, apparently, of the Earl of Oxford, one of the two generals to whom the military powers of the whole kingdom were at this time intrusted; but it was suspected, perhaps owing to the application made to him on her account, that after my lord's departure from the king he had been with the Viscountess Lovel, whose husband was among the rebel leaders. 'But wrath said never well,' adds Bedingfield in reporting this rumour to John Paston himself. It was evident that he had enemies, and it was necessary to conduct himself at such a critical period with extreme discretion.[4]

Fear of invasion on the East Coast. At this time the rebels had not yet landed in England. Nothing had been known of their movements till very lately; but the Earl of Lincoln had been in Flanders with the Lady Margaret of Burgundy, the chief organiser of the conspiracy. The East Coast, it was supposed, was chiefly threatened; and

[1] No. 1008.   No. 1010.   [3] No. 1012.   [4] No. 1014.

INTRODUCTION

the king had made a progress through Suffolk and Norfolk to animate the people to loyalty. Commissions of array had been issued for the Eastern Counties on the 7th April. On the 15th Henry kept his Easter at Norwich; after which he went on to Walsingham, and thence to Coventry.[1] News came, however, that seemed to show the East Coast was in no immediate danger. The rebels had left the Low Countries, but they had gone to Ireland. The gentlemen of the Eastern Counties were informed that the king would put them to no further charge at that time, but hoped the country would be ready on reasonable warning.[2]

Battle of Stoke. John Paston knighted. The extraordinary farce enacted in Ireland—the recognition of Lambert Simnel as the son of Clarence, his coronation in Christ Church Cathedral, Dublin, and his enthusiastic and universal reception by a people to whom political truths have been at all times unimportant, and rebellion a mere amusement,—these were facts that could not have been easily realised by sober-minded Englishmen. The news, indeed, could scarcely have reached England very much in advance of the rebel hosts themselves, which presently crossed the sea and landed at Furness in Lancashire.[3] In less than a fortnight they penetrated into the heart of England, where they were met by the king's forces and suffered a complete overthrow in the battle of Stoke. In that battle John Paston was with the king's army, and seems to have done some distinguished service, in recognition of which he was knighted by the king upon the field of battle. The same honour was conferred at that time upon fifty-one persons besides himself, while thirteen others were made knights bannerets.[4]

Deputy to the Earl of Oxford as Admiral. Sir John Paston, as he was now called, continued to maintain his influence with the Earl of Oxford and the king. The earl was Lord High Admiral, and he made Sir John his

[1] See Spedding's Notes in Bacon's Henry VII.—*Works of Bacon*, vi. 55, 56.
[2] No. 1015.
[3] It was but on the 5th May, as Spedding has pointed out (*Bacon*, 56) that the principal party of the rebels landed in Ireland. On the 4th June they had crossed the Channel and landed in Lancashire. The coronation of Lambert Simnel took place on Ascension Day, the 24th May.—*Rolls of Parl.* vi. 397.
[4] No. 1016 and Note at p. 187 (vol. vi.).

THE PASTON LETTERS

deputy; in which capacity we find letters addressed to him about a whale taken off the coast of Norfolk,[1] and deputations waiting upon him at Caister from the corporation of Yarmouth,[2] besides some correspondence with the earl as Admiral.[3] He got his brother William into the earl's service; and though ultimately the earl was obliged to dismiss him as being 'troubled with sickness and crased in his mind,'[4] William Paston certainly continued many years in the earl's household. He became, in fact, a means of communication between the earl and his brother, and in one case we have an important letter addressed to the earl by the king on the subject of the war in Britanny, copied out by William Paston and forwarded to Sir John.[5]

The war in Britanny. The eager interest with which this war in Britanny was watched by Englishmen—the anxiety to learn what had become of English volunteers, and of the forces sent thither afterwards by the king's authority—is shown in several of the letters.[6] The facts relating to the whole affair, and their true chronology, had been a good deal confused and mis-stated until the late Mr. Spedding, in editing Lord Bacon's *History of Henry VII.*, compared the testimony of the Paston Letters with that of other original sources.[7] But it would take up too much space, and involve writing a complete history of the times, to show what important light is thrown upon this and other subjects of interest in the reign of Henry VII. by the scattered notices of political events contained in these letters; and we must be content, for the remainder of the period, briefly to indicate the matters of public interest referred to.

The rising in the North, in which the Earl of North-

[1] Nos. 1029, 1030.   [2] No. 924.   [3] Nos. 1049, 1050, 1051.
[4] No. 940.   [5] No. 913.
[6] Letters 1026, 1030, 1036. An allusion to this war occurs in Barclay's *Ship of Fools*, f. 152 b.:

'The battles done, perchance in small Britain,
In France, in Flanders, or to the worldes end,
Are told in the quere, of some, in wordes vain
In midst of matins in stead of the Legende,
And other gladly to hear the same intend
Much rather than the service for to hear.'

[7] Spedding's *Bacon*, vi. 68, 72, 84, 97-8, 101-2.

INTRODUCTION

The Earl of Northumberland. umberland was slain, is the subject of two letters;[1] and, closely connected with this subject, if our chronology is to be relied on, is an intended progress of the king into Norfolk a few weeks earlier, which was abandoned for some reason not explained. The Great Council which Henry had summoned on the affairs of Britanny appears to have been dissolved on the 3rd March 1489. Two days before it separated, the Earl of Northumberland was appointed to protect the kingdom against the Scots, and entered into indentures with the king at Sheen 'for the keeping out of the Scots and warring on them.' But instead of having an outward enemy to contend with, before two months had elapsed he found himself called upon to put down the revolt in Yorkshire, and he was killed on the 28th April.

Intended royal visit to Norfolk. The king, if his original designs had been adhered to, would by this time have passed through the Eastern Counties, 'kept his Easter at Norwich, and gone on to Walsingham. In the course of his progress he was to have visited the Earl of Oxford at his mansion at Hedingham in Essex, where William Paston, Sir John's brother, was staying in the earl's service. Sir John himself had notice from the earl to come to him with the same number of men 'defensably arrayed' as he had before granted to do the king service;[3] and in anticipation of the royal visit to Norfolk, William Paston sent orders to the Bailiff of Mautby to have his horse Bayard well fed, whatever it cost, that the animal might look fat and sleek when the king came.[4] This order, however, it must be observed, is provisional, 'if Bayard be unsold'; and perhaps the proviso may point to the reason why the royal progress was abandoned. The subsidy which caused the rising in Yorkshire was heavily felt over the whole kingdom besides; and though at another time a royal progress might have been very popular, the king doubtless saw that it would be unadvisable to add to the expenses of his subjects at a time when they were so severely taxed already.

Creation of Prince Henry as Duke of York. In No. 1058 we have a list of the persons who were made Knights of the Bath on the creation of Henry, the king's

[1] Nos. 1037, 1039.   [2] No. 1031.   [3] No. 1032.   [4] No. 1033.

THE PASTON LETTERS

second son (afterwards Henry VIII.) as Duke of York, in November 1494.[1]

Perkin Warbeck.

In July 1495, the corporation of Yarmouth write to Sir John Paston about the capture of five captains of Perkin Warbeck's host, who landed at Deal with about 140 men, when an invasion was attempted by the pretender. Whatever encouragement was given to Perkin abroad, his appearance off the coast of Kent gave little satisfaction to the inhabitants, who killed or took prisoner every man that set foot on the land. Perkin, leaving his friends to their mercy, sailed away, only creating a little disquietude as to where he would next make his appearance. One of the captains taken, whose name was Belt, said he knew he had no hope of mercy, and therefore did not mind revealing the plans of his comrades. They meant to gain possession of Yarmouth or to die for it.[2] If this was said in good faith, the rebels must have been so discouraged by their reception at Deal, that they changed their plans and went to Ireland. But it may of course have been said purposely in order to mislead. It was, however, effectual in creating some alarm about the safety of the town. The corporation received a promise from Sir John Paston that aid should be forthcoming, if required; but the very next day intelligence was received that the rebel fleet had sailed westward,[3] and doubtless before many days more all serious alarm was at an end.

Edmund de la Pole.

The next political letter refers to Edmund de la Pole, Earl of Suffolk, whose first escape from England was made in the summer of 1499. The king was then staying at Godshill, in the Isle of Wight, where the Earl of Oxford was with him; and the latter wrote to Sir John Paston on the 20th August to make inquiry what persons had accompanied the fugitive, or were privy to his departure, commanding him to take into

[1] No. 1058.—This list agrees pretty well with the names given in the description of the ceremony printed by me in *Letters and Papers of Richard III. and Henry VII.*, vol. i. p. 390. But besides some variations in spelling and a difference in one place as to the Christian name, this list includes the names of Lords Harington and Clifford, who are not only not mentioned in the other as having been made Knights of the Bath on this occasion, but who seem to be excluded by the statement that there were only twenty baths and beds provided besides those of the prince himself.

[2] No. 1059. [3] No. 1060.

INTRODUCTION

custody every one whom he could find to have been any way concerned in the matter, or any 'suspect' person who seemed to be 'of the same affinity,' found hovering near the sea coasts.[1] Writs were issued the very same day to the sheriffs of the Eastern Counties to prevent persons leaving the kingdom without a licence.[2]

Coming of Catherine of Arragon to England.

The next letter after this is a notification from the king to Sir John Paston, given on the 20th May 1500, that Catherine of Arragon, the affianced bride of Arthur, Prince of Wales, was expected in England in the following May. Sir John Paston was required to be ready to give his attendance at her reception at that date; but owing to a change of plans, she did not arrive before October 1501.[3]

Meeting of Henry VII. and Philip of Castile.

After this there is nothing more relating to public matters during Sir John Paston's life; but we must not pass over without notice the very curious account given in No. 1078—a letter which, though among the Paston papers, has no obvious connection with the Paston family at all—of the meeting between Henry VII. and Philip, King of Castile, at Clewer, near Windsor, in January 1506. It is well known how Philip, who until the death of his mother-in-law, Isabella of Spain, was only Archduke of Austria, had set out from Flanders to take possession of his new dominions, when, meeting with a storm at sea, he was driven upon the coast of England, and was for some time entertained by Henry at his court. This letter gives a minute description of the meeting between the two kings, and of the persons by whom they were accompanied, noting the apparel and liveries of all present, after the fashion of court newsmen. The scene unquestionably must have been a striking one; but we must refer our readers for the particulars to the letter itself.

Social Aspect of the Times

State of society.

Thus far have we followed the fortunes of the Paston family and the history of the times in which they lived, as

[1] No. 1065.
[2] *Letters and Papers Ric. III. and Hen. VII.*, vol. ii. p. 377. [3] No. 1066.

THE PASTON LETTERS

illustrated by their correspondence. The reader must not, however, imagine that we have by any means exhausted the materials before us, either in their social or in their political bearings. Indeed, to whatever length we should prolong these observations, we could not but leave an ample harvest of facts to be gathered in by others, nor have we attempted more than to bring the leading points of the story into one connected narrative. Of the general condition of society revealed to us by this remarkable correspondence, we have left the reader to form his own impressions. But a few very brief remarks upon this subject may perhaps be expected of us before we conclude.

Education.

The first thing which strikes the most casual observer on glancing over these letters, is the testimony they afford to the state of education among the people at the period in which they were written. From the extreme scarcity of original letters of such an early date, we are too easily led to undervalue the culture and civilisation of the age. But these letters show that during the century before the Reformation the state of education was by no means so low, and its advantages by no means so exceptionally distributed, as we might otherwise imagine. For it is not merely that Judge Paston was a man of superior cultivation, and took care that his family should be endowed with all those educational advantages that he had possessed himself. This was no doubt the case. But it must be remembered that the majority of these letters were not written by members of the Paston family, but were only addressed to them; and they show that friends, neighbours, lords, commoners, and domestic servants possessed the art of writing, as well as the Pastons themselves. No person of any rank or station in society above mere labouring men seems to have been wholly illiterate. All could write letters; most persons could express themselves in writing with ease and fluency. Not perhaps that the accomplishment was one in which it was considered an honour to excel. Hands that had been accustomed to grasp the sword were doubtless easily fatigued with the pen. Old Sir John Fastolf evidently feels it a trouble even to sign his name, and in his latter years invariably allows

INTRODUCTION

others to sign it for him. Men of high rank generally sign their letters, but scarcely ever write them with their own hands. And well was it, in many cases, for their correspondents that they did not do it oftener. Whether, like Hamlet, they thought it 'a baseness to write fair,' and left such 'yeoman's service' to those who had specially qualified themselves for it; or whether, absorbed by other pursuits, they neglected an art which they got others to practise for them, the nobility were generally the worst writers of the day. Their handwriting and their spelling were on a par, and were sometimes so outrageous, that it requires no small effort of imagination to comprehend the words, even if we could be sure of the letters.[1]

Eton College.

Education, nevertheless, was making undoubted progress, both among high and low. Eton College and King's College, Cambridge, had been founded by Henry VI. only a few years before old Judge Paston died. His grandson and namesake, William Paston, as we have seen, was sent to the former place for his education, and was learning to construct Latin hexameters and pentameters there in 1479. His progress, it is true, seems to have been but indifferent. What was to be expected of a young gentleman of nineteen, whose attention, even while at school, was distracted by the thought that he had already met with one who might be a partner for life? Nevertheless, in that same letter in which he writes to his brother John what he knows of Mistress Margaret Alborow, he sends him also a specimen of his performances in Latin versification. It is not a very brilliant production, certainly, but the fact of his sending it to his elder brother shows that John Paston too had gone through a regular classical training on the system which has prevailed in all public schools down to the present day.

Oxford.

It has, moreover, been remarked that the illustrations both of Eton and of Oxford life in the fifteenth century bear a

[1] A notable example of this is afforded by the letters of Edmund de la Pole, Earl of Suffolk, which will be found printed in my *Letters and Papers of Richard III. and Henry VII.* His successor in title, Charles Brandon, Duke of Suffolk, the favourite of Henry VIII., wrote quite as barbarous a hand, and outraged orthography in a manner equally bewildering.

striking resemblance to the well-known usages of modern times. It is true Walter Paston's expenses at Oxford were not great, even if we take into consideration the much higher value of money in that day. For a period of probably half a year they amounted to no more than £6 : 5s. : 5¾d.[1] Yet when he became B.A. he gave a banquet, as graduates have been accustomed to do since his day, for which he was promised some venison from Lady Harcourt, but was disappointed.[2] Even the expenses attending the graduation, however, do not appear to have been very heavy. 'It will be some cost to me, but not much,' wrote Walter Paston in his own case, though he had been disappointed in the hope of passing at the same time as Lionel Woodville, the queen's brother, afterwards Bishop of Salisbury, who apparently would have borne a portion of the expenses of his fellow-graduates.[3]

From the letters just referred to we are reminded that it was at this time usual for those who received a liberal education not only to take a degree in arts but to proceed afterwards in the faculty of law. At the universities, unfortunately, law is studied no longer, and degrees in that faculty are now purely honorary.

Mode of computing dates. Some other points may be suggested to us, even by the most superficial examination of the contents of these volumes. The mode in which the letters are dated by their writers shows clearly that our ancestors were accustomed to measure the lapse of time by very different standards from those now in use. Whether men in general were acquainted with the current year of the Christian era may be doubted ; that was an ecclesiastical computation rather than one for use in common life. They seldom dated their letters by the year at all, and when they did it was not by the year of our Lord, but by the year of the king's reign. Chronicles and annals of the period, which give the year of our Lord, are almost always full of inaccuracies in the figures ; and altogether it is evident that an exact computation of years was a thing for which there was considered to be little practical use. As to months and days, the same remark does not apply. Letters were very

[1] No. 931. [2] No. 946. [3] No. 945.

320

frequently dated in this respect according to what is the general usage now. But even here, as the reader will not fail to observe, there was a much more common use of Festivals and Saints' days, and when a letter was not written on a day particularly marked in the Calendar, it was frequently dated the Monday or Wednesday, or whatever day of the week it might happen to be, *before* or *after* such a celebration. Agnes Paston even dates a letter during the week by the collect of the Sunday preceding :—'Written at Paston in haste, the Wednesday next after *Deus qui errantibus.*'[1]

Mode of reckoning. Of their modes of computing other things we have little indication in these volumes except in money accounts, which are always kept in Roman figures. No separate columns are set apart in MSS. of this date (although for the convenience of the reader this has sometimes been done in print) for the different denominations of pounds, shillings, pence, and marks, so that it would have been impossible for the best arithmetician easily to cast up totals after the modern fashion. The arithmeticians of that day, in fact, had a totally different method of reckoning. They used counters, and had a counting-board or abacus, on which they set up the totals.[2] An instance of this occurs in the first volume, where John Paston, in superintending the works at Caister Castle, or, as we now rather suspect, at Mautby, thought it advisable to change the room in which his coffers and his 'counterwey' should be set. In connection with this incident one other point is worthy of observation. On taking the measure of the new room, John Paston's wife reported that he would find it less convenient than the former one. 'There is no space,' she wrote, 'beside the bed, though the bed were removed to the door, to set both your board and your coffers there, and to have space to go and sit beside.'[3] When it is considered that the room in question was a 'draught chamber,' that is to say, that it contained a privy in

[1] No. 34.
[2] The modern mode of adding up columns of arabic numerals was called *Algorism* or *Awgrym*. Thus Palsgrave gives as an example of the use of the word—'I shall reken it syxe times by aulgorisme, or you caste it ones by counters.'—*Promptorium Parv.* i. 18.
[3] No. 224.

VOL. I.—X

321

addition to the furniture which Paston intended to introduce, want of space ought certainly to have been a very serious objection.

Manner of living. The neglect of sanitary considerations in domestic architecture—indeed, in domestic matters generally—was no doubt a prolific source of disease and pestilence. Yet the general plan of daily life pursued by our ancestors was, it must be owned, more wholesome than that of the nineteenth century. It is well known that they were early risers. Innumerable patent kinds of artificial light did not tempt them to waste the natural hours of rest either in study or in dissipation. Their meals too were earlier. Their dinner was at noon, if not before ; and after dinner, in the long summer days, it was customary to take some additional repose. Thus Henry Windsor concludes a letter to John Paston—'Written in my sleeping time at afternoon, on Whitsunday.'[1] This practice of sleeping in the daytime was so universal that in the case of labourers it was only thought necessary to keep it within certain limits, and to restrict it by Act of Parliament to a quarter of the year, from the middle of May to the middle of August.[2]

Sending dinners out. A curious practice in relation to dining mentioned in Letter 423 has already been incidentally alluded to. It was the year after Sir John Fastolf's death, and John Paston's wife had gone out of Norwich to reside at Hellesdon. Paston's increased importance in the county was shown by the Mayor and Mayoress of Norwich one day *sending their dinners out* to Hellesdon, and coming to dine with Margaret Paston. Of this kind of compliment we have another illustration in More's *History of Richard III.* It is well known how, when just after the death of Edward IV. the Earl of Rivers and Lord Richard Grey were conducting the boy king Edward V. up to London, they were overtaken by the Duke of Gloucester at Stony Stratford, and placed under arrest. As the story is reported by More, Gloucester at first treated his prisoners with courtesy, and at dinner sent a dish from his own table to Lord Rivers, praying him to be of good cheer, for all

[1] No. 332. [2] Statute 6 Hen. VIII. ch. 3.

322

should be well enough. 'And he thanked the duke,' continues the historian, 'and prayed the messenger to bear it to his nephew the Lord Richard with the same message for his comfort, who he thought had more need of comfort as one to whom such adversity was strange ; but himself had been all his days in ure therewith, and therefore could bear it the better.'

Chivalry and courtesy. The courtesies of life were certainly not less valued in those rough unquiet days than in our own. Although men like Caxton lamented the decline of chivalry, its civilising influence continued, and its most important usages were still kept up. Among the books which William Ebesham transcribed for Sir John Paston at the rate of twopence a leaf, was one which was called *The Great Book*, treating of 'the Coronation and other Treatises of Knighthood,' 'of the manner of making joust and tournaments,' and the like.[1] His library, or that of his brother John, contained also 'the Death of Arthur,' the story of Guy of Warwick, chronicles of the English kings from Cœur de Lion to Edward III., the legend of Guy and Colbrand, and various other chronicles and fictions suited to knightly culture ; besides moral treatises, like Bishop Alcock's *Abbey of the Holy Ghost*, and poetical and imaginative books, such as the poems of Chaucer—at least his *Troilus and Cressida*, his *Legend of Ladies* (commonly called *The Legend of Good Women*), his *Parliament of Birds, the Belle Dame sauns Mercie*, and Lydgate's *Temple of Glass*. Books like these formed part of the recreations of a country gentleman. They contained, doubtless, the fund of ideas which fathers communicated to their children around the winter fire. And the children were the better qualified to appreciate them by an education which was entirely founded upon the principles of chivalry.

The training of the young. It was in accordance with these principles, and to maintain a true sense of order in society, that the sons of knights and gentlemen were sent at an early age to serve in other gentlemen's houses. Thus John Paston the youngest was sent to be brought up in the family of the Duke of Norfolk ; and so

[1] Nos. 695, 987.

323

THE PASTON LETTERS

common was this practice, so necessary was it esteemed to a young gentleman's education, that, as we have seen, his father was reproached for keeping his elder brother at home and unemployed. In a new household, and especially in that of a man of rank, it was considered that a youth would learn something of the world, and fit himself best for the place he was to fill in it. It was the same also, to some extent, with the daughters of a family, as we find Margaret Paston writing to her son Sir John to get his sister placed in the household either of the Countess of Oxford or of the Duchess of Bedford, or else 'in some other worshipful place.'[1] This we have supposed to be his sister Margery, who (no doubt for want of being thus taken care of) shortly after married Richard Calle, to the scandal and disgust of the whole family. His other sister, Anne, was placed in the household of a gentleman named Calthorpe, who, however, afterwards desired to get rid of her, alleging that he wished to reduce his household, and suggested that she 'waxed high, and it were time to purvey her a marriage.' It is curious that the prospect of her being sent home again does not seem to have been particularly agreeable even to her own mother. Margaret Paston wonders why Calthorpe should have been so anxious to get rid of the young lady without delay. Perhaps she had given him offence, or committed some misdemeanour. Her mother therefore writes to her son John the youngest in London to see how Cousin Clere 'is disposed to her-ward,' that she may not be under the necessity of having her home again, where she would only lose her time, and be continually trying her mother's patience, as her sister Margery had done before her.[2]

Want of domestic feeling. And was this, the reader may well ask, the spirit of domestic life in the fifteenth century? Could two generations of one family not ordinarily live together in comfort? Was the feeling of older people towards children only that they ought to be taught the ways of the world, and learn not to make themselves disagreeable? Alas! I fear, for the most part it amounted to little more than this. Children, and especially daughters, were a mere burden to their parents.

[1] No. 704.   [2] No. 766.

324

INTRODUCTION

They must be sent away from home to learn manners, and to be out of the way. As soon as they grew up, efforts must be made to marry them, and get them off their parents' hands for good. If they could not be got rid of that way, and were still troublesome, they could be well thrashed, like Elizabeth Paston, the aunt of the last-mentioned young ladies, who, as will be remembered, was allowed to speak to no one, was beaten once or twice a week, and sometimes twice in one day, and had her head broken 'in two or three places' in consequence.[1]

Such a state of matters, however repulsive to our feelings, is by no means unaccountable. That age was certainly not singular, however much mistaken, in its belief that a sense of what is due to the State is more important than a sense of what is due to the family. Our ancestors forgot the fact—as we too, in this age of enforced schooling are too apt to leave it out of account—that the most important part of education, good or bad, must inevitably be that which a child receives at home. They were rewarded for their forgetfulness by a loss of natural affection, for which their high sense of external order afforded but imperfect compensation. Admirable as the feudal system was in maintaining the necessary subordination of different classes, it acted most injuriously upon the homes, where all that makes up a nation's real worth must be carefully tended in the first instance. The very *Wardships.* foundation of domestic life was in many cases vitiated by a system which put the wardship and marriage of heirs under age at the disposal of their superior lords. In the case of an important landowner who held of the Crown, it was a regular matter of bargain and sale. The wardship and marriage were granted away to such a person as could offer the Treasury a satisfactory sum for the privilege; and if the heir took it upon himself to marry without licence of such person, he incurred a heavy fine.[2] Thus was the most sacred of all

[1] No. 94, and p. 155 of this Introduction.
[2] We have already referred, at p. 154, to the case of Stephen Scrope, whose wardship was sold by his stepfather, Sir John Fastolf, to Judge Gascoigne, but was afterwards bought back again to prevent the judge marrying him to one of his own daughters, both the original sale and the redemption being equally against the will of

325

THE PASTON LETTERS

human relations made a matter of traffic and sale, and the best feelings of the human heart were systematically crushed by considerations the most sordid.

Remarks of a Venetian on the English. The absence of domestic affection among the English people generally was, in fact, a subject of observation to foreigners in that day. The earliest extant report of a Venetian ambassador on the state of this country was written in the reign of Henry VII., and in this we find some very strong comments on the subject, showing that the coldheartedness of parents towards their children, the want of tenderness in husbands towards their wives, the mercenary way in which marriages were contracted by parents or guardians for the young people under their charge, was such as to shock the sensibility of strangers from the warmer lands of the South. To the Italian mind it seemed as if there was no real human nature in Englishmen at all. There was licentiousness among them, to be sure, but our Venetian almost doubted whether in high or low society an Englishman was ever known to be in love. He had witnessed nothing of the sort himself. On the contrary, he had seen young noblemen content to marry old widows for the sake of fortunes, which they hoped to share soon with younger partners; and he suspected that although Englishmen were very jealous husbands, the most serious offences against married life might be condoned for money.[1]

Freedom of manners. It is impossible to deny that these comments, except the last, which we would fain hope was a mistake, must have been largely justified. The Paston letters bear strong additional testimony to the general truth of what our Italian critic saw in England. Yet, acute as his observation was, an ambassador from the stately Signory of Venice was perhaps not altogether

Stephen Scrope himself, who complained that Fastolf had 'bought and sold him like a beast.' The particulars of these transactions are not obtained from the Paston Letters, but there will be found several notices of another wardship, viz. that of Thomas Fastolf of Cowhaw, kinsman of Sir John Fastolf, which was bought by Sir John of the king, and committed by patent to John Paston and Sir Thomas Howes, and which became the subject of a good deal of controversy.—*See* Nos. 248, 263, 266, 267, 271, 292, and 352.
[1] *Italian Relation of England* (Camden Soc.), pp. 24-27.

326

INTRODUCTION

in a position to read the deepest mysteries of the English heart. To this day the warmth of the English nature lies covered by a cold exterior; yet even in the external manners of the people the genial Erasmus found touches which our Venetian cared not for, and did not deign to notice. While feudalism still kept down the natural emotions, insisting on a high respect for order, there was a freedom in social intercourse, and in England more than elsewhere, which has long ago been chilled among ourselves by the severity of Puritanism. In his own amusing way Erasmus tells us how in this delightful island ladies and gentlemen kissed each other freely whenever they met, in the streets or in their houses. There were kisses when you came, and kisses when you went away—delicate, fragrant kisses that would assuredly tempt a poet from abroad to stay in England all his days.[1] So the witty Dutchman informed a friend in the unrestrained freedom of epistolary correspondence. And we may believe that in most cases the severity of home was mitigated by a greater freedom of communication with the world outside. Only in cases of very severe displeasure were the daughters of a family shut up for a time, like Elizabeth Paston, and forbidden to speak to any one. For the most part, they received the salutations of strangers, and conversed with them without reserve, as marriage was quite understood to be a thing which depended entirely upon arrangements made by their parents.

Urbanity. With all this, there was an urbanity of manners, a courtesy of address, and a general external refinement, on which more recent times have not improved. And in these things England was pre-eminent. Our Venetian could not help noticing that the English were a very polite people. Another Italian of that day, Polydore Vergil, has recorded that in this respect they resembled his own countrymen. The hard schooling which they received at home, the after-training elsewhere in the houses of 'worshipful' persons, had taught them from their early years to consider above all things what was due to others. In every relation of life, in the freest social intercourse, the honour due to parents, to strangers, to noblemen, or to kings,

[1] *Erasm. Epp.* lib. v. 10.

327

THE PASTON LETTERS

was never for a moment forgotten. In the most familiar letters the son asks his father's or mother's blessing, and the wife addresses her husband as 'right worshipful.' When people talked to each other on the street, they did so with heads uncovered. Even kings at the mention of other potentates' names took off their hats with reverence.[1]

Import-
ance of
maintain-
ing
authority. An age which, with all its many drawbacks, cultivated ideas such as these cannot be looked upon as despicable or barbarous. We could have wished to see something more of the element of love in families—something more of the easy rule of natural affection occasionally superseding the hard notions of feudal or parental discipline. But the anxiety to uphold authority, to preserve honour for whom it was due, to maintain social and political order in spite of influences which were conspicuously at work breaking it up before men's eyes, was a true and wholesome feeling, to the strength of which we owe a debt unspeakable even in these days of progress. At no time in England's history was there a stronger feeling of the needful subordination of the different parts of society to each other ; but under a king incapable of governing, this feeling bred a curse, and not a blessing. The great lords, who should have preserved order under the king, fell out among themselves, and in spite of the fervid loyalty of the age, the greatest subject became a kingmaker.

The
Earl of
Warwick's
household. That civil war should have broken out in a state of society like this need occasion no surprise. The enormous retinues of feudal noblemen were in themselves sufficiently dangerous to the peace of the kingdom, and when the sense of feudal subjection to one sovereign was impaired, the issue could not be doubtful. At the table of the great Earl of Warwick, Stow informs us that the flesh of six entire oxen was sometimes consumed in a single meal. With the profuse hospitality of the Middle Ages, he entertained not only all his regular dependants, but all chance comers who had any acquaintance in his house-

[1] *Italian Relation*, pp. 22-32; Polydore Vergil, 14-15. Henry VII., in conference with the Spanish ambassador, De Puebla, always took off his hat when the names of Ferdinand and Isabella were mentioned (Bergenroth's *Spanish Calendar*, vol. i. p. 10). I have also seen notices of the same custom elsewhere.

328

INTRODUCTION

hold. Visitors were also allowed to carry off joints from his table, and the taverns in the neighbourhood of Warwick's inn were actually full of his meat.[1] Such a nobleman had no difficulty in obtaining friends to fight for him in the day of battle. He maintained, in fact, what might be called a little standing army at all times, and if an emergency arose, doubtless many who had dined at his table would flock to his standard, and take his wages.[2]

The
Tudor
policy. The causes which had produced the wars of the Roses were carefully watched by the Tudor sovereigns, and one by one rooted out. Laws were passed against noblemen keeping large retinues, and were not suffered to remain a dead letter. The nobility of England learned to stand in awe of the Crown in a way they never did before, and never have done since. Every branch of the royal family, except the reigning dynasty, was on one pretext or another lopped away. Every powerful nobleman knew that just in proportion as he was great, it was necessary for him to be circumspect. Under Henry VIII. and Elizabeth, birth and rank counted for very little, and the peers became submissive instruments, anxious, and indeed eager, to carry out the sovereign's will. In short, the unity of a divided nation was restored under a set of politic kings, who enforced the laws, kept down the nobility, and, in spite of their despotism, were generally loved by the people.

[1] Stow's *Chronicle*, 421.   See No. 760.

329

APPENDIX TO PREFACE AND INTRODUCTION

I. WILL OF PETER LE NEVE.—See p. 3

THE following extracts from the will of Peter Le Neve, as contained in the principal register at Doctors' Commons, are curious in other respects besides their bearing on the history of the Paston MSS.

Item, I give and bequeath unto the Reverend Doctor Tanner, Chancellor of Norwich, and Mr. Thomas Martin of Palgrave, all my abstracts out of records, old deeds, books, petigrees, seals, papers, and other collections which shall only relate to the antiquityes and history of Norfolk and Suffolk, or one of them, upon condicion that they, or the survivor of them, or the executors or administrators of such survivor, do and shall, within twelve months next after my decease, procure a good and safe repository in the Cathedral Church of Norwich, or in some other good and publick building in the said city, for the preservation of the same collections, for the use and benefitt of such curious persons as shall be desirous to inspect, transcribe, or consult the same. And I doe hereby give full power to the said Doctor Tanner and Thomas Martin, and to the survivor of them, and to the executors or administrators of such survivor, to fix and prescribe such rules and orders for the custody and preservation of the said collecions as they shall think proper. . . .

Item, my will and mind is, that if my said wife Frances shall at any time hereafter intermarry with Thomas Allen, my late clerk, then I will that she shall have and enjoy but the annuity or summe of forty pounds per annum from the time of such her intermarryage, and noe more shall be paid unto her by my aforesaid trustees; and I strickly charge and forbid her, the said Frances, to permitt the said Thomas Allen to come into any of my studys, or to lend or give him any of my books or papers, or to suffer him in any respect to intermeddle with my affairs. Item, I give unto my said wife Frances such goods and things att Bow and Wychingham as I shall mencion and sett down in a certain paper to be signed and left by me for that purpose. Item, I give unto my said wife Frances my crown, silver gilt, my collar, silver party, my jewell, my herald's coat and chain. Item, I give unto Henrietta Beeston the summe of twelve pence per week, to be paid to her from the first day of August last for so long time as she shall continue with me at Wychingham. Item, I will that all my shelves, presses, drawers, and boxes now in my

330

APPENDIX

study att Wychingham shall goe along with my Norfolk and Suffolk collections to Norwich. . . .

Item, the residue of my printed or manuscript books, arms, and things relating to antiquity, I give them unto such person and persons, and bodyes, politic or corporate, as I shall direct and appoint, in a paper to be signed and left by me for that purpose.

The above will was proved 7th November 1729.

II. JULIAN HERBERD.—See pp. 33, 34

The following documents in the case of Julian Herberd *v.* William Paston are preserved in the Record Office among 'Chancery, Parliamentary and Council Proceedings.' The date, it will be seen, must be after 1432 :—

MEMBRANE 1

William Paston.
    Sr Rauf, parson of Bronham, steward with my maister Cromwell.
    Austinne Bange of Norwiche.
    John Roppys with hem priour of the Abbey of Norwiche.
    Rob't Chapelleyn of Norwiche.
    Rob't Grygge of litel Plomstede in the cuntie of Norwiche.
    Sr William, the vicaire of Seint Stephenes Chirche in Norwiche.

MEMBRANE 2

Please it to youre moste hie and habundant grace to graunte un to youre pouere and continuel bedwoman Julian Herberd, that William Paston one of youre Juges of the cõe benche may come with alle his affinite and appere bifore youre hie and gracious presence with alle youre worthy and right wyse counsail, and that of youre hie goodnesse comaunde the seide William Paston to bringe bifore yow and to schewe alle the evidences and munimentes, whiche that the modere of youre seide pore bisechere schulde have yeve un to the seide William Paston state or to any man that had it bifore hym or eny man for here seide moder or eny of the seide blode, fro the tyme youre seide pore bisechere modere was borne un to this oure. For the seide William Paston knowleched bifore my lorde of Warewyk and youre Chaunceller of Inglonde, youre Tresorer, youre chef Juge of the Kynges benche, and afore other of yoᵗ sergeantz of lawe, beynge to gidere, how he radde diversez evidences of xix acres londe that schulde longe un to youre seide pore bisechere every yere vjs. viijd.; so that sche wolde holde here plesed and content. Up on the whiche sche wolde nat holde here so agreed with oute youre gracious advis in this matere. Besechinge to youre hie and habundant grace, for oure right worthy and gracious Kynge youre fadere soule, and for oure right worthy and gracious quene youre moder soule, whos soules God of his grace assoille, that youre seide pore bisecher may have here evidences, so that here trewe right might be opinly knowen. For there ys twies so good behinde as the saide William Paston knowleched of

331

the seide xix acres, and youre seide pore bisecher wol nat assent that he schulde take his otthe, laste he wol suere that he have nat here evidences. For it may nat be but he moste nedes have hem or summe of his, and that ys opinly knowen. That it like un to youre good Grace to considere this matere above wretyn, and thereuppon to graunte, that the seide William Paston with alle his affinite and youre seide bisecher may alle be bounden to yow in a simple obligacion in what somme that liketh youre hie wysdome, demene so that they may abide youre awarde, with the assent & consent of youre fulle wys and discrete councell and youre worthy and gracious jugement in this mater for the love of God and yn wey of charitee.

MEMBRANE 3

TO OURE RIGHT GRACIOUS LORDE THE KYNGE

Please it to youre right high and gracious lordeshipe to considere the grete wronges that William Paston hath done to Julian Herberd, youre pore wydowe and continuell bedewoman, for with holdynge of diverses evidences and wrongefulle prisonmentes that he hath done to the seide Julian ayenst youre lawes, whiche been here under wretyn yn article wise, whiche the seide Julian bisechith un to youre moste hie and gracious lordeshipe oversee, and that remedie may be putte therynne by youre gracious hondes atte Reverence of God and in wey of charitee.

These been the wronges and extorcions done to Julian Herberd doughter and heir of Herry Herberd of lytel Plumstede yn the Counte of Norff. and Margarete his wyf, doughter and heir to William Palmere, sometyme of the seide Plumstede, by William Paston, and of othere by his assent.

Firste, there as the seide Margarete died sesid yn here demene as yn fee taille of a mesuage of xix. acres of londe with thappourtenance yn Plumstede, the whiche to the same Juliane schulde discende be right of heritage, as doughter and nexte heir of the seide Margarete. The whiche William Paston the seide Juliane of the seide mees and londes now be xl. wynter hath witholden, the whiche been yerly worth xxx*ī*. and better, the sōme ys now owynge lx*lī*.

Memorandum, quod Juliana Herberd de Norwico, que fuit filia Margarete Palmere de Plumstede produxit Robertum Bresyngham et Johannem Colton, Cives Norwici, coram Willelmo Paston apud Norwicum in Camera sua ad recordandum coram eo et aliis circumstantibus quod Johannes Thornham optulit prefate Juliane pro tribus acris terre in campis de Plumstede predictis xl*ī*. pro jure suo hereditario, que tres acre jacent in placito inter dominum Johannem Thornham, petentem, et Robertum Grigge tenentem. Et prefatus Robertus Bresyngham et Johannes inquirebant per viciñ vill' adjac̃, qui dixerunt quod Margareta Palmere, mater dicte Juliane fuit recta heres illius terre; Et quod post decessum ejusdem Margarete discendere debuisset prefate Juliane ut de feodo talliato. Et postea dictus Willelmus in presencia Radulphi Rectoris de Brunham, Johannis Roppys, Henrici Pye de Brixston, Thome Marchall et aliorum ibidem existencium publice legebat cartas et evidencias pertinentes dicte Juliane, et optulit eidem Juliane pro suo jure habendo etc., xij*d*., et postea xx*d*. Et eciam pro majore evidencia dicta Juliana produxit duodecim legales homines

ville de Plumstede Magna et Parva coram Thoma Erpyngham milite, qui dixerunt quod prefata Margareta, mater dicte Juliane, fuit recta heres predictarum terrarum etc., et quod per totam patriam bene est cognitum quod prefata Juliana est recta heres ejusdem Margarete. Ac eciam alia vice predictus Willelmus optulit dicte Juliane pro jure suo xx*ī*. in presencia Ricardi Gegge, Gentilman, sibi solvendos quandocunque vellet, prout idem clericus omni tempore recordare voluerit.

Also there as the seide Julian poursued ayenst the seide William atte a parlement holden atte Westminstre, and there the seide William did here arrest yn to the Countour of London, and there kepte here yn prisone to the seide parlement was ended thretnynge here to holde here there terme of here lyf, but yf sche wol relesse to hym here right and make acquitaunce generall.

Also the seide Paston, be nightes tyme bituene ix. or x. of the belle, did do bringe the seide Julian prisoner under warde to his ynne in Fletestrete, and there constreined here to seale a blanke chartre, yn whiche he dide write a relesse atte his owne devys, and sent here ayene to prisone, and there kepte here iij. daies, and sent ayene for here to hire the relesse radde, and profred for here right vj. marke.

Also the seide Paston, the Saturday nexte bifore the feste of Saint George, the vj. yere, etc., profred the seide Juliane in presence of the Chaunceller vj. marke yn playne court and iij. acres of the seide londe, and so moche ys the seide Juliane refused that profre, did arreste here newe in the seide Countoure and helde here there from the vij. day of Feverere, etc., and there wolde make here swere on a book or be bounde by obligacion never more to poursue here right.

Also the seide Paston atte Counsell holden atte Redynge the seide Juliane poursued to the lorde of Bedford, and he comaunded to write his lettres to the seide Paston chargynge hym to aggre with here, the seide Paston havynge knowleche that sche sewed for the lettres, made a false sugestion to the Chaunceller, wherby sche was by a sergeaunt of armes committed to Flete, and there beten, fetered and stokked, and so there holden by an hole yere, to that entent that no man schulde wete where sche was by come tille sche hadde be dede in prison. Of whiche false prisonment Sr Thomas Erpyngham poursued here deliveraunce, comaunded here to be atte the nexte Cessions to be justefied there, consideringe to here grete damage as well in here body as losse of goodes by so longe tyme continued, whiche prisonment the seide Julian wolde nat have hadde for xl*lī*. beside alle other losse of goodes.

Also the seide Paston with holdeth alle the evidences to here seide right longinge, and wastynge the seide mesuage and londes in that he may.

Also the seide Paston kepte here iij. yere in the pitte withynne the Castell of Norwiche in grete meschef, in so moche that scho hadde nat but a pynte of mylke yn x. daies and x. nightes, and a ferthinge loffe, standinge under the jugement and ordenance of the Duke of Norffe now late passed to God.[1]

Also, the seide Paston scith hadde youre seide suppliant in prisone in the Kynges benche, and there sche lay xij. monthes and more in harde payne and distresse nye dede for colde hunger and thurste.

[1] John Mowbray, second Duke of Norfolk, who died in 1432.

Item, the seide Paston dede to bringe here oute of the Roundehows yn to youre paleys and brought here afore youre chef Justice, and than the saide Paston comaunded certeines persones to bringe here to prisone to youre Benche, and badde atte his perille certeines persones to smyte the brayne oute of here hede for suynge of here right, and there beynge in grevouse prison durynge half yere and more fetered and cheined, suffringe colde, hunger, thurste, in pointe of deth, God and ye, gracious Kynge, helpe here to here right.

(*Membranes* 1 *and* 2 *are sewn on to the face of membrane* 3, *one at the top, the other at the bottom.*)

III. PARMINTER'S INSURRECTION.—See p. 75.

In the bundle of Privy Seals for the year 29 Henry VI. is a pardon to James God, dated on the 4th March, and delivered to the Chancellor for execution on the 5th. Attached to it is the following record of his indictment:—

'*Kent sc.*—Jur' dicunt quod Jacobus God nuper de Feversham in com' prædicto, plummer, et alii, ac quamplures alii proditores, rebelles et inimici illustrissimis Principis Henrici Regis Angliæ Sexti post Conquestum ignoti et nuper complices et de societate falsi proditoris Will'i Parmynter, smyth, qui se ipsum nominavit Secundum Capitaneum Kanciæ, eidemque adhærentes et de ejus covina et assensu in omnibus proditionibus suis mortem dicti Regis et destructionem regni sui Angliæ confœderantes, machinantes, compassentes et proponentes, ultimo die Augusti anno regni dicti Regis vicesimo nono[1] apud Feversham et alibi in com. Kanciæ se adinvicem congregaverunt ad numerum quadringentorum hominum et amplius, dicentes et confidentes quod ipsi essent de eorum covina et assensu ad eorum libitum et voluntatem xl. milia hominum armatorum et modo guerrino arraiatorum ad præbendum et percussiendum bellum contra dictum Regem seu quoscumque alios in proditionibus suis prædictis eis contravenientes, et falso et proditorie insurrexerunt et mortem dicti Regis imaginaverunt et compassi fuerunt, ac guerram adtunc et ibidem et alibi per vices infra dictum com. Kanc. falso et proditorie contra dictum Regem, supremum dominum suum, levaverunt, in destructionem ipsius Regis et Regni prædicti.

BENET.'

There is a note of the trial of Parmynter in Hilary term, 29 Hen. VI., on the Controlment Roll of that year, rot. 9.

IV. PARDON TO JOHN PAYN.—See p. 78.

On the Patent Roll 30 Henry VI., p. 1, m. 23, occurs the following entry:—

De Pardonacione.—Rex omnibus ballivis et fidelibus suis ad quos, &c.,

[1] So in the record, but evidently an error. It should have been *vicesimo octavo*.

salutem. Sciatis quod cum nonnulli rebelles nostri in comitatu nostro Kanciæ, paucis ante diebus contra pacem nostram insurrectionem gravem concitantes, quasdam factiones proditorias contra nostram personam detestabiliter machinati fuerint, nonnullaque proditiones, murdra, felonias et facinora, aliasque transgressiones perpetraverint; quia tamen, cum nuper per civitates, oppida atque villas in eodem comitatu nostro ad eorum hujusmodi insolencias et rebelliones coercendos iter faceremus, plurimi ex eisdem, spiritu sanioris consilii ducti, plurimum humiliati, etiam usque femoralia nudi, suorum immanitates criminum coram nobis confitentes, veniam a nobis effusis lachrymis anxie postularunt; Nos, ad singulorum hujusmodi ligeorum nostrorum submissiones humillimas nostros misericordes oculos dirigentes, ac firmiter tenentes quod de cætero in nostra obedientia stabiles permanebunt, fidem ligeanciæ suæ erga nos inantea inviolabiliter servaturi, ad laudem, gloriam et honorem Omnipotentis et misericordis Dei ac gloriosissimæ Virginis matris Christi, de gratia nostra speciali pardonavimus, remisimus et relaxavimus Johanni Payn de Pecham in comitatu prædicto, yoman, alias dicto Johanni Payn, nuper de Estpekham in comitatu prædicto, smyth, qui inter cæteros se submisit nostræ gratiæ, quocumque nomine censeatur, sectam pacis nostræ quæ ad nos versus eum pertinent, seu poterit pertinere, pro quibuscumque proditionibus, feloniis, murdris et transgressionibus per ipsum a septimo die Julii anno regni nostri vicesimo octavo usque decimum diem Junii ultimo præteritum factis sive perpetratis; acetiam utlagarias, si quæ in ipsum Johannem occasionibus prædictis seu earum aliqua fuerint promulgatæ; necnon omnimodas forisfacturas terrarum, tenementorum, reddituum, possessionum, bonorum et catallorum, quæ idem Johannes nobis occasionibus prædictis seu earum aliqua forisfecit aut forisfacere debuit, et firmam pacem nostram ei inde concedimus: Ita tamen quod stet recto in curia nostra si quis versus eum loqui voluerit de præmissis seu aliquo præmissorum. Proviso semper quod ista nostra pardonacio, remissio sive relaxacio se non extendat ad aliqua malefacta supra mare et aquas aliquo modo facta sive perpetrata. In cujus, &c. Teste Rege apud Westmonasterium secundo die Novembris.

Two similar patents were granted on the same date to Richard Doke, yeoman, and William Souter, labourer, both of Peckham.

V. THE DUKE OF YORK AT DARTFORD.—See p. 99.

The most minute account of the encampment of the Duke of York at Dartford is contained in the following extract from the Cottonian Roll, ii. 23.

At Crayfford, myle from Dertfford.

Primo die mensis Marcii anno regni Regis Henrici Sexti xxx^{o} ther was my Lord of Yorkes ordynaunce iij$^{mill.}$ gownner, and hym selff in the middell ward with viij$^{mil.}$, my Lord of Devynsher by the southe side with vj$^{mil.}$, and my Lord Cobham with vj$^{mil.}$ at the water side, and vij. shippus with ther stuff. And sith that tyme, and sith was poyntment made and taken at Dertfford by embassetours, my Lord the B. of Wynchester, my Lord B. of Ely, my Lord the Erle of Salusbury, my Lorde of Warrewik, my Lord Bewcham, and my Lord of Sydeley, &c., whiche poyntment was, &c. And soon after was Chatterley, yeman of the Crown, maymed, notwithstondyng he was takyn at Derby with money making and ladde to London. Then after the Kynges yeman of his chambur, namyd Fazakerley, with letteris was sent to Luddelowe to my Lord of Yorke chargyng to do forth a certeyn of his mayny, Arthern, squier, Sharpe, sqier, &c. ; the whiche Fazakerley hyld in avowtry Sharpes wiff, the which Sharpe slewe Fitzacurley, and a baker of Ludlow roos and the Commyns, &c., the whych baker is at Kyllyngworth Castell, &c. After this my Lord of Shrousbury, &c., rode in to Kent, and set up v. peyre of galowes and dede execucion upon John Wylkyns, taken and brought to the towne as for capteyn, and with other mony mo, of the whiche xxviij. were honged and be heded, the whiche hedes were sent to London; and London said ther shuld no mo hedes be set upon there; and that tyme Eton was robbyd, and the Kyng beyng at Wynsor on Lowe Sonday, &c

VI. THE DUKE OF YORK AND THE COUNCIL.—See p. 132.

The following document is enrolled on the Patent Roll, 32 Henry VI., membrane 20:—

Pro Ricardo Duce Ebor.—Rex omnibus ad quos, &c., salutem. Inspeximus tenorem cujusdam actus in consilio nostro apud Westmonasterium tento facti, venerabili patri Johanni Cardinali et Archiepiscopo Cantuariensi, totius Angliæ primati, Cancellario nostro, per Thomam Kent, clericum ejusdem consilii nostri, ad exemplificationem tenoris prædicti sub Magno Sigillo nostro in forma debita fiendam nuper deliberatum et in filaciis Cancellariæ nostræ residentum, in hæc verba:—

The xxj. day of Novembre, the yere of the regne of oure Souverain Lorde King Henry the VIth xxxijti. at Westmynstre, in the Sterred Chambre, being there present the Lordes, the Cardinal Archebisshop of Canterbury and Chaunceller of England, th' Archebisshop of Yorke, the Bisshops of London, Winchestre, Ely, Norwich, Saint Davides, Chestre, Lincoln, and Carlisle, the Duc of Buckingham, th'Erles of Salisbury, Pembroke, Warrewik, Wiltshire, Shrovesbury, and Worcestre, Tresourer of England, the Viscount Bourchier, the Priour of Seint Johns, the Lordes Cromwell, Suddeley, Duddeley, Stourton, and Berners. The Duc of York reherced unto the seid Lordes that he, as the Kinges true liegman and subgit, was by commaundement directed unto him undre the Kinges Prive Seal, come hidre to the Kinges greet Counsail, and wolde with all diligence to his power entende to the same, and to all that that sholde or might be to the welfare of the King and of his subgettes; but for asmoche as it soo was that divers persones, suche as of longe tyme have been of his Counsail, have be commaunded afore this tyme, by what meanes he watte never, not to entende upon him, but to withdrawe thaim of any counsail to be yeven unto him: the which is to his greet hurte and causeth that he can not procede with suche matiers as he hath to doo in the Kinges courtes and ellus

where, desired the Lordes of the counsail abovesaid that they wolde soo assente and agree that suche as have been of his counsail afore this tyme might frely, without any impediment, resorte unto him and withoute any charge to be leide unto theim, yeve him counsail from tyme to tyme in suche matiers as he hath or shal have to doo. To the which desire alle the Lordes abovesaide condescended and agreed, as to that thing that was thought unto them juste and resounable, and fully licenced all suche persones as he wolde calle to his counsail frely withoute any impediment to entende unto him; and commaunded this to be enacted amonge th'actes of the Counsaill. Actum anno, mense, die et loco ut supra, præsentibus dominis supradictis. T. Kent.

Nos autem tenorem actus prædicti ad requisicionem carissimi consanguinei nostri prædicti, Ricardi Ducis Ebaracensis, duximus exemplificandum per præsentes. In cujus, &c. Teste Rege apud Westmonasterium, vj. die Decembris.

VII. DEFENCE AGAINST THE EARL OF WARWICK.—See p. 185.

The following commissions are found on the Patent Roll 38 Henry VI., p. 2, m. 21. They afford remarkable evidence of the terror inspired in the Queen's Government by the capture of Lord Rivers at Sandwich.

De advocando et debellando.—Rex carissimo consanguineo suo Johanni Duci Norff' ac dilecto et fideli suo Philippo Wentworth militi, necnon dilectis, sibi Roberto Willoughby, Johanni Hopton, Willelmo Tyrell, Thomæ Brewes, Gilberto Debenham, Johanni Clopton, Willelmo Jenney, et Reginaldo Rous, salutem. Quia satis manifestum est quod quidam rebelles nostri Ricardo nuper Comiti Warr' proditori et inimico nostro adhærentes, villam nostram Sandewici jam tarde intrarunt et ibidem mala quamplurima nobis et fidelibus ligeis nostris fecerunt et perpetrarunt, et alia mala prioribus pejora in diversis partibus comitatus nostri Suff', si eas ingredi poterint, facere et perpetrare proponunt, ut veraciter informamur, nisi eorum maliciæ citius et celerius resistatur: Nos, tam maliciæ ipsius inimici nostri ac complicum suorum prædictorum (*sic*), quam pro defensione partium ibidem providere volentes, ut tenemur, assignavimus vos, conjunctim et divisim, ac vobis et vestrum cuilibet plenam potestatem et auctoritatem damus et committimus ad advocandum coram vobis [omnes] et singulos ligeos nostros comitatus prædicti, cujuscunque status, gradus seu condicionis fuerint, de quibus vobis melius videbitur expedire, ad proficiscendum vobiscum contra præfatum inimicum nostrum ac complices suos prædictos, ac ad assistenciam et auxilium suum vobis seu vestrum cuilibet in eorum resistenciam dandum et impendendum in casu quo idem inimicus noster ac complices sui prædicti dictum comitatum vel partes adjacentes ingredi præsumant, ac ad eos et secum comitantes ut hostes et rebelles nostros debellandum, expugnandum, et destruendum, ac ad omnia alia et singula quæ juxta sanas discretiones vestras in hac parte in repressionem prædictorum inimicorum nostrorum ac complicum suorum et eorum maledicti propositi fore videritis necessaria et oportuna, facien-

dum, exercendum et exequendum. Et insuper assignavimus vos conjunctim et divisim ad omnes personas partem prædicti nuper Comitis Warr' seu aliorum rebellium nostrorum et complicum suorum verbis vel operibus defendentes et tenentes, vel aliqua verba contra majestatem nostram regiam habentes et dicentes, similiter capiendum et arestandum, et in prisonis nostris in forma prædicta custodiendum, et custodiri faciendum. Et ideo vobis et vestrum cuilibet mandamus quod circa præmissa diligenter intendatis et ea faciatis et exequamini in forma prædicta. Damus autem universis et singulis vicecomitibus, majoribus, ballivis, constabulariis, ac aliis officiariis, ministris, fidelibus legiis et subditis nostris quibuscunque, tam infra libertates quam extra, tenore præsentium, firmiter, in mandatis, quod vobis et vestrum cuilibet in executione præmissorum intendentes sint, assistentes et auxiliantes in omnibus diligenter. In cujus, &c. Teste Rege apud Westmonasterium, x. die Februarii. Per Consilium.

Consimiles literæ Regis patentes diriguntur carissimo consanguineo suo Johanni Duci Norff' ac dilectis et fidelibus suis Thomæ Tudenham militi, Willelmo Chamberleyn militi, Miloni Stapulton militi, et Philippo Wentworth militi; necnon dilectis sibi Willelmo Calthorp, Johanni Heydon, Henrico Inglose, Johanni Wymondham, et Thomæ Claymond in comitatu Norff'. Teste ut supra.

Consimiles literæ Regis patentes diriguntur dilectis et fidelibus suis majori et aldermannis ac vicecomitibus villæ suæ de Kyngeston super Hull, et eorum cuilibet in villa prædicta. Teste Rege apud Westmonasterium, xvj. die Februarii.

VIII. WILLIAM WORCESTER.—See p. 199.[1]

1460 AUG. 28 *De scripto irrotulato, Worcestre.*—Universis et singulis Christi fidelibus ad quos præsens scriptum pervenerit, Willelmus Worcestre, alius dictus Botoner, de Castre juxta Yermouth in com' Norff., gentilman, salutem in Domino. Noveritis me, præfatum Willelmum, dedisse, concessisse et hoc præsenti scripto meo confirmasse Henrico Everyngham armigero, Hugoni Fenne gentilman, Henrico Wyndesore gentilman, Roberto Toppes juniori, gentilman, et Johanni Bokkyng, gentilman, omnia et singula bona mea et catalla, mobilia et immobilia, viva et mortua, ubicumque et in quorumcumque manibus, tam infra comitatu prædicto quam alibi infra regnum Angliæ existentia seu[2] inveniri poterint; acetiam omnia debita quæ mihi quacumque de causa a quibuscumque personis ubilibet debentur; habenda et tenenda omnia prædicta bona, catalla et debita præfatis Henrico, Hugoni, Henrico, Roberto et Johanni, executoribus et assignatis suis, ad inde faciendum, ordinandum et disponendum liberam suam voluntatem, ut de bonis, catallis et debitis suis propriis, sine contradictione, perturbatione, seu reclamatione aliquali imperpetuum; Ita, videlicet, quod nec ego, prædictus Willelmus, nec executores mei, nec aliquis alius per nos, pro nobis, seu nomine nostro, aliquid juris, proprietatis, seu clamei in prædictis bonis, catallis et debitis, nec in aliqua parcello eorundem, de cætero exigere,

[1] [From *Close Roll* 39 Henry VI., m. 13 *d.*] [2] *Sic.*

clamare seu vendicare poterimus nec debemus in futuro; sed ab omni actione juris, proprietatis et clamei inde petendi totaliter simus exclusi imperpetuum per præsentes. In cujus rei testimonium huic præsenti, scripto meo sigilium meum apposui. Datum vicesimo octavo die Augusti, anno regni Regis Henrici Sexti post Conquestum Angliæ tricesimo octavo. 1460 AUG. 28

Et memorandum quod prædictus Willelmus venit in Cancellariam Regis apud Westmonasterium primo die Septembris anno præsenti et recognovit scriptum prædictum et omnia contenta in eodem in forma prædicta.

IX. JOHN PASTON CLAIMED AS THE KING'S 'NATIVUS.'—See p. 225.[1]

FROM THE FIRST ASSEMBLY BOOK OF THE CITY OF NORWICH (fol. 65).

[Assembly on Friday after the Epiphany, 5 Edw. IV.]

Eodem die publicata fuit per Maiorem et Recordatorem Civitatis causa adventus domini de Scales ad civitatem secunda vice infra xviijcim dies; est et fuit pro bonis et catallis Johannis Paston quem dominus Rex pro suo nativo seisivit, ad dicta bona et catalla in quorumcumque manibus comperta fuerint nomine domini Regis seisiend', et mesuagium[2] ipsius Johannis Paston infra Civitatem intrand' et seisiend' cum omnibus bonis et catallis in eodem inventis. Unde super et de materiis predictis per Recordatorem et Consilium legis peritorum Civitatis responsum fuit dicto domino de Scales omnibus viis modis et forma secundum eorum erudicionem prout poterunt (? potuerunt) pro libertate Civitatis salvand' et custodiend' illesa. Et quia materia predicta tangit libertatem Civitatis et privilegia, et dictus dominus de Scales per aliquod responsum ei factum non vult satisfieri, pro eo quod dictus dominus de Scales intendit omnino dictum mesuagium intrare et clausuras eiusdem frangere; Id circo presens communis congregacio summonita fuit, consilium et avisamentum communis Consilii et Constabulariorum[3] Civitatis audire et inde habere. Post vero diversas com- 1466 JAN. 10

[1] For this extract from the Assembly books of the City of Norwich I am indebted to the Rev. William Hudson of Eastbourne, who further adds the following particulars:—

The Mayor this year was Thomas Elys who is mentioned in the Paston Letters (iv. 139) as a great supporter of the Duke of Suffolk and opponent of Paston.

The Recorder apparently was John Damme, I suppose the same who occurs so often as a friend of the Pastons.

What with this divergence of feeling and the difficulty of satisfying Lord Scales as well as their own duty towards the City the case was a delicate one and was rather ingeniously dealt with.

There is no other reference to the matter in the Norwich documents so far as I am aware.

[2] The house is supposed to have been in the parish of St. Peter Hungate, but it is not certainly known.

[3] About this period the 24 Ward Constables were associated in an Assembly with the 60 Common Councillors. This is why they are mentioned here, not with any reference to 'police' action.

THE PASTON LETTERS

municaciones communicare petierunt deliberacionem; matura deliberatione habita sic est deffinitum, quod introitus factus erit per assensum totius communis congregacionis per feoffatores ipsius Johannis Paston, quia bene suppositum est quod tam certi Aldermanni quam Cives Communarii[1] Civitatis sint cofeoffati cum ipso Johanne Paston; et sic per feoffatores dictum mesuagium erit apertum sine fractura vel ad minus nomine ipsorum feoffatorum vel feoffati unius.

X. A CHRONOLOGICAL NOTE.

It is desirable here to correct an error in the text, which unfortunately was discovered too late. Letters 1020-1022 are out of their proper place. No. 1020 is certainly a letter of Elizabeth Woodville, Edward IV.'s queen, not of her daughter Elizabeth, who was Henry VII.'s. No. 1021 was placed after it as being about the same time, which no doubt it was; and the fact that the Earl of Oxford was out of favour for a considerable part of Edward IV.'s reign made it appear as if both letters belonged to that of Henry VII., to which they were accordingly relegated in previous editions. But this Earl of Oxford was in favour under Edward IV. till the restoration of Henry VI.; and No. 1022, a letter which only appeared in the Supplement of the last edition of this work, was written by John Daubeney, who was killed at the siege of Caister in 1469. The reference to the Queen's confinement, moreover, which was so perplexing in the case of Elizabeth of York, fits exactly with the August of 1467, in which month Elizabeth Woodville gave birth to a daughter named Mary. This letter, therefore, was written on the 8th August, which would be the 'Saturday before St. Laurence' day' in that year: and it must be noted that the footnotes on p. 107 are entirely wrong. The Archbishop of York referred to in the letter was George Nevill, and the Treasurer was Richard, Earl Rivers.

No. 1021 is perhaps before A.D. 1467, as Howard and Sir Gilbert Debenham are believed to be intending 'to set upon Coton,' of which apparently Sir Gilbert was in possession in April 1467 (see vol. iv. No. 664, p. 274).

[1] Members of the Common Council.

END OF VOLUME I

Printed by T. and A. CONSTABLE, Printers to His Majesty
at the Edinburgh University Press

The
Paston Letters
Volume 2

THE PASTON LETTERS

Early Documents

BEFORE entering upon the correspondence of the Paston family, in the reign of Henry VI., we have thought it well to give the reader a brief note of such deeds and charters of an earlier date as appear either to have been preserved in the family, or to have any bearing on its history. The following is a list of those we have been able to meet with either in the originals or in other quarters, such as Blomefield's *History of Norfolk*, where notices are given of several documents, which appear now to have got into unknown hands. The documents seen by Blomefield, and those from the Paston and Dawson-Turner collections, now in the British Museum, were probably all at one time part of the Paston family muniments. The three Harleian charters seem to have been derived from a different source.

A Deed is cited by Blomefield (*Hist. Norf.* vi. 480), by which Anselm, Abbot of St. Benet's, Hulme, and the Convent there, gave to Osbern, the priest (said by Blomefield to have been a son of Griffin de Thwait, the founder of the Paston family), the land of St. Benet's of Paston (*terram Sancti Benedicti de Paston*), in fee, for half the farm of one *caruca*, as his ancestors used to pay for the same.

Also a Deed of William the Abbot (who lived in King Stephen's reign), granting to Richer de Pastun, son of Osbern, son of Griffin de Thwete, all the land that the Convent held in Pastun, with their men, and other pertinencies.

Also a Deed of Covenant between Richer de Paston and Reginald the Abbot, and Convent of St. Benet's, Holme, that when peace should be settled in England, and pleas held in the Court of our Lord the King, the said Richer would, at the request and at the expense of the Abbot, give him every security in Court to release the lands in Pastun.

'Ralph de Paston was son, as I take it' (says Blomefield) 'of this Richer, and appears to have had two sons, Richard and Nicholas.

VOL. II.—A   I

THE PASTON LETTERS

'Richard, son of Ralph de Paston, by his deed, *sans* date, granted to Geoffrey, son of Roger de Tweyt, lands in this town (Oxnead), paying 9d. per ann. for his homage and service, 40s. for a fine (*in gersumam*), and paying to him and his heirs on the feasts of St. Andrew, Candlemas, Pentecost, and St. Michael, on each feast, 2s. *ob.* He sealed with one *lis.* Laurence de Reppes, William and John, his brother, William de Bradfield, &c., were witnesses.'—Blomefield, vi. 480-1.

'There was also another branch of this family, of which was Wystan, or Wolstan, de Paston, which I take to be the lineal ancestor of Sir William Paston, the Judge, and the Earls of Yarmouth. This Wolstan lived in the reign of Henry II. and Richard I., and married, as is probable, a daughter of the Glanvilles, as appeared from an impalement of Paston and Glanville in the windows of Paston Hall in Paston. His son and heir styled himself Robert de Wyston and Robert de Paston; who, dying in or about 1242, was buried at Bromholm, and left Edmund de Paston. To this Edmund, son of Robert, son of Wolstan de Paston, Sir Richard de Paston gave the land in Paston which Robert, his father, held of him and Nicholas, his brother, by deed *sans* date.'—Blomefield, vi. 481.

Undated Deed of Nicholaus filius Radulfi Diaconi de Paston, granting to Robert, son of Wistan de Paston, two parcels of lands—one of them abutting on the lands of Eudo de Paston. Witnesses—Richard de Trunch; Will. Esprygy; Ralph de Reppes; Roger de Reppes; Richard, s. of Ralph de Baketon; John de Reppes; Roger, s. of Warin de Paston; Hugh, s. of Will. de Paston, &c.—Add. Charter 17,217, B.M. (Paston MSS.).

Undated Deed of Richard, son of Ralph de Pastune, granting to Edmund, son of Robert Wistan de Pastune, lands in Pastune, &c.—(*Seal attached, in fine condition.*)—Add. Charter 17,218, B.M. (Paston MSS.).

Blomefield also mentions (vi. 481) that Nicholas, son of Ralph de Paston, gave lands to Robert, son of Wystan de Paston, by deed *sans date.* Witness, Roger de Repps.

Undated Deed Poll, by which Richard, the son of Ralph, Deacon of Paston, grants to Edmund, the son of Robert Wiston of Paston, certain lands at Paston.—Add. Charter 14,810, B.M. (D. Turner's Collection of Deeds relating to Norfolk).

Richard, son of Ralph de Paston, according to Blomefield (xi. 24), gave 12d. a year rent in Paston to the Priory of Bromholm. This gift is also mentioned by Richard Taylor in his Index Monasticus of the Diocese of Norwich, p. 15, where the purpose of the endowment is said to be 'to keep their books in repair.'

Deed, cited by Blomefield (vi. 481), by Richard, son of John, son of Richard de Paston, granting to the Priory of Bromholm, Alan de Tilney, with all his family, &c. (*cum tota sequela*), and 7 acres of land in Paston and Knapton, with messuages, &c., for 4 marks of silver *in gersumam*, and a rent of 22d. a year.

Undated Deed Poll, whereby William, the son of Robert Barrett, grants to Edmund, the son of Robert Whiston of Paston, certain lands in the Common Field of Paston.—Add. Charter 14,813, B.M. (D. Turner's Coll.).

EARLY DOCUMENTS

Undated Indenture between Clement Parcerit of Gimmingham, and Cecil, his wife, and Edmund, the son of Robert de Paston, concerning lands in Paston Field.—Add. Charter 14,814, B.M. (D. Turner's Coll.).

Undated Deed Poll, by which Richard de Lessingham grants to William, son of Robert de Paston, certain lands in the Common Field of Paston.—Add. Charter 14,812 (D. Turner's Coll.).

Ancient Deed of Nich. Chancehose of Baketun granting to Edmund, fil. Roberti Wistan de Pastun, and his heirs, for 30s., a *tresroda* of land in Pastun.—Add. Charter 17,219, B.M. (Paston MSS.).

Undated Deed Poll, by which Richard, son of John de Paston, grants to Roger, his brother, certain lands in Paston Field.—Add. Charter 14,811, B.M. (D. Turner's Coll.).

Undated Deed Poll, whereby Hugh, son of William de Pastun, grants to Walter, son of Edmund de Pastun, and his heirs, a *tresroda* of land in the fields of Pastun, 'inter terram quæ fuit Osberti Salr. (?), ex parte Austri, et terram quæ fuit Ricardi Chaumpeneys ex parte Aquilonis, et abuttat super forreram quæ fuit Roberti Carpentar' versus Orientem, et super liberam et terram ecclesiæ de Past' versus Occidentem.'—Add. Charter 2004, B.M.

A.D. 1313, 16 Oct. 'William de Paston obtains a pardon as an adherent of the Earl of Lancaster for his participation in the death of Gaveston, and the disturbances occasioned thereby.' 16 Oct., 7 Edw. II.—Palgrave's Parliamentary Writs, vol. ii. div. iii. p. 1262.

A.D. 1324, 22 Jan. Deed Poll, dated on Sunday after the Feast of St. Agnes, 17 Edward II., whereby Henry de Mundham, parson of Oxnead, and another, grant to William Hautayne and Alice, his wife, a certain messuage and premises in Oxnead.—Add. Charter 14,804, B.M. (D. Turner's Coll.).

A.D. 1324, 19 Feb. Quit-Claim by Edmund, son of Robert de Neketone, to Robert de Paston, Tabernarius, of lands in the fields without the West Gate of Bury St. Edmund's. Sunday after St. Valentine's Day, 17 Edw. II. Seal attached.—Harl. Charter 54 A. 31, B.M.

A.D. 1329, 24 Dec. Deed Poll of Margery, daughter of Robert de Neketon, granting to Robert de Paston lands in the fields of St. Edmund's. St. Edmund's Bury, Sunday, Christmas Eve, 3 Edw. III.—Harl. Charter 54 A. 32, B.M.

A.D. 1330. Petition to Parliament 4 Edw. III. of John de Claveryng, complaining that John Payne of Dunwich, Constantine de Paston, Austin Fitzwilliam, and others of Dunwich, took by force and arms five ships and a boat belonging to him, at Wallerswyke, and goods to the value of £300, after having beat, shipwrecked, and imprisoned (*baterent, naufrerent, et emprisonerent*) the said John's servants. The king's answer: 'Eyt en Chauncellerie oyer et terminer pur le horibilite du trespas, devant covenables justices.'—Rolls of Parl. ii. 33.

A.D. 1333, 29 April. Deed Poll, dated Thursday next before the Feast of the Invention of the Holy Cross, 7 Edward III., whereby Alice, widow of William Hautayne, grants to Henry de Colby and others a messuage, with the appurtenances in Oxnead.—Add. Charter 14,805, B.M. (D. Turner's Coll.).

A.D. 1341, 28 Aug. Deed Poll of Robert de Paston granting to William

---

THE PASTON LETTERS

de Bradeleghe and William Child, Chaplains, lands in the fields of St. Edmund's Bury, without the West Gate at Stanywerp, &c. St. Edmund's Bury, Tuesday after St. Bartholomew, 15 Edw. III.—Harl. Charter 54 F. 37, B.M.

A.D. 1341. Indenture of 15 Edw. III. between John de Knapeton, rector of Freugges, and Clement de Paston and Will. his son.—Add. Charter 17,221, B.M. (Paston MSS.).

A.D. 1361. Charter of Sir Rob. de Mauteby to the Prior of St. Olave's, Herlyngflet, 35 Edw. III.—Add. Charter 17,222 (Paston MSS.), B.M.

Notes of Proceedings in Outlawry of the time of Edward III. Judgment by Sir John Hody, mentioned in a more modern hand.—Paston MSS., B.M.

A.D. 1382, 5 Oct. Deed Poll, dated on Sunday next after the Feast of St. Michael, 6 Richard II., by which Robert de Paston grants to John Gant certain lands in Paston field.—Add. Charter 14,817, B.M. (D. Turner's Coll.).

A.D. 1404, 1 Oct. Deed by which Mary, Lady Mortimer, mother of Sir John Fastolf, grants to her said son her manors of Caister and Caister Hall, together with her manor of Repps and the advowson of the free Chapel of St. John, within the said manor of Caister, to hold to him and his heirs for ever. 1 Oct., 6 Henry IV.—Add. Charter 14,597, B.M. (D. Turner's Coll.).

THE PASTON LETTERS

Henry V

I

HENRY V.'S CONQUESTS IN FRANCE[1]

THESE be the names of Townes, Castell, Citees, and Abbeys that the [King did][2] gete in his secund viage :— *1417-*

The Town of Cane and the Castell.
The Town of Valeis [*Falaise*] and the Castell.
The Town of Argenton and the Castell.
The Town of Bayeux and the Castell.
The Town of Alawnsom and the Castell.
The Town of Frezsne le Vicont and the Castell.
The Town of Seint Savers de Vive and the Castell.
The Town of Seint Jakes de Beueron and the Castell.
The Town of Seint Jakes de Burvam and the Castell.
The Town of Seint Low and the Castell.
The Town of Valence and the Castell.
The Cytee of Averense and the Castell.
The Cytee of Sees.
The Cytee of Leseaux.
The Cytee of Everose.
The Town of Louerse.
The Town of Counsheux.
The Town of Vire.

[1] [From Paston MSS., B.M.]   [2] Parchment mutilated.

THE PASTON LETTERS

1417-9 The Town of Karentine.
The Town of Chyrbourgh and the Castell.
The Town of Vernoile and ij. Castell.
The Town of Morteyn and the Castell.
The Town of Powntlarche and the Castell.
The Town of Esey and the Castell.
The Town of Dounfrount and the Castell.
The Town of Pountedomer and the Castell.
The Town of Turve and the Castell.
The Town of Costaunce and the Castell.
The Cytee of Roon and the Castell.
The Town of Galion and the Castell.
The Town of Galdebek [*Caudebec*].
The Town of Mustirvilers.
The Town of Depe.
The Town of Ve and the Castell.
The Town of Vernoile suz Seyne and the Castell.
The Town of Mawnt and the Castell.
The Castell of Towk.
The Castell of Morvile.
The Castell of Overs in Awge.
The Abbey of Seint Savers suz Deve.
The Abbey of Seint Peers suz Dive.
The Abbey of Seint Stevenis of Cane.
The Bole Abbey of Cane.
The Castell of Cursy.
The Castell of Gundy.
The Castell of Nevylebeke.
The Castell of Vermus.
The Castell of Garcy.
The Castell of Oo [*Eu*].
The Castell of Vileine.
The Castell of Egyll.
The Castell of Regyll.
The Castell of Curton.
The Castell of Fagernon.
The Castell of Chamberexs.
The Castell of Ryveers.

HENRY V

The Castell of Bewmanill.   *1417-9*
The Castell of Bewmalyn.
The Castell of Harecourt.
The Abbey of Behelwyn.
The Castell of Parlevesque.
The Castell of Semper.
The Castell of Tracy.
The Castell of Tylly.
The Castell of Groby.
The Castell of Carsell.
The Castell of Hommbe.
The Castell of Seynt Denise.
The Castell of Bonvile.
The Castell of Grennevile.
The Castell of Perers.
The Castell of Seint Gilerinz.
The Castell of Bewmound.
The Castell of Asse la Rebole.
The Castell of Tanny.
The Castell of Antony.
The Castell of Balon.
The Castell of Mountfort.
The Castell of Tovey.
The Castell of Lowdon.
The Castell of Noaus.
The Castell of Seynt Romains in Plaine.
The Castell of Daungell.
The Castell of Peschere.
The Castell of Bolore.
The Castell of Keshank.
The Castell of Turre.
The Castell of Seint Imains.
The Castell of Seint Germains.
The Castell of Bomstapyll.
The Castell of Croile.
The Castell of Bakuile.
The Castell of Bellacombyr.
The Castell of Douyle.

417-9 The Castell of Likone.
The Castell of Ankyrvile.
The Abbey of Seint Katerinz.

These er the gates names of Roon, and how the lordys lay in sege, and to fore what gate, and also the derth of vitailes withyn the forseyd Cytee of Roon.
Le Port Causches. To fore thys gate, lay my Lord of Clarense[1] vnto riversyde of Seyne with mykyl of hys howsold and a grete market ; and then fro that gate upward lay my Lord of Urmound,[2] my maistre Corwayle[3] with the Lord Talbotts meyne. *Le Port de Castell.* At thys gate my Lord Marchall,[4] the Lord of Haryngton. *Le Port de Bewvoisyn.* At thys gate lay my Lord of Excester. *Le Port de Vowdelagate.* To fore thys gate lay the Lord Roos, the Lord Wylleby, the Lord Fyhew,[5] Sir John Gray, and Sir William Porter. *Le Port Seint Yllare.* To fore thys gate lay the kyng and my Lord of Glowcestyr. *Le Port de Martynvile.* To fore thys gate lay my Lord of Warwyk and Sir Phelip Leche. *Le Port debut de Pount.* To fore thys gate lay my Lord of Huntyngdon, my Lord of Sawlisbyry, my maistre Nevile, and my mayster Umphirvile. *Le Port de Vicount.* Thys ys the chefe Water-gate of the town, and at thys gate cometh in al maner marchawndys and vitailes.
Furthyrmore as towchyng to the derth of vytayles withyn this forseyd Cytee, j. [one] Buschell of Whete was worth v. scutys, j. lofe j. frank, j. dog j. frank, j. kat ijs. sterlinges, j. rat vjd. sterlinges. And as towchyng all other vitailes, it was spendit or that we com in to the Cytee.

Urbis Rotomagi Wulstano captio claret,
Quam Rex Henricus Quintus sexto capit anno.

[1] Thomas, Duke of Clarence, the King's brother.
[2] James Butler, Earl of Ormond.
[3] Sir John Cornwall, afterwards Lord Fanhope.
[4] John Mowbray, Earl Marshal, afterwards Duke of Norfolk. [5] Fitz-Hugh.

8

2

AMYE BOWET TO —— [1]

TRESCHER et mon tresfiable amy je vous salue tres- 1417-9 souvent de tout mon cuer, desirant pur savoir et oier bons noveles de vous, et que vous soiez en prosperitee. Et, mon tresfiable amy, vous face assavoir que monsieur mon baron covient sey apparailler et ordenyier envers le Roy ore en y ceste proschein viage en la presence oue le Duc de Excestre, pur la quelle luy covient faire graundes expenses entour son arraie en salvacion de son honour, lequel je vorreie faire ma diligence pur saluer et encrescer a mon poair, come je suy graundement tenuz ; et vous estez la persone en la quelle je plus graundement maffie devaunt aucune altre ore vivant. Pur quey je vous emprie tresespecialment de trestout mon cuer que vous please pur faire a tant pur moy quant a ore pur moy faire chevyceance de xl. marcz come pur voie dapprompt ore en y ceste nostre graunde busoigne, promittant de certeyne que sereez bien et loialment repaiez a aucune jour reisoignable que vous veuilliez assigner ; et si vous ne osez pleignement affier en y ceste ma promys pur peril quent purra avenir en temps avenir, vous auerez tiel seuretee come vous veuillez deviser. Trescher et mon tresfiable amy, pluisours a vous nay escrier au present, mays que vous veuillez doner foie et credence a une gentile feme portour dycestes. Et pri al Saint Espirit qil vous ait touz jours en sa tressaintisme garde. Escript en haste a Wrentham, le xxviij^me jour de Mars.
AMYE BOWET.

On the back is written in a different hand :—
' Thomas Lente et Matillda uxor mea petunt de Galfrido Somerton xiij. iiijd. quos Willelmus Lyster et dicta Matillda, circa xxiiij. annos elapsos quum ipsi levaverunt finem de tenementis in Castre inter ipsos et Walterum Gase ; et dicit quod dicta Matillda quando ipsa examinata fuit per Justiciarios apud Jernemuth qui sedebant super Rayes (?) in ecclesia Fratrum Carmelitarum,

[1] [Add. MS. 34,889, f. 141.] This letter appears to be of a very early date. If its contents refer, as seems probable, to the preparations for Henry v.'s expedition in France, it is of the year 1417, and so earlier than No. 1 ; which, however, it may follow as bearing on the same subject.

9

1417-9 dictus Justiciarius dedit dictos xiij. iiijd. quos ipse habere debuisset pro labore suo dictæ Matilldæ, et dictus Galfridus dictos xiij. iiijd. posuit in loculo suo proprio et nullatenus illos dictæ Matilldæ solvit : et ad festyngong per iiij. annos elapsos le boteler apud Somerton audivit quod dictus Galfridus promisit dictæ Matilldæ et dicto Thomæ tunc viro suo dictos xiij. iiijd.'

3

[THE PARSON OF EDINGTHORPE] TO WILLIAM SEWARDBY[1]

A mon trescher et honure sieur, William Sewardby.

TRESCHER et honure sieur, jeo me recomaund a vous si tresentierement de t . . . . doyere et de savore bonez novells de vous et de vostre entiere estat et souereyn . . . . tres bonz de vous auore et savore com vous mesmes lez sauera meltz devisere ou . . . . . . et si de moy le vostre. Vous plese savore, a la fesaunce de cestez j'estoy en bon saunte. [Et quant a] vostre boys de denz le boys de Baketon vous plese savore que le Prieur de Bromholm est (?) [nostre] parochen, et nous ade prie pur avore vostre dit boys dissevere et departie a son boys issint . . . . boys que est parcel a vostre boys pur lour profit et saunz damage de vostre dit boys, mes Richa[rd] . . . . disseveryng fere saunz vostre volunte ou autre maundement de vous, come le portour de t . . . . . . ment que jeo ne puis ore escrire. Et touchant vostre manere illuques si longuement com . . . . . . maynez de dit priour, vous, ne null de voz bien voliauncez y aueroyent nulle conyschaun[ce] . . . de vostre manere as autrez de lours seigneuries, et ensi vous et vostrez serrount en temps avenir . . . . . . que vous les tenez en voz maynez proprez et sure tiele colour si vous plese Richard Causton . . . . . . et payr omez a vous si taunt come le priour avaundit fet a termes et jours par vous assign[ez]

[1] [Add. MS. 34,889, f. 142.] This letter appears also to be of a very early, but quite an uncertain date. It is unfortunately mutilated, some words being lost on every line on the right hand side of the MS.

10

. . . . . pur avore par voz tenauntz lez ditz terez, rentz et 1417-9? tenementz, boys et autres comoditez . . . . disseverez et departez. Et vous covyent avore i. seneschal pur tenire vostres courtez iluque[s] . . . . . . de dit priour ne en son daungere, mes tiel homme que nad null dom de eux et tiele . . . . . . vous luy voliez bien rewardere pur son travail. Trescher et honure sieur, de ceste matere et de . . . . . . par le portour de cestz, et nous ferrous nostre powere et diligence de lez accomplere a vostre . . . . . . Sieur, jeo prie a Dieux quil vous doyne tresbon vie et long honour et souereyn joye de . . . . A Edythorp juxta Bromholm, le primer jour de Jul'.

4

ABSTRACT[1]

Marriage Settlement of William Paston, dated the Eve of the Annunciation 1420 of the Virgin, 8 Henry v.—It is agreed between Sir Edmund Berre, Kt., on 24 MARCH the one part, and William Paston of Paston on the other, that the latter shall marry Agnes, daughter of the said Sir Edmund, and that his trustees of the manor of Oxenede, Norf., shall demise the same to the said William and Agnes, and the heirs of their bodies, &c. Also Sir Edmund's trustees, either of the manor of Estodenham, co. Norf., or of the manor of Hollewellebury, Herts, at the option of William Paston, shall deliver one or other manor to the said William and Agnes, and the heirs of their bodies, &c. If Estodenham be chosen, Paston is to make to Sir Edm. and his wife Alice an estate for life, either in the manors of Marlingford, Norf., and Stanstede, Suff., or in the manors of Elghe and Willyngham, Suff., &c.

5

ABSTRACT[2]

Inspeximus of a Deed of Thos. Pecke, clk., dated 10 Hen. v., granting 1422 the reversion of the manors of Breydeston, Caston, &c., then held by Sir John Carbonell and Margery, his wife, to Sir Rob. Brewys, John Fitz-Rauff, and others.—(*See* Blomefield's *Norfolk*, ii. 285.)

[1] [Add. Charter 17,225, B.M.]   [2] [Add. Charter 17,243.]

11

THE PASTON LETTERS

Henry VI

6

INFORMATION AGAINST WALTER ASLAK [1]

1424 BE it remembered that where, on the nyght next biforne the feste of the Circumcision of owre Lord Jesu, the [second] [2] yeer of the regne of Kyng Henry the Sexte, certeyns maffaisours, felons, and brekeres of the kynges peas vnknowyn, to the noumbre of iiijxx [*four score*] and more by estimacion, of malice and imaginacion forne thowght felonowsly, the dwellyng place of John Grys of Wyghton, in Wyghton, in the shyre of Norffolk, brokyn, and with carpenteres axes the yates and the dores of the seyd place hewen, and the seyd John Grys, and hys sone, and a servaunt man of hese by here bodyes tokyn, and fro the seyd dwellyng place by the space of a myle to a payre gawles ledden, there hem for to have hangyd ; and by cause hem fayled ropes convenient to here felonowse purpos, the seyd John Grys, hese sone, and hys man there felonowsely slowen and mordered in the most orrible wyse that ever was herd spoken of in that cuntre. Wher up on Walter Aslak, purposyng and imaginyng to

[1] [From Paston MSS., B.M.] This paper refers to proceedings as late as the fourth year of Henry VI., and therefore cannot be earlier than 1426 ; but as it mainly relates to outrages committed in the second year of Henry VI., i.e. 1424, we have arranged it under that year.
[2] This word is omitted in the MS.

12

HENRY VI   1424

putte William Paston in drede and intollerable fere to be slayn and mordered in the seyd forme with force and ageyn the kinges peas, on the shyre day of Norffolk, halden at Norwiche, the xxviij day of August, in the seyd secunde yeer, beyng there thanne a grete congregacion of poeple by cause of the seyd shyre, in hese owne persone, and by Richard Kyllynworth, that tyme hese servaunt, to the seyd William Paston swiche and so many manaces of deth and dismembryng maden and puttyn by certeyns Englische billes rymed in partye, and up on the yates of the Priorie of the Trinite chirche of Norwiche, and on the yates of the chyrche of the Freres Menures of Norwiche, and the yates of the same Cite called Nedeham yates and Westewyk yates, and in othre places wyth inne the seyd Cite by the seyd Walter and Richard sette, makyng mension and beryng this undyrstondyng that the seyd William, and hese clerkes, and servauntes schuld be slayn and mordered in lyke forme as the seyd John Grys in the seyd forme was slayne and mordered : conteynyng also these too words in Latyn, *et cetera*, by which wordes communely it was undyrstandyn that the forgeers and makers of the seyd billes imagyned to the seyd William, hese clerkes and servauntes, more malice and harm than in the seyd billes was expressed. Wherfore the seyd William, hese seyd clerkes and servauntz, by longe tyme aftyr were in gret and intollerable drede and fere by the sayd maffaisours and felons to be slayn and mordered. Wherfore the seyd William, hese clerkes and servauntes, ne durst not at here fredom nothyr goon ne ryde.

Wher up on the seyd William, for hese owyn persone, affermyd a pleynt of trespas ageyn the seyd Walter and Richard, processe contynued ther up on til the seyd Walter and Richard were founden gilty of the seyd trespas by an inquisicion ther of takyn in dwe and lawefull forme, by whiche inquisicion the damages of the seyd William for the seyd trespas were taxed to cxxli [£120]. Aftyr which pleynte affermyd, and to fore ony plee up on the seyd pleynt pleded, the seyd Walter and William, by Thomas Erpyngham, Knyght, a myghty and a gret supportour of the seyd Walter in alle these matiers and circumstaunces ther of ageyn the seyd

13

THE PASTON LETTERS

1424 William, were induced to trete in the same matier in the forme that folwith : That is to seyne, that the seyd William schuld sue forth the seyd pleynt and the execucion ther of at hese owne will, and the seyd Walter schuld defende hym self in the seyd pleynt at hese owne will, except that he schuld no benefice take by noon proteccion, ne wrytte of *corpus cum causa*, ne of no lordes lettres up on the seyd sute. And what so ever fortunyd in the seyd pleynt, the proces, execucion, or the sute ther of, the seyd Walter and William schuld stonde and obeye to the ordinaunce of certeyns persones by the seyd William and Walter arbitratores that tyme named, if thei myghten accordyn, and ellys of anoonpier also that same tyme named, of alle the seyd trespas, pleynt, and sute, and alle the circumstaunces ther of, so that the seyd arbitrement and ordinaunce of the seyd arbitratores, or ellys of the seyd nounpier, were made withinne xl. dayes next folwyng aftyr the jugement geven in the seyd pleynt.

And aftyrward, the Thursday next biforn Pentecost, the thrydde yeer of the regne of the seyd kyng, at London, in the presence of the right excellent, high and myghty prynce, the Duc de Gloucestre,[1] and by hese commaundement, atte sute and instaunce of the seyd Thomas Erpyngham, it was accordyd bytwen the seyd William and Walter that thei schuld stande and obeye to the ordinaunce and award of alle the seyed matiers of twenye of these iiij. persones, William Phelip, Knyght, Henry Inglose, Knyght, Oliver Groos, and Thomas Derham, chosen on the partye of the seyd William Paston, and tweyne of those iiij. persones, Symond Felbrygge, Knyght, Bryan Stapilton, Knyght, Roberd Clyfton, Knyght, and John of Berneye of Redeham, chosen on the partie of the seyd Water, and elles the decree and jugement of a nounpier to be chosen by the same arbitrores. The whiche William Phelip, Bryan Stapilton, Roberd Clyfton, Oliver Groos, John of Berneye, and Thomas Derham, takyng up on hem the charge of the makyng of the seyd award and ordinaunce by the assent of the seyd Thomas Erpyngham, the Fryday next aftyr the feste of the Assumpcion of Owre Lady, in the seyd

[1] Humphrey, Duke of Gloucester, Protector of England.

14

HENRY VI   1424

thrydde yeer, at Norwiche, tokyn ensurans of the seyd William and Walter by here fayth and here trowthez to stande and obeye to here ordinaunce of alle the seyd matiers, and the same day biforne noon, maden here full ordinaunce and arbitrement of alle the same matiers in the chyrche of the Greye Freyrys at Norwich ; and aftyrward, up on the same award and ordinaunce mad, hadden a communicacion ther of with the seyd Thomas Erpyngham ; and aftyr the same communicacion, the same day aftyr noon, the same ordinaunce and award wretyn was red byforn the seyd arbitrores and the seyd Walter and William, and examyned, agreed, and assented, and by the seales of the same vj. arbitrores and the seyd Walter and William, was affermed and ensealed and left in the handes of the seyd Sir Bryan, saveliche to be kept in playne remembraunce of the seyd award and ordinaunce ; the whiche award and ordinaunce the seyd William was at all tymes redy to obeye and performe, on to the seyd feste of Michelmesse, that the seyd Walter to holde or performe the seyd award pleynly refused.

And where the seyd Walter, by jugement of the Chaunceller of Inglond, the xvj. day of Jull' the seyd thrydde yeer, was remytted to the kynges prison at Norwich by cause of the seyd sute, the seyd Walter yede at large owt of warde fro the seyd xvj. day of Jull' to the seyd day of the makyng of the seyd arbitrement and award, and fro that day in to Michelmesse thanne next aftyr ; the seyd William that meene tyme evermore supposyng that the seyd Walter wolde have holde and performyd the sayd ordinaunce, arbitrement, and award. And at the comyng of the right high and myghty prynce the Duc of Norfolk fro his Castell of Framyngham to the Cetie of Norwyche, aftyr the seyd day of the makyng of this arbitrement and ordinaunce, and to fore the feste of Michelmesse than next folwyng, the seyd Walter by hese sotill and ungoodly enformacion caused the seyd Duke to be hevy lord to the seyd William. Where the seyd William the tyme of the seyd enformacion was with Sir John Jermy, Knyght, and othre of the counseill of the seyd Duk of Norffolk in hys lordshipes in Norffolk and Suffolk, thanne to hym falle [*fallen*] by the deth of the right worthy and noble lady hys modyr,

15

1424 occupied abowte the dwe service of wryttes of *diem clausit extremum*[1] aftyr the deth of the seyd lady. And where as the seyd William Paston, by assignement and commaundement of the seyd Duk of Norffolk, at hese fyrst passage over the see in to Normandye, in the kynges tyme Henry the Fyfte, was the Styward of the seyd Duc of Norffolk, of alle hese lordshipes in Norffolk and Suffolk fro hys seyd passage un to the seyd feste of Michelmesse; [And[2] over that as sergeaunt of lawe, thow he be unworthy, withholdyn with the seyd Duc of Norffolk alle the tyme that he was sergeaunt bifore the same feste of Michelmesse. And all be it that the fees and the wages of the seyd William for hys seyd service unpayed draweth a gret some to hys pouere degree, if the seyd Duk of Norffolk lyked, of hys noble and plentifous grace, to graunte to the seyd William, in right, ony part of the favour of hese good lordship, the seyd William wolde evere be hys pouere and trewe bedeman, and evere in hys herte thenke alle hys seyd service, and alle the service that ever he dede to the seyd [Duke] of Norfolk, plentefeously weell rewarded.[3]]

And where the seyd Walter, the tyme of the seyd trespas and of the seyd bylles makyng ne long to fore, ne never aftyr biforn the seyd comyng of the seyd Duc of Norffolk to Norwich, ne no tyme hangyng the seyd sute, ne the tyme of makyng of the said arbitrament and ordinaunce, never was servaunt to the seyd Duc of Norffolk at fees, ne at wages, ne wythhaldyn in hese service, ne to hym sued to be supported by hese high Lordship in this seyd matier, to the knowleche of the seyd William, ne to no commune knowleche, in the shyres of Norffolk, Suffolk, ne Norwiche; the sute that the seyd Walter made for supportacion in this seyd matier was be the meene of the seyd Thomas Erpyngham to the seyd Duk of Gloucestre, by whose reule and commaundemente the seyd

---

[1] These were writs issued on the death of a tenant *in capite* of the Crown, and directed to the escheators in the different counties in which his lands lay, directing them to inquire by jury what lands he held, and of what value, and who was his nearest heir, and what was the heir's age.
[2] Over this word is written 'va,' the first syllable of *vacat*, showing that the passage is cancelled.
[3] Here is written 'cat.'—*See* Note 2.

16

arbitrement and award was mad in the forme aforn seyd. 1424 And not with stondyng the seyd trespas and grevaunce by the seyd Walter doon the seyd William, ne that the seyd William ne is not satisfied of the seyd cxx[li], ne no peny therof, and hath absteyned hym of al maner of execucion, sewyng of godes or catelles, that by force of the seyd processe, or ony othyr, he myght have had ageyn the seyd Walter or hese borwes [*sureties*], ne that the seyd William hath suffred the seyd Walter to gon at large by long tyme whan he myght have had hys body in warde in lawfull forme : The seyd Walter, be billes in the too last parlementz holden at Westminster and at Leycestre, and at divers tymes in divers other maneres hath noysed and skaundered the seyd William ungoodly and othyr wyse than othyr [either] gentilnesse or trowthe wolde ; and, overmore, caused the seyd William orribly to be manassed of hys deth, betyng and dismembryng of hys persone by certeyns servauntz of the Lordes Fitz Wauter and othre persones, and by ferefull and overe felle lettres and sondes. Wherfore the seyd William, nothyr hese frendes, ne hese servauntz in hys companye, at here fredam sithen the seyd parlement at Leycestre durst not, ne yet ne dar not rydyn ne goo abowte swyche occupacion as he arn used and disposed, to here grete and unportable drede and vexacion in here spirites, and gret harme and damage and losse of here pouere goodes.

[Overmore,[1] the seyd Walter hath sued, and yet rigorously suethe a wrytte of *decies tantum*[2] ageyns x. persones of the seyd Inquisicion and ij. of the servauntz of the seyd William and iiij. othre persones ; supposyng by hese seyd sute hem to have taken of the seyd William in hys seyd syte lxij[li] [£62] and more of moneye. The whiche sute of *decies tantum* the seyd Walter, betwyx God and hym, knewith verraly is untrewe. And also the seyd Walter hath sued, and yet persuyth Adam Aubre, on of the seyd Inquisicion in the court of the said Duc

---

[1] Here is written 'va.'—*See* p. 16, Note 2.
[2] A writ against a juror who had been bribed, by which the prosecutor could recover from him ten times the amount of the bribe, dividing the proceeds with the King.

17

1424 of Norffolk of hys manoir of Fornsete, by cause and occasion of the seyd matiers, in whiche sute in the seyd court it is proceded ageyn the seyd Adam in other maner thanne othyr lawe, conscience, or good fayth wolde.[1]]

Overmore the seyd William, atte commaundement of the seyd Duc of Norffolk, hath submytted hym to stonde to the ordinaunce of divers persones of alle the seyd matiers : ones at Leyceetre, the Wednesday next biforn Palm Soneday, the iiij. yeer of the regne of the syd kyng ; anothyr tyme at Reed clyf in Aprill the same iiij. yeer, aftyr the forme of certeyns billes endented ther of made. The whiche submission, with alle the circumstaunces ther of, the seyd William hath be at alle tymes redy to obeye. The cause why the seyd Walter, by the seyd Englishe bylles, and in othyr forme, putte and sette the seyd William, and hys seyd clerkes and servauntz, in drede and fere intollerable to be slayn and mordered, and to hem trespaced in the forme aforn seyd, was onely for as moche as the seyd William was with the prior of Norwiche of counseille in hese trewe defence ageyn the entent of the seyd Walter in a sute that he made ageyn the seyd priour of a voweson of the chyrche of Sprouston in the counte of Norffolk, wher to the seyd Walter hath nothyr title suffisaunt ne right in no maner wyse by ony matier by hym declared byforn thys tyme.

This scrowe is mad only for the informacion of the worthy and worshipfull lordes the arbitrores ; savyng evere to the maker the benefice reasonably to adde and amenuse, his ignoraunce in swiche occupation and defaute of leyser also tendrely considered.

---

[1] Here is written 'cat.'—*See* p. 16, Note 2, and p. 17, Note 1.

18

7

WILLIAM PASTON TO JOHN STAYNFORD[1]

To my weel beloved John Staynford of Furnyvales Inne.

THE instruccion to comune of to John Robynson of 1425 Carleton bysyde Snayth.

To enquerre and wyte whether the stoon may be sawed or nought. Whether it wille chippe or chynne or affraye with frost or weder or water.

Also that every pece of the stoon be iij. foote longe, and that xv. tunne tyght of the stoon be every stoon weel bedded into the walle and a foote thikke that it ryse in heighte a foote in the walle ; and x. stones of the stoan must be ii. foote broad, and at the lest a foote and an half thikke. A stoon wil drawe the wighte of a pipe, as I suppose ; the gret stones and nought the smallere stones shuld be sawed, so that every pece sawed shud holde the seid lengthe of iij. foote, and the seid brede of ij. foote, and to be, after it is sawed, half a fote or lesse on thikkenesse, and thenne the brode sawed stones shulde evere stond in the werk betwen the seid weel bedded stonys that shuld ryse but a fote in the walle and ben ankered iche of hem with other ; and this werk shal be strong j nowe, as werkmen seyn, and drawe but litill cariage. I wold have swiche stoan a xx[ti]. tunne tight caried to Moneslee[2] in Norffolk between Crowmere and Bromholm, and but a myle from Bromholm.

To reporte plein answere of this bylle writen and how sone I myght have the seid stone caried to Monesle aforn seid, and for what price.

This werk is for a . . .   W. PASTON.

On the back is written, also in the Judge's hand :—
'Sount due a mon sieur Will. Bardolf de ses gages en les lyueres a . . .

---

[1] [Add. MS. 34,889, f. 213.] This letter appears from the postscript to be of the year 1425, as Bardolf's wages, due on the 4th February in that year, had not yet been paid.   [2] Mundesley.

19

THE PASTON LETTERS

1425 de mon tres honneure seigneur le Count de Warrwick, capitayn illeoqes, iusques al iiij.ᵉ jour de febr. lan de Roy Henri Sysme tierce, ccccxiiij̄i. xvjs. xd. qᵘ'
  Below this is written in Fenn's hand: ' 14 Febʳ 3 H. 7. 1487'—a great misreading of the date.

8

NICHOLAS PRIOR OF BROMHOLM TO WILLIAM PASTON[1]

A Will' Paston soit donne.

JULY 5 Dere Syre and weel be loved, I grete yow weel, and do yow to wetyn that Dawn John Pastone was atte Norwiche on Munday last passed, and dede settyn on Cryste Chyrche gates divers litteres, a lytyl tyme, and ij. copiis wheche stondyn ther yet, for somounnyn me to the curt of Rome. And we supposyn to have hym at Bromholm, or sum man in hys name wyth inne a lytyl tyme ; for dawn Robert of Yorke was atte Norwiche be sendynge of my lady of Murlee, and spak wythe hym in hyre hous on Munday afornseyd, and ther he told the forseyd dawn Robert that he wolde nedys ben Priour of Bromholm, to levyn and deyin ther upon. Also he seyde, as for the composissioun of Bromholm, he hadde do sherchyd att Clunye ; and ther inne he standyth clere as he seythe ; and as for provisyoun, he seyde he hadde spokyn wyth the Chaunceler and the chef Justyse and Ascam, and thei demptyne hym clere as ther inne, and he seyth ; and other dowte is ther none inne be hys tale. And after this the forseyd dawn John askyd obedience of the forseyd dawne Robert in my ladyis presens, and dawn Robert seyde agayne he xulde noghte done that atte that tyme, but he badde hym provyn owt hys purpos as for the composissioun and provisioun to an hende, and than he wolde do hys dever to hym ; and thus he departyd. Where for, yif ony thing may be don whyl ye arn

[1] [Add. MS. 34,888, f. 1.] This letter is evidently of the year 1425. Comp. No. 10.

20

now atte Londone for oure helpe and his lettyng, gode Syre, **1425** helpythe atte this tyme if it maybe godely, we be seche yow. **JULY 5** Dawn Thomas of Cane was atte my lord of Norwiche for helpe in this matier, and he seyde he was inhibytyd and alle hys clerkes be the curt of Rome in this matier, and he seyde by yowre advys, yif it lyke yow, wryttes may ben taken agens hym, and that is best remedye ther inne ; j. [one] wrytte is *ne ingrediatur manu forti.* The Holy Trinite have yow in governaunce. Wretyn atte Bromholm the v. day of July,

per Nich. Priorem de Bromholm.

9

ABSTRACT[1]

Bill witnessing a concord made 24 Sept. 4 Hen. vi. between John **SEPT. 24** Kertelyng, clerk, general attorney to Sir John Fastolf, on the one part, and Richard Boson, Esq., on the other, viz. : That Fastolf shall have in fee-simple the manor of the said Richard in Castre called Bosons of the gift of the said Richard before Easter next, and that the said Richard shall have Fastolf's manor in Titeleshale called Peekhalle, in fee-simple, of the gift of Fastolf, paying to Fastolf £60 within the next four years.

10

WILLIAM PASTON TO ——[2]

Right worthy and worshepefull Sir, I recommaunde **NOV. 5** me to yow, and thank yow for the good, trew, and diligent labour ye have hadde for the matier betwen the Priour of Bromholme[3] and his commoigne[4] apostata, Johne

[1] [From a Bodl. MS.]
[2] [From Paston MSS., B.M.] This letter, being dated in November, was probably written before Nos. 11 and 12 which follow, though evidently very near them in point of date. The chief evidence of the time when they all must have been written will be seen in No. 12.
[3] Who this Prior was we cannot say, the list of the Priors of Bromholm being very defective. Blomefield says, that a Prior John has been met with in the 11th of Edward III., and Robert, in the 14th of Henry VI.—that is to say, in 1435 or 1436, just ninety-nine years later. Nothing is known of the Priors between these dates, even by the latest editors of Dugdale.
[4] 'Commoigne,' *i.e.* brother monk. The writer also calls him *apostata, i.e.* a monk who has run away and renounced his order.

21

THE PASTON LETTERS

1425 Wortes, that namythe hym self Paston, and affermith hym **NOV. 5** untrewely to be my cousyn. [I have many pouere men of my kyn, but so fals, and so pouere,—but he was nevere of my kyn.][1] God defende that any of my saide kyn shuld be of swyche governaunce as he is of ! Maister John Ixworthe told me that he hadde lettres fro a frende of yowres in the courtt of Rome, that is of the seyd priores counseill in this mater as ye be, whos name I knowe nought, specifyeng that the seyd John Wortes adversarius prioris desperat in causa et concordiam quærit. It is told me sithen that the seyd John Wortes is in the cite of Rome, sacred a bysshop of Irland, videlicet episcopus Corcagensis, wherby it is seyd here that his pretense of his title to the priourie of Bromholme is adnulled, and voide in your lawe. The seyd John Wortes, and a contreman of myne in the seyd court, Maister John Urry, have sent me lettres, wherof I sende yow copies and a trewe instruccion of the seyd matier closed with this bille, the whiche lettres and the matier ther of me semyth mervaillous and straunge. A prest of Norffolk, that spak with yow in Julle or August last passed, told me that he yede with yow to the cardinales hous, Trikaricensis,[2] to espie if any swyche processe were sued ageyn me as the seyd lettres specifien, and that ye told the same prest at alle tymes ther was than no swiche processe sued, ne had ; the whiche relacion I trust and beleve bettre than the seyd lettres. I have, by advys of counseill, in makyng a procuracie *ad agendum, defendendum, provocandum, et appellandum* to yow and the seyd Maister John Urry and the Wynsalaw (?) de Swysto ; and also a general appelle, the engrossyng of wyche the messager of this bill myght nought abide ; the whiche procuracie and appelle I shal sende to yowr persone, tantummodo [cum pecuniis],[3] with moneye onward, on trust. My will is, ye have the chief governaunce of this matier, and that this article be counseille [*i.e.*, secret] ; wher upon I prey yow hertily to be saddely avysed in these matiers, and, as nede is, so to governe

[1] These words occur in the draft, but are crossed out.
[2] Thomas Brancaccio, Cardinal Bishop of Tricarico. He was made a cardinal by his uncle, Pope John XXIII., and is said to have been a man of very bad morals.
[3] Interlined, and afterwards erased.

22

hem by your wysdom, that the seyd prioures estat and honeste, **1425** and myn also, to yowr worshepe be saved ; and that, in alle **NOV. 5** haste resonable, ye lyke to sende me redes lettres of alle the seyd matier, and the circumstances ther of, and who ye w᷃ be governed in this mater. I was nevere somouned, ne nev̄ hadde tydynges of this matier but by seyd lettres and othe̅. fleyng tales that I heve herd sithen, I nevere hadde to do more with the seyd John Wortes than is specified in the seyd instruccion. Al myghty God have yow in His governaunce. Writen at London, the v. day of Novembre.

Yowre frend unknowen.[1]

A Instruccion and Informacion of the verray trewe matier betwen the Priour and the Covent of Bromholm and the seyd John and me, as I am enformed, and as I knowe touchant my persone and the[2] ——.

Ista litera
missa non
fuit. Right worthy and worshepefull Sir, I recomaunde to yow, preyng yow to wite that I have resceyved yowr goodly lettres makyng mencion that Sir John Paston,[3] ut asserit, hath optyned me condempnyd to hym in CCC[vij.][4] marcz and C.s. ; and that the same John, atte reverence of your right worthy persone, hathe cesed of his sute of certeins processes ageyns me up on the seyd condempnacion, takyng continuance[5] of the same matier unto Cristemasse next comyng ; by which lettres ye conseille me to make ende with the seyd John, ne deterius inde contingat. I [s]end yow, closed with this bille, [the][6] copie of un frendly lettre that the seyd John hathe sent to me late, touchant the same matier. The seyd priour hath sent also to yow, and to

[1] Above these words, and in the place where the signature might have been expected, occur these names, one above another—
  'Thomas Abbas de Leyston, in Com' Suff.
  'Ricardus Fremelyngham, concanonichus ibidem.'
They do not, however, appear to be connected with the letter. The following words are also scrawled between this letter and the next :—'N. persona ecclesiæ de Testerton in Com' Norff. Gees Cuttyng. Joh' persona ecclesiæ de Yermuth (?), Alicia Gosloth (?).'
[2] *Sic.*
[3] The title 'Sir' was at this time commonly prefixed to a priest's name.
[4] The 'vij.' is struck out.
[5] Contiat̄ce, MS. here and after.
[6] Struck out.

23

THE PASTON LETTERS

1425
NOV. 5

Mayster William Swan, whiche longe hathe be his procurator, a procuracie for my person, and v. marcz of moneye onward. Wher up, in the seyd prioures name, and in myn own also, I prey yow hertily to sette al these matieres in continuaunce un to yowr comyng in to Ingeland ; and because ye arn here beneficed, owr cuntreman, and of worshepe and cunnyng worthyly endowed, the seyd priour and his brether, and I also, willen gladdely in these matieres be treted by yow ; and if this mesure be accepted, and we may have knowyng here ther of, it shall cause the attemptacion of diverses matiere a geyn summe frendes of the seyd John to cese. And if this continuance be refused, I prey yow, with al my power, that of your wysdom and good discrecion ye wille, in the seyd prioures name, and myn, defenden the seyd sutes, and alle other that the seyd Johne sueth ageyn the seyd priour and me, in your best maner, and to be of owr counseill in these matieres ; and as ye lyke resonablely to write to us, so we wil be governed in yowre rewarde, and al other circumstaunces of the same matieres.[1] I conceyve by your seyd lettres that the grece of the matier conteigned in the same ye have of the informacion and assercion of the seyd John, and as he hath enformed yow, I wot weel ye trewely writen ; but I hope and trust verrayly the matier of his informacion is untrewe [for he hathe no cause to swe to me, ne I was nevre somouned ne cited].[2] The priour of Bromholm sued ageyn the seyd John and other in Ingeland a wryt of *præmunire facias*, and I was therin of the same prioures counseill as the lawe of Ingelond and myn office willen, and more I have nought hadde to do with the seyd Johne, and I can nought beleve that in this cas the same Johne myght by your lawe any swich sute have ageyn me as your lettre specifieth. Also William, the prest specified in yowr [letter],[3] told me that he, after that ye told hym of this matier, lyke as yewrce (?), he comuned with Maister William Swan, and he told the seyd prest ther no processe in the courte ageyn me in no maner ——.[4]

[1] Here occur the following words, crossed out :—' Ferthermore, touchant my persone, I mervaille that the seyd —— Ferthermore.' [2] Struck out. [3] Omitted in MS. [4] The draft here ends abruptly.

24

HENRY VI

1425
NOV. 5

The above two documents are from a corrected draft, written on one side of a broad sheet of paper. On the other side is a long Latin pleading, also much corrected, relative to the Abbey of Bermondsey ; prefixed to which are the following words, in the same hand as the preceding letters :—

' Sir, do writen ij. copies of this note in papier, wyde writen, and gete a copie of the writte in the Eschekyr ageyn.'

The pleading referred to is in a different hand, and begins as follows :—

' Et prædictus abbas dicit quod ipse de præmissis domino Regi compotum reddere non debet ; quia dicit quod diu ante erectionem, fundationem sive erectionem prioratus de Bermundeseye qui nunc erectus est in prædictam Abbatiam, Willielmus Rufus filius Willelmi Conquestoris nuper Rex Angliæ fuit seisitus d emanerio de Bermundeseye,' etc.

I I

JOHN PASTON *ALIAS* WORTES[1]

Venerables et discretes persones les courtesans demorans en l'ostel du Templebar en la cité de Londres, Mes treschiers et treshonnourés seigneurs et amis.

TRESCHIERS et treshonnourés seigneurs et grans amis, 1426 toutte recommendation premise, plaisir vous soit de scavoir que je vous notifie et avertich pour le present que Wilhelmus Paston le Sargant est denunciés escommuniés, que plus plainement poes perchevoir per Instrument que vous envoye. Et pour tant, mez treschiers seigneurs, que je disire moult le salut de votre ames et l'onneur de cascun de vous, comme faire le doy, je affin que vous u [ou] aucun de vous n'ayes aucune conversation u participation auvecquels le dit Wilhelmus, car il est aggrevés a cloquettes sonans, et tant que pour faire cesser en touttes eglises leur il voldroit aler. Mais jou suy homme d'eglise et sur touttes choses desire et convoite l'onneur et le bien dou Royaulme, car gy suy tenus, je ne envoye point pour le present les dittes aggravances, ne ossi voillans faire si grand mal que poroye jusquels a che que j'aray certaines

[1] [From Paston MSS., B.M.] William Paston, who is here spoken of as a Serjeant, attained that degree in 1421, and was made Judge of the Common Pleas in 1429. But a closer approximation to the date of this letter may be made by comparing it with that which follows, which is certainly much about the same time.

25

THE PASTON LETTERS

1426

novelles et responses comment li dis Wilhelmes se voldra ordonner en mes affaires, car nous avons en le loy que nuls os excumeniés ne puet et ne doit estre admis devant juge quelconque. Mes treschiers seigneurs, se aucune chose vo plaise que faire puisse, mande le me et le feray de bon cuer. E le sancte Dieuls qui vous ait tous et cascun de vous en sa sancte garde. Et osy, mes treschiers et treshonourés seigneurs, plaise vous scavoir que encelle meyme cause li dis Wilhelmes est redevaules et enquews envers moy, par sentence diffinitive que j'ay obtenu pour moy, en mille deuls cens et trente ducas, et que li dis Wilhelmes ne puet yestre jamays absols sy non qu'il soit d'acort auvecquels moy. Escript a en la ville de Bruges le xxiije jour de Janvier.

JOHANNES PASTON,[1] en temps passé Priour de Broholm, et pour le present evesquels de Corkagen, le tout vostre.

1 2

WILLIAM PASTON TO WILLIAM WORSTED AND OTHERS[2]

A mez treshonnourés Meistres Will'm Worstede, John Longham, et Meistre Piers Shelton soit donné.

MARCH 1

RIGHT worthy and worshepefull sires and maistres, I recomand me to yow, and thank yow with al my herte, of the gret tendrenesse ye lyke to have of the salvacion of my symple honeste, preying yow evermore of your good continuance. I have, after the advys of your lettre, doon

[1] William Paston, as appears by Nos. 12 and 14 following, disputed this writer's right to call himself Paston, and asserted that his real name was Wortes. It is curious that neither in the list of the Bishops of Cork, nor in that of the Priors of Bromholm, is the name either of Paston or Wortes to be met with.

[2] [From Paston MSS., B.M.] About the year 1425 the question of the validity of the Duke of Gloucester's marriage with Jacqueline of Hainault was before the Court of Rome. This letter must have been written in the spring of the year following, when Parliament was sitting at Leicester. The original is slightly mutilated at the edge in one place.

26

HENRY VI

1426
MARCH 1

dewely examyned the instrument by the wysest I coude fynde here, and in especial by on Maister Robert Sutton,[1] a courtezane of the Court of Rome, the which is the chief and most chier man with my Lord of Gloucestre, and his matier in the said court for my lady, his wyff ;[2] and here aunswere is that al this processe, though it were in dede proceded as the instrument specifieth, is not suffisant in the lawe of Holy Cherche, and that hem semyth, by the sight of the instrument and by the defautes [that] ye espied in the same and other, and in maner by the knowelech of the notarie, that the processe, in gret part ther of, is fal[se and un]trewe. I have taken advys of Maister Robert Bruus, chauncellor with my Lord of Cantirbury,[3] and Maister Nicholl Billesdon,[4] cha[uncellor] of my Lord of Wynchestre,[5] and Maister John Blodwelle,[6] a weel lerned man holden, and a suffisant courtezan of the seyd court, and all these acorden to the seyd Maister Robert Sutton. Nought with stondyng that I herde nevere of this matier no maner lykly ne credible evidence unto that I sey your lettre and the instrument, yet I made an appell and a procuracie, and also a provocacion, at London, longe biforn Cristemasse, by the a[dvys] of Maister David Aprys, Maister Symond Kempston, and Maister James Cole, and sent al this, with an instruccion of al the matier, w[ith] my procuratours to Rome by your frere, my Maister Suppriour, and geff hym gold that he was content : and, overmore, nowe here by advys I make this day a newe appelle and a newe procuracion, and upon this alle the seyd worthy men here seyn and informe me pleynly I have no maner cause in lawe ne in conscience to drede aught in this matier. Myn adversarie[7] is become Bysshop of Cork in Irland, and ther arn ij. other persones provided to the same bysshopriche yet lyvyng, beforn my seyd adversarie ; and by

[1] Prebendary of Lincoln, 1435-9. Died 1439.
[2] Jacqueline of Hainault, whom Humphrey, Duke of Gloucester, married, pretending that her former marriage with John, Duke of Brabant, was void by consanguinity. The question which of the two marriages was valid was at this time before the Pope.
[3] Archbishop Chicheley. [4] Dean of Salisbury, 1435-41. Died 1441.
[5] Henry Beaufort, Bishop of Winchester, afterwards Cardinal.
[6] LL.D. Prebendary of Hereford about 1433, and of Lichfield 1432-43.
[7] John Paston or Wortes, the writer of the preceding letter.

27

THE PASTON LETTERS

this acceptacion of this bysshopriche, he hath pryved hym self of the title that he claymed in Bromholm, and so adnulled the ground of his processe ageyn me, and also the tyme 'of his grevaunce pretendid, and the tyme of his sute he was *apostata*, and I trowe is yet, and so unable to sue any swich processe. I purpose me to come homward be London, to lerne more in this matier, if I may. I prey the Holy Trinite, lord of your cherche and of alle the werld, delyvere me of my iij. adversaries, of this cursed bysshop for Bromholm, Aslak for Sprouston,[1] and Julian Herberd for Thornham. I have nought trespassed ageyn noon of these iij., God knowing, and yet I am foule and noysyngly vexed with hem, to my gret unease, and al for my lordes and frendes matieres, and nought for myn owyn. I wot not whether it were best in any sermon or other audience, in your cherche or elles where, to declare aught of this matier in stoppyng of the noyse that renneth in this case. I submitte me and alle this matier to your good discrecion ; and evere gremercy God, and ye, who ever have yow and me in His gracious governance. I suppose to see yow on Palm Sunday. Writen at Leycestre, the Friday the thredde wyke of Lente.

Alle the seyd lerned men telle me trewely ther is nother perill ne doubte in the takyng doun of the instrument and the bille to no creature. Which instrument and bille I send yow ageyn by the berare of this, which I prey you to kepe as pryve as ye may.

Yowr man,   W. PASTON.

I have preyed my Maister Hammond to write yow tydyngges, and smale (?) lesynges among.

[1] A lordship in Sprouston was acquired by John Aslake of Bromholm in 14 Richard II., and seems to have continued some time in that family. Blomefield notes that a Walter Aslake, Esq. of Sprouston, had a protection in the 10th of Henry VI., being in France in the retinue of John, Duke of Bedford (Blomefield's *Norfolk*, x. 462). Probably this was the same Walter Aslak mentioned in No. 6 preceding.—*See* p. 18.

THE PASTON LETTERS

15

ABSTRACT[1]

—— TO WILLIAM PASTON.

1426 (?)   'Dear and well-beloved Cousin.'—Is in good health, but ill at ease, being informed that she is in debt to Steyard for my lord's debt, whose soul God assoil, £7 and a pipe of wine. Knew nothing of it in my lord's life, except of 2 pipes for herself, and one for her mother-in-law, of which she has paid 20s. Since my Lord's death, Steyard has never asked her for it. 'For which time, as I was at Jernemouth abiding in the Frere Carmes the time of the pestilence, his wife came unto me,' asking the writer to be good lady to him ; and he asked no more then than the above 3 pipes. He asked no more last harvest when he was sick and like to die, when John of Berneye was present. Thinks, therefore, his asking is untrue. My Lord would have made me or some of his council privy to such a debt. Hopes Paston, whom my Lord made one of his feoffees, will see 'that ye and I be discharged anemps the King as for the debt of Steyard.'—Dated Castre, the day after the Conversion of St. Paul. Addressed, 'A mon tres cher et bien ame cousin, Will'm Paston soit donné.'

[This letter is endorsed in another hand, 'W. Paston, j. feoffatorum et executorum Johannis Rothnale per lit' Cz.(?)' It seems, therefore, to have been written by the Lady Elizabeth, widow of Sir John Rothenhale, whose name occurs in No. 8 in connection with William Steyard of Great Yarmouth. She was the daughter of Sir Philip Branch, Kt., and had been previously married to John Clere of Ormesby. She died at Caister, the place from which this letter is dated, in 1440; and by her will, which was dated at Caister, 16th October 1438, she bequeathed all her goods at Ormesby to her son Robert Clere, and all her goods at Horning Hall, in Caister, to her son Edmund.—*See* Blomefield's *Norfolk*, iv. 35, vi. 392, xi. 210.]

16

ABSTRACT[2]

1426-7   Depositions on the —— day of ——, 5 Hen. vi., by Richard Wyoth, executor of Margery, daughter and heir of Edmund Bakon, touching the manor of Gressam which Bakon purchased, *temp.* Edw III. After the death of two brothers, Margery became sole possessor, and gave it to Wyoth and other executors to perform her will, with proviso that Philip Vache and Eliz., his wife, should have it during their lives, but that the reversion of it should be

[1] [From Paston mss., B.M.]   [2] *Ibid.*

HENRY VI

13

ABSTRACTS[1]

(1) *Capias* against William Stayard of Great Yarmouth, late lieutenant of Thomas Chaucer,[2] chief butler of Henry v., for debts to the Crown.

(2) Release by William Steyard of Great Yarmouth, to Elizabeth, widow of John Rothenhale, Knight, of all personal actions against her as her husband's executor. 7 April, 4 Hen. vi.

14

ABSTRACT[3]

JOHN PASTON *alias* WORTES.

i. Draft writ to the Sheriff of Norwich to attach and bring before the Council DEC. 1 John Paston *alias* Wortes and others for violation of the statutes of Provisors 25 Edw. iii. and 16 Ric. ii., on the complaint of John Brundale, prior of Bromholm that although he, Brundale, was canonically elected prior, the said Paston or Wortes had crossed the sea without royal license, obtained a provision of the said priory in the Court of Rome, and got himself installed as prior, and the other expelled. Also the said John Paston or Wortes, and John Gees, a Carmelite friar of Norwich, Edmund Alderford, late of Norwich, clerk, Barth, Waryn, parson of Trunche, William Cuttyng of Worsted, clerk, John Gees of Crowemer, merchant, and Ralph Gunton of Norwich, scrivener, received the said instruments at Bakton, and put them into execution.—Dated 1 Dec.

ii. On the back of the preceding is another draft writ of the same date against the same parties for endeavouring to draw the prior out of the kingdom by a suit in the Court of Rome.

The paper is endorsed—'S. (?) Billæ vis. Veneris prox. post diem antedictum (?) Anno H. vj. v^to, et non necessario festinant'. Iterum supervidendum.'

Endorsed in a later hand—'Towchynge Sir John Fastolffes landes in Norffolk and Surrye.'

[1] [From Paston mss., B.M.]
[2] He is believed to have been son of Geoffrey Chaucer, the famous poet, and his daughter Alice married William De la Pole, at this time Earl, afterwards Duke, of Suffolk.
[3] [From a Bodl. ms.]

HENRY VI

sold, giving William, son of Robert Moleyns, the first option of purchase. It was accordingly offered to him, but he refused to buy. On the death of said Eliz., however, he bought the manor for 420 marks, and held it two years, when Wyoth re-entered because part of the purchase-money was unpaid. W. Moleyns's wife, however, induced him to accept security from Thos. Fawkoner, merchant of London, whose daughter the said William agreed that his son should marry, when he came of age ; and it was arranged that meanwhile Fawkoner and Wyoth should be jointly enfeoffed of the manor, which was to be given in jointure, if the marriage took effect. The marriage did not take effect, and Fawkoner re-entered upon the manor according to the enfeoffment, but paid Wyoth nothing, till Thos. Chawsers,[1] Esq., a kinsman of the said Margery, made him understand that Wyoth might enter on his own portion, and had even a prior right to himself. At length Fawkoner sold his right to Chaucers and Wyoth, and released the manor on security for the payment. Wyoth then said he should have little advantage by the bargain, except in having easy days of payment ; 'et quod dictus Thomas Chaucers, pro bona voluntate quod (*sic*) erga dictum Willelmum Paston gessit, episcopum Londoni de emptione ejusdem manerii per longum tempus dilatavit, intentione ut idem Willelmus illud emeret si voluerit.'

17

ABSTRACT[2]

RAUF, Parson of Cressyngham, to WILLIAM PASTON, Justice.

Is he to deliver to John Halleman Paston's evidences belonging to the 1427-43 manor of Wodhalle in Pagrave, and under what form ? Hopes to see him at Norwich, on Tuesday or Wednesday after Michaelmas-day. Cressingham, 20 Sept.

On the back are written, in William Paston's hand, some notes of a case touching 'Frater Kensale.'

[Ralph Wolman *alias* Harple was incumbent of Cressingham from 1427 to 1460 ; but this letter could not have been written later than 1443, as William Paston died in August of the following year.]

18

ABSTRACT[3]

Mutilated Letter in French, from JOHN VAUX, Parson or Edythorp, to ——.

Only the right-hand half of the letter remains. Names mentioned—Richard 1426 de Causton, William Coule. Date lost.

[John Vaux was Rector of Edingthorp in Norfolk, in 1388. His successor was

[1] *See* Note 2 on page 29. *See also* Blomefield, viii. 127.
[2] [From Paston mss., B.M.]   [3] *Ibid.*

1429   John Prentys, who was presented to the living in 1429 by the feoffees of the duchy of
Lancaster.—Blomefield, xi. 29.]

19

ABSTRACT[1]

DEC. 7   'A grant of the Monastery of Bury to make William Paston, justice,
brother of the Chapter-House.' Day of St. Ambrose 1429.
[The description is taken from an endorsement. The document itself is printed
in Yates's *Bury St. Edmunds*, p. 156.]

20

WILLIAM PASTON TO THE VICAR OF THE ABBOT OF CLUGNY[2]

1430(?)   MY ryghte worthy and worshopeful lord, I recomaunde
me to yow. And for as meche [as I] conseyve
verrayly that ye arn Vicar general in Inggelond of
the worthy Prelate, the Abbot of Clunie, and have hys power
in many grete articles, and mong other in profession of monkes
in Inggelond of the seyd ordere. And in my cuntre, but a
myle fro the place where I was born, is the poure hous of
Bromholm of the same ordre, in wheche arn divers vertuous
yongge men, monkes clad and unprofessyd, that have abedyn
there. . . . Abbyte ix. or x. yeer; and be lenger delaye of
here profession, many inconvenientez arne lyke to falle. And
also the priour of . . . hath resigned in to your worthy handes
by certeins notables and resonables causes, as it apperyth by an
instrument, and a symple lettre under the comune seal of the
seyd hous of Bromholm, which the berare of this hath redy to
shewe yow, wher up on I prey yow wyt al my herte, and as I
evere may do yow service, that it lyke to your grace to graunte

1 [Add. Charter 17,226, B.M.]
2 [From Paston MSS., B.M.] This letter is printed from a rough draft written
on paper, corrected in William Paston's own hand, and scribbled over, after his
fashion, with numerous other drafts and jottings on both sides. Some of these occur
upside down between the lines of this letter. At the head of the memoranda on
the back are the words, ' In parliamento, anno H. vj. viij°.' from which we may infer
the date to be at least as early.

32

of your charite, by yowr worthy lettres to the prior of Thet- 1430(?)
ford in Norfolk, of the seyde ordre of Clunye, autorite and
power as your ministre and depute to professe in dwe forme
the seyd monkes of Bromholm unprofessed. And that it lyke
yow overmore to accepte and admitte the seyd resygnacion by
your seyd autoritie and power, wyth the favour of your good
lordshepe in comfort and consolacion of your pouere prestes,
the monkes of the seyd hous of Bromholm, and there up to
graunte your worthy lettres, wittenessyng the same acceptacion
and admyssion of the seyd resignacion, and al your seyd lettres
to delyvere to my clerke, to wham I prey yow to gyve feith
and credence touchant this matier, and to delivere it hym in
alle the hast resonable. And I am your man, and evere will
be by the grace of God, which evere have yow in his kepyng.
Writen at Norwich the   1 of Aprill.

          Yowres,   WILL. PASTON.

21

ABSTRACT[2]

A Memorandum, dated 8 Henry VI., that Sir Simon Felbrigge, William 1429-30
Paston, &c., recovered certain land in Edithorp, Bakton, and Northwalsham,
against Richard, Abbot of St. Benet's, Hulme, John Roys, and others.

22

ABSTRACT[3]

ROBERT, LORD OF WILLUGHBY AND BEAUMESNIL, TO WILLIAM PASTON, ESQ.

Notifying that he has granted to Sir William Oldhall and Margaret, our 1431
sister, his wife, for moneys which Oldhall has lent and paid for him at need, JAN. 8
an annuity of 120 marks on lands in Norfolk and Suffolk, in which ye (William
Paston, Esq.) stand enfeoffed, to our behoof. Pont de l'Arche, 8 Jan. 1430,
9 Hen. VI.—*Signed. Fine seal, mutilated.*

1 Blank in MS.
2 [From Paston MSS., B.M.]   3 [Add. Charter 17,227, B.M.]
VOL. II.—C   33

23

ABSTRACT[1]

1432   Deed Poll, whereby Robert York, Prior of the church of St. Andrew of
MAY 1   Broomholme, and the Convent of the same place, grant to Sir Simon Felbrygg,
Knt., William Paston of Paston, and others, certain lands in Bacton Wood,
&c., 1 May, 10 Henry VI. (*Fragment of seal.*)

24

EDUCATION OF HENRY VI[2]

*Articles de Monsr. de Warrewyk[3] touchant le bon regime du
Roy, etc.[4]*

NOV. 9   FOR the goode reule, demesnyng and seuretee of the
Kynges persone, and draught of him to vertue and
connyng, and eschuyng of eny thing that mighte yeve
empeschement or let therto, or cause eny charge, defaulte, or
blame to be leyd upon the Erle of Warrewyk at eny tyme
withouten his desert, he, considering that perill and besinesse
of his charge aboute the Kinges persone groweth so that
that auctoritee and power yeven to him before suffiseth him
nought without more therto, desireth therfor thees thinges that
folowen.

Furst, that considering that the charge of the reule,
demesnyng, and governance, and also of nourture of the
Kinges persone resteth upon the said Erle whiles it shal like
the king, and the perille, daunger, and blame if eny lak or
defaulte, were in eny of thees, the whiche lak or defaulte mighte
be caused by ungodely or unvertuous men, if eny suche were
aboute his persone; he desireth therfore, for the goode of the

1 [Add. Charter 14,313, B.M. (Dr. Turner's Coll.)]
2 [Add. Charter 17,228, B.M.]
3 Richard de Beauchamp, Earl of Warwick, who died in 1439.
4 This title is taken from a contemporary endorsement.

34

King, and for his owne seuretee, to have power and auctoritee 1432
to name, ordeigne, and assigne, and for cause that shal be NOV. 9
thought to him resonable to remoeve thoo that [shal] be
aboute the Kinges persone, of what estate or condicion that
thei be, not entending to comprehende in this desir the Stuard,
Chamberlein, Tresoror, Controrellor, ne Sergeantz of offices,
save suche as serve aboute the Kinges persone and for his
mouth.

Responsio. As toward the namyng, ordeignance, and assignacion beforesaid, it is agreed, so that he take in noon of the
iiij. knightes ne squyers for the body without th'advis of my
Lord of Bedford,[1] him being in England, and him being out,
of my Lord of Gloucestre[2] and of the remenant of the Kinges
Counsail.

Item, the said Erle desireth that where he shal have
eny persone in his discrecion suspect of mysgovernance, and
not behoveful nor expedient to be aboute the King, except
th'estates of the hous, that he may putte hem from excercise
and occupacion of the Kinges service till that he shal mowe
have speche with my Lordes of Bedford or of Gloucestre, and
with the other Lordes of the Kinges Counsaile, to that ende
that, the defaulte of eny suche persone knowen unto him, shal
mowe ordeigne therupon as theim shel thenke expedient and
behoveful.

Responsio. It is agreed as it is desired.

Item, the said Erle desireth that, for sikenesse and other
causes necessaries and resonables, he may, by warnyng to my
Lordes of Bedford or Gloucestre and the Kinges Counsail, be
and stande freely discharged of the saide occupacion and
besinesse about the Kinges persone, under the favour and
goode grace of the King, my Lordes of Bedford and Gloucestre, and other Lordes of the Kinges Counsail.

Responsio. It is agreed as it is desired.

1 John, Duke of Bedford, Regent of France, the King's uncle, brother of the late
King Henry V.
2 Humphrey, Duke of Gloucester, Protector of England, another uncle of the
King, being the youngest brother of Henry V. He was called 'the Good Duke
Humphrey.'

35

THE PASTON LETTERS

1432
NOV. 9

Item, that considering howe, blessed be God, the King is growen in yeers, in stature of his persone, and also in conceite and knouleche of his hiegh and royalle auctoritee and estat, the whiche naturelly causen him, and from day to day as he groweth shul causen him, more and more to grucche with chastising, and to lothe it, so that it may resonably be doubted leste he wol conceive ayeins the said Erle, or eny other that wol take upon him to chastise him for his defaultes, displesir, or indignacion therfore, the whiche, without due assistence, is not easy to be born : It like, therfore, to my Lord of Gloucestre, and to alle the Lordes of the Kinges Counsail, to promitte to the said Erle, and assure him, that thei shul fermely and trewely assisten him in the excercise of the charge and occupacion that he hathe aboute the Kinges persone, namely in chastising of him for his defaultes, and supporte the said Erle therinne ; and if the King at eny tyme wol conceyve for that cause indignacion ayeins the said Erle, my said Lord of Gloucestre, and Lordes, shul do alle her [*i.e.* their] trewe diligence and power to remoeve the King therfro.

Responsio. It is agreed as it is desired.

Item, the said Erle desireth that for asmuche as it shal be necessarie to remoeve the Kinges persone at diverse tymes into sundry places, as the cases mowe require, that he may have power and auctoritee to remoeve the King, by his discrecion, into what place him thenketh necessarie for the helthe of his body and seuretee of his persone.

Responsio. It is agreed as it is desired.

Item, sith the said Erle hath take upon him the governance of the Kinges persone, he desireth that alle th'estates, officers, and servantz of the Kinges hous, of what estate and condicion thei be, have special commandement and charge yeven by my Lordes of Bedford and Gloucestre, and by the Lordes of the Kinges Counsail, that in alle manere thinges seyn and advised by the said Erles descrecion, that is, for the Kinges estate, worship, helthe, and profit, by his commande-

36

1432
NOV. 9

ment and ordeignance, thei be attendant and obeissant in accomplisshing therof.

Responsio. It is agreed as it is desired.

Item, for asmuche as the said Erle hath knouleche that in speche that hath be had unto the King at part and in prive, not hering the said Erle nor eny of the knightes set aboute his persone, nor assigned by the said Erle, he hath be stured by summe from his lernyng, and spoken to of diverse materes not behovefull, the seid Erle doubting the harme that mighte falle to the King, and the inconvenientz that mighte ensue of suche speche at part if it were suffred, desireth that in al speche to be had with the King, he or oon of the iiij. knightes, or sum persone to be assigned by the said Erle, be present and prive to it.

Responsio. This article is agreed, excepting suche persones as for nieghnesse of blood, and for their estate, owe of reson to be suffred to speke with the King.

Item, to th'entent that it may be knowen to the King that it procedeth of th'assent, advis, and agreement of my Lord of Gloucestre, and alle my Lordes of the Kinges Counsail, that the King be chastised for his defaultes or trespasses, and that for awe therof he forbere the more to do mys, and entende the more besily to vertu and to lernyng, the said Erle desireth that my Lord of Gloucestre, and my said other Lords of the Counsail, or great part of hem, that is to say, the Chanceller and Tresorer, and of everych estate in the Counsail, spirituell and temporell, summe come to the Kinges presence, and there to make to be declared to him theire agreement in that behalve.

Responsio. Whan the King cometh next to London, all his Counsail shal come to his presence, and there this shal be declared to him.

Item, the said Erle, that all his dayes hath, aboven alle other erthely thinges, desired, and ever shal, to kepe his trouthe and worship unblemysshed and unhurt, and maye not

37

THE PASTON LETTERS

1432
NOV. 9

for all that lette malicious and untrewe men to make informacions of his persone, suche as thei may not, ne dare not, stand by, ne be not trewe, bescheth therfore my Lord of Gloucestre, and alle my said Lords of the Counsail, that if thei, or eny of hem, have be enformed of eny thing that may be or soune to his charge or defaulte, and namely in his occupacion and reule aboute the Kinges persone, that the said Erle may have knowleche therof, to th'entent that he may answer therto, and not dwelle in hevy or synistre conceit or opinion, withoute his desert and without answere.

Responsio. It is agreed.

CROMWELL.

H. GLOUCESTRE.

J. EBOR.   P. ELIEN.

W. LINCOLN.   J. BATHON., Canc.   J. ROFFEN.

SUFFOLK.   H. STAFFORD.

J. HUNTYNGTON.

The foregoing document is written on a skin of parchment docqueted with the words printed in italics at the head. The following memorandum is also endorsed—'xxix^e die Novembris anno undecimo apud Westm. lecti fuerunt præsentes articuli coram dominis infra et subscribentibus et ad eosdem Responsiones dabantur secundum quod infra patet, præsentibus dominis infrascriptis.' There are also other endorsements, but of a later date.

25

DALLING'S PETITION [1]

1433(?)

Prefixed to this document in Fenn is the following title :—'A Petition to the Commons of England against Sir William Paston, Knight, a Judge of the Common Pleas, by William Dalling.' This heading, however, has been taken from a more modern endorsement. No contemporaneous document, so far as I am aware, gives Judge Paston the designation of knight, or speaks of him as Sir William. In this petition itself he is called simply William Paston, one of the Justices; and although his name occurs frequently on the Patent Rolls, in commissions of the peace, of gaol delivery, and the like, down to the year of his death, the word 'miles' is never appended to it.

The original commencement of this document has been crossed out. It was in these words :—

Plesit to the righte sage and wyse Communes of this present Parlement,

[1] [From Fenn, iii. 14.]

38

1434(?)

that wher every Justice of the Kyng is sworne that he shulde not take no fees ne reward for to be of councell with noo man, but oonly wyth our Soverayne Lorde the Kyng, and therto thei be swore. And ther is oon Will' Paston, one of the Justice of our Soverayne Lorde in the Comene Place, taketh fees and rewarde.

On the back of the original document is written, in a hand of the time, 'Falsa billa Will'i Dalling, ad Parliamentum tempore quo-Henr. Grey fuit vicecomes ante annum terciodecimum Regis Henr. vj^ti.' Henry Grey was sheriff of Norfolk in 1430, and again in 1433-4. The Parliament referred to must either have been that of 8 Hen. VI. (1429-30) or that of 12 Hen. VI. (1433), which sat till 21st December. Probably the latter.

PLESE it to Commines of the present Parlement, that William Paston, on of the Justice of oure Saverayne Lorde Kyng, takyth diverse fees and rewardes of diverses persones withinne the shir of Norffolk and Suffolk, and is with holde with every matere in the sayde contrees, that is for to sey :—Of the Toune of Yernemuth, ls. yerly ; of the Abot of Seyn Benetys. xxvjs. viijd. ; of the Prior of Seyn Feithes, xxs. ; 'and of my Lady Rothenhale,[1] xxs' ; and of the Prior of Norwich, xs. ; and of the Prior of Penteney, xxs. ; and of the Toun of Lenn, xls. ; and of the Prior of Walsyngham, xxs. ; and of Katherine Shelton,[2] x. mrc. ayeins the Kyng for to be of hir councell for to destroye the right of the Kyng and of his warde, that is for to sey, Raf,[3] soon and eyer of John Shelton.

26

ABSTRACT [4]

1435
SEPT. 26

Lease made at Castre, on Monday before Michaelmas 14 Henry VI., by Geoffrey Walle, surveyor of the manors of Sir John Fastolf, to John Rakesond, son of Geoffrey Rakesond of Ormesby, of a messuage of Fastolf's in Ormesby, called Reppes Place, etc.

[1] This sentence in the original has a line drawn over it. She was a widow of Sir John Rothenhale, Knight, and dying at Caister, by Yarmouth, in 1440, was buried in Norwich Cathedral.—F. *See* Nos. 13 and 15, ante.

[2] Catharine, widow of William Shelton, Esq., and daughter of Simon Barret, was grandmother to Ralph, and died in 1456.—F.

[3] Sir Ralph Shelton, Knight, son and heir of John Shelton, Esq., was born in 1430. He married Margaret, daughter of Robert Clere, Esq. of Ormesby, and was High Sheriff of Norfolk.—F.

[4] [Phillipps MS., 9,735, No. 264.]

39

27

ABSTRACT[1]

1435
SEPT. 30
A *vidimus* or official attestation of two indentures relative to the custody of the castle of Le Mans between Sir John Fastolf, governor of Anjou and Maine, and captain of Le Mans under the Duke of Bedford, and Matthew Goth [Gough] and Thomas Gower as his lieutenants. The first indenture is for the quarter from 1st October to 31st December 1434, the second for the three quarters following, to 30th September 1435. A retinue is to be maintained of twenty-four lances and the 'archiers de la personne dudit Mathieu,' viz., sixty mounted and fourteen on foot, and 222 archers besides. Mounted archers to have 12*d*. a day, etc.

The document is authenticated by the *garde du scel des obligations de la Viconté de Rouen*, on the 8th March 1448 (*i.e.* 1449).

28

NOTE[2]

1432-5
Building accounts of William Granere, master of the works at Caistre in 11, 12, and 13 Henry VI.

29

JOHN GYNE TO JOHN PASTON[3]

To the worthy and worshipful sir and my good maister,
John Paston of Trynyte hall in Cambrigge

1435-6
RIGHT worthy and worshipfull sir, and my good maister, I comaund me to yow. Like it yow to witte that on the Soneday next after the Ascencion of oure Lord, in the high weye betwex Cambrigge and the Bekyntre toward

---

[1] [Add. Charter 17,237, B.M.]
[2] [Add. Charters 17,229-31, B.M.]
[3] [Add. MS. 34,888, f. 4.] Fenn has written on the MS. of this letter the date 'circa 1435-6,' which, I agree with him, must have been about the time that it was written.

Newmarket, I fonde a purs with money ther inne. Th'entent 1435-6 of this my symple lettre is this, that it please to your good Maistership by weye of charite, and of your gentilnesse, to witte if ony of youre knowleche or ony other, swich as yow semeth best in your discrecion, have lost swich a purs, and, the toknes ther of told, he shal have it ageyn, what that ever he be, by the grace of oure Lord, Who ever have yow in his blissed kepyng. Wretyn at Sneylewell the Moneday next after the seid Soneday. By youre pover servaunt,

JOHN GYN.

30

WILLIAM PASTON TO LORD —— [1]

PASTON recomaund hym to youre good lordeship, 1436 willyng with all his herte to doo yow servise to his symple power. And as touching the maner of Walsham he seyth that at your comaundement he wille be redy to shewe yow and preve that the seid maner and all the vesture and crop therof this yeer by trewe title in lawe and conscience is his owen trewly, bowth and in gret party payed for, and that John Roys never hadde non estate in the seid maner, but oonly occupied it by suffraunce of the seid Paston and other feffes in the seid maner, and that be bargayn of the seid maner th'estate that the seid Roys shuld have hadde in the seid maner and in stoor therof shul have be condicionel to be voide and nought for defaute of payement, and that the seid John Roys ne kept not his dayes of the payementz, &c.; and that the seid William Paston, in the lyve of the seid John Roys, for defaute of payment entred in the seid maner with the seid the crop and the vesture of this yeer therof than therupon, and that the seid John Roys never at noo tyme payed to the seid John Baxtere sith the seid bargayn, nother for the seid bargayn ne for the dette he aught to hym, more

---

[1] [Add. MS. 34,889, f. 140.]

1436 thaune an C. and xl. marcz, wherof he borwed ageyn of the seid John Baxtere xl*li*.; and over that he oweth and beforn the seid bargeyn aught by his obligacion to the seid John Baxtere, of trew dette of mony borwed, other xl*li*., and hath hadde and taken the profitz of the seid maner by iij. hool yer before his deth to the value of xxx*li*. and more, and that he receyved in his said bargayn of the seid John Baxtere xl. marcz worth of stoor; the which iiii^xx*li*. of dette and xxx*li*. of the profitz of the seid maner, and xl. marcz worth of stoor, maketh the somme of Cxxxvi*li*. xiij*s*. iiij*d*. Wherof, thogh the lawe wille it not, were abated, if conscience required it, Cxl. marcz payed by the seid John Roys and x*li*. for the value of the seid crop, over the value of the verray ferme of the seid maner for this yeer, yet remanyneth dwe to the executoures of the seid John Baxter liij*li*. vj*s*. viij*d*., and all the title and interesse of the seid John Roys his heyres and assignes in the seid maner lawfully and in conscience extincted and adnulled. Wher upon the said Paston lowly besecheth your good lordeship that if it may be preved this mater be trew that ye wille not be displesed thogh he desire to have his fre disposicion of the seid maner.

On the back of this letter are the following memoranda:—

'Hæc billa . . . . . . [testatur][1] quod Johannes Baxtere vendidit Johanni Roys mesuagium suum [vocatum][1] Walccham place, cum toto stauro ibidem vivo et mortuo in Bryanes, cum omnibus aliis terris et tenementis suis, liberis et nativis, cum pertinentiis, ex parte occidentali ecclesiæ North Walsham, et molendinum ventriticum et mesuagium nuper Rogeri atte Hille, cum omnibus redditibus et servitiis pertinentibus dictis mesuagio et tenemento ubicumque fuerint in comitatu Norffolk, pro iijC. marcis et l. marcis; unde dictus Johannes Roys solvit dicto Johanni Baxtere die Jovis proximo ante festum Apostolorum Simonis et Judæ anno regni regis Henrici vi. xij., C. m., et habet diem solvendi residuum, videlicet ad festum Nativitatis Domini et festum sancti Michaelis proximo futurum xl. marcas annuatim, quousque dictæ CCC. marcæ et l. marcæ plenarie persolvantur. Datum die Jovis prædicta. Hæc prædicta de manu Thomæ Whitewelle.'

Then after two further imperfect entries relating to the same matter:—

'Memorandum, quod licet esset concordatum quod W. Roys haberet barganium, &c., quod, ut credo, non ita erit, tunc in festo Nativitatis Domini anno

---

[1] Mutilated.

---

regni regis Henrici vi. xv° debentur executoribus de eodem barganio C. marcæ 1436 præter et ultra Cxl. marcas per Johannem Roys in vita sua solutas et xl*li*. de antiquo per dictum Johannem Roys Johanni Baxter debitas, videlicet per obligacionem suam xxxv*li*. inde, et ex mutua sua obligacione v*li*. de Perey Noble (?), ut patet per papirum dicti Baxter, et ultra xl*li*. per dictum Johannem Baxter post dictum barganium dicti Johanni Roys per obligacionem . . . ejusdem Johannis Roys præstitas. Memorandum eciam quod dictus Johannes Roys nec uxor ejus unquam protulerunt aliquem denarium solvendum dictis . . . dicti Johannis Baxter nec Willelmo Paston post mortem dicti Baxter. Set circa Nativitatem Domini anno regni dicti regis xiiij° et in quadragesima tunc proximo sequente uxor dicti Roys apud Paston dixit quod habuit xx. marcas paratas ad solvendum. Et sic dixit Johannes Roys tempore quo Domina Skales fuit apud Paston, videlicet ix. die Januarii dicto anno xiiij° et sic omnibus temporibus quibus dictus J. Roys et uxor ejus ut prædicitur dixerunt quod habuerunt xx. marcas paratas ad solvendum semper fuerunt arretro xl*li*. absque dictis xl*li*. novi debiti et xl*li*. antiqui debiti.'

31

NOTE

Fenn mentions an indenture, dated 19th May 1436, 14 Henry VI., and 1436 signed by the Earl (afterwards Duke) of Suffolk, from which he has given a MAY 19 facsimile of Suffolk's signature. See vol. i. p. 36.—The original of this indenture I have not met with.

32

ABSTRACT[1]

Sir H. Inglose notifies his agreement with John Topy of Wyndham, jun., 1438 in an action for trespass done to him at Stalham. Dilhams, Monday after the AUG. 18 Assumption of Our Lady, 16 Henry VI.

---

[1] [Add. Charter 17,232, B.M.]

33

JOHN WILLOUGHBY TO LORD BEAUMONT[1]

To my ryght noble and ryght [dra]dde lord, my Lord Beaumont.

1432-40

RYGHT wursshipfull sire, my ryghte noble, and ryghte
dradde lorde, after dyw recommendacion to yowr
reverens, please hit yow to know that yowr lordes-
ship luste to empointe me to abyde yowr noble avys touching
the landis of Latemer, which my Lorde Latemer holdith ate
this day. My lord, I muste, and owe of dywte, abyde yowre
empoyntement, and shall; how be hit I have be confortid to
complaine me to my lordis and yow of the grete wronge that
I have. But, sir, y have soe verray truste one yowre lordes-
ship that I refuse all counsaille, abyding yowre empointemente
and rewell, as my diwte is to doo; byseching yow, my lord,
to remembre yow and compasse of yowre servaunt, and that
ye lust of yowr grace to comyne with my Lord of Salisbury,
and to fele him in the mater, and as ye fele him, hit please
yowre lordeship I may have knowlege; and whate yowre
pore bedman may do to yowre plesire, I ame redy ate yowre
comaundement ate all howris, which knowith God, Hoe have
yow, my ryghte noble lord, in His blessid gouvernauns.
    Write ate Broke, the v. day of Marche.
        Your pore bedman and servant,
                JOHN WYLUGHBY.

[1] [From Paston MSS., B.M.] The writer of this letter was the father of Robert,
first Lord Willoughby de Broke, who afterwards laid claim to the barony of Latimer,
as being descended from Elizabeth, sister and sole heir of John Nevill, fifth Lord
Latimer, who died in 1430. He was, however, unsuccessful, as the title had been
revived in 1432 by a writ of summons to George Nevill, a son of Ralph, first Earl of
Westmoreland. This George died in 1469, and was succeeded by his grandson,
Richard Neville, then an infant of two years old, who had summons to Parliament as
Lord Latimer in 1492. The Lord Latimer here spoken of seems to be George
Nevill, and it is probable that the letter was written between 1432 and 1440, as John,
Lord Beaumont, was created Viscount in the latter year, while he is not so addressed
here.

44

THE PASTON LETTERS

35

ABSTRACT[1]

About
1440

Draft Lease by Sir Simon Felbrygge; Oliver Groos, Esq.; John Berney
of Redham, Esq.; William Paston of Paston; Thomas Stodhagh; Roger
Taillour of Stafford Bernyngham; and Thomas Newport of Runham, executors
of Robert Mawteby and John his son, to Margery, widow of the said John,
of 'two parts of manors, &c.' and the reversion, &c., which they lately held
along with Sir Miles Stapleton, Sir William Argenten, Sir John Hevenyngham,
Sir John Carbonell, Sir William Calthorpe, John Boys, Esq., and William
Caston, Esq., now deceased, by deed of Robert Mawteby. The remainder,
after Margery's death, is to go to Margaret, daughter of the said John and
Margery, and the heirs of her body; then to Peter Mauteby, son of Robert and
uncle of Margaret; then to Alianora, widow of Robert; then to Alianora,
widow of William Calthorp and sister of Robert Mawteby, with reversion to
the trustees to fulfil the will.

[This paper is addressed to John Berney of Reedham, and appears, by an
endorsement, to have been transmitted along with a letter of William Paston.
The date is fixed by the contents within pretty narrow limits, for it is after the death
of John Boys, Esq., which was in August 1439 (Inquis. *post mortem*, 18 Hen. VI.,
No. 2), and before that of Sir Simon Felbrig in 1442 (Inquis. *p. m.*, 21 Hen. VI.,
No. 33). It is easy to see, in fact, that the document had something to do with
the marriage settlement of John Paston and Margaret Mauteby, which was about
1440.]

36

ROBERT REPPS TO JOHN PASTON[2]

A mon tresreverent et treshonerable Maister John Paston soit doné.

1440
NOV. 1

SALVETE, &c. Tytyngs, the Duk of Orlyawnce[3] hath
made his oath upon the Sacrement, and usyd it, never
for to bere armes ayenst Englond, in the presence of
the Kyng and all the Lordes, except my Lord of Gloucestre.[4]

[1] [From Paston MSS., B.M.]
[2] [From Fenn, i. 4.] This letter was written in 1440, the year of the release
of the Duke of Orleans.
[3] Charles, Duke of Orleans, who was taken prisoner at the battle of Agincourt in
1415, and had never since been released.
[4] Humphrey, Duke of Gloucester, uncle of the King, and before this time
Protector.

46

34

AGNES PASTON TO WILLIAM PASTON[1]

To my worshepefull housbond, W. Paston, be this letter takyn

DERE housbond, I recomaunde me to yow, &c. Blessyd 1440(?)
be God I sende yow gode tydynggs of the comyng,
and the brynggyn hoom, of the gentylwomman[2] that
ye wetyn of fro Redham, this same nyght, acordyng to poynt-
men [*appointment*] that ye made ther for yowr self.
    And as for the furste aqweyntaunce be twhen John Paston[3]
and the seyde gentylwomman, she made hym gentil cher in
gyntyl wise, and seyde, he was verrayly your son. And so
I hope ther shall nede no gret trete be twyxe hym.
    The parson of Stocton[4] toold me, yif ye wolde byin her a
goune, here moder wolde yeve ther to a godely furre. The
goune nedyth for to be had; and of colour it wolde be a
godely blew, or erlys a bryghte sangueyn.
    I prey yow do byen for me ij. pypys of gold.[5] Your
stewes[6] do weel.
    The Holy Trinite have you in governaunce.
    Wretyn at Paston, in hast, the Wednesday next after *Deus
qui errantibus*,[7] for defaute of a good secretarye. Yowres,
                AGN. PASTON.

[1] [From Fenn, i. 2.] This letter must have been written some little time before
the marriage of John Paston and Margaret Mauteby, which seems to have been about
1440.
[2] Margaret, daughter and heir of John Mauteby, shortly afterwards married to
John Paston, Esq.
[3] Son of William and Agnes Paston.
[4] Laurence Baldware was rector of Stockton 'about 1440.'—Blomefield, viii. 49.
[5] Gold thread on pipes or rolls, for needlework or embroidery.—F.
[6] Ponds to keep fish alive for present use.—F.
[7] The Collect for the Third Sunday after Easter.

45

HENRY VI

And proving my seyde Lord of Gloucestre agreyd never to 1440
hys delyveraunce, qwan the masse began he toke his barge, &c. NOV. 1
    God yef grace the seide Lord of Orlyaunce be trewe, for
this same weke shall he to ward Fraunce.
    Also Freynchmen and Pykardes, a gret nowmbre, kome to
Arfleet,[1] for to arescuyd [*have rescued*] it; and our Lordes
wyth here smal pusaunce manly bytte [*beat*] them, and pytte
hem to flyte, and, blyssyd be our Lord, have take the seide
cite of Arflet; the qwych is a great juell to all Englond, and
in especiall to our cuntre.
    Moreover there is j. [*i.e.* one] kome in to Englond, a
Knyght out of Spayne, wyth a kercheff of plesaunce i wrapped
aboute hys arme; the qwych Knyght wyl renne a cours wyth
a sharpe spere for his sovereyn lady sake; qwom other [*either*]
Sir Richard Wodvyle[2] or Sir Christofore Talbot[3] shall delyver,
to the wyrchip of Englond and of hem selff, be Goddes grace.
    Ferthermore, ye be remembryd that an esquyer of Suffolk,
callyd John Lyston, recoveryd *in assisa novæ disseisinæ*[4] vij{c}
[700] marc in damages ayenst Sir Robert Wyngfeld, &c. In
avoydyng of the payement of the seid vij. c. marc, the seide
Sir Robert Wyngfeld sotylly hath outlaywed the seide John
Lyston in Notyngham shir, be the vertue of qwch outlagare,
all maner of chattell to the seide John Lyston appertynyng,
arn acruwyd on to the Kyng, &c. And anon as the seide
utlagare was certyfyed, my Lord Tresorer[5] graunted the seid
vij. c. marc to my Lord of Norffolk, for the arrerag of hys
sowde [*pay*] qwyl he was in Scotland; and, acordyng to this
assignement forseide, taylles [*tallies*] delyvered. And my Lord
of Norffolk hath relesyd the same vij. c. marc to Sir Robert
Wyngfeld. And here is greet hevyng an shovyng be my Lord
of Suffolk and all hys counsell for to aspye hough this mater
kam aboute, &c.
    Sir, I beseche recomende me on to my mastres your modyr,
to my mastres your wyff, and to my mastres your suster, *et
omnibus alijs quorum interest*, &c.

[1] Harfleur.   [2] Afterwards Earl Rivers, father of Elizabeth, Queen of Edward IV.
[3] Third son of John, the famous Earl of Shrewsbury.
[4] *i.e.*, in an assize of novel disseisin—an ancient law process.
[5] Ralph, Lord Cromwell.

47

THE PASTON LETTERS

1440
NOV. 1

Sir, I pray you, wyth all myn hert, hold me excusyd that I wryte thus homly and briefly on to you, for truly convenable space suffycyd me nowt.

No more atte this tyme, butte the Trynyte have you in proteccion, &c.; and qwan your leysyr is, resorte ageyn on to your college, the Inner Temple, for ther ben many qwych sor desyr your presence, Welles and othyr, &c.

Wretyn in le fest de touts Seynts, entre Messe et Mateyns, *calamo festinante*, &c.   Yours,   ROB. REPPES.

37

ABSTRACT [1]

—— —— TO FRIAR BRACKLEY (?).

About
1440(?)

Touching a suit of Reynold Rowse against William Burgeys. This suit was instituted originally for 5*s.* 4*d.* of rent; but when Rouse found he could not prevail by right, he maliciously sued the other for trespass in having fished his water, and driven him away by force. He afterwards got him arrested for treachery upon an obligation (*i.e.*, a bond). Burgeys complained to Justice Paston, who counselled him not to plead; 'For zyf thu do, he seyd, thu xalte hafe the werse, be thi case never so trewe, for he is feid with my Lord of [N]orthfolke, and mech he is of he [*sic*] counsel; and also, thu canst no man of lawe in Northfolke ne in Sowthfolke to be with the azens hym; and, for [s]othe no more myth I qwan I had a ple azens hym; and therfor myn counsel is, that thu make an end qwat so ever the pay, for he xal elles on do the and brynge the to nowte.'

[This letter is mutilated, and in part defaced. It is addressed on the back—'Be this take to Mayster Brele (?) of the Greye Freres.' Although the name seems to be written Brele, it was probably intended for Friar Brackley of Norwich, of whom we have several letters of a later period. The date must be between the year 1429, when William Paston was made a judge, and 1444, when he died; and as the name of Reginald Rows occurs in Blomefield (*Hist. of Norfolk*, ix. 441) 'about 1440,' this letter will probably not be far out of its true place if inserted in that year.]

[1] [From Paston MSS., B.M.]

48

38

MARGARET PASTON TO JOHN PASTON [1]

To my worshepfull husbond, John Paston, abidyng at Petyrhous in Cambrigg.

After
1440

RYTH reverent and worsepful husbon, I recomawnde me to zow with alle myn sympyl herte, and prey zow to wete that there come up xi. hundyr Flemyns at Waxham, quereof wer takyn, and kylte, and dronchyn [*drowned*] viij. hundryte. And thei had nowte a be, ze xul a be atte home this Qwesontyde, and I suppose that ze xul be atte home er owte long be.

I thanke yow hertely for my lettyr, for I hadde none of zow syn I spooke with zow last of for the matyr of Jon Mariot; the qwest passyd nowte of that day, for my Lorde of Norfolke was in towne for Wedyrbys matyr,[2] qwer for he wolde nowt latyd pase off, for further (?) of I kowe [*know?*] Fynch ne Bylbys makethe no purwyans for hys gode.

No mor I wryte to zow atte this tyme, but the Holy Trenyte hawe zow in kepyng. Wretyn in Norweche, on Trenyte Sune day.   Yowr,   MARKARYTE PASTON.

[1] [From Fenn, iii. 18.] The date of this letter is uncertain. From the fact of John Paston's residence at Peter House in Cambridge, it would appear, as Fenn remarks, to have been written early in his married life, and we know that he was married as early as 1440.
[2] Probably Thomas Wetherby, who was Mayor of Norwich in 1432-3, is referred to. He took offence at the Aldermen and Commons of the city for not naming the person he wished as his successor, and for some years afterwards showed his hostility by instigating prosecutions against the city, causing their attorneys to abandon their pleas, and so forth.

THE PASTON LETTERS

39

SIR JOHN FASTOLF TO HENRY INGLOSE AND JOHN BERNEY [1]

To my ryght wel belovyd cosyns, Herry Inglese and Johan Berney, Escuiers.

After
1440(?)

RYGHT wel belovyd cosyns, I comaund me to yow. And please you to hafe in knoulege that at whyche tyme ye were delyvered out of pryson by the moyen of ij. prysonners that y delyvered yow, whyche, as ye know wel, one was Burd Vynollys and the other Johan de Seint Johan dit Dolot, and in lyke wyse I boughte anothyr prysonner clepyt Johan Villers for the delyveraunce of Mautbye[2] Sqwyer, whyche mater ye knowythe welle. And for as moche as my wrytynges that makyth mencion of that delyveraunce of the said Mautbye be not in my warde, y pray you that ye wolle undre your seelys certyffye me the trouthe how the said Mautbye was delyveryd by my moyen. Y hafe found a cedule that makyth mencion of that prysonner, of whyche I sende you a double, to be better avertysed of the mater. And therfor, as my trust ys yn yow that ye sende me your gode remembraunce in as goodly haste as ye may. And our Lord kepe you. Wryt at Londone the v. day of November.

JOHN FASTOLF, *Chevalier.*

40

ABSTRACT [3]

1441
MAY 7

Letters Patent, dated 7th May 19 Henry vi., by which Richard, Duke of York, Earl of March, etc., lieutenant and governor of France, grants to his beloved councillor, Sir John Fastolf, an annuity of £20.

[1] [MS. in Pembroke College, Cambridge.] The date of this letter is quite uncertain; but as Fastolf is believed to have returned from abroad about 1440, we presume it was not earlier than that year.
[2] No doubt John Mauteby, son-in-law of John Berney and father of Margaret Paston. *See* Blomefield's *Norfolk*, xi. 228.
[3] [Add. Charter 14,598, B.M. (D. Turner's Coll.)]

50

41

ABSTRACT [1]

1441
OCT. 14

Sir Thoma. Keryell, lieutenant of Calais, notifies that his servant, John à Bekkes, mariner, master of his ship *Bonaventure*, has sold it to Sir John Fastolf, and that he agrees to the sale. Calais, 14th October 1441. Signed 'R. Wenlok.' (*Fine seal, mutilated.*)

42

NOTE

1442

A proviso occurs for William Paston and Robert and Esmond Clere in an Act of Parliament 20 Henry vi., securing to them certain copyhold lands with two mansions thereon in Paston and Edithorp, Norfolk, held by the feoffees of the duchy of Lancaster, in exchange for other lands, called Charterhold, with two mansions thereon, in the same places.—*Rolls of Parliament*, v. 59.

43

ABSTRACT [2]

JOHN AND MARGARET PASTON.

APRIL 15

Indenture tripartite, whereby Sir Simon Felbrigge, Oliver Groos, Esq., and William Paston, feoffees of Robert Mauteby, Esq., deceased, at the request of Margaret, wife of John Paston, daughter and heir of John Mauteby, son and heir of said Robert, and in consideration that the said John Paston and Margaret now have issue a son, John, whereby John Paston the father is by the law of England, for term of his life of the inheritance of his said wife, —— grant and confirm to the said John Paston the manors of Mauteby, Sparham, Basyngham, Westbekham, Matelask, and Briston, the manor of Salle called Kirkehalle, and the manor called Fleghalle in Wynterton, Somerton, Ormesby, Martham, Horseye, Waxstonesham, and Pallyng, and 100s. rent in Castre by Norwich and Merkeshale, Norfolk; and the manor of Freton in Suffolk; with certain reversions on the death of Eleanor, wife of Thomas Chambre, Esq., formerly wife of the said Robert Mauteby, Margery, wife of Ralph Garneys, Esq., mother of the said Margaret, formerly wife of John Mauteby, and of Edward Mauteby, Esq., and Thomas Mauteby, Esq., sons of the said Robert. To hold to the said John Paston, with remainder to Margaret and the heirs of her body; with contingent remainders in tail to Edw. Mauteby, Thomas Mauteby, &c.

Dated Mauteby, 15 April, 20 Hen. vi.

[1] [Add. Charter 17,233, B.M.]   [2] [From a Bodl. MS.]

51

44

ABSTRACT [1]

1442
APRIL 20

Grant by John, Duke of Norfolk, to William Berdewell, Esq., of an annuity of 10 marks out of Stonham, Suffolk. Framlingham, 20th April 20 Henry VI.

45

ABSTRACT [2]

ELEANOR CHAMBRE TO WILLIAM PASTON.

About
1442

Thanks him for what he did for her at Sparham at their last interview. He then expected to have more leisure to attend to her affairs at London after this Hallowmass, when he would ordain that she should have lawful estate for life in the partition made 'betwixt you and me, to for such that was there for my husband and for me at that time.' Begs him to do it now, and deliver it to her brother, John Chambre, or her servant, John Coke, the bearer. Sends the deed of annuity under her husband's signet and hers, which she must pay to Paston's children.

Welouby, Sunday after St. Martin.

[Alianore, widow of Robert Mauteby, Esq., remarried Thomas Chambers, Esq., lord of Sparham in her right, in 20 Henry VI. Her son, John Mauteby, was the father of Margaret, wife of John Paston.—*See* Blomefield, xi. 228.]

46

DEPOSITION AGAINST JOHN HAWTEYN [3]

1443
SEPT. 8

PRIMO suggessit Sanctissimo Papæ mentiendo quod coactus et constrictus [fuisset] metu parentum ordinem [4] intrare ; secundo quod in insufficienti et prohibita ætate et in eodem ordine invite esset professus ; Et tertio, quod ita fuerat invallatus et inclusus in ordinis arctitudine ut sibi tempus opportunum exeundi acquirere nequiret. Contra

[1] [Add. Charter 17,234, B.M.]   [2] [From Paston MSS., B.M.]
[3] [From Paston MSS., B.M.]
[4] The Order of Carmelites.—*See* Note 1 on page 54.

quæ sic depono, non per ficta et fantastice ymaginata, sed per visa et audita a fide dignis denunciata. Et primo, contra primum articulum, viz., quod metu parentum etc. quia, ut asserunt fide media quam plures fide digni quorum nomina perlongum esset enarrare, quod alter parentum, suple pater, neci submersionis suffocatus fuerat in Themisia diu antequam ordinem ingressus est prænotatus Johannes ; ergo, dissonum videtur quod metu parentum ingressus est, sed tantum alterius parentis. Secundo, contra secundum articulum, scilicet quod ex insufficienti etc., quia per vere visa et audita a fide dignis personis contra illud testimonium perhibere volentibus verum est asserere quod xiiij^cim annorum fuerat ætatis antequam indutus esset ; quod sic evidet, quia natus erat in Swapham Markett, in loco qui Delgate dicitur, ubi parentes ejus commorabantur, quando primo intraverant villam antedictam pro annuali stipendio dato Thomæ Delgate, cujus erat ipsa mansio, et istud ad testimonium Adæ Ram, Roberti Sergaunte, Agnetis Ymay commatris [1] sæpedicti Johannis Hawteyn et Katerinæ Gannok, uxoris compatris [1] Johannis Hawteyn prædicti, viz. Johannis Gannok qui obiit anno Domini mccccxxxiiij^o. Istis transactis, parentes dicti Johannis, viz. Haymundus Hawteyn, pater ejus, et Claricia Hawteyn mater ejus, conjunctim emerunt mansionem in eadem villa, viz. Swapham Markett, a Martino Waron anno regni Regis Ricardi Secundi post conquestum xxij^o, quod datum, suple Regis Ricardi, præcessit nativitas Johannis Hawteyn in Delgate per testimonia præallegata. De facili ergo, probatur quod sit ætatis annorum xliiij^or ad minus, enumerando a xxij^o anno regni Regis Ricardi Secundi post conquestum usque ad annum xxj^m Henrici Sexti.

1443
SEPT. 8

Omnia in hac cedula quo ad Hawteyn dicta fuerunt Jacobo Gresham viij^o die Septembris anno Regis Henrici vj^ti xxij^o, prout scribuntur. Frater Johannes Alburugh dicit quod hoc medio intravit Johannes Hawteyn in ordinem. Circa xij. annum ætatis suæ missus fuit London' essend' cum quodam

[1] *Compater* and *commater* (in French *compère* and *commère*) correspond in meaning to the old English word *gossip, i.e.* god-sib, or related in baptism—generally applied to godfathers and godmothers.

1443
SEPT. 8

Thoma Brown modo apprenticii ; quod actum fuit, quodque sibi non bene complacuit, et cucurrit ad Fratres et dixit quod fuit nepos Alburugh, et ea de causa Reverendus Magister Walden [1] interrogavit eum si vellet esse frater, et dixit quod vellet et humiliter rogavit ex caritate. Et veraciter scit quod fuit ætatis xiiij. annorum et amplius tempore professionis suæ et moram traxit ibidem per iij. vel iiij. annos. Et postea fuit apud Maldon per duos annos, et ab illo loco exiit. Deinde captus et Norwico incarceratus per dimidium annum. Et postea in domo de Blakney per iiij^or annos mansit, et ibidem fuit terminarius et hospes ; et cucurrit ab inde cum vestibus officii de domo hospicii furtive et cepit librum (?) Alburugh avunculi sui et canciavit illum apud Aylesham pro iiij. marcis et dimidia, quas dictus Alburugh solvit pro libro rehabendo.

Et addidit idem Johannes Hawteyn vel Alburugh frater et avunculus dicti Johannis Hawteyn quod Johannes Hawteyn apostata fuit natus apud Swafham Market circa iiij. annum post transitum patris sui a Scheryngton usque Swafham. Et dicit quod Robertus frater ejus fuit pluris ætatis quam Johannes fuit per iiij^or annos, et dictus Robertus fuit natus apud Scherynton.

Et serviens Daubeney dicit quod Hamond Hawteyn transivit a Scheryngton usque Swafham tempore quo Thomas Erpyngham custodivit Regem R. in Turre London.[2]

Stephanus Plattyng de Aylesham pro vero dicit quod ad Festum Purificationis Beatæ Mariæ anno regni Regis Henrici vj^ti xxj^o elapsi fuerunt xxviij^o anni postquam ipse primo habitavit in dicta villa de Aylesham ; quo tempore Claricia quæ fuit uxor Hamonis Hawteyn fuit vidua et commorans in messuagium nunc Johannis Draper de Aylesham, et postea nupta fuit Petro Fysch, cæco, qui insimul vixerunt vj. vel vij. annos, et post obitum dicti Petri dicta Claricia cepit in virum Willelmum Punyant de Aylesham. Et ad dictum festum Purificationis Beatæ Mariæ dicto anno xxj^o dicti Ponyant et Claricia insimul in matrimonio cohabitaverunt per xxij. annos.

[1] The celebrated Thomas Netter of Walden, provincial of the Carmelite order in England ; a great opponent of Wycliffe.
[2] Richard II. was committed to the Tower in 1399, just before his formal resignation of the crown.

1443
SEPT. 8

Hoc de Pounyant cum Claricia affirmant. Et dicit idem Ponyant quod frater Johannes Hawteyn professus fuit post matrimonium inter ipsum et præfatam Clariciam et quod ipse ad ultimum exitum suum de ordine prædicto dimisit capam suam in domo dicti Ponyant apud Aylesham.

Willelmus Barbour dicit quod quo ad nativitatem Johannis Hawteyn penitus ignorat, sed dicit quod habet quendam (sic) filiam ætatis xliiij^or annorum, et ultra vel circa, et dicit quod Johannes Hawteyn est talis ætatis. Et dicit quod Tiphania soror Hawteyn est manens in villa ultra London vocata Hawehunte, sed in quo comitatu ignorat.

This paper is endorsed, 'Hauteyn, Oxened.'

47

MARGARET PASTON TO JOHN PASTON [1]

To my rygth worcheful husbond, John Paston, dwellyng in the Inner Temple at London, in hast.

SEPT. 28

RYTH worchiful hosbon, I recomande me to yow, desyryng hertely to her of yowr wilfar, thanckyng God of yowr a mendyng of the grete dysese that ye have hade ; and I thancke yow for the letter that ye sent me, for be my trowthe my moder and I wer nowth in hertys es fro the tyme that we woste of yowr sekenesse, tyl we woste verely of your a mendyng. My moder be hestyd a nodyr ymmage of wax of the weytte of yow to oyer Lady of Walsyngham, and sche sent iiij. nobelys to the iiij. Orderys of Frerys at Norweche to pray for yow, and I have be hestyd to gon on pylgreymmays to Walsingham, and to Sent Levenardys [2] for yow ; be my trowth I had never so hevy a sesyn as I had

[1] [From Fenn, iii. 20.] This letter was written after the birth of John Paston's eldest son, who was born in 1442, and cannot be later than 1443, as William Paston, who is mentioned, died in August of the year following.
[2] St. Leonard's Priory, Norwich.

1443
SEPT. 28
from the tyme that I woste of yowr sekenesse tyl I woste of yowr a mendyng, and zyth myn hert is in no grete esse, ne nowth xal be, tyl I wott that ze ben very hal. Your fader [1] and myn was dysday sevenyth [*this day se'nnight*] at Bekelys for a matyr of the Pryor of Bromholme, and he lay at Gerlyston that nyth, and was ther tyl it was ix. of the cloke, and the toder day. And I sentte thedyr for a goune, and my moder seyde that I xulde have dan [*then*], tyl I had be ther a non, and so thei cowde non gete.

My fader Garneyss [2] senttee me worde that he xulde ben her the nexch weke, and my emme [*uncle*] also, and pleyn hem her with herr hawkys, and thei xulde have me hom with hem; and so God help me, I xal exscusse me of myn goyng dedyr yf I may, for I sopose that I xal redelyer have tydyngys from yow herr dan I xulde have ther. I xal sende my modyr a tokyn that sche toke me, for I sopose the time is cum that I xulde sendeth her, yf I kepe the be hest that I have made; I sopose I have tolde yow wat it was. I pray yow hertely that [ye] wol wochesaf to sende me a letter as hastely as ze may, yf wryhyn be non dysesse to yow, and that ye wollen wochesaf to sende me worde quowe your sor dott. Yf I mythe have had my wylle, I xulde a seyne yow er dystyme; I wolde ye wern at hom, yf it wer your ese, and your sor myth ben as wyl lokyth to her as it tys ther ze ben, now lever dan a goune zow [*though*] it wer of scarlette. I pray yow yf your sor be hol, and so that ze may indur to ryde, wan my fader com to London, that ze wol askyn leve, and com hom wan the hors xul be sentte hom a zeyn, for I hope ze xulde be kepte as tenderly herr as ze ben at London. I may non leyser have to do wrytyn half a quarter so meche as I xulde sey [*say*] to yow yf I myth speke with yow. I xall sende yow a nothyr letter as hastely as I may. I thanke yow that ze wolde wochesaffe to remember my gyrdyl, and that ze wolde wryte to me at the tyme, for I sopose that wrytyng was non esse for yow. All myth God have yow in his kepyn, and sende yow helth.

[1] William Paston.
[2] Perhaps her godfather. The family of Garneys were Lords of Gelderstone, the place called by Margaret Paston Gerlyston, a few lines above.

56

Wretyn at Oxenede, in ryth grete hast, on Sent Mikyllys Evyn.   1443
SEPT. 28

Yorys,   M. PASTON.

My modyr grette yow wel, and sendyth yow Goddys blyssyng and hers; and sche prayeth yow, and I pray yow also, that ye be wel dyetyd of mete and drynke, for that is the grettest helpe that ye may have now to your helthe ward. Your sone [1] faryth wel, blyssyd be God.

48

ABSTRACT [2]

LAND IN PASTON.

Warrant to Sir Roger Frenles, Knight, Chief Steward of the Duchy lands OCT. 17
in Norfolk and other counties, and Sir Thomas Tudenham, particular Steward of the lordship and manor of Gymyngham, to demise (*dimittere et tradere*) to the undertenants (*bassis tenentibus*) specified in an act of Parliament, certain charterhold land in Paston and Edithorp granted to the King by William Paston, Robert Clere, and Edmund Clere in exchange for certain parcels of copyhold land, in accordance with an act of the last Parliament holden at Westminster. The copyhold land granted to them consisted of $36\frac{1}{2}$ acres 9 perches $1\frac{1}{2}$ qr. of a perch and 1 pekke of land, pasture, heath, and marsh, with two houses built on certain parcels thereof, with $\frac{1}{3}$ of a rood of waste land [not belonging to the Duchy?] in Paston; and it was given in recompense for $36\frac{1}{2}$ acres $26\frac{1}{2}$ perches and half a quarter of a perch, half a 'pekke' and one 'naylle' of land, pasture, and heath, called 'Chartrehold,' with two houses built on certain parcels thereof, in Paston and Edithorp, which are to be annexed to the Duchy. These parcels are specified in an inquisition dated 18 May 18 Hen. VI., remaining in the treasury of the Duchy, which was taken by virtue of letters of the Cardinal to Lord Bardolf and others.

17 Oct. 22 Hen. VI.

[1] Almost certainly his eldest son, John, afterwards Sir John Paston.
[2] [From the Chancery Roll of the Duchy of Lancaster, 22 Hen. VI., Y. 2 c., No. 79.]

57

THE PASTON LETTERS   HENRY VI

49

WILLIAM PASTON AND WILLIAM JOYE [1]

1444
HEC sunt hostilmenta et vutensilia domus, bona et catalla, que Willelmus Paston, in indentura presentibus annexa nominatus, tradidit et dimisit Willelmo Joye in eadem indentura nominato, secundum formam ejusdem indenture, ex communi assensu eorundem Willelmi et Willelmi, per Robertum Gynne, Johannem Albon de Paston et alios appreciata, assignata et specificata, modo subsequenti, videlicet: tres equi precii quinque marcarum; quatuor vacce, quelibet precii vij*s*. vj*d*.; una juvenca brendyt precii v*s*.; unus tauriculus, precii iiij*s*.; una juvencula dowet precii iiij*s*.; due sues, quelibet precii iij*s*. iiij*d*.; tres porculi, quilibet precii xvj*d*.; tres porcelli, quilibet precii xij*d*.; quatuor alii porcelli, quilibet precii viij*d*.; una carecta, precii vj*s*. viij*d*.; apparatus carette, videlicet una sella, unum par des stroppys; duo paria dez trayses, precii ij*s*.; due caruce cum les hokys et stappilles; unum par rotarum; due herpice, precii v*s*.; quatuor paria dez trayses ad aratrum, precii viij*d*.; due furse fimose, precii vj*d*.; una vanga, precii iij*d*.; unus tribulus, precii iij*d*.

Hec sunt blada et alia hostilmenta et utensilia domus, bona et catalla, per predictum Willelmum Paston predicto Willelmo Joye secundum formam dicte indenture similiter dimissa et non appreciata, videlicet: sex quarteria frumenti; xxv. quarteria ordei; viij. quarteria avenarum; quidam tassus pisarum in fine australi antique grangie messuagii predicti, qui est altitudinis iij. virgarum et iij. quarteriorum unius virge, et quidam alius tassus vescarum in boriali fine ejusdem grangie, altitudinis iij. virgarum et j. quarterii unius virge; qui quidem duo tassi fuerunt vesture xij. acrarum et dimidii, et dimidii rode terre; iij. vasa vocata Kelerys; j. Gilyngsat; iiij. stondes pro servitio; j. stonde in coquina; ij. patelle cum ligaminibus ferreis; j.

[1] [From Douce Charters in Bibl. Bodl., No. 18.]

58

parva patella cum ligamine ferreo; j. magna olla ennea [*ænea*]; 1444
alia olla ennea minor; j. parva olla ennea; j. tabula; j. par des trostelles; j. longum hostium jacens in boteria; j. par des trestelles, j. trow, ij. bolles, j. morter, j. thede, j. temse, j. mashsterell, j. tankard cum ligamine ferreo; j. bultyngpoke, j. magna trow pro farina, cista pro farina, j. fleshoke, j. tripes ferreum, j. veru ferreum; j. aunderun, j. par de tongys, j. lach'gres ennua, j. seturis, j. magnum lavacrum pendens, j. kynderkyn, ij. soos leeke, j. par de belwes, j. magnum planke super mensam coquine hargour; iij. perapsides; iij. disci; iij. sauserys de pewter; iij. perapsides; iij. disci; j. magnus discus, vj. sissorn, iij. ciphi de ligno, j. chayer; duo longa scanna, j. scannum mediocre longitudinis; ij. scanna vocata buffet stoles; ij. bankar; j. gladius, ij. ferra vocata aplates; j. chirne; j. chyrnyng staf; j. curta falx; j. candelabrum ferreum; j. parvum salerium; j. beryngsceppes, unum par dez pepyrquens, ij. uteri, j. cadus cum vergous; j. parva cista in boteria; j. selura supra servisiam; j. metesetell; j. pykforke; iij. longa bordclothis; j. towayll, j. san . . . et j. walet pro autumpno; j. lucerna; ij. vomeri et ij. cultri que ponderant xvij. li. et dim.; j. carectula, Anglice, a carre; j. sunvectorium (?); ij. novi rowintrees et j. curtur 'ignum in le carthows; ij. veteres bige; j. par rotarum rerratarum; ij. kemell cum hopys ferreis; j. frena, j. pelvis; viij. sacci; iiij. longa ligna fraxinora in pistrina; j. fetyrlok.

In dorso—

Summa catall' infrascriptorum et appreciat', v*li*. 19*s*. 8*d*.
Summa granorum infrascriptorum ultra persas (?) et vesias, iiij*li*. xviij*s*. iiij*d*.
   Quarterium frumenti ad iiij*s*., quarterium ordei ij*s*. iiij*d*., et querterium avenarum ad ij*s*.
Item, vestura xij. acrarum et di., et di. rod. pisarum et vescar'.
Item, dicta vestura piseii et vescar. ad *li*., lacr' ad iiij*s*. de xij. acr' et di. rod. non lax.

Summa totalis, xiiij*li*. viij*s*.

59

50

OXNEAD AND FRIAR HAWTEYN[1]

1443-9 THIS day at x. of the clok Edmund Paston and the parson of Oxened went owth of the Manor doun to Wantown Gapp, for thei herd tydynges that the freyr[2] was comyng; and with the seyd frier came John Cates and on Whalter Herman of Wheytte, and Wylliam Yemmys of Burgh, the frieres man. And Edmund Paston seyd to John Cates Welcome, and he askyd hem what here[3] cause was in commyng. The Frier seyd he cam for to speke with the gode lady, and Edmund seyd that he shuld speke with her. At this tyme sche was so ocupied he myth not speke with her. And he seyd that he shuld assay; and he cam redyng fro Wantown Gappe to the grete Cate; and there he lyted and knokkyd on the gate; and we folwyd as yarn as we myth; and ther was with in John Jaallere and John Edmundes, and asked the friere what he wold; and he seyd that he wuld comyn inne for to speke with the gode ladi of the hows. And thei seyd nay, he shuld not come in. And than cam on Edmund Paston and the parson, and asked hym what was cause of his comyng at this tyme. And he seyd for to entre in the maner of Oxened, the which his fader was possessid of and his auncestres from kyng Edward the thred on to Colbys tyme, and that he had fownd a tayll ther of in the kynges bokes. And than Edmund Paston answeryd hym and seyd that it wher best declaryng of his evydence in Westminster hall. And he seyd a geyn, so he shuld whan he myth. And he seyd to hem that come with hym, 'Serys, I chargge yow ber record now that I am kept owth with stronge hand, and may not take poscession.' And evyn forth with he presyd to the

[1] [Add. MS. 34,888, f. 19.] This paper, like No. 63, which also refers to Friar Hauteyn's claim to Oxnead, can be assigned to no definite year; but its date must be before the death of Edmund Paston in 1449. It is indorsed in a later hand: 'A Frier came to take possession of the mannor of Oxned.'
[2] John Hauteyn.   [3] *here* (or *her*) for *their*.

60

1444 or may for yow. He hath hadde a cyetica [*sciatica*] that hath letted hym a gret while to ride, and dar not yet come on non horses bak, and ther for he hath spoke to the Lordes of the Conseill, and enformed hem of your sekenesse and his also, that he may not ride at these next assizes to Estgrynsted; and though thoe assizes discontynue *puer noun venue dez Justicez*, he hopeth to be excused and ye also. And as for the remenant of the assizes, he shall purvey to be ther by water. And Almyghty Jesu make yow heyle and strong.

Wretyn right simply the Wednesseday next to fore ye Fest of the Purificacion of Our Lady at London.

By your most symple servaunt,
JAMYS GRESHAM.

52

JOHN GYNEY TO WILLIAM PASTON[1]

To the worthy and worshipfull Sir and good Lord and Maister, William Paston, on of the Justices of oure Sovereign Lord, of his Commone Benche at Westminster.

Not later than 1444 RIGHT worthy and worshipfull Sir, and my good Lord and Maister, I recomaund me to yow. And where as ye, by your lettre direct to my Lady, your wyf, wold that my seid Lady shuld have Robert Tebald and me to geder, as sone as she myght, and the evidences which the seid Robert receyved of yow at your last beyng at Norwich, and that I shuld amende the defautes therinne, and that that doon there shuld of Baxteres Place of Honyng be taken estate to yow and to other, as your seid lettre requireth: Prey and beseche yow to witte that, on the Friday next after your departyng fro Paston, Thomas Walysh and William Burgh, in his owen per- sone, and the seid Thomas by William Inges and William Walsyngham, his attornies, by his lettre under his seal, where

[1] [From Fenn, iii. 28.] There is nothing to be said of the date of this letter, except that it is not later than 1444, when William Paston died.
62

gate ward to a leyd hand on the gate. And than the seyd 1443-9 Edmund put hym fro the gate and seyd, 'Ne wer for reverence of thy lord and myn, and thow leyst any hand on the gate I xall sey thye hert blod or thow myn.' And than the seyd frier seyd scornfully that he myth thanke his mayster. And than the seyd Edmund seyd that he myth sey his lord ryght wele; and than he stowpyd doun and toke up herd and delivered to his man, seying to hem that come with hym, 'I charge yow all of the kynges behalffe ye bere record that I take here poscession of myn inheritance.' And Edmund seyd that this takyng of poscession skylled nowgt. And than the friere seyd that sen he myth not have it nowe, he shuld come a geyn a nothir tyme. Edmund is rede forth to Heydon. It was told us this afternon that ther wer iij. men come fro Skeyton and mette with the frier in the feld and spoke with hym a gode while, and than redyn the same wey that they come.

51

JAMES GRESHAM TO WILLIAM PASTON[1]

To my right worthy and worshepfull Lord, William Paston, Justice, in hast.

PLEASE it your good Lordship to wete that the Chief 1444 Justice of the Kynggs Benche[2] recomaundeth hym to JAN. 29 yow, and is right sory of the matier that is cause of your noun comyng hedir, but he wole do al that he can

[1] [From Fenn, iii. 26.] 'From a memorandum,' says Fenn, 'on the back of this letter, dated in April 1444, it is probable that it was written on the 30th of January 1443.' Did Fenn mean the 30th of January 1443-4? In the side-note immediately below the letter, he dates it in his usual exact manner, 'Wednesday, 30th of January 1443, 22 H. VI.' But unfortunately there is an error here. January in the 22d year of Henry VI., means January 1444 according to the modern computation, or 1443 in the style formerly in use, by which the year was reckoned from the 25th of March. But the 30th of January was a Wednesday in 1443, only according to the modern computation of the year,—that is to say, it was a Wednesday in the year 1442-3, not in 1443-4. I imagine, however, that the '30th of January' should have been '29th of January,' and that Fenn really meant 1443-4, corresponding with the 22nd year of Henry VI.; for the memorandum to which he refers is a draft agreement, dated on Passion Sunday, 22 Hen. VI., A.D. 1444.
[2] The celebrated Sir John Fortescue.

61

[were] at Honyng, and delyvred to my Lady Scarlet seson Not [*seisin*] in the seid place, and Colbyes and Donnynges in later Walsham. And the seid Thomas Walyssh, as the seid than Tebald told me, wold not enseale the seid lettre of attornie 1444 til the parson of Ingeworth come to hym therfore, and required hym to don it. Wychyngham in his owen per- sone in the nyght next befor the seid Friday, as the seid Tebald infourmeth me, come to the same Tebaldes hows, and desired hym to enseale acquytaunce, as he seid, and the same Robert refused to don it.

Nertheless, whether it were acquytaunce or were not, the same Robert kan not seye, for he myght noo sight have there of. And the seid Wychyngham the same nyght rood to John Willyot, and desired of hym the same, and refused also to don it. What is the best to be don in this matier my seid Lady, your wyf, kan not thynke with owt your advis and counseile. Wherfore as touchyng the takyng of th'estate to yow and other, as in your seid lettre is conteigned, is yet right nought doon.

The Holy Trinite have yow in his blissed kepyng. Wretyn at North Walsham, the Thursday next after the Purificacion of oure Lady.

My seid Lady, your wyf, preyeth yow to be remembred of here grene gynger of almondes for Lente, and of the leche of Orwelde, for here seknes encreseth dayly upon here, whereof she is sore a ferd.

By youre servunt,   JOHN GYNEY.

53

ABSTRACT[1]

Indenture between the Prior and Convent of the Monastery of St. Andrew, 1444 Bromholme, impropriators of the Church of St. Margaret, Paston, and John MARCH 15 Partrik, vicar of the said church, of the first part, William Paston of Paston, of the second part, and Edmund Palmer of Wytton, of the third part, relative to lands in Baketon and Wytton, and containing amongst other things a grant by the Prior and Convent to the said John Partrik, at the instance of the said

[1] [Add. Charter 14,571, B.M. (D. Turner's Coll.)]
63

1444 William Paston, in consideration of which masses, called *certeynes*, are to be performed every Friday for the souls of William Paston and Agnes his wife, and the obit of Clement Paston, William's father, is to kept yearly on St. Botolph's day (17th June). Dated 15th March 22 Henry VI. Confirmed by Walter, Bishop of Norwich, and John, the Prior of the Cathedral of Norwich, and the chapter of that church, 11th and 21st March 1446[-7].

54

ABSTRACT [1]

JOHN MARYOT TO WILLIAM PASTON, Justice.

Before 1444 — Is ready to fulfil the indentures of Becham made by W. P. with his late mother, if W. P. will send 'the indenture of our part,' that Maryot may know the terms and his own title. Will make no bargain else.—Crowmer, Monday after Our Lady's Nativity.

55

ABSTRACT [2]

WILLIAM WOTTON DE PAGRAVE TO JUSTICE PASTON.

Sends his wife to him to explain some business about lands in Lytyl Pagrave, of which a woman of Sporle has already spoken to him; also touching some land at Castleacre.—*On parchment.*

56

—— TO JOHN PASTON [3]

1444 RIGHTE reverent and my most worshipful maister, I recomaund me to yow. Please it yow to wite that I sende yow a copie of a verdite take before my maister Roberd Clere by vertu of a writ *diem clausit extremum*,[4] whiche

[1] [From Paston MSS., B.M.] This and the following letter are quite uncertain in point of date, except that they were of course written before the death of William Paston, to whom they were addressed.
[2] [From Paston MSS., B.M.]
[3] [From Paston MSS., B.M.] This letter is without a signature or address, and who the writer was does not appear. It was evidently written soon after the taking of the inquisition on the death of William Paston, the Judge, the date of which is given in the extract as 2nd November 23 Henry VI., *i.e.* 1444.
[4] *See* p. 16, Note 1.

64

writ I sende yow also with this, of whiche verdite the wordis 1444 arn as it folwith :—

Inquisicio capta apud Wynterton, secundo die Novembris anno regni Regis Henrici vj[ti] post conquestum vicesimo tertio, coram Roberto Clere escaetore domini Regis in com. Norfolk et Suffolk, virtute brevis domini Regis sibi directi et presenti Inquisitioni consuti, per sacramentum Johannis Berkyng, Nicholai Pikeryng, Johannis Chapell, Johannis Jekkys, Willelmi Stiwardson, Roberti Hosele, Johannis Topy, Johannis Wacy, Johannis Rychers, Thomæ Broun, Walteri Heylok, Willelmi Stotevyle, Thomæ Mason, Roberti Marche, Johannis Kechon, legalium et proborum hominum in hac parte pro domino Rege juratorum: Qui dicunt super sacramentum suum quod Willelmus Paston nominatus in dicto brevi nulla terras et tenementa tenuit de domino Rege in capite die quo obiit in comitatu predicto. Et quod obiit quarto decimo die mensis Augusti, anno regni domini Regis predicti xxij. Et quod Johannes Paston filius ipsius Willelmi est hæres ejus propinquior, et ætatis xxiij. annorum.

Ther is founde more of other thyngges be the same verdite touchyng other matieris, whiche he will not certifie yet. And for as moche as my maister Clere wetyth well that the seid verdite touchyng my maister your fader, hoes soule God assoyle, must have other maner of makyng thanne he kan make, he recomaundith hym to my maistres your moder, and yow also; and prey yow that ye will do it make as effectuel and availeabill for the wel of my maister your fader and yow as ye kan, and sele it with your seall, or what seall ellys ye will, in his name, and sealle it also with as many of other seales as ther be jerores, and delyvere it to William Bondes, his depute, to delyvere into the Chauncelre. And if William Bondes be fro London or this may be redy, thanne purveye ye for the speed of this matier in youre best wise ; and what so ever ye do, or sey, or write, or seale, or avouche in this matier in my maister Cleris name, he shall avowe it, and [*i.e.* if] it shulde coste hym gret parte of his good.

Sir, ther is noon enquerre take in Suffolk, for as moche as my maister your fader helde no londe ther but be my maistres your moder ; but if ye will that he shall inquere ther as sone as he may wete it, it shall be doo ; and if this forseide verdite

65

1444 may serve for bothe, he is right glad therof. He tolde me that he seide to the jurores, whiche have sealed her verdite : ' Seris, I wot well this verdite after my makyng is not effectuel in lawe, and therfore may happe it shall be makid newe at London, and ellys peraventure I shulde be amercied in the Kyngges Courte ; and therfore I truste yow, and [*i.e.* if] it be newe mad and newe sealed, ye will avowe it.' And thei seide with a good herte ya ; these wordes wern seide *in secreta confessione* to v. or vj. of the reuleris of the seide jurre whiche he kan truste righte well. He preyith yow to holde hym excused that he writyth not to yow for this matier, for he is ocupied in other wise. He badde me write in this fourme to yow, which he supposith ye will beleve, and he knoweth alle this writyng, and is well concented and agreed therto. Sir, ther arn xv. jurores abowe to certifie ye, as many as ye will : but lete these men that be tottid be certified, for thei be the rewleris and t . . . . he spk (?) &c. Sir, atte reverence of God, if I shall make ony purvyaunce in this cuntre for my maistres comyng hom, lete me have reson[able] warnyng, and so God me helpe, and I shall do my dever. I here no tydyngges of Thom' yet. My maistres Garneys, your moder, ...[1] Berney, and my maisteris your sonys and my maister your brother arn heyle and mery, and recommend hem to yow. And I beseche your [mastership][1] that this sympil skrowe may recomaund me to my reverant and worshipful maistres, your moder. And I prey our Lord of this . . . . . .[1] bothe moche worship and wilfare, and graunte me to do and labour that is to your bothererys pleaser.[2]

Writen the Saterday next. . . . . . .[3]

This letter appears to have been used as a wrapper for others. It is endorsed, ' Literæ diversorum directæ J. Paston receptæ apud London per diversos annos ante festum Michaelis anno xxxiiij Hen. vi. Literæ Fastolff pro Costid (?). Literæ W. Wayt pro tempore suæ tribulationis. Literæ Windham.'

[1] Mutilated. [2] *I.e.*, that which is to the pleasure of you both (?).
[3] A little mutilated at bottom.

66

57

WILL OF EDMUND NORMAN [1]

IN Dei nomine, amen. Ego Edmundus Norman de Fylby, 1444 compos mentis, die Dominica in festo sancti Nicholai DEC. 6 Episcopi, anno domini M[lmo] iiij[c] xl. iiij.[to], condo testamentum meum in hunc mundum (*sic*). In primis do et lego animam meam Deo Patri, &c., corpusque meum sepeliendum in ecclesia sancti Petri de Crowmere. Item, summo altari ecclesiæ prædictæ xl*d*. vjs. viijd.[2] Item, emendacioni ejusdem ecclesiæ vjs. viijd.[3] xl*d*. Item, summo altari ecclesiæ de Fylby xl*d*. Item, emendationi ecclesiæ de Fylby prædictæ vel fenestræ de novo faciendæ et intrando in parte boriali ecclesiæ prædictæ in fine occidentali, x. marcas. Item, Edmondo, capellano sancti Johannis Baptistæ in eadem ecclesia, xl*d*. Item, volo quod omnes feoffati in terris et tenementis remittant jus suum Edmundo Clere armigero, magistro meo, ut ipse vendat et disponat cum aliis executoribus meis pro salute animæ meæ, et patris, matris, et omnium quibuscumque teneor. Item, cuilibet ordini fratrum de Jernemoth, vjs. viiijd. Item, fratribus ordinis Minorum de Walsyngham vjs. viiijd. Item, lego Willelmo Bondis omnia bona mea existentia in hospicio meo de Clifforde London', videlicet lectum et indumenta mea. Item, lego Roberto Baketon et uxori ejus, firmario meo in Fylby, omnia utencilia mea infra mansionem meam ibidem præter lectum plumale postea legatum. Item, Edmundo filio dicti Roberti, filiolo meo, xl*s*. Item, filiabus ejusdem Roberti, Elizabethæ et Margaretæ, cuilibet xx*s*. Item, Edmundo filio Roberti Norman de Ormesby, vjs. viiijd. Item, Ricardo Kemp, xxvj*s*. viiij*d*. Item, Johanni Grave, sonam meam deargent'.[3] Item, Nicholao Pekeryng de Fylby, meum optimum lectum plumale infra mansionem meam apud Fylby. Item, Johanni Spencer de Crowmere, xx*s*. Item, uxori Johannis Couche, pro labore et diligentia suis circa me dum infirmabar, vjs. viiij*d*. Item,

[1] [Add. MS. 34,888, f. 10.] [2] Interlineations by another hand.
[3] Here occurs an illegible interlineation, in which only 'xs.' is visible.

67

THE PASTON LETTERS

¹⁴⁴⁴
^{DEC. 6} Edmundo Bataly capellano vj*s*. viii*d*. Item, lego Thomæ Stalham et uxori ejus meum lectum plumale apud Norwicum. Item, die obitus mei ad exequias, cuilibet capellano iiij*d*. et clerico, j*d*. Item, ad distribuendum inter pauperes die sepulturæ, xl*d*. Residuum vero bonorum meorum non legatorum do et lego executoribus meis, quos ordino et constituto Edmundum Clere, armigerum, Magistrum meum Robertum Clere, Willelmum Bondes, Nicholaum Pekeryng, Magistrum Johannem Semecrofte et Ricardum Kemp, ut ipsi disponant pro salute animæ meæ.

²Et lego dicto Edmundo Clere pro labore suo xl*i*. si vult. Et Roberto Clere C*s*., et similiter cuilibet aliorum executorum xl*s*.

Item, lego Pers. de Crowmere iij*s*. iiij*d*.

Item, volo quod in fenestra ecclesiæ de Fylby tres³ ymagines, videlicet, una ymago sancti Edmundi, alter[a] Sancti Johannis Baptistæ, alia Sanctæ Mariæ, et ibidem fiat scriptio : —*Orate pro animabus Johannis Norman seniori, Margaretæ uxoris ejus, et Edmundi filii prædicti* et tale armo (*sic*). [*Here follows a sketch of a shield, the upper part marked as silver and the lower black, with the word 'Katerwole' (?) upon it.*]

58

THE DUKE OF NORFOLK TO JOHN PASTON [4]

To our right trusti and welbelovid John Paston, Squier.
The Duc of Norff.

Before
1444(?) TRUSTI and right welbelovid, we grete you weel, lating you witte that for the trust that as weel we, as the heires of Edmund Swathyng, have unto you, we have appointed you to be one of the makeres up indifferently of the

¹ Interlineations by another hand.
² What follows is in a different hand, apparently the same as that of the interlineations noticed above. ³ Corrected from 'quatuor.'
⁴ [From Fenn, i. 10.] Fenn thinks this letter must have been written before 1444, when Yelverton was made a judge. This is, doubtless, most probable. There is, however, an Edmund Swathing, Esq., mentioned by Blomefield (*Hist. of Norfolk*, viii. 42) as alive in 1446, and if it be his executors who are referred to, the date would appear to be later.

68

THE PASTON LETTERS

After
1444 et fidelis nobis Willelmus Paston, nuper unus Justiciariorum nostrorum, defunctus, nobis in vita sua inpendyit, consessimus et hac presenti carta nostra confirmavimus, in quantum in nobis est, Johanni Paston armigero, filio et heredi dicti Willelmi, viginti tria mesuagia, quingintas triginta et iiij. acras pasture, bruere et marissy in villis de Paston, Edythorp, et Bakton, in comitatu nostro Norff. quas diversi tenentes nostri ibidem de nobis separatim native tenent ad voluntatem nostram per virgam sive copiam et per serta redditus et servissia, nativa annualia inde nobis reddend., que ad valorem novem librarum annuatim exeunt vel infra. Concessimus eciam eidem Johanni curiam lete, seu visus franciplegii nostri, in villis de Paston et Edithorp predictis, que est annui valoris viij. solidorum per estimacionem ; ad quatuor libratas, quatuor solidatas et octo denariatas redditus. Redditum octo boschellorum avenarum et trium caponum cum pertinentiis in villis predictis, ac in villis Wytton et Easewyk in comitatu predicto, percipiendum anuatim de omnibus et singulis liberys tenentibus nostris ibidem pro tenementis suis qui de nobis separatim tenent in eisdem villis, una cum fidelitatibus et aliis serviciis eorundem tenentium et eorum cujuslibet, de, seu pro, tenementis illis et eorum qualibet parcella nobis debitis sive pertinentibus. Concessimus etiam eidem Johanni et heredibus suis officium parcarie ac costidie¹ parci nostri de Grymgham in com. nostro predicto, una cum proficuo agistamenti bestiarum ejusdem parci pro vadiis suis pro officio predicto annuatim percipiend : salvis no . . et hodierna sufficienti pastura ferarum nostrarum ibidem ut tempore nostro prius usitatum fuit ; quod quidem proficuum agistamenti ad valorem x. marcarum extendit per annum. Habenda, tenenda et percipienda predicta messuagia, terram, pasturam, brueram, mariscum, curiam lete, et visus franciplegii, redditus, et servissia, officium et agistament' proficu' cum pertinentiis, prefato Johanni et heredibus suis de nobis et heredibus nostris, per fidelitatem et redditum unius rose rubie ad Festum Nativitatis Sancti Johannis Baptiste annuatim nobis solvendum, si petatur, pro omnibus serviciis, exaccionibus et demandis. Eo quod

¹ *Sic, pro custodiæ.*

70

HENRY VI

evydences betwix us and the seide heires. Wherfor we pray Before you hertily, that ye wil yeve attendaunce at such day and place 1444(?) as ye and our right trusti and welbelovid frende William Yelverton, with oure welbelovid servaunt Jenney, shal mow attende to the making up of the seide evidencez ; and we shal send summe of our servauntz to awayte upon you for your reward and costis, that ye shal be pleasid with by the grace of God, who have you ever in his keping.

Wreten undir our signet in oure Castel of Framlyngham, the xviij. day of ——.

{JOHN¹
MOWBRAY.}NORFF.

59

JOHN PASTON'S PETITION [2]

To the Kyng our Soverayn Lord.

PLES your Hyghnes of your abundante grace, an con- After syderacion of the servys and plesure that your Hyghnes 1444 knowyth to yow don by William Paston, late one of your judgys, and old servaunt to that nobyll Prinse your fadyr, to graunte onto John Paston, Esquyer, sonn and heyir of the seyd Wylliam, your lettrys patents under the seel of yowr Duche of Lancastre, being in the keping of Thomas Chesham, aftyr affecte of note folowyng ; and he schall pray to God for yow.

REX, etc. Sciatis, quod de gracia nostra speciali et ex mero motu nostro, ac pro bono et laudabyli servicio quod dilectus

¹ The name 'John Mowbray' is represented by a curious monogram, in which every letter both of the Christian and the surname can be traced.
² [From Tanner MS. 95, f. 82.] This is a draft in the handwriting of William Worcester, very illegible from the number of the corrections, and also from the ink being very much faded. Of its date I cannot tell except that it was clearly written in the reign of Henry VI, and after the death of Judge Paston in 1444.

69

HENRY VI

messuagia, terra, pastura, bruera, mariscus, curia lete, redditus, After servicia predicta, officium et agistament' profic', valorem supra 1444 specificatum excedant, vel valorem illum non attingant, aut aliquo actu, restriccione seu mandato facto, edito aut proviso non obstante. Volumus etiam et assignavimus quod omnes illi qui per nos seu ad usum nostrum, jus, titulum, seu statum in premissis, seu aliquo premissorum habuerunt seu habent, nobis antehac non relaxatum, jus, titulum et statum illa prefato Johanni et heredibus suis dimittent et relaxent. In cujus . . .

60

CATHERINE, DUCHESS OF NORFOLK, TO JOHN PASTON [1]

To our right trusty and hertily welbeloved John Paston, Squier.

{Kateryn, Duchesse
of Norff.}

RIGHT trusty and entierly welbeloved, we grete you wel After hertily as we kan. And for as moche as we purpose 1444(?) with grace of Jesu to be at London within bryff tyme, we pray you that your place ther may be redy for us, for we wole sende our stuff thedir to for [*tofore, i.e. before*] our comyng ; and siche agrement as we toke with you for the same, we shall duely performe yt with the myght of Jesu, who haff you in his blissed keping.

Wretyn at Eppeworth, ij^{de} day of Octobre.

¹ [From Fenn, iii. 16.] The writer of this letter was the widow of John Mowbray, second Duke of Norfolk, who died in 1432. After the Duke's death, she married again no less than three times ; and Fenn thinks this letter, which is dated from Epworth in Lincolnshire, a seat of the Duke of Norfolk's, was probably written during her first widowhood. It must be remarked, however, that in 1432 John Paston was only twelve years old at the utmost, so that this letter could hardly have been written till at least ten years after. It is, besides, hardly probable that John Paston would have been addressed as the owner of a 'place' in London, before his father's death in 1444. The exact year, however, is quite uncertain.

71

61

ABSTRACT[1]

ROBERT, LORD WYLUGHBY [of Eresby], TO JOHN PASTON.

Between
1444
and
1451

Desires him to favour Reginald Balden who 'hath ado with you for certain lyflode which was his father's, wherein your father was enfeoffed.' Boston, 16th December.

[The date of this letter is probably after the death of William Paston in 1444, and cannot be later than 1451, as the writer died on St. James's day (25th July) 1452.]

62

AGNES PASTON TO EDMUND PASTON[2]

To Edmond Paston of Clyffordis Inn, in London, be this Lettre take.

1445
FEB. 4

TO myn welbelovid sone, I grete yow wel, and avyse yow to thynkk onis of the daie of youre fadris counseyle to lerne the lawe, for he seyde manie tymis that ho so ever schuld dwelle at Paston, schulde have nede to conne defende hym selfe.

The Vikare[3] of Paston and yowre fadre,[4] in Lenttyn last was, wher [*were*] thorwe and acordidde, and doolis[5] sette howe broode the weye schulde ben,[6] and nowe he hath pullid uppe the doolis, and seithe he wolle makyn a dyche fro the corner of his walle, ryght over the weye to the newe diche of the grete

1 [From Paston MSS., B.M.]
2 [From Fenn, iii. 32.] This letter must have been written in February 1445, as it appears from the contents that William Paston was dead, but had been alive in the preceding Lent.
3 John Partrick of Swathfield was Vicar of Paston, from 1442 to 1447.—F.
4 William Paston, the Judge.
5 Landmarks. 'Dolestones' are still spoken of in Norfolk in this sense.—*See* Latham's Edition of Johnson's *Dictionary.*
6 On the 6th July 1443 a licence was granted to William Paston to enclose a portion of the highway at Paston, and another at Oxnead, on his making two other highways in place thereof.—*Patent Roll,* 21 Henry VI. p. 1, m. 10.

72

closse. And there is a man in Truntche, hyzht Palmer to, that hadde of yowre fadre certein londe in Truntche over vij. yere or viij. yere agoone for corn, and trewli hathe paide all the yers; and now he hathe suffrid the corne to ben with sette for viijs. of rentte to Gymmyngham, wich yowre fadre paide nevere. Geffreie axid Palmere why the rentte was notte axid in myn husbonddis tyme; and Palmere seyde, for he was a grete man, and a wyse man of the law, and that was the cawse men wolde not axe hym the rentte.

1445
FEB. 4

I sende yow the namis of the men that kaste down the pittis, that was Gynnis Close, wretyn in a bille closid in this lettre.

I sendde yow not this lettre to make yow wery of Paston; for I leve in hoope, and ye wolle lern that they schulle be made werye of her werke, for in good feyth I dar welseyne it was yowr fadris laste wille to have do ryzht wel to that plase, and that can I schewe of good profe, thowe men wolde seye naye. God make yow ryzht a good man, and sende Goddis blessyng and myn.

Wrettyn in haste, at Norwich, the Thorsdaie aftir Candelmasse daie.

Wetith of yowre brothere John now manie gystis [*joists*] wolle serve the parler and the chapelle at Paston, and what lenghthe they moste be, and what brede and thykknesse thei moste be; for yowre fadris wille was, as I weene veryli, that thei schuld be ix. enchis on wey, and vij. another weye. And porveythe therfor that thei mow be squarid there, and sentte hedre, for here can non soche be hadde in this conttre. And seye to yowre brothir John it weer wel don to thinkke on Stansted Chirche;[1] and I praye yow to sende me tydynggs[2] from be yond see, for here thei arn a ferde to telle soche as be reportid.

By yowr Modre,

AUGNEIS PASTON.

1 Stansted Church in Suffolk.—Dame Agnes had possessions in that parish.—F.
2 These tidings relate to our foreign transactions, the giving up of Maine, Truces, &c. &c. on the King's marriage, which had taken place in November.—F.

73

63

JOHN HAWTEYN TO THE ARCHBISHOP OF CANTERBURY[1]

To the most reverent Fader in God the Archebisshop of Caunterbury, Chanceler of Englond.

1444-9

BESECHETH mekely zour gracious Lordship, zour owne servant and oratour John Hauteyn, chapeleyn, that wher he hath dyvers seutees and accions in lawe to be sewed a zent A., that was the wife of W. Paston, of the maner of Oxenedes, in the countee of Northfolk; and for as meche as zour seid besecher can gete no counsell of men of court to be with hym in the seid matiers, by cause that the seid W. P. was one of the Kynges Justices, and John P., son and heir to the seid W. P., is al so a mon of court; that hit plese zour good Lordship to assigne, and most streytly to comaund John Heydon,[2] Thomas Lyttylton,[3] and John Oelston to be of counsell with zour seid besecher in the seid matiers, and oder that he hath to do azenst the seid Anneys and oder; and zour said besecher shal contente hem well for their labour. And that this be doo in the reverence of God, and wey of charite.

JOHN HAUTEYN, Chapeleyn.

1 [From Fenn, iii. 36.] This is a petition addressed to John Stafford, Archbishop of Canterbury, as Chancellor, after the death of William Paston in 1444. Stafford was made Archbishop in 1443. His appointment as Chancellor was even earlier, and he held the office till the 31st of January 1450.
2 A lawyer and recorder of Norwich.—F.
3 Afterwards the famous Judge Lyttelton.—F.

74

64

SIR ROGER CHAMBERLAIN TO AGNES PASTON[1]

To my right worchepfull Cosyn, Agnes Paston.

After
1444

RIGHT worchepfull cosyn, I comand me to you. And as for the mater that ye sent to me fore, touchyng the maner callid Walshams, in Walsham, the trouth is, youre husbond soldyt to my moder upon condition that she shuld never sel it but to youre sones, John or William; and for the suerte of the seid condition, youre seid husbond, as I conseyve, ded the seid maner be charged with a gret annuyte upon the same condition, or the tyme that my seid moder toke estate, of the whech I suppose ye shall fynde sufficiant evydens, if ye serge youre evydences therfor. And I be seche almyty God kepe you.

Wretyn at Geddyng, the xv. day of September.

Your Cosyn,

SIR ROGER CHAMBERLEYN.

65

THE DUKE OF BUCKINGHAM TO THE VISCOUNT BEAUMONT[2]

To the right worshipful, and with all myn herte right entirely belovid brother, the Viscounte Beaumont.

Between
1442
and
1455

RIGHT worshipful, and with all myn herte right entierly beloved brother, I recomaunde me to you, thenking right hertili youre good brotherhode for your gode and gentill letters, the whiche it hath liked you to sende unto me

1 [From Fenn, iii. 38.] Nothing can be said as to the date of this letter, except that it is evidently after the death of William Paston.
2 [From Fenn, i. 16.] There appear to be no means of ascertaining the exact year when this letter was written; but as the writer was created Duke of Buckingham on the 14th September 1441, and his son, the Earl of Stafford, was killed at the battle of St. Albans on the 22nd May 1455, the date must lie between these two limits.

75

THE PASTON LETTERS

Between 1442 and 1455

Between nowe late; and like it you to knowe I perseeve by the tenor of the seid lettre, your gode desire of certein dubete that I owe unto you. In gode faith, brother, it is so with me at this tyme, I have but easy stuffe of money withinne me, for so meche as the seison of the yer is not yet growen, so that I may not plese youre seide gode brotherhode, as God knoweth my will and entent were to do, and I had it.

Nevertheles, and like you, I sende you, bi my sonne Stafford,[1] an obligacion wherof, of late tyme, I have rescevid part of the dubete therinne comprisid; the residue of whiche I prai you to resceve bi the seid obligacion, and that I may have an acquitance therof, and to yeve credence unto my seid sonne in such thing as he shall say unto your gode brotherhode on my behalve.

Right worshipfull, and with all myn herte right entirely belovid brother, I besecche the blissed Trinite, preserve you in honor and prosperite.

Writen at my Castell of Makestok,[2] the xvij. day of Marche.

> Yowre trew and fethfull broder,
> H. BUKINGHAM.

66

WILLIAM YELVERTON TO JOHN PASTON[3]

To my ryght wurchepfull cosyn, John Paston, Esquier.

Between 1444 and 1460

RIGHT worchepful cosyn, I recomaunde me to yow, thankyng yow as hertyly as I kan for my selff, &c., and specially for that ye do so moche for Oure Ladyes hous at Walsyngham, which I trust veryly ye do the rather

[1] Humphrey, Earl of Stafford, the Duke's eldest son, who was slain at St. Albans in 1455.
[2] In Warwickshire.
[3] [From Fenn, i. 20.] The date of this letter is not earlier than 1444, when William Yelverton was appointed a Justice of the King's Bench; and, as Fenn remarks, it is probably not later than 1460, when he was made a Knight of the Bath, otherwise he would have signed himself Knight as well as Justice.

76

Between 1444 and 1460

for the grete love that ye deme I have therto; for trewly if I be drawe to any worchep or wellfare, and discharge of myn enmyes daunger, I ascryve it unto Our Lady.

Preyng yow therfore that ye woln ben as frendly to Our Ladyes hous as I wote well ye have alwey ben, and in especyall now, that I myght have of yow the report certeynly be your letter of that, that Naunton your cosyn informyd yow, and told yow be mouth of all maters towchyng Oure Ladyes hous of Walsyngham.

For me thynkyth be that I have herde be Oure Ladys prest of Walsyngham, if I understode weel that mater, that it shuld do moch to the gode spede of the mater; and dought yow not our Lady shall qwyte it yow and here poer priour here aftyr, as he may, &c.

Preyng yow also, cosyn, and avysyng for the ease of us both, and of our frendes, and of many other, that ye be at London be tymes this terme, and if we spede well now, all well all this yere aftir; for I knowe veryly ther was nevyr made gretter labour thanne shall be made now, and therfore I pray to Our Lady, help us, and her blissid Sone, which have you in His holy kepyng.

Wreten at your poer place of Bayfeld, on Sent Fraunces day,[1] in hast.

> Your cosyn,
> WILLIAM YELVERTON, Justis.

67

ABSTRACT[2]

OCT. 30 1446

Indenture, dated 30 Oct. 25 Henry VI., by which Agnes Paston grants a lease to John Downing, miller, and others, of the mill called Woodmill, in Paston.

[1] St. Francis' day is the 4th of October.
[2] [Add. Charter 14,819, B.M. (D. Turner's Coll.)]

77

THE PASTON LETTERS

68

THE BAILIFF AND JURATS OF JERSEY TO VISCOUNT BEAUMONT[1]

A nos treshonorés et nobles Signours Visconte Beaumont, Connestable d'Engleterre et Seigneur de Sudele, grant mestre de hostel de nostre Souverayn Seigneur le Roy d'Engleterre et France.

1447

TRESHONORABLEZ et noblez seigneurs, nous nous recommandous tant que faire le povons a voz honnorablez seignouriez. Et vous plese savoir que le samedy xvme jour du moys de Aprille nous avons receu unez lettrez patentes de nostre Souverain Seigneur le Roy d'Engleterre et de France, contenant comme il vous a donné la guarde dez islez de Jersey et Guernesey durant le non aage de l'er de mon Seigneur de Warwyk, et unez aultrez lettrez a nous directes de par vous, presentées de par voz servitours Jean Morin et Robert Haxby. Et pour cause que eulx n'avoyent point de procuracions, ou feisions difficultey, et non obstant a voz ditz servitours a estey delivrée et baillie la pocession de la dicte isle de Jersey, et ont juré et promis par lours serementz de guarder le loys et coustumez et anciens usagez de la dicte isle, et nous envoier lettrez soubz lez seaulx de voz armez, comme voz promettez tenir en fermete ce que eulx ont promis, et de ce nous ont bailly plege Sire John Bernard, cappitaine desdictez islez, quer aultrement nous ne lez eussons point receus, comme il apparest par le certificat a eulx par nous donné, quer tous lez seigneurs, guardes, cappitaines, juges, et aultrez officers de audevant de cez hourez ont estey jurez a nous lois, coustumez et anciens usagez, lez queilz ont estey

[1] [From Paston MSS., B.M.] The custody of the islands of Jersey and Guernsey, &c., during the minority of Ann, daughter and heir of Henry de Beauchamp, Duke of Warwick, was granted in 25 Henry VI. to John, Viscount Beaumont, and Sir Ralph Butler, Lord Sudley.—*See* Dugdale's *Baronage*, ii. 54.

78

1447

guardéz et seront en tempz advenir avecquez l'aide de Dieu, qui vous ayt en sa sainte guarde.

Escript en Jersey le xvij^me jour du moys de April.

> De par lez vostrez le Balliff [et]
> Jurés de l'Isle de Gersy.

69

EDMUND PASTON TO JOHN PASTON[1]

Tradatur Johanni Paston, of the Inner In in the Temple, att London.

1447(?)

RYTH worschipfull brothir, I recomaund me to yow, &c. I preye write to myn modre of youre owne hed as for to consell her howh that sche kepe her prevye, and tell no body ryth nowth of her counsell; for sche woll tell persones many of her counsell this day, and to morwe sche woll sey be Goddis faste that the same men ben false. I have seen parte of the evydence, and the maner[2] hath be pourchasid be parcell, and certeyn feffement mad of the avowson, and certeyn pecis of lond enterlessaunt the maner; and I wote well ye have on collaterall rellesse wyth a warente of on of the wyffys of Hauteyn[3] of all the holl maner.

Steward, the chiffe constable, told me he was enpanellyd up on the assise be twex yow and Fraunncesse; he axyd me counsell what he myght do ther inne, for he told me it was take in Sir Thomas Tudham name. He wold fayne be chalengyd. I concellyd him swere the trewthe of the issue that he shall be swore to, and thanne he nedyd never to drede hym of noon

[1] [From Paston MSS., B.M.] From the conversation here reported touching the anticipated ascendancy of Daniel and the Marquis, afterwards Duke, of Suffolk, this letter may be referred to the year 1447. In April of the year following, the influence of Suffolk was paramount, and Daniel was said to be out of favour, as will be seen by Letter 75 following.
[2] The manor of Oxnead.—See Blomefield, vi. 478.
[3] Probably Robert, father of John Hauteyn, the friar.

79

1447(?) atteynte. I yave him this counsell, and noon othir. He enqueryd me of the rewle of myn master Danyell[1] and myn Lord of Suffolke,[2] and askyd wheche I thowte schuld rewle in this schere ; and I seyd bothe, as I trowh, and he that survyvyth to hold be the vertue of the survyvyr, and he to thanke his frendes, and to aquite his enmyys. So I fele by him he wold forsake his master, and gette him a newh yf he wyste he schuld rewle ; and so wene I meche of all the contre is so disposyd. The holy Trenyte kepe yow.

Wrete at Norwiche, on the Wednysday after Seynt Peter[3] in hast.　　　　Your Brother,　　　　E. PASTON.

70

ABSTRACT[4]

1447
SEPT. 3
　　Deed by which William Pope, perpetual Vicar of Paston, confirms to Agnes, widow of William Paston, and John Bakton, their estate in a piece of land, particularly described ; and also binds himself to celebrate mass every Friday for the souls of said William and Agnes, &c. &c., exhort his parishioners to put up prayers for them every Sunday, called ' certeynys,' and celebrate William Paston's obit on the 13th August.

Dated at Paston, 3rd September 26 Henry vi.

71

ABSTRACTS[5]

Oct. 21, 26
　　21 Oct., at London.—Letter from Fastolf to Thomas Howys and John Grene, desiring them to procure information about one Robert Eccles, cousin and heir to John Eccles, whom the counsel for the prior of Hickling propose to call to give evidence about the rent of 25 marks.

1447, [26 Oct.] 'Thursday byfore S. Symond and Jude,' 26 Hen. vi. at Castre. Long letter from Thomas Howys in reply to the preceding, with the

[1] Thomas Daniel.
[2] William de la Pole, at this time Marquis, afterwards Duke, of Suffolk.
[3] St. Peter's day is the 29th June.
[4] [Add. Charter 17,235, B.M. (Paston mss.)]
[5] [From mss. Hickling, 130, 140, in Magd. Coll., Oxf.]

results of searches made in the Bishop's registry for wills of the Eccles family, with particulars about various members of the family, etc.　　1447
Oct. 21,
26

[For these abstracts I am indebted to Mr. Macray, and also for those immediately following, which are from the same source.]

72

ABSTRACTS[1]

THE PRIOR OF HICKLING.

Hickling 71.
[14 . .]　At Westminster.
Letter [on paper, in English] *from two counsel, William Wangeford and William Jenney,* to Sir John Fastolf, giving their opinion on his claim against the prior of Hickling. Sir John cannot recover the £20 forfeit, because the condition of the obligation only extended to the heirs of Sir Hugh Clifford, and not to his assigns, and Sir John is only an assign ; but the rent of 25 marks is sure to him, and he can recover it, if denied by the prior, by process of law ; they will consult with justices and serjeants whether he can recover it by distraint.

Hickling 74.
[14 . .]　Friday in the 2nd week after Easter at Lenne.
Letter, [in English, on paper] *from Henry Notyngham* to Sir Henry Barton, Alderman of London. Has counselled with Paston, and finds him more friendly and ready to help in Barton's matter than ever before ; supposes that the cause is, that the prior that was obstinate is dead, and another appointed, who Paston trusts will be more easy to stir. Desires that Paston may be thanked. Sends a letter which he desires ' a child of zours' may carry to Mistress Jenkin Leventhorpe the younger ; and ask at my lord's inn of Doreham or of Ratclyff or some other which he may think best, if he (*i.e.* my Lord of Durham) shall be at this Parliament. Send to Thomelin Grys, spicer at Norwich, some ' loder,' as soon as he can goodly buy it, which comes each week to Rossamez Inn in St. Laurence's Lane.

Hickling 75.
[14 . .]　14 Apr., at Norwich.
Letter, [in English, on paper] from H[enry] Notyngham to Sir Henry Barton, alderman of London. Delivered Paston the copy of the deeds ; shewed his letter to the prior and convent, but gained nothing ; they said they would please Barton full fain, but all their counsel are full against their binding themselves by any such confirmation ; they were bound to the former owner and his

[1] [From mss. in Magd. Coll., Oxf.]

heirs, but not to his assigns. Advises him to get good counsel, and thinks nothing can be done unless he gets Paston's assent and grant to help the matter.

Hickling 89.
[1450 or 1451 ?]　18 Aug. Norwich.
Letter [in English, on paper] *from ' W.* [*Hart*]*, Bisshope of Norwich,'* to Sir John Fastolf. Has put himself greatly in his devoir to put an end to the controversy between Fastolf and the house of Hykelyng, and has been so importunate that Lord Scales has advised him not to meddle in the matter, because he is taken as a suspect person ; if he could do him more profit, he would not spare labour or cost, on account of Fastolf's towardness and gentleness to condescend unto right and reasonable mean, the which he conceives not in the other party. Had hoped his good and devout purpose towards the place of St. Bennet's would have grown to some good conclusion ; was there the Sunday before St. Laurence's Day, and greatly rejoiced at such work and cost as he has done there. Heartily desires him to come here to the air of his natural birth, where he will find my Lord of Norfolk and such attendance as the Bishop and other gentles of the country may do, ready unto him at all times ; his coming would be to his health and heart's ease, and the cause of much peace in the country.

Small seal, fastened *on* the letter ; a stag ; a straw round it.

Hickling 104.
[　]
Letter, [in English, on paper] from *Lord Scales* to Sir John Fastolf, asking him to withdraw an outlawry which has been issued against John Dowebegyng, servant of the former, for a debt of £100 due to Fastolf by Thomas Danyell, Esq., for which Dowebegyng had become bound.

Signed by Lord Scales, who adds a postscript in his own hand that Fastolf has been as faithful and kind to him since he came into England as he was in France, and that there is no one of his estate for whom he would do so much.

Small seal, on the paper, with a straw round it.

73

ABSTRACT[1]

1447
NOV. 29
　　Indenture, dated St. Andrew's Eve, 26 Henry vi., between Agnes Paston and Waryn Baxter, the former agreeing that Baxter shall have, at the will of the lord of the manor of Knapton, the lands, &c. that were Richard Redys [Rede's], with reservations.

[1] [Add. Charter 17,236, B.M. (Paston mss.)]

74

JAMES GRESHAM TO JOHN PASTON[1]

To my right worshipfull mayster, John Paston.

WORTHY and worshipful sir, and my right good　1448
maister, I recomaund me to yow. And do yow　MARCH 11
wete that this nyght at soper I was with my maistresse your wyff at my maistresse Cleres, and blissed be God thei fare weel and hopyn that [you[2]] shall sende themme good tidyng of your matier, Whanne ye knowe the certeynte therof, &c. And my maistresse your modir come thedir and fareth well and sendeth yow Goddis blissyng and heris, and she bad me write to yow that she hath verey knowelage by a trewe and trusty man, whos name she shall telle yow by mouthe atte your next metyng, that ther was purposed a gret meyne of a wondir gaderyng of shipmen abowte Conorhithe for to have come to Oxened, and putte me owt there in a wers wyse thanne ye were put owt at Gresham ; and this was purposed for to have ben at Oxened and a ryfled and put in the preest[3] there, but this purpose helde not, for thei were countermandet, by what mene I can not knowe yeet. And[4] it is do hir to wete that thei be purposed to be at Ox[n]ede a bowt midlent, and I am promitted that I shall have ii. days warnyng by a good freend. And therfor she prayeth yow that ye aspie besily if the preest come into thir countre or noght. For if ought shall be doo I trowe the Frere wole be there atte doyng. And if ye can aspie that he come hider, send my maistresse word as hastily as ye may, and of your avyse and of all other thyngges as ye seme, &c. And God have yow in his kepyng. Wretyn at ix. on the clokke at evyn the noneday (*sic*) nex to fore Sent Gregory day in hast.

[1] [Add. MS. 34,889, f. 178.] St. Gregory's Day is doubtless that of St. Gregory the Pope (12 March), and this letter may be referred with certainty to the year 1448, just after Paston's first expulsion from Gresham. The Monday before St. Gregory's Day in that year would be the very day preceding.
[2] Omitted in MS.　　　　[3] Friar John Hawteyn.　　　　[4] 'and' repeated in MS.

THE PASTON LETTERS

My brother Bekke and his felawship shall telle yow more
by mowthe thanne I can telle yow now.—Your servaunt,

J. GRESHAM.

75

MARGARET PASTON TO JOHN PASTON [1]

*To my ryth wyrchypful hwsbond, Jon Paston, be this lettyr
delyveryd in hast.*

1448
APRIL
RYTH wyrchypful hwsbond, I recomawnd me to zw,
desyryng hertyly to heryn of zour wel fare, praying
zw to wete that I was with my Lady Morley [2] on the
Satyrday next after that ze departyd from hens, and told here
qhat answer that ze had of Jon Butt, and sche toke it ryth
straw[n]gely, and seyd that sche had told zw, and schewyd zw
i now [*enough*], qher by ze myth have knowleche that the
releve owt [*ought*] to ben payd to her. And sche seyd sche
wyst wel that ze delay it forthe, that sche xuld nowth have
that longyth to her ryth. And sche told me hw it was payd in
Thomas Chawmbers tym, qhan her dowther Hastyngs [3] was
weddyd ; and sche seyd sythyn that ze wyl make none end
with her, sche wyl sew therfore as law wyl.

I conseyvyd be here that sche had cwnsel to labore azens
zw therin withyn ryth schort tym. And than I prayd her that
sche wuld vwche save nowth to labowr azens zw in this mater
tyl ze kom hom ; and sche seyd nay, be her feyth, sche wuld
no more days zeve [*give*] zw therin. Sche seyd sche had sett
zw so many days to a kord with her, and ze had broke them,

---

[1] [From Fenn, iii. 54.] The date of this letter is fixed by an endorsement in
these words, 'Literæ termino Paschæ anno xxvj.,' showing that it was written in
Easter term, in the 26th year of Henry VI. Easter term in that year lasted from the
10th of April to the 6th of May.

[2] Isabel, widow of Thomas, Lord Morley, who died in 1435. She was the
daughter of Michael de la Pole, Earl of Suffolk. Fenn confounds her with the
widow of the Lord Morley who died in 1417, who was a daughter of Edward, Lord
Dispencer, and had previously married Sir Hugh Hastings. But this lady died about
1426 (Blomefield, ii. 440), and cannot be the lady mentioned in the text.

[3] Ann, married to John Hastyngs.—*See* Blomefield, ii. 430.

84

HENRY VI

that sche was ryth wery therof ; and she seyd sche was but a 1448
woman, sche must don be her cownseyl, and her cwnseyle had APRIL
avysyd her, so sche seyd sche wyld do. Than I prayd her
azyn that sche wuld teryn [*tarry*] tyl ze kom hom, and I seyd
I trostyd veryly that ze wuld don qhan ze kom hom, as itt
longeth to zw to don ; and if ze myth have very knowleche
that sche awyth of ryth for to have itt, I seyd I wyst wel that
ze wuld pay it with ryth gode wyl, and told her that ze had
sergyd to a fownd wrytyng therof, and ze kwd non fynd in
non wyse. And sche sayd sche wyst wele there was wrytyng
therof inow, and sche hath wrytyng therof hw Syr Robert of
Mawthby, and Sir Jon, and my grawnsyre, and dyverse other
of myn awncesterys payd it, and seyd nevyre nay therto. And
in no wyse I kwd not geyn no grawnth of her to sesyn tyl ze
kom hom ; and sche bad me that I xuld don an erand to my
moder, and qhan I kam hom, I dede myn erand to her. And
sche axyd me if I had spokyn to my lady of this forseyd mater,
and I told her hw I had do, and qhat answer I had ; and sche
seyd sche xuld gon to my Lady Morles on the nexst day, and
sche xuld speken to her therof, and a say to getyn grawnt of
her to sesyn of the forsayd mater tyl that ze kom hom. And
truly my moder dede her dever ryth feythfully therin, as my
cosyn Clare [1] xal tellyn zw qhan that he speketh with zow ;
and sche gete grawnt of my seyd lady that there xuld nowth
ben don azens zw therin, and ze wold acordyn with her, and
don as ze owyn to do be twyx this tym and Trinyte Sunday.

Laueraw[n]ce Rede of Mawthhy recommawndeth hym to
zu, and prayt zw that ze wyl vwchesave to leten hym byn
[*buy*] of zw the ferm barly that ze xuld have of hym, and if ze
wyl laten hym have it to a resonabyl pris, he wyl have it with
ryth a gode wyl ; and he prayit zw if ze wyl that he have it,
that ze wyl owche save [*vouchsafe*] to send hym word at qhat
pris he xuld have the kowmb as hastyly as ze may, and ellys he
must be purvayd in other plase.

As twchyng other tydyngs, I sopose Jon of Dam xal send

---

[1] Probably William, eldest son of Robert Clere of Ormesby, who died in 1446.—
See Blomefield, vi. 336.

85

THE PASTON LETTERS

1448
APRIL
zw word in a letter. As it is told me veryly, Heydon xal not
kom at London this term.

It is seyd in this contre that Danyell [1] is owth of the Kyngs
gode grase, and he xal dwn and all hys mene, and all that ben
hys wele wyllers ; there xal no man ben so hardy to don
nether seyn azens my Lord of Sowthfolk, [2] nere non that
longeth to hym ; and all that have don and seyd azens hym,
they xul sore repent hem. Kateryn Walsam xal be weddyd
on the Munday nexst after Trinyte Sonday, as it is told me, to
the galaunte with the grete chene ; and there is purvayd for
her meche gode aray of gwnys, gyrdelys, and atyrys, and
meche other gode aray, and he hathe purcheysyd a gret
purcheys of v. mark be zer to zevyn her to her joynture.

I am aferd that Jon of Sparham is so schyttyl wyttyd, that
he wyl sett hys gode to morgage to Heydon, or to sum other
of ywre gode frendys, but if [*i.e.* unless] I can hold hym inne
the better, ere ze kom hom. He hath ben arestyd sythyn
that ye went, and hath had moche sorw at the sewte of mayster
Joh Stoks of London for x. mark that Sparham owt to hym ;
and in gode feyth he hath had so moche sorow and hevynesse
that he wyst nowth qhat he myth don. I fell hym so disposyd
that he wold asold and asett to morgage all that he hath, he
had nowth rowth to qhom, so that he myth an had mony to
an holpyn hym self wyth ; and I entretyd hym so, thatt I
sopose he wyll nother sellyn ner sett to morgage, nother catel
ner other gode of hese, tyl he speke with zw. He soposeth
that al that is don to hym is att the request of the Parson of
Sparham and Knatylsale. I sopose it is almas to comfort hym,
for in gode feyth he is ryth hevy, and hys wyf al so. He is
nowth nw under arest, he hath payd hys feys, and goth at
large ; he was arestyd att Sparham, of on of Knatysales men.

Hodge Feke told me thatt Sym Schepherd is styl with
Wylly, [3] and if ze wyl I xal purvey that he xal be browth hom
er ze kom hom. It is told me that he that kept zour schep
was owth lawyd on Munday at the swth of Sir Thomas

---

[1] Thomas Daniel. [2] *See* p. 80, note 2.
[3] William Paston, son of the Judge (?).

86

HENRY VI

Todynham, and if it be so, ze arn nowth lyk to kepe hym 1448
longe. And as twchyng that that ze badeyn me spekyn for to APRIL
Bakton, he seyth he is wel avysyd that sche seyd sche wuld
never have to don with all, ner he kan not pek that sche seyd
sche hath non ryth to have it, and he wyl say lyche as he hath
herd her seyd ; and if sche speke to hym therof, he wyll rather
hold with zw than with her. I pray ye that ze wyl vwche save
to send me word hw ze spede in zour matter twchyng Gressam,
and hw Danyel is in grace. Harry Goneld hath browth to me
xls. of Gressam syn ze zede, and he seyth I xal have more or
Qhythson tyd, if he may pyk it up.

I sopose Jamys Gressam hath told zw of other thyngs
that I have sped syn ze zedyn hens. If I her any strawnge
tydyngs in this contre, I xall send zw word. I pray zw that I
may ben recommawndyd to my Lord Danyel.

The Holy Trynyte have zw in hys kepyng, and send zw
helth and gode spede in al zour maters twchyng zour ryth.

Wretyn at Norwyche, on the Wedenys day nexst after
thatt ze partyd hens.

Yors, MARGARETE PASTON.

76

LORD SCALES TO THOMAS GNATESHALE [1]

To Thomas Gnateshale.

Thomas Gnateshale, I wul ze wite it was oute of my remembrance that Date
Paston hade pout in my determinacion the discort betwene you and hym. I uncer-
was the more favourable to your entent, but in so mych as I had forgete that tain
beforesaid, I praye you that ye suffre the cornes in mene hand til that I have
determined the matier betwene you too be the advis of lerned men whech han
knowelich in such causses, the which thing I wul do in as short tyme as may,
wherof ze shal have knowelich.

Writen at Myddelton, the xiiij. day of August.

THE LORD SCALES.

---

[1] [From Paston MSS., B.M.] The person to whom this is addressed is probably
the same 'Knatysale' mentioned in the preceding letter, and as it contains no evidence
of any definite date, we think best to insert it here.

87

THE PASTON LETTERS

77

ABSTRACT[1]

MARGARET PASTON TO HER HUSBAND (*not addressed*).

1448
MAY 19

On Friday last, the Parson of Oxened 'being at messe in one Parossh Chirche, evyn at levacion of the sakeryng, Jamys Gloys had been in the town, and come homeward by Wymondam's gate,' when he was attacked by Wymondham who had two of his men with him, and driven into 'my mother's place' for refuge. With the noise of this, my mother and I came out of the church from the sakeryng, and Wymondham 'called my mother and me strong whores, and said, ye Pastons and all her kin were . . . . . . yngham said he lied, knave and churl as he was.' After noon my mother and I reported this to the Prior of Norwich, who sent for Wymondham; and Pagrave came with us. While Wymondham was with the Prior, and we at home, Gloys was assaulted again in the street, 'as he stood in the Lady Hastyngs' chamber,' by Thomas Hawys, one of Wymondham's men. This last assault the Parson of Oxened saw. Sends Gloys to her husband for fear of further trouble. The Lady Morle 'would have the benefice of her obligacion,' as her counsel tells her it is forfeit, and she would not have the relief till she have your homage. The Lord Moleyns' man is collecting the rent at Gresham 'a great pace,' as James Gresham will report to you.

Trinity Sunday, at even.

Further statement about the assault added in a different hand (qu. Agnes Paston's?).

[From the fact of Lord Molyns being in possession of Gresham, and collecting rents there, it is clear that the date of this letter is 1448. This date also agrees with what is said in Letter 75 about a relief claimed by Lady Morley.]

78

JOHN NORTHWOOD TO JOHN, VISCOUNT BEAUMONT[2]

To my worschypful and reverent Lord, John, Vicont Beaumont.

MAY 28

RYGTH worschypfull, and my reverent and most spesiall Lord, y recomaund me un to yowr good grace in the most humble and lowly wyse that y canne or may, desyryng to her of your prosperite and well fare [as to my][3] most syngeler joy and spesiall comfort.

[1] [From Phillipps ms. 9735, No. 256.]
[2] [From Fenn, i. 12.] The date of this letter will appear by a foot-note.
[3] The bracketed words are noted by Fenn as 'imperfect in the original, the paper being chafed.'

88

THE PASTON LETTERS

1448
MAY 28

the Pees of Coventre of thys riot, be caws the shreffe of Warwyk shyre is dede,[1] and they may not sytt in to the tyme ther be a new shreve.

And all thys myschef fell be cawse of a nold debate that was be twene heme for takyng of a dystres, as hyt is told.

And All mygthty Jesu preserve yowr hye astat, my spesiall Lord, and send yow long lyve and good hele.

Wryten at Coventre on Tewusday next after Corpus Christi day, &c.

Be yowr own pore Servant,   JOHN NORTHWOD.

79

LORD MOLYNS TO THE BISHOP OF WINCHESTER[2]

To the worschypful Fader yn God, and my ryth gode Lord, the Bysshop of Wynchestyr.[3]

JUNE 13

WORSCHYPFUL Fader yn God, and my rythe gode Lord, as hertely as y canne, y recomaund me to your gode Lordschyp; to the wyche plese hyt to wyt that y have resayvyd your lettre, by the wyche y oundyrstond the dayely sute to your Lordschyp as of Pastun, as for the mater betwyx hym and me, wer yn also y fele that he ys wyllyd that comynycasyon and trete schold be had betwyxt hys counsayle and myne, now at Mydsomer ; to the wyche, my Lord, y am at the reverens of your Lordschyp wel agreyd, and have send to my counsayle at Loundon, aftyr the seyng of thys your last letter, as for the trete by twyxt hym and me, and that they schold yeve ful attendauns to the end of the mater

[1] Thomas Porter was sheriff of the counties of Warwick and Leicester in 26 Henry VI., and died in his year of office on Monday after Corpus Christi day (27th May 1448), the day before this letter was written.—Inquisition *post mortem*, 27 Henry VI., No. 13.
[2] [From Fenn, i. 190.] It appears, by John Paston's petition presented to Parliament two years later, that after he had been dispossessed of Gresham by Lord Molyns in February 1448, communications passed between his counsel and that of Lord Molyns on the subject until Michaelmas following. This letter must refer to the first overtures.   [3] The celebrated William of Waynflete.

90

HENRY VI

1448
MAY 28

And gyf hyt plees your Hygnes, as towchyng the soden aventuer that fell latly at Coventre, plees hyt your Lordshyp to her that, on Corpus Christi Even[1] last passed, be twene viij. and ix. of the clok at a[fternon],[2] Syr Umfrey Stafford[3] had browth my mayster Syr James of Urmond[4] towa[r]d hys yn [*inn*] from my Lady of Shrewesb[ery,[5] and][2] reterned from hym toward hys yn, he met with Syr Robert Harcourt[6] comyng from hys moder towards hys yn, and pass[ed Syr][2] Umfrey ; and Richard, hys son, came somewhat be hynd, and when they met to gyder, they fell in handes togyder, and [Sir Robert][2] smot hym a grette st[r]oke on the hed with hys sord, and Richard with hys dagger hastely went toward hym. And as he stombled, on of Harcourts men smot hym in the bak with a knyfe ; men wotte not ho hyt was reddely. Hys fader hard noys, and rode toward hem, and hys men ronne befor hym thyder ward ; and in the goyng downe of hys hors, on, he wotte not ho, be hynd hym smot hym on the hede with a nege tole, men know not wyth us with what wepone, that he fell downe ; and hys son fell downe be fore hym as good as dede. And all thys was don, as men sey, in a Pater Noster wyle. And forth with Syr Umfrey Stafford men foloed after, and slew ij. men of Harcowrttus, on Swynerton, and Bradshawe, and mo ben hurt; sum ben gonne, and sum be in pryson in the jayll at Coventre.

And before the coroner of Coventre, up on the sygth of the bodyes, ther ben endited, as prynsipall for the deth of Richard Stafford, Syr Robert Harcourt and the ij. men that ben dede. And for the ij. men of Harcourts that ben dede, ther ben endited ij. men of Syr Umfrey as prynsipall. And as gytte ther hath ben no thyng fownden before the Justice of

[1] 22nd May.
[2] The bracketed words are noted by Fenn as 'imperfect in the original, the paper being chafed.'
[3] Killed in an engagement with Jack Cade in June 1450.
[4] Probably Sir James Butler, son and heir-apparent of James, fourth Earl of Ormond, who in 1449 was created Earl of Wiltshire.
[5] Wife of John Talbot, the famous Earl of Shrewsbury.
[6] He signalised himself in the wars of Henry VI. and Edward IV., was a Knight of the Garter, and in November 1470, 10 Edward IV., was slain by the Staffords, perhaps in revenge for this murder of Richard Stafford.—F.

89

HENRY VI

1448
JUNE 13

by twne the sayde Pastun and me, as thow y were present with hem.

And, my Lord, hyt were to grete a thyng, and hyte laye yn my power, but y wold do at the reverens of your Lordschyp, yn las than hyt schold hurt me to gretly, wyche y wote wel your Lordschyp wol nevyr desyr.

And God for hys mercy have you, rythe worschypful Fadyr yn God, and my rythe gode Lord, yn hys blessyd kepyng.

Wrytyn with my noune chaunsery hand, yn hast, the xiij. daye of June, at Teffaunt.

Vere hartely your,   MOLYNS.

80

ANONYMOUS TO JOHN PASTON[1]

WORCHEPEFUL mayster I recomend me to yow : and I pray yow to wete I was at Katefeld in Cobbes place for to se the armes as ye comaunded me, and the feld is gold wyth iii. bukkeles of sylver mad on the wyse as it is her, wyth floweris of sylver on the bukkelis mad of iiij. lyke a trew-love. Also, syr, I have spoke to a fryer that is conversaunt at Wykelwode wyth Randolffis dowter and he hath behestid me for to gete me Randolffis armes of hese dowter Wyltones wyf ; but I have not yet spoke wyth the frier a yen. Also I pray yow to wete that I was at Mauteby and ye have there CC. combz of malt if ye wyl gef for xiiijd. a combz in the comes and xxi. for xx. ye shal have redy mony, as I suppose, for Pykeryng sellyth for xid. and xiid. the lest that hath, as the parson of Mauteby tellyth me. And the parson

[1] [Add. ms. 34,889, f. 143.] This letter is neither signed nor addressed, but there is no doubt the person for whom it was intended was John Paston the eldest, who possessed property at Mautby in right of his wife. The reference to Laurence Reede seems further to show that it is of the year 1448. See p. 85.

91

1448
MAY 28

1448
JUNE 13

1448

1448 and I have do throche your qwete for it was ete wyth myse to petowsly for to se ; and if it plese yow I pray yow that ye wyl send me word qwhedyr ye wyl selle your malt and your qhete aftyr the pryse of the countre or (?) it shal be purveyid for to kepe it til ye may sett. And I have spoke to Lawrauns Reede for the ferme ; but he wyl not take it, as I conseyve, til he speke wyth yow. I suppos for to a made a covienaunt wyth hym, but he hath no sewerte yet, and the londis shal not be in your handis til myhelmes as he seyeth ; ther for he is the mor terying, &c. I beseche all myti Jhesu spede yow and kepe yow. [*Not signed.*]

On the back are some names of families in a contemporary hand, and five shields of arms tricked in a modern hand, the latter being apparently the armorial bearings of ancestors of the Earl of Yarmouth, to whom there is a letter addressed by ‘Wm. Smyth’ upon this subject at f. 146 of the MS.

81

JAMES GLOYS TO JOHN PASTON[1]

To my Ryght Wurchepfull master John Paston be this deliuered in hast.

DEC. 3   RIGHT reverent and wurchepfull sir, I recommande me to yow, desyryng to here of yowr welfare, the which gracyows God contynually preserve and kepe to yowr gostly hele and bodily welfare ; praying yow to wete that as for the broke sylver that my mastres wend for to a sent yow whan she dede wryte her letter, ther is none in your forcer ; she supposyd that ye left it at Norwiche in yowr cofere, wher of ye have the key. Also my mastres yowr moder grete yow wele, and pray yow to send her word how she shall do with Edward of Whode of Paston ; for she dede seys his corn on the lond the last hervest, and he led it a wey after that it whas

[1] [Add. MS. 34,888, f. 57.] This letter bears upon the dispute about Gresham, and is probably of the year 1448, for it is to be presumed that Edmund Paston died shortly after the date of his nuncupative will, 21st March 1449.

seysyd with awth licens and leve of here or any of here offyceris. Item, my mastres yowr syster recommand her hertly to yow, and pray yow that and ye wold wochesaff to speke to my master Edmund, and pray hym if that he hath bowth here ger that she sent to hym fore, that he wold send it her home ; in cas that[1] he have not bowth it, that he wold be it and sent it here in all the hast that he may goodly. Furthermore if it plese yow to her of my master Berney, he was at Gresham with my mastres on the Tuysday next after Halwemasday, the same day that we dystreynyd Jamys Rokkysson, and I had mette a litill a fore with Pertrych, and he thrett me, and sayd that we shuld not long kepe the dystresse, and there for my mastres dede us don on owr jakkys and owr salettis. My master Berney cam in and the parson of Oxened with hym and sey us in owre jakkis, and he wexe as pale as any herd and wold right fayn a ben thens. So my mastres dede hym dyne, and whill thei wher at dynar Herry Collys told my mastres openly among us all that the same tyme that Pertrych entryd a geyn up on yow, his master was at Causton to yow ward, and there it was told hym that Pertrych had putt yow owth and all your men, and that ye and my mastres wher redyn a geyn to Norwhich, and all your howshold, and that causyd hym that he cam no forther that tyme ; and my Master Berney confermyd all this and seyd that it was so. Whan thei had etyn he had mych hast to a be thens, so my mastres desyryd and prayd hym that he wold come a geyn or aght long ; and so with mych praying he be hest her if he mythe. And Herry Collys stode ther bysyde and seyd to my felachep, ‘ What shuld my master do here,’ quod he, ‘ lete yowr master send after his kynnysmen at Mautby, for thei have nowth that thei mawn lese.’ And so thei redyn her wey. And with in a sevenyght after my master Berney sent Davy to my mastres, and prayd my mastres that she wold hold his master excusyd, for he had hurt his owyn hors that he rode up on ; and he dede Davy sadillyn an oder hors ; and he stode by and made water whill he sadyllyd hym, and as Davy shuld a kyrt the hors, he slenkyd behynd and toke his master on the hepe suyche a stroke that

[1] The word ‘ that ’ is repeated in the MS. by inadvertence.

1448
DEC. 3   never man may trust hym after, and brake his hepe. And he had sent Herry Collys to Norwhich for medycynys, so he must ryde hom the same nygt ; for his master had no man at home. So my mastres was rygth sory, and wend that it had be trowth, but I know wele that it was not so. It happyd that I rod the next day to Norwhich, and I rood in to my mastres your moder, and she dede aske me after my master Berney, and I told here how he was hurt. And she askyd the parson of Oxened if he wer hurt, and he seyd nay ; for Davy lay with hym the same nygt a fore and told hym that he was heyll and mery, and prayd hym that he wold be with hym the Sonday next after ; and so Davy lay the same nygt after that he had told my mastres the tale with the parson of Oxened. I beseche yow of yowre gode masterchep that ye wold not do wreythe this letter, for and my mastres knew that I sent yow suyche a letter I were never abyll to loke up on her, nor to abyde in her heysyte. My mastres yowr moder hath sent yow ij. letteris ; she hath in dosyd hem to my master Edmunde, and she wuld wete if ye had hem or nawth. The Holy Trynyte have yow in kepyng. Wrytyne at Norwhich on Sent Clementis evyn. In hast.—Your servaunt,   JAMIS GLOYS.

82

MARGARET PASTON TO JOHN PASTON[1]

To my ryght worchippfull hosbond, John Paston, be this delyveryd in hast.

1449(?)
JAN. 31   RIGHT worchipfull hosbond, I recommand me to yow, praying yow to wete that I have receyvyd your letter this day that ye sent me be Yelvertonys man. As for your signette, I fond itt upon your bord the same day that ye

[1] [From Fenn, iii. 408.] Fenn thinks this was written about 1460, but I do not see on what evidence. From the reference to Gresham, I should rather suppose it belongs to 1449. By the subscription, it would appear that the writer was very near the time of lying in ; but we cannot tell the exact date of the birth of any of her children. Lord Molyns dispossessed John Paston of the lordship of Gresham on the 17th February 1448. After repeated remonstrances on the subject to no purpose,

went hens, and I send it yow be Richrad Heberd, bringer 1449(?) herof. As for your eronds that ye wrete to me fore, Richard JAN. 31 Charles is owte abough your eronds abowte Gresham, and for his awyn maters also, and I suppose he komyth not hom tyll it be Tesday or Weddenesday next komyng ; and alssone as he komyth hom, he shall go abowte your eronds that ye wrete to me fore.

I sent yow a letter wreten on Tesday last past, whiche, as I suppose, Roger Ormesby delyveryd yow. I toke it to Alson Pertryche. She rod with Clyppysbys wyff to London.

I pray yow if ye have an other sone that you woll lete it be named Herry, in remembrans of your brother Herry ;[1] also I pray yow that ye woll send me dats and synamun as hastyly as ye may. I have speke with John Damme of that ye bad me sey to hem to sey to Thomas Note, and he sey he was wel payd that ye seyd and thowgh therin as ye dede. Ner’les I bad hym that he shuld sey to the seyd Thomas therin as it wer of hymself with owte your avys or any others ; and he seyd he shuld so, and that it shuld be purveyd for this next weke at the ferthest. The blyssed Trinyte have yow in his kepyng.

Wretyn att Norwyche, in hast, the Fryday next befor Candelmesse day.

Be your gronyng wyff,   M. P.

83

MARGARET PASTON TO JOHN PASTON[2]

Begs him not to be displeasid though she be out of the place he left her in ; 1449 for she heard such tidings that she durst not abide there. Divers of my Lord FEB. 28 Moleyns' men said if they might get her they would steal her and keep her in the castle ; ‘ and than they said they would that ye should fetch me out. They

Paston went and took up his quarters there again on the 6th October 1449, and succeeded in keeping possession till the 28th January 1450, when the place was attacked, in his absence, by Lord Molyns' men, who undermined the walls, and drove out Paston's wife. The ‘ errands about Gresham ’ probably refer to the time of Lord Molyns' first occupation.

[1] No notice is taken elsewhere of John Paston having a brother named Harry.

[2] This abstract was made from one of the Roydon Hall MSS. shown to the Editor in 1875. Since that date he has not seen the original.

1449
FEB. 28

said it should be but a little heartburning to you.' After that I could have no rest till I was here. I did not venture out of the place till I was ready to ride, and no one knew an hour before but the good wife, whom I told that I was coming here to get gear made for me and the children. I beg you will keep secret the cause of my coming away till I see you. I spoke with your mother on my way hither, who offered to let me abide in her place if you wished me to stay in Norwich, and to give me such gear as she could spare till you can be purveyed of a place of your own. Let me know what to do. I should be sorry to dwell so near Grassam as I did, till the matter between you and the Lord Moleyns is settled. Barow said there was no better evidence in England than Lord M. had of Gresham. I said I supposed they were such as William Hasard spoke of, the seals of which were not yet cold, and that you had evidence with seals 200 years older. Do not on any account trust Lord Moleyns and his men, or eat or drink with them, though they speak ever so fair. Roger Foke of Sparham dare not leave his house for the suit Heydon and Wyndham have against him. Watkin Shipdam wishes you to speak to Sir J. Fastolf about the harness you had of him, etc

Norwich, Friday after Pulver Wednesday.

84

ROBERT, PRIOR OF BROMHOLM, TO JOHN PASTON [1]

To my Sovereyn, John Paston.

449(?)
MARCH 5

I RECOMEND me hertily, thankyng yow for the tydings, and the good awysse that ze sent me be the Parson of Thorpe; [2] latyng zow wittin that the Byschope of the todir syde of the see sent laate to me a man, the qwych wuld abydin uppon my leyser, for to an had me ovyr wyt hym to the seyd Byschope, and so forth to the Courte. [3] So the seyd

---

[1] [From Fenn, iii. 80.] There is no distinct clue to the date of this letter; but Fenn throws out a conjecture which, in default of any better guide, may be accepted as not improbable, that 'the Bishop of the other side of the sea' was Walter Lyhert, Bishop of Norwich, who in the beginning of 1449 must have been in Savoy, having been sent thither by the King to persuade the anti-pope Felix v. to renounce his claim to Nicholas v. for the peace of the Church. This Felix actually did in the beginning of this year, and Wharton considers Bishop Lyhert to have been the cause of his doing so (Angl. Sac. i. 418). Fenn, however, dates this letter 1450, on the supposition that the Bishop would have been still abroad in the beginning of that year, which is a mistake, as his name appears in the Rolls of Parliament as a trier of petitions as early as February.

[2] Robert Rogers was parson of Thorpe from 1445 to 1476.

[3] Court of Rome.

96

THE PASTON LETTERS

85

NUNCUPATIVE WILL OF EDMUND PASTON [1]

1449
MARCH 21

OMNIBUS Christi fidelibus ad quos præsens scriptum pervenerit, Nos, Willelmus May, Magister Novi Templi, London', Johannes Bakton gentilman, Thomas Parker, civis et cissor Londoni, et Johannes Osbern, salutem in Domino sempiternam. Sciatis quod xxj. die Martij Anno Domini mccccxlviij. [2] Edmundus Paston de comitatu Norff., armiger, in bona memoria ac sana mente existens, languens in extremis, in nostra præsentia, condidit et declaravit testamentum suum nuncupativum in hunc modum :—In primis, legavit animam suam Deo Omnipotenti, Beatæ Mariæ Virgini et omnibus Sanctis, corpusque suum ad sepeliendum in ecclesia Templi prædicti, sive in ecclesia Fratrum Carmelitarum London' [ad electionem sui confessoris [3]]. Item dictus Edmundus, pro eo quod noluit circa bona sive negocia temporalia mentem sive animam suam affligere seu occupare, set ad æternam felicitatem se præparare, dedit, legavit ac commisit omnia bona et catalla sua prædilecto fratri suo Johanni Paston, ex magna confidencia in ipso habita ut ea disponeret pro bono animæ suæ, prout melius videret Deo placere ac animæ suæ prodesse. Et dictum Johannem Paston ordinavit et constituit executorem suum. In cujus rei testimonum præsentibus sigilla nostra apposuimus.

Endorsed—Copia ultimæ voluntatis Edmundi Paston.
Endorsed in a later hand—Testamentum Edmundi Paston secundi filii Willelmi Paston Justiciarii.

---

[1] [From Paston MSS., B.M.]

[2] This is 1449 according to the modern computation, which begins the year on the 1st of January instead of the 25th March.

[3] These words are erased.

98

---

man and I arryn a poynted that he schal comyn ageyn a purpose 1449(?) fro the Byschope, to be my gyde ovyr the see, and so I purpose MARCH 5 me fully forthe a noon aftir this Estryn. I mak me evyre day fulli redy as privyli as I can, be sekyng zow, as I trost on zow, and as I am zour trow bede man, as labor for me her that I mythe haf a wyrte of passagche directid un[to] swyche men as zow thyng that schyd best yife me my schargche.

The best takyng of schepynge is at Yernemuthe er Kyrley, or som othir place in Norfolk syde. I schal haf favour he now [enough] wyt ther seergiours [searchers]; bod all my goode spede and all my wel lythe in you heer, for ther on I trost fully.

Som cownsel me to haf a letter of exschawnge, thow it wer bode of xls. er lees, bod I comitte all my best in this matir to zour wysdam, and qwat at evyr ze pay in this matir, I schal truly at owr metyng repay ageyn to zow. Bod for Godds love purvey for my sped her, for ell [else] I lees all my purvyans, and ther too I schyd jaape [1] the Byschope man, and caus hym to com in to Yngland, and lees all his labour. For Goddis love, send me down this wyrte, er ell bryng it wyt zow, that I mythe haf fro zow a letter of tydings and comforthe ; for I had nevyr verray need of zour labor til now, bod my hert hangithe in gret langor.

All my brethir wenyth that I schyd no forthir goo than to the Byschope, and undir that colour schal I weel go forthe to the Courte. I haf gret stody til I haf tydings fro zow. Avyr mor All mythi Good haf zow in kepyng, bodi and soule.

Writtin in hast, the Wednesday in the fyrst week of clen Lent. [2]

Your Orator,   ROBT., P. of B.

I sent zow a letter, bod I hade non answer ageyn.

---

[1] Deceive.

[2] The first week in Clean Lent means the first *entire* week in Lent beginning on a Sunday.

HENRY VI

86

LORD MOLYNS TO THE TENANTS OF GRESHAM [1]

To my trusty and wel belovyd, the Vycary and Tenaunts of my Lordschepe of Gressham.

1449
MARCH 24

TRUSTY and welbeloved frendys, I grete yowe well, and putte yowe all owte of doute for all that ye have doon for me ; and the money that ye pay to my welbeloved servaunt, John Partrich, I will be your warant as for your discharge, and save yowe harmeles ayenst all thoo that wold greve yowe, to my power. And, as hertly as I can, I thanke yow of the gud wyl ye have had, and have, toward me. And as to the tytyll of rigth that I have to the Lordship of Gressam schal with in short tyme be knoweyn, and be the lawe so determynyd, that ye schall all be glad that hathe ought me youre gud wyll therin.

And All Myghty God kepe yow ; and, be His grace, I schall be with yowe son aftyr the Parlement es endyd.

Wrytten atte London, on Oure Lady evyn last past.

R. H., LORD MOLYNS.

87

MARGARET PASTON TO JOHN PASTON [2]

To my rytz wurschipful Mayster, Jon Paston, be this delyverid in hast, dwelling in the Inner Tempill.

APRIL 2

RYTZ wurschipful hosbond, I recommawnd me to zu, praying zu to wete that my kosyn Cler [3] dynyd with me this day ; and sche told me that Heydon was with her yister evyn late, and he told her that he had a letter from

---

[1] [From Fenn, i. 192.] Lord Molyns took possession of Gresham, as already shown—see page 94, note 1,—on the 17th of February 1448 ; but the reference to Parliament as sitting at the date of this letter proves it to belong either to 1449 or 1450. The latter date, however, is not very probable.

[2] [From Paston MSS., B.M.] The date of this letter is evidently both after Paston's expulsion from Gresham by Lord Molyns in February 1448, and after the death of Edmund Paston in 1449. It cannot, however, be so late as 1450, else Hauteyn would not have expected to obtain possession of Oxnead through the Duke of Suffolk's influence.   [3] Elizabeth, widow of Robert Clere of Ormesby.

99

1449
APRIL 2

the Lord Moleynys, and schewyd her the same letter, praying hym that he wold seyn to his frends and wele willerres in this contre that he thanketh hem of her godewill, and for that thei have done for hym ; and also praying Heydon that he wold sey to Rychard Ernold of Crowmer that he was sory and evyl payd that his men maden the afray up on hym, for he seyd it was not be his will that his men xuld make afray on noman in this contre owth rytz grett cause. And as for that was don to zu if it mytz ben prevyd that he had don otherwise to zu than rytz wold as for the mevabyl godis, ze xuld ben content, so that ze xuld have cawse to kon hym thank ; and he prayd Heydon in the letter that it xuld ben reportid in this kontre that he wold don so, if he had don otherwyse than he owth to don.

The frere[1] that cleymyth Oxned was in this town zastyrday and this day, and was ledgid att Beris, and this afternon he rod, but qhedder I wote not. He seyd pleynly in this town that he xal have Oxnede, and that he hath my lord of Suffolkes[2] good lordship, and he wol ben his good lord in that mater. There was a persone warnyd my moder with in this to days that xuld ben bewar, for thei seyd pleynly sche was lyk to ben servyd as ze were servyd at Gressam with in rytz schort tyme. Also the Lord Moleyns wrott in his forseyd letter that he wold mytyly, with his body and with his godis, stand be all tho that had ben his frends and his wel willers in the mater towching Gressam, and preyd Heydon that he wold sey to them that thei xuld not ben aferd in non wyse, for that was don it xuld ben abedyn by.

My moder prayith zu that ze wil send my brother Willyam to Kawmbrege anomynale[3] and abok of sofystre of my brother Emundes,[4] the qheche my seyd brother Willyam the last tyme he spak with her, that he xuld asent [*should have sent*] to my brother Willyam. The blisseful Trinyte have zu in his keping.

[1] John Hawteyn.—*See* Nos. 46 and 50.
[2] William De la Pole, Duke of Suffolk.
[3] A *nominale*.
[4] Edmund Paston, who must have died very shortly after declaring his will on the 21st of March 1449.

100

Wretyn at Norwyche in hast, on the Wodenysday next be for Palm Sonday.   Zowres,

M. P.

1449
APRIL 2

88

[MARGARET PASTON] TO [JOHN PASTON][1]

1449(?)

RYT wurchipful hwsbond, I recomawnd me to zu, and prey zw to gete som crosse bowis, and wyndacs[2] to bynd them with, and quarrels ;[3] for zour hwsis her ben so low that ther may non man schet owt with no long bowe, thow we hadde never so moche nede.

I sopose ze xuld have seche thyngs of Ser Jon Fastolf, if ze wold send to hym ; and also I wold ze xuld gete ij. or iij. schort pelleaxis to kepe with doris, and als many jakkys, and ye may.

Partryche[4] and his felaschep arn sor aferyd that ze wold entren azen up on them, and they have made grete ordynaw[n]ce with inne the hwse, as it is told me. They have made barris to barre the dorys crosse weyse, and they have made wykets on every quarter of the hwse to schote owte atte, bothe with bowys and with hand gunnys ; and the holys that ben made forr hand gunnys, they ben scarse kne hey fro the plawncher [*floor*], and of soche holis ben made fyve. There can non man schete owt at them with no hand bowys.

Purry felle in felaschepe with Willyum Hasard at Querles, and told hym that he wold com and drynk with Partryche and with hym, and he seyd he xuld ben welcome, and after none

[1] [From Fenn, iii. 314.] 'The direction of this curious letter,' says Fenn, 'is obliterated, but it is plainly from Margaret Paston to her husband ; and the paper is likewise so completely filled with writing, that she has not even either subscribed or dated it, but by the mentioning of Sir John Fastolf it must have been written before 1459.' It appears to us most probably to belong to the year 1449, when Paston was making preparations to re-enter Gresham, which he actually did in October of that year.
[2] Windacs are what we now call grappling irons, with which the bow-string is drawn home.—F.
[3] Properly *quarreaux*. They were square pyramids of iron shot out of cross-bows.—Grose's *Milit. Antiq.* i. 149.
[4] John Partrich, one of Lord Molyns's retainers.

101

1449(?)

he went thedder for to aspye qhat they dedyn, and qhat felachep they hadde with them ; and qhan he com thedder, the dors were fast sperid [*fastened*], and there wer non folks with hem but Maryoth, and Capron and hys wyf, and Querles wyf, a[n]d another man in ablac (?) zede sum qhate haltyng, I sopose be his words that it was Norfolk of Gemyngham ; and the seyd Purry aspyde alle this forseyd thyngs. And Marioth and his felaschep had meche grette langage that xall ben told zw qhen ze kom hom.

I pray zw that ze wyl vowche save to don bye for me j. li. [*1 lb.*] of almands and j. li. of sugyr, and that ze wille do byen sume frese to maken of zour child is gwnys ; ze xall have best chepe and best choyse of Hayis wyf, as it is told me. And that ze wyld bye a zerd of brode clothe of blac for an hode fore me of xliiij*d.* or iiij*s.* a zerd, for ther is nether gode cloth ner god fryse in this twn. As for the child is gwnys, and I have them, I wel do hem maken.

The Trynyte have zw in his keping, and send zw gode spede i[n] alle zour materis.

89

WILLIAM COTYNG TO JOHN PASTON[1]

To the right reverent sir my most worshiful maister, my maister John Paston.

About
1449
APRIL

RIGHT reverent and my most worshipful maister, I recomaund me to yow. Please it yow to wete that the man whiche I wolde have hadde to a be youre fermour at Snaillewelle hath tolde me that he will not therof, and this he makith his excuse ; he seythe that he shall dwelle with his wyffes fader and fynden hym for his good as longe as he levyth and he will no forther medill in the werde. I fele well by hym that he hath inquered of the maner, for he coude telle me well that olde Briggeman aught my maister, your

[1] [Add. MS. 34,889, f. 164.] This letter must have been written about the year 1449, when William Paston, son of the Judge, was a student at Cambridge.

102

fader, whom God assoile, moche good, and how that he hadde al that was ther whanne Briggeman was ded ; and that this Briggeman owith yow moche good at this tyme. I answered therto, as for olde Briggeman, I seide that it was his will that my maister shulde have his good, be cause he was a bonde man and hadde no childer. And as for this Briggeman, I seide that he hath bought a faire place sithe he was your fermour, and payed therfor ; but for this I kan not turne hym. Wherfor, and it like yow to sende to me a bille of the value of the maner, I shall inquere if any other may happe to be gete, and sende yow worde therof ; and in this and what ye will comaunde me ellys I shall do my parte by the grace of our Lord, Who ever have yow in His kepyng. Amen. Writen at Cambrigge the Sunday nexte before the fest of Seynt George.

My maister your brother[1] recomaundeth hym to yow, as me semyth he is in right febill hele. he will not telle me qwy, save he seyth he compleyned onys and hadde no remedy, and therfor he seythe he shall suffer for a seoson. Forsothe I suppose he is not intreted as he aught to be.—Your servaunt and bedeman,

W. COTYNG.

About
1449
APRIL

90

ROBERT WENYNGTON TO THOMAS DANIEL[2]

To my Reverend Mayster, Thomas Danyell, Squier for the Kyngs Body, be thys letter delyverd in haste.

1449
MAY 25

MOST reverent mayster, I recomaund me on to yowr graceus maystreschup, ever deseryng to her of yowr wurschupfull ustate, the whyche All myghte God mayntayne hyt, and encrese hyt on to hys plesans : Plesyng

[1] William Paston.
[2] [From Fenn, i. 208.] On the 3rd April 1449 royal letters were issued in favour of Robert Wynnyngtone of Devonshire, who was bound by indenture to do the King service on the sea 'for the cleansing of the same, and rebuking of the robbers and pirates thereof, which daily do all the noisance they can.'—Stevenson's *Letters and Papers illustrative of the Wars of the English in France*, i. 489.

103

1449
MAY 25

yow to know of my wellfare, and of all yowr men, at the makyng of thys letter, we wer in gode hele of body i blessyd be God.

Mo over, mayster, I send yow word, by Rauly Pykeryng, of all maters, the whyche I be seche yow yeve hym credens, as he wyll enforme yow of all; so, sur, I beseche yow, in the reverens of God, that ye wyll enforme owr Soverayn Lord the Kyng of all maters that I send yow in thys letter, lyke as I have send a letter to my Lord Chaunseler and to all my Lordys by the sayd Pykeryng; the whyche letter I beseche yow that ye take and delyver to my Lord and all my Lordys by yowr awne handys, and lete the sayd Pykeryng declare all thyngs as he hath sayn and knoweth.

Furst, I send yow word that when we went to see, we toke ij. schyppys of Brast comyng owte of Flaundrys; and then after, ther ys made a grete armyng in Brytayne to mete with me and my felyschyp, that ys to say, the grete schyp of Brast, the grete schyp of the Morleys, the grete schyp of Vanng, with other viij. schyppis, bargys, and balyngers, to the number of iij. m^{ll} [3000] men; and so we lay in the see to me[te] with them.

And then we mette with a flotte of a c. [a hundred] grete schyppys of Pruse, Lubycke, Campe, Rastocke, Holond, Selond, and Flandres, betwyte Garnyse [Guernsey] and Portland; and then I cam abord the Admirall, and bade them stryke in the Kyngys name of Englond, and they bade me skyte in the Kyngys name of Englond; and then I and my feleschyp sayd, but [unless] he wyll streke don the sayle, that I wyld over sayle ham by the grace of God, and God wyll send me wynd and wether; and dey bade me do my wurst, by cause I had so fewe schyppys and so smale, that they scornyd with me. And as God wuld, on Fryday last was, we had a gode wynd, and then we armyd to the number of ij. m^{L} [2000] men in my felyschyp, and made us redy for to over sayle them; and then they lonchyd a bote, and sette up a stondert of truesse, and com and spake with me. And ther they were yolded all the hundret schyppys to go with me in what port that me lust and my felawys; but they faothe with me the day

104

1449
MAY 25

before, and schotte atte us a j. m^{L} [1000] gonnys, and quarell[1] owte of number, and have slayn meny of my felyschyp, and meymyd all soo. Wherfor me thyngkyt that they haye forfett bothe schypps and godys at our Soverayn Lord the Kyngys wyll. Besechyng yow that ye do yowr parte in thys mater, for thys I have wrytyn to my Lord Chaunseler[2] and all my Lordys of the Kyngys Counsell; and so I have brofte them, all the c. [hundred] shyppys, within Wyght, in spyte of them all.

And ye myght gete leve of owr Soverayn Lord the Kyng to com hydder, hyt schall turne yow to grete wurschup and profett, to helpe make owr a poyntement in the Kyngs name, for ye sawe never suche a syght of schyppys take in to Englond this c. wynter; for we ly armyd nyght and day to kepe them, in to the tyme that we have tydengs of our Soverayn and hys counsell. For truly they have do harme to me, and to my feleschyp, and to yowr schyppys more [than] ij. m^{L} li.[3] worth harme; and therfor I am avesyd, and all my feleschyp, to droune them and slee them, withoute that we hafe tydyngs from owr Soverayn the Kyng and hys counsell. And therfor, in the reverens of God, come ye yowr self, and ye schall have a grete avayle and wurschup of yowr comyng to see a suche syght, for I der well sey that I have her at this tyme all the cheff schyppys of Duchelond, Holond, Selond, and Flaundrys, and now hyt wer tyme for to trete for a fynell pese as for that partyes.

I writ no more to yow at this tyme, but All myghty Jesus have yow in hys kepyng. I writ in hast, within Wyght, on Soneday at nyght after the Ascencion of owr Lord.

By yowr owne Servant, ROBT. WENYNGTON.

[1] See p. 101, Note 3.
[2] John Stafford, Archbishop of Canterbury.
[3] Fenn says the reading of the original is indistinct, and he could not determine whether £2000 or £3000 was meant.

105

91

WILLIAM PASTON TO JOHN PASTON[1]

To myn most reverent and [w]urchepful broder, Jon Paston.

About
1449

TO myn most reverent and wurcheful brodur, I recummend me hartely to zow, desiryng speciali to hare of zowre wellefare and prosperite, qweche Almyty God contenu to zowre gosteli hele and bodili welfare. And if it plase zowre goode broderod to here of myn wellefare, at the makyng of this bylle I was in good hele. And if it leke zowre good broderod to remembre the letter that I sent to zow of the noyse that was telde of zow, that ze schuld a be on of the capetayns of the ryserse in Norfolk, and how that j. scholere of Cambryg, qweche is parsone of Welle, schuld an utteryd ferthere to zowr grete schalndyr [slander]; besechyng zow to undyrstond that the seyde parsone of Welle was sone [after ?][2] that tyme at Lundon, were he harde sey of j. swyr of ij. c. marc be zere [of one squire of 200 marks by year] that ze and Master Thomas Wellys wolde sewe the seyd Parsone Welle for zowre schalndyr; and the seyde parsone come to Cambryg sothyn, and hathe pekyd a qwarell to on Mastyr Recheforthe, a knythys sone of Norforfolke,[3] and seyd to Rychechefor[3] that he had because that ze schuld sewe hym; and the seyd Parsone Welle thretyd Rycheferthe that wat some ever that ze causyd Parson Welle to lese be zowre sewtes, that Rycheferthe schul lese the same to the Parson oñ Welle. Werefor this jeltylmon Rycheforthe taketh grete thowt, and pray me to wrythe to zow that ze wulde sese zowre suthe tylle the tyme that ze wulde asyne that I mythe speke wythe zow, and odyr sundry have speke with zow of the same mater; for yt ware pithe that Rycheforthe chuld have ony hurthe thereby. I beseche

[1] [From Paston MSS., B.M.] As it appears from Margaret Paston's letter of the 2nd April 1449 that William Paston was a student at Cambridge in that year, the date of this must be about the same period.
[2] Word omitted.   [3] So in MS.

106

About
1449

zow holde me excusyd, thow I wryt no better to zow at thys tyme, for in good feyth I had no leysere. The brynggar of thys letter can telle zow the same. God have zow in hys kepyng. Wretyn at Cambryg, on Fryday [sa]nyth[1] nexste before Mydsommer Evyn.

In case ze come ba come [back home ?] be Cambryg, I schal telle zow mo of it. I am sory I may wrythe no bettyr at this tyme, but I trust ze wylle [have] paciens.

Be zowre pore Broder, W. PASTON.

92

SIR JOHN FASTOLF TO JOHN PASTON[2]

To the Worshypful Sir, and my ryght well beloved cosen, John Paston.

1449(?)
JULY 10

WORSHYPFULL and ryghte welbelovyd cosyn, I comaund me to you. Please you to here that the Pryore and Convent of Norwyche have wythholden certeyn rent for landes that they halden of me wythinne my maner of Haylysdon, and the ij. tapers of wax of ij. lbs. wyght, by the space of xviij. yere, that mountyth xxjs.[3] valued in money. And the lordes of the seyd maner beyng before me, and y yn my tyme, have been seised and possessed of the seyd rent. Prayng you to speke wyth the Pryore, or comaundyng me unto hym. And that ye lyke to move hym to make me payment as his dewtee ys, so as y have no cause to gowe further, and to do as justice requyreth. He hahyth xxx. acres lande or more by the seyd rent, and whyht ought to pay me othyr rent more by myn evidence. More over y pray you, cosen, that I may speke with you or [before] y ryde, and that on Thursday by the ferthest; and then y shall tell you

[1] This is written 'sanyth,' but there is a stroke through the a, which was perhaps intended to have been carried through the s also.
[2] [From Palmer's Foundacion and Antiquity of Great Yermouthe, p. 61.]
[3] 'xxj.o,' as printed by Palmer, but the 'o' no doubt should be 's.'

107

THE PASTON LETTERS

tydyngs off the Parlement, and that ye fayle not, as my trust ys yn you. I pray God have you in Hys guidance.

Wreten at Castor, the x. day off Julie 1449.[1]—Your Cosen,
JOHN FASTOLFE.

93

AGNES PASTON TO JOHN PASTON[2]

To John Paston be this letter delyveryd.

Not after 1449 SOON, I grete zow wel with Goddis blyssyng and myn, and I latte zow wette that my cosyn Cler[3] wrytted to me that sche spake with Schrowpe[4] after that he had byen with me at Norwyche, and tolde her what cher that I had made hym, and he seyde to her he lyked wel by the cher I made hym.

He had swyche wordys to my cosyn Cler that lesse than ze made hym good cher, and zaf hym wordys of conforth at London, he wolde no mor speke of the matyr.

My cosyn Cler thynkyth that it were a foly to forsake hym lesse than ze knew of on owdyr as good or better; and I have assayde zowr suster,[5] and I fonde her never so wylly to noon as sche is to hym, zyf it be so that his londe stande cleer.

I sent zow a letter by Brawnton for sylke, and for this

---

[1] So the date is given in the book from which this letter is copied, but the year is certainly wrong, as the writer did not go to reside at Caister till 1454. The date indeed would have been suspicious apart from this, as the mode of dating is quite unusual in these letters. Probably in the original ms. (which the Editor has not seen) '1449' was inserted after 'Julie' in a later hand.

[2] [From Fenn, iii. 202.] This letter is dated by Fenn 1454, with some others relating to matches proposed for Elizabeth Paston; but the date of this cannot be later than 1451, as Sir Harry Inglos died that year. Moreover, it cannot be either 1451 or 1450, as 'the Saturday next after Midsummer,' when this letter is dated, preceded 'the Wednesday next after Midsummer day' in both these years. Thus 1449 is the latest possible date.

[3] Elizabeth, widow of Robert Clere of Ormesby, Esq.

[4] Stephen Scrope, a son of Sir John Fastolf's wife by a former husband.

[5] Elizabeth Paston.

108

HENRY VI

matyr befor my cosyn Cler wrote to me, the qwyche was wrytten on the Wednysday nexzt aftyr Mydsomer day. Not after 1449

Sir Harry Ynglows is ryzth besy a bowt Schrowpe for one of his dozthers.

I prey zow, for zette nozth to brynge me my mony fro Horwelbery, as ze com fro London, edyr all or a grete parte. The dew dette was at Crystemesse last paste, no thynge a lowyd, vij*li*. xiiijs. viij*d*., and at this Mydsomer it is v*li*. more; and thow I a low hym all his askyng, it is but xxvjs. vj*d*. less, but I am nozth so avysyth zytt. As for the Frer,[1] he hath byen at Sent Benetts, and at Norwyche, and made grete bowste of the sewte that he hath azens me, and bowzthe many boxes, to what intent I wett never. It is wel doen to be war at London, in drede gyf he bryng ony syse at Sent Margarets tyme.

I kan no more, but Almyzty God be owr good lorde, who have zow ever in kepyng. Wryten at Oxnede in grete hast, on the Satyr next aftyr Mydsomer.

By yowr Modyr, A. P.

94

ELIZABETH CLERE TO JOHN PASTON[2]

To my Cosyn, John Paston, be thys letter delyvered.

Not after 1449 TRUSTY and weel be loved cosyn, I comaunde me to zow, desyryng to here of zowre weelfare and good spede in zowre matere, the qwech I prey God send zow to his plesaunce and to zoure hertys ease.

Cosyn, I lete zow wete that Scrope[3] hath be in this cuntre to se my cosyn zoure sustyr, and he hath spoken with my cosyn zoure moder, and sche desyreth of hym that he schuld

---

[1] John Hawteyn.—*See* Nos. 46, 50, and 63.

[2] [From Fenn, iii. 204.] This letter appears from the contents to be of the same year as the preceding.

[3] Stephen Scrope.—*See* p. 108, Note 4.

109

THE PASTON LETTERS

Not after 1449 schewe zow the endentures mad be twen the knyght that hath his dowter and hym, whethir that Skrop, if he were maried and fortuned to have children, if tho children schuld enheryte his lond, or his dowter, the wheche is maried.

Cosyn, for this cause take gode hede to his endentures, for he is glad to schewe zow hem, or whom ze wol a sygne with zow; and he seith to me he is the last in the tayle of his lyflode, the qweche is CCCL. marke and better, as Watkyn Shipdam seith, for he hath take a compt of his liflode dyvers tymes; and Scrop seith to me if he be maried, and have a sone an eyre, his dowter that is maried schal have of his liflode L. marke and no more; and therfore, cosyn, me semeth he were good for my cosyn zowre sustyr, with[out] that ye myght gete her a bettyr. And if ze can gete a better, I wold avyse zow to labour it in as schort tyme as ze may goodly, for sche was never in so gret sorow as sche is now a dayes, for sche may not speke with no man, ho so ever come, ne not may se ne speke with my man, ne with servauntes of hir moderys but that sche bereth hire an hand[1] otherwyse than she menyth. And sche hath sen Esterne the most part be betyn onys in the weke or twyes, and som tyme twyes on o day, and hir hed broken in to or thre places. Wherfor, cosyn, sche hath sent to me by Frere Newton in gret counsell, and preyeth me that I wold send to zow a letter of hir hevynes, and prey yow to be hir good brothyr, as hir trost is in zow; and sche seith, if ze may se be his evydences that his childern and hire may enheryten, and sche to have resonable joynture, sche hath herd so mech of his birth and his condicions, that and ze will sche will have hym, whethyr that hir moder wil or wil not, not with-standyng it is tolde hir his persone is symple, for sche seyth men shull have the more deyute of hire if sche rewle hire to hym as sche awte to do.

Cosyn, it is told me ther is a goodly man in yowre Inne, of the qweche the fadyr deyed litte, and if ze thynk that he were better for hir than Scroop, it wolde be laboured, and yif Scroop a godoly answere that he be not put of tyl ze be sure of a bettyr; for he seid whan he was with me, but if [*i.e.* unless] he

---

[1] To bear one on hand, means to assert or insinuate something to a person.

110

HENRY VI

have som counfortable answer of zow, he wil no more laboure in this mater, be cause he myght not se my cosyn zoure sustyr, and he seyth he myght a see hire and sche had be bettyr than she is; and that causeth hym to demyr that hir moder was not weel willyng, and so have I sent my cosyn zowre moder word. Wherfore, cosyn, thynk on this mateer, for sorow oftyn tyme causeth women to be set hem otherwyse than thei schuld do, and if sche where in that case, I wot weel ze wold be sory. Cosyn, I prey zow brenne this letter, that zoure men ne non other man se it; for and my cosyn zowre moder knew that I had sent yow this letter, sche shuld never love me. No more I wrighte to zow at this tyme, but Holy Gost have zow in kepyng. Writyn in hast, on Seynt Peterys day,[1] be candel lyght. Not after 1449

Be youre Cosyn, ELIZABETH CLERE.

95

JOHN DAMME TO JOHN PASTON[2]

To my ryght worshepfull master John Paston at London in the Inner Temple.

1449 NOV. 30 PLESE it your good maistershep to knowe that my maisteresse your wyff recomaundeth here to yow and fareth well, blyssed be God, and all your menye faren well also and recomaunde hem to yaw, &c. I was with my lord of Oxenford and dede myn erand, and I found his good lordshep well disposed towardys yow, for he seid if he were sent to for to come to, &c., if it kepe faire weder he wold not tarye, and if it reygned he wold not spare. More over I spak with Pertrych as touchyng the letter sent to my lord Moleyns; he seyth that he was privy to the wrytyng and wele a vowe it by record of xx. persons, but he wold name to me no persone; and so he and I accorded not fully. And I bad hym remembre

---

[1] June 29.

[2] [Add. 34,888, f. 32.] This letter was evidently written in 1449, after John Paston had re-entered Gresham, and his wife was keeping it for him. See No. 88.

111

1449
NOV. 30

hym that he myght not abyde there if ye wold have hym owt. And he seid he knewe well that. But he seid, if ye put heem out, ye shuld be put owt sone after a geyn. And I seyd if it happe it so thei shuld not longer reste there. And Mariot stod by and seyd that were no merveyll whill thei were but ij. men, but it shuld not be best so. And I seyd that I lete them wete it shuld be so if ye wold, thow they made all the strenght which they coude make. And ther to Mariot seyd stately, that myght not be performed ; and more langage ther was, to long to wryte at this leyser. Pertrych and his felaw bere gret visage and kepe gret junkeryes and dyneres, and seyn that my lord Moleynes hath wrytyn pleynly to hem that he is lord there and well be, and shall be, and ye not to have it ; but I trust to Goddes ryghtwysenes of better purvyaunce. Lyke it yow to remembre what Heydon doth and mayde by colour of justice of the pees, beyng of my lordes councell and not your good frend nor weell wyller, and to comon with your sad councell what ye must suffre by the lawe, and where inne ye may resiste. On Sunday last passed Gunore and Mariot and John Davy and other dyned with Pertrych, &c.; and after eveson [*evensong*] Gonore spake to my maisteresse that she shuld make here men to leue here wyfeles and here jackes ; and she answered that thei purposed to hurte no man of here owyn sykyng ; but for it was seid that she shuld be plukkyd owt of here howse, she were loth to suffre that ; and therfore she sayde thei shuld goo soo til ye come hom. And he seid stately, but if thei left here aray it shuld be plukked from them. I trust he must have a better warant, from his stately langage, or ells he shall not have it from hem esily. All this I remitte to your good remembrauce with Goddes help, to Whom I pray to gyde your ryght to his worshep and your hertes desire.

Wrytyn at Sustede on Seynt Andrewe day, &c.—Yowres,
J. DAMME.

Were but well, as me semyth, that ye myght ordeygne now a fetys jacke defensable for your self, for there con they do best and best chep, &c.

112

96

JAMES GRESHAM TO [JOHN PASTON][1]

'The King is now into the Marches of Wales, as it is said, to the intent he may be near the country if my Lord of Buckingham, which is commissioner now in Wales for divers offences done there to the Crown, would sue to have his commission to be enlarged, if he were repyned.' It is not known when the King will be in London again, but he is expected here at the beginning of the Parliament. I have your writs of error, but can see nothing wrong. Thos. Denys asked me why you did not follow his suggestion about the removing of the strength at Gresham, and thinks it should be done yet. Francis Costard is not yet well at ease, for his *venire facias* between Will. Prentys and him and Hen. Halman comes in very inopportunely. You had better come hither as soon as possible and get the favor of the sheriff that shall be next year.
London, 16 Oct.

1449 (?)
OCT. 16

97

SIR JOHN FASTOLF TO JOHN FASTOLF AND JOHN KIRTELING[2]

To my ryght tristy and welbelovede Cosin and Frende, John Fastolf, and Sir John Kirtelinge, Parson of Arkesay.

TRUSTY and welbeloved frendz, y grete yow wel. And for as moche as y have appointed with my sone, Stephen Scrope, lyke as y sende yow the appointement writen hereafter in this letter, the whiche appointement y woll ye fulfylle be the avys of my counsel in that at longeth to my party, like as hit ys writen.

Thys ys the appointement made be twene Sir John Fastolf, Knight, and Stephen Scrope, Squier, in the maner as here after hit ys writen :—

OCT. 31

[1] This abstract was made from one of the Roydon Hall MSS. shown to the Editor in 1875. Since that date he has not seen the original.
[2] [From the Castlecombe MSS. in the B.M., Add. MS. 28,212, No. 21.] According to the endorsement, this letter should have been written in the year 1449; but the reader will see by the footnotes that there are grounds for doubting the accuracy of this date.

1449 (?)
OCT. 31

Fyrst, for as moche as the mariage of the saide Stephen Scrope was solde[1] to Sir William Gascoyng, the Chefe Justice of Englonde, for v^c [500] marke, with the whiche mariage was deliverd in hande to the sayde Gascoyng the maner of Wyghton on the Wolde, in Yorke schyre, with the apertenance of the saide maner ; and whan the sayde Gascoyng hade hym, he wolde have solde hym agayn, or maried the saide Stephen Scrope ther [*where*] he schulde have byn despareiged : wherefore, at the request of the sayde Scrope and hys frendes, the saide Fastolf boght the ma[ri]age of the saide Scrope of the saide Sir William Gascoyng for v^c marke, wherby the saide Fastolf hath mariage of the saide Stephen Scrope, or elles to have the saide somme of v^c marke that he payde for hym, like as hit ys above sayde.

Item, for as moche as the sayde Stephen Scrope ys comyn to the saide Fastolf, sayinge that he hath fownde wey to be maried at his lyst, and also for his worschippe and profyt, so that the saide Fastolf woll consent therto, that ys to say, to Fauconeris doughter of London, that Sir Reynalde Cobham[2] had weddid.

Item, for as hit ys the saide Fastolf ys wille to further and helpe the saide Scrope in any wize ther he may be fortherede, the sayde Fastolf consenteth that the sayde Scrope marie hym to the Fauconeris doughter, with that that the sayde Fauconer gyf to the sayde Fastolf the saide somme of v^c marke, the whiche he payde for the saide Scrope.

Item, yf that the sayde Stephen Scrope pay or do pay the somme afore sayde of v^c marke sterling, than the sayde Sir John Fastolf and Dame Mylicent,[3] his wyf, schall make astate of the said maner of Wyghton on the Wolde in Yorke schyre,

[1] The marriage of wards in those days used to be sold to men of property, who would compel them to marry their own sons or daughters, or whatever other persons suited them. The only restriction to this right was, that the ward might, on coming of age, have an action against his guardian in case of *disparagement*, that is to say, if he was married beneath his station.
[2] Sir Reginald Cobham of Sterborough, in Surrey, who died in 1446. He was the father of the notorious Eleanor Cobham, the mistress, and afterwards wife, of Humphrey, Duke of Gloucester.—Brayley's *Hist. of Surrey*, iv. 159.
[3] Milicent, wife of Sir John Fastolf, is known to have been alive in the 24th year of Henry VI. (1446). William Worcester says the allowance for her chamber was
114

with the apertenaunce of the sayde maner, to the saide Stephen Scrope and to the woman, the whiche schalbe his wyf, and to here eyres of here bodyes begete be twix hem two.

Item, yef the sayde Stephen dye with oute eyre of his body begeten, than the sayde maner of Wyghton, after the descece of the saide hys wyf, schall retourne agayne to the sayde Fastolf and Dame Mylicent, his wyf, and to the eyres of the sayde Mylicent.

Item, yf so be that the sayde Fauconer wilnot pay the sayde somme of v^c marke, bot peraventure wolde gyf a lesse somme, then the sayde Fastolf wyl deliver to the mariage of the saide Scrope certayn londe, havynge rewarde to the somme that the sayde Fauconer wil gyf, havyng rewarde to the afferrant of xl. pounde worthe land and v^c mark of golde.

Item, if that the sayde Fauconer wilnot gyf no somme of golde for the sayde mariage, the sayde Fastolf wyl take the mariage of the childe that ys eyre to the forsaide Sir Reynolde Cobham, and that the sayde Scrope forto conferme the estat hys moder has made to the saide Fastolf, yf so be that the consel of the saide Fastolf se by thaire avys that hit be for to do, and that the said mariage may be [as] moche worth to the said Fastolf as v^c mark.

Item, ze sende me be Raufm[an an] answare o[f] the letters that y sende yow, that I may have ve[ray] knolage how that hit standys with me ther in al maner of thynges, and that I [h]ave an answare of every article that y wrote to yow.

Item, for as moche as that I am bonden for my Lord Scales[1] to my Lord Cardnale[2] in v^c mark, the qu[ech] somme he kan not fynd no way to pay hit, on lese then that he sel a parcel of his land ; quer fore he sendis ower a man of his called Pessemerche, with whom I wil that ze spek, and se be

1449 (?)
OCT. 31

paid until that date ; but as he says nothing more, it has been supposed she did not live longer. Mr. Poulett Scrope also believes her to have died in 1446, on the authority of a contemporary MS., which says she and Fastolf lived together thirty-eight years.—*Hist. Castlecombe*, 263.
[1] Thomas de Scales, 8th Lord.
[2] John Kemp, Archbishop of York, afterwards of Canterbury ; or, if this document be some years earlier, Cardinal Beaufort, Bishop of Winchester.

THE PASTON LETTERS

1449(?)
OCT. 31

zore avis whech of the places of my said Lord Scales that standis most cler to be solde; and if the place that is beside W[a]lsyngham stand cler, I have hit lever then the tother ; and therfore I pray [z]ow that ze make apointement with the said Pesemerche in the best wise that ze may, athir of the ton place or the tother, and or ze let take hit after xx. zere, havyn[g] rewarde to the verray val[u] therof, and as ze don send me worde be the next massager.

Item, my Lord of Hungerford[1] has writen to me for to have the warde of Robert Monpyns[on]is sone, wher of I am agreed that he schal [have] hit like as I has wretyn to hym in a letter, of the whech I send zow a cope closed here in : wher fore I pray zow to enquere of the verray valu of the land that Monpynson haldis of me, and sendis me word in hast ; for my said Lord Hungerford sais in his letter that hit is worth bot xls. a zere aboufe the rentis, as ze may se the letter that he sent me, the q[uec]h I send zow be my son Scrope. And I pray zow to demene zow to my said Lord as eesely as ze may in this mater and al other that I have to do with hym, as ze may se be the cope aforesaid. And or (sic) have zow in his kepyng. Wretyn at Roan (?)[2] the last day of October.

J. FASTOLFE.

Endorsed—Appunctuamentum factum pro Stephano Scroope anno xxviij° Regis H. vj. ad maritandum.

[1] Walter, 1st Lord Hungerford, died in August 1449, and was succeeded in the title by his son Robert.
[2] The name is a little indistinct from the decay of the paper, but the first and last letters are clear, and it is scarcely possible to doubt that Rouen was the place here intended. Yet if this be so, the letter must be much earlier than the date assigned to it in the endorsement.

116

HENRY VI

98

RICHARD, EARL OF WARWICK, TO SIR THOMAS TODENHAM[1]

To owr ryght trusty and welbelovyd Frend, Ser Thomas Todenham.

RYGHT trusty and welbelovyd frend, we grete you well, hertely desyryng to here of yowr welfare, which we pray God preserve to yowr herts desyr ; and yf yt please yow to here of owr welfare, we wer in goud hale atte the makyng of this lettre, praying you hertely that ye wyll consider owr message, which owr Chapleyn Mayster Robert Hoppton shall enforme yow of. For as God knowyth we have gret besynesse dayly, and has had here by for this tyme. Wherfor we pray you to consyder the purchas that we have made wyth one John Swyffhcotte, Squier of Lyncolnshyr, of lxxx. and viij*li.* by yer, whereuppon we must pay the last payment the Moneday nexte after Seynt Martyn' day, which sum ys CCCC. and lviij*li.* ; wherfor we pray you wyth all owr herte that ye wyll lend us x*li.*, or twenty, or whet the seyd Maister Robert wants of hys payment, as we may do for you in tym for to com ; and we shall send yt you ageyn afor Newyers day wyth the grace of God, as we ar trew knyght. For there is nonne in your cuntre that we myght wryght to for trust so well as unto you ; for, as we be enformyd, ye be owr well wyller, and so we pray you of goud contynuaunce.

Wherfore we pray you that ye consyder our entent of this mony, as ye wyll that we do for you in tym to com, as God knowyth, who have you in hys kepyng.

Wreten atte London, on All Salwyn [*All Souls'*] day, wyth inne owr loggyng in the Grey Freys [*Friars*] wyth inne Newgate. RIC., ERLE WARWYKE.[2]

1449(?)
NOV. 2

[1] [From Fenn, i. 84.] Richard Nevill, Earl of Warwick, afterwards famous as the 'King-maker,' succeeded to the title in 1449, and this letter is not unlikely to have been written in that very year. Certainly it is not many years later. In 1449 and 1450 Warwick was probably in London to attend the Parliament.
[2] 'The seal of this letter,' says Fenn, 'is of red wax, on which is the Bear and Ragged Staff, the badge of this nobleman, with his motto,—the whole very fair and curious, and around it is a braid of twine.'

117

THE PASTON LETTERS

99

ABSTRACT[1]

1449
DEC. 11

Copy of a Grant from the Crown to John Bray for services against the King's enemies. Caen, 11th December 14[4]9, 28 Henry vi.

[This document is very mutilated and decayed. It is written in French, the spelling of which is very peculiar, and is probably a bad copy by some one who did not know the language.]

100

WILLIAM TAILBOYS TO VISCOUNT BEAUMONT[2]

To my right honorabull and right wurshipful Lord, my Lord Viscont Beaumont.

Before
1450

RIGHT honorabull and my right wurshipfull Lord, I recomaund me unto your gode Lordship with all my service, evermore desireng to here of your prosperitie and welfare, the which I pray God encres and contynue to his plesur, and after your oone herts desire ; thankyng you of the gode Lordship that ye have shewed me at all tymes, beseching you alway of gode contynuance.

Plesid your gode Lordship to be remembred how afore this tyme Hugh Wythom hath said he wold be in rest and peese with me, and not to maligne agayn me otherwise than lawe and right wold ; that notwithstandyng, upon Munday last past, he and iij. men with him come unto a servaunt hous of myn in Boston, cald William Shirref, and there, as he sete at

[1] [From Paston MSS., B.M.]
[2] [From Fenn, iii. 282.] This letter is dated by Fenn between 1455 and 1460, but cannot be later than the former of these years, as Lord Cromwell died in the beginning of 1456. It seems, further, beyond a doubt that the Lord Willoughby, mentioned along with him, was Robert, Lord Willoughby of Eresby, who was connected by marriage both with Lord Cromwell and with Lord Welles ; and if so the date cannot be later than 1451, as this Lord Willoughby died in July 1452. Indeed, I have very little doubt it is before 1450, as both Tailboys and Beaumont were of the Duke of Suffolk's party, and it is not likely that the former would have ventured to complain of his powerful neighbours, Lords Willoughby, Cromwell, and Welles after the Duke's fall, especially as we know that in the beginning of 1450 he was in prison for an attempt to murder Lord Cromwell.

118

HENRY VI

his werke, stroke him upon the hede and in the body with a dagger, and wondet him sore, and pulled him out of his hous, and set him in prison without any cause resonabull, or without writ, or any other processe shewid unto him ; and that me semes longs not for him to do, bot as he says he is endited, and as your gode Lordship knawes wele, I and all my servaunts are in like wise ; bot and any man shuld have done hit, it longs either to the shirref or to your baliff as I conceyve, and other cause he had non to him as fer as I kan knawe, bot awnly for the malissiousness that he hath unto me, ne I kan think non other bot it is so. And now yistre nyght my Lord Welles[1] come to Boston with iiij^xx [*four score*] horses, and in the mornyng foloyng toke hym out of prison, saying afore all peepll, 'Fals thefe, you shall be hanged, and as mony of thy maistre men as may be goten '—as your servaunt John Abbot kan report unto your gode Lordship,—and hath taken him away with him to Tatessall, what to do with him I kan not say, bot as I suppose to have him to Lincoln Castell : wherfor I besech your gode Lordship in this matier to be my gode Lord, and it please your gode Lordship to write a letter to the kepere of the Castell of Lincoln, that it liked him to deliver him out of prison undre a sufficient seurety had for him, for and thai may kepe him still be this meyne, thai may take all the servaunts that I have, and so I may do agayn in like wise.

Before
1450

And also, as I am enformed, without he be had out of prison in hast, it will be right gravewis to him to heile of his hurt, he is so sore streken ; and if there be any service that your gode Lordship will comaund me to do in any cuntre, plesid you to send me word, and it shal be done to my power with the grace of God, which have you, my right honorabull and wurshipfull Lord, alway in his blessid kepyng. Writen at Kyme,[2] upon Wednesday next after our Ladi day the Assumpcion.[3]

Also plesid your gode lordship to wit, after this letter was

[1] Leo, Lord Welles.
[2] In Lincolnshire, between Tattershall and Sleaford.
[3] 15th August.

119

Before made, there come a man fro Tatessall into my fenne, which
1450 owght me gode will, and be cause he wold not be holden
suspect, he speke with wemen which were mylkand kyne, and
bad theme goo to a preest of myn to Dokdike, and bid him
fast goo gif me warnyng how that my Lord Wilughby,[1] my
Lord Cromwell,[2] and my Lord Welles[3] proposid theme to
set a sessions, and hang the said William Shirref, and thai
myght bryng ther entent abowte; and so, as I and your servaunt
John Abbot stode to geder, the prest come and gaf me warnyng
herof, which I trust to for my worship your gode Lordship wold
not shuld happen, for it wer to me the grettest shame that
myght falle; bot and it plese your gode Lordship to write to
all your servaunts in this cuntre, that thai will be redy upon
a day warnyng to come when I send theme word, I trust to
God thai shal not hang him agayn the lawe, bot I, with help of
your gode Lordship, shall be abull to let hit.

By your Servaunt,

WILLIAM TAILBOYS.[4]

101

IMPEACHMENT OF THE DUKE OF SUFFOLK[5]

To the King oure Soverayn Lord.

1450 SHEWETH and piteuously compleyneth youre humble
FEB. 7 trewe obeisantes Comunes of this youre nobile reaume,
in this youre present Parlement, by your high autorite
assembled for the seurte of your moste high and royall per-

[1] Robert, Lord Willoughby of Eresby, who married Maud Stephen, a niece of
Lord Cromwell. [2] Ralph, Lord Cromwell.
[3] Leo, Lord Welles, whose son Richard married Joan, a daughter of Robert,
Lord Willoughby of Eresby.
[4] William, afterwards Sir William, Tailboys of South Kyme, in Lincolnshire,
who was attainted under Edward IV. as an adherent of the House of Lancaster. His
family was afterwards ennobled as Barons Talboys. He was most unfavourably
mentioned in the impeachment of the Duke of Suffolk, of whom he appears to have
been a great adherent, and is accused of having made an attempt to murder Lord
Cromwell in the Star Chamber at Westminster, on the 28th November 1449.—See
Rolls of Parliament, v. 181-200.
[5] [From Fenn, iii. 62.] These are the articles of impeachment exhibited against
the Duke of Suffolk, as printed by Fenn from a contemporaneous copy among the

120

sone, and the welfar of this your nobile reaume, and of your 1450
trewe liege peple of the same, that William de la Pole, Duke FEB. 7
of Suffolk, late of Ewelme, in the counte of Oxenford, falsly
and treyterously hath ymagined, compassed, purposid, fore-
thought, done, and commytted divers high, grete, heynous,
and horrible treasons ayenst your most roiale persone, youre
corones of your raumes of England and Fraunce, your duchiee
of Guyan and Normandie, and youre holde enheritaunce of
your countee of Anjoye and Mayne, the estate and dignite of the
same, and the universall wele and prosperite of all your trewe
subgettes of raumes, [duchies] and counte in maner and in
forme ensewyng.

First, the seid Duke the xx[ti] day of Juy[ll] the xxv. yere[1] of
youre blissid regne, in youre citee of London, in the parich of
Sepulcr, in the ward of Faringdon infra, ymagynyng and
purposing falsly and treyterously to distroy your moste roiall
persone, and this your seid realme, thenne and ther trayterously excited, councelled, provoked, and comforted the Erle
of Donas[2] [bastard][3] of Orliaunce, Bertrande, Lord Pressigny,
Maister William Cusinet,[4] enemys to you Soverayne Lord,
and other your enemies, subgettes and ambassiators to Charles,[5]
calling hem selfe king of Fraunce, your grettys adversarie and
enemey, to meve, councell, ster, and provoke the same Charles
to come in to this your realme, to leve, reise, and make open
werr ayenst you, Soverayne Lord, and alle this your reaume
with a grete puissaunce and arme to distroy your most roiall
persone, and your trewe subgettes of the same realme, to the
entente to make John, sone of the same Duke, [King] of this
your seid realme, and to depose you of your heigh regalie
therof; the same Duke of Suffolk havyng thenne of your
graunte the ward and mariage of Margarete, doughter and
heire to John, the late Duke of Somerset, purposing here to

Paston MSS., endorsed 'Coumpleyntys ayens the Dewke of Suffolk.' Another copy
will be found in the *Rolls of Parliament*, v. 177. The day of the Duke's impeachment was the 7th February 1450. [1] A.D. 1447.
[2] John, Count of Dunois, one of the most renowned warriors of the times. He
was a grandson of Charles V. of France, a natural son of Louis, Duke of Orleans, and
half-brother of Charles, Duke of Orleans, who was prisoner in England.
[3] Blank in Fenn. [4] Cousinot. [5] Charles VII.

121

1450 marey to heis said sonne, presuming and pretendyng her to be
FEB. 7 nexte enheritable to the Corone of this your realme, for lak
of issue of you Soverayn Lord, in accomplishement of heis
seid traytours purpose and entent, wheroppon the same Duke
of Suffolk, sith the tyme of heis areste, hath do the seid
Margarete to be maried to heis said sonne.

Item, the seid Duke of Suffolk being most trostid with
you, and prevyest of your councell of fullong tyme, prepensing
that your seid grete enemeye and adversarie Charles schuld
conquerr and gete be power and myght your seid realme of
Fraunce, duchies, and countee, the xx[ti] day of January the
xvij. yer[1] of your regne, at Westminster, in the shir of
Middlesex, and divers othir tymes and places within your
seid realme of Engeland, falsly, trayterously, by sotel menes
and ymaginacyons, for grete corrupcion of good, taking of
money, and other excessyf promises to him made by Charles,
Duke of Orliaunce,[2] your enemye, councelled and stered of
hym selfe only, your heighnesse to enlarge and deliver out of
prison the same Duke of Orliaunce, enemye to you Soveren
Lord, and to the most victorious noble prince of blyssid
memory, the king youre fadir, whom God assoile! takyn be
hem prisonere, to th'entent that the seid Charles, calling hym
self king of Fraunce, schuld recover, gete, and have be false
conqueste, and other desayvabile menes ayenst you, your
heirz and successors, your seid realme of Fraunce, duches
and counte, be the wyle, subtill councell, might, and ayde of
the seid Duke of Orliaunce.

Notwithstanding that be the late wylle and ordinaunce of
your seid fadir, for divers thingis moveyng his grete wysdome,
contrary ther of was avysed and declared, by wiche councell
and stering only of the seid Duke of Suffolk the seid Duke of
Orliaunce was soverd [suffered] at his liberte to departe of this
youre realme to the partee of Fraunce.

Afore wich departer the first day of May the seid xvij.
yerr[1] of your regne, at London, in the parich of Sent Martyne,
in the ward of Farindon infra, the same Duke of Suffolk,
trayterously adherent to the seid Charles, calling hym selfe

[1] A.D. 1439. [2] Charles, Duke of Orleans.—See p. 46, Note 3.

122

kyng of Fraunce, then and ther falsly and trayterously coun- 1450
seiled, coumforted, stered, and provoked the seid Duke of FEB. 7
Orlyaunce to excite and moeve the same Charles, calling hym
selfe kyng of Fraunce, your grete enemeye and adversarie,
to make and reyse open werr ayenst you in your seid realme
of Fraunce and duchie of Normandy, to conquer, and to
opteyn falsly be force, myght, and other menes ayenst you,
your heiriz and successors, your seid realme of Fraunce and
duche of Normandy, Uppon wich adherence, councell, and
counfort of the seid Duke of Suffolk, the seid Charles calling
hym selfe kyng, hath made open werr a yenst you in your
seid realme of Fraunce, and hath it attrochid unto hym,
and the most party of your duchie of Normandy, and takyn
prisonyrs the ful nobile Lordys and coragyouse Knytys, the
Erle of Schrouesbery[1] and the Lord Faconberge,[2] with many
othir nobles and people of your trewe leiges, to ther likly
fynall ondoing, your gretest disheritaunce, and oure grete
lamentable losse that ever comen a fore this to you, or ony of
your ful noble progenitors, or to your trewe subgettes.

Item, wher the seid Duke of Suffolk late was on of your
ambassitours with othir to youre seid adversarie Charles, calling
hem self kyng of Fraunce, he, above heis instruccion and
power to hym be you committyng, promised to Reyner,[3] King
of Cesile, and Charles Daungers,[4] heis brothir, your grete
enemeys, the deliveraunce of Maunce and Mayne, without
the assent andvyse or knowyng of other your seid ambassitours with him thenne accompanyd; and theroppon after
heis comyng in to this realme from the same ambassiate, in
performing of heis seid promyse, he falsly and trayterously,
for grette rewardes and lucre of good to hym yeven by your
enemes, caused the said Reyner and Charles Daungers to have
deliveraunce of Maunce and Mayne aforeseid, to your over
grete disheritaunce and loss irreparable, enforsing and en-

[1] John Talbot, first Earl of Shrewsbury, the great hero of the French wars, slain
at Castillon in 1453.
[2] William Nevill, Lord Fauconberg.
[3] René, Duke of Anjou, father of Queen Margaret.
[4] Charles of Anjou, Count of Maine.

123

1450
FEB. 7
rychyng of your seid enemes, and grettest mene of the losse of your seid duche of Normandye ; and so was the seid Duke of Suffolk falsly and trayterously adherent, aidant, and confortant to your grete enemeys and adversaries.

Item, the seid Duke of Suffolk being reteyned with you in your wages of werr in your seid realme of Fraunche and duchie of Normandye, and therby strostid be you and alle your councellers to knowe the privite of your councell ther, and the purviaunce of your armes, the defence and keping of your townes, forteresses, and places, sieges, purveaunce, and ordinaunce of werr in the same parties for you to be mad, knowyng all [such] private, and being adherent to your seid grete enemeye, calling hem self kyng of Fraunce, hath eften and many divers tymes falsly and trayterously discoverd and opennd to hym, and to heis capytaynes and conductors of heis werr, your enemes, the privite, ordinaunce, and provision of your seid councell, purveaunces of armes, defence keping, townes, forteresses, places, syeges, and ordinaunce, werby your grete adversarie and enemeys have geton and takyn, be the menes of this is treason and falshode, ful many lordchepes, townnes, casteles, fortesses, and places within your seid realme of Fraunce and duchie of Normandie, and letted your capitaynes of your werres to conquer, keppe, and acheve your rithfull enheritaunce ther.

Item, the seid Duke of Suffolk beyng of your grete Privey Councell, and with you best trostid, knowyng the secrenesse therof and of this your realme, the xvj. day of Juyll xxv[ti] yerr[1] of your regne, at London, in the parich of Sent Laureaunce Pulteney, in the ward of Sandewyke [Candewyke] Stretke, and at othir divers tymes and places, falsly and trayterously beyng adherent and aidant to the seid Charles, calling hem selfe king of Fraunce, your grete enemeys, the seid xvj. day, and in the parich of Sent Laurence aforeseid, openned, declarid, and discovered to the seid Erle of Danas, Bastard of Orlyaunce, Bertrand, Lord Presigni, Maister William Cosinet, your enemeys, subgettes, ambassiatours and conncellours to the seid Charles, calling hem self king of

---

[1] A.D. 1447.

124

1450
FEB. 7
Fraunce, the privitees of your councell, aswell of this your realme for the comyn wele of the same, as for the governauns and ordinaunce for the conquest, conservacion, saufgard, tuycyon of your seid realme of Fraunche and duchie of Normandy ; [whereby the great part of your said realm of France and duchy of Normandy][1] at that tyme being in your in handys, as [should be, is] the seid Charles, calling hem selfe kyng of Fraunce, and [his] armes goton and takyn out of your handes.

Item, suth the matier first moeved of the convencyon of trewes and pees by twenne you and your seid grette enemeye Charlys, callyng hem selfe kyng of Fraunche, wheroppon by grete diberacyon ye, by the advyse of your Councell, have send many solempne ambassatours to the same Charles for the god of pees to be hadde be twyn you and this your realme, and your subjettes in your realme of Fraunche, duchie of Normandye, and othir places under your obeysauns, and the same Charles and heis subgettes, the seid Duke of Suffolk being next and grettest of your Councell, havyng knowlach of the power and auctorite comytted to alle your ambassiatours send in this be half, hath deseyvably and trayterously by heis lettres and messages discovered and opened to your seid grete enemeye Charlys, calling hym self kyng of Fraunce, alle ynstruccions and informaciouns yeven to your seid ambassatours afore their comyng in to Fraunce, werby the effectuale concord and trewes that schuld have folowed of suche ambassiat by tywnne both the seid realmes and subgettes, have take non effectualle conclusyon, but by his fals, fraudelent, traiterous werkes, dedes, and deceyvable yma gynacyons, your grete enheritaunce, seygnyouries, lordshippis, townes, castell, forteresses, and possessions in your seid realme of Fraunche and duchie of Normandye, by cause of heis false messages, sendyngs, and wrytyngys have be takyn by reft, and gotten fro you be your seid enemeys.

In proof of the wich treson the seid Duke of Suffolk, sitting in your Councell in the Stere Chambre, in your pales

---

[1] These words are omitted in Fenn, and are supplied from the *Rolls of Parliament*.

125

1450
FEB. 7
of Westminster, seid and declarid openly be for the Lordis of your Councell ther being, that he had his place in the Councell hows of the French kyng as he had ther, and was ther as wel strostid as he was here, and couth remeve from the seid French kynge the prevyest man of heis Councell yf he wold.

Item, whan in this your roialme ful oftyn tymes provicyon hath be mad for divers armes to be sent in to your seid realme of Fraunche, duches of Normandy and Gyand, the seid Duke of Suffolk, by the instaunce and meenes mad to hym be your seid enemeys and adversareys for grette outeragyous yeftes and rewardes of them takyn, trayterously hath restrayned, and utterly lettyd the passage of such armees in favour and supporte of your seid enemeys.

Item, the seid Duke of Suffolk, as your ambassatours by twene you and Charles, callyng hym self kyng of Fraunche, in fortefyeng of hem and enchresing of his myght, hath not comprised in trewes, taken in your party the Kyng of Arregon,[1] your old allye and frend, nother the Duke of Breten,[2] but sufferd and causid the seid Duke of Bretayne to be compremysid of the party of the seid Charles as his subget, frende, and allye, wherby ye have ben estraunged from the god loffe and assistence of the seid King of Arregon, and therby and be othir on trewe and falce conjectours of the seid Duke of Suffolk, the seid Duke of Breteyn is become your enemeye ; and Gyles[3] of Breten, his brothir, the wiche is, and of long tyme hath ben, your trewe and welvylled man and servaunt, put in gret dures of pricon, and likely to be potte to the dethe or distroid for his trewe feith and welle that he hath to you.

And of alle tresons and offensys in alle theis seid arteculys specyfied and conteynyd, we your seid Comens accuse and empeche the seid William de la Pole, Duke of Suffolk, and pray that this be enacte in this your High Courte of Parlement, and theroppon to procede in this your High Courte of Parlement, as the mater and caas aforeseid requireth for the surete

---

[1] Alfonso v., King of Arragon. [2] Francis I., Duke of Brittany.
[3] Giles of Brittany, the duke's brother, who was murdered in April 1450, after having been kept four years in prison by the duke.

126

1450
FEB. 7
and welfar of your most roiale person, and savacyon of this your realme, &c.

102

JOHN PASTON'S PETITION[1]

To the Kyng, oure Soverayn Lord, and to the right wyse and discrete Lordis, assemblyd in this present Parlement.

1450
BESECHITH mekly your homble liege man, John Paston, that where he, and oder enfeffed to his use, have be pecybily poscessyd of the maner of Gresham, within the counte of Norffolk, xx. yere and more, til the xvij. day of Februarij, the yere of your nobill regne xxvi.,[2] that Robert Hungerford, Knyght, the Lord Molyns, entred in to the seyd maner ; and how be it that the seyd John Paston, after the seid entre, sued to the seid Lord Molyns and his councell, in the most louly maner that he cowde, dayly fro tyme of the seid entre on to the fest of Mihelmes than next folwyng, duryng which tyme divers communicasyons were had betwix the councell of the seid Lord and the councell of your besecher. And for asmych as in the seid communicasyons no titill of right at any tyme was shewed for the seid Lord but that was fully and clerly answeryd, so that the seid Lords councell remitted your seid besecher to sewe to the seid Lord for his finall and rightfull answer. And after sute mad to the seid Lord be your seid besecher, as well at Salysbery as in other places to his gret coust, and non answer had but delays, which causyd your seid besecher the vj. day of Octobre last past to inhabite hym in a mansion with in the seid town, kepyng stille there his poscession, on tille the xxviij. day of Januarij last past, the seid Lord sent to the seid mansion a riotous peple, to the nombre of a

---

[1] [Add. Charter 17,240, B.M.] The date of this petition must be during the sitting of Parliament, in the beginning of the year 1450. The first expulsion of John Paston from Gresham is here clearly dated in February 1448. The 'October last' in which he re-entered might, so far as appears in this petition, have been in the same year, but the letters referring to this dispute in 1449 compel us to put it a twelvemonth later. [2] A.D. 1448.

127

1450 thowsand persones, with blanket bendes[1] of a sute as riseres ageyn your pees, arrayd in maner of werre, with curesse, brigaunders, jakks, salettes, gleyfes, bowes, arows, pavyse,[2] gonnes, pannys with fier and teynes brennyng therein, long cromes[3] to drawe doun howsis, ladders, pikoys, with which thei myned down the walles, and long trees with which thei broke up yates and dores, and so came in to the seid mansion, the wiff of your besecher at that tyme beyng ther in, and xij. persones with her ; the which persones thei dreve oute of the seide mansion, and myned down the walle of the chambre wher in the wiff of your seid besecher was, and bare here oute at the yates, and cutte a sondre the postes of the howses and lete them falle, and broke up all the chambres and coferes within the seid mansion, and rifelyd, and in maner of robery bare awey all the stuffe, aray, and money that your seyd besecher and his servauntes had ther, on to the valew of ccli. [£200], and part therof sold, and part ther of yaffe, and the remenaunt thei departed among them, to the grete and outrageous hurt of your seid besecher, sayng openly, that if thei myght have found ther yowr seid besecher and on John Damme,[4] which is of councell with hym, and divers oder of the servauntes of your seid besecher, thei shuld have died. And yet divers of the seid mysdoeres and ryotous peple onknowyn, contrary to your lawes, dayly kepe the seid maner with force, and lyne [i.e. lien, lie] in wayte of divers of the frendis, tenauntes, and servauntes of your seid besecher, and grevously vexe and trobill hem in divers wise, and seke hem in her howsis, ransakyng and serchyng her shevys and strawe in her bernes and other places with bore speris, swerdis, and gesernys,[5] as it semyth, to sle hem if thei myght have found hem ; and summe have bete and left for ded, so that thei, for doute of here lyves, dare not go home to here houses, ner occupy here husbondry, to the gret hurte, fere, and drede, aswele of your seid besechere as of his seid frendis, tenauntes, and servauntes.

1 Bands of white woollen cloth ? 2 Pavises were large shields.
3 Crome is a Norfolk word, signifying a staff with a crook at the end of it.
4 This person was returned to Parliament for Norwich in October 1450.
5 Battle-axes.

And also, thei compelle pore tenauntes of the seid maner, now 1450 within ther daunger, ageyn ther wille, to take feyned pleyntes in the courtes of the hundred ther ageyn the seid frendis, tenauntes, and servauntes of your seid besecher, whiche dare not apere to answere for fere of bodily harme, ne can gete no copiis of the seid pleyntes to remedi them be the lawe, because he that kepyth the seid courtis is of covyn with the seid misdoers, and was on of the seid ryseres, which be coloure of the seid pleyntes grevously amercy the seid frendes, tenauntes, and servauntes of your seid besecher, to the[ir] outrageous and importabille hurte.

Please it your hynesse, consideryng that if this gret insurreccyon, ryottis, and wrongis, and dayly continuans ther of so heynosly don a geyn your crowne, dignite and peas, shuld not be your hye myght be duly punysshed, it shall gefe grett boldnesse to them, and alle other mysdoers to make congregacyons and conventicles riottously, on abille to be seysed, to the subversyon and finall distruccyon of your liege peple and lawes : And also, how that your seid besecher is not abille to sue the commone lawe in redressyng of this heynos wrong, for the gret myght and alyaunce of the seid Lord : And also, that your seid besecher canne have non accyon be your lawe ageyn the seid riotous peple for the godis and catellis be hem so riottously and wrongfully take and bore awey, because the seid peple be onknowe, aswelle here names as here persones, on to hym ;—To purvey, be the avyse of the Lordis spirituall and temporall assembled in this present Parlement, that your seid besechere may be restoryd to the seid godis and catellis thus riottously take away ; and that the seid Lord Molyns have suche comaundment that your seid besecher be not thus with force, in maner of werre, hold oute of his seide maner, contrary to alle your statutes mad ageyn suych forcibille entrees and holdyngs ; and that the seid Lord Molyns and his servauntes be sette in suche a rewle, that your seid besechere, his frendis, tenauntes, and servauntes, may be sure and saffe from hurt of here persones, and pesibly ocupy here londs and tenements under your lawes with oute oppressyoun or onrightfull vexasioun of any of hem ; and that the seid riseres and causeres

1450 therof may be punysshed, that other may eschewe to make any suche rysyng in this your lond of peas in tyme comyng. And he shalle pray to God for yowe.

103

MARGARET PASTON TO JOHN PASTON[1]

To my rytz wurchipful mayster, Jon Paston, be this delyvered in hast.

FEB. 21 RYT wurchipful hosband, I recommawnd me to zu, desyryng hertyly to heryn of zour wele fare, preying zu to weten that I commawndyd Herry Goneld to gon to Gunnore to have copys of the pleyntes in the hundrede, and Gunnore was not at home ; but the seyd Herry spake with his clerk, and he told hym pleynly he wost wele his mayster wuld not late hym have no copys, thow he wor at home, tyl the nexst hundred ; qher for I send zou that byl that ws wownd abowt the relefys. Custans, Mak, and Kentyng wold adysavowyd here swtes rytz fayn the last hundred, as I herd sayn of rytz thryfty men ; but the Lord Moleynys men thrett hem that bothe they xuld ben betyn and lesen here hows and lond and alle here goods, but if [unless] they wold avow it ; and after that Osborn was gon, Hasard[2] intretyd Kentyng and Mak to avow the swtys after that they hadde disavowyd itt, and zave hem mony to zef to the clerkes to entren azen the pleyntes. But if[3] ze seke a remedy in hast for to remeve itt, I soppose they wyl distreyn for the mersymentes er the nexst hundred.

As for Mak, he gate respyt that he xuld not sew tyl the nexst hundred. As for Herry Goneld, he was dystreynyd zysterday for rent and ferm, and he must pay it to morue, xxijs., or elles lesyn his dystresse. They gadder mony fast

1 [From Paston MSS., B.M.] From an allusion in the latter part of this letter, it is evident that it was written in 1450, after Margaret had been driven out of Gresham, as mentioned in John Paston's petition, No. 102 preceding.
2 William Hasard.—See Letter No. 88. 3 But if, i.e. unless.

of all the tenawntes. All the tenawntes ben chargyd to pay al 1450 her rent and ferm be Fastyngong Sonday.[1] It ys told me FEB. 21 that the Lord Moleynys xuld kepe his Fastyngong att Jon Wynters plase.

The seid Lordes men haddyn a letter on Thursday last past ; qhat tydyngs they hadde I wote nott ; but on the nexst moruenyng be tymys Thomas Bampton, a man of the Lord Moleynys, rod with a letter to his lord, and they that ben at Gressam waytyn after an answer of the letter in hast. Barow, and Hegon, and all the Lord Moleynys men that wer at Gressam qhan ze departyd hens bene there styll, save Bampton, and in his stede is kom another ; and I here sey thei xul abyd here styll tyl her lord kom . . . .[2] to Barow as ze komawndyd me to weten quhatt the cawse was that thei thrett men . . . .[2] Goneld and other of zour servawnts and wele willers to zow, the qheche wer namyd to hym that were thrett . . . . .[2] [s]wore pleynly that they were never thrett ; but I know veryly the contrary, for of his owyn felaschep lay[d] in awayt sondery dayis and nytis abowt Gunnelds, Purrys, and Bekks plasis, and som of them zedyn in to Bekks and Purrys [ho]usys, bothen in the hallys and the bernys, and askyd qher they were, and thei were answeryd that they were owth ; and thei seydyn azen that they xuld meten with hem another tyme. And be dyvers other thyngs I know, if thei mytz aben kawt, other [either] they xuld aben slayn or sor hurt.

I sent Kateryn on this forseyd masage, for I kowd geten no man to do it, and sent with her Jamys Halman and Herry Holt ; and sche desyryd of Barow to have an answer of her masage, and if these forseyd men mytz levyn in pese for hem, and seyd ther xuld elles ben purveyd other remedy for hem. And he made her grett chere, and hem that wer ther with her, and seyd that he desyryd for to spekyn with me, if it xuld ben non displesans to me ; and Kateryn seyd to hym that sche supposyd that I desyryd not to spoken with hym. And he seyd he xuld com forby this plase on huntyng after non, and

1 Fastyngong was a popular name for Shrovetide. Fastingong Sunday I believe to have been the Sunday after Shrove Tuesday, which would be the 22nd of February in 1450. 2 Mutilated.

1450
FEB. 21

ther xuld no mor com with hym but Hegon and on of his owyn men; and than he wold bryng seche an answere as xuld plese me. And after none they come hydder, and sent in to me to weten if thei mytz speken with me, and praying that thei mytz speken with me, and they abedyn styl with owtz the zatys; and I kam owth to hem, and spak with hem with owt, and prayid hem that thei wold hold me exkusyd that I browth hem not in to the plase. I seyd in as meche as thei wer nott wele wyllyng to the gode man of the plase, I wold not take it up on me to bryng hem in to the jantylwoman. They seyd I dede the best, and than we welk forthe, and desyryd an answer of hem for that I hadde sent to hem for. Thei sayd to me thei had browtz me seche an answer as thei hopyd xuld plese me, and told me how thei had comownd with all her felaschep of soche materis as I had sent to hem fore, and that thei durst under take that ther xud no man ben hurt of hem thatt wer rehersyd, ner no man that longeth to zu, nother for hem ner non of her felaschep, and that they answeryd me be her trowthis. Never lese I trest not to her promese, in as meche as I fend hem ontrew in other thyngs.

I conseyvyd wele be hem that they wer wery of that thei haden don. Barow swor to me be his trowth that he had lever than xls., and xl. tha: his lord had not comawndyd hym to com to Gressam; and he seyd he was rytz sory hidderward, in as meche as he had knowleche of zw before, he was rytz sory of that that was don. I seyd to hym that he xuld have compascion on zu and other that wer disseysyd of her lyvelode, in as meche as he had ben dissesyd hym self; and he seyd he was so, and told me that he had sewyd to my Lord of Suffolk dyvers tymys, and wold don tyl he may gete his gode azen. I seyd to hym that ze had sewyd to my Lord Moleynys dyvers tymys for the maner of Gressam syth ze wer dissesyd, and ze cowd never gete no resonabyl answer of hym; and ther fore ze entred azen, as ye hopid that was for the best. And he seyd he xuld never blame my Lord of Suffolk for the entre in his lyvelode, for he seyd my seyd lord was sett ther up on be the informacion of a fals schrew; and I seyd to hym in lyke wyse is the matier be twyx the Lord

132

1450
FEB. 21

Moleynys and zu. I told hym I wost wele he sett never ther upon be no tytyl of rytz that he hadde to the maner of Gressam, but only be the informacion of a fals schrew.[1] I rehersyd no name, but me thowt be hem that thei wost ho I ment. Meche other langage we hadde, qhyche xuld taken long leysyr in wrytyng. I rehersyd to hem that it xuld abe seyd thatt I xuld not longe dwell so ner hem as I dewe and they for swer it, as thei do other thyngs more that it was never seyd, and meche thyngs that I know veryly was seyd.

I here seyn that ze and Jon of Damme ben sore thrett alway, and seyn thow ze ben at London, ze xul ben met with ther as wele as thow ze were her; and ther for I pray zu hertyly be ware how ze walk ther, and have a gode felaschep with zu qhan ze xul walk owt. The Lord Moleynys hathe a cumpany of brothell with hym that rekk not qhat they don, and seche ar most for to drede. Thei that ben at Gressam seyn that they have not don so moche hurte to zu as thei were commawndyd to don. Rabert Lauerawns is wele amendyd, and I hope xall recure. He seyth pleynly he wyl compleyn of his hurt, and I soppose Bek wyl compleyn also, as he hath cause. Bek and Purry dare not abyd att hom tyl thei here other tydyngs. I wold not Jon of Damme xuld com hom tyl the cuntre be storyd otherwyse than it is. I pray Godde grawnt that it mot sone ben otherwyse than it is. I pray zu hertyly that ze wil send me word how ze don, and how ze spede in zour materis, for be my trowth I kan not ben wel att ese in my hert, ner not xal ben tyl I here tydynges how ze don. The most part of zour stuff that was at Gressam is sold, and zovyn away. Barow and his felaw spak to me in the most pleasawnt wyse, and me semyth be hem thei wold fayn plese me. Thei seyd thei wold do me servyse and plesans, if it lay in her powres to don owth for me, save only in that that longeth to her lordes rytz. I seyd to hem, as for seche servys as they had do to zw and to me, I desyr no mor that thei xuld do nother to zw ner to me. Thei seyd I myt an had of them att Gressham qhat I hadde desyryd of hem, and

[1] John Heydon, Esq. of Baconsthorpe, appears to have been the person referred to.—*See* No. 135 following.

133

THE PASTON LETTERS

1450
FEB. 21

had as moche as I desyryd. I seyd, nay; if I mytz an had my desyr, I xuld nother a departid owth of the place, ner from the stuff that was ther in. Thei seyd, as for the stuff it was but esy. I seyd ze wold not a zoven the stuff that was in the place qhan thei com in, not for Cli. Thei seyd the stuff that thei sey [*saw*] ther was skars worth xxli. As for zour moder and myn, sche faryth wel, blissid be God, and she had no tydynges but gode zett, blissid be God. The blissyd Trynyte have zou in his kepyng, and send zou hele, and gode spede in al your maters. Wretyn at Sustede,[1] on the Satyrday next after Seynt Valentynys day.

Here dare no man seyn a gode wurd for zu in this cuntre, Godde amend it.

Yowres,   M. P.

104

ABSTRACT[2]

MARCH 7

The beginning of this letter, which is more than half lost by mutilation, speaks of 'a bill in the Parliament of the extortions done [to me]' from the 17th year [of Henry vi.] hitherto. The rest seems to be partly memoranda of things to be entered in this 'bill,' viz. of sheep distrained at Drayton, of a matter of trespass between Lady Bardolf and Fastolf, of 'Chevers mater in Blyclyng,' of an unpaid annuity at Hiklyng, of decays at Tichewell, etc. They are to learn from Nich. Bokkyng, to whom the £100 for Busshop was paid. Thinks two men should occupy Castre and Wynterton which Broun holds alone. It is too much for one to occupy well; 'and in the same wise at Heylesden and Drayton.' Let me know what Lampet has done in my matter, and if you find him friendly. Both my ships have arrived in safety, thank God.

London, 7 March 28 Henry vi.   *Signed.*

[1] Sustead was John Damme's place (*see* Blomefield, viii. 168). It is in the immediate neighbourhood of Gresham.
[2] [Ms. Phillipps, 9735, No. 225.]

134

HENRY VI

105

AGNES PASTON TO JOHN PASTON[1]

*To John Paston, dwellyn in the Inder In of the Tempyll, att
London, be thys letter delyverd in hast.*

SON, I grete yow, and send yow Godds blyssyng, and myn; and as for my doughtyr your wyfe, che faryt well, blyssyd be God, as a woman in hyr plyte may do, and all your sonys and doughtrys.

1450
MARCH 11

And for as meche as ye will send me no tydyngs, I send yow seche as ben in thys contre. Rychard Lynsted cam thys day fro Paston, and letyt me wete that on Saturday last past Dravale, halfe brother to Waryn Harman, was takyn with enemyis, walkyn be the se syde, and have hym forthe with hem; and they tokyn ij. pylgremys, a man and a woman, and they robbyd the woman, and lete hyr gon, and ledde the man to the see, and whan they knew he was a pylgreme, they geffe hym monei, and sett hym ageyn on the lond. And they have thys weke takyn iiij. vesselys of [*i.e.* off] Wyntyrton; and Happysborough and Ecles men ben sore aferd for takyn of mo [*i.e.* more (?)], for ther ben x. grete vesselys of the enemyis; God yeue grace that the see may be better kepte than it is now, or ellys it chall ben a perlyous dwellyng be the se cost.

I pray yow grete well your brethyrne, and sey hem that I send hem Goddis blyssyn and myn; and sey William that if Jenett Lauton be not payd for the krymson cort wheche Alson Crane wrote to hyr for in hyr owyn name, that than he pay hyr, and see Alson Cranys name strekyn owt of hyr boke, for che seithe che wyll aske no man the money butt Alson Crane. And I pray yow that ye wyll remembr the letter that I sent yow last, and God be with yow.

Wretyn att Norwyche, the Wedenesday next before Sent Gregory.   AUGNES PASTON.

[1] [From Fenn, iii. 304.] Fenn assigns this letter to the year 1458, but not very confidently. The similarity of its contents, in part, to those of the letter immediately following, appears to me to render the year 1450 the more probable date.

135

106

MARGARET PASTON TO JOHN PASTON[1]

To my rytz worchipful maystyr, Jon Paston, be this delyveryd in hast.

1450 MARCH 12 RYTZ worchipful hosbond, I recomawnd me to yow, desyring hertyly to her of zour wellfar, &c.[2] . . . . Wyllyam Rutt, the whiche is with Sir Jon Hevenyngham, kom hom from London zesterday, and he seyd pleynly to his master, and to many other folks, that the Duke of Suffolk is pardonyd, and hath his men azen waytyng up on hym, and is rytz wel at ese and mery, and is in the Kyngs gode grase, and in the gode conseyt of all the Lords, as well as ever he was.

Ther ben many enemys azens Yermowth and Crowmer, and have don moche harm, and taken many Englysch men, and put hem in grett distresse, and grettely rawnsommyd hem ; and the seyd enmys been so bold that they kom up to the lond, and pleyn hem on Caster Sonds, and in other plases, as homely as they were Englysch men. Folks ben rytz sore afred that they wel don moche harm this somer, but if [*i.e.* unless] ther be made rytz grett purvyans azens hem.

Other tydyngs know I non at this tym. The blysseful Trinyte have zow in his kepyng.

Wryten at Norwyche, on Seynt Gregorys day.

Yowrs,   M. P.

[1] [From Fenn, i. 28.] The reference to the Duke of Suffolk's pardon proves this letter to have been written in the year 1450.
[2] Here Fenn has omitted a passage, relating, as he says, to some common business about Paston's farms and tenants.

107

ABSTRACT[1]

SIR JO. FASTOLF TO SIR THOS. HOWYS, PARSON OF CASTLCOMBE, WILL. COKE, AND WATKIN SHYPDAM.

Bids 'Sir Parson' send in all haste 'the utmost knowledge of all grievances' done to him by John Heydon this thirteen years. You have sent me the costs of the pleas, but not declared particularly how often I have been wrongfully distrained by the enforcing of the said Heydon. 'I took never plea in the matter because the world was alway set after his rule, and as I would have engrossed up [*upon*] my bill.'   **1450 APRIL 16**

London, 16 April 28 Henry VI.

Search the accounts of Drayton Heylesdon, &c., these thirteen years.

108

LORD SCALES TO JOHN PASTON[2]

To my right trusty and right enterly welbeloved frend, John Paston, Squier.

RIGHT t[r]usty and enterly welbeloved frend, I grete you welle, and wyll ze wite that a man of Osberd Monford hath declared me how the said Osberd is infourmed that Danyelle shuld be pourposed to enter in the place of Braystone. And as fer as I can undirstande, Danyelle is come in to this cuntre, for none other cause but for to have suche as the Kyng hath gifen hym in Rysyng, which lieth not in me ner in none of the Kynges subgectes to go ageyns hise graunte and plesaunce. And in cas the said Danyelle wold enter upon the said Osberd otherwise than lawe wold, seyng the said Osberd is my tenaunt and homager, it is my part to   **APRIL 22**

[1] [From a modern copy by Blomefield on the fly-leaf of a Letter addressed to him. Headed, 'Gave this original letter of Sir John's to Sir Andrew Fountain.'—MS. Phillipps, 9735, No. 229.]
[2] [Douce MSS. 393, f. 100.] It appears by a paper, which will be found further on (No. 119), that Daniel entered the manor of Braydeston or Brayston during the Parliament which was held at Leicester in the spring of 1450. This letter must have been written at that time.

1450 APRIL 22 holde with hym rather than with Danyelle in hise right, which I wylle do to my pouer. And as zet I can not apperceyve that Danyelle wylle labore in any maters in this cuntre ; and if he wylle be of good governance, I am wel paied. And in cas that he wold do wrong to the lesse gentilman in the chirre, it shal not lye in hise pouer be the grace of God. He letethe me wite that he wylle be wel governed in tyme commyng.

Right trusty and enterly wel beloved frend, I pray God have you in hise governance. Writen at Midelton, the xxij. day of Aprille.

SCALES.

109

LORD SCALES TO JOHN PASTON[1]

To my right trusty and welbeloved frende, John Paston, Squier.

Year uncertain Right trusty and welbeloved frend, I grete you hertly wel, and wul ye wite that Wotton is ever creyng and callyng upon me to write un to you for hise londe ; wherfore at the reverence of Good, consideryng the symplenesse of hem all, I pray you that ye put hem at a certen, and lete hem all that they aught to have of right, for thaire creyng cause men to thinke ye do hem grete wrong, which I wote wel ye wold be sory to do.

Oure Lord have you in hise governance. Writen at Midelton, the xvj. day of October.

Youre frende,   SCALES.

110

LORD SCALES TO JOHN PASTON[2]

To my right trusty and enterly welbeloved frend, John Paston, Squier.

Year uncertain Right trusty and enterly welbeloved frend, I grete you welle ; and for as mych as there is vareaunce betwene William Wotton and hise moder and the fermour there, wherfore I pray you that ze wyll [fynde][3] a weye accordyng to

[1] [From Fenn, iii. 364.] This and the six letters following, all but one of which are, like the last, written by Lord Scales to John Paston, are placed here merely for convenience, the years in which they were written being quite uncertain, though probably not very far apart. The one letter among them of which Lord Scales is not the writer, is inserted in abstract on account of its bearing on that which immediately precedes it.
[2] [Douce MS. 393, f. 99.]   [3] Mutilated.

right for to put hem in rest and pees. For in as mych as they be yo[ur] tenantes, ze aught to have the reule of them before any other, praying you to do youre part to put hem oute of trouble.   **Year uncertain**

I pray God have you in hise governance. Writen at Midelton, the xiij. day of Aprille.

Youre frend,   THE LORD SCALES.

111

LORD SCALES TO JOHN PASTON[1]

To my ryght trusti and wel beloved frend, John Paston, Sqyer.

Right trusty and wel beloved frend, I comande me to you, and for certain maters that I have for to do, for the which ma[ters I] sende unto you a squier of myne called Elyngham ; praying you to gefe hym faythful credence of that he shall declare you on myne behalfe as for this tyme. God have you in Hise keping. Writene at Midelton, the xviij. day of Julle.—Yowre frend,   **Year uncertain**

SCALES.

112

LORD SCALES TO JOHN PASTON[2]

To [my] right trusty and welbeloved frend, John Paston, Squier.

Right trusty and welbeloved frend, I grete you welle ; and as touchyng the mater that Elyngham and ze comuned to giders of the last tyme he was with you, I pray you that ze wylle assigne such a day as yol liketh best, so that it be with inne this viij. dayes, and sende me worde what day ze wylle be here be the bringer herof.   **Year uncertain**

I pray God have you in governance. Writen at Midelton, the iij. day of August.

Youre frend,   SCALES.

[1] [MS. in Pembroke College, Cambridge.] This letter evidently was written in the same year as the next, but there is no evidence what that year was. Below the signature is a note in a modern hand erroneously identifying the writer with Anthony Woodville, Lord Scales. He was certainly Thomas, Lord Scales, of Henry VI.'s time.   [2] [Douce MS., f. 101.]

113

LORD SCALES TO JOHN PASTON[1]

To my right trusty and welbeloved frend, John Paston, Squier.

Year uncertain

Right trusty and welbeloved frend, I grete you wel ; and for as myche as there is certayn vareaunce betwene Elizabeth Clere and a servaunt of myne, called William Stiwa[r]desson, prayng you feithfully that ze wylle labore and intrete the said Elizabeth to such appointemente as the brynger of this letter shal informe you of, and do your trewe dilligence in this mater, as ze wyll I do for you in any thyng ze may have ado in this cuntre, whiche I will do with al my herte.

Oure Lord have yow in hise keping. Writen at Myddelton, the last day of August.

SCALES.

114

ABSTRACT[2]

ELIZABETH CLERE TO JOHN PASTON.

Year uncertain

Stywardesson came to her on Easter even to church, and made a very humble submission. He at first denied having slandered her, or said that he was beaten, only that he was sore afraid ; but at last acknowledged he had untruly charged her men with coming into his place with force and arms, and that he was beaten, for which his master took an action against her. Called her tenants to bear witness to his recantation. Said she would give him no answer now but by advice of her friends, and his master must leave his maintenance. Promised him an answer on Saturday in Easter week. He told another man that Heidon promised his master it should be put in award by Palm Sunday ; 'for he is double both to him and to me, and so is William Geney and mo of my counsel.' He is willing to make a release. His barn which his men entered to distrain, he says, is frank, and he may give the rent when he pleases. Wishes Paston's advice what answer to make.—Easter Monday.

[1] [Douce MS. 393, f. 102.]   [2] [From Paston MSS., B.M.]

140

115

LORD SCALES TO JOHN PASTON[1]

To my right trusty and wel be loved frend, Jhon Paston, Squier.

Right trusty and wel beloved frend, I grete you wel, thankyng you hertely for the gentilnes and good wylle I have founde in you at alle tymes. And for as myche as I and other stonde feffed in the landes of Thomas Canon, which is in vareaunce betwene you and hym, if ye wylle do so myche as for your part chese ij. lerned menn and the said Canon shal chese other ij., they to juge this mater as they shal seme of right and resoun. And if so be that the said Canon wylle not do so, I wylle not lete you to suye hym after the forme of the Kynges lawe. And if ze thinke it to many lerned men, take ze one, and he another ; and if they may not accorde, ze and I to be umpere, for we stande bothe in like cas. And we shal make a good ende be the grace of oure Lord, which have you in hise governance.

Writen at Midelton, the ix. day of Octobre.

Zowr frend,   SCALES.

Year uncertain

116

LORD SCALES TO JOHN PASTON[2]

To my right trusty and welbeloved frend, John Paston, Squier.

Right trusty and welbeloved frende, I grete you hertly well, praying you that ye wyll sende me a coppie of the awarde that was made be you and my cousyn Sir Miles[3] betwex my cousyn Bryan Stapylton and Elizabeth Clere, and that ze wyll sende me the said awarde be the bringer herof. I pray God have you in governance.

Writen at Midelton, the ix. day of Novembre.

SCALES.

Year uncertain

[1] [Douce MS. 393, f. 103.]   [2] [From Paston MSS., B.M.]
[3] Sir Miles Stapleton.

141

THE PASTON LETTERS

117

THE DUKE OF SUFFOLK TO HIS SON[1]

The copie of a notable Lettre, written by the Duke of Suffolk to his Sonne,[2] giving hym therein very good counseil.[3]

1450 APRIL 30

MY dere and only welbeloved sone, I beseche oure Lord in Heven, the Maker of alle the world, to blesse you, and to sende you ever grace to love hym, and to drede hym ; to the which, as ferre as a fader may charge his child, I both charge you, and prei you to sette alle spirites and wittes to do, and to knowe his holy lawes and comaundments, by the which ye shall with his grete mercy passe alle the grete tempestes and troubles of this wrecched world. And that also, wetyngly, ye do no thyng for love nor drede of any erthely creature that shuld displese hym. And there as any freelte maketh you to falle, be secheth hys mercy soone to calle you to hym agen with repentaunce, satisfaccion, and contricion of youre herte never more in wille to offend hym.

Secondly, next hym, above alle erthely thyng, to be trewe liege man in hert, in wille, in thought, in dede, unto the Kyng oure alder most high and dredde sovereygne Lord, to whom bothe ye and I been so moche bounde to ; chargyng you, as fader can and may, rather to die than to be the contrarye, or to knowe any thyng that were ayenste the welfare or prosperite of his most riall person, but that as ferre as your body and lyf may strecche, ye lyve and die to defende it, and to lete his highnesse have knowlache thereof in alle the haste ye can.

Thirdly, in the same wyse, I charge you, my dere sone, alwey, as ye be bounden by the commaundement of God to do, to love, to worshepe youre lady and moder, and also that ye

[1] [From Fenn, i. 32.] The date of this letter is sufficiently clear from the last words of it.
[2] John de la Pole, who succeeded him as Duke of Suffolk.
[3] This heading looks as if copied by Fenn from an endorsement, which is probably not quite contemporaneous.

142

HENRY VI

obey alwey hyr commaundements, and to beleve hyr councelles and advises in alle youre werks, the which dredeth not, but shall be best and trewest to you. And yef any other body wold stere you to the contrarie, to flee the councell in any wyse, for ye shall fynde it nought and evyll.

1450 APRIL 30

Forthe[rmore],[1] as ferre as fader may and can, I charge you in any wyse to flee the company and councel of proude men, of coveitowse men, and of flateryng men, the more especially and myghtily to withstonde hem, and not to drawe, ne to medle with hem, with all youre myght and power. And to drawe to you and to your comp[any good][1] and vertuowse men, and such as ben of good conversacion, and of trouthe, and be them shal ye never be deseyved, ner repente you off. [Moreover never follow][1] youre owne witte in no wyse, but in alle youre werkes, of suche folks as I write of above, axeth youre advise a[nd counse]l ;[1] and doyng thus, with the mercy of God, ye shall do right well, and lyve in right moche worship, and grete herts rest and ease. And I wyll be to you as good lord and fader as my hert can thynke.

And last of alle, as hertily and as lovyngly as ever fader blessed his child in erthe, I yeve you the blessyng of oure Lord and of me, which of his infynite mercy encrece you in alle vertu and good lyvyng. And that youre blood may by his grace from kynrede to kynrede multeplye in this erthe to hys servise, in such wyse as after the departyng fro this wreched world here, ye and thei may glorefye hym eternally amongs his aungelys in hevyn.

Wreten of myn hand,

The day of my departyng fro this land.[2]

Your trewe and lovyng fader,   SUFFOLK.

[1] These words in brackets were chafed and illegible in the original MS.
[2] According to William Worcester, the Duke embarked on Thursday, the 30th April.

143

118

THE EARL OF OXFORD TO JOHN PASTON [1]

*To owre Ryght trusty and right welbeloved Frend,
Johan Paston, Esquier.*

The Erle of Oxenford.

1450(?)
APRIL 30

RIGHT tristy and welbeloved frend, we grete you right
hertily well. And for asmuche as we be enformed
that on [*one*] Thomas Kecham, a servaunt of owre
right welbeloved brothir, Sir Richard de Veer, knyght, hath to
done with Sir Henry Inglose knyght in a certeyn matier in wich
youre good maisterschep may cause his singuler ease and a vaile
as anenst the said knyght, as Thomas Kecham hath enformed
us ; We pray you hertily that, at the reverence of us and this
oure writyng, ye woll take the labour upon you to speke unto
the said Sir Henry, conceyving a mene and the weye of an
ende to be had be twix thaym of right, causyng the said knyght
to sease of hese malice and wrongful suette as a nenst the said
Thomas. And ferthermore we pray you to see that the said
knyght take no benefeys ne prevayle not as a nenst the Gaoyler
of the Castell of Norwich for the suerte of the said Thomas
Kecham, as we verily trust ye will ; in wich feithfully doyng
we shall kun yow hertily thanke. And right trusty and welbeloved, the Trynitie have yow in Hese kepyng. Wreton at
oure Manour of Wevenhoo, the last day of Aprill.

Below the text of this letter is written in another hand, 'Smalwode
Sparhawk.'

[1] [Add. MS. 34,888, f. 164.] This letter cannot be later than 1451, as Sir Henry
Inglose died in June of that year. The date may be about 1450, like that of some
other letters of the Earl of Oxford.

144

119

ABSTRACT [1]

A paper of memoranda in William Worcester's handwriting, of which the 1450-2
principal contents are as follows :—

A commission of *oyer* and *terminer*, dated 1 August 28 Henry VI.—A session
at Swaffham, on Thursday after the Exaltation of the Holy Cross, 29 Henry VI.
(17 September 1450).—A note of six other sessions :—1. At Norwich before
the Duke of Norfolk, the Earl of Oxford and Yelverton, Tuesday after St.
Mathias' day, 29 Henry VI. (2 March 1451) ; 2. At Norwich, before Oxford
and Yelverton, Monday after St. Martin in Winter, 29 Henry VI. (16 November
1450) ; 3. At Norwich, before Oxford and Yelverton, Wednesday after the
Conception of St. Mary (15 December), continued seven days ; 4. At Lynn,
before Oxford, Scales, and Yelverton, Tuesday after Epiphany (13 January) ;
5. At Norwich, before John Prysot and Yelverton, Thursday in Easter week,
29 Henry VI. (29 April 1451) ; 6. At Walsingham, before Scales and Prysot,
Monday *in crastino clausi Paschæ* (3 May 1451).

'Parliamentum apud Leyseter —— anno xxviij'.—Durante illo Parliamento
intravit T. Daniell manerium de Braydeston.—Will'us, Dux Suff' obiit tertio
die Maii anno xxviij' Regis Henry vi[ti].—Jak Cade, proditor de Kent, fugit de
le Blakheth xxij. die Junii anno xxviij. H. vi., [   ] Julii mense decapitatus
fuit.—Injuria Plumbsted post hoc (?)' — Mundford and Heydon entered
Braysto[ne] on the eve of the Nativity of St. Mary anno 29 (7 September
1450). Thomas Danyell entered Braydeston a second time, 30 Henry vi.

Between Mich. 30 and 31 Henry VI. (1451 and 1452) Norfolk, Oxford,
Scales, and a great number of others were at Norwich holding sessions. The
same year 'John P.' was with John, Earl of Oxford, at Whevenho on the
Nativity of St. Mary (8 September). The same year, before all these things,
Thomas Danyell was married at Framlyngham.

'Testimonium Commissionariorum et cognitio Milonis Stapulton quo ad
impanellationem juratorum.

'Item, testimonium concilii quoad mutationem actionum in indictamentis et
recordum apparet et declaratio Johannis Geney facta Thomæ Gurney.

'Item, testimonium concilii et Thomæ Grene quoad absenciam Johannis
Porter. Et testimonium hominum de Bliclyng. Item, missio pro Johanne
Porter pro pecunia et placito proprio. (Memorandum, quando Porter fuit
juratus, J. Andru fuit extractus de indictamento.)

'Item, testimonium juratorum de non procuratione. Et indictamentum
Johannis Andrew in Suff. causa fugationis ejus.

'Item, antiquum debat' supposit' inter Andrews et Porter erat pro districti-
one capta de Johanne Andrews apud Weston pro debito domini Bardolf ; pro
qua causa idem Johannes Andrews implacitare vellet dictum Johannem Porter
ad terminum (?) nisi pro dicto domino Bardolf ; sic dictus Andrews continuavit

[1] [From Paston MSS., B.M.]

145

1450-2 maliciam suam erga prædictum Johannem Porter, et e contra quod et malicia
Heydon erat causa conspiracionis per ipsum. . . . '

[As this document is a key to the dates of several of the letters during the years
1450 to 1452, we have thought it best to insert it in the beginning of the period to
which it refers, instead of the date at which it may be supposed to have been written.]

120

WILLIAM LOMNER TO JOHN PASTON [1]

To my ryght worchipfull John Paston, at Norwich.

1450
MAY 5

RYGHT worchipfull sir, I recomaunde me to yow, and
am right sory of that I shalle sey, and have soo wesshe
this litel bille with sorwfulle terys, that on ethes ye
shalle reede it.

As on Monday [2] nexte after May day there come tydyngs
to London, that on Thorsday [3] before the Duke of Suffolk
come unto the costes of Kent full nere Dower with his ij.
shepes and a litel spynner ; the qweche spynner he sente with
certeyn letters to certeyn of his trustid men unto Caleys warde,
to knowe howe he shuld be resceyvyd ; and with hym mette a
shippe callyd Nicolas of the Towre, with other shippis waytyng
on hym, and by hem that were in the spyner, the maister of
the Nicolas hadde knowlich of the dukes comyng. And
whanne he espyed the dukes shepis, he sent forthe his bote to
wete what they were, and the duke hym selfe spakke to hem,
and seyd, he was be the Kyngs comaundement sent to Caleys
ward, &c.

And they seyd he most speke with here master. And soo
he, with ij. or iij. of his men, wente forth with hem yn here
bote to the Nicolas ; and whanne he come, the master badde
hym, ' Welcom, Traitor,' as men sey ; and forther the maister
desyryd to wete yf the shepmen wolde holde with the duke,
and they sent word they wold not yn noo wyse ; and soo he was
on the Nicolas tyl Saturday [4] next folwyng ;

[1] [From Fenn, i. 38.] The date of this letter is perfectly determined by the events
to which it relates.
[2] 4th May.   [3] 30th April.   [4] 2nd May.

146

Soom sey he wrotte moche thenke [*thing*] to be delyverd 1450
to the Kynge, but thet is not verily knowe. He hadde hes MAY 5
confessor with hym, &c.

And some sey he was arreyned yn the sheppe on here
maner upon the appechementes and fonde gylty, &c.

Also he asked the name of the sheppe, and whanne he
knew it, he remembred 3tacy that seid, if he myght eschape
the daunger of the Towr, he should be saffe ; and thanne his
herte faylyd hym, for he thowghte he was desseyvyd, and yn
the syght of all his men he was drawyn ought of the grete
shippe yn to the bote ; and there was an exe, and a stoke, and
oon of the lewdeste of the shippe badde hym ley down his
hedde, and he should be fair ferd wyth, and dye on a swerd ;
and toke a rusty swerd, and smotte of his hedde withyn halfe
a doseyn strokes, and toke awey his gown of russet, and his
dobelette of velvet mayled, and leyde his body on the sonds of
Dover ; and some sey his hedde was sette oon a pole by it, and
hes men sette on the londe be grette circumstaunce and preye.
And the shreve of Kent doth weche the body, and sent his
under shreve to the juges to wete what to doo, and also to the
Kenge whatte shalbe doo.

Forther I wotte nott, but this fer (?) is that yf the proces
be erroneous, lete his concell reverse it, &c.

Also for alle your other maters they slepe, and the freer [1]
also, &c.

Sir Thomas Keriel [2] is take prisoner, and alle the legge
harneyse, and abowte iij. m[l] [3000] Englishe men slayn.

Mathew Gooth [3] with xv[c] [1500] fledde, and savyd hym
selffe and hem ; and Peris Brusy was cheffe capteyn, and hadde
x. m[l] Frenshe men and more, &c.

I prey yow lete my mastras your moder knowe these
tydyngis, and God have yow all yn his kepyn.

I prey yow this bille may recomaunde me to my mastrases
your moder and wyfe, &c.

[1] An allusion to Friar Hauteyn's suit or Oxnead.
[2] Sent to France to carry succours to the Duke of Somerset, but defeated and taken
prisoner at the battle of Fourmigni, 15th April 1450.
[3] Matthew Gough, a celebrated captain in the French war.

147

1450
MAY 5

James Gresham hath wretyn to John of Dam, and re-comaundith hym, &c.

Wretyn yn gret hast at London, the v. day of May, &c.

By yowr wyfe.[1]   W. L.

121

JOHN CRANE TO JOHN PASTON[2]

To my right worshupfull cosygne, John Paston of Norwyche, Squyer.

MAY 6

RIGHT worshupfull sir, I recomaunde me unto yow in the most goodly wyse that y can ; and forasmuche as ye desired of me to sende yow worde of dyvers matirs here, whiche been opened in the Parliament openly, I sende yow of them suche as I can.

First moost especiall, that for verray trowthe upon Sater-day[3] that last was, the Duke of Suffolk was taken in the see, and there he was byheded, and his body with the appurtenaunce sette at lande at Dover, and alle the folks that he haad with hym were sette to lande, and haad noon harme.

Also the Kyng hath sumwhat graanted to have the resump-sion agayne in summe, but nat in alle, &c.

Also yef ye purpose to come hydre to put up your bylles, ye may come now in a good tyme ; for now every man that hath any, they put theme now inne, and so may ye, yif ye come with Godds grace to your pleasur.

Ferthermore, upon the iiij[th] day of this monthe, the Erle of Devenesshire[4] come hydre with iij[c] [300] men wel byseen, &c.

And upon the morow after my Lord of Warrewyke[5] with iiij[c] [400] and moo, &c.

[1] This singular subscription Fenn believes to have been owing to a momentary forgetfulness on the part of the writer, William Lomner, who had been in the habit of acting as Margaret Paston's secretary in writing to her husband.

[2] [From Fenn, i. 44.] The date of this letter, as of the preceding, is clearly proved by internal evidence.   [3] 2nd May.

[4] Thomas Courtenay.   [5] Richard Nevill.—*See* Letter 98.

148

Also, as hyt ys noysed here Calys shal be byseged withynne this vij. dayes, &c.

God save the Kyng, and sende us pees, &c.

Other tithyngs be ther noon here, but Almyghty God have yow in his kepyng.

Writen at Leycestre, the vj. day of May.

Your cosigne,   JOHN CRANE.[1]

1450
MAY 6

122

ABSTRACT[1]

SIR JOHN FASTOLF TO SIR THOS. HOWYS, Parson of Castlecombe, 'being at Castre.'

MAY 7

Begs him to solicit the expedition of the matters of which he wrote since Easter.—Debts of Thos. Symmys for rents and sale of wools not yet paid to F. in Dedham.—As for the matter of Rydlyngfold and Hykele, 'seth it ys soo the world is changed gretely over it was, y pray you, and charge you, parson, labour ye to my frendz Lampet and others' to get a copy of their evidences ; for 'howbeit the said prioress say that her evidence be in the Duke of Suffolk's keeping or his counsel,' she had a book in which all the evidence is copied. The thing would have been sped long ere this, if 'my Lord Norwich['s] Chancellor' or Master Pope, had labored as they promised. For God's sake send me a good answer. 'If an inordinate book be made, remembering the deliverance' of cloths, &c. into F.'s wardrobe, let the indentures be engrossed. Wonders Howys cannot furnish him with a full account of the damages sustained by F. and his tenants these ten or twelve years past. He has only sent a declaration of costs in defending some of them. Get a letter of Nich. Bokkyng of the £100 to whom it was paid.

London, 7 May 28 Henry VI.   *Signed.*

[1] Probably John Crane of Woodnorton, of whom there are some notices in Blomefield (*Hist. Norf.* viii. 313, 316 ; x. 282).

[2] [MS. Phillipps, 9735, No. 223.]

149

THE PASTON LETTERS

123

THOMAS DENYES TO JOHN PASTON[1]

To my maister Paston.

1450
MAY 13

I RECOMAUND me unto your good maistership ; and as for tidings, Arblaster come home to my Lord[2] on Mun-day, at sopertyme ; and my Maister Danyell[3] is Styward of the Duche of Lancastre by yonde Trent, and Arblastr seith he hath made him his undirstyward.

And as for the Chamberleynship of Inglond, the Lord Beamond[4] hath it, and the Lord Rivers[5] Constable of Inglond.

As for the Duche on this side Trent, Sir Thomas Tuden-ham had a joynte patent with the Duke of Suffolk,[6] which, if it be resumed, Sir Thomas Stanley hath a bille redy endossed therof.

My lord wole not to Leicestre.[7]   My Maister Danyell desireth yow thedir. I shall ride thiderward on Friday by tymes.

Wretyn in hast at Wynche,[8] the xiij. day of May.

I pray yow to thynk upon my mater to my mastresse your wyf, for my mastresse Anne, for in good feith I haf fully

[1] [From Fenn, i. 162.] This letter, which Fenn vaguely assigned to the latter part of the reign of Henry VI., may be pretty safely attributed to the year 1450. The mention of Lord Rivers and the Duke of Suffolk could not have been earlier than 1449, as the one was only created lord, and the other duke in 1448, and at a later date than the 13th of May. The reference to the Duke of Suffolk again is not likely to have been long after his decease. Had it been on a Tuesday or Thursday, Monday would have been spoken of as 'yesterday,' or Friday as 'to-morrow.' Now, the 13th of May was a Wednesday in 1450. The changes in officers of state mentioned in this letter are, therefore, those consequent on the fall of the Duke of Suffolk. There is, besides, as will be seen by a foot-note, an allusion to the Parliament at Leicester.

[2] John de Vere, 12th Earl of Oxford.   [3] Thomas Daniel.—*See* p. 80.

[4] John, Viscount Beaumont.

[5] Richard Woodville, created Baron Rivers 29th May 1448 ; afterwards earl.

[6] William de la Pole.—*See* p. 80, Note 2.

[7] Parliament was sitting at Leicester in May 1450.

[8] A seat of the Earl of Oxford, near King's Lynn, in Norfolk.

150

HENRY VI

conquered my lady sith ye went, so that I haf hir promisse to be my good lady, and that she shall help me by the feith of hir body.

1450
MAY 13

Your servant,   DENYES.

124

THE EARL OF OXFORD TO JOHN PASTON[1]

To our right trusty and intierly welbeloved John Paston, Esquyer.

RIGHT trusty and right intierly welbeloved, we grete you hertly wele. And it is so, as ye know wele your self, we haf and long tyme haf had the service of Thomas Denyes, by continuance wherof we wend to haf had his atten-daunce at our lust ; and nevertheless we haf so strictly examynid his demenyng that we fele and pleynly conceyve that the love and effeccion which he hath to a gentilwoman not ferre from yow, and which ye be privy to, as we suppose, causith hym alwey to desire toward your cuntre, rather than toward suych ocupacion as is behovefull to us. We write therfore to yow, prayng yow hertly as ye love us, that it like you to do that labour at our instaunce be suych men [mean] as your wisdom can seme, to meve that gentilwoman in our behalf for the wele of this mater, undirtakyng for us that we wole shew our bounte to thaym bothe, if it plese hir that this mater take effect, so that be reason she shall haf cause to take it in gree. And it the comyng thider of our persone self shuld be to plesir of hir, we wole not leve our labour in that : wherfore we pray you that ye wole do your part heryn, as ye wole we do for yow in

Year uncer-tain

[1] [From Fenn, iii. 360.] This letter cannot well be of the same year as the last, but is probably not many years earlier, and certainly not many years later. The reasons against its being of the same year are—first, that it seems to be implied in the letter preceding that the Earl of Oxford was at Winch, near Lynn, in Norfolk, on the 13th May 1450, which makes it improbable that he would be at Wivenhoe in Essex four days after ; and, secondly, that he is not likely to have offered to go into Norfolk (especially after having just come out of Norfolk) on a matter touching the private affairs of one of his own adherents, when he declined to go to the Parliament at Leicester.

151

VOL 2

THE PASTON LETTERS

Year
uncer-
tain

tyme comyng, and that ye se us in hast.   The Holy Trinite
kepe yow.   Wretyn at Wevenho, the xvij. day of May.
The Erle of Oxenford.

OXENFORD.

125

SIR JOHN FASTOLF TO SIR THOMAS HOWYS[1]

*To my trusty and welbelovyd frende, Sir Thomas Howys, Parson of
Castellcombe.*

1450
MAY 27

TRUSTY and welbelovyd frende, I grete you well.[2] . . . .
And I pray you sende me word who darre be so hardy
to keck agen you in my ryght.   And sey hem on my
half that they shall be qwyt as ferre as law and reson wolle.
And yff they wolle not dredde, ne obey that, then they shall
be quyt by Blackberd or Whyteberd ; that ys to sey, by God
or the Devyll.   And therfor I charge yow, send me word
whethyr such as hafe be myne adversaries before thys tyme,
contynew still yn her wylfullnesse, &c.

Item, I hyre oft tymys manye straunge rapports of the
gouvernaunce of my place at Castre and othyr plasys, as yn
my chatell approvyng,[3] yn my wynys, the kepyng of my
wardrobe and clothys, the avaylle[4] of my conyes at Haylysdon,
&c., and approwement[3] of my londys ; praying you hertly as
my full trust ys yn you to help reforme it, and that ye suffre no
vityouse man at my place of Castre abyde, but well gouverned
and diligent, as ye woll aunswer to it.

Allmyghty God kepe you.   Wryt at London, xxvij. day of
Maij anno xxviij° regni Regis Henrici VI.

JOHN FASTOLF, Kt.

[1] [From Fenn, i. 52.]
[2] Here, says Fenn, follow some orders respecting his affairs at Caister.
[3] Approving lands or chattels meant turning them to profit, and in the former case
commonly implied increasing the rents.   [4] Use or profit.

152

HENRY VI

126

J. PAYN TO JOHN PASTON[1]

To my ryght honurabyll maister, John Paston.

RYGHT honurabyll and my ryght enterly bylovyd
maister, I recomaunde me un to yow, with al maner
of due reverence, in the moste louly wyse as we ought
to do, evermor desyryng to here of your worshipfull state,
prosperite, and welfar ; the which I beseke God of his
aboundant grace encrece and mayntene to his moste plesaunce,
and to your hartis dssyre.

Pleasyth it your gode and gracios maistershipp tendyrly to
consedir the grete losses and hurts that your por peticioner
haeth, and haeth jhad evyr seth the comons of Kent come to
the Blakheth,[2] and that is at xv. yer passed, whereas my maister
Syr John Fastolf, Knyght, that is youre testator,[3] commandyt
your besecher to take a man, and ij. of the beste orsse that wer
in his stabyll, with hym to ryde to the comens of Kent, to gete
the articles that they come for.   And so I dyd ; and al so sone
as I come to the Blakheth, the capteyn[4] made the comens to
take me.   And for the savacion of my maisters horse, I made
my fellowe to ryde a wey with the ij. horses ; and I was
brought forth wit befor the capteyn of Kent.   And the
capteyn demaundit me what was my cause of comyng thedyr,
and why that I made my fellowe to stele a wey with the horse.
And I seyd that I come thedyr to chere with my wyves
brethren, and other that were my alys and gossippes of myn
that were present there.   And than was there oone there, and
seid to the capteyn that I was one of Syr John Fastolfes men,

1450
(written
in
1465)

[1] [From Fenn, i. 54.]   This letter was actually written in the year 1465 ; but as
the circumstances to which it relates belong to the year 1450, and are connected with
the memorable insurrection of Jack Cade, we have thought it right, as Fenn did, to
place it under the earlier year.
[2] Jack Cade and his followers encamped on Blackheath on the 11th June 1450,
and again from the 29th of June to the 1st July.   Payn refers to the latter occasion.
[3] Sir John Fastolf (who is dead at the date of this letter) left Paston his executor,
as will be seen hereafter.   [4] Jack Cade.

153

THE PASTON LETTERS

1450
(written
in
1465)

and the ij. horse were Syr John Fastolfes ; and then the capteyn lete cry treson upon me thorought all the felde, and
brought me at iiij. partes of the feld with a harrawd of the
Duke of Exetter[1] before me in the dukes cote of armes,
makyng iiij.   Oyes at iiij. partes of the feld ; proclaymyng
opynly by the seid harrawd that I was sent thedyr for to espy
theyre pusaunce, and theyre abyllyments of werr, fro the
grettyst traytor that was in Yngelond or in Fraunce, as the
seyd capteyn made proclaymacion at that tyme, fro oone Syr
John Fastolf, Knyght, the whech mynnysshed all the garrisons
of Normaundy, and Manns, and Mayn, the whech was the
cause of the lesyng of all the Kyngs tytyll and ryght of an
herytaunce that he had by yonde see.   And morovyr he seid
that the seid Syr John Fastolf had furnysshyd his plase[2] with
the olde sawdyors of Normaundy and abyllyments of werr, to
destroy the comens of Kent whan that they come to Southewerk ; and therfor he seyd playnly that I shulde lese my hede.

And so furthewith I was taken, and led to the capteyns
tent, and j. ax and j. blok was brought forth to have smetyn
of myn hede ; and than my maister Ponyngs, your brodyr,[3]
with other of my frendes, come and lettyd the capteyn, and
seyd pleynly that there shulde dye a C. or ij. [*a hundred or
two*], that in case be that I dyed ; and so by that meane my
lyf was savyd at that tyme.   And than I was sworen to the
capteyn, and to the comens, that I shulde go to Southewerk,
and aray me in the best wyse that I coude, and come ageyn to
hem to helpe hem ; and so I gote th'articles, and brought
hem to my maister, and that cost me more emongs the comens
that day than xxvijs.

Wherupon I come to my maister Fastolf, and brought hym
th'articles, and enformed hym of all the mater, and counseyled
hym to put a wey all his abyllyments of werr and the olde

[1] Henry Holland, Duke of Exeter.   During the civil war which followed, he
adhered to the House of Lancaster, though he married Edward IV.'s sister.   His
herald had probably been seized by Cade's followers, and pressed into their service.
[2] Sir John Fastolf had a residence in Southwark.
[3] Robert Poynings, who, some years before this letter was written, had married
Elizabeth, the sister of John Paston, was sword-bearer and carver to Cade, and was
accused of creating disturbances on more than one occasion afterwards.

154

HENRY VI

1450
(written
in
1465)

sawdiors ; and so he dyd, and went hymself to the Tour, and
all his meyny with hym but Betts and j. [*i.e.* one] Mathew
Brayn ; and had not I ben, the comens wolde have brennyd
his plase and all his tennuryes, wher thorough it cost me of
my noune propr godes at that tyme more than vj. merks in
mate and drynke ; and nought withstondyng the capteyn that
same tyme lete take me atte Whyte Harte in Suthewerk, and
there comandyt Lovelase to dispoyle me oute of myn aray,
and so he dyd.   And there he toke a fyn gowne of muster
dewyllers[1] furryd with fyn bevers, and j. peyr of Bregandyrns[2]
kevert with blew fellewet [*velvet*] and gylt naile, with leg-
harneyse, the vallew of the gown and the bregardyns viij*li.*

Item, the capteyn sent certeyn of his meyny to my chamber
in your rents, and there breke up my chest, and toke awey j.
obligacion of myn that was due unto me of xxxvj*li*. by a prest
of Poules, and j. nother obligacion of j. knyght of *xli.*, and my
purse with v. ryngs of golde, and xvij*s*. vj*d*. of golde and
sylver ; and j. herneyse [*harness*] complete of the touche of
Milleyn ;[3] and j. gowne of fyn perse[4] blewe furryd with
martens ; and ij. gounes, one furryd with bogey,[5] and j.
nother lyned with fryse ;[6] and ther wolde have smetyn of
myn hede, what that they had dyspoyled me atte White
Hart.   And there my Maister Ponyngs and my frends savyd
me, and so I was put up tyll at nyght that the batayle was at
London Brygge ;[7] and than atte nyght the capteyn put me
oute into the batayle atte Brygge, and there I was woundyt,
and hurt nere hand to deth ; and there I was vj. oures in the
batayle, and myght nevyr come oute therof ; and iiij. tymes
before that tyme I was caryd abought thorought Kent and
Sousex, and ther they wolde have smetyn of my hede.

[1] 'A kind of mixed grey woollen cloth, which continued in use to Elizabeth's
reign.'—Halliwell.
[2] A brigandine was a coat of leather or quilted linen, with small iron plates sewed
on.—*See* Grose's *Antient Armour.*   The back and breast of this coat were sometimes
made separately, and called a pair.—Meyrick.
[3] Milan was famous for its manufacture of arms and armour.
[4] 'Skye or bluish grey.   There was a kind of cloth so called.'—Halliwell.
[5] Budge fur.
[6] 'Frieze.   A coarse narrow cloth, formerly much in use.'—Halliwell.
[7] The battle on London Bridge was on the 5th July.

155

↓

THE PASTON LETTERS

1450
(written
in
1465)

And in Kent there as my wyfe dwellyd, they toke awey all oure godes mevabyll that we had, and there wolde have hongyd my wyfe and v. of my chyldren, and lefte her no more gode but her kyrtyll and her smook. And a none aftyr that hurlyng, the Bysshop Roffe[1] apechyd me to the Quene, and so I was arestyd by the Quenes commaundment in to the Marchalsy, and there was in rygt grete durasse, and fere of myn lyf, and was thretenyd to have ben hongyd, drawen, and quarteryd; and so wold have made me to have pechyd my Maister Fastolf of treson. And by cause that I wolde not, they had me up to Westminster, and there wolde have sent me to the gole house at Wyndsor; but my wyves and j. coseyn of myn noune that were yomen of the Croune, they went to the Kyng, and got grase and j. chartyr of pardon.

Per le vostre,   J. PAYN.

127

JAMES GRESHAM TO JOHN PASTON[2]

To my right worshipfull [mai]ster John Paston at Wynchestre be this delyuered.

1450
JULY 3

AFTER al due recomendacion had, I recomaunde me to yow and prey yow to wete that Heydon seweth in his accion a geynst Osebern x. *tales* retournable xv[a.] Johannis. *Ideo mittetur vel loquatur Vicecomiti Norffolk,* &c. And I suppose that as for Costardis accions thei wole have *nisi prius,* &c. As touchyng the matier of Oxened the frere[3]

---

[1] Fenn gives this name 'Rosse' with two long s's, but translates it Rochester, from which I presume it was written 'Roffe' for *Roffensis.* The Bishop of Rochester's name was John Lowe.
[2] [Add. MS. 34,888, f. 73.] The legal proceedings mentioned in this letter show that the year is the same as that of Gresham's other letter immediately following (No. 128).
[3] John Hauteyn.

156

THE PASTON LETTERS

128

JAMES GRESHAM TO MASTER WHITE[1]

To my Maister Whyte, Esquyer, with my Lord Cardynall,[2] for to take to John Paston.

1450
JULY 8

AFTER al due recomendacion, I recomaund me to yow, and do yow wete that this same Wednesseday I receyved your lettre whiche was wretyn on Saterday last passed, wherby ye willed me to send yow worde of your matiers, &c. As touchyng the frere,[3] he abydeth in lawe up on our plee of profession, like as I sent yow word by wrytyng, whiche I sent yow in a box with other stuf by a man of the Archedeken of Rychemond. I endorsed it thus, 'To William Plumstede, with my Lord of Winchestre,[4] or to John Paston.'

We shuld have amendet our plee of profession, but thanne your counseyll fereth he wolde take an issue that he is not professed, and that shuld[5] be tried by the certificat of the Dean of Poulys, *sede vacante*; and therfore we abide in lawe, and wole not amende our plee. The day of th'assises in Norffolk is *aie Veneris proximo post Festum Nativitatis Beatæ Mariæ apud Norwicum,* and Costards *nisi prius* is take owt ageynst that day, and Prentis *nisi prius* ageynst Halman also.

As touchyng the sute ageyns Osebern and Foke, he hath geve day xv. Johannis with x. *tales,* as I have wretyn to yow to fore this tyme; and I suppose that he wole have a *nisi prius* of the same atte seid assises. As touchynge the fyn in the Kyngs Benche for Osebern and Foke, the fyne were cessed this terme, but I hadde no leyser to talke with Croxton ther of

---

[1] [From Paston MSS., B.M.] This letter appears to have been written in the year 1450, when Gresham was in London looking after John Paston's interests in various lawsuits. Mr. White, to whom it is directed for the purpose of being conveyed to Paston, was a servant of Cardinal Kemp, who had been made Lord Chancellor in the beginning of the year. It is evident from other letters that John Paston took counsel of the Lord Chancellor's servant in his causes.
[2] Cardinal Kemp.   [3] John Hawteyn.—*See* Nos. 46 and 63.
[4] William of Waynflete, Bishop of Winchester.
[5] The word 'it' is interlined in the original after 'shuld,' but is clearly superfluous.

158

HENRY VI

leveth his delagacie a bideth up on our plee of profession by as meche as we sey that long to fore the writte purchaced he was professed a frere and sey not and yet is professed, &c. And Sotyll and other of your counseill thynk the law is on our syde. Brampton brought me a lettre and a clowt sowed clos with thynggis therin, and a letter endorsed to yow from my maistresse your moder, whiche I sende yow with this. The lord Moleyns man brought ij. writtes to the Shirrefis depute of Norfolk, oon a geynst yow, myn eme[1] and James Gloys *quare clausum suum apud Gresham fregerunt,* &c., the othir writte a geynst yow and J. Gloys *quare vi et armis in hominis et servientes ipsius apud Gresham insultum fecerunt,* &c. And whanne the seid lord Moleyns man delyvered these wrettys, Lomnour stode be side and aspied it. And thanne the seid man desired to have ageyn the writtis, and toke hem a geyn; and whanne he had theym he seid they shuld not come in their handes a vii. nyght after. And so he kepeth theym stille. And Caly and Yates also have promysed me that ther shall no writte be retourned a geyn yow but that ye shall have copies ther of at reasonable tyme to make your avantage as the law wole, &c., to caste your esson[2] or suyche other, &c. Sir, I prey God yeld yow for your letter ye sent me by Lethom, whiche I receyved yistereuyn right late. Wherby I hope and conceyve that ye be in good cas for your maner of Gr[esham], for truly I was right weel comforted therof. As touchyng Skyner and his borwys the attachementes may not be wretyn but by the recordes of the reconysance, and alle the recordes of Chauncerye be at Wynchestre. *Ideo,* &c. I prey God for your good speed in all your matiers, Amen. Wretyn in hast at London the Friday next after seint Petir day.—Your servant,   J. GRESHAM.

1450
JULY 3

---

[1] 'eme,' *i.e.* uncle.
[2] *Essoin,* a legal expression, meaning an excuse admitted for non-appearance in Court.

157

HENRY VI

yet, &c. Your bedfelawe seigh bothe my other writynge and this, and he recomaundeth hym to yow, and shuld have wretyn to yow, if he had not be prevy to my writyng. Ye ar meche hold to hym, for he is diligent for yow, &c.

1450
JULY 8

As touchyng Drewe Barantyn, I myght not yet speke with hym, &c. *Circumspecte agatis,* and be war of lordis promysses, for it is tolde me in counseil ther is a writte of forcyble entre[1] in framyng ageynst yow.

Almghty God be your gyde. Wretyn in hast with inne an hour after the resceyte of your lettre, at Wesminster, the Wednesseday next after Seint Thomas day.[2]

Yours JAMES GRE.

129

ABSTRACT[3]

JAMES GRESHAM TO [JOHN PASTON?].

Inquiry made as to the injury of Sporle wood for lack of hedging. The three years' growth of the wood availeth no man. The farmers now cannot sell it the better, so it must be either to your hurt or Halman's. Hopes the wastes at Cressingham will be amended. Your tenants are treated unfairly about the Sheriff's turn by those of the Prior of Norwich and John Coo. Can get no money, for Fulchier hopes he is not so far in arrear as you think. Halman can get no money; his corns are so cheap he will not sell, but he hopes to make purveyance at Michaelmas.

Calybut says he never asked the Vicar of Sporle to be bound for him. They will meet with me at Gressenhale on St. Bartholomew's day and seal the other part, so that they have notice from you at Swaffham Market, Saturday next before.

Accounts of Sneylewell, Cressingham, and Sparham on the back.

About
1450

[We have placed this letter after the preceding as being probably not many years apart from it in date, if not the very same year. The name of Halman occurs in both, and also in a letter of the Vicar of Sporle, which will be found a little further on.]

---

[1] For Gresham?
[2] The translation of St. Thomas was on the 3rd July.
[3] [From Paston MSS., B.M.]

159

THE PASTON LETTERS

130

ABSTRACT[1]

Sir J. Fastolf to Sir Thomas Howys, Parson of Castlecombe, at Caister.

1450
AUG. 8

Has sent home letters by John Bedford. Sends by the bearer Thomas Medew eight writs of 'green wax'[2] for certain processes he has in Norfolk, with a *distringas* for Sir John Shypton, which he must get served with the advice of Thomas Grene and other of Fastolf's trusty friends. The inquest must be certified of the truth and Shypton's falsehood proved. Will give his testimonial, when needful, 'that I never sealed none such quittance.' Let Greene correct the roll of articles I send by Bedford. I hear you have omitted several of the extortions done to me (*in margin*, 'eyer and determiner'). London, 8 August 28 Henry vi.

Let Master Doket have a copy of the evidence of Rydlyngfeeld.

'Item, purvey me at the leest v. doseyn long bowes, with shot longyng thertoo. And purveyeth also quarell[3] hedys to be made ther, for the price ys derer heer then ther; and let no langage be had of ordenances makyng.'

Signed.

131

JAMES GRESHAM TO JOHN PASTON[4]

To my right especiall maister, John Paston,[5] in hast.

AUG. 19

RYGHT worthy worshipfull sir, and myn especiall maister, I recomaund me to yow, and pray yow wete that I was [yesterdaye atte][6] . . . .[6] my lord Chauncellers[7] hous, and there I spake with White; and he tolde me that he hadde the letter that ye sewed for from

[1] ms. Phillipps, 9735, f. 224.]
[2] Writs under the seal of the Court of Exchequer, which was of green wax, directing the sheriff of a county to levy certain fines.
[3] *See* page 101, Note 3.
[4] [From Fenn, iii. 86.] The date of this letter is ascertained by the news contained in the last paragraph of the fall of Cherbourg, besides other internal evidence.
[5] 'After John Paston had received this letter,' says Fenn, 'it seems as if he had sent it to my Lord Oxford, for on the back of it, in John Paston's handwriting, is the following direction: "To the rith worspfull and my rith speciall lord, my Lord of Oxenford."'
[6] These passages, in which the text is broken by brackets or dots, are indicated by Fenn as illegible in the original.
[7] John Kemp, Cardinal Archbishop of York, afterwards of Canterbury.

160

HENRY VI

. . . .[1] directed to the Lord Moleyns of that substance that ye hadde sued to hym for an especiall assise[2] and an *oier* and *determiner*,[3] [and][1] . . . . .[1] that he shuld comaunde his men beyng at Gresham to departe thens, and that the profitez thereof shuld be receyved by an endifferent [person][1] . .[1] saufly to be kepte til the right were determyned be twen yow and my Lord M., &c., whiche letter White sente forthe [by][1] a man of my Lord Chaunceller to the Lord Moleyns. And he sent his answer in writyng of this substance, that it shuld not like my Lord Chaunceller to graunte assise, &c., for als moche as the Lord M. hadde sore be laboured in his cuntre to peas and stille the poeple[4] there to restreyngne them from rysyng, and so he was dayly laboured there abowt in the Kynggs servyce, and that considered, he trustid veryly that there shuld non assise be graunted to your entent. And he seid forther in his answer, if he myght attende to be in Norffolk, and leve the necessary servyce that he dede to the Kyng now in Wyltshire, he wolde be but weel pleased that ye hadde your assise; for he knewe his title and his evydence so good for his part, that he durst weel putte it in my Lord Chaunceller, and in what juge he wolde calle to hym. And wher my Lord Chaunceller desired hym to avoyde his men from Gresham, he trustid that my Lord wolde not desire that, by cause he hadde his possession, and that it was his wyffs ryght, and so hym thought it a geynst reason that he shuld a voide utterly his possession.

This same Moneday goth my Lord Chaunceller and my Lord of Buk[5] into Kent to sytte up on an *oier* and *determyner*[6]

1450C
AUG. 19

[1] These passages, in which the text is broken by brackets or dots, are indicated by Fenn as illegible in the original.
[2] A writ directed to the sheriff for recovery of possession of things immoveable, whereof yourself or ancestors been disseised.—F.
[3] Is a commission especially granted to certain persons for the hearing and determining of causes, and was formerly only in use upon some sudden outrage or insurrection in any place.—F.
[4] These disturbances among the people were the remains of Cade's rebellion, which had been lately suppressed.—F.
[5] Humphrey Stafford, Duke of Buckingham, fell in the battle of Northampton in July 1460.—F.
[6] These commissions of *oyer* and *determiner* were to try those who had been concerned in the late rebellion under Cade.—F.

161

THE PASTON LETTERS

1450
AUG. 19

at Rorchestre; and Whyte told me that there is wretyn an generall *oier* and *determyner* to be in Norffolk, and what ther[fore][1] and for the Lord Moleyns writyng, hym semyth it is not to your avayll to sewe for an especiall assise, ne for an *oier* and *determyner*.

Whan I come hiddirward, I mette with my Lord of Norffolk betwen Berkewey and Baburgham homward, and whethir he shall come agayn hiddir or noght I wot not, but I trowe rather yes thanne nay; for it is seid that alle the Lordes be sent for to be here on Moneday or Tuysday next comyng for a counseyll.

The Chief Justice[2] is not here, ne noon other Justice, except Danvers[3] is now made Juge of the Comune Place, and is forth into Kent with the Lords, &c.

Al this tofore was wretyn on the Moneday next after our Lady day. And this same Wednesseday was it told that Shirburgh[4] is goon, and we have not now a foote of londe in Normandie, and men arn ferd that Calese wole be beseged hastily, &c.

Pynchamour shall telle yow by mowthe more thanne I have leyser to write now to yow. I wrot to myn em'[5] that there were ix. or x. m[l] [*nine or ten thousand*] men up in Wiltshire, and I halde it of the report of Whittocks mede; but I trowe it is not so, for here is now littel speche therof; ner the lesse, if I here more, I shall sende yow worde her after by sum loders that come to Seynt Bertilmews [fayre].[1]

Wretyn in hast at London, the Wednesseday next after our Lady day, &c.

Your own symple servaunt,

JAMES GR.

[1] See Note 1, p. 161.
[2] John Hody was at this time Chief Justice of the King's Bench.—F.
[3] Robert Danvers became a Judge of the Common Pleas 14th of August 1450.—F.
[4] Cherbourg surrendered to the French on the 12th August 1450.—See Stevenson's *Reductio Normanniæ*, p. 367.
[5] 'Quære this abbreviated word,' says Fenn. It is probably *eme*, meaning uncle.

162

HENRY VI

132

THE EARL OF OXFORD TO JOHN PASTON[1]

To my right trusty and intierly welbeloved John Paston, Squyer.

RIGHT trusty and intierly welbeloved, I grete yow wele, and wole and pray yow that ye dispose your self to be with my Lord of Norffolk in al hast goodly, to that intent that where it was desired by dyvers gentilmen of this shire[2] that I shuld my self a be with his Lordship at Framyngham, to excuse me to his Lordship; for truly I haf suych writyn to my said Lord for myn excuse, which writyng I send to yow by Thomas Denyes, to whome I pray you to gif credens. And the Trinite kepe yow. Wretyn at Bury Seynt Edmond, the xxj. day of August.

I pray you to speke with Sir Miles Stapilton and Brewes, and to delyver to thaym my lettres, wherof I send yow copies, and make Brewes to send over a man to me with th'entent of my Lord of Norffolk, and with th'effect of your deligens, with a more credible message than Brewes ded to my wif; for I had never a wers jurney for a jape in my lif, ne a lewder, as ye shal wele conceyve.

OXENFORD.

1450(?)
AUG. 21

[1] [Douce ms. 393, f. 88.] From the similarity of the contents of this and the two following letters, it is evident that they belong to the same year; and the mention of Thomas Denyes, from whom the Earl of Oxford was afterwards estranged, proves that it must have been before 1454. In the summer of 1450, there was disaffection in Norfolk, which led to the issuing of a special commission of *oyer and terminer* in September. These three letters may, therefore, have belonged to that year.
[2] 'This shire' should be Suffolk, as the Earl dates from Bury St. Edmunds, but I should think Norfolk was intended, which the Earl had probably just left on his way up to London. Compare next number.

163

VOL 2

THE PASTON LETTERS

133

THE EARL OF OXFORD (?) TO SIR MILES STAPLETON AND THOMAS BREWES[1]

To my ryght trusti and wyth all myn hert intyerly welbelovyd Sir Mylys Stapelton, Knyght.

1450(?)
AUG. 21

RYGHT trusty and wyth all myn hert entierly welbelovyd, I grete yow wele, and wol that ye wete that a gentelman of your ally ·haghe [*hath*] ben wyth me, at whos instans and steryng and by hese good avyes I wold ful fayne amet [*have met*] wyth yow at Framyngham; but I may no lenger abyde here for the strayte comaundment that I have to be wyth the Kyng. Wherfore I pray yow to comown wyth Brews and Paston, and to put in artycles be ther avyses and be your wysdom the indisposicion of the people of this counte, and what were most necesary to be desierid of the Kyng and of my Lordis of the Councell for the restreynte of ther mourmour and the peas, and to sende it me be the brynger herof, to whom I pray yow gef credens. And the Holy Ternyte kepe yow. Wretyn at Wynche, the xxj. day of August.

To my ryght trusty and entierly welbelovyd Thomas Brewes, Squyer.

RYGHT trusty and intyerly welbelovid, I grete yow wele. And for as mouche as ye were with my wyf at Wynche in the name and behalve of the substaunce of the gentelys of this shyer, and cause my wyf to wryte to

---

[1] [From Paston MSS., B.M.] The two letters following are from contemporaneous copies written on the same paper. Being dated the same day as the preceding letter of the Earl of Oxford, and addressed to the two persons named in the postscript, we should have every reason to suppose they are the copies there mentioned, were it not for the circumstance that the Earl of Oxford's seat at Wynche, near Lynn, in Norfolk, must have been a good day's journey from Bury St. Edmunds. The internal evidence, however, is in other respects so strong that we have no doubt at all upon the subject. The difficulty as to the date may be accounted for by supposing that these two letters were really written at Wynche the day before, but that the date 21st August was filled in by the Earl at Bury St. Edmunds at the time he despatched his letter of the same date to John Paston.

164

THE PASTON LETTERS

1450
[AUG.]

feytfull servaunts; and I trost to God to se youre good Lordship at Framyngham as I shall . . . . . And yf your Lordshep seme necessary that I now beynge at Westminster shall any thynge laboure or des[ire for the rule] and governaunce of the counte forsayd, or for reformacion of suche wronge as the peples herts most agrugge as . . . . lyke that I meve to the Kynge and the Lordes of the Counceyll, so wyll I meve, and none otherwyse as . . . . Wheryn I beseche your grace to know your entente by the brynger her of. And my service is redy to your Lords[hip] . . . . . mercy who kepe who kepe[1] nebbey (?) for hese grace.

135

JOHN PASTON AND LORD MOLEYNS[2]

Un to the right reverent fadir in God and my right gracious Lord, the Cardinal Archebisshop of York, Prymat and Chaunceller of Inglond.

1450(?)

BESECHETH mekely John Paston that where Robert Hungerford, Knyght, Lord Molens, and Alianore, his wyff, with force and strength, and grete multitude of riottous peple, to the noumbre of a thousand persones and mo, gadered by th'excitacion and procuryng of John Heydon[3] a yenst the Kynggs pees, in riotous maner entred up on your seid besecher and othir enfeoffed to his use in the manoir of Gresham with th'appurtenaunces in the shire of Norffolk; whiche riotous peple brake, dispoiled, and drew doun the place of your seid besecher in the seid toun, and drafe out his wiff

---

[1] So in MS.
[2] [Add. Charter 17,239, B.M.] This is a bill addressed to Cardinal Kemp as Lord Chancellor, to which reference will be found to be made in the succeeding letter. Kemp was appointed Lord Chancellor on the 31st January 1450. The acts here complained of were therefore those connected with Paston's second expulsion from Gresham.
[3] John Heydon, Esq. of Baconsthorpe, a lawyer, who was recorder of Norwich from 1431 to 1433, and sheriff in 1431-2.

166

HENRY VI

1450(?)
AUG. 21

me for to turne agayn into Norffolk, be wheche wrytyng, and be your report it semyd to me that a gret asemble had be purposid wythin the counte heer. I therfore sayd unto yow, wolyng and mevyng yow aftyr your trowth, and as ye know, that ye do put in artycles the indisposicion of the people, and what your avyce is to be do for the restreynyng of the same; and this articles I pray yow set to your seal, and cause other gentelmen with wham ye have comonyng set ther seales, for this is necessary, and that I may schew it to the Kyng and to my Lordis of hese Councell, and that I fayle not here of for your honeste and myn excuse. And the Ternyte kepe yow. Wreten at Wynche, the xxj. day of August.

134

[THE EARL OF OXFORD TO THE DUKE OF NORFOLK][1]

1450
[AUG.]

RYGHT high and myghty Prynce and my right good Lord, I recomaunde me un to youre good Lordshep. And for asmouch as I am enformed [that] certeyn notable knyghtis and squyers of this counte dispose thaym self to be with youre Lordshep in hasty tyme at Fram[yngham], theer to have comonyngs with youre good Lordshep for the sad rule and governaunce of this counte, wych standyth ryght . . . . indisposyd, God amend it; for qwych sad rule and governaunce to be had I wold full fayn a ben with your good [Lordship]. But for asmouch as the Kynge hath geve to me straitly in charge to be with hys Highnesse at Westminstre on Saterda[y]. . . . . . [I must] departe towards London. Therfore therof I beseche your good Lordship that ye vouchesaf to comon with the seyd k[nyghtes and squyers] as with your

---

[1] [From Paston MSS., B.M.] This would seem by internal evidence to be the letter of excuse written by Oxford to the Duke of Norfolk, which the Earl mentions in his letter to John Paston of the 21st August. The original from which it is taken is a copy without signature or address, and mutilated in the margin.

165

HENRY VI

1450(?)

and servauntes there beyng, and ryfled, took, and bare awey alle the goodes and catalx that your seid besecher and his servauntes hadde there to the value of ccli. [£200] and more; and the seid manoir, after the seid riottous entre, kept with strong hande in manere of werre, as weel ayenst your seid besecher and his feffees, as ayenst oon of the Kyngges justicez of the pees in the seid shire, that come thedir to execute the statutes ordeigned and provyded ayenst suche forcible entrees and kepyng of possessions with force, as it appiereth by recorde of the seid justice certified in to the Chauncerie; and yet the seid Lord Molens the same manoir kepith with force and strengthe ayenst the fourme of the seid statutes: Please it your reverent Faderhood and gracioux Lordship, these premisses considered, to graunte on to your seid besecher for his feffees by hym to be named a special assise[1] ayenst the seid Lord Molens, Alianore, and John Heidon, and othir to be named by your seid besecher, and also an oyer and determyner[2] ayenst the seid Lord Molens, John Heidon, and othir of the seid riotous peple in like fourme to be named, to enquere, here and determyn all trespaces, extorcions, riottes, forcible entrees, mayntenaunces,[3] champerties,[4] embraceries,[5] offenses, and mesprisions[6] by hem or ony of hem doen, als weel atte sute of our sovereign Lord the Kyng, as of your seid besecher and his seid feffees, and every of hem, or of ony othir of the Kyngges lieges: atte reverence of God, and in weye of charite.

---

[1] See p. 161, Note 2.
[2] See p. 161, Note 3.
[3] Unlawful support given to a disputant by one not concerned in the cause.
[4] Bargains made with litigants for a share in what may be gained by the suit.
[5] Attempts to corrupt juries.
[6] Treason or felony committed by oversight or wilful neglect of a duty.

167

136

JOHN PASTON TO JAMES GRESHAM[1]

The copie of the letter of J. P.

1450
SEPT. 4

JAMES GRESHAM, I prey yow laboure forth to have answer of my bille for myn especial assise, and the oyer and termyner,[2] accordyng to my seid bille that I delyvered to my Lord Chanceler,[3] letyng hym wete that his Lordship conceyved the graunt of suyche a special matier myght cause a rumour in the cuntre. Owt of dowte the cuntre is not so disposed, for it is desired ageyn suche persones as the c[untre] wolde were ponysshid; and if they be not ponysshid to refourme that they have do amysse, by liklynesse the cuntre wole rise up on th[em]. Men talke that a general oier and termyner is graunted to the Duke of Norfolk, my Lord of Ely, the Erll of Oxenford, the Lord Scales, Sir John Fastolf, Sir Thomas Fulthorp, and William Yelverton, and men be right glad therof. Yet that notwithstondyng, laboure ye forth for me. F[or] in a general oyer and termyner a *supersedeas* may dassh al, and so shall not in a special. And also if the justicez come at my request, they shall sytte als long as I wole, and so shall thei not by the generall. And as for commyssioners in myn, &c., Sir John Fastolf must be pleyntyf als weel as I my self, and so he may not be commyssioner; and as for alle the remenant, I can thynke them indifferent inow in the matier, except my Lord Scales, whos wyff is aunte to the Lady Moleyns.

And as for that the Lord Moleyns hath wretyn that he dar put the matier in awarde of my Lord Chanceler, and in what juge he wole take to hym, &c. (which offre as I suppose shall be tolde to yow for to make yow to cesse your labour), thanne

[1] [From Paston MSS., B.M.] It is evident that this letter was written partly in answer to Gresham's of the 19th August 1450. The year is therefore the same. The letter is printed from a copy in Gresham's handwriting.
[2] *See* p. 161, Note 3.   [3] Cardinal Kemp.—*See* last No.

lete that be answerid, and my Lord Chaunceller enfourmed thus : The matier was in trete by th'assent of the Lord Moleyns a twene his counseil and myn, whiche assembled at London xvj. dyvers dayes, and for the more part there was a sergeant and vj. or vij. thrifty apprentisez ; at whiche tyme the Lord Moleyns title was shewed, and clerly answerid, in so meche that his own counseil seide they cowde no forther in the matier, desiryng me to ride to Salesbury to the Lord Moleyns, promyttyng of their part that thei wolde moeve the Lord Moleyns, so that thei trusted I shuld have myn entent or I come thens ; of whiche title and answer I send yow a copie that hath be put in to the Parlement, the Lord Moleyns being there present, whereto he cowde not sey nay. Also by fore this tyme I have agreed to put it in ij. juges, so thei wolde determyne by our evydences the right, moevyng nother partie to yeve other by ony mene, but only the right determyned, he to be fully recompensed that hath right. Whereto he wold not agree, but alle tymes wolde that thoe juges shulde entrete the parties as they myght be drawe to by offre and profre to my conceyte as men bye hors. Whiche matiers considerid, my counseil hath alwey conceyved that the tretees he offred hath be to non othir entent but to delaye the matier, or ellis to entrete me to relese my damages, for title hath he non. And he knowith weel the title shall never better be undirstond thanne it hath be by his counseil and myn atte seid comunyca-cions. And also my Lord Chanceler undirstond that the Lord Moleyns men toke and bar away more than ccli. [£200] worth of my goodes and catalles. Wherof I delyvered hym a bylle of every parcell, wherto al the world knoweth he canne make no title. And if he were disposed to do right, my counseill thynketh he shuld restore that, for therfor nedith nowthir comunycacion nor trete. And with owt he wole restore that, I trowe no man can thynk that his trete is to no good purpose.

I preye yow hertily laboure ye so to my Lord Chaunceller that owther he wole graunte me my desire, or ellis that he wole denye it. And lete me have answer from yow in wrytyng how ye spede. If my Lord Chanceler hath lost my bille that I

1450
SEPT. 4

1450
SEPT. 4

delyvered hym, wherof I sende yowe a copie, that thanne ye put up to hym an othir of the same, takyng a copie to your self.

Recomand me to my cosyn William Whyte,[1] and prey hym to gyf yow his help in this, and lete hym be prevye to this letter. And lete hym w[ete] that my cosyn his suster hath childe, a doughter. Wretyn at Norwich, the iiij. day of Septembre.

Dyverse men of my freendis avyse me to entre in to the maner of Gresham by force of my writte of restitucion, whiche I wole not do by cause the maner is so decayed by the Lord Moleyns occupacion, that where it was worth to me l. marks clerly by yeer, I cowde not now make it worth xxli.; for whiche hurt, and for othir hurtis, by this special assise I trust to have remedye.

137

ABSTRACT[2]

SIR JOHN FASTOLF TO SIR THOMAS HOWYS, THOMAS GRENE, AND WATKYN SHYPDAM.

SEPT. 7

Has no word from them of the correction and engrossing of the damages done to him by divers men in Norfolk, of part of which he sent a roll to them at Castre a month ago. Sends John Bokkyng for an answer. Was often damaged by the Duke of Suffolk's officers in Lodylond, both by undue amerci-ments and distraining cattle at Cotton, and by the officers of Cossey, of which there should be remembrances at Castre. Wrote also that they should see the Bishop of Norwich about the letter left with him concerning the award of Dedham. Is particularly anxious to know what they have done about Ryd-lyngfeld, &c.

London, 7 Sept. 29 Hen. vi.   *Signed.*

[1] Cardinal Kemp's servant.—*See* No. 128.
[2] [From MS. Phillipps, 9735, No. 245.]

138

ABSTRACT[1]

SIR JOHN FASTOLF TO SIR THOMAS HOWYS, at Castre, or at Pokethorp in Norwich, or at Haylydon Manor.

1450
SEPT. 15

Has received his letter by Thomas Fastolf touching his diligence about the recovery of the letter with the Bishop of Norwich, and of the evidences of Rydlyngfeld, with a copy of a certain indenture which F. has already sealed. Has no answer of the correction of the articles F. sent home to him two months ago. As my Lord of Norfolk is at Norwich to sit upon the oyer and terminer, you must labor to shew forth my grievances. Nothing can be done till after Michaelmas about the *venire facias* for the jury of Sybton. Has written this week by the Parson of Estharlyng to Berney, who, he hears, has been shewing favor to his adversaries. Refers him further to John Bokkyng, who is now in Norfolk.

London, 15 Sept. 29 Hen. vi.

139

HENRY VI. TO JOHN PASTON[2]

To oure trusty and welbeloved John Paston, Squier.

By the King.

TRUSTY and welbeloved, for asmuche as oure right trusty and welbeloved the Lord Moleyns is by oure special desire and comaundement waitting upon us, and now for divers consideracions moeving us, we purpose to sende hym in to certaine places for to execute oure commaunde-ment, for the whiche he ne may be attendant to be in oure countees of Northfolk and Suffolk at the time of oure Commis-sioners sitting upon oure commission of oier determiner within the same oure counties : We therfore desire and praye that

SEPT. 18

[1] [From MS. Phillipps, 9735, No. 253.]
[2] [From Fenn, iii. 362.] The bearing of this letter upon the contents of Nos. 135 and 136 proves it to be of the same year.

1450
SEPT. 18
considering his attendance upon us, and that he must applie hym to execute oure commaundement, ye wol respite as for any thing attempting ayenst hym as for any matiers that ye have to do or seye ayenst hym, or any other of his servants, welwillers, or tenaunts, by cause of hym, unto tyme he shal mowe be present to ansuere there unto ; wherein ye shall ministere unto us cause of pleasure, and over that, deserve of us right good thanke. Yeven under oure signet at oure Palois of Westmynster, the xviij. day of September.

140

ABSTRACT[1]

THE VICAR OF SPORLE TO JOHN PASTON.

1450(?)
SEPT. 29
Reports the disposition of 'my master,' the Provost. Francis Costard brought his evidence to my master's presence, where it was examined. He wondered what title you would claim to the land. I said, men said it was once free till it was soiled by a bondman. He gave more weight to the evidence of John Aleyn and Nicholas Waterman. Aleyn says he was steward of the manor, in Garleke's days, forty years, and never knew it claimed for bond ground ; and the said Nicholas says it was he who moved your father to buy the manor. Many others have set their seals to corroborate this. Asked him to be good unto Henry Halman, who was amerced in his court for chastising a servant of his, a bondman of yours. My master asked mockingly if a man might not beat his own wife.

Sporle, Michaelmas morning.

[This letter would seem to belong to the same year as No. 128, in which 'Costard's *nisi prius*' and an action against Halman are referred to. No. 129 also mentions Halman and the writer of this letter.]

[1] [From Paston MSS., B.M.]

141

THOMAS DENYES TO JOHN PASTON[1]

To my maister Paston in hast.

RIGHT worshipfull and my right good maister, I recomaund me to you. And like you wete that it is now . . . . I haf for Danyels sake put my self withynne the maner of Rydon ; and her is with me a kynnesman [of] my mastres your wifes, John Bendyssh. And as yestirday cam John Wodehous with a xij. hors to Geyt[on] ; on the othre side cometh Fitz William with xx. hors ; and on the third parte, oon Hoberd of Midelton hath redy a xx. felaws ; and on the fourth parte, stant the toune of Lynne redy with Herry Wodehous ; and thei all be gon thedir this nyght. This day folwyng cometh to thaym Herry Tudenham, William Narburgh, Thomas Trusbut, Thomas Kervile, and Shuldham servauntez, Salesbury and William Owayn. It is so that of my lorde[2] gete I no socour, and lever I had to dy than gif up the place sith I am ther yn. And I wene if thei gete the place upon me ther helpith my lif no pardon. Wherfore I lowly beseche yow, maister Paston, advertise in your wisdom that this was the first purpose of Tudenham and Heydon whils thei regned, to gete this place ; and to that intent thei brought hider the lord Roos, which now is full simpely thought on with my maister that I serve. And ye wete wele that I have most encountred the entent of Tudenham and Heydon of ony pouer man on lyve ; And if I be lost or put to an ungoodly rebuke heryn my service is the lesse of valu to you that be gentils of the shire. Wherfore I requyre your maistership to come hider in your persone with suych as ye seme not to that intent to take party in the mater, but to that intent to help to set peas in the shire, and to stire my lord for his honour. For yister-

1450
OCT. 4

[1] [Add. MS. 34,888, f. 45.] This is evidently the same year as No. 142, in which William Wayte writes to Paston that Denyes ought to withdraw his garrison from Roydon. The MS. is slightly mutilated at the top in the right-hand corner.
[2] The Earl of Oxford.

1450
OCT. 4
day my lord sent to Lynne and made a cry to be made that he wold be named in the writ of the statute of Northampton, and that cry hath caused the common pople of the toun of Lynne to stere the more. Neverthelesse all the substaunce of the toun is in peas and peasid by the wisdam of the Meir theer, but not for than sum of thaym come with Harry Wodehous, so that I deme he hath a vj[xx.] persones in all on all sides. I beseche you to send me hider sum socour beside forth, with John Osbern and John Lister with thaym, and come ye aftir a parte by your good wisdome soukyng (*sic*) their demenynges, and send me your advyse. Wretyn the nyght of the Sunday a forn seynt Feithesday.—Your servaunt, THOMAS DENYES.

This day I deme thei come beforn us. If ye help not now, Tudenham and Heydon shal achieve in their desese the conquest that thei coude never achieve in their prosperite.

142

WILLIAM WAYTE TO JOHN PASTON[1]

To my mayster, John Paston, in ryght gret hast.

OCT. 6
SYR, and it plese, I was in my Lord of Yorks[2] howse, and I herde meche thynge more thanne my mayster[3] wrytyth un to yow of ; I herde meche thynge in Fletestrede. But, Sir, my Lord was with the Kynge, and he vesaged so the mater that alle the Kynges howshold was and is aferd ryght sore ; and my seyd Lord hayth putte a bille to the Kynge, and desyryd meche thynge, qwych is meche after the Comouns desyre, and all is up on justice, and to putte all thos that ben indyted under arest with owte suerte or maynpryce, and to be tryed be lawe as lawe wyll ; in so meche that on Monday Sir William Oldhall was with the Kynge atte Westminster more

[1] [From Fenn, iii. 154.] This letter must have been written just after the Duke of York came over from Ireland in 1450, when he demanded that justice should be fairly administered against persons accused. A Parliament was summoned, which met on the 6th November, and Sir William Oldhall was chosen as Speaker.
[2] Richard, Duke of York, afterwards Protector, the father of King Edward IV.
[3] The writer was clerk to Judge Yelverton.

thanne to houres, and hadde of the Kynge good cher. And the Kynge desyryd of Sir William Oldhall that he shuld speke to hese cosyn York, that he wold be good Lord to John Penycock, and that my Lord of York shuld wryte un to hese tenance that they wold suffyr Peny Cocks officers go and gader up hys rentes fermes with inne the seyd Dukes lordsheps. And Sir William Oldhall answherd ayen to the Kynge, and preyed hym to hold my Lord escusyd, for thow my Lord wrotte under hese seale of hys armes hys tenantez wyll not obeyet ; in someche that whanne Sir Thomas Hoo mette with my Lord of Zork be yon Sent Albons, the Western men felle upon hym, and wold a slayne hym, hadde [not?] Sir William Oldhall abe [*have been*], and therfor wold the Westerne men affalle up on the seyd Sir William, and akyllyd hym. And so he tolde the Kynge.

Sir Borle Jonge and Josse labour sore for Heydon and Tudenham to Sir Wilem Oldhall, and profyr more thanne to thowsand pownde for to have hese good Lordshep ; and therfor it is noon other remedye but late Swhafham men be warned to mete with my seyd Lord on Fryday nest comyng atte Pykenham on horssebak in the most goodly wyse, and putte sum bylle un to my Lord of Sir Thomas Tudenham, Heydon, and Prentys, and crye owte on hem, and that all the women of the same town be there also, and crye owte on hem also, and calle hem extorcionners, and pray my Lord that he wyll do sharp execucyons up on hem. And my mayster counceyll yow that ze shuld meve the Meyer and all the Aldermen with all her Comoners to ryde ayens my Lord, and that ther ben madde byllez, and putte them up to my Lord, and late all the towne cry owte on Heydon, Todenham, Wyndham, and Prentys, and of all here fals mayntenours, and telle my Lord how meche hurte thei have don to the cetye, and late that be don in the most lamentabyl wyse ; for, Sir, but yf [*unless*] my Lord here sum fowle tales of hem, and sum hyddows noys and crye, by my feyth thei arne ellys lyke to come to grace. And therfor, Sir, remember yow of all these maters.

Sir, also I spake with William Norwych, and asked hym

1450
OCT. 6

1450
OCT. 6

after the Lord Moleyns how he stod to my Lord ward; and he told me he was sor owte of grace, and that my Lord of York lovyth hym nought. William Norwych tolde me that he durste undertake for to brynge yow un to my Lord, and make hym your ryght good Lord; and, Sir, my mayster counceyllyd yow that ze shuld not spare, but gete yow hese good Lordshep.

Sir, be war of Heydon, for he wold destroyed yow be my feyth. The Lord Scales and Sir William Oldhall arne made frendys.

Sir, labour ze for [to] be knyth of the shire, and speke to my Mayster Stapulton[1] also that he be yt; Sir, all Swafham, and they be warned, wyll zeve yow here voyses. Sir, speke with Thomas Denys, and take hese good avys therin. Sir, speke to Denys that he avoyde hys garyson atte Rydon, for there is non other remedy but deth for Danyell, and for all thos that arne indyted. Sir, labour ze to the Meyer that John Dam[2] or Will Jenney be burgeys for the cetye of Norwych, telle them that he may be yt as well as Yonge is of Brystow, or the Recordor is of London, and as the Recordour of Coventre is for the cite of Coventre, and it so in many places in Ingland. Also, Sir, thynk on Yernemouth that ze ordeyne that John Jenney, or Limnour, or sum good man be burgeys for Yernemouth. Ordeyne ze that Jenneys mown ben in the Parlement, for they kun seye well.

Sir, it wore wysdam that my Lord of Oxenford wayte on my Lord of Yorke. In good feyth, good Sir, thynke on all these maters; meche more I hadde to wryte on to yow, yf I kowde a remembryd me, but I hadde no leyser be my fyth. Hold me escused of my lewde rude wrytyng. Late John Dam be ware for the Lorde Moleyns; and, Sir, late the cetye be ware, for he wyll do hem a velony, but yf he may have hese men; and, Sir, yf he come to Norwych, look there be redy to wayte up on the Mayer a good fellawshep, for it is seyd her that they arne but bestys.

[1] Sir Miles Stapleton.
[2] John Dam actually was returned to Parliament for the city of Norwich in November 1450.

176

1450
OCT. 6

Sir, my mayster bad me wryte un to yow that ze shuld store the Mayer and alle the Alderman to crye on my Lord that they mown have justyce of these men that be indyted, and that my Lorde wyll speke un to the Kynge therof. And, Sir, in divers partes in the town there [where] my Lord comyth, there wolde be ordeyned many porcions of Comeners to crye on my Lord for justice of these men that arne indyted, and telle her nammes, in speciall Todenham, Heydon, Wyndham, Prentys. Sir, I cende yow a copy of the bylle[1] that my Lord of Yorke putte un to the Kynge; and, Sir, late copyes go abowte the cetye i now, for the love of God, wy[c]he have yow in hese kepyng.

Wretyn on Seynt Feyth daye, in hast.

Be your Servaunt,   W. WAYTE.

143

RICHARD, DUKE OF YORK, TO KING HENRY VI[2]

Richard, Duke of York, his Peticion to Kyng Henry for the punyshement of Treytors, &c.

1450

PLEASE it your Hyghnes tendirly to consider the grett grutchyng and romer that is universaly in this your reame of that justice is nouth dewly ministred to such as trespas and offende a yens your lawes, and in special of them that ben endited of treson, and other beyng openly noysed of the same; wherfore for gret inconveniens that have fallen, and grett is lyke to fallen her after in your seid reame, which God defende, but if [*unless*] be your Hyghnesse provysion convenable be mad for dew reformacion and punyshment in this behalf; Wherfore I, your humble suget and lyge man, Richard, Duke of York, willyng as effectually as I kan, and desiryng suerte and prosperite of your most roiall person, and

[1] See next No.
[2] [From Fenn, i. 64.] The MS. from which this was printed by Fenn was doubtless the copy of my Lord of York's 'bill' which William Wayte sent to John Paston, as mentioned in the end of the last letter.

VOL. II.—M   177

1450

welfare of this your noble reame, councel and advertyse your excellent, for the conversacion [*conservation*] of good tranquillite and pesable rewle among all trew sogetts, for to ordeyn and provyde that dewe justice be had a yenst all such that ben so endited or openly so noysed: wher inne I offre, and wol put me in devour for to execute your comaundements in thes premises of such offenders, and redresse of the seid mysrewlers to my myth and power. And for the hasty execucion herof, lyke it your Hyghnes to dresse your letteres of prevy seale and writts to your officers and ministres to do take, and areste all soch persons so noysed or endited, of what astatte, degre, or condicion so ever thei be, and them to comytte to your Tour of London, or to other your prisons, there to abyde with outen bayle or maynprice on to the tyme that they be utterly tryed and declared, after the cours of your lawe.

144

SIR JOHN FASTOLF TO SIR THOMAS HOWYS AND WILLIAM BARKER[1]

To my ryght trusty freende, Sir Thomas Howys, Parson of Castellcombe, beyng at Castre, and William Barker, in haste, at Castre Yn, by Jermuth.

OCT. 15

RYGHT trusty and welbelovyd freende, I grete you well. And as for Hygham place to be sold, as ye avysen me to bye it at the some of C. mark or wythynne, and reserve yn the said payment myne oune dewtee, and pay the remenant in wolle to the said Hygham credytes as your lettre makyth mencion; I hafe undrestand that William Jenney shall be her thys wek, and I shall veele hym how neere it may be sold; for yff the wydow wolle sylle it after xiiij. yeer or xv. yeere that it may be leten, sendyth me utterly word, for I wolle not melle of it ellys thus avysed. And sende ye me word how mech more yn value yn a stoon shall I syle my

[1] [From Fenn, iii. 92.]

178

1450
OCT. 15

wolle, and how [*much?*] anothyr chapman wole gefe me for the place when I hafe bought it; but after xiiij. yeer I wold by the place.

Wretyn at London, the xv. day of October anno xxix. regni Regis Henrici vi.

J. FASTOLF.

145

ANONYMOUS TO JOHN PASTON[1]

To my cosyn, John Paston.

OCT. (?)

I RECOMAWNDE me un to yow the best wyse I kan. Whanne I cam to Ware, ther herd I furst tydynges that the Lord Moleyns shuld come in to Norfolk in hast with grette pupyll, and, as on of hys men seyd ther, with the vij^xx [*sevenscore*]. Also a man of the Lady Morles[2] cam thedyr owte of Wyllshire ther thanne, and seyd that the seyd Lord was comyng thedyrward with grette pupyll. And atte London a man of hys hedde large langage, and seyd that my Lord shuld come to Norffolk, and do meche thyng agayns hem that hadde do indite hym and hys men, and also for the personyng of hys men atte Norwych. This is sopposyd verely to be Heydons werke that wyll sette hym verely to do the utterst ayens yow and John Dam in the werst wyse that he can. Ze have both lordshep and frendshep in your countre, and also good inow to reciste hym yf he wyll do yow wronge, and peraventur that shuld brynge thys matier nyer and ende thanne it is now. Whedder it be to be done or not, I remitte that to youre counceyll.

Also, my Lord[3] shall be atte Walsyngham on Sonday nest comynge, a from thens he shall go to Norwych. For any thynge in the werd [*world*] meve my Lord of Oxenford and

[1] [From Paston MSS., B.M.] The tone of this letter so closely resembles that of William Wayte of the 6th October 1450, especially in its warnings to Paston and John Damme, and in the information it contains as to Lord Moleyns not being in favour with the Duke of York, that it may be safely inferred to have been written about the same period.
[2] See page 84, Note 2.   [3] Probably the Duke of York.

179

THE PASTON LETTERS

1450
OCT. (?)
my cosyn Sir Miles Stapulton that they awayte up on my seyd Lord in the most wurchepfull wyse that they kun, and do hym as good attendaunce and plesaunce as they mown. And ye do the same also ; and that the cyte of Norwych mete with hym in the best wyse also ; and also that they and ze also cherse and wirchep well Sir William Oldhalle. And ther be good informacion made ayens T. T. and H.,¹ for they wyll spend mᴸ mᴸ li. [£2000] for to come in ther, and that were petye. Spende sum what of your good now, and gette yow lordshep and frendshep ther, *quia ibi pendet tota lex et prophetæ.* And send som man to aspye of the governaunce, and of the comyng of the Lord Moleyns, and take hed to your self. And byd John Dam be war of hym self. Sum men suppose that my Lord of York cherse not meche the seyd Lord Moleyns. And send sum men hedyr often to London that mown he them here and brynge yow tydynges. And I pray God spede yow in alle youre werkes.

Youre Cosyn,
NAMELES ATTE THIS TYME.

Endorsed: Literæ Fastolff, Yelverton, circa le oyrdeterminer.—Memorandum de billa actus justic' apud Walsingham.

146

JAMES GRESHAM TO JOHN PASTON²

To my worshipfull Maister Paston, at Norwich, in haste, be this delyvered.

[OCT.] PLEASE it yow to wete that I come to London the Wednesseday at even late next after my departyng from yow, and it was told me that my Maister Calthorp hadde writyng fro my Lord of York to awayte on hym at his

¹ Thomas Tuddenham and Heydon.
² [From Fenn, iii. 94.] This letter, though it has no date except of the day of the week, must have been written about October 1450, after the Duke of York had come over from Ireland, and before the elections for the Parliament which met in November, and the appointment of sheriffs in the different counties for the ensuing year. The references to the affair of Lord Moleyns and to the indictment of Heydon cannot belong to a later year.

180

HENRY VI

comyng in to Norffolk to be oon of his men, and that no gentilman of Norffolk had writyng to awayte on hym but he ; and sum folke wene that it is to th'entent that he shuld bo outhir shiref or knyght of the shire, to the fortheryng of othir folks, &c.

1450
[OCT.]

The Kyng is remevid from Westminster, summe men sey to Fysshwick,¹ and summe sey to Bristowe. And it is seid that he hath do wretyn to alle his men that be in the chekroll² to awayte on hym atte Parlement in their best aray ; why, no man can telle. Heydon³ was with my Maister Yelverton,⁴ and desired hym to see the recordes of his endytementz, and axed of hym if he were indited of felonye ; and my Maister Yelverton told hym it was. And thereto H. seide ' Sir, ye wole recorde that I was never thef ; ' and he seid he trowed right weel that he cowde telle why he took Plumpsteds goods, and othir words whiche were long to write. And my Maister Y. seid to hym he cowde not knowe the laborer of th'endytement, and H. seid ageyn he knewe weel the laborer thereof ; and my Maister Y. conceyte is H. ment yow. Wherfor he advyseth yow that in onywyse ye make Plumpsted to take apell accordyng ; for if he so do, thanne is H. barred of his conspirace, and also of his damages, though that he be nonn-sewed therin, or though it be afterward discontynued, &c., and ellis are ye in jopardy of a conspirace, for H. hopeth to have the world better to his entent thanne it is nowe. For it is told me that rather thanne he shuld fayle of a shiref this yeer comyng for his entent, he wole spende mᴸli. [£1000].

This communicacion be twene them was on Moneday last passed, and on Tewisday last passed H. mette with Maister Markham,⁵ and he tolde H. his part how that he levid un-goodly in puttyng awey of his wyff, and kept an other, &c. ; and therwith he turned pale colour, and seid he lyved not but

¹ In Lancashire, now in the suburbs of Preston.
² The check-roll is a roll or book, containing the names of such persons as are attendants, and in pay to the King, or other great men, as their household servants, &c.—F. ³ *See* page 166, Note 3.
⁴ William Yelverton, a Justice of the King's Bench.
⁵ John Markham, one of the Judges of the King's Bench, who became Chief Justice in 1461.

181

THE PASTON LETTERS

1450
[OCT.]
as God was pleased with, ne dede no wrong to no person. And therupon Maister Markham reherced how he demened hym a genst men of Court, and named yow and Genneye ; and H. seid, as touchyng the peple that rifled yow, and the doyng thereof, he was not privy therto, for he was that tyme here at London ; and as touchyng the Lord Moleyns title, H. enforced gretly, and seid his title was better thanne yours.

Yisterday was my Maister Yelverton at dyner with my Maister Fastolf,¹ and there among other thei were avysed that my Maister F. shall write to my Lord of Norffolk that he certifie the Kyng and his Counseill how the cuntre of N. and S. [*Norfolk and Suffolk*] stonde right wildely, withowt a mene may be that justice be hadde, whiche wole not be but if a man of gret byrthe and lyflod there be shiref thes yer comyng, to lede the peple in most peas ; and therto thei named Maister Stapilton,² if it wole happe, &c. Also that my Lord Norffolk shall certifie the Kyng and his Counseill that but if the day of the oyer and termyner stonde, it wole be full harde, by cause the peple is so wylde.

Also that alle knyghtes and escuyers of the same cuntre shuld certifie the same, for summe of H. part have boosted that all . . . . at Norwich shuld not be worth an haughe. *Ideo,* &c.

Item, Prentise is now in the Mydle Inne, and Dynne . . . . .

Almyghty God have yow in his kepyng. Wretyn the Thursday next after my departyng. . . . .

Your,
J. GRESHAM.

¹ Sir John Fastolf. ² Sir Miles Stapleton.

182

HENRY VI

147

JAMES GRESHAM TO JOHN PASTON¹

To my worshipfull maister, John Paston, Escuyr, dwellynge att Norwich, in hast.

AFTER that myn letter was wretyn, I spak with Maister Yelverton, and tolde hym the substance of my letter to yow. And he bad me write to yow that as touchyng the matier of my Lord of Oxeford, he shall lette the awardyng and th'entre therof als long as he may ; and he demyth veryly that H. Wodehous coude never have take up on his knowelage to have called up on the matier with owt counseil and enformacion of Heydon, and it were weel do that my Lord of Oxeford knewe it.

1450

Item, Maister Yelverton told me that the Lord Moleyns was enfourmed that he and alle his men wern endited of felonye in Norffolk, whiche caused hym and his to be right wroth toward my maister and yow. And Maister Yelverton hath tolde a man of the Kyngges Benche called Styrop, whiche is a man of the Lord Moleyns, the trouth that nothir he ner noon of his is endited, and Stirop is now in to Wiltshire, and shall telle it to the Lord M. ; for that shall squage weel his hete of wrethe. And as touchyng Germyn,² if he be Shiref, William Genney wole undirtake for hym that he shall and wole be ruled weel inow, &c.

¹ [From Paston MSS., B.M.] This letter is anonymous, but is in the handwriting of James Gresham. It must have been written in the autumn of the year 1450, while Lord Molyns was in Wiltshire, and when the nomination of John Jermyn as Sheriff of Norfolk was expected, but had not yet been decided on, or at least not known to the writer. It was therefore certainly written after the preceding number, though the latter is probably not the letter to which it was intended to serve as a postscript.
² John Jermyn was actually appointed Sheriff in the end of the year 1450.

183

148

THE DUKE OF NORFOLK TO JOHN PASTON[1]

To oure trusti and welbelovid John Paston, Squier.

The Duc of Norffolk.

1450(?)
OCT. 16

RIGHT trusti and welbelovid, we grete you well. And forasmoche as oure unkill of York and we have fully appoynted and agreed of such ij. persones for to be knightes of shire of Norffolk as oure said unkill and we thinke convenient and necessarie for the welfare of the said shire, we therfor pray you, in oure said unkill name and oures bothe, as ye list to stonde in the favour of oure good Lordshipp, that ye make no laboure contrarie to oure desire. And God have you in his keping.

Wreten at Bury Seynt Edmondis, the xvj. day of Octobr.

149

THE EARL OF OXFORD TO JOHN PASTON[2]

To owr welbeloved John Paston.

OCT. 18

RIGHT welbeloved, I grete yow well. And as towchyng for tydyngs, I can none, savyng that my Lord of Norffolk met with my Lord of York at Bury on Thursday, and there were to gedre til Friday, ix. of the clokke, and than they departed. And there a gentilman of my Lord of York toke unto a yeman of myn, John Deye, a

[1] [Douce MS. 393, f. 92.] This letter and that which follows clearly refer to the same matter. The time of year and the part taken by the Duke of York in the election are circumstances which in themselves create a pretty strong presumption in favour of the year 1450. And this presumption almost becomes a certainty, when we observe that the date of this letter—16th October—was a Friday in that year; for the meeting of York and Norfolk is stated in the next letter to have been on a Thursday and Friday, and this letter would doubtless have been written as soon as a decision had been come to between the two Lords.
[2] [From Fenn, i. 98.] For evidence of date, see note to preceding letter.

184

1450(?)
OCT. 18

tokene and a sedell of my Lords entent, whom he wold have knyghtts of the shyre, and I sende you a sedell closed of their names in this same lettre, wherfore me thynkith wel do to performe my Lords entent.

Wretyn the xviij° day of Octobr, at Wynche.

OXENFORD.

Com. Norff', { Sir William Chambirlayn.[1] }
            { Henry Grey. }

150

THE DUKE OF NORFOLK TO JOHN PASTON[2]

To oure right trusty and welbeloved servaunt, John Paston, Squier.

The Duc of Norffolk.

OCT. 22

RIGHT trusti and right welbelovid, we grete yo hertily well, prayng you specially that ye will make you redy to awayte upon us at Yippiswich toward the Parlement the viij. day of Novembre in youre best aray, with as many clenly people as ye may gete for oure worship at this tyme; for we will be there like oure estate in oure best wise without any delay. Yeven under oure signet in oure Castell of Framlyngham, the xxij. day of Octobre.

[1] The names actually returned by the Sheriff of Norfolk and Suffolk for this Parliament were—for Norfolk, Sir Miles Stapleton and Henry Gray; for Suffolk, Sir *Roger* Chamberleyn and Sir Edmund Mulso.
[2] [Douce MS. 393, f. 93.] This letter must have been written either in 1449 or in 1450, in both of which years Parliament met on the 6th of November; and as we have other letters, both of the Duke of Norfolk and the Earl of Oxford, relating to the Parliament of 1450, we are inclined to think this also belongs to the later year. Framlingham, the seat of the Duke of Norfolk, is not more than thirty-two miles from Bury, from which he wrote on the 16th.

185

151

JOHN DAMME AND JAMES GRESHAM TO JOHN PASTON[1]

To my worshipfull and good maister, John Paston, Escuyer.

1450
NOV. 11

PLEASE it yow to wete that Sir William Oldhall is chosyn Speker of the Parlement, and admytted by the Kyng, &c. Item, the day of oier and termyner shall holde at Norwich on Moneday next comyng, and by that cause my Lord of Oxenford shall be disported of his comyng to the Parlement for to attende to the Sessions of oier, &c.

Item, the Lord Moleyns hadde langage of yow in the Kynggs presence as my Maister Yelverton can telle yow by mouthe. Your presence shuld have do meche ease here in your own matiers and other, as your weel willers thynkyn, and your absence do non ease here; netheles my Maister Yelverton shall telle you all, &c.

It is seid here that the Duke of York and the Duke of Norffolk shulln not come here this vii. nyght.

Item, it is supposed that an oier and determyner shall come hastily into Norwich. William Dynne abydeth therfore.

As touchyng Shirefs, ther arn none chosyn ne named, and as men suppose, non shall be chosyn til my Lord of Yorks comyng, &c.

Wretyn in hast at Westminster, Mercur' in Festo Sancti Martini. Yours,

J. D. and GR.

It is apoynted that who shall sue any bille in the Parlement, thei must be put into the Commone Hous by for Seint Edmunds day[2] atte ferthest, &c.

[1] [From Fenn, iii. 100.] The date of this letter is determined by the fact mentioned in the first sentence. Sir William Oldhall was chosen Speaker of the Parliament which met on the 6th November 1450. John Damme represented Norwich in this Parliament. Moreover, the date at the end of the letter shows that St. Martin's day fell on Wednesday in the year it was written, which was the case in 1450.
[2] 20th November.

186

152

RICHARD CALLE TO JOHN PASTON[1]

To my ryght reverent and most wurschipfull Maistre my Maister John Paston the eldre, esquyer, at London in the Inner Tempyll.

1450
NOV. 11

RYGHT reverent and my mooste wurschipful maistre, I recommaunde me unto youre goode maistership. Like you to witte that I have taken astate in the londe at Gresham as your maisterschep aviced me; wherfore I besche you that ther may be taken an axion in my feffes name and myn a yenst Jamys Gatte, as you semeth beest, and as hasty processe as may be had a yenst hym, with your goode avice I wold; for what tyme as I had taken astate he labored to men of the toun to have putte it in a ward, but I wold not tyll I had spoken with your mastership, &c. Also John Warles schal gather the rente and ferme of Basyngham this yere. Item, William Smythe schal occupie hes ferme this yere, and Croumer. And as for the yeris aftre I have founde a meane that all your landis schall be letten as weele as ever they weere in that maner, with helpe of one Robert Coole, weche Robert fereth hym sore of the affence weche he ded a yenst John Herbynger; for he is informed that your maisterschip hath taken a axion a yenst hym, and John Herbynger hath du hym lost in the hundred xld., and he hath hym in the scheryffis turne. Wherfore that it like you to withdrawe if any axion ye have a yenst hym for he will a bide any ij. men award ther aboute; and more over he is the most able man to take a ferme of lond that I knowe in your lordeship, and he schal be a gret fermour of your the next yere. Ferthermore, ther is on Robert Wyghte, otherwise Farbusschour, aftre that your officer of Matelask had seased al Lyghtfot catell for suche

[1] [Add. MS. 34,889, f. 160.] This letter must have been written in 1450. We know already that John Paston recovered possession of Gresham between September 1450 and March 1451 (see pp. 170, 219). Here we find that he deputed Richard Calle to take possession for him in November.

187

1450
NOV. 11

dwtees as whas owynge the seid Robert Wyght, come upon your bonde grounde, and brak doun the gardeyn dike of the seid Lyghtfotes and toke a wey a bullok of ij. yere age and hath caryed it a wey out of your lordschip; wherfore the tenauntes desireth your maistership that ye well take an axion a yenst hym that he may be punyssched. Item, as for a dey at Mauteby we can non geete, for Wynston woll not of it in no wice. And as for tidinges here we here non but my lord of Wurcestre lithe at Blakney and kepith housold there in the Frieri. Item, Wymondham had entred in to Felbryge and he whas put out be the comens and like if had beden to have lost hes heed. My ryght wurschipful mastre, All myghty Jhesu preserve and kepe you. Wreten at Heyneford on Sein Marteyn Day. Be your pore servaunt and bedman,

RIC. CALLE.

153

ABSTRACT[1]

SIR JOHN FASTOLF TO SIR THOMAS HOWYS, Parson of Castlecombe.

NOV. 11

'Right trusty and welbeloved friends,' I thank you for the quittance of Richard Sellyng you have sent me by Worcestre, with a quittance of Fauconere for the purchase of Davyngton, and another of Roys for the purchase of Tychewell. Ask my cousin Herry Sturmer's wife to search for an indenture and other writings between me and Sellyng or Lady Wiltshire. As you inform me that Sir Thomas Todenham has sent to John Clerc to be at London, you must ask him and his wife to go before the bailiffs of Yarmouth, and certify how it was Bysshop's wife did not receive the £100 I was ruled to pay her. John Clerc must not come up till I send for him.—(In margin, 'eyer and determiner.') Special labour has been made that Justice Yelverton should not come down this Martinmas, but the King and Lords have determined that he shall keep his day; 'and the labour that ye, with my cousin Paston, made late to my Lord Norfolk was right well avised, in case that the Justice should be countermanded.' Urge my friends to do their very best for me now in the matters 'labored last at the oyer and terminer,' that they may take a worshipful end. Thank Nicholas Bokkyng for what he did about the certificate of the jury in the office[2] of Tychewell, and beg him to get it sealed in time, which

[1] [From MS. Phillipps, 9735, No. 226.]
[2] An inquisition taken by the escheator of a county by virtue of his office was frequently called an 'office.' Its object was to ascertain the King's title to certain lands.

188

1450
NOV. 11

will be a great evidence for the recovery of my manor. Sends home some horses 'to be occupied in the cart.' Commendations to his cousin John Berney.
Signed.

Send for William Cole about the accounts, and thank the Parson of Hayledson[1] for the three writings of Wiltshire's will and Gorney he sent me by Worcester; but say I prayed him to search for more.

London, St. Martin's day.

[This letter is dated on Martinmas day, at which date in the year 1450 it will be seen by the preceding number that Justice Yelverton was going down into Norfolk, and an oyer and terminer was going to be held at Norwich. The reference to the 'office,' or inquisition, of Tychewell also proves the year to be 1450.—See Nos. 162 and 164, pp. 199-201.]

154

JUSTICE YELVERTON TO SIR JOHN FASTOLF[2]

A Lettre to Sir John Fastoff from Justice Yelverton.[3]

MY moste worshypfull and best betrusted maister, I recommaund me to yow, thankyng yow for manye grete gentlenesse and kyndnesse that ye hafe showed unto me, and for the grete ease that I had of your man and your horsys also.

As for tydyngs owte of thys contree, here ys a marveyllous disposed contree, and manye evylle wylled peple to Sir Thomas Tuddenham and Heydon, and but yff they been putt in comfort there by the meene of a good shyreve and undreshyreve, they may hafe remedye now by the ordre of lawe, and ellys grete inconvenices arn lyke for to folowe ther off. Therfor, Sir, for the weele of all our gode contree, mewyth the Kyng,

[1] Thomas Hert was presented to Hayledson by Sir John Fastolf in 1448.
[2] [From Fenn, iii. 50.] This would appear to have been written in 1450, just after Yelverton's arrival in Norfolk, whither, it will be seen by the last two letters, he was going in November. The nomination of sheriffs had not yet taken place, and was anxiously expected by many, in the hope that it would lessen the influence of Sir Thomas Tuddenham and Heydon, who had hitherto been very powerful in Norfolk.
[3] This is only an endorsement on the MS., and is not even contemporaneous. The MS. itself is not addressed, being, as shown in the margin, only a copy, marked 'Copia' in the same hand as the document.

189

1450
NOV.

my Lord Chaunceller,[1] and all othyr Lordes as ye thynk best for thys matier on thys behalf.

Also, Sir, yff they noysse me by thee meene of my Lord Scalys, or by anye othyr meene, or by onye bylle sewed by Brygg, or by onye othyr man by her [*i.e. their*] craft, that it please yow to sey for me yn savacion of my pore worshyp, whych I wote well they may not hurt but they doo me wrongs, to the Kyng, my Lord Chaunceller, my Lord of Wynchester,[2] my Lord Cromewell, and in othyr places, as ye semyth, that no credence be goven to myne hurt yn myne absence.

Also, Sir, that William Geney and Brayn, the clerks of the Sessions, ben hastyed hedreward as well as they may; and, Sir, my cousyn Paston and my brothyr Cleere can tell yow moch more thyng that I shuld wryte off to yow, and I had leyser; but I shall wythynne short tyme sende yow more tydyngs owte of thys contree, by the grace of God, whych hafe yow yn hys holye kepyng.

By your old Servaunt,
WILLIAM YELVERTON, Justice.

155

JUSTICE YELVERTON TO JOHN BOCKING[3]

To my welbeloved cosyn, John Bockyng.

WORSHIPFULL and right welbeloved cosyn, I comaunde me to you, prayng you to recomaunde me to my Maister Fastolf, and thank hym in my name hertily for his man and his hors. And also for to meve hym for that we may have a good shereve and a good undershereve that neythir for good favore no fere wol returne for the Kyng, ne betwix partie and partie, none othir men but such

[1] Cardinal Kemp.
[2] The celebrated William de Waynflete, Bishop of Winchester.
[3] [From Paston MSS., B.M.] The correspondence of this letter with the last is such as to leave no doubt that they were written at the same period. The MS. is a contemporaneous copy.

190

1450
NOV.

as ar good and trewe, and in no wyse will be forsworne; for the pepil here is loth to compleyne til thei here tidynges of a good shereve. And that William Jenney and Brayne, the clerk of the Cessions, and Thomas Denys, ben hastid hydirward as fast as thei may, and than men supposen he nedith not to dowghtyn his materes. And also that my cosyn Paston be so hastily holpen in his maters that he may sone come hedir ageyn. And also that my maistir be my sheld and my defense ageyns all fals noyses and sclaundres meved ayens me by her menes in myn absens.

At Walsyngham, and in othir places in the duche of Lancastre, men shal be redy to seche Heydon at hom in his own hous, if he come home; and in lyke wyse standith Sir Thomas Tudenham his neighburs to hymward as the more part of the pepil seth in this cuntre. His men have told here the falsest tales of Sir William Oldhall and of me that evere I herd speke of. It wer ful necessarye and profitable to the Kyng and to his pepil for to have othir officers in his duche.

Asay how ye can sett hem a werk in the Parlement, for if this maters be sped as it is aforn desired, thei ar lyke to be sett a werk here well inough, by the grace of God, which have you in holy kepyng.

By your cosyn,
WILLIAM YELVERTON, Justice.

156

ABSTRACT[1]

SIR JOHN FASTOLF TO SIR THOMAS, Pastor of Castlecombe, JOHN BOKKYNG, and WATKIN SHYPDAM.

NOV. 23

Thanks the Parson for a letter by Robert Botiller, and one by John Clerc, advising that Bokking and William Jenney be 'in that parties' betimes for the oyer and terminer. Has received instruction of the first purchase of Haylysdon. Is glad John Clerc is come. Much strange labour has been made to him by Tasborough and Swolle. Complains of the untruth of Appulzerd of Norwich in the Lady Bardolf's matter. A bailly of Hikelyng maintains the Prior in his

[1] [From an original, sold by Messrs. Puttick and Simpson on the 2nd March 1870.]

191

1450
NOV. 23
wrong against Fastolf. William Barker had a box of evidences of the farm of Lady Bardolf's lands, and a deed of Norman's feoffment with evidences of Saxthorp, which cannot be found here, and must have been left at Norwich or Castre. Don't forget Norman's matter, and the maintainers of the false inquest of Beyton Bradwell. Wyndham wants to be friends with me about the Lady Bardolf's matter. The master of St. Giles has been with me for the purchase of Mundham Maner with appurtenances in Cyselond, and I have agreed with him for 200 marks. Don't forget the bailly of Hykelyng, who said I should forge [i.e. had forged] evidence, &c.

London, 23 Nov. 29 Hen. VI. *Signed.*

[An extract from the latter part of this letter is printed by Blomefield, *Hist. Norf.* iv. 388-9 (Note 9).]

157

ABSTRACT[1]

NOV. 28
Power of attorney by John, Cardinal Archbishop of York, and others, to John Est and others, including William Worcestre and Geoffrey Sperlyng, to deliver seisin to Walter Leyhert, Bishop of Norwich, and others, of and in the manor of Mundham, &c.—28 Nov. 29 Hen. VI.

20 *Seals, of which three are lost.*

Endorsed by Blomefield—'Sir John Fastolff's Feoffees Release,' &c., with a reference to his *History of Norfolk*, vol. ii. 762 (fol. ed.).

158

ABSTRACT[2]

DEC. 2
Thanks them for their diligence. Has respited the matter against Wyndham touching the Lady Bardolf till next term, as he offers to come to an agreement.[3] Is ready to agree with all persons who will find sufficient surety, except Sir Thomas Tudenham, Heydon, and *Pykering* (underlined). Master John Botewright has sent him a letter of great loss and damage done by Tudenham and Heydon to the 'comyn' of Swaffham, 'benymmyng (?) 600 acres lond of her

[1] [From Add. Charter 17,238, B.M.]
[2] [From MS. Phillipps, 9735, No. 235.]
[3] Fastolf's signature is placed here, near the beginning of the letter, after the first paragraph.

192

---

comyn.' Has written to 'my brother Yelverton,' and would write also to my Lord of Oxford, but that he is so vexed in spirit 'in thys trouble seson,' that at times he cannot abide the signing and sealing of a letter. Prays them to see well to the accountants and auditors' charges.

1450
DEC. 2

London, 2 Dec. 29 Hen. VI.

'And because I might [not] abide till the writing of the matters that I commanded Worcester to write, I signed the letter so near the beginning; but I will ye tender, nevertheless, my letter and articles for my most profit and avail.'

159

ABSTRACT[1]

Memoranda signed by Sir John Fastolf (*mutilated at the head*) viz. about the Prior of Hikelyng; that John Ulveston and John Andrew be indicted for forging the office of Boyton, as well as for Bradwell in Suffolk; Brayn to deliver copies; if they sit in Suffolk, to take heed of Sypton's matter. Nicholas Apleyard will doubtless appear to the bill of maintenance; so the Prior and Sacristan and Sir H. Inglose must be 'laboured' to give information. Process against Dynne, Prentis, &c. Obligation of 200 marks that Brian Stapleton has in keeping. The Parson of Castlecombe to speak with John Emond of Taverham secretly about one who pretended title to Dedham, &c. 'That ready word come alway atwix Norwich and this of the tidings that are there.' Matter of Margaret Brygge, &c. 'That Paston conceive the crossed letter, and say therein to my Lady Felbrigg.' To speak to Paston and Jenney about various matters. To speak to Reppys 'that he feel my Lord Scales and the Prior of Hikelyng jointly if they will yet treat, as my Lord Scales and my master were agreed at London,' &c.

1450

[From the reference to Sypton's matter, it would appear that this paper is a little before the two following in point of date.]

[1] [From MS. Phillipps, 9735, No. 277.]

VOL. II.—N
193

160

SIR JOHN FASTOLF TO SIR THOMAS HOWYS AND JOHN BOCKING[1]

To my ryght trusty frende and servaunt, Sir Thomas, Parson of Castellcombe, and John Bokkyng, at Prynce Inne yn Norwych, or at Beklys.

1450
DEC. 4
RYGHT trusty and welbelevyd servaunt, I grete you well. And forasmoch as I undrestand that on Monday next the oyer and terminer shall be holden at Beklys, and ye avysen to sende yow a certificat for cause of the forged quytaunce by Sir John Sypton, whych wrytyng I scende you by the berer here of, prayng you that ye solicit to my councell that the said Sir John Sypton be endited thereuppon, and that ye foryete not Ulveston, Andreus, and the othyrs that forged a fals office[2] to cast my maner of Bradwell yn to the Kyngs hand.

Item, I sende you a copie of Sibieton ple and quytaunce forged to grounde your bille by it.

No more for haste, but God kepe you. Wryt at London, iiij. day of December, anno xxix° regni Regis H. VI.

Item, Sir John Bukk, Parson of Stratford, physshed my stankys at Dedham, and holp brake my damme, destroyed my new mille, and was ayenst me allwey at Dedham, to the damage of 20l., which may be endyted allso.

Item, he and John Cole hath by force this yeer, and othyr yeers, take off my waters at Dedham, to the nombre of xxiiij. swannys and signetts, and I pray you thys be not foryeted. J. FASTOLF.

[1] [From Fenn, iii. 102.] [2] See p. 188, Note 2.

194

161

ABSTRACT[1]

SIR JOHN FASTOLF TO SIR THOMAS, Parson of Castlecombe, and JOHN BOKKING, in haste, at Princes Inn, in Norwich.

As the oyer and terminer in Suffolk is to be on Monday next, desires them to get Sir John Sypton indicted for forging the false acquittance, and Bury his advocate also. Has inquired of his tenants at Dedham who were the chief counsel of breaking his mill-dam, and they say Sir John Squyer was chief, but John Waryn was of counsel and court-holder there; also Sir John Buk, Parson of Stratton, who fished his stanks, &c. John Cole of Stoke has also taken in years past more than twenty of his swans. Let them be presented. The late Parson of Cotton got F.'s late bailly, Henry Holm (now dead), pledged out by false representations of the sufficiency of his bail, &c.

1450
DEC. 5

London, 5 Dec. 29 Hen. VI. *Signed.*

162

FASTOLF TO SIR THOMAS HOWYS[2]

To my ryght trusty and welbelovyd frendys, Sir Thomas, Parson off Castellcombe.

RYGHT trusty frendys, I grete you well. And lete you wete that I have resseyved your lettre thys day, which was wryt xv. day of December, and undre[stand] well your ryght gode mocions and causes shewed of inconvenients that myght fall, yff the shyreve have not a gode undreshyreff whyche were not enclynyng to the partie of T. H.[3] And there as ye meoffe me to wryte to ij. Lordys for the said cause, they be both forth to theyr contre, and shall therfor wryte unto hem upon the tenor of your lettrez in that at y

DEC. 20

[1] [From MS. Phillipps, 9735, No. 247.]
[2] [From Paston MSS., B.M., and MS. Phillipps, 9735, No. 248.] The original of this letter has been torn in two, and the first portion is now among the Paston MSS. in the British Museum, while the latter part is in the library of Sir Thomas Phillipps at Cheltenham. [3] Tuddenham and Heydon.

195

1450
DEC. 20

can or may, as forre as reson and justice wolle, for such an officer as woll not, for no mede, hate, or losse, execut[1] dewlye his office to the weele of the contre.

Item, the day of thys lettre wrytyng, John Bokkyng ys com to me, and hath expressley enformyd me by mouth as by wrytynges the greete labour and diligence whych ye have take uppon yow, seth Martismasse, in especiall, abowte the expedition of my processe of *oyer and terminer* before the Kyngs Commyssioners attained ; and I vele ryght well by the avauncement of my processe your faithfull diligence, for whych y can you ryght gode thank, and trustyng uppon your gode continuance. And seth the Commissioners shall sytt at Lynne after the Epiphanye, such of my maters as have take none ende, but hang yn processe for deffaut of aunsuer or apparaunce of my partie, I pray you that the said maters may be called uppon of the new, and dew processe had as ferre as justice and gode concience wolle.

Item, it ys so, as I undrestand, that the Lord Scalys woll be at Lynne thys Cristmasse, and at the oyer and terminer halden there, and Sir Thomas Tuddenham and Heydon wolle appere, of which I am well content ; and it ys lyke that grete labour and speciall pursute shall be made to the Lord Scalys that he wolle meynteyn the said Tuddenham and Heydon in all he can or may, and thus I have herd sey. Wherfor such persones as have founde hem soore greved by extorcion as I have ben, and have processe or wolle hafe processe before the Commissioners, they most effectuelly labour to my Lord Oxford, and to my brothyr Zelverton, Justice, that they wolle as ferre as justice, reson, and concience do that justice may [be] egallie mynistred, and not to wythdrawe theyr couragez well sett from the pore peple ; for and they hald not the hand well and stedfast yn thys mater from hens forth whyle it shall dure, as they have herebefore, the pore peple and all the grete part of both shyres of Norffolk and Suffolk be destroyed. For it shewyth well by what manyfold undewe menys of extorcion they have lyved yn myserie and grete pouverte by manye yeers contynewed that the moste part of the comyners

1 ' Forbear to execute ' doubtless was intended.

1450
DEC. 20

have litill or nought to meynteyn their menage and housold, ne to pay the Kyngs taskys, nothyr theyr rents and servises to the Lordz they be tenants un too, as it shewyth daylie to all the world, whych ys overe a grete pitie to thynk. And when the said pore peple have be by such injuries overladd and so undoon, nedz most the gentlemen that have they pore lyvelode amongs hem be gretely minisshed and hyndered of their increse and levyng.

Item, where as I undrestand by a lettre sent to me from my welbelovyd frende Maister John Botewryght, that grete extorcion have be don by the officers of the duchee in takyng awey cxl. acres pasture at Swaffam, whych ys of the Kyngs demeynz and of hys enheritaunce as of the duchee of Lancaster, for whych pastures, yff it com not ynne ayen, it woll be grete disheritaunce to the Kyng, and fynall destruccion of the tenauntes there, for whych the said Maistre John desyryth and prayeth of remedie yn the name of all the toune of Swaffam. As to thys such as wold here the encrese and wellfare of hym, of hys parysshons, and off all thoose mysdon untoo, most by the avice of som lerned man to put theyr oppressions and grevaunces in wrytyng, well grounded, and as the trouth of the mater ys, and that the said wrytyng or bille may be enseled wyth the seles of such gentlemen that have lyvebode there, and wyth the men that be cowthest knowen,[1] and that wrytyng so enseled be directed to the Kyng, and to the Lordz of hys Councell. And then it ys and woll be of more credence to the Kyng and the Lordys then a simple lettre. And thys doon wyth the labours that they may make there in shewyng theyr grevaunces to the Commissioners ; and the seid grevaunces shewed also here amongs the Kyng and the Lordz, it ys verraily to thynk that they shall be purveyd of a remedie. And foryete not to sende or wryte to Maister Botewryght in goodly haste of thys article wyth your correccion to be had where the avertisementes of you and my frendz that have more particuler knowlege yn such maters.

Item, I have grete mervaylle that yong Jenney, whych ys of my Lord Cromewell councell, and Robert Ledam, also off

1 Most publicly known.

1450
DEC. 20

hys councell, and hys man be not spoke with there, that they doo not attaine an accion ayenst Sir Thomas Tudden[ham], Heydon, and John Gent, whyche have and wold dayly labour to disseise my Lord Cromewell of a knyghten service in Saxthorp, which ye have ryght suffisaunt evidenses by an endentures of Kyng Edward iij[d] dayes enseled, as of Kyng Herry dayes the iiij[the], that the seid maner ys hald by the iiij[the] part of a knyzt fee[1] of my Lord Cromewell as of the maner of Tateshale. And the seid Tuddenham and Heydon wold after theyr voulente have it hald yn meen of the maner of Hetersete, whych sufficient evidenses that ye have specifyeth no thyng soo. And I have lost xx[li.] yeerly yn approwement[2] of my chatell, for cause my Lord Cromewell, throw neglecence of hys officers in Norffolk, have not meynteyned hys ryght. And there as John Bokkyng seith that John Jenney hath no commaundment of my Lord to pursue hys ryght, it shewyth off reson that seth he ys of hys councell in especiall for that shyre, he ought doo hys ryzt to be savyd and kept of hys dewtee. And thertoo he knouyth well that my said Lord hath commaunded hym dyvers tymys to take kepe hys ryzt be savyd in thys mater. Wherfor I pray you requyre hym on my Lord ys behalf[3] to compleyn to Justice at thys *oyer* [*and terminer* for a] remedie, and that the [bi]lle be made yn my Lordys name. And then to. . . . . . have commaundment ryzt sone of my Lord eftsonys, and [*i.e.* if] he wolle sende unto hym by suche as goth dayly into that contre to Tateshale. And I had send hym hys speciall [com]maundment, had he sent me suche word betyme whyle he was here. I pray you remembre ye so John Jenney and Robert Ledham as I have no cause to [wri]te more, ne to compleyn to my Lord of theyr neclgence.

Item, Sir Parson, where it ys soo that my cosyn Boys ys passed to God, whoos soule God assoyle, ye shall fynde amonges my bokes of accomptes at Castre, or amonges othyr wrytynges, he owed me money for a ferm he heeld of me, as

1 A knight's fee was an amount of land sufficient to maintain a knight, and held subject to a knight's service.
2 *See* p. 152, Note 3.   3 Here begins the portion in the Phillipps MS.

Watkyn Shypdam ys remembred ; and also I lent hym xl[s.] whych I shuld have an obligacion at Castre off, praying you to inquire off thys dewteez, and see recuvere may be made off it.

1450
DEC. 20

Item, I seende a lettre at thys tyme to my cosyn Wychyngham, to hys modre also, for a mater that touchyth my cosyn Robert Fitzrauff ys amercement, and the partie also. Whych lettre I woll ye breke to undrestand my wrytyng and the substaunce off it the more. And y pray you hertly to speke wyth the partie at Norwych as well as wyth my ryght welbelovyd cosyn Sir Herry Inglose, and wyth my cosyn Wychyngham assone as ye goodly may. And meoffe ye the said mater yn such wyse as your discrecioun can well consider that the rathyr the said mater may take a gode ende, yff it may be yn ony wyse ; yn whych mater ye shall do me ryght singler plesyr, and that thys be not slewthed, for taryeng drawth perell. I wryte but briefflye, for I . . . .[1]

Item, where as Brome ys not well wyllyng yn my maters, whych for the wrong takyng and wyth haldyng my shepe I ought take a accioun ayenst hym ; for declaracioun in whate wyse he dyd it, John Bele my sheperefe can enforme you best, for he laboured about the recuvere of it. My Lady Norfolk sent me a lettre viij. yere goon, whych I shuld hafe, desyryng that the processe I was purposed take ayenst hym shuld be respited, and all that reson wold he shuld obbey. I am avysed therfor let som man about my Lord Norfolk and my Lady have wetyng, or I begynne. Yhyt I wold ye had declaracioun before of the conduyt and grounde of thys mater.

Item, where my cosyn Inglose avyse me fully to take a speciall assise on the priorye of Hykelyng for my rent, I have abydden upon my cosyn Paston that he and I shuld take one to ghedyr, and I vele hym no thyng spede in it. Let me know how he woll doo thys next terme, for elles am I fully avysed to take myne owt, and to traverse all iij. offices[2] for Beyton, Bradwell, and Tychewell, wyth the help of my frendz, Not elles at thys tyme ; but I pray you comfort all thoo that

1 Three words indistinct.   2 *See* p. 188, Note 2.

1450
DEC. 20

fynde hem greved to abyde by theyr ryzt, and that ye woll contynew forth for my worshup and proffyt as ferre as ryzt wolle. Whych I trust to God shall better have, hys cours then it hath beforn ; who have you in hys kepyng. Wryt at London, the xx. day of Decembre anno xxix° regni Regis H. vi.

Item, that thys lettre commaund me to my cosyn John à Berney.   J. FASTOLF.

(*On the back*)—Item, I have sende ij. lettres to my Lord Erle of Oxford, the ton by Robson ys man, a squyer of my Lordys. And the grete substaunce of the lettre ys that the issues forfeted may be sent upp be tyme to my Lord Tresorer ; for there shall be none assignment made, ne may not, till it com yn wrytyng ; it be don, had it be sent. Grete sute ys made to pardon it, but the Kynges Councell woll not suffre it. The ij. lettre Nicholas Bokkyng beryth for excuse of my cosyn Inglose, because grete labor hath be made to my Lord York ayenst my cosyn Inglose and Seggeford, that they shuld endyte the Priour of Walsyngham tenaunt yn Salle. Wher-uppon my Lord York, unadvertised of the trouth, sent a lettre to my Lord Oxford to support the Pryor ys tenaunt ayenst Seggeford namely.

Item, I desyre that and John Berney or onye man can mete wyth Dallyng, that fals undre eschetor, in onye place proviable, that he may by force brought to Castre without damage of hys bodye, and there to be kept yn hold, that he may confesse the trouth of the fals office he forged off my maner of Tychewell.

Item, forasmoche as ye shall have to doon at Lynne for my maters there as for Tychewell and othyr, therfor I wolle that yee doo purvey of gode frendys as be aboute Flegg that passen yn jureez, that they may wayt uppon yow there at Lynne, and other suche trusty men that ye can ghete to spede my processe. And that ye do hem goode chier and cost uppon hem after that the case shall requyre. I commyt thys mater to be ruled by your wysdom, that it be net forzeten.

200

1450
DEC. 27

and there seye myn evydence, and than made the office therby, and for Suffolk also, the fals offices found there in likewise, &c.' You must sue him to the utmost.

[The date of this letter is determined by the reference made in it to the Sessions held at Lynn, in the January following, before the Earl of Oxford and Justice Yelverton.—*See* No. 167. At the foot of the original ms. is this inscription:—'Donum Rev. Fra. Blomefield, 10 Dec. 1735.']

165

ANONYMOUS TO —— [1]

1450

I PREY zu if ze have any old gownys for lynynges and old schetys and old schertys that may non lenger seven zu, I prey zu send hem hom in hast, for I must okupye seche thyngis in hast. Wyndham hath medyd the juryorys and yaf hem mony that xuld passe on the qwhest be twyn zour modyr and hym ; if ther myt ben purveyd any mene that it myt ben dasched in cas wer that it xuld passe azens zour modyr, it wer a good sport ; for than he wold ben wode. He sent with his men to the afray iij. gunnys in very trowth. I have inquiryd veryly ther after. He is wode wroth that Daniel is amrel, for it is told me that on of his men is indytyd in the amrellys cort sythyn that Danyel was made amerel. I pray zu bewar in qhat felaschep ze ryd qhan ze com homward, for ther gon many fals shrewys and thevys in this contre.

Thomas Skipping rod to Londonward on Friday last past in gret hast and purposyd hym for to ben at London on Sonday be none on erandys of his maysterrys : qhat the cawse is I wote nott. On sent me word her of that knowth it for trowth.

[1] [Add. ms. 34,889, f. 150.] The date of this letter seems to be towards the close of the year 1450 ; for though I have not met with the date of Daniel's appoint-ment as Admiral, which would prove the year, it will be seen by the last paragraph of No. 142 that Wyndham was indicted at that time along with Toddenham and Heydon, as one of the makers of disorder in Norfolk.

202

163

THE EARL OF OXFORD TO JOHN PASTON [1]

To our welbeloved John Paston.

Th'erl of Oxenford.

RIGHT trusty and welbeloved, we grete you well. And for as moche as the qwene and my Lord of York have writyn to us for a matier that is depending betwix the toun of Salle and on [*one*] Sechforth of the same toune, we pray yow that at such tyme as we purpose yow to be with us now this Cristemesse at Wynche that ye lete the sayd Sechforth have wetyng ther of, and that he may be with us that same tyme, for diverse matiers wich that we have to speke with hym ; and that ye fayle not, as we trust yow. Wretyn in owr manor of Wynche, the xxiij[th] day of Decembre.

1450
DEC. 23

164

ABSTRACT [2]

SIR JOHN FASTOLF TO JOHN BERNEY AND SIR THOMAS HOWYS.

Begs them to have heed to his matters to be sped on Tuesday after the Twelfth, especially 'to labor the jury that was supposed to 'a past in the office found for Tychewell,[3] that they may appear at Lynne, and there make a certificate before my Lord of Oxford, and the Justice William Yelverton, that they were never privy nor consenting to such an office-finding.' On this an action may be founded against Dallyng, 'the false harlot.' Would like Berney rewarded for his labor, if it were secretly done, and Dynne also. 'Ye wete what I mean. I pray you see well forth, for *Mitte sapientem*, &c.'

London, in haste, St. John's day in Christmas ;[4] 'for he cam to Castre,

DEC. 27

[1] [Add. ms. 34,888, f. 168.] The subject of this letter is evidently referred to in the postscript of the last.
[2] [From ms. Phillipps, 9735, No. 237.]
[3] *See* No. 153 ; also *PS.* to No. 162.
[4] This, which is written after the date, would appear to apply to Dallyng.

201

166

SIR JOHN FASTOLF [1]

Item, that Sir John Ingelose and the Meyer be spoke to for here worship that the man weche that herd Heydon seye the langage upon wheche he is endyted, be sent heder ; for that aught not to be kept prevye but oplyshed, seyng any thyng towchyng or sownyng to treson. And, on the other part, it is to grett necye (?) to noyse any man with ought cause, &c. Hit is not here worship this mater, if hit be trew, is so longe kept prevye with theym, &c.

J. FASTOLFE.

167

THE EARL OF OXFORD TO JOHN JERMYN [2]

To my ryght trusty and intierly welbeloved John Jermyn, Shirreve of Norffolk.

RIGHT trusty and intierly welbeloved, I grete yow wele. And where late by the Kyngs comaundment in the tyme of his Parliament, holden now last at West-minster, I was in persone at Norwich, holdyng Sessions of oir determyner [3] with Yelverton, on of the Kyngs Jüges, by greet space and greet attendaunce, which for to a do with suych diligence in the Parliament tyme I wold a be right lothe, but for the pupplyk wele of all the shire.

It is also not oute of your remembraunce what indisposicion

1451
JAN. 2

[1] [From Paston mss., B.M.] This is a mere fragment, containing nothing but the postscript of a letter, the date of which must be either towards the end of the year 1450, or the beginning of 1451. A passage to the same effect will be found in a letter of Fastolf's, written on the 7th January 1451.
[2] [From Fenn, iii. 106.] As this letter was written in the year that John Jermyn was Sheriff of Norfolk, the date must be 1451.
[3] *See* page 161, Note 3.

203

THE PASTON LETTERS

the Commons of bothe countes in the ende of somer last passed wer of, and how the Kyng, by the hole advyse of all the greet Councell of Ingland ; send hider his said Commission ; and how I have do my part therynne, I reporte me to all the world. I here a gruggyng, neverthelesse, that trow favour in your office to the pople that hath compleyned by many and grete horible billes agayn certeyn persones shuld not be shewid at this next Sessions at Lenn, ne ferther in the said Comission, which, if it so were, as God defend, myght cause a latter errour wurs than the first.

I pray yow, therfore, that ye wole write to me your disposicion how ye purpose to be demened, and how I shal take yow for th'execucion of the Kyngs Comission, and the pupplik wele of all the shire ; and aftir that that ye write to me, so wole I take yow, latyng yow wete that I were lothe to labour ferther but if I wist that the Commons shuld be easid as Godds law wold ; and if ony errour grow, the defaute shal not be founde in me.

I pray yow more over to gif credence to the berer her of, and the Trinite kepe yow. Wretyn at Wynch, the second day of January.

THE ERLE OF OXENFORD.

168

THE EARL OF OXFORD TO SIR JOHN FASTOLF[1]

To my right trusty and intierly welbeloved Sir John Fastolff, Knyght.

RIGHT trusty and intierly welbeloved, I grete yow wele, and pray yow to be right sadly advysed of the contynue of a bille of instruccion closid her ynne ; and therupon, as I trust yow, to comon with suych my Lords of the Kyngs Councell as be present now at this tyme, in especiall

---

[1] [From Paston MSS., B.M.] This letter, which is dated at the same place and on the same day as the preceding, was probably written in the same year also.

204

THE PASTON LETTERS

Commissioners my Lord the Duc of York, Bouchier, my mayster,[1] that will not come there, *de prodicionibus*, &c., but Kent praeth hem to hang no men when thei come.

Other tydyngs as yett can I non tell you, save Ulveston is Styward of the Mydill Inne, and Isley of the Inner Inne, be cause thei wold have officz for excuse for dwellyng this tyme from her wyves, &c. Sir T. T.[2] lost hes primer at the Tour Hill, and sent his man to seche [*fetch* (?)] it, and a good felaw wyshed hit in Norffolk, so he wold fetch hit there, &c. Men ween that Norffolk men wer hardier thanne thei be.

God graunte, and at the reverence of God help too that an outas[3] and clamour be made upon the Lord Scalez,[4] preying hym for well of the cuntre, neyther susteyn ner help hym ner Heydon in no wyse, and that ye crye upon my mayster and yours that he obeye not the syrcorar [*certiorari*] as yett, as ye may se be hes lettre from my mayster, rudely and in hast be me endited, of which I pray excuse, &c. And pray Blake[5] to do Swafham men sey sum what to the matier.

I wote well T. and H.[6] wil not come there at this tyme, as it is verily reported, &c. *Mitte sapientem, &c.* Brayn and I shalbe with you on Saturday nest at evyn, with the grace of Jesu, to whom I be take you. In hast, at London, the ij[de] day of Januar.

By J. BOCKYNG.

---

[1] Sir John Fastolf, whose servant Bocking was.
[2] Sir Thomas Tuddenham.
[3] An outcry.
[4] *See* p. 196.
[5] Elsewhere mentioned as bailiff of Swaffham.
[6] Tuddenham and Heydon.

206

HENRY VI

my Lord Chaunceller, and that ye wole send me instruccyon agayn of their avise, and how I shal demene me. And the Trinite preserve yow. Wretyn at Wynch, the second day of January.

THE ERLE OF OXENFORD.

169

JOHN BOCKING TO WILLIAM WAYTE[1]

To William Wayte.[2]

RITH feithful and welbelovyd brother, Wiliam Wayte, I comaunde me to yow as the lord may to his tenant, praying you effectualy to recomaunde me to my singuler gode mayster and yours, excusyng me that I write not to hym, for I dar not envolde me in the same. And as for tydyngs her, I certifye you that all is nowght, or will be nowght. The Kyng borweth hes expense for Cristemesse ; the Kyng of Aragon,[3] the Duc of Myleyn,[4] the Duc of Ostrich,[5] the Duc of Burgoyn[6] wolde ben assistent to us to make a conquest, and nothyng is aunswered, ner agreed in maner, save abydyng the grete deliberacon that at the last zall spill all to goder, &c.

The Chief Yistice[7] hath waited to ben assauted all this sevenyght nyghtly in hes hous, but nothing come as yett, the more pite, &c. On *oyr and determiner*[8] goth in to Kent, and

---

[1] [From Fenn, iii. 134.] The evidence on which this letter has been assigned to the year 1451 will be seen in a footnote.
[2] This is supplied by the Editor, there being no address in the MS. itself.
[3] Alfonso V.
[4] Francis Sforza, one of the most able and successful generals of the time. He was a soldier of fortune, of peasant origin, and succeeded to the Duchy of Milan by his marriage with Bianca Maria, natural daughter of Philip Maria, the preceding Duke, whose interests he had at one time opposed as general of a league formed by the Pope and the Venetian and Florentine Republics against the Duchy.
[5] Albert, surnamed the Prodigal, brother of the Emperor Frederic III.
[6] Philip the Good.
[7] Sir John Fortescue.
[8] A commission of *oyer and terminer* for Kent and Sussex was issued in December 1450 to Richard, Duke of York, Lord Bourchier, Sir John Fastolf, and others.—Patent Roll, 29 Hen. VI. p. 1, m. 16 *indorso*.

205

HENRY VI

170

WILLIAM WAYTE TO JOHN PASTON[1]

To my Ryght seuere ana ryght worchepfull mayster, my mayster Paston, in hast.

RYGHT Reverent and ryght wurchepfull sir, I re- comaunde me un to youre good maysterchep. Late yow wete that Blake the baly of Swafham cam hom from London on the Saterday after that my mayster departed from yow atte myn lord of Oxenfordis. And he told my mayster that he cam to London on Seint John day atte nyte. And he yede streyt to my lord Chaunceler and told my seyd lord that yf the Kyng pardoned ser Thomas Tudenham and Heydon her issewes that the shire of Suffolk wold paye no taxe ; for what nedyth the kynge for to have the taxe of hese pore puple whanne he wyll not take hese issues of thos rych extorssioners and oppressours of hese puple. And also he told my seyd lord Chaunceler and many more lordes that yf the kynge pardon hym or grauntted any *supersedeas*, London shuld with inne short tyme have as moche for to do as they hadde for to kepe London Brygge whanne the Capteyn[2] cam thedir ; for he told hym that ther was up in Norffolk redy to ryse V M[l.] comons yf they have not execucion of the *oyre* and *terminer*. And whanne my lord Chaunceler herd this he was ryte glade therof, and dede Blake telle all this and moche more a forn the kynge and all hese lordes, that they blyssed him whanne they herden yt. And yf he hadde not a seyd this they shuld an hadd and *supersedeas* and pardon also, for ther was made a gret suggestion that it hadde be don of grette malyce. And so the lord Scales meyntenyth Sir Thomas Tudenham in all that he may goodly, but he wyll not avow

---

[1] [Add. MS. 34,888, f. 63.] The date of this letter is sufficiently evident.
[2] Jack Cade.

207

1451
JAN. 3

yt; but he shall come don to the *oyre determiner* sekerly, and for to make anende atwex sir T. Tudenham and Swafham; for [he] hayth made and genttyl letter un to the parson, the bayly and the inhabitaunce of Swafham, and seth that he wyll do hese parte to sette them in reste and peas. And so my mayster understande that yf Swafham and he werne accorded that thei shuld sette lytyll be Norwych. And therfore my mayster prayeth yow that ye wyll speke with the Mayer and hese brethern that they purvey that ther be atte Lenn a sufficiaunt fellawshep to gedyr, and that ther be madde a grette noyse up on the lord Scales, bothe of Tudenham and Heydon, and for all thos that arne of that sekt, and that wyse purvyaunce ordenance he hadde how they shull be demened; for this same day was the parson of Swafham with my mayster, and they arne accorded that ther shall be of here lordshep and sufficiaunt fellawshep and they shall have here loggyng atte the Frere Menours atte Lenn. And they wyll not assentte to noone ende but as the Cety doyth. And it is here avyse that the meyre shuld purveye for hem in sum other Freres. For Tudenham and H[eydon] wyll brynge with hem sufficiaunt counceyll as any kun they gete in London; And also the Cetye must purvey that as many sufficiaunt mene as can be gette or spoke to, that they be redy yf it happe of any tryall. Also the Cetye hadde nede to have Sir Miles Stapulton ther show they shuld helpe to hese costys. Ware, Sir, atte the reverens of God be thenke yow well of all these maters. Blake was atte London on Thursday and herd no word of the stretes,[1] ne of Robson my lord of Oxffordis man, and or Blake cam to London Sir T. Terell hadde labored to Sir John Fastolf that Sir T. Tudenham shuld ave [been[2]] bownde to Sir John Fastolf in foure thowsand pounde to stande to hese rule and ordenance; and so whanne Blake cam and deysshsed all to gedyr, and so he dede Sir John Fastolf labor to the kynge and to the Chaunceler for to lette the *supersedeas* and the pardon; and ther was grette langage atwex Blake and Tudenham; it wor to moche to wryte yt un to yow, but he hayth sore noyssed my mayster to the Kynge and to the lordes. Also Tudenham

[1] I.e. the *estreats*.   [2] Omitted in MS.

208

1451
JAN. 3

is owte of the kynges hows, and Cotton is Warderopper, my mayster shall on Monday dyne with. Also, sir, it wore grette wysdam that my mayster hadde knowleche atte Walsyngham on Fryday nest comyng how the Maire and ze be accorded, for my mayster wyle be recaled therafter. William Geney sent un to my mayster for to ascuse hym that he shuld not come to Lenn un to the Wedenesday. And, Sir, that were agrette hurte bothe to the Cyte of Norwych and for Swafham; and therfor my mayster wold that the Mayer shuld send for hym, that he be ther be tyme on the Tuesday, and that moo bille be made ayens Tudenham and Heydon, what so ever falle. The Holy Gost have yow and yours in hese kepyng. Wretyn atte Rougham, the Sonday nyte nest after newe zers day in hest as it semyth.—Be your servaunte,

W. WAYTE.

171

ABSTRACT[1]

SIR JOHN FASTOLF TO JOHN A BERNEY AND SIR THOMAS HOWES.

JAN. 7

Sends John Bokkyng on matters to be sped at the oyer and terminer. They must remember a *certiorari* is out of the King's Bench, and a *procedendo* was granted at one time 'for certain which had not appeared in the place and pleaded.' Has received all the stuff contained in a bill dated 28th November, made by John Davye of Yarmouth, and delivered to one Roger Metsharp, master of the little boat called *The Blythe*. Wonders they did not send the great ship with malt. Desires provisions for Lent by next ship. Remind my cousin Inglos that the man that 'appeched' Heydon be sent hither, if he dare stand by his words. All the indictments against Heydon are not worth a halfpenny. Howes must take John à Berney's advice about this matter.

London, Thursday after Twelfth, 29 Hen. VI.

Let all who were on the inquest for Bardolf's matter be indicted, whatever it cost.   *Signed.*

[1] [From MS. Phillipps, 9735, No. 246.]

172

WILLIAM WAYTE TO JOHN PASTON[1]

*To my ryght reverent and ryght worchepfull mayster,
my mayster Paston in hest posybyll.*

1451
JAN. 9

SYR, lyke yt yow to know that my lord Scalys sent hese pursevaunt unto my mayster[2] on the Twelthe day, that my mayster shuld mete wyth hym atte Wynche aforn my Lord of Oxenford on the Thursday nest folwyng. And whanne my mayster cam thedyr, he delyvered my mayster a letter from my Lord Chauncheler, quych my mayster wyll shew yow atte Lenn. I shuld send yow a copy therof, but it is so longe that I had no leyser to wryte it. My mayster rode to Walsyngham on the Fryday folwyng, and ther he mette with the shereve, and the shereve lyveryd my mayster a letter from my Lord of Norffolk, qwych I send yow a copy of. And atte Walsyngham my mayster resceyvyd a letter from Osberne youre man. And ther Heydonis man made hese avaunte that he was the Justice of the Pease on Caustonheythe; and so it semyth be here contenaunce that they trost of a good zere. And, Syr, whanne my mayster cam hom on Saterday ther was lyvered my mayster a letter from Sir John Fastolf, and a neyther letter cam to me from John Bokkynge,[3] qwych I send you a copy of. Sir, God send us a fayre day atte[4] Lenn. And that ther may be pople jnow to crye up on the Lord Scales that he mayntene not Sir T. T. and H. in here wronges, as the copy of B letter makyth mencion. And, Sir, atte the reverens of God, laborth youre materis wysely and secretely, for Wyndam noysed yow sore aforn my Lord of

[1] [Add. MS. 34,889, f. 230.] This letter was evidently written on the Saturday after the same writer's letter of the 3rd January immediately preceding.
[2] Judge Yelverton. He was lord of the manor of Rougham, from which this letter is dated.
[3] No. 169.   [4] *Atte* repeated in MS.

210

1451
JAN. 9

Oxenford and my Lorde Scales that ze shuld reyse meche puple with grette arey owte of Norwyche. And therfor, Sir, late the puple be wysely and manly gydyd in here frekynge and demenynge. Also my Lord Scales sent for the parson of Sw[a]tham and divers men of the same town to mete with hym aforn my Lord of Oxenford the seyd Thursday, for to trete with hem for Sir Thomas Tudenham; and ther was the baly of Swafham and Sir Thomas Tudenham prest. And so my Lord Scales yave the parson of S. grette langage and to men of same towne. Y. and the parson answherd my Lord Scales manly in the best wyse. And ther was grette langage twexen Blake the baly and Tudenham prest that my lordys and my mayster worne acornberd therof. And so it is lyke that my Lord Scales shall make ther no loveday; and so Swafham wylbe ther in here best array. Also, Sir, Brygge was atte Walsyngham; and ther he craked grette wordes, and seyd to many divers men that it shuld be thanked alle tho that labored a yens hem. And he seyd that it worne but viij. personys, and yf men be men now it shuld be thanked hym and told hym atte Lenn. In the lest wysse he is now with the Lord Scales; the Lord Scales wyte Thomas Denyes, John Lyster and me all those indytementis. And the Lord Scales seyth that I made all the bylles and the panell; and so he is hevy lord to me and to Thomas Denyes. Prentys is atte hom with the Lord Scales; the shereve told me that he wyll do for the Cyte of Norwych as meche as he may. Sir, I wold ther worne a thowsand of good Maudby men to crye owte on Tudenham, Heydon, Prentys and Brygge for here falsse exstorciones. Also, Sir, atte the reverens of God, make an ende atwexen Sexeford and men of Salle; it lyeth in your power. I shall make redy youre forsebyll entres ayens Lenn, with the grace of God, Qwych have yow in Hese kepynge. Wretyn atte Rougham on Saterday nyte in hest.

Sir, I send yow and lewde letter be Richerd Yenneys. I beseche yow be ware to whom ze shew your letters; lete them be brente.—Be your servaunt,

W. WAYTES.

211

THE PASTON LETTERS

173

ABSTRACT[1]

SIR JOHN FASTOLF TO THOMAS HOWYS, Clerk, and JOHN BOKKYNG, in haste.

1451
JAN. 12

Begs them to labour his matters, and forget not 'that old shrew, Dallyng, for he is sore at my stomach.' Sends by the Parson a *procedendo* against Tudenham, which he has got out with great labour, with a letter to my brother Yelverton. 'And as to an assize for Hikkelyng, I shall be there on in the beginning of this term; and for Tichewell in like wise.' Bokkyng must remind my cousin Inglos about the indictments for treason of Heydon, 'that the man might be sent up to preve the said matter.' Fears it has slept too long. Wishes his ship *The Blythe* sent to him.

London, 12 Jan. 29 Hen. VI.   *Signed.*

Get my Lord [Oxford] and Yelverton to write a letter to Blake of the King's house, thanking him for his friendliness to the country; 'and forget not that Dallyng be had before my Lord and Yelverton, and make his confession before hem, &c. And let the great men that have most matters against [him] help somewhat to this good end.'

174

ABSTRACT[2]

SIR J. FASTOLF TO SIR THOS. HOWYS AND JOHN BERNEY at Castre, in hast; or at his place in Pokethorp, at Norwich.

JAN. 28

Master Hue Acton has been with him for the new evidences ensealed for the manor of Mundham, which F. has sold to the use of the Church of St. Giles that he is master of, &c. Thanks them for what they have done for him in his causes before the Commissioners of *oyer and terminer* at Lynne, &c. Hears Appulzerd's son expects the inquest of Mancroft in Norwich to be reversed. Speak to my cousin Inglose about this. Fastolf's audit books. My cousin John Berney puts me in great comfort by seeing to the safeguard of my place in my absence. Would be sorry he should be injured by having respited his entry into Rokelond Tofts at my request.

Make friends in Norwich against Easter when the *oyer and terminer* is to be held again, for I must proceed in the matter against Appulzerd.

London, 28 Jan. 29 Hen. VI.   *Signed.*

[1] [From MS. Phillipps, 9735, No. 230.]
[2] [From MS. Phillipps, 9735, No. 236.]

HENRY VI

Begs them to send his grain and malt in a good vessel, well accompanied, with a good wind, as he has had great losses before. Speak to the Mayor of Norwich about Appulzerd's matter; 'for there was no city in England that I loved and trusted most upon, till they did so unkindly to me and against truth in the Lady Bardolf's matter.'

1451
JAN. 28

[This letter is referred to by Blomefield (*Hist. of Norf.* iv. 388, Note 9), and two short extracts are given from the beginning, relating to the Hospital of St. Giles.]

175

MEMORANDA FOR PROSECUTIONS[1]

Præsentationes factæ et fiendæ in audiendo et determinando.[2]

FOR as meche as the *oyer and termyner* is thus restreynyd, not vythstandyng the wrytyngs and all the materis utterid be my Lord of Oxenford, but if ther folow sumwhat lyke to the perell lyke to be conceyved be maters that so wern utterid and be the seyd wrytyngs, ellis shall it gretly sowndyn ageyns the worchep and the weel of all the personys, lordis, and other that eyther have wreten or utterid owght, and lyke wyse of hem in whos name seche materis hath ben utterid, soo that hereaftyr, whan they have ryght gret nede to be herd, and to be wel spedde, they shul the rather fayle thereof bothen, and here enemyes the heyer up and the more bold, &c. And therfore herein men must hold fote as manhod woll wyth wysdom; and ellis *novissimus error pejor priori.*

Item, in the cyte of Norwyche must the falshodys and the fals getyngs of good ther don ben fowndyn, and thow summ maters ben not presentable, or peraventure in seche forme not corigyble ther, yet so that the mater in the self be orible and fowle, and so that summe other be sufficient, yet it semyth summe men best that all go forthe and be taken, and namely [especially] in this werd [world] that now is, &c.

Item, in lyke wyse must it be in the shier, ther me thynkyt

[1] [From Paston MSS., B.M.] This paper must belong to the early part of the year 1451, when it was proposed to indict Tuddenham and Heydon at Norwich.
[2] This title is taken from a contemporaneous endorsement.

1451

THE PASTON LETTERS

1451

it is reson that my Lordys sett bothe the day and the place of the Sessions, and all men kepe that wern the robberis at Gresham and to Plumstede, the shippyng of wolle ageyn the statute, that is felonye, and the lycence than, if ony be, ther shull come to lyght and disputed, and I suppose veryly be other statutes and be lawe fownde voyde, and the leveryes that Heydon hatht yoven to hem that arn not hese menyall men.

Item, the presonment of John Porter of Blykelyng.
Item, the presonment of John Langman of Swafham.
Item, the presonment of Robert Patgrys of Burnham.
Item, the extorcions in her [their] cortes.
Item, the prisonynge of Dallynge, and of hese obligacion mad to Sir Thomas Todenham, and howe he was presonyd at Norwyche, at Thetforthe, at Lynne, and also of many other that ben don soo too.
Item, to remembre T. Denyes of the tale that Fyncheham told whan he cam hom for Sir T. Todeham, that he be ware therof, &c.
Item, for to indyte Pryntys of a voluntary eschete that where on Symond Hamond of Patesle wheche was indyted of felonye, and because of hese goods he lete hym owte of the castell *anno xvj*[e] *Regis nunc.*
Item, for to indyte the same Prentys and William Goodwen of Swafham for the robbynge of Geffrey Sowle.
Item, the same Prentys and Goodwyn robbed Thomas Irynge of Myleham *anno xx*[e] *Regis nunc.*
Item, the same Prentys toke of Wylliam Dallynge at Norwyche v. mark for smytynge of of hese feteris whan he was there in prison *anno xix*[e] *Regis nunc.*
Item, to indyte the baly of Swaffham, T. Todenham, Heydon, Prentys, of felonye as excercarys [accessaries].
Item, to speke to Feraris for hese mater at Thyrnyng.
Item, to indyte a cowper at Geyton wheche slow a tenaunt of Danyell at Geyton. Hese name is Thomas Dowce that was slayn; and ther kan no man indyte hym, for Sir T. Todenham mayntteynyth hym, and therfore he were worthy to be indyted as excercary, *anno xxv*[e] *Regis nunc.*

HENRY VI

Item, to indyte Heydon, because he rydyth armyd ayens the statute and the commyssion of the peas.
Item, for takyng awey of John of Berneys haborjoun at Walsyngham.
Item, to inquere what they dede to Alexaunder Reve of Cokely Clay.
Item, what they dedyn to Shragger, and to hese sone, for they stokked hym and hese sone at Swafham.
Item, what they deden to Gachecroft at Methewold.
Item, to enquere what they deden to a chanon of Ingham; he was arestid, and set in prison at Swafham, and [they] dede hym make a obligacioun [*forced him to give a bond*].
Item, how that be her comaundment Emond Wyghtton was arestid at Hempton, and put in the stokks at Fakenham more than iij. dayis, till he made a fyn of v. marks, and yet he spent and yave xls. besyde.
Item, for to endyte Knatesale, John of Woode, Robert of Woode, for Ferers mater.
Item, that William Kelynge of Castlelaker under eschetor, how that he rydyth armed, and reysith many men ayens the peas; he met wyth the Byschop at West Dereham with x. men of armys.
Item, of extorcious amerciaments take of the Prior of Westacre at Narforthe and Swafham, and hese man there set openly and shamefully and gret oppression in stokks, and a flok of hoggs taken; and be whyche appressions and extorcions was the Prior of Westacre compellid to yeven Sir T. Todenham a fee of xls. a yere, and to make Shuldam her styward, and yeven hym a fee of xls. a yere there. W. Yelverton and all other aforn hym had but xxvjs. viijd.; but of these and of many mo wers it is a gret foly to laboren in as for any indytements, but if ye be ryght seker of the sherefes office; for if he lyst, he may returne men i nowe of Swafham, and seche as ye wold have for the enquest of the hunderid, and it is the more to drede of the undyrschereff that they arn asented, and drawe all aftyr her draught. And that they wold that no sessions shuld be because of the massage that he sent to my mayster be Nicholas Dowyldays clerks, and therfore ther must be the

1451

THE PASTON LETTERS

1451 begynnynge of all these maters, as ye wold save your worchepis, and eschewe shame and the peryll, &c.

(*At the bottom of the page*)—M^{dm} of [*blank*] groond and of the extorcions of Sporlle.

On the back of this document occur the following further memoranda in two columns :

Maters steried to hurt of both parties.		Ambidexter.[1]	
Sir John Fastolf,	} Est'.[2]	Dux Norff.	} Stockton,
Bisshoppis Wif.		Dux Suff.	} Est'.
The Priour of Norwich,	}	Ed. Wynter,	}
The Cite.		John Mariot.	}
The Abbot of Wendlyng,	} Est'.	Ferrers,	} Est'.
The Cite.		Hobbes Wif.	}
The Abbot of Leiston,	} Est'.	Prior Walsyngham,	} Est'.
William Jeney.		Ric. Doget.	}
Gregory Guybon,	}	Mondford,	} Est'.
—[3] Perpoynt.	}	Danyell.	}
John Tatleshale,	}	Sir John Curson,	} Est'.
Robert Mortymer.	}	Maister John Selet.	}
The Lady Bardolf,	}	Sir John Curson,	} Est'.
Sir John Fastolf.	}	Will. Thurton.	}
The Lord Moleyns,	}		
John Paston.	}		

176

OPPRESSIONS OF TUDDENHAM AND HEYDON [4]

THESE be names of men that arne myschevesly oppressed and wronged by Sir T. Tudenham and Heydon and here adherentes :—

Yelverton.   Gregorius Gybon.
Fastolf.   Joh. Maryot.

---

[1] This term is applied to a juror who receives money of both parties in a suit.
[2] This abbreviated word is probably *Estreat*, indicating that an extract or official copy of the indictment had been made.   [3] Blank in MS.
[4] [From Paston MSS., B.M.]   This paper no doubt belongs to the same period as the last.

216

1451   Paston.   Ferrers.   1451
Berney.
Straunge.
Framyngham.
Trenchemer.
Joh. Jenney, Senior.
Joh. Damme.
Nicholaus Grome.
Joh. Ode.
Joh. Knevet.
Robert Clyfton.
Thomas Hypgame.
Homines de Swafham.
Joh. atte Howe of Helloughton.
Simon Blake.
Joh. Botwryghe, Clerk.
Item, many men indyted in Norffolk and Suffolk be Tudenham and Heydon, &c.
Ric. Wryght of Saham.

177

FRIAR BRACKLEY TO JOHN PASTON [1]

PRIMO.   Sciat vestra veneranda discretio quod Episcopus 1451(?) hujus diocesis est Thomæ Danyell et suis fautoribus maxime benevolus et in ipso episcopo T. T., J. H.,[2] et suis complicibus est ipsius confidentia maxima, &c.

2° Si justiciarii pacis hujus comitatus omnes et singuli debeant sua autorite pacis media pro eorum posse per totum Norfolch. comitatum diligenter conservare et pacis ejusdem

---

[1] [Add. MS. 34,889, f. 158.]   This undated letter may have been written in February or March 1451, when Tuddenham and Heydon hoped to regain their ascendency. Though not addressed, we may presume that it was written to John Paston.   [2] Sir Thomas Tuddenham and John Heydon.

217

THE PASTON LETTERS

451(?) perturbatores carceri vel castro proprio mancipari facere, quæritur quare dictus episcopus, pacis, ut creditur, justiciarius, non vult in hac parte hujusmodi pacis perturbatoribus resistere ; sed magis eisdem in talibus insolenciis favorem et auxilium in omnibus præbere.

3° Si quærantur consiliarii dicti Episcopi, certum est quod Prior monachorum, M. J. Celot, J. Bulman, T. T.,[1] J. H.,[2] J. W.,[3] Johannes Yates cum consimilibus ceteris sunt etiam consiliarii dicti Danielis.

4° Cum, secundum Apostolum,[4] furta, homicidia et talia vicia eis similia sunt abhominabilia Deo et hominibus, ac utriusque legis divinæ et humanæ contraria sacratis sanccionibus, in tantum quod non solum qui talia agunt digni sunt morte, sed etiam qui conscenciunt agentibus ; ex quibus certe verisimiliter concluditur quod non solum Kervere, latro, et Daniel famulus, furator equi ac murre satis notorius, puniretur una cum fautoribus ejus.

5° Vestra discretio dicta Christi in Ewangelio diligenter consideret, ‘ Si in viridi ligno hæc faciant, in arido quid fiet ? ’[5]

6° Non solum hæc pensare debetis pro vestræ personæ defensione seu vestræ familiæ, sed magis movere vos debet zelus et amor rei publice totius vestræ patriæ.

7° Si ista indilate et cum omni possibili celeritate citius non reformaveritis, timendum valde supponitur de insurreccione plebis, quod absit omnino.

8° Novitque discretio vestra ex paucis indigestis plura politice percipere. Statui pro præsenti tempore finem scribendi imponere.

---

[1] Sir Thomas Tuddenham.   [2] John Heydon.   [3] John Wyndham.
[4] The reference appears to be to Romans i. 29-32.   [5] Luke xxiii. 31.

178

JAMES GLOYS TO JOHN PASTON [1]

To my right reverente and wurchepfull Mayster, John Paston, Esquyer, be this delivered in hast.

RIGHT reverent and wurchepfull Sir, I recomand me to 1451 you, besechyng you to wete that Wharles told me that MARCH 1 Partrych seid that his lord [2] knewe wele that ye were entred pesibily in the maner of Gresham ; where fore, he seid, thow the tenauntes and fermors pay you the rents and fermes the tyme that ye be in possession, his seid lord, thow he entre ageyn, wuld never aske it them. Item, the seid Partrych seid to Wharles that his lord wull come down hym self and entre in the seid maner within short tyme. Wharles wull not discharge your baly of xvvjs. and viijd., which he toke the seid baly enseled in a purs. The seid Wharles told my mayster, John of Berney, at the court, that he repented hym that he payd you any peny till he had be distreyned ; and he seid than pleynly that he wull nomore pay till he were distreyned. I have be there divers tymes for to distreyn hym, and I cowde never do it but if [*unless*] I wuld a distreyned hym in his moders hous, and there I durst not for her cursyng. The baly of the hundred told me that Wharles spake to hym in cas he had be distreyned that he wold have gete hym a replevy ; and the baly bad hym kete a replevy of his mayster and he wold serve it.

Item, the maner londs at Gresham, with othre tenaunts londs that be fallyn in your hands ben letyn to ferme. I can gete no tenaunte to dwell in the maner hous. And if the rede shuld be caryed thens, the tenaunts shuld thynk that ye fered sum new entre, and it shuld sore discomfort hem, for thei whisshed whan it was caried to the maner that it had be leyd ther thus pesibly ij. yer afore. Asfor the obligacyon that ye shuld have of the parson of Cressyngham, he seth he cam never

---

[1] [From Paston MSS., B.M.]   This letter was written in the spring of 1451, when John Paston had re-entered Gresham.   [2] Lord Molyns.

THE PASTON LETTERS

1451
MARCH 1 at Cressyngham syth he spake with you, and that he be heste it you not till Fastyngong.[1] His hors ben stolyn, and therfore he may not ryde.

Item, Gonnore kept a court at Routon the Thursday[2] next after Seynt Mathy[3] the Appostell, and it was told me that Bettes was ther with hym ; wherefore I rode theder. And be cause that it was a fraunchised town and within the Duchye,[4] and also that Gonnor had gret rewle in the seid town, I toke with me the baly of the hundred and set hym with me in my Lord of Norffolks warant, and than yede in to the court ther as Gonnor and Bettes wern. The seid baly told Gonnor of this warant, and Gonnor rebuked hym so that he durst not a rest the seid Bettes. Than I toke it up on me and arested hym myself as he sate be Gonnor. Gonnor desired than to se my warant, and I shewed it hym, and he seid he wold obey it as the lawe wold. And he proferyd me suerte, men of the seid town of Routon. Than I told hym, and [i.e. if] he wold be bownd hym self with othre I would agre ther to, but I wuld have no shipmen that had nought, ner such men that rought [cared] never, and thei were onys on the see, wheder thei come ageyn or noght. Than Bettes toke Gonnor a supersedias that he had of Wychyngham twelmoneth ago for anothre man that asked suerte of the seid Bettes. I wold have had it, and he wold not lete me have it, ner shewe it me but in his hands. Than I told hym that it was noght, and he seid it was gode i nowe. I bad hym take it me for my discharge, and he seid pleynly I shuld not have it. Than I told hym I wold have my prisoner. The seid Gonnor seid I shuld not have hym, and dede set alle the tenaunts up on me and made a gret noyse, and seydyn alle pleynly I shuld not have hym yf he wold abyde with hem. Than I told Gonnor that I shuld certifie a rescuse, and prayd the baly of the hundred that he wold record the same. Item, the seid Gonnor seid I myght have favoryd the seid Bettes the more be cause the seid Bettes was my mayster Stapylton man, and that his men shuld not be bownd and I

[1] Fastingong, or Shrove Tuesday, fell upon the 9th March in 1451.
[2] 25th February. [3] St. Matthias, whose day was the 24th February.
[4] The Duchy of Lancaster.

220

1451
MARCH 1 shuld go lose. He seid I shuld be tyed or aght longe and alle my feleshep bothyn ; but, God yeld hym, he hath yovyn me iiij. days respyte. Than I told hym it shuld never ly in his power to bynde me, ner non of my feleshep so fast but that it shuld be in your power to make hym to losyn us, and if that he abode in Norffolk he shuld be made to seke the skyrts of his sadill or Esterne. And if he had kept his wey that nyght I shuld have kept hym trewe covenaunte, for I lay on wayte up on hym on the heth as he shuld have comen humward, and if I myght have met with hym I shuld have had Bettes from hym ; but he had leyd such wetche that he had aspied us or he cam fully at us ; and he remembered Wyndhams manhood, that iiij. swyft fete were better than ij. hands, and he toke his hors with the spores and rode to Felbrygge Hall as fast as he myght rydyn, and I suppose he lay ther all that nyght.

Item, the seid Gonnor manased and thret John of Beston for he wuld not warn hym her of ; and he dede sease alle his lond in Routon, and warned hym that he shuld not occupy his lyme kyll ner no lond that he had in Routon ; and he mad his avaunte whan I was gon, if that I had not brought the baly of the hundred with me I shuld never have go thens ; and yet, not withstandyng that I brought the baly with me, and thei had wust where myn hors had stond I shuld have be wele betyn. All this language had thei whan that I was gon.

Item, the seid Gonnor seid after that I was gon to the tenaunts of the seid town, that his supersedias was noght, and as for the rescuse, he shuld purvey a mene to excuse it. Where fore and it pleasyd you to send my mastres word how that I shuld be demened with the seid Bettes, and wheder that ye wuld I shuld a rest hym ageyn or nought, and to purvey such a mene for Gonnor that he myght ley his bost, it shuld be gret comfort to all yowr frendes and tenauntes ther abowtyn.

Item, I have be at my mayster Stapilton with your writtes, and he made it right straunge for to ensele hem. He seid that he knew of nown such inquiscion takyn at Swafham beforn hym ; he seid if it were presented ther, it was presented in his absens, whill that he was in his inne ; wherfore he seid

221

THE PASTON LETTERS

1451
MARCH 1 he wold not ensele hem till he sey the bokes. Whan I had answeryd hym ther to, than he seid he wold comown with my mayster Yelverton her of whan he come home, and til he had spok with hym he wold not ensele hem. I told hym my mayster Yelverton had enseled hem. Thann he seid he knew not my mayster Yelverton seale. He shewed it to Gonnor, and asked hym wheder it was his seall or noght. Gonnor seid it was his sealle. Than my mayster Stapilton brake ought of this mater and spake to me of the a restyng of Bettes and makyng of affray up on Gonnor. He seid Gonnor cam to hym to compleyn up on me. I told hym that Gonnor had enformed hym as it plesyd hym, for I had yove hym no cause to compleyn of me, and if it pleased hym to her myn excuse he shuld fynd me in no defaute. Whan he had herd myn excuse, he cowde not blame me. Meche othre langage we had, for I was with hym ner an ower. Than he asked me wheder the inquisicion was taken be fore the justice of the peas or the justice of the oyer determyner. I told hym be for the justic of the peas, for I seid it was the cessyons of the peas at Swafham. Than he bad me put up my warants, for he seid he wold not ensele hem till he had comowned with my maister Yelverton. I told hym it shuld not nede to comown with my mayster Yelverton, ner labor hym therfore, for I seid it myght not hurt thow he enseled hem not ; for I seid the writts were executed, and that the shereff had mad ought warants of them, and his warants were executed, and so the seid writts shuld stand you in litill avayll, save only, I told hym, ye desiryd his sealle, because it was fownd before othre lords with hym, and that he stode in the teste of the said writts, and that was cause of my comyng theder. Than he wend I had comyn for to assayn hym, for forthwith he enseled hem, but me thynk be his langage he hath labored of the toder part.

Item, and it pleased your gode maystershep to gete of my mayster Yelverton a supersedias for John Osborn and an othre for me. We suppose that Gonnor and Bettes wull do us arest, and we wuld the supersedias that we haue ought of the Chauncery were kept till more nede were. My mastres[1]

[1] Margaret Paston.

222

recomand her to you, and prayth you to hold her excused that she write yow no letter, for myche of the mater that she shuld have wrete to you I had wrete in my letter or she knew ther of ; and also she knew not of so redy a massanger as I had. And it plesyd your gode maystershep to send us a pardon for to assoylyn Gonnor this holy tyme of Lentyn, the rather be cause of this gret bulle,[1] we shuld leve in the more reste and peas, and kepe the more our pacyence than we do. The Holy Trynyte have you in His kepyng. Wretyn on the Monday next after Seynt Mathie[2] the Appostell, in hast.

Your pore servaunte,

JAMES GLOYS.

179

JAMES GLOYS TO JOHN PASTON[3]

To my right reverent and wurchepfull mayster, John Paston, Esquyer, be this delivered in hast.

RIGHT reverent and wurchepfull Sir, I recomaund me to you, prayng you to wete that I have labored divers men that ben enpaneld atwix my mastres, your moder, and Wyndham.[4] Ther be many of them woll do her parte, and ther ben summe that wull not passe ther upon, for thei ben aferd that the werd [world] shuld turne. It is noysed in Norwhich that my Lord of Oxenford, my mayster Yelverton, and ye, and John Damme shuld be endited in Kent for mayntenaunce of the oyer determyner in Norffolk ; and this, with othre feryth sore men of Norwhich. I trow my mastres writyth to you here of more clerly. Item, Wyndham hath be divers tymes at my mastres Cler, and mad hym erands to her,

[1] Probably a bull of indulgence issued at the close of the year of jubilee 1450, for the benefit of those who had not been able to visit Rome that year.
[2] St. Matthias. His day was the 24th February.
[3] [From Paston MSS., B.M.] From what it mentions about Gonnor, this letter will be seen to be of the same year as the last. The fears entertained of Heydon recovering his influence are also indicative of the spring of 1451. The letter is slightly mutilated in the margin at the bottom.
[4] John Wyndham, Esq. of Felbrigg.

223

MARCH 1

MARCH 1

MARCH 2

THE PASTON LETTERS

1451
MARCH 2

and told her that he was sued in my mastres, your moders name but he supposyd that she knew not there of. He thought that ye and James Gresham had do it un malyce, my mastres your moders unknowyng. But whan he knew that I labored the enqueste, than he sent my mastres Clere word how that he knew wele that it was my mastres your moders labore. Item, he told my Lady of Morle[1] of this sute, and he seid that he wend that my seid lady had mad an hend a twix them for the seid sute. Item, Heydons men brought his awyn hors and his sadyll thourgh Aylsham on Monday, and thei comyn in at the Busshoppes gates at Norwich and comyn over Tomelond and in to the Abbey. Thei a bedyn there all that nyght, and ij. days after, wenyng to men of the town that Heydon had go over the fery, and so in to the Abbey; and sythyn thei seid thei shuld go to London for Heydon. Item, sum seyn that Heydon shuld be mad a knyght, and myche othre langage ther is which causyth men to ben aferd, wenyng that he shuld have a rewle ageyn. Item, there were ij. men at John Betes of Holt; thei had langage of the Lord Moleyns. If it please yow to enquere of Symond, brynger of this letter, he shall enforme you of her langage. Item, Gonnor was wetched at Felbrygge Halle with xl. persones of the Lady Felbryggs[2] tenaunts and mor that night that I lay on wayte up on hym, and he durst not go home on the next day till they brought hym home. Thei mad a compleynt to my Lady Felbrygge, and my mastres had excused it. Item, the manase Burflet, and wull sease his lond. Symond shall telle yow how thei wer answered. Item, as for the subsidy that Sir Herry I[nglos] and the Lady Felbrygge shuld payn, the meyr knowe not yet veryly what thei schuld pay, for thei have not cast the valew of her londs. The bill closyd in this letter maketh mensyon of the valew of divers gentelmens londs that [ben] examyned in Norwhich. We can not know what Calthorp payth, for we can not speke with the shereffe,

[1] See p. 84, Note 2.
[2] Catherine, widow of Sir Simon Felbrigg, was lady of the manor of Felbrigg, of which Wyndham only had the lease at this time, though he afterwards became the proprietor.—See Blomefield, viii. 112.

224

ner the undre [shereffe], ner no man that gadered that hundred 1451 ther as Calthorp dwellytht. The Holy Trynyte have you in MARCH 2 his kepyng. Wr[etyn] the Tuesday next after Seynt Mathie,[1] in hast. Your pore servaunt,

JAMES GLO[YS].

180

MARGARET PASTON TO JOHN PASTON[2]

To my rith wurshepfull hosbond, Jon Paston.

RITH worchipfull hosbond, I recommawnd me to yow, MARCH 3 praying you to wete that ther is a gret noyse in this town, that my Lord of Oxforth and Yelverton and ye ben endytid in Kent for mayntenyng of the oyer determyner; and Jon Dame is endytyd ther also of treson, be cawse that he dede Heydon endytyn[3] of treson for takyng down of the quarter of the man. And the pepyll that ben ayens Ser Thomas Todenham and Heydon ben sore aferd be cawse of this noyse, and of other langage that is had bothe in this town and in the contre, that these seyd Todenham and Heydon shuld ben as well at ese, and have as grett rewill as ever they hadde.

Jamys Gloys tellith me that he hath sent yow word of Heydonys hors and of other thyngs, mor of whiche I was purposid to asent yow word of. The Holy Trinyte have yow in kepyng. Wretyn at Norwiche, the Weddenysday next after Seynt Mathy.[1]

Yowris, M. P.

[1] St. Matthias.—See p. 223, Note 2.
[2] [From Fenn, iii. 288.] It will be seen that this letter contains a distinct reference to the last which was written the day before it. Indeed, the information contained in this letter is nearly all anticipated in that of Gloys.
[3] i.e. caused Heydon to be indicted.

THE PASTON LETTERS

181

DENYES TO JOHN PASTON[1]

To my maister Paston.

1451
MARCH 4

RIGHT wurshipfull sir, and my right good maister, I recomaunde me to yow. It is so that up on an hasty sodeyn warnyng I departid from London and spake not with yow at my departyng, Wherof I was full sory. I pray yow, neverthelesse, that ye wole eftsones speke to William White with my Lord Cardinall, for I desire his maistership and good will and wole do to my power. And as touchyng to that that he semith I haf don agayn hym, in good feith I wole abide your rule or, by Seynt Kateryne, his owen rule. He is a gentilman and I wole don it with good will. I am right sory ye had not set me thorgh with hym erst I went, for I haf prayed yow ther of, as ye know your self dyvers tymes. The Holy Trynite preserve yow. Wretyn at Wevenho the iiii. day of Merche.—Your servaunt, DENYES.

Sir, my Lord[2] hath kept sessions at Colchestre, and my maister Yelverton with hym, and he desired me to write to yow to be wel ware if ony fals suggestion or lesynges wer made by Tuddenham and Heydon and that to your power thei be answerd in his absence. As for my Lord Scales, her be seven of housold meny indited of felony, which are strong thefes. Item, I pray yow, write in hast to the Meir of Norwich to gif credens to me whan I come to hym, and if ye so do I shal shape their articles in billes in to a nother facion I trust, and make thaym redy and delyver thaym resonably wele. My

[1] [Add. MS. 34,889, f. 169.] This letter must have been written in a year when Easter fell after the 20th April, as Lent does not appear to have begun on the 4th March; and as it was during the life of Cardinal Kempe, we may pretty safely fix it to the year 1451. The year 1454, indeed, might be possible as regards Easter, but there is no indication here of those troubles of which the writer complains so bitterly in that year on the 20th March. See No. 239.
[2] The Earl of Oxford.

226

Lord purposeth to be at London the ende of the first weke of 1451 Lent, and not erst. I pray your maistership, se sum meane MARCH 4 that White do me not that harme in the Chauncery wherof ye sent me word by Brayn, for, as God sauf my soule at the day of Jugement, I fonde surete for the pees, but the Maister of the Rolles[1] ful untruly recordeth that surete takyn as a baile, wher of treuth it was otherwise, and ful synnefully ruleth that mater, and never wold suffir me to execute the acte but lettid me, notwithstandyng it is a law private in the self as I shal clerly declare whan I come. The Holy Trinite preserve yow. I write to yow thus that ye may kyt awey this lower part of this lettre.

182

MARGARET PASTON TO JOHN PASTON[2]

To my Ryth worshipfull hosband, John Paston.

RITH wurchipfull hosbond, I recommawnd me to yow, MARCH 15 desiring hertily to her of yowr welfar; preying you to wete that Herry Halmannys wif sent to me word on Saterday last past that Prentys thretyth her hosbond sor, and John Robyns, for suche thynges as Prentys seyth that they haue donn ayens hym; he seyth he shall make hem so besy or he leve hem that he shall make hem not wurth apeny; and they ben aferd that he woll hold hem conuawnt if he have powyr ther to. It is seyd her that the kyng shuld com in to this contre, and sir Thomas Todenham and Heydon arn well cheryeshid with hym. And also it is seyd they shall have as grett rewill in this contre as evyr they hadde, and many more folkes arn sory therfore than mery. Sir Thomas Todenhamys man and Heydonys sowyn this sedde all abowte the contre, that here maysteris shull cum hom in hast in here prosperite and be als well att esse as ever they wer. As for that ye

[1] Thomas de Kirkeby.
[2] [Add. MS. 34,888, f. 55.] This letter would appear to be of the same year as No. 184, written a fortnight later. Both letters speak of rumours that Tuddenham and Heydon will regain their ascendency.

227

THE PASTON LETTERS

1451
MARCH 15
dessyryd that I shuld enquyr wher any stuff is of yowris, I wot not how to don ther with, for if ever wer aspyid that hath of yowr stuff, and we had it from hym, other that have more ther of wold ben ware be hym, and avoyd seche stuff as they have of yowris. I suppose John Osbern shall tell yow whan ye com hom agode meen to wete wher meche ther of is becom. Jamys Gloys is ayen to Gressam and I suppose John Damme shall tell yow what he hath donn ther. Yowr tenawntis wold fayn that summe mene of yowris shuld abyde amongis hem, for they ben in gred diswyr what they may do ; the langage is so grett on the tother party that it maketh the tenawntis sor afferd that ye shuld not regoyse itt. I send to yow a letter be Colynys of Frawnceys Costard what dedis he woll don. It was told me also that the Lord Molyns was lyke to have aday ayens yow att Thetford at the next assyse. On [one] that loueth yow ryth-well told me how it was told hym so, and warnyd me therof in secrete wyse. Itt is gode to ben war of ther falsed. I pray yow that ye woll send me word in hast, if ye woll have red to your levery as ye wer avysid, and if ye woll not, &c. And also I pray yow that ye woll do bey ij. gode hattis for your sonys for I can none getyn in this town. Mor tydynges can I not send yow yett. The Holy Trinyte have yow in his kepyng. Wretyn att Norwiche on the fyrst Monday of Lent.

Yowris,   M. P.

shuld cawse yow for to be displeasid ; and if I have do, I am sory therof, and will amend itt. Wherefor I beseche yow to forgeve me, and that ye bere none hevynesse in your hert ayens me, for your displeasans shuld be to hevy to me to indure with.

1451
[MAR. 2

I send yow the roll that ye sent for, in selyd, be the brynger her of ; it was fownd in your trussing cofor. As for hering, I have bowt an horslode for iiij[s.] vj[d.] I can gett none ell [eels] yett ; as for bever [i.e. drinkables], ther is promysid me somme, but I myt not gete it yett. I sent to Jone Petche to have an answer for the wyndowis, for she myt not come to me. And she sent me word that she had spoke therof to Thomas Ingham, and he seyd that he shuld speke with yow hymself, and he shuld accord with yow wel jnow, and seyd to her it was not her part to desyr of hym to stop the lyts ; and also he seyd itt was not his parte to do itt, be cawse the place is his but for yeris.

And as for all other eronds that ye have commandid for to be do, thei shal be do als sone as thei may be do. The blissid Trynyte have yow in his keping. Wretyn at Norwyche, on the Monday next after Seynt Edward.

Yowris,   M. P.

referred to were intended as provision for that season. This conjecture may be correct ; but it must be noted that John Paston was at home at Norwich, if not in the beginning of Lent, at least on the fourth Sunday of Lent in 1454. Moreover, if the date of this letter, 'Monday next after St. Edward,' means after the 18th March, which was the day of St. Edward the King and Martyr, the year 1451 would suit rather better than 1454 ; for, in the former year, the Monday after St. Edward's day would be the 22nd of March, and Ash Wednesday the 10th, while in the latter the Monday after St. Edward would be the 25th, and Ash Wednesday the 6th, so that the provision of herrings would be very late.

183

MARGARET PASTON TO JOHN PASTON[1]

To my right wurchipfull husbond, John Paston, be this delyverid in hast.

1451(?)
[MAR. 22]
RIGHT wurchipfull hosbond, I recomawnd me to yow, beseching yow that ye be not displeasid with me, thow my symplenesse cawsed yow for to be displeasid with me. Be my trowth, it is not my will nother to do ne sey that

[1] [From Fenn, iii. 238.] The date of this letter is quite uncertain. Fenn assigns it to the year 1454, when Lent began very late, as it is evident the herrings and eels

228

229

THE PASTON LETTERS

184

MARGARET PASTON TO JOHN PASTON[1]

To my right wurchepfull husbond, John Paston, [be]yng in the Inner Tempill, be this delivered in hast.

1451
MARCH 30
RIGHT wurchepfull husbond, I recomaund me to you, prayng you to wete that myn unkyll Phylyp Berney[2] was at Lynne this last weke, and he was at inne at the baylyffes hows of Lynne, and Partrych[3] came in to the same place whill myn unkyll was ther. And the seid Partrych was wele aqueyntyd with the balyffe, and the balyffe told hym that he sent a letter to the Lord Molyns, and that the Lord Molyns had sent hym a nother letter, letyng hym wete that he purposyd hym to be at Lynne thes weke. Than Partrych seid that he had word that the seid lord purposyd hym to be ther at that tyme ; but he seid summe men supposyd that he wuld not come here ; and the balyffe seid that he was right glad that he shuld come in to this countre. On of myn unkyll men herd all this langage, and told it myn unkill. The baly ner Patrych knewe not at that tyme what myn unkyll was to us ward. Also I purposyd me to have sent to Stapylton, as ye sent me word be James Gresham, and it is told me that he is to London. Item, it is noysed abowte Gresham and all that contre that the Lord Molyns shuld be there in hast. Item, Gonnore had right gret langage, and he trostyd that the word [world] shall turne sumwhat after ther entent. Othre tydynges have we non, but that Tudenham and Heydon shuld have ageyn the rewle in this contre, assmych as ever thei had or more. The Holy Trynte have you in kepyng. Wretyn at Norwhich un the Tuesday next before Mydlentesonday.[4]

Yowre,   M. P.

[1] [From Paston MSS., B.M.] This letter, like several of those preceding, speaks of a juncture in which it was expected that Tuddenham and Heydon would regain their influence. The adherents of Lord Molyns were also in hopes that he would shortly be in Norfolk and re-enter Gresham. The date must therefore be 1451.
[2] Philip Berney, Esq. of Caston. He was a brother of Margaret Mauteby, who was Margaret Paston's mother.   [3] See p. 101, Note 4.
[4] Mid-Lent Sunday fell on the 4th April in 1451.

230

185

PETITION FROM THE TOWN OF SWAFFHAM[1]

To the ryght wise, noble, and discrete Comons of this present Parlement.

1451
MEKELY besechyn, bewailyn, and shewyn the pouer and simple inhabitaunts in the toun of Swafham, in the counte of Norfolk, that where Sir Thomas Tudenham of Oxburgh, knyght, this xvj. yeeris last passid before the day of the Acte of Resumpcion in the last Parlement before this,[2] hath ocupied and governed the lordship and maner of Swafham forsaid, with the appertenauncez, as styward and fermer of the same ; in which ocupacion and governaunce the said Sir Thomas, and othre his servauntz and adherentz in a rolle to this peticion annexed named, han petously and synnefully don and comitted the trespasez, offencez, wronges, extorcyons, mayntenauncez,[3] imbraceryes,[4] oppressions, and perjuryes in the seid rolle conteyned ; and of dyverse and many articles ther of, and of many othre wrongs, and of that that the said Sir Thomas is a comon extorcioner, the same Sir Thomas be fore the ryght noble, true, and pleyn lord, our good and gracious lord the Erle of Oxenford, and othre the Kyngs commissioners of *oire determyner* withynne the same shire, the said Sir Thomas Tudenham, and othre his servauntz and adherentz arn indited.

Please it your noble wisdamis to conceyve that it hath be the comon law of the land of long tyme that if a comon theef were, in ony cuntre, so often indited or detect of so many

[1] [From Paston MSS., B.M.] This is a rough draft of a Petition which seems to have been intended for presentation to Parliament in the beginning of the year 1451. Parliament was prorogued on the 18th December 1450 till the 20th January following, but it did not actually meet again for despatch of business till the 29th April. It would appear from this Petition that Sir Thomas Tuddenham and his adherents were indicted before the Earl of Oxford at the sessions of *oyer and terminer* which sat on the 2nd March 1451.
[2] This must be the Act of Resumption of 28 Henry VI.—See *Rolls of Parliament*, v. 183.   [3] See p. 167, Note 3.   [4] See p. 167, Note 5.

231

1451 offencez he shuld not, by the law of the lande, be late to baile ne meynprise, but be kept in prison til he were put to answere of swich crymes as he were so detect of. And also please your greet wisdams to conceyve that all the Juges of the Kynges Benche, of long and late tyme sittyng in their place, laudabely han usid to comitte to prison, with oute baile or meynprise, for a tyme, al persones that han be detecte before theym of any ryot or greet cruel offence agayn the peas, which offence myght a be subvercyon of the law by ony liklynesse ; and advertisyng the greet mischeves that this noble roialme hath oftyn standyn in for the greet extorcyons and oppressions that hath be don in the same,[1] and how greet a subvercyon of the lawe and of the polityk governaunce of the land suych extorcyon is ; and of your prudent and sage wisdams lyke yow to make requisicion to the Kyng our soverain Lord, and to the Lords espirituallx and temporelx in this present Parlement assembled, that by the consideracion that the said Sir Thomas wold never apere, in his persone, ne by his atturney, at no sesions of *oir determyner* holden in the said counte ; plese the Kyng and Lords forsaid, to comitte the said Sir Thomas Tudenham to preson, ther to abide til in to the tyme that he to the said inditements hath answerid, and to the billes and compleynts of the said inhabitauntz in fourme of law.

And more over, where that the said Sir Thomas Tudenham hath, among many othre greet wrongs, ful synnefully causid a writte of assise of novell dissessyn[2] to be brought ageyn John Aleyn and xxiij othre of the said toune, in the name of the Abbot of Sawtre,[3] and causid that assise to passe by perjury, as in the first article in the rolle to this peticion annext it is more opinly conteyned, please your greet wisdams, for the reverens of God by that concideracion, that the jurry of the said assise durst not, for drede of the horrible menaces of the said Sir Thomas, othrewise do but be for sworn in gevyng their verdite in the same assise, in which case the said inhabitauntz, for pyte and remorce of their concyencez, wer lothe to

[1] [Original note here in margin.] Answer neyther to the billes ne inditeing forsaid, ne to non of theym.
[2] *See* p. 47, Note 4.   [3] A Cistercian monastery in Huntingdonshire.

232

sew a writ of atteynte,[1] to pray the Kynge and Lords forsaid 1451 to ordeyn, by auctorite of this present Parlement, that the said writ of assisse, verdit, recoverer, and the jugement ther of, with every othre circumstaunce therof, be voide, revokd, and adnulled, for the love of God.

[2] Item, compleyneth John Bladsmyth of Swafham of that that where John, late Pryour of Penteney,[3] predecessor of the prior that now is, and the covent of the same place, the Munday next aftir the fest of Seynt Mathew the Evangelist, the xiij. yeer of the kyng, our soverain lord that now is, at Swafham forsaid, lete to ferme to the forsaid John Bladsmyth certeyn londs, rents, tenements, and pasture,[4]——

186

ABSTRACT[5]

Sir John Fastolf to Sir Thos. Howys, Parson of Castlecombe, at Castre.

Received a letter from them, 3rd April, with the last account of Sir Jo. APRIL 13 Kyrtelyng and Intewod. Understands Rob. Norwych will not occupy as undersheriff, because Jenneys had given him language not to his pleasure, and so Aleyn is to occupy, who is not F.'s wellwiller ; but Howys has provided a remedy with the sheriff. When the *venire facias* is made out, I will try and get it sent you, and I shall have Paston's advice. Knows well the obstinate will of false Dallyng, but Bokkyng must speak with him, and entreat him in his best manner.—Margaret Bryg's matter.

As to the oyer and terminer, it is certain Heydon and Tuddenham will be at Norwich with all the maintenance and fellowship they can. It is said Justice Prysot will be there. You must do your best to keep your friends steadfast ; and I in the meantime will labour here, and send you word how the world is set. Men of the city of Norwich have good audience and favour among the Lords, and are waiting an answer of their matters. Has delivered up the shipmen, and left the ship here for causes which he will write ; 'for the rayse hath been full costuys, except they came in saufftee.'

London, 13 April, 29 Hen. vi.

[1] A writ to inquire whether a jury gave a false verdict.
[2] This is written on the back.
[3] John de Tyrington. He was succeeded in 1449 by Richard Pentney.
[4] The sentence breaks off thus abruptly in the MS.
[5] [From MS. Phillipps, 9735, No. 231.]

233

187

MARGARET PASTON TO JOHN PASTON[1]

To my right wurchepfull howsbond, John Paston.

1451   R IGHT wurchepfull howsbond, I recomand me to yow, APRIL 16   prayng yow to wete that the Parson of Oxened[2] told me that Wyndham told hym that Sweynnysthorp[3] is hold of the Kyng be the therd part or the fourt part of a knyt fye, and ho so ever had the maner of Sweynsthorp, he shuld fynde an armyd man, in tyme of werre in the castell of Norwhic, xl. days to his owyn cost, and that ye shuld pay xxx[s.] to the Kyng yerly owth of the seyd maner ; and it is fond also that your fader shuld a died seysyd, and that ye shuld a entyryd ther in as heyr after your fader dysseys, and that ye shuld be now up on the age of xxx. wynter.

The Trinite have yow in hys kepyng. Wreten at Norwhic, the Friday next a fore Seynt George.—Yowrs,

           M. PASTON.

188

ABSTRACT[4]

Sir John Fastolf to Sir Thos. Howys, at Castre in Flegg.

APRIL 21   Sends two *venire facias* for Beyton in Norfolk and Bradwell in Suffolk, returnable *in quindena Pasche*, which is a short day. You must deliver them in

[1] [From Fenn, iii. 84.] The date of this letter depends upon the age of John Paston, who, in November 1444, was found to be twenty-three years old. As he is now ' upon the age of thirty winters,' this letter was probably written in 1451.
[2] His name was Laurence Baldewar.
[3] In 1444, according to Blomefield (*Hist. of Norf.* iv. 40), a rent-charge out of the manor of Swainsthorp was settled by John and Agnes Paston, the eldest son and the widow of William Paston, the Justice, to find a priest to sing for the soul of the said William in the chapel of our Lady the Great in Norwich Cathedral.
[4] [From MS. Phillipps, 9735, No. 243.]

234

haste to the Sheriff by Paston's advice, by whom I send them. Labour to the 1451 Sheriff for the return of such panels as will speak for me, and not be shamed, APRIL 21 for great labour will be made by Wentworth's party. 'Entreat the Sheriff as well ye can by reasonable rewards, rather than fail,' for they have taken as false an issue as can be with me ' by H. [*i.e.* Heydon's] advice for cold love.' I had traversed the plea in the inquisition that I had disseised Sir Hue Fastolf ; but they put it now that I had only a joint interest in the manor. The names you sent for Bradwell are like to do well, except Hopton, who has married with the Lady Wentworth. I am also in doubt of one Reppes of Heringflete, who is Heydon's man. Had purposed to have been at the oyer and terminer this time, but cannot, &c.

Horshighdoun, 21 April, 29 Hen. vi.   *Signed.*

189

DEBENHAM, TYMPERLEY, AND WHITE TO JOHN PASTON[1]

M AISTER Paston, we comaund us to you, lattyng you MAY 2   witt that the Sheriff [is] noght so hole as he was, for now he wille shewe but a part of his frendeshippe. And also there is grete prese off pepill, and fewe frendes, as ferr as we can feel yitt. And therfore be ye sadly avised wheder ye seme best to come your self, or send or, &c., for we will assay in as much as in us is to prevaile to your entente. And yett, if it neded, we wolde have a man to giffe us informacion, or shewe evidence after the case requireth. Also the Shereffe enformed us that he hath writyng from the Kyng that he shall make such a panell to aquyte the Lord Moleynes. And also he tolde us, and as ferr as we can conceyve and feel, the Shereff wille panell gentylmen to aquyte the Lorde, and jowroures to a quyte his men ; and we suppose that it is be the mocion and meanes of the othir party. And yif any meanes of tretie be proferd, we know not what meane shulde be to your pleasir. And therfore we wolde fayne have mor knowlege, yiff ye think it were to doo.

No more at this tyme, bot the holy Trinite have you in his

[1] [From Paston MSS., B.M.] As this letter speaks of the indictment and expected acquittal of Lord Molyns, the date must be 1451. This letter is written on parchment.

235

1451
MAY 2

kepyng. Wretin at Walsyngham, in hast, the secund day of May.—Be your trewe and feithfull frendes,

DEBENHAM, TYMPERLEY, AND WHITE.

And also, Sir, as we conceyve, the Lord Moleynes shall not be quyte before Thursedey; in as muche as he was indyted before the Justice, we undirstand he shall not be quyte but before the Justice. Wherfore we avise you, iff ye think it be to doo, to send your frendes in the meane tyme, and come your self to your place at Sperham, and there abyde unto tyme that we have knowlege how the saide mater will drawe, and till that we may have worde from you, and ye from us, &c.

190

W. LOMNOR TO JOHN PASTON[1]

MAY (?)

RYGHT worchipfulle Sir, yours goode cosynes and frendes avyse yow to come to Walsyngham, and that ye be there to morw betymes at vj. on the clok; for the Lord Moleyns offreth a trete for the goodes, and amendes to be made, or he goth ought of this contre, and if it be not taken, his men shulle justifie; wherupon your title might be hurte. The Lord Skales, the Justis, and other knyegtes and squyeres merveyle grettly ye come not, and thow they that have not so true and evident mater as ye have concelle yow to be absent; yet I wolde ye dede as ye be desyrd be that felaship, for many wolde yow right welle. Whanne ye come, I shalle telle yow more.

The Lorde Moleyns shulde not have be aquyte of his comaundement, hadde he not sworen on a boke, sweche evidens was ayens hym; and ther is no jentelman wolde aquite his men for no goode, &c.   W. LOMNOR.

[1] [From Paston MSS., B.M.] This letter has no address, but there can be no doubt from the contents it was intended for John Paston. It was evidently written about the same time as the last, while the Sessions was sitting at Walsingham, and Paston's suit against Lord Molyns was still pending.

192

SIR THOMAS HOWYS TO SIR JOHN FASTOLF[1]

To my reverent and worchepfull mayster, Sir John Fastolf, Knyght, be this lettre delyvered.

1451
MAY 9

RIGHT reverent and worchipfull maister, I recomaunde me louly un to yow. Please you to wete the Sonday next after the Fest of the Invencion of the Cros,[2] the ix. day of May, at Castre, I receyved a lettre from you by your clerk, W. Barker, the tenure wherof I shall do goode in all hast goodly. But for the more special cause of my wrytyng at this tyme is to gef you relacion of the un true demenyng of this oure determyner, by the parcialte of the Jugez of it; for whan the Counsell of the cite of Norwich, of the toun of Swafham, youres, my Maister Inglose,[3] Pastons, and many other playntyfs had put in and declared, bothe by writyng and by woord by fore the Jugez, the lawfull excepcions in many wise, the Juges by ther wilfulnesse myght nat fynde in ther hert to gef, not als moche as a bek nor a twynclyng of ther eye toward, but toke it to derision, God reforme such parcialte; and by cause Prisot[4] thought that yf the Sessions of the oyer determyner had be holden at Norwich as they bygonne, he supposed it shuld nat so fast passe to th'entent of Tudenham and Heydon and ther felawes, as it shuld do ell[es] in other place, but enjorned to Walsyngham, wher they have grettist rule, ther to be holden on Tuesday, iiij[te] day of May.

This knowing, my Maister Yelverton,[5] Genney, and other myght weel conceyve how the governaunce of the oyer deter-

[1] [From Fenn, iii. 116.]
[2] The 3rd of May.
[3] Sir Harry Inglos.
[4] John Prisot, Chief Justice of the Common Pleas.
[5] William Yelverton, Justice of the King's Bench, afterwards knighted by Edward IV.

191

SIR JOHN HEVENINGHAM TO MARGARET PASTON[1]

To my ryght worchipffull cosyn, Margarete Paston, be this letter delivered.

1451 (?)
MAY 7

RYGHT worchipffull and welbeloved cosyn, I comaunde me to you as herteli as I can, thankyng you off your goode chere the last tyme I was with you. And, worchippffull cosyn, please that you to calle un to your remembrauns I wrote un to you for my cosyn Anneys Loveday to have ben in your service, and I reseyved from you a letter that your wyll was goode, but durst not to in to the tyme ye hadde spoke with my cosyn your husbonde.

Worchippffull cosyn, I have labored for hir in othir placez, but I can not have my entent as yet. Wherffor yff that hit please you to have hyr with you to in to the tyme that a mastris may be purveyeid for hir, I pray you ther off, and I shall contente you ffor hir boarde, that ye shal be wel pleased; for, cosyn, and I hadde a wyff, I wolde not care for hir. And ther as she is, she is not well at hir ease, for she is at Robert Lethum; and therfor I pray you herteli that ye wyll tendre this my writyng, and I beseche you that in cas be that ye wyll fulffylle hit that ye wel sende my cosyn Will Staunton for hir, and I shal kepe you trewe promys, as I have be for wretyn. And I beseche Almyghti Jesu preserve you. Wretyn at Hevenyngham, on the vij. day off May, &c. —Your oune cosyn,

JOHN HEVENYNGHAM, Knyght.

[1] [From Fenn, iii. 144.] The date of this letter is doubtful, but it was evidently written at a time when John Paston had been for some considerable time absent from Norwich, which appears to have been the case in the beginning of May 1451. The writer of this letter died in July 1453.

1451
MAY 9

myner shuld procede, for it was the most parcial place of alle the shire, and thedre wer cleped alle the frendez, knyghteys, and esquiers, and gentilmen that wolde in nowise do other wise than they wolde. And the seid Tudenham, Heydon, and other oppressours of ther set come doun theder, as I understand, with iiij[c] [400] hors and more; and consideryng how ther wellwillers wer ther assembled at ther instaunce, it had be right jowpertous and ferefull for any of the pleyntyfs to have be present, for ther was nat one of the pleyntyfs ner compleynuantez ther, but your right feithfull and trusty weel willer John Paston. And my Maister Yelverton seid full discretly, and countrolled the seid Prisot when he seid, sittyng, in the Guyhalle of Norwich, these wordys to the Meyre and Commonalte, 'A, Sir Meyre and your brethren, as to the processe of youre compleyntez, we wole put them in contynuance, but in all other we wole procede;' which wordys Yelverton thought right parciall. And by side this the seid Prisot wolde suffre no man that was lerned to speke for the pleyntyfs, but took it as a venom, and took them by the nose at every thred woord whiche myght weel by knowe for open parcialte.

And as for the Lord Scalys, ye knowe well what he is toward you, and namely for Hikelyng matter. Also to knowe som of your feynt frendes, at that tyme that my Lord Norffolk sat at Norwich up on the oyer determyner, Sir John Hevyngham myht nat fynde it in his hert to go iiij. furlong from his duellyng place to the shirehouse, but now he cowd ryde from Norwich to Walsyngham to syt as one of the Commyssioners. As to the rule of other, that ye wolde have supposed your wellewillers, how they have byhavyd them at Walsyngham, I shall sende yow woord in all hast whan Bernay[1] come hom to Castr, for he is nat yet come from Walsyngham. But this I knowe well, that they founde none obstacle ner impedyment in ther consciens in all your matter; but how they have do with Norwich, Swafham, and Paston, I am nat yet clerly informed; I suppose they arn put in respite. I here sey Heydon seweth for an ende to be had with the cite of

[1] Probably Philip Berney.

1451
MAY 9

Norwich, and as to the namys of them that passed on ther acquitaile ayenst yow, Broyn can weell informe yow. I understand that Sir Robert Conyers, Calthorp, Mundford wer capteyns, and Maister Ric. Doget also.

Item, as for the ij. *venire facias* ye sent to be retorned for your manorz of Bradwell and Beyton, I have do them to be retorned of suche namys as I have sent woord before, savyng sume be take, and except out. Moreover, as for the mater of Sir John Sibton, Geney and Raulyns gef ful counsell that it shuld abyde tyl the mater of Bradwell myght procede, so that bothe maters myght take up on a day, for they sey it wold drawe xx. marc to labour the Jure to London, and yet it wer hard to bryng about. And they gef you counsell in all wise that ye labour to have Yelverton Juge at that tyme, and in all wise bothe in that materz and in all other, that ye be war that Prisot have not to have do in any wise, for than all wole be nought. Of alle other materz I shall send you woord in all hast goodly, for at thys tyme I had no leyser by cause of the hasty comyng up of Hug Fen, whom I beseche yow to fele of the demenyng of the oyer determyner, for he can telle yow moche and [*i.e.* if] he wole ; whether he wole or nay, I can nat sey, for I know wele he was at Walsyngham. And I beseche All myghty Jesu have yow in his mercyfull governaunce. Wrete at Castre, the Sonday, ix. day of May anno xxix° Regis Henrici vj^{ti}.

On the back of the letter is written—

I prey yow be nowth displesed thow I have nowt subscribed my name withinne forth, for it is of neclygens, quoth Howys, Parson of Castlecomb.

193

JOHN OSBERN TO JOHN PASTON[1]

To my ryght reverent and worcheful Master, John Paston, be this delyverid.

PLESE it your masterchep to wete that I have spoke wyth the Shereff[2] at hese placez, mevyng to hym, as for that that was left wyth hese Under shereff, it is your wyl he shuld send a man of hese for it ; for thow it were more ye wold gladly he shuld take it ; he thanked yow, and sayde hese Under shereff was at London, and hymselff had non deserved, and if he had he wold a take it. And whan I departyd from hym, I desyerid hym a yen to send therffore, and than he seyde it shuld abyde tyl ye come hom, wherby I conceyve he wold have it, and be gladde to take it. Moreover, I remembred hym of hese promyses made before to yow at London, when he took hese oth and charche, and that ye were wyth hym when he toke hese oth, and oder dyvers tymes ; and for tho promyses made be hym to yow at that tyme, and other tymes at the oyer determyner at Lynne, ye proposed yow be the trust that ye have in hym for to atempte and rere accions that shuld be to the avayle of hym and of hese office. He wold a know what the accions shuld be. I sayde I coude not telle hym, and than he seyde he wold do for yow that he may, excepte for the aquitell of the Lord Molyns men, in so meche as the Kyng hath wrete to hym for to shewe favour to the Lord Moleyns and hese men, and as he seyth the indytement longyth to the Kyng, and not to yow,

1451
MAY 27

---

[1] [From Fenn, iii. 308.] At the date of this letter Lord Molyns had probably been acquitted, but the action against his men was still pending. The year must therefore be 1451. The date 'Thursday next after St. Austin' is understood by Fenn to be after the Feast of St. Austin, or Augustine, Bishop of Hippo, which was celebrated on the 28th of August ; but the dates of the preceding letters make it more probable that the writer means St. Augustine, the apostle of England, whose day was the 26th of May.
[2] John Jermyn.—*See page* 183, Note 2.

1451
MAY 27

and the Lord Molyns a gret lord. Also, as he seyth, now late the Lord Molyns hath sent hym a letter, and my Lord of Norffolk anoder, for to shew favour in these indytements, he darnot abide the joporte of that, that he shuld offende the Kinges commaundment. He know not how the Kyng may be informed of hym, and what shal be seyde to hym.

And than I sayde as for any joporte that he shuld abyde in any thing that he doth for yow, or be your desyre, you have offered hym, and wol performet, sufficient sewerte for to sawe hym harmeles, and therfore I supposid ther wold non resonable man thynk but that he myght do for yow wyth owte any joporte. And then he seyde he myth non sewerte take that passid *Cli.* ; and the Lord Molyns is a gret lord, he myght soon cause hym to lese that, and meche mo. Than I sayde, be that meane, in defawte of a Shereff, every man may be put from hese lyvelod ; and thann he seyde iff it were for the lyvelode, men wold take hem the nerer for to abyde a joporte ; but be hese feyth, as he swore, if the Kyng wryte ayan to hym he wol no lenger abyde the joporte of the Kyngges wrytyng, but he trustyth to Godde to inpanell seche men as shuln to hise knowleche be indeferent, and non comon jurors. As me semyth it wold do goode and [*if*] ye wolde gett a comaundment of the Kyng to the Shereff for to shew yow favour, and to inpanell jantelmen, and not for to favour non seche riotts, &c. ; for he seyde that he sent yow the letter that the Kyng sent hym, and ye seyde a man shuld gete seche on for a noble.

Item, I remembred hym of the promyses that he hath made to Temperley, and that if he wold make yow very trew promys, ye wold rewarde hym as meche as he wold desire, or any other resonable man for him, and asmoche and mor then any adverserry ye have wold gef hym ; than he seyde he toke never no mony of non of hem alle. There was proferid hym at Walsyngham for the Lord Molyns xx. nobles, he had not a peny ; moreover, I proferid hym, if he wold make yow promys that ye myght veryly trust upon hym, ye wold geff hym in hande as he wold desire, or to leve a summe if he wold a named it in a mene mannys hand, and seche as he hath trust

to. And then he seyde, if he myght do for yow, or if he do any thyng for yow, then he wol take yowre mony wyth a good wyl ; and other promys I coude not have of hym, but that he wol do for yow all that he may, excepte for the inditements. I conceyve veryly he hath made promys to do hese part that they shul be a quytte, but I suppose he hath made non other promys ayens yow for the lyvelode ; but he lokyth aftyr a gret brybe, but it is not for to trust hym veryly wyth owte that he may not chese. I suppose he had no wrytyng fro my Lord of Norffolk as he seyde.

I was at Framyngham for to a spoke wyth Tymperley, Debnam, or Berry, and they were all ought. My Lord, as he came from London, he was at Yepysweche on Moneday, and when he wythowth the town toward Framyngham, he had all hese men ryde forth afore a gret pase, for he wolde felwe softely ; and when hese men were owte of syght, he rode wyth v. men to a squieris place of hese therby, and on Tewsday, rodde my Lady to hym ; and so I dede nought at Framyngham. No more at thys tyme, but All myghty Jesu spede yow, and have yow in hese kepyng. Wrete at Norwiche, the Thursday next aftyr Sent Austyn, &c.

Be your servunt,   JOHN OSBERN.

1451
MAY 27

194

AGNES PASTON TO JOHN PASTON[1]

To [Herry][2] Barker of Synt Clements Parys, in Norwych, to delyver to my Master John Paston, in haste.

ON Thursday the wall was mad zarde hey, and a good wylle be fore evyn it reyned so sore that they were fayne to helle the wall, and leve werke. And the water is fallyn so sore that it standyt ondyr the wall a fote

1451
or later

---

[1] [From Paston MSS., B.M.] As this letter refers to the 28th year of Henry VI., seemingly as a past date, it cannot well be earlier than 1451. But probably it is not much, if at all, later.
[2] The Christian name *Herry* is crossed out, and *Meye* (?) appears to be written over.

1451
or later
deppe to Ballys warde [i.e. *towards the land of a neighbour named Ball*]. And on Friday after sakeryng, one come fro cherch warde, and schoffe doune all that was thereon, and trad on the wall and brake sum, and wente over ; but I cannot zet wete hoo it was. And Warne Kynges wyfe, as she went over the style, she cursyd Ball, and seyde that he had zevyn aweye the waye, and so it prevyt be John Paston is words. And after, Kyngs folke and odyr come and cryid on Annes Ball, seying to her the same. Zystyrnevyn wan ı xul goo to my bede, the Vycare¹ seyde that Warne Kyng and Warne Harman, betwyxte messe and matynsse, toke Sir Roberd² in the vestry, and bad hym sey to me, verely the wall xulde doun a gayne. And wan the Vycar tolde me I wyste ther of no worde, nor zet do be Sir Roberde, for he syth he were loth to make any stryfe. And wan I com out of the cherch, Roberd Emundes schowyd me how I was amercyde for seute of corte the laste zer vj*d.*, and seyd it was xij*d.* tylle Warne Kyng and he gat it awey vj*d.*

I send zou word how John Jamys was demenyd at Cromere, to send to Jamys Gressham how he xall be demenyd. Gaffrey Benchard, Alexander Glover, heywards,³ tokyn a dystresse of John Jamys or the bond tenent of A. Paston, calde Reynalds, in Cromer, the xxviiij*ti* yer of thys Kyng, and W. Goodwyn, Baly of Cromer, with the seyd J. Jamys, with forsse toke awey the dysstres, wech was ij. horsse and a plowe. And Good be with zou.

Be ANNES PASTON, your Modur.

¹ William Pope was vicar of Paston from 1447 to 1455.
² Probably the Vicar's Curate.
³ Haywards were (originally) persons who guarded a farm and crops in the night, and blew a horn on an alarm of robbers.—Halliwell.

195

AGNES PASTON TO JOHN PASTON¹

To John Paston be thys byll deliverd in hast.

I SPACKE thys day with a man of Paston syde, and he told me that a man of Paston told hym that Paston men wold not goo presessyon ferther than the chyrche yerde on Sent Markys day,² for he seyd the presessyon wey was stoppyd in, and seyd with in chort tyme men hopyd that the wall chuld be broke doun ageyn. Item, he seyd that I was amercyid for stoppyng of the seyd [way]³ at the last generall court, butt he cowd not tell who meche the mercyment was. And he that told it me askyd the man that told it hym if he had the mercyment in hys exstrete for to distreyn there fore ; and he seid nay, but seyd he that chuld do it chuld bettyr doe take it up on hym than he chuld. Item, the same man told me that he mett with a man of Blyclyng, hyght Barker, that cam late fro London, and he told hym that I had a sute att London ageyn Wareyn Herman of Paston, and seyd that Roberd Branton was hys attornnye, and seyd he seygh hym ryght besy for hym att London. And for yete not yor sustyr ;⁴ and God have yow in kepyng. Wretyn att Norwyche the xij. day of May,

1451
or later

Be yor modyr, A. PASTON.

¹ [From Paston MSS., B.M.] This letter has the appearance, to judge from its contents, of being perhaps a few weeks later than the preceding one. It is, however, in a different hand.
² April 25. ³ Omitted in MS. ⁴ Elizabeth Paston?

196

AGNES PASTON TO JOHN PASTON¹

To John Paston, dwellyng in the Tempyll at London, be thys letter delyverd in hast.

1451
or later

I GRETE yow wele, and lete yow wete that on the Sonday befor Sent Edmond, after evyn songe, Augnes Ball com to me to my closett and bad me good evyn, and Clement Spycer with hyr. And I acsyd hym what he wold ? And he askyd me why I had stoppyd in the Kyngs wey ? And I seyd to hym I stoppyd no wey butt myn owyn, and askyd hym why he had sold my lond to John Ball ? And he sor [*swore*] he was nevyr a cordyd with your fadyr ; and I told hym if hys fadyr had do as he dede, he wold a be a chamyd to a seyd as he seyd. And all that tyme Waryn Herman lenyd ovyr the parklos² and lystynd what we seyd, and seyd that the chaunge was a rewly chaunge, for the towne was un do therby, and is the werse by an Cli. And I told hym it was no curtese to medyll hym in a mater butt if he wer callyd to councell ; and prowdly goyn forthe with me in the cherche, he seyd the stoppyng of the wey xuld coste me xx. nobylls, and zet it shuld downe ageyn. And I lete hym wete he that putte it downe chull pay therfor. Also he seyd that it was well don that I sett men to werke to owle³ meney whyll I was her, butt in the ende I chale lese my coste. Than he askyd me why I had a wey hys hey at Walsham, seyng to me he wold he had wyst it whan it was karryd, and he chuld a lettyd it ; and I told hym it was myn owyn grownde, and for myn owyn I wold holde it ;

¹ [From Fenn, iii. 44.] This letter of Agnes Paston's refers to the same subject of dispute as the two preceding, and was probably written after them ; but the exact year is not certain.
² The half door of her 'closet' or pew in church.
³ 'To owl,' says Fenn, 'may signify to deceive, as an owler is a person who carries contraband goods in the night ; though I rather think it means in this place to oil, that is, to smooth to her purpose ; but q. ?' The explanation certainly is not very satisfactory. From the definition of 'owler' we might perhaps conjecture with more probability that 'to owl' was to work in the night time. Did Agnes Paston, to avoid interruption, set men to build the wall by night ?

and he bad me take iiij. acre and go no ferther. And thus churtly he departyd from me in the cherche zerde. And syt [*since*] I spacke with a serteyn man, and acsyd hym if he herd owt sey why the dyner was mad att Norfolkys howse, and he told me [he] herd sey that serteyn men had sentt to London to gete a commyssyon owt of the chaunstre to putt downe ageyn the wall and the dyk.

1451
or later

I receyvyd yor letter by Robert Reppys thys day after thys letter wretyn thus far. I have red it, butt I conn yeve yow non aunswer mor than I have wretyn, save the wyfe of Harman hathe the name of owr Lady, whos blyssyn ye have and myn. Wretyn at Paston, on the day after Sent Edmond,¹

Be yowyr modyr, AUGNES PASTON.

197

MARGARET PASTON TO JOHN PASTON²

To my rygth worshipfull hosbond, John Paston, be this delyverid in hast.

RYGTH wurchipfull hosbond, I recommawnd me to yow, desyring hertyly to her of your welfar, preying yow to wete that itt was told me this weke that ther is afayr plase to sell in Seynt Laueransis parysch, and stant ner the chirche, and by the water syde, the whiche place Toppis hath to sell. Pyte alyster [*a dyer*] bowgth itt of Toppis and now, for defawt of payment, Toppis hath enterid ayen therinne, and shall selle itt in hast, as it is told me. The seyd lyster dwellyth therinne at this tym, but he shall owte, for he is hald rygth apore man. I suppose if ye lyke to bye itt when ye com hom, ye shall mowe have itt of Toppis als godechepe or better than another shuld. Als for tydyngs, we have none gode in this

1451
[JUNE 3]

¹ St. Edmund's day was the 16th November.
² [From Fenn, iii. 424.] Reference is made in this letter to the forcible entry of Daniel into Brayston in 1450, and from the terms of the allusion, that event must have been pretty recent. The date of this letter, however, cannot be earlier than 1451, as Lady Boys must have been a widow at the time, and she only became so in December 1450.—*See* Letter 162, p. 198.

1451
[JUNE 3] contre; I pray God send us gode. Itt was told me that Rychard Sowthwell hath enterid in the maner of Hale,[1] the whiche is the Lady Boysys,[2] and kepyth itt with strength with seche another felashep as hath be att Brayston, and wastyth and dispoylyth all that theris ; and the Lady Boys, as it is told me, is to London to compleyn to the Kyng and to the Lordys ther of. Itt semyth it was not for nowgth that he held with Charlys and his felashep. I prey yow that ye wol vowchesawf to speke to Jamys Gloys to bye the Ungwentum Album that I spake to hym for ; and that ye woll remembr your fayr dowgteris gyrdyl. I hope ye shull be at hom so sone that I woll do wryte nomor tydyngs to yow. The blyssid Trinte have yow in his keping, and send yow gode spede in all that ye woll spede well inne. Wretyn at Norwyche on the Asencion day.   Yours,   M. P.

198

JAMES GRESHAM TO [JOHN PASTON][3]

JUNE ? PLEASE it your maistership to wete that, as touchyng Blake of the Kyngges hous, I spak with hym, and he told me that if the Lord Molyns wold take suyche appoyntement as ye agreed to, that he shuld lete me wete therof on Satirday after noon, as I tolde yow whanne ye dyd on your botes, &c. And sith that tyme I herd no word of hym. Item, there is laboured a supersedeas for alle them that th'exigend[4] is ageyn, that arn convycted by record of my Lord

[1] Holm Hale.
[2] Sibilla, daughter and heir of Sir Robert Ylley, and widow of Sir Roger Boys, Knight. She was alive after 1450.—F.
[3] [From Paston MSS., B.M.] This letter is anonymous, but it is in James Gresham's handwriting. In Letter 190 we have Lord Molyns offering to treat with Paston for the injury done to his property at Gresham. Apparently Paston has now mentioned what terms he would accept. From what is said of the supersedeas, it would seem that this letter was written not long before the next, which is dated on Trinity Sunday.
[4] A writ of exigent lies where the defendant in a personal action cannot be found, or anything of his to distrain. The sheriff is therein directed to proclaim him on five county court days, requiring him to appear on pain of outlawry.

248

200

NOTE

1451
JUNE 28 A letter of Sir John Fastolf to Sir Thomas Howes, dated 28th June 1451, 29 Henry VI., is mentioned by Fenn in vol. iii., p. 133, in a footnote, and the following sentence extracted :—'The untrouthe of the Pryour of Hykelyng draweth away my devotion in such causes.' The original of this letter I have not met with.

201

MARGARET PASTON TO JOHN PASTON[1]

To my rygth worshypfull hosbond Jon Paston, be this delyverd in hast.

JULY 1 RYGTH worchypfull hosbond, I recommawnd me to yow, desyryng hertyly to her of yowr wellfar, preying yow to wete that I have spoke with my Lady Felbrygg[2] of that ye bad me speke to her of, and she seyd pleynly to me that she wold not, ne nevyr was avysyd, neyther to lete the Lord Moleyns ne non other to have ther intents as for that mater, whyll yet she levyth. And she was rygth evyll payd with Sawtr that he shuld reporte as itt was told yow that he shuld have reportyd ; and she made rygth moche of yow, and seyd that she wold nowgth that no servaunte of herys shuld reporte no thyng that shuld be ayens yow otherwyse than she wolld that your servawnts shud do or seyn ayens her ; and if other your servawnts dede ayens her, or any of her ayens yow, she wold that itt shuld be reformyd be twyx yow and her, and that ye mygth ben all on ; for she seyd in good feyth she desyryth your frendshep ; and as for the report of Sawtr, she

[1] [From Fenn, iii. 124.] The mention made of the death of Sir Harry Inglos at the end of this letter proves it to have been written in the year 1451. According to the inquisition *post mortem* 29 Hen. VI., No. 9, he died on the 1st July 1451, which corresponds exactly with 'the Thursday next after St. Peter,' the day this letter was written.
[2] *See* p. 224, Note 2.

250

---

of Oxenford, except ij. men which the Lord M. gyveth no fors of. Item, I send yow Treshams letter and a copie of the same. Item, I send yow the *cerciorari* for my maistresse your modir. Item, I send yow the *scire facias* for Osbern and Foke *versus* Heydon and Wyndam. Item, I send yow a *distringas* ageynst Tudenham, &c. Item, I beseche yow if it may be in cas my Lord of Oxenford have not Holt hundred, that ye wole take it to suyche on as yow seme best, for it is told me that Pertriche laboureth therfore. And that is by the setting on of Heydon, &c. As touchyng the *capias* ageynst Pertrich, and the *pros.* a geynst Costard, &c., it wole not be hadde, &c.

1451
JUNE ?

199

JOHN BERNEY TO JOHN PASTON[1]

To the Ryght worshpful John Paston, Esquyer.

RYGHT worshipfull, &c. Please zou to comfort and help my pouer tenaunt, Symond Sparre, whech ys a restyd by warant, at the sute of the Lord Scalys, for Sir T. Tudynham shepp. And, Sir, uppon Fryday last passyd, Blake, the Kynges secratory, tolde me that there was delyveryd a *supersedyas* for all men in that sute. But, Sir, as my verry trust is in zou for this, lat it be easyd, as I may doo for zou, &c.; for, Sir, I may not attent, by cause I am occupyed with my suster, for hir husbond, Sir Rychard Veuuter,[2] dessessyd upoon Fryday last, &c. Wretyn in gret hast upon Trenyte Sunday.

JUNE 20

Be zoure pouer cosyn,   JOHN BERNEYE.

[1] [From Paston MSS., B.M.] For the date of this letter see Note 3 on last page. Trinity Sunday fell on the 20th of June in 1451.
[2] Blomefield mentions a Sir Richard Veutre, who presented to the living of Cockthorp in 1450.—*Hist. Norf.* ix. 218.

249

seyd she supposyd that he wold nowgth reporte so ; and if she mygth know that he dede, she wold blame hym therfor. I told her that itt was told me syth that ye reden [? yeden, *i.e.* went], and that itt grevyd me mor that the seyd Sawtr shuld reporte as he dede than itt had be reportyd of another, in als moche as I had awgth hym goodwyll befor ; and she prayid me that I shud not beleve seche reports tyll I knewe the trowth.

1451
JULY 1

I was att Toppys at dyner on Seynt Petyrs day ; ther my Lady Felbrygg and other jantyll women desyryd to have hadde yow ther. They seyd they shuld all abe [*have been*] the meryer if ye hadde ben ther. My cosyn Toppys hath moche car tyll she her goode tydyngs of her brotheris mater. Sche told me that they shuld kepte a day on Monday next komyng be twyx her brother and Ser Andrew Hugard and Wyndham. I pray yow send me word how they spede, and how ye spede in yowr owyn materys also. Also I pray yow hertyly that ye woll send me a potte with treacle in hast ; for I have ben rygth evyll att ese, and your dowghter bothe, syth that ye yeden hens, and on of the tallest younge men of this parysch lyth syke and hath a grete myrr'. How he shall do God knowyth. I have sent myn unkyll Berney[1] the potte with treacle that ye dede bey for hym. Myn awnte recommawndeth her to yow, and prayith yow to do for her as the byll maketh mencion of that I send you with this letter, and as ye thenk best for to do therinne.

Ser Henry Inglose is passyd to God this nygth, hoys sowle God asoyll, and was caryid forthe this day at ix. of the clok to Seynt Feythis, and ther shall be beryid. If ye desyer to bey any of hys stuff, I pray you send me word therof in hast, and I shall speke to Robert Inglose and to Wychyngham therof ; I suppose thei ben executors. The blyssyd Trinte have you in his kepyng. Wretyn at Norwyche in hast on the Thursday next after Seynt Peter.

I pray yow trost nott to the sheryve[3] for no fayr langage.
      Yours,   M. P.

[1] Philip Berney.   [2] St. Peter's day was the 29th June.
[3] John Jermyn was sheriff of Norfolk and Suffolk this year.

251

THE PASTON LETTERS

202

ABSTRACT[1]

SIR J. FASTOLF TO SIR THOMAS HOWYS, Parson of Castlecombe.

1451(?)
JULY 20
Has received his letter by Herry Hansson. Does not think he authorised Howys to have Andrews and his other adversaries noted and corrected at *oyer and determyner* ; but if there was any letter to that effect, F. will bear him out. Thinks even if there was any letter to that effect sent by negligence, Howys should have taken counsel, and he would not have been sued for conspiracy. If Andrews and the others had been sued in Suffolk instead of Norfolk, they could have had no grounds of action.

London, 20 July.

[John Andrews was one of Heydon's adherents who gave trouble to Fastolf and his friends on more than one occasion ; but this letter seems to have reference to the proceedings taken against several of that faction in 1451.]

203

ABSTRACT[2]

SIR JOHN FASTOLF TO JOHN BERNEY, SIR THOS. HOWYS, AND WALTER SHIPDAM.

1451
SEPT.
Begs them to hasten Rob. Boothe to London. Hears that the *oyer and termyner* is to be at Norwich on Thursday[3] after Holyrood day, and that Will. Yelverton, justice, is to be there. Ascertain, therefore, how the substantial men of Norwich are inclined in my matter against Appulzerd, and take Paston's advice in proceeding. Is advised to send John Bokkyng or Will. Barker to them before the time. Bids them send an indenture of Cornelys Floryson about wheat and malt. Has arrested the ship. As to the matter against Applierd, if Todenham, Heydon, Wymondham, &c., or any of them, will labour for their acquittal against me in the Lady Bardolf's matter, you must oppose it. Trusts the present mayor and his predecessor know what he has done for the town, and Will. Jenney and his brother can testify to Applierd's demeanour. You must get a copy of the indictment, lest he deny the presentment. Sends a lease of Lady Sterburgh's part and Bardolf's, made by Wichingham and Blake, and a

[1] [From MS. Phillipps, 9735, No. 258.]
[2] [From MS. Phillipps, 9735, No. 233.] From the reference to the date of the *oyer and termyner* mentioned in this letter, it is clear that it was written in the same year as the letter following, and probably a few days earlier.
[3] September 16th, Holy Rood day being the 14th.

HENRY VI

confirmation of Sir Reynold Cobham,[1] and the said Lady Sterburgh his wife, **1451** &c. Commend me to my Lord of Ely[2] and my Lord of Oxford if they be **SEPT.** there, and my coz. Yelverton, and ask my Lord of Norwich for tidings of Hikelyng. 'Item, blessed be God of his visitation ! I have been sore sick and am well amended, and trust to our Lord to see you hastily and other of my friends.'

(Signature not F.'s own.)

204

ABSTRACT[3]

SIR JOHN FASTOLF TO JOHN A BERNEY, JOHN PASTON, AND SIR THOMAS HOWYS.

As the *oyer and termyner* is to be at Norwich on Thursday next,[4] sends **SEPT. 14** John Bokkyng to wait upon his counsel there to see to his matter against Appulzerd. They are to spare no cost to bring it to a good end, especially the bill of maintenance against Appulzerd, who was the greatest cause that the inquest passed against F. so untruly.

London, 14 Sept. 30 Hen. VI.

(Signature not F.'s own.)

205

SIR JOHN FASTOLF TO SIR THOMAS HOWES[5]

To my trusty frendys, Sir Thomas Howys, Parson of Castellcombe, beyng at Castre.

RYGHT trusty frendys, I grete you well. Item where **SEPT. 23** as the Bysshop of Norwych[6] makyth but delayes in my resonable desyre for an eende to be had in the xxv. marc of Hykelyng, y am upon a appoyntement and throw wyth the heyr of Clyfford, that he shall entree in the hole maner that ys chargeable wyth my xxv. marc rent, which the Pryour and Convent have forfeted the seid hole manor to the heyers undre her Convent seele of record, because of myne nonne payment of xxv. marc ; and so then the Pryour

[1] Sir Reginald Cobham of Sterborough in Surrey, father of the notorious Eleanor Cobham.
[2] Thomas Bourchier, afterwards Archbishop of Canterbury.
[3] [From MS. Phillipps, 9735, No. 251.] [4] 16th September.
[5] [From Fenn, iii. 132.] [6] Walter Lyhart or Hart.

THE PASTON LETTERS

1451 shall lese for ever iiij[xx] [*four score*] marc of rent, and that **SEPT. 23** wythout onye concience, for they have be fals both to the Clyffordys and to me thys vij. yeere day. And y trust to God to correct hem so by spirituell law and temporell law, that all othyr Relygyoux shall take an example to breke the covenant or wille of anye benefactor that avauncyth hem wyth londs, rents, or gode ; and my confessours have exorted me gretely ther too. And Almyghty God kepe you. Wryt at London, the xxiij. day of September anno xxx° R. H. VI.

JOHN FASTOLF, Kt.

There is one Walsam wold desyre acquitaunce of pardon for the wydow of Hygham, I hafe no cause, for hyr husband left hyr whereoff to pay hyr debts suffisaunt, and for me he ferre the better. The wydow noysyth you, Sir Thomas, that ye sold a wey salt but for xxs. that she might hafe had xls. for every wey, I pray you aunswer that for your acquytaille.

Item, sende me the value of Goold ys tenement in Drayton, wyth xx. acres lond therto, what it was worth yeerly when it stode hoole ; for Sellyng seith it was worth but j. noble by yeer.

206

RICHARD SOUTHWELL TO JOHN PASTON[1]

To my mastir, John Paston, Esquier.

DEC. 18 RIGHT worshipfull sir, I recomaunde me unto you. And please it you to witte of oure newe tydinges here ; as this day com writing both to my Lorde[2] and to my Lady from London, that there be certein lettres directed

[1] [From Fenn, iii. 366.] This letter must have been written in 1451. It appears from No. 119 that Daniel entered the manor of Brayston or Braydeston during the sitting of the Parliament at Leicester in the spring of 1450. He was dispossessed by Mundford and Heydon on the 7th September following, but he entered the place a second time in the 30th year of Henry VI., *i.e.* some time between the 1st September 1451 and the 31st August 1452. In this letter it is anticipated that he will be enabled to enter the place by his influence with Lord Scales and the Duke of Somerset. This cannot refer to his first entry, as Somerset was in France for a long time before.
[2] John Mobray, Duke of Norfolk, married Ellenor, daughter of William Bourchier, Earl of Ewe, in Normandy.—F.

HENRY VI

to my Lorde from my Lady his moder,[1] and diverse other **1451** Lordes for to have Danyell[2] in his favour a geyne, and as it **DEC. 18** is supposed by the meanes of the Duc of Somersette,[3] for he hath ben right conversaunte with hym all this quarter of this yere. And also thei that sente this writing sayn playnly that the Lorde Skales is gode lorde to hym, and that he hath promysed hym to make Sir Thomas Tudenham, Heydon, and hym accorded, and other men in the cuntre, and that he shall be suffred to entre in to Brayston, and kepe it to th'entente that the cuntre shall thinke, and my Lord also, that he hathe grete favour amonge the Lordes of the Counsell, and cause men to fere hym the more. Whethir it be thus or non I can not say ; never the lesse me thinketh ye shall sone knowe if Mounford will agree that he shall entre in to Brayston, and if that be trewe, all the remenant shall seme the more likly.

I pray you brenne this letter when ye have redde it. My Lorde and my Lady sayn ye shall be right welcome and ye will se theym this Crisemasse. I reporte me to your wisdom, and God have you in his keping. Writon at Framlyngham, the xviij. day of Decembre.

RIC. SOUTHWELL.

207

AGNES PASTON TO JOHN PASTON[4]

To John Paston dwyllyng in the Tempyll at London be this letter delyverid in haste.

I GRET zou well, and lete zou wete that Warne Harman **1451** on the Sonday after Hallumesse after ensong seyd or later **NOV.** oponly in the cherch zerde that he wyst wyll that and the Wall were puddoun, thou he were an hundryd myle fro

[1] Catharine, daughter of Ralph, Earl of Westmoreland, and widow of John Mowbray, Duke of Norfolk.—F.
[2] Thomas Daniel, Esq., was Constable of Rising Castle, and married Margaret, sister of John Howard, afterwards Duke of Norfolk.—F.
[3] Edmund Beaufort.
[4] [Add. MS. 34,888, f. 76.] This letter is evidently of the same year as Nos. 194 and 196, which must be 1451 at the earliest.

1451
or later
NOV.

Paston he wyste well that I wolde sey he ded yt and he xuld bere the blame, seying Telle yte here ho so wyll, thou it xuld coste me xx. nobyllys it xall be puddoun azen. And the seyd Warnys wyfe with a lowd vosse seyd All the deuyllys of hell drawe her sowle to hell for the weye that she hat mad. And at euyn a sertyn man suppyd with me and tolde me that the patent[1] grantyt to closse but a perch on bred, and that I had clossyd more than the grant of the patent is as men seyd. And John Marchall tolde me that there was a thryfty woman come forby the watteryng and fond the weye stoppyde and askyd hym ho had stoppyd the weye, and he seyd, they that had pore to zeue it, and askyd here Wat was freer than zyfte, and he seyd she sey the day that Paston men wold not asofferyd that. And God be with zou. Wretyn at Paston on Monday after Hallumys day.—Be zour modyr,

ANNES PASTON.

208

OSBERT MUNDFORD TO JOHN PASTON[2]

To Right Worshipful sir and my gode maister Johan Paston, escuier, &c.

1452
FEB. 9

RIGHT worshipful Sir, and my Right gode Maister, I Recommaunde to yow with al myne hert. Plese yow that I have understanden that Daniel hath entred in to Brayston, and put owte my servantes and dispoiled my godes, notwithstandinge I am here in the Kinges service and under his proteccion, which was shewed him; for the whiche owtrage I write to the King at this tyme and to other my gode lordes, for to be kepte in my pocession, and to be

[1] The patent granted to her husband in 1443 (21 Hen. vi.). See Introduction.
[2] [Add. 34,888, f. 79.] It appears by No. 119 that Daniel entered the manor of Braydeston, or Brayston, first during the time of the Parliament at Leicester, 28 Hen. vi. (i.e. May or June 1450), and a second time during the thirtieth year of the King, i.e. 1451-2. As this letter is dated February, 1452 must be the year.

256

1452
FEB. 9

restored again to my godes. And if so be that I may not have my pocession ayene and be restored to my godes as I desire, I wol take an accion be your avis of forsable entre in my name and my wifes for owre title, &c., and an accion of trespasse for dispoiling of my godes ayenst him and al tho that were helpinge or consenting therto, &c., and assisse of a novel Disseson in my sonnes name, Johan of Berney, for to trye the title and ende debate with Goddes help and youres, &c.; for the whiche matere I write unto my fader, to myne Eme[1] Adam, to my Cosyn Fyncheham, to Edmond Piers, and to other divers of my frendes to be my helpers in thes mater in myne absence. For I may not come nor I wol not come, though I shulde lese al Brayston, and it were myne, considering that the enemyes drawen dailly hedirward, as it is openly said, &c. Wherfore I praye yow, as my ful trust is in yow, to tendre this matere in myne absence. And that it shal plese yow to recommaund me to my worshipful maistresse and gossip, your wif. And my maistresse recommaundes her vnto yow, and to her worshipful nece, and to al youres. Prayinge Almighty God to have yow in his kepinge and sende yow right gode lif and longe, after your awne hertes desire. And, Sir, if it plese yow to come to Calais with the king, ye shul have a stope of bere to comforte yow after your travaille of the see. And if ther be any service that ye wol commaund me to do for you here, ye shul fynde me your owne man. Written at Calais, the ix[th]. day of Feveree, &c.—Your awne seruant,

OSBERNE MUNDEFORD.

[1] 'Eme,' i.e. uncle.

209

JOHN CLOPTON TO JOHN PASTON[1]

Unto myn right worshipfull sir, John Paston.

1452
APRIL 1

RIGHT worshipfull Sire and myn good maister, I recomaund me unto you, thankyng you of your gentilness chewed unto me; praying you of contenuance as myn full trust is. Furthermore, and it please you to be atte aleyser un Seynt Markis day next comyng and to be at Thetford, myn brodir Tyrell and I wole awayte uppon you ther for the matere ye woet of. And I praye you to hold me excused that I myght not kepe myn day in the Passion wike, for in good feight I was so occupied I myght not. And, Sire, yif this day may be hol . . I praye you sendith me woord that I myght send warnyng to the todir party. Also, Sire, I have warned your atteynt accordyng to your comawndment. Sir, the kyng hath sent unto me by Howard to be frendly to the lord Moleyns; not with stondyng myn service shall be redy at your comawndement in that matere er any othir by the grace of God, Who preserve you, body and sowle. Wreten at Melford, the furste day of Aprill.—Be youris,

J. CLOPTON.

210

PROCLAMATION BY THE DUKE OF NORFOLK[2]

The Duc of Norffolk

1452
[APRIL]

BE hit knowen to alle the Kyngs trewe liege peple, the cause of our comynge in to this contre ys, by the comandement of the Kynge our soverayn Lorde, for to enquer of suche gret riotts, extorcyons, oryble wrongis and

[1] [Add. MS. 34,888, f. 60.] The date of this letter must no doubt be referred to the year when the writer was Sheriff of Norfolk and Suffolk, which he was from November 1451 to 1452.
[2] [From Fenn, iii. 248.] The intended royal visit to Norfolk mentioned in the end of this proclamation appears to tally best with the date of April 1452, when, it will also be seen from the letters following, the Duke of Norfolk was at Framlingham, hearing complaints from the gentlemen of Norfolk.

258

1452
[APRIL]

hurts as his Highnesse ys credybyly enformyd ben don in this contre, and to know in serteyne, by yow that knowe the trowthe, by what persone or personys the seyde gret riotts, extorcions, oryble wrongis and hurts be done. Wherfor we charge yow alle, on the Kyngs behalve our soverayne Lorde, that ze spar neyther for love, drede, ne fer that ze have to any persone of what estat, degre, or condicion he be, but that ze sey the soth by whome suche offences de done, and that ze spar no man that ze knowe gilty; and be the feyth that we owe to our soverayn Lorde, they schal be chastysid after ther desert, and hit reformyd as lawe requyrith.

Also hit ys opunly puplysschid that serteyne servaunts of the Lord Scales schulde in his name manasse and put men in feer and drede to compleyne to us at this tyme of the seide hurts and greves, seynge that we wolde abyde but a schort tyme her, and aftir our departynge he wolde have the rewle and governaunce as he hath had affore tyme. We lete yow wete that nexst the Kynge our soverayn Lord, be his good grace and lycence, we woll have the princypall rewle and governance throwh all this schir, of whishe we ber our name whyls that we be lyvynge, as ferre as reson and lawe requyrith, hoso ever will grutche or sey the [contrary[1]]; for we woll that the Lord Scales, Sir Thomas Tudenham, Sir Mylis Stapylton, and John Heydon have in knowleche, thowh our persone be not dayly her, they schal fynde our power her at all tymes to do the Kynge our soverayn Lord servyse, and to support and mayntene yow alle in your right that ben the Kyngs trewe lige men. For hit may non ben seyde nay, but that her hath ben the grettest riotts, oryble wrongs and offences done in thise partyes by the seide Lord Scales, Thomas Tudenham, Mylis Stapilton, John Heydon, and suche as ben confedred on to theym that evir was seen in our dayes; and most myschiffe throwh ther maliciouse purpose lyke to have fallyn amonge the Kyngs trewe liege peple now late at Norwiche, ne had we better providid therfor. And also that God fortunyd us to withstande ther seyde malicious and evill disposid purpose. Wherfor makith billiz of your grevance, and come to us,

[1] Indicated by Fenn as illegible in MS.

259

THE PASTON LETTERS

1452
[APRIL]
and we schal brynge yow to the Kynges presence our selfe, whos presence wyll be her in all the hast with the mercy of God, and see the reformacion ther of his owyn persone.

211

SOME GENTLEMEN OF NORFOLK TO [THE SHERIFF?][1]

APRIL 23 RIGHT wurchipfull, we commawnd us to yow. Please it yow to wete that we and other jentilmen of the shyer of Norffolk hath be in purpose assewyd [*have sued*] to the hygh and myghty Prynce and owr ryght gode Lord the Duke of Norffolk to Framlyngham, to have enformyd his Highnesse of dyvers assaughtes and ryottes made be Charles Nowell and other ageyn the Kyngs lawe and peas, withowte any cause or occacion, up on John Paston and other of owre kynne, frendes and neyghborys, ne had be that dayly this x. days it hath be do us to wete that his Highnesse shuld come in to Norwych or Claxton, we not beyng in certeyn yet whedyr he shall remeve ; praying yow as we trust, that ye woll tender the welfare of this shyer and of the jentylmen ther in, that ye woll lete owr seyd Lord have knowyng of owr entente in this, and after to send us answher wheder it please his Highnesse we shuld come to his presens, and in what place, or to send owr compleynt to hym if mor informacion be thowth behoffull, trostyng to his gode Lordshep of remedy in this mater ; whiche do [i.e. *done*], semyth us, shall be owr seyd Lordys honur and gret rejoyng to all the jentylmen of the shyer, and cause the peas to be kept her after be the grace of God, how have yow in hys blyssed kepyng. Wretyn at Norwyche, on Seynt Georgys day.

SIR JOHN HEVENYNGHAM. JOHN FERRERS. THO. GURNAY.

[1] [From Paston MSS., B.M.] There are two copies of this paper, besides a draft written on the back of that which follows. The date both of this and of the two following letters will be seen by comparing them with No. 217 following.

260

THE PASTON LETTERS

1452
APRIL 23
my seyd Lord that his Hyghnes wold se this punischichid (*sic*), and desirid my master (?) H . . . . . . mi cosin (?) Tymperle, the dene and odir to (?)[1] and dayly hath be redy with such jentilmen as dwelle here abought that can record the trought to have come (*sic*) compleyn to my Lord ; but we have had contynually tydynges of my Lordes comyng heder that causid us for to abide ther up un, besechyng your gode maystershep that ye wull lete my Lord have knowlech of my compleynt. And that ye wull tender the gode spede of the entente of the letteris wretyn to you fro jentilmen of this shire. Prayng yow that ye woll yeve credens to the berer herof, and be his gode mayster in cas any man make any qwarell to hym. And what that I may do be your comaund-ment shall be redi with the grace of God, how have in his blissid kepyng. Wretyn at Norwhich, un Seynt Georges day.

213

JOHN PASTON TO ——[2]

APRIL RYTH worchefull sir and cosyn, I recommaund me to yow, [and] pray yow that ye will in mi behalf inform my Lord of the domag of Charlis Nowell to meward, withow occacion gef on min part, as the berer herof knoweth (?).[3] I am and was my Lords man and homagier, or the seyd Charlis knew my Lord, and will do my Lord sech servis as I can, and that ye will tendre the god sped of the mater of the letter direct to you fro serteyn jentilmen of thes shir, with whech jentilmen or odir to bere recor of

[1] The preceding words from 'and desirid' are a peculiarly illegible interlineation, and do not appear to form a consecutive sense along with the passage following. Perhaps the words 'and daily hath' should have been erased, which would make the connection intelligible.

[2] [From Paston MSS., B.M.] This letter, like the preceding, is from a rough draft in Paston's handwriting. It is clearly of the same date as the two last, or perhaps a day or two later. There is nothing to show with certainty who was the person addressed ; but we should think it was probably Sir John Fastolf.

[3] The reading is very uncertain, being partly interlined in a very cramped hand, partly corrected in the text.

262

HENRY VI

JOHN GROOS. W. ROKEWODE. JOHN BAKON, Senior. JOHN BAKON, Junior.[1]
1452
APRIL 23

J. PAGRAVE. ROBT. MORTIMER. NICHOLAUS APPILYARD.

212

JOHN PASTON TO [THE SHERIFF OF NORFOLK?][2]

REVERENT and ryth wurshepfull sir, and my god maister, I recommaund me to yow. Plese yow to wete that Charles Nowell with odir hath in this cuntre mad many riot and sautes ; and, among othir, he and v. of his felachip set upon me and mo (?) of my servants at the Chathedrall church of Norwich, he smyting at me, whilis on of his felawis held myn armes at my bak, as the berer herof shall mor playnly inform yow. Whech was to me strawnge cas, thinking in my conseyth that I was my Lords man and his homagier, or Charlis knew hys Lordschipe, that my Lord was my god Lord, and that I had be with my Lord at London within viij. [days?][3] bey for Lent, at which tyme he grantyd my his god lordship, so lagerly [*largely*] that it must cause me ever to be his trew servant to myn pow[er]. I thowt also that I had never geff cawse to non of my Lords hous to ow me evill wil, ne that ther was non of the hows but I wold have do fore as I cow (*sic*) desir anioone (?) to do for me, and yet will except my adversare ; and thus I and my frendes haff miusid of this and thowt he was hard to do thus. And this notwithstanding, assone as knolech was had of my Lords coming to Framlingham, I never attemptid to procede ageyns hym as justis and law wuld, but to trust to

[1] The names subscribed thus far are in the same handwriting as the document. Those below may perhaps be autograph signatures, although the names of Pagrave and Mortimer are in a hand much like that of John Paston.

[2] [From Paston MSS., B.M.] This is printed from a rough draft in John Paston's handwriting, on the back of which is a draft of the preceding letter. The date of both letters is the same. The reading of particular words in this draft is very uncertain, owing to the cramped handwriting used in corrections and interlineations, and the manner in which several of the words are abbreviated.

[3] Word omitted.

261

HENRY VI

this thowt, I have bene dayly toward my Lord to compleyne to his Lorship, but the continuall tydyngs of my seyd Lords coming heder hath cawsid us to awayt ther opon. Beseching yow, cosine, as my trust is in yow, that ye will help to kepe the god rewll of thes shir, and my por honeste, and geff credens to the berer herof, and be his god master if any querel be mad to him. And what I may do for you, I am and ever shall be redi to do it be the grace of God, hoo ——
1452
APRIL

214

THE SHERIFF OF NORFOLK TO THE KING AND COUNCIL[1]

To the Kyng and the Lordes of his Councell.

I JOHN CLOPTON, Shereffe of Norffolk, certifie that wher oon John Falyate and othre were take within the hundred of Blofeld in the seid shire, and led to the castell of Fram-lyngham in the counte of Suffolk, I, the forseid Shereffe, be the comaundement of my Lord of Norffolk, the last day of Aprill receyved at the seid castell a bille of divers knowlech and confessyons which were enformyd me shuld have be mad in the presens of my seid Lords Councell be Roger Chirch and othre, which the seid John Falyate, as it was enformed me, shuld have confessid to have be trewe. After which bille receyved and be me red and understand, callyng befor me the seid John Falyate and alle othre that where examyned, except the seyd Roger Chirch, in the presens of divers of my Lords Councell there, I red to the seid John Falyate the tale comprised in the seid bille seid be the seid Roger Chirch, demawndyng hym of the trought her of ; wherto he answered, and seid that he wust wele ther was no wey with hym but deth, and therfore, as he wuld answer afore God, he wuld sey the trought, and seid that the substaunce of the tale told be
[APRIL 30]

[1] [From Paston MSS., B.M.] John Clopton was Sheriff of Norfolk from Michael-mas 1451 to Michaelmas 1452.

263

THE PASTON LETTERS

the seid Roger Chirch was untrewe, and feyned and imagyned be the same Chirch, and that he never had knowleched that the tale to be trewe. Neverthelesse he seid that he was with a felesshep gadered undre Possewykwode be the prokeryng of the seid Chirch, which feleshep, whan thei were all togeder, passid not the nombre of xv. persones. And that the seid Chirch wast the furst that ever mevid hym for to come theder, seying that he shuld have feleshep i nowe and do goode, for he was balyffe of the hundred, and be colour of his office he shuld send in men i now, and that he knew a gode name for her capteyn, that shuld be John Amend Alle. More over I the seid Shereffe asked the seid Falyate if thei whan thei wer to geder spoke of Paston and othre gentilmen named in the seid bille to have assisted hem ; and he seid pleynly nay, but that thei and othre thryfty men were noysid be the seid Chirch and be his councellores sith the tyme of the gaderyng of the seid feleshep, and never was spokyn of ther. In like wyse seid othre that were examyned in the seid bille.

215

JOHN OSBERN TO JOHN PASTON[1]

To my right reverent and worchepful maister John Paston in the Iner In of the Temple be this delyverid in hast.

PLEASE it your maisterchep to weete that John Reyner and Nicholas Strecok of Sparham have gete a respyte of Nicholas Byschop for the distresse that the seid Byschop had take, as ye knowe wele, tyl seche tyme as ye may speke wyth Symond Blake for the trought of the mater ; not wythstandyng this respite myght never be gete tyll that Byschop had a reward of mony ; it is told me he toke viij*d.* for hese reward. The dryvers ought of the catell fro Sparham ground

[1] [Add. MS. 34,888, f. 83.] The reference to the outrages of Charles Nowell, the bailiff of Bradeston, and the trouble about that manor, show that this letter must be of the year 1452.

264

THE PASTON LETTERS

216

MARGARET PASTON TO JOHN PASTON[1]

To my rygth wirchipfel hosbond, John Paston, be this delyverid in hast.

RYTH worshipfull hosbond, I recommawnd me to yow, desyryng hertyly to her of your welfar, praying yow that ye woll send me word in hast how ye be agreid with Wychyngham and Inglose[2] for that mater that ye spake to me of at your departyng ; for if I shuld purvey other wood or hey, it shuld be bowgth best chepe be twixt this and Seynt Margretys messe,[3] as itt is told me. As for Applyard, he com not yett to this town syn he com from London. I have sent to Sir Bryse to lete me have knowleche when he comyth to town, and he hath promysid that I shall have knowleche, and when he comyth I shall do your commawndement. My moder bad me send yow word that Waron Herman hath dayly fyshid hyre water all this yer, and therfor she prayith yow to do therfor while ye be att London as ye thynk best.

Chyrche[4] of Byrlyngham was toke and browte to the castell yisterday be the Beshopys men, and all his godys ben seysid for that he owyth to the Boshop. And the seid Chirche seyth as for that he hath seyd of hem that he hath appelyd befor this tyme, he woll awow itt and abyd therby ; and seyth that he woll appele one that hath mor nobelys than they have all that he hath spoke of yett, and that shall avayll the King more than they have all that he hath speke of yett ; but what he is, he woll not name tyll he know mor. I trow but if that be the grett labour made ayens hym, he is lyke to have grett favour of hem that have be his supportors. Men thenk that have spoke with hym that he hopeth to have good helpe. I pray God that the trewth mote be knowyn.

[1] [From Fenn, iv. 14.] What is said in this letter about Church of Burlingham clearly shows that it belongs to the same year as the last and the letters following.
[2] *See* p. 251. [3] 20th July. [4] Roger Church.—*See* p. 263.

266

HENRY VI

to Lyng grownd were Hugo Sadde of Baldeswell, Byschoppis man, Nicholas Gatesend, Roberd Joye, Jacobis Baxter of Lyng. James Gloys hath a bill of the tyme and day. I pray your maisterchep to know that on Fryday in the afftyr none I spak with my lord of Norwiche in hese chamber more than the space of j. owre and ther I dede to hym myn erand that ye commaunded me for to a do to chalanches, and when my lord woost that ye were to London he was right sory that he had not a spoke wyth yow or that ye reden ; he told me that he had iij. letters fro my lord of Norffolk the day before. Alle I wet wel were they not for yowre mater of Charlys Nowell. Aftyer that he had told me of these letteris he askid me how ye dede. I sayde wel, for I trostid to my lord of Norffolkis lordchep and ritewesnesse that he wold see that Charles shuld be sharply correctyd for hese trespasse and mysrewle, or ellis the jentelmen of the shire must to giddyer purvey anodyer meane ; and he seid it wold never odyerwyse be, but if he had spoke wyth yow or ye redyn to London he hopid be your avys he shuld a perveyd a meane to a set that in correccion, and also the trobyl for the maner of Brayston, for that was cause of all. For he seide he had spoke wyth my lord Skales and he is wel disposid to yow and vn the best wyse and wel do . . . yow that he can, so that he wold forsake Danyell. This was seyde in a diswere, savyng he told me he must . . . . pleayne he told me many more thyngges and tales I pray you of your maistechep (*sic*) hold me excusid that I wryte hem [not], but they were not alle of gret substans, &c. I had gret cher, he comaunded me to be had into the seler, and for to drynk wyne and ale bothe ; and so I had and goode chere. My mastras recomendith her to yow and pray yow that ye wol do the cost vn my mastras Margery for to do make her a new gyrdyl a yens Witsontyde, for she shal never have, my mastras seith, till she hath nede ; and my mastras prayith yow to send her tydyngges, as hastely as ye may, how ye do in your maters. The Holy Trenyte have yow in hese kepyng. Wrete at Norwiche the xiiij. day of Maii.—Be your seruaunt,

JOHN OSBERN.

265

HENRY VI

I pray yow that ye woll vouchesaff to send me an other sugor loff, for my old is do ; and also that ye well do make a gyrdill for your dowgter, for she hath nede therof. The blyssid Trinyte have yow in his kepyng. Wretyn at Norwyche in hast, on the Tewysday next befor Seynt Thomas day.[1]

Paper is deynty.[2]

Yours, M. P.

217

INFORMATION OF OUTRAGES[3]

CHARLYS NOWEL, Otywell Nowell, Robert Ledeham, John the sone of Hogge Ratkleff, Robert Dallyng, Herry Bangge, Roger Cherche, Nicholas Goldsmyth, Robert Taylor, Christofer Grenescheve, ——[4] Dunmowe, Elis Dokworth, Christofer Bradle, Jon Cokkow, assemblyng and gadderyng to hem gret multitude of mysrewled people, kepe a frunture and a forslet at the hows of the seid Robert Ledeham, and issu ought at her pleser, sumtyme vj., sumtyme xij., sumtyme xxx[ii] and mo, armed, jakked, and salattyd with bowis, arwys, speris, and bylles, and over ride the contre and oppresse the people, and do many orible and abhomynable dedis lyke to be distruccion of the shire of Norffolk, wythoute the Kyng owre Sovereyn Lord seth it redressid.

Un Mydlent Soneday[5] certeyn of the seid felechep in the chirche of Byrlyngham made a fray upon tweyne of the servauntes of the reverent fadyr in Godde, Byschop of Norwiche,[6] the seid servaunts at that tyme knelyng to see the

[1] Translation of St. Thomas, Apostle, 7th July.
[2] Fenn says that the letter is written upon a piece of paper nearly square, out of which a quarter had been cut before the letter was written.
[3] [From Paston MSS., B.M.] The misdemeanours of Roger Church, who is here complained of among other malefactors, must refer to the same period as Letter 214. The date is rendered even more certain by a comparison with the letter following.
[4] Blank in MS.
[5] Midlent Sunday fell on the 19th March in 1452.
[6] Walter Lyhart or Hart.

267

THE PASTON LETTERS

1452 usyng of the Masse; and there and than the seid felechep wold have kelled the seid two servauntes at the prestis bakke, ne had they be lettyd, as it semed.

[1][Item, un the Moneday[2] next before Esterne daye, sex of the seid persones made a saute upon John Paston and hese two servauntes at the dore of the cathedrall cherche of Norweche, wyth swerdes, bokeler, and dagareis drawe smet at the seid Paston, on of them holdyng the seid Paston be bothe armes at hese bakke, as it semyth purposyng there to have morderid the seid Paston and they had not a be lettyd; and also smet on of the servaunts of the seid Paston upon the naked hed wyth a swerd, and poluted the seynteware.]

Item, on the Monday[2] next before Esterne day, x. of the seid persones lay in awayte in the hey weye undyr Thorp Woode up on Phelep Berney, Esquier, and hese man, and shet at hem and smet her hors wyth arwes, and then over rede hym and brake a bowe on the said Phelippis hed and toke hym presoner, callyng hym traytor. And when they had kepte hym as long as thei lyst, thei led hym to the seyd Byshop of Norwiche and askid of hym swerte of the peas, and forwyth relessid her suerte and went her way.

Item, iij. of the seid felechep lay unawayte upon Emond Brome, jentelman, and with nakid swerds fawte wyth hym be the space of a quarter of a owre and toke hym presoner; and when they had kepte hym as long as they lyst, lete hym goo.

Item, xl[ti] of the same felechep come rydyng to Norwiche jakked, and salettyd, with bowys and arwys, byllys, gleves, un Maundy Thursday,[3] and that day aftyr none, when service was doo, they, in lyke wyse arrayid, wold have brake up the Whyte Freris dores, where,[4] seying that they came to here evesong; howbeit that they made her avaunt in towne they shuld have sum men owt of town (?), qwhyke or deede; and there made a gret rumor, where the mayre and the aldermen, with gret multitude of peple, assembled, and therupon the seyd felischep departid.

[1] This paragraph is crossed in the MS.
[2] April 3, Easter day being the 9th April in 1452. [2] April 6.
[4] After the word 'where' the original text had 'the seid Paston dwellith,' but these words have been struck out, and other alterations made in the paragraph.

268

HENRY VI

Item, dyvers tymes serteyn of the seid felechep have take 1452 fro John Wylton, wythoute any cause, hese net, hese shep, and odyr cattell, and summe there of have saltyd and eten, sume thereof have aloyned,[1] so that the seid Wylton wot not where for to seke hese bestes; and un the morwe[2] next aftyr Esterne day last past, they toke fro hym xj. bestis, and kepte hem two dayis wythowte any cause.

Item, in lyke wyse they have do to John Coke and Kateryn Wylton.

Item, in lyke wyse they have take the goodys and catelles of Thomas Baret and many odyr.

Item, certeyn of the seid felechep late made a sawte upon John Wylton in Plumsted cherche yerd, and there beete hym so the [that] he was [in] dowth of his liff.

Item, in lyke wyse upon John Coke of Wytton, brekyng up hese dores at xj. of the clok in the nyght, and with her swerdis maymed hym and gaf hym vij. grete woyndis. Item, smet the modyr of the seid Coke, a woman of iiij[xx] [four score] yeres of age, upon the crowne of the heed wyth a swerd, wheche wownde was never hol to the daye of her deth.

Item, the seyd Dunmowe, on of the seid feleche[p], now lete beet the parson of Hasyngham, and brake hese hed in hese owne chauncell.

[3][Item iii[xx] [three score] of the seid felechep, arayid as men of werre, now late enterd with fors upon Phelep Berney and disseisid hym of the maner of Rokelandtoftys, wheche darnot, for feer of mordyr, reentre hese owne londe; how be it, he and hese aunseters have be pesibely possessid therof many yeris.]

Item, Alredis sone of Erll Some, fast be Framyngham, un the Saterday[4] next before Palme Soneday last past was pullid ought of a hows and kyllid. Whedyr any of the seid felechep were there or not men kan not sey, there be of hem so many of wheche many be unknowe people.

Item, the seid felechep make seche affrayis in the contre abowte the seid Ledehams place, and so frayith the people that

[1] Eloined (French *éloigne*), removed to a distance. [2] April 10.
[3] This paragraph is crossed out. [4] April 1.

269

THE PASTON LETTERS

1452 dyvers persones for feer of mordyr darnot abyde in her howses, ne ride, ne walke abowte ther ocupacions, wyth owte they take gretter people abowte hem then acordith to her degre, wheche they wol not do in evel exaumple gevyng.

Item, the seid felechep of a fer cast maleys and purpose now late toke Roger Cherche, on of ther owne felechep, be hese owne assent, wheche Roger Cherche be her assent had movid and and sterid a rising in the hundred of Blofeld, and hath confessed hym self to be at that arysyng, and hath enbylled, as it is seid, divers jentelmen and the most part of the trysty yomen and husbondis and men of good name and fame of the hundred abowte the seid Ledehams place, where the seid felechep is abydyng, and nameth hem wyth odyr suspecious people for risers, to the entent to hide and cover her awn gylt, and to holde them that be trw men and innosent in that mater in a dawnger and feer that they shuld not gader peopell, ner attempte to resiste ther riotows governauns of the seid reotows felechep.

[1][Item, it is conceyved that if the seyd riotows felechep, and they that drawe to them were dewly examyned, it shuld be knowe that if there were any seche rysyng, it was conjectyd, don, imagened, and labored be the seid reotows felechep and be ther meanes; for aswele the seid Cherche, as dyvers of the most suspecious persones be the seid Cherche enbelled for rysers, as it is seid, be and have be of long tyme dayly in compeny wyth the seid reotows felechep.

Item, on of the seid felechep of late tyme, as it is seide, to encresse her malicious purpose, hath proferid rewardis and goode to anodyr persone for to take upon hym to apele certeyn persones, and afferme the seying of the seid Roger Cherche.]

In wytnesse of these premesses, dyvers knytes and esquiers, and jentelmen whos names folwen, wheche knowe this mater be seying, heryng, or credible reporte, to this wrytyng have set her seall, besechyng your Lordcheppis to be meanes to the Kyng owre sovereyn Lord for remedy in this behalve. Wrete, &c.

[1] These paragraphs are crossed through.

270

HENRY VI

On the lower margin of this paper, and on the back are scrawled a few additional 1452 memoranda, of which the following are the most important. One paragraph, which is in the handwriting of John Paston, is so carelessly written that the names contained in it are quite uncertain.

Memorandum, that Jon, sone of Roger Ratkliff, bet T. Baret, and Beston and Robyn Taylor tok and imprysonyd Thomas Byrdon of Ly[n]gwode. Item, Robert Dalling bet Nicholas Chirch at Stromsaw Chirch. Memorandum of manassing of the quest at Hengham. Item, Robert Dallyng bete Thomas Dallyng.

Roger att Chirche, Robert Dallyng and Herry Bang with other went with fors and armys, and fechid William Clippisby oute of his faders hous, and brought hym to the town of Walsham, and kept hym there ij. days and ij. nytys, and fro thens had hym to Romgey (?), and there impresonyd hym and made hym [give] to Eusdale (?) an oblygacion of C. libr. made after her owyn desyr.

218

A PETITION TO THE LORD CHANCELLOR[1]

To the right reverent fader in God, Cardynale Archebusshop of York[2] and Chaunceler of Inglond.

PLEASE it yowre gode Lordeshep to know that oon Roger Cherche, other wyse callyd Roger Bylaugh, Roger Wryte, and Roger Baly, late[3] was at a gaderyng and assemble of xv. persones in a feleshep under a wode in the town of Possewyke, in the counte of Norffolk, which feleshep, as it is seid be hem, was procured and gaderyd be the seid Roger Cherche and his councelores, the same Roger seyng to summe of the same feleshep,[4] he had remembrid a gode name for her capteyn, that shuld be John Amend Alle; and the seyd Roger aftyr the seyd gaderyng aggreyd hym self to be take and examyned be persones of his own covyne, and be color of his seid feleshep of xv. persones be hym gaderyd, enbilled divers gentilmen, and many thryfty and substanciall

[1] [Add. Charter 17,241, B.M.] The date of this petition will be seen by a footnote. [2] Cardinal Kemp.
[3] Here the words 'before Crystmasse last past' originally stood in the text, but are crossed out.
[4] Here occurs a caret referring to some illegible words in the margin.

271

1452 yomen, and thryfty husbondes, and men of gode name and fame, noysyng and diffamyng to the Kyng and his Councell that the seid gentilmen, yomen, and thryfty husbondes, with other, to the nombre of ccc. persones, shuld have mad a gaderyng and a risyng ageyn the Kynges peas under the seid wode, contrary to the trought ; which is veryly conceyved to be don of malyce to put the seid gentilmen and yomen in feer and trobill that thei as wele as alle the contre shuld not be hardy to attempt, ne lette the purposyd malyce of the seid Cherche and his councellores in divers riottes, extorcious, forsibil entreys and unlawfull disherytauns of gentilmen and other of the Kynges liege peple in the seid shire that thei dayly use, which riottes, extorcions, aswele as the seid untrewe diffamacions, causyth gret grudgyng, trobill, and comocyon in the seid shire. Please it yowre gode grace, these premysses considered, not to suffre the seid Cherche to have no pardon of the comune grace graunted be the Kyng owre soverayn Lord un Gode Fryday last past,[1] un to the tyme that he hath fownde sufficient suerte of wel namyd persones of the seid shire of his gode beryng ; and to direct a comyssion un to such notabill persones in the seid shire as please you, to take and examyn the seid Roger Cherche, as wele as othre that them semyth necessary to examyn in this behalf, so that thei that be giltes in this may be so declared, and that thei that be gilty may be ponysshed acordyng to her demerytes ; and to beseche the Kyng owre soverayn Lord in the behalf of the gentilmen of the seid shire that his Hignesse wull not take hem, ne any of hem, in conceyt to be of such rewle and disposicion up un enformacion of such a mysse rewled and encredibill man as the seid Roger. And thei shall pray to God for you.

[1] On Good Friday the 7th April 1452, Henry VI. offered general pardons for offences against himself to all who would sue them out of Chancery.—*See* Whethamstede, 317, 319.

219

PARTIES IN NORFOLK[1]

ITT is to remembre under hos rule that the gode lord is 1452 at this day, and whiche be of his new cownseyll.

Item, that Debenham, Lee, Tymperle, and his old cownseyl and attendans, as well as the gode ladijs servawntys, be avoydyd, and Tymperle of malys apelyd of treson.

Item, that the sescionys of the pees wyth owte cause was warnyd in the myddys of hervest, to grette trobill of the contre, whiche was never se in Norffolk at seche tym of the yere ; and itt was unlawfully warnyd to appere with inne iiij. or v. days after the warnyng. Howbeitt the contre was before warnyd at the shyer day to have had the sescionys the Tewysday befor Michelmes.

Item, that at the seid sescionys was non other cawse of settyng thereof declaryd but a commysyon beryng date before Estern, &c., to arest, take, and expungne traytorys and rebellys, of whiche, be Goddis grace, is no nede in this contre at this tyme, &c.

Item, be the demenyng of the seyd sescionys was verily conseyvid be the jantylmen of the shyer that it was set of purpose to have, be indytements, defowlyd seche personys as wer of the old counseyl with the seid Lord, and seche as kepe Wodhows lond, or seche as help or confort Osbern Munford, marchale of Kalys, in his rygth of the maner of Brayston, of whiche he is now late wrongfully dyssesyd,[2] and generally to have hurt all other that wold not folwe the oppynyons of the seyd new cownseyll ; whiche malysiows purposid oppynyon the jantylmen of the seyd shyer that wer sworyn att the seyd

[1] [From Paston MSS., B.M.] This paper bears upon the same matters as the last, and must be attributed to the same date. The MS. is a draft, with corrections in John Paston's handwriting.
[2] The Duke of Norfolk.
[3] Mountford was disseised of Brayston by Daniel in the spring of 1450, but recovered possession on the 23rd September. I find no note of his having been disseised again, but I should think he must have been, as this paper is certainly two years later.

1452 sescions kowd not fynde in her conciens to observe, but dede the contrarye as it apperyth be here verdyte if itt be shewyd, &c. Remembre the verdyt of Brayston, &c.

And where on Roger Chirche, wyth on Robert Ledham, Charlys Nowell, John son of Hodge Ratcleff, and on Robert Dallyng had the rewle and kepyng of the seid maner of Brayston to the use of Thomas Danyell after the dyssesing of the seyd Osbern Monford, the seyd Roger be the comon ascent of his seyd felashep, be the colowre of xv. personys gadderid be the exitation of the seyd Roger Chyrche and his felashep, accusid many notable and thryfty men that were well willid to the seyd Munford for the seid maner of Brayston, to be ryseris, wher as the seyd thrifty men, as well as all that contre, hath at all tymys be pesyble and of no seche disposicion : It was purposid after the seid sescions, whan the intents of the seyd new cownseyl mygth not be executyd be indytements, than to have had the seyd Roger Chirche owte of the Kyngs gayle, seying that he shuld appele for the Kyng, and wold have do the sheryff delyverid hym owt of prison, howbeit he was comyttyd thidder be the justyse of assyse and gayle delyvere be cawse he was indyted of fellonye, and that ther apperid not suffycient inquest to delyver hym.

Item, day seth thei labour feynid materis to hurt jentilman and odir be soch acusements, &c.

Memorandum, as it semyth be the confession of dyvers of the seid xv. personys that thei were innocent and knew not whi thei assemelyd but only be the excitacion of the seyd Chirche and his menys, and after the tyme of that they conseyvid itt was do to no good intent, thei never medillid forther in the mater. Item, to remembre how suttely the seyd Chirche was, be his owyn assent, led to my Lord of Norffolk be his owyn felashep to the entent to accuse and defame seche as they lovyd not.

Memorandum, of the session at Norwich. Memorandum, of my Lord of Somerset and of the Blak frers.

Memorandum, that Charlys Nowell is baly of Brayston, and hath ther ijd. on the day, and of that mater growyth his malys.

Item, memorandum of them that for fer of disclosid of

her falsenes acusid odyr that they shuld not be thowth gilti 1452 hemself, and labour to have the mater handlid be her frends that the trowth shuld not be triid owt.

220

EDMUND WYCHYNGHAM TO JOHN PASTON[1]

To my ryth trusty Cosyn, John Paston, escwier.

RYTH reverent and trusty Cosyn, I recomande me to 1452-3 zow, thankyng zow of zour good wil and counseill. OCT.

Like zow to wete, I cam hom be myn Lord of Oxeford and told hym of the greet labour of Sir Thomas Tudenham and Heydon for schirevez of owr schire, and namyd the personez quom thei laboryd fore, and myn Lord agreeyth not to tweyne of hem ; to the knyth he seyd not moch to, but I felt my lord he wold labore for William Dorward, myn neview.[2] And thanne I answerd, Sir, he may not profite me in myn matere for he hath weddyd myn nece. Also I felt myn Lord that myn Lord Crumwell laboryth for Stonham of Huntyngton schire, Sir John Tirell howe [who] weddyd hese modir, hese sone executour to my Lady Clyfton, with Heydon and othir memento, &c. And to fore I cam to Framyngham myn lord of Norffolk hadde wrytyn for Sir Robert Conyers, takyng promys of hym to be rewlyd in alle matterez as myn Lord of Norffolk wil avyse hym, and as an undirschireve ze schall be acounseill therof. And as touchyng Lee, as I am enformyd, ther ys no man that he wil do lesse for thanne for Sir Thomas Tudenham. And as touchyng myn seyd Lord of Norffolk, he hath wrytyn, or I cam, be Debenham, as he may not wel returne, and the personez ben Sir Robert Conyers, Henry Gray, Thomas Brews. And I

[1] [Add. MS. 33,597, f. 1.] The year when this letter was written is not exactly certain, but seems to have been either 1452 or 1453. It might be 1450, except that one would have expected in October of that year to hear something about the parliamentary election, as well as the election of sheriffs.
[2] William Dorward, according to Blomefield (*Hist. of Norf.* vi. 519), married Margaret, daughter of Nicholas Wichingham, who thus appears to have been a brother of Edmund the writer of this letter.

THE PASTON LETTERS

1452-3 suppose as for Thomas Brews he schall be translate in to
OCT. myn brothir John Blake, but myn seyd Lord of Norffolk
hath previly (?) wrytyn to the Kyng for Sir Robert Conyers
promisyd[1] be the seyd Sir Robert that he schall non undir-
shireve, ne non othir officer make, but be the avyse of myn
seyd Lord of Norffolk counseill, to qwhom ze schall be prevy
to And I have no dowte zour owyn materez schall ben speed
aftir zour entent myn seyd Lord of Norffolk wil with alle
hese herte that Blake schuld be it, or ellez the seyd Sir Robert
with alle hese herte. And yf myn Lord of Norffolk, to for
myn comyng, hadde be a vertysyd, he wold a do hese trew
parte ther to, as I suppose he schall have vere knalich from
myn Lord. I preye zow remembre William Bury for myn
venire facias. And yf it likyd myn brothir Blake to remembre
my welbelovyd mayster Sir John Bawryte (?, of myn mater I
trust he wold remembre the Kyng ther of atte hese leyser;
for he knowyth the matere, and that Debenham hath greet
charge to labore myn seyd Lordys materez of Norffolk, levying the favour of Sir Thomas Tudenham. Aftir I here I
schall send zow be wrytyn. I preye zow in like forme. God
preserve zow to Hese grace. Wrytyn atte Framyngham the
Fryday next to fore the feste of Simon and Jude.

E. WYCHYNGHAM.

221

MARGARET PASTON TO JOHN PASTON[2]

*To my right worchepful husbond, John Paston,
be this delyverid in hast.*

1452(?) RIGHT worchepful husbond, I comaund me to yow. I
NOV. 5 pray yow that ye wol do bye ij. doseyn trenchors, for
I can none gete in this town. Also I pray yow that
ye wol send me a booke wyth chardeqweyns[3] that I may

[1] The sentence here is a little confused, and we forbear to supply punctuation.
[2] [From Fenn, iii. 168.] This letter was written during the life of Philip Berney,
most probably in 1452, while he lay sick of the wounds, of which he afterwards died.
See No. 227 further on.
[3] A preserve made of quinces.—*See* Index to Furnivall's *Manners and Meals in*

276

have of in the monynggs, for the eyeres be nat holsom in this 1452(?)
town; therfor I pray yow hertely lete John Suffeld bryng it NOV. 5
hom wyth hym.

No more but the blyssid Ternyte have yow in Hese
kepyng, and send yow good sped in all yowre maters. Wrete
on Sent Leonard even.

My uncle Phelyppe[1] commaund hym to yow, and he
hath be so seke sith that I come to Redham, that I wend he
shuld never a askapid it, nor not is leke to do but if he have
redy help; and therfore he shal into Suffolk this next weke
to myn aunt, for there is a good fesician, and he shal loke to
hym.

My Lady Hastyngs[2] told me that Heydon hath spoke to
Geffrey Boleyn[3] of London, and is a greid wytht hym that he
shuld bargeyn wyth Sir John Fastolff to bye the manor of
Blyklyng as it were for hymselff, and if Boleyn byet in
trowght Heydon shal have it.   Yowr,

M. P.

I cam to Norwiche on Sowlemesday.

Olden Times. In the ordinances of the household of George, Duke of Clarence,
'charequynses' occur under the head of spices, their price being five shillings 'the
boke,' or £2, 10s. for 10 lbs.—See *The Society of Antiquaries' Collection of Ordinances
for the Royal Household,* p. 103. The word also occurs pp. 455, 471 of same volume.
[1] Philip Berney.
[2] Margery, widow of Sir Edward Hastings of Elsing, Norfolk, who styled himself Lord Hastings and Stutvill.—*See* Blomefield, viii. 112, and ix. 513, 514.
[3] An ancestor of Anne Boleyn and Queen Elizabeth. He was Mayor of London
in 1457.

277

THE PASTON LETTERS

222

AGNES PASTON TO JOHN PASTON[1]

*This lettre be delyvered to John Paston, beynge at London,
in the Innere In of the Temple.*

1452(?) I GRETE you well, and sende you Goddes blissyng and
NOV. 16 myn. And as touchyng the mater wheche ye desyryd
my cosyn Clere shulde write fore, she hath doo, and I
sende you the copy closed in this lettre. As for the enquerre
I have sent by Pynchemore to enquere and sent myn owen
men to William Bakton, and don hem enquered in dyverse
placs, and I can here no woord of noon suych enquerans; I
wot not what it menyth. Roberd Hill was at Paston thys
wyke, and the man that dwelled in Bowres place is oute ther
of, and seid to Roberd he durst no lenger abyde ther in, for
Waryn Herman seyth to him it is his place. As for Cokets
mater, my doughter your wyf told me yester even the man
that suyth him will not stonde to your awarde.

Bertilmow White is condemnyd in Forrenecet Court in
xl. marc, as it is seid.

Item, as for Talfas, the Sherevis hav be hest to do all
the favour thei may. I sente the Parson of Seynt Edmundes
to Gilberd, and he seide ther was come a newe writ for to
have him up by the xv. day of Seynt Martyn, and how Caly
hadde ben at hem,[2] and desired to carye up Talfas on his
owen cost, and yeve hem goode wages.

Item, John Osbern seide to me this day that he supposed
thei will not have him up be forn Estern, and Margerete
Talfas seide to me the same day that men tolde hire that he
shulde never have ende till he wer at London, and asked me

[1] [From Fenn, iii. 162.] This letter is certainly not earlier than 1451 or later
than 1453; for it was written some time after Lady Boys became a widow, which
was in December 1450 (*see* p. 198), and before Sir John Fastolf's removal from
London into Norfolk, which will be seen hereafter, was in the autumn of 1454.
Probably the true date is 1452, for in the summer following, owing to Gurney's utter
inability to pay his rent, we find Agnes Paston urging her son seriously to look out
for another tenant for Orwellbury.
[2] The modernised version in Fenn reads 'at home.'

278

counsell wheder she myte yeve the Sherevys sylver or non; 1452(?)
and I tolde hire if she dede, I supposed she shulde fynde hem NOV. 16
the more frendly.

Item, as for Horwelbur, I sende you a bill of all the
rescyts syn the deth of your fader, and a copy wrete on the
bak how your fader lete it to ferme to the seide Gurnay. I
wulde ye shulde write Gurnay, and charge him to mete with
you fro London warde, and at the lest weye lete him purveye
x*li*. for [he] owyth be my reknyng at My helmesse last passed,
be syde your faddes dette, xviij*li*. xiiij*s*. viij*d*. If ye wolde
write to him to brynge suerte for your fadyrs dette and myn,
and pay be dayes, so that the man myte leven and paye us,
I wolde for yeve him' of the olde arreragis x*li*.; and he myte
be mad to paye xx. marc be yer, on that condicion I wolde
for yeve him x*li*., and so thynketh me he shulde hav cause
to praye for your fader and me, and was it leten in my fadres
tyme. I fele by Roberd, his wif is right loth to gon thens,
she seide that sche had lever I shulde have all her gode after
her day, than thei schulde go out ther of.

Item, John Dam tell me that the Lady Boys[1] will selle
a place called Halys,[2] but he seith sehe speketh it privyly,
and seith it is not tayled, as John Dam kno, wech will she
hath seide as largely of other thyngs that hath not be so.

Item, he tolde me, as he herd seyn, Ser John Fastolf
hath sold Heylysdon to Boleyn[3] of London; and yf it be
so, it semeth he will selle more. Wherfor I praye you, as
ye will have my love and my blissyng, that ye will helpe
and do your devoir that sumthyng were purchased for your
ij. bretheren. I suppose Ser John Fastolf, and he wer spake
to, wold be glader to lete his kensemen have parte than
straunge men. Asay him in my name of suych placs as ye
suppose is most cler.

It is seid in this contre that my Lord of Norfolk seith
Ser John Fastolf hath yoven him Castr, and he will hav [it]
pleynly. I sende you a bill of Osbern hand, whech was the
ansuer of the Sheref and John of Dam.

[1] *See* p. 248, Note 2.   [2] Holm Hale.—*See* p. 248.
[3] Geoffrey Boleyn.—*See* p. 277, Note 3.

279

THE PASTON LETTERS

1452(?)
NOV. 16

Jon, brynge me my lettre hom with you, and my cosyn Cler is copy of her lettre, and the copy of the reseyth of Horwelbury; and recomaunde me to Lomnor, and tell him his best be loved fareth well, but sche is not yet come to Norwich, for thei deye yet, but not so sor as thei dede. And God be wyth you. Wreten at Norwych, in right gret hast, the xvj. day of Novembr.

By your moder,

ANNEYS PASTON.

223

THE DUKE OF YORK AND SIR JOHN FASTOLF [1]

1452
DEC. 18

THIS endenture witnesseth that where Richard, Duc of York, by his lettre of saal [*sale*] bering date the xv. day of the monneth of Decembre, the xxxj^{ti} yere of the regne of oure soverain Lord Kyng Henry the Sext, hath bargaigned, aliened, solde, graunted, and confermed unto John Fastolf, Knyght, the jowelles undrewriten:—That is to wite, a nowche of gold with a greet poynted diamand sette up on a roose enameled white; a nowche of gold in facion of a ragged staf, with ij. ymages of man and woman garnysshed with a ruby, a diamande, and a greet peerle; and a floure of gold, garnysshed with ij. rubyes, a diamande, and iij. hanging peerles. To have, holde, and rejoyce the same jowelles to the saide John, his executors and assignees, frely, quietly, and pesibly for evere more, like as in the saide lettre of saal more openly is conteened. Nevertheles the saide John wolle and graunteth herby that yif the saide Duc paie or doo paie to the same John or to his attornee, his heires or to his executors, in the Fest of the Nativitee of Sainte John Baptist next commyng, iiij^c xxxvij*li*. [£437] sterlinges withouten delay, that than the saide letter of saal to bee hold for notht; but he to delivere ayein unto the saide Duc, or to his attornee paieng the saide iiij^c xxxvij*li*. sterlinges in the saide Fest, the saide jowelles. And yif defaulte bee made in the paiement of the saide iiij^c xxxvij*li*.

280

¹ [Add. Charter 17,242, B.M.]

in partie or in all ayenst the fourme aforesaide, than wolle and graunteth the saide Duc herby that the forsaide lettre of saal, by him as is abouve saide made, stande in ful strengh and vertu, this endenture notwithstanding. In witnesse wherof, to the parte of this saide endenture remaynyng towards the saide John the saide Duc hath sette his seel. Yeven at Fodringey, the xviij^e day of the saide monneth of Decembre, the xxxj^{ti} yere of the regne of oure saide souverain Lord King Henry the Sext.

1452
DEC. 18

R. YORK.

Seal attached mutilated.

224

MARGARET PASTON TO JOHN PASTON [1]

To my right worchippfull hosbond, John Paston, be thys delyveryd in hast.

RIGHT worchipfull hosbond, I recommand me to yow, desyring to here of your welfar; praying yow to wete that Sir Thomas Howes hath purveyed iiij. dormants² for the drawte chamer,³ and the malthouse, and the browere, wherof he hath bought iij., and the forte, that shall be the lengest and grettest of all, he shall have from Heylesdon, whiche he seyth my Mayster Fastolf shall geve me, be cause my chamer shall be made ther with. As for the laying of the seyd dormants, they shall be leyd this next weke, be cause of the malthous, and as for the remenant, I trow it shall abyde tyll ye come hom, be cause I can nother be purveyed of pysts [*posts?*], ne of bords not yette.

1453
JAN. 30

I have take the mesure in the draute chamer, ther as ye wold your cofors and cowntewery⁴ shuld be sette for the

¹ [From Fenn, iii. 324.] The beginning of this letter refers to building operations, which I presume to be the same as those to which the next letter relates, and therefore of the same date. They were probably at Caister Castle.
² Large beams.
³ Draught chamber. A withdrawing-room.—Halliwell.
⁴ Cowntewery must mean his counter, desk, or board to sit and write, etc., at.—F.

281

THE PASTON LETTERS

1453
JAN. 30

whyle; and ther is no space besyde the bedd, thow the bedd wer remevyd to the dore, for to sette bothe your bord and your kofors ther, and to have space to go and sitte be syde. Wherfor I have purveyd that ye shall have the same drawte chamer that ye had befor ther, as ye shall ly to your self; and whan your gerr is removed owte of your lytil hous, the dore shall be lokkyd, and your baggs leyd in on of the grete koforis, so that they shall be sauff, I trost.

Richard Charles and John Dow have fetched hom the chyld¹ from Rokelond Toftes, and it is apraty boy; and it is told me that Wyll is att Blyklyng with a pore man of this town. A yonge woman that was sometyme with Burton of this town sent me word therof; I pray yow send me word if ye woll that any thyng that ye woll be do to hym or ye com hom. Richard Charles sendeth yow word that Wylles hath be at hym here, and offerd hym to make hym astate in all thyngs according to ther in dentur, and if he do the contrary ye shall sone have word.

My moder prayith yow to remembr my suster, and to do your parte feythfully or ye com hom to help to gette her agode mariage. It semyth be my moders langage that she wold never so fayn to have be delyveryd of her as she woll now.

It was told here that Knyvet the heyer is for to mary; bothe his wyff and child be dede, as it was told here. Wherfor she wold that ye shuld inquyr whedder it be so or no, and what hys lyvelode is, and if ye thynke that it be for to do, to lete hym be spoke with therof.

I pray yow that ye be not strange of wryting of letters to me be twix this and that ye come hom. If I myght I wold have every day on from yow. The blyssed Trinyte have yow in his kepyng. Wrete att Norwyche, on the Tesday next after the Convercion [of] Seynt Poull.

Be yours,

M. P.

¹ Probably a member of the Berney family (*see* Sir John Fastolf's letter of the 28th. January 1451). Philip Berney, as will be seen by No. 217, was disseised of the manor of Rockland Tofts during the year 1452.

282

225

JOHN PASTON TO JOHN NORWODE [1]

To John Norwode.

I LETE you wete that Hache hath do no werk of myn wherfore he aught to have receyvid any mony, savyng only for the makyng of the litill hous above the halle wyndownes, for the remenaunte was that fell down in his diffaute. And as for the makyng of that litill hous, he toke that in a comenaunte [*covenant*], with makyng of too chymnyes of Sir Thomas Howys for xls., which comenaunte may not hold, be cause that I must have thre chymnyes and in a nother place.

1453

Item, the seid litill hows drawyth not v. thowsand tyle, which after xvj*d*. the thowsand shuld drawe vjs. viij*d*. Notwithstandyng, if Sir Thomas thynk that he shuld be alowyd mo, he shall be. And ye must remembre how that he hath receyvid vjs. viij*d*. of you, and of Robert Tolle before Halwe-messe, as apperith in his accompt, viijs. And he hath receyvid of Tolle sith Halwemesse vs. iiij*d*. And than be this rekenyng he shuld be xiijs. iiij*d*. a fore hand, which I wold ye shuld gader up in this newe werk aswele as ye myght, for I am be hold to do hym but litill favour.

Item, be war ther leve no firsis in the deke that ye reparre, and that the wode be mad of fagot and leyd up forthwoth as it is fellid for taking away. I wold ye wer her on Satirday at evyn thow ye yed ageyn on Moneday.

JON PASTON.

The following memoranda occur on the back of this letter:—

Rec' W. Hach.
Rec' de Joh'e Paston, anno xxx°, vjs. viij*d*.
Item, de Roberto Telte, xiijs. iiij*d*.
De Thoma Howis, xxd.
Item, de Joh'e Norwod, anno xxxj. pro camino ls.
Summa, lxxjs. viij*d*.

¹ [From Paston MSS., B.M.] From the memoranda on the back of this letter, it would appear to belong to the 31st year of Henry VI.

283

THE PASTON LETTERS

1453 · Will' Hach fecit quandam kaminam v. mark, et pro le closet xs.
Summa, lxxvjs. viijd.
Sic debentur dicto Hach, per Joh'em Paston, vj.; et dedit ei xvs. in recompensationem cujusdam billæ ibe (?) et omne jus ipsum et Mo (?) Unde tradidi ei xiiijs. iiijd. per plegios Thomæ Howis qui manusepit (sic) quod dictus Will' perimplot [perimpleret?] barganium suum et in fine operis haberet de me vjs. viijd. residuum.

226

MARGARET PASTON TO JOHN PASTON[1]

To my right wurshipfull Mayster, Jon Paston, be this delyveryd in hast.

APRIL 20

RIGHT wurshipfull hosbond, I recommand me to yow, preying yow to wete, &c.[2] . . .

As for tydyngs, the Quene[3] come in to this town on Tewysday last past after none, and abode here tyll itt was Thursday, iij. after none; and she sent after my cos. Elysabeth Clere[4] by Sharynborn, to come to her; and she durst not dysabey her commandment, and come to her. And when she come in the Quenys presens, the Quene made ryght meche of her, and desyrid here to have an hosbond, the which ye shall know of here after. But as for that, he is never nerrer than he was befor.

[1] [From Fenn, i. 68.] According to Blomefield (*Hist. of Norf.* iii. 158), Margaret of Anjou, Queen of Henry VI., visited Norwich in the spring of 1452; but by the same authority, it would appear that she had returned to Westminster before the 17th of March in that year, which would not suit the date of this letter. Besides, John Paston at Norwich in April 1452, and dates a letter at Norwich on St. George's day, complaining of the assault made upon him at the door of Norwich Cathedral on Monday before Easter. It is impossible, therefore, that Margaret Paston could have written to him from Norwich two days before St. George's day in that year. From an undated entry in the Norwich city records, which bears internal evidence of having been made in the year 1453, it would appear that the King's half-brothers, Edmund, Earl of Richmond, and Jasper, Earl of Pembroke, visited Norwich in that year.—(See fol. 19 of a volume, entitled *An Old Free Book*, in the Norwich city archives.) As to the Queen's visit I find no direct evidence, but I think it possible she may have come with *one* of the King's brothers, and that the other may have come a little later.
[2] Here (says Fenn) follows some account of money received, etc.
[3] Margaret of Anjou.
[4] Widow of Robert Clere, Esq. of Ormesby, who died in 1446. Fenn says his daughter, but no notice is found of a daughter of that name, while the widow occurs frequently in this correspondence.

284

HENRY VI

1453
APRIL 20

The Quene was right well pleasid with her answer, and reportyht of her in the best wyse, and seyth, be her trowth, she sey no jantylwoman syn she come into Norffolk that she lykit better than she doth her.

Blake, the bayle[1] of Swaffham, was here with the Kyngs brother,[2] and he come to me, wenyng that ye had be at hom, and seyd that the Kyngs brother desyrid hym that he shuld pray yow in his name to come to hym, for he wold right fayn that ye had come to hym, if ye had ben at home; and he told me that he west wele that he shuld send for yow when he come to London, bothe for Cossey and other thyngs.

I pray yow that ye woll do your cost on me ayens Witsontyd, that I may have somme thyng for my nekke. When the Quene was here, I borowd my coseyn Elysabeth Cleris devys, for I durst not for shame go with my beds among so many fresch jantylwomen as here were at that tym. The blissid Trinyte have yow in his kepyng.

Wretyn at Norwych on the Fryday next befor Seynt George.

Be yowrs, M. PASTON.

227

AGNES PASTON TO JOHN PASTON[3]

To my welbelovyd Son, John Paston.

JULY 6

SONE I grete yow well and send you Godys blessyng and myn, and lete you wete that Robert Hyll cam homward by Horwelle bery, and Gurney tellyd hym he had byn at London for mony and kowd nat spedyng, and behestyd

[1] Bailiff.
[2] Either Edmund Tudor, who was created Earl of Richmond about November 1452, or Jasper, who was created Earl of Pembroke at the same time. They were half-brothers to the King, being sons of his mother, Catherine, Queen of Henry V., by her subsequent marriage to Sir Owen Tudor.
[3] [From Fenn, iii. 182.] Sir John Hevenyngham, whose death is mentioned in this letter, was found, by an inquisition taken on the 29th September 32 Henry VI., to have died on the 3rd of July preceding, which was in the year 1453.—(Inquis. *post mortem*, 31 Hen. VI., No. 7.) He left a son named John, over twenty-three years old, who was afterwards knighted.

285

THE PASTON LETTERS

1453
JULY 6

Robert that he shuld send me mony be you. I pray for getyt not as ze com homward, and speke sadly for i. nothyr fermor.

And as for tydyngs, Phylyppe Berney[1] is passyd to God on Monday[2] last past wyt the grettes peyn that evyr I sey man; and on Tuysday Ser Jon Henyngham zede to hys chyrche and herd iij. massys, and cam hom agayn nevyr meryer, and seyd to hese wyf that he wuld go sey a lytyll devocion in hese gardeyn and than he wuld dyne; and forthwyth he felt a feyntyng in hese legge and syyd don. This was at ix. of the clok, and he was ded or none.

Myn cosyn Cler[3] preyt you that ze lete no man se her letter, wheche is in selyd undir my selle. I pray you that ze wyl pay your brothir William for iiij. unces and j. half of sylke as he payd, wheche he sende me by William Tavyrner, and bryng wyt yow j. quarter of j. unce evyn leke of the same that I send you closyd in thys letter; and sey your brothyr William that hese hors hath j. farseyn and grete rennyng sorys in hese leggis. God have you in kepyng. Wretyn at Norwyche on Sent Thomas evyn in grete hast.[4]

Be your modyr, A. PASTON.

228

MARGARET PASTON TO JOHN PASTON[5]

To my ritht worchipfull Mayster John Paston, be this delyveryd in hast.

RYTHT worchipfull hosbond, I recommawnd me to yow, praying yow to wete that I have spoke with Newman for his place, and I am thorow with hym therfor, but he wold not lete it in no wyse lesse than v. marc. I told hym

[1] Third son of John Berney, Esq. of Reedham, who was the father of Margaret Paston's mother.
[2] July 2.
[3] Elizabeth, widow of Robert Clere, Esq. of Ormesby.
[4] The Translation of St. Thomas the Martyr (Becket) was celebrated on the 7th July.
[5] [From Fenn, iii. 186.] This letter chronicles the same two deaths as the preceding, and is therefore of the same date.

286

HENRY VI

1453
JULY 6

that sekyrly ye shuld not know but that I hyrid it of hym for iijli. I seyd as for the noble,[1] I shuld payt of myn owyn purse, that ye shuld no knowlech have therof. And this day I have had inne ij. cartfull of hey, and your stabyl shall be made I hope this next weke. I kowd not gette no grawnt of hym to have the warehows; he seyth if he may in any wyse forber itt her after, ye shall have itt, but he wull not grawnt itt in no convawt [*covenant*]. He hath grawntyd me the hows be twix the vowte and the warehows, and that he seyd he grawntyd not yow.

And as for the chamer that ye assygnyd to myn unkyl,[2] God hath purveyd for hym as hys will is; he passyd to God on Monday last past, at xj. of the clok befor none, and Sir John Hevenyngham passyd to God on Tewysday last past; hois sowlys both God assoyle. His sekenesse toke hym on Tewysday, at ix. of the clok befor none, and be too after none he was dedd.

I have begonne your inventare that shuld have be made or this tym, if I had ben well at ease. I hope to make an ende therof, and of other thyngs both this next weke, and ben in that other place, if God send me helth. I must do purvey for meche stuff or I come ther, for ther is nother bords ne other stuff that must neds be had or we come there. And Richard hath gadderid butt lytill mony syth he come from yow. I have sent John Norwod this day to Gresham, Besigham, and Matelask to gete als meche mony as he may. The blissid Trinyte have yow in his keping. Wretyn at Norwych, on the Utas day of Peter and Powll.[3]

Yowrs, M. P.

[1] A noble was a coin of the value of 6s. 8d. A mark was 13s. 4d. Five marks therefore were equal to £3, 6s. 8d.; but Margaret said she would pay the odd noble, or 6s. 8d., out of her own purse, and not let Paston know but that he had the place for £3. A little artifice for accepting terms which she had doubtless told Newman her husband could never agree to.
[2] Philip Berney.—See p. 251, Note 1.
[3] The day of St. Peter and Paul is the 29th of June. The *utas* or octave of a feast is the eighth day of the feast—that is to say, the seventh day after, which in this case is the 6th of July.

287

THE PASTON LETTERS

229

MARGARET PASTON TO JOHN PASTON[1]

RYTH worchepfull howsbonde, I recomende me on to yow. Plesyt yow to wete that I sent Tomas Bon to Edwarde Coteler to have one ansuer of the mater that ye spak to hym of, and he sent me worde that he hade spok to hys man therof, and he tolde hym that he hade no wrytynge nor evidens of no swyche thyng as ye spak to hym of, ner not wyst were he scholde have cnowlage of no swyche thyng, save that he tolde hym that he receyvyd onys j.c.s. [100s.] of the same rent; but and he may have cnowlage of ony man that havyth ony wrytyng or ony thyng that may out prevayle, he schal late yow have cnoulage therof.

As for Wylliam Yellverton, he come here never syn ye yede. As for my Lady Stapullton, att the wrytyng of thys letter sche was not come home. Wyndhamys[2] erand to my Lady of Southefolk[3] was to desiyr hyr gode Ladychep and to beseche hyr that sche wold spek to my cosyn Evenyngham[4] that he myt have hys gode wyll, for he levith in hope to have hys modyr, and he hath made menys to have her by John Gros and hys wyf, and by Bokynham and by odyr dyvers, and profuryth hyr to find suerte to acquitt hyr housbondys dettes, the qwyche is CCC. marc, and to payit doune on j. day. And by thys mene, as he seyth, he hathe bargeynid with j. marchande of London, and hath solde to hym the mariage of hys son, for the qwyche he scal have vij. C. [700] marc, and of that the iij. C. [300] marc schoulde be payd for the forseyd dettes; and also he proforyth to yeve hyr the maner of Felbryg to hyr.

[1] [From Paston MSS., B.M.] There is neither signature nor address to this letter, but it is undoubtedly from Margaret Paston to her husband. The handwriting is the same as that of her other letters. The date seems to be after the death of Sir John Heveningham in 1453, and is not likely to have been a later year, as the Duchess of Suffolk's influence must have been diminished when the Duke of York came into power, though it may possibly have been powerful again in 1456.
[2] John Wyndham, Esq. of Felbrigg.
[3] Alice, widow of William de la Pole, Duke of Suffolk.
[4] John, son of Sir John Heveningham.—See p. 227, Note 3.

HENRY VI

joyntour, and odyr la[r]ge profors as ye schal here eraffter. As for the good wyll of my cosyn Hevenyngham, he seyth Wyndh[am][1] he schall never have hytt, nott for to have hyr gode konyth he [abydyth][2] hys soull hevy therof, for he is aferde that and if the large profors may be perfor[m]yd, that sche wyll have hym. My seyd cosyn preyith yow, att the reverens of Gode, that ye wyll do yowyr [devoir][3] therin to brec it and ye can. He schall be here ayen on Mychaell mas evyn. He was full sory that ye wer outt att thys tyme, for he hopyd that ye schoulde have do myche goode att this tyme. He hathe seyde as myche ther ageyns as he dar do to have hyr gode modyrchep. My Lady of Southfolce sent j. letter to hyr yesterday by Stanle, the qwyche is callyd j. well cherysyd man with my seyd Lady, and desyiryng hyr in the letter that sche wolde owe hyr godde wyll and favor to Wyndham in that that he desyiryd of hyr, and of more matterys that ye schall here er after, for I suppose sche wyll schew yow the same letter and mak yow of hyr counsel in many thyngys, and I schall do my part as feythfully as I can to lett Wyndhamys purpose tyl ye come home. I pray yow sende me a copy of hys petygre, that I may schew to hyr how worchepphull it is, for in goode feythe sche is informyd bi hyr gentyll son Gros and Bokenham that he is mor worcheppfull in berthe and in lyvelode therto than they or ony odyr can preve, as I suppose. I pray yow lett nott thys mater be discuyryd tyl ye her more therof or after, for my cosyn Hevenyngham tolde myche here of in secret wyse, and of odyr thyngis qwyche ye schall have cnoulage of qwan ye come home, &c.

In hast, all in hast.

[1] Mutilated.
[2] Erased in MS. Apparently some further correction should have been made.
[3] Omitted in MS. 'Do your devoir,' i.e. endeavour, seems to have been the phrase intended.

THE PASTON LETTERS

230

THE DUKE OF NORFOLK'S PETITION[1]

MY Lordes, ye know well ynough the grete peynes, labours, and diligences that before thys tyme y have doon, to th'entent that the over greete dishonneurs and losses that ben come to thys full noble royaume of England by the fals menes of som persones that have take on theym over grete autoritee in thys royaume shulde be knowen, and that the persones lyvyng that have doon theym shulde be corrected aftyr the merites of her desertes. And to that entent y have denounced and delyverd to you in wrytyng certeyn articles ayenst the Duc of Somerset, whych ys one of theym that ys gylty thereoff, whertoo the Duc of Somerset have aunsuerd; and to that that he hath aunsuerd y have replyed yn such wyse that y trowe to be sure ynough that there shall no vayllable thyng be seyd to the contrarie of my seyd replicacion, and asmoch as he woold sey shall be but falsnesse and lesyngs, as be the probacions that shall be made thereuppon shall mow appiere; how be it that to alle people of gode entendement, knowyng how justice owyth to be ministred, it ys full apparaunt that the denunciacions ayenst hym made ben sufficiently preved by the dedes that have folowed thereoff; whereuppon y have requyred to have ouverture of justice by yow, whych ye have not yhyt doon to me, whereoff y am so hevy that y may no lenger beere it, speciallie

[1] [From Fenn, iii. 108.] This paper is headed 'Copia' in the MS. It is entitled by Fenn, 'The Speech of John Mowbray, Duke of Norfolk, against Edmund Beaufort, Duke of Somerset, in the House of Lords.' This title, however, is clearly no part of the original document, which has much more the character of a petition to the Privy Council than of a speech in parliament. The paper itself professes to be a 'bill' signed by its author, who demands that the conduct of the Duke of Somerset in France and in England should be made the subject of investigation by separate tribunals according to the laws of either country. Now the House of Lords, being only a branch of the English Legislature, would have had no right to authorise a judicial investigation in France. The date of this petition must have been in the end of the year 1453, after the loss of Guienne. The Duke of Somerset appears to have been committed to the Tower a little before Christmas in that year; for, after his liberation on the 4th March 1455, he declared before the Council that he had been confined there 'one whole year, ten weeks, and more.'—See Rymer, xi. 362.

HENRY VI

seth the mater by me pursued ys so worshipfull for all the royaume, and for you, and so greable to God, and to alle the subgettys of thys royaume, that it may be no gretter. And it ys such that for anye favour of lignage, ne for anye othyr cause there shulde be no dissimulacion, for doubt lest that othyr yn tyme comyng take example thereoff, and lest that the full noble vertue of justice, that of God ys so greetly recommaunded, be extinct or quenched by the fals oppinions of som, that for the grete bribes that the seyd Duc of Somerset hath promysed and yoven them, have turned theyr hertys from the wey of trouth and of justice; some seyeng that the cases by hym committed ben but cases of trespasse, and othyr takyng a colour to make an universell peas. Whereoff every man that ys trewe to the seyd Coroune auyth gretely to marveylle, that anye man wold sey that the losse of ij. so noble duchees as Normandie and Guyen, that ben well worth a greet royaume, comyng by successions of fadres and modres to the seyd Coroune, ys but trespasse; where as it hath be seen in manye royaumes and lordshyps that, for the losse of tounes and castells wythoute sege, the capitaynes that hav lost theym han be deede and beheded, and her godes lost; as in Fraunce one that lost Chyrborough; and also a knyght that fledd for dred of bataille shulde be byheded, soo that alle these thyngs may be founden in the lawes wryten, and also yn the boke cleped *L'arbre de Bataille*. Wherfor, for to abbregge my langage, y requyre you that forasmech as the more partie of the dedes committed by the seyd Duc of Somerset ben committed yn the royaume of Fraunce, that by the lawes of Fraunce processe be made thereuppon; and that all thyng that y have delyvered and shall delyvere be seen and understand by people havyng knoulige theroff, and that the dedes committed by hym in thys royaume bee yn lyke wyse seen and understand by people lerned yn the lawes of thys land; and for preffe thereoff to graunt commissions to inquere thereoff, as by reason and of custom it owyth to be doon, callyng God and you all my Lordes to wytnesse of the devoirs by me doon in thys seyd matere; and requyeyng you that thys my bille and alle othyr my devoirs may be enacted before you. And that y may have

THE PASTON LETTERS

1453 it exemplified undre the Kyngs grete seele for my discharge and acquytaille of my trouth, makyng protestacion that in case ye make not to me ouverture of justice upon the seyd caas, y shall for my discharge do my peyn that my seyd devoirs and the seyd lak of justice shall be knowen through all the royaume.

Einsi signé,   J. M. Norff.

231

WILLIAM REYNOLDS, OF CROMER, TO AGNES PASTON[1]

To my ryght reverent and wourchipfull mastras, my Mastras Paston, the modyr of my maister John Paston, be this delyvered.

RYGHT reverent and wourchipful Mastras, with most humble and louly servyce in moste goodly wice I recomaund me to your contynuell supportacion. Please it your good grace to have notycion that I have late a place of yours in quiche John Rycheman dvellyd, for it stode at a grete dyspeyr and I have late it for xvs., but up your good grace, for the lockis of the dores arn pulled of and born a waye, and the wyndowes ben broken and gone and other bordys ben nayled on in the stede of the sayd wyndowes. Also, the swynysty ys doun, and all the tymbyr and the thatche born a way ; also the hedge ys broken or born a wey, quiche closed the gardeyn ; querthorgh the place ys evyl apeyred to the tenaunt. On Sent Marckes daye I entred the seid place and lete it to your be hove, and on the day after cam Henry Goneld and seyd my latyng schald not stond, and went and seled the dores ; querfor I beseche your gracious favor that my latyng may stond, for I have late alle your londis everychone. I know not oon rode unlate, but alle

[1] [Add. ms. 34,889, f. 225.] This letter is shown by the memoranda on the back to be of the year 1453, i.e. 31 Henry vi. Agnes Paston had tenants at Cromer, and her property there descended to her grandchildren, as she outlived her son John.

292

ocupyed to your profyghte. The tenaunt quich by your lycens schuld have youre place to ferme by my latyng ys gretely be hated with oon Johane, the wyfe of Robert Iclyngham, chapman, quich ys voysed for amysse governyd woman of hyr body by the most parte of owr town wel recordyth the same, and sche dvellyth al by your seyd place ; and by cause this seid tenaunt ys gretely ayens hir for hir ungoodly governaunce, therfor sche mad menys to one Abraham Whal, quiche ys one of hir supportores, and he hath spoke with the seyd Henry Gonelde that he myght seke a remedye to cause this seyd tenaunt to be a voydyd and kept oute your seid place and not come ther inne.

He that is bryngger of this bylle ys the man to quich I have late to ferme by the licens of you ; therfore I beseche your gracaus favor to be schewed onto hym, and mekeli I beseche your contynuell supportacion that ye wuld send me wrytyng under your seele how I schal be demened. Nomor, &c. Wrytin at Crowmer the nest day after Sent Marc.—Be your servaunt at alle tymes,

WILLIAM REYNOLDES of Crowmer.

The following memoranda are written on the back :—

Firmale terræ ten' Roperes in Crowmer Anno xxxj°.

In primis Gylmin (?) tenet ad firmam ij. acras ad terminum ——[1] annorum et reddit per annum	xxd.
Item, Johannes Parnell tenet iij. rodas ad terminum xij. annorum et reddit per annum	xijd.
Item, Willelmus Reynoldes pro iij. rodis in ij. peciis ad terminum x. annorum et reddit per annum	ixd.
Item, Thomas tenet pars (sic) terræ et reddit per annum	ijd. ob.
Item, Ricardus Child pro prato et j. inclausura vocata Longclos ad terminum annorum et reddit per annum	iijs. iiijd.
Item, Rogerus Caryour pro j. orto per annum	xd.

[1] Blank in ms.

293

THE PASTON LETTERS

232

THE COUNTESS OF OXFORD TO JOHN PASTON[1]

[To my] right trusty and welbeloved Jon Paston, Esquier.

About 1454

RIGHT trusty and intierly welbelovyd, I grete you wele. Prayng you as I specially trust you that ye wole be good frend to James Arblaster in his mater touchyng the maner of Smalbergh, as I wote wele ye haf ever be to hym ryght especial frend ; and thogh it so be that the sayd James had gret trobles, losses, and adversite herbeforn, nevertphelesse he shall not be so bare of frendys ner goodes but that I wole se hym holpyn with the mercy of God. In performmyng wherof the berer of this shal enforme you of myn inten and disposicion more largely than I wole put in wrytyng. And the Trinite have you in hys kepyng. Wretyn at Wefnow,[2] the vij. day of August.

ELIZABETH VER, Countes of Oxenford.

233

THE COUNTESS OF OXFORD TO JOHN PASTON[3]

To John Paston, Sqwyer, dwellyng in Norwich.

Year uncertain

RYGHT entierly welbeloved, I grete yow well, and pray yow that ye woll be good frende un to Arblaster in suche matiers as he shal enfo[rme] yow, and I thanke yow for the good frendship that ye have shewed to hym. And

[1] [From Paston mss., B.M.] At the bottom of the letter is a contemporary note which appears to show that it was filed along with others of various dates before Michaelmas 1454 :—'Literæ de diversis annis ante Michaelem xxxiij.' More precise evidence of its date does not seem to be attainable.
[2] Wivenhoe, near Colchester, in Essex.
[3] [From Paston mss., B.M.] This and the letter immediately following are inserted here merely on account of their similarity to the last. Their dates are quite uncertain.

294

I sent a letter to Margaret Gurnay byfore Cristemesse of certeyn langage that I herd, wich plesed me nowght, and so I prayed my Lord to gif me leve to wrytte to hir ; and therfore and ye here any thyng, answere, as my trust is in yow. Right entierly welbeloved, the Holy Gost have yow in his kepyng. Wretyn in hast the first day of February.

Year uncertain

        OXENFORD,
        ELYZABETH DE VEER. }

234

THE COUNTESS OF OXFORD TO JOHN PASTON[1]

To my right entiery welbeloved John Paston of Norwich, Squyer.

Right entierly welbeloved, I grete yow well, thankyng yow of the gret jentylnesse that ye have shewed un to my right welbeloved James Arblaster, prayng yow of contynuaunse ; and if ther be any thyng that I may doo for yow or any of yowres, here or in any other place, I pray yow let me wete and I shall be redy to do it, with the grace of God, ho have yow in his kepyng. And I pray yow to be frendly unto my right welbeloved Agneys Arblaster, wich is to me gret plesier and hertes ease and ye so be. Wretyn at Wevenho the xiij° day of Aprill.

        OXENFORD.
        ELYZABETH.

235

NEWSLETTER OF JOHN STODELEY[2]

1454 JAN. 19

AS touchyng tythynges, please it you to wite that at the Princes[3] comyng to Wyndesore, the Duc of Buk' toke hym in his armes and presented hym to the Kyng in godely wise, besechyng the Kyng to blisse hym ; and the Kyng yave no maner answere. Nathelesse the Duk abode stille with the Prince by the Kyng ; and whan he

[1] [Douce ms. 393, f. 82.]
[2] [Egerton ms. 914, B.M.] There is no evidence that this letter had anything to do with the Paston correspondence, but as a very interesting political letter of the period we have thought it right to give it a place in the collection. The date is quite certain, being after the birth of Prince Edward in October 1453, and before the death of Cardinal Kemp in March 1454.
[3] Edward, only son of Henry vi., born 13th October 1453.

295

1454
JAN. 19
coude no maner answere have, the Queene come in, and toke the Prince in hir armes and presented hym in like forme as the Duke had done, desiryng that he shuld blisse it ; but alle their labour was in ‚veyne, for they departed thens without any answere or countenaunce savyng only that ones he loked on the Prince and caste doune his eyene ayen, without any more.

Item, the Cardinalle[1] hathe charged and commaunded alle his servauntz to be redy with bowe and arwes, swerd and bokeler, crossebowes, and alle other habillementes of werre, suche as thei kun medle with to awaite upon the saufgarde of his persone.

Item, th'erle of Wiltshire[2] and the Lord Bonvile have done to be cryed at Taunton in Somerset shire, that every man that is likly and wole go with theym and serve theym, shalle have vjd. every day as long as he abidethe with theym.

Item, the Duk of Excestre[3] in his owne persone hathe ben at Tuxforthe beside Dancastre, in the north contree, and there the Lord Egremond[4] mette hym, and thei ij. ben sworne togider, and the Duke is come home again.

Item, th'erle of Wiltshire, the Lord Beaumont, Ponynges, Clyfford, Egremond, and Bonvyle, maken all the puissance they kan and may to come hider with theym.

Item, Thorpe[5] of th'escheker articuleth fast ayenst the Duke of York, but what his articles ben it is yit unknowen.

Item, Tresham,[6] Josep,[7] Danyelle,[8] and Trevilian[9] have

[1] John Kemp, Cardinal Archbishop of Canterbury.
[2] James Butler, Earl of Wiltshire and Ormond.   [3] Henry Holland.
[4] Thomas Percy, third son of Henry, Earl of Northumberland.
[5] Thomas Thorpe, one of the Barons of the Exchequer, who was also Speaker of the House of Commons, but was at this time imprisoned in the Fleet in consequence of an action brought against him by the Duke of York.—(See *Rolls of Parl.* v. 239.)
[6] Thomas Tresham, who as 'Sir Thomas Tresham, Knight,' was attainted under Edward IV. for fighting on the Lancastrian side at Towton, but his attainder was afterwards reversed in Parliament 7 and 8 Edw. IV., on the ground that he was a household servant of Henry VI. and had been brought up in his service from a child.—*Rolls of Parl.* v. 616-617.
[7] William Joseph, who, with Thorpe, was frequently accused by the Yorkists of misleading the King.—*Rolls of Parl.* v. 280, 282, 332, 342.
[8] Thomas Daniel, Esq.—*See* p. 255, Note 2.   [9] John Trevilian.

296

made a bille to the Lordes, desiryng to have a garisone kept at Wyndesore for the saufgarde of the Kyng and of the Prince, and that they may have money for wages of theym and other that shulle kepe the garyson.

Item, the Duc of Buk' hathe do to be made M[i]. M[i]. [2000] bendes with knottes, to what entent men may construe as their wittes wole yeve theym.

Item, the Duke of Somersetes herbergeour hath taken up all the loggyng that may be goten nere the Toure, in Thamystrete, Martlane, Seint Katerines, Tourehille, and there aboute.

Item, the Queene hathe made a bille of five articles, desiryng those articles to be graunted ; wherof the first is that she desireth to have the hole reule of this land ; the second is that she may make the Chaunceller, the Tresorere, the Prive Seelle, and alle other officers of this land, with shireves and alle other officers that the Kyng shuld make ; the third is, that she may yeve alle the bisshopriches of this land, and alle other benefices longyng to the Kynges yift ; the iiij[th] is that she may have suffisant lyvelode assigned hir for the Kyng and the Prince and hir self. But as for the vth article, I kan nat yit knowe what it is.

Item, the Duke of York wole be at Londone justly on Fryday next comyng[1] at night, as his owne men tellen for certain, and he wole come with his houshold meyne, clenly beseen and likly men. And th'erle of Marche[2] cometh with hym, but he will have a nother feliship of gode men that shall be at Londone before hym . . . that he is come ; and suche jakkes, salettes, and other herneys as his meyne shulle have, shalle come to Londone with hem, or before hem in cartes. The Erle of Salesbury[3] wille be at Lon[don] on Monday[4] or Tywesday next comyng with seven score knyghtes and squyers, beside other meynee. The Erles of Warwyk,[5] Richemond,[6]

[1] 25th January.
[2] Afterwards Edward IV., the Duke of York's eldest son.
[3] Richard Nevill, Earl of Salisbury, father of Warwick the King-maker.
[4] 21st January.
[5] Richard Nevill, Earl of Warwick, afterwards known as 'the King-maker.'
[6] Edmund Tudor, the King's half-brother. He was the father of King Henry VII.

297

THE PASTON LETTERS   HENRY VI

1454
JAN. 19
and Pembroke[1] comen with the Duke of Yorke, as it is seide, everych of theym with a godely feliship. And natheles th'erle of Warwyk wole have M[i]. men awaityng on hym beside the feliship that cometh with hym, as ferre as I can knowe. And as Geffrey Poole seithe, the Kynges bretherne ben like to be arrested at their comyng to Londone, yf thei come. Wherfore it is thought by my Lordes[2] servauntz and welwillers here that my Lord, at his comyng hider, shalle come with a gode and clenly feliship, suche as is likly and accordyng to his estate to have aboute hym ; and their harneys to come in cartes, as my Lord of Yorkes mennes harneys did the last terme, and shalle at this tyme also. And over that, that my Lord have a nother gode feliship to awaite on hym and to be here afore hym, or els sone after hym, in like wise as other Lordes of his blode wole have.

And for the more redynesse of suche feliship to be hade redy, that my Lord send sadde and wise messagers to his servauntz and tenauntz in Sussex and elswhere, that they be redy at London ayenst his comyng, to awaite on my Lord ; but lete my Lord beware of writyng of lettres for theym, lest the lettres be delivered to the Cardynalle and Lordes, as one of my Lordes lettres was nowe late, for perill that myght falle, for that lettre hathe done moche harme and no gode.

And as for suche tydynges as ben contened in the lettre sent home by John Sumperman, I can nat hiderto here the contrarie of any of theym, but that every man that is of th'opynion of the Duke of Somerset[3] makethe hym redy to be as stronge as he kan make hym. Wherfore it is necessarie that my Lord loke wele to hym self and kepe hym amonge his meyne, and departe nat from theym, for it is to drede lest busshementes shuld be leide for hym. And yf that happed, and my Lord came hiderward, as he hathe ben used for to come, he myght lightly be deceyved and betrapped, that God defende. And therfore lete my Lord make gode wacche and be sure.

[1] Jasper Tudor, brother of the Earl of Richmond, and half-brother to the King.
[2] Probably the Duke of Norfolk.
[3] *See* p. 255, Note 3.

298

HENRY VI

1454
JAN. 19
The Duke of Somerset hathe espies goyng in every Lordes hous of this land ; some gone as freres, som as shipmen taken on the sea, and som in other wise ; whiche reporte unto hym all that thei kun see or here touchyng the seid Duke. And therfore make gode wacche, and beware of suche espies.

And as touchyng the priveé seale and my Lordes seurtee, it is necessarie that my Lord be advertised that yf the Chaunceller,[1] or any other, make any question to my Lord of his comyng contrarie to the teneur of the seid priveé seall, that my Lord by his grete wisdom make answere that he was credibly enformed that aswele the Duke of Somerset beyng prisoner, as other beyng at large, holdyng his opynyon ayenst the wele of the Kyng and of the land, made grete assemblees and gaderyngs of people, to mayntene th'opinion of the seid Duke of Somerset and to distrusse my Lord ; and that the comyng of my Lord in suche forme as he shalle come is onely for the saufgarde of his owne persone, and to none other entent, as my Lord hym self can sey moche better than any that is here kan advertise hym.

Thise thinges aforseid ben espied and gadred by my Lord Chaun   ,[2] John Leventhorpe, Laurence Leventhorpe, Maister Adam, William Medwe, Robert Alman, John Colvyle, Richard of Warderobe, and me, John Stodeley. And as sone as we kun knowe any more in substance we shull send home word. Writen at London, the xix. day of Janyvere.

The meire and merchauntz of London, and the mair and merchauntz of the staple of Caleys, were with the Chaunceller on Monday last passed[3] at Lamhithe, and compleyned on the Lord Bonvile for takyng of the shippes and godes of the Flemmynges and other of the Duke of Burgoynes Lordships, and the Chaunceller yeve theym none answere to their plesyng ; wherfore the substaunce of theym with one voys cryed alowde, ' Justice, justice, justice ! ' wherof the Chaunceller was so dismayed that he coude ne myght no more sey to theym for fere.

[1] Cardinal Kemp was at this time Chancellor.—*See* p. 296, Note 1.
[2] So in MS.   [3] 14th January.

299

THE PASTON LETTERS

236

MARGARET PASTON TO JOHN PASTON[1]

*To my right wurshipfull hosbond, John Paston,
be this delyveryd in hast.*

1454(?)
JAN. 29

RIGHT worshipfull hosbond, I recommawnd me to yow, praying yow to wete that I spak yistirday with my suster,[2] and she told me that she was sory that she myght not speke with yow or ye yede ; and she desyrith if itt pleased yow, that ye shuld yeve the jantylman, that ye know of, seche langage as he myght fele by yow that ye wull be wele willyng to the mater that ye know of ; for she told me that he hath seyd befor this tym that he conseyvid that ye have sett but lytil therby, wherefor she prayth yow that ye woll be here gode brother, and that ye myght have a full answer at this tym whedder it shall be ya or nay. For her moder hath seyd to her syth that ye redyn hens, that she hath no fantesy therinne, but that it shall com to a jape ; and seyth to her that ther is gode crafte in dawbyng ; and hath seche langage to her that she thynkyt right strange, and so that she is right wery therof, wherefor she desyrith the rather to have a full conclusyon therinne. She seyth her full trost is in yow, and as ye do therinne, she woll agre her therto.

Mayster Braklee[3] be her yisterday to have spoke with yow ; I spak with hym, but he wold not tell me what his erond was.

It is seyd her that the cescions shall be at Thetford on

---

[1] [From Fenn, iii. 170.] The request made at the end of this letter that John Paston would procure his wife an ornament for her neck, is noted by Fenn as one that she had made in April 1452, and of which this was probably a repetition nine months afterwards. There seems no better evidence of date to go by, so we follow the same mode of inference ; but as we have placed the letter containing the first petition for the necklace in 1453 instead of 1452, we must attribute this letter to the year 1454.
[2] Elizabeth Paston.
[3] John Bracklee or Brackley was a brother of the Convent of Grey Friars, or Friars Minors, in Norwich. He took a Doctor of Divinity's degree, and was a famous preacher.—F.

300

HENRY VI

Saterday next komyng, and ther shall be my Lord of Norffolk **1454** and other with grette pupill [*people*], as it is seyd. **JAN. 29**

Other tydyngs have we none yett. The blissefull Trynyte have yow in his kepyng. Wretyn at Norwyche, on the Tewysday next befor Candelmasse.

I pray yow that ye woll vowchesawf to remembr to purvey a thing for my nekke, and to do make my gyrdill.

Yowris,   M. P.

My cosyn Crane recommawndeth her to yow, and praytth yow to remembr her mater, &c., for she may not slepe on nyghtys for hym.

237

AGNES PASTON TO JOHN PASTON[1]

*Thys letter be delyverd to John Paston, dwellyn in the
Inder In of the Tempyll at London, in hast.*

I GRETE yow well, and lete yow wete that thys day I was **About** with my doughtyr yor wyfe, and che was in good hele att **1454** the makyn of thys letter, thankyd be God ! and sche lete yor sustyr and me wete of a letter wheche ye sent hyr, that ye have be laboryd to for Ser William Oldhall to have your sustyr, and desyryng in the seyd letter to have an answer in schort tyme, who [*how*] sche wyll be demenyd in thys mater.

Yor suster recomaundyt hyr to yow, and thankyt yow hertyly that ye wyll remembyr hyr, and lete hyr have knowleche ther of, and prayt yow that ye wyll do your dever to bryng it to a good conclusyon ; for sche seythe to me that sche trystyt that ye wyll do so, that it xall be bothe for hyr worchup and profyt. And as for me, if ye can thynke that hys lond standyt cler, in as meche as I fele your sustyr well wyllyd ther to, I hold me well content.

---

[1] [From Fenn, iii. 188.] This letter refers to a proposal for Paston's sister which was probably in or a little before 1454, as in a letter of the 15th July in that year Paston states that several such offers had been under consideration.

301

THE PASTON LETTERS

About
1454

And as for the oblygacyon of the persen of Marlynferthe, wheche I sent yow by John Newman, I pray yow lete it be suyd ; and as for the Parson and Lyndesey, they be a cordyd. And God have yow in kepyn, and send yow hys blyssyn and myn. Wretyn at Norwyche on Pulver Wedenesday.[1]

Be yor moder,   AUGNES PASTON.

238

INGHAM'S PETITION[2]

1454

FUL mekely bisecheth your humble liege man, Walter Ingham of youre schire of Norffolk, gentylman, that where the seide Walter was in Goddes pees and youres at Dunston in the seid shire the xj. daye of the monthe of January, the yere of youre rengne the xxxij., oone Thomas Denyes,[3] of ful grete malice, prepensed ungodely soore agaynste gode feithe and concience, imagynyng utterly to destroye youre seyde besecher, contryved a lettre in the name of my Lord of Oxenforde, he not knowyng of ony soch lettre comaundyng youre seide besecher to be with the seide Lorde at Wevenho, in your shire of Essex, the xiij. day of the seide monthe of January, for divers grete maters towchyng my seide Lorde. The seide Thomas, thenkyng in his conceite that youre seid besechere wolde in noo wyse disobeye the seide wrytyng, but that he wolde putte hym in his devoyre to fulfill my seide Lords desyre, layde dyvers folks arraied in maner of werre with jakkes, saletts, langedebiefs,[4] and boore speres in ij. busshements for youre seide besecher in ij. places, knowyng wele that youre seide besecher must come oone of thes ij. weyes for, tho [*there*] were no moo, to that intent that they

---

[1] If in 1454, Ash-Wednesday was the 6th of March.
[2] [From Paston MSS., B.M.] This is a petition to the King in Parliament which, supported by the influence of Cardinal Kemp, appears to have met with a favourable hearing from the House of Lords. The date will appear by the letter following.
[3] *See* Nos. 123 and 124.
[4] The *langue-de-bœuf* was a kind of glaive with a double edge half down the blade.

302

HENRY VI

[might] murdre your seide besecher be cause he had laboured **1454** for his fadir in a wryte *sub pena* agaynst the seide Thomas Denys and Anneys his wyf for a notable somme of money that the seide Anneys shulde have payede to the fadir of your seide besecher ; the seide Thomas comaundyng the seide mysdoers in any wyse whech of theym that mette first with youre seide besecher shulde sle hym, and they shol be nota[b]ly rewardet for ther laboure, and the seide Thomas shulde kepe and save theyme harmeles. Bicause of whech comaundement oone of the seide busshements mette with the forsaide besechere the xij. day of the seide month, as he came toward my seide Lorde of Oxenforde acordyng to his lettre at Dunstone afore seide, and hym than and there grevosly bette and woundet, aswell upon his hede as upon his leggs, and other ful grevous strokes and many gaf hym upon his bakke, so that youre seide besecher is mahamed upon his ryght legg, and feyne to goo on crucches, and so must do al dayes of his lif to his utter undoyng ; notwithstandyng the seide mysdoers and riotous peple in this conceite [lef]te youre seide besecher for dede. Upon the whech ryot it was complayned to my Lord Chauncelere[1] by the frends of yowre besecher, desyryng of hym by ca[use of th]e grete ryote doone by the seide Thomas, and also for the sauf garde of youre seyde besechere, that oone of your serjantes of armes myght be comaundement [go][2] and areste the seide Thomas to appere before you in your Chauncerie for the seide ryot, because the seide Thomas was at that tyme at London ; bi force of [whech com]aundement oone of youre serjants of armes went to Lyncolne Inne to arreste the sayde Thomas. The whech areste the seide Thomas utterly diso[beyed in] grete contempte of your highnesse ; nevertheles he is now in the warde of the Wardeyne of the Flete by the comaundement of my Lorde Chaunceler. [Wher]fore plese it your highnes of youre most noble and habundante grace, by the assente of your Lordes Spirituel and Temporel, and of your Comons in this your present Par[lement assem]bled, and by auctorite of the same, to ordeyne and estabelessche that the seide Thomas Denys may abide in the seide prisone of the Flete, and not to

---

[1] John Kemp, Archbishop of Canterbury and Cardinal. [2] Mutilated.

303

1454 be [admitted to bayl] nor meynprise in noo wyse in to soch tyme that the seide Thomas have answered to soch accion or accions as youre seide besecher schal take agaynst hym for the seide mahayme and betyng, and also unto soch tyme as the same accions ben folly discussed and determyned bi twene your seide besecher and the seide Thomas Denys, consideryng that if the same Thomas scholde go at large, he wolde never answere your seide besecher but hym delay by protecions and other weies, so that the same besecher schulde never be content nor agreed, for the exhorbitant offence done to hym ; and also un to the tyme the seide Thomas fynde sofficient suerte of his gode beryng fro this tyme forthe. And he shal pray to God for youre moste noble astate.

239

THOMAS DENYES TO JOHN PASTON[1]

To my right wurshipfull maister, John Paston.

MARCH 20 RIGHT wurshipfull and myn especiall good maister, I recomaund me to you with all service and prayer to my power. And like it you to wete that how be a full straunge acte is passid agayn me in the Higher House before the Lords, wherof I send you a copie. Neverthelesse I hope to God that it shal not passe in the Comon House ; but me is be falle the most sorwful infortune that ever por man had, standyng in suych case as I do, for my Lordis the Cardenale and of Oxenford haf imprisoned my wif in the countour, and how thei shal guyde hir forth, God knoweth. Which standith to nygh myn hert, if Godds will were ; but wel I know that by thes vengeable malics don to hir and me thei wole [not ?] be content, for Ingham lithe beside that to take

[1] [From Fenn, iii. 174.] This letter is without a signature, and the writer was unknown to Fenn ; but a comparison with the letter which follows (now printed for the first time) leaves no doubt that it was written by Thomas Denyes, whom we have already met with as a dependant of the Earl of Oxford (*see* Letters 123, 124, and 132). The date is fixed by the reference to the death of Cardinal Kemp in the postscript.

304

1454 awey my wyves doughter out of Westminster to make an end MARCH 20 of my wif if he can, and also to arest my servauntz, that I drede that she nor I shal haf no creature to attend us ne help us ; and suych malice haf I never herd of herbeforne. And it is told me that beside that thei wole dispoil, if any good thei can fynde of myn in Norwich or Norffolk, and imprisone my servauntz there. Wherfore I lowly beseche your maistership, for our Lords mercy, that ye vouchsauff to socour theym in this necessite ; and if ony entree be made or shuld be made upon myn wifes place in Norwich, that ye vouchsauff to socour my servauntz, and do ther inne after your wisdam for Crists love and seynt charite.

Beside this, a frend and kynnesman of myn, oon Robert Clement of Betele, hath writen to me that he is arestid, and like to be imprisoned bi a writte of dette, take agayn hym upon an obligacion of C*li.* [£100] in which he and I and other wer bounde to my Lorde of Oxenford xiiij. yeer agone, wherof I haf many acquitaunces. Wherfore I pray your good maister-ship to send to the Shirreve that my said kynnesman may ben easid, and no retourne made ageyn hym, but that he may answer the next tyme bi attourney ; for truly that writte was take oute in the end of the terme aftir I was arestid, and aftir it was aperid to.

I pray your maistership, for Godds sake, to be not displesid, ne wery to do for me in these materes of your charite, for I had lever gif the said Robert suych good, litell if it be, as I haf, than he wer undone for me, or ony man ellis that ever ded for me. And I hope, if God vouchsaf that the mater may come to reson, to sauf hym harmles, and all other with Godds mercy, ever prayng you of your maistership and socour for Godds love, who ever kepe for his mercy.

Wretyn in Flete, the Wednesday the second weke of Lent.

Mor over, in augmentyng of my sorwe, I wend my wif shuld a dyed sith, for aftir she was arestid she laboured of hir child, that she is with all, waityng either to dye or be delyvered, and she hath not gon viij. weks quykke. What shal be falle Almighti God knoweth, and shull dispose mercifully.

VOL. II.—U
305

1454 Aftirward my wif was sum dele easid bi the labour of the MARCH 20 Wardeyn of Flete, for the cursed Cardenale had sent hir to Newgate. God forgif his sowle. Now she is take to baile til Tuesday. The Cardenale is dede, and the Kyng is relevid.[1]

240

JOHN PASTON TO [THE EARL OF OXFORD][2]

MARCH 31 RIGHT wurchepfull and my right especiall Lord, I recomaund me to your gode Lordshep, besechyng your Lordshep that ye take not to displesauns thow I write you, as I here say that Agnes Denyes, be the menes of your Lordshep and of my Lord the Cardynall,[3] hos sowle God assoyle and forgeve, was set in preson, beyng with child —which, and the sorough and shame there of, was nygh her deth—and yet dayly is vexed and trobled, and her servauntes in like wyse, to the uttermest distruccion of her person and godes. In which, my Lord, at the reverens of God, remembre sche was maried be you and be my menes, be your comaunde-ment and writyng, and draw therto full sore ageyn her entent in the begynnynge ; and was worth v.ᶜ [500] marc and better, and shuld have had a gentilman of this contre of an C. marc of lond and wele born, ne had be your gode Lordshep and writyng to her and me. And this considered in your wise discrecion, I trost, my Lord, thow her prisonyng were of oderes labore, ye wuld helpe her ; and if she be destroyd be this mariage, my conscyens thynketh I am bownd to recompense her after my pore and sympill power. My

[1] This last sentence must have been added a few days after the date of the letter, for Cardinal Kemp died on the 22nd of March 1454. Wednesday in the second week of Lent was the 20th March.
[2] [From Paston MSS., B.M.] This letter was so manifestly written on the receipt of the last, that there can be no question about the date. It bears no address upon the back, so that it is probably only a copy, or, if an original, it certainly was not sent ; but the person for whom it was intended was evidently the Earl of Oxford.
[3] Cardinal Kemp.

306

1454 Lord, ye know I had litill cause to do for Thomas Denyes, MARCH 31 savyng only for your gode Lordshep. Also, my Lord, I know wele that Water Ingham was bete, the mater hangyng in myn award, right fowle and shamefully ; and also how the seid Thomas Denyes hath, this last terme, ageyn your nobill estat, right unwysely demened hym to his shame and grettest rebuke that ever he had in his lyve. Where fore it is right wele do his person be ponysshed as it pleaseth you. But this not withstondyng for Godds love, my Lord, remembre how the gentilwoman is accombred only for yowr sake, and help her ; and if aught lyth in my power to do that that myght please yowr Lordshep, or cowde fynde any way for Water Ingham avayll and wurchep, I wull do it to my power ; and the rather if your Lordshep support the jentilwoman, for I know the mater and that longe plee is litill avayll, and every thyng must have an ende. I have told my brother Mathew Drury more to enforme yowre Lordshep than I may have leyser to write for his hasty departyng. Right wurchepfull and my right especiall Lord, I besech All myghty God send you asmych joy and wurchep as ever had any of my Lords yowr aunceters, and kepe you and all yowres. Wretyn at Norwich the iiij. Sonday of Lent.

Yowre servaunte to his powr,

JOHN PASTON.

241

INFORMATION AGAINST ROBERT LEDHAM[1]

1454 THEES be the persons that enformyd the Justicez of the Kyngis Benche the last terme of suche ryottis as hath be done be Robert Ledham : The Lord Skales, Sir Thomas Todenham, Sir John Chalers, Edmond Clere, Water George, John Alyngton, Gilbert Debenham, John Denston, William Whit, William Alyngton, Reynald Rows, John

[1] [From Add. Charter 16,545, B.M.] This paper refers mainly to events of 1452 and 1453, but was probably drawn up in 1454, after the Duke of York had come into power.

307

THE PASTON LETTERS

1454 Berney, Richard Suthwell, John Paston, John Henyngham, Raff Shelton, Henry Grey.

These be the names of the knyghtes and esquyers that endittyd Robert Ledham :—Thomas Todenham, knyght, Androw Ogard, knyght, John Henygham, knyght, William Calthorp, esquyer, Bryan Stapelton, esquyer, Osbert Mondford, esquyer, John Groos, esquyer, William Rokwod, esquyer, Thomas Morle, esquyer, Thomas Scholdham, esquyer, John Wyndham, esquyer, John Berney, esquyer, William Narbow, esquyer, John Chippysby, esquyer, William White, esquyer, John Bryston, esquyer, John Paston, esquyer.

These be dyvers of the ryottis and offensis done in the hundred of Blofeld in the counte of Norffolk, and in other townys be Robert Lethum, otherwyse callyd Robert Ledham of Wytton, be Blofeld in the counte of Norffolk, and by his ryottys men and by other of his affinitez and knowleche, whos names folowyn, and that they contynually folow and resorte unto his hous, and ther be supported and maynteynet and confortid.

These be the principall menealle men of the sayd Robert Ledham ys hous be the whiche the sayd ryottys have be done, that use in substaunce non other occupacion but ryottys :—In primis, John Cokett, Thomas Bury, Thomas Cokowe, Cristofer Bradlee, Elys Dukworth, William Donmowe, Cristofer Grenesheve, Roger Chirche. Notwythstondyng the sayd Robert Ledham kypith dayly many mo in his house and chaungeth such as have be oppenly knowyn for riottis and takith other for hem as evill as they. And these be the most principale persons comyng and resortyng unto the house of the sayd Robert Ledham, and ther be supportid and mayntened in ryottes be whom the sayd ryottes have be don, that ys to sey : In primis, Robert Taillor, Henry Bang, Robert Dallyng, John Beston, Charles Navell, John, the sone of Roger Ratclyff, Robert Berton; notwythstondyng ther be money moo whos names ben unknowyn. With the which persons, and many moo unknowyn, the sayd Robert Ledham kept atte his hous in maner of a forcelet and issith ouute atte here pleaysour and atte his lust, the sayd Ledham to assigne,

308

somtyme vj. and sometyme xij., somtyme xxxᵗⁱ and moo, 1454 armyd, jakkid, and salettyd, with bowys and arrowys, speris, billys, and over ryde the countrey and oppressid the Kyngs peple, and didde mony oryble and abhomynable dedes, like to have be destruccion of the enhabitantes in the sayd hundred, in the forme that folowyth, and warse.

In primis, on the Monday [1] next before Ester day and the shire daye, the xxx. yere of oure soverayne Lord the Kyng, x. persons of the sayd riottors, with a brother of the wyff of the sayd Robert Lethum, laye in awayte in the hyght way under Thorpe Wode upon Phillip Berney, esquyer, and his man comyng from the shire, and shette atte hym and smote the hors of the sayd Phillipp with arowes, and than over rode hym, and toke hym and bette hym and spoillid hym. And for thayr excuse of this ryot, they ledde hym to the Bysshopp of Norwiche, axyng seuerte of the peas wher they hadde never waraunt hym to areste. Which affray shorttyd the lyffdayes of the sayd Phillippe, whiche dyed withynne shorte tyme after the said affray. [2]

Item, iij. of the sayd riottys feloshippe the same day, yere, and place, laye on awayte uppon Edmond Broune, gentilman, and with naked swerdes and other wepyng faght wyth hym be the space of on qaurte (sic) of an houre, and toke and spoillyd hym, and kepte hym as long as them lyst, and after that lette hym goo.

Item, xlᵗⁱ of the sayd riottys felowshipp, be the comaundement of the same Robert Lethum, jakket and salettyd, with bowes, arowys, billys, and gleyves, oppon Mauyndy Thursday, [3] atte iiij. of the clokke atte after nonne, the same yere, comyn to the White Freres in Norwyche, and wold have brokyn theyr yates and dorys, feynyng thaym that they wold hire thayre evesong. Where they ware aunswered suche service was non used to be there, nor withyn the sayd citee atte that tyme of the daye, and prayd them to departe ; and

[1] 3rd April 1452.
[2] Philip Berney died, as we have seen, on the 2nd July 1453, fifteen months after the date assigned to the outrage.
[3] 6th April 1452.

309

THE PASTON LETTERS

1454 they aunswered and sayd that affore thayre departyng they wold have somme persons ouute of that place, qwykke or dede, insomuch the sayd freris were fayn to kype thaire place with forsse. And the mayr and the sheriffe of the sayd cite were fayn to arere a power to resyst the sayd riotts, which to hem on that holy tyme was tediose and heynous, consedryng the losse and lettyng of the holy service of that holy nyght. And theroppon the sayd ryotors departid.

Item, the sayd Robert Lethum, on the Monday [1] nest after Esterne day, the same yere, toke from on John Wilton iiij. neet for rent arere, as he said, and killed hem and layd them in salte, and afterward ete hem.

Item, the sayd Robert Lethum, with vj. of his sayd ryottes, the same yere made assaute upon John Wilton in Plumstede churche yerde, and theer so bete hym that he was in doute of his lyff ; and also dede to hym many grete wronggys and oppressioun, unto the undoyng of the sayd John Wilton.

Item, in lyke wyse the sayd Robert Lethum and his men assauted on John Coke of Witton, in brekyng uppe his dorys atte a xi. of the cloke in the nyght, and wyth thaire swerdys maymed hym and gaff hym vij. grete wondys, and toke from hym certayn goodys and catalls, of the whiche he hadde, nor yitte hath, no remedy nor restitution.

Item, the same day and yere they bete the moder of the same John Coke, she beyng iiijˣˣ [four score] vere of age and more, and smote hure upon the crowne of here hed with a swerd ; of the whiche hurte she myght never be helyd into the day of hure deth.

Item, John, the sone of Hodge Ratleffe, and other of the sayd felowshipp, toke on Thomas Baret of Byrlygham out of his house, and bete hym and wondid hym that he kept his bedde a month, and toke from hym certayn goodes and catells.

Item, the sayd Robert Taillor, because the sayd Thomas Baret complayned of the same betyng, lay in awayte oppon hym, with other of his feloushippe, and bete hym agayn.

Item, John Beston and the sayd Robert Taillor, and other

[1] 10th April 1452.

310

of the sayd riottes felowshipp, toke on Thomas Byrden of 1454 Lyngewod and bete hym and prisoned hym till unto such tyme that he was delyvered by the mene of my Lord of Norwych ; and for that sorow, distres, and grete payne and betyng, the sayd Thomas Byrden toke suche kynesse that he dyed.

Item, the sayd Robert Dallyng and Herry Bange, and other of the sayd felowshippe, toke and bete on Nicholas Chirche atte Strumpeshawe, beyng in the church of the same towne, that he was [in] dout of his lyff.

Item, the sayd Robert Dallyng lay on away upon on Thomas Dallyng, and hym grevously bete.

Item, on Middleynt Sunday, [1] the xxxᵗⁱ yere of oure soveraigne Lorde the Kynge that now ys, Robert Dallyng, Robert Churche, Robert Taillor, Herry Bang, Adam atte More, with other unknowyn, be the comaundement and assent of the sayd Robert Ledham, made affray uppon Herry Smyth and Thomas Chambre atte Suthbirlyngham, the sayd Herry and Thomas and that tyme knelyng to see the usyng of the masse, and than and ther wold have kyllyd the sayd Herry and Thomas atte the prestys bakke, ne had they be lettyd.

Item, the sayd Robert Lethum, with his sayd ryottis felawshipp, the same yere dide and made so many ryottes in the hundred where he dwellyth that dyvers and many gentilmen, frankeleyns, and good men, durst not abyde in here mansyon place, ne ryde, nother walke aboute thaire occupacions without mo persons, arrayd in maner and forme of werre attendyng and waytyng uppon them than thayr lyvelode wold extende to fynde hem. And so, for savacion of thaire lyves, and in eschewyng of suche inordinat costys as never was seen in that countrey befor, many of them forsoke and leffte thaire owyn habitacion, wyff and childe, and drewe to fortresses and good townes as for that tyme.

In primis, Phillipp Berney, esquyer, Edmond Broom to Castre ; Thomas Holler, John Wylton to Norwych ; Oliver Kubyte to Seynt Benetts ; Robert Spany to Aylesham ; Thomas

[1] 19th March 1452.

311

1454 Baret, with many others, to Meche Yermouth and to other placys of strenght.

Item, the sayd Robert Ledham, contynuyng in this wyse, callyd unto hym his sayd mysgoverned felowshipp, consydryng the absence of many of the well-rewlyd people of the sayd hundred of affere cast malice, and congected, purposed and labored to the sheriff of the shire that the sayd Roger Chirche, on of the sayd riottous felawshipp, was made bailly of the hundred ; and after causid the same Roger to be begynner of arysyng and to take oppon hym to be a captayn and to excite the peple of the countrey therto. And ther oppon, be covyne of the sayd Robert Ledhaum, to appeche all these sayd well rewlyd persones, and as well other divers substanciall men of good fame and good governaunce that were hated be the sayd Robert Ledhaum, and promittyng the sayd Roger harmeles and to sew his pardon be the mene of Danyell ; to the which promyse the sayd Rogger aggreed, and was arested and take be the sayd Ledham be covyne betwixt hem, and appeched suche persons as they lust, to the entente that the sayd substanciall men of the countre shuld be by that mene so trowblyd and indaungered that they shuld not be of power to lette and resist the mys rewle of the sayd Ledham and his mysgoverned felawshipp, the whiche mater ys confessid by the sayd Roger Chirch.

Item, William Breton and John Berton, and other of the sayd ryottes, come into the place of on Robert Spany of Poswyke and serched his housez, hous be hous, for to have bete hym yf they myght have founde hym.

Item, William Donmowe, servaunt of the sayd Robert Ledham, and by his comaundement, the same yere bete the parson of Hashyngham, and brake his hede in his owyn chauncell.

Item, the sayd Thomas Bery, Elys Dukworth, Thomas Cokowe, George of Chamer, the v. day of Novembre last past, with divers other onknowyn men, onto the nombre of xx. persons, and noman of reputacion among hem, comen, under color of huntyng, and brake uppe gatys and closys of Osburne Monford atte Brayston ; and xij. persons of the same

312

felowshipp, with bowys bent and arowys redy in thair handys, 1454 abode alone betwixt the maner of Brayston and the chirche, and there kept hem from vij. of the clokke on the mornyng unto iij. of the clokk after none, lyyng in awayte oppon the servauntez of the sayd Osburne Monford, lorde of the sayd maner, so that nonne durst comen ouut for doute of thair lyves.

Item, viij. of the sayd felowshipp, on the Wennesday next after, prevely in an hole layn in awayte oppon William Edworth and Robert Camplyon, servauntz to the sayd Osburn Montford, comyng from Okill[1] market, till that tyme that the said William Owell and Robert come uppon hem onwarre, and theruppon chasid hem so that yf they had not be well horssyd and well askapped, they had ben dede and slayne.

Item, vj. or vij. of the sayd Ledamys men dayly, boyth werkeday and haly day, use to goo aboute in the countrey with bowys and arowys, shotyng and playng in mennys closis among men catall, goyng from alhous to alhousez and manassyng suche as they hated, and soght occasion and quarels and debate.

Item, notwithstandyng that all the lyvelod that the sayd Ledham hath passith not xx*li.* [£20], be sydes the reparacion and outcharges, and that he hath no connyng ne trew mene of getyng of any good in this countre, as for as any man may conceyve, and yette xypith in his house dayly xx. men, besydes women and gret multitude of such mysgoverned peple as ben resortyng to hym, as ys above sayd, to the whiche he yevith clothyng, and yitte bysyde that he yevith to other men that be not dwellyng in his household ; and of the sayd xx. men ther passith not viij. that use occupacion of husbondrye ; and all they that use husbondrye, as well as other, be jakked and salettid redy for to werre, which yn this countrey ys thoght ryght straunge, and ys verely so conceyved that he may not kepe this countenance be no good menes.

Item, the sayd Ledham hath a *supersedias* oute of the chauncerie for hym and divers of hys men, that no warant of justice of pees may be served agayn hem.

[1] Acle.

313

1454 Item, please unto your Lordshipp to remembre that the sayd Ledham and his sayd mysgoverned feloushipp be endited of many of these articles and of many moo not comprehendit here, and in especiall of the sayd rysyng agayn the Kyng. Wherfore, though the sayd Ledham can prove the sayd enditement of treson voyde in the lawe for symplenesse of them that gaffe the verdit, that it lyke you, for the Kyngs availl, not redely to suffre the sayd Ledham to departe atte large unto the tyme that the mater of the sayd enditement be better enquered of for the Kyngs avayll, and that the sayd Ledham fynde surte of his good aberyng ; and the inhabitauntz of the sayd hundred of Blofeld shall pray for you. And els they be lyke to be destruyd for ever.

242

JOHN CLOPTON TO JOHN PASTON[1]

Un to ryth reverent Sir, and my good mayster, John Paston.

About 1454

RYTH wurthy and wurchypfull Sir, and my ryth good mayster, I recomaunde me on to you, thankyng you evermore of your gret jentylness and good maystyrhod shewyd on to me at all tymys, and specyally now to my herthys ease, qwyche on my part can nowt be rewardyd, but my sympyll service is ever redy at your comaundement. Ferthemor, as for the mater that ye wete of, I have laboryd so to my feydr that your entent as for the jointoure xal be fulfellyd ; and, Sir, I besheche you sethyn that I do my part to fullefelle your wyll, that ye wolle shew me your good maystyrhod in here chambyr, as my full trust is, in so moche that it xall nowth hurthe you nor non of youris, and the profite ther of xal be on to the avayle of my maystress your suster, and to me, and to non odyr creature.

And also my maystress, your modyr, xall nouth be charchyd the with her bourd aftyr the day of the mariage,

[1] [From Fenn, iii. 192.] The exact year of this letter is uncertain, but from what John Paston writes to Lord Grey on the 15th July 1454, about proposals having been recently made for his sister, it is not unlikely to be that year.

314

but I to discharge her of here persone, and to ease me that About hat here chambyr may be non contradiccion. 1454

And, Sir, I am redy, and alwey wolle to performe that I have seyd on to you, &c.

Ferthe.nor, lykyd you to wete I was a Thursday last passyd at Cavendyshe, to dylyver an astate to Wentworth in the londe that was my brothyr Cavendyche, as I tolde you wan I was last with you. And ther I spak with Crane ; and he be sowthe me that I wolde sende over to my maystress your modyr for his excuse, for he myth nowth be with here at this tyme, but on the Saterday in Esterne wyke he wolle nouth fayll to be with her. So he counsellyd me that I and my brothyr Denston xulde mete with hym there ; and so, withoute your better avyse, I and my brothyr purpose us to be with you ther at that tyme ; for the sonner the levyr me, for, as to my conceythe, the dayys be waxyn wondyrly longe in a scorte tyme. Qwerfor I besheche you sende me your avyse how ye wolle have me rewlyd, &c.

No more I wrythe to you at this present tyme, but be schechyng you to recomaunde in the lowlyest wyse. And the Trinite preserve you body and sowle.

Wretyn with my chauncery hand, in ryth gret haste, on the Fryday be forn Palmesoneday.

Your,

JOHN CLOPTON.

243

JOHN CLOPTON TO JOHN PASTON[1]

Maryage Artycles betwix Anneys Paston, &c. on the one partie, and William Clopton, Squyer, on the other partie.

THIS indenture, made betwix Anneys that was the wyfe of William Paston, John Paston hir sone, and John Dam on the one partie, and William Clopton, Squyer, on the other partie, witnesseth that accord is take attwyn the

[1] [From Fenn, iii. 196.] The date of this draft settlement is no doubt about the same period as that of the preceding letter, whatever may have been the exact time that it was written.

315

THE PASTON LETTERS

seid parties that John Clopton, sone and heir of the seid William Clopton, by the grace of God, shall wedde Elizabeth, the doughter of the seid Anneys. For which mareage the seid Anneys, &c. shall paye to the seid John Clopton CCCCth marc in hand of lawfull mony of England; and over that, yf the seid mareage be holdyn with the seid Anneys, the seid Anneys shall bere the costages therof the day of the weddyng, with swech chaumbeyr as shall be to the plesir of the seid Anneys; and the seid William Clopton shall do his feffees make a lawfull estate to the seid William of londs, tenementz, rentz, and servysez to the yerly value of xl*li.* over all chargez born, to have and to hold to hym terme of his lyfe, withoutyn empecement of wast, the remaindr therof to the seid John and Elizabeth, and to his heirs male of hir body lawfully begotyn, withoute impechement of wast, withynne xij. dayes after the seid weddyng.

And over that, withynne the seid xij. dayes the seid John shall do lawfull estate to be made to the seid William of londs, tenementz, rentz, and servysez to the yerly value of xl. marc over all charges born; to have and hold to the seid William terme of his lyfe, withoute empechement of wast; the re-mayndre therof to the seid Elizabeth, to have and hold to hir terme of hir lyfe withoute empechement of wast.

Also it is accorded that the seid William shall make estate of all the residue of his londs which he is sesid of, or any other man to his use, to swech personys as the seid John shall name, to the use of the seid John.

Also the seid John Clopton shall do lawfull estate to be made to the seid Elizabeth of londs, tenementz, rentz, and servysez to the yerly value of xxx*li.* over all chargez born, to have and hold to hir duryng the lyfe of the seid William.

And moreover the seid John permytteth and ensureth be the feith of his body that he shall leve, over the xl*li.* worth lond aboveseid to his heirs and issue male of the body of the seid Elizabeth begotyn, londes in fee symple or in taill to the yerly value of xl. marc, in cas the same issue male be governyd to the seid John as the sone oweth to be to the fadir. And, &c.

316

THE PASTON LETTERS

245

THOMAS DENYES TO JOHN PASTON[1]

To my Maister Paston.

1454
MAY 3

RIGHT reverent and wurshipfull Sir, and myn especiall good maister, I recomaund me to you. And for as moche as oon Lord above giffeth and takith as hym plesith, I thank His grace of every thyng; and for the bounte that ye shew to me in this troble, I haf no spirite to thank you as I shuld. Sir, as for certeyn evidence of myn touchyng your place in Seint Andrues Parissh, my wif tellith me that she lefft thaym in a chest at Ovyes shette; the key ther of she hath sent now to Ovy also. And as for more evidence, sum is in the kepyng of Frere John Mendham, wherto I beseche your maistership that ye wole se for the sauf and secreet kepyng therof. God wote my wif delyvered all, myn unwetyng; ever therfore I doute, trustyng with such hope as is be lefft me to the best, with Godds grace.

Othre evidence of myn is at Folsham, I wote not with whome. I thank God of my conyng; but as sone as I may know, I shal write to you. Wherfore, sith it is thus, I beseche your maistershep disdeigne not, but for our Lords love ye vouchsauf to take it to you, or to se that it be sauf, if it plese you. And that ye wole send for John Maile, for I conceyve hym right feithfull to me, and I am enfourmed that he is gretly manasid for me. And that ye vouchsauf to do put hym in comfort that I lese not his good wille, and that ye shew hym your good maistership and favor that he be holpen and not hurt for me. Ferthermore, I wrote to you for such smal thynges as I had leid to plegge to you for such good as that I

¹ [From Paston MSS., B.M.] For the date of this letter it may be sufficient to refer the reader to Letters 238 and 239 preceding. Both Denyes and his wife are here still in prison, but he expresses himself grateful to Paston for efforts made in his behalf.

HENRY VI

244

THOMAS DENYES TO JOHN PASTON[1]

To my maister Paston.

1454
APRIL 8

RIGHT Reverend and wurshipfull Sir, myn especyall good maister, I recomaund me to you. And for as moch as adversite and prosperite bothe ly in the disposicion of o [*one*] man above, I thank God, and late you wete that I stand yet in as greet troble as ever I dede or gretter; praying you ever to be my good maister and to contynue your benyvolens as I am ever bounde to you. Myn hevynes is sum whet incresid, for a fals harlot, sauf your reverens, one James Cook, a servaunt of myn, falsly and traitourously is hired bi Watte Ingham and hath accused and diffamed me and my wif of settyng up billes agayn lordis, that, Almighti God I take to record, I not am ne never was gilty therof; but the same theef and Asshcote han made an appoyntement to come and robbe me of suych littel goodis of myn as thei can gete in Norffolk or Norwich. Wherfore I beseche your maistership for charite of your help and socour to my servauntz if such case falle. For I trowe this is a troble that never man suffrid non like in such case, and ther-fore, gentill Sir, as God hath indued you of myght and power to socour suych troubles, shew your bounte to me in this nede, and that for Goddes love, Who Almighti preserve you. Wretyn in Flete the viij. day of Aprill.—Your wofull servant, DENYES.

The said Asshcote can counterfete my hand and therfore I drede he wole stele by sum fals letters suych as he myght gete. I haf wretyn my servantz theraftir.

¹ [Add. MS. 34,888, f. 94.] That the year in which this letter was written was 1454 is evident from its being dated from the Fleet. *See* Nos. 239 and 245.

317

HENRY VI

borwid of you. Wheryn I beseche your maistership that if my frends pay you accordyng to my writyng, that ye than vouchsaf to do the said plegges be sent hider to me by such conduyte as your wisdam like to avise, and that they myght be here by the iiij^{to} die of the xv^{cim}[1] of Ester, for than is my grettest jouparte touchyng myn imprisonement; for sith myn enmyes coude not avail to send me to the castel of Bristow (which was their purpose, whan thei undirstood the disposicion of the Comons Hous agayn their billes), ever sith they make a privy labor to haf me remevid, and I wote not whedir, ne wethir that tyme I shal be sent to the Kynges Bench, and abide ther, or remittyd hider agayn.

1454
MAY 3

Nevertheless, if I haf releve of such pouer godes as shuld be myn by reson, than I hope to do better, and sumwhat to aquyte, wherby I hope to put my frends in gretter corage to do for me. And if I haf no releve, than can I nomore, but all refere to God as I do daily. Wherefore, if ye be not paied, I pray you to councell my said frendes to send me suche mony as thei may gete of myn agayn that day, ever your maistership and wisdam seyng to the conduyte therof. More over, I doute lest that Richard Davy of his untrouth enfourme myn enmys wher such pouer thyng as I haf is, to that intent that thei may riffel and dispoil all. Wherof, if such case hapne, I can no ferthre, but I besech your help in every thyng. It is yours all, ther is a dede of gifft therof to you among myn evidence, as ye vouchsauff to do or do to be don in every thyng I holde me content. And Al myghti God preserve you.

Wretyn in non hertis ease at Flete, the iij. day of Maii.

WOFUL DENYES.

¹ The fourth day of the quinzaine of Easter.

THE PASTON LETTERS

246

LORD SCALES TO JOHN PASTON[1]

To my right and welbeloved frend, John Paston, Squier.

1454
MAY 17

RIGHT trusty and welbeloved frend, I grete you wel; and for as mych as I have understande that ze have do take a distresse of certayn bestes upon certayn land, which I stande inffeffed in, in the town of Pagrave, for what cause I knowe not; wherfor I pray you that ze wyll make deliverance ageyn of the said bestes, and if any thyng ze can axe be dute of right, setteth a day, and lete your evydences and right be shewed, and I shall assigne conceill of myn to be there to se it; and all that reson or lawe wyll, I wyll be right glad ze have, and otherwise I trowe ze wold not desire. And if ze wyll do this, I wyll be wel paied, and elles ze constreyn me to pourveye other wise, as lawe may gyde me. Oure Lord have you in governance. Writen at Walsyngham, the xvij. day of May.

Youre frend,   THE LORD SCALES.

247

BOTONER TO JOHN PASTON[2]

To my Maister Paston.

JUNE 8

WORSHYPFULL Syr, and my gode maister, after dewe recomendacion, wyth alle my trewe servyce precedyng, lyke you wete that as to nouveltees, &c., the Prince shall be create at Wyndesour, uppon Pentecost

[1] [From Fenn, iii. 200.] This letter is dated by a contemporary note at the bottom of the original, which is given thus in Fenn : 'Li't āā Mich. xxxiij.' But for 'āā,' according to the Errata in vol. iii., we should read 'āē,' i.e. 'Litteræ *ante* Mich. [Festum S. Michaelis] xxxiij.' [i.e. anno Regis xxxiii.].
[2] [From Fenn, i. 76.]

320

THE PASTON LETTERS

1454
JUNE 8

I sende a lettre to Maister Berney to lete you see for the gouvernaunce yn Yorkshyr.

BOTO-H.R.-NER.[1]

248

R. DOLLAY TO JOHN PASTON[2]

Un to my ryght worshypfull Mastyr Paston, be thys byll delyveryd in haste.

JUNE 29

RYGHT trusty and well belovyd master, I recomande me un to yow, desyryng to her of your good prosperite and wellfar. And as towchyng for Ser Phylyp Wentforde, he rood on to London ward up on Seynt Jon ys day, and on the evyn afor he sent to my master for to have sum of hys men for to ryd with hym to Colchester; and for be cawse he shulde not have no suspesion to me, I rod myself and a felaw with me; and he rood with an C. [*hundred*] hors with jakks[3] and saletts,[4] and rusty habyrjons;[5] and ther rood with hym Gyboun of Debnem, and Tympyrle, and all the felashyp that they cowd make. And Gyboun seyde that he wolde

[1] William Worcester, or Botoner, as he called himself indifferently, secretary to Sir John Fastolf. He frequently introduces the letters 'H. R.' into or above his signature, and sometimes at the top of his letter. Fenn reads the name 'Botener,' which is certainly wrong according to the facsimile given of the signature in this place.
[2] [From Fenn, iii. 210.] This letter gives an account of certain proceedings for taking possession of the person of a minor in opposition to the claims of Paston and Sir John Fastolf as guardians. Fenn supposes the ward in question to have been Thomas Fastolf of Ipswich; but it appears, by a petition afterwards presented to Parliament (see *Rolls of Parl.* v. 371), that he was another Thomas Fastolf, viz. the son of John Fastolf, Esq. of Cowhawe, Suffolk, whose wardship was granted on the 6th June 1454 to John Paston, Esq., and Thomas Howes, clerk. The St. John's day mentioned in this letter is therefore St. John the Baptist's day, 24th June, not St. John the Evangelist's, 27th December.
[3] The jack or jacket was a military vestment, calculated for the defence of the body, composed of linen stuffed with cotton, wool, or hair quilted, and commonly covered with leather.—F.
[4] A salet was a light helmet of various construction.—F.
[5] The haubergeon was a coat composed either of plate or chain-mail without sleeves. For a fuller account and view of these, the reader is referred to Mr. Grose's accurate *Treatise on Ancient Armour and Weapons*, 4to, 1785.—F.

322

HENRY VI

Sonday,[1] the Chaunceller,[2] the Duc of Bokyngham, and manye othyre Lordys off astate, present wyth the Quene.

1454
JUNE 8

As to my Lord Yorke, he abydyth aboute Yorke tille Corpus Crist Feste[3] be passyd, and wyth grete worship ys there resseyved.

And certeyn Justices, Prysot,[4] Byngham,[5] Portyngton,[6] and &c., be thedre for execucion of justice uppon such as hafe offendended yn cause creminall.

It ys seyd the Duc of Exceter[7] ys here coverdtlye. God send hym gode councell hereafter.

And the Pryvee Sele[8] ys examynyd how, and yn whate maner, and be whate autorite prevye selys were passed forthe in that behalf, whych ys full innocent and ryght clere yn that mater, as it ys welle knowen.

The Frenshmen hafe be afore the Isles of Gersey and Gernessey, and a grete navey of hem, and v^c. [500] be taken and slayn of hem by men of the seyd trew Isles, &c.

Syr Edmond Mulso ys come from the Duc of Burgoyne;[9] and he seyth, by hys servaunts rapport, that he wolle not discharge the godes of the mrchaunts of thys land, but so be that justice be don uppon the Lord Bonevyle, or els that he be sent to hym to do justice by hym self, as he hath deserved, or satisfaccion be made to the value.

Yowr mater[10] is enseled as of the thyng ye wote of.

I can no more for haste and lak of leyser, but our Lord kepe you. Wryt hastly viij. of June.

[1] June 9 in 1454.
[2] Richard Nevill, Earl of Salisbury, was appointed Chancellor on the 2nd April 1454.
[3] June 20 in 1454.
[4] John Prisot, Chief Justice of the Common Pleas.
[5] Richard Bingham, a Justice of the King's Bench.
[6] John Portington, a Justice of the Common Pleas.
[7] Henry Holland, Duke of Exeter. On the 11th May this year he had been ordered to appear before the Council on the following Thursday (16th May).—See Nicolas's *Privy Council Proceedings*, vi. 180.
[8] His name was Thomas Lyseux.—See *Patent Roll*, 32 Hen. VI., m. 14.
[9] Philip the Good, Duke of Burgundy.
[10] Doubtless the grant of the wardship of Thomas Fastolf of Cowhawe.—See p. 322, Note 2.

HENRY VI

endyte as many as he cowde understonde that wer of the toder party; and longe Bernard was ther also; and he mad Ser Phylyp Wentforde to torne ageyn, and maad every men to beende her bowys, and lyth down of hier hors for to wyte and ony man wolde come ageynstem, and he seyde how he shulde not let hys wey nor for Ser John Fastolf nor for Paston, nor for noon of hem all.

1454
JUNE 29

And as for the ward,[1] he was not ther, but ther was had anoder chyld lyk hym, and he rood next hym, and whan that he was ij. myle be zonde Colchester, he sent hym hoomageyn with a cer tey[n] meyny. And Ser Phylyp Wentforde, and Gyboun of Debnem, and Tymperle, and Bernard, they took a man of Stratford, a sowter,[2] and hys name ys Persoun; and they enqueryd hym of every manys name of the toder party, and he tolde hem as many as he cowde; and they bad hym enquer ferther for to knowe all, for they desyryd of hym for to enquer as fer as he cowde, and he shulde have well for hys labor.

No mor to yow at thys tyme, but the Holy Gost have yow in hys kepyng.

Wretyn at Hadley, the Saturday after Seynt John ys day. And I beseeche yow hertyly recomande me to my Master Alblaster.

By yowr man,   R. DOLLAY.

249

WILLIAM BOTONER TO JOHN PASTON[3]

To my gode maister, John Paston, Escuier, in Norwich, and yn hys absence, to John Berney, at Caister, Squyer.

JULY 5

WORSHYPFULL Sirs, I recomaund me to yow. Lyke yow wete that as to the waraunts and copes that ye remembrd to be gheten owt, it ys laboured for, &c.

[1] Thomas, son of John Fastolf, Esq. of Cowhawe.   [2] A shoemaker.
[3] [From Fenn, i. 140.] The year in which this letter was written must be that of the mayoralty of Robert Sturmy at Bristol, as shown in p. 324, Note 2. It certainly could not be 1457, Fenn's date, as Lord Cromwell died in January 1456.

323

THE PASTON LETTERS

1454
JULY 5
And as to the assisse, it shall hald at Norwych, the Monday next com fortendayes.

The Duc of York, the Lord Cromewell, and othyr Lordys of the North that were wyth my seyd Lord York, comen hedre by Monday next, as it ys credybly seyd. The Lordys that be appoynted to kepe the see maken hem redye yn all haste; and the Tresourer also, the Lord Wyltshyre [1] for the west coost. And a stately vessell, only for the warre, ys made new at Brystow by the Mayr, called Sturmyn.[2] And the seyd toune with the west coosts wolle do her part, and [i.e. *if*] they may be supported or favoured.[3]

Mastere Pownyngs [4] hath day tille the next terme by a

[1] James Butler, Earl of Wiltshire and Ormond. He was appointed Lord Treasurer of England on the 15th March 1455 (Patent, 33 Henry VI., p. 2, m. 20), but on the 29th May following the office was taken from him, and given to Henry, Viscount Bourchier (*Ib.* m. 12). But this letter, which is dated in July, cannot be in 1455; indeed, we have positive evidence that it is in 1454. How, then, are we to explain the manner in which Wiltshire is referred to above? It is just possible—though not likely, as Wiltshire was a Lancastrian—that his appointment may have been enrolled in the wrong year, and that he was really made Lord Treasurer on the 15th March 1454. A difference in punctuation will perhaps solve the difficulty best:—'The Lords that be appointed to keep the see maken hem ready yn all haste, and the Treasourer also: the Lord Wyltshyre for the west coast.' John Tiptoft, Earl of Worcester, is mentioned as Lord Treasurer on the 11th February 1454.—See *Rolls of Parl.* v. 238.

[2] The name was printed by Fenn 'St'myn,' and in the modern version on the opposite page, 'St. Myn.' Robert Sturmy was Mayor of Bristol in the year 1453-4. It was probably this very ship that was captured by the Genoese in 1457, of which disaster there is the following notice in the MS. Calendars of Bristol:—'Mr. Robert Sturney [*alias* Sturmey], who was Mayor in 1453, had this year a ship spoiled in the Mediterranean Sea by the Genoese, which ship had gotten much wealth as having been long forth. She had spices fit to be planted here in England, as was reported, but the men of Genoa in envy spoiled her. Which wrong, when King Henry understood, he arrested the Genoa merchants in London, seized their goods, and imprisoned their persons, until they gave security to make good the loss; so that they were charged with £6000 indebted to Mr. Sturney.'—Seyer's *Memoirs of Bristol*, ii. 189.

[3] 'The said town,' it would appear, did 'do her part' on the occasion; for besides this ship fitted out by the Mayor, Bristol subscribed £150 to a loan raised by the Duke of York from the seaports for the protection of trade. This sum may appear insignificant for a flourishing seaport; but London itself only subscribed £300, and Southampton, which was the next largest contributor, only £100, while Norwich and Yarmouth contributed the latter amount between them.—Seyer's *Bristol*, ii. 188; see also *Rolls of Parl.* v. 245. We must remember, however, that these sums probably represent about fifteen times their value in modern currency. At all events, by comparison with other places, Botoner had no cause to be ashamed of his native town.

[4] Robert Poynings.—*See* p. 154, Note 3.

324

remayner. Manye a gode man ys hert he hath.[1] God comfort hym in ryght!

And justice ys don dayly uppon thevys and malefactours, and people be glad that justice may procede.

The Lord Bourchier hath a gode renomee of hys wyse demenyng at Calis, but he ys not yhyt comen.

The Soudeours be more temperat then they were. Not ell[es] for lak of leyser, but our Lord kepe yow.

Wryt at L. [London], the v. day of Jullet.

Gressam qwyts hym well yn your erandys doyng to me.

Your, W. BOTONER.

1454
JULY 5

250

EDMUND, LORD GREY OF HASTINGS TO JOHN PASTON [2]

To my trusty and wele belovid John Paston, Squyer, be this lettre delivered.

TRUSTY and welebelovid frend, I comaund me to zow, certifying zow that and zour sustyr be not zit maried, y trust to God y know that where she may be maried to a gentylman of iii. C. [300] marc of lyvelod, the which is a grete gentylman born, and of gode blode; and yf ze think that y shall labore ony ferder therynne, y pray zow send me word by the bringer of this lettre, for y have spoke with the parties, and they have granted me that they wolle procede no ferder therynne tyll y speke with hem azen; and therfore, y pray zow, send me word in hast how that ze wylle be desposed therynne; and God have zow in hys kepyng. W[r]ettin at Ampthill, the xj. day of July last past.

JULY 11

BY EDMOND GREY, LORD OF HASTYNGES, WAIFFORD, AND OF RUTHYN.

[1] 'Many a good man's heart he hath.'—We should have thought this explanation unnecessary, but that Fenn, in his modern version, gives the following most extraordinary rendering:—'Many a good man is hurt (*that*) he hath.'

[2] [From Fenn, iii. 214.] This letter is dated by a memorandum at the bottom of the original, in the handwriting of John Paston—'Liberat. per Will. Aleyn, valetum dicti domini xiiij. die Julii anno xxxij°. H. vi.'

325

THE PASTON LETTERS

251

SIR JOHN FASTOLF TO THOMAS HOWYS [1]

To my ryght trusty frende Sir Thomas Howys, Parson of Castelcombe.

1454
JULY 12
RYGHT trusty frende, I grete you well, and wolle ye wete that I thynk it to greete merveylle of your trouth and wysdom that ye shuld haf, that ye hafe noysed me, and seyd to John Andreus at Yeppyswych, in presence of dyvers men, that ye have suffisaunt waraunts undre my lettre and sele to safe you harmlese, in case ye be condempned yn the somme this Andreus sewyth you for. And know for certeyn, there passed no such warauntis undre my sele; nothyr I comaunded you not for to labour ne do thyng that shuld be ayenst the law, nether unlawfully ayenst ryght and trouth. And therfor y ought not ne wolle not pay for yow. Wherfor I charge you sende me your warauntis and lettres or acomp of them, and of whoos hand wrytyng they ben; and whate evidences, instruccions and informacions ye had and by whom, as well as of my lerned councell as of othyrs. And also that ye comyn with my cosyn John Paston, &c., and take his gode avice whate remedie ys best, whethyr to sew an atteynt ayenst th'enquest a *decies tantum* in your oune name or by the parlement; for y wolle do seke all the remedies that may be had ayenst the seyd Andreus. And kepe ye close and sure from hym in all maner wyse, for your oune welfare; for know ye for certeyn that Andreus wolle ley all the wayt and aspies of such as ye wene to take for your true frendys to arrest you; and then be ye as it were be thout remedie, for ye not be tyme to sende me the materes abofe specyfyed.

Item, Robert Inglose hath spoke wyth me and hath offred me to by lond to satisfye my dewtee that lyeth in Rakhyth, and y am avysed to by it, if ye can send thedre som trusty man that can telle whate it ys worth cleerly, and off whome

[1] [Add. MS. 34,888, f. 102.]

326

it ys halde, and also yf it be sure lyvelode, and your avice wythall; but beware that ye com not owt, God kepe you. Wryt at London in haste the xij. day of Julle, A° xxxij do. Regni Regis Henrici vj. JOHN FASTOLF, ch'l'r.

1454
JULY 12

252

JOHN PASTON TO LORD GREY [1]

Dominus de Grey.

RIGHT worshipfull and my ryght gode Lord, I recomand me to yowr gode Lordship. And where as it pleasyd yowr Lordship to dyrecte yowr letter to me for amaryage for my por suster to a jantylman of yowr knowleth of CCC. marc lyflod, in cas she wer not maryd; wherfor I am bownd to do your Lordship servyse; forsothe, my Lord, she is not maryd, ne insurid to noman; ther is and hath be, dyvers tymys and late, comunycacion of seche maryages wyth dyvers jantylmen not determynyd as yett, and whedder the jantylman that yowr Lordchip menith of be on of hem or nay I dowth. And wher as your seyd letter specyfyith that I shall send yow word whedder I thowght ye shuld labour ferther in the mater or nay, in that, my Lord, I dare not preswme to wryte so to yow wythowte I knew the gentylmans name,—notwythstandyng, my Lord, I shall take uppe on me, wyth the avyse of other of here frendys, that she shall nother be maryd ner inswryd to no creatwr, ne forther prosede in no seche mater befor the fest of the Assumpcion of owr Lady next comyng, dwryng whyche tyme yowr Lordship may send me, if itt please yow, certeyn informacion of the seyd gentylmanys name, and of the place and contrey where hys lyfflod lyth, and whedder he hath any chylder, and, after, I shall demene me in the mater as yowr Lordship shall be pleasyd; for in gode feyth, my Lord, it were to me grette joy that my seyd pore

JULY 15

[1] [From Fenn, iii. 216.] This letter is the answer to No. 250, originally printed from a copy in Paston's own handwriting, without signature.

327

1454
JULY 15
suster were, according to hier pore degre, marijd be yowr avyse, trustyng thanne that ye wold be here gode Lord.

Ryght wurchipfull and my ryght gode Lord, I beseche Almghty God to have yow in His kepyng. Wrete att Norwych, the xv. day of Jull.

253

THOMAS PLAYTER TO JOHN PASTON[1]

To my ryght reverent and worshipfull maister, John Paston, be this dylyverd at London, and ellys sent to hym to Norwic.

JULY 20 RYGTH worshipfull Sir, and my rygth good maister, I recomend me to you. Lyke you to wete I have spoken wyth my lord Chanceler[2] and put the bylle by for hym and all the lordis upon Wednesday at after non last past, wenyng to me to have an answer upon Thursday. And my lord Chanceler told me that they sped no partycler mater yet syn they cam, nor han no leyser to attend swych maters. I have spoken to my Lord Wylchyre,[3] and he promysed to help forth that he can, and my Lord Beauchamp[4] bothe. Fenyngley cam but on Thursday at evyn. Item, Sir, I have do made a new bylle whyche I purpose to delyver to the kyng. And, Sir, the lordes merveyle sore of the entre that was made by th͛ straunge man or my lord entred; they thynk that was a straunge werk and a sotyll. Item, I spake to my Lord Chanceler how my maister[5] and ye and your frendis were pute owte of the comyssyon of pees; neverthe les he hath not graunted yet non newe. And as for the questyon that ye wylled me to aske my lord, I fond hym yet at no

[1] [Add. MS. 34,889, f. 217.] The reference to Lord Wiltshire proves the date of this letter to lie between 1449 and 1460, and it would seem to be 1454 when the 20th July was a Saturday, Wednesday and Thursday being spoken of as past dates and Monday as a future one.
[2] Richard, Earl of Salisbury.
[3] James Butler, Earl of Wiltshire and Ormonde.
[4] John, Lord Beauchamp.   [5] Sir John Fastolf.

328

good leyser. Item, Sir, after the lordys seying, the Councell schuld breke up on Monday next comyng. And as for the Archebysshop of York[1] is heyll and mery, &c. Wretyn the xx. day of July.—By your man and servaunt, 1454
JULY 20

THOMAS PLAYTER.

254

WILLIAM PASTON TO JOHN PASTON[2]

To his wurchypfull Brodyr, John Paston.

[JULY] RYTH wurchypfull broder, I recomande to yow; and as for tedyng, my Lord of Yorke hathe take my Lord of Exsater[3] in to hys awarde. The Duke of Somerset[4] is styll in prison, in warse case than he was. Syr Jon Fastolf recomande hym to yow, &c. He wyll ryde in to Norfolke ward as on Trusday, and he wyll dwelle at Caster, and Skrop[5] wyth hym. He saythe ye ar the hartyest kynysman and frynd that he knowyts. He wolde have yow at Mawdeby dwellyng.

I had gret cher of Byllyng be the way, and he told me in cownsayle wathe he sayd to Ledam.

Ledam wulde a do hys wyse to a mad a complent to Pryothe[6] in the scher-howse of yow, and Byllyng consallyd hym to leve, and tolde Ledam ye and he wer no felawys, and sayd to Ledam, 'That is the gyse of yowr contre men, to spend

[1] William Booth was Archbishop of York from 1452 to 1464. If the letter had been earlier Cardinal Kemp would have been Archbishop of York, and would have been called 'Cardinal of York.'
[2] [From Fenn, i. 72.] The date of this letter is fixed by the fact referred to in Note 3, and by Sir John Fastolf's going into Norfolk, which, though delayed a little later than is here projected, certainly did take place in 1454. See another letter of William Paston further on, dated 6th September.
[3] Henry Holland, Duke of Exeter. On the 24th July the Duke of York was charged by the Privy Council to convey him to Pomfret Castle.—*See* Nicolas's *Privy Council Proceedings*, vi. 217.
[4] Edmund Beaufort, Duke of Somerset, who was committed to the Tower in the end of the year 1453.—*See* p. 290, Note 1.
[5] Stephen Scroope, Sir John Fastolf's ward, son of Lady Fastolf, by her former husband.
[6] John Prisot, Chief Justice of the Common Pleas.

329

1454
[JULY]
alle the good they have on men and lewery gownys, and hors and harnes, and so beryt owth for j wylle [*bear it out for a while*], and at the laste they arn but beggars; and so wyll ye do. I wylde ye schull do wyll, be cause ye ar a felaw in Grays In, wer I was a felaw. As for Paston, he ys a swyr [squire] of wurchyp, and of gret lyvelode, and I wothe he wyll not spend alle hys good as [*at ?*] onys, but he sparyt yerly C. mark, or j. C. *li.* [£100]; he may do his ennemy a scherewd turne and never far the warse in hys howsholde, ner the lesse men abowthe hym. Ye may not do so, but if yt be for j. [*one*] sesun. I consayll yow not to contenu long as ye do. I wulle consalle yow to seke reste wyth Paston.'

And I thankkyd Byllyng on yowr behalfe.

God have yow in hys kepyng.

Be yowr por Brodyr,   WYLLYAM PASTON.

Meche odyr thyng I can telle an I had lesur. Recomande me to my suster Margeth [and] my cosyn Elizabeth Clyr, I pray yow.

255

WILLIAM PASTON TO MARGERY PASTON[1]

To his rythe worchypfull and harthy wellebelovyd suster, Margere Paston, dwellyng in Norwyche.

[1454]
AUG. 10
RYTHE harthely well belovyd suster, I recomand me, &c. And I have received zowre letteres. And as for my nevewes, they lerne rythe well bothe, and there gownys and there gere schall be mad for hem a cordyng the enthenthe of zowre letter, and all oder thynggis that behovyth on to here profythe harddely to my powere.

[1] [Add. MS. 33,597, f. 5.] This letter is in the handwriting of William Paston, son of the judge; but the 'Margery' Paston to whom it is addressed seems to be his brother John's wife, Margaret. His nephews, John Paston's sons, were at school in London. His sister Elizabeth, who was married to Robert Poynings in 1458, is here said to be upon the point of marriage, but no doubt this refers to the negotiations of the year 1454, as the eldest of John Paston's sons must have been sixteen in 1458. St. Laurence's day, on which the letter was written, is the 10th August.

330

And, Suster, God zelde zow for zowre labore fore me, for gaderyng of my mony. And I pray, as sone as ze receyvyth, send it heder be some trusty man; and that I plese to calle ther on, &c. My suster and my broder recomand hem to zow bothe, and I may say to zow in counsayll sche is op on poyn of mariage, so that moder and my broder sett frendely and stedfastely there on, leke as I wothe well ze wolld, and it lay in zow as it dothe in hem, &c. I pray zow do zoure parthe to kall theron. It were to long to wrythe on to zow all the maner of demenyng of this mater; and therfor I have spoke to Wyllyam Worseter and to Wethewell to tell it zow holly as it is. I wothe ryth well zow (*sic*) good labore may do moche; and send me word how ze here as hastely as ze may. Item, Howard spak of a mariage betwex his sone and my neece Margery, zowr dother: it wer well do such materes wer nawthe sclawfully laboryd; it is wurchypfull, &c. Send me word, and Gog (*sic*) have zow in His kepyng. Wretyn at London on Sent Lawrens day in hast.—Be zowre brodyre,
[1454]
AUG. 10

WYLLYAM PASTON.

Item, send zow a letter directyd to Wollysby. I pray zow lethe it be delyvered hym as hastely as ze may; and if ze come to this contre I am leke to se zow, and we schall make rythe mery I trust.

256

RICHARD, DUKE OF YORK, TO JOHN PASTON[1]

To our right trusty and welbeloved John Paston, Esquire.

The Duc of York.

RIGHT trusty and welbeloved, we grete yow hertily wel. And of your benivolence, aide, and tendre love by yow, at th'instance and at the reverence of us, to our right trusty and welbeloved in God, the prior and convent of
1454
AUG. 19

[1] [From Fenn, i. 92.] This and the following letter could hardly have been written in any year except 1454 or 1455, when the Duke of York was in power. In the former year he is very likely to have been at his own castle of Sandal on the 19th August, seeing that on the 24th July he was commissioned to convey the Duke of Exeter to Pomfret Castle.

331

1454
AUG. 19 the hows of Our Lady of Walsingham, of our patronage, in such matres as they had adoo for certain lyvelood by tham claymed to belonge unto the seid hows, favorably and tendrely shewed,—as hertily as we can we thank yow, and desire and pray yow of your good continuance; and as far as right, lawe, and good conscience wol, to have in favorable recommendacion suche personnes as been or shal bee committed to take possession and saison, in the name and to the use of our ful worshipful nepveu, th'erl of Warrewic, in and of the manoirs and Lordeships of Boules and Walcots,[1] with th'appertenauntes in Litel Snoring in the countee of Norffolk, as our grete trust is unto yow. And God have yow in His keping.

Yeven undre our signet at our castel of Sandhall the xix. day of August.

R. YORK.

257

THE EARL OF WARWICK TO JOHN PASTON[2]

*To the worshipfull and my right trusty frende
John Paston, Squyer.*

AUG. 23 WORSHIPFULL and my right trusty and welbeloved frende, I grete you well. And forasmuch as I have purchased of the worshipfull and my welbeloved frende, Priour of Walsyngham, ij. maners in Lityl Snoryng, with thappurtenants, in the Counte of Norffolk, which maners

---

[1] According to Blomefield (vii. 186), Catherine, widow of John Cokerell of Albergh Wykes in Suffolk, died seised of the manors of Walcotes and Boles in 6 Henry VI., which she left, with others, to Catherine, daughter of John Cokerell, junior, her son, who died before his father. This younger Catherine died a minor in 10 Henry VI., and the jury knew not who was her heir. In 29 Henry VI. George Heath of Mildenhall released to Humphrey, Duke of Buckingham, all his rights in Walcotes and Boles; but in the 18th of Henry VII. Christopher Conyers and Alice his wife conveyed it to the Heydons. Of its having been purchased by the Earl of Warwick or having belonged to the Prior of Walsingham, as stated in the next letter, Blomefield tells us nothing except that Richard, Earl of Warwick, presented to the rectory of Snoring Parva in 1460 and 1466.

[2] [From Fenn, i. 88.] See preliminary note to the last letter (p. 331, Note 1).

be cleped Bowles and Walcotes,—I desir and hertily praye 1454
yow, that ye woll shewe to me, and my feoffes in my name, AUG. 23
your good will and favour, so that I may by your frendship the more peasably rejoy my forsaid purchase.

And more over I praye you to yeve credens in this mater to my welbeloved chapellayn, Syr John Suthwell, berer of this my lettre, and in the same mater to be my feithfull frende, as my gret trust is in you, wherin ye shall do to me a singular pleasir, and cause me to bee to yow right good lord, which sumtyme shall be to you available by the grace of God, who preserve you and sende you welfare.

Yeven under my signet at Midilham, the xxiij. day of August.

RICHARD, ERL OF
WARREWIK. } R. WARREWYK.

258

WILLIAM WORCESTER TO JOHN PASTON[1]

To my Maister Paston.

H. R.

AFTYR dewe recomendacion wyth my simple service 1454(?
precedyng, please your maistershyp to wete, that SEPT. 2
as to such remembrance that ye desyre me to contynew forth to the uttermost, I shall wyth gode wille, so as my maister wille licence me, as oft as I can, th'officer to hafe

---

[1] [From Fenn, iii. 318.] This and the next letter were certainly written on the same day, but the precise year may be questioned. From a comparison of the two together, with William Barker's letter of the 3rd Nov. following (No. 265), I am inclined to think all three belong to the year 1454, when Sir John Fastolf had just come to settle for the rest of his days in Norfolk. Sir John Fenn, I think rightly, considers this first letter to have been written between jest and earnest; and this tone may be very well explained by the supposition, that on Fastolf's settlement at Caister, Worcester expected to have had some position of importance assigned to him in his master's household. That such would be his fortune was probably the expectation of others as well as himself, and apparently John Paston had written to him in the belief that Worcester's influence with Sir John might occasionally be of value to him.

The
Paston Letters
Volume 3

THE PASTON LETTERS

Henry VI

260

WILLIAM PASTON TO JOHN PASTON[1]

To my rith wurchipfull brodir, Jon Paston, be this delyveryd.

RYTH wurchyfull brodyr, I recomande me to zow, desiryng to her of zowr willefar. Byllyng[2] the serjant hathe byn in his contre, and he come to Lundon this weke ; he sent for me and ast me how I fared ; I tolde hym her is pestelens, and sayd I fard the better he was in good hele, for it was noysyd that he was ded. A toke me to him and ast how my suster dede, and I answeryd wyll, never better. He seyd he was with the Lord Gray,[3] and they talkyd of j. jantilman qweche is ward to my Lord—I remember he sayd it was Harry Gray that thei talkyd of ; and my Lord sayd, 'I was besy with jn this fewe days to a maryd hym to a jantyllwoman jn Norfolke that schall have iiij. C.

1454
SEPT. 6

---

[1] [From Fenn, iii. 220.] There is abundant evidence that the year in which this letter was written was 1454. The references to Lord Grey's offer of a husband for Elizabeth Paston, and to Sir John Fastolf's going into Norfolk, of which William Paston had before written by anticipation, though a little prematurely, in No. 254, are in themselves sufficient to fix the chronology ; but the mention of fealty having been done by a new Archbishop of Canterbury and a new Bishop of Ely removes any possible doubt on the subject.

[2] Thomas Billing was made a serjant in 1453, and about 1469 was appointed Chief Justice of the King's Bench.

[3] Edmund, Lord Grey of Ruthyn.—*See* Letter 250.

VOL. III.—A

I

THE PASTON LETTERS

1454
SEPT. 6

marc to hyr mariage, and now a wyll not be me, for iiij. C. marc wulde do me hese ; and now he wulde have his mariage mony hymself, and therefore (quoth he) he schall mary hym self for me.'

This wurds had my Lorde to Byllyng, as he tollde me, he understod that my Lord laboryd for his owne a vayle, and consaylyd to byd her be wyse ; and I thanlkeyd hym for hys good consayll.

I sent zow an answer of zowr letter of Sir Jon Fastolf comyng hom, as he told me hem self ; neverthe lesse he bode longer than he sayd hymself he schull a do.

He tolde me he schulde make j. [*one*] ende be twix Skroop[1] and my suster wulle he is in Norfolke. Many wulde it schulde not prove, for thei say it is an onlykkely mariage.

In casse Cressener be talkyd of ony mor, he is countyd a jantyllmanly man and a wurshepfull. Ze knowe he is most wurchipfull better than I. At the reverens of Good, drawe to sume conclusyn ; it is time.

My Lord Chanseler[2] come not her sone I come to Lundon, nether my Lord of Yorke.[3]

My Lord of Canterbury[4] hathe received hys crosse, and I was with hym in the kynggs chamber qwan he mad hys homage. I tolde Harry Wylton the demeanyng betwix the kyng and hym ; it war to long to wrythe.

As for the prist that dede areste me, I can not understand that it is the pryste that ze mene.

Her is gret pestelens. I purpose to fle in to the contre. My Lord of Oxforthe is come azen fro the se, and he hath geth hym lytyll thank in this countre. Much more thyng I wulde wrythe to zow, but I lak lysore.

Harry Wylton sey the Kyng. My Lord of Ely[5] hathe

---

[1] Stephen Scroope.—*See* vol. ii. p. 108, Note 4.

[2] Richard Nevill, Earl of Salisbury, was appointed chancellor in April 1454.

[3] Richard, Duke of York, at this time Protector.

[4] Thomas Bourchier, who was translated from the Bishopric of Ely to Canterbury in April 1454.

[5] William Grey. He received his temporalities by a patent of the date of this letter, 6th September 1454, which shows that he had by that time done fealty.

2

HENRY VI

do hys fewthe [*his fealty*]. God have zow in his blyssyd kepyng.

1454
SEPT. 6

Wretyn at Lundon on the Fryday be for owr Ladys day, the Natyvite, in gret hast. I pray recomand me to my suster, and cosyn Cler.

Be yowr broder, WM. PASTON.

261

ABSTRACT[1]

Sir John Fastolf to John Paston.

Has searched among his evidence, and found a release of Nycolas Bockyng of his messuage and lands in Castre, 'sometime Fraunceys and afterward John Barboures, and Cassandre his wife,' which is enrolled *in Banco, Rotulo primo de cartis scriptis, de termino Sc. Trin. anno r. R. Henr. Sexti, 23°.* Send me the copy of it. (*Signature not in his own hand.*)

1454-9
SEPT. 19

Castre, 19 Sept.

[The year in which this letter was written is uncertain, but it cannot be earlier than 1454, when Fastolf came to Caister, nor later than 1459, as he died in November of that year.]

262

RICHARD SOUTHWELL TO JOHN PASTON[2]

To the right reverent and worshippfull John Paston, in haste.

RIGHT reverent and worshippfull Sir, and my right trusti and welbelovid cosin, I recomaund me unto you, praiyng you hertily to remembr me unto my Master Radclyff, so that by your gode meanes I shall mowe

1454(?)
OCT. 6

---

[1] [From MS. Phillipps, 9735, No. 227.]

[2] [From Fenn, iii. 376.] This letter must have been written during one of the periods of the Duke of York's ascendency, and on a comparison of possible years I am inclined to assign it to 1454. The date 1460, to which Fenn ascribes it, would have been highly probable but for the fact that John Paston, who was returned to Parliament in that year, does not appear to have arrived in London even on the 12th October, so that probably he had not left Norwich on the 6th.

THE PASTON LETTERS

1454(?)
OCT. 6

have his gode mastershipp, the whiche I have effectuelly to [m]y power sewed fore iij. yer, and never deserved the contrarye to my knowlege, by my trouth ; and if it can or may be founden that I have, I will obeye me, and offre me to abyde the rewle of you and my cosin your brothir, &c.

Also my Lord of Caunterbury [1] Master Waltier Bl[a]kette will help forthe, if nede be ; and as to the remenant of the Lordes, if the case requir that ye may understand by your wysdum thei be displeased with me—as I trust to God thei be not,—I beseche you to remembr that I have aforetyme b[en] accused unto the Kings Highnesse and the Quenes for owyng my pore gode will and service unto my Lord of York and other, &c. Wherof I suppose that Thomas Bagham is remembred that I brought hym oones from my Lady a purs and v. marc therin, and to Sir Phelipp Wenteworth an other and a Cs. [100s.] therin for their gode will and advise therin to my Lady and all us that were appelled for that cause, notwithstanding the King wrote to my Lord by the meanes of the Duc of Somersette, [2] that we shuld be avoyded from hym, &c. And within this ij. yer we wer in like wise laboured ageyns to the Quene, so that she wrote to my Lord [3] to avoyde us, saiyng that the King and she coude nor myght in no wyse be assured of hym and my Lady as long as we wer aboute hym, with much other thing, as may be sufficiently proved by the Quenes writing under herr own signett and signe manuell, the whiche I shewd to my Lord of Caunterbury and other Lordes, &c.

I prey you have me excused that I encombr you with thees matiers at this tyme, for me thinketh ye shuld will and desire me to do any thing to your honour and pleaser at any tyme, wherto I shal be redy and welwilled to my power by the grace of God, who have you ever in his keping, and all youres.

Writon at Norwiche, on Seint Feithes day, in haste.

Youres,   RIC. SUTHWELL.

[1] Thomas Bourchier.
[2] Edmund Beaufort, Duke of Somerset.
[3] John Mowbray, Duke of Norfolk, in whose household R. Southwell had an appointment.—F.

4

263

THOMAS HOWES TO [JOHN PASTON ?] [1]

1454
OCT. or
NOV.

PLEASE your maistreship to wete, for as mych as the wryt directed to the exchetor cam not tyl in the Vigil of Symond and Jude, [2] at viij. of the clocke at evyn, whiche coude in no wyse profit us that day ; notwithstondynge we had a yoman of my Lords chamber, and were at Cowhaw, havyng Bertylmeu Elys with us, and ther was Long Bernard sytting to kepe a court. And we at the furst Noy come in the court, and Bertylmeu havynge this termys to Bernard, seying, 'Sir, forasmych as the Kyng hathe grauntyd be hese lettres patent the wardship with the profites of the londes of T. Fastolf duryng hese nun age to you [3] and T. H., wherfor I am comyn as ther styward, be ther comaundement, upon ther pocession to kep court and lete, whiche is of old custum usyd upon thys day ; wherfor I charge you, be the vertu herof, to seas and kepe nouthir court nor lete, for ye have non autoryte.' Quod Bernard, 'I wyll kepe bothe court and lete, and ye shal non kepe here ; for there is no man hath so gret autoryte.' Than quod Bertylmeu, 'I shal sytte by you, and take a reconysaunce as ye do.' 'Nay,' quod Bernard, 'I wyl suffre you to sytte, but not to wryte.' 'Well,' quod Bertylmeu, 'thanne forsybly ye put us from our pocession, whiche I doute not but shalbe remembryd you anothir day,' &c. 'But, Seres,' quod he, 'ye that be tenaunts to this manoyr, we charge you that ye do nowthir seute nor servise, no[r] paye ony rents or fermys but to the use of John Paston and T. ; fo[r] and ye do, ye shal paye it ageyn ; and as for on yeer past, we have sewyrte of Skylly, whiche hath resevid it of you to ther use.' And thus we departid, and Bernard kept court and lete.

[1] [From Paston MSS., B.M.] This letter is anonymous, but appears to be in the handwriting of Thomas Howes. It must belong to the year 1454, when the wardship of Thomas Fastolf of Cowhaw was granted to Howes and John Paston.
[2] St. Simon and St. Jude's day is the 28th October. The Vigil is the 27th.
[3] So in MS. The writer seems to be confusing the direct and indirect mode of reporting a speech.

5

THE PASTON LETTERS

1454
OCT. or
NOV.

And ther was Ser P. Wenteworth and hise brothir, yong Hopton, yong Brewse, yong Calthorp, with xxiiij. horse ; and we spoke with non of hem, nor they with non of us, for we wold not seke upon hem. And we have enteryd in all othir plasis undir this forme. I wold we had had the wryte betymes lever than xxs. of myn owne, but it farith thus in many othir maters, God amende hem.

Memorandum.—To sende hom wyn and ij. quart botelys.

264

ABSTRACT [1]

SIR JOHN FASTOLF to his right well-beloved Brother, RICHARD WALLER.

1454-7
OCT. 30

My Lord is and hath been always my good lord, especially now that he is chief officer under the King. Commend me to his grace, and beg him to favor my matters 'as far as conscience will, ... now in mine old age.' Desires his favor and credence for Henry Fylongley and John [Pa]ston, whom he has desired to wait on Waller.

Castre, 30th Oct.

Endorsed.—'A John Paston et John Bokkyng ou William Barker.'

[This letter is written in Botoner's hand. The date is probably between 1454 and 1457, as in 1458 Botoner appears to have been in London,—at least he was so in November, and in the summer also he was away from Norfolk ; and in 1459 the 30th October would have been within a week of Fastolf's death, when he must have been ill inclined, even if capable, to dictate letters, unless of very special urgency.]

265

WILLIAM BARKER TO SIR J. FASTOLF [2]

To myn ryght worshipfull mayster, Sir John Fastolf.

1454
NOV. 3

PLEASE youre maystership, the cause of myn teryyng is that I must ben at Norwyche on Monday at the shyre to stoppe the oughtlawrye of John Porter, wheche but if be holpen, he shalben dowble oughtlawed bothe atte the sewt

[1] [From MS. Phillipps, 9735, No. 273.]
[2] [From Paston MSS., B.M.] For the date of this letter, see preliminary note to No. 258 (vol. ii. p. 333, Note 1). John Porter, who was at this time in Fastolf's service, seems to have gone immediately after into that of the Duke of Norfolk.—*See* Nos. 268, 278.

6

of the Kyng for a reskuse, as for serteyn money he oweth to on Hewghe, a man of court. And also the next day I shuld ben, if it please yow, at Saxthorp with a certeyn person, as I shal telle youre maystership here after, of whom I shuld have certeyn evydences of the maner of Saxthorp, and rentall, and fyrmall as I am promysed. And, Sire, as for alle the maters that I went fore in to Essex and Suffolk, I have spedde theym, as I shal declare to youre maystership at myn comyng, and brought wryghtyng from theym. And as for myn Lord of Norffolk, towchyng your money, he seyth ye shal have hit with inne this xiiij. dayes. Hit was his fyrst mater to me after I hadde delyvered his rynge. The money is redye, but he seyd that he must have stoor with inne hym, for he loked dayly whan the Kyng wold send for hym. But as sone as Barette, his tresorer, come home—whom he hath sent for money,—ye shall in contynent after have your Cli. [£100]. I made to his Lordship as I hadde no thyng know in the mater for onely for the excuse of Sir Thomas, &c. And I beseche the blessed Trinyte preserve yow, myn ryght wurshipfull mayster, after his pleasaunce and youre herts desyre, &c.

Wreten in hast at Wroxham, the Sonday after Allehallwen day.

Youre bedeman and servaunt,   WILLIAM BARKER.

1454
NOV. 3

266

SIR JOHN FASTOLF TO JOHN PASTON [1]

To the worshypfull and my ryght welbelovyd cosyn, John Paston.

NOV. 11

WORSHYPFULL and ryght welbelovyd cosyn, I comaund me to yow. Lyke you to wete that I have resseyved a lettre at thys tyme from John Bokkyng, wyth a copie of the patent concernyng the wardeshyp that ye wote off, by whych y understand that ye have both wrought and holpen by your grete wysdom to bryng thys matier aboute, whych y desyred your frendshyp and gode avice

[1] [From Fenn, iii. 224.]

7

1454
NOV. II

for the suertee of the seyd waarde ;[1] and for expedicion of whych y thank you ryzt hertlye, and pray you to contynew foorth your gode labours in the same yn such wyse as it may be made sure ynall wyse, thoy it cost me the more of my gode.

And where as it ys remembred me by the seyd lettres that y shuld labour to ghete the seyd ward yn to my gouvernance, truely y can not see how y coude do it to be doon, for y have none acqueyntaunce in that contree that y coude trust too, wythoute the Shyreve myght be my tender frende in thys cause, or othyr such as ye thynk best. Wherfor y pray you hertlye to take thys mater tenderly to hert, and that ye lyke seke a moyen of such frendys as ye can best avyse, and may verrayly trust uppon, to gyde thys mater yn such wyse as myne entent myght be sped for the possession of it ; for now that y have go so ferre yn the matier, I wold not it faylled for no gode, but it preved well, and toke to a gode conclusion.

And where as y have understand late, by certeyn well willers to you warde, whych have meoved me, that yn case the seyd warde myght be had, that ye desyre an alliaunce shulde take atwyx a doughter of yours and the seyd waard, of whych mocion y was ryght glad to hyre off, and wylle be ryght well wylling and helpyng that your blode and myne myght increse yn alliaunces. And yff it please yow that by your wysdom and gode conduyt that ye wolde help beere owte thys mater sub-staunciallie ayenst my partie contrarie and eville willers, that I myght have myne entent, I ensure you ye and y shuld appoynt and accorde yn such wyse as ye shuld hale you ryght well plesed both for the encresyng of your lynage and also of myne. And y pray you be ware whom ye make of your counsaille and myne yn thys mater, and that it may be well bore owte er ye com thens, and yn a sure wey ; and yff y had knowe rathyr [*i.e.* earlier] of your entent, it shuld hafe cost me more of my gode before thys, to hafe com to a gode conclusion, whych y pro-mysse yhyt shall bee, and the mater take, by the fayth of my bodye.

Worshypfull and ryght welbelovyd cosyn, y pray God spede you yn thys matier, and sende you your gode desyrs.

[1] Thomas Fastolf of Cowhawe.—*See vol. ii. p. 323, Note 1.*

8

Wreten at Castr, the xj. day of November anno xxxiij° R. H. vi.

1454
NOV II

Your cosyn, JOHN FASTOLFE.

Item, cosyn, I pray yow when ye see tyme that my Lord of Caunterbury[1] and my Lord Cromewell[2] may be spoke wyth for the godes of my Lord Bedford, beyng yn dyvers men handz, be compelled to be brought ynne, as ye shall see more along of thys mater, wyth the wrytyngs that I have made mencion, and left wyth John Bokkyng and William Barker.

267

THOMAS HOWES TO JOHN PASTON[3]

To the wurshepfull Sir, and my good Maystyr John Paston, at London, in haste.

WURSHEPFULL and reverent Sir, and my good maistyr, I recomaund me to zow in as delygent wyse as on my part apperteineth, and p[le]a[s]e yow to wete that my maistyr[4] was right well pleasyd with youre feithefull labour in fulfellyng the patent for the warrd ot A. B. C., and he wyll feithefully labour as ye have avysed hym be wrytyng of John Bokyng. And putte my maistyr in more corage, I meovyd to hym upon myn hed that encas be the child wer wyse, that thanne it wer a good maryage be twen my wyff youre doutir and hym ; and, Sir, my maistyr was glad whan he herd that moyen, cosetheryng that youre doutyr is desendyd of hym be the modyr syde. And, Sir, I have enqwerid aftyr the seyd child, and no dout of but he is lykly and of gret wyt, as I her be report of sondr personez. And it is so, as I am credebly enformyd, that Jeffrey Boleyn maketh gret labour for maryage of the seyd child to on of hese douterez. I wold well to hym, but bettyr to yow. Wherfor that ye

NOV. 13

[1] Thomas Bourchier.
[2] Ralph, Lord Cromwell.
[3] [From Fenn, iii. 230.]
[4] Sir John Fastolf.

9

1454
NOV. 13

delygently labour for expedecyon of this mater, that encas ye can fynde ony moyan ther to have the seyd child, and we shal do feithefully owre delygens in lyke wyse her, as ye avyse us, &c.

And, Sir, as ye thynke with avyse of my Maistyr Yelverton, Jenney, and otherez my maisterez counsell therin, that the Shereff may be rewardyd, and yif my seyd maisterez counsell thynke it be to do'n, that thanne ye lyke to take an actyoun upon anenteynt [*an attaint*],[1] wheche ye most with them take upon yow at thys tyme in my maisterez absence ; for as ye do in that mater, he woll hold hym content, for Wyllyam Barker hathe an instruccyon of my maisterez intent upon the same. And I send John Bokyng a copy of the panell, wheche I shewed yow at Castr, &c. Almyghty Jesu have yow eternally in hese mercyfull governaunce.

Wretyn at Castr, the Wednysday next aftyr Seynt Martyn, anno xxxiij.

TH. HOWYS.

268

SIR THOMAS HOWYS TO JOHN PASTON[2]

To the wurshepfull and reverent Sir, my good Maystir John Paston, in all goodly haste.

NOV. 18

REVERENT and wurshepfull Sir, and my good maistyr, I recomaund me to yow in as louly wyse as on my part aperteineth. And plese yow to wete that my maistyr is fully purposed to sewe ateynte, whereupon he wrytethe a lettere directyd to yow and otherez, for the wheche I beseke yow to be my good maystyr in pursewyng the seyd ateynte ; and also my maistyr is agreed what reward ye geve the Shereff he holdeth hym content. Wherfor, that youre reward may be the larger, so he woll[3] ther upon returne the panell for the seyd ateynte ; and thanne yef Jenney wold meove my Lord of

[1] This is an action against a jury that has given a false verdict.
[2] [From Paston MSS., B.M.]
[3] *Woll corr from wold.*

10

1454
NOV. 18

Norffolke that he wold be my good Lord, amyttyng me for hese chapeleyn, and Jhankyn Porter for hese servaunt, wheche is hese chek roll, it shuld cause the matere to have the redyer expedecyon, as well be the Shereff as be the gret jury. And yef the processe may have so redy sped that it myght be had be fore my Maystyr Yelwerton in this vaccacyon tyme, it wer a gret counfort, &c. Beseking yow at the reverence of God, and as ever my power servyse may be at your comaundement, that ye effectualy labour this matere in the most spedfull wyse, as youre descrecyon, with Jenneyes avyse, thinketh most exped-yent ; for I ferre gretly to be outlawed or the seyd processe shuld be brought to a conclucyon withoute redy processe in the seyd ateynte. And I here no sewer tydinges of a parlement ; but rather thanne I shuld be outlawed, I wold yeld my self to preson, wheche shuld be myn undoyng, and thanne to be with oute remedy. My refformacyon and counforte in eschewyng that lythe holly in your helpe and Jenneyez at thys tyme, be cause my maystyr hathe comytted the governaunce of the seyd matere to yow, and what expense it draweth he agreyth to bere it, &c.

I beseke Almyghty Jesu have yow, my good maystyr, eternaly in hese me[r]cyfull governaunce, and inspyre yow with hese speryt of remembraunce effectualy to procede in this matere.

Wretyn breffly at Castre the Monday next be fore Seynt Edmond the Kyng,[1] anno xxxiij. Regis H. vj[th.]

Item, Sir, as for mony to the sped of this matere, Bokkyng hathe redy in comaundement to make delevery to yow what that ye nede, so there shall be no defaute in that, &c.

T. HOWYS.

[1] The day of St. Edmund the King was the 20th November.

11

269

SIR JOHN FASTOLF TO JOHN PASTON [1]

To my right welbilovyd cosyn, John Paston.

1454-9 · · · · . . . .
. . . . wise, and for asmoche as it is
. . . . the Lady Hastinges [2]
doughter, as I undrestande . . . . . . is
lyneally descendid of my Lady Felbrig [3] is sustre . .
· · · · · · . she was maried to Sir Hug' Fastolf,
graunsir to this same Thomas; and the Lady Hastinges is
comen of Sir Robert Clyfton, which dwellid besyde Lynne.
I prey yow, cosyn, enquere of my Lady Felbrigge how nygh
they bethe of kynrede, and whethir they mow marie to ghedre
or not, and how many degrees in lynage they bethe a sundre,
for I reporte me to yowr wyse discrescion what the law wol
sey ther ynne.

Item, it is so that Wyndam [4] came yesterday to Jernemouth,
and is at Stapletons; and this day a man of Stapletons came
to me to wete if they sholde come speke with me or not, and
I have sent Sir Thomas to hem to know ther entent and what
they meane; and also he shal sey unto theym that I woll not
medle ther with but as law and consciens will.

This is the tydinges that I have; I pray yow send me
some of yours. As towching the North cuntre, Sperling hathe
tolde yow. And God kepe yow. Wretyn at Castre this same
day.   J. FASTOLF.

---

[1] [From Paston MSS., B.M.] This letter is mutilated and its date is uncertain,
except that, being dated at Caister, it must have been written between 1454 and
1459.

[2] Margery, widow of Sir Edward Hastings of Elsing, and daughter of Sir Robert
Clifton. After her first husband's death she married John Wymondham, who bought
the manor of Felbrigg from Lord Scales and the executors of Sir Simon Felbrigg.—
See Blomefield, viii. 112.

[3] Catherine, widow of Sir Simon Felbrigg. She was the daughter of Anketill
Mallory, Esq. of Winwick, in Northamptonshire.

[4] John Wymondham or Wyndham.—*See* Note 2.

12

1455
JAN. 9
he wold all the Lords were. And now he seith matyns of Our
Lady and evesong, and herith his Masse devoutly; and Richard
shall tell yow more tidings by mouth.

I pray yow recomaund me to my Lady Morley,[1] and to
Maister Prior,[2] and to my Lady Felbrigge,[3] and to my Lady
Hevenyngham,[4] and to my cosyn your moder, and to my
cosyn your wife.

Wreten at Grenewich on Thursday after Twelftheday.

Be your cosyn,

EDMUND CLERE.

271

ABSTRACT [5]

SIR JOHN FASTOLF TO HENRY FYLONGLYE AND JOHN PASTON.

JAN. 24
Must pay £40 to the Exchequer this term for the ward of Thomas Fastolf,
in part payment of £80, and other great payments at the same time, amounting
to £200 or more. Desires him, therefore, to speak with my Lord of Canterbury, whose day of payment is long past, that he may have 'the rather ready
payment' of his duty; 'for he is one of the Lords earthly that I most trust
upon.' Hopes he will consider the great loss Fastolf already sustains by
'the great good the King oweth me, and other divers Lords to my great
discomfort.'

Castre, 24 Jan.

[This letter could not have been written before the year 1455, as Sir John Fastolf
only came to reside at Castre in the autumn of the year preceding. The wardship of
Thomas Fastolf was procured by Sir John for John Paston in June 1454, so that it is
highly probable he had to pay for it in the beginning of next year. In the year following, again, Fastolf was endeavouring to make good those claims against the Crown,
which he here merely mentions as a ground of indulgence to himself.]

---

[1] *See* vol. ii. p. 84, Note 2.   [2] Probably the Prior of Bromholm.
[3] *See* p. 12, Note 3.
[4] Sir John Heveningham married Elizabeth, daughter of Sir John Reedesham.
Unless he married a second time, this Elizabeth was now his widow.
[5] [From MS. Phillipps, 9735, No. 260.]

270

EDMUND CLERE TO JOHN PASTON [1]

To my welbeloved cosyn, John Paston, be this delivered.

RIGHT welbeloved cosyn, I recomaund me to you, latyng
you wite such tidings as we have.   1455
JAN. 9

Blessed be God, the Kyng is wel amended, and hath
ben syn Cristemesday, and on Seint Jones day [2] comaunded
his awmener [*almoner*] to ride to Caunterbury wyth his offryng,
and comaunded the secretarie to offre at Seint Edwards.

And on the Moneday after noon the Queen came to him,
and brought my Lord Prynce with her. And then he askid
what the Princes name was, and the Queen told him Edward;
and than he hild up his hands and thankid God therof. And
he seid he never knew til that tyme, nor wist not what was
seid to him, nor wist not where he had be whils he hath be
seke til now. And he askid who was godfaders, and the Queen
told him, and he was wel apaid.

And she told him that the Cardinal [3] was dede, and he seid
he knew never therof til that tyme; and he seid oon of the
wisist Lords in this land was dede.

And my Lord of Wynchestr [4] and my Lord of Seint Jones [5]
were with him on the morow after Tweltheday, and he speke
to hem as well as ever he did; and when thei come out thei
wept for joye.

And he seith he is in charitee with all the world, and so

---

[1] [From Fenn, i. 80.] There is no doubt about the date of this letter. The King
fell ill at Clarendon in the autumn of 1453, and remained in a state of utter imbecility
during the greater part of the year 1454, so that in March a deputation from the
House of Peers, sent to communicate with him on the death of his Chancellor, Cardinal Kemp, was obliged to report that they had been utterly unable to obtain from him
any answer or sign that he understood the least thing said to him. It appears from
this letter that his recovery was about Christmas, when he heard for the first time of
the birth of his son fourteen months before, and of the death of Cardinal Kemp nine
months before.

[2] Dec. 27.   [3] John Kemp, Cardinal Archbishop of Canterbury.
[4] William Waynflete, Bishop of Winchester.
[5] Robert Botyll, prior of the Order of St. John of Jerusalem

13

272

SIR JOHN FASTOLF TO JOHN PASTON

*To my right trusty and welbelovyd cosyn, John Paston,
in goodly haste.*

RYGHT trusty and welbelovyd cosyn, I comaund me to
yow. And please yow to wete that I am avertysed
that at a dyner in Norwiche, wher as ye and othyr   1455
FEB. 7
jentylmen wer present, that that ther were certeyn personez,
jentylmen, whiche utteryd skornefull language of me, as in
thys wyse, with mor, seyeng, 'War the, gosune [*cousin?*] war,
and goo we to dyner; goo we wher? to Sir John Fastolf, and
ther we shall well paye ther fore.' What ther menyng was,
I knowe well to no good entent to me ward; wherfor, cosyn,
I prey yow, as my truste is in yow, that ye geve me knowelege
be writing what jentylmen they be that had this report with
more, and what mo jentylmen wer present, as ye wold I shuld
and wer my deute to do for yow in semblabyll wyse. And I
shall kepe yowr informatyon in this mater secret, and with
Godds grace so purvey for hem as they shall not all be well
pleasyd. At suche a tyme a man may knowe hese frendes and
hese fooes asonder, &c. Jesu preserve and kepe yow.

Wretyn at Caster, the vij. day of Feverer, anno xxxiij.
R. H. vj^ti.   JOHN FASTOLF, Knyght.

---

[1] [From Fenn, iii. 232.]

THE PASTON LETTERS

273

THOMAS HOWYS TO JOHN PASTON[1]

To the right wurshepfull Sir, my good Maystyr John Paston.

1455

RIGHT worshepfull Sir, and my good maistyr, I re-comaund me louly unto you, thankyng youre good maystyrshep for your good remembraunce for the cherche of Stokysby, wherupon I have desyred my trusty frend, Wylliam Worcestre, to come be the Abot[2] homward, besekyng you to avertyse hym youre good avyse how he may be have hym best in this mater to the seyd Abot, etc. And, Sir, en cas ye myght be at a leyser to be with my mayster upon Thursday next comyng, forasmyche as Maistyr Yelvyrton and Jenney shal be her, ye shuld do my maistir ryght gret pleasure. And I beseke you the rather for my sake, for at that tyme the conveyaunce of al materez shal be comounyd of ; and I know verely your avyse shall peyse depper in my maisterys conceyt thanne bothyn thers shal do. Ye have dayly gret labour for me, God reward yow, and my pore preyer ye shall have, &c. I beseke Almyghti Jesu have you in hese mercyfull governaunce, and graunt you evyr that may be to your most herte plessaunce, &c.

Your chapeleyn and bedeman,

THOMAS HOWYS.

[1] [From Paston mss., B.M.] The rectory of Stokesby in Norfolk was vacant in the year 1455. The right of presentation ought to have belonged to Sir John Fastolf, as John Fastolf—doubtless of Cowhawe—had presented in 1444 ; but it was allowed to lapse to the Bishop, who presented Simon Thornham, LL.D. Afterwards it appears that James Gloys was rector, who must have been presented by John or Margaret Paston. This letter was probably written a few days before that which comes next.

[2] Of St. Benet's, Hulme. His name was John Martin.

16

THE PASTON LETTERS

276

SIR JOHN FASTOLF TO JOHN PASTON, ESQ.[1]

To myn ryght weel beloved cosyn, John Paston, Squier.

1455
MARCH 29

WORSHIPFULL cosyn, I recomaunde me to yow. And lyke yow to wete that at this tyme I sende to yow myn welbeloved frende and servant, Sir Thomas Howys, to have youre good councell and advyse how and in what wyse he may best be demened there at this tyme in hys yeldyng to the Sheref upon his exigend, wheche is and shal be v. tymes called as on Monday next comyng, as I understande ; and, the same by good and discrete advyse con-cluded and sette in a good weye by sewertes found to appere at London the day of the retorn of the wrytte or otherwyse, that thenne if ye thenke hit be to do'n [*to do*], ye lyke to take upon yow to comon with myne Lord of Norwyche,[2] recomaundyng me to hys good and tender Lordship, and declaryng to hym how and in what wyse the seyd Sir Thomas was demened in the *oyer and determyner*, and sethe how he hath wrongously and with ought cause be vexed by John Andrews and other, and greetly trowbled, wherupon this atteynt now is grownded, in such wyse as ye thenk best to be done ; and that his Lordship by youre medyacion here after geve not any favore to any persone or persones on myne contrarye partye for any synystre informacion geven other wyse than the trought in the mater shal require, as he shal weel understande by youre good reporte, for ye know the same mater weel. Wherfore, cosyn, I praye yow that ye wole tender the same for the weel and good speed therof, as myne syngler trust is in yow. And the blessed Trynyte preserve yow to his pleaser.

In hast, at Castre, the xxix. day of Marche.

Youre, JOHN FASTOLF, Chr.

[1] [From Paston mss., B.M.] The reference here made to the process of attaint, which Fastolf had resolved to sue in November 1454 (*see* No. 268), shows that this letter must belong to the month of March following. It is written in Barker's hand.

[2] I suspect ' Norwyche ' is here a slip of the pen, and that ' my Lord of Norfolk ' was intended.

18

HENRY VI

274

THE ABBOT OF ST. BENET'S TO JOHN PASTON[1]

To my ryght well be lovyd John Paston, Esquyer, be this delivered.

WURCHEPEFULL Sire, and right well be lovyd, I grete yow well, desyryng to here of youre well fare, praying you interlych to bie with me at dyner on Seynt Benett day, the whiche xall be on Friday next comyng, or ell[es] in brief tyme covenable to your ease, to th'entent that I may commoun wyth yow of divers maters, the whiche I purpose to have a doo in be your good advyse, and in on especyall as for the chirche of Stokesby, whiche I understand xall moche be reulyd after your advyse and con-tent ; tristyng our communicacion had in the seyd [matters] xall cause pees and pleaser to all parties be leve of our Lord, the whiche Lord mote preserve you in all goode.

Wreten in my Monastery the xvij. day of Marche.

Be your good frend,

THE ABBOT OF S. BENETTS.

1455
MARCH 17

275

ABSTRACT

SIR JOHN FASTOLF TO JOHN PASTON AND —— YELVERTON.

Thanks them for speeding his action against Thomas Fauconere. Begs them to sue it out, as Fauconere is obstinate, and has wrought against Byckwod right unjustly, who owes great sums to divers creditors, etc.

Castre, 20th March.

Between
1455-9

[The date of this letter must be during Sir John's residence at Caister between 1455 and 1459.]

[1] [From Fenn, iii. 236.] This letter was written by John Martin, Lord Abbot of St. Benet's of Hulme. The heads of this monastery were mitred abbots, and sat in Parliament. The date may be assigned to the year 1455 for two reasons—first, that in that year St. Benet's day (the 21st of March) fell on a Friday ; and second, that in the same year the living of Stokesby lapsed to the Bishop of Norwich.

17

HENRY VI

Item, cosyn, I sende youre a lettre to delyver to myne seyd Lord with a copye of the same, wheche I praye yow to se, and if ye thenk hit be to do'n, delyveret [*deliver it*] youre self, &c., to th'entent he myght know the disposicion of the pepul how they be sette, &c.; for he weel advertysed in this mater shalbe a greet supporter of trought in this be half, for the partye contrarye wole do'n that they can to labore the jure, and don to have theym rewled after theyr entent and contrary to trought ; wheche mater I remytte ondly to youre ryght wyse discrecion.

1455
MARCH 29

277

SIR JOHN FASTOLF TO THE DUKE OF NORFOLK[1]

RIGHT hy and myghty Prynce, my right gode and gracyous Lord, I recomaund me to your gode Lord-ship, etc. And please itt your Hyghnesse to wete that Sir Philip Wenteworth purchasid the Kyngs patentis of the ward of the heyer and londes of a por kynnesman of myne called John Fastolf of Cowhawe, late passed to God, to the grett hurte and distruccion as well of the inherit-ance of the seyd heyer as interrupcion and breking of the last will of the seyd John, and also to my grett troble and dammage ; and for asmoche as it fortowned be grase the seyd patentes to be mystake, so that they were not laufull ne suffycyent, be avyce of conceyll, certeyn persones,[2] to myn use, purchesid be the Kyngs letters patentes suffycyent and laufull of the ward of the seyd londes. And the rigth of thes bothe patentes hath be putte in juges and lerned men, affor

MARCH (?)

[1] [From Paston mss., B.M.] The ms. of this is a corrected draft. Although the person addressed is not named, the style in which he is addressed, and particu-larly the last sentence, leave no doubt that it is the Duke of Norfolk. Indeed, this is not unlikely to be the letter mentioned in the postscript to the last, of which a copy or draft was sent along with the original to John Paston that he might deliver the latter, only if he approved of its contents. If so, it is probable that Paston withheld it, as we find by the letter immediately following that Fastolf addressed another memorial to the Duke on the subject of his dispute with Wentworth four days later.

[2] They were John Paston and Thomas Howes, and their patent was dated 6th June 32 Hen. vi. (1454).—See *Rolls of Parl.* v. 371.

19

THE PASTON LETTERS

1455
MARCH (?)

hom the seyd Sir Philipp ne his conceyll cowd never prove hes tytill lawfull be his seyd patents, and this notwithstanding intendith be fors, as I understand, to take the profytes of the seyd londes ageyns all lawe and concyence. Beseching your Lordchip to tender me in myn age and sekenesse that may not ryde ne help myself, and of your habundant grace to supporte me in my right, that I be not be fors ageyns lawe and concyence kepte from the possescion of the seyd londes in this contre, wher ye be Prynce and Sovereyn next owr Sovereyn Lord.

The following memoranda occur on the back :—

Br[adwe]ll juxta Jernemut.
Kirley juxta Leystoft, viij*li*.
Foxhole . . . .
Cowhaw in Nakton } —xviij*li*.
  on this side Yepiswich, iij. myl,
Langston in Brustall, } iij*li*.
  ij. myle beyond Yepiswich,
Bentele, ij. mile beyond Brustall, xiiij*li*. (?)

278

SIR JOHN FASTOLF TO THE DUKE OF NORFOLK [1]

APRIL 2

RIGHT high and myghty Prynce, my right noble and good Lord, in my right humble wyse I recomaunde me to your good grace. And for the noble lordship and supportacion shewid unto me at all tymes, I beseche our Lord God guerdon yow, where as I may not, but only as yowr daily and contynuell bedeman, now in myn age, pray for

---

[1] [From Fenn, iii. 338.] Although there is no direction upon this letter, it was evidently addressed to the Duke of Norfolk, as it speaks of 'your Castle of Framlingham.' The absence of any written address Fenn accounts for by supposing the letter to have been enclosed in a cover; but as it appears that the original contained at least one passage which was crossed out (*see* page 341 in Fenn), we may with greater probability consider it to have been a corrected draft, like the last, sent to John Paston for his approval. The dispute with Sir Philip Wentworth and the matters of John Porter and Sir Thomas Howes, here referred to, both point to the year 1455 as the date of this letter.—*See* Nos. 265, 268.

20

THE PASTON LETTERS

279

ABSTRACT [1]

SIR JOHN FASTOLF TO JOHN PASTON.

1455
MAY 3

Thanks him for his letters, and the answer he made to Bokkyng. Does not know how to answer him concerning the ward,[2] the suit against William Jenney and Sir Thomas, etc. If Paston could be at London this term, even for three days, it would speed better than Fastolf's writing, and Fastolf will pay his costs. If he cannot, Paston must use his own discretion, and Fastolf will abide by what he does. It would be a great rebuke if the matter of the ward went against us, 'for nowadays ye know well that law goeth as it is favored, and after that the attorneys be wise and discreet in their conduct.' Castre, 3 May.

[This letter, being dated at Caister in the month of May, cannot be earlier than 1455, and the references to the matter of the ward and the suit against Sir Thomas Howes seem to fix it to that year.]

280

ABSTRACT [3]

RICHARD CALLE TO JOHN PASTON.

1455(?)
MAY 8

Thorne did not come to him, nor could he learn anything about him from Sir Thomas Howes, except that Howes had informed him of what Paston commanded Calle to tell his wife. Will not distrain till he hear from Paston. Howys trusts to have sufficient reckoning of all things touching Fastolf, so that neither he nor Paston be hurt. He will do nothing in future without Paston's advice. Desires him to remember John Elger, Bocking, and others 'for the rescues which was made for Jankyn Porter.' Remember James Gresham to withdraw the suit for W. Magges. No News.

8 May.

[The allusion to John or Jankyn Porter in this letter makes it probable that it was written in the year 1455.—*See* No. 278.]

---

[1] [From MS. Phillipps, 9735, No. 244.]
[2] Thomas Fastolf.—*See* vol. ii. p. 323, Note 1.
[3] [From Paston MSS., B.M.]

22

1455
APRIL 2

the good prosperite of youre right highe and noble estate, as I am gretly bounde to doo; prayng tendirly yowre Highnesse to contynue yowre good lordship and supportacion in the materes touchyng your servaunt John Porter and my pore Chappelleyn Sir Thomas Howes, trustyng verily to God that, with the supportacion of your good Lordship, there mater shall yette come to a good conclusion in punisshyng of perjure and embracery that many yeris hathe ben and yette is usid in this shire, whiche were grete merite, and to my conceyte, in yow that ar soo noble a Prynce, a singler renoune, as for the beste dede that may be doo for the weel of bothe shires.

And in like wise that it please youre right good grace to contynue youre noble favour and supportacion to me in remedyeng the force doon by Sir Philip Wentworth, kepyng now wrongful possession of certeyn londes in Suffolk, nygh youre Castel of Framyngham; whiche londs certeyn of my frendes, to myn use, have of the Kyngs graunte by his lettres patent byfore ony patent that the seid Sir Philip hathe, whiche is my singler matier in myn owen parte that I have now to doo, as my cosyn Paston can enforme yowr Lordship, for he knowith the mater and myn hole entente, to whom your good grace lyke to yife credence. He cometh to awaite upon your Lordship at this tyme, as I understande, by my cosyn youre servaunt Richard Suthwell, youre Lordship desired.

Right highe and myghty Prynce, my noble and right good Lord, I beseche the Holy Goste be with yow, and evere more sende yow the accomplisshment of youre right noble desires to his plesir and youres.

Writen at my pore place of Castre, the ij^{de} day of Aprill.

Your humble man and servaunt,

J. FASTOLF.

21

HENRY VI

281

ABSTRACT [1]

'THOMAS CANON, THE HELDER, OF MEKYLL PAGRAVE,' TO JOHN PASTON.

1455
MAY 16

Desires to hear of his 'durat prosperite and welfare.' Hopes he will protect him as he has done, if any man will put him to any wrong. Has land in Lytyl Pagrave and in Lytyldonham, called Strangys, which he wishes to sell to Paston before any other, on condition that he will 'keep it counsel' from John Pagrave till he and the writer have accorded.

At Sporle, Friday, after Ascension Day, 33 Hen. VI.

282

MEMORIAL TO HENRY VI [2]

Tradatur J. P.

MAY 21

MOSTE Cristen Kyng, ryght hygh and myghty Prince, and our mooste redoubted souverayn Lorde, we recomaunde ws as humblye as we suffice unto your hygh excellence, where unto please it to wete that for so moche as we hyre and understande to our grettyst sorowe erthlye that our ennemyes of approuved experience, such as abyde and kepe theym sylf under the whyng of your Magestee Royall, have throwen unto the same ryght stedyousely and ryght fraudulentlye manye ambyguytees and doubtes of the fayth, lygeaunce, and dewtee that, God knowyth, we beere unto your Hyghnesse, and have put theym yn as grete devoyr as they coude to enstraunge ws from your mooste noble presonce and from the favour of your goode grace; whych

---

[1] [F.om MS. Phillipps, 9735, No. 252.]
[2] [From Fenn, iii. 178.] This is a copy of the memorial drawn up by the Duke of York and the Earls of Warwick and Salisbury just before the first battle of St. Albans, which the Duke of Somerset and his friends would not allow to be presented to the King. Although this copy is without date, the original was dated at Ware, the 21st May.—*See Rolls of Parl.* v. 281, where the whole document is cited.

23

1455
MAY 21
goode grace to ws ys and owe to be our singuler and mooste desyred yoie and consolacion: We at thys tyme be comyng wyth grace as your true and humble liege men, toward your seyd Hygh Excellence to declare and shew therto at large owr sayd fayth and ligeaunce, entendyng wyth the mercye of Jesu yn the seyd comyng, to put ws yn as diligent and hertye devoyr and dewtee as onye your lyege men on lyve to that at may avaunce or preferre the honnour and wellfare off the sayd Mageste Royalle and the seurte of the sayd most notable person; the whych [we] beseche our blessed Creature to prosper [in] as grete honnor, yoie, and felicitie as ever had onye prince erthlye, and to your sayd Hyghnesse so to take, accept, and repute ws, and not to plese to geve trust or confidence unto the sinistrez, maliciouse, and fraudulent laboures and rapportes of our sayd ennemyes unto our comyng to your sayd moste noble presence; where unto we beseche humblye that we may be admitted as your liege men, to th'entent to show ws the same; wheroff yerstenday we wrote our lettres of our entent to the ryght reverent fadre yn God, the Archebysshop of Caunterburye,[1] your Chauncellr of England, to be shewed to your sayd Hyghnesse, whereoff, forsomoch as we be not acerteyned whethyr our sayd entent be by hys fadrehode shewed unto your seyd goode grace or not, we sende thereoff unto thys closed a copy of our said lettres of our disposicion toward your sayd Hygh Excellence and the honnour and weele of the land, whereynne we wolle persevere wyth the grace of our Lorde.

[1] Fenn states that on the margin of the MS., in a hand nearly coeval with the letter itself, is written, 'Memorandum quod dict' literæ (?) Dominorum direct' Archiepiscopo Cant. est apud . . . . .' What followed is lost, the paper being torn. The letter to the Archbishop of Canterbury, however, will be found quoted at full length in the *Rolls of Parliament*, v. 280-1.

283

THE BATTLE OF ST. ALBANS[1]

Bellum apud Seynt Albons.

BE yt knowen and hadde in mynde that the xxj. day of May the xxxiij. zere of the regne of Kyng Herry the Sext, our sovereigne Lord Kyng toke his jurnay from Westmynster toward Seynt Albones, and rested at Watford all nyght; and on the morwe be tymes he cam to Seynt Albones, and wyth him on his partye assembled under his baner the Duyke of Bockingham, the Duke of Somersete, the Erle of Penbrok, the Erle of Northumburlond, the Erle of Devynsshire, the Erle of Stafford, the Erle of Dorsete, the Erle of Wyltsshire, the Lorde Clyfford, the Lord Dudley, the Lord Burneys, the Lord Rose, wyth other dyversse knyghtes, squyeres, and other gentilmen and yemen to the nounbre of ij^{ml} [2000] and moo. And upon the xxij. day of the seyde moneth above rehersed assembled the Duyk of Yorke, and wyth hym come yn companye the Erle of Salesbury, the Erle of Warrewyke with diverse knyghtes and squyers unto ther partye into the felde, called the Key Feld, besyde Seynt Albones. Fyrthermore, oure seyd sovereyne Lord the Kyng, heryng and knowyng of the seyde Dukes comyng with other Lordes afore seyde, pygth his baner at the place called Boslawe in Seynt Petrus Strete, whych place was called afore tyme past Sandeforde, and commaundeth the warde and barrers to be kepte in stronge wyse; the for seyde Duyk of York abydyng in the feld aforeseyde frome vij. of the clokke in the morn tyl yt was al most x. without ony stroke smeton on eyther partye. The seyde Duke sende to the Kyng our sovereyne Lord, b? the avyse of his councell, prayng and be sekyng hym to take him as his true man and humble suget; and to consider and to tender at the reverence of Almyghty God, and in way of

[1] This paper is reprinted from the *Archæologia*, vol. xx. p. 519, to which it was communicated by Mr. Bayley, keeper of the records in the Tower, in 1822.

1455
MAY 21-22
charite the true entent of his comyng—to be good and gracyous soveryne Lorde to his legemen, whech with al ther power and mygth wille be redy at alle tymes to leve and dye with hym in his rigth. And to what thyng yt shoulde lyke his Mageste Ryall to commaunde hem, yf yt be his worsship, kepyng right of the Croune and welfare of the londe; 'More over, gracyous Lord, plese yt zour Majeste Ryall of zour grete goodnesse and ryghtwesnesse to enclyne zour wille to here and fele the ryghtwyse partye of us zoure sugettes and legemen; fyrst, prayng and besechyng to zoure Lord Jesus of his hye and myghty power to geve un to zou vertu and prudence, and that thorugh the medyacyon of the glorious martyr Seynt Albon to geve zou very knowleche to knowe the entent of oure assembleng at this tyme; for God that is [in] Heven knoweth than our entent is rightful and true. And there fore we pray unto Al myghty Lord Jesus these wordes—*Domine sis clipeus defensionis nostræ.* Wherefore, gracyus Lord, plese it your hyghe Majeste to delyvere such as we wole accuse, and ze to have lyke, as they have deserved and done, and ze to be honorabled and worsshepyt as most ryghtffull Kyng and oure governour. For and we shall now at this tyme be promysed, as afore this tyme ys not unknowen, of promes broken whech ful fayth fully hath ben promysed, and there upon grete othes made, we wyll not now cesse for noon such promysse, surete, ne other, tyl we have hem whych hav deserved deth, or elles we to dye there fore.'

And to that answered the Kyng our sovereyne Lord, and seyde: 'I, Kyng Herry, charge and comaund that no maner persone, of what degre, or state, or condicyon that evere he be, abyde not, but voyde the felde, and not be so hardy to make ony resystens ageyne me in myn owne realme; for I shall knowe what traytor dar be so bold to reyse apepull in myn owne lond, where thorugh I am in grete desese and hevynesse. And by the feyth that I owe to Seynt Edward and to the Corone of Inglond, I shal destrye them every moder sone, and they be hanged, and drawen, and quartered, that may be taken afterward, of them to have ensample to alle

such traytours to be war to make ony such rysyng of peple withinne my lond, and so traytorly to abyde her Kyng and governour. And, for a conclusyon, rather then they shall have ony Lorde here with me at this tyme, I shall this day, for her sake, and in this quarrell my sylff lyve or dye.'

Wych ansuere come to the Duke of Yorke, the wheche Duke, by the avyce of the Lordes of hys Counceill, seyde unto hem thise wordes: 'The Kyng our sovereyne Lord will not be reformed at our besechyng ne prayer, ne wylle not understonde the entent that we be comen heder and assembled fore and gadered at this tyme; but only ys full purpose, and there noon other wey but that he wole with all his power pursue us, and yf ben taken, to geve us a shameful deth, losyng our lyvelode and goodes, and our heyres shamed for evere. And ther fore, sythe yt wole be noon othere wyse but that we shall ootterly dye, better yt ys for us to dye in the feld than cowardly to be put to a grete rebuke and asshamefful deth; more over, consederyng yn what peryle Inglonde stondes inne at thys owre, therefore every man help to help power for the ryght there offe, to redresse the myscheff that now regneth, and to quyte us lyke men in this querell; preyng to that Lord that ys Kyng of Glorye, that regneth in the kyngdom celestyall, to kepe us and save us this day in our right, and thorugh the helpe of His holy grace we may be made strong to with stonde the grete abomynable and cruell malyse of them that purpose fully to destrye us with shameful deth. We ther fore, Lord, prey to The to be oure confort and Defender, seyng the word afore seyde, *Domine sis clipeus defensionis nostræ.*'

And whanne this was seyde, the seyde Duke of Yorke, and the seyd Erle of Salesbury, and the Erle of Warrewyk, betwene xj. and xij. of the clocke at noon, the broke into the toun in thre diverse places and severelle places of the fore seyd strete. The Kyng beyng then in the place of Edmond Westby, hunderede of the seyd toun of Seynt Albones, comaundeth to sle alle maner men of lordes, knygthtes, end squyeres, and zemen that mygth be taken of the for seyde Dukes of York. Thys don, the fore seyde Lord Clyfford

THE PASTON LETTERS

1455
MAY 21-22 kept strongly the barrers that the seyde Duke of York myght not in ony wise, with all the power that he hadde, entre ne breke into the toun. The Erle of Warrewyk, knowyng ther offe, toke and gadered his men to gedere and ferosly brake in by the gardeyne sydes betuene the signe of the Keye and the sygne of the Chekkere in Holwell strete; and anoon as they wer wyth inne the toon, sodeynly the blew up trumpettes, and sette a cry with asshout and a grete voyce, 'A Warrewe! A Warrewyk! A Warrewyk!' and into that tyme the Duke of York mygth nevere have entre into the toun; and they with strong hond kept yt, and myghttyly faught to gedere, and anoon, forth with after the brekyng in, they sette on them manfully. And as of Lordes of name were slayn the Lord Clyfford, the Duke of Somersete, the Erle of Northumberlond, Sir Bartram Entuwysselle, Knynght; and of men of courte, Wyllyam Zouch, John Batryaux, Raaff of Bapthorp and hys sone, Wyllyam Corbyn, squyers; William Cotton, receyver of the Ducherye of Lancastre; Gylbert Starbrok, squyer; Malmer Pagentoun, William Botelore, yomen; Rogere Mercroft, the Kynges messanger; Halyn, the Kynges porter; Raufe Wyllerby; and xxv. mo, whych her names be not zet knowen. And of hem that ben slayn ben beryed in Sent Albonos xlviij. And at this same tyme were hurt Lordes of name—the Kyng, our sovereyne Lord, in the neck with an arrowe; the Duke of Bukingham, with an arrowe in the vysage; the Lord of Stafford in the hond, with an arowe; the Lord of Dorsette, sore hurt that he myght not go, but he was caryede hom in a cart; and Wenlok, Knyght, in lyke wyse in a carte sore hurt; and other diverse knyghtes and squyers sore hurt. The Erle of Wyldsshyre, Thorpe, and many other flede, and left her harneys behynde hem cowardly, and the substaunce of the Kynges partye were dyspoyled of hors and harneys. This done, the seyde Lordes, that ys to wote, the Duke of Yorke, the Erle of Salesbury, the Erle of Warrewyke, come to the Kyng, our sovereyne Lord, and on here knees be soughte hym of grace and foryevenesse of that they hadde doon yn his presence, and be sought hym of his Heynesse to take hem as hys true legemen, seyng that they

28

HENRY VI

never attendyde [*intended*] hurt to his owne persone, and ther **1455** fore [the] Kyng oure sovereyn Lord toke hem to grace, and **MAY 21-22** so desyred hem to cesse there peple, and that there shulde no more harme be doon; and they obeyde hys commaundement, and lote make a cry on the Kynges name that al maner of pepull shulde cesse and not so hardy to stryke ony stoke more after the proclamacyon of the crye; and so cessed the seyde batayle, *Deo gratias*.

And on the morwe the Kyng and the seyde Duke, with other certeyn Lordes, come in to the Bysshops of London, and there kept resydens with joye and solempnyte, concludyng to holde the parlement at London, the ix. day of July next comyng.

284

THE BATTLE OF ST. ALBANS[1]

THE solecytouriz and causerys of the feld takyng at [**MAY 22**] Seynt Albonys, ther namys shewyn her aftyr:—

> The Lord Clyfford.
> Rauff Percy.
> Thorpe.
> Tresham and Josep.

The inony [*enemy's*] batayle was in the Market-place, and the Kynges standard was pight, the Kynge beynge present with these Lordes, whos namys folwe:—

The Duke of Bokyngham.	
The Duke Somyrcete.	With many Knyghtes and
The Erle Devynshire.	Squyeriz, to the noumbre
The Erle of Northeombirlond.	in alle that faught that day
The Erle Stafford.	iij[ml.] [3000], and it was done
The Erle Dorcete.	on Thursday last past atwyx
The Lord Clyfford.	xj. and xij. at mydday.
The Lord Ros.	

[1] [From MS. Phillipps, 9735, No. 278.]

29

THE PASTON LETTERS

1455
[MAY 22] The namys of the Lordes that were on the othir party shewyn here aftyr:—

The Duke of York.	
The Erle of Salesbury.	With many otheriz, to
The Erle of Warwyk.	the noumbre of v[ml.] [5000]
The Lord Clynton.	men.
Sir Robert Ocle.	

And Sir Rober Ocle tok vj[c] [600] men of the Marchis, and tok the Market-place or ony man was war; than the larum belle was ronge, and every man yed to harneys, for at that tyme every man was out of ther aray, and they joynid batayle anon; and it was done with inne di. [i.e. *one half*] houre, and there were slayn the men, whos namys folwyn:—

The Duke Somyrcete.	With many othir men, to
The Erle Northombirlond.	the noumbre of iiij[c] [400],
The Lord Clyfford.	and as many or mo hurt.
The Lord Clynton.	The Kynge was hurt with
Sir Bartyn at Wessyll.	an harwe in the necke. The
Babthorpe and hese sone.	Duke of Bukkyngham hurt,
Cotton, Receyvour of the Duchye.	and fled in to the Abbey. The Erle Devynshire hurt.
Gryphet, Ussher of Hall.	The Erle Stafford and Dorcetyr gretly hurt. Fylongley
Herry Loweys.	faught manly, and was shet
Wyllyam Regmayde.	thorwe the armys in iij. or
John Raulyns. Asple.	iiij. placys.
Harpour, Yoman of the Croune.	

The Duke of Norfolke come a day aftyr the jurney was done with vj[ml.] [6000] men.
And the Erle of Oxinford also.

The Erle of Shrewysbury,	
Lord Crumwelle,	with x[ml.] [10,000] men were
And Sir Thomas Stanley,	comynge.

The Kynge with all the Lordes come to London to Westmenstyr on Fryday, at vj. of clocke at aftyr none, and London went a generalle processyon the same day.

30

HENRY VI

285

JOHN CRANE TO JOHN PASTON[1]

Unto my worshipfull and welbeloved cosyn, John Paston,
be this lettre delivred in hast.

RIGHT worshipfull and entierly welbeloved Sir, I re- **1455** commaunde me unto you, desiring hertly to here of **MAY 25** your welfare. Furthermore lettyng you wete, as for such tydinges as we have here, such [*these*] thre Lordes be dede, the Duke of Somerset, the Erle of Northombrelonde, and the Lord Clyfford; and as for any other men of name, I knowe noon save only Quotton of Cammbrigeshire. As for any other Lordes, many of theym be hurt; and as for Fenyngley, he lyveth and fareth well, as fer as I can enquere, &c.

And as for any grete multytude of people that ther was, as we can tell, ther was at most slayn [x][2] vj. score. And as for the Lordes that were with the Kyng, and her men wer pilled and spoyled out of all their harneys and horses; and as for what rule we shall have yit I wote nett, save only ther be made newe certayn officers.

My Lord of Yorke, Constabil of Englande; my Lord of Warweke is made captayn of Calyes; my Lord Burgchier is made Tresorer of Englande; and as yit other tydinges have I none.

And as for our soverayn Lorde, thanked be God, he hathe no grete harme.

No more to you at this tyme, but I pray you send this lettyr to my Maistresse Paston, when ye have sene hit; preyng you to remembre my systir Margrete ageyne the tyme that she shal be made nonne.

Written at Lamehith, on Witsonday, &c.

By your cosyn,

JOHN CRANE.

[1] [From Fenn, i. 100.] This letter relates to the first battle of St. Albans and the principal changes which took place immediately after it.
[2] In the original letter, the x is struck out, and vj. placed after it in the same line.—F.

31

THE PASTON LETTERS

286

ABSTRACT [1]

SIR JOHN FASTOLF TO JOHN PASTON.

1455
MAY 28

Thanks him for his pains in speeding his causes at London this term. Understands the Sheriff of Norfolk's officers are at Norwich, and now the writ of attaint is sent home by William Barker, which Fastolf sends again to Paston that he may consult with the Sheriff or his officers what to do. Both William Barker and Seffrey (sic) Spyrlyng are now at Norwich, and one of them, if need be, shall wait on Paston.

Castre, 28 May.

'And I trust to God, as the world goeth now, the said attaint shall do right well.'

[The postscript of this letter seems to refer to the change of administration after the battle of St. Albans. As to the action of attaint sued by Fastolf, see Nos. 268 and 276.]

287

WILLIAM BARKER TO WILLIAM WORCESTER [2]

To William Worcester, be this lettre delyvered in hast.

JUNE

SIR, I recomaunde me to yow; and as for tydyngs, ye may enforme myn mayster, there is non but that he hath knowleche of, but that the Kyng, the Quene, and the Prynce remeven to Hertford to morwen withoughit faute; myn Lord York to the Fryres at Ware; myn Lord Warwyk to Hunesdon; the Erle Salysburye to Rye; and there they shall abyde to tyme the Parlement be gynne.

The Duk Buk is come inne, and sworn that he shal be rewled, and draw the lyne with theym; and ther to he and his brethern ben bounde by reconysaunce in notable summes to abyde the same.

The Erle of Wylts sent to the Lordes from a place of his, called Peterfeld, a lettre desyring to know if he shuld come,

[1] [From MS. Phillipps, 9735, No. 255.]
[2] [From Fenn, i. 104.] This letter relates entirely to occurrences after the battle of St. Albans. The writer here only signs with his initials, but from the facsimile given by Fenn of his 'W. B.,' he can be clearly identified with William Barker.

32

HENRY VI

and abyde aboughit the Kynges persone as he dede be fore; and if he shuld not, than that they wold lycence hym to goon in to Erland, and leve there upon his landes, &c., and before this don, the Lordes were advysed to have made hym to don as the Duk Buk hath don, and no more; but what that wolle falle now therof, no man can telle as yet.

1455
JUNE

The Baron of Dudley is in the Towre; what shal come of hym, God wote. The Erle of Dorsete is in warde with the Erle of Warrwyk.

Hit was seyd, for sothe, that Harpere and ij. other of the Kynges chamber were confederid to have steked the Deuk York in the Kynges chamber; but hit was not so, for they have clered theym therof.

But London upon the same tale areysen, and every man to harneys on Corpus Christi even, and moche adoo there was.

Syr William Oldhall a bydeth no lenger in Seyntwery than the Chef Juge come, for that tyme he shal goo at large, and sewe all his maters himself, &c.

The Baron Dudley hath appeched many men; but what they ben, as yet we can not wete. Sir Phillyp Wentworth was in the feld, and bare the Kynges standard, and kest hit down and fled. Myn Lord Norffolk seyth he shal be hanged therfore, and so is he worthy. He is in Suffolk now. He der not come aboughit the Kynge.

Edmond Stendale was with Wenlok there in the feld, and ffowly hurt.

Fylongley is at home at his owen place with his wyf, and shal doe ryght weel; but we have a greet losse of his absence this terme, for hit wole be longe er he come this terme, I am a ferde.

Alle the Lordes that dyed at the jorney arn beryed at Seynt Albones.

Other thinges ben non here, but ye shal sene by Thomas Scales lettre the rewle of the Frenshemen, &c.

God spede us weel in our matres this terme, I praye to God, who have yow in his kepyng, &c.

W. B.

33

THE PASTON LETTERS

288

THE DUCHESS OF NORFOLK TO JOHN PASTON [1]

To oure right trusti and welbelovid John Paston, Esquier.

The Duchesse of Norffolk.

1455
JUNE 8

RIGHT trusti and welbelovid, we grete you hertili weel. And for as muche as it is thought right necessarie for divers causes that my Lord have at this tym in the Parlement suche persones as longe unto him, and be of his menyall servaunts, wherin we conceyve your good will and diligence shal be right expedient, we hertili desire and pray you that at the contemplacion of thise oure lettres, as our special trust is in you, ye wil geve and applie your voice unto our right welbelovid cosin and servaunts, John Howard and Syr Roger Chambirlayn, to be Knyghts of the shire, exorting all suche othir as be your wisdom shal now be behovefull, to the good exployte and conclusion of the same.

And in your faithful attendaunce and trewe devoyre in this partie, ye shal do unto my Lord and us a singlere pleasir, and cause us herafter to thank you therfore, as ye shal holde you right weel content and agreid, with the grace of God, who have you ever in his keping.

Wreten in Framlyngham Castel, the viij. day of June.

289

ABSTRACT [2]

SIR JOHN FASTOLF TO JOHN PASTON.

JUNE 11

Thanks him for his letter sent from London. Bokkyng writes that a writ of *ravishment de garde* is taken, and Wentworth's counsel 'call sore upon the action of 200 marks in the Common Pleas, and John Andreus is ready there,

[1] [From Fenn, i. 96.] From the time of year at which it was written, this letter must refer to the parliamentary election of 1455.
[2] [From MS. Phillipps, 9735, No. 269.]

34

HENRY VI

and writs of *capias* ayenst John Porter as well as ayenst Sir Thomas.' Begs him to hasten to London, as there is great labour against our intent. Wentworth has got Debenham, Radclyff, and others in my Lord's house against us. Would rather he were at London two days too early than too late; for he trusts no man's wit so much as Paston's.

1455
JUNE 11

Castre, 11 June.

[The references in this letter to the affair of the wardship, and to the actions against John Porter and Sir Thomas Howes, all show that it belongs to the year 1455.]

290

SIR JOHN FASTOLF TO JOHN PASTON [1]

1455(?)

.   .   .   .   .   J. FASTOLF.

More overe, cosyn, I pray yow concyder . . . that yff the plees for the mater ye [wit off] may be engroced be tyme or the Courtys remefe, hyt may stand yn more suertee; and ellys hyt wille stand yn a jubardye as to alle that hathe be spended and doon heere before. And therfor, savyng your better avice, I had lever ye were at London a weke the rather and tymelyer then a weke to late. I pray yow doth somwhate aftyr my councell as I wolle do by youres.

[1] [From Paston MSS., B.M.] This is only the mutilated postscript of a letter without any address, though it was doubtless directed to John Paston. The anxiety expressed that Paston should be in London in good time corresponds so closely with the contents of the preceding letter that we may refer this to the same period, especially as both the preceding letter and this are in the handwriting of William Worcester. The matter, which was to be engrossed before the Courts removed, had reference probably to the wardship of Thomas Fastolf of Cowhawe.—*See* No. 292 following.

35

291

WILLIAM PRYCE TO JOHN PASTON[1]

*The copy of a Letter sent to John Paston be the Undir-
Shreve[2] of Norff.*

1455
JUNE 19

RYGHT worchepfull Sir, I recomaund me on to you, &c.
And, Sir, as for the eleccion of the Knyghts of the
shire here in Norffolk, in good feyth her hath ben
moch to do ; nevir the latyr, to lete yow have knowlech of
the demenyng, my Master Berney, my Master Grey and ye
had grettyst voyse, and I purpose me, as I woll answer God,
to retorne the dieu eleccion, that is aftir the sufficiente, yow
and Mastir Grey ; nevir the latyr I have a master.
Wretyn at Hederset, the Thursday next befor Midsomer.
By   WILL'M PRYCE.

292

ABSTRACT[3]

JUNE 21

Writ to the Treasurer and Barons of the Exchequer in pursuance of patent,
12th December last, granting to John Bokking and William Worcester the
wardship, etc., of the heir of John Fastolf of Cowghawe.

Above in William Worcester's hand :—'Bre. ad allocand. Vicecomitem de
proficuis terr. Thomæ Fastolf in custodia Johannis Bokkyng.'
Inrolled, Trin., 33 Hen. vi., rot. 3.

[Memoranda below in William Worcester's hand as to certain statements of Hugh
Fenn about the form of the writ of livery directed to the Sheriff.]

---

[1] [From Fenn, iii. 452.] The evidence of date in this letter is the same as in
No. 288. Notwithstanding Pryce's efforts, not one of the persons named in this letter
was actually elected, the knights returned for Norfolk in 1455 being the Duke of
Norfolk's nominees, Sir Roger Chamberlain and John Howard.—*See* Nos. 294 and
295 following.
[2] *Shieve* in Fenn is almost certainly a misreading.
[3] [From MS. Phillipps, 9735, No. 261.]

36

1455   gouverned, and com to London yff ye sende me worde,
JUNE 22 and that I hafe word from yow yf nede be bytyme from
London.

294

JOHN JENNEY TO JOHN PASTON[1]

To my wurshipfull maister, John Paston, Esquier.

JUNE 24

MI Maister Paston, I recomaunde me to you. And
wher ye shulde be enformed that I shulde sey to
Howard[2] that ye labored to be Knyght of the
shire, I seid never soo to hym. I tolde my Lord of Norffolk
atte London that I labored diverse men for Sir Roger Chaum-
berleyn, and they seid to me they wolde have hym, but not
Howard, in asmeche as he hadde no lyvelode in the shire, nor
conversement [*i.e.* acquaintance ?] ; and I asked them hom
they wolde have, and they seid they wolde have you, and thus
I tolde hym. And he seid on avysely, as he kan doo full well,
I myght not sey ye labored ther, for I herde never sey ye
labored therfor, be the feithe I vowe to God.
As for this writ of the Parlement of Norwich, I thanke
you that ye will labour ther in ; as for my frendys ther, I
truste right well all the aldermen, except Broun[3] and sech
as be in his dawnger.[4] I prey you spekith to Walter Jeffrey[5]
and Herry Wilton,[6] and maketh them to labour to your entent.
I prey you that yf ye thenke that it wull not be, that it like
you that to sey that ye meve it of your self, and not be my

---

[1] [From Fenn, iii. 240.] The parliamentary election to which this letter refers is
evidently the same as in Nos. 288 and 291. The election of Howard and Chamberlain actually took place on the 23rd June, the day before this letter was written, as I
find by the original returns in the Record Office.
[2] John Howard, the Duke of Norfolk's cousin. He was afterwards created Duke
of Norfolk himself by Richard iii., in whose cause he fell fighting at the battle of
Bosworth.
[3] Richard Brown was Mayor of Norwich in 1454, and member for that city in
1460.—F.
[4] This means *in his debt*, and therefore under his influence.—F.
[5] Walter Jeffrey was Under-Sheriff of Norwich in 1451, 1452, and 1459.—F.
[6] Henry Wilton was returned with John Jenney in 1477.—F.

38

293

SIR JOHN FASTOLF TO JOHN PASTON[1]

To my ryght trusty cosyn, John Paston.

WORSHYPFULL Sir and cosyn, I commaund me to
yow. And lyke yow wete that accordyng to your
desyre I sende John Russe to yow to hafe your
informacion of such materis as shall be thought exspedient to
be laboured yn your absence for the mater of Wentworth, and
hafe geve hym in commaundment to entend it in all that he
can or may. And, Cosyn, he hath a lettre of credence to the
baylly of Dedham because of doubt of syght of the baylly ys
lettre ther for disclosyng, &c., to do after the wrytyng of
T. Denys. And y sende yow ij. lettres com to me from
London that maketh mencyon of grete besynesse ayenst us,
and an accion toke ayenst yow, Howys, Bokkyng, &c., that
most nedys be tendred ; in case an essoyn[2] can be take, so
moche the better. And therfor, cosyn, at reverence of God,
dispose yow to London yn all the haste that ye can. For the
atthacment can not be tille ye com. And on partie adverse
besyeth hem sore in your absence, *facies hominis facies leonis.*
And I have worde yn a nothere lettre that my Lord Chauncellor ys yn the lyke wyse disposed yn owre one syde, and
therfor that ye kepe hym ynne to helpe bere the favour of
thys mater yn all wyse ; And Byngham Justys ys full well
disposed also. Dyvers new processe ys ayenst Sir Thomas.
And all othere materis I commyt to your discrecion ; yf nede
be, I com thedre my sylf. Y pray God kepe yow. Wryt
hastly uppon Sonday before Seynt John Baptiste.— Your
cosyn,   J. FASTOLF.

Item, after that I have word from yow, so wolle I be

---

[1] [Add. MS. 34,889, f. 171.] There can be no reasonable doubt that this letter is
of the same date as Nos. 289 and 290, *i.e.* of the year 1455.
[2] An excuse allowed for not appearing in Court.

37

desire. Sum men holde it right straunge to be in this Parle-   1455
ment, and me thenketh they be wyse men that soo doo.   JUNE 24
Wreten atte Intewode,[1] on Sceint John day, in hast.
Your servaunt,
JOHN JENNEY.

295

JOHN JENNEY TO JOHN PASTON[2]

To my wurshipfull maister, John Paston, Squier.

MI wurshipfull maister, I recomaunde me to you ; and I   JUNE 25
thanke you that it plesith you to take seche labour
for me as ye doo. My servaunt tolde me ye desired
to knowe what my Lord of Norffolk seid to me whan I spake
of you ; and he seid in asmeche as Howard[3] myght not be, he
wolde write a lettre to the Under-Shreve that the shire shulde
have fre eleccion, soo that Sir Thomas Todenham wer not,
nor none that was toward the Duc of Suffolk ; he seid he
knewe ye wer never to hym ward. Ye may[4] sende to the
Under-Shreve, and see my Lord lettre. Howard was as
wode as a wilde bullok ; God sende hym seche wurshipp as
he deservith. It is a evill precedent for the shire that a
straunge man shulde be chosyn, and no wurshipp to my
Lord off Yorke, nor to my Lord of Norffolk to write for
hym ; for yf the jentilmen of the shire will suffre sech inconvenyens, in good feithe, the shire shall not be called of
seche wurshipp as it hathe be.
Wreten atte Intewode, this Wednesday next after Sceint
John, in hast.   Your servaunt,
JOHN JENNEY.

---

[1] This estate came to Jenney by his marriage with Elizabeth, daughter of Thomas
Wetherby, a rich alderman of Norwich, who, after having twice served as Mayor,
quarrelled with the city about the election of his successor in that office in 1433, and
instigated various prosecutions against them. He died in 1445.
[2] [From Fenn, iii. 380.] This letter clearly refers to the same matters as the preceding, and was written the day after.
[3] *See* p. 38, Note 2.
[4] The modern version in Fenn reads, ‘The Mayor sent to the Under-Sheriff, and
saw my Lord's letter.’

39

296

ALICE CRANE TO MARGARET PASTON[1]

To my cosyn, Margeret Paston, be this letter delyvred.

About
455 (?)
JUNE 29

RYGHT worshipfull cosyn, I recomaund me unto you, desyryng to here of youre welfare; and if it like you to her of my welfar, at the makyng of this letter I was in good hele, loved be God. The cause of my wrytyng to you at this tyme is this, praying you to send me word of youre welfare, and how ye do of youre seknesse, and if the medycyn do you ony good that I send you wrytyng of last; thankyng you of the grete frenship that ye have do to my moder with all my hert.

Also I pray you that ye wyll be good meyn to my cosyn youre husbond, that he wyll se that my fader be well ruleyd in his lyvelode for his worship and his profett.

Also prayng you to hold me exschusyd that I have wryten no ofter to you, for, in good feth, I had no leysir; for my Lady hath be seke at London, ner hand this quarter of this yere, and that hath be grete hevinesse to me; but now, blesyd be God, she is amendyd and is in the contre agayne.

Also thankyng you of the grete chere that I had of you when I was with you laste with all my herte, prayng you of good contenuanse, for I had never gretter nede than I have now, and if I had leyser and space, I wolde write to you the cause.

No more at this tyme, but the Holy Trenite have you in his kepyng.

Wryten at Wyndesore, the xxix. day of June,

By youre pore bede oman and cosyn,

ALICE CRANE.

Also, cosyn, I pray you to sende me sum Norfoke threde to do a boute my nekke to ryde with.

[1] [From Fenn, iii. 146.] John Crane of Woodnorton, whom we suppose to have been the writer of Letters 121 and 285, had a wife of the name of Alice, who was apparently a widow in 1457, when she presented to the living of Woodnorton (*see* Blomefield, iv. 313). But the writer of this was more probably a daughter, serving in the household of a lady of rank according to the custom of the times. If so, the date is before John Crane's death, which must have happened between 1455 and 1457.

40

297

WILLIAM WORCESTER TO JOHN PASTON[1]

To my Maister Paston.

PLEASE your gode maistership to wete, that as yersten-day came lettres from London that the Parson[2] most nedys up to London to safe the next amerciement; and so ys forth to appiere, yff he nedys most, xv. Johannis,[3] as ye shall see by Barkers lettre, and shall be to morne at London, and with Goddes grace he shall be releved by the meene of the Parlement; by Sonday yee shall hafe weetyng.

1455
JULY 7

As for my maister,[4] he departyth not to London tille the next weke after thys, and [*i.e.* if] he ryde.

As for tydyngs be none couthe [*i.e.* publicly known], but Ponyngs[5] ys qwyt and delyvered of all tresons; and Sir William Oldhale ys process yn the Kyngs Bynche reversed; and the Priest that acoused Lordz Cromewell,[6] Grey,[7] and my

[1] [From Fenn, iii. 128.] At the date of this letter, William Worcester and his master, Sir John Fastolf, were both at Caister, though the latter was thinking of going up to London. This, being in July, cannot have been before 1455. Fenn supposes the pardon to Poynings to have been on account of his participation in Cade's rebellion, and accordingly dates this letter 'about 1451.' But Poynings was accused of raising disturbances in 1453 and 1454. The reversal of Sir William Oldhall's outlawry in 1455; for we have seen in No. 287 that he was obliged to remain in sanctuary for some little time after the battle of St. Albans. It appears by an *inspeximus* on Patent Roll, 34 Hen. VI., m. 16, that he presented a petition to the King in Parliament on the 9th July, 33 Hen. VI. (1455), setting forth how he had served the King in France, and yet had been pronounced a traitor by the Parliament of Reading in 31 Hen. VI., but that his outlawry had been reversed in the King's Bench.

[2] Thomas Howes.

[3] *Quindena Johannis*, or on the quinzaine of St. John, *i.e.* 8th July, the 15th day from St. John the Baptist's day.

[4] Sir John Fastolf.

[5] Robert Poynings.—*See* vol. ii. p. 154, Note 3.

[6] Ralph, Lord Cromwell. He was accused of treason by a priest named Robert Colynson—See Nicolas's *Privy Council Proceedings*, vi. 198.

[7] Probably Edmund, Lord Grey of Ruthin; but there were at this time also a Lord Grey of Codnor and a Lord Grey of Wilton.

41

1455
JULY 7

maister wolle confesse who caused hym to do it, so that he may have hys lyve, &c.

Assone as ye goodly may to see my maister, it shall be to hym a singuler pleasir. Sir, a baylly of my maister ys yn Drayton. John Eimond brought a lettre to yow, and he sent me wetyng he was shent [*abashed*] uppon som mater, as he supposyth, conteyned yn the lettre. Y pray you yn ryght be hys gode maister, and that y may wete the cause, for y doubt he shall and most obbey, yff he hath offended.

At Castr, the noneday,[1] vij. day Jullet.

Your, W. WORCESTRE.

On the top of this letter, in a different hand, is written:—

Prove ontrouthe in the Undir-Sherif, or that he dede othir wise thanne your counsell avysid hym, and Paston shall demene hym accordyng.

298

SIR J. FASTOLF TO JOHN PASTON[2]

To the worshypfull and my ryght welle belovyd cosyn, John Paston.

JULY 10

WORSHYPFULL and ryghte welbelovyd cosyn, I comaund me to you. Please you to wete that the pryour and convent of Norwych have wyth holden certeyn rent for londes that they holden of me wythynne my maner of Harlyston, and the ij. tapers of wax of ij*lb.* wyghte by the space of xviij. yeers that mountyth . . . . xxj*s.* valued in money; and the lordes of the seyd maner beying before me, and also y yn my tyme have be seisid and possessed of the sayd rent. Praying you to speek wyth the pryour, recomaundyng me unto hym, and

[1] The day of the Nones.—F.

[2] [From a modern copy by Gough in Bodl. Library.] This letter was evidently written in the year 1455, as appears by the reference to the Parliament and to the intended journey of Sir John Fastolf up to London (see No. 297).

42

that ye lyke to meave hym to make me payment, as hys dewtee ys, so as y have no cause to stirre further, and to doo as justice requyryth. He holdyth xxx. acres land or more by the sayd rent, and yhyt ought to pay me othyr rents more by myne evidents of more ade. Y pray you, cosyn, that y may speke wyth you or y ryde, and that on Thrysday by the farthyst, and then y shall tell you tydyngs off the Parlement, and that ye fayle not, as my trus ys yn you. Y pray God have you yn Hys governance.

1455
JULY 10

Wreten at Castre, the x. day of Julle.

Your cosyn,

JOHN FASTOLFE.

299

HENRY WINDSOR TO BOKKYNG AND WORCESTER[1]

Unto my moost faitfull brethern, John Bokkyng and William Worcestre, and to eyther of theym.

WORSHIPFULL Sir, and my most hertely and best be loved brother, I recommaund me unto you in more loly wise than I can other thenk or write; and with al my service and trewe herte thank you of your gentill lettres, full brotherly written unto me at mony tymes of old, and especiall of late tyme passed. And trwly, brother, I thank Almyghty God of your welfare, of the which the berer of this my pour lettre certified me of, &c.

JULY 19

And, Sir, as touchyng al maner of newe tithinges, I knoo well ye are averous; truly the day of makyng of this letter, ther were nonn newe, but suche I herd of, ye shalbe served with all.

As for the first, the Kyng our souverain Lord, and all his trwe Lordes stand in hele of there bodies, but not all at

[1] [From Fenn, i. 108.] As this letter refers to the disputes which arose after the battle of St. Albans as to who should bear the blame of that occurrence, the date is certain.

43

THE PASTON LETTERS

hertes ees as we. Amonges other mervell, ij. dayes afore the
writyng of this letter, there was langage betwene my Lordes
of Warrewikke and Cromwell afore the Kyng, in somuch
as the Lord Cromwell wold have excused hym self of all the
steryng or moevyng of the male journey of Seynt Albones;
of the whiche excuse makyng, my Lord Warrewikke had
knolege, and in hast wasse with the Kyng, and sware by his
othe that the Lord Cromwell said not trouth, but that he was
begynner of all that journey at Seynt Albones; and so betwene my said ij. Lordes of Warrewikke and Cromwell ther is
at this day grete grugyng, in somoch as the Erle of Shrowesbury hath loged hym at the hospitall of Seynt James, beside
the Mewes, be the Lord Cromwells desire, for his sauf gard.

And also all my Lord of Warrewikke men, my Lord of
York men, and also my Lord of Salesbury men goo with
harnes, and in harnes with strang wepons, and have stuffed
their Lordes barges full of wepon dayly unto Westminster.
And the day of makyng of this letter, ther was a proclamacion made in the Chauncerie, on the Kyngs behalf,
that noman shuld nether bere wepon, ner were harnes defensible, &c.

Also, the day afore the makyng of this letter, ther passed
a bill[1] both by the Kyng, Lordes, and Comens, puttyng
Thorp, Josep, and my Lord of Somerset in all the defaute;
be the which bill all maner of actions that shuld growe to any
person or persones for any offenses at that journey doon, in
any maner of wise shuld be extynt and voide, affermyng all
thing doon there well doon, and nothing doon there never
after this tyme to be spoken of; to the which bill mony a
man groged full sore nowe it is passed.

And if I myght be recommaunded unto my speciall
maister and youres, with all loliness and trewe service I
beseech you hertely as I can.

And also to my brethren Th. Upton,[2] Lodowick of Pole,
William Lynd Calyn [*Lincoln* ?], and John Merchall.

---

[1] See *Rolls of Parl.* v. 280.
[2] *Upon* in Fenn, but Upton in the modern version on the opposite side of the
page.

44

HENRY VI

No more, but our Lorde have you both in his perpetuell
kepyng.

Writen at London, on Seynt Margarete Even,[1] in hast;
and after this is rede and understonden, I pray you bren or
breke it, for I am loth to write any thing of any Lord. But
I moost neds; ther is no thing elles to write. Amen.

Your awn,

H. WYNDESORE.

300

JAMES GLOYS TO JOHN PASTON[2]

*To the right wurchepfull Sir, ana my goode mayster, my Mayster
John Paston, be this delivered.*

REVERENT and right wurchepfull Sir, and my gode JULY 25
mayster, I recomaund me to you, prayng you to wete
that ther is reysed a slandrows noyse in this countre
up on my Mayster Yelverton and you and my Mayster
Alyngton, which I suppose is do to bryng you ought of the
conceyte of the pepyll, for at this day ye stand gretly in the
countreys conceyte. It is seyde be Heydon and his disciples
that my Mayster Yelverton and ye and my Mayster Alyngton shuld have doo oon Sir John Tartyssale, parson of the
Estchurche[3] of Warham and chapeleyn to the priour[4] of
Walsyngham, to put in to the Parlement, a bille of divers
tresons don be my Lord of Norwich,[5] Sir Thomas Tudenham,

---

[1] St. Margaret's day is the 20th July, the eve the 19th.
[2] [From Fenn, iv. 32.] This letter is attributed by Fenn to the year 1461, but
that date is certainly inaccurate, as it was answered by John Paston at Norwich the
very day it was written, whereas in July 1461 Paston was in London. Moreover, it
certainly could not have been *after* 1461, as Sir Thomas Tuddenham was beheaded in
February of the following year. It must therefore belong to the reign of Henry VI.;
and considering the time of the year, 1455 is the only date at which it is at all likely
that any one would have ventured to attempt the impeachment of Tuddenham and
Heydon in Parliament, or could have been plausibly accused of such a design against
persons of so much influence.
[3] There were three churches in the parish of Warham.
[4] Thomas Hunt. [5] Walter Lyhert, Bishop of Norwich.

45

THE PASTON LETTERS

and John Heydon, and ye shuld have set to your seales; and
if that Heydon had be vj. howrs fro the Parlement lenger
than he was, ther had be granted an *oyer determiner* to have
enquer of hem, &c. This was told yesterday in right wurchepfull audience, and a mong the thrifties men of this countre;
and thei seyd right shrewdly, for my lord of Norwich hath so
flatered the lay pepill as he hath redyn a bought his visitacion
that he hath thers herts. Wherfor, and it plese you to lete
me have knowlech what ye wuld I shuld sey to it, wher as I
her any such langage, I wull do my parte, and have do hed
toward as I have thought in my conceytes best, &c. And if
ther be any other servyce that ye wull comaund me, I am and
wull be redy at yowr comaundment with the grace of God,
how [*who*] ever have you in his blyssed kepyng.

Wretyn at Wighton in hast, on Sent James day,

Be your servaunte, JAMES GLOYS.[1]

301

JOHN PASTON TO JAMES GLOYS[2]

To Sir James Gloys.

THER be dyvers thynges in your letter sent to me; one
that a slaw[n]derus noyse shuld renne ageyns Yelverton, Alygton and me, to brynge us owte of the
conceytes of the puple be Heydon and his dyscyplis, of a bill
that shuld have do put uppe in to the Parlement ageyns my
Lord of Norwich and odir. I lete yow wete this is the furst
day that I herd of any seche, but I wold wete the namys of
hem that utter this langage and the mater of the bill. As for
my Lord of Norwych, I suppose ye know I have not usid to
meddel with Lordes maters meche forther than me nedith;
and as for Sir Thomas Todynham, he gaff me no cawse of late

---

[1] He was a priest, and a dependant of the Pastons.
[2] [From Paston MSS., B.M.] This letter, which is printed from a draft in John
Paston's hand, was written in answer to the preceding, to which the reader is referred
for the evidence of its date.

46

HENRY VI

tyme to labor ageyns hym, and also of seche mater I know
non deffaut in hym. And as for Heydon, when I putte a bill
ageyns hym I suppose he shall no cause have, ne his discyplis
nother, to avante of so short a remedy ther of, as ye wrygth
they sey now. As for that ye desyr that I shuld send yow
word what I shuld sey in this mater, I pray yow in this and
all other lyke, ask the seyeres if thei will abyd be ther langage,
and as for me, sey I prupose me to take no mater uppon me
butt that I woll abyde by; and in lek wys for Yelverton and
Aligton. And that ye send me the namys of them that ye
wryte that herd this langage seyd shrewedly, and what they
seyd; and that ye remember what men of substance wer ther
that herde itt; for if this can be dreve to Heydon or his
dissyplis, as ye wryte, it wer a gode preve that they fere to be
appelyd of seche materes. And I thank yow for your godwill.
Wrete att Norwych, on Seynt James day.

302

JOHN CHEDWORTH, BISHOP OF LINCOLN,
TO JOHN PASTON[1]

To the worshipfull and welbeloved John Paston, Esquyer.

RIGHT worshipful and welbeloved Sir, I comaunde me JULY 26
unto you, and with all my hert thank you for the
grete labours that ye oftymes have diligently doon for
my welbeloved servant John Ode, to th'entent that he shuld
mowe atteyne to entre and enjoy peasible his inheritaunce, as I
am enformed dew unto him; and pray you of youre goode contynuaunce, certifieng you that I have written unto Yelverton,
the justice, that he wol, at some sesonable tyme, common with
Sir Thomas Tudenham, knyght, and to offre him asmoche
reason as it shal be thought unto him and to you, that lawe

---

[1] [From Fenn, iii. 246.] The date of this letter is ascertained by a contemporaneous memorandum at the bottom of the original in these words, 'Litt. direct.
Joh'i Paston inter Michaelem xxxiij. et xxxiiij. Henr. Sexti.'

47

1455
JULY 26

wol in that behalf require, prayng you that ye wol common
with the saide Yelverton, and to conceyve betwix you such
lawful meones of gyding of this matier that my said servaunt
may have peasebly with owten grete trouble his said enheritaunce, as I shal in case semblable do my labour unto your
pleasaunce. And pray you that of the disposicion of the said
Sir Thomas Tudenham in this behalf, I may be certified. And
Jesu preserve you.

Written at London, the xxvj. day of July.

J., BYSSHOPP OF LINCOLN.

303

JAMES GRESHAM TO JOHN PASTON[1]

*To my right worshipfull maister, John Paston, at Norwiche,
be this delyvred.*

OCT. 28

PLEASE it your maistership to wete[2] . . . .
Here be many marvaylos tales of thynggs that shall
falle this next moneth, as it is seyd ; for it is talked
that oon Doktor Grene, a preest, hath kalked [*calculated?*] and
reporteth, that by fore Seynt Andreu day next comyng shall
be the grettest bataill that was sith the bataill of Shrewisbury,[3]
and it shall falle bytwene the Bisshoppes Inne of Salesbury
and Westminster Barres, and there shall deye vij. Lords,
whereof iij. shuld be bisshoppes. Althis and meche more is
talked and reported. I trust to God it shall not falle so.

Also there is gret varyance bytwene the Erll of Devonshire
and the Lord Bonvyle, as hath be many day, and meche debat
is like to growe therby ; for on Thursday at nyght last passed,

[1] [From Fenn, i. 114.] This letter was written in 1455, at the time of the
King's second attack of illness, which happened while he was under the control of
the Duke of York and the Earls of Warwick and Salisbury, as mentioned at the end
of the letter. In the latter part of the letter some words are lost by the decay of the
original MS.
[2] Here, says Fenn, follows an account of some law business, etc.
[3] Fought in 1403 between King Henry IV. and the rebel Percies.

48

HENRY VI

1455
OCT. 28

the Erll of Denshyres sone and heir come with lx. men of
armès to Radford's[1] place in Devenshire, whiche was of counseil with my Lord Bonvyle ; and they sette an hous on fyer at
Radfords gate, and cryed and mad an noyse as though they
had be sory for the fyer ; and by that cause Radfords men
set opyn the gats and yede owt to se the fyer ; and for with
th'erll sone forseid entred into the place and intreted Radford
to come doun of his chambre to sp[e]ke with them, promyttyng hym that he shuld no bodyly harm have ; up on whiche
promysse he come doun, and spak with the seid Erll sone.

In the mene tyme his menye robbe his chambre, and ryfled
his huches,[2] and trussed suyche as they coude gete to gydder,
and caryed it awey on his own hors. Thanne th'erll sone seid,
' Radford, thou must come to my lord my fadir.' He seid he
wold, and bad oon of his men make redy his hors to ride with
hem, whiche answerd hym that alle his hors wern take awey ;
thanne he seid to th'erll sone, ' Sir, your men have robbed my
chambre, and thei have myn hors, that I may not ride with
you to my lord your fadir, wherfor, I pray you, lete me ride,
for I am old, and may not go.'

It was answerid hym ageyn, that he shuld walke forth with
them on his feete ; and so he dede till he was a flyte[3] shote or
more from his place, and thanne he was . . . softly, for cawse
he myght not go fast. And whanne thei were thus departed,
he turned . . . oon ; forwith come ix. men ageyn up on hym,
and smot hym in the hed, and fellid . . . of them kyt his
throte.

This was told to my Lord Chaunceler[4] this fornoon
. . . . . . messengers as come of purpos owt of the same
cuntre. This matier is take gretly . . . . . passed at ij.
after mydnyght rod owt of London, as it is seid, more thanne
. . . . the best wyse. Summe seyne it was to ride toward

[1] ' Nicolas Radford,' says Fenn in a note, ' was an eminent lawyer, and resided at
Poghill, near Kyrton.' In Pole's *Description of Devonshire*, p. 219, we find that one
Nicolas Radford dwelled at Upcot in Henry VI.'s time, ' after whose death controversy arose betwixt John Radford of Okeford and Thomazin, sister of the said Nicholas,'
who had married Roger Prous.
[2] A hutch was a coffer or chest standing on legs.
[3] A flight was ' a light arrow formed for very long and straight shots.'—Halliwell.
[4] Archbishop Bourchier.

49

1455
OCT. 28

my Lord of York, and summe . . . . . k, so meche rumor is
here ; what it menyth I wot not, God turne it . . . . . . at
Hertford,[1] and summe men ar a ferd that he is seek ageyn.
I pray God . . . . . . my Lords of York, Warwyk, Salesbury
and other arn in purpos to conveye hym . . . . &c.
The seid N. Crome, berer her of, shall telle you suche tydynggs . . . . in hast, at London, on Seint Simon
day and Jude.

Yowr poer   J. GR.

304

ABSTRACT[2]

SIR JOHN FASTOLF ' TO MY RIGHT TRUSTY BROTHER, NICHOLAS MOLYNEUX.'

OCT. 30

As I come not to London this winter, I beg you to see to my Lord's
matters, and labour to my Lord of Canterbury and Master John Stokys for the
recovering of my Lord's[3] [good]s. No man can say more in the matter than
you where his goods are, ' and where they be disposed,' especially those that
Sir Rob. Whytynham[4] had. Also the Lord Cromwell had ' a certain number
of plate.' Your costs shall be paid out of the first money received. Hears
from Duke de Leawe, one of Lord Willoughby's executors, that they will
labour to my Lord Beaumont to advance the process for recovery of his part of
the reward for the taking of the Duke of Alençon. Fendykes, a learned man
of the Temple, will help with his advice. Commend me to my sister your
wife.

Castre, 30 Oct.

In Worcester's hand, and endorsed by him.—' A John Paston et John
Bokkyng.'

[During the winter of 1455-56 we find several allusions to this claim put forward
by Fastolf to the goods of the late Duke of Bedford. Unless we are to infer from
the manner in which Lord Cromwell is mentioned that he was dead when this letter
was written, it is probably of the year 1455.]

[1] The King was at Hertford, as appears by the Privy Seals, in August and
September 1455, and not improbably in October also.
[2] [From MS. Phillipps, 9735, No. 228.]
[3] The Duke of Bedford.
[4] Sir Robert Whityngham died on the 4th November 1452.—*Inq. post mortem*,
31 Hen. VI., No. 47.

50

HENRY VI

305

WILLIAM WORCESTER TO JOHN PASTON
AND JOHN BOCKING[1]

*To the ryght worshypfull Sir, John Paston, and
to my brothyr, John Bokkyng.*

1455
NOV. 13

PLEASE it yow to have yn knowlege that y veele well my
maister takyth gretely to hert the materes whych he
hath wryt to you upon the execucion of my Lord
of Bedford ys godes, and in especiall for the recuveryng of
hem, as well as of Sir Andreu O.[2] executors as of Sir Robert
Whytyngham, &c. to th'entent that it myght be opynly knowe
yn hys lyve tyme that they be not yn his gouvernaunce no part
of it, and that hys factors after hym shuld not be troubled ne
charged for it. And seth the seyd mater ys of so grete wyght
and charge, and that he takyth it so gretely to hert, puttyng
hys grettist trust yn yow, to remembre thys seyd mater by
avyse of hys councell lerned, both spirituell as temporell, that
ye wolle not delay it, but wyth all your entencion remembred
there, as ye by your wysdoms shall thynk it moste expedient,
that som fruyt may grow of it.

There ys ynowgh whereoff, and it myght be recuvered,
John Bokkyng, ye know ryght moch yn thys mater, and
mooste of my maister ys entent hereynne. And therfor, for
myne acquytaille, y wryte to you to shew the chieff wrytynges
of the copy of endentures of Sir Robert Whytyngham, and of
othyr wrytynges concernyng that to Maister Paston, that he
may be more rypelyer grounded yn the seyd mater when he

[1] [From Paston MSS., B.M.] On the 11th November 1454 Sir John Fastolf wrote
to Paston about the goods of the Duke of Bedford, but the subject recurred to his
thoughts for more than a year afterwards, and particularly in January 1456, when all
the other executors of the Duke were dead. This letter is certainly before the death
of Lord Cromwell, and therefore not later than 1455 ; but it seems to indicate much
greater solicitude on the subject than Fastolf showed in the preceding year.
[2] Sir Andrew Ogard, who died on the 13th October 1454.—*Inq. post mortem*, 33
Hen. VI., No. 25.

51

1455
NOV. 13
shall comyn wyth my Lordz of Caunterburye, Cromewell, and with onye of my maister councell. And our Lord kepe you.

My maister carpyth so oft on it dayly, and that meovyth me to wryte to yow both. Att Castre, xiij. day of November.

Your, W. WOR-H.R.-CESTRE.

306

MARGARET PASTON TO JOHN PASTON[1]

To my right wurshipfull husbonde, John Paston, be this delivered, in hast.

NOV. 25 RIGHT wurshipfull husbonde, I recomaunde me unto you. Plesith you to witte that myn aunt Mondeforthe[2] hath desiryd me to write to you, besechyng you that ye wol wochesafe to chevesshe for her at London xx[ti] marke for to be payed to Mastre Ponyngs, outher on Saterday or Sonday, weche schalbe Seint Andrwes Daye, in discharchyng of them that be bounden to Mastre Ponyngs of the s[ei]de xx[ti] marke for the wardeship of her doughter, the weche xx[ti] marke she hath delyvered to me in golde for you to have at your comyn home, for she dare not aventure her money to be brought up to London for feere of robbyng ; for it is seide heere that there goothe many thefys be twyx this and London, weche causeth her to beseche you to content the seide money in dischargyng of the matre, and of them that be bounden, for she wolde for no goude that the day were broken. And she thankyth you hertely for the greet labour and besynesse that ye have had in that matre, and in all others touchyng her

[1] [From Fenn, iii. 252.] St. Andrew's day fell on Sunday in 1455 and 1460. This letter must be written in one of these two years, and the probabilities are greatly in favour of the former, as John Paston and William Worcester were not on good terms after the death of Sir John Fastolf.

[2] Osbert Moundford, Esq. of Hockwold, married Elizabeth, daughter of John Berney, Esq., and by her had Mary, their daughter and sole heir, who married Sir William Tindale, Knight of the Bath.

52

and hers, wherfore she seithe she is ever bounden to be your bed-woman, and ever wolle be whyle she levethe.

1455
NOV. 25

My cosyn, her sone, and hese wife recomaundethe them unto you, besechyng you that ye woll weche safe to be her goode mastre, as ye have ben a fore tyme ; for they be enformed that Danyell is comen to Rysyng Castell, and hes men make her bost that her mastre shal be a yene at Brayston withinne shorte tyme.

Ferthermore, as for the matre that my sone wrote to me for the boxe wheron wreten *Falce Carte Sproute* that I shulde enquer of William Wurcestre wher it were, the seide William was not at home sen that I had hes letter ; but as sone as he comethe home, I shall enquere of hym, and sende you an answer.

As towchyng for your leveryes, ther can noon be gete here of that coloure that ye wulde have of, nouther murrey, nor blwe, nor goode russets, undrenethe iijs. the yerde at the lowest price, and yet is ther not j nough of on clothe and coloure to serve you. And as for to be purveid in Suffolk, it wul not be purveide nought now a yenst this tyme, with oute they had had warnyng at Michelmesse, as I am enformed. And the blissed Trenyte have you in his kepyng.

Wreten at Norweche, on Seint Kateryn Day.

Be your,

MARGARET PASTON.

307

ABSTRACT[1]

SIR JOHN FASTOLF TO JOHN PASTON.

Thanks him for his pains in the advancement of his 'chargeable matters.' Was never so much bound to any kinsman as to Paston, who tenders so much his worship and profit. Sends Worcestre with important letters to my Lord Privy Seal and the Abbot of Bermundsey, and would like Paston to common with them. Thanks him for informing him of the answer made to the bill of Wentworth, 'which I know had stand in great jeopardy had not ye be.' Sends

[1455]
DEC. 11

[1] [From MS. Phillipps, 9735, No. 262.]

53

[1455]
DEC. 11
his evidences concerning Bradwell, that the Judges and Parliament may have better consideration of his right, and of the patents granted to Paston and Howys in that behalf. Desires credence for William Worcestre.

Castre, 11 Dec.

[The date of this letter must be between the year 1454, when Sir John Fastolf settled at Caister, and 1458, as he was not alive in December 1459. The reference to Parliament fixes it more precisely, as 1455 was the only year during this period in which Parliament sat in December.]

308

RICHARD BINGHAM TO SIR JOHN FASTOLF[1]

Copie of my fader Bynghames lettre to my fadre F.

About
1455
RIGHT honorable and reverend maistre, after due and hertely recomendacion, I thank yow als hertily as I can that it likith your gode maistership, of your godnesse, to let to ferme to my son Scrope the pouer enheritance that he schal enherit after your decesse, if God will that he life therto. And I hafe for my saide son comonde with my maistres of your counsell, that is to sey, Paston and other, and I fynde them not straunge, bot right streyte to dele with in the mater ; and therfore my saide sone, and I for hym, must sue to the well of mercy, that is to say, to your honurable person, where is special refuge for my saide son in this cas. My saide son is and hath be, and will be to hys lifes ende, your true lad and servaunt, and glad and well willed to do that myght be to your pleaser, wirschip, and profit, and als loth to offend yow as any person in erth, gentill and well disposid to every person. Wherfore I besech your gode grace that ye will vouchesafe remember the premissez, my saide sons age, his wirschipfull birth, and grete misere for verrey povert, for he hath had no liflode to life opon sithen my lady his moder deed, safe x. marc of liflode that ye vouched safe to gife hym this last

[1] [From Castlecombe MSS., Add. 28,212, f. 26, B.M.] This letter has been printed by Mr. Poulett Scrope in his privately printed *History of Castle Combe.* From evidences contained in other of the family muniments, Mr. Scrope supposes it to have been written about the year 1455, which is probably not far from the true date. Compare Letter 349 following.

54

yer, and therfore to be his good maister and fader. And thof he be not worthy to be your son, make hym your almesman, that he may now in his age life of your almesse, and be your bedeman, and pray for the prosperite of your noble person. And if I durst, for your displesaunce, I wolde besech yow that ye wolde vouchesafe lat my saide son hafe the saide lifelode to ferme for terme of your life, payng to yow therfore yerely CC. marc at ij. festes of the yere, that is to say, Cristemasse and Middesomer, and ye schall be paied hit truly at London, in Hillary terme for the feste of Cristemasse, and Trinite terme for the feste of Midsomer ; and I will be bounden for hym and [*i.e.* if] your maistership will vouchesafe to take me, and he and I schall ever pray for yow. And thof the saide lifelode be better to yow in availl yerely then I offer yow therefore, this summe of CC. marc schal be truly paid to yow yerely ; and God, that rewardeth every gode dede, schal pey for hym the remenant to yow, for every peny an C., in relesyng of yow in Purgatory, or ellys encresyng of your merite in Heven. And how your maistership will that my saide son schall do in this mater, I besech yow that he may be certified be your writing.

About
1455

309

FASTOLF'S CLAIMS AGAINST THE CROWN.—I.[1]

Billa de debitis Regis in partibus Franciæ Johanni Fastolf militi debitis.

THESE ben the injuries, losses, and damages that the seyd Fastolf hath had, as well withynne this royaume of England as in othir parties in maner and fourme as it ensewith.

1455

First, it is to consider how that the seyd Fastolf hath ben

[1] [From Fenn, iii. 260.] The date of this paper is determined by the last paragraph, showing that it was composed fifteen years after Sir John finally left France in 1440.

55

1455 vexed and troubled seth he came last into this lande by the myght and power of the Duc of Suffolk, and by the labour of his counseill and servaunts in divers wyses, as in grete oppressions, grevous and outrageous amerciemants and manye grete horrible extorcions, as it may appere more pleynly by a rolle of articles thereupon made, the damages of which entenden to the somme of . . . V. m¹. marc.

Item, the seyd Fastolf hath be gretely damaged and hurt by the myght and power of the seyd Duc of Suffolk and his counseill, in disseising and taking awey a maner of the seyd Fastolf, called Dedham, in the counte of Essex, to the value of C. marks of yerly rent which was halden from the seyd Fastolf by the terme of iij. yere day and more, to his grete hurt, with CC. marks in costs expended in recouvere of the same, the some in all, . . V^c. marc.

Item, there ys cast in to the Kyngs hands by untrew forged offices and inquisicions, supposed to be founde by dyvers eschetours in the countees of Norffolk and Suffolk, iij. certeyn maners of the seyd Fastolf, to the value of C. marks yeerly, which seyd offices and inquisicions were never dewly founde,

56

but forged by untrue imaginacions and meenys of certeyn persones hys eville willers, as it hath be confessed by thos that were appoynted and named to be upon the enquestys; and by the maliciouse labour of his seyd evylle willers, the seyd maners have ben troubled and put in plee this iiij. yere day and more, to the damage and costs of the seyd Fastolf, the somme . . . . . V^c. marc.

Item, the seyd Fastolf hauuing the yeft of the Baronyes and Lordshipp of Sillie Guillem[1] and Lasuze, in the countee of Mayn, to hym and to his assignes for ever, the which weren goten by the seyd Fastolf, and no charge to the King, for the value and denombrement [number] of iiij. m¹. saluz[2] of yerly rent, he was commaunded by the Kinges lettres to deliver upp the sayd baronyes and lordshipps to the Kyngs commissioners, promyssyng hym, by the Kyngs commaundement to have be recompensed therefor, as the seyd Fastolf hath to shewe, and he not recompensed nor rewarded no thing for the levyng of his seyd baronyes and lordship, to

[1] Sir John took the castle of Sillie le Guillem in 1425, and from which he was dignified with the title of baron.—F.
[2] The salute was a gold coin of Henry VI. current in France for £1, 5s. English.—F.

57

1455 the damages of the seyd Fastolf of the somme of . . . m¹. m¹. v.^c [2,500] marc.

Item, wher as the seyd Fastolf had a prisonner of his owen taking, called Guill'm Remond,[1] which was raunsonned, and agreed to pay hym for his raunson with the marks the somme of xxxij. m¹. saluz, the prisonner, withoute knowelege or licence of the seyd Fastolf, was take awey from hym by the Duc of Bedford, then beyng the Kyngs Regent of Fraunce; and with the seyd prisonner he caused the towne of Compyn, than leyng in the Frensh partye ys gouvernaunce, for to be yeldyn to the Kyng, and to his seyd Regent in his name; and the seyd Fastolf, after long pursewts made to the Kyng and his conseill, was recompensed but to the value of m¹. vj^c. saluz in lands in Normandye, when they fortuned to falle into the Kyngs hands, which lands he hath also lost. And also the seyd Fastolf hath lost the residue of the seyd raunson, besyde the seyd lands, to the somme of . . . . m¹. m¹. m¹. m¹. marc.

Item, the seyd Fastolf ys yhyt owyng for his porcion and part for the recompens and reward that shuld grow

[1] In 1423 he took the castle of Pacy, the governor whereof was Guillaume Reymond.—F.

58

and be dewe to hym for the takyng of John, callyng hym Duc of Alauncon, at the batayle of Vernell,[1] which that payd for hys raunson xl. m¹. marks, which rewarde, besyde the Lord Wyllughbye ys part, shuld extend to the somme of . . m¹. m¹. m¹. m¹. marc.

Item, ys dewe to the seyd Fastolf, by the execucion of the last wylle and testament of John, Duc of Bedford, whos soule God assoyle, for prestys and othir charges for saufgarde and keping of certeyn forteresses, castellys, and townes, and for othir costs, prests, and charges by hym born in his service, as it may appiere in certeyn articles writen in a rolle partic'lerly of the same, the somme of . . . iiij^m¹. D^c. iiij^xx. xix. [4,599] marc, vs. 6d.

Summa totalis xxj^m¹. iiij^xx xix. [21,099] marc, vs. 6d.

Item, seth the last comyng over of the seyd Fastolf into this royaume, as by the space of xv. yere and more, he hath born grete costs, charges, and expenss, at alle tymes intending upon the Kyngs highnesse and the Lordes of his counseille, as he hath had in commaundement, and was his part to doo; for the which and for all the service that he hath doo to the right noble Kyng Herry the iiij^the, ayle [grandfather] to our Souvragn Lord that now ys, and to the most victorious Prince and Kyng, his fader, whos soulys God assoyle, and also to our seyd Souvereyn Lord, he hath had, nouther fee, wagys, reward, ne recompense in this his royaume of England, but hath born it of hys own propre godys, at all tymys to the Kyngs honour and prouffit as to his power, which ys to hym

[1] This battle was fought in 1424.—F.

59

THE PASTON LETTERS

1455 right grevouse and chargeable, trusting to have be considered and rewarded as othir men of suche deservyng have be in the tymes of the right noble progenitours of our seyd Souvreyn Lords, late Kyngs of this seyd reaume.

There is a corrected draft of the above paper, in William Worcester's handwriting, among the Paston MSS. in the British Museum, on the back of which are the following additional memoranda:—

Thees been the prestys and sommes of money that the [sic] Sir John Fastolf, knyght, hath lent to oure seid Soverayn Lorde that now is, at his commaundement in his grete necesitees, at divers tymes with in this his reaume of England :—

Item, the seid Fastolf lent to oure seid Soverayn Lorde, in the moneth of September, the xv. yer of his seid regne, as it appereth at the seid recept of Westminster, the somme of . . . . m¹ li.

It is also to be remembred that the seid Fastolf hath lent to oure seid Soverayn Lord, in the moneth of Feverer, the seid xv. yer of his noble regne, as it appereth at the Kynges receyt of Westminster, the somme of . . . . . m¹ marc.

Item, the seid Fastolf lent to our seid Soverayn Lorde, for the viage of Sir Thomas Kiriel, and of his retinue in to the Duchie of Normandye, in the xxviij. yer of his noble regne the somme of CC. marc. Also afore that tyme in the Kynges grete necessite ageyn the coronacion of the Quene, at his forseid commaundement, the somme of Cli. Somme of bothe . iij^c. xxxiij li. vj s. viij d.¹

Item, the seyd Fastolf lent to the voyage that Thomas Danyell made in to Breteyn, as it is notorily knowen, of which he ys not yhyt payd, the somme of . . . . Cli.

Item, the seyd Fastolf hath born grete charge and cost of a lone made for the spede and help of a voyage whych the Erle of Shrewysbury now last made in to the Kynges Duchee of Gyen, . ————²

¹ So in MS. The total should be £100 less. ² A blank.

HENRY VI

310

FASTOLF'S CLAIMS AGAINST THE CROWN[1]

A Declaracion of the Costs which Sir John Fastolf was at, ben without this royaume.

THE declaracions of certeyn prests, costys, and chargys don and born by Sir John Fastolf, aswel in the tyme of the moste noble and victoryouse Princes of blessed memorie, Kyng Herry the iiij^the, Kyng Herry v^th, as in the tyme of our Souvereyn Lord Kyng that now is, in hys werrys by yend the see, as by the articles that folowen more pleynly apperyth :—

First, it ys to be remembred that to the sayd Fastolf ys owyng for divers costys and chargis by hym born for the tyme that he occupied th'office of the Constabulrye of Burdeux for the saufgarde of the Kyngys Duchie of Guyen, as it apperith pleynlye by accompt made of the sayd office of Constabulrye, remaynyng in the Kyngs Cheker at Westminster of record, wherof he yet nouther had payement nor assignement of, the somme of . . . . . ij^c. xxvij li. xv s. iij d. ob.

Item, in like wyse there ys owyng to the seyd Fastolf for wagys for hys service don to the Kyng, and to the Duc of Clarence, beyng the Kyng ys

¹ [From Fenn, iii. 268.] This appears to be a supplementary paper to the preceding. Two other copies or drafts of this paper exist among the Paston MSS. in the British Museum.

THE PASTON LETTERS

Lieutenant in the seyd Duchie of Guyen, as it may appere under suffisaunt writing, the somme of . . . . ij^c ij li. x s.

Item, in lyke wyse ys owyng to the seyd Fastolf for costys and chargys that he bare when he was Lieutenant of the towne of Harflew¹ in Normandie, as yt shewith by a debentur made to the seyd Fastolf, with hym remaynyng, ... Cxxxiij li. vj s. viij d.

Item, in lyke wyse ys owyng to the seyd Fastolf for the keping and vytaylyng of the Bastyle of Saint Anthoyne in Paris, as it apperith by writing suffisaunt and by the creditours of Sir John Tyrell, Knyght, late Tresourier of the Kyngs house, remaynyng in the Escheker of Westminster of record, the somme of . . . . . xlij li.

Item, there ys owyng to the seyd Fastolf for the saufgarde of the toune of Pount Melank² in the parties of Fraunce, as it apperith by accompt therof made in the Kyngs Escheker of England of record, the somme of . . . . iiij^xx ix li. x s. iiij a. ob. q.

Summa xlij. marc ix s. q.

And in semblable wyse, over all this ys owyng to the seyd Fastolf for prests and wagys of hym and his reteneys beyng

¹ Sir John Fastolf was Lieutenant of Harfleur in 1415.—F.
² Pont Meulent was taken in 1422.—F.

HENRY VI

in the Kings service in his royaume of Fraunce and duchie of Normandie, as wel abowte the saufgarde and gouvernaunce of his tounys, castell, and forteresses of Alaunson, Fresney Le Vicounte, Vernell, Honneflete, as for othir grete causys and charges born and payd in the Kyng our Souvereyn Lord ys dayes that nowys, for the avauncement of his conquest, the good and utilite of hym, of his seyd royaume and duchie forseid, as it apperyth oppenly by accomptys made in the Chambre of Accompts of Paris and Roon, wherof the vidimus remaynen with the seyd Fastolf, and also by certeyn debentur conteynyng the seyd sommes, redy to shewe, wherof the seyd Fastolf hiderto hath had nouther payement nor assignacion, the somme of . . . . v. m¹. iiij^xx ij. marc, xiij s. iij d. ob. sterling.

Summa totalis vj. m¹. cxxv. marc, ix s. ob. q.

There are two drafts of the preceding statement among the Paston MSS. in the British Museum, besides an imperfect draft hereafter mentioned. These appear to have been drawn up as early as the year 1452. One of these is in William Worcester's handwriting; the other is a fair copy from it, with further corrections, in his hand. The document printed above embodies all the corrections in the second paper, and corresponds with it almost exactly in every point, except that the latter places the second item relating to the Duke of Clarence at the very end of the account, and contains the following additional entries :—

And beside all this, there is yet owyng to the sayd Fastolf upon the voyage that Thomas Danyell made into Bretayn, as it is openly knowen, the somme of . . . Cli.

THE PASTON LETTERS

Item, overe this the seyd Fastolf lent to the voyage that Sir Thomas Kyryell made into Normandye, in the xxiiij. yere of the regne of the Kyng our Souverain Lorde, the somme of CC. marc; also lent to the Kyng afore that tyme in his necessite the somme of C*li*. The somme of both, ... ij^c. xxxiij*li*. vj*s*. viij*d*.

And also the seyd Fastolf hath borne grete charge and cost of alone made for the spede and helpe of the voyage whiche the Erle of Shrowysbury [1] now last made into the Kynges duchie of Guyenne, to whom God graunte good expedicion, as it shewith by suffisaunt writyng, for whiche at the commaundement of my Lord Cardynalle [2] the seyd Fastolf made a chevyssaunce and leyd to wedd [*i.e.* pawned] the substaunce of his pore juellys, in the whiche chevyssaunce the seyd Fastolf hath lost xxxvij*li*., and is like to lese more herafter, by cause he is not of poer to quyte hem oute; the seyd juellys lyne as yet to plegge for the somme of . . iiij^c*li*.

Somme of the prestys and debtys abofe rehersed, ... ij^{ml}. xlv. markes, vj*s*. *v*d. *ob*.

The following is written on a separate paper, on the back of which occurs the imperfect draft above referred to.

Item, overe all thys grete debtes dew at thys day to the seyd Fastolf, he desyryth and prayth that it may be pondered and concydered the grete lossez and damages that he hath susteyned and born, as well in the parties of Fraunce as in thys land; as at one tyme lost the somme and value of iiij^{ml}. mark for Guillem Remond, hys prysonnere, that agreed to pay for hys raunsom xxxij^{ml}. salux. The seyd prisonnere was take awey from hym, and delyvered the toune of Compyne in to the obbeissaunce of our Souvereyn Lord. Also the reward that the seyd Fastolf shuld hafe hys part for the takyng of the Duc off Allaunson, whych shuld mount for hys seyd part iiij^{ml}. [4000] markes, the grete losse that he hath in delyveryng upp the baronye of Syllye Guillem, in the counte of Mayn, be thout [*without*] recompense or reward, whych was gevyn to hym and hys assigneez in the value of m^l. m^l. [2000] salux off yerly rent. Also the lesyng of hys pore lyvelode in Normandie that was of the yerly

[1] John Talbot, first Earl, sent to France in 1452 to recover Guienne for the English; killed the following year in endeavouring to relieve Castillon.
[2] Cardinal Kemp.—*See* vol. ii. p. 160, Note 7.

64

HENRY VI

value of . . . . . ¹ mark. The grete importune lossez and damages that he hath had seth he came into England, whych hys evylle wyllers the officers and servauntes of the Duc of Suffolk have, be thout [*without*] cause resonable, made hym leese, as in causyng hym to be disseised wrongysly of iiij. of hys maners of Dedham, Beyton, Bradwell, Hykelyng, and Tychewell, to the value of ij^c. [200] mark of yerely rent; besyde othyr damages and lossez by colours of the lawe, and by menys of extorcions, as it may shew by a rolle of articles to the value of vj^{ml}. [6000] markes.

311

NOTE

'Many of the letters in this collection,' says Fenn (iii. 261, Note 1), 'mention the disputes between the Duke of Suffolk and Sir John Fastolf concerning different manors and estates.' This remark is made with reference to the complaints against Suffolk in No. 309 preceding. Only two of these letters have been seen by the present editor.

312

ABSTRACT [2]

Sir John Fastolf to John Paston.

Sends by his servant an instruction to be engrossed, corrected by Paston's advice, and a remembrance concerning Walsingham, which I .:ope by your help 'shall be corryged.' Certain friends of yours and mine have been here, and desire me to write to you 'for your friendship and go:d will, passing all other men's.'

1 [The date of this letter is quite uncertain, but it was probably written some time during those later years of his life when Sir John Fastolf resided at Caister. The signature, like some others during that period, is not in Fastolf's own hand.]

1 Blank in MS.
2 [From MS. Phillipps, 9735, No. 239.]

THE PASTON LETTERS

313

LORD CROMWELL TO JOHN PASTON [1]

To my right trusty ffrend, John Paston, Squier.

Before 1456

TRUSTY and welbeloved frend, I grete you wele. And for as much as hit is don me to understande that there is a greet straungenesse betwix my right trusty frend John Radcliff and you, withoute any matier or cause of substaunce, as I am lerned; wherfore, in as much as I love you wele bothe, I am not content hit shulde so be.

Praying you hertly to forbere the said straungenesse on your partie to suche tyme as I speke with you next my self, leting you wite I have wreten to him to do the same; and that ye faile not herof, as I may do any thing for you herafter. And our Lorde have you in His keping. Wretin at London, the x. day of Fevrier.

CROMWELL.

314

BOTONER TO JOHN PASTON [2]

To my maister, John Paston.

1456 JAN. 6

PLEASE your maistershyp to wete that I had sent yow word of the god chiere that the persons ye wote off had here upon New Yeer Day, and how well they toke it, but W. Barker coude playnly enforme yow. And

1 [From Fenn, ii. 290.] This letter was attributed by Fenn to Humphrey Bourchier, who was created Lord Cromwell in the first year of Edward IV., and it was accordingly placed by him in that reign. The signature, however, of which Fenn gives a facsimile, is not that of Humphrey Bourchier, Lord Cromwell, but of Ralph, Lord Cromwell, who died on the 4th January 1456.
2 [From Fenn, iii. 256.] By the reference to the Duke of Bedford's will as having been in dispute for twenty years, it would appear that this letter was written in the beginning of the year 1456. Bedford died at Rouen on the 14th September 1435.

66

HENRY VI

John Sadler of Ocle told me how they avaunted of it when he of Lynne came by hym at nyzt lyeng, that he had neider better chier, &c.

1456 JAN. 6

My maister demaundyth me sondry tymes when ye shall be here. I coude not sey till thys day be passed. William Geney shall be here to morn, so wold Jesus ye were her then. I asked licence to ryde yn to my contree, and my maistr dyd not graunt it; he seyd hys wille was for to make, &c. Y aunsuerd it fyt not me to know it. God gefe hym grace of holsom councell, and of a gode disposicion; *non est opus unius diei, nec unius septimanæ.*

My Lord Bedford wylle was made yn so bryeff and generall termys, that yn to thys day by the space of xx. yeer can neider hafe ende, but all wey new to constrewe and oppynnable; so a generallte shall ne may be so gode as a particuler declaracion.

I wryte blontly. I had foryete to hafe told yow Maister Fylongley meoved me to enforme my maister to hafe a generalle pease, so it myzt be worshypfull. Y hafe seyd no word, for I can not medle yn hygh maters that passyth my wyt; and therfor yff ye and W. Geney mete to gheders, ye know and can devyne best what ys to be doon. Our Lord be with yow.

Wryt hastly, vj. day Januar.

W. BOTONER, H.R.

315

BOTONER TO JOHN PASTON [1]

Please yow to wete that my maister [2] yn allwyse wille that I ryde to Dedham to speke with Broke as well as wyth the stuard, and to gefe aunsuer to Broke yn whate wyse he wille depart for the reuersyn; he was ryd or I came home. And my maister wille comyn with yow for the moyens of a chauntuarye to be founded of the place ye wote off; y seyd hym such chargeable maters wold be doo betyme to know the certeyntee. And a greter lak ys

1456(?)

1 [From Paston MSS., B.M.] From the desire expressed by the writer in this letter to visit his own country, we may refer it to the same period as the last.
2 Sir John Fastolf.

67

1456(?) yn hym, he taryeth so long to put all thynges of charge yn a sure wey; hyt ys for lake of sad councell to moove hym. And I most be at Castre by Thursday next; and I pray yow let me not be lete of my voyage yn to my contree, and I shall kepe Yorkesshyre with Spyrlyng, or such as shall ryde. The parson [1] with yow shall do well sort my maister evidences, and that ys one the grettist thyng nedefull for the seurtee of hys lyfelode; and so it wold be remembred hym, for now all thyng ys sett at appoynt, how it standyth with hys debtys and officers, except that mater of grettist charge, and also to provyde for the approowement of hys lyfelode. W. BOTONER.

And, syr, yff ye thynke to done (*think it to be done*), to meofe Cler of the acre lond, but gefe hym no credence yn the contrarye, for I shall preffe it trewe yn my seyng for onye man lyvyng. He that wille dysseyve hys servaunt yn maryage for so litell a thyng, he wold disseyve another frende yn a gretter thyng. He sekyth occasyons and querell to colour hys brekyng off.

316

BOTONER TO JOHN PASTON [2]

About 1456

Please yow to wete that as for ease of my maisters [3] tenaunts in Dedham, yff a lettre were devysed by Maister Geney yn my maister name or youres to Thomas Hygham, one of the justices of pease in Suffolk that toke the veredyt, he myzt do grete ease, as yn disavowyng of it or yn wythdrawyng it onute of the bokes. Robert Dene, clerk of the pese, seyth that lete my maister councell avise that whych he may do undammaged hymsylf, and he wille with all hys hert. John Bokkyng ys well remembred that my maister caused the seyd Thomas Hygham, by Maister Geney mocion, to be one of the justice of pease, and one Jermyn of Suffolk also. Whych both Hygham and Jermyn hath suffred my maister hafe, savyng your reverence, tweyn shrewde tornys seth that they mizt hafe letted, as now the seyd Thomas Hygham myzt hafe letted the presentment or a moderated othyrwyse, &c.

At reverence of God, beyth as sone as ye may with my maister to ease hys spyryttes. He questioneth and desputyth with hys servauntes here, and wolle not be aunsuerd ne satysfyed som tyme but after hys wylfulnesse, for hyt suffysyth not our simple wyttes to appease hys soule; but when he spekyth wyth Maister

---

[1] Sir Thomas Howes.
[2] [From Paston MSS., B.M.] There is no address to this letter, but it seems to have been intended for John Paston. The exact time when it was written is uncertain, but we have placed it after the last on account of the reference to Deddam. The true date cannot be many years before or after 1456.
[3] Sir John Fastolf.

68

Zelverton, yow, or wyth William Geney and suche othyrs as be auctorised yn the law, and wyth haboundance of godes, he ys content and haldeth hym pleased wyth your aunsuers and mocions, as reson ys that he be. So wold Jesus, one of yow iij., or som suche othyr yn your stede, myzt hang at hys gyrdyll dayly to aunsuer hys materes.

About 1456

I had but litille thyng to done when I scrybled thys bille.

Your,　　W. BOTONER.

317

ABSTRACT [1]

SIR JOHN FASTOLF ' TO THE WORSHIPFUL LADY AND MY RIGHT WELLBELOVED SISTER, WHYTTYNGHAM.'

As all the executors of my Lord Regent, except himself, are dead, and as he would not have her troubled in her age 'for execution of my said Lord's goods,' nor for the evidences of his purchased lands, etc., which were left in keeping 'with my brother your husband,' sends John Paston and other his attorneys to common with her, and settle the matter, which will be a great discharge for her husband's soul.

1456 JAN. 20

Castre, 20 Jan.

[This letter must have been written after the death of Lord Cromwell, who was one of Bedford's executors, and who died on the 4th January 1456.—*See* his Epitaph in Dugdale's *Baronage*, ii. 46.]

318

ABSTRACT [2]

SIR JOHN FASTOLF TO JOHN BOKKING OR WILLIAM BARKER, TO DELIVER TO JOHN PASTON AT LONDON.

Copy of a letter of Fastolf's to the wife of Sir Robert Whytyngham (the copy examined by Botoner) to the same effect as the preceding No., but with some slight differences in the wording, and dated 25th January instead of 20th.

JAN. 25

On the back is written :—'Cousin Paston, I pray you take Nicholas Molyneux, Thomas West, or Robert Waryn, whether ye may hafe at leyser, with you, to go speke with the gentlewoman.'

---

[1] [From MS. Phillipps, 9735, No. 266.]
[2] [From MS. Phillipps, 9735, No. 275.]

69

319

SIR JOHN FASTOLF TO JOHN PASTON AND OTHERS [1]

To my right trusty frendes, John Paston, Nicholas Molyneux, and Thomas West, Escuiers.

1456 JAN. 26

WORCHIPFULL Sirs, and my right trusty frendis, I commaunde me to you. And lyke you to wite that I desire to knowe in certayn, or evere I laboured to London, by whate menys in the lawe spirituell or temporell I might labour, or ellys my frendes and atturneys in my name and in myne absence myght laboure best, for the recuvere of the goodes of my Lord of Bedford, whos soule God assoyle, and that his purchased londes might be sold to fulfille his wille and pay his debtes. And if it were thought that the most spedyest and seurest wey were to have it doon by act of Parlement, than I desire and pray you, as my singuler trust is in you, that ye wille do make a substanciall bille in my name upon the said mater and for the said cause, to be grounded and devysed by avis of substanciall lerned man, as Thomas Yonge and othir suche, and of civille lawe, and the said bille to be put up to the Kyng, whiche is chief supervisor of my said Lordis testament, and to the Lordes Spirituelle and Temporelle, as to the Comyns, of this present Parlement, so as the iij. astates may graunte and passe hem cleerly. And the said bille may be grounded with so grete resons by your wysdomes and good enformacion, and so rightfull and of conscience that it shall not be denyed, ne letted to passe amonges the Lordes Spirituell and Temporell, neythir amonges the Comyns, whan it comyth before hem. And if this said bille, after it is devised and made, and sent me a copie of hit, hit shold be to me a singuler confort; for evere I came to London, I wold that alle thing shuld be made redy to my hande. And it were exspedient

---

[1] [The original of this letter is the property of W. A. Tyssen Amhurst, Esq. of Didlington Park, Brandon.] As this letter was written during Sir John Fastolf's residence at Caister, and Parliament appears to have been sitting at the time, the date must be 1456.

70

and according that my Lord Chaunceller [1] were meoved that it might please his good Lordship to write a lettre to me, in case I must come up for the said cause, and that by as muche he is in the mater as souverain juge and ordinarie principalle under the Pope in a cause testamentarie, and also by cause the wille of my said Lord is aproved in his court before his predecessour. And Alle myghty God kepe you.

1456 JAN. 26

Writ at Castre, the xxvj. day of Januar.

Your,

J. FASTOLF.

And I wolde this bille were devised by my Lord of Caunterbury is avis and agreement, to th'entent that he may tender the mater the more whan it shalle come in revolucion before hym. And I pray you hertely to take this mater tendirlye to hert, for it shall be to me my most singuler comfort, and for my discharge a grete record as of myne acquitayle to my said Lordis soule. Also ye must make frendes of suche as be nere aboute my said Lord of Caunterbury, and may do, as Maister John Stokys and his styward, for to remembre hys good Lordship as ofte as nede is. And that Davy Breknok ne Sir Robert Whitingham wyffe be not foryeete.

320

WILLIAM WORCESTER TO JOHN PASTON [2]

To the worshypfull Sir, John Paston, Escuier.

WORSHYPFULL, aftyr dew recomendacion, please your gode maistershyp to wite that where as my maister wrytith to yow so homelye of so manye materes to yow of hys, to be remembred unto hys councell lerned by mene of yow and of hys frendz and servauntz there,

JAN. 27

---

[1] Thomas Bourchier, Archbishop of Canterbury.
[2] [From Paston MSS., B.M.] This letter must have been written the day after the last, as this also speaks of a bill being presented to Parliament for recovery of the Duke of Bedford's goods. The passage in which the writer proposes visiting the west country confirms the date of Letter 314.

71

THE PASTON LETTERS

**1456
JAN. 27**

y pray yow and requyre yow not to wyte [*impute*] it me that y am the causer of it that my seyd maister noyeth yow with so manye materes, for, be God, hym sylf remembryth the moste part of hem ; albe it the particler rehersell of the materes be fressher yn my remembraunce then yn hys. And, Sir, yn trouth he boldyth hym to wryte to yow for the grete lofe and singler affeccion he hath yn yow before all othyr yn hys causes spedyng, and that ye wille moste tendyrlye of ony othyr re-membre hys servauntes as well as othyrs to whom belongyth to spede the materes. He desyryth my Lord Chauncellor shuld wryte to hym specially yff he most nedes com upp, and a bille to be made yn to Parlement for recuvere of my Lord Bedford godes.

Sir, there ys one Haryngton of Doncastre, a besye soule, that damagyth my maistre to gretely in Bentley. And Herry Sotehille ys of my maister councell, but no thyng that ys pro-fytable ys don to hym to remedye it, ye shall see by one Sir John Vincentes letter sent to yow now, and W. Barker can enforme yow. Yn the ende of thys terme y suppose to be at London, and yn to west contre. My maistre wrytith to yow for a rent of viij*li*. of annuite charged of a touneshyp called Batham Wyly, that Maister Scrope he shall be beneficed yn the ryzt of it. Ye have nede fare fayre with hym, for he ys full daungerouse when he wille. Y gate hym gode evidensis of the seyd rent that my maister ne my lady had nevere, and he can not know it, &c. Also my maister hath wreten to yow for avice of a new feffement to be made for the maners of Tychewell and Beytone, and betyme he desyryth to be sent hym. Y pray yow, and ye se Maister Yng at a leyser to commaund me to hym, and trustyng hys gode maistershyp that he wille be of my councell ayenst one William Fouler of Bokyngham thath kepyth from me a litelle lond. And yff he wille contynew hys gode maistershyp to me, ye may sey hym that I cast duelle yn my contree, and wayt uppon hym to help ghete ayen a pore gode of myn, for heere y thryve not, but lose my tyme. Y pray our Lord have yow yn hys kepyng.

Wryt hastlye, the xxvij. day of Januare.

Your, W. WYRCESTRE.

72

321

SIR JOHN FASTOLF TO JOHN PASTON[1]

To the worshypfull Sir, and my ryght welbelovyd cosyn, John Paston ; and in hys absence, to John Bokkyng and William Barker.

WORSHYPFULL Sir and cosyn, I recomaund me to yow. And lyke yow to wete that y have a taylle[2] with my cosyn Fenne[3] of v^c [500] marc and more, for to be chaunged uppon such places as a man myght have moste spedye payment ; and I pray yow hertlye to comyn wyth the seyd Fenne, that y myght be ensured of the seyd taylle to be eschaunged ; and for whate rewarde competant to be yeven uppon the same, I wolle agree it.

**1456
FEB. 5**

Item, I desyre to know who ben the residew, the remenant of the co-executors of the Lord Wyllughbye,[4] now the Lord Cromewell[5] ys deceased ; for thys cause. Hyt was so, that there was dew to the Lord Wyllughbye and to me x. m^{l.} [10,000] marc for a reward, to be payd of my Lord Bedford ys godes, for the takyng of the Duc of Allauncon.[6] And the seyd Lord Wyllughbye had but one thowsand marc payd, and I m^{l.} [1000] mrc, soo viij. m^{l.} [8000] levyth [*remains*] yhyt to pay ; of whych somme iiij. m^{l.} [4000] most grow to the executors of the seyd Lord Wyllughby to dispose. And ther-for y desyre that the executors, and such as most have intrest in the Lord Wyllughby goodes, may be comyned wyth ; that they may [make] pursuete for payment of the seyd iiij. m^{l.}

1 [From Fenn, i. 120.]
2 A tally. This was a cleft stick, in both parts of which notches were cut to represent sums of money due ; on which one part was given to the creditor, the other being retained by the debtor.
3 Hugh Fenn.
4 Robert, Lord Willoughby of Eresby.
5 Ralph, Lord Cromwell.
6 John, Duke of Alençon, taken prisoner at the battle of Verneuil in 1424.

73

THE PASTON LETTERS

**1456
FEB. 5**

[4000] marc, for hys part to be had, and y shall make for my part.

And [*i.e.* if] Maister Nevyle,[1] the whych hath wedded my Lady Wyllughbye, have power or intrest to resseyve the Lord Wyllughby ys debts, then he to be labured untoo. And my Lord of Salysburye woll be a grete helper yn thys cause.

The Kyng, whych ys Supervisor of my Lord Bedford testament, hath wreten and comaunded by sondry lettres, that the seyd Lord Wyllughbye shuld be content for hys part. And so moch the mater ys the furtherer.

And ther ys one Yon', a servaunt of the Lord Wyllugh-bye, whych pursewed thys mater ; yff he were yn London, he coude geve gode enformacion uppon thys mater.

Y pray yow wryte to me how my maters doth, and of such noveltees as ye have there. And our Lord have yow yn hys kepyng.

Wreten at Castr hastlye, v. day of Feveryer, anno xxxiiij^{to} Regis Henrici vi.

Your cosyn, J. FASTOLF.

322

JOHN BOCKING TO SIR JOHN FASTOLF[2]

To the right reverent and worshipful Sir, and my right good maister, my maister Sir John Fastolf, at Castre.

FEB. 9

RIGHT reverent and my right worshipful maister, I recomaunde me to yow in my right humble wise. Please hit your right good maistership to wyte that on Sonday laste I sent yow many and divers lettres and writynges, by Lampet, of all matiers that I hadde knowlege at that tyme redy to answere. And now suche tidinges as ar here, but fewe that ar straunge, excepte that this day my

1 Sir Thomas Nevill, a younger son of Richard, Earl of Salisbury, married Maud, the widow of Robert, Lord Willoughby.—Dugdale, ii. 86.
2 [From MS. Phillipps, 9735, No. 265.]

74

Lordes York and Warwik comen to the Parlement in a good aray, to the noumbre of iij^c [300] men, all jakkid[1] and in brigantiens,[2] and noo lord elles, wherof many men mervailed. It was seid on Saterday my Lord shuld have ben discharged this same day. And this day was seide, but if he hadde come stronge, he shuld have bene distrussid ; and no man knoweth or can sey that ony prefe may be hadde by whom, for men thinken verily there is no man able to take ony suche enterprinse.

**1456
FEB. 9**

The Kyng, as it was tolde me by a grete man, wolde have hym chief and princepall counceller, and soo to be called hise chef counceller and lieutenant as longe as hit shuld lyke the Kyng ; and hise patent to be made in that forme, and not soo large as it is by Parlement. But soome men thinken it wil ner can otherwise bee ; and men speke and devyne moche matere of the comyng this day in suche array to West-minster. And the Lordes speken this day in the Parlement of a greet gleymyng sterre that but late hathe be seen diverse tymes, mervelious in apperyng. The resumpsion, men truste, shall forthe, and my Lordes of Yorkes first power of protec-torship stande,'and elles not, &c. The Quene is a grete and strong labourid woman, for she spareth noo peyne to sue hire thinges to an intent and conclusion to hir power.

I have seid to the bringer here of more to declare yow alle a longe. And as for hise comyng, ye like to understande that your nevew, my Maister Filongley, hathe laboured and doon that he cowde or myght to hise preferraunce ; but as for to make hym freman and at hise ease, to hise profite and worship, it can not bee with owte William Lyne be here, that boughte hise prentishode of his maister, to hise grete hurte and castyng of bakke by ij. or iij. yere of tyme loste ; and ne were it that the maister and wardeyns of the Taillours tendre hym, be cause of yow and of Fynynglee, hise firste maister, that solde hym to William Lyne, as weel as the seide Lyne and Richard, shuld alle lese ther fredoms, as ye shall more pleinly under-stande by the reporte of the seid Richard, &c.

1 *i.e.* in coats of mail.—See vol. ii. p. 322, Note 3.
2 See vol. ii. p. 155, Note 2.

75

THE PASTON LETTERS

This day was my Lord Devenshire at Westminstre, and shuld have apperid, but he was countermaundid. As to youre matier of Wentworthe, the trety contynueth, and is putte by the arbitrours in Fortescue and Yelverton, and we have day of newe til Friday come sevenyght. God graunte it take a good ende. The lawe is with us clerly, as weel in th'atteynte as therinne as yette, blessid be our Lord, hoo have you in hise most noble governaunce.

Written in your place this Moneday of Fastyngange,[1] m̃ ccccl̃v. Your humble servaunt, J. B.

And that ye like to write a good lettre for Richard Fastolf to Sir Roger Chamberleyn, and to Thornton, Chamberleyn of London, and to both of hem, &c.

323

ABSTRACT [2]

Sir John Fastolf to John Paston

Thanks him for the pains he takes in his 'chargeable matters,' especially the ward of T. F., and his advice for the recovery of my Lord of Bedford's goods. My servants Bokkyng and Barker have written to me for writings making mention of the jewels and goods of my Lord delivered to Sir Robert Whitingham that they cannot find there. I send, therefore, W. Worcestre with a copy of Whitingham's account, which, however, is not a complete statement.

Castre, 12 Feb.

P.S.—Has just received a letter from Paston, for which he thanks him.

[This letter was evidently written in the same year as No. 317.]

---

[1] Fastingong was Shrovetide.—See vol. ii. p. 131, Note 1.

[2] [From ms. Phillipps, 9735, No. 270.]

HENRY VI

324

HUGH A FENNE TO JOHN PASTON [1]

To the right worchepfull Sir, John Paston, at Norwich.

RYGHT worchepfull Sir, I recumaunde me un to you. Leke you to wete my Maister Fastolf compert [2] is spedde and demyd in the Eschequyer for hym a yens the Kyng, wher in was crafti labour and cloos to the seid spede, and laked no dylygence, for the matter was defused and dubble intendementz after dyverse mennys appynyons.

Her is Williem Brandon, late Eschetour,[3] and wold have a *non molestando* [4] for Fulthorp; and be cause ye spake to me that no mo shuld be sued owte, and I can gete no lybarate [5] in that case, therfore, as it is tolde me, he wyll have oon up on Wenteworth is patente, and that wer to my maister bothe velleny and hurte. I pray you send me heryn your avyse. It is no grete maistre to gader up that mony, if it wer wele labord. I have somwhat affrayed them, and made hem spend mony, as I wot well ye shall her therof. Ye and I been discharged of our maynprys.

Now, Sir, for Goddis sake, as I have meved you a fore,

---

[1] [From Fenn, iii. 332.] The first paragraph of this letter seems to relate to Fastolf's claims against the Crown set forth in Nos. 309 and 310, and as these seem to have been drawn up in the end of 1455, this letter probably belongs to the year following. The reference to William Brandon as 'late escheator' confirms this date; and also, perhaps, the mention, at the end, of William Norwich, who was Sheriff of Norwich this year.

[2] Compertorium is a judicial inquest in civil proceedings made by Commissioners to find out, etc., the truth of a cause.—F.

[3] An Escheator was a county officer who certified into the Exchequer the King's escheats, *i.e.* lands which fell to the King, either for a time or altogether, as by the death of tenants *in capite*, minority of heirs, etc. William Brandon was Escheator of Norfolk and Suffolk from 13th November 33 Hen. VI. to 4th November 34 Hen. VI., *i.e.* from 1454 to 1455.

[4] A writ which lies for him who is molested contrary to the King's protection granted him.—F.

[5] A writ of *liberate* is a warrant either for the payment of annual pensions, etc., granted under the Great Seal, or for delivery of possession of certain lands or goods in the custody of a sheriff.

THE PASTON LETTERS

help to sette my maister in a worcheful dyreccion of his maters to his honour, his profyte, and his hertis ease, that which so doon he shall have the better leysour to dysspose hym self godly, and be sette his londs and his goodys to the plesour of God, and the wele of his sowle, that all men may sey he deyeth a wyse man and a worchepfull. Yf ye wyste what worchep shuld growe to you in favour and conseyte of all men thus to do, I wot well ye wolde be right spedy therin, for I beleve fully ye ar ryght well wylled therto; and if owte I cowde helpe therto at myn nexte comyng, yf I knew your entent, I wold do that I cowde. Yf it like you to wryte your avyse in a bylle that I myght have it by Good Fryday at Seint Benettys, Williem Norwyche wol send it theder. The Holy Trinyte conserve you in honour and prosperite.

From London, the furst day of Marche.

Your, HUGH A FENNE.

325

JAMES GRESHAM TO JOHN PASTON [1]

To my right worshipfull Maister, John Paston.

AFTER due recomendacion had, please it your maistership to wytte that William Yelverton was mevid by me to comene with my maister his fadir, as I wrot to yow from Norwich. And now he tellith me that he hath comened with his fadir; and he undirstondith that his fadir seyth that he hath not knowelaged Fennes [2] obligacion. And he seyth that Maister Fastolf undirstood that Fen hadde title to the maner of Haryngby, and therfor wold he that Fen shuld have it after Maister F. lyve; and, by liklynes, ther shall be labour made by Fenn to have releses of Maister Yelverton, &c., but he hath not yet relesed. He can no more

---

[1] [From Paston mss., B.M.] As this letter relates to money matters of Fenn and Sir John Fastolf, it may most probably be referred to the same year as Nos. 321 and 324.

[2] Hugh Fenn.—See No. 324.

HENRY VI

undirstond of hym as yet. If he can undirstond ony more pleynly this day, I shall have knowelage at Norwich on Friday or Saterday next comyng. Please it you to have pacience, though I write so brefly.

In hast, at Walsyngham, the Wednesseday next to fore Esterne.

Youre pouere servaunt, JAMES GR.

326

ARCHBISHOP BOURCHIER TO SIR JOHN FASTOLF [1]

To the right worshipfull, and my right entierly welbeloved Sir John Fastolf, Knight.

RIGHT worshipful, and my right entierly welbeloved, I grete you right hertly wele, thanking you specialy, and in full herty wise, for the verray geantle goodnesse that ye have shewid unto me at all tymes, praying you of good contynuance.

And as touching suche matiers as ye sente unto me fore, I truste to God verraly, insomuche as the rule is amendid heer, and the wedder waxeth seesonable and pleasante, to see you in thise parties within short tyme, at whiche tyme I shal commune and demeene unto you in suche wise, that ye shal be right wele pleasid.

And as for the matier concernyng my Lord of Bedford, thinketh nat contrarye, but that ye shal finde me hertly welwillid to doo that I can or may for th'accomplesshment of youre desire, as wel in that matier as in other, like as your servaunte John Bokking, berer hereof, can clierlier reporte unto you on my behalve; to whom like hit you to yeve feith and

---

[1] [From Fenn, i. 124.] The date of this letter will appear tolerably certain on a comparison with No. 319. In that letter Fastolf talks of coming up to London, if necessary, about the matter of my Lord of Bedford's goods, but expresses a wish that if he is to come, my Lord Chancellor—viz. the Archbishop of Canterbury—should be got to write him a letter about it.

1456
MARCH 27
credence in this partie. And the blissid Trinitee have you everlastingly in His keping.

Written in my Manoir of Lamehith, the xxvj. daie of March.

Your feithfull and trew, Th. Cant.

327

DAME ALICE OGARD TO JOHN PASTON[1]

To my right wurshipfull cosyn, John Paston, Esquyer.

MARCH 30 RYGHT worshippfull and enterly belovyd cosyn, I comaund me to yow hertly; latyng yow wete that there ys a contraversie mevyd be twix my cosyn John Radeclyff[2] of Attylburgh and me for the advoweson of the chirch of Attylburgh, the whech ys now voide, wheroff the title is myn veryly as God knowith, the whech shall be oppenyd unto yow; and upon Thursday next atte Wymondham, there shall be take an enquerre *de jure patronatus* afore Master Robert Popy and Master Symond Thornham, atte whech day I may nought be my selff as God knowyth, and thow I myght, yt were not convenyent.

And therfore, ryght trusty cosyn, consideryng that I am a wedowe impotent as of body, tendyrly and hertily I pray you, yf yt lyke yow, to be there assistyng my councell in my right as reson and lawe will upon Thursday next, be viij. of the clokke; and Fyncham,[3] Spelman, and othir of my councell shall be than there waytyng upon yow. And, jentyll cosyn, have me excused thowh I wryte thus brefly and homly to yow, for in trouth I do it of a synguler trust and affection, the

[1] [From Fenn, iii. 290.] This letter would appear to have been written in the year 1456, as Thomas Fairclowe, D.D., was presented to the church of Attleborough on the 2nd August in that year by Dame Alice Ogard as patron.
[2] John Radcliff, Esq., married Elizabeth, daughter and heir of Walter, Lord Fitz-Walter. He was in her right called Lord Fitz-Walter, and was killed at Ferrybridge in 1461.
[3] Simeon Fincham, of Fincham, Esq. His son John married Agnes, daughter of John Spelman, of Beckerton, Esq., I suppose the person here mentioned. He died in 1460, and Simeon in 1458.—F.

80

THE PASTON LETTERS

1456(?)
APRIL 25
at the loong, but wroong shal he nor any other do me, wher I may gete remedy by the lawe in any place throw Goddis mercy. Wherfor, sir, if he be stille in your servyse, lyke you I myght have knowlech, and thanne if your discreccion semith any thyng that I owe to do, by you I wil be advertysed and ruled; and if I coude conceyve that I owe to pay ageyn, as I understonde clerly the contrary, forsothe in right hasty seson wold I provyde and send hym from my seid lorde a sufficient discharge for myn more availl, that he shuld noght lose by me. And that is reson aswele, for that I wil not, by Goddis grace be hurted by hym, nor geve hym cause by my wil. I deserve my lordis good lordeship as wele as any other of my simple poer her. I besech you that by this simple bille I may be recommaunded to my worchepful maistresse. The blissid Trinite have you in His holy governaunce. Written, London xxv. day of Aprill.

Youris owen, Hugh a Fenne.

329

SIR JOHN FASTOLF TO JOHN PASTON[1]

To my worchepfull Cosyn, John Paston, Esquyer, in hast goodly.

1456
MAY 2
WORCHEPFULL Cosyn, I comaunde me to yow. Lyke yow to wete that for als moche as my lord of Norwich shal the next wyke visite the hous of Hykelyng, as on Thursday, as I understand, I pray yow that ye lyke to informe my lord how it is appoynted atwix the prior of the said hous and me that my title of xxv. marc of yerly rente is put in the ordynaunce of yow and Fyncheham, and if any variaunce fortune by twix yow that thanne we shall stand to the rule and ordynaunce of my lord of Caunterbury

[1] [Add. MS. 35,251, f. 24, B.M.] This letter seems to be of the same year as No. 341.

82

wheche I have in yow, consideryng the goode nome and fame 1456 MARCH 30 of trouth, wysdom, and good conducte, the which I here of you. And therfor, and ye may to youre well, I beseche you hertyly to be there, and ye shall nought lese therby with the grace of Almyghty Jesu, the wheche evyr preserve and promote you, gentill cosyn, in moche worship to youre hertys ease.

Atte Bokenham Castell, on Teuysday in Pache weke, in hast. D. A. Ogard.[1]

328

HUGH FENN TO JOHN PASTON[2]

To the worchepfull sir, John Paston esquyer.

WORCHEPFULL Sir, my reverent and right trusty 1456(?) APRIL 25 maister and cosyn, I recommaunde me to you. Lyke you to wyte that wher I have made my fyne of Ikburgh with Nicholas Waterman, thanne beyng feodary to my Lorde of Yorke, as the same Nicholas wil recorde, wherof sufficient writyng is had; the which payment, so made, is sufficient in the lawe; in the which caas noo newe feodary is chargeable nor I demaundable, but the seide Nicholas owe to answere therof in his accompt; and if he concele, my Lorde may have good remedy ageyns hym, and so owe to do. The which not withstandyng, oon I trowe called Osbarn, som tyme your servant, now my Lordis feodary, hath often meved to do I wote not, and now late hath distreyned my cattel, and seith he wil dryve hem awey, &c., and wil have Cs. for fyne, wher my uncle paied xxvjs. viijd., Herry Somer xxs., and so many other ded. Sir, he may do me a pety shame in distreyning and dryvyng awey to make me hevy, and hym not glad I hoop

[1] Dame Alice Ogard was the widow of Sir Andrew Ogard, Knight, whose first wife was Margaret, the daughter of Sir John Clifton, Knight, of Bokenham Castle. He died in 1454, and Alice, his relict, in 1460.—F.
[2] [Add. MS. 34,889, f. 173.] The year of this letter is uncertain, but it must belong to the latter part of Henry VI.'s reign, and there is great probability that it was written in 1456, like No. 324, which is also written by Hugh Fenn from London.

81

and of my seid lord of Norwich, they callyng to them ij. temporall juges suche as them please, the ij. chef juges only except. Wherfor that it please his good lordship to commaunde the seid priour to be bound by obligacion to stand to the seid appoyntement in lyke form as I at all tymes lefull am redy soe to do, to th'entent that my lord may verily knowe that the complysshyng of the seid appoyntement is nat deferred ner delayed by me. Forthermore, Cosyn, I understand that ye have a feodary concernyng all the knyght fees in this shire, and for als moche as the lord Scalys cleymeth an homage of my place called Essex in Hikelyng I pray yow that ye lyke to sende me woord if it can be understand by the seid feodary if suche an homage owe to be do or nay. Moreover like yow to remembre that lateward I meved unto yow that I wold do kyt out a litell fleet rennyng by twix the Comouns of your lordship of Maulteby and Castre ther it was of old tyme, and now is over grounded and growen by reedes. Wherfor lyke yow to write on to your baly of Mauteby to take your tenauntes with hym to have a sight of the seid water and ground, and that they bere half costes for ther part, and I wole bere the other part. And all though my wrytyngges put yow many tymes to gret labour and besynesses, I pray yow to take it that I do it for the synguler affiaunce and feythful trust unto yow. Besehyng All myghty God have yow, my worchefel Cosyn, in his merciful governaunce. Writ at Castre, the ijde. day of Maij.

And that ye lyke to come in to these partyes byfore ye ryde to London, I pray yow hertely that I may speke with yow for dyvers maters that I have to comowne with yow, &c.

J. Fastolf.

1456
MAY 2

83

330

JOHN BOCKYNG TO JOHN PASTON[1]

To my worshipful maister, John Paston, Squier.

1456
MAY 8

SIRE, please it your maistership to wyte that on Wednesday, the v. day of Maij, I received a lettre from you by the prestis man of Walsyngham, and the Ascencion Day,[2] in the mornyng, I received a lettre from yow bi the handes of John Frays, my maisteris man, in whiche bothe moche thinge is conteyned whiche alle at this tyme I may not answere un to my comyng the nexte weke. And as to our atteynte,[3] the Chief Justice hathe, sithe this day sevenyght, kept the Gildehalle in London with alle the Lordes and Juges, sauf one in eche place. My Maister Markham yesterday rode owte of London be tymes. Notwithstandyng we called ther upon, and hadde at the barre Chokke,[4] Letelton,[5] Jenney,[6] Illyngworth,[7] John Jenney, and Dyne, and remembrid the longe hangyng and the trouthe of the matier, with the grete hurte of the partie in the tyme ; and we have rule the next terme betymes, and non otherwise, for to morwe the juges sitten ayen in the toune. Mayster Yelverton can not be myry for Wyrmegey, and as for the distresse, it is a *non omittas*, and therfore Poley may and wil retorne what isseus he will. If thei be smale, we shall suffre at this tyme ; if thei be grete, we must appere for Wyngfelde ; and moche labour we have to conceyve a goode warant of attorney. We shal plede the next

1 [From Paston MSS., B.M.] The date of this letter is quite certain, not only from the circumstance of the 5th May being a Wednesday in 1456, as mentioned in the beginning, but also from Ascension Day falling between that and the 8th, the day on which this letter was written.
2 Ascension Day was the 6th May in 1456.
3 See Nos. 267, 268, etc.
4 Richard Choke, Serjeant-at-law, afterwards Judge of the Common Pleas.
5 Thomas Lyttelton, the great lawyer, at this time King's Serjeant, afterwards Judge of the Common Pleas, famous for his treatise on *Tenures.*
6 William Jenney.
7 Richard Illingworth, afterwards Chief Baron of the Exchequer.

84

1456
MAY 8

none erste. I wolde Arblaster and he spoke with yow this vacacion. I write noo more til my comyng.

As for tidinges, noon othere thanne I sent yow laste ; but forthe on the same, all is as it was with the Quene,[1] the Prince and myn Lord York ar stille at Tutbury and Sandale, and my Lord of Warrewick at Warrewick. My Lord Bukingham rode on Ascencion Even to Writell, noo thing wel plesid, and sumwhat on easid of herte to his purpose ; for the King hathe ley in London Friday, Saterday, Sonday, Monday, Teusday, and Wednesday remevid to Westminster agen. In alle whiche tyme, men of London that wer chargid and sworne wolde not nor hadde noo thing presentid sauf trespas ; this day thei shal sitte ayen. The peas is weel kepte, but the straungiers[2] ar soore a dradde, and dar not come on brode. Here is alle that I knowe as yet. Our Lord Jesu be with yow.

Writen at Suthwerk the viij. day of Maij.

I have paied to Dory C*s.*, and with moche peyne made hym to ghete day of the other C*s.* til the nexterme.

Your owen   J. B.

Endorsed in a seventeenth-century hand.—L'ra Joh'is Bokking, Attorn. in Communi Banco.

1 A full stop after 'Quene' would improve the grammar of this sentence, but the original is entirely without punctuation. The writer evidently meant that the Queen and Prince were at Tutbury, and the Duke of York at Sandal.
2 The foreign merchants. A riot took place about this time in London, in which the houses of foreigners were attacked.—*See* Fabyan's *Chronicle* ; also Brown's *Venetian Calendar*, i. 81, 84.

331

JOHN BOCKING TO JOHN PASTON[3]

To my Maister Paston.

MAY 15

WORSHIPFUL Sir, and my good maister, I recomaunde me to yow. This day I come home ; and as to our materes, I shall be with yow on Monday and Teusday next, be my maisters advys, and enforme

3 [From Fenn, i. 130.] Whitsun Eve, the day on which this letter is dated, fell on the 15th May in 1456, just a week after the date of last letter ; and no one can doubt that they both belong to the same year.

86

terme, for as at this tyme we wold on Monday enparle and we may.

1456
MAY 8

Ye must suerly entrete the shireve, for we have moche to doo with hym, as yesterday hadde we a grete day also in th'eschequer. Myn maister[1] is moche bounde to Haltofte, and there we ar assigned day over to the next terme, and dwelle in law. Our counsail was longe or thei come, but at the laste thei acquitte them weel. The bille was thought not by all that stode at the barre that wer of nother partie. We ar joyned in the sute of the obligacion in the Comon Place ayenst Jenney and Howes. As for attachement, ye may none have withowte ye or on of yow make your othe in propre persone before the barons. I wolde have doon it ; I cowde not be amytted. And as for other processe, it is advised that by the cors of th'eschequer I shall take a *venire facias* ayenst Wentworthe, Andrews, longe Barnard, and Deyvill *ad respondendum quare in possessionem, &c. ingressi sunt.* And we must telle where other Coughawe or Kirkeley, I suppose ; and therupon a distresse and an attachement ; nevertheles by your othe, &c., hereafter. And it is thought good that the same men shal be in the writte of ravyshment. Jenney hath advised us to ley it in Blithinges hundred, and I have taken of hym names ; for as for London it is nyghe enbracerye, as ye thought well, and soo is Middlesex. Maister Yelverton conceyvith it weel to your entent. There are aboughte and in Suffolk but fewe men as of gentilmen and men of substance, but if [*unless*] it be in Blithing hundre, were Hopton is grete ; but Jenney dredeth it not we may have good men at large ; and as for the hundre, he wil doo inow thereinne.

As for the tailes of iiij^{xx}*li.* [*four score pounds*], as yette we shal doo weel inowghe and thei were contentid ; or thei that shal have the silvere, the noyse were the lesse, for it shall, in pledyng, alwey be rehersid by our contrarie party that for x. marc we have alle that evere ther is, &c. I can not here now Wentworthe takith this matier by no meane ; what he meneth I wote not. He is no thing pleasid with the matier of the bille in th'eschequer. Thomas Denys come yesterday, and

1 Sir John Fastolf.

85

yow of all, and of suche as I will not write. Your cofre is at the Prinse Inne ; sende for it whane ye like, be the token, I hadde of Margret Goche a boke of lawe that Wigge brought me. As for tidyngs, my maistys your brother faren weel, and recomaunde them to my maistresse, there moder, to yow, and to all, &c.

1456
MAY 15

As for tidings elles, the Kyng is at Shene, the Quene and Prince at Tutbury, but if it be the latter remevyng. Tidings were that the Lord Beaumont was slayn, and my Lord Warrewik sore hurte, m^l. [1000] men slayn, and vj^{xx}. [*six score*] knyghts and squiers hurte, and no thing trewe, blessed be God. As for the Lumbards,[1] ij. of the trespasers were hanged on Monday, and there ar be this tyme proclamacions made, or shall be, thorwe London, the pees to be kepte up on grete peynes ; and the Lumbards to occupie the merchaundizes as thei dide til the Counsail or Parlament have otherwise determyned. And noo more as yet.

The atteynte abidith unreuled til the next terme, as I shal telle yow, and it shal doo weel with God is grace, hoe have yow in kepyng and all youres.

Writen at Caster *vigilia Pentecosten.*

Your owen   J. B.

1 *See* Note 2, preceding page.

332

HENRY WINDSOR TO JOHN PASTON[2]

AFTER humble and due recommendacion, please it your gode maistership to understand that atte makyng of this my pour letter ther were no noveltees with us, but suche as yee understode full well afor your departyng, except the Kyng woll in to Scotland in all maner wyse of

1456(?)
[MAY 16]

1 [From Fenn, iii. 278.] The date of this letter is doubtful. The two pieces of intelligence at the beginning were certainly both false rumours, as the writer, indeed, seems to have suspected. Henry VI. never went to Scotland in manner of war, and the Earl of Wiltshire never was made Chancellor. But the time when those rumours seem most likely to have arisen was in the year 1456, when the Duke of York had

87

1456(?)
[MAY 16] werre, and that my Lord of Weltshire shal be made Chaun-celler. I suppose the better is but a sclaunder, and therfore be ye avised howe ye delyver theym as tidynges.

Also I wotte ful well where I lefte you in suche matiers as it pleassyd you to make me of your counsell, as touchyng oon matier specially; and howe that ye said unto me whenne I desired your goode maistership to shewe favour in suche as ye best myght yf any thing shuld be shewed *ad lumen*, my Maister F. except; and howe that ye answered and said as it pleassyd you that I was conquered, in trouth, that shuld preve but a full grete unstabulnes in me with more, &c. But, Sir, I pray you howe some ever my maister rekeneth with any of his servaunts, bring not the matier in revolution in the open Courte, for and it were ones opened afore the Juges howe that any lettre patentes shuld be purchased of an ante date,[1] and the defaute faunde in me, he wold be a m^l [*thousand*] tymes avised, and my Maister F. both, or that ye wold amend me soo much as I shuld be appered therbe. And therfor I beseche you be well avised howe that matier be oponed for myn ease.

I was not desired to write unto you of no on persone, so God be my help, yourself except; but I wold ye wold take avise and counsell of the Preest that hadde you soo long under hand on Shorthursday,[2] whenne I and my feleship, God thank

been deprived of the Protectorate. The Earl of Wiltshire, being of the opposite party to York, was not unlikely to have been talked of as Chancellor, although the Chan-cellorship was given on the 7th of March to the Archbishop of Canterbury. As to the rumoured expedition against Scotland, we know that in the preceding year James II., in defiance of the truce, laid siege to Berwick, which offered a gallant resistance (Nicolas's *Privy Council Proceedings*, vi. 248). This, however, does not appear immediately to have led to open war between the two countries. Diplomatic relations were still carried on till, on the 10th of May 1456, James II. despatched Lyon Herald to the King of England to declare plainly that the Truce of 1453 was injurious to Scotland, and that he did not mean to abide by it (Lambeth MS. 211, f. 146 b). No reply was made to this message till the 26th of July, when an answer was despatched by the Duke of York in the King's name (*see* Rymer, xi. 383); but there can be little doubt the desire to punish the insolence of the Scots must have been very general long before.

[1] A law was passed in the eighteenth year of Henry VI. to put a stop to the abuse of persons making interest about the Court procuring antedated letters patent, by means of which they were enabled to claim the emoluments of lands or offices granted to them from a date anterior to the actual passing of the grant.—See Hardy's Introduction to the *Patent Rolls of King John*, p. xxx.

[2] Shere or Shore Thursday, Maundy Thursday, the day before Good Friday.

1456(?)
[MAY 16] you, hadde of you right grete chere to our grete comfort and your grete coste, howe that the same Preest understandeth this letter of the Gospell underwriten : ' Jesus dixit Simoni Petro, Si peccav[er]it in te frater tuus, vade et corripe eum inter te et ipsum solum ; si te audierit lucratus es fratrem tuum. Si autem te non audierit, adhibe tecum adhuc unum vel duos, ut in ore duorum vel trium testium stet omne verbum. Quod si non audierit, dic ecclesiæ ; si autem ecclesiam non audierit, sit tibi sicut ethnicus et publicanus,' etc. And in another place, ' Tunc accedens Petrus ad Jesum dixit, Domine, quotiens petevit [*peccabit*] in me frater meus, [et] dimittam ei ? usque septies ? Dicit illi Jesus, Non dico tibi, usque septies, set usque septuagesies septies.'[1]

My maister can doo no thing, the which shall come in open audience at thise deies, but it shalbe called your dede. Hit is not unknoon that cruell and vengible he hath byn ever, and for the most parte with aute pite and mercy ; I can no more but *vade et corripe eum*, for truly he cannot bryng about his matiers in this word [*world*], for the word is not for hym. I suppose it wolnot chaunge yetts by likelenes, but I beseche you, Sir, help not to amend hym onely, by [*but?*] every other man yf ye kno any mo mysse disposed.

I canno more, but as I can or mey, I shal be his servaunt and youres unto such tyme as ye woll comande me to sursese and leve of, yf it please hym.

Sir, I pray you take this copy[2] of your statute, it is not examined be me, for I found hit thise v. yeres pessed.

Writan in my slepyng tyme at after none, on Wytsonday. Also, Sir, yf I have rehersed wyttyngly the text of the Gospell syngularly unto your maistership, I beseche you to be had excused.

Your own,

H. W.

[1] St. Matthew's Gospel, chap. xviii. ver. 15, 16, 17, and ver. 21, 22.
[2] This relates to papers sent with this letter, and accounts for there being no direction, as the whole was enclosed in a parcel.—F.

333

JOHN RUSSE TO JOHN PASTON

To my Maister Paston, in haaste.

1456
JUNE I Please your good maistirship to wete that my Lord of Norffolk yaf in comaundement to Cristofre and to the balif of Colneise to laboure with us acording to your mocion. And as to Skilly, fermour of Cowhaugh, we enteryd there, and seyd we wold have payment for the half yeer past, and sewrete for the half yeer comynge, or ellys we wold distreyne and put hym out of pocession, and put in a newe fermoure ; and soo oure demenyng was suche that we toke no distresse, and yit we have hym bounde in an obligacion of xviij*li*. payabil at Michelmesse without condecion, and vj*s*. viij*d*. we receyvid of hym for opocession, for the ferme as yit remayneth on gatherid in the fermourez handes. But I seyd hym I wold be ther ageyn for the recedu of the half yeer ferme past withinne this xiiij. dayes ; and he seyd he wold do hise delygence to gather it up. But he spak with Wentworth sethyn, whiche yef hym an uttyr rebuke, as he swor to me, and seyd he wold have hys payment of Skylly, and therfor this next terme whiche he is bounden in to Wentworth for the yeerly payment of the same ferme ; and the seyd Wentworth seyd he wyll takyn an accyon of trespas this next terme ageyn us that were there ; and Devyle seyd ye were hender the londes at the begynning of your sute thanne ye be now, and that shalbe knowe be Lammesse next comyng, for he hathe thynges to shewe ye saw nevyr yit. Skilly offerid me xl*s*. to have delyvered hym ageyn hise obligacion, and he wold have put me in pocession of a distresse, and [*i.e.* if] I wold have delyvered it hym ; he seithe he dede nevyr so mad a dede, for Wentworth wold no bettyr mean thanne we had takyn a distresse. He shuld sone have remedyed that ; but now he seith Skylls is withoute remedy, but he will be payd, &c.

Item, Sir, as to the fermourez of the manor of Langston in Brustal, we have also sewyrte be oblygacion withoute condecion payabil at Michilmesse, and toke no distresse but enteryd the londes ; but we had gret peyne to brynge hem ther to, for ther is one John Cook of Braunford hath it in ferme of Wentworth all, and he leteth it out ageyn be parcelles to iij. sondre persones. But he was not at home, where for we have the same fermourez bounde for payment, and they had no mony redy, but they have promysed to delyvere Herry Deye at Yepiswiche this day xxx. in party of payment.

Item, Sir, as to the fermour of the maner of Bentley, clepid Bentley Houses, we have hym bonde in lyke wyse for the ferme of the seyd maner from Michilmesse last past tyl Mychelmesse next comyng, in an obligacion of x. marks payabil at Michilmesse next comyng, without ony condecyon ; and in party of payment I have receyvid of hym xiij*s*. iiij*d*., and he promyseth me iiij*l*.

[1] [From Paston MSS., B.M.]

1456
JUNE I markes at Lammesse next comyng. And as for Bradwell, my maistir[1] hathe sewyrte ; and as for Kyrley Hawe, I was with the fermour yistirday, but he wyll paye no peny, nor be bounde neithir. Wherfor my maistir shal sende us to take a distresse tomorwyn, and I truste we shal fynde sum meanys to have hym bounde, &c.

Item, John Andrewe hathe in fee yerly of the maner of Coughaugh xxs., and Thomas Denys xiij*s*. iiij*d*. of the maner of Foxhole, but as ferre as I can enquere there is payd no more feez out of non of the maneris to none othir men but to these tweyne.

Item, as for the endenturis, I sende here with a copy of Skyllyez endenture and a copy of Deynis endenture, fermour of the maner of Bentley, clepid Bentley Houses ; and Herry Deye shal brynge a copy of John Cooks endenture of the ferme of the maner of Langston in Brustall ; and as for Wareyn Bonde, he mad nevyr endenture for the ferme of Kyrkley Hawe, for he hathe ocupyed it but sethin Michilmesse last past ; and so he holdith it but be promyse upon compnaunt [*covenant* ?]. And we shal gete a copy of Sewalys endenture, fermour of Bradwelle, and me semyth, savyng your bettyr avyse, it war right expedient that ye shuld for the sped of this mater be at London in al haste.

Primo die Junii anno xxxiiij.[2]

Youre humble servaunt and bedeman,

JOHN RUSSE.

334

JOHN BOCKING TO JOHN PASTON[3]

To my right good maister, John Paston, Squier, at Norwiche, in haste.

JUNE 7 SIR, please it your maistership to wyte, I have my attache-ments graunted in open Courte with helpe of Litelton[4] and Hewe at Fen, and was bide to make redy the names, &c. before the Barons, of which Haltoft[5] was one.
. . . .[6]

[1] Sir John Fastolf.
[2] The thirty-fourth year of the reign of Henry VI. This date is added in a different hand, apparently that of John Paston, to whom the letter is addressed.
[3] [From Fenn, i. 134.] On comparing this with the previous letters of Bocking, Nos. 330 and 331, it will be seen that they must all three be of the same year.
[4] Thomas Lyttelton.—See p. 84, Note 5.
[5] Gilbert Haltoft.
[6] Here, in the original, followed various passages relating to law business, which Fenn has not printed.

THE PASTON LETTERS

1456
JUNE 7

As for tidings, the Kyng is at Shene, the Quene at Chestre; the Duc of Buk was, as I come hiderward, at Writell, the Erle of Warrewyke at Werrewyke, and the Lords Chaunceller,[1] Tresorier,[2] and th'Erle of Sar' [*Salisbury*] in London, and noo more Lords at the begynyng this day of the grete Counsail. Many men say that there shuld be, but thei wote not what. The sege shall, as men say, come to Caleys and to Guynes, for moche puple come overe the water of Somme, and grete navies on the see.

Th'Erle of Penbroke[3] is with the Kyng, and noo more Lordis. Th'Erle of Richemond[4] and Griffith Suoh (?) are at werre gretely in Wales. The Comons of Kent, as thei werre wo[n]tte, er not all weel disposid, for there is in doyng amongs hem what evere it bee. Of Scotts is here but litell talkyng. My Lord York is at Sendall stille, and waytith on the Quene and she up on hym.

I dide my maistress your moderis erands, as ye have herde of, for Maister William hath writen his entente, and he and Clement faren weel.

Writen at Horshighdone, vij^mo die Junij.

Rokewode and Crane faren weel, and thei and I re-comaunde hem to my maistress your wif.

And as I understande, the Clerke of the Rolles is owte of charite with Maister Yelverton, and my Lord Chaunceller a litell mevid, &c.

Your owen, J. B.

[1] Archbishop Bourchier.
[2] Henry, Viscount Bourchier, was appointed Lord Treasurer on the 29th May 1455 (*Patent Roll*, 33 Hen. VI., p. 2, m. 12), and so continued till the 5th October 1456, when the office was taken from him and given to the Earl of Shrewsbury (*Patent*, 35 Hen. VI., p. 1, m. 16).
[3] Jasper Tudor.—*See* vol. ii. p. 298, Note 1.
[4] Edmund Tudor.—*See* vol. ii. p. 297, Note 6.

92

THE PASTON LETTERS

1456
JUNE 24

about the process of Hykelyng that has been so many years and days driven off.

St. John Baptist's Day.

[From the reference to 'the matter of my Lord of Bedford,' this letter was most probably written in the year 1456.]

337

ABSTRACT[1]

SIR JOHN FASTOLF TO JOHN PASTON.

'First it is to remember that, upon St. John's day, there was Sir Symond Brayles, chaplain of my Lady of Suffolk, and in presence of Sir Miles Stapleton and Edward Grymston, said that the 200 marks was paid before in the Duke of Suffolk's days.' Can prove by writings that this was not so, and that he 'offered to put it upon my Lord Chancellor and upon one or two of Lords of the King's council as my said Lord Chancellor will call unto him,' that it may be known whether my Lady is wronged or Fastolf. The £100 of the above sum was not paid by assignment to Clyffton. Sir Simon complains that the suit was stolen against Sir Thos. Tuddenham, and judgment given without my Lady's counsel knowing of it ; which can be disproved.

Castre, St. John Baptist's Day.

'Item, I remembered Sir Simon for the restitution of my revenues of Dedham 3 year day, and my damage of a mill put down,' etc. I paid 500 marks for the ward of Sir Rob. Harlyng's daughter for my Lord to Sir John Clyfton, of which the Duke had no right to receive one penny, for there was no land held of the King.

[This letter corresponds so closely with the last that it must have been written the same day.]

[1] [From MS. Phillipps, 9735, No. 238.]

94

HENRY VI

335

ABSTRACT[1]

SIR JOHN FASTOLF TO JOHN PASTON, ESQ.

As to the matters on which Paston sent to him by Will. Barker to desire his advice, Paston knows that Fastolf has put his whole confidence in him, and begs he will do with the advice of Fastolf's learned counsel whatever they jointly think for his weal ; 'for ye know well I am so visited by the hand of God that I may not deal with such troublous matters, without it should be to great hurt of my bodily welfare, which I trust ye would not desire.' If you find my Lady of York disposed to visit this poor place, commend me to her, and tell her how it is with me that I cannot receive her as I ought.

Castre, 18 June.

1456
JUNE 18

[As it will appear a little further on that the Duchess of York visited Caister in 1456, this letter is probably of that year.]

336

ABSTRACT[2]

SIR J. FASTOLF TO JOHN PASTON.

To-day my cousin Sir Miles Stapleton, Sir James Braylyes, Andrew Grygges, 'hyr resseyvor,' and Grymston have been with Fastolf at Castre, and brought him 253 marks, which they would have paid if he had had the obligation here. Sends therefore a letter by his servant Colyn how Sir S. and he are agreed for its deliverance, etc. Sir S. made many strange insinuations that the money was paid before, partly by assignment to Clyffton, etc. On the 18th and 19th inst. 'long Bernard, with a priest of Kent, to the number of 16 horse, hafe, at Nacton, Bentley, and other places of F., and entered by colour of a deed of feoffment made to the Lady Roos and others, and hafe right proud language to the farmers, that they will obtain their intent.' Russe has written more plainly by Nich. Colman.

'Item, I charge right greatly the matter of my Lord of Bedford for my discharge, and for the recovery of my Lord's goods.' Begs Paston to common with the Lord Chancellor and others about it ; and desires him to give 'mine attorney, Raulyns, and my serjeants' a warning 'to take more tenderness'

JUNE 24

[1] [From MS. Phillipps, 9735, No. 242.]   [2] [*Ibid.*, No. 263.]

93

HENRY VI

338

FRIAR BRACKLEY TO JOHN PASTON[1]

Honorabili viro Johanni Paston armigero ac confratri suo Willelmo germano uterino.[2]

RYTE reverent Syre, &c. I am informyd credybily of a secrete frend that S. T. T. [*Sir Thomas Tuddenham*] and J. H. [*John Heydon*], with J. A. [*John Andrews ?*] and other of cursyd covy, wyl bryng with hem many gentylmen of here bende to compleyn upon me at the next chapitle, &c. And there fore, by the grace of God, I dispose me, with help of zour good maysterschip and my Mayster Willyam, zour brother. Where fore, at the reverens of God, that ze do speke with the clerk men clepyn Brayn, that kepyth the bokys of here inditementes at the *oyer determyner*, anno xxix° regni Regis ; and that an extret or a copy myte schortly be wrytyn owt of as many namys as dedyn indyte T. T. and J. H. for trespas, extorsyones, and oppressyonys done to other men, as wele as to my Mayster Fastolff, etc., that I may be redy to schew to my ordre, lyk a kalender, a legende of here lyvys and here rewlyng of the cuntre, in destruccyon and gret myschef of the cuntre in here dayes. At the reverens of

1456(?)
[JUNE 29]

[1] [From Paston MSS., B.M.] Dr. John Brackley, the writer of this letter, was a Grey Friar of Norwich, of considerable celebrity as a preacher. Several letters of his are found in this collection, written in the years 1459 and 1460. This, however, must be a few years earlier, as in 1459 Brackley writes of William Worcester in very different terms. The handwriting also is not so close as that of his later letters. We cannot, however, carry the date further back than 1455, as it seems that Worcester and Howes were at this time together, which must have been at Caister. Nor will the year 1455 itself suit all the circumstances of the letter, for it is evident that John and William Paston were also together, and as the writer asks John Paston to speak to Yelverton, it may be presumed they were in London. Now, John Paston was certainly not in London within a week after St. John the Baptist's Day in 1455. We have therefore placed the letter in 1456. It will be observed that, on the 1st of June in that year, John Russe advised Paston to go up to London.
[2] This address is in William Worcester's hand. The letter itself is in Brackley's own.

95

1456(?)
JUNE 29] Jesu, forzet not this mater, ne the mater of Dedham, etc. I wolde ze askyd my good lord and mayster, Yelverton, yf I sent hym ony letter in the same mater, &c. Dicente Davitico Psalmo :[1] *Ne obliviscaris voces inimicorum tuorum, nam superbia eorum ascendit semper* in psalmo ; qui et si nunquam ascendant in cœlos, utinam nunquam desendant ab [*ad*] abissos, &c., etsi anima eorum in malis tabescebat, &c. Scriptum festinacione (?) feria 3ª post festum Natalis Sancti Johannis Baptistæ.[2] Recommendetis me magistro meo W. Paston, confratri vestro, et Thomæ Playter cognato meo, cui dicite quod faciat Willelmum Geneye sibi benivolum quia Sampson filius et heres J. Sampson desendant ab (?) abissos, &c. Owlton mortuus, et ibi sunt duæ viduæ, major et minor, senior et junior. Eligatur quæ sibi melius placet.

Magister Thomas Howys vobis amantissimus se cordialissime recommendat vobis, etc. Item, Willelmus Wigorniensis recommendat se vobis ex toto corde. Scribo vobis, utinam ad placitum.

Vester ad vota,
F. J. B., *Minorum minimus.*

I hafe a rolle redy of the inditements, that they were indityd for trespase and extorsyon and oppressyon done to my Mayster Fastolff, in the keping of W. Worceter, &c.

Visa frangatur et in ignem post jaciatur. Si dignemini loqui cum effectu magistro Ricardo Fysscher, secretario domini mei comitis Warwicensis, pro cujus nomine et amore promptissimus sum adhuc plura pati, ut mittatur pro me litera magistro provinciali et diffinitoribus.

[1] *See* Psalm lxxiii. (or lxxiv.) 23.
[2] St. John the Baptist's Day is the 24th June. *Feria tertia* means Tuesday.

339

FRIAR BRACKLEY TO JOHN PASTON[1]

Magistro meo venerabili Johanni Paston Armigero detui.

Dixi enim magistro meo gardiano ante meum exitum quod magistri mei generosi et amici alii vellent me juvare pro die Jovis pro pascendo doctores, patres ac cæteros confratres nostri provincialis capituli ; et in exitu meo consentire noluit, quia Gurnay suus socius et procurator, frater juvenis nostri conventus et unus sacerdos simplex, curatus de Worsted, et Bukle, cocus, super se diem prædictum assumpserunt. Et ego dixi, 'Olim fuit modus quod unus ejusdem loci magister esset præferendus in tali diei eleccione. Sed unum scitote, si magistri mei certi generosi et ego cum eis habere non potuerimus diem quem elegimus, certe pro hoc tempore nullum alium diem habere volumus.' Utinam placeret vobis ut magistra mea, uxor vestra, vellet mittere pro magistro gardiano, et dicere sibi quod ipsa quæsivit a me qualem diem ego haberem pro fratribus pascendis in tempore capituli et quod ego dixi me habiturum illum vel certe nullum aliter. Quæcumque ego potero procurare de pecuniis seu victualibus ego singula venderem et expendere vellem in reparacionibus, &c. Rogo vos ex caritate ut magistræ meæ matri vestræ ac aliis amicis vestris vobis notis, insinuetis nostram indigenciam pro faciliori relevamine capituli provincialis. Sic enim ad vestri et mei magistri mei specialem instanciam præsencialiter habere residenciam teneo, ut alia loca pro præsenti negocio accedere non valeam, &c. Non plura pro præsenti sunt calamo præsentanda, nisi quod vos, vestros et vestra Jesus Christus graciose conservet in prosperis et graciosius dirigat in agendis. Amen.

Recommendetis me, si placeat, uxori et matri et confratribus vestris W., &c. et domino meo Rectori de Blofeld, utinam de Hadle, &c.; cui dicatis quod hac nocte jacuit Colinus Gallicus cum pulcherima Amasia sua in camera conducta per eum, &c. Utinam nunquam vigeat, &c. Ipse proponit in vestra præsentia dicere dicto rectori satis perversa verba. Et spero quod dominus Rector faciat de sua speciali gratia meum negocium per Ricardum famulum suum crastina die summo mane expediendum, quia dies ista est dies ultima, &c. Ex manerio de Castre, Sabbato circa tempus prandii festinantissime.

Magister meus[2] valde gavisus est quando audivit de vobis quomodo scienter, audacter, viriliter et veraciter respondistis adversariis vestris coram Domino Cancellario aliisque dominis, &c.

Vester præ cæteris orator,
F. J. B., *Minorum minimus.*

[1] This letter was copied by the Editor from one of the Royden Hall MSS. in 1875.
[2] Sir John Fastolf.

340

HENRY FYLUNGLEY TO SIR JOHN FASTOLF[1]

To my ryght worshipfull unkle, and my ryght good master, Syr John Fastalf, Knyght.

1456(?)
JULY 17
RYGHT worshipfull unkull, and my ryght good master, I recomaund me to yow wyth all my servys. And, Sir, my brother Paston and I have comened togeder as touchinge to your colage that ye wold have made ; and, Sir, hit ys to gret a good that ys axed of yow for youre lycens ; for they ax for every C. marc that ye wold amortyse D. marcz, and woll gefe hit noo better chepe.

And, Sir, y told my brother Paston that my Lady of Bargeveney[2] hath, in dyvers Abbeyes in Lecestershyre, vij. or viij. prestes singinge for her perpetuell, by my brother Darcyes and my unkle Brokesbyes meanes, for they were her executors ; and they acorded for money, and gafe a cc. or ccc. marc, as they myzt acord for a prest. And for the suerte that he shuld synge in the same abbey for ever, they had maners of good valew bounden to such persones as plesed the sayd barthern [*brethren*], Brokkesby and my brother Darcy, that the sayd servyse shulde be kept. And for lytell moore then the Kynge axed hem for a lycence, they went thorgh with the sayd abbots. And y hold this wey as sure as that other. Ye may comen with youre councell therof.

[1] [From Fenn, i. 166.] This letter must have been written about the time Sir John Fastolf first began to make inquiry on what terms he could obtain a licence for establishing a college at Caister,—a project which he had much at heart during the latter years of his life. A letter from Sir John himself upon this subject will be found a little further on, dated the 18th November (No. 351), and we think it probable that this is of the same year, 1456.
[2] Edward Nevill, Lord Abergavenny, was twice married. His first wife, to whom he owed his title, was Elizabeth, daughter of Richard Beauchamp, Earl of Worcester. His second was Catherine, daughter of Sir Robert Howard. The Lady here mentioned is probably the former, for though Dugdale says he obtained a dispensation for his second marriage in 1448, that date is inconsistent with the age of his son and other facts mentioned.

And yf there be any servyse that I can do for yow, hit shall be redy at all tymes, with the grace of God, who have yow in his kepynge.

1456(?)
JULY 17

Wryten at London, the xvij. day of Juyll.
Your nevew and servaunt,
HENRY FYLUNGLEY.

341

SIR JOHN FASTOLF TO JOHN PASTON[1]

To my worshipful cousyn, John Paston.

1456
JULY 31
RIGHT trusty and worshipful cousyn, I recomaunde me to yow. And like it yow to wyte, myn attorny, Raulyns, hathe enformed me that the Jugis have ruled processe to goo owte ayenst the priour of Hikelyng of distresse *per omnia bona et catalla*, of whiche the writte and other ar not yet come fro London. I trust whan thei come, be your good counsail and meane, the Shireve wil doo his devoir ; how be it, as I understande, thei have sente the Lord Scales all there evidences, and he wil come and dwelle there hym silf. And I am also enformed, for certeyn, that the Bushop of Norwiche, for all the truste I hadde to hym, that by his meane I shulde have knowen there fundacion, he hathe warned his officeres not to have adoo therinne, by cause of the Lord Scales, &c. Cousyn, I pray yow, in as moche as the matere, by agrement, was putte in you and Fyncham, and how that ye, for the same cause, specially kepte your day at London, and toke not in there defaute and not myn, that ye wil soo in caas ye see Fyncham remembre, and to othere there as ye seme it shulde profite to be knowen, and that yet nevertheles my sute soo serforthe I wole yet, as I wolde thanne, and at all tymes am redy ; and soo I wolde the priour knewe, and all othere, as weel his weelwillers as otheres, as the bringer

[1] [From Paston MSS., B.M.] This letter is doubtless of the same year as No. 336, in the end of which Fastolf wishes his attorney, Rawlyns, urged to greater activity in the matter of Hickling.

THE PASTON LETTERS

1456
JULY 31 herof shall declare you more pleinly. As for tidinges, my folkes ar not yet come fro London. The abbot of Seint Benettes hathe ben with me, and suche as he tolde me the bringer shall enforme you. And our Lord Jesu have you in governaunce.

Writen at Castre, the last day of Julle.

Your cousyn,   J. F.

342

LORD SCALES TO JOHN PASTON[1]

To my right trusty and intierly welbeloved frend,
John Paston, Squier.

AUG. 10 RIGHT trusty and entierly welbeloved frend, I grete you well, and wull ze wite that Danyell[2] hath required me to write un to you, praying you that ze wyll kepe the day upon Thursday[3] vij. dayes nexst comyng, which shal be for the best, as I trust; not with standyng I suppose lerned men wyll not be easy for to gete be cause of this besy tyme of hervest. Almyghty God have you in Hise governaunce.

Writen at Mydelton,[4] the x. day of August.

Your frend,   SCALES.

343

LORD SCALES TO JOHN PASTON[5]

To my right trusty and welbeloved frend, John Paston, Squier.

About
1456(?) Right trusty and welbeloved frend, I grete you hertly well. And for as mych as I u[ndyrstond] a bill was made at Yermuth ageyns my cousyn Bryan

---

[1] [From Fenn, i. 158.] This letter is dated by a memorandum at the bottom of the original, in the handwriting, as Fenn believes, of John Paston : 'Lettera inter Mich. xxxiiij. et xxxv.'
[2] Thomas Daniel of Rising.—*See* vol. ii. pp. 79, 80, 103, etc.
[3] 19th August.   [4] In Norfolk.
[5] [From Paston MSS., B.M.] This letter is placed immediately after another letter of Lord Scales, dated like this from his seat at Middleton in Norfolk, as probably belonging to the same period, though the exact year is uncertain.

100

HENRY VI

Stapylton and hise wy. . . . have set up the said bill in the Kynges About Bench, which bill is in your kepyng, pray[ing] you that ye wyll sende me the 1456(same bill be the bringer herof, to the entent I m[ay] se it. And as I am informed be my said cousyn, ye shewed hym grete gentilnesse and benyvolence, wherof I thanke you right hertely. I pray God have you in governance.

Writen at Midelton, the xx. day of Septembre.

Zowr frend,   SCALES.

344

ARCHBISHOP BOURCHIER TO JOHN PASTON[1]

To our right truste and right welbeloved John Paston, Esquier,
and William Norwiche,[2] and to either of theym.

RIGHT truste and right welbeloved, we grete you hertly 1456 wel. And where as Sir Nichol Bowet, Knight, sueth SEPT. 7 an appeelle in the countee of Norffolk ayenst oon Robert Offord of Berking for the deeth of oon Sir Henry Bowet, clerc, we being enformed that the matier is pitevous, praie you hertly that ye wul in our behalve moeve and entreete the Shirreve of the saide countee to surceese of the execucion of any processe upon the exigent[3] to hym directed in that behalve unto the next terme, so that resonable meanes maye be founden to save the saide Robert harmelesse; lating hym wite that we have written to the saide Sir Nichol for a convenient treetie to be taken in that behalve, as shalbe thought according to right. And God have you ever in his keping.

Written in our Manoir of Mortelake, the vij. daie of September.

T., ARCHBYSSHOPP OF CANTERBURY.

---

[1] [From Fenn, iii. 276.] This letter may be presumed to have been written during the time that Archbishop Bourchier was Lord Chancellor, viz. between 7th March 1455 and 11th October 1456, when the Great Seal was given to Bishop Waynfleet. William Norwich, also, was Sheriff of Norwich in 1455, and is doubtless addressed in that capacity, but his year of office would not have begun so early as September. The letter therefore belongs to the following year.
[2] Sheriff of Norwich, 1455; Mayor, 1461. Died, 1463-4.—Blomefield.
[3] *See* vol. ii. p. 248, Note 4.

101

THE PASTON LETTERS

345

JOHN BOCKING TO JOHN PASTON[1]

To my right worshipful Maister, John Paston.

1456
OCT. 8 RIGHT worshipful Sir, and my good maister, I recomaunde me to yow, and have receyvid a lettre from yow by Sir Thomas is man, berer herof. And as for the accions,[2] bothe of ravishement and th'attachement, the declaracions ar made *tunc solvend'* and not *solut'*, and as moche amendid as we can or may be favour have amendid. We hadde be beguyled and they hadde not be sen in Norffolk, for here til this day come noo counsaill; and to have *per manus Johannis Wyngfelde* it wole not be, for we can not bringe it inne, and also it is to late.

And as for iiij^xx^li. [*fourscore pounds*],[3] Fenn and I mette with Worsop this day, and he spake soore to Fenn and me, and we put hym overe, saying we wolde doo as moche as we myghte. I thinke verily that Fenn wole deserve ther inne a thanke, but I can not understande hym what he wolde be doon to, or how rewardid, for whanne I speke of it he is desplesid, and seithe he desirith noo rewarde; but he farith as a man wole sey he wold noo silvere, and lokith awaywardes and takith a noble. And he hath written to yow of the matere of Sir Philip Wentworthe touching this writte of *liberate*,[4] whiche is but a color and noo warant sufficient, ner we owe not to doo no thinge that shuld obeye it, ner the Shireve nother dothe but of favor that he dothe to hem, and hym liste otherwise to doo, as Fenn writeth yow more pleinly. And as

---

[1] [From Paston MSS., B.M.] The body of this letter relates entirely to proceedings in the dispute between Sir John Fastolf and Sir Philip Wentworth about the wardship of Thomas Fastolf. The postscript alone relates to public matters. The date will appear by the footnotes.
[2] Against Sir Philip Wentworth.
[3] This sum was to be paid by John Bocking and William Worcester for a patent of the wardship of Thomas Fastolf.—*See* Letter 347 following.
[4] *See* p. 77, Note 5.

102

HENRY VI

for a *supersedies* [*sic*], there lithe noon, as he seith, up on a 1456 *liberate*. OCT. 8

And as for entryng in Bradwell, thei doo opyn wronge, for after myn patent opteyned, there was a writte to sease it into the Kynges hande, and soo it was and is. And as to your patent, it is counsailled me to have a writte to th'eschetor *de custodia liberanda*, whiche may not be denyed. And if we myght have *una cum exitibus a tempore mortis*, it were a sovereigne writte. It shalbe assaied, and doo thertoo what can lete; the fermours be promised to be saved harmeles and chargid not to paie ony thing to them.

And as for the iiij^xx^li. [*fourscore pounds*] to be sette on Olivere is taile, I can not see it wole be, for there is noo suche worlde to bringe it abowte. It is faire, and we can ghete it on Fulthorp is dette by grete labor for agrement, for I drede it wole be moste agayn us that it is of recorde soo longe unpaied. And Hue at Fenn sueth now to Nailer to ghete owte moo *liberates*, suche as the last were to the last eschetor. And this God graunte thei take good spede.

And as to your isseus, I shal accordyng to your lettre speke with Gresham whanne he cometh, and the Juges and Barons bothe shalbe enformed of the title of Wentworthe, as ye write, and how it is up on a feyned dede upon surrender, and a patent cancelled, &c., which Fenn hath promisid to doo.

And as to Sir Thomas matier, I write un to yow and hym joinctly what hathe be doon therinne at this tyme. And Jesu have yow in kepyng.

Writen at Suthwerk, the viij. day of Octobre.

As to tidinges, the Kyng and the Quene ar at Coventre.[1] The Counsail be ganne there yesterday, and my Lord Shrewyshbury,[2] Tresorier of England, and John Wode shalb [*shall be*] Under-Tresorer. Thus thei say in the Chequer.

Your owen,   J. B.

---

[1] The Privy Seal dates show the King to have been at Coventry between the 20th September and the 14th October 1456.
[2] John Talbot, second Earl of Shrewsbury, was appointed Treasurer on the 5th October 1456.—*Patent Roll*, 35 Hen. VI., p. 1, m. 16.

103

346

BOTONER TO JOHN PASTON[1]

To my Maister Paston.

1456(?) OCT. 12 PLEASE yow to wete that I hafe remembred of the langage that I hafe late lerned W. Barker had to yow and othyrs of his accomptes apposyng,[2] and of that they be not hole bethyn [*between*] ws, but yn division, &c. Sir, as I may sey yow, hyt was nevere othyrwyse, ne nevere ys lyke to be; for now they hafe do with Lowys, he that ys next shall be yn the same as he was yn gelosye; for when my maister comaundyth such as of force, by reson of her occupacion, most be nere hym, to do a message to hys felow, or question of hym, hyt shall be ymagyned amonges our felyshyp that he doth make maters to my maister. And so it ys ymagyned of me when I wryte lettres to London, to Bokkyng or Barker, that yn such maters as please hem not, then it ys my doyng; yff it take well to theyr entent, then it ys her [*their*] doyng. And yn gode feyth, so it was ymagyned of me and othyrs that wrote, by my maister comaundment, to Castre, to the parson of Blofeld, Geffrey Spyrlyng, and othyrs, that of such maters as was lykyng to hem and coude be sped by help of my maister frendes as by theyr solicytyng, then it was seyd that it was theyr avice, labour, and doyng. And yff the maters went not to my maister entent, ne that they coude not bryng aboute the mater, then it was imagyned and jangled that it was my wrytyng and doyng. I bare nevere my maister purs, ne condyt nevere chargeable mater alone of hys yn lawe, for my discrecion ne connyng know not whate such maters menyth.

[1] [From Paston MSS., B.M.] The date of this letter is uncertain, but must be between the years 1454 and 1459, when Botoner was apposyng. Bocking and Barker seem to have been in London at the time, which we know was the case in February 1456; and as we have evidence that Bocking at least was still there in October, we may perhaps attribute this letter to the October of 1456.
[2] The *apposing* of accounts was the charging of an accountant with the balance due by him to his employer.

104

I knew nevere of *oyer* ne *terminer*, ne rad nevere patent 1456(?) OCT. 12 before, ne my maister knew nevere the condyt of such thynges; and when he wrote of hys grevonse to hys frendys, he commaunded no man to be endyted, for he wyst not whate belonged to such thynges, ne the parson neyther, but remitted it to hys councell lerned. There was no man gretter at hert with hym, as Andreus wyth Heydon, because of castyng Bradwell and Tychewell yn the Kynges handes, and toke awey the waarde. And I came nevere at the *oyer and terminer*.

By God, my maister lost c. marc by a seute of Margyt Bryg upon a defence of atteynt, because a quest passed ayenst hyr of xij. penyworth lond by yeer; and I dar sey and prefe it, my maister never spake of hyr, ne knew hyr not, ne wrote to sew hyr at the *oyer and terminer*, as I am remembred. Yhyt yt was well deffended, at my maister grete cost and labour, and myne pore labour also. Yhyt ought not I, ne none such yn my stede, beer the wyte [*blame*] wyth Sir Thomas, ne none othyr; he that takyth the tolle most take the charge, hyt ys hys negligence that wille take the labour more then he may awey. I wold the parson ys wellfare asmoch as man lyvyng, to my wreched power; and yff, or when, ye hyre onye froward ymagynacions, I pray yow gefe no credence tille ye hyre it aunsuerd. I am eased of my spyrytes now that I hafe expressed my leude [*ignorant*] menyng, because of my felow Barker, as of such othyr berkers ayenst the mone, to make wysemen laugh at her foyle. Our Lord kepe yow.

Wryt at Castre the xij. day of October.
Your   W. BOTONER.

I hafe and do purchasse malgre to remembre of evidenses lakkyng by negligence, &c. And therfor I most be muet and suffre gretter losses but [*unless*] it be othyrwyse concydered. I sende yow the copie of your patentes,[1] in parchement, and I hafe remembred as well as I can both the stuard and Bertilmeu Elys for execucion ayenst the pleggs of your seyntuarye, car-

[1] Probably the patent of 6th June 1454, granting the wardship of Thomas Fastolf to John Paston and Thomas Howes.—*See* No. 248 (in vol. ii.), also the letter following.

105

1456(?) OCT. 12 penter (?) Snow, that evere ys disposed to breke promysses. Foryefe me of my leude lettre wrytyng, and I pray yow laugh at it.

347

SIR THOMAS HOWES TO JOHN PASTON[1]

To my right goode maister, John Paston.

1456 or 457 REVERENT Sir, &c. Please yow to wete that it [is] so that my maister, of his owen frowardness, and of non other mannys mevyng, hat sent a warent to Cristefor that he shuld delyver me no mony tyll the iiijxxli. [*fourscore pounds*] where payed for Bokkyng and Wurcestre patent;[2] and yf the seyd Cristefore delyvered me any mony, that he shuld take a sewerte of me therfor, nowthwithstandyng my maister preyed me that I shuld reherce alle thynge in my name, where of I held me content. And now I fele this traytour wrytyng under nethe, and I nowth prevy ther to, at my comyng owt causet me to thynk the more hevynes, &c. Nevertheles, I prey yow that a mene may be taken of trety by the mene of Clopton or Ellys. Sende me word, and I shal seke menys of trety, for, be God, I shal trust no more no fayre wordes; and there to I shall lete alle the Lords of this lond knowe what wrytyngs I have, and his disposicion. Save yowre reverens, Cristyfor sal (?) have swyche a maister, &c. I prey yow, as ever I may do yow service or be yowre bede-

[1] [From Paston MSS., B.M.] This letter is dated by the writer in the 35th year of Henry VI., but he does not say in what month it was written. The 35th of Henry VI. was reckoned from the 1st September 1456 to the 31st August 1457. Taken in connection with the postscript of Botoner's letter immediately preceding (the date of which letter this partly confirms), it is not unlikely that this was written about October. Perhaps 'Wednesday after messe' should have been 'Wednesday after Michaelmesse.' If so, the exact date would be October 6th.
[2] The wardship of Thomas Fastolf was at first granted to John Paston and Thomas Howes, by patent of the 6th June 1454, and for this they agreed to pay 100 marks into the Exchequer. But, for some reason or other, a new arrangement was made, and the wardship was granted by another patent, dated 12th December 1454, to John Bokkyng and William Worcestre, who offered the King 20 marks over what Paston had offered, *i.e.* £80 in all.—See *Patent Roll*, 33 Hen. VI., p. 1, m. 10.

106

man that ye wele sende me yowre avise. I had lever paye 1456 xx. marke, or xli. in hande and xli. yerely furthe, with myn or enemyndz good love, than to yelde me to preson ayens here 1457 entent, and sewe forth the tyncte. And no trost what my maister wele do, for I can right evele beleve that he wele bere owt the cost of the tyncte whan he maket straunge to ley dowun the condempnacion, &c.

Wretyn brevely at Horseydown the Wenesday after messe, anno xxxvto.   T. Howys.

I shal nowt leve this mater to serve the most enemy that he hat in Inglond. I wele non of his good. I have lever other men go to the Dille [*Devil?*] for his good than I do.

348

JAMES GRESHAM TO JOHN PASTON[1]

To the right worshipfull and myn especiall maister, John Paston, Esquyer, in hast be this delivered.

1456 OCT. 16 AFTER al due recomendacion, like it you to wete, that the day of your assise is *die Lunæ proximo post tres septimanas Sancti Michaelis*, whiche is on Moneday come vij. nyght; at whiche tyme I trost ye wole be here, or ellis can I do lytell or nought there inne.

As touchyng your mater ageynst Gunnore, that dwelleth in lawe, I have spoken to Lyttelton,[2] and comuned with hym there in, but it is not yet spoke of atte barre. Gunnore hath waged his lawe[3] of that he haade his day to wage it of, &c.

[1] [From Fenn, i. 24.] This letter is assigned by Fenn to the year 1449, but the true date is 1456, as will be seen by the footnotes.
[2] See p. 84, Note 5.
[3] Wager of law was an ancient process by which a defendant cleared himself in an action of debt. He gave sureties that on a certain day he would 'make his law,' then took oath that he did not owe the plaintiff anything, as alleged, and called eleven compurgators to swear they believed him.

107

THE PASTON LETTERS

1456
OCT. 16

As touchyng your issues at Wentworth sute, it is ijs., and it was retourned er I come here. My Maister Fastolfs councel taketh heed thereto, &c.

As for tydynges, my Lord Chaunceler [1] is discharged. In his stede is my Lord of Wynchestre.[2] And my Lord of Shrewisbury [3] is Tresorer, and Broun [4] of your Inn is Undertresorer. If ye wold sende to hym to graunte you the namyng of th'escheterorship of Norffolk, &c., it were weel do, for it is told me he wold do moche for you.

Maister Lawrence Bothe [5] is Prive Seall. And it is seid that my Lord of York [6] hath be with the Kyng, and is departed ageyn in right good conceyt with the Kyng, but not in gret conceyt with the Whene [*Queen*]; and sum men sey, ne hadde my Lord of Buks [7] not have letted it, my Lord of York had be distressed in his departyng.

On Moneday last passed was a gret affray at Coventre bytwene the Duke of Somersets men and the wechemen [*watchmen*] of the toun, and ij. or iij. men of the toun were kylled there, to gret disturbance of alle the Lords there; for the larom belle was ronge, and the toun arose, and wold have jouperdit to have distressed the Duke of Somerset, &c., ne had the Duke of Buks not have take a direccion therein.

Also it is seid the Duke of Buks taketh right straungely that bothe his brethren [8] arn so sodeynly discharged from ther offices of Chauncellerie and Tresoryship; and that among other causeth hym that his opynyon is contrary to the Whenes [*Queen's*] entent, and many other also, as it is talked. Item, sum men seyn, the counseil is dissolved, and that the Kyng

[1] Thomas Bourchier, Archbishop of Canterbury, afterwards Cardinal.
[2] William Waynflete, Bishop of Winchester, was appointed Chancellor in Archbishop Bourchier's place on the 11th October 1456.
[3] John Talbot, second Earl. He was appointed Treasurer on 5th October 1456.—Patent Roll, 35 Hen. vi., p. 1, m. 16.
[4] John Brown.—*See* William Wyrcestre's *Annals* under the year 1468.
[5] Afterwards Bishop of Durham, and finally Archbishop of York.
[6] Richard, Duke of York.
[7] Humphrey Stafford, Duke of Buckingham.
[8] The two Bourchiers, viz. Thomas Bourchier, Archbishop of Canterbury, and Henry, Viscount Bourchier, the former of whom had been Lord Chancellor and the latter Lord Treasurer (*see* Notes 1, 2, and 3 above), were the Duke of Buckingham's half-brothers by the mother's side.

108

is forth to Chester,[1] &c. Also summe sey that many of the Lords shall resorte hiddir to London ageynst Alhalwen tyde.

1456
OCT. 16

And as touchyng th'eleccion of Shirefs, men wene that my Lord of Canterbury shall have a gret rule, and specyall in our countre.

I can no more, but Almyghty God send us as his most pleaser is.

Wretyn al in hast, the Saterday next after Seint Edwards day.

Your Servaunt, JAMES GRESHAM.

349

ABSTRACT [2]

SIR JOHN FASTOLF TO JOHN PASTON.

Begs him in the end of the term to come home by Dedham, along with William Worcester and Barker, to see to the accounts of barley and such husbandry as is used there. As to Wighton in Yorkshire, Bokkyng reminds me you spoke to me that my son Scrope and his father-in-law [3] should have all the lyvelode of my wife's in farm, to which I agreed, or else that Lord Vesey would have Wighton, as he once had, at a rent of £34—much more than I make it worth yearly. Do as you think best for me. I had rather my son Scrope had it with sufficient surety.

NOV. 10

Castre, 10 Nov.

Begs him to common with William Worcester that by means of my Lord of Canterbury, or otherwise, Master William Clyf and others of the executors of John Wellis may be spoken to for the recovery of great good that William Worcester knows Wellis owed to Fastolf.

[The date of this letter appears to be 1456. Of the years when Fastolf resided at Caister, it is not 1454, because in that year Barker could not have been in London on the 10th November (*see* No. 265). It is not 1455, because Worcester appears to have been at that time at Caister (*see* Nos. 305 and 306). The same appears to have been the case in 1457, though we can only judge by a letter of the 29th October; and although Worcester certainly was in London in November 1458, Sir John Fastolf was then in London with him.]

[1] The Court had been staying at Coventry.
[2] [From MS. Phillipps, 9735, No. 241.]
[3] Richard Bingham, Judge of the King's Bench.

109

THE PASTON LETTERS

350

ABSTRACT [1]

SIR JOHN FASTOLF TO JOHN PASTON AT THE TEMPLE.

1456
NOV. 15

Received certain letters by Henry Hanson on Thursday last, including one from William Barker written in Lukett's hand, and two bills of supplication, one of which, in the name of the tenants of Cotton, he has sent to Paston, as he has already written. John Russe and Geoff. Spyrlyng have ridden to Cotton in consequence, and will inform Paston how they speed. Thinks the bill 'right good and well spoken according to the truth of their riotous demeaning.' Received at the same time a bill written in his own name, of which he approves. Hears that young Henry Wentworth, young Calthorpe, and young Brews were at the distress-taking, among others. Has perfect confidence in Paston as to the treaty, and hopes to obtain again the manor of Bradwell by some means, as clear as he had it before his unhappy release. Hears that the Chief Justice 'rectid the matter' in Parliament before the Lords, and showed how Fastolf was wronged in that it was untruly found by the office that he had disseised Sir Hue Fastolf of the manor, whereas he has documents proving a true sale. My Lady of York has been here, 'and sore moved me for the purchase of Castre.' Begs him to devise means for the licence of mortising of certain buildings for the foundation of a college, 'as ye and I have commoned of before.' William Worcester can show him a copy of one passed by the King, and signed ready to the late Chancellor Stafford. Desires him to make himself acquainted with two chaplains about my Lord of Canterbury and my Lord Chancellor. William Barker writes of a general treaty, to which he can make no answer further than he has already done to Yelverton and Paston.

Castre, Monday after St. Martin.

[In this letter, as in the last, we have Worcester and Barker both in London, which, we have seen, points to the year 1456. It is clear also that this letter was written just before that which follows.]

[1] [From MS. Phillipps, 9735, No. 259.]

110

351

SIR JOHN FASTOLF TO JOHN PASTON [1]

To the worshipful and my right welbeloved cosyn, John Paston, at the Temple, or to William Barker, at Suthwerk, be this delvered.

WORSHIPFUL cosyn, I comaunde me to yow. And where as I late wrote unto yow in a lettre by Henre Hansson for the fundacion of my college, I am soore sette therupon; and that is the cause I write now, to remembre yow agayn to meve my Lords of Canterbury [2] and Wynchestre [3] for the licence to be opteined, that I might have the morteisyng withowte ony grete fyne, in recompence of my longe servise contynued and doon un to the Kyng, and to his noble fader, whom God assoile, and nevere yette guerdoonned or rewarded.

1456
NOV. 18

And now sithe I have ordeyned to make the Kyng founder, and evere to be prayed fore, and for his right noble progenitors, hise fader, and uncles, me thinketh I shuld not be denyed of my desire, but the rather to be remembrid and spedde.

Wherfore, as I wrote un to yow, I pray yow acqueynte

[1] [From Fenn, i. 164.] This letter, as printed by Fenn, bears no date in itself, but in the editorial note at the foot it is dated: 'Caister, 18th of November.' Probably this date is expressed in the original, but has been accidentally omitted in the printing. If so, the year in which it was written must be either 1456 or 1457, and most probably the former. In 1455 the Archbishop of Canterbury and my Lord Chancellor were one and the same person, which they evidently are not here; and in 1458 it appears by the Castlecombe MSS. that Sir John Fastolf was in London on the 26th November, so that he is not likely to have been expecting a visit from the Duke of Norfolk at Caister eight days before. On the other hand, if this was written in the year 1456, it must be remembered that Archbishop Bourchier had been just recently discharged of the office of Lord Chancellor, which was given to Bishop Waynflete on the 11th October, and it is highly probable that the Archbishop had been already spoken to on the subject in his capacity of Chancellor.
[2] Thomas Bourchier, Archbishop.
[3] William Waynflete, Bishop.

111

THE PASTON LETTERS

1456
NOV. 18

me and yow, for the rather spede here of, with a chapelleyn of my Lord of Caunterbury, that in your absence may re-membre me, and in like wise with my Lord Chaunceller;[1] for seyng the Kyngs disposicion, and also hise, un to the edyfyeng of God is service, it myght in noo bettyr tyme be mevid, &c.

My Lord of Norffolk is remevid from Framlyngham on foote to goo to Walsyngham,[2] and deily I wayte that he wolde come hidre.

Your cosyn,

J. FASTOLF.

352

ABSTRACT[3]

PROCEEDINGS IN A SUIT IN MICHAELMAS TERM, 35 HEN. VI.

NOV.

I. Writ to the Sheriff of Suffolk to attach John Andrewe of Boylom, and bring him before the Barons of the Exchequer on the morrow of All Souls to answer, along with Sir Philip Wentworth and Thos. Deyvill of Netlestede, to the suit of John Paston and Thomas Howys.

II. Pleadings. The King committed the wardship of Thomas, son and heir of John Fastolf of Cowhawe, to Paston and Howes by patent, 6th June 32 Hen. VI.; but on the 8th June 32 Hen. VI., Andrewe and Deyvill, with force and arms, entered Sholond Hall, Suffolk, and Foxhole, and Bentley Houses, etc., and took rents to the sum of £360, and underwood to the value of £40. Imparlance granted till 26th Nov., when the parties were not agreed. *Venire facias* was then awarded *a die Sancti Helarii in xv. dies.*

[1] William Waynflete, the Bishop of Winchester before mentioned.
[2] On pilgrimage to the famous shrine of Our Lady at Walsingham.
[3] [Add. Charter 17,244, B.M.]

HENRY VI

353

JOHN DORY TO JOHN PASTON[1]

*To my ryth wurchepfull sovereyn and master, John Paston,
be this delyveryd in hast.*

RYTH wurshepfull master and sovereyn, I recomaunde me to you, besechyng you to pardon me that I cum not to awayte up on you like as Barkere wrote to me. For I have notable and grete causis syth the lettere cam from hym, the qweche hath chaungyd my purpos, and be my master the Schreve is wrytyng, on to weche I must aplie me, all excusis leyd apart. And as for the wrytyng Barkere wrote to me, be the qweche he directyth a gret default in my deputys for return of the *habeas corpus* with *ducens tecum*, ther as is none, I dar seye, for John Rede spek to all my master Fastolfs councell to advyse hym in the return, and to have returnyd hit after ther conceyt, and thei wuld gyf hym non advys. Nevertheles I now understande ther entent be Barkere is wrytyng; for thei wuld put alle juparte up on me to myn utter ondoyng, and yit to do my trewe part in execu-cion of ther entent, for ye knowell my master hath put the juparte and the losse, if any growe, to me on his part. And ther for I may repent the tyme that ever I promysyd my trewe and good wyll to that entent. For alle the malesse and evyl-will that is owyng to me in alle the Schere ys for that mater and non other, the qweche hath grettely hurt me, and in tyme comyng schall hurt more. But lete them hold me excusyd, thei schall not have my goodwill so feythfully as thei have had, be my troweth, and I schall helpe my sefl [*sic*] as I may. And, Sire, I be seche you, thynke not that I pyke this be waye of qwarell, that I myth be this querell owe my good wyll to the toder part, for thei schall never have yt in that

About
1456(?)

[1] [Add. MS. 34,889, f. 170.] The name of Dory occurs only once elsewhere in these letters, and then without a Christian name; but the person so referred to (at the end of No. 330) is probably the under-sheriff of Norfolk; and this letter, which is likewise concerned with Fastolf's business, may have been written about the same period.

VOL. III.—H

THE PASTON LETTERS

About mater, nor in non other. And for good the qweche I have receyvyd yff be thowth I have not deservyd yt I am abill to content yt a geyn. And on Friday nexst foluwyng I schall be with you atte Norwich be Goddys grace, and knowe your entent in this mater.

No more, &c., but &c.—Be your man and servaunt,

JOHN DORY under Schreve of Norffolk.

1456(?)

354

JOHN BOCKING TO JOHN PASTON[1]

1457(?)
APRIL 2

SIRE, lyke it your maistership to wete that I sende you at this tyme the rolle of the copies of all patentes, and the appoyntement with Wentworth laste, and also a abstracte drawen as it come simply to my remembrance. And I shalbe with you sumtyme the next weke. All men ar owte at this tyme, as the Parson,[2] Worcester, and Barker; and therfore til thei come, I may not owte. H. Wyndesore departid on Monday, and will doo that he can. He telleth me Lumleys patent is in his awarde, but it is of noo force. And also he hathe Constable is ij. [*second?*] patente, and that is moste ayenst us, &c. He wil purveie therfore as ye knowe myn maister[3] comaundit hym to yow.

Here hath ben Wilton with the dede of feffement yester-day, and all men hadde ensealed sauf myn maister that now hathe ensealed, and H. Inglose is right soory. I can no newe tidinges, but that myn maister hath put his matier of Issabells in Scroudeby, and the rente of the priour of Norwiche dieu to Heilesdon in your hande and Thomas Grene. Ye shal the next weke have the evidences. And Jesu kepe you and youres.

[1] [From Paston MSS., B.M.] The date of this letter is very uncertain. In 1456 the writer dates from Southwark on the 8th of May, and in 1458 from London on the 14th of March, so that there is rather a presumption against his being at Caister on the 2nd of April in either of these years. But these points, it must be owned, are little to be relied on, as Bokking certainly passed to and fro a good deal between London and Norfolk. The date must, however, be between 1455 and 1459. The letter has no address, but was doubtless intended for John Paston.
[2] Thomas Howes. [3] Sir John Fastolf.

HENRY VI

I sende myn Maistres Crane a lettre fro hir brother, but I have the credence, whiche I can not say but if she appose me for certein materes of hir brotheres.

Writen at Castre, the ij. day of Aprill.

Your owen servaunt,

J. B.

1457(?)
APRIL 2

355

BOTONER TO JOHN PASTON[1]

To my Maister Paston.

PLEASE you to wete that, after dew recommendacion, hyt yt so that my maister sendyth me to London for the mater of Rochestr, as for dyvers of hys oune particuler maters which concern not the lawe, &c.; and I am lyke to tarye till ye com, in case ye com wythynne iij. wekys.

Sir, at reverence of God, seth my maister ys fully yn wille to renew hys fefment, that it may be do be tyme by the surest grounde that may be had, for, be it nevyr so suerly don, hyt shall be thought lytille ynowgh to kepe hys lond owte of trouble; and to spare for no councell ne cost to make sure, for a peny yn seson spent wille safe a pounde. I comyned with my broyder Spyrlyng, which seyth he wille do hys attendaunce, and to kepe it ryzt close of the namys. Taryeng drawyth parell.

And ye meved a gode mater to the Parson and to me at your last beyng at Castr, that my maister shud be lerned whate hys housold standyth uppon yerlye, seth he kept it holye to ghedr at one place; and that don, then to see by the revenues of hys yeerly lyfelode whate may be leyd and assigned owte for that cause to meynteyn hys seyd housold, and over that, whate may be assigned to beere owte hys plees, and also do pay for hys foreyn chargs[2] and dedes of almes to a con-venyent somme.

1457
APRIL 20

[1] [From Fenn, iii. 294.] It appears from the contents of this letter that it was written two and a half years after Sir John Fastolf came to live in Norfolk, which he did in the autumn of 1454. The date therefore is certain.
[2] Charges not connected with his household accounts.—F.

1457
APRIL 20

And seth the grettist ordynarye charge most be hys housould kepyng, hyt were moste exspedyent that ye wold note well to remembre specially my maister to do hys audyt[or]es cast up and make rollys of hys accompts concernyng the seyd housould seth he came yn to Norffolk thys ij. yer and half, whych was nevyr so long to doo thys xl. wynter as ye now. And it ys pytee that hys audyt ys none ethyr wyse yn that entended; ye must nedys, yff ye wille my maister know how hyt stand with hym yerly of hys chargs, that thys be do fyrst, as it was allwey accustomed. My maister wille acord it to be don, but it ys forgete throwgh negligence of men yoven to sensualite, as Thomas Upton, me, and othyrs. My maister can not know wheder he go backward or forward till thys be doon.

I can not elles, but ye wille not foryete thys that the audyt[or]es go verraily aboute it to an ende. And Haylysdon accompts be behynde for ij. yeer to [too] grete pite ys, and it wer yours or yn any wyseman gouveraunce.

At Norwich hastly, the Wenstay in Ester weke.

BOTO-H.R.-NER.

356

BOTONER TO JOHN PASTON[1]

*To the ryght worshypfull Sir, John Paston, Escuier,
beyng in Norwych, yn haste.*

MAY 1

RYGHT worshypfull Sir, aftyr dewe recommendacion, please yow to wete that I wrote a remembraunce to yow the day that I departed owte of Norwich, by Rychard, the Parson ys servaunt of Blofeld, concernyng

[1] [From Fenn, iii. 298.] That this letter was written in the year 1457 appears pretty clear from its agreement with the last, in which Botoner speaks of the expediency of getting the accounts of Fastolf's household audited, and mentions that his master was sending him up to London. A further confirmation of the date may be found in the dates of the Privy Seals of the 35th year of Henry vi., which show that the King was at Hereford during April, though he had removed to Worcester on the 4th of May.

116

1457
MAY 1

certeyn maters to be remembred by your wysdom for my maister ys avaylle, whych your grete wysdom can well undrestand ys ryght nedefull, as one thyng yn especiall, that Shypdam and Spyrlyng ought to labour, fyrst of onye thyng that belongyth, to audyt the accompts of the resseyt and despense of my maister housold at Castr seth he came last in to Norffolk, whych aswell for the provisyons that ys had of hys oune grownyng as in money payd; for (till the seyd accompts be made ordynatlye, whych be of a grete charge yeerlye, wete ye for certeyn my maister shall nevere know whethyr he goth bakward or forward. And manye othere accomptants that maken lyvere of provysyons of cornys and catell to the household by the resseyvour and by the bayllyfs can not approve theyr liberatz just tille the seyd housold bokes be made upp; and seth it hath be kept ordynarylye seth my maister begen to kepe house thys l. yeer almoste, and when he hath be absent beyond see, &c., hyt ought to be more redelyer be doon and made upp whyle he is present, and well the rathere that hys housold menye were not so hole to ghedr thys xl. yer as be now at Castr. Also hyz minustrs of accompts of hys chieff maner of Haylysdon for iij. yeer to make upp and to examyn; and I ensure yow full simplye approwed hys wollys and hys fermys.

And the iij[d] ys that so wold Jesus my maister audytors wold faythfully and playnlye enforme my maistr of the trouth of the yeerly grete damage he beryth in debursyng hys money aboute shyppes and botes, kepyng an house up at Jermuch [*Yarmouth*] to hys grete harme, and resseyvyth but chaffr and waare for hys cornys and wollys, &c. and then most abyde along day to make money; of such chaffr takyng he shall nevere[1] be monyed, ne be aunsuerd clerly of hys revenues yeerly but [*unless*] those thyngs abofeseyd be amended be tyme. Yn Lowys days xij. yeer to gheder my maister was wont to ley upp money yeerly at London and Castr, and now the contrarye—*de malo in pejus*.

I dar not be know of thys bille, but ye may question and

[1] The left-hand copy in Fenn reads 'neide,' but the modern version 'never,' which is clearly the true reading.

117

1457
MAY 1

vele of the disposicion of thys maters of otheres, and then undrstand yff I wryt justlye or no; and ye, as of your mocion for my maister worshyp and profyt, exortyng hym, the stuard, Shypdam, and Spyrlyng to take a labour and a peyn that thys be reformed.

I pray yow, and require yow kepe thys mater to your sylf.

Yowr,   BOTONER.

As for nouveltes none comth,[1] but yt ys seyd the sege shall com to Calix. The Erle of Warwyk[2] ys yhyt at Caunterbury with the Archbyshyp,[3] and the Erle younger brothere[4] maryed to Sir Eadmund Yngylthorp doughter uppon Seynt Marks Day. The Erle of Worcestr[5] broght aboute the maryage. The Queen and the Kyng at Herford,[6] the Lordes Bokyngham,[7] Shrewsbury,[8] and otheres ther. And now it ys seyd Herbert[9] shall com ynne, and apper at Leycester before the Kyng and the Lordes, hys lyfe graunted and godes, so he make amendys to theym he hath offended. Manye be endyted, som causelese, which makyth Herbert partye streng, and the burgeys and gentlemen aboute Herford wille goo wyth the Kyng wyffe and chylde, but a pease be made or the Kyng part thens, for ell[es] Herbert and hys affinite wille acquyt them, as it ys seyd.

The Erle of Warwyk hath had the folks of Caunterbury and Sandwych before hym, and thanked hem of her gode herts and vytaillyng of Calix, and prayeth hem of contynuaunce.

I sende a bille of the namys endyted to my maister and

[1] So in Fenn, but qu. 'couth.'—*See* p. 41.
[2] Richard Neville, Earl of Warwick.
[3] Thomas Bourchier, Archbishop of Canterbury.
[4] John Neville, afterwards Marquis Montague, married Isabel, daughter and heir of Sir Edmund Ingoldesthorpe of Burgh Green, in Cambridgeshire, by his wife Jane, sister, and at length co-heir of John, Lord Tiptoft, first Earl of Worcester. He was slain in the battle of Barnet in 1471.
[5] John Tiptoft.
[6] Hereford.
[7] Humphrey Stafford.
[8] John Talbot, second Earl.
[9] Sir William Herbert, afterwards Earl of Pembroke, a steady Yorkist.

118

1457
MAY 1

yow, to see and laugh at theyr Wellsh names descended of old pedegris. Our Lord be with yow.

Wryt hastly at London, the fyrst day of May.

BOTONER.

357

SIR JOHN FASTOLF TO JOHN PASTON, ESQUIRE[1]

To myne worshipfull cosyn, John Paston, Squier.

About
1457
AUG.

Ryght worshipfull cosyn, I recomaunde me to yow, and thanke yow of youre greet peyn and labores that ye daylye take for me in alle myn causes, for wheche I am greetly holden to yow, God yelde hit yow. And, cosyn, hit is so, as I am enformed, that a fermore of myn maner in Saxthorp, called John Bennes, shuld come be fore yow for to appoynte for suche dewte as he oweth to me upon his ferme. I sende to yow the bokes of his accompt to th'entent that Spyrlyng may awayte upon yow at his comyng, and declare hym his dewte, wheche, as myn receyvore seyth, hit wole drawe to the summe of xlvli. [£45], and more money at Michelmasse now next comyng. And the ferme is but xxli. [£20] yerly, by wheche ye may understande that he hadde greet favore in his payementes to his weel and myn greet hurt, as I reporte me to youre greet wysdome. Nevertheless, sethe hit is so that he hath hadde this advayle upon me, I wold seen now that suche dewte as shal ben dewly founde upon hym by accompt to be made at this day, that I may ther of have payement in hande as reson wole, or of as moche as the day is ronne of; and for the resydewe to have greable sewerte, that is to sey, of xxli. growen at Mihelmasse next comyng, to have payement theref at the Festes of Seynt Andrew and the Annunciacion of our Lady next comyng by even porcions, as in his endenture made of the seyd lees more pleynerly is conteyned. And this don, I am content that he goo at large, and elles that Spyrlyng take a rekenyng of hym, so as I may be aunswered accordyng to the statute, &c. And, cosyn, that overe this ye lyke to yeve credence to the brynger her of of that he shal declare yow in this be half be mouth. And oure Lord kepe yow.

Wreten in hast, at myne manoir of Castre, the Saterday next after our Lady Day the Assumpcion.

And, cosyn, I praye yow that he have none favore other wyse than lawe wole, seyng he is so contraryows for any fayer promyse of his behalf, &c.

Youre cosyn,   JOHN FASTOLF, Ch'r.

[1] [From Paston MSS., B.M.] This is a letter of pure business, and the date is uncertain; but as John Paston had been giving advice about money matters and the affairs of Fastolf's household in 1457, we may insert it here.

119

THE PASTON LETTERS

358

ABSTRACT[1]

1457
OCT. 2

Copy of a charter granted by John Paston, [patron?] of the church of Gresham, and Robert Miller, ... allowing the prior and convent of St. Sepulchre of The[tford] to distrain for a pension on the vicarage.

2 Oct. 36 Hen. VI.

[This document is mutilated. In the margin is the following note in a modern hand : 'E. Coll. Fr. Blomefield, *Hist. Norf.* vol. i. fo. 436.']

359

ABSTRACT[2]

SIR JOHN FASTOLF TO 'MY BROTHER' WILLIAM YELVERTON, JUSTICE.

OCT. 29

Begs him to continue his kindness especially, now that the Parson, Sir Thomas, comes up to appear before him and other the King's judges 'by the cruel and hasty suit of Androus and his affinity.' Hopes the process sued by him so eagerly 'upon the unjust condemnation shall be reformed and holpen by the attaint in chastising of perjury that reigneth so much now a days.' It were a blessed deed if it were reformed by Yelverton. Desires credence for 'my cousin Paston' and Sir Thomas in the matter.

(Signature not Fastolf's own.)

Castre, 29 Oct.

[This letter is written in William Worcester's hand. The suit of Andrews against Howes appears to have been in 1457, as it is referred to afterwards in a writ of the 1st September 1458, which will be found noticed under that date.]

360

SIR JOHN FASTOLF TO STEPHEN SCROOPE[3]

A Stevyn Scrope.

OCT. 30

WORSCHEPEFUL and my right wel beloved Sone, I comaund me to yow, and hertily thank yow for your good avertismentys, and right well avysed lettres to me sent from tyme to tyme, and so pray yow of your good continuance.

[1] [Add. Charter 17,245, B.M.] [2] [From MS. Phillipps, 9735, No. 268.]
[3] [From Fenn, iii. 42.] The date of this letter is clearly the same as that of the last, with only a day's difference.

120

THE PASTON LETTERS

458(?)
AN. 24

chambre, I am desirede to come unto his Highnesse to London ; wherunto for suche grevous diseas and infirmitees as it hath liked oure Lord to visit me with, wherof Robert Danby can at large declare unto yow, I can ne mowe dispose me, without feynyng, by the trouth I owe unto the King, but that therby I doubt not, I shulde not rekever, daies of my lyfe, suche hurt as, by the reason of the said diseas, wolde grow unto me, the which hath right fervently and sore holden me in many diversez bihalvez, so that, sith my last comyng from London I had not, by the space of vj. daies togidiez, my helth.

Wherfore, brothre, I pray yow, with al myn hool hert, that it like yow to cal tofore yow the said Robert Danby, and to take of him the vray trouth in the premissez, and therupon to bee my good and tendre moyen, as by your wysdome can best bee thought convenable, unto the Kinges goode grace, for th'excuse of my nown comyng ; prayng yow hertly to certifye me, by comers bitwen, suche tidings as ye shal have in thos partiez, with othre your good pleasir to be performed at my power, as knoweth oure Lord, to whom I biseche to ever have yow in his blissed proteccion and keping.

Wryten at Shirrifhoton, the xxiiij. day of Januare.

Your trew brodir, wich prayth you hertely to excuse me to the Kings Heghnesse.

R. SALISBURY.

illness given by Salisbury is, of course, a mere pretence, and, moreover, was not adhered to, for within a week after it was penned Salisbury actually was in London with a company of 400 horse and 80 knights and squires (*see* Botoner's letter of the 1st February). This sudden change of tactics on the part of the Earl seems to me hardly probable, and I see no reason why the letter should not refer to a genuine illness upon a different occasion. Nevertheless, as there is no positive evidence on the subject, I leave the date suggested by Fenn, with a query, on which the reader may use his own judgment.

HENRY VI

Plese it yow to wete that, for as mech as the parson Sir Thomas Howes cometh up at this tyme by the grevous pursewte of John Andreus and Heydon, to apere be fore the right worschepeful Sir, my right wel be loved brother, your fadir,[1] and other the Kynges Juges of the Kynges Benche,—I pray zow hertily that ye wille have in remembraunce for to recomaund me to hym whan ye speke with hym, and for to thank hym for his rightful favour shewed in Sir Thomas matier, and in alle other maters that toucheth me, wheche ben attained in that hey courte ; and so it lyke yow, pray hym of his good continuance, and I shall doo serve it unto hym to my symple power for his good wyl to me shewed, and to myne ; and I trust to God that he shal hold hym plesid. And that it like yow to geve credence to the seid Sir Thomas of that he shal sey to zow for my worschepe and profyte, and that this lettre may recomaund me to my doghtir your wyf, besechyng the blissed Trinite to sende yow the acomplyshment of your good desyre.

1457
OCT. 30

Wretyn at Castre, the xxx. day of Octobr.

J. F.

361

RICHARD, EARL OF SALISBURY, TO VISCOUNT BEAUMONT[2]

To the right worchiful and with al myn hert rigt entierly welebiloved Brother, the Viscount Beaumont.

RIGHT worshipful, and, with al myn hert, right entierly wele bilovede brothre, I recomaunde me unto yow. And for somoche as by the Kings moste noblez lettrez brought me late by Hagreston, oon of the gromes of his

1458(?)
JAN. 24

[1] On comparing this letter with the last, the person here referred to would seem to be Justice Yelverton. Mr. Poulett Scrope, however, in his privately printed *History of Castlecombe* (p. 277), says it was Sir Richard Bingham, whose daughter Joan Stephen Scrope had by this time married. It is quite possible that Fastolf sent a similar message to Bingham by Scrope, and to Yelverton by Paston and Howes.
[2] [From Fenn, i. 146.] Fenn considers this letter to have been called forth by the summons sent by the King to the Lords of both parties to come to London, in the beginning of 1458, with a view to a reconciliation. On this view, the excuse of

121

HENRY VI

362

AGNES PASTON[1]

Erands to London of Augnes Paston, the xxviij. day of Jenure, the yer of Kyng Henry the Sext, xxxvj.

TO prey Grenefeld to send me feythfully word, by wrytyn, who Clement Paston hath do his dever in lernyng.

1458
JAN. 28

And if he hathe nought do well, nor wyll nought amend, prey hym that he wyll trewly belassch hym, tyl he wyll amend ; and so ded the last maystr, and the best that ever he had, att Caumbrege. And sey Grenefeld that if he wyll take up on hym to brynge hym in to good rewyll and lernyng, that I may verily know he doth hys dever, I wyll geve hym x. marcs for hys labor, for I had lever he wer fayr beryed than lost for defaute.

Item, to se who many gownys Clement hathe ; and the that be bar, late hem be reysyd. He hathe achort [*a short*] grene gowne, and achort musterdevelers[2] gowne, wer never reysyd ; and achort blew gowne that was reysyd, and mad of a syde gowne, whan I was last at London ; and asyde russet gowne, furryd with bevyr, was mad this tyme ij. yer ; and asyde murry gowne was mad this tyme twelmonth.

Item, to do make me vj. sponys, of viij. ounce of troy wyght, well facyond and dubbyl gylt.

And sey Elyzabet Paston that she must use hyr selfe to werke redyly, as other jentylwomen done, and sumwhat to helpe hyr selfe ther with.

Item, to pay the Lady Pole . . . xxvjs. viijd. for hyr bord.

And if Grenefeld have do wel hys dever to Clement, or wyll do hys dever, geffe hym the nobyll.

AGNES PASTON.

[1] [From Fenn, i. 142.] [2] *See* vol. ii. p. 155, Note 1.

123

363

AGNES PASTON TO JOHN PASTON[1]

Tho my wele be lovyd son, John Paston,
be this delyvered in haste.

SONNE, I grete zow wele, and lete zow wete that for as
myche as zoure brothir Clement leteth me wete that ze
desyre feythfully my blyssyng,—that blyssyng that I
prayed zoure fadir to gyffe zow the laste day that ever he
spakke, and the blyssyng of all seyntes undir heven, and myn
mote come to zow all dayes and tymes ; and thynke veryly
non other but that ze have it, and shal have it, with that that
I fynde zow kynde and wyllyng to the wele of zoure fadres
soule, and to the welfare of zoure bretheren.

Be my conseyle dypose zoureselfe as myche as ze may to
have lesse to do in the worlde ; zoure fadye sayde : In lityl
bysynes lyeth muche reste. This world is but a thorough fare,
and ful of woo ; and whan we departe therefro, rizth nouzght
bere with us but oure good dedys and ylle. And ther knoweth
no man how soon God woll clepe hym, and therfor it is good
for every creature to be redy. Qhom God vysyteth him he
lovyth.

And as for zoure bretheren, thei wylle I knowe certeynly
laboren all that in hem lyeth for yow. Oure Lorde have zow
in his blyssed kepyng, body and soule.

Writen at Norwyche, the xxix. day of Octobyr.

Be zoure modir, A. P.

[1] [From Fenn, iii. 40.] As there is no distinct evidence of the date of this letter,
I have placed it after another paper written by Agnes Paston, and making mention
of Clement, though I rather suspect it may be a little later. It certainly cannot have
been, as Fenn supposes, written within a short time after William Paston's death in
1444, as Clement Paston was then only two years old. From some of the expressions
we might be led to suspect that John Paston was in trouble at the time.

1458
FEB. 1

Rygt worshypfull Sir, I beseche the blessed Trinite hafe
yow yn hys gouvernaunce.

Wrete at London, the fyrst day of Feverzer, anno 36 R.
H. vi.

Moreover, please you to wete that William Canyngs the
merchaunt wryteth an aunsuer of your lettre. I trust it shall
be the better for your wrytyng.

My brother promytted me a certeyn somme when I maryed,
and I shall hafe it of my sister yff I may.

Your humble servauntte,

W. BOTONER, *dit* WORCESTYR.

365

ABSTRACT[1]

WILLIAM BOTONER TO SIR JOHN FASTOLF

1458(?)
[FEB.]

You shall know the governance here on Paston's coming to you better than
I can write. The King is gone to Berkhamstead, 'and it is said my Lords
Somerset, Exeter, Clifford, and Egremont, that rode upon Thursday last to
the King, they come again to London ; and the Lord of Northumberland is
come to the King at this time after the Lords' departing out of London with
3000 or 4000 people, as it is said, but all toke (?) to a good peace, and re-
conysances made to keep the peace in great sums till Michaelmas, and in the
mean time to make a throw peace final by means of all the Lords.' John
Vyncent of Bentley was at the Priory of Lewes in Sussex this week, and says
that sixty sail of Frenchmen were sailing before the coasts, keeping the sea.
The Lord Fauconberg is at Hampton with his navy. Edmund Clere of the
King's house has heard from a soldier of Calais that Crowmer and Blakeney is
much spoken of among Frenchmen. 'The King's safe conduct is not holden
but broken, as it is voiced here, and that will do no good to merchants till it
be amended.' Figs and raisins are dear at 18s. the croc (?), 'wherte' at 10s.
the qr., malt 5s. Remains here awaiting for the com[ing of your] officers of
Castlecombe to bring up your money. Expects to send £40 by Master Paston.
. . . . *(Mutilated at the bottom ; date lost.)*

[The King was at Berkhamstead in the end of June and beginning of July 1450 ;
also on the 3rd March 1453 (from Reading, whither he returned immediately) ; also
in February and March 1458 (from 20th February to 13th March). This letter must
have been written in February 1458.]

[1] [From MS. Phillipps, 9735, No. 274.]

364

WILLIAM BOTONER TO SIR JOHN FASTOLF[1]

To my ryght worshypful master, Sir John Fastolf.

1458
FEB. 1

RYGHT worshypfull Sir, and my ryght gode maister, I
recomaund me to yow yn my full humble wyse. Please
yow to wete, as to nouveltees here both[2] Christofr
Barker wryteth to you more along.

The Kyng came the last weke to Westminster, and the
Duk of Yorke came to London with hys oune housole onlye
to the nombre of cxl. hors, as it ys seyd ; the Erle of Salysburye
with iiijᶜ [400] hors yn hys companye, iiijˣˣ [*fourscore*] knyghts
and sqwyers.

The Duke of Somerset came to London last day of Janyver
with ijᶜ [200] hors, and loggyth wythoute Temple Barre, and
the Duc of Excestr shalle be here thys weke with a grete felyshyp and strong, as it ys seyd.

The Erle of Warwyke ys not yhyt com, because the wynde
ys not for hym.

And the Duke of Excester takyth a grete displesir that my
Lord Warewyke occupyeth hys office, and takyth the charge of
the kepyng of the see uppon hym.

Item, as for tydyng of beyend see, I hyre none certeyn, but
that the Frensh Kyng[3] shulde hafe maryed hys doughter to the
Kyng of Hungerye,[4] whych had the descomfytur uppon the
Turks, and the seyd Kyng ys decesed wythynne thys vj. wekes,
or the spouselle was made ; but he ordeyned or he dyed that
the Frensh Kyngs doughter shuld be named Quene of Hungerye
duryng hyr lyffe.

[1] [From Fenn, i. 150.] Fenn states that he has omitted, as of no consequence,
the first part of this letter relating to the holding of some courts and some other law
matters wherein Yelverton, Fylongley, and others were concerned.
[2] The modern version in Fenn reads 'here being.' [3] Charles VII.
[4] Ladislaus v., who died on the 23rd November 1457, when on the point of
marriage with Magdalen, daughter of Charles VII. of France. He is believed to have
been poisoned.

366

JOHN BOCKING TO SIR JOHN FASTOLF[1]

To my Maister Fastolf, at Castre, in haste.

1458
MARCH 15

LYKE it your maistership to wyte that, as for tidings,
the Counsell is, the fornone, at the Blake Frires, for
the ease of resorting to the Lordys that are withinne
the toun ; and at afternone at the White Frirers in Fletstrete,
for the Lordis withowte the toun ; and all thing shall come to
a good conclusion with God is grace, for the Kyng shall come
hidre this weke, and the Quene also, as some men sayn, and
my Lord Buk,[2] and Stafford[3] with hire, and moche puple.

My Lord of Caunterbury takith grete peyne up on hym
daily, and will write un to yow the certeynte of suche tidings
as falle ; and shuld have doon or this tyme, saf for that he
wolde knowe an end of the matter.

Other tidings here are none, sauf my Lord of Excestre[4]
is displesid that the Erle of Warwyk shall kepe the see,
and hath therfore received this weke mˡ. li. [£1000] of the
Hanupere.[5]

The messenger was on horsbak whanne I wrote yow this
bill, and therfore it was doon in haste ; and our Lord Jesus
kepe yow.

Writen at London the Wednesday after Midlenton.

And my Lord of Caunterbury tolde me that the Frenche
men have ben before yow, and that ye shotte many gonnes ;
and so he tolde all the Lords. I have desirid hym to move

[1] [From Fenn, i. 154.] This letter relates to the temporary reconciliation effected
between the Lords of the opposite parties in the spring of 1458.
[2] Humphrey Stafford, Duke of Buckingham.
[3] Henry Stafford, Earl of Stafford, grandson of Buckingham, who succeeded him
in the Dukedom in 1460.
[4] Henry Holland, Duke of Exeter.
[5] The Hanaper of Chancery.

1458
MARCH 15 the Counsell for refreshing of the toun of Yermowth with stuff of ordnance and gonnes and gonne powdre, and he seid he wolde.

Your humble servaunt,

J. BOKKING.

367

WILLIAM CALTHORPE TO JOHN PASTON [1]

To my worshipfull Cosyn John Paston.

1458(?)
MAY 11 ?] RIGHT worshipfull Cosyn, I recommaund me unto you, certifying you that your man John Osberne of Walsyngham hath be with me and lete me have knowlage of a commyssion chuld be doun from my lord Chaunceler to Sir Robert Conyers, you other and me, and that ye wold have your day upon Munday or Tewesday at Crowemer, Blakeney or Walsyngham, &c. And after that he was departed from me, ther cam a servaunt from my cosyn Twyer, and seid that his maister hade a letter from you that ze have set to be at Blakeney uppon Munday next comyng. And for as much as I stande in nonn certeyn be cause of variaunce of the massangeres, therfore I send a man of myne to you, praying yowe to sende me verray certeynte and a copy of the commyssion, that my neybures may have knowlage of the kingis entent yf the case requyreth so, &c.

I hold Blakeney a resonable place, and if ye kepe youre purpose at Blakeney uppon Munday next comyng I shall mete ther with you, with Goddis grace, Wheche have you ever in His intyer kepyng, &c. Wretyn at Brunham upon the Assencion day of our Lord, &c., By W. CALTHORPE.

[1] [Add. MS. 34,889, f. 163.] The date of this letter is by no means certain, but may be 1458, after the reconciliation of parties. The reference to 'the King's intent' shows at least that it was not when the Duke of York was Protector; and it is not likely to have been under Somerset's rule or in the reign of Edward IV. If 1458 was the year, the day (Ascension Day) was the 11th May.

128

368

ABSTRACT [1]

JOHN PASTON AND T. HOWYS [2] TO FASTOLF AT CASTRE

1458
MAY 24 Yesterday 'I and other of yours' were at your manor of Bentlay—a right fair manor, in the shrewdest rule and governance. You have had many officers there who, for ill-will, have put out the tenants, and let the lands to your hurt. Some owe for six, some for seven years, etc.

Yesterday Harry Sotehill, of your learned counsel, was with us, and has taken ways in the law, etc. As Barker sends word that the attaint held not, we shall stay the longer. The Lord Egremont sent for my brother, and told him 'he would see you homeward, as he supposed.' Take care, therefore, you make no more grants, for you have made too many. Could let Bentlay, with surety, for 500 marks a year; but will not venture, because of the trouble of letting Wyghton, 'and also till Scrope hath spoken with you,' who will be with you now, etc.

Doncaster, Wednesday in Pentecost week.

[It appears from an account of Paston's expenses, of which an abstract is given farther on, that he was at Doncaster in the 36th year of Henry VI.]

369

JOHN JERNYNGAN TO MARGARET PASTON [3]

Unto my ryght wurchipfull Cosyn, Marget Paston, this lettre be delyvered in haste.

JUNE 1 RYGHT wurchipfull and my moste beste beloved maystres and cosyn, I recommaund me unto you as lowly as I may, evermor desyring to here of your gode welfar; the whiche I beseche Almzthy Jesus to preserve you and kepe you to his plesur, and to your gracious herts desyre.

And yf it please you to here of my welfar, I was in gode hele at the makyng of this lettre, blessed be God.

[1] [From MS. Phillipps, 9735, No. 267.]
[2] John Paston signs for both.
[3] [From Fenn, i. 156.] The engagement at sea described in this letter is dated by Fabyan on Trinity Sunday or Monday 1458.

129

1458
JUNE 1 Prayng you that it plese you for to send me word yf my fadyr wer at Norwiche with you at this Trenite Masse or no, and how the matyr dothe be twene my Maystres Blawnche Wychynham and me, and yf ze sopose that it shall be brought a bowte or no; and how ze fele my fadyr, yf he be wele wyllyng thereto or no; prayng you lowly that I may be recomaund lowly unto my maystres, Arblastres wyfe, and unto my Maystres Blawnche, her dowzther, specially.

Ryght wurchipfull cosyn, yf it plese you for to her of suche tydings as we have her, the basset [*embassy*] of Burgoyne schall come to Calleys the Saturday [1] eftyr Corpus Christi day, as men say v. hondred horse of hem. Moreover, on Trenite Sonday, [2] in the mornyng, came tydings unto my Lord of Warwyke that ther were xxviij[te] sayle of Spaynyards on the se, and wherof ther was xvj. grete schippis of forecastell; and then my Lord went and manned fyve schippis of forecastell, and iij. carvells, and iiij. spynnes [*pinnaces*], and on the Monday, [3] on the mornyng eftyr Trenite Sonday, we met to gedyr afore Caleis, at iiij. at the clokke in the mornyng, and fawz thet gedyr till x. at the clokke; and ther we toke vj. of her [*their*] schippis, and they slowe of oure men aboute iiij[xx] [*four score*], and hurt a ij. hondred of us ryght sore; and ther wer slayne on theyr parte abowte xij[xx] [*twelve score*], and hurt a v. hondred of them.

And haped me, at the fyrste abordyng of us, we toke a schippe of iij[c] [300] ton, and I was lefte therin and xxiij. men with me; and thei fawzthe so sor [4] that our men wer fayne to leve hem, [5] and then come they and aborded the schippe that I was in, and ther I was taken, and was prisoner with them vj. houris, and was delyvered agayne for theyr men that wer taken beforne. And as men sayne, ther was not so gret a batayle upon the se this xl. wyntyr. And for sothe, we wer wele and trewly bette; and my Lord hathe sent for mor scheppis, and lyke to fyzthe to gedyr agayne in haste.

[1] June 3rd. [2] May 28th. [3] May 29th.
[4] 'for' in Fenn; seemingly a printer's error, as the word is 'sore' in the modern version.
[5] Here, according to Fenn, the words 'and go the' occur in the original, struck out.

130

1458
JUNE 1 Nomor I write unto you at this tyme, but that it plese you for to recomaund me unto my ryght reverent and wurchipfull cosyn your husband, and myn ownkll Gournay, and to myn awnte his wyfe, and to alle gode maysters and frends where it schall plese yow; and eftyr the writyng I have from you, I schall be at you in alle haste.

Wretyn on Corpus Christi day in gret haste, be your owne umble servant and cosyn,

JOHN JERNYNGAN.

370

HENRY WYNDESORE TO JOHN PASTON [1]

To my full speciall gode Maister, John Paston.

1458(?)
[AUG. 27] WORSHIPFULL Sir, and my full speciall goode maister, after humble recommendacion, please it you to understand that such service as I can doo to your plesir, as to myn understadyng, I have shewed my diligence nowe this shorte season sithen your departyng, and in especiall aboute suche a copie of a foundacion as your maistership commaunded me to gete you a copie of, of the which I sende unto you at this tyme, by my broder William Worcestre, iij. copies writen by Luket, because I had no leisir, but somoch besems in settyng forth my Maistr of the Rolles. [2] At this tyme, and in all this Kyngs deies, ye can have noon oder accordyng any thing to your entent.

[1] [From Fenn, i. 170.] At the date of this letter Sir John Fastolf must have been in Norfolk, and William Worcester in London. From the time that the former went into Norfolk in 1454, till the end of the year 1457, Worcester seems generally to have resided with him; but in the beginning of 1458 he was in London, and it appears by the Castlecombe MSS. (Add. MS. 28,208, B.M. pp. 39, 42) that he was holding courts at Castlecombe in Wiltshire in June and July of that year, and that, in November of the same year, he and Fastolf were both together in London. It is probable, therefore, that he was in London in August, before Fastolf had come up. Indeed, he appears not to have returned to Norfolk till January following; so that in August he might quite well have devoted himself to the study of French in the expectation of a lengthened stay.

[2] Thomas de Kirkeby.

131

THE PASTON LETTERS

1458 (?)
[AUG. 27]
And as for the names of the Poles,[1] William hath more wrytyng than ye and I coude fynde, foundon by labor made by hym and me. And also, Sir, he hath caused me to examyn olde and mony records, writen by some Frenshman, concernyng the manour of Dedham; that was a comborous labour, for these copies were full defectif, as it apereth by the correctyng of them.

Item, Sir, I may sey to you that William hath goon to scole, to a Lumbard called Karoll Giles, to lern and to be red in poetre or els in Frensh; for he hath byn with the same Caroll every dey ij. tymes or iij., and hath bought divers boks of hym, for the which, as I suppose, he hath put hymself in daunger to the same Karoll. I made a mocion to William to have knoen part of his besines, and he answered and seid that he wold be as glad and as feyn of a good boke of Frensh or of poetre as my Mastr Fastolf wold be to purchace a faire manoir; and therby I understand he list not to be commynd with all in such matiers.

Item, Sir, as for any tidings, William can tell you here at London ar but full fewe; but Henry Bourghier is ded sodenly at Ludlowe; my Lord of Caunterbury and my Lord Bourgchier shall be this wyk at Hunnesdon, and hunte and sporte theym with Sir William Oldhall.

At this tyme nothyng els to your maistership; but and it please you to remembre my maister at your best leiser, wheder his old promise shall stande as touchyng my preferryng to the Boreshed in Suthwerke. Sir, I wold have byn at a noddr place, and of my maisters owun mocion he said that I shold sett uppon the Boreshed, in the which matier I reporte me to William Worcestre, Bokkyng, and William Barker, and most specially to my maisters awun remembraunce.

I know full well ther cann noo conclusion be taken to myn asayle [*avayle* ?] without help of your maistership, unto the which I utterly submitte me in this, and in all oder. And

[1] Apparently William Worcester was examining the pedigree of the De la Poles, ancestors of the late Duke of Suffolk, who had disputed with Fastolf the right to the manor of Dedham.

132

HENRY VI

our Lord Jesu preserve you and all youres, and send you your herts desire with right.

1458 (?)
[AUG. 27]

Writen at London on Sonday next after Seynt Bartholomu Dey in hast.

By your servaunt,   HENRY WYNDESORE.

371

ABSTRACT[1]

Writ of *pone* procured by Thomas Howes, clerk, of Castre, against John Wyndham, Thomas Danyell of Rysyng Castle, Edmund Bukenham of Snyterton, Robert Lethum of Wytton by Blofeld, Simon Gunnor of Estbekham, and sixteen others, for maintaining a plea begun at Westminster without the King's writ by John Andrew of Beylom, Suffolk, against Howes, whom he had maliciously procured to be indicted.

1458
SEPT. 1

[1] Sept. 37 Hen. vi.

On the back are the words : ' Manutenencia facta fuit iiij[o] die Julii anno xxxv[to].[2] Dampna Cli.

372

BOTONER TO JOHN PASTON[3]

To my Maister Paston.

SIR, as I went to my horsward by Lincoln Coke ys place, hyt fortuned that Wymondham and H. Fenne talked to gedre, and called me by my name, and both asked how my maister[4] fard, &c. Then Fen desyred me abyde to see astate taked yn Lyncoln place by hym boght of Markham. In the meene tyme the seyd Wymondham sent hys man to speke with hym, and yede yn talkyng of Sir Thomas[5] how he

[1] [From Paston mss., B.M.]
[2] A.D. 1457.
[3] [From ms. Phillipps, 9735, No. 249.] This letter clearly relates to the subject of the preceding No.
[4] Sir John Fastolf.   [5] Howes.

133

THE PASTON LETTERS

wille help labour to an ende, and had spoke with Heydon yersten efe for the seyd cause. I seyd the cruell amerciementes by their labour, and the [*they* ?] not beneficed, shewed to grete a malice to undo a preest innocent yn such a cause, &c. After my takyng leefe, he called me ageyn, and seyd that he desyred Sir Thomas to be gode meene to my maister to hafe affeccion to the chylde, &c. I aunsuerd, yff my maister had before the maryage be laboured [*i.e.* if my master had been applied to before the marriage], hyt had [been] moche esyer to bryng aboute then now. And because hys fadre was so maryed ayenst my maister wille, he nevere wold hafe affeccion to hym all hys lyfe dayes. He seyd that Thomas[1] was with hys modre ther she duellyth, and yff it please my maister to sende for hym by Sir Thomas meene, &c.

I ensure yow by my soule I brake no mater to hym but of Sir Thomas undoyng, and hys adversaries nevere the better, whych to my power wold help make it knowen to Lordes and all othyrs of the cruell amerciementes, the cruell juge to be knowen as he ys, for I am of hys contrey, and know hys rysyng and maryages as well as hym sylfe. At ix. at clok to hors bake. I pray yow breke my bille (?).

Your,   H. R.

373

ABSTRACT[2]

ROLL OF THE PERSONAL AND OTHER EXPENSES OF JOHN PASTON IN THE 36TH AND 37TH YEARS OF HENRY VI.

For dress and cloth, various.

' Liberat' hospitio,' £57, 17*s*. 7*d*. ' Item, uxori et pueris domi,' £8, 19*s*. 1*d*. ' Item, pueris Cantabrig' cum v. marke (?) per Wekeys,' 101*s*. ' Item, eisdem et sosiis (*sic*) suis in regard',' 4*s*. 2*d*. ' Item, eisdem apud London,' etc.

' Item, Henr' Bolte, capellano pro stipendio usque Pascha, xxxv[to].' 13*s*. 4*d*. ' Et 17 die Julii pro ij. quart',' 26*s*. 8*d*.

' Expencæ forinsecæ.'—' Pro fine Domino Regi facto quod Johannes

[1] Apparently Thomas Fastolf.
[2] [From Add. Charter 17,246, B.M.]

134

HENRY VI

Paston non sit miles.' Expenses with Munford at Thetford, 2*s*. 1*d*. ' Item, in exemplificatione Ecclesiæ de Gresham, Magistro Bulman,' 3*s*. 8*d*. ' Item, expenc' equorum Fastolf Norwici ij. vic. et Alexand' apud Forncet,' 3*s*. 1*d*. ' Item, præsentatio angnellorum data Radclyff,' 18*d*. To Alexander coming from Cambridge. ' Item, in coltellis apud Dancaster datis servientibus Fastolf et meis,' 3*s*. 4*d*. Glazing Chapel at Mauteby, 10*s*. ' Pro arrestatione Carroli Nowell apud Bury septimana Matthiæ,' 3*s*. 8*d*. Expenses of Ball's horse at Berkwey for six weeks, 10*s*. ' Item, expenc' meæ versus Snaylwell et redeundo de Bury,' 5*s*. 4*d*. ' Item, expenc' Norwici ad cess' hospic' existent' apud Heylysdon,' 18*d*. ' Item, expenc' meæ apud Sweynsthorp,' 8*d*.

In Easter and Trinity terms.—Paid to William Wyrcester ' equitanti super negotia maritagii sororis,' 10*s*. For wine and spice with Fortescu and Wentworth, 23*d*.

Hilary term.—Lent to James Arblaster at London, 40*s*. ' Item, exequiæ Edmundi Paston,' 2*s*. 4*d*. To divers poor people of Norwich for relief of their charge ' circa reparationem murorum civitatis,' 7*s*.

374

ELIZABETH POYNINGS TO AGNES PASTON[1]

To my right worshypfull moder, Agnes Paston.

RIGHT worshipfull and my most entierly belovde moder, in the most louly maner I recomaund me unto youre gode moderhode, besekeyng you dayly and nyghtly of your moderly blissing, evermore desiryng to her of your welfare and prosperite, the which I pray God to contynw and encresce to your herts desyre. And yf it lyked your gode moderhode to here of me and how I do, at the makyng of this lettre I was in gode hele of body tanked be Jesu. And as for my mayster, my best-beloved that ye call, and I must nedes call hym so now, for I fynde noon other cause, and as I trust to Jesu non shall; for he is full kynde unto me, and is as besy

1459
JAN. 3

[1] [From Fenn, iii. 328.] The writer of this letter is Agnes Paston's daughter Elizabeth, for whose marriage, as we have seen, there had been a good deal of negotiating in past years (*see* Nos. 93, 94, 236, 250, 252), and who has now become the wife of Robert Poynings. As the 3rd of January, the day on which this letter is dated, was a Wednesday, the year must be 1459. The 3rd of January did not fall on a Wednesday again till 1470, by which time Elizabeth Paston and Robert Poynings must have been married several years, as will be seen by No. 126 preceding (vol. ii. p. 154, Note 3).

135

THE PASTON LETTERS

1459
JAN. 3

as he can to make me sur of my joyntor, wherto he is ibounde in a bonde of m'li. to you mother, and to my brother John, and to my brother William, and to Edmund Clere,[1] the which neded no such bond. Wherfore I beseke you, gode moder, as our most synguler trost is yn your gode moderhode, that my maistr, my best beloved, fayle not of the C. marc at the begynnyng of this terme, the which ye promysed hym to his mariage, with the remenant of the money of faders wille; for I have promytted faithfully to a gentilman, called Bain, that was oon of my best beloved suertees, and was bounde for hym in CC*li*., of which he reherseth for to ryseyve at the begynnyng of thys terme Cxx*li*., and yf he fayle therof at this tyme, he wille clayme the hool of us, the which were to us to grete an hurt; and he con not make an ende with noon of hys other suertees withoute this seyd sylver, and that con my brother John telle yow wel i nough, and it lusteth hym to do soo, and in all other thyngs. As to my Lady Pool,[2] with whom I sojerned, that ye wul be my tendr and gode moder that she may be payde for all the costes doon to me before my maryage, and to Christofre Houson, as ye wrote unto my brother John that I shuld have ben so; and that it plese your gode moderhode to yeve credence to William Worcestr. And Jesu for his grete mercy save yow.

Written at London, the Wendysday the iij. day of Janyver.

By your humble doughter,

ELYZABETH PONYNGGS.

[1] Edmund Clere was the second son of John Clere, Esq. of Ormesby, and died in 1463.
[2] See p. 123.

HENRY VI

375

JOHN PASTON, THE ELDER SON, TO HIS FATHER[1]

To my ryght wyrschypful fadre, John Paston, Esquyer, be thys letter delyveryd in hasty wyse.

RYGHT worschypful Syr, in the most lowly wyse, I comaund me to yowr good faderhod, besechyng yow of yowre blyssyng. Mut it plese yowr faderhod to remembre and concydre the peyn and hevynesse that it hath ben to me syn yowr departyng owt of thys contre, here abydyng tyl the tyme it please yow to schewe me grace, and tyl the tyme that by reporte my demenyng be to yowr plesyng; besechyng yow to concydre that I may not, ner have noo mene to seke to yow as I awght to do, and savyng under thys forme, whych I besech yow be not take to no dysplesur, ner am not of power to do any thynge in thys contre for worschyp or profyht of yow, ner ease of yowr tenantys whych myght and scholde be to yowr pleasyng. Wherfor I besech yow of yowr faderly pyte to tendre the more thys symple wryghtyng, as I schal owt of dowght her after doo that schal please yow to the uttermest of my power and labor; and if ther be any servyce that I may do if it please yow to comaund me, or if y maye understonde it, I wyl be as glad to do it as any thyng erthely, if it wer any thyng that myght be to yowr pleasyng. And no mor, but Allmyghty God have yow in kepyng.

Wretyn the v. day of Marche.

By your older sone,

JOHN PASTON.

1459
MARCH 5

[1] [From Fenn, iii. 336.] By Letter 377 following, it will be seen that the writer of this letter had given displeasure to his father in the early part of the year 1459. There can be no doubt that this letter refers to the same occasion.

THE PASTON LETTERS

376

ABSTRACT[1]

SIR JOHN FASTOLF TO JOHN PASTON AND SIR THOMAS HOWES, PARSON OF BLOFELD

1459
APRIL 13

As you desire me to write letters to certain lords, etc., on 'such matters as ye beth now to London for,' and as you know best what it would be most expedient for me to write, I send my servant Colyn Newman to you with my signet sealed in a little leather bag, under a signet of a ram, that you and William Jenney, or two of you, may make out letters in my name as you think fit, keeping copies of those you write. When Sir Thomas comes home again, let him bring back my signet sealed under your signets and the copies you have sent. 'And also peradventure I might as well write to them that ben away as to those that been present. And among others ye may say to my nephew, Henry Filongley, I trust right greatly in my Lord Treasurer's good Lordship that he will be my good Lord's supporter to me in my right.'

Castre, 13th April 37 Hen. VI.

(*Signature not Fastolf's own.*)

377

MARGARET PASTON TO JOHN PASTON[2]

Tho my ryth worschopfful hossebond, John Paston, in hast.

APRIL 29

RYTHE worchefpwl hosbond, I recommawnd me onto yow. Plesyth you to wete that on Thorisday last was ther wer browt unto this towne many Prevy Selis, and on of hem was indosyd to yow, and to Hastynggs, and to fyve or

[1] [From ms. Phillipps, 9735, No. 254.]
[2] [From Fenn, i. 174.] The only years during the married life of John and Margaret Paston (except when their eldest son was a mere child), in which the Sunday preceding Ascension Day fell some time before the 10th of May, were 1456 and 1459. In the former year the King could not either have been or have intended to be at Leicester on the 10th of May. In 1459 the Privy Seals show that he was at Northampton on the 14th, 18th, and 19th of May, and it is quite possible he may have been at Leicester on the 10th. In 1464 Edward IV. was at Leicester in May, and the Sunday before Ascension Day was the 6th of May; but it is not probable this letter was written in that year, for two reasons. In the first place, Margaret Paston could hardly have hoped for an answer from her husband—who may be presumed to have been in London—in time to have sent his son to be at Leicester on the 10th; secondly, Letter 375, which is evidently of the same year as this, would probably have been signed 'John Paston, K.' (*i.e.* Knight).

HENRY VI

sexe odyr gentylmen; and anodyr was sent onto yowr sone, and indosyd to hym selfe alone, and asynyd wythinne wyth the Kynggys howyn hand, and so wer bwt fewe that wer sent, as it was told me; and also ther wer mor specyal termys in hys then wern in oderys. I sey a copy of thoo that wer sent onto odyr gentylmen. The intent of the wrytyng was, that they sshuwlde be wyth the Kyngg at Leycester the x. day of May, wyth as many personys defensebylly arayid as they myte acordyng to her degre, and that they schwld bryng wyth hem for her expensys for ij. monythis. As for the lettyr that was indosyd to yow and to odyr, it was delyveryd to Welyam Yelvyrton, for ther aperyd no mor of the remwlawnt. Hastynggs is forthe into Yorke schyr.

1459
APRIL 29

I prey yow that ye vowchesaf to send word in hast how ye wyl that yor sone be demenyd herin. Men thynk her, that ben yowr wel wyllerys, that ye may no lesse do than to send hym forthe. As for hys demenyng, swn ye departyd, in god feythe, it hath ben ryth good, and lowly, and delygent inn ovyr sythe of yowre servawntys, and odyr thinggys, the whiche I hope ye wold abe plesyd wyth, and ye had be at hom. I hope he wyl be well demenyd to plese yow heraftyrward. He desyryd Alblaster to bemene[1] to yow for hym, and was ryte hevy of hys demenyng to yow, as I sent yow word also be Alblaster, how I dede to hym aftyr that ye wer go; and I beseche yow hartyly that ye wochesaf to be hys god fadyr, for I hope he is schastysyd, and wil be the worher [*worthier?*] heraftyr.

As for alle odyr tynggys at hom, I hope that I and odyr schal do howr part ther inne, as wel as we may, bwt as for mony it comyth bwt slowly. And God have yow in hys kepyng, and sen yow good sped in alle yowr matteris.

Wretyn in hast at Norwece, on the Sonday next before the Assencyon Day.

Ser, I wold be ryte glad to he [*hear*] swmme gode tydynggys fro yow.

Be yorys,   M. P.

[1] To be mean, *i.e.* to be a mediator. Fenn has not apprehended the phrase, which he has modernised 'to bemoan.'

THE PASTON LETTERS

378

OSBERT MUNDEFORD TO JOHN PASTON [1]

A mon treshonnoure Seigneur, Jehan Paston, Escuier.

1459(?)
MAY 25

TRESHONNOURE Sire, je me recommande a vous tant que je puis, et vous prie qu'il vous plaise me recommander a ma maistresse vostre noble espouse et a tous voz enffans, et que ne soit point mis en oubly mon petit homme d'armes. Et oultre vous plaise me recommander a mon Maistre Yelverton et mon Maistre Caulthorpe, et a touz mes autres maistres et amis de pardela ou sera vostre bon plaisir. Et vous mercie des grans plaisirs et amitiez que avez faitz et monstrez a moy et aux miens, lesquelz Dieu me doint deservir. Treshonnoures Sire, plaise vous savoir que mon frere Jehan a Bernay ma escript dune matere dont me touchastes, moy estant parde la, a laquelle vostre desir vouldroit l'onneur des deux pars, et de laquelle matere le porteur de cestes vous informera, et des nouvelles de pardeca s'il vient a voz bons plaisirs. Et vouldroye bien que vous et mon dit frere Jehan a Bernay voulsissez communiquer avecques la personne aqui la matere touche, et que je peusse savoir son entente, affin dy otemperer, car je luy vouldroye faire plaisir et service ; car je y suis tenu, et la chose sera en partie reglee par vous et par mondit frere, mais je veil estre le tiers, et une autre personne sera le quart. Treschere et treshonnoure Sire, je vous recommande tout mon fait de pardela, et sy faiz je la petite Marie, pour laquelle je vous mercie, et especiallement ma damoiselle vostre fame et noble espouse, et me desplaist de la grant paine et charge que avez pour elle ; mas Dieu me doint grace que je le puisse aquicter.

¹ [From Paston MSS., B.M.] The writer of this letter was put to death at Calais on the 25th June 1460, having been taken at Sandwich when about to go thither in aid of the Duke of Somerset against the Earl of Warwick. The date cannot be in that year, and how much earlier it may be is quite uncertain, unless we suppose 'mon petit homme d'armes' to be Paston's eldest son, who, as we have seen, was summoned to perform military service in 1459.

140

HENRY VI

Priant nostre Seigneur qui soit garde de vous, et vous doint bonne vie et longue, et joyeulx acomplissement de touz voz desirs. 1459(?) MAY 25

Escript a Calais, le xxvme jour de May.

Le tout votre serviteur,

OSBERNE MUNDEFORD.

379

WILLIAM BARKER TO JOHN PASTON [1]

To myn ryght worshypfull [m]ayster, John Paston, at London, atte the Temple.

PLEASE youre maystership that as to morwen a newe *inquirendum* shal be taken at Wycham Markette for the parsonage of Rendelesham for one Mayster John Clerke, a chapeleyn of the Lady Roos ; and Sir Thomas [2] shuld a ben there, but he is hurte of an hors, and also hit was so late warnyng that we myght not ben there ; and, as Mayster Steven seyth, hit should not a avayled, thow one hadde bene there, and elles I wold a labored theder myn self. But he seyth and [i.e. if] ye wold speke to myn Lord Norwych, and enforme hym of the trought of the mater, he shal never presente ner inducte non tyl the ryght of the patentes be discussed, and also we may after wardes hald a *melius inquirendum*. Mayster Steven hath wreten to Sir John Bulman all the tytles and presentacions, and therefore, if hit please yow to comon with hym, ye shall understande all the mater by hym how myn Lord is disposed. And [if] Mayster Robert Eppeswell is now at London, hit were shame that they shuld have ther entent. Sir Phillip Wentworth groundeth not 1459 JUNE 24

¹ [From Paston MSS., B.M.] It appears by the Bishops' Registers at Norwich that John Clerk was instituted to the living of Rendelsham on the 20th June 1459 on the King's presentation. This letter must have been written four days later in ignorance of the fact. Clerk's predecessor was John Sybton, administration of whose goods was granted on the 19th May 1450.
² Sir Thomas Howes.

141

THE PASTON LETTERS

1459
JUNE 24

his presentacion by the patent, but by the endenture a twyxt the wedewe and hym, &c. Myn mayster is as freshe as ever he was this ij. yere, thanked be God. And youre mater that ye have meved of to Sir Thomas for the porchase, &c., myn mayster is weel agreed therto, but fyrst hit was taken strangely, &c. Almyghty Jesu preserve yow, myn worshipfull mayster, to youre desyre after his pleser and youre trewe entent.

Hastly at Norwyche, on Seynt John Day, at vij. of the clokke at even. Youre owen man,

W. BARKER,
Per mandat' T. H.

380

ABSTRACT [1]

SIR JOHN FASTOLF TO JOHN PASTON

JULY 3

'Hit is to remember my cousin, John Paston, that where as he desired to have the names of the new feoffment of the manor of Dedham that William Geney might see to ground such matter upon as might be for the surety of the said manor, I sent a copy of the said feoffment by John Daunson the last week.' Gives other points of information asked for. Has caused the patent to be written and sealed for Rauff Alygh's fee. Paston is to oversee the evidences of Fastolf's tenement by St. Olave's Church, which one Laurence Donne has summoned. Philip Grocer on London Bridge is a great maintainer of Donne. As to the matters moved by Stephen Scrope and Richard Byngham has lately written by Daunson 'to my said cousin' and to William Yelverton of his intent, and given them full power to appoint with them.

(Signature not his own.)

Castre, 3 July 37 Hen. VI.

Would like Paston and Hue at Fenne to see a speedier mean for the recovery of the 300 marks adjudged to Fastolf to be received of the Lady Fulthorp for the ward of Thomas Fastolf.

¹ [From MS. Phillipps, 9735, No. 250.]

142

HENRY VI

381

JOHN, LORD LOVEL, TO VISCOUNT BEAUMONT [1]

To my right worshipfull, and my moost best beloved Lord Fadre, my Lord Beaumont.

Right worshipfull and my moost best beloved Lord Fadre, I recomaunde me unto youre good Lordship. Please it yow to wit, I have consayvid your writyng right well ; and for asmoche as ye desure the stiwardship of Baggeworth for youre wilbeloved Thomas Everyngham, which y trowe verely be right a good and a feithfull gentilman. How be it, my Lord, youre desire shall be had in all that is in me ; and at the instaunce of your Lordship, y by th'avise of my counceill, shall gyf it hym in writyng undre suche fourme as shall please yow, wheryn y wold be glad to doo that at might please youre good Lordship, prayng yow right hertly ye wold be myn especiall good lord and fadre in all suche [matters] as ye can thynk shuld growe to my worship or profite in any wise, as my synguler trust is moost in yow. And y alwey redy to doo yowe servyse with Goddes grace, who have yow, my right worshipfull and my moost best beloved Lord Fadre, ever in His blessid kepyng. Between 1454 and 1459

Written at Rotherfild Gray, the xxiiij. day of Juyle, &c.

Furthermore, my Lord, and it like yow, my Lady my modre recommaundid her unto your good Lordship, yn whom her moost feith and trust is in, prayng yow, ye woll be good brother unto her, for she hath taken yow for her chief counceill, &c.

JOHN, LORD LOVELL.

382

ELIANOR, DUCHESS OF NORFOLK, TO VISCOUNT BEAUMONT [2]

To my right worshipfull and right entierly welbelovid cousin, the Viscount Beaumont.

Right worshipfull and right entierly welbelovid cousin, I comaunde me to 1444-1460

¹ [From Fenn, i. 128.] The writer of this succeeded to the barony of Lovel in 1454, and married Jane, the daughter of John, first Viscount Beaumont, the person addressed. As Beaumont was slain at the battle of Northampton on the 10th July 1460, this letter cannot be later than 1459, but may be some years earlier.
² [From Fenn, i. 194.] Here we have another letter, of uncertain date, addressed to the same person as the last. The year when it was written is quite immaterial, but must have been between 1444, when John Mowbray, the writer's husband, was confirmed in the dignity of Duke of Norfolk (which had belonged to his grandfather in the time of Richard II.), and 1460, when Viscount Beaumont was slain at the battle of Northampton.

143

THE PASTON LETTERS

HENRY VI

you with alle my herte, desiring to here, and verile to knowe of your worshipfull estate, profite, hele and good prosperite, the whiche I beseche our Lord Jesu ever to mayntene and preserve in alle worship, to his plesaunce, and to your herts ease.

Please it you, cousin, to witte that your welbelovid servaunt, Roger Hunt, and a servaunt of my moost dred Lord my husbond, on William, yoman of his ewry,[1] have comend to gedre, and been fully thorgh and agreed that the said William shall have his office, if it may please your good Lordship. Wherfore, cousin, I pray you, as my speciale truste is in you, that ye will, at th'instaunce of my proier and writing, graunte by your lettres patents to the said William the forsaid office, with suche wages and fees as Roger your said servaunt hath it of you ; trustyng verile that ye shall fynde the said William a faithfull servaunt you, and can and may do you right good service in that office.

And, cousin, in th'acomplesment of my desire in this mater, ye may do me a right good pleaser, as God knowith, whom I beseche for His merci to have you ever in His blessed gouvernaunce, and send you good lyfe and long, with muche good worship.

Writen at Framlynham, the viij[th] day of Marche.

ELIANORE, the Duchess of Norfolk.

383

FRIAR BRACKLEY TO JOHN PASTON[2]

To my Mayster, Jon Pastone, Esqwyer, be this letter presentid.

Jesu mercy.

1459 RYTE reverent mayster, &c., as sone as ze may goodly, comyth to Castre, and Zelverton[3] with zow, and ze think it to be done ; and sendyth home zowr men and hors, tyl ze haf do here, &c. And by grace of God and zour polityk wisdham, ze schal conclude more effectually in gret matyers of substans, to my maysterys[4] and zour worship and profyte. It is hey tyme ; he drawyt fast home ward, and is

[1] An officer who had charge of the table linen, etc.
[2] [From Fenn, iii. 342.] No signature appears to be attached to this letter as Fenn has printed it, but the style is unmistakably that of Brackley, to whom he attributes it. The original was endorsed in an ancient hand, according to Fenn, 'Littera fratris Doctoris Brackley per quam patet Jo. Fastolf valde desiderasse presentiam consanguinei sui Jo. Paston.' The date seems to be shortly before Sir John Fastolf's death, which happened on the 5th November 1459.
[3] William Yelverton. [4] Sir John Fastolf.

144

THE PASTON LETTERS

384

WILLIAM JENNEY TO JOHN PASTON[1]

To my worshipful and right gode mayster, John Paston, Squyer.

1459(?) WURSHIPFUL sire, and my right gode mayster, I
AUG. [22] recomaunde me to zou, and hertely I thanke zour gode maystership that ze liked to sende my mayster zour sone to Sporle with suych felaship as ze dede, for which I am ever bounde to doo zou service, prayeng zou of zour gode contenuaunce.

Sire, the cause why I kam not was this : I was falle seek with an axez [*ague*], and truly that caused me that I and my felaship taryed ; and so be cause theroffe I caused my lady to wryte a specyall lettre to my Lord Scales. But for al that Blake hath hoom the corn in my Lady of Suffolkys name. And the cause why I sent no wurd of my seknes was, that I wuld not myn enmy shuld be rejoysed be the knowlych of my seknesse. So God help me, the felaship that was redy to goo was right sory that thei myght not goo furth with me ; and my lordes and my ladyes wyl was that thei shuld have goon further. But if I had been heil and not seek, there shuld have kome a wurshipful felaship out of Suffolk of so litel warnyng ; but truly I lay seek at Ipeswych of the axez bothe Sunday and Monday. But, sire, syn ze have shewed me so kyndely zour gode maystership, I praye zou I may have your felaship

[1] [From Fenn, iv. 38.] This letter is referred by Fenn to the beginning of Edward IV.'s reign, but on a careful examination I think it must be earlier, as William Jenney's proceedings, even in the first year of Edward IV., were by no means friendly to John Paston. The Lord Scales here mentioned must therefore be the Lord Scales of Henry VI.'s time, who was murdered in July 1460, and the letter, having been written in August, cannot be later than 1459. In that year, as will be seen by Letter 377, John Paston's eldest son had already begun active life, and I am inclined to think that it is the precise year in which the present letter was written. John Paston, the second, was at that time not more than nineteen years of age, and we hear nothing of his doings earlier. The manor of Sporle was inherited by John Paston, senior, from his father the judge.

146

ryte lowe browt, and sore weykid [*weakened*] and feblyd, &c. 1459 And ze must bryng with zow a forme of a supplicacyon made at London in what maner wyse Mr. R. Popy, a cunnyng and a crafty man, schal presentyn and purposyn to the Kyng for the inmorteysing of Castre to Seynt Benet, &c., which he promittyd up [*promised upon*] a certeyn mony, &c., and undirtoke it, &c., and fond that tyme no bonys in the matere, &c. And now he seyth he wil labour and ryde and do hise part, &c. And he wold haf me to help hym, &c., quod non fiet, &c., or elles a man of credens of my masterys, &c., quod dubito fieri, &c. God bryng zow sone hidyr, &c., for I am weri tyl ze come.

Sir Thomas the parson, zowr owne most trewe, &c., be myn trewthe, and I zour bedeman and zowrs at zour comaundement, in zour letter haf no more towchid of the mater, &c., to my mayster, &c. Every day this v. dayes he seyth, 'God send me sone my good cosyn Paston, for I holde hym a feythful man, and ever on man.' Cui ego, 'That is soth,' &c. Et ille, 'Schew me not the mete, schew me the man.' Hæc verba replicat sæpius cum magno stomacho, &c. Colinus Gallicus dicit in Jernemuta et aliis locis se esse executorem, &c. Dixit etiam heri coram pluribus, si semel fuerit London' nunquam vult videre Norfolchiam, &c. Dicit etiam, ubi executores credunt se habituros claves, &c., post mortem alii habebunt claves, ita bene sicut illi, &c. Falsissimus est, et ego bene dixi in partem suam inter ipsum et me, &c. Propter Deum, faciatis Spirlyng venire juxta promissum in f'cū [*factum?*], &c. Gallicus ipse maxime odit rectorem et vellet supplantare eum, &c. Item, valde desiderat suum, quietus est quia absit, &c.

Henricus Todyham continue aspirat post mortem magistri cum mille habeat oculos nocendi, &c., si quorum duos deperderit, nullus cæteros timeret, &c.

HENRY VI

redy at a nothir tyme to help to execute a commyssion touchyng 1459(?) Blake, and that thei may be redy withinne ij. dayez after ze AUG. [22] have warnyng. And, sire, my service is redy to zou at alle tymys, as ze shewe me gret cause to doo zou service. Wreten at Thelton,[1] the Wednysday next before Seynt Bertilmew Day in haste.

Your servaunt, WILLIAM JENNEY.

385

WILL OF SIR JOHN FASTOLF[2]

In the name and the wurship of the holy, blyssydfull Trynite [in the year] 1459 of our Lord Jesu Crist, M[t]CCCCLIX., and in the xxxviij. yeer of [our NOV. 3 souerayn Kyng] of Englonde and of Fraunce, Herry the Sexte, the iij. day of the moneth [of] Novembre,[3] I, John Fastolf of Castre, be Gret Jernemuth, of the counte of [Norfolk], Knyght, beynge in good remembraunce, albeit I am sykly and thorwh age infeb[led], bryngyng to mende and often revolvynge in my soule how this world is tra . . . and how, amongs all e[r]thely thynges that is present or for to come, there is noe thynge in this onstable world so serteyn to creature of man kende as is departynge out of this world be dethe, the soule from the wrechyd body ; and noo thynge erthely so onserteyn as the oure and tyme of deth—Therefore I, willynge and desyrynge that of suche goodes of substaunce worldly, mevabill and onmevable, that God of hise bounteuous grace hathe sent me in my lif to dispose and ocupye, that they be disposed as it may be thowght best for the helthe of my soule and to the plessaunce of God, and also for the relyf, soccour, and helpe of the soulez that I am most oblygid and bounde to purveye and doo . . . for, as the soule of John Fastolf, my fadyr, Dame Mary, doutyr of Nicholas . . . . . my modir, and the soule of Dame Milcent, my wiff, the dautyr of [Sir Robert] Tibtot, knyght, and for the soulez of othyr of myn . . . . . . kynsefolke and speciall frendes here undir wretyn,—I ordeyn and . . . . . this my last will in fourme and maner folwyng :—

[*First Draft.*]   [*Second Draft.*]

*[Fyrst, I will and ordeyne that, if   *Firste*, Forasmyche as for the wel-
it plese oure sovereynge lord Kynge   fare of my soule and of the soules
Herry the Sexte, or hese heyre Kynges,   forseyd, and for ese, support, and helpe

[1] Thelveton, near Diss, in Norfolk.
[2] [From Paston MSS., B.M.] This document is printed from the original draft, in which a great part of the text has been crossed out, and other paragraphs substituted in the margin. The passages thus cancelled are enclosed within brackets with asterisks. Those substituted for them or inserted in a later hand are printed in a parallel column on the right. The passages bracketed without asterisks, and also the dotted columns, are lost by mutilation.
[3] The date was originally 'the xiiij. day of the moneth of June.'

147

THE PASTON LETTERS

for the longe contynwyd servise be me in the daye of strengthe and helthe of my body, to hym and to the noble Kynge Herry the Forthe and Herry the Fifte, hise progenitoris, and to hise noble uncles John Duke of Bedford, Thomas Duke of Clarence, whill they were in the werrys of oure seyd sovereyng Lord and hise noble progenitoris forseid, in Fraunce and Normandy as in cuntreez and othyr placis, consederynge my many gret labourys, peynis, and perilis in the seyd servise of oure sovereyn Lord and hise noble pro- genitoris forseyd, and hise pleyntyuous grace withoutyn ony other . . . . . of myn executores namyd in my testament, or ellys for a resonable sume of [money] whiche oure seyd sovereyn Lord owith me, or in othir wise, or be ony othyr meane, so as myn executores therein shall accorde with oure seyd sovereyn Lord and hise counsell, or with hise heire Kynges and here councell, to lycence and graunte to them that be feffyd to myn use in my Lordshepis manerez, londes, tenementes, rentes, servisez, with here appurtenaunces, or to here assigneez aftyr the effecte and forme of the lawe, by the avyse of myn executores, to ordeyne, founde, and stablishe, withinne the gret mancion or dwelynge place late be me newe edified and motid in the town of Castre, be Gret Jernemuth, in the counte of Nor- ffolk, whiche mancion or dwellyng place I was born in, a collage of a priory of vj. religeous personis, monks of the ordir of Seynt Benett, and to inmorteise and graunte to the seyd priour and vj. religeous personis, or to here succes- sorys, the forseyd mancion or dwellynge place, with all the appurtenauncez and othir sufficent and cleer lyflode of the forseyd lordshepis, maneres, londes, and tenementes, rentes, and servisez, with here appurtenauncez, for the sustenta-

of the pore inhabitantes in the cuntre of Flegge, and for to avoyde that noo lord nor gret astat shuld inhabit in tyme comyng withinne the gret mancion be me late edified and motid in Castre forseid, I have of long tyme been in purpose to stablishe and founde a col- lage withinne the seyd gret mancion, and soo to purveye that suche as I lovyd and thought behoffefull for the seyd cuntre, and that noon othyr, shulde inhabite in the seyd mancion with the collagyens of the seyd collage : Ther- for, and for the senguler love and trust that I have to my seyd cosyn John Paston, [abov]e all othyr, beyng in veray beleve that he will execute my will here in, I will and ordeyne, as he and I have covinauntyd and been ac- cordyd that he shall, with inne reson- able tyme aftyr my deseas, founde or do founde . . . . and indewe withinne the seid mancion a collage of vij. religeous monkys or pristes, to preye for the soulis above seyd in perpetuite, of whiche one to be cheif governour of hem, and he to have xli., and iche othyr prist or monk [of the said co]llage x. marks yeerly for here sustenaunce and fynding, clerly paid in mony, and that the seyd collagyens shull be soo indewyd that be syde here seyd pencions for here propir levynge to be grauntyd hem, they . . . . . inmorteysid to hem to fynde vij. pore folke yeerly in perpetuite in the seyd mancion of Castre to preye for the soulis above seyd in perpetuite. Of whiche pore folk iche of hem to have xls. a yeer or th . . . . ere levynge, fynding, and sustentacion ; and that the seyd John Paston shall ordeyne and make swyr to the seyd collagyens, and to the seyd pore folke a sufficent summe, and a competent and an esy dwellynge place . . . . . seid collag- yens nor here successorys beryng no

148

cion of the seyd priour and vj. religeous personys and here successorys, and for here othyr chargys and reparacionis, and for vij. pore men in the seyd collage in perpetuite, be the avise and discrecion of myn executores forseid, to be foundyd and susteynid ; and that thanne the forseyd feffees or her assig- nees if they . . . . grauntes of othyr havyng entresse in this be halve requisit lawefully shul make, founde, and stab- lishe, or doo be made, founde, and stablishid in the seyd collage, with the seyd priour and vj. religeous men, ever to endure, for to prey for my soule and for the soulez of my fadir and my modir, and of all my kynsefolk and good doeres, and for the soulez of the blissyd memorye Kynges forseyd, Herry the Forthe and Herry the Fifte, and the seyd noble Dukys, and for the good astat and prosperite of oure sovereyn Lord durynge hese lyf tyme, and aftyr for hese soule, and for all Cristeyn soules, therefor to synge and sey dayli devyne servise and preyeris in perpetuite ; and to be of the orderis, proffession, obedyence, and governaunce of the ordyr of Seynt Benettes, and of the same ordyr and profession as been the monkes of Seynt Benettes in Holme, in the counte of Norffolk, and shalbe stablyshid be the good avyse of myn executorys : And thoo feffeez forseyd, or here assygnez, inmorteyse and graunte, or do been inmorteised and grauntid, feffe sufficiently swyrly and lawfully to the seyd pryour and religeous, [and to their] successores, the forseyd mancion and dwellynge place, with the appurte[nances], ... sufficient, swyr, and cleer lyflode of the for seyd lordshepis maneres . . . . rentes, servisez, with here appurtenauncz in Castre forseyd, and in all othir placis . . . . . lithe next the seyd mancion or dwellynge place, for the sustenaunce [of the] seyd priour and vj. religeous men and here successoris, here servauntis, and the [seyd] vij. pore men : And for the chargys and reparacionis forseyd, to the yeerly valew of thre hundryd markes starlyng over all chargys ; to have and to holde to the forseyd religeous men and to here successoris for ever ; providid alwey that the seyd priour and religeous men and here successoris be bounden and compellabill sufficiently in lawe be the discrecion of my seyd executoris, to susteyne the for- seyd vij. pore men contynwally, sufficiently, and convenyently in all thyngis withinne the seyd collage for ever, and for to preye for the soulys afore seyd.]*

*[Item, I will and graunte that if outhyr the forseyd licence and graunte of

reparacion there of, for whiche and for othyr consyderacionis above seyd, I will, graunte, and ordeyne that the seyd John Paston shall have in fee symple, to hy[m and his heirs] all the manerez, londes, and tenementes in Norffolk, Suffolk, and Norwiche in whiche the seyd John Paston or ony othyr to myn use are or were feffyd in or have title to, and that all feffeez feffyd in the seyd manerez, londes, and . . . er astat of the seyd manerez, londes, and tenementes to suche per- sonys, and at suche tymes and in suche fourme as the seyd Paston, hise heyris or his assigneez, shall requyre hem, or ony of hem. And the seyd John Paston . . . . . seyd collage shal bere and paye to my behoff, towardes the paymentys of my dettes and othir thynges, be my present will assygnid to be do, m¹m¹m¹m¹ [4000] mark, in suche fourme and at suche tyme as in this my present will . . . . . . here aftir folwyng :—

149

THE PASTON LETTERS

oure seyd sovereyn Lord, or of hise heyre Kynges, or the licence or graunt of ony othyr . . . . entresse in this behalve be not lawefully, swyrly, and suffe- ciently . . . . . . that thanne my seid executorys shall geve or do be gove to . . . . . . of the monastery of Seynt Benettes of Holme for seyd, lysflode or mony competent . . . . seyd abot and covent or here successorys, and my seyd executores shal accorde there in be here wise discrecionis, for the indewe- ment and sustentacion of vj. monkes in the seyd monastery and vij. pore men in the same monastery, to prey for the soulys forseyd in perpetuite, to be foundyd, susteynid, and kept, providid that the vj. monkes forseyd be aumentyd above the noumbre of monkes of here ferst fundacion, and over the noumbre that they now use to kepe in the seyd monastery, and that lawefull and agreable swyrte perpetualy be made be the avyse of myn seyd executores, aswell for the augmen- tacion, susteyning, and kepynge of the seyd vj. monkys, as for the convenyent and sufficient sustentacion, fyndyng, and kepyng of the seyd vij. pore men in perpetuite, to preye as is afore seyd.

[First Draft.]

*[It]em, I will and ordeyne that all and singuler lordshepis, maneres, londes, and tenementes, [ren]tes, and servisez, with here appurtenauncez, in whiche ony persone or personys are feffid in or have astat and possession to myn use, in whiche sum ever counteez or townez the said lordshepis, maneres, londes, and tenementes, rentes, and servisez bein withinne the ream of Englond ; and that all the forseyd and senguler lordshepys, maneres, tenementes, rentes, and servisez, with here appurtenaunce, in whiche ony person or personys been intitlyd to myn use be the lawe, shall be sold be my seyd executores, except manerez, londes, and tenementes, rentes, and servisez, with here appurtenauncez, as shall be morteysyd to the seyd collage, if the fundacion thereof take effecte : And that the mony of the sale or salys comynge be disposed be my seyd executores in executyng of thys my last wyll and testament, and in othyr dedes of almesse as my seyd executores be here discrecion shal seme best to plese God for the helthe of my soule and for the soulys forseyd : And that happe the fundacion of the seyd collage

[Second Draft.]

Item, I wyll, ordeyne, and graunte that all othir lorshepis, manerez, londes, and tenementes, rentes, and servisez, with here appurtenaunce, in whiche ony persone or personis been feffid in, or have astat or possession, or be in titlid to myn use be the lawe, except the seyd manerez, londes, and tenementes, rentes, and servisez, with here appur- tenauncez, in the shirez of Norffolk, Suffolk, and Norwiche, in the article next presedent specified, shull be sold be the seyd John Paston and Thomas Howys, ij. of myn executoris. And I will, graunte, and ordeyne that the seyd John and Thomas, and noon othir while they leve, shall have the sengler rewle, sale, and disposecion of all my londes forseyd, except before except, and execucion of this my last will and of every article there in ; and I will that the seid John and Thomas shall have all the profitez and avaylez and emolwements of the seyd maneris, londes, and tenementes, rentes, and servisez, with all othir comoditeez thereof comyng, til be them they be sold, and the mony of the profites and salis thereof comynge, be them to be disposed for the welfare of my soule

150

to take to noon effecte, nor the seyd collage foundyd, that thanne the lord- shepis, londes, and tenementes, rentes, and servise, with here appurtenaunce, whiche shul bee assygnid to the seyd morteysyng, also shull be sold [be my]n executores, and the mony there- of comyng to be disposed be [myn] executores in executyng and parform- ynge of my will and testament, and in othyr dedes of mercy, pite, and almesse as shal seme best to my seyd executores for the soulez of me and the soulys undyr wretyn.]*

[Item, I will and ordeyne that my seyd executoris shull take and have all the issewys, avaylez, profitez, and emolwements of all and senguler lord- shepys, manerez, londes, tenementes, rentes, and servisez forseyd, with here appurtenaunce, excepte before except, to be geve to the seyd collage, on to tyme they be sold feithefully and trewly be my seyd executores ; and on to tyme that they that shull be purchasorys be feithefull and trewe bargeyne thereof made be twene hem and my seyd executorys, shull take and have the issewes, profitez, avayles, and emolwements, withoute fraude or male ingyne. And also I wyll and ordeyne that my forseyd executores shull take and have all the issewys, profitez, avayles, and emolwementes of all and senguler aforn except l . . . . . londes, tenementes, rentes, servisez, with here appurtenauncez, on to tyme . . . . . and vj. religeous men or here successoris, if the forseyd admynistracion . . . . . shull have and take lawefull and feithfull estat beforce of the seyd inmorteys[yng], or ellys that they be feithfully and trewly accordid with my seid executorys for the takyng and havyng of the issewes, profitez, and avayles, and emolwementes withoute fraud or male ingyne. And if the seyd inmorteysyng take noon effecte, I will and ordeyne that my seyd executores shull have and take all and senguler issewys, profitez, avayles, and emolwementes of the forseyd except lordshepys, londes, manerez, and tenementes, rentes, and servicez, with here appurtenauncez, tyl they be feithefully and trewly sold be my seyd executores, unto tyme that they that shalbe purchasorys thereof, be feithefull and trewe bargayne be twene them and my seyd executores thereof made, shull take thoo issewys, profitez, and avaylez, and emolwements thereof, withoute fraude or male ingyne. And I will and ordeyne that my seyd executores shull dispose all and senguler issewys, profitez, avaylez, and emolwe- mentes afornseyd for my soule, and for the soulys aforn rehersyd, as they shall seme beste to the plesure of God.]

Item, forasmyche as it is seyd that dyverse personis of dyverse desentes pretende . . . . . . at this day to be next heneritere [inheritor] to me aftyr my deseas, where . . . . knowe that no creature hathe title or right to inheryte ony . . . . londes and tenementes, rentes, and servisez that ever I hadde, or ony persone or personys . . . . . have to myn use ; therfor I will and ordeyne that no persone nor personis as hey . . . me for no douteful or obskure materes conteynid in this my present will, nor for noon othyr, shall take ony maner of avauntage, benefice, or profit be ony

and of the soulez forseyd duryng the lyf of the seyd John and Thomas ; and in cas this my will be not executyd in theyre [liv]es, that thanne the exe- cucion be thereof doon be othyr myn executores that aftyr hem too shal have the mynistracion of my goodes.

151

HENRY VI

1459 NOV. 3

manner meanys or weyes, of ony manerez, lordshepis, londes, tenementes, rentes, servisez, goodes, or catellys that were myn at ony tyme.

Item, I will and ordeyne and graunte that myn executoris [before namyd], or the more part of them[1] and noon othir, shall have the decleracion and interpretacion of all and senguler articles, chapetris, clausis, whiche and wordes in this my last will hadde and wretyn, in whiche articlis, chapetris, clausis, and wordes ony doute or doutez, dirknesse or dyversite of undirstondyng shall falle or happe to be founde, and that no persone or personys be reson of suche articlys, chapetris, clausys, or wordes, have or take ony profit or avauntage othyr wise thanne aftyr the maner and fourme of declaracion and interpretacion of my seyd [too namyd][2] executors.

Item, I will, ordeyne, and comaunde that all my dettes that is owynge [be] me be dewe examynacion be fully payd and contentyd to the creditoris, which can be foundyn dewe that is owynge be me; and also that all wronges, trespacis, offencis, and grevys be me doon or comyttid, if ony bee, that ony maner persone hathe been hyndryd or damagid wrongfully, if ony suche bee that can suffeciently and lawefully be previd and knowe, I wyll fyrst be fore all othyr thinges it be speed that myn executores do make amendes, restitucion, and satisfaction to thoo personys or to here executorys by me damagyd and hyndred as concience and good feithe requyreth.

Item, I will and ordeyne that in every town in which I or ony to myn use have lordshepys, manerez, londes, and tenementes that the pore pepyl of the tenure of the seyd town have ij. yeer to gethyr in reward after theyre afferaunt and quantite of the x. part of oon yeerly valewe and reveneuse of the seyd [lor]dshepis, manerez, londes, tenementes, and rentes, halfe to be departyd to . . [par]ishe cherchis for werkys, ornamentes, and othyr thynges necessarye to the seyd chyrchis, and half to be departyd amonges the seyd pore pepil that be tenauntes[3] of the seid lordshepis, maneres, londes, and tenementes soo to be disposed aftyr the discrecion of myn executores [before namyd],[4] aftyr my will approvid, and my dettes payd.

Item, I will and ordeyne that the pryour of the prioury of the parishe cherch of Jernemuth for the tyme beynge, and hese covent and hise successorys, observe and kepe yeerly and perpetualy to endure an annversary in the seyd parishe cherche for to preye for the soule of my fadyr, John Fastolf, Squyer, that lythe buryed there in the seyd chyrche, with *placebo* and *derige* and messe, be note the vigyl and day of hese obit, with the noumbre of prystes and clerkes accordyng in such a cause; and for to susteyne the kepyng of the seyd annversary, I will that be the avise of myn executorys [before namyd][4] that londes or teneme[ntes] . . . . ordeynid to the yeerly valewe of xx*s*., and that to be inmorteis . . . . swyr to the seyd prioury or

[1] *Or the more part of them.*—These words are crossed out. The words 'before namyd' are an interlineation substituted for them by the second hand.

[2] Interlineation by second hand.

[3] 'fermors' inserted in a different hand.

[4] Interlined by second hand.

1459 NOV. 3

parishe chyrche, oonly to susteyne and bere . . . . . and chargys of the perpetuall kepyng and susteyning of the seyd annversary.

Item, I will and ordeyne that if I have ony reliquis of Seyntes, also suche ornamentes for the chirche, that I have left as vestmentes, garlementes of sylke or velwet, of robis, and my gownys, that parcell of hem be yovin to the seyd monastery cherche of Seynt Benettes, where I shal be buryed, to remayne for ornament of the chapell there be me late edified; and also part of hem to be distrubited amonges the parishe chyrchis that be in suche townes that I have ony lordshipis, manerez, londes, tenementes, and rentes, provided that a resonable and a competent part of the seyd reliquis and ornamentes be kept and govyn to the seyd collage to be made at Castre, and this to be doon be the avise of myn executores be fore namyd.[1]

Item, I will and ordeyne that suche of my consanguinite and kynred whyche be pore and have but litil substaunce to leve by, that they be relevyd of my goodes . . . . . havyng consederation to thoo that be nerrest of my kyn and of . . . . . Also of here good disposecion too God ward and to me in here . . . . . othir of my kyn, that a consyderacion be hadde and yovyn to the relyf and prefer[ment] of my cosyn Robert Fitzraf, for hese good, trewe and long servise to me doon and contynwyd, and alsoo be reson of my consanguynite and kynred.

Item, I will and ordeyne that if ony persone make ony compleynt to myn executores that I have purchasyd ony taylid londes be this my will ordeynid to be sold,[2] and that thoo personys that so compleyne doo suffeciently and evydently prove and shewe withoutyn ony collucion, fraude, or male ingyne suche londes taylid; thanne I will that the right heyris purchase as be suche taylid londes, if ony be in my possession or in my feffeez handes, and that for a . . . . . . is thanne ony othir persone after the avyse and discrecion of the seid John Paston and Thomas Howis, clerk, and where there be no lawefull answere nor debarre of the tayle.[3]

Item, I will and ordeyne that the holy place of monastery and abbathye of oure Ladyiz chirche of Langley, in the diocise of Norwiche, for my soule to be more specialy recommendyd, and also for to kepe and susteyne, one day in the yeer, myn annversary solempnely be note the *derige* and messe of requyem for ever to endure for the helthe of my soule and for the soule of Dame Milcent, my wif, the doutyr of Sir Robert Tibetot, Knyght, whiche was of the consanguynite and kyn to the foundorys of the seyd monastery, and she owyng a senguler affeccion and love of devocion to the preyeris of that place, that the Abot and Covent have a reward and a remuneracion of my mevable goodes aftyr the discrecion of myn executores before namyd.

Item, I will and ordeyne that be the avise of myn executorys before namyd, that prevecion and ordenaunce be made that the obit and annversary may be yeerly inperpetuite kept with *placebo* and *derige* and messe of requiem benote for the soule of Dame Mary, my modir, in the chirche of Attil-

[1] *be fore namyd.*—These words are an interlineation by another hand.

[2] *be this my will ordeynid to be sold*, interlined by another hand.

[3] *after the avyse—tayle.*—These words are an interlineation by the second hand.

1459 NOV. 3

burgh, *[and a fundacion of a messe there, or in othyr convenyent place to be morteysid, for ever to seye and preye for here soule and for here auncetryez aftyr the discrecion of myn executorys.]*

[*Second Draft.*]

*and that oon of the monkis or pristes in the collage be me ordeynid in the mancion of Castre forseid shall synge specialy in perpetuite for the soule of my modir and all here auncestryez, and good dooerys.

Item, I will and ordeyne that it be provided by myn executores before namyd a reward as a yefte be made to the chapell of Seynt Jorge in the Castill of Wyndishore, and to the collagyens of the same collage for to have my soule recomendid amonges . . . . . with an annversary to be kept yeerly and perpetualy amonges hem with *placebo* and [*derige* and] messe of requyem be note.[1]

Item, I will, ordeyne, and comaunde that myn [executores and][2] feffeez* porsewe lawfully my right and title that I have in xxv. marke of yeerly rente, with all the areragis that of right and concience is dewe to my feffeez feffyd there in to myn use to dispose for my soule helthe chargyd and payable out of a maner in Hiklyng, callid Nethyrhalle, with the priour and covent of Hiklyng for the tyme beyng, be bounden and astrict be wryting undyr here covent sealys to paye yeerly. And on lyke wise I wyll that pursewt be made be Parlement or othyrwise lawefull for redressyng of the wrong doon to me in the maner of Bradwell, in the hundrid of Lodynglond in Suffolk, whiche I purchasid trewly, and hadde a lawefull astat in the same maner, as myn evydence woll shewe of record, xl. yeer past; and for to redresse the wrong full entre doon . . . . . my feffeez in the maner of Dedham Nethirhalle by Willyam, late Duke of Suff[olk], as well as for the wrongfull entre eftsonys and late made upon serteyn personys feffyd to myn use in the seyd maner, now of latter tyme; And that myn executores doo dewly here deligence aboute the recovery and getyng ageyn of the seyd manerez, lond[es], and tenementes and rentes above seyd of my goodes to be born.

[*Second Draft.*]

*be the avise of myn executores before namyd

Item, I will and ordeyne that the wardeyn and the procutoris for the tyme beyng of the parishe chirche of Seynt Oloff in Suthewerk, be London Brege, beyeng to the use of the seyd chirche of Seynt Oloff, be preferryd, in beyeng and purchasyng of myn executorys before namyd, a tenement with a warff thereto longyng, set be the seyd chirche, callyd the Bukheed, before ony man, and for a lesse valewe than it is worthe withine the sum of xx*li*.

Item, I will that a convenyent stoon of marbill and a flat fygure, aftyr the facion of an armyd man, be made and gravyn in the seyd stoon in laton in memoryall of my fadyr, John Fastolf, Squyer, to be leyd upon hese toumbe in the chapell of Seynt Nicholas, in the parishe chirche of Jernemuth, and with my skochonys of armys of hym and hese auncestryez, with a scripture aboute the stoon makynge mencion the day and yeer of hise obite.

[1] *with an annversary—note*, erased.

[2] Erased.

1459 NOV. 3

Item, I will that in semblable wise a marble stoon of a convenyent me . . . . made to be leyd upon the toumbe of Dame Mary, my modyr, in the . . . . foundid in the parishe chyrche of Atilburgh, and that a figure . . . . of a jentilwoman with here mantil, with a scripture made of laton in on . . . . iiij. skochonys of armys of here iij. husbondes, as the skochon of Thomas Mortimer, Knight, [John] Fastolf, Squyer, the seconde husbonde, and of John Farwell, Squyer, the thridde husbonde, auncetryez in the seyd toumbe, and the day and yeer of here obite to be wretyn aboute.

* [Item, I will that a provecion be made for swerte of the maner of Cowlynge in Suffolk, accordyng to the last wyll of Dame Marget Braunche, my sustir, in whiche maner I stond enfeffed in to here use, and serteyn londes in the seyd Cowlynge that Dame Mary, my modir, purchasyd to here and to hire heirez, that Herry Braunche, my neweu, here son . . . . seyd maner, provided that he be oblygid to preye for hise fadir, Sir Philip Br[aunche, and his] modir, Dame Marget, serteyn preyeris and messez, with a prist, to be contynw[aly] seyd [be] the discrecyon of myn executorys.]*

[*Second Draft.*]

Item, that myn executores before namyd helpe that the maner of Cowlynge be disposed and guydid aftyr the will of Dame Marget Brannche, my sastir, if my executoris thynke it be to doo.

Item, I will and ordeyne that the executores of John Wellys, aldreman of London, whiche hadde gret goodes of myne in hise governaunce whil I was in the partyez of Fraunce and Normandye, and hadde never opyn declaracion to whos handes of my resseyvoris atturnyez, or servauntes of myne the seyd goodes were delyvered particlerly, and for that cause to be aserteynid of the trouthe in this be halve, as well as for the dyscharge of the seyd John Wellys soule, his executores and attornyez may yeve accompt, soo declaryng of my seyd goodes accordyng to the trouthe and concience.

* [Item, to be providyd, if it be thowght comodiously that it may be doon be myn executores, that a chauntry may be foundyd in the chyrche of Seynt Oloff, be London Brege, in Southewerk, to prey for my soule perpetualy.] *

Item, I will and requyre that it be knowyn to all pepill present and for to come that where afore thys tyme whil I dwellyd and excersysed the werrys in Fraunce, Normandye, Angoy, and Mayne, as in Gyen, havyng undir the Kyng, myn sovereyn Lord, officez and governauncez of cuntreez and placis, as of castilys, fortreys, citeez, and townes be xxx. yeer and more contynwed, be reson of whiche officez . . . . . many sealis of myn armys gravyn with my name wretyn aboutyn . . . . course (?) in the seyd castilys and fortreycez that my lef tenauntes and . . . . . officerz beyng in dyverse suche placis ocupied undyr me the sealys and sygnettes to seale saf conduytez and billettes of saf gardes, and othyr wrytinges of justice longyng to suche officez of werre; and I doutyng that summe of the forseyd sealys of armys or sygnettes remayne stille amonges myn officeres or personys not delyvered to me ageyn, and that with the sealys of armys and signettes ony monwements, chartrys,

THE PASTON LETTERS

dedes, letterys patentes, blankes chartrys in parchemyn or paper, or othyr evydence forgyd and contryved withoute my knowynge or assent, myght soo be sealyd ageyn all concience and trouthe and ryghtwisenesse; and for these causez, and for doute of ony inconvenyent that myghte falle be this my wrytinge, I sertefie for trouthe and afferme on my soule, I swere and proteste that sethe I cam last out of Fraunce and Normandye, xix. yeere passed, I never sealyd wrytinge of charge, yefte, nor graunte with noon othyr seal of armys nor sygnet thanne *[with this same seal of armys and sygnet . . . . this my present will and my last testament],* and overmore that I have enselyd no [charge] yefte, nor graunte be the space of xix. yeer with noo seal nor sygnet, of noo lordshype, maner, nor manerez, annuite, reversionis, nor of no yiftes nor grauntes of goodes and cattellys, mevable and on mevable, nor mony, excepte suche as I have made opynly to be knowyn, executyd, and put in pocession be fore this day. Wherfore I requyre . . . . . . all Cristyn peple to yeve noo feithe nor credence to ony pryvat wryting not opynly declarid nor provid in my lif tyme, nor to blanke chartrys sealyd in my . . . . whereof I remembre me well that oon John Wyntir, Esquyer, late my servaunt, hadde (?) in kepyng a blanke letter in parchemyn ensealyd ondyr my seal, and never delyvered it me ageyn, but seyde he hadde lost it at hyse confecion, as wryting ondyr hise owyn hande maketh mencyon or he deyde.

Item, I will and ordeyne that myn houshold be holdyn and kept with my menyal servauntz be the space of half yeer aftyr my deseas, soo as they wyll be trewe to me and obedyent to myn executorys, and here wages for that tyme payd, and that in the meane tyme they purvey hem for othyr servise as they lyke best to avise to leve in trouthe; and if ony servaunt be well governyd and holde ageyns my . . . or ageyn myn executores to breke my good disposecion, I wy[ll that he shall be?] remevyd, and that he abyde noo lenger among the fel . . . . trewly avoydid withoutyn ony reward of me or of myn ex[ecutores].

* [Item, I will and ordeyne that amonges othyr lordes, frendes, and kynesmen that I desyre, [for] the discharge of my concience, be put in remembraunce of preyeris for the [good] affeccion I hadde on to them that I desyre shuld be preyed fore, is the soule of that blyssyd prynce, Thomas Bedford,[1] late Duke of Excestre, the soulys of the Lord Tibtot, Rauff, Lord Crumwell, Sir John Radclife, my brothyr-in-lawe, and

[Second Draft.]
* I have usyd this ij. yeer day last passed.

[Second Draft.]
Item, I will and ordeyne that amonges othir that I have put in remembraunce be this my will to be preyed fore that suche as shalbe bounden to preye for me, and be rewardid of myn almesse, shalbe chargid be myn executoris be fore namyd to preye for the welfare of m[y] soverayn Lord the Kyng, and for the soulys of all my good lordes and kynsefolk, and of thoo I am b[ounden] to preye fore

156

[1] Beaufort.

HENRY VI

Dame Cisly, late hyse wiff, my sustyr, whiche lithe buryed at Burdeux; Sir Philip Braunche, Knyght, my brothyr-in-law, that deyde and was slayn in Fraunce, and Dame Marget, late hyse wif, my sustyr, buryed at Cowlynge; also John Farwell, Squyer, my fadyer-in-lawe; Sir Herry Inglose, Knyght, of my consangwynite; Sir Hewe Fastolf, Knyght, that deyde in Cane in Normandye; Sir Robert Harlynge, Knyght, my neveu, that was slayn at the sege of Seynt Denys in Fraunce; John Fitzraf, Squyer, my neveu; Cisly, late the wif of Herry Fylongley, my nese, also late desesyd; Dame [Dan] Willyam Fastolf, of my consaguynite, prophessyd in the monastery of Seynt Benettes, and aftyr Abot of Fescamp in Normandye, whiche deide at Parys; Mathew Gowgh, Squyer, Thomas Gower, Squyer, John Sak (?), marchaunt of Paryse, my trusty frend and servaunt, and for the soule of John Kyrtlyng, parson of Arkesey, my right trusty chapeleyn and servaunt domysticall xxx. wynter and more, Thomas Hoddeson, a trusty servaunt of myne, John Lyndford, and William Gunnour.]*

Item, I, will, ordeyne, and streyghtly charge myn executorys that noon of hem shall [give] quyetaunce nor rellesse in no wise be hym self, nor be noon othir, to noon of my detorys, nor to dettour of myn executoris, of what so ever of astat or condecion that he be of, withoute the *[knowynge, plessaunce, and assentynge of al myn executorys, or the more part of hem.]*

Item, I, will, ordeyne, and streightly charge that none of myn executorys, be him self, nor be noon othyr, in ony maner or condecion cautelous, colour . . . . . . shall sell, nor doo selle, alyen, nor doo alyen, withdrawe, or do be [withdra]we, my londes and tenementes, jowellys of gold or sylvir, dettes or cattelys, vesselys or vestmentes of sylke, lynen, or wollyn, or ony othyr utensylez, to my persone or houshold perteynyng, nor noon othyr goodes of myne, mevable or on mevablys, quyk or ded, generaly or specialy, withoute *[the knowyng, plessaunce, and assentynge of all myn executorys, or the more part of hem; and if it be soo that ony of myn executores attempte maleciously the contrary in effecte, he fallith in the centense of excommunicacion, doyng the contrary to my last will.]*

Item, I, will, ordeyne, and streyghlty charge that all my feffeez feffyd of trust on to myn use of and in all my

[Second Draft.]
* full wyll and assentynge of the seyd John Paston and Thomas Howys, clerk.

[Second Draft.]
* the very will and assentyng of the seyd Paston and Howys, and that noon othyr attempte there in nor in noon othir cause in this my will to doo the contrarye to hem in effecte I require hem in Goddes be halve.

157

THE PASTON LETTERS

manerez, lordshepis, londes, tenementes, and rentes, and servisez, and profitez, be me or othyr to myn use purchasyd *[in all maner of counteez, citeez, or burghes or townes with in the ream of Eng[lond] . . . . .]* they that have astat, pocession, or tythe to myn use, with all the goodly haste, ... and withoute delay aftyr they be requyred be myn executores * aftyr my deseas, that they shall feffyn and make lawefull astat in fee symple *[of and in all maner lordshipys, londes, tenementes, meswages, rentes, servisez, and profitez forseyd, or of every parcell of the same]* to that persone or personys to whom or to whiche *[my seid executores in accomplisment of my last will, the said maneres, lordshepys, londes, tenementes, mecis, rentes, and servisez, or ony parcell of the same,* shall sell, or doo sell aftyr the declaracion of this my last will * for the helthe of my soule, *[Dame Milcent, my wif, with all my progenitorys, cosynes, and benefactorys, and all my frendes.]*

* [Item, I will, ordeyne, and streightly charge, aftyr be the grace of God I be desesed out of thys world, also myn executores willynge in effecte to accepte the charge upon hem of execucion of my testement and of mynistracion of my last will, all the articlis there in conteynid they shall ransakyn besyly and discussyn soo discretly in here remembraunce, that both in will . . . . shal not omyttyn for to complishe the seyd articles in . . . . Seynt Poule the Appostyll seithe he that is ignoraunt . . . . . . God Almighty shall hym not knowyn to hise savacion[1] . . . . . . this article to otherys that ignoraunce shuld not been on to myn execu[torys] in hurtynge of my soule, occacion of trespacynge, nor God offendyng.]*

* [Item, I wyll, ordeyne, and hertely desyr, that if it soo be be the grace of the Holy Gost, or of my good Aungill, or ellys be the verteuous devocion of ony good man, or be lyberte of fredam of myn owyn will, it happe ony good werkes and profitable to the helthe of my soule necessarye or avayleable to come be favour or swetnesse in to my remembraunce, as oftyn as I wryte or doo wryte suche thyngs worthy to be remembryd in ony codicill or codicilles for to

[Second Draft.]
* except before except, be me grauntid to the seyd John Paston or hese assygnes.

* before namyd.

[Second Draft.]
* the seid John Paston and Thomas Howys.

* except before except.
* to dispose.
* and for the soulis above seyd.

[1] See 1 Cor. xiv. 38. The translation of this verse in the Vulgate—'Si quis autem ignorat ignorabitur '—conveys a materially different sense from that of our English version.

158

HENRY VI

be conyoinid to my testament or to my last will, thanne I will and preye with gret instaunce of al myn executorys that alle thoo poyntes or articlys be me expressyd and conteynid in the seyd my codicill or codicillys that they may have strenghe and vertwe of observaunce in effecte, as if the hadde be wretyn in the code of my testement and my last will.]*

* [Item, I will, I ordeyne, and I hertely desyre, sethe that every mortall creature is soget to the lymitez or merkys of mutabelyte and chaungeableness, and mannys levynge in frelte and condecion is caduke and casewell, therfor on the behalve of Almyghty God, and be the weye of entyer charyte, I exhorte, beseche, and preye all myn executorys, in the vertwe of oure Lord Jesu Cryst, and in the vertwe of the aspercion of Hise holy blood, shed out graciously for the savacion of al man kende, that for the more hasty delyveraunce of my soule from the peynefull flawmes of the fyre of Purgatory, on suche maner and wise they dele and departe my goodes feithfully be here discrecion and prudence and polytik,]* the yeer of my buryeng, in exspence of myn entyrement and othyr almesse, the same yeer, and dedys of pyete (?) for the holsum estat of my soule amonges pore parple and nedy to [be p]artyd and distributid plenteuously and hastely, the sum of m^{ll} marke *[. . . . . . . the space of v. or vij. yeer immediatly folwyng by yeer Dxxxiij<i>s</i>. vj<i>s</i>. viij<i>d</i>. in almessefull deds and charitable wirkys, with all goodly possibelyte that they shall soo dispose my goodes in effecte feithefully that my soule, vexid in peynefull angwyshis, with holy Job, be not compellyd to sey with gret lementacion and mornyng, Have mercy on me, have mercy on me, namely yee that my frendes shuld bee, for the hande of Goddes punysshynge hathe grevously touchyd me. These be the articlys, xxxj. be noumbre, concernith the intent and purpose of my last will be the handes of myn executores, whiche I charge hem streytly, prey hem, and beseche hem enterly feithefully to execute, as they will have helpe of God and of hise holy Gospell. And soo I requyre hem as wysdam, justice,

[Second Draft.]
* Item, I wyll and ordeyne that John Paston and Thomas Howys, clerk, geve and dispose.

[Second Draft.]
* . . . . of the salis of my londes and my goodes be my will . . sygnid to be sold, be fully disposid for the well of my soule in almessefull dedes [and] charitable werkes with all goodly possibelite.

[The following new clause at the end.]
Item, I will and ordeyne that the seyd John Paston, for the payment of iiij. m^{ll} marke forseid, shal bere and paye to the seyd Thomas Howys, clerk, or to suche as shall aftyr them have the mynistracion of my my goodes, the seid sum [of] viij^c marke iche othyr yeer of the forseyd yeerrys in whiche

159

1459 NOV. 3 and concience to doo for me as they wolde I shuld doo for hem in cas lyche. In tokene and witnesse whereof, to this my last will I, Sir John Fastolf, above[1] . . . .] *

that sum is ordeynid to be distributid til he . . . . . be tho paymentes born and payd the seyd sum of iiij^{ml} markes, and that soo paid to be disposed be the seyd [John Pa]ston and Thomas Howys, or be hem that shal aftyr them have the mynistracion of my goods in executyng [my] will in awmesse full dedes in fourme afore seyd soo that my mevable goodes be mean of that . . . . shall the lenger indure in dedis of almesse.

386

WILL OF SIR JOHN FASTOLF[2]

Anno Domini millesimo quadringentesimo quinquagesimo nono, mensis Novembris, videlicet, die Sabbati proximo post Festum Omnium Sanctorum, Johannes Fastolff, miles, de comitatu Northfolch, Norwicen Dioc', in manerio suo de Castre, dictæ Diocesis, quoad bona sua immobilia suam ultimam declaravit voluntatem prout sequitur:

John Fastolff, Knyght, the secunde and the thirde day of the moneth of Novembre, the yere of the reigne of King Henry the Sexte after the Conquest, xxxviij. yers, being of longe tyme, as he said, in purpos and wille to founde and stablissh withynne the gret mansion at Castre, by hym late edified, a college of vij. religious men, monkes or seculer prestes, and vij. pore folke, to pray for his soule and the soulys of his wife, his fader and modir, and other that he was beholde to, imperpetuite. And forasmuch as he had, as he rehercid, a very truste and love to his cosyn, John Paston, and desired the performyng of the purpoos and wille forsad to be accomplisshed, and that the said Sir John shulde not be mevid ne sterid in his owne persone for the said accomplisshing of the said purpoos and wille, ne with noon other wordly maters, but at his oune request and plesire, wolde, graunted, and ordeyned that the said John Paston shalle, withynne resonable tyme aftir the dissese of the said Sir John, doo founde and stablisshe in the said mansion a college of vij. monkes or prestes and vij. pore folke, for to pray for the soulys above said imperpetuite; so that one of the said monkes or prestes be maister, and have x*li.* yerely, and ich othir monke or preste x. marc yerely, and ich of the pore folke xl*s.* yerely; and that the said John Paston shalle make sure to the said collegions a sufficient roume and a competent and an esy duelling place in the said mansion, the said collegions nor her successours bering no charge of reparacion therof. For which, and for othir charges and labours that the said

[1] The original draft ends with this word at the bottom of the page. Apparently the last few words of the draft were written on a flyleaf, which is now lost.

[2] [From Add. MS. 22,927, B.M.]

John Paston hath doon and take uppon hym, to the eas and profite of the said John Fastolf, and for othir consideracions by hym rehercid, the said Sir John Fastolff wolde, graunted, and ordeyned that the said John Paston shalle have alle the maners, landes, and tenementes in North[folk], Southfolk, and Norwich, in which the said John Paston or any other are or were enfeffed or have title to the use of the said Sir John Fastolf; and at [*that*] alle the feffees infeffed in the said maners, londes, and tenementes shalle make and deliver astate of the said maners, landes, and tenementes to such persones, at such tymes, and in such forme as the said John Paston, his heirs, and his assignes shalle requere thaym or any of thayme. And that the said John Paston shall pay to othir of the said Sir Johns executours iiij$^{ml.}$ [4000] marc of laufulle money of England in the forme that folweth, that is to say: Where the said Sir John hadde apointed and assigned that his executours shalle, the first yere aftir his disses, dispoos for his soule and performyng his wille a m$^{l.}$ marks or a m^{l}*li.* [£1000] of money, and yerely aftir, viij$^{c.}$ [800] marc, tille the goodes be disposed, the said John Paston shalle pay iche othir yere the said summe of viij$^{c.}$ marc till the summe of iiij$^{m.}$ [4000] be paid; so that the said mevabill goodes shall the lenger endure to be disposed, by th'avise of his executours, for the said soulys: And also the said Sir John said, forasmuch as it was the very wille and entent of the said Sir John that the said John Paston shulde be thus be avauntaged and in no wise hurte of his propir goodes, therfore the said Sir John wolde graunted that if the said John Paston, aftir the dissese of the said Sir John, by occasion and unlaufulle trouble in this reame, or by mayntenaunce or myght of Lordes, or for defaute of justice, or by unresonable exaccions axid of hym for the licence of the said fundacion, withoute coveyne or fraude of hym selve, be lettid or taried of the making or stablesshing of the making of the said fundacion, that thanne he fynde or doo finde yerely aftir the first yere of thus dissese of the said Sir John, vij. prestes to pray for the said soulys in the said mansion, if he can purvey so many, or els for as many prestes as faile, yeve yerely aftir the said first yere, by th'avise of his executours, to bedred men and othir nedy true pepille, as much money in almose for the said sowlys as the salary or findyng of the prestes so faillyng is worthe or amounteth to, unto the tyme he may laufully and peasably founde the said college and doo his true devir for the said fundacion in the meane tyme. And the said Sir John Fastolf wolde, graunted, and desired faithfully alle the residewe of his executours and feffees to shewe the said John Paston favore in the said paymentes and daies, and help hym for the Kinges interesse and the eschetours, and furthir hym in that they may in alle othir thinges as they wolde doo to hym selve, and not vex ne inquiete hym for the said fundacion in the meane tyme. Ande where the said Sir John Fastolf made his wille and testament the xiiij. day of June in somer last passed, he wolde, graunted, and ordeyned that this his wille touching thes premissez, as welle as the said wille made the said xiiij. day, except and voided out of his said wille, made the said xiiij. day, alle that concerneth or perteyneth to the fundacion of a college, priory, or chauntery, or of any religious persones, and all that concerneth the sale or disposing of the said maners, landes, and tenementes, wherof this is the very declaracion of his full wille, stand and be joyntly his very enteir and last wille, 1459 NOV. 3

1459 NOV. 3 and annexed and proved togedir. Also the said Sir John Fastolf, Knyght, the Tuysday next before the fest of Alle Saintes, and in the moneth of Septembre the said yere, and the iij. day of Novembre, and diverse other tymes, at Castre aforesaid, wolde, ordeynyd, and declared his wille touching the making of the said college, as welle as the graunte of the said maners, landes, and tenementes in Norffolk, Suffolk, and Norwich, in fourme, manere, and substance aforeseid. Also the said Sir John wolde and ordeyned that if the said John Paston, by force or myght of any othir desiring to have the said mansion, were letted to founde the seid college in the said mansion, that thanne the said John Paston shulde doo poule down the said mansion and every stone and stikke therof, and do founde iij. of the said vij. prestes or monkes at Saincte Benettes, and one at Yermuth, one at Attilbrugh, and one at Sainte Oloves Church in Southwerke. Also the said Sir John Fastolf, the iij. and iiij. daies of the moneth of Novembir abovesaid, desired his said wille or writyng, touching the fundacion of the said college and the graunte of the said maners, landes, and tenementes to the said John Paston, to be redde unto the said Sir John; and that same wille redde and declared unto hym articulerly, the said Sir John Fastolffe wolde, ordeyned, and graunted that the said John Paston shulde be discharged of the payment of the said iiij$^{ml.}$ markes, and noght pay therof in case he did execute the remenaunte of the said wille.

Also the said Sir John Fastolf, Knyght, aboute the tyme of hervest the yere of the reigne of King Henry the Sexte, xxxvth yere at Castre faste by Mikel Yermuth, in the shire of Norffolk, in presence of divers persones that tyme called to by the said Sir John, did make astate and feffement and liverey of the seasin of the maner of Castre aforesaid, and othir maners, landes, and tenementes in Norffolk, to John Paston, Squier, and othir; and at that lyverey of season therof delivered, as welle by the handes of the said Sir John as by other, the said Sir John Fastolfe by his owne mouth declared his wille and entente of that feffement and liverey of season made to the use of the said Sir John asfor during his live onely, and aftir his decese, to the use of the said John Paston and his heirs. And also the said Sir John said and declared that the said John Paston was the best frende and helper and supporter to the said Sir John, and that was his wille that the said John Paston shulde have and enherite the same maners, landes, and tenementes and othir aftir his decese, and there to duelle and abide and kepe householde; and desired Daun William Bokenham, Priour of Yermouth, and Raufe Lampet, Squier, Bailly of Yermuth, that tyme present, to recorde the same. Also the said Sir John Fastolf, the vj. day of July next aftir the tyme of the sealing of his wille made the xiiij. day of June, the xxxv. of King Henry the Sexte, and aftir in the presence of Daun William Bokenham, that tyme Prioure of Yermouth, and other, wolde, ordeyned, and declared by wille that the said John Paston shulde have alle thynges as the said Sir John had graunted and declared to the said prioure and othir at the tyme of the said [asta]te and feffement made to the [said] John Paston, the said xxxv. yere of King Henry the vj$^{th.}$ the said John seyng [*saying*] that he was of the same wille and purpoos as he was and declared at the tyme [of the] said astate takyng. Also the said Sir John wolde that John Paston and Thomas Howes, and noon othir of his executours, shulde selle

alle maners, landes, and tenementes in whiche any persones were enfeffed to the use of the said Sir John, excepte the said maners, landes, and tenementes in Norffolk, Suffolk, and Norwich; and the same John Paston and Thomas Howes shalle take and receyve the profites, ysshueys, and emolumentes commyng of the said maners, landes, and tenementes, excepte before except, tille they may resonably be solde; and that the said John Paston and Thomas, the money comyng of the same sale, as welle of the said proufites, ysshuys, and emolumentes, shulde dispoos in dedys of almose for the soule of the said Sir John and the soulys aforesaid, and in executyng of his wille and testament: And also the said Sir John wolde that alle the feffees enfeffed in the said maners, landes, and tenementes assigned to be sold, whanne thay be required by the said John Paston and Thomas Howes, shall make astate to persone or persons as the said John Paston and Thomas shalle selle to, the said maners, landes, and tenementes, or any parte therof, and that noon othir feffe [*feoffee*] nor the executours of the said Sir John shall make any feffement, relece, ne quitance of any londes befor assigned to be solde that wer at any tyme longing to the said Sir John, withoute the assente of the said John Paston and Thomas Howes. Datum anno Domini, mense, die et loco supradictis. 1459 NOV. 3

387

SIR JOHN FASTOLF'S WILL[1]

Anno Domini [millesimo][2] quadringentesimo quinquagesimo nono, mensis Novembris, videlicet, die Sabbati proximo post Festum Omnium Sanctorum, Johannes Fastolffe, miles, de com' Norfolk, Norvicen' dioc', in manerio suo de Castre, dict' dioc', suum condidit testamentum, et ipsius ultimam declaravit voluntatem, prout sequitur:—In primis, commendavit et commisit animam suam Deo Omnipotenti, Creatori suo, ac gloriosæ Virgini Mariæ, matri Domini nostri Jesu Christi, et omnibus Sanctis. Item, legavit corpus suum, postquam ab hac luce migraverit, sepeliendum in ecclesia conventuali monasterii Sancti Benedicti in Hulmo, Norvicen' dioc', sub arcu novæ capellæ per ipsum ibidem de novo constructæ, ex parte australi chori sive cancelli, sub tumba marmorea, juxta corpus Milicenciæ olim consortis suæ ibidem sepultæ; ac voluit quod abbas et conventus monasterii prædicti, antequam corpus suum ibidem sepeliretur, securitatem facerent quod dabunt et concedent Johanni Paston et aliis per ipsum nominandis, licentiam dandi et concedendi septem monachis vel presbyteris et

[1] From a modern copy among the MSS. at Narford, in the possession of Andrew Fountaine, Esq. The original of this document has not been met with, and the copy from which it is printed is unfortunately very corrupt; but no other text is obtainable. The more obvious inaccuracies have been corrected, but some obscurities remain, on which the reader may exercise his own judgment. For a knowledge of this document I am indebted to Mr. Tyssen Amhurst, of Didlington Hall, Brandon, to whom it was lent by the owner.

[2] Omitted in MS.

VOL 3

THE PASTON LETTERS

1459 NOV. 3 eorum successoribus in quodam collegio apud Castre prædict' per prædictum Johannem Paston stabiliendo et dotando, terras et tenementa quæ idem Johannes Paston et alii feoffati per ipsum Johannem Fastolf seu suos feoffatos de dictis abbate et conventu tenent, vel tantum inde quantum idem Johannes dictis monachis vel presbyteris dare voluerit. Item legavit, ordinavit, et præcepit omnia debita sua fideliter persolvi et quæcumque per ipsum forisfacta de quibus constare poterit, emendari, restitui,[1] et satisfieri cum effectu. Item legavit ad reparationem et sustentationem portus villæ Magnæ Jernemuth', ac ad renovationem et sustentationem murorum dictæ villæ pro bono commodo reipublicæ, salva tuitione villæ prædictæ et patriæ adjacentis, centum marcas sterlingorum, sub conditione quod burgenses seu gubernatores dictæ villæ sine mora seu dilatione perficiant[2] reparationem portus et murorum prædictorum quamdiu dicta summa a se extendet, ut gentes ibidem commorantes habeant animam suam in suis orationibus specialiter recommendatam. Item, cuilibet ecclesiæ parochiali singularum villarum in quibus habuit, aut aliquis ad suum usum habet, domum seu manerium, terras, et tenementa pro speciali recommendatione animæ suæ, unum vestimentum de serico panno pro missis ibidem celebrandis, et quod fiat in eodem scutum armorum suorum brodinatum secundum discretionem executorum suorum et indigentiam dictarum ecclesiarum. Item, legavit et ordinavit servientibus[3] suis et familiaribus domesticis remunerationem condignam seu competentem de bonis suis mobilibus juxta statum suorum [*sic*] ad summam tres centum marcarum, ita quod quilibet generosus habeat duplicem ad valentiam, et sic descendendo successive juxta statum eorum seu exigentiam meritorum ministrorum suorum ac fidelium laborum, habita tamen consideratione ad certos servientes[4] circa personam suam attendentes diebus et noctibus in laboribus, angustiis et vigiliis, tam in sanitate quam in infirmitate, circa præservationem corporis sui ac sanitatem celerius obtinendum. Item, legavit cuilibet ordini Fratrum religiosorum et domorum Mendicantium, tam in villa Magnæ Jernemouth quam in civitate Norwici, pro recommendatione animæ suæ, summam competentem secundum discretionem executorum suorum limitandum, cum nihil in proprio habeant unde sustentari valeant nisi de caritate et elemosina devotorum Christianorum. Residuum vero omnium bonorum suorum mobilium legata sua excedentium, ac catallorum suorum vivorum et mortuorum, ac debita singula quæ sibi debeantur, dedit et legavit executoribus suis infrascriptis juxta modum, formam et potestatem eisdem per eum superius limitatam, specificatam et ascriptam, ut ipsi eisdem modo et forma, per inde omni pondere discretionis et sani consilii, ea distribuant pro salute animæ suæ inter maxime debiles et pauperes, claudos et cæcos, ac alios impotentes in eorum lectis decumbentes, se et suos sustentare commode non valentes; habita consideratione speciali ad pauperes de consanguinitate et affinitate sua intimos et propinquos, et præsertim in locis ubi quondam possessiones, prædia, redditus et sua dominia fuerunt situata, et præsertim in villis et locis ubi habent, seu aliquis ad usum suum habet, dominia, maneria, terras, tenementa, et etiam ad emendationem pauperum ecclesiarum villarum prædictarum, viarum turpium et pontium communium reparationem, et in aliis piis elemosinariis usibus et caritatis operibus, specialiter in comitatibus Norfolk' et Suffolk'; et

[1] restum, MS. [2] proficiant, MS.
[3] finentibus, MS. [4] finentes, MS.

HENRY VI

quod circa funeralia et legata sua ac elemosinas supradictas primo anno post decessum suum mille marcæ seu mille libræ disponantur, et annuatim postea quingentæ libræ, triginta tres libræ, sex solidi et octo denarii, quousque bona sua mobilia et pecuniæ de venditione terrarum ac bonorum suorum vendendorum provenientia modo et forma prædictis plenarie disponantur, sicut coram Deo in die extremo Examinis voluerint respondere; et ad hoc eos exhortabatur in Domino Jesu Christo taliter pro[1] ipso singula fideliter peragere vellent cum pro eis in casu consimili faceret juxta conscientiam, rationem, et justitiam. Et prædicti testamenti ac ultimæ voluntatis suæ suos executores ad exequendum, disponendum et ministrandum modo et forma per eum inferius limitatis et subscriptis, constituit, ordinavit, fecit et elegit Willelmum Wintoniensem episcopum; Johannem, Dominum de Beauchamp; Nicholaum, abbatem de Langle; Johannem Stokes, legum doctorem; Fratrem Johannem Brakley, doctorem theologiæ; Willelmum Yelverton, unum justiciariorum Domini Regis; Johannem Paston, armigerum; Henricum Filongley, armigerum; Dominum Thomam Howes, presbyterum; et Willelmum Worcester; quos modum et formam executionis et administrationis bonorum suorum per executores suos fiend' sic limitavit, voluit, disposuit, et modificavit; videlicet, quod prædicti Johannes Paston et Thomas Howes solum et ante alios executores prædictos subeant et habeant administrationem et dispositionem omnium bonorum mobilium, catallorum ac denariorum ex venditione omnium terrarum et tenementorum suorum vendendorum et proficuorum eorundem terrarum et tenementorum provenientum, ut ipsi duo soli ea disponant pro salute animæ suæ, et quod alii executores supradicti abstineant se ab omni administratione dictorum bonorum suorum, nisi pro modo, forma, causa, loco, et tempore quibus per ipsos Johannem Paston et Thomam Howes ad eorem juramenta pro dicta administratione fuerint evocati pariter et rogati; et quod nullus dictorum aliorum executorum suorum sine consensu et voluntate ac advisamento dictorum Johannes Paston et Thomæ Howes capiat aliquid seu distribuat de bonis suis mobilibus et catallis prædictis, nec venditionem eorundem neque terrarum nec tenementorum prædictorum faciat, nec aliqua sibi debita recipiat, neque aliquos creditores suos quovis modo acquiet et, neque, prædictis Johanne Paston et Thoma Howes viventibus et administrare bona sua volentibus, aliquis alius executorum prædictorum administrationem bonorum suscipiat suorum, sed quod quantum dicti alii sui executores ad [*sic*] eorem singuli prædict' Johanni Paston et Thomæ Howes in quibuscunque egibilibus [*sic*] quæ hujusmodi testamentum et ultimam voluntatem concernentibus, favorabiliter assistant et succurrant cum per eosdem fuerint ad hoc requisiti. Voluit tamen quod si alter prædictorum Johannis et Thomæ recusaverit onus administrationis bonorum hujusmodi subire, vel ante administrationem functam obierit, quod tunc ille dictorum duorum executorum suorum administrare volens eligat unum de executoribus prædictis sibi associandis quem putaverit in hiis sibi magis idoneum, et ita voluit fieri de omnibus aliis executoribus præscriptis; videlicet, quod uno moriente vel deficiente de duobus, alter loco ipsius ad electionem administrationem incumbent' substituatur et assumatur. Si autem ambo executores prædicti onus recusaverint subire administrationis prædictæ, vel ambo executores administrationem incumbentes moriantur antequam substituantur executores alii, voluit quod tunc illi duo

[1] per, MS.

THE PASTON LETTERS

1459 NOV. 3 executores viventes prædictam administrationem subeant et habeant quos major pars executorum viventium sui testamenti duxerit eligendos, et quod illi duo administrationem subeuntes ad dictos Dominum Episcopum et Dominum de Beauchamp, Nicolaum Abbatem de Langley, Johannem Stokes, Fratrem Johannem Bracley, Willelmum Yelverton, Henricum Filongley, et Willelmum Worcester recursum habeant pro eorum consilio et advisamento obtinendo in causis arduis et materiis requisitis. Supervisores vero dicti testamenti reverendissimum in Christo patrem et dominum, Dominum Thomam Dei gratia Cantuariensem Archiepiscopum, Walterum Episcopum Norwicensem, Magistrum Robertum Popy clericum, et Hugonem Fenn, Domini Regis auditorem, ordinavit et constituit, et voluit quod dicti duo executores onus administrationis subeuntes remunerarentur secundum merita laborum suorum et diligentiam in præmissis expediendis juxta discretionem dicti Domini Episcopi Wintoniensis et Magistri Johannis Stokes, seu majoris partis aliorum executorum viventium. Supervisores vero prædicti et cæteri executores remunerarentur secundum merita laborum suorum per discretionem duorum executorum dictæ administrationi incumbentium. Et voluit quod si quis prædictorum per eum superius nominatorum dictos Johannem Paston et Thomam Howes in officio suo hujusmodi seu circa administrationem bonorum ejusdem defuncti quoquomodo impediverit, turbaverit, vexaverit, molestaverit, vel inquietaverit, aut aliquid prædictorum facere præsumpserit vel conatus fuerit, ab administratione bonorum suorum omnino removeatur, et si quid præmissorum ante susceptionem administrationis hujusmodi attemptaverit, ipsum ad administrationem hujusmodi nullatenus admitti voluit et declaravit. Datum anno Domini, mense, die, loco supradictis.

388

INVENTORY OF SIR JOHN FASTOLF'S GOODS[1]

1459 Memorandum that here aftir foloweth an inventarye of the gold and silver in coyne and plate, and othir godes and catelles that sumtyme were Sir John Fastolf, Knyght, whiche the said Sir John Fastolf gaf to John Paston, Squier, and Thomas Howys, clerk, of trust and confidence, that the same godes shuld the more saufly be kept to the use of the said Sir John duryng his lif, and aftir his decesse to be disposed in satisfiyng of the duetees and dettes to God and Holy Chirche, and to alle othir, and in fulfillyng and execucion of his legate last wille and testament without eny defraudyng of the said Holy Chirche or of eny creditours or persones.

[1] [From Add. Charter 17,247, B.M.] The MS. from which this document is printed is a roll which appears to have been at one time in the possession of Blomefield, the historian of Norfolk. At the end is the following note in his handwriting:—'March 7, 1743.—A true coppy of this roll given to Sr. Andr. Fountain, Kt., by me, Fra. Blomefield.'

HENRY VI

First, in goold and silver, founden in th'abbey of Seynt Benet aftir the decesse of the said Sir John Fastolf, m^{l}m^{l} iiij^{xx} xiij*li.* iij*s.* iiij*d.* 1459

Item, founden atte Castre, lxj*li.* vj*s.* viij*d.*

Item, receyved atte Bentlee by the handes of William Barker in money by hym receyved of John Heryngton, xx*li.*

Item, receyved atte London, CCCClxix*li.*

Summa M^{l}M^{l}DCxliij*li.* x*s.* in coyne.

First, two peces of golde, weiyng xlviij. unces.
Item, two ewers of golde, weiyng xxvij. unces.
Item, j. flaget of silver, weiyng xxxviij. unces.
Item, ij. prikettys of silver, weiyng xxvij. unces et di.

Summa of golde, lxxv. unces, and of silver, lv. unces.

Item, iij. chargeours of silver, weiyng vij^{xx} iij. unces.
Item, xij. platers of silver, weiyng ix^{xx} ix. unces.
Item, xij. disshes of silver, weiyng vij^{xx} viij. unces.
Item, xij. sausers of silver, weiyng iiij^{xx} xv. unces.

Summa v^{c} lxxv. unces.

Item, xij. flat peces bolyond in the bothom, weiyng viij^{xx} ix. unces.

Item, vj. bolles with oon coverecle [*lid*] of silver, the egges gilt, my maister helmet enameled in the myddes, weiyng viij^{xx} iiij. unces.

Item, a candilstik, a priket and ij. sokettys of silver, weiyng xvij. unces.

Item, ij. potell pottes of silver wrethyn, the verges gilt with braunches enameled, with j. tree in the lyddys, weiyng vj^{xx} xij. unces.

Item, ij. galon pottes of silver wrethyn, the verges gilt, enameled in the lyddes with iij. floures, weiyng xj^{xx} ix. unces.

Item, j. roste iron with vij. staves and j. foldyng stele of silver, weiyng lxxiij. unces.

Item, ij. flagons of silver, with gilt verges, and the cheynes enameled in the myddes, with j. hoke, weiyng ix^{xx} unces.

Summa, ix^{c} lxiiij. unces.

Item, a saltsaler like a bastell [*a bastille or small tower*], alle gilt with roses, weiyng lxxvij. unces.

Item, a paire of basyns, alle gylt, with an antelope in the myddes, weiyng xj^{xx} unces.

Item, ij. ewers, gilt, pounsed with floures and braunches, weiyng xxxix. unces.

Item, j. spice plate, well gilt like a double rose, my maister helmet in the myddes, with rede roses of my maisters armes, weiyng v^{xx} x. unces.

THE PASTON LETTERS

Item, ij. galon pottes, all gilt, enameled in the crownes with violet floures, weiyng x^{xx} xiij. unces.

Item, vj. bolles, with oon coveracle gilt, with my maisters helmet enamelled in the myddes, weiyng viij^{xx} vj. unces.

Item, j. stondyng cuppe, all gilt, with a coveracle, with my maisters helmet enamyled in the myddes, weiyng xlj. unces.

Item, another cuppe of the same facione, all gilt, weiyng xlij. unces.

Item, iiij. cuppes, gilt like founteyns, with j. columbyne floure enameled in the myddes, weiyng iiij^{xx} xvj. unces.

Summa, DCCCClxv. unces.

Item, j. grete flagon, with stuf theryn, weiyng xvij^{xx} xj. unces.

Summa, CCClj. unces.

Item, vj. platers, weiyng vij^{xx} unces.

Item, xiiij. disshes, weiyng ix^{xx} unces.

Item, xij. peces of dyvers sortes, weiyng vij^{xx} xiij. unces.

Item, ij. grete galon pottes, playn, with gilt verges, my maisters helmet in the kever, weiyng xij^{xx} xij. unces.

Item, j. paire basyns, the verges gilt, Harlyngs[1] armes in the bottom, weiyng v^{xx} xv. unces.

Item, ij. quart potts, with gilt verges, with the same armes in the lydde, weiyng lxx. unces.

Item, ij. ewers, the oon demi gilt, and the othir the bordures gilt, weiyng lj. unces.

Item, j. spice plate demi gilt, my maisters terget enamyled in the myddes, weiyng lxxj. unces.

Summa, DCCCCCxxxij. unces.

Item, j. stondyng cuppe gilt, with j. kever, with j. rose in the toppe, weiyng xl. unces.

Item, anothir cuppe of the same facion, gilt, weiyng xlj. unces.

Summa, iiij^{xx} j. unces.

Item, iij. grete chargeours, weiyng vij^{xx} ij. unces.

Item, xij. platers, weiyng xj^{xx} xij. unces.

Item, xij. disshes, weiyng ix^{xx} viij. unces.

Item, xj. sausers, weiyng lxxvj. unces.

Summa, DCxxxviij. unces.

Item, j. paire basyns, with gilt verges and j. rose, with my maisters helmet enameled and gilt in the myddes, weiyng viij^{xx} vj. unces.

---

[1] Sir Robert Harling of East Harling, in Norfolk, was a companion in arms of Fastolf, and was killed at Paris in 1435.

HENRY VI

Item, ij. ewers, gilt and enameled in like wise, weiyng lxxv. unces.

Item, xij. flatte peces, pounsed in the bottom, the verges gilt sortely, weiyng vij^{xx} xvj. unces.

Item, j. spiceplate demi gilt, wrethyn, weiyng lxxij. unces.

Item, vj. bolles, with oon kever, the verges gilt, my maisters helmet in the myddes, weiyng viij^{xx} iiij. unces.

Item, ij. grete pottes, eche of a galon, wrethyn the verges of bothe gilt with popy leves, with j. tre levedroses in the lidde, enameled, weiyng xj^{xx} xvj. unces.

Item, ij. potelers, with gilt verges, enameled in the liddes, weiyng iiij^{xx} ix. unces.

Item, ij. flagons, with gilt verges, and the cheyne enameled in the myddes, weiyng viij^{xx} j. unces.

Item, j. candelstik, with j. priket and ij. soketts, weiyng xvij. unces.

Summa, xj^c xxxvj. unces.

Item, j. saltsaler, with j. kever, well gilt, with many wyndowes, weiyng iiij^{xx} vj. unces.

Item, vj. bolles, all gilt, with j. kever and j. rose in the toppe, eche enameled in the bottom with my maisters helmet, weiyng viij^{xx} vj. unces.

Item, ij. galon pottes, gilt playn, anameled in the lyddes with my maisters target, weiyng vij^{xx} xiiij. unces.

Item, j. stondyng cuppe, pounsed with floures, well gilt, weiyng xlij. unces.

Item, j. gilt cuppe, stondyng covered, pounsed with j. rose in the toppe, weiyng xlvij. unces.

Item, vj. gobelettes, wele gilt, with j. columbyne floure, weiyng vij^{xx} vj. unces.

Summa, DCxlj. unces.

Chapell.

Item, vij. prikettes, with gilt verges, weiyng iiij^{xx} vj. unces.

Item, ij. stondyng candilstikkes, with gilt verges, weiyng iiij^{xx} j. unces.

Item, j. ship, with gilt verges, weiyng ix. unces.

Item, j. box for syngyng brede,[1] weiyng iiij. unces.

Item, j. haly water stop, with j. sprenkill and ij. cruettes, weiyng xij. unces.

Summa, C iiij^{xx} xij. unces.

Item, j. brode pryket, all gilt, weiyng xlv. unces

Item, j. paire basyns, all gilt, enameled in the bottom with roses, weiyng xl. unces.

---

[1] The round cakes or wafers intended for consecration in the Eucharist.

THE PASTON LETTERS

Item, j. pyx, demi gilt, weiyng xxx. unces.

Item, j. crosse, all gilt, weiyng xlj. unces.

Item, j. ewer, all gilt, weiyng xvij. unces.

Item, j. chalice, alle gilt, weiyng xxvij. unces.

Item, j. lesser chalice, all gilt, weiyng xiiij. unces.

Item, j. roses over gilt, weiyng xv. unces et di.

Item, j. ymage of Seynt Michell, weiyng viij^{xx} x. unces.

Item, j. ymage of oure Lady and hir Childe in hir armes, weiyng v^{xx} x. unces.

Summa, D^cxxix et di unces.

Item, j. grete flagon, weiyng xviij^{xx} viij. unces.

Item, j. almesse disshe, weiyng vj^{xx} xij. unces.

Summa, D^c unces.

Item, j. sensour of silver, and gilt, weiyng xl. unces.

Item, j. ship, weiyng xviij. unces.

Item, j. pece with j. kever, weiyng xx. unces.

Item, j. gobelet, gilt, weiyng xj. unces.

Item, j. stondyng cup, with j. kever, weiyng xij. unces.

Summa, Cj. unces.

Item, iij. grete chargeours, of oon sorte, weiyng xj^{xx} xviij. unces.

Item, j. chaufer, to sette upon a table for hote water, weiyng iiij^{xx} xiij. unces.

Item, iiij. holowe basyns, wherof oon is bolyons, weiyng all x^{xx} xiij. unces.

Item, iij. botelles, of oon sorte, weiyng vij^{xx} xiiij. unces.

Item, vj. grete peces, of oon sorte, weiyng v^{xx} xvij. unces.

Item, xij. peces, all of oon sorte, weiyng xj^{xx} xiiij. unces.

Item, iiij. smale peces, weiyng xxv. unces.

Item, j. grete bolle, with j. kever, weiyng lxij. unces.

Item, iij. gobelettes, pounsed, weiyng xiiij. unces et di.

Item, j. powder box, and j. kever to j. cup, weiyng xxij. unces.

Item, ij. basyns, the verges gilt with popy leves, enameled with my maisters helmet in the bottom, weiyng viij^{xx} ix. unces.

Item, ij. ewers, gilt, enameled in the same wise, weiyng iiij^{xx} unces.

Item, iiij. ewers, of the olde facion, weiyng lxxvij. unces.

Summa, xv^c xxij. unc' et di.

Item, j. litill flat pece, gilt, with j. kever, weiyng xxvij. unces.

Item, j. stondyng pece, all gilte, with j. kever, weiyng xxxviij. unces.

Item, j. litill stondyng pece, gilt, with j. kever, weiyng xxj. unces et di.

Summa, iiij^{xx} vj. unc' et di.

HENRY VI

Apud Sanctum Benedictum.

Item, ij. basyns with gilt verges, and my maisters helmet in the botom, with ij. ewers, with gilt verges, and my maisters helme on the lyddes, weiyng togider CCxxxj. unces.

Item, iiij. prikettes, with gilt verges, weiyng xxxj. unces.

Item, ij. lesser prikettes, weiyng v. unces.

Item, j. basyn and j. ewer, with my maisters armes in the botom, weiyng lxij. unces.

Item, ij. litill ewers, of ij. sortes, weiyng xxiiij. unces.

Item, j. spiceplate, with gilt verges, weiyng xliiij. unces.

Item, ij. galons, with gilt verges, with my maisters armes in the liddes, weiyng iiij^{xx} xvj. unces.

Item, ij. potellers, of oon sorte, weiyng iiij^{xx} iiij. unces.

Item, ij. othir potellers, of oon sorte, weiyng iiij^{xx} xiij. unces.

Item, j. potell potte, of anothir sorte, weiyng xxxv. unces.

Item, j. quartelettes, of dyvers sortes, weiyng xlviij. unces.

Item, j. litill botell, with j. cheyne and j. stopell, weiyng xxxviij. unces.

Item, j. brode priket, with gilt verges, weiyng xxiiij. unces.

Item, ij. candilstikkes, ij. prykettes, and iiij. sokettes, weiyng xxxvij. unces.

Item, vj. gobelettes, of dyvers sortes, weiyng xxviij. unces.

Item, xiij. peces, of dyvers sortes, weiyng vj^{xx} xv. unces.

Item, j. old pece, with j. kever and j. knop, weiyng xxxij. unces.

Item, ij. chargeours, of oon sorte, weiyng lxxviij. unces.

Item, vj. platers, of oon sorte, weiyng vij^{xx} vij. unces.

Item, xviij. disshes, of dyvers sortes, weiyng x^{xx} xvj. unces.

Item, vj. sawsers, of oon sorte, weiyng xxviij. unces.

Summa, xv^c xvij. unces.

Item, j. saltsaler, alle gilt, with j. kever, weiyng xxxvij. unces.

Item, j. pese, with j. kever, all gilt, with j. knop, weiyng xxxj. unces.

Item, j. playne pece, gilt, with j. kever, weiyng xxvj. unces.

Item, j. litill pece, gilt, with j. kever, weiyng xvij. unces.

Summa, v^{xx} xij. unces.

Item, j. chargeour, weiyng xlv. unces.

Item, viij. platers, weiyng ix^{xx} xj. unces.

Item, viij. disshes, weiyng vj^{xx} v. unces.

Item, viij. saucers, weiyng xlix. unces.

Item, j. potell potte, with gilt verges, enameled in the top with violet leves, weiyng xlix. unces.

Summa, CCCC iiij^{xx} iij. unces.

Item, j. stondyng cup, with j. kever, all gilt, weiyng xxxviij. unces.

Item, j. founteyn, all gilt, with j. columbyne floure in the bottom, weiyng xxiij. unces.

Summa, lxj. unces.

THE PASTON LETTERS

Item, ij. saltsalers, weiyng xxxix. unces.
Item, j. candilstik, with ij. sokettes, weiyng xxj. unces.
Item, iiij. flat peces, pounsed in the bottom, weiyng xl. unces.
Item, ij. gobelettes, pounsed, weiyng ix. unces.
Item, j. ewer, with j. knop, weiyng xiij. unces.
Item, xiij. spones, wherof oon is gilt, weiyng xvij. unces.
Item, ij. potellers, with my maisters armes on the liddes, weiyng lxxji. unces.
Item, j. potell potte, with braunches on the lidde enamelid, weiyng xlix. unces.
Item, iij. pottes, enameled with j. garlond, weiyng v^{xx} vij. unces.
Item, j. quart pot, weiyng xxix. unces.
Item, j. grete chargeour, weiyng lxxix. unces.
Item, iij. lesser chargeours, weiyng v^{xx} xj. unces.
Item, v. platers, of oon sorte, weiyng v^{xx} xv. unces.
Item, xij. disshes, of oon sorte, weiyng x^{xx} ix. unces.
Item, ix. sausers, of oon sorte, weiyng lxiij. unces.

Summa, M^{l} iiij^{x} xij. unces

Item, j. gobelet, gilt, with j. columbyne in the bottom, weiyng xxiiij. unces.
Item, j. stondyng cup, with j. kever, weiyng xxxv. unces.

Summa, lix. unces.

Castre.

Item, ij. prykettys, with gilt verges, weiyng xvij. unces.
Item, ij. cruettes, oon lakkyng a lydde, weiyh viij. unces.
Item, j. litill crosse, with j. fote, all gilt, weiyng vij. unces.
Item, j. sakeryng bell, weiyng xj. unces.
Item, j. chalice, weiyng xviij. unces.
Item, j. saltsaler, weiyng v. unces.
Item, j. paxbrede,[1] weiyng   [2]unces.
Item, j. grete saltsaler, with j. kever, weiyng xxvij. unces.
Item, j. playn basyn, with j. ewer, weiyng liij. unces.
Item, ij. flat peces, of oon sorte, weiyng xxij. unces.
Item, xvij. spones, of ij. sortes, weiyng xviij. unces.
Item, iiij. platers, weiyng iiij^{xx} xiij. unces.
Item, vj. disshes, weiyng iiij^{x} xiiij. unces.
Item, iiij. sausers, weiyng xviij. unces.
Item, j. candilstik, withoute sokettes, weiyng xviij. unces.

Summa, CCCCx. unces.

---

[1] A small tablet with a representation of the Crucifixion on it, presented to be kissed during the mass.
[2] Blank in MS.

172

THE PASTON LETTERS

Item, j. knoppe, for a covere, gilt, weiyng j. unce.
Item, j. flagon, of silver and gilt, accordyng with the olde inventarie, weiyng x^{xx} xviij unces.
Item, anothir flagon, of the same sorte and of the same weight, x^{xx} xviij. unces.

Summa, DCxliiij. unces di.

Item, j. paire of olde flagons, iij. pyntes, fayleth j. stopell, weiyng iiij^{xx} x. unces.
Item, j. grete sawser, weiyng vj. unces di.
Item, ij. olde cruettes, weiyng vj. unces.

389

SIR JOHN FASTOLF'S WARDROBE[1]

Memorandum.

That the last day of Octobre, the   yere of the reyne of King Henri the Sixt, Sir John Fastolf, Knyght, hath lefte in his warderope at Castre, this stuffe of clothys, and othir harnays that followith, that is to wete :—

Togæ remanenciæ hoc tempore in Garderoba Domini.

First, a goune of clothe of golde, with side slevis, sirples wise.
Item, j. nothir gowne of clothe of golde, with streyght slevys, and lynyd withe blak clothe.
Item, halfe a gowne of red felwett.
Item, j. gowne of blewe felwett upon felwet longe furrid withe martyrs, and perfold[2] of the same, slevys sengle.
C. Item, j. gowne, clothe of grene, of iij. yerds.
Item, j. side scarlet gownys, not lynyd.
Item, j. rede gowne, of my Lorde Coromale[3] is lyverey, lyned.
Item, j. chymere[4] cloke of blewe satayne, lynyd with blake silke.
Item, iij. quarters of scarlet for a gowne, di. quarter of the same.
Item, j. broken gowne of sangweyne, graynyd with the slevys.
Item, j. gowne of Frenche russet, lynyd with blak clothe.

---

[1] [From Archæologia, xxi. 252.] This roll and the preceding are both printed in the Archæologia from transcripts made by Blomefield, the Norfolk historian, for his friend Sir Andrew Fountaine. The original of this second roll we have not met with.
[2] Trimmed. The word is more commonly written 'purfled.'
[3] Cromwell.
[4] The *chammer* or *shamew* was a gown cut in the middle.—*See* Strutt's *Dress and Habits of the People of England*, ii. 359.

174

HENRY VI

M^{d} of xlvj. unces gold and ij^{ml.} Dxxv. unces of silver plate taken from Bermondesey.

Sold by John Yong of London.

In primis, a peson[1] of gold, it fayleth v. balles, weyng xxiij. unces gold.
Item, j. paire basons, beyng[2] bothe weiyng v^{xx} ij. unces.
Item, j. paire ewers, beyng[2] bothe weiyng xlv. unces.
Item, j. paire of newe flagons, cheyned, everyche weiyng lxxiiij. unces —vij^{xx} xiij. unces.
Item, iiij. platers, parcell of ix. platers not sortely, weiyng in all x^{xx} ix. unces; so iche wcieth xxiij. unces. Soo the weight of the same iiij. platers, iiij^{x} xiij. unces.
Item, xij. disshes, weiyng in all ix^{xx} ix. unces.
Item, xij. sausers, weiyng in all iiij^{x} xvij. unces.

Summa unciarum argenti, DClxxiij. unc' et de auro, xxiij. unc'.

Item, j. cup of golde, with an ewer, weiyng xxiij. unces.
Item, ij. spiceplates, weiyng bothe iiij^{x} xij. unces.
Item, ij. olde chargeours, of oon sorte, weiyng iiij^{x} viij. unces.
Item, j. grete plater, weiyng xxxviij. unces.
Item, v. olde disshes, weiyng in alle lxxvj. unces.
Item, v. sausers, weiyng xxix. unces.
Item, ij. quart pottes, weiyng liiij. unces.
Item, ix. platers, weiyng xvj^{xx} iij. unces.
Item, a flat pece, playne, of silver, weiyng xvj. unces.
Item, a quart pot, of silver, with gilt verges, weiyng xxvj. unces.
Item, an holowe basyn, of silver, weiyng xxviij. unces.

Summa unciarum de auro, xxiij. unc'; et de argento, DCClxx. unc'.

Item, ij. stondyng cuppes, gilt, of oon sorte, iche weiyng xxiiij. unces—lxvij. unces.
Item, vj. gobelettes, uncovered, weiyng xxiij. unces et di.
Item, j. layer, weiyng xviij. unces.
Item, j. saltsaler, gilt, weiyng xxxiiij. unces.
Item, j. lesse chargeours, weiyng lxx. unces.
Item, v. platers, not sortely, parcell of ix. platers, weiyng in all x^{xx} ix. unces; so iche plater weyeth by estymacion xxiij. unces. So the weight of v. platers, Cxv. unces.

Summa, CCCxxxiiij. unces di.

Item, j. saltsaler, gilt, with a cover, weiyng xxxj. unces.
Item, iiij. peces, gilt, with ij. coveres, weiyng lxxiiij. unces.
Item, vj. Parys cuppes, of silver, of the Monethes, with lowe fete, the bordures gilt, weiyng iiij^{xx} x. unces.
Item, j. white stondyng cuppe, with a cover of silver, weiyng xij. unces di.

---

[1] An instrument in the form of a staff, with balls or crockets, used for weighing, before scales were employed for that purpose.
[2] The word 'beyng' in these two places seems to have been altered to 'weyng,' which was unnecessary.

173

HENRY VI

Item, j. chemer of blak, lynyd with blak bokerame.
Item, j. gowne of blak, lynyd with blak lynyng.
Item, iij. quarters of a russet gowne with ought slevys.
Item, j. jagged huke[1] of blakke sengle, and di. of the same.

U.

Tunicæ Remanentes ibidem.

Item, j. jakket of blewe felwett, lynyd in the body with smale lynen clothe, and the slevys withe blanket.
Item, j. jakket of russet felwett, lynyd with blanket clothe.
Item, j. jakket of red felwet, the ventis bounde with red lether.
Item, j. jakket of blakke felwet upon felwet, lynyd with smale lynen cloth.
Item, j. jaket, the bret and slevys of blak felvet, and the remanent of russet fustian.
Item, ij. jakketts of russet felwet, the one lynyd with blanket, t'other with lynen clothe.
Item, ij. jakketts of chamlettes.
Item, j. jakket of sateyne fugre.[2]
Item, j. dowblettis of red felwet uppon felwet.
Item, j. jakket of blak felwet, the body lynyd with blanket and the slevys with blak clothe.
Item, j. dowbelet of rede felwet, lynyd with lynen clothe.
Item, ij. jakketts of derys lether, with j. coler of blak felwet.
Item, j. dowbelet of white lynen clothe.
Item, j. pettecote of lynen clothe stoffyd with flokys.
Item, j. petticote of lynen clothe, withought slyves.
Item, ij. payre hosyn of blakke keyrse.
Item, iij. payre bounden with lether.
Item, j. payre of blake hosyn, vampayed with lether.
Item, ij. payre of scarlet hosyn.

U
V

Capucia et Capelle.

Item, j. russet hode, with owgt a typpett, of satyn russet.
Item, j. hode of blakke felwet, with a typpett, halfe damask and halfe felwet, y jaggyd.
Item, j. hode of depe grene felwet, jakgyd uppon the rolle.
Item, j. hode of russet felwet, with a typpett, half of the same and half of blewe felwet, lynyd with the same of damaske.

---

[1] A kind of mantle.—*See* Strutt's *Dress and Habits*, ii. 363.
[2] Figured or branched satin.

175

1459

Item, j. hood of depe grene felwet, the typpet blake and grene felwet.
Item, j. hood of russet felwet withougt a typpet.
Item, j. hode of damaske russet, with j. typpet, fastyd with a lase of silke.
Item, j. rydyng hode of rede felwet with iiij. jaggys.
Item, j. hode of skarlet, with a rolle of purpill felwet, bordered with the same felwet.
Item, j. hode of blake satayne, the rolle of blake felwet.
Item, j. of purpill felwet, with owten rolle and typpet.
Item, j. hode of russet felwet, the typpet lynyd with russet silke.
Item, j. typpet, halfe russet and halfe blake felwet, with j. jagge.
Item, j. rydynghoode of blakalyere, lynyd with the same.
Item, j. rydyng hoode of blakke felwet, i-lynyd with blakke clothe.
Item, j. hatte of bever, lynyd withe damaske gilt, girdell, bokkell, and penaunt, with iiij. barrys of the same.
Item, j. gret rollyd cappe of sangweyn, greyned.
Item, ij. skarlet hoodys.
Item, iiij. hodys of sangweyn, graynyd.
Item, ij. hodys of perce blewe. Item, ij. hodys blakalyre.
Item, j. knitte cappe. Item, j. unsette poke.
Item, ij. poyntys of a hood of skarlot.
Item, j. blake rydyng hoode, sengle. Item, ij. strawen hattis.
Item, j. blewe hoode of the Garter.
Item, j. gowne of my ladys, sengle.

Alia res necessaria ibidem.

Inprimis, j. canope of greene silke, borderyd with rede.
Item, iij. trapuris, with iij. clothis of the same sute.
Item, ij. old cheses plis [charubles] of rede.
Item, ij. pokkettis stuffyd and embraudyd with white rosys after his devyce, of rede with crossis leten with silver.
Item, j. pece of scarlot, embraudit in the myddell, containing in length iij. yerds and di.
Item, j. pece of blewe, contaynyng in length iij. quarters, and in brede v. quarters.
Item, j. pece of skarlot for trappars for horsys, with rede crossis and rosys.
Item, ij. stripis of the same trappuris sutly.
Item, j. pece of Seynt George leveray, for j. hode.
Item, j. ball of coper gilt, embrauded rechely with j. skogen [scutcheon] hongyng therbi.
Item, ij. pencellis of his armys.
Item, ij. yerds and j. quarter of white damaske.
Item, j. pece of white felwet ij. yerdis longe.
Item, j. pece of rede satayne, brauden [embroidered] with Me faunt fere.
Item, ij. strypes of the same.
Item, ij. cote armours of silke, aftir his own armys.

176

1459

Item, j. cote armour of whyte silke of Seynt George.
Item, ij. pecys of clothe of golde of tyssent.
Item, j. pece of blak kersey with rosys, and embraudit with Me faunt fere.
Item, ij. stripis of the same sute.
Item, ij. peces of blewe canvas of xlij. yerds.
Item, j. pece of linnen cloth, steyned.
Item, j. pece of grene wurstet xxx. yards longe.
Item, iiij. clokys of murry [1] derke.
Item, j. bollok haftyd dager, harnesyd wyth sylver,[2] and j. chape [3] thertoo.
Item, j. lytyll schort armyng dager, withe j. gilt schape.
Item, ij. payre tablys of cipris, being in casys of lether.
Item, j. parre tablys of G., enrayed withowght, and here men in baggys longyng thertoo.

E.

Imprimis, v. pellowes of grene silke.
Item, j. pellow of silk the growund white wyth lyllys of blewe.
Item, ij. pellowes of rede felwet and the growund of ham blakke.
Item, v. pellowys of rede felwet.
Item, ij. pellowys of rede felwet beten upon satayne.
Item, j. littill pellow of grene sike, full wythin of lavendre.
Item, j. pellow of purpyll silke and golde.
Item, ij. pellowes of blew silke, with a schelde.
Item, v. large carpettys.

Imprimis, j. longe pillowe of fustian.
Item, iij. brode pillowes of fustyan.
Item, ij. pillowys of narwer sorte and more schorter, of fustyan.
Item, j. longe pellow of lynen clothe.
Item, j. pellow of a lasse sorte.
Item, j. brode pyllow of lynen clothe.
Item, ij. pillowes of lynen clothe of a lasser assyse.
Item, viiij. pelowes of lynen clothe off a lasser assyse.
Item, v. of the lest assyse.

In primis, j. cover of grene silke to a bedde, lynyd with blewe silke.
Item, j. close bedde of palle grene and whyte, with levys of golde.
Item, j. covyr of the same.
Item, j. covyr of rede silke lynyd with bokerame.
Item, j. cover of white clothe, fyne and well-wrought, purpeynte [pourpointé or stitched] wyse.
Item, j. cover of raynis, wrowght with golde of damaske.
Item, j. donge [mattress or feather bed] of purle sylke.

---

[1] Dark or brownish red. [2] Silver twisted round the haft.
[3] The schape or chape was the ferule of the scabbard.—Dr. Meyrick.

VOL. III.—M   177

1459

Item, j. seler of white lynen clothe.
Item, j. testur of the same. Item, ij. curtaynys sutely.
Item, iij. cartaynyes of lynen clothe.
Item, iij. blankettis of fustian

Clothis of Arras and of Tapstre warke.

Inprimis, j. clothe of arras, clyped the Schipherds clothe.[1]
Item, j. of the Assumpsion of Oure Lady.
Item, j. newe banker of arras, with a bere holdyng j. spere in the middys of the clothe.
Item, j. tester of arras with ij. gentlewomen and ij. gentlemen, and one holdyng an hawke in his honde.
Item, j. clothe with iiij. gentle women.
Item, j. testour of arras with a lady crouned and a grete rolle aboughte her hede, the first letter N.
Item, j. clothe of ix. conquerouris.
Item, j. cover for a bedde, of newe arras, and a gentlewoman beyng ther in the corner with a whelp in hir honde and an Awnus Day abought hir nec.
Item, a seler of arras frangyd with silke, red, grene, and white.
Item, j. testir of the same, red, grene, and white.
Item, j. testur frangyd with grene silke. Item, j. seler of the same.
Item, j. clothe for the nether hall, of arras, with a geyaunt in the myddell, beryng a legge of a bere in his honde.
Item, j. clothe of arras for the dese [daïs] in the same halle, with j. wodewose [a savage] and j. chylde in his armys.
Item, j. clothe of the sege of Faleys for the west side of the halle.
Item, j. clothe of arras with iij. archowrys on scheting [shooting] a doke in the water with a cross bowe.
Item, j. clothe of arras withe a gentlewoman harpyng by j. castell in myddys of the clothe.
Item, j. cover of arras for a bedde, with a mane drawyng water in the myddel of the clothe ought of a welle.
Item, j. lytell tester of arras, whith j. man and a woman in the myddyll.
Item, j. banker [2] of arras with a man schetyng at j. blode hownde.
Item, j. clothe of arras with a lady crouned, and j. rolle aboughte her hedde with A. N., lynyd with gray canvas.
Item, j. clothe of arras with a condyte in the myddill.
Item, j. clothe of arras, with a gentlewoman holding j. lace of silke, and j. gentlewoman a hauke.
Item, ij. clothis portrayed full of popelers.
Item, j. testyr of blewe tapistry warke with viiij. braunchys.
Item, j. blewe hallyng [3] of the same sute.

---

[1] Probably representing the Adoration of the Shepherds.
[2] Covering for a bench.   [3] Hanging for a hall.

178

1459

Item, j. rede clothe of v. yerds v. dim. of lenthe.
Item, j. banker of rede, with iij. white rosys and the armys of Fastolf.
Item, j. nothyr clothe of rede, with v. roses sutly.
Item, j. hallyng of blewe worstet, contaynyng in lenthe xiij. yerds, and in bredthe iiij. yerds.
Item, j. hallyng with men drawen in derke grene worsted.
Item, ij. pecys of whyte worsted, bothe of one lenthe.
Item, j. hallyng of depe grene, contaynyng in lenthe xj. yerds, and in bredthe ij. yerds and one halfe.
Item, j. hallyng of the same sute, lenthe, and brede.
Item, j. tester of grene and whyte, wyth braunchis sutely.

F.

Clothis of Arras.

Item, ij. clothis of arras for the chamboure over the nether halle, of huntyng and of haukyng.
Item, iij. clothis of grene and whyte, withe braunchis sutely to the other wreten before.
Item, a coveryng of a bedde of aras, withe hontyng of the bore, a man in blewe, with a jagged hoode, white and rede.

G.

Canvas in the Warderop and fyne Lynen Clothe of dyvers sortes.

First ix. berys for fetherbeddys.
Item, iiij. transomers.
Item, j. pece of lynen clothe, countyng lenthe and brede iiij^xx. ellys, and the tone ende kit and nought enselyd and the other ende hole.
Item, j. pece of lynen clothe, yerde brode, contaynyng xiiij. yerds and more, and not sealed.
Item, j. pece of grete lynen clothe, yerde brode, of xxij. yerds.
Item, j. pece of yerde brode, xxiv. yerds iij. quarters, pro Willelmo Schipdam.
Item, j. pece of a yerde and a halfe quarter brode, of xxv. yerds and iij. quarters, pro Willelmo Schypdam.
Item, j. pece of yerde brode, of xij. yerds and j. quarter.
Item, j. pece of fyne lynen clothe, yerd brode, of lvj. yerdys of lenthe.
Item, j. pece of grete clothe, yerde brode, of lvij. yerds.
Item, j. pece of grete clothe of xxiiij. yerds.
Item, j. pece of clothe of xxviiij. yerds.
Item, j. pece of clothe of xxxvij. yerds et dim.
Item, j. pece of grete clothe of xxij. yerdys per Willm. Schypdham.
Item, j. pece of clothe lyke of xxxij. yerds and j. quarter.
Item, j. pece of lyke clothe of xxxvj. yerds, per Willm. Schypdam.

179

THE PASTON LETTERS

Item, j. pece of clothe of xxxiij. yerds and j. quarter, per Willm. Schypdam.

Item, j. pece of xxvij. yerds j. quarter. Item, j. pece of x. yerds dim.

Item, j. pece of viij. yerds. Item, j. pece of xxviij. yerds iij. quarters.

Item, j. pece of xix. yerds dim. Item, j. pece of xxij. yerds j. quarter.

Item, j. pece of xiij. yerds j. quarter. Item, j. pece of xxiij. yerds.

Item, j. pece of xxvij. yerds j. quarter. Item, j. pece of xxx. yerds dim.

Item, j. pece of xxxij. yerds dim. Item, j. pece of xlj. yerds and j. quarter.

Item, j. pece of xxxj. yerds dim. Item, j. pece of xviij. yerds iij. quarters.

Item, j. pece of xiij. yerds. Item, j. pece of xiiij. yerds.

Item, j. pece of xlv. yerds. Item, j. pece of viij. yerds dim.

Item, j. pece of xiij. yerds dim. Item, j. pece of xxij. yerds j. quarter.

Item, j. pece of xxxix. yerds.

Item, j. pece of xxxiij. yerds j. quarter of beter clothe.

Item, ij. rollys of lynen clothe, both not moten. Item, lx. yerds of clothe.

Item, j. pece of Seland clothe, with dyvers sealys at the endys.

Summa totalis, xl. peces.

Summa totalis istius folij ultra ij. rolles conc' lx. virg' et in pece sigillat' cum Domini secreto sigillo uti in fine paginæ, ml. xxxvij. virg. ij. quart. dim. per C. que re.

Manent, cum tribus pecijs restitutis.

H.

Adhuc in Garderoba in domo Superiori.

Item, iij. grete brasse pottys of Frenche makyng.

Item, j. grete chafron of brasse. Item, ij. chafernes of a lase sorte.

Item, iiij. chafernes of the French gyse for sewys. Item, j. panne.

Item, j. litell potte of brasse. Item, ij. chamber basons of pewter.

Item, iiij. chargeourys. Item, vj. platowres. Item, vj. sawsers of pewter.

Item, iiij. candylstykkeys of my mayster is armys und my ladyes, copper and gilt.

Item, j. fountayne of latayne to sette in pottys of wine.

Item, ij. hangyng candylstykkes. Item, ij. maundys [baskets].

Item, j. basket of wykers. Item, xxj. bowys.

Item, viij. schefe arrowys of swanne.

HENRY VI

Camera ultra Buttellarium pro extraneis.

Item, j. fedder bedde. Item, j. bolster. Item, j. pillowe.

Item, ij. blankettys. Item, j. payre of schetys.

Item, j. purpeynt of white. Item, j. seloure. Item, j. testoure.

Item, ij. curtaynys of the same sute. Item, j. cobbord clothe of the same.

Magna Camera ultra Aulam Estevalem.

In primis, j. fetherbedde. Item, j. bolster. Item, j. seler.

Item, j. tester, withe one gentlewoman in grene, taking a mallard in hir hondes.

Item, j. coveryng, with j. geyaunt smytyng a wilde bore with a spere.

Item, iij. courtaynes of grene silke.

Item, j. clothe of arras, of the Schipherds.

The White Chambour next the Gret Chaumbur, sumtyme Nicholas Bokkeyng is Chambre.

In primis, j. fedder bedde. Item, j. bolster. Item, j. pyllowe of doun.

Item, ij. blankettys bon.

Item, j. payre of schetys, every schete iiij. schete iiij. webbes.

Item, j. coveryng of whyte lynen clothe. Item, j. purpoynt.

Item, j. tester. Item, j. seler. Item, iij. curtaynys of whyte.

Item, j. fedder bedde. Item, j. bolster. Item, ij. blankettys.

Item, ij. payre of schetys. Item, ij. coverlettes of grene warke.

Item, j. cobbord clothe.

The Chaumboure, sumtyme for Stephen Scrope, hangyng clothys portrayed with the Schipherds.

Item, j. federbedde. Item, j. bolster.

Item, ij. fustian blanketts, every of hem vj. webbys.

Item, j. pyllowye of downe. Item, j. pyllowe of lavendre.

Item, j. cover of apres [ypres ?], lynyd with lynen clothe.

Item, j. tester and j. seler of the same. Item, iiij. curtaynes of rede saye.

Item, j. clothe hangyng of Schovelers.

Item, j. rede curtayne o saye for the chayre.

Item, iiij. cosschonys of rede say. Item, j. cobbord clothe.

Item, j. rynnyng bedde with a materas.

Item, j. bolster. Item, ij. blankettis. Item, j. payre of schetys.

Item, j. coverlet of yellow clothe.

Raffman is Chambour.

Item, j. fedder bedde. Item, j. bolster. Item, j. blanket.

Item, j. payre of schetys. Item, j. redde panne of kinyng skynnys.

THE PASTON LETTERS

Item, j. testour. Item, j. selour of rede saye.

Item, j. hangyng clothe of popelers. Item, ij. tapettis with clowdys.

Item, j. coveryng of grene saye. Item, j. coverlet of other warke.

The Yeomen is Chambur for Straungers.

In primis, iij. fether beddys. Item, iij. bolsterys. Item, j. materas.

Item, v. blankettys. Item, iij. payre of schetys.

Item, j. coverlet of grene warke.

Item, ij. coverynges of white, grene, and blewe.

Item, ij. hangyng clothys of the same.

The White hangyd Chambre next Inglose is Chamboure.

In primis, j. feddebedde. Item, j. bolster. Item, ij. blankettys.

Item, j. payre of schetys. Item, j. pillowe of downe.

Item, j. purpoynt white hangyd. Item, j. hangyd bedde.

Item, j. selere. Item, j. testoure. Item, iiij. curtaynys of white.

Item, j. curtayne of the same.

Inglose Chambre.

In primis, j. fedder bedde. Item, j. bolster.

Item, ij. blanketts of fustian, everyche of them vj. webbes.

Item, j. peyre of schetys, every schete iij. webbys. Item, j. hed schete.

Item, j. pillowe of downe. Item, j. pillowe of lavendre.

Item, j. covering of aras. Item, j. testoure.

Item, j. seleure of the same. Item, j. pane furryd with menevere.

Item, iij. courtaynys of rede saye. Item, v. clothes of tapserey warke.

Item, j. bankere clothe of the same. Item, j. cusschen of redde silke.

Item, iiij. of rede saye. Item, j. cobbordclothe. Item, j. paylette.

Item, j. bolster. Item, j. blanket. Item, j. payre of schetys.

Item, j. coverlyte. Item, j. grene carpette.

The White hangyd Chambour next the Warderobe.

In primis j. fedderbedde. Item, j. bolster. Item, ij. blankettys.

Item, j. payre of schettys. Item, j. hed schete. Item, j. pillow of downe.

Item, j. pillow of lavendre.

Item, j. purpuont white, with a scuchon after an horse wyse, visure and braunchis of grene.

Item, j. selour. Item, j. testour. Item, iiij. curtaynys of lynen clothe.

Cole and Watkyn is Chamboure that was for the two auditourys.

Item, ij. materasse. Item, ij. blankettys. Item, ij. schetys.

Item, j. bolster. Item, j. coverlet of white warke withe burdys.

Item, j. testour of red saye. Item, j. seler of canvas.

HENRY VI

The Porter is Chambour.

In primis, j. fedder bedde. Item, j. bolster. Item, j. payre of schetys.

Item, j. blankett. Item, j. coveryng cloth.

Item, j. curtayne of rede saye.

The Chambour agenest the Porter is Chamboure.

In primis, j. fedder bedde. Item, j. bolster. Item, j. payre of schetys.

Item, j. payre of blankettys. Item, ij. coverlettys of grene and yolowe.

Item, j. seler of blewe panes and white. Item, ij. pecys of saye.

The Chamber over the Draught Brigge.

In primis, j. fedder bed, covered withe gray canvas. Item, j. bolster.

Item, ij. blankettys, j. payre of schettys.

Item, j. rede pane furryd withe connyngs.

Item, j. testour, and j. selour of rede saye with Me faunt fere.

Schipdam is Chambre.

In primis, j. fedderbedde. Ijem, ij. blangettis. Item, ij. schetys.

Item, j. bolster.

Item, j. coverlet of white rosys, at every corner iiij., and one in the myddell.

Item, j. seler of rede say.

Item, j. testour of rede say, lynyd wythe canvas. Item, j. chayre.

Item, j. pece of rede say for accomptyng borde.

Item, iiij. cosschonys rede say. Item, j. aundiren. Item, j. firepanne.

Item, j. payre of tongus. Item, iij. formys. Item, j. junyd stole.

The Inner Chaumbour over the Gatis.

In primis, j. federbedde. Item, j. bolster. Item, ij. blankettes.

Item, j. gardevyaunt [meat safe]. Item, ij. cosschonys of blewe say.

Item, j. junyd stole.

The Myddell Chambour.

In primis, j. feder bedde. Item, j. materas. Item, j. quylt.

Item, ij. coverletts of rede say. Item, j. testour withe a selour.

Item, ij. courtaynys of rede say. Item, j. testoure of the same.

Item, j. payre of tongys.

Camera Bokkyng in le Basecourte.

In primis, j. fedderbedde. Item, j. bolster.

Item, ij. payre of schetys. Item, ij. blankettys.

Item, j. coverlete of popelers, lynyd with whyte lynnyng clothe.

Item, j. selour. Item, j. testour of rede saye.

THE PASTON LETTERS

The Coke is Chambour.

Item, j. feder bedde. Item, j. bolster. Item, ij. schetys.
Item, j. redde coverlyte of rosys and blood houndys hedys.

Feraufe [or Fitzrauf] is Chambre.

Item, j. fedderbedde. Item, j. bolster. Item. j. payre of schetys.
Item, ij. blankettys. Item, j. coverlyte. Item, j. testour.
Item, j. selour of blewe clowded.

Thomas Fastolff Chamboure.

Item, j. fedderbed. Item, j. bolster. Item, j. payre of schetys.
Item, ij. blankettis. Item, j. rede coverlet.
Item, j. coveryng of worstet. Item, j. testour.
Item, j. selour of rede say, withe the armys of Fastolf.

The Bedde in the grete Stabull.

Item, j. materas. Item, j. payre of schetys.
Item, j. coverlyt of blewe and rede.

The Bedde in the Sumer Stabull.

Item, j. materas. Item, j. payre of schetys.
Item, j. coverlyte of blewe and rede.

The Gardinares Chambre.

In primis, j. bolster. Item, j. materas. Item, j. payre of schetys.
Item, ij. blankettys. Item, j. coverlet of blewe.
Item, j. nother of better blewe. Item, j. materas. Item, j. bolster.
Item, j. carpet. Item, j. coveryng of grene say.
Item, j. coveryng of popelerys. Item, j. selour of blewe.

My Maister is Chambre and the withe draughte withe the Stable.

In primis, j. fedderbedde. Item, j. donge of fyne blewe.
Item, j. bolster. Item, ij. blankettys of fustians.
Item, j. payre of schetis. Item, j. purpeynt.
Item, j. hangyd bedde of arras. Item, j. testour. Item, j. selour.
Item, j. coveryng.
Item, iij. curtaynes of grene worsted.
Item, j. bankeur of tapestre warke.
Item, iiij. peces hangyng of grene worsted.
Item, j. banker hangyng tapestry worke. Item, j. cobbord clothe.
Item, ij. staundyng aundyris. Item, j. feddefflok.
Item, j. chafern of laten. Item, j. payre of tongys.

184

HENRY VI

Item, j. payre of bellewes. Item, j. litell paylet. Item, ij. blankettys.
Item, j. payre of schetys. Item, j. coverlet.
Item, vj. white cosschynes. Item, ij. lytell bellys.
Item, j. foldyng table. Item, j. longe chayre. Item, j. grene chayre.
Item, j. hangyng candylstyk of laton.

In Camera and Warda nuper pertinentibus Dominæ Mylcentiæ Fastolf.

In primis, j. fedder bedde. Item, j. bolster. Item, j. materas.
Item, j. quelte. Item, smale pyllowes of downe.
Item, j. hongyd bedde of fyne whyte. Item, ij. smale payletts.
Item, j. rede coverlet. Item, j. leddre pyllewe. Item, j. basyn.
Item, j. ewer. Item, ij. pottys.
Item, ij. lyttyll ewers of blew glasses, powdered withe golde.

The Chambure there Margaret Hodessone laye.

Item, j. fedderbedde. Item, j. bolster. Item, ij. fustians.
Item, j. chayre withe j. pece of palle white and grene.

The utmost Chambur nexte Winter Halle.

Item, j. fedder bedde. Item, j. bolster.
Item, j. coveryng of grene worsted. Item, ij. staundyng aundeirys.
Item, j. hangyng candylstyk of laton.
Item, j. cobbord clothe. Item, j. rede chayre.

The White Draught Chamber for Lewys and William Worcester.

In primis, j. fedder bedde. Item, j. donge. Item, j. bolster.
Item, j. hangyd bedde. Item, j. testour.
Item, j. selour of rede worsted, i-hangyd with clothe of pale, blake, white, and grene. Item, j. arstellawe.

G

In primis, ij. pecys of satayne after the fassion of a dowblet to were under gownes.
Item, viij. quarters of silk, the slevys of the same rolled to gedder for jakketts.
Item, j. jakke of blakke lynen clothe stuffyd with mayle.
Item, vj. jakkes stuffyd with horne.
Item, j. jakke of blake clothe lyned with canvas mayled.
Item, xxiiij. cappes, stuffed withe horne, and sum withe mayle.
Item, vj. payre glovys of mayle, of schepys skynne, and of doos.
Item, iij. grete crosbowes of stele, with one grete dowble wyndas ther too.
Item, j. coffyre, full of quarrellys of a smale sorte.
Item, xij. quarrellis of grete sorte, feddered with brasse.
Item, vj. payre curassis. Item, j. payre of breggandires.

THE PASTON LETTERS

Item, iij. harburyones of l'Milayne.
Item, v. ventayletts for bassenetts. Item, vj. peces of mayle.
Item, j. garbrasse. Item, j. polleson. Item, vj. payre grevys.
Item, iiij. payre thyes. Item, xj. bassenetts. Item, j. payre coschewes.
Item, j. payre bregandines, helyd with rede felwet. Item, j. spere.
Item, ij. bassenetts. Item, ij. saletts withe ij. visers.
Item, viij. saletts, white, white oute vesoure. Item, v. payre vambras.
Item, iij. spere heddys. Item, j. swerde with a gyld chape.
Item, j. prikkyng hat, covered withe blake felwet.
Item, ij. tarcellys on hym be hynde. Item, iij. gonnes, called serpentins.
Item, ij. white payre of brigaundiris. Item, ij. payre hosyn of blak kersey.
Item, payre bounde wyth lether. Item, ij. payre of skarlat.
Item, j. payre of blake vampayed withe lether.
Item, ij. jakketts of russet felwet. Item, ij. aundyrys, grete, of one sorte.
Item, ij. lasse, of anothyr sorte. Item, iij. lesser aundiris.
Item, xi. aunderis for lecchen. Item, j. iren spitte.
Item, ix. barrys of iren for curtaynes.
Item, ij. chaynes for the draught brigge.

Magna Aula.

xj. crosbowes whereof iij. of stele, and v. wyndas. Item, j. borespere.
Item, vj. wifles. Item, j. rede pavys. Item, j. target.
Item, xxj. speris. Item, j. launce gay. Item, iij. pecys of rede worsted.
Item, j. grene chayre. Item, j. red chayre.
Item, j. pece of rede worsted in the toure parloure.
Item, j. banker of tapestry worke.
Item, j. nothir of tapestry warke newe, in the hall wendewe.
Item, vij. cosschenys of tapestre.

Aula Yemalis.

Item, j. clothe of arras, of the Morysch daunce.
Item, ij. chayrys fraungyd. Item, j. rede chayre di. dos (?).
Item, di. dosn. of tapestrye warke. Item, j. banker of aras.
Item, ij. andyris stondyng.

Celar.

In the seler, certayn vessell whiche John Ouresby is chargid withe by an endenture, wherof the copy is annexed to this lese.
Item, ij. pypes of rede wyne.

The Bottre.

Item, ij. kervyng knyvys.
Item, iij. kneyves in a schethe, the haftys of every, withe naylys gilt.

186

HENRY VI

Item, j. payre galon bottels of one sorte.
Item, j. payre of potell botellys of one sorte.
Item, j. nother potell bottell. Item, j. payre quartletts of one sorte.
Item, iiij. galon pottis of lether. Item, ij. potteleris of lether.
Item, j. trencher knyfe. Item, j. grete tankard.
Item, ij. grete and hoge bottelis. Item, xiiij. candylstykkys of laton.
Item, certayn pecys of napre, accordyng to a bylle endentyd annexed to this lese.
Item, j. quartelet for wine.

In primis, ij. chargeres argenti de parvo sorte. Item, v. platers argenti.
Item, xij. dissches argenti unius sortis.
Item, viij. dissches argenti minoris sortis.
Item, xj. sawseris argenti unius sortis.
Item, iij. crateras argenti, quarum, j. data Margaretæ Hoddsone.
Item, iij. covertorijs argenti enamelid and borage floures in les botimes.
Item, vj. chacyd pecys gilte bi the bordurys, with the towche of Paryce.
Item, ij. pottis argenti potlers, percell gilte and enameled with violetts and dayseys.
Item, ij. pottis of sylver, of the facion of goods enamelyd on the toppys withe hys armys.
Item, j. quarteler argenti, percel gift withe j. chase a bought of rosys and levys.
Item, j. rounde salt seler, gylt and covered with a wrethe toppe with this wordys wreten, Me faunt fere, a bowght.
Item, j. salt seler, pacell of the same fassion sengle.
Item, ij. salt selers of sylver, playne and smale with a dowble rose graven withe armys.
Item, j. basyn of sylver, percell gylte, with a dowble rose, his armis enamelid in the bottom be with his helme and his crest.

Liberat' London' cum Domino.

Item, j. nother bacyn, white, of the same facion, enamilid with his armys in the bottom.
Item, ij. ewars ther withe.
Item, j. lytyll sylver bacyn playne, with j. flat ewer.
Item, j. goboleit chaced, the bordours gilt.
Item, xvj. sponys of sylver, withe knappys gylt lyke perle.
Item, j. candylstyk of sylver, percell gylt, dowble nosyd.
Item, j. rounde basyn argenti cum, j. ewer argenti playn.
Item, ij. grete bacyns of sylver, the bourdour is gylt and wretyn abought, Me faunt fere.
Item, ij. ewers accordyng ther to. Item, j. lytyll stert panne of sylver.
Item, ij. disschys of sylver founden in my lady is chambre.
Item, ij. smale pecys.
Item, j. saltseler bolltouned inwarde, covered and gylt.
Item, j. stondyng coppe gylte, with j. knappe in maner like perle.

1459

Item, ij. playn borde clothys for my maister is table, counte ix. yerds in lengthe.
Item, ij. playne clothis for my maisters table, ece counte vj. yerds.
Item, vj. napkyns playn.
Item, iiij. tewelles playn warke, eche cont' in lenthe ij. yerds, dim'.
Item, iiij. playne clothis for the hall, eche of vj. yerds.
Item, ij. wasschyng tewellys of warke, eche of x. yerds.
Item, j. pocter (?).   Item, j. overpayn of Raynes

Capella.

Inprimis, ij. antyfeners.   Item, j. legande of hoole servyce.
Item, ij. myssayles, the one noted and closyd wyth sylver, and the other not noted.
Item, j. sauter claspyd with sylver, and my mayster is armys and my ladyes ther uppon.
Item, j. mortellege covered withe white ledes.
Item, j. vestement covered withe crownes gilt in the myddes, with all the apparayle.
Item, j. vestement hole of redde damaske warke.
Item, j. vestement of blak clothe of golde, with the hole ornaments.
Item, j. auter clothe, withe a frontell of white damaske, the Trynete in the myddys.
Item, j. vestement of tunekell.   Item, j. cope of white damaske, withe the ornaments.
Item, j. awbe.   Item, j. stole.
Item, j. favon, encheked white and blewe.   Item, j. auter clothe.
Item, ij. curtaynes of white sylke, withe a frontell of the same, with fauchouns of golde.
Item, j. vestement of divers colurys, withe a crosse of golde to the bakke, iiij. birdys quartelye.
Item, j. crosse of sylver and gylt, with oure Lady and Seynt John.
Item, j. chales sylver and gylt.   Item, j. pax brede.
Item, j. crucyfyxe, thereon withe oure Lady and Seynt John enamelyd, and full of flour delys.
Item, ij. candylstykkys of sylver, the borduris gylt.
Item, j. cruettys of sylver, percell gylt.
Item, iiij. pyllowes stondyng on the autre off rede felwet withe flowrys enbrawderid.
Item, ij. carpettis.   Item, iiij. cosschenys of grene worstede.
Item, j. chayre in the closet of Fraunce, fregid.
Item, j. cosschon of redde worsted.   Item, j. sakeryng bell of sylver.

Pistrina.

Item, j. bulter.   Item, j. ranell.   Item, ij. payre wafer irens.
Item, ij. basketts.   Item, j. seve.   Item, j. payre trayes cum j. coler.
Item, j. materas.   Item, j. blanket.   Item, j. payre of chetis.
Item, j. coverlyte.

188

Brewhousee.

Item, xij. ledys.   Item, j. mesynfate [*mashing tub*].   Item, j. yelfate [*ale vat*].
Item, viij. kelers, &c.

Coquena.

Item, j. gret bras pote.   Item, vj. cours pottys of brasse.
Item, iiij. lytyll brasse pottis.   Item, iiij. grete brasse pottis.
Item, ij. pike pannys of brasse.
Item, ij. ladels and ij. skymers of brasse.
Item, j. caudron, j. dytyn panne of brasse, j. droppyng panne.
Item, j. gredyren, iiij. rakkys, iiij. cobardys, iij. trevitts.
Item, j. fryeyng panne, j. sclyse.
Item, ij. grete square spittys, ij. square spittys cocnos.
Item, ij. lytyll brocchys rounde, j. sars of brasse.
Item, j. brasyn morter cum j. pestell, j. grate, j. sarche of tre.
Item, j. flessche hoke, ij. potte hokys, j. payr tongys.
Item, j. dressyng knyfe, j. fyre schowle, ij. treys, j. streynour.
Item, j. venegre botell.

Larderia.

Item, iij. grete standere pannes, j. bochers axe.
Item, ij. saltyng tubbes.   Item, viij. lynges.   Item, iiij. mulwellfyche.
Item, j. barell, dim. alec. alb. di.
Item, j. barrell. anguill., unde car. cc. anguill.
Item, j. ferkyn anguill. hoole.   Item, j. barrell.
Item, j. busschell salt albi.   Item, j. quart. alb sal.

390

FASTOLF'S COLLEGE [1]

ULTIMA exitacio domini Johannis Fastolf ad concludendum festinanter cum Johanne Paston fuit quod vicecomes Bemond, Dux Somerset, comes Warwyk, voluerunt emere, et quod intendebat quod executores sui

[1] [From Paston MSS., B.M.] This paper is a very rough draft, full of errors in grammar and spelling. Additions have been made to the text here and there in the handwriting of John Paston. It was evidently written after Sir John Fastolf's death, possibly several years later.

189

THE PASTON LETTERS

HENRY VI

desiderabant vendere et non stabilire colegium; quod totaliter fuit contra intencionem sui dicti Johannis Fastolf; et considerabat quod certum medium pro licencia Regis et dominorum non providebatur, et sic tota fundatio colegii pendebat in dubiis; et ideo ad intencionem suam perimplendam desideravit dictum barganium fieri cum Johanne Paston, sperans ipsum in mente voluntate perficiendi dictum colegium et ibidem manere ne in manibus dominorum veniat.

Item, plures consiliarii sui dixerunt quod licet fundaret regulos seu presbiteros, aut eicientur per clamia falsa aut compellantur adherere dominis pro manutinencia, qui ibidem ad costus colegii permanerent et morarent[ur] et colegium destruerent; et hac de causa consessit eos ditari in pencionibus certis ad modum cantariæ Heylysdon, sic quod dictus Johannes haberet ad custus proprios conservacionem (?) terrarum erga querentes et clamatores; et ne executores diversi propter contrarietates et dissimulaciones se favores——[1]

Item, considerabat quod ubi monechy et canonesi [*monachi et canonici*] haberent terras seu tenementa ad magnam [*sic*] valorem, scilicet m[l] [1000] vel ij. m[l] [2000 *sc. librarum*], tam singulares monachi et canoneci tantum per se resiperent [*reciperent*] xl*s.* per annum et prandium, et quod abbas, officiarii et extraequitatores expenderent residuum in mundanis et riotis; et ideo ordinavit dotacionem prædictam in annuetatibus.

Et quod non fuit intencio dicti Johannis Fastolf in convencione prædicta mortificare CCC. marcas terræ, quia prima convencio Johannis Paston est solvere v. m[l] [5000] marcas in tribus annis et fundare colegium quod in intencione dicti Johannis Fastolf constaret m[l] [1000] libr., et semper dedit Johanni Paston mancionem suam in manerio et tota terra [*sic*] in Northefolk et Southefolk assessa ad v. C. [500] marcas annuatim, tunc Johannes Paston emeret revercionem CC. marcarum terræ quæ valet iiij.[2] m[l] [4000] marcas ad suam propriam adventuram pro vj. m[l] v. C. [6500] marcis.

Item, pro tranquillita[te] et pace tempore vitæ, ita ut non perturbetur per servos hospicii, ballivos, firmarios seu attornatos placitorum.

[1] *Sic*—the sentence left unfinished.   [2] The figures 'iiij.' are blurred.

190

Item quod abbas de Sente Bede [1] potuit resistere fundationi, intentione ut tunc (?) remaneat sibi et suis.

Endorsed :—' Causa festinæ barganiæ inter Fastolf et Paston.'

391

WILLIAM PASTON TO JOHN PASTON

To my Maistr Jon Paston in Norffolk.

RYTHE will belovyd broder, I recomand me to zow, sertefyeng zow that on Fryday last was in the mornyng, Wurceter and I wer come to London be viij. of the clok, and we spak with my Lord Chanceler,[3] and I fund hym well disposyd in all thyng, and ze schall fynd hym ryth profytabyll to zow, &c.   And he desyred me to wrythe zow a letter in hys name, and put trust in zow in gaderyng of the good togeder, and pray zow to do so and have all his good owthe of every place of his, and his awne place, qwer so ever they wer, and ley it secretly wer as ze thowth best at zowr assynement, and tyll that he speke with zow hym selff, and he seyd ye schuld have all lawfull favor.   I purpose to ryde to him this day ffor wryttis of *diem clawsit extremum*,[4] and I sopose ze schall have a letter sent from hym selff to zow.

As for the good of Powlis, it is safe j now [*enough*]; and this day we have grant to have the good owthe of Barmundsey with owthe avyse of any man, sawyng Worseter, Plomer, and I my selff, and no body schall know of it but we thre.

My Lord[5] Treasorer[6] spekyth fayr, but zet many avyse me to put no trust in hym.   Ther is laboryd many menys to intytill the Kyng in his good.   Sothewell[7] is Eschetor, and he is

1459
NOV. 12

[1] Apparently St. Benet's is intended.
[2] [From Fenn, iii. 352.] This letter gives an account of the steps taken by William Paston in behalf of his brother, who was Sir John Fastolf's principal executor, to secure the goods of the deceased knight immediately after his death.
[3] William of Waynflete, Bishop of Winchester.
[4] *See* vol. ii. p. 16, Note 1.
[5] The left-hand copy in Fenn reads 'brod,' which seems to be a misprint.
[6] James Butler, Earl of Wiltshire and Ormond. Beheaded in 1461.—F.
[7] Richard Southwell.

191

THE PASTON LETTERS

1459
NOV. 12

rythe good and well disposyd. My Lord of Exsater[1] cleymyth tytill in myn master plase, with the aportynancys in Sothewerk, and veryly had purposyd to have entrid ; and his consayll wer with us, and spak with Wurseter and me. And now afterward they have sent us word that they wold meve my Lord to sue be menys of the lawe, &c. I have spoke with my Lord of Canterbury and Master Jon Stokys, and I fynd hem rythe will disposyd bothe, &c.

Item, to morow ar the nexst day ze schall have a noder letter, for be that tyme we schall know mor than we do now.

My Lord Chanceler wold that my master schuld be beryed wurchyply, and C. mark almes done for hym ; but this day I schall holly know his enthent. Master Jon Stokys hathe the same consaythe and almes gevyng. Harry Fenyngley is not in this towne, ner the Lord Bechamp.

Item, we have gethe men of the speretuall law with haldyn with us, qwat casse some ever hap. We have Master Robert Kenthe, but in any wyse have all the good ther to gedyr, and tary for no lettyng, thow ze schuld do it be day a lythe [*daylight*] opynly, for it is myn Lord Chanceler ffull in thenthe that ze schuld do so.

As for Wyllyam Worceter, he trustythe veryly ze wold do for hym and for his avaylle, in reson ; and I dowthe nott and he may veryly and feythefully understand zow so disposyd to hym ward, ze schall fynd hym feythefull to zow in leke wysse. I understand by hym he will never have oder master butt his old master ; and to myn consaythe it were pete butt iff he schull stand in suche casse be myn master that he schuld never nede servyce, conseryng [*considering*] how myn master trustyd hym, and the long zers that he hathe be with hym in, and many schrew jornay for his sake, &c.

I wrythe zow no mor, be cawse ze schall [have] a noder letter wretyn to morow. Wretyn at Lundon the xij. day of Novembr, in hast, be

WILLYAM PASTON.

[1] Henry Holland, Duke of Exeter.

HENRY VI

392

SIR JOHN FASTOLF AND JOHN PASTON[1]

MEMORANDUM, that I Robert Fytzrawff, Esquyer, recorde that I, beyng in my Master Fastolff chambre, lenyng upon the gret bedde, at suche tyme as John Paston, Esquyer, Master John Brackeley, Master Clement Felmyngham, weere in comonycacion with my seid master of dyvers gret maters towchyng his will, and serten appoyntmentes a twyx my seid master and the seid John Paston, in the weke next be ffor my seid master dissesid, I hard my seid master and the seid John Paston appoynte and conclude that the seid John Paston shulde take upon hym the rwle of my masters howsold and of all his lyflod in Norffolk and Suffolk duryng his lyve ; and aftir his dissese the seid John Paston shulde do ffounde a colage at Caster of vij. monkes or prestis, and pay iiij. m^l. mark of money be yeres to my seid masteres executoris, at eche payment viij^c marke, till the seid som wer paid ; and that the seid John Paston shulde have all the lyvelode that was my seid masters in Norffolk and Suffolk to hym and to his heyres in fee. And aftir this seid mater rehersed my seid master seide these wordes, ' Cosyne, I pray you and requere you, lete this be settled in all hast withowte tarying, for this is my very last wille.' Also be it knowe to all men that I had knowlege of this bargayne dyverse tymes halfe-yere past, and how my seid Master Fastolff and the seid John Paston wer nye at a conclucion of the seid maters a quarter of a yere be fore this last bargayne was made.

Wrete at Caster the xxvj. day of Novembre the xxxviij. yere of Kyng Herry the Sexte. In witnesse wherof, I have syngnyd this bull with myn own hand and sette to my seale.

ROBT. FETZRAWFF.

1459
NOV. 26

[1] [From a Bodl. MS.]

THE PASTON LETTERS

393

BISHOP WAYNFLETE'S ADVICE[1]

BE it remembred that forasmoch as Sir John Fastolf late decesed, of grete affeccion, hath put me yn trust to be one of hys executors, and seth hyt ys desyryd me to know my disposicion hereynne, myne advyse is this, that fyrst an inventorie be made holye of hys godes and catell yn all places, and thayt they be leyd yn sure waard by your discrecions, tille the executors, or the moste part of tho that he put hys grete trust uppon, speke wyth me and make declaracion to me of hys laste wille, to the accomplyshment whereoff I wolle be speciall gode Lord.

Ferthymore, as touchyng hys buryeng and month ys mynde[2] kepyng, that it be don worshyplye, accordyng to hys degree and for the helth of hys soule, and that almesse be yeven yn mass seyng, and to pore peple to the some of a hundred mrcks tille that othyrwyse we speke to geder ; and I can agree ryzt well that hys servaunts haf theyr rewardes be tymes accordyng to hys wylle, to th'entent that they may be better disposed and to pray for the wellfare of hys soule, takyng avyse of a lerned man yn spirituell lawe, for no charge of administracion till the executors com to ghedr, or the moste part that hys trust was most uppon, to tak the administracion.

W. WINTON.

394

ABSTRACT[3]

ROBERT SPANY OF POSSEWYKE TO THE WIFE OF JOHN PASTON, ESQUIRE

Between 1459 and 1466

Begs her influence with her husband and Sir T. Howes, executors of Sir J. Fastolf, for reparation of a wrong done by Sir John, who refused to ratify a purchase made by the writer from his surveyor, Sir John Kyrteling, of a

[1] [From Fenn, iii. 358.]
[2] A monthly celebration in memory of a deceased person, when prayers were said and alms offered for the good of his soul.
[3] [From Paston MSS., B.M.]

HENRY VI

place and lands in Tunstale, sometime called Wrightes of Smalbergh, without receiving 10 marks over what was bargained.

Between 1459 and 1466

[This letter must have been written between the death of Fastolf in 1459 and that of Paston in 1466.]

395

FRIAR BRACKLEY TO JOHN PASTON[1]

Carissimo suo magistro, Johanni Paston, armigero.

Jesus, Maria, &c.

RYTE reverent mayster and most trusty frend in erthe, as lowly as I kan or may, I recomaunde me, &c. Syr, in feyth I was sore aferd that ze had a gret lettyng that ze come not on Wednysday to met, &c. Be myn feythe, and ze had be here, ze schuld haf had ryte good chere, &c., and hafe faryd ryte wele after zour pleser, &c., with more, &c.

Sir John Tatirshall is at one with Heydon, &c., and Lord Skalys hathe made a lofeday[2] with the prior and Heydon in alle materys except the matere of Snoryng, &c. And the seyd pryor spake maysterly to the jurrorys, &c., and told hem and [*i.e.* if] they had dred God and hurt of here sowlys, they wold haf some instruccyon of the one party as wele as of the other. But they were so bold they were not aferd, for they

1459

[1] [From Fenn, iii. 346.] This letter belongs to the latter part of the year 1459. After the dispersion of the Duke of York's army near Ludlow in October of that year, commissions were granted to various persons to arrest and punish his adherents. Even as early as the 14th of October, Lord Rivers and others were commissioned to seize their lands and goods in different counties (see *Patent Roll*, 38 Hen. VI., p. 1, m. 12, *in dorso*). But this letter, we are inclined to think, was written about six or seven weeks later, for it will be seen by the next that Bocking, who is here stated to have been with my Lord Chancellor 'this term,' must have been in attendance on him before the 7th December, and therefore, we may presume, during Michaelmas term, which ended on the 28th November. It is, however, difficult to judge, from the very slender allusion to Sir John Fastolf, whether this letter was written before or after the old knight's death. Brackley here speaks of having been quite recently in Somersetshire, which is not unlikely to have been in the middle of October, when the Earls of March, Warwick, and Salisbury withdrew into the West. Brackley, as will be seen, was a great partisan of these Lords, and may very well have accompanied them ; but not long before Fastolf's death he appears to have been at Norwich.

[2] Love days were days appointed for the settlement of disputes by arbitration.

THE PASTON LETTERS

HENRY VI

fownde no bonys to sey in her verdyte, as T. T.[1] and J. H.[2] wold, &c.

A lewde [*i.e.* illiterate] doctor of Ludgate prechid on Soneday fowrtenyte at Powlys, chargyng the peple that no man schuld preyen for these Lords traytorys,[3] &c. ; and he had lytyl thank, as he was worthy, &c. And for hyse lewd demenyng his brethir arn had in the lesse favour at London, &c. Doctor Pynchebek and Doctor Westhawe, grete prechowrys and parsonys at London, bene now late made monkys of Charterows at Schene, one at the on place and an other at the other place, &c.

The Chaunceler[4] is not good to these Lords, &c., for he feryth the Erle of Marche wyl cleyme by inheritans the Erldam of Ha . . . . .[5] &c., of which mater I herd gret speche in Somercede schyre, &c. Wyndham, Heydon, Todynham, Blake, W. Chambirleyn, Wentworth, have late commyssyonys to take for tretorys and send to the next gayl all personys fawtorys and weelwyllerys to the seyd Lords, &c. Mayster Radclyff and ze haf none of commyssyonys directid to zow, &c., for ze bene holdyn favorabil, &c. Wyndham and Heydon bene namyd here causerys of the commyssyonys, &c.

On Moneday last at Crowmere was the ore and the bokys of regystre of the amrelte takyn a wey from my Lord Scalys men be a gret multitude of my Lord Rossys, &c. The Lord Skalys is to my Lord Prince,[6] &c., to wayte on hym, &c. He seyth, per Deum Sanctum, as we sey here, he schal be amrel or he schal ly there by, &c. Be my feyth, here is a coysy werd [*unsettled world*]. Walsham of Chauncery, that never made lesyng, told me that Bokkyng was with my Lord Chaunceler this terme, but I askyd not how many tymys, &c.

As I haf wrytyn to zow oftyn byfor this, *Facite vobis amicos de mammona iniquitatis*, quia de facto. T. T., J. H., et J. W. [*J. Wyndham*] cum ceteris Magistri Fastolf fallacibus famulis magnam gerunt ad vos invidiam, quod excelleritis eos

---

1 Sir Thomas Tuddenham.   2 John Heydon.
3 Meaning the Earls of March, Warwick, and Salisbury.
4 William Waynflete, Bishop of Winchester.
5 The original letter is here defective.—F.
6 Edward, Prince of Wales.

---

in bonis, &c., Judas non dormit, &c. *Noli zelare facientes iniquitatem, quoniam tanquam fenum velociter arescent et quemadmodum olera herbarum cito per Dei gratiam decident.* Ideo sic in Psalmo : *Spera in Domino et fac bonitatem et pasceris in divitiis ejus et delectare in Domino, et dabit tibi petitiones cordis tui.*[1] Et aliter : *Jacta cogitatum tuum in Domino et ipse te enutriet.*[2] *Utinam*, inquit Apostolus, *abscindantur qui vos conturbant*,[3] &c. Et alibi : *Cavete vos a malis et importunis hominibus.*[4] Precor ergo Deum qui vos et me creavit et suo pretioso sanguine nos redemit, vos vestros et vestra gratiose conservet in prosperis et gratiosius dirigat in agendis.

Scriptum Walsham, feria quarta[5] in nocte cum magna festinatione, &c. Utinam iste mundus malignus transiret et concupiscentia ejus.

Vester ad vota promptissimus,
Frater J. BRACKLEY,
Minorum minimus.

396

JOHN BOCKING TO YELVERTON, PASTON, AND FILONGLEY[6]

To my right worshipful maistris, William Yelverton, Justice, John Paston, and Herre Filongley, and to eche of them.

RIGHT worshepful Sers, I recomaunde me to yow. And like it yow to wete, that my Lord Chaunceller[7] is right good and tendre Lord in all your materes, and soo wil contynue, and my Lord Tresorier[8] in like wise; which bothen have answerid Wyndham, not aldermoste to hise plesir, becaus of his noiseful langage, seyng [*saying*] how he myght have noo lawe, and that my Lord Chaunceller was not made executor but for meigntenaunce,[9] with many othir

---

1 Psalm xxxvi. (or xxxvii.) 1-4.   2 Psalm liv. (or lv.) 22.
3 Gal. v. 12.   4 2 Thess. iii. 2.
5 'Feria quarta' means Wednesday.
6 [From Fenn, i. 178.] This letter was written at Coventry during the Parliament which sat there in 1459, when the Duke of York and his adherents were attainted.   7 William Waynflete, Bishop of Winchester.
8 James, Earl of Wiltshire, was made Treasurer of England on the 30th October 1458.—*Patent Roll*, 37 Hen. VI., p. 1, m. 21.   9 *See* vol. ii. p. 167, Note 3.

DEC. 7

THE PASTON LETTERS

HENRY VI

woordis noo thing profitable ner furtheryng his entents. As for ony particuler materes, the parlament as yet abideth upon the grete materes of atteyndre and forfetur ;[1] and soo there be many and diverse particuler billes put inne, but noon redde, ner touchyng us, as nygh as we can herken ; to whiche Playter and I attenden daily, trustyng on my Lords aboveseid, my Lord Privy Seall,[2] and other good Lords, and many also of your acquayntaunce and owres, that and ony thing be, we shall sone have knowlege.

The Chief Justice[3] is right herty, and seith ful wel and kyndely of my maistr, whom Jesu for his mercy pardonne, and have yow in His blessid governaunce.

Writen at Coventre the morwne after Seint Nicholas.[4]

And as to money, I delyvered unto the Under-tresorier[5] a lettre from Maister Filongley, and I fonde hym right wele disposid to doo that may please yow in all our materes ; and take noo money of hym as yette, for we have noo nede to spend ony sumes as yette, ner with Gods grace shall not have. I come to this town of Coventre suche day sevenyght as the parlement byganne ; and as for suche things as I coude herken aftyr, I sende to William Worcetre a grete bille of tidings to shewe yow and all.

Yesterday in the mornyng come inne th'erle of Pembroke[6] with a good felechip ; and the Duchesse of York[7] come yestereven late, as the bringer here of shall more pleinly declare yow, to whom ye like to gif credence. The Bushop of Excester[8] and the Lord Grey Ruthyn[9] have declarid them ful worshipfuly to the Kings grete plesir. Playter and I writen you a lettre by Norffolk, yoman for the Kyngs mouth.

Your   JOHN BOKKING.

---

1 Against the Duke of York and his adherents.   2 Lawrence Booth.
3 Sir John Fortescue.   4 St. Nicholas' Day is the 6th December.
5 'Undertresouer' in Fenn must, I think, be a misprint.
6 Jasper Tudor.—*See* vol. ii. p. 298, Note 1.
7 Cecily, daughter of Ralph Nevill, Earl of Westmoreland.
8 George Nevill, son of Richard, Earl of Salisbury, brother of Richard, Earl of Warwick. He was afterwards Archbishop of York.
9 Edmund, Lord Grey of Ruthin, afterwards created Earl of Kent.

The following list of those of the Duke of York's party who were attainted by Parliament was found by Fenn pinned to the above letter :—

The Duc of York.	Edward Bourghcier, sq.
Therle of Marche.	A brother of his.
Therle of Rutland.	Thomas Vaughan.
Therle of Warrwyk.	Thomas Colte.
Therle of Salusbury.	Thomas Clay.
The Lord Powys.	John Denham.
The Lord Clynton.	Thomas Moryng.
The Countesse of Sarr.	John Oter.
Sir Thomas Nevyle.	Maistr Ric Fisher.
Sir John Nevyle.	Hastyngs and other that as yet we can not know the names, &c.
Sir Thomas Haryngton.	
Sir Thomas o Parre.	
Sir John Conyers.	
Sir John Wenlok.	As for the Lord Powys, he come inne, and hadde grace as for his lyf, but as for hise gods the forfeture passid.
Sir William Oldhall.	

397

SIR PHILIP WENTWORTH'S PETITION[1]

MEKELY besechith Phelip Wentworth, Knyght, that where the warde and mariage of Thomas, sone and heire of John Fastolf, late of Cowhaugh in the [county] of Suffolk, squyer, and of the lond of the same John, belonged to the Kyng of rigth, and among other by reason of the nonnage of the sayd heir, the maner of Bradwell in the said counte was sesed in to his handes by vertu of an enquest take a fore his Eschetour of the seid counte. The whiche offices[2] John Fastolf, Knyght, and other tented to

---

1 [From Paston MSS., B.M.] This petition was presented to the Parliament which sat at Coventry in 1459, and received the Royal assent. It has already been printed in the *Rolls of Parl.*, v. 371.
2 An inquisition taken before an escheator, by virtue of his office, was frequently called an office.

NOV. or DEC.

traverse, and by that meane had the sayd maner to ferme, accordyng to the statute in that case made, and it was founden and jugement yoven for the Kyng in the said traverse by the labour of the said Phelipp, which, the xviij. day of Novembre, the yer of the regne of the Kyng the xxvj.,[1] bought of Marmaduke Lampney, than Tresorer of Englond, the said ward and mariage for an C. marc, as it appereth in the Kynges receyte, be syde all other costes and charges that the said Phelipp hath don uppon the same, as weel in fyndyng of the Kyngges title of the said ward, as in the meyntenauns of all other sewtes dependyng uppon the same, to the costes of the said Sir Phelypp more than D. marc. And the said John Fastolf, Knyght, was adjuged in the Kynges eschequer to pay an C.ixli xiijs. viijd. ob. for the issuez and profites which he had take of the londes of the same warde. And where the Kyngges lettres patentes be entred in the remembrauns on the Tresorer parte in the said eschequyer in this fourme:

Rex omnibus ad quos, &c., salutem. Sciatis quod per manucaptionem Thomæ West de London armigeri, et Willelmi Barker de Norwico gentilman, commisimus Johanni Paston armigero et Thomæ Howes clerico custodiam omnium terrarum et tenementorum cum pertinentiis quæ fuerunt Johannis Fastolf de Cowhaugh in com Suffolk armigeri die quo obiit et quæ per mortem ejusdem Johannis Fastolf ac ratione minoris ætatis Thomæ, filii et hæredis dicti Johannis Fastolf, ad manus nostras devenerunt et in manibus nostris ad huc existunt; habendam a tempore mortis præfati Johannis Fastolf usque ad plenam ætatem dicti hæredis, una cum maritagio ejusdem hæredis, absque disparagatione; et si de hærede illo humanitus contingat antequam ad plenam ætatem suam pervenerit, hærede illo infra ætatem existente non maritato, tunc dicti Johannes Paston et Thomas Howes habeant custodiam et maritagium hujusmodi hæredis, simul cum custodia omnium terrarum et tenementorum prædictorum; et sic de hærede in hæredem quousque aliquis hæres hæredum prædictorum ad plenam ætatem suam pervenerit: Reddendo

[1] A.D. 1447.

200

nobis prout concordari poterit cum Thesaurario nostro Angliæ citra festum Paschæ proximo futuro, ac sustentando domos clausuras et ædificia, necnon supportando alia onera dictis terris et tenementis cum pertinentiis spectantia sive aliquo modo incumbentia quam diu custodiam habuerint supradictam, ac inveniendo dicto hæredi compententem sustentationem suam: Eo quod expressa mentio de vero valore annuo præmissorum in præsentibus minime facta existit, aut aliquo statuto, actu sive ordinacione in contrarium edito sive proviso non obstante. Proviso semper quod si aliquis alius plus dare voluerit de incremento per annum pro custodia et maritagio prædictis, quod tunc prædicti Johannes Paston et Thomas Howys tantum pro eisdem solvere teneantur si custodiam et maritagium habere voluerint supradictam. In cujus &c. Teste Rege apud Westmonasterium vj[to] die Junij anno H. vj[ti] xxxij[do].

And after that an accorde is entred in the sayd Eschequer in thys forme:—In Hillarii record', anno xxxvj[to] Regis H. vj[ti] ex parte Remembr' Thesaurarii:

Et modo, xx. die Februarii hoc termino, prædicti Johannes Paston et Thomas Howys venerunt hic in propriis personis suis et optulerunt se ad concordandum cum Thesaurario Angliæ pro custodia omnium terrarum et tenementorum, una um maritagio ejusdem hæredis. Et super hoc concordatum est inter Johannem Comitem Wigorniæ, Thesaurario Angliæ et præfatos Johannem Paston et Thomam Howys quod ipsi solvent domino Regi pro custodia omnium terrarum et tenementorum prædictorum, videlicet a tempore mortis præfati Johannis Fastolf usque ad plenam ætatem dicti hæredis ac maritagium ejusdem hæredis, decem marcas tantum; de quibus quidem x. marcis consideratum est per Barones quod prædicti Johannes Paston et Thomas Howys et manucaptores sui prædicti pro custodia et maritagio prædictis erga Regem onerentur prætextu Regis literarum patentium et concordiæ predictorum ac aliorum præmissorum.

So by the sayd lettres patentez and the sayd accorde the sayd John Paston and Thomas Howys schuld have the sayd C.ixli. xiijs. viijd. ob. and the sayd ward and mariage, the

201

whiche is worthe CCli., for the sayd x. marc only. And also, for as moche as the sayd Tresorer recordeth in the Kyngges High Court of Parlement begonne at Westminster the ix. day of Jule the yer of the Kyngges noble regne xxxiij., that he made never no suche accord wyth the sayd John Paston and Thomas Howys of the sayd ward, the whiche mater is of record in the Kyngges chauncerye certefyed by the sayd Erle of Worceter, as weell as by other his lettres to dyvers persones directed, sealed with his signet, wretyn and signet with hys owen hand, as plenerly dooth appere: Where for plese it your gret wysdams, the premisses considered, to pray the Kyng oure soverayn Lord, that, by the advys and assent of his Lordes spirituelx and temperelx, and by you hys comunes in the present parlement assembled, stablysshed and inacted that the sayd entre of accord and jugement theruppon be anulled and of non effect. And the sayd Phelyppe schall pray to God for you, &c.

398

ABSTRACT[1]

G. SPERLYNG TO JOHN PASTON

Paston was misinformed as to what Sperlyng said of his late master's[2] will. What he said was that about Hallowmas was twelvemonth he was about eight weeks with his said master, who one day examined him about the conveyance of his lands, and said there was no man of worship in Norfolk had so many auditors as he, yet he could never get the certainty how his livelode was disposed; but he had found a means to be quiet, 'whereof,' he said, 'I am as glad as a man had geve me 1000 mark,' by granting his cousin Paston all his livelode in Norfolk and Suffolk, on condition he should amortise sufficient lands to maintain a master and six secular priests at Castre. Paston was to take the risk of any counter claim and trouble hereafter, etc.

Norwich, Epiphany Day.

[The date of this letter must be 1460, as it is after Fastolf's death, and speaks of a conversation the writer had with him about the management of his lands a twelvemonth before Hallowmas preceding the date of the letter. At Hallowmas 1459 Sir John was dying, and quite unable to support any conversation for want of breath, so that the reference must be to Hallowmas 1458.]

[1] [From Paston MSS., B.M.]   [2] Sir John Fastolf.

202

399

WILLIAM BOTONER TO JOHN BERNEY[1]

To the ryght worshypfull Sir, John Berneye, Scuier, at Castre beyng.

RYGHT wohypfull Sir, I recommaund me to yow.[2] . . . . As for tydyngs here, I sende som of hend wreten to you and othyrs how the Lord Ryvers,[3] Sir Antonye, hys son, and othyrs hafe wonne Calix[4] be a feble assault made at Sandwich by Denham,[5] Squyer, with the nombre of viij[c] men, on Twyesday betwene iiij. and v. at cloks yn the mornyng. But my Lady Duchesse[6] ys stille ayen receved yn Kent. The Duke of York ys at Debylyn [Dublin], strengthed with hys Erles and homagers, as ye shall see by a bille. God sende the Kyng victorie of hys ennemyes, and rest and pease among hys Lordes.

I am rygt gretly hevyed for my pore wyfe, for the sorow she takyth, and most leefe hyr and hyr contree. Y shall nothing take from hyr more then a litell spendyng money, tille better may bee. And the Blessed Trinite kepe and sende you helth.

Wret at London hastly, the Monday after I departed from you, 1459, x.

Your,

W. BOTONER, called WYRCESTER.

[1] [From Fenn, i. 182.] The date of this letter is ascertained partly by the reference in the suppressed passage to Sir John Fastolf's interment, and partly by the allusion to the capture of Rivers and his son by John Denham. Compare the letter following.

[2] 'Here,' says Fenn, 'follow complaints against Frere Brakle, etc., concerning Sir John Fastolf's interment, affairs, etc.'

[3] Richard Widville, Lord Rivers, afterwards created an Earl by King Edward IV., who married his daughter Elizabeth.

[4] This must be a sneer. The truth, as recorded by Botoner himself in his annals, was that John Denham and others secretly sailed from Calais, and surprised Sandwich, where they took Lord Rivers and his son Anthony prisoners, and carried them back to Calais.

[5] John Denham or Dynham, afterwards Lord Dynham.

[6] Cecily, Duchess of York.

203

THE PASTON LETTERS

400

WILLIAM PASTON TO JOHN PASTON[1]

*To his right worshipfull brother, John Paston,
be this lettre delyvered.*

1460
JAN. 28

AFTER dewe recomendacion had, please you to wete that we cam to London upon the Tewysday by none, nexst aftr our departour fro Norwich, and sent our men to inquyre after my Lord Chaunceler,[2] and Maister John Stokys, and Malmesbury.

And as for my Lord Chaunceler, he was departed fro London, and was redyn to the Kyng ij. dayes er we were come to London; and as we understand he hasted hym to the Kyng by cause of my Lord Ryvers[3] takyng at Sandwyche, &c.[4] . . . .

As for tydyngs, my Lord Ryvers was brought to Caleys, and by for the Lords with viij^xx. [*eight score*] torches, and there my Lord of Salesbury reheted [*rated*] hym, callyng hym knaves son, that he schuld be so rude to calle hym and these other Lords traytors, for they schall be found the Kyngs treue liege men, whan he schuld be found a traytour, &c. And my Lord of Warrewyk. rehetyd hym, and seyd that his fader was but a squyer, and broute up with Kyng Herry the Vte, and sethen hymself made by maryage, and also made Lord, and that it was not his parte to have swyche langage of Lords, beyng of the Kyngs blood. And my Lord of Marche reheted hym in lyke wyse. And Sir Antony[5] was reheted for his langage of all iij. Lords in lyke wyse.

¹ [From Fenn, i. 186.] This letter, like the last, refers to the capture of Lord Rivers and his son at Sandwich, an incident dated by William Worcester in his annals shortly after the Christmas of 1459, which probably means just after the New Year.
² William de Waynflete, Bishop of Winchester.
³ *See* p. 203, Note 3.
⁴ 'Then follows,' says Fenn, 'a long account of private business, which is here omitted.'
⁵ Sir Anthony Widville, afterwards Lord Scales and Earl Rivers.

204

HENRY VI

Item, the Kyng cometh to London ward, and, as it is seyd, rereth the pepyll as he come ; but it is certayn ther be comysyons made in to dyvers schyres that every man be redy in his best aray to com whan the Kyng send for hem.   1460 JAN. 28

Item, my Lord Roos is com fro Gynes.

No more, but we pray to Jesu have you in his most mercyfull kepyng. Amen.

Wretyn at London, the Munday next after Seynt Powle day.[1]   Yowr broder,

WILLIAM PASTON.

401

WILLIAM BOTONER TO ——[2]

1460
FEB. 7

A VERY frende at nede experience will schewe be deede, as wele as be autorite of Aristotle in the Etiques that he made of moralite. Also by the famous Reamayn Tullius in his litell booke *De Amicicia* ; thangyng you for olde contynued frendschip stidffastely grounded, as I wele [*qu.* feel?] be your letter of a goode disposicion made, as it appereth. Where as it schewith to the understandyng of suche as you write uppon that I schulde, be crafty councell of some men sodenly have departed in to these parties, &c., and that I straunched me from sertein persones to moche, &c. ; as for the furste, it schalbe to openly knowe that I departed not hedre be councell of suche persons as they ymagyne, for in trowthe no creature levyng, when I departed from Norwich, knewe it, saffe one that hath and evermore schal be next of my knowlege in viagis makyng, alle be it I will not alwey disclose the cause. I herde sey sith I come to London theye weche ye dempte to be of my councell thanne . where at

¹ The Feast of the Conversion of St. Paul is on the 25th of January.
² [From Paston MSS., B.M.] The MS. of this letter is not an original, but a copy in the handwriting of John Paston. It appears to be written on the cover of a letter from his wife, addressed on the back, 'To my ryght wurschipfull husbond, John Paston, be this delyvered in haste.' The date must be 1460, as it is clearly not long after the death of Sir John Fastolf ; and as the writer speaks of having recently left Norwich, it was probably not many days or weeks after No. 399.

205

THE PASTON LETTERS

1460
FEB. 7

Wolsyngham or Thepala (?) when I departed. I have wrete the cauce to hym that of nature schulde be my beste frende, that for as much I had labored as weele as W. Paston do my maister frendes, chevised, and leyd money content out of his purse to the some of C*li.*, and more for clothe and other thynges for my seide maister entencion, promyttyng payment be fore Cristemesse, or right soone aftir, or to be at London, and acquytyng me that I put me my dever. And be cause my maister attorneys in that parties toke not to herte to make the payementes here so hastely as they ded there, I had no comffortable answere of spedyng the seid paymentes here. And also I was not put in truste a mong the seid attorneys there to yeve on peny for my maister sowle, but I paid it of myn owne purse befoore ; nother in trust ne favour to geve an almesse gowne, but that I praid for it as a straunger schulde doo, alle be it myn autorite is as grete as theris, and rather more as I tolde you. And also my Lorde of Canturebury and Maister John Stookes, his juge, had geve autorite to ministre to a certein somme till the testament were proved. And these preseidents consedred wolde discorage any man to a bide but a litel amonges hem that so straunged hem self from me and mistrusted me, be thut any cauce ye knowe wele how that my maister man servauntes were put in gretter truste and familiarite to handell, geve, and telle out of the bagghes my maister money bothe at Seint Benetts and in Norwich in divers places by grete summes and litell. And ye as other my maister servauntes and I that helped gete my maister goode and brynge it togedre were straunged, and as it semyd by there demenyng mistrusted to oure grete vilanye and rebuke, wheche muste be answerd the causes why, and we declared [i.e. *exculpated*], and so shal I make it for my pore person, and for my maister sowle heele. It is not soilied (?) knowen that I was one of the cheeffe that kepte bothe my Maister Paston and myn oncle[1] in my maister favour and truste, and if I wolde have labored the contrary, by my sowle—that is the grettest othe that I may swere of my silff—they had never be

¹ Botoner's wife, whose Christian name was Margaret, was a niece of Thomas Howes, parson of Blofield. He therefore calls Howes his uncle.

206

HENRY VI

nygh my maister in that case they stonde nowe. And if they woll labour to damage or hendre me, all the worlde woll mysreporte of hem and litel truste hem, nowther they schal not have wurschip nor profight bi it. I wolde be to them as lowyng and as wele willyng as I gan, so I fynde cause, and other I wolnot be to my fadre, and he weere a liffe. I requere you a[n]swere for me as I wolde and have do for you whan som of hem have seid ful nakedly of you, and suche as ye deeme hafe mysereported causeles of me, I pray you that they see my letter as weele as my frendes. My maister also (God yelded is sowle) graunted to me a liffelode accordyng to my degre, that I, my wiffe, and my childre, schulde have cause to prey for hym. My wiffes uncle[1] was present in his chapell at Castre as wele as my wiffe, and comaunded her oncle to chese the londe. This is trowthe be the blissed Sacrament that I receyved at Pasch [*i.e.* Easter]. And because I demaunded my right and dwte of my Maister Paston, he is not plesed. I have lost more thanne x. mark worthe londe in my maister servyce, by God, and not [*unless*] I be releved, alle the worlde schal knowe it elles that I have to gret wrong. Wolde God I kowde plese bothe Maister Paston and my oncle in reson, who preserve you.   1460 FEB. 7

Wrete hastely the vij. day of Feveryere.
Your,
W. BOTONER, *dit* Wurcester.

¹ *See* Note on last page.

207

THE PASTON LETTERS

402

W. LOMNER TO JOHN PASTON[1]

To the right worchipfull and reverent and myn good
mayster Paston, Squyere, be this taken.

1460
APRIL 6

MY ryght worchipfull mayster, I recomaunde me to yow, besechyng yow to hold me excusyd that I awaytyd noon otherwyse opon yow and my mastras at my comyng from Norwich; for yn good feyth I was soo seke that I hadde moche labour to come home, and sythen that tyme I have hadde my parte, &c. And, Sere, as for Berney, he begynnyth to falle ought of the popell conceyte faster than ever he fell yn, for serteyn causez, &c. I shalle telle yow yn haste. But, Sere, blyssyd be God, as for yow, your love yncresith amonge hem, and so I prey God it mot, for and I herde the contrarie, ye shuld sone have wetyng. The undershrefe dothe Mortoft favour, and lete hym goo yn Norwich as hym lyst, and al the contre abought me sey right evyll of hym for a mayntenor of the Kynges enime; for ther ben an C. [*hundred*] purposid to ride to the Kyng for hym, and he come neer this contre, for they sey thow he hadde never doo with his handes he hath seid a now to die. I have warend the under-shreffe ther of, &c. Sere, forther, I am yn bildyng of a pore hous. I truste God that ye shulle take your loggyng ther yn here after whan ye come to your lordshippis on tho partes. And I durste be soo bolde on your maystershep to aske of yow xij. copill of oken sparris, I wold hertilly prey yow not to have them, but ther they may be for bore beste, and that is at a yard of yourz yn Saxthorpe, callid Barkerz. I have eshe but noon oke, but litell now comyth the fellyng ther of, &c. And me semyth ye myght take mony for wood ther that stant and seryth and doth no good but harme, and

1 [From Paston MSS., B.M.] The date of this letter must be after the death of Sir John Fastolf, and before John Paston had gone to take possession of his lands in Norfolk. Saxthorpe was one of Fastolf's manors which so came to him. The year may therefore be presumed to be 1460.

208

HENRY VI

with yn fewe yeres ye shulnot wete where it is become, &c. 1460 Also ther be serteyn materz betwyn soom of your tenuantez APRIL 6 and me. I abide your comyng and doo not [*naught?*] at the reverens of yow; they be knowelle yn the contre. And God have yow yn his kepyng.

Wretyn on Palme Sunday.

Be your servaunt,

W. LOMNER.

403

FRIAR BRACKLEY TO [WILLIAM PASTON][1]

1460
[before
Easter]

JESU mercy, Marie help, cum Sanctis omnibus, trewe menyng executorys ffro fals terrauntes and alle tribulacyons. Amen. Ryte reverent Sire, &c., W. Y.[2] Judex and hise wyf were here with here meny and here hors in our ladyes place, &c. on Saterday at evyn, and yedyn hens on Monday after none, whan summe had drunkyn malvyseye and tyre,[3] &c. And I prechid on the Sonday byfore hem, not warnyd tyl after mete. And than for lak of M. Vergeant, or our wardeyn Barnard, I sodeynly seyd the sermon. And byfore I had ryte ovyr and soleyn chere of hem bothe, &c.; but after the sermon he seyd opely to the priour, heryng myche folk in the chirch, 'I haf herd hym oftyn here and ellys where, but [this][4] is the best that ever I herd hym sey,' &c., and at evyn drank to me, and made me good chere, half on the splene, &c.

But on Moneday, whan he had ny etyn and drunkyn a now, he gan to rollyn hym in hise relatyvis, and we eldyd hym, as many men thowtyn, ryte ongayly in hise gere, &c.; hise wyf begynnyng the communicacyon with rite a sootyr (?) chere. And he heeld on so sore he cowd not cese, &c. tyl

1 [From Paston MSS., B.M.] From what is said of the expectation of a descent of Warwick upon the coast, it appears that this letter was written in the spring of 1460.
2 William Yelverton.
3 Tier, a bitter drink or liquor.—Halliwell.
4 Omission in MS.

THE PASTON LETTERS

1460
[before
Easter]

he went to his hors, &c. And the pryor demenyd hym gentylly in hise talkyng. And there was not forgetyn non unkyndnesse of my Mayster J. P., zour brother, of sleyn [*slaying*] of hise man Wormegey, and of mariage of hise dowghtyr, whiche now schal solempnely be maryed to Conerys,[1] a knytes sone, &c. And now last at Seynt Benettes, where he so worschipful a justise and as kunnyng in lawe as ever was zour fadyr, &c. as alle men knowyn, &c. I shalle telle yow zour brother J. P. brokyn owt be occasyon of zour langage, and takyn wytnesse of Malmysbury, a man of my Lord of Caunterbury, whiche hath spokyn with the seyd justise the last terme in Westmyster Halle. And there he seyd more tymes than one, 'Sire, this the fyrst tyme that ever I spake with zour Lordschip, &c.' And sythe after ze weryn at Seynt Benettys forseyd, ze komyn not gentylly but ryte malicyously disposid to myn Lady Felbrygg, and dede your devoyr to haf put hym out of hir conceyt, and it wolde not be, &c. And what vyolens my Mayster J. P., germanus vester, dede to W. Wayt,[2] &c. up on hise owne grownd at Musshold, &c. And after al these materys, bare me on hand[3] that I had seyd to on of the worthiest of the schyre that the seyd justise be gan the brekyng at Seynt Benettes; for I suppose I seyd thus to my Lord Fyz Water, *alias* my Mayster Radclyff, to whos in I went to, and zaf hym a potel of swete wyne, he demaundyng me of that brekyng, &c., as I remembre me, and suppose I seyd, 'W. Y., justise, began to myn knowlache and understondyng.' Whan he seyd so fumowsly, 'Who so ever sey that of me, he lyeth falsly in hise hede, &c.' And my Mayster Radclyff rode forthe with owt of towne to Dokkyng and Brumham, and with hym rode W. Y., sone to the justise. And yf the seyd Radclyff teld this to W. Y., I wote never. And yf he dede I merveyle sore. But and al go to al, as is like to go, I may not sey nay, but I trow I seyd so. Radclyf and ze bene grete frendes. I wold ze wold lat hym knowe the trowth, &c.

1 John, son of Sir Robert Conyers, knight, married Eleanor, daughter of William Yelverton, Justice of the King's Bench.—Blomefield, i. 483.
2 Judge Yelverton's clerk, the writer of No. 142. *See* vol. ii. p. 174, Note 3.
3 *See* vol. ii. p. 110, Note 1.

210

HENRY VI

1460
[before
Easter]

This mater mevyd the justisis wyf, and than he be gan hise mater more boldly, seyng to me be fore the pryour and miche pepyl, that it was told hym the same day that I seyd, as for the brekyng, the justise began. 'Forsothe,' seyd I, 'whan I came into the chambre there, the fyrst word I hard was this, that ze seyd to my mayster J. P., "Who that ever seyth so, I sey he lyeth falsly in hise hede," &c.' 'Ya,' quod the justise, 'ze schuld haf told what mevyd me to sey so to hym.' And I seyd I cowde not tellyn that I not herd, &c. Et Judex—'Ze schuld haf examyned the mater,' &c. And I seyd, 'Sire, it longyd not to me to examyne the mater, for I knew wele I schuld not be juge in the mater, and alonly to a juge it longyth to sene and stodyen illam Sacræ Scripturæ clausulam, whiche holy Job seyd, *Causam quam nesciebam diligentissime investigabam.*'

And than, 'No,' seyth he hardyly, 'ze schal not be juge, but yf ze had owt me as good wil as ze dede and do to Paston, ze wold than have sergyd the cause of my gret greef, why I seyd as I seyd, &c. But I haf sey the day, ze lovyd me bettyr than hym, for he yaf zow never cause of love as I haf done,' &c. 'Sire,' I sey, 'he hath yovyn me cause swyche as I am behold to hym for,' &c. 'Ya,' seyth he, 'ze schal bere wytnesse, &c., and the other Mayster Clement and W. Schipdham.' Cui ego—'As for the wytnesse I schal bere, I schal say and writyn as I knowe,' &c. Cui ille—'I made hise testament,'[1] and I knowe,' &c. Cui ego—'I saw nevir testament of your makyng; and as for on testament that he made, and I knowe bothe the writer and maker, after hise wyl and intent, ze stonde stille there in as ze dede than,' &c. Et tunc gavisus est, &c. Et ille—'I knowe ze haf a gret hert, &c., but I ensure zow, the Lordes above at London arn infoormyd of zow, and they schal delyn with zow wele anow.' Cui ego—'He or they that hafe infoormyd the Lordes wele of me, I am behold to hem; and yf they be otherwyse infoormyd, I schal do as wele as I may. But be myn trowthe I schal not be aferd to sey as I knowe for none Lord of this lond, if I may go saf and come, quod non credo, per Deum, propter evidencias multas,' &c. Tunc prior

1 This seems to refer to the will of Sir John Fastolf, though he is not named.

211

THE PASTON LETTERS

1460
[before
Easter]
—'Domine, non expedit nec rationi seu veræ conscientiæ congruit, quod vos contendatis cum Magistro Paston, vel ipse vobiscum, pro bonis defuncti, quæ solum sua et non vestra sunt. Miror valde,' inquit, 'cum prioribus temporibus tam magni fuistis amici, et non sic modo, quare valde doleo.' Cui Judex—'There is no man besy to bryng us to gyder, &c., so that I kan wele thynk it were lytil maysteri.' But in feyth I knowe wele the Juge, W. Wayte his mawment [*i.e.* puppet], hise boy Yimmys, with here hevedy and fumows langage, have and dayly do uttyr lewd and schrewd dalyauns, &c.

I sent zow bode of dyvers thinges be M. Roger Palle, and I haf no answer, &c. I schuld go to Castre, and a man of my Lordes Norfolk told here he came fro London, and there he had commonly voysid that the Duke of Norfolk schuld be the Kynges comaundement kepe hise Esterne at Castre for safe gard of the cuntre ayens Warwyk and other swich of the Kinges enmyes whiche may lytely be lyklynesse aryve at Waxham, &c. My mayster zour brother, J. P., ne ye, ne M. T. Howys, ne I may not esily be brokyd in the Jugys conscyens, &c. Sir Jon Tatirshales man spake with yow at London, and than ye seyd to hym to hafe comyn in your owne persone to our Lady or this tyme, whiche was cause of myn abidyng here, &c. I schal, be the grace of Jesu, be at Castre on Soneday next, &c. W. W., J. B., junior, Colinus Gallicus, et T. Upton multum, ut suppono, fuerunt assidui ad informationem malam dandam dominis diversis hujus regni contra vestrum germanum J. P., M. T. Howes, me, etc.; sed confido in vobis quod vos confiditis in Christo Jesu et Sanctis omnibus, qui vos vestros et vestra dirigat in agendis. Recommendetis me, si placeat, Magistro meo Johanni P., uxori, et matri, cum filiis suis nepotibus vestris, et Thomæ Playtere vestro dilecto amico. Et quare vobis jam scribo et non vestro germano J. P. alias scietis, etc.

Vester orator continuus,
F. J. B., Minorum minimus.

212

THE PASTON LETTERS

1460
man schuld not trusty on a broke swerd, ne on a fool, ne on a chyld, ne on a dobyl man, ne on a drunke man,' &c., thow that he were an amewse and a notarye be W. W. Hibernicus he schal knowe al, and be hym Colyn and Spirlyng the same knowe schal, &c. Hoc ideo dicite W. P., Cavete, &c., quia, Deo teste, bona fide et conscia non ficta, hæc suprascripta sunt in toto vera, &c. Feria secunda ad minus in prandio vos videbo, &c. Scriptum festinissime infra quarterium horæ, præsentis latore nimis sponsalium causa festinante. Recommendo vos vestros et vestra Deo.

vester totus prius notus,
Frater J. B. Minorum minimus.

405

ANONYMOUS TO H. B. OF LINCOLN[1]

To my good Maister, H. B. of Lincoln.

APRIL 9
RIGHT worcheful sir, after my recommendation, like you to wete I wold yisterday have spoken with you if ye had be allone at good leiser, for my aquytaile to God and to you, and for the wele of my maister, God pardon hym. I have many thynges to remembre you if ye wol. Wherof diverse specialtes that I wold sey, I may not write. For I meved you at your chamber wyndow at Lammes homward from London some thynges of my good wil, and me thought ye toke it gretely to displeisur; the which caused me to sey the lesse of thynges that had be worchepfull to have be doon. But, Sir, as I remembred you late at Norwich of the variaunce by twix the worchepfull man and you, for Goddes love and your most ease, folwe the meanes of his good wil by help of holsom gentilmen, and also the feithfull love of other that grucchen to you warde, as I fele moche thof thei speke litil

[1] [Add. ms. 34,888, f. 143.] This letter is mysterious, but seems to have some bearing on Sir John Fastolf's will, and may be assigned with tolerable certainty to the year 1460, as the 9th April, the day it was dated, was a Wednesday, and one expression in it shows that it was written immediately before Easter, which in that year fell on the 13th April.

214

HENRY VI

404

FRIAR BRACKLEY TO JOHN PASTON[1]

1460
JHESUS Maria, &c.,—Reverende domine et præ omnibus mortalibus amantissime. Super omnia omnino oblivioni non tradenda faciatis ut W. P.[2] germanus cum sua ac vestra prudenti industria sagaciter et secrete informet H. Fylongley de W. W.[3] Hibernico ac Colino Gallico, qui suo malicioso proposito confederati sunt, adversusque dominum et magistrum suum militem defunctum et executores ejus ad dampnificandos eos et bona defuncti per ostensionem literarum secretarum olim dicto militi missarum, ex confidentia speciali, sicut solito more amicus amico solet scribere. Si hæc enim proditoria condicio esset insinuata per H. Fylongley vel per me, forsan Domino Comite Wilschirie, idem fallax et deceptorius Colinus Gallicus non esset cum dicto comite tam magnus et intimus cum dicto domino, sicut credit se esse unum de suis secretioribus, vel cum Regina per laborem sui germani ad magistrum Ormond ut ipsum faciat introduci ad favorem et servicium Reginæ. Si habueritis amicos circa Reginam, cito poteritis Colinum frustrare suo a proposito. Si W. P. vester germanus posset per subtilia media adquirere et adquiri facere casketum C. Gallici ac casketum W. W. Hibernici, audiretis et videretis aliqua non laude sed fraude plena, &c. Mitte sapientem et nihil ei dicas, &c. Prudenti viro pauca scribenda pro presenti propono quia scio vos ex paucis plura colligere et ex præambulo plura concludere. Item, propheta clamat, 'Nolite confidere in verbum mendacii,'[4] &c., et secundum eundem prophetam, 'Non est confidendum super baculum arundineum confractum,'[5] &c., et est commune et vulgare dictum: 'A

[1] [Add. ms. 34,888, f. 161.] This letter is evidently holograph. The date might be at the very end of the year 1459, after the death of Fastolf and after the attainder of the Yorkists at Coventry; but is more probably in the early part of 1460, between January and May. Indeed, though the language is mysterious, its substance is probably not unconnected with that of the preceding letter.
[2] William Paston, son of the judge.
[3] The initials 'W. W.' suggest the name of William Worcester; but he was not an Irishman, and before this letter was discovered he was believed to be Brackley's 'Colinus Gallicus,' who, however, is here mentioned as a different person. [4] Jerem. vii. 4.
[5] Referring apparently to Isaiah xxxvi. 6—not 'the same prophet.'

213

HENRY VI

1460
APRIL 9
therof to you, rettyng in you singuler fastnesse ageyns kyndenesse and reson ; for with love and unyte ye shal do moost good for oure maister to your worchep. And with the contrary many mysse dispenses as han be and thanne moche lette in doyng of good dedis to the causers perill and slawnder God hath sent you wysdham grete that telleth you the best is to drede God. A man shal never have love of God nor love nor drede of good men for myskepyng of moche good thof it wer his owen, for it is dampnable ; but wher it is truly delt with and godly disposed, thanne folwith bothe grete meryte and worchep. Pety it is that mo more is do for hym. At the gate is nowther mete, drynke nor money, *ut dicitur*, no man wele spekyng thof thacte above be not do necessary almesse to the nedy that peynen wold and myght be do dayly. And, Sir, be ware what ye talke to som men of the lordes your coexecutours, and what is spent for the man, and what he was worth. Thei reporten you unfavorabely and withoute credence, as men seyn, and some I have herd. Also your entretyng and other for you with them that have entres with you for to have your entent sped, is tolde oute whow, and your iournay to lorde Beauchamp to Cambrig is taken as men like, and your associacion is seid made by your witt to your purpos. As somme fer of and grete that may nor peraventur wiln not medle, somme ye wold thei left, somme havyng no conduyt, somme no stomak, and somme glosours and witnesses for lucre ; this is not my seyyng, I have often herd it. Therfor to have such a post as the seid man is that ye be in variaunce ; so he do wele, as I fully beleve, he shuld help you to bere moche, and cause eschuyng of moche of this noyse. This variaunce grew of mater of noght and japes ; the soner may be accorde. And thynke not, Sir, that any persone hath stered me herto ; for by the good Lorde I trist to receyve this holy tyme it is my owen steryng and good hert to you warde, for that I her and see, and moost of your wele willers, in eschuyng of inconvenyentz as right many talke must ensue to you ward. For I fonde you pleyn at Cristemesse, and I toke you that ye loved me, wher to fore, withoute cause truly, to my seid maister moch ye hyndred me, as parte he tolde me, and thanne I praied you in that your good

215

1460
APRIL 9
maistership and amendement, and sith I have be pleyn and wol be. And I require you as ye arn a gentilman, kepe thees maters secrete by twix God, you and me ; for by Almyghty Jhesu of me knoweth this non erthely creatur, nor shal knowe. Other thynges been that sounden not wele, but as I fele your wisdham take me in this, so herafter I wil demene me with you in maters. I am urke of variaunces, for parties waxen wrooth if men hold not with there oppynyons whan thei in angre trotte over fer by yon hem self. I may not come by you to London ward, I trow I must by Suffolk ; elles I had not writen this. Oure Blissed Lorde have you in His governaunce and be your conduytour to His pleisur, Amen. This Wednesday, ix. day Aprill.

As ye arn a veray gentilman, be my true confessour as I am youres and take me as I mene, thof my termes been not discreet. Brenne this scrowe or kepe it pryvy, as ye like and I beseche you, if ye wil trist me, wil me pleyn, &c.—Your owen, &c., to my power.

406

WILLIAM PASTON TO JOHN PASTON [1]

To hys rythe wurchyp[full] broder, Jon Paston, [dwell]yng at Castre.

MAY 2
BRODER, I comand me to zow, certhefieng zow that Playter is redyn to Lundon ward this day abowthe ij. afternone. And he teryed here, and schulde abedyn styll till he had had an horse that Master Thomas Howys schuld have lent hym. And so I thowthe he schuld have taried to long ; and so he hathe bowthe on off myn hors. And iff it nede, he schall send zow word be his man fro Lundon how he felythe the disposycyon off men ther, &c. ; and he schall send

[1] [From Paston MSS., B.M.] The date of this letter is certainly in the year 1460, for it was written after the death of Sir John Fastolf, and before the deposition of Henry VI., Margaret of Anjou being still spoken of as 'the Queen.'

216

his man hom be Newmerket wey. And I have infurmyd hym acording after the ententhe of zowr letter.

1460
MAY 2

I spak this day with Bokkyng. He had but few wurdes, but I felt be hym he was rythe evyll disposyd to the parson and zow, but coverthe langgage he had. I wene he be assentid to the fyndyng of this offyce [1] takyn at Bokynham, and Recheman schall bryng zow the namys of the men that mad the verdythe on Soneday nexst comyng. I pray send to myn broder Clements fermor of Somerton for money for my broder Clement, for to have sent to hym to Lundon. I schuld have done it qwan I was at Caster ; myn moder desyryd me, and I sent a letter after to the parson, and prayed hym to receve it, &c.

Item, I prayd the parson to wrythe a letter in his name to myn suster Ponyngges,[2] as ze and I comunyd onys togeder, cownsellyng her to take good avyse befor sche sold her wood at Wrenham ; and he schuld knowe ther by weder Ponyngges wer in Kent ar nat, &c. I understond that this Bokkyng and Worceter have grett trust in ther awne lewd consaythe, wathe some ever it menythe, &c. Bokkyng told me this day that he stood as well in consaythe with myn Maister Fastolff iii. days befor he dyed as any man in Englond. I sayd I soposyd nay, ner iij. zere before he dyed. I told hym that I had hard dyveres talkynges of hym as men sayd, qweche I soposyd schuld nat easly be browthe a bowthe, and he swore that he talkyd never with no man in no mater that schuld be a zen zow, &c. It is he that makythe William Wurceter so froward as he is.

I wold ze had a witnesse of Roberd Ingglows, thow he wittnessyd no more but that myn master had his witthe, becawse he was so lathe with myn master Fastolff. Worceter sayd at Castre it schuld be nessessary for zow to have good witnesse, as he saythe it schuld go streythe with zow wytheowt zowr witnesse were rythe sofycyent. Myn cosyn Berney can tell zow, &c.

Item, remenbre to make the parson to make an instrument

[1] See p. 199, Note 2.
[2] Elizabeth Paston, now wife of Robert Poynings.

217

1460
MAY 2
up on his sayyng. I funde hym rythe good qwan I spak with hym at Caster ; and remembre the newe evydens.

Item, Arblaster and I spakk togeder. I felle hym rythe feythefully disposyd to zow ward, and he schall mow do myche good and he go to Lundon, for he can labore will a monge Lordes. He and I comunyd to geder of myn Lord Awbre ; [1] lethe hym tell zow qwat it was, for he will speke with zow to morow. It is full nessessary to mak zow strong be lord chep, and be oder menys. Myn Lord Awbry hathe weddit the Duke of Bokyngham dowter,[2] and he was lathe with Master Fastolff be fore he dyed, and he is gret with the Qwene.

God have zow in His kepeng. Wretyn at Norwyche the secund day of May.

Be zowr broder,   W. PASTON.

Omnya pro pecunya facta sunt.

407

THE ABBOT OF LANGLEY TO JOHN STOKES [3]

To the ryght worchepfull Sere, Mayster John Stokes.

MAY 8
RYGHT worshypfull Sere, I recomaund me to yow ; and for asmyche as it is informyd me that it was appoynted that alle the executors of the worshepfull knyght, Sere John Fastolf, whos soule God asoyle, shuld be at London as on Monday next comyng, of wheche executors I am namyd for on, as I ondyrstond ; wherfore, in as myche as ye be ordenary and on of the same executors, I prey yowre tendre my laboure, withoute my comyng, be youre dyscrecion, myght be more profyt to the dede ; for I conseyve it shuld be but charge to the dede, and lytell avayleable, consyderyng that John Paston, Squyere, and Thomas Howys, parson of Blofeeld, schall come up at this time, wheche were[4] the persones above

[1] Aubrey de Vere, son of the Earl of Oxford, who suffered death, with his father, in February 1462.
[2] Anne, eldest daughter of Humphry, Duke of Buckingham.
[3] [From Fenn, iii. 398.]
[4] This word is omitted in the literal transcript in Fenn.

218

all other that the seyd Sere John Fastolf put in hys most sengulere love and trust, and wold they shuld have the kepyng and dysposicion of hys goods, as wele in hys lyve as after hys deseas, to dyspose for the well of hys soule ; and that non other namyd hys executors, but only they tweyn, shuld have ony kepyng or dysposyng of ony part of hese goods duryng ther lyves ; and that alle other namyd executors shuld supporte them and geve them to the seyd John Paston and Thomas Howys here good avyse in performyng of hys desyre in that behalve. Wherfor that it lekyth yow in ony thyng ye desyre me to do in thys cause or matere to geve yowre feyth and credence to the seyd John Paston and Thomas Howys ; and so desyred me the seyd Knyght feythefully to do, that knowyth God, whom I be seke preserve yow from alle adversyte.

1460
MAY 8

Wretyn in the Abbey of Langeley, the viij. day of the monyth of May, the yeere of oure Lord m¹cccc.lx.

Youre preest,   ABBOT OF LANGELEY.[1]

408

JOHN PASTON TO MARGARET PASTON [2]

To my trusty cosyn, Margaret Paston, at Norwich, be this delyvered.[3]

JUNE 19
I RECOMAUNDE me to you, letyng you witte that I sent a letter to John Russe and Richard Kalle that thei, by th'advyse of Watkyn Shipdam and William Barker shuld send me word of whom alle the maneres, londes, and tenementes that were Sir John Fastolffes wern holde, preyng you that ye wold do them spede them in that matier ; and if my feodaryes, whiche lye in the tye of my gret cofyr, may ought wisse therin, lete them se it.

[1] His name was Nicholas.
[2] [From Paston MSS., B.M.] This letter appears to have been written the year after Fastolf's death.
[3] Below this address is written, in another hand, 'To Richard Calle, at Caster, be this deliverid in hast.'

219

THE PASTON LETTERS

1460
JUNE 19
Item, I wolde that William Barker shulde send me a copye of the olde traverse of Tychewell and Beyton. And lete Richard Kalle spede hym hidderward, and come by Snaylwel, and take suyche mony as may be getyn there, and that he suffre not the mony that the tenauntes owe to come in the fermours handes.

Item, that he come by Cambrigge and bryng with hym Maister Brakkeles licence from the provynciall of the Grey Freres. I prey you recomaunde me to my modir.

Wretyn at London the Thursday next to fore Midde-somer.   JOHN PASTON.

409

FRIAR BRACKLEY TO JOHN PASTON[1]

Venerabili armigero, Johanni Paston seniori, detur hæc litera.

JULY 6   HONORIS superni amorisque interni indissolubile vin-culum tam venerabili viro in Christo condignum, præcordialissime magister ac amice singularis, non solum quales debeo sed quales valeo vobis refero grates cordiales pro vestris beneficiis quampluribus michi multi-formiter exhibitis, pro quibus omnibus recompenset vos Altissimus. Honorabilis domine, causa motiva præsentis scripturæ est hæc. Ex magno cordis affectu audire desidero de vestra expeditione prospera in materia concernente testa-mentum et voluntatem venerabilis viri J. F.[2] militis per Ricardum Calle vel Johannem Pampyng, vestros fideles ser-vientes ; qood si fieri non possit per relationem latoris præ-sentium, michi certificare dignemini. Cujus verbis audienciam credulam præbere curetis, sicut et michi dare velletis si vobis-cum personaliter interessem. Scire insuper dignetur vestra caritas quod iste frater, præsentium lator, est meus spiritualis

[1] [Add ms. 34,888, f. 147.] This is a letter of Friar Brackley, apparently written the year after Fastolf's death. It is in a large and regular handwriting, different from some of his other letters.
[2] Sir John Fastolf.

220

filius, eo quod in ordinem per me indutus et professus et ad gradum sacerdotii promotus, jam per biennum continuum, fuit socius et servitor meus satis solaciosus in tempore meæ gravissimæ infirmitatis, in laboribus et vigiliis continuis, tam diurnis quam nocturnis, quorum occasione a suo libro et studio fuit multiformiter impeditus ; sicque ad suos amicos non potuit habere recursum ad sui victus et vestitus adquirendum sub-sidium. Cui si placet intuitu caritatis elemosinam per vos graciose collatam Willelmo nepoti meo ingratissimo, utinam non infidelissimo, latori prædicto dare curetis, qui vobis suam indigenciam fideliter explanabit et dicti nepotis viciosa demerita certissime declarabit. Unum enim scitote, si frater prædictus circa meam personam non fuisset multiformiter solicitus ego pluries fuissem mortuus. Spero enim per Dei graciam circa festum ad Vincula Petri vestram graciosam visitare presenciam, et de dicti fratris gratitudinem clariorem dare noticiam. Cui propter Deum ad mei cordis multiforme solacium dicti beneficii ne denegetis suffragium, sicud in vobis gero confidenciam singularem. Non plura pro præsenti vobis offero calamo digna, sed vos, vestros et vestra defendat Trinitas alma, Quæ vos graciose conservet in prosperis et graciosissimis dirigat in agendis. Scriptum Donewici, in vigilia Translacionis Sancti Thomæ Martiris.

1460
JULY 6

Vester ad vota promptissimus ac orator pauperculus.
                    FRATER J. B., Minorum minimus.

410

THE YORKIST LORDS TO THE AUTHORITIES IN NORFOLK[1]

The Erlys of Marche, Warwyke, and Salysbury.

RYGHT welbeloved, we grete you wele ; and wher, for JULY 23 the tendre love that we have to the concervacion of the Kyngs peas, lawes, and justice in this his realme of Englonde, we have comaunded the Kyngs peeple in his

[1] [From Fenn, iii. 244.] This manifesto must have been issued in July 1460, after the battle of Northampton, when the King was in the hands of the confederate

221

THE PASTON LETTERS

1460
JULY 23
name, be oure letters and diverse writyngs, that no man shulde robbe or dispoile Sir Thomas Todenham, Knyght, John Heyden, John Wyndham, Herry Todenham, and John Andrws, and other weche have sued to us for oure seide letters ; we, wolyng to eschewe that any person shulde have colour be oure seide letters to noyse us, or any of us, that the seide Sir Thomas, John Heyden, John Wyndham, Herry, and John Andrws, or any other of suspecte fame, be accorded with us, or any of us, for suche wrongs as they, or any of ham, have do to us, our servaunts and tenants or wellweļlers, or that we shulde hafe hem in tendrenesse or favour to dis-corage trewe people to swe a yen hem be the lawe ; We therfore notyfie to yow, as we woll that it be notyfid to all people, that we, ne noon of us, intende not to favour or tendre hem, or any other of suspecte fame, but rather to corecte suche be the lawe, for we made our seid letters soly for kepyng of the pease and justice, and not for favour of suspecte con-dicione. And the Holy Trynyte kepe yow.

Wreten at London the xxiij[th] day of Jule.

To all Meyers, Sceryves, Balyfys, Constables, and all the Kynges Offecers and Ministres in Norffolk, and eche on of hem.

411

ABSTRACT[1]

THE KING TO JOHN NEDHAM AND THOMAS LITILTON, JUSTICES OF THE COUNTY PALATINE OF LANCASTER

1460(?)
JULY 26
Desires them to show favour to the defendants in an appeal of robbery sued before them out of malice by Thomas Bury against John Berney of Redham, Norf., Junior, Esq., John Paston of Norwich, Esq., John Berney of Redham, Norf., Senior, Esq., John Hevenyngham, of Norwich, Esq., and Christopher

Lords. It certainly was not, as Fenn supposes, in 1455, after the battle of St. Albans, when the Earl of March was only thirteen years old and the Duke of York, his father, was made Protector. York had not come over from Ireland in July 1460, and is consequently not named in this document.
[1] [From Paston mss., B.M.]

222

Norwich of Brundehale. They are to receive no writ returned in the name of the Sheriff of Norfolk touching that matter except by the hands of the sheriff himself, or of John Bernarde his under-sheriff.

1460(?)
JULY 26

London, 26 July.

II. Another letter, similar in substance, in which no justices' names are given.

[These documents cannot be later than 1460, as the younger John Berney died in July of that year (see next letter). But as Judge Littleton was only made a King's Serjeant in 1455, they cannot be many years earlier, and they are not unlikely to be of the year 1460 itself.]

412

JOHN PASTON TO MARGARET PASTON[1]

To my wurschipfull coysyn, Margaret Paston, be this delyvered in haste.

I RECOMAUNDE me unto you, letyng you witte that your unkyll, John Berney, is deed, whoos soule God have mercy ; desyryng you to sende for Thomas Holler,[2] and enquere of hym wher his goode is, and what he is wurthe, and that he take goode eede to all suche goods as he had bothe meveable and on mevable ; for I undre stande that he is wurthe in money v[c.] [500] marke, and in plate to the valwe of other v[c.] marke, beside other goods. Wherfor I wolde ye schulde not lete hym wete of his dissese unto the tyme that ye

1460
JULY 28

[1] [From Fenn, iv. 36.] According to Fenn, Margaret Paston's uncle, John Berney, second son of John Berney, Esq. of Reedham, died in July 1461, and he accordingly places this letter in that year. It is evident, however, that John Berney was dead at the date of Nos. 431 and 462, the former written in January 1561, the latter certainly not so late as the 28th July in the same year, for Thomas Denys was murdered at the very beginning of the month. Indeed, it is clear that in No. 462 Margaret Paston wishes to arrange about the approaching anniversary of her uncle's death. John Berney must therefore have died in July 1460, although from the troubled character of the times his will (which is preserved in the Principal Registry at Somerset House), made on the 2nd June 1460 (Monday after the Feast of St. Petronilla the Virgin), was not proved till the 1st December 1461.
[2] When Berney's will was proved at Lambeth, 1st December 1461, administration was granted provisionally to Thomas Hooler, who was to send in accounts before the morrow of the Conversion of St. Paul (Jan. 26) following. Power was, however, reserved of committing administration to John Paston. But John Paston did not appear on the day, and left the undivided administration to Hooler.

223

1460
JULY 28

had enquered of the seide Thomas Holler of all suche maters as be a bovyn wreten, and whan he hathe enformed you therof, than lete hym wete verely that he is deede, desiryng hym that no man come on to his place at Redham but hym selfe, unto the tyme that I come.

Item, I lete you witte that gret parte of his goode is at William Taverners, as I undrestande. Thomas Holler woll telle you justely the trouthe as I suppose, and deseyre hym on my behalfe that he doo soo, and ther is writyng therof ; and telle Thomas Holler that I and he be executours named, and therfore lete hym take heede that the goods be kept saffe, and that nobody knowe wher it shall lie but ye and Thomas Holler. And Thomas Holler, as your unkyll tolde me, is prevy wher all his goode lithe and all his writyng, and so I wol that ye be prevy to the same for casualte of deethe, and ye too shal be his executours for me as longe as ye doo trewly, as I trowe verely ye woll.

Wreten at London, the xxviij[t] day of Jule.

I requer yow be of god cumfort and be not hevy, if ye wil do owth for me.

Yowr,   JOHN PASTON.

413

ABSTRACT[1]

AUG. 1

'Soutwerk cum membris,' No. 50 a.—'Inquisitio post mortem Johannis Fastolf militis capta per escheatorem Regis, ubi mentio fit quorundam tenementorum, viz., the Berehouse, Boreshead, Hartshorne, et 2 molendinorum aquaticorum. Aug. 1, Hen. vi. 38.'

[1] [From MS. Index in Magd. Coll., Oxford.]

414

ANONYMOUS TO YELVERTON AND PASTON[1]

To the right worshipful Seres, my right welbeloved and trusted cosyns, William Yelverton, Justice, and John Paston.

SIR, please yowr right worshipfull maystership that 1460(?) Mayster Paston come to London as on Thursdaye att none last past, and I trust verelye all maters here were resonablye labored to his comyng, and now they shal be better. Neverthelesse, I have ben mevid of tretye by dyvers personez sith I came hidre, as wele for Tudenham, Wentworth, Heydon, and other at this tyme not wel willed to yow and yourez, seyng that such money as is spent a twix yowe is but wastfully expendid and to non use vertuouse. I fele by theym they be not right corageous in theyr werkes, ner nought wold if they myght have a resonable trete. I meve not this that ze shold thenk that they had conquered me by noyans, but I do it to avertyse yow for th'eschewyng of the importable costes that hath ben born by yow, and yet lyke to bee, aswele in the elde maters hangyng as in newe at this tyme to be grownded, if this werre shal rest and hold a twyx yowe, and specially for the ease of hym that shalbe solicitour in the same. Ye nede at this terme rather to have had thre solicitours than in any other terme past this iij. yere, on concyderyng the maters hangyng, &c. ; of which please yow to send yowr gode advyse and wille yf ye thenk it to be don, and els not, for this is but a mocion, &c.

[1] [From Paston MSS., B.M.] This letter is by an unknown writer, and very uncertain as to date. It shows that Tuddenham, Wentworth, and Heydon, all adherents of the House of Lancaster, were desirous of a compromise with Yelverton and Paston. The year 1460, some time after the battle of Northampton, is perhaps as likely a period as any.

415

FRIAR BRACKLEY TO JOHN PASTON[1]

To my Mayster Jon Pastone, Esqwyer, be this letter presentid.

Jesus, Maria, &c.

1460
OCT.

RYTE reverent Sire, after du recommendacion, we sey in this cuntre that Heydon is for Barkschir in the Comon Hows. And the Lady of Suffolk[2] hath sent up hyr sone[3] and hise wyf to my Lord of York to aske grace for a schireve the next yer, Stapilton, Boleyn, or Tyrel, qui absit. God send zow Ponyng, W. P., W. Rokewode, or Arblaster. Ze haf myche to done ; Jesu spede zow. Ze haf many good preyers, what of the covent, cyte, and cuntre. God safe our good Lords, Warwik, alle hise brether, Salisbury, &c., fro al fals covetyse and favour of extorcyon, as they wil fle uttyr schame and confusyon. God save hem, and preserve fro treson and poyson ; lete hem be war her of for the pite of God ; for yf owt come to my Lord Warwik but good, far weel ze, far weel I, and al our frends ! for be the weye of my sowle, this lond wer uttirly on done, as God forbede. Her [*their*] enmyes bostyn with good to come to her favour ; but God defende hem, and zeve hem grace to knowe her frends fro her enmyes, and to cherisch and preferr her frends and lesse the myte of alle her enmyes thorw owt the schiris of the lond. And [*i.e.* if] my good Lord Warwik, with my Lord his brother Chaunceler[4] and my Lord her fadyr[5] woldyn opposyn, as dede Danyel, Fortesku, Alisaunder, Hody, Doctor Aleyn, Heydon, and Thorp, of the writyng made be hem at Covyntre Parlement, they schuld answer wers than sub

[1] [From Fenn, iii. 382.] This letter appears to have been written just before the sitting of the Parliament of October 1460, of which John Paston was a member. Warwick's brother was then Chancellor. No signature is attached to this letter in Fenn's literal copy, although the name is appended to the modern transcript.
[2] Alice, widow of William, Duke of Suffolk.
[3] John de la Pole, second Duke of Suffolk. He married Elizabeth, the Duke of York's daughter.
[4] George Nevill, Bishop of Exeter.   [5] Richard Nevill, Earl of Salisbury.

cino or sub privo (?), and this generaly wold I sey at Powlys 1460 Cros, etc., and [*i.e.* if] I schuld come there, &c. It is veryfyed OCT. of hem, 1° Jeremiæ, 8°, *Vere mendacium operatus est stilus mendax scribarum*, &c. And think of two vers of zour Sawter, *Scrivoantur hæc in generatione altera* (hujus scilicet parliamenti) *et populus qui creabitur laudabit Dominum*,[1] &c. *Deleantur etiam tales perversi scriptores de libro viventium et cum justis non scribantur.*[2] Et non plura, sed vos, vestros et vestra conservet Jesus graciose in prosperis et graciosius dirigat in agendis.

Ex Norwico, feria quarta,[3] nuncio festinante.

And I prey zow for Godds sake to be good mayster to Jon Lyster, &c. And I prey zow think, in this Parlement, of the text of Holy Scripture, *Quicunque fecerit contra legem Dei et contra legem Regis judicium fiet de eo, vel in condemnationem substantiæ ejus, vel in carcerem, vel in exilium, vel in mortem* (Primo Esdræ, vij., et parti 2° Esdræ 8°).

416

FRIAR BRACKLEY TO [JOHN PASTON]

[OCT.

Jesus, Maria, &c. Reverende domine, si contingat ut sitis Londoniæ hoc termino in principio parliamenti, hæc poteritis in secretis dicere domino Warwik ac domino Cancellario, quomodo Johannes W.[4] apud Felbrigg jacet cum manu forti contra pacem domini Regis et patriæ, qui quantum valere potest est hostis publicus et inimicus capitalis domini Regis et suorum fidelium dominorum utilitatem rei publicæ et communitatem Angliæ diligentium, pro quo taliter esset modo indilate et cum omni festinacione possibili providendum quod esset commissio directa sub pœna ligeanciæ et pœna mortis et privatione bonorum vicecomiti, domino M. Stapilton, domino W. Chambirleyn, W. Yelverton justiciario, W. Calthorp, Johanni Twyre, Johanni Geney, T. Gurnay, Johanni Fyncham, Johanni Yelverton Juniori, Edmundo Bokyngham, Johanni Gros, Johanni Dam, Johanni Lomenour, Jacobo Arblaster, T. Denys, ut assistant sub pœna prædicta sex primis militibus et armigeris ad excitandum populum de patria pro domino T. T.,[5] J. H.,[6] P. Wentworthe, J. A.,[7] T. Danyel, H. Hunton, J. Wode, W. Prentys, S. Gunnor, H. Todynham, Joh. Wyndham, Palmere Ballivo de Costsey, T. Brygge, et suis complicibus subito et secretiori modo capiendo et versus London adducendo cum manu forti, et in Turri vel Newgate firmiter

[1] Psalm ci. (or cii.) 18.   [2] Psalm lxviii. (or lxix.) 28.
[3] 'Feria quarta' means Wednesday.   [4] John Wyndham.
[5] Sir Thomas Tuddenham.   [6] John Heydon.
[7] John Andrews. *See* p. 222.

THE PASTON LETTERS

1460
[OCT.]

cum Thorp de Scacario carcere collocando, &c. Et tunc eorum clientes et eis adhærentes non possent, ymmo nec auderent, nocere populo patriæ bonæ disposicionis. Certe si in hac parte fideliter laborare in effectu volueritis, dominus Comes Warwic, et omnes sibi et suis benivoli essent vobis multiformiter obligati, et tunc esset in Norffolchia mansio concors et valde pacificus. Utinam bona voluntas vestra non sit in hac materia pigra, &c.

2°. Item, quod Episcopus Norwicensis esset in curia Regis ad tempus, vel in parliamento omnino, quia hic parvum bonum facit, nisi supportando iniquos et paci patriæ contrarios ; est enim satis dives ad comprestandum pecunias Regi in necessitate sua. Ipse enim cum ducissa Suff. et aliis personis prænominatis sunt Reginæ et principi maxime favorabiles cum totis suis viribus ; et ideo maxime expediens est parti Regis et comitis Warwic subtrahere, diminuere, et pocius opprimere, vires omnium illorum prædictorum eis et suis continue malignantium ex adverso, &c.

3°. Item, vos et vestri præmunire poteritis, si placeat, Doctores Kyrry et Godard quomodo fama communis hic volat continue per Boreales et eorum fautores quod Regina ac sui firmiter statuerunt unanimi decreto ipsos doctores et me non solum morti ignominiose tradere sed etiam generaliter omnes Fratres Minores citra flumen Trent commorantes interfici facere. Sed Magister Vergeant cum socio qui in sermonibus Reginam cum principe solempniter recommendat et in suis missis Reginam nominatim specificat per instanciam Ducissæ Suff. erit cum socio privilegiatus ab hac punicione.

4°. Item, bonum esset quod juvenis dux Suff. cum suis militibus et armigeris uteretur suis calcaribus et jam probaretur in bello cui esset fidelis, an caro vel piscis. Si T. T. cum suis prius recitatis essent unde memorati in parliamento a dominis et communibus, non dubium quin puniti essent causatores insurrectionis falsorum Regis contra Comitem Warwic apud pontem Westmonasterii, &c.

5°. Item, memorari dignetur dominus Comes Warwic quomodo T. T., J. H., J. A., et H. T.,¹ J. W. et cæteri gravissime comminantur priorem Wals' [Walsingham], &c.

6°. Item, caveant Comes Marchiæ et Comes Warwic ne quovis modo sit inter eos controversia, sed sint omnino unanimes et concordes, nec aliqua cupiditas consiliariorum suorum faveat alicui eorum adversario propter lucrum bonorum in finalem deperdicionem ipsorum et amicorum suorum.

7°. Item, fiat per decretum parliamenti diminutio juris peritorum ac legis attornatorum Suff. et Norff. punicique taxata singulorum oppressorum, generosos ac eorum liberos, nativosque tenentes cotidie et annuatim gravissime infestancium.

8°. Continue ac continue cordialiter cogitate ac scrutinio diligenti sæpius revolvite quomodo inimici vestri et adversarii antiqui, spiritu rancoris et invidiæ maliciose agitati, nituntur pro posse suo, et totis viribus, vos, et vostros vobis benevolos funditus destruere et finaliter deperdere, quod absit omnino ; quare ex naturali legis dictamine potestis et debetis vim vi volenter ac potenter reprimere ac repellere et eorum maliciis inveteratis virili congressu rigorose resistere, quia minus malim incomparabiliter videtur existere quod eorum obstinata malicia potestate politica sit diminuta et quasi dejecta quam vos et vestri affines, propinuqi et amici essetis nimis depauperati, et quasi, quod absit, finaliter abjecti.

228

¹ Henry Tuddenham.

417

FRIAR BRACKLEY TO JOHN PASTON [1]

*Reverendo magistro meo et amico singulari
Johanni Paston armigero detur.*

JHESUS, Maria, Raphael, Johannes Baptista, Johannes 1460
Ewangelista, Franciscus Guardianus, cum Sanctis om- OCT. (?)
nibus, succurrant mæstis in tribulationibus. Amen.
Præcordialissime domine et amice maxime singularis, Omissis
pro præsenti vestri gratitudinis beneficiis mihi sæpius impensis,
me humilime vestræ reverenciæ recommendo. Pensetis,
quæso, cum omni festinatione possibili instabilem virum,
utinam Hibernicum² non ingratissimum, cujus nacionis ali-
quales proprietates sunt istæ :—animo sæva, vultu ferox, torva
affatu, versupellis moribus et inconstancia in omnibus bonis
viis suis ; qui inter cætera magistro Clementi retulit quod
expensæ annuales magistri Johannis Fastolff, bonæ memoriæ,
secundum fidelem compotum se extendunt omni anno ad
octingentas marcas in Norfolch et Suffolch, &c., et quod idem
miles vobiscum faciens pactum pro iiij. M¹, &c., fuit purus
fatuus ; et quod idem vobis donatorum literarum faciens fuit
major fatuus, &c., et quod idem Hibernicus scit deteriorare,
et diminuere bona militis ad summam viginti m¹ marcarum,
&c. Ob reverentiam Jhesu Christi, cavete quod impediatur
omnino a suscipiendo onus testamenti quousque verum et
integrum compotum reddiderit de defuncti bonis per eum
receptis tot annorum evolutis et transactis curriculis, &c.
Item, quod non vendat nec alienet maneria, terras, tenementa
cum pertinentiis, nec commutat jocalia nec evidenciales literas,
nec pecunias per vestrum germanum, W. P., et per ipsum receptas London, Bermondyseye, &c., cum jam sciat de multis ubi
sunt, &c. Videtur mihi, salvo saltem vestro meliori judicio, quod
de aliis personis et locis est cum omni celeritate possibili pru-
denter providendum et politice, ne idem W. W. oculis luscus
et denigrato colore, in facie fuscus, sit cum W. Yelverton judice

¹ [Add. MS. 34,888, f. 158.] This letter appears to be holograph. If we are right
that it was written just before No. 418, we may place it early in October 1460.
² See p. 213.

229

THE PASTON LETTERS

1460
OCT. (?)

confederatus, et per Ducem Exoniæ satis tiranizantem sup-
portatus et per suos complices, &c. Sapienti loquor ; nam
philosophorum princeps ait ' Cave ab hiis quos natura signavit' ;
et metrice dicitur :

'Nam fallax faciens mens, mores ac pariformes
Concludunt mutuo quod sit quasi fraudis ymago.'

Dixi vobis quod non esset pro vobis nec vestris utile in W.
W. aliquam confidentiam gerere. Post vestrum didici reces-
sum in 4ᵒʳ nostri collegii famulis duplicibus et falsis cum omni
perfidia contra voluntatem militis et ejus executores iniquitatis
vinculo confederatis et astrictis, scilicet Colino Gallico, coquinæ
clerico, W. W., militis secretario et W. Eton ; nunc in promp-
tuario propter Jhesum Christum deleantur de libro vertuose et
unanimiter viventium et a modo cum justis nequaquam con-
scribantur, &c. Est vulgare proverbium ' Accordyng to ryte
reson that to oftyn it is in ceson, that in trust is gret treson.'
Ideo cavete quod Sapiens dicit ' Qui cito credit, levis est
corde.'¹ Et audite scripturæ sacræ sententiam ' A malo inquit
consiliario serva animam tuam,'² &c. Nam alibi Sapientis pro-
clamat eloquium : ' Non est sapientia, non est prudentia, non
est consilium contra Dominum.'³ Hæc ibi. In alienis negociis
velox, nec vivax erit, qui in propriis causis piger existit. Rogo
attendite et menti imprimite diligenter quod revolvite quomodo
poteritis resistere homini tam perverso noxam volenti et nocu-
mentum executoribus inferre. Mens mea particulam evangelii
retinet : ' Si in viridi ligno hoc faciunt in arido quid fiet ?'⁴
Quasi diceret, si iste W. W. executorum ultimus et merito
novissimus et per vestram et magistri Thomæ Howes dili-
genciam inscriptus tantam proterviam gerit, in hoc quasi ex-
ordio, quid in fine malicios sit facturus ? Hoc penitus ignoro.
Deo vos vestros et vestra commendo et præsentem causam.
Recommendetis me si placeat recommendandis, &c. Scriptum
festinanter, hora prima post prandium. W. B., lator præsentis, intendit vobis si placeat humilime et verissime servi-
turum. Ex Castre in die Sabbathi.
Vester ad vota promptissimus,

FRATER J. B., Minorum minimus.

¹ Eccles. xix. 4.   ² Ibid. xxxvii. 9 (8).   ³ Prov. xxi. 30.   ⁴ Luke xxiii. 31.

230

418

FRIAR BRACKLEY TO JOHN PASTON [1]

Venerando suo magistro, Johanni Paston.

Jesus, &c.

REVERENDE domine, &c. Propter Deum caveatis a 1460
confidentia in illo nigro Hibernico² oculis obliquo
et lusco, qui utinam corde, ore et opere non esset
obliquior ; qui heri misit literam Colino Gallico ; de quibus
dicitur quod singuli caccant uno ano. Et parvus Adam hodie
portavit (?) magistro suo responsum. Idem enim luscus dicit
vos esse cupidissimum, quia multum afflixistis debitores patris
vestri, persequendo eos cum omni rigore, &c. Item dicit
quod cum pater vester fuerit judex ditissimus, quasi nihil
fecistis pro eo in distribuendo elemosinam pro anima ejus, et
cum nihil feceritis pro patre vestro, quomodo pro magistro
Fastolf aliquid facietis ? Item dicit ' Utinam fuissem in morte
magistri mei, quia in me ultra omnes homines mundi maxime
confisus est,' &c. Item dicit quod in hora qua obiit magister
suus, obviavit sibi unus albus bubo, qui eodem tempore juxta
unam ecclesiam continuo clamavit mirabiliter et volavit sæpius
iteratis vicibus sub equo suo inter tibias equi sui &c. Item
dixit cuidam fratri conventus mei, ' Magister Brakle accipit
super se magnum regimen, &c., et certe, si pecunia legata in
ultima voluntate suis servientibus non fuerit in larga habun-
dancia distributa, erit ad magnum dedecus et verecundiam
personæ meæ,' &c. Utinam caveritis ita bene de eo sicut
ego cavebo, quia cum sit filius Hibernicus, ego de eo semper
minus curabo. Ipse vellet habere bona ex parte sua, &c.

¹ [From Paston MSS., B.M.] This letter appears by the contents to have been
written about the beginning of the Parliament of 1460, to which it would seem
Paston did not immediately repair to take his place, thus giving occasion to an insinuation that he did not wish to be called upon to vote money for the King and
Queen.
² See p. 213.

231

THE PASTON LETTERS

460 Deo teste non fecit (?)[1] vos magistri sui, &c. Hæc omnia et plura dixit idem miser magistro Clementi, a quo hæc omnia et plura didici &c. Item dicit quod vos timetis adire locum parliamenti quia non vultis præstare pecunias Regi nec Reginæ et aliis ; et ideo pigritia vestra in hoc passu erit bonis mortui satis nociva, &c. Ego tot et tanta audivi de illo quod, per Deum, nunquam confidam in illo, &c. ; est enim miser multum malencolicus et in toto colericus, et, salva patientia vestra, reddat compotum de singulis antequam capiat onus testamenti, &c.

Judex[2] cras venturus est, &c., et sicut se hic gerit vestra caritas notitiam habebit, &c. Rogo detis mihi licentiam recedendi ad conventum Norwici, ad mutandum vestimenta mea propter sudores, &c., et ad studendum pro sermone, &c., ad honorem Dei, &c., qui vos vestros et vestra salvet in sæcula. Amen. Vester orator,

FRATER J. B.

On the back :—Item dixit magistro Clementi quod ipse non vult esse Frere, veni mecum, nec canta secum, nec Dacok, nec facok, nec Frater, tu va pedes, &c. Item dicit vos instruxisse magistrum suum contra eum de auferendo evidencias, &c., et ipse plures labores habuit pro eo quam vos vel aliquis alius, &c. Custodite literam ultimo a me vobis missam, &c. Utinam Upton et ipse essent extra locum, &c., quia hic fiunt consumptiones maximæ, &c.

Endorsed in a 16th century hand :—A lettre much dispraising W. Wircester, from Doctor Brakley.

[1] The word is 'ft' in the MS. And to make sense of the passage, I must suppose another word to be omitted. 'Non fecit vos *amicum* magistri sui,' *i.e.* he did not make you out to be any friend of his master.
[2] William Yelverton.

HENRY VI

419

CHRISTOPHER HANSSON TO JOHN PASTON[1]

To the right worshipfull Sir and Maister, John Paston, Escuier, at Norwiche, be this delyvered in hast.

RIGHT worshipfull Sir and Maister, I recomaund me un to you. Please you to wete, the Monday after oure Lady Day[2] there come hider to my maister ys place,[3] my Maister Bowser, Sir Harry Ratford, John Clay, and the Harbyger of my Lord of Marche, desyryng that my Lady of York[4] myght lye here untylle the comyng of my Lord of York and hir tw sonnys, my Lorde George[5] and my Lorde Richard,[6] and my Lady Margarete[7] hir dawztyr, whiche y graunt hem in youre name to ly here untylle Mychelmas. And she had not ley here ij. dayes but sche had tythyng of the londyng of my Lord at Chestre. The Tewesday next after, my Lord sent for hir that sche shuld come to hym to Harford [*Hereford*], and theder sche is gone. And sythe[8] y left here bothe the sunys and the dowztyr, and the Lord of Marche comyth every day to se them.

Item, my Lord of York hath dyvers straunge commissions fro the Kyng for to sitte in dyvers townys comyng homward ; that is for to sey, in Ludlow, Schrrofysbury, Herford, Leycetre, Coventre, and in other dyvers townys, to punych them by the fautes to the Kyngs lawys.

As for tythyngs here, the Kyng is way at Eltham and at Grenewych to hunt and to sport hym there, bydyng the Parle-

[1] [From Fenn, i. 198.] This letter must have been written in the year 1460, when the Duke of York came over from Ireland, his party having been victorious at the battle of Northampton, and gained possession of the King's person.
[2] The Nativity of Our Lady is on the 8th September. The Monday following was in this year the 15th.
[3] Probably Sir John Fastolf's place in Southwark.
[4] Cecily, Duchess of York.   [6] Afterwards Duke of Clarence.
[6] Afterwards Richard III.   [7] Afterwards Duchess of Burgundy.
[8] The modern version in Fenn reads : 'And she hath left here.'

THE PASTON LETTERS

460 ment, and the Quene and the Prynce byth in Walys alway. ct. 12 And is with hir the Duc of Excestre and other, with a fewe mayne, as men seythe here.

And the Duc of Somerset he is in Depe [*Dieppe*] ; withe hym Maister John Ormound, Wyttyngham, Andrew Trollyp, and other dyvers of the garyson of Gyanys, under the Kyng of Fraunce safcondyte, and they seythe here, they porpose hym to go to Walys to the Quene. And the Erle of Wyltschyre[1] is stylle in pece at Otryght at the Frerys [*Friars*], whiche is seyntwary.

Item, Colbyne ys come home to my maister is place, and seyth that, at your departyng[2] ouzt of London, ze send hym word that he schuld come hedder to the place, and be here un tylle your comyng a zene ; and so he is here it, and seith he wolle take no maister but be your avyce, nether the leese [*nevertheless*] awaytythe uppon Maister Oldhall the most parte at Redre[3] at his place.

Item, Maister Ponyngs hathe enteret on an two or iij. placys uppon the Erle of Northomberlond, and he stondyth in good grace of the Kyng, my Lord of Marche, my Lord Warwyk, and my Lord of Salysbury. Most parte of the contre abought his lyflod hold aythe withe hym. And my maisteras your sister[4] is not delyverd as yet ; God yef hir god delyveraunce.

No more to you at this tyme, but and ze wolle comaund me any servyce y may doo, it is redy. And Jesu have you in his blessid kepyng ; and I beseche you this letter may comaund me to my maisteras your moder, and my maisteras your wyfe, and alle your houshold.

Wreten at London the xij. day of Octobre.

Your owne Servaunt, CHRISTOFER HANSSON.

[1] James Butler, Earl of Wiltshire and Ormond.
[2] Paston must have left London and gone to Norwich not long before the Parliament, which began on the 7th October ; and, as we have already observed, he did not return in time for its commencement.
[3] Redriff or Rotherhithe.
[4] Elizabeth, wife of Robert Poynings.—No. 406, p. 217.

HENRY VI

420

ABSTRACT[1]

ROBERT CALL TO [JOHN PASTON].

Has delivered the horse-litter to Robert Lynne according to his message. 1460(?) Cannot get a farmer for Mauteby. Sends John Deye. He will not pass one oct. 17 combe barley for an acre. He has fourteen acres 'reasonably well dight to sow on wheat.' None will take the close at Mauteby at the price agreed upon with Calle by Lynne and Robert Butler. Caister, St. Luke's Eve.

P.S. on the back, unimportant.

[From what is said in Margaret Paston's letter of the 20th October following about the lands at Maultby being unlet, this may perhaps have been written in the same year three days earlier.]

421

THOMAS PLAITER TO JOHN PASTON[2]

To my rygth worchipfull and my good maister, John Paston, Esquyer, in hast.

RYGTH worchipfull and my most speciall synguler good maister, I recomend me to you, besechyng your maistership not to be dysplesed with my long taryans, and also to take it to no gref thou it were long or I wrot to you ; for in good feyth I wend my self with in sevenygth after Seynt Feythesmesse[3] to have ben at London, and for asmoche as Suthwell[4] desyred me to tarye for evydens gevyng, &c. I promysed hym so to do and tarye tyll the Munday after Seynt Feythesmesse, or tyll the Tewysday sevenyth after at the

[1] [From Paston mss., B.M.]
[2] [From Paston mss., B.M.] The writer of this excuses his delay in coming to London, as he had been asked to stay and give evidence before the under-escheator, who was to sit at Acle on Tuesday after St. Luke's Day. This refers to the inquisition on the lands of Sir John Fastolf, which was taken at Acle on that day in 1460.   [3] St. Faith's Day is on the 6th October.
[4] Richard Southwell, Escheator of Norfolk.

THE PASTON LETTERS

1460
OCT.]

ferthest, and at tho dayes I hard no word fro hym. And so uppon the Thursday after had I word that the under-eschetour schuld sytte at Ocle[1] the Tewysday after Seynt Luce;[2] and so I tarye as yette, and trust verely to be with you the Saterday at the ferthest after Seynt Luce. Item, Sir, if my Maister of the Rolles[3] be not come, I trust to God to com tydely i now, as for the traversys; and if ye besi you to the innyng ther of or I com, Richard Ley schall delyver hem you, if ye send to hym for it; for I left hem with hym to gete hem in if he mygth, and promysed hym a reward for his labour. Item, my maistres[4] and all folkes be heyll and mery, blyssed be Jesu, ho have you in his blyssed governans and proteccion.

By your, THOMAS PLAITER.

422

THOMAS PLAITER TO JOHN PASTON[5]

To my maister, John Paston, Esquyer.

[OCT. 21]

A[FTER] my most speciall recomendacion, like your maisterchip wete that the office[6] is taken at Ocle in lyke forme as Suthwell[7] can chew you, for Fraunceys Costard hath sent it hym, and the jentylmen that passed upon the office wold fynd nor medyll nouther with the tenurs nor ho is next here [*heir*]. Wherfor if ye wol have other wyse found, Fraunceys Costard hath under take it, but it schal not be suche men of worchip [as] is yn this. Item, the under-chryf was at Ocle, and ded and sayd to the jentylmen al that ever he cowde to the lette of the matter. And as for Suffolk, I understand they have no warant, so I tarye as yet what cas that ever

[1] Acle in Norfolk.
[2] St. Luke's Day is the 18th October. The Tuesday after it was the 21st in 1460.
[3] Thomas de Kirkeby. [4] Margaret Paston.
[5] [From Paston MSS., B.M.] This letter must have been written immediately after the taking of the inquisition referred to in the preceding. The list of the jury who took it is on a separate paper found apart from this letter, in which it was enclosed. The names of those indicated as sworn are identical with those on the official record (Inquisitions *post-mortem*, 38 and 39 Hen. VI., No. 48), but seven additional names are included, besides one that is struck out.
[6] The inquisition.—*See* p. 199, Note 2. [7] Richard Southwell.—*See* p. 191.

236

HENRY VI

1460
[OCT. 21]

falle. And if ye wold that I tarye not, that it lyke you by the brynger her of to send me hasty wurd.

I send you the names of the jure here in.

Your, THOMAS PLAITER.

On a separate paper formerly enclosed in the preceding is the following List:—

Jurati pro Domino Rege.[1]

Willelmus Rokewood, armiger, jur'.
Johannes Berney, armiger, jur'.
Radulphus Lampytte, armiger, jur'.
Johannes Byllyngford, armiger, jur'.
[Jacobus Arblaster, armiger, jur'.][2]
Willelmus Deymayne, armiger, jur'.
Willelmus Dawbeney, armiger, jur'.
Willelmus Julles, jur'.
Christofre Norwiche, jur'.
Thomas Holler, jur'.
Johannes Berkyng, jur'.
Robert Bryghtlede, jur'.
Robertus Spany, jur'.
Johannes Bernard, jur'.
Rogerus Iryng, jur'.
Robertus Townesende.
Johannes Grygges de Ranworth, jur'.
Robertus Regestre, jur'.
Johannes Maunvyle, jur'.
Willelmus Rysyng.
Johannes Doke.
Robertus Jekkes, jur'.
Johannes Why[te].
Henr[icus] . . . ratte.
Car[ol]us Barker.
Johannes Cappe.
Thomas Paternoster.

[1] This is a panel of the jury drawn up before the inquisition was taken. The heading and the word 'jur'.' opposite the names of those sworn have been added afterwards. [2] This name is scored out with the pen.

237

THE PASTON LETTERS

423

MARGARET PASTON TO JOHN PASTON[1]

To my ryth worchepfull husbond, Jon Paston, be thys delyveryd in hast.

1460
OCT. 21

R YTH worchepfull husbonde, I recomand me to yow. Plesyth it yow to weet that I receyvyd yowyr letter that ye sent me by Nycolas Colman on Sonday last past. And as for the mater that ye desyiryd me to breke of to my cosyn Rokwode, it fortunyd so that he came to me on Sonday to dyner sone aftyr that I had yowyr letter; and when we had dynyd, I mevyd to hym ther of in covert termys, as Playter shall informe yow eraftyr. And as I thowt by hym, and so ded Playter also by the langwage that he had to us, that he wold be as feythfull as he kowd or myte be to that good Lorde that ye wrot of, and to yow also, in ony thynge that he kowde or myte do in case wer that he wer set in offsye, so that he myth owte do; and ther to he seyd he wolde be bownde in a m[l] *li.* [£1000] and he was so myche worthe.

As for the todyr that ye desyiryd I scholde meve to of the same mater, me semyth he is to yonge to take ony swhyche thyngys up on hym; and also I knowe veryly that he scholl never love feythfully the todyr man that ye desyiryd that he schuld do, for when he rem[em]bryth the tyme that is paste, and ther for I spak not to hym ther of.

Thys day was holde a gret day at Okyll[2] befor the undyr schreve and the undyr exchetor, for the mater of Syr Jon Fastolfys londys; and ther was my cosyn Rookwod and my cosyn Jon Berney of Redham, and dyvers odyr jentylmen and thryfty men of the contre; and the mater is well sped aftyr your intent (blyssyd be God!) as ye schall have knowlage of in hast.

[1] [From Fenn, iv. 194.] Reference is made in this letter, as in the preceding, to the holding of the inquisition on Sir John Fastolf's lands at Acle, which was on Tuesday the 21st October 1460, the day this letter was written.
[2] Acle, in Norfolk.

238

HENRY VI

1460
OCT. 21

I suppose Playter schall be with yow on Sonday or on Monday next comyng, if he may. Ye have many good prayers of the poer pepyl that God schuld sped yow at thys Parlement, for they leve in hope that ye schold helpe to set a wey that they myte leve in better pese in thys contre thane they have do befor, and that wollys schold be purveyd for, that they schuld not go owt of thys lond as it hathe be suffryd to do be for, and thane schall the poer pepyll more leve bettyr thane they have do by her ocwpacion ther in.

Thomas Bone hathe salde all yowyr wole her for xx*d.* a stone, and goode swerte fownd to yow ther for, to be payid a Myhellmas next comyng; and it is solde ryth well aftyr that the wole was, for the moste part was ryte febyll. Item, ther be bowt for yow iij. horse at Seynt Feythys feyer, and all be trotterys, ryth fayir horse, God save hem, and they be well kepyd. Item, your myllys at Heylysdon be late [*let*] for xij. marke, and the myller to fynde the reparacion; and Rychard Calle hathe let all yowyr londys at Caster; but as for Mawtby londys, they be not let yet. Wylliam Whyte hathe payid me a geyne thys daye hys x.*li.*, and I have mad hym a qwetans ther of, be cause I had not hys oblygacion.

Ther is gret talkyng in thys contre of the desyir of my Lorde of York.[1] The pepyll reporte full worchepfully of my Lord of Warwyk. They have no fer her but that he and othyr scholde schewe to gret favor to hem that have be rewyllers of thys contre be for tyme.

I have done all yowyr erandys to Syr Thomas Howes that ye wrote to me for. I ame rythe glade that ye have sped welle in yowyr materys be twyx Syr Fylyp Wentworthe and yow, and so I pray God ye may do in all othyr materys to hys plesans. As for the wrytyngys that ye desyirid that Playter schulde sende yow, Rychard Call told me that they wer at Herry Barborys, at the Tempyll gate.

The mayir[2] and the mayires sent hedyr her dynerys thys day, and Jon Dame came with hem, and they dynyd her. I am beholde to hem, for they have sent to me dyvers tymys

[1] The claim made by Richard, Duke of York, to the Crown in Parliament on the 17th October 1460.
[2] John Gilbert, Mayor of Norwich.

239

1460
OCT. 21

sythe ye yed hense. The meyr seyth that ther is no jentyl-man in Northefolk that he woll do more for than he wole for yow, if it laye in hys poer to do for yow. J. Perse is stylle in prisone, but he wolle not confese more thane he ded when ye wer at home. Edmond Brome was with me, and tolde me that Perse sent for hym for to come spek with hym, and he tolde me that he was with hym and examynyd hym, but he wold not be a knowe to hym that he hade no knowlage wher no goode was of hys masterys more thane he hade knowlageyd to yow. He tolde me that he sent for hym to desyir hym to labor to yow and to me for hym if ye had be at home; and he tolde me that he seyd to hym ayen that he wold never labor for hym but [*unless*] he myth know that he wer trwe to hys mastyr, thow it lay in hys power to do ryth myche for hym. I suppose it schulde do none harme thow the seyd Perse wer remevyd ferther. I pray to Gode yeve grace that the trowthe may be knowe, and that the dede may have part of hys owne goode. And the blissyd Trynyte have yow in Hys kepyng.

Wretyn in hast at Heylysden the Tuesday next aftyr Seynt Lwke.

Be yowyrs,   M. P.

424

PIERS TO MARGARET PASTON[1]

To myn right reverent and worchipphull Maisterez Paston, be this delivered.

1460

RIGHT reverent and wurchippfull maisteres, I recom-aunde me un to yow, beseching yow of your good maisteresshipp to be myn good maisteres to help wit your gracious woord un to myn right reverent and wurchip-

[1] This and the letter following appear to have been written by the prisoner spoken of in the end of Margaret Paston's letter immediately preceding. We have accord-ingly placed them here as belonging to the same period, though from a subsequent letter (No. 462) we may rather surmise that this first of the two was written in 1461.

240

phull maister and your to take of me, his pore presoner and   1460
your, suerte queche I xall fynd to be bounde for me to brynge me un to all answere, in to the tyme that myn maister and ze have dimisse me wit myn suerte. And bescheche your good maistereschipp to prey myn mayster that he will yeve yow lycense wit his wurchippfull counsaill and youre, in case that myn maister may nout tarie, that ze in his absence may take myn seid suerte. And if it please his heyghnesse and youre, that I may have answere ayene be the bryngere of this, and here up I xall send for myn suertes, queche I trust in Good xul be to your plesure. No more att this tyme. I prey God evyr have yow in kepyng.

Be your pore presonere,

PIERS, sum tyme the servaunt of
John of Berneye.

425

PERSE TO SIR ROBERT ROKESBY[1]

To my right worschipfull Sir, Robert Rokysby.

RYGHT wurshipfull Sir, I recomaunde me to you, besechyng you, of your goode mastership, that ye wol wechesafe to speeke to Richard Kowven that he myght brynge me or sende me the money that is betwen hym and me in all the haste that he maye, for in goode feythe I hadde never more neede for to have help of my goode as I have at this tyme, for, Godwot, it stonde right straunge with me; for the false chayler that kepeth me entretethe me worse thanne it weere a dogge, for I am feterid worse thanne ever I whas, and manacled in the hands by the daye and nyght, for he is a feerde of me for brekyng a weye. He makethe false tales of me, throw the means of a false qwene that was tendyng to a Frensheman that is presoner to my Lord Roose,[2]

[1] [From Fenn, iii. 432.]
[2] Thomas, Lord Roos. He fled to Scotland with Margaret of Anjou after the battle of Towton in 1461, and was beheaded at Newcastle after the battle of Hexham in 1464.

VOL. III.—Q   241

1460

and for be cause of that he bronde me every day be John of Berney, that is goone to the tother Lords;[1] but I truste to God oonys to qwite hys meede. And, Sir, I thanke you mekel of that ye have doone for me or seide; and, Sir, I shal deserve it a yenst yow, be the grace of God, for i' feythe I am be holden to you more thane to all men that ever I founde syn I cam in preson.

No more to you at this tyme, but God have you in His kepyng.

Be your servaunt and bedman,   PERSE.

426

FRIAR BRACKLEY TO JOHN PASTON[2]

To the rite worshipful esqwyr, John Paston, be this presentid.

Jesus, Maria, Johannes Baptista. Franciscus, cum Sanctis omnibus, assistant vobis vestris in laboribus. Amen.

OCT. 24

WORSCHIPFUL and most interely bitrustid mayster and specyal frend, after dute of al lowly recomen-dacyon, ze schal conceyve that I certefye zow for trewthe. I comonyd late with a worschipful and a wele namyd, a good thrifty man of this cuntre, whiche told me in secrete wyse that he herd Doctor Aleyn seyn after the Parlement of Covintre[3] that yf the Lords that tyme reynyng and now discessid myte haf standyn in governans, that Fortesku the justise, Doctor Moreton, Jon Heydon, Thorp and he, schuld be made for evir; and yf it turnyd to contrary wyse, it schuld

[1] The Lords of the Duke of York's party.
[2] [From Fenn, iii. 386.] This letter was clearly written after the battle of Northampton in 1460, by which the state of parties at the Parliament of Coventry in 1459 was exactly reversed.

With regard to this and other letters of Dr. Brackley, the original editor, Sir John Fenn, has expressed a misgiving that he may in some instances have misread the contractions used in the Latin words. This was certainly the case in the present letter, in which misreadings have been corrected, and some passages supplied from the Ms.
[3] Held in December 1459.

242

growe to her fynal confusyon and uttyr destruccyon; for why,   1460
the parlyows [*perilous*] writing and the myschevous inditing   OCT. 24
was ymaginid, contrivid, and utterly concludid by her most vengeable labour, &c., and her most malicyows conspiracye ayens the innocent lords, knytis, gentilis, and comonys, and alle her issu perpetuel, &c. And as I wrote last to zour maystership the text of Jeremiæ c° 8° *Vere mendacium operatus est stilus mendax scribarum*; it folwith in the same place, *Confusi sunt sapientes, perterriti et capti sunt; verbum Domini projecerunt, et sapientia nulla est in eis. Propterea dabo mulieres eorum exteris; agros eorum hæredibus alienis, &c.* I wolde myn Lord Chanceler and my specyal Lord Erl, utinam Duke, of Warwyk, with al her trewe affinyte, schuld remembre this text, which is Holy Scripture, &c., as I wold do by for the Kyng and hise Lords at the Cros;[1] for the principil of this text hath be contynued in dayly experiens sithe before the Parlement of Bury;[2] but the conclusyon of this text came never zet to experiens, and that is gret rewthe. Consideret discretio vestra singulorum annorum curricula, et percipietis tunc perplurima exempla de dominorum fidelium atque com-munium morte satis injuriosa multiformiter lamentanda dis-currendo per singula, &c. Ex paucis scit discretio vestra perpendere plura, &c. Et ubi ego semel in ecclesia Pauli palam prædicavi hunc textum, *Non credas inimico tuo in æternum* (Ecc. 12°), et quidam hujus regni doctor et episcopus, utinam non indignus, asseruit eundem textum Scripturæ Sacræ non incorporatum, quid doctor Nicholaus de Lira super eundem textum dicit, contra audietis. *Non credas, &c.*, id est, Nun-quam credas ei quem probasti inimicum, &c. Sequitur in textu:—*Sicut æramentum æruginat malicia illius*, id est, rubigi-nem odii servat interius, licet contrarium ostendatur exterius. Ideo in textu sequitur:—*Etsi humiliatus vadat corvus [curvus]*, tibi magnam reverenciam exhibendo, *affirma, abice [abjice] animum tuum ab illo, nullo modo credendo ei, et custodi te ab illo. Non statuas illum penes te* (id est, ipsum tibi familiarem exhibendo); *ne conversus stet in loco suo* [should be *tuo*] te supplantando; *et in novissimo agnoscas verba mea esse vera*, sed

[1] Paul's Cross.   [2] In 1447.

243

THE PASTON LETTERS

1460
OCT. 24

nimis tarde. Sequitur : *Quis miserebitur incantatori a serpente percusso, &c. ; et qui comitatur cum viro iniquo et obvolutus est in peccatis ejus ?* Una hora tecum permanebit ; at autem declinaveris non supportabit. *In labiis suis indulcat inimicus, et in corde suo insidiatur, ut subvertat te in foveam. In oculis suis lacrimatur inimicus, et si invenerit tempus non saciabitur sanguine. Si incurrerint tibi mala* [invenies] *eum illic priorem*, &c. In finem rogo, videte textum et postillatores super eodem, ex quibus potestis plane considerare episcopum modernum aliquando Scripturam Sacram ignorare, &c. Utinam dominorum fidelium provida discrecio amicorum dileccionem sapienter sic pensaret quod inimicorum dileccionem nequaquam sic amaret, ut inimicis mortalibus confidenciam exhiberet ; quare ut prius sic replico Jesu Sirach sanum et salubre consilium, *Non credas inimico tuo in æternum*. Sapienti, non insipienti scribo. Plura habeo vestræ reverentiæ scribere quæ jam non expedit calamo commendare. Uxor Johannis Berney de Redham jam infra triduum peperit filium, &c. Magistra mea uxor vestra sana est cum filiis vestris et filiabus ac tota familia. Conventus noster inter cæteros habet statum vestrum specialissime recommendatum in missis ac orationibus, consuetisque suffragiis ; et cum jam sitis in parliamento præsenti pro milite electo, uti vobis consulo verbis Pauli Apostoli, *Labora sicut bonus miles Jesu Christi* ;[1] et alibi, Job utendo verbis, *Militia super terram est vita hominis* (Job 7). *Viriliter igitur agite et confortetur cor vestrum quia speratis in Domino* (in Psalmo).[2] *Quis*, inquit Sapiens, *speravit in Domino et confusus est, et permansit in mandatis Dei et derelictus est ?*[3] quasi diceret, nullus.

Ex Norwico feria sexta post festum Sancti Lucæ Evangelistæ.

[*Not Signed.*]

[1] 2 Tim. ii. 3.   [2] Psalm xxx. (xxxi.) 24.
[3] Eccles. ii. 11, 12 (v. 10 of our English version).

244

HENRY VI

427

MARGARET PASTON TO JOHN PASTON[1]

To my ryth welbelovyd brodyr, Clement Paston, for to delyver to hys brodyr Jon, in haste.

RYTH w[urshepfu]ll husbonde, I recomande me to yow. Plesyth yow to weet that I receyvyd a lettyr on Seynt Symondys evyn and J[w]d, that came frome Jon Paston,[2] in the wyche lettyr he wrot that ye desyryd that I scholde do Jon Paston or Thomas P[layter] looke in the gret standyng chyste in on of the gret canvas baggys whyche standyth ageyns the lokk, for the copys of the fals inqwest of ofys that was fownde in Northefolk, and for the kopy of the comyssyon that came to Jon Andrewys and Fylpot and Heydon, and othyr thyngys towchynge the same mater, I have do. Jon Paston sowte all iij. grete baggys in the seyd kofyr at ryth good leyser, and he can non swhyche fynde. Plesyth it yow to remembre ye sent me word in the fyrste lettyr that ye sent me, that ye wolde that Playter scholde asent hem up to yow to London, and I schewyd hym yowyr wryttyng howe that ye wrote to me ther in. I suppose be cawse he purposyd to come up to London hym selve hastely, he sent yow none answer ther of. Rychard Calle tolde me that alle swhyche thyngys were lefte with Hery Barbore at the Tempyle Gate when the last terme was doo, and soo I sent yow worde in a lettyr whyche was wretyn on the Twesday next aftyr Seynt Looke,[3] and ther in was an answer of all the fyrst lettyr that ye sent me. I sent itt yow by yonge Thomas Elys. I sent yow anothyr lettyr by Playter, the whyche was wretyn on Saterday[4] last past.

Item, I receyvyd a lettyr frome yow on Sonday,[5] of the

1460
OCT. 29

[1] [From Paston MSS., B.M.] The date of this letter is ascertained by the statement at the end that, on the morrow, a 'day' was to be kept at Bungay for Fastolf's lands. The inquisition on Fastolt's lands in the county of Suffolk was held at Bungay on Thursday before All Saints, 39 Henry VI., i.e. 30th October 1460.—(Inquisitions *post mortem*, 38 and 39 Hen. VI., No. 48.)
[2] The elder son of that name.
[3] See No. 423.   [4] October 25th.   [5] October 26th.

245

THE PASTON LETTERS

1460
OCT. 29

wyche I sent yow an answher of ma lettyr on Seynt Symondes Evyn and Jwde by Edmunde Clere of Stokysby ; and as sone as I hade the seyd lettyr on Sonday, I sent to Syr Thomas Howes for the mater that ye desyryd that he scholde inqwer of to Bokyng, and I sent a yene sethe to the seyd Syr Thomas for to have knowlage of the same mater yesterdaye, and I have non answher of hym yet. He sent me worde he scholde do hys part there in, but othyr answer have I none yet of hym. I sende yow in a canvase bage, inslyd by Nycolas Colman, as many of Crystofyr Hansonys acomptys as Jon Paston can fynde ther as [*where*] ye sent worde that they were. Rychard Harbard recomawndyth hym to yow, and prayth yowe that ye wole wychesave to remembre the lettyr that scholde be sent fro my Lorde of Warwyk to a man of hys beyng at Lowystofete ; and if it be not sent to hym, that it plese yow to do purvey that it may be sent to hym in haste, if it maye be, as to morow ther schall be keppyd a day at Bowunggey for Mastyr Fastolfys londys be for the exchetore, and there schall be Wylliam Barker and Rychard Call. Ye schall have knowlage in haste what schall be do ther. And the blyssyd Trinite have yow in Hys kepyng.

Wretyn in haste at Norwyche on the Wednysday next aftyr Seynt Symond and Jwde,

Be yowyr   M. P.

428

SIR GEOFFREY BOLEYN TO JOHN PASTON, ESQ.[1]

To my ryght wurschypfull Ser, John Paston, Esquyer.

1460 (?)
DEC. 5

RYGHT wurschypfull Ser, after ryzth hertely recomendacion, lyke it yow to wete that my Maister Fastolf, hoose sowle God asoyle, whan I bowth of hym the maner of Blyclyng, consideryng the gret payment that I payed

[1] [From Paston MSS., B.M.] This letter was probably written in the year 1460. It is evident some time had elapsed since Sir John Fastolf's death, but as the subject was one which the writer wished to bring early before Paston's notice, it is not likely that he allowed much more than a twelvemonth to pass by.

246

HENRY VI

therfor, and the yerly annuyte duryng his lyfe after his entent, was to me gret charge ; and the same tyme, in his place at Southwerk, by his othe made on his primer ther, grauntted and promitted to me to have the maner of Guton, with all the apportenaunce for a resonable pris afor ony other man. And, Ser, as I understande ye be that person that my seid maister, consideryng your gret wysdom, most trosted to have rewle and dyreccion of his lyfelode and goodes,—and, Ser, trewly, yf I hed ben nere unto yow, I wold have spoken to yow herof be for this tyme ; neverthelasse I wolde desyre and pray yow to schewe me yowr goode wyll and favour in this by halve, wher inne ye schall dyscharge my seid maistres sowle of his othe and promyse, and I schall do yow servyce in that I can or maye to my power. And of yowr goode wyll and favour herynne I pray yow to late me have wetyng, and I schall be redy to wayte on yow at ony tyme and place wher ye wull assyne. And owr blyssyd Lord have yow in his kepyng.—Wret the v. day of Decembre.

Be youer owyn,   GEFFREY BOLEYN.[1]

1460 (?)
DEC. 5

429

FRIAR BRACKLEY TO [JOHN PASTON][2]

JHESUS help, Marye mercy, et Franciscus cum Sanctis subveniant defuncto et suis in tribulationibus. Amen. Præcordialissime in Jhesu Christo prædilecte, et omissis pro præsenti singulis vestram amicabilem benevolentiam concernentibus, propter quasdam materias mihi a fidedignis personis nuper relatas, &c., equitetis quam cito potestis secure pro corporis vestri conservatione. Scitote quod commissionarius J.

1461 (?)
JAN. (?)

[1] The subscription and signature only are in Boleyn's hand.
[2] [Add. MS. 34,889, f. 156.] This letter has no date, except that it was written on a Friday (*feria sexta*). It might, perhaps, be a little hazardous to date it Friday the 2nd January 1461, just after news of the defeat and death of the Duke of York reached Norfolk ; but this date agrees well with the warning to John Paston to ride to London with all haste for his safety, which can hardly mean anything else than that the Lancastrian party, with their Norfolk supporters (several of whom, indeed, are expressly named here), were now sure to bear rule.

247

461(?) Heydon, vester ac meus capitalis inimicus, Philippus Wentworth
JAN. (?) et J. Andrw malignantur maxime contra vos et M. T. H.[1] et me et
alios vestros. Et magister Clemens et ego sequemur vos usque
Colcestriam, ibidem expectando donec vos aliquem nuncium de
London illuc miseritis, et tunc ad vos veniemus cum duobus
vel tribus famulis nostro proposito necessariis, R. Botilere
Matthæo Gowh vel Johanne Lore. Sumus nempe equestres
pessimi, nec ascensum equi seu descensum scientes, sed adju-
torium ad minus duorum est nobis duobus necessarium, &c.
Certe si non esset aura tam contraria, et pluvialis nimis, quare
equitare est nobis omnino necessarium ; aliter vere melius pro-
fecissem pro me in itinere per ambulare quam per equitare.
W. Y.[2] judex cum omni consilio Johanni Heidon faciet contra
vos et me et M. T. H. quicquid potest ; quare dicit Gregorius,
' Minus jacula feriunt quæ prævidentur.' Si W. P., vester
germanus, et T. Playtere, cum associatis antecederent, plura
percipere possent quæ jam non cognoscent, &c., utinam velletis
hoc instancia cordiali considerare in effectu. Notate q. .[3]
literam a me primo vobis scriptam de pigricia, &c., quanta
mala proveniunt ex illa, &c., W. Rokewode est rogatus a
W. Y. judice ut faveat sibi et Tendale contra Wyndham armigerum pro manerio de Felbrigge, cum pertinenciis, &c., et tunc
scietur utrum J. H. favebit Wyndham vel Judici, &c., cum ejus
flatus olim calidus, olimque frigidus existat, et aliquando nec
calidus nec frigidus sed satis tepidus. Sed oretis cum propheta, ' Confundantur qui me persequuntur et non confundar
ego, paveant illi et non paveam ego ; induc super eos diem
afflictionis et duplici contritione contere eos,'[4] domine Deus.
Et Psalmista ait ' Averte mala inimicis meis,et in veritate tua
disperde illos '[5] et sequentia. Et [super] inimicos meos de-
spexit oculus meus. Valete in Christo Jhesu. Scriptum
festinantissime, feria vj[a]. Recommendetis me specialissime
magistro T. H. et J. Berneye, &c.—Vester ad vota,

F. J. B.

[1] Magistrum Thomam Howys.   [2] William Yelverton.
[3] A contraction perhaps meant for *quandam* and blurred. If so, it should have
been struck out altogether ; for the words *a me primo* (which are an insertion in the
margin) make the sense definite.   [4] Jer. xvii. 18.   [5] Ps. liii. (liv.) 5.

248

430

CLEMENT PASTON TO JOHN PASTON[1]

To hys rythe worchypfwll broder, John Paston.

RYTHE reverent and worchypfwl broder, I recomawnde   1461
to yow, certyfyyng yow that yowr letter was delyveryd   JAN. 23
to me the xxiii. day of Januar abowthe none seasson,
and Rychard Calle rode in the mornyng, and therfor I brak
[*opened*] yowr letter, if ther wer any aftr mater ; and I dede
Christofer Hauswan goo to my Lord of Cawnterbure[2] to tell
him, as yowr letter rehersyd, and my Lord seyd he hadde
spokyn with yowr man ther of the day be fore, and if the
Byshop of Norwyche wod not doo so mwche for him, he hys
the les behold to him. Notwithstandyng, he sayd, he wold
save yow harmles agens John Yowng ; but and ye do well
remember thys Lord have many maters to thynge on, and if it
be forgeten, the harm is yowrs, and also if the word [*world*]
torn, John Yong will not doo at hys prayer.

And my Lord Fitzwater[3] is ryden northewards, and it is
sayd in my Lord of Cawnterberys howse that he hethe takyn
ij[c] [200] of Andrew Troloppys[4] men. And as for Colt,[5]
and Sir Jamys Strangwysse, and Sir Thomas Pykeryng, they
be takyn or ellys dede. The comyn voysse is that they
be de dede. Hopton[6] and Hastyngs[7] be with the Erle of
Marche, and wer no at the fewlde.[8] Wat word that ever he
have fro my Lords that be here, it is well doo, and best for
yow, to see that the contre be allweys redy to come bothe fote

[1] [From Fenn, i. 202.] This letter appears to have been written after the battle
of Wakefield, when the victorious army, led on by Margaret of Anjou, was marching
southwards.   [2] Archbishop Bourchier.
[3] Sir John Radcliff of Attleborough, styled Lord Fitzwalter in right of his wife,
only daughter and heiress of Walter Fitzwalter, seventh lord. This John was at the
battle of Ferrybridge on the 29th March 1461, and died, probably of his wounds, on
the 6th April following.—*See* G. E. C.'s *Complete Peerage.*
[4] Andrew Trollope, whose desertion of the Duke of York at Ludlow in 1459 caused
the dispersion of the Yorkist leaders. He was killed at the battle of Towton in
March 1461, fighting on the Lancastrian side.
[5] Thomas Colt.—See *Rolls of Parliament*, v. 348.
[6] Walter Hopton.—See *Rolls of Parliament*, v. 368.
[7] William, son of Sir Leonard Hastings.—See *Rolls of Parliament, ib.*
[8] The battle of Wakefield.

249

1461   men and hors men, qwen they be sent for ; for I have herd seyde
JAN. 23   the ferthere Lords will be here soner that men wen, I have
arde sayde, er iij. weks to an ende ; and also that ye xwld come
with more men, and clenlier arayed than anoder man of yowr
cwntre xwld, for it ly the more up on yowr worchyp, and
towcheythe yow more nere than odermen of that cwntre, and
also ye be mor had in favor with my Lords here. In this cwntre
every man is well wyllyng to goo with my Lords here, and I hope
God xall helpe hem, for the pepill in the northe robbe and styll,
and ben apoyntyd to pill all thys cwntre, and gyffe a way
menys goods and lufflods in all the sowthe cwntre, and that
wyll ask a myscheffe. My Lords that ben here have as moche
as they may do to kep down all thys cwntre more than iiij. or v.
schers, for they wold be up on the men in northe, for it ys for
the welle of all the sowthe.

I pray yow recomawnde me to my moder, and that I prayed
her of her blyssyng. I pray yow exscwse me to her that I
wryte her no letter, for thys was y now a doo. I dare not
pray yow to recomawnde me to my swster yowr wyff, and the
masenger I trow be so wysse he can not doyt. Ye mwst pay
him for hys labor, for he taryd all nyt in thys town for thys
letter.

Wrytyn the xxiij. day of Janware in haste, wan I was not
well at hesse. God have [you] in Hys keping.

By CLEMENT PASTON,   Yowr broder.

431

THE PRIOR OF BROMHOLM TO JOHN PASTON[1]

Amicabili magistro nostro, Johanni Paston, armigero.

JAN. 31   FUL reverent and worshipful, after all dewe reverence
and recommendacion, your pore Preste besecheth
humble it plese your good maystirship to understande
be this simple bylle that on the Friday next after the Feste of

[1] [From Fenn, iii. 404.] As executor to Sir John Fastolf, Paston must have
taken possession of Caister soon after his death. The Duke of Norfolk, however,
pretended a title to it, and, as we shall find hereafter, had dispossessed Paston by June

250

the Conversion of Seynt Poule laste paste I was at your place   1461
at Castre to a tolde yow what answer I hadde of Sir Thomas   JAN. 31
Howis, parson of Blofeld ; and in as moche as ye wer not at
hoom, I tolde it to my mastras your wyfe ; and God thanke
her of her jentilnes, she made yow grete cher, and mor over a
vysed me to sende yow a bille ther of to Lundon. This was
his answer, whan I had talked to hym as I cowde in lyke wyse
as ye averted me to do. He answered a geyn in these wordes,
' Nere is my kyrtyl, but nerre [*nearer*] is my smok.' And this
was his menyng that ye schulde be mor ner us and tender to
us than he, and that ye schulde rather owe us good wyl than
he, and that we schulde labour rather to yowr maystirship than
to hym ; and also that good that he had to dispose he had be
sette it, and of passel he tolde me he had delyvered the Abbot
of Langele fourescor li., wher of, as he seyd to me, ye grutched
and wer in maner displesed, not withstandyng ye seyd a geyn
to hym ye shulde geve as moche. And he seyd to me ye
named the places wher ; and therfor he avysed me to labour
effectualy to your good maystirship, for ye mych [*might*] helpe
us[1] wele. For he seyd ye had moche good of the dede to
dispose, what of your fader, God blisse that sowle, what of
Berney, and what now of his good Mayster Fastolfe. And as
for Sir John Fastolfe, on hoose soule Jesu have mercy ! he seyd
to me ye had of his good four, four, and four mor than he in
these same termes with owte ony summe.

And after all oder talkyngs he tolde me he shulde be with
yow at Lundon hastyly, and that he wolde sey good worde to
yow to releve our poor place. Sir, I beseche bethe not displesed, for truly and I woste to have your hevy maystership
therfor, I had lever it had bene on thoght. And is this that
whan Sir Thomas Howes and ye be saunne at Lundon, we
myght be so in your good grace, that our place myght be
broder to Langele, for that shulde glade us mor than the commission that the Bysshop of Norwich sente us on Thrusday

1461. This letter, dated on Saturday after the Feast of the Conversion of St. Paul,
must therefore have been written in January 1461, as in 1460—the only other probable
year—that feast (25th January) fell on Friday, and a letter written on Saturday after
the feast would not have referred to the Friday after the same feast as a past date.
[1] *us.* The word is *no* in Fenn's literal copy, which must be a misprint.

251

THE PASTON LETTERS

1461
JAN. 31

laste paste to gader the dymes, for that is a shrewde labour for us, a grete coste and a shrewe juparde.

Over mor that hy and myghty celestial Prince preserve yow body and sowle, and sende yow coumforte of the Holy Goost wele to performe all your hertis desir in all your materes to his plesaunce, and your wurship, and solace to alle your welle wyllers.

Wretyn at Bromholm, on the Saturday next after the Feste of the Conversion of Seynt Poule laste paste.

From your Preste and Bedeman,
JOHN, PRIOUR OF BROMHOLM.

432

MARGARET PASTON TO JOHN PASTON[1]

A Lettre to J. Paston, ar., from his wife.[2]

MARCH 1

PLEASE it you to wytte that it is lete me witte by on that owith you good wyll that there is leid awayte up on you in this cuntre, yf ye come here at large, to bryng you to the presence of syyche a Lord in the north as shall not be for your ease, but to jopardie of your lyf, or gret and importable losse of your goods. And he that hath take up on hym this enterprise now was undr-shireff to G. Sayntlowe. He hath gret favour herto by the meanes of the sone of William Baxter that lyth beryed in the Grey Freres; and, as it is reported, the seid sone hath geve gret sylver to the Lords in the north to bryng the matier a bowte, and now he and alle his olde felaweship put owt their fynnes,

[1] [From Fenn, iii. 412.] 'This letter,' says Fenn, 'has no direction, and lest it should be opened, the paper which fastens the seal is, along the edge, marked with lines by a pen, which communicate with the latter (*qu.* with the *letter*?), by which means the receiver might easily have discovered any attempts to have opened it, as the lines would not then have exactly coincided again. On the back of it, but in a later hand, is written, "A lettre to J. Paston, ar., from his wife."'

Fenn considers, I think with great probability, that this letter was written 'just before the important crisis that finished Henry's reign, and placed Edward on the throne,' when Margaret of Anjou was expected in London after winning the second battle of St. Albans. Giles Saint Loe was sheriff of Norfolk and Suffolk in 1458.

[2] This title is taken from an endorsement in a later hand.

252

and arn ryght flygge and mery, hopyng alle thyng is and shalbe as they wole have it. Also it is tolde me that the fadr of the bastard in this cuntre seid that now shuld this shire be made sewir for hym and his heires hens forward, and for the Baxsteris heyres also, wherby I conceyve they thynke that they have none enemy but you, &c.

1461
MARCH 1

Wherfor like it you to be the more war of your gydyng for your persones saufgard, and also that ye be not to hasty to come in to this cuntre til ye here the world more sewer. I trowe the berar of this shall telle more by mowthe, as he shall be enformed of the rewell in this cuntre. God have yow in His kepyng.

Wretyn in hast, the secund Sunday of Lent by candel light at evyn.

By yours, &c.   M.

433

JOHN DAVY TO JOHN PASTON[1]

On to my Maystyr Pastone, be this lettre delyveryd.

RYTH wurchopful Sere, I recomaund me on to you. And iff it lyke you I have spokyn with Bussard, and demaundyd hym iff he had ony evydens, dedys, or copyis, or ony other evydens of ony place or off ony lyflod that longget on to my mayster,[2] and seyth, Nay, be is feyth, and be is trowthe, for, if he hadde, he wold send hem on to you with a good wyl; for he seyth it xud don hym non ese. And, Ser, iff it plese you I askyd hym if he knew ony evydens that he had delyveryd on to William Wossetyr, bill, or deds, or ony other evydens that xuld longgyn on to ony purchas or off ony lyfflod on to my maystrys, and he seyth, Nay trewly; for he seyth the last tyme that he wrot on to William Wusseter,

[1] [From Fenn, iv. 78.] This letter was written some time after the death of Sir John Fastolf—not unlikely, as Fenn imagines, in the reign of Edward IV.; but the exact date is immaterial.
[2] Sir John Fastolf.

253

THE PASTON LETTERS

it was be ffor myssomyr, and thanne he wrot a cronekyl of Jerewsalem, and the jornes that my mayster dede whyl he was in Fraunce (that God on his sowle have mercy!); and he seyth that this drow more than xx. whazerys [20 *quires*?] off paper, and the wrytyng delyveryd on to William Wursseter, and non other, ne knowyth not off non other be is feyth.

Be your man,   J. DAVY.

434

THOMAS SHOTBOLT TO JOHN PASTON[1]

To my worshipfull maister, Maister Paston of the Temple.

WORSHIPFULL Sir, soo ye will send a polletik person to Ludgate in secrete wise to comune with me, and lete hym not in no wise speke of you to hove (?) youre good maistership, and a resonable remedy shall ease you of a gret part that the criour cleymeth of you for Maister Fastolffs detts of xiij. or xiiij. yere at the lest, and be that perave[ntu]re of the hole *qui in uno est reus morbus [in omnibus] reus* . . . . . . Sir, remembreth your worship if y doo to ease you, lete me not be discoveryd, for ye knewe not your worship y wold not doo thus. What ever ye have of me, ye may sey it is found in the stywardes boks, and y know that ye have desired favour to have hym seese for your worship that procur hym ageyns you; whoo so shall kom to me, he may kom in Maistre Nevills name, for with hym have y a doo. As for your own servaunts, y ferd me lest they be knowyn whethir it be servaunt or othir, send knowleche of my reword and a bille under your seall or your own hands, or bothe on your worship to have it close that y be not blamyd for that; y shall telle you her after. Wretyn in Ludgate.

Your servaunt and there prisoner,
THOMAS SHOTBOLT.

[1] [From Paston MSS., B.M.] Beyond the evident fact that this letter was written between the death of Sir John Fastolf in 1459 and that of John Paston in 1466, there is not much clue to the date.

254

435

MARGARET PASTON TO JOHN PASTON[1]

To my ryth worcepful husbonde, John Paston.

RYTH reverent and worcepfful husbonde, I recomande me to yow, desyryng hertely to here of yowre welle fare, thankyn yow for yowr letter and for the thyngys that ye sent me ther with. And towchyn John Estegate, he com nowdyr non sent hedyr nowt zyt; wer for I sopose I must borrowyn money in schorte time but zyf [*unless*] ye come sone home; for I sopose I xal non have of hym, so Godd helpe me. I have but iiijs. and I howhe nerr as meche mony as com to the for seyd some. I have do yowr herrendys to my modyr and my hunckyl and as for the feffeys of Stokysby, my hunckyll syth that ther be no mo than he wrot to yow of that he knowit. And also I hauwe delyvyrit the todyr thyng that ye sent me inselyd in the boxe as ye comaundit me, and the man seyt, that I delyverid it to, that he wylle nowt of the bargeyne that ye sent hym, but sweche thynggys be do or he come ther that ye sent hym worde of, he seyth that he wold nowt be noysyd with no sweche thyngis of that is, that it wer do in hesse tyme for xx. marke. I sopose he xal send yow word in shorte time ho he wylle do. I pray yow that ye wylle weche save to beyn for me swech lacys os I send yow exsaumpyll of in this letter and j. pesse of blac lacys; as for cappys that ye sent me for the chylderyn they be to lytyl for hem. I pray yow bey hem feyner cappys and larger than tho wer. Also I pray yow that ye wylle weche save to recomaunde me to my fadyr and my modyr and tellyth heer that alle herr chyldyrryn ben in gode hele, blyssyd be Godd. Heydonis wyffe had chyld on Sent Petyr day. I horde seyne that herr husband wylle nowt of her, nerr of her chyld that sche had last nowdyr. I herd seyn that he seyd,

Year
uncer-
tain

[1] [Add. MS. 34,889, f. 199.] The date of this letter is not clear, and we place it at the end of Henry VI.'s reign. It is probably much earlier.

255

THE PASTON LETTERS

Year uncer- tain

zyf sche come in hesse precence to make her exkewce that he xuld kyt of her nose to makyn her be know wat sche is ; and yf her chyld come in hesse presence, he seyd he wyld kyllyn he wolle nowt be intretit to have her ayun in no wysse, os I herde seyn. The Holy Trinite have yow in Hesse kepyn and send yow helth. Wretyn at Geldiston on the Wedynisday nexte after Sent Thomas.—Be yowris,   M. PASTON.

436

A WHITSUNDAY SERMON OF FRIAR BRACKLEY[1]

FRENDS, this holy tyme, as owr moder Holy Chirch maketh mension, the Holy Gost came from hevyn, and lighted in the disciples of Crist, inflamyng them with connyng, and strenghyng them with grace. And be cause the doctrine and prechyng of them shuld go thurgh-ought all the werd, furst thei wer to be enfourmed and taught connyng, and to be strenth with awdacide and grace, and than to be endewed and yovyn all manner of langags that thei myght prechyn to all maner of naciones, so that tho naciones that thei preched to myght understond them, and every naciones his owyn tonge ; and so thees Appostilles, after that thei wern enspired with the Holy Gost, wher so ever thei preached, were ther never so many naciones present, ich nacion thought that thei spokyn in ther owyn langage—etenim illud loquebantur variis linguis Apostoli.

Frends, iij. thyngs be necessary in prechyng to hym that shall prechyn thurgh the werd as the Appostell dede—that is to sey, connyng, boldnesse, and langags. If thei had had connyng and none audacite, but have fered to have preched, it shuld litill a profited, as we have exampiles dayly at Cam-brige, exempli [gratia][2] de Clerico quis studuit sermonem,

---
[1] [From Fenn, iii. 392.] The original ms. of this sermon was endorsed, of course in a much later hand than the document, 'An ancient Whitsunday sermon preached by Frier Brackley (whose hand it is) in the Friers Minors Church, in Norwich.' Of this and the remaining papers of Henry VI.'s time the dates are very uncertain.   [2] Omitted in Fenn's literal transcript.

256

HENRY VI

&c. And if thei have bothyn connyng and audacite, and have none eloquensye ner copiousnesse of langage, so that he preche that his audiens is most excercised in, that thei may understand hym, elles it profiteth not.

Therfor thes holy Appostill[es], be for thei shuld prechyn, furst thei wer to be confirmed and strenghed. Our Lord strenghed them be under nemyng,[1] enformyng, and helpyng, culpando ut in Evangelium recumbentibus, &c. He strenghed them with his help and grace whan he brethed in them, seyng 'Accipite Spiritum Sanctum ; et quorum remiseritis peccata, remittuntur eis, et quorum retinueritis retenta sunt,'[2] &c. He strenghed them also be his doctrine whan he seid 'Petite et accipietis ; si quid petieritis Patrem in nomine meo, dabit vobis.'[3] How that ye shuld prayn to God and askyn, I taught you on Estern day. Therfor ye shall pray to God be good werkyng, right full lebyring, and in good deds perseveryng.

Frends, ye owe for to ask of God that your joy may ben a full joy and perfight ; we may never have a full joy in this werd, wher as ever among folwyth hevynesse. A man joyth sumtyme in gold and sylver, and in gret substaunce of erdly gods, in bewte of women, but this joy is not perfyght—but this joy is not stabill, but it is mutabill as a shadow ; for he that this joyth in the bewte of his wyffe, it may fortune to morwyn he shall folwyn her to chirch up on a bere. But if ye wull knowyn what is a full and a wery joy, truly forgeve-nesse of synne and everlestyng blisse, wher as is never sike-nesse, hunger, ner thurst, ner no maner of disseas, but all welth, joy, and prosperite, &c. Ther be iij. maner of joys, the on void, a nother half full, the thred is a full joy. The furst is plente of werdly gods, the seconde is Gostly grace, the threde is everlestyng blisse. The furst joy, that is affluens of tem-porall gods, is called a veyn joy, for if a man wer set at a bord with delicate mets and drynks, and he sey a cawdron boyllyng a forn hym with pykke and bronston, in the which he shuld be throwyn naked as sone as he had dyned ; for he shuld joy mych in his deliciose mets, it shuld be but a veyn joy.

Right so doth the joy of a covetouse man, if he sey what

---
[1] i.e. reproving.   [2] John xx. 22, 23.   [3] John xvi. 23, 24.
VOL. III.—R   257

THE PASTON LETTERS

peyn his sowle shuld suffre in helle for the myskepyn and getyn of his good, he shuld not joy in his tresore, ut in Libro Decalogorum, 'Quidam homo dives,' &c.

Semiplenum gaudium est quando quis in præsenti gaudet et tunc cogitans de futuris dolet, ut in quodam libro Græco, 'Quidam Rex Græciæ,' &c. Her ye may se but half a joy ; how [who] shuld joy in this werd, if he remembred hym of the peynes of the toder werd ? 'Non glorietur fortis in fortitu-dine sua, nec sapiens in sapientia sua, nec dives in divitiis suis.'[1] De quibus dicitur, qui confidunt in multitudine diviti-arum suarum, quasi oves in inferno positi sunt.[2] 'Qui glori-atur, in Domino glorietur.'[3] Therfor lete us joy in hope of everlestyng joy and blis. 'Gaudete quia nomina vestra scripta sunt in cælo,'[4] ut gaudium vestrum sit plenum. A full joy is in hevyn. Et in hoc apparet quod magnum gaudium est in cælo, quoniam ibi est gaudium quod 'oculus non vidit, nec auris audivit, et in cor hominis non ascendit, quæ Deus præ-paravit diligentibus,'[5] et ideo, fratres, variis linguis loquens [precor] ut gaudium vestrum sit plenum, vel habeatis gaudium sempiternum.

437

THE EARL OF OXFORD TO JOHN PASTON[6]

To owre right Trusty and welbeloved John Paston

RIGHT Trusty and welbeloved we grete yow well. And where as it is not unknowen to you that we wrot a bille to Maister Brakle, and yaf hym in comaunde-ment to delyver yow a bille indentyd of x. mark owyng to John of Fen, as it apperith by a bille indentyd under the seall of Robert Reppis, jentylman, wich by the will of John of Fen is due un to us, wher of the sayd Robert shuld paye v. mark by his owne instaunce at Lammesse next comyng ; We pray

---
[1] Jer. ix. 23.   [2] Psalm xlviii. (xlix.) 6, 14.
[3] 1 Cor. i. 31.   [4] Luke x. 20.
[5] 1 Cor. ii. 9.   [6] [Add. MS. 34,888, f. 166.]
258

HENRY VI

yow that ye woll receyve the forsayd money for us and delyver it un to Maister Brakle as we trust yow. Wretyn in owr manor of Wevenho the xxv[th] day of Julij.

438

THE EARL OF OXFORD TO JOHN PASTON[1]

To my right trusty and right welbeloved John Paston.

Right trusty and right welbeloved, I grete yow wele. And I am enformed that William Mathew of Norwich, Bocher, hath brought an accion of dette agayn Nicholas Hert, a tenaunt of myn, berer hereof, and hath supposid by his accyon that my said tenaunt shuld ow hym lxxx. for his hire of tyme that he shuld a ben servaunt to my said tenaunt ; wher it is said to me for trouthe that he was aprentyce to my said tenaunt, and never othrwise with holde but as aprentice, and owith no mony to haf of hym. I send to yow my said tenaunt to gif yow clere informacyon of the mater, and I pray you that ye wole calle the jurry before yow that arn impanellid betwen thaym, and opne thaym the mater at large at myn instaunce, and desire thaym to do as concyens wole, and to eschue perjury. And the Trinite kepe yow. If ye take the mater in rule, I pray therof, and wole be content.

Wretyn at Wevenho, the xxviij. day of Decembr.

THE ERLE OF OXENFORD.

439

SIR JOHN WINGFIELD TO JOHN PASTON[2]

To my welbelovyd brother, John Paston, Squier.

Brother Paston, I recomaunde me unto you, praying you that ye take the labour to speke with Thomas Ratclef of Frammesden for the delyveraunce of part of an hous which lythe in his wode at Fraumesden, which hous the owener hath caryed part therof to Orford, which so departed, the remenant that remayneth ther in his wode schall do hym lytell good, and yt schall hurte gretly the warkeman and the owener therof also, which is my tenaunt, and [i.e. if] the hous schuld be set upon my ground.

I wright unto you in this halfe, be cause I understond he woll be moche avised by you, and yf he do ony thynge at my request, I schall do as moche that schall plese hym ; and also the pore man schall gef hym ij. nobles or xxs. rather than fayle. I pray you be as good a mene for hym as ye may in this be halfe, as my verry trust is in you, and I schal be redy at all tymes to doot that

---
[1] [From Fenn, iii. 138.]   [2] [From Fenn, iii. 140.]
259

may be to your plesur. I trust to Jesu, who have you in His kepyng, and sende you joy of all your ladyes.

Wretyn at Lederyngham, the Tewesday in Whisson weke.

Your brother and frende,
WYNGEFELD J.

440

[JOHN PASTON ?] TO [RICHARD] SOUTHWELL [1]

BROTHER Suthwell, I comand me to yow, sertifiing yow that, on Thursday be the morwe, I spak with my cosine Wichingham at London, where he lete me wet of the letter sent to Lee, wherby I conseyve the stedfast godlordship and ladiship of my Lord and my Lady [2] in this mater, &c., whech gevith cause to all her servaunts to trost verily in them and to do hem trew servise. I lete yow wete that the seid Wychyngham, when I departid from hym, had knowleche that Jane Boys shuld that nyght be come to London, and he put in a bylle to the Lordis for to have delyverauns of hyr and to have hese adversarys arestid. And this nyght at Norwiche was told me newe tydyngges that she shuld on Thursday after my departyng a be before the Lordis and there asaide untrewly of her selff, as the berer hereof shal informe yow if ye know it not before ; of wheche tydyngges, if they be trew, I am sory for her sake, and also I fere that her frendys schuld sewe the more feyntely, wheche Godde defende. For her seyng untrewly of her selff may hurt the mater in no man but her selff ; and thow she wol mescheve her selff, it wer gret pete but if the mater were laborid forth, not for her sake, but for the worchepe of the estatys and

[1] [From Paston MSS., B.M.] This letter is printed from a corrected draft in a hand which may be that of Margaret Paston, writing in her husband's name. The beginning may perhaps refer to the impending marriage of Richard Southwell with Amy, daughter of Sir Edmund Wichingham, which took place, according to Blomefield (x. 274), about the beginning of Edward IV.'s reign. From the mention made of Osbert Mundford, however, the letter cannot be later than 1460. The ravishment of Jane Boys, as here related, corresponds so closely with that of Dame Joan Beaumont, of which notice will be found in the *Rolls of Parl.*, v. 269, that we might almost surmise the same person is spoken of ; but this can hardly be.

[2] Probably the Duke and Duchess of Norfolk.

other that have laboryd therin, and in ponyshing of the gret oryble dede. Wherfore I send yow dyvers articlis in a bill closid herin, wheche preve that she was raveshid ayens hyr wel, what so ever she sey.

Thes be provis that Jane Boys was ravischig [*sic*] ageyn her wil, and not ber awn assent.

One is that she, the tyme of her takyng, whan she was set upon her hors, she revyled Lancasterother [1] and callid hym knave and wept, and kryid owte upon hym pitewly to her, and seid as shrewdly to hym as coud come to her mende, and fel doune of her hors unto that she was bound, and callid him fals t[r]aytor that browth her the rabbettes.

Item, whan she was bounde she callid upon her modyer, wheche folwyd her as far as she myght on her feet, and whan the seid Jane sey she myght goo no ferther, she kryid to her modyer and seid that what so ever fel of her, she shuld never be weddyd to that knave, to deye for it.

Item, be the weye, at Shraggarys hous in Kokely Cley, and at Brychehamwell, and in all other places wher she myght see any people, she kryid owte upon hym, and lete people wete whos dowtyr she was, and how she was raveshid ayens her wyll, desyeryng the people to folwe her and reskew her.

Item, Lancasterotherys prest of the Egle in Lyncolne shire, wheche shroff her, seid that she told hym in confession that she wold never be weddyd to hym, to deye for it ; and the same prest seid he wold not wedde hem togedyr for M[l] *li*.

Item, she sent divers tokenes of massage to Sothwell be Robert Inglose, wheche previth welle at that tyme she lovyd not Lancasterother.

Item, a man of the master of Carbrokes come dyvers tymes in the weke before she was raveshid to Wychynghams hous, and inquerid of her mayde whedyr her mastras was insuerid to Sothwell or nay, the wheche prevyth well that Lancasterother was not suere of her godwill ne knew not of her

[1] According to Blomefield (viii. 299) Joan (or Jàne), one of the four daughters of Edmund de Wichingham, married, first, Robert Longstrather, and afterwards Robert Boys of Honing, in Norfolk.

counseyl, for if he had, he ne nedid not to have sent no spyes.

Whech seen, I avyse yow to move my Lord and my Lady to do in this mater as affettualy as they have do before, for this mater touchyth hem, consideryng that they have begonne ; and dowt not, what so ever falle of the woman, well or evel, my Lord and my Lady shal have worchep of the mater if it be wel laborid, and also ye shall have avayl therof and the advers parte chall gret trobil.

Also it were necessarie that Wychyngham were sent to and cofortyd in hese seute, and that he avysid hym of seche articlis and preves of the mater as I have sent to yow and put hem in writing, but not to disclose non tho preves to non creature unto that tyme that it fortune the mater to be tried be enquest, or other wyse take end, but avyse hym for to seye to the Lords and all (?) in generall termes that what so ever Lancasterother or hese douter seyn nowh, it shal be wel prevyd she was reveshid ayens her wyll ; and let him desire of the Lordis that hir dowter mith be in his kepyng, and at large fro Lancasterother un tylle the mater were duly examynd. I wold this mater sped the bety[r] be cause my Lady spoke so feythefully to me therin, and that mevyth me to wryte to yow this long symple lettyr of myn intent. [1] [Also wher ye be informyd that vj. men of Osbern Monforthes shuld a be at the seid raveshing, I certifie yow verily it was not soo ; for Osbern Mondeford wol do in the mater all that ever he can or may to help to punisse the doer, and desirith to know the grownd of that tale, of whech I pray send me word if and what ye will ellis.] God kepe yow.

Wret at Norwich the Soneday nex before the fest of Sent Margret.

Item, [if] she had be of hes assent affter the time she was in hes possescion in Lynkoln shire, hit had be bett—[2]

[1] This passage is crossed out in the MS.
[2] Sentence left incomplete.

441–448

ABSTRACTS [1]

The following letters and papers cannot be referred to any certain date, though probably of the reign of Henry VI. Being of very little interest, they are noticed as briefly as possible merely for the sake of completeness.

441.—W., Bishop of Norwich, to William Yelverton, steward of his lands, and John Intwode, his surveyor.—Desires them to inquire at Bacton into the demand made by Richard Blake in a bill enclosed, and minister to him as right and law will.—London, 8 Nov.

442.—Memoranda of John Berney against Simon Corbrygg, who obtained lands by a charter forged by Broke, a scrivener, late owner of Weggs, and has injured Berney for eight years past or more in the possession of the manor of Cleyhall.

443.—William Jenney to John Paston, Esq.—Has been shown by his neighbour, Robert Tylyard, a piece of evidence of certain 'lyfelode' he has in Whetacre, by which it appears that Lord Wellys should have no ward of the same, unless he can produce contrary evidence. As Paston is of my Lord's council, and has the rule of his 'lyflode' in this country, desires he will write to him that the matter be indifferently seen.—Theberton, 13 Dec.

444.—J. Burton to Margaret Paston.—Sends hogsheads of wine by Plumton the carter, etc. Desires her to send the money to 'dawn' William Dallyng.—Dated, 'Wednesday after I parted from you.'

445.—W. Cotyng [2] to Margaret Paston.—Has received to-day £9:0:2 from Simon Miller, her farmer at Tichwell, for Midsummer payment. Sends it by Roger, servant of the Parson of Thorp. Simon has paid five shillings for finding a man to the King for Tichwell, and but for me you would have paid a mark. Charges for repairs. As for your lining cloth, my brother is still beyond the sea.—Brankaster, 31 July.

[1] [From Paston MSS., B.M.]
[2] He was rector of Swainsthorp, to which he was presented by William Paston and John Dam in 1444, and which he exchanged for the living of Tichwell in 1450. —Blomefield, v. 63.

THE PASTON LETTERS

446.—— to ——.—My father and I bought the reversion of Olton, etc., of Ralph Lampet and Alexander Kyngyston. They have now made a new sale of it to William Jenney without giving notice to me or my father. We ask your mediation with Jenney, whom we trusted most.

447.—Eliz. C[lere] to John Paston.—Concerning a pasture in the town of N. overgrown with whins. Wants advice as to the conditions of the right of pasturage. Your mother prays you to think on Horwellebery.—25 May.

448.—Memoranda to inquire :—(1) If William Cofe were enfeoffed in Rothnall Hall? (2) If Tylerd knew William Cofe of Northcofe[1] before the day of his death two years, one year, half a year, or a quarter, etc.; what seal he used? (3) If Tylerd were not about him, to common with Gernyngham and such as were about him. (4) Item, in case it can be understood that he made none estate, ' than lete Wodesyde goo to Robert Prymer in his owyn name, saying that John P. (Paston) is his good mayster in hys mater,' etc.

1 William Cove of North Cove, Suffolk.—*See* Suckling's *Hist. of Suffolk*, i. 48.

THE PASTON LETTERS

Edward IV

449

JOHN PASTON THE YOUNGEST TO ——[1]

I RECOMAND me to yow, and lete yow wete that not-wythstandyng tydinggs come down, as ye know, that pepill shuld not come up tyll thei were sent fore, but to be redy at all tymes ; this notwithstandyng, most pepill owt of this cuntre have take wages, seying thei woll goo up to London ; but thei have no capteyn, ner rewler assigned be the commissioners to awayte upon, and so thei stragyll abowte be them self, and be lyklynes are not like to come at London half of them. And men that come from London sey, there have not passid Thetford, not passyng CCCC. ; and yet the townes and the cuntere that have waged hem shall thynk thei be discharged, and therfore if this Lords above wayte aftyr more pepill in this cuntre, be lyklynes it woll not be easy to get with owt a newe comission and warnyng. And yet it woll be thought ryght straunge of hem that have waged pepill to wage any more, for every towne hath waged and sent firth, and are redy to send forth, as many as thei ded when the

1461

1 [From Fenn, i. 226.] According to Fenn, this letter is in the original ' without either date, name, or direction,' the contents only proving it to have been written by ' one of John Paston's sons.' Nevertheless, in a very misleading way, the signature ' John Paston ' is inserted at the foot of the right-hand copy, with a reference to a facsimile of the signature of John Paston the youngest. There is every appearance, however, that John Paston the youngest really was the writer, and that the date is, as Fenn supposes, just after the accession of Edward IV.

THE PASTON LETTERS

1461 Kyng sent for hem be fore the feld at Lodlowe ;[1] and thei that ar not go, be goyng in the same forme.

Item, ther was shrewd rewle toward in this cuntre, for ther was a certeyn person forth wyth after the jurney at Wakefeld, gadered felaship to have mo[r]dered John Damme, as is seyd ; and also ther is at the Castell of Rysyng, and in other ij. plases, made gret gaderyng of pepill, and hyrryng of harneys, and it is wele undyrstand they be not to the Kyng ward, but rather the contrary, and for to robbe. Wherfore my fadyr is in a dowte, whedir he shall send my brother up or not, for he wold have his owne men abowte hym, if nede were here ; but not-wythstandyng, he wyll send up Dawbeney, hys spere and bowes with hym, as Stapilton and Calthrop or other men of worship of this cuntre agree to doo. Wherfore demene yow in doyng of yowr erandes ther aftyr, and if ye shall bryng any masage from the Lords, take writyng, for Darcorts massage is not verely beleved be cause he browt no wrytyng.

Item, this cuntre wold fayne take these fals shrewes that are of an oppynion contrary to the Kyng and his Counsell, if they had no auctorite from the Kyng to do so.

Item, my brother is redy[n] to Yarmowth for to lette brybers that wold a robbed a ship undyr color of my Lord of Warwyk, and longe nothyng to hem ward.

450

W. PASTON AND THOMAS PLAYTERS TO JOHN PASTON[2]

To my maister, John Paston, in hast.

APRIL 4 PLEASE you to knowe and wete of suche tydyngs as my Lady of York hath by a lettre of credens, under the signe manuel of oure Soverayn Lord King Edward, whiche lettre cam un to oure sayd Lady this same day, Esterne

1 The battle of Mortimer's Cross, near Ludlow, gained by Edward IV. before he was king, on the 3rd February 1461.
2 [From Fenn, i. 216.] The date of this letter is sufficiently apparent from the contents.

EDWARD IV

Evyn,[1] at xj. clok, and was sene and red by me, William Paston.

1461
APRIL 4

Fyrst, oure Soverayn Lord hath wonne the feld,[2] and uppon the Munday[3] next after Palmesunday, he was resseved in to York with gret solempnyte and processyons. And the Mair and Comons of the said cite mad ther menys to have grace be Lord Montagu[4] and Lord Barenars,[5] whiche be for the Kyngs coming in to the said cite desyred hym of grace for the said cite, whiche graunted hem grace. On the Kyngs parte is slayn Lord Fitz Water, and Lord Scrop sore hurt ; John Stafford, Horne of Kent ben ded ; and Umfrey Stafford, William Hastyngs mad knyghts with other ; Blont is knygth, &c.

Un the contrary part is ded Lord Clyfford, Lord Nevyle, Lord Welles, Lord Wyllouby, Antony Lord Scales, Lord Harry, and be supposyng the Erle of Northumberland, Andrew Trollop, with many other gentyll and comons to the nomber of xx.^{mi.} [20,000].

Item, Kyng Harry, the Qwen, the Prince, Duke of Somerset, Duke of Exeter, Lord Roos, be fledde in to Scotteland, and they be chased and folwed, &c. We send no er [*no sooner*] un to you be cause we had non certynges tyl now ; for un to this day London was as sory cite as myght. And because Spordauns had no certeyn tydyngs, we thought ye schuld take them a worthe tyl more certayn.

Item, Thorp Waterfeld is yeldyn, as Spordauns can telle you. And Jesu spede you. We pray you that this tydyngs my moder may knowe.

Be your Broder,   W. PASTON.
                    T. PLAYTERS.

' On a piece of paper pinned to the above letter,' says Fenn, ' is a list of the

1 4th April.
2 The battle of Towton, fought on Palm Sunday, the 29th March 1461.
3 30th March.
4 John Nevill, Lord Montague, brother of the Earl of Warwick.
5 Sir John Bourchier, Lord Berners.

THE PASTON LETTERS

names of the noblemen and knights, and the number of soldiers slain at the above battle of Towton, as follow :—'

Comes Northumbriæ.	Millites.
Comes Devon.	Sir Rauff Gray.
Dominus de Beamunde.	Sir Ric. Jeney.
Dominus de Clifford.	Sir Harry Bekingham.
Dominus de Nevyll.	Sir Andrew Trollop.
Dominus de Dacre.	With xxviij.ml. [28,000]
⌠Dominus Henricus de	nomberd by Harralds.
⌡ Bokyngham.	
Dominus de Well[es].	
⌠Dominus de Scales	
⌡ Antony Revers.	
Dominus de Wellugby.	
⌠Dominus de Malley	
⌡ Radulfus Bigot Miles.	

451

THOMAS PLAYTERS TO MASTER JOHN PASTON[1]

To my maister, John Paston, Esquyer.

PLEASE your Maisterchep to wete, that I have spokyn with Essex, in the matter that ye wete of, and fynd him be his talkyng wel dysposed, not withstandyng he woll not falle to no conclusyon to engrose up the mater, tyll the chef baron[2] be com to London, and that he be maad privy to the mater, which we loke after this same secund Saterday[3] after Esterne ; and as for Notyngham he is not yet comyn to London.

Item, as for tydyng, it is noysed and told for trouth of men of worchip, and other, that the Erle of Wylchyr is taken,

---

[1] [From Fenn, i. 222.] This letter relates mainly to occurrences just after the battle of Towton in April 1461.
[2] Peter Arderne.   [3] 18th April in 1461.

268

THE PASTON LETTERS

452

THOMAS PLAYTERS TO JOHN PASTON[1]

To my rigth reverent and worchipfull John Paston, Esquyer, or to my maytres his wyf.

AFTER my most special recommendacion, lyke your maisterchip wete that the mater for you and my maistrez, your moder, ayens Powtrell and Tanfeld hath ben called upon as dylygently and as hastely this terme as it mygth be ; and al way dayes yeven hem by the Court to answer, and than thei toke smale excepcions, and trifeled forth the Court, and al wey excused them by cause the bylle is long, and his councell had no leysur to se it. And they prayed heryng of the testament of my maister your fader,[2] and therof made a nother mater, and argued it to putte hem fro it, be cause they had emparled to us by fore ; and than Hyllyngworth to dryve it over this terme, allegged varians be twyx the bille and the testament that John Damme was named in the testament John Dawme, in whiche cas now the Court must have sigth of the said testament. Where fore ye must send it up the begynnyng of the next terme, or elles we schall have no sped in the mater. And therfor, Maistres, if my maister be not cum hom, and ye have not the sayd testament in your kepyng, that than it plese you to speke un to my maistres, your moder in lawe,[3] for the seyd testament, that I mygth redely have it here, and that it be sealed in a box, and sent to me, and I schall kepe it safe, with Godds grace.

---

[1] [From Fenn, iv. 2.] The reference to the Earl of Wiltshire's head having been set on London Bridge shows this letter to have been written not very long after the battle of Towton. The exact date is probably about the beginning of May, as it appears, by the Privy Seal dates in the Record Office, that Edward IV. was at Middleham on the 6th of that month on his way southwards, having gone on to Durham and Newcastle after the victory.
[2] William Paston, the Judge, who died in 1444.
[3] Agnes Paston, the widow of the Judge.
270

EDWARD IV

Doctor Morton,[1] and Doctor Makerell, and be brougth to the
kyng at York. Maister William also spak with a man that sey hem.

Item, sir, I herd of Sir John Borceter and Christofer Hanson, that Herry the sext is in a place in York schire is calle Coroumbr ; suche a name it hath, or muche lyke. And there is sege leyde abowte, and dyvers squyers of the Erle of Northumbrelands, and gadered them to geder, a v. or vj.ml. [five or six thousand] men, to byger [bicker] with the sege, that in the mene while Herry the sexte myght have ben stole a way at a lytyll posterne on the bak syde ; at whiche byker ben slayn iij.ml. [3000] men of the North. Sir Robert of Ocle and Conyrs leyth the sege on our syde, and thei it is that have do this acte. Sum say the Qwen, Somerset and the Prince schuld be there. Item, it is talked now for trouthe, the Erle of Northumberland is ded. Item, the Erle of Devenshire is ded justely.[2] Item, my Lord Chaunceler is to York. Item, the King and the Lords com not here before Whitsontyde, as it is sayde. Item, sir, sone uppon the chef baron comyng I schall send you a lettre, with Godds grace, who preserve you, and have you in His blyssed kepyng. Your,

THOMAS PLAYTERS.

At Cokermouthe was the Erle of Wylchire taken, and these other Doctors. Item, som men talke Lord Wellys, Lord Wyllouby, and Skales ben on lyve. Item, Sir Robert Veer is slayn in Cornewayll, as it is tok for trouthe.

---

[1] Afterwards Cardinal, the Minister of Henry VII.
[2] He was beheaded at York after the battle of Towton.

269

EDWARD IV

And as for tytyngs, in good feyth we have non, seve the
Erle of Wylchir[1] is hed is sette on London Brigge.

Mayster William is reden hom to my Maistrs Ponyngs ; and as for Maister Ponyngs hymself, sche letteth as thow sche wyst not where he were. A gentylman that kam fro York told me my maister was heyl and mery, and rode to mete the Kyng comyng fro Mydlam Castell.

Berwyk[2] is full of Scottys, and we loke be lyklyhod after anoyther batayll now be twyx Skotts and us.

And I pray Jesu have you in His blyssed kepyng.
Your,   THOMAS PLAYTER.

453

JOHN SMYTH TO JOHN PASTON, SENIOR[3]

To hys worschepfull mayster, John Paston the Eldest, Esquier.

RYGHT worschepfull and my synguler mayster, I recomaunde me to you. If it plese your maysterschepe to wete, the cause of my wryghtyng is thys. I have understande be comunyng with othyr credybell men that many and the more part of the feffeys of the landys late Sir John Fastolf, and also thei that pretende to ben executores of the seyd Sir John, purpose them to sell to my Lord of Suffolk, thow he recuver not be tayle, or to othyr myghty lordys, a gret part of the landys of the seyd Sir John, to the entent that ye schal not have them ; upon wech sale thei wole make astate and entre and put you to your accion, and thow ye recuver in the lawe, as I am enformyd, ye schall recuver of hard and but

---

[1] James Butler, Earl of Wiltshire and Ormond.
[2] Henry VI. and his Queen after the battle escaped to Berwick, and from thence retired to Edinburgh.—F.
[3] [From Paston MSS., B.M.] This letter was evidently written in the beginning of Edward IV.'s reign ; and as it appears by No. 458 that Paston had already been dispossessed of Caister, not indeed by the Duke of Suffolk, but by the Duke of Norfolk, as early as the 5th June 1461, we may presume that this letter, dated in May, belongs to that year. The margin of the letter is slightly mutilated, but the words which are lost are obvious, and have been supplied in brackets.
271

1461
MAY 10

a part, the qwech schuld be dere of the sute. Qwer it semyth to me, yt wer necessarye to you to se remedy for thys mater, and eyther putt it in award or elles that my Lord of Wa[rwick], the qwech is your good Lord, may meve that the Kyng, or hym sylf, or my Lord Chawmbyrleyn or sum othyr wytty me[n], may take a rewle betwexe you and your adversaryes; for yf ye may not holde the forseyd landys ther schal growe [great] losse bothe to the dede and to you, and men schal putt you in defawte therof; your frendys schal be sory. It is [better to] bere a lyttell losse than a gret rebuke. Your mater hangyth longe in the audyens. Yf ye hadde ther your entent your ad[versaries should] cese the rather. I beleve veryly yf ye do your part to have pees, God of Hys gret grace schal graunte it to you, the q[wech give] you the speryte of wysdam to gyde you on to Hys pleser. Amen.

We desyre to se your maysterschep in Norffolk; your pr[esens] there be necessarye.

From Norwych the x. day of May.

Your clerk,   [JOHN] SMYTH.

454

THOMAS DENYES TO JOHN PASTON [1]

To my maister Paston.

I LOWLY recomaund me to your maistership, thankyng you as a pouer man may do his maister for soccuryng my wyf, which I wete wele is wo begone; praying you for love of our Lord Jhesu Criste to take no displesir though I not sent ne wrote to you herbeforn in this troble that I haf. For parde ye may conceyve that I was besy j nogh to shifft my self til now. Truly the noise cam sodeynly and I was withynne the walles of your Cite, God sauf the governour therof, for he was besy to trappe me, more besy than he wole be a know, *et per fenestram in sporta dimissus sum per murum, et*

[1] [Add. MS. 34,888, f. 175.] The date of this letter is probably a little earlier than that of the next (No. 455).

272

sic effugi manus ejus; but he shal abye, by God, if I lyf, for serchyng myn house. And, Sir, as for the fals noise, sauf your reverence, that he leyth on me and on tweyn servauntz of myn, he lyeth falsly, your reverence savid; for I may haf an C. persones notable and thrifty, whan tyme comyth, that wole prove and make good by every meane, that my servauntz, which he nameth, wer that same our at Brisle which is thens more than xvj. myle, and that the same our and the same day and a greet space bothe beforn and afftir. But ever I besech your maistership of contynuaunce, and that ye like to do my wif help and comfort in hir dissese; for if she wer not, God knowith, I should soone shyfft. And truly I haf no thought ne sorwe but for hir. Wherfore I beseche you lowly for His love that all socourith and susteyneth to be good maister and comfort to her. It shal not be long to but that I shall send to hir to labour hir to other place, as for ony thyng touchyng me ellis but that. I pray you also, if the boy that is hurt dey, to meve your tenauntz in that hundrid wher he was bete to do for me and myn; ellis can I not desire ne write at this tyme for lak of remembraunce, for I am not yet myn own man. Besechyng yow alwey of good maistership, for Almyghty God knowith that the mater was falsly begunne on me and usurie it is and acursid, so wold our Lord I never had knowyn it; but sith I delid therwith I myght never reche it to handle the mater to trouth or reson. Wherfore I am compellid to do therwith unresonably. But, gentill Sir, socour my wif, and be not displesid with me, and than shal I do wele with Goddis mercy, Who Almyghty preserve yow for His mercy. Wretyn onavised, &c.

I pray you socour my wif, for she is wedow yet for me, and shal be til more is done, sith I se that neyther plee, trety ne werre may make my peas; for I leve hir undir your proteccion til I write to hir to go thens, which shal be hastily, I suppose, praying you to be alwey hir good maister, for I purpose not to se hir of a while, though she remeve. Wrete with sorwfull hert, &c.—Yours,   DENYES.

1461
APRIL (?)

VOL. III.—S   273

455

THOMAS DENYES TO JOHN PASTON [1]

To my Maister Paston.

1461
MAY

R IGHT wurshipfull and myn especiall good maister, I recomaund me to yow with all my service, besechyng you hertily, at the reverence of God, to helpe me now in the grettest extremite that I cam at sith my greet trobil with Ingham.[2] It is not oute of your remembraunce how Twyer in Norff[olk] vexith me bothe by noise and serchyng myn house for me, so that theer I can not be in quyete; and all that, I am verily acerteyned, is by Heydens crafft. And heer in the Kyngs house annenst Howard,[3] wher I had hopid to a' relevid myself, I am supplanted and cast oute from hym by a clamour of all his servaunts at onys, and ne wer oonly that his disposicion acordyth not to my pouer conceyte, which maketh me to gif lesse force, be cause I desire not to dele ther [where] bribery is like to be usid, ellis by my trouth this unhappy unkyndenes wold I trow a' killed me. I pray yow, at the reverence of Jesu Criste, to enfourme my Lord of Warwyk of me. Parde I haf do hym service; I was with hym at Northampton, that all men knew; and now agayn at Seynt Albones, that knowth James Ratcliff; and ther lost I xx*li*. wurth horse, herneys, and mony, and was hurte in diverse places. I pray yow to gete me his good Lordship, and that I may be toward hym in Norffolk in his Courts holdyng, or ellis, if ony thyng he haf to do; and that ye wole gete me a letter to Twyer to late me to sit in rest. For now if I made any

[1] [From Fenn, iv. 10.] The writer of this letter speaks of having served with the Earl of Warwick at the battle of Northampton in July 1460, and again at the second battle of St. Albans in February 1461. We know from later letters that he was murdered in the beginning of July following. As he dates from York, and speaks of being 'here in the King's house,' the date would appear to be about the 10th of May, on which day we find by the dates of the Privy Seals that Edward IV. was at York.

[2] *See* vol. ii. Nos. 238, 239.

[3] Sir John Howard, who was sheriff of Norfolk this year.

274

felaship agayn Twyer, I can haf no colour now the Shirref and I be oute, so I must kepe me aparte, which I am lothe to do, be God, if I myght better do.

I besech yow to send me your intent by the next man that come from yow. I shuld a' come to zow, but, so help me God, my purs may no ferther. The Holy Trinite preserve yow.

Wretyn hastily at York, &c.

Your to his power,   DENYES.

1461
MAY

456

THE EARL OF OXFORD TO JOHN PASTON [1]

To owre right trusty and welbeloved John Paston.

TH'ERL OF OXENFORD.

R IGHT trusty and welbeloved, we grete yow well, and pray yow, as oure trust is in yow, that if ye or any of yowre men here that Howard purposith hym to make any aray at owre manor of Wynche, that ye woll lete John Keche, owre kepere ther of, have wetyng by tymes, for and he have warnyng he will kepe it in to the tyme that we come thedir, with the grace of God, wiche have yow in His kepyng. Wretyn in owre manor of Wyvynho the last day of May.

OXENFORD.

MAY 31

[1] [Douce MS. 393, f. 85.] The date of this letter may, with great probability, be attributed to the year 1461. It certainly cannot be later, as the writer was executed for high treason in February 1462. He was found to have been corresponding with Margaret of Anjou for the restoration of Henry VI., but the discovery must have been much later than May 1461. Sir John Howard, who, for his services to the House of York, was afterwards made Duke of Norfolk, appears to have had great influence just after the accession of Edward IV., which he used in a very overbearing manner; and we have already seen, by the last letter, that the Earl of Oxford's servant, Thomas Denyes, was at this very time suffering much persecution at his hands.

275

457

THOMAS PLAYTER TO JOHN PASTON[1]

To my right good maister, John Paston, in all hast.

1461　AFTER my most special recommendacion, please your maisterchip wete, the Kyng, be cause of the sege a boute Carelylle, chaunged his day of Coronacion to be upon the Sunday[2] nexst after Seynt John Baptyste, so the'ntent to spede hym northward in all hast ; and how be it, blyssed be God, that he hath now good tydynggs, that Lord Mountagu hath broken the sege, and slayn of Scotts vj.ml. [6000] and ij. knyghes, whereof Lord Cliffords brother is one, yet not wythstandyng he wol be crowned the sayd Sunday. And John Jeney enformed me, and as I have verely lerned sethen, ye ar inbylled to be made knygth at this Coronacion.[3] Wheder ye have understandyng before hand, I wot not ; but and it lyke you to take the worchip upon you, consyderyng the comfortable tytynggs afore seyd, and for the gladnesse and plesour of al your welwyllers, and to the pyne and dyscomfort of all your ille wyllers, it were tyme your gere necessarye on that by halfe were purveyd fore, and also ye had nede higth you to London, for as I conceyve the knygthes schuld be made upon the Saterday by for the Coronacion ; and as moche as may be purveyed for you in secrete wyse wythouten cost I schall by speke for you, if nede be, ayens your comyng, in trust of the best ; nevertthelesse, if ye be dysposed, ye had nede send a man by fore in all hast, that no thing be to seke. William Calthorp is inbylled, and Yelvertoun is inbylled, whiche caused Markham ; because Yelverton loked to have ben chef juge, and Markham thynketh to plese hym thus. And as for the mater ayens Poutrell, we can no farther pro-

[1] [From Fenn, i. 230.]　It is evident from the contents that this letter was written some time before the coronation of Edward IV.　[2] 28th June.
[3] John Paston was not made knight at the coronation of Edward IV., but his eldest son was made knight, probably as a substitute for himself, within two years after.

276

cede, tyl we have my maister your faders testament.　I sent 1461 my maistres a letter for it.　No more, but I pray Al myghty Jesu have you in His kepyng.
　　　　　Your,　　　　THOMAS PLAYTER.

458

RICHARD CALLE TO JOHN PASTON[1]

To my right reverent worschipfull master, my Master John Paston.

RIGHT reverent and worschipfull master, I lowly re-　JUNE 5 comande me unto your good masterschip.　Plesith you to witte that I have ben at Framelyngham, and spake Ric Sothwell to hafe hes advice in this mater ; wherin he wolde geve me but litell councell, and seide ze were straungely disposed, for ye trusted no man, and had moche langage, weche the berer herof schal enforme your masterschip.

And as for the letters, they were delivered my Lorde[2] at the Logge, but I cowde not speke with hese Lordeschip.　And suche tyme as they were delyvered Fitz William whare there, weche is now keper of Castre ; and what tyme as my Lorde had sene the lettres, he comaunded hym to avoide, and so he did.　And thanne my Lorde sent for Sothwell.　And in the meene tyme my Lorde sent a man to me, and axed me where ye were, and I tolde hem ye were with the Kyng ; and so he sent me worde that an answere schulde be made be Sothwel to the King, seyng that ii. or iij. eyers [*heirs*] had ben with my Lorde, and shewed her [*i.e.* their] evidence, and delyvered it to my Lorde, seyng they have had gret wrong, besechyng my Lorde that it myght be reformed.　Wherfor he comaunded me that I shulde go hom, for other answer cowde I non have.　So I aboude upon Sothwel to a' know my Lordes answer to the

[1] [From Fenn, iv. 6.]　The date of this letter, like that of the last, is shown by a reference to the approaching coronation of Edward IV.
[2] The Duke of Norfolk, who appears by this time to have taken possession of Caister, and appointed a keeper for it.

277

1461　Kyng ; weche answere Sothwel tolde me was, that he writeth to JUNE 5 the Kyng that certeine points in your lettres be untrew, and that he schal prove suche tyme as he cometh befor the Kyng, besechyng the Kyng to take it to no displesur ; for he is advised to kepe it still unto the tyme that he hath spaken with his Highnesse, for he trusteth to God to schewe suche evidence to the Kyng and to the Lords, that he schulde have best right and titill therto ; and so he sent a man forthe to the Kyng this day.　It were right wele don ye awayted upon hes man comyng, that ye myght knowe the redy entent of my Lordes writyng.

Berthelmew Elysse hathe ben with my Lorde, and made a relesse to my Lord ; and Sir Will Chamberleine was ther ij. dayes afore I come thirder, I can thynke for the sam mater. And Thomas Fastolf whas there the same tyme that I was ther ; and as I am enformed, they have delyvered my Lorde serteine evidence.　Wherfore me semeth it were right wele don, savyng your better advice, to com hom and sele up your evidence, and have hem with you to London, to prove his titill noght.　Ther be but ii. or iij. men with in the place, and if ye thynke it best to do it, send word, and I suppose a remedy schal be had.

Also I here no word of Master William, nor of the writts for the Parlament.　Also it is tolde here that Tudenham[1] and Heydon have a pardon of the Kyng, and that they schal come up to London with the Lady of Suffolk to the Coronacion. Also as for the letter that ye sent to Thomas Wyngfeld, I have it still, for he is at London.　Some men sey he meved my Lord for to entre, and some sey Fitz William is in defaute.　So I can see ther is but fewe goode.　Also my master Sir Thomas Howys schol send a letter to the person ye wote of, for to deliver you the gere at London the next week.　My right wourschipfull and reverent master, Almyghti God preserve you.

Wreten at Norweche, on the morwe after Corpus Christi Day.

　　　　Your pore servant and bedman,　　　R. C.

[1] Sir Thomas Tuddenham was beheaded in February following.

278

459

ROBERT LETHUM TO JOHN PASTON[1]

A tres reverent Sire, John Paston, Esquier, demouraunt ou lostell le Roy soit d[onne].

RIGHT worshipfull sir, I recomaund me to you.　And, 1461 sir, yesterday I resceived of you a lettre from oure JUNE 19 sovereign lord the Kyng directe to John Fulman, dyvers othir, and me, by the quych, for certeyn causes that meved hym, and for the well and save gard of his person and this his realme, he desired we chuld fynd men for kepyng of the see.　I said to you that I hade beyn dyvers tymes spoled and robbed, as ye have herd, and also gretely vexed and sued to me [*my*] unportab[l]e [charges] ; [2] nevir the les, to my pouer, with my body and my gode, I chall be redy to do hym servyce in resistyng his enmyse and rebelles.　Also I said I dwelled upon the cost of the see here, and be langage hit were more necessare to with hold men here than take men from hit.　The said the Kyng hade wreton to dyvers persones here quych hade promysed men, queruppon I promysed a man, quych chall be redy at such tyme I have knowelege quere the shippyng chall be, to waite upon yow, or quane the Kyng comaundes.　I write to you of my promyse as ye comaund me, and pray you I may have a copy of the said lettre.　And I pray Godd kepe you.　Wrete at Plumsted on the Fest of Seynt Gervaise and Prothase.[3]
　　　　　Your,　　　　ROBT. LETHUM.

[1] [From Paston MSS., B.M.]　As we find by the last letter that John Paston was with the King in the beginning of June 1461, this may with great probability be attributed to the same year.　[2] Omitted in MS.　[3] 19th June.

279

THE PASTON LETTERS

460

JAMES GRESHAM TO JOHN PASTON[1]

To my right worshipfull maister, John Paston, at Heylesdon in Norffolk, in hast.

1461
JNE 21

AFTER due recomendacion hadde; please it your Maistership to witte, that as for Plaiter he shall excuse the writte of the parlement, &c. As touchyng my maister Howard,[2] I cannot yet speke with hym, ne with Moungomerye[3] nether. But as for the day of Coronacion of the Kyng, it shall be certeynly the Moneday next after Mydsomer, and it is told me that ye among other ar named to be made knyght atte Coronacion, &c.

Item, it is seid that the Coronacion do, the Kyng wole in to the north part forthwith; and therfor shall not the parlement holde, but writtes shall goo in to every shire to gyve them, that ar chosyn knyghtes of the shire, day after Michelmesse; this is told me by suyche as arn right credible. Maister Brakle shall preche at Poules on Sunday next comyng as he tolde me, and he told me, that for cause Childermesse day[4] fal on the Sunday, the Coronacion shall on the Moneday, &c.

Wretyn in hast at London, the Sunday next tofore Mydsomer,

Your right pouere servant,
JAMES GRESHAM.

[1] [From Fenn, i. 232.] Like Nos. 457 and 458, this letter refers to the approaching coronation of Edward IV.
[2] Sir John Howard.   [3] Sir Thomas Montgomery.
[4] Childermas, or Holy Innocents' Day, the 28th of December, fell on Sunday in the year 1460. The day of the week on which it fell used to be considered ominous or unlucky during the whole ensuing year. This superstition seems to have continued as late as the beginning of the eighteenth century, and is alluded to by Addison in the seventh number of the *Spectator*. It is not true, however, that Edward's coronation was put off till Monday. It took place on the Sunday which had been originally appointed for it, but the processions and pageantry were deferred till next day. The following is the account of the matter given in a contemporary chronicle in the Cottonian MS., Vitellius, A. xvi:—

'And upon the morn, Sunday, which was St. Peter's Even, and the 28th day of

280

EDWARD IV

461

CLEMENT PASTON TO JOHN PASTON[1]

To my rythe worchypfull broder, John Paston, be thys delyveryd in hast.

1461
JUNE 26

BRODER, I recomawnde me to zow, desyeryng to here of yowre welfare, the qwyche I pray God mayntene. Plesse yow to wette that I have sent my moder a letter for mony for my swster;[2] and if ze wyll agre that I may have xx^{li}li. [£20], I xall zeve zow acowmpts ther of, and ze xall be payyd azen of the obligacyon that my moder hathe, or ellys I xall take a swerte of my suster. I wysse obligacion mwste nedes be swyd, and a doseyn accions more in her name, and sche doo well thys terme; and it wyll be doo with in fowertenyut. The Cowntas of Northumberlond[3] and Robarde Fenus[4] ocupie all her lond, and that is a gret myscheffe. I prey zow spe[ke] to my moder her of, and lat me have a awnswer within thys sevenyut. Also, broder, Wyndham is come to town, and he seyd to me he wyll goo gett hym a mayster, and me thowte by hym he wold be in the Kynges servise, and he saythe that he wyll have Felbryg azen or Myhelmes, or ther shal be v.^{c} [500] heds broke ther fore. Broder, I pray zow delyver the mony that I xwld have in to swm prior of swm abbey to swm mayster of swm colage to be

June, he was crowned at Westminster with great solemnity of bishops and other temporal lords. And upon the morn after, the King went crowned again in Westminster Abbey, in the worship of God and St. Peter. And upon the next morn he went also crowned in St. Paul's in the worship of God and St. Paul; and there the angel came down and censed him. At which time was as great a multitude of people in Paul's as ever was seen afore in any days.'

[1] [From Paston MSS., B.M.] Elizabeth Paston, who, as we have seen (No. 374), had been married to Robert Poynings by the beginning of the year 1459, became his widow in 1461, her husband having been killed in the second battle of St. Albans on the 17th February. It would appear by this letter that she was immediately after dispossessed of her husband's lands by Eleanor, Countess of Northumberland, who was Baroness Poynings in her own right.
[2] Elizabeth Paston, now widow of Robert Poynings.
[3] Eleanor, widow of Henry Percy, third Earl, who was slain at Towton in 1461.
[4] Fenys.

281

THE PASTON LETTERS

1461
JUNE 26

delyveryd qwan I can espy ony londe to be porchasyd. I pray zow send me word wyder ze wyll doo thus or no. No more, but owre Lord have zow in Hys kepyng. Wrytyn on Fryday nexst after Seynt John is day.

By zour broder,
CLEMENT PASTON.

462

MARGARET PASTON TO JOHN PASTON[1]

To my right worchepfull hosbond, John Paston, be this letter delyveryd in hast.

JUNE

RIGHT worchepfull hosbond, I recommand me to you. Please you to wete that thys day in the mornyng the parson of Snoryng came to Thomas Denys and fechyd hym owt of hys hows, and beryth hym a hand,[2] that he shuld a mad a byllys agayns Twyer and hym, and hathe a leed hym ferthe with hem. Hys wyf hathe no knowlege of it. Ferther more the seid parson seythe that the seyd Thomas Denys shuld a take sowdyors owt of hys felachep whan he went to Seynt Albons;[3] that hys a nother of hys compleynts. Item, anothyr of hys compleynts ys, a beryth the seyd Thomas a hand,[2] that he had awey a hors of John Coppyng of Bryslee, and a nother of Kyng of Donham, the wyche hors were stole be the seyd ij. personys. Wher for the seyd Thomas toke hem as a comyshaner and delyveryd hem to the exchetor, Frances Costard, and one of them he bowt of the seyd Fraunces. And the seyd parson hathe a wey the seyd hors,

[1] [From Paston MSS., B.M.] This letter appears from internal evidence to have been written some time after the second battle of St. Albans, which was fought in February 1461, and before the murder of Thomas Denys in July following. But to all appearance it was not very long before the latter date. The MS. is mutilated, and a few words are lost in eight consecutive lines.
[2] *i.e.* accuses him. *See* vol. ii. p. 110, Note.
[3] Thomas Denys was at the second battle of St. Albans in February 1461. *See* No. 455.

282

EDWARD IV

1461
JUNE

and seyth that he wolle the seyd thevys shuld be recompenst be Thomas Denys. Thys I am enformyd of all thesse maters be hys wyffe, and sche prayythe yow in the reverence of God ye wolle be hyr good maister, and helpe that hyr hosbond may have sume remedy be your labor in thys mater, [for she] seythe syn that hyr hosbond ys the Kyngs offycer, that they owt to spar hym the rather. But they that hathe hym take no . . . . . . told me that they hope to have a newe chonge in hast.

Item, Pers that was with my unkyll Barney[1] sent you a l[etter] . . . . . . er desyryng to have your good masterchep, and he woll fyynd sufficient suerte[2] for hym for to com . . . . . . whan som ever ye woll require hym. I' good feyth it ys told me hys leggs ar all . . . . . . [Send] me word, encas the suerte be sufficient, in what sum ye woll have hem bownd for hy . . . . . . te in bayle. Item, it ys told me that ther be many Freynche shyppys of se a geyns Yamothe, a[nd . . . . t]hey woll do harme on the coste. I pray yow hertely that ye woll send me word in hast howe that ye do with my [Lord] of Norffolk, and with your adversaryys. Item, I have do purveyed in thys wareyn xj.$^{xx.}$ [eleven score] rabets and sent up be the berer herof. The blyssyd Trinite have yow in Hys kepyng, and send yow the better of all your adversariis, and good sped in all your maters. Wretyn in hast, the same day that ye departyd hens.

Item, I pray yow that ye wolle remember my unkyll Barneys mater tochyng the executyng of his wylle, and how ye wolle that we be demenyd for kepyng of hys yerday, and that it lekyth you to send me word be Mr. John Smy[th].

[1] John Berney.   [2] *See* Letter 424.

283

THE PASTON LETTERS

463

THOMAS DENYES TO MARGARET PASTON[1]

To my right noble and wurshipfull mastresse, my Mastresse Paston, or to William Paston if she be absent.

1461
JULY

RIGHT noble and wurshipfull mastresse, I recomaund me to yow with my pouer servise. And for so moche as I here no thyng of my maister your husbonds comyng hastly home,—and though he cam or come not, it were expedient that the Kyng were informed of the de-menyng of the shire,—therfore I send to yow a testymonyall, which is made by a greet assent of greet multitude of comons, to send to the Kyng. I pray yow for the good spede therof that in all hast possible ye like to send it to my said maister, if he be with the Kyng; ellis fynde the meane to send it to the Kyng, thogh my maister be thens; beside forthe that ye vouchsauf to late diligent labour be made to a sufficient nombir to assele for my Maister Paston allone, for if bothe holde not, I wolde oon helde.

I pray yow that it lyke you to send for my Maister William Paston, and shew hym all thys, and that it were hastid; for on the adversaire parte Judas slepith not.

Berney promised to a' sent, but for our Lords love trust not that; for I se his slouthe and sely labour, which is no labour. And I wold ful fayn speke with yow, &c.

My maister your husbond wole peraventure blame us all, if this mater be not applied; for he may not of reson do so largely heryn by his myght, be cause he is elyted, as the

---

[1] [From Fenn, iv. 18.] This letter speaks of the county of Norfolk as being in an unquiet state, and of John Paston as having been elected knight of the shire. It will be seen by No. 458 that writs for an election were expected as early as the 5th of June in 1461, and as I find that the writer of this letter was murdered on the 4th of July following, the date is probably about the very beginning of that month. From what is said at the beginning of the letter about Paston's absence from home, it was evidently some time after the last, which was written on the very day of his departure.

284

THE PASTON LETTERS

465

WILLIAM LOMNER TO JOHN PASTON[1]

To the right worchipfull and my good maister John Paston.

1461
JULY 6

RYGHT worchipfull and my good mayster I recomaunde me to yow. And, sir, yf the Coronacion had be on Relik Sunday,[2] as it was apoyntyd, I shuld have waytid on yow. And as for my Lord of Norffolks mene, I told my mastres your wyfe, here disposission as I coude know, the wheche I sopose she told yow, as I can espye some of his meny was grette cause of T. D.[3] deth, &c. Also ye have knowlych how Fastolff[4] is com yn to my Lord of Norffolks hous, for ij. causez, as I understande; on is to enfors my Lords entre yn Castre be his cleym; an other is to helpe his fader yn lawe[5] ayens Felbrigge, &c. For love of Good take good awayte to your person, for the word [*world*] is right wilde, and have be sythyn Heydonz sauffe gard was proclamyd at Walsyngham; for yn good feyth I trow, but if [*i.e.* unless] he be ponysshid the countre wille rise and doo moche harme, and also for the comyssion Sir Miles Stapilton and Calthorp, that arn among the comunes ought of conseite and reputid the Kyngs enmez, as the brenger of this bille can telle yow, to whom I beseche yow to be good mayster, for he hath doo the Kyng good servyse as ony pore man of our contre, and yet is he callid traitor be sweche as he can telle yow, soportid be Roger Bolwer and Aleyn Roos, Heidonz owyn men [chif constablez].[6] And it plese yow that John Yve and John Brigge myght have your warentez for cheffe constable, &c., for they ocupye yn Kyng Herris name. Further, sire, I am gretly yn your danger and dette for my pension, for it is told

---

[1] [From Paston MSS., B.M.] From the reference to the coronation, it is quite evident that this letter must have been written in the first year of King Edward the Fourth. [2] 12th July in 1461.
[3] Thomas Denys. [4] Thomas Fastolf of Cowhaw.
[5] This would seem to be John Wyndham, but I find no mention of such a relationship between him and Fastolf.
[6] Interlined.

286

EDWARD IV

Comons myght wisely do with help of his favour, if it wer wisely wrought. If my Maister William Paston ride hastly from a x. daies to London, I wole with hym, if he send me word. The Holy Trinite preserve yow. Wretyn rudely in hast the Sunday, &c.

1461
JULY

Men sey, send a wiseman on thy erand, and sey litell to hym, wherfor I write brefly and litell.

THOMAS DENYES.

464

RICHARD CALL TO MARGARET PASTON[1]

To my most reverent and worshipfull mastresse, my Mastresse Margaret Paston, this be delyuered.

PLESITH it your mastresseship that my mastre[2] wolde that ye alowe the berer hereof for hes costs, in asmoch as he come hether for that matre, and for non other; but ye must lete Thomas Denys wif be prevy therto, for my mastre wol that she bere the cost, for it is her matre; and that ye make her goode cheere, and if ye wol have her hom to you for a seacon, unto the tyme sche be out of her trouble, my mastre is agreed. And if sche sende to my mastre for any matre, let her sende her owne man upon her owne coste, thowe ye paye the money for a secon, unto the tyme that sche may pay you a yein, mastre holdeth hym content. My right wurshipful mastresse, Almyghti Jesu kepe you. Wreten at London the iij. day of Jul.

JULY 3

Your poore seruaunt and bedman,

RIC. CALL.

On the back of this letter is the following memorandum:—'Memorandum of j. comb whete, whereof was mad iiij.ˣˣ· and x. [*fourscore and ten*] brown lovis and iiij.ˣˣ· and xvj. white lovis, after vj. j.ᵈ· price the   . .'

---

[1] [From Paston MSS., B.M.] This letter seems to have been written in 1461, just before Thomas Denys was murdered, in consequence of the occurrences mentioned in No. 462. [2] John Paston.

285

EDWARD IV

me ye have paied, and at your comyng I shalle make amendez with your good maistreship, and suche servyse as lith yn my pore powere is, and shalbe, redy at alle tymez with Godds grace, how have yow yn His kepyng. Wretyn yn hast at Dallyng, on Sent Thomas Even, &c.

1461
JULY

Be your Servaunt,

L.

466

MARGARET PASTON TO JOHN PASTON[1]

To my ryth worchepfull hosbond, John Paston, be thys deliverid in hast.

RIGHT worcheful hosbond, I recommand me to yow. Please yow to wete that I have spoke with Thomas Denys wyffe, and she recommand hyr to your good masterchep, and she prayeth yow to be her good master, and prayet yow of your good masterchep, that ye myght geve her your advice howe to be demenid for hyr person and hyr goodes. For as towchyng hyr owne person, she dare not goo home to hyr owne place, for she is thret if that she myght be take, she shuld be slayne or be put in ferfull place, in shortyng of hyr lyve dayes, and so she standyth in gret hevynes, God her helpe. Ferther more she is nowe put be her brother in Norwich with Awbry, and she thynkyth the place is right conversaunt of pupyll for hyr to abeyd in, for she kepyth hyr as close as she may for spyyng. Item, as I went to Seynt Levenard ward, I spake with Maister John Salet, and commonyd with hym of hyr, and me thowgt be hym that he howyth hyr ryght good wylle. And than I haskyd hym howe she myght be demenyd with hys[2] goodes and hyr. He cownseld me that she shuld get hyr a trosty frend, that war a good, trewe, poor man, that had not moche to lese, and wold

JULY 9

---

[1] [From Paston MSS., B.M.] This letter clearly relates to the affairs of Thomas Denys's wife, after the murder of her husband in 1461. John Paston and William Rokewood were trustees of his lands, and Margaret's cousin, John Berney of Witchingham, it will be seen, wrote more than one letter to them about this time. [2] *i.e.* her husband's.

287

1461
JULY 9

be rewlyd after hyr, and to have a letter of ministracion ; and so I told hyr. Than she seyd she wold have hyr broder advice therin. Item, she seyth ther be no mor feffes in hys londes but ye and Rokwood, and she prayeth yow that it please yow to speke to Rokwood that he make no relesse but be your advice, as she trostyth to yowr good masterchep. Item, the last tyme that I spake with hyr she mad suche a petows mone and seyd that she wost ner howe to do for mony, and so I lent vjs. viijd. Item, I sent my cosyn Barney the bylle that John Pampyng wrot be yowr commanddement to me, and he hath sent a letter of hys entent to yow and to Rokwod therof, and also but if it please yow to take better hed to hys mater than he can do hym self, I can thynk he shall ellis fare the wors for i' feyth he standyth daly in gret fere, for the false contrary party ageyns hym. Item, at the reverence of God, be ware howe ye ryd or go, for nowgty and evyll desposyd felacheps. I am put en fere dayly for myn abydyng here, and cownsellyd be my moder and be other good frendes, that I shuld not abeyd here but yf the world wher in mor quiete than it is. God for hys merci send us a good world, and send yow helthe in body and sowle, and good speed in all your maters. Wreten in hast the Thursday next after Seynt Thomas.

By your,   M. P.

467

JOHN BERNEY TO JOHN PASTON AND WYLLIAM ROKEWODE[1]

To the worshipfull John Paston and Wylliam Rokewode, Squyeris, and to everych of them.

JULY 10

RIGHT worshipfull cosynes, I recummaund me to yow. And for as mech as I am credybilly informyd how that Sir Myles Stapylton knyght with other yll dysposed persones, defame and falsly noyse me in morderyng of Thomas

[1] [From Fenn, i. 236.]

1461
JULY 10

Denys the Crowner, and how that I intend to make insurexyones contrari unto the law ; and that the seyd Stapylton ferthermore noyseth me with gret robries ; in whech defamacyones and fals noysyngs the seyd Stapylton, and in that his saying he is fals, that knowith God, &c. And for my playn acquitayll, yf he or any substancyall gentylman wyll say it, and avow it, I say to it contrari, and by lisens of the Kyng to make it good as a gentylman. And in this my playn exskeus, I pray yow to opyn it unto the Lords, that the seyd Stapylton, &c., makyn gret gaderyngs of the Kyngs rebelyones, lying in wayte to morder me. And in that I may make opyn proff. Wretyn in hast the x. day of July anno regni Regis E. iiij. primo.   JOHN BERNEYE.

Remembre to take a wryht to chese crowneres in Norffolk.

468

JOHN PASTON TO MARGARET PASTON[1]

To my cosyn, Margaret Paston.

JULY 12

I RECOMAUND me to yow, letyng yow wete tha the Undershreve doughtyth hym of John Berney ; wherfore I pray yow bryng hem to gedyr, and set hem acord, if ye can, so that the seyd Ondershreve be sure that he shall not be hurt be hym, ner of hys cuntrymen. And eyf he woll not, lete hym verely understonde that he shall be compellyd to fynd hym suerte of the pes to agry in thys heed, and that shall nowther be profitabyll, ner worcheful. And lete hym wete that there have be many compleynts of hym be that knavyssh knyght, Sir Miles Stapilton, as I sent yow word before ; but he shall come to hys excuse wele inow, so he have a mannys hert, and the seyd Stapylton shall ben ondyrstand as he ys, a fals shrewe. And he and hys wyfe and other have blaveryd

[1] [From Fenn, iv. 20.] This letter and the next, which is an answer to it, are evidently of the same year as No. 471. Relic Sunday (the third Sunday after Midsummer Day) was the 12th July in 1461.

VOL. III.—T

1461
JULY 12

here of my kynred in hedermoder ;[1] but, be that tyme we have rekned of old dayes and late dayes, myn shall be found more worchepfull thanne hys and hys wyfes, or ellys I woll not for hys gilt gypcer.

Also telle the seyd Berney that the Shreve ys in a dought whedyr he shall make a newe eleccion of knyghts of the shyre, be cause of hym and Grey ; where in it were bettyr for hym to have the Shreves good wyll.

Item, me thynkyth for quiete of the cuntre it were most worchepfull that as wele Berney as Grey shuld get a record of all suche that myght spend xls. ayere, that were at the day of eleccon, whech of them that had fewest to geve it up as reson wold. Wretyn at London, on Relyk Sonday.

Item, that ye send abowght for sylver acordyng to the old bylle that I sent yow from Lynne.   JOHN PASTON.

469

MARGARET PASTON TO JOHN PASTON[2]

JULY 15

I RECOMAND me to yow. Please yow to wete that I have sent to my cosyn Barney, acordyng to your desyr in the letter that ye deed wright on Relec Sonday to me, wheropon he hathe wreten a letter to yow and anothyr bylle to me, the wyche I send yow. He tolde the masanger that I sent to hym that the Undershereve nedyth not to fer hym nor non of hys ; for he seyd, after the aleccion was doo, he spak with hym at the Grey Fryers, and prayyd hym of hys good masterchep, and seyd to hym that he feryd no man of bodely harme, but only Twyer and hys felachep.

Item, Sir John Tatersalle and the baly of Walsynsham and the constabyll hathe take the parson of Snoryng and iiij. of hys men, and sete hem fast in the stokkys on Monday at nyght ; and, as it is seyd, they shulde be carryyd up to the Kyng in hast. God defend yt but they be shastysyd as the lawe wolle. Twyer and hys felachep beryth a gret wyght of Thomas Denys

[1] In hugger-mugger, i.e. clandestinely.
[2] [From Fenn, iv. 24.] See note to preceding letter, p. 289, Note 1.

1461
JULY 15

dethe in this contry abowght Walsynham ; and it is seyd ther yf John Osberne hade owght hym as good wylle, as he deed befor that he was acqueyntyd with Twyer, he shuld not adyyd [*have died*], for he myght rewlyd al Walsynham as he had lyst, as it ys seyd.

Item, Will Lynys, that was with Master Fastolf, and swyche other as he is with hym, goo fast abowght in the contr, and ber men a hand,[1] prests and others, they be Skotts, and take brybys of hem and let hem goo ageyn. He toke the last wek the parson of Freton, and but for my cosyn Jarnyngham the younger,[2] ther wold a led hem forthe with hem ; and he told hem pleynly yf they mad any suche doyngs ther, but [*i.e.* unless] they had the letter to schewe for hem, they shuld aley on her bodyys. It wer welle do that they wer met with be tymys. It is told me that the seyd Will reportyth of yow as shamfully as he can in dyvers place. Jesu have yow in Hys kepyng. Wreten in hast, the Wednysday after Relec Sonday.

Yf the Undershereve come home, I woll a say to do for hym as ye desyryd me in your letter. As for mony, I have sent abowght, and I can get non but xiijs. iiijd. syn ye went owght. I wolle do my parte to get mor as hastely as ye may.

By yowr,   M. P.

470

JOHN BERNEY TO JOHN PASTON[3]

To the worshipfull John Paston, and to my cosyn, Wylliam Rokewode, Squyer, with my Lord of Cantyrburi.

JULY 16

RIGHT worshipfull sir, I recummaund me to yow, prayng yow hertyli to labour for that the Kyng may wryte unto me, gevyng me thankyng of the good wyll and servyse that I haff doo unto hym, and in beyng with hym a

[1] That is to say, make imputations against them. *See* vol. ii. p. 110, Note 1.
[2] John Jerningham, junior, son of John Jerningham, senior, of Somerleyton, Suffolk.
[3] [From Fenn, i. 238.]

THE PASTON LETTERS

1461
JULY 16

yens his adversaries and rebelyones, as well in the North, as in this cuntre of Norffolk. And in that the Kyng shold please the Comynnes in this cuntre; for they grudge and sey, how that the Kyng resayvith sych of this cuntre, &c. as haff be his gret eanemyes, and opresseors of the Comynes; and sych as haff assystyd his Hynes, be not rewardyt; and it is to be consederyd, or ellys it wyll hurt, as me semyth by reason. And in ayd of this chaungebyll rewle, it wer nessessary to move the good Lords Spiretuall and Temperall, by the whech that myght be reformyd, &c. And in cas that any of myn olde enemyes, Tudynham, Stapylton, and Heydon, with thyr affenyte labur the Kyng and Lords unto my hurt, I am and wylbe redy to come to my souverayn Lord for my exskeus, soo that I may come saff for unlawfull hurt, purveyed by my seyd ennemyes. No more at this tyme, but God preserve yow in gras. Wretyn at Wychyngham the xvj. day in the moneth of July, anno regni Regis E. iiijᵗʰ primo.   JOHN BERNEYE.

Please it yow to move this unto my Lords Cauntyrburi, Ely, Norwych, &c.

471

JOHN BERNEY TO JOHN PASTON[1]

To the ryght worshipfull John Paston, Squyer, in hast.

JULY 17

SIR, I recomaund me to zow, &c. And as for my playn dysposyssyon towards the Undyrshrewe, I wyll hym no bodyli hurt, nor shal not be hurt by me nor by noo man that I may rewle. But the Comynnes throw all the schyer be movyd agayn hym, for cause of his lyght demeanyng towards them for this elexsyon of knygtts of the shyer for the Parlement. And I suppose yf that he wyll, he may be hastyli easyd as thus :—lat hym make notys unto the seyd Comynnes that this theyr eleccyon shall stande, or ellys lat hym purchas a new wryt, and lat hym make wrytyng unto them what day

[1] [From Fenn, iv. 28.]

292

EDWARD IV

1461
JULY 17

they shall come, and they to make a new eleccyon acordyng unto the law. And, sir, I pray zow, sey to hym that it is nott his oneste to lye upon too many men, noysyng them rebyliones of Norff [olk], and Berney theyr c . . . No more to zow at this tyme, but I haff sent zow ij. letteris within this viij. dayes. Wretyn the xvij. day of July anno regni Regis E. iiijᵗʰ 1ᵐᵒ.   JOHN BERNEY.

472

MARGARET PASTON TO JOHN PASTON[1]

To my worchepful hosbonde, Jon Pastun, this letter be delyvered in hast.

RYTH worchepful husbond, I recomawnd me to yow. Plesyt yow to wete that I am desyrid be Sir John Tatersale to wryte to yow for a comyssyon or a noyr in termyner [*oyer and terminer*][2] for to be sent down in to this cuntre to sit uppon the parson of Snoryng, and on soche as was cause of Thomas Denyssys dethe, and for many and gret horebyl robbryys; and as for the costs ther of the cuntre wele pay therfor, for they be sor aferd but [*i.e.* unless] the seyd dethe be chastysed, and the seyd robbryys, they ar aferde that mo folks xal be servyd in lyke wyse.

JULY 18

As for the prest and vj. of hese men that be takyn, they be delyveryt to Twer [*Twyer*], and iiij. be with hem of the cuntreys cost, for to be sent with to the Kyng; and yf they be browt up at the reverens of God, do yowr parte that they schape not, but that they may have the jugement of the lawe, and as they have deservyd, and be comytyt to prison, not to departe tyl they be inqueryd of her forseyd robery be soche a comyssion that ye can get, that the Keng and the Lords may hondyrstonde wat rewle they have be of, not hondely for the moderys and the robbryys, but as wele for the gret insurrexsin

[1] [From Fenn, iv. 30.] The date of this letter is certain, as it refers to the murder of Thomas Denys.
[2] *See* vol. ii. p. 161, Note 3.

293

THE PASTON LETTERS

1461
JULY 18

that they were lyke amade within the shyre. The preests of Castyr they be streytely take hede at be Roberd Harmerer and hoder, so that the seyde prestys may have no thyng out of ther owne, ne of hodyr menys, but they be rassakyt, and the plase ys watchyd bothe day and nyth. The prestys thynk ryth longe tyl they tydynggs fro yow. At the reverens of God, be ware hou ye goo and ryde, for that ys told me that ye thret of hem that be nowty felawys that hathe be inclynyng to them, that hathe be your hold adversarys.

The blyssyd Trenyte have yow in hys kepyng. Wretyn in hast, the Saturday nex be fore Sent Margarete.

Be yours,   M. P.

473

GRANT FROM THE CROWN[1]

Pro Johanne Paston.

JULY 27

REX omnibus ad quos &c. salutem. Cum Nos indebitati sumus Johanni Paston armigero et Thomæ Hows clerico in septingentis marcis legalis monetæ regni nostri Angliæ eisdem Johanni et Thomæ solvendis juxta formam cujusdam billæ manu nostra signatæ cujus tenor sequitur in hæc verba :—

Edward, Kyng of Inglond and of Frauns, Lord of Irlond, recorde and knoweleych that we have receyvyd of John Paston, Squyer, and Thomas Hows, clerk, be the assent of oure trusty and welbelovyd cosyn Thomas Archebysshop of Caunterbury, [and?] Mayster John Stokys, clerk, an nowche of gold with a gret poynted diamaunt set upon a rose enamellid white, and a nowche of gold in facion of a ragged staff with ij. ymages of man and woman garnysshed with a ruby, a dyamaunt and a gret perle, which were leyd to plegge by oure fader, whom Crist assoyle, to Sir John Fastolff, knyght, for CCCC. xxxlvij*li.*; and also an obligacion wherby oure seid fader was bound to the seid Sir John Fastolff in an C. marc; for which we graunt

[1] [From *Patent Roll*, 1 Edw. IV., Part 3, No. 13.]

294

EDWARD IV

1461
JULY 27

and promitt in the word of a kyng to pay to the seid John Paston and Thomas Hows, clerk, or to her assignez, D.CC. mark of lawfull money of Englond at days underwritte, that is to sey; att the Fest of All Seyntes than next folowyng after the date of thys bille CC. mark, and other CC. mark at the Fest of All Seyntis than next folowyng, and other CC. mark at the Fest of All Seyntes than next folowyng, and an C. mark at the Fest of All Seyntys thanne next folowyng. And also we graunte that the seid John Paston and Thomas Hows shall have a signement sufficient to hem aggreabill for the seid payment. And if it fortune that the same John and Thomas be unpayd by the seid assignement of any of the seid paymentis at any of the seid Festis, thanne we graunt upon notice made to us therof by the same John or Thomas to pay hem or her assignez that payment so behynd onpaid oute of oure cofirs withoute delay. In witnesse werof we have signed this bill with oure hand the xij. day of Jule the first yere of [our] reign.

Nos solutionem summæ illius præfatis Johanni et Thomæ fieri et haberi volentes, ut tenemur, concessimus et per præsentes concedimus eisdem Johanni Paston et Thomæ Hows septingentas marcas monetæ prædictæ percipiendas modo et forma subsequentibus, videlicet, centum marcas inde annuatim percipiendas de primis denariis provenientibus et crescentibus de feodi firma civitatis nostræ Norwici et de omnibus aliis firmis, exitibus, proficuis et reventionibus de eadem civitate provenientibus per manus majoris, custodis, vicecomitum, civium seu ballivorum ejusdem civitatis pro tempore existentium aut aliorum receptorum, firmariorum seu appruatorum eorundem feodi firmarum, exituum, proficuorum et reventionum dictæ civitatis pro tempore existentium, et centum marcas inde annuatim percipiendas de firmis, redditibus, exitibus, proficuis et aliis commoditatibus quibuscumque de comitatibus nostris Norff' et Suff' provenientibus per manus vicecomitum eorumdem comitatuum pro tempore existentium quousque septingentæ marcæ eisdem Johanni Paston et Thomæ Hows plenarie persolutæ fuerint. In cujus &c. Teste Rege apud Westmonasterium, xxvij. die Julii.

Per ipsum Regem oretenus.

295

474

THOMAS PLAYTER TO JOHN PASTON[1]

To maister John Paston Esquyer in hast.

1461
AUG. 1 (?)
PLEASE your maistership wete that Danyell of Grayes In enfourmed me that Kyng of Dounham whiche slewe Thomas Denys is arested and in hold at Wysbyche and had ben delyvered nor had Fraunceys Costard a taken suerte of pees of hym; and so he is kept in by non other meane but al onely by suerte of pees. And as I felt by the said Danyell if he be craftyly handeled he woll accuse many other; but Danyell is loth to name hem, but I suppose he ment by Twyer and yet other mo, right sufficient, and kalled of substans. Item, Haydon hath payed cccc. marks and is delivered. Item it is talked the parlement schal be proroged tyl the iiij. day of Novembre and the kyng wol in to Scotland in al hast. Wretyn in hast uppon the day of the Advencion.[2]
—Youris,   THOMAS PLAITER.

475

JOHN PASTON TO MARGARET PASTON[3]

To my mastres Paston and Richard Calle.

AUG. 1
FIRST, that Richard Calle fynde the meane that a distresse may be taken of such bestes as occupie the ground at Stratton, and that cleyme and contynuauns be made of my possession in any wise, and that thei be not suffrid to

[1] [Add. MS. 34,888, f. 181.] The year in which this letter was written is certain, not only from the reference to the murder of Thomas Denys, which was in July 1461, but also from the mention of the prorogation of Parliament to the 4th of November.
[2] Probably meaning the Feast of St. Peter ad Vincula (1st August).
[3] [From Paston MSS., B.M.] This letter is printed from a draft which is partly in John Paston's own hand. The contents clearly refer to, first, the Norfolk election of 1461, which it was proposed to confirm by a new meeting of the electors at the shire-house; and secondly, the necessity of electing a new coroner after the murder of Thomas Denys. The date is therefore certain.

296

occupie withowt thei compoune with me; and that aftir the distresse taken the undirshreve be spoke with all that he make no replevyn with out agrement or apoyntement taken, that the right of the lond may be undirstand.   1461 AUG. 1

ij. Item, I here sey the peple is disposed to be at the shire at Norwich on Sen Lauerauns Day for th'affermyng of that thei have do afore, wherof I hold me wele content if thei do it of her owne disposicion, but I woll not be the cause of the labour of hem, ner bere no cost of hem at this tyme, for be the lawe I am suer befor, but I am wel a payed it shall be on han halyday for lettyng of the peples werk. I undirstand ther shall be labour for a coroner that day, for ther is labour made to me for my good wyll here, and I wyll nothyng graunt withowt the under shreves assent, for he and I thought that Richard Bloumvyle were good to that occupacion. Item, ye shall undirstand that the undirshreve was some what flekeryng whill he was here, for he informyd the Kyng that the last eleccion was not peasibill, but the peple was jakkyd and saletted, and riottously disposid, and put hym in fere of his lyfe. Wherefore I gate of hym the writte whech I send yow herwith, to that entent, thow any fals shrewe wold labour, he shuld not be sure of the writ, and therfore ye most se that the undirshreve have the writ at the day, in case the peple be gadered, and thanne lete th'endentures be made up or er they departe.

iij. Item, that ye remembyr Thomas Denys wyfe that her husbond had divers billes of extorcion don be Heydon and other, whech that he told me that his seid wyfe beryid whan the rumour was, so that thei were ny roten. Bidde her loke hem up and take hem yow.

iiij. Item, as for the seyd distreynyng at Stratton, I wold that Dawbeney and Thomas Bon shuld knowe the closes and the ground, that thei myght attende ther to, that Richard were not lettyd of other occupacions, and I wold this were do as sone as is possibill, or I come home. Notwithstandyng, I trowe I shall come home or the shire, but I woll nat it be knowe till the same day, for I will not come there with owt I be sent fore be the peple to Heylisdonne. Notwithstandyng,

297

1461
AUG. 1
and the peple were wele avertised at that day, they shuld be the more redy to shewe the oribyll extorcions and briberys that hath be do upon hem to the Kyng at his comyng, desyring hym that he shuld not have in favor the seyd extorcioners, but compelle hem to make amendes and sethe [*satisfaction*] to the pore peple.

v. Item, that Berney and Richard Wright geve suche folkys warnyng as wyll compleyne to be redy with her billes if thei list to have any remedy.

vj. Item, that the maters ayens Sir Miles Stapilton may at Aylesham be remembyrd.

vij. Also if ye can be any craft get a copy of the bille that Sir Miles Stapilton hath of the corte rolles of Gemyngham, that ye fayle not, but assay and do yowr devyr, for that shuld preve som men shamefully fals. Master Brakle seyd he shuld a get oon of Freston. I wold he shuld assay, or ellys peraventure Skypwith, or ellys Master Sloley; for if Stapilton were boren in hande that he shuld be founde fals and ontrewe, and first founder of that mater, he wold bothe shewe the bille and where he had it.[1]

viij. Item, I wold the prestis of Caster were content for Midsomer term.

ix. Item, ther is a whith box with evidens of Stratton, in on of the canvas baggis in the gret cofir, or in the spruse chest. Ric. Calle knowith it well, and ther is a ded of feffement and a letter of atorne mad of the seyd londs in Stratton to John Damm, W. Lomner, Ric. Calle, and John Russe. I wold a new dede and letter of atorne were mad owth theroff be the feffees of the same laund to Thome Grene,[2] Thome Playter, the parson of Heylisdon, Jacobo Gloys, klerke,[3] Johanni Pamping, and that the ded bere date nowh, and that it be selid at the next shire; for than I suppose the seyd feffes will be ther if it may not be don er that tyme. I wold have the

[1] Between this and the next paragraph is the following sentence crossed out:—'Item, I send yow a writ direct to the Meyer and Shreves of Norwich for to receyve of hem an C. [*hundred*] mark yerly for suche jowellys as the Kyng hath of me.'
[2] This name is substituted for three others crossed out, viz. 'John Grenefeld, Thomas Playter, Water Wrottisle, Squyer.'
[3] Here occurs the name, 'Christofere Grenacre,' crossed out.

298

seyd dedis leyd in a box, both old and new, and left secretly at Ric. Thornis hows at Stratton, that whan I com homwar I mygh fynd it ther, and mak seson [*seisin*] and stat to be take whil I wer ther. Wret at London on Lammes Day.   1461 AUG. 1

476

JOHN RUSSE TO JOHN PASTON[1]

*To my right worshypfull and reverent maistyr,
John Paston, at Norwich.*

RYGHT worshypfull sir, and my right honourable maister, I recomaunde me louly to you. And plese youre maistirshyp to wete that my Maister Clement, youre brothyr, and Plater, wrot a letter to my mayster yore sone[2] yistirday, the tenure of whych was how ye were entretyd there. And as ye desyred me, so I enformyd hem the mater along, for they wist not of it til I told hem; and they wrete the more pleynerly inasmych as a worshypfull man rood the same day, and bare the letter to my seyd maister youre sone.   AUG. 23

The Lord Bourgcher is with the Kynge, and my Lord Warwyk still in the North, &c.

Item, sir, thys day cam on John Waynflet from the Kyng streyt weye, and he is of myn aquyntaunce; and he teld me there was no voyse nor spekyng aboute the Kyng of that mater; and I teld hym all the mater along hou ye were intretyd, whych he wyll put in remembraunce in ony place that he cometh in in Suffolk or Esex as he goth homward, for he owyth no good wil to youre adversary. And the seyd Waynflet teld me that he knowyth for serteyn that the Kyng cometh not to Northefolk til he hathe been upon the Marchys

[1] [From Fenn, iv. 42.] Edward IV. went into the Marches of Wales, as mentioned in this letter, in the autumn of 1461. He was at Gloucester on the 11th September, and at Ludlow on the 21st, as appears by the dates of his privy seals. The matter mentioned in the postscript is doubtless Howard's contention with Paston in the shire-house at Norwich, to which allusion is made in the letter following.
[2] John Paston, the eldest son.

299

1461
AUG. 23
of Walys, and so there is no serteynte of hyse comyng thys many dayez. He teld me he lefte the Kyng with a smal felashyp aboute hym.

And I enqueryd hym of the gydyng of my maystyr yore sone, whiche he comendyd gretly, and seyd that he stood well inconseyt, and dayly shuld increse; and he was well in acqueyntaunce and be lovyd with jentilmen aboute the Kyng. But he seyd ther shal no thyng hurte hym but youre streytnesse of mony to hym, for withoute he have mony in hyse purse, so as he may resonably spende among hem, ellys they wyll not sette by hem; and there be jentilmen sones of lesse reputacion that hath mony more lyberal x. tymez than he hath, and soo in that they seyd Waynflet seyd it were full necessary for you to remembre, &c.

As for tydyngs here bee noon newe, &c. I truste I shal brynge you a letter from my mayster youre sone, or thanne I come, for whych I shal rather thanne fayle abyde on day the lenger. And Jesu have you, my right honourable maister, in Hyse mercyfull governaunce, and preserve you from adversyte. Wretyn at London, on Seynt Bertylmewys Evyn.

I can speke with noo man but that thynke the gydyng of youre adversary hath bee.1 in many causez ryght straunce, and as it is soposyd that he shal undyrstonde at the Parlament; but for Gods sake have men inow aboute yow, for ye undyrstonde is on manerly dysposecion.

Your bedeman and servaunt,

JOHN RUSSE.

300

477

JOHN PASTON, THE ELDEST SON, TO HIS FATHER[1]

To my rythe reverent and worchypfoll fader, John Paston, Esquyer, dwellyng in Heylysdon, be thys letter delyvered in haste.

MOST reverent and worschepfull fadyr, I rekomawnd me hertyly, and submytt me lowlely to your good faderhood, besechyng yow for cheryte of yowr dayly blyssyng. I beseche yow to hold me ascewsyd that I sente to yowe none erste no wrythgtyng, for I kowd not spede to myn intent the maters that ye sent to me for. I have laboryd dayly my Lord of Essexe, Treserer of Ynglond, to have mevyd the Kyng bothe of the maner [of] Deddham and of the byll copye of the Corte Roll, everye mornyng ore he went to the Kyng, and often tymys inqueryd of hym and he had mevyd the Kyng in these matyers. He answeryd me naye, seyyng it was no tyme, and seyd he wold it war osse fayne spedd os I myselfe, offed tymys de layding me that in trouthe I thowt to have send yowe word that I felyd by hym that he was not wyllyng to meve the Kyng ther in. Neverthe lesse I lawberyd to hym contynually, and prayed Barronners hys man to remembyr hym of it. I told offten tyms to my seyd Lord that I had a man teryyn in town, that I schuld a sente to yow for othyr sundry maters, and he teryid for no thyng but that I mythg send yowe by hym an answer of the seyd matyers; othyr tyms besechyng hym to spede me in theys matyers for thys cawse, that ye schulde thynke no defawte in me for remembryng in the seyd maters.

And nowe of late, I, rememberyng hym of the same mater, inqueryd if he had mevyd the Kyngs Hythgnes therin; and he answeryd me that he hadde felte and mevyd the Kyng ther

1461
AUG. 23

1461
AUG. 23

1 [From Fenn, iv. 46.] Allusion is made in this letter, as in the last, to Edward IV.'s going into Wales in 1461. The writer appears to have been with the King, and expecting to accompany him on the journey. Edward was at Battle on the 21st August 1461, according to the dates of his privy seals.

301

1461
AUG. 23
in, rehersyng the Kyngys answer therin; how that, when he had mevyd the Kyng in the seyd maner of Dedham, besechyng hym to be yowr good Lord ther in, konsyderyng the servyse and trewe part that ye have done, and owthg to hym, and in espesyal the rygth that ye have therto, he seyd he wold be your good Lord therin as he wold be to the porest man in Inglond. He wold hold with yowe in yowr rygth; and as for favor, he wyll nogth be under stand that he schal schewe favor mor to one man then to anothyr, nowgth to on in Inglond.

And as for the bille copyd of the Cort Rolle, when he mevyd to him of it, he smylyd and seyd that suche a bylle ther was, seyyng that ye wold an oppressyd sundreys of yowr contremen of worchypfull men, and the for he kepyd it styll. Never the lesse he seyd he schuld loke it uppe in haste, and he schuld have it.

Baronners undertoke to me twyes ore thryes that he schuld so a' remembred hys lord and master,1 that I schuld au had it with inne ij. or iij. dayes. He is often tyms absent, and therfor I have it nowthg yyt; when I kan gete it, I schall send it yowe, and of the Kyngs mowth, hys name that take it hym.

I scend you home Pekok a geyn. He is not for me. God send grace that he may do yow good servyse, that be extymacion is not lykelye. Ye schall have knowleche aftyrward how he hathe demenyd hym her with me. I wold, savyng yowr dysplesure, that ye were delyvered of hym, for he schalle never do yow profyte ner worchyp.

I suppose ye understand that the monye that I hadde of yowe att Londun maye not indur with me tyll that the Kyng goo in to Walys an kome ageyn, for I under stand it schall be long or he kome ageyn. Wher for I have sent to Londun to myn onkyl Clement to gete an Cs. of Christofyr Hansom yowr servaunt, and sene [*send*] it me be my seyd servaunt, and myn herneys with it, whyche I lefte at Lundun to make klene.

I beseche yowe not to be dysplesyd with it, for I kowd make non othyr cheysaunce [*arrangement*] but I schuld a

1 Henry Bourchier, Earl of Essex.

302

boruyed it of a strange man, sum of my felawys, who I suppose schold not lyke yowe, and ye herd of it a nothyr tyme. I ame in suerte wher as I schall have a nothyr maun in the stede of Pekoke.

My Lord of Estsexe seythe he wyll do as myche for yowe as for any esquyer in Inglond, and Beronners hys man telht me, seyy[n]g, 'Yowr fadyr is myche be holdyng to my Lord, for he lovyth hym well.' Bernners mevyd me ons, and seyd that ye must nedys do sum wate for my Lord and hys, and I seyd I wost well that ye wold do for hym that laye in yowre powar. And he seyd that ther was a lytyl mony be twyxe yowe and a jantylman of Estsexe, callyd Dyrward, seyyng that ther is as myche be wern [*between*] my seyd Lord and the seyd jantylman, of the wyche mony he desieryth yowr part.

It is talkyd here how that ye and Howard schuld a' strevyn togueder on the scher daye, and on of Howards men schuld a' strekyn yow twyess with a dagere, and soo ye schuld a ben hurt but for a good dobelet that ye hadde on at that tyme. Blyssyd be God that ye hadde it on. No mor I wryth to yower good faderhod at thys tym, but All myghty God have yowe in Hys kepyng, and sende yowe vyttorye of yowr elmyes [*enemies*], and worschyp in cressyng to yowr lyvys end yn. Wrytyn at Lewys, on Seynt Bertylmwes Eve.

Be yowr servaunt and elder sone,

JOHN PASTON.

1461
AUG. 23

478

CLEMENT PASTON TO JOHN PASTON[1]

To hys rythe reverent and worchypfwll broder, John Paston.

RYTHE reverent and worchypfwll broder, I recomawnde me to yowr good broderhood, desieryng to herre of zour welfar and good prosperite, the gwyche I pray God encresse to His pleswr and zowr herts hesse [*heart's ease*];

AUG. 25

1 [From Fenn, iv. 52.] The references to Howard's conduct, and to John Paston the son being with the King, prove this letter to be of the year 1461. Compare the last paragraph of the letter immediately preceding with the first of this.

303

1461
AUG. 25

certifyyng zow that I have spok with John Rwsse, and Playter spok with him bothe, on Fryday be for Seynt Barthelmw. He tolde us of Howards gydyng, gwyche mad us rythe sory tyl we herde the conclusion that ze hadde non harme.

Also I understood by W. Pekok that my nevew hadde knowleche ther of also up on Saterday nexst be for Seynt Barthelmwe, in the Kyngs howse. Not with standyng, up on the same day Playter and I wryte letters on to him, rehersyng al the mater, for cause if ther wer ony questionys mevyd to hym ther of, that he xwlde telle the trowthe, in cas that the qwestions wer mevyd by ony worchypfwll man, and namyd my Lord Bowcher,[1] for my Lord Bowcher was with the Kyng at that tyme.

I fele by W. Pekok that my nevew is not zet verily aqweyntyd in the Kyngs howse, nor with the officers of the Kyngs howse he is not takyn as non of that howse; for the coks [*cooks*] be not charged to serve hym, nor the sewer[2] to gyve hym no dyche, for the sewer wyll not tak no men no dyschys till they be comawndyd by the cownterroller. Also he is not aqweyntyd with no body but with Weks;[3] and Weks ad told hym that he wold bryng hym to the Kyng, but he hathe not zet do soo. Wherfor it were best for hym to tak hys leve and cum hom, til ze hadd spok with swm body to helpe hym forthe, for he is not bold z now to put forthe hym selfe. But than I consyderyd that if he xwld now cum hom, the Kyng wold thyng [*think*] that wan he xwld doo hym ony servie som wer, that than ze wold have hym hom, the qwyche xwld cause hym not to be hadde in favor; and also men wold thynke that he wer put owte of servic. Also W. Pekok tellythe me that his mony is spent, and not ryotesly, but wysly and discretly, for the costs is gretter in the Kyngs howse qwen he rydythe than ze wend it hadde be, as Wyllam Pekok can tell zow; and therof wee must gett hym jCs. at the lest, as by Wyllam Pekoks seyyng, and zet

[1] Henry, Viscount Bourchier, who had been created Earl of Essex on the 30th June preceding. The writer had forgotten his new dignity.
[2] An officer who had the ordering of the dishes, etc.
[3] John Wykes was an usher of the King's chamber, and a friend and cousin of J. Paston's.—F.

304

that will be to lytill, and I wot well we kan not get xl*d*. of Christifyr Hanswm. So I xall be fayn to lend it hym of myn owne silver. If I knew verily zour entent wer that he xwld cum hom, I wold send hym non. Ther I wyll doo as me thynkithe ze xwld be best plesyd, and that me thynkythe is to send him the silver. Ther for I pray zow hastely as ze may send me azen v. mark, and the remnawnte, I trow, I xall get up on Christofir Hanswm and Lwket. I pray zow send me it as hastely as ze may, for I xall leve my selfe rythe bare; and I pray zow send me a letter how ze woll that he xull be demenyd. Wrytyn on Twsday after Seynt Barthelmwe, &c. Christus vos conservet!

1461
AUG. 25

CLEMENT PASTON.

479

LORD BEAUCHAMP TO SIR THOMAS HOWES[1]

To myn welbeloved frende, Sir Thomas Howys,
Parson of Blofeld.

WELBELOVED frende, I grete you well. And for as muche as I understonde that William Wurcester, late the servant unto Sir John Fastolf, Knyth, whois soule God assoyle, ys not had in favour ne trust with my right welbeloved frende, John Paston, nether with you, as he seyth, namely in such maters and causes as concerneth the wylle and testament of the said Sir John Fastolf; and as I am informed the said William purposeth hym to go into his cuntre, for the whiche cause he hath desired me to wryte unto you that ye wolde ben a special good frend unto hym, for his said mastris sake, to have alle suche things as reason and consciens requireth, and that ye wolde be meane unto Paston for hym in this mater to schewe hym the more favour at thys tyme for this my writyng in doyng of eny truble to hym, trusting that he wole demeane hym in suche wyse that he shal

AUG. 28

[1] [From Fenn, iv. 96.] This letter was probably written in the year 1461, if not in the year preceding. The disputes about Fastolf's will came before the Spiritual Court in the year 1465; but at the date of this letter they could not have proceeded very far.

305

1461
AUG. 28

have no cause unto hym, but to be his good master, as he seyth. And yf ther be eny thing that I can do for you, I wole be right glad to do it, and that knoweth Almyghty God, whiche have you in his keping. Wretin at Grenewyche, the xxviij[th] day of August.

J. BEAUCHAMP.

480

LORD HUNGERFORD AND ROBERT WHITYNGHAM TO MARGARET OF ANJOU[1]

A la Reyne D'Engleterre [en] Escote.

AUG. 30

MADAM, please it yowr gode God, we have sith our comyng hider, writen to your Highnes thryes. The last we sent by Bruges, to be sent to you by the first vessell that went into Scotland; the oder ij. letters we sent from Depe, the ton by the Carvell in the whiche we came, and the oder in a noder vessell. But, ma dam, all was oon thyng in substance, of puttyng you in knolege of the Kyng your uncles[2] deth, whom God assoyll, and howe we sta[n]de arest [*arrestea*], and doo yet; but on Tuysday next we trust and understande, we shall up to the Kyng, your cosyn germayn.[3] His Comyssaries, at the first of our tarrying, toke all our letters and writyngs, and bere theym up to the Kyng, levyng my Lord of Somerset in kepyng atte Castell of Arkes,[4] and my felowe Whityngham and me, for we had sauff conduct, in the town of Depe, where we ar yete. But on Tyysday next we understand, that it pleaseth the said Kyngs Highnes that we shall come to hys presence, and ar charged to bring us up, Monsieur de Cressell, nowe Baillyf of Canse, and Monsieur de la Mot.

Ma dam, ferth [*fear*] you not, but be of gode comfort,

[1] [From Fenn, i. 246.] That this letter was written in the year 1461 is sufficiently evident from its contents. The MS. from which it was printed by Fenn was a copy in the handwriting of Henry Windsor, and was manifestly the enclosure referred to in his letter No. 483. It bore the same paper-mark as that letter.
[2] Charles VII. of France. He died on the 22nd July 1461.
[3] Lewis XI., son of Charles VII.
[4] Arques, in Normandy, south of Dieppe.

306

and beware that ye aventure not your person, ne my Lord the Prynce,[1] by the See, till ye have oder word from us, in less than your person cannot be sure there as ye ar, [and] that extreme necessite dryfe you thens; and for God sake the Kyngs Highnes be advysed the same. For as we be enformed, Th'erll of March[2] is into Wales by land, and hath sent his navy thider by see; and, Ma dame, thynketh verily, we shall not soner be delyvered, but that we woll come streght to you, withaut deth take us by the wey, the which we trust he woll not, till we see the Kyng and you peissible ayene in your Reame; the which we besech God soon to see, and to send you that your Highnes desireth. Writen at Depe the xxx[ti] dey of August.

1461
AUG. 30

Your true Subgettes and Liege men.

HUNGERFORD.
WHITYNGHAM.

At the bottom of the Copy of the Letter is added:—

These ar the names of those men that ar in Scotland with the Quene. The Kyng Herry is at Kirkhowbre with iiij. men and a childe.

Quene Margaret is at Edenburgh and hir son.

The Lord Roos and his son.

John Ormond.	Sir Edmund Hampden.
William Taylboys.	Sir Henry Roos.
Sir John Fortescu.	John Courteney.
Sir Thomas Fyndern.	Myrfyn of Kent.
Waynesford of London.	Dauson.
Thomas Thompson of Guynes.	Thomas Burnby.
	Borret of Sussex.
Thomas Brampton of Guynes.	Sir John Welpdalle.
John Audeley of Guynes.	Mr. Roger Clerk, of London.
Langheyn of Irland.	John Retford, late Coubitt.
Thomas Philip of G[i]ppeswich.	Giles Senctlowe.
	John Hawt.

[1] Edward, son of Henry VI.
[2] Edward IV., whom the Lancastrians did not yet recognise as king.

307

THE PASTON LETTERS

481

JOHN PAMPYNG TO JOHN PASTON, SENIOR [1]

To my right worshipfull master John Paston, the older, Squier.

1461
SEPT. 6

PLEASE your mastirship to wete that I have be at Cotton, and spoke with Edward Dale, and he told me that Yelverton and Jenney were there on Friday,[2] and a toke distresse of xxvj. or more bullokks of the seid Edwards in the Park, and drofe hem to a town therby; and a neygh-bore there understandyng the bests were Edward Dalis,[3] and bond hym to pay the ferme, or ellis to bryng in the bests be a day. And whan the seid Edward undirstod the takyng of the seid bests he went to Yelverton and Jenney, and bond hym in an obligacon of xli., to pay hem his ferme at Mighelmes; whech I told hym was not well do, for I told hym ye had be abill to save hym harmeles. And because of discharge of his neyghbour he seid he myght non other wise do. Nevirthelesse as for mony thei get none of hym redely, ner of the tenaunts nowthyr, as he can thynk yet. The seid Yelverton dyned on Friday at Cotton, and there chargid the tenaunts thei shuld pay no mony but to hym, and hath flaterid hem, and seith thei shall be restorid ayen of such wrongs as thei have had be Sir Philip Wentworth and other for Master Fastolff; and because of such tales, your tenaunts owe hym the bettir will. And I purposid to have gon to Cotton and spoke with the tenaunts, and Edward Dale told me he supposid thei wold be this day at Nakton. And because [I desired][4] to speke with hem as ye comaundid me, I terid not but rod to Ipwich to my bed, and there at the Sonne was the seid Yelverton and Jenney and Thomas Fastolff; and myn ost told me, that the same aftir

[1] [From Paston MSS., B.M.] In the letter of James Gloys, which follows (No. 482), will be found an allusion to a recent 'revel done in Suffolk' by Yelverton and Jenney. That the affair alluded to was the same which is described in this letter will appear beyond doubt if the reader will refer to Letter 487.
[2] 4th September. [3] Apparently the writer has omitted a word or more here.
[4] Omitted in MS.

308

none thei had be at Nakton, but what thei ded there I can not telle, and whan I was undirstand your man, Hogon, Jenneys man, askyd suerte of pes of me; and Jenney sent for an officer to have hed me to prison; and so myn ost undirtoke for me that nyght. And this day in the mornyng I wente to Sen Laurerauns Chirche; and there I spak to hem and told hem ye merveylid that thei wold take any distresse or warne any of your tenaunts that thei shuld pay yow no mony. And Yelverton seid ye had take a distresse falsly and ontrewly of hym that ought yow no mony ner hem nowther. And he seid he was inffifd as well as ye; and as for that I told hym he wost odre [knew the contrary], and thow he were it was but your use, and so I told hym that men were inffifd in his lond, and that he shuld be servid the same withinne fewe dayes. And he seid he wost well ye were not inffifd in his lond, and if ye toke upon yow to make any trobill in his lond ye shall repente it. And also he seid that he wold do in like wise in alle maners that were Sir John Fastolffs in Norfolk as thei have begonne, and other langage as I shall telle yow. And so I am with the gayler, with a clogge upon myn hele for suerte of the pees; wherfore please your mastirship to send me your avise.

Item, John Andrews was with hem at Cotton, and thei have set a man of the seid Andrews to kepe the plase.

Item, Wymondham, Debenham and Tympirle come to Yelverton this day at masse and speke with hym; and I speke to Tymperle in your name that he wold not comforte ner be with hem ayein in this mater; and he seid he undirstod no such thyng, ner it was not his comyng hedir. Wretyn at Ipwych the Sonday next before the Nativite of Owr Lady.

Yowr servaunt, JOHN PAMPYNG.

The back is covered with some rough memoranda in Richard Calle's hand, of moneys received at different times of year by Richard Charlys, Thomas Howys, William Berton, baker, of Southwark, Ralph Lovel, John Prentyng, Richard Coomber, and John de Dorylot. Some of these payments are made through Dawbeney, John Paston, junior, and John Paston, senior (*per manus Johannis Paston Senioris*).

309

THE PASTON LETTERS

482

JAMES GLOYS TO JOHN PASTON [1]

To the right reverent and wurchepfull Sir, and my gode mayster, John Paston, Esquyer.

1461
SEPT. 24

RIGHT reverent and wurchepfull sir, I recomand me to your gode maystershep, prayng you to wete that I was at Blakkes, and spake with his wiffe; and she seth he was not at hame this iij. weks,—he ridith up the countre to take accompts of balys [*bailiffs*],—and that this day sevennyght he shuld have satyn in Caystr by you up on accounts, and fro thens he shuld have redyn to Lynne, and that he shall be at home un Monday at nyght next comyng. Wherfor I have left my heraund with her. But she seth that he shall not mown comyn [*be able to come*] to you, for my Lady[2] have sent for hym in gret hast, bothyn be a letter and be a tokyn, to comyn to her as hastly as he may; notwithstandyng she shall do the herand to hym.

As for Yelverton, I dede a gode fele to enquer of Yemmys Skynner whan the seid Yelverton shuld go to London. He seid not this sevynnyght. He cowde not tell what day till he had spokyn with his son. His sone shuld come to hym or his master shuld ridyn. I shall enquer mor at Walsyngham. And for Godds love be not to longe fro London, for men seyn ther, as I have be [told], that my Lord of Glowcetir[3] shuld have Caystre, and ther is gret noyse of this revell that was don in Suffolk be Yelverton and Jeney; and your wele willers thynkyn that if thei myght prevayle in this, thei wold attempt you in other. But seas ther pore and malyce, and preserve

[1] [From Fenn, iv. 58.] On the back of this letter is the following memorandum in a contemporaneous hand:—'De Ric'o Calle pro ordio (*i.e.* hordeo) ibidem pro ij. annis terminatis ad Mic' anno primo regni Regis E. iiij., xxvj. viijd.' This shows that the letter itself could not have been written later than 1461, and as there was no 'Lord of Gloucester' before that year, it could not have been earlier.
[2] Alice, Duchess of Suffolk.
[3] Richard, the King's brother, afterwards Richard III.

310

EDWARD IV

you from all evill. And at the reverence of God lete sum interposicion go a twix you and my mastres your moder or ye go to London, and all that ye do shall spede the better; for she is set on gret malyce, and every man that she spekith with knowith her hert, and it is like to be a fowle noyse [over] all the countre with aught it be sone sesid.

1461
SEPT. 24

Also, sir, it is told me that my Lord of Norfolk is comyn to Framlyngham, and that ye be gretly comendyd in his hows-hold. Therfor it wer wele do, me semyth, that ye spake with hym. The Holy Trynyte kepe you.

Wretyn at Norwich, the Thursday next after Sent Mathewe.

Your pore prest, JAMES GLOYS.

483

HENRY WYNDESORE TO JOHN PASTON [1]

To my full worshipfull, speciall gode maister, John Paston, Squyer, abidyng at Norwich.

OCT. 4

RIGHT worshipfull sir, and some tyme my moost speciall gode master, I recommaunde me unto your gode mais-tership, with all my pour service, if it may in any wise suffice; and farthermore, sir, I beseche you, nowe beyng in your countre, where ye may deily call unto you my maister Sir Thomas Howys, ones to remembre my pour mater, and by your discretions to take such a direction theryn, and so to conclude, as may be to your discharge and to my furtherance, accordyng to the will of hym that is passed unto Gode, whose saull I pray Jesu pardone! for truly, sir, ther was in hym no faute, but in me onely; yf it be not as I have remembred your maistership affore thy[s] tyme. For truly, sir, I der say I shuld have had as speciall and as gode a maister of you, as any pour man, as I am, withyn England shuld have hadd of a worshipfull man, as ye ar, yf ye had never medulled the godes of my maister F., and as moche ye wold have done, and labored fore me, in my

[1] [From Fenn, i. 240.] For the date of this letter, compare No. 480.

311

1461
OCT. 4

right, if it hadde byn in the handes of any oder man than of your self anely. But, I truste in Gode, at your next comyng to have an answere, such as I shalbe content with. And yf it may be so, I am and shalbe your servaunt in that I can or may, that knoith our Lord Jesu, whom I besech save and sende you a gode ende in all your maters, to your pleiser and worship everlastyng. Amen. Writton at London, iiijᵗᵒ die Octobris.

As fore tidyngs, the Kyng wolbe at London withyn iij. deies next comyng ; and all the castelles and holdes in South Wales, and in North Wales, ar gyfen and yelden up into the Kynges hand. And the Duc of Excestre [1] and th'erle of Pembrok [2] ar floon and taken the mounteyns, and dyvers Lordes with gret puissans ar after them ; and the moost part of gentilmen and men of worship ar comen yn to the Kyng, and have grace, of all Wales.

The Duc of Somerset, the Lord Hungerford, Robert Whityngham, and oder iiij. or v. Squyers are comen into Normandy out of Scotland, and as yette they stand strete under arest ; and as merchauntes that ar comen late thens sey, they ar like to be demed and jugged prisoners. My Lord Wenlok, Sir John Cley, and the Dean of Seynt Severyens, have abiden at Cales thise iij. wikes, and yette ar there, abidyng a saufconduit, goyng uppon an ambassate to the Frenshe Kyng ; and Sir Wauter Blount, Tresorer of Cales, with a grete feleship of souldeours of Cales, and many oder men of the Marches, have leyn, and yette doo, at a seege afore the Castell of Hampmes, by side Cales, and deily make gret werre, either parte toother.

Item, I send unto you a copy of a letter that was taken uppon the see, made by the Lord Hungerford and Whytyngham.

Item, we shall have a gret ambassate out of Scotland in all hast of Lordes.

At your comaundement, and Servaunt,
HENRY WYNDESORE.

[1] Henry Holland. He married Anne, sister of King Edward IV., but remained a steady Lancastrian, and was attainted this year in Parliament.
[2] Jasper Tudor, half-brother of Henry VI.

484

CLEMENT PASTON TO JOHN PASTON [1]

To his right reverent and worshipfull broder, John Paston, Esquier, be this delivered in great haste.

1461
OCT. 11

BROTHER, I recommende me to you. After all dewe recommendacions, &c. Sir, it was tolde me by rythe a worshipfull man that loveth you rythe well, and ye him, and ye sall knowe his name hereafter, but put all things out of doubt he is such a man as will not lye : on the xjᵗʰ day of October the Kinge said, ' We have sent two privy sealys to Paston by two yomen of our chamber, and he disobeyeth them ; but we will send him anoder tomorrowe, and by Gods mercye, and if he come not then he sall dye for it. We will make all oder men beware by him how they sall disobey our writinge. A servant of our hath made a complainte of him. I cannot thinke that he hath informed us all truely, yet not for that, we will not suffer him to disobey our writinge ; but sithen he disobeyeth our writinge, we may beleve the better his gydinge is as we be informed.' And therwith he made a great avowe that if he [ye] come not at the third commandement ye xulde dye therefore. This man that told me this is as well learned a man as any is in England ; and the same xjᵗʰ day of October, he advised me to send a man to yow in all the hast that might be to lett yow have knowlache, and that ye xulde not lett for none excuse, but that ye xulde make the man good cheere and come as hastily ye might to the Kinge, for he understandeth so much that the King will keep his promise. Notwithstanding, by mine advice, if ye have his letter or the messenger come to you, come to the Kinge wards or ye meet

[1] This letter is reprinted from the *Norfolk Archæology*, vol. iv. p. 26, where it is edited from a transcript contained in a MS. genealogy of the Paston family drawn up by Sandford, author of the *Genealogical History of England*. The references to Howard's animosity against Paston, and to an approaching Parliament, prove clearly that this letter is of the year 1461.

1461
OCT. 11

with him, and when ye come ye must be suer of a great excuse. Also if ye doe well, come right stronge, for Howards wife made her bost that if any of her husbands men might come to yow ther yulde goe noe penny for your life ; and Howard hath with the Kinge a great fellowship.

This letter was written the same day that the Kinge said these words, and the same day that it was told me, and that day was the xjᵗʰ day of October as abovesaid ; and on the next morning send I forth a man to yow with this letter, and on the same day send the Kinge the third privye seale to you. Also he that tolde me this seid that it were better for yow to come up than to be fotte out of your house with streingth, and to abide the Kings judgement therin, for he will take your contumacy to great displeasure. Also, as I understand, the Duke of Norffolk hath made a great complaint of yow to the King, and my Lord of Suffolk [1] and Howard and Wyngfelde helpe well to every day and call upon the King against yow. The Kinge is at this day at Grenewich, and ther will be still till the Parliament beginne. Some say he will goe to Walsingham, but Mr. Sotyll seid in the aulle in the Temple that he harde no worde of any such pilgrimage. No more, &c. Writton the xjᵗʰ day of October at midnight.

My nevew John tolde me also that he supposed ther were out proclamacions against yow, &c. the same day.

By CLEMENT PASTON,
your broder.

[1] John de la Pole, son and heir of William, Duke of Suffolk, who was attainted in 1450, was not restored to the Dukedom till the 23rd of March 1463 ; but being in favour at court, and having married Edward IV.'s sister, he seems even at this time to have been popularly called ' my Lord of Suffolk.'

485

RICHARD CALLE TO JOHN PASTON

To my ryght reverent and wurschipfull maystre, my mastre John Paston.

1461
OCT. 13

PLESITH it your maystreschip to witte that Mr. John and I, with other mo, have ben at Cotton on Friday [2] last passed, and there Jenney had do warned the corte there to be the same Friday, and he was at Eye at the cescions the Thorsday before ; and on the Friday in the mornynge he was comyng to Cotton to hoolde the corte there. And it fortuned we had entred the place or he come ; and he herd therof and turned bac a yein to Oxon [3] to my Lorde of Norwiche, and there dyned with hym. And my Lorde sent Mr. John Colleman to Cotton Halle to speke with you ; and at hes comyng he undrestode ye were not there, and if ye had, my Lorde desired you to come and spoken with hym, and that my Lorde desired to put your matre in a trety ; in so moche that Mr. John Colleman tolde to my master, John Paston, that diverse of your elmees [enemies] had labored to my Lorde to have a trety if he cowde brynge it aboute, &c. And as for the tenaunts they wolde not come at the place on to the tyme that I sent for hem, for they sey pleynly they woll not have a do with hem ; and so the corte whas holden in your name, and the tenaunts ryght weele plesed ther of, excepte Thurnberne and Agas, and as for any socour, they have there ryght noone at all. And so Mr. John whas ther Friday all day and Saterday tyll none ; and than he toke hes horse with xxx. men with hym and rode to Jeney place, and toke there xxxvj. heede of nete, and brought hem in to Norfolk ; and so whas I left still at Cotton with xij. men with me, be cauce they reporte and we abode there ij. dayes we

[1] [From Paston MSS., B.M.] On comparing this letter with No. 481, no one will doubt that both were written in the same year.
[2] 9th October. [3] Hoxne.

THE PASTON LETTERS

1461
oct. 13

schulde be pult out be the heeds. And so we a mode [? *abode*] there v. dayes and kepte the place, and I walked aboute all the lordeschippes and spake with all the fermours and tennaunts that longen to the maner to undrestande her disposessyon and to receyve money of hem ; and I fynde [them] ryght weele disposed to you. And be cauce the corte whas warned in her name and not in youre, therfor they purvey no money ; but they have promysed me to pay no money to no man but to you, so that ye woll safe hem harmeles ; and I told hem ye wold safe hem harmeles. They have apoynted with me to make redy her money withinne a fornyght aftre Halowemesse, &c. I have receyved of the tenaunts that I undrestod out [*owed*] you werst wyll viij. marc, &c. And as for Edward Dalys money it is redy, so that your maistreschip woll se that he be not hurt be hes obligacion. Ferthermore, plesit your maistreschip to sende worde if they entre into the maner ayein, how we schall be rwled and gidyd ; for the tenaunts fere hem they wol entre whan we be gon, and than wol they distreyne the tenaunts, for they sey there that my Lorde of Cauntyrbury and other Lords woll relese to hem, notwithstandyng that I have enformed hem other wice ; wherfore, savyng your better advice, me semethe it were ryght weele doo that ye had a letter of my Lorde of Cauntirbury, and other to the tenaunts of Cotton that it is her wyll and entent that ye schulde have the rwle and gouernaunce, and receyve the money of that maner, and other that were Sir John Fastolff, on whom God have mercy, for I dought not and suche a lettre came downe to the tenaunts there schulde no man sey nay to it. Beschyng your maystreschup to have an answere of how we schall be gided and rwled, &c. Item, to sende worde howe we schall doo with the geere that wee toke out at the Wyght Freris, wether it schall be sent to you or nought. And Jesu preserve you. Wreten at Norwiche upon Sein Edwards Day.

Be your servaunt and bedman,
RIC. CALLE.

Endorsed in a hand nearly contemporaneous: 'Litter' *sirca anno (sic)* E. 4 iij. *vel* iiijo.'

316

486

WILLIAM NAUNTON TO JOHN PASTON, SENIOR [1]

To my Master Paston, the elder, be thys letter delyveryd in hast.

1461
oct.

RYGHT wurchypful sir, I recommend me to zour good masterchyp. The cause qwy I wryth I let zour have knowlech of the mene that be in Cotton Halle, how they be strangely dysposyd ageyns zow ; for, as I here say, they make revell there. They melt led and brek down zour bregg, and make that no man go in to [the] place but on a ledder, and make them as strong as they kan a geyns zow be the supportacion of Jeney and Debenham, and hys sone ; for they seye ther that Jeney hath sold the lyflod on to Debynham, and that hys son the knyth shall dwell ther, and ther forr they have warnyd a cort ageyns Munday, and now they ar a vysed to kepyt on Saturday be forr Munday. Qwat they mene therby I wot never, but as for the felechyp in the place that ys there now, and have be here al thys weke, there ys no man of substans, as we here, and there have be but vij. or viij. al thys wyke ; but there wyll be a gret felechyp thys nyth or to morwe up on Saturday, for than they wyl kepe the cort. And as for Edward Dale, he dar not abyde wyl at hom, they thret hym so, be cause he wyl send them no vytaly. And as for me self, Edward Dale dar not let me wyll [*well*] be there for takyng in suspecyon. And jas for the tenaunts, they be wel dysposyd except j. or ij., so that ze wyl support them in hast, for they may nowt kepe of ther katel of the ground long ; and specyally they desyr to have zowr owne presens, and they wold be of gret cownfort. No mor I wryth to zour, but the Holy Gost have zour in kepyng. Wretyn on the Fryday after my departyng. Be your Servaunt,

WYLLYAM NANTON.

[1] [From Fenn, iii. 414.] This letter corresponds so closely with the next in what is said about the occupants of Cotton Hall, that it is clear they were both written about the same time.

317

THE PASTON LETTERS

487

RICHARD CALLE TO JOHN PASTON, JUNIOR [1]

To the right worschipfull sir and maistre, John Paston jun., esquyer.

1461
oct.

RYGHT worschipfull sir, I recomaunde me unto your mastreschip, certifiyng you that Jenney and Yelverton hathe certified up in to the Kynges Benche insurrecions [and] congregacions a yenste me ; wherupon they have sente to the scheryff a writte chargyng hym in peyne of C*li.* to brynge me in to the Kyngs Benche the morwe after Sein Marteyn. And this daye the seide Jenney hathe sent doune to the scheryff an other writte called an *habeas corpus* retornable *crastino Animarum*, weche schalbe on Twesday next comyng be cauce they were in dought and in greete feere that I schulde have ben aquytte of the inditement of fellony now at this gayle delyverye. And also my maistre hathe sente an other writte for me retornable at the seid *crastino Animarum*. And so I am like to ride to London warde to morwe. And the scheryff wold make me to fynde suerte that I schulde appere in the Kyngs Benche the seid daye ; and yet, that notwithstandyng, he wolde send me with strenghe of men as a presoner ; and if any thynge schall cauce me that I goo not up to London, it schalbe be cauce I woll fynde no' suerte ; for in cas he wold have suffred me to have gon up be my selfe at myn owne coste, I wolde have founde hym suerte. And so at the makyng of this bille we were not fully condesended hough we schulde doo. My mastre is in goode hele, blissed be Godd, and dothe and schall doo ryght weele in alle hes maters. Ther

[1] [From Paston mss., B.M.] This letter was written in a year in which the morrow of All Souls' Day (*i.e.* the 3rd November) fell on Tuesday. The Dominical letter of the year must therefore be D. This was the case in 1461, and no other year will suit a letter addressed to John Paston, junior. For if we go back there is no earlier year in which D was the Dominical letter till we come to 1450, when John Paston, junior, was only ten years old ; and if we go forward the next is 1467, which was after John Paston the father's death.

318

1461
oct.

is an ongracious felaschip of hem and a fals. They have sent for Fitzraff and Schipdam, be a citacion for the proffe of the testement, and alle is but for to delay it ; yet it were weele done ye rode over to Fitzraff and felte hes disposicion how he woll be disposed, and in like wice with Schipdam, for I have spoken with hem of that matre, in cas that any citacion come doun for hem, how they wolde be disposed, and I have founde the too straunchely disposed. God send us a good scheryf thys yere, and thanne we schalle do weele inough, be the grace of God.

And, sir, your man tolde me that ye desired to knowe the demenyng at Cotton of the tenaunts and other. I lete you wete the moste parte of alle the tenaunts have bene here with me for to see me, and they have tolde me all the demenyng as it is undrewrete. Furst, as for the money that they receyved there it drwe upon a xxiiij[ti] *li.* and more silver, for the tenaunts myght not cheese but they moste nedes paye, for they distreyned on my Lords of Suffolk fee, my Lords of Norwich fee, and on all men grounde, so that they myght not have her catell in reste, weche caused hem to paye her money. I knowe weele i nough who payed and wo paied not. All the grete fermours have payed. And as for the kepyng of the place ther be therin iiij. men, and on of Debenham men, called Sokelyng, and hes wyff, and on Mannyng, a tenaunt, a fals knave ; and they have enforced them as stronke as they kan, and they have broken doune the brigge and have leide a planke over, in cas that ye go theder ye may not come at Dale is howce in no waie, for he have had meche trouble for my mastre and for me ; but and ye wolde gete my Lords meane and pulle the knaves out be the heede, it were weele done. I purpose to com hom warde that same wey. Item, I lete you witte that the gayle delyverye holdeth not this daye, and alle is doone be cauce of mee, Jenney wolde not lete the clerke of peas come hether this daye for feere that I schulde have ben aquytte of the felonye, for in trouthe and tho it had holden, I had founde the meane for to have ben quytte, for I whas through with the scheryff and panel made aftyr myn avice ; but though the

319

THE PASTON LETTERS

1461
OCT.

gayle delyver had holden, I cowde not have ben delyverd, becauce of thes writtes that be come downe. Item, the scheryff hathe a grete losse that this daye holdethe not, for ther schulde have ben quytte xl. men this daye. Item, the scheryff tolde me that my maistre tolde hym that I whas assent to my takyng at Scoolys, weche was to me ryght greete hevynes and discomforture nough in my trouble. And God knoweth it was never my wylle ner myn entent, as I mot be saved at the dredful day of Dome ; for ther is no man so sore hurte as I am be the takyng, bothe in losse, and also in reprefe of myn owne persoune and of my frends, withoute that my mastre be my good maistre, as I truste he wolle be, or elles I am disseyved. He hathe my trewe servyce and shal have whylle that I leve, what so ever his mastreschip do to me, but I can thynke he hathe be enformed be myn elmyes [*enemies*] that wold make hym disp[l]esed with me, and to be myn evy [*heavy*] mastre, but dissimulacion dothe muche harme, &c. I reporte me, &c. No more to you at this tyme, but Jesu kepe you, and send you as much fortune and grace as I wolde ye had, &c. I beseche [you] to be my goode mastre as ye have be, for I never deserved nor wol deserve the contrary.

Your servaunt, RIC. CALLE,
presoner.

END OF VOLUME III

Printed by T. and A. CONSTABLE, Printers to His Majesty
at the Edinburgh University Press

The
Paston Letters
Volume 4

THE PASTON LETTERS

Edward IV

488

MARGARET PASTON TO JOHN PASTON[1]

A Lettre to J. Paston, Armig., from his wife, shewing his imprisonment in the Fleete.[2]

RYTH worchepfull husbond, I recomand me to yow. Plesyt yow to wet that I receyvyd yowyr lettyr that ye sent me by John Holme on Wednysday last past, and also I receyvvd a nothyr lettyr on Fryday at nyt,

1461 NOV. 2

[1] [From Fenn, iv. 232.] This letter is ascribed by Fenn to the year 1465, in consequence of the allusion to John Paston's imprisonment in the Fleet. But there were more occasions than one on which he was confined there. Fenn himself knew of two. Paston was committed to the Fleet, as we know from William Worcester, on Saturday, the 3rd November 1464. He was also confined there in August and September 1465, and may very possibly have been released by the beginning of November. But I am inclined to think this letter refers to an imprisonment prior to either of these. For, in the first place, the news of it seems only to have been recent. It had become general subject of conversation at Norwich, 'on Saturday last,' whereas in 1465 it must have been known two months earlier. Secondly, Sir William Chamberlain, whose influence Sir Thomas Howes hopes will be of service, must have died in the spring of 1462. According to Blomefield (*Hist. of Norfolk*, i. 321), his will was dated the 3rd March 1461 (which would be in the modern computation 1462), and was proved on the 21st April 1462. It may be presumed, therefore, that on receiving the letter from his brother Clement (No. 484), written on the 11th October 1461, John Paston hastened up to London and was immediately thrown into prison. By this letter, however, we find that he was soon afterwards released, and his great enemy Howard sent to prison in his stead.

[2] There is no direction to the letter, but the words above inserted are written in an ancient hand upon the back of it.—F.

VOL. IV.—A   I

THE PASTON LETTERS

1461 NOV. 2 that ye sent me by Nycolas Newmanys man, of the whyche lettyrs I thanc yow; for I schold ellys a' thowt that it had be wers with yow than it hathe be, or schal be, by the grace of Almyty God. And yet I kowd not be mery, sethyn I had the last lettyr tyll thys day that the Meyir sent to me, and sent me werd that he had knowlege for very trowthe that ye wer delyveryd owt of the Flet, and that Howard was comytyd to ward for dyvers gret compleynts that wer mad to the Kyng of hym. It was talkyd in Norwyche and in dyvers othyr plasys in the contre on Saterday last past, that ye wer comytyd to Flet, and in good feyth, as I herd sey, the pepyle was ryth sory ther of, bothe of Norwyche and in the contre. Ye ar ryth myche bownde to thank God, and all tho that love yow, that ye have so gret love of the pepyll as ye have. Ye ar myche behold to the Meyir[1] and to Gylberd,[2] and to dyvers othyr of the aldyrmen, for feythfully they owe yow good wyll to ther porys.

I have spoke with Syr Thomas Howys for swyche thyngys as ye wrot to me for, and he promysyd me that he schold labour it aftyr yowyr intent as fast as he kowd; and in good feyth, as my brodyr and Playter kan tell yow, as be hys seying to us, he is and wole be feythfull to yow. And as for Wylliam Wyrcestyr, he hathe be set so up on the hone, what by the parson and by othyr, as my brodyr and Playter schall telle yow, that they hope he wole do well i now. The parson seyd ryth well and pleynly to hym. The parson tolde me that he had spook with Syr Wylliam Chambyrleyn,[3] and with hys wyfe, and he thynkyth that they wole do well i now aftyr yowyr intent, so that they be plesantly intretyd. The parson tolde me that he wyst well that Syr Wylliam Chambyrleyn cowd do more ese in swyche matyers as ye wrot of, towchyng my Lord of Bedford,[4] than ony man kowd do that leveyth at

[1] William Norwich was Mayor of Norwich in 1461.
[2] John Gilbert was Mayor in 1459 and in 1464. He died in 1472.
[3] Sir William Chamberlain of Gedding, Suffolk, a Knight of the Garter, who had served under the Regent Bedford in the French wars. He married Anne, daughter and heir of Sir Robert de Herling, who, though she long survived him, and had two husbands after him, the second of whom was John, Lord Scrope of Bolton, was buried by her own desire beside her first husband, in the chancel of Herling Church.
[4] John, Duke of Bedford, Regent of France, died at Paris in 1435.—F.

EDWARD IV

1461 NOV. 2 thys day. Also he tolde me that he felt by hem that they wold owe yow ryth good wyll, so that ye wold owe hem good wyll. The parson hopyth verily to make yow acordyd when he comyth to London.

Item, my brodyr and Playter wer with Calthorp[1] to inquer of the mater that ye wrot to me of. What answer he gave hem, they schall tell yow. I sent the Parson of Heylysdon[2] to Gurnay[3] to spek to hym of the same mater, and he seyth feythefully ther was no swyche thyng desyiryd of hym, and thow it had be desyiryd, he wold nowthyr a' seyd nor done a yens yow. He seyd he had ever fownde you lovyng and feythfull to hym, and so he seyd he wold be to yow to hys power, and desyiryng me that I wold not thynk hym the contrary. As for John Gros, he is at Slole; ther for he myth not be spok with.

I pray yow that ye wole send me word whedyr ye wole that I schall remeve frome hens, for it begynyth to wax a cold abydyng her. Syr Thomas Howys and John Rus schall make an end of all thyngys aftyr yowyr intent, as myche as they can do ther in this week, and he purposyth to come forward to yow on the Monday next aftyr Seynt Leonardys Day.

My brodyr and Playter schold a be with yow er thys tym, but that they wold a byd tyl thys day wer past, be cause of the schyer. I spok to my brodyr Wylliam as ye bad me, and he told me, so God hym help, that he hyryd ij. horse ij. dayis be for that ye redyn, that he myth a' ryde forthe with yow; and be cause that ye spak not to hym to ryde with yow, he seyd that he wend[4] ye wold[5] have had hym with yow.

Thomas Fastolfys modyr was her on the next day aftyr ye wer redyn, to have spoke with yow for hyr sone. Sche[6]

[1] *Query*, if Sir William Calthorpe, Knight, High Sheriff of Norfolk, etc., in 1464, and died very old in 1494.—F.
[2] Thomas Hert was instituted to the Rectory of Hellesdon in 1448.—F.
[3] Thomas Gurney of Norwich, Esq., died in 1471.—F.
[4] 'Woud' in Fenn in the original text, but this is evidently a misprint. The right-hand copy reads 'wend,' *i.e.* weened or thought, and the note immediately following shows that this was the reading intended.
[5] The word 'not' seems here to have been omitted in the original letter.—F.
[6] The word 'He' occurs in the text before 'Sche,' but is evidently a mistake.

THE PASTON LETTERS

1461
NOV. 2

prayith yow, at the reverens of God, that ye wole be hys good mastyr, and to help hym in hys ryth, that he may have hom hys lyvelod owt of ther handys that have had it in hys nownage. Sche seyth that they wold mak hym a yer yonger than he is, but sche seyth that he is more thane xxj., and upon that sche dare take an othe.

And the Blyssyd Trynyte have yow in Hys kepyng, and send yow good sped in all yowyr matyrs, and send the vyctary of all yowyr enmyis.

Wretyn in hast, on Sowlemas Daye.[1]

By yowyrs,   M. P.

489

MARGARET PASTON TO JOHN PASTON[2]

To my ryth worchepfull [hus]bond, John Paston, be thys delyveryd in hast.

NOV. 20

RYTH worchepfull husbond, I recomand me to yow. Plesyt yow to wet that I receyvyd yowyr lettyr that ye sent by the gold smyth, as thys day in the mornyng. As for Syr Thomas, he sent me word he schold to yow ward as on Twysday last past; if he fayle ony thyng that ye sent word he schold bryng with hym, it is not for no lak of remembrans, for I sent to hym thryis or fowyr tymys ther for, and that he schold hast hym ther in. As for Rychard Call, he was not at home thys fortnyth. When he comyth I schall do yowir erendys to hym; and as for all yowyr odyr erendys I schall do hem as well as I can. I sent yow a byll yestyrday by old Taverham, and a byll of Jone Gaynys mater, the whyche bylle I pray yow may be delyveryd to Thomas Playter. I spak to hym of the same mater or he yed hens, and I pray yow, if it plese yow, to geve hym yowyr avyse what ye thynk is best to do ther in. Sche seyth sche is ryth

[1] All Souls', otherwise Soulmas Day, and of November.—F.
[2] [From Paston MSS., B.M.] This letter seems to have been written in 1461, the year of John Paston's great dispute with Howard.

4

THE PASTON LETTERS

Year
uncertain

remayn be the grace of God all the days of myn liff. And, sir, I suppose I shall never see yow no more, nor non of myn frendes, whiche is to me the grettest lamentacion that myght come un to myn herte; for, sir, by the grace of God, I shall go to Rome and in to oder holy places, to spende myn dayes of this present liff in the servise of God. For I hadde lever liffe in gret tribulacion in the service of God in this present liff, than for to folowe the wretchednesse of this worlde.

And, syr, of on thing I be seche specially your good maysterchep that ye wolle shew your good maistershep un to my fader in tyme of his nede, and that ye wolle recomaunde me in the most lowly wise with all reverence un to his good faderhode, be sechyng hym that he wole yeff me every day, during the dayes of his liff, his paternall blissing. And I have marvayle san that I have writen so many letters un to hym be for this tyme, that I hadde never non letter ageyn, whiche is to me the grettest lamentacion that ever come to my hert; and nowe knowing that I shall never see hym more, nor you, nor non other of my frendes, marvayle ye not thow sorowe is imprended in myn hert.

But, reverent maister, myn singuler trust remayneth nowe in your person, for, sir, and it please you, I most nedes write un to your good maisterchep, in the whiche my most trust remayneth. For, syr, and it please you, as for myn inheritaunce and other things whiche shulde come to me after the deth of my fader, whoes liff God preserve to his long plesauns, knowing that I shall never com ther, I hadde lever that by your good a vise that ye wolde take it unto you, for I hadde lever that ye hadde it rather than any person in the worlde during my liff, with all the profites ther of; and if that ye wole make as good evidences for you in that partye as ye can, and I shall a seale hem. And as you semeth best, and in the most secret wise, rewle you in this mater.

And, sir, I be seche you to recomaunde me in the most lowly wise to myn reverent Maister William Lumnour, seyeng hym that I am and shall be his perpetuall bedman, and as ye thenk best, ye may telle hym of all these maters. And, syr, I be seche you to recomaunde me with all reverence un to my

6

EDWARD IV

1461
NOV. 20

sory, and if hyr old mastyr demene hym not well to yow sche prayith yow that ye wole be hyr good mastyr, and I that sche fare never the werse for hys defawtys. And also I pray yow that ye wele be John Lysterys good mastyr in hys mater. He spak to Playter ther of, and Playter seyd he hopyd to fynd a mene aftyr that he had spook with yow, that schold ese hym ther in. I thank yow hertly for yowyr lettyr, for it was to me gret comfort to her fro yow. God knowyth my modyr and I thowt ryth longe tyll we herd tydyngys fro yow. And the blyssyd Trinite have yow in Hys kepyng. Wretyn in hast on Seynt Edmundys Day the Kyng.

By yowyr M. P.

The pepyll was nevyr bettyr dysposyd to yow than they be at thys owyr. The byll that Howard hathe mad a yens yow and odyr hathe set the pepyll in thys contre a rore. God yeve grace it be no worse than it is yet.

490

ROGER TAVERHAM TO JOHN PASTON[1]

To my reverent and most be trusted maister, John Paston, Esquyer, duelling in the Inner Temple, be this delyvered.

Year
uncertain

RYGHT reverent and most be trusted maister, I recommaunde me in the most lowly wise un to your good and prevyd maysterchep, and desiring many days to here of your welfare, whiche I be seche God encrese un to his plesauns and un to the prosperite and welfare of your person, and of all youres. And I be seche you of the good contynuaunce of your maysterchep at diverses tymes befor this writing shewed un to me; and, sir, ther is non man a lvye that I trust more to than I doo un to you, and I am your bedman, and so shall

[1] [From Fenn, iv. 252.] This letter and the next are placed here merely for convenience. The two are evidently some years apart in point of date, and nothing is quite clear about the date of either, except that the latter must have been written in the reign of Edward IV., and of course before the death of John Paston in 1466. This, which is several years earlier than the other, was almost certainly written in the reign of Henry VI. The writer was probably the 'old Taverham' mentioned by Margaret Paston in the last letter.

5

EDWARD IV

Year
uncertain

masteras your wiff, and to all other maysters and frendes ther. And, sir, that ye wolle thank the bringer of this letter, whiche hathe ben in my gret tribulacion my good frende; and, sir, whan ye speke with my fader, recomaunde me un to hym with all reverence, and sey un to hym I shall send hym a letter in all hast possible.

And, syr, as for this mater, demene you as ye wolle, and I shall doo your plesauns as moche as in me is. And, reverent maister, remitte me summe letter by the bringer her of of all thes maters, for he duellith with my Lorde, and he is ryght moche be trusted, for I knowe wele he wole yef a tendaunce un to you for to have summe letter from you; for, syr, it shall not be longe or that I go to Rome, by the grace of God. And as sone as I have a letter from you at this tyme, I shall send you a noder ageyn.

No more at this tyme, but the Holy Trinite have you in His blissed keping. Wreten at Sarum, the Monday aftyr Mydsomer Day. And lete these maters be kept secrete by your best a vise.

Be youre poure servaunt,   ROGER TAVERHAM.

491

ROGER TAVERHAM TO JOHN PASTON[1]

To my right wourshipful maister, John Paston, Esquyer, be this letter delyvered.

RIGHT wourshipful maister, I recommaunde me un to
1461(?) your maistership, and I thank your maistership that hit pleased your maistership to sende me wourde a yen of my letter that I sende you by the brynger herof. Sir, as I am enformed, ye sent me wourde how that my fader was dede long tyme passed, and also ye desired to knowe my tittylle of ryght. Sir, I am very heyre, by the disceas of my fader, to a

[1] [From Fenn, iv. 253.] The mention of Lord Wenlock in this letter proves that it cannot be earlier than 1461; but if the writer be, as we have surmised, the 'old Taverham' mentioned by Margaret Paston in No. 489, it is most probably of that year.

7

461(?) place called Keswyk, in Taverham, with all the apportenauncez, and that comyth by enherytaunce and discente to me, for I am the helder and heyre; and though my Lorde Cromwell[1] hath taken Thomas Taverham, my yonger brother, as warde for the same enheritaunce, that maketh no mater to me, in so moche I am helder brother. Wher for I beseche you to sende me a letter of attourney made to you in my name in the strengest wise that ye can, for to entre in to the same lyvelode, and I shall asseal that, and than I shall do my service and feaute to the seid Lorde Cromwell in all thing as by the tenure of the same lyvelode of olde tyme aught to be done. And herin I kno well the King shal cause my Lorde Cromwel to do me bothe lawe and right; and also my Lorde Chanceler, with oder Lordes diverse, shall do the same. And, sir, I beseche your maistership to do and to take possession in the saide place with the apportenaunce in short tyme, for losyng of the rent this yer passed.

And, sir, as for the place of Attylbrigge that my moder in lawe now duellith in, sir, your maistershep shal right not [naught] attempte ther now in; for my Lorde of Warwik[2] hath seen how the same place was yeven me by testament by Sir Roger Dallyng after the disease of my fader, whiche is redy to be shewed. And therupon my Lorde of Warwik hath comaunded certeyn gentilmen to entre in the same place, and your maistership hadde be moved ther in or this, but for cause that ye love wel Lumpnour,[3] and that my moder in lawe is his sister; but I knowe wel hit woul cost CCCli., but that she shal be dispossedded of that place in short tyme. And, maister, how ye woul be rewled in the seid place of Keswyk, I be seche you to sende me wourde, as my sengler trust is in you; for and ye woulde not take possession in the saide place, my Lorde Wenlok[4] woulde have that ful fayne, for all the

[1] Humphrey Bourchier, Lord Cromwell, so created in 1461.
[2] Richard Neville, Earl of Warwick.
[3] William Lumner, of Mannington, in Norfolk.—F.
[4] John Wenlock was created Baron Wenlock in 1461 by Edward IV.; but he afterwards left the York party, and joined that of Lancaster. He was cleft down with a battle-axe by the Duke of Somerset for not coming up in time at the battle of Tewkesbury in 1471, whereby that battle was lost.—F.

8

contray knowith while that while I leve, I am heyr and non 1461(?) other. And therfor I beseche you in all hast sende me wourde by the bryngger herof in hast, quia mora trahit periculum. And, sir, I would come speke with you. I am seke, and may not goo; but telle the bryngger heroff all your entent. For my liff duryng I hadde lever that ye hadde that place for jd. than a nother man, thow he woulde yeff me meche mony, for your maistership ther shewed to me in my yong age. And God kepe you, &c.

Your chapeleyn, ROGER TAVERHAM.

492

ABSTRACT[1]

RICHARD CALLE TO JOHN PASTON.

Since I left you I have received at Cotton £4 : 2s., with which I have made 1461 purchases of linen shirts, &c. for you. Shall have more money before Christmas. NOV. 20 Debenham, Jenney, nor none of his men 'come not there sen' that I was there.' A letter of attorney is made for Nakton in your name to Sir John Hevenyngham, and a rental and fermal sent him. We kept a court this week at Calcotte but could get little money, not so much as I paid my Lady of Suffolk's officers. Farmers will not occupy there till appointment be made between Paston and Debenham; nor Risynge till he hear from Paston. Can get no day for Mautby. They will not give a noble, nor even 6 shillings, for a cow. Dey occupies your lands there till you come home. Risynge would take them and the closes at Castre if he is not to have Calcotte. The prests shall be paid as soon as we get money, I hope this week. Wheat 12d. a comb, barley 8d., malt 9d. and 10d. No good price for malt, 'saving, as we understand, it is good Flanders.' John Russe and Robert Glover are sending a ship with corn over, and we have ventured with them 100 comb malt. You should make some bargain with your beer brewers. Can get no money from Aleynes, farmer of Gresham, since ye rode, but 40s. Has laid in sufficient beef for Paston's household till 'Faste-gang' (Lent). Sir Thomas Howys advises my mistress not to send Edmund Paston to Cambridge or elsewhere till after Christmas. Please ask Clement, your brother, to get a writ against Geoffrey Clerk of West Somerton for the 20s. that Belys gave him to pay Clement. Remember the letter I sent you last week.

Caister, St. Edmund's Day.

[From what is here said of the levying of rents at Cotton, and from the mention of Debenham and Jenney in connection with it, we may presume this letter was written in 1461. With this supposition agrees the reference to John Paston's brother, Clement, who, as we see by No. 484, was in London in October.]

[1] [From Paston MSS., B.M.]

9

493

AGNES PASTON TO JOHN PASTON[1]

To John Paston, at London, be this delyverd in hast.

1461 I grete you welle, and lete you wete that this day Berth' Elys of Paston DEC. 1 come to Norwych to me, and shewet me a rentall for the terme of Seynt Mich., the yer of Kyng H. vj. xxxix°; and in the ende of the seyd rentall, of Waryn Kynges hand is wretyn 'Agnes Paston vijd. ob. [7½d.]. Item, the same Agnes for v. acre lond xxd.' Item, Aleyn Bayfeld askyth the same rent for the yer last past at Mich. Item, I have knowlech be a trew man that whan Sharpe the reseyvor was at Gemyngham last, Waryn Herman was dyvers dayes with hym, and put hym in mynde that the mercyment for makynge of the walle chuld be askyd ageyn and be distreynyd ther for. Item, I sent you be Doctor Aleyns man the restew [residue] of Waryn Herman, and seche names as Cullynge and Sammys putt in of her owyn fre wylle befor John Northales, shereve of Norwyche,[2] under her selis. God be with you and send you His blyssyng and myn. Wretyn at Norwych the Tuisday next after Seynt Andrew.

Item, the seyd Berth' Elis seyth that the seyd reseyver wold not alowe the rent in Trunche nor the mercyments for my sute to the curt. Gonnor wold suffyr no man to answer for me.

Be your moder, AGNES PASTON.

494

SIR JOHN HEVENYNGHAM TO JOHN PASTON, SENIOR[3]

To myn ryght worchipffull cosyn, John Paston the elder, Esquyer, be this letter delivered in hast.

DEC. 12 Ryght worchipffull cosyn, I recomaunde me to you in as hertely wyse I can, desyryng ever to here off your welffare, whiche I beseche our Lord Jesu

[1] [From Paston MSS., B.M.] The year in which this letter was written is deter-mined by the mention of John Northale as Sheriff of Norwich.
[2] He was Sheriff of Norwich in the first year of Edward IV.
[3] [From Paston MSS., B.M.] This letter is evidently of the same year as No. 492. The contents, moreover, seem to show that the date cannot be far distant from that of Richard Calle's letter of the 1st of February following.

10

to preserve to your hertes pleaser, &c. Sir, ye sent me a letter of atorney to 1461 reseyve and to ocupye in your name the maner called Burnevyles in Nakton. DEC. 12 Sir, as for that ocupacion, I can litil skylle en, ne I wel not take up on me non suche ocupacionis; wherffor I beseche you holde me excused, for it is no werd [world] for me to take suche ocupacionis. I have as moche as I may to gader myn ownne lyfflode, and truli, cosyn, I can not gader that well. And therffor, cosyn, I pray you take it to non displeaser. Sir, that I may worchepfulli doo for you, ye shal fynde me redy be the grace of Jesu, whom I hertely beseche to have you in Hise mersyfull kepyng. Wretyn at Hevenyngham on Seynt Lucye Even.

Be your cosyn,

JOHN HEVENYNGHAM, knyght.

495

ANONYMOUS TO JOHN PASTON[1]

RYGHT worchefull master, I recommend me on to yow, 1461(?) &c. The cause of my wrytyng is this; I was at DEC. Blofeld on Sent Andruys Day[2] wyt the person,[3] and he understode non noder but that I cam to se is master chepe, for it was hese cheve day,[4] and that I mevyd in to hym of the lond in Sochewerk, how I hard sey qwan I was in Sochefolk that Geney mad hys avaunt that he had zon [given] zow and hym a choppe of xx. pownd of lond. And in contynent he telde me al the mater beter than I cowde telle hym, and as I cowde understond in hym be my sympyl wyt, that he was of knoleche of alle the mater; for he seyd that Yelverton cam don fro the benche, and plete the mater, and for cause ye wer to laches, and cam not in tyme, the mater yede a mys. And so I understode be hym that he is dysposyd to excuse Yelverton in al materys rather than yow; but never de les make good cher to the person, as thow ye understode that he wer your frend, tyl tyme ye have your in tente. But be warr

[1] [From Fenn, iv. 64.] The date of this letter is a little uncertain, but it seems to have been written at the beginning of the dispute between Paston and Yelverton, about Fastolf's will, and the year 1461 appears to me on the whole most probable.
[2] 30th November.
[3] Thomas Howes.
[4] The day of his *chief* or patron saint. Blofeld Church is dedicated to St. Andrew.

11

THE PASTON LETTERS

1461(?)
DEC.

and trost hym not, but make yow so strong in lorchepe and in the lawe, that ye reeke not meche qwder he be good or bad, &c.

Item, ye meche be held on to Tomas Grene and Edmund Wydewel, broder to Heu à Fen, for thei reporte meche worchepe of your master chepe in al maters, and that cause the substans of the towne to howe yow servese, and be wel dysposyd on to yow masterchepe, and that understonde I hevery day. And yf that plese yow, qwan we partyt at Norwyche in yowr plase, ye seyd on to me ye wold som qat do be my sympyl a wyse; and this is myn a wyse that in ony wyse ye make Heu à Fen and Tomas Grene on your consel, yf ye can fyne in yow herte. For I dare sey, as I her and understonde, that thei how yow ryth good well and servyse, for a man may her be the halfe qwat the hole menyth, and therfor for Godds lowe remember yow wel in this mater; for and it stode on myn lyfe, I wold do as I awyse yow, &c.

Item, for howr Lords love, goo tharow with Wyll Weseter, and also plese Chrewys as ye thynke in yow hert best for to do; for it is a comon proverbe, 'A man must sumtyme set a candel befor the Devyle'; and therfor thow it be not alder most mede and profytabyl, yet of ij. harmys the leste is to be take.

Item, ye xul oonderstonde that the parson telde me that dey wer somuned to cum for the probat of the testement at Convercyon of Sent Powle;[1] and therfor I wolde avyse yow in ony wyse that ye xuld understond the mater wysely her ye com hom, for I sopose that Yelverton and he is confydett and acorde to geder.

Item, qwan I was at Blofeld with the parson, ther cam Robert Fyrass to hym, seyyng that he is compeld be the Kyngs Commycyoners to have harnes after is degre, and that the parson sent hym to my mastras that che xuld delyver hym harnes, and I understond che wylle not tylle ye com hom. But ye xul understond it is an halmes dede to do hym good, understondyng is nesessyte and nede that he stond in, and also understondyng that he was kynnyes man to my master, and it

[1] Jan. 25.

12

EDWARD IV

1461(?)
DEC.

is a comon proverbe, 'A man xuld kepe fro the blynde and gevyt to is kyn'; and hevery man wyl sey wel ther of, the mor cause he is a gentylman, and of is kyne, and in gret penur. And therfor, for the love of God, remembyr seche maters.

No mor at this tyme, but God have yow in Hys kepyng, bothe body and sowle, and sqede yow in yowr maters as wel as wel as I wolde ye xulde do.

496

MARGARET PASTON TO JOHN PASTON [1]

To my right wurchepfull husband, John Paston.

RIGHT wurchepfull husbond, I recomaund me to you. Please it you to wete that myn awnte is dissesid, whos sowle God assoyll. And if it please you to send word how ye wull that we do for the lifflode that she had at Walcote, wheder ye wull that any body take possession thir in your name or not. And if it like you to have with you my cosyn William her sone, I trow ye shuld fynde hym a necessary man to take hede to yowr howshold, and to bye all maner of stuffe nedefull therto, and to se to the rewle and gode gidyn therof. It hath be told me be for that he can gode skill of such thyngs; and if ye wull that I send for hym and speke with hym ther of, I shall do as ye send me word, for in feyth it is tyme to crone your old officers for diverse thyngs wher of I have know parte be Dawbeney, and more I shall telle you whan ye come hame.

Also it is thought be my cosyn Elizabeth Clere, and the viker[2] and other that be your frends, that it is right necessary

DEC. [3]

[1] [From Fenn, iv. 106.] Except that it seems to be of the reign of Edward IV., the date of this letter is about as uncertain as that of the last; but as they are both written about the same time of year, and both recommend John Paston to use the counsel of Hugh Fenn, it is highly probable that they are of the same year. Perhaps the last letter may have been written by the vicar mentioned in this.

[2] The vicar of Paston? Robert Williamson was vicar of Paston at this time.

13

THE PASTON LETTERS

1461(?)
DEC. [3]

for you to have Hew of Fen to be your frende in your maters; for he is callid right feythfull and trosty to his frends that trost hym, and it is reported her he may do myche with the Kyng and the Lords, and it is seid that he may do myche with hem that be your adversaryes: and therfor, Godds sake, if ye may have his gode wille, forsake it not. Also it is thought the more lerned men that ye have of your owyn contre of your councell, the more wurchepful it is to you.

Also if ye be at home this Cristmes, it wer wele do ye shuld do purvey a garnyssh or tweyn of powter vesshell, ij. basanes, and ij. hewers, and xij. candlestikes, for ye have to few of any of thes to serve this place. I am a ferd to purvey mych stuffe in this place till we be suerrer therof. The Blissid Trinyte have you in His blissid kepyng.

Wretyn the Thursday next after Sent Andrew.

Be yowr   M. P.

497

MARGARET PASTON TO JOHN PASTON [1]

*To my ryth worchepful husbond, Jonhn Paston,
be thys delyveryd in hast.*

1461
DEC. 29

RYTH worchepfull husbond, I recomande me to yow. Plesyt yow to wete that I receyvyd the lettyr that ye sent me by a man of Seynt Mychell parysche on Fryday next aftyr the Consepcion of owyr Ladi;[2] and anon as I had it, I sent my modyr[3] the lettyr because of swyche materys as longyd to hyr in that same lettyr. And sythyn that tyme I kowd gete no massanger to London but if I wold have sent by the Scheryfys men; and I knew nowthyr her mastyr nor them, not whedyr they wer well wyllyng to yow or not; and therfor methowt it had be no sendyng of no lettyr by hem.

[1] [From Paston mss., B.M.] The date of this letter will appear by comparison with No. 500. A few words in the margin of the original letter are illegible, the writing having been injured by damp.
[2] The Conception of Our Lady was on the 8th December.
[3] Margaret always speaks of Agnes Paston as her mother.

14

EDWARD IV

1461
DEC. 29

And as for swyche materys as John Geney and Jamys Gresham spak to me, I sped hem as well as I kowd; and they bothe told me that ye schold veryly a ben at home before Crystmas, and that causyd me that I wrot not to yow now non answer. For if I had know that ye schold not have ben at home er thys tyme, I schold a sent some man to yow; for I thynk ryth longe tyll I have some god tydyngys fro yow. I fer me that it is not well with yow that ye be fro home at thys good tyme. And many of yowyr contre men thynk the same; but they be hertty inow to yow-ward, and full fayn wold her god tydyngys fro yow. The wer no byllys put to the Scherryf[1] at hys beyng her, ner non opyn playnt mad that I . . . . . of no persone, be cawse they had so lyttyll knowlage of hys comeyng in to thys contre. He demenyd hym full . . . . . and indeferently, as it was told me, and Yelverton mad a fayir sermone at the Sesschyonys, and seyd . . . . . so that the Kyng was informyd that ther was a ryotows felawschep in thys contre, wer for the Kyng was gretly dysplesyd, and that the Kyng undyrstood well that it was not of ther owne mosyon, boot of cownselyng of one or ij. that ben evyll dysposyd folk. And also he seyd if ony man wold put up ony byllys of compleynts of ony extorcion or brybery don be ony men of thys contre to them, they wer redy to receyve them, and to make a-kord be twyx hem; and if they cowd not mak the acord, that than the schold tak the byllys to the Kyng, and he schold set hem thorow. And the Scheryfe seyd that he wold he . . . . . them that wold compleyne and dorste not for fer put up ther byllys.

And Yelverton preyid the Scheryfe that if he had for get onythyng that the Kyng seyd to hem at ther departtyng, that he wolde rehersyt [*rehearse it*] ther. And than the Scheryf seyd that he had seyd all that he remembryd, save only [that] the Kyng . . . . to hem ij. personys, Syr Thomas Todenham and Heydon. And than Yelverton seyd, 'A, that is trowthe, as th . . . . that J[ohn of] Dame told me that he spak with the Scheryf aftyrward, and let hym h . . . . . . the rewylle [and] demenyng of thys contre, and what cawsyd the

[1] The Sheriff was Sir Thomas Montgomery.

15

1461
DEC. 29

pepyll for to grwge ayens swyche folkys as had the reuyll be fortyne ; and he was pleyne to hym in many thyngys, as he told me ; and he fond the Scheryfe ryth pleyne ayen to hym, and well dysposyd in that that myth growe to the welfar of the schere. The Scheryfe seid he undyrstood by swyche informacion as he had, syns he came into thys contre, that they had not all gydyd hem well that had the rewyill of thys contre be for ; and therfore he seyd feythfully, and swore by gret othys that he wold nowthyr spar for good, nor love, nor fer, but that he wold let the Kynge have knowlage of the trowthe, and that he wold do asmyche for thys contre as he cowd or myth do to the welfare therof, and seyd that he lekyd the contre ryth well. And John of Dame seyd if the contre had had knowlage of hys comyng, he schold have had byllys of compleyntes and knowlage of myche more thyng than he myth have knowlage of that tyme, or myth have because of schort abyng ; and he seyd he wold not be longe owt of thys contre.

And also Yelverton seyd opynly in the Seschyons they to come downe for the same cause to set a rewyll in the contre. And yet he seyd he woste well that the Kynge myth full evyll have for bor ony of hem bothe ; for. as for a knyth ther was none in the Kyngys howse that myth werse a be for bore than the Scheryfe myth at that tyme. I have myche mor to wryt to yow of than I may have leyser at thys tyme ; but I troste to God that ye schall be at home yowyr selfe in hast, and than ye schall knowe all. And but if ye come home in haste, I schall send to yow ; and I pray yow hertly, but if ye come home, send me word in hast how ye do. And the blyssyd Trinyte have yow in hys kepyng. Wretyn in hast on Seynt Thomas day in Crystmas.[1]

By yowyr, MARGARET PASTON.

Here was an evyll rewlyd felawschep yestyrday at the schere, and ferd ryth fowle with the Undyr Scheryfe, and onresnably as I herd sey.

[1] The day of St. Thomas of Canterbury (Becket), 29th December.

16

498

RICHARD CALLE TO JOHN PASTON[1]

To my right reverent and my moost wurschipful maystre, my Maystre John Paston.

RIGHT wurshipfull and my mooste reverent mastre, I recomaunde me unto your goode maystreship. Like you to witte that on Childremasse daye[2] there were moche people at Norwich at the shire, be cauce it was noyced in the shire that the Undresheriff had a writte to make a newe aleccion ; wherfore the people was greved be cauce they had labored so often, seying to the Sheriff that he had the writte, and pleynly he shulde not a wey unto the tyme the writte were redd. The Sheriff[3] answerd, and seyd that he had no writte, nor west who had it. Hersuppon the people peacyd, and stilled unto the tyme the shire was doone, and after that doone, the people called uppon hym, ' Kylle hym ! Heede [*behead*] hym ! ' And so John Dam, with helpe of other, gate hym out of the schire-hows, and with moche labour brought hym unto Sporyer Rowe ;[4] and ther the people mett a yenst hym, and so they a voided hym unto an hows, and kept fast the dore unto the tyme the meyer was sent fore, and the Sherif, to strenght hym, and to convey hem a wey, or ell he had be slayne. Wherfor divers of the thrifty men came to me, desiryng that I shulde writte unto your maistreship to lete you have undrestandyng of the gidyng of the people, for they be full sory of this trowble ; and that it plese you to sende hem your advice how they shal be gided and rwled, for they were purposed to a gathered an c. or cc.[degree] of the thriftyest men, and to have come up to the Kyng to lete the Kyng have undrestandyng of ther mokkyng. And also the people fere hem sore of you and Mastre Berney,[5] be cauce ye come not home.

[1] [From Fenn, iii. 150.] The contents of this letter clearly refer to the matter alluded to in the postscript of the preceding letter of Margaret Paston, so that the date must be the same. [2] 28th December. [3] Sir Thomas Montgomery. [4] Spurrier Row, as I am informed by Mr. L'Estrange, was what is now called London Street. [5] John Berney of Witchingham.

17

1461
DEC. 29

Plese you that ye remembr the bill I sent you at Hallowmesse for the place and londs at Boyton weche Cheseman had in his ferme for v. mark. Ther wol no man have it above xlvj^t. viij^d., for Alblastre and I have do as moche therto as we can, but we can not go a bove that. And yet we can not lete it so for this yere, with owte they have it for v. or vj. yere. I wrote to your mastreship herof, but I had non answre ; wherfor I beseche you that I may have an answere of this be Tlwelthe, for and we have an answre of this be that tyme, we shall enfeffe hem with all, &c.

My right wurshipfull and my moost reverent maistre, Almyghty Jesu preserve you, and send you the victorye of your elmyes, as I truste to Almyghty Jesu ye shall. Wreten at Norwich on Seyn Thomas daye after Cristemasse daye.

Your pore servant and bedman, R. CALL.

499

RICHARD CALLE TO JOHN PASTON[1]

To my moost reverent and wurshipfful mastre, my Master John Paston of the Enner Temple, this be delyvered.

Plesith your maystership to understande that as for the ferme that Cheseman had in Boyton, that is to sey, xl. acre lond erable, j. medwe, and other smale parcell, payng yerly for it iiij^li., weche I can not lete the xl. acre lond abowe xl. comb barly or xl^s., and ye to bere al charges of the reparaucion and fense aboute the place, weche shulde be gret cost. The lond is so out of tylthe that a nedes [*uneath, i.e.* scarcely] any man wol geve any thyng for it. Ther can no man lete it to the walwe that it was lete before, and that I reporte me to my master, Sir Thomas Howys, not be gret gold. Wherfore I wol not do therin unto the tyme that I have answere from your mastership, weche I beseche you it may be hast. And as for Spitlynges, I have lete som of the lond in smale parcell, because I cowde gete no fermor for it. And as for Sir T. H., in good feythe I fynde [him] weele disposed in all thynges, excepte for Sir W. Chamberleyn for Rees in Stratton. And so the blissid Trinite preserve and kepe you from all adversite. Wrete at Blofeld, the Thorsday next after Hallowmesday.

Your pore servaunt and bedman, R. CALLE.

[1] [From Paston MSS., B.M.] The date of this letter is uncertain. Its contents are mere matter of business, and as relating to the same farm mentioned in the last may be supposed to belong to the same year, especially as in the last Calle mentions having written to Paston on the subject 'at Hallowmass.' There is, however, a discrepancy in the value assigned for the farm.

18

500

THOMAS PLAYTER TO JOHN PASTON[1]

To John Paston, the older, in hast, and if he be not at London, than to be delyvered to Clement Paston in hast.

LYKE your maisterchip wete that at the last cessyons Erpyngham hundred and other hundredys ther aboute were not warned, and the schreff excused hym be cause he cowde not knowe who was officer there. Item, Yelverton lete the pepoll understand that the Kyng wold have his lawes kept, and that he was dysplesed with the maner of ther gaderyng, and that he wold have it amendyd ; for he conceyveth that the hole body of the shire is well dysposed and that the ille dysposed pepoll is but of a corner of the hole shire ; and yet that ther mysdoyng growyth not of ther owyn dysposysyon but of the abbettement and steryng of sum ille dysposed persones whiche is understand and knowe to the Kynges hygthnesse. Item, he lete hem wete that the Kyng had commandyd hym to sey if ther were any man, pore or ryche, that had cause to complayne of any person that he schuld put up hys bylle to the shref and hym, and they schuld set a reule be twyx hem ; and if he wold not abyde ther reule they schuld delyver the sayd bylle of compleynt to the Kynges hignesse, and he schuld set the rewle and suche dyreccion that the party compleynaunt or defendaunt schuld be punysshed for his dysobeysauns of the said rewle if the case requyred ; and also more over, if ther were ony person that put up ony suche bylle, and it mygth apere to them by ther examinacion or other wyse fals or untrewe, or elles be cause of malyce, that than suche compleynaunts schuld sharpely be punysshed. And than

[1] [From Paston MSS., B.M.] The mention of Tuddenham and Heyden in this letter proves that it cannot be of later date than the year 1461, as the former was executed in February 1462. At the same time the reference to John Paston, Junior, could not be much earlier, and the message from the King to the people of Norfolk certainly could not have come from Henry VI. only a year or two before. The date must therefore be 1461 precisely.

1461
DEC.

19

THE PASTON LETTERS

1461
DEC.

whan he had sayd this and moche more, in dyscoragyng to the pepoll to put bylles, as after my conseyt, he reported hym to the schref ther present, that the Kyng thus comanded hem thus to sey, desyreng the said schref if ony thyng of the Kyngs comaunded were be hynd unspoken by hym self that he wold remembre and helpe forthe to telle it. And than the schref said, lyke as he rehersed the Kyng comanded, and more over that the Kyng named ij. men, by name Tudenham and Haydon, and if ony man wold put bylles a yens them, he said in feythfull wyse he wold help hem, and ferther the mater to the Kyng higthnesse. And for his demenyng ther every man thougth hym rigth wel dysposed ; but Yelverton had for yeten to expresse the names of Tudham and Haydon.

Item, the schref desyred the jentylmen to go with [him] to Felbryg Halle, and specially he requyred Mr. John P., the younger ; but he cowde no pepoll gete, and so he cam not there. Item, there was a bylle set up on the shirehous dore, and the content ther of was but of the favour to you ward, Barney, Knyvet and Felbrygge, and of the hatered of other ; it was but of sum lewde dysposed person it semeth. Item, sir, at the last shire was moche pepoll and ille governed for they wold not be rewled be no body, they had almost a slayne the underschref, for they told hym wryttes of eleccion was sent doun and he kept it on syde to be gyle hem, and to make hem labour ayen, and ther for he that kepyth it is to blame, me thynketh. Item, sir, please you to telle Mr. Clement, we have goten a reles of al maner accions and appelles of Margret Clerk, made to Gymmyngham, on of the pryncypalles, and that he woll inquyre wheder it be suffycyant for alle, and send me word, and weder it dyvers fro trespas and dette, wher damages is to be recovered, for in this appell is no damages to be recovered, but only an execucion, whiche non of them may be contributory to other execucion as is in other cases. Nevertheles, I hope it be sufficiant for all, for sche is in the cas to have the lyf in stede of damages.

Your THOMAS PL.

501

ANONYMOUS TO MARGARET PASTON [1]

To my right worchepfull Mastres Paston.

I RECOMAWNDE me to your good mastreschep, besech- 1461(? yng yow in the weye of charyte, and as I maye be your bedeman and servaunt, that ye wyll lete me have wetyng hoghe I maye be rewelyd ageyns the next schyer. It is seyd that ther xal be mych more pepyll than was the last ; and also if I be in my Ladys place, or in ony other in the town, I xall be takyn owte. Also, mastres, that my Maystyr Radclyffs xal take all my catell and all other pore good that I have, and so but I maye have helpe of my mayster and of yow, I am lost. Also my servaunt Maryot wyll go fro my wyfe to my ryght gret hurte. Wherfore, mastres, I besech your help in all thes, and I xal content the costs as ye xall be plesyd, be the grace of God, hoo ever preserve yow, &c.

Also, mastres, I can not be with owte your contynuall help, but I must selle or lete to ferme all that I have.

Mastres, my Lady sent to Cawnbrygg for a doctour of fesyk. If ye wyll ony thyng with hym, he xal abyde this daye and to morwe. He is ryght a konnyng man and gentyll.

[1] [From Fenn, iv. 104.] This letter appears to have been addressed to Margaret Paston at a period when her husband was a man of some influence, and perhaps the year 1461 is not far from the true date. It is not unlikely to have been written about the same time as No. 500, which also refers to a meeting at the shire or county court.

20

21

THE PASTON LETTERS

502

ELIZABETH MUNDEFORD TO JOHN PASTON [1]

To my right worchipfull sir, and my right good neveu,
John Paston, Squyer, be this lettre delyvered, &c.

1461-6

R IGHT worchipfull sir, and my right good neveu, I recomand me un to you with all myn herte. Plece it you to undyrstande the grete nessessyte of my wrytyng to you is this, that ther was made an exchaunge be the graunsyre of my hosbonds Mundeford, un hose sowle God have mercy, of the maner of Gressenale with the aunsetrys of Rows for the maner of Estlexham, the qwych is parte of my juntor, and my grauntfadyr Mundeford recoweryd the said maner of Estlexham be assyze [2] a geyne the aunsetrys of Rows, and so madyt clere ; and nowe have Edmund Rows [3] claymyt the seyd maner of Estlexham be the verteu of a tayle [*an entail*], and hathe takyn possesseon, and made a feffment to my Lord of Warewyke, [4] and Water Gorge, [5] and to Curde. [6] And un Fryday be for Seynt Walentyne is Day Water Gorge and Curde enteryd and toke possessyon for my seyd Lord of Warewyke, and so bothe the forseyd manerys were ontayled, and at the tyme of the exchaunge made, the tayles and evydens of bothe for seyd manerys were delyvered un to the partyes indeferently be the avyse of men lernyd. Qwerfor I besech you that it plese you to take the grete labor upon you to

[1] [From Fenn, iv. 108.] The date of this letter must lie between the years 1461 and 1466. The writer's husband, who is spoken of as dead, was put to death in June 1460, and John Paston, the person addressed, died in May 1466.

[2] Assize is a writ directed to the sheriff of the county for recovery of the possession of things immovable, whereof yourself or ancestors have been dispossessed.—F.

[3] Edmund Rous was second son of Henry Rous, Esq. of Dennington, in Suffolk, the ancestor of the present Earl of Stradbroke.

[4] Richard Neville, Earl of Warwick.

[5] Walter Gorges, Esq., married Mary, the daughter and heir of Sir William Oldhall, and was at this time Lord of the Manor of Oldhall, in Great Fransham. He died in 1466. His son and heir, Sir Edmund Gorges, afterwards married a daughter of Sir John Howard, Knight, the first Duke of Norfolk of that family.—F.

[6] John Curde was Lord of the Manor of Curde's Hall, in Fransham.—F.

22

informe my Lordys good Lordchep of the trowthe in the 1461-6 forme a bowyn wreten, and that it plese you to undyrstand qwedyr that my Lord wyll a byde be the feffment made to hym or not ; and that it shall plese my Lord that I may have right as lawe requeryt, for I trust to God be soche tyme as my Lord shall be informyd of the trowthe be you, that hese Lord-chip wyll not supportt the forseyd Rows a geyne my right. And if I hadde very undyrstandyng that my Lord would take no parte in the mater a bowe seyd, I would trust to Godds mersy, and to you, and other of my good fryndes, to have possession a geyne in right hasty tyme, beshechyng you to pardon me of my symple wrytyng, for hadde no leyser. Right worchipfull and my right good neveu, I beshech the Blyssed Trenyte have you in Hese gracyous kepyng.

Wreten at Norwych in gret hast, the Tewysday aftyr Seynt Walentyne is Day.

Youre ouyn, ELIZABETH MUNDEFORD. [1]

503

SIR ROBERT WILLIAMSON TO AGNES PASTON [2]

To my right reverent mastras, Agnes Paston,
be this lettre delyveryd in haste.

R YGH wurcheful mastres, I recomaund me un to yow, 1460-4 thankyng yow of the gret chere that ze made me the last tyme that I was with zow. Mastres, in alle zour godys and ocupacyons that lyth in my simpil power to do in wurd, wil and dede, I have do my dylygens and my power therto, so I be savyd be fore God, and have owyn to your person ryght herty love ; for the qwych I am ryght ille

[1] Elizabeth Mundeford was the widow of Osbert Mundeford, Esq. of Hockwold, in Norfolk, and was daughter of John Berney, Esq., by which means she was aunt to J. Paston.—F.

[2] [From Fenn, iii. 48.] The writer of this letter was Vicar of Paston from 1460 to 1464, and as he dates from Bromholm, which is in the immediate neighbourhood of Paston, we may presume that it was written during the time he held that benefice.

23

460-4 aqwyt, and it be as I understande yt; for it is do me to wete that I am swid with mor of my paryshchons for a reskuse makyng up on the offycers of the shrewys [*sheriff*], and I take God to record that it is wrongfully do on to us. And the gret fray that the [*they*] mad in the tyme of masse it ravyched my witts and mad me ful hevyly dysposyd. I pray Jesu gef hem grace to repent hem therof that the [*they*] that caused it may stand out of perel of soule.

Maystras, at the reverens of God, and as evyr I may do servyce that may be plesyng on to yow, send me justyly wurd be the brynger of this bylle ho ze wil that I be gydyd; for it is told me that if I be take I may no other remedy havyn but streyth to prison. For the whiche I have sold away xxs. wurth of stuffe; and the reswd [*residue*] of my stuff, I have put it in swier hande, for trwly I wil not abyde the joparte of the swth, —I have levir to go as far as my fet may ber me. Nevir the less as ze komand me to do, so it be not to my gret hurt, I wil fulfille it. Nomor to zow at this tyme, but God send yow that grace that ze may kome to His blyss.

Wreten at Bromholm in gret haste,

Be your   Sir ROBERT WILLYAMSON.

504

MARGARET PASTON TO JOHN PASTON [1]

To my ryth worchepfull husbond, John Paston,
be thys delyveryd in hast.

1462
JAN. 7

RYTH worchepfull husbond, I recomand me to yow. Plesyt yow to wet that I sent yow a lettyr by my cosyn Barneys man of Wychyngham wyche was wretyn on Seynt Thomas Day in Crystmas,[2] and I had no tydyngys nor lettyr of yow sene the wek before Crystmas;

[1] [From Paston MSS., B.M.] The contents of this letter clearly show that it was written in January 1462, nine days after No. 497.

[2] *See No. 497.*

24

wher of I mervayle sore. I fere me it is not well with yow be cawse ye came not home or sent er thys tyme. I hopyd verily ye schold have ben at home by Twelthe at the ferthest. I pray yow hertly that ye wole wychesave to send me word how ye do as hastly as ye may, for my hert schall nevyr be in ese tyll I have tydyngys fro yow. Pepyll of this contre begynyth to wax wyld, and it is seyd her that my Lord of Clarans and the Dwek of Suthfolk and serteyn jwgys with hem schold come downe and syt on syche pepyll as be noysyd ryotous in thys contre. And also it is seyd here, that there is retornyd a newe rescwe up on that that was do at the scher. I suppose swyche talkynge comyth of false schrewys that wold mak a rwmor in this contre. The pepyll seyth here that they had levyr go up hole to the Kynge and compleyne of siche false screwys as they have be wrongyd by a fore, than they schold be compleynyd of with owt cause and be hangyd at ther owne dorys. In good feyth men fere sore here of a comone rysyng but if [*i.e.* unless] a bettyr remedy may be had to a pese the pepyll in hast, and that ther be sent swyche downe to tak a rewyll as the pepyll hathe a fantsy in, that wole be indeferent. They love not in no wyse the Dwke of Sowthfolk nor hys modyr. They sey that all the tretourys and extorsyonerys of thys contre be meynteynyd by them and by syche as they get to them with her goodys, to that intent to meynten suche extorsyon style as hathe be do by suche as hathe had the rewyll undyr them be fore tyme. Men wene, and the Dwke of Sowthfolk come ther scholl be a schrewd reuell but if [*unless*] ther come odyr that be bettyr belovyd than he is here. The pepyll feryth hem myche the more to be hurt, because that ye and my cosyn Barney come not home; they sey they wot welle it is not well with yow and if it be not well with yow, they sey they wot well, they that wole do yow wronge wole sone do them wronge, and that makyth them all most mad. God for Hys holy mersy geve grace that ther may be set a good rewyll and a sad in this contre in hast, for I herd nevyr sey of so myche robry and manslawter in thys contre as is now within a lytyll tyme. And as for gadyryng of mony, I sey nevyr a werse seson, for Rychard Calle seyth he can get

25

THE PASTON LETTERS   EDWARD IV

1462
JAN. 7

but lytyll in substans of that is owyng, nowthyr of yowyr lyvelod nor of Fastolfys th'eyr. And John Paston seyth, they that may pay best they pay werst; they fare as thow they hopyd to have a newe werd [*world*]. And the blyssyd Trinite have yow in Hys kepyng and send us good tydyngys of yow.

Yelverton is a good thredbare frend for yow and for odyr in thys contre, as it is told me.

Wretyn in hast on the Thorsday nex aftyr Twelthe.

By yowyr   MARGARET PASTON.

505

MARGARET PASTON TO JOHN PASTON [1]

JAN. 27

RYTH worchepfull husbond, I recomand me to yow. Plesyt yow to wet that Perse was delyveryd owt [of] preson by the generall pardon that the Kynge hathe grantyd, whyche was opynly proclamyd in the Gyld Hall. A none as he was delyveryd he cam hedyr to me, God wote in an evyll plyte, and he desyiryd me wepyng that I wold be hys good mastres and to be mene to yow to be hys good mastyr, and swore sore that he was nevyr defawty in that ye have thowte hym defawty in. He seyd that if ther wer ony coyne in the cofyr that was at Wylliam Tavernerys it was ther withowt hys know-lage, for hys mastyr wold nevyr lat hym se what was in that cofyr, and he told me that the keyis wer sent to Thomas Holler [2] by mastyr John Smyth. What Holler leyd in or took owte he wot not as he sweryth. He offyrd me to be rewlyd as ye and I wold have hym, and if I wold comand hym, to go ageyn to preson, whedyr I wold to the Castyll or to the Gyld Hall, he wold obey my comandment. And seth that he came of hys owne fre wyll withowt ony comandment of ony man or desyir,

[1] [From Paston MSS., B.M.] This letter relates to the prisoner Piers mentioned in Nos. 423, 424, and 426. He seems to have been delivered by a general pardon issued at the commencement of the reign of Edward IV. The letter bears no address. It is endorsed, but in a much later hand:—' A lettre to J. Paston, Ar., from his wife.'

[2] He was John Berney's executor.

26

I seyd I wold not send hym ageyn to preson, so that he wold abyde yowyr rewyll when ye came home. And so he is here with me and schall be tyll ye send me word how ye wole that I do with hym. Where fore, I pray yow that ye wole lete me have knowlage in hast how ye wole that I do with hym.

Item, I have spok with John Dame and Playter for the lettyr testymonyall, and John Dame hathe promysyd to get it, and Playter schall bryng it to yow to London. Item, I have purveyd yow of a man that schall be here in Barsamys sted and ye wole, the wyche can bettyr cherysch yowyr wood, bothe in fellyng and fensyng there of than Barsam can; and he schall mak yow as many hyrdyllys as ye nede for yowyr fold, of yowyr owne wood at Drayton, and schall tak as lytyll to hys wagys as Barsam dothe; and he is holdyn a trew man. Item, Playter schall tell yow of a woman that compleynyd to the Dwk of Sowthefolk of yow, and the sey[d] Playter schall tell yow of the demenyng and answeryng of the scheryfe for yow, and also of the demenyng of the seyd Dwke, and of othir materys the wyche wer to longe mater to put in wryttyn. The pepyll of that kontre be ryth glad that the day yed [*went*] with yow on Monday as it ded. Ye wer nevyr so welcome in to Norfolk as ye schall be when ye come home, I trowe. And the blyssyd Trynyte have yow in Hys kepyng. Wretyn in hast on Wednysday next aftyr Seynt Augnet the Fyrst.

By yowyr M. P.

Item, Ric. Calle told me that he hathe sent you a answer of all erands that ye wold shuld be do to Sir Thomas Howes. Sir Thomas Howes cam nowther to me nor sent syn that he cam home from London.

Will Worceter was at me in Cristemes at Heylysdon, and he told [me] that he spake with you dyvers tymys at London the last terme; and he told me that he hopyd that ye wolle be hys good master, and seyd he hopyd ye shuld have non other cause but for to be hys god maister. I hope and so do my moder and my cosyn Clere, that he wolle do well inowe, so that he be fayre fare with Dawbeney and Playter. Avise me to lete Peers go at large and to take a promys of hym to

27

THE PASTON LETTERS

com to me a mong unto your comyng hom, and in the mene while his demenyng may be knowyn and espyed in mo thyngs.

506

JOHN DOWBIGGING TO JOHN PASTON [1]

To the ryght reverent and worship sir, John Paston, sum tyme Lord of Gresham, and now fermour therof, as hit is seide.

PERYS of Legh come to Lynne upon Cristynmesse Even in the fresshest wise, and there he dyned so as was; bot when my Lorde of Oxenforde herde hereof he with his feliship and suche as I and other your presoneres come rydyng unto Lynne, and even unto the Bysshop gaole where the seid Perys dyned with other of his feliship. My Lorde pulled hym oute of the seid gaole and made to kest hym upon an horse, and tyed an halter by his arme, and so ledde hym furth like hym selff. And even furthwith the seid Bysshop, the Mair, and other their feliship mette with my seide Lorde and your presoneres, and also the seide Perys tyed by an halter, the Bysshop havyng thies wordes unto my Lorde with his pillion [2] in his handes, 'My Lordes, this is a presoner, ye may knowe by his tepet and staff. What will ye do with hym?' Therto my Lorde seide, 'He is my presoner nowe.' Wherto the Bysshop seid, 'Where is youre warraunt or commission therto?' My Lorde seide, 'I have warraunt sufficiaunt to me.' And thus they departed, the Mair and all the cominaltie of Lynne kepyng theire silence. Bot when we weren goon, and Perys of Legh fast in Rysyng Castell, then the yates of Lynne, by the Bysshop comaundement weren fast sperred [*shut*] and keped with men of armes. And then the

---

[1] [From Paston MSS., B.M.] This letter is evidently earlier in date than the last, and may perhaps have been written at the close of the year 1460, but as it refers to the same prisoner as the preceding No. we place it here for convenience. It is printed in the fifth volume of Fenn's edition as a letter of Henry VII.'s time owing to a misreading of the address, which might easily convey the impression that it was directed to 'Sir John Paston.'

[2] The hat worn by a Doctor of Divinity.

28

EDWARD IV

Bysshop and his squyers rebuked the Mair of Lynne and seid that he hade shamed both hym and his toun for ever, with muche other langage, &c.

The Bysshop shulde have keped his Cristenmesse at Gaywode, bot yet he come not oute of Lynne. In faith, my Lorde dyd quyte hym als curageousely as ever I wist man do. The Bysshop come to the toun with lx. persones the same tyme, and made to sper the yates after hym, bot when we mette, ther bode not with hym over xij. persones atte the most, with his serjaunt of armes; whiche serjaunt was fayn to lay doun his mase; and so atte the same yates we come in we went oute, and no blode drawen, God be thanked.

Yf ye will any thyng atte I may do, send me worde; hit shall be doon to my power, &c. Comaunde me to my maistresse your wyff, &c. And yf ye dar joperdie your suyrtie of C. marc I shall come and se you. And elles have me excused, for, &c.

From your oune,

JOHN DOUEBIGGYNG.

507

RICHARD CALLE TO JOHN PASTON [1]

To the ryght reverent and my mooste worschipful master, my Master John Paston, in the Inner Tempyll.

Plesith it your maistership to witte that I have been at Burnewyll in Nacton to receyve the rentes and fermys of the tenauntes. And I undrestande be them, and be Robert Goordon that Mastre Jenney whas there and helde a coorte on the Mondaye next aftre Tlwelthe, and warned the tenauntes that they

---

[1] [From Paston MSS., B.M.] The manor of Burneviles in Nacton, near Ipswich, was part of the lands of Sir John Fastolf which Paston inherited by his will; but his claim was disputed by Jenney, one of the executors. As Jenney is here said to have complained that his fee was two years in arrear, we may presume that it was little over two years since Fastolf's death when this letter was written. For further evidences of date compare No. 494. It may also be observed that we find undoubted evidence that John Paston was residing in the Inner Temple six weeks later (*see* No. 511), whereas in the preceding year he was in Norfolk, where his brother Clement wrote to him news from London (No. 430).

29

THE PASTON LETTERS

schulde pay no money to no man onto the tyme they had worde from hym, seyng that he whas on of the feffeys of the same maner, and that he whas feed with Sir John Fastolff, of weche fee he was be hynde for ij. yere; wherfore he desired the tenauntes that they schulde not be redy in payement onto the tyme they had word from hym, but that he myght be payed of his seide fee, lyke as the wylle of the deede was. Wherfore I can gete no money of them unto the tyme they have knowleche how it stond be twyx your maistership and Mr. Jenney; for withoute Jenney write to hem or come hom ward that wey, and have the tenauntes together and lete hem witte that ye ought to have the rentes and fermes of the seid maner, I can not see that ye be like to have but litell money there, withoute ye woll do distreyne throuout all the lordeschip. I have sette dayes to purvey but [*their*] money ayenst the first weke of cleene Lenton, and than they schul have an answere who shal receyve it. Wherfore that it please your maistership to remembre to speke to Mastre Jenney. The blissed Trinite preserve you and kepe you from all advercyte. Wreten at Yebbyshep [1] the furst daye of Februare.

Your pore servaunt and bedman,

R. CALLE.

Item, the maner of Stratton shuld paye of rente xxvjs. viijd., weche the fermour seythe my mastresse Brandon is acorded with you. He is be hynde for certeine yeres, &c.

508

JOHN PASTON TO ——— [2]

RIGHT trusty and welbeloved, I grete yow hartily well, and will ye wite that where hit is so, that Sir John Fastolf, whom God assoyle, with other, was sum tyme by Sir Herry Inglose enfeffed of trust of his maner offe Pykewurthe in Rutlande, the which made his wille, proved, that the seid maner sholde be solde by Robert Inglose and Edmunde Wychingham his executours, to whom the seid Sir John hath

---

[1] Ipswich?

[2] [From Paston MSS., B.M.] The MS. is a rough draft signed by John Paston the eldest, and corrected in his hand. It seems to have been written on the cover of a letter addressed to himself; for on the back is this direction in another hand :— 'To my most reverent and worchefull maister, John Paston the eldest, Esquier, be this deliveryd in hast.'

We have inserted this letter in the year 1462 as this was the first year after Fastolf's death, when John Paston appears to have been residing in London in the beginning of February. The only other possible years are 1463, 1465, and 1466.

30

EDWARD IV

relesed, as his dute was to do; now it is so that for John Browne [1] ther is shewed a dede under seall of armes berynge date byfore his reles made to the Duke of Norffoke, Henry Inglose and other, contrarie to the wille of the seid Sir Herry and the trust of the feoffement that the seid Sir John Fastolff was infeffed inne. And a letter of Attorney under the same seale of armes to yow, to deliver seison acordynge to the same feffement, to the gret disclaundre of the seid Sir John and all his, yef this be true. Wherfore I preie yow hertili that ye feithfully and truly rescribe to me in all the hast ye may what ye knowe in this mater such as ye wull stonde by with outen glose, and how ye can imagine that this crafte shulde be practised, and specially whether ye yourself delivered seison in Rutlond or noo. And this and what incedentes ye knowe, I preie yow by wrytinge certefie me in all hast, that I may be the more ripe to answer to this, to the wurship of the seid Sir John, that was your maister, so that thorowh your defaute your seid maisters soule ther for lie not in perell, but this disclaundre may be eesed and cesed as reson requireth, to the wurship of hym and all that longe to hym. And this I pray yow faile not offe as I truste yow. Wret at Londo[n] the ix. day of Februar.

Yowr frend,

JON PASTON.

509

SIR THOMAS HOWES TO JOHN PASTON [2]

To the ryght wurshipfull sir and meyster, myn Mayster John Paston, Squier.

RYGHT worshipfull sire and mayster, I recomaunde me to yow. And please yow that the chirche of Drayton is or shal be resyngned in hast in to the Bysshopys hands by Sir John Bullok, desyryng yow hertly that ye lyke I

---

[1] This name is substituted for 'Herry Inglose,' struck out.

[2] [From Fenn, iv. 68.] For evidence of the date of this letter, Fenn quotes the

31

1462
[FEB.]
may have the presentacion of the next avoydaunce for a newew of myn, callyd Sir Reynold Spendlove, whiche I truste youre maystership wold agree to make in youre name and myn as was last, &c. And, sir, please yow also that I have hadde diverse communicacions with Worcestr sethe Crystmesse,[1] and I fele by hym otterly that he wole not appoynt in other fourme than to have the londs of Feyrechildes and other londes in Drayton to the sume of x. marc of yow proprely, by syde that that he desyreth of myn mayster, whom God assoyle, whiche mater I remytte to your noble discrecion.

And as for answere of the bylles that I have, I have ben so sekelew seythe Crystmasse that I myght not yette don hem, but I shal in alle hast, wher inne ye may excuse yow by me if ye please tyl the next terme, at whiche tyme alle shal be aunswered, be Godds grace, who preserve yow and send yow th' accomplyshement of youre desyres, &c.

Item, sere, please youre maystership hit was leten me wete in ryght secrete wyse that a pyssaunce is redy to aryve in thre parties of this londe, by the meane of Kyng Herry and the Quene that wes, and by the Dewk Somercete and others, of vi.ˣˣ. m.ˡ [120,000] men; and here day, if wynde and weder hadde servyd theym, shuld a' ben here sone upon Candelmasse; at Trente to London werdes thei shuld a' ben by Candelmasse or sone after, one parte of theym, and another parte comyng from Walys, and the thredde fro Yernessey and Garnesseye. Wher fore it is weel don ye enforme myn Lord Warwyk, that he may speke to the Kyng that good provy[s]ion be hadde for withstandyng there malicyous purpose and evyl wylle, whiche God graunt we may our come theym; and so we shuld, I

following extracts from the Institution Books in the Registry of the Bishop of Norwich:—

'Draiton

'Reg. xi. 124. 29 January 1460-1. Johannes Bullock ad præsentationem Joh'is Paston arm. et Tho. Howys capellani.

'Reg. xi. 131. 15 March 1461-2. Joh'es Flourdew ad præsentationem eorundem.'

It thus appears that the living was resigned by John Bullock in 1461-2, and on the 15th March John Flourdew was presented to it, not the person here recommended by Howes.

[1] This word is indicated by Fenn as indistinct in the MS.

---

dought not, if we were alle on [one]. There ben many medelers, and they ben best cheryshed, whyche wold hurt moche if these come to, as God diffende, &c.

T. HOWYS.

1462
[FEB.]

510

MARGARET PASTON TO JOHN PASTON[1]

*To my ryth worchepfull husbona, John Paston,
be this delyveryd in hast.*

PLESYTH yow to wete that John Wellys and his brodyr told me thys nyth that the Kyng lay at Cambryge as yestyrsnyth to Sandwyche ward, for ther is gret dyvysyen be twyx the Lordys and the schypmen ther, that causyth hym to goo thedyr to se a remedye therfor.   MARCH

I thank God that John Paston yed non erst [*went no earlier*] forthe, for I trust to God all schall be do er he comyth. And it is told me that Syr John Howard is lek to lese hys hed.

If it plese yow to send to the seyd Wellys, he schall send yow mor tydyngys than I may wryt at thys tyme. God have yow in Hys kepyng.

Wretyn in hast at Thetford, at xj. of the clok in the nyth, the same day I departyd fro yow.

I thank Pampyng of hys good wyll, and them that wer cause of changyng of my hors, for they ded me a bettyr torne than I wend they had do, and I schall aquyt them anothyr day, and I maye.

By yor   M. P.

[1] [From Fenn, ii. 288.] It appears by the dates of the Privy Seal writs that Edward IV. was at Cambridge on the 2nd and 3rd March 1462, and this is probably the visit alluded to, although we do not find that the King went on to Sandwich afterwards.

511

JOHN PASTON, THE ELDER, TO HIS FATHER[1]

*To myn ryth reverent and worschypfull fader,
John Paston, beyng in the Inder Temple.*

1462
MARCH 13
RYGHT reverent and wyrshypfull fader, I recomand me un to you, be sychyng you of your blessyng and gode faderhode. Pleasyt it you to understond the grete expens that I have dayly travelyng with the Kyng, as the berour here of can enforme you; and howe long that I am lyke to tary here in thys country or I may speke with you a gayn, and howe I am chargyd to have myn hors and harnys redy, and in hasty wyse, besykyng you to consyder theys causes, and so to remembr me that I may have suche thynges as I may do my mayster servys with and pleasur, trusting in God it schall be to your wyrshyp and to myn and vayll [*avail*]. In especiall I besyche you, that I may be sur where to have mony somwhat be fore Estern, ether of you, or by myn uncle Clement, when nede ys. Of othir causes the berour hereof can enforme you. No more to you at thys tyme, but God have you in Hys kepyng.

Wryten at Stamford, the xiij. day of March.

Be yowr sone and servant,

JOHN PASTON, THE OLDER.

[1] [From Fenn, iv. 126.] It appears by the dates of the Privy Seal writs that Edward IV. was at Stamford, from the 9th to the 17th March, in the second year of his reign, i.e. in 1462. This letter belongs therefore to that year.

512

REPORT OF FRENCH PRISONERS[1]

Memorandum. This is the confessyon of xvj. Frenshemen with the Mastyr, takyn at Sheryngam, the iij. wek of Lent.

RIGHT worshipfull sir, I recomaund me to you, and lete you wytte, that I have be at Shiryngham, and examyned the Frenshmen to the nombre of xvj. with the maister. And thei telle that the Duke of Somerset is in to Scotland; and thei sey the Lord Hungyrforthe was on Monday last passed afore Sheryngham in to Scotland ward, in a kervyle [*carvel*] of Depe, no gret power with hym, ne with the seid Duk neyther. And thei sey that the Duk of Burgoyn[2] is poysened, and not like to recovere. And as for powers to be gadered ayenst our welfare; thei sey, there shulde come in to Seyne CC. gret forstages[3] owt of Spayne, from the Kyng there;[4] and CCC. shippes from the Duk of Bretayne[5] with the navy of Fraunce, but thei be not yet assembled, ne vitayll there purveyd, as thei sey, ne men. And the Kyng of Fraunce[6] is in to Spayne on pilgrymage with fewe hors as thei sey; what the purpose is thei can not telle certeyn, &c. In hast at Norwich.   MARCH

The Kyng of Frauns hath comitted the rewle of Bordews on to the marchaunds of the toun, and the browd[7] tha[t] be therin to be at ther wages; and like as Caleys is a Stapole of wolle here in England, so is that made staple of wyne.

John Fermer, presoner, seyth, on [*one*] John Gylys, a clerk that was with the Erle of Oxforthe, wych was some tym in Kyng Herrys hows, was a prevy secretary with the Erle of

1462
MARCH

[1] [From Fenn, i. 250.] This letter evidently refers to the state of matters in the beginning of the year 1462, when Henry VI. and Margaret of Anjou were in Scotland, and when the Earl of Oxford had just been beheaded for conspiring against Edward IV. The date of Oxford's execution was the 20th of February. This confession of the Frenchmen is dated in the third week of Lent, that is to say, between the 14th and the 20th of March.   [2] Philip the Good.

[3] Large ships with forestages or forecastles.   [4] Henry IV., King of Castile.   [5] Francis II., the last Duke.   [6] Lewis XI.

[7] This word, says Fenn, is imperfect in the original.

THE PASTON LETTERS

1462
MARCH

Oxforthe ; and if any wrytyng wer made by the seyd Erle, the seyd Gylys knew ther of in this gret matyeres.

513

JAMES GRESHAM TO JOHN PASTON[1]

To my right singler maister, J. Paston, Squyer, in hast, &c.

MARCH 24

AFTER due recomendacion, please it your maistership to wyte Maister Yelverton, justice, seid in the Sessions that the Kyng shulde kepe his Estern at Bury, and from thens come unto this cuntre and se suyche riottes as have be in this cuntre punyshed in suche fourme as happely summe shulde hange be the nekke. And he tolde what thank he had of the Kyng at Cambrigg for cause he declarid so well the charge of extorcions doon by Shirefs and other officers, &c., for the whiche declaracion the Kyng tooke hym by the hand, and seid he cowde hym grett thanke, and prayed hym so to do in this cuntre, &c.

In hast, at Norwich, the Wednesseday next tofore th'Annunciacion, &c.

Your povere,   J. GRESHAM.

514

JOHN WYKES TO JOHN PASTON[2]

To my right trusti and welbelovid frend, John Paston, Esquier.

MARCH 25

RIGHT worshipfull, and myn enterly welbelovyd frend, I recomaund me un to you, hertely thankyng yow of your gret present of fisch, and of the felyshipp that my cosyn your sonne shewid unto me att Norwiche, purposyng

[1] [From Fenn, iv. 76.] It does not appear that Edward IV. ever did spend an Easter at Bury, as here projected. He was, however, at Cambridge in the beginning of March 1462 ; from which he proceeded to Peterborough, Stamford, Newark, and Lincoln, and at Easter (18th April) he seems to have been at Leicester.

[2] [From Fenn, i. 252.] As this letter relates to the arrest of a confederate of the Earl of Oxford and his son, who were executed in February 1462, for conspiring against Edward IV., the date must be referred to that year.

36

THE PASTON LETTERS

1462
APRIL (?)

whom I truste ye stonde right wel in conseit, with whiche God contynwe. Wherfor I beseke youre maistirshipp that if my seid Lord have the seid office, that it lyke you to desyre the nomyncacion of on of the officez, eythyr of the countroller or serchorship of Jernemuth, for a servaunt of yowrez, and I shuld so gyde me in the office as I truste shuld be most profit to my seyd Lord. And if youre maistirshyp lyked to gete graunt thereof, that than it plesyd you to lycense on of youre servaunts to take out the patent of the seyd office ; and if it cost v. or vj. or viij. marke, I shal trewly contente it ageyn ; and yeerly as longe as I myght have the officez, or any of hem, I shal geve my maister youre sone v. marke toward an haukeney.

It shuld be to me right a good mean to stondyn as well in the trust as in the conseyt amongs marchaunts, with whom and with alle men I calle myself a servaunt of yourez, and soo wil do, if it plese you, which boldyth me the more to calle upon youre right wurshipful maistyrshyp in this mater, where in I beseke you to forgeve me my boldneyse in thys behalve. And if I knew that my Lord shuld have the office in sertayn, than I wold wayte upon youre good maystyrshyp there to opteyne the patent, if it plesyd youre good maystirship to gete me the graunt, &c.

No more on to you, my right honourable maister, at thys tyme, but Jesu I beseke sende you a good conclucyon in all yore maters, and graunt you ever youre herts desyre.

Yore contynwal servaunt and bedeman,

JOHN RUSSE.

38

EDWARD IV

be the grace of God to deserve it un to you in tyme to come, in such place as I may do for you.

1462
MARCH 2

Desiryng you specyally, wher as a tenaunt of myne of Lavenham, called John Fermour, is sesid and arestid with in the towne of Yermowth, be cause he dwellid with the Erle of Oxonfords son, and purposid to have passid the see withou[t] lycence, and stondyth out of the conceyte of much peple, I wold desyre you, that ye wold wryte to the Baylyffs of Yermouth to delyver the seid John Fermor to my servaunt John Brenerigg, brynger of this, with an officer of the seid Towne, to be caried unto the Kyngs Castell of Rysing at my cost ; ther to be examynid of certeyne Artycules, which I may not disclose, til I have spoke with the Kyngs Highnes : praying you to wryte to the seid Baylffs, that I shall be her suffisant discharge ayenst the Kynge. Desyryng yow to geve credence to the brynger herof, as my verray trust is in yow.

Wretyn at Lavenham, the xxv[th.] day of Marche.

Your trew and feithfull frend, havyng no blame for my gode wylle.   JOHN WYKES,

Ussher of the Kyngs Chambre.

515

JOHN RUSSE TO JOHN PASTON[1]

To the rigth reverent and worshipfull sir, and my right honourable maystyr, John Paston.

APRIL (?)

RIGHT worshipfull sir, and my right honourable maistir, I recomaunde me to you in my most humble wise. And plese it youre good maistirshyp to wete that it is seyd here that my Lord Worcestre is lyk to be Tresorer, with

[1] [From Fenn, iv. 112.] This letter must have been written before the 14th of April 1462, on which day the Earl of Worcester was appointed Treasurer of the Exchequer (*Patent Roll*, 2 Edw. IV., p. 1, m. 19).

37

EDWARD IV

516

W. C. TO JOHN PASTON[1]

To myn ryght worshipfull and ryght singler good mayster, myn Mayster John Paston.

Myn ryght worshipfull mayster, I recomaunde me to yow in myn ryght homble wyse. And please your maystership that I have ben at Wetyng and there hald the court and lete on Hokmonday[2] as hit hath bene of olde tyme accostomed ; and the tenauntes have attorned and bene full gladde that myn lady shuld rejoyse hit and kepe here possession. The priour of Bromhill that was fermoure his terme is expired, and wole sewe to myn lady and hir councell to have a newe terme ; but lete myn lady be ware, for, as I here seyn, he bydeth but a tyme that he myght gete a summe of money to geders of myn ladyes lyflode, and to gone ther with[3] a love of his sojornyng as yette in Hokehold. She hath bene dreven fro town to town for his sake. Hit is wele done ye advertyse myn lady, if she be in that cas that she hath governaunce of hir owen londes, that she do no thyng to that lyflode ner non other in Norffolk, with ought advyse of theym that have vysyted and overseen theym ; for there hath bene straunge rewle, bothe in woodsales and sale of londes helde at wylle for fre rent, as ye shal knowe here after. Thoresby, a man that was generall attorney for myn Lord Oxenford that was, told me that the Kynge hadde made Keche generall receyvoure by priveseale of alle londes that were the Erle of Oxenford and Dame Elyzabet, ecept tho that Howard hadde entered and Lanham and an other graunted to Wykes, and certeyn lyflode in Kent that was assigned to the tresorer of howshold of the Kynges hows ; and she shuld have be Keches hande v.[c] [500] mark, ij.[c] and l. [250] mark to bene payed at this Estern and the remulant at Mihelmasse. And of the remulant the Kyng shuld be answered. Ye shal sone understande how it is ; and if hit be so, hit [is][4] but foly to laboure ayenst eny ferther. I wold fayn knowe, for the courtes for the half yere wold bene holde for nede. And our Lord be with youre maystership and sende yow th'accomplyshement of youre noble desyres. Wreten hastely at Norwyche, the iiij[te] day of May.

1462
MAY 4

Youre servaunt to his power, W. C.

And whan ye comon with myn ryght worshipfull lady I beseche yow remembre myn pore maters in whiche is greet concyens, &c.

[1] [From Paston MSS., B.M.] The manor of Weeting, in Norfolk, came to John Vere, twelfth Earl of Oxford, by his marriage with Elizabeth, daughter and heir of John Howard, Esquire, son and heir of Sir John Howard, Knight. This Earl was beheaded in February 1462, for treason against Edward IV., and the present letter seems to have been written in May following.

[2] Hock Monday was a fortnight after Easter Monday. In 1462 it fell on the 3rd May, the day before this letter was written.

[3] *With* repeated in MS.

[4] Omitted in MS.

39

517

MARGARET PASTON TO JOHN PASTON[1]

To my ryght wurschipful maister, John Paston.

1462
MAY 18

I RECOMAUNDE me unto you. Plesith it you to witte that I have spoken with Furbuschour and other of the matre that ye spake to me off, and they have promysed me to be as feythefull in it as it where for hem selfe. Also I have spoken with my modre and seide to here as ye desired me to doo, and sche seide sche knewe the massache weele inowe before be other persones in like wice as ye comaunded hem to sey to her; and sche seide she wode fayne that ye dede weele what so ever ye sey and fille forthe in other talkyng. Me semethe che is displesed that ye came not to her or than ye roode foorthe. I schall telle you more whan that ye come home. Thomas Denys wyff whas at me, and desired me that I schulde sende to you and desire you that che myght have knowleche from you how ye woll that sche schall doo with her matre; sche seithe her brother and other of her frendes thynke that she schulde up to London and calle uppon her matre there, but she seithe pleynly she woll nought doo therin withoute your advice. It whas toolde me that Bacon and Gonnor whas here to speke with me for the matre that Bacon spake to you of, and at that tyme I whas at Norweche and I herde no more of hem sethen. And as for my brother William, he is not purposed to come to London tyll aftre Pentecost; but my brother Clement is purposed to come forward on Monday or on Twesday next comyng at the

[1] [From Paston MSS., B.M.] This letter is evidently not far removed in date from No. 489, in which 'Joan Gayne's matter' is also mentioned. The year, however, cannot be 1461, as William Paston was in London that year as early as the 4th April. It seems also from this letter that John Paston had recently left home, which could not have been the case in 1461 if No. 453 be of that year. We have therefore little doubt that the true date is 1462, and that the substance of the letter relates to proceedings taken by the widow of Thomas Denys against her husband's murderers.

40

ferthest. No more at this tyme but the blissed Trinite preserve you. Wreten the xviij. day of May.
Your MARGARET PASTON.

1462
MAY 18

I prey yow that ye woll wete safe to remembre Johane Gayne matre, and that ye woll take John Paston that he remembre you of it, for Dawbeney and Pampyng woll sone for gete it.

518

JOHN PASTON, JUNIOR, TO HIS FATHER[1]

To my ryght wurschipull fadre, John Paston.

MAY

PLESIT you to wete that I am at Leyn, and under stande be dyvers personys, as I am in formed, that the Mayster of Carbroke[2] wold take a rewle in the *Marè Talbot* as for capteyn, and to yeve jaketes of his levery to dyvers personis qwych be waged be oder men, and nouth be hym, beyng in the said shep. Qwerfor in as moch as I have but few sowdeors in myn levery her, to strenketh me in that qwych is the Kynges commandement, I kepe with me yowr too men, Dawbenney and Calle, qwich I purpose shall seyle with me to Yermeth; for I have purveyed harneyse for hem. And ye shall well understande, be the grace of God, that the said Mayster of Carbroke shall have non rewle in the sheppes, as I had purposid he shuld have had, because of his besynesse, and for this is on of the specyall causes I kepe yowr said men with me, besechyng you ye takyt to non dysplesur of ther taryng

[1] [From Fenn, iv. 100.] On the 29th May 1462 a commission was granted to Sir John Howard and Sir Thomas Walgrave to arrest the ships, the *Mary Talbot* and the *Mary Thomson*, both of Lynn, and other vessels in Norfolk, Suffolk, and Essex, for a fleet which the King was fitting out (see *Patent Roll*, 2 Edw. IV., p. 1, m. 14, *in dorso*). Sir Thomas Walgrave may perhaps have been the person designated in this letter as the Master of Carbroke. At all events, the date is clearly about this time.

[2] At Carbrooke, in Norfolk, was a commandry formerly belonging to the Knights Templars, which, like most of the possessions of the order, when it was suppressed in Edward II.'s time, was given to the Knights of St. John.

41

1462
MAY

with me. Nat withstandyng, ther herden[1] at Wyggenalle shall be don this day be the grace of God, Whoo have you in kepyng.

Wreten at Leynn, the morow after my departyng from you.

Item, as far such tydynges as be here, Th. shall in forme you. JOHN PASTON.

519

ABSTRACT[2]

JUNE 6

Inventory of household stuff remaining at Castre, 6 June 2 Edward IV., viz. of robes, jewels, arras, etc.

520

NOTE

Among some MSS., which seem formerly to have belonged to the Paston Collection in the Bodleian Library at Oxford, is one endorsed—'A Pedigree showing how the manor of Caister was divided,' tracing its descent from earlier owners to Sir John Fastolf.

521

J. DAUBENEY TO JOHN PASTON[3]

To my most reverent and worchepfull maister, John Paston, dwellyng at Heylysdon, be this delyveryd.

Ih's.

JULY 3

MOST reverent and worchefull master, I recommaund me onto your god masterchep. Please you to have knowlage, on the Fryday at afternoon next after Seynt Peter, there was at the taveran in London old Debnam

[1] I do not understand the meaning of the word 'herden.'—F.
[2] [From MS. Phillipps, 9735, No. 354.]
[3] [From Fenn, iv. 138.] The date of this letter is shown by an entry on the *Patent Roll*, 2 Edw. IV., p. 1, m. 7, *in dorso*. On the 27th June 1462 a commission was given to Gilbert Debenham, Jun., Esquire, Walter Alderiche, master of the *George* of Yarmouth, and John Childe, to arrest for the King's service a ship called *The Barge of Yarmouth, alias The George*, with victuals, masters, and mariners for the same.

42

and young Debnam, Thomas Edmonds, and I; and ther the seyd Thomas Edmonds fell in communicacion with old Debnam, and seyd that my Lord Tresorer[1] had put hym to a gret charge for the vetelyng of *Mary Talbot*,[2] seyyng to old Debnam that he hard sey that he had a C. bullocks to selle, the wyche the seyd Edmonds wolle bey so that they may a cord the price. Than the seyd old Debnam answerd ageyn, and seyd he wold, so that he myght have good payment, or elles the seyd Edmonds to be bound in abligacion to pay hym at suche dayys as they myght a cord. And noon upon thys same langwage, yong Debnam spake to hys fader, 'Sir, I pray you that ye wolle take avisment of this mater tille to morowe, for I trost to your good faderhod that ye wolle late me have a serteyn of your bullocks for the vetelyng of the *Barge of Yermothe*, and I shall fynd you sufficiant suerte for the payment therof for Edmonds. I wolle that ye knowe I have be ther, and spoke with the owner and with the maister of the seyd barge, and they knowyn myn oppoyntment.'

1462
JULY 3

Than the seyd Edmonds answered to yong Debnam, and told hym that the sety of Norwic and Yermothe hathe grauntyd, and send wrytyng to the Kynge and to the Lords that they wolle manne and veteylle the seyd barge of hyr owne cost fro the tym of hyr goyng owt tylle hyr comyng home; and thus the seyd Edmonds told hym that my Lord Tresorer and all the Lords that be at London thynk they do ryght well her devyer, and be worthey moche thanke of the Kyng. 'Well,' quod yong Debnam, 'I had in commaundment for to have the rewle of the seyd barge, and I wolle be at Yermothe as thys day iiij. dayys, and man hyr and bryng hyr downne to the Gylys of Hulle, for that ys my chype.'

Also he seyd mor, with out that he myght have the seyd barge, he wolle note goo to see but hym self and hys xxiiij. men. And thus, yf please your maisterchep, he departyd from the taveran; and at hys departyng, he told the seyd Thomas Edmonds, 'Thys ys Paston labor.' Than the seyd Edmonds answerd hym ageyn, and seyd playnly he was to

[1] John Tiptoft, Earl of Worcester. He was beheaded in October 1470.—F.
[2] See Preliminary Note to No. 518, p. 41, Note 1.

43

THE PASTON LETTERS

1462
JULY 3
blame for to reporte so of your masterchep, for he knoythe veryly he seyd on trewly of you and of my master your son bothe, and ther on he wold take a bothe. And so, yf it please your good masterchep, late the cety of Norwic and Yermothe have knowlage of hys gret crakyng and bost, and let hym of hys purpose by the autorite that they have.

Item, my master your son wolle have to hys jakets murry[1] and tany [*tawny*], and that it please yow sum of my felachep may spek to on of the drapers for to ordeyn yt ageyns hys comyng hom, for I trowe it shall be thys day sevenyght ar he comithe home.

Item, sir, if please you, Skrowpe hathe sent to you to London be Byngham for the mony that ye knowe of, zit I spake not with hym; but I shall telle hym that I suppose ye shall be here in the last end of the terme, and I shall send your masterchep word what answer I have of hym.

Item, sir, if pleese suche tydyngs as I her of, I send you word. My Lord of Warwek hathe be in Skotlond, an take a castell of the Skoots; and upon thys ther came the Quene of Skoots[2] with other Lords of her contre, as ye shall her the namys, in basetry [*embassy*] to my seyd Lord of Werwek, and a trews is take betwyx thys and Seynt Bertylmew Day in Auguste. Thes is the last tydyngs that I knowe. No mor to your god masterchep at this tyme, but Jesu have [you] in kepyng.

Wretyn on the Saturday next after Seynt Peter.

By your por servaunt,

J. DAUBENEY.

---

[1] Dark red or purple and yellowish colour.—F.
[2] Mary, daughter of Arnold, Duke of Gelders, and mother to James III., King of Scotland.

EDWARD IV

522

RICHARD CALLE TO JOHN PASTON, JUNIOR[1]

To my maistre, John Paston the yonger, be this delyvered.

SERE, I have receyved your lettre, wherin I undrestand 1462 that my maistre desired that my maistre your brother myght have the gidyng and governaunce of the *Barge of Yermouthe*. As to that, and men of Yermouthe had knowen my maistre entend a fornyght a goo, he had ben swer of it, but nough it is so that Debenham hathe a comyscion of the Kyng expressed oonly for that schip named in hes comyscion; and he hathe ben here at Yermouthe, and spoken with the balyffs and with the owners of the seide schip, and takyn suche a direccion that they may graunted it ne man but hym. And moreover he hathe endented with the owners of the schip what daye it schulbe redy as well vetaylled as manned; and also he hathe brought downe letters from my Lord Tresorer to all priours and gentlemen in this contre to helpe hym and assiste hym to vetayle and manne the seide schip, and hes men is here dayle, and gothe abought and gathereth whete, malt, money, and what so ever any man woll geve, &c.

The blissed Trinyte preserve you. Wreten at Castre, the Friday next aftre I receyved your lettre.

Item, is talked here that my maistre your brother and Debenham were at words at London, and that Debenham shuld have streken hym, had nought Howard a' beene, &c., wherof I am ryght sory, &c. Neverthelesse I trust to God all schul be weell.

Your servaunt, RIC. CALLE.

---

[1] [From Fenn, iv. 144.] This and the next letter were evidently written not very long after the last.

THE PASTON LETTERS

523

RICHARD CALLE TO JOHN PASTON[1]

To my maistre, John Paston.

PLESITH your maistership to wit that I whas at Scole, and spake with Alblastre, John Sadeler, and with other good yomen of the contre to undrestonde how they were gided for the vetelyng of the *Barge of Yermouth*. And I undrestonde be them that there [*their*] hundred have payed; nevertheles it is but litell. Ther was gatherd in that hundred xviijs. and certein corn, and some other hundred vj. marc and corne, and so they have payed in all the hundreds and townys here a boute, that is to sey, Est Flegge and West Flegge and up to Blofeld, Tunsted and up to Stalom, I undrestand, be the comiscion that Debenham hath. It is more large thanne master John is, as ye schal undrestand, wherof I send you a copy, weche causeth me that I labour no ferther therin. Notwithstandyng your maistership schal have knowleche what every hundred geve, and Yermeth bothe.

Wreten at Wynterton, the morwe aftre I departed from your maistership.

Youre poore bedman, RIC. CALLE.

524

ABSTRACT[2]

RICHARD CALLE TO JOHN PASTON

1462(?)
[JULY 5]
Cannot inform him how much malt he has at Castre, 'for the malters have not moten all up yet,'—probably 400 quarters new and 160 comb old malt of Castre and Mauteby, of which 40 quarters will be spent in the household by Hallowmas. At Yarmouth it is now 2s. 2d. a bushel—it was 2s. 6d. But London is a better market. Thinks the price will fall here, as the fields are

---

[1] [From Fenn, iii. 430.]
[2] [From Paston MSS., B.M.]

EDWARD IV

reasonably fair in Flegge, and so up to Norwich. The carriage from Yarmouth 1462(?) to London will be 6d. per quarter, 'and I understand j. quartre of Yermothe [JULY 5] mette makethe at London but vij. busschell.'

Norwich, Monday after St. Peter's Day.

[As John Paston does not seem to have been in undisturbed possession of Caister before 1462, and we have evidence of Richard Calle having been there in that year about the time of year when this letter was written, we may with great probability refer it to that year.]

525

JOHN RUSSE TO JOHN PASTON[1]

To the right worshypful my right honourabyl mayster, John Paston.

RIGHT worshipfull sir, and my right honourabill maister, JULY 15 I recomaund me to you in my most humble wyse, and please your maistirship to wete that her is on Thomas Chapman, an evyl disposyd man al wey ayens you, as I have informyd youre maistirship many tymes, and now he hathe labouryd to my Lord Tresorer to subplante me, and brought down wryghting from the Kyng and my Lord Tresorer; but or hise wryting cam, Wydwell fond the meanys, be the supportacion of Maistir Feen, that we had a discharge for hym out of the Chauncery; wherfor the seyd Chapman proposyth to be at London in all haste, and to avertise the Kyng and my Lord Tresorer ageyn me to the grettest hurt he can imagyne. Wherfor I beseke youre maystirship, consedryng is evyl disposecion to yow, and also the rather at my pore instaunce, that ye lyke that my Lord Tresorer mygth undyrstonde that the seyd Chapman is of no reputacion, but evyl disposyd to brybory of straungers, and be colour of hise office of supervisor of the searche shal gretly hurte the port. The seyd Chapman supportors is Blakeney, clerk of the sygnet, and Avery Cornburght, yoman of the Kynges chaumbre. He hathe here of Avereyes xxiiij. tune wyn, whereof at the long wey he shal

---

[1] [From Fenn, iv. 120.] The precise year in which this letter was written is a little uncertain, but from the date and contents it would appear that Russe was now in possession of the office which in No. 515 he had asked Paston to procure for him; so that it cannot be earlier than 1462.

THE PASTON LETTERS

EDWARD IV

462(?)
JULY 15
make the seyd Averey a lewd rekenyng. The seyd Chapman lovyth not you, nor no man to yow wards, &c.

Sir, I prey God brynge you onys to regne amongs youre cuntre men in love, and to be dred. The lenger ye contynwe there the more hurt growyth to you. Men sey ye will neyther folwe the avyse of youre owyn kynred, nor of youre counsell, but contynwe your owyn wylfullnesse, whiche, but grace be, shal be youre distrucion. It is my part to enfourme youre maistirshyp as the comown voyse is, God betir it, and graunt yow onys herts ease; for it is half a deth to me to here the generall voyse of the pepyll, whiche dayli encreassyth, &c.

Sir, I beseke youre maistirshyp to remembre my maystresse for the lytil sylvir, whiche for serteyn thyngs delyverid to youre use is dewe to me. I have nede of it now. I have bought salt and other thyngs, whiche hathe brought me out of myche sylvir. I wold trust, and I nedyd to borwe xx*li.*, your maistirshyp wold ease me for a tyme, but thys that I desyre is myn owyn dute. And Jesu graunt yow ever yowr herts desyre to youre worshyp and profyt, and preserve yow my right honourabyll maister from all adversyte.

Wretyn at Jernemuthe, the xv. day of July. Here is a kervyl [*carvel*] of Cane in Normandy, and he takyth Duchemen, and raunsumyth hem grevously.

Yore servaunt and bedman, JOHN RUSSE.

526

WILLIAM PASTON TO JOHN PASTON[1]

To myn wurchipfull broder, Jon Paston.

1462
JULY
RYTHTHE wurchipfull broder, I recomand [me] to zow. Lekit it zow to wethe [*wit*], Jon of Dam is come to towne, and purposit hym to tary here a day ar ij. ar longar, I can thynk, and he be desyryd. Were fore I pray

[1] [From Paston mss., b.m.] The reference to the death of Christopher Hanson proves this letter to have been written in July 1462, as the precise date of his death is given in Letter 528.

48

zow, and as I have afore this tyme desiryd zow the same, that
1462
JULY
suche materis as hathe be comunyd now lathe be twyx myn moder, zow and hym, may take some good conclucyon be twyx owre selff here at hom. And in myn consayt, savyng zow better avyse, it were so most convenyent and wurchipfull for us all, and comforthe to all owre fryndis. And for this ententhe I wold tary here the lengar; for I wold be as glad as any man a lyve that suche an en mythe be take be twix us that iche off us all schuld inyoy the wylleffar off odyr, qweche I trust with zowr good help schall be rythe wyll, and I dowthe nat myn mastyr Markam wyll be will plesyd thus.

I have tydynges from London, and a monge odyr tydynges I have knowlage that Cirstofre Hanson is passid to God on Saterday last past, at ij. of clok after mydnythe. It is good to take hede there to, &c.

Item, I sent to zow to have had zowre avyse qwat menys were best to make for the mater towchyng the Lord Scrop, qwere in I had an answer, but me thowthe it was not to the poynthe. I sopose, and I purposyd to make the labore that ze sent me word I schuld do towchyng me, I can thynk I schuld sone be answerid, meche sonar than he. I must send some answer to hym, were in I wold have zowr consayll; for he desirid the same, and I wold not he schold thynk that he were forgotyn be us.

Be zowr pore broder,
WILLIAM PASTON.

I can thynk and he were here he wold be a feythfull frynd to zow; but and so were that ze thowthe that it were for to labore for any oder man, me thynkit it were for zow to remembre myn nevew. That were somewat lykly, and there to wold I be glad to help and lene to the toder. For as for me, I know so moche that sche will none have but iff he have, ar be leke to have, meche more lond than I have; and iff I knewe the contrary, it schuld nat be left for the labore, but I wold not be in a folis paradyce, and ze be myn good brodir. I trust thow to do rythe will, &c.

VOL. IV.—D
49

THE PASTON LETTERS

EDWARD IV

527

THOMAS PLAYTER TO JOHN PASTON[1]

To my rigth good maister, John Paston the oldest, beyng at Heylesdon, besyde Norwiche, in hast.

1462
JULY
PLEASE your maistership wete that Christofer Hanson is ded and beryed; and as for executor or testament, he mad non.

As for tydyngs, the Erles of Warrewyk, of Essex, Lord Wenlok, Bysshop of Dereham, and other go in to Scotland or inbassat. And as for the sege of Kaleys, we here no mor ther of, blyssed be God, ho have you in His kepyng.

Item, as for Christofers papers that longeth to your tenants, I have goten of William Worcester; and as for all the remnaunt of Christofer good, William Worcester hath the reule as hym semeth most convenient.

Your, THOMS PLAYTER.

528

PLAYTER TO JOHN PASTON[2]

To my maister, John Paston, at Heylesdon.

ITEM, plese you wete of other tytyngs. These Lords in your other letter,[3] with Lord Hastyngs and other, ben to Karlyle to resseve in the Qwen of Scotts;[4] and upon this appoyntement, Erle Duglas[5] is comaunded to come thens, and as a sorowfull and a sore rebuked man lyth in the Abbey

[1] [From Fenn, iv. 124.] This letter, like the last, is dated by the letter following.
[2] [From Fenn, i. 270.] This letter seems to have been penned immediately after the last was sent off.
[3] *i.e.* the other letter to you—meaning No. 527.
[4] Mary of Gueldres, widow of James II.
[5] James, Earl of Douglas, who had been banished from Scotland, but was made by Edward IV. a Knight of the Garter.

50

of Seynt Albons; and by the said appoyntement schall not be
1462
JULY
reputed, nor taken, but as an Englysseman, and if he come in the daunger of Scots, they to sle hym.

Item, Kyng Harry and his Aderents in Scotland schall be delyvered; and Lord Dakres of the Northe is wonne and yelden, and the seid Lord, Sir Richard Tunstall, and on Byllyngham in the said Castell ben taken and heded.

Item, the Qwen and Prince ben in Fraunce and ha mad moche weyes and gret peple to com to Scotland and ther trust to have socour, and thens to com in to Inglond : what schall falle I can not sey, but I herd that these appoyntements were take by the yong Lords of Scotland, but not by the old.

Your, PLAITER.

Christofer dyed on the Saterday next be for Seynt Margret,[1] Anno . E . ij*do.*

529

JOHN RUSSE TO JOHN PASTON[2]

To my right honorabil and worshypfull maister, my Maister Paston.

1462
SEPT.
PLEASE it youre worshipfull maistyrshyp to wete, that it is informyd me thys day scretly, that there is dyrected out a commyssyon to mayster Yelwyrton and maister Jenney, which shall tomorwyr syttyn be vertu of the same at Seynt Oleffes;[3] and the substaunce of jentilmen and yemen of Lodyngland be assygned to be afore the seyd commesyoners; and it is supposed it is for my maisters londs, for as the seyd

[1] St. Margaret's Day was the 20th July. The Saturday before it in 1462 was the 17th.
[2] [From Fenn, i. 260.] This letter must have been written in the year 1462 before the Duke of Somerset was received into favour. Proclamations similar to those mentioned in this letter were issued on the 6th March 1461 and the 11th May 1464; but neither of these can be the case referred to. The coming of the King to London must have been in the beginning of September 1462. He was in London on the 14th of that month, and had been at Fotheringay on the 1st, as the dates of Privy Seals inform us.
[3] St. Olave's, in Suffolk.

51

1462
SEPT.
persone informyd me, the seyd comesyoners have been at Cotton, and there entred, and holdyn a court. I can not informe youre maystyrship that it is thus in serteyn, but thus it was told me, and desyryd me to kepe it secret ; but be cause I conseyve it is ageyn your maistyrship, it is my part to geve you relacion thereof.

I sende you a letter which cometh from Worcestyr[1] to my maister youre brothyr. I wold ye undyrstod the intente of it, for as for Worcester, I knowe well he is not good. Sum men ar besy to make werre, for p'[2] the absentyng of my maister, the parson comyth not of hyse owyn mocyon, but I wold youre maistyrship knewe be whom it is mevyd. I herd you never calle hym false pryst, be my trouth, nor other language that is rehersyd hym, but Gode sende a good accord, for of varyaunce comyth gret hurt of tyn tyme, and I beseche Jesu sende youre maistyrship youre herts desyre, and amende hem that wold the contrary.

Sir, yesterevyn a man came from London, and he seyth, the Kyng cam to London on Satyrday, and there dede make a proclamacion that all men that were be twyx lx. and xvj. shuld be redy to wayte upon hym whan so ever they were callyd ; and it is seyd, that my Lord Warwyk had sent to the Kyng, and informyd hyse Hyghnesse that the Lord Summyrset had wretyn to hym to come to grace ; but of the fleet of shyppis there is no tydings in serteyn at London on Monday last past.

Youre bedman and servaunt,
JOHN RUSSE.

[1] William Worcester.
[2] p'.—So in Fenn's left-hand copy. The word seems to have been ambiguous in the original MS., and is rendered 'by' (in italics) in the modern version.

52

530

JOHN PASTON TO THE LORD CHANCELLOR[1]

SHEWYTH and lowly compleynith on to your good 1462(?) Lordship John Paston, the older, Squier, that where Sir John Fastolf, Knyght, cosyn to your seid besecher, was seasid of diveris maners, londs, and tenements in Norfolk, Suffolk, and Norwich, the xxvij. yere of Kyng Herre that was, and therof infeffid diveris persones to execute and performe his will, and mad his will in especiall that a college of vij. monks shuld be stabilissid, founded, and indewed withinne a plase late be the seid Sir John edified at Caster be the see in Norfolk, and certeyn livelode to be immortesid[2] therto, to prey for his sowle, his faders and moders, in forme and maner as in his will mad at that tyme more pleynly specifyth ; whech will and feffment continued till the xxxv. yere of the seid late Kyng. And aftir, upon divers communicacions had be divers personis with the seid Sir John Fastolff, and upon divers consideracions mevid to hym, the seid Sir John Fastolff conceyvid that such be monkys hym there to be indewed shuld not be of power to susteyne and kepe the seid plase edified, or the lond that shuld be immortesid ther to, acordyng to his seid entent and will ; wherfore, and for good will that the seid Sir John Fastolff had to the proferryng of your seid besecher mevyd hym to have the seid plase and certeyn of his livelode of gretter valew than the charge of the seid college schuld drawe, and to found the seid college and to bere the reparacion and defens therof. Upon which mocion the seid Sir John Fastolff and your seid besecher apoynted be word withowt writyng at that

[1] [From Paston MSS., B.M.] This is a draft bill in Chancery prepared by John Paston with a view to the commencement of a suit against Yelverton and Jenney for their entry into the manor of Cotton and other lands of Sir John Fastolf in Suffolk. The document may have been drawn up in the latter part of the year 1461 ; but from the contents of the preceding letter it is not unlikely to have been a year later. Two copies of this document exist, with the very same corrections and interlineations in both.
[2] Amortized, or granted in mortmain.

53

1462(?) tyme mad that your seid besecher shuld, aftir the decese of the seid Sir John Fastolff, have the seid plase in Caster, and all the maners that were the seid Sir John Fastolffs or any other to his use in Norfolk, Suffolk, and Norwich, up trust that the same John Paston shuld founde there a college of vij. monkes or prestes havyng a certeyn pension for her sustenacion payid clerly in mony withowt any charge, cost, reparacion, or joperde of defens of the seid plase or of any other livelode to be bore be the seyd collegians, and more over to paye a certeyn somme of mony of the revenews of the seid maners, londes and tenementes to be disposid yerly be certeyn yeres for the sowle of the seid Sir John Fastolff till the summe of v.ml. [5000] mark were so disposed. Upon wech apoyntement it was acordyd be thwyx the seid Sir John and your seid besecher, for as moch as your seid besecher had non astate in the seid maners and londes and tenementes, that for his more suerte, and upon trust that the seid Sir John had to your seid besecher in this behalfe that a newe feffement shuld be mad of the seid plase and of the maner of Caster, and all the seid maners, londs and tenements to your seid besecher, and divers other personys to the use of the seid Sir[1] John, terme of his lif, and aftir his decese to the use of your seid besecher. And moreover, for as moch as your seid besecher was in dowte whedir God wold send hym tyme of life to execute the seid apoyntement, intendyng that th'effect of the old purpose of the seid Sir John Fastolff schuld not be all voyded, thow it so fortuned your seid besecher cowd not performe the seid apoyntement, mevid the seid Sir John Fastolff that, not withstandyng the seid apoyntement, that he aftir the seid feffement mad shuld make his will for the seid college, to be mad in all maner wise as thow the seid Sir John Fastolff and your seid besecher shuld not make[2] the seid apoyntement ; and that aftir that, the seid apoyntement to be ingrosid and made so that the seid college shuld hold be the same apoyntement of your seid besecher, and ellis this seid will of the seid Sir John

[1] 'Sir.'—This word is omitted in the first copy.
[2] 'Shuld not make.'—These words are interlined in place of the word 'left,' which is erased.

54

Fastolff to stand in effect for executyng of his seid purpose. 1462(?) And sone aftir this comunicacion and apoyntement the seid feffement was mad acordynge, and season deliverid to your seid besecher at the seid plase edified in Caster, as well as at the seid maners, londs, and tenements, the seid Sir John Fastolff beyng present at delivery of season mad to your seid besecher of the seid plase and maner of Caster, where the seid Sir John, more largely expressyng the seid will and entent, deliverid your seid besecher possession with his owne hands, declaryng to notabill personys there the same feffement to be made to the use of the seid Sir John as for terme of his lif only, and aftir his decese to the use of your seid besecher and his heyrs ; and divers tymes in divers yeres aftir declared his entent in like wise to divers personys. And aftir, be gret deliberacion and oft communicacion of the seid mater, the seid Sir John Fastolff and your seid besecher comenauntyd[1] and apoynted be writyng thoroughly for the seid mater so that your seid besecher shuld have the seid plase and all the seid maners, londs, and tenements in Norfolk, Suffolk, and Norwich, to hym and to his heyrs ; and that he shuld found a college of vij. monkes or prestes withinne the seid plase perpetually as is before seid, and to pay iiij.ml. [4000] mark to be disposed in certeyn yers for the sowle of the seid Sir John Fastolff ; the whech apoyntement declarid and red before the seid Sir John Fastolff, be good deliberacion was be the seid Sir John fully concludid, agreyd and stabilisshid for his last will in that behalve.

And also the seid comenauntes and apoyntementes eftsonis callid to remembraunce be the seid Sir John Fastolff, the same Sir John, for certeyn consideracions movyng hym, be his word, withowt writyng, dischargid your seid besecher of the seid somme of iiij.ml. mark, desiryng hym so to ordeyne that ich of the seid monkes or prestes shull yerly have as the prestes of the chauntry of Heylesdon had, and that vij. pore men shull also be founde yerly in the seid plase inperpetuite to pray for the sowles above sayd.

[And aftir, that is to sey the Satirday, Sonday, and Monday

[1] So spelt in both copies.

55

THE PASTON LETTERS

462(?) next before the decese of the seid Sir John, the same Sir John, remembryng divers maters and intents in his mynd necessary for the wele of his sowle, wheche were not expressid in the seid will and apoyntement, nowther in his testament, and that he wold have one will mad and wrete conteynyng the seid apoyntements, as well as the seid other maters not declarid in his intent and will acordyng, comaundid to have it so ingrosid and wrete.]¹ And where your seid besecher hath don his part acordyng to the will and apoyntements of the seid Sir John, as well in fyndyng of the seid prestes and pore men as in all other thyngs that to hym belongyth to do in that behalfe; and, this not with standyng, William Yelverton, Knyght, and William Jenney, wheche be infeffid joyntly with your seid besecher in divers of the seid maners, londs and tenements, have ² mad a sympill entre in all the seid maners in Suffolk, and chargid the baylifs, fermors, and tenaunts of all the seid maners to pay hem the profitez and revenews of the same maners, londs, and tenements; and thus, contrary to th'entent of the seid feffement, and contrary to the will of the seid Sir John Fastolff, thei trobill and lette your seid besecher to take the profitez of the seid maners, londs, and tenements; of whech your seid besecher hath no remedy at the comen lawe. Wherfore please your good and gracious Lordship to direct severall writts of subpena to the seid William and William, chargyng hem severally upon a peyne convenient to appere before your Lordship in the Chauncery at a certeyn day be your Lordship to be limityd, to answer to these premisses, and to do as right and consiens requirith. And your seid besecher shall pray God for yow.

The following article is added in the first copy with many corrections :—

And aftir, late before the discese of the seid Sir John Fastolff, he wold and ordeynid that on wrytyng shuld be mad of the fundacion of the seid college aftir the forme of the seid apoyntement mad with your seid besecher, and of diverses othir articles conteynid in his seid former willes, not concerning the seyd colegge and also of divers maters wheche he remembrid necessary for the wele of his sowle, that were nevir expressid in writyng before, joyntly to geder expressyng his hole and inter and last will and intent in all.

¹ The clause between brackets is cancelled in the first copy.
² This word is interlined in the second copy only.

56

EDWARD IV

531

JOHN RUSSE TO JOHN PASTON¹

To my right honourabyl and worshypfull maister, my Maister John Paston.

PLESE your worshypfull maistership to wette, here is a ship of Hith, wyche seith that John Cole cam from the west cost on Wednysday last past; and he seyth that the fleet of shippis of this londe met with lx. seile of Spanyards, Brettenys, and Frenshemen, and there tok of hem l. [50], wherof xij. shyppys were as gret as the *Grace de Dewe*; and there is slayn on thys partyes the Lords Clynton² and Dakyr,³ and many jentilmen juve (?) ⁴ and othyr, the nombre of iiij.ᵐˡ. [4000]; and the seid Spanyards were purposyd with marchaundise in to Flaundres. My Lord of Warwyks shyp, the *Mary Grace* and the *Trenyte*, hadde the grettest hurt, for they wer formost. God send grace, thys be trew. On Thursday last past at London was no tydings in serteyn where the fleet was, nor what they had doon, and therfore I fere the tydings the more.

Item, sir, as for tydings at London, ther were arystyd be the tresorer xl. seyles lyeng in Temse, wherof many smale shyppis; and it is seyd it is to carye men to Caleyse in all haste, for feer of the Kyng of Fraunce for a sege. And it was told me secretly there were CC. in Caleyse sworn contrary to the Kyngs well, and for defaute of there wages; and that Qwen Marget was redy at Boleyn with myche sylver to paye the soudyers, in cas they wold geve here entresse. Many men be gretly aferd of thys mater, and so the tresorer hath mych to do for thys cause.

¹ [From Fenn, i. 261.] This letter was evidently written not very long after No. 529. The fleet mentioned here and in that letter is that referred to in the preliminary note to No. 518, p. 41, Note 1.
² John, Lord Clinton. The rumour was false, as he was summoned to Parliament in 1463. Nicolas supposes he died about 1465.
³ Richard Fynes, Lord Dacre of the South, who was Lord Clinton's father-in-law. He did not really die till 1484.
⁴ This word, Fenn says, is doubtful in the original MS.

1462

57

THE PASTON LETTERS

1462 Item, sir, as for tydings out of Ireland, ther wer many men at London at the feyre of the contres next them of Ireland, and they sey thys iij. wyks came there neythyr shyp nor boot out of Irelond to bryng no tydings; and so it semyth there is myche to doo there be the Erle of Pembrook.¹ And it is seyd that the Kyng shuld be at London as on Satyrday or Sonday last past, and men deme that he wold to Caleyse hym selfe; for the soudyors are so wyld there, that they wyll not lette in ony man but the Kynge or my Lord Warwyk.

Othyr tydings the were come to London, but they were not publyshyd; but John Wellys shal abyde a day the lenger to know what they mene.

No mere un to yow, my right honourable maister, at thys tyme, but Jesu send yow youre herts desyre, and amende hem that wold the contrary.

Your bedman and conty[n]wal servaunt,
JOHN RUSSE.

532

JOHN PASTON, JUNIOR, TO HIS FATHER²

To my ryth reverent and worchepfull fadyr, John Paston, be thys delyveryd in hast.

NOV. I RYTH reverent and worchepfull fadyr, I recomand me on to yow, beseechyng yow lowly of your blyssyng. Plesyt you to have knowlage that my Lord³ is pur-posyd to send for my Lady, and is lyke to kepe his Crystmas here in Walys, for the Kyng hathe desyered hym to do the same. Wherfor I beseche yow that [ye]⁴ wole wychesave to send me some mony by the berer herof; for, in good feythe, as it is not on knowyng to yow that I had but ij. noblys in my purse, whyche that Rychard Call took me by your

¹ Jasper Tudor, Earl of Pembroke, half-brother to Henry VI.
² [From Fenn, i. 266.] In the month of October 1462, as we learn from William Worcester, Margaret of Anjou came out of France, whither she had fled in spring, with a force of 2000 men, landed on the coast of Northumberland, and laid siege to Bamborough, which she took and placed in the keeping of the Duke of Somerset.
³ The Duke of Norfolk. ⁴ Omitted in original.

58

EDWARD IV

comandement, when I departyd from yow owt of Norwyche. The berer herof schuld bye me a gowne with pert of the mony, if it plese yow to delyver hym as myche mony as he may bye it with; for I have but on gowne at Framyngham and an other here, and that is my levere gowne, and we must were hem every day for the mor part, and one gowne with-owt change wyll sone be done.

As for tydyngs, my Lord of Warwyk yed forward in to Scotland as on Saterday ¹ last past with xx.ᵐˡ. [20,000] men; and Syr Wylliam Tunstale is tak with the garyson of Bamborowth, and is lyke to be hedyd, and by the menys of Sir Rychard Tunstale ² is owne brodyr.

As sone as I here any more tydyngys, I schall send hem yow by the grace of God, who have yow in Hys kepyng. Wretyn in hast, at the Castle of the Holte,³ upon Halowmas Daye.

Your sone and lowly servaunt,
J. PASTON, Junior.

1462
NOV. I

533

JOHN PASTON THE YOUNGEST TO JOHN PASTON THE ELDER⁴

To my ryth worchepful brodyr John Paston, the elder, sone of John Paston, Esquyer, be thys delyveryd in hast.

RYTH worchepfull brodedyr, I recomaunde me to yow. Plesyt yow to wet, that as thys day we had tydyngs here, that the Scottys wyll come in to Ingelnd with in vij. days aftyr the wrytyng of thys lettyr, for to rescue these iij. castellys, Alnewyk, Donsamborowe⁵ and Bameborowe, whyche castellys wer besegyd, as on yesterdaye. And at the

DEC. II

¹ 30th October.
² Sir Richard Tunstal was on Queen Margaret's side, while his brother William, it seems, was on that of King Edward. ³ In Denbighshire.
⁴ [From Fenn, i. 272.] The sieges mentioned in this letter took place, according to Warkworth, in December of the *first year of Edward IV., i.e.* 1461; but according to William Worcester in 1462. The dates of the Privy Seal writs prove that the latter is right, and that Edward IV. was at Durham in December 1462.
⁵ Dunstanborough.

59

THE PASTON LETTERS

1462
DEC. 11

sege of Allnewyk lythe my Lord of Kent and the Lord Scalys; and at Donsameborow castyll lythe the Erle of Wyrcetyr [and] Syr Rafe Grey; and at the castyll of Bameborow lythe the Lord Montagwe and Lord Ogyll, and othyr dyvers Lordys and gentylmen that I knowe not; and ther is to hem owt of Newe Castyll ordynans inowe, bothe for the segys and for the feld, in cas that ther be ony feld takyn, as I trow there shall none be not yet, for the Scottys kepe no promes. My Lord of Warwyk lythe at the castyll of Warcorthe, but iiij. myle owt of Alnewyk, and he rydyth dayly to all thes castelys for to overse the segys; and if they want vataylys, or any othyr thyng, he is redy to pervey it for them to hys power. The Kyng comandyd my Lord of Norfolk[1] for to condyth vetaylys and the ordynans owt of New Castyll on to Warcorthe Castyll, to my Lord of Warwyk; and so my Lord of Norfolk comandyd Syr John Howard, Syr William Peche, Syr Robert Chamberlyen, Rafe Ascheton and me, Calthorp and Gorge, and othyr, for to go forthe with the vytalys and ordynans on to my Lord of Warwyk; and so we wer with my Lord of Warwyk with the ordynans and vytalys yesterdaye. The Kyng lythe at Durham, and my Lord of Norfolk at New Castyll. We have pepyll inow here. In cas we abyd here, I pray you purvey that I may have here more mony by Crystmas Evyn at the ferthest, for I may get leve for to send non of my wagyd men home ageyn; ne man can get no leve for to go home but if they stell a wey, and if they myth be knowe, they schuld be scharply ponyschyd. Mak as merry as ye can, for ther is no joperte toward not yet. And ther be any joperte, I schall sone send yow word, by the grase of God. I wot well ye have more tydyngys then we have here, but thes be true tydyngys.

Yelverton and Jeney ar lek for to be gretly ponyschyd, for because they came not hedyr to the Kyng. They ar morkyn [markea] well inowe, and so is John Bylyngforthe and Thomas Playter; wherefor I am ryth sory. I pray yow let them have wetyng therof, that they may purvey their excuse

---

[1] John Mowbray, who succeeded his father in the dukedom of Norfolk in 1461. He was at this time only eighteen years of age.

60

in hast, so that the Kyng may have knowlage why that they come not to hym in ther one personys; let them come or send ther excuse to me in wrytyng, and I schall purvey that the Kyng schall have knowlage of ther excuse; for I am well aqueyntyd with my Lord Hastyngys, and my Lord Dakarys,[1] whyche be now gretest abowt the Kyngys person; and also I am well aqueyntyd with the yonger Mortymere, Fererys, Hawte, Harpor, Crowmer, and Bosewell, of the Kyngys howse.

1462
DEC. 1

I pray yow let my grandam[2] and my cosyn Clere[3] have knowlage how that I desyryd you to let hem have knowlage of the tydyngys in thys letyr, for I promysyd for to send them tydyngs.

I pray yow let my modyr[4] have cnowelage how that I, and my felawscep, and your servauntys ar, at the wrytyng of this lettyr, in good hell, blesyd be God.

I pray yow let my fadyr have knowlage of thys lettyr, and of the todyr lettyr that I sent to my modyr by Felbryggys man; and how that I pray bothe hym and my modyr lowly of her blyssyngys.

I pray yow that ye wole send me some lettyr how ye do, and of your tydyngys with yow, for I thynk longe that I here no word fro my modyr and yow.

I pray yow that thys bill may recomand me to my systyr Margery, and to my mastres Jone Gayne, and to all gode mastyrys and felawys within Castyr. I sent no lettyr to my fadyr, never syn I departyd fro yow, for I kowd get no man to London, and never sythe.

I pray yow in cas ye spake with my cosyn Margaret Clere, recomande me to hyr; and Almythy God have yow in Hys kepyng.

Wretyn at Newcastyll on Saterday next aftyr the Consepsion of owyr Lady.

Your,   JOHN PASTON, the
                          Yongest.

I pray yow let Rychard Call se thys lettyr.

---

[1] See p. 57, Note 3.   [2] Agnes Paston.
[3] Elizabeth, widow of Robert Clere of Ormesby.   [4] Margaret Paston.

61

THE PASTON LETTERS

534

[JOHN] PASTON TO [THE DUKE OF SUFFOLK][1]

1462-3

THAT it please my lordis good grase to be good lord and supporter of Paston in his right and possession of the maner till his right can be lawfully or be trete dispreved by his adversaries, consideryng that the said Paston is my lordis homager and was nevir ayens his lordship and that my lord is not gretly behold to do for the seid Pastons adversaries as he understandith.

And in case my lord woll not supporte the seid Paston in his right but be indifferent athwyx bothe partyes, that thanne it please my lorde to have consideracion to the right of the mater as folowyth in articles and ther upon to be remembird whedir it be resonably desired by William Jenney or by Debenham as his waged man or for his sake that Paston shuld leve the possession or the takyng of the profitez of the seid maner.

First to be remembird that the seid maner aswell as the maner of Nakton were Sir John Fastolffis, and that the seid Paston of the seid maners toke estatis at Cotton and attornement of the tenauntis viij. or ix. yere goo, in such wise as the tenauntes can reporte, and continued there in possession aswell in the live of the seid Sir John as sithen, and hath take the profitez therof sith the discese of the said Fastolff, except for the terme of Mighelmes a yere passed, whech tyme the tenauntes were compellid by fors of distresses to pay ayens ther willes part of the seid profitez.

And that also the title of the seid Paston to the seid maner is not all only by the seid feffement but aswell by a graunt and bargeyn made a thwyx the seid Fastolff and the

---

[1] [Add. MS. 34,889, f. 182.] This petition must have been drawn up at the end of 1462 or in the beginning of 1463, which would be considered still 1462 in the old computation. It must have been fully three years after Fastolt's death, which took place on the 5th November 1459, and the imprisonment of Richard Calle in 1461 (see No. 487) is referred to as having taken place 'at Michaelmas the year past.' The nobleman to whom the petition is addressed seems to be the Duke of Suffolk.

62

seid Paston as by the last will of the seid Fastolff, where by the seid Paston ought to take the hole profitez of the seid maner, and also it is lefull to the seid Paston to kepe the seid maner with fors, consideryng he hath be in possession iij. yere and more; hough be it, the seid Paston intendyth to kepe the seid maner pesibly and non otherwise. And that the pretense and cleyme of the seid Jenney is that he schuld be inffeffed with the seid Paston in the seid maner; by whech pretense, if it were trewe, yet the seid Paston by reason shuld not be put out of the seid maner, for who som evir had titell therto by feffement or by executrie, Paston shuld be on that had title; hough be it, the seid Paston cleymyth not in that forme, but by the titell of his bargeyne and by the seid Fastolffis will.

1462-3

Item, to be remembird, whech tyme as my lord had wretyn his lettirs and sent his servauntes for the eyde and supporte of the seid Paston to take the profitez of the seid maner of Nakton as of the maner of Cotton, desyryng the tenauntes to the seid Paston, the seid Jenney wold have no consideracion therto; hough be it, though he were a feffe he had no titell to take the seid profitez, consideryng he is non executor, but presumptuously, havyng no consideracion to my lordis lettir ner sendyng, compellid the tenauntis by distresses to pay hym more besely thanne any feffe or executor, and now at this same tyme hath be at Nakton and reseyvid as moch mony as he coud gader there.

Item, where at Mighelmesse the yere passed the seid Paston sent his sone, a servaunt of my Lordis, and also Richard Calle, servaunt to the seid Paston put to hym by my Lordis fader,[1] to reseyve the profitez of the seid maner as thei had do many yeres before, the seid Jenney ded arest the seid Calle for a thef and as a thef caried hym to th'entent that the tenauntes shuld be discoraged to pay the seid Paston. Whech tyme, at the request of the said Calles kynred, it pleased my lord to write to the seid Jenney and Debenham

---

[1] William de la Pole, the unfortunate Duke of Suffolk, murdered in 1450. It is a piece of information which we do not meet with elsewhere, that Richard Calle entered the service of the Pastons by this duke's recommendation.

63

THE PASTON LETTERS

462-3 for the deliverauns of the seid Calle; to which letteris they nouther toke hede nor reputacion, but by that sotilte reseyved the profitez of the seid maner, the seid Paston havyng non help by my seid Lordis writyng nor sendyng.

Wherfore please my Lordis good lordship to supporte the seid Paston in kepyng of his right and possession till it be dispreved or knowe onlawfull, and the seid Paston will applye to such meanes as it pleasith my Lord to take wherby the right of the mater may be undirstond and determined.

And also that it like my lord to remembir that it is not behofefull for any prinse lightly to geve trust or to applye to the desires of any persones that have geve hym cause of mistrust.

535

[JOHN PASTON TO MARGARET PASTON][1]

463 (?)
JAN. 14
I RECOMAND me to yow and have reseyvid your lettir, which causith me to write in the lettir that I send to yow, Daubeney and Richard Calle, certeyn articles touchyng the rewle of myn hows and myn livelode, as ye shall undirstand whanne ye see hem. Also, I send yow in the same lettir a bille of all the malt that remaynd at Mighelmes. I suppose ye have non such of it. Nevirthelesse it had be convenient it had be had amongis your servauntis and yow. Also I woll that ze warne both Daubeney and Richard Calle that thei disclose nat what malt I have, ne what I shall selle, ne that on marchant knowe nat what an other hath, for ther is gret spies leid her at London for ingrosers of malt to heyghne the prise; hough be it myne is not but of myn owne growyng and my tenauntis.

[1] [Add. MS. 34,889, f. 183.] The MS. of this letter is a rough draft in John Paston's hand, and there can be no doubt to whom it was addressed. As to the year in which it was written there is no positive evidence; but Daubeney and Calle were both with Margaret Paston in the beginning of 1463 (see No. 536), and the only thing against that date is that Margaret, writing to her husband (then in London) on the 19th, acknowledges only a letter of the 9th. This, however, might well be owing to the disturbed state of the country, or it may be that the present letter, which is only a draft, was not really despatched.

64

EDWARD IV

Also I lete zow wete, I faile mony here and must nedys 1463(?) have up mony at this tyme for sped of my maters, so that JAN. 14 it may come up savely whanne James Gresham and other attornes come up at the begynnyng of this terme, with whom Richard Calle may come the same tyme. And peraventure some trusty carier . . . at this tyme; and with hym myght some mony come trussid in some fardell, not knowynge to the carier that it is no mony but some other clothe or vestement of silk or thyng of charge. Wherfore take avise of such as ye trust, and purvey that I may have up at this tyme j. c. li. of gold after the old coynage and xx li. in grotes.

Item, if I[1] myght have sur cariage, I wold have heder all the gylt plate that Richard Calle leyd up, he can tell wer and I trowe ye know also; and ij. potell pottis and a rosting iron of silver (?) lyth at the same place, for it shuld[2] stand me in gret stoher if it mygth be do closly and suerly. Item, take trew men of yowr counsel.

Wret the morwe next after Sent Hillary.

Item leve a bill indorcid what ye take awey if ye take any. —Your own, &c.

[1] 'Item, I I,' MS. [2] 'Shuld shul,' MS.

536

MARGARET PASTON TO JOHN PASTON[3]

To my right worchepful hosbond, John Paston, be this letter deliveryd in hast.

RIGHT worchepfull hosbond, I recommand me to you. 1463 Please you to wete that I received a letter frome you JAN. 19 on the Sonday[4] next after Twelfthe day, weche was sent be a prest of Seynt Gregorys paryche of Norwic; and wher as ye mervaylyd I sent you no wrytynggs of suche letters as ye sent me be for, I sent you a answer of the substauns of suche

[3] [From Fenn, iv. 150.] This letter refers to a coming election of knights of the shire, which seems to be for the Parliament which met on the 29th April 1463. No other general election of Edward IV.'s time will suit the date, and it is quite certain that it was written during Edward's reign. [4] 9th January.

VOL. IV.—E

65

THE PASTON LETTERS

1463 maters as ye have wretyn of me be for (be Playter), the weche JAN. 19 he told me a sent hem to you to London. And as towchyng the erands that ye sent to me for to do to Richard Calle, I have do as ye command me to do, and callyd upon hym therfor, bothe be for your writyng and sithyn; he thar have non excuse for defaute of leyser, for he hathe be but ryght litill her syn ye departyd hens. He is owght at this tyme, and whan that he comythe home I shall make hym make yow a cler bylle of the receyt of your lyvelod, and Fastolf bothe; and I shale send yow a cler bylle of my receyts, and also of my payments owght thereof ageyn; and as for suche erands that shuld be do to Sir Thomas Howys, I have shewyd Richard Calle your writyng, and told hym your entent, and as for suche thyngs as ye wold he shuld sey to hym on hys none heed. Also I have do your erands to my moder and to my cosyn Cler[1] after your writyng. Item, I have spoke to John Adam and to Playter of your entent of the last bylle that ye sent me, and they sey they wolle do after your entent as moche as they may, and ye shall have a answer therof in hast.

Item, Sir Robert Coniors dinid with me this day, and shuyd me a letter that came frome the Kyng to hym, desyryng hym that he shuld a wayt upon hys welle be lovyd broder the Duke of Suffolk, at Norwiche, on Monday next comyng, for to be at the alection of knyghts of the chyer [shire]; and he told me that every jentylman of Norffolk and Suffolk that arne of any repetacion hathe writyng from the Kyng in lyke wyse as he had. I felle hym be his seyyng that he ys right welle disposyd to you ward; he seythe ther shall no man make hym to be a geyns you in no mater. Skypwith shall telle you suche tydyngs as bethe in this contre, and of Thomas Gornay and of his man; hym self is clerk convicte, and hys man is hangyn; ye shall here her after what they and oder wer purposyd a do to her master.

I thank you hertely of your writyng to me be for that John Paston came home, for God knowith I thowght right longe tyle I hard from you; I shalle send word in writyng of suche tydings as we have her on Monday in hast. Daubeney

[1] Elizabeth, widow of Robert Clere of Ormesby.

66

EDWARD IV

deseyryht to wet what tyme that it please you that he shuld 1463 come ageyn to you. JAN. 19

My moder and many other folkys makyth moche of your son John, the elder, and right glad of hys comyng hom, and lekyth reght welle hys demenyng. Heydon[1] son hathe bor owght the syyd stowtly her this Cristemes, and whan that he rydyth, he hathe iiij. or v. men with hym in a clothyng; but he hathe but lytyl fafor in this contre but yf [unless] it be of the Bischop[2] and of the Prior of Norwic.[3] The seyd prior hathe grauntyd hym the stewerdchep that hys feder had . . . . he hathe it under the Covent Seals, and Spylman,[4] his tutor, to lerne hym howe he shuld be demenyd . . . . it is seyd abowght Bakynstorp that Herry Heydon shuld a seyd that it wer welle do that men of the . . . . shuld make redy her [their] bald batts[5] and her clot shon[6] and go feche hom her knygts of chyer [shire] . . . . Barney; and it is promysyd hym that he shall be met with be cause of hys langage . . . . us a good world and a pesybyll. I shall purvey for all thyngs that ye have sent to me for, so that I ween ye shal be pleasyd. The blyssyd Trinite have you in Hys kepyng. Wretyn in hast, the Wednysday next . . . . Seynt Agnet.

Your, M. P.

537

ABSTRACT[7]

THOMAS PLAYTER TO JOHN PASTON

Please your maistership wete, that as for my Lord of Norwich cosyns deth, JAN. Thomas Gurneys man hath confessed that he slewe hym by commaundment of

[1] This must be Henry, son of John Heydon, Esq., Recorder of Norwich.—F.
[2] Walter Lyhert, Bishop from 1445 to 1472.—F.
[3] John Molet or Mowth, Prior from 1453 to 1471.—F.
[4] Henry Spilman, afterwards Recorder of Norwich; he was the founder of the Spilmans of Narborough, by marrying Ela, daughter and heir of William de Narborough.—F.
[5] Bald batts seem to mean here ball bats, or bats to play at ball with.—F.
[6] Clot shon, clouted shoes—shoes shod with thin plates of iron.—F.
[7] These extracts are quoted by Fenn from a letter now lost, in reference to what is said in the last letter about Thomas Gurney and his man.

67

THE PASTON LETTERS

his maister, and confessed over that the same dager he slewe hym with, he kest it in a sege [*a jakes*] whiche is founden and taken up al to-bowyd [*bent together*], for he cowde not breke it, and in prison is bothe he and his maister.

Also on Thursday next after Cristemasse was a man slayn, by whom no man woot, nor what he is that was slayn no man knowe, his face is so mangled.

538

RICHARD CALLE TO JOHN PASTON [1]

To my ryght reverent and wurschip[full] mayster, my Mayster John Paston in the Ynner Temple at London.

[FEB.] PLESITH your goode maystrechip to witte that ther comen doune to the undrescheryff of Norwiche, a writte a tache Mr. John P. the yongere, wherof I sende you a copy closed herin, but they woll not a reeste hym within Norwich; but I undrestande ther is comen an other writte to the undrescheryff of Norfolk bothe for hym and me, and for all thoo that ben indyghted. Wherfore I purpose me to ride to Hoonyng to the scheryff thys day, to undrestande how he is disposed, and to desire hym to shewe favour to your pore tenaunts; and as I feele hym disposed I schall send your maystreship answer.

And as for tidyngs here in this contre, we have noon but that ther be many Frenchemen upon the see and do moche answer upon the coosts. Mr. Yelver[ton] knew of the comyng up of the *teste* within ij. dayes after they were goon, &c. My ryght reverent and wurschipful maystre, the blissed Trinite preserve and kepe and ferther you in all your maters.

Sir William Wyllugby whas at Risynge Castell, and yester-day he come home a yenne. On Tentale hathe entred in to a parte of Felbregge lyvelod, and a corte holden, and the tenaunts retorned. Item, as for the cort that Deben[ham] schuld holde at Calcot we here not of it.

Your pore servaunt and
bedman, R. C.

[1] [From Paston MSS., B.M.] As the writ, of which a copy is subjoined to this letter, is dated on the 31st January in the second year of Edward IV. (1463), the letter itself must have been written in February.

EDWARD IV

Rex vi[ce]comitibus Norwici, salutem. Præcepimus vobis quod capiatis Johannem Paston juniorem, nuper de Norwico, armigerum, si inventus fuerit in balliva vestra, et eum salvo custodiatis, ita quod habeatis corpus ejus coram nobis a die Paschæ in unum mensem ubicunque tunc fuerimus in Anglia, ad respondendum nobis de quibusdam feloniis et transgressionibus unde in comitatu nostro Suffolchiæ indictatus est. Et si prædictus Johannes in balliva vestra inveniri non poterit, tunc ad duos comitatus in balliva vestra citra terminum prædictum proximo tenendos juxta formam statuti in hujusmodi casu provisi proclamari faciatis quod idem Johannes sit coram nobis ad præfatum terminum ad respondendum nobis de præmissis. Et habeatis ibi hoc breve. Teste Johanne Markham apud Westmonasterium, xxxj° die Januarii, anno regni nostri secundo.

CROXTON.

Rotulo xxvj° R. Per contr' Anno secundo Regis Ed. iiijti r. xiij. Irrotulatur coram Rege de recordo, termino Hillarii anno secundo Regis Ed. iiijti, prout patet in rotulo infrascripto.[1]

539

MARGARET PASTON TO JOHN PASTON [2]

PLEASE you to wet that Will. Jeney and Debham cam to Calcote on Wednysday before none, and ther they spake with Rysyng and John Smythe, and haskyd hem rent and ferme, and they seydyn they had payed you, and so they myght not paye hem. Also, ferthermore, they told hem that ye had hold a corte ther syn that they enteryd there. Than Jenney answerd ageyn 'Be cause he held a corte here we mad hym hold corte at London, and so shall we make the to hold a corte at Ipysweche withowt thow wolt pay us the rent and ferme.' 'Sir,' quod Rysyng, 'I toke the ferme of my master and of Sir Thomas Howys.' Jenney seyd, 'And as for Sir Thomas, he and we schall acord well i nowe.' And so they hahte seled up the berne dore and woll dryve a wey the catell

FEB. or MARCH

[1] This note is to imply that the writ is enrolled among what are called the Records on the Coram Rege Roll of Hilary term, 2 Edw. IV., rot. 26, a former writ against John Paston, junior, being enrolled in the Controlment Roll, 2 Edw. IV., rot. 13.
[2] [From Paston MSS., B.M.] This letter, though not addressed, seems to have been written by Margaret Paston to her husband. The election referred to must have been that for the Parliament of 1463. From one expression used it is clear that it was written some time before Easter, and the dispute with Jenney and Debenham about Calcote proves the date to a certainty. Compare Nos. 538 and 540.

THE PASTON LETTERS

bothe of the fermores and of the tenauntes, withowt the fermor and John Smythe woll fynd hem suerte to pay hem at Esterne, and Jenney and Debham woll [be] bownd ageyn to hem in a obligacion of xlli. to save hem harmelese ageyns you. And so as yet Rysyng standythe under award at Leystofte. So Rysyng hathe sent word to me that I shall knowe thys nyght or ellis to morowe what end they hathe mad.

Item, as towchyng the burges of Yermothe they wer chosyn on Wednysday. The Baly Wydwell ys on; and as for the todyr the Bischoppe sent to the towne for to have a man of hys owne, and so they be not acordyd yit of hym; en cas they may not acord, John Rus shall be the todyr.

Item, as towchyng Grene, a came not to Caster on Thursday, for he went to Norwich the same day, and so he is yet ther. Daubeney hathe spokyn with Watkyn Shypdam for to be at Beyton on Monday to kepe a corte ther; and so he woll be at Caster on Sonday and spek with you, for he seythe that Fastolfe[1] hathe mad a cleyme ther to; that is the cause he wolle comon and speke with you ther of hym selff.

Item, I can not, ner Daubeney nowther, fynd your wyght boke; it is not in the trussyng cofyr, ner in the sprucheste nothyr. Jon Walsham toke me a quayer, I suppose it lo[n]gythe to the same boke, that same I send you, and the byllis of Walcote with ale sealyd. Wretyn thys day.

By your, M. P.

On the back are the following accounts, written, in a very careless hand, by Richard Calle :—

Forene' Recept'.

De Johanne Prentice de Castelaere ad festum Sanctæ Fidis per manus vicarii de Sporle,	lxs.
De Roberto Wylley clerico post Nativitatem Domini,	cs.
De Willelmo Whyte, vigil' Conversionis Sancti Pauli,	vjli. xiijs. iiijd.
De Edmundo Wynter, mason, de Bermynghem circa Conversionem Sancti Pauli,	vjs. viijd.
De Willelmo Elys de Wynterton ad Pascha,	vjs. viijd.
De Warino Herman ad Pascha,	xiijs. iiijd.
De Johanna Bakeney uxore Gerard,	xiijs. iiijd.

[1] Thomas Fastolf of Cowhawe.

EDWARD IV

Item, de Johanne Russe.

Rec. de Willelmo Norwich et M. Johanne Smythe venditio jocalium Johannis Berney de Redham pro tant' denar' pro me pro debito ipsius Berney apud Redham solut',	xxli. xvjs.

Recept' de Tesauro.

Inprimis, pro viagio Johannis Paston, Jun. cum Rege et aliis causis (?) versus Annewyke de denariis receptis de debito prioris Norwicensis,	lli.
Item, de auro remanente de Coppes in eadem baga,	lxs.
Item, de baga pecuniæ prestandæ eodem tempore,	viij. marc'.
Item, de remanent' in forcerio tesaur' li'berat'[1] frater meus Will' Yelv'n,	xs. iiijd.

Termino Michaelis.[2]

Item, de pecunia remanente cum Thoma Gresham apud London; termino Michaelis xxli., termino Hillarij, xxxiijs. iiijd.,	xxjli. xiijs. iiijd.
Item, de tesauro London termino Michaelis, l. marc', termino Hillarij l. marc', termino Paschæ l. marc',	cli.
Item, de tesauro Norffolk cariat' versus London termino Paschæ, ultra xlli. remanens (sic) apud terminum Trinitatis,	xl. marc'.

540

ABSTRACT [3]

[JOHN PASTON] TO JOHN PAMPYNG, RICHARD CALLE, AND WILLIAM WYKES.

1463

Remember my instructions about bills and actions against Debenham by my tenants at Calcote. Make a 'remembrance apart' of the ground on which every trespass has been committed, whether it be in my lands or in those of my tenants, and whether the land was holden of me by Calcote Hall fee, or Freton Hall fee, lest Debenham justify [on the plea that] he took them elsewhere. As my tenants at Cotton have been compelled to pay much money to Jenney and Debenham against their wills, I would, as I have told John Paston the younger, that he should ride to Cotton with Richard Calle and such friendship as he can get, and demand my duties, except from those who had been compelled to pay the others. The latter to take actions next term against Debenham. Will respite them for this once all they have paid, till it may be recovered by law ;

[1] The words 'tesaur' liberat'' are interlined and apparently intended to be inserted here. I must leave the grammar of the sentence as it stands in the original. The word at the end, which I believe stands for 'Yelverton,' is very ambiguous from the careless writing.
[2] These words are inserted between the lines, but whether they were intended for a heading is a little uncertain.
[3] [From Paston MSS., B.M.]

1463 that is, provided they ask it: otherwise, will politicly put them in jeopardy of losing their farms. Desires Calle to make a roll of the tenants and when he comes to Cotton enter therein how much cattle has been distrained from each.

It appears by the last letter that a writ was issued, evidently at the suit of Debenham, against John Paston, junior, and the other agents of his father in Suffolk. From the present paper it would seem that John Paston also instituted a prosecution on behalf of his tenants against Debenham. We shall find by later letters that these suits were going on in 1463, and were not terminated in the beginning of the following year. The ms. from which the above abstract has been made is a draft with a heading in John Paston's hand. On the back are notes of the Statutes of Westminster and of Richard II. touching *scandalum magnatum*, etc.

541

RALPH LAMPET'S TESTIMONY[1]

ARCH 19 TO all tho to whom this present wrytyng shall come, Rauff Lampet, Squier, sendyth gretyng in our Lord. And forasmoch as it is meritory to bere witnesse of trought, and that I knowe and herd the disposicion and will of Ser John Fastolff, knyght, aftir the forme folowyng, and am requered to sey the trought, I record and testifie, and bere witnesse that Ser John Fastolff, knyght, aboughte the tyme of hervest was v. yere, that was the yere of our Lord M[l]ccclvij. at Caster, fast by Mekyll Yarmouth, in the Shire of Norffolk, in presens of divers persones that tyme callid to by the seid Ser John, ded make estat and feffement and livery of seison of the maner of Caster aforeseid, and other maners, londs, and tenements in Norffolk to John Paston, Squier, and other. And at that livery of season thereof delivered, as well by the hands of the seid Ser John as be other, the seid Ser John Fastolff by his owne mouth declared his will and entent of that feffement and livery of season, mad to the use of the seid Ser John as for duryng his life only, and aftir his decese to the use of the seid John Paston and his heyrs. And also the seid Ser John seid and declared, that the seid John Paston was best frend, and helper, and supporter to the seid Ser John, and that it was his will that the seid John Paston shuld have and inherite the same

[1] [Tanner ms., 106, f. 35 b.]

72

THE PASTON LETTERS

1463 Paston, to have Caister and all his other livelode in Norfolk and Suffolk in
APRIL 6 order to endow a college of seven priests and seven poor men. My Lord said, many thought Sir John would make Paston his heir; to which he replied that there was no man living that he would like better to be his heir, and begged my Lord to be his good lord if it so fortuned, which the Duke promised to do. Has heard the Duke since often acknowledge that Sir John had declared plainly he would make Paston his heir. Not having his own seal present, has sealed this with that of the prior of Ixworth, and requested him to put his seal to it besides. Ixworth, 6 April 1463.

544

MARGARET PASTON TO JOHN PASTON[1]

To my rytz wurchepfull mayster, Jon Paston, in hast.

MAY 6 RYT wurschipfull hosbond, I recommand me to zou, desyring hertyly to her of zour wellfar, praying zou to wete, that I [have] spoken with Strawngs wyf of the matter that ze spoken to me of; and sche seyth pleynly to me, be her feyth, that sche knew never non seche ne never herd of non scheche, and told to me in lyk wyse as sche had seyd to Jamys Gloys. And sche seyd to me if sche kowd inquier of any other that sche thinght xuld have knowleche of any seche, sche xuld wetyn of hem, and letyn me have knowleche therof; and if ze soppose that any other be in this contre that ye thync xuld have knowleche of this forseyd mater, yf ye wyll send me word ther of, I xall do my part ther in.

Also I have ben att Sweyngsthorp and spoken with Kokett, and he seyth that he woll don lyche as ye bad me that I xuld sey to hym for to don. And I have spokyn with the sexteyn, and seyd to hym as ye bad me that I xuld don, and he axid me ryt feythfully hw ye sped in zour materys.

I teld hym that ze haddyn fayr be hests, and I seyd I hopyd that ze xuld don rytz well therin; and he seyd that he

[1] [From Fenn, iv. 188.] Our reason for believing this letter to have been written in the year 1463 will be seen in a footnote.

74

maners, londs, and tenements, and other, aftir his decese, and 1463
ther to dwelle and abide, and kepe howsold, seying that he MARCH 19
knew well that the disposicion of the seid Paston was to do
good in the contry, and be non oppressor of the pore pepill.
And the seid Ser John desired me, and Daune William Bokenham, that tyme Prior of Yarmouth, beynge presente, to record
as he had seid to us. And this I record and witnesse for
trought be the feyght that I owe to God and all Seynts. In
witnesse wherof to this my writyng I have set to my seall and
signe manuell the xix. day of March, the third yer of the reigne
of Kyng Edward the Fourth.

R. LAMPET.

542

ABSTRACT[1]

RAFF LAMPET TO HIS COUSIN DAUBENEY

Reminds him that he spoke to him at Redham, in the church, about certain Date
lands ' which John of Berney bought of me,' and for which there is still owing uncer-
to him 13s. 4d., and a rent of 6d. four years in arrear. Begs him to speak to tain
Master Paston to get him the money.

We place this letter immediately after another document signed by Ralph Lampet,
the exact date being uncertain and immaterial. It is probably, however, about this
period, as it may be surmised to be after the death of John Berney.

543

ABSTRACT[2]

Testimony of Sir Roger Chamberlain, witnessed by Reginald Tylneye, 1463
prior of Ixworth, and Sir John Rose [a brother of the house], that he was with APRIL 6
the Duke of Norfolk in September before Sir John Fastolf died, when my
Lord urged Fastolf to sell him the reversion of Caister, or (as he wished to
give it to the Abbey of St. Benet's) to exchange it for a manor of my Lord's
in South Walsham, which lay more convenient for the Abbey. Sir John,
however, begged him not to press it, as he had appointed with his cousin, John

[1] [From Paston mss., B.M.]
[2] [From ms. Phillipps, 9735, No. 280.]

73

EDWARD IV

supposyd that D.[1] wold don for zou; but he seyd he was 1463
no hasty laborer in non mater. He seyd be hys feyth he wost MAY 6
qher a man was that laboryd to hym for amater ryth along
tym, and alwey he be hestyd that he wold labor itt effectualy,
but qhyll he sewyd to hym that he kowd never have remedy
of his mater; and than qhan he thowth that he xuld no
remedy have to sew to hym, he spak with Fynys,[2] that is now
Speker of the Parlment, and prayid hym that he wold don for
hym in hys mater, and zaf hym areward; and withinne ryth
short tym after his mater was sped. And the seyd sexteyn[3]
and other folkys that ben yowr ryth wele willers have kownselyd me that I xuld kownsell zou to maken other menys than
ye have made to other folks, that wold spede your materys
better than they have don thatt ye have spoken to therof be
for this tym. Sondery folks have seyd to me that they thynk
veryly, but if [*unless*] ye have my Lord of Suffolks[4] godelorchyp, qhyll the werd [*world*] is as itt is, ye kan never leven in
pese with owth ye have his godelordschep; therfor I pray that
with all myn herth, that ye wyll don yowr part to have his
godelordschep and his love in ese of all the materis that ye
have to don, and in esyng of myn hert also; for be my trowth
I am afferd ellys bothen of these materys the qhyche ye have
in hand now, and of other that ben not don to yett, but
if he wyl don for zou and be your godelord. I pray yow
hertylye send me werd how ze don, and how ye speden in
zour materys; and I pray you as for seche thyngs as Jamys
hath a byll of, that I may have hem as hastyly as ze may; and

[1] Possibly John Damme.
[2] This looks like a mistake, for no Speaker of the name of Fynes is met with during this period. The expression, however, suggests that the letter was written about the beginning of a new Parliament, which could only have been that which met on the 29th April 1463. On the following day the Commons elected John Say as their Speaker, whose name Margaret Paston seems to have confounded with the family name of William Fenys, Lord Say, the trusty friend of Edward IV. who accompanied him into exile when he fled from his kingdom in 1470. It does not appear, however, that John Say, the Speaker, was related to that family.
[3] The Sacrist or Sexton of the Priory of Norwich was the officer who had the care of Sacra, or Holy Things, as the Church Plate, Copes, etc.; he was likewise Secretary, Auditor, and Chancellor of the Convent, and had a Sub-sacrist or Deputy to perform the servile parts of his office. In 1444 Brother Richard de Walsham was appointed Sacrist.—F.
[4] John de la Pole, Duke of Suffolk.—F.

75

1463
MAY 6
that ze wyll vowchesave to bey apese of blak bukram for to lyn with a gown for me, I xuld bey me amurrey gown to gon in this somer, and leyn in the koler the satyn that ze zeve me for an hodde; and I kan gettyn non gode bokeram in this town to lyn it with. The Holy Trinyte have yow in His kepyng, and send zou helth and good spede in all yowr maters.

Wretyn att Norwyche, on ye Fryday nexst after Crowchemesse Day.[1]

Yours,   M. P.

545

[JAMES GRESHAM] TO JOHN PASTON[2]

To mygth rigth gooa and speciall maister, John Paston, dwellyng at Heylesdon be syde Norwich.

JULY

RIGTH reverent, &c. Please your maisterchip wete that I resseived your letter whiche ye sent by Crome, and as for the examinacion of, &c. that I wrot to you of in my former letter to be taken on the Munday or on Tewysday, &c. this was the cause. Ye yaff me informacion at my last departyng fro you that the murdre was don upon the day nexst after Seynt Petre. And for doute lesse ye had be ougth at the comyng of my seid letter, and for dowte that I supposed that my maistres, your wyf, had not be remembred of the day, it caused me, accordyng to your informacion, to wryte the uttermost day for her remembrans. Nevertheless, if ye certifie that ye toke the examinacion with in the yere and day, and sette the day in certayn, your certificat is sufficient in

---

[1] Crouchmas Day, or the Invention of the Cross, was on the 3rd of May.—F.

[2] [From Paston MSS., B.M.] This letter seems to be in James Gresham's handwriting. It is evident that it was written shortly after Midsummer. Rather more than a year and a day had elapsed since a murder committed on the morrow of St. Peter's Day (*i.e.* on the 30th June), and it is mentioned that Convocation was to sit some little time after Relic Sunday, which always falls in the middle of July. Further, the King is said to be at Northampton, which he was in July 1463, and no other year appears to suit.

1463
JULY
lawe and shall bynd any of the parties to sey the contrary. And also the writte is that ye schuld certefie *sine dilatione*, and no day expresly yoven you whan to certifie it; wherfor ye may kepe uncertefiet tyl the nexst terme. And so do sir, for it schal do no hurt; but if ony questions or jangelyng schuld be mad when the examinacion was, let a sufficiant day with inne the yere be noysed, and if the *teste* be to schort we schal fynd the mene it schal be amendyd by hym that wrot it. For after the informacion that I had of Crome the Sunday was the uttermest day, and therefor it was happy that sche was examined thenne. And where that ye wold I schuld tak the advice of Maister Markham, &c., if all thyng were laufull, and elles not, it is full hard to my self to determine the certaynte of every circumstans of the mater, and it is not gretely to be comuned of with other, nor to comune of casez lyke; for whan the mater schuld come in revelysshon it wold cause prevy titlers and flaterers ougth of suche questions to ymagyn, and contryve mater of distourbans. Wherfor upon the certeynte of myn determinacion I brak the mater to Master Markham, which called to hym Master Byngham, and so thei ij. meved Y.[1]; and after that mocion he kept not his owyn councell but brak to every man of it. Hou be it he was sore mevyd with it, I wote it well, and glad to take avyse and comfort of other personez than of Masters Markham and Byngham. Al circumstans were to long to wryte, but I hope to speke with you be tymes i nough or ye schall nede to certefye, &c. And, sir, in conclucion, Masters Markham and Byngham thynk it sufficiant i nougth to take his promys and his othe with ougth obligacion that he schal mak amends if profe here after can be mad uppon hym. And to this Maister Markham prayed you to agre by the same token ye mevyd hym to sette an ende be twyx you and my masters your brethern. Nevertheless if ye thynk this wey not sufficiant, ye may lete sum other handele the mater at hom to hym if that ye hope to gete good pref in the mater, for with ougth evydent proffe the mater schall be but noysefull to you, and cause men to thynk that it growyth of your ille wyll to hym

---

[1] Yelverton.

1463
JULY
ward, &c.; for he noyseth and seyth, because of ille wyll ye have caused a mad woman to take apell a yens hym.

Item, sir, as for Leukenore he is not at London, but peraventure I schal make hym to be meved in the mater here after.

Item, I dede your erand to my maister your son.

Item, as for John Say,[1] he recomendyth hym to you, bothe for your billes and for your labour, and prayeth you if ony land that lyth for the priour ease mygth be aspyed, that ye wold help to gete it hym and send hym word; and as for the morteysyng . . . . . . and at his cost and labour.

Item, as for tydyngs, the Kyng and the counsell is at Northampton,[2] and the Convocacion schall be . . . . after Relyk Sunday. And ther be ij. marchaunts come fro Caleys, and they mygth no leve have to com[e] . . . . schuld bere the Kyng certeyn lettres and juste tytyngs that sege is comyng to Caleys. And trew[s] . . . . [ou]re Lady Day, as I herd sey.

Item, it is talked that Duchemen and Englysshemen ben at contraversie with in . . . . . .

546

JAMES GRESHAM TO MARGARET PASTON[3]

To my right wurshepfull mastres, my Mastres Margret Paston, at Caster.

1463

PLEASE it your good mastressship to wete that a *fieri facias* is come out of the Exchequir for Hue Fen to the Shireff of Norffolk to make levy of CC. mark of the propir goods and catels of my masters, as executor of Sir

---

[1] Probably the Speaker of the Parliament of 1463, whom Margaret Paston named Fynes in Letter 544. *See* p. 75, Note 2.

[2] According to the dates of the Privy Seals the King was at Northampton from the 8th to the 28th July 1463; also on the 2nd May, 1464.

[3] [From Fenn, iv. 130.] John Paston's eldest son appears to have been knighted in the course of the year 1463. The earliest notice which I find of him as knight is in a writ dated 11th July, 3 Edward IV., entered on the Coram Rege Roll of Trinity

1463
John Fastolf; of whech *fieri facias* we sent my master word, whech sent us word ayen by Berney that we shuld lete the Shiref undirstand that my master nevir toke upon hym as executor, and so for that cause that writte was no warant to take my masters goods; and also that my master mad a dede of gift of all his goods and catels to Master Prewet and Clement Paston and other, so that my master hath no goods whereof he shuld make levy of the forseid summe; and if the Shireff wold not take this for non answere, that thanne my master wold he shuld be lettid in Master Prowetts and Clement Pastons name. Nevirthelesse we spak with the Shireff this day, and lete hym undirstand the causes aforeseid, and he agreid, so that he myght have suerte to safe hym harmeles, to mak such retorne as my master or his counsell coud devise. And because my master wrote by Berney that he wold not fynd the Shireff no suerte, we wold not apoynt with hym in that wyse; and so we toke avyse of Thomas Grene, and by cause the Undir-Shireff shall be on Monday at Hygham, by Bastewyk brygg, and he and we thought that it was best that Master Prewet shuld mete with the Shireff there, and require and charge hym that by colour of the foreseid *fieri facias* that he make no levy of any goods and catels of the seid Prowetts and Clement Pastons ayens the seid John Pastons, letyng hym vete that such goods as the seid Paston had, be now the seid Prowetts and Clement Pastons by vertu of a dede of gift mad to hem almost ij. yere agoo; and if the Shireff woll be besy aftir that to take any catell, that he be lettid in Master Prowetts name and Clement Pastons by Daubeney and other; whech besines of the Shireff shall be on Tuisday or Wednesday, and as we understand at Heylesdon. Wherfor ye must send thedir Daubeney with Pecok, and the may gete hym here more felasep by the avise of Master Sir John Paston. JAMES GRESHAM.

---

term, 3 Edward IV. This letter is not unlikely to have been written about that time, as it appears by a subsequent letter (No. 550) that Sir John Paston remained for some time at home in Norfolk, when the friends of the family thought he ought to be abroad in the world.

THE PASTON LETTERS

547

ABSTRACT[1]

1463
UG. 15

Deed poll whereby Elizabeth, widow of John Vere, Earl of Oxford, Lady of the manor of Knapton, Norfolk, grants to Agnes, widow of William Paston, the right of removing obstructions in two watercourses belonging to the mill called Wodmyll in Bacton; the first of which watercourses flows out of Knapton Fen, and the second from the mill of the Abbot of St. Benet's of Holme.

Stratford of the Bowe, 15th Aug. 1463, 3 Edward IV.

Fine Seal.

548

THE DUKE OF NORFOLK TO JOHN PASTON, SENIOR[2]

To oure right trusty and entierly welbelovid servaunt, John Paston, th'elder.

THE DUC OF NORFF.

UG. 31

RIGHT trusty and entierly welbelovid servaunt, we grete you hertily well, and specially praying you that ye will be with us at Framlyngham on Sonday next comyng, that we may comon with you there, and have youre sadde advise in suche matiers as concernyth gretly to oure weel, whiche shall be mynestred unto you at youre comyng. Prayng you that ye fayle not herof, as our speciall trust is in you. And our Lord preserve you in His keping.

Written at Framlyngham the xxxj. day of August.

NORFF.

[1] [From Add. Charter 14,514, B.M., D. Turner's Coll.]
[2] [From Fenn, iv. 250.] John Mowbray, Duke of Norfolk, the writer of this letter, succeeded his father in the dukedom in November 1461, being at the time only seventeen years of age. A year afterwards, in November 1462, we find him living at his castle of Holt in Denbighshire, where he proposed to spend Christmas (*see* No. 532), but before that season came he was sent for by the King to serve against the Scots (No. 533). I am inclined to think this letter was written in the August of 1463; for although the Duke was again living at Holt in March following, it seems probable that he would have visited his chief family seat at Framlingham in the meanwhile. John Paston, the youngest, who was attached to his household, was certainly at home with his family in the latter part of this year (*see* No. 560).

80

THE PASTON LETTERS

550

R. C. V. C. TO JOHN PASTON THE ELDEST[1]

To my worcheppefull master, Master Paston the heldest.

63(?)

RYTH worchepfull master, I recommend me on to zowr masterchepe. And of on mater at reverens of God take hede, for in trowth I her meche talkyng therof, and that is both in Norffolk, Suffolk, and Norwyche, among halle men of worchepe, as welle that love zow as oder, and that is of my master, your son, Syr Jon, causse he is so at home, and no noderwyse set for. Summe sey that ze and he both stond howth of the Kyngs good gras, and summe sey that ze kepe hym at home for negard chepe, and wyll no thyng ware [*spend*] up on hym; and so heche man sey is avyse as it plese hem to talke. And I have hanqwerryd [*inquired*], and seyd the most cause is inparty for cause ze har so meche howte, that he is the rather at home for the save gard of the costs. But at the referens of God, excheuyng of common langage, se that he may worchepfull be set for, heyder in the Kyngs servyse, or in maryache; for as towchyng the Lady Chaberlen[2] that mater is don, for I spake with the parson therof, and I hard be hym that that mater wyll not pre [*proceed?*].

No more, but God spede zow as well in all maters, as I wold ze xuld do, I be seche zow that this leter be kept secrete.

Be zow[r] bede man,

R. C. V. C.

[1] [From Fenn, iv. 128.] In the preceding letter Sir John Paston seems to have been at home; in Letter 552, we find that he had left home without leave. It is very probable, therefore, that the present letter was written in the interval between them, seeing that the writer complains of Sir John being kept at home.
[2] This Lady Chamberlayne was Anne, daughter and sole heir of Sir Robert Herling, Knight, by Jane, daughter and heir of John Gonvile, Esq. Her first husband was Sir William Chamberlayne, Knight of the Garter, a renowned and

82

EDWARD IV

549

THE ABBOT OF LANGLEY TO SIR JOHN PASTON[1]

To the ryght worcheppful Sere John Paston, Knyght, be this delyvered.

1463
SEPT. 4

RYGHT worchepful ser, and tendyrly belovyd in our Lord God, I comend me to you, sendyng you know-yng that I dede your erand to my brother, the persoon of Blofeeld, on Wednysdaye was sevenyght, after the undyr-standyng that I had of you and from you be this brynger; whech man I felte ryght wele and favorabelye dysposyd to you ward, and more favorable wole be than to ony other jentylman levand, the wylle of the dede performyd, and his conscyens savyd; and more thinges seyd favorably for yow which I entytelyd in a scrowe to a' certyfyed to your servaunt Calle, yf he had come, as ye sent me woord he sculd ado, and xuld, as ye behestyd me, abrowte me our ferme for Heylesdon, which not don, causeth me to wryte, prayng your jantylnesse that I send no more therfore, for it is unpayed for the zeer afore the Halwemesse that my Mayster Fastolf deyed, and for the same zer that he deyed in, and sythen for ij. zer, and vs. unpayed of a zer, and come Myhelmesse nexte xal be another zer unpayed. Thus is iiij. zer unpayed and vs., and at Myhelmesse next xal be v. zer and vs.

This thus kepte from Holy Chirche that is Holy Chirchez good, may not be withoute grete parelle of soule; wher the parelle is God knoweth, I pray God amend it, and geve hem grace that have his goods so to dyspose them, that thei and the dede both may be oute of parelle. And the Trynyte have you in His mercyful kepyng. Wretyn at Langle, on Soneday, at evyn late, next after Seynt Johne Daye Decollacion.[2]

Be your welewylland,

ABBOT OF LANGELEYE.

[1] [From Fenn, iv. 146.] The date of this letter is clear, from the statement it contains as to the length of time which has elapsed since the decease of Sir John Fastolf.
[2] The Decollation of St. John the Baptist was observed on the 29th August.

81

EDWARD IV

551

MARGARET PASTON TO JOHN PASTON[1]

To my ryght worchipfull hosbond, John Paston, be thys letter delyveryd in hast.

1463
NOV. 13

RIHT worchepfull husbond, I recommand me to you. Please you to wete that I was at Norwic this wek to purvey suche thyngs as nedythe me ageyns thys wynter; and I was at my modder, and wille I was ther, ther cam in on Wrothe, a kynnysman of Elysabet Clers, and he sey your dowter, and preysyd hyr to my moder, and seyd that she was a goodly yong woman; and my moder prayd hym for to gett for hyr on good mariage yf he knewe any; and he seyd he knewe on shuld be of a CCC. mark be yer, the wyche is Sir John Cley son, that is Chamberleyn with my Lady of York,[2] and he ys of age of xviij. yer old. Zyf ye thynk it be for to be spok of, my moder thynkyth that it shuld be get for lesse mony nowe in thys world than it shuld be her after, owthyr that j. [*one*], or sum other good mariage.

valiant soldier, who died in 1462. She was at this time his widow, and inherited from her father a very considerable fortune.
She afterwards married Sir Robert Wingfield, and after his decease she became the wife of John, Lord Scroop of Bolton.
By the name of Lady Scroop she founded and endowed a Fellowship in the College of Gonville and Caius at Cambridge, originally founded by an ancestor of her Ladyship's.
She was born in 1426, and was alive in 1502.
At the time this letter was written she must have been nearly forty years old, when Sir John Paston could not have been much above twenty.—F.
[1] [From Fenn, iv. 88.] I have found no letters of Margaret Paston dated from Caister before the year 1463; but I am inclined to think that this and the letter following both belong to that year. The latter, being addressed to Sir John Paston, at least cannot be earlier, and my reasons for believing it to be of that very year will be seen in the note to it (p. 84, Note 2). It is just possible that this letter may be of a different date, but considering that both were written in November, and both certainly between the 12th and the 19th, and that in both Margaret Paston not only dates from Caister, but speaks of Daubeney as being with her, the presumption, I think, is pretty strong that they are of the same year.
[2] Cecily, Duchess of York, widow of Richard Plantagenet, Duke of York, and mother of Edward IV. She died in an advanced age, at her castle of Berkhamstead, in May 1495, and was buried near her husband, in the Choir of the Collegiate Church of Fotheringhay, in Northamptonshire.—F.

83

THE PASTON LETTERS

1463
NOV. 13
Item, I spake with Master John Estgate for Pekerynes mater after your entent of the mater of the letter that ye sent home, and he seyd to me he shuld write to yow howe he had don ther in ; and so he sent you a letter, the wyche was sent you be John Wodows[1] man with other letters.

As for answer [of] other mater, Daubeney tellythe me he wret to you. I be seche Alle myghty God have you in Hys kepyng. Wretyn at Caster, the Sonday next after Seynt Marteyne.

Be your   M. PASTON.

552

MARGARET PASTON TO SIR JOHN PASTON[2]

*To my welbelovyd son, Sir John Paston,
be this deliveryd in hast.*

NOV. 15
I GRET yow welle, and send yow Godds blissyng and myn, latyng yow wet that I have receyved a letter from you, the wyche ye deliveryd to Master Roger at Lynne, wherby I conseyve thar ye thynke ye ded not well that ye departyd hens withowt my knowlage. Wherfor I late yow wett I was ryght evyll payed with yow. Your fader thowght, and thynkyth yet, that I was asentyd to your departyng, and that hathe causyd me to have gret hevinesse. I hope he wolle

[1] John Wodehouse, Esq. of Kimberley, son of the renowned John Wodehouse, Esq., who gained so much honour at the battle of Agincourt ; he died in 1465, and lies buried in Kimberley Chancel.—F.

[2] [From Fenn, iv. 168.] As Sir John Paston was knighted in the year 1463, and his father died in May 1466, the date of this letter must lie between the years 1463 and 1465. I think the first of these years is probably the true date. Sir John Paston, it seems, had left home without letting his mother know of his intention. Whither had he gone? Not to London, because he addressed a letter to his father there ; besides he had passed by Lynn. One would naturally suppose, therefore, that he had gone to wait upon the King, at a time when Edward was at a distance from the capital. And in this view we are confirmed by the passage in which Margaret desires her son to speak with Wykes, who, as we know by Letter 514, was an usher of the King's Chamber. Now Edward IV. was in Yorkshire, staying, for the most part, at Pomfret, during October and November 1463, while about the same time of year in 1464 he was at Reading, and in 1465 at Greenwich. Sir John would naturally have passed through Lynn on his road to the North.

84

THE PASTON LETTERS

1463
NOV. 15
It wer welle do that ye sent a letter to hyr howe ye do, as astely as ye may. And God have you in Hys kepyng, and make yow a good man, and zyf yow grace to do as well as I wold ye shuld do.

Wretyn at Caster, ye Tewisday next befor Seynt Edmund the Kynge.

Your moder,   M. PASTON.

I wold ye shuld make mech of the parson [of] Fylby, the berer herof, and make hym good cher yf ye may.

553

MARGARET PASTON TO JOHN PASTON[1]

*To my ryth worchepfull husbond, Jon Paston,
be thys lettyr delyveryd in haste.*

1462-3
DEC.
RYTH worchepfull husbond, I recomand me to yow. Plesyth it yow to wet that Jon Jeney was here with me thys daye and told me that ye desyiryd that I shold do make a dyche at Heylysdon, and the seson is not for to do make no new dechys, nor to repare non old tyll it be aftyr Crystmas, as it is told me, and so I sent yow word in a lettyr more thane a monythe goo ; I wot not whedyr ye had the lettyr or not, for I had non answer ther of fro yow. Jone Dyngayne recomandyth hyr to yow, and prayith yow for Goddys sake that ye wole be hyr good mastyr, and that ye wole wychesave to spek to Hwe of Fen for hyr, for it is so that serteyn lyvelod whyche hyr husbond had in Engham was cast in the kyngys hand in hyr husbandys lyve, and, as she undyrstandyth, it was do in hys fadyrys lyve ; of the whyche

[1] [Add. MS. 34,889, f. 198.] This letter must lie between the years 1459, when Sir John Fastolf died (as Hellesden belonged to him), and 1465, as John Paston died in May 1466. The most probable year is either 1462 or 1463, for it is mentioned here that Paston's farmer at Swainsthorpe had found security for the payment of his rent, and Richard Calle had levied four marks rent of him in February 1464. *See* No. 558.

86

EDWARD IV

be your good fader hereafter, yf ye demene you welle, and do 1463 as ye owe to do to hym ; and I charge you upon my blyssyng NOV. 15 that in any thyng towchyng your fader that shuld be hys worchep, profyte, or avayle, that ye do your devoyr and dylygent labor to the fortherans therin, as ye wulle have my good wille, and that shall cause your fader to be better fader to you.

It was told me ye sent hym a letter to London. What the entent therof was I wot not, but thowge he take it but lyghtly, I wold ye shuld not spar to write to hym ageyn as lowly as ye cane, besechyng hym to be your good fader ; and send hym suche tydyngs as be in the contre thir ye bethe in, and that ye war [*beware*] of your expence bettyr and I have be befor thys tyme, and be your owne purse berer, I trowe ye shall fyndyt most profytable to you.

I wold ye shuld send me word howghe ye doo, and howghe ye have schevyfte for yourself syn ye departyd hens, be som trosty man, and that your fader have no knowlage therof. I durste not late hym knowe of the laste letter that ye wrot to me, be cause he was so sor dyspleasyd with me at that tyme.

Item, I wold ye shuld speke with Wekis, and knowe hys dysposysion to Jane Walsham. She hathe seyd, syn he departyd hens, but [*unless*] she myght have hym, she wold never maryd, hyr hert ys sor set on hym ; she told me that he seyd to hyr that ther was no woman in the world he lovyd so welle. I wold not he shuld jape hyr, for she menythe good feythe ; and yf he wolle not have hyr, late me wete in hast, and I shall purvey for hyr in othyr wysse.

As for your harneys and ger that ye left here, it ys in Daubeneys kepyng ; it was never remevyd syn your departyng, be cause that he had not the keyes. I trowe it shall apeyer [*get injured*], but if it be take hed hate [*unless it be taken heed at*, or *to*] be tymys. Your fader knowythe not wher it is.

I sent your grey hors to Ruston to the ferror, and he seythe he shull never be nowght to rood, nowthyr ryght good to plowe nor to carte ; he seyth he was splayyd, and hys shulder rent from the body. I wot not what to do with hym.

Your grandam wold fayne here sum tydyngs from yow.

85

EDWARD IV

hyr husband spok to Hwe of Fen ther of in hys lyve to 1462-3 helpe that he myth be dyschargyd ther of, and Hwe of Fen DEC. promysyd hym verily that he had mad an ende ther in and dyschargyd hym, and that he shold never be hurt nor trublyd ther for ; and now the laste wek Barnard the undyr scheryfe sent downe a warant to sese the lond for the Kynge, and so, but [*unless*] he have xxs. for a fyne within shorte tyme he wol not suffyr her to have the avayle of the londys. Wher fore she prayith yow, for Goddys sak, that ye wole purvey a mene that Hwe of Fen may save hyr harmles, in as myche as he promysyd hyr husbond to purvey ther fore in hys lyve ; and if it plese not yow to speke to hym ther of, that it plese yow to do John Paston or Thomas Playter or sume othyr, that ye thynk that cane undyrstande the mater, for to spek to the seyd Hwe of Fen ther of in hyr name, and to serge the kyngys bokys ther fore, if ye thynk that it be for to do, and sche woll ber the cost ther of. As for the mater that ze wold I schold spek to Wylliam Worcester of towchyng the false forgyd evydens, I can not spek with hym yet ; hys wyfe seyth allwe that he is oute when that I send for hym. Yowyr fermore of Sweynysthorpe hathe fownde suerte for yowyr dute, as Rychard Calle tellyth me, so that ye scholl be plesyd when ye come home. And the blyssyd Trinite have yow in Hys kepyng. Wretyn in hast on the Monday next aftyr Seynt Andrew.—By yowyr,   M. P.

554

ABSTRACT[1]

Indenture, 10th Dec. 3 Edward IV., between Robert Wodlark, Provost of 1463 the College of St. Mary and St. Nicholas, Cambridge, and John Paston, Esq., DEC. 10 witnessing a loan by Paston to the college of 100 marks till the octaves of St. Hilary, 1464 [*i.e.* 1464-5], upon certain plate.[2]

Note below in a different hand :—'Memorandum quod Mr. Alexander Lye erit apud Norwicum in die Martis pro[ximo] post diem Carniprivii.'

[1] [From Paston MSS., B.M.]
[2] The plate specified in this document is the same as that contained in the *second* list in No. 561, at p. 98.

87

THE PASTON LETTERS

555

JAMES GRESHAM TO JOHN PASTON[1]

To my right worshipfull mayster, John Paston,
at Castre, in Norfolk.

AFTER due recomendacion hadde, please it your maister-ship to wytte that this day the plee by twene Ogan and yow was sore argued in the Kynggs Bench by your counsell, in lettyng of the jugement, and to morwe have they day to argue ageyn. And for lak of copies of the plee, I am fayn to sewe for newe copies therof for your counsell. Your counsell hopeth to do weel therin. These argued for yow, Maisters Grenefeld,[2] Catesby,[3] Pygot,[4] Notyngham,[5] and Starky,[6] &c. And yesterday was the matier by twene Deben-ham and yow called by Geney[7] for an answer. I have spoken onto Catesby, and delyvered hym your enfromacion, and to be advysed, and to commune with Maister Grenefeld, &c.

The two Chefe Juges[8] and Maister Lyttleton[9] arn awaytyng up on the Kyng, for the Kyng is purposed in to Gloucestreshire, &c.

[1] [From Fenn, iv. 156.] The date of this letter is abundantly evident, first from the circumstance that the 26th of January (the morrow of St. Paul) was a Thursday, and secondly, from the mention of the King's going into Gloucestershire. In January 1464 Edward IV. was at Northampton, and on the 9th of February he was at Gloucester.

[2] John Greenfield. He and the two next named were made serjeants-at-law in November 1463.

[3] John Catesby. He was appointed Judge of the Common Pleas in 1481.

[4] Richard Pygot.

[5] William Nottingham. He was appointed Chief Baron of the Exchequer in 1479.

[6] Humphrey Starkey. He was made a serjeant in 1478.

[7] William Jenney was made a serjeant in 1463, and a Justice of the King's Bench in 1481.

[8] John Markham, Chief Justice of the King's Bench, and Robert Danby, Chief Justice of the Common Pleas, both appointed in 1461.

[9] Thomas Lyttelton, the famous lawyer, was created a serjeant in 1453, and appointed a Judge of the Common Pleas in 1466. He died in 1481, aged seventy-nine, as Fenn here tells us in a footnote; but Foss, in his *Judges of England,* says nothing of his age.

EDWARD IV

It is seid that my Lord Chaunceller[1] shull be here on Saterday on on Moneday next comyng, as the maisteres of the Chauncerye sayn. I write to yow this by cause ye seid to me if ye wyst that my Lord Chaunceller shuld be here, thanne wolde ye come hidder, and ell[es] wolde ye not come here this terme.

As touchyng Rysyng, he hath his day, Utas[2] Purificationis, but I have that weye that his presence is recondet for al this terme.

Maister Clement[3] tellyth me that Wysseter hath put excepcion on to your wyttenesseres,[4] &c.

It is seid that the Kyng wold ride Sussex, Kent, Essex, Suffolk, and Norffolk, and so to the Parlement, for he hath sent for alle his feed men to awayte up on hym in their best aray in al hast.

Wretyn at London, the Thursday in the morwe after Seynt Poule.

Your owen poure man,

JAMS GRESHAM.

556

HENRY BERRY TO JOHN PASTON[5]

To my Rygth worsschipful cosyn, John Paston, Squyer,
be this Letter delyveryd, &c.

RYGHT worsschypfull and reverent cosyn, I recomaunde me on to you wyth al myn hert, as your feythful kynnesman and oratour, desyrynge to here of the goode prosperite and welfare of your worsschipfull modyr

[1] George Neville, now Bishop of Exeter, but soon after the writing of this letter translated to York.

[2] The Utas or Octave of a feast is the seventh day after it.

[3] Clement Paston, brother to John Paston.

[4] This relates to the disputes concerning Sir John Fastolf's will.

[5] [From Fenn, i. 278.] By the mention of Sir John Paston it is evident that this letter was written after 1463, but of course the date cannot be later than 1466, in which year John Paston the father died, to whom the letter is addressed. It appears also to have been written shortly after the death of James Sevenoke, Abbot of St. Augustine's, Canterbury, which Fenn, I know not on what authority, says occurred in 1463. Even the new edition of Dugdale does not give the date; but Fenn's date is in all probability right.

THE PASTON LETTERS

my Lady and cosyn, wyth your wyff, Sir John Paston, your brethern Wyllyam and Clement, with all your sonys and doughters, to whom I beseche you hertely that I may be recomaundyd. God of His hyghe mercy preserve you all un to Hys mercy and grace, and save you from al adversite.

Worsschipfull cosyn, my speciall writynge and hertys desire afore rehersyd, nature naturaly so me compellyth,

Watt thou I be putt fer ought of conceyte and syght,
I have you all in remembrance both day and nyght;

besechynge you, gentyll cosyn, to tender my writynge. I take God to my wyttnesse, I wold as fayn do that myght be un to your honor, worsschippe, and profit as any herthly man can thynke.

Worfor now late deyde the Abbot of our Monastery, and lefte us in grete ded [*debt*]; the brynger heroff is my speciall frende : the holdyst brother in our place never hard nor saw our chirche in that mysere that is now; we have cast the perellys amongys us, and there is nowne other helpe, butt every brother that hath any worsschipfull kynne or frendys, every man to do his part to the well fare, socour, and releve of our monasteri; therfor, worsschipfull cosyn, I, a brother of that worsschipfull monastery, wer inne begoon the feyth of all thys lond, mekely besechyth you in the reverence of Allmygty God to render help, and socour us in our grete necessite; for in London lyth to wedde many ryche jowells of ouris, with other grete detts, wych my brother wyll enforme you of.

Plesyth your goodnesse, for Godys sake, and all the Seyntts of evyn, and att my sympyll request, to have compassion upon us, ye havynge dooe swerte [*due surety*] both in obligacions and pleggs; in the reverens of All myghti God, do your allmesse and charite; hitt schall cause you to be prayed for, and all your kynne as long as the chirche stantt; and be this menys, I trust to All myghty God, to se my cosyn William, or Clement, to be stward of our londys, and so to have an intresse in Kentt, to the worsschippe of God and you all, wych ever have you in His kepynge. Amen.

Writyn at Caunterbury in hast the xxviij[t] day of Januare.

EDWARD IV

Also I beseche you, schew the brynger of this letter sum humanite and worsschipe, that when he comyth home, he may reporte as he fyndeth.

[1][This is the cause every wele thi putt my kynne in my berd, seyinge, I am come of lordys, knygtes, and ladys. I wold they wer in your daunger a m[l] merke, that they mygte know you, &c.]

Be your cosyn and bedman, HENRY BERRY.

557

CLEMENT PASTON TO JOHN PASTON SENIOR[2]

To hys rythe worchyfull broder, John Paston thelder,
Sqwyer be this delyveryd.

BRODER, I recomawnde me to zowe. After all dew recommendacions, &c. Az for Hew Fennys obliga-cion, Zelverton knowlacheyd it to be Sir John Fastolfe is dede opynly in the Escheker, and ther he hadde is jugement to receive the mony and xli. for domages. And they report here that they have a schreve after her entent that wyll mak hem execucion, or ellis return that ye have wastyd the godis of the dede; so that they wyll have execucion of zowr own goodis, or ellys a wryt to tak zowr body. Thus ze may se they zeve no fors wat they doo, thow they xwld lesse and stroy all the goodis of the dede; And ther for, for savacion of goodis of the dede, better it wer to suffer tak sum trete than to suffer the goodis thus to be lost. Also Zelverton hathe ben at all the tenauntis of Sowthewerk and chargid hem to pay no mony but to hym. Also the kyng hathe ben in Glowcetescher and pwnyssede hys rebellious a zens the lawe, and so he enten-dithe to doo in Norfolk, and after that in oder contreez. God zeve grasse and good spede in hys jornay. No more but I

[1] This last paragraph is crossed out in the original ms.

[2] [Add. MS. 34,889, f. 2.] For the date of this letter and the King's going to Gloucestershire, see preliminary note to No. 555, p. 88, Note 1.

THE PASTON LETTERS

1464
FEB. 15
pray Gode have zow in hys kepyng. Wretyn on Hasse Wednysday in haste.

Also I pray zou, send me xls. that I tok James Gressam and John Pampyng for zowr materis. Also ther is no man that hathe contentyd ony thyng in the Kyngis Benche of all thys term for zour materis, and that makythe the clerkis and zowr Aturnay wery. I trow I xall be fayn to contente hem or ellys they xall be unpayyd.

Zowr broder, CLEMENT PASTON.

558

RICHARD CALLE TO JOHN PASTON[1]

To my mooste reverent and wurchipfull mastre, my Mastre John Paston, be this delyverd.

FEB. 27

PLESITH it your goode mastreschip to undrestande that I have receyved a byll of John Boteler, weche speketh of your heygh at Heylesdn, and of your barly in other places, but I undrestand not what ye wold I schulde do therin; nevertheles I schal do make it redy. And as for your heygh I schull tell you whan I come hume; and as for money at Heylesdon I can non gete, and at Sueynesthorp I have take iiij. marc.

Item, as for tidyngs the Sessions schal be at Thetford on Wednesday next comyng, where I undrestande Mr. Berney wol be with moche people, be cauce ther is come to hym a

[1] [From Fenn, iv. 72.] This letter and the next both mention assizes at Thetford. The latter, which is dated on Wednesday, the last (29th) day of February, and which was certainly written in the year 1464, mention them as being held on that very day. The present letter, dated on the second Monday in Lent, says they are *to be* held on Wednesday following. Now the second Monday in Lent 1464 fell on the 27th of February, that is to say just two days before that particular Wednesday on which we know that the assizes really were held. This alone seems almost sufficient evidence of the date of the letter. As for the King's going up to London, it appears by the dates of the Privy Seals that on the 9th February he was at Gloucester, on the 16th and 17th at Kimbolton; and it is stated in the next letter that he was at Waltham on the 27th, which shows that he really was moving towards the capital. This was not the case in 1462, the year to which Fenn assigns the letter; nor do I know his authority for stating that there was a Burgundian Embassy in the beginning of that year.

92

Prevy Seale that he schuld be with the Kyng within vj. dayes that the Prevy Seale whas delyverd hym, weche he can not doo, for the vj. day is to morwe. Ther is on comen to Felbrigge, to William Yelverton on other, and to Robert Rough an other, and non of them wol goo to the Kyng ; and the Undrescherif tolde me that ther is comen a comyscion doun to hes maistre, that in cas they come not up to the Kyng be ther Prevy Seales, that than he rere the contre and take hem and bryng hem to the Kyng wher so ever he be.

1464
FEB. 27

Item, Jamys Gresham tellethe me the same, and as for tidyngs fro London we here non, but that John Colman telleth me that if Berney or Robert Rough come up they are like to die.

Ther be come to London Embasetors from the Duke of Burgundy, weche cauced the Kyng to spede hym the rather to London.

Item, as for any newe assises at Thetford ther is non but that hathe hanged this v. yere, as the Scherif tellethe me.

I whas purposed to be at home this nyght tell I had your bille, weche causeth me to ride on to Drayton for divers thyngs, &c. Almyghty Jesu preserve you.

Wreten at Norwiche, the ij. Munday of clene Lente.

Your pore beedeman and servaunt, RIC. CALLE.

559

JOHN PAMPYNGE TO JOHN PASTON, SENIOR[1]

To my right worshipfull master, John Paston, the elder, Squier.

FEB. 26

PLEASE your mastership to wete that the Assise holde this day at Thetford ; and as for any newe Assise, that ye spak of, ther is non, ner non other savyng on for a man a bought Brunham.

[1] [From Fenn, iv. 158.] The circumstance of the last day of February falling on a Wednesday fixes the date of this letter to the year 1464. There is no evidence in

93

THE PASTON LETTERS

1464
FEB. 29

I spak with Herward, and I askyd hym if ther was any gret day at Bury, and he seid ther was but a small day, and as for any assises ther wer non but old ; and he told me that Debenham and the Undershireff were falle ought. Debenham bare the Shireff on hand[1] that he had do indited an hundred men son he cam in to hys office, and the Shireff told hym that the Kyngs bokkes apperid whedir it was so or nought ; and he told Debenham that he coud indite an hundred at on tyme whan ye wer indited, and named yow the cause of ther brekyng.

Ther was a man kyllid now late in Suffolk, and he that ded it was on of Debenhams men ; and Herward told me that the Shireff seid to hym he wold do Debenham a shrewd turne and he coud.

Item, it was told me at Norwich that Master Berney shuld have be here with a gret felaship, and it is not so, ner no man heryth of hys comyng, ner her is but litell pepill nowther, ther wer not so few this iij. yer, as men say.

Item, Herward askyd me where John Gayn was, and I askyd why, and he seid ther is a *capias* ought ayens hym upon the condempnaceon,[2] and the Shireff hath it, he bad me geve hym warnyng ; it is retarnabill xv. Pasch.[3]

Item, thei sey here that the Kyng was on Monday at Waltham.

Item, Nicholas Colman hath brought home your fardell ; it is at Norwich.

Item, ther be no more Juges here but Sir Pers Ardeyn.[4]

Wretyn at Thetford, the Wednesday the last day of Februar.

the dates of Privy Seals that the King was at Waltham in the end of February, or that he had previously visited Cambridgeshire, in any year during the period when this letter must have been written ; but it is quite possible that he was at Waltham on the 27th February 1464, and if so, that he had passed through Cambridgeshire on his way from Kimbolton, where he had been on the 17th.
[1] *i.e.* accused him. *See* vol. ii. p. 110, Note 1.
[2] Query, as to this word, it being not perfect in the original.—F.
[3] Quindena Paschæ, the fifteenth day after Easter.
[4] Sir Peter Ardern, Knight, was appointed Chief Baron of the Exchequer, and also a Justice of the Common Pleas, in 1448 ; but in 1462 a new Chief Baron was appointed, and Ardern retained only the judgeship in the Common Pleas. He died in 1467.

94

Item, Wymondham[1] is here, and was at the shirehows this day, and the Kyngs livery abaught his nekke, and ther stood be the Juge, whill a lettir of the Kyngs was red. The effect was, as it was told me, that the Kyng will that justice be had, and that all risers ayens the pees, and oppressers of the pepill, be chasteised, letyng hem weet[2] that he was late in Cambridge Shire, and there such as had offendid askyd grace, whech thei had, savyng such as wer rewlers, whom he woll somwhat bee punyshid, purposyng to be in this contry abought Estern, &c.

1464
FEB. 29

Your servaunt, &c., JOHN PAMPYNGE.

560

JOHN PASTON THE YOUNGEST TO JOHN PASTON, HIS FATHER[3]

To my rygte reverent and worchepfull fadyr, John Paston, dwellyng in Castyr, be thys delyveryd.

RYTH reverent and worchepful fadyr, I recomand me on to yow, besechyng yow lowly of your blyssyng, desyryng to here of yowyr wellfar and prosperyte, the whyche I pray God preserve on to Hys plesans, and to yowyr hertys desyir ; besechyng yow to have me excusyd that ye had no wrytyng fro me syth that I departyd frome yow ; for so God me helpe, I send yow a lettyr to London anon aftyr Kandylmas, by a man of my Lordys ; and he forgat to delyver yt to yow, and so he browt to me the lettyr ayen ; and sythe that tyme I kowd get no messenger tyll now.

MARCH

[1] John Wymondham, Esq., the purchaser of Felbrigg ; he died there in 1475, and was buried in the Augustine Friars at Norwich.—F.
[2] The word 'weet' is omitted in Fenn's original text, but occurs in the modern copy.
[3] [From Fenn, i. 284.] 'The Duke of Somerset's going' here referred to cannot well be his flight to Scotland in 1462 (*see* No. 512), though the time of year at which this letter is dated would agree very well with that supposition ; for it appears by Letter 511 that John Paston, the father, was at that time residing in the Temple and not at Caister ; nor indeed have we distinct evidence of his being at the latter place before 1464. Moreover, in the beginning of 1463, Somerset had just made his peace with King Edward and been received into favour, but early in 1464 he rebelled again. There can be little doubt, therefore, that this year is the true date.

95

THE PASTON LETTERS

As for tydyngs, syche as we have here I send yow. My Lord and my Lady[1] ar in good hele, blyssyd be God, and my Lord hathe gret labore and cost here in Walys for to take dyvers gentyllmen here whyche wer consentyng and helpyng on to the Duke of Somersettys goyng ; and they were apelyd of othyr se[r]teyn poyntys of treson, and thys mater. And bycause the Kyng sent my Lord woord to keep thys contre, is cause that my Lord terythe here thus longe. And now the Kyng hathe geve my Lord power, whedyr he wole do execusyon upon thes gentyllmen, or pardon hem, whedyr that hym lyst ; and as fertheforthe as I kan undyrstand yet, they shall have grase. And as sone as thes men be come in, my Lord is perposyd to come to London, whyche I supose schall be within thys fortnyght. The menys namys that be apechyd ar thes, John Hanmer, and Wylliam hys sone, Roger Pulyston, and Edward of Madok ; these be men of worchepe that schall come in.

The Comenys in Lancasher and Chescher wer up to the nombyr of a x. m^{l.} [10,000] or more, but now they be downe ayen ; and one or ij. of hem was hedyd in Chestyr as on Saterday last past.

Thomas Danyell[2] is here in Chesscher, but I wot not in what plase, he hathe sent iij. or iiij. letyrys to Syr John Howard, syne my Lord come hedyr.

And othyr tydynggs her we none here, but that I supose ye have herd before ; I supose veryly that it schall be so nye Esterne[3] er ever my Lord come to London, that I schal not move [q. *mowe*? *i.e.* be able] come home to yow before Estern ; wherfor I besech yow, that ye wole wyche save [*vouchsafe*] that one of your men may send a byll to myne oncyll Clement, or to som othyr man, who that ye wole, in youyr name, that they may delyver me the mony that I am

---

[1] John Mowbray, Duke of Norfolk, and Elizabeth, his wife.
[2] This gentleman had a reversionary grant of the constableship of Rising Castle in 1448, 27 Hen. VI. He married Margaret, daughter of Sir Robert Howard, and sister of Sir John, afterwards Duke of Norfolk. He is said to have been attainted in the 1 Edw. IV., but fully restored both in blood and possessions in the 14th of the same King. He was esquire of the body to Henry VI.—F.
[3] In 1464 Easter Day fell on the 1st of April.

EDWARD IV

behynd of this quarter syn Crystmas, and for the next quarter, in parte of that some that it plesid yow to grant me by yer ; for by my trowthe, the felawchep have not so myche mony as we wend to have had be ryth myche ; for my Lord hath had gret costs syn he came hedyr. Wherfore I besech yow, that I may have this mony at Estern, for I have borowyd mony that I must paye ayen after Estern : and I pray to Allmyty God have yow in kepyng.

Wretyn in the Castyll of the Holte, in Walys, the fyrst day of Marche.

Your sone and lowly servant,
JOHN PASTON, the yongest.

561

ABSTRACT[1]

Copy of an indenture bearing date 11th April, 4 Edward IV., witnessing the delivery to Richard Calle, servant of John Paston, Esquire, by John, prior of the monastery of Holy Trinity, Norwich, by virtue of the King's writ, of a red box containing seventeen bundles of evidences, with £40 of silver in groats, and 80 nobles of gold, in a bag, and other valuables.

An inventory of the articles referred to in the foregoing indenture is contained in a separate paper mutilated in the right-hand margin, which we give verbatim as follows :—

This is the parcell be endenture received by Richard Calle of . . . . day of Aprile the forthe yere . . . . . . as it apperit by the copye that the seyde Richard sendeth me by John Threcher.

Unam cistam rubeam cum xvij. bundellis evidenciarum in eadem cista contentis.
Quadraginta libras argenti in grossis et iiij^{xx} nobil.
Duo turribula[2] argenti et deaurata.
Unam pixidem argenti et deauratam.
Unum osculatorium cum imagine Sancti Jacobi et . . . . . .
Unum cruett argenti et deauratum.
Unum crismatorium rotundum.
Unum calicem argenti et deauratum.
Unum alium calicem cum imagine Sanctæ Trinitatis.

Md.[3]

I left no cruet in the cofer.[3]
I left non soch in the cofer but chalis of gold.[3]

---

[1] [From Paston MSS., B.M.]
[2] Thuribula, censers, from *thus*.
[3] These marginal notes are in John Paston's hand.

THE PASTON LETTERS

This is the copy of a bille drawin in Englyche that I sent home [of all] manner of suche stuff as was in myne coffre in the abb[ey] . . . . . . by a letter sent with the same bylle that he chowlde take hede that . . . yf he fonde aney more, wele be it, as it aperit in the seyd lett[er] . . . woulle be lokyd [*locked*] uppe.

Unum calicem de auro playne ponderis duas li[bras].
Unum alium calicem de auro cum scriptura 'Cal[icem salutaris accipiam,'[1] ponderis xix. unc'].
Unam tabulam de auro cum imagine Sancti J[acobi positam cum lapidis pretiosis,] ponderis xiij. unc' et iij. quarteria.
Unum par turribulorum argenti et deaurat' cum scriptura, viz., in prima parte 'Dat' est eis,' &c. ; et in secunda parte 'Ascendit fumus,' pond' xiij. lb. et [x. unc'].
Unam pixidem argenti pro sacramento deaurat' cum cruce [in summitate ac chased cum] liliis, pond' v. lb. et iij. unc' di'.
Unam ampullam argenti deaurat' pond' i. lb.[3]

[4] All this was put in a paner togyddre and . . . . for to berit in to the coffre.
Item, xl. mark in noblis and xl. li. in gro[tis].
Item, evydens.

(margin notes:)
hes to alis after e unc'
orth iij. li.[2]

his is orth iiij. xv. s.[2]

hes be orth, after d. the ach viij. li.
j s. ix. d.[2]

562

SACRED VESSELS[5]

This is the plate that was in my cofir at Norwich.

A CHALEYS of goold playne, weyng ij. pound.
Item, a nother chaleys of goold, with this writynge 'Calicem salutaris[6] accipiam,' weyng xix. unces.
Item, one table of gold, with an image of Sen James set with precious stonys, weyng xiij. unce iij. quarter.
Item, one peyre of sensers of silver and gilt, with scripture,

---

[1] Psalm cxv. [cxvi.] 13.
[2] *See* Note 3 on last page.
[3] The plate in this list is the same as that described in No. 554, by which the words lost in this MS. have been supplied.
[4] Added in John Paston's hand.
[5] [From Paston MSS., B.M.] This list of articles is in the handwriting of Richard Calle, writing, I presume, as John Paston's secretary, and in his name. It will be seen that it corresponds with a Latin list contained in No. 561, and must therefore be the 'bill drawn in English' there referred to.
[6] Salutularis, MS.

EDWARD IV

viz., in the first part, 'Dat' est eis,' &c., and in the second parte, 'Ascendit fumus,' &c., weyng xiij*li*. et x. unc'.

Item, one box of silver and gilt for the sacrement, with a crosse in the heyght, and chased with liliis, weyng v*li*. iij. unc' di.

Item, one potte callid a crismatorie to put in holy creme and oyle, of silver and gilt, weyng j*li*.

563

A LIST OF GILT IMAGES[1]

AN image off Owr Lady with ij. awngellis sensyng, gilthe, viij^{xx} unc', viz., xiiij*li*. et. iiij. unc'.
Item, a crosse with a fott, lx. unc', gilthe in to cassys and gilt, viij^{xx} & xvij. unc', viz., xiiij*li*. & ix. unc'.
Item, an image of Sent Jon Vangelist, gilthe, weyng vij^{xx}x. unc', viz., xij*li*. vj. unc'.
Item, an image of Sent Jon Baptist, gilthe, with the Lamb, lviij. unc', viz., iiij*li*. x. unnc'.
Item, an image off Sent Jamis with his staff, gilthe, weyng xxxvj. unc', viz., iij*li*.
Item, an image off Our Lady, gilthe, with a crowne and a lely, weyng iij^{xx}vj. unnc', viz., v*li*. vj. unc'.
Item, an image of Sent Denys, gilthe, weyng l. unc', viz., iiij*li*. ij. unc'.
Item, an image off owr Savyowr, gilt, with His crosse, His diademe, and His fane, v^{xx}xj. unc', viz., ix*li*. iij. unc'.

Summa unciarum xl^{xx}viij. unc'.
Summa lxvij. lib. iiij. unc'.
Sum in markis Cj. mark ij. unc', di.

Memorandum, j. lib. continet xij. unc' ; j. marc continet viij. unc'.

Endorsed—Episcopus Cantuariensis.

---

[1] [From Paston MSS., B.M.] This list is likewise in the handwriting of Richard Calle, and was perhaps drawn up about the same time as the preceding one.

THE PASTON LETTERS

564

CLEMENT PASTON TO JOHN PASTON[1]

To my rygth worchepful broder John Paston Sqwyer.

1464
APRIL 18

RYGHT worshypfull brothyr, I recomawnde me to zow. After all dew recomendacions, &c., plesse it zow to wett that after that I had harde say that the person of Blowfelde[2] wasse com to town I went to hym to his in, and he bade the mesenger say that he wasse not within, and I bad hym say a gayn that I come thyder to hym for hys own worchep and avayle and that I wasse sory that I com so fer for hym; and after that he sent for me and he cowde not fynde me, and I harde say ther of. And than I wrott a letter, resytyng how that he wasse sworn yesterday for to say the trowthe of al maner of materis consernyng Sir John Fastolfe, avysyd hym to remember qwat hys wytnesse hadde sayd for hys sake, and wat schame it xwlde be to hym to say the contrary; And also, if he sayde the contrary, ze wold heraffter prove the trowthe and contrary to hys sayyng, and prove hym in a perjuri. And also I badde hym remember with wat maner of men he delt wythe; and I rehersyd how untrwly they hadde don. And not with standyng thys, after I met with hym in the strett and spak with hym, and I fownde hym passyng strawngely disposyd and sor mevyd with consiens that ze xwld have the lond and fownd the colage but with an C. marcs, not with stondyng he myth fynde in hys consiens by the well that the colage xwld be fowndyd in a noder plasse but with an C. marcs, and the reminaunt of the lylode sold so that he myth pwroe the mony; so I felt by hym that all hys strawngenes from zow is for he demythe that ze wold parte from no thyng; and I told hym the contrary ther of to be

[1] [Add. MS. 34,889, f. 7.] This letter was written in April 1464, when witnesses began to be examined about Fastolf's will. *See* No. 565. The Privy Seals of Edward IV. show that he was in Kent (at Dartford) on the 15th and 18th of that month, and immediately after started for York.

[2] Thomas Howes.

EDWARD IV

1464
APRIL 1

trwe, az this day he is exaymined up on a bok to sey the trowthe of all thynges as the juge will[1] aske hym, for the jugeis informacion; wych I trowe wyll not be good. Also they have pwt in *testes* azens zow iij^{xx} or iiij^{xx} men. Mayster Robard Kent wold sayn that ze xwle gett zow ij. lycens of the prioris of zowre wytnes, Mayster Clement and the monke, with an A[2] datt beryng before the comyng up; for that must ye nedis have. Also he wold sayn that ze xwld com to thys towne. Me thowte by Sir Thomas that they have aswerte in maner that ze xall have no lycens for zour fundacion. And [*i.e.* if] they be abowte to gett a lycens to fownde the colage in a noder place, me thynkythe that wold hurte; her colour is for cause ze can gett no lycens to fownde it at Caster; werfor thow zour wyll wer trwe, they myth lawfully fownde it in a noder place. My Lord Chawnceler[3] is gone to Zork and wyll not be her of all thys term. Wrytyn on Wednisday nexst be for Saynt George.

The Kyng hathe ben in Kent and ther ben endityd many for Isleis dethe; and he wyll com to town this day azen and he wyl not tary her but forthe to Zork straytt.

By CLEMENT PASTON.

565

ABSTRACT[4]

DEPOSITIONS TOUCHING SIR J. FASTOLF'S WILL

'Primum testes reprobatorii producti per Yelverton, contra testes Paston principaliter productos &c.

'Facta fuit sequens examinatio testium subscriptorum secrete et singillatim,

[1] 'will.' In MS. 'w',' which ought to read 'with'; evidently a slip of the pen.
[2] Apparently meaning an *ante* date.
[3] George Nevill, Bishop of Exeter, afterwards Archbishop of York.
[4] [From MS. Phillipps, 9309.] These depositions, of which we shall only attempt to give some of the principal points, were produced in the Spiritual Court by Sir William Yelverton and William Worcester in opposition to the claim of John Paston and Thomas Howes to be Sir John Fastolf's executors. The examinations were taken at intervals during the years 1464, 1465, and 1466, and the suit was not terminated when John Paston died. The MS. volume here referred to contains three distinct bundles of these depositions bound up in a wrong order. A volume containing similar matter among the Paston MSS. in the British Museum will be found entered in the year 1465.

THE PASTON LETTERS

1464
APRIL-
NOV.

videlicet, Domini Johannis Davy capellani vicesimo octavo die mensis Aprilis, Thomæ Upton quinto, Johannis Bockyng duodecimo, Nicholai Newman xvj^{to} diebus mensis Maii; Johannis Loer, Willelmi Eton quarto, Roberti Lynne quinto, diebus mensis Junii; Bartholomei Elys tercio, magistri Roberti Wylly sexto, Johannis Marshall, Johannis Davy terciodecimo et Willelmi Lyne ultimo, diebus mensis Julii; Anno Domini millesimo quadringentesimo sexagesimo quarto, Indictione duodecima, pontificatus Sanctissimi in Christo patris et domini nostri, domini Pii Divina prudencia Papæ Secundi anno sexto, In Domo Thesaurarii ecclesiæ Cathedralis Sancti Pauli, London, infra parochiam Sancti Gregorii civitatis London situat', per venerabilem virum magistrum Johannem Druell, utriusque juris doctorem, examinatorem et commissarium ad infra scripta specialiter deputatum. In præsentia mei Nicholai Parker notarii auctoritate Apostolica, publici scribæ in hac parte de et super exceptionibus infra scriptis, par partem domini Willelmi Yelverton et Willelmi Worceter productorum.'

1. John Davy chaplain, staying at the University of Cambridge, *liberæ conditionis*, 30 years old and more, examined *super exceptionibus infrascriptis* of which the tenors are quoted, viz., on the part of Yelverton and Worceter against John Russe, Robert Cutteler clk., Master Clement Felmyngham, Rob. Boteler, Ralph Lampet, Brother Will. Bokyngham, and Master Robert Popy, witnesses on the opposite side, whose testimony is discredited 'eo quod parte sua non præsenti juraverunt et super non juratis deposuerunt, ac in depositionibus suis fuerint et sint varii, contrarii, singulares negativam asserentes, causas dictorum suorum minime reddentes, unumque et eundem præmeditatum sermonem proferentes, a testatore non vocati aut rogati perhibere testimonium, nec sufficienter probantes in hac parte, prout ex inspectione depositionum suarum liquere poterit intuenti.' Further, John Russe was illiterate, and did not understand Latin when he made his deposition, and he contradicted the other witnesses on his own side: viz., to the 9th interrogatory he said, Sir J. Fastolf's will was not written before his death, which Clement Felmyngham and Robt. Cutteler in their reply to the 3d said it was. Moreover he expected advantage to himself from his testimony, and was discharged by Howys of £300 that he owed Fastolf. He had also secretly abstracted certain muniments and charters of the testator, which were in the custody of Will. Worceter, in the house of John Tovy, at Castir, Norwich dioc., in Nov. 1459. Moreover he was *supravisor et locator* of the testator's lands called Akethorpe, yearly value 9 marks, appointed by Paston or Howys, who promised to sell them to him much under value for his testimony. Further, his statement that he was present *in quadam bassa camera* at Caister between 8 and 9 A.M. on the Saturday before Sir J. Fastolf's death, a perjury, for he was really all that time in other places a long way off. His declaration that he was no servant or tenant of those who brought him forward was untrue: he had hired a house of Howys in the town of Yarmouth, value 40s. a year. He was inconsistent in his testimony about the hour Sir J. declared his will. He also pretended never to have seen Fastolf's will before his death, although he wrote the said pretended will with his own hand with the date at the head, which at the beginning of this suit he caused to be cut off from the writing and hidden.

EDWARD IV

1464
APRIL-
NOV.

Also the said Rob. Cutteler chaplain, when he made his deposition, was 'levis opinionis, malæ conscientiæ et de mensa Joh'is Paston ac tenens ipsius, prout ad primum interrogatorium examinationis suæ primæ et secundæ respondebat.' Also he was perjured: because in April 1457 in par. of Holy Trin., Castir, he beat and maimed one Jo. Flemyng, and boasted of it (*ac sic factum nomine suo ratum habuit*), but being taken before Sir J. Fastolf, justice of the peace, he swore he had not done so.—Proofs that he was not disinterested.

Exceptions to Rob. Popy: He was a tenant of Paston's, &c. &c.

Davy says John Rus was at Yarmouth on the Saturday in question, as he usually was on Saturdays, to buy victuals for Fastolf's house, &c. (Proof declared insufficient in the margin.) Sir J. Fastolf was so ill, that, as Davy had heard he was unable to speak from 22d Oct. 'Quæ quidem infirmitas vocabatur judicio medicorum, *sincope*, quæ ipsum vexabat singulis horis et ipsum deduxit ad extasim de scientia istius jurati, qui continue conversabatur cum eo usque ad ipsius mortem.'

2. Thos. Upton, one of the clerks of the King's kitchen, *literatus*, 'liberæ conditionis,' forty years old and over; 2d. witness.

Mentions that W. Worceter gave Jo. Rus a casket to keep containing certain documents, which Rus delivered to Howys after Fastolf's death. Was clerk of the kitchen to Fastolf when Rus used to go on Saturday to Yarmouth, &c.

9 May. Jo. Bokkyng produced by Jo. Naseby, proctor of Yelverton and Worceter, before Master Tho. Wynterton, LL.D., auditor of Thomas Archbishop of Canterbury, at his house in the parish of St. Martin, in presence of Robert Kent, proctor of John Paston.—Examination committed to John Druell, LL.D. who on the 12th May examines him secretly in the house of the treasurer of St. Paul's.

'Dicit quod Johannes Tovy quædam munimenta et evidencias[1] in certis bagis et pixidibus contenta quæ Willelmus Worceter eidem Johanni Tovy liberavit custodienda.' Rus was and is Howys' tenant for the house he lives in. After Fastolf's death Upton delivered to Clement Felmyngham a signet or gold ring, 'ad signandum sigilla dicti domini Johannis Fastolf,' in a little bag, which was to be returned 'post signacionem hujusmodi,' but afterwards he said he had lost it. Touchyng brother W. Bukyngham, it was publicly noised at Yarmouth that Robert Brown, a chaplain of that town, had killed one Seman Burton, that Bukyngham knowingly received him, and that by his advice he fled. To the last exception he says he believes Fastolf did not release Paston from the payment of the said 4000 marks, 'quia iste juratus non intellixit in tota vita sua tantam liberalitatem in dicto domino Johanne Fastolf.' Fastolf had such difficulty in breathing for five or six days before his death that he could hardly speak.

Interrogatories proposed on the part of Paston and Howys, and administered to witnesses.

'In primis, interrogetur quilibet testis hujusmodi cujus sit conditionis et an

[1] There is no verb in the MS. to govern *munimenta et evidencias*.

THE PASTON LETTERS

sit famulus, [1] serviens aut tenens partis eum producentis, et cui parti magis favet partium prædictarum.' Secondly, whether he be in the pay of any one. There are six interrogatories in all, and they are numbered.

Then follow answers of some one, whose name does not appear, to each of these six interrogatories; and other answers by—

1. Nich. Newman, Usher of the Chamber to Lady Catherine, Duchess of Norfolk.

2. John Loer, servant of the Abbot of Langley.

3. Will. Eton.

4. Rob. Lynne of Bucklande.

5. Barth. Elys of Yarmouth, 'literatus liberæ conditionis,' fifty years old and more (proves Rus's absence, but his testimony is declared in the margin to be improbable, and not to agree with Davy's).

6 July. Naseby produces Rob. Wylly on the part of Yelverton and Worcester. Examined on the 9th.—Says he was required by Paston and Howys to see Fastolf's will, and 'ad impediendum [impendendum] consilium suum:'—that on a Sunday in the summer after Fastolf's death, John Paston showed him, at Fastolf's house in Southwark, Sir John's will written on paper, in presence of Clement Felmyngham and John Bracley, and asked his opinion if it was valid. Thought it insufficient to overthrow any previous will. A clause mentioning Tudenham and Heydon as executors was cancelled by this deponent's advice, 'eo quod erat contra caritatem.'

13 July at Bow Church. Naseby produces John Marshall and John Davy, whose examinations follow.

19 Oct. 1464. Druell examines Hen. Wenstall at the treasurer's house of St. Paul's.

15 Nov. 1464. Druell examines Rob. Hert.

1 Dec. Naseby produces Rob. Fyztrauf, whose production Kent opposes; who tries to prove Rus's absence (insufficiently, as remarked in the margin), because he was constantly with Fastolf, except half an hour that morning, when he held the basin while Henry Barbour lathered the beard (lavit barbam) of the said Sir John Fastolf.

'Responsiones personaliter factæ per dominum Thomam Howys unum executorum domini Joh'is Fastolf, ultimo die mensis Aprilis Aº Dⁿⁱ 1464,' &c., 'coram Ven. viro Mag'ro Thoma Wynterbourne, LL.D.,' &c., 'in camera ejusdem infra manerium Revᵐⁱ patris apud Lamehith, Winton dioc' situat', in præsenncia mei Nicholai Parker,' &c.

Howys says he did not see Coteler or Rus in Fastolf's chamber that Saturday before he went to dinner. On Saturday and Sunday before his death Fastolf spoke so low he could hardly be heard by any one, and Howys heard him only by putting his ear close to his mouth. Fastolf's mind was clear.

---

[1] The text is continued here at another part of the volume, the leaves being misplaced.

EDWARD IV

566

ABSTRACT[1]

Power of attorney by Roger Fidyon, clerk, and William Bondys to Richard Lynstede, John Holme, and John Brikkes, to enter and take possession of the manor of Hornynghall, in Castre, by Yarmouth, with appurtenances in Castre, Maudeby, Ormesby, Filby, and Scroudeby, or elsewhere in the hundred of East Flegge, Norfolk, which the said Roger and William have of the gift of Edmund Clere; and thereafter to deliver seisin therein to Agnes Paston, William Paston, Elizabeth, Countess of Oxford, John Veer, Earl of Oxford, John Scroop, Knight, Lord Scroop, Sir William Yelverton, Elizabeth Cleere; William Jennay, John Grenefeld, John Catesby, Serjeants-at-Law; John Hastynges, John Clopton, John Calthorp, Hugh Fen, Thomas Cornewaleys, Thomas Howes, clerk, Roger Marchall of London, Henry Spilman, William Lomnour, Bartholomew Whyte, William Whyte, John Applyerd, James Arblaster, William Wurcetyr, and Richard Maryot, according to a charter granted to them by the said Roger and William.

Castre, 12th May, 4 Edward IV.

567

MARGARET PASTON TO JOHN PASTON[2]

To myn ryght worshypful hosbond, John Paston, be thys delyveryd in haste.

RYGHT worshypful hosbond, rekomaund me on to you. Pleasyth you to wete that I sent yesterday Loveday to Norwyche to speke wyth the Vykyr of Derham[3] for the mater betwen Master Constantyn and hym; and he seyth that as for that mater, Master Constantyn sewyd hym for

---

[1] [From MS. in the Bodleian Library.]

[2] [From Fenn, iv. 176.] The commission to Lord Scales and Sir John Howard mentioned in this letter seems to have reference to a proclamation dated the 11th May 1464, by which all men between the ages of sixty and sixteen were ordered to attend the King. The date is confirmed by the reference in the postscript to the death of 'Rous of Suffolk,' for Reginald Rous of Denington died in 1464. (See Weever's *Funeral Monuments*, p. 782.)

[3] Constantine Dalby was instituted to the Vicarage of East Dereham in 1451, and was succeeded in 1458 by Robert Sheringham.

THE PASTON LETTERS

feyth and trowth brekyng, and he sewed Master Constantyn in the Temporall Curte uppon an obligacion of xli.; and ther was made appoyntment be twen hem by the advyce of bothe ther Conceylis, be for Master Robert Popy, that eche of hem shuld relece othyr, and so they dede, and the sewtys wer wythdrawyn on bothe partyes, and iche of hem aquyttauncyd othyr; and as for any copy of the plee, he had never non, ner he ner Master John Estegate, that was hys atornay, remembryth nat that it was regestryd; and Master John Estegate seythe, if it schuld be scergyd in the regester it wold take a fortenyght werk, and yit peraventur never be the nerer.

Syr Thomas Howes hathe ben ryght besy thys weke at Blofeld, in wrytyng and lokyng uppe of ger, and John Russe hathe ben with hym ther the moste parte of alle thys weke, and thys day was Robert Lynne ther with hym; what they have do I wote nat, but I schal wete if I may.

It was told me that Syr Thomas desyryd of John Russe to make hym a new inventory of Syr John Fastolffs goods. John Russe myght not be spoke with yit, for the letter that he shuld a wretyn, whych ye sente me word of.

Item, it is tolde that the Dwke of Suffolk[1] is kome home, and owthyr he is ded, or ellys ryght seke, and not lyke to eskape; and Syr John Howard is kome hom; and it is seyd that the Lord Skalys[2] and he have a comyssyon to enquer whye they of this contre that were sent for kame not hastylar uppe afftyr they wer sent for. It is reportyd that the Kyng is gretly dyspleasyd ther with. At the reverence of God, arme yowr selve as myghtyly as ye kan ageyn yowr enmyes, for I know verrayly that they wyl do ageyn yow as myghtyly as they kan with all ther power.

It is told me that Syr Thomas shal kom uppe in haste, and othyr, suche as he kan make for hys partye.

Also for Goddys sake be war what medesyns ye take of any fysissyans of London; I schal never trust to hem be cause of your fadr and myn onkyl, whoys sowlys God assoyle.

The blissyd Trynyte have yow in Hys kepyng, and sende

---

[1] John de la Pole, Duke of Suffolk.

[2] Anthony Widville was created Lord Scales in 1461.—F.

EDWARD IV

yow helthe and good spede in all yowr materis. Wretyn in haste, on the Fryday next befor Sceynt Bernabye.

By yowrs, M. P.

Alle the jentylmen of thys contre that went uppe to the Kyng ar contrmaundyd, and ar com hom ageyn. It is told me that Rowse of Suffolk[1] is ded. If John Gayn myght have any releese of his sone, if it myght do hym ese, it wer a good torne for hym.

568

RICHARD CALLE TO JOHN PASTON[2]

To my ryght wurschipfull my mastre, John Paston, be this delyverd in haste.

PLESITH it youre goode maisterchippe to witte that I have be with my Mastre Calthorppe for the matre ye wrote to hym fore, wherin I have founde hym ryght weele disposed and favorabley; nevertheles he tolde me that William Jenney hath bene hes goode frende and have ben of hes councell this ij. yere in all hes matres towchyng the lawe, but he seide lever he hadde lose the lesser frende than the greete frende, and so he hathe graunted favour accordyng to youre desire, and wrote a lettre to the undrescheryff of Norfolk that he schuld take suerte sufficient to save hym harmeles, and that done to write a lettre to the undrescheryff of Suffolk and lete hym witte that he hath taken suerte that ye schall appere in the *crastino Animarum* upon the exigents returnable, or elles

---

[1] Reginald Rous, Esq. of Denington, in Suffolk, died in 1464. He was the ancestor of the present Earl of Stradbroke.

[2] [From Paston MSS., B.M.] This letter refers to the suit brought by Jenney against Paston in 1464, in which, as will be seen hereafter, Paston failed to appear at four successive county courts held at Ipswich, and was at last outlawed in Michaelmas term. See No. 572.

THE PASTON LETTERS

1464
JUNE 28 to bryng a *super sedias*[1] lauful before that daye, chargyng hym that he do sece [*cause to cease*] the callyng of the writts, and to retorne that ye appered the furst day. Weche suerte is taken, and a letter wreten to the undrescheryff of Suffolk acordynge herto.

Item, as for Sir Thomas Howes, he lythe most at Norwiche. I can thynke he come not up to London tyll Michelmes.

Item, I rode over to Techewelle whan that I whas at Mastre Calthorppes for to have money of the fermours, and Yelverton and Sir Thomas hathe sent to hem that they schol pay to you no more money, for that they had payed to you they schulde payed [*pay it*] ayene to them; and so I gane [*can*] gete no money of hem. Wherfore I went for to distreyne hem; and so they seide that I myght not distreyne hem, for I come before the daye, for her [*their*] day is at Midsomer. Nevertheles I wold not lette, for that Simond Miller and other promysed to Mr. William Cotyng and to me that I schuld have the money aftre Midsomer, so that I brought with me a quetaunce of suche money as ye have receyved of hem, or elles a generall quetaunce; and the tone I purposed to do in haste be the advice of the seide Mastre W. Cotynge. For, and I torned, I can thynke it schuld hurte. I am purposed to lete it in youre name to other folks or to them ayen, and suerte founde to you, &c. And Almyghty God preserve and kepe you. Wreten at Norwiche on Sen Petres Even.

Your pore servaunt and bedman,

RIC. CALLE.

[1] *Super sedias.* So spelt in MS.

THE PASTON LETTERS

1464 the seid maners, with a clause of distresse for defaut of payment of the seid rente, and vj. acres of lond in the seid towne of Caster, and the avowsons of the chirches of the same town, and the fourth part of the seid mancion, or any part therof for the habitacion of the seid prestes and porefolk, to be reparid at the costes of your seid besecher, and his heires or assignes for evir. And also by your seid lettirs patentes to graunt the same prestes to be one body incorperate and to have succession perpetuall, and a comon seall, and to be persones abill to plede and to be impletid, and to purchase and alienyn all maner londes, goodes and catell, by the name of the master and his brethyrn of the college of Sen John Baptist of Castre aforeseid. And also by your seid lettirs patentes to licence the seid prestes to take and reseyve, and to hold to them and to ther successours the seid annuite, rent charge, vj. acres of lond, avousons, and the seid ———[1] part of the seid mancion, for evir. And to geve your Chaunceler of Inglond for the tyme beyng, comaundement, power, and auctorite that where as in this petision is not comprehendid the certeynte of termes, maters, clauses, and other circumstaunces convenient and requisite after forme of lawe for licens of the seid fundacion, that your seid Chaunceler, that notwithstandyng, do make your seid lettirs patentes in forme of lawe effectuall and sufficient in that behalf after the very entent aforeseid, not excedyng the valew and somme before specifyd, without any fyne or fee other thanne is afore specifyd to be payd for the seid lettirs patentes, licens, or grauntes by your seid besecher or by the seid prestes; and thei shall pray hertly to God for yow.

Endorsed in a later hand:—Supplicatio Jo. Paston [pro] fundacione Collegii apud Caistor [secundum] formam testamenti Jo. Fastolf, mil.

[1] A blank on an erasure.

569

JOHN PASTON TO EDWARD IV.[1]

To the Kyng, our Liege Lord.

BESECHYTH lowly your humble servaunt, John Paston the older, squier, that it please youre good grace, for such a fyne as your highnes hath apoynted your seid besecher to content yow, wherof ye be put in suerte, to graunt on to your seid besecher your gratious lettirs patentes of licence to found, stabilissh, and endewe in the gret mancion of Caster in Flegge in Norffolk, that late was John Fastolffs, knyght, cosyn to your seid besecher, a college of vij. prestes, wherof one to be master, and of vij. porefolk, to pray for your noble astate and for the soule of the seid John Fastolff and such other as he was behold to inperpetuite, aftir ordinauns by your seid besecher in that behalff to be made; and to inmortese, geve and graunt to the seid prestes and to ther successours, for the sustentacion of hem and of the seid porefolk CXX. mark of annuite and rent charge, or annuites and rentes charge, yerly goyng out of the maners callid Redhams, Vaux, and Bosomes, in Caster forseid, Begviles in Wynterton, Reppis in Bastewyk, Spencers in Heryngby, Loundhall in Saxthorp, Heylesdon, Drayton, Heynesford, Guton in Brandeston, Beyton, Techewell, and of the thrid part of the maner of Runham with th'apportenauns in the shire of Norffolk, and of the maners of Hemnales in Cotton, Burneviles in Nakton, Akthorp in Leystoft, Calcotes, Havelound, Spitlyngges, with th'apportenauns in the shire of Suffolk, and out of any part of

1464

[1] [From MSS. in the Bodleian Library.] This, and the alternative petition which follows, seem to have been drawn up in the year 1464, as one or other of them must have been the subject of the agreement of the 10th September in that year (No. 571). The two are printed from two parchment MSS. in the Bodleian Library. There is also, among the Paston MSS. in the British Museum, a third copy, fair written on parchment like the other two, of which the text corresponds in the beginning to the second petition, and in the latter part to the first.

EDWARD IV

II.

To the Kyng, our Sovereyn Lord.

Please it yowr highnes to graunte unto yowr humble servant John Paston the older, Squier, yowr gracious lettres patents of licence to fownde, stabelysh, and endewe in the gret mancion of Castre be Mekyll Yermowth in Norffolk, that late was John Fastolffs, knyght, cosyn to yowr seyd besecher, a colage of vij. prystes wheroff on to be master, and vij. pourmen, to praye for your noble astate, and for the sowle of the said Fastolff and suche othir as he was holde to inperpetuite, and to inmortese and gyve to the seyd prystes, and to ther successours for the sustentacion of hem, and of the seyd pourmen C. marke of annuite and rent charge, yerly goyng owt of all maneres, londes, and tenementz that were the seyd Fastolffs within the Shyres of Norffolk and Suffolk, and vj. acres of londe in the sayd town of Castre, and the iiij. parte of the sayd mancion for the habitacion of the sayd prystes and pourmen, to be repared at the costes of your seyd besecher and hys heyres and assignes for ever, as suerly and lawfully as your seyd besecher can devise. And also be your letters patentz to graunt the same prystes to be one bodie incorperate, and to have succession perpetuall, and a comon seall, and to be persones abyll to plede and be impletid, and to purchase and alienyn all maner londs, tenements, godes, and catell, be the name of the master and hys brethyrn of the collage of Saynt John Baptiste of Castre aforsayd. And also be your letters patentz to licence the sayd prystes to take and receyve, and to holde to theym and to ther successours the sayd annaunite, rente charge, vj. acres of lond, avowsons, and the seyd iiij. parte of the said mancion for ever, with owte eny ffyne or fe to be payde for the sayd lettres patentz, licens or grauntes be your sayd besecher, or be the said pristes. And thei shall pray hertly to God for you.

Endorsed in a later hand:—Peticio Joh'is Paston Arm' ad Regem pro collegio in Caister.

1464

570

ANONYMOUS TO MASTER ROTHEWELL[1]

MAISTER Rothewell, please you to remembre, as for the mater that John Paston and Sir Thomas Howys comownyd with you of, in whiche they desyred specialy the good lordship, support and helpe of my Lordis of Wynchestre and Beauchamp for acomplishement of the will

1464(?)

[1] [Add. MS. 33,597, f. 6.] This letter would seem to be of about the same date as No. 569.

1464(?) of here testatour [1] and in esshewynge of costis. And where as ye meovyd to knowe the materys that were contraryed be otherys, we undirstonde and have knowlege of late tyme it [2] stondeth in these materys folwyng.

Fyrst, the seyd Testatour be hise testament namyd the seyd Lordys and the seyd John Paston and Thomas Howys and othyr executorys, and wolde as for the admynistracion, kepyng and execucion of his goodis shuld be takyn and doo be the seyd Paston and Howys duryng here lyves, if they will take admynistracion ; and if ony of hem too desese or refuce the admynistracion, the tothyr to chese to hym on of the remnaunt of the executorys to execute, &c. And if bothe deye, noon chosyn, thanne tweyne to be chosyn be the executorys levyng, or the more part of hem, to admynistre in lyk wise. And they too that do occupye to have recourse to my seyd lordis and the othyr executorys in takyng here good avyse chargeable and requysit materys. And this is oon matere that othyr namyd in the Testament gruche with. Notwithstandyng, as for ony avauntage that we cleyme to have by it, we wyll be agreable to ony mean resonable that oure seyd lordis wyll ordeyne to the good disposecion of the goodys accordyng to oure testatorys intent, or to ony meane that may concyensly or lawefully be meovyd.

Item, as for hise wyll touchyng hese goodis on mevable, as hese londis and tenamentis, the seyd testatour hathe at all tymes this xx. yeer, in all wyllis that he hathe made, ordeynid that a gret part of hyse seyd londis shuld goo to the fundacion of a collage at Castre of vij. monkys or pristis and vij. pore folke ; and he by hyse last wyll ordeynid that the seyd John Paston shuld have all the londis and tenementis in Norffolke, Suffolke and Norwyche ; and that the seyd Paston shuld at hese cost inmorteyse and indewe the seyd Collage and paye iiij [ml] mark to be dysposed for the testatouris soule, as is declaryd in the seyd wyll more pleynerly. And as for the remnaunt of the lyflode to be sold, and the mony thereof comynge to be disposed be thoo personys that he hathe ordeynid to have the execucion of hise wyll and testament.

[1] Sir John Fastolf.   [2] it. MS. reads 'in.'

112

And as for thys matere of the Collage, there shall, be the 1464(?) mene hereof, more mony growe to the handis of the mynistrorys, what soo ever they bee, and also lesse labour thanne shuld have doo and thys hadde not bee, in cas the seyd mynistroris wolde intende to parforme ony will that the seyd Testatour made thys xx. yeer. And also it shalbe well provyd that the seyd Testatour was dysposed to have doo more largely to the seyd Paston thanne is conteynid in the seyd wyll if he hadde levyd the tyme to have expressyd and parformyd hise wyll and entent.

Wherfor, plese my seyd lordis to take suche a direccion that the may undirstonde the trouthe of these materys, and to shewe here good lordshepys and favour accordyng to the trouthe in parformyng of the Testatourys wyll, and in sesynge of voyd costis of hese goodis. And that they will geve noo credence to suche as wyll upon here owyn imagynacionys for maleyse or invye intendyng to contrarye the dedys wyll or mys spende hese goodis . . .

Endorsed by another hand :—
     A letter to Rothwell or Worcester or of Watkyn Schyddam.

571

FOUNDATION OF CAISTER COLLEGE [1]

Apunctuament' Regis pro fundacione Collegij apud Caistre, &c.

THE Kyng, for the soume of CCC. mark of lawfull mony 1464 of Inglond, or of silver plate to the valew therof, SEPT. 10 grauntith to John Paston the older, Squier, to have licens, lawfully mad, to make and found a College of vij. prests and vij. pore folk at Caster, in Flegge in Norffolk, for the soule of Sir John Falstolf, Knyght ; thei to be indued with certeyn rent, and otherwise aftir the intent and effect as is specifijd in a bille therof, signed by the Kyng ; and that he

[1] [From Fenn, iv. 182.]

THE PASTON LETTERS

1464 shall showe his good grase, favour, and assistence to have the SEPT. 10 said fundacon inacted and autorised in the parlement next holden, and discharge the seid John Paston and the seid prests of any other fyne or fee to be mad in the Chauncerie for the seid fundacion ; and that the Kyng shall signe and graunt warants for seid licens, and shewe his good grace and favour in the expedision therof, what tyme he be sued to therfore by the seid John Paston.

Also, the Kyng grauntith to be good and favorabill Lord to the seid John Paston, and inespeciall in all thyngs touchyng the execucion of the will of the seid Sir John Fastolf, and also to be good and favorabill Lord to the seid John Paston, in supportyng and helpyng hym, in that the Kyngs Highnesse may lawfulle do, in such maters as are in debate athwyx the seid John Paston and William Yelverton, or William Jenney, or any other, concernyng the londs and tenements, goods or cattell, that were the seid Sir John Fastolfs. Also the Kyng grauntith to help and support the seid John Paston to opteyne and have to the use of the seid Sir John Fastolf such goods as were the seid Fastolfs deseitfully aloyned out of the possession and knowlech of the seid John Paston ; and that the Kyng shall graunt the seid John Paston such lawfull writynggs and lettirs from the Kyng, directed to such persones as shall be behovefull for the same, what tyme the seid John Paston suyth to the Kyngs Highnesse therfore.

Also where Yelverton, or Jenney, or any Justise of the Peas of the Shire of Suffolk hath recorded any riot, trespas, or offenses to be do ayens the Kyngs peas, by the seid John Paston, his servauntis, or tenaunts, or frends ; or where any inditement or presentment is found ayens them, or any of them, before any of the seid Justises, for any such riot, offenses, trespas, or for any other mater remaynyng of record in the Kyngs Benche, or in any other plase, the Kyng grauntith to the seid John Paston, and all other persones named in the seid records or inditements, or in any of hem, and to alle her boroughs [*sureties*] and plegges, and to ich of hem that woll sue it, a pardon of all riotes, trespas, offenses, felonys, forfetures doon ayens the Kyngs peas, and of fynes therefore

114

dempt [*adjudged*], or to be dempt, and of all other thyngs 1464 generally, treason except, and that the Kyng shall signe warants SEPT. 10 lawfull of the seid pardons, what tyme his Highnesse be requerid by the seid John Paston or his attornys.

And also that his Highnesse shall do inquere and examinacion be mad whedir the seid record of the seid Justises and presentments, and other informacions or compleynts mad ayens the seid John Paston, were do trewly and lawfully or nought ; and if it be found that thei were do otherwise thanne trought, lawe, or consiens woll, thanne the Kyng grauntyth to cause the doers therof to recompense the seid John Paston and the seid other persones, as far as lawe and good consiens woll in that behalf.

And that if it fortune any compleynt to be mad ayens the seid John Paston, by any persone in tyme comyng, to the Kyng, that he shall take no displeasir to the seid John Paston till the tyme he come to his answer, and be found in defaut.

And that the Kyng shall receyve an *Cli.* of the seid CCC. mark, what tyme he send for it, and the remnaunt as sone as the seid fundacion take effect ; and also that his Highnesse shall gete the assent of the reverent fader in God, the Archebisshop of Caunterbury, in such apoyntments as is mad athwyx the Kyng and the seid John Paston, of such goods as were the seid Sir John Fastolfs, for the delivere therof ; and that if the seid John Paston refuse the administracion of the goods and catell that were the seid Sir John Fastolfs, sufferyng other to take it opon hem, the Kyng, at the instauns of the seid John Paston, grauntith to be good and favorabill Lord to such other as the coors of the lawe, and assent of the seid John Paston, shall take the seid administracion in execucion of the seid Fastolfs will, touchyng the administracion of the goods and catell forseid, acordyng to the same wyll ; and that the Kyng shall not cleyme nor desire any of the londs or tenements, goods or catell, that were the seid Sir John Fastolf, ayens the seid John Paston, or any other executor, administror, or feffe of the seid Sir John Fastolf, nor support or favour any other persone in cleymyng any of the seid londs or tenements, goods or catell, ayens any the seid administers, executores, or feffes.

115

THE PASTON LETTERS

And the Kyng grauntith that where as this bille is not sufficiently mad in clauses and termes accordyng to th'entent therof, that his Highnesse woll take and execute the very entent therof, notwithstandyng the insufficiens of any such termes and clauses in thes bille. Wretyn at Marleburgh, the Monday next after the Nativite of oure Lady, the fourthe yere of the reigne of the Kyng.

572

ABSTRACTS[1]

Outlawry of John Paston.

NOV. 20   The following writs and copies of writs stood originally on a file in the order in which they are here noticed.

I. Edward IV. to the Prior of Norwich.—Orders him to deliver to the bearer all goods in his hands belonging to John Paston, Esq., who is outlawed. Reading, 20 Nov.

II. Writ to Edmund Clyre, Escheator of Norfolk, touching the above outlawry.—John Paston is here called 'the elder.' Dated 20 Nov.

III. Supersedeas addressed to the Escheator of Cos. Cambridge and Hunts to stay confiscation of the goods of John Paston, who has been outlawed, first for trespass against William Jenney, and secondly for trespass against William Hogan; of which he was convicted in Suffolk on Monday, 10 Sept., 4 Edw. IV. Both cases are removed by writs of error into the King's Bench.—Teste J. Markham apud Westin., 28 Nov., 4 Edw. IV.

IV. Copy of supersedeas on the exigent issued at Jenney's suit to the Sheriff of Suffolk.—Teste J. Markham apud Sekbrok, 24 Aug., 4 Edw. IV. With the return on the writ of exigent, notifying Paston's non-appearance when proclaimed at the county courts held at Ipswich on Monday 21 May, Monday 18 June, Monday 16 July, and Monday 13 Aug., 4 Edw. IV. The supersedeas was delivered to the sheriff by Richard Calle in Paston's name on the 29 Aug.

V. Edward IV. to Sir John Markham, Chief Justice of the King's Bench.

[1] [From Paston MSS., B.M.]

116

THE PASTON LETTERS

such jeopardies as by the lawe myght ensue to youre over gret damage, which I ne wold. And of your disposicion herin it like yow I may be certified in writing by the berour herof. And Oure Lord have you in his keping. Wryten at London the xxvij. day of Novembre anno lxiiij[o].

By the Tresorer of Ingland,

SYR WATER BLOUNT.

574

ANONYMOUS TO JOHN PASTON[1]

*To my ryght worshipfull maister and brother,
John Paston, this letter be taken.*

R YGHT worshipfull and reverend mayster and brother, with alle my service I recommaunde me on to yow. Please nit onto your grete wysedom to have yn your descrete remembrauns the streite Ordre on which we ben professid, and on which ze er bownden to kepe your residens,

[1] [From Fenn, iii. 418.] It is difficult to assign with confidence either a date or a meaning to this strangely worded epistle. The signature itself is a mystery. The order of the Temple of Sion is unknown to archæologists, and the place from which the letter is dated cannot be identified. From the peculiar device used as a signature, resembling what in heraldry represents a fountain, Fenn threw out a suggestion that Fountaine was the writer's name, remarking that a family of that name resided at Salle, in Norfolk, and might have been related to Paston as the writer claimed to be. But there seems to be an air of irony about the whole communication which forbids us to construe any of its statements seriously; nor do we find the slightest allusion to this letter or its contents in all the rest of the correspondence. For my part, I am inclined to think it was a mocking letter addressed to John Paston by one of the prisoners in the Fleet, where Paston had himself been confined in 1464. His imprisonment on that occasion was probably of short duration, but I cannot tell the precise date of his release. He was committed to the Fleet, as we are informed by William Worcester (*Itinerary*, p. 366), on Saturday the 3d November. If I am right in my conjecture about this letter, he had, perhaps, been already liberated; but some of his late fellow-prisoners, probably members of the Inner or Middle Temple like himself, who had formed themselves into a fancy 'Order of the Temple of Sion,' amused themselves by speculating on the probability that he was not yet quite clear of the toils of the law, and that he would be obliged to come back and spend Christmas in gaol, among the jolly companions whom he had recently deserted. I may remark that the name of Thomas Babington occurs in Dugdale's *Origines Juridiciales*, p. 163, as having been elected a reader in the Inner Temple in 22 Hen. VII., when he seems to have been an old man; for, owing to his sight failing, he was excused from reading, and John Port, who was afterwards Attorney General, and, later still, Justice of the King's Bench, read in his place.

118

EDWARD IV

—Commands him to make supersedeas upon the exigents. For, as the King understands, Jenney obtained judgment against Paston for £23 : 10s., and William Hogan by the support of Jenney took another action, and obtained a judgment of £16 : 13 : 4 'against conscience and law, as we be informed.' If Paston has delivered to the sheriff any writs of error to send the actions to our court of parliament, he is to comply, according to the usual course in such cases.—Fotheringay, 3 Aug.

VI. Edward IV. to Thomas Croxton, Clerk of the Crown.—Commanding him to search the records and see that the processes of outlawry against John Paston have been well and sufficiently made out.—Reading, 3 Oct.

Memorandum subjoined, 'that William Jenney's counsel hath openly vaunted in Westminster Hall that the King hath sent another letter to the sheriff, commanding him to certify John Paston outlawed.'

* V. and VI. are copies on the same paper.

573

SIR WALTER BLOUNT TO THE
PRIOR OF NORWICH[1]

To the Prior of Norwich.

R EVEREND fader in God, I recomaunde me to you. NOV. 27
And for so muche the Kyngs hyghhnesse is advertysed ye shuld have in . . . .[2] certayn goodes of John Pastons to the value of vij. or viij. m[l] mark wherin the Kyng is entytilled by such processe of owtlawry as is awarded ayenst the said Paston; Wherefor in the Kynges name I charge you that if any such good be in your governance[3] or within your monastery, ye suffer noon of thayme to passe oute of your garde, but suerle to kepe thaym unto the Kynges behouffe, unto ye tyme ye have otherwise in comaundment, as ye will answer at your perille and in eschewing his gret displeasur and

[1] [MS. in Pembroke College, Cambridge.]
[2] A word or two illegible.
[3] So the word seems to have been originally, but the writing is faded, and a modern hand has attempted to restore the beginning as 'no . . .'

117

EDWARD IV

and specially on this tyme of Crystmas amonggis your con- 1464(?)
frerys of this holy Ordre, the Temple of Syon; for ynlesse DEC. 3
than ze kepe dewly the poynts of your holy Religion, owr Maister Thomas Babyngton, maister and soverayn of owr Order of th'assent of his brythryn ben avysed to awarde azenste yow ryght sharp and hasty proces to do calle yow to do your obcervauns, and to obeye the poynts of your Religion, which wer on to me grete hevynesse. Wherfore I, as he that hath most grettest cause, and ys most bownden on to your grete gentylnesse, and also whom nature and kynde most specially byfore every of alle owr breth[r]yn bynden me to owe and wilne yow goode wylle and trewe hert, consyderyng the grete tyme of penawns that ze havyn ben yn fro sone upon Mighelmas hederto, that ys to say, yn relevyng and sustenawns of your evyn Crysten,[1] and also yn the charytable and meritory dede of almyssdoyng, that ys to say yn plenteous and liberall zeftis, which ys more precyusseur than goolde er sylver, which hath nat be at alle tymys to your grete ease, neyther hertis plesauns, but rather to your grete desese and yntollerable peyne. And wher Godds lawe and manys lawe acorden that hit shall nat be lawful to non erthely man to be so lyberall and plenteous of that that God sendith hym, that he sholde so despose hit so that he sholde nowgch have to lyve by; and forasmych as I have perfite knowlich of your freel[2] [frail] and naturall disposiseon so set on to theym that ben nedy and hunggery that of your selfe ze have no myght, neyther power to absteyne and rewle yourself, but also long as God sendith and zevyth yow whereof to dispose and help your evyn Crysten ze most nedis despose hit forth a monggus your evyn Cristen, I conseile yow that yn also hasty and goodely tyme as ze kan to come on to your holy brytheryn that ben of that devowt and clos conversacion, to th'entent that ze myght ben advertysid and lernyd by theym the goode rewle and messur that ze owght and sholde have yn the despociscion and delyng of your almys.

[1] i.e. your fellow-Christians.
[2] Fenn interprets this word *free will*, which I cannot think to be the meaning intended.

119

THE PASTON LETTERS

1464(?)
DEC. 3
And also, sethnys ze haven chosen zow a place yn this seson of Avent, yn which ze have had a resonable leysour and space to do your penauns yn, which drawith fast to a ende; which hath been a convenyent place as for the ceson of the yer; and now hit drawith fast on to Cristmas, on which tyme every trewe Crysten man sholde be mery, jocunde, and glad. And sethnys ther is no place which by lyklyhod of reason ze shulde fynde yn your hert to be so gladde and yocunde yn as ze sholde be yn the place of your profession a mounggis your holy brytheryn; yn which place yn this ceson of the yer hit ys a custumyd to be alle maner of desport, lyke as hit is nat unknowe to your wisse descrescion; wherfore, as my symple reason ledith me your grete descrescion sholde rewle you that ze sholde approche nygh the plase of your holy relegion yn also hasty tyme as ze code er myght, of whos comyng alle your saide bretheryn wolde be glade and fayn, and yn especiall I, your servaunt and brother, lyke as I am most syngguler bownden to th'encresse of your prosperite and welfar, which I shall ever desir with Godds mersy, which have yow undir His blessid and favorable proteccion. Wrytten yn the Temple of Syon, iij^d. day of December, yn grete hast.

By your Servaunt and brother,

120

575

[JOHN PASTON] TO MARGARET PASTON AND OTHERS[1]

To my mastres Margrete Paston, and to my welbelovid Frendis, John Daubeney and Richard Calle.

1465
JAN. 15
I PRAY yow, see to the god governaunce of my housold and guydynge of other thynges touchyng my profite, and that ye, with Daubeney and Richard Calle, and with other such of my frendis and servauntis as can avise yow aftir the mater requireth, wekely take a sad comunecacion of such thynges as be for to do, or oftenner and nede be, takyng avise of the master, and of the viker[2] and Sir Jamis,[3] that is for to say, as well for provision of stuffe for myn howsold as for the gaderyng of the revenew of my livelode or greynes, or for setting awerk of my servauntis, and for the more poletik meane of sellyng and carryng of my malt, and for all other thynges necessari for to be do; and that whanne I come home I have not an excuse, seying that ye spoke to my servauntis and that Daubeney and Calle exskue them that thei wer so besy thei myght not attende; for I woll have my mater so guided that if on man may not attende a nother shall be comaunded to do it; and if my servauntis faile I had lever wage some other man, for a jorny or a season, thanne my mater should be on sped.

As for my livelode, I left with Daubeney a bille of many of my dettis, wherby ye alle myght have be insured whedir ye shulde have sent for silver.

---

[1] [Add. MS. 34,889, f. 15.] The contents of this letter show it to be of the year 1465, when Daubeney and Calle, as we know, were with Margaret Paston (*see* No. 576). Reference is made to the displeasure Sir John Paston had given to both his parents in 1463 (*see* No. 552), and what his mother writes about his return home in May of this year (No. 579) goes to confirm the date. Further proof will be found in the footnote at p. 126.
[2] If this be the vicar of Paston, it was William Warner, who succeeded Robert Williamson in 1464.   [3] James Gloys, the priest.

121

THE PASTON LETTERS

1465
JAN. 15
It liketh me evill to here that my prestis and pore men be onpaiid, and that no mony sent to me more thanne x. markis be Berney of alle this season, and yet therof telle Richard Calle he sent me viii. nobils in goold for v. markis, and that as longe as gold was better payment thanne silver I had nevir so moche gold of hym at onys; and telle hym that I wolle nat that he shall kepe that use, for I trowe my tenauntis have but litell gold to pay.

Also remembir yow in any housold, felaship or cumpany that will be of good rewle, purvyauns must be had that every persone of it be helpyng and furtheryng aftir his discrecion and powyr, and he that woll not do so without he be kept of almes shuld be put out of the houshold or felachep.

Item, where ye desire me that I shuld take your sone[1] to grase, I woll for your sake do the better, and will ye knowe he shall not be so oute of my favour that I will suffir hym to mischefe without he be eftsones his owne defaut. And hough be it that in his presumptuouse and ondiscrete demenyng he gaf bothe me and yow cause of displeasir, and to other of my servauntis ille exaumple, and that also guided hym to alle mennes undirstandyng that he was wery of bidyng in myn hows, and he not insurid of help in any other place; yet that greveth nat me so evill as doth that I nevir coud fele nor undirstand hym poletyk ne diligent in helpyng hym self, but as a drane amongis bees which labour for gaderyng hony in the feldis and the drane doth nought but takyth his part of it. And if this myght make hym to knowe the better hym self and put hym in remembrauns what tyme he hath lost, and hough he hath leved in idelnes, and that he coud for this eschewe to do so heraftir, it myght fortune for his best. But I here yet nevir from no plase that he hath be in of any poletyk demenyng or occupacion of hym. And in the kynges hows he coud put hym self foorth to be in favour or trust with any men of substauns that myght forther hym; nevertheless as for your house and myne I purpose not he shall come there, ner be my will non othir but if [*i.e.* unless] he can do more thanne loke foorth and make a fase and countenauns.

[1] Sir John Paston.

122

1465
JAN. 15
Item, send me word whedir my glasier hath do at Bromholm and at the friers of the South Towne,[1] and whedir he be paiid such mony as I sent home word he shuld be paiid, and if he have do all he must have more mony, but I remembir not certeynly what, till I come home, for I remember nat what his bargeyn was for the werk at the Southtowne. I trowe Mr. Clement can telle, and also fele hym self and send me word. Also that ye and Richard Calle and Daubeney see that Mr. Clement and Mr. Braklee[2] which hath grete nede I wote well, and my prestis and pore men be paiid and also all othir men. And that ye see that I be not callid on for that is my dewte. Also that ye see amongis yow that that is owynge me be not lost ne forborn for lewdnes, for that shall bothe hurt me and do my tenauntis harme. Lete Richard Calle remembir that my fermour of Sweynesthorp is falle in gret dette for defaut of callyng upon but be on [*one*] yere; And I deme that bothe John Willeys and my new fermour of Snaylewell arn like to be in the same case, and peraventure Aleyn of Gresham and other.

Item, remembir yow or evir I had a doo with Fastolffis livelode, whill I toke hede to my livelode my self, it both served myn expenses at home and at London and all other charges, and ye leid up mony in my cofirs every yere, as ye knowe. And I wote well that the payment of my prestis and other charges that I have for Fastolffis livelode is not so gret as the livelode is, thow part therof be in trobill. And thanne consider that I had nought of my livelode for myn expenses at London this twol monyth day; ye may verely undirstand that it is not guided wittely nor discretly; and therfore I pray yow hertly put alle your wittes to gedir and see for the reformation of it. And ye may remembre be this how ye shuld do if this wer yowris alone, and so do now.

And that ye woll remembir I have sent yow all many lettirs touchyng many maters, and also a bille now last by Pecok of erandis, desiryng yow to see hem alle to gedir and send me an answere articlerly; and such as ye can not spede at this tyme,

[1] South Town, Yarmouth, where there was a house of Austin Friars.
[2] Dr. John Brackley, the Grey Friar.

123

THE PASTON LETTERS

1465
JAN. 15

lete hem be sped as sone as ye may, that ye se over my seyd lettiris oft tymes til they be sped.

Item, I remembir that myn heygh at Heylisdon the last yere was spent and wasted fwll recklesly and colored under my shep.[1] I pray yow see that I be not servid soo this yere.

Item, Pecok told me of a fermour that wold have had Mautby Mersh, paying xij. markis as it went afore ; and Richard Calle told me of on [one] that wold pay more. Burgeys paiid me first xij. markis vjs. viijd., and I had the reed and the rushis, and he found the shepherdis hyre in shakke tyme for my fold ; and sithen he brigged awey the shepherdis hyre and thanne the nobill, and I trowe he occupyth ne lenger hym self. And I remembir he told me vij. yere goo that my merssh shuld alwey apeyr [impair] till the prime were past the nombre of xix., and thanne it shuld amend a ix. or x. yers, promittyng me he wold thanne amend my ferme. I praye yowe help to lete it aswell as ye can, rather to hym thanne a nother man if he woll do aswell, and that ye comon with Pecok.

Item, as for the mater that I wrote of to the viker and other goode felaws, desire hem that thei be not to excessive hasty in the mater for non nede, but to do that the may do therin [goodly][2] and wittely as sone as thei may ; And as for the respite of the mater here, lete hem not care therfore. I shall do well ineugh, telle hem ; for certeyn, the mater is in as good case as any such mater was this xx. wynter, as my counsell tellyth me ; but I will be sure of all weyes that I may have, and specially the declaracion of the trought of my mater and of my frendis.

Item, as for the mater athwyx the parson of Mautby, Constantine[3] and the viker of Derham,[4] whedir it were smalle mater or gret I care not, but I am sure that too witnesse which I knowe were apposed therin before a juge spirituall, whech as

[1] Meaning, that the waste was attributed to his sheep.
[2] This word 'goodly' has been lined out, and a very illegible word inserted above it.
[3] Constantine Dalby had been rector of Mautby from 1453 to 1460, and appears also to have held the vicarage of East Dereham from 1451 to 1458. He was succeeded at Mautby by Thomas Howes from 1460 to 1465, and then by Robert Cutler or Cotteler, who must be the 'parson of Mautby' spoken of just before.
[4] Robert Sheringham was vicar of East Dereham from 1458 to 1467.

124

1465
JAN. 15

I suppose was Master Robert Popy or some other ; the viker of Derham can telle, and as I trowe can John Wynter of Mautby, or othir parysshons telle, where the sute was athwyx hem, and I can think it was in the chapitell ; if ye can easely gette me what the witnesse seid, I wold nomore ; but do no gret cost over it.

Item, recomaund me to Master Robert Popy, and telle hym, as for any thyng seid ayens hym in my mater then myn adversaris ment ontrewly, they proved nought but that he is a good man and a worshipfull and a trewe.

Item, if I have any otis beside my stuffe, or may any bye aftir xiiijd., spare not, and take good mesure of bartirre for some other chafers, and send me word hough moch ye may bye.

Item, it is told me ye make no wood, nowther at Caster nor Mautby, wherof I merveyle ; remembir yow we must brenne wood a nodir yere.

Item, I send yow a titelyng that I mad whill I was at home, what malt I had by estimacion set at the lest ; wherfore see that Brigge make a reknyng of his malt, and cast ye my book and loke what ye can amend it ; and apeyre [impair] it shall not if alle folkis have do trewly ; but I suppose fewe of you have take any heed at it as moch as I ded.

Item, I may selle here for vjs. viija. a quarter clene fyed after Royston mesure, whech is lesse thanne the water mesure of London. Cambridge shire malt is here at xs. Cast ye what I may selle of new and old, savyng stuffe for myn hows. Item, to remember that Guton malt must be shipped at Blakeney. Item, Lynstedis malt at Wolcote may be shipped there ; therfore cast amongis yow what malt may best be sold.

Item, if on [one] man may not attende to gader silver, sende a nother, and send me word what hath be reseyved and spent.

Item, that I have an answer of alle my lettirs and of every article in hem.

Item, but if ye make such purvyauns that my prestis be paiid and pore men, beside other charges, and purvey

125

THE PASTON LETTERS

1465
JAN. 15

mony for me beside ; owther ye gadir shrewdly or ellis ye spend lewdly.

Item, I sent a lettir by Rauff Greneakyr to James Gresham and to yow, which he promised me shuld be at Norwich on Wednesday aftir Thwelth day, and therin wer divers maters ; and in especiall of a mater that shuld be in communication on Teusday last past bethwyx Yelverton and Robert Wyngfeld, as in the seid lettir is specifiid. It is so that the seid Robard shall be here within this ij. dayes ; if any thyng ye have aspied of it send me word. Item, yonge Knevet tellith me that he is my good frend, and he is come rydyng homeward on Friday last was. I pray yow, ley wetche whedir ye here any thyng that he medillyth hym at that mater, and send me word ; for I wold understande whedir he wer just and trew or nought, and that do [done] it shall not ligh in his power to hurt me. But take ye hed and inquere and knowe other mennes purpos, and kepe your intent as close as ye can ; and what some evir boost be mad, werk ye wisely and set not by it but send me word what ye here.

Item, Calle sendyth me word that Sir Thomas Howes is seke and not like to askape it, and Berney tellyth me the contrary ; wherfore I pray yow take hed therat, and lete me have knowleche, for though I be not behold to hym I wold not he were ded for more thanne he is worth.

Item, take the viker the bille that I send yow herwyth.

Item, that ye, if ye can fynd the meane, to aspie what goodis Edmond Clere eschetith of any mannes.[1]

Item, remember well to tak heed at your gatis on nyghtis and dayes, for theves, for thei ride in divers contres with gret felaship like lordis, and ride out of on [one] shire in to a nother. Wretyn at London, the Tuisday next aftir Sent Hillary.

Item, that Richard Calle bryng me up mony, so that my prestis [i.e. borrowings] be paiid, and that he come up suerly with other men and attornis.

Endorsed in a later hand :—' Some speciall lettres towching John Paston's trowbells and sute for Fastolfs landis by the Duke of Suffolk.'

[1] Edmund Clere, as appears by evidences in the Record Office, was escheator of Norfolk and Suffolk from November 1464 to November 1465.

126

576

JOHN WYKES TO MARGARET PASTON[1]

Unto my maystres, Margareget Paston, be thys letter delyveryd in hast, &c.

RYGHT wyrshypfull maystres, I recomaund me un to your gode maystresshyp. Please it you to wyte that my mayster your hosbond, my maystres youre moder, my mayster Sir John, Mr. Wyllyam, Mr. Clement, and all ther men, wer in gode helth, whon thys letter was wryten, thankyd be Jesu, and also ther maters be in a gode wey, for my Lord Chaunseler ys ther syngeler gode Lord in thys mater at thys tyme ; and that it provyth, for he was yesterday in the Escheker, and ther he had a foren hym alle the Juges, all the Barons of the Escheker, and all the Shurgents, and ther argued wher that the Barons of the Escheker shold award any such Comyssyon or not, and uppon that the seyd Comyssyon shull be broght uppon Fryday unto the Chaunsery, and ther to be provyd, wher it be lafull or not, &c.

Item, and yf it please it you to gyve Daveney[2] knowlych that ther ys jugement gyven uppon the condempnacion a yenst Hall,[3] that he claymed for hys bond man, and the jugement ys gyven a yenst Daveney, Ric. Call, and Thomas

[1] [From Fenn, iv. 134.] This letter must be later than the year 1463, as Sir John Paston does not appear to have been knighted so early as February in that year. But as John Paston, the father, was at Caister and not at London in the early part of the year 1464, it cannot be that year. Neither can we assign it to 1466, the last year of John Paston's life, as it appears by a letter written on the 17th February in that year that although John Paston was in London, his son Sir John could not have been there for some time before. We are therefore shut up to the year 1465 as the only possible date for this letter.
[2] So in Fenn, but the name ought certainly to be Daubeney, perhaps spelt Dabeney.
[3] Robert Hall. I find that he brought an action in Trinity term, 3 Edward IV., against John Daubeney of Norwich, gentleman, and Thomas Boon and Richard Call of Norwich, yeomen, for having, in conjunction with William Daubeney of Sharyngton, Norfolk, Esq., unlawfully imprisoned him at Norwich for three hours on the 20th February, 39 Hen. VI. (1461), until he gave them a bond of £100 for his ransom.

1465
FEB. 7

127

Bon, and ther ys comen owte proces for to take ther bodys thys same day, and if thay or any of them be taken thay shull never gon oute of prison on to the tyme that they have satesfyed the party of viij** marc, and ther for lete them be ware. And the Holy Trinyte have you in Hys kypyng. Wryten at London, uppon Thursday next after the Purificacion of our Lady, &c.

By your Servaunt,   JOHN WYKS.

577

WILLIAM WORCESTER TO ——— [1]

PLEASE your maistershyp to wete that aftyr recomendacion that I sende Thomas More to myne oncle the parson [2] wyth certeyn credence to hafe aunsuer uppon by hym for myn acquytaille another day, yff onye thyng falle sinistrely only yn theyr deffaut, as God defend, not be my wille, for I hafe as feythfulle demensed me seth I rode to London thys terme, and hedertoo as anye maner creatur yn reson coude desyre me; and hafe demened me at London accordyng to the message sent me by the baylly of Drayton, and I vele but littille that my gode wille ys allowed.[3] I hafe also, seth I came to Norwiche, enformed hym whate proffyt ease and avaylle I may help stand hem both yn my maister godes and yn hys lyvelode; yff he or hys frendys set littille by it, I may nat do wyth all. And the blessed Trinite be with yow, because ye wolle the wellfare off my maister, whoos soule God hafe pytie on and bryng hym owte of peyn, as the wellfare of the parties it meovyth me wryte to yow the rathyr. I enformyd yow for trouth, and as I wille prefe, that I was the

[1] [From Paston MSS., B.M.] In this letter reference is made to a 'testament' drawn up by Sir John Fastolf eight years previously. This, however, cannot be his last will, as that would carry the date to a year after John Paston's death, who seems to be here spoken of as living. The settlement referred to is doubtless the testamentary declaration of 1457 mentioned in No. 541.
[2] Sir Thomas Howes.
[3] i.e. Little credit is given me for my good will.

128

THE PASTON LETTERS

Item, the seyd Edmond seythe, yf he may fynd any other thyng that may do yow ease in that mater he wolle do hys part therin.

Item, Jon Russe sent me word that Barker and Herry Porter told hym in councell that the Duk of Suffolk hathe bowght one Brytyeff ryghte, the wyche makythe a cleyme on to Heylysdon, and the seyd Duke is proposyd to entere within shorte tyme after Esterne, for in so moche the seyd Russe felle be the seyd Barber and Porter that all the feffees wolle make a relees on to the Duk and helpe hym that they can in to her power, for to have hys good lorchep.

Item, yf it please you, me thynkythe it war ryght nessessary that ye send word howe that ye wolle your old malte be purveyed for; for and any hote weder come affter that it hathe leyne this wynter season, it shall be but lost but yf [unless] it be sold be tymys, for as for the pryse [price] here, it is sore falle. I have sold a C. comb of malt that came fro Guton, to Jamys Golbeter, clenefyed, and strek met, and non inmet (?), for ijs. ijd., the comb, and to be payed at Mydsomer and Lammes.

Item, ther be dyvers of your tenantrys at Mauteby that had gret ned for to be reparyd, at [? but] the tenaunts be so por that they ar not a power to repare hem; wherfor yf leke you, I wold that the marche that Bryge had myght be kept in your owne hand this yer, that the tenaunts myght have ruschis to repare with her howsys. And also ther is wynfall wod at the maner that is of noo gret valewe, that myght helpe hem with toward toward the reparacion, yf it leke you to late hem have it that hathe most need therof. I have spoke with Borges

that he shuld heyne [raise] the price of the mershe, or ellis I told hym that he shuld no lenger have it, for ye myght [have] [1] other fermors therto that wold geve therfor as it was late befor, and yf he wold geve therfor as moche as another man wold, ye wold that he shuld have it befor any other man; and he seyd he shuld geve me answer be a fortenyght after Esterne. I can get non other fermor therto yet.

Item, I understand be Jon Pampyng that ye wolle not that

[1] Omitted in MS.

130

---

principall doer and cause that both Maister Paston and myne oncle came fyrst yn the testament viij. yeer goon, to a gode entent; and yff they wold wyrke ayenst me to minussh my power, theyr disposicion woll be construed ferther than they wille it were, and they not so avaylled as they weene yn all thynges. The blessed Trinete be wyth yow. Wryt on Passyon Sonday.

Your W. WYRCESTRE.

Memorandum to Thomas More that because ye myzt foryete myne erand to Maister Bernay, I pray you rede hym my bille, and that he wille take it to a gode entent; for how so evyr I wryte I meene well, and so shall.

578

MARGARET PASTON TO JOHN PASTON [1]

*To my ryght worchepfull hosbond, Jon Paston,
be this deliveryd in hast.*

RIGHT worchefull hosbond, I recomand me to you. Please you to wet that I send you a copy of the deed that Jon Edmonds of Taveram sent to me, be the menys of Dorlet. He told Dorlet that he had suche a deed as he supposyd, that wold don ease in prevyng of the tytyll that the Duk of Suffolk cleymythe in Drayton; for the same deed that he sent me, the seale of armys is lyke onto the copy that I send you, and noo thyng leke to the Duk of Suffolks auncesters.

[1] [From Paston MSS., B.M.] The claims laid by the Duke of Suffolk to Drayton and Hellesden occupy a prominent place in this correspondence during the year 1465, and I do not find them alluded to in any letter of an earlier date. Moreover, the purchase by virtue of which the Duke laid claim to the latter manor, which is reported here as a secret, is mentioned again as a piece of news in a letter undoubtedly written on the 10th May 1465. There can be little doubt therefore that this letter is of the same year. The apostyle, or set of marginal notes appended, is in the handwriting of John Paston.

EDWARD IV

your sone be take in to your hows, nor holpe be you, tylle suche tyme of yere as he was put owt therof, the wiche shall be abowght Seynt Thomas messe.[1] For Gods sake, sir, a pety on hym; remembre yow it hathe bed a long season syn he had owt of your to helpe hym with, and he hathe obeyed hym to yow and wolle do at all tymis, and wolle do that he can or may to have your good faderood. And at the reverence of God be ye hys good fader, and have a faderly hert to hym; and I hope he shall ever knowe hymselff the better here after, and be the more ware to exchewe suche thyngs as shuld dysplease you, and for to take hed at that shuld please you. Pecoke shalle telle you be mothe of more thyngs than I may write to you at this tyme. The blyssyd Trinite have you in Hys kepyng. Wretyn at Caster in hast, the Monday next after Palme Sonday.   Your M. P.

579

MARGARET PASTON TO JOHN PASTON [2]

*To my ryght wyrshypfull husband, John Paston,
be thys delyveryd in hast.*

RYGHT wyrshipful husband, I recomaunde me unto you. Pleasyd you to wyte that I have spokyn thys wyke wyth dyvers of youre tennaunts of Drayton and put hem in comfort that all shalbe well hereafter by the grace

[1] This might be the translation of St. Thomas the Martyr, 7th July, or St. Thomas Apostle's Day, 21st December; but most probably it means the day of St. Thomas à Becket, 29th December.
[2] [From Paston MSS., B.M.] Holy Rood Day, on which this letter is dated, commonly means the 14th of September (feast of the Exaltation of the Holy Cross). Here I suspect it is the 3rd May (Invention of the Holy Cross), as the contents of the letter suit that date in the year 1465. It will be seen that Margaret Paston dates from Caister, and proposes next week to be at Hellesden. Her next letter, dated the 10th May, is from Hellesden, and shows that she carried out the intention here expressed of sending men to collect money at Drayton, and had left her eldest son at Caister to keep the place. There is also a close agreement between that letter and this, in what is said about the demeanour of the tenants and Mr. Philip's conduct. The apostyle of this letter, as of the preceding, is in the hand of John Paston, very ill written, and occasionally ambiguous.

131

1465
MAY 3

of God; and I fyle well by hem that they wylbe ryght glad to have ayen there olde mayster, and so wold they all except j. or ij. that be fals shrewys. And thys next wyke I purpose on Wensday or Thursday to be at Haylesdon, and to a byde ther a wyke or ij., and send oure men aboute to gedere money at Drayton and Haylesdon; and yf ye wyll I woll do kepe a corte at Drayton or I com thens. I pray yow send me word how ye wyll that I doo there in. I recevyd ij. letters from you of Nicholl Tolman yesterday, werin ye desyre that we shuld purvey for your malte and barley; and soo shall we doo as well as we cann, and send you word howe that we may doo therewith in hast.

Malt,
barly.

Item, yesterday Master Phylyp[1] toke Dorlets hors upon Drayton lond as they went to the plowe for the hole yere ferm; and as it ys told me the tenaunts of Drayton tolde hym that he dyde hym wrong to make hym pay for the hole yere, for non of the tenaunts had payd hym but for the di' [half] yere and he say thohg they had not payd but for the di' yere, Paston shuld pay for the other di' yere, and for moo yers also yf he lyvyd. But I trow to gyte Dorlet ayen hys hors or els Mr. Phylyp ys lyke to be unhorssyd ons, and we lyve all. Your son[2] shall com hom to moryn, as I trowe, and as he demenyth hym hyr after I shall lete you have knowlych; and I pray you thynk not in me that I wyll supporte hym ne favour hym in no lewdnesse, for I wyl not. As I fynd hym hereafter, soo I wyll lete you have knowlych. I have put your evydens that com owte of the abbay[3] in a seck and enseylyd hem under Ric. Call ys seall that he shal not say but they eryn as he left hem; but as for the place where they ern kypt he hath no knowlych . . . .

Dorlat et
verba
M.P.

J. P., sen.

Rotuli
prioris (?)

. . . . As for the gentylwoman that ye wrote to me for yn youre lettere, I . . . . there, yf it lykyd all folks as well as it shold doo me, I trow . . . . a bowte yf her frends were as well a gryed therto, and as they . . . . parte,

[1] Philip Lipgate, the Duke of Suffolk's bailiff.
[2] Sir John Paston.
[3] See No. 561.

132

1465
MAY 3

yf ye wyll that it be movyd of more hereafter I wyll . . . . wyll make a newe parson, at Drayton. Also it ys sayd that . . . . there, by cause it hath stond so long voyd; yet and any sh. . . . . had lever that he com in by the Byshop then by a . . . . doo therein. yf ye wyll send hom any presentacion selyd . . . . we shall a say to gyte som gode priste and sette hym . . . . Wryten in haste at Caster on Holy Rode Day &c.
As . . . . doo therein as well as I cann. I have gyte a replevyn . . . . CC shype, and yf they may not be hadde ayen, then he grau[nteth] . . . . We fynd hym ryght gode in that we desyre of him for you, and therfore yf it lyke you I wold he were th . . . .

Data
obliga-
cione (?)
pro ovibus

580

JOHN RUSSE TO JOHN PASTON[1]

To the right worshipfull sir, my right honourabyll maister, John Paston, at London.

RIGHT worshipfull sir and my right honorabyll maister, I recomaund me to you in the most humble wise. And please youre maistir ship to wete that my maistresse hathe dyverse tymes spokyn to me to helpe to purvey a merchaunt for sum of youre malt; but in good feyth I can gete no man that wyll geve at the most more than xxij d. for a quarter, for soo men selle dayli at the moste, and sumtyme xx d. a combe. My maistresse is right hevy therfor, but I can not remedy it; if ony good marchaunt were there, after my sympil conseyt it were good to take hym, for the yeer passith faste and the [feldes][2] be right plesaunt to wards, &c. Sir, at

MAY 6

[1] [From Paston MSS., B.M.] As this letter refers to the Duke of Suffolk's claim to the manor of Drayton, the date must be 1465. The original MS. is mutilated to some extent in both margins.
[2] The tops of the letters f, l, d visible.

133

1465
MAY 6

the reverence of Jesu, laboure the meanys to have peas; for be my trowth the contynwaunce [of this] trobill shall short the dayez of my maistresse, and it shall cause you to gret losse, for serteyn she is in gre[t hevi]nesse as it apperith at . . . . ll covertly she consederith the gret decay of youre lyflode, the gret detts that hange in detours hands and h . . . . [she speaket]h not thus to me, but I conceyfe this is cause of here gret hevynesse; me semyth of ij. hurts the leste is mos[t] . . . . well the dayli contynewyng maleyse of youre insessiabyll enemyes, how they contryve and seke occacions to . . . . informyd, more wyll doo every foot of grownd withinne fewe dayez, and rather to geve it awey for nowght tha[n] . . . . . . it. Where as they many tymes have meovyd a trety and never it taketh to noo conclucion, and as they have seyd in youre d . . . . . . Sir, after my sympyll conseyt it were well doon to agree to a trety, and be that ye shuld knowe ther desyre and the uttir . . . . . . the lond were dubyll the valwe that it is. Worsestyr shewyth hem presedents what every maner cost at the fyrst byeng, and ther . . . . rekne the bargeyne shuld avayle you foure tymes mor than it shall; and in thys they be gretly blyndyd; my maister the parson hathe . . . . . to rellesse in serteyn londs whiche he refus[eth to] doo, but I conseyve, and ye drawe not to a conclucion thys terme that he wyll be as redy to rellesse . . . . men, truste ye thys for serteyn; and soo he [told] me serteynly. He hathe be meovyd to revoke Maister Roberd Kente and to take the avoket or proctor [that] Maister Yelwirton hathe. What it myght hurtyn if he soo dede I knowe not, but they have made gret labour to hym therfor. He gaf me a gret reb[uke] . . . . the bill that was put in ayens Elyse Davy and otheris, to whiche I answeryd hym as me thowght and soo in maner made my peas, &c. Maister . . . . . . was here and in presence of men of the most substance in Jeremuth he be havyd hym to you wards in full goodly termys, soo God helpe . . . . and after my conseyt he wyll not be redy to relesse in ony of

134

1465
MAY 6

the londs. A man of hyse teld me secretly that Maister Yelwyrton and otheres blamyd hym and seyd . . . . to hym be cause he was so redy be hym self to agree to trete and make hyse peas with yow, neyther he seyd to me to trete nor the contrary nor had but langwage to me as he had to othyr. I askyd my maister the parson if he undyrstod that Maister Yelwyrton yaf ony favour to my Lord of Suffolk in Drayton, and he seyd he supposyd Maister Yelwyrton was not cler of that mater, but Mayster Jenney was in nowyse pleasyd with all, &c. Sir, as for the wytnesse that were desyred to be redy whan nede requirith in thys mater, R. Calle can avertise youre maistirshyp. Sir, at the reverence of Jesu consedre how many yeers it is past that my good lord and maister deseasyd and how lytill is doon for . . . . . of the grete substaunce that he hade it is hevy to remembre; ye sey the defaute is not in yow after your conseyt, but I can here no . . . . in that of youre openyon, for thys I knowe for serteyn and it had pleasyd you to have endyd be the meanys of trety, ye had ma[de] . . . peas to the gret well of the dede with the forthe part of the mony that hathe be spent, and as men sey only of very wylful[nesse of your] owyn person. For the mercy of God remembre the onstabylnesse of thys wold hou it is not a menut space in comparyson to ever . . . . leve wylfullnesse whyche men sey ye occupye to excessifly. Blyssyd be God ye had a fayre day laste whiche is noysyd cost yow . . . . to iiij. lords, but a newe mater anewe cost and many smale growe to a gret summe, and summe mater on recurabyll, formen seyd . . . is lyk to stonden in a perplextif if ye take not a conclucion in haste, and if it were doo it were hard to have recovery; but as my [maister] the parson seyd, thys terme they wyll prove if ye wyll agree to trete, and if ye refuse they all wyll do the uttirmest. I conseyve well [your] maistirshyp hathe a conseyt that if a man of good will meove yow or remembre you to trete, that that man, what soo ever he be, shuld be meovyd be youre adversaryez to meove you in that mater, and soo in that it hertyth you gretly that they shuld seke to you for peas. Be my trowth, sir, there was nor is no man, savyng onys, as

135

1465
MAY 6

I teld you, Maister Jenney spake to me, that ever I knewe wold seke or feythefully desyre to have peas with yow, savyng because of the exspence of the good so onprofitably in the lawe, and that is the prynsypal cause of meovyng of ther peas, &c. I wold well God helpe me soo it grevyth me to here that ye stonde in no favour with jentylmen nor in no gret awe with the comowns. Ye truste the jury of Suffolk; remembre what promyse Daubeney hade of the jury and what it avaylid; it is a dethe to m[e] to remembre in what prosperite and in what degre ye myght stonde in Norfolk and Suffolk and ye had peas and were in herts ease, and what worshyp my maisters your sones and my maistresse youre douters myght have be preferryd to if ye had be in reste. A day lost in idyll can never be recoveryd, &c. Sir, I beseke youre maistershyp for yeve me that I wryte thus boldly and homly to you; me thynkyth my hert . . . . not be in ease but if I soo doo, for ther was, nor never shal be, no mater that ever was soo ner myn herte, that knowy[th God,] whom I beseke for Hese infenyt mercy preserve you and my maistresse and all youres from all adversyte and graunt yow . . . . herts desyre. Wretyn at Jernemuthe the vj. day of may.

Your contynw[al bedesman]
and servaunt, JOHN [RUSSE].

581

MARGARET PASTON TO JOHN PASTON [1]

To my mayster, John Paston the oldest be thys delyveryd.
in hast.

MAY 10

RYGHT wyrshypfull husbond I recomaund me unto you. Pleysed you to wyte that on Wensday last passyd Dabeney, Naunton, Wykes and John Love werr at Drayton for to speke with your tenaunts ther to put hem iu

[1] [From Paston MSS., B.M.] The date of this letter is rendered certain by the mention of Thomas Ellis as having been elected Mayor of Norwich. He was so elected for the second time in 1465. He had been Mayor before in 1460-61, and was again after this in 1474-75; but neither of these latter dates will suit the other contents of this letter. Like some others of this year, this letter is apostyled by John Paston.

comfort and for to aske money of hem also. And Pyrs Waryn, otherwyse callyd Pyrs at Sloth, whych ys a flykeryng felowe and a besy with Mr. Phylyp and the Bayly of Cosshay, he had a plowe goyng in your lond in Drayton, and ther your seyd servaunts at that tyme toke hys plowe ware, that ys to say ij. marys, and broght hem to Heylysdon, and ther they be yet. And on the next mornyng after Mr. Phylyp and the Baylly of Cosshay com to Haylysdon with a grete nomber of pepell, that ys to say viij.ᵡᵡ men and mor in harnysse, and ther toke from the persons plowe ij. hors, pris iiij. marc and ij. hors of Thomas Stermyns plowe, pris xls., saying to hem that ther was taken a playnt ayenst hem in the hunderd by the seyd Pyrs for takyng of the forseyd plowarre at Drayton, and but they wold be bond to com to Drayton on Tewysday next comyng to awnswer to such maters as shalbe sayd to them ther they shold not have ther bests ayens; whych they refusyd to do on to the tyme that they had an awnswer from you; and so they led the bestes forth to Drayton, and from Drayton forth to Cosshay. And the same after none folwyng the parson of Haylesdon send hys man to Drayton with Stermyn for to speke with Mr. Phylyp to know a waye yf they shuld have ayen ther cattell or not; and Master Phylyp awnsweryd them yf that they wold bryng home ther destresse ayen that was taken of Pyrs Waryn, that then he wold dylyver hem thers, or els not; and he lete hem playnly wyte that yf ye or any of your servaunts toke any dystresse in Drayton that were but the valew of an hen, they wold com to Haylesdon and take ther the valew of an ox therefore, and yf they cannot take the valew therof there, that then they wyll do breke your tenaunts howsys in Haylesdon, and take as moch as they cowd fynd therein; and yf they be lettyd therof, wych shall never lye in your power for to do, for the Duck of Suffolk ys abyll to kepe dayly in hys hows more men then Dabeney hadde herys on hys hede, yf hym lyst; and as for Dabeney he ys a lewde felowe, and so he shalbe servyd herafter, and I wold he were here. And therfore yf ye take uppon you to lette them so for to do, that then they wold goo in to any lyflode that ye had in Norfolk or Suffolk, and to take a destresse in lykewysse

1465
MAY 10
Petr'.
Warin.

Distr'
Sturmyn
et rectoris
de Heylis-
don.

Crak.

1465
MAY 10

Accio
rectoris et
sturmyn.

as they wold do at Haylysdon. And other awnswerr cowde they non gyte, and so they departyd. Ric. Calle axid the parson and Stermyn yf they wold take an accyon for ther catell, and the parson [1] seyd he was agyd and syklow, and he wold not be trobelyd herafter; he sayd he had lever lose hys catell, for he wyst well yf he dyde so he shold be endytyd, and so vexid with hem that he shold never have rest by hem. As for Stermyn, he sayd at that tyme he durst not take no sute ayenst hem nother; but after that Ric. was rydyn, I spake with hym, and he sayd he wold be rulyd as ye wold have hym, and I fond hym ryght herty and wel dysposyd in that mater; and he is bownde to you an obligacyon of xli. sengyll with outen condycyon that he shall abyde by such accyons as shalbe takyn by your advyse in hys name; wherfore I have send you a tytelyng therof in a byll closyd herin. I axyd Thomas Gryne avyse when they had take the dystresse hyre, and he avysyd me that herre destresse shold be delyveryd a yen to them so that we myzt have ayen ours; and me thoght it was non awnswer after myn entent, and wold not therof but axyd avyse of Skypwith what hym thoght that were best to doo there in, and most wyrshypfull. He seyd by hys avyse that I shold send to you in al the hast that I cowde, and that ye shuld fynde a mene therfore above, by the avyse of youre lernyd counsell to have a wrytte from above for to delyver yt of lesse then the undershyrff werre other wysse dysposyd to you then we fynde hym, for it symyth that he ys made of the other party. And as for the replevyn for the CC. shype ys not yet servyd. Skypwith thynkyth that ye myzt have a wrytte both for the shype and the destresse now taken at Haylysdon, I pray you that ye wyll send word in hast how [ye] woll that we doo in thys mater. Skypwith went with me to the Byshop of Norwych, and I lyte hym have knowlych of the ryotous and evyll dysposycyon of Master Phylyp, desyryng hys Lord-shyp that he wold see a mene tha[t] a correccyon myzt be

Replevin.

Episcopus
Norwic'.

[1] Thomas Hert, perhaps a relation of the Bishop of Norwich, was presented to the rectory of Hellesden by Sir John Fastolf in 1448, but how long he held it is uncertain, as the list of rectors is very defective, and the next name that appears on it is George Gardiner in 1579.

hadde, in as moch as he was chef Justic of the Peas and hys ordynare, and inasmoch as he was a prest [1] and under hys correccyon that he shold have understondyng of hys dysposi-cyon; and I made Dabeney to tell hym all the mater howt it was; and he seyd he wold send for hym and speke with hym. And he told me of dyvers thyngs of the demenyng of hym, wherby I understode he lykyd not by hys dysposicyon nor demenyng in thys mater nor in no nothyr; for it symyd he had provyd hym what he ys in other maters. My lord seyd to me that he wold ryght fayn that ye had a gode conclusyon in your maters, and seyd by hys trouth, that he ought you ryght gode wyll, and wold ryght fayn that ye wer com home, and seyd to me that it shold be a grete comfort to your frends and neghbors, and that your presens shold do more amongs hem, than a C. of your men shold do in your absens, and more, your enmys wold ferr to do ayens you yf ye myght be at home, and steryng amonges hem, and seyd full playnly in meny other thyngs it wer to long to wryte at thys tyme, as Skypwith shall tell you when he comyzt to you. I pray you thanke Skypwith of hys gode wyll, for he was ryght well wyllyd to go with me and yeve me hys avyse, me thynkyth he ys ryzt well wyllyd to you.

Item, I pray you send hastely word how tʰᵃᵗ ye wyll that we be gydyd with thys place, for as it ys told me, it ys lyke to stond in as grete jupardy in hast as othere don. On Thursday al day there were kept in Draton logge in to lx. persons, and yet as it ys told me, ther be within dayly and nyztly in to a xvj. or xx. persons.

Item, it ys told me that Thomas Elys of Norwych, whych nowe ys chosyn Mayer, seyd at Drayton that yf my Lord of Suffolk nede a C. men he wold purvey hym therof, and yf any men of the town wold go to Paston he wold do lay hem faste in prison. I wold youre men mygh have a *supersedias* [3] owte of the chauncere, and be owte of the danger of ther men here; and I pray you let not Wyll Naunton be foryete therin.

1465
MAY 10

Episcopus
Norwic'.

Skipwith.

Per'
Heyl'd.[2]

Elys.

Super-
sedeas.

Ric. Naunton.

[1] Philip Lepeyate was presented to the rectory of Salle in Norfolk, in 1460, by Thomas Brewse, Esq., afterwards father-in-law of John Paston, the youngest.
[2] *i.e.* Periculum Heylesdon.
[3] So in MS.

THE PASTON LETTERS

1465
MAY 10

Calle and other can tell you of hys demenyng ; and I pray you that ye be not dysplesyd for his abydyng with me, for in gode feth he hath ben a grete comfort to me syn ye departyd hens, as I wyll lete you wyte hereafter. I pray you yf hys brother com to you for a relesse of hys londe, lette him non have on to the tyme that ye see hys faderes wyll, the whych I wote wher it ys, and that it like you to desyre hym to be gode brother to him.

J. Paston at Castre. M. P. at Heylisdon.

Item, I have left John Paston the older at Caster, to kype the place there, as Ric. can tell you; for I had lever, and it pleasyd you, to be captensse here then at Caster; yet I was nothyng purposyd to abyde here when [I] come from home but for a day or ij., but I shall abyde here tyll I here tydyngs from you.

Brightled.

Item, it ys told me that the Duck of Suffolk hath boght or shal by in hast the ryzt that on Bryghtylhed hath in Haylesdon, &c.

Evidens. Pekering.

Item, as for the evydens that Watkyn Shypdam hadd, he delivered to hys wyffe a box enselyd with hys owyn seall by hys lyffe for to be delyveryd to you, whych box she delyveryd to Ric. Call under the same seall after hys dessesse. Ric. can tell you of the gydyng of the cofere with other boks that were

Evidens. Norwic'.

at Shypdams. And as for all your other evydens ye ther not feer as for the syzt of hem, for ther hath nor shall no man sen hem tyll ye com hom. I can not fynd that ye send to me fore to have oute of the rolle.

Colt. Malt.

Item, I here no word of Colte of New Castell, nor of no nother from you that shold have your malte, but I have spoken to the Viker, John Rus and Robert Boteler, to help for to sell your malte, and as we can do therein, we shall send you word.

Præpositus de [Cantab].¹

The Provest of Cambrygge ys com into thys contry and Dabeney shall receve of hym that longyth to you on Monday or Tewysday, and he shall have hys delyveryd accordyng to your wrytyng.

Mater. Clere.

Item, my moder told me that she thynkyth ryght strange that she may not have the profects of Clyre ys place in peasabyll wyse for you, she seyt it ys hers and she hath payd most ther-

¹ This word is left blank by Paston.

140

EDWARD IV

1465
MAY 10

fore yet, and she sayth she wyll have the profects therof, or ells she wyll make more folk to speke therof. She seyth she knowyt not what ryght ne titell that ye have therin but yf ye luste to trobell with herre, and that shold be no wyrshep to you ; and she sayth she wylbe ther thys somer and repayre the housyng ther. In gode feyth I hyre moch langage of the demenyng betwene you and herre. I wold ryght fayn, and so wold many moo of youre frendes, that it were otherwyse bytwene you then it ys, and yf it were I hope ye shold have the beter spyde in all other maters. I pray God be your gode spyde in all your maters, and yef yow grace to have a gode conclusyon of hem in haste for thys ys to wyry a lyffe to a byde for you and all youre. Wryten in haste at Haylysdon the x. day of May.

The cause that I send to you this hastely ys to have an awnswer in haste from you.

> Your M. P.

582

MARGARET PASTON TO JOHN PASTON¹

To my ryght wyrshypfull mayster, John Paston the oldest, be this delyveryd in haste.

I RECOMAUND me, &c.

MAY 13

Yf it pleasyd you, I wold ryght fayn that John Jenney werre putte oute of the Comyssyon of the Peas, and that my brother Wyll. Lumner wer set yn hys stede, for me thynkyth it wer ryght necessere that ther were such a man

¹ [From Fenn, iv. 164.] There can be little doubt this letter was written in the year 1465, when Margaret was troubled by Mr. Philip Lipgate and the Duke of Suffolk's bailiff of Cossey. It may be observed also that Margaret here dates from Hellesden, and speaks of having been recently at Caister. Compare Nos. 579 and 581. Further, the name of John Jenney is found on the Commission of the Peace for Norfolk, dated the 1st April 1465 (Patent, 5 Edward IV., p. 1, m. 32), but it is not on the commission issued on the 20th February following (ib., m. 27); so that John Paston seems to have acted on his wife's suggestion and been successful in getting him removed.

141

THE PASTON LETTERS

1465
MAY 13

in that county that oght you gode wyll, and I knowe verely he owyth you ryght gode wyll ; he was with me at Caster but late. Yf ther be made any labour for Doctour Alyn to be Justice of the Peas, I pray you for Gods sake let it be lettyd yf ye may, for he wyll take to moch upon hym yf he werr. I wold not that he wer remembyrd of your parte but yf [unless] he be spokyn of of other parts : he ys ryght grete with Master Phylyp Lypzate and the Baylyf of Coshay.

Yf it please yow to wyte that Wyks dyde a reste one Wyll. Dylmyn of Norwych, as Pampyng can enforme you of, for sertyn harnys wych he delyveryd hym at New Castell for to cary to Yarmoth by water, and ther to delyver it to hym ayen ; whych harnys he kypt styll, and may not be delyveryd ; and now ther ys com down an *habeas corpus* for hym, and most appyr at the Comyn Place [*Common Pleas*] on Fryday next comyng. Wherfor yf it pleasyd you that ther myght be taken an accyon in Wyks name of trespas under such forme as ther may be a *capias* a wardyd a yenst hys comyng ; for after that he was arestyd he dyde Daubeney to be mayntenyng ; and as for the harnys Wyks delyveryd it to hym the x. day of Januar, the ij. yer of Kyng E.¹ in Pylgryme strete, at New Castell : Inprimis, a peyr brygandyrs, a salet, a boresper, a bawe, xviij. arwys, ij. payr polronds [*shoulder pieces*], a standard of mayle, a payr slyvys of plate, to the valew of v. marc. And at the reverens of God, slowth not your maters nowe, and make any end of hem, other purvey you to make hym or to marre hem in haste, for thys ys to orybyll a coste and trobell that ye have and have had, for to endur any whyle, and it ys grete hevenys to your frends and welwyllers, and grete joy and comfort to your enemmyes. My Lord of Norwych seyd to me that he wold noth abyde the sorow and trobell that ye have abyden, to wyn all Sir John Fastolf ys gode. And God be your spede in all yor maters. Wryten at Haylesdon the xiij. day of May.

I thynk ryght long to hyr tydyngs tyll I have tydyngs from you.

> Your M. P.

¹ A.D. 1463. This was at the time the King was in the north, when Alnwick Castle surrendered to him.

142

EDWARD IV

583

MARGARET PASTON TO JOHN PASTON¹

To my ryght wyrshypfull husbond, John Paston, by thys delyvery[d] in hast.

PLEASE it you to wyte that on Satourday last your

1465
MAY 20

servaunts Naunton, Wyks, and other, wer at Drayton, and ther toke a dystresse for the rent and ferm that was to pay, to the nomber of lxxvij. nete, and so broght them hom to Hayllesdon, and put them in the Pynfold, and so kept hem styll ther from the seyd Satour day mornyng un to Monday,² at iij. at clok at after non. Fyrst on the same Satour day the tenants folwyd uppon, and desyryd to have ther catell ayen ; and I awunsweryd hem, yf they wold do pay such dewts as they oght for to pay to you, that then they shold have ther catell delyveryd ayen ; or els yf they wer not a power to pay redy money, that then they to fynd suffycyant suerty to pay the money at such a day as they mygh agrye with me, and therto to be bonden to you by obligacyon ; and that they seyd they durst not for to take uppon hem for to be bonden, and as for money they had non for to pay at that tyme, and therfor I kept stylle the bestys.

Harleston was at Norwych, and send for the tenants the seyd Satour day at after non, and ther, by the menys of the Bayllyf of Coshay, put the tenants in such feer, sayng that yf they wold pay such dewts, or els for to be bonden to pay, that then they wold put hem owte of such londs as they huld bondly of the Lordshyp, and so to dystrayn hem and trobell hem, that they shuld be wery of ther part ; and that put hem [in] such feer that they drust nother pay nor be bonden.

And on the same day at evyn-song time Harleston com to

¹ [From Fenn, iv. 200.] A comparison of this letter with No. 581 will leave no doubt that they were both written in the same year.
² This was the day the letter was written.

143

465
AY 20

me to Haylesdon, desyryng me that I wold delyver a yen the seyd dystresse; and as for such dystressys as they had taken here of your tenants shold be delyveryd a yen in lyke forme; and I seyd I wold not delyver hem soo, and I told hem that I wold delyver hem as ys wryten a fore and other wyse not, and other wyse I wold not delyver hem but by the form of lawe. And other comynycacyon was had by twene us at that tyme of dyvers maters whych wer to long to wryte at thys tyme, but ye shall have knowlych therof in hast.

And on Monday next after at ix. at clok ther com Pynchemor to Haylesdon with a replevyn,[1] whych was made in Harleston ys name as Understewerd of the Duche [Duchy], sayng that the bests were taken upon the Duche Fee, wherfor he desyryd me to mak hym levery of the seyd bests so taken; and I seyd I wold not delyver hem on to the tyme that I had examenyd the tenants of the trough [truth]. And so I send theder Wyks with Pynchemor to understond what they wold say; and the tenants seyd that ther was taken non upon the Duche at ther knowlych, save only Pyrs Warryn the yonger. And Paynter seyd that ther catell was taken upon the Duche, whych they connot prove by non record, save only by ther awyn sayng; and so we wold not a bey that replevyn, and so they departyd. And at iij. at clock at after non Pynchemor come to Haylysdon a yen with ij. men, whych broght with hem a replevyn from the Shyryff, whos namys be John Whytherley and Robert Ranson, whych requyryd me by the same replevyn to make them delyvery of the seyd bestys taken at Drayton; and so I, syyng the Shyryffs replevyn and under hys seale, bade my men delyver hem, and soo they wer delyveryd.

And as for all other maters that ye have wretyn to [me] of, I wyll spede me to send you a awnswer as hastely as I may, for I may no leysor have to wryte no more to you thys tyme. The blyssyd Trynyte have you in His kepyng. Wryten at Haylesdon, the xx. day of May.

By yours,　　M. P.

[1] This is a writ for restitution of cattle that have been distrained or impounded. It was commonly granted by the sheriff on security being given that the party would bring the matter to an issue at law.

584

MARGARET PASTON TO JOHN PASTON[1]

To my ryght wyrshypfull husbond, John Paston,
be thys delyveryd in haste.

1465
MAY 27

RYGHT wyrshypfull husbonde, I recomaunde me to you. Please it you to wyte that I have send to Master John Smyth and to Master Stephyn to have a vyse for the church of Drayton; and they send me word that ther moste be had a comyssion from the Byshop to calle in the person Flowredew,[2] and that most be proclaymyd in the church of Drayton iij. tymes by a Deen,[3] and after that yff he appyre not with in vj. monthys after the fyrst proclamacion, that then he for to be depryvyd, and the patron to present whom he luste, and ells your presentacyon ys not sufficyant. And I have so purveyd that a comyssyon ys hadde, and shal be servyd as hastely as it may be.

As for John Rysyng, I have sent to hym to wyte the cause that he ys not broght up to London, and he sayth that he callyd upon the Shyrff that he myght be had up for [to] com to hys awnswer, and the Shyrff told hym that he wold not bryng hym up at hys owyn coste; and John Andres seyd that he wold not have hym up, and so he ys styll in prison at Ipswych; and so shall he be but yf ye canne fynde the beter mene for to have hym oute. I have sent to hym xiij[s.] iiij[d.] to help hym sylf ther with; he payth for hys borde wykely xx[d.] And Hopton and Smyth be ther styll allso, and they have money ynogh, wher som ever that they have it. Rysyng

[1] [From Fenn, iv. 206.] What is said here about the tenants of Hellesden and Drayton, and about Master Philip Lipyate, leaves no doubt that this letter was written in 1465. It contains, moreover, a distinct reference to Letter 582.
[2] John Flowerdew was instituted to the Rectory of Drayton on the 15th of March 1461, on the presentation of John Paston, Esq., and Thomas Howes, Clerk.—F.
[3] This means the Rural Dean, who had a district of ten churches in the country, wherein he exercised a jurisdiction of great advantage to ecclesiastical discipline, and the sentences of superior Ecclesiastical Courts were to be executed by him.—F.

1465
MAY 27

dymeth that they have confort of the other party; and I send you a copy of the warant that they wer a restyd by, &c.

I spake not with my moder syn Rychard Calle broght me the letter from you tochyng her mater, for I myght have no lesor. While I speke with her at leysure I wyll remember her in that mater, acordyng to your wrytyng. And as for your tenants of Drayton, as I canne understond by hem, they be ryght gode and trew hertyd to you to ther powers, and full fayn wold that ye had it a yen in peasse, for they had as leffe al most be tenants to the Devell as to the Duke, except Wyll. Herne, Pers at Sloth, and on Knott of the same towne, for they be not gode.

All your tenants at Haylesdon and Drayton, except thes iij., be ryght glad that we err ther a mongs hem, and so be many other of our olde nebers and frends; and but yf [unless] ye com hom by Wensday or Thursday[1] in Wytson wyke, I purpose me to ssee you in secrete wyse by Trynyte Sonday,[2] but yf [unless] ye send to me contrary comaundement er that tyme; and I pray you send me yeur avyse how ye wyll that we doo a yenst the next shyr, whych shulbe the Monday next after Trynyte Sonday, as for callyng upon the replevyn that the bests of Drayton wer delyveryd by.

Item, Richard Calle told me that ye desyryd to have Master Phylyp ys name, and hys name ys Phylyp Lypzeate, and I send you a letter[3] by Henre Wylton ys man, wherin I wrote Master Phylyp ys name; and in the same letter I wrote to you for Wyll. Lumnor. I pray you send me word yf ye have it. And the Blysshyd Trynyte have you in Hys kypyng. Wryten the Monday next after Assencyon Day.[4]

By yours,　　M. P.

[1] 5th or 6th of June.　　　　[2] 9th of June.
[3] No. 582.　　　　　　　　　[4] 23rd of May.

585

MARGARET PASTON TO JOHN PASTON[1]

To my ryght wyrshypfull husbond, John Paston,
be thys letter delyveryd.

1465
JUNE 11

RYGHT wyrshypfull husband, I recomaunde me unto you. Please it you to wyte that I recevyd letters from you on Wensday laste passyd, the were wryten the Monday next before, wherof I thanke you of the letter that ye send to me. I wolde fayn doo well yf I cowde, and as I canne I wol doo to youre pleasure and profet; and in such thyngs as I cannot skyle of, I wyll take a vyse of such as I know that be youre frendes and doo as well as I canne. Wher as ye wrote to me that I told hym that the Ducks men werre not so besy as they had be by fore, no more thay were not at that tyme, but sythen thay have be bysyer. What confort that thay have I canne not have no knowlych as yet, but I suppose and all your felshyp were gode, thay shold not have so grete confort as they have, or ells they wold not be so besy as thay have be. Grete bost thay make that the Duck shold have Drayton in peas, and after thys Haylesdon, and that with in short tyme; thay er moch the bolder, I suppose, by cause that ye be wher as ye be. At the reverens of God, yf ye may by any wyrshypfull or resonabell mene, com oute therof as sone as ye may and come home amonges your frends and tennaunts, and that shold be to hem the grettyst confort that thay myzt have and the contrary to your enmys.

It ys sayd here that the Duck of Suffolk shall com to Coshay in haste and logge ther for a season; I fyle well by your tenaunts that yf ye were peaseabyly possessyd and your cort holden in peaseabyll wyse, and that they myzt be in pease

[1] [From Paston MSS.] This letter, in which it is anticipated that the Duke of Suffolk will obtain possession, first of Drayton, and then of Hellesden, is evidently a little later in date than Nos. 578 and 581, and can only be of the year 1465.

THE PASTON LETTERS

1465
JUNE 11

a yenst the other many, than they wold take accyons a yenste hem for such wrongs as have be don to hem, and ells they say that they thernot [*dare not*] take it uppon hem, for they dwelle so ney to the other many that thay knowe well thay shold never be in ease yf thay dyde soo whyle that thay dele amongs hem. On Thursday last John Doket, the bayly ys son y lawe, and Thomas Ponte, with other, erly in the mornyng, an owre by fore the sonne rose, com to your fold, and drove away the flock at Drayton, both Colyet and other, in to Coshay fee, or ever that the shipherd myght have knowlych therof and then he fowlyd one and desyryd to have hem a yen, and thay wold not suffer hym to have them no more but the Colyet and ther were c. and j. of yours and tho had thay forth with hem to Coshay, and the same day we had a replevyn for the cc. shype and replevyn for the hors that wer taken at Haylesdon, and how that thay were obbeyd Ric. Calle shall enforme you, and of other maters also, the whych I may not wryte to you of at thys tyme.

Item, I have spoke with [John] Strange of the mater that ye wrote to me of, and in gode feyth I[1] fynd hym, as me symyth, ryght well disposyd to you wards ; and he hath, acordyng to your desyre, spoken with Yelverton yesterday to fyle his dysposicion in that mater, and Yelverton, as it symyth by hym, roght not gretely thogh the mater brake, so that he myght have any resonabell colour to breke, he ys so callyd uppon by Wayte and other of the Duck of Suffolk ys counsell that he ote [*wot*] not where to hold hym, and he ys put in so gret confort, as I am enformyd, to receve money for the lond, and that temptyth hym ryght sore ; for with money he wold fayn be in handelyng, as ye know he hath nede therof. He told John Straunge that it ys informyd hym that ye have up an enquest to depreve ther wytnesse and ther with ys he sore movyd . . . . that yf any thyngs be don in temporall maters other in spyryt[uall] . . . . . . maters tochyng executors or feoffeys or wyttnes tyll the day of . . . . trety be passyd, he wyll not abyde no trety therin, but do as . . . . thynkyth best

[1] The ms. has 'in' instead of 'I,' evidently by mistake.

148

for to do therein. I told John Straunge that I kn[ew] . . . . thogh it were soo that shold passe any such enquest it shol n . . . . of them in provyng of her trothys, the whych shold be no hurt . . . . for John Straunge desyryd me that I shuld send to you in al haste that . . . . any such folks that thay shold not doo in the mater till the day of . . . . may have knowlych howe he and other wold doo in such maters as sh . . . . . . he wold be loth that he shold have any colour to breke for any thyng . . . . and Yelverton sayth it shall not breke thorf his defaute yf ye wyll n[ot] . . . . . be ryght glad to have your gode wyll and to goo thorgh in all maner mate[rs] . . . . eschewyng of wastfull expens of the dede ys godes and that the godes myzt be dyspendyd to the welle of the dede. Straunge desyryd to knowe what appoyntements he desyryth to have in the trety, and he sayd he wold not let that be understand tyll the tyme of trety cam. Me symyth, save your beter avyse, it were wel do that thay that be com up for you myzt be kypt in som secryte place and not do [*naught done ?*] in the mater tyll the tyme of the trety were passyd. The cost there of shall not be grete to that it myzt hurte yf the trety were broken by that meane and then ye may have hem nyer ; and yf ye thynk it be to doo ye may have hem to go to ther mater after the seyd tyme, for of ij. hurtes the grettyst ys best to be eschewyd.

Item, as for youre houshold at Caster, savyng your beter avyse, me thynkyth that v. or vj. of your folkes, such as ye wyll assyngne, were [enough to?][1] kype the place, and they for to go to bord with the prustes, and ye not to kype no houshold ther yet ; and that ye shall fynd more profettabyll than for to doo as we do nogh ; for ther expens, as I understond, have not be moch the lesse by fore Wytsontyde than it shold be thogh I had be at home by cause of resortyng of pepell theder ; and yf the houshold were broke thay myzt have a gode excuse in that, whosome ever come. Ric. Call shall enforme you of thys maters, and mo other, more playnly than I may do wryte

[1] Paper decayed.

149

THE PASTON LETTERS

1465
JUNE 11

at thys tyme. It is necessary that possessyon be kypt hyre yett tyll ye be more ferther forth in other maters. The Blessyd Trynyte have you [in] Hys kypyng, and send you gode spyde in all your maters, and send you grace to have a gode conclusyon in hem in haste. Wryten on the Tewysday nex before Corpus Christi.

By your faynt houswyff at thys tyme,
M. P.

586

JOHN PASTON THE YOUNGEST TO HIS FATHER[1]

JUNE 15

RYTH reverent and worchepfull fadyr, I recomand me on to yow, beschyng yow lowly of your blyssyng. Plesit yow to have knowlage how that I have be in Sowthefolk for syche materys as my cosyn Dawbeney took my modyr a byll of, towchyng the materys be twyx yow and Jenney. And of all the jentylmen that ye wold my modyr schold send to for thys mater ther ar no more at home bot John Alyngton ; and I schewyd hym the byll of the namys of the Inqwest and knew no more of hem all bot thes, John Depden, Thomas Wodborne, John Donemowe, Herry Chesten, and Adam Wrene. And to all them Alyngton sent a man of hys for to fele hem how they wer dysposyd. Thys was the answer of John Depden and Thomas Wodborne, they sayd the last tyme they wer at London iche of ther costys stood hem on xs., and they seyd they wold no mor come at London bot if[2] they knew who schod pay for ther costis ; but me thowt by Alyngtonys man that they wold have had a brybe of yow be syd the payment for ther costys for to have bedyn at home, for they have non othyr levyng but brybys. As for John Donemow and Herry Chesten, so that ther issuys may be payd they wyll not come ther ; nor in trowthe they scholl not

[1] [Add. ms. 34,889, f. 190.] This letter refers to the dispute with Jenney in 1464-5, and seems to belong to the latter year.
[2] 'But if,' the old familiar expression for 'unless,' occurs in this letter with peculiar frequency.

150

come ther. Wher for Alyngton prayith yow that ther issuys may be payid. Adam Wrene was not spoke to, for he is Jenneys baly or hys fermour. As for the quest they ar not yet somoned to aper, and but if[1] they be somonyd ther scholl non of hem all aper. The most part of the todyr dwell a bowt Ippyswyche and they be Debnamys tenauntys and Brewsys, and I knowd get no man to spek with hem but if[1] I schold have spok with hem my selve ; and my spekyng with hem schold rather aperyd [*have impaired*] the mater than a mendyd it. And also I hyid me the faster home a geyn, for I lay at my cosyn Lovedays on Corpus Christi Day at nyth ; and he told me that the Duches of Sofokys consell wold entre in to Calcot Hall, and they wold kep it tyll the Duches knew who schold be her tenaunt, owthyr ye or Debnam. Thus told one of the men of the seyd cowncell to Loveday ; whyche man schold ryd thedyr with hem. And thys schold be do as to morow at aftyr non ; bot I trow they wole but tak a distres for the servys of the maner, whych is dwe ; but I have sent word to Rysyng and to the tenauntis that they schold dryve a wey ther catell. And as for the maner, my brodyr and I scholl kepe it so that they schall not entyr as that daye, by the grase of God, nor aftyr nowthyr and [*i.e.* if] we may knowe of it, but if[1] ye send us othyr wys word. As for the namys that ye wold have for to pase upon the mater betwyx yow and Hogan, I spok to Alyngton and Loveday therof, and Loveday seyd he knew non that wold pas up on ony inquest for hym, for he medylyd with no syche men ; and Alyngton seyd that he kowd assyne me none men for serteyn, not tyll he had spok with some, whyche he seyd wold aske gret leyser, for he knew bot fewe in Sofolk ; if it had be in Cambrygge schyre he kowd have get you j now. My modyr spak with old Banyard of Sibton Abbey for the same mater, and he knew none that wold pase upon the mater at hys desyer, but he asygnyd dyvers men that love not Jeney, whyche he kowd thynk wold pase upon it at yowr desyer if ye spok with hem your selve ; or at the lest iche of hem kowd get yow ij. or iij. men that wold sey as they wold in cas ye spok with hem your selve, whoys

[1] See footnote 2 on preceding page.

151

1465
JUNE 15 namys I send you in a byll by Loveday. Item, as for the gape at Nakton Rychard Calle seyth that it was a thorn busche was leyd in with owt a stake betwyx ij. thornys that grew; and as for Jeneys netes, ther was not one lost her calfe that I can inquer of. And I pray God farther yow in all youyr materys to Hys plesans and to youer hertys desyir. Wretyn in hast at Hallysworthe the Saterday next aftyr Trinite Sonday.

My cosyn Hevenyngham is at London, and he kowd asygne you men that wold say as he wold mor than Syr John Wyngfeld, Alyngton, and all.—Your sone and lowly servant,
JOHN PASTON THE YONGEST.

587

RICHARD CALLE TO SIR JOHN PASTON [1]

*To my ryght reverent and worschippfull master,
Sir John Paston, Knyght.*

JUNE 15 PLESITH it your gode mastership to wete that as for the examynacion of Master Robert Popy, his examinacion was wreten in a longe bille of parchemyn accordyng to the deposicion in the Spirituall Coorte. And Master Robert come into the Chauncery, and was sworne that all that was wreten in the seide bille was trewe, and so delyverd the same bille to the Mastre of the Rolles; and he bare it forthe with hym in his hande, for it was delyverd hym at the risyng of the Coorte. Tounesende was by and I bothe, &c. And as for delyveryng of money to Dawbeney, I do that I may do, and more thenne I may weele doo, for I have put my selfe in gret daunger for that I have borwyd, &c. Almyghty God spede you in all your maters, &c. Wreten the Saterday next after Corpus Christi Daye. Your servaunt R. C.

[1] [From Paston MSS., B.M.] This letter seems to have reference to the depositions touching Sir John Fastolf's will in the suit brought by Sir William Yelverton and William Worcester against John Paston and Thomas Howes. Robert Popy seems to have been examined in the spring of 1464 (*see* No. 565); but the suit was still going on in 1465, and in a letter of Margaret Paston's, of the 24th June following, Richard Calle is mentioned as having recently left her and gone to her husband in London.

152

588

JOHN RYSYNG TO JOHN PASTON [1]

*Onto my ryght reverent and worchipfull maister, John Paston,
Esquyer, be this letter delyvered.*

RYGHT reverent and worchipfull sir, I recomende me onto your good maisterchip in the moste lowly wise that I can or may, letyng your masterchippe understonde howe that John Smyth, of Freton, and John Hopton, of Freton, and I were attached and led onto Gippeswich, and there putte into the Kynges pryson by cawse of the fyn which was sessed upon the forsaid John Smyth, John Hopton, and me, as your maisterchippe knowith well. And as for John Smyth and John Hopton, they had labored the meanes onto Master Jenney, that they were delyvered owt of pryson or than the massenger come ageyn to theym which they sent onto yow; and I remayne stille in pryson, and I can not knowe but that they labour the meanes to make me to paye the money for theym. And so I can not se non other meane but that I shall ly stille in pryson, and been ondo for ever withoute your good masterchippe shewed to me at this tyme; for as I am enformed that Jenney hath promysed theym that I shall paye the fyne for theym, and also alle the costes that haith be spent ther upon, and shall be spent, for thei say that I am sufficient to bere the hole daunger. And my keper yafe me licence to goon home, and thei had hevyed the peple that dwelle ther, and that gretly, and said playnly how that ye myght not beere the dawnger a geyns Jenney for your self; therfor the seiden that ye myght not helpe them owt of dawnger when thatte ye myght not helpe your self. Wherfor I pray your masterchippe to lete me have word in as hasty tyme as ye may, to knowe whether that I shall abyde her stylle or not, and if I myght do yow any

1465
JUNE 18

[1] [From Paston MSS., B.M.] The imprisonment of John Rysing is referred to in Margaret Paston's letter of the 27th May 1465 (No. 584), and in another of the 24th June following (No. 590). There can be no doubt this letter is of the same year.

153

1465
JUNE 18 good at London, I pray your mastershippe that ye will sende for me, and I will come up to yow. And if ther be non other remedy but that the money most nedys be paid, I pray your masterchippe that ye will make such purveyaunce therfor that it may be to myn delyveraunce at the reverence of God, and in the weye of charite as myn hole truste is in your masterchippe, for I can not seke to no man, nor will not but only to yow. Wherfor I pray yow that ye will tenderly understand this letter, as I may pray for yow onto God, who have yow in His kepyng. Wretyn at Gippeswich the xviij. day of June.

These ar the names of theym that have parte of my catell, Gilbert Nicoll, of Sprowton, William Merssh and John Woode of Gippeswich, bocher.

By your man and feithfull servant,
JOHN RYSYNG.

589

ABSTRACT [1]

JUNE Examinations taken at the house of the treasurer of St. Paul's Cathedral, London, of the following witnesses in the matter Sir John Fastolf's will, viz. :—of Thomas Torald and Robert Lawe on the 18th ; of William Waterman on the 19th ; of John Osbern and John Heydon on the 20th ; of William Pykeryng, John Symmys and John Shawe on the 21st days of June 1465.

590

MARGARET PASTON TO JOHN PASTON [2]

*To my ryght wyrshipfull husbana, John Paston,
be thys delyveryd in hast.*

JUNE 24 RYGHT wyrshypfull hosbond, I recomaund me to you. Please it you to wyte that the same Wensday that Ric. Call departyd hens I send Ric. Charlys to speke wyth the undershryf, requyryng hym that he shold serve the replevyn

[1] [From MS. Phillipps, 9309.]
[2] [From Paston MSS., B.M.] As this letter refers to Paston's disputes with the Duke of Suffolk and his officers, the date must be 1465.

154

for the shype and hors that were take, &c.; and the shryf sayd playnly that he wol not, nor derst not serve it, not thogh I wold yeve hym xx *li.* to serve it. And Ric. Charlys axhyd the cause why, and he sayd, for he wold not have to doo with that felshyp, and so it ys yet unservyd. I supyose that Ric. Calle hath told you what revell ther was by the Bayllyf of Coshay and his felaw upon your men that shold have servyd the replevyn.

1465
JUNE 24

Item, the same Wensday that Ric. Call rode from hens the were indytyd v. of men by the enquest of Fourhoo hunder, as Crome can enforme you, and on Fryday last paste John Paston, the yonger, Wykes and Thomas Honewerth were endytyd at Dyram, by what menys the berour herof Crome shall [en]forme you. I send theder Ric. Charlys, John Seve, and iij. or iiij. other gode felows, for to have don other folks as gode atorne; but it wold not be, for the Juge ys soo parcyall with the other party that I trowe ther shalbe sped no maters before hym for you, nor for non of yours tyl it be otherwyse by twene you than it ys. Crome shall tell you of hys demenyng at the last sessyons at Dyrham. I send you a copy of both the endytements. Your son John Paston the yonger, I hope shal be with you thys wyke and enforme you of mo thyngys, and howe myn hors and hys sadell and harnys ys prysoner at Coshaye Halle and have ben ever syn Wensday last.

Item, I recevyd a letter from you on Satorday last, whych was wryten on Monday next before and I have sent to Sir Thomas Howys the same day for such maters as ye wrote to me of, and he sent me word that Wyllyam Worceter had a boke of remembraunce of recaytys that hath be recevyd by Sir John Fastolf or any of hys sythen the iiij.[te] yere Kyng Harry, both of hys owyn lyflode or of any other mannys that he had to doo wyth all. He sayd, yf ye wold send to Wyll. Worceter to loke therfore he sayd he wyst well he wold lete you have knowlych yf any such thyng may be founde, and also he sayd that he wold sende to the seyd Wyll. to serche therfore, and as for such bokys as he hath hyre at hom he wol doo loke yf any remembraunce canne be founde therof, and ye shall have knowlych ther of, as he hath promysyd, by Satorday next comyng.

155

THE PASTON LETTERS

1465
JUNE 24

And as for the woman that made the clayme that ye wrote of he ys wellwyllyd that she shold be seyn to in the way of almys. And as I here say, it symyth by hym that in any thyng that he canne doo tochyng the savacyon of the dedys gode,[1] other in lyflode, other in other godys, he sayth that he wyll doo. I canne not have no knowlych that Haydon mellyth in the mater of Drayton ; yf he do oght therin, he doyth it closely, as he ys wont to doo, and wayshyth hys hondys ther of as Pylate dyde. It shalnot be long to or that I send to yow ; of such tythynges as we have I shall lete you have knowlych ther of. I fynd Crome ryght welwyllyng to you in such thyngys as lyth in hym for to do. I pray you lete hym be thankynd therfor, and that shall cause hym to be the beter wylled ; he hath not be rewardyd as yet but by Ric. Call, as he canne tell you. The Blyssyd Trynyte have you in His kepyng and send you gode spyde in all your maters. Wryten in hast on Mydsomer day.

As for Rysyng, but yf [*unless*] ye purvey for hym he canne no helpe have at home.

By yours, M. P.

591

[JOHN PASTON] TO MARGARET PASTON AND OTHERS[2]

To my cosyn Margret Paston and to John Dawbeney and Richard Calle.

JUNE 27

I RECOMANDE me to yow, and have received a letter from yow and a nother for Richard Calle be John Colman, and . . be Roos ; and I have received of Colman the plate and mony acording Richard Callis letteris. Item, I con yow thonk ye send me word the prise of corn.

---

[1] *i.e.*, the dead man's goods.
[2] [Add. MS. 34,889, f. 9.] This letter, which is in the handwriting of John Paston, refers to the proceedings of the Duke of Suffolk to enforce his claim to Drayton and Hellesden, and was clearly written in the summer of 1465 on Thursday before St. Peter's Day, *i.e.* before the feast of SS. Peter and Paul (29th June).

156

THE PASTON LETTERS

1465
JUNE 27

hurt not, for it was laufully bowth and sold, and he never kleymid it after. Item, I am in purpose to tak assise ageynse hem at this tyme, and elles I wold have sent thedir streyt be a letter of attorney to entre in my name ; never the les ye be a gentilwoman, and it is worshep for you to confort yowr tennauntis ; wherfor I wold ye myth ryd to Heylisdon and Drayton and Sparham, and tari at Drayton and speke with hem, and byd hem hold with ther old master til I com, and that ye have sent me word but late, wherfore ye may have none answer yet, and informe me as I ha (*sic*) wrete to ye within ; and sey oupinly it is a shame that any man shuld set anny lord on so ontrwe a mater, and speciall a preste ; and lete hem wete, as sone as I am com hom I shall see hem. Item, that as for distreyn for rent of ferm, thow the Dewk had tytill, as he hath not, he may non ask til the next rent day after his entre, that is Michelmes, and seye that ye will be paiid everi peni and asken hem it. And make mech of men of Cossey, becawse they wer owr welwillers when we wer neyboris ther ; and lete hem wete that the begyningis of shech mater had never worchip nor profite of me, ne shall, and desyr god will of yowr neyboris, &c., and suyn all othir menes that ye kan to plese the pepill. And lete yowr tenaunts wete that the Dewke may never be lawe compel hem to torn from me ; and do all so well as ye can, and if any entyr be made in Heylisdon shuff him owt and set sum man to kepe the place, if ned be, not withstandyng it longith not to the manere. Item, I wold fayn have sum man to be bayle of Heylisdon and Drayton, &c., that myth go amongis the tenauntis. And elles I wold han Richard Chyllins (?) to go amond [*q.* among?] hem tyl I com hom and also Richard Calle whan home. Item, he sent me word that the tenauntis of Drayton wold not come to the Dewkis cort and that they will be stefast to me and kepe hem straunge and froward from the Dewkis cowncell ; all this mater shall turne to a jape and not hurt hem ; ner, and if ye be wavering it shall hurt hem. Item, I let yow wete this is do to cause me to loose my labor ayens hym for Dedham, which I wil not for it. God kepe yow. Wret the Thursday befor Sent Petres day.

158

1465
JUNE

Item, as for yowr sone,[1] I lete yow wete I wold he dede wel, but I understand in hym no disposicion of policy, ne of governans as man of the werle owt to do, but only levith and ever hath as man disolut with owt any provision, ne that he besiith hym nothinge to understand swhech materis as a man of lyvelode must nedis understond ; ne I understond nothing of what disposicion he porposith to be, but only I kan thynk he wold dwell ayeyn in yowr hows and myn, and ther ete and drinke and slepe.[2] Therfor I lete yow wete, I wold know hym or he know myn entent, and how wel he hath ocupiid his tym now he hath had leyser. Every pore man that hath browt up his chylder to the age of xij. yer waytyth than to be holp and profited be hes chylder, and every gentilman that hath discrecion waytith that his ken and servantis that levith be hym and at his coste shuld help hym forthward. As for yowr sone, ye knowe well he never stode yow ne me in profite, ese or help, to valew of on grote, savyng at Calkot Hall whane [he[3]] and hes brothir keptid on day ayeyns Debenham, and yet was it at iii. [times[3]] the coste that that ever Debenham sones put hym to. For be her police [*by their policy*] they kepe Cotton at my cost and with the[4] profitis of the same. Wherfor geff hem no favor tyle ye feel what he is and will be.

Item, Calle sendith me word that Master Phylip[5] hat entrid in Drayton in my Lord of Suffolk's name, and hat odir purpose to entre in Heylisdon, and he askith my avyse ; whech is that ye confort my tenantis and help hem til I com hom, and lete hem wet I shall not lese it, and that the Dowk of Suffolk that last diid wold have bouth it of Fastolff, and, for he mygth not have it so, he claymyd the maner, seying it was on Polis [*one Pole's*], and, for his name was Poole, he claymed to be eyr. He was ansueryed that he com nothing of that stok, and how somever[6] wer kyn to the Polis that owth[7] it it

---

[1] Sir John Paston.
[2] A later hand has here written in the margin : 'Hic postea fuit Sir John Paston senior, miles.' But the *postea* is wrong.
[3] These words omitted in MS.
[4] *the* repeated in MS.
[5] Philip Lipgate, the Duke of Suffolk's bailiff.
[6] 'How somever' for 'whosomever,' or 'whoever.'
[7] 'Owth' for 'ought,' *i.e.* owned.

157

EDWARD IV

1465
JUNE 2

Item, tel Richard Calle to have wittenses redy. I wol spede this mater spirituall befor Estern.

592

MARGARET PASTON TO SIR JOHN PASTON[1]

JULY 6 (

I GRETE yow wele, letyng yow wetyn that I am informyd for certeyn the Duc of Suffolk reysyth grete pepyl bothe in Norffolk and Suffolk to comyn doune with hym to putte us to a rebeuc and thei may ; querfor I wold in ony wyse that ze make yow as strong as ze can wyth inne [*in the*] place, for I and other moo suppose that zyff they fynd zow not here they wyl seke yow there ze arn. I wold John Paston the zonger schuld ryde azyn to my Lady of Norffolk and be wyth hyr stylle tyl we haff other tydyngs, and ther may he do sum good, after that he heryth tydyngs, in goyng forth to hys fadyr or in to sum other place quere we may hafe remedy ; for yt [is] told me that there ar come to Cossay onward more than ij. hundred, and ther ys comyng, as yt ys seyd, more than a thowsand. I wold that ze sende hyder Lytyl John that I mygth sende hym abowte on myn errandys. Sende me worde how that ze doo by summe of the tenantes that be not knowyn.

Item, byd Richard Calle send me word in a bylle, of how many materys that he hath sent myn husbond an answere of, the quych he sendt hom in divers letters for to be sped here and of the fermours of Tychwelle.

Item, zyf Sir Jamys Gloys may come to Norwych to Adam Taylours how I wold he come on Munday bytymys, and I schal sende to hym thyder. God kepe yow alle. Wretyn in hast on Satyrday. BY YOUR MODYR.

---

[1] [From Paston MSS., B.M.] This letter is not addressed on the back, nor is the handwriting that of Margaret Paston, but from the subscription it would appear to have been written by her to one of her sons ; and as John Paston the younger is mentioned in the body of the letter, the person addressed was evidently his elder brother. The letter seems to have been written shortly before the Duke of Suffolk's attempt on Hellesden mentioned in the next No., probably on the Saturday preceding it.

159

1465
ᴜʟʏ 6 (?)
Item, yt ys told me that zong Heydon reysyth mych pepyl in the sokyn and in other place.

Item, I wold ze schuld do Rychard Calle hye hym of makeng of alle the acountes and, zyf nede, lete hym gete help and kepe Thomas Hunnworth stille wyth yow, and be war of of Pykyng [*Pickering ?*]

593

RICHARD CALLE TO JOHN PASTON [1]

To my mastre, John Paston, in hast.

ᴜʟʏ 10

PLESITH it youre maysterschip to witte of the rwle and disposicion of the Master Philip and the Balyf of Cossey, with others of my Lorde of Suffolkes men. On Monday last past, at aftrenoon, [they] wer at Heylesdon, with the nombre of CCC. men, for to have entred, notwithstandyng they seyde they come not for to entre; but withoute dought, and they had been strong inough for us, they wolde have entred, and that we undrestonde nough, but we knowyng of ther comyng and purveyed so for hem, that we wer strong j nough. We had lx. men withinne the place, and gonnes, and suche ordynauns, so that if they had satte upon us, they had be distroyed. And ther my mastres was withine, and my mastre, Sir John, and hathe gate hym as grete worship for that day as any gentleman myght doo, and so is it reported of the partye and in all Norwiche. And my Lorde of Norwiche sent theder Master John Salett and Master John Bulleman for to trete, and so they ded; and the Duc men seide they had a warant for to attache John Dawbeney, Wyks, Calle, Hunewrthe, and Bliclyng and other, weche they wuld have; and my master, Sir John, answerd them, and seide that they were not withine, and though we had ben, they shuld not have had hem; and so they desired oon of our men. And so

[1] [From Fenn, iv. 212.] From what has been already said about the Duke of Suffolk's claim to the manor of Hellesden, it is clear that this letter is of the year 1465. Later it cannot be, as John Paston was dead before July 1466.

160

Naunton stede by my mastres and haxed hem whom they wold have, and seyde if they wold have hem he wold go with hem, and so he ded. And on the next day they caryed hym forthe to my Lord of Suffolk to Claxton, through Norwich; and ther we had founde a remedy for hym for to heve lette hym; and he wold not, but nedys go forthe with hem; but like a jentelman he was entreated amongs hem. And Harleston desyred at Heylesdon to speke with my mastre, Sir John, and so he ded, and seyde to hym it were ryght weele don that he rode to my Lord of Suffolk and desired hym in any wice that he schulde do so, and seyde that it was hes dwte so for to do, in asmoche as my Lorde was come to contre, and that he wolde ryde with hym, and brynge hym to my Lorde; and he answerd and seide to hym, whan that he undrestode that my Lord were hes fathers goode Lord and hes, that thanne he wolde se hes Lordship, and [ell]es he had non aronde to hym; and so they departed. And thanne appoyntement was taken that they shull sende home ther men, and we schuld send home oure. And nough my Lord of Suffolks men come from Claxton to Norwich, and face us and fray upon us, this dayly. Ther fylle uppon me befor Sevayne dore xij. of hes men, viij. of them in harneys, and ther they wold have myscheved me and the Scheryf letted hem and other, and they make ther awaunte were that I may be goten I schul dye; and so they lye in a wayte for to myscheve me, Dawbeney, and Wyks; and so I dare not ryde out alone withoute a man with me. And I undrestonde ther is comyn an Heyre Determyner [1] to enquer of all ryots, and my Lord of Suffolk and Yelverton be Comyscioners; and so they sey as money of us as can be taken shal be endyted and hanged forth with; and so the people here are dysmayed with ther rwle. Wherfore that it like yow to sende werd how my mastres schal do at Heylesdon, and we in all other maters; and wether ye wol that we feche a yene the flok of Heylesdon, for they are nough dreven to Causton, and there go they on the heyth; and my Lord of Suffolk wolbe at Drayton on Lames Daye, and kepe the Coort ther; wherfor ye must seke an remedy for it, or ell[es] it woll not do weele.

1465
ᴊᴜʟʏ 10

[1] An Oyer and Terminer, or Special Commission.

VOL. IV.—L
161

1465
ᴜʟʏ 10
If my Lord of Norffolk wold come, he schulde make all weele, for they feere hym above all thyngs, for it is noyced here that my Lord of Norffolk hathe taken partye in thes mater, and all the cuntre is cladde of it, seyng that if he come they wooll hooly go with hym.

And me senethe it were wele don to meve my Lord in it, though ye schuld geve hym the profyghts of Heylesdon and Drayton for the kepyng, and som money be side; for ye must seke som other remedy than ye do, or ell[es] in my conseyte it schull go to the Divell, and be distroyed, and that in ryght schort tyme. And therfore at the reverence of God take som appoyntement with Master Yelverton, suche as ye thynke schuld most hurt.

I beseche you to pardon me of my writyng, for I have pitte to se the trybulacion that my mastres hathe here, and all your frends, &c.

Almghty Jesu preserve and kepe you. Wreten the Wednesday next Seint Thomas Daye.

Your pore servaunt and bedman,
Rɪᴄ. Cᴀʟʟᴇ.

594

MARGARET PASTON TO JOHN PASTON [1]

To my right worschipfull husbond, John Paston, in hast.

ᴜʟʏ 12

RYGHT worshypful husbond, I recomaund me to yow, preyeng you hertyly that ye wyl seke a meen that yowr servauntys may be in pees, for they be dayly in fer of ther lyvys. The Duke Suffolks men thretyn dayly Dawbeney, Wykys, and Richard Calle, that wher so ever they may gete them they schold dye; and affrayes have ben made on Rychard Calle this weke, so that he was in gret jupperte at Norwych among them; and gret affrayes have ben made uppon me and my felashep her on Monday last passyd, of

[1] [From Fenn, iv. 218.] It is needless to point out that this letter must have been written in the same year as the last.

162

whych Rychard Calle tellyth me that he hath sent yow word of in wryghtyng, mor pleynly than I may doo at thys tyme, but I shal informe yow mor pleynly heraftyr.

1465
ᴊᴜʟʏ 12

I suppose ther shal be gret labor ageyn yow and yowr servauntys at the Assysis and Cescions her; wherfor me semyth, savyng your better advyce, it wer wele do that ye shold speke with the Justicys or they com her; and yf ye wol that I compleyn to them or to any other, if Good fortune me lyfe and helth, I wol do as ye advyse me to do, for in good feyth I have ben symply intretid among them; and what with syknesse, and troble that I have had, I am browte ryght lowe and weyke, but to my power I wyl do as I can or may in your maters.

The Duk of Suffolk and both the Duchessys shal com to Claxton thys day, as I an informyd, and thys next weke he shal be at Cossey; whether he wol com ferther hyddyr ward or not, I wot not yit. It is seyd that he schold com hyddyr, and yet hys men seyd her on Monday that he cleymyd no tytyl to thys place; they seyd ther comyng was but to take out such ryotus peple as was her within thys place, and suche as wer the Kyngys felonys, and indytyd and outlawyd men. Neverthe lesse they wold schew no warauntys wherby to take non such, thow ther had suche her; I suppose if they myght have com in pesably, they wold have made an other cause of ther comyng.

Whan alle was doo and they scholde departe, Harlyston and other desyryd me that I schold com and se myn olde Lady, and sewe to my Lorde, and if any thyng wer amysse it schold be amendyd. I said if I scholde sewe for any remedye, that I scholde sewe ferther, and lete the Kynge and alle the Lordys of thys lond to have knowlech what hathe be don to us, if so wer that the Deuk wolde meynten that hathe be don to us by hys servauntys, if ye wolde geve me leve.

I pray yow sende me worde if ye wyl that I make any compleynt to the Duke or the Duchesse; for as it is tolde me, they know not the pleynesse that hathe ben don in such thyngys as hathe ben don in her [*their*] namys.

163

THE PASTON LETTERS

1465
JULY 12

I schold wryght muche mor to yow but for lak of leyser. I comaundyd my Mayster Tom thys day to have com ageyn by me from Norwych, when he had spokyn with Rychard Calle, but he cam not. I wolde he wer qwyte of hys indytments, so that he wer qwyte of yowr servyce ; for by my trowthe, I holde the place the mor ongracyous that he is in, for hys dysposycion in dyverce thyngys, the whych ye schal be informed of her after.

The Trynyte have yow in kepyng. Wretyn the Fryday next after Seynt Thomas.

By yowr,   M. P.

595

JOHN PASTON TO MARGARET PASTON[1]

To my cosyn, Margaret Paston.

JULY 13

I RECUMMAND me to yow, I thank of yow of yowr labour and besynes with the unruly felechep that cam befor yow on Monday last past, wherof I herd report be John Hobbis. And in god feyth ye aquyt yow rygth wel and discretly and hertyly to yowr wurchep and myn, and to the shame of your adversarijs, and I am wel content that ye avowid that ye kept possession at Drayton and so wold doo. Wherfor I pray yow, make yowr word god if ye may, and at the lest, let myn adversarijs not have it in pees if ye may. Jon Hobbys tellith me that ye be seekly, whech me lekith not to here ; praying yow hartyly that ye take what may do yowr eese and spar not, and in any wyse take no thowth no to moch labor for thes maters, ne set it not so to yowr hert that ye fare the wers for it. And as for the mater, so they overcome yow not with fors ne bosting, I shall have the maner sewrlyer to me and myn, than the Dewk shall have Cossey, dowt ye not. And in cas I come not home within thre wekis,

[1] [From Paston MSS., B.M.] As this letter is dated on a Saturday, and refers to the Duke of Suffolk's attempt on Hellesden as having been made on the Monday preceding, there can be no difficulty in fixing the precise date, both of day and year.

164

THE PASTON LETTERS

1465
JULY 13

gentilmen ner of other ; it is god a lord take sad cowncell, or he begyne any sech mater.

And as for the Pools that owth Drayton, if ther wer C. of hem levyng, as ther is non, yet have they no tytill to the seyd maner. God kepe yow. Wret the Satirday, &c.

                                    Yowr Jon PASTON.

I pray yow be as mery with yowr felachep as ye kan.

Item, I send hom writt and prasens for yowr servaunts and myn.

Item, I may sell you woll for xld. the ston, redi mony, as Arblaster can tell yow, and malt for iiijs. the quarter at days xxj. for xx. delivered of Yermouth mesur. If ye fayle mony ye most make it of yowr wole or malt.

I send you hom writts of replevin for the shep and the horses that wer take, and avise yow lete the writtis be delivered be fore my Lord of Norwich, and god rekord ; and if ye may make men with fors to take the catell agey[n] be waran of replevyn, spar not rather than fayle.

On the back of the letter is the following memorandum in a different hand :—

Md. there lefte behynde of Heylesdon folde of my mastre schepe xlj. modreschep. Item of lambes xxxiiij. Item of my mastres xij. modreschep. Item of her lambes xij.

596

MARGARET PASTON TO JOHN PASTON[1]

[JULY ?]

R IGHT worcheful hosbond, I recommand me to yow, and pray yow hertely at the reverence of God that ye be of good comfort, and trost veryly be the grase of God that ye shall overcome your enemys and your trobelows maters ryght welle, yf ye wolle be of good comfort, and not take your maters to hevely that ye apeyr not your self, and

[1] [From Paston MSS., B.M.] Margaret Paston, as will be seen by subsequent letters, was in London with her husband in September 1465. This letter seems to have been written not long before, when she first entertained the thought of going thither.

166

EDWARD IV

1465
JULY 1.

I pray you com to me, and Wykes hath promisid to kepe the plase in yowr absens. Nevertheles whan ye come set it in seche rewle as ye seme best and most suer, bothe for Castre and Heylisdon if the werr hold. In cas ye have pees send me word.

As for that it is desyrid I shuld show my tytill and evydens to the Dewk, me thynkyth he had evyll cowncell to entre in opon me, trusting I shuld shew hym evydens. And [if] ye seme it may do yow god or eese, lete my Lord of Norwich wet that the maner of Drayton was a marchants of London callid Jon Heylisdon longe er any of the Polis that the seyd Dewk comyth of wer borne to any lond in Norfolk or Suffolk ; and if they wer at that tyme born to no lond, how may the seyd Dewk klaym Drayton be that pedegre ? As for the seyd John Heylisdon, he was a por man born, and from hym the seyd maner dessended to Alice his dowtyr, hos estat I have, and I soppose the seyd Dewk comyth not of hem.

Item, as for the pedegre of the seyd Dewk, he is sone to William Pool, Dewk of Suffolk, sone to Mychell Pool, Erl of Suffolk, sone to Mychel Pool, the furst Erl of Suffolk of the Polis, mad be King Richard seth my fader was born ; and the seyd furst Mychell was sone to William Pool of Hull, whech was a wurchepfull man grow be fortwne of the werld. And he was furst a marchant, and after a knygth, and after he was mad baneret ; and if any of thees hadde the maner of Drayton I will los Cli. so that any persone for the Dewk will be bond in as moch to prove the contrary ; and I wot weel the seyd Dewkis Cowncell wil not claym the seyd maner be the tytill of the fader of the seyd William Pool. And what the fader of the seyd William was, as be the pedegre mad in the seyd last Dewkis fadirs daijs I know rygt weell ; wherof I informyd Herry Boteler to tell my old Lady of Suffolk, becawse he is of her cowncell ; and more will I not tell in thes mater, but if [unless] I be desyrid or compellid.

Item, let my Lord of Norwich wete that it is not profitabe ner the comen well of gentilmen that any jentilman shuld be compellid be an entre of a lord to shew his evidens or tytill to his lond, ner I wil not begine that example ne thralldam of

165

EDWARD IV

1465
[JULY ?]

thynk veryly that ye be strong inowe for alle your enemys be the grace of God. My moder is your good moder, and takyth your maters ryght hertely. And zif ye thynnk that I may do good in your maters yf I come up to you, after I have knowlage of your entent it shall not be longe or I be with you be the grace of God. And as for any othyr thyngs of sharge that be in this contre, I hope I shall so ordeyn therfore that it shall be safe. I have delyveryd your older sonne xx. mark that I have received of Ric. Calle, and I kowd no more of hym syn ye departyd. [And I send yow another bage of mony that was in your square cofyr.[1]] And I pray God hertely send us good tydyngs of yow, and send the victory of your enemys. Wretyn in hast on Saterday.   Your M. P.

Item, I take your sonne of your faders oode mony, that was in the lytyll trussyng cofyr x. mark, for my broder Clement seythe that xx. mark was to lytyll for hym.

[1] This sentence is struck out.

597

[MARGARET PASTON ?] TO ———[2]

Cosyn, I recommaunde me to yow, letyng yow wete that I am informid that the parson of Brandeston is take be yowr sowdiors and led forth with hem, and they have ryfelid his godis, and summe of myne husbondes also, and of his ballyes, weche were left with the seyd parson to kepe. Wherfore I avyse yow, and praye that he maye be lete go agayn, and to have ower godes as were take fro hym ; for and yowr sowdioris be of sweche disposicion that they wyll take that they may gete, it shall no wurchip be to you, nor profite in tyme to come ; and therof wolde I be sory. And if the seyd parson be othirwyse disposid thanne he owth to be, I wyll helpe that he shall be

[1] [The words appear in brackets]
1465(?

[1] [From Paston MSS., B.M.]

[2] [From Paston MSS., B.M.] The MS. of this letter seems to be a draft in a hand like that of James Gresham. It is anonymous and without address. Even the writer is very uncertain. But it may not unlikely be a draft letter from Margaret Paston to some neighbour who, while the Duke of Suffolk was laying claim to Hellesden and Drayton, was not too mindful of John Paston's rights. Brandeston is about eleven miles from Norwich, eight miles beyond Drayton. Thomas Hoop was parson of Brandeston from 1448 to 1475. He was presented to the living by Sir John Fastolf.

167

465(?) chaysteysid as conciens and lawe requerith.   I wolde ye shulde remembre yt ye have bore blame for sweche thynges before this tyme that hath be do othirwise thanne lawe hath requerid.   And God have yow in His kepyng. Wrete at Norwiche.

598

JOHN WYKE TO SIR JOHN PASTON[1]

To my ryght wyrshypfull mayster, Sir John Paston, be thys letter delyveryd.

1465
JULY 30

PLEASE it your maistershyp to wyte, uppon Satourday last, Mayster Wyll. Paston and I werre with my Lord the Byshoppe of York, and enformyd hys Lordshyp of the entre that was made at Haylesdon in the Duk of Suffolks name.   And my Lord asked of ous whether the C. marc wer payd or not, and we awnswered that it was payd many day a goon.   And than he sayd, 'I dar swer uppon a boke that the Duchesse of Suffolk hath no knowlych therof.'   And so he comaundyd ous to a wayte uppon hym, for he wold be at London a yen uppon Tewysday next; and soo we have non awnswer as yet.

Item, I have spoken with Mayster Robert Kent for your maters, and byddeth that ye shold not dowte therof; and as for the neglygens of your wytnes, Mayster Robert sayth it ys but a jape, and shall be no hurt.   And the copys therof wer deliveryd or than I cam hom from Parker ys hands, and that causyd me to spake no word to hym therof.

Item, the Lord Scales sayd at a soper wher as he soped within thys iiij. nyztys that he wold ryde home and enter in ij. fayre maners in hys contray, and desyred Stanhope that shall wed Gernyngham ys suster to ryde with hym.   I suppose it be to entre in to Caster and Cotton; wherfor maketh gode wache be tyme, for it ys mery to plede in possession, &c.

[1] [From Paston mss., B.M.]   The date of this letter is sufficiently apparent from the reference in the beginning to 'the entry made at Hellesden in the Duke of Suffolk's name.'

Item, I have send you an unce of myvers (?) by the beror   1465
JULY 30
of thys letter, and thay cost me iiijs. iiijd.

Item, your gesseren[1] and gaunteletts shall be send hom by the next caryours, for ther be non hyre yete, &c.   No more to you at thys tyme.   The Holy Trynyte have you in Hys kypyng.   Wryten at London uppon Tewysday next after Seynt Anne.

By youre servaunt, JOHN WYKE.

599

MARGARET PASTON TO JOHN PASTON[2]

To my ryght worschipful husbond, John Paston, be this delyverd in hast.

RIGHT wurchepfull husbond, I recomaund me to you.   AUG. 7
Please it you to wete that I sent on Lammesse day[3] to Drayton, Thomas Bonde and Sir James Gloys to hold the court in your name, and to clayme your tytill; for I cowde gete none other body to kepe the court, ner that wuld go theder but the seide Thomas Bonde, be cause I suppose thei were a ferd of the pepill that shuld be there of the Duke of Suffolks parte.   The said Thomas and James, as the Duke of Suffolks men, that is to sey, Harlesdon, the parson of Salle, Mayster Phillip and William Yelverton, the which was styward, with a lx. persones or more be estymacion, and the tenauntes of the same town, sum of hem havyng rusty pollexis and byllys, comyn in to the maner yard to kepe the courte, met with them, and told them that thei were comyn to kepe the court in your name, and to clayme your titill.   Wherfore the seid Harlesdon, with ought any mor words or occasion yovyn of your men, comytted the seid Thomas Bonde to the kepyng

[1] A sleeveless coat of mail.
[2] [From Paston mss., B.M.]   This is another of the series of letters relating to Paston's dispute with the Duke of Suffolk about Drayton and Hellesdon in 1465.
[3] August 1.

1465
AUG. 7
of the new Baly of Drayton, William Dokett, seyng that he shuld go to my lord and do his herand hym self, notwithstandyng that Sir James dede the erands to them, and had the words; wherfor thei toke the seid Thomas with ought occasion. Thei wuld have mad the seid Thomas to have had the words, and the seid James told hem that had hem, because he was the more pesibill man, whan afterward thei bade avoyde, and sithen led forth Thomas Bonde to Cossey, and bownde his armes be hynde hym with whippe cord like a theffe, and shuld have led hym forth to the Duke of Suffolk, ner had be that I had spokyn with the juges in the morwyn or thei yede to the shirehous and enformed hem of such ryottes and assaugthis as thei had mad up on me and my men; the baly of Cossey and all the Duke of Suffolks councell beyng ther present, and all the lerned men of Norffolk, and William Jenney and my[che] pepill of the contre; the juge callyng the baly of Cossey befor them all, and yaffe hym a gret rebuke, comaundyng the shereffe to se what pepill thei had gadred at Drayton; which came after to Helesdon to se the pepill ther, with weche [pe]pill he held hym wele content; and fro thens he rode to Drayton to se ther pepill, which wer avoyded or he came.   And ther he desired to have delivered the seid Thom. Bonde to hym; and thei excusid hem and seid thei had send hym to the Duke of Suffolk. Notwithstandyng, afterward thei sent hym to Norwhich to hym, desiryng hym that he shuld delivere hym not withought he mad a fyne, be cause he trobilled the Kynges lete; for which thei mad l . . . . to juges.   But after that I understod it, I sent Danyell of Mershlond and Thomas Bonde[1] to enforme the juges how the seide Thomas was entreted amonges hem, and so he ded.   And the juges were gretly . . . . . with the Dukes men, and forwith comaunded the sheryf to delyver the seide Bone withoute any fyne m[aking], seyng that he out non to make.   And in goode feythe I founde the juges ryght gentell and forborable to me

[1] At this point the letter is continued in a different ink upon a new sheet of paper, which was formerly stitched to the first sheet.   A line which was formerly covered by the sewing shows that Margaret Paston intended at first to have written: 'to the justice, and he . . . . . . (five words illegible, the paper being cut) thei toke the seid Thomas with ought warant, afftre trobillyng of the lete.'

in my matres, notwithstandyng the Duckes councell had made   1465
AUG. 7
her compleynt to them or I come in ther werst wice, noysyng us of gret gatheryng of peopell and many riotes thynges don be me and your men.   And after I enformed the juges of ther untrouthe and of ther gidyng, and of our gidyng in like wice. And after the juges undrestod the trouthe he gave the baly of Cossey befor me and many other a passyng gret rebuke, seyng without he amended hes condicion and governaunce, thei wuld enforme the Kynge and helpe that he schuld be punyschet. And wher as ye avyced me . . . . . a felaschip to kepe the coorte at Drayton with easy cost, it was thought be your councell it wer better otherwise, and not to gather no people, for it was told me that the Dukes men had to the nombre of v. C. men, and your councel avised me to gete a felischip to kepe my place at Heylesdon, for it was told me that they schuld come and pulle me out of the place, weche cauced me to kepe the place the strenger at that tyme.   And as for kepyng of any coort for you at Drayton, I can not wete how it cowde be brought a boute withoute helpe of other but if there schuld growe gret inconvenyence of it.   And at the ass[izes] . . . . . made gret labor to endite your men, notwithstandyng it was letted.   And as for the writtes of replevyn, they were delyverd openly be for the juges to the scheryf, and also other writtes wech Jamys Gresham brought; and aftre that Ric. Calle spake with the high scheref for the servyng of hem.   And so he promysed to serve it and to send men of hes owne to serve it; and so he sent ij. of his men with Ric. Lynsted, and with ij. of Scheperdes to Cossey for the schepe.   And ther they wer answer that Yelverton cleymeth the properte, and so wer they answerd in all other places wher as any catell was.   And so they departed and come to the scheryf and enformed hym; and I undrestande the scheryf taketh it for an answere; notwithstandyng I send hym word withoute that Yelverton had ben ther in hes owne persone he myte not cleyme the properte, and aviced hym to be ware what retorne he made that he were not hurte by it.   And so he hathe made no retorne yet.   What he wul doo I wat ner.   He is stylle in this contre yet and schal be this iiij. or v. dayes, but

THE PASTON LETTERS

1465
AUG. 7

your councell thynketh it were well don that ye gete an *allias*[1] and a *pluries* that it myght be sent don to the scheryf and than he can mak non excuse but nedys . . . . .[2] it well (?) to make a retorne as he wol abide by. I can not wete how the catell woll be goten ayen withoute other processe be had more than we have yet.

Item, on Tuesday next comyng schal the sessions of the pees be at Wolsyngham. What schal be do ther I wot not yet; for as for any indytementes that we schuld labor a yenst them it is but wast werk; for the scheryf ner the jerrours wol no thyng do ayenst them.

Item, wher as ye desire to knowe what gentelmen wolde do for you at this tyme, in goode feythe I founde Herry Greye, Lomnor, Alblastre, Wer . . . . (?), Berney of Redham, Skyppewith, and Danyell of Merchelond, ryght weele disposed to you ward at this tyme in helpyng and in zevyng ther goode avice to me for suche maters as I had to doo. Ye schal have more pleyne undrestondyng of all thynges her after than I may write to you at this tyme.

Item, the *supersedias*[3] and the *supplicavit*[3] is delyverd to Alblastre and to Wechyngham, and they have mad out bothe warantes and *supersedias*;[4] nevertheles ther is non servyd yet.

Item, I received the box with the writt and the letter that Berney sent to me on Friday last and non er [*no earlier*].

Item, as for the pris of malte it is fallen here sore, for it is worthe but ij*s.* viij*d.* j. quarter at Yermoth.

Item, as for your wolle, I may selle a stoone for xld., so that I wol geve halfe yere day of payment. I prey you sende me word how I shal do in this matre and in all other, &c. And God kepe you. Wreten in haste the Wednesday next aftre Lammes daye.

Your   M. PASTON.

[1] So in MS.   [2] A word illegible.
[3] So in MS.
[4] *Supersedias* is a writ to stay certain proceedings; *supplicavit* a writ for taking surety of the peace when violence is threatened by any one.

EDWARD IV

600

JOHN PASTON TO MARGARET PASTON[1]

To my cosyn, Margaret Paston, at Heylisdonn.

I RECOMAUND me to you. And as for the letter that I send yow touchyng John Russe, I will that ye and your counsell see it openly; and kepe this bille to your self or to some secret frend of yours. And I pray yow remembir ij. thynges; on, if ye fynd hym in any maner wise disposed to leve his bargeyn, take it at his offer, and take ayen the writyng that he hath of that bargeyn, or a writyng of his owne hand of relesyng his bargeyn to me; for peraventure at this tyme he woll be glad to leve his bargeyn, as I undirstand, and whanne he sethe that I have peas he wolle calle theron ayen. Wherfore I pray yow werk wisely herin, for he may in no maner wise aske the money of me and kepe his bargeyn, for he hathe divers tymes desired me to have take of hym more masse (?) therfore. Another, as sone as ye may, or ye breke this mater with John Russe, make due serche with the fermours at Akthorp what mony Russe hath reseyved ther in my tyme, that is to sey, for Mighelmes the first, the ij., iij., iiij. yeres of Kyng E., of whech he hath reseyved ij. payments, that is xij*li.* at the lest, or er the maner was trobelid by Jenney or Yelverton. And I deme that he hath reseyvid some sithen, but that he kepith counsell.

Item, for as moch as Sir Thomas Howes gaderid for the xxxix. yere of Kyng Herry, the seid John Russe woll, under colour of that surmytte, that he reseyvid in my tyme was therfore, wherfore ye must make a serche what he hath reseyvid sith Sir John Fastolff dyed, and what tyme; and therupon ye shall undirstand what he hath reseyvid for me, and what for hym; and in case he hathe reseyvid xiij*li.*, and Richard hath payd hym his dute as he promised, thanne growyth nat to John

[1] [From Paston MSS., B.M.] It is sufficiently clear from the reference to accounts of the 4th year of Edward IV., that this letter cannot be earlier than 1465, which is the last year of the writer's life.

THE PASTON LETTERS

1465
AUG. 7

Russe past iiij. or v*li.*; notwithstandyng fare fayre with hym and resonabilly, so that he leve his bargeyn, and lend hym the remnaunt of the xx*li.* upon suerte for xx*li.* He desireth to have outher his dewte or borowyng at this tyme.

Item, he that shall speke with the fermours of Akthorp, whos name is Langham, he must inquere generally what mony he hath payd to all men sith Sir John Fastolff dyed, and see his billes of payment, and take therof a titelyng. Ric. Calle hath a bille of parcellis of every mannes ferme, and he can serche this best, in case he be not so favorabill to John Russe, wherfore I remitte this to your discrecion; but I suppose John Russe woll telle yow what he hath reseyvid for hand bifore this tyme wretyn by his seying what he had reseyvid, and I suppose and he remembird that he seid to me, he wold not aske his mony in this forme; nevirthelesse it shall do good, so he leve his bargeyn by this meane.

I mervyll that I here no tidyngges from yow hough ye have do at the assisses. The berer of this letter is a comon carier, and was at Norwich on Satirday, and brought me lettirs from other men, but your servaunts inquere nat diligently after the comyng of cariers and other men. Wretyn at London the Wednesday next after Lammes day.

Ye shall have lettirs of me this weke.

JOHN PASTON.

601

JOHN PASTON TO MARGARET PASTON AND OTHERS[1]

To my mastresse, Margret Paston, James Gresham and Ric. Calle.

I RECOMAUND me to yow, and have reseyvid ij. lettirs from John Russe, wherin he remembirth me that I shuld owe hym xix*li.*, or therupon, for divers parcelles whech he seith he shuld have deliverid in to myn hows, wherof he seith

[1] [From Paston MSS., B.M.] This is evidently the letter referred to in the beginning of the last.

EDWARD IV

1465
AUG. 7

xiiij*li.* was deliverid in to myn howse ij. yere g[oon], and that I had a bille deliverid me therof, and the remnaunt sithen, and desireth of me payment of the seid xix*li.* Wherfore I certi[fye] yow as I undirstand in the mater; ye may lete John Russe come to yow and take such a direccion in the mater as reason and trought woll. I lete yow wete that abought ij. yer goo the seid John Russe deliverid me first a bille of the seid xiiij. [*li.*], and I examined the parcelles; and as I remembir xj*li.* was my dewte, wherof the certeyn somme is writen in my blak book of foreyn reseytes that yere, and the remnaunt was Ric. Calles dewte, wherof he was allowed, savyng apart was Elys dewte. And as for the seid xj*li.*, I offerid the seid John Russe payment in hand at that tyme, and desired hym he shuld no more send in to myn howse, and warnyd yow and Richard that ye shuld no more stuffe take in to myn hows without ye peyd in hand, nowther of hym ner of non other. And the seid John Russe prayd me to remembir that I had grauntyd hym the maner of Akthorp in Leystoft, at a certeyn prise, as it apperyd by writyng undir my seall, and desired me that I wold take the seid somme in party of payment. And I told hym that as for such mony that shuld com from hym for that lond, I wold take it of hym and ley it up by the self, that I myght purchase other lond therwith, bicause I wold lesse Fastolffs lyvelode for the college, but I wold pay hym his dewte without any stoppage. And he thanne desired me to take that same xj*li.*, and ley it up to the same use, seying to me that it was as good to do so as I for to take it hym, and he to take it me ayen. And thus he and I agreed, and departed, and thanne he prayd me to take more chafar of hym, whech I denyed. And nough I merveyll what shuld cause hym to aske mony for that dewte; neverthelesse I deme he supposith that he coud not opteyne his bargeyn by me, bicause of the trobill that it standyth in; and for that or for some other cause he repentyth his bargeyn and woll nomore of it. Wherfore send for hym, and take James Gresham or some of your frends and Richard Calle, and fele what he menyth; and if ye can fynd hym disposed to leve his bargeyn yet, though I myght kepe stille the seid mony I wold he shuld

1465
AUG. 7
not lese therby. Nevirthelesse if he woll refuse his bargeyn, thanne take ayen the writyng that he hath of that bargeyn and a writyng of his hand that he dischargyth me of the graunt that I mad hym of that same bargeyn. And thanne loke that ye enquere what mony he hath reseyvid of the seid maner in my tyme, wherof the ferme is vj*li*. yerly whech I suffird hym to occupie to his owne use by fors of the seid bargeyn all my tyme; and aftir the parcellis cast what I have had of hym; abbate therof the mony that he hath reseyvid of the seid maner, and also as moch of the xiiij*li*. as the seid Ric. Calle and Elys owen, wher of he is alowid ; and thanne see that the seid John Russe be content of the remnaunt of his parcellis that is dew by me, but loke ye pay non other mennes dewtes.

Also the seid John Russe writyth in his littir that rather thanne he shuld fayle this mony that I wold lend hym asmoch to pay ayen at Cristemasse ; wherfore, if he leve his bargeyn I woll ye lend hym asmoch mony over his dewte as shall make up xx*li*., takyng of hym suerte to pay ayen at Cristemasse, as he writyth ; in case be that he will kepe stille his bargeyn, thanne ye may answere hym it is no reason that he shuld aske me any part of that mony ayen, for he owyth that and moch more.

Item, the seyd John Rus sent me heder a man for this mater only with in thes ij. daijs. Wherfor let him know an ansue letyng (?) for I fel well (?) he hath mad agret bargen but late, wherfor he hath mor nede of mony now, and I wol do for hym that I may resonably. Nevertheles his wryting merveylith me that he askith thes mony as dewte, wheche he toke me for parte of my payment. I deme it comith not all of his owne disposicion. Inquier ye that ye can what it menith. God kepe yow. Wret the Wednisday nex Lammes.

Yowr JOHN PASTON.

In cas ye han Drayton in any quiete take sewertie of yowr tenants for paiment as I have wret befor.

176

THE PASTON LETTERS

603

WILL OF NICHOLAS PICKERING[1]

1465

To alle trewe Cristen pepill the wiche these present letteres schall se or here, Roberd Banyngham, confessour to Nicholas Pekeryng of Filby, Alson the wyfe of the seide Nicholas, Roger Silveryn, John Herte of Cowteshall, Robarde Yoxsale, Richarde Hawe, Robarde Manufrac (?), John Case, servaunt of the forseid Nicholas, and Henry Becham, servaunt of the seide Nicholas, and Thomas Page of Beston, sende gretyng in oure Lorde. Where it is mery-tory nedefull to bere wytenesse of troughthe, alle ye mot knowe us that we herde the forseide Nicholas Pekeryng seyn, lying on his dede bedde, these wordes folwyng, as we willen answere before God, that whanne William Pekeryng, sone of the seide Nicholas rekenyd with his fadir for xx. quarteres barly that the seid William cleymed of his faderys yifte to his mariage ; and for vij. dayes cariage of corne in hervest, and for als a thousande waltyle that his fadir had fro ye seide Williams wyfes place, the wiche reknyng greved the seide Nicholas his fadir, and seide, 'Thou comyst in with many bak reken-yngges. Remembre the that thou hast be the costlyest childe that evere I hadde, and how that I yaf ye x. acres of fre londe aftir my discesse ; and me thynketh be the thou heldest the not lowest, but woldest have all. But on thyng I shall sey to the; if thou trouble John, thy brother, or ony of myn executores, or cleyme ony more londes or goodys that evere were myne, I shal yeve ye Goddys curse and myn, for thou hast be ever frowarde to me.' In witnesse and recorde herof we have sette oure sealys.

To alle trewe Cristen pepill the qwiche these presente letters shal see or here, John Herte of Couteshale, Roberd Yoxhale, Roger Silveryn, Thomas Dawes, and Thomas Drye, sende gretyng in oure Lorde. Where it is mery-tory, nedefull and medefull to bere witnesse of trought, all ye mot knowe us, that we herde William Pekeryng, sone of Nicholas Pekeryng, seyn that his fadir wolde he shulde have but x. acres of fre londe aftir his decesse be syde other x. acres of fre londe that he yaf hym in maryage. In wittenesse and recorde heer of we have setto oure seales.

Endorsed: A Testymonyall.

---

[1] [From Paston MSS., B.M.] From the contents of the preceding letter it is pro-bable that this document was drawn up in 1465. Blomefield, indeed, states (vol. ii. p. 221) that Nicholas Pickering was buried in the steeple of Filby church in 1466. But the date may be an error, for he certainly seems to have been dead in or before 1465.
[2] *and* repeated in MS.

178

602

JOHN ESTGATE TO ——[1]

1465

SER, ze sent to me a letter conteynyng the substaunce of the processe off Mr. Robert Ippyswell for the mater off the codicill of Nicholas Pykeryng, &c. Me mervelyt gretly off the certificat off Mr. Robert in that be halve, for this is the truthe as forth forth as I kan remembre me. The codicill had nether day nor place lymyte, qwer or qwan it xuld a ben mad; qwerfor to a reprovyd that that nether was qualifyid with day nor place it had be gret foly, &c. Therfor I askyd off the juge hys accounts, and specy-ally the deposicionys and attestacionys off the wytteness that wer swor in the seyd codicill, &c.; by the qwyche it mowth appere clerly qwan and qwere this codicill xuld a be made and wrete. And this sen I mad protestacion to for the seyde Mr. Robert that I wolde impugne the mater as lawe requiryd. The qwych peticion I made diverse tyme to fore moche recorde, judicialy syttyng the seyde M. R.,[2] &c. The qwyche peticion he wold not her, but seyde expresse that nether Will. Pyker-yng nor non other man xuld sen his accounts nor knowe qwat the deposicion wer in that parte ; this mater was comownyd to for Mr. John Selet and my mayster and yours diverse tymys, and ever he seyde we xuld not sen the seyde deposicions. And so qwat sum ever he hath certyfyid, this is the truthe, God to wetenesse and all Seynts, qwo preserve zow evermore.

And I pray zow to declare this to my mayster and zours ; and comende me hertly to hys good maysterchep. And God sende hym victorye off all hys elmyes, and so pray all hys well wyllers at Norwich. JOHN ESTGATE.

---

[1] [From Paston MSS., B.M.] The writer of this letter is reported to be dead in No. 604, which was written on the 18th August 1465. We have little doubt, how-ever, that this belongs to the same year, as the names of Robert Ippeswell and John Salet occur in the correspondence more than once about this time.
[2] Master of the Rolls.

177

604

MARGARET PASTON TO JOHN PASTON[1]

*To my ryght wyrshypfull mayster, John Paston,
be thys letter delyveryd in haste.*

RYGHT wyrshypfull husbond, I recomaund me to you. Please it you to wyte that the cause that I wrote to you non er [*earlier*] than I dyde after the sessyons was by cause that Yelverton held sessyons at Dyrham and Walsyngham the next wyke after the assyses, and to have knowlech what labour that was made ther, and to have send yow werd therof. Ther was grete labours made by the bayly of Coshay and other for to have endytyd your men both at Dyrham and at Walsyngham, but I purvayd a mene that her [*their*] purpose was lettyd at thos ij. tymes.

Hugh a Fen ys in Flegge. Richard Call spake with hym thys wyke, and he sayd to Richard that he and his wyff wold be with me here thys wyke toward a place of hys that he hath purchasyd of Godehreds. Yf he come I shall make hym gode chyre, for it ys told me of dyvers folks that have spoke with hym sythen he com in to Norffolk as thay fele by hys saryng that he awyth you ryght gode wyle.

Item, as for my comyng to you, yf it please you that I come, y hope I shull purvey so for al thyngs or I com that it shull be sayff y nogh by the grace of God tyll I com ayen ; but at the reverens of God, yf ye may purvey a mene that ye may com hom your sylf; for that shall be most profortabell to you, for men cut large thongs here of other mens lether. I shull wryte to you ayen as hastely as I may. God have you in

---

[1] [From Fenn, iii. 370.] That this letter was written in the year 1465 appears clearly by the reference to the Assizes held at Walsingham (*see* No. 599), and the in-tention which the writer intimates of visiting her husband in London. Moreover, the first sentence of the letter, and also the postscript, are evidently written in answer to her husband's complaint in No. 600, that she had not written to him what she had done at the Assizes.

179

THE PASTON LETTERS

1465
AUG. 18

Hys kypyng. Wryten in haste at Haylesdon, the Sonday next after the Assumpsyon of our Lady.

Item, my cosyn Elysabeth Clere ys at Ormesby and your moder purposyth to be at her place at Caster thys wyke, for the pestylens ys so fervent in Norwych that thay ther [*dare?*] no lenger abyde ther, so God help; me thynkyth by my moder that she wold ryght fayn that ye dyde well and that ye myght spyde ryght well in your mater. And me thynkyth by my cosyn Clere that she wold fayn have youre gode wyll, and that she hath sworyn ryght faythfully to me that ther shall no defaute be founde in her, nor noght hath be yf the trogh myght be understond, as she hopyth it shull be herafter. She sayth ther ys no man a lyff that she hath put her truste in so moch as she hath doon in you. She sayth she wote well such langage as hath be reportyd to you of her other wyse then she hath deservyd causyth you to be other wyse to her then ye shuld be. She had to me thys langage wypyng, and told me of dyvers other thyngs the whych ye shall have knowlych of herafter.

As for the hygh shyrf [*sheriff*] he demenyd hym ryght well her to me, and he sayd to me, as for replevyns he wold aske counseyll of lernyd men what he mygt doo therin, and as largely as he mygt do ther in, or in any other mater touchyng you, savyng hymsylf harmlys, he wold doo for you and for yours that he mygt do.

Item, I have do layd in [*caused to be laid in*] the presenta-cyon of Drayton, and have presentyd Sir Thomas Hakon, parson of Felthorp, the whych is hold ryght a gode man and wel dysposyd, and the Duck of Suffolk hath layd in a nother; and ther shall be take an inquisicyon ther upon, and Mr. Styven ys your a voked [*your advocate*] therin. Mr. John Estgade ys passyd to God on Thursday last passyd, whos sawle God assoyle! Wherof in gode feyth I am ryght sory, for I fynd hym ryght ryth full to you. They deyy ryght sore in Norwych.

John Rus sayth the profets that hath be take of the maner of Caister syn Sir John Fastolf deyd hath be take by Sir Thomas Howys and Jenney.   By yours, M. P.

180

I mervayll that ye had no tythyngs from me at that tyme that your letter was wryten, for I send you a letter by Chytockys son that ys prenteys in London, and the seyd letter was of the demenyng at the assyes at Norwych and of divers other maters. I pray you send me word yf ye have it. As for the replevyns Richard Calle sayth he hath send you a awnswere of hem, and also the copys of them.

1465
AUG. 18

605

NOTE

In the Introduction in Volume I., will be found a document entitled ' A remembrance of the worshipful kin and ancestry of Paston, born in Paston in Gemyngham Soken.' This paper, which was printed in the preface to vol. v. of the original edition, p. xliv., appears to have been composed during the lifetime of John Paston by some one who owed the family no good will, not unlikely by Sir William Yelverton. The contents agree very well with the imputation made on John Paston, for which he was imprisoned in 1465, that he was a bondman to the King. The original of this document I have not met with.

606

ABSTRACT[1]

EXAMINATIONS TOUCHING FASTOLF'S WILL

John Paston examined by a commission of Thomas, Archbishop of Canter-bury, addressed to John Druell, LL.D., in the cause between Sir William Yelverton, Knight, and William Worcester, pretensed executors of Sir John Fastolf, and John Paston, Esq., and Thomas Howys, executors, as is said, dated 8 July 1465.

AUG.

[1] [From Paston MSS., B.M.] Among the Paston MSS. in the British Museum is a small volume (Addit. MS. 27,450) of 132 pages, with a contemporary parchment cover, consisting entirely of examinations of witnesses touching Sir John Fastolf's Will. It is in two parts, separated by a blank page, the first containing the deposi-tions of John Paston, taken in 1465, and the second those of the witnesses brought forward by Yelverton and Worcester, which were taken in 1466. We give here the substance of Part I. only. An abstract of Part II. will be found under its proper date.

181

THE PASTON LETTERS

1465
AUG.

1. Whether Sir John Fastolf made his will, dated 14 June 1459, in English, and sealed by him with his seal of arms ? Answer. He made a note of articles in his will, deponent thinks in Latin, probably on that day, but it was not then sealed, and no executor was named.

2. Whether before the will was fair copied an original note of it was made on paper, and corrected and interlined by Paston ? And whether that note fair copied was the true will which was sealed by Fastolf ?—There was such a note, which being made, Paston went to London and waited some time, when William Worcester informed him it had been fair copied in the beginning of July. Had seen an old will long before, in which some of the articles were the same, but Fastolf altered them from time to time in consultations held with this deponent. Does not know if he did interline, but the note will show, which was then in the keeping of William Worcester, Fastolf's clerk; nor does he know if the will was drawn up from it, as he was not present at the engrossing or sealing, but hears there were several things altered.

3. Where the will is, in whose custody, and whether he have power to execute it ?—The parchment sealed by Fastolf, which Worcester says was his will, was kept some time after his death at Caister, and afterwards produced in audience of the Archbishop, and there remains.

28 Aug. Examined in the Fleet.—Said he was a prisoner, wished first to speak with his counsel, and desired another notary joined with Nicholas Parker, who was not indifferent.

10, 11, 12 Dec. Appeared before the commissary in the treasurer's house of St. Paul's Cathedral, London. Examination continued.

4. Whether the said will was kept in the tower called the treasury of Sir John Fastolf at Caister till his death, and whether Paston and Howys after-wards entered and took it, and what was then done with it ? Whether, since Fastolf's death it was exemplified in Latin, and sealed with Fastolf's seal, and by whom ? And whether the Latin contained more or less than the English ? Who exhibited the English will in audience of Canterbury ? Was it the true will, or was it written and sealed after Fastolf's death ?—Soon after Fastolf's death the said parchment was exhibited to Paston by Howes and Worcester. It afterwards remained in the keeping of Howes and Paston, and has since been exhibited in the audience of Canterbury. It was not translated into Latin after Fastolf's death, nor sealed, to Paston's knowledge. Does not know any will, Latin or English, to have been sealed after Fastolf's death.

5. Whether Paston exhibited any English will sealed in the audience of Canterbury ?—The note made in June contained an article relative to Fastolf's college, and lands in Norfolk and Suffolk granted conditionally on their being refused by Paston. When Paston went to London, and after a time Worcester came to him, Worcester told him this note was put in parchment and sealed, with the other articles, by advice of Master John Brakley, about the beginning of July. William Bukman, now Abbot of Wymondham, then Prior of Yarmouth, was present when it was sealed, and named as a witness. He and Thomas Ingham reported that Fastolf told them at the time it was his will that Paston should have those things he had granted at the time of the seisin of the said feoffment delivered, whatever was written in the parchment. The said

182

parchment (English) remains in the court. As to the Latin, Fastolf made on paper a schedule of executors for the Latin parchment, and told Paston and Howys that he did not mean all the executors to have administration of his goods. He also told Paston, Bracley, and Clement Felmyngham, after Paston returned from London, that he was informed the Latin will gave equal powers to all the executors, which he never intended. Fastolf made his last will in November, not altogether the same.

1465
AUG.

6. Who kept Fastolf's seal of arms and signet after his death, how long did it remain whole, and how many writings did Paston seal with them ?—At Fastolf's death his seal was in a purse sealed with his signet, and placed in a chest. The signet was on his finger at death, but was afterwards placed in the chest in presence of deponent and Thomas Howys, Master John Bracley, Master Clement Felmyngham, and three servants of Fastolf's chamber, and sealed with the seals of deponent, Howys, and others. The chest remained in Fastolf's chamber, sometimes in custody of his servants, and sometimes in that of Howys. Afterwards the seals were placed in a white box sealed in the presence of divers men in the hall of the manor, which box was delivered along with certain rings to John Stokys, who opened the box, and after inspecting the seals and rings, sealed it up again and delivered it to Roger Malmesbury, in whose custody they now remain. This deponent sealed nothing with them.

7. Whether, after Fastolf's death, Paston or any other wrote on a schedule of paper a certain grant or bargain, viz., that Paston should have Fastolf's lands and tenements in Norfolk, Suffolk, and Norwich, for 4000 marks, and that Paston and Howys should have sole administration of his goods so long as Paston was alive ; and whether after Fastolf's death it was so recently written that Paston, to dry the writing, scattered ashes over it ? And if he say it was written during Fastolf's life, by whom was it written ? By himself, or John Russe, or Friar Brakley, or whom ? And how long before Fastolf's death, and in whose presence ? And whether that sum was specified in the schedule or a blank left for it ? And whether the contents of this schedule were extracted and put in a new one ? and by whom was that written ? Whether by J. Russe ? And what time elapsed between the two writings ? And whether the second schedule contained more than the first, and what the additional matter was, and by whom added ? And whether this asserted will of Fastolf, made, as Paston pretends, on Saturday, 3 Nov. 1459, was extracted or imagined from the contents of the said bills, or either of them ? And what was the matter in the said will added to the matters in the schedules ? And how long it was before the said pretended will could be formed to the satisfaction of John Paston ?

For two years before his death Fastolf had granted that Paston should have the above lands after his death, without any condition, but for the purpose that he should found a college at Caister of seven monks or priests, and pay 5000 marks to be distributed for the soul of Sir John Fastolf ; and about that time he enfeoffed Paston and others in the said lands, declaring that that enfeoffment was to the use of the said Sir John for life, and afterwards of Paston After this, viz., in the said month of June, Fastolf made the said articles in certain paper notes in Latin and English. Master John Brakley kept copies, which

183

1465
AUG.

he showed to Paston after his return to London. After that, viz., in September and October, Fastolf several times requested Paston to engross the agreements made between them about the college, saying he would remit to him 1000 marks of the said 5000 marks. And in October and November he recited in certain writings that in order that he might not be disquieted with worldly affairs he had bargained with this deponent that he should have the control of all his lands from which any profit might be derived in England, and of the households and foreign expenses belonging to him, so that he should put aside as much of his dues as he could spare for the college; and that he should have all his lands in Norfolk, Suffolk, and Norwich, for 4000 marks, which he was to pay on certain stated days to Fastolf's executors for the benefit of his soul. Two paper writings were made of the premises, one by the hand of Paston and the other by Mr. John Brakley, which are severally remaining with them. This agreement Brakley, by Fastolf's order, got written out in parchment indented, and read to Paston, who sealed it in his presence as Brakley reported to Paston. Afterwards, another of the said writings was read to Fastolf in the presence of Paston, Brakley, Mr. Clement Felmyngham, and others, several times in October and November. Comments were made on the reading of it by Fastolf on one occasion, when he said a certain clause was not consistent with his intention, which was that Paston and Howys should be sole administrators of his goods, and that as to his lands in Norfolk, Suffolk, and Norwich, and the college to be founded, he would dispose of them according to his agreement with Paston,—the master to have a stipend of £10, and each of the fellows of 10 marks, and that seven poor men should be found with 40s. a year each, as stated in the will. Fastolf desired his will dated in June to be corrected in these particulars, and written anew by Walter Shipdam, for whom he frequently sent on this business. Meanwhile Brakley and Paston wrote another paper in English as a memorial of Fastolf's intention, of which deponent delivered a copy under his own hand in Court. The last two lines this deponent wrote and dried with ashes in presence of Thomas Howys. The will of 14 June and that exhibited by Paston and Howys differ little or nothing in effect, except in these articles touching the college, and the sole administration given to Paston and Howys.

As to new writings after Fastolf's death. Brakley translated those words about the sole administration from English into Latin, partly before his death and partly after. After Fastolf's death Paston, Howys, and Brakley caused the said Walter Shipdam to put into form (*fecerunt dictum W. S. formare*) the last will and testament of the said Fastolf, both of the said college and of the said single administration (*de dicta singulari administratione*), and of other things in the will of June not contrary to his last will and declaration, of which several writings were drawn by Shipdam, first in paper and afterwards in parchment. As to the writing of the agreements, Brakley kept it during Fastolf's whole life, and a year after, and a copy remained with this deponent after Fastolf's death; at which time deponent and Howys were sitting in the hall of the manor of Caister at supper when William Worcester came into the hall, and Paston and Howys, rising from supper, had a talk with Clement Felmyngham, John Brakley, and William Worcester, immediately after Fastolf's death. At

184

1465
AUG.

that time, by the advice of Brakley, a copy of the agreement was delivered to William Worcester, at his request, folded up and sealed that night by Brakley, Clement Felmyngham, and Howys. It remained in Worcester's keeping till he rode to London, and then he left it with the said Master John Brakley, Clement Felmyngham, and Thomas Howys. Its tenor was transcribed on parchment by Shipdam shortly afterwards.

607

JOHN PASTON THE YOUNGEST TO MARGARET PASTON[1]

To my mastras, Margaret Paston, be this deliveryd in hast, at London.

SEPT. 14

AFTYR all humbyll and most dwe recomendacion, as lowly as I can, I beseche yow of your blyssyng. Plesyt yow to wet that I have sent to my fadyr to have an answer of syche maters as I have sent to hym for in hast, of whyche matyrs the grettest of substans is for the maner of Cotton, besechyng yow to remembyr hym of the same mater, that I may have an answer in the most hasty wyse.

Also I pray yow that myn Ante Poonyngys[2] may be desyiryd to send me an answer of syche materys as sche wotyth of, by hym that schall brynge me an answer of the mater of Cotton.

Also, modyr, I beseche yow that ther may be purveyd some meane that I myth have sent me home by the same mesenger ij. peyir hose, j. peyir blak and an othyr payir roset, whyche be redy made for me at the hosers with the crokyd bak, next to the Blak Freyrs Gate, within Ludgate; John Pampyng knowyth hym well jnow I suppose. And [*if*] the blak hose be payid for he wyll send me the roset un payd

[1] [From Fenn, iv. 224.] It appears by Letter 610 following that Margaret Paston was in London in September 1465. This letter must therefore have been written in that year.

[2] Elizabeth Paston, now widow of Robert Poynings; afterwards married to Sir George Brown of Betchworth Castle, Surrey.

185

1465
SEPT. 14

for. I beseche yow that this ger be not forget, for I have not an hole hose for to doon; I trowe they schall cost both payr viijs.

My brodyr[1] and my sustyr Anne,[2] and all the garyson of Heylysdon fare well, blyssyd be God, and recomand hem to yow everychon.

I pray yow voysyt the Rood of Northedor[3] and Seynt Savyour, at Barmonsey,[4] amonge whyll ye abyd in London, and lat my sustyr Margery[5] goo with yow to pray to them that sche may have a good hosbond or sche com hom ayen; and now I pray yow send us some tydyngys as ye wer wonte to comand me; and the Holy Trinyte have yow in kepyng, and my fayir mastras of the Fleet. Wretyn at Norwyche on Holy Rood Daye.

Your sone and lowly servaunt,
J. PASTON THE YOUNGEST.

608

ANONYMOUS TO MARGARET PASTON[6]

To my mestresse, Margaret Paston, by thys letter delivered.

SEPT. (?)

PLEASE your good mastreschep to have knowlage that as thys day was Master Stevyn of Norwich at Caster, and ther he told me he was yesterday at Hoxhon with the Byschop of Norwych; and ther he seythe that ther is gret labor mad be Master Phylyp[7] and be the baly of Cossey; in

[1] Sir John Paston.—F.
[2] Anne Paston, afterwards the wife of William Yelverton.—F.
[3] The Cross at the north door of St. Paul's.
[4] The Abbey of Saint Saviour at Bermondsey, in Surrey, was founded in 1081, 15th William the Conqueror, by Alwin Child of London; it was surrendered in 1539, 31 Hen. VIII., when it was pulled down, and a Fair House built on the site by Sir Thomas Pope, Knight.—F.
[5] Margery Paston; she afterwards married Richard Calle.—F.
[6] [From Paston MSS., B.M.] This letter was probably written about or before the beginning of September 1465, as the proceedings of Salet and Ipyswell on the commission of inquiry here referred to are alluded to in a letter of Margaret Paston to her husband on the 27th of that month.
[7] Doubtless Philip Lipgate.

186

so moche ther is mad a comission on to Master John Salet and Master Robert Ipyswell for an inquerry that the parson[1] that my master[2] mad last at Drayton ys deed, as they sey, and in so moche they purpose to put in the parson of Felthorp, as he hard sey, for the Duk of Suffolk. And thes he thynkyth it were a gret urt to my master tytyll. And also another inquerry howe [*who*] ys patorne of the seyd chyrche; and thys is leke to come in revelicion but yf [*unless*] ther be gret labore mad to morowe be tymys and that ye have a man at Hoxhon in all hast for a newe comicion; and in that commysion Master Stevyn wold that ye shuld have Master Jon Salet, Master Symond Thornaham, Master Nicholl Stanton. And that it be mad be the avice of Master Jon Bulman; for he told Master Stevyn he wold do for you that he may, in so moche Master Stevyn hathe promyssyd hym a nobyll; and so the seyd Master Stevyn wold ye shuld send hym a letter and late hym have knolage that Master Stevyn shall reward hym that he shall hold hym pleasyd.

Item, a told me that a sent a letter to Sir William Maryys of all this mater yesterday, weder ye have er not he can not sey, but in noo wyse that ye dyskure not Master Stevyn, for he wold not for an *Cli.* that it ware knowe that ye knewe ther of by hym, for he seythe gold gothe gret plenty at Hoxhon on ther part. And yf it be labord be tymys it may be remevyd to Caunterbury. Also yet it is good to send to Norwich to the seyd Sir William for the letter ar the massanger goth, &c.

[1] This must be John Flowerdew, presented by John Paston and Thomas Howes in 1461.
[2] John Paston.

609

JOHN PASTON TO MARGARET PASTON [1]

To my Cosyn Margret Paston.

1465
SEPT. [21]

MYN owne dere sovereyn lady, I recomaund me to yow, and thank yow of the gret chere that ye mad me here to my gret cost and charge and labour. No more at thys tyme, but that I pray yow ye woll send me hedir ij. clue of worsted [2] for dobletts, to happe me thys cold wynter; and that ye inquere where William Paston bought his tepet of fyne worsted, whech is almost like silk, and if that be mech fyner thanne that he shuld bye me after vij. or viij.ˢ, thanne by me a quarter and the nayle therof for colers, thow it be derer thanne the tother, for I wold make my doblet all worsted for worship of Norffolk, rather thanne like Gonnores doblet.

Item, as for the mater of the ix.ˣˣ·*li.* askyd by my Lady of Bedford [3] for the maner of Westthirrok, where as Sir Thomas Howes saith that he hath no wrytyng therof, but that Sir John Fastolf purchased the seid maner, and payd serteyn money in ernest, and aftirward grauntted his bargeyn to the Duc of

¹ [From Fenn, iv. 90.] From the mention of 'this cold winter' at the beginning of this letter we might naturally suppose that the feast 'of Sent Mathe,' on or about which it was written, was that of St. Matthias, which occurs on the 24th of February. But we believe the day of St. Matthew to have been intended, so that the expression must have had reference to some unusually cold weather in September. It is clear from the contents of the letter that Margaret Paston had recently been with her husband in London, and had just left him in company with Richard Calle on her return towards Norfolk. Letters for her and Richard Calle on her return towards Norfolk. Letters for her and Richard Calle on her return towards Norfolk. Now the only time, so far as I can find, that Margaret Paston ever visited her husband in London—at all events when her sons were grown up—was in September 1465 ; and on that occasion Calle was with her, and everything else agrees. Indeed, no one can doubt that the latter portion of the letter immediately following was written in answer to this letter.

² Worsted is a small market-town in the most east part of the county of Norfolk, formerly famous for the manufacture of those stuffs which still bear its name, and of which, for the worship of Norfolk, J. Paston desired his doublet to be made.—F.

³ Jaquetta, daughter of Peter of Luxembourg, Earl of Saint Pol, was the second wife of John, Duke of Bedford, the Regent of France during Henry VI.'s minority. She was married to him in 1433, and after his decease, in 1435, she became the wife of Sir Richard Wydvile, and died in 1472.

188

Bedford, and so the money that he toke was for the mony that he had payd. Peraventure Sir Thomas hath writyng therof, and knowyth it not ; for if ther be any such mony payd upon any bargeyn he shall fynd it in Kyrtlyngs bocks that was Sir John Fastolfs reseyver, and it was abought such tyme as the Duc of Bedford was last in Inglond, whech, as it is told me, was the viij. yere of Kyng Herry the fift, or the viij. yere of Kyng Herry the sext, and the somme that he payd for the seid bargeyn was CCC. marks. Also he shall fynd, the xxij. yere of Kyng Herry or ther abought, in the acompts of on of Fastolfs Reseyvors at London, that ther was take of Sir Thomas Tyrell, and of the Duchesse of Excestre,[1] that was wif to Sir Lowes John, fermours of the seid maner, serteyn mony for repayment of part of the seid CCC. marks. Also he shall fynd in yeres after that, or in that yere, or ther aboutes, that Sir John Fastolf reseyved mony of my Lord Revers [2] that now is, by the name of Richard Wydevile, for his owne dette dew to Sir John Fastolf; wherfore, if Sir Thomas be trewe to his master, lete hym do his devoir to make that Worseter, whech is uphold be hym with the deds goods, to be trewe to his master, or ellis it is tyme for Sir Thomas to forsake hym, and helpe to punyssh hym, or men mast sey that Sir Thomas is not trewe ; and more over lete

1465
SEPT. [21]

¹ Anne, eldest daughter of John Montacute, third Earl of Salisbury, married, 1st, Sir Richard Hankford, Knight; 2ndly, Sir Lewis John, Knight (whose will was proved in 1442); and 3rdly, John Holland, who was created Duke of Exeter 6th January 1443, and died in 1446. Fenn erroneously supposed the lady to have been the widow of Thomas Beaufort, a previous Duke of Exeter, who died in 1426. This Beaufort, Duke of Exeter, married Margaret, daughter and heir of Sir Thomas Nevill, but his wife did not survive him, as Fenn supposed, for at his death he was found to have been tenant of her lands for life by the law of England. Fenn's note on this passage is, however, so interesting that we must quote a part of it. Beaufort, Duke of Exeter, was buried in the Abbey of Bury St. Edmunds. 'On digging,' he says, 'amongst the ruins of this Abbey, the body of the Duke was found, on the 20th of February 1772, wrapt in lead, and entire. The face, hair, and every part were perfect, and the flesh solid, but being exposed to the air, the body soon became offensive . . . . . I procured some of the hair, which was of a fine brown colour, and very flexible.'

² Sir Richard Wydvile, in 1448, was created Baron Rivers of Grafton, in North-amptonshire, and elected a Knight of the Garter. His daughter Elizabeth afterwards became the Queen of Edward IV., who then advanced her father to the dignity of Earl Rivers. He was seized by the Lancaster mutineers, and beheaded at Banbury in 1469.—F.

189

1465
SEPT. [21]

Sir Thomas examine what he can fynd in this mater that I sent hym werd of, whech mater he shall fynd in the seid Reseyvours bocks, if he list to seke it.

Item, on the day after your departyng, I reseyved letters by Will. Ros from your sones to me, and to yow, and to Ric. Calle, &c.

Item, I shall telle you a tale,
Pampyng and I have picked your male [1]
And taken out pesis [2] v.,
For upon trust of Calles promise, we may soon onthryve ;
And, if Calle bryng us hedir xx*li.*,
Ye shall have your peses ayen, good and round ;
Or ellis, if he woll not pay yow the valew of the peses, there
To the post do nayle his ere ;
Or ellis do hym some other wrongs,
For I will no nore in his defaut borough ;
And but if the reseyvyng of my livelod be better plyed
He shall Crists ours and mine clene tryed ; [3]
And loke ye be mery and take no thought,
For thys ryme is cunnyngly wrought.
My Lord Persy [4] and all this house
Recomaund them to yow, dogge, catte, and mowse,
And wysshe ye had be here stille,
For the sey ye are a good gille. [5]
No more to you at this tyme,
But God hym save that mad this ryme.
Wret the of Sent Mathe,[6]
Be yowr trew and trustie husband, J. P.

¹ Male, or Mail, is a trunk or portmanteau. It is to be observed that in the original letter the verses do not finish the line but are written as prose.—F.

² Pieces of money.

³ I do not understand this line.—F. Surely 'ours' must be a misreading of 'curs' (curse) ?

⁴ Henry, Lord Percy, son and heir of Henry Percy, Earl of Northumberland, who was killed at the Battle of Towton in 1461, by Eleanor, granddaughter and heir of Robert, Lord Poynings.
His father having been attainted, he continued to be called Lord Percy ; but he was afterwards fully restored both in blood and title.—F.

⁵ An agreeable companion.—F.

⁶ St. Matthew's Day is the 21st September.

190

610

MARGARET PASTON TO JOHN PASTON [1]

RYGHT wourchipful husbonde, I recomaunde me to yow, dyssyryng hertely to here of yowr welfare, thankyng yow of yowr grett chere that ye made me, and of the coste that ye dede on me. Ye dede more cost thanne my wylle was that ye choulde do, but that it plesyd yow to do so, God gyf me grase to do that may plese yow. Plesyt yow to wet that on Fryday after myn departyng frome yow I was at Sudbury and spake with the schreve, and Ric. Calle toke hym the ij. writts, and he brake them, and Ric. hathe the copes of them ; and he seyde he wolde send the writts to hys undre-schryf and a leter therwyth, chargyng hym that he schowlde do ther ine as largely as he owt to do. And I and Ric. informyd hym of the demenyng of hys undrchryf, how parciall he hade be with the other partye, bothe in that mater, and also for the accionnys beyng in the scher ; and he was nothyng wel plesyd of the demenyng of hys undreschef, and he hat wretyn to hym that he choulde be indeferent for bothe partyes acordyng to the lawe, bothe for that materys and for alle other. What the undreschryf wylle do therin I wot ner, for he is not yet spokyn with.

Item, as for Cotton, I entryd in to the plase as on Sunday last was, and ther I abode tyll un Wednysday last pasyd. I have left ther John Paston the yonger, Wykes, and other xij. men for to receive the profyttes of the maner ; and ayenst the day of kepyng of the corte, I hope ther shall be more to streynkyth them, yf it nede. John Paston hath be with my lorde of Norfolk seyth [*since*] we entryd, and dyssyryd his

1465
SEPT. 27

Vic.
Norfolk
pro ovibus.

Answer of
the writts
and of the
replevyn.

Margareta
Paston
intravit
manerium
Cotton die
Dominica
proxima
ante
festum
Michaelis.

¹ [From Paston MSS., B.M.] This letter is apostyled in the handwriting of John Paston, and numbered 'IIII.' at the head, showing that it is of the same sequence as the next, which is numbered 'V.' and dated on the very same day. In fact, the latter is clearly nothing but a postscript to this, and bears the address upon the back, which this does not.

191

Left column (p. 192)

1465
SEPT. 27
hank
w of
ur de-
nyng at
tton.

membir
kton.

okenge
Jenney
]
benham
Calcotes

aisday
xt before

gchell.
w your
t is
on, con-
eryng
r
nds be
ayges
d your
emyes
cor-
d,
lir up
profits
ll
dly

good lorchyp to streynth hym with hys howsolde men and other yf nede be; and he hath promysyd he would do so. And I sent Ric. Calle on Tusday to Knevett, dysyryng hym that he woulde sende to hys baley and tenaunts at Mendlesham, that thei choulde be redy to come to John Paston whan he sent for them; and he sent a man of his forthwith, chargyng them in aney wyse that they choulde do so. And he sent me wourde be Ric. and hys sonne also, yf wee were not stronge inough, that owther he or hys sonne, or bothe yf nede were, would come with suche feleschipp as they coude gett abowt them, and that thei woulde do as feythfully as they kowde for yow, bothe in that mater and in alle other.

Item, on Saterday last was, Jenney ded warne a corte at Calcotte to be holde ther in hys name as on Tusday last was, and Debenham de[d] charge another court ther the Sunday next after to be holde ther the same Tusday in hys name. And Daubeney had knowleche ther of, and he dede send on Sunday at nyght to yowr elder sonne, for to have some men fro thens; and so he sent Wykes and Bernay to hym on Monday in the mornyng. And assone as thei were come to Castre thei sent for men ther in the contre, and so they gett men and to a iij.xx. men; and Daubeney and Wekes and Bernay rod to Calcott the same Munday at nyght with ther felechyp, and ther kept them prevye in the pl[a]se, so that non of alle the tenaunts kneue them ther, saf Rysyngs wyff and her how-solde, tylle the Theusday at x. of the cloke. And than Sir Thomas Brews, Debenham the fadre,[1] and the knyt hys sonne,[2] Jenney, Mykelfylde younger, Jermyn, and younge Jernyngham, and the Baley of Motforde, with other to the noumbre of a iij.xx. persones, coum fro the sessionnys at Becklys, the whech thei hade keppt ther on the day byfor, coume to Seynt Olevys, and ther thei teryed and dynyd. And whan thei had dynyd, Sir Gylberde Debenham came to Calcott with xx. hors for to wett what felechipp ther was in the plase. And than Wekes aspyed them commyng; and he and Bernay and ij. with them rode owt to a' spoke with them. And whan Sir Gilberd aspyd them comyng, he and his felechipp flede and rode ayen to Seynt

[1] Gilbert Debenham, senior, Esq.   [2] Sir Gilbert Debenham.

192

Right column (p. 193)

1465
SEPT. 27
hast, and
that I may
see
acompt
for this
trobill
tyme.

Olovys. And than they sent young Jernyngham and the Baley of Mottforde to yowr men lettyng hem wete that the Justice of the Pese wer coum doune with Debenham and Jenney, to se that the pese choulde be kepte, and that thei choulde entre and kepe the courte in pesible wyse. And yowr men answeryd and seyd that they knewe no man was pos-sessyd ther in, ner hade no ryght therin but ye, and so in your name, and in your ryght they seyd they woulde kepyt. And so they yede ayen with thys answer, and wer put fromme ther purp[o]se that day. And all the tenaunts bestes wer put fro Calcalcott[1] fee, and challe be tylle other remedy maye be hadde. Yowr men woulde not kepe ther a cort that daye by cause it was warnyd by the tother parte, but we wyl do warne a corte and kepyt, I hope in hast. Ye wyll laugh for to here alle the processe of the demenyng ther, wheche wer to longe to writt at thys tyme. Bernay challe telle yow whane he come; but he challe not come to yow tylle after Seynt Feythesmesse,[2] that he maye bryng yowr answeres of other materys. It is tolde me the sessionys choulle be her at Norwiche on Tusday next comyng, and in Suffolk the Ses-sionys challe be the same Tusday owther at Dounwyche or at Ypswyche. I suppose ther challe be labowr ayenst soume of our folks ther, but we cholle assay to lete ther pourpose yf we maye. It is tolde me yf ther hade no folks a' be left here in thys plase whyll I have be owt, they choulde a' be neue masters her by thys tyme; therfor it is not good to leve it alone yett.

Veneat(sic)
Barney.

Cessiones
Norwici
et Dunwici
Martis
proximo
post
festum
Michelis.

Deprudentia custodiendi Heylesdon.

Item, Arblaster hathe sent a letter to myn Lorde of Oxene-fords tenaunts that be nerrest abowt Cotton to help John Paston yf they be sent to, &c.

Tenentes
Oxoniæ
pro
custodia
Cotton.

Item, I was thys daye with myn Lorde of Norwyche at Thorppe, and informyd hym of the demenyng of the mater for Drayton chyrche, and of alle the demenyng and parcialte of Master John Solatt and Ypswell; and also I informyd what disposission that they were of that were upon the quest. And in good feyth me thynkyth by hym that he is ryght ille plesyd that the mater was so gydyt. He seyde to me ryght

Episcopus
Norwici
pro
ecclesia de
Drayton.

Lete yowr
counsell
comone

[1] So in MS.   [2] 6th October.

Lower left column (p. 194)

1465
PT. 27
h hym,
thei
sey
y
owe not
n
dens
titell,
have
mor to
by my
tynge
t I sent
w
anne
avyse
ugh I
all take
n
ion,
that
that
tion I
ve as
od titell
my Lord
Norwich
h to
chirch
Thorp.

iscopus
d
ndon.

rnwayle

pleynly that the Jugis dede not therin as thei owght to do, and he seyd thowe I hadde hade noo councell, the he howght of ryght to have assyngyd me councell suche as I hadde dyssyrid; but he seyde he wyst well he dede in that mater as he have do in other materys byfor. Me thynkyth by suche thynges I harde ther that the seyd Master John ner the tother is not grettly in conseyt at thys tyme; and so tolde me Aschefylde in councell. What the cause was he myght have no leyser to telle me. I mevyd my lorde in the mater acordyng to the intent of yowr wrytyng yf aney axcion wer take; and he seyd feythefully yf it myght prevayle yow, he woulde with ryght good wylle that it choulde be doo; and ellys he woulde not in noo wyse that it choulde be doo. And he dyssyryde me to sende to hym suche as be of yowr councell lernyd, that they myght comune with hym therin, for he seyd he woulde not ye choulde take non axcion therin withowt it myght provayle. He was well payed that I tolde hym that ye woulde not do therin withowt hys knowleche and assent; and he seyd he woulde do therin as he woulde do yf the mater wer hys owne. Be avyse of yowr councell, I purpose to sende Loumnowr and Playter to commone with hym therin. He seyd he woulde feyne that ye were owt of troble; and he seyd, yf he myght doo owght to helppe yow forwarde in aney of yowr materys, he swore by heys feythe he wode do hys parte feythfully therin. He purp[o]syd to be at London thys terme, and thanne he seyd he woulde speke with yow of maney thyngs; he wycheyd herteley that he myght have spoke with yow on owr. He mevyd to me of a mater of a jentyllman of Cornale. He seyd he woulde speke with yow therof her after; yf it myght be browt to, it myght do meche good in maney thyngis. I harde yow onys speke of the same; ye tolde me ye hade be mevyd to therof by other.

Item, I received at letter frome yow yesterday, wherof I thanke yow hertely, and I pray yow that I maye be as ye writt. And as for suche materys as Sir Thomas Howys choulde be spoke to for[1] I sent Ric. Calle this day to speke with hym, but he myght not speke with hym; but as hastely

[1] See No. 609.

194

Lower right column (p. 195)

1465
SEPT. 27
Ecclesia de
Mautby.

as I may I challe do myn parte to spede the erands and other. It is tolde me that Sir Thomas wyll ressyng Mautby chyrche, and yf it plesyd yow to geve it to on Sir Thomas Lyndis, I truste verely that ye choulde leke hym ryght well, for he is rit a prystly man and vertusly dysposyd. I have knowe hym this xx. yer and mor; he was brother to the goode parsone of Seynt Michellys that ye lovyd ryght well; and yf he myght havyt he woulde kepe an howsolde therupon and bylde (?) well the plase (?); and therof have it grete nede, for it is now rit evyll reparyd, and I wott well he woll be rulyd and gydyt as ye wyll have hym. I praye yow, yf it plese yow that he have it, that it lekyth yow to sende me an answer by the berrer herof.

Wursted.

Item, I have do spoke for yowr worstede[1] but ye may not have it tylle Halowmesse; and thane I am promysyd ye challe have as fyne as maye be made. Ric. Calle challe bryng it up with hym.

Wretyn the Fryday next before Michelmas day.

611

MARGARET PASTON TO JOHN PASTON[2]

To my ryght worschipfull husbond, John Paston, in haste.

To get a
copy [of]
that he
hath
hed;
notwith-
standyng
[I] wote
well thei
have found
no such
evidens as
ye wene.

ITEM, it was tolde me thys day that Master John Sclatt hathe made a serge in the regestre this monethe aftre the wylles and testements of suche as hought the maners of Heylesdon and Drayton this c. yere, and be that hathe they founde suche evidence as schal be gret strenghthyng to the Duks tittle, as it is seide. I undrestonde verely that Mastre John Salet is all on that partye, and no thyng with you.

[1] See No. 609, p. 188, Note 2.
[2] [From Paston MSS., B.M.] This letter is apostyled in the handwriting of John Paston, and numbered 'V' at the head. As it refers to Paston's dispute with the Duke of Suffolk about the manors of Hellesden and Drayton, it must belong to the year 1465. The reader will also perceive that it contains an allusion to John Paston's imprisonment in the Fleet, and to my Lord Percy, who is mentioned in Letter 609, and who must have been a fellow-prisoner of Paston's.

195

1465
SEPT. 27
Item, as for the bill that ye sent to Sir Thomas Howys touchyng on Edmond Carvyll and on Fraunces, I wote ner whether he had hem or nought, for he is not spoken with yett in the maters. As wee spede owr materys, we chall sende yow answers of them as hastely as we maye. At the reverense or God, spede ye yowr materys that ye maye come owte of that loggyng that ye ar in as hastely as ye maye, for I have non fansey with some of the felechipp. I tolde yow, as me thowth, I praye yow be ware, &c.

I praye yow yf it plese yow that I may be recommaundyd to my Lorde Percy, and to myn mastres, and to my Lorde Abott. And I pray God bryng yow and them owt of troble, and send yow good spede in alle yowr materys. Wretyn in hast, the Fryday next afor Michellmes.

Be yowr,   M. P.

Yf it plese yow to send aney thyng by the berer herof, he is trusty inough.

612

SIR JOHN PASTON TO JOHN PASTON[1]

[To] his ryght worschypful [fa]dre John Paston, beyng [in i]he Flete at London, be thys delyvered.

RYGHT Worschypful Syr, in the most lowly wyse I recomand me to you. Pleasyth it you to wet that I sente you a letter but late agoo, in whych letter I lete you have understondyng that if it pleasyd yow to grante and assente therto, Syr Thomas Howes wolde resyngne the benefyse of Mawteby to a ful prestly man of Norwych callyd Sir Thomas Lyndys, whom I suppose ye have knolech of. Neverthelesse I wote wele he hath not ben grettly aquentyd with you. But I and he have ben moch aquentyd to geder, and I

[1] [MS. in Pembroke College, Cambridge.] This letter, as will be seen, was written in 1465 on the same day as Margaret Paston's two letters, Nos. 610, 611.

196

---

understond and knowe hys vertews levyng and dysposicion ryght wele; whyche heraffter, I wote wele, sholde please you ryght wele. And that letter whyche I sente you as I understode syns Nycholas Calman the berer ther of came not owte of Norwych iiij. or v. dayes after that the bylle was delyveryd hym; wherefor I am in dowte whyther it is come to your handes.

Whych causyth me to wryght to you ageyn in thys wyse, besechyng yow, if it plese yow that the seyd Sir Thõs Lyndys schal be of your promotynge in the wyse above wretyn that there it lyke you that I may have answer by the berer herof; whych schal tary at London a day or ij., and not passynge No more to yow at thys tyme, but Alle myghty God have yow in guydynge. Wretyn at Heylesdon the Fryday next byfore Seynt Mychell.

By yowr older sone,   JOHN PASTON.

1465
SEPT. 2[...]

613

SIR JOHN PASTON TO JOHN PASTON[1]

To my ryth reverrend and worchepfull fadre, John Paston, be thys delyveryd.

AFTYR all humbyll and most due recomendacion, as lowly as I can, I beseche yow of your blyssyng. Plesyst yow to have knowlege that as on Sonday next be for Myhelmas Day, as my modyr came fro London ward, sche cam homward by Cotton, and sche sent for me to Heylysdon to come to hyr thedyr, and so I have ben in the plase ever sethyn. And as sone as' Myhelmas Day was past, I begane to dystreyne the tenants, and gadryd some syllvyr, as myche, I trowe, as wyll pay for our costs; and yet I cepe here ryth a good felawschep, and mor wer promysyd me, whyche

oct. 3

[1] [From Fenn, iv. 80.] The signature of this letter, according to the fac-simile referred to by Fenn, is that of Sir John Paston, the eldest son of the person addressed. The date is undoubtedly 1465, as it will be seen by Letter 610 that Margaret Paston entered Cotton on Sunday before Michaelmas in that year.

197

1465
OCT. 3
that came not to me, wherby I was ner deseyvyd. For when Debnam herd sey how that I began to gadyr sylvyr, he reysyd many men with in j. daye and an halfe, to the nombyr of iij[c] men, as I was credebly assartaynyed by a yeman of the chambyr of my Lordys[1] that owythe me good wyll, whech yeman, as sone as he had sene ther felauschep, rod streyth to my Lord and informyd hym of it; and also he informyd my Lord how that I had gadryd a nothyr gret felashschep, whyche felawschep he namyd more than we wer by j[c] and an halfe and yett more. And he seyd on to my Lord and my Lady, and to their consell, that with owt that my Lord took a dyrectyon in the mater, that ther wer leek to be do gret harme on bothe oure pertyes, wheche wer a gret dysworchep to my Lord, conselderyng how that he takyth us bothe for hys men, and so we be knowyn well inow. Upon whyche informacion, and dysworchep to my Lord, that tweyn of hys men schold debat so ner hym, contrary to the Kyngs pese, consedryd of my Lord and my Lady and ther cownsell, my Lord sent for me and Syr Gylberd Debnam to come to hym to Framlyngham bothe, and as it fortunyd well my modyr come to me to Cotton not half an owyr be for that the mesenger came to me fro my Lord, wheche was late upon Twysday last past at nyth; and the next day on the mornyng I rod to my Lord to Framlyngham, and so ded Syr Gylberd also. And as sone as we wer come, we wer sent for to come to my Lord, and when we come to my Lord, he desiryd of us bothe that we schold neythyrthyr gadyr no felawschep, but syche men as we had gadryd that we schold send hem home a yen, and that the coort schold be contenuyd in to the tyme that my Lord, or suche as he wold asyngne, had spok bothe with yow and Yelverton and Jenney, and that on indeferent man chosyn by us bothe schold be assynyd to kepe the plase in to the tyme that ye and they wer spook with.

And then I answed my Lord, and seyd how that at that tyme I had my maistyr within the maner of Cotton, whyche was my modyr, and in to the tyme that I had spook with hyr I cowd geve none answer; and so my Lord sent Rychord Fulmerston, berer hereof, to my modyr thys day for an

[1] The Duke of Norfolk.

198

---

answer, whyche answer he schold bryng to my Lord to London, for my Lord rod to Londons word as yesterday, and the soner be cause he trustyd to have a good end of this mater and alle othyr be twyx yow, whyche he takyth for a gret worchep to hym, and a gret avantage bothe, and he cowd bryng this mater abowt, for then he wold trust to have your servyse, alle whyche wer to hym gret tresour and avantage.

And this was the answer that my modyr and I gave hym, that at the instans of my Lord and my Ladye we wold do thus myche as for to put the coort in contenuans, and no more to receyve of the profyts of the maner than we had, and had dystresid for tyll in to the tym that sche and I had werd ayen fro my Lord and yow, if so wer that they wold neythyr mak entreys nor dystreyn the tenantys, nor chepe no coort mor then we wold do. And we told Rychord Fulmerston that thys my modyr and I ded at the instans and gret request of my Lord, be cause my Lord intendyd pes, whyche resonably we wold not be ayenst, and yet we seyd we knew well that we schold have no thank of yow when ye knew of it, with owt it wer be cause we ded it at my Lordys instans. But be for thys answer we had receyvyd as myche sylvyr full ner as Rychord Calle sent us bokys of for to gadyryt bye; and as for the possessyon of the plase, we told hym that we wold kepe it, and Syr Gylberd agreyd, so that Yelverton and Jeney would do the same; for it was tyme for hym to sey so, for my Lord told hym that he wold hym fast by the feet ellys, to be suyr of hym, that he schold make non insurreccions in to the tyme that my Lord came ayen fro London.

I wene, and so dothe my modyr bothe, that thys appoyntment was mad in good tyme; for I was deseyvyd of bettyr than an C. men and an halfe that I had promyse of to have come to me when I sent for hem. Thys promes had I befor that I sent to yow the last lettyr the daye aftyr Seynt Myhell. Jenney herd seye that I cepyd Cotton, and he rod to Nacton, and ther held a cort and receyvyd the profytys of the maner.

I beseche yow that I may have knowlage in hast fro yow ye wyll that I be demenyd in thys mater and in al othyr, and

1465
OCT. 3

199

THE PASTON LETTERS

I schal aplye me to fulfyll your intent in them to my power by the grace of God, whom I beseche have yow in guydyng, and sende yow yowyr herts desyir. Wretyn at Hemnalle Halle, in Cotton, the Thursday next befor Seynt Feythe.

My modyr recomandyth her to yow, and preyith yow to hold hyr excusyd that sche wrytyth not to yow at thys tyme, for sche may have no leyser. The berer her of schall informe yow whedyr Jeney wyll agre to thys appoyntment or not. I thynk he dar do non othyr wyse.

Your sone and lowly servaunt,

JOHN PASTON.

614

THE DUKE OF NORFOLK TO JOHN PASTON, THE YOUNGEST[1]

To owr trusty and enterly beloved servaunt, John Paston, Esquyr.

THE DEUKE OF NORFF.

RYGHT welbeloved servaunt, y grete yow hertly welle, sertefyng that we shulle be at fulle age on Fryday nexst comyng. Wherfor, wele consayled be the Lordes of owr Consayle and oder of owr Consayle, that ye, on of owr servauntes of howsholde, with oder, be with us at London on Fryday or Saterday nexst comyng at the ffurdest, too a companye us thann too owr worshyp, for we shull have thann levery of owr landes and offyces; and that ye ffayle us

[1] [From Fenn, iv. 62.] John Mowbray, third Duke of Norfolk, died on the 6th November 1461. It appears by the Inquisitions *post mortem*, 1 Edward IV., No. 46, that John, his son and successor in the title, was seventeen years old on St. Luke's Day (18th October) in that year. He must therefore have been born on the 18th October 1444, and would have been of full age on Friday, 18th October 1465. The John Paston, Esq., to whom this letter was addressed, must have been the youngest of that name, who, as we have seen already, had been serving in the Duke's household. His father was at this time a prisoner in the Fleet, so that the letter could not have been intended for him.

200

EDWARD IV

not, as ye woll have owr good Lordeshyp in tyme comyng; and also that ye doo warne owr ffeede men[1] and servaunts, suche as be nye too yow, that they be ther thann in owr leverey. Y wreton the xij. day of October.

NORFF.

615

THE DUKE OF SUFFOLK'S ATTACK ON HELLESDON[2]

THYS be the parcell underwryten of such godys as were taken and beren away at Haylesdon, of John Pastons, hys sones and hys servaunts by the Duk of Suffolk servaunts and tenaunts the xiiij. day of October the v. yere of Kyng E. the iiij[te], the whych day the place of Haylesdon was broken and pullyd dowyn, &c.

In primis, ther was lost of John Pastons ther at that tyme in beddyng ij. ffeder bedds with ij. bolsters, iiij. materas, with iiij. bolsters; a grete seler with the testor, and iij. corteyns of whyte lynen cloth, and a coverlyte of whyte werstede longyng therto.

Item, a selere with a testore, and iij. corteyns of blewe bokeram with a coveryng of blew werstede longyng therto; v. pylowys of dowyn, vj. coverlyts of werk of dyvers colors, vj. payr blankettys, ij. payr shytes of iij. webbys, ij. hedshytes of ij. webbys, vj. payre shytes of ij. webbys, ij. basons of pewter, and iij. candelstykks of latyn for the chamber.

The Botere.

Item, in primis, vj. bord clothys, vj. towellys, xij. napkyns, vj. candelstykks of laton, ij. saltsalers of sylver, ij. saltsalers of pewter, ij. basons of pewter with j. ewers, a barell of vyneger, a barell of vergyous, xij. ale stondys, ij. pantre knyves, a pyce of sylver, a pype for brede, a ale stole, xij. spones of sylver, &c.

[1] Those who held lands of the Duke as their superior.
[2] [From a Bodl. MS.]

201

THE PASTON LETTERS

The Browhern.

Item, a grete lede to brew v. comb malte with one plawyng, a mayshsate, ij. kylyng sates, vj. kylers, ij. clensyng sates, a taptrogh, a temps to clense, with a scyppe to bere malte, a syff to syft malte, a bultyng pype, ij. knedyng satys, a moldyng bord.

The Kychyn.

Item, ij. dosyn pewter vessell, iiij. grete bras pannes, iij. potts of bras, j. greddyron, ij. broches, j. dressyng knyff, j. morter of marbell with a pestell, j. litell panne of bras of di. galon, ij. pothoks, ij. rakks of yron, ij. brendeletts, a almary to kepe in mete, j. axe to clyve wode, ij. saltyng satys to salte in fflesh.

Gere taken owt of the Chyrch.

Item, in the stepell, ix. sheffe arwys, ix. bawys, ij. handgonnes, iiij. chambers for gonnys, ij. mallys of lede, ij. jakks.

Item, in the church, a purs and iij. gold ryngs, a coler of sylver of the Kyngs lyvery and a nobyll of viijs. iiijd. the whych was Wykys.

Item, a syde gowne of blewe of Wyks.

Item, a stokke gonne with iij. chambers.

Gere taken owte of the Chaumber of Ric. Calle.

Item, a syde morrey gowne, a dobelet of blak satyn, a payre hosyn, a jakks, the polronds of a payr bryganders of rede sateyn ffugr.

Item, a payr of large tabelles of box, pris vjs. viijd.

Item, a staffe, pris iijs. iiijd.

Item, boke of Frensh, pris iijs. iiija.

Gere taken away of Margeret Pastons.

Item, an unce of gold of Venyse, di. pype of gold damask, di. unc' of gold of Gene, an unc' of sylk, a li. of threde, a close glasse of yvery, a grete combe of yvere, a fyne kerchy of fyne Holond cloth, a quarter of blak velwet.

202

EDWARD IV

Gere of Johanne Gayns.

Item, a ryng of gold with a dyamonics, a typet of sarsenet, a nobyll of xs., a nobyll viijs. iiijd.

Gere of John Wyks.

Item, a dobelet of blak fusteyn, a hers harnys, vjs. a gray hers, pris xls., ij. shertys, pris iiijs.

Will. Bedford.

Item, a Normandy byll and a bawe, pris of them both vjs.

John Boteler.

Item, a payr botys, a payr sporys, a shert, a cappe, a hatte, a dobelet, a payr hosyn, a brydell, ij. crepers, v. ston of wall, xxx. welfellys, a spere staff.

Shepe.

Item, taken away uppon Draytun grounde at on tyme by the baylly of Cossey and others, CC. shepe callyd hoggys.

Item, at a nother tyme, upon the same ground, iiij[xx.] hoggys and xl. theyves.

Item, at a nother tyme, at Haylesdon, by the baylly of Cossey and Bottesford and other, iviij[cc.] moder shype and CCCC. lambes.

Memorandum, a gowne of Richard Calle, pris ixs., j. peyr hosen, iijs., j. swerd, iijs., ij. bonets, ijs. . . . . j. jakk, xxvjs. viijd., j. schert, iijs. iiijd.

Memorandum, the pullyng downe of the place at Heylesden, to the hurts and skathes of ———

Item, the pullyng downe of the logge of Heylesden.

Item, the distroyng of the waryne at Heylesdon.

Item, ... the maner and the warreyn.

Item, memorandum, the rydyngs and costs off suthe.

203

THE PASTON LETTERS

1465
OCT. 14
Memorandum, the assaw made uppon Marg. Paston, Sir John Paston, at Heylysdon beeffor the place was . . . .

. . . .

Memorandum, the imprisonment off Sir John Paston in the Flet and in the Kyngs Benche.

616

MARGARET PASTON TO JOHN PASTON[1]

OCT. 17

ON Tuesday in the morwyn whas John Botiller, otherwyse callid John Palmer, and Davy Arnald your cook, and William Malthows of Aylsham, takyn at Heylesdon be the balyf of Ey callid Bottisforth, and led for to Cossey, and ther thei kepe hem yet with ought any warant or autoryte of Justice of Peas. And thei saye thei will carie hem forth to Ey preson, and as many as thei may gete more of your men and tenaunts, that thei may know that owe yow good wyll or hath be to you ward, thei be thret to be slayn or presoned. The Duke came to Norwich[2] on Tuesday at x. of clok with the nombre of v. hundred men. And he sent after the Meyr and Alderman with the Sherefs desiryng hem in the Kyngs name that thei shuld take an enqueraunce of the constablys of every ward with in the cyte what men shuld a go on your party to have holpyn or socowryd your men at any tyme of thes gaderyngs, and if any thei cowde fynde, that thei shuld take and arest hym and correct hym, and also certifie hym the names on Wyndenesse day [*Wednesday*] be viij. of clok. Which the Meyr dede, and wull do anythyng that he may for hym and his. And her up on the Meyr hath arestid on that was with me callid Roberd Lovegold, braser, and threte hym that he shall be hanged be the nek; wherfor I wuld that ther

myght come down a writ to remeve hym if ye thynk it be to do. He was not with me not save that Harleston and other mad the assaught up on me and Lammesse; he is right good and feythfull on to you, and therfore I wuld he had help. I have non man at this tyme to avayte upon me that dare be avowyd but Litill John. William Nawton is here with me, but he dare not ben avowyd, for he is sore thret. It is told me the old Lady and the Duke is set fervently ageyn us be the enformacion of Harlesdon, the Bayly of Cossey and Andrewys and Doget the balys sone, and suych other fals shrewys the which wuld have thes mater born ought for ther owyn pleser; the which causith an[1] evyll noyse in this contre and other places. And as for Sir John Hevenyngham, Sir John Wyndefeld and other wurchepfull men ben mad but her doggeboldes;[2] the whiche I suppose wull turne hem to diswurchep here after. I spake with Sir John Hevenyngham and enformed hym with the trough of the mater, and of all owyr demenyng at Drayton, and he seid he wuld that all thyng wer wele, and that he wuld enforme my lord as I seid to hym, but Harleston had all the words and the rewle with the Duke here, and after his avyse and Doctor Aleynes he was avysed here at this tyme.

The logge and the remenaunte of your place was betyn down on Tuesday and Wednesday, and the Duke rode on Wednysday to Drayton and so for to Cossey whille the logge at Heylesdon was in the betyng down. And this nyght at mydnyght Thomas Sleyforth, Grene Porter, and Joh. Botesforth the Baly of Eye, and other, had a cart and fetched awey fetherbeddes, and all the stuffe that was left at the parsones, and Thom Wateres hows to be kept of owrs. I shall send you billes er after, as ner as I may, what stuffe we have forborn. I pray you send me word how ye will that I be demened, wheder ye wull that [I][3] abide at Cayster or

[1] [From Paston MSS., B.M.] This letter is not addressed, but seems undoubtedly to have been intended for the writer's husband. The attack upon the lodge at Hellesden here referred to was in 1465, as appears by the letter immediately following.
[2] 'Norwich.'—This word is interlined, the writer having originally written 'this town,' and afterwards struck out the word 'town.'
204

[1] *an—&c*, MS.
[2] The old word 'dogbolt' seems to have meant a servile follower, or one bound to wait the commands of another. Thus in Lilly's *Tragicall Comedie of Alexander and Campaspe*, where Manes complains that he serves a master whose house is a tub, Granichus remarks 'That Diogenes that dog should have Manes that dogbolt it grieveth nature and spiteth art.' [3] Omitted in MS.
205

THE PASTON LETTERS

1465
OCT. 17
come to you to London. I have no leyser to write more. God have yow in His kepyng. Wretyn at Norwich on Sent Lukes Evyn.
M. P.

617

MARGARET PASTON TO JOHN PASTON[1]

To my ryght wyrshypfull hosbond, John Paston, be thys delyveryd in hast.

OCT. 27

RYGHT wyrshypfull hosbond, I recomand me to you. Please it you to wyte that I was at Haylesden upon Thersday laste passyd, and sey the place ther, and in gode feyth ther wyll no cryatur thynke how fowle and orubelly it ys arayed but yf they sey it. Ther comyth moch pepyll dayly to wonder ther upon, both of Norwych and of other placys, and they speke shamfully therof. The Duck had be beter then a m^{l}.*li.* that it had never be don; and ye have the more gode wyll of the pepyll that it ys so foylle don. And they made youre tenauntys of Haylesdon and Drayton, with other, to help to brede down the wallys of the place and the logge both,—God knowyth full evyll ayenst ther wyllys, but that they derst no notherwysse don for ferre. I have spoken with your tenauntys of Haylesdon and Drayton both, and putte hem in comfort as well as I canne. The Duck ys men rensackyd the church, and bare a way all the gode that was lefte ther, both of ours and of the tenaunts, and lefte not so moch but that they stode uppon the hey awter, and ransackyd the images, and toke a way such as they myght fynd, and put a way the parson owte of the church till they had don, and ransackyd every mans hous in the towne v. or vj. tymys. And the chyff maysters of robbyng was the Baylly of Ey, the Baylly of Stradbroke, Thomas Slyford, and Porter; and Slyford was the chyff robber of the cherch, and he hath

most of the robbery next the Baylly of Ey. And as for lede, bras, pewter, yren, dorys, gatys, and other stuffe of the hous, men of Coshay and Causton have it, and that thay myght not cary, thay have hewen it a sonder in the most dysspytuose wyse. Yf it myght be, I wold som men of wyrshop myght be send from the Kyng to see how it ys both ther and at the logge, or than any snowys[1] com, that they may make report of the troth, ellys it shall not mo be seyn so playnly as it may now.

And at the reverens of God, spyde your maters nowe, for it ys to orybell a cost and trobell that we have now dayly, and most have tyll it be other wyse; and your men dar not goo abowte to geder uppe your lyfflode, and we kype here dayly more than xxx. persons for savacyon of us and the place, for, in very trowght, and the place had not be kypyd strong, the Duck had come hether. Arblaster thynketh verely that Hugh a Fen may do moch in your maters, and he thynkyth that he wole do for you faythfully, yf ye wyll, &c.

At the reverens of God, yf any wyrshypfull and profetabile mene may be take yn your maters, for sake it not in eschuyng of our trobell and gret costs and charges that we have, and may growe here after. It ys thoght here that yf my Lord of Norffolk wolld take uppon hym for you, and that he may have a comyssyon for to enquer of such ryotts and robberyes as hath be don to you and other in thys contray, that then all the contray wyll a wayte uppon hym, and serve your entent; for the pepyll lovyth and dredyth hym more then any other lord except the Kyng and my Lord of Warwyk, &c.

God have you in Hys kypyng, and send ous gode tydyngs from you. Wryten in haste, upon the Sonday Seynt Symon and Jude ys Evyn.

By yours,
M. P.

618

MESSAGE TO SIR WILLIAM YELVERTON [1]

This is the Instruccion for the Messenger.

THAT ye grete well Sir William Yelverton, letyng hym wete in our behalf we be informed that certeyn persones, in the name of the right worshipfull our cosyn the Duc of Suffolk, have enterid in the manoir of Drayton that was Fastolffes, and have dreven from the seid manoir and other xiij^c shep and other bestes pastured upon the seid manoir. Notwithstandyng, we merveyle gretly that the seid Sir William, his sones and servauntes, as it is seid, assiste and comfort the seid persones so entryng and with-drawyng the seid catell, seying that he is named both feffe and executour. And all be it so that there is variaunce bithwene hym and our welbelovid John Paston in our coort, consernyng as well the seid manoirs as other goodes that were Sir John Fastolffes, whom God assoyle, yit is may not acorde with worship and consiens for the seid Sir William to assiste the distruccion of the seid manoirs and goodes in the meane tyme. Wherfore we desire hym that he woll do his devoir effect-ually to help to save the seid manoirs from all such pretense of titell, and to cause the seid catels to be restored to the manoirs aforeseid, and not to be withdrawen and distroyed as they be ; and that he do his feithfull part in this behalf acordyng to the trust that he was put in, as we may do for hym in tyme to come.

[1] [From Paston mss., B.M.] This appears to be a message from the King rebuking Judge Yelverton for partizanship in assisting the Duke of Suffolk against Paston in his entry into the manor of Drayton. The date is therefore 1465. The ms., however, is only a corrected draft, and it is not certain that such a message was actually sent.

208

619

JOHN WYMONDHAM TO JOHN PASTON [1]

To my worchipful cosyn, John Paston.

RYGTH worshipful cosyn, I comaunde me to yow. And forasmoch as ther was a child ded at Asteles, and on other lik to be ded in the same place, what tyme that I rode oute aboute my litil livelod, my lady and I bothe thoughte pite on my mastres your wif to se her abide ther, and desirid here to com to my pore hous on to soch tyme as ye shuld a be othirwise avised, wyche, if it plese yow, I am right wel apaied.

Sythen, I undirstande be my lady that ye desire to knowe whedyr that I shulde abide here stille or nowe [*or no*]. As to that, I have non other place that I wold abide at, and my lady seith how she is avised to ende hir lif here. Also she seith how ye desire to have a stabil with inne my plas ; and as to that, afeith, sir, I have none, but that must nedis serve for my wode. As for a chambre, ye shall have on for your men al redy, and as touching a stabil, Sir John Sparham and I have gote yow on ther [*where*] your hors stode the last tyme ye

1465(?)
NOV. 10

[1] [From Fenn, iv. 240.] As to the date of this letter, we can only reproduce what is said of it by Sir John Fenn : 'John Wymondham, Esq., the writer of this letter, married Margery, the daughter of Sir Robert Clifton, Knight, of Denver, in Norfolk, and widow of Sir Edward Hastings, of Elsing, Knight. He therefore calls her "My Lady." He died in 1475.

'He purchased the manor and estate at Felbrigg, of the trustees of Sir Simon Felbrigg, where he had resided ; but once in his absence Sir John Felbrigg made a forcible entry, and dragging out his Lady by the hair of her head, who had locked herself up in a chamber to keep possession, got into possession, and retained it till Wymondham obtained the King's order to Thomas Montgomery, Esq., High Sheriff of the county, to put him again into possession. The dispute was then settled with Sir John Felbrigg, and upon Wymondham's paying to him 200 marks [£133 : 6 : 8] he released his claims, &c.

'This letter seems to have been written during the time that he was dispossessed of Felbrigg, and which must have been either before the year 1461 or 1466, those being the years in which Sir Thomas Montgomery was Sheriff of Norfolk, and as J. Paston at this time seems to have been under misfortunes, it was probably near the latter year. I have therefore ventured, though doubtfully, to date the letter in 1465.'

1465(?)
NOV. 10

were in this town, and an hows to ley inne hey and straw, and cost yow not but making of a rak and a mangeour, and more to your ease there than here ; and yf ye wyl that it be made redy for yow, send werd be the bringer of this letter. And, cosyn, as towching to paiment, I can not sey how ye shal be pleasid with my pore fare, but aftir that ye arn com home, and arn aqweintid there with, we shal so acorde as shal be plesir to us bothe, with the grace of God, which have [you] in His blissid governaunce, and send yow your moderis blissing.

Wreten at Norwich, on Seint Martyn is Even.

     Your poer cosyn and ffrend,

         J. WYMONDHAM.

And how that ever ye do, hold up your manship.

620

MARGARET PASTON TO JOHN PASTON [1]

*To my Rightwurshipfull hosbond, John Paston,
be this delyveryd in hast.*

RIHT worchipfull hosbond, I recomand me to yow, praying yow to wete that I have receyvid the mony that Mayster Brakle had of yow, wherof he hath ageyn v. marc. uppon pledgis of the too basonys that ye had of hym tyll ye come hom. As for cloth for my gowne, I can non gete in this town better than that is that I send yow an exsample of, whiche me thynkith to symple bothe of colour and of cloth. Wherfor I pray yow that ye woll vouchesauf to do bey for me iij. yerdis and j. quarter of seche as it pleasith yow that I shuld have, and what colour that pleaset yow, for in gode feyth I have do sowte all the draperis schopis in this town, and her is right febill cheys. Also I pray yow that ye woll do bey a loff of gode sugour and di. j. lb. [*half one pound*] of holl synamun, for ther is non gode in this town ;

1441-
65
NOV.

[1] [Add. ms. 33,597, f. 2.] The year in which this letter was written is altogether uncertain.

210

and as for mony, ther is non of your tenantis ne fermouris bryngith non as yett. As for tydyngis in this countre, Herry Ingloses men have slayn ij. men of Tonsted on Thursday last past, as it is seyd, and all that countre is sore trobelid ther-with ; and if he had abedyn at home he had be lyke to have be fechid owte of his owyn hows, for the peple ther abowght is sor meved with hym. And on Saterday last past he come ryding thorow this town toward Framyngham ; and if he had abedyn in this town he shuld have ben arestyd ; for men of Tonsted and of the countre pusewid after hym in to this town, and made agrett noyse of hym, and required the mayre and sheryves that he ne his men shuld not pas the town, but that they shuld do as it longed to there parte to do, and told hem the cause why ; and as it is seyd the sergeantis were fals, and lete hym have knowleche ther of, and he hythid hym hens in hast, &c. The blyssyd Trynyte have yow in His keping. Wreten att Norwyche on the Weddenesday next after Seynt Martyn.—Be yowris,

            M. P.

1441-
65
NOV.

621

NOTE

The letter of John Payn to John Paston (No. 126 in vol. ii.), which, on account of the circumstances to which it refers, we have placed in the year 1450, was written, as appears by the contents, fifteen years later, *i.e.* in 1465. We therefore call the reader's attention to it in this place.

622

FUNERAL OF LADY KATHARINE HOWARD [1]

THIS wrytenge, made at Stokeneylond the vth yer of Kynge Edward the iiiith and the morowe next affter Sowlemesse day, wytnesseth that this day and yer a bove said my lady, dame Kateren Howard, departed to God,

1465

[1] [Add. ms. 34,889, f. 38.] 'Soulmas,' or All Souls' Day, is the 2nd November, and it appears that Lady Katharine died on the morrow of that day in 1465. As these expenses run into December, we place them at the end of the year.

211

THE PASTON LETTERS

1465 and my master spent uppon her at this day a bove wreten at her beryinge, and also at her vij^th day, more than   xxli.

Also my master spent uppon her at her xxx^ti day, in almesse and in odre costes, in primis to v.m^l. and ccc. of pore folke every pece takenge i d.   Summa   xxijli. vs.

Item, my master gaff to vi^xxix. prestes and clerkes every pece vj d.   Summa   iijli. iiijs. vj d.

Item, my master gaff to lxviij. cheldren in the quere every pece ij d.   Summa   xs. iiij d.

Item, my master paid for blakke cloth for gownes for his men vij^xx yerdes prise of every yerde iiijs. iiij d.   Summa   xxjli.

Item, my master bout as myche waxe for torches and taprys as cost hym   viij. markis. iijs. ij d.

Item, my master paid for xiij. pore mennes gownes for the clothe and for the makengs   lijs.

Item, my master spent in all maner of spyces as myche as drew   liijs. xj d.

Item, my master spent in wyne at the said day   iij. pypes.

Item, my master spent in maltt for brewenge   viij. seme.

Item, my master spent in bere at the same day   xxxij. barelles.

Item, my master spent in whete to make brede and odre bakenge   xiij. seme.

Item, my master spent at the said day in brawne   ij. gret bores.

Item, in beff	. xij. gret oxsen.
Item, in moton	xl. shepe.
Item, in porke	xij. hogges.
Item, in pygges	lxx.
Item, in swannes	xij.
Item, in geese	iiij^xx.
Item, in conyis	c. cowple.
Item, in capons	xxiiij.
Item, in chekens	vij^xx.
Item, in venyson	xxx. dois.

EDWARD IV

Item, in pertryches	.	.	.	iiij. doseyn. 1465
Item, in fesauntis .	.	.		xiv.
Item, in pekokkes	.	.	.	vij.
Item, in mallardes	.	.		iij. doseyn.
Item, in plovers	.	.	.	iij. doseyn.
Item, in eggis	.	.	.	viij. C.
Item, in mylke	.	.	.	xxx. galons.
Item, in hony	.	.	.	iij. galons.

623

MARGARET PASTON TO JOHN PASTON THE YOUNGER[1]

To John Paston the younger.

I GRETE you wele, letyng you wete that as for[2] your Before sustrys[3] beyng with my Lady, if your fader wull aggrey 1466 therto I hold me right wele pleasyd; for I wuld be right clad that she shuld do her servyse be for any other, if she cowde do that shuld pleas my ladyes good grace. Wherfor I wuld that ye shuld speke to your fader therof and lete hym wete that I am pleasid that she shuld be ther if he wuld, for I wuld be right glad and she myght be preferrid by mariage or be servyce, so that it myght be to her wurchep and profight in dischargyng of her frendis; and I pray you do your parte therin for your owyn wurchep and herys. And assone as ye may with ought daunger, purvey that I may have ageyn the vj. marks that ye wote of, for I wuld not that your fader wust it. Item, if ye pas London, send me ageyn my chene and the litill chene that I lent you be for, be sum trusty person; and if ye wull have my good wille, eschewe such thyngis as I spake to you of last

[1] [Add. MS. 34,889, f. 208.] This letter was written at a time when John Paston, the writer's husband, and one of his sons, was in London, while the other, to whom this letter is addressed, was going thither. The date must therefore be before May 1466, but what particular year or month it is impossible to say.

[2] 'affor,' MS.

[3] This may be either Anne or Margery Paston. Who 'my lady' was does not appear.

THE PASTON LETTERS

Before 1466   in owr parisch chirch. I pray God make you as good a man as ever was any of your kynne, and Goddis blissyng mote ye have and myn, so that ye do wele, &c. Wretyn the Sonday next after your departyng.

And I pray you, send me sum tydyngis as sone as ye may after that ye be comyn to London, how your fader spedyth and your brother in here materes.

Be your moder.

624

JOHN RADCLIFF OF ATTLEBOROUGH TO JOHN PASTON[1]

To my ryght trusty and welbelovyd Frend, John Paston.

R YGTH trusty and welbelovid, I cummaund me un to zow, lattyng zow wytte that there ys a tenawnt off Thyrnyng, on [one] Wyllyam Rust, whos dur ys selyd be a offycer off zowrys. Wherffor I pray zow that ze wyll se that the forsay tenawnt be not hurt; and yff there be oni thyng that ys dw for to pay, I wyll se that hyt schall be content. And therfore I pray zow that hyt may be repytyd un tyll the tyme that I speke with zow. No more at thys tyme, but the Hole Trinite hawe zow in kepyng. Wretyn at Attylburgth the xvij. day off Dyssembyre.

JOHN RADCLYFF DE ATTYLBURGTH.

[1] [Add. MS. 34,889, f. 223.] The principal lordship in the manor of Thurning belonged to the Radcliff, or Ratcliff, family, afterwards Earls of Sussex; but it seems there was another lordship which belonged to John de Mauteby in the ninth year of Edward II. From this very likely Margaret Paston derived some claims, and John Paston through his wife. *See* No. 634. The year of this letter, however, cannot be ascertained.

EDWARD IV

625

SIR JOHN FELBRIGGE TO JOHN PASTON[1]

To my Cosyn Paston, be thys letter delyverd yn haste.

R YGHT reverent and worshyppeful cosyn, y comawnd 1466(?) me on to you, desyryng to her off your welfare, the JAN. [20] whyche Almyghty Jesu preserve to Hys plesawns, and to your own herts desyres. Forthermore and yff yt please your gentylnesse to be my trusty frend, as my ful truste ys yn you, as for swyche materys as the brynger off this lettre shall enforme you, and beth effectualy my frend, and brynge yt abowte, and by my trowthe y shall geve you an C. marke for your labowr. For yn trowthe y am aferde that Roberd Radclyff hathe deseyvyd me, for he laboryd to me dayly by my Lords comawndement off Warwyk, and brought with hym Yllyngworthe and oder off my Lords counsel, and seen my evydens; and so we stoden uppon apoyntement, and y for to have had an unswere sent to Felbrygge Halle, and yff ne had be for ffendyng off my Lords lordschyppe, y myght have had my money for my ryght or y cam owt off London, as my man schall enforme you. For yn trowthe y muste now make an schiffte, for Wyndham hathe sold hys ryght, and rathere than yt schuld go that way to, y had lever my Lord had yt ij. C. marke with yn the pryse that y grawnt yt laste, and therfor y be scheche you to labowr to my Lord that y may have an unswer. And thies many townes longithe thereto, Felbrygge, Aylinton, Ronton, Colby, Bannyngham, Ingworthe, Styrston, besyde hamelets.

No mor to you at this tyme, but the Holy Trinyte have

[1] [From Fenn, iv. 242.] The date of this letter cannot be ascertained with very great precision; but as it belongs most probably to about the same period as Letter 619, which we have referred to November 1465, we may assign this to the January following.

466(?)
AN. [20] you yn His kepyng. Wryten at Felbrygg, the Monday affor Seynt Augnetes Day.[1]

By your cosyn,   JOHN FELBRYGGE.

626

JOHN WYKES TO SIR JOHN PASTON[2]

Un to the ryght wyrshypfull mayster, Sir John Paston, Knygt, be thys letter delyverya.

1466
FEB. 17

RYGHT wyrshypfull and my especyall gode mayster, I recomaund me unto your gode maystershyp, letyng you wyte that the berour herof told me that ye had grete mervyll that I send to you no word ne letter of awnswer of the letters that ye had send to me to London. As for on letter ye send to me by Rychard Playtorys man, and therof I send you an awnswer in a letter by a man of the Prior of Bromholm; and as for other letters, ther com no more to me but that on.

Item, Mayster Flemmyng lokyth dayly for hys hors, and at every tyme that I mete with hym, he askyth of me when hys hors shuld com, and when I here any word from you. Wherfore I pray you send me word in a letter how he shall be awnswerd, and yf the hors shall com, lette me knowe when; for and he had not trustyd theruppon, he wold have purveyd hym in a nother place, &c.

Item, John Oter ys not yet payd, but as I suppose it shall

[1] The modern version in Fenn reads 'the Monday *after* Saint Agnes's Day,' and the date subjoined at the bottom of the page is in accordance with this reading. But it is more likely the text as printed in the old spelling is correct. St. Agnes' Day is the 21st January. The Monday before it would have been the 20th in 1466.

[2] [From Fenn, iv. 246.] As this letter was written after Edward IV.'s marriage, and before the death of John Paston the father, the date must be either 1465 or 1466. Fenn assigns it to the latter year, and I think he is right, though he does not state his reasons. I find that John, Lord Lovel, died on the 9th January 1465, leaving his son and heir, Francis, only nine years old, so that even if we date this letter 1466, the young lad was married at the early age of ten. This was probably owing to his wardship having been obtained by Lord Fitzhugh, or some person interested; but as the inquisition on his father's death (*Inq. p. m.*, 4 Edw. IV., No. 27) was not taken till October 1465, there seems no ground for believing that he could have been forced into wedlock a month after he was left an orphan.

216

not be long to tyll he have it, for he hath spoken to my mayster your fader a yer therfor; and as for Gylmyn, he hath not spoken to my mayster as yet, &c.

1466
FEB. 17

Item, I truste he wylbe your gode fader, for John Say hath told hym playnly of hys demenyng ayenst you, and told hym that he had the lasse favour for your sake, &c.

Item, the Erle of Arundell ys[1] son hath weddyd the Quyne ys suster.

Item, the Lord Lovell ys son[2] hath weddyd my Lady Fytzhugh ys doghter, &c.

Item, Jenney desyryth a trety with my mayster, and spake to my mayster therof hym sylf in Westminster Hall.

Item, all felaws in the Kyngs hows fareid well, and wold have you ther.

No more to you at thys tyme, but the Holy Trynyte have you [in] kepyng. Wryten at London, the Monday next after Seynt Volentyn.

Your servant,   JOHN WYKYS.

627

CLEMENT PASTON TO JOHN PASTON[3]

To hys rythe worchypfwll mayster, John Paston, Sqwyer.

RYTHE worchypfwll broder, I recomawnde me to zow. MARCH 18 And as for zour letter to my Lorde Chawnceler I have not delyveryd it; for I askyd avysse there in, and I was aunsweryd there in that sythen he was takyn to baylle, the Chawncelerer[4] cowde not compelle the swertes to bryng hym in

[1] Thomas Fitz Alan, Lord Maltravers, eldest son of William Fitz Alan, Earl of Arundel, married Margaret, second daughter of Richard Widville, Earl Rivers, and sister to Elizabeth, Queen of Edward IV. He succeeded his father as Earl of Arundel in 1487, 3 Hen. VII., and died in 1524, 16 Hen. VIII.—F.

[2] Francis Lovel, son and heir to John, Lord Lovel, married Anne, daughter of Henry, Lord Fitz Hugh. It is curious that she is here called 'Lady Fitz Hugh's daughter,' when her father was alive.

[3] [From Paston Letters, B.M.] The reference to the dispute between Elizabeth Poynings and the Earl of Kent, which is alluded to in a subsequent letter, proves this letter to have been written in the year 1466. The earl in question was only so created on the 3rd of May 1465, and John Paston, to whom the letter is addressed, died in May 1466. [4] So in MS.

217

1466
MARCH 18

befor hys day. Also me thowte zour letter was not most plesauntly wrytyn to take to swyche a lorde. And as for the tresorer, hys name is Syr John Fooge, but he is not in London nor wythe the Kyng, so I kan [not] have the letter sent hym but if I hyeryd a man to bere it. And as for zour question of the patentes, Grenfeld and Catesby and Sterkey holdyn it a good question, for the statute is, *Patentes dez tenements dount null titill est trouve pur le roy de recorde sount voydez,* anno xviij. H. vi. ca. vj. But I trowe in zour cas that be ther opiniounis the Acte of the Parlement is a tytyll of recorde. It is said to the contrary intent, thow the londs be forfetyd of record, yet ther is no certificacion of recorde qwat londes they be, nor wer [where] nor in qwat place they lye; but and thys clawse be in the patents, *Non obstante quod nulla inquisicio pro nobis inde est inventa,* by Grenfelde is consayle the patents xwld be clerly goode. But me semythe that amendyt not the mater, for be for the makyng of the statute above sayde, patents graunttyd of londs be fore inquisicion were goode and effectuell and the statute is generall :—*Patents dount null tytill, &c. sount voydez.* Thanne it folowyt well if the Acte of Parlement be no tytyll for the Kyng thann is ther no tytyll for the Kyng of recorde, for that clawse in the patente is no tytyll; than if ther [be] no tytyll, ergo the patents voyde.

My suster[1] standythe in the same casse with my Lord of Kent.

Broder, I pray zow send mor mony for my nevew John, for he mwst ellys com hom azen; for the Kyng gothe into Scotlonde, and he is nowther horsyd nor harneysyd, for his grett hors is lykly to dye; and if ze wyll sende it to me or to Christofyr Hanyngton it xall be save for hym. I send zow a letter from hym closyde herin. And I pray spek to my moder that my hors faylle not on Passyon Swnday,[2] for thann xall I be redy and thanne xall ower redyng be don. Wrytyn on Twesday nexst after Seynt Gregory is Day.   Zowr broder,

CLEMENT PASTON.

On the back.—The man wold not tak my letter but I wass fayen to gyve hym ijd. for the beryng.

[1] Elizabeth, widow of Robert Poynings.   [2] 23rd March.

218

628

FRIAR JOHN MOWTH TO JOHN PASTON[1]

To my worchepful mayster, John Paston the holdest, be this letter delyveryd in hast.

RYTH reverent and worcheful sire, I hartyly recomende 1466 me on to your reverens, thankyng yow for the gret MAY 12 cher and comfortabyll words that ye yovyn on to me wat tyme that I was last yn yowr presens; desyryng ful specyaly of Almity God, owt of al your wordly tribulacyonys and adversyte, gracyowus delyverans, and yn al vertuows prosperite, good encres and contynuans. If yt like your maysterchep to know the cause of thys wrytyng, it ys thys; it is nowth unknow[2] on to yow that Mayster Brakle (Cryst rest hys sowle !), delyveryd to Wyllam Paston, your broder, certayn oblygacyonys, of the weche the dute xuld grow to my convent yn Norwyche. I have spoke on to Wyllam Paston her of, and he excuseth hym and seyth on this wyse; that be the wyl of Mayster Brakle, wat tyme that Sire Tomas Todenham,[3] Knyth, xuld be put on to hys deth, he delyveryd hem on to hys confessor; the weche, as he seth, xuld a be Grey fryer, hows name he knowyth nowt; also he seyth that after the deth of the forseyd Knyt, he spake with the Fryer, confessor on to the Knyth, and hasked hym aftyr the forseyd oblygacyonys, and as he seyth, the Fryer seyd on to hym that he had delyveryd hem on to [the] Knyth Marchall. Werfor I beseche you, as specyaly as I may, that, now wyl your broder is at London, that ye of your grace wyl know the trowthe in this mater, for the comfort of the dede, and profyth of my

[1] [From Fenn, i. 256.] Friar Brackley, who is here mentioned as dead, is spoken of in John Paston's deposition of December 1465, without any indication that he was at that time deceased (*see* No. 606). We may presume, therefore, that he died between that time and May 1466, in which month and year died John Paston, to whom this letter is addressed.

[2] *Nowth unknow.* I believe this to be the true reading of the original MS. Fenn prints it 'nowthn know.'

[3] He was beheaded on Tower Hill in February 1462.

219

THE PASTON LETTERS

1466
MAY 12

convent. Nomor at this tyme, but that I be seche Almyty God in Trinyte conserve your, and kepe yow in all vertuows prosperite. Amen.

Wretyn at Heylysdon in gret hast, the xij. day of May, in your maner aftyr mete. The cause wy the mayster delyveryd hem to hym mor than to yow, was, as he seyd on to me, for as meche as ye had so many maters yn hand for yowr self, and also for the dede, that he durst not attempt yow with all ; and al so be cause he had lesse for to do hys hope was that he xuld asped yt mor redyly.

Fr[e]re Willam Thorp dwellyng at Salisbury.

By yowr pore orator and bedman,
FRIER JAN MOWTH.

629

MARGARET PASTON TO SIR JOHN PASTON [1]

1466(?)
NOV. 13(?)

I GRETE you wele and send you Goddis blissyng and myn ; letyng you wete that I send you be the berer herof xl*li*. of Ryall which I have chevysshed and borwed for you, be cause I wuld not take that was leyd ought for you at Norwich ; for, as I am enformed be Mayster John Smyth, the Chaunceller, and other that we ben all a cursed that we have thus mynystred the dedis godes with ought licence or auctorite, and I wene we spede all the wers there fore. At the reverence of God, gete you a licens of my Lord of Caunterbery in dyschargyng of my conscyens and yowris, to mynystre a certeyn summe of iij. or iiij^c marcs, enfourmyng hym how that your lyffelod hath stond this ij. yer in such trobill that ye myght right nought have of it, ner yet can take of it with ought ye shuld hurt your tenauntis, thei have so ben vexid be on trew meanes before this tymes, And ye have many grete

[1] [Add. MS. 34,889, f. 99.] This letter was written before administration had been obtained of John Paston's will; presumably therefore in the year in which he died, 1466. It may be observed, likewise, that in 1467 'my lord of Canterbury' would probably have been called 'my lord Cardinal.'

220

EDWARD IV

materis on hand and may not have to bere them ought, ner to save your ryght, withaught ye myght for a tyme takyn of your faderis godes. And this I hope shall discharge owr conscyens of that we have mynystred and spend be fore. For we have nomor to acquite this xl*li*. and bere all other charges but the xlvii*li*. that your unkyll and ye is privy to, that was leyd up at Norwich. I wuld ye were ware of large theftis and rewardis gevyng, as otheris folkis avyse you to do, for though ye have nede thei wull not be right redy to help you of ther owyn ; and that ye may understand be that that thei have taken a wey from you be for this tyme. I wuld not in no wyse ye shuld put your self in no daunger to hym but as litill as ye may ; for if ye do, it shall be right wele remembred you her after. And be ware how ye ben bownd in any obligacion to any creature but if it be leyd in endifferent handis and trosty for yowr part. And remembre to gete the obligacion that ye mad to the Duchesse of Suffolk ; for though it be in my Lord Chancelleris hande it is jepartows, be cause of perell of deth. Item, understand wele the poyntis that ben in my cosyn Arblasteris letter that arn wretyn in yowrs, and purvey redily ther for for your owyn a vayll. Item, send me home answeris of sueche materis as arn now sent you bethen (*sic*) mowth and wrytyng at this tyme as hastly as ye can, or ells it shall hurt yow mor than ye or I can yet understand. Item, me semyth, if ye shall not comyn home this Crystmesse, or if ye shuld be at my Lady of Suffolk, it [were [1]] necessary to have Playter there with you if ye shuld engroos any appoyntementis with here at that tyme. For she is sotill and hath sotill councell with here ; and therfore it were wele do ye shuld have summe with you that shuld be of your councell. If John Paston be with you at London desire hym to take hede to yowris materis and in what case thei ben left at your departyng, that if nede be he may help you to labore for such causes as Wykes shall telle yow be mowth ; and if he be not with yow, and ye wull I shall send hym to you. Item, spare of [2] the xl*li*. as mych as ye may that ye may perfourme be the mony that the Duchesse of Suffolk shuld have, in cas that it may not be gadered of the

[1] Omitted in MS.   [2] *of* repeated in MS.

221

1466(?
NOV. 13(

THE PASTON LETTERS

1466(?)
NOV. 13(?)

lyvelode. Send home Wykes a sone as ye can, and how ye will that I do in your materis and lyvelode at home. God have you in His kepyng. Wretyn the Thursday next Sent Martyn.

Be your Moder.

630

MARGARET PASTON TO JOHN PASTON [1]

To my right wurchipfull husbond, John Paston, be this deliverd in hast.

Year uncertain
NOV.

R YTH worchepfull husbonde, I recomande me to yow. Plesyth yow to weet that Thomas Grene was with me as on Saterday last paste, and let me have knowlage that the scherre schold be as thys day at the Gyld Hall in Norwyche, and be desyiryd me that the swte that ye have ageyns Thomas Jeryng and othyr myth be sesyd as for thys schere ; and I seyd that I durste do ryth not there in. And he tolde me that Thomas Jeryng was with yow in Flegge the laste tyme that ye wer ther, and ye seyd to hym that he scholde not be hurte by the swte. And Thomas Grene told me that if the seyd Jeryng and othyrs in the same wryte mad not an end with yow by the nexte schere, the whyche schall be thys day monyth, that he the seyd Thomas Grene wole purchese a new wryte of hys owne coste ayens that daye. I

[1] [From Paston MSS., B.M.] I find no very satisfactory evidence touching the date of this letter. Allusion is made to John Paston having been at Lincoln. The occasion referred to might have been in 1458, when, as we know by No. 373, he went into the North as far as Doncaster; or it may have been in the spring of 1461. (See Nos. 452 and 458.) It is not probable, however, that this letter was earlier than the latter date, as there is no appearance at that time of any dispute having arisen between John Paston and his brother William. On the contrary, William Paston is in correspondence with his brother in April 1461 (No. 450). On the other hand, if the occasion referred to when John Paston was at Lincoln was in the spring of 1461, this letter could hardly have been written in the same year; for it cannot be supposed that he left books at Caister on his return south, when Caister was in the possession of the Duke of Norfolk. The date, however, being so uncertain, I prefer to place this letter at the end of John Paston's correspondence rather than assign it doubtfully to any particular year.

222

EDWARD IV

Year uncertain
NOV.

woste not that the scher shuld be so sone when I wrote to yow yowyr laste lettyr. And he remembyryd the trobulus werd [*world*] that is nowe, and also that they wer nowtye felawys that ye suyd, and ther fore he thowte that it war best to let it be respyte at thys tyme, and so they schall be respyth at thys tyme. I have sent to Jaferay Spyrlyng for the bokys that ye sent to me fore, and he seyth that he hathe none there of, for he seyth he lefte hem with yow when he was with yow in the Northe contre ; for he seyth ye left hym behynd yow at Lynkcolne. He supposyth they be at Kaster.

Item, my cosyn Crane recomandyth hyr to yow, and prayith yow that ye wole wychesave to spek to Jamys Gresham for to swe ferthe the mater betwyx Dame Margaret Spurdans and hyr ; and sche prayith yow at the reverens of God that ye wole tendyr that mater well, for all hyr troste is in yow.

Item, the tenauntys at Sweynysthorp prayid me for to wryte to yow for to pray yow for Goddys sake that ye wole help for to get hem a good baly of the hundyryd that they be in ; for they sey that they have be gretly hurte by swyche offyserys as they have had ther be fore tyme. Folk wold fayne in thys contre that Heydon scholde be purveyd for, that he goo not so at large as he dothe, for he is in thys towne nere every wek, and hathe be ever syne ye yd hens. And also it is seyd in thys towne that ye have be good maister thys terme to Yatys, and many be ryth sory ther of, and that he dothe so well as it [is] seyd here that he dothe. It is seyd that he is scapyd all dangerys, and he hathe tak new accionys ageyns hys neyborys, as it is seyd. Othyr tydyngys have we none here but that ye have more pleynly there. And the Blyssyd Trinyte have yow in Hys kepyng, and send yow good sped in all yowyr materys. Wretyn in haste at Norwyche the Monday next be fore Seynt Edmunde the Kynge.

Be yowyr,   M. P.

My modyr wold ryth fayne know how that ye and my brodyr Wyllam wer acordyd, sche wold ryth fayne that all wer well betwene yow.

223

THE PASTON LETTERS

631

B. D. M. S. TO JOHN PASTON[1]

Be this delyvered to Mastyr John Paston.

I RECOMAUNDE me unto you as unknowyn. And as for the wryting I send unto you, the cause why yt was nate endossed was, for the berer ther of knew yow wel i now. And as for youre Cossyn Mary, she ys no longer with us, as a pon Seynt Mathewys Evyn she departyd from me, and went to Awdry Croxeston, and she told me that ye wold pay for her borde ther. But on thyng I let you know ; she hathe demenyd her ful symply bothe for youre worship and also for her awne. Ther ys but few within oure plasse but they know how yt is with her, and al by her awne bessynes of her tunge. And I had knowyn as myche at the begynnyng as I have don sythe, I wold not have delt in the mater nat for xl. pound ; for I wys she ys no thyng so sadde as I wold she wer.

No more to you at thys tyme, but the Holy Gost have you in His kepyng, and send you youre hertys esse. I pray you hertly that I may sp[e]ke with you.

B. D. M. S.

632

ABSTRACT[2]

RICHARD SUTHWELL TO JOHN PASTON, ESQUIRE.

Thanks him for speaking to the Mayor and Recorder for the appearance of certain persons at this last session, as he wrote from Walsingham. Thomas Wolvesby and Colyns make great labor for the poor men's undoing. Begs him to move the Mayor to have pity, considering their trouble at Walsingham, when they were prisoners.

Thetford, Shere-Thursday.

[1] [From Fenn, iv. 262.] There is no evidence of the date either of this or of the four following letters beyond the fact that this and the two next are addressed to John Paston, while the two last are addressed to Margaret Paston during her husband's life. None of them, therefore, can be later than 1466.

[2] [From Paston mss., B.M.]

224

EDWARD IV

633

ABSTRACT[1]

JOHN PASTON, JUNIOR, TO HIS FATHER, JOHN PASTON

Has spoken 'with Warwyk and Stwkle' for the place and lands in Arleham. Declined their offer of 6d. an acre, they keeping the place in repair ; but Stwkle has promised all the lands shall be purveyed for, as for this year. Warwyk this day offered my mother 7d. an acre for the lands in Arleham, but I counselled her to hold out for a longer term. Kook will no longer hold the place for 7d. or 8d. an acre, and will only give 6d., if he is to keep it in repair. Has spoken with Dame Alice Weche and Geoffrey Spyrlyng, who have agreed to set a tenant to occupy the lands in dispute till Paston comes home.

St. Martin's Even.

634

ABSTRACT[2]

THOMAS GNATYSHALE TO MRS. PASTON

I hope the young man I sent will please 'my master and you.' I hope you will not receive him at this time, and when my master comes home refuse him. As for your lands at Sparham, there are not many lands to let. Has inquired at Salle. Master Edward[3] is clearly answered of £18 a year and 7s. or 8s. more. Bryston, Thyrnyng, and Owleton are let, which belong to the manor of Salle. So he is clearly answered twice a year at London, besides the fees, viz., of the receiver 26s. 8d., of the steward 20d., and of the bailliff 26s. 8d.

Sparham, Wednesday before Ascension.

635

ABSTRACT[4]

T. GNATYSHALE TO MRS. PASTON

James and Robert Radclef mean to take away my goods, and I shall be taken if I be at Norwich at next shire. Pray let my master know. I suppose

[1] [From Paston mss., B.M.]   [2] *Ibid.*
[3] Probably Edward, son of Robert Mauteby. He was Margaret Paston's uncle.
[4] [From Paston mss., B.M.]

VOL. IV.—P

225

THE PASTON LETTERS

it was by their commandment that my two neat were taken on Saturday last at Lyng, 'for one that is under bailly of Richmond took hem.' John Everyton will tell you more. The receipts of the manor of Sparham with costs are £10, 3s. 11½d. If any man of yours come to Norwich please send me your advice.

(Signed) 'T. GNAT.'

636

ABSTRACT[1]

JAMES ARBLASTER TO JOHN PASTON, [SQUIRE][2]

John à Berney of Wychyngham wishes to disinherit him of his liberty of faldage in Colyette. Desires the help of one of Paston's men. As for my Lady of Oxford, 'I have get you a trusty man against Tuesday or Wednesday next.'

[There is no distinct evidence of the date of this letter, except that it is probably not later than 1466, when John Paston died, though it may have been addressed to his younger son John. Compare Nos. 232, 233, and 234, in vol. ii.]

637

JOHN PASTON'S FUNERAL[3]

Expences paid by Gloys at Norwich the day the Cors was ther and befor.

FYRSTE. The iiii. orders of fryers, viii*l.* Item, almesse, iis. viid. Item, to xxiii. susters of Normandys,[4] with the gardian eche of them, iiii*d.*, and the gardian, viii*d.* —viiis. Item, in offering on Pentecost Tuesday[5] for my master, id. ; for the herse, xls. For xxiiii. yerdes of brod wythtys for gowns, xxviis. viii*d.* ; for dyeng of the same, iiii*s.*

[1] [From Paston mss., B.M.]
[2] This designation is added on the address, but is struck out.
[3] [From Blomefield's *Norfolk*, vi. 483. Folio edition, iii. 692.] The original of this document was probably among the Paston mss. when Blomefield composed his *History of Norfolk*, but where it is at present cannot be ascertained. It is cited by Blomefield, or perhaps by his continuator, Mr. Parkin, as 'a very long but narrow roll,' then in his possession. The text, however, does not seem to be printed entire, as the Editor only professes to give 'several particulars therein.'
[4] At Norwich.   [5] 27th May 1466.

226

EDWARD IV

For settyng on the tents, vi*d.* For xxii. yerdes and iii. quarters of brod wythts, xxxiiiis. iii*d.* For grownedyng, iiis. iiii*d.* For dyeng, iiiis. To xxxviii. prests at the dyryge at Norwyche, when the cors lay ther, xiis. viii*d.* To xxxix. schyldern with surplyces within the schurche and without, iiis. iiii*d.* To xxvi. clerks with iiii. kepers of the torches, eche of them iid., iiis. iiii*d.* To the clerks of St. Peters and St. Stevens for the ryngers ageyn the cors, iis. To the iiii. orders of fryers that rede ageyn the cors——. To the Prioress of Carow, vis. viii*d.* To a maide that came with her, xx*d.* To the ancors [*anchoress* ?] xl*d.* In almesse, xvs. To a woman that came from London with the cors to Norwyche, vis. viii[*d.*]

Payments be Gloys and Calle at Bromholme.

Fyrste. To the Prior, be my masters bequest, xls. To ix. monks, eche of them vis. viii*d.*, iii*l.* To an other monke, who was of the same place, xx*d.* For brinnyng of the Abbes with the torches, xx*d.* To the Priors boteler for bred, iis. x*d.* For wasshyng of napry, xii*d.* To the boteler for hys reward, xx*d.* To the baker for cccx. eggs, xix*d.* To hym for hys reward, iiii*s.* iiii*d.* To xxviii. bedds with —— of clothys, and wasshyng of the same, vs. To ii. men that fyllyd the grave, viii*d.* To brueng of v. kome malte, xx*d.* For ix. pownd candyl, xi*d.* To the clerks of Bromholm, viii*d.* For viii. peces of peuter lost of the Priors, xx*d.* Geven among the men of the bakhouse, xx*d.* To the parisshe schyrche of Bromholm, xs. To xii. schyrchys, ls. viii*d.* To the prest that cam with the cors from London, iiis. iiii*d.* To servytors that awaytyd upon hym by the komawndment of W. Paston, xxi*d.* To Playters for hys offering, iiii*d.* To the vyker of Upton, iis. To the sexton of Bromholm for xxii. crossys geven to Marget and Modeley, *per* John Paston, iiii*s.* vi*d.* To xiiii. rynggars, viis. To xxiiii. servertors, eche of them iiiid., viiis. To lxx. servertors, eche of them iii*d.*, xviis. vi*d.* Paid to Dawbeny for servertors, viis. For fyshh the day after the enterment, vis. x*d.* For vi. barells bere, xiis. For a roundlet of red wine of xv. gallonys, &c., xiis. xi*d.* To

1466

1466

227

THE PASTON LETTERS

1466 a hors hyer for iii. days for Sir James, xii*d*. For a quarter malte, v*s*. For iiii. bushels wete, xxxii*d*. For a quarter of otys, ii*s*. viii*d*. For x. kombe malte brueng, xl*d*. For the boord of Rychard Hermer, wrythe, iii. days, and for hys hyer the sayde tyme, xiii*d*. *ob*. For William Yonge, barbor, v. days mete and drynke, and hys hyer the sayde tyme, xvi*d*. For vi. pownd candyl, vii*d*. *ob*. To xii. pore men beryng torches from London to Norfolk be vi. day, i*s*., takyng eche of them on the day iiii*d*., and for iii. dayes in goyng homer-ward, takynge every day vi*d*. Geven to Martyn Savage and Denschers awaytyng upon my master at London be vii. dayes before that he was caryed, ii*s*. x*d*. For bred bowthe, xxiii*s*. For vii. barels bere, xvii*s*. vi*d*. For a barel of the grettest assyse, iii*s*. iiii*d*. For iiii. barells of alee, xiii*s*. iiii*d*. For bred and alee for xii. men that bare torches, xiii*d*. *ob*. To a dole at Bromholm, vl. xiii*s*. iiii*d*. To William Colens, one of the botelers at Bromholm, xii*d*. To Wate Webster, another bote-ler, xii*d*. To Greg. Worsteler, one of the porters at Brom-holm, iiii*d*. The parson at Mauteby,[1] and Sir Thomas Lynes, to the prestes at the deryge at Bromholm, xliii*s*. In almesse, xlvii*s*. vi*d*.; more, xx*s*. To the glaser for takyn owte of ii. panys of the wyndows of the schyrche for to late owte the reke of the torches at the deryge, and sowderyng new of the same, xx*d*. [This part of the roll, according to Blomefield, or his continuator, seemed to be written by Gloys, above mentioned, in an indifferent hand. The remainder is in a very neat and curious old hand, which was supposed to be that of Margaret Paston.]

Vittelles bought by Richard Charles.

First. For xxvii. gees, xvii*s*. For xxvii. frankyd gees, vi*s*. viii*d*. lxx. caponnes, xvii*s*. vii*d*. For xxix.[2] xvii*s*. chekons, xvi*s*. vi*d*. For x. chekons, x*d*. For xli. pygges, xiii*s*. x*d*. For xlix. calvys, iiii*l*. xiii*s*. iiii*d*. For xxxiiii*s*.

[1] Robert Coteler, who was presented to the living by John Paston in 1465, on the resignation of Thomas Howys.
[2] A short blank occurs in Blomefield after 'xxix.' and before 'xvii.'

228

EDWARD IV

lambys, xxvii*s*. ii*d*. For xxii. shep, xxxvii*s*. v*d*. x. nete, 1466 iiii*l*. xvi*s*. i*d*. For ii. napronnes to Richard Lynstede, x*d*. For claretts and fawcetts, vi*d*. MCCC. eggs, vi*s*. vi*d*. For xx. galons milk, xx*d*. For viii. galons creme, ii*s*. viii*d*. For iiii. pints of butter, iiii*d*. For i. quarter and ii. bushels of whete mele, vii*s*. x*d*. To the parson of Crostweyt for i. quarter of whete, vi*s*. For xiii. galons of ale, ii*s*. To a labourer for iii. days, xii*d*. To xxiii. galons of ale, iiii*s*. For xiii. salt fysshe, iiii*s*. iiii*d*. For the purveying of bred, ale, and fysshe, iii*s*. iiii*d*. To William Reynolds for lodgyng of Master Prowet, the Prior of the White Freres, the parson of Mautby, Sir Thomas Lynds, and other, by ii. nyghtis, vi*d*. For bred, ale, and possets to the same persons, vi*d*. To Herman, fleying bests by iii. days, ii*s*., and to John Foke, by iii. days, xx*d*. For purveying of all the velys, lambes, x. beefins, certain piggs and polaly [*poultry*], xl*d*.

BILL OF THE PRIOR OF BROMHOLM.

Memorandum. The Prior toke to bord diverse persons laboryng abought the enterment, begynnyng the Thursday in Pentecost weke, the vi. yere of Kyng Edward the iiiith.

On Thursday I[1] find 3 persons who had xii*d*. for their board and hire; on Friday 5 who had xv*d*.; on Saturday 8 who had xxiii*d*. On Monday all were employed; and on the day after I find 4 to be allowed for their board iiii*d*. *ob*., and for their hires v*d*.,—ix*d*. *ob*. Delivered by the Prior to Richard Charles:—Fyrst, v. quarters of otes, xiii*s*. iiii*d*.; v. swyne, xii*s*. vi*d*.; ii. bushel of mestlyn, xv*d*.; v. pownd of candell, v*d*.; xx. quarters of malte, xiii*s*. iiii*d*., and with gryndyng and brewyng, xviii*s*. For a cartfull of hey, iii*s*. iiii*d*. For ii. swyne, v*s*. For ii. bushel otes, viii*d*. For a quarter of herryng, vi*d*. For half a quarter makerell, vii*d*. *ob*. To the parson of St. Peters for his fee of the wax abought the coors, beside ii. candels of i. *lb*. and i. hert candel of a pound, xx*d*. At my masters xxx. day for offeryng, i*d*. Geven to churches and in almes by Gresham, toward Bromholm, v.

[1] Blomefield or his continuator here speaks in his own person.

229

THE PASTON LETTERS

1466 *marks*. To the clerk of St. Peters of Hungate[1] his felaship for ryngyng when the coors was in the church, xii*d*. To Dawbeney for bests and other stuffe for the enterment, xx*l*. To him in gold for to chaunge into small mony for the dole, xl*l*. To W. Pecok, in iii. bags to bere to Bromholm, in copper, the 20th day, xxvi. *marks*. To Medeley for his reward, iiii. *marks*, and the same to Maryot. To Maryot for costs he bare by the way to Bromholm, iii*l*. xii*d*. More to Medeley for mony paid by him, xli*s*. x*d*. To the keper of the inne where myne husband dyed, for his reward, xx*s*. To Paston chirch, x*s*. To Bakton chirch, vi*s*. viii*d*. To Gresham the London carrier, in full payment for the Chaundeler of London, v*l*. xix*s*. More in almes mony, vi*s*. viii*d*. More for wyne and bere, vii. *marks*. To the parson of St. Peters, vi*s*. viii*d*. For wyne for the seingers when the coors was at Norwich, xx*s*. To Skolehouse in part of his bille for torches and wax made at Bromholm, for to brenne upon the grave, iiii. *marks*. For x. yerds of narow blak for the viker of Dallynge and Robert Gallawey, and for iii. yerds and quarter of brod cloth for Illee, xx*s*. x*d*. To Freton chirch, vi*s*. viii*d*. For a cope called a frogge of worsted for the Prior of Brom-holm, xxvi*s*. viii*d*. For bred at the enterment, ix*s*. In almes, viii*s*. iiii*d*. In wyne and spices, l*s*. To Dom. John Loveday for cloth for a ridyng cope for himself, xiii*s*. ii*d*. To the makyng of Redham Stepill, viii*s*. iiii*d*. To John Orford, wax chandeler, for xii. torches and one candell of i. *lb*., lv*s*. ii*d*. *ob*. To John Dewe for grey lynen cloth and sylk frenge for the hers, vi*l*. xvi*s*. ii*d*. Given to the Austeners at the chapter at the . . . . . . of Yarmouth, lxxv*s*. To Daubeney for to kepe the yere day at Bromholm the first yere after his dethe, viii*l*. ii*s*. iiii*d*. Given at Castor to xxv. howsholders, every houshold iii*d*. the said tyme, vi*s*. iii*d*. To viii. pore men the said tyme, xviii*d*. To the master of the College the said tyme, vi*s*. viii*d*. To Mastkr Clement Felmyngham the said tyme, vi*s*. viii*d*. To viii. prests at Castor the said tyme, ii*s*.

[1] A church in Norwich, rebuilt by John Paston in 1460, the advowson having been acquired by him and Margaret, his wife, in 1458. The date of the rebuilding is engraved in stone on a buttress by the north door.

230

EDWARD IV

viii*d*. To childern in surplices and other pore folk at the said 1466 tyme, xiii*d*. To the parson of Hungate, vi*s*. viii*d*. To the said parson for a certeyn[1] unto Mighelmesse next after the said yere day, viii*s*. viii*d*. To Skolous, wax chandeler, for makyng of the hers at Bromholm, xxii*l*. ix*s*. viii*d*. To Philip Curson, draper, for cloths, ix*l*. iii*s*. *ob*. To Aubrey, draper, xxxiiii*s*. For a quarter of makerell, xii*d*. To the Prior of Bromholm for malte spent at the enterment, xl*s*. For light kept on the grave, x*s*. Geven at Cristemasse next after the said yereday, to eche of the iiii. orders of friers, x*s*.,—xl*s*. To the vyker of Dallyng for bryngyng home of a pardon from Rome, to pray for alle our frends sowles, viii*s*. iiii*d*. For a black gowne to the said viker, viii*s*.

638

FASTOLF'S GOODS[2]

DECLARACIO bonorum mobilium Johannis Fastolf militis ad manus Johannis Paston armigeri de-veniencium et possidencium tam ex liberacione Thomæ Howys, Rectoris de Pulham, unius executoris dicti militis, quam ex Rapto aliorum hominum serviencium et tenencium suorum. Ac valorem in possessione dominiorum maneriorum terrarum et tenementorum suorum in eorum prima perquisicione per dictum militem solutorum et per heredem dicti Paston clameatorum pro nichilo solvendo, cum custubus edificacionis eorundem. Et pro quibus omnibus supra specificatis executores dicti militis petiunt de heredibus et executoribus dicti Johannis Paston, solucionem restitucionem ac satisfacionem de dampnis occasione hujusmodi retencionis.

In primis.

Die octava mensis Novembris anno xxxviij. Regni Regis Henrici Sexti, videlicet tercio die post obitum Johannis Fastolf

[1] Masses called 'certeynes' are referred to in No. 53 (vol. ii. p. 64).
[2] [From a ms. in the Tower of Magd. College, Oxford.] This is a paper drawn up by William Worcester after John Paston's death in 1466. The errors in grammar are characteristic of the writer.

231

1466 militis, Thomas Howys clericus, co-executor dicti Johannis Fastolf, deliberavit Johanni Paston armigero de bonis dicti Johannis Fastolf existentibus ad tunc sub salva custodia in abbathia Sancti Benedicti de Hulmo de parte majoris summe in auro, videlicet in nobilibus antiquis boni et justi ponderis ij^{ml.} cccc. nobilia, precii nobile viij*s.* iiij*d.*, faciunt m^l*li.*, et alia vice in moneta argenti xxiiij*li.* xvij*s.* ij*d.*; unde summa

. . . . m^lxxiiij*li.* xvij*s.* ij*d.*

Item, idem Thomas liberavit Johanni Paston dicto mense Novembris apud Norwicum, de vasis argenti diversarum specierum ad tunc habitarum extra thesauraium dicti militis manerij de Castre, iiij^{ml.} xxiij. unciarum ponderis Troie, precium uncie ij*s.* x*d.*, faciunt v^c·lxix*li.* xviij*s.* vj*d.* Et eidem Johanni apud Norwicum alia vice, de vasis argenti, ponderis lvij. unciarum, precium uncie ut supra, vij*li.* iiij*s.* x*d.* Et eidem Johanni alia vice apud dictum Castre liberantur de vasis argenti Cxij. unciarum precium ut supra xv*li.* xvij*s.* iiij*d.*; unde summa . . . . v^c·iiij^{xx}·viij*li.* viij*d.*

Item, idem Thomas liberavit eidem Johanni Paston apud Norwicum dicto mense Novembris, in cyphis et vasis auri triati et finati, iij^{xx}·xv. unciarum ponderis Troie, precium uncie xl*s.* . . . . Cl*li.*

Item, idem Thomas liberavit dicto Johanni ad faciendum certum prestitum comiti de Salysberye de bonis dicti Johannis Fastolf, unde idem Johannes Paston habet sufficientem securitatem et obligacionem Episcopi Norwicensis xxxiij*li.* vj*s.* viij*d.* Et consimili modo liberavit dicto Johanni ad faciendum certum prestitum   domino de Fitzwater, unde idem Johannes habet sufficientes securitates, xxxiij*li.* vj*s.* viij*d.* . . lxvj*li.* xiij*s.* iiij*d.*

Item, dictus Johannes Paston cepit de bonis dicti militis existentibus sub custodia Willelmi Worcetyr, contra agreamentum suum, et tradita per ipsum ad salvo custodiendum Thome Plummer de London scryvaner et Johanni Gressham de eadem capper, videlicet in vasis argenti diversarum specierum m^l·viij^c·iiij^{xx}·x. unciarum, precium uncie ut supra, CClxviij*li.* v*s.* Et consimiliter cepit cyphum coopertum de

puro auro ponderis Troie xxiij. unc', j. quart. di., precium 1466 uncie xl*s.*, xlvj*li.* xv*s.* Et similiter cepit unam cathenam auri puri, ponderis Troie xxiij. unc' et dimidii, precium unc' ut supra xlvij*li.* . . . . CCClxij*li.*

Item, idem Johannes Paston cepit consimili modo de bonis dicti militis traditis Willelmo Worcetyr ad custodiendum, dicto mense Novembris, videlicet London, apud domum dicti Thome Plummer, ultra Cxl*li.* per dictum Worcestre solutas pro panno nigro pro liberatis togarum datis erga funeralia dicti militis, et pro serico pro baneretis pictis cum armis, necnon pro vino et speciebus, videlicet viij^c·j. nobilia antiqua boni et justi ponderis, precium nobile viij*s.* iiij*d.*, iij^c·xxxiij*li.* xv*s.* Et liberantur dicto Johanni Paston per manus dicti Thome Howys, London, de moneta tradita in custodia dicti Thome Plummer lxij*li.* xj*s.* iiij*d.*; pro toto. . . CCCiiij^{xx}·xvj*li.* vj*s.* iiij*d.*

Item, dictus Johannes Paston cepit consimili modo de Willelmo Worcestre certa notabilia monilia et jocalia auri cum lapidibus preciosis garnizata, videlicet unum monile ditissimum vocata Anglice *a White Rose* nuper domini ducis Eborum [1] cum magno precioso lapide vocato *a poynted dyamant*, qui in prima empcione constabat, ut dicitur iiij^{or} m^l·marcarum, ac alia duo jocalia nuper dicti domini ducis tradita in plegio quando dictus Johannes Fastolf obligatus fuit pro dicto duce in tribus milibus libris executoribus cardinalis Anglie [2] super certis denariis prestitis dicto duci, et unde idem, dominus dux debebat dicto Johanni Fastolf in denariis prestitis CCCClxvj*li.* xiij*s.* iiij*d.* Et pro aliis justis causis CClxvj*li.* xiij*s.* iiij*d.* Et predicta tria jocalia per assensum dicti domini ducis sub sigillo armorum in scriptis tradita assignata fuerunt dicto Johanni Fastolf ut bona sua propria ad vendendum et disponendum in recompensacione debiti sui et aliis magnis laboribus et vexacionibus dicti militis pro dicto duce sustentatis et habitis dum modo locum tenens pro Rege fuit in Francia, ac postea in Anglia. . . . vij^c·xxxiij*li.* vj*s.* viij*d.*

[1] Richard, Duke of York, father of Edward IV.
[2] Probably Cardinal Beaufort; but it may be Cardinal Kemp.

1466   Item, predictus Johannes Paston recepit exitus et proficua omnium maneriorum, terrarum et tenementorum dicti militis in comitatibus Norffolk, Suffolk, Essex et Surrie per manus ministrorum et servorum sine consensu executorum dicti militis, diversis annis ex quo obiit, per propinquam estimacionem . . m^l·vj*s.*·lxvj*li.* xiij*s.* iiij*d.*

Item, dictus Johannes Paston recepit diversa alia catalla et bestias dicti militis, videlicet equos et palefridos principales suos valoris xxx*li.* ac oves et animalia minuta cubancia in pasturis de Castre et aliis maneriis, videlicet ij^m·iiij^c·lvj. oves diversorum generum precium capitis xiiij*d.* Cxliij*li.* v*s.* iiij*d.* Et in precio xiij. magnarum bestiarum vj*li.* Et in valore vj^{m.} cuniculorum apud Warennam de Haylysdon anno quo dictus miles obiit per Warennarios ibidem per propinquam estimacionem assessato precium m^l· xv*s.*, xlv*li.* Similiter in precio vellerum lane ovium de stauro suo apud Haylysdon ante obitum suum remanencium, xxvj*li.* xiij*s.* iiij*d.* per ipsum recept' . . CCl*li.* xiij*s.* iiij*d.*

Item, idem Johannes Paston recepit apud Castre predictam stuffuram et ordinacionem pro defensione patrie in artilleria, videlicet colubrinas librillas [1] diversorum magnitudinum cum cameris in decem carectis oneratis ac in curassys, brigandinis jakkis, salectis, basnetes, habourjonnys, lanceis, crossebowes de calibe [*chalybe*], longbowes, arcubus, sagittis, gonnepowder, gonnestonys, et cetera hujusmodi defensibilia valoris. Cl*li.*

Item, recepit apud Castre per supervisum dicti Thome Howys in valore librorum pertinencium capelle ac in utenciliis garderobe dicti militis ibidem, videlicet in costeris et lectis de pluma et coopertoria de arras et tapestria ac penulis de martys cum togis necnon utencilia aule camerarum coquine et cetera hujusmodi, ut per billam de particulis patet, Cxxj*li.* vij*s.* iiij*d.* Et simili modo de utenciliis Warderobe et camerarum remanencium apud manerium suum in Suthwerk, valoris xx*li.*, ... Cxlj*li.* vij*s.* iiij*d.*

Item, dictus Johannes recepit per manus dicti Thome Howys, Willelmi Paston, Thome Playter, Thome Plummer

[1] *colubrinas librillas, i.e.* culverins.

de London, scryvaner, Christofori Hansson armigeri et Luce 1466 Nantron ad diversas vices tam Londoniis quam in Suthwerk, ut patet per billam de parcellis, ... Ciiij*li.* xj*s.* viij*d.*

Item, idem Willelmus Worcestre mense Julii anno v^{to} regni Regis Edwardi quarti solvit uxori dicti Thome Plumer pro debito dicti Johannis Paston ut pro panno nigro ac prestita facta et liberaciones argenti fact' suo mandato diversis personis, ... xxxij*li.*

Item, idem Johannes recepit in valore et precio panni lanei nigri coloris per ipsum dati diversis hominibus de affinitate sua propria, ultra Clij*li.* ut in precio panni lanei nigri coloris provisi et dati amicis et servientibus dicti Johannis Fastolf erga funeralia sua tenenda, xl*li.* Et similiter idem Johannes Paston fecit prefatum Thomam Howys exponere et tradere diversis hominibus in regardis et solucionibus circa propria negocia dicti Paston expedienda London' et alibi xxx*li.* xvj*s.* j*d.* Et consimiliter idem Johannes fecit dictum Thomam exponere et solvere in expensis victualium hospicii tenti apud Castre anno primo quo idem miles obiit, tam circa extraneos et notos supervenientes de affinitate et amicicia sua sine causa apud Castre Maner trahentes ibidem moram inutilem, ad summam iiij^{xx}·xl*li.*, prout evidenter patebit per certam declaracionem, ... Clxl*li.* xvj*s.* j*d.*

Item, ultra predicta bona sic sibi applicata, prefatus Johannes Paston pretendebat habere et possidere, sine racione et scripto autentiquo, omnia dominia, terras et tenementa dicti militis in comitatibus, Norffolk, Suffolk et Norwico, ac sine solucione alicujus summe que constabant dicto militi in prima empcione ultra edificaciones et repparaciones dictorum maneriorum, ... ix^{ml.}·viij^c·*li.*

Item, considerandum est quod, ultra dictas perquisiciones, edifficacio manerii de Castre velut fortalicium defensionis patrie constabat in triginta annis vj^{ml.}·*li.* Et edifficacio manerii de Haylysdon, cum clausura bosci et warenne, ac edifficacione duarum domorum vocatarum *lez logges* apud Haylysdon et Drayton, v^c·xlviij*li.* xiij*s.* iiij*d.* Et custus imparcacionis parci in Cotton cum repparacione manerii iiij^c·*li.*

VOL 4

THE PASTON LETTERS

1466 Et repparacio principalis mesuagii sui in villa de Jernemouth CC*li*. Edifficacio et repparacio tenementorum suorum in civitate Norwici CCxl*li*. . . vij^{ml}·CCCiiij^{xx}·viij*li*. xiij*s*. iiij*d*.

Item, ultra ista, prefatus Johannes Paston retinet in custodia sua principales evidencias maneriorum dicti militis vocatorum Dedham Netherhall et Dedham Overhall in comitatu Essex; que quidem maneria, in defectu dictarum evidenciarum per ipsum non prosequutorum a tempore obitus dicti militis pro recuperacione eorundem, et hucusque, existunt extra possessionem, in maximum prejudicium defuncti, pro eo quod dictum manerium vocatum Dedham Netherhall constabat dicto militi in prima empcione m^{l}·*li*., et predictum manerium vocatum Dedham Overhall Clx*li*. Et exitus et proficua dictorum maneriorum que ad manus executorum dicti militis medio tempore non devenerunt secundum ratam xl*li*. per annum ascendunt ad CCiiij^{xx}·*li*. Sic in toto, . . . m^{l}·iiij^{c}· xl*li*.

639

ABSTRACT[1]

EXAMINATIONS TOUCHING SIR JOHN FASTOLF'S WILL

MAY and JUNE A.D. 1466. The following witnesses were examined secretly and apart on behalf of Sir William Yelverton, 'deceased,'[2] in the house of the treasurer of St. Paul's Cathedral by John Druell, LL.D.:—

May 17. John Monke *alias* Smyth.
19. John Dawson and John Gyrdyng.
20. William Boswell, Robert Inglys, Ric. Horne, and Thos. Pykeryng.

[1] [From Paston MSS., B.M.] The following examinations are contained in the same volume as the depositions of John Paston of which an abstract will be found in No. 606. They begin at page 21, immediately after Paston's depositions, a single blank page intervening.

[2] By a singular mistake in the record, Sir William Yelverton is here spoken of as deceased instead of John Paston:—'per partem venerabilis viri domini Willelmi Yelverton militis defuncti contra testes Johannis Paston armigeri et domini Thomæ Howys.' Yelverton certainly lived for some years after this, and was continued as judge by Henry VI. on his restoration (*see* Foss), but John Paston died on the 26th May 1466.

EDWARD IV

May 21. Henry Clerke, John Tovy, Thos. Hert, William Shawe, and Nich. Cherche. 1466 MAY and JUNE
22. Thos. Newton, Th. Spycer, and Thos. Neve.
23. John Rugge, John Clerke, and Rob. Bunche.
June 10. Stephen Scrope.
11. Ric. Fastolf.

I. John Monke, a smith of the parish of St. James, Pokethorpe, in Norwich, illiterate, of free condition, thirty-two years old and over, alleges bribery of witnesses by Paston and Howys, who offered to sell John Russe lands at Leystofte at little more than half their value. Howes made Russe a present of salt, barley, and malt to the value of £20, and promised him a full discharge of his account for goods of the testator in his custody to the value of £200 and over. He paid Robert Cutteler, vicar of Caster, 'colore cujusdam ultimi *vale* dicti testatoris prius non debite' (*sic*), money and corn to the value of 20 marks, and promised to present him to the living of Mawdeby whenever Thomas Howse resigned it. They gave Felmyngham an annuity of 8 marks, and 40s. to a boy who is his servant. They gave Robert Boteler a fee (*feodum*) of 5 marks [a year] for life, and the farm of a close called Mawdeby close, besides some other gifts which are specified. Hence the said John Russe, Rob. Cutteler, Clement Felmyngham, and Rob. Butteler, falsely deposed in answer to the second interrogatory that on the Saturday before the testator's death they were present in a certain low room (*bassa camera*) in the manor of Caister, where the testator was principally between the hours of 8 and 11 A.M., and that with them were the said John Paston and John Brakley, and no others; for in reality there were present in the chamber with the testator on that day, and especially during those hours, the said Rob. Fitzrauf, Nich. Newman, and John Loer continually, and the said Dan John Davye, Dan Thomas Howys, Friar John Bernard, physician, and Henry Barbour, and several others [at intervals]. Moreover, Cutteler, Felmyngham, and Butteler, said Russe was present on that occasion, whereas both he and Cutteler were in other places. Moreover, bribes were given by Paston and Howes in various forms during the months of January, February, and March 1462[-3], and at other times in the parishes of Caister and Yarmouth, and in the city of London, to Ralph Lampet, brother William Bukenham, and the said Rob. Cutteler. Paston promised to promote Bukenham to the priory of Yarmouth, and also, as a reward for his testimony, to give him 13 acres of the testator's land in Scroudby and Caister called Isabell, to the use of the prior and convent of Norwich. Hence the testimony of these witnesses was false, that Fastolf, about the beginning of Autumn five years ago, had made to John Paston estate and feoffment and livery of seisin of his manor of Caister, and other lands in Cos. Norf. and Suff., and the city of Norwich, to the use of the said testator while he lived, and afterwards to that of the said John Paston and his heirs; for if any such thing was done (which is not admitted) it was on the 16th October 1457, in the 36th year of Henry VI., after the Autumn of the said year, and not to the use of Paston and his heirs, but to the use of Fastolf himself, and for the accomplishment of his will. Further, the testimony of Russe, Cutteler, Bukenham, Felmyngham, and Butteler was untrue as to the alleged will of Fastolf that John

THE PASTON LETTERS

1466 MAY and JUNE Paston should obtain the King's license for the foundation of a college at Caister. It was in truth Fastolf's will that the executors should obtain the King's license to found a college there of seven Benedictine monks of the same profession as the monastery of St. Benet at Hulme, of whom one should be prior, and of seven poor men, and that they should be endowed out of his lands to the extent of 300 marks a year, all charges deducted, to pray for the soul of Lady Milicent, his wife, his parents and benefactors; and if the executors were unable to obtain this license, they were to give the abbot and convent of St. Benet's lands and money for the maintenance of six new monks and seven poor men in that monastery with a like object. Further, it is not true as alleged that on Saturday before his death, viz., 3rd Nov., between eight and eleven A.M., the testator openly declared his will with a clear voice in the hearing of bystanders, for he was so ill and weak from want of breath that he was unable to speak distinctly at any time that whole day, especially during the hours above mentioned.

Moreover, bribes were offered by Paston and Howes in May and June 1465, in the parishes of Caister and Yarmouth, and in the city of London, to Thomas Thorald, Robert Lawes, Will. Waterman, John Osbern, John Heydon, Will. Pykeryng, John Symmys, and John Shawe, for their testimony in this matter, viz. that they should have 20s. besides travelling expenses and divers other sums which were offered to them in Paston's name by Cutteler, vicar of Caister, and Ric. Calle; and John Paston promised the said William Pykeryng that he should recover certain lands in the tenure of his brother John Pykeryng, in Fylby, to the value of 40s. Influenced by these bribes, Thos. Thorald deposed that on the Saturday before Fastolf's death, Bartholomew Elys and John Davys came to his house in Belton, two miles and more from Yarmouth, about eight A.M., when he was in his grange, and asked him to come with them to divers manors of the said Sir John, to receive certain grain from his farmers; after which they drank in Thorald's house, and he went with them to Freton, and to the manor called Calcote hall, and other places in Lothynlond until midday. Robert Lawes also deposed that on Friday before Fastolf's death he went to Becclys, and next day, viz. Saturday, returning homeward (*rediens domorsum*), met on the way the said Bartholomew Elis, John Davy, and Thomas Thorald going to Freton, when Davy called him and bade him tell Thomas Howys or John Rus that on Monday or Tuesday next he would go to Caister and give an account of his stewardship. Afterwards, about two P.M., Lawes came to Caister and told John Rus his business in the absence of Howys. But the said William Waterman, being bribed as aforesaid, falsely declares that on the Saturday before Fastolf's death Barth. Elys and John Davy came to his house at Gorlyston about seven A.M., and that he went with them to Thorald's house, and that they went and spoke with Thorald at the grange while he waited for them at the gate. Afterwards they all entered the hall of Thomas Thorald and drank beer together, and all four went together to Calcote-halle and waited there till ten A.M., when Watyrman left the other three and returned home. And about two P.M. Elys and Davy returned and drank beer at Watyrman's house. But the truth is that Elys and Davy were at Yarmouth that day from seven till past eleven A.M.

EDWARD IV

Further, John Osberne, Will. Pykerynge, and John Heydon were corrupt witnesses. John Osberne said that on Saturday before the Feast of St. Leonard, when Fastolf was ill of his last illness, the said Osberne, Pykerynge, and Heydon came to Caister to receive certain monies of John Rus for barley sold to him by Osberne; that about eight A.M. they entered the hall of the manor and found Robert Hert and others, servants of Fastolf, sitting at breakfast; and that John Russe immediately came to Osberne and talked to him about the payment. At last Russe took them into the *claustrum*, and leaving them, entered Fastolf's chamber; then, after remaining two hours and more, returned into the *claustrum* and delivered the money to Osbern. This testimony was confirmed by Heydon and Pykeryng; but the truth is that Russe that Saturday, from seven till near twelve o'clock (*a principio horæ septimæ usque ad finem horæ undecimæ*), and Robert Hert from seven to ten A.M., were at Yarmouth, three miles off. 1466 MAY and JUNE

Further, John Symmys and John Shawe were corrupt witnesses, the former saying that Robert Hert was present in the said manor-house of Caister at eight A.M. on the said day, and even at nine o'clock at dinner-time (*tempore prandii*), and that he saw the said Robert Hert sitting among Fastolf's other servants at breakfast (*jentaculum*); and that he (Symmys) and Henry Wynstall, Fastolf's barber, were occupied together in shoeing horses in the said manor from breakfast-time aforesaid to dinner-time, and that at dinner-time Symmys saw the said Henry sitting in the hall with others; and that on the said Saturday, about eight A.M., and even at noon, Symmys saw John Rus in the hall of the said manor. Also John Shawe deposed that on the Saturday before Fastolf's death he saw John Rus and Henry Wynstall in the hall of the said manor, both at eight A.M. at breakfast and at dinner at midday, and he also saw Robert Hert, porter at the gate of the manor, at those hours; and that between breakfast and dinner Shawe and Wynstall were occupied along with John Symmys in shoeing Sir John's horses. But the truth is that both Rus and Hert were absent as above-mentioned, and Wynstall was with Fastolf in his chamber from nine A.M. to half-past ten. Also Symmys, William Pykeryng, Heydon, Osberne, and Lawes were all absent the whole of that Saturday, and certainly between eight and eleven A.M. And notwithstanding that the contrary is alleged against them, John Davy, Barth. Elys, John Bokkyng, John Davy, chaplain, Thos. Upton, Nich. Newman, John Loer, Wm. Eton, Robert Lynne, John Marshall, Wm. Lynne, Henry Wynstall, Robert Hert, and Robert Fitzrauff, gave honest testimony in behalf of Yelverton and Worcester, being men of good repute, sufficiently rich, and well worthy of credit.

Additional exceptions on the part of Yelverton and Worcester to the testimony of John Rus and Clement Felmyngham, showing that Paston had offered to let to the former a tenement in Yarmouth for less than its true value, and had promised the latter 100 marks for the Austin Friars at South-Town,[1] which was not bequeathed in Fastolf's will; also that he had given Master Robert Popy, besides his expenses, 20 marks for his testimony, and remitted to him 10*s*. of the rent of a fishery which was five years in arrear, and that he had

[1] South-Town, Yarmouth, sometimes called Little Yarmouth.

1466
MAY
and
JUNE

also released to him 40 marks of a penalty of 100 marks due by Popy upon a bond; in consequence of which Popy deposed that on the 30th October three years previously,[1] John Paston had reported to him at Caister that he had made an agreement with Fastolf by which he was to have all Fastolf's lands in Norfolk, Suffolk, and the city of Norwich, after his death, paying for the same 4000 marks, and was to found a college in the manor, etc.; on hearing which Popy returned to Fastolf, and related to him what Paston had said to him, and Sir John confirmed it, requesting him to show the same goodwill towards Paston, as he had done to himself. But in truth Fastolf never asserted or confirmed any such thing.

Answers to interrogatories by the same deponent, viz.—1. As to his knowledge of the parties and witnesses.

2. As to the alleged instances of bribery, and the absence of Rus on the day referred to. The latter fact deponent says he knows, because he and Rus lay together in the chamber of Thomas Howys, and on Friday before Fastolf's death Rus went to Yarmouth to buy victuals, and left with him the key of the chamber, Howys being then at Blowfeld; and Rus remained at Yarmouth all that Friday and the Saturday following, and returned on Sunday.

4. As to the condition of Fastolf on the Saturday before his death. He was so weak for want of breath that he could not speak distinctly; those about him could not hear what he said without inclining their ears to his mouth, and even then they could hardly understand him. And this deponent says he knows, because on Friday and Saturday before his death he was frequently in Sir John's chamber, and when people spoke to him to comfort him in his illness he only answered by sighs, so that deponent and others could not tell what he meant. Moreover, Sir John was accustomed when in health daily to say certain prayers with his chaplain, but on that day the chaplain said the service alone, while Fastolf lay on his bed and said nothing.

6. As to Russe and Hert being at Yarmouth, he says he heard Thomas Howys that Saturday morning order the latter to take horse and ride thither to get provisions for the household, and he saw him ride out of the manor accordingly about seven A.M., and also saw him return with the provisions about ten A.M. [In the margin here is written 'Nititur deponere de absencia Hert, sed non probat.']

7. Knows that Henry Wynstall was absent from the hall of the manor from about nine to half-past ten, for he saw him enter the chamber with his instruments to shave Sir John, and wait there an hour and a half, and he could not have left without deponent seeing him. Moreover, John Symmys did not shoe horses in the manor that Saturday, for deponent had the custody of the forge and kept the keys.

Answers to another set of interrogatories proposed on behalf of Paston and Howes, and here quoted at length, to the following effect, viz.: 1. Where each witness has lived since he was born, and whether he be in the service of the party producing him? 2. As to his knowledge of the witnesses on the

---

[1] 'Quod dictis Johannes Paston apud Castre penultimo die Octobris ultimo præterito ad tres annos proxime elapsos sibi retulit.' It would seem by this that Popy's testimony must have been given within three years of Fastolf's death.

1466
MAY
and
JUNE

other side? 3. What particulars he can give as to any bribery he imputes to them, and what was its special object? 4. By what means he knew it, and by whom he has been asked to give testimony, and whether he has conferred with his fellow-witnesses; whether they have received instructions what to depose; how often he has come up to London to give evidence and returned without being called; and how much he was promised for coming? 5. Each witness is to declare how he knows the facts, and to be charged not to reveal to the others on what subjects he was questioned.

The only point of interest in these replies is that deponent was asked by William Worcester in the city of Norwich on Sunday eight days to give his testimony in the cause. He denies all communication with his fellow-witnesses, &c.

Note.—The evidence of this first witness runs to five or six times the length of any other, and we have noted all the material points in it. Of the depositions of the others we shall not give any summary, but mention briefly any new statements that seem to be of interest:—

II. John Dawson, husbandman (agricultor), of Blowfeld, where he has been for four years, having formerly lived five years in the manor of Caister, and before that in Cambridge three years, literatus, liberæ conditionis, about thirty years old.

His testimony generally agrees with that of Monke, and he says the covenant of Akethorpe was made in the February before Fastolf's death. Between Christmas and Easter after his death deponent heard Howes in the manor of Caister say to Robert Cutteler the vicar that he should have 6 marks for his labour in giving evidence about Fastolf's will; and afterwards Howes in his chamber in the said manor paid him 6 marks. Paston also promised him a benefice worth 40 marks. He says, about a month before Fastolf's death, he heard Howes and Paston frequently repeat publicly in the household the tenor of Sir John Fastolf's will. About St. John Baptist's day last he was at Yarmouth, and heard John Symmys and John Shawe say they were hired by Paston and Howes to give evidence in the proving of Fastolf's will.

III. John Gyrdynge of Fretenham, where he has lived four years; before which time he lived with the Prior of St. Faith's two years, before that in the manor of Caster four years, before that with John Emeryngale of Wroxham two years, and before that in Norwich as an apprentice with Henry Toke five years; a cook, illiterate and of free condition, thirty-two years old and over.[1] Agrees with the evidence of corruption against Rus and others. Was present in Fastolf's room that Saturday forenoon, and saw the two chaplains celebrating mass. H. Wynstall the barber was present till ten A.M.

IV. William Boswell of Thetford, who was four years with Friar Bracley, &c., literatus, of free condition, thirty years old and more. Heard Howys, Paston, and Rus frequently confer at Caister about the sale of a house in Yar-

---

[1] The residences of every one of the witnesses are given from the time of his birth; but we have given these details only in one or two cases as specimens.

1466
MAY
and
JUNE

mouth, which Howys, at the request of Paston, at length granted to Rus at £20 less than its value, to the end that Rus might bear witness in their favour in the proving of Fastolf's will. [Here occurs a marginal note by another hand, 'Male sonat. Quod alius consensit non probatur.' At the head of this deposition also it is said that this witness has been proved corrupt.]

V. Robert Inglys of Lodon, gentleman, who has lived there two years, and before that in the parish of Hopton three years, before that with Henry None, Esq., for more than a year, before that with Sir John Fastolf two years, before that with the Abbot of Langley two years, and before that in Hopton with his father; illiterate, and of free condition, thirty years old and more.

VI. Richard Horne of Brundall, Norwich diocese, husbandman (agricultor), who has lived there four years, and before that with Thomas Howys six years, and before that in the parish of St. George, Southwark, three years; illiterate, of free condition, twenty-six years old.

VII. Thomas Pykeryng of Wroxham, Norwich diocese, who has been a schoolmaster at Norwich and Aylesham, and is now clerk to Robert Norwich, steward of the Abbot of St. Benet's, Hulme.

VIII. Henry Clerke of Blowfeld, husbandman (agricultor), once in the service of Sir John Fastolf, illiterate, twenty-eight years old, of free condition. Says that on the Saturday before Fastolf's death Howys sent him and John Shawe to Yarmouth about seven A.M., with a cart-load of malt to one named Chirche; that they arrived about eight, and were spoken to by John Rus and Robert Cutteler in the market-place; that they waited with their cart till two P.M., when deponent took leave of Russ and Cutteler in the street, having repeatedly seen them there in the interval. Also that at eight and nine A.M. he saw Robert Hert in Yarmouth, who soon after his arrival delivered him a sack containing meat, bought, as he said, by Rus for Fastolf's household. He says also that between eight and nine he spoke with the said John Symmys, William Pykeryng, and John Osbern in Yarmouth.

Marginal notes are appended to the above statements, affirming that bribery had been proved against this witness by four others, and that he stood alone in his testimony.

IX. John Tovy of Caister, where he has lived ever since he was born, agricultor, literatus, of free condition, twenty-four years old and more; cannot depose of his own knowledge to the bribery of John Rus and the others. He says John Rus was not present in the manor on the said Saturday, having to be at Yarmouth to provide victuals for the household. About eight A.M. witness conveyed to the said manor some linen, which his mother had washed, for she was Sir John's washerwoman, and waited there, sometimes in the hall and sometimes in Sir John's chamber, till after midday, but did not see John Rus or any of the others named, as he would have done if they had been present.

X. Thomas Hert of Caister, agricultor, who has lived there from his birth, illiterate, of free condition, twenty-three years old. Cannot depose to bribery except from hearsay. Was sent to Caister by his father on the Saturday before Fastolf's death with capons to be sold to John Rus, purveyor of victuals for the household, but on inquiring for him, found he was absent, and delivered the

1466
MAY
and
JUNE

capons to Sir Thomas Howes. Waited till nine A.M. and saw neither Rus, Cutteler, Boteler, nor Robert Hert, but was told Rus was at Yarmouth, and Boteler sick in his chamber. John Symmys had nothing to do with the shoeing of Sir John's horses that day. Was asked to bear witness in this cause a fortnight ago by Sir William Yelverton's servant at Caister.

XI. William Shave, roper of Yarmouth, illiterate, of free condition, fifty-eight years old. On the Saturday before Fastolf's death, was at the house of John Balle, at the sign of the Cock, in Yarmouth, in a parlour near the public street, when Sir Thomas Howes informed John Rus, there present, that he had been desired by John Paston to remit to him £20 of the price of a house sold to Rus by the said Thomas, and thereupon he remitted to him the said £20 and 5 marks, in which he was bound to Sir John Fastolf. He also promised him the lands of Akethorp Hall for 40 marks less than any other, provided he would favour the intention of Howes and Paston. [It is remarked in the margin that witness does not say what intention.] William Lynde, a servant of Sir John Fastolf, was present, besides others. He saw Russ and Cutteler that Saturday at Yarmouth, between nine and twelve A.M., and spoke with them and drank in the house of Thomas Lounde. As to Thomas Torald, witness was at Yarmouth one Saturday, when he heard Robert Cutteler and Torald conversing; and the former told the latter that Sir Thomas Howes loved him well, and that John Paston could do him much good, and in the name of Paston and Howes he promised Torald 20s. for his labour, besides expenses, if he would depose for them. Knows that on the Saturday before Fastolf's death Bartholomew Elys was in Yarmouth from half-past eight to eleven A.M., for he and witness bought fish called roches together, sold some, and divided others in Elys's house. That day he saw John Rus in Yarmouth several times every hour from seven to eleven A.M., for he was in the market-place all that time on his business, and at vespers he saw John Rus in the parish church of the said town. Next day, Sunday, he also saw him there at matins and at mass.

XII. Nicholas Chirche of Yarmouth, merchant, literatus, of free condition, forty years old and more. Testifies concerning a conversation held in John Balle's parlour at the Cock in Yarmouth after the Christmas following Fastolf's death, with Sir Thomas Howes, John Paston, John Rus, Friar Clement Felmyngham, Dan Robert Cutteler, Robert Boteler, Thomas Neve, and others, when Howes remitted to John Rus £20 of the price of a house he had sold him, and 5 marks of the arrears of his accounts. He also testifies to other acts of the same nature on that occasion, and to the absence of Rus and Cutteler at Yarmouth on the Saturday above referred to, &c.

[In the margin it is remarked that this witness has been proved corrupt by three others.]

On the 22d May John Naseby, proctor for Yelverton and Howes, produced as a witness one John Rugge, in presence of Master Robert Kent, Paston's proctor.

XIII. Thomas Newton of Burgh, agricultor, illiterate, of free condition, fifty years old and more.

XIV. Thomas Spycer of Southtown, by Yarmouth, tailor, illiterate, of free condition, fifty years old and more.

THE PASTON LETTERS

XV. Thomas Neve of Jernemuth [*Yarmouth*], merchant, *literatus*, of free condition, forty years old and more.

XVI. John Rugge, mariner, of Yarmouth, illiterate, of free condition, fifty years old.

XVII. John Clerke of Gorlaston, *agricultor*, illiterate, of free condition, fifty years old. Heard Clement Felmyngham report to him at the Austin Friars in Southtown that Paston and Howes had given him a pension of 8 marks a year for life, and 40s. for his servant, to say masses for the soul of Sir John Fastolf. Cannot witness of bribery otherwise. A little after Michaelmas, two years before Fastolf's death, William Worceter in Fastolf's name delivered possession of six of his manors in Lodylond, viz. Spytlyng in Gorlaston, Bradwell Hall in Bradwell, Hadlounde in Bradwell, Calcotes in Freton, Beytons in Belton, and Akethorpe in Leystoft, to Sir Thomas Howes and others, his co-feoffees named in a charter of enfeoffment, to the use of Sir John during his life, and to execute his will afterwards. This he knows, because he rode with Howes to the said manors when he took possession, and saw and heard Worceter deliver possession thereof. Thomas Torald reported to witness in Lent last that Paston and Howes had promised and paid him 20s., besides his expenses, to give evidence in the proving of Fastolf's will, and had given each of his fellow-witnesses as much.

XVIII. Robert Bunche of Yarmouth, mariner, *literatus*, of free condition, fifty years old. Swears to having seen John Rus that Saturday at Yarmouth between seven and eight. [A marginal note says that being afterwards produced as a witness by Paston, he admitted having been suborned, and having deposed falsely.]

On the 22d July Yelverton's proctor, Naseby, produced in presence of Paston's proctor, Kent, two witnesses, viz.—Stephen Scrope, Esq., and Richard Fastolf.

XIX. Stephen Scrope, Esq., of free condition, seventy years old or about. Says he was several times with Sir John Fastolf in his manor of Caister within the two years before his death, when Sir John told him he had made his will, and had ordered his executors to erect a college of six or seven monks and seven poor men at Caister, and that they should have lands and goods to the value of 300 marks a year, if a license could be obtained from the King to that effect; otherwise that the number of monks at St. Benet's should be increased, and seven poor men supported in the monastery. [In the margin it is remarked that this witness proves nothing against the accused witnesses, but only endeavours to depose concerning the will of the deceased.]

XX. Richard Fastolfe, of the parish of St. Mary Eldermary, in London, tailor, where he has lived for two years, and before that in the parish of St. Michael, Crokydlane, London, for a quarter of a year, formerly with the Duke of York, *literatus*, of free condition, thirty-two years old. Went to Caister about the Feast of the Exaltation of the Holy Cross preceding Fastolf's death, along with one Thomas Plummer, *scriptor*, of London, now deceased. Found Sir John walking about his chamber led by two servants, when Plummer petitioned him to help deponent with goods that he might marry, as he was one of Sir John's relations. To this Sir John made answer that he had within a

244

EDWARD IV

few [days] preceding made his will, which he would not alter, and that he had made mention of deponent therein. He also said to Plummer that if he had come in good time, he should have written his will.

[Throughout all the above depositions will be found marginal comments in another hand, a few of which we have noticed incidentally, tending to show that the testimony given is insufficient to prove the bribery of Paston's witnesses, or to invalidate their statements.]

'Responsiones personaliter factæ per Johannem Paston, armigerum, xxix° die mensis Julii anno Domini M°CCCClxv°, Indictione xiiiⱼᵐᵃ, pontificatus sanctissimi in Christo patris et domini nostri, domini Pauli Divina providentia Papæ Secundi anno primo, in domo habitationis venerabilis mulieris Elisabethæ Venor in le Flete vulgariter nuncupat' infra parochiam Sanctæ Brigidæ Virginis in suburbeis civitatis London' situata, [et] x., xj., et xijᵐᵒ diebus mensis Decembris anno Domini supradicto, Indictione xiiijᵐᵃ, pontificatus dicti sanctissimi patris domini Pauli Papæ Secundi anno secundo, in domo thesaurarii ecclesiæ Cathedralis Sancti Pauli London' in parochia Sancti Gregorii civitatis London' situata, coram venerabili viro Magistro Johanne Druell, utriusque juris doctore, commissario et examinatore in hac parte specialiter deputato, in præsentia mei, Nicholai Parker, notarii publici, scribæ in ea parte assumpti et deputati, de et super interrogatoriis per partem venerabilis viri domini Willelmi Yelverton militis et Willelmi Worceter, executorum testamenti domini Johannis Fastolf militis ministratis, productum.'

640

NOTE

EXTRACT FROM 'AN INDEX TO DEEDS AND WRITINGS IN THE TOWER, MAGDALEN COLLEGE, OXFORD'

'34. The testimony of Th. Howes concerning the testament of Sir John Fastolf, touching which controversies arose between John Paston the elder, and Thos. Howes of the one party, and William Yelverton, Knight, and William Worcetyr on the other.'

245

THE PASTON LETTERS

641

EDWARD IV. TO THE BAILIFFS OF YARMOUTH[1]

BY THE KINGE (EDWARD THE FOURTH)[2]

TRUSTY and welbeloved, we greet yow well, letting yow wete that our trusty and welbeloved knight Sir John Paston, our welbeloved William Paston, and Clement Paston, with other, have been before us and our councell worshipfully declared of the surmise of great charge that was laid on our behalfe unto John Paston deceased and them, jointly and severally; so that we hold them and every of them sufficiently declared in that matter, and take and repute them as gentlemen descended lineally of worshipfull blood sithen the Conquest hither; and over that, have commanded that plenare restitution of the mannor of Castor, and of all other lands and tenements, with goods and cattell, that the said John Paston deceased had of the gift and purchase of Sir John Fastolfe, Knight, shall wholly be restored unto our said Knight Sir John Paston, like as the said John Paston deceased had in any time of his daies. Wherefore, in as much as our said Knight intendeth to make his abideing in Castor, we desire and pray yow that, for our sake and contemplation, ye will be friendly and neighbours unto him in his right; and such other things as may be to his profitt and ease, wherein ye shall do unto us full and good pleasure. Yeaven under our signet in our Castle at Windsore the xvijᵗʰ day of July.

Subjoined to the above in Sandford's Genealogy is 'the coppie of a warrant sent

[1] This letter is reprinted from the *Norfolk Archæology*, where it was first published by Mr. Worship from a transcript made by Sandford in his MS. Genealogy of the Paston family, compiled in 1674. Sandford states that 'the originall under the King's seale remaineth in the custody of Edward Paston, Esq.' The date is rendered certain by the warrant subjoined.

[2] We have placed the words 'Edward the Fourth' in parentheses, though they are not so printed by Mr. Worship, and are probably not so written in Sandford's MS., because we suspect that they were not in the text of the original document, but were added by Sandford by way of explanation.

246

EDWARD IV

from Kinge Edward the Fourth to restore Sir John Paston to the lands and possessions which he purchased of Sir John Fastolfe, whereof the originall remaineth in the custody of Edw. Paston, Esq.' It is addressed 'To all tenaunts, fermors, or occupiers of all the lands and tenements, and of every part of them, that late were John Paston's, Esq., now deceased, by way of inheritance, or Agnes Paston, Margaret Paston, William Paston, and Clement Paston, or any of them, and to all such persons what so they be, now being in the mannor or place of Castor, or in any lifelode that was the said John Paston, Esq., by way of gifte or purchase of late Sir John Fastolfe, or of any other, within our counties of Norff., Suff., and Norwich, and to all the tenants, fermors, baylies, or occupiers of the same, and of every part thereof; and to all mayers, shreves, eschetors, bayliffs, and other our officers, as well within franchise as without our counties aforesaid, hereing or seeing these our letters.' The King mentions in this warrant that 'great part of the said lands, tenements, and manors had been seized into our hands'; and the tenants, farmers, bailiffs, and occupiers of these lands are charged thenceforth to pay the whole issues and profits thereof to Sir John Paston; and the mayors, sheriffs, escheators, and others the King's officers are charged to be 'assisting, helping, and strengthening.' The warrant is 'Yeven under our signet at Windsore, the xxvijᵗʰ day of July, the sixth yeare of our reigne.'

642

ABSTRACT[1]

Latter clause of a writ of *supersedeas* to an escheator directing him not to make inquisition *post mortem* on the lands of John ——, until further notice. Westminster, 20 July.

[From the time of year at which this writ is dated, it may have been issued after the death of John Paston, who died in May 1466, the inquisition on his lands not having been taken till October following. But it may possibly have applied to the lands of Sir John Fastolf, who died in November 1459, the inquisition after his death not having been taken till October 1460.]

643

ANCESTRY OF THE PASTONS

The following document is derived from a transcript made by Sandford in the Genealogy mentioned in No. 641, and some previous papers, and is likewise reprinted from Mr. Worship's article. Prefixed to it in Sandford's MS. are these words:—'The Briefe followinge was delivered to Edward Paston, Esq., amonge other evidence, by his uncle Clement Paston, and it is written in an old hand.' It would appear, however, from the wording, not to be a 'brief' or abstract, as Sandford considered it,

[1] [From Paston MSS., B.M.]

247

THE PASTON LETTERS

but an extract from some certificate made in the King's name in behalf of Sir John Paston, setting forth what had been proved on examination as to the gentility of his ancestry.

THEY shewed divers great evidences and court rolles, how that they and their ancetors had been possessed of a court and seniory in the town of Paston, and of many and sundry bondmen, sithen the time that no mind is to the contrary; and how that Agnes Paston, wife to the said William Paston, father to the said John, William, and Clement, in title of her dower, is in possession of bondholders, and also of bondmen, whose ancetors have been bondmen to the ancetors of the said John Paston sithen the time that no minde is to the contrary. And they shewed divers fines, some leavyed in the time of the begining of the reigne of our noble progenitor, Edward the First, son of Kinge Henry, son of King John, of liveloude whereof they and theire ancetors have been possessed ever since to this day.

Also they shewed divers inquests which is matters of record. Also they shewed divers deeds and grants before time of mind, how that their ancetors had licence to have a chaplen and have divine service within them. And that divers of their ancetors had given lyvelyhood to houses of religion to be prayed for, and confirmacions under the Great Seale of our noble ancestor Kinge Henry the Third, son of Kinge John, confirming the same grants.

Also they shewed divers olde deeds, some without date, insealed under autenticke seales, of divers particular purchases in the town of Paston, reciting in the said deeds that the land was holden of the ancetors of the said . . . . Paston, as of the chiefe lord of the fee, and by homage, and had ward, marriage and reliefe. Also they shewed how their ancestors were infeoffed in divers men's mannors and lands in trust. Also they shewed a great multitude of old deeds, without date and with date, wherein their ancetors were alwaies sett first in witness, and before all other gentlemen. Also they shewed how their ancetors had, in old time and of late time, married with worshipfull gentlemen; and proved, by deeds of marriage and by other deeds, how their ancetors had indowed

248

their wives, and by discents of livelyhood, and by testaments and wills of their ancestors under seale; and made open by evident proofe, how they and their ancetors came lineally descended of right noble and worshipfull blood, and of great lords, sometime liveing in this our realme of Ingland. And also they made open proofe how they were nere of kin and blood to many of the worshipfullest of the country, and also nere to many and sundry great estates and lords of this realme, and was openly proved and affirmed, without contradiction or proofe to the contrary.

They shewed how they had kept pl'ce with divers . . . . and with Plays that had wedded the Earle Warren's daughter, the third yeare of Edward the First. They shewed a lineall discent, how their first ancetor, Wulstan, came out of France, and Sir William Glanvile together, his kinsman, that after founded the pryory of Bromholme by the towne of Paston and the towne of Bentley; and how Wulstan had issue Wulstan, which bare armes gould flowret azure; and how he had issue, Raffe and Robert; which Raffe, senior, bare armes as his father, and Robert the younger bare silver flowret azure. And Robert had issue Edmund and Walter; which Edmund the elder bare as his father; and his brother, because he married Glanvile's daughter, a cheife indented gold, the field silver, flowret azure; and how their ancestors after bare with lesse number; and how Sir John Paston was heire to all those, for they died sans issue. And this was shewed by writinge of olde hand, and by old testaments and evidences.

644

WILL OF AGNES PASTON [1]

TO all to whom this present writting xal come, I, Agnes Paston, late the wife of William Paston, Justice, send greting in God everlasting, lating hem know that I, the forseid Agnes, of goode and hole mende, the xvj. day of

1466 SEPT. 16

[1] [From Paston MSS., B.M.]

249

THE PASTON LETTERS

1466 SEPT. 16 Septembre, the vj. yere of the reigne of Kyng E. the iiij[th] and the yere of our Lord a M'CCCClxvj., make and ordeyne my last will in al the maners, londes, tenementes, rentes, services, mesuages, and places, that ony person or persones bene seased of to myn use and behof with in Norwiche, Norffolk, Suffolk, Essex, Hertfordshere, or in any other shere with in Englond, praying and desiring al the personez so feffed to myn use, after this my will, writtyn and inceled under my seale, be shewed unto them, that they wol make astate to the persones lemited in my seid will according.

And inasmoche as myn husband, whos soule God assoile, dyverse tymes, and specialy among other the day of the moneth, rehersed to me that the lyvelod whiche he had assigned to his ij. yongest, William and Clement, by his will in writting, was so littill that they mizt not leve thereon, withouzt they shuld hold the plowe to the tayle; and ferthermore, seying that he had dyvers oder maners, that is to say, the maner of Sporle, Sweynsthorp, and Bekham; which maner of Bekham he was purposed to chaunge with the maner of Pagrave; and if he myzt bring it abouzt, then xuld on of his ij. yongest sones have the seid maners of Sporle and Bekham, and no more, and the other yongest sone xuld have al the remenaunt. And he that had the maner of Sweynsthorp xuld be bound in a gret some to the prior of the Abbey of Norwiche, to paie dayly for ever to the monke that for that day singeth the masse of the Holy Goste in our Lady Chapell in Norwiche, where he purposed to leye his body, every day iiij d., to sing and pray for his sowle and myn, and al the sowles that he and I have hade any goode of or be beholdyn to pray for. And after that the ——[1] day of ——[1] next folowing my seid husbond lying seke in his bed, in the presens of John Paston, his sone and myn, John Bakton, John Dame, and of me, declared his will towching certein of his children and me, at whiche tyme he assigned to the seid John Paston the maner of Gressham in honde, and the revercion of suche lyvelode as he zave me after my decesse, askyng hym the question wheder he held hym not content so, seying to him in these termes, 'Sir, and

[1] Blanks in MS.

250

thow do not I doo, for I will not geve so mekyll to on that the remenaunt xal have to littill to leve on. At the whiche[1] . .'

1466 SEPT. 16

645

WILL OF AGNES PASTON [2]

B.—And after that the —— day of the monethe my seyd husbond lyyng seke on hys bede sent for me, John Paston, Bakton, and John a Dame, to here hiis wyll rede; and in owr presens all he began to reede hiis wylle, and spak fyst of me, and assynyid to me the maners of Paston, Latymer, and Schypden and Ropers, in Crowmer, for terme of my lyffe, and the manerys of Merlyngforthe, Stonsted, and Horwelbury, whyche wasse myn owne enheritans, and Oxned, whyche wasse my jontor, and [prayd me to hold me contente so, for][3] hadde do to lityll to ony it wasse to me, for somme he faryd the better, and so devedede (?) he ded for not of hem all, but he hadde more to care for, wyche myn as well as hys. And than he red John parte, and assynyd to hym and to hys wyffe the maner of Gressam, and after my desesse the maner of Oxned; and he, thynkyng by John Pastons demenyng that he wasse not plesyd because . . . .

C.—Swynne of slowyth that hiis wyll wasse not made up, but wot swm ever cwm of me, Dame, I wyll ze know my wyll, and seyd that swyche lond as he hadde not wrytyn in hiis wyll wott xwlde he do with all, he wold his ij. yongest sonnys, Wyllam and Clement, xwlde have, and owte of Sweynthorpe to have hiis perpetuell masse. And of thys prayd me to reporte recorde and berre wyttnesse; in qwyche disposicion and intent he continuyd in on to the day of hiis dethe, and I

[1] Here the fragment ends at the bottom of a leaf written only on one side.
[2] [From Paston MSS.] The following appear to be three separate fragments of an original draft of Agnes Paston's will, written on two sides of a small scrap of paper. Two of these fragments have the letters B and D prefixed to them, showing that they were intended as insertions in a part of the text now lost.
[3] These words are struck through with the pen.

251

THE PASTON LETTERS

darre rytgh largely deposse that that same wasse hiis last wyll the tyme of hiis dethe; qwyche wyll immediatly after my husbondes decesse I hopynd and declaryd to John Paston and al the other executores of my husbond, desyeryng hem to have performyd it. And the seyd John Paston wold in no wysse agree ther to, seyying that by the lawe the seyd manerys xulde be hiis, in as moche as my husbonde made no wyll of hem in wrytyn, and gatte the dedis owte of my possession and estat of the feffees in the seyde manerys, myn unknowyng.

And after that swyche tresowre of my husbons as wasse leyde in the Abbey of Norwyche by the seyd John Paston, John Bakton, John Dam, and me, to delyvere azen to us all, the seyde John Paston owte of the seyde Abbey unknowyn to the priour or ony oder person of the seyde Abbey, and with-owte my wetyn[g] and assente, or ony of owre felawys, toke and bare awey all, and kepyng it styll azens my wyll and all the tother executores wyllys, nothere restoryng the seid Wyllam and Clement to the forseyd land, nother recompensyng them of my husbonds tresor, and ordeynyng for my husbonds sowle in havyng of hiis perpetuell masse acordyng to his wyll. Werfor, in as moche as I know and understonde verrely that it wasse my husbands wyll the tyme of hys dethe, that the seyd Wyllam and Clement xwlde have the seyd manerys of Sporle, Sweynsthorp, and Bekham, and the annuyte for hys perpetuell masse to be going owte of the seyde maner of Sweynthorp, and that the possessioneres of the seyd manerys at thys day wyll in no wysse by any fayer menez or spekyng tender my seyd husbonds sowle and myn, ner perform the wyll of my seyd husbond, I wyll have and xall by the gras[e] of swyche lyvelode as I have in my possession, that is for to sey, the maners of Stonsted, Marlyngforthe, and Horwellbury, that swm tym wasse my faders and my moders, and cwm on to me by them as myn enheritance. And after my decesse if I wolde soffer it to desend, xwld goo to the wronge posses-sioners of the seyd manerys of Sporle, Sweynsthorp, and Bekham, qwyche xall not be lettyd for me, but if it be thorow her owne defaute, make, sta[b]lesse and ordeyn myn husbonds perpetuell masse and myn, and of the remenaunt, as swerly as

252

EDWARD IV

can be made by the lawe, I wyll the seyd Wyllam and Clement be recompensyd to the valew of the seyde manerys of Sporle, Sweynthorpe, and Bekkam, zerly [*yearly*], on to the tyme that they be restoryd to the forseyd manerys of Sporle, Sweynthorp, and Bekkam, in lik forme, and lyke astat as xall be afterwards lymytyd in thys my last [will; chargyng and requiryng the seyd Wyllam and Clement that after that they be restoryd to the manerys of Sporle, Sweynsthorp, and Bekam, they restore myn heyres to Marlyngforthe, Stons[ted], and Orwelbury.]

646

NOTE

In the Paston Genealogy drawn up by Sandford, to which we have several times before alluded, occurs another extract from the will of Agnes Paston, as follows :—

'Also I bequeath to the Whight Fryers of the said city of Norwich, for I am there a suster, to helpe to pay hir [*their*] debts, xx*li.*, which I will be gathered of the arrerage of my lyvelode. Also I bequeath to the auter of Gracion of the said House, whereas mine husband and I have a perpetuall masse, a vestment which they have for a prist to judge in or [*of?*] rede satern. Also to the mendinge of the chappell of our Ladie within the said place, whereas Sir Thomas Gerbrege, my grandfather, and Dame Elizabeth his wife, and Sir Edmond Berrye my father, and Dame Alice his wife, be buried, and Clement Paston my sonn.'

647

WILLIAM PASTON'S WILL [2]

ON the Thurseday at nyght before Our Ladys Day the Assumpcion,[3] betwixt xj. and xij. of the clokk, in the yer of Our Lord God MCCCC. and xliiij., the Sondays lettre on the D., died my husbond, God assoyle his

[1] The word 'will' is omitted in the MS., and the words 'my last' repeated. What follows is crossed out.
[2] [From Fenn, iii. 15.] The following memorandum relative to the death of her husband was written by Agnes Paston, probably about the time she made her will.
[3] The Assumption of Our Lady was the 15th August.

253

THE PASTON LETTERS

sowle. And on the Fryday after I sent for John Paston, John Dam, &c. And on the Wedynysday after cam John Paston, &c. And on the Fryday John Paston, John Dam and I yede into the chambre, and they desyred of me to see the wyll. I lete them see it. And John Dam redde it; and when he had redde it, John Paston walkyd up and down in the chambere. John Dam and I knelyd at the beddys fete.

648

ABSTRACT [1]

Roll of paper containing a draft in English of part of the inquisition on the death of John Paston, relating more especially to the foundation of Fastolf's college. In the latter part the jury find that John Paston died on the 22nd May [2] last, and that Sir John Paston, Knight, is his son and next heir, and is of the age of 24 years and more.

** Copies of the original inquisition, as returned into Chancery, and of that on the death of Sir John Fastolf, exist among the Paston MSS. in the Bodleian Library.

649

MARGARET PASTON TO JOHN PASTON [3]

To my ryght wyrshypfull mayster, Sir John Paston, Knyzt, be thys letter delyveryd in hast.

I GRYTTE you well, and send you God ys blessyng and myn, desyryng you to send me werd how that ye spede in youre maters, for I thynk ryght leng tyll I here tydyngys from you; and in alwyse I avyse you for to be ware that ye kepe wysly your wrytyngys that ben of charge, that it com not in her [*their*] handys that may hurt you herafter. Your fader, wham God assole, in hys trobyll seson set more

[1] [Addit. Roll, 17,258, B.M.]
[2] The date in the inquisition returned into Chancery (6 Edw. IV., No. 44) is 21st May.
[3] [From Fenn, iv. 272.] The date of this letter is shown by the contents to be shortly after John Paston the father's death, probably in the same year.

254

EDWARD IV

by hys wrytyngys and evydens than he dede by any of hys moveabell godys. Remember that yf the wer had from you, ye kowd never gyte no moo such as the be for your parte, &c.

Item, I wold ye shold take hyde that yf any processe com owte a yenst me, or a yenst any of tho that wer endyted a fore the coroner, that I myght have knowlych therof, and to purvey a remedy therfor.

Item, as for your fader ys wyll, I wold ye shold take ryght gode counsell therin, as I am enformyd it may be prevyd, thogh no man take no charge thys twelfmonth. Ye may have a letter of mynystracyon to such as ye wyll, and mynyster the godys and take no charge. I avyse you that ye in no wyse take no charge therof tyll ye know more than ye doo yet; for ye may verely knowe by that your unkell Will. seyd to you and to me, that thay wyll lay the charge uppon you and me for moo thyngys then ys exprest in your fader ys wyll, the whych shud be to grete for you or me to bere; but as for me, I will not be to hesty to take it uppon me, I ensure you.

And at the reverens of God, spede your maters so thys terme, that we may be in rest herafter, and lette not for no labour for the season, and remember the grete cost and charge that we have had hedyr toward, and thynk verely it may not lenge endur. Ye know what ye left when ye wer last at hom, and wyte it verely ther ys no mor in thys countray to bere owte no charge with. I avyse you enquer wysely yf ye canne gyte any more ther as ye be, for els by my feth I feer els it will not be well with ous; and send me word in hast hough ye doo, and whether ye have your laste dedys that ye fayled, for playnly they er not in thys contrey. It ys told me in consell that Ric. Calle hath nyer conqueryd your uncle Will. with fayre promyse twochyng hys lyflode and other thyngs, the whych shold pre-vayll hym gretly, as he sayth. Be ware of hym and of hys felowe be myn avyse. God sende you gode spede in all your maters.

Wryten at Caster, the moreu next after Symon and Jude, wher as I wold not be at thys tyme but for your sake, so mot I ches.

By your Moder.

255

THE PASTON LETTERS

650

ABSTRACT[1]

SIR JAMES GLOYS TO SIR JOHN PASTON

1466(?)
NOV. 10

Was at Snaylwell on Sunday, but could get no money. Most of the tenants away at Canterbury or elsewhere. The rest said when you were there last you had given them till Candlemas, 'so that thei myght malt ther corn and brynge it to the best preffe.' Warned them to be ready by Tuesday before St. Edmond the King, when Richard Calle would visit them. A thrifty man beside Bery is willing to take the farm; but every one says the last farmer was undone by it. Advises Paston not to overcharge his farms. I have seen Catelyn's corn, and your tenants say it is sufficient to content you. Your shepherd wishes to know if you will continue him, for no one has spoken to him since my master your father died. Men of Fordham have occupied your ground these two years that my master has been in trouble. I think you should speak to my Lord of Worcester, as he and Woodhous are lords of the town. I have bid the farmers at Snaylwell sow some wheat land, and have warned the tenants at Sporle, Pagrave, and Cressingham to be ready to pay. Advises him to keep up his place at Langham's. If 'my master' had lived he would have exchanged it for the parsonage. Supped on Monday night at a place of the Duke of Suffolk's with the parson of Causton, a chaplain of the Duchess, 'and they talked over my Lady's bargain, and were right sorry that she should forsake it.' The parson asserted that the feoffees had put her in possession of the manors. Talk over this with your counsel; for if the feoffees be compelled to release in Chancery it will be nought, because of the estate they made before; so when you expect to be most quiet you will be most troubled. There was also the parson of Brampston, and he said W. Yelverton had sent a letter to the bailiff he has set at Guton, but what it meant I could not find out. W. Yelverton has put the parson of Heynford out of his farm. I did not speak with your mother before writing this, as she was at Caister.

Norwich, St. Martin's Even.

From the mention of John Paston the father as dead, and the trouble he had been in for two years, it would appear that this letter must have been written in 1466, the year of his death. The letter is endorsed in a contemporary hand: 'Literæ anno vj. et vij. Edwardi iiij^ti.'

---

[1] [From Paston MSS., B.M.]

THE PASTON LETTERS

Date
uncer-
tain

krotte abovyn in the toppe, lesse that he hathe ben ondoone. And also the other ij. pottys be prentyd with that marchauntys marke too tymes on the coveryng, and that other pott is butt onys morkyn but with on prente, notwithstondyng I hadde lyke othe and promyse for on as well as for alle.[1]

653

ABSTRACT[2]

EDWARD MAWDBY TO HIS NIECE MARGARET PASTON

Has a tenant, a widow in Sall, building a house on his ground. She has been threatened with having it pulled down. Send for Aleyn Roos, my receiver, and take his counsel what is to be done.

London, 24 Nov. Signed 'By your nevew Edward Mawdby'; although addressed 'my most trusty and well beloved niece.'

654

ABSTRACT[3]

E. CLERE[4] TO MARGARET PASTON

My little cousin your son[5] is a fair child. Wishes certain evidences of Frethorp, which she delivered to Margaret Paston's husband to make award between her and Rammesbury, a paper book of the customs of Ormesby and a roll called 'domysday,' &c. Your father-in-law[6] was of counsel both with my mother[7] and with my mother-in-law.[8] Supposes there may be other evidences, as of Tacolneston, Therston, Reynthorp, Rusteynes in Wymondham, Kesewik, and Stratton. Sends back some rolls brought by a man from Norwich, which belong to Margaret Paston and not to the writer.

---

[1] The signature of this letter, Fenn says, is torn off the original MS.
[2] [From Paston MSS., B.M.]
[3] [From Paston MSS., B.M.]
[4] Elizabeth, widow of Robert Clere of Ormesby. She died in 1492.
[5] This must be one of the younger sons of John and Margaret Paston.
[6] William Paston, Justice.
[7] Margaret, wife of Thos. Owydale or Dovedale, of Tacolneston, daughter and heir of William Reeves.
[8] Elizabeth, daughter of Sir Philip Branch, and wife of John Clere, Esq. of Ormesby; after whose death she married again Sir John Rothenhale. *See* No. 15 in vol. ii.

EDWARD IV

651

ABSTRACT[1]

THOMAS GRENE TO WILLIAM YELVERTON, ESQ.

Desires his favour for Frere John Chesteyn and John Russe of Yarmouth, who are suspected by Lord Scales of having treasures or jewels of my Master Paston's. He never trusted them with any, knowing they were familiar with William Jenney and Sir Thomas Howes. Is sure he put no treasure into any place in that town, religious or other, for he often said he wondered any thrifty man would live in it, 'there were so much riotous people therein.' Begs his favour for my mistress Paston, 'which is now under your governance.' Hopes to see her hereafter 'as worshipful and well at ease as ever she was, and a great deal better when these troubles be passed; for I am sekir whan God woll that she be passed them she would not suffer them again for right great riches.'

Norwich, morrow of St. Thomas Apostle.

[This letter has a great appearance of having been written shortly after John Paston's death. We place it therefore in the year in which he died.]

1466
DEC. 22

652

SIR JOHN PASTON TO MARGARET PASTON[2]

To Mestresse Margrete Paston, be thys delyveryd.

PLEASE it yow to weete that I sende yow by Barker, the berer heroff, iij. tracle pottes of Geane [*Genoa*] as my potecarie sweryth on to me, and mooreovyr that they weer never ondoo syns that they come from Geane. Wheroff ye shalle take as many as pleasyth yow; neverthe lesse my brother John sente to me for ij., therfor I most beseche yow that he maye have at the lest on. Ther is on potte that is morkyn ondre the bottome ij. tymes with thyes letteris M. P., whyche potte I have best truste on too, and nexte hym to the wryghe potte; and I mystruste moost the potte that hathe a

Date
uncer-
tain

---

[1] [From Paston MSS., B.M.]
[2] [From Fenn, iv. 264.] This and the two letters following are without any certain date, but they are all addressed to Margaret Paston, most probably after her husband's death.

EDWARD IV

655

SIR JOHN PASTON TO JOHN PASTON[1]

ITEM, Arb[l]aster must mak a proctyr by yowr advyce, and iff he lyst to make the seyd Master John Halfnothe he maye, elles he must sende uppe an other; and he most also make a letter of waraunt to the seyde Master John Half-nothe undre hys selle by yowre advyce in thys forme :—

1466(?)

Master John, &c. I recomande me, &c., letyng yow weet that I have made yow my proctor towchyng the testement off John Paston, Esquier; wherffor I praye yow that ye on my behalve reffuce the admynystracion of hys seyde testamen, fur I woll nowt have ado ther with. Wherffo[r] loke that ye on my behalve reffuce all admynestracion, entresse or besynesse, that I myght have there by. And thys shewys yow my wyll here in, and shall be to yow a dyscharge att any tyme. No moor, &c.

Yowr frend, JAMES ARBLASTER.

I wolde nat that myn oncle William scholde cawse hym to take on hym as hys felawe, for iff myn oncle William doo thus moche in the corte I suppose it may here afftre doo ease. For as God helpe me I cannot sey verrely iff my fadre (God have hys sowle !) agreyd that he shold be one, but in my sowle he never thowt that he sholde be, for he never namyd no moor butt my modre and me, and afftre, yow, whan I rehessyd myn oncle Clement, yow and Arblaster, and than he chase yow, seyng he thoght that ye were good and trewe. Kepe thys secrett. Iff myn oncle be noon executor, it maye happely brynge ageyn a trussyng coffre with CC. old peyse noblis, whyche he toke from me as executor.

---

[1] [From Paston MSS., B.M.] The MS. from which this letter is printed is a draft in the handwriting of Sir John Paston. There can be little doubt it was addressed to his brother John, and as it refers to the administration of their father's will, we place it in the year of his death.

656

JOHN RUSSE TO MARGARET PASTON[1]

*To the worshypfull and my right honorabyll maistresse,
Maistresse Marget Paston.*

After
1466 RIGHT worshipfull and myn right honourable and good
maistresse, I recomaund me to you in my most
humble wyse, besekynge youre maistresshyp to take
no dyspleasure of the longe forberyng of youre mony, whiche
is ix*li*. xvj*s*. viij*d*. now. Be my trouthe, Maister Fen had of
me l. marke at hyse beyng here fore custum, wherof a gret
part is owyng me tyl I may be leysere[2] gather it up. I thynke
of every day a wyke tyl ye be content, and I thanke God I owe
not al the world so myche as I do you. In as goodly haste as
I can, youre maistresship shal have it with ever my servise and
preyer, for ye do a meritory dede ; it hathe savyd my pore
honestie and gretly avayled me ; wher as if it had leyn in youre
coferys, as, I doute not, a M'*li*. more dothe, no profit shuld
have growe to any man ; it is a meritory dede to helpe them
that mene trewly, whiche, for Godis sake, maistresse consedre.
I truste I am of that substans that, what soever caswelte fortunyd, yourre maistressbip shuld not lese on pene of yourre
dute. Every ourre (?) may be distreynid of myn the value of
C. marke in shyppis and literys, and owe not but to you C*s*., I
dare afferme. Also, maystresse, ye have an obligacion of me
of xl*li*. a byll of xx*li*., and abil of xx*li*., and a byll of xl*li*. ; for
Godis sake, maistresse, spare me for a tyme, the rather for the
affeccion that my maister[3] had to me, whos soule Jhesu assoyle.
Hyse maistirshyp grauntyd me many tymez to have lent me of
the dedys goodis xl*li*., to have payd hym ageyn in v. yeer ; and
so I doute not but I shuld have had if hyse maistirshyp had
levyd. I lost a gret losse of hese departyng ; for hyse sake,

---

[1] [Add. MS. 34,889, f. 226.] This letter must have been written some time after
John Paston's death, but probably not many years later. Compare No. 651.
[2] *Sic.*   [3] John Paston.

260

maystresse, shewe me the more favour. I intende not to After
debarre you of oon peny, so Jhesu helpe me, but in as goodly 1466
haste as I can to contente you ; be my trouthe, at thys seasun
I have not in my pocession x. marke which is right litil, what
casewelte that ever fortune. I am deseyvid of many men ; be
my trouthe there is owyng me in thys town xl. marke of iij.
yeer passyd, that thow I shuld go to prison I knowe not to
have xxs. of ony of hem. Right worshypfull and my right
honourable maistresse, I beseke Almyghti Jhesu, ever preserve
you from adverste. Maistresse, for the servise that to my
pore powyr I aught my maister youre husbonde I am the werse
by xx*li*. and more sylvir ; for Godis sake therfor, maistresse,
yit favour me a season ; I aske not ellys.

Yourre bedeman and servaunt,   JOHN RUSSE.

657

J. STRANGE TO SIR JOHN PASTON[1]

*To my rith worchipfull and good master,
Ser John Paston, Knyght.*

RYTH worchupful ser, after dewe recomendacion, plesyt Betwen
zow to understond the cause of my wrytyng ys for a 1467-9
maryage for my Masterys Nargery, zowr suster. For
my nevyewe, John Straunge, wold make her sur of xl*li*. joynture
and CC. marke be zer of inherytaunce ; and yf zee and zour
frendes wole agreve herto, I trost to God that xall take a conclusion to the plesur of God, and worchup to both partyes.

Moreover, yt plesyth zow to wete, I am sore troblyd
with Bedston, as wele as the wey of tachements owte of the
Chauncer as oderwyse. I must beseche zow of zowr good
mastershepe and help in secrete maner as the Ser Thomas

---

[1] [From Fenn, iv. 286.] This letter being addressed to Sir John Paston touching
a proposal of marriage for his sister, must have been after the death of his father in
1466, and, of course, before the actual marriage of Margery Paston to Richard Call,
which seems to have taken place towards the close of 1469.

261

Between Lynes, the brynger of thys, shall enforme zow. I xall be att 1467-9
London in the begynnyng of thys terme, be the grace of God,
qwych preserve zowe.

Wretyn att Norwych in hast, the Monday after Twelthe
Day.

By yowr,   J. STRANGE.

658

SIR JOHN AND LADY HOWARD[1]

1467
JAN. 22 THIS wrytenge made at London the vj*te* yer of Kynge
Edward the iiij. and the xxij. day of Jenever wytnesseth what stoffe my master Sir John Howard hath
delyverd to my Lady his wyfe in this monyth of Jenever.

Ferst ij. rynges of goolde set with good dyamawntes, the
wyche the quene yaff my master.

Item, a rynge of goolde with a fyne rubye.

Item, a nowche of goolde set with a fyne safyre, a grete
balyse and v. perles.

Item, my master yaff here a fyne pece of holand clothe as
good as Reynes conteynenge in length xl. yerdes, the yerde
was wele worth iiijs.

Item, my master gaff her a noder pece of holand clothe,
corser, conteynenge in lengthe more than xl. yerdes, the yerde
was worthe ijs. iiijd.

Item, my master gaff her a longe gowne of fyne cremysen
velvet furred with menyver and purfeled with ermynes.

Item, my master gaff her a longe gowne of fyne grene
velvet furred with menyver and purfeled with ermynes.

Item, my master gaff her vij*xx* scynnes of fyne ermynes.

Item, my master gaff her vij. yerdes and di. of fyne grene
velvet.

Item, my master gaff here vij. yerdes of cremyson velvet.

---

[1] [Add. MS. 34,889, f. 51.] The date is taken from the head of the document,
but there are additions of later dates to January 1468.

262

Item, my master gaff here a devyse of goolde with xiiij. 1467
lynkes and the ton halffe of the lynkes enamyled set with iiij. JAN. 22
Rubyis iij. dyamawntes and vij. perles.

Item, my master gaff her an nothe devyse of goolde of the
same fassyon with odre xiiij. lynkes, and theryn vij. Rubyis
and vij. perles.

Item, my master gaff her a gyrdyll of clothe of goolde and
the harneys of goolde.

Item, my master gaff her a gyrdyll of grene damaske and
the harneys of sylver and gylte.

Item, my master gaff her iij. edges of blak velvet set with
lviij. perles.

Item, my master gaff here a longe gowne of blak velvet
furred with martrys and purfeled with marteres.

Item, my master gaff her a longe gowne of murrey furred
with menever and purfeled with ermynes.

Item, my master gaff here a coler of goolde with xxxiiij.
roses and sonnes set on a corse of blak sylke with an hanger of
goolde garnyshed with a saphyre.

Item, my master gaff her iiij. owches of goolde garnyshed
with iij. rubyis, a saphyre, an amytes, an emerawde and xv.
perles.

Item, my master gaff here a peyr of bedes for a gentyl-
womannes nekke gawdeid with viij. gawdeid of goolde and
viij. perles.

Item, a rynge with a grete saphyre.

Item, my master gaff her a nother ryng with an amytes.

Item, my master gaff her iij. Agnus Dei of goolde.

Item, my master gaff her a gret sygnnet of goolde with
the vernycle.

Item, my master gaff her v. odre ryngis of goolde withowt
stones.

Item, my master gaff her a cheyne of goolde with a lokke
of goolde gernyshed with a rubye.

Item, my master gaff her a lytell gerdyll of sylke and
goolde called a demysent and the harneys of goolde.

Item, my master gaff her a longe of vyolet engreyned
furred with martres and purfeled with martres.

263

THE PASTON LETTERS

1467
AN. 22

Item, the xviij. day of Feverer my master delyverid to my Lady to have to Braye a bed of cremysen damaske embrowdered with Cyle counterpoynte and testour all affter one.

Item, the same day my master delyverid my Lady a bede, a cyle, a counterpeynt and a testor of Aras with out goolde.

Item, a pece of Aras for hangenge conteynenge in length xj. yerdes and iij. quarters.

Item, a nother pece of Aras conteynenge in length viij. yerdis and iii. quarters.

Item, a nother pece conteynenge vij. yerdis a quarter and di. in length.

Item, a nother pece of Aras conteyneng v. yerdes and iij. quarteres in length.

Item, delyverd to my said Lady iiij. peces of new Aras wyche cam late fro Caleys wereof on is a covertore fore a bedde and the todde [sic] iij. ar tapettes conteynenge all iiij. peces in flemesh elles square C iiij^xx xij.

Item, my master left at London at his departynge to Braye in his place in Bathe Rowe the xx. day of feverer ij. brede clothes of Blewe.

Item, the vij^th yer of Kynge Edward the iiij^th and the xvj. day of March, my master sent to my Lady to Bray a longe coshon of cremesen velvet and iij. schorte coshones of cremesen velvet. Item, a longe coshon of grene velvet and ij. short cushones of grene velvet.

Item, the same tyme my master delyverd her a cheyne of goold of the olde facyon prise iiij. markis.

Item, the yere above said and the xvj. day of Apryll, my master delyverd to my Lady v. sylver spones.

Added in Sir John Howard's own hand:—And the vij. zere of the kenge and in the monithe of Janever I delyvered my wyffe a pote of selver to pote in grene genger that the kenge gaffe.

On the back of this MS. is the following unfinished memorandum:—
'M^d that I John Legge hawe bownde mey self to John Osberne yn an oblygacyon—'

264

THE PASTON LETTERS

1467
MAN. 27

that they shuld ryd to tak a dystres in sertayn maners that wer Syr John Fastolffys; wherfor I suppose veryly that they be to Gwton and Saxthorp. Wher for to morrow I purpose to send Dawbeney thedyr to wet what they do, and to comand the ¹ tenauntis and fermors that they pay no mony to nobody bot to yow. John Grey, othyrwyse callyd John Delesbay, and John Burgeys they be Yelvertons kapteyns, and they ryd and go dayly, as well in Norwych as in othyr plasys of yours and othyr menys, in the contre in ther trossyng dowblettis with bombardys and kanonys and chafeveleyns, and do what so ever they wyll in the contre; ther dar no pore man dysplese theym, for what so evyr they do with ther swordys they make it lawe; and they tak dystressys out of mens howsys, hors or catell, or what they wyll, thow it be not on that for that they ask the dwte for. Wher for, me thynkys with esy menys ye myth get a prevy seall of the Kyng to be dyrectyd to the meyer of Norwyche, as for the towne of Norwyche, and for the countre a nothyr prive seall, dyrect to me and to som othyr good felaw, Syr William Calthorp, for he hatyth Grey,² for to arest the seyd felaws for syche ryot and to bryng hem to the next prison, ther to abyed with out bayle tyll syche tym as the Kyng sendyth othyrwyse woord, and they that the prive sale shall be dyrect to, to be chargyd vpon peyne of ther alegeans to execut the Kyngis comandement; and, this done, I warant your lyvelod that my lord delys not with shall be gadyrd pesybylly. As to that lyvelod that my lord clemys I shall do my dever, our logyng kep, to tak as myche profyt of it as I may be the grase of God, Whom I pray send you the acomplyshement of your hertys desyir, and other por folys thers. All my felawshep ar mery and well at ease, blyssyd be God, and recomandyth hem all on to yow. Wretyn the Tweysday next befor Kandylmas.—Your brodyr,

J. P.

¹ 'the' repeated in MS.
² 'Syr William—Grey' is an interlineation.

266

EDWARD IV

659

JOHN PASTON TO SIR JOHN PASTON ¹

To my mastyr, Sir John Paston, logyng in Fletstret, be thys delyveryd.

SYR, lyekyth it yow to wet that thys day my modyr sent me your lettyrs, wer by I undystand, blessyd be God, all thyng standyth in good wey. Also I undyrstand by your lettyr sent to my modyr and me that ye wold have your lyvelod gadyrd as hastyly as we myght do it. Syr, as to that, and othyr folk do no wers ther dever [*devoir*] in gaderyng of othyr manerys then we have don in Caster, I tryst to God that ye schall not be long unpayid; for thys day we had in the last comb of barly that eny man had owyth in Caster towne, not with standyng Hew Awstyn and hys men hathe crakyd many a gret woord in the tym that it hathe ben in gaderyng. And twenty comb Hew Awstyns man had doun cartyd redy for to have led it to Yarmowth. And when I herd ther of I let slype a sertyn of whelpys that gave the cart and the barly syche a torn that it was fayn to tak covert in your bakhous systern at Caster halle, and it was wet within an owyr aftyr that it cam hom, and is nye redy to mak of good malt all, ho ho! William Yelverton hathe ben at Gwton and hathe set in a new bayly ther and hathe dystreynyd the tenauntis, and hathe geve hem day till Candyllmas to pay syche mony as he axyth of hem. Also the seyd Yellverton hathe ben at Saxthorpe, and hathe dystreynyd the fermour ther and takyn of hym swerte to paye hym. And thys day the seyd Yelverton and viij. men with hym, with jakys and trossyng dobletis all the felawshep of hem, wer redy to ryd; and one of the same felawschep told to a man that sye hem all redy

1467
JAN. 27

¹ [Add. MS. 33,597, f. 3.] This letter appears to have been written in the year 1467, like No. 661, which bears date eleven days later. Besides what is said here of Yelverton, note the reference to John Grey and John Burgeys, whose names appear in the other letter also.

265

EDWARD IV

660

T. DAVERSE TO SIR JOHN PASTON ¹

To my right good mayter, Sir John Paston, Knyght.

MY right especiall good mayster, I recomand me to yow, thankyng you right hertely of your gentell letter late send to me. And as to Pynchester mater, &c., I wulde I were youre nygh kynnesman, yef hit plesed God, and than shuld I know yef hit shuld greve your herte asmeche as hit dothe other of my kynne and frendes to see me thus cowardly hurte and maimed ² by Pynchester, causeles; and of myn entente in that mater, Wylliam Rabbes shall telle you more. All so I beseche yow to recomand me to my Lordes good grace, as to hym whom of erthely estates, next my dewte, I moste love and drede, and that shuld he well knowe and hit lay in my power, praying you hertely to declare his Lordship such mater as Wylliam Rabbes shall enfourme yow, and to send me my Lordes answere.

All so in asmoche as I understode by yow that money shuld cause you conclusion in your mater this next terme, and ye wull be at London on Monday at nyght or Tewsday by none, I truste that I have studyed such a mene that, up on surete as ye may make, to gete yow an *Cli.* or CC. mark to be lante un to yow for an halfe yere, with oute any chevysshaunce or losse of good by yow, as Wylliam Rabbes shall telle you more, &c.

1467(?)
JAN. 29

¹ [From Fenn, iv. 172.] The precise date of this letter is by no means certain. Fenn dates it merely between 1463 and 1469; but if it be 'my Lady of Oxford,' and not 'my Lord,' who is spoken of near the end (*see* page 268, footnote 2), it may be many years later. The Earl of Oxford was committed to the Tower in the latter part of the year 1468. In 1470 he took part in the brief restoration of Henry VI., and on the return of Edward IV. he was obliged to quit the country. If the Earl, therefore, is alluded to as living in England, the date cannot well be later than 1468. Probably it is about the year 1467. In that year the 29th January fell on a Thursday, which would allow a reasonable time for the writer to suggest to Sir John Paston the expediency of his being in London on Monday or Tuesday following.

² The words 'and maimed' are inserted from the right-hand copy in Fenn. They are not in the left-hand copy, having been overlooked, apparently, by the transcriber.

267

THE PASTON LETTERS

1467 (?)
JAN. 29

And as to Ovyde 'De Arte Amandi,' I shall send hym you this next weke, for I have hyt not now redy ; but me thenkeyth Ovide ' De Remedio ' were more mete for yow, but yef [*unless*] ye purposid to falle hastely in my Lady Anne P.[1] lappe, as white as whales bon, &c. Ye be the best cheser of a gentell woman that I knowe, &cc. And I pray you to re-comaunde me to my Lord of Oxford,[2] and to my goods Maysters Nedeham, Richemond, Chyppenham, Stavely, Blox-ham, Stuard, and Ingulton in speciall, and all other good masters and frendes in generall, &c. And, sir, Maystres Gaydade recomand me [? *her*] to yow and said bessyng fare for charite, and she said me she wuld fayne have a new felet, &c.

Wreten at London, this xxix. day in Janyver.

With herte and servyse your,

T. D.[3]

661

JOHN PASTON TO SIR JOHN PASTON[4]

1467
FEB. 7

SYR, it is so that thys Saterday John Rus sent me word by Robert Botler, that William Yelverton hathe ben thys iij. dayis in Yermothe for to get new wytnessys up to London ; and, as it is thowt by the seid John Rus and Robert Botler, ther wytnessyng is for to prove that it was Sir John Fastolfs wyll that ther schold be morteysyd iij.[c] mark by yer to the colage, and also that syche astat as my fadyr took

[1] Who my Lady Anne P. was I cannot tell. The expression 'as white as whale's bone' is rather a strange one.
[2] The modern version in Fenn reads 'my Lady of Oxford,' but 'my Lord of Oxford' is right.
[3] Fenn says this subscription is explained by 'T. Daverse' being written under the direction, as he believes, in the hand of the receiver.
[4] [From Fenn, iv. 276.] This letter must have been written in February 1467. It was evidently after Sir John Paston had succeeded to his father's estates, but before any arrangement had been come to between him and Yelverton. It will be found hereafter that on the 11th January 1468 Sir John Fastolf's executors, including Yelverton, released their rights in Caister and other manors to Sir John Paston. On the back of this letter, Fenn says, is written in an ancient hand, 'Testes idonei ad negandum veritatem, ut patet infra.'

268

THE PASTON LETTERS

662

SIR JOHN PASTON TO JOHN PASTON[1]

To my brother, John Paston.

1467
MARCH

RYGHT worschypful and verrely welbelovyd brother, I hertely comande me to yow, thankyng yow of yowr labor and dylygence that ye have in kepyng of my place at Castr so sewerly, both with yowr hert and mynde, to yowr gret bisynesse and troble ; and I ageyn warde have hadde so lytell leyser that I have not spedde bot fewe of yowr erendys, ner kannot befor thys tyme.

As for my Lady Boleynes[2] dysposicion to yow werds, I kannot in no wyse fynde hyr a greable that ye scholde have her dowter, for all the prevy meanes that I kowde make, inso moche I hadde so lytell comfor by all the meanes that I kowde make, that I dysdeyned in myn own p[e]rson to comon with hyr ther in. Neverthelesse, I undrestande that sche seythe, 'What if he and sche kan agre I wyll not lette it, but I will never advyse hyr therto in no wyse.' And uppon Tewesday last past, sche rood hom in to Norfolke. Wherfor as ye thynke ye may fynde the meane to speke with hyr yowr selfe, for with owt that, in myn conceyt, it wyl not be.

And as for Crosseby, I undrestand not that ther is no maryage concluded betwen them, nevertheless ther is gret langage that it is lyke to be. Ye be personable, and per-aventure yowr beyng ones in the syght of the mayde, and a lytele descuveryng of your good wyl to her, byndyng hyr to kepe it secret, and that ye kan fynde in yowr hert, with som comfort of hyr, to fynde the meane to brynge suche a mater abowt as schall be hyr pleasur and yowrs, but that thys ye

[1] [From Fenn, iv. 326.] This letter is evidently of the same year as No. 666 following, and a little earlier in point of date.
[2] Anne, widow of Sir Geoffrey Boleyn. She was daughter of Thomas, Lord Hoo and Hastings. Sir Geoffrey had by her three daughters, of whom the youngest, Alice, is here referred to. This Alice was afterwards married to Sir John Fortescue.

270

her at Caster at Lames next befor that Sir John Fastolf dyid, was delyveryd to my fadyr to the intent for to perform the seyd wyll.

1467
FEB. 7

Bartholomew Elys, John Appylby, and John Clerk ar the wytnessys ; and as for Barthew Elys, he is owtlawyd, and also men say in Yermowthe that he is bawde betwyx a clerk of Yermowthe and hys owne wyfe ; and as for John Appylby, he is half frentyk, and so take in the towne, notwithstandyng he is an attorny, as Barthew Elys is, in the Baylys Coort of Yermowthe ; and as for John Clerk of Gorleston, he is owt-lawyd at Sir John Fastolfys swte, and at dyvers othyr menys, notwithstandyng he is thorow with Sir T. Howys[1] for Sir John Fastolf, for thys cause, that the seyd Clerk was on of Sir T. Howys[1] last wytnessys befor thys.

I trow John Loer shall be anothyr wyttnesse. As for Barthew Elys and John Appylby, they lye thys nyht at Blyborowgh onward on her wey to Londonward. Make good weche on hem.

I pray yow send us some good tydyngs. Wretyn the Saterday, lat at nyght, next aftyr Kandylmas Day.

I pray yow remembyr John Grey and John Burgeys. We have hom the most part of your barly, save fro Wynterton, and that I trost to have thys next wek, or ellys we wyll strat [*distrain?*] for it by the grace of God, whom I besеche mak yow good.

I thynk ther comyng up is for to dysprove your wyttnessys that he had in to the Chancery.

J. P.[2]

[1] Fenn has 'Sir Thowys' in his left-hand copy, which we cannot help thinking a misreading of 'Sir T. Howys.'
[2] Fenn says this letter 'has neither subscription nor date '; nevertheless these initials stand at the foot of the text as he has printed it.

269

kannot do with owt som comfort of hyr in no wyse ; and ber yor selfe as lowly to the moder as ye lyst, but to the mayde not to lowly, ner that ye be to gladde to spede, ner to sory to fayle. And I always schall be your herault bothe her, if sche com hydder, and at home when I kome hom, whych I hope hastly with in xl. dayes at the ferthest. My modre hathe a letter, whych can tell you mor, and ye may lat Dawebeney se it.

1467
MARCH

JOHN PASTON, K.

I suppose and ye kall welle upon R. Calle, he schall purvey yow mony. I have wretyn to hym inow.

663

RICHARD CALLE TO SIR JOHN PASTON[1]

To my ryght reverent and worschipfull mayster, Sir John Paston, Knight.

PLESITH it you to wete that I have spoken with Henre Inglouse, and I fynde hym disposid weele ; hough be it he hath be labored to nough of late be divers, never-theles he woll not come withoute he have a suppena, and if he come up be suppena, he can sey nor nought woll sey, any thynge that schulde be prejudice or hurte to your mater, and so he hathe tolde them that hath labored to hym for it, weche hym thynkyth causith them to have no grete hast to have hym up. He tellith me that the Abbot of Langley schal come up and Wichyngham. Thes have her writtes of suppena delyverd unto them. Also ther cometh up Doctor Vergraunt and Frier Bernard. And as for Robert Inglouse, I have spoken with hym, and I fynde hym no thyng so weele disposid as his brother is ; he hath be sore labored be the meanes of my Lord

APRIL 3

[1] [From Paston MSS., B.M.] This letter seems to relate to the summoning of witnesses to London for the probate of Fastolf's will, and being addressed to Sir John Paston, we may presume that it was written in the year after his father's death, and before the final settlement of the dispute.

271

467
PRIL 3
of Norffolk and of my Lord of Suffolk; he seyth largely that he knoweth moche of this mater, seyng to me that if he schulde be examyned be for a juge, he wolde my master your uncle[1] wer his juge, for he knoweth the mater as weele as any man. He seith if he be sworn be fore my Lorde Chaunceler, he woll desire of my Lord that Maister William schulde be sworn as weele as he; nevertheles I have so mevyd hym that withoute ther come a suppena for hym he woll not come, as he seth it is hard to truste hym. It were weele doo if ther were no suppena out for hym to cauce that ther schulde non come, nouther to hym nor to hes brother, &c. I can not undrestonde of no moo that schulde come up yet, but I schal enquere, and sende you word as hastely as I can. I have not spoken with John Maryot yet, but I schall speke with hym within this iij. dayes and sende you worde. &c.

Ferthermore, sir, like you to remembre the lees of the maner of Sporle; your fermours goth out at Michelmes next comyng. Henry Halman wolde have it for his sones, and if be schulde have it he wolde wete at this tyme, be cauce he wolde somerlay[2] and tylle the londe, otherwise then it is; it were tyme to lete it, wo so ever schulde have it. Henry woll geve for it but xx*li.*; wherfor, if ye wol that he have it, plese you to sende word how we schal do with all, &c. Almyghty Godde spede you in all youre maters, and sende you hastely a goode ende in hem. Wreten at Castre on Friday next after Esterne Day.

Your own Servaunt, RIC. C.

[1] William Paston.
[2] Halliwell gives the expression 'to summerland a ground' which is used in Suffolk, meaning to lay it fallow a year. For this he refers to Ray.

272

664

[WILLIAM PASTON] TO SIR JOHN PASTON[1]

To my right worshipfull nevew, Sir John Paston, knyght.

MYNE suster,[2] Arblaster[3] and I have apoyntyd that we chall kepe no howsold this terme,[4] but go to borde; wer for we avyse zow to purvay for us a logyng ner a bowt my lord Chanseler that be honest, for Arblaster will non oder.

1467
APRIL (?)

Item, as for zow, we avyse zow in any wyse gete zowr chamer assynyd with in my Lordis place, and gete chamer a lone iff ze may, that Arblaster and I may have a bed ther in ziff it fortune us to be late ther with zow.

Item, take hed to get suyrtees for the pore men that come up and that they may be sent hom a zen forthe with owt taryyng, and take avyse so that the proses may so go forthe that they may be qwett at the next assyssys; take avyse of Townysend.

As for Yelverton, fynd the menys that he speke not with my Lord till we come.

Iff any labore be mad to my Lord to asyne men to here the mater indefferently, make labore to my Lord that the men be nat namyd till we come, for we can inffurme hym soche as be parciall be ther dedis here affore, qweche peraventure my Lord wold thynk wer indefferent i now till he be infurmyd; it may be answerid be my Lord that he will nat prosede no

[1] [Add. MS. 33,597, f. 8.] This is not a formal letter but a set of memoranda on a long slip of paper. It is in the handwriting of William Paston, son of the judge, and addressed to his nephew, Sir John. The date may be about April 1467. *See* No. 663.
[2] This must be his brother John's widow, Margaret, who was in London in the spring of 1467. *See* No. 662, p. 271.
[3] James Arblaster, a confidential friend of the family.
[4] Easter term began on the 15th April in 1467.

467
RIL (?)
ferther in the mater till Arblasters comyng and myn for we can best infurme the mater.

Item, send a letter to Richard Kalle and to Sir Jamys Gloys to come up to London in any wyse. For ther is no man can do in dyvers materis that they can do in answeryng suche mater as Zelverton wyll ley a zen zow. And also they can best mak the bill that ze schuld put a zens hem; and ther for remembre.

Item, wrythe a letter to myn suster for the C. marcs for my Lady Soffolk, for we have no verry dyrect answer of her weder sche wyll send it ar nat.

Item, speke to zowr atorney in the Kyngis benche that he take hed to all maner indytamentis both old and new and to all oder materis that hangyng ther.

Item, do Pampyng comyn with owr sperituall concell suche mater as nedyn ther. And have newe wretyn the attestacion that lakkyn. The same man that wrott the oder may wrythe that. For Zelverton mad gret avawnt that ye schuld be hyndrid in that.

Wrythe a letter to myn nevew John zonger to come up to prove the wyll.

Speke with Sir Gilberd Debenham qwill he is in cownt to leve uper Cotton.

Item, Zelverton, Howys and Worceter make meche that we have put them owt off possescyon of the lond; qweche they sey is contrary to my Lord Chanseler comandement, and in trowth Sir Jamys and Calle meche spokyn to the tenantis in my lordys name; For Zelverton thynketh that he may now breke the trete. Qwer for, take a vyse her in off M[r] Tresham and of Master Staneley, and informe my Lord how my broder[1] qwas all way in possession till he was put owt for the mater of bondage, and how ze fynd the colage, and qwat an hurt it wer to zow in noyse off contre iff any oder man schuld now receyve any proffitis off the londis. They will labor that indefferent men schuld receyve, and that wer nat good. My Lord may say that he will end the mater, but as for the possescyon, he will nat put zow owt. Labor this in all hast posible.

[1] John Paston, son of the judge. Dead in 1466.

274

665

SIR JOHN PASTON TO JOHN PASTON[1]

MY hand was hurte at the torney at Eltham upon Wednesday last. I would that you had been there and seen it, for it was the goodliest sight that was sene in Inglande this forty yeares of so fewe men. There was upon the one side, within, the Kinge, my Lord Scalles, myselfe, and Sellenger; and without, my Lord Chamberlyn, Sir John Woodvyle, Sir Thomas Mountgomery, and John Aparre, &c.

APRIL

By your brother,

JOHN PASTON, Mil.

666

JOHN PASTON TO SIR JOHN PASTON[2]

SYR, plesyth yow to weet that my modyr and I comonyd this day with Freyr Mowght to undyrstand what hys seying shall be in the coort when he cometh up to London, wheche is in this wyse:—He seyth at syche tyme as he had shrevyn Master Brakley, and howsyllyd hym bothe, he let hym wet that he was enformyd by dyvers personys that the seyd Master Brakley owt for to be in gret consyens for syche thyngys as he had doone and seyd, and causyd my fadyr, whom God asoyle, for to do and seye also, in proving of Sir

1467
APRIL (?)

[1] This extract from a letter of Sir John Paston to his brother is quoted in Sandford's MS. Genealogy of the Paston family, and is here reprinted from Mr. Worship's article on that genealogy in the *Norfolk Archeology*. The original letter I have not been able to find. The tournament here referred to probably took place shortly after Easter. The next letter is evidently written in reply to this.
[2] [From Fenn, iv. 330.] This letter appears by the contents to have been written more than a week after Easter. The year must be 1467, as the dispute with Yelverton touching Sir John Fastolf's will seems to have come to an end before the January following (*see* No. 680). In 1467 Easter Day fell on 29th March.

275

THE PASTON LETTERS

John Fastolfys wyll. To whom the seyd Mastyr Brakley answerd thus agayne: 'I am ryght glad that it comyth to yow in mynd for to meve me with thys mater in dyschargyng of my consyens ayenst God,' seying ferther mor to the seyd Freyr Mowght, be the wey that hys sowle shold to, that the wyll that my fadyr put into the coort was as veryly Syr John Fastolfys wyll as it was trew that he shold onys deye. This was seyd on the Sonday when the seyd Brakley wend to have deyid then. On the Monday he revyvyd a yen, and was well amendyd tyll on the Wednysday, and on the Wednysday he sekyned a yen, supposyng to have dyeyd forthe with. And in hys syknes he callyd Freyr Mowght, whyche was confessor on to hym, of hys owne mosyon, seyng on to hym in thys wyse :—'Syr, wher as of your owne mosyon ye mevyd me the last day to tell you aftyr my consyens of Sir John Fastolfys wyll lyek wyse as I knew, and now of myn owne mocyon, and in dischargyng of my sowle, for I know well that I may not askape, but that I must dye in hast, wharfor I desyr you that wyll report after my dethe, that I took it upon my sowle at my dying that that wyll that John Paston put in to be provyd was Syr John Fastolfys wyll.' And the seyd Brakley dyid the same Wednysdaye.

And wher as ye wold have had Rychard Calle to yow as on Sonday last past, it was thys Twysday I or I had your lettyr; and wher as it plesyth yow for to wyshe me at Eltam, at the tornay, for the good syth that was ther, by trowththe I had lever se yow onys in Caster Hall then to se as many Kyngs tornay as mygth be betwyx Eltam and London.

And, syr, whar as it lyekyth yow to desyir to have knowlage how that I have don with the Lady Boleyn,[1] by my feythe I have don nor spokyn nowght in that mater, nor not wyll do tyll tyme that ye com hom, and ye com not thys vij. yer. Not withstandyng, the Lady Boleyn was in Norwyche in the week aftyr Estern, fro the Saterday tyll the Wednysday, and Heydons wyfe[2] and Mastras Alys[3] bothe, and I was at Caster, and wyst not of it. Hyr men seyd that she had non othyr

---
[1] See Note 2, p. 270.   [2] Anne, second daughter of Sir Geoffrey Boleyn.
[3] Third daughter of Sir Geoffrey Boleyn.

THE PASTON LETTERS

comynge of the Bastard of Burgoyne attende to th'execucion off myn offyce, as my wyll and duete were to, in myn owne persone. Wherfor of verray necessite I must depute suche a person in all goodly hast to ocupye as my deputee and to have my full power undere me at that season as is bothe of byrthe honorable and one all other wyse lykly. How be it that of long tyme contynnuynge I have ben enured of your stedfaste and preved feythful good cosyngnage and tendyrnesse to me shewed unfeyned to my gret refute[1] and hertes ease at all seasons. Wiche emboldeth me to call uppon you now; and also remembrynge the honour of the offyce doynge and the neighnesse of blode that ye be of to me, I thenke no person so convenable to ocupye in myn absence as you. For myn excuse, therfore, I specyally pray you, as my feythfull truste is holy in you, to take the labour uppon you and to do theryn be your discrecion to the most honour of the kynge, the realme, and be lyke as I am asured that ye can and wyll, puttynge you in surete that I wull become tributary to your costes and charges in that behalve. And as for all suche duteis as schall belonge to me at that tyme by reason of myn offyce, I gyff theme you for parcell of your said costes; and at such tyme as ye and I and myn counsell mete next ye schal not fayle to be agreid with, to your pleasure for the residue, by Goddis grace, Wiche ever preserve you. And, cousyn, I sende you be the berer herof the double of this lettre, prayng that ye will subscribe it with your owne hande and send it me a geyn be hym. Wryten under my signet the xviij. day of May.

To my rigth trusty and rigth enteerly belovyd cousyn,
Sir John Howard, knygth.

And this letter is assigned with my lordes own hande.

---
[1] Sic in ms.

EDWARD IV

erend to the towne but for to sport hyr; bot so God help me, I suppose that she wend I wold have ben in Norwyche for to have sen hyr dowghter. I beseche yow with all my hart hye yow hom, thow ye shold tery but a day; for I promyse yow your folk thynk that ye have forgetyn hem, and the most part of them must depart at Whytsontyd at the ferthest, they wyll no lenger abyd. And as for R. Calle, we can not get half a quarter the mony that we pay for the bare housold, besyd menys wagys. Daube nor I may no mor with owt coynage.   Your,   J. PASTON.

667

ABSTRACT[1]

'Bill indented' 1 May, 7 Edw. IV., between Sir John Paston and Thomas Lomnor, whereby the latter sells to the former an ambling horse 'upon this condition, that if the marriage betwixt the Lord Charles, son and heir to the Duke of Burgon, and the Lady Margaret, sister to our Sovereign Lord the King' take effect within two years, Sir John agrees to pay 6 marks for the horse on the day of the marriage; but if it do not take effect within that period he will pay only 40 shillings.

[There is a modern copy of this document in the Heralds' College, in the collection called Brooke's *Aspilogia*, vol. i. f. 47, where a drawing is given of Sir John Paston's seal, which seems to have been attached to it when the transcript was made. It has been since removed at some time or other.]

668

THE DUKE OF NORFOLK TO SIR JOHN HOWARD[2]

The Duc of Norffolk.

RYGTH trusty and enteerly beloved cousyn I comaunde me to you with all myn herte. And lyke it you to wete that God hath vyset me with grete infirmite and dissease, wherthurgh I neyther can nor may at this season and

---
[1] [From ms. Phillipps, 9735, No. 192.]
[2] [Add. ms. 34,889, f. 59.] The famous tournament between Lord Scales and the Bastard of Burgundy took place at Smithfield on the 11th and 12th June 1467. See *Excerpta Historica*, 176 This paper is evidently a copy of the original letter.

EDWARD IV

669

SIR JOHN HOWARD[1]

THIS wrytenge made at London the vij[th] yer of kyng Edward the iiij[th] and the ——[2] day of June wytnessyth what Jakettes my master Sir John Howard geveth at the fytenge betwyx my Lord Scales and the Bastard of Burgoyne.

John Alpherde	John de Spayn
Brome	Jenyn Saunpere
William Noryse	John Kyngton
Herry Straunge	Lytell Edmond
Robert Cumberton	John Coles
Hastynges	Thomas Mershe
John Fowler	Rechard Leder
John Nyter	John Gylder
Thomas Moleyns	Rechard Waleys
John Waleys	Ravensbye
Robart Thorppe	Thomas a Chambre
John Bleaunt	Thomas Whytenge
Thomas Thorppe	Thomas Grymston
Davy Horell	Roger Jewell
Robert Cooke	Colson
Robart Clerke	John Squyre[3]
John Hobbes	Scarlett[3]
Wynche	William West[4]
John Wady	John Dykynson
William Fernwale	Thomas Bowden
Raff Barlyscose	William Denny
Thomas Seynclew	John Starkeweder
Whyttebye	George Hardwyn
Kechyn	Thomas Caunterbury

---
[1] [Add. ms. 34,889, f. 61.]   [2] Blank in ms.
[3] These two names, John Squyre and Scarlett, are bracketed together, and the name 'Alford' written opposite.
[4] Opposite this name is written 'Wal' in the margin.

1467
JUNE

Dyott	William Yngram
Robart Messeden	John Brodebryge
John Mynshe	Aleyn Cowper
Richard Pulton	Rechard Roger
John Wakeleyn	Herry Cooke
Nicholas Shakerley	Edward Holman
Hew Flynte	Rechard Halbroke[1]
Thomas Newton	Robart Sleper
William Clerke	John Cheynour
Robart Nosbet	John Hylle
Herry Nudygate	

670

JAMES GRESHAM TO SIMON DAMME[2]

To my worshipfull cosyn, Symond Damme, [at] Lyncoln Inne, at London, [be] this delyvered.

1467(?)
JULY 2

RIGHT worshipfull sir, and as in my trost my veray speciall good maister, I recomande me to you with al the servyce I can and may. Lyke it you to wytte that I have do my bysynes to enquere for suyche dedes as ye wrot for on to me, and, so God me helpe, I can not wytte where I shuld spede to have ony suyche dedes. I spak to a persone that is your good lover, the whiche tolde me that ther was a gret plee bytwene my Lord of Suffolk and Sir John Fastolf for the maner of Drayton, for whiche matier William Wysetre was sent to enquere for evydencez touchyng the Pooles lyvelond in suyche places as thei were lords of in their

[1] Opposite this name is written 'chad' in the margin.
[2] [From Paston mss., B.M.] As this letter has reference to the disputes between the Duke of Suffolk and the Paston family about Drayton, it might be supposed to have been written about the year 1464, but that the entire absence of any mention of John Paston the father makes it probable that the true date is after his death. It is therefore not unlikely to be of the same year as No. 671, in which Margaret Paston mentions the probability of Hellesdon being taken again out of their hands, and also desires an answer to a letter that she had sent to her son, Sir John, 'by James Gresham's man.'

280

dayes. And the seid Wysetre fonde evydencez that touched a maner called Mundham maner, sum tyme longyng to the Pooles that were owenners of Drayton, the whiche evydences eased meche Sir John Fastolf; but the seid persone that enfourmed me of this can not telle the armes, ne what evydencez tho shuld be in certeyn, savyng he thynkyth indoubted that William Worcetre shuld not be unremembred of this. Wherfore it is thought to the same persone that enfourmed me of this and by me also, that it shuld be expedyent for you to comune of this matier by your wysdam with the same William Wysetre, now beyng at London, for he by lyklyhod can telle you a certeynte. And as touchyng my maister, Sir Thomas Mongomery, I trost veryly that he nothyr hath ne shall have cause of grudger by my defaut, for I can not understand ony cause of grudger; for ever whanne my cosyn Damme[1] hath spoken with my seid maisters attourne to have knowelage by writyng of what thyng shuld be the cause of callyng on you, he answerith that my maister, W. Paston, hath a bille therof, but my cosyn can non gete. Wherfor I deme that the seid attourne meneth not weel. I entende noon other but in als meche as in me is to se your indempnyte with the grace of God, who ever mote be your guyde and protector. Wretyn at Norwich the ij. day of Juylle.

1467(?)
JULY 2

Your servaunt in that he can and may to his powar,
I, JAMES GRESHAM.

Cosyn, an noon after this was wretyn, had I knowelage of the massageris comyng to London berar of this, and I had thought to have wretyn the letter above wretyn newe, by cause of the foule wrytyng and interlynyeng, but now I lakke leyser. Wherfor I pray you understond the pyth of my seid wrytyng, and enfourme my seid maister Sir John P. of the same, for I wold fayne do that shulde please hym, &c. And the

[1] As it appears by the postscript that this letter was hurriedly despatched, we may perhaps presume that it was intended in the first instance for Sir John Paston, but that as 'my cousin Damme' required to be informed of the same particulars, it was afterwards addressed to him, with instructions to communicate the contents to Sir John.

281

1467(?)
JULY 2

persone that enfourmed me dar not be a knowe of his name, he wold not it shuld be understood to them that be of counsell ageyn my maister. It was the parson of Heylesdon, &c. More over, as I have wretyn to you of late, Palmer, undershireve of Norffolk, hath sent his letter to his depute to acomplyssh our entent for Chyldes matier as ye and I were accordet. This told Wykes me for verray certeyn, &c., the ij. day of Juylle.

On the back of this letter are some scribblings in another hand, viz.:—First, a partial copy of the address; second, the name 'John Dode'; third, the following inscription, 'Orate pro anima Johnnes (sic) de Boys armenger de Londoun.'

671

MARGARET PASTON TO SIR JOHN PASTON[1]

To Sir John Paston, Knyght, be this delivered in hast.

1467
JULY 11

I GRETE you wele, and send you Godds blissyng and myn, letyng you wete that Blykklyng of Heylesdon came fro London this weke, and he is right mery, and maketh his bost that with in this fourtnyght at Heylesdon shuld be bothe new lords and new officers. And also this day was brought me word fro Caystr that Rysyng of Freton shuld have herd seid in diverse places, ther as he was in Suffolk, that Fastolf of Coughawe maketh all the strenght that he may, and proposith hym to assaught Caystr, and to entre ther if he may, in samych that it is seyd that he hath a v. score men redy, and sendyth dayly aspies to understand what felesshep kepe the place. Be whos power, or favour, or supportacion that he wull do this, I knowe not; but ye wote wele that I have ben

[1] [From Fenn, iv. 294.] This letter must have been written some time after Sir John Paston had obtained possession of Caister by virtue of the King's warrant of the 17th July 1466 (No. 641), and before the Duke of Norfolk laid claim to it again in 1469. Thus the date is certainly either 1467 or 1468. But in the latter year Sir John Paston and his brother were both in Flanders at the marriage of the Princess Margaret to the Duke of Burgundy; and Daubeney could not have been with them, as he was when this letter was written, for John Paston the younger says he had sent him five shillings by Calle's man. Thus 1467 appears to be the only year possible.

282

affrayd ther befor this tyme, whan that I had other comfort than I have now, and I can not wele gide ner rewle sodyours, and also thei set not be a woman as thei shuld set be a man. Therfor I wold ye shuld send home your brothers, or ell[es] Dawbenye, to have a rewle, and to takyn in such men as wer necessary for the saffegard of the place; for if I wer ther withought I had the mor sadder or wurchepfull persones abought me, and ther comyn a meny of knavys, and prevaylled in ther entent, it shuld be to me but a vylney. And I have ben abought my liffelode to set a rewle ther in, as I have wretyn to you, which is not yet all performed after myn desyre, and I wuld not goo to Caystr till I had don. I wull no mor days make ther abowtyn if I may; therfor in any wyse send sume body home to kepe the place, and whan that I have do and performed that I have be gunne, I shall purpose me thederward if I shuld do ther any good, and ell[es] I had lever be thens.

1467
JULY 11

I have sent to Nicholas, and such as kepe the place, that thei shuld takyn in sume feles [fellows] to assiste and strengh them till ye send hame sume other word, or sume other man to governe them that ben therin, &c.

I marvayll gretly that ye send me no word how that ye do, for your elmyse [enemies] begynne to wax right bold, and thet puttith your frends bothyn in grete fere and dought. Therfor purvey that thei may have sume comfort, that thei be no more discoraged; for if we lese our frends, it shall hard in this troubelous werd [world] to kete them ageyn.

The blissid Trynyte spede you in your mater, and send you the victory of your elmyse, to your herts eas and ther confusyon. Wretyn at Norwich, the Saterday next befor Relyke Sonday,[1] in hast.

I pray you remembre wele the maters that I wrote to you for in the letter that ye had be James Greshames man, and send me an answer ther of be the next man that comyth, &c.

Be your moder,

M. P.

[1] Relic Sunday (the third Sunday after Midsummer Day) was the 12th July in 1467.

283

672

DECLARATION OF SIR THOMAS HOWYS[1]

1467
JULY 21

BE it knowen to all men that this present wrytyng shall rede, see, or hyre. Forasmoche as I understande nowe late ther ys a newe contryved processe concernyng the variaunce uppon my maister Sir John Fastolf is testament and last will, whos soule God assoyle, made by Sir John Paston, Knyght, and his counsell in the seyd Pastons name and myne, ayenste Sir William Yelverton, Knyght, and William Worcetter, that is exhibited and putte in my lordys courte of Audience be fore his auditoure, me unwetyng or assentyng, in the vigille of Seint John Baptiste; in wheche processe ys surmyttyd and made mencion that William Worcetter in his owne persone, and by others in his name, hathe promysed and gevyn money to corupte certayne wytnesse to depose untreuly in a processe exhibit in John Pastons lyf tyme by Sir William Yelverton, Knyght, the sayd William Wissetter ayenste John Paston decesed and me; and wheche witnesse were Stephan Scrope, Squier, Richard Fastolf, gentilman, Thomas Neve, gentilman, William Boswell, clerk, John Monke, Nicholas Churche, John Rugge, John Daunson, Richard Horne, Thomas Pykeryng, Harry Clerk, John Tobye, Thomas Hart, Thomas Neuton, John Gyrdyng, Thomas Spycer, and others, frome the moneth of August into the moneth of March, the yere of Cryst M$^{il.}$CCCClxv., yn Yermouthe, Castre, Fretenham, Bloofeld, Thetford, Brundale, Wroxham, Borough, Southetoune, Yermouthe, Gorleston, Suthewerk, Norwych, and London; so they to be corupted in all the forseyd named tounes wyth prayer, price, and money to hem promised and gevyn, be syd har expences, her costs, and her labours, to be conducted to depose with Sir William Yelverton and William Worcetter partye ayenste the seyd John Paston and mee: I the sayd Thomas Howys so made partye, and unwetyng and assentyng, a yenste the [said][2] Sir William Yelverton and William

[1] [From a MS. in the tower of Magd. Coll., Oxford.] [2] Omitted in MS.
284

Worcestre, sey and afferme for trouth in this matyer to be 146 knowen, that for declaracion of trouth in this processe and JULY mater, and for the discharge of my conscience and the trewe acquietall to my sayd Master Fastolf that putte me in grettyst charge of hys testament, and for grete remorse I have in my soule of the untrewe forgyng and contryvyng certayne testamentes and last wyll by naked wordes in my sayd Maister Fastolf name aftyr he was desesyd; y, in the name of the seyd Sir William Yelverton and William Worcetter, required and prayed the sayd above named witnesse and alle other wytnesse produced in Sir William Yelverton and William Wyssetter name before that tyme, excepte the forsayd Stephan Scrope, Esquier, and Richard Fastolf, to come to London, and appere in my lords house of audience before his auditour, and there to say, depose, and witnesse the trouthe as they knewe in especiall, in the absense of John Russe, Sir Robert Cotiler, late vycar of Castre, Robert Botyler beyng oute of the chamber of Sir John Fastolf, Knyght, there he lay seke in his maner of Castre, the Saterdaye next before the seid Sir John Fastolf discesyd, namely, from viij. tylle xj. atte belle affore mydday, and present in other placez, where diverse of the sayd named wytnesse and diverse other witnesse sawe ham. And the sayd Worcestre nother promysed ne yave hem gode, money, nother reward, neyther relessed no debtes, not soo nought payed not for har costes, nother dispenses by the wey comyng to London, taryeng, ne returnyng a yen, that lawe and reson wold understonde the sayd witnesse ought have for har costes and labours, weche was payed by my handes, I beyng present dayly and tymely diverse tymes most conversaunt at Jermuth wyth hem; and in especiall whan they taryed more than xxiiij. dayes in London or they coude be examyned; and I knowe well the sayd Sir William Yelverton, nouther the seyd William Worcestre promysed ne payed no maner money ne godes worth, nouther relessyng har dutes, yf any they axed they knowe yt not, as the seyd named witnesse wylle sey and certyfye the trouth. And as for ij. witnesse called Bunch and Shave, lete hem be examynyd, yf the seyd Sir William or William Worcestre fyrst procured, moved, or excited hem

285

1467
JULY 21

at Yermouth, or any other place, to come to London to depose in the said maters, or promysed or payed hem ony money, or any man for ham promysed or payed; and yf they be of trewe disposicion, they woll discharge the seyd Sir William Yelverton and William Worcestre, for ther was none in especiall but I, that labored hem alle to come to London to my lordis audience yn the seyd Yelvertons and Worcestres names; but I pryncipally required them to depose treuly as they knewe, be the owte promyse, mede, rewarde, or money, yn the discharge of my conscience, and for the trouthe of the mater to be knowen to all the worlde, as I am redy to preve, whyle God lendeth me lyffe, and yn the same quarell to dye. And I evyr seth that I understode the seyd John Paston is untrewe demenyng in the contryvynge of my Maister Fastolf testament and last wille, and was compellyd to appere before my lord ys auditour at Lambyth, to be sworn atte my ffree will to declar the trouth of my seyd maister trewe testament and last wyll befor my seyd Lord of Canturbury is auditur of his courte of audience, I nevyr varyed ne held aftyr wyth John Paston, but alwey have ben stedfast wyth the processe that I have enfourmed my Lord of Canterbury, and divers others astates also in like wyse have declared to the sayd Sir William Yelverton and William Worcestre to procede, and soo evyr woll be stedfaste. And in witness for trouth, I sele this declaracion wyth my signet, and subscrybe it wyth my hand and name, in presence of Maister John Prentyse, Sir Edmond Hall, John Smyth, John Robynson, Thomas Hoore, John Bullok, and Richard Batilmewe, the xxjth day of Jule the yer of Crist M$^{il.}$CCCC^{mo} lxvij°.

                                              T. Howys.

286

673

JOHN PASTON TO HIS MOTHER[1]

RYGHT worchepfull modyr, I recomand me onto you, 1467 lowly besechyng yow of your blyssyng. Plesyt yow to we [sic] that my brodyr and I be in good hele, blyssyd be God, and all our felawshep; and as for me I tryst to God to . . . yow by Halowmes or within iiij. dayes aftyr at the ferthest; at whyche tyme I tryst to fynd the menys . . . dyscharge yow of syche folk as ye kepe of my brodyrs, and that must I do by myn owne menys; for as for my brodyr, by my trowthe he is not of power to do it; for this I ensure yow, so God help me, he hathe at thys season not a peny in hys purs, nor wotys not wher to get eny. And as for Bekham I warant, and ye wyll send the plate whych ye and I comond of for to helpe to paye hys dettis, and for to swe forthe for hys jwgement thys terme, it sholl neythyr be morgagyd nor sold. Wherfor, modyr, I and he bothe beseche yow that ye wyll send hym the plate by Jwde; or ellys, so God help me, I wot not how he shall do; for by the feythe that I ow to God he lokyth every day to be arestyd, and so I wene he sholl, so God helpe me. Jwde had ned to be sped hastyly lest syche arestys falle in the tyme. And as for my Lord of Norffolk, it is promysed me to have hys good lordshep, but I must tery a whylle, as my Lady told yow, for the maners sake. And as for tydynges her, so God help, neythyr the Kyng nor the Lordis can as yet undyrstand no serteynte, whedyr they shall go togedyr ayen by the werre or not. When I here the serteynte I shall send yow word. Ye may send mony by Jwde for my sustyr Annys hood and for the tepet of sersenet, viijs. a yerd of damask and vs. for sarsenet;

[1] [Add. MS. 34,889, f. 196.] The date of this letter is difficult to fix, but from the two brothers being together (which was rather a rare occurrence), and both in good health, the summer of 1467 seems not improbable. (See No. 671.) The date must at least be earlier than Nov. 1469, when Sir John Paston, as we shall hereafter find, actually executed an indenture for the sale of East Beckham. It seems quite impossible, moreover, that this letter can be of the year 1469.

287

467(?) hyr hood wyll take iij. quarters. No mor for lak of leyser, but I pray God send yow your hertis desyir and othyr pore folys thers.—Your sone and humbyll servant,

J. PASTON.

674

SIR JOHN PASTON TO LORD BEAUCHAMP[1]

To the Lord Bechampe[2]

AND forasmuch as I am credibly enformed that my lord of Winchestre hath sent to you desiring that ye shold ensele dyvers writinges of graunt and relesse of your estat in alle such maners, londes and tenementes as late wer of J. Fastolf knyght, and wheryn ye togider with other be jointly enfeffed to th' use of the seid J. Fastolf, I, considering the honorable disposition and great sadnesse of my seid lord of Winchestre which[3] hath now taken upon [him][4] th' administracion of testament of the seid J. F., trusting veryly that my seid lord wol as conscience requireth consider my title and interest in that behalf, praie you right hertely that not withstonding any labour or mocion on my part or for me in tyme passed made to you to ensele any writyng of graunt or relesse of your seid estat to me or to myn use, that ye wol now ensele and perfourme the entent and desir of my seid lord of Winchestre now made unto you.

SIR JOHN PASTON, K.

Indorsed : Dominus de Bewchamp.

---

[1] [Add. MS. 35,251, f. 25, B.M.] This letter apparently was written in 1467, probably in August, just before No. 675. The original is a corrected draft.
[2] This address is written in the margin, with a note a little way below : ' To myn oncle Wylliam in lyke forme.'
[3] Here occurs an interlineation of an incomplete clause : ' is feffe of the seid—— (*word crossed out*) and also therein as——.'
[4] Omitted in MS.

288

675

NOTE

The following is an extract from ' An Index to Deeds and Writings in the Tower, Magdalen College, Oxford ':—

Documents relating to Norf. and Suffolk, No. 47.

' Thomas Archiep. Cant., Willielmus Episcopus Winton., et Johannes Beauchamp dominus de Beauchamp, juxta formam barganiæ et effectum ultimæ voluntatis Johannis Fastolf in curia Audientiæ, &c., concedunt Johanni Paston militi totum jus in maneriis de Castre vocatis Vaux, Bosoms, et Redhams, Spensers in Heringby, Reggisley, Reps, cum aliis terris in diversis villis; necnon in manerio de Guton cum advocatione ecclesiæ de Heinford in Saxthorp vocat. Loundhall, cum aliis terris in diversis villis, et in manerio de Caldecots et Akethorp, Spitlings, Habeland, &c., habit. ex feoffamento Rad. dom. de Sudley et aliorum.

Aug. 28. Edw. IV. 7.' 1467 AUG. 28

676

ABSTRACT[1]

A small slip of paper close written on both sides with accounts of wages. AUG. 31 In the margin on one side is the name John Braham, with the memorandum, ' Thys wrytynge, made the iiijth yere of Kynge Edward the iiijth, and in the monyth of Novembre, wytnessez of the wagez that my master payith to his men.' A blank seems to have been left below this at first, but it was afterwards filled up in a different hand : ' Memorandum that the vᵉ yer of Kyng Edward the iiijᵗ I rekenyd wyth my master at Stoke; and on the v. day of Aprylle for the yerys that I have be wyth my mastyr, whesche shal be at Hocke Monday next cumyng vᵉ yer and an halfe; for the whesche yerys I have reseyyyd at sondery tymeys *vli.* and iiijᵈ., and thys seyd v. day I reseyyyd of my master v. marcs.'

On the other side, in the first hand, is an account extending from the 11th April, 5 Edw. IV. (1465) to the last day of August, 7 Edw. IV. (1467), of payments to a female named Rose,[2] for wages by ' my master,' Braham and Thorpe. These sums vary from 3s. 4d. to 8s. 4d., at a time; but there are also two items for presents made to her, viz. for 4 ells of Holland cloth at 8½d. the ell, 2s. 10½d., and for a pair of hosen, 12d. On the 7th Oct. 6 Edw. IV. (1466) it is said, ' My master toke her for wages at Stoke, 5s.'

---

[1] [From Paston MSS., B.M.]
[2] It appears by other letters that she was a servant ' dwelling before Mrs. Paston's gate.'

289

677

NOTE

The following is another extract from the Index referred to in No. 675 :—

' 12. Concessio Joh. Paston militis Johanni Duci Norfolk et aliis manerii sui vocati Hemnales in Cotton in Com.' Suff., ac manerii sui de Haynford, et advocationis ecclesiæ ejusdem in Com.' Norff., habit' ex dono Th. Archiepisc. Cant. et Willielmi Episc. Wynton., cum littera attor. ad deliberandum seisinam. Oct. 2. Edw. IV. 7.' 1467 OCT. 2

678

ABSTRACT[1]

PETITION OF JOHN HERLYNG OF BASYNGHAM TO ' LADY' PASTON

Requests ' her Highness' to confirm some grants of her late husband to him of land at Basyngham. William Swan claims, and has taken from him 2 perches of ground in breadth near his (Swan's) gate, which has always been parcel of Herlyng's tenement of Greyve's during his and his father's time. John Pykerell, too, has made mean to the Abbot of St. Benet's to remove a boundary stone which has stood there sixty years. Pykerell also took the writer's horse and used it in his field without leave, on Friday before the Exaltation of the Holy Cross, 6 Edw. IV., which made the beast unserviceable till Fastegong next following. Pykerell has also done him other injuries.

[As this petition refers to the ' Fastegong' or Shrovetide after Holy-Rood Day 6 Edw. IV. as a past date, it cannot have been drawn up earlier than the year 1467. The manor of Basingham, in Norfolk, belonged to the Mauteby family, and came to John Paston by marriage. This paper, therefore, was addressed to his widow Margaret.]

---

[1] [From Paston MSS., B.M.] 1467 later

290

679

CECILY DAWNE TO SIR JOHN PASTON[1]

To the right worshipfull, and with my faithful hert and service full entyerly beloved gode maister, Sir John Paston.

RIGHT worshipfull Sir, and with my faithfull herte and service full entierly beloved gode maister, in my moste humble wyse I recommaund me unto your goode maistreship. Pleace it the same to wite that I thenke right longe to I have veerey knolege of your welfare, the which undrestande wil be to me right grete comfort. And that causeth me to write unto you as nowe. And also to late you wite that I herde reperte ye shuld be wedded unto a Doughter of the Duchez of Somerset, which mater, and I spake with you, I couth enforme your maistership that were to longe to write as nowe. But I shal and do pray God dayly to sende you such one unto your worldes make that wil drede and faithfully unfeyned love you above alle othir erthely creatures. For that is most excellent richesse in this worlde, as I suppose. For erthely goodes bene transsitory, and wedding contynues for terme of lyfe, which with some folke is a full long terme. And therfore, Sir, savyng your displeasir, me semez wedding wolde have goode avysement. Moreover, Sir, like it your maistership to undirstond that wynter and colde weders draweth negh, and I have but fewe clothez but of your gift, God thanke you. Wherefore, Sir, and it like you, I besech your gode maistership that ye will vouchsafe to remembre me your servaunte with some lyverey, such as pleaseth you, ayens this wynter, to make me a gown to kepe me from the colde wedders. And that I myght have it and such answare as ye pleace in the premisses sente unto me be the bringer herof. And I schal contynuwe your oratrix and pore servaunte and 1463-7 NOV. 3

---

[1] [Add. MS. 34,889, f. 166.] This letter is of course not earlier than 1463, when Sir John Paston received his knighthood, but probably belongs to a period before his flirtations with Anne Haute, who first appears on the scene in the summer of 1468.

291

THE PASTON LETTERS

1463-7 hertely pray to God for your prosperite, Whom I besech have
NOV. 3 you, Right worshipful Sir, and with my faithful herte and service
full entierly beloved gode maister, in His blessed governaunce.
Writen at Hellowe the iij[de.] Day of Novembre.

CECILE DAUNE.

680

ABSTRACT[1]

1468   Release by William, Bishop of Winchester, John, Lord Beauchamp, Sir John
JAN. 11 Howard, Sir William Yelverton, Justice of the King's Bench, Thomas Lytelton,
Justice of the Common Pleas, William Jenney, Serjeant-at-Law, William Paston,
Esq., Thomas Howys, clerk, and William Grene, to Sir John Paston, Knight, of
the manors of Castre, in Flegge, called Vaux and Bosoms, and the lands in
Castre called Redham, the manors or tenements in Heryngby called Spensers and
Fennes, a third part of the manor of Runham, the manor of Wynterton, called
Begyyles, with a windmill, the manor of Reppes in Bastewyk, and messuages,
&c., in Yarmouth ; the lands called Billes in Stokesby and Cattes in Heryngby,
&c. ; the manors of Guton in Brandeston, Heynford, the manor of Saxthorp,
called Loundhalle, with a watermill, the manor of Lincolnhalle, in Boyton, &c.,
in Norfolk ; and the manor called Caldecotes in Freton, Suff. ; the manors of
Akethorp in Lowestoft and Spitlyngges in Gorleston, and lands called Havelound in Bradwell, &c. ; also in the manor of Tichewell, &c., in the hundred
of Smethedon, Norf. ; and the manor of Hempnales in Cotton, and Burnevyles
in Naketon, Suff. ; all which the said Bishop and the others had, *inter alia*, of
the gift of Ralph, Lord Sudeley, Sir William Oldhall, Richard Waller, Esq.,
Thomas West, Esq., William Wangford, and Nicholas Girlyngton.
Dated 11th Jan. 7 Edw. iv.

1 [MS. in Bodleian Library.]

681

WILLIAM WORCESTER TO MARGARET PASTON[1]

*To my ryght worshypfull maistras, Margyt Paston,
wedowe.*

RYGHT worchypfull maistras, aftyr dew recomendacion, 1468
please your gode maistrasshyp to wete that I comyned
late wyth your entier welbelovyd son, Sir John Paston,
of the fundacion of my Maister Fastolf Collage myght ben at
Cambrygge, yn case hyt shall nat bee at Castre, nether at Seynt
Benetts, because that Universyte lyeth neere the cuntree ot
Norffolk and Suffolk ; for albe it my Lord of Wynchestr ys
disposed to found a Collage yn Oxford for my seyd maister to
be prayd for, yhyt wyth moch lesse cost he myght make som
othyr memorialle also yn Cambrygge, and yt weere of ij. clerkys,
iij. or iiij. scolers, founded at leest wyth the value of gode
benefices and ryche parsonages, that myght be purchased the
advowsons, wyth moch lesse goodes then lordshyppes or maners
may ; and I fonde your son well disposed to meofe and excyte
my seyd Lord. Also now the Cristmasse weke next before the
feest att London, my Lord Wynchester called me to hym yn
presence of Sir John, and desyrid hym effectually to be my
gode wyller ; and maister wold hafe no wordes rehersed on my
behalf, and he seyd full welle.   Wold Jesu, Maistras, that my
gode maister that was som tyme your husbond, yn my seyd
Maister Fastolf lyfe dayes, as he shewed to me, their coude hafe
founded yn hys hert to hafe trusted and lovyd me as my
Maister Fastolf dyd, and that he wold not hafe geven credence
to the malyciouse contryved talys that Frere Brakley, W.
Barker, and othyrs ymagyned ontruly, savyng your reverence,

1 [From Fenn, iv. 280.]   It seems probable that this letter was written about the
beginning of the year 1468.   As to the time of year, we may judge by one expression
that it was not very long after Christmas ; and as the writer congratulates Margaret
Paston that Caister is to be at her command, we may with great probability suppose
the date to be about the same as that of the preceding document.

THE PASTON LETTERS

1468(?) of me.   And now ye may opynly ondrestand the sothe, and
your son Sir John also ; and yhyt for all that I put nevyr my
Maister Fastolf lyfelode yn trouble, for alle the unkyndnesse
and covetuse that was shewed me, as I hafe declared to the
berer heroff, that I know ye trust welle, to whom yn thys ye
may gefe credence at thys tyme.

God amend J. Russe.   I wold he had ben at Irland for one
day ys sake.

Your,   W. W.

And I thank you hertly for my pore woman, she shuld
com to you at your commaundment late or rathe, but for
gelosye and mysdemyng of peple that hafe me yn greete
awayt ; and ye know welle, maistras, better ys afrende unknow
then knowen ; the world ys to mysdemyng and redy to make
dyvysyon and debate that comyth of an envyouse disposicion.
And I am ryght glad that Castr ys and shall be at your
comaundment, and yowres yn especialle.   A ryche juelle yt ys
at neede for all the cuntre yn tyme of werre ; and my Maister F.
wold rather he had nevyr bylded yt then hyt shuld be yn the
gouvernaunce of eny sovereyn that wole oppresse the cuntree.
And I fynde the relygyoux of Seynt Benetts full unkynde toke
away a chambre, the elder Abbot had put me yn possessyon
for my solace, when I myzt com thedr and desport me, and
toke that chambre to Maister John Smyth, that Sir Thomas
Howys seyd to me, was none holsom counceller yn the reformacion of the last testament made but ij. executors to hafe the
rule allone.   I wold he had nevyr medled of yt, that councell
made moch trouble.   I pray you kepe thys letter close to your
sylf, as I trust you and Sir Jamys, and also yn R. Toly that I
undrestand hym close and just.

I had no tyme to speke withyn now late, when I was but
one day at Norwych. W. Barker sclaundred me yn certeyn
maters of gode to the some of v[c.] mark that Reynold Harneys
shuld kepe and take me half.   Wold Jesu B[a]rker had seyd
true, hyt myzt hafe do me moch gode !   And, Maistras, as I
dar desyre you, I pray you recomaund me to my best maistras,
your moder Agnes, for she favoured me and dyd me grete

cherytee, to be the better disposed to hyr son, Maister John, 1468
and by my soule yt made me the hertyer to safe the lyfelode
fro trouble or from claymes, as I support me to alle the world,
I put nevyr maner ne lyfelode of my Maister Fastolf yn trouble,
ne entitled no crettur to na place, and ye may speke wyth hyr
herof when ye be allone.

682

HUGH FENN TO SIR JOHN PASTON[1]

To the right worchepfull Sir John Paston, Knyght.

RIGHT worchepfull sir, I recommand me to you.   Like 1468
you wete a distresse was take in Caster by Thomas [APRIL 1]
Pekok, I trowe your servant, a besy man, called of a
full true sowle, John Hadynet of Haryngby, a pore man his
plow hath loyn ever sith, he seith ; I understonde it is for Catts
landes.   I sent my clerk to my mastresse, your moder, and the
seid John with hym therfor ; and my mastresse wold hym
come ageyn a nother day, for Pecok was not thanne at home ;
so he ded, and can not have it, as he seith, but that ye wold I
shuld speke with you at Castr therof, and or other maters he
tolde me this day.   And by cause of my moders yereday
holden this day, God have hir sowle, and to morwe shal be a
good day, I wol by Goddes grace dispose me to His mercy
ageyns Thursday, as I have used ; therfor I pray you pardon
my comyng.   In the weke after Ester, I entende to se you and
my seid mastresse certeynly ; it is loong seth I sy hir, me semeth.
And if ye be not thanne at Castr, I pray you send me worde
that I may come soner to you to comon with you in this mater,
and in all other what ye wil, and sone departe to London fro
thens ; and therfor I wil abide with you a good while.

1 [From Fenn, iv. 290.]   This letter was written on the Tuesday before Easter,
probably in the year 1468, *i.e.* after the other executors of Fastolf had released to Sir
John Paston.   The date could hardly be later than 1469, when Sir John was driven
out of Caister by the Duke of Norfolk ; and in 1469 he does not seem to have been
residing there about Easter.

1468
APRIL 12] Sir, as to Catts ye be remembred what I seid to you at London at ij. tymes. I am the same man ; I have sith I cam geten th'evidences in to myn handes, and I am redy to shewe them what lerned man her that ye wol assigne. The mater is cler to my thynkyng. Titleshale that solde it to Sir J. Fastolf myght as wele a solde hym your lande or myn ; and if the sale be lawfull, I shal leve my hands at the first as I said at London. The distresse to be kept for that, I wisse it nede not, and it was unlawfully taken. Like it you to do delyvere the pore man his goods ageyn, I am redy to answer you for elde and new as right wol. I shal breke no day to be assigned, for to leve all other thyngs.

By the blissed Lady I beleve that ye wol dispose you wele, and so I pray God ye do, and have you in His blissed gover-naunce. Wretyn at the hede town of Norffolk this Tuysday.

Your owen,　　　H. atte FENNE.

683

EDWARD IV. TO SIR JOHN PASTON[1]

To our trusty and welbeloved Sir John Paston, Knight.

BY THE KING.

APRIL 18 TRUSTY and welbeloved, we greet yow well. And where it is accorded betwixt us and our cozen the Duke of Burgundye that he shall wedde our derrest sister, Margaret, and that in shorte while we intende to sende her into the parts of Flanders for the accomplishment and solempnizacion of the marriage so concluded ; at the which time it behoveth her to be accompanied with great nobility of this realme, for the honour thereof, of us and our said sister : We therefore, wele understanding and remembering the good

[1] This letter is reprinted from Mr. Worship's article on Sandford's genealogy of the Paston family in the *Norfolk Archæology*. The original was transcribed by Sandford, but is not now to be found. Margaret, sister of Edward IV., was married to Charles the Bold, Duke of Burgundy, at Bruges, on the 3rd July 1468.

296

affection ye bere towards us all, our pleasure is, and our said 1468 sister, whereupon we greatly trust, desire and pray yow right APRIL 18 effectuously that, every excuse or delaye laide aparte, ye will dispose yourselfe to the saide intent and purpose against the first day of June next cominge, according to your honour and degree, and that ye faile not so to doe, as we singularly trust yow, and as ye intend to do us justys, pleas![1] Yeven under our signet at our mannor of Greenwich, the xviij. day of Aprill.

684

JOHN PASTON THE YOUNGER TO MARGARET PASTON[2]

To my ryght reverend and worchepfull modyr, Margaret Paston, dwellyng at Caster, be thys delyvered in hast.

RYTH reverend and worchepfull modyr, I recomaund JULY 8 me on to you as humbylly as I can thynk, desyryng most hertly to her of your welfare and herts ese, whyche I pray God send yow as hastyly as my hert can thynk. Ples yt yow to wete, that at the makyng of thys byll, my brodyr and I, and all our felawshep, wer in good helle, blyssyd be God. As for the gydyng her in thys contre, it is as worchepfull as all the world can devyse it, and ther wer never Englyshe men had so good cher owt of Inglong that ever I herd of.

As for tydyngs her, but if it be of the fest, I can non send yow ; savyng my Lady Margaret[3] was maryd on Sonday[4] last past, at a towne that is callyd the Dame, iij. myle owt of Brugys, at v. of the clok in the mornyng ; and sche was browt the same day to Bruggys to hyr dener ; and ther sche was

[1] So, as printed in the *Norfolk Archæology*.
[2] [From Fenn, ii. 2.] As this letter gives an account of the marriage of the Princess Margaret to Charles, Duke of Burgundy, there is no doubt of the year in which it was written.
[3] Margaret, sister of King Edward IV.　　　[4] 3rd July.

297

1468
JULY 8 receyvyd as worchepfully as all the world cowd devyse, as with presession with ladys and lordys, best beseyn of eny pepyll, that ever I sye or herd of. Many pagentys wer pleyed in hyr wey in Bryggys to hyr welcomyng, the best that ever I sye. And the same Sonday my Lord the Bastard,[1] took upon hym to answere xxiiij. knyts and gentylmen, with in viij. dayes at jostys of pese ; and when that they wer answeryd, they xxiiij. and hym selve schold torney with othyr xxv. the next day aftyr, whyche is on Monday next comyng ; and they that have jostyd with hym into thys day, have ben as rychely beseyn, and hymselve also, as clothe of gold, and sylk and sylvyr, and goldsmyths werk, myght mak hem ; for of syche ger, and gold, and perle, and stanys, they of the Dwkys coort, neythyr gentylmen nor gentylwomen, they want non ; for with owt that they have it by wyshys, by my trowthe, I herd nevyr of so gret plente as ther is.

Thys day my Lord Scalys[2] justyd with a Lord of thys contre, but not with the Bastard ; for they mad promyse at London that non of them bothe shold never dele with othyr in armys ; but the Bastard was one of the Lords that browt the Lord Scalys in to the feld, and of mysfortwne an horse strake my Lord Bastard on the lege, and hathe hurt hym so sore, that I can thynk he shalbe of no power to acomplyshe up hys armys ; and that is gret pete, for by my trowthe I trow God mad never a mor worchepfull knyt.

And as for the Dwkys coort, as of lords, ladys and gentyl-women, knyts, sqwyers, and gentylmen, I hert never of non lyek to it, save Kyng Artourys cort. And by my trowthe, I have no wyt nor remembrans to wryte to yow, half the worchep that is her ; but that lakyth, as it comyth to mynd I shall tell yow when I come home, whyche I tryst to God shal not be long to ; for we depart owt of Bryggys homward on Twysday next comyng, and all folk that cam with my Lady of Burgoyn owt of Inglond, except syche as shall abyd her styll with hyr, whyche I wot well shall be but fewe.

[1] Anthony, Count de la Roche, commonly called the Bastard of Burgundy, a natural son of Duke Philip the Good.
[2] Anthony Woodville, Lord Scales, afterwards Earl Rivers.

298

We depart the soner, for the Dwk[1] hathe word that the 1468 Frenshe Kyng[2] is purposyd to mak wer upon hym hastyly, JULY 8 and that he is with in iiij. or v. dayis jorney of Brugys, and the Dwk rydyth on Twysday next comyng, forward to met with hym ; God geve hym good sped, and all hys ; for by my trowthe they are the goodlyest felawshep the ever I cam among, and best can behave them, and most lyek gentylmen.

Othyr tydyngs have we non her, but that the Dwke of Somerset,[3] and all hys bands depertyd welbeseyn owt of Brugys a day befor that my Lady the Dwches cam thedyr, and they sey her, that he is to Qwen Margaret that was, and shal no more come her ayen, nor be holpyn by the Dwk. No more ; but I beseche yow of your blyssyng as lowly as I can, whyche I beseche yow forget not to geve me ever day onys. And, modyr, I beseche yow that ye wolbe good mastras to my lytyll man, and to se that he go to scole.

I sent my cosyn Dawbeney vs. by Callys man, for to bye for hym syche ger as he nedyth ; and, modyr, I pray yow thys byll may recomend me to my sustyrs bothe, and to the mastyr, my cosyn Dawbeney, Syr Jamys,[4] Syr John Style, and to pray hym to be good mastyr to lytyll Jak, and to lerne hym well ; and I pray yow that thys byll may recomand me to all your folkys, and my wellwyllers. And I pray God send yow your herts desyr.

Wretyn at Bruggys the Fryday next aftyr Seynt Thomas.

Your sone and humbyll servaunt,

J. PASTON, the yonger.

685

ABSTRACT[5]

General pardon to William Paston, son of the judge, for offences com- JULY 16 mitted before the 15th April last. The grantee is described by different *aliases*, as William Paston of London, of Caster, of Norwich, and of Wymondham, gentleman. Westminster, 16th July, 8 Edw. IV. *Great Seal attached.*

[1] Charles the Bold, Duke of Burgundy.　　　[2] Lewis XI.
[3] Edmund Beaufort, Duke of Somerset.　　　[4] Sir James Gloys, a priest.
[5] [From Add. Charter 17,248, B.M.]

299

THE PASTON LETTERS

686

THE EARL OF OXFORD TO SIR JOHN PASTON[1]

To Sir John Paston, Knyght.

1468(?)
JULY 18

RIGHT worshipfull, and my especiall true hertid frende, I commaunde me un to you, preying you to ordeyne me iij. horsse harneys as godely as ye and Genyn kan devyse, as it were for yourselfe; and that I may have thyme in all hast, ordere. Also Skerne saith ye wolde ordeyne ij. standarde stavys; this I pray you to remembre, and my wife shalle deliver you silver,—and yit she most borowed it; vj. or vij*li*. I wold be stowe on a horsse harneys, and so Skerne tolde me I might have. The Lord Hastings had for the same price, but I wolde not myne were lik his; and I trust to God we shalle do right welle, who preserve you. Wreten at Canterbury in hast, the xviij. day of Juyll.

OXYNFORD.

687

SIR JOHN PASTON TO MRS. ANNE[2]

To Mastresse Annes.

1468
JULY 22

RYTHE it is so that I may not, as oft as I wold, be ther as [*i.e.* where] I might do my message myselff, myn owne fayir Mastresse Annes, I prey yow to accept thys byll for my messanger to recomand me to yow in my

[1] [From Fenn, ii. 26.] The writer of this letter was committed to the Tower in November 1468, and though afterwards released, it was not long before he became a declared enemy of Edward IV.; so that, after the brief restoration of Henry VI. in 1470, he was obliged to leave the kingdom. The date of this letter, therefore, is not likely to be later than the present year, but it may be a year or two earlier.

[2] [From Fenn, ii. 294.] The Mrs. Anne to whom this letter was addressed seems to have been a Mrs. Anne Haute, to whom Sir John was for a long time engaged. That it was written before the year 1469 will appear probable on referring to Margaret Paston's letter written on Easter Monday (3rd April) in that year, in which she wishes to know for certain if he be engaged; and we have therefore

300

EDWARD IV

most feythfull wyse, as he that faynest of all other desyreth to knowe of yowr welfare, whyche I prey God encresse to your most plesure.

1468
JULY 2

And, mastresse, thow so be that I as yet have govyn yow bot easy [*i.e.* little] cause to remembyr me for leke of aqweyntacion, yet I beseche yow, let me not be forgotyn ye rekyn up all yowr servaunts, to be sett in the nombyr with other.

And I prey yow, Mastresse Annes, for that servyse that I owe yow, that in as short tyme as ye goodly may that I myght be assarteynyd of yowr entent and of your best frends in syche maters as I have brokyn to yow of, whyche bothe your and myn ryght trusty frends John Lee, or ellys my mastresse hys wyff, promysyd befor yow and me at our fyrst and last beyng togedyr, that as sone as they or eyther of theym knewe your entent and your frendys that they shold send me woord. And if they so do, I tryst sone aftyr to se yow.

And now farewell, myn owne fayir lady, and God geve yow good rest, for in feythe I trow ye be in bed.

Wretyn in my wey homward on Mary Maudeleyn Day at mydnyght. Your owne,

JOHN PASTON.

Mastresse Annes, I am prowd that ye can reed Inglyshe; wherfor I prey yow aqweynt yow with thys my lewd [*uncouth*] hand, for my purpose is that ye shalbe more aqweyntyd with it, or ellys it shalbe ayenst my wyll; but yet, and when ye have red thys byll, I prey yow brenne it or kepe it secret to yoursylff, as my feythefull trust is in yow.

little difficulty in referring it to the year 1468, when Sir John was over in Flanders at the marriage of the Princess Margaret to Charles of Burgundy. Mrs. Anne appears to have been a lady of English extraction, who was either born abroad or had passed most of her life on the Continent. She was, moreover, related to Lord Scales, and is therefore not unlikely to have been the daughter of one William Haute of Kent, who married at Calais, in 1429, the daughter of a certain Richard Wydeville. (See *Excerpta Historica*, p. 249.) But she could speak and even read English; and Sir John, who was now returning homewards to England, designed in this letter to open a correspondence with her. He appears, howver, not to have despatched it, as the original remained among the papers of the Paston family; or else perhaps it was returned to him on the breaking off of the engagement.

301

THE PASTON LETTERS

688

THOMAS HOWES TO CARDINAL BOURCHIER[1]

To my moste honorabyl Lord Cadenall, and Archibushop of Caunterbury.

1468
OCT. 10

MOSTE reverent and my ryght good Lord, I recomaund me to your gracyous Lordshyp yn my moste humble wyse. Please your Lordshyp to wete that my Lord Norffolk councell hath now late mevyd Sir Wylliam Yelverton, Knyght, and me to be preferryd for to purchasse the maner of Castre, and certeyn other lordshypps that wer my Maystyr Fastolf, whom God pardon, owt excepted the maner of Gunton that yowr Lordshyp desyryth to purchasse, and othyr certeyn maners that my Mastyr Fastolf frendys hafe desyred to be preferryd. And be cause the pretens bargayn that John Paston yn hys lyffe surmytted, bye colour of whych he entended to hafe all my Mastyr Fastolf londes in Norffolk and Suffolk for nought, savyng the hygh reverence of your astate, was not juste ne trew; and be cause that I wyth othyr of my Master Fastolf executors may have wher of to dyspospose yn cheryte full dedys to do for hys sowle; I have condescended the rather that my seide Lord of Norffolk shall be preferryd to the purchasse of the seyde maner of Castre, and othyr maners that may be sparyd to th'encresse of hys lyfelode yn thys land; and thys covenantys to be engroced upp wythynne shorth tyme, as by all Halowaunce, in case yowr Lordshyp be agreed and plesyd wyth all; wher uppon I wold beseche yowr nobyll Lordshyp to lete my wete your good plesur and avice yn thys behalfe.

And be cause my seyd Lord Norffolk ys so nere of blode to yowr hyghnesse knyghted, that meevyd me to be the more wyllyng to condescend to the forseyd purchasse, and so trust-

[1] [From Fenn, iv. 298.]

302

EDWARD IV

yng your Lordshyp wold be ryght well pleased wyth alle. Wretyn at Norwich the x. day of Octobyr, anno viij. R. E. iiij*t*

1468
OCT. 10

Yowr pore chapleyn, T. HOWYS.

689

ABSTRACT[1]

[*Circa* 1468.] Long declaration in English (on a paper roll) by Thomas Howes, 'for the discharge of his conscience,' impugning the authenticity of the will nuncupative, said to have been made by Sir J. Fastolf on the day of his death, and propounded by John Paston and the said Thomas in opposition to an earlier will propounded by Sir W. Yelverton and W. Worcetyr; containing details intended to prove that the alleged will was fabricated by Paston. Amongst other things, Howes says that at Paston's desire he did, a year before Fastolf's death, move Fastolf that Paston might buy three of his manors and live in his college, 'and the seyd Fastolf, mevyd and passyoned gretely in his soule, seyd and swar by Cryst ys sides, "And I knewe that Paston woolde by ony of my londes or my godes he shulde nevyr be my feffe, nother myn executor." Albeyt he seyde that he wolde suffer that the said Paston for terme of hys lyf shall have a loggyng yn a convenyent place yn the seyd maner of Castre withoute denyance of ony havyng intrest yn the seyd maner.'

690

ANONYMOUS TO SIR JOHN PASTON[2]

To Maistyr Syr John Paston, Knyght, at London, with my Lorae the Archebisshop of Yorke, be this letter delyverid.

1468
OCT. 28

I RECOMMAND me unto you. It is tolde me that the man that ye wote of cam ridyng by my Lady Suthfolk and by Cotton, which is in gret decay; and Barnay tolde him that Edward Dale tolde hem he durst no lenger serve him of

[1] [From a MS. in Magdalen College, Oxford.] This Abstract is derived from Mr. Macray's Report on the Muniments of Magdalen College, printed in the Fourth Report of the Historical MSS. Commission.

[2] [From Paston MSS., B.M.] The reference to the Earl of Pembroke, who was only so created in 1468, and who was beheaded in July 1469, fixes the date of this letter to the former year.

303

1468
OCT. 28

ale, for it was warnid hym that my Lady Suffolk[1] wolde entyr, and whan she shulde enter few men shulde knowe, it shulde be do so sodenly. She taryeth but of tythynges fro London. He spak nat with hyr. I pray you speke to my Lorde of Zorke[2] for the subpena in the Chanceri ayen William Paston that he take noon hurte. He desyrith to write to yow for it. My Lorde of Northfolk men have warnid the tenantis to pay you no mony, and thai speke alle in the Kynges name. Ye may tell my Lorde of Yorke that it is open in every mannys mouth in this contre the language that my Lorde of Yorke and my Lord of Warwik had to my Lorde of Norfolk in the Kings chambre, and that my Lorde of Yorke saide, rathir than the londe shulde go so, he wolde com dwell ther hym sliff. Ye wolde mervaile what harts my Lords hath goten, and how this language put peeple in comforte. My Lorde of Norffolk answerde that he wolde speke to my Lady his wiff, and entret hir. And your adversarys reherce that my Lorde shall never be Chanceleer til this mateer be spede,[3] for ther bargans ar made condicionall, to holde and nat holde as afftir my Lorde be Chaunceler and nat. Sothwell is all the doar, and he hath saide that my Lorde of Zorke licensid hym to labour in the mateer. My Lorde of Norwich shuld by xl. marke of the same lond. Thai entende to have a man of my Lady of Suthfolks sheryve, and specially Harcort. My Lorde coude nat bileve it but if [i.e. unless] he harde it, how it is rejoysshid in som place that he is nat Chaunceleer. Ther cam oo man into the contre with a newe patent, saying that my Lorde was Chanceler, and at that was the first patent that was sealid sithen he was officeer. The tythandes did goode *pro tempore*. Ther are witnes labourid, as it is said, to witnes and swere ageyn you of men of *cli.* a yeer, and many oder men, som that knew never of the mateer nor never harde Sir John Faskolff speke; ye know what jure is in this contre in maters that ar favoured by them that ar now ageyn you. It is harde whan a mateer restid by jure in this contre, som of the

1 Alice, widow of William de la Pole, Duke of Suffolk.
2 George Nevill, Archbishop of York.
3 The Great Seal was taken from Archbishop Nevill on the 8th June 1467. Apparently in 1468 he was hoping to be made Chancellor again.

1468
OCT. 28

same quest that founde you bondeman shall witnesse ayens you. Syr Thomas Howys comyth to London, and if my Lorde of Zorke wolde entret frendely my Lorde of Ely,[1] and get feithfully his promyse that my Lorde of Ely sende for Hawys, he shulde make Hawys to go home ageyn and leve all his fellowis post allon; and that my Lorde wolde entret my Lorde Tresaurer, my Lord Penbrok,[2] my Lady Bedford,[3] and remembre the bargan is not yit made, it may be better lettid affor than afftyr; and if the mateer spede my Lorde getith gret worshipp and gret thanke. I doute not he undirstondyth it, for it is well undirstonde what he hath saide. And pray his Lordeshipp to remembre a shereve this yeer, for ther is mych to be undirstonde in the shereve. And sende me worde if my Lorde Penbrok be go, and if my Lorde be Chaunceler. Et memorandum, Sir William Terell your testimoniall. Et memorandum, my Lorde Cardynall to sende answer to Sir Thomas Howys; and though my Lorde Cardynall be nat ther now, yit lat Townysende make it redy ageyns my Lords commyng. If Sir Thomas Howys wer handelyd by Maister Tressam and made byleve and put in hope of the moone shone in the water and I wot nat what, that such labor wer made that eythir he shulde be a pope or els in dyspeyr to be depryved *de omni beneficio ecclesiastico* for symony, lechory, perjory, and doubble variable pevyshnesse, and for admynystryng without auctoryte; and how he promisid bi his feith to my Lord t'obey his rewle and brak it, and what he hath saide to my lords in this mateer; and if ye recur in the courte, he shall be undo, and this mateer tolde hym by my Lorde of Ely and Maister Tresham, halff in game and halff in ernest, it shulde make hym to departe, for Yelvyrton and he ar halff at variance now. And entret my Lords servaunts to speke in your maters to all such persones as nede is. And I shall be hastyly with you by the grace of God, whom have yow in kepyng. Writen on Seynt Simonde Day and Jude.

By your owne.

1 William Grey, Bishop of Ely.
2 William Herbert, Earl of Pembroke.
3 *See* page 188, Note 3.

691

SIR JOHN PASTON TO JOHN PASTON[1]

To my ryght welbelovyd brother, John Paston, Esqer, beyng at Caster, or to John Dawbeney there, be this letter delyvered.

1468
NOV. 9

RYGHT welbelovyd brother, I comand me to yow, letyng yow wete that I have wagyd for to helpe yow and Dawbeney to kepe the place at Castr, iiij. wel assuryd and trew men to do al maner of thyng what that they be desyryd to do, in save gard or enforcyng of the seyd place; and mor ovyr they be provyd men, and connyng in the werr, and in fetys of armys, and they kan wele schote bothe gonnys and crossebowes, and amende and strynge them, and devyse bolwerkys, or any thyngs that scholde be a strenkthe to the place; and they wol, as nede is, kepe wecche and warde. They be sadde and wel advysed men, savyng on of them, whyche is ballyd, and callyd Wylliam Peny, whyche is as goode a man as gothe on the erthe, savyng a lytyll he wol, as I understand, be a lytel copschotyn [*high-crested*], but yit he is no brawler, but ful of cortesye, meche uppon James Halman; the other iij. be named Peryn Sale, John Chapman, Robert Jakys Son, savyng that as yit they have non harneyse comyn, but when it komyth it schall be sent to yow, and in the meane whyle I pray yow and Dawbeney to purvey them some.

Also a cople of beddys they most nedys have, whyche I pray yow by the help of my modre to purvey for them, tyl that I com home to yow. Ye schall fynde them gentylmanly, comfortable felawes, and that they wol and dare abyde be ther takelyng; and if ye undrestond that any assawte schold be towardys, I sende yow thes men, becawse that men of the

1 [From Fenn, iv. 302.] The original of this letter, Fenn informs us, was written upon a whole sheet of paper, of which a quarter was cut away before the letter was finished, so that the bottom part of it was only half the width of the upper. Roger Ree was made Sheriff of Norfolk in 1468, which fixes the date.

1468
NOV. 9

contre ther about yow scholde be frayed for fer of losse of ther goods; wherfor if ther wer any suche thyng towards, I wolde ye take of men of the contre but few, and that they wer well assuryd men, for ellys they myght discorage alle the remenant.

And asfor any wryghtyng fro the Kyng, he hathe promysyd that ther schall come non; and if ther do his unwarys [*without his knowledge*], yowr answer may be thys, how the Kyng hathe seyd, and so to delay them tyll I may have worde, and I schall sone purvey a remedye.

I understond that ye have ben with my Lorde of Norfolke now of late. What ze have done I wete not; we se that he shal be her ageyn thys daye. Mor ovyr, I trow John Alforde schall not longe abyde with my Lorde; I schall sende yow tydyng of other thyngys in haste, with the grace of God, who, &c. Wretyn on Wednysday nexte befor Seynt Martyn.

JOHN PASTON.

I fer that Dawbeney is not alther best storyd to contenew howsold longe; lete hym send me worde in hast, and I wyll releve hym to my power, and or longe to I hope to be with yow.

Roger Ree is scheryff of Norfolke, and he schall be good jnow. Th'exchetter I am not yit assertaynyd of.

Also, that thes men be at the begynnyng entretyd as corteysly as ye can.

Also, I pray yow to sende me my flowr[1] be the next massanger that comyth.

Also, as for my Lorde Fytz Waters oblygacion, I know non suche in myn adward as yit.

Also, the obligacion of the Bisshop of Norwychys oblygacion, I never sye it that I remembre; wherfor I wolde and prey my modre to loke it up.

Also, as for the Byble[2] that the master hath, I wend the

1 This may mean flour for household use; or it may signify his flower, his device or cognisance.—F.
2 This must mean some MS. copy, for at this time there was only one printed edition of the Bible, which would have sold even then for a much greater sum than is here mentioned. I mean 'Biblia Latina Mogunt. per J. Fust et P. Schoiffer, 1462.'—F.

THE PASTON LETTERS

1468
NOV. 9 uttermost pryse had not passyd v. mark, and so I trowe he wyl geve it : wet, I pray yow.

Also, as for Syr Wylliam Barber and Syr Wylliam Falyate, I wolde, if they kan purvey for them selfe, folfayne be dyschargyd of them.

692

ELIZABETH POYNINGS TO SIR JOHN PASTON[1]

To the worshipful Sir John Paston, Knyght, be thys delveryd in hast.

1468(?)
DEC. 15 WORSHIPFULL and with all myn hert interly wilbeloved nevoue, I recomaunde me to yow, desyryng to here of your prosperite and wilefayr, which I pray All mighti God maynteyn and encres to His plesour and your herts desir, thankyng God of your amendyng and helth ; forthermore, certefying yow that Sir Robert Fenys hath doon grete hurte in the lyvelode whiche perteyned to my husband and me in the Shire of Kent, wherein William Kene and other persones arn enffeid, and gretly troubleth hit, and receyveth the issuez and profitez of gret part of theym. And as of my seid husbonds lyvelode, aswell in the same shire as in other

[1] [From Fenn, iv. 266.] Elizabeth Paston, as we have seen (No. 374), had married Robert Poynings by the beginning of January 1459. We must, however, correct a slight inaccuracy in the preliminary note to that letter, where it is said that by the year 1470 they must have been married several years. Their union, in fact, lasted little more than two years ; for Robert Poynings was slain at the second battle of St. Albans on the 17th February 1461. The inquisition *post mortem*, taken some years afterwards (9 and 10 Edw. IV., No. 49), gives that day as the date of his death. His son and heir, Edward, named in this letter (who was afterwards Lord-Deputy of Ireland in the reign of Henry VII.), was probably born towards the close of the year 1459, for he is mentioned at the date of the inquisition (31st Jan. 49 and 1 Hen. VI., *i.e.* 1471) as eleven years old and over. Elizabeth Poynings must have remained a widow some years ; but before 1472 she had married Sir George Browne of Betchworth, Surrey. This letter is certainly of later date than No. 627, for the lands which she was then endeavouring to recover from the Earl of Kent were now occupied by the Earl of Essex. It may perhaps have been a year or two after 1466, but it was probably not later than 1469, as in 1470 Henry VI. was restored, and Essex, being a Yorkist, would not have been so powerful. The year 1468 must be a tolerable approximation to the true date.

308

THE PASTON LETTERS

1468(?)
DEC. 15 utterly of the menuraunce, occupacion, and receyt of the revenuez of the said maners of Tyrlyngham and other, accordyng to the tenour of the lettres labored by Sir Edwarde, for the maners assigned to hym from the Kyngs Highnes, directyd to the same Robert Fynes, or strayter if hit may be, and that I and myn assignez may peasseble rejoie theym ; and if eny person wold attempt to do the contrarye, that a comaundement, yf it ples the Kyngs Hignes, by hym myght be yevyn to my Lorde Chaunceller to seall writtyngs sufficiaunt with his gret seall, in eydyng and assisting me and myn assignez in this same.

And as for the maners of Esthall, Faukham, Asslie, and Chelsfeld, with th'appurtenauntez in the seid schire of Kent, whereof my hysbond at his departur was seassed, and my son sethens, unto the tyme that the Erle of Kent[1] without eny inquission or title of right for the Kyng, by colour of the Kynges lettres patentes, entret into theym, and hym therof put owte, and now my Lorde of Essex[2] occupieth them in lyke maner and forme ; yf eny remedy therin wilbe hade, I pray yow attempt hit.

Also, forther more, I hertely pray yow that if eny generall pardon be grauntyd, that I may have on for John Dane my servaunt, whom the said Robert Fenys of gret malice hath endyted of felonye, and that ze secretly labour this, and send me an aunswer in writtyng in as godly hast as ze may. As soon as that may ples yow to send me passels of costes and expences ze bere and pay for the said causez, I will truely content yow hit of the same, and over that rewarde yow to your plessour by the grace of Jesu, quo have yow in His blessed keping. Wretten in Suthwerk the xv^th daie of Decembyr.

Be your awnt, ELIZABETH PONYNGS.

[1] Edmund Grey, Lord Grey of Ruthin, and Baron Hastings, who was created Earl of Kent in 1465.
[2] Henry, Viscount Bourchier, created Earl of Essex in 1461.

310

EDWARD IV

shirez, besyde myn jounter, my seid husbond, whan he de- 1468(
partyd towarde the feld of Saint Albons, made and ordeyned DEC. 1
his wille, that I shuld have the rewell of all his lyvelode, and of Edwarde his soon and myn, and to take the issuez and profitez of the seid lyvelode, to the fyndyng of his and myn seid son, to paie his dettez, and to kepe the right and title of the same lyvelode, which I myght nat accordyng occupie for Sir Edwarde Ponyngs, myn seid husbonds brother ; and so sith myn seid husbonds departyng, I assigned that the seid Sir Edwarde for certeyn yereez shuld have and take the revenuez of the maners of Westwode, Estwell, Levelond, Horsmonden, Totyndon, Eccles, Staundon, and Combesdon, parcell of the seid lyvelode, which arn clerely yerely worth lxxvj*li.* xiijs. iiij*d.*, to the entent that the seid Sir Edwarde shuld paye myn husbonds dettez, for he wold not suffer me to be in rest without that he myght have a rewell in the lyvelode ; and after the seid assignement made, the seid Robert Fenes, contrary to trowth, and withoute cause of right, interupted me and the seid Sir Edwarde, aswell of and in the seid maners as of other maners undirwretyn ; wher uppon the same Sir Edwarde suet unto the Kyngs Highnesse, and hade the Kyngez honorable lettres undir his signet, directed to the said Sir Robert Fenys, the tenour wherof I send unto yow herin inclosid ; and as for residue of the lyvelode of myn seid husbonds and myn, within the same shire of Kent, wherin the said William Kene and other arn enffeed, that is to say, the maner of Tyrlyngham, Wolverton, Halton, Newyngton, Bastram, Rokesley, and Northcray, with th'appurtenauncez, I of them, by myn seid husbonds wille, shuld have residue, and take the issuez and profitez of theym, contrarye to right and conciens, takyng away my ryght, and brekyng my said husbonds wille, the seid Robert Fenys hath doon gret wast and hurte ther, and long tym hath take upe the revenuez and profitez of the same, wher thorough I have not my ryght, and the seid wille may not be performed.

Wherfor I hertely pray yow that ze will labour unto the Kynges Highnes, at yt lyketh hym addres his honorable lettres to be directed to the seid Robert Fenys, dischargyng hym

309

EDWARD IV

693

ABSTRACT[1]

THE KING TO SIR ROBERT FYNYS

Commanding him not to levy the rents of Westwode, Estwell, Levelond, 1468
Horsmonden, Totyngdon, Eccles, Stondon, and Comebesdane in Kent.

[This was evidently the copy of the writ obtained by Sir Edward Poynings referred to in the preceding letter. Below is written, 'The copie of the lettre myssyve endossid by the Kynges awn handes.']

694

SIR GEORGE BROWNE TO JOHN PASTON[2]

To my trusty and welbelowyd cosyn, Jhon Paston, Esquyer, in haste.

Loyawlte Ayme.

Be zowr howne

G. BROWNE.

Hyt schal newyr cum howt for me.

[1] [From Paston MSS., B.M.]
[2] [From Fenn, iv. 100.] The writer of this brief and enigmatical letter was the Date uncersecond husband of Elizabeth Paston, as mentioned in the preliminary note to No. 692 preceding. If the John Paston, Esquire, to whom it is addressed be the first of that name, that is to say, Elizabeth Paston's brother, the date is not later than 1466 ; but as it was certainly some years later before the writer became connected with the Pastons by marriage, the person addressed is more probably John Paston the youngest, brother of Sir John. The date of this communication, however, is unimportant. Its purport, of which Fenn has suggested rather a complicated explanation, appears to me simply a promise of secrecy on some subject : ' *Loyauté, aimé* (*i.e.* Honour bright, my dear friend). It shall never come out for me.'

END OF VOLUME IV

Printed by T. and A. CONSTABLE, Printers to His Majesty
at the Edinburgh University Press

The
Paston Letters
Volume 5

THE PASTON LETTERS

Edward IV

695

WILLIAM EBESHAM TO SIR JOHN PASTON[1]

To my moost worshupfull maister, Sir John Paston, Knyght.

MY moost woorshupfull and moost speciall maister, with all my servyce moost lowly I recomande unto your gode maistirship, besechyng you most tendirly to see me sumwhat rewardid for my labour in the Grete Booke[2] which I wright unto your seide gode maistirship. I have often tymes writyn to Pampyng accordyng to your desire, to enforme you hou I have labourd in wrytyngs for you; and I see wele he speke not to your maistership of hit. And God knowith I ly in seint warye [*sanctuary*] at grete costs, and amongs right unresonable askers. I movid this mater to Sir Thomas[3] late, and he tolde me he wolde move your maistir-

1469 (?)

---

[1] [From Fenn, ii. 10.] By the date of one item in the account subjoined to this letter it must have been written after the year 1468, probably in the year following.
[2] This 'great book' has been identified, on evidence which at first sight seems conclusive, with MS. 285 in the Lansdowne library in the British Museum. But probably this latter is only another transcript by Ebesham of a very similar volume. *See* Account of this MS. in 'Sailing Directions for the Circumnavigation of England,' published by the Hakluyt Society in 1889.
[3] Sir Thomas Lewis, a priest.

VOL. V.—A

I

THE PASTON LETTERS

ship therein, which Sir Thomas desirid me to remembir wele what I have had in money at soondry tymes of hym.[1]

And in especiall I beseche you to sende me for almes oon of your olde gownes, which will countirvale much of the premysses I wote wele; and I shall be yours while I lyve, and at your comandement; I have grete myst of it, God knows, whom I beseche preserve you from all adversite. I am sumwhat acqueyntid with it. Your verry man,
W. EBESHAM.

Folowyng apperith, parcelly, dyvers and soondry maner of wrytyngs, which I William Ebesham have wreetyn for my gode and woorshupfull maistir, Sir John Paston, and what money I have resceyvid, and what is unpaide.

First, I did write to his maistership a litill booke of Pheesyk, for which I had paide by Sir Thomas Leevys[2] in Westminster . . . . . . xx*d.*

Item, I had for the wrytyng of half the prevy seale of Pampyng . . . . viij*d.*

Item, for the wrytynge of the seid hole prevy seale of Sir Thomas . . . . . . ij*s.*

Item, I wrote viij. of the Witnessis in parchement, but aftir xiiij*d.* a peece, for which I was paide of Sir Thomas . . x*s.*

Item, while my seide maister was over the see in Midsomerterme — Calle sett me a warke to wryte two tymes the prevy seale

---

[1] Here (according to Fenn) follows the account as stated more at large in the subjoined Bill.
[2] Fenn's modern transcript reads Lewis. Is 'Leevys' in the other a misprint for 'Lewys'?

2

EDWARD IV

in papir, and then after cleerely in parchement . . . . iiij*s.* viij*d.*

And also wrote the same tyme oon mo of the lengist witnessis, and other dyvers and necessary wrytyngs, for which he promisid me x*s.* whereof I had of Calle but iiij*s.* viij*d.* car. v*s.* iiij*d.* . . . . . . vs. iiij*d.*

I resceyvid of Sir Thomas at Westminster, penultimo die Oct., anno viij. . . . . . iij*s.* iiij*a.*

Item, I did write to quairs of papir of witnessis, every quair conteynyng xiiij. leves after ij*d.* a leff . . . . iiij*s.* viij*a.*

Item, as to the Grete Booke —First, for wrytyng of the Coronacion, and other tretys of Knyghthode, in that quaire which conteneth a xiij. levis and more, ij*d.* a lef . . . . ij*s.* ii*a.*

Item, for the tretys of Werre in iiij. books, which conteyneth lx. levis aftir ij*d.* a leaff . . . x*s.*

Item, for *Othea*[1] pistill, which conteyneth xliij. leves . vii*s.* ij*a.*

Item, for the Chalengs, and the Acts of Armes which is xxviij*ti* less . . . . . . iiij*s.* viij*a.*

Item, for *De Regimine Principum*, which conteyneth xlv*ti* leves, aftir a peny a leef, which is right wele worth . . . . iij*s.* ix*d.*

---

[1] *Othea* means a treatise on Wisdom.—F. The name is derived from the Greek 'Ω θεά, but was used in the Middle Ages as a proper name. See a poem beginning
'Othea of prudence named godesse,'
mentioned in the Third Report of the Historical MSS. Commission, p. 188.

3

THE PASTON LETTERS

1469(?)   Item, for Rubrissheyng of
all the booke . . . . . .   iiis. iiijd.
Summa rest' . . .   xxijs. iiijd.
Summa non solut' . . .   xljs. jd., unde
pro magno [1] libro scripto xxvij[e] cum diu'
chal.[2]
Summa Totalis . . .   iijli. iijs. vd.

WILLIAM EBESHAM.

In further illustration of the payments made in that age for writing, etc., Sir John Fenn gives the following extracts from an original quarto MS. then in his possession, containing—

The various expences of Sir John Howard, Knight, of Stoke by Neyland, in Suffolk (afterwards Duke of Norfolk), page 136.

Item, the vij[th] yere of Kynge Edward the iiij[th], and the xxviij. day of July (1467). My master rekened with Thomas Lympnour of Bury, and my master peid hym—

For viij. hole vynets . . . prise the vynett, xiid., ... viijs.
Item, for xxj. demi vynets . . . prise the demi vynett, iiijd. . . . . vijs.
Item, for Psalmes lettres xv[c.] and di' . . . the prise of C. iiijd. . . . . vs. ijd.
Item, for p'ms letters lxiij[c.] . . . prise of a C., jd. . . . . . v. iijd.
Item, for wrytynge a quare and demi . . . prise the quayr, xxd. . . . . ijs. vjd.
Item, for wrytenge of a calender, ... xijd.
Item, for iij. quayres of velym, prise the quayr, xxd. . . . . . vs.
Item, for notynge of v. quayres and ij. leves, prise of the quayr, viij[d.] . . . . iijs. vijd.
Item, for capital drawynge iij[c] and di', the prise, ... iijd.
Item, for floryshynge of capytalls, v[c.] . . . . vd.
Item, for byndynge of the boke, ... xijs.

cs. ijd.

The wyche parcellis my master paid hym this day, and he is content.

This is an account of a limner or illuminator of manuscripts, who resided at Bury.

1 *magno*, 'm°' in Fenn.
2 So in Fenn. Qu. *cum diurnali challengiorum*? Fenn omits the whole of this clause, *unde . . . . chal'*, but notices its occurrence in a footnote.

THE PASTON LETTERS

697

ABSTRACT [1]

1469   W. COTING to JOHN COOK, draper of Norwich, 'and that he deliver or
JAN. 9   send this bill to Richard Kalle in all goodly haste, for the matter is of substance.'
This day in the grey morning three men of my Lord of Norfolk with long spears carried off three good horses from John Poleyn, 'one of your farmers at Tichewell,' telling him to treat with my Lord of Norfolk. Wishes to know what to do, 'for such an open wrong unremedied knew I never.' Saturday after Epiphany.
'Anno viij°' is written below.
[The signature of this letter is written in an abbreviated form, 'W. Cot.' According to Blomefield, W. Cotyng was rector of Titchwell from 1450 to 1457, and he had been previously rector of Swainsthorp, to which he was presented by Judge Paston in 1444. This letter is twelve years later than the date at which his incumbency of Titchwell is said to have terminated; but doubtless he is the writer. He is referred to as living even in the year 1485, in a letter written by Dame Elizabeth Browne, who says that he and James Gresham were clerks to her father Judge Paston.]

698

EDWARD IV. TO SIR JOHN PASTON [2]

To our trusty and welbeloved Sir John Paston, Knight.

BY THE KINGE.

JAN. 18   TRUSTY and welbeloved, we grete yow well. And how be it that we late addressed unto yow our letters, and commanded yow by the same, for the consideracions in them conteined, to have ceased of makinge any assemblye of our people for the matter of variance de-

1 [From Paston MSS., B.M.]
2 This letter is reprinted from the Paston Genealogy in the *Norfolk Archæology*, to which we have already several times referred (*see* Nos. 484, 641, 643, etc.). Edward IV. was at Salisbury in January 1469, one of his privy seals being dated there on the 16th of the month.

EDWARD IV

696

THE EARL OF OXFORD TO SIR JOHN PASTON [1]

To the worshipfull, and with alle myn hert right entierly bilovyd Sir John Paston, Knyght, this lettre be delivered.

TH'ERLE OF OXINFORD.

RIGHT hertly welbilovyd, I grete you wele. And where   1469(?)
I am for trowth enformyd that the Duchesse of   JAN. 7
Suffolk wolle hold a court on Monday next commyng at Coton, to th'entent that she wolle fynde the maner of Thempnals holde of hir by knyghts service and they that ben possessioners of the same shulde payle certeine of the Parke of Weverston; and by cause this is nat performyd nor don, thoo that ben possessioners shall at the said court be amersid. And it is agreed that Sir William Yelverton, Sir Thomas Hoo, shalle be at the said court and wolle pay the amercyment, and to delyver the said Duchesse possession of the said service and palyng, and so by this meane to be come tenauntes to the said Duchesse. And what wolle falle more herof I kan nat sey. Wherfor me thinkith it were welle don ye were at the said court with your councell, and to do therin as they wolle avise you. Also as ye come to the said court take your wey by the said Duchesse to th'entent that ye come to se hir welfare, &c. Do herin as your councell wolle avyse you. I wolde ye dud welle. And to my power I wolle help yow. And our Lorde kepe yow. Wrytyn at Tatyngston the vij. day of Januer.

Endorsed: Th'Erle off Oxenfford.

1 [From Paston MSS., B.M.]   It will be seen by No. 690, that in October 1468 the Duchess of Suffolk had a design of suddenly entering the manor of Cotton and dispossessing Sir John Paston. This letter, in which it is said she proposes to hold a court there, was probably written in the beginning of the following year.

EDWARD IV

pendinge betwixt yow on that one partie, and our right   1469
trustie and right entirely beloved cosin the Duke of Norffolk   JAN. 18
on that other, and to have appeared before the Lords of our Councell at our Palleys of Westminster at a certeine day in our said letters specified; yett nevertheless we understonde not as yet if ye have conformed yow to the performinge of our said commandement or not. We therefore eftsones write unto yow, willing and straitly charging yow to cease of the said ryotts and assemblies; and that incontinent upon the sight of these our letters that ye dispose yow personally to appear afore the said Lords of our Councell at our said Pallis, there to answere to such thinges as in that behalfe by them shall be laid and objected against yow, not failinge hereof, all excuses laid aparte, as ye will avoide our displeasure. Yeven under our signet at our citye of Salesbury, the xviij. day of January.

699

SIR JOHN PASTON TO ROGER TOWNSEND [1]

To the ryght worshypfull and hys best betrustyd Frende, Roger Townesende.

RIGHT worshipfull sir, I comaunde me to yow, praying   1467-9
yow hertly to remembre that by the award made by-   FEB. 12
twen yow and me by Roger Townesend for a tenement in Stratton in Norfolk callid Rees, I shuld delyver yow all the evydens apperteynyng to the said plase, and not from thens forth to chalenge nor interupte my lady your wyfe ner yow of the said tenement; And that for thes said causes ye shuld and therto were agreyd to geve me an horse and xli. to an harneys. And moreovir before Cristemasse in the kynges chambre ye ther ageyn promysed me that ye wold such tyme as I send to yow home to yowre plase by any servant of myne er any man

1 [Add. MS. 34,889, f. 186.]   This letter was probably written after the death of John Paston, the writer's father, but the precise year is uncertain.

from me, that ye wold delyver it hym and send it to me by hym. My brothir John hath send me word that he remembird yow therof on my behalfe and that you answerid hym that ye wold gyfe hym or me a fayre harneys at your comyng to London. I deme in yow that ye thynke par case to bye a fayre harneys here for x. markz; but, cosyn, as God help me, I bowte an harneys syn that tyme for my self, which cost me xx*li.* But I con not desire of yow so moch. Wherfore, cosyn, with all myn hert I pray yow accordyng to yowre promyse that it like yow to send me by my servaunt, berer herof, the said somme of x*li.*, as my trust is in yow, and as I wolde in like case have don to yow, and as in the premysses I delt feithfully with yow and evir so shall dele, with the grase of God, Who have yow in Hys kepyng. Wretyn at London the xii. day of Feveryer.—Youris,

JOHN PASTON, K.

700

JOHN PASTON TO SIR JOHN PASTON[1]

To my mastyr, Sir John Paston, knyght, in Flet stret.

SYR, &c. It is so that, with owght ye have hasty reparacyon doon at Caster, ye be lyek to have doubyll cost in hast, for the reyn hathe so moystyd the wallys in many plasys that they may not tylle the howsys tyll the wallys be reparyd; or ellys ye shall have doubyll cost for to untylle your howsys ayen at syche tyme as ye shall amend the wallys. And if it be not do thys yer, many of the wallys wyll lye in the moot or longe to; ye knowe the febyllnesse of the utter coort of old. John Pampyng hathe had hame to Caster as good as x^ml. tylle fyr the plase at Yermeuthe, and it wer pete that the tyll wer lost; and the lenger that it lythe unleyd the wers it wyll be. I have thys day bespok as myche lyme as wyll serve for the tyll. Wherfor I prey yow re-

[1] [Add. MS. 33,597, f. 4.] The year in which this letter was written is doubtful, but it was most probably either 1468 or 1469, at the beginning of Lent.

8

membyr the cost of the werkmanschep and purvey the money by oo mean or othyr, what shefte so evyr ye make. And, for your owne profyte, remembyr to goo thorow with Hwghe of Fen; for by my trowthe ye wyll ellys repent yow er owght longe. For bothe ye shall loose hys good wyll and lett peraventure that avantage that he myght do yow in your lond recoveryng; wher as he may do yow harme and [*if*] he wyll and then, to late wyse. Item, that ye remembyr your relesys and gounys of my Lord of Norffolk er ye com hom. Item, I send yow by the berer herof a lettyr dyrect to yow that a man of my Lord of Oxenfortheys delyverd me; whych lettyr comyth fro the Kyng. Item, that ye remembyr in eny wyse to serche for the fyne in syche plasys as my modyr sent you woord of in a lettyr; for myn oncyll and my grauntdam report that they have serchyd in all plasys thar as it shold be, but they can not fynd no thyng of it. Also that ye look whedyr the fyne was reryd to eny feeffeys mor then to my grauntfadyr and my grauntdam and ther issu; for and ther wer eny feoffeys namyd in the fyn, it is the bettyr for yow. My Lady and my grauntdam be com to London for the same mater; wherfor it wer well do that the jwgys wer enformyd of your mater befor they spok with theym. I prey yow hye yow hom hastyly and se your owne profyte your sylf. Pampyng and I shall clowt up your howsys as we may with the money that we have tyll more come, but ye shold do bettyr your sylf. I prey red thys byll onys on a day tyll ye have sped thes maters wretyn her in; thowe it be to your peyne to labore theym, remembyr your profyt. Nomor, &c., but God kep yow thys Lent fro lollardy of fleshe. Wretyn at Norwyche the Twysday next aftyr that I departyd fro yow.

J. P.

9

701

MARGARET PASTON TO SIR JOHN PASTON[1]

To Sir John Paston, knyght, be this delivered in hast.

I GRETE you wele and send you Goddes blyssyng and myn, desiryng you to recomaund me to my brother William, and to comune with hym and your councell in such materis as I wryght to you, that ther may be purveyd be some writyng fro the Kyng that my Lord of Norffolk and his councell seas [*cease*] of the wast that thei done in your lordsheps, and in especiall at Heynford; for thei have felled all the wood, and this weke thei wull carie it a wey, and lete renne the wateris and take all the fyssh. And Sir William Yelverton and his sone William, John Grey and Burgeys, William Yelvertons men, have ben at Guton and takyn distresses, and with ought that [*unless*] thei wull pay them thei shall not set ought no plow to till there lande; thei byd them lete there land lye on tilled but if [*unless*] thei pay them. So that if the tenauntes have no remedy that thei may pesibly, with ought assaught or distresse takyng, be the seid Yelverton or his men, or of any other in there names, at there liberte herye there landis, with in this vij. days there tylth in the feldis be lost for all this yere and thei shall be on doon; and though ye shuld kepe it here after pesibilly ye shuld lese the ferme of this yere, for thei may not pay you but if [*unless*] thei may occupie there landis; thei set not so sone a plow ought at ther gatis but ther is a felesship redy to take it. And thei ride with speris and launyegays, like men of werre, so that the seid tenauntis arn a ferd to kepe there owyn howses. Therfore purvey an redy remedy, or ellis ye lese the tenauntis hertis and ye gretly hurt; for it is gret pety to here the swemefull[2] and petowse compleyntis of the pore tenauntis that come to me for comfort and socour sometime vi. or vij.

[1] [Add. MS. 34,889, f. 202.] This letter must have been written in 1469, after the Duke of Norfolk and Sir William Yelverton had taken possession of Fastolf's lands.   [2] *swemeful*, sorrowful.—Halliwell.

10

to geder. Therfore, for Goddis love, se that thei ben helpyn and desire my brothere William to geve you good concell here.

Also it is told me that my Lady of Suffolk hath promysed you here good will, if your bargayn of the mariage[1] holdyth, to do as largely as she shall be disired, or largelyer if there be any appoyntment takyn a twix you for any materes a twyx her and you. And [*i.e.* if] thei wuld avyse you to geve any money to here to make here refuse or disclayme here titill, me semyth ye may wele excuse you be the money that she had last, and be the wrongis that were don be here and here men in fellyng of wood and pullyng doune of your place and logge at Heylesdon, and takyn a wey of the shep and your faderis goodis, which were takyn a wey at the pullyn don of the seid place; wheche wele considered, she were wurthy to recompense you. And [*if*] the Kyng and the lordis were wele enformed thei wuld considere the redilyer your hurtis. It semyth this Sir William Yelverton hath comfort that he is so bold, for [he[2]] hath ryght prowde and fowle langage and ryght slaundrows to the tenauntis, as thei have reported to me. Therfor be ryght ware that ye bynde not your self nor mak non ensurance till ye be suer of a pesibill possession of your lande; for oftyn tyme rape rueth, and whan a man hath made such a covenante he must kepith it, he may not chese; there[fore[2]] be not to hasty till your londe be clere. And labore hastly a remedy for thes premysses, or ellis Sir John Fastolffis lyvelode, though ye entre it pesibilly, shall not be worth to ye a grote this yere with ought ye wull on do your tenauntis. I pray you remembre a kerchye of Cremyll for your suster Anne. Remembre to labore some remedy for your faderis will whill my Lord of Caunterbury[3] lyvyth, for he is an old man and he is now frendly to you and if he happed to dye, how [*who*] shuld come after hym ye wote never; and if he wer a nedy man, in asmych as your fader was noysed of so greet valew he wull be the mor straunge to entrete. And lete this be not for gete; for [if] ther were on [*one*] that aught us no good wyll he myght calle us up to make accounte of his

[1] With Anne Haute.   [2] Omitted in MS.   [3] Cardinal Bourchier.

11

THE PASTON LETTERS

1469
MARCH 12 goodis, and if we had not for to showe for us where by we have occupied, he myght send doun assentence to curse us in all the diosyse and to make us to delivere his goodis ; which were to us a gret shame, and a rebuke. There fore purvey hastly and wyssely therfore whill he lyvyth, and do not as ye dede whill my Lord of York[1] was Chanceller make delays, for if ye had labored in his tyme as ye have do sith, ye had be thurgh in your materis ; be ware be that, and lete slauth nomor take you in such diffaught ; thynk of after clappes and have provysion in all your work, and ye shall do the better. God kepe you. Wretyn on Myd Lent Sonday in hast.

Be your moder, M. P.

702

CARDINAL BOURCHIER'S DECLARATION[2]

1469 TO all cristen men to whom this present writyng shall come, Thomas, by the providence of God, Preeste Cardinall Archiebisshopp of Caunterbury, Primat of all Inglond and Legat of the Appostallic See, gretyng. Where now late Alice, Duchesse of Suffolk, come to us and desirid of us to dismysse us of oure estate and to enseall a deed of a relees of the maner of Haylysdon with the appurtenaunce in the counte of Norffolk ; which we denyed, in as myche as wee stode infeoffyd in the seid maner with othirs to the use of Sir John Paston knyght, sone and heire to John Paston sqwyer ; to the whiche the seid Duchesse replied, seying and affermyng that she was accordyd and agreed with the seid Sir John Paston by the meane of the ryght Reverent fader in God, George Archebysshop of York, and that the seid Sir John Paston was fully assented and agreed that the seid Duchesse shuld have the seid manere wyth th'appurtenaunce to hir, hir

[1] George Nevill, Archbishop of York. He surrendered the Great Seal on the 8th June 1467.
[2] [Add. MS. 34,889, f. 127.] From what Margaret Paston writes to her son Sir John in the end of the last letter about his father's will, and also from what she says a little later about the Duchess of Suffolk (*see* page 15), we may assign this document with great probability to the year 1469.

12

heyris and assignes for ever more, and that all the feoffees 1469 enfeoffid and seisid in the seid manere wyth the appurtenaunce shuld relees and make astate to hir or such as shee wolde assigne of the seid manere wyth th'appurtenaunce ; the wehych we answerde and seid upon condicion that the seid Sir John Paston weere so agreed we wold relees wyth a goodwyll, and els not ; and yff so were that we cowde understand hereafter by the seid Right reverent Fadir in God, George Archebisshop of York, or by the seid Sir John Paston, that ther ware noon such accorde made by twex the seid Duchesse and the seid Sir John, that than oure deed and relees by us so ensealed off the seid maner wyth th'appurtenaunce shuld stond as voyd, and of no force nor effecte ; to the wehyche the seid Duches agreed, and prayd us that we wold sealle hir a deed of the same maner, wyche shee had theere redy, uppon the same condicion and uppon noone other. And wee than, at hir specyall request upon the condicion aforeseyd rehersid, sealid the seyd deed and delyvered it ; and the seid Duchesse at the same tyme promitted us that she wold use and kepe the seid writyng noo notherwise, nor to noon othir use but uppon the same condicion as is aforeseid. In witnesse whereoff, to this oure present writyng we have sette oure seall.

703

SIR JOHN PASTON TO JOHN PASTON[1]

To myght' well belovyd brother, John Paston, or to John Dawbeney, in his absence.

RYGHT worschypful and well belovyd brother, I comand MARCH me to yow, letyng you wete that Sir Thomas Howes hadde a free chapell at Castr, wher of the gyfte longyth to me, whyche chapell, as I understande, scholde be in the olde tyme, er the place at Caster wer bylte, with in the motte, wher-

[1] [From Fenn, iv. 308.] Sir Thomas Howes appears to have died in the latter part of the year 1468. Before the end of that year his living of Pulham was vacant, and his death is alluded to in a letter of Margaret Paston's, written on the 30th September 1469, as having occurred 'within this twelvemonth.' It would appear by

13

THE PASTON LETTERS

1469
MARCH 17 for I ame but the better pleased ; and soo it is now that at the speciall request of the Qwen and other especiall good Lordes of myn, I have gevyn it to the berer her of, callyd Master John Yotton, a chapleyn of the Qwenys. Neverthelle[ss] in tyme passyd I proposyd that the master of the colegg scholde have hadd it, and so er longe to I hope he schall, wherfor I thynke he most take possession, and that is the cawse of hys comyng. Wherfor I pray yow make hym good cher. He is informyd that it scholde be worthe Cs. be yer, whyche I belyve not ; I thynke it der jnow xls. by yeer. He most have it as it was hadde befor.

Item, thys daye I understonde that ther be comen letteris from my moder and yow, and Dawbeney, wherin I schall sende yow answer when I have seyn them.

No mor at this tyme, for within this iij. dayes I shall lette yow have kneleche of other maters.

Wretyn the xviij. day of Marche.

Whether he nedyth indoccion, or institucion, or non, I wot not ; if it nede, brother, ye may seale any suche thynge as well as I. Master Stevyn kan tell all suche thynges.

JOHN PASTON, K.

704

MARGARET PASTON TO SIR JOHN PASTON[1]

To Sir John Paston.

APRIL 3 I GRETE you wele, and send you Godds blissyng and myn, thankyng you for your seall that ye sent me ; but I am right sory that ye dede so grete cost ther up on, for on of xld. should have served me right wele. Send me ward

the following extract, quoted by Fenn, from the Institution Books of the Bishop of Norwich, that Sir John's presentation referred to in this letter was not allowed, or was not made out in time, and that the Bishop presented by a lapse :—

'Cantaria in Cayster-hall.
'Lib. xi. p. 170, 21 March 1468. Mr. Joh'es Yetton, S.T.P. ad col. Ep'i. per laps'.'

[1] [From Fenn, iv. 312.] Allusion is made in this and the next letter to the expected visit of Edward IV. to Norfolk in 1469. Owing to the proposed marriage of Sir John Paston with his kinswoman, Anne Haute, Lord Scales appears at this time

14

EDWARD IV

what it cost you, and I shall send you money therfor. I send 1469 you a letter be a man of Yarmoth ; send me word if ye have APRIL it, for I marveyll ye sent me non answer ther of be Juddy.

I have non very knowleche of your ensuraunce [*engagement*], but if ye be ensured I pray God send you joy and wurchep to geder, and so I trost ye shull have, if it be as it is reported of her[1] ; and a nemps God, ye arn as gretly bownd to her as ye were maried, and therfor I charge you up on my blissyng, that ye be as trew to her as she wer maried on to you in all degrees, and ye shall have the mor grace and the better spede in all other thyngs.

Also, I wuld that ye shuld not be to hasty to be maried til ye wer more suer of your lyvelode, for ye must remembr what charge ye shall have, and if ye have not to mayntene it, it wull be gret rebuke ; and therfor labour that ye may have releses of the londs, and be in more suerte of your lond, or than ye be maried.

The Duchesse of Suffolk[2] is at Ewhelm, in Oxford shir, and it is thought be your frends her that it is do that she myght be ferr and ought of the wey, and the rather feyne excuse be cause of age or sikenesse, and if that the Kyng wuld send for her for your maters.

Your elmyse [*enemies*] be as bold her as thei wer befor, wherfor I can not thynk but that thei have sume comfort. I sent to Cayster that thei shuld be war in kepyng of the place, as ye dede wright to me. Hast you to spede your maters as spedily ye can, that ye may have lesse felesshep at Cayster, for the expences and costs be grete, and ye have no nede therof and [*if*] ye remembre you wele what charges ye have beside, and how your liffelode is dispoyled and wasted by your adversaries.

Also I wuld ye shuld purvey for your suster[3] to be with

to have interested himself in Sir John's behalf. On the back of this letter, as Fenn tells us, is a note : 'The L. Scales is now frend to Sr. J. Paston.' But the handwriting is not contemporaneous.
[1] The lady here referred to is Anne Haute.
[2] Alice, widow of William de la Pole, Duke of Suffolk.
[3] This was most probably Margery Paston, with whom the whole family were, very soon after the writing of this letter, so much displeased for having without their consent contracted herself in marriage to Richard Calle.—F.

15

469
PRIL 3
my Lady of Oxford,[1] or with my Lady of Bedford,[2] or in sume other wurchepfull place, wher as ye thynk best, and I wull help to her fyndyng, for we be eyther of us werye of other. I shall tell you more whan I speke with you. I pray you do your devyr her in as ye wull my comfort and welefar, and your wurchep, for diverse causes which ye shall understand afterward, &c.

I spake with the Lord Skales at Norwich, and thanked hym for the good lordshep that he had shewed to you, and desired his Lordship to be your contynuall good lord ; and he swore be his trought he wold do that he myght do for you ; and he told me that Yelverton the Justice had spoke to hym in your maters, but he told me not what ; but I trow, and ye desired hym to telle you, he wuld. Ye ar be holdyng to my Lord of his good report of you in this contre, for he reported better of you than I trow ye deserve. I felt be hym that ther hath be profered hym large proferes on your adversaries parte ageyn you.

Send me word as hastly as ye may after the begynnyng of the terme, how ye have sped in all your maters, for I shall thynk right long till I her sume good tidyngs.

Item, I pray you recomaund me to the good mayster[3] that ye gaffe to the chapell of Cayster, and thank hym for the gret cost that he dede on me at Norwych ; and if I wer a gretter lady he shuld understand that he shuld far the better for me, for me semyth be his demenyng he shuld be right a good man.

Item, I send you the nowche[4] with the dyamaunch, be the berer herof. I pray yow forgate not to send me a kersche[5] of Cr'melle for nekkerchys for your syster Anne, for I am

[1] Elizabeth, the daughter of Sir John Howard, Knight, and widow of John de Vere, Earl of Oxford, who was beheaded in 1461-2.—F.
[2] See vol. iv. p. 188, Note 3.
[3] Dr. John Yotton. See No. 703.
[4] An ouch is a collar of gold, formerly worn by women ; a gold button, set with some jewel, is likewise so called, but that most probably was the ornament here mentioned to be sent to Sir John by his mother; we may suppose it was intended as a present to his betrothed bride.—F.
[5] A kersche of Cr'melle, perhaps means a kerchief of Cremell, crewel or worsted, to be made into neck-handkerchiefs for her daughter Anne, who appears to have been for education and board with some lady of consequence.—F.

16

1469
APRIL 3
schente of the good lady that sche is with, be cawse she hathe non, and I can non gette in all thys towne.

I xuld wrythe mor to yow but for lakke of leyser. God have yow in Hys kepyng, and send yow good spede in alle your maters. Wryten in haste on Eestern Munday.

Be your Moder.

705

JOHN PASTON TO SIR JOHN PASTON[1]

To Master Syr John Paston.

SYR, I pray yow recomand me to my Lord Scalys good lordshep, and to let hym weet that, in lyek wyse as hys Lordshep gave me in comandement, I have enqweryd what the gentyllmanys answer was that my Lord of Norfolk sent to to awayte up on hym at the Kyngs comyng in to thys contre. Hys answer was to my Lord of Norfolks messenger, that he had promysyd my Lord Scalys to awayte up on hym at the same seson, and in as myche as he had promysyd my Lord Scalys, he wold not false hys promesse for no man on lyve. I fond the menys that the seyd gentylemanys wyfe mevyd hyr husbend with the same mater as thow she had axyd hym of hyr awne hed,[1] and he told hyr that he had gevyn thys answer. Thys gentylman is Sir William Calthorp ;[2] but I pray yow tell my Lord Scalys that ye undyrstand not who it is, for he preyid me to be secret ther of.

I pray with all my hart, hye yow hom in hast, for we thynk longe tyll ye coome. And I pray yow send me woord whedyr ye shall be mad a Crysten man or ye com home, or nowt ; and if so be that ye send eny man hom hastly, I pray yow send me an hat and a bonet by the same man, and let hym bryng the hat upon hys hid for mysfacyonyng of it. I have

APRIL 7

[1] [From Fenn, iv. 318.] For the date of this letter see preliminary note to the last (p. 14, Note 1).
[2] Sir William Calthorpe, Knight, had been High Sheriff of Norfolk and Suffolk, both in this and the preceding reign, and died very old in 1494. His second wife was Elizabeth, daughter and co-heir of Sir Miles Stapleton, Knight, of Ingham.—F.

VOL. V.—B

17

469
PRIL 7
ned to bothe, for I may not ryd nor goo owt at the doorys with non that I have, they be so lewde [*shabby*]. A murry bonet, and a blak or a tawny hat. And God send yow your desyr. Wretyn at Caster, the viij. day of Apryll.

Your J. PASTON.

706

LORD SCALES TO THE COUNCIL OF THE DUKE OF NORFOLK[1]

Ih's.

WYRSHYPFULL and my ryght gode frend, I comaund me to you. And where as I am enformed that my Lorde of Norffolk pretendeth title to serteyn londys of Sir John Pastons whych were late of Sir John Fastolf, it is sayd that by the comaundement and supportacyon of my sayd Lord, sertayn hys servaunts felleth wode, maketh grete wast, and destrayned the tenants of the seyd lands, to the grete damage of the seyd Sir John Paston and hys sayd tenants ; and also that my sayd Lord entendyth to entre sertayn places of the same. And for asmoch as maryage ys fully concluded by twyx the seyd Sir John Paston and on of my nerrest kynneswomen, I dout not that your reason wele conceyveth that nature must compelle me the rather to shewe my gode wylle, assystens, and favour unto the seyd Sir John in such thyngs as concerne hys enherytans. And because I am on of my said Lordys councayll, and must and will tendre hys honour, I hertely pray you that it may lyke you to advertyse and avyse my sayd Lord and yourys, that all such entres, fellyng of wode, destraynyngs of tenants, and all such maters lyke touchyng the seyd londes or any part

[1] [From Fenn, iv. 322.] This and the following letter were printed by Fenn from contemporaneous copies, written on the same paper without signature or address. On the back, however, is the following memorandum :—'Copea literæ Dñi de Scales;' to which has been added in a later handwriting : 'ad Conciliũ Duc' Norff' et aliis (sic) in favore J. Paston mil. eo quod maritaret cognatã suam Annã Hawte.' The date is clearly in the year 1469, when the Duke of Norfolk laid claim to Caister.

18

1469
APRIL 10
of them, be cessyd unto such tyme as a resonabell meane may be founde by my sayd Lords counsayll, my Lord my faders[1] and other cousyns and frendes of my seyd kynneswoman thys next terme, as may be to my sayd Lordys honour, and to the savyng of the ryght tytle of the seyd Sir John Paston.

Over thys I pray you that ye wille enforme my gode frend James Hobard of the premysses, that he may advertyse my seyd Lord in lyke wyse ; and that ye will yeve credens unto William Paston, and I shal be welwilled to do that may be to your plesur, with Godds mercy.

Fro Westmynstre, the x. day of Apryll.

707

LORD SCALES TO ————[2]

RYGHT trusty and welbelovyd, I grete you well. And for asmoch as a maryage ys fully concluded bytwyx Sir John Paston and my ryght nere kynneswoman Hawte, I will that ye and all other my servaunts and tenants understand that my Lord, my fader,[3] and I must of nature and reason shewe unto hym our gode assystens and favour in such maters as he shall have a doo. Wherfor I pray you hertely that ye will take the labour to come to Norwych, to comen with William Paston, and to yeve credens unto hym in such maters as he shall enforme you of myne entent, and of sertayn persones with whom ye shall comen by th'avyse of the seyd William Paston, of such maters as touch the sayd Sir John Paston ; prayng you to tendre thys mater as ye wolde do myne owne.

Fro Westmynstre, the x. day of April.

[1] Richard Woodville, Earl Rivers.
[2] [From Fenn, iv. 324.] See preliminary note to the last letter (p. 18, Note 1).
[3] See Note 1, supra.

19

708

ABSTRACT [1]

1469
MAY 5   Citation by Thomas, Cardinal Archbishop of Canterbury, to William [Waynflete], Bishop of Winchester, and John Beauchamp, Knight, Lord Beauchamp, to appear before the Archbishop in fifteen days after being summoned, and take upon them the charge of the execution of Sir John Fastolf's will, if they so will to do.

Lambeth, 5th May 1469, in the 15th year of the Archbishop's translation.

[The MS. belongs to the Castle Combe Collection.]

709

ARCHBISHOP NEVILL TO SIR JOHN PASTON [2]

To my right trusty and welbeloved Sir John Paston.

Ih's.

1469 (?)
MAY 7   RIGHT trusty and welbeloved, I grete you hertely well, and sende you by Thomas your childe xx.ˡⁱ, prayng you to spare me as for eny more at this tyme, and to hold you content with thessame, as my singlr truste is in you; and I shalle within bref tyme ordeigne and purveye for you such as shalbe unto your pleasir, with the grace of Almightty God, who have you in His proteccion and keping.

Writen in the manoir of the Mor [3] the vijth daye of Maye.
                G. EBORAC.

[1] [Add. Charter, 18,249, B.M.]
[2] [From Fenn, ii. 34.] This letter was almost certainly written between the years 1467 and 1469, and is not unlikely to be of the latter year, before the Nevills and the Archbishop had come to be regarded as open enemies of Edward IV.
[3] The Moor in Hertfordshire, a seat of Archbishop Nevill.

20

710

JOHN PASTON TO SIR JOHN PASTON [1]

1469
[MAY]   SYR, plesyth it to undyrstand, that I conceyve, by your lettyr whyche that ye sent me by Jwde, that ye have herd of R. C.[2] labor whyche he makyth by our ungracyous sustyrs [3] assent; but wher as they wryet that they have my good wyll ther in, savyng your reverence, they falsly lye of it, for they never spake to me of that mater, ner non othyr body in ther name. Lovell axyd me onys a qwestyon whedyr that I undyrstood how it was betwyx R. C. and my suster. I can thynk that it was by Callys menys, for when I axyd hym whedyr C. desyird hym to meve me that qwestyon or not, he wold have gotyn it aweye by humys and by hays, but I wold not so be answeryd; wherfor at the lest he told me that hys oldest sone desyird hym to spere [*inquire*] whedyr that R. C. wes swyr of hyr or nowt, for he seyd that he knew a good maryage for hyr, but I wot he lyeyd, for he is hole with R. Cale in that mater. Wherfor to the entent that he nor they sholl pyck no comfort of me, I answerd hym, that and my fadyr, whom God asoyle, wer a lyve, and had consentyd ther to, and my modyr, and ye bothe, he shold never have my good wyll for to make my sustyr to selle kandyll and mustard in Framlyngham; and thus, wythe mor whyche wer to longe to wryet to you, we departyd.

And wher as it plesythe you in your lettyr to crye me mercy for that ye sent me not syche ger as I sent yow mony for, I crye yow mercy that I was so lewde [*bold*] to encomber yow with eny so sympyll a mater, consyderyng the grette maters and weyghty that ye have to doo; but need com-

[1] [From Fenn, iv. 344.] This letter appears by the contents to have been written a little before Whitsuntide after the death of Sir Thomas Howes, and when the Duke of Norfolk was preparing to make good a claim to the manor of Caister, which, as we shall see, he regularly besieged and took in September 1469. The date is therefore certain.
[2] Richard Calle's   [3] Margery Paston.

21

1469
[MAY]   pellyd me, for in thys contre is no syche stuffe as I sent to yow for.

Also, wher as it plesyth yow to send to Rychard Calle to delyver me monye, so God help me, I wyll non axe hym for my sylfe, nor non had I of hym, nor of non othyr man but of myne owne, syne ye depertyd; but that lytyll that I myght forbere of myne owne, I have delyveryd to Dawbeney for howsold, and pay it for yow in menys wagys; and ther for who ever sendys yow word that I have spent yow eny mony syne ye went hens, they must geve yow an othyr reknyng, savyng in met and drynk, for I eete lyek an horse, of purpose to eete yow owte at the dorys. But that nedythe not, for ye com not within them; wherfor, so God help me, the felaushep her thynkys that ye have forgetyn us alle. Wherfor and eny thyng be ille rewlyd when ye come home, wyet it [*impute it to*] your selfe for defawt of oversyght.

Also, I undyrstand for verry se[r]teyn, and it is sent me so woord owt of my Lordys howse, that thys Pentcost is my Lordys consell at Framlyngham, and they purpose thys week and the next to hold coortys her at Caster, and at all othyr maners that wer Sir John F.,[1] and purchasyd of Yelverton and of Syr T. H.,[2] whom God asoyle, and how that my demenyng sholbe, it is to late to send to yow for avyse; wherfor, and I do well I axe no thank, and if I do ille, I pray yow leythe the defawt on over lytyll wyte, but I purpose to use the fyrst poynt of hawkyng, to hold fast and I maye; but so God help me, and they myght pulle downe the howse on our hedys, I wyet [*blame*] hem not, whyche I trust to God to help hem from; for by God that bowght me, the best Erle in Inglond wold not dele so with my Lord and my Lady as ye do, withowt makyng of some menys to them; so God help me, whoso ever avyse yow to do so, he is not your frend. And I may, I trust to God to se yow abowght Mydsomer or befor, for in good feythe I wene ye purpose yow that it shall be Estern er ye come hom, for all your servants her wen [*here ween*] that ye purpose ne more to dele with them, but to leve hem her [*here*] in ostage to my Lord of Norfolk.

[1] Fastolf's.   [2] Sir Thomas Howes.

22

Also, syr, I pray yow purvey what Ine that my brodyr   1469
Edmund shall be in, for he losythe sore hys tyme her, I   [MAY]
promyse yow; I pray yow send me word by the next messenger that comyth, and I shall eythyr send hym or bryng hym up with me to London.

Also, syr, we pore *sanz deners* of Castr have brook iij. or iiij. stelle bowys; wherfor we beseche yow, and ther be eny maker of steele bowys in London whyche is very kunnyng, that ye wyll send me woord, and I shall send yow the bowys that be broken, whyche be your owne greet bowe, and Roberd Jacksonys bowe, and Johon Pampyngs bowe; thes iij. have kast so many calvys, that they shall never cast qwarellys[1] tyll they be new mad.

I praye yow fynd the menys that my Lord have some resonable meane profyrd, so that he and my Lady may undyrstand that ye desyr to have hys good lordshep. I promyse yow it shall do yow ease and your tenaunts bothe, and God preserve.
                  J. P.

711

ROBERT BROWNE TO SIR JOHN PASTON [2]

To the right worshipful Sir John Paston knyght be this delivered.

RIGHT worshipfull Sire, I recommaunde me to you, &c.,   1469
certefying you for certeyn that the kyng sent a lettre unto my Lord of Norffolk for to contenue all maner of materes unto suche tyme as he sholl take a direction therin, as I am enformed by Master Haute, and by a messenger of his owne [it was sent[3]], &c. Acordyng to the same entent and

[1] See vol. ii. p. 101, Note 3.
[2] [Add. MS. 33,889, f. 70.] The date of this letter is fixed by Roger Ree being Sheriff of Norfolk, which he was from November 1468 to November 1469. The time would seem to be April or May 1469, when the Duke of Norfolk was proposing to take forcible possession of Caister.
[3] These words are interlined before '&c.,' but possibly are intended to be read with the next sentence, which is difficult to construe, there being no punctuation in the MS.

23

1469 the rehersall by estimacion by cause the Secretary of his Clerkes was with the Kyng the Quene hath sent a[1] lettre unto my Lady of Norffolk and a nother lettre unto my Lady of Suffolk the elder, desyeryng theym to common with my lordis that all such materis as the Kyng wrote unto them fore mabe kept so that no defaute be founden in them, as ye may understand by youre lettre sent frome the Quene, &c. Also Roger Ree the Shirereve of the Shire wilbe at Caster, as my Lord Tresourer told me, upon Tuesday or Wedynsday, to se that goode rule be kept. Also my Lord of York[2] sendis you a lettre, &c. My Lord Scalez is with the Kyng, &c. I take unto the brynger herof xxs. that is sufficaunt as he wille telle you, also the secretarye, vjs. viijd. As for all othere materes for haste I contenue unto that I may have leyser to write to you. I pray you to recommaunde me to my mastres your moder. At London upon Sonday in hast.

ROBERT BROWNE.

The letter is endorsed in another hand :—
'The Counsell of my Lord of Suffolk, Robert Harlesdon. The Counsell of my Lord of Norffolk, Sir Thomas Walgrave, knyght [sergeant at] lawe and Richard Southwell and to everiche of them.'

712

ABSTRACT[3]

RICHARD CALLE TO SIR JOHN PASTON

MAY 22 I would have been with you on Sunday before Ascension Day, had I received any command to that effect. Henry Wheler told me my day of the surety of peace was *quindena Trinitatis*, 'and thereof he made me a bill. He is foully to blame to serve me so.' I am much bound to you, nevertheless, for the safeguard of my sureties. Gives an account of monies disbursed since parting with Sir John at London. Repaid 'my mistress' 66s. 8d., part of 100s. she lent for Mariot's matter. Paid Dawbeney for household since Midlent, 30s. Received from the farmer of the dairy, £11, 11s. 4d.

[1] Before the word 'a' 'nothere' is interlined, probably by inadvertence.
[2] Archbishop Nevill.
[3] [From Paston MSS., B.M.]

24

Delivered 'to the master of the college onward for his hire,' 50s. Has received of Paston's 'lifelode' since he came from London but £18, 10s. Has spent £12, 10s. more than he received, and has borrowed of John Wellys and others. Could borrow nothing of Mr. William. 'And of all this twelvemonth I have not had one penny for my wages. There is none of them that hath purveyed nor chevised have so much as I have done. Here is no man paid of their wages, but all spent in household.' Cannot get a penny in all Suffolk or Flegge, of Paston's 'lifelode,' nor in Boyton nor Heyneford. Can get money only at Gughton, which I must gather myself, for the bailiff will not come there. Much malt made, which had better be sold to pay the men's wages, who complain grievously, 'and the master of the college and Sir John Stille both.' Will obtain for Dawbeney in ten days 6 or 7 marks more, which should keep the household for the next seven or eight weeks. The price of malt is but 20d. a quarter, but it would be better to sell some than that the men should be unpaid. Wonders he has no word from him about letting Spoorle. Cannot give Mariot an estate in Bekham as Paston directs, for Paston has the deed which James Andrewes sealed, but will talk with him and see how he is disposed; for it would be well that Paston were through with him. He is not trusty, but seeks pretexts for delay. Jekson's crossbow is broken. Shall he send it to London to be mended?

Caster, Monday in Pentecost week.

[The mention of Jekson's crossbow being broken proves this letter to be of the year 1469. Compare No. 710, p. 23.]

1469
MAY 22

713

RICHARD CALLE TO MARGERY PASTON[1]

MYN owne lady and mastres, and be for God very trewe wyff, I with herte full sorowefull recomaunde me unto you, as he that can not be mery, nor nought shalbe tyll it be othewise with us then it yet is, for thys lyf that we lede nough is nowther plesur to Godde nor to the worlde, consederyng the gret bonde of matrymonye that is made be twix us, and also the greete love that hath be, and as I truste yet is be twix us, and as on my parte never gretter; wherfor I beseche Almyghty Godde comfort us as sone as it

1469

[1] [From Fenn, iv. 350.] This letter was evidently written about the same period as No. 710. The original appears to have had no address, although Fenn prints one in the right-hand copy; but on the back was the following memorandum, evidently not quite contemporary: 'Litera Ric'i Calle Margeriæ Paston filiæ Joh'is Paston ar'i quam postea duxit in uxorem.'

25

1469 plesyth Hym, for we that ought of very ryght to be moost to gether ar moost asondre; me semyth it is a m[ll.] [*thousana*] yere a goo son that I speke with you. I had lever thenne all the goode in the worlde I myght be with you. Alas, alas! goode lady, full litell remembre they what they doo that kepe us thus asundre; iiij. tymes in the yere ar they a cursid that lette matrymonye; it causith many men to deme in hem they have large consyence in other maters as wele as herin. But what lady suffre as ye have do; and make you as mery as ye can, for I wys, lady, at the longe wey Godde woll of Hys ryght wysnes helpe Hys servants that meane truly, and wolde leve accordyng to Hes lawys, &c.

I undrestande, lady, ye have hadde asmoche sorwe for me as any gentylwoman hath hadde in the worlde, aswolde Godd all that sorwe that ye have hadde had rested upon me, so that ye hadde be discharged of it, for I wis, lady, it is to me a deethe to her that ye be entreted other wise thene ye ought to be. This is a peyneful lyfe that we lede. I can not leve thus withoute it be a gret displesure to Godde.

Also like you to wete that I had sent you a letter be my ladde from London, and he tolde me he myght not speke with you, ther was made so gret awayte upon hym and upon you bothe. He told me John Threscher come to hym in your name, and seide that ye sent hym to my ladde for a letter or a token, weche I shulde have sent you, but he truste hym not; he wold not delyver hym noon. After that he brought hym a rynge, seyng that ye sent it hym, comaundyng hym that he schulde delyver the letter or token to hym, weche I conceyve sethen be my ladde it was not be your sendyng, it was be my mastres and Sir Jamys[1] a vys. Alas, what meane they? I suppose they deeme we be not ensuryd to gether, and if they so doo I merveyll, for thenne they ar not wele avised, remembryng the pleynes that I breke to my mastres at the begynnyng, and I suppose be you bothe, and ye dede as ye ought to do of very ryght; and if ye have do the contrare, as I have be enformed ye have do, ye dede nouther concyensly nor to the plesure of Godde, withoute ye dede it for feere, and

[1] Sir James Gloys, a priest.

26

for the tyme to please suche as were at that tyme a boute you; and if ye so dede it for this service it was a resonable cause, consederyng the grete and importable callyng upon that ye hadde, and many an on trewe tale was made to you of me, weche God knowt I was never gylty of.

My ladde tolde me that my mastres your modre axyd hym if he hadde brought any letter to you, and many other thyngs she bare hym on hande,[1] and a monge all other at the last she seide to hym that I wolde not make her prevy to the begynnyng, but she supposyd I wolde at the endyng; and as to that, God knowt sche knewe furst of me and non other. I wott not what her mastreschip meneth, for be my trowthe ther is no gentylwoman on lyve that my herte tendreth more then it dothe her, nor is lother to displese, savyng only your person, weche of very ryght I ought to tendre and love beste, for I am bounde therto be the lawe of Godde, and so wol do whyle that I leve, what so ever falle of it. I supose, and ye telle hem sadly the trouthe, they wold not dampne ther soules for us; though I telle hem the trouthe they woll not be leve me as weele as they woll do you; and ther for, goode lady, at the reverence of Godde be pleyne to hem and telle the trouthe, and if they woll in no wise agree therto, betwix God, the Deelf, and them be it, and that perell that we schuld be in, I beseche Godde it may lye upon them and not upon us. I am hevy and sory to remembre ther disposicion, God sende them grace to gyde all thyngs weele, as wele I wolde they dede; Godde be ther gide, and sende them peas and reste, &c.

I mervell moche that they schulde take this mater so heedely as I undrestonde they doo, remembryng it is in suche case as it can not be remedyed, and my desert upon every be halfe it is for to be thought ther shulde be non obstacle a yenst it; and also the worchipfull that is in them, is not in your mariage, it is in ther owne mariage, weche I beseche Godde sende hem suche as may be to ther worship and plesur to Godde, and to ther herts ease, for ell[es] were it gret pety. Mastres, I am aferde to write to you, for I undrestonde ye have schewyd my letters that I have sent you be for this tyme;

[1] See vol. ii. p. 110, Note 1.

27

THE PASTON LETTERS

1469 but I prey you lete no creatur se this letter. As sone as ye have redde it lete it be brent, for I wolde no man schulde se it in no wise ; ye had no wrytyng from me this ij. yere, nor I wolle not sende you no mor, therfor I remytte all this matre to your wysdom. Almghty Jesu preserve, kepe, and [give] you your hertys desire, weche I wotte weele schulde be to Goods plesur, &c.

Thys letter was wreten with as greete peyne as ever wrote I thynge in my lyfe, for in goode feyth I have be ryght seke, and yet am not veryly weele at ease, God amend it, &c.

714

JAMES HAWTE TO SIR JOHN PASTON [1]

To my worchypfull brother, Sir John Paston,
be thys byll delyvered in hast.

MAY 22 RYGTH worchipfull brother, I recomaund me onto you, lettyng you to wytte, that my Lorde Stafford [2] was made Erle of Deveneschere apon Sonday ; and as for the Kyng, as I understond, he departyt [*departeth*] to Walsyng-game apon Fryday com vij. nygth, and the Quene also, yf God send hyr good hele.

And as for the Kyng [he] was apoyntyd to goo to Calys, and now hyt ys pute of. And also as for the goyng to the see, my Lord of Warwyke schyppys gothe to the see, as I understond. None other tydynggys I can none wryte unto you, but Jesu have you in Hys kepyng.

Wretyn at Wyndysore on Monday after Whytsonday, in hast, &c.

By your brother, JAMES HAWTE.

[1] [From Fenn, ii. 16.] The King's visit to Norfolk and the creation of Lord Stafford as Earl of Devonshire both fix the date of this letter as 1469. The writer seems to be the brother of Anne Hawte, to whom Sir John Paston was engaged, and he accordingly calls him his brother.

[2] Humphrey Stafford, Lord Stafford of Southwick, was created Earl of Devonshire on Sunday, 7th May 1469 ; so that the writer ought to have said, not 'upon Sunday,' but 'upon Sunday fortnight.'

28

715

SIR JOHN PASTON TO JOHN PASTON [1]

To my Modr, and to my brother, John Paston.

BROTHER, it is so that the Kyng schall come in to Norffolk in hast, and I wot nat whethyr that I may come with hym or nowt ; if I come I most do make a livere of xx[ti] gownes, whyche I most pyke owt by your advyse ; and as for clothe for suche persones as be in that contre, if it myght be had ther at Norwyche, or not, I wot not ; and what persones I am not remembryd.

If my modre be at Caster, as ther schall be no dowt for the kepyng of the place whyl the Kynge is in that contre, that I may have the most parte at Caster ; and whether ye woll offre your selfe to wayte uppon the Lorde of Norfolk or not, I wolde ye dyde that best wer to do ; I wolde do my Lorde plesur and servyse, and so I wolde ye dyde, if I wyst to be sur of hys gode lordeschyp in tyme to kome. He schall have CC. in a lyverye blewe and tawny, and blew on the leffte syde, and bothe darke colors.

I pray yow sende me worde, and your advyse by Judd of what men and what horse I cowde be purveyd off, if so be that I most nedys kome, and of your advyse in all thyngs be wryghtyng, and I schall send yow hastely other tydyngs. Late Sorell be well kept.

JOHN PASTON, Kt.

146 JUNE

[1] [From Fenn, ii. 22.] This letter must have been written in the beginning of June 1469. Edward IV., as appears by the dates of his privy seals, was at Windsor on the 29th May and at Norwich on the 19th June in that year. Fenn says he was also in Norfolk in the year 1474, but I can find no evidence of the fact.

29

THE PASTON LETTERS

716

JOHN PASTON TO SIR JOHN PASTON [1]

1469 JUNE

TO begyn, God yeld yow for my hatys. The Kyng hathe ben in this contre, and worchepfully receyvyd in to Norwyche, and had ryght good cher and gret gyftys in thys contre, wherwythe he holdyth hym so well content that he wyll hastyly be her agayn, and the Qwen allso, with whom, by my power avyse, ye shall com, if so be that the terme be do by that tym that she com in to this contre. And as for yowr maters her, so God help me, I have don as myche as in me was, in laboryng of theym, as well to my Lord Revers [2] as to my Lord Scalys, [3] Syr John Wydwyll, [4] Thomas Wyngfeld, and othyr abowt the Kyng. And as for the Lord Revers, he seyd to myn oncyll William, Fayrfax, and me, that he shold meve the Kyng to spek to the two Dukys of Norffolk and Suffolk, that they shold leve of ther tytyls of syche lond as wer Syr John Fastolfs. And if so be that they wold do nowt at the Kyngs reqwest, and then the Kyng shold comand theym to do no wasts, nor mak non assawtys nor frayis upon your tenants nor plasys, tyll syche tym as the lawe hathe determynd with yow or ayenst yow ; this was seyd by hym the sam day in the mornyng that he depertyd at noon. Whedyr he meved the Kyng with it or nowt I can not sey, myn oncyll Wyllyam thynkys naye. And the same aftyr none folowyng I told my Lord Scalys that I had spokyn with my Lord hys fadyr, in lyek forme as I

[1] [From Fenn, iv. 334.] Edward IV. arrived at Norwich in the middle of the month of June 1469. There are privy seals dated at Bury on the 15th and 16th of the month, at Norwich on the 19th and 21st, at Walsingham on the 21st and 22nd, at Lynn on the 26th, and at Stamford on the 5th July. Edward did not return with the Queen as he intended, but she visited Norwich without him a little later. See a paper on the subject of her visit by Mr. Harrod, in the *Norfolk Archæology*, vol. v. p. 32.

[2] Richard Woodville, Earl Rivers, father to the Queen, Lord Treasurer and Constable of England.

[3] Anthony Woodville, Lord Scales, eldest son of the Earl Rivers.

[4] A younger son of Earl Rivers.

30

have rehersyd, and axyd hym whedyr that my Lord hys fadyr had spokyn to the Kyng or nowt, and he gave me thys answer, that whedyr he had spokyn to the Kyng or nowt, that the mater shold do well inow.

Thomas Wygfeld told me, and swore on to me, that when Brandon meuvyd the Kyng, and besowght hym to shew my Lord favour in hys maters ayenst yow, that the Kyng seyd on to hym ayen, 'Brandon, thow thou can begyll the Dwk of Norffolk, and bryng hym abow the thombe as thow lyst, I let the wet thow shalt not do me so ; for I undyrstand thy fals delyng well inow.' And he seyd on to hym, more over, that if my Lord of Norffolk left not of hys hold of that mater, that Brandon shuld repent itt, every vayn in hys hert, for he told hym that he knew well inow that he myght reauyll [*rule*] my Lord of Norffolk as he wold ; and if my Lord dyd eny thyng that wer contrary to hys lawys, the Kyng told hym he knew well inow that it was by no bodys menys but by hys ; and thus he depertyd fro the Kyng.

Item, as by wordys, the Lord Scalys and Syr John Wydwyll tok tendyr your maters mor then the Lord Revers.

Item, Syr John Wydvyll told me, when he was on horsbak at the Kyngs depertyng, that the Kyng had comandyd Brandon of purpose to ryd forthe fro Norwych to Lyne, for to tak a conclusyon in your mater for yow ; and he bad me that I shold cast no dowghtys but that ye shold have your entent, and so dyd the Lord Scalys also ; and when that I preyd them at eny tyme to shew ther favor to your mater, they answered that it was ther mater as well as yours, consyderyng, the alyans [1] betwyx yow. Comon with Jakys Hawt, and he shall tell yow what langage was spekyn betwen the Duk of Suffolks consell, and hym, and me ; it is to long to wryght, but I promyse yow ye ar be held to Jakys, for he sparyd not to spek.

Item, the Kyng rod thorow Heylysdon Waren towads Walsyngham, and Thomas Wyngfeld promysyd me that he wold fynd the menys that my Lord of Glowsestyr [2] and hym sylf bothe shold shew the Kyng the loge that was breke down,

146 JUNE

[1] This refers to the contract between Sir John Paston and Anne Hawte.—F.

[2] Richard, Duke of Gloucester, afterwards King Richard III.—F.

31

and also that they wold tell hym of the brekyng down of the plase. Contrary to thys maters, and all the comfort that I had of my Lord Scalys, Sir John Wydvyll, and Thomas Wyngfeld, myn oncyll Wylliam sethe that the Kyng told hym hys owne mowthe, when he had redyn for by the loge in Heylysdon Waren, that he supposyd as well that it myght fall downe by the self as be plukyd downe, for if it had be plukyd down, he seyd that we myght have put in our byllys of it, wehn hys jugys sat on the *oyeer determyner* in Norwyche, he beyng ther. And then myn oncyll seythe how that he answered the Kyng, that ye trustyd to hys good grace that he shold set yow thorow with both the Dwkys, by mene of trete ; and he seythe that the Kyng answerd hym that he wold neythyr tret nor spek for yow, but for to let the lawe proced, and so he seyth that they departyd. And by my trowthe, and my Lord Tresorer encorage you not more than he dyd us her, ye shall have but esy [*indifferent*] help as on that party. Wherfor labor your maters effectually ; for by my trowthe it is nedy[s], for, for all ther wordys of plesur, I cannot undyrstand what ther labor in thys contre hathe don good ; wherfor be not ovyr swyft tyll ye be swyr of your lond, but labor sore the lawe, for by my trowthe tyll that he passyd with yow, ye get but esy help as I can undyrstand.

I had with me on day at dener in my modyrs plase, she beyng owt, the Lord Scalys, Sir John Wydvyll, Sir John Haward, Nicolas Haward, John of Par, Thomas Gornet, Foscwe, Cheyny, Trussell, the Knyghts son, Thomas Boleyn, *qua propter*, Brampton, Barnard, and Broun, Perse, Howse, W. Tonstale, Lewes Debretayll, and othyr, and mad hem good cher, so as they held them content.

Item, my Lord of Norffolk gave Bernard, Broom, nor me no gownys at thys seson, wherfor I awaytyd not on hym ; notwithstandyng I ofyrd my servyse for that seson to my Lady, but it was refusyd, I wot by avyse ; wherfor I purpose no more to do so. As for Bernard, Barney, Broom, and W. Calthorp, ar sworn my Lord of Glowsetyrs men, but I stand yet at large ; not withstandyng my Lord Scalys spok to me to be with the Kyng, but I mad no promes so to be, for I

32

told hym that I was not woorthe a groote withowt yow, and therfor I wold mak no promes to nobody tyll they had your good wyll fyrst ; and so we depertyd.

It was told me that ther was owt a preve seall for yow to attend upon the Kyng northeward ; and if it be so, I thynk veryly it is do to have yow fro London be craft, that ye shold not labor your maters to a conclusyon thys terme, but put them [in] delaye. I pray yow purvey yow on it to be at hom as sone as the terme is doone, for be God I take gret hurt for myn absence in dyvers plasys, and the most part of your men at Caster wyll deperte withowt abod, and ye be not at hom within thys fortnyght. I pray yow bryng hom poynts and lasys of sylk for yow and me. J. P.

717

ABSTRACT[1]

RICHARD CALLE TO SIR JOHN PASTON

Has arranged with Mariot's debtors at Bekham, and discharged him of the debt of £16. Has thus taken an open estate in the manor, as Paston desired. Had much trouble to bring Mariot, and especially his wife, [to reason], but with fair words and money got her out of the house. Lord Scales has sent to-day to Mr. Roos and others for men to come to Middleton on Wednesday,—short warning enough ; and we were in doubt 'what purveyance ye had made at London.' I believe my mistress and my master your brother have sent you word of the demeaning of the King and the Lords here.   JULY 3

Norwich, Monday after St. Peter's day.

[The reference to the King's being in Norfolk fixes the date of this letter to the year 1469.]

_____

[1] [From Paston MSS., B.M.]

718

JOHN AUBRY[1] TO SIR HENRY SPELMAN[2]

To the right reverent Sir Henry Spelman, Recordor of the Cite of Norwich, be this Letter delivered.

RIGHT reverent sir, I recomaunde me to you. Plese it you to knowe, this same day com to me the Shirreve of Norffolk[3] hymself, and tolde me that the Quene shall be at Norwich up on Tuysday[4] cometh sevenyght suyrly. And I desired to have knowe of hym, by cause this shuld be hir first comyng hedir, how we shuld be rulyd, as well in hir resseyvyng, as in hir abidyng here. And he seide, he wold nat ocupie hym ther wyth, but he councelid us to wryte to you to London, to knowe of hem that ben of counsell of that cite, or wyth other wurshepfull men of the same cite, that ben knowyng in that behalf, and we to be ruled ther aftir, as were acordyng for us ; for he lete me to wete that she woll desire to ben resseyved and attendid as wurshepfully as evir was Quene a forn hir. Wherefore, sir, I, be the assent of my Bretheren Aldermen, &c., prey you hertily to have this labour for this cite. And that it plese you, if it may be, that at that day ye be here in propre persone ; and I trust in God, that outher in rewardis, or ellys in thankynges, both of the Kyngs comyng, and in this, ye shall ben plesid as worthy is.

Wrete in hast at Norwich the vj. day of Juyll Anno ix° Regis E. quarti.

By your weelwyller, JOHN AUBRY, &c.

[1] Mayor of Norwich in 1469.   [2] [From Fenn, ii. 18.]
[3] Roger Ree was Sheriff of Norfolk this year.   [4] 18th July.

719

EDWARD IV. TO THE DUKE OF CLARENCE, &c.[1]

These iij. letteres undirwreten, the Kyng of his own hand wrote unto my Lords Clarence, Warrewyke, and Archbishop of York. The credence wherof in substaunce was, that every of them shulde in suech pesibil wise, as thei have be accustumed to ryde, come unto his Highness.   1469
JULY 9

R. E.   *To our Brother of Clarence.*

BRODIR, we pray you to yeve feight [*faith*] and credence to our welbeloved Sir Thomas Montgomery and Morice Berkly, in that on our behalf thei shal declare to you. And we truste ye wole dispose you accordyng to our pleser and comaundement. And ye shal be to us right welcome. At Notyngham the ix. day of Jull.

To our Cosyn Th'erl of Warr'.

COSYN, we grete you well, and pray you to yeve feight and credence to Sir Thomas Mongomery and Morice Berkley, &c. And we ne trust that ye shulde be of any suech disposicion towards us, as the rumour here renneth, conseryng the trust and affeccion we bere in yow. At Notyngham the ix. day of Jull. And, cosyn, ne thynk but ye shalbe to us welcome.

To our Cosyn Th'archbyshop of Yorke.

COSYN, we pray you that ye wul, accordyng to the promyse ye made us, to come to us as sone as ye goodely may. And that [ye] yeve credence to Sir Thomas Mongomery and Morice Berkly, in that un our behalve thei

[1] [From Fenn, ii. 40.] The dates of Edward the Fourth's privy seals show that he was at Nottingham in July 1469. He was not there in 1470, the year to which Fenn assigns these letters ; and both Clarence and Warwick were then in France. It would appear, therefore, that these letters were written at the time of Robin of Redesdale's rebellion, which the King was going northwards to suppress.

THE PASTON LETTERS

1469
JULY 9

shal sey to you ; and ye shalbe to us welcome. At Notyng-ham the ix. day of Jul.

720

MARGARET PASTON TO SIR JOHN PASTON[1]

To Sir John Paston, be this delivered in hast.

AUG. 31

I GRETE you wele, and send you Godds blyssyng and myn, letyng you wete that Sir John Hevenyngham was at Norwich this day, and spake with me at my moders, but he wuld not that it shuld be understand, for my Lord hath mad hym on of the capteynes at Caystre of the pepill that shuld kepe the wetche abaught the place, that no mann shuld socour them, if my Lord departed. I desired hym to favour them, if any man shuld come to them fro me or you, and he wuld not graunte it, but he desired me to write to you to understand if that my Lord myght be mevyd to fynde suerte to recompense you all wrongs, and ye wuld suffre hym to entre pesibilly, and the lawe after his entre wuld deme it you. Be ye avysed what answer ye wuld yeve.

Item, sith that that I spake with hym, and the same day a feythfull frende of owrs came on to me and mevyd me if that my Lord myght be entreted to suffre endifferent men to kepe the place, and take the profites for bothe parties till the right be determyned be the lawe ; and my Lord for his parte, and ye for your parte, to fynde sufficient suerte that you nowther shuld vex, lette, ner trobilled the seid endifferent men to kepe pesibiley the possession of the seid place, and to take the pro-fights on to the tyme to be determyned be the lawe, to his behowe that the lawe demeth it. And the seid persones that so endifferently kepe possession befor ther entre into the seid place, to fynde also sufficient suerte to answere the parte that the lawe demeth it to, of the profits duryng ther posses-sion, and to suffre hym pessibilly to entre, or any in his name,

[1] [From Fenn, iv. 366.] This letter was written after the Duke of Norfolk had begun to besiege Caister, which he did in the year 1469.

36

whan so ever thei be required be the parte to whom the right is demyd of all thes premyses. Send werd how ye will be demened be as good advyse as ye can gete, and make no longer delay, for thei must neds have hasty socour that be in the place, for thei be sore hurt, and have non help. And if thei have hasty help it shall be the grettest wurchip that ever ye had, and if thei be not holpen it shall be to you a gret dis-wurchep ; and loke never to have favour of your neybors and frends but if this spede wele ; therfor pretend it in your mend, and purvey therfor in hast. How so ever ye do, God kepe you, and send yow the vittory of your elmyse, and geve yow and us al grace to leve in peas. Wretyn on Sent Gyles Evyn,[1] at ix. of the belle at nyght.

Robyn came home yester evyn, and he brought me nowther writyng from you, ner good answer of this mater, which grevyth me right ill that I have sent you so many messangers, and have so febill answers ageyn.

Be your Moder.

1469
AUG. 3

721

MARGARET PASTON TO SIR JOHN PASTON[2]

I GRETE zow wel, and send zow Godds blyssyng and myn, letyng zow wete that on Thurysday last was my moder and I wer with my Lord of Norwych,[3] and desyerd hym that he woold no mor do in the mater towscheyng zowr syster, tyl that ze and my brother and other that wern executers to zowr fader mythe beyn her to geder, for they had the rule of her as weel as I ; and he sayde playnly that he had be requeryd so oftyn for to exameyn her, that he mythe not nor woold no longar delay yt, and schargyd me, in peyn of cursyng, that sche schuld not be deferred, but that she xuld a per beforn hym the

[1] St. Giles' Day is the 1st September ; St. Giles' Eve the 31st August.
[2] [From Fenn, iv. 358.] This letter has reference to the contract of marriage between Richard Calle and Margery Paston in 1469. See No. 710, preceding. The last paragraph seems to have reference to the propositions mentioned in the preceding letter. [3] Walter Lyhert.

1469

37

THE PASTON LETTERS

1469

nexte day ; and I sayd pleynly that I woold nowder bryng her nor send her ; and than he sayd that he woold send for her hym sylfe, and schargyd that she schuld be at her lyberte to cume wan he sent for her ; and he seyd be hys trowthe that he woold be as sory for her and [if] sche ded not welle, as he wold be and sche wer ryth ner of hys kyn, bothe for my moder ys sake and myn, and other of her frendds, for he woost welle that her demenyng had stekyd soor at our harts.

My moder and I in formyd hym that we kowd never onderstond be her sayyng, be no language that ever sche had to hym, that nether of hem wer bownd to other, but that they myth schese bothe. Than he seyd that he woold sey to her as wele as he kowde, before that he exameynd her ; and so that was told me be dyverse persones that he ded as welle and as pleynly as sche had be rythe ner to hym, wych wer to long to wrythe at thys tyme : her aftyr ye xalle wete, and hoo wer laberers ther in. The schanseler[1] was not so gylty her in as I wend he had ben.

On Fryday the Bysschope he sent for her be Asschefeld and other that arn ryth sory of her demenyng. And the Bysschop seyd to her ryth pleynly, and put her in remem-berawns how she was born, wat kyn and frendds that sche had, and xuld have mo yf sche wer rulyd and gydyd aftyr hem ; and yf she ded not, wat rebuke, and schame, and los yt xuld be to her, yf sche wer not gydyd be them, and cause of for-sakyng of her for any good, or helpe, or kownfort that sche xuld have of hem ; and seyd that he had hard sey, that sche loved schecheon [such one] that her frend[es] wer not plesyd with that sche xuld have, and therfor he had her be ryth weel avysyd how she ded, and seyd that he woold undyrstand the woords that sche had seyd to hym, whether that mad matri-mony or not. And sche rehersyd wat sche had seyd, and seyd, yf thoo woordds mad yt not suher, she seyd boldly that sche wold make that suerher or than she went thens, for she seyd

[1] Fenn thinks this was Dr. John Saresson, otherwise Wigenhale, who, he tells us, was Chancellor to the Bishop from 1435 to 1471, and had other Church preferment in the Diocese. But I am a little doubtful whether he lived so long, as it does not appear that he kept any other of his preferments to so late a date. We know that Dr. William Pykenham was Chancellor in 1471.

38

sche thowgthe in her conschens sche was bownd, wat so ever the wordds wern. Thes leud wordds greveth me and her grandam as myche as alle the remnawnte. And than the Bysschop and the Schawnseler bothe seyd that ther was neyther I ner no frend of hers wold reseyve [her].

And than Calle was exameynd aparte be hym sylfe, that her wordds and hys acordyd, and the tyme, and wher yt xuld a be don. And than the Bysschop seyd that he supposyd that ther xuld be fownd other thynggs ageyns hym that mythe cause the lettyng ther of ; and ther for he say he wold not be to hasty to geve sentens ther upon, and sayd that he wold geve overe day tyl the Wednsday or Thursday aftyr Mykylmes, and so yt tys delayyd. They woold an had her wyl performyd in haste, but the Bysschope seyd he woold non other wyse than he had seyd.

I was with my moder at her plase whan sche was exameynd, and wan I hard sey what her demenyng was, I schargyd my servaunts that sche xuld not be reseyved in my hows. I had zeve hir warnyng, sche mythe a be war a for, yf sche had a be grasyows ; and I sent to on or ij. mor that they xuld not reseyve her yf sche cam ; sche was browthe a geyn to my place for to a be reseyved, and Sir Jamys[1] tolde them that browthe her that I had schargyd hem alle and sche xuld not be reseyved ; and soo my Lord of Norwych hath set her at Roger Bests, to be ther tyle the day befor sayd, God knowyth fule evel ageyn hys wyle and hys wyvys, yf they durst do other wyse. I am sory that they arn a cumyrd with her, but zet I am better payed that sche isther for the whyle, that sche had ben in other place be cause of the sadnes and good dysposysion of hys sylfe and hys wyfe, for sche xal not be sou'd [*suffered ?*] ther to pleye the brethele.[2] I pray zow and requer zow that ye take yt not pensyly, for I wot wele yt gothe ryth ner zowr hart, and so doth yt to myn and to other ; but remembyr zow, and so do I, that we have lost of her but a brethele,[2] and set yt the les to hart, for and sche had be good, wherso ever sche had be, yt xuld not aben as it is, for and he wer ded at thys owyr, she

[1] Sir James Gloys.
[2] *Brethele* or *brethelyng* signified a worthless person.

146

39

1469 xuld never be at myn hart as sche was. As for the devors [*divorce*] that ze write to me of, I supose wat ze ment, but I scharge zow upon my blyssyng that ze do not, ner cause non other to do, that xuld offend God and zour conschens, for and ze do, or cause for to be do, God wul take vengawns ther upon, [and] ye xuld put zour sylfe and other in gret joparte; for wettyt wele, sche xal ful sor repent her leudnes her aftyr, and I pray God sche mute soo. I pray zow for myn hard ys hese [*heart's ease*], be ze of a good cownfort in alle thynggs; I trust God xal helpe ryth wele, and I pray God so do in alle our maters. I wuld ze toke hed yf ther weher any labor mad in the kort of Cawntrybery for the leud mater forsayd.

But yf [*i.e.* unless] the Duke[1] be purveyd for, he and hys wyse kow[n]sel xalle lefe thys cuntre; yt is told me that he seythe that he wul not spar to do that he is purposyd, for no Duke in Ynglond. God helpe at nede.

722

SIR JOHN PASTON TO MASTER WRITTILL[2]

To Mastyr Wryttyll.

[SEPT.]

MASTER WRYTTYLL, I recomande me to yow, besechyng yow hertely, as myn holl trust is in yow, that ye doo yowr devoyr to contynew trews tyll Fryday or Saturday in the mornyng, by whych tyme I hope the massanger shall come, and that ye be not dryven to take an appoyntment if ye kan undrestand by any lyklyed that itt be able to be abydyn and recystyd, and that ye fele my brotherys dysposycion therin, as my trust is in yow, prayng yow to remembre that it restythe, as God helpe me, on all my well. For as God helpe me, I hadd levyr the place wer

---

[1] The Duke of Norfolk.
[2] [From Fenn, iv. 370.] Master Writtill, to whom this and the next letter are addressed, is mentioned later as a servant of the Duke of Clarence, by whose means Sir John was endeavouring to arrange a suspension of hostilities with the Duke of Norfolk, who was now besieging Caister.

brennyd, my brother and servants savyd, than the best 1469 appoyntment that evyr ye and I comonyd of scholde be my [SEPT.] goode wyll be takyn, if this massage from the Kynge may reskwe it. And if it be so, that my Lorde be remevyd by the Kynges comandement, whyche restythe with hys honour, I may in tyme to kome do hym servyse, as schall recompence any grodge or dysplesur that he evyr had, or hathe to me or myn; and ye, if it the rather by your wysdam and polesye the moene above wryten may be hadd, schall be as sewr of the servyce of my trewe brother and servantys, and me, as ye kan devyse by my trowthe; for in goode feythe thys mater stykyth mor nyghe myn hart and me than I kan wryght on to yow, and to my brother and servaunts mor ner than as God knowyth they wot off. Wherfor, Master Wryttyll, all owre welfare restyth in yow, besechyng yow to remembre it. For thys mater is to all usse eyther makyng or marryng.

Item, asfor Arblaster or Lovell, I kan not thynke that they or any of them may be with yow. Wherfor in yow is all, and God have yow in kepyng.

Wretyn at London, the day next affor yowr departyng. I schall sende yow mor knowleche to morrow, with Godds grace.   Yowrs,   JOHN PASTON, K.

723

SIR JOHN PASTON TO MASTER WRITTILL[1]

RYGHT wershypfull syr, I recomaund me to you, thank- SEPT. 10 yng you of your grete labour whych I have nozt as yet, but I shall deserve to my power; and ferthermore lyke yow to wyte that I have thoght ryght long after you; nevyrthelesse I remember well that ye delt wythe ryght delayous peple. My Lord Archbyshop and other of my Lords, and I, dempte by cawse of your long tarryng, that by youre sad dyscrescyon all hadde ben sett thorow.

---

[1] [From Fenn, iv. 372.] See preliminary note to last letter. We have adopted a different punctuation from that of Fenn in some parts of this letter.

1469 Neverthelesse I understend by your wrytyng that my Lord SEPT. 10 of Norffolks concell thynketh that hys entent, whych ye sertefyed me by your wrytyng, sholde be more to hys wyrshep than the appoyntements and rewll made by the Lords of the Kyngs concell whych be to my seyd Lord of Norffolk ner kyne [*near kin*]; whych appoyntements sythen yourr departyng hath be largely remembryd amongs the seyd Lords here, thynkyng it in hem self so honorabyll to my Lord of Norffolk, that ther shuld non of my Lords concell well avysed mevyd to the contrary.

Jamys Hobard[1] was sent fro my [Lord] of Norffolk heder, and spake with my Lord Archbyshop,[2] and answer he had of my seyd Lord; and howe my Lord tendryd the mater yet and wyll I trowe he have told you, and yf he have not, the brynger her of schall informe you; and he broght thys same appoyntement from my Lord, that my Lord was well agryed that I shulde ocupye. For my parte, iff I shud take no other apoyntement but acordyng to your letter, it wer hard for me and for my tytell to putte my Lord in that possessyon; for ther ys thyngs in erthe [*uneath, i.e.* scarcely] to myn esse in your letter, goode for me in that appoyntement, savyng the suerty of my brothers lyffe and my servants, whych ye thynke dowtefull yf so be that thay lakke stuff, shotte, and vytayll; mervaylyng sore, and thynk it impossybell in thys shorte season, or in iiij. tyme the season heder towards, that thay shuld lakk other [*either*], with owte it soo be that my Lords men have enterd owght the place, and so had ther stuffe from hem, whych I cannot thynk. Also, sir, for [*fore*] the tyme of your comyng to my Lord of Norffolk, servaunts of [my Lords wer with][3] my moder at Norwych, mevyng to send to my brother hyr sone, to delyver the place under such a forme as youre lettere specefyeth, and so I cannot understand what regard my Lords concell takyth to my Lords letter, and to your labour in thys behalf, but that

---

[1] This most probably was James Hobart, who, in 1478, was Lent-Reader at Lincoln's Inn, and in 1487 Attorney-General.—F.
[2] George Neville, Archbishop of York.
[3] The original MS. was indistinct in these places.

they offeryd as largely afore. Ze wryteth in your letter that 1469 ye durst not passe your credens; please you to remember that SEPT. 10 seyd your credens affore the Lords was ryght large, and as large as myght well be in thys mater, both to my Lords councell of Norffolk to withdrawe the seege, with moor other mater as ye knowe; and to the Justice of the Peas and to the Shyryff and hys offycers, your awtoryte was grete inow to iche of them.

Wherfor, Mayster Wretell, I never for this, nere zet wyll, take appoyntement in thys mater, but as my Lords wyll and my Lord Archbyshop, whych, as well as I my self, have holy putte our tryst to youre dyscrete dyreccyon; and my seyd Lord sythen youre departer, zour zoyng,[1] thynkyng you alls mete a man in executyng ther comaundement as cowde be chosyn. Neverthelesse for awnswer to your at thys season, my Lord Archbyshop ys north wards towards the Kyng; how be it, it ys seyd, upon a metyng with my Lord of Clarens, my Lord shuld retourne a yen; and as zester evyn he send a servaunt of hys to me, wenyng to hys Lordship that Sir Humfray[2] and ye wer in Caster as was appoynted, and ye shuld send to hys Lordshyp answer of the gydyng ther by wrytyng, comaundyng me that yff any such wrytyngs cam from you, yf hys Lordshyp wer not past xx. myle fr[om] Lond]on,[3] to com to hys Lordshyp with the same. Understandyng for sertayn that he ys nott yet so ferr, wherfor I will in althe hast possybell ryde nygt and day till I see hys Lordshyp, and after comunicacyon had with hys Lordshyp, as sone as ys possybell that a man may go be twext, ye shall have an answer of hys dysposicyon; for hys intres is such that, as I have wryten, I shall never do therin withoute hym, as my cosyn, brynger herof, more playnly shall enforme you; for I canne thynke ryght well, that as ze wryteth to me, my broder wyll not delyver the place to non erthly person, but yf he see wrytyng fro my Lord.

It semyt be yowr wrytyng that my Lord of Norffolk

---

[1] The words 'zour zoyng' (your going) seem to be redundant.
[2] Sir Humphrey Talbot was a Captain at this siege, under the Duke of Norfolk.—F.
[3] The original MS. was indistinct in these places.

THE PASTON LETTERS

1469
SEPT. 10

conseyll intende not that my Lord Archbyshop shuld dele in thys mater, for he ys not named in your letter, wherof I mervayle; for it was movyd to you at your departyng hens, the Kyngs concell shuld have take dyreccyon in thys mater, or els my Lord Cardenall,[1] my Lord of Clarens, my Lord Archbyshop, and my Lord of Essex,[2] &c. Neverthelesse, Mayster Wryttyll, all profytht, maner, or lyflod, leyd apart, if it be so that thorow reklesnese my brother and servaunts be in such joperte as ye have wryten to me (whych shold be half impossybell in my mynd that thay shold myssuse so mech stuff in iiij. tymes the space), and that ye have evident knowlych by my seyd brother hym self therof, I woll praye yow to se hym and them in suerte of ther lyffys, what so ever shold fall of the lyfflode; how be it I wold not that my brother and servaunts shold gyff upp the place not for a m'li., yf thay myght in any wyse kepe it and save ther lyves. And therfor, at the reverens of God, sycht it ys so, that my Lord Archbyshop and my Lords all, and I, have putte our trust in you, that ye wyll do your devoyer to have the verrey knowlech of my brother hymself, and not of my Lords men, wheder he stante in such jopertye as your letter specefyeth or net, for I dowte not uppon the syzth of thys letter, and of the letter that ye had before, that my brother will put no mystrust in you, consyderyng that he knowyth that ye com from my Lords, and my Lord Archbyshop, and have my wrytyng ; and as for my Lord Archbyshop wrytyng and aunswere, such as it shalbe, ye shall have it in all the haste possybell. But I thynke veryly that my Lord eschewyth to telle you any thyng without that he myght speke with you allone, and me thynketh veryly that thay ought not to lette [*hinder*] you to speke with hym allone, consyderyng that ye have auctoryte and wrytyng from the Lords so to do. And as for the justificacyon of entryng the place, and sege layng to [the same][3] and the comaundement of the Justice of the Pease and the Sherewe to assyste my Lord in thys gydyng, I wote

1 Thomas Bourchier, Archbishop of Canterbury, and Lord Cardinal.
2 Henry Bourchier, Earl of Essex.
3 Here the original MS. was indistinct.

44

EDWARD IV

1469
SEPT. I

ye understond that the Lords knowe all that mater, and ye herd it comened, and how thay toke it in ther consayts.

Ther ys no more, Mayster Wryttell, but I commyth all thys wrytyng unto your dyscrescyon ; and as ye thynk best acordyng to such menys desyre as have entretyd you therin, and for my moyst avayle, I pray you, sir, soo doo, and I shall se un to your besynes and labour, that ye shall have cause to do for me in tyme comyng, and as the brynger herof shall tell you. And I pray God have you in Hys kepyng.

Wryten at London, the x. day of Septembr.

By your frend for ever,

JOHN PASTON, K.

724

MARGARET PASTON TO SIR JOHN PASTON[1]

I GRETE you wele, letyng you wete that your brother and his felesshep stand in grete joperte at Cayster, and lakke vetayll; and Dawbeney[2] and Berney[3] be dedde, and diverse other gretly hurt; and they fayll gunne-powder and arrowes, and the place sore brokyn with gonnes of the toder parte, so that, but thei have hasty help, thei be like to lese bothe ther lyfes and the place, to the grettest rebuke to you that ever came to any jentilman, for every man in this countre marvaylleth gretly that ye suffre them to be so longe in so gret joperte with ought help or other remedy.

The Duke hathe be more fervently set therup on, and more

SEPT. I

1 [From Fenn, iv. 382.] This and the other letters relating to the siege of Caister are all rendered certain in point of date by the documents touching its surrender on the 26th September.
2 John Dawbeney, Esq.
3 Osbert Berney, the other person here mentioned as dead, was not killed at the siege. He survived, and died without issue some years after, when he was buried in Bradeston Church in Norfolk, there being a brass plate in the chancel having the following inscription to his memory :—'*Hic jacet Osbertus filius Joh. Berney, Armig. de Redeham Dni. et de Brayston.*' He was the son of John Berney, Esq., by Catherine, daughter of Osbert Mundeford of Hockwell, Esq.—F.

45

THE PASTON LETTERS

1469
SEPT. 12

cruell, sith that Wretyll, my Lord of Claraunce man, was ther, than he was befor, and he hath sent for all his tenaunts from every place, and other, to be ther at Cayster at Thorysday next comyng, that ther is than like to be the grettest multitude of pepill that came ther yet. And thei purpose them to make a gret assaught—for thei have sent for gannes [*guns*] to Lynne and other place be the seeys syde—that, with ther gret multitude of gannes, with other shoot and ordynaunce, ther shall no man dar appere in the place. Thei shall hold them so besy with ther gret pepill, that it shall not lye in their pore within to hold it ageyn them with ought God help them, or have hasty socour from you.

Therfor, as ye wull have my blyssyng, I charge you and require you that ye se your brother be holpyn in hast. And if ye can have nonmeane, rather desire writyng fro my Lord of Clarens, if he be at London, or ell[es] of my Lord Archebusshop of York, to the Duke of Norffolk, that he wull graunte them that be in the place her lyfes and ther goodes ; and in eschewyng of insurreccions with other in convenyens that be like to growe within the shire of Norffolk, this trobelows werd [*world*], be cause of such conventicles and gaderyngs within the seid shire for cause of the seid place, thei shall suffre hym to entre up on such appoyntment, or other like takyn be the advyse of your councell ther at London, if ye thynk this be not good, till the law hath determyned otherwyse; and lete hym write a nother letter to your brother to deliver the place up on the same appoyntment. And if ye think, as I can suppose, that the Duke of Norffolk wull not aggre to this, be cause he graunted this aforn, and thei in the place wuld not accept it, than I wuld the seid massanger shuld with the seid letters bryng fro the seid Lord of Clarence, or ell[es] my Lord Archebusshop, to my Lord of Oxenford, other letters to rescue them forth with, thowghe the seid Erle of Oxenford shuld have the place duryng his lyfe for his labour. Spare not this to be don in hast, if ye wull have ther lyves, and be sett by in Norffolk, though ye shuld leys the best maner of all for the rescuse. I had lever ye last the lyffelode than ther lyfes. Ye

46

EDWARD IV

1469
SEPT.

must gete a massanger of the Lords or sume other notabill man to bryng ther letters.

Do your devoir now, and lete me send you no mor massangers for this maters ; but send me be the berer her of more certeyn comfort than ye have do be all other that I have sent be for. In any wyse, lete the letters that shall come to the Erle of Oxenford comyn with the letters that shall comyn to the Duke of Norffolk, that if he wull not aggree to the ton, that ye may have redy your rescuse that it nede no mor to send therfor. God kepe you.

Wretyn the Tuesday next befor Holy Rood Day, in hast.

Be your Moder.

725

SIR JOHN PASTON TO MARGARET PASTON[1]

M OODR, uppon Saterday last was, Dawbeney and Bernay wer on lyve and mery, and I suppose ther com no man owt of the place to yow syn that tyme that cowde have asserteynyd to yow of ther dethys. And as towchyng the fyrsenesse of the Duke or of hys peple schewyd syn that tyme that Wryttel departyd, I trowe it was concludyd that trews and abstynence of werre scholde be hadd er he departyd, whych shalle dewr tyl Monday next comyng ; and by that tyme I trow that trews shall be takyn tyll that day vij. nyght aftr, by whych tyme I hope of a goode dyreccion schall be hadde.

And wher as ye wryght to me that I scholde sewe for letteris from my Lordys of Clarans and Yorke, they be not her, and if they wrot to hym as they have don ij. tymes, I trow it wolde nat advayle ; and as for to labor thois letteris and the rescu to gedre, they ben ij. sendry thyngys, for when the rescu is redy, that the cost ther of is don. For if I be drevyn therto to rescu it er they com ther that scholde do it, it shall cost a m'l. escuys, and as meche after, whyh wey wer

SEPT. 15

1 [From Fenn, iv. 386.] This letter was clearly written in reply to the last.

47

1469
SEPT. 15

harde for me to take, whyll that I maye do it otherwise; but as to sey that they schall be rescuyd if all the lands that I have in Ingelond and frendys maye do it, they shall, and God be frendly, and that as schertly as it may goodlely and wele be brout abut. And the grettest defawt erthly is mony and som frendys and neyborys to helpe; wherfor I beseche yow to sende me comfort with what money ye coude fynde the menys to get or chevysche uppon suerte sufficient, er uppon lyflod to be inmorgage er yit solde, and what peple by lyklyed yowr frendys and myn kowde make uppon a schort warnyng, and to send me worde in all the hast as it is need-full. But, moodre, I fele by yowr wryghtyng that ye deme in me I scholde not do my devyr withowt ye wrot to me som hevye tydyngs; and, modre, if I had nede to be qwyk-ynyd with a letter in thys nede, I wer of my selfe to slawe [too slow] a felaw; but, moodre, I ensur yow that I have herde x. tymes werse tydyngs syn the assege by gan than any letter that ye wrot to me, and somtyme I have herde ryght goode tydyngs both. But thys I ensure yow that they that be within have no werse reste than I have, ner castyth mor jupperte; but whethyr I had goode tydyngys er ill, I take Gode to wittnesse that I have don my devoyr as I wolde be don for in case lyke, and schall doo tyll ther be an ende of it.

I have sent to the Kynge to Yorke, and to the Lordys, and hope to have answser from them by Wednysday at the ferthest, and after that answer shall I be rewlyd, and than send yow word, for tyll that tyme kan I take non dyreccion. And to encomfort yow, dy[s]peyre yow not for lak of vytayle ner of gonne powder, ner be natt to hevy ner to mery therfor; for and hevynesse or sorow wolde have be the remedy ther of, I knew nevyr mater in my lyfe that I kowde have ben so hevy or sory for, and with Goddys grace it schall be remedyed well inow; for by my trowhe I hadde lever lose the maner of Caister than the symplest mannys lyfe therin, if that may be hys saveacion. Wherfor I beseche yow to sende me worde wat mony and men ye thynke that I am lyke to get in that contre; for the hasty purchace of mony and men schall be the

48

getyng and rescu of it, and the sauevacion of most mennys lyfys, if we take that weye.

1469
SEPT. 15

Also thys daye I porpose to sende to Yorke to the Kyng for a thyng, whych same only maye by lyklyod be the savacion of all. Ye must remembre that the rescue of it is the last remedy of all, and how it is nat easy to get; and also ye sende me worde that I scholde nat kome hom withowt that I kome stronke. But if I had hadd on other stronge place in Norfolke to have comen to, thowe I have browt ryght fewe with me, I scholde, with Godds grace, have rescued it by thys tyme, er ellys he scholde have ben fayne to have besegyd bothe placys or yit, and the Duke had not kept Yarmoth owthe. But, mother, I beseche yow sende me som mony, for by my trowth I have but xs. I[1] wot not wher to have mor, and moreovyr I have ben x. tymes in lyke case or werse within thys x. wekys. I sent to Rychard Call for mony, but he sendyth me non.

I beseche yow to gyde the evydence that Pekok can tell yow of, and to se it saffe; for it is tolde me that Richard Call hath hadd right large langage of them. I wolde nat they com in hys fyngrys. I have no worde from yow of them, ner whether ye have yit in yowr kepyng the evydence of Est Bekham owt of hys handys, ner whethyr ye have sent to my manerys that they schold not paye hym no mor mony or not. Also that it like yow to geve credence to Robyn in other thyngs.

Wret the Fryday next after Holy Roode Day.

JOHN PASTON, K.

[1] *I.* The right-hand copy in modern spelling reads 'and.'

726

WRITTILL TO THE BESIEGERS OF CAISTER[1]

Sir John Hevyngham,[2] Th. Wyngfeld,[3] Gilbert Debenham,[4] Wil. Brandon,[5] and to everych of them severally in otheris absence.

1469
[SEPT.]

HIT is so that accordyng to such direccion as was mevid to be desird of my Lords beyng heer, as for such as heere bee they marveil gretly therof, thynkyng and remembring in themself that such offre as was made by my credence to my Lorde,[6] and to fore you reported, shuld have sownyd more to his pleasure and honour than this his desire. Nevirthelesse my Lords thenke where as they wrote and desirid joyntly that such credence as ye remembre myght be observyd and taken, and by you refusid, nowe yif they shuld assent to the desire of this direccion, hit is thought in them not so to doo; for it is so fortuned that dyvers of my Lords, from whome I brought both wrytyng and credence, be at the Kyngs high commaundement hastely departed unto his High-nesse, trustyng in God to have heeryng in brief tyme of their hasty ayen comyng, atte which tyme my Lords that heere be, and they that shal come ayen, shal comon and speke to gyder of this desire and direccion, and such answere as they geve and make shall be sent unto you than with haste possible. Ovir

[1] [From Fenn, iv. 404.] This letter is anonymous, but was evidently written by Writtill during his negotiations for a suspension of hostilities.
[2] Sir John Heveningham, Knight and Banneret, was a descendant of an ancient family situated at the town of Heveningham, in Suffolk. His son Thomas became owner of the estate at Ketteringham, in Norfolk, where this family continued for several generations.—F.
[3] Sir Thomas Wingfield was a younger son either of Sir Robert or Sir John Wingfield of Letheringham, in Suffolk.—F.
[4] Sir Gilbert Debenham, Knight, was descended of an ancient and knightly family in the county of Suffolk.—F.
[5] Sir William Brandon married Elizabeth, daughter of Sir Robert Wingfield, and was ancestor to Charles Brandon, afterwards Duke of Suffolk.—F.
[6] The Duke of Norfolk.

50

this, me thenkith for your excuse of burden and charge such as I hier will be leid unto you concernyng the grete werks that dailly be and ar at the maner of Castre, yif ye thenk that God shuld have pleasir, and also the Kyng oure sovereign Lorde, and that my seide Lords shuld thenk in you gode avise or sad, and that ye entendid to avoide the sheddyng of Cristyn blode and the destruccion of the Kyngs liege people, that at your politik labour and wisedome ye myght bryng my Lord to th'abstynence of warre, and a trieux to be had and contynued unto tyme of the retourn of my seid Lords, or els knowlege of their entent; certifeng you for trouth that ther be messengers sent unto my seid Lords with lettrez of such answere as I had of you to your desire to gyder, knowyng certeinly that ther shal be hasty relacion of ther entents in the premisis, which answers ye shall have atte ferthist by Monday cometh sevenyght. Ferthirmore lettyng you wit that I understond for certein that my Lords that be heere eschewe, for such inconveniense that myght fall, to conclude any answere by them self, consideryng that my credence was geven by all the Lords; prayng you, as shal be doon to the continuaunce of this trieux aforesaid, that I may be acerteyned, or yif at this houre ye coude yit thenk my credence resonable and honour-able to be accepted and taken, sendith me woorde in wrytyng from you by my servant, brynger of this, al delaies leid aparte. For I acertein you, as he that owe you service, I was and yit am gretly blamed for my long taryng with you, for dyvers of my Lords taried heere for me, by th'assent of al my Lords, lenger than they wold have don, to know myn answere and guydyng from you.

1469
[SEPT.]

And ovir this I certyfie you that ye cannot make my Lords heere to thenk that yif ther be inconvenient or myshief, murdre, or manslauter had or done, but and your wills and entents were to the contrarye, my Lord is notid so well disposid that, with oute your grete abettement, he neither will doo nor assent to non such thyng; prayng you therfor, as your frende, to remembre wele your self, and so to rule you, as my Lords may have in tyme to come knowlege of your more sadd disposicion than as yit I feele they thenk in you.

51

THE PASTON LETTERS

And how that my Lords note sum of you, James Hobert, beyng of my Lords counsel, can enforme you ; wherefor for Godds sake remembr you, and delyver my servant, and yif ye thenk my first credence or this advertisement shal be taken to effect, than I pray you that my servaunt, brynger hereof, may have sure condyte to speke with John Paston, and to report to hym these direccions, and upon that to delyver hym a bill certifyng the same.

727

WRITTILL TO THOMAS WINGFIELD[1]

MR. WYNGFELD, I recomande me to you. Please you to wit I have sent a lettre joyntly to you and to al my Lordes[2] counsel ; nevirtheles, for the special favor and service that I bere and owe to you, I write to you aparte, praying you to put your hasty devoir to the delyverans of my servaunt, with th'answere of the same ; and ovir that for Goddis sake remember you hou that ye stond my Lordes nygh kynnesman, and by whom my Lordes wulle gretly be steerid, that ye eschewe and avoide to be non of those that my Lordes here thenk shuld set or cause my Lord to do thynges otherwise than accordith to the pleasir of my Lordes ; for it is so that there be dyvers of my Lordes counsel stond in hevy report of my Lordes, of which I wold ye were non ; certifeing you that I know so ferre that yif ye any thyng doo in this mater to the pleasir of my Lordes, it will neither be unremembrid ne unrecompensid, not doutyng but that hereafter to have a large thonk of you for this my counsel ; praying you ferthermor to move Sir John Hevyngham, and such as ye knowe wele disposid, to assist you in this ; and that this bille be kept secrete, as my trust is in you. Wreten at London.

[1] [From Paston MSS., B.M.] This and the letter following are corrected drafts upon the same paper, and both evidently written at the same time, and by the same writer, as the last letter.
[2] The Duke of Norfolk's.

52

THE PASTON LETTERS

ventur within vij. dayes. And iff ye maye kepe it so longe, I wold be gladde, and aftr that iff ye have nott from me other wryghtyng, that than ye do ther in for yowr saffgarde and yowr felaschep only, and to yowr worschypys ; and as for the place, no force therfor. Ye knowe thys hande, therfor nedythe no mencion from whem it comythe ; and more ovyr, they that be abut yow be in obloquy of all men, and mor ovyr they have ben wretyn to by alse speciall wryghtyng as myght be, after the worlde that now is, and promyse yow that the Dukes concell wolde that they had nevyr be gon it ; and more ovyr they be chargyd in payne of ther lyvys, that thow they gate the place, they scholde not hurt on of yow. Ther is nowther ye ner none with yow, but and he knewe what is generally reportyd of hym, he or ye, and God fortewne yow wele, may thynke hym iiij. tymes better in reputacion of all folk than evyr he was. Be war whom ye make a concell to thys mater.

Also I lete yow wete that I am in moche mor comfort of yow than I maye wryght, and they that be about yow have cawse to be mor ferde than ye have ; and also bewar of spendyng of yowr stuffe of qwarellys, powdr, and stone, so that if they assaut yow er we come, that ye have stuffe to dyffende yow of over, and than of my lyfe ye get no mor, and that your felaschyp be evyr ocopyed in renewyng of your stuffe.

Wretyn the Mondaye next aftr Holy Roode Daye.

I trow, thow ye not prevy ther to, ther is taken a trews new tyl thys day vij. nygh.

54

EDWARD IV

728

WRITTILL TO JOHN PASTON[1]

MR. PASTON, it is so that sith tyme I spake with you I sent you a bill which concludith an abstinence of werre to be had unto Fryday last was, trustyng in that season that by the menes of my Lordes heere a conclusion shal be taken ; lettyng you wit that before my comyng hider certein of my Lordes were departid hens towards the Kyng northwards. And for asmich as I cannot in this season have no hasty answere of such lettrez as were sent unto them concernyng this mater, I have wretyn by the menes of my Lordes heere I have wretyn a lettre to my Lordes counsell a lettre,[2] and amonges other thynges movid them in the seid lettre to advertise my Lord for abstynence of werre til Monday come sevenyght ; and yif my Lordes and his counsell so agree, I have comaundid my servaunt, brynger hereof, to geve you knowlege of the same, avisyng you that contenuyng the seid seson to absteyne yow from werre gevyng outward in like wise ; and by that season I hope to have knowlege of my Lordes ententes.

729

SIR JOHN PASTON TO JOHN PASTON[3]

To John Paston, and to non othyr.

I RECOMAND me to yow, and promyse yow that I have
and schall labore and fynde the meane that ye schall have honor of yowr delyng as ye have hyddr towards, as all Ingelond and every man reportythe ; and moreover I am in weye for it by many dyverse weys, wherof ther schall be one exicutyd by thys day xiiij. nyght at the ferthest, and pera-

[1] [From Paston MSS., B.M.] See preliminary note to last letter.
[2] So in the MS., the redundant words being left uncancelled.
[3] [From Fenn, iv. 394.] See preliminary note to No. 724.

53

EDWARD IV

730

PASSPORT TO THE BESIEGED ON SURRENDER OF CAISTER[1]

The Duc of Norffolk.

WHERE John Paston, esquier, and other divers per-
sones have, ageyn the peas, kepte the manoir of Caster with force, ageyne the wille and entent of us the Duc of Norffolk, to oure grete displeaser ; whiche notwithstanding, at the contemplacion of the writing of the moost worshipfull and reverent Fader in God the Cardenall of England, and our moost trusty and entierly beloved Unkel the Archbisshop of Canterbury, the right noble Prince my Lord of Clarence, and other Lords of oure blood, and also at the grete labour and enstaunce of our moost dere and singler belovid wiffe, we be agreed that the seid John Paston and his seid fellaship, beyng in the seid maneur, shall depart and goo out of the seid maneur without delay, and make therof deliveraunce to suche persones as we will assigne, the seid fellaship havyng their lyves and goods, horsse, and harneys, and other goods beyng in the kepyng of the seid John Paston ; except gonnes, crossebows, and quarells, and alle other hostelments, to the seid maneur annexed and belonginge. And to have xv. dayes respyte aftir their seid departing out, to goo in to what place shall like theim, without any accions or quarell to be taken or made by us, in our name to theim, or any of theim, within our fraunchise or without, duryng the seid tyme.

Yoven under our signet at Yermouth the xxvj. day of Septembr the ix[te] yere of King Edward the iiij[th].

NORFF'. (L.S.)

[1] [From Fenn, ii. 24.]

55

THE PASTON LETTERS

731

JOHN PASTON AND THE SURRENDER OF CAISTER[1]

The Duc of Norff'.

1469
SEPT. 26

JOHN, Duke of Norffolk, Erle Marshall of Sussex, Surrey, and of Nottyngham, Marshall of Inglonde, Lorde Mowbray of Segreve, Bromfelde, and Yalle, to al our frendes, servauntes, and othir Crystyne people, gretyng. Wher John Paston, esquier, and othre diverse persones forseble hath kepte the manoir of Castre, contrary to our will and pleaser, and aftirwarde by his lowly labour and gret meanese to us maade, the seide John Paston hathe maade deliveraunce of the seide manoir to such persons as we have assignede, and he and his seide felowship by our lycence to departe out of the same. Wherefore we pray, wil, and charge you and everysche of you, that ye ne vexce, trouble, manase, ne greve the forseid persones, nor eny of them, for the kepyng of the seide manere contrary to the Kynge our Sovereynge Lordes lawyes, for we have takyne them in our safe garde. Yevin undir our signet and signmanuell the xxvj[t] day of Septembre, the ix[th] yere of Kynge Edward iiij[t].

NORFF'. (LS)

732

JOHN PASTON TO SIR JOHN PASTON[2]

Caystr yelded.—J. P.

[SEPT.]

RYGHT werchepfull sir, I recomand me on to yow. And as for the serteynte of the delyverance of Caster, John Chapman can tell yow how that we wer enforsyd therto, as wel as mysylf. As for John Chapman and his iij.

[1] [From a MS. in the College of Arms.] The original of this document, signed and sealed by the Duke of Norfolk, is inserted in the MS. volume called Brooke's *Aspilogia*, vol. i. p. 35.
[2] [From Fenn, iv. 410.]

EDWARD IV

felaws, I have purveyd that they be payid ache of them xls., with the mony that they had of yow and Dawbeney; and that is inow for the seson that they have don yow servys. I pray yow geve them ther thank, for by my trowthe they have as well deservyd it as eny men that ever bare lyve; but as for mony, ye ned not to geve hem with owt ye wyll, for they be plesyd with ther wagys. Wryttyll promysyd me to send yow the serteynte of the apoyntment. We wer sor[1] lak of vetayl, gonepowdyr, menys herts, lak of suerte of rescwe, drevyn therto to take apoyntement.

1469
[SEPT.]

If ye wyll that I come to yow, send me woord, and I shall pervey me for to tery with yow a ij. or iij. dayis. By my trowthe, the rewardyng of syche folkys as hathe ben with me dwryng the sege hathe putt me in gret danger for the monye. God preserve yow, and I pray yow be of good cher tyll I spek with yow, and I trust to God to ese your hert in some thynggys.

J. PASTON.

733

MARGARET PASTON TO SIR JOHN PASTON[2]

To Sir John Paston, in hast. A matre.

I GRETE zow wele, and send zow Godds blyssyng and myn, letyng zow wete that me thynke be the letter that ze sent me Robeyn, that ze thynke that I xuld wryte to zow fabyls and ymagynacyons; but I do not soo. I have wrytyn as yt have be enformed me, and wulle do. It was told me that bothe Daubeney and Berney wer dedee, but for serten Daubeney is dede, God asoyle hys sowle; wher of I am rythe sery, and yt had plesyd God that yt mythe abe other wysse.

SEPT. 23-30.

Remembyr zow, ze have had ij. gret lossys withyne thys towylemonth, of hym and of Sir Thomas.[3] God wysyth

[1] *sor.* So the word stands in Fenn, and 'sore' in the copy in modern spelling; but I suspect a misreading of 'for.'
[2] [From Fenn, iv. 396.] This is written, as will be seen, in reply to No. 725.
[3] Sir Thomas Howes.

THE PASTON LETTERS

1469
SEPT. 23-30

[*visiteth*] zow as yt plesythe Hym in sundery wyses; He woole ze xuld know Hym, and serve Hym better than ze have do be for thys tyme, and than He wull send zow the mor grace to do wele in ale other thynggys. And for Godds love, remembyr yt rythe welle, and take yt pacyentely, and thanke God of Hys vysitacyon; and yf ony thyng have be a mysse ony other wyse than yt howte to have ben befor thys, owther in pryde or in laves expences, or in eny other thyng that have offendyd God, amend yt, and pray Hym of Hys grace and helpe, and entende welle to God, and to zour neybors; and thow zour poor heraftyr be to aquyte hem of her maleys, zet be mersyfulle to hem, and God xale send zow the mor grace to have your entente in other thynggys.

I remembyr thys clawsys, be cause of the last letter that ze sent me. I have sent to Hary Halman of Sporylle to helpe to gete as ze desyerd me, and he canne not gette passyd v. or viij. at the most, and zet yt wule not be but yf [*unless*] he cume that ze trust upon that xuld cume, for they long a parte to hym. And Ryschard Sharman hathe asayed on hys parte, and he cane not gette passyd v.; for thoo that long to us, thei long also to our adversarys, and they have be desyerd be them, and they woold nowte do for hem, and ther for they thynke to have magery of the toder parte.

As for the jantylman that ye desyerd me to speke with, I spake with hys wyfe, and sche told me he was not in thys cuntre, ner nowte woost wan he xuld be her; and as for the toder man, he hath bowthe [*bought*] hym a livery in Bromeholme Pryery, and have geve upe the woord [*world*], &c.

Item, as for mony, I kowde getee but xli. upon pledges, and that is spent for zour maters her, for payeng of zour men that wern at Caster, and other thyngys, and I woot not wer to gette non, nowther for suerte ner for pleggs; and as for myn owyn lyvelod, I am so sympely payed ther of that I fer me I xale be fayn to borow for my sylfe, or ell[es] to breke up howsold or bothe.

As for the zeddyng [*yielding*] of the place at Caster, I trowe Wretyll hathe told of the pawntements [*appointments*] how ytts delyvered. I woold that [it] had be so her [*ere*] thys tyme,

EDWARD IV

and zan [*then*] ther xuld not a ben do so mykyle herte as ther is in dyverse weyes; for many of our welewyllers arn putte to loosse for our saks, and I fer me that [it] xale be long her yt be recumpensyd ageyn, and that xale cause other to do the lesse for vus her aftyr.

1469
SEPT. 23-30

I woold ze xuld [send] zour brother woord, and sum other that ze truste, to see to zour owyn lyelod to sette yt in a rule, and to gader ther of that may be had in haste, and also of Sir John Fastolf lyoeld that may be gadyrd in pesybyle wyse. For as for Ryschard Calle, he wulle no mor gadyr yt but yf ze comaund hym, and he woold fayn make hys . . acowntte, and have zour good maystyr schepe, as ytts told me, and delyvere the evydens of Bekkeham, and alle other thynggys that longyth to zow, that he trustythe that ze wylle be hys good mayster heraftyr. And he sethe he wylle not take non newe master tyle ze refuse hys servyse.

Remembyr that zowr lyvelod may be set in soche a rule that ye may knowe how ytts, and wat is owyn to zow; for be my feythe I have holpyn as mysche as I may and mor, savyng my sylfe, and therfor take hede er yt be weers.

Thys letter was begune on Fryday was vij. nythe, and enddyd thys day nexte afftyr Mychylmes Day. God kepe zow, and yeve zow grace to do as wele as I woold ze dede; and I scharge zow be war that ze sette no lond to mortgage, for if eny avyse zow ther to, they arn not zowr frendds. Be war be tymes myn avyse, &c. I trow zowr brother wyll geve zow tydyngs in haste.

734

NOTE[1]

Inventory of household goods (including guns) left at Caister by Sir John Paston at the entry of my Lord of Norfolk.

[1] [MS. Phillipps, 9735, No. 201.]

THE PASTON LETTERS

735

JOHN PASTON TO SIR JOHN PASTON[1]

To my master, Sir John Paston, in Flett-Stret.

1469
OCT. 5

RYGHT worchepfull sir, I recomand on to you, praying yow that ye wyll in all hast send me word how that ye wyll that Sir John Style, John Pampyng, W. Mylsent, Nycolas Mondonet, T. Tomson shall be rwlyd, and whedyr that they shall sek hem newe servysys or not; and Mathewe Bedford also, for he hathe be with me this seson, and is fro my modyr. And if so be that ye wyll have thes to abyde with yow, or eny of them, send word whyche that they be; for betwyx thys and Halowmas my modyr is agreyd that they shall have met and drynk of hyr for syche a serteyn wekly as my modyr and yu and I can acord when we met. Notwithstandyng, if ye kowd get Barney or eny of thes seyd folkys, whyche that ye wyll not kepe, eny servyse in the mene seson, it wer more worchep for yow then to put them from yow lyek masterles hondys [*hounds*]; for by my trowthe they ar as good menys bodys as eny leve, and specyally Sir John Stylle and John Pampyng. And I wer of power to kepe them and all thes befor rehersyd, by trowthe they shold never depert fro me whyll I leveyd.

If ye send me word that I shall come to yow to London for to comon with yow of eny mater, so God help me, I have neythyr mony to com up with, nor for to tery with yow when I am ther but if [*unless*] ye send me some; for by my trowthe thes werkys have causyd me to ley owt for yow bettyr then x. or xij*li.*, besyd that money that I had of my modyr, whyche is abowt on viij*li.* God amend defowts; but this I warant yow, with out that it be Mathew, whyche ye sent woord by John Thressher that ye wold have to awayt on yow, ther is no man

[1] [From Fenn, iv. 412.] This is a letter desiring instructions about the garrison of Caister after its surrender.

60

EDWARD IV

that was hyryd for the tyme of thys sege that wyll axe yow a penny.

1469
OCT. 5

Also I pray yow send downe acomandment to Stutvylle, or to some awdyter, to take acomptys of Dawbneys byllys; for hys executors ar sore callyd upon for to admynyster by the Byshop, or ellys he seythe that he wyle seqwester. Dawbeney set in hys dett that ye owt hym xij*li.* and xs. Whedyr it be so or nowt, hys byllys of hys owne hand wyll not lye, for he mad hys byllys clere or then the sege com abowt us.

As for the evydence of Bekham, my modyr sent to Calle for hem; and he sent hyr woord that he wold make hys acompts, and delyver the evydence and all to gedyr. My modyr hathe sent to hym ayen for hem thys day. If she sped, they shall be sent to yow in all hast, or ellys, and ye send for me, I shall bryng hem with me. Send my modyr and me word who ye wyll that have the rwyll of your lyvelod her in thys contre, and in what forme that it shall be delt with. I wyll not make me mastyrfast with my Lord of Norff., nor with non othyr, tyle I spek with yow; and ye thynk it be to be don, get me a mastyr.

Dell corteysly with the Qwen and that felawshep, and with Mastras Anne Hawte for Wappys,[1] tyll I spek with zow. Wretyn on Seynt Feythys Evyn.

J. PASTON.

By Sent George, I and my felawshep stand in fer of my Lord of Norff. men, for we be thret sore, not withstandyng the save gardys[2] that my felawshep have. As for me, I have non, nor non of your howsold men, nor non wyll have; it wer shame to take it.

[1] This expression 'for Wappys' I do not understand.—F. Perhaps Wappys may be a proper name.
[2] *Save gardys.* This is printed 'same gardys' in Fenn, but is evidently a misreading; in the right-hand copy the word is 'safeguards.'

61

THE PASTON LETTERS

736

SIR JOHN PASTON TO MARGARET PASTON[1]

To Mestresse Margret Paston, be thys delyveryd.

1469
[OCT.]

RYGHT worchypfull Moodre, I comand me to yow, and beseche yow of yowr blyssyng and Gods. Thanke yow for yowr tendrenesse and helpe bothe to me, my brother, and servants.[2]

.   .   .   .   .   .

The Kynge is comyn to London, and ther came with hym, and roode ageyn hym, the Duke of Glowcestr, the Duke of Suffolke, the Erle of Aroundell, the Erle of Northumbreland, the Erle of Essex, the Lordes Harry and John of Bokyngham, the Lord Dakres, the Lorde Chambreleyn, the Lorde Montjoye, and many other Knyghtys and Sqwyers, the Meyr of London, xxij. Aldremen, in skarlett, and of the Crafftys men of the town to the nombre of CC., all in blewe. The Kynge come thorow Chepe, thowe it wer owt of hys weye, be cawse he wold not be seyn, and he was accompanyed in all peple with m^t horsse, som harneysyd and som nat. My Lorde Archebysshop[3] com with hym from Yorke, and is at the Moor,[4] and my Lorde of Oxenfford roode to have mett the Kyng, and he is with my Lorde Archebysshop at the Moor, and come nat to town with the Kynge; some sey that they wer yesterday iij. myle to the Kyng wards from the Moor, and that the Kyng sent them a massangr that they scholde com when that he sent for them. I wot not what to suppose

[1] [From Fenn, i. 292.] The allusion in an unprinted passage in this letter to the approaching marriage of Richard Calle with Margery Paston proves it to be of the year 1469. In that year it appears by the dates of the privy seals that Edward IV. remained during the whole of September in Yorkshire, having been detained by Warwick at Middleham as a prisoner during the month of August; but he was in London as early as the 13th October.
[2] Here, according to Fenn, follow passages touching 'an account of monies, debts, &c., a dispute with his uncle William, and a desire to defer his sister Margery's marriage with Richard Calle till Christmas.'
[3] George Nevill, Archbishop of York.
[4] See p. 20, Note 3.

62

EDWARD IV

therin; the Kyng hymselffe hathe good langage of the Lordes of Clarance, of Warwyk, and of my Lords of York [and] of Oxenford, seyng they be hys best frendys; but hys howselde men have other langage, so that what schall hastely falle I cannot seye.

1469
[OCT.]

My Lorde of Norffolke schall be her thys nyght. I schall sende yow mor when I knowe mor.

Item, iff Ebysham come not home with myn oncle W., that than ye sende me the ij. Frenshe bookys that he scholde have wretyn, that be may wryght them her,

JOHN PASTON, Kt.

737

ABSTRACT[1]

[JOHN PASTON] TO [SIR JOHN PASTON]

Has reckoned with Maryot. Accounts of Bekham. Has not spoken with W. Bakton, but will before returning to Norwich. Means to visit Bekham on his way thither. Sends copy of the condition wherein ye be bound to John Maryot. As for Sir T. Mongomere's man, etc.

1469

Richard Calle says he has delivered to me all writings he had of you except an endenture for letting Saxthorpe, which is but a jape. All but a rental of Snaylwell are but accounts, etc. He has delivered me four or five court rolls of Sir J. Fastolff's lands, of his own hand. He has done reasonably well about showing me the arrears of your lifelode. 'As for his abiding, it is in Blakborow nunnery, a little fro Lynn, and our unhappy sister's also. And as for his service, there shall have no man have it before you, and ye will. I hear not speak of none other service, of no lord's that he shall be in.' Has not yet spoken with Daubney's executors, but will on his way homewards. Sends copy of the inventory[2] he [John Paston] made on leaving Caister. Means to be at Sporle to-morrow or Thursday, to see what may be made of the wood, and who will give most for it. . . . . (*MS. mutilated at the bottom.*)

[This letter is in the handwriting of John Paston, but the signature is lost. It is quite certain that it was written in 1469 after the surrender of Caister. Allusion is also made to the unpleasant subject of the engagement of Richard Calle and Margery Paston, who seem to have retired to Blackborough nunnery prior to their marriage.]

[1] [From Paston MSS., B.M.]   [2] *See* No. 734.

63

738

ABSTRACT[1]

1469
NOV. 6

Indenture between Sir John Paston, of the one part, and Roger Townsende, gent., of the other part, containing covenants for the sale of the manor of Est Beckham, and of all Paston's other lands in Est Bekham, West Bekham, Bodham, Sherryngham, Beeston near the Sea, Runeton, Shipden, Felbrigg, Aylmerton, Sustede, and Gresham, which the said Sir John had of the gift of John Mariet the elder of Est Bekham, for 100 marks, of which he has received already £54, leaving £12, 13s. 4d. to be paid by the said Roger at the Feast of St. Luke next coming. Dated 6th Nov. 9 Edw. IV.

Seal, with inscription, ' Si Dieu vuet.'

739

ABSTRACT[2]

1469, 25 Nov. 9 Edw. IV. 'In the priory of Saynt Marye Overy in Suthwarke.' Acknowledgment (in English) by Will. Yelverton, Knt., Just. of K. B., of the receipt from Bishop Waynflete of £87, in full satisfaction of all claims on Sir J. Fastolf by Jaquet, Duchess of Bedford; solemnly promising also that he will not hereafter receive any sums, great or small, on account of Fastolf's goods, debts, or possessions, without the assent of the Bishop, that he will at all times be ready to seal such grants, &c., as the Bishop may require to be sealed, and that he will not himself make or seal any grant, etc., without the Bishop's will and agreement.

---

[1] [Add. Charter, 14,526, B.M.]
[2] The following abstract is taken from Mr. Macray's Report on the MSS. in Magdalen College, Oxford.

740

JOHN PASTON TO SIR JOHN PASTON[1]

To Master Syr John Paston, Knyght.

RYGHT worchepfull syr, I recomand me to you, &c. It is so that thys day ther cam a good felaw to me, whyche may not be dyscoveryd, and let me wet that my Lord of Norff. consayll hathe this Crystmas gotyn the two wydows, whows husbands wer slayn at the sege of Caster, and have hem bowndyn in a gret some that they shall swe a peel ayenst me and syche as wer ther with me within the plase, and they be bownd also that they shall relese no man within the apell namyd tyll syche tyme as my Lord of Norff. wyll lycence them.

1469
DEC.

Item, the cawse is thys, as it is told me by dyvers, that ye meke no more swte to my Lord for yourself than ye do, and therfor they do the wors to me for your sake.

Item, as for my comyng up to London, so God help me, and I may chese, I com not ther, for *argent me fawlt*, without apell or an inkyr [*inquiry?*] of som specyall mater of your cawse it. Item, I pray yow remembyr Caleys, for I am put out of wagys in thys contre.

Item, I pray yow send me some tydyngs how the world gothe *ad confortandum stomacum.*

Item, ye must purvey anewe atorny in thys contre. As for me, for our maters and clamore is to gret, and our purse and wytte to slendyr, but I wyle rubbe on as long as I maye bothe with myn owne, and other menys that wyle do for me tyll better pese be.

Wretyn thys Saturdaye, at Norwcyche.   J. P.

---

[1] [From Fenn, iv. 416.] It appears by the contents that this letter was written about Christmas after the siege of Caister. An appeal of murder was a process sued by the nearest relative of a person killed. It was quite independent of any prosecution for murder by the Crown, and no royal pardon was of any avail against it ; but the appeal had to be brought within a year and a day of the fact.

741

JOHN PASTON TO SIR JOHN PASTON[1]

1470
MARCH 1

RYGHT worchefull Syr, I recomand me to yow aftyr the old maner, sertyfyng yow that I have comonyd with my modyr for your coming hom, but I can not fynd by hyr that she wyll depert with eny sylvyr for your costis, for she and hyr cwrate[2] alegge mor poverte then ever wasse. Item, as for your clok at Harcortis it wyll be nye Estern er it be redy, for ther is stolyn owt of hys chaumbyr some of the ger that belongyd therto, and that must have leyser to be mad ayen. Item, the caryer forgat your byll behynd hym, but it was delyveryd all to gedyr, but it shall be browght yow and the wyndas with the teles by the next caryer, as myn orangys shall com to me I tryst. Dame Elyzabet Calthorp is a fayir lady and longyth for orangis, thow she be not with chyld. Item, I pray yow that ye wyll make aqwetance on to the person of Mawtby[3] and to John Seyne as executors to John Dawbeney, for they wyll take non admynystracyon of hys goodis tyll they be aqwetansyd of youre and my modyr. Ye maye do it well j nough, so God help me ; for I wot well ye owt hym mony, and he nat yow, if so be that he wer trewe when he dyid, and I wot well we fond hym nevyr on trew in hys lyve ; but hys frendys and othyr of the contre putt grett defawt in me that ther is no thyng don for hym, seying that he myght do no more for us but lose hys lyfe in your servyse and myn ; and now he is half forgotyn among us. Wherfor I pray yow let thys be sped.

Item, as for Doctor Pykenham, J. Pampyng can tell yow he is not in Norwyche. When he comyth I shall spek with hym and send yow hys answer. Item, as for myn oncyll Wylliam, I have grant to have a byll of hym what every thyng lythe for ; but all thyng is not yet in rest ayen that was

---

[1] [Add. MS. 34,889, f. 192.] This letter may be dated 1470, by comparing the postscript with the postscript of No. 742, which seems to have been written in answer to it. John Daubeney was killed at the siege of Caister in 1469. See Nos. 725, 733.
[2] James Gloys.
[3] Robert Cutler or Cotteler. See next page.

remevyd for the chyrchyng of my Lady Anne. As sonne as I have the byll I shall send it yow and hys answer, whyche he wyll fyrst have plegyd owght, and also whethyr he purposyth to do as he seyd by my graundamys lond.

1470
MARCH 1

Item, Gefrey Spyrlyng hathe ofte spokyn to me to send to yow for to undyrstand how ye will deell with hym for hys place in Norwyche, for he seythe that he had lever have your good mastyrship ther in then eny othyr manys good lordshep ; for and ye wyll be hys good mastyr he wyll swe no ferther, or ellys he must.

Item, a for (*sic*) myn old reknyng, I shall make it up in hast and send it yow for your bettyr remembrance, for as me thynkyth by your wrytyng ye have nye forgetyn it ; but I am rype j now in it for myn owne dyscharge. Item, I pray yow, take in to your a ward a short murry jornade[1] of myn whyche Jacobyn, Wykis woman, hathe lest that she be flyttyng and that it be exchetyd. Item, I pray yow send me swyr tydyngis of the world in hast.

As for the bysheop of Wynchestyr, W. Wyrceteyr told my modyr that he had takyn charge x. dayis or then Pampyng cam hom ; but he wenyth that the bysshop wyll be a yenst yow, in so myche that [he[2]] avysyd my modyr to consell yow that ye sholl labor to my Lord Cardynall[3] that the seyd byshop shold not be amytted to take admynystracyon. No mor, &c.

Wretyn at Norwyche the fyrst daye off Marche.   J. P.

I pray, get us a wyfe somwher, for *Melius est nubere in Domino quam urere.* (ca° primo.)[4]

Noveritis universi per presentes me J. P. mylitem remisisse, &c. Roberto Cotteler personæ ecclesiæ de Mawtby in comitatu Norfolk et Johanni Seyne de Rollysby in eodem comitatu, executores testamenti et ultimæ voluntatis Johannis Dawbeney armygeri, nuper defuncti, omnimodas acciones, tam reales, &c. quos versus eundem Robertum sive Johannem Seyne habui, habeo, &c., racione alicujus debyti dicti Johannis Dawbeney,

---

[1] Halliwell gives 'jornet' as 'a kind of cloak' ; 'murrey' was a dark red colour.
[2] Omitted in MS.
[3] Cardinal Bourchier.
[4] The reference is as inaccurate as the quotation. The text referred to is 1 Cor. vii. 9 : 'Melius est enim nubere quam uri.'

THE PASTON LETTERS

1470
MARCH I

jam defuncti, mychi dicto J. Paston debite (*sic*) a principio mundi usque in diem, &c. In cujus, &c. Datum, &c.

As for the yer of the Kyng, let it be set in, but as for the daye and the monyth let it be owt, for the day must be aftyr probate of the wyll and the admynystracyon takyng. I pray you, let thys be sped in all hast possybyll ; and as for your obligacyon and syche ger as belongyth to yow, I shalbe swyr of it er they have the aqwetance.

Item, as for owyr afrayis her, J. Pampyng can tell yow ; but and they get me, ye loose a brodyr, *quod juratum est*.

It is good to do by the comandment of your mastyr whyll I am so well boryn owte ; thys my lord of Norffolk galantis send me woord dayly *ad confortandum stomacum*. Ye must spek with your mastyr and comon some remedye hastyly, or be God I enswyr yow, whyll owyr Dwk is thus cherysheid with the kyng, ye nor I shall not have a man unbetyn or slayn in thys contre, nor our sylfe nowthyr, as well ye as I, *quod juratum est* onys ayen. The Dwke, the Dwches and ther consell ar wrothe that ye make no meanys to them your sylfe.

Item, I send yow Townysendis endentwre by John Pampyng.

742

SIR JOHN PASTON TO JOHN PASTON[1]

*To John Paston, Esquier, beyng at Norwyche,
be thys letter delyveryd.*

MARCH

I COMANDE me to yow, letyng yow wete, &c.[2]

Item, as for Mestresse Kateryn Dudle, I have many tymes recomandyd yow to hyr, and she is noo thynge dis-

[1] [From Fenn, ii. 28.] From the reference to the King's being about to go into Lincolnshire, and what is said of the Earl of Warwick, it may be clearly inferred that this letter was written on the outbreak of the insurrection of Sir Robert Welles in the beginning of March 1470.

[2] Here (according to Fenn) follows an account of bills and receipts, etc.

68

1470
MARCH

pleasyd with itt. She rekkythe not howe many gentylmen love hyr ; she is full of love. I have betyn the mater for yow, your onknowleche, as I told hyr. She answerythe me, that sche woll noon thys ij. yer, and I beleve hyr ; for I thynke sche hathe the lyffe that sche can holde hyr content with ; I trowe she woll be a sore laboryng woman this ij. yer for mede of hyr sowle.

And Mestresse Gryseacresse is sure to Selenger, with my Lady of Exestre, a fowle losse.

Item, I praye yow speke with Harcort off the Abbeye, for a lytell clokke, whyche I sent hym by James Gressham to amend, and that ye woll get it off hym, and it be redy, and sende it me ; and as for mony for hys labor, he hathe another cloke off myne, whyche Sir Thomas Lyndes, God have hys sowle ! gave me ; he may kepe that tyll I paye hym. Thys klok is my Lordys Archebysshopis, but late not hym wete off it, and that itt [be] easely caryed hyddre by yowr advyse.

Also as for orenges, I schall sende yow a serteyn by the next caryer. And as for tydynge the berer hereoff schall insforme yow ; ye most geve credence to hym.

As for my goode spede, I hope well. I am offryd yit to have Mestresse Anne Haulte, and I schall have help i nowe, as some say.[1]

.   .   .   .

Item, it is soo that I am halffe in purpose to com home with in a monythe her afftr, or abowt Med Lente, or beffor Esterne, ondyr yowr coreccon, iff so be that ye deme that [my] modre wolde helpe me to my costys, x. mark or ther abowt ; I praye feele hyr dysposicion and sende me worde.

Item, I cannot tell yow what woll falle off the worlde, for the Kyng verrely is dysposyd to goo in to Lyncoln schyr, and men wot not what wyll falle ther off, ner ther afftre ; they wene my Lorde off Norffolke shall[2] brynke x.ml. men.

Item, ther is comen a newe litell Torke, whyche is a wele

[1] Here (according to Fenn) follows an account of some disputes between Sir William Yelverton and Sir John Paston, his uncle William, etc., of no consequence.

[2] *shall.* This word is not in Fenn's left-hand or literal transcript, but is given as part of the text in the right-hand copy.

69

THE PASTON LETTERS

1470
MARCH

vysagyd felawe, off the age off xl. yere ; and he is lower than Manuell by a hanffull, and lower then my lytell Tom by the schorderys, and mor lytell above hys pappe ; and he hathe, as he seyde to the Kynge hymselffe, iij. or iiij. sonys, chyldre, iche one off hem as hyghe and asse lykly as the Kynge hymselffe ; and he is leggyd ryght i now, and it is reportyd that hys pyntell is as long as hys legge.

Item, I praye yow schewe, or rede to my moodre suche thynges as ye thynke is for her to know, afftre yowr dyscression ; and to late hyr undrestond off the article off the trete between Syr Wylliam Yelverton and me.

Item, my Lorde of Warwyk, as it is supposyd, schall goo with the Kynge in to Lyncolne schyre ; some men seye that hys goyng shall doo goode, and som seye that it dothe harme.

I praye yow evyr have an eyghe to Caster, to knowe the rewle ther, and sende me worde, and whyther my wyse Lorde and my Lady be yit as sottyt [? *besotted*] uppon it as they were ; and whether my seyd Lorde resortythe thyddre as offte as he dyd or nott ; and off the dysposycion off the Contre.

J. P., K.

743

ANONYMOUS TO JOHN PASTON[1]

To my Cosyn, J. Paston.

MARCH 27

THE King camme to Grantham, and ther taried Thoresday all day ; and ther was headed Sir Thomas Dalalaunde, and on John Neille, a greate capteyn ; and upon the Monday next after that at Dancastr, and ther was headed Sir Robert Wellys, and a nothr great capteyn ; and than the King hadde warde that the Duk of Clarence and the Erle of Warwick was att Esterfeld [*Chesterfield*], xx. mile from Dancastre.

[1] [From Fenn, ii. 36.] This letter gives an account of the suppression of the rebellion in Lincolnshire in 1470.

70

1470
MARCH 27

And upon the Tewesday att ix. of the bell, the King toke the feld, and mustered his people ; and itt was seid that wer never seyn in Inglond so many goodly men, and so well arreiyed in a feld. And my Lord was whorsshupfully accompanyed, no lord ther so well ; wherfor the King gaffe my Lord a greate thanke.

And than the Duk of Clarence and the Erle of Warwik harde that the King was comyng to them warde, in contynent they departed and wente to Manchestre in Lancasshire, hopyng to have hadde helpe and socour of the Lord Stanley, butt in conclucion ther hadde litill favor, as itt was enformed the King, and so men sayn they wente westward, and sommen demen to London. And whan the King harde they wer departed and gon, he went to York, and came theder the Thoresday next aftr, and ther camme in to hym all the gentilmen of the shire ; and uppon our Lady Day [he] made Percy Erle of Northumberland, and he that was Erle affore Markeys Muntakew. And [so][1] the King is purposed to come southwarde, God send hym god spede.

Writen the xxvij. day of March.

FOR TROWYTH.

[1] This word is not in the text of Fenn's literal transcript, but it is given in brackets in the transcript in modern spelling.

744

ABSTRACT[2]

WILLIAM WORCESTER TO ———

1470

Letter in English, on paper (signed W. W., but unaddressed), desiring some one to propose to 'my Lord' [the Bishop of Winchester ?] the obtaining of a letter from Sir John Paston to the tenants of Titchwell that he will not claim any rents from them, and another from 'my Lord,' to the same effect, on behalf of Sir William Yelverton ; and the sending a warrant to expend 4 or 6 marks upon making up the sea banks before the Titchwell pastures, because at

[2] [From MS. Titchwell, 120, in Magdalen College, Oxford.] From internal evidence it would seem that this letter must have been written shortly before that which follows it. The abstracts of these two letters have been kindly supplied to me by Mr. Macray.

71

THE PASTON LETTERS

1470   Spring the sea breaks in upon them. Desires to know whether Sir W. Yelverton's advice shall be taken upon business matters. 'Frere' Geffrey Westvale is going to be created Doctor in Theology at Cambridge, at the Feast of St. John, who twenty years past, when at Yarmouth convent, belonged to 'my Maister Fastolf'; and Sir Thomas Howys, a month before his decease, promised to help him on Mr. Fastolf's order. He would have come now to 'my Lord' to ask his alms had not the writer letted him. Desires to be informed whether 'my Lord' will help him. 'Maister Briston yn lykewyse Maister Spicer, and Maister Stevyns, trustyn appon me and dyvers others to speke to my Lord for a relyeve,' and Thomas Fastolf and Milcent Fastolf, and many others, 'that make me noyed and werye.'

745

ABSTRACT[1]

MAY 17   Letter in English from W. Wyrcestre to Bishop Wayneflete.—Has been at Tychewell to endeavour to let the manor and farm, but none of the farmers there will take it without guarantees from Sir John Paston and Sir William Yelverton in writing against any distraint. . . . . the younger, who owes £9, will come to the Bishop about the letting. The writer represents his own poor condition. Has been at charges ten years in London, and in riding on the infinite process of 'my Maister Fastolf's testament yn the court of audience.' Is now obliged to retire from London to Cambridge in order to live cheaply. Had been promised 25 marks on Paston's behalf, 20 marks for ever of Fastolf's lands, 5 marks of fee for his life, and £15 worth of land for ever. Has not had clearly 8 marks.

746

JOHN PASTON TO SIR JOHN PASTON[2]

To Syr John Paston, Knyght, or to Thomas Stompys,
to delyuer to the seyd Syr John.

JUNE 22   RYGHT worchepfull syr, and my specyall good brodyr, I recomand me to yow; and for as myche as I can not send yow good tydyngs, ye shall have syche as I knowe.

[1] [From MS. Titchwell, 199, in Magdalen College, Oxford.]
[2] [From Fenn, iv. 428.] As this letter refers to an incident in the siege of Caister as having taken place 'in August last,' there can be no doubt about the date.

It is so that on Wednysday last past ye and I, Pampyng, and Edmund Broom were endyttyd of felonye at the Sessyons her in Norwyche for shotyng of a gonne at Caster in August last past, whyche goone slowghe two men, I, Pampyng and Broom as pryncypall, and ye as accessary; notwithstandyng Townysend[1] and Lomner held an oppynyon that the verdytt is voyd, for ther wer ij. of th'enqwest that wold not agre to th'endyttment. And in as myche as they ij. wer agreyd in othyr maters, and not in that, and that they two wer not dyschargyd fro the remnant at syche tym as that verdyth of yowyr endytment was govyn, ther oppynyon is that all the vordyght is voyde, as well of all othyr maters as of yowyr. Whedyr ther opynyon be good or not, I can not determyne, nor them sylf neythyr.

I pray yow let not thys mater be slept, for I can thynk that my Lord of Norff. consaylle wyll cawse the wedows to tak an apell, and to remeve it up in to the Kyngs Benche at the begynyng of this term. Townysend hathe promysyd me that he shall be at London on Twysday next comyng, and then ye may comon with hym in that mater, and take hys avyse.

Item, Townysend and Lomner thynk that and ye have good consayll, ye may justyfye the kepyng of the plase for the pesybyll possessyon that ye have had in it mor then iij. yeer; but in conclusyon, all thys is doo for nowght ellys but for to enforse yow to take a dyreccyon with my Lord of Norff.

I undyrstood by R. Sothewell—for he and I comonyd in thys mater ryght largely betwyx hem and me—in so myche he tellyth me that and I be at London in the wek next aftyr Seynt Petyr, at whych tyme he shall be ther hym sylf, he seyth that my Lady hathe promysyd me hyr good ladyshep, and sent me woord by hym, in as myche as he spak for me to hyr, that she wold remembyr myn old servyse, and for get the gret dysplesyr in syche wyse that I shall undyrstand that the swtte that I have mad to my Lord hyr husbond and hyr shall torne to your avantage and myn, more then we weene as yett or shall undyrstand tyll syche tyme as I have spokyn with hyr good grace. And upon thys promesse I

[1] Probably Roger Townsend, afterwards Justice of the Common Pleas.

THE PASTON LETTERS

1470   JUNE 22   have promysyd Sothewell to meet with hym at London that same weeke next aftyr Seynt Petyr; wherfor I wold passyngly fayne that ye wer in London at that season, or nye abowght London, so that I myght undyrstand at your plase wher that I myght spek with yow or then I spek with my Lady.

I propose to go to Canterbery[1] on foot thys next week, with Godds grace, and so to com to London fro thense. I pray yow se that I be safe for Parker and Henry Coletts mater.

Sothewell[2] told me thys, that if so be that ye wyll your sylf, ye shall have bothe goode lordshep and ladyshep, and mony or lond, or both, and all your maters set cler. What that he menyth, I can not sey. As for all othyr maters in thys contre, I shall do as well as I may for fawt of monye tyll I spek with yow. I have many collars on, as I shall tell yow when I come.

No more, but God preserve yow and yours. Wretyn at Norwyche, Fryday next aftyr Corpus Christi Daye.

            J. P.

I ded as myche as I kowd to have lettyd th'endyttment, but it wold not be, as I shall enform you; and Townsend knowyth the same.

747

JOHN PASTON TO SIR JOHN PASTON[3]

To Syr John Paston, Knyght, or to Thomas Stomppys,
to delyuer to the seyd Syr John.

JUNE 25   AS I sent yow woord by a lettyr that John Wymondham browght to London, J. Pampyng is endyghtyd of felony, and Edmund Broon as princypallys, and ye as axcessary, for schotyng of agonne in Awgust last past, whyche

[1] On pilgrimage to the shrine of Saint Thomas Becket, I suppose.—F.
[2] Richard Southwell, Esq. of Wood-Rising. He acquired this estate by marrying Amy, daughter and co-heir of Sir Edmund Wichingham, Knight.—F.
[3] [From Fenn, iv. 434.] This letter, it will be seen, refers in the beginning to the same matter as the preceding.

gonne kyllyd ij. men; and I trowe that my Lord of Norff. consayll wyll make on of the wedows, or bothe, to swe an apell up on the same endyghtment thys terme. Wherfor I pray yow se well to thys mater, that when it is sertyfyid in to the Kyngys Benche, Broom and Pampyng may have warnyng that they may purvey for hem self, if ther com eny *capyas* owght for hem. Townysend can tell yow all the mater.

Also ye must in eny wyse be ware, for my grauntdam[1] and myn Lady Anne[2] and myn Oncyll Wyllam shall be at London within thes viij. or x. dayis, and I wot well it is for nowght ellys but to make myn Oncyll Wyllam swyr of hyr lond, notwithstandyng she hath reryd affyn of it be for Goodreed,[3] the Justyse, in my grauntfadyrs dayis, and my modyr tellyth me that ye have the copye of the same fyne; I wold avyse yow to have it redy, what so evyr betyd. I trow they wyll be the more besy abowght the same mater, because they thynk that ye dar not com in London, nor at Westmenstyr to lett [stop] them; but if so be that ye have not the copy of the same fynne, look that ye spare for no cost to do serche for itt, for it wyll stand yow on hand, I feell by the werkyng.

Thys day sevennyght I trust to God to be forward to Caunterbery at the ferthest, and upon Sater·· ··y com sevennygh I tryst to God to be in London; wherfor I pray yow leve woord at yowr plase in Fleet Strett wher I shall fynd yow, for I purpose not to be seyn in London tyll I have spook with yow.

I pray yow remembyr thes maters, for all is doon to make yow to drawe to an ende with thes Lordys that have your lond fro yow. No more, but I pray God send yow your herttys desyir in thees maters and in all othyr.

Wretyn at Norwyche, the Monday next aftyr Seynt John Baptyst.   J. P.

[1] Agnes Paston, widow of William Paston, the Judge.
[2] Anne, daughter of Edmund Beaufort, Duke of Somerset, married William Paston, the uncle of Sir John Paston.
[3] William Goodrede was created a Serjeant-at-Law in 1425. In 1431 he was appointed King's Serjeant, and in 1434 became a Justice of the King's Bench.—F.

748

ABSTRACT[1]

1470
JULY 3   Indenture between Sir John Paston and Edmund Shaa, goldsmith, London, concerning 20 dishes and a saucer of silver pledged to the latter, 3rd July 10 Edw. IV.

749

ABSTRACT[2]

JULY 8   Indenture, dated London, 8th July 10 Edw. IV., whereby Sir John Paston places in pawn to Stephen Kelke, goldsmith, of London, 16 pottingers, weighing 22 lb. 10½ oz. Troy weight, for £40, till Whitsuntide following.

750

ABSTRACTS[3]

FASTOLF'S LANDS

JULY 14   '11. A triparted indenture betweene William Bishop of Winton and John Paston, Knight, and others, touching the intent of two feoffmentes of the Bishop of Wynton, the one of the mannors of Drayton and Tolthorp, in the county of Norfolk and the city of Norwich, which were somtymes Sir John Falstofs; the other of the mannors of Wynterton, cald Bregmiles (?), of Reppys in Bastwyke, the third part of the mannor of Rowneham, londes and tenementes cald Cutts in Haringby, and lands cald Buley in Stokesby, to Guy Fairfax, John Paston, Squier, et aliis. July 14, Edw. IV. 10.'

'17. Relaxatio Johannis Paston, Georgii Arch. Cant. et aliorum Willielmo Wayneflet totius juris de et in omnibus maneriis, terris, &c. quæ fuerunt Johannis Falstolf in comit' Norf., exceptis manerio de Castre et Spensers in Haringby, ac

---

[1] [From Paston MSS.]
[2] [From Add. Charter 17,249, B.M.]
[3] The following entries are taken from the old index of deeds and writings relating to Norfolk and Suffolk, preserved in the tower of Magdalen College, Oxford.

terris vocat' Vaux, Redham, et Bosoms, et maner' de Hayleydon, Drayton, et Tolthorp. Julii 14, Edw. IV. 10.'   1470 JULY 14

'28. An indenture contayning mutuall releases of the Bishop of Wynton to John Paston, Knight, et c[a]. July 14, Edw. IV. 10.'

'29 and 61. An indenture containing the agreement betweene Wylliam Wainflet, Bishop of Wynton, and Sir John Paston, concerning Sir John Fastolfes landes and goods. July 14, Edw. IV. 10.'

This last document, of which there is another copy or draft, numbered 36 in the Index, is more fully described, as follows, by Mr. Macray, in the Fourth Report of the Historical MSS. Commission :—

1470, 14 July, 10 Edw. IV. Indenture tripartite (very long, in English) between Bishop Wayneflete and Sir John Paston, Knight, containing an agreement for the termination of disputes between the executors of the will of Sir John Fastolf, whereby the property of the latter has been much wasted ; dividing the manors between the Bishop and Paston, and providing for the foundation of seven priests and seven poor scholars in Magdalene College ; Paston to deliver up all deeds and muniments to the Priory of St. Mary Overy, in Southwark, to be put in a chest, locked with two locks and two keys, of which the Bishop to have one and Paston the other, and the Bishop to bring thither also all his deeds ; one part of this indenture to remain with each of the parties, and the third with the Prior of St. Mary Overy.

751

PAMPYNG TO SIR JOHN PASTON[1]

*To my most reverent and worshipfull master, Sir
John Paston, Knyght.*

RIGHT worshipfull sir and my good master, I recomaund   JULY 15 me unto yow in my moost lowly wise. And please yow to wete I have with the mony ye sent me by Judy rewardid my felashyp as ye comaundid, wretyn in a bille closid herin ; and as for William Milsent I lete hym wete hough he undirstood he was disposed to goo hoom to his fadere, wherof ye were pleasid and wold he shuld do so. He

---

[1] [From Paston MSS., B.M.] Reference is made in this letter to the appeal which the two widows were to sue against Sir John Paston. See Nos. 746, 747.

1470
JULY 15   said he intendid not to be with his fadir, ner it was not in his power so to do ; nevirthelesse he is home to his fadir and ther abidith, but what he purposith to do I wote not. Davy is at home and takyth heed to his lond. Homeworth is content and gooth to his labour. As for Stompis, I have be with the Abbot of Sen Benetts for hym as ye comaundid. And he recomaundith hym to yow, and said to me he was right glad that ye wold send to hym for any servaunt ye had, saying that if he coud do any thyng for yow, and for any servaunt of yours, he wold do it feithfully. And also he said he wold not fayle yow whill he levid in that he coud and myght do, trustyng heraftir to have your help and favour in that he shall have a do. And he told me and Stompis bothe, whanne so evir he come he shuld be welcome, and that he wold do as welle to hym as to fewe servauntes he had for yowr sake, and that he wold kepe hym for yow. As for my self my mastres saith she woll geve me mete and drynk for a season ; nevirthelesse I am warnyd to be ware, for it is told me that ther is processe out upon the appele ayens me and other ; wherfore I beseche yow that that mater may be take heed to as ye may, that we myght have knowlech of any processe ther be, that we may be ware, for I thynk verely, and I or any other come in ther hands this world, we shuld not escape without shame at the leest.

Item, as for the remnaunt of the mony biside this bille, ye owe to the parson of Sent Edmondes Caster for iiij. combe malt, and ij. combe whete, xs. whiche I promysid hym to pay ; and Rob. Newton lymebrenner for lyme, xiijs. iiijd., calling upon me for it ; and Robert Bery for shoyng, xs. ; and if it please yow that I make payment herof there shall remayne in my handes xxiijs. iiijd. And what ye woll I do herin, I beseche yow to send me word. Judy hath be with Thom Fastolff, he can telle yow answer in that mater. As for the rewle at Caster, they selle and make mony of such stuffe as they fond there, and kepe other rewle that the contre is full sory and irk of, and of my lordes men resortyng to hem, and riden about the contry onknowen, and by berynges on hand[1] take large

---

[1] See vol. ii. p. 110, Note 1.

bribys. I pray God be your spede and send yow some good   1470 meane for your wele and ease to them that owe yow servise.   JULY 15 Wretyn at Norwich the Monday next aftir Relik Sonday,
Your pore servaunt,

PAMPYNG.

752

MARGARET PASTON TO SIR JOHN PASTON[1]

I GRETE yow well and send yow Goddes blissyng and   JULY 15 myne, letyng yow wete that your fermours have brought me a gret bille of reparacion, the which I send yow, with lxs. in mony. I wold have had the residue of the mony of them, and they said it was your agrement that this reparacion shuld be do and alowed now at this payment, and so I coud get no more mony of them. And they say that the parson[2] was prevy to the reparacion. If ye were thus agreed and woll have the reparacion examined ye may send word ; but I wold ye shuld purvey for your self as hastely as ye may, and come home and take heed to your owne and to myn therto, otherwise thanne ye have do bifore this, bothe for my profite and for yours, or ellis I shall purvey for my self otherwise in hast, so that I trust shall be more ease and avayle for me and non ease nor profite to yow in tyme to come. I have litell help nor comfort of non of yow yet, God geve me grase to have heraftir. I wold ye shuld assay whedir it be more profitable for yow to serve me thanne for to serve such masters as ye have servid afore this, and that ye fynde mooste profitable theraftir do in tyme to come. Ye have assayed the werld resonabilly, ye shall knowe your self the bettir heraftir. I pray God we may be in quyete and in rest with oure own from hens forth. My power is nat so good as I wold it were for your sake and other ; and if it were, we shuld not longe be in

---

[1] [From Paston MSS., B.M.] This letter, although subscribed 'By your mother,' is neither signed nor addressed. It is, however, undoubtedly from Margaret Paston to her son Sir John. It is written in Pampyng's hand, and seems to be of the same year as his own letter immediately preceding, which is dated on the same day.
[2] Sir Thomas Howes.

1470
LY 15

daungere. God brynge us oute of it; who have yow in His
kepynge. Wretyn with onhertes ease the Monday next aftir
Relike Sonday. By your Modir.

1470
AUG. 5.

have answer off every thynge. Other thynges Bacheler Walter,
berer heroff, schall informe yow

Wretyn at London, the Sondaye nexte beffor Seynt
Lawrence Daye.[1]

Also my brother Edmonde is not yet remembryd. He
hathe not to lyff with, thynk on hym, &c.

JOHN PASTON, KT.

753

SIR JOHN PASTON TO JOHN PASTON[1]

. . . . . *Paston, &c.*

UG. 5

BROTHER, I comand me to yow, &c. . . .[2] Also
telle John Pampyng that the mayde at the Bulle at
Cludeys at Westminster sent me on a tyme by hym to
the Moor a rynge of goolde to a tookne, whyche I hadde not
off hym. Wherffor I wolle he scholde sende it hyedre, ffor
sche most have itt ageyn, or ellys *vs.*, ffor it was not hyrrys.
Item, I praye yow be redye; the mater qwykennythe bothe
ffor yowe and yowres as well as ffor us and howrys.

As ffor tydynges, my Lorde Erchebysshop[3] is at the Moor,
but ther is belesfte with hym dyverse off the Kynges servantes,
and as I understond he hathe lysence to tarry ther tyll he be
sente ffor. Ther be many ffolkes uppe in the northe, soo that
Percy[4] is not able to recyst them; and soo the Kynge hathe
sente ffor hys ffeeodmen to koom to hym, for he woll goo to
putt them downe. And soom seye that the Kynge sholde
come ageyn to London, and that in haste, and as it is sayde
Cortenayes be londyd in Devenschyr, and ther rewle.

Item, that the Lordes Clarance and Warwyk woll assaye
to londe in Inglonde evyrye daye, as ffolkes ffear.

I praye yow late not John Mylsent be longe ffrom me, with
as moche as can be gaderyd: and also that ye wryght to me
off all thynges that I have wretyn to yow ffor, so that I may

---

[1] [From Fenn, ii. 46.] This letter, as it will be seen from the contents, was
written at the period just before the restoration of Henry VI.
[2] Here follows an order about searching for some writings, etc.—F.
[3] This must mean George Neville, Archbishop of York, and brother to the Earl
of Warwick, who seems to have been suspected by the King, and left at the Moor as
a kind of state prisoner.—F.
[4] Henry Percy, who was restored to the Earldom of Northumberland this year on
its surrender by John Nevill, Lord Montague. *See* No. 743.

80

754

ABSTRACT[2]

AUG. 7

Indenture, dated London, 7th Aug., 10 Edw. IV., whereby Sir John Paston
puts in pawn to Ric. Rawlyn of London, grocer, 2 chargers and 4 potengers,
weighing 11 lb. 1¾ oz silver, for £20, till Whitsunday following.

755

ABSTRACT[3]

1470, 10 Aug., 10 Edw. IV., at Eshher. Undertaking in English by John
Paston, Esq., son of John Paston, Esq., who was one of the feoffees and executors
of Sir John Fastolf, that whereas Bishop Waynflete, also one of the feoffees, and
now sole executor, has taken upon him to perform the will of the said Sir John,
so far forth as it may be performed (it being in most substance not yet performed,
and his property wasted and devoured), out of his manors and lands in Essex,
Surrey, Norfolk, Suffolk, and the city of Norwich, he (the said John Paston) will
do true and faithful service to the said Bishop, and will be aiding and assisting to
him and Magdalen College, in order that the lands may be let to their greatest
profit, he being rewarded by the Bishop, to show his very good will to the due
performing of Fastolf's will; and that before the Feast of All Saints next he
will deliver up to the said Bishop all charters, deeds, evidences, rentals, accounts,
etc., pertaining to any of the said manors, excepting such as concern solely the
manor of Castre, which by covenant of the said Bishop with Sir John Paston,
Knight, brother of the said John Paston, Squire, must remain with the same
Sir John.

---

[1] St. Laurence's day is the 10th of August.
[2] [From Add. Charter 17,250, B.M.]
[3] The following abstract, like some others preceding, is taken from Mr. Macray's
Report to the Historical MSS. Commission on the Records of Magdalen College,
Oxford.

VOL. V.—F

81

756

ABSTRACTS[1]

PAINTER'S WORK

1470

1. Account of payments to Robert Spery, servant of Vyol, and others, for
working at the Frerys[2] in June and July; also for varnish, lead, earthen pans,
yellow ochre, oil, bristles to make brushes, etc., for painter's work.

Endorsed: 'Vialles byll comprisid in the iij. rolles of stuff and werkmanship
to A. P.[3] place and the Freris, which, as Clargynet understondith, is paid to
Viall.'

'Memorandum: j. copy of this bill remayneth amonges the billes of werkmanship at the White Freres and Baretts place, and a noder among the billes of
plate and Vialles plegis.'

2. 'Bill indented,' 15th Aug. 10 Edw. IV., between William Paston, Esq.,
and Thomas Vyall of Norwich, painter, relative to the pledging of certain coral
beads and plate to the former, for £5.

3. Account of sums owing to one Vyall for certain persons 'at the Freris,'
during August, September, and October. Total, 32s. 10d.

Endorsed: 'Viall's reckoning written in the roll of the Freris werke not
paid, and must be allowed of the £5 that was lent to Viall not yet content
again.

'Memorandum: one copy of this bill remaineth amongs the bills of work-
manship at the White Freris and Baretts place, and another bill amongs the
bills of plate and pledges.'

757

FASTOLF'S COLLEGE[4]

G. 27

'4. John Paston, Squier, bindes himself to doe true and faithfull service to
the Bishop of Winton, and to be ayding to his college and other his officers and
tenants, for the landes of Sir John Falstolf, and to deliver to him all deedes,
evidences, etc., except such as concerne the manor of Castre. Aug. 27,
Edw. IV. 10.'

---

[1] [From Paston MSS., B.M.]
[2] Apparently the White Friars at Norwich. [3] Agnes Paston's?
[4] This entry is from the same old index of deeds in Magdalen College, Oxford,
referred to in previous Nos.

82

758

EDWARD IV. TO WILLIAM SWAN[1]

To oure welbelovid William Swan, Gentilman.

R. E. BY THE KING.

1470
SEPT. 7

TRUSTY and welbeloved, we grete you well. And for
soo muche as we be credibly acertayned that our
auncient ennemyes of Fraunce and our outward
rebells and traitors be drawe to gadre in acorde, and entende hastily to lande in our countre of Kent, or in the parties
therof ner adjonyng, with grete might and power of Frenshemen, utterly to destroie us and our true subgietts, and to
subverte the comon wele of the same our royalme: We
straitly charge and commaunde you, upon the feyth and
liegeaunce that ye bare unto us, that ye arredie you with
alle the felaship ye can make, and as sone as ye may undrestonde that thay lande in our said countie or nerbye, that you
draw thider, as we have comaunded othere our subgietts to
doo, and put you in uttremost devoir with thaim to resiste the
malice of our said ennemyes and traitours; and if thai and ye be
not of power soo to doo, that thanne ye drawe you to our citie
of London, by which tyme we trust to be there in our owne
personne or nerby; and if we be not that, that thanne ye do
farther all ye shal bee commaunded by our Counsail there,
upon the payne above said.

Yeven undre oure signet at oure citie of York, the vij. day
of Septembr.

---

[1] [From Fenn, iv. 438.] This letter does not properly belong to the Paston
correspondence. It was copied by Fenn from an original in the library of Brigg
Price Fountaine, Esq. of Narford, in Norfolk, nephew and heir of the celebrated
antiquary, Sir Andrew Fountaine. The MS. was contained in a volume of State
Papers, some of them originals, and some copies, of various dates, which had belonged
to Sir Edward Coke.

The date of the document is undoubtedly in September 1470, when Edward was
at York, anticipating the invasion of Clarence and the Earl of Warwick, aided by the
King of France.

83

THE PASTON LETTERS

Henry VI. Restored

759

JOHN PASTON TO MARGARET PASTON[1]

*To my ryght worchipfull Modyr, Margaret Paston,
be thys delyuered.*

1470
OCT. 12

AFTYR humbyll and most dew recommendacyon, as lowly as I can, I beseche yow of yowr blyssyng. Plesyt yow to wet that, blyssyd be God, my brodyr and I be in good hele; and I tryst that we shall do ryght well in all owyr maters hastyly; ffor my Lady of Norff.[2] hathe promyssyd to be rewlyd by my Lord of Oxynforthe[3] in all syche maters as belonge to my brodyr and to me; and as for my Lord of Oxynforthe, he is bettyr Lord to me, by my trowthe, than I can wyshe hym in many maters; for he sente to my Lady of Norff. by John Bernard only for my mater, and for non othyr cause, my onwetyng [*i.e.* without my knowledge], or wythout eny preyer of me, for when he sente to hyr I was at London, and he at Colchestyr, and that is a lyeklyod he rememberthe me.

The Dwk and the Dwchess swe to hym as humbylly as evyr

[1] [From Fenn, ii. 50.] The contents of this letter clearly refer to the state of matters on the restoration of Henry VI.
[2] Elizabeth, daughter of John Talbot, first Earl of Shrewsbury, was the wife of John Mowbray, fifth Duke of Norfolk.
[3] John de Vere, a staunch Lancastrian.

84

THE PASTON LETTERS

760

THE DUKE OF SUFFOLK'S MEN[1]

*To the Baillies, Constables, and Chamberleyns of our
Burgh of Eye, and to everch of them.*

THE DUKE OF SUFF.

1470
OCT. 22

FOR asmuche as Edmond Lee and John Barker, which were waged for your town to awaite upon us in the Kings service to Lincolne Feld, and from thens to Excestre and ayen, and for that season, as we be enformed, thei ar not yet fully contented and paied of their wages; wherfore upon the sighte herof we woll and charge that ye, with oute any lenger delay, paie them their hooll duties acording the covenants that ye made with them, and ye faille not herof as ye entende our pleaser.

Wreten at Wyngefeld, the xxij.th day of Octobr.

SUFFOLK.

761

MARGARET PASTON TO [JOHN PASTON][2]

OCT. 28

I GRETE you wele and send you Goddis blyssyng and myn, and I sende you be the berere herof all the sylver vessell that your graundam[3] makyth so mych of, which she seid I had of myn husband, and myn husband shuld have had it of his fader. And wher as she seid that I shuld have had a garneys, I had ner see never more than I send you, that

[1] [From Fenn, iv. 448.] The battle here referred to as 'Lincoln Field' is what is commonly called the battle of Stamford, in which the insurrection of Sir Robert Welles in Lincolnshire was completely defeated in March 1470. Just before the date of this document, Edward IV. had left the kingdom, and Henry VI. had been restored; but perhaps Suffolk was not aware of the situation, or did not recognise it.
[2] [Add. MS. 34,889, f. 206.] This letter was written by Margaret Paston to one of her two sons, Sir John or John, at a time when they were both together. That was the case in October 1470, as appears by a letter of the younger brother, written on the 12th (No. 759), to the postscript of which this seems to be an answer.
[3] Agnes Paston, the judge's widow.

86

HENRY VI RESTORED

1470
OCT. 1

I dyd to them; in so myche that my Lord of Oxynforth shall have the rwyll of them and thers, by ther owne desyirs and gret meanys.

As for the ofyces that ye wrot to my brodyr for and to me, they be for no poore men; but I tryst we shall sped of othyr ofyseys metly for us, for my Mastyr the Erle of Oxynforthe bydeth me axe and have. I trow my brodyr Syr John shall have the Constabyllshep of Norwyche Castyll, with xxli. of ffee; all the Lordys be agreyd to it.

Tydyngs, the Erle of Wyrcestyr[1] is lyek to dye this day, or to morow at the ferthest. John Pylkyngton, Mr. W. att Clyff, and Fowler ar takyn, and in the Castyll of Pomfrett, and ar lyek to dye hastyly, with owte they be dead. Sir T. Mongomere and Joudone be takyn; what shall falle of hem I can not sey.

The Qwen[2] that was, and the Dwchess of Bedford,[3] be in seyntuary at Westmestyr; the Bysheop of Ely[4] with othyr Bysheopys ar in Seynt Martyns. When I here more, I shall send yow more. I prey God send yow all your desyrs. Wretyn at London on Seynt Edwards Evyn.

Your sone and humbyll servant, J. P.

Modyr, I beseche yow that Brome may be spoken to, to gadyr up my syllvyr at Gwton in all hast possybyll, for I have no mony. Also that it lyek yow that John Mylsent may be spoken to, to kep well my grey horse, and he be alyve, and that he spare no met on hym, and that he have konnyng lechys to look to hym. As for my comyng hom, I knowe no serteynte, for I terry tyll my Lady of Norff. com to go thorow with the maters, and she shall not be here tyll Sonday.

[1] John Tiptoft, Lord Treasurer and Chief-Constable of England. He was beheaded on a charge of cruelty, 18th October 1470.
[2] Elizabeth Woodville, Queen of Edward IV.
[3] Jaquetta of Luxemburg, Duchess-Dowager of Bedford, widow of Sir Richard Woodville, the mother of Edward's queen.
[4] William Gray.

85

HENRY VI RESTORED

1470
OCT. 28

is to say, ij. plateris, vj. dysshes and vj. sawceris. The ij. playteris weyn xliij. unces di., and the vj. dysshes weyn lxxiiij. unces di. and the sawcers weyn xvij. unces j. quarter. And I marvayl! that ye sent me not word what an unce of sylver is werth at London; for it had be lesse joparte to have sold it here and have sent you the money than the plate. I myght have sold it her for iijs. an unce, sum xxli. iiijs. iijd. Be ware how that ye spend it, but in acqutyng you ageyn such as ye be in daunger to, or abought the good speed of your materis; for, but if ye take odere heed to your expensis, ye shall do your self and your frendis gret diswurchep and enpoveryssh so them that non of us shall help other, to owr elmys [*enemies'*] grete comfort. It is understand ryght now in this countre be such as cleyme to be frendly to you in what grete daunger and nede ye stande in, bothe to diverse of your frendis and to your elmyse. And also it is noysed that I have departed so largely with you that I may nowhere help yow, my self nor none of my frendis; which is no wurchep, and causeth me to set the lesse be us; and at this tyme it compellith me to breke up howshold and to sogeorn; which I am right loth to have to do if I myght otherwyse have chosyn; for it caused gret clamour in this town[1] that I shall do so; and it shuld not have neded if I had restreyned whan I myght. Therfore for Goddis sake take hede here to, and be ware from hens forth; for I have delivered and sent you bothyn my parte the dedis and yowris, and not restreyned nowhere for my self nor the dede. Where fore I thynk we spede and fare all the wers; for it is a fowle slaunder that he was so wurcheful beried and his qwethword not performed, and so litill do for hym sithen. And now though I wold do for hym, I have right not [*naught*] beside my lyffelode that I may make any chevysans with, with ought grete slaunder; and my lyffelode encreasith evill, for I am fayn to takyn Mautby in myn owyn hand, and to set up husbandry ther; and how it shall profite me God knowyth. The fermour owyth me lxxxli. and more. Whan I shall have it I wete never. Therfore be never the bolder in your expenses for any help ye trust to have of me. For I will fro

[1] Norwich.

87

1470
CT. 28 hens forth bryng my self ought of such daunger as I stand in for your sakes, and do for the dede and for them that I have my goodis of; for till I do so, I know for certeyn that I shall fayll grace and displeas God, How [*who*] have you in His kepyng. Wretyn on Sent Symondis day and Judes in hast.— Be your Moder.

Item, I send zow ij. sherte clothys, iche of iij. zardis of the fynest that is in thys towne. I xuld a dohem mad here[1] but that xuld a be to long here [*ere*] ze xuld a had hem. Zour Awnte[2] or sum other good woman wule do her almes up on zow for the makyng of them. I thank zow for the gowne that ye gave me Halowmesse day I hope [I[3]] xole be wur-shuped ther with. At reverence of God, be ware and take hed to soche thynggis as is wretyn with ynne thys letter. Telle your brother that the mony is not zet cownyd that I xuld send hym for thersarsenet (*sic*) and damaske that I spake to hym foor. As for the damaske that may be forebore tylle the nexte terme, but as for the sarsenet I woold have yt and yt mythe be, for I goo in my rentis. Late zour brother[4] see thys letter. As fore your syster[5] I can send zow no good tydyngges of her, God make her a good wooman.

762

SIR JOHN PASTON TO JOHN PASTON[6]

To John Paston, Esquyere, in haste.

OV. 15 BROTHER, I comand me to yow, praying yow that thys be yow guydyng, if other folkys wy[ll] agree to the same, that Mr. Roos, olde Knevett, ye, and the wor-shypfullest that wyll do for owr sake, as Arblaster, John

[1] 'I xuld a dohem mad here' = I should have got them made here.
[2] Elizabeth, widow of Robert Poynings.   [3] Omitted in MS.
[4] Sir John Paston, if this letter be to the younger brother.
[5] Margery Paston, now probably married to Richard Calle.
[6] [From Fenn, iv. 450.] From what is said in this letter about the Earl of Oxford, it is impossible that it can have been written at any other time than during the brief restoration of Henry VI., which only lasted from October 1470 till April following.

88

Gyneye, Wodhows, and al other gentelmen that at the daye 1470 wyll be in Norwyche, that ye all holl as on bodye come to NOV. 15 geder, that my Lorde of Oxenforde maye ondrestande that som strenkethethe restyth ther by, whyche if it be well handely[d] and prove in the handely[ng], I trow Heydonnes parte woll be but an easy comparyson. Nevertheless ye than most ye be war of on [*one*] payn, and that is thys: Heydon wyll of crafte sende amonge yow per case vj. or mor with harneyse for to sclandre yowr felawschep, with seyng that they be ryotous peple, and natt of substance. Requer the gentel-men above wretyn that if any men be in Norwyche of the contre that ber any suche harneyse, to do them leve it or any glysteryng byll.

The Meyr and siteseynes of Nowyche wher wonte to have asertayne[1] in harneyse of men of the town to the nombr of ij. or iij. or v.c, whyche if they now do in lyke case, those wole owe better wyll to Mr. Roos and yow than to other folkys; and if it be so that the thowt nat to have non suche at thys tyme, I thynke the Meyr woll do it at the request of Mr. Roos and yow, if lak of tyme cawse it not.

Item, be well war of Clopton, for he hathe avysed my Lorde to be all to gydre rewled by Heydon, in so moche he hathe reportyd that all thyng and all materys of my Lordes, and in all the contre, scholde guydyd by Heydon. If Clopton or Hygham or Lowes John be besy, prese in to my Lorde byfor them, for the be no Suff.[2] materys, and tell the raylyng; prayng them not to cawse my Lorde to owe hys favor for the pleser to som folkys ther present. For if my Lorde favoryd or theye owther, by lykelyed my Lorde and they myght lose vj. tyme as many frendes as he scholde wynn by ther meanes. Also if ye cowde fynde the meanes, Mr. R. and ye, to cawse [the] Meyr in my Lordes ere to telle hym, thow he scholde bynde my Lorde to concell, that the love of the contre and syte restyth on owr syde, and that other folkys be not belovyd, ner nevyr wer, thys wolde do

[1] *A certain*, i.e. a number.
[2] I retain this word in the abbreviated form in which it is printed in Fenn's literal transcript; the copy in modern spelling reads *sufficient*.

89

1470
OV. 15 nonn harme, if it be soo that that all thynge go olyver currant (?); with mor to remembre that ther is owt of that contre that be nat at Norw. besyde me, that be ryght worshyp-full, and as worshypfull as few be lengyng to Norff., that woll and schall do my Lorde servyse the rather for my sake and Master Rossys, and the rather if my Lorde semyth nat moche thynge to Heydon guydyng.

Also, the godely menes wherby ye best can entrete my cosyn Sir W. Calthorpe at the seyde day, wse them to cawe hym, if itt wyll be, to come, ye in hys companye, and he in yow in cheff at yow cheff schew, and Mr. Roos and he in company, latyng my seyde cosyn wete that I tolde hym ones that I scholde meve hym of a thyng I trostyn scholde be encressyng bothe to hys honor and well.

I sende yow a lettyr, com to Norwyche by lyklyed to yow on Monday last past. It come some what the lattre, for I wende have dyed nat longe by foer it. Also I receyved on from yow by Mr. Blomvyle yister evyn. Tell my cosyn W. Yelverton that he may not appyr of a whylle in no wyse. I trow my cosyn hys fadr schall sende hym worde of the same. Do that ye can secretly that my Lorde be nat hevy Lorde on to hym. It is undrestande that itt is doon by the craffte of Heydon. He gate hym in to that offyce to have to be ageyn me, and nowe he sethe that he hathe don all that he can ageyn me, and now may doo no mor; nowe he wolde remeve hym. The daye is comen that he fastyd the evyn for, as an holye yonge monke fastyd mor than all the covent, aftr that for hys holynesse and fastyng hopyd to be abbott, whyche afterwarde was abbott; than lefte he hys abstynens, seyng, 'The daye was come that he fast the evyn for.'

Brother, I pray yow recomand me to my Lord of Oxford gode Lordshyp. And wher as I told my Lord that I shuld have awaytyd uppon hys Lordsyp in Norff., I wold that I myght soo have don lever then a hundred *li.*; but in gode-feth thos maters that I told my Lord trewed shold lette me war not fynyshed tyl yesterday. Wherfor yf that cause, and also syn Halowmasse every other day myst not hold uppe

90

myn heed, nor yet may, in semech that sythen the seyd day, 1470 in Westminster Halle and in other place, I have goon with a NOV. 15 staffe as a goste, as men sayd, more lyke that I rose owte of the erth then owte of a fayr laydys bedd; and yet am in lyke case, savyng I am in gode hope to amende. Wherfor I be-shyche hys Lordshyp to pardon me, and at a nother tyme I shall make dobell amends; for by my trouth a man cowyd not have hyred me for v. mark with so gode will to have ryden in to Norff. as to have at thys season ther to have awaytyd in hys Lordshyp, and also I wold have ben glad for my Lord shold have knowyn what servys that I myght have don hys Lordshyp in that contray.

Item, your geer ys send to you, as Thomas Stampes sayth, savyng Mylsents geer and the shafeson,[1] whych I cannot entrete Thomas Stampes to goo therfor thys iij. or iiij. days, wherfor I knokkyd hym on the crowne, &c.

Item, loke that ye take hyde that the letter wer not broken or that it com to your hands, &c. Wryten at London, on Thursday next after Seynt Erkenwolds Day, &c.

JOHN PASTON, K.

763

ABSTRACT[2]

[1470] 6 Dec., on paper. Notice in English from the Duke of Norfolk DEC. 6 to Philippe Cosard, William Dux, and other of his servants and tenants in the counties of Norfolk and Suffolk, to depart out of the manor of Castre, and all other manors and lands which he bought of Sir W. Yelverton and other executors of Sir J. Fastolf, as soon as they can conveniently remove all his stuff and their own which is therein, he having consented, at the desire of the Archbishop of Canterbury, the Chancellor of England, and the Bishop of Winchester, to give up the said manor, etc. Signed by the Duke, 'Norff.' Small seal of arms, three lions passant, in chief, a label of three points, a straw round the seal.

[1] *Chevron*, a covering for a horse's head, made of iron and leather.
[2] The following abstract is taken from Mr. Macray's Report on the Documents in Magdalen College, Oxford, already referred to.

91

THE PASTON LETTERS

764

ABSTRACT [1]

1470
DEC. 11

1470, 11 Dec., 49 Hen. vi., 'and of the readepcion of his roiall power 1.' Release (in English) from John, Duke of Norfolk, to Bishop Wayneflete, of the manors of Castre, Wyntertone, Baytone, Bastwik, and Tolthorpe, in Norfolk, and of Caldecote, Burneviles or Burnegyles, in Suffolk, which had been sold to him by Nicholas, Abbot of Langle, Will. Yelverton, Knight, Justice, Thomas Howes, clerk, and Will. Worcetre, and of which the said Yelverton, Howes, and Will. Jenney, as feoffees with others, for Sir J. Fastolf, of the said manors, enfeoffed the said Duke and others by deed, dated 1st. Oct., 8 Edw. iv. [1468], the said Duke being informed by the Archbishops of York and Canterbury, and by the said Bishop of Winchester, that the said bargain was made contrary to the will of the said Sir John Fastolf. Covenants also to deliver up all evidences concerning the same, specially the said deed of feoffment and two papers, one with four seals specifying the said bargain, and another with three seals specifying a license to enter on all Fastolf's manors till the bargain be performed. And for this reconveyance the said Bishop pays to the said Duke 500 marks.

765

ABSTRACT [2]

DEC. 24

1470, 24 Dec., 49 Hen. vi., 'and of the readepcion of his royall power, the first.' Acknowledgment by 'the highe and myghti Prynce, John, Duke of Norff.,' of the receipt of 100 marks from the Bishop of Winchester, being part of 250 marks which the said Bishop has promised to pay upon knowledge of the delivery of the manor of Castre, and other lordships specified in a writing between the said parties, unto the feoffees of the said Bishop.

[1] This abstract is also taken from Mr. Macray's Report on the Documents in Magdalen College.
[2] This abstract is from the same report as the two last.

THE PASTON LETTERS

767

ABSTRACT [1]

1471
FEB. 12

Norfolk and Suffolk Deeds, No. 50. 'John Paston, Knight, binds himself to performe all appoyntments made betweene him and W. Wanflet, Byshop of Winton, concerning certayne landes which were Sir John Fastolfes. Feb. 12, Hen. vi. 49.'

768

ABSTRACT [2]

FEB. 14

Release by John Beauchamp, Knight, Lord Beauchamp, to John Paston and Roger Townesend, Esqs., of his interest in the manors of Castre called Redhams, Vaus, and Bosoms; and in the manors of Begviles in Wyntirton, Spensers in Heryngby, Reppes in Bastwyk, and a third part of the manor of Runham; and in all lands called Billes in Stokesby, Cattes in Haringby, a messuage called Dengayns in Yarmouth, and all lands and tenements in the hundreds of East Flegge and West Flegge in Norfolk; which premises Lord Beauchamp lately had in conjunction with Thomas, Archbishop of Canterbury, William Yelverton, Justice, William Jenney, Serjeant-at-law, and William Paston, now surviving, and John Radclyff of Attylburgh, John Paston, Hen. Fylongley, Esqs., Thomas Howes, clerk, and Thomas Grene, now deceased, of the gift and feoffment of Ralph Boteler, Knight, Lord Sudeley, Sir William Oldhall, Ric. Waller, Esq., Thos. West, Esq., William Wangford, and Nich. Girlyngton.

Dated 14th Feb., 49 and 1 Hen. vi.

769

THE EARL OF OXFORD TO THOMAS VERE [3]

To my right dere and welbeloved brother, Thomas Veer.

MARCH 14

RIGHT dere and welbeloved brother, I command me hertly unto you; certifying you that I have receyved your writing, directed now laste unto me, by my servant William Cooke, by which I understande the faithfull gwydyng

[1] [From ms. Index in Magd. Coll., Oxford.]
[2] [From a ms. in the Bodleian Library.]
[3] [From Fenn, ii. 54.] It is sufficiently apparent from the contents that this was written during the restoration of Henry vi., and in anticipation of the attempt by King Edward, which was very soon afterwards successful, to recover his throne. Edward in fact landed at Ravenspur the very day this letter was written.

HENRY VI RESTORED

766

MARGARET PASTON TO JOHN PASTON [1]

To John Paston the yonger, be this delivered in hast.

I GRETE you wele, and send you Godds blyssyng and myn, latyng you wete that sith ye departed my Cosyn Calthorp sent me a letter, compleynyng in his wrytyng that for asmych as he can not be payd of his tenaunts as he hat be befor this tyme, he purposith to lesse his howshold, and to leve the streytlyer. Wharfor he desireth me to purvey for your suster Anne; he seth she waxeth hygh, and it wer tyme to purvey her a mariage.

I marveyll what causeth hym to write so now; outher she hath displeased hym, or ell[es] he hath takyn her with diffaught. Therfor I pray you comune with my Cosyn Clere at London, and wete how he is dysposyd to her ward, and send me word, for I shall be fayn to send for her, and with me she shall but lese her tyme, and with ought she wold be the better occupied she shall oftyn tymes meve me, and put me in gret inquietenesse. Remembr what labour I had with your suster, therfor do your parte to help her forth, that may be to your wurchiep and myn.

Item, remembr the bill that I spake to you of, to gete of your brother of such money as he hath receyvid of me sith your faders disseas. Se your Unkyll Mautby, if ye may, and send me sume tydyngs as sonee as ye may. God kepe you.

Wretyn the Fryday next befor Sent Thomas of Caunterbury, in hast.

By your Moder.

1470
DEC. [

[1] [From Fenn, iv. 288.] This letter was probably written in or about the year 1470. Anne Paston, the sister of John Paston, here mentioned, was married to William Yelverton, a grandson of the Judge, in 1474 (Itin. W. Wyrc. 369), and the match had been already determined (as will appear in a future letter) before June 1472. At the date of this letter she was still staying in Calthorpe's household, into which, after the manner of the times, she had been sent for her education; and Calthorpe desiring to reduce his establishment, suggested, somewhat earlier than her mother anticipated, that it was time to provide a husband for her.

HENRY VI RESTORED

and disposicion of the cuntre, to my gret cumfote and pleaser; which I dowbte not shall redunde to the grethest presyng and worship that ever dide till eny cuntre; certifying you ferdermore that by Nicheson of your other tydyngs laste send unto me; also thes by Robt. Porter. I have disposed me with all the power that I can make in Essex and Suffolk, Cambrygeshire, and other places, to be on Monday next comyng at Bury, which purpose I intende to observe, with Godds grace, towards you in to Norffolk, to the assistence of you and the cuntre, in case Edwarde with his companye had aryved ther, and yete I shall do the same noughtwithstandyng; for if he aryve northwarde, like as ye wete by likelyhode he shulde, I caste to folow and porsew hym. And where ye desire that I shulde send you woorde what disposicion shalbe take in the cuntre wher ye be, I desire you that ye, by theadvyse of the gentilmen which ben there, chese iij. or iiij., and send theym to me at Bury on Monday next; and than I and they, with my Counceyle, shall take a direccion for the suretie of all that cuntre, by Godds grace; by whome I shall send than to you relacion, wheder ye shall remayne still ther your selff, or resorte to me with all thos that be accompanyed with you. And Jhesu preserve you. At Hithingham [*Hedingham*], the xiiij. day of Marche.

By your lovyng brothyr,

OXYNFORD.

147
MARCH

770

THE EARL OF OXFORD TO HENRY SPILMAN AND OTHERS [1]

To my right trusty and welbelovyd Henry Spilman, Thos. Seyve, John Seyve, James Radclif, John Brampton the older, and to eche of them.

TRUSTY and welbeloved, I comende me to you, lettyng you witte that I have credible tydyngs that the Kyngs gret enemys and rebellis, accompanyed with enemys estraungers, be nowe aryved, and landyd in the north parties

MARCH

[1] [From Fenn, ii. 58.] This letter was evidently written five days after the last.

THE PASTON LETTERS

1471
ARCH 19 of this his land, to the utter destruction of his roiall persone, and subversion of all his realm, if they myght atayne ; whom to encountre and resiste the Kings Highnesse hath comaunded and assigned me, under his seall, sufficient power and auctorite to call, reyse, gader, and assemble, fro tyme to tyme, all his liege people of the shire of Norff., and other places, to assiste, ayde, and strenght me in the same entent.

Wherfor, in the Kyngs name, and by auctorite aforesaid, I straitly charge and command you, and in my owne byhalf hertly desire and pray you, that, all excuses leid apart, ye, and eche of you in your owne persones defensibly araied, with asmony men as ye may goodly make, be on Fryday next comyng at Lynne, and so forth to Newark, where, with the leve of God, I shall not faile to be at that tyme ; entendyng fro thence to goo foorth with the help of God, you, and my fryndes, to the recountr of the said enemyes ; and that ye faill not hereof, as ye tendre the weele of our said sovereygne Lord, and all this his realme.   Written at Bury, the xix^th day of Marche.   OXYNFORD.

771

JAMES GRESHAM TO SIR JOHN PASTON [1]

To the right worshipfull and speciall singler maister,
Sir John Paston, Knyght, be this delyvered.

1471 AFTER due recomendacion hadde with all my service, &c. . . . . . . [2]
      As for tydyngs, here in this cuntre be many tales, and non accorth with other.   It is tolde me by the Undir-shireve that my Lord of Clarence is goon to his brother, late Kyng ; in so moche that his men have the Gorget [3] on their

[1] [From Fenn, ii. 60.]   The political news in this letter show that it was written after the landing of Edward IV. in Yorkshire.
[2] 'Here,' according to Fenn, 'follow copies of indictments and appeals procured against Sir John Paston and his servants ; and likewise other law business.'   The indictments and appeals in question are doubtless those referred to in the next No.
[3] A collar worn round the neck.—F.

96

THE PASTON LETTERS

Wykes, Edmund Brome, John Dawebeney, and Thurstan, etc., for Easter. 'Per Contr. de Anno viij.   Ro. xxviij.   Vynter.'

Capias against John Pampyng, late of Castre, Edmund Brome, late of Redeham, William Bedford and Edmund Mason, late of Bychamwelle, laborer, and Alex. Cok of Norwich, yeoman, 'xv. Pasch.,' appealed by Christiana, widow of Thos. Mylys, in Easter term, as principals in the death of her husband.   Also *capias* against William Paston of Norwich and Ralph Lovell of Bychamwelle, gent., appealed as accessaries.   Ro. lxix.   Registrum Sonde.'

⁎ All the above writs are for the county of Norfolk.

773

ABSTRACT [1]

1471
APRIL 10 '30. Relaxatio Johannis Paston facta episc. Winton, et aliis totius juris in maneriis vocat. Akethorp in Leyestoft, Spitlings in Gorleston, Habland in Brad-well, etc., quæ quondam fuerunt Johannis Fastolf.—April 10, Edw. IV. 11.'

[1] This is another entry from the old index of deeds in Magdalen College, Oxford.   There is probably some slight error in the date, as Edward IV. was not acknowledged as King on the 10th April, in what would otherwise have been the eleventh year of his reign.   He was so acknowledged a few days later—*i.e.* after the battle of Barnet, which was fought on the 14th April—so that if the date had been, say, April 20, instead of April 10, it would have been quite consistent.   It is impossible, however, to say where the error lies, so we place the document under the date actually expressed in it.

98

HENRY VI RESTORED

breests, and the Rose over it.   And it is seid that the Lord 1471 Howard hath proclamed Kyng E. Kyng of Inglond in Suff., &c.

Yours, and at your comandement,
                                    JAMES GRESHAM.

772

ABSTRACT [1]

A Register of Writs, etc., which was probably sent with the preceding letter.   It is addressed on the back, 'To Sir John Paston,' and endorsed 'James Gresham.'

Distringas against Sir John Paston, late of Castre, for his appearance in the King's Bench, Easter, 8 Edw. IV.   'Per Contr. de Anno viij° E. iiij^ti.   Ro. xxviij. [2]   Vynter.'

Distringas against Sir John Paston and Ric. Calle, late of Castre, with *capias* against William Wykes, late of Castre ; Edmund Brome, late of Redeham ; and John Dawebeney, late of Castre ; Thurstan Cokesson, *alias* Starky, late of Castre ; John Pampyng, late of Castre ; and Henry Swete, late of Castre, yeoman, for their appearance in the King's Bench in Easter to answer for offences against the statute *de ingressibus manu forti.*   'Per Contr' de Anno viij° E. iiij^ti.   Ro. xxviij.   Vynter.'

'Of these ij. writtes ar *supersedeas* delyvered to the Undirshirreve.'

Writ of exigent against John Pampyng, late of Castre, gent., and Edmund Brome of Castre, gent., 'Oct' Joh'is,' appealed by Cecilia, widow of John Colman, as principals in the death of her husband.   Ro. 67.   'Breve istud deliberatur de recordo, Hill. xlix.   Sonde.'

Another writ of exigent against Pampyng and Brome at the King's suit for divers felonies and murders.   'Ro. xvj.   Per Contr' de Anno x° E. iiij^ti.   Ro. xij°   Vynter.'

Distringas against Sir John Paston and Ric. Calle for their appearance in the King's Bench in Easter term, on an indictment for forcible entry.   'Per Contr' de Anno viij° E. iiij^ti.   Ro. xxix.'

Distringas against Sir John Paston and Ric. Calle, with *capias* against John Wykes, late of Castre, Edmund Brome, John Dawebeney, and Thurstan Cokesson, *alias* Starky, late of Castre, for their appearance in the King's Bench in Easter term, on an indictment of forcible entry.   'Per Contr' de Anno viij. E. iiij^ti.   Ro. xxviij.   Vynter.'

Distringas against Sir John Paston and Ric. Calle, with *capias* against John

[1] [From Paston MSS., B.M.]
[2] The Controlment Roll 8 Edw. IV. is now missing.

97

THE PASTON LETTERS

Edward IV.

774

SIR JOHN PASTON TO MARGARET PASTON [1]

To my Moodre.

MOODRE, I recomande me to yow, letyng yow wette 1471 that, blyssed be God, my brother John is a lyffe and APRIL 18 farethe well, and in no perell off dethe.   Never the lesse he is hurt with an arow on hys ryght arme, be nethe the elbow ; and I have sent hym a serjon, whyche hathe dressid hym, and he tellythe me that he trustythe that he schall be all holl with in ryght schort tyme.   It is so that John Mylsent is ded, God have mercy on hys sowle ! and Wylliam Mylsent is on lyffe, and hys other servants all be askepyd by all lyklihod.

Item, as ffor me, I ame in good case, blyssyd be God ; and in no joparte off my lyffe, as me lyst my self ; for I am at my lyberte iff nede bee.

Item, my Lorde Archebysshop [2] is in the Towr ; neverthe-lesse I trust to God that he schall do well i noghe ; he hathe a saffe garde for hym and me bothe.   Neverthelesse we have ben

[1] [From Fenn, ii. 62.]   This letter, as shown by the contents, was written just four days after the battle of Barnet, by which Edward IV. recovered his throne.   It is not signed, but the writer is Sir John Paston.
[2] George Neville, Archbishop of York.   It was from the custody of this prelate that Edward escaped, after having been surprised and taken prisoner by the Earl of Warwick, in 1470 : perhaps the kind treatment of his then prisoner now procured his pardon.—F.

99

THE PASTON LETTERS

troblyd syns, but nowe I undrestande that he hathe a pardon ; and so we hope well.

Ther was kyllyd uppon the ffelde, halffe a myle ffrom Bernett, on Esterne Daye, the Erle of Warwyk, the Marqweys Montacu, Sir William Terrell,[1] Sir Lewes Johns, and dyverse other Esquiers off owr contre, Godmerston and Bothe.

And on the Kynge Edwardes partye, the Lord Cromwell,[2] the Lord Saye,[3] Sir Omffrey Bowghsher[4] off owr contre, whyche is a sore moonyd man her, and other peple off bothe partyes to the nombre off mor then a m[l].

As for other tythynges, is undrestande her that the Qwyen Margrett is verrely londyd and hyr sone in the west contre, and I trow that is to morow, or ellys the next daye, the Kynge Edwarde wyll depart ffrom hense to hyr warde, to dryve her owt ageyn.

Item, I beseche yow that I may be recomendyd to my cosyn Lomner, and to thanke hym ffor hys goode wyll to me wardes, iff I had hadde nede, as I undrestoode by the berer heroff ; and I beseche you on my behalve to advyse hym to be well ware off hys delyng or langage as yit, ffor the worlde, I ensur yow, is ryght qwesye, as ye schall know with in thys monthe ; the peple heer feerythe it soor.

God hathe schewyd Hym selffe marvelouslye lyke Hym that made all, and can undoo ageyn whan Hym lyst ; and I kan thynke that by all lyklyod schall schewe Hym sylff as mervylous ageyn, and that in schort tyme ; and, as I suppose, offter than onys in casis lyke.

Item, it is soo that my brother is on purveyed off monye. I have holpyn hym to my power and above. Wherffor as it pleasythe yow remembre hym, ffor kan not purveye ffor my selffe in the same case.

Wretyn at London the thorysdaye in Esterne weke. I hope hastely to see yow.

[1] Sir William Tyrell was cousin to Sir James Tyrell, the afterwards supposed murderer of Edward V. and his brother the Duke of York.—F.
[2] Humphrey Bourchier, third son of Henry, Earl of Essex, had summons to Parliament, in 1461, as Lord Cromwell, in right of his wife.—F.
[3] William Fienes, Lord Say. [4] Son of John, Lord Berners.

EDWARD IV

All thys bylle most be secrett. Be ye not adoghtyd off
the worlde, ffor I trust all schall be well. Iff it thusse contenewe, I ame not all undon, nor noon off us ; and iff otherwyse, then, &c. &c.

775

[THE EARL OF OXFORD] TO A LADY[1]

To the ryght reverent and wyrchypfull Lady.[2]

RYGHT reverent and wyrchypfull Lady, I recomande me to yow, lettyng yow wete that I am in gret hevynes at the makyng of thys letter ; but thankyd be God, I am eschapyd my selfe, and sodenly departyd fro my men ; for I undyrstand my chapleyn wold have detrayed me ; and if he com in to the contre, let hym be mad seuer, &c. Also ye shall gyff credence to the brynger of thys letter, and I beseke yow to reward hym to hys costs ; for I was not in power at the makyng of thys letter to gyff hym, but as I wass put in trest by favar of strange pepyll, &c.

Also ye shall send me in all hast all the redi money that ye can make, and asse mone of my men asse can com well horsyd ; and that they cum in dyverse parcellys. Also that my horsse be sent, with my stele sadelles ; and byd the yoman of the horse cover theym with ledder. Also ye shall send to my moder,[3] and let hyr wete of thys letter, and pray hyr of hyr blessyng, and byd hyr send me my kasket, by thys tokyn ; that she hathe the key theroff, but it is brokyn.

Also ye shall send to the Pryor of Thetford,[4] and byd hym

[1] [From Fenn, ii. 68.] The signature of this letter is composed of flourishes which were probably devised on purpose to make it unintelligible. Fenn suggests that the first character may be taken for an O, and the last for a D ; but to our thinking the resemblance is rather difficult to trace. There is, however, great probability in his conjecture that the writer was the Earl of Oxford, and the date just after the battle of Barnet.
[2] Margaret, daughter of Richard Neville, Earl of Salisbury, sister to the late Earl of Warwick, and wife of John de Vere, Earl of Oxford.—F.
[3] Elizabeth, daughter and heir of Sir John Howard, Knight, who was the grandfather of John Howard, first Duke of Norfolk of that name. She was now the widow of John de Vere, late Earl of Oxford.
[4] John Vescey, Prior of Thetford, from 1441 to 1479.—F.

THE PASTON LETTERS

send me the sum of gold that he seyd that I schuld have. Also sey to hym by thys token, that I schewyd hym the fyrst Prive Seale, &c. Also lete Pastun, Fylbryg, Brews, come to me. Also ye shall delyver the brynger of thys letter an horsse, sadell, and brydell. Also ye schallbe off gud cher, and take no thowght, for I schall brynge my purpose abowte now by the grace of God, Qwhome have yow in kepyng.

O . . . . D (?).

776

JOHN PASTON OF GELSTON TO MARGARET PASTON[1]

AFTYR humbyll and most dew recomendacyon, in as humbyll wyse as I can, I beseche you of your blyssyng, preying God to reward you with as myche plesyer and hertys ease as I have latward causyd you to have trowbyll and thowght ; and, with Godys grace, it shall not be longe to or then my wronges and othyr menys shall be redressyd, for the world was nevyr so lyek to be owyrs as it is now ; werfor I prey you let Lomnor no be to besy as yet. Modyr, I beseche you, and ye may spare eny money, that ye wyll do your almesse on me and send me some in as hasty wyse as is possybyll ; for by my trowthe my leche crafte and fesyk, and rewardys to them that have kept me and condyt me to London, hathe cost me sythe Estern Day[2] more than v*li.*, and now I haue neythyr met, drynk, clothys, lechecraft, ner money but up on borowyng ; and I have asayid my frendys so ferre, that they be gyn to fayle now in my gretest ned that evyr I was in. Also, modyr, I beseche yow, and my horse that was at lechecraft at the Holt[3] be not takyn up for the Kynges hawkys,[4] that he

[1] [From Paston MSS., B.M.] This letter was printed by Fenn in his fifth volume, of which the original MSS. are now recovered. It was evidently written in April 1471, when the writer was recovering from the wound he had received at the battle of Barnet (*see* No. 774. It is not addressed, but is endorsed in another hand, 'Litera Johannis Paston armigeri matri suæ.'
[2] The battle of Barnet was fought on Easter Day, 14th April 1471.
[3] A pasture so called, and means the groves, or lands full of wood.—F.
[4] This may signify, in jocular language, if he be not dead.—F.

EDWARD IV

may be had hom and kept in your plase, and not to go owght
to watyr, nor no whedyr ellys, but that the gat be shet, and he to be chasyd aftyr watyr within your plase, and that he have as myche met as he may ete ; I have hey i new of myn owne, and as for otys, Dollys will purvey for hym, or who that dothe it I wyll paye. And I beseche yow that he have every wek iij. boshell of otys, and every day a penyworthe of bred ; and if Botoner be not at Norwyche, and Syme kepe hym, I shall geve hym well for hys labore. Also that Phelypp Loveday put the othyr horse to gresse ther, as he and I wer acordyd.

Item, that Botoner send me hyddyr the two shyrtys that wer in my casket, and that he send me hydyr xls. by the next messenger that comyth to London.

Item, that Mastress Broom send me hedyr iij. longe gownys and ij. doblettes, and a jaket of plonket chamlett, and a morey bonet out of my cofyr. Sir Jamys hathe the key, as I sent hyr werd be for thys.

Item, that syche othyr wryghtynges and stuff as was in my kasket be in your kepyng, and that no body look my wryghtynges.

Item, that the horse that Purdy hathe of myne be put to some good gresse in haste ; and if it plese yow to have knowlage of our royal person, I thank God I am hole of my syknesse, and trust to be clene hole of all my hurttys within a sevennyght at the ferthest, by wyche tym I trust to have othyr tydynges ; and those tydynges onys had, I trust not to be longe owght of Norfolk, with Godys grace, Whom I beseche preserve you and your for my part.

Wretyn the last day of Apryll. The berer herof can tell you tydynges, syche as be trew for very serteyn.

Your humbylest servaunt,

J. OF GELSTON.

777

THE BATTLE OF TEWKESBURY[1]

Ded in the Feld.

Edward that was called Prynce.
Lord John of Somerset.
Erle of Devenshire.
Lord Wenlok.
Sir William Vaus.
Sir Edmond Hamden.
Sir John Seymour.
Sir William Bermoth.
Water Barrow.
Mr. William Henmar.
Mr. Feldyng.[2]
Hervy, recorder.[3]
Mr. Herry, capteyn of Brystowe.
Sir Roberte Whetyngham.
Knoyll.

Thes be men that were heveded.[4]

The Duke of Somerset.
The Lord of Sent Jones.[5]
Sir Jerveys Clyfton.
Humfrey Awdeley.
Lowes Miles.
Forey of Fraunce.
Sir John Delvys.[6]
Lord Foskew on lyffe.

[1] [From MS. Phillipps 9735, No. 279.] This paper is in a contemporary hand-writing, and undoubtedly refers to the battle of Tewkesbury.
[2] Sir William Fielding, according to Warkworth's Chronicle.
[3] These words, 'Hervy, recorder,' are written over 'Herry, capteyn,' as a correction; but the latter are not erased. Warkworth mentions Sir Nicholas Hervy.
[4] Beheaded. [5] Sir John Longstruther, Prior of St. John's.
[6] Originally written 'Mr. Delvys,' and corrected.

Sir William Carre.
Sir Hew Courteney.
Sir Thomas Tressham.
Sir Herry Tressham.
Sir William Newbery.
Mr. Gower.[1]
Mr. Awdeley.[2]
Robert Clerke.
Lechefeld, mason of Westmynster.
Sir William Grymesby yet on lyffe.

Thes be the Knyghtes that the Kyng mad in the Feld.

Lord Cobham.	Sir Richard Croft.
Sir George Nevel.	Sir John Pylkyngton.
Sir Philip Courtenay.	Sir John Byngham.
Sir Herry Bemonde.	Sir John Harley.
Sir Moreys of Barkley.	Sir John Boteler.
Sir Richard Hastynges.	Sir Christofer Morysby.
Sir Roberte Haryngton.	Sir John Clay.
Sir Thomas Gray.	Sir Robert Wylleby.
Sir James Terell.	Sir Robert Grene.
Sir John Feres.	Sir Roger Ree.
Sir Herry Feres.	Sir Richard Radclyffe.
Sir Herry Purpeynt.	Sir John Saundes.
Sir John Parre.	Sir Thomas Strikelande.
Sir John Downe.	Sir George Browne.
Sir Roger Kyngstone.	Sir William Motton.
Sir John Crokere.	Sir Tery Robsert.
Sir —— Skerne.	Sir Thomas Cromewell.
Sir James Crowmere.	Sir Robert Corbet.
Sir William Sandalle.	Sir Nicholas Langford.
Sir John Deverys.	Sir John Seyntlowe.
Sir Herry Grey.	Sir William Brandon.
Sir Edward Wodehous.	

[1] James Gower, according to Warkworth. [2] Sir Humphrey Audeley.

778

JOHN PASTON TO MARGARET PASTON[1]

MOST worchepfull and my ryght specyall good modyr, as humbylly as I can, I recomand me on to yow, besechyng yow of your blyssyng. Please it yow to undyrstand that thys day I spake with Batcheler Water, whiche let me have undyrstandyng of your welfare, wherof I thank God with all my hert. Also he leet me have knowlage that the Lord Scalys had grauntyd yow to be my good lord, wherof I am no thyng prowd, for he may do lest with the gret mastyr; but he wold depert ovyr the see, as hastyly as he may; and because he wenyth that I wold go with hym, as I had pro-myseyd evyr, and he had kept foorthe hys jornay at that tyme, thys is the cause that he wyll be my good lord and help to get my pardon. The Kyng is not best pleasyd with hym for that he desyerthe to depert, in so myche that the Kyng hathe seyd of hym, that wen evyr he hathe most to do, then the Lord Scalys wyll sonest axe leve to depart, and weenyth that it is most cause of kowardyese. As for pardon, I can never get, withowght I schold paye to myche money for it, and I am not so purveyd. As for Herry Hallman, my brodyr wyll axe hym no sylver tyll ye be payeyd; therfor ye may send to hym and have it.

Item, I am sory that ye have fadyrd my hors that was at Caster to be my Brodyr Edmundys, for I had leever that they

[1] [From Fenn, iv. 116.] From the mention of Lord Scales in this letter it might be supposed that it was written not later than the year 1469, when Anthony Wood-ville, the last Lord Scales, became Earl Rivers by the death of his father; but I believe the date to be 1471, and that the writer is simply speaking of Earl Rivers by his old title. In the first place there is no appearance of either of the John Pastons requiring a royal pardon before the year 1471; secondly, it is not probable that either of them would have spoken so slightingly of the value of Lord Scales's intercession at an earlier period; and thirdly, it seems doubtful whether Edmund Paston could have been old enough to own a war-horse many years before. Finally, we find by Letter 780 following that John Paston, the youngest, succeeded in obtaining a pardon signed by the King on the 17th July 1471. If the reference to the autograph plate in Fenn is correct, this letter was in the hand of his elder brother, Sir John Paston, Knight; but as it is not signed, like most of his letters, 'John Paston, K.,' we are inclined to suspect that it was really written by the younger brother, like No. 780.

had hym style then owght ellys; wherfor thow they profyr hym yow from hense foorthe, let not my brodyr Edmund take hym, but let him sey whedyr they wyll let hym have hym or not, that I have promyseyd my brodyr Edmund a bettyr hors for hym, so that he wyll not cleyme the same for hys. As for tydyngs her be non but that the Scottys and Walyshe men be besy; what they meane I can not seye. My cosyn John Loveday can tell yow, and ther be eny odyr flyeyng talys, for he hathe walkyd in London, and so do not I. When I may I wyll come hom with Godys grace, whom I beseche to sende you your hertys desyeyr. Wretyn the v. daye of Julle.

Be yowr humblest sone and servant,

J. P.

779

ABSTRACT[1]

Norff. and Suff. Deeds, No. 5. ' Relaxatio Johannis Paston militis, Davidi Husband et Will. Gyfford totius juris in maneriis de Saxthorp, Tichwell, Haineford, Essex in Hickling, etc., Calcote, Leystoft, Habland, Broweston, Gorleston alias Spitlings, quæ quondam fuerunt Johannis Fastolf mil., et quæ Will. Waynflet episcopus Winton' habuit ex dono Rad. Boteler domini de Sudley, et prædicti David et Willielmus ex dono episc. prædicti, necnon de et in 25 *markes redd.* precipiend. de priori de Hickling. Julii 12, Edw. IV. 11. With a scedule annexed touching the same release.'

780

JOHN PASTON TO MARGARET PASTON[2]

To my most worchepfull Modyr, Margaret Paston, be thys delyveryd in hast.

RYGHT worchepfull modyr, I recomand me to yow, and as lowly as I can, I beseche yow of yowr blyssyng. Please yow to undyrstand that thys Wednysday Sir Thomas Wyngffeld sent to me, and let me wet that the Kyng

[1] [From MS. Index in Magd. Coll., Oxford.]
[2] [From Paston MSS., B.M.] This letter refers to a pardon granted by the King to John Paston the younger, for having taken part with the Lancastrians at the battle of Barnet. Though the 'bill' for this pardon was signed by the King on the 17th July, the pardon itself did not pass the Great Seal till the 7th February following, under which date it is enrolled on the Pardon Roll of 11 Edw. IV., memb. 9.

THE PASTON LETTERS

1471
JULY 17

had syngnyd my bylle of perdon, whyche the seid Sir Thomas delyveryd me; and so by Fryday, at the forthest, I tryst to have my perdon ensealyd by the Chanceler, and soone aftyr, so as I can fornyshe me, I tryst to se yow, if so be that eny of the Kynges hows com in to Norwyche. I wold fayne my gray horse wer kept in mewe for gnattys. Also, modyr, I beseche yow that Dollys and his felawe may be sent to, that I may have my money redy ayenst that I come home, whyche is dew to be payid, for thys mater hathe cost me the settyng over. Also that it may please yow that Purdy at Heylysdon maye be sent to for the horse that he hathe of myne, and that the horse may be kept well, and have as myche mete as he wyll eate be twyx thys and that I come home, and that Jakys nage have mete i now also. Also, and Syr Thomas Wyngfeld come to Norwyche, that he may have as good chere as it please yow to make on to that man that I am most behold to for hys gret kyndnesse and good wyll, for he takyth full my part ayenst my gretest enmyeys, Brandons and hys brodyr William; for at my fyrst comyng to Sir Thomas Wyngfeld, bothe William Wyngfeld and William Brandon the yonger wer with Sir Thomas, and had gret wordys to myn owne mowthe, and in cheff W. Wyngfeld; and wher so evyr he may met me on evyn grownd he wyll do myche; but and we met evynly, no fors, so I have yowr blyssyng. I prey yow, with owght it be to my Lady Calthorp, let ther be but fewe woordys of thys perdon. No more, but I prey God preserve yow and yours.

Wretyn the Wednysday next before Mary Mawdelen,

By your humblest sone, J. P.

108

EDWARD IV

781

SIR JOHN PASTON TO JOHN PASTON[1]

To Mestresse Margret Paston, or to John Paston, Esqier, hyr sone, in hast.

RYGHT well belovyd brother, I comende me to yow, letyng yow wete that I am in wellffar, I thanke God, and have ben evyr syns that I spake last with yow; and mervayle for that ye sent never wryghtynge to me syns ye departyd; I herde nevyr synes that tyme any worde out off Norffolk; ye myght aft Bertlemai Feyr[2] have had messengers i nowe to London, and iff ye had sent to Wykys, he scholde have conveyed it to me. I herde yisterdaye, that a Worsted man of Norffolk, that solde worstedys[3] at Wynchester, seyde that my Lord of Norffolk and my Lady wer on pylgrymage at Our Lady[4] on ffoot, and so they went to Caster; and that at Norwyche on scholde have had large langage to yow, and callyd yow traytor, and pyked many quarellys to yow. Sende me worde ther off; it wer well doo, that ye wer a lytell sewrer off yowr pardon than ye be: avyse you, I deme ye woll her afftr ellys repent yow.

I undrestonde that Bastarde Fauconbryge[5] is owther hedyd or lyke to be, and hys brother bothe; some men seye he wolde have deservyd it, and som sey naye.

I purpose to be att London the ffyrst daye off the terme; send me worde whethyr ye schall be ther or nott.

Item, I wolde wete whether ye have spoken wyth my Lady off Norffolk or not, and off hyr disposicion and the howsoldys

1471
SEPT.

1 [From Fenn, ii. 72.] Apart from the reference to John Paston's pardon, the date of this letter is fixed by what is said of the bastard Falconbridge.
2 Bartholomew Fair, in Smithfield.
3 Worsted, in Norfolk, a town formerly famous for the spinning of the fine thread with which the yarn called Worsted is made.—F.
4 Of Walsingham.
5 Thomas Nevill, a natural son of William, Lord Fauconberg. He was beheaded in 1471, and, as mentioned in Letter 782 following, his head was placed on London Bridge.

109

THE PASTON LETTERS

1471
SEPT. 15

to me and to yow wardes, and whether it be a possible to have Caster ageyn and ther goodewylles or not; and also I praye yow undrestande what ffelaschyp and guydyng is in Caster, and have a spye resortyng in and owt, so maye ye know the secretys among them. Ther is moche adoo in the Northe, as men seyn; I pray yow be ware off yowr guydyng, and in cheff off yowr langage, and so that ffro hense fforthe by yowr langage noo man perceyve that ye ffavor any person contrary to the Kynges plesur. I undrestonde that the Lord Ryvers hathe lycence off the Kynge to goo to Portyngale now within thys vij. nyght. I pray yow recomande mo to my modre, and beseche hyr off hyr blyssyng on my be halve.[1]

Item, I praye yow sende me worde iff any off owr ffrendys or wellwyllers be dede, ffor I feer that ther is grete dethe in Norwyche, and in other Borowgh townese in Norffolk, ffor I ensur you it is the most unyversall dethe that evyr I wyst in Ingelonde; ffor by my trowthe, I kan not her by pylgrymes that passe the contre, nor noon other man that rydethe or gothe any contre, that any Borow town in Ingelonde is ffree ffrom that sykenesse; God sease it whan it pleasyt Hym. Wherffor, ffor Goddysake, let my moodre take heede to my yonge brytheren that they be not in noon place wher that sykenesse is regnyng, nor that they dysport not with noon other yonge peple whyche resortythe wher any sykenesse is, and iff ther be any off that sykenesse ded or enffect in Norwyche, ffor Goddes sake, lete hyr sende them to som ffrende off hyrse in to the contre, and do ye the same by myn advyce; late my moodre rather remeve hyr howsesolde in to the contre.

Even now Thyrston browt me word ffro London that it was Doctor Aleyn that cawsyd yowr troble that ye had at Norwych; and that John Pampyng roode ffor a dyscharge ffor yow, and that he hathe sped well, but howghe, that wot I nott; iff ye be cleer owt off Doctor Aleyn danger, kepe yow ther, and her afftr ye maye schoffe as well at hys carte. I praye yow sende me worde off all the fforme off hys delyng with yow.

1 Here follow, says Fenn, some directions about payments of money.
110

EDWARD IV

I had almost spoke with Mestresse Ann Hault, but I dyd not; nevyrthelesse thys next terme I hope to take on weye with hyr or other; sche is agreyd to speke with me, and sche hopythe to doo me ease as sche saythe.

I praye yow sende me worde hoghe ye doo with my Lady Elysabeth Boghscher; ye have a lytell chaffyd it, but I can not tell howe; sende me worde whether ye be in better hope or werse. I her seye that the Erle off Oxenffordys bretheryn be goon owt off Sceyntewarye. Sir Thomas Fulfforthe[1] is goon owt off Sceyntewarye, and a gret ffelaschyp ffettchyd hym, a iij.xx., and they sey that with in v. myle off London he was CC. men; and no man watethe wher he is become not yit.

The Lordes Hastyngs and Howerd be in Caleys, and have it pesebely; and Sir Walter Wrettesle and Sir Jeffrey Gate be comyn thense, and woll be at London thys daye as it is seyde.

Wretyn at Waltham besyd Winchester the daye nex Holy Roode Daye.[2]

J. P., K.

1471
SEPT. 1

782

SIR JOHN PASTON TO JOHN PASTON[3]

To hys well belovyd John Paston, Esquier, at Norwyche, or to Mestresse Margret, his Modre.

I COMANDE me to yow, letyng yow weet that, &c.[4] I wolde ffayne have the mesur wher my ffadre lythe at Bromholm; bothe the thyknesse and compace off the peler at hys hed, and ffrom that the space to the alter, and the

SEPT. 2

1 Sir Thomas Fulford was son of Sir Baldwin Fulford, beheaded at Bristol in 1461; he likewise ended his life on the scaffold.
2 Holyrood Day, 14th of September.
3 [From Fenn, ii. 80.] The evidences of date in this letter are the same as in the last.
4 Here follows an account that the Duchess of Suffolk and Duke of Norfolk intend again commencing appeals against Sir John Paston and his brother, etc., concerning Caister, etc.—F.

111

1471
SEPT. 28

thyknesse off that alter, and imagery off tymbre werk ; and what hyght the arche is to the grounde off the ilde, and how hye the grounde off the qwyr is hyer than the grownde off the ilde.

Item, I praye yowe late the mesur by pekthred be taken or elt mesured by yerde, how moche is ffrom the northe gate, ther the brygge was, at Gressham to the sowthewall, and in lyke fforme ffrom the este syde to the west, also the hyght off the estewall, and the hyght off the sowthest towr ffrom the grownde, iff ye maye easely. Also what bredde every towr is within the wall, and whych towr is moor then other within.

Allsso how manye ffote, or what brede eche towr takythe within iche corner off the quadrate[1] ovyrthwert the dorys, and how many taylors yards is from the moote syde, wher the brygg was, to the hyghe weye, or to the heddge all a longe the entre, and what brede the entre is be twyen the dykys. I praye yow, iff ye have a leyser in any wyse, se thys doone yowrselffe iff ye maye ; or ellys iff Pampyng do it, or who that ye thynke can doo it, I wolle spende xxd. or as ye seme to have the sertayn off every thyng her in. And as for my ffaders tombe, I charge yow se it yowr selffe, and when I speke with yow I woll tell yow the cawses why that I desyr thys to be doon.

As ffor tydyngs, the Kyng, and the Qwyen, and moche other pepell, ar ryden and goon to Canterbery, nevyr so moche peple seyn in Pylgrymage hertofor at ones, as men seye.

Allsso it is seyde that the Erle of Penbroke[2] is taken on to Brettayn ; and men saye that the Kynge schall have delyvere

[1] A drawing is here given in the original letter, apparently designed as a plan of the quadrangle of Gresham, of which the subjoined is a facsimile.

[2] Jasper Tudor.

112

1471
SEPT. 28

off hym hastely, and som seye that the Kynge off France woll se hym saffe, and schall sett hym at lyberte ageyn.

Item, Thomas Fauconbrydge hys hed was yesterdaye sett uppon London Brydge, lokyng into Kent warde ; and men seye that hys brother was sor hurte, and scope to seyntwarye [sanctuary] to Beverle.

Sir Thomas Fulfforthe escaped owt of Westminster with an C. sperys, as men seye, and is in to Devenshyr ; and ther he hathe strekyn off Sir John Crokkers hed, and kylt an other knyght off the Corteneys, as men seye. I wolde ye hadd yowr verry pardon at onys ; wherfor I praye yow ffayle not to be at London within iiij. daye afftr Seynt Feythe ;[1] ye schall do goode in many thynges, and I praye yow sende me worde heroff by the next messenger ; and iff it come to Mestresse Elysabeth Hyggens, at the Blak Swan, sche schall conveye it to me, ffor I woll not ffayle to be ther at London ageyn within thys vj. dayes.

Mestresse Elysabeth hathe a son, and was delyveryd within ij. dayes afftr Seynt Bertelmew ;[2] and hyr dowtr A. H. was the next daye afftr delyveryd off an other sone, as sche seythe, xj. weks er hyr tyme ; it was crystened John, and is ded. God save all ! No mor tyll I speke with yow.

Wretyn at London on Mychellmesse Evyn.

J. P., K.

Item, I praye yow late some wytty felaw, or ellys yowr-selff, goo to the townes ther as thes ij. women dwelle, and inquire whether they be maryed syns and ageyn or not, ffor I holde the hoorys weddyd ; and iff they be, than the appelys wer abbatyd ther by. I remembr not ther names ; ye knowe them better then I. Allsso in the Schreffvys bookys ther maye ye ffynde off them.

[1] 5th of October.   [2] 24th of August.

783

R. L. TO JOHN PASTON[1]

To hys worshipful master, John Paston, Esquier.

1471
OCT. 21

RYGHT wurchupfull ser, I comaund me to your good maysterchepe, &c. Plese it you to understond that Redford desyryd me on your byhalfe that I chuld goo and comon with the woman that was the fullars wyfe of South Walsham, whech woman is now maryed to on Thom Styward, dwellyng in the parysch of Seynt Gyll in Norwych, whech woman seyd to me that che sewyd never the pele, but that she was by sotyle craft brought to the New In at Norwych, and ther was Maystir Southwell, and he entretyd hyr to be my Lords wewe [widow],[2] by the space of an hole yer next folwyn, and therto he mad hyr to be bowne in an obligacyon. And whan that yer was past he desyred hyr to be my Lords wedow another yer ; and than she seyd that she had lever lose that that she had do, than to lose that and meer ; and therfor she seyd pleynly that she wold no mor of that mater. And so she toke hyr an husbond, whech is the seyd Thom Styward ; and she seyth that it was full sor ageyn hyr wylle that ever the mater went so forforth, for she had never non avayle therof, butt it was sewyd to hyr gret labor and losse, for she had never of my Lords councell, but berely hyr costs to London. No mor, but God have you in Hys kepyng.

Wretyn at Norwych, the Monday next after the Fest of Seynt Luke.

By your servant,

R. L.

[1] [From Fenn, iv. 440.] In the postscript to the preceding letter, Sir John Paston intimates his belief that the two widows who had appealed his brother of the murder of their husbands had married again, and that thereby the appeals were abated. It appears by the present letter that this intelligence was correct as regards one of them.
[2] The widow of a tenant in chivalry was called the Lord's widow.

114

784

JOHN PASTON TO MARGARET PASTON[1]

1471
OCT. 28

RYGHT worchepfull m[other, as lowly as] I can I re-comand me to yow, besechyng yow of your dayly blyssyng, praying yow to take thys key, and Sir Jam[ys] . . . . [m]y broder E., or J. Pampyng, and to ondo the kofyr that standith at my bedys feet, and ther in a ly[tyl sqw]are box ye shall fy[nd two de]dys, wher of the seallys be wownd in whyght paper ; my brodyr E. sye [saw] when I wond them up. The tone [begy]nyth 'Sciant, &c., quod ego *Matilda Bigota* ' ; and the todyr begynyth 'Sciant, &c., quod ego *Rogerus* . . . .' [I pray y]ow lett [them be] sealyd and sent me by *Radley* with the deedes there in. Sir Jamys knowyth the . . . . But [if so] be that ye fynd not thys box with thes two deedes in that cofyr, then I prey yow take the k[ey] . . . . teye of the same cofyr, and opyn the cofyr that standyth in the utter chambyr, and ther ye shall fynd . . . . [d]edes. My brodyr, Sir John, recomandyth hym to yow, and besechyth yow of your blyssyng ; and as for hys mater [there is yet no conclu]syon of no poynt, but I tryst ther shall be with in thes ij. dayeys. Jenney, W. trowbly[th] . . . . [my] brodyrs servauntes with old accyons and all syche thynges as he can renew to stoppe the oblyga-cio[ns w]hyche he is bownd in on to my broder ; but all shall be easeyd, I tryst. As for Mrs. A. Hawlt, the mater is mevyd [by div]ers of the Qwenys consayll, and of ferre by R. Hault, but he wold it shold be fyrst of our mocyon, and we wold [it] shold com of theym fyrst ; our mater shold be the bettyr.

[2] [From Paston MSS., B.M.] There was a general pardon in the latter part of the year 1471, and both John Paston and his brother took advantage of it, as appears by the *Pardon Roll*, 11 Edw. IV., membranes 9 and 25. The date of this letter is also shown by the answer to it, written by Margaret Paston on the 5th November. Many of the words in this letter are lost by the mutilation of the original MS., which is full of holes, from having been exposed at one time to damp. The address is almost completely lost, but a portion of the word ' [Ma]rgaret ' is visible, and a small fragment of an endorsement below in which the word ' Paston ' is legible.

115

THE PASTON LETTERS

Tydynges, ther is a generall pardon mevyd whyche my brodyr J. trystyth to have the preve[lege] of as soone as it is grantyd, whyche shall bee a bowght All Halow tyed at the ferthest. I have spok with my L[ord Rive]rs and with all myn old aqweyntance, and have good cheer of theym, hold as it maye. When we be conclud[yd in] eny poynte of our maters, ye shall have knowlage ther howhe to put yow in [comfort] er we have eny . . . but in veyn when we have comfort ye shall have parte. Newe tydynges, datys s . . . [s]ugyr of Mr. Kwte (?) x*d*. di.lb., and bettyr I tryst. No more, but I beseche God preserve yow and yours.

Wretyn on [Seint] Symondes Day and Jwde.

Your humblest sone and servaunt,

J. PASTON.

785

SIR JOHN PASTON'S DEEDS[1]

In the square trussyng coffre.

A boxe with evydence off my place in Fletstrett.

A lytell box with obligacions off the Archbisshop off York and W. Jennyes oblygacion.

A box with evydence of Tytlyshall.

A box with the letter of attorney off Fastolffes londes by Sir John Paston.

j. A box de actis inter episcopum Wynt' et J. P. militem. Item endentur' de argento mutuato termino Trinitatis anno x°. et testamentum W. Paston, Justic'.

Item, ij. pixides de novis cartis de terris Fastolffes.

Item, a litell box with the obligacion off T. Fastolff and one off James Gresham.

Item, a box with the dede off gyfft off J. P., and the byll assygnyd for the dyamant.

Item, the bagge de placitis in usu.

Item, the bagge with ger taken owt off my caskett.

Item, a bagge with the bondell where on was wreten 'London.'

Item, a bagge with evydence off Est Bekham.

Item, a bondell de actis parlimenti et de excambia in Paston.

[1] [From Paston MSS., B.M.] The following inventory is in the handwriting of Sir John Paston. The date at which it was drawn up must, from internal evidence, be later than the tenth year of Edward IV.; so perhaps it may be a list of the contents of the coffer mentioned by John Paston in Letter 784.

EDWARD IV

Item, a bondell de actis Cantuariensis.

Item, a bondell de fyrma Caster Berdolffis.

The endenture off Snaylwell by Wylleys.

A bondell of Gresham Moleyns.

A bondell off processe off th'eschekyr letter and byllys sirca (*sic*) festum Johannis anno ix°.

Item, th'endenture off W. Jeney. Item, a bondell off letteris and byllis anno x°.

A bondell with inquisicions not returnyd in to the Chanceri.

Copia voluntatis Fastolff ultima et probata.

Enventorium (*sic*) apud Caster per Episcopum Norwic' et dominum de Scales et alia ad rediseisinam (?)

Apunctuamentum Regis et litera amici. Endentura de Fennes per patrem Hugonis Fenne.

The verray endenture off my mariage.

Item, a bondell off letteris from my brother John.

Item, iij. billis, the endenter off W. Jenney for Bacton, a byll of Wylleys and one off J. Owdin (?)

Item, a bondell with the names off them that had stoff from Heylesdon.

Item, a byll off Sweynesthorp. Item, a byll off Brok off Dedham off the purchace theroff, a quitance pro Scaccario.

A bonde towchyng the probatt off Fastolffes will, with mi olde testament.

A copie off a generalle releffe de terris Fastolffes.

786

ABSTRACT[1]

WILLIAM PEKOC TO SIR JOHN PASTON

Has received Wheteley's letter, but though he has spoken to Sir John's tenants at Paston, Bakton, etc., has obtained no money to send him. They are better pleased to pay Sir John than Master 'Will. P.,' so they be saved harmless. Has put them in good comfort, and Sir John must take care that they be not sued this term. The fishing was never worse. No herring to be got under 13*s*. 4*d*. a barrel, and 8*s*. 4*d*. a sale. The swans were sent the week after your departure. John Osborn and Munde are merry. None dead at Caster and Mawteby since Michaelmas, but much mortality still at Fylby, Ormysby, and Scrowby.

Mawteby, 4 Nov.

[This letter most probably belongs to the year 1471, which it will be seen by the letter immediately following was a year of great mortality.]

[1] [From Paston MSS., B.M.]

THE PASTON LETTERS

787

MARGARET PASTON TO JOHN PASTON[1]

I GRETE you wele, and send you Goddes blyssyng and myn, letyng you wete that myn Cosyn Clere hathe sent to me for the C. marc that I borwed of her for your brother. It fortuned so that a frend of her of late hath loste better than CCC. marc, and he sent to her for money, and she had non that she myght comyn by, and ther for she sent to me for the seyd C. marc ; and I know not how to do therfor, for by my trowth I have it not, nor I can not make shyft therfor, and I shuld go to preson ; therfor comune with your brother her of, and send me word how that he wull make shyft ther for in hast. I must elles nedes sell all my woods, and that shall dysse avayll him better than a CC. marc, and I dey ; and if I shuld selle them now, ther wull noman gewe so myche for them be ner an C. marc as they be worth, be cause ther be so many wood sales in Norfolke at thys tyme. Therfor lete hym make purvyaunce therfor in hast, as he wull have my good wyll, and wull that I save hym the seyd woods to the better a wayll, and send me word here of in hast if ye wull my welfare, for I shall never be in quiete tille I k[n]owe an ende in thys, for she hath therfor an obligacion of an C*li*. And it is not kepte cloos, ther be many persones now k[n]owyn it, which me semyth a greet rebuke to me that I departyd so largely with yowr brother that I reservyd not to pay that I was endaungered for hym, and so have dyverse seyd to me which of late have k[n]owyn it ; and whan I remembre it, it is to myn hart a very spere, consideryng that he never gave comforte therein, ner of all the money that hath be reseyvyd wull never make shyft therfor. And he had yet be for thys tyme have sent me l. marc thereof, yet I wuld have thought that he had had summe consideracion of myn daungers that I

[1] [From Paston MSS., B.M.] This letter is not addressed, and the MS. is in fact only a corrected draft, of which a fair copy has since been found. The fair copy is not addressed either. The letter was evidently written to John Paston in answer to No. 784. The date is ascertained by the fact that John Berney of Witchingham died in the year 1471.

EDWARD IV

have put me in for hym. Remembre hym how that I have excusyd hym of xx*li*. that the Prior of Bromholm had, which shuld elles have be in that daunger that it shuld have be to us a grete rebwke, with hought that he myght a ben holpyn wyth shuch money as he shuld have had of your fadyrs bequest ; and I payd to the shereffe for hym also money. All thes shuld have holpe me wele therto, be syde other thynges that I have bor thys yeres that I speke not of ; there fore lete hym helpe me now, or elles it shall dysawayll hym better than the trebyll the money, wheder that I leve or dey, with ought he hath better consideracion to the daungers that I stond in. Also I wulde ye shuld meve hym to take John Pampyng to hym, or elles to gete hym a servyce in the Chauncery, or in sume other place where as he myth be preferryd, for it ys pety that he lesyth hys tyme so her, and it is non a wayll to non of ws, and for diverse othyr thyngs whesch ye shall knowe her after, I wolde that I war hens in haste, for all maner of happys, constrw ye, &c. I can yw thanke for ywyr lettyr that ye sente me, and that ye have inquiryd of shwch thynges as ye thynk that shwld plese me. I send yow the boxe and the dedes that ye sente to me for, but as for the key of the cofyr in the wtter chambyr I can not fynd yt ; yf the boxe had be ther in, ye cwdnat not have hadd yth but yf [*unless*] I had broke wp the cofyr ; ther for remembre yw wer ye have do the key ; I kep styll the key that ye sente me tyll that ye cwm home.

As for the tydynges here, ywr cosyn Barney of Wych-shynggham ys passyd to Gode, hwm Gode asoyle. Veylys wife, and Lodonys wife, and Pycard the bacar of Twmlond, ben gone also ; all thys hwlsold and thys parych ys as ye leftyd, blyssyd be Gode ; we lewyn in fer, but we wut not qweder to fle, for to be better than we ben here. I send yw demi a riale for to by wyth swger[1] and dates for me. I pray yw do as wel as ye can, and sende it me as hastely as ye may, and sende me word qwat price a *li*. of peppyr, clowys, masis, gingyr, and sinamun, almannys, ryse, ganyngal,

[1] In Fenn's edition this is printed 'swgar, feg, and dats.' The word 'feg' is not in the MS. It seems to be a misreading of 'swg'' (sugar), which the transcriber forgot to cancel.

1471
NOV. 5
safrwn, reysonys of Corons, grenys,[1] of ych of these sende me the pryce of ych of these,[2] and yf that it be bettir shepe at London than it is here, I shal sende yw mony to bye wyth soch stwfe as I wull have. Remember that I spake to yw to spek to ywyr brother for the seyd C. marc wan ye departed hens. I trow ye had forgettyt, that ye sent me non answer ther of in ony wys. Lete me have an answer ther of in hast, and sende me woord how ywyr brother and ye spede in ywyr maters; and Goddes blissyng and myn mut ye have both, and send yw good sped in all ywyr maters.

Wretyn in hast on Sent Levnards Eve.[3]

By ywyr Moder.

788

BILL OF COSTS [4]

Termino Sancti Michaelis Anno xj° E. iiij[a] pro Ricardo Calle deff' versus Willelmum Huggan q. in placito trans'.

NOV.

In primis, for a copy of the bill, ...	iiij*d.*
Item, for makyng of the awnswer to Mr. Pygot, Mr. Fayrefax, and to Mr. Hosy, ...	x*s.*
Item, wyne and perys at tavern ij. tymes, ...	xiiij*d.*
Item, for a copy of record in the Kynges Bench, . .	iij*s.* iiij*d.*
Item, for pledyng of the record in the Kynges Bench a yenst Wyll. Huggan, ...	x*s.*
Item, gyven to Hosey, the xxvij. day of the same moneth, for to enparle[5] to the bill, ...	iij*s.* iiij*d.*
Item, the xxx. day of October, for the copy of the tytelyng of Huggans plee, ...	iiij*d.*
Item, for wyne at [the] Cardenall Hatte[6] the same day, .	vj*d.*
Item, the iiij. day of November, gyven to Mr. Fayrfax and Mr. Hosey for puttyng yn of the replicacyon, . .	vj*s.* viij*d.*
Item, the x. day of November, gyven to Mr. Fayrfax, Mr. Pygotte, and Mr. Hosey, for the seyng of the paper, and comenyng of the issewe a yenst Wyll. Huggan, . .	x*s.*

[1] F. adds 'and comfytys,' but the words are not in the MS.
[2] F. reads 'the price of a *li.*,' but this is not in the MS.
[3] The following sentence is added in the fair copy: 'I warn yw kepe this letter clos and lese yt not; rather brenyt.'
[4] [From Paston MSS., B.M.]
[5] To *imparl*, a technical expression, meaning to obtain time to plead.
[6] A tavern in Southwark. The name is still preserved in Cardinal Hat Alley.

120

Item, for the wyne at the Cardenall Hatte, . . .	[1] viij*d.*	1471 NOV.
Item, for the entre of the aunswere a yenst Huggan by Ric. Calle, payd to Sandys, ...	vj*s.*	
Item, to Nedersole for makyng of the paper, . . .	ij*s.* vj*d.*	
Item, for the copy of the same, ...	ij*s.* vj*d.*	

Summa totalis, lvj*s.* iiij*d.*

789

EDMUND PASTON TO JOHN PASTON [2]

Tho my rytgh wurshepfull brother John Paston, in hast.

RYGH wurshipful brother, I recumawnd me to zow, prayeng zow hartely that ze wyl remembyr soche maters as I wryth to zow. I send zow now be the brynggar her of mony, wycche mony I pray zow that [ye [3]] be stowe yt as I wryth to zow. I wend a don yt my sylf but consyderyng costis and other dyvers thyngis I may not bryng yt abowthe. Wher for I pray zow hartely to take the labour up on zow, and I trust to deservyt. I pray zow be stow thys mony thus: to Christofyr Hanyngton v*s.*: to the prynspall of Stapylin[4] v*s.* in parte of payment. Also I pray zow to bye me iij. zerddis of porpyl schamlet, price the zerd iiij*s.*, a bonet of depe murry, pryce ij*s.* iiij*d.*, an hose clothe of zelow carsey of an ellyn, I trow yt wyl cost ij*s.*; a gyrdyl of plunkket ryban, price vj*d.*; iiij. lacis of sylke ij. of one color and ij. of ane other, price viij*d.*; iij. doseyn poynttis wythe red and zelow, price vj*d.*; iij. peyer of pateyns. I pray zow late

NOV. 18

[1] *N.B.*—Under viij*d.* is written '46*s.* 4*d.*' in a different hand.
[2] [Add. MS. 34,889, f. 130, and Add. MS. 27, 445, f. 52.] The MS. of this letter is in two fragments, from which it is now printed entire. The letter in which it was written is shown by Margaret Paston's letter to the writer's brother John Paston, on the 29th November 1471 (No. 791), in which she apologises for not sending him money for a runlet of wine she had desired him to purchase for her, on account of the number of thieves stirring. It will be seen that she made the request by means of her son Edmund in this letter.
[3] Omitted in MS.
[4] Staple Inn.

121

1471
NOV. 18
Wylliam Mylsant purvey for them. I was wonte to pay but ij*d.* ob. for a payer, but I pray zow late them not be lefte behyng thow I pay mor; they must be lowe pateyns; late them be long inow and brode up on the hele. Among all other I pray zow recumawnd me to Mastres Elyzabet Hygons. I may sey poverte pames feleschepe. Yf that I had ben so well purveyde as I wend I trowst to have ben with zow her thys; also I pray zow recumawnd me to my brother Sir John. I fer lasse he wyl take a dysplesur with me that I send hym no mony. I pray zow excuse me as ze can. I trust to send hym sum a bowth Candylmesse. I had a promyse of Masteres Elyzabeth of a typet of welvet; but and I myth have a hatlase I woold thynk me well. I pray zow sey thus myche on zour owyn hed, and yf ze can not sped of the hatlase I pray zow bye me one of xij*d.* or xvj*d.* Also Sir I send Parkar hys mony be the brynggar har of and I have desyered hym to lend me a gown of puke, and I have send hym a typet of welvet to boredyr yt [round,[1]] a bowthe; and I pray zow be at schesyng there of; and yf that he wyl not be cryst calkestowe over hys hed that is schoryle in Englysche, yt is a terme newe bròwthe up with my marschandis of Norwych. Sir John Pampyng recummawnd hym to zow and pray zow that ze wyl remembyr hys harnes, and yf that ze can get the mony he pray zow to delyver Parkar x*s.* that he howyth hym. Also, sir, my modyr gretis zow wel and send zow Goddis blyssyng and heres, and prays zow that ze wyl bye her a runlet of Malmesey owthe of the galey; and yf ze have no mony sche byd that ze schuld borow of my brother Sir John, or of sum other frend of zowers, and send [he]r[1] woord as hastily as ze have it, and sche schale send zow mony; and yf that ze send it home sche byd that yt schuld be woond in a canivasse for brochyng of the caryars, for sche sethe that sche hath knowyn men served soo befor. Also I pray zow, if ze speke with Master Roger, tell hym that yf he cum in to thys cuntre thys crystemas, he schal have hys x*s.*, and yf that he cum not I schal send yt hym be xij. day [*Twelfth Day*] at the fardest. I pray zow, hartely remembyr

[1] Mutilated.

122

1471
NOV. 18
my gere, and that ze wyl desyere Wylliam Mylsant on my be halve to purvey for the caryage in as hasty wyse as yt can. Also I pray zow that the welvet that levyt of my typet may be send hom a geyn, for I woold strype a dobelet ther with. As for Masteres Blakenye, I trowe sche in zour quarters. I woold I had the same entyrpryce up on hyr that John Bramppton of Atylborowe had up on master Byrston. Alle the Coorte recommawndes hem tow zow. I pray zow, and ze can get me any profytable servyce, a saye. My brother Sir John was meved of my hawnt Ponyngges to have ben with here. I woold have rytgh an hesy servyse tyl I were owthe of detis. God zeve zow in Hys kepyng. Wretyn at Norwyche, the Monday nex be fore Sen Edmond the Kyng.

EDMOND PASTON.

On the back of the letter are the following memoranda:—

In primis, to the pryncypall of Stapyll In . .	v*s.*
Item, for iiij. lasys	viij*d.*
Item, for iij. doseyn poyntes	vj*d.*
Item, for a plonket ryban	vj*d.*

790

ABSTRACT [1]

[MARGARET PASTON] TO HER SON [SIR JOHN PASTON]

Wonders she has no answer to her letter by Ric. Raddeley. Wants him and his brother to get a discharge from my Lord of Canterbury, 'for occupying of your father's goods.' If my Lord died before we got it, his successor might be 'more hasty upon us than he hath been.' My Lord knows the great charges we have had since he deceased, which have caused the goods to be spent. If any of us were to die, no one would take charge for us unless we have a discharge. Remember the spices and malmsey I have sent to you for. St. Edmund's Day the King.

Sealed.

1471(?)
NOV. 20

[At the date of this letter, Sir John Paston and his brother John were together in London, and apparently the Archbishop of Canterbury was seriously ill. Of the latter fact we have no certain knowledge, but it appears by a subsequent letter that there was a report of his death in June 1472, and the two brothers were certainly in London together in November of the year preceding. It is probable therefore that the Archbishop was ill of the epidemic which prevailed in the latter part of 1471 and the spring of 1472. The two brothers were not together in November 1472.]

[1] [From Paston MSS., B.M.]

123

THE PASTON LETTERS

791

MARGARET PASTON TO JOHN PASTON[1]

To John Paston, Esquier, be this delyverd in hast.

1471
NOV. 29

I GRETE zow welle, and send zow Goddes blyssyng and myn, letyng zow wete that I have a letter from zour brother, wherby I undyrstand that he cannot, ner may, make no porveyans for the C. mark ; the wyche causythe me to be rythgh hevy, and for other thynges that he wrytht to me of that he is in dawnger. For remembering wat we have had befor thys and ho symppylly yt hath be spente and to lytyl profythe to any of us, and now arn in soche casse that non of us may welle helpe other with owte that we schuld do that wer to gret a dysworschip for us to do, owther to selle wood or lond or soche stuffe that were nessessary for us to have in owr howsys ; so mot I answer a for God, I wot not how to do for the seyde money, and for other thyngges that I have to do of scharge, and my worshup saved. Yt is a deth to me to thynk up on yt. Me thynkyth be zour brothers wrythtyng, that he thynkyth that I am informed be sume that be a bowthe me to do and to sey as I have be for thys, but be my trowthe he demyth a mysse ; yt nedyth me not to be informed of no soche thengges. I construe in my owyn mend, and conseyve i now and to myche, and whan I have brokyn my conseyte to sume that in happe ne deniythe yt too, they have put me in cownforth more than I kowde have be any imajynasyon in my owyn conseythe. He wrythetyth to me also, that he hath spend thys terme xl*li.* Yt is a gret thyng ; me thynkyth be good dyscresyon ther mythe myche ther of aben sparyd. Zour fadyr, God blysse hys sowle, hathe had as gret maters to do as I trowe he hathe had thys terme, and hath not spend halfe the mony up on them in so lytyl tyme, and hath do ryth well. At the reverens of God, avyse hym zet to be war of hys expences and gydyng that yt be no schame to us alle. Yt is a schame

[1] [From Paston MSS., B.M.] St. Andrew's Eve, the 29th November, fell on a Friday in 1471. It will also be seen that the beginning of this letter refers to the same subject as the beginning of Letter 787.

124

THE PASTON LETTERS

792

MARGARET PASTON TO JOHN PASTON, ESQUIRE[1]

To John Paston, Esquyer, be this deliuered.

1471(?)
DEC. [1]

I GRETE you wele, and send you Goddis blyssyng and myn. Desyryng you to send me word how that your brother doth. It was told her that he shuld have be ded, which caused many folkis and me bothyn to be right hevy. Also it was told me this day that ye wer hurt be affray that was mad up on you be feles disgysed. Ther fore, in any wyse send me word in hast how your brother doth and ye bothyn ; for I shall not ben wele at eas till I know how that ye do. And for Goddis love lete your brother and ye be ware how that ye walken, and with what felesshep ye etyn or drynkyn, and in what place, for it was seid here pleynly that your brothere was poysoned. And this weke was on of Drayton with me and told me that there were diverse of the tenauntis seid that thei wost not what to do if that your brothere came home ; and ther was on of the Duk of Suffolkis men by, and bad them not feryn, for hys wey shuld be shorted and [*i.e.* if] he shuld come there. Wherfore, in any wyse be ware of your self, for I can thynk thei geve no fors what to do to be wenged and to put you from your entent, that thei myght have her wyll in Ser John Fastolffis land. Thy[nke]² what gret sor[ow]² it [shu]ld² be to me and any . . . . I had lever ye had never know the lond ; remembre it was the distruccion of your fadre ; trost not mych up on promyses of lordis now a days that ye shuld be the suerer of the favor of there men. For there was a man, and a lordis sone, seid but late, and toke it for an exampill that Sir Robert Harecourt had the good will of the lordis after ther comyng in, and yet within shorte tyme after here men kylled hym in hys

[1] [Add. MS. 34,889, f. 211.] This letter may be of the year 1471, when it would seem by No. 791 that the two brothers, Sir John and John, were both together (in London, no doubt) about St. Andrew's Day. If so, it was written just two days after that letter, on the receipt of unpleasant news, which was evidently false.
[2] Mutilated.

126

EDWARD IV

and a thyng that is myche spokyn of in thys contre that zour faders graveston is not mad. For Goddes love, late yt be remembyrd and porveyde for in hast. Ther hathe be mych mor spend in waste than schuld have mad that, me thynkyth be zour brother that he is wery to wrythe to me and there fore I wyl not a kumbyr hym with wrythtyng to hym. Ze may telle hym as I wryth to zow. Item, I woold ze schuld remembyr zour brother of Pekerngges mater, if he cum not hom hastely, that ze and Townesend and Lumnor may examyn and sette yt thorow. The pore man is almost on don ther by, and hys brother suethe hym and trobylyth hym sor zet ; and also for the plesur of my koseyn Clere and the Lady Bolen, I woold yt were sette thorow.

1471
NOV. 29

As for my rowndlet of wyne, I schuld send zow mony there fore, but I dar not put yt in joperte, ther be so many theves stereng. John Lovedayes man was robbyd in to hys schyrte as he cam home ward. I trow, and ze assaye Towneshend or Playter, or sum other good kuntery man of owrys to lend yt zow for me tyl they cum hom, they wyl do so myche for me and I schal contente them a geyn. Item, Jamys Gressham hath ben passyng sekke and ys zet. Judy tellythe me that zour brother is avysed for to sue hym. For Goddes sake, late non onkyndnesse be schewed to hym, for that woold sone make an hend of hym. Remembyr ho keynd and true hartyd he hath ben to us to hys powre ; and he had nevere take that offyce upon hym that he is in dawnger for, ne had be for owr sakkes. He hathe sold a gret parte of hys lond there for, as I suppose ze have knowlache of. Late yt be remembyrd, and ellys owr enmyes wyl rejoysyt, and ther wyl no wurshup be ther in at long way.

I schuld wryth mor but I have no leyser at thys tyme. I trow ze wyl sone kum hom, and there fore I wryth the lesse. God kepe zow and send zow good speede, &c. Wretyn the Fryday, Sen Andrue Ev.

Be zour modyr.

The following note is written on the back of the Letter in Sir John Fenn's hand:— 'This letter was fastened by threads brought through with a needle and made fast by the seal. The threads being cut on the directed side, the letter is opened without breaking the seal.'

125

EDWARD IV

owyn place. A mannes deth is litill set by now a days. Therefore be ware of symulacion, for thei wull speke ryht fayr to you that wuld ye ferd [*fared*] right evyll. The blissid Trynyte have you in his kepyng. Wretyn in gret hast the Saterday next after Sent Andrewe.

1471 (?)
DEC. [1]

Lete this letter be brent whan ye have understond it. Item, I pray you send me iiij. suger lofis, ich of them of ij*li.*, and iiij*li.* of datis if thei be newe. I send you x*s.* be the berer hereof ; if ye pay more I shall pay it you ageyn whan ye come home. And forgete not to send me word be the berere hereof how ye don ; and remembre the bylles and rembrauns for the maner of Gresham that I wrote to your brother for.

Be your moder.

793

JOHN PASTON TO SIR JOHN PASTON[1]

. . . . the very valew of Sporlewood passyth not C. mark of no manys mony that I can spek with, and to be payid by dayis as the byll that Jwde shall delyv[er] . . . rehers ; and ther ayenst ye shold loose ij*li.* of the ferme of the maner yerly, whych standyth by undyr wood ; and yet the fense must stand yow over on xij. mark by the lest wey ; but, by God, and I wer as ye, I wold not sell it for C. mark more then it is woorthe. Syr John Styll recomandyth hym to your good mastyrssheppe, and seyth pleynly if ye wyll he wyll com up to yow and awayte on yow whersoever ye be, coort or othyr. By Seynt Mary, he is owyng more mony than I wend ; for he is owyng for a twelmonthe and a quarter at thys Crystmas, savyng for hys boord, xij*d.* a wek for iij. quarters ; and he seythe pleynly that ye and R. Calle both bad hym syng styll for Syr

1471

[1] [From Paston MSS., B.M.] This seems to be only a portion of a letter, beginning in the middle of a sentence. Probably it was a second leaf added to a more lengthy epistle. It is written on one side of a slip of paper and is in the hand of John Paston the younger. It is endorsed 'John Paston' in that of his brother Sir John, to whom it was doubtless addressed. The date must be towards the end of the year 1471, as it appears by the letter immediately following that Lord Rivers embarked for Portugal that year on Christmas Eve.

127

471 John Fastolf as he dyd before; but I have bodyn hym that he shall get hym a servyse now at thys Crystmas; and so he shall, withowt that ye send hym othyr wyse woord, or ellys that ye or I may get hym som benefyse or fre chapell, or som othyr good servyse whych I praye yow enqwer for.

Item, and ye werk wysly your mater myght com in with othyr maters of the lordes in ther apoyntmentes with the Kyng, but it wold be labord to a porpose this Crystmas whyll ye have leyser to spek with your mastyr. Item, myn aqweyntans with the Lord Revers is none othyrwyse but as it hathe ben alweys; savyng and he go no to Portygall to be at a day upon the Serasyns, I porpose and have promysyd to be ther with hym; and that jorney don, as Wykys seythe, farwell he. He porposyth to go forward a bowt Lent, but Fortune with hyr smylyng contenans strange of all our porpose may mak a sodeyn change. I ensuer yow he thynkyth all the world gothe on ther syd ayen; and as for my comyng up at the begynnyng of thys next term, with owt ye send me othyrwyse woord that I myght do yow som good when I wer com, by my feyth I com not ther, for it shold put yow to a cost, and me to a labor and cost bothe; but [if] ye send for me I com streyght, thow I tery the lesse whyll ther, and so I shall withowt I may do yow som good. By my feythe I porpose to make up my byllys clere, and send yow the copyse as hastyly as I can. Yonge Wyseman othyrwye callyd Foole, told me that Sir W. Yelverton is abowt to make a bargayne with the Dwches of Suffolk or with my Lord of Norfolk, whyche he may get fyrst, for the maner of Gwton. I reseyve all yet, God hold it.

I praye yow recomand me to my brodyr Molynewx, and all othyr good felaws.

J. P.

794

MARGARET PASTON TO SIR JOHN PASTON[1]

I GRETE you wele; letyng you wete that ther was told me 1471 a thyng in your absens that goth right nere myn hert, be a wurchepfull man and such an as ye wuld beleve and geffe credence to, and that owyth you right good wille; which if it had comyn to myn remembraunce at your departer I wuld have spoke to you of it most specially befor all other materis; but I am so trobilled in my mende with your materis that thei be so delayd and take no better conclusion, and with the ontrowth that is in servantis now a days but if the maysteris take better heed to ther handis, that such thyngis as I wuld rathest remembre I sonest for gete. It was told me that ye have sold Sporle wood of a right credebill and wurchepful man, and that was right hevy that ye shuld be know of such disposicion, consederyng how your fader, whos sowle God assoyl, cherysshed in every manor his woodis. And for the more preffe that this shuld be trought, the forseid person told me that it was told hym of on [one] that was toward Sir William Yelverton, to whom Richard Calle shuld have seid in thes termes, that Sporle Wood shuld be sold, and that it shuld comyn now in to Cristen mennes handis. Which if it were knowyn shuld cause bothyn your elmyse [enemies] and your frendis to thynk that ye dede it for right gret nede, or ellis that ye shuld be a wastour and wuld wast your lyvelod. If ye had do so in Sir John Fastolfes lyffelode, men shuld have supposid that ye had do it of good pollice, be cause of the onsuerte that it stoonit (?) in, to have takyn that ye had myght of it duryng your possession, to have boryn ought the daungere of it with the same; but for to do this of your owyn lyffelode, men shall thyng that ye do it for pure nede. And in asmych as it is so nere your most elmyse ere, it shall be to you the gretter vylney and shame to all your frendis, and the grettest

[1] [Add. MS. 34,889, f. 116.] This letter would seem to have been written about the end of the year 1471 or the beginning of 1472, when we first hear of Sir John Paston's design to sell Sporle Wood. See Nos. 793, 798.

471 coragyng and plesere that can be to your elmyse. For if ye be thus disposid ye shall make them and all othere certeyn of that that befor this tyme thei haue ben in dought, and cause them to purpose the more cruelly agayn you. Where fore, in eschewyng of the greet slaundre and inconveniens that may grow ther of, I require you, and more over charge you upon my blissyng and as ye wull have my good will, that if any such sale or bargany be mad, be your assent or with ought, be Calle, or any othere in your name, that ye restreyn it; for I wuld not for a M[l] marcs that it wer understond that ye were of that disposicion, ner that ye were comyn to so gret nede which shuld cause [y]ou to do so; for every [man[1]] shuld thynk that it were thurgh your owyn mysgovernaunce. Therefore I charge you, if any such bargayn be mad, that ye send a bill as hastly as ye can to Herry Halman, that he do all such as have mad or takyn that bargayn seasse and felle non of the wood, upon peyn that may falle ther of. And how [who] so ever wull councell you the contrary, do as I advyse you in this behalffe, or ellis trost never to have comfort of me; and if I may knowe ye be of such disposicion, and I leve ij. yer it shall disavayll you in my liffelode ccc. marcs. There fore, send me word be the berere here of wheder ye have assent to any such thyng or nought, and how that ye be disposid to do ther in, for I shall not be quiete in myn hert till I understand yow of the contrary disposicion.

Be your more moder.

795

SIR JOHN PASTON TO MARGARET PASTON[2]

To my most honorabl and tendre modre, Margrete Paston, be thys letter delivered.

1472 M OST worschypfull and kynde moodre, I comande me JAN. 8 to yow, and beseche yow off yowr dayly blyssyng and remembraunce. Please it yow to wete thatt I have my pardon,[3] as the berer heroff can informe yow, for

[1] Omitted in MS.   [2] [From Fenn, ii. 86.]
[3] His pardon passed the Great Seal on the 21st December 1471. *Pardon Roll* 11 Edward IV., m. 25.

comffort wheroffe I have been the marier thys Crystmesse, and 1472 have been parte theroff with Sir George Browen,[1] and with my JAN. 8 Lady myn aunte, hys wyffe,[2] and be ffor Twelthe[3] I come to my Lorde Archebysshope,[4] wher I have hadde as greete cheer, and ben as welkom as I cowde devyse; and iff I hadde ben in sewerte that Castr weer hadde ageyn, I wolde have comen homewards thys daye.[5]

. . . .

And I beseche yow to remembr my brother to doo hys deveyr thatt I maye have agayn my stuffe, my bookes and vestments, and my beddyng, how so evyr he doo, thoghe I scholde gyffe xx[ti] scutes by hys advyse to my Lady Brandon, or some other goode felawe.

As for any tydynges ther be noon heer, saffe that the Kyng hath kept a ryall Crystmesse; and now they seye that hastelye he woll northe, and some seye that he woll into Walys, and some seye that he woll into the West Contre. As ffor Qween Margrett, I understond that sche is remevyd from Wyndesor to Walyngfforthe, nyghe to Ewhelme, my Lady of Suffolk Place in Oxenforthe schyre.

And men seye that the Lorde Ryverse schyppyd on Crystmesse evyn in to Portyngale warde; I am not serteyn.

Also the schalle be a convocacion off the Clergye in all haste, whyche men deeme will avayle the Kynge a dyme and an halffe, some seye. I beseche God sende yow goode heele and greater joye in on year then ye have hadde thys vij.

Wretyn att the Moor the viij. daye off Janever, A° E. iiij. xj.

By yowr soone,   JOHN PASTON, K.

[1] Sir George Browne, Knight, of Betchworth Castle, in Surrey.—F.
[2] Elizabeth Paston, formerly married to Robert Poynings.
[3] Twelfth day, 6th of January.—F.
[4] George Neville, Archbishop of York.—F.
[5] Here follow directions about Caister, and a hope that it might be had again by the latter end of the term, when he would come home, and put his lands and houses into order.—F.

796

JOHN PASTON TO SIR JOHN PASTON[1]

*To my ryght worchefull brodyr, Syr John Paston, Knyght,
be thys delyveryd.*

1472
JAN. 23

RYGHT worchepfull syr, I recomand me to yow in my
best wyse, lykeyth yow to wet[2]
that I have thys day delyveryd yowr mantyll, yowr
ray gowne,[3] and yowr crosbowys, wyth telers and wyndas, and
yowr Normandy byll to Kerby to bryng wyth hym to London.

Item, in eny wyse, and [*if*] ye can axe the probate of my
fadyrs wyll to be gevyn yow wyth the bargayn that ye make
wyth my Lord of Canterbery, and I can thynk that ye may
have it, and as soone as it is prevyd ye or I may have a lettyr
of mynystracyon upon the same, and a qwetance of my Lord
Cardinalle evyn foorthe wyth; and thys wer one of the best
bargaynys that ye mad thys ij. yer I enswyr yow, and he may
make yow aqwetance or get yow one of the Bysheop of Wynchestyr for Syr John Fastolfys goodes also, and in my reson
thys wer lyght to be broughyt a bowght wyth the same bargayn.
And ye purpose to bargayn with hym ye had need to hye yow,
for it is tolde me that my Lord of Norffolk wyl entyr in to it
hastyly, and if he so doo, it is the wers for yow, and it wyll
cawse them to profyr the lesse sylvyr.

Item, I pray yow send me some secret tydyngs of the
lyklyed of the world by the next messenger that comyth
between, that I may be eyther myryer or ellys mor sory then I
am, and also that I may gwyd me ther aftyr.

Item, as for Sir R. Wyngfeld, I can get no x. *li.* of hym,

[1] [From Fenn, iv. 420.] It appears by a letter of the 17th February following
(No. 798), that at the beginning of the year 1472 the Pastons were endeavouring to
come to an understanding with the Duke of Norfolk by the intercession of the
Duchess. For further evidence of date, see the next letter.

[2] A blank occurs here in Fenn's left-hand, or literal copy, which is not explained.

[3] This means a gown made of cloth that was never either coloured or dyed.—F.
But according to Halliwell ' ray ' means striped cloth.

132

797

MARGARET PASTON TO JOHN PASTON[1]

To John Paston, Esquyer, be thys delivered.

1472
FEB. 5

I GRETE you wele, and send you Godds blyssyng and
myn, letyng you wete that the woman that sewyth the
appell ageyn your brother and his men is comyn to
London to call ther up on. And whan that she shuld come
to London ther was delivered her C. *s.* for to sewe with, so
that be that I here in this countre she wull not leve it, but
that she shall calle ther up on such tyme as shall be to your
most rebuke, but if [*unless*] ye ley the better wetch. She hath
evill councell, and that wull see you gretely uttered, and that
ye may understand be the money that was take her whan she
came up, and ye shuld fynd it, I knowe it wele, if ther myght
have you at avauntage; ther for, for Godds sake make diligent
serge be the advyce of your councell, that ther be no necglicens
in you in this mater ner other for diffaught of labour, and call
upon your brother, and telle hym that I send hym Godds
blyssyng and myn, and desire hym that he wull now a while,
whill he hath the Lords at his entent, that he seke the meanes
to make an ende of his maters, for his elmyses arn gretly
coraged now of late; what is the cause I knowe not. Also, I
pray you speke to Playter that ther may be fownd a meane
that the shereffe or the gaderer of grene wax[2] may be discharged of certeyn issues that renne up on Fastolf for Mariotts
mater, for the balyfe was at hym this weke, and shuld have
streyned hym, but that he promysed hym that he shuld with
in this viij. days labore the meanes that he shuld be discharged

[1] [From Fenn, iv. 424.] As anticipated in the preceding letter we here find that
steps are being taken by one of the two women whose husbands were killed at the
siege of Caister, to prosecute the appeal against Sir John for her husband's death.
The other woman, as will be seen by Letter 783, had married again during the year
1471, and was thus disqualified from pursuing the same course.

[2] Estreats delivered to the Sheriff out of the Exchequer, to be levied in his
county under the Seal of that Court, made in green wax, were from thence called
green wax.—F.

134

but he seyth that I shall have the fayirest harneys that I can
bye in London for sylvyr, but money can I non get. I can
not yet make my pesse wyth my Lord of Norffolk nor my
Lady by no meane, yet every man tellyth me that my Lady
seyth passyngly well of me allweys notwithstandyng. I trowe
that they wyll swe the apell[1] thys term, yet ther is no man of
us indytyd but if it wer doon a for the crowners er then
we cam owt of the plase; ther is now but iij. men in it,
and the brygges alwey drawyn. No mor, but God lant yow
myn her.[2]

1472
JAN. 23

Wretyn the Twysday next aftyr Seynt Agnet the fyrst.[3]

J. P.

Item, yestyrday W. Gornay entryd in to Saxthorp and ther
was he kepyng of a coort, and had the tenaunts attou[r]nyd
to him, but er the coort was all doon, I cam thedyr with a
man with me and no more, and ther, befor hym and all hys
feluwschep, Gayne, Bomsted, &c., I chargyd the tenaunts that
they shold proced no ferther in ther coort upon peyn that
myght folle of it, and they lettyd for a seasen. But they sye
that I was not abyll to make my partye good, and so they
procedyd ferther; and I sye that, and set me downe by the
stward and blottyd hys book wyth my fyngyr as he wrot, so
that all tenaunts afermyd that the coort was enterupte by me
as in yowr ryght, and I reqwered them to record that ther was
no pesybyll coort kept, and so they seyd they wold.

[1] This must be the appeal of the two widows, though one of them is said to have
married again. *See* No. 783.

[2] This sentence I wish to have explained.—F.

[3] The festival of St. Agnes, the first (and the most noted of the two), was kept
on the 21st of January; her second festival was on the 28th of the same month,
which it is to be observed was not the octave of the former, but a distinct feast upon
a different occasion, and it is sometimes written ' Agnetis Nativitas '; but it was on
account of a miracle wrought at her tomb that this second feast was instituted.—F.

133

or ell[es] he must content hym, &c. Also, I send you be the
berer herof, closed in this letter, *v. s.* of gold, and pray you
to bey me a suger loyfe, and dates, and almaunds, and send it
me hame, and if ye bewar [*lay out*] any mor money, whan ye
came hame I shall pait you ageyn. The Holy Gost kepe you
bothyn, and deliver you of your elmyse [*enemies*]. Wretyn on
Sent Agas Day, in hast.

1472
FEB. 5

Item, I pray you speke to Mayster Roger[1] for my sorepe,
for I had never mor nede therof, and send it me as hastly as
ye can.

Be   M. P.

798

SIR JOHN PASTON TO JOHN PASTON[2]

A Johan Paston, Esquier, soit doné.

FEB. 17

BROTHER, I comande me to yow, and praye yow to
loke uppe my *Temple of Glasse*,[3] and send it me by
the berer herof.

Item, as for tydyngs, I have spoken with Mestresse Anne
Hault, at a praty leyser, and, blyssyd be God, we be as ffer
fforthe as we weer toffoor, and so I hoope we schall contenew;
and I promysed hyr, that at the next leyser that I kowd ffynde
therto that I wolde come ageyn and see hyr; whyche wyll take
a leyser as [I] deeme now; syn thys observance is over doon,
I purpose nott to tempte God noo moor soo.

Yisterday the Kynge, the Qween, my Lordes of Claraunce
and Glowcester, wente to Scheen to pardon; men sey, nott
alle in cheryte; what wyll falle, men can nott seye.

The Kynge entretyth my Lorde off Clarance ffor my
Lorde off Glowcester; and, as itt is seyde, he answerythe,

[1] Master Roger was, I suppose, some leech famous for his syrups, etc.—F.

[2] [From Fenn, ii. 90.] After the death of Prince Edward, the son of Henry VI.,
who is said to have been murdered just after the Battle of Tewkesbury in May 1471,
Richard, Duke of Gloucester, married his widow Anne, who was the daughter of
Warwick the Kingmaker. The reference to the proposed sale of Sporle wood goes
further to fix the date. *See* Letter 793, and Nos. 819 and 820 following.

[3] A poem of Lydgate's.

135

1472
EB. 17 that he may weell have my Ladye hys suster in lawe, butt they schall parte no lyvelod, as he seythe; so what wyll falle can I nott seye.

Thys daye I purpose to see my Lady off Norffolk ageyn, in goode howr be it!

Ther is proferyd me marchaunts ffor Sporle woode. God sende me goode sale whan I be gynne; that poor woode is soor manashed and thrett.

Yitt woote I nott whether I come home beffoor Esterne or nott, I schall sende yow worde. No moor, &c.

Wretyn the ffyrst Tewesdaye off Lenton.

                         JOHN PASTON, K.

799

ABSTRACT[1]

RIL 10   Norfolk and Suffolk Deeds, No. 38.—'Relaxatio Johannis Paston facta Willielmo Wainflet et aliis totius juris in manerio vocat' Pedham Hall in Beyton, etc., in omnibus terris, tenementis, redditibus, etc., in villis de Beyton, Akle, Birlingham, et Hykling, quæ quondam fuerunt Johannis Fastolf.— April 10, Edw. IV., 12.'—There is a similar deed of the same date including the manor of Titchwell, numbered 'Titchwell, 5,' in the collection.

800

SIR JOHN PASTON TO HIS BROTHER, JOHN PASTON[2]

To Master John Paston, or to my mestresse, hys Modre, be this letter delyveryd in hast.

PRIL 30   **B**ROTHER, I comand me to yow[3]

      By Juddy I sende yow a letter by Corby with in iiij. dayes byffor thys; and ther with ij. potts off oyle for saladys,

---

[1] [From MS. Index in Magd. Coll., Oxford.]

[2] [From Fenn, i. 288.] The date of this letter is ascertained by the fact that Sir Thomas Waldegrave died on the 28th April 1472.—See Inquisition post mortem, 12 Edw. IV., No. 4.

[3] Here (according to Fenn) follows an order for making out an account and receiving some rents, etc.

136

whyche oyle was goode as myght be when I delyveryd itt, and   1472 schall be goode at the reseyvynge, iff it be nott mysse handelyd,   APRIL 30 nor mysse karryd.

Item, as ffor tydyngs, the Erle of Northomberlonde is hoome in to the Northe, and my Lord off Glowcester schall afftr as to morow, men seye. Also thys daye Robert of Racclyff weddyd the Lady Dymmok at my place in Fleet-street, and my Ladye and yowrs, Dame Elizbeth Bowghcher,[1] is weddyd to the Lorde Howards soon and heyr.[2] Also Sir Thomas Walgrave is ded off the syknesse that reygnyth, on Tewesday, now [no] cheer ffor yowe. Also my Lorde Arche-bysshope[3] was browt to the Towr on Saterday at nyght, and on Mondaye, at mydnyght, he was conveyd to a schyppe, and so in to the see, and as yitt I can nott undrestande whedyr he is sent, ner whatt is fallyn off hym; men seye, that he hathe offendyd, but as John Forter seythe, some men sey naye; but all hys meny ar dysparblyd [*dispersed*], every man hys weye; and som that ar greete klerkys, and famous doctors of hys, goo now ageyn to Cambrygge to scoolle. As ffor any other tydyngs I heer noon. The Cowntesse off Oxenfford[4] is stylle in Seynt Martyns; I heer no word off hyr. The Qween hadde chylde, a dowghter, but late at Wyndesor; ther off I trow ye hadde worde. And as ffor me, I am in lyke case as I was. And as ffor my Lorde Chamberleyn,[5] he is nott yitt comen to town; when he comythe than schall I weete what to doo. Sir John of Parr is yowr ffrende and myn, and I gaffe hym a ffayr armyng sworde within this iij. dayes. I harde somwhat by hym off a bakke ffreende off yowr; ye schall knowe moor her afftr.

Wretyn the last daye of Apryll.

---

[1] Elizabeth, daughter and heiress of Sir Frederic Tilney, Knight, and widow of Sir Humphrey Bourchier, son of John, first Lord Berners. Her husband was slain at the battle of Barnet.

[2] Thomas Howard, afterwards created Duke of Norfolk, by Henry VIII., for his victory over the Scots at Flodden. He was son and heir of John, Lord Howard.

[3] George Nevill, Archbishop of York.

[4] Margaret, wife of John de Vere, Earl of Oxford, daughter of Richard Nevill, Earl of Salisbury, and sister of Warwick the Kingmaker.

[5] William, Lord Hastings.

137

801

JOHN PASTON TO SIR JOHN PASTON[1]

To Mastyr Syr John Paston, Knyght, in hast.

1472
AY 14   **S**YR, I recomande me to yow, &c. W. Gorney and I ar apoyntyd that ther shall no mony be takyn at Saxthorp tyll thys terme be past, for he hathe promysyd me to spek with yow and your consell, and that ye shall tak a wey betwyx yow so that ye shall be bothe plesyd. He had warnyd a coort at Saxthorp and to have be kep upon Holy Rood Day last past, and ther he wold have gadyrd the half yere ferm; but it fortunyd me to be there ere the coort was half done, and I took syche a wey with hym that the qwest gave no verdyt, ner they procedyd no ferther in ther cort, nor gadyrd no mony ther, nor not shall do, tyll syche tym as ye spek to gedyr, and [*if*] ye be at London thys term; but and ye be not at London, I wold avyse yow to let Townsend tak a wey with hym, for it lyeth not in my power to keep werre with hym; for and I had not delt ryght corteysly up on Holy Rood Day I had drownk so many oystyrs, for yowng Heydon had reysyd as many men as he kowd mak in harneys to have holp Gornay; but when Heydon sye [*saw*] that we delt so corteysly as we ded he withdrew hys men and mad hem to go hom a yen, not-withstandyng they wer redy, and ned had be. And also my Lord of Norffolks men wyll be with hym ayenst me I wet well as yet, tyl bettyr pesse be.

Item, as for myn ownkyll William, I have spook with hym, and he seyth that he wyll make a byll in all hast of iche percelle be twyxt yow and send yow word in wryghtyng how that he wooll dyell with yow; but I can not se that he besyth hym abowght it, notwithstandyng I calle upon hym dayly for it. As for mony, I can none get, neyther at Snaylewell nor at

---

[1] [From Paston MSS., B.M.] What is here said of the attempt of Gurney to collect the rents at Saxthorpe, seems to show that this letter is of the same year as No. 796. Also the mention of Maryot's annuity and the green wax agrees very well with the previous allusion to these matters in No. 797.

138

Sporle tyll mydsomer, thow I wold dryve all the catell they   1472 have. I was bond to the shrevys for gren wax[1] and for a   MAY 14 *fyeri facias* that is awardyd owt of yowr lond, wyche drawyth in alle bettyr than v. mark, and I am fayn to borow the mony to pay it by that Lord I beleve on, for I cowd not gadyr a nobyll of areragys syn I was with yow at London of alle the lyve-lod ye have. As for John Maryot, he is payid of hys anuyte in to a nobyll or xs. at the most, but as for all hys dettors I can not pay hem tyll I can gadyr more mony, so God help me. I pray yow send a byll to John Pampyng that he may ryed with me ovyr all your lyvelood, and tak a clere reknyng what is owyng and what that I have receyvyd, that ye may have a cler reknyng of all that ye owe in thys contre, and what your tenauntes owe yow. Item, I pray yow send me word as hastyly as ye can, how the world goethe. No more, but God lant yow lansmann,[2] and rather then to stand in dowght, remembyr what peyn it is a man to loese lyberte. The Flet is a fayir preson, but ye had but smale lyberte ther in,[3] for ye must nedys aper when ye wer callyd. Item, I have fownd Jamys Greshamys oblygacyon. Item, he comyth to London-ward thys day.

Wretyn the xiiij. day of Maye.   J. P.

---

[1] *See* p. 134, Note 2.

[2] So in MS. What does this mean? Compare similar expression at p. 133.

[3] I have found no other mention of Sir John Paston having been imprisoned in the Fleet.

802

JOHN PASTON TO SIR JOHN PASTON[4]

  RYGHT worchefull syr, I recomande me to yow, sertyfy-   MAY 25 ing yow that I was purposyd to have com to London to have made my pese with my Lady of Norffolk, but I undyrstand she is not in London; notwithstandyng that

---

[4] [From Paston MSS., B.M.] This letter seems to have been written in 1472, when, as before observed, the Pastons were endeavouring to make peace with the Duke of Norfolk by means of the Duchess. The date is confirmed by the reference to James Gresham's obligation at the end. Compare last No. There is no address on the back.

139

THE PASTON LETTERS

1472
MAY 25

is no cause of myn abydyng at hom, but thys is the cause, so God help me,—I can get no mony, neythyr of your lyvelod ner of myn, to pay for my costes, nor for to ease yow with at my comyng. Notwithstandyng I am promysyd som at Snayle-well, and if so be that John can take eny ther, he shall bryng it yow with thys bylle. I send yow here ij. of my reknynges that I have receyvd and payd syn I delt with yowr lyvelod, and by thes ij. and by that reknyng that I sent yow to Lon-don ye may know what is receyvyd by me, and what I have payid ; and howgh and when so evyr ye wyll let your ten-auntes and fermours at alle plasys be examynd, ye shalle fynd it non othyr wyse. So God help me, as your lyvelod is payid, it cannot paye your dettes in thys contre ; for it drawyth up on a xli. that ye owe yet in thys contre, besyd the xiili. to Dawbney ; and with in thes vij. dayis I shall send yow a clere byll what ye owe, for ther are axyid many thynges that I knewe not of when I was with yow.

Also I enswyr yow by my trowthe I saw my modyr nevyr sorer mevyd with no mater in hyr lyve then she was when she red the byll that ye gave me warnyng in that Perker had atainyd an axyon ayenst yow and me, for she supposyth veryly that it is doon by myn oncyll William meanys, to mak yow to sell your lond. But thys she comandyd me for to send yow word, that and ye sell eny lond, but paye your dettes with syche good as my Lord Archebyshopp owyth yow, and eny law in Inglond can put fro yow eny of hyr lond, she sweryth by that feyth that she owyth to God she wyll put fro yow dobyll as myche lond as ye selle. And therfor I wold avyse yow, calle sharply upon my Lord, the Archebyshop, for ye ar not bond to undo your sylf for hym.

Item, I pray yow se that I tak no hurt by Parker. As for myn oncyll W., I can not mak hym to send you the byll of syche stuff as he hathe of yowrs. He seyth he woll, but he comyth no of with it.[1] He and I ar fowly fallyn owght thys same day for a mater betwyx Lovell and Johne Wallsam and hyr sustyr. Lovell hathe bowt Jone Walshamys part of hyr lyvelod, and maryd hyr to a knave, and myn oncyll W. hathe

[1] So in MS.

140

EDWARD IV

oft spok with my modyr and me for to delyver Jone Wals-hamys evydence to Lovell, whyche I have in kepyng ; and be cause I wyll not delyver Lovell the evydence therfor we fyll owt, in so myche that he seyth he wyll stryppe me fro the maner of Sweynsthorpe. Wherfor I pray yow in eny wyse send me by John Mylsend a copye of the deed that I sent yow to London. Ther is in the same deed Gresham and Snayle-well, and Sporle and Sweynsthorpe, alle to gedyr I trow. And I prey you let the date and the feoffeys namys, and alle be set in. And I trust to God to mak yt so sewyr that he shall do me lytyll harm. Gefrey Spyrlyng callyth oft up on me to undyrstand how ye wyll delle with hym for hys plase in Nor-wyche. I pray you send me woord by John what answer I may geve hym ; he delyth alwey ryght frendly with yow.

Item, I send yow here wyth Jamys Greshamys oblygacyon.

Item, I pray yow send serteyn woorde how the world gothe.

Wretyn the xxv. day of May. J. P.

1472
MAY

Endorsed—John Paston.

803

MARGARET PASTON TO SIR JOHN PASTON[1]

To Sir John Paston, Knythe, be thys delyverid.

I GRET zow welle, and send zow Godds blyssyng and myn, latyng zow wet that I spakke with frends of myn with yne thys fewe days that told me that I am leke to be trobyld for Sir John Fastolles goodes, the whyche were in zour fadyrs possessyon, and as for me I had never none of them. Where fore I pray zow send me a kopy of the dysse-

1472
JUNE

[1] [From Paston MSS., B.M.] It is evident that Henry Heydon's purchase of Saxthorpe, mentioned in this letter, must have been subsequent to his support of Gurney in the possession of that manor, as mentioned in Letter 801. No doubt the year is the same. The letter is endorsed by Sir John 'Per matrem.'

141

THE PASTON LETTERS

1472
JUNE 5

charge whyche ze have of my Lord of Wynchester that ze told me that ze had, bothe for my dyscharge and zowyrs wat sum ever that be callyd upon of eyther of us here after. Item, yt ys told me that Harry Heydon hat bowthe [*bought*] of the seyd Lord bothe Saxthorpe and Tychewelle, and hathe takke possessyon there in. We bette the busschysse and have the losse and the disworschuppe and ether men have the byrds. My Lord hathe falsse kownselle and sympylle, that avyseythe hym thereto ; and as yt ys told me, Guton ys leke to goo the same wey in hast. And as for Heylysdon and Drayton, I trow yt is ther yt schalle be. Wat schalle falle of the rem-naunt, God kowythe,—I trow as evelle or whersse. We have the losse among us. Yt owythe to be remembyrd, and they that be defawty to have konsyens there in. And so mot I thryve, yt was told me but latte that yt is seyd in kownselle of them that ben at Caster, that I am leke to have but lytylle good of Mauteby yf the Duke of Norfolke have possessyon stylle in Caster ; and yf we lesse that, we lesse the fayereste flower of owr garlond. And ther for helpe that he may be owte of possessyon there of in haste be myn a vyse, wat so ever fortune here after. Item, yt is seyde here that my Lord Archebysschoppe is ded ; and yf yt be so, calle up on hys sueretes for the mony that is owyng to us, in hast be myn avyse ; and at reverens of God helpe that I mythe be dys-chargyd of the C. mark that ze wet of, owder be that mene or sum other, for yt ys to myche for me to bere, with other charges that I have besyd, that I am to hevy wan I thynk up on yt. As for your syster Anne, Master Godfrey and his wyffe and W. Grey of Martyn, arn up on a powntment with me and your brother John, so that ze wylle a gre there to and be her good brother ; sche schalle have to joyntor hys modyrs lyvelod after the dyssese of her and her husbond, and I to pay xli. be zere to the fynddyng of her and her husbond tylle cli., be payed. And yf hys grawntsyers lyvelod falle to hym here after, he hathe promysed to amend her joyntyr. Master God-frey hathe promysyd hym for hys parte xls. be zere, and than lakkythe but iiij. nobyls of xx. mark be zere, the wyche they hope ze wylle make upe for zour parte. Wylliam Grey told me

142

EDWARD IV

he schuld speke with zow here in wan he kam to London thys terme. God kepe zow.

Wretyn in hast on Fryday next after Sen Pernelle.[1]
Be your modyr.

1472
JUNE

804

JOHN PASTON TO SIR JOHN PASTON[2]

To my ryght worchepfull brodyr, Sir John Paston, Knyght.

RYGHT worchepfull sir, I recomand me to yow.[3]
. . . .
Item, Mastyr John Smythe tellyth me that Sir T. Lyneys goodys ar not abyll to paye a quarter of hys detts that be axyd hym ; wherfor syche money as is be left it most be devydyd to every man a parte aftyr the quan-tyte, whyche dyvysyon is not yet mad, but when it is mad he hathe promysyd me that your part shalbe worthe iij. the best, &c.

Item, as for J. of Barneys hors, whoso have leest need to hym he shall cost hym xx. marks, not a peny lesse.

Ye send me woord of the maryage of my Lady Jane ; one maryage for an other on, Norse and Bedford were axed in the chyrche on Sonday last past. As for my syster Anne, my modyr wyll not remeve fro W. Yellverton for Bedyngfeld, for she hathe comend ferther in that mater, syn ye wer in this contre, as it aperyth in hyr lettyr that she sendyth yow by Thyrston.

Tydyngs her, my Lady of Norffolk is with chyld, she wenyth hyrsylf, and so do all the women abowght hyr, inso-myche she waytys the qwyknyng with in thes vj. wekys at the ferthest. Also W. Gernay wenyth that Heydon is swyr of

[1] St. Petronilla the Virgin or St. Pernell. Her day was the 31st May.
[2] [From Fenn, ii. 92.] This letter, like the last, is dated by the reference to Gurney and Heydon. The date is confirmed by the allusion to the proposal to sell Sporle wood.
[3] Here follows an account of some money transactions, etc.—F.

143

THE PASTON LETTERS

1472
JUNE 5

Saxthorp, and that Lady Boleyn of Gwton. John Osberne avysythe yow to take brethe for your wodsale at Sporle, for he hathe cast it, that it is woorthe as good as ix.ˣˣ.*li.* Bewar of Montayn, for he may not pay yow so moche mony with hys ease.

I prey yow recomand me to Sir John Parre with all my servys, and tell hym by my trouthe I longyd never sorer to see my Lady than I do to se hys Mastershepe; and I prey God that he aryse never a mornyng fro my Lady hys wyff, with owght it be ageyn hyr wyll, tyll syche tyme as he bryng hyr to Our Lady of Walsyngham.

Also I prey yow to recomand me in my most humbyll wyse unto the good Lordshepe of the most corteys, gentylest, wysest, kyndest, most compenabyll, freest, largeest, most bowntesous knyght, my Lord the Erle of Arran,[1] whych hathe maryed the Kyngs sustyr of Scotland. Herto he is one the lyghtest, delyverst, best spokyn, fayrest archer; devowghtest, most perfyghte, and trewest to hys lady of all the knyghtys that ever I was aqweyntyd with; so wold God, my Lady lyekyd me as well as I do hys person and most knyghtly condycyons, with whom I prey yow to be aqweyntyd, as yow semyth best; he is lodgyd at the George in Lombard Street. He hath a book of my syster Annys of the *Sege of Thebes;* when he hathe doon with it, he promysyd to delyver it yow. I prey lete Portland bryng the book hom with hym. Portland is loggyd at the George in Lombard Street also.

And thys I promyse yow, ye schall not be so longe ayen with ought a byll fro me, as ye have ben, thow I shold wryght how ofte the wynd changyth, for I se be yow wryghtyng ye
crosse it.

·–+–·–+–·

can be wrothe and ye wyll for lytyll.[2]   Wretyn the v. day of

·–+–·–+–·

June.   J. PASTON.

1 Thomas Boyd, Earl of Arran, in 1466, married Mary, daughter of James II. and sister of James III., Kings of Scotland. He was appointed Regent, but becoming unpopular, was banished, and died in exile before 1474.—F.

2 These two words are crossed as here represented, and over them is written, 'crosse it.'

144

EDWARD IV

805

JOHN PASTON TO SIR JOHN PASTON[1]

To my ryght worchepfull brodyr, Sir John Paston, Knyght.

RYGHT worchepfull sir, I recomand me to you, sertyfying yow that I have spokyn wyth Mastyr John Smyth[2] for Sir T. Lyndys, and he hathe shewyd me your byll whyche ye axe to be content of. Your byll a lone drawyth iiij. mark and ode monye, for ye have set in your byll for wax a lone xxs., whyche to Mastyr John S. imagynacyon, and to all other ofycers of the coort, shold not drawe past xxd. at hys berying. The bylls that be put into the coorte of Syr Thomas Lynys dettes drawe xxxli. xviijs. vjd., and all the money that can be mad of hys house and goodes in this contrey drawyth but vli. Mastyr J. Smyth wold ye shold send hym into the coort an inventory of syche goodys as Syr T. had at London when he dyeid, and that inventory onys had, ye shall have as comyth to your part and more also. Ye must send the serteynte whedyr the wax be xxs. or xxd.; and as for the Freers, Master John wyll not alowe theym a peny, for he seyth wher the dettes may not be payeid, set the beqwestes at nowght. He is agreid to pay the potycarye aftyr that he have the inventory fro yow. Rysyng I trowe hathe be with yow.

Item, as for John Maryot, I have sent to hym for the xls. but I have non answer.

Item, I have spok with Barker, and he hathe no money, nor non can get tyll harvest, when he may dystreyn the cropp upon the grownd; he seyth there is not owyng past v. mark, and on Saturday next comyng he shall send me a vewe of hys

1472
JULY 8

1 [From Paston MSS., B.M.] The references to the affairs of the deceased Sir Thomas Lynde, the Duchess of Norfolk's pregnancy, and other subjects mentioned in the letter immediately preceding, prove clearly that this letter belongs to the same year.

2 Master John Smyth was, at this time, an officer in the Bishop's Court; he became afterwards Chancellor of the Diocese of Norwich, and died about 1491.

THE PASTON LETTERS

1472
JULY 8

acompte whyche I shall send you as sone as I have it. As for Fastolffes v. mark, J. Wyndham hathe be spokyn to by me half a doseyn tymys to send to hym for it, and he seyth he hathe doon so.

Item, Sir John Styll hathe told Jwde when ye shall have the chalys; ax Jwde of your crwets allso.

Item, the prowd, pevyshe, and evyll disposyd prest to us all, Sir James, seyth that ye comandyd hym to delyver the book of vij. Sagys to my brodyr Water, and he hathe it.

Item, I send you the serteynte her with of as myche as can be enqweryd for myn oncyll W. cleym in Caster; thase artyclys that fayle, the tenaunts of Caster shall enqwer theym, and send theym to me hastyly; they have promysyd, and they com, ye shall have theym sent yow by the next messenger that comyth to London.

Item, my modyr sendyth you woord that she hathe neyther Master Robard Popyes oblygacyon nor the Byshopys.[1]

Item, my modyr wold ye shold in all haste gete hyr aqwetance of the Byshop[2] of Wynchester for Sir John Fastolffes goodes; she preyid you to make it swyr by the avyse of your consayll, and she wyll pay for the costes.

Item, she preyith you to spek to the seyd Byshop for to get Master Clement Felmyngham the viij. mark be yer dwryng hys lyffe that Sir J. Fastolff be set hym; she preyid you to get hym an asygnement for it to som maner in Norffolk or in Lothynglond.

Item, she wold ye shold get yow an other house to ley in your stuff syche as cam fro Caster. She thynkyth on of the Freerys is a fayir house; she purposeyth to go in to the contre, and ther to sojorn onys ayen.[3] Many qwarellys ar pyekyd to get my brodyr E. and me ought of hyr howse; we go not to bed unchedyn lyghtly, all that we do is ille doon, and all that Sir Jamys and Pekok dothe is well doon; Sir Jamys and I be tweyn. We fyll owght be for my modyr,

1 Walter Lyhert, Bishop of Norwich, from 1445 to 1472.
2 William de Wainfleet, Bishop of Winchester from 1447 to 1486.
3 Fenn reads 'onys a yer,' which may have been intended; but I think the true reading is 'ayen.'

146

EDWARD IV

with 'Thow prowd prest' and 'Thow prowd sqwyer,' my modyr takyng hys part, so I have almost beshet the bote, as for my modyrs house; yet somer shal be don or I get me ony mastyr. My modyr proposeith hastyly to take estate in all hyr londys, and upon that estate to make hyr wyll of the seyd londys, parte to geve to my yonger brethyrn for term of ther lyvys, and aftyr to remayn to yow, pert to my syster Annys,[1] maryage, tyll on Cli. be payid, part for to make hyr ile at Mawtby, parte for a prest to syng for hyr and my fadyr, and ther ancestrys. And in thys aungyr betwen Sir Jamys and me, she hathe promyseid me that my parte shall be nowght; what your shal be, I can not sey. God sped the plowghe; i feythe ye must purvey for my brodyr E. to go over with you, or he is on don; he wyll bryng xx. noblys in hys purse. My modyr wyll nowthyr geve nor lend non of you bothe a peny forward. Purvey a meane to have Caster ayen or ye goo ovyr; my Lord and Lady (whyche for serteyn is gret with chyld), be wery ther of, and all the housold also. If ye wyll eny othyr thyn to be don in thys contre, send me woord, and I shall do as well as I can with Godes grace, Who preserve yow.

Wretyn the viij. day of Julle.   I pray yow recomand me to my Lord of Aran,[2] Sir John Par, Sir George Browne, Osbern Berney, R. Hyd, Jhoxson my cosyn, hys wyfe Kate, W. Wood, and all.   I pray brenne thys by[ll] for losyng.

Your,   J. P.

1472
JULY 8

806

ABSTRACT[3]

A paper endorsed 'The copy of the request to the Bishop of Winchester by Sir John Paston, Knight.'

Complains of my Lord not making him an acquittance of 4000 marks which he has often claimed, etc.

[Sir John Paston is desired in Letters 796 and 805 to procure from the Bishop of Winchester an acquittance for Sir John Fastolf's goods, and this paper may be presumed to be of the same year.]

1 She afterwards married William Yelverton, Esq.
2 *See* p. 144, Note 1.   3 [From MS. Phillipps 9735, No. 271.]

147

1472(?)

THE PASTON LETTERS

807

ABSTRACT[1]

1472
AUG. 12 Norf. and Suff. Deeds, No. 63.—'Relaxatio Willielmi Paston Will. Wainflete et aliis totius juris in manerio de Caldecots in Freton, in Akethorp, in Lowestoft, Spitlings in Gorleston, tenementi vocat' Habland in Bradwell, et tenementi vocat' Broweston in eadem villa, et aliis terris infra hundred de Loddinglond Aug. 12, Edw. iv. 12.'

808

JAMES ARBLASTER TO THE BAILIFF OF MALDEN[2]

To my ryght trusty ffrend John Carenton,
Baylye of Maldon.

SEPT. 20 RYGHT trusty frend, I comand me to yow, preying yow to call to your mynd that, lyek as ye and I comonyd of, it were necessary for my Lady and you all, hyr servaunts and tenaunts, to have thys Parlement as for one of the burgeys of the towne of Maldon, syche a man of worchep and of wytt as wer towardys my seyd Lady ; and also syche on as is in favor of the Kyng and of the Lords of hys consayll nyghe abought hys persone. Sertyfying yow, that my seid Lady for hyr parte, and syche as be of hyr consaill be most agreeabyll, that bothe ye, and all syche as be hyr fermors and tenauntys, and wellwyllers, shold geve your voyse to a worchepfull knyght, and one of my Ladys consayll, Sir John Paston, whyche standys gretly in favore with my Lord Chamberleyn ; and what my seyd Lord Chamberleyn may do with the Kyng and with all the Lordys of Inglond, I trowe it be not unknowyn to you most of eny on man alyve. Wherefor, by the meenys of the seyd Sir John Paston to my seyd

[1] [From ms. Index in Magd. Coll., Oxford.]
[2] [From Fenn, ii. 98.] The date of this letter is ascertained by the reference made to it in that which immediately follows it.
148

THE PASTON LETTERS

1472
SEPT. 21 And I thankyd hem in your name, and told them that ye wold have noo voyse as thys day, for ye supposyd not to be in Inglond when the Perlement shold be, and so they cam not at the sherhous [*shire-house*] ; for if they had, it was thought by syche as be your frends here, that your adversarys wold have reportyd that ye had mad labor to have ben one, and that ye koud not bryng your purpose abowght.

I sent to Yermowthe, and they have promysyd also to Doctor Aleyn and John Russe to be mor then iij. wekys goo.

Jamys Arblaster hathe wretyn a lettyr to the Bayle of Maldon, in Essex, to have yow a bergeys ther ; howe Jwde shall sped, let hym tell yow, when ye spek to gedyr.

Syr, I have ben twyis at Framlyngham sythe your departyng, but now, the last time the consayll was ther, I sye [*saw*] yow lettyr whyche was bettyr then well endyghtyd. R. C.[1] was not at Framlyngham when the consaill was ther, but I took myn owne avyse, and delyvered it to the consayll with a propocysion ther with, as well as I kowd spek it, and my wordys wer well takyn, but your lett[yr] a thousand fold bettyr. When they had red it, they shewd it to my Lady.[2] Aftyr that my Lady had sen it, I spok with my Lady offryng to my Lord and her your servyse, and besyd that, ye to do my Lord a plesur[3] and hyr a bettyr, so as ye myght depert wyth ought eny some specyfyid. She wold not tell in that mater, but remyttyd me ayen to the consayll, for she seyd, and she speke in it, tyll my Lord and the consayll wer agreed, they wold ley the wyght [*blame*] of all the mater on hyr, whyche shold be reportyd to hyr shame ; but thys she promyseid to be helpyng, so it wer fyrst mevyd by the consayll. Then I went to the consayll, and offyrd befor them your servyse to my Lord, and to do hym a plesure, for the haveing ayen of your place and londys in Caster, xl*i*. not spekyng of your stuff nor thyng ellys. So they answerd me your offyr was more then resonabyll ; and if the mater wer thers, they seyd, they wyst what conscyence wold dryve hem to. They seyd they wold meve

[1] Richard Calle.
[2] Elizabeth, Duchess of Norfolk.
[3] Make him a present.—F.
150

EDWARD IV

Lord Chamberleyn, bothe my Lady and ye of the towne 1472 kowd not have a meeter man to be for yow in the Perlement, SEPT. 2 to have your needys sped at all seasons. Wherfor, I prey yow labor all syche as be my Ladys servauntts, tenaunts, and wellwyllers, to geve ther voyseys to the seyd Sir John Paston, and that ye fayle not to sped my Ladys intent in thys mater, as ye entend to do hyr as gret a plesur, as if ye gave hyr an C*li*. And God have yow in Hys keping.

Wretyn at Fysheley, the xx. day of Septembyr.

J. ARBLASTER.

I prey yow be redy with all the acomptanttys belongyng to my Lady, at the ferthest within viij. dayes next aftyr Perdon Sonday, for then I shall be with yow with Gods Grace, Who have yow in keepyng.

809

JOHN PASTON TO SIR JOHN PASTON[1]

To my ryght worchepfull brodyr, Sir John Paston, Knyght.

RYGHT worchepfull sir, I recomand me to yow, letyng SEPT. 2 yow wet that your desyer as for the Knyghts of the Shyer was an impossoybyl to be browght abowght ; ffor my Lord of Norffolk and my Lord of Suffolk wer agreid i mor then a fortnyght go to have Sir Robert Wyngfeld, and Sir Rychard Harcort, and that knew I not tyll it was Fryday last past. I had sent or I rod to Framlynham, to warne as many of your frends to be at Norwyche as thys Monday, to serve your entent as I koud ; but when I cam to Framlynham, and knew the apoyntment that was taken for the ij. knyghts, I sent warnyng ayen to as many I myght to tery at hom ; and yet ther cam to Norwyche thys day as many as ther costs dreave to ix*s. id. ob.*, payid and reknyd by Pekok and R. Capron, and yet they dyd but brak ther fest and depertyd.

[1] [From Fenn, ii. 102.]
149

EDWARD IV

my Lord with it, and so they dyd, but then the tempest aros, 1472 and he gave hem syche an answer that non of hem all wold tell SEPT. 2 it me ; but when I axid an answer of them, they seyd, and [*if*] som Lordys or gretter men mevyd my Lord with it, the mater wer your (kepe consaile), and with thys answer I depertyd. But Syr W. Brandon, Sothewell, Tymperley, Herry Wentworthe, W. Gornay, and all other of consayll, undyrstand that ye have wronge, insomyche that they mevyd me that ye shold take a recompence of other lond to the valew ; but they wold not avowe the offyr, for I anserd hem that if they had ryght they wold have ofred no recompence. Dyscovyr not thys, but in my reason, and [*i.e.* if] my Lord Chamberleyn[1] wold send my Lady a letter with some privy tokyn betwyx theym, and allso to meve my Lord of Norffolk when he comyth to the Parlement, serteynly Caster is yours.

If ye mysse to be burgeys of Maldon, and my Lord Chamberleyn wyll, ye may be in a nother plase ; ther be a doseyn townys in Inglond that chesse no bergeys, whyche ought to do, and ye may be set in for one of those townys, and ye be frendyd. Also in no wyse forget not in all hast to get some goodly ryng, pryse of xx*s.*, or som praty flowyr of the same pryse, and not undyr, to geve to Jane Rodon, for she hathe ben the most specyall laborer in your mater, and hathe promysyd hyr good wyll foorthe, and she doeth all with hyr mastresse. And my Lord Chamberleyn wyll, he may cause my Lord of Norffolk to com up soner to the Parlement then he shold do, and then he may apoynt with hym for yow, or the ferm corn[2] be gadryd. I profyrd but xl*i.*, and if my Lord Chamberleyn profyr my Lady the remenaunt, I can thynk it shall be taken. My Lady must have somwhat to bye hyr kovercheff[3] besyd my Lord. A soper that I payd for, wher all the consayll was at Framlyngham, ij*s.* iij*d.*, and my costs at Framlyngham twyis lying ther by viii. dayis, with ix*s. id.* ob., for costs of the contre at Norwyche drawyth abowght xx*s.*, I trowe more : by our Lady, i it be lesse, stand to your harmys, and *sic remanet* v*li.* xiij*s.* iiij*d.*

[1] William, Lord Hastings.
[2] Corn paid in part of rent.—F.
[3] A head-dress, or handkerchief.—F.
151

THE PASTON LETTERS

I axe no more gods of you for all the servyse that I shall do yow whyll the world standyth, but a gosshawke,[1] if eny of my Lord Chamberleyns men or yours goo to Kaleys, or if eny be to get in London; that is, a mewyd hawk, for she may make yow sporte when ye com into Inglond a doseyn yer hens, and to call upon yow owyrly, nyghtly, dayly, dyner, soper, for thys hawk. I pray noo more but my brother E., J. Pampyng, Thyrston, J. Myryel, W. Pytte, T. Plattyng Jwde, lityll Jak, Mastyr Botoner, and W. Wood to boote, to whyche persons I prey yow to comand me; and if all thes lyst to spek to yow of thys mater when Sir George Browne, W. Knyvett, R. Hyd, or eny folk of worchepp and of my aqweyntanse be in your compeny, so that they may helpe forthe, for all is lytyll i nowe, and ye be not very well wyllyng, I shall so pervey for hem, and ever ye com to Norwyche, and they with yow, that they shall have as deynte vytayll and as gret plente therof for id. as they shall have of the tresorer of Caleys for xvd., and ye, peraventure, a pye of Wymondham to boote. Now thynk on me, good Lord, for if I have not an hawke, I shall wax fatt for default of labor, and ded for default of company by my trowthe. No more, but I pray God send you all your desyrs, and me my mwyd gosshawk in hast, or rather then fayle, a sowyr hawke. Ther is a grosser dwellyng ryght over ayenst the well with ij. boketts a lytyll fro Seynt Elens, hathe evyr hawkys to sell.

Wretyn at Norwyche the xxj. day of September, Anno E. iiij[ti] xij°.

J. P.

Rather then faylle, a tarsell provyd wyll occupy the tyme tyll I com to Caleys.

[1] From the anxiety here expressed for a hawk, we may judge of the attention which was paid to the diversion of hawking. Latham, in his book of Falconry, says that a goshawk is the first and most esteemed kind of hawk; that a sore hawk is from the first taking of her from the eyry till she hath mewed her feathers. The tassel, or tiercel, is the male of the goshawk, so called because it is a tierce or third less than the female; it appears here, that a 'grosser,' or dealer in foreign fruits, etc., sold hawks. —F.

EDWARD IV

810

JOHN PASTON TO SIR JOHN PASTON[1]

A Monsieur J. Paston, Chevaller.

RYGHT worchepfull sir, I comand me to yow, sertyfying yow that Pekok hath receyvyd of Sir John Stylle by a bylle all suche stuff as he had of your. And as for Kendallys mater, he hathe doon as myche in it as can be doon: but as for Richard Calle, he hathe gevyn hym a pleyn answer that he wyll not seale to the lease that ye have mad to Kendalle, for he seyth he wottyth not whether it be your wylle or not, notwithstandyng he sye yore sealle up on it. I wold be sory to delyver hym a subpena and ye sent it me.

I send you herwith the endenture betwyx yow and Townesend. My modyr hathe herd of that mater by the reporte of old Wayte, whyche rennyth on it with opyn mowthe in hys werst wyse. My modyr wepyth and takyth on mervaylously, for she seythe she wotyth well it shall never be pledgyd ought; wherfor she seythe that she wyll purvey for hyr lond that ye shall none selle of it, for she thynkys ye wold and it cam to yowr hand. As for hyr wyll and all syche maters as wer in hand at your last being here, they thynk that it shall not lye in all oure porys to let it in on poynt.

Sir Jamys is evyr choppyng at me, when my modyr is present, with syche wordys as he thynkys wrathe me, and also cause my modyr to be dyspleased with me, evyn as who seyth he wold I wyst that he settyth not by the best of us; and when he hathe most unfyttyng woordys to me, I smylle a lytyll and tell hym it is good heryng of thes old talys. Sir Jamys is parson of Stokysby by J. Bernays gyft. I trowe he beryth hym the hyeer.

Item, ye must sende in haste to W. Barker a warrant to

[1] [From Paston MSS., B.M.] The date of this letter is shown by a contemporaneous endorsement 'Anno E. iiij[ti] xij°,' as well as by the repetition of the writer's request for a goshawk.

THE PASTON LETTERS

pay John Kook xxxs., and to the woman of Yermothe for otys xx., and Syr John Styll hys money, for they call dayly up on it.

Item, I prey yow send me some tydynges howgh the world gothe, and whether ye have sent eny of your folk to Caleys. Me thynkes it costyth yow to myche money for to kepe hem all in London at your charge.

Item, whethyr ye have eny thyng spokyn of my going to Caleys.

Item, as for a goshawk or a terssell, I wend to have had on of yours in kepyng or thys tyme, but fere [far] fro iee fer fro hert; by my trowthe I dye for defawlt of labore. And it may be by eny meane possybyll, for Godes sake let on be sent me in all hast; for if it be not had by Halowmesse, the seson shall passe a non, *Memento mei*, and in feythe ye shall not loose on it. Nor yet myche wyne on it by God, Who preserve yow.

Wretyn on Seynt Mychell Day, in Monte Tomba.[1]

J. P.

811

MARGARET PASTON TO JOHN PASTON[2]

To John Paston, esquyer.

I GRETE you wele; letyng you wete that on Saterday last past within nyght the felesshep at Cayster tokyn ought of Mawtby Cloos xvj. shep of diverse mennes that were put therein to pasture, and thei ledde them a wey, so that every man ferith to put any bestis or catell therin, to my grete hurt and discoragyng of my fermour that is now of late come theder. And the seid evill disposed persones affraid my seid fermour as

[1] The feast of St. Michael in Monte Tomba was the 16th October.

[2] [Add. MS. 34,889, f. 108.] This letter was clearly written between the surrender of Caister in 1469 and its recovery by Sir John Paston after the death of the Duke of Norfolk in 1476. The year 1472 may be considered very probable from what Margaret Paston writes in June of that year (No. 803).

EDWARD IV

he came from Yarmoth this weke and shotte at hym that if he had not had a good hors he had belike to have ben in joparte of his lyfe; so that be thes rewle I am like to lese the profite of the lyfelode this yere but if there be purveyed the hastyere remedy. Thei threte so my men I dar send non theder to gader it. Thei stuffe and vetayll sore the place, and it is reported here that my Lady of Norffolk seth she wull not leas it in no wyse. And the Duchesse of Suffolkis men sey that she wull not departe from Heylesdon ner Drayton,—she wuld rather departe from money; but that shuld not be wurchepfull for you; for men shull not than set be you. There for I will avyse you to have rather the lyvelod than the money; ye shall mown excuse you be the College which must contynue perpetuall, and money is sone lost and spent whan that lyfelode abideth. Item, I lete you wete that Hastyngis hath entred ageyn in to his fee of the Constabyllshep of the Castell of Norwich be the vertu of his patent that he had of Kyng Harry; and I here sey he hath it graunted to hym and his heyeris. There was at his entres your unkill William and other jentilmen dwellyng in Norwich. This was do be fore that ye sent me the letter be Pers I had forgetyn to have sent you word ther of. God kepe you. Wretyn the Friday next after Sent Luke.

Be your moder.

812

SIR JOHN PASTON TO JOHN PASTON[1]

A Johan Paston, Esquyer, soit done.

WORSHYPFULL and weell belovyd brother, I recomand me to yow, letyng yow weet that I sente yow a letter and a rynge with a dyamond, in whyche letter ye myght well conceyve what I wold ye scholde do with the same rynge, with menye other tydyngs and thyngs whyche

[1] [From Fenn, ii. 112.]

THE PASTON LETTERS

1472
NOV. 4

I prayed yowe to have doon for me, whyche letter Botoner[1] had the beryng off. It is so nowe that I undrestond that he is owther deed or ellys harde eskapyd, wheroff I am ryght hevye, and am not serteyn whethyr the seyd lettyr and rynge come to yowr handys or nott. I wolde nott that letter wer seyn with some folkys; wherffor I praye yow take good heede hoghe that letter comythe to yowr handys, hooll or brokyn, and in especiall I praye yow gete it, iff ye have it nott.

Also I praye yow feele my Lady off Norfolks dysposicion to me wards, and whethyr she toke any dysplesur at my langage, or mokkyd, or dysdeyned my words whyche I hadd to hyr at Yarmothe, be twyen the place wher I ffyrst mett with hyr and hyr lodgyng, ffor my Lady Brandon and Syr William[2] also axhyd me what words I had had to hyr at that tyme. They seyd that my Lady seyde I gaff hyr ther off,[3] and that I sholde have seyde that my Lady was worthye to have a Lords soon in hyr belye, ffor she cowde cheryshe itt, and dele warlye with it; in trowthe owther the same or words moche lyke I had to hyr, whyche wordys I ment as I seyde. They seye to that I seyde she toke hyr ease. Also I scholde have seyde that my Ladye was off satur [stature] goode, and had sydes longe and large, so that I was in goode hope she sholde ber a fayr chylde; he was nott lacyd nor bracyd ine to hys peyn, but that she left hym rome to pleye hym in. And they seye that I seyde my Lady was large and grete, and that itt sholde have rome inow to goo owt att; and thus whyther my Lady mokk me, or theye, I woote nott. I mente weell by my trowthe to hyr, and to that she is with, as any he that owythe heer best wyll in Ingelond.

Iff ye can by any meed weete whethyr my Ladye take it to dysplesur or nowt, or whether she thynke I mokkyd hyr, or iff she wyght it but lewdnesse off my selffe, I pray yow

[1] William Botoner, otherwise Worcester. He certainly was alive some years later than this.
[2] Sir William Brandon, Knight, was standard-bearer to the Earl of Richmond, and was slain in Bosworth Field by Richard III. He was father to Charles Brandon, Duke of Suffolk.—F.
[3] Meaning apparently, as Fenn suggests, 'I paid her off, or treated her with unceremonious language.'

156

sende me worde; ffor I weet nott whethyr I maye trust thys Lady Brandon or nott.

1472
NOV. 4

Item, as ffor tydyngs nowe, heer be but ffewe, saff that, as I undrestande, imbassators off Bretayne shall come to London to morawe, and men seye that the Lorde Ryverse[1] and Scayls, shall hastelye come home; and men seye that ther is many off the sowders that went to hym into Bretayne been dede off the fflyxe, and other ipedemye [epidemics], and that the remenant sholde come hom with the Lorde Skalys. And som seye that thees imbassators come ffor moor men. And thys daye rennyth a tale that the Duke of Bretayne[2] sholde be ded. I beleeff it not.

I sent yow worde off an hawke; I herde nott from yow syns; I do and shall doo that is possible in suche a neede.

Also I canne nott undrestand that my Lord off Norffolk shall come heer thys tyme; wherffor I am in a greet agonye howe is best ffor me to sue to hym ffor rehavyng off my place; that goode Lorde weet full lytell how moche harme he doothe me, and how lytell goode or worshyp it dothe hym. I praye yow sende me yowr advyce. No moor to yow at thys tyme, but God have yow in Hys kepyng.

Wretyn at London the viij. daye off Novembre, anno E. iiij[d] xij[o]. I feer me that idelnesse ledyth yowr reyne; I praye yow rather remembre Sir Hughe Levernoys tyll yowr hauke come. JOHN PASTON, K.

[1] Anthony Woodville, Earl Rivers, etc., went to endeavour to obtain the possession of the Earls of Pembroke and Richmond, who were detained as prisoners by the Duke of Brittany.—F.
[2] Francis II., the last Duke of Brittany, was born in 1435, and died in 1488.—F.

157

THE PASTON LETTERS

813

SIR JOHN PASTON TO JOHN PASTON[1]

A John Paston, Esquyer, soyt done.

1472
NOV. 8

BROTHER, I comend me to yow, letyng yow weet, &c.[2] As for the delyverance off the rynge to Mestresse Jane Rothone, I dowt nott but it shall be doon in the best wyse, so that ye shall geet me a thank moor than the rynge and I ar worthe or deserve.

And wheer ye goo to my Laydy off Norffolk, and wyll be theer att the takyng off hyr chambre, I praye God spede yow, and our Ladye hyr, to hyr plesur, with as easye labor to overkome that she is abowt, as evyr had any lady or gentyllwoman, saff our Lady heer selffe, and soo I hope she shall to hyr greet joye, and all owres; and I prey God it maye be lyke hyr in worship, wytt, gentylnesse, and every thynge excepte the verry verry thynge.[3]

No moor to yow at [this] thyme, but I woll sleepe an howr the lenger to-morrow by cawse I wrote so longe and late to nyght.

Wretyn betwen the viij. and the jx. daye off Novembre anno xij[o] E. iiij[d].
J. P., K.

[1] [From Fenn, ii. 118.]
[2] The first part of this letter treats of some money transactions of no consequence, etc.—F.
[3] Fenn, in his modernised text, makes this 'except the sex.'

158

814

MARGARET PASTON TO JOHN PASTON[1]

To John Paston, Esquyer.

I GRETE you wele and send you Goddes blyssyng and myn, letyng you wete that I have sent to Doctor Aleyn wyffe to have spoke with her as ye desired me, and she was so syke that she myght not comyn; but she sent her broder elaw to me, and I lete hym wete the cause why that I wuld have spoke with her as ye desired me. And he told me that he shuld have brought me wrytyng this day from her be vij. of the belle, how that she wull that ye shuld have labored or do for her; but he came no mor at me. Nevertherlesse she sent me an nother massenger, and lete me wete[2] that her husband had sent her the same nyght from London that she shuld come up as fast as she cowde to labor to the Lordes there in her propre person; wherfor she myght geve me non answer, ner send you word how that ye shuld do till [that] she had spokyn with her husband, or had other wrytyng from hym.

1472
NOV. 19

Therfore I thynk t[hat s]he hath other councell that avysseth her to labour to other than to you. I wuld not that [you be] to besy in no such maters [ty]ll the werd [world] were mor suer, and in any wyse that w[hile my] Lord the Chaunceller is in [occu]pation, labore to have an ende of your grete materes and . . . macion, and abide not up [on] trost of an nother seson, for so shall ye be disseyved a[s ye hav]e ben befor this tyme. I have understand sith that ye departed that ther . . . . mad to supplant you; therfore, for Goddes sake, in this onstabill werd [world] labore

[1] [From Paston MSS., B.M.] From the time of year and other circumstances, it seems probable that the election here referred to was that of the year 1472. A circumstance which confirms this date will be found noticed in a footnote. The original letter is mutilated in the middle by the decay of the paper, in more than one place.
[2] The words after 'Neverthelesse' originally stood 'her seid brother-in-law told me that tyme that he was with me,' but are crossed out.

159

THE PASTON LETTERS

er[nestly your] maters that thei may have summe good conclusion, and that shall make y[our enemies] fere you, and elles
thei shall . . kepe you low and in trobill. And if any
mater . . . be Act of Parlement and pro . . . .
lete your bill be mad redy, and lese not your [ma]teres for
other mennes ; for if your elmyse [enemies] may profight now
at this tyme, ye shall be [in] wers case than ever ye were
befor. All the cou[ntry] wenyth that ye shuld now over-
comyn all your trobill, which if ye do not ye shall fall o[ug]ht
of conceyte. I write as well this to your brother as to you ;
therfore lete no diffaught be in you nowther.

Item, it was lete me to wete syth ye departed of such as
were your frendes and were conversaunte with the toder parte
that ther was mad labor and like to be concluded, that the
eleccion of the knyghtes of the shire shuld be chaunged, and
new certificat mad and John Jenney set there in ; ther for do
your devoir to understond the trought as sone as ye can, for
the seid Jenney this day rideth up to London ward, and I
suppo[se be]cause of the same. I pray you remembre your
brother to send me the evydence and remembrance towchyng
the maner of Gresham, which that I wrote to hym be Juddy,
and send them be sum suer man.

Item, take hede to the labour of your unkyll, for he hath
had right straunge langage of your brother of late to right
wurchepfull persones ; therfor werk wysely and bewar wham
that ye lete know your councell.

Item, remembre Lomnors mater as ye may do therin, and
send me werd in hast. Mayster Roos shall be at London the
next weke ; therfore ye shall not nede to make my Lord to
write, but whan that he comyth, if my Lord can make hym to
put it in indifferent and wurchepfull men, than that it pleasith
my Lord to write to them that thei shuld take it upon them to
set a rewle therin, with ought better advyse, me semyth it wer
wele do. The Holy Gost be your gyde and send yow good
spede and councell, and delivere you ought of all trobill and
disseas to his pleser.

Wretyn the Thursday next be for Sent Kateryn,[1] in hast.

[1] St. Catherine's Day is the 25th of November.

EDWARD IV

Recomaund me to my Mastres Kateryn, and send me
werd how ye don, &c.

Be your Moder.

Do my Lord[1] on Sonday send for the shereffes debute
[deputy] to wete how thei be disposid for certificate of the
knyghtes, and I shall understand if thei be eschaunged ; for
on Sonday at nyght, or on Monday, it shall be put in, and
[if i]t is put in, ther is no remedy. Geney seth he wull
attempt the law therin.

815

SIR JOHN PASTON TO MARGARET PASTON[2]

*To Mestresse Margret Paston, or to John Paston, Esquier,
or to Roose dwyllyng affor ther gate, to delyver to them.*

PLEASE it yow to weete that I have opteyned letterys NOV. 22
from the Kynge to my Lorde off Norffolke, to my
Lady of Norffolk, and to ther concell, whyche letter
to ther concell is nott superscrybyd, for cawse we wyst nott
serteyn whyche of the councell sholde be present when the
massenger cowme. I therffor thynke that thoos namys most
be somwhatt by yowr advyce ; and for get nott Gornaye, nor yitt
Brome, iff ye thynke so best, nor Sowthewelle. I trust to my
cosyn Gornaye, and on to Brome and Barnard in cheffe ; and
as to Bernarde, brother, I praye yow to take hys advyce, for I
hope he is my welwyller, as ye know, and iffe he do me perffyght ease in thys mater, I thynke verrely in tyme to come to
gyff him xx. scutys, and yit a goode turne whan so ever it
lythe in my power.

The Kynge hathe specially doon for me in thys case, and

[1] The Duke of Norfolk. It will be seen by the preceding letter that John Paston
was going to Framlingham in the beginning of November 1472.
[2] [From Paston MSS., B.M.] In this letter, as in the last, allusion is made to the
visit paid by John Paston to the Duchess of Norfolk in November 1472.

THE PASTON LETTERS

hathe pitte me, and so have the Lordys, in ryght greete comfort, that iff thys fayle, that I shalle have ondelayed justyce ;
and he hathe sente a man of worship and in greet favor wyth
hym on thys massage, whyche hathe nott ofte ben seyne,
whyche gentylman kan well do hys mastrys massage and
brynge trywe reporte. I have gevyn hym vli. for hys costes :
God sende hym and yow goode spede in thees werkes. I feer
thatt he shall nott speke with my Lady, for that she hathe
takyn hyr chambre. Iff she be my verry goode Ladye, as she
hathe seyde hertoffor that she wolde be, I hope that she wolle
speke with hym. Neverthelesse I praye yow by the meanes of
Mestresse Jahne Rothen that [you][1] will have my Ladye mevyd
for me, and wher that herr to fore I wolde have departyd with
C. marke to have hadde hyr goode helpe and to be restoryd
to my place ; whyche nott acceptyd, I tolde my seyde Lady
that I feeryd that my power sholde natt be ther aftre to gyff
so large a plesyr, for at that tyme I was in hope that the
Bysshop of Wynchester sholde have payd it, thoghe it hadde
drawen a Cli. Yet for as moche as men may nott lure none
hawkes with empty handys, I wolde yitt agre to gyffe my
Lady xxli. for an horse and a sadell, so that I be restoryd to
my place, and that doone, to have a relesse of my Lorde, and
my gounes and bokes to be restoryd, iff it maye bee. Neverthelesse thys mony is nott yit redy with me. I remytte thys
to yowr dyscressyons.

Item, iff it be soo that itt be thowte behovefull, I thynke
that thoghe nowther Slyfelde, nor ye, brother John, maye
come in to my Ladyes chambre, that my moodre, iff she weer
at Norwyche, she myght speke with hyr, for that she is a
woman and off worshyppe. I thynke that my moodre sholde
meve my Lady moche. I thynke that ther most be some body
for me, havyng auctoryte to conclude for me, or ellys knowyng myn entente, they myght make delaye, and seye they
wolle at the Kynges enstance comon with me ; never the lesse
I was nott ther present. Wherffor, rather than fayle, yff
neede be, I wolle with owte any abode, iff I heer from yow,
come home ; and Slyfelde is agreyd to tary the a vij. nyghte

[1] Omitted in MS

EDWARD IV

for my sake, so that the mater take effecte. I praye yow make
hym goode cheer, and iff it be so that he tarye, I most
remembre hys costes ; therffor iff I shall be sent for, and he
tery at Norwyche ther whylys, it wer best to sette hys horse
at the Maydes Hedde, and I shalle content for ther expences.

Item, ye maye largely sey on my behalve for suche servyse
that I sholde do to my Lorde and Lady hereaffter, whyche by
my trowthe I thynke to doo ; nevertnelesse to sey that I woll
be hys sworyn man, I was never yitt Lordys sworyn man, yit
have I doone goode servyce, and nott leffte any at hys most
neede ner for feer. But as Gode helpe me, I thynke my Lady
shalle have my servyce above any lady erthely, wheche she
scholde weell have knowyn, had I been in suche case as I
hadde nott been alweye the werse welkome ; for that on of
my herandes alweye was undrestande that it was for Caster,
whyche was nott acceptable, and I evyr the werse welkome.

Item, brother, I ame concludyd with my Lorde for yow,
that ye shalle be at Caleys if ye list, and have iij. men in wages
undre yow, wheroff my Lorde seythe that William Lovedaye
most be on, tyll tyme that he have purveyed other rome for
hym. Iff ye be dysposyd to goo, as I tolde hym that ye weer,
yett wer it nott best that ye lete it be knowe tyll thys mater
be doone, and then ye maye acordyng to yowr promyse lete
my Ladye have knowleche ther off. Never the lesse my
Lorde shalle be here with in xx. dayes or ther abowt ; iff ye
come thys weye ye maye speke with hym ; nevertheles se ye
shall nott lose no tyme, iff ye weer at Caleys at thys owr, for
my Lorde promysed me that he wolde wryght to Elkenhed the
tresorer at Caleys for yow by the next massenger thatt went.

Item, ther hathe Perauntes wyffe wryte to me that Bernaye
servyth hyr onkyndely. He owythe hyr xxxijs. and she is in
noon hope that evyr he will come ther ageyn ; sende me
worde iff he wyll. He shall nott lyf so weell and trywly to
geedre, I trowe, but iffe he goo thyddre.

I hadde comen home, butt that I ame nott yitt verrely
purveyd for payment for my oncle William the xxvj. daye of
thys monythe, and he dothe me harme. He delythe so on-
curteysly with Towneshende, for he wille nott yitt paye hym

THE PASTON LETTERS

1472
NOV. 22

the C. marke, payable at Halowmesse, whyche he hadde a monythe affore; wherffor I feer that Towneshende wille nott do for me ageyn. I shall doo as I kan.

Wretyn on Sondaye next Seynt Clement.

JOHN PASTON, K.

816

MARGARET PASTON TO JOHN PASTON [1]

To John Paston, Esquyer, be this delivered.

NOV. 23

I GRETE you wele, letyng you wete that Doctor Aleyns wyffe hath be with me and desired me to write to you to desire you to be good mayster to her husband and to her in her materes, for she tellith me that her trost is full in you, and if she myght have walked she shuld have come to have spoke with you or than ye departed; therfor, I pray you do your devoir for her, for I conceyve that she feyneth not, notwithstandyng that I had her in suspecion as I have wretyn to you before, be cause that she came not, but I conceyve now the trought and that sikenesse caused thatt she absent her. Therfore I pray you help her, for, so God help me, I have right gret pete on her, and it is right grete almes to help her, and I trow she wull put her most trost and sewe specialle to you. Also I wuld ye shold desire your brother to be good mayster on to her, for I suppose be that tyme ye have herd her excuse in such materes as he shuld be displeased with her husband, ye shall hold you pleased. God kepe you and send you Hes blyssyng, with myn. Wretyn on Sent Clementes Day at nyght, in hast,

Be your Moder.

[1] [From Paston MSS., B.M.] It is evident that this letter was written in the same year as No. 814.

164

THE PASTON LETTERS

1472
NOV. 24

stand, if ye have owght to do, wherin she may be an helper; for ther was never knyght dyd so myche cost on hyr as ye have doon.

I mervyall that I her no woord of the lettyrs that my Lord Chamberleyn shold send to my Lord and my Lady for Caster. It is best that my Lord Chamberleyn wryght to my Lady by som prevy tokyn betwyx theym, and let a man of hys com with the lettrys. My Lord Chamberleyn may speed with my Lady what maters he wyll, savyng the gret mater; and if ye inbyll me for a solysitor, I shal be *a vouster comandment a touz jours.*

Item, me thynkyth that ye do evyll that ye go not thorewgh with my Lady of Suffolk for Heylysdon and Drayton; for ther shold growe mony to you, whyche wold qwyte yow ayenst R. T. and all other, and set yow befor for ever.

I prey you for your ease, and all others to you ward, plye thes maters. As for alle other thynges, I shall send yow an answer, when I com to Norwyche, whyche shall be on Thorsday, with Godes grace. I have teryd her at Framlyngham thys sevennyght, for [my] Lady took not hyr chambyr tyll yersterday. Adewe.

Wretyn on Seynt Kateryns Evyn. J. P.

[1] I sye the pye, and herd it spek; and, be God, it is not worthe a crowe; it is fer wers then ye wend; be God, it wer shame to kep it in a cage.

818

ABSTRACT [2]

NOV. 26

'Soutwerk cum membris,' No. 17a.—'Literæ patentes concessæ a Rege ad petitionem Domini Fundatoris pro ponte fiendo in vico vocato le Bermoseystret. Dat. 26 Novembris anno regni Regis Ed. IV. 12°.'

[1] This *P.S.* is written on the back of the letter.
[2] [From MS. Index in Magd. Coll., Oxford.]

166

EDWARD IV

817

JOHN PASTON TO SIR JOHN PASTON [1]

To Master Sir John Paston, Knyght.

RYGHT worchepfull syr, I recomand me to yow, thankyng yow most hertly of your dylygence and cost whyche ye had in gettyng of the hawk, whyche ye sent me, for well I wot your labore and trowbyll in that mater was as myche as thow she had ben the best of the world; but, so God help me, as ferforthe as the most conyng estragers [*falconers*] that ever I spak with can imagyn, she shall never serve but to ley eggys, for she is bothe a mwer de haye, and also she hathe ben so brooseid with cariage of fewle that she is as good as lame in boothe hyr leggys, as every man may se at iee. Wherfor all syche folk as have seen hyr avyse me to cast hyr in to some wood, wher as I wyll have hyr to eyer [*lay eggs*]; but I wyll do ther in as ye wyll, whedyr ye wyll I send hyr yow ayen, or cast hyr in Thorpe wood and a tarsell with hyr, for I weit wher on is. But now I dar no more put yow to the cost of an hawke, but, for Godes sake, and ther be eny tersell or good chep goshawk that myght be gotyn, that the berer herof may have hyr to bryng me, and I ensuer yow be my trowthe ye shall have Dollys and Browne bonde to paye yow at Kandyllmas the pryse of the hawke. Now, and ye have as many ladyse as ye wer wont to have, I reqwere yow for hyr sake that ye best love of theym all, onys trowbyll yowr syllf for me in thys mater, and be owght of my clamor.

Item, as for the ryng, it is delyverd, but I had as gret peyn to make hyr take it as ever I had in syche a mater; but I have promyseid yow to be hyr knyght, and she hathe promyseid me to be more at your comandment then at eny knyghtes in Inglond, my Lord reservyd; and that ye shall well undyr-

1472
NOV. 2

[1] [From Paston MSS., B.M.] At the foot of this letter is written, in a different but contemporary hand, 'A° E. iiij^ti xij°.' The date is besides abundantly evident from other circumstances.

165

EDWARD IV

819

JOHN OSBERN TO SIR JOHN PASTON [1]

To the right worshepfull my master, Sir John Paston, Knyght.

A° xij. E. R. quarti.

Please it your masterschep to knowe that Johon Shawe and I have goten a carpenter fro Walsyngham to Sporle to valewe your wod the[2] the wheche carpenter hese costis there Sondaye at nyght next before the Assencion off owre Lord Jesu Cryst, Mondaye, Tewesdaye, Wednesdaye, Assencion Daye, Frydaye and Saterdaye, and for hese labor iijs. iiijd. And upon the syte of your seid wode he hath valewid the launde wythin the dykes xij. fote inward fro the cop of the dyke and wythowte at liiijs. vijs. xd. And wythin the wode xij. fote wythin alle the dykes vj^xx. li. vijs. viijd. the valewe of the dykes abowte the woode fro xij. fote fro wythin owtewardis arn prysid at xli. grete chepis the valew of the trees in the maner and in the closes azens the seid manor toward Swaffham xx. marc gret chepe; there off be ware and be not to hasty, &c., the cloos at the tow . . . . toward Pykenham not valewid nor not spoken of, &c. The summa totall ix^xx·li. & xviijs. ijs. viijd.

And if ze shuld selle all this wode togedyr for redy sylver never lesse in the summa paste v. marc, if ze woll sell the wode . . . . the lawnde wythin the dykes and the standardis thoo I shall wryte aftyr in this bille for to stande in any wyse less . . . . all the hole sum at the most paste xli. for who so ever shall by it he maye so leve and gete goode, &c.

The summa of your standardis for certeyn reconyd the Mondaye and the Tewsdaye whill I was at Sporle wyth in . . . . and xij. fote wythin the dykes in forme above rehersid xj^xx and iche standarde a zard [*yard*] above the grownde . . . . . abowte an . . lesser till we come xij. inche and viij. inche besyde all odyr smale that arn of lesse mesure . . . . growe the wheche arn many and resonabely sufficient, &c., the nowmber off the standardis wythin your . . . . . cowntid and summe be estimacion of the mesures and formes above rehersid CCCC^ma xxxvj^th . . . .

As for your undyrwode I can not fynde the meane to valewid to your avayle, be cause it were necessary to knowe the purpose off your fellyng, where off beware, &c.

As for the fensyng of your dykes, and ze shuld felle your bordorys off your wode the Suthsyde, viz., toward Pykenham fro the Wonges to Walsyngham Weye is lxxx. rodde at leste, the price of the rodde iiijd., dyggyng, plashyng, and heggyng. Summa, xxvjs. viijd.

The Est syde toward Neyghton and Sparham vij^xx. rodde at the leste, Summa, xls.

[1] [From Paston MSS., B.M.]
[2] *Sic*, qu. 'there'?

167

1472
The Northende toward Dunham lxxx. rodde,   Summa, xxvj*r*. viij*d*.
The West syde toward Sporle be the Loyes
vj*xx*. rodde,   .   .   .   Summa, xl*s*.

        Summa, vj*li*. xiij*s*. iiij*d*.

Where off sum is repayrid, sum maye be sperid, but at the lest it woll coste yow a vj. marc, &c.

If it please yow to take myn symple avyse in your wode sale, selle non in gret, but make fagottes and astell and lete alle your grete and goode tymber and trees stande, and ze shall make resonably mony to your worchep, and to your best avayle as John Shawe your servaunt shall telle yow, if I maye do zow any service in this c . . . . ze shall ffynde me redy, so that ze sende sufficient warant be the grace off Jesu, Who haue y[ow in His] kepyng. Wrete in hast, at Walsyngham, the Sundaye next aftyr the feest off the Assencion off owr [Lord] Jesu Cryste.

            Be your   JOHN OSBERN.

I praye yow geff credens in alle these materes to Shawe, for he can telle yow more shortlyer then I shuld wryte, and I hold hym trewe to yow in hese menyng.

Endorsed—Per John Osbern, pro Sporl Wood.

820

RICHARD CALLE TO MARGARET PASTON[1]

To the ryght reverent and worshipffull my mastres,
Margaret Paston, in haste.

NOV. 27   Plesith it you to wete that I have receyved your letter, wherin I conceyve ye wolde undrestonde how I do with the sale of Sporle Wode. It is so that I have begonne to felle asshe at the townes ende for to sette the contre on werke, and be that I shall undrestonde how the remnaunt wol doo. I have sette suche a classe [*glass*] before here ien [*their eyes*] ther, that they are madde upon it, so that I truste be Ester to make of money, what with the barke and with the asshe, at the leest l. marke for to retayle the wode our selfe, and be Cristemas next after that, other l. marke, and so yerely l. marke at Cristemesse as longe as the wode lasteth, to the some that I tolde you, and I truste more; and to this I durste be bound. Nevertheles, I am a bowte to selle it all a grete and to brynge it to all moste to as goode proffe as thowe we retayled it oure silffe, for it is so that ther is a man of Carbroke, they calle hym Saunders, I may have of hym for all the wode and barke that is in Sporle xj*xx*. marke, to paye at suche dayes a fore reherseyd, we to bere the costes of the fense and of the tithe ; but we are not throw yet, nor nought shal be tille I have worde from you a yene, weche I

---

[1] [From Paston MSS., B.M.] It is evident that this letter must have been written some time after the preceding, but very probably in the same year.

168

---

must have be Sonday come sevenyte at the fertheste, for on the Wednesdaye 1472 nexte after that we shal mete a yene at Sporle. Wherfore I beseche you sende NOV. 27 ne your avice how ye thynke herein, and I shal doo that in me is be Godes grace ; if I can do better with hym I shall. It shal be harde werke, but if I haunse hym som what, for ther is moche money be twix us, and therfore spare not to sende my master, Sir John, worde to take suche dayes of payment as is a bove wreten, for it shalbe performed what wey som ever we take be Godes grace.

Item, mastres, as for your write [*wright*] ye may not have hym tille after Cristemas, for he had taken an howse to make while I was with you, it wolbe this iij. wekes yet or then he make an ende, &c.

Item, I mette with Robert at Heythe of Matelaske at Norwiche, when I come from you. I felle on hande with hym for Matelaske Kerre, I myght have had of hym for that vij. marke and xx*d*. Dele nogh as ye thynke.

Item, as for money of the fermour of Sporle, he telles me he is bounde to Tounesende to pay hym at this Candelmesse. And he seythe if he may be discharged a yenst hym your money shalbe redy at hys daye, be Godes grace, Who have you in His blissed kepyng.

Wreten at Sporle, the Friday next after Seint Edmund the Kynge.

         Your servaunt,   R. CALLE.

821

JOHN PASTON TO SIR JOHN PASTON[1]

To Sir John Paston, Knyght.

SYME recomandyth hym to your good mastyrshep, and NOV. preyeth yow that ye wyll not forget, though he be a or boye, to let hym were the same lyvere that your men DEC. do ; and if it pleased yow to lete hys gowne clothe be sent hym home, that it myght be mad ayenst your comeing in to thys contre, he wold be as prowd as eny man ye have. Sir, as hertly as I can, I thank yow for the hatt, whyche is comyng, as I undyrstand by your wrytyng, sent by John, the Abottys man of Seynt Benet.

My modyr sendys you Godes blyssyng and hyrs, and preyes yow to get a new lycence of my Lord of Norwyche

---

[1] [From Paston MSS., B.M.] The date of this letter is shown by the reference to the situation of the Duchess of Norfolk. Compare Letter 817. There is an old, and nearly contemporary, endorsement, 'Anno xv*o*, mens. Novemb.,' but this is clearly erroneous.

169

1472   that she may have the sacrement in hyr chapell. I gat a NOV.   lycence of hym for a yere, and it is nyghe woryn ought. Ye or   may get it for the Byshoppys lyve, and ye wylle. DEC.

As for the lettyrs that Slyfeld shold get newe of the Kyng, whyche ye shold bryng to my Lord of Norffolk, it is myn avyse that ye shall come home your sylff as hasty ly as ye maye, so that ye may be at the crystenyng of the chyld that my Lady is with ; it shall cause yow gret thank, and a gret fordell [*advantage*] in your mater. And as for the lettres, leve a man of yowr to awayte on Slyfeld to bryng theym after yow ; of whyche lettres I avyse yow to have one dyrect fro the Kyng to yow, comandyng yow to be the messenger and brynger of the other lettres to my Lord, my Lady, and ther consayll, for your owne mater ; and thys me thynkyth shall do well, for then shall the man shewe to my Lordes consayll the lettre dyrect to yow that ye have awtoryte to be your owne solycy-tour, and also it shall be thought that the Kyng tendryth yow and your mater, when he wryghtyth to your sylf for it.

My Lady wayteth hyr tyme with in viij. dayes at the ferthest.

822

ABSTRACT[1]

DEC. 7   1472, 7 Dec.—'Vigill of Concepcion of oure Lady,' 12 Edw. IV. Indenture of agreement (in English) between Bp. Waynflete and William Worceter, by which the latter undertakes to deliver to the Bishop all deeds, charters, rolls of courts, and accounts, and all other muniments which are in his hands relating to the manors and lands of the late Sir John Fastolf, excepting lands, etc. in Norfolk, called Fairchilds, and two tenements and two gardens called Walles, in Suthwerk, of which he himself is seised ; and also, as executor of the will of Sir Thomas Howes, to deliver up all money and goods of Fastolf, and obligations for property, etc., sold by the said Thomas, which he can recover, over the sum of £40 due to him, the said William Worceter, for his marriage, and also to assist the said Bishop and his College at Oxford in all matters relating to Fastolf's lands ; in return for which the Bishop covenants to pay him £100, and also an allowance upon all sums of money recovered by him.

---

[1] This abstract is taken from Mr. Macray's account of the MSS. in Magdalen College, Oxford, printed in the Fourth Report of the Historical MSS. Commission.

170

823

JOHN PASTON TO SIR JOHN PASTON[1]

To my Mastyr, Sir John Paston, Knyght, be thys delyveryd.

RYGHT worchepfull Syr, I recomand me to yow, thank- 1472 yng yow most hertly of your gret cost, whyche ye dyd DEC. 18 on me at my last being with yow at London ; whyche to my power I wyll recompence yow with the best servyse that lythe in me to do for your plesure, whyll my wytts be my owne.

Syr, as for the mater of Caster, it hathe be mevyd to my Ladys good grace by the Byshope of Wynchester, as well as he kowd imagyn to sey it, consederyng the lytyll leyser that he had with hyr ; and he told me that he had rygyt an agreabyll answer of hyr, but what hys answer was, he wold not tell me. Then I axyd hym what answer I should send yow, in as myche as ye mad me a solysyter to hys Lordship for that mater ; then he bad me that undyr consayll I shold send you woord that hyr answer was more to your plesure than to the contrary, whych ye shall have more pleyn knowlage of thys next terme, att whyche tyme bothe my Lord and she shall be at London.

The Byshop cam to Framlyngham on Wednysday at nyght, and on Thursday by x. of the clok befor noon, my yong Lady was krystend, and namyd Anne. The Byshop crystend it and was godfader bothe, and with in ij. owyrs and lesse aftyr the crystenyng was do, my Lord of Wynchester departyd towards Waltham.[2]

And I let you pleynly weet, I am not the man I was, ffor I was

---

[1] [From Fenn, ii. 42.] Fenn informs us that this letter is dated on the back in a contemporaneous handwriting, 'Anno x*o*,' which seems to mean 10 Edw. IV. This date however, is certainly erroneous ; for in the inquisitions taken on the death of the Duke of Norfolk, Anne, Lady Mowbray, his daughter and heir, was found to have been four years old on the 10th December 1476. She was born, therefore, on the 10th December 1472.

[2] Then follows the substance of a conversation between the Lady of Norfolk and Thomas Davers, wherein she promises to be a friend to Sir John Paston concerning Caister ; but J. Davers swore J. Paston not to mention her goodwill to any person, except to Sir John.—F.

171

THE PASTON LETTERS

1472
DEC. 18

never so roughe in my mastyrs conseyt as I am now, and that he told me hymselff before Rychard Sothewell, Tymperley, Sir W. Brandon, and twenty more, so that they that lowryd, nowgh[1] laughe upon me ; no moor, but god look.

Wretyn at Framlyngham, the Fryday next aftyr that I departyd fro yow. Thys day my Lord is towardys Walsyngham, and comandyd me to overtake hym to morow at the ferthest.

J. P.

824

JOHN PASTON TO THE DUKE OF NORFOLK[2]

To the right hyghe and myghty Prince, and my right good and gracious Lord, my Lord the Dwke of Norffolk.

1472

MEKLY besechyth your hyghness, your poore and trew contynuall servaunt and oratour, John Paston, the yonger, that it myght please your good grace to call on to your most discret and notabyll remembrance that lateward, at the cost and charge of my brodyr, John Paston, Knyght, whyche most entendith to do that myght please your hyghness, the ryght nobyll Lord, the Bysshop of Wynchester entretyd so, and compouned with your Lordshepp, that it liekyd the same to be so good and gracious Lord to my seyd brodyr, that by forsse of serteyn dedys, relessis, and lettrys of attorney selyd with the sealys of your good grace, and of other serteyn personys infeoffyd to your use in the maner of Caster, late John Fastolffes, Knyght, in the conte of Norffolk, my seyd brodyr and I, with other enfeoffyd to my seyd brodyrs use in the seyd maner, wer peasably possessyd of and in the same tyll syche tyme as serteyn personys, servaunts on to your good grace, entred in to the seyd maner, and therof have takyn the

---

[1] In the modern version Fenn reads, 'so that they that *loved not*, laugh upon me.'

[2] [From Paston MSS., B.M.] This petition is shown by internal evidence to have been drawn up towards the end of the year 1472, as it sets forth that the Duke had been more than three years in possession of Caister, which was surrendered to him in September 1469. There can be no doubt therefore that it was presented or prepared for presentation at the time of John Paston's visit to Framlingham.

172

EDWARD IV

1472

issuses and profitys in the name of your seyd hyghnesse by the space of thre yer and more, to the gret hurt of my seyd brodyr and me your seyd servuantes and oratour : wherfor, as I have oft tymys befor thys, I beseche your good grace, at the reverence of God, and in the wey of charyte, that my seyd brodyr may by your hyghness be ayen restoryd in to the possessyon of the sey[d] maner, acordyng to the lawe and good conscyence ; and wee shall prey to God for the preservacyon of your most nobyll estate.

825

MARGARET PASTON TO SIR JAMES GLOYS(?)[1]

I RECOMAUND me to you, and thanke you hertyly of your letteris, and delygente labour that ye have had in thoes materis that ye have wretyn to me of, and in all other, to my profette and worschep, and in esspeciall atte this sesons towchyng the mater that I sent you the indenture of. Ye have lyghtyd myne hert therin by a pound, for I was in fere that it wold not have bene doo so hastyly with oute danger. And as for the letters that Thom Holler son schuld have brought me, I see nother hym ne the letters that he schuld have brought ; wherfor, I pray you hertely, yeve it be no dysese to you, that ye will take the labour to bryng Walter theyr he schuld be, and to purvaye for hym that he may be sette in good and sad rewle. For I were loth to lese hym, for I trust to have more joye of hym than I have of them that bene owlder ; though it be more coste to me to send you forth with hym, I hold me plesed, for I wote wele ye schall best purvaye for hym, and for suche thynges as is necessar to

1473
JAN. 18

---

[1] [From Paston MSS., B.M.] The allusion by the writer to her cousin Berney's sickness makes it probable that this letter was written in 1471, when the Monday after St. Hilary would be the 18th of January. John Berney of Reedham died on the 20th January in that year (Inquis. *post mortem*, 13 Edw. IV., No. 17). The letter has neither signature nor address, but was probably written by Margaret Paston to her priest, Sir James Gloys, who died in the course of this year.

173

THE PASTON LETTERS

1473
JAN. 18

hym, than another shuld doo, after myne intent. And as for ane hors to lede hys gere, me thynke it were best porvaye one atte Camberage, lesse than [*unless*] ye canne gytte onye carreours from thens to Oxynforth more hastyly ; and I mervell that the letters come not to me, and whether I may laye the defaute to the fauder or to the son therof. And I wold Water schuld be copilet with a better than Holler son is, there as he schalbe ; howe be it I wold not that he schuld make never the lesse of hym, by cause he is his contre man and neghbour. And also I pray you wryte a letter in my name to Watere, after that ye have knowne myne entent be fore this to hym ward ; so that he doo welle, lerne well, and be of good rewle and disposycion, ther shall nothyng faylle hym that I may helpe with, so that it be nessessare to hym ; and bydde hym that he be not to hasty of takyng of orderes that schuld bynd hym, till that he be of xxiiij. yeere of agee or more, thoff he be consaled the contrare, for oftyn rape [*haste*] rewith. I will love hym better to be a good secular man than to be a lewit prest.

And I am sore that my cosyn Bernay is seke, and I pray you yeff me white wine, or ony of my wateris, or ony other thyng that I have that is in your awarde, may doo hym ony comforth. I lette hym have it ; for I wold be right sory yf ony thyng schuld come to hym botte good. And for Godsake advise hym to doo make hys will, yeve it be not doo, and to doo well to my cosyn, hys wiff, and els it were pete ; and I pray you to recomaunde me to hyr, and to my nawnte, and to all the gentill men and gentil women there. And as for John Daye, and he be dede I wold be sory, for I know not howe to come by my mony that he oweith me ; and I porpose that Pacoke schall have les to doo for me another yeres than he haith had, if I may be better porvayed with your helpe, for he is for hym self, bott not for me.

And as for ony marchandes to my corn, I can gytte none here ; therfor I pray you, doo ye als wele therein as ye canne ; also I send you by the berear hereof the bill of myne resaytes. And yef ye go forth with Walter, I pray you come to me als sone as ye may after ye be commyn home ; and me lyketh

174

EDWARD IV

1473
JAN. 18

myne abydyng and the contre here[1] right well, and I trust whan sommer comith and fayre wether, I schall lyke it better, for I am cherysed here botte to wel.

And I construe your letter in other materis well i nough, whereof I thanke you ; and if it nede not to send forth Walter hastyly, I wald ye myght come to me, thowe ye schuld com opon one day and goo agayne on the next day, than schuld I comon with you in all materis ; and I hold best if ye have not the letteris that Holler son schuld have brough me, that ye send Sym over for them this nyght that I may have them to morowe, and yif ye may combe your self, I wold be the better playsed.

And I remember that water of mynte or water of millefole were good for my cosyn Bernay to drynke, for to make hym to browke,[2] and yeve thei send to Dame Elesebeth Callethorppe ther ye shall not fayill of the tone or of both, sche haith other wateris to make folkis to browke. God kepe you.

Wrytyn on the Monday next after Sent Hiller.

I have no longer leyser atte thys tyme.

826

SIR JOHN PASTON TO JOHN PASTON[3]

To John Paston, Esquyer, or to Mestresse Margret Paston, hys Modre be thys letter delyveryd.

FEB. 3

WEELL belovyd Brother.[4] . . . . As ffor tydyngs heer, ther bee but fewe, saff that the Duke of Borgoyen[5] and my Lady, hys wyffe farethe well. I was with them on thorysdaye last past

---

[1] I think this must have been written at Maltby, where Margaret Paston certainly lived during her later years, and where she was doubtless staying when she desired a license of the Bishop to have the Sacrament in her private chapel. See No. 821.

[2] *i.e.* to enable him to retain food in his stomach.

[3] [From Fenn, ii. 120.]

[4] Here follows an account of letters sent to him from Calais—of farme barly in Fledge, and of olde stuffe at Norwich, etc.—F.

[5] Charles the Bold, and Margaret, sister to Edward IV.

175

THE PASTON LETTERS

1473
FEB. 3

at Gawnt.[1] Peter Metteney ffarethe weell, and Mestresse Gretkyn bothe and Rabekyn recomend hyr to yow ; she hathe ben verry seke, but it hathe doon hyr goode, ffor she is ffayrer and slenderer than she was, and she cowde make me no cheer but alwey my sawse was 'How ffaret Master John, yowr brother ?' wher with I was wrothe, and spake a jalous worde or too, dysdeynyng that she sholde care so moche ffor yow, when that I was present.

Sende me worde to Hoxons in wrygtyng, what goode the Bysshop ded ffor me at Framynham, and howe my Lorde, my Ladye, and all the cort or [are] dysposyd to me wards.

I here also seye that my Ladye and yowrs, Dame Margret Veer[2] is ded, God have hyr sowle ; iff I weer not sorye ffor herr, I trowe ye have been.

No moor to yow at thys tyme, but All myghty Good have yow in kepyng.

Wretyn at Caleys the iij. daye of Februarye Anno R. R. E. iiij. xij°·   J. P., K.

827

NOTE

FEB. 10

In Blomefield's History of Norfolk, vol. xi. p. 208, it is stated that 'on February 10 in the 13th of Edward iv., an indenture was made between Sir William Yelverton, William Jenney, serjeant-at-law, and William Worcester, executors of Sir John [Fastolf] on one part, and Thomas Cager and Robert Kyrton on the other, whereby the said Robert was appointed surveyor of the lands and tenements in Southwark and other places in Surrey, late Sir John's, to perform his last will ; and also receiver of rents ; who was to have 6 marks per ann., and to be allowed besides all reasonable costs that he shall do in the defence and keeping out John Paston, Esq., and of all others claiming by him.'

---

[1] Ghent, in the Netherlands.
[2] Daughter and heir of Sir William Stafford, and wife to Sir George Vere. Their son, John Vere, was afterwards Earl of Oxford.—F.

176

EDWARD IV

828

ABSTRACT[1]

'J. P.' [John Paston] to Sir John Paston

As I promised in the letter that Playter sent, Playter and I have been with my mother to get her to make chevesance for the £100, but she bade us send you word, you need look for no other comfort from her. Jwde can tell you Barker's answer. As for John Kook you promised him payment yourself and to Sir John Styll 5 marks in part payment. My mother has sold her barley for 14d. I never meet John Smyth but I speak of it to him. He keeps his courts here at Norwich all the week. As for Fastolf, I can only speak to Wymondham his father-in-law, which I do as often as I see him. Would be sorry the great matter which requires hasty answer 'lest the kok be in perayle ' should be delayed by his negligence. Thinks Edmund Fastolf 'was a reason-' able man to Robert of Lyne. Wherefore, let my brother Edmund sue for ' the same, for one wife may serve for us both till better peace be. So God ' help me ye may allege a plain excuse that these dyrk wars have so hindered ' me that her lyvelode and mine both should be too little to live at our ease till ' I were further before the hand than I could be this two year, and she found ' after her honor and my poor appetite.' Would rather forbear what he would have than bring them in pain. 'Say better for me, for ye can and ye will. ' This matter must be honestly handled, for I wot well my young lady of ' Oxenforthe shall hear of it. We have here no tidings, but a few Frenchmen ' be whyrlyng on the coasts, so that there dare no fishers go out but under safe ' conducts. I pray you, and ye have any more oranges than ye occupy, that ' poor men may have part for a great bellied lady.' First Monday of Clean Lent, 13 Edw. iv.

1473
MARCH 8

Addressed—'A Mys' John Paston, schevaller, soyt done.' *Endorsed*—'Mens' Marcii Anno xiij°.'

829

JOHN PASTON TO SIR JOHN PASTON[2]

To my Master, Sir John Paston, Knyght, be thys delyverd in hast.

A

S I was wryghtyng this bylle, Mastresse Jane Harsset comandyd me streyghtly that I shold recomand hyr to yow in hyr best wyse, and she sendyth yow word she wold be as fayne to here fro yow as an other poore body.

MARCH 26

---

[1] [From MS. Phillipps 9735, No. 257.]
[2] [From Paston MSS., B.M.] This letter is endorsed with what appears to have been the date of its receipt—'xxviij° die Marcii A° xiij¹ E. iiij¹¹.'

VOL. V.—M   177

THE PASTON LETTERS

1473
ARCH 26

Syr, it is so that my cosyn John Blenerhasset[1] is enformyd that for verry serteyn he is chosyn to be on of the colectours of the taske in Norffolk, wher in verry trowthe he hathe not a foot of lond with in the shyer ; wherfor I beseche yow that, as hastyly as ye may aftyr the syght of thys bylle, that it may please yow to take the labore to comon with Sir Rychard Harrecorte, and to let hym have knowlage that thys gentyll-man hathe nowght with in the shyer, and that ye tweyne may fynd the meane to get hym owght of that thanklesse offyce, for I promyse yow it encomberthe hym evyll, and my mastresse hys wyffe, and alle us hys frendys here ; and if so be that ye and Sir R. Harcorte may not fynd the meane betwyx yow, that then it may please yow to meve my Lord Chamberleyn with thys mater, and so Master Harsset prayithe yow, and Mastresse Jane, hys wyff also, for she lyekyth no thyng by the ofyce.

It is thowght her amonge us that Heydons be the causers that he was set in. I prey yow enqwer of Sir R. Harcort who was the cause, and that it may be wyst in the next byll that ye send me ; for if they wer the causers, it lythe in my cosyn Harsettes power to qwytte theym.

We have no tydynges to send, but that our Frenshemen[2] whyche kepte our costs her ar home into France, for lake of vytayll, we saye.

Hogan[3] is put in the Gyld Halle in Norwyche, and shalbe browght up to London for reportyng of hys old talys. He varythe not. No more, but I prey God send yow the Holy Gost amonge yow in the Parlement Howse, and rather the Devyll, we sey, then ye shold grante eny more taskys.

Wretyn the day next aftyr our Lady Day, the Anuncya-cyon, Anno xiij. E. iiij¹¹.

Yong Heydon laborythe alle that he can to mary on

---

[1] John Blennerhasset, Bleverhasset, and (for shortness) often called Harsset, of Frens, married first Jane, daughter of Thomas Higham, Esq., and secondly Jane, daughter of Sir Thomas Tindal of Hockwold, Knight. He died in 1510, aged 87.—F.
[2] The French vessels that infested the coast, as mentioned in the preceding letter.
[3] Hogan pretended to foretell commotions and rebellions, etc.—F.

178

EDWARD IV

of hys doughtyr to yonge John Barney[1] by the mean of W. Calthorpp.   J. P·

1473
MARCH 26

830

SIR JOHN PASTON TO JOHN PASTON[2]

A son trescher & bon ame Freer, John de Paston, Esquier.

W

EELL belovyd brother, I recomand me to yow, letyng yow wete that at the request of Mestresse Jane Hassett and yow, I have laboryd the knyghtys off the sheer off Norffolk, and the knyghtys off the shyre off Suffolk. I understond ther had ben made labor that suche a thing shulde have ben as ye wrotte to me off, but now it is saff.

APRIL 2

Raff Blaundrehasset wer a name to styrte an hare. I warrant ther shall come no suche name in owr bokys, ner in owr house ; it myght per case styrt xx¹¹ harys at onys ; ware that jd. perse.[3] I redde ther in the bille off Norffolk, off one John Tendall, Esquier, but I suppose it be not ment by owr Tendall, and iff it be, he shall not rest theer, iffe I maye helpe it.

As for tydyngs, the werst that I herde was that my moodre wyll not doo so moche ffor me as she put me in comffort off.

Other tydyngs, I herd sey ffor serteyn that the Lady Fitz-water is ded, and that Master Fytzwater shall have CCCC. mrke a yer more than he had. I am not sory therffor.

As ffor the worlde I woot nott what it menyth, men seye heer, as weell as Hogan, that we shall have adoo in hast ; I know no lyklyhod but that suche a rumor ther is.

Men sey the Qwyen with the Prynce shall come owt off Walys, and kepe thys Esterne with the Kyng at Leycetr, and some seye nowther off them shall com ther.

Item, off beyond the see, it is seyd that the Frense Kyngs

---

[1] This marriage never took effect.—F.
[2] [From Fenn, ii. 122.]
[3] 'Ware that penny purse '—*qu.* that penurious fellow ?

179

THE PASTON LETTERS

1473
APRIL 2

host hathe kyllyd the Erle of Armenak[1] and all hys myry mene; some seye undre appoyntment, and some seye they wer besegyd, and gotyn by pleyn assault.

Ferthermoor men seye that the Frenshe Kynge is with hys ost uppon the water off Some a lx. myle froo Caleys; I leve them wheer I ffond them.

I made yowr answer to the ffrends off Mestresse Jane Godnoston accordyng to yowr instrucions. As for me, I am nott serteyn whether I shall to Caleys, to Leysetr, or come home into Norffolk, but I shall hastely send yow worde, &c.

Wretyn the ij. daye of Aprill, Anno E. iiij. xiij°.

831

SIR JOHN PASTON TO JOHN PASTON[2]

To John Paston, Esquier.

APRIL 12

BEST belovyd brother, I recomend me on to yow, letyng yow weet that I receyvyd on Wednysday last past yow angery lettre towchyng the troble that Sandre Kok is in, wherein I have largely comonyd with John Russe, and advysed hym to take a curteys weye with Sandre, for yowre sake and myn. He seythe he wold not dysplease yow by hys wyll, and that he purposythe to entrete yow and wolde deserve it to yowe. He undrestod that ye had large langage to the jurye that passyd again Saundre. I lete hym weete that ye weer wrothe, and that he shall nowther please yowe ner me, but iff he dele curteyslye with Saundre. I tolde hym as for the condempnacion uppon the accion off trespasse I thoght it nowther good ner worshypfull. Also I have wretyn to the person of Maultby to dele curteyslye with Saundre, iff he woll please yow or me.

[1] John, Count of Armagnac, assassinated on the 6th March 1473.
[2] [From Paston MSS., B.M.]

180

1473
APRIL 12

Item, I sende yow herwythe the *supercedyas* for Saundre; so that iff ye fynde any meane for the condempnacions that than ye maye ease therwith the suerte off pease. John Russe, as I suppose, is att home thys daye.

Item, as for tydynges heer, the Kynge rydeth fresselye thys daye to Northamton warde, there to be thys Esterne, and after Esterne he purposythe to be moche at Leysettre, and in Leysettre shyre. Every man seythe that we shall have a doo or Maye passe. Hogan the prophet is in the Tower; he wolde fayne speke with the Kyng, but the Kynge seythe he shall not avaunt that evyr he spake with hym.

Item, as for me, I most nedys to Caleyse warde to morowe. I shall be heer ageyn, if I maye, thys next terme. John Myryell, Thyrston, and W. Woode be goon from me, I shrewe them.

My modre dothe me moor harme than good; I wende she wolde have doon for me. Playter wroot to me that she wolde have leyde owt for me C*li.*, and receyvyd it ageyn in v. yer of the maner of Sporle, wherto I trustyd, whyche if she had performyd, I had nott ben in no juperte of the maner of Sporle. Neverthelesse I shall do whatt I kan yitt. I preye yow calle uppon hyr for the same, remembre hyr of that promyse.

Item, I preye yow remembre hyr for my fadrys tombe at Bromholme. She dothe ryght nott [*naught*]; I am afferde of hyr that she shall nott doo weell. Bedyngfelde shall mary Sir John Skottes doghtre, as I suppose.

Item, Janore Lovedaye shall be weddyd to one Denyse, a ffuattyd (?) gentylman, with Sir G. Brown, nowther to weell ner to ylle.

Item, as for me, iff I had hadd vj. dayes leyser more than I hadd, and other also, I wolde have hopyd to have ben de-lyveryd of Mestresse Anne Hault. Hyr frendes, the Quyen and Attclif agreyd to comon and conclude with me, if I can fynde the meanes to dyscharge hyr concyence, whyche I trust to God to doo.

i. Item, I praye yow that ye take a leyser thys Estern halydayes to ryde to Sporle and sende for John Osberne, and

181

THE PASTON LETTERS

1473
APRIL 12

I wolde ye sholde conclude a bergayn with one Bocher, a woode byer, whyche Mendham that was my fermor ther can fecche hym to yow.

ii. And thys is myn entent. I wolde have the dykes to stonde stylle, acordyng as John Osberne and I comonyd, I trow xij. foothe with in the dyke.

iij. Item, that the standardes off suche mesur as he and I comonyd off maye also be reservyd. I suppose it was xxx. inche, abowt a yerde from the grownde.

iiij. Item, that it be surely fencyd at the cost off the woode byer in any wyse with a sure hedge, bothe hyghe and stronge.

v. Item, that ther be a weye taken with the fermores for the undrewood, so that I lesse not the ferme therffore yerly. Item, John Osbern can telle yow the meanys howe to entrete the fermores, for Herry Halman hath pleyed the false shrowe and fellyd my woode uppon a tenement off myn to the valew off xx. marke, as it is tolde me. I praye yow enquire that matre and sende me worde and dele with hym ther afftre.

vj. Item, iff the seyde wood clere above alle charges excep as is above, be made any better than CC. marke, I wolle seye that ye be a good huswyff. John Osberne seythe that he woll do me a frendes turne ther in and yitt gete hym self an hakeneye.

vij. Memorandum, that he have nott past iij. or iiij. yere off untraunce at the ferthest.

viij. Item, thatt I have payement off the holl as shortly as ye kan, halffe in hande, the remenaunt at halffe yeer, or ellys at ij. tymes with in one yere at the ferthest by mydsomer xij. monyth.

ix. And that ye make no ferther bergayn than Sporle woode and the lawnde, not delyng with noon other woode, nowther in the maner, nor ellys wher in none other tenement.

x. Item, that ye have sufficient sewerte for the monye, with penaltes iff nede be, some other men bonden with hym for the payement.

xj. Item, I wolle well be bownde to waraunt it to hym.

Item, I sende yow herwith a warant to yow and John

182

1473
APRIL 12

Osberne joyntlye to bergayn. Comone and conclude that bergayn.

xij. Item, I suppose he woll, iff he conclude with yow, desyre to felle thys Maye, and I to have mony soon afftre. I reke not thowe he fellyd not tyll thys wynter; but iff he woll nedes begyn thys Maye, therffor I wryght yow thus hastely entrete hym, iff ye can, that he felle not tyll wynter.

xiij. Item, be ware how ye bergeyn, so that he felle nott butt in sesonable tyme and sesonable wood, for he maye felle no undrewood thys Maye, as I trowe

Item, as for yowr costes late th . . . . . . newe fynde yow mete, and I woll allow it there, or ellys make me a bylle what it dra[weth to] . . . . yow.

Item, I praye yow iff ye g . . . . . for me as ye can. I made my Lady heer but easy cheer, neverthelesse I gaff hyr . . . . . ys.

I promysed hyr to purveye hyr . . . . weselys, but I was deseyvyd; yit I wend to have had one.

My Lord of Norffolk hathe ben mevyd for Caster by my Lord Cardenall and the Bysshop of Wynchester, but it woll take non effecte . . . my Lady come. God gyff grace that she brynge auctoryte when she comythe thys next terme to common ther in and conclude, and so I prey yow advyse hyr. Itt may haply paye for hyr costes.

No mor to yow, but wretyn at London, the xij. daye of Aprill, Anno E. iiij[ti] xiij°.

I sende yow her with ij. letteris from John Osbern to me, wherby and by hys billes ye may undrestond the verry valewe off the wood.

I praye yow sende me wryghtyng ageyn by the Mondaye vij. nyght afftre Ester; iff Hoxon or the goode man off the Goot have it, they shall conveye it welle.

183

THE PASTON LETTERS

832

SIR JOHN PASTON TO JOHN PASTON[1]

To John Paston, Esqer, in Norffolk.

1473
APRIL 16

WYRSSHYPFULL and ryght hertyly belowyd brother, I recomande me on to yow, letyng yow wete that on Wednysdaye last past I wrote yow a letter, wheroff John Carbalde had the beryng, promyttyng me that ye shold have it at Norwyche thys daye, or ellys to morowe in the mornyng, wherin I praye yowe to take a labor accordyng afftr the tenur off the same, and that I maye have an answer at London to Hoxon, iff any massenger come, as ene I maye doo ffor yow.

As ffor tydyngs, ther was a truse taken at Brussellys about the xxvj. daye off Marche last past, be twyn the Duke off Borgoyn and the Frense Kyngs imbassators and Master William At Clyff ffor the Kyng heer, whyche is a pese be londe and water tyll the ffyrst daye off Apryll nowe next comyng, betwyn Fraunce and Ingelond, and also the Dukys londes. God holde it ffor ever and grace be.

Item, the Erle of Oxenfford was on Saterdaye at Depe, and is purposyd into Skotlond with a xij. schyppys. I mystrust that werke.

Item, ther be in London many fflyeng talys, seiyng that ther shold be a werke, and yit they wot not howe.

Item, my Lorde Chamberleyn[2] sendyth now at thys tyme to Caleys the yonge Lorde Sowche[3] and Sir Thomas Hongreffords dowtre and heyr,[4] and some seye the yonge

1 [From Fenn, ii. 130.]
2 William, Lord Hastings.—F.
3 John, Lord Zouch of Harringworth; he was attainted in the first year of Henry VII.—F.
4 Mary, daughter and heir of Sir Thomas Hungerford; she afterwards married Edward, son and heir to William, Lord Hastings, who in her right became Lord Hungerford, her uncle's attainder being reversed.—F.

EDWARD IV

Lady Haryngton, thes be iij. grett jowelles, Caleys is a mery town, they shall dwell ther I wott not whylghe [*how long*]. 1473 APRIL 16

No mor, but I have ben, and ame troblyd with myn over large and curteys delyng with my servants, and now with ther onkynd nesse; Plattyng, yowr men wolde thys daye byd me ffar well to to morow at Dover, notwithstandyng Thryston yowr other man is ffrom me, and John Myryell, and W. Woode whyche promysed yow and Dawbeney, God have hys sowle, at Castre, that iff ye wolde take hym in to be ageyn with me, that then he wold never goo ffro me, and ther uppon I have kepyd hym thys iij. yer to pleye Seynt Jorge and Robyn Hod and the Shryff off Notyngham, and now when I wolde have good horse he is goon into Bernysdale, and I withowt a keeper.

Wretyn at Canterburye, to Caleys warde on Tewesday and happe be, uppon Good Frydaye the xvj. daye off Apryll, Anno E. iiij^{ti} xiij°.

Yowr,   J. P., K.

Item, the most parte off the sowdyors that went over with Sir Robert Green have leeff, and be comyn hom, the hyghe weye ffull ; my cariage was behynd me ij. hours longer than I lokyd afftr, but I wysse I wende that I myght have etyn my parte on Good Frydaye all my garees [*finery*] and pryde had ben goon, but all was saffe. I pray yow iff W. Mylsent go ffroo yow, that he myght come to me at Caleys, I will have hym.

THE PASTON LETTERS

833

SIR JOHN PASTON TO JOHN PASTON[1]

To John Paston, Esquyer, in Norwich.

1473
MAY 18

RYGHT wershypfull brother, I recomand me to yow, &c.[2]

As for tydyngs, the Erle of Wylshyr[3] and the Lord Sudele[4] be ded, and it was seyd that Sir W. Stanle was deed, but nowe it is seyd naye, &c.

Item, as ffor your goyng to Seyn James,[5] I beleve it but atwyen ij., &c.

I herd seye that a man was thys daye examyned, and he confessed that he knewe greet tresor was sende to the Erle off Oxenfford, wheroff a m^{le} li. [£1000] sholde be conveyd by a Monke off Westminster, and some seye by a Monke off Chartrehows.

Item, that the same man schulde acuse C. gentylmen in Norffolk and Suffolk that have agreyd to assyst the seyd Erle at hys comynge thyder, whyche as itt is seyd, sholde be within viij. dayes afftr Seynt Donston, iff wynde and weddyr serffe hym—fflyeng tales. No mor at thys tyme, but God have yow in kepyng.

Wretyn at London on Seynt Donstones daye, xviij. daye of Maye, Anno, E. iiij^{ti} xiij°.

JOHN PASTON, K.

1 [From Fenn, ii. 136.]
2 Then follow some orders concerning servants, debts, securities, etc.—F.
3 John Stafford was created Earl of Wiltshire in 1470. He was uncle to Henry, Duke of Buckingham.
4 . . . . . . Butler, Lord Sudley.—F.
5 Apparently John Paston had talked of making a pilgrimage to the shrine of St. James of Compostella in Spain.

EDWARD IV

834

SIR JOHN PASTON TO JOHN PASTON[1]

To John Paston, Esqer, be thys delyveryd.

1473
JUNE 3

RYGHT wyrshypfull brother, I comand me to yow, letyng yow weet that thys daye I was in very purpose to Caleys ward, all redy to have goon to the barge, saff I teryed ffor a yonge man that I thoght to have had with me thyddr, on that was with Rows, whyche is in the cowntre ; and because I cowde not geet hym, and that I have no mor heer with me butt Pampyng, Edward, and Jak, therffor Pampyng remembryd me, that at Caleys he tolde me that he purposed to be with the Duchesse off Norffolk, my Lady and yowrs. And Edward is syke and semythe nott abydyng ; he wolde see what shold falle off thys worlde ; and so I am as he that seythe ' Come hyddr John, my man.' And as happe was yesterday, Juddy went affor to Caleysward ; wherffor I am nowe ille purveyd, whyche ffor owte that I knowe yit is lyke to kepe me heer thys Wytsontyd.[2] Wherffor iff ye knowe any lykly men, and ffayr condycioned, and good archers, sende them to me, thowe it be iiij. and I wyll have them, and they shall have iiij. mrks by yer, and my levere [*livery*].

He maye com to me hyddr to the Gott [*Goat*], or yit to Caleys with a riall[3] iff he be wyse, whyche iff nede bee, I wolde that Berker toke hym to come uppe with, iff it be suche one as ye tryst.

Item, I suppose bothe Pytte and Kothye Plattyng shall goo ffrom me in hast ; I wyll never cherysshe knaves soo as I have don, ffor ther sakys.

Item, I praye yow sende me a newe vestment off whyght damaske ffor a dekyne, whyche is among myn other geer at Norwiche, ffor he shall ther too as ye woot off : I wyll make

1 [From Fenn, ii. 138.]
2 Whitsunday fell on the 6th June in 1473.
3 A royal, a gold coin of 10s. value.

THE PASTON LETTERS

1473
JUNE 3

an armyng doblett off it, thow I sholde an other tyme gyff a longe gown of velvett ffor another vestment, and send it in all hast to Hoxon to send me.

I hopyd to have been verry mery at Caleys thys Whytsontyde, and am weell apparayled and apoyntyd, saff that thes ffolks ffayle me soo, and I have mater ther to make off ryght excellent. Som man wolde have hastyd hym to Caleys thowe he had hadd no better erand, and som men thynke it wysdom and profyght to be theer now weell owt off the weye.

Item, as ffor the Bysshop[1] and I, we bee nerrer to a poynt than we weer, so that my part is nowe all the londes in Flegge Holly, the maner off Heylesdon, Tolthorpe, and tenements in Norwyche and Erlham, excepte Fayrechylds, but ffarweell Drayton ; the Devyll do ytt them.

Item, large and fferr comynycacion hathe ben bytwyen Sir John Fogge, Ric. Haulte, ffor ther suster and me, byffor Doctor Wyntborne and ellys wher, so that I am in better hope than I was, by Seynt Lawrens[2] that I shall have a delyveraunce.

Item, as ffor tydyngs heer, I trow ye have herde yowr parte, howe that the Erle off Oxenfford landyd by Seynt Osyes in Essexe, the xxviij. daye off Maye, saff he teryed nott longe, ffor iff he had, the Erle off Essexe[3] rod to hym wardys, and the Lords Denham and Durasse, and other mor, whyche by lyklyod sholde have dystrussyd hym ; but yit hys comyng savyd Hogan hys hed, and hys profesye is the mor belevyd ffor he seyde that thys troble sholde begyn in Maye, and that the Kynge sholde northwards, and that the Scotts sholde make us werke and hym batayle.

Men loke afftr they wot not what, but men by harneys ffast ; the Kyngs menyall men and the Duke off Claraunces, ar many in thys town ; the Lord Ryverse[4] com to daye, men seye to purveye in lyke wyse.

Item, how that the Cowntesse off Warwyk[5] is now owt

[1] Waynflete, Bishop of Winchester.   [2] 10th of August.
[3] Henry Bourchier, Earl of Essex, Lord Treasurer.
[4] Anthony Woodville, Earl Rivers, beheaded at Pontefract, 1483.
[5] Anne, widow of Richard Neville, the great Earl of Warwick, sister and heir to Henry Beauchamp, Duke of Warwick, and mother of Isabel, the wife of George, Duke of Clarence.

188

EDWARD IV

off Beweley Seyntwarye, and Sir James Tyrell conveyth hyr northwarde, men seye by the Kynges assent, wherto som men seye that the Duke off Clarance is not agreyd.

1473
JUNE 3

Item, men seye that the Erle off Oxenfford is abowt the Ilde off Tenett hoveryng, som seye wyth grett companye, and som seye, with ffewe.

No mor, but God kepe yow.

Wretyn at London the iij. daye off June, Anno E. iiijti xiijo.

JOHN PASTON, K.

835

ABSTRACT[1]

Norf. and Suff. Deeds, No. 67. ' Relaxatio Willielmi Paston facta Will. Wainflet et aliis de toto jure suo in manerio vocat' Caldecots, Akethorp, Spitlings, Habland, Broweston, etc. Jun. 13, Edw. iv. 13.'

JUNE 13

836

SIR JOHN PASTON TO EDMUND PASTON[2]

A Edmond Paston, Esquyer, a Caleys soyt donne.

BROTHER Edmond, I grete yow weell, letyng yow weete that abowt thys daye vij. nyght I sende yow a letter by Nycholas Bardeslee a sowdyer, whyche is wont woute[3] to be at border [*brother*] Perauntys,[4] and also an hoseclothe[5] off blak ffor yow. I wende that ye sholde have hadde itt within ij. dayes, but I am afferde that he deseyved me.

JULY 5

Item, I lete yow weet that Plattyng is comen hyddr, and he seythe that ye gaffe hym leve to ffetche hys geer and Pittys, and that is hys erande hyddr and noon other, ner he thowt never to goo ffro me, ner he wyll nott goo ffro me as he seythe,

[1] [From MS. Index in Magd. Coll., Oxford.]
[2] [From Fenn, ii. 146.]   [3] So in Fenn.
[4] Fenn suggests a fanciful explanation of the expression ' border Perauntys,' presuming the latter word not to be a proper name ; but see page 163.
[5] Cloth for hosen.

189

THE PASTON LETTERS

1473
JULY 5

wherffor, I praye yow sende me worde off hys condycions, and whyghe ye thynke that he sholde never do me worshypp.

He seythe also that he and Pytte weer at the takyng off the Esterlyngs, and that he was in the *Pakker*, and Pytte in the *Crystoffre*. I praye yow sende me worde howe bothe he and Pytte quytte them, by the report off some indyfferent trewe man that was ther, iff they quytte them weell, I wolde love them the better, wherffor the next daye afftr the syte of thys letter, I praye yow wryght ageyn, and sende it by the next passage.

Item, I sende a lytell praty boxe herwith, whyche I wolde that Juddy sholde delyver to the woman that he wetyth off, and praye hyr to take it to the man that she wetyth off ; that is to seye, as moche as ye knowe all well i now, but ye maye nott make yow wyse in no wyse.

Item, I praye yow sende me worde as ye wer wont to do off heer wellffar, and whether I weer owt and other inne or nott ; and whether she shall fforsake Caleys as sone as ye sende me worde off or nott.

By God I wolde be with yow as ffayne as yowr selff, and shall be in hast with Godds grace.

Item, as ffor my brother John, I hope within thys monyth to see hym in Caleys, ffor by lyklyhod to morowe or ellys the next daye he takyth shyppe at Yarmothe, and goothe to Seynt James[1] warde, and he hathe wretyn to me that he wyll come homwarde by Caleys.

Item, I suppose that James Songer shall come with me to Caleys, the rather ffor yowr sake.

Item, Mestresse Elysabett ffareth well, but as yit Songer knoweth nott so perffytly all that ye wolde weet, that he woll nott wryght to yow off thees ij. dayes tyll he knowe moor, but iff she hadde ben bolde, and durst have abydyn styll at hyr gate, and spoken with me, so God helpe me, she had hadd thys same that I sende nowe wher ye woot off, whyche ye shall see woryn heer afftr, itt is a praty ryban with praty agletts[2] and goodlye.

[1] *See page 186, Note 5.*
[2] Pendant ornaments of metal, like tags or points, etc.—F.

190

EDWARD IV

Make yow not wyse to Juddy, nowther not that ye wolde weet any thynge, ffor I maye sey to yowe at hys comyng ovr, he browt goodly geer reasonablye.

1473
JULY 5

Item, as ffor my byll[1] that is gylt, I wolde it weer taken head too ; ther is one in the town, that can glaser weell i nowe, as I herde seye. Also, ther is on comythe every markett daye ffro Seynt Omerys to Caleys and he bryngethe dagers, and ffetchyth also, he may have it with hym, and brynge it ageyn the next markett daye ffor xijd. or xvjd. at the most, and ellys late it be weel oylyd and kepte tyll I come. No more.

Wretyn at London the v. daye of Julle, Anno E. iiijti xiijo.

837

SIR JOHN PASTON TO MARGARET PASTON[2]

To my ryght wyrshypful moodre, Margret Paston.

RYGHT wyrshypfull and my ryght tendre modre, I recommaunde me to yow, besechyng yow of yowr dayly blessyng. Please it yow to weet that I herde not from yow off longe tyme, whyche cawsythe me to be ryght hevye ; ner at the last tyme that I sende to yow in wryghtyng I hadde from yowr selffe noo wryghtyng ner answer ageyne, saff by Playter one tyme and by my brother one other tyme ; whyche answer off Playter was noo thyng acordyng but contraryaunt to other wryghtyng more comfortable that he hadde sent me nott longe byffore that on yowr behalve, as he wrott, whyche God amende. Nevertthelesse to my more hevynesse, I herde seye that ye sholde have been passhyng hevy for my sake, and in cheffe for that I was lyke to late goo the maner off Sporle, wherin I was pytte in comfort

JULY 30

[1] A warlike instrument of offence.—F.
[2] [Add. 34,889, f. 125.] This letter appears to be of the year 1473, as in that year Sir John Paston writes on the 5th July that he hopes to be in Calais within a month (No. 836). Later in the year (22 Nov.) he writes that the citations here referred to were not ready (No. 842, p. 199). The date is further confirmed by what is said of the manor of Sporle (comp. pp. 181, 182).

191

THE PASTON LETTERS

to have had relyffe by the meanes off yow; and syns it was tolde me that iff I leete it goo that ye wold therfore dysavauntage me more lond in tyme to come, off syche as by poscybylyte myght come to mee of yowris. Uppon whyche corage my grauntdame[1] and myn oncle[2] togedre gaffe me an answer on hyr part moche lyke, and so my fadre, God have hys sowle, leffte me scant xl*li.* londe in reste, and ye leffe me as pleasythe yow, and my grauntdame at hyr plesur; thus may I have lyttel hope off the worlde. Neverthelesse I beseche yow to be my good moodre, how so ever ye do with yowr londe; for I feell weell that iff I have one losse I am lyffe [*q.* like ?] therfor to have three. But as for Sporle, it shall nott goo iff I maye, ner by my wyll; and iff ther hadde been performed me as largelye as was promysed me by Playter, I were sewre it sholde nott have goon, nor yit sholde nat goo. Neverthelesse iff ye and all my frendys and yowris in Norffolk myght have lende me so moche monye and to have takyn it uppe in v. yere, I suppose they sholde peraventure have ben payed ageyn in a yer or ij. iff I had solde any woode. Neverthelesse, plese yow to weet that I have provyd my fadres wyll and testement, wherin I maye nowt dele on to the tyme that all the executoris have reffused; wherffor ther most be sende sitatacions (*sic*) to yow and alle other that weer namyd my fadris executoris. Wherin iff ye list not to take admynystracion, as I woot well ye woll nott off olde, ye most than make a proctor that must, on yowr behalve, byffor my Lorde of Canterbury, with a sufficiaunt warant and autoryte, undre a notarys syngne ther in the corte, reffuse to take admynystracion. And this instrument and aultoryte I beseche yow maye be redy and att London by the fyrst daye of the terme ; and iff yow be not aqueynted with none suche at London, iff it please yowe to take and avowe for your proctor and sende hym auctoryte, on [*one*] Master John Halsnothe whyche was a clerke off Master Robert Centis[3] and was so trusty to my fadre, God have hys sowle, and to sende me a letter off yowre

[1] Agnes Paston. [2] William Paston.
[3] Robert Kent, who had been John Paston the father's proctor in the Court of Archers. *See* vol. iv. pp. 243, 244.

192

EDWARD IV

wylle ther in, I undertake that he shall not do but as ye sende me worde. Plese it yow to gyff credence to Juddy herin.
No more to you att thys tyme, but Jhesu have yow in Hys kepyng. Wretyn att Caleys, the last daye saff one off Julle.—
Yowr sone,   J. P., K.

838

MARTIN RONDELLE TO SIR JOHN PASTON[1]

Monseigneur Jehan Paston, chevalier d'Engleterre.

MON treschier et honnore seigneur, je me recomande a vous outant que je puis ne scay. Et vous plaise savoir que je ay oy novelles de vous par ung de vo marchans de Calais touchant unne armura de unna sella que je vous doy, et de una barbuta, laquelle est en diferansce entre vous et moy, de laquelle je vous ay aultre foix dist que je estoie contant de fere toute rexon [*raison*], et en quore le vous dige prexentement que je suis prest de fer tout chou qu'il apartient en tout rexon, set [*c'est*] asavoir de la barbute et de l'armura de sella. D'aultre chiox ne vous suis en riens tenut, forque en toute les chiox que me seroint posible de faire pour l'amour de vous a vostre honneur et a vostre profit, je suis tout jour prest a vostre comendement.

Item, en houltre, je ay entendut que vous voulles avoir unng harnax complet. Com je prins vostra mexure dernierement quant vous fustes en ceste ville de Bruges, saichies que je ay en quor vostre mexure de toutes lez piesces ; pour quoy, se il vous plaist que je la vous fasa, je la vous faray de bon ceur, et tout cella que il vous plaira avoir fait ; et au regard du pris, je faray tellement que vous seres content de moy pour tant quant il vous plaira lesiem savoir queles piesses que vous voles avoir, et la faisson et le jour que vous la voles avoir par quelcun aqui je puis in chauder en nom de vous, et qui me ballia argant de sus, je feray si bien que se Dieu plaist vous vous loeres de moy. Aultre chiox ne vous say que

[1] [From Paston MSS., B.M.]

VOL. V.—N   193

THE PASTON LETTERS

mander pour le prexent, senon que je prie a Dieu que il vous doint ce que vostre ceur desir.
Escript a Bruges, le xxviij. jour de Ahoust, l'an lxxij.
                                   Le tout vostre serviteur,
                                        MARTIN RONDELLE,
                                        Armurier de Monsire le
                                        Bastart de Bourgogne.

Endorsed—Par Martyne Rowndell, armorer de Bruggys. Anno E. iiij*ti* xiij°.

839

LORD HASTINGS TO SIR JOHN OF MIDDLETON AND SIR JOHN PASTON[1]

To my right hertily beloved frends and felaws, Sir John of Middelton, and Sir John Paston, Knights.

AFTER herty recommendacion, I thank you of the gode attendance that ye yeve unto the Kings counsail at Calais ; and the gode and effectuelle devoires that ye putte you to assiste my depute Sir John Scot, in alle suche things as mowe concerne the saufgarde of my charge there. Leting you wite, that if ther be any thing that I can and may do for you, I shal with right gode wil performe it to my power.

And I preye you to recommaunde me to my Lady Howard,[2] my Lady Bourghier,[3] and all othre ladies and gentilwomen of the saide towne. And in likewise to the Mayre, Lieutenant, and felaship of the staple ; my felaws the souldeours, and all othre suche as ye shal seme gode. And oure Lord sende you your desires.

[1] [From Fenn, ii. 152.] This letter, Fenn tells us, is endorsed in a hand of the time, '²E. (?) Hastyngs, Anno xiij°.,' showing that it was written in the thirteenth year of Edward IV.
[2] Margaret, wife of Sir John Howard, Lord Howard, and afterwards Duke of Norfolk. She was daughter of Sir John Chedworth, Knight, and died in 1490, 5 Hen. VII.
[3] Lady Bourchier was probably the wife of a son of Sir John Bourchier, Lord Berners.

194

EDWARD IV

Writen at Notyngham, the xvj. day of Septembre.
Sir Joh Paston, I pray you to yeve credens to suche thing as my depute shall shew you fro me, and conforme you to the same.

                    Your felaw,   HASTYNGS.

840

NOTE

On the Close Roll 13 Edw. IV. m. 5, is an indenture tripartite bearing date 1 Nov., 13 Edw. IV., between Thomas Byllyng, Chief-Justice, and others, including William Paston on the one part ; Jane Ingaldesthorp, late wife of Edmund Ingaldesthorp, Knight, William Norys, Knt., and Isabel, Marquesse Montague, his wife, of the second part ; and William Parker, citizen and tailor, London, of the third part.

841

SIR JOHN PASTON TO JOHN PASTON[1]

To John Paston, Esquier, at Norwych, be thys delyvered.

WYRSHYPFULL and well belovyd brother, I comand me to yow, letyng yow weet that the worlde semyth qweysye heer ; ffor the most part that be abowt the Kyng have sende hyddr ffor ther harneys, and it [is] seyd ffor serteyn, that the Duke off Clarance makyth hym bygge in that he kan, schewyng as he wolde but dele with the Duke of Glowcester ; but the Kyng ententyth, in eschewyng all inconvenyents, to be as bygge as they bothe, and to be a styffeler atweyn them ; and som men thynke that undre thys ther sholde be som other thynge entendyd, and som treason conspiryd ; so what shall falle, can I nott seye.

Item, it is seyde that yisterdaye ij. passagers off Dovr wer takyn ; I ffer that iff Juddy had noon hasty passage, so that iff he passyd nott on Sondaye or Mondaye, that he is taken, and som geer off myn, that I wolde not for xx.*li.*

[1] [From Fenn, ii. 126.] This letter is misdated in Fenn as of the 15th April. St. Leonard's Day is the 6th November.

195

THE PASTON LETTERS

I hope and purpose to goo to Caleys warde on Sondaye or Mondaye or nyghe bye, ffor I am nott accompanyed to do any servyse heer; wherffor it wer better ffor me to be owt off syght.[1]

. . . .

Item, Sprynge, that wayten on my ffadre when he was in Jowel hous [*gaol house*], whom my ffadre at hys dyeng besett xl*s*. he cryethe evyr on me ffor it, and in weye off almess, and he wolde be easyd, thow it wer but xx*s*. or x*s*.; wherffor he hathe wretyn to my modr, and most have an answer ageyn; I wolde that my moodr sende hym, as thoghe she lende hym som whatt, and he woll be pleasyd, and ellys he can seye as shrewdely as any man in Ingelonde.

Item, the Kynge hathe sent ffor hys Great Seall; some seye we shall have a newe Chauncelor, but som thynke that the Kynge dothe as he dyde at the last ffeldys, he wyll have the Seall with hym; but thys daye Doctor Morton, Master off the Rollys, rydethe to the Kynge, and berythe the Sease [*Seals*] with hym.

Item, I had never mor nede off mony than now; wherffor Fastolffes v. mrks and the mony off Master John Smythe wolde make me holl, &c.

Wretyn on Seynt Lenards Daye, Anno R. R. E. iiij^ti xiij°.

Item, sende me my vestment acordyng to the letter I sent yow by Symond Dam, in all hast. J. P., K.

842

SIR JOHN PASTON TO JOHN PASTON[2]

To John Paston, Esquyer, be thys delyvered.

RYGHT wyrshypfull and hertyly belovyd brother, I comand me to yow, letyng yow wet that I receyvyd a letter that come from yow, wretyn circa viij. Mychaelys,[3] wherin ye leet me weet off the decesse off

[1] Here follow some money transactions relative to a Doctor Pykenham, his mother, and others.

[2] [From Paston MSS., B.M.]

[3] i.e. *circa octabas Michaelis*—about the Octaves of Michaelmas, or 6th October.

EDWARD IV

Syr James, and that my moodre is in purpose to be at Norwyche, and I am ryght glad that sche wyll now doo somwhat by yowr advyce; wherffor be war fro hense forthe that noo suche felawe crepe in be twyen hyr and yow, and iff ye lyst to take a lytell labore, ye may lyff ryght well, and she pleasyd. It is as good that ye ryde with a cople off horse at hyr cost as Syr James or Richard Calle.

Ye sende me worde also that she in noo wyse wyll purveye thyr C*li*. for the redemyng off Sporle. Late it goo. As towchyng that mater, John Osbern tolde me that he comonyd with yow at Sporle of that mater; ferr he devysed that Kokett, or suche an other man, sholde, to have it the better cheppe, leye owt the valewe off vj. yere for to have it vij. yere, wherto I wolde agre; and for Goddys sake, if thatt maye be browt abowt, late it be doon. As ye woot of, it is laten for xxij*li*. be yere, yit the fermor graunt but xxj.; but to Kokett it wolde be worthe xxv*li*., yea and better. Neverthelesse, if Kokett wyll delyver vj^xx-*li*., I wolde he had it for vij. yeer, with thys that my moodre be agreable to the same, by cawse of th'entresse that she hathe for my brother William, whyche shall nott be off age thys vij. yeer; nevertheless, as ye know myn olde entent, I purpose to purvey for hym in an other plase better than ther; whyche graunte off my moodre I praye yow to be my solycytor in, whyche [and] it be browt abowt, Sporle shall be in as goode case as evyr he was.

John Osbern willyd me to make yow a sufficiaunt waraunt to selle and felle wood at Sporle, whyche I remembre ye have in as ample forme as can be; neverthelesse iff thys meane above wretyn off letyng to ferme maye be hadde, it shall, I hope, nat nede to felle ner selle moche. But I remytte that geer to yowr dyscrescion, but iff ye have suche comforte, I praye yow sende me worde. I maye seye to yow, John Osbern flateryd me, for he wolde have borowyd mony off me.

Item, in retaylyng of woode theer, it weer harde to tryst hym; he is nedye. If Kokett, or whoo so evyr had that maner to ferme for vij. yere, and payd therffor but vj^xx-*li*., he sholde, to lete it ageyn, wynne xxxvj*li*., whyche we[re] moche; wherffor, iff it myght bee, yt wer more resenable vj^xx. vij*li*. to

THE PASTON LETTERS

be reseyvyd, and yit is ther lost xxix*li*., or ellys iff ye take lesse mony and fewer yerys, so it be aftre the rate, so ther be purveyd C*li*. at the lest; send worde.

Item, ye wroot that lyke a trewe man ye sende me xviij*s*. by Richarde Radle. Ye weer to trewe; but he semys to be a false shrewe, for he browt me noon yitt. Whethyr he be owt of town or nott, kan I nott seye.

Ye prayed me also to sende yow tydynges how I spedde in my materis, and in cheff of Mestresse Anne Hault. I have answer ageyn fro Roome that there is the welle of grace and salve sufficiaunt for suche a soore, and that I may be dyspencyd with; neverthelesse my proctore there axith a m^L docatys, as he demythe. But Master Lacy, another Rome renner heer, whyche knowyth my seyde proctor theer, as he seythe, as weell as Bernard knewe hys sheeld, seythe that he menyth but an C. docates or CC. at the most; wherffor afftre thys comythe moor. He wrote to me also, *quod Papa hoc facit hodiernis diebus multociens.*

Item, as towchyng Caster, I tryst to God that ye shall be in it to myn use or Crystmesse be past.

Item, yowr ost Brygham recomand hym to yow, and when he and I rekenyd, I gave hym ij. noblis for yowr borde, whyll ye weer theer in hys absence; but in feythe he wolde, for nowth that I kowde doo, take j*d*. Wherffor ye most thanke hym or charge me to thanke hym on yowr behalve in some nexte epystyll that ye wryght to me to Caleys. He leete me weet that he wolde do moor for yow than soo.

Item, my Lady Bowgcher was almost deed, but she ys amendyd. I trowe they come in to Norffolk.

Item, as for W. Berker, I heer no worde from hym. I praye yow comon with Berney ther in, he knoweth myn conceyt; and also I praye yow hast Berney ageyn. I wold not that he played the fooll, ner wastyd hys tyme ner hys sylver.

Item, as for the brace of growndes [*greyhounds*], or one verry goode, or in especiall the blak of Germynes, I can nott seye but ye be a trewe man, but William Mylsent isse a false shrewe, so mote I thee, and I trow hys master ys too.

EDWARD IV

Item, I most have myn instrumentes hydder, whyche are in the chyst in my chambre at Norwyche, whyche I praye yow and Berney to gedre joyntly, but natt severally, to trusse in a pedde,[1] and sende them me hyddre in hast, and a byll ther in how many peces. Thys most be had to avoyde idelnesse at Caleys.

Item, I preye yow take heed among thatt my stuffe take noon harme, ner that myn evydence, wher ye wott of, be owt of joperte.

Item, I praye yow doo for Berneye as ye kan, so that he maye be in sewerte for hys annywyte, and that it be nott costious fro hense forthe to hym any mor to come, or sende for it. I pray yow wynne yowr sporys in hys mater.

Item, I purposed to have sent heer with the testament off my fadre and the scytacions to my moodre to yow and Arblaster; but they be nott redy. Within ij. dayes aftre the comyng off thys, I suppose they shall be with yow, and than I shall wryght mor to yow.

As for other tydynges, I trust to God thatt the ij. Dukes of Clarans and Glowcester shall be sette att one by the adward off the Kyng.

Item, I hope by the means of the Duke of Glowcester that my Lord Archebyshop[2] shall come home.

Item, as towchyng my sustre Anne,[3] I undrestand she hathe bene passyng seek; but I wende that she had ben weddyd. As for Yelverton, he seyde but late that he wold have hyr, iff she had hyr mony, and ellis nott; wherffor me thynkyth that they be nott verry sewre. But, amonge alle other thynges, I praye yow be ware that the olde love of Pampyng renewe natt. He is nowe fro me; I wott nat what he woll do.

No more. Wretyn at London, the xxij. daye of Novembre Anno R. R. E. iiij^ti xiij°. JOHN PASTON, Kt.

[1] A kind of basket.

[2] George Neville, Archbishop of York, though formerly pardoned, had been accused of holding correspondence with the Earl of Oxford, for which he was imprisoned at Guines.

[3] Anne Paston married William Yelverton, grandson of Sir William Yelverton, the Judge.

THE PASTON LETTERS

843

SIR JOHN PASTON TO JOHN PASTON[1]

To John Paston, Esquier.

1473
ov. 25

RYGHT wyrshypfull and well belovyd brother, I re-comaund me to yow, letyng yow weet that I sende yow her with j. sitacion, where in ben my moodre and yee, wheroff I praye yow that I maye have hasty answeer. The effecte theroff is no moor, but ye bothe most sende answer, and make yow a proctor heer, and that most come hyddre ondre a notaryes syngne, affermyng that ye make suche a man, Master John Halsnothe, or ellis, yf ye will do the cost, to sende some other hyddre ; yowr proctor to take admynystra-cion or to reffuse, and what so he dothe, ye to holde it for ferme and stable. Than most my moodre and ye wryght a lettre, undre my moodre seall and yowr syngne manuell, to me and Master John Halsnothe in thys forme :—'We gret yow well, letyng yow weet that we have made yow, Master John Halsnothe, our proctor in the testament of John Paston, husband and fadre to yow, wherin we wyll that on owr be-halff ye refuse the admynestracion of the seyde testament. And thys wryghtyng is to yow warant and dyscharge, and also the verry wyll of usse.' Thys most we have for owr dyscharge.

Item, I pray yow take good hedde to my soster Anne, lesse the old love atwyen hyr and Pampyng renewe.

Item, I pray yow sende me worde howe my moodre is dysposyd to hyr wardes, and iffe so weer that a good mariage myght be had, what she wolde depart with.

Item, I praye yow that ye remembre hyr for the tombe off my fadr at Bromholme, and also the chapell at Mauteby, and sende me worde how she is dysposyd her in.

[1] [From Paston MSS., B.M.] The year in which this letter was written is clearly shown, partly by the allusions made in it to several matters mentioned in previous letters, and more especially by what is said of the Earl of Oxford. That nobleman was besieged in St. Michael's Mount, Cornwall, by Sir Henry Bodrugan during October and November 1473.

200

EDWARD IV

Item, iff I have Caster ageyn, whethyr she wolle dwelle ther or nott, and I wyll fynde hyr a prest towardes at my charge, and geve hyr the dovehowse and other comodytes ther ; and if any horsekeper on myn lye ther, I wolle paye for hys borde also, as weell as for the prestes.

1473
nov. 25

Item, iff my modre sholde have a new prest, I thynk that my brother Syr J. Goos weer a metly man to be ther. He wolde also doo, as ye wolde have hym nowe, ber the cuppe evyn, as What-calle-ye-hym seyde to Aslake.

Be war of Myneres fro hense forthe, and sende me worde how ye trist Doctor Pykenham. I wolde, if he wolde doo owght for my moodre, that he hastyd the soner to paye me the C*li.*, so that I myght pledge owt Sporle.

Item, as for other tydynges, the Erle of Oxenforthe is stille besegyd. Neverthelesse, onys he issued owt, and toke a jentylman, and hant [*draggea*] hym within ; but now off late he was besye, and one espyed hym, and shott at hym and strake in the verry fase with an arowe. I sye thys daye the same man, and theere I leef hym.

Iff Arblaster come to yow, ye maye see hys letter sente to hym by me, wherin I have wretyn that he scholde take yowr advyce ; but I praye you, above all thynges, that me make hast so that I heer from yow ageyn by thys day vij. nyght.

At London, the xxv. daye of Novembre.

JOHN PASTON, K.

844

THE TENANTS OF SPORLE TO SIR JOHN PASTON[1]

To oure specyall good lord and mayster, Syr John Paston, Knyght, be this delyvered in hast.

RIGHT worchepfull and oure specyall good mayster and loord, after oure dewe recomendacion with owre servyce. Please it yow to knowe that we arn grevously troubled, and not lyke to kepe oure tenourys, the whiche we holde of

Date
uncer-
tain

[1] [From Paston MSS., B.M.] The date of this letter is very uncertain, but as a good deal is said about this time of the manor and wood of Sporle, we insert it here for convenience.

201

THE PASTON LETTERS

Date
uncer-
tain

you, but yf ye helpe us ; for we wer bete at the boordourys syde, and afterwarde our servauntes wer bete at the plowe in Spoorle felde, and somme of them be lyke to dey. And we redyn to Maister Shereve and to Mayster Southwell for remedye, and thei advysed us to ryde to Mayster Wyngfeld ; and thenne we understode that Mayster Wyngfeld was reden to London, &c. And so we stonden withoute remedye, and in grete doute of owr lyves, and losse of owr goodys. Wher-for we beseche you to socoure us accordyng to your right and owres. And ellys we kan nott abyde it, &c. Cryst kepe your good lordshep.

Be your poore tenauntes of Spoorle.

845

NOTE

1474
FEB. 9

It appears by the Early Chancery Proceedings printed by the Record Commission (vol. i. p. xc.), that a decree was given in Chancery in Hilary term, 13 Edw. IV. compelling William Paston and other trustees to fulfil a covenant between Richard, Duke of Gloucester and Elizabeth, Countess of Oxford. On the Close Roll, 13 Edw. IV. memb. 1, is a release by William, Bishop of Ely, Sir Thomas Montgomery, John Wentworth, clk., William Paston, Esq., Roger Townesend and Jas. Arblaster to Richard, Duke of Gloucester, of all their right in Ocle Magna and Parva, etc., in Essex, which they have by enfeoffment of Eliz., Countess of Oxford, and in other manors in Norfolk and Suffolk which they lately had of the gift of the same. This release is dated 9th Feb. 13 Edw. IV., and was acknowledged in Chancery on the 11th Feb. Below it are enrolled three other deeds by the Countess and her feoffees to the Duke, dated 9th June, 12 Edw. IV., and acknowledged in Chancery, 25th June, 14 Edw. IV.

202

EDWARD IV

846

SIR JOHN PASTON TO MARGARET PASTON[1]

Mestresse Margrett Paston, at Norwyche.

RYGHT honorable and most tendr good moodr, I re-comand me to yowe, besechyng yow to have, as my tryst is that I have, yowr dayly blessyng ; and thanke yow off yowr good moderhood, kyndenesse, cheer, charge, and costes, whyche I had, and putte yow to, att my last beyng with yow, whyche God gyffe me grace her afftr to deserve !

1474
FEB. 20

Please it yow to weet, that I thynge longe that I heer nott ffrom yow or ffrom Pekok yowr servaunt, ffor the knowlege howe he hathe doon in the sale off my fferme barlye, ner whatt is made theroff ; wherffor I beseche yowe, if it be not answeryd by that tyme that thys bylle comythe to yowe, to hast hym and itt hyddre wards ; ffor iff that had nott taryed me, I deme I had been at Caleys by thys daye ; ffor it is soo, as men seye, that the Frense Kynge with a gret hoste is at Amyans, but iij[xx.] myle from Caleys ; and iff he, or hys, roode byffor Caleys, and I nott theer, I wolde be sorye.

Item, men seye that the Erle of Oxenfford hathe ben con-streynyd to sewe ffor hys pardon only off hys lyffe ; and hys body, goodes, londes, with all the remenaunt, at the Kynges wyll, and soo sholde in all haste nowe come in to the Kyng ; and some men seye that he is goon owt off the Mounte,[2] men wot not to what plase, and yit lefte a greet garnyson theer, weell ffornysshyd in vytayll, and all other thynge.

Item, as ffor the havyng ageyn off Castre, I trust to have good tydyngs theroff hastelye.

Item, my brother John ffarethe weell, and hathe doon ryght delygentlye in my cosyn Elizabet Berneys mater, wheroff hastely I trust he shall sende hyr tydyngs that schall please hyr ; and as to morow he purposyth to take hys jurneye to Walys warde to the Lorde Ryverse. No mor at thys tyme, but Jeswe have yow in Hys kepyng.

[1] [From Fenn, ii. 154.] [2] St. Michael's Mount in Cornwall.

203

THE PASTON LETTERS

1474
FEB. 20   Wretyn at London the xx. daye off Feverer, Anno E. iiij^{ti}
xiij°.

Yowr sone,   J. PASTON, K.

847

LORD HASTINGS TO JOHN PASTON [1]

To my right trusty and welbeloved servaunt,
John Paston, Squier.

1474(?)
APRIL 26   JOHN PASTON, I recommaunde me unto you. And whereas I appointed and desired you to goo over unto Guysnes to yeve youre attendaunce and assistaunce upon my brother Sir Rauf Hastings in all suche things as concerne the suretie and defense of the Castell of Guysnes during his infirmyties; it is shewed unto me that ye have full truely and diligently acquyted you unto my saide brother, in all his besynesses sithe your comyng thider. Whereof I thanke you hertly. And as I conceive to my grete comfort and gladnesse, my saide brother is wele recovered and amended, thanked be God. And soo I truste he may nowe spare you. Wherupon I have writen unto him, if he may soo doo, to licence you to come over unto me ayen. Wherefore I woll and desire you, th'assent of my saide brother had, to dispose you to come over in all goodly haste, as well for suche grete maters, as I fele by youre ffrends, ye have to doo here, as to yeve youre attendaunce upon me. And your retourne ye shall be to my welcome.

From London, the xxvj. day of Avrill.

[2] I pray you in no wise to depart as yet without my brother Roaf asent and agrement; and recommaund me to my syster, all my nieces, to the constabyll, and to all Ryves [*reeves*].

Your tru frend,   HASTYNGES.

[1] [From Fenn, ii. 296.] I cannot discover in what year John Paston could have been staying at Guisnes during the month of April at the request of Lord Hastings, unless it was in the year 1474. There seems no other probable year in which we have not distinct evidence of his being elsewhere.

[2] This postscript is in the writer's own hand, the preceding part of the letter being in that of a clerk. A fac-simile of the postscript is given by Fenn.

204

848

SIR RALPH HASTINGS TO JOHN PASTON [1]

To my feithful lovyng gode cousyn, Johan Paston.

COUSYN Paston, I recommaunde me to you in as speciall   1474
wise as I cane. And like you to witte, on Sondaye at   MAY 9
even last I hadde writing and evedence frome my lorde
by Punche of tidyngis and have understonde them wel al a
longe. And on Monday erly in the mornyng I came to Calais
to have spoken with you, but I came to late. Praying you to
advertise my lord [2] to se wel to him self, etc. And at my
comyng home the same nyght I felle doune syke, and have
ever sith kept my bedde and yitte do. And, as you knowe
wel, the Connestable sykened with you in his goyng to Calais,
of whome I doubt me, and so I do of my self bothe. So that
here amongis us nowe is no man to stirre about and see qwykly to
alle thingis as ther aught to be and is nede to be, which hevieth
me gretly; and though I were up and might somwhat stire
myself, yitte I am not seure so to contynue ij. daies to-geder,
etc. As for moo men, my Lord hathe praied me and advised
me to holde me content with thoo that I have, and that I
shulde make as litel coste in reparacions as I maye, because he
cannot se wel howe the monney cane be goten to content them.
Cousyn, as for moo men ye knowe right wel thoo that we have
are to fewe, and we have nede; notwithstonding I shal do as
wel as I may with thoo that I have. But as [for] [3] eny ferther
reparacions, might I ones for oure seurte have this fournisshed
that I am about, I kepe not to make moo, for I doubt me that
this we are about, that parte therof wil reste in my nekke,
because we cane not be seure of oure assignement. I pray you,
cousyn, brekes to my Lord all suche maters that ye cane remembre and thinke [4] may be for the wele of us and the seurte of

[1] [Add. MS. 34,889, f. 122.] This letter was clearly written in the same year as No. 847, which was apparently 1474.

[2] Lord Hastings.   [3] Omitted in MS.

[4] 'thinke' repeated in MS.

205

THE PASTON LETTERS

1474(?)   this place, as my ful speciall truste and alle othir mennes here
MAY 9   is in you. I hadde thought to have writton to my lord to
have sente some othir seure man hidre to have assisted and
holpen us during oure infirmitees, but I fele by Punche that
my Lord saith I write always so plainly to him that hit fereth
him, and therfore I dar not but shal forbere to write any more
so; howe be hit, it were ful necessarye and behoffull so to do,
that knoweth God, Who ever preserve you. Writton at
Guysnes, the ix^e daye of May.

I praye you to sende us some of your tidingis by this berer
as oft as ye may. And if ther be anything I may do to your
plesir, I shal do it with as good hart as ye cane desire.

Your tru luffuyng coussen,

RAUFF HASTYNGIS.

849

ABSTRACT [1]

1474   Letters patent, dated at Westminster, 24 July, 14 Edw. IV., for levying a
JULY 24   subsidy in the county of Norfolk for a war against France.

850

JOHN PASTON TO SIR JOHN PASTON [2]

To Sir John Paston, Knyght, or to hys brodyr Edmund in hys
absence, lodgyd at the George by Powlys Wharff, in London.

JULY 25   RYGHT worchefull sir, I recomand me to yow, preying
yow to remembyr, or ye depert ought of London, to
spek with Herry Ebertonys wyf, draper, and to
enforme hyr that I am profyrd a maryage in London, whyche
is worth vj^c [600] mark and bettyr; with whom I preyid yow

[1] [Add. Charter 14,973, B.M.]

[2] [From Paston MSS., B.M.] This letter is endorsed in a contemporaneous hand 'Anno xiiij°,' showing that it was written in 1474, the 14th year of Edward IV. We also find Sir John writing to his brother in November following that his brother Edmund had heard nothing more of Eberton's daughter.

206

to comone, in as myche as I myght not tery in London myself,   147
alweys reservyng that if so be that Mastresse Eberton wyll   JULY 2
dele with me, that ye shold not conclud in the other place, thow
so wer that Eberton wold not geve so moche with Mastress
Elyzabet, hys dowghtyr, as I myght have with the other, for
syche fantazy as I have in the seyd Mastress Elyzabet Eberton.
And that it lyek yow to sey to Ebertons wyff that syche as I
spak to hyr of shalbe bettyrd rather then enpeyred as for my
part; and if it lyek hyr to deale with me, I wylbe at London
for that cawse only with in xiiij. dayis aftyr the wryghtyng of
thys byll, with Godes grace, Who preserve yow and yours

Wretyn at Norwyche, on Seynt Jamys Day.

Also, sir, I prey yow that ye wyll, as I desyerd yow, comon
with John Lee or hys wyf, or bothe, and to undyrstond how
the mater at the Blak Freerys dothe, and that ye wylle see and
spek with the thyng your sylf, and with hyr fadyr and modyr,
or ye depert; and that it lyek yow to desyer John Lee is wyff
to send me a byll in all hast possybyll, how fer forthe the mater
is, and whedyr it shalbe necessary for me to come up to London
hastyly or not, or ellys to kast all at the Kok.

Also, sir, I prey yow that Pytt may trusse in a male, whyche
I left in your chambyr at London, my tawny gowne furyd with
blak, and the doblet of porpyll sateyn, and the doblet of blak
sateyn, and my wryghtyng box of syprese, and my book of the
Metyng of the Dwke and of the Emperour, and when all thys
gere is trussyd in the male, to delyver it to the berer herof, to
brynge me to Norwyche.

Item, I send yow herwith the pylyon for the male, and x^s.
for the hyer, whyche is usery, I tak God to rekord.

Also, that it lyek yow to spek with your apotycary, whyche
was som tyme the Erle of Warwykes apotycary, and to weet
of hym what the wedow of the Blak Freiris is woorthe, and
what hyr husbondes name was. He can tell all, for he is
executore to the wedous husbond. I prey yow forget me not,
no more then I do yow. I have spokyn thys day with Jamys
Hubberd and Herry Smyth, and to morow I shall have an
answer of theym.

207

THE PASTON LETTERS

Also, my modyr wyll labore thys mater with effect, that the CC. mark may be had for the wood.

Also, brodyr Edmund, I prey yow, and my brodyr Sir John be not in London, that ye wyll labore all thys maters with effect, as my trust is in yow in every poynt as is above wretyn.

Also, I assartayn yow that I was with Ferrour thys day, and he had no leyser to comon with me ; but I wyll be with hym ayen to morow by apoyntment betwyx hym and me, and so as I speed I shall send yow woord by the next man that comyth to London.

Also, I sent John Lee is wyff a lettyr by on Crawethorn dwellyng in Wood street, or ellys in Sylver street at the end of Wood street. I prey yow weet whedyr she had it or nought ; and she had it not, brodyr Edmund, I prey yow go to the same Crawethorn, and tak the lettyr of hym, and delyver it hyr in all hast.

J. PASTON.[1]

851

ABSTRACT[2]

'Bill' dated 24 Oct., 14 Edw. IV., relative to the pledging of certain parcels of plate by William Paston, Esq., to Elizabeth Clere of Ormesby. The parcels amount in all to 250 oz. 4 dwt., and are pledged for £40. *Sealed.*

ii. Fair copy of the preceding.

852

ABSTRACT[3]

THE VICAR OF PASTON TO MARGARET PASTON

When my master Sir John's baily was at Paston he scared your tenants, bidding them pay no rents to Mr. William. On which Harry Warns wrote to Mr. William, who bade him warn them not to pay money to any one else ; otherwise he would meet them at London 'as the law would,' or at some market or fair, and make them pay arrears to Midsummer. Beware of Warns,

---

[1] This signature stands in the middle of the postscript.
[2] [From Paston MSS., B.M.]   [3] *Ibid.*

208

EDWARD IV

for he made Master William privy to all the examinations of the tenants by my master your son. He also charged the tenants not to sell as my master desired, else Master William would undo them. '*Ideo*, putte no trost in hym, *quia duobus dominis nemo potest servire.*' Pastun, 3 Nov.

[This and the letter following both appear to have been written at the time of Sir John Paston's dispute with his uncle William, at the end of the year 1474.]

853

ABSTRACT[1]

[THE VICAR OF PASTON] TO MRS. [MARGARET PASTON]

John Qwale, farmer of Paston, is distressed by things that Herry Warns has done and said against him. Warns carried home 'an esse' [*ash*] blown down by the wind, and says it is your will, because Master John Paston has given him power over all that he has in Paston. 'More awre he stondes in grete dowte to ery or to sawe' [*to harrow or to sow*], for John of Bactun says he shall have no land, unless he find surety, 'and it were no resun that he suld somerlay and compace hys londes to a noder mans hand.' Warns says if Qwale put out any cattle at the gates, he will take it for the grain that Master William delivered to him. He says Mrs. Margaret Paston[2] has no rule there, and shall have none; also that John Qwale shall not have Gyns close nor the Chyrche close, as he has taken them to farm. 'Qwere fore, bott ze gyfe hym oderwas power, he wyll gefe up all.'

854

[WILLIAM PASTON] TO SIR JOHN PASTON[3]

[*To*] *my right worshipfull neview* [*Sir J*]*ohn Paston, Knyghte, be* [*this*] *lettre delivered in hast.*

[Right] worshipful neview, I recommaund me to you. And, sir, I pray you . . . . that ther was none

---

[1] [From Paston MSS., B.M.]
[2] Mrs. Margaret Paston is here spoken of by name and in the third person, but the letter can hardly be addressed to any one else.
[3] [From Paston MSS., B.M.] Of this letter only two fragments remain, giving, as will be seen, a very mutilated text. Little more can be said about the contents than that they refer to money matters between William Paston and his nephew Sir John, which are probably those referred to in succeeding letters. The handwriting is that of William Paston. A mutilated endorsement, apparently in the handwriting of John Paston the younger, shows merely the words ' . . . . . to Sir J. P. for . . . . .'

THE PASTON LETTERS

obstacle ner lettinge that ye found in me to . . . .
. . . . . . save me harmeles ; at whiche tyme it was thought aswel . .
. . . . Johns by obligacioun
was not inow to save me harm[eles] . . . .
. . . . . [i]n the meane seasoune ; for as your reasoun will give . .
. . . . ght fell of yow but goode. And if the caas
so fill that . . . . ys will take it
on them, than I to bere the losse. Wherupp[on] . . . . .
. . . . [b]ound to me to save me harmeles. And for as
muche . . . . m by obligacioun of statute
merchaunt for you the . . . . in
myne oune kepinge for my discharge, and after a . . . .
. . . . . . [r]estorid me ageyn at this Michelmas. And m . . .
. . . . shuld hange still till Candilmas, and me thinke it is by con . . . . . . obligacions paiable
at . . . . [Candle]mas I did at the begynny[ng] . . . . . will
kepe still the . . . .
. . . . or sufficient and that . . . .
. . . . . as wold pay at th. . . . .
. . . . with me than thus . . . .
. . . . indenture wherby
. . . . for be cause
that ye w . . . .
. . . . experyens.
Also I wold avyse you . . . .
. . . . my Lord of Norfolk.
Also, nevew, there is onne Fr . . . .
. . . . but hym silf and his wif and . . . . . .
. . . . wherfore I have writin to . . .
. . . . in this matier ; and I
trust I . . . . And
I pray yow that may ha . .

855

ABSTRACT[1]

Fragment of a draft deed by which Sir John Paston and John Paston, Esq., mortgage certain premises not named to the use of Master John Morton, William Paston, Thomas Playter, and Thomas Lovell, for £114.

[Nothing is clear about the date of this document, but we place it here, as bearing, like the last, on money matters between Sir John Paston and his uncle William.]

---

[1] [From Paston MSS., B.M.]

210

EDWARD IV

856

SIR JOHN PASTON TO MARGARET PASTON[1]

To Mestresse Margrett Paston at Norwyche, or to J. Paston in hyr absence.

RYGHT wyrshypfull and my moste kynde and tendre moodre, I recomaund me to yow, thankyng yow off the grete cost and off the greet chere that ye dyd to me and myn at my last beyng wyth yowe ; whyche cheer also hath made me perfyghtly hooll, I thanke God and yow, in so moche that where as I feeryd me that for weykenesse, and so green recuveryd off my syknesse, that I scholde have apeyryd by the weye ; but, God thanke yow, I toke so my crommys whyls I was wyth yow, that I felyd my sylfe by the weye that God and ye had made me stronger than I wenyd that I had ben, in so myche that I feell my selffe every daye holler than other.

It was soo that I mett wyth myn onkle William by the weye, and there in the felde I payed hym the iiij*li.* whyche I had borowyd off hym ; and he was passyng inquisytyff howe that I was purveyd for recompensyng off Towneshend. I tolde hym I hopyd weell ; he tolde me that he undrestood that I had the C*li.* of the Bysshopys executores, and he had herde seye that I had also borowyd another C*li.* of a marchaunt, and so I lakyd but an C. marke. I deme he herde thys of T. Lovell, for I tolde hym that I was in hope to fynde suche a freende that wolde lende me C*li.* He axed me, who was that ? I answeryd hym, an olde marchaunt, a freende of myn, but myn oncle thowte that shold be by weye of chevyshanse [*usury*], and to myn horte ; wherffor I was pleyne to hym, and tolde hym that ye wer sewerte therffor, and purveyed it off suche as wolde doo for yowe. And as for the forte [*fourth*] C. mark, he seyde to me that as for that he

---

[1] [From Paston MSS., B.M.] It is evident from the contents that this letter must have been written shortly before that which follows.

211

THE PASTON LETTERS

1474 wolde, rather than joperte sholde be, purvey it by weye off chevyshaunce at London, in so moche that, er he come fro London, he had for my sake leyde v. C. markes worthe of plate with Hewghe Fenne. The place at Warwykes Inne is large, and my grawntdame is agyd; it had ben jopertous to leve moche plate wyth hyr, thoghe halffe were hyr owne. But if I maye do other wyse, I purpose nott to chevyshe any mony by hys meane.

Item, I have delyveryd yowre botell to Courbye the caryer thys same daye, and he promysed me to be with yow on Mondaye nyghte, or ellys on Touesday tymely. He hathe also xld. to paye for the thryd hyryd horse, and he bryngythe the iij. horse wyth hym, and is contente for hys labor and for the mete largely. They be delyveryd hym in as good, and rather better plyght, than whan I had them forthe, and not gallyd nor hurte. He hate also ij. sadelys, one of my brotheres, and one other hyred, as ye woot off.

Item, he hathe a peyre botys off Edmond Reedes, the shomaker, whyche Saundre borowyd off hym. I beseche yowe that William Mylsent or Symme maye se that every man have hys owne.

Item, as for my brother Edmond, blyssyd be God, he is weell amendyd.

Item, as for Hankyn owr dogge, I am a fferde never to see hym, but if [*unless*] yowr good helpe bee.

Item, as for the bookes that weer Sir James, iff it lyke yow that I maye have them, I ame not able to by them; but somwhat wolde I gyffe, and the remenaunt with a goode devowte herte, by my trowthe, I wyll prey for hys sowle. Wherffor iff it lyke yow by the next messenger or karyer to sende hem in a daye, I shall have them dressyd heer; and iff any off them be claymyd here aftre, in feythe I wyll restoor it.

Wretyn on Saterdaye.   John Paston, K.

212

EDWARD IV

857

SIR JOHN PASTON TO MARGARET PASTON[1]

To Mestresse Margrete Paston, or to Roose, dwellyng byffore hyr gate at Norwyche.

AFTRE dew recomendacion, my most tendre and kynde moodre, I beseche yow off yowr dayly blessyng. Please it yow to weete that I reseyvyd a lettre thhat come from yowe, wretyn the xxvj. daye of Octobre, none erst but[2] on Wednysday last past, wherby I conceyvyd that, at the wryghtyng off that letter, ye weer nott serteyn of the delyng betwyn Towneshende and me. It was so that, God thanke yow, I receyvyd the xxli. broght by Syme, and also the mony browght by my brother, with whyche mony, and with moor that I had my selff, I redemyd the maner of Sporle, and payed Towneshend bothe the CCCC. marke ther ffor, and also xli. that I owte hym besyde, and have off hym aqwytaunce off all bargaynes and off all other dettes. Nevertheless, I assayed hym iff he wolde, iff nede hadde ben, gyvyn me a xij. monyth lenger respyght, whyche he grauntyd to do; but in conclusyon I can nott entrete hym, but that he woll have the uttremest of hys bargayn, and thys xxli. payeable at Candelmesse and Esterne. I kan entrete hym noon other wyse as yit; wherffor I thynke, iff I had passyd my daye, it had ben harde to have trustyd to hys cortesye, in so moche I ffynde hym also ryght loose in the tonge. For Bekham, he spekyth no thyng comfortably ther in ; what he wyll doo, can I nott seye.

Item, as for Castre, it nedyth nott to spore nor prykke me to doo owghte ther in. I doo that I can with goode wyll, and somwhat I hope to doo hastely ther in that shall doo goode.

Item, as for the bokes that weer Syr James, God have hys sowle, whyche it lykethe yow that I shall have them, I beseche yow that I maye have them hyder by the next massenger, and

1 [From Paston mss., B.M.]   2 No earlier than.

213

THE PASTON LETTERS

1474
NOV. 20 iff I be goon, yit that they be delyveryd to myn ostesse at the George, at Powlys Wharffe, whyche wolle kepe them saffe, and that it lyke yow to wryght to me whatt my peyne or payment shall be for them.

Item, it lyked yow to weet of myn heelle. I thanke God nowe that I am nott greetly syke ner soore, but in myn heele, wherin alle men know nott whatt peyne I feele. And wher ye advysed me to hast me owt of thys towne, I wolde full fayne be hense. I spende dayly mor than I sholde doo, if I wer hense, and I am nott well purveyed.

Item, blessyd be Good, my grauntdam is amendyd by suche tyme as myn oncle W. come hyddre. But my yongest cosyn Margret, hys doghtre, is ded and beryed er he come home.

I am as moche afferde off thys londe that is in hys hande as I was off that that was in Towneshendes hande. I hope to wryght yow moor serteynte within iiij. or v. dayes. No more, &c.

Wretyn the xx. daye of Novembre, anno E. iiij. xiiij°.

            Yowr Sone,   J. Paston, K.

858

SIR JOHN PASTON TO JOHN PASTON[1]

To John Paston, Esquyer, at Norwyche, or to Roose, awellyng affor Mestresse Pastonys gate, in Norwych.

RYGHT wyrshypful and weell belovyd brother, I recomaunde me to yow, letyng yow weet that I have comonyd with yowr ffreende Dawnson, and have receyvyd yowr rynge off hym, and he hathe by myn advyce spoken with hyr[2] ij. tymes ; he tellythe me off hyr delyng and answers, whyche iff they wer acordyng to hys seyng, a

1 [From Fenn, ii. 164.]
2 Apparently Lady Walgrave, hereafter referred to. She was the widow of Sir Richard Walgrave, Knight.
214

EDWARD IV

ffeynter lover than ye wolde, and weell aghte to, take therin greet comffort, so that he myght haply slepe the werse iij. nyghtys afftr. And suche delyng in parte as was bytwyen my Lady W. and yowr ffreende Danson he wrote me a lyghte theroff, whyche I sende yow herwith; and that that longythe to me to doo therin, it [*I?*] shall nott ffayle to leeve all other bysynesse a parte. Neverthelesse within iij. dayes, I hope so to deele herin, that I suppose to sette yow in serteynte hoghe that ye shall fynde hyr ffor evyr her afftr. It is so, as I undrestande, that ye be as besy on yowr syde ffor yowr ffreende Dawnson, wheer as ye be, I praye God sende yow bothe goode spede in thees werkys, whyche iff they be browte abowte iche off yowe is moche beholden to other; yit were it pyte that suche crafty wowers, as ye be bothe, scholde speede weell, but iff ye love trewly.

Item, as ffor Stoctons doghtr, she shall be weddyd in haste to Skeerne, as she tolde hyrselffe to my sylke-mayde,[1] whyche makyth perte off suche as she shall weer, to whom she brake hyr harte, and tolde hyr that she sholde have hadde Master Paston, and my mayde wende it had been I that she speke off; and with moor that the same Mester Paston kome wher she was with xx. men, and wolde have taken hyr aweye. I tolde my mayde that she lyed off me, and that I never spake with hyr in my lyff, ner that I wolde not wedde hyr to have with hyr iij^ml. marke.

Item, as for Ebortons dowghtr, my brother Edmonde seythe, that he herde never moor speche theroff syns yowr departyng, and that ye wolde that he sholde nott breke, nor doo no thynge therin, but iff it come off theer begynnyng.

Item, I had answer ffrom my Lorde[2] that he is my speciall goode lorde, and that by wryghtyng ; and as ffor Bernaye he sette hym in hys owne wages ffor my sake, and that whan so ever I come to Caleys, I shall ffynde all thyng ther as woll have it, and rather better than it was heretoffor.

1 A person who made gowns of silk, etc., for both men and women, as appears from the manner in which she is here mentioned.—F.
2 I am not certain whether the Duke of Norfolk is here meant, or Lord Hastyngs, the then Governor of Calais.—F.

215

Item, the Kyng come to this towne on Wednysdaye; as ffor the Frenshe Embassate that is heer, they come nott in the Kynges presence, by lykehod, ffor men seye that the chyeff off them is he that poysonyd bothe the Duke off Berry[1] and the Duke off Calabr.[2]

Item, ther was never mor lyklyhod that the Kyng shall goo ovyr thys next yer than was nowe.

I praye yow remembre that I maye have the pewter vessell heddr by the next karyer by the lattr ende off thys weke.

Item, I praye yow remembr so that I may have the bokys by the same tyme, whyche my moodr seyde she wolde sende me by the next carier.

Wretyn at London, the Sondaye the xx. daye off Novembr, anno E. iiij[ti] xiiij°.

JOHN PASTON, K.

859

ABSTRACT[3]

Norfolk and Suffolk Deeds, No. 33. 'The agreement and accord between the Bishop of Winton and John Paston, Knight, touching the building of the College at Castre of seven priests and seven poor men, translated by dispensation of the Pope to seven priests and seven poor scholars in Magdalene College, and touching the lands of Sir John Fastolf.   November 29, Edw. iv. 14.'

860

SIR JOHN PASTON TO JOHN PASTON[4]

To John Paston, Esquier.

BROTHER, I recomaunde me to yow, letyng yow weete that I have, lyke as I promysyd yowe, I have doon my devoyr to know my Lady Walgraves stomacke, whyche, as God helpe me, and to be pleyn to yowe, I ffynde

[1] Charles, Duke of Berry and of Guienne, who was supposed to have been poisoned by order of his brother Lewis XI. in May 1472.
[2] Nicholas of Anjou, Duke of Calabria and Lorraine, who died about the same time as the Duke of Guienne.
[3] [From MS. Index in Magd. Coll., Oxford.]
[4] [From Fenn, ii. 170.]

216

in hyr no mater nor cawse, that I myght tak comfort off. Sche will in nowyse receyve, ner kepe yowr rynge with hyr, and yit I tolde hyr that sche scholde not be any thynge bownde therby; but that I knew by yowr herte off olde that I wyst weel ye wolde be glad to fforber the lesvest [*dearest*] thynge that ye had in the worlde, whyche myght be dayly in her presence, that sholde cawse hyr onys on a daye to remembr yow, but itt wolde not be. She wolde nott therby, as she seyde, putte yow ner kepe yow in any comffort therby. And mor ovyr, she preyed me, that I sholde never take labor moor heer in, ffor she wolde holde hyr to suche answer as she hadd geven yow to ffoor, werwith she thowght bothe ye and I wolde have holde us contente, had nott been the words off hyr suster Geneffyeff.

When I undrestood all thys, and that over nyght she bad hyr that weent bytwyen hyr and me byd me brynge with me hyr muskeball[1] which, &c., than I aftr all thys axid iff she weer dyspleasyd with me ffor it, and she seyde, naye.

Than I tolde hyr, that I had nott sent it yowe, ffor synne off my sowle; and so I tolde hyr all, how I had wretyn to yow why that I wold nott sende it yow, by cawse I wyst weell ye sholde have slepyd the werse; but nowe, I tolde hyr, as God helpe me, that I wolde sende it yow, and gyffe yow myn advyse nott to hope ovyr moche on hyr, whyche is ovyr harde an hertyd lady ffor a yonge man to tryst on to; whyche I thowght that ffor all my words, ye cowde nott ner wolde nott do ffor all myn advyce.

Yitt ageynwards she is nott dyspleasyd, nor fforbad me nott but that ye sholde have the kepyng off hyr muskball; wherffor de ye with itt as ye lyke. I wolde it hadd doon weel; by Good, I spake ffor yow soo, that in ffeythe I trowe I kowde nott seye so weel ageyn.

Wherffor I sende yow herwith yowr rynge, and the on-happy muskeball. Also make ye mater off it herafftr as ye kan, I am nott happy to wow nowther ffor my selff ner noon

[1] This muskball, or ball of perfume, seems to have been taken from Lady Walgrave by Sir John Paston in a jesting manner, to send to his brother as a present from her.—F.

217

other. I tolde hyr all the processe off the Lorde Howarde and off yowr grewnds [*greyhounds*] as I kowde; all helpys nott.[1]

I her no worde off my vessell, ner off my boks; I mervayll. No moor.

Wretyn at London, the xj. daye of Decembr, anno E. iiij[ti] xiiij°.

J. P., K.

861

SIR JOHN PASTON TO JOHN PASTON[2]

To the ryght worshypfull John Paston, Esquier, at Norwych, or to hys modr, Margreet Paston, in hys absence, in haste.

I RECOMANDE me to yow, praying yow hertely, that I maye have weetyng when that my Lorde and Lady of Norffolk shalle be at London, and howgh longe they shall tery theer, and in especiall my Lorde of Norffolk; ffor uppon ther comyng to London wer it ffor me to be guydyd. Neverthelesse I wolde be soory to come theer but iff I neds most. I thynke it wolde be to yow ovyr erksom a labor to solycyte the maters atwyen them and me, but iff I weer theer myselffe; wherffor, iff ye thynke it be convenyent that I com thyddr, I praye yow sende me worde as hastely as ye maye, and by what tyme ye thynke most convenyent, that I sholde be theer; and off all suche coumfforte as ye ffynde or heer off the towardnesse theroff, and when also that ye shall be theer yowr selffe. For it is so that as to morow I purpose to ryde in to Flaundrys to purveye me off horse and herneys, and percase I shall see the assege at Nwse[3] er I come ageyn, iff I have tyme; wherffor, iff I so doo, by lyklyhod it woll be a

[1] 'Here follows,' says Fenn, 'some displeasure at his uncle William's proceedings in matters between them, etc., of no consequence.'
[2] [From Fenn, ii. 174.] 'Though this letter,' says Fenn, 'has no signature, yet it is written by Sir John Paston, Knight.'
[3] Neuss, not far from Düsseldorf, in the territory of Cologne, at this time besieged by Charles the Bold, Duke of Burgundy.

218

xiiij. dayes er I be heer ageyn; and afftr, as I heer ffrom yowe and other ther uppon, that at the next passage, and God woll, I purpose to come to London warde: God sende me goode spede; in cheff ffor the mater above wretyn; and secondly, ffor to appoynt with the Kyng and my Lorde, ffor suche retynwe as I sholde have now in thees werrys in to Frawnce; wherffor I praye yow, in Norffolk and other places, comon with suche as ye thynke lykly ffor yow and me, that ar dysposyd to take wages in gentylmenns howsys and ellys wher, so that we maye be the moor redy, when that nede is; neverthelesse at thys owr, I wolde be gladde to have with me deyly iij. or iiij. mor than I have, suche as weer lykly; ffor I lakke off my retynwe, that I have neer so many. I praye yow sende me som tydyngs, suche as ye heer, and howghe that my brother Edmonde dothe.

For as ffor tydyngs heer, ther be but ffewe, saffe that the assege lastyth stylle by the Duke off Burgoyn affoor Nuse, and the Emperor[1] hathe besegyd also, not fferr from these, a castell, and an other town in lyke wyse, wher in the Dukys men ben. And also, the Frenshe Kynge, men seye, is comyn ryght to the water off Somme with iiij[ml]. [4000] spers; and som men trowe that he woll, at the daye off brekyng off trewse, or ellys byffoor, sette upon the Duks contreys heer. When I heer moor, I shall sende yowe moor tydyngs.

The Kyngs inbassators, Sir Thomas Mongomere and the Master off the Rolls[2] be comyng homwards ffrom Nuse; and as ffor me, I thynke that I sholde be sek but iff I see it.

Syr John off Parre and William Berkeley com thys weye to Flaundrs ward to by them horse and herneys, and [I] made Sir J. Parr goode cheer as I cowde ffor yowr sake; and he tolde me, that ye made hym haulte cheer, &c. at Norwyche. No moor.

Wretyn at Caleys, the xvij. daye off Janever, anno Edwardi iiij[ti] xiiij°.

[1] Frederick III. of Austria, Emperor of Germany.
[2] Dr. John Morton, afterwards Bishop of Ely, Lord Chancellor, Archbishop of Canterbury, and Cardinal.

219

THE PASTON LETTERS

862

MARGARET PASTON TO JOHN PASTON [1]

To John Paston, Sqwyer, be thys delyveryd in hast.

Jh's.[2]

1475
JAN. 29

I GRET yow well, and send yow Goddes blyssyng and myn, letyng yow wet that my cosyn Robard Clere was her with me thys weke, and told me that he was nowt payd of the mony that ye know that was borowd of hys modyr and of hym, but iiij^{xx}*li*. The xx*li*. that my plegges ly for ys on payd. He seyd that he was desyryd to delyvere my plegges, and to have be payd the xx*li*.; but he wold not, tyll he had spokyn with me, because of the promys that he had mad to me befor that he shuld not delyver them to non withowt my assent. I seyd to hym that I suppose veryly that yowyr brodyr hys a greyd with yowyr hunkyll that he shuld paye all the hole, for I suppose he hath a swerte for ale that and more. I wold undyrstond how yt ys, and how that my seyd cosyn shall be content, for I war loth to lese my plegges; I wot yt well, yowyr good hunkyll wold ben in possessyon with good well, but I wol not soo. I wold that ye shuld speke with yowyr hunkyll ther in, and send me word in hast what he seet [*saith*].

I marvyll, be my trowth, that I had no wrytyng fro yowyr brodyr, er he departyd fro London, as he promysyd in the last lettyr that he sent me, the wych was wretyn be for the Kynges comyng to Norwych; I went [*expected*] veryly to have hard from hym ar[*ere*] thys tyme. I wold ye shuld send hym word of yowyr hunkyles delyng in thys seyd mater, and send me an answwer ther off.

Recomaund me to yowyr grauntdam. I wold she war her in Norffolk, as well at es as evyr I sy hyr, and as lytyll rewlyd

---

[1] [From Paston MSS., B.M.] This letter was evidently written on the same day as that immediately following.
[2] This is the customary contraction of the name Jesus, which was frequently written at the head of a letter.

220

---

be hyr son as evyr she was, and than I wold hope that we alle shuld far the bettyr for hyr. Yt ys told me that yowyr hunkyll hath mad gret menys and larg profyrs to John Bakton to make a relesse to hym of Oxinhed. Whedyr that be don or nowt, I wot nowt yet, but I shall wot in hast, yf I may.

1475
JAN. 29

I wold ye shuld spekyn with my Lord of Norwych, and a say to get a lysen of hym to that I may have the sacrement her in the chapell, because yt ys far to the chyrche, and I am sekly, and the parson ys oftyn owt. For all maner of casweltes of me and myn, I wold havyt grauntyd, yf I myth.

Send me word yf ye her ony tydynges from yowyr brodyr how he doth of hys seknes, and in odyr thynges, as farforth as ye know, as astely as ye may. I thynk long tyll I her from hym for dyvers causys. God kepe yow.

Wretyn in hast at Mawdby, on the Satyrday next be for Candelmes Day.

Send me an answwer of thys lettyr in hast, and odyr tydynges, &c.

Be yowyr modyr.

My cosyn Robard told me that ther was mor than vij*li*. of the mony that was payd hym that was ryght on rysty, and he cowd nowt havyt chaungyd. He was on goodly servyd ther in.

863

MARGARET PASTON TO SIR JOHN PASTON [1]

To Ser John Paston, Knyght, be thys delyveryd in hast.

Jh's.[2]

R YGHT welbelovyd son, I gret yow well, and send yow Goddes blyssyng and myn, letyng yow wete that I marveyle that I have had no wrytyng from yow sethyn ye sent me the lettyr that ye sent me be for the Kynges comyng

---

[1] [From Paston MSS., B.M.]   [2] See p. 220, Note 2.

221

THE PASTON LETTERS

1475
JAN. 29

to Norwych; in the whyche lettyr ye wrot to me that ye shuld a wretyn azeyn to me or ye shuld de part owt of London. It ys so that yowyr hunkyll William hath do payd to my cosyn Robard Clere but iiij^{xx}*li*. of the Cli. and he wol no mor pay but yf [*unless*] he hath delyveraunc of my plegges, the wych was leyd to plegg for xx^{ti}*li*.; the wych ben bettyr. I wot well, be cause of the good well that he owyt to me, as ye know, he wold ben in possessyon therof. My cosyn, Robard Cler, was her with me thys weke, and told me, that yf he wold a delyveryd them, he myth an had the seyd xx*li*.; but he seyd he wold nowt, tyll he had spokyn with me; be my trowth I fynd hym ryght kyndly dysposyd to yow, and to me bothe; and so I have desyryd hym to kepe styll the plegge in hys possessyon, tyll I have word from yow how ye ar agreyd with yowyr hunkyll for the payment of the seyd mony; I wen veryly that ye have fownd hym swerte for alle, and yff ye have soo do, I wold ye shuld wryt to yowyr hunkyll therfor, that I myth have my plegges ageyn, for I war loth that they shuld com in hys fyngyers.

Item, as for Sporyl wood, be ffor the Kynges comyng into Norffolk, I myth an had chapmen to abowtyd [*have bought it*] a gret [*in whole*] for xij^{xx} [*twelve score*] mark, and now ther wol no man by yt a gret, bycause of the gret good that the pepyll ys leyd to for the Kyng; werfor we ar a bowth to retaylyt as well as we may, and as well as yt can be browth too; and I send yow word how we shall do as astely as I may. As for yowyr barly in thys cuntre, yt cannot be sold above x*d*. or xj*d*.; that ys the gretest prys of barly her, and but yt be at a bettyr prys, I purpose for to do yt malt. And as for mony, I cowd not get yet of Pecok but iij*li*.; and he seth that be than that the owt chargys be boryn, and the repracion of the myll at Wyntyrton, we ar lyke to have but lytyll mor mony besyd the barly. Malt ys sold her but for xiij*d*. and whet ij*s*. or xxvj*d*. at thys time, and otys xij*d*. Ther ys non owtlod suffyrd to goo owth of thys cuntre as yet; the Kyng hath comaundyd that ther shuld non gon owth of thys lond. I fer me that we shall have ryth a straung ward [*world*]; God a mendyd, whan Hys wyll ys. I thank yow for the flakons

222

EDWARD IV

that ye sent me; they be ryght good, and plesyth me ryght well: I shall be as good an huswyff for yow as I can, and as I wold be for myselff. Send me word how ye doo of yowyr syknes that ye had on yowyr hey [*eye*] and yowyr lege; and yff God wol nowt suffyr yow to have helth, thank Hym therof, and takyt passhently, and com hom a geyn to me, and we shall lyve to geddyr, as God woll geve us grase to do; and as I have seyd to yow beffor thys, I wold ye war delyveryd of my mastres A. H.,[1] and than I wold trost that ye shuld do the bettyr.

1475
JAN. 29

As for the bokys that ye desyryd to have of Syr Jamys,[2] the best of alle and the fayrest ys cleymyd; ner yt ys not in hys inventory. I shall a say to get yt for yow, and I may; the prys of the todyr bokys, besyd that, ys xxs. vj*d*. the wych I send yow a byll of. Yf ye lyk be the prys of them, and ye wol have them, send me word. And also I pray yow send me an answere of thys lettyr, be cause I thynk long seth I hard from yow. God have yow in Hys kepyng.

Wretyn at Mawdby, on the Sattyrday nex be forn the Purificacion of owyr Lady, the xiiij. yer of Kyng Edward the iiij^t.

Yowyr Modyr.

Endorsed—Anno xiiij°.

864

SIR JOHN PASTON TO JOHN PASTON [3]

To hys brother John Paston, or to hy[s] oncle William Paston, in Werwyk Lane, or to Edmond Paston, at the George, at Powlys Wharfe, to deliver any of them.

FEB. 5

R YGHT worshypffull, I recomaunde me on to yow, letyng yow weete that I thynke longe that I heer nott from yow syns Crystmesse, ner have no serteyn knowleche whether that Towneshend hathe performyd hys promysse or nott, ner off my brother Johnys beyng at London, ner off

---

[1] Anne Haulte.   [2] Sir James Gloys.
[3] [From Paston MSS., B.M.]

223

my Lord or Lady off Norfolkes comyng to London, at whoys comyng sholde be the cheffe labor and sewte that I or or any for me sholde labor. It was soo, God thanke yow bothe, that iche off yow, at my last beyng with yow, grauntyd me to take labor uppon yow; and iche off yow, for the havyng ageyn off my place in Castre. Now is it soo, that wher my verry purpose was to have comyn to London now with the Master of the Rollys[1] and Sir Thomas Mongomere, demyng to fynde the Kyng at the Parlement; and also that my Lorde and Lady off Norffolk sholde nott by lyklyhod fayle to be theer also: wherffor me thoght the tyme was convenyent; but it happyd so that suche tydynges come hyddre off the Frenshe Kynges hasty comyng in to thees marchys of Pykardye, whyche cawsyd my Lordes Depute and Cownsell heer to desyr and charge me soo streyghtly, that in noo wyse I maye, tyll I heer other tydynges, departe from hense. Notwithstondyng the Marchall and Counsell heer have wretyne to my Lorde Lywetenant for me, and moor over desyryd bothe the Master of the Rollys and Sir T. Mongomere to remembre my materes bothe to the Kynge and to my lorde, in so moche that, iff the season be convenyent, both the seyd Master and Syr T. Mongomere wille labore bothe the Kynge and my lorde to entreate my Lorde off Norffolk, my lady hys wyff, and ther consell, to do for me all that reason wyll; of whoys good willes and labor her in I ame better ensuryd off, than I kan for lakke of leyser at thys tyme wryght yowe wetyng off; wherffor I praye yow and iche of yow, iff the season be convenyent, to take the labor, that theese jentyllmen maye do for me, and to my proffyght, like as I feelle them dysposyd to doo; and moore over I have somwhatt informyd them bothe ther in; and also that I maye hastyly heer from yow, and iff it come to that any mony most be gevyn to my Lorde or Lady off Norffolk ffor a plesyr herffor, I woll, uppon as I heer from yow, come to yow in alle hast possible, all thynges leyde a parte.

Item, iff any letter be requesyth to be hadde, in lyke forme as oonys ther was from the Kyng to my Lorde off

[1] John Morton, afterwards Bishop of Ely.

Norffolk, Sir T. Montgomere will by your advyces opteyne yow suche one off yowr entents to my proffyghte in the premyssys, and by thys my wryghtyng I bynde me to repaye yowe, iff any suche letter or wryghtyng be opteynyd, what so ever it coste. No more for lakke off leysor.

Wretyn at Caleys, the v. day of Feverer, Anno E. iiij. xiiij°.

As for tydynges heer, my masteris th'embassatores, Sir T. Mongomere, and the Master of the Rollys, kom streyght from the Duke at hys assege at Nywysse, whyche wyll nott yitt be wone.

Yowr JOHN PASTON, K.

865

SIR JOHN PASTON TO MARGARET PASTON[1]

To Mestresse Margret Paston, at Norwyche, be thys delyveryd.

PLEASE it yow to weete that I receyvyd a letter from yow, wretyn the Saterdaye next byffor Candelmesse; for answer wheroff, lyke it yow to weete, that as for the bokys that weer Sir James (God have hys sowle!), I thynke best that they be styll with yow, tyll that I speke with yow my selffe. My mynde is now nott most uppon bokes.

Item, as for xxli. that ye sey that yowr plate lythe for, it is so, that I fownde my oncle William no sewerte therffor, as Playter and my brother John bothe cowde ensforme yow; it was never desyryd of me, ner the tolde me nott that any suche pledge laye for it, but that ye hadd dyschargyd me of xxli. and chevysshyd it, and that ye sholde repaye it in hast; wherin I woll do as ye woll, and as it pleasyth yow to sende me wetyng.

Item, I ame sory that ye be no better payd off the xxli. that I had off yowe, whyche ye sholde have receyvyd ageyn off my londes in Flegge. Iff the markett be nott goode yit, I hope it shall be better; never the lesse my wylle is that ye

[1] [From Paston MSS., B.M.]

sholde have yowr holl xxli. ageyn, and not lose jd. Wherffor if it be so that ye be mysse servyd ther, I beseche yow off pacyence tyll the begynnyng of the next yeer, and iff aught be behynd, ye shall receyve uppe the remenaunt then, for, as God helpe me, I wolde be sory that ye lost moor for me; I have pytte yow to cost, charge, and losse i nowge, God thanke yow of it, thoughe ye lose no more. Wherffor iff Sporle woode sprynge any sylver or golde, it is my wyll that fyrst of alle ye be yowr owne payer off all that is be hynde; and next thatt, to paye myn oncle William vij××vjli. xiijs. iiijd. and besyd that, xvjli. lost uppon the chevysshaunce of iiij××li.; and so I owe viij××ijli. xiijs. iiijd. Wherffor I beseche yow to make hast in repayment heroff as fast as it wolle growe, as my trust is in yowe.

Item, wher it pleasyd yow to weete of myn heele and amendyng; I thanke Godde I ame in goode case, and as goode a full hooll, bothe off the fevre, agwe off myn ie, myn legge, and myn heele, saff that I ame tendre off all theese; and were nott goode rewle, full like to feell off iche off them ryght soone; nevertheless, God thanke yow off yowr large profre, wheroff I wolde be ryght gladde iff I myght, for trobles and other labor that I have takyn on me nowe in to Fraunce warde; for the goode spede off me, and that jorneye, I beseche yow off yowr preyeres and remembrance; and thatt jorney, with Goddes grace, ones doon, I purpose verrely, with Goddes grace, therafftree to daunce atendaunce most abowt yowr plesure and ease: and with Goddes grace, soone uppon Esterne, er evyr I goo forthe, I hope to se yow, and fecche your blessynge. No moor at thys tyme, but Jesus have yow in Hys kepyng.

Wretyn at Caleys, the xxij. daye of Feverer, anno E. iiijti xiiij°. Yowr Sone,

JOHN PASTON, K.

On the back of the preceding letter is written in another hand, as follows:—
Memorandum, that Syr John Paston owthe to William Paston, acordyng to the endenture made be twex them,—

viij××ijli. xiijs. iiijd.

Wheroff payable the firste day of Octobre for Townsend, C. marke.
Item , the xxvj. day off Novembre,— iiij××xvjli

866

MARGARET PASTON TO JOHN PASTON[1]

JOHN PASTON, I send yow Godds blyssyng and myn, letyng yow wete, that I hadd non er thys lettyr than on Sent Matheus Evyn; yf I myth a had an massenger or thys tym I had sent yt yow. I con yow thank for the lettyr that ye sent to my cosyn Calthorpp and me of the tydyngs; I wold ye shuld do soo mor. As ye may remembyr that I spak to yow for the xxtili. for my cosyn Clere, spek to yowr hunkyll therof, and send me an answer therof in hast. And for the lycens that I spak to yow for, to have the Sacrement in my Chapell, yf ye cannot getyt of the Busshop of Norwych, getyt of the Busshop of Caunterbery, for that ys most swyr for all plase. God kepe yow.

Wretyn on Mydlent Sunday.

867

RICHARD SOUTHWELL TO JOHN PASTON[2]

To the right worshippfull, and my right feithfull gode cosin, John Paston, Esquier.

RIGHT worshippfull and my right feithfull gode cosin, I recomaunde me unto you, and, as hertily as I can, thanke you of your right gentill and kynde remembraunce, that I consceyve well by your late writyng that ye have to me wardes, undeserved in dede, but not in will, so God helpe me, as ye shuld weell knowe, if my power might accorde with my will. And, cosin, in the mater that it liked you to remembre me in, bothe to my worship and pleaser, I

[1] [From Fenn, ii. 178.] This letter was written on the back of Letter 861.
[2] [From Paston MSS., B.M.] Fenn thinks the gentleman here referred to was John Berney of Reedham, Esquire, who married Alice, daughter of Richard Southwell, Esquire, of Wood Rising, the writer of this letter. He accordingly dates it about the year 1475, and I see no reason to question his opinion.

THE PASTON LETTERS

1475
MARCH 26

feere me that nouther my pouere doughter nor pouere purs can nor may be to his pleaser; wold God outher might; and I shuld take me right neere to his pleaser, savyng myself, I ensure you by my truth. And howe to understand his pleaser and disposicion therin, I see no mean as thus advised, but if [*unless*] it might please you by your wisdam to attempte it forther, as ye seme moste conveniente, and therupon I to be guyded by your gode advise, as the cas shall require; wherin ye shall bynde me herefter to do that may be to your pleaser to my power, and yette with no better will than I have had, so God help me, Who have you ever in His kepinge, and sende you your hertes desire to His pleaser; and if it pleas you to remembre further in the premisses, I trust ye shall leese no labour on my pouere parte; howe be it I fere me sore, as I be gan, bothe of my pouere doughter and purs.

Writon at Woderysyng, the morn efter Our Lady Day, in haste.

I require you this bill may be secrete.

By your trewe cosin,
RIC. SUTHWELL.

868

JOHN PASTON TO MARGARET PASTON[1]

To my ryght worchepfull modyr, Margaret Paston, at Mawtby.

1475(?)
[MAR. 29]

RYGHT worchefull modyr, aftyr all humbyll recomendacyons, as lowely as I can I beseche yow of your blyssyng. Pleasyt yow to wete that late yester nyght I cam to Norwyche, purposeing to have been as thys day with yow at Mawtby, but it is so that I may not hold my purpose, for he that shall pay me my quarter wagys for me and my retenew, is in Norwyche, and waytyth ourly when hys

[1] [From Fenn, iv. 444.] This letter was evidently written in 1475, when John Paston and one or more of his younger brothers were about to go over to France with the King's army.—*See* Letter 871. Margaret Paston was at that time continually resident at Mautby.

228

THE PASTON LETTERS

869

WILLIAM PASTON TO MARGARET PASTON[1]

To my right worshupfull sistir, Margaret Paston.

1475
APRIL 7

RIGHT worshupfull sustir, I recomaunde me to you, praying you to undirstonde, the priour of Bromeholme hath sent ayen to me for xx*li.*; and my cosyn William Whyte desired me to wryte to you for the rewarde that was offird hym to his churche and xx*li.* of my brothirs goodys to be lent hym upon sufficient suertee, and by a yeeris ende payd ayen; he hath and may doo for you and for my neveue, Sir John, in many thynges, and is his kynnesman, and it were a gode frendely dede and no jopardy nor hurt. The Abbot of Wymondham hath sent to me too tymes. Frendship may not hang by the wynde, nor for faire eyne, but causis must be shewid; men wene that I hadd your coffers and my brothirs and maistir Fastolffes in myne awarde, and that ye wote wele, &c. Send your avise to my neveue, Sir John, by the next messynger. Ye sent me oonys for the same mater, but I may not leene my money to defende othir men is causis; your discrecion (?) thenkith that it were no reason. I have tolde them your saying; and as it is s[o] that ye may nat come to the coffers but all be togedir. Therfor ye must sende to my neveue and to Arblastir how ye will have this answerd; for the Abbot will be heere on Monday at the sene, and labour must bee desired the next terme. Hit nedis nat to put you in remembrance of my mater touchyng my Fadirs soule, my modir and me, and God kepe you. Wreton at Norwich the vij[th] day of Aprill.

I have tolde thes folkis, as ye have seid to me all weys, that your will is gode, but that ye may not come theretoo withoute th'assent of all your felowes.

[1] [Add. MS. 34,889, f. 215.] As Margaret Paston, at the date of this letter, is not at Norwich and her son Sir John seems to be there, we may infer that it was written in the year 1475. *See* No. 868 (preliminary note).

230

EDWARD IV

money shall com to hym. It is oon Edmund Bowen of the Cheker, a specyall frend of myn, and he avysyth me to tery tyll the money be com, lest that I be unpayed, for who comyth fyrst to the mylle, fyrst must grynd.

1475(
[MAR. 2

And as I was wryghtyng thys byll, on of the gromys of my lords chambyr cam to me, and told me, that my lady wyll be here in Norwyche to morow at nyght towards Walsyngham, whyche shall, I wot well, be a nother lett to me; but I had more need to be other wyse ocupyed then to awayte on ladyse, for ther is as yett, I trowe, no sperre that shall go over the see, so evyll horsyd as I am. But it is told me that Rychard Call hathe a good horse to sell, and on John Becher of Oxborough hathe an other; and if it myght please yow to geve Syme leve to ryd in to that contre at my cost, and in your name, seying that ye wyll geve on of your sonys an horse, desyryng hym that he wyll geve yow a penyworthe for a peny, and he shall, and the pryse be resonabyll, hold hym pleasyd with your payment ought of my purse, thow he knowe it not or hys horse depert fro hys lands. Modyr, I bese[che] yow, and it may please yow to geve Syme leve to ryde on thys message in your name, that he may be here with me to morow in the mornyng be tymys, for wer I onys horsyd, I trowe I wer as ferforthe redy as some of my neyghborows. I herd a lytyll word that ye purposeid to be here in Norwyche thys next week. I prey God it be thys week. Modyr, beseche yow that I may have an answer to morow at the ferthest of thys mater, and of eny other servyse that it please yow to comand me, whyche I wyll [be] at all seasons redy to acomplyshe with Gods grace, Whom I beseche to preserve yow and yours.

Wretyn at Norwyche, thys Wednysday in Estern Week.

By your sone and servaunt,
J. P.

229

EDWARD IV

Item, I pray you remembre the obligacion that Wix hath, and that I may have my money of the parsone of Maudeby.— By your brothir,
WILLIAM PASTON.

147
APRIL

870

EDMUND PASTON TO JOHN PASTON[1]

To John Paston, Esquyer.

SYR, I recummawnd me to zow. Please yt zow to wette that my modyr hathe causyd me to putte Gregory owte of my servyse, as, God help, I wrythe to zow the very cause why. Yt happyd hym to have a knavys loste, in pleyn termes to swhyve a quene, and so dyd in the Konyneclosse. Yt fortunyd hym to be a spyed be ij. plowemen of my modyrs, whyche werne as fayne as he of that mater, and desyerd hym to have parte, and as kompany requeryd, seyd not nay; in so myche that the plowemen had her alle a nythe in ther stabylle, and Gregory was clere delyvered of her, and as he swherys had not a do with her within my modyrs place. Not with standdyng my modyr thynkks that he was grownd of that matier; wherfor ther is no remedy but he moste a voyde. And in so myche that at the laste tyme that ze wer her, [ye] desyerd hym of me, yf that he schuld departe from me, I send zow the very cawse of hys departyng, as my modyr sethe; but I am in serteyn the contrary is true. Yt is nomor but that he can not plese all partys. But that jantylman[2] is hys woords Lord, he hathe seyd that he woold lyfte them whom that hym plese, and as that scheweyt welle, he lyftyd

1475
[MAY

[1] [From Fenn, iii. 426.] This letter was wrongly attributed by Fenn to Edmund Paston, son of the Judge. It is in the hand of the Judge's grandson, also named Edmund, and was written at a time when his mother Margaret was living at Mautby, where he, the writer, was also at the time, though he expected to join his brother John, to whom he writes, in the following week. These circumstances strongly suggest that it was written in 1475, when Margaret Paston certainly was residing at Mautby, as we find Edmund Paston with his brother John in London a month later preparing to go over to Calais. *See* No. 873. Whitsun Eve in 1475 would be the 13th May.

[2] Fenn supposes the person alluded to to be the priest, James Gloys.

231

875(?)
MAY 13] on [one] xiiij. myle in a mornyng, and nowe he hath ben caw
sar of hys lyfte, I wot not how far, but yf that ze be hys better
master ; but and we a mong us geve not hym a lyfte, I pray
God that we never thryve. And that is hys intente, I trowe,
to bryng us to ; wherfor I requer zow, yf that yt plese zow to
have hym, that ze wylle be the better master to hym for my
sake, for I am he that is as sory to departe from hym as any
man on lyve from hys servant, and be my trowthe, as far-
forthe as I knowe, he is as true as any on lyve.

I troste my fortune schale be better than ever to leve
thus her ; but yf I wer hens wards, I ensuer zow I wold not
schange for none that I knowe. He is profytabylle on dyvers
thynggs as ze knowe welle.

Ther has ben a gret breke be twyx Calle and me, as I
schal enforme zow at my coming, wyche schalle be on
Wedynsday next be the grace of God, who preserve zow.
Wretyn at Mawteby, on Wyteson eve.

EDMOND PASTON.

871

MARGARET PASTON TO SIR JOHN PASTON [1]

Un to Syr John Paston, be this delyvered in hast.

1475
MAY 23
RYGHT welbelovyd son, I grete you well, and send you
Cristes blissyng and myne, desyringe to know how ye
faire. I mervaile that I have herd no tydynges from
you sythe ye sent me the lettyr of an answere of the xxli.
the which I have layde pleages for to my cosyn Cleere, the
which letter was wryten the xxijᵗʸ day of Februar ; and as for
that money, I can not gete no lenger day therof than Mydsomer, or fourte nyght after ; and towardys that money, and
the xxᵗʸli. that I send yow by syde to London by Sym, I have

[1] [From Paston mss., B.M.] This letter is endorsed 'Mens' Maii, anno xvᵒ.'
The date is confirmed by the fact that in 1475 the Tuesday after Trinity Sunday was
the 23rd of May.

232

receyved no mor money of yowres, but as moch as I send 1475
yow wryten in this letter. And as for any discharge that I MAY 23
promysed at the boroeng off the xxᵗⁱli. when I leyde the
pleages ther fore, I thought not but that your uncle shuld a
boroed them owte, and I to have had my pleages, as well as
he his ; never the less I shall be the warer how I shall dele here
aftyr. By my trowth, I wote not how to do ther fore ; the
Kyng goth so nere us in this cuntre, both to pooer and
ryche, that I wote not how we shall lyff, but yff [*unless*] the
world amend. God amend it, whan His wyll is. We[1] can
nother sell corne ner catell to no good preve. Malt is here
but at xd. a comb ; wheete, a comb xxviijd. ; ootes, a comb xd. ;
and ther of is but lytell to geet here at thys tyme. William
Pecok shall send you a byll what he hath payde for yow for ij.
taskes at this tyme ; and how he hath purveyde for the rem-
naunte of your corne ; and also off other thynges that be
necessary that shuld be purveyd for in your absence. Send
me word also whome ye wyll desyre to do for yow in this
contre, or ellys where in your absence ; and wryte to them to
do for yow, and they wyll be the better wylled to do for yow ;
and I wyll do my devyr for yow also, as well as I can.

The somma off money that I have receyvyd off Wylliam
Pecok :—First, xls. off Runnham. Item, off Bastwyk, xxs.
Item, off Runnham, xxs. Item, off him for barly at Runn-
ham, xxs. Item, off the fyschynge at Bastwyke, xiijs. iiijd.
Item, for barely sold at Runnham, viijs. Summa totalis, vjli.
xvjd.

Item, I have receyvyd of Ric. Calle, of Sporle wodd, xxvjs.
viijd., and more shall I hope here aftyr within short tyme ; as
I receyve for yow, I hope to yeff yow a trew acownt ; and
this is all that I have receyvyd for yow zytt, sen ye departyd
hens. God bryng yow well ageyn to this contre, to His
pleasans, and to your wurshyp and profyzt.

Wryten at Mawteby, the xxiijᵗʸ day of May, and the
Tewsday next afftyr Trinyte Sonday.

For Goddes love, and your brether go over the see, avyse
them as ye thynk best for her [*their*] save garde. For some

[1] *We.* Originally written *I*, and corrected.

233

1475
MAY 23
of them be but yonge sawgeres, and wote full lytyll what yt
meneth to be as a sauger, nor for to endure to do as a sawger
shuld do. God save yow all, and send me good tythynges of
yow all. And send ye me word in hast how ye doo, for I
thynk longe to I here off yow. Be youre Modyr.

Item, I wold not in no wyse that ye shuld nother sell
nor sett to pleage that ye have in Runnham, what som ever
fortune of the remnaunt ; for yt is a praty thyng, and resonable well payde, and nere thys towne. I wold be ryght sory
that ye shuld for bere that ; I had lever ye for bore that your
uncle hath to morgage than that.

872

ABSTRACTS [1]

NORFOLK AND SUFFOLK DEEDS, No. 13.

MAY 28
'Johannes Paston miles relaxat Willielmo Wynton' episc. et aliis totum
jus de et in manerio de Tichwell, Essex in Hickling, Guton, Beyton, Newton,
Calcotes in Fretton, Leyestoft, Habeland, Brodeston, et Gorleston. Maii 28,
Edw. IV. 15.'

No. 32.

'Charta Johannis Paston militis de terris Johannis Fastolf pert. prædict.
Johanni, et continens concessionem quarundam evidentiarum episcopo Winton',
et relaxationem orationum, actionum, et demandarum versus prædictum episcopum. Maii 28, Edw. IV. 15.'

[1] [From ms. Index in Magd. Coll., Oxford].

234

873

SIR JOHN PASTON TO JOHN AND EDMUND
PASTON [1]

*To John Paston, or to hys brother Edmond Paston,
at the George, at Powles Wharf.*

1475
JUNE 13
BROTHER Edmonde, it is soo that I heer telle that ye
be in hope to come hyddre, and to be in suche wages
as ye schall come lyve lyke a jentylman, wheroff I
wolde be gladde. Wherffor, for yowr better speede, I lete
you weete that Heugh Beamond is deed ; wherffor I wolde
ye had hys roome nowe or never, iff ye can brynge it abowt ;
ellys iff ye dispose yowe to abyde in Inglonde, syns it is so
that the Bysshop of Lynkolne [2] is Chauncelee, hys servyse is
the meter for yow ; he is next neyghbour to Norffolk off any
astate. God sende yow some good warde of hys.

I praye you, iff yowr leyser be ther aftre to remembre
Towneshende, that he, with the advyse and assystence of my
Master of the Rollys, [3] have one daye off marche with the
slawe Bysshop of Wynchester, that he maye kepe me hys
promyse, that is to seye, to entrete the Duke and Duchesse of
Norffolk for Caster. He promysed to doo it, and to ley owt
an Cli. for the same.

Item, I praye yow sende me some tydynges within v.
dayes aftre that ye see thys bylle.
Wretyn at Caleys, the xiij. daye off June.

JOHN PASTON, K.

[1] [From Paston mss., B.M.] This letter must have been written in the year
1475, when, as will be seen by No. 871, some of Sir John Paston's brothers, among
whom doubtless were both John and Edmund, to whom this letter is addressed, were
going over to Calais. The Bishop of Lincoln (Rotherham) was Chancellor in 1475.
It is true the Great Seal was taken from him on the 27th April, and given to Alcock,
Bishop of Rochester, until the 28th September, when it was restored to Rotherham.
But it is certain this letter could not have been written in a later year, as the Duke of
Norfolk died in January 1476.
[2] Thomas Rotherham. [3] *See* p. 219, Note 2.

235

THE PASTON LETTERS

874

MARGARET PASTON TO SIR JOHN PASTON[1]

To the right worshipffull Sir John Paston, Knyght,
in haste.

1475
AUG. 10

RIGHT welbeloved sone, &c. . . . .
. . . .
. . . .
. . . .[2]

As for tidyngs here in this contre, we have non, but that
the contry is bareyn of money ; and that my Lady of Yorke[3]
and all her howsold is here at Sent Benetts,[4] and purposed to
abide there stille, til the Kynge come from be yonde the see,
and lenger if she like the eyre ther, as it is seide.

I thynke ryght longe tille I here some tidyngs for [*quære,*
from ?] you and from your brethren. I prey God sende you
and al your company goode spede in your journeys, to His
plesure, and to your worshippes and profights.

Wreten at Mauteby, on Sen Lawrens Even, the xv. yere
of the regne of Kyng E. the iiijth.

Be yor Moder.

---

[1] [From Fenn, ii. 180.]
[2] The chief part of this letter relates to Sir John Paston's private affairs, his rents
and lands, and informs him that William Jenney had entered into Holme Halle, in
Filby, 'in the ryght and titell of his douterlawe, weche was Boys doughter,' etc.—F.
[3] Cecily, Duchess of York, daughter of Ralph Neville, Earl of Westmoreland,
was the widow of Richard Plantagenet, Duke of York, and mother of King Edward
IV., etc. She died in 1495, and was buried near her husband in the college of
Fotheringay.—F.
[4] The Abbey of St. Bennet at Holm.

236

THE PASTON LETTERS

1475
SEPT. 11

that danger have been, I mygh yit have ben at home with yow
at thys daye, or with in vij. dayes aftre. No more, but I
beseche Jesus have yow in kepyng.

Wretyn at Caleys, the xj. daye of Septembre.

JOHN PASTON, K.

876

JOHN PASTON TO SIR JOHN PASTON[1]

To the ryght worchepfull Sir John Paston, Knyght, lodgyd
at the George, by Powlys Wherf, in London.

OCT. 10

RYGHT werchepfull sir, I recomand me to yow, sertyfying yow that I have comonyd with Barnard and other
your wellwyllers with my Lord of Norffolk, whyche
avise me that ye shold, for your nyghest meane to get Caster
a yen, labore to get a lettre fro the Kyng dyrect to R. Sothewell,
Jamys Hubbard, and other of my lordys consayll being, and to
iche of theym ; and in the seyd letter to lete theym have knowlage that the Kyng mevyd to my lord of the seyd mater beyond
the see, and hough my lord answerd the Kyng that at hys
comyng in to Inglond he wold meve to hys seyd consayll of the
seyd mater, and geve the Kyng an answer. Wherfor the Kyng
in the seyd lettyr must streyghtly charge theym, and iche of
theym, to comon with my lord in the seyd mater in syche
wyse that the Kyng may be sertyfyed of an answer fro my lord
and theym at the ferthest by *crastino Animarum* ;[2] for Suthewell
nor Jamys Hubbard shall not be at London befor Halowmass,
and thys is the best wey that ye may take, as we thynke here.

My lady sweryth, and so dothe Barnard on hyr behalff,
that she wold as fayne ye had it as eny body ; notwithstandyng
she seyd not so to me, sythe I cam hom, for I spak not with
hyr but onys sythe I sye yow last. Yet she lythe in Norwyche,
and shall do tyll she be delyverd ; but I have be seek ever sythe
I cam on thys syd the see, but I trust hastyly to amend for all
my seknesse that I had at Caleys, and sythe I cam over also,

---

[1] [From Paston MSS., B.M.]
[2] The Morrow of All Souls, *i.e.* 3rd November.

238

EDWARD IV

875

SIR JOHN PASTON TO MARGARET PASTON[1]

To Mestresse Margret Paston, at Norwyche.

1475
SEPT. 1

RYGHT reverend and my most tendre and kynde moodre,
I recomaunde me to yow. Please it yow to weete that,
blessyd be God, thys wyage of the Kynges is fynysshyd
for thys tyme, and alle the Kynges ost is comen to Caleys as
on Mondaye last past, that is to seye, the iiij. daye of Septembre ; and at thys daye many of hys host be passyd the see in
to Inglond ageyn, and in especiall my Lorde off Norffolk and
my bretheryn.

Item, I was in goode hope to have hadde Caster ageyn.
The Kynge spake to my Lorde off Norffolk for it, and it was
full lyke to have comyn ; but in conclusyon it is delayed tyll
this next terme, by whyche tyme the Kynge hat comaundyd
hym to take advyce off hys councell, and to be sywer that hys
tytle be goode, or ellys the Kyng hathe asserteynyd hym that
for any favor he most do me ryght and justyce, &c.

And iff Caster hadde comen, by my feythe I had comyn
streyhte home. Notwithstondyng, iff I may do yow servyce
or eese, as ye and I have comonyd heer to foor, aftre as I heer
from yow, as God helpe me, I purpose to leeffe alle heer, and
come home to yow, and be yowr hosbonde and balyff ; wher in
I spake to my brother John to telle yow myn advyce.

I also mysselyke somwhat the heyr heer ; for by my trowte
I was in goode heele whan I come hyddre, and all hooll, and
to my wetyng I hadde never a better stomake in my lyffe, and
now with in viij. dayes I am crasyd ageyn. I suppose that I
most be at London at Mychelmesse, and ther to purveye for
payment for myn oncle William, by whyche tyme I praye yow
that I may heer from yow and off yowr advyce and helpe, iff
any thynge be growyn off Sporle woode. For had nott yit

---

[1] [From Paston MSS., B.M.] It is evident that this letter was written after the
return of King Edward IV. from France in 1475.

237

EDWARD IV

1475
OCT. 10

cam but of cold. But I was never so well armyd for the werre
as I have now armyd me for cold ; wherfor I avyse yow, take
exampyll by me, if it happyn yow to be seek, as ye wer when I
was at Caleys, in eny wyse kepe yow warme. I weene Herry
Woodhous nor Jamys Arblaster ware never at onys so many
cotys, hose, and botewx as I doo, or ellys by God we had gone
therfor. What we shall yet I can not sey, but I bere me bold
on ij. dayes amendyng.

My modyr sendyth yow Godes blyssing and hers, and she
wold fayne have yow at home with hyr ; and if ye be onys
mette, she tellyth me ye shall not lyghtly depart tyll dethe
depart yow.

As I was wryghtyng thys lettyr, on told me that the Kyng
shold be at Walsyngham thys next.[1] If it be so, it wer best
for yow to awayte on the Kyng all the wey, and if ye have not
men and horse i nowghe I shall send yow. Do as ye thynk
best ; and as ye wyll have me to do, send me your avyse, and
I shall accomplyshe it to my power, with Godes grace, Who
preserve yow.

Wretyn at Norwyche, the x. day of October, anno xv°
E. iiij[ti].

P. J.[2]

877

JOHN PASTON TO SIR JOHN PASTON[3]

To Sir John Paston, Knyght, lodgyd at the
George, by Powlys Wherff, in London.

OCT. 23

AFTYR all dwtes of recomendacyon, please it yow to
undyrstand that I have spoken with my lady[4] sythe I
wrot to yow last ; and she told me that the Kyng had
no syche woordys to my lord for Caster, as ye told me ; but
she seyth that the Kyng axid my lord at hys departyng fro
Caleys, how he wold deele with Caster, and my lord answerd
nevyr a woord.

---

[1] So in MS. Qu., the word 'week' omitted ?
[2] It is curious that John Paston has here reversed his initials.
[3] [From Fenn, ii. 182.]
[4] The Duchess of Norfolk.

239

THE PASTON LETTERS

Sir W. Brandon[1] stood by, and the Kyng axid hym what my lord wold do in that mater; seying that he had comandyd hym befor tyme to meve my lord with that mater, and Sir W. Brandon gave the Kyng to answer that he had doone so; then the Kyng axid Sir W. B. what my lordys answer was to hym, and Sir W. B. told the Kyng that my lords answer was that the Kyng shold as soone have hys lyff as that place; and then the Kyng axid my lord whedyr he seyd so or nought, and my lord seyd, yee. And the Kyng seyd not a woord ayen, but tornyd hys bak, and went hys wey; but my lady told me, and the Kyng had spokyn any woord in the world aftyr that to my lord, my lord wold not have seyd hym nay. And I have gevyn my lady warnyng that I wyll do my lord no more serveys; but er we partyd, she mad me to make hyr promess that I shold let hyr have knowlege er I fastonyd myselff in eny other servysse; and so I departyd, and sye hyr not syness, nor nought purpose to doo, tyll I spek with yow.

I prey yow bryng home some hattys with yow, or and ye come not hastyly, send me on, &c., and I shall pay yow for it a comb otys[2] when ye come home.

My modyr wold fayn have yow at Mawtby; she rode thydyr ought of Norwyche on Saturday last past, to purvey your lodgyng redy ayenst your comyng.

I have been ryght seek ayen sythe I wroote to yow last, and thys same day have I ben pessyng seek; it wyll not ought of my stomak by no mean. I am undon. I may not ete halff i nough, when I have most hungyr, I am so well dyettyd, and yet it wyll not be. God send yow heele, for [I] have non iij. dayes to gedyr, do the best I can.

Wretyn at Norwyche, the Monday next be for Seynt Simone and Jude,[3] anno E. iiij. xv°.

J. P.

[1] Sir William Brandon was the grandfather of Henry VIII.'s favourite, Charles Brandon, Duke of Suffolk. Footnote 2 on p. 156, taken from Fenn, is wrong. Charles Brandon's father, who was slain at Bosworth, was another Sir William, knighted by the Earl of Richmond before the battle.
[2] In 1475 a comb of oats sold for 11d.; we have therefore the value of a hat in this reign.—F. In No. 871 the price of oats is given as 10d. a comb, but the markets are considered to be bad. [3] 28th of October.

240

EDWARD IV

878

JOHN PASTON TO MARGARET PASTON[1]

AFTYR all dewtes of recomendacyon, in as humbyll wyse as I can, I beseche yow of your blyssyng. The cheff cause that I wryght to yow for at thys season is, for that I undyrstand that my lady[2] wold be ryght glad to have yow a bought hyr at hyr labore; in so myche that she hathe axyd the questyon of dyvers gentylwomen whedyr they thought that ye wold awayte on hyr at that season or nought, and they answerd that they durst sey that ye wold, with ryght good wyll, awayte on hyr at that tyme, and at all other seasons that she wold comand yow. And so I thynk that my lady wyll send for yow; and if it wer your ease to be here, I wold be ryght glad that ye myght be here, for I thynk your being here shold do gret good to my brodyrs maters that he hathe to sped with hyr. Wherfor, for Godes sake, have your horse and all your gere redy with yow, wheresoever ye be, ought or at home, and as for men, ye shall nott need many, for I wyll come for yow, and awayte on yow my sylf, and on or ij. with me; but I had need to undyrstand wher to fynd yow, or ellys I shall happyly seeke yow at Mautby, when ye be at Freton, and my lady myght then fortune to be ferforthe on hyr jorney or ye cam, if she wer as swyfte as ye wer onys on Good Fryday.

And as for the mater in the latter end of my brodyr Sir Johnys lettyr, me thynk he takyth a wronge wey, if he go so to werk; for as for the peopyll here, I undyrstand non other but that all folkys here be ryght well dysposyd towardes that mater, fro the hyghest degre to the lowest, except Robart Brandon and John Colvyll; and it is a grete lyklyhod that the grettest body is well dysposyd towardes that mater, in as myche as they wold put yow to the labore above wretyn, and if they wer not, I thynk they wold not put yow to that labore.

[1] [From Paston mss., B.M.] This letter seems to have been written shortly before the confinement of the Duchess of Norfolk in December 1475.
[2] The Duchess of Norfolk.

241

THE PASTON LETTERS

Also here was here with me yesterday a man fro the Priour of Bromholme to lete me have knowlage of the ille speche whyche is in the contre now of new, that the tombe is not mad; and also he seythe that the clothe that lythe over the grave is all toryn and rotyn, and is not worth ijd., and he seythe he hathe pachyd it onys or twyis. Wherfor the Pryour hathe sent to yow at the leest to send thedyr a newe clothe a yenst Estern.

Also Mastyr Sloley prayith yow, for Godes sake, and ye wyll do non almess of tylle [tile] that he myght borow some of yow tyll he may bye some, and pay yow ayen; for on [one] the fayrist chambyrs of the Fryers, standyth half oncoverd for defaulte of tylle, for her is yett non to get for no money. And the Holy Trynyte have yow in kepyng.

At Norwyche, thys Twysday.

Your sone and humbyll servaunt,

J. Paston.

879

SIR JOHN PASTON TO EDWARD IV.[1]

[To the King] our souverain Lord.

[Sheweth] unto your highnesse your feythful liegeman and servaunt, John Paston, Knight, that wher Sir William Yelverton, William Jenney, and Thomas Howes were inffeffed in certain . . . . [to the] use of your said suppliaunt, they of grat malice confeterd with oon or ij. of the counsell of my lord the Duc of Norffolk, caused the same Duc to clayme tytle unto [the mano]ir of Caster and other lands of your said supplant, wherinne the said Yelverton and his coofeffees wer

[1] [From a ms. in the Bodleian Library.] The Castle of Caister was surrendered to the Duke of Norfolk in September 1469, but he must have been taking the rents of the manor for a year or two before. From what is stated in this petition, the Duke must have given it up again in the end of the year 1470, i.e. during the restoration of Henry VI.; but he entered again after half a year, and the date of this second entry is given by William Worcester as the 23rd June 1471. After this, the petition says, he kept possession for four years and more, so that the date of the document must be towards the close of the year 1475. The Duke died on the 17th January 1476.

242

EDWARD IV

inffeffed, contrary to th'entent and wille that thei wer enfeffed for; upon whiche title the said Duc with great force asseyed and entred the said manoir of Castre and other lands of your said suppliant, putting hym from the lawful possession and estate that he had in the same, and also take from him vjc. shepe and xxx. nete, and the same, with other stuf and ordinaunces longing to the same manoir, of the value of Cli. toke and caryed awey, and the said manoir diffaced, hurt, and appeired, so that it coude not be repaired with CC. marc. Also the revenues of the said lands by the space of iij. yeres, to the value of vijxxli., the same my lord the Duke receyved, and the owtrents of the same never payed, whiche great trouble was like to be the undoing of your said suppliant; wherfor he was fayn to sue to the said Duc and lord by the meanes of his godsip the Bisshop of Wynchestre, whiche was in his special favour; at whos contemplacion, and for vc. [500] marc whiche the same your suppliant payed unto the same Duc, he graunted him to have agen his said manoir and lands, and to restor him to the possession of the same, whiche was so doen. And your said suppliant being in peasible possession, my said lord the Duc and his cofeffees, Sir William Brandon, Thomas Hoo, Rauf Ashton, and other, at the desir of my said lord, relessed their estate and interesse, as wel under my said lordes sele as under their own sele. Wherupon your said besecher continued in possession but half a yer; at whiche time he was chargid in reparacions to the somme of C. marc, and payed the owt rents dewe by the space of the said iij. yer to the some of xlli. That doon, my said lord, by sinistre motive and advice, with force agen entred the said manoir and other lands aforsaid with alle stuf of howshold being in the same manoir to the value of C. marc, and so long time hath kept and rejoysed the revenues of the said lands, and in chief the said manoir, to the value of vjxxli. by the space of iiij. yer and mor; for redresse wherof yor said suppliant hath this said space of iiij. yer sued to my said lord and his counsell, and of alle that time the same my lord wold never suffre him to come in his presence, ne here him, ne noon other for him to declair or shewe his grief. And furthermor whanne your said besecher

243

THE PASTON LETTERS

1475 hath sued to the counsel of my said lord, and desired them to move his lordship therinne, and to answer him resonably and according to right, they answered that thei have shewed my said lord his request, and that he was, and is alwey, so moved and displesed with them, that thei dar nomor move him therinne. And thus yor said suppliant hath loste alle his coste and labour, to his charge by his feyth this iiij. yer in his sute, the somme of vᶜ marc, and now is owt of remedye, without your habundant grace be shewed in that behalve, in somoche as he is not of power t'attempt your lawes ayenst so mighty and noble estate, nor t'abide the disples of him. Wherfor please it your moost noble grace, at the reverence of God, to move my said lord to withdrawe the affeccion whiche he so hath to the said manoir and lands, and to suffre your said besecher to have and enjoye the possession of the same according to right; and he at your commandment shal relesse unto my said lord alle the damages above wretyn, whiche amount to the somme of mᴸ.ccc.liij*li*. vjs. viij*d*., and in time to come, with Goddes grace, be the mor hable to do you service, and also specially preye to God for the conservacion of your moost noble persone and estate royall.

Endorsed in a later hand— . . . . Paston mil. Regi pro . . . .
. . . . . Norff. in . . . . . de Caister.

880

ABSTRACT[1]

ROBERT WHYNBERGH TO SIR JOHN PASTON

Has ridden 100 miles to get out the obligation of Craksheld and Salter. Has been opposed by Mr. Lovell, as they are his tenants. Understands it is in my lord's closet, and the tenants are warned to pay no money without it. They keep from him the farm of the Priors Maner as well as Strehalle.[2] Desires him to write to Mr. William Paston to inform my lord of a wrongful

[1] [From Paston mss., B.M.]
[2] Street-Hall or Straw Hall, in Great Cressingham, was one of the manors which belonged to Judge Paston. In 1451, Blomefield tells us that Walter Paston, clerk, gave it to his brother John. In the reign of Henry VIII. Sir William Paston sold it to Dame Elizabeth Fitzwilliams.—Blomefield, vi. 99.

244

THE PASTON LETTERS

1476
JAN. 17 Item, as ffor other means, I have sente my servaunt Richard Toring to London, whyche I hope shall brynge me goode tydyngs ageyn, and with in iiij. dayes I hope to see yowe.

Wretyn on Wednysdaye, xvij. daye off Janyver, anno E. iiij*ti* xvᵒ.

JOHN PASTON, K.

882

JOHN PASTON TO MARGARET PASTON[1]

To my ryght worcheful modyr, Margaret Paston.

JAN. 21 AFTYR all dewtes of recomendacyon, pleasyt yow to weet that as yesterday att noon my brodyr Sir John departyd fro Norwyche towardes London; for as now all the sped is with the Kyng for the swerte of the maner of Caster, consyderyng the dyeing seasyd of my Lord of Norffolk. He trustyth to be in thys contre ayen with in x. or xij. dayes. And at hys departyng he seyd to me that ye sent hym woord to selle the clothe of gold, if he myght selle it well, whyche clothe I thynke may be sold, iff ye wyll agre; not withstandyng I wylle make no bargayn for it, tyll ye send me woord of the serteyn some what ye wyll have for it, or ellys ye to have it ayen. Sir Robard Wyngfeld offyrd me yesterday xx. mark for it, but I wot well ye shall have more for it, if ye wyll sell it; wher for, as ye wyll deele in this mater, I prey yow send me woord to morew be tymys, for if thys bargayn be forsakyn, I trow it wyll be longe er ye kan get an other bargayn to selle it eny thyng aftyr that is woorthe.

Modyr, in as humbyll wyse as I can, I beseche yow of your blyssyng. I trust fro hense foorthe that we shall have our chyldyr in rest with ought rebwkyng for ther pleying wanton; for it is told me your ostass at Freton hathe gotyn hyr syche a

[1] [From Paston mss., B.M.] This letter is shown by internal evidence to have been written shortly after the Duke of Norfolk's death, which, as we have seen, took place on the 17th January 1476. It was written on a Sunday, and states that Sir John Paston had left Norwich the day before. The letter following, which is of the 23rd January, is dated by John Paston, 'Tuesday next after your (Sir John's) departing,' so that the Sunday on which this was written must certainly have been the 21st.

246

EDWARD IV

distress taken by John Markham at Strehall in Cressingham, which is held of 1475 the King's manor of Necton. They took cattle in lambing time in March, in the 14th year of this King, 'and put Craksheld and Salter in such fear of losing of their cattle that they were bound to my lord by obligation, and Craksheld is dead for thought.' Will take the letter to Mr. William though it cost him fourteen days' labor. Was five weeks riding 'to Canterbury, and again I will no longer drive, for in winter I may not ride,' etc.

[From the reference to 'the 14th year of this King,' it is evident that this letter was written after 1474, the 14th year of Edward IV. It may, perhaps, be of the reign of Henry VII.; in which case it was addressed to the younger John Paston, who was then a knight, his brother being dead, about the year 1500.]

881

SIR JOHN PASTON TO JOHN PASTON[1]

LYKE it yow to weete, that not in the most happy season 1476 ffor me, it is so ffortunyd, that wher as my Lorde off JAN. 17 Norffolke, yisterdaye beying in goode heele, thys nyght dyed abowte mydnyght, wherffor it is ffor alle that lovyd hym to doo and helpe nowe that, that maye be to hys honoure, and weell to hys sowele. And it is soo, that thys contre is nott weell purveyd off clothe off golde ffor the coveryng ffor hys bodye and herse; wherffor every man helpyng to hys power, I putte the cowncell off my lorde in cowmffort, that I hoped to gete one ffor that daye, if it weer so that it be nott broken, or putt to other use.

Wherffor please it yow to sende me worde iff it be so, that ye have, or kan kom by the clothe off tyssywe that I bowte ffor our ffaders tombe, and I undretake it shall be saffyd ageyn ffor yowe on hurt at my perell; I deeme herby to gete greet thanke, and greet assystence in tyme to come; and that owther Syme or Mother Brown maye deliver it me to morow by vij. off the clokke.

[1] [From Fenn, ii. 186.] This letter is not addressed, but must have been intended for the writer's brother John, or else, as Fenn suggests, for his mother, Margaret. Sir John, however, ends by saying, 'Within four days I hope to see you'; and it appears by next letter that he was actually with his brother at Norwich within *three* days, whereas he paid no visit to his mother, who seems to have been living, as she had done for some time, at Mautby. This letter must have been written from Framlingham, whither Sir John had doubtless gone to petition the Duke of Norfolk about Caister.

245

EDWARD IV

thyng to pley with, that our other chyldyr shall have leve to 1476 sporte theym. God send hyr joye of it. JAN. 28

Wretyn at Norwyche, thys Sonday.

Your sone and humbyll servaunt,

JOHN PASTON.

883

JOHN PASTON TO SIR JOHN PASTON[1]

To Sir John Paston, Knyght, at the George, at Powlys Wharffe.

AFTYR all dewtes of recomendacyon, lyeketh yow to weet JAN. 23 that I ensuer yow your sendyng to Caster is evyll takyn among my lordes folkes, in so myche that some sey that ye tendryd lytyll my lordes dethe, in as myche as ye wold so sone entre upon hym aftyr hys dysseace, with ought avyse and assent of my lordes consayll; wherfor it is thought here by syche as be your frendes in my lordes house that if my lady have onys the graunt of the wardshepp of the chyld,[2] that she wyll ocupye Caster with other londes, and ley the defaute on your unkynd hastyness of entre with ought hyr assent. Wherfor in eny wyse get yow a patent of the Kyng ensealyd be for hyrs, and ye may by eny meane possybyll.

Also I prey yow comon with my Lord Chamberleyn for me, and weet hough that he wyll have me demeanyd.

It iss told me for serteyn that ther is none hey to gete at Caleys; wherfor if I mygh be pardond for eny kepyng of horse at Caleys till Myd somer, it wer a good torne.

The berer herof shall come home ayen fro London with in a day aftyr that he comyth thedyr, if ye wyll ought comand hym. I prey yow send me woord by hym hough ye do with your maters, and I prey yow in eny wyse lete me undyrstand,

[1] [From Paston mss., B.M.]
[2] This child was Ann, who soon after was betrothed to Richard Plantagenet, Duke of York, the second son of King Edward. She died very young, and the Duke was, as it is supposed, smothered in the Tower by the command of his uncle Richard III.—F.

247

THE PASTON LETTERS

by the berer heroff, hough Bowen of the Cheker wyll dele with me ; vj^{xx}. and x*li*. it is nough, and I wold have vij^{xx}*·li*. and x*li*. and I to plege it ought in iiij. or v. yer, or ellys to forfet the maner.

Wretyn at Norwyche, the Twysday next aftyr your departyng thens, xxiij. die Januarii, anno E. iiij^{ti} xv°.

JOHN PASTON.

884

SIR JOHN PASTON TO JOHN PASTON[1]

To John Paston, Esquier, at Norwyche, be thys delyveryd.

I RECOMAUNDE me to yow, letyng yow weete that I was infformyd by Ric. Radle, that on Scarlett, that was undrescheryff to Hastyngs,[2] wolde sywe to me on yowr behalff, ffor that ye weer dyspleasyd with a returne off Nichill[3] uppon yow in the seyde Hastyngs tyme ; wherffor Ric. Radle thoghte that the seyde Scarlett wolde be gladde to gyff yow a noble or a riall ffor a sadell to amends, so that ye wolde sease and stoppe the bylle, whyche ye entende to putt into the corte ageyn hys Master Hastyngs.

Wherffor the seyde Scarlett com to me, and prayed me to helpe in the same, and so I have don my devoir to ffeele off hym the most that he can ffynde in hys stomake to depart with to please yow ; and in conclusyon I trowe, he shall gyff yow a doblett clothe off sylke, price xx*s*. or therabout ; whyche uppon suche answeer as I heer ffrom yowe, I deme that Bysshop the atornye shall, iff I conclude with hym on yowr behalve, paye in mony or otherwyse, to whom that ye woll assynge heer.

---

[1] [From Fenn, ii. 190.]
[2] John Hastyngs was Sheriff of Norfolk the preceding year.—F.
[3] Nihils, or Nichils, are issues which the sheriff that is apposed in the Exchequer says are *nothing worth* and illeviable, through the insufficiency of the parties from whom due.—F.

248

THE PASTON LETTERS

Item, as ffor my mater heer, itt was thys daye beffoor alle the lordes off the cowncelle, and amonge them all, it was nott thowght, that in my sendyng off Whetley thyddr, in mediately afftr the dycesse off the Duke, that I dalt onkyndly or onfyttyngly, but that I was moor onresonably dalte with ; wherffor, late men deme what they wylle, grettest clerkys are nott alweye wysest men ; but I hope hastely to have on weye in it or other.

Item, I wende [*expected*] to have ffownde a gowne off myn heer, but it come home the same daye that I come owte, browght by Herry Berker, loder [*carrier*]. I wolde in alle hast possible have that same gowne off puke ffurryd with whyght lambe.

Item, I wolde have my longe russett gowne off the Frenshe russett in alle hast, ffor I have no gowne to goo in here.

Item, I praye yow recomande me to my moodr, and lat us alle prey God sende my Lady off Norffolk a soone, for upon that restythe moche mater ; ffor if the Kyngys soone[1] mary my lords dowghtr, the Kynge wolde that hys soone sholde have a ffayr place in Norffolk, thowhe he sholde gyffe me ij. tymes the valywe in other londe, as I am doon to weete. I praye yow sende me worde off my ladyes spede as soone as ye kan.

Item, as ffor Bowen I shall ffele hym, and sholde have doon, thowghe ye hadde nott sente.

Item, ther is offryd me a goode marriage for my suster Anne Skypwithys sone and heyr off Lynkolneshyre, a man v. or vj. mrke by year. No mor.

Wretyn at London, the xxvij. daye off Janyver, anno E. iiij^{ti} xv°.

Item, my Lady off Excester[2] is ded, and it was seyde

---

[1] Richard, Duke of York, second son of King Edward IV., in or before January 1478, married Anne, sole daughter and heir of John Mowbray, late Duke of Norfolk.—*Rolls of Parliament*, vi. 168. She was at that time only in her sixth year, and she died early.
[2] Anne, daughter of Richard, Duke of York, sister of Edward IV., and widow of Henry Holland, the last Duke of Exeter, her first husband ; she died 14th of January 1475, and lies buried with Sir Thomas Saint Leger, Knight, her second husband, in a private chapel at Windsor.—F.

250

EDWARD IV

I shall by the means of Raddele weet at whoys sywte it was takyn owte ; I deme it som thynge doon by craffte, by the means off them that have entresse in your lond, to th'entent to noyse itt therys, or to make yow past shame off the sellyng theroff.

Item, I have receyvyd a letter ffrom yowe wretyn on Tywesdaye last.

Item, wher that som towards my Lady of Norffolk noyse that I dyd onkyndely to sende so hastely to Caster as I dyd ; there is no dyscrete person that so thynkyth, ffor iff my lorde hade ben as kynde to me as he myght have ben, and acordyng to suche hert and servyce as my grauntffadr, my ffadr, yowr self, and I, have owght and doon to my Lords of Norffolk that ded ben, and yitt iff I hadde weddyd hys dowghtr, yitt most I have doon as I dydde.

And moor ovyr, iff I had hadde any demyng off my lordys dethe iiij. howrs or he dyed, I most neds, but iff I wolde be knowyn a ffoole, have entryd it the howr byffor hys dycesse ; but in effecte, theygh that in that mater have always ment onkyndely to me, they ffeyne that rumor ageyn me ; but ther is noon that ment truly to hym that dede is, that wolde be sory that I hadde itt, and in especiall suche as love hys sowle.

Item, wher it is demyd that my lady wolde herafftr be the rather myn hevy lady ffor that delyng, I thynke that she is to resonable so to be, ffor I did it nott onwyst to hyr cowncell ; there was no man thoght that I sholde doo otherwysse ; an as to seye, that I myght have hadde my ladyes advyce or lyve [*leave*], I myght have teryed yitt, or I cowde have speken with hyr, or yitt have hadde any body to have mevyd hyr there on my behalve, as ye wote I dydde what I cowde. Moreovyr I taryed by the advyce off Sir Robert Wyngffelde iij. dayes there, ffor that he putte me in comffirt that the Lord Howard,[1] and hys brother Sir John, sholde have comen to Norwyche, att whoys comyng he dowtyd nott but that I sholde have a goode dyrection takyn ffor me in that mater, they leyhe to me onkyndenesse ffor ovyrkyndenesse.

---

[1] Afterwards Duke of Norfolk.—F.

249

EDWARD IV

that bothe the olde Dywchesse off Norffolk,[1] and the Cowntesse off Oxenfforde[2] weer ded, but it is nott soo yitt.

Item, I shall remembr Caleyse bothe for horse and alle, &c.

885

JOHN PASTON TO SIR JOHN PASTON[3]

To Sir John Paston, Knyght, at the George, by Powlys Wharf, in London.

A FTYR all dwtes of recomendacyon, lyeketh yow to wete, that with in thys owyr past, I receyd your letter wretyn the xxvij. day of Januar, by whyche I undyrstand that Scarlet wold have an end with me ; but lesse then xl*s*. is to lytyll, for iff I wold do the uttermost to hym, I shold recover by the statwte, I trow xl*li*. or more, but lesse then xxxiij*s*. iiij*d*. I wyll in no wyse ; and ye may sey that ye of your owne hed wyll geve hym the ode nobyll of xl*s*., and if ye have the v. noblys I prey yow let Parker of Flett stret have therof xxx*s*. and lete Pytte and Rychard and Edward drynk the xl*d*. As for your gownys, they shalbe sent yow in as hasty wyse as is possybyll. Thys must be consayll :—It is promysyd my lady by my Lord Chamberleyn that the *diem clausit extremum* for my lord shall not be delyverd tyll she be off power to labore hyr sylff her most avauntage in that mater, wherfor ye ned not to dele ov r largely with thexchetoures. Also consayll :—Robard Brandon and Colevyle have by meanys enformyd my lady that ye wold have gotyn Caster fro hyr by stronge hand, now thys frost whyll the mote is frosyn, in so myche that she was posposed to have

---

[1] Ellenor, only daughter of William Bourchier, Earl of Ewe, in Normandy, and widow of John Mowbray, Duke of Norfolk.—F.
[2] Margaret, daughter of Richard Nevile, Earl of Salisbury, and wife of John de Vere, Earl of Oxford, now a prisoner in the Castle of Hammes, in Picardy ; or it may refer to Elizabeth, widow of the late Earl of Oxford, and daughter and heir of Sir John Howard, Knight.—F.
[3] [From Paston MSS., B.M.]

251

THE PASTON LETTERS

1476
FEB. 3

sent thedyr R. Brandon and other to have kept the place tyll syche tyme as she made axe me the questyon whedyr ye entendet that wey or not, and I avysed hyr that she shold rather sofyr R. Brandon and hys retenew to lye in Norwyche of hys owne cost then to lye at the taverne at Yermouthe on hyr cost, for I lete hyr have knowlage that ye never entendyd non entre in to that place, but by hyr assent and knowlage I wast well. Syr, for Godes sake, in as hasty wyse as is possybyll, send me woord how ye feele my Lord Chamberleyn and Bowen dysposed to me wardes, for I shall never be in hertes ease tyll I undyrstand ther tweys dysposysyon. Also, I prey yow, let Symond Dame have knowlage as soone as ye have red thys lettyr that I wold in eny wyse that he swe forthe the axions a yenst Darby and other for Byskley, notwithstandyng the bylle that I sent hym to the contrary by Edmund Jeney, for Darby and I are brokyn of, of our entrete whyche was apoyntyd at Thettford. God sped yow in thes maters, and in all other. Ye send me woord of a good maryage for my syster Anne. I prey yow aspye some old thryfty draff wyff in London for me. Thomas Brampton at the Blak Fryers in London wyth syche other as he and I apoyntyd wyll helpe yow to aspye on for me on ther part. I prey yow that I may be recomandyd to hym, and prey hym that he wyll, in as hasty wyse as he can, comforte me wyth on letter fro hym, and fro the other persone that he and I comond of, and I prey yow as ye se hym at the parvyse[1] and ellys where, calle on hym for the same letter and telle hym that ye most nedys have on to me, and when ye have it breke it and ye lyst or ye send it me.

Endorsed—iij. Februarij, anno xv°.

---

[1] The church porch. In London it commonly meant the portico of St. Paul's Cathedral, which is doubtless the place here intended.

252

886

JOHN PASTON TO LORD HASTINGS[1]

To my Lord.

MY most doughtyd and singuler good lord, aftyr most humble and dew recomendacyon, please it your good lordshepp to have knowlage that, accordyng to your comandement, in my wey homeward, I remembred me of a persone whyche to my thynkyng is meetly to be clerk of your kechyn, whyche persone is now in servyse with Master Fitzwater, and was befor that with Whethyll at Gwynes, and purveyor for hys house, and at syche tyme as the Kynges grace was ther last in hys vyage towardes France. Thys man is meane of stature, yonge inough, well wittyd, well manerd, a goodly yong man on horse and foote. He is well spokyn in Inglyshe, metly well in Frenshe, and verry perfite in Flemyshe. He can wryght and reed. Hys name is Rychard Stratton; hys modyr is Mastress Grame of Caleys. And when I had shewyd hym myn intent, he was agreable and verry glad if that it myght please your lordshepp to accept hym in to your servyse; wherto I promysed hym my poore helpe, as ferforthe as I durst meve your good lordshepp for hym, trustyng that I shold have knowlage of your plesure her in, or I departed towardes your lordshep ought of this contrey. Wherfor I advysed hym to be redy with in xiiij. dayes of Marche at the ferthest, that if it pleasyd your lordsheppe to accept hym or to have a syght of hym be for your departyng to Caleys, that ther shold be no slaughthe in hym.

He desyred me to meve Master Fitzwater to be good mastyr to hym in thys behalve, and so I dyd; and he was verry glad and agreable ther to, seiyng if hys sone had ben of

---

[1] [From Paston mss., B.M.] Although the lord to whom this letter was addressed is not named, it was undoubtedly intended for Lord Hastings, Lieutenant of Calais, who, as will be seen hereafter, was preparing to go over to Calais in March 1476.—*See* No. 888.

253

THE PASTON LETTERS

1476
MARCH 2

age, and all the servauntis he hathe myght be in eny wyse acceptabell to your lordshepp, that they all, and hym silff in lyek wyse, shall be at your comandment, whyll he leveth.

And at my comyng home to my poore house, I sent for Robart Bernard, and shewid on to hym that I had mevyd your lordshepp for hym; and he in lyek forme is agreable to be redy by the xiiij. day of Marche to awayte on your lordshepp, be it to Caleys or ellys where, and fro that day so foorthe for ever, whyll hys lyff wyll last, with ought grugeing or contrarying your comandement and plesure, in eny wyse that is in hym possibyll t'accomplishe.

I shewed on to hym that I had preyed Master Talbot to be a mean to your good lordshepp for hym, and if so wer that Mastyr Talbot thought that your lordshepp wer content to take hys servyse, then that it wold please Mr. Talbot to meve my Lady of Norffolkes grace to wryght or send to Bernard, puttyng hym in knowlage that hyr grace is content that he shall become your menyall servaunt. Wherof he was passyng well pleasyd; but, that notwithstandyng, as I enformed your lordshepp, he is not so reteyned, neyther by fee nor promess, but that he may let hym sylff loose to do your lordsheppe servyse when ye wyll receyve hym, and so wyll he do; but, your lordshepe so pleasid, leve wer bettyr. Rychard Stratton told me that whyll he was in servyse with Whethyll, John Redwe mocyond hym onys myche aftyr thys intent, but at that tyme Whethyll wold not be so good mastyr to hym as to meve your lordshepe for hym.

My lord, I trust that your lordshepe shall lyek bothe ther persones and ther condicyons; and as for ther trowthes, if it may please your good lordshepe to accept my poore woord with thers, I wyll depose largely for that. And as it pleasyth your good lordshepe to comand me in thes maters, and all other, if it may please your lordshepe to shewe the same to my brodyr Nessfeld, he knowith who shall sonest be with me to putt me in knowlage of your plesure, whyche I shall be at all seasons redy t'accomplyshe to my poore power, with Godes grace, Whom I beseche longe to contenue the prosperous astate of your good lordshepp.

254

EDWARD IV

Fro Norwyche, the seconde daye of Marche, with the hand of your most humble servaunt and beedman,

JOHN PASTON.

1476
MARC

887

JOHN PASTON TO [MARGERY BREWS][1]

MASTRESSE, thow so be that I, unaqweyntyd with yow as yet, tak up on me to be thus bold as to wryght on to yow with ought your knowlage and leve, yet, mastress, for syche pore servyse as I now in my mynd owe yow, purposyng, ye not dyspleasyd, duryng my lyff to contenu the same, I beseche yow to pardon my boldness, and not to dysdeyn, but to accepte thys sympyll byll to recomand me to yow in syche wyse as I best can or may imagyn to your most plesure. And, mastress, for sych report as I have herd of yow by many and dyverse persones, and specyally by my ryght trusty frend, Rychard Stratton, berer herof, to whom I beseche yow to geve credence in syche maters as he shall on my behalve comon with yow of, if it lyke you to lystyn hym, and that report causythe me to be the more bold to wryght on to yow, so as I do; for I have herd oft tymys Rychard Stratton sey that ye can and wyll take every thyng well that is well ment, whom I believe and trust as myche as fewe men leveing, I ensuer yow by my trowthe. And, mastress, I beseche yow to thynk non other wyse in me but that I wyll and shall at all seasons be redy wythe Godes grace to accomplyshe all syche thynges as I have enformyd and desyerd the seyd Rychard on my behalve to geve yow knowlage of, but if [unless] it so be that a geyn my wyll it come of yow that I be cast off fro yowr servyse and not wyllyngly by my desert, and that I am and wylbe yours and at your comandmen in every

1476

---

[1] [From Paston mss., B.M.] This letter is printed from a draft in the hand of John Paston the younger. I suppose it must have been written about the year 1476, and intended for Margery Brews, whom he afterwards married. It will be seen that Richard Stratton, whom in his last letter he recommended to Lord Hastings, is here the bearer of a confidential message to the lady.

255

476(?) wyse dwryng my lyff. Her I send yow thys bylle wretyn with my lewd hand and sealyd with my sygnet to remayn with yow for a wyttnesse ayenste me, and to my shame and dyshonour if I contrary it. And, mastress, I beseche yow, in easyng of the poore hert that somtyme was at my rewle, whyche now is at yours, that in as short tyme as can be that I may have knowlage of your entent and hough ye wyll have me demeanyd in thys mater, and I wylbe at all seasons redy to performe in thys mater and all others your plesure, as ferforth as lythe in my poore power to do or in all thers that ought wyll do for me, with Godes grace, Whom I beseche to send yow the accomplyshement of your most worchepfull desyers, myn owne fayer lady, for I wyll no ferther labore but to yow, on to the tyme ye geve me leve, and tyll I be suer that ye shall take no dysplesur with my ferther labore.

888

SIR JOHN PASTON TO JOHN PASTON[1]

To John Paston, Esquier, or to Mestresse Margrett Paston, hys moodre, in Norffolk.

1476 MARCH 12 I RECOMANDE me to yow, letyng yow wete that, blessyd be God, upon Saterdaye last past my lorde[2] and wee toke the see, and come to Caleyes the same daye, and as thys daye my lorde come to Guynesse, and theer was receyvyd honourablye with owt any obstaklys; wheer as I fownde Master Fytzwalter and othre, whyche wer ryght hevye for the dethe of the noble man thatt was theer to foor, itt happyd soo that my seyd Master Fytzwalter axid me ryght hertely for yow, and I lete hym weete that I demyd ye wolde be heer in haste, wheroffe he seyde he was ryght soory, for soo moche that he entendyth to come in to Englonde, and as I conceyve he wyll come to Attylborogh, and brynge my mestresse hys wyffe with hym, and theer to stablysshe hys howse

¹ [From Paston MSS., B.M.]   ² Hastings.

256

1476 RCH 21 ryght gladde, ffor I hope that I ame fferre moor in ffavor with my lorde then I was to ffoor.

Item, I sende yow, brother John, a letter herwith, whyche was browte hyddr to Caleys, ffrom the George at Powles Wharff; I deme it comethe ffrom my brother Water.

Item, iff ye entende hyddrewarde, itt weer weell doon that ye hygthed yowe, ffor I suppose that my lorde wille take the vywe off alle hys retynywe heer, nowe byffoor hys departyng; and I thynke that he woolde be better contente with yowr comyng nowe, than an other tyme; doo as ye thynke best, and as ye maye.

Item, wher Master Fytzwalter made me to wryght to yowe to advyse yow to tarye, I remytte thatt to yowr dyscrecion.

As ffor tydyngs heer, we her ffrom alle the worlde; ffyrst, the Lorde Ryverse was at Roome right weell and honorably, and other Lords off Ynglonde, as the Lord Hurmonde,¹ and the Lord Scrope,² and at ther departyng xij. myle on thysehalff Roome, the Lorde Ryverse was robbyd off alle hys jowelles and plate, whyche was worthe mˡᵉ marke or better, and is retornyd to Rome ffor a remedy.

Item, the Duke of Burgoyne hath conqueryd Loreyn, and Quene Margreet shall nott nowe be lykelyhod have it; wherffor the Frensche Kynge cheryssheth hyr butt easelye; but afftr thys conquest off Loreyn, the Duke toke grete corage to goo uppon the londe off the Swechys [Swiss] to conquer them, butt the [they] berded hym att an onsett place, and hathe dystrussyd hym, and hathe slayne the most parte off hys vanwarde, and wonne all hys ordynaunce and artylrye, and mor ovyr all stuffe thatt he hade in hys ost with hym; exceppte men and horse ffledde nott, but they roode that nyght xx. myle; and so the ryche saletts,³ heulmetts, garters, nowchys⁴ gelt, and alle is goone, with tents, pavylons, and alle, and soo men deme hys pryde is abatyd. Men tolde hym that they weer ffrowarde karlys, butte he wolde nott beleve it, and yitt men seye, that he woll to them ageyn. Gode spede them bothe.

¹ John, sixth Earl of Ormond.   ² John, Lord Scrope of Bolton.
³ Light head-pieces.—F.   ⁴ Embossed ornaments, chains, buckles, etc.—F.
258

---

contynuall. Wherffor he thynketh that he sholde have as grete a lakke off yow as off any one man in that contre, willyng me to wryght on to yowe, and to late yow weete off hys comynge. He also hathe tolde me moche off hys stomake and tendre faver that he owythe to yow; wherffor I asserteyn yow that he is your verry especiall goode master, and iffe ye weer abydynge in thatt contre, whylse he weer theer, he is dysposyd to doo largely for yowe in dyverse wyse, whyche weer to longe to wryght, in so moche that I feele by hym that he thynkyth that itt sholde be longe er he scholde be wery of yowr expences of horse or man. Now I remytte alle thynge to your dyscresion; ye woote best what is for yow.

As for my lorde, I undrestande nott yitt whethyr he wylle in to Ingelonde the weke to foor Esterne, or ellys aftre.

I pray yow recomande me to my moodre. I wolde have wretyn to hyr, but in trowthe I ame somewhatt crased, what with the see and what wythe thys dyet heer.

No moor to yow, but wretyn at Gynes, the xij. daye off Marche, anno E. xvj.

            By JOHN PASTON, K.

1476 MARCH 12

889

SIR JOHN PASTON TO MARGARET PASTON[1]

To Mestresse Margrete Paston, at Norwyche, or hyr sone, John Paston, Esquyer, and to everych off them.

I RECOMANDE me to yowe. Like it yow to weete that I am nott sertayne yitt whether my lorde² and I shall come into Ingelonde the weke byffoor Est[er]ne, or ellys the weke afftr Est[er]ne; wherffor, moodr, I beseche yow to take noo dysplesyr with me ffor my longe tarynge, ffor I most doo noon otherwyse ffor dysplesyng off my lorde. I was noo thynge gladde off thys jornaye, iff I myght goodely have chosen; nevertheless, savyng that ye have cawse to be dyspleasyd with me ffor the mater off Kokett, I am ellys

MARCH 21

¹ [From Fenn, ii. 198.]   ² Hastings.
VOL. V.—R   257

Item, Sir John Mydelton toke leve off the Duke to sporte hym, but he is sett in pryson att Brussellys.

I praye yowe sende me som worde iff ye thynke likly that I may entr Caster when I woll, by the next messenger.

Wretyn at Caleys, in resonable helthe off bodye and sowle, I thanke Good, the xxj. daye off Marche, anno E. iiijᵈ xvjᵒ.

            J. P., K.

1476 MARCH 21

890

JOHN PASTON TO SIR JOHN PASTON[1]

To the ryght worchepfull Sir John Paston, Knyght, lodgyd at the George, by Powlys Wharf, in London.

AFTYR all dewtes of recomendacyon, lyeketh yow to wet, that to my power ye be welcom ayen in to Inglond. And as for the Castell of Shene, ther is no mor in it but Colle and hys mak, and a goose may get it; but in no wyse I wold not that wey, and my modyr thynkyth the same. Take not that wey, if ther be eny other.

I undyrstand that Mastres Fytzwater hathe a syster, a mayd, to mary. I trow, and ye entretyd hym, she myght come into Crysten menys handys. I prey yow spek with Mastyr Fytzwater of that mater for me, and ye may telle hym, synse that he wyll have my servyse, it wer as good, and syche a bargayn myght be mad, that bothe she and I awaytyd on hym and my mastress hys wyff at oure owne cost, as I a lone to awayt on hym at hys cost; for then he shold be swer that I shold not be flyttyng, and I had syche a qwarell to kepe me at home. And I have hys good wylle, it is non inpossybyll to bryng a bowgh.

I thynk to be at London with in a xiiij. dayes at the ferthest, and peraventure my mastress also, in consayll be it clatryd. God kepe yow and yours.

At Norwyche, the vj. day of May, anno E. iiijᵈ xvjᵒ.

               J. P.

MAY 6

¹ [From Paston MSS., B.M.]
259

THE PASTON LETTERS

891

SIR JOHN PASTON TO MARGARET PASTON[1]

*To Mestresse Margret Paston, in Norwyche, or to hyr
sone John Paston, Knyght.*

1476
MAY 27

PLEASE it yow to weete that as for my materes, and
theye appeyre nott,[2] the doo, blessyd be Godde, as
weell as I wolde they dyd, saffe that it shalle cost me
grett mony, and it hathe cost me moche laboor. It is soo
that the Kynge most have C. marke, and other costes will
drawe xl. marke. And my mater is examynyd by the Kynges
Cowncell, and declaryd affoor alle the Lordes, and now lakkythe
noo thynge but [the Pry]vy Seals, and wryghtyng to Master
Colv[ill][3] to avoide; for the[3] [Kyng hath p]romysed me as
moche as I wolde he sholde fullefille, and alle the Lordes,
Juges, Serjauntes, have affermyd my title goode. Nott withstandyng Sowthewell, James Hubberde, and Sir W. Braundon,
where at ther owne desyrs, offryd to afferme and advowe my
tytell for goode, and that my Lorde off Norffolk that ded is
had noo tytell, thatt they knywe, they tolde my tale as ille as
they cowde, and yitt a lye or too to helpe it, and yit it servyth
them nott, they be knowen as they ar (in Cowncell be it seyde,
and so most all thys letter be).

I have moche payne to gete so moche mony. Neverthelesse, but iff myne oncle schewe hym selfe werse than ever he
was, I shalle nott fayle, if he kepe me promyse, and thatt is
but as he dyde last, that is butt to be my sywerte, and I to
make hym sywerte ageyn.

The Kynge departythe thys daye, and wille nott be heer
tyll Fryday, whyche lettyth me, or ellys by thatt daye I wolde

---

[1] [From Paston MSS., B.M.] This letter relates to Sir John Paston's claim to
Caister after the Duke of Norfolk's death, which claim he succeeded in establishing
in June 1476, as appears by the letter following. The date 26th May at the end of
the letter is an error. The 'Monday next Holy Thursday' was the 27th.
[2] *i.e.* if they do not get worse.
[3] Paper decayed.

260

THE PASTON LETTERS

1476
JUNE 30

bynde me in no suche clawse, butt iff it be for xx*li.* by a resonable daye, and xx. marke aftre the dyssease off my moodre.
Take example at Derby.

Item, ye make yow sywerer than I deme yow bee, for I
deme that her frendes wyll nott be content with Bedyngfeldes
sywerte, nor yowres. I deme thys mater will ocopy lenger
leyser than ye deme for.

Item, I remembre thatt thys mony that she sholde have is
nott redy, but in the handes of marchauntes of the Estaple,
whyche at a prove ye shall fynde per case so slakke payeres,
that ye myght be deseyvyd ther by. I knowe dyverse have
lost mony er they cowde gete ther dywtes owte off the Staple.
God spede yow, and sende yow that ye wolde have.

I sende yow the obligacion here with acordyng to yowr
desyr, and a letter to Bedyngfelde, thankyng hym for yow,
and more over letyng hym know of myn entent. Opyn it,
and close it ageyn, if ye lyst.

Item, where I tolde yow that the gowne clothe off olde
chamlott, I wolde have it hoome for my suster Anne; ye for
gate it. I praye yow sende it home by the next messanger,
and a letter with it of suche tydynges as ye knowe.

Item, blissed be God, I have Castre at my will. God holde
it better than it doone her to foore.

No moore, but wretyn the next daye aftre Seynt Petre,
anno E. iiij[ti] xvj°. J. PASTON, K.

893

SIR JOHN PASTON TO MARGARET PASTON[1]

To Mestresse Margret Paston.

[AUG. 30]

PLEASE it yow to wete that I was upon Tywesdaye, the
daye that I departyd froo yowe, with my brother John
at Atelborow by viij. of the clokke at evyn, and founde
hym in suche case as iff ye had seyn hym than ye wolde have

---

[1] [Add. MS. 34,889, f. 188.] Strangely enough there is no mention elsewhere of
the serious illness of young John Paston mentioned in this letter, by which we might
fix the year when it was written. But perhaps we may surmise that it was 1476,

262

EDWARD IV

have hopyd to have comen homeward, and erst per aventure.
No moor, but Jesus have yow in kepyng.

147
MAY

Wretyn at London, the xxvj. daye of Maye, the Mondaye
next Holy Thurrysdaye, the Assencion.

The Kynge wold have bowte it, but he was ensformyd off
the trowthe, and that it was nott for a prynce, and off the
greet pryse that I wolde selle it att; for that I myght nott
for bere it, for he scholde have payed m[l.]m[l.] marke or moor, iff
he hadde hadde it.

Your sone, J. PASTON, K.

892

SIR JOHN PASTON TO JOHN PASTON[1]

*To John Paston, Esquier, beyng at the Syngne of the
George, at Powles Wharffe.*

JUNE

I RECOMAUNDE me to yow, letyng yow weete that I
hav receyvyd yowr letter, wretyn the next daye aftre
Mydsomer; for answer wheroff I thynke that to be
bownde in v[c.] [500] marke, I thynke it is to moche, where as
I felt by yow ye sholde have with the gentylwoman but iiij[c]
[400]; nevertheelesse I agree. But ye shall undrestande that
I wyll not be bownde for yow that ye shall make hyr joyntour
past xx*li.* by yer, within a sertayne daye lymyted; be it j. yere
or ij., that is the largest that ye maye performe. For as for
the maner of Sparham, my moodre and ye acorde notte in
yowr saynges; she wyll nowght graunte yow ther in, whylse
she levyth, saff, as she seythe to me, she hathe grauntyd yow
x. marke by yer tyll xl*li.* be payed, that is but vj. yeer; and
aftre hyr dyscease she woll agree with goode will, so that it
maye be yowr proferment, that ye sholde have that maner in
joynture with yowr wyffe to the lenger lyver off yow bothe,
payng x. marke by yeer, soo or th . . . as she wyll that
it shall be. Therfore, as for l. marke joynture, I pray yow

---

[1] [From Paston MSS., B.M.]

261

EDWARD IV

be as gladde of hym osse off a nywe sone. I wenyd nott that
he sholde nott have levyd tyll the mornyng; in so moche that [AUG.
by my trowthe I dare seye that iff it had nott fortunyd us to
have comyn to hym, he had not been on lyve on Wednysdaye.
For syns Saterday slepyd he nott iiij. howris, and yitt iij. of
them was syns I come thydyr, on to thys nyght; and thys
nyght, blessyd be God, he hathe slepyd well, and with Goddys
grace I dowte not but thatt he shall do well. For his agywe
is goone, and alle that laye in hys stomak and undre hys syde
it weryth aweye, and within a daye or ij. I hope he shall be so
stronge that I maye come frome hym; and he hopyth to see
yowe with in fewe days affter, as he seyth. On Wednysdaye
I wysshed to hym that he and I hadde been at Norwyche;
wheruppon he harpyd all that nyght, and for cawe (*sic*) he
hadde not so goode rest as he wolde, it fylle in hys brayne to
come to Norwyche; and he in an angyr wolde nedys to horse.
He wolde non horsse litter, he was so stronge. Neverthelesse
we wenyd nott that he sholde have been able to have redyn a
myle, and wenyd that it had nott been possible to have passid
Wyndham; bott whan he was uppe for that, we seyde he
roode so welle he ledde uss a dawnce faster than alle we cowde
weell folowe. He was at Wyndham, by my trowthe, in lesse
than an howr by a large quarter, and ther restyd hym an
howre, and to horse ageyne and was heer in lesse than an
howr and one halffe. And now he dowteth nott to slepe
weell, for he seyth that he never ffaylyd to slepe weel in that
bedde that he hathe chosyn now at Frenshys, and thusse I
hope he be sauffe. And I am in dowte whethyr I shall within
ij. dayes owther come home to yow or ellis to goo forthe as
ye woote off. No moore, &c. Wretyn on Frydaye next the
Decollacion of Seynt John Baptyst.

Item, I have the wrythynges off Richard Calle.

Your sone, J. PASTON, K.

---

after he had been at Calais, where he was expected in the spring. The fact that he
was ill at Attleborough agrees with this supposition, for that was the seat of the
Fitzwalter family, and 'Master Fitzwalter' is mentioned in No. 888 as at Calais
showing much interest in the Paston family. It may be observed also that in 1476,
Friday 'next' the Decollation of St. John Baptist (29th August) would be the very
next day.

263

894

DAME ELIZABETH BREWS TO JOHN PASTON[1]

*To my wurschypfull cosyn, John Paston, be thys bill
delyvered, &c.*

476
or
477

RYGHT wurschypfull cosyn, I recommande me un to yowe, thankyng zowe hertely for the grette chere that ze made me the last tyme that ze were with me at Norwych, &c.

And, cosyn, as for the mater·that was put in my nowncle Hastynges and Henry Heydon, I ondyrstand be myn uncle, that ther was made non ende therin, whech I am ryght sory for. Cosyn, ze be remembred what ze promysed me that, and so were that myn uncle and Herry Heydon made none ende therin, that ze wold put the mater in me; and if it please zowe so for to do, in good faith, cosyn, I schall goo as wele and as ryghtfully and consciensly as I can for both the partyes. And, cosyn, if it please zowe to com to Topcroft, and poynt ze what dey when ze will com, I schall sende for my cosyn to be ther the same day. And, cosyn, I pray zowe to sende me worde agayn be the brynger of thys letter, howe ze will do, &c.

And Almyghty Jesus hafe zowe in kepyng, &c.

Be zour cosyn,
Dame Elizabeth Brews.

[1] [From Paston mss., B.M.] This is the first of a series of letters, some of which were certainly written in February 1477, relating to the engagement of John Paston to Margery Brews. How early they began it is not easy to say precisely. On the back of this letter is written, apparently in the hand of John Paston, to whom it is addressed, 'Letræ dominæ Elyzabethæ Brews et Margariæ filæ (*sic*) ejus.'

895

DAME ELIZABETH BREWS TO JOHN PASTON[1]

*Un to my ryght wurschypffull cosyn, John Paston, be
thys lettur delyvered, &c.*

RYGHT wurschypfull cosyn, I recommande me un [to] yowe, &c. And I send my husbonde a bill of the mater that ze knowe of, and he wrote an other bill to me agayn towchyng the same mater; and he wold that ze schuld go un to my maistresse yowr modur, and asaye if ze myght gete the hole xx*li.* in to zowr handes, and then he wolde be more gladd to marye with zowe, and will gyffe zowe an C*li.* And, cosyn, that day that sche is maryed, my fadur will gyffe hyr l. merk. But and we acorde, I schall gyffe yowe a grettere tresur, that is, a wytty gentylwoman, and if I sey it, bothe good and vertuos; for if I schuld take money for hyr, I wold not gyffe hyr for a m*li.* But, cosyn, I trust zowe so meche that I wold thynke her wele besett on zowe, and ze were worthe meche more. And, cosyn, a lytylr after that ze were gone, come a man fro my cosyn Derby, and broght me wurde that suche a chance fell that he myght not come at the day that was set, as I schall let zowe undyrstond more pleynly, when I speke with zowe, &c. But, cosyn, and it wold please zowe to come agayn what dey that ze will set, I dare undyrtake that they schall kepe the same daye; for I wold be glad that, and myn husbond and ze myght acorde in thys maryage, that it myght be my fortune to make and ende in thys mater betwene my cosyns and zowe, that yche of zowe myght love other in frendely wyse, &c. And, cosyn, if thys byll please not zowr entent, I pray zowe that it may be brent, &c.

No more unto yowe at thys tyme, but Almyghty Jesus preserve zowe, &c.

By zowr cosyn,
Dame Elizabeth Brews.

[1] [From Paston mss., B.M.] *See* preliminary note to last letter.

896

DAME ELIZABETH BREWS TO JOHN PASTON[1]

*To my wurschypfull cosyne, John Paston, be this bill
delyveryd, &c.*

77
B.

COSYN, I recomande me un to yowe, thankyng yowe hertely for the grette chere that ye made me and all my folkys, the last tyme that I was at Norwych; and ye promysyd me, that ye wold never breke the mater to Margrery unto suche tyme as ye and I were at a point. But ye hafe made hyr suche advokett for yowe, that I may never hafe rest nyght ner day, for callyng and cryeng upon to brynge the saide mater to effecte, &c.

And, cosyn, uppon Fryday is Sent Volentynes Day, and every brydde chesyth hym a make [*mate*]; and yf it lyke yowe to come one Thursday at nyght, and so purvey yowe, that ye may abyde there tyll Monday, I trusty to God, that ye schall so speke to myn husband; and I schall prey that we schall bryng the mater to a conclusyon, &c. For, cosyn,

It is but a sympill oke,
That [is] cut down at the first stroke.

For ye will be resonabill, I trust to God, Whech hafe yowe ever in Hys mercyfull kepyng, &c.

Be yowr cosyn, Dame Elizabeth Brews,
otherwes schall be called be Godds grace.

[1] [From Fenn, ii. 208.] It is clear from internal evidence that this letter was written between the 7th and the 12th of February, and the fact that St. Valentine's Day (the 14th) fell on Friday, proves the year to have been 1477. Besides which, we have distinct references to the matter further on in the dated correspondence.

897

MARGERY BREWS TO JOHN PASTON[1]

*Unto my ryght welebelovyd Voluntyn, John Paston,
Squyer, be this bill delyvered, &c.*

1477
FEB.

RYGHT reverent and wurschypfull, and my ryght welebeloved Voluntyne, I recomande me unto yowe, ffull hertely desyring to here of yowr welefare, whech I beseche Almyghty God long for to preserve un to Hys plesur, and yowr herts desyre. And yf it please yowe to here of my welefar, I am not in good heele of body, nor of herte, nor schall be tyll I her ffrom yowe;

For there wottys no creature what peyn that I endure,
And for to be deede, I dare it not dyscure [*discover*].

And my lady my moder hath labored the mater to my ffadur full delygently, but sche can no mor gete then ye knowe of, for the whech God knowyth I am full sory. But yf that ye loffe me, as I tryste verely that ye do, ye will not leffe me therefor; for if that ye hade not halfe the lyvelode that ye hafe, for to do the grettest labur that any woman on lyve myght, I wold not forsake yowe.

And yf ye commande me to kepe me true wherever I go,
I wyse I will do all my myght yowe to love and never no mo.
And yf my freends say, that I do amys,
Thei schal not let so for to do,
Myne herte me bydds ever more to love yowe
Truly over all erthely thing,
And yf thei be never so wroth,
I tryst it schall be better in tyme commyng.

No more to yowe at this tyme, but the Holy Trinite hafe yowe in kepyng. And I besech yowe that this bill be not seyn of none erthely creatur safe only your selffe, &c.

And thys letter was indyte at Topcroft, with full hevy herte, &c.

By your own, Margery Brews.

[1] [From Fenn, ii. 210.]

THE PASTON LETTERS

898

MARGERY BREWS TO JOHN PASTON[1]

*To my ryght welebelovyd cosyn, John Paston,
Swyer, be this letter delyveryd, &c.*

1477
FEB.

RYGHT wurschypfull and welebelovyd Volentyne, in my moste umble wyse, I recommande me un to yowe, &c. And hertely I thanke yowe for the lettur whech that ye sende me be John Bekarton, wherby I undyrstonde and knowe, that ye be purposyd to come to Topcroft in schorte tyme, and withowte any erand or mater, but only to hafe a conclusyon of the mater betwyx my fader and yowe; I wolde be most glad of any creatur on lyve, so that the mater myght growe to effect. And ther as ye say, and ye come and fynde the mater no more towards you then ye dyd afortyme, ye wold no more put my fader and my lady my moder to no cost ner besenesse, for that cause, a good wyle aftur, wech causyth myne herte to be full hevy; and yf that ye come, and the mater take to none effecte, then schuld I be meche mor sory and full of hevynesse.

And as for my selfe, I hafe done and undyrstond in the mater that I can or may, as Good knowyth; and I let yowe pleynly undyrstond, that my fader wyll no mor money parte with all in that behalfe, but an C*li.* and l. marke, whech is ryght far fro the acomplyshment of yowr desyre.

Wherfore, yf that ye cowde be content with that good, and my por persone, I wold be the meryest mayden on grounde; and yf ye thynke not yowr selffe so satysfyed, or that ye myght hafe mech mor good, as I hafe undyrstonde be yowe afor; good, trewe, and lovyng volentyne, that ye take no such labur uppon yowe, as to come more for that mater, but let is [*it?*] passe, and never more to be spokyn of, as I may be yowr trewe lover and bedewoman duryng my lyfe.

[1] [From Fenn, ii. 214.]

EDWARD IV

No more un to yowe at thys tyme, but Almyghty Jesus preserve yowe, bothe body and sowle, &c.
Be your Voluntyne,
MARGERY BREWS.

147
FEB

899

THOMAS KELA TO JOHN PASTON[1]

*Un to my ryght wurschypfull maister, John Paston,
Swhyer, be this bill delivered, &c.*

RYGHT wurschypfull sir, I recomande me un to yowe, lettyng yowe knowe, as for the yonge gentylwoman, sche owyth yowe hyr good herte and love, as I knowe be the comynicacion that I hafe hade with hyr for the same.

And, sir, ye knowe what my maister and my lady hath profered with hyr CC. merke. And I dar sey, that hyr chambr and areyment schall be worthe C. merk. And I harde my lady sey, that and the case required, both ye and sche schuld hafe yowr borde with my lady iij. yer aftr.

And I understand by my lady, that sche wold that ye schuld labur the mater to my maister, for it schuld be the bettr.

And I harde my lady sey,

That it was a febill oke,
That was kit down at the first stroke.

And ye be beholdyng un to my lady for hyr good wurde, for sche hath never preysyd yowe to mech.

Sir, lyke as I promysyd yowe, I am yowr man, and my good will ye schall hafe in worde and dede, &c.

And Jesus hafe yowe in Hys mercyfull kepyng, &c.
Be yor man,   THOMAS KELA.

[1] [From Fenn, ii. 216.]

THE PASTON LETTERS

900

SIR JOHN PASTON TO JOHN PASTON[1]

To John Paston, Esquyer, at Norwyche, in hast.

1477
FEB. 14

I RECOMAUNDE me to yow, letyng yow weete, that yisterdaye beganne the grete cowncell, to whyche alle the astats off the londe shall com to, butt if it be ffor gret and reasonable excusis; and I suppose the cheffe cawse off thys assemble is, to comon what is best to doo, now uppon the greet change by the dethe off the Duke of Burgoyne, and ffor the kepyng off Caleys and the Marchys, and ffor the preservacion off the amyteys taken late, as weell with Fraunce as now with the Membrys off Flaundres; wher to I dowt nott ther shall be in all hast bothe the Duks off Clarance and Glowcestre, wheroff I wolde that my brother E.[2] wyst.

Item, I ffeele butt litell effecte in the labor off W. Alyngton; neverthelesse I deme it is nott for yow. She shall not passe CC. mark, as fferr as I can undrestand aparte.

Item, I will nott fforget yow otherwyse.

Itt is so that thys daye I heer grett liklyhood, that my Lorde Hastyngs shall hastely goo to Caleys with greet company; iff I thynke it be for yow to be on [*one*], I shall nott fforgeet yow.

Item, thys daye the mater by twyen Mestresse Anne Haulte and me hathe been soor broken bothe to the Cardinall,[3] to my Lorde Chamberleyn,[4] and to my selffe, and I am in goode hope. When I heer and knowe moor, I shall sende yow worde.

It semythe that the worlde is alle qwaveryng; it will reboyle somwher, so that I deme yonge men shall be cherysshyd; take yowr hert to yow. I ffeer that I can nott be excusyd, but that I shall fforthe with my Lorde Hastyngs ovyr the see, but I shall sende yow worde in hast, and iff I goo, I hope nott to tary longe.

[1] [From Fenn, ii. 204.]   [2] Edmund Paston, who was in the garrison of Calais.
[3] Thomas Bourchier, Archbishop of Canterbury.—F.
[4] William, Lord Hastyngs.—F.

EDWARD IV

Item, to my brother Edmond. I am like to speke to Mestresse Dyxon in hast, and som deme that ther shall be condyssendyd, that iff E. P. come to London that hys costs shall be payed ffor.

147
FEB.

I shall hastely sende yow worde off moor thyngs.

Wretyn at London, the xiiij. day off Feverer, anno E. iiij[ti] xvj. the Fryday a for Fastyngong.

JOHN PASTON, K.

901

JOHN PASTON TO MARGARET PASTON[1]

To my ryght worchepfull modyr, Margaret Paston.

RYGHT worschepfull modyr, aftyr all dwtes of recommendacyon, in as humble wyse as I can, I beseche yow of your dayly blyssyng. Modyr, please yt yow to wett, that the cause that Dame Elizabeth Brews desyreth to mete with yow at Norwyche, and not at Langley, as I apoyntyd with yow at my last being at Mawtby, is by my meanys, for my brodyr Thomas Jermyn, whyche knowyth nought of the mate [*match*], telyth me, that the causey or ye can comme to Bokenham Fery is so over flowyn that ther is no man that may on ethe passe it, though he be ryght well horsyd; whyche is no mete wey for yow to passe over, God defend it. But, all thyngs rekynyd, it shalbe lesse cost to yow to be at Norwyche, as for a day or tweyn, and passe not, then to mete at Langly, wher every thyng is dere; and your horse may be sent home ayen the same Wednysday.

Modyr, I beseche yow for dyvers causys, that my syster Anne may come with yow to Norwyche; modyr, the mater is in a resonable good wey, and I trust with Gods mercy, and with your good help, that it shall take effect bettyr to myn avauntage then I told yow of at Mawtby; for I trow ther is

MARCH

[1] [From Fenn, ii. 220.] This letter evidently refers to a meeting arranged between Margaret Paston and Dame Elizabeth Brews on the subject of John Paston's approaching marriage, which took place in the latter part of the year 1477.

1477
MARCH 8
not a kynder woman leveing then I shall have to my modyr in lawe, if the mater take, nor yet a kynder fadyr in lawe then I shall have, though be he hard to me as yett. All the cyrcumstancys of the mater, whyche I trust to tell yow at your comyng to Norwyche, cowd not be wretyn in iiij. levys of paper, and ye know my lewd hed well i nough, I may not wryght longe, wherffor I ffery over all thyngs tyll I may awayte on yow my selff. I shall do tonnen[1] in to your place a doseyn ale, and bred acordyng, ayenst Wednysday. If Syme myght be forborn it wer well done, that he war at Norwyche on Wednysday in the mornyng at markett.

Dame Elizabeth Brewse shall lye at Jon Cookys; if it myght please yow, I wold be glad that she myght dyne in your howse on Thursday, for ther shold ye have most secret talkyng. And modyr, at the reverence of God, beware that ye be so purveyd for, that ye take no cold by the wey towards Norwyche, for it is the most peraylous marche that ever was seyn by eny manys dayes that now lyveth ; and I prey to Jesu preserve yow and yours.

Wretyn at Topcroft, the viij. day of Marche.

    Your sone and humbyll servaunt,   J. P.

902

SIR THOMAS BREWS TO SIR JOHN PASTON[2]

To my ryght wurschypfull cosyn, Syr Jhon Paston, Knyght, be this letter delivered, &c.

RYGHT wurschypfull, and my hertely welebelovyd cosyn, I recommande me unto yowe, desyring to here of yowr welefar, whech I pray God may be as contynuall good as I wolde hafe myn own. And, cosyn, the cause of my wryting un to yow, at thys tyme, is, I fele wele be my cosyn John yowr broder, that ye hafe undyrstondyng of a mater,

[1] *i.e.* cause to be tunned.
[2] [From Fenn, ii. 224.] The date of this letter, as of the last, is fixed by the subject.

272

whech is in comynicacyon tochyng a maryage, with Godds 1477 grace, to be concluded betwyx my saide cosyn yowr broder, MARCH 8 and my doghter Margery, wheche is far commonyd, and not yyt concluded, ner noght schall ner may be tyll I hafe answer from yowe agayn of yowr good will and asent to the seid mater ; and also of the obligacyon weche that I sende yowe herewith ; for, cosyn, I wold be sory to se owther my cosyn yowr broder, or my doghtr, dryvyn to leve so meane a lyff as thei schuld do yf the vj.xx.*li.* [£120], schuld be payde of ther maryage money.

And cosyn, I hafe takyn my selfe so nere in levyng of this vj.xx.*li.*, that wher as I hade layde upp an C*li.* for the maryage of a yonger doghter of myn, I hafe nowe lent the saide C*li.* and xx*li.* over that, to my cosyn yowr broder, to be paide ageyn be suche esy days as the obligacyon, weche I sende yowe herwyth, specyfyes. And, cosyn, I were ryght lothe to be stowe so mech uppon one doghter, that the other her susters schuld far the wars ; wherfor, cosyn, yf ye wyll that thys mater schall take effect undyr suche forme as my cosyn yowr broder hath wretyn unto yowe, I pray yowe put therto yowr good wylle, and sum of yowr coste, as I hafe done of myn more largely then ever I purpose to do to any tweyn of hyr susters, as God knowyth myn entent, Whom I besech to send yowe yowr levest herts desyr.

Wretyn at Topcroft, the viij. day of March, &c.

    Be your cosyn,
    THOMAS BREWS, Knight.

903

SIR JOHN PASTON TO JOHN PASTON[1]

To John Paston, Esquyer, in haste.

I HAVE received yowr letter, and yow[r] man, J. Bykerton, MARCH 9 by whom I knowe all the mater off Mestresse Brews, whyche iff it be as he seythe, I praye Godde brynge it to a goode ende.

    [1] [From Paston MSS., B.M.]

1477
MARCH 9
Item, as for thys mater of Mestresse Barly,[1] I holde it but a bare thynge. I feele weell that itt passyth nott . . . marke. I syghe hyr for yowr sake. She is a lytell onys ; she maye be a woman heer aftre, iff she be nott olde nowe ; hir person semyth xiij. yere off age ; hyr yerys, men sey, ben full xviij. She kowyth nott off the mater, I suppose ; neverthelesse she desyryd to see me as gladde as I was to se hyr.

I praye yow sende me some wryghtyng to Caleys off yowr spede with Mestresse Brewys. Bykerton tellyth me that she lovyth yow weell. Iff I dyed, I hadde lever ye hadde hyr than the Lady Wargrave ; neverthelesse she syngeth weell with an harpe.

Clopton is aferde off Sir T. Greye, for he is a wydower now late, and men sey that he is aqueyntyd with hyr of olde.

No more. Wretyn on Sondaye, the ix. daye off Marche, anno E. iiij.ti xvij° to Caleys warde.

Iff ye have Mestresse Brews, and E. Paston Mestresse Bylyngford, ye be lyke to be bretheryn.

    J. PASTON, K.

904

JOHN PASTON TO SIR JOHN PASTON[2]

Thys bylle be delyverd to Thomas Grene, good man of the George, by Powlys Wharffe, or to hys wyff, to send to Sir John Paston, wherso evere he be, at Caleys, London, or other placys.

RYGHT worchepfull sir, and my most good and kynde brodyr, in as humbyll wyse as I can, I recomand me to yow. Syr, it is so that I have, sythe John Bekurton departyd fro hens, ben at Toppcrofft at Syr Tohmas Brewse ; and as for the mater that I sent yow word of by Jon Bekurton, towchyng my sylff and Mastress Margery Brews, I am yet at no serteynte, hyr fadyr is so hard ; but I trow I have the good wyll of my lady hyr modyr and hyr ; but as the mater

[1] Fenn reads this name Burly, but I think erroneously.
[2] [From Paston MSS., B.M.]

274

provyth, I shall send yow woord, with Godes grace, in short 1477 tyme. MARCH 9

But as for John Bekurton, I prey yow dele with hym for suerte as a soudyor shold be delt with ; trust hym never the more for the bylle that I sent yow by hym, but as a man at wylde, for every thyng that he told me is not trewe ; for he departyd with ought lycence of hys mastyr, Syr Thomas Brewse, and is fere endangeryd [*indebted*] to dyvers in thys contrey. I prey God that I wryght not to yow of hym to late ; but for all thys I knowe none untrowthe in hym ; but yet I prey yow, trust hym not over myche upon my woord.

Syr, Perse Mody[1] recomandyth hym to your mastyrshep, and besecheth yow to send hym word in hast, hough he shall be demeanyd at your place at Caster ; for he is asygnyd to no body as yet, to take of mete and drynk, nor yet wher that he shall have money to paye for hys mete and drynk ; and now is the cheff replenysheing of your warenn there, the avauntage of the dove howse wer well for hym, tyll ye come hom your sylff.

Sir, I prey yow pardon me of my wryghtyng, hough so ever it be, for carpenters of my crafte that I use now, have not alderbest ther wyttys ther owne. And Jesu preserve yow.

Wretyn at Norwyche, the ix. day of Marche, anno E iiij.ti septimo decymo.   J. P.

905

SIR THOMAS BREWS[2]

MEMORANDUM. — To let my cosyn, Margaret 1477 Paston, ondyrstand that for a jontor to be mad in Sweynsthorp in hand, and for a jontore of no more but x. mark ought of Sparham, I wylle depart with CC. mark

[1] Perse Moody was a servant of Sir John Paston's, now at Caister.—F.
[2] [From Paston MSS., B.M.] This paper is evidently drawn up about the same time as the last letter. It is a draft in John Paston's handwriting, but is evidently written as in the name of Sir Thomas Brews. It is endorsed in a more modern hand : 'A determinacion of Sir Tho. Brews how much he would gyve with his daughter Margery in mariage.'

275

1477 in hand, and to give theym ther boord free as for ij. or iij. yer in serteyn, or ellys CCC. mark with ought ther boord, payable by l. mark yerly tyll the some of CCC. mark be full payed.

Item, I wyll geve CCCC. mark, payable l*li.*, in hand at the day of maryage, and l*li.* yerly tyll the some of CCCC. mark be full payed upon thes condycyons folowing.

Wher of on condycyon is thys, that I wyll lend my cosyn John Paston vj*xx.li.*, besyd hys maryage money, to pledge ought the maner of Sweynsthorpe, so that he may fynd syche a frend as wyll pay me a yen the seyd vj*xx.li.* by xx. mark a yer, so that it be not payed of the maryage money, nor of the propre goodes of my seyd cosyn John.

Or ellys, an other condycyon is thys, if it be so that my seyd cosyn John may be suffred, fro the day of hys maryage to my doughter, to take the hole profites of the maner of Sparham, besyde the maner of Sweynsthorpe, for terme of ther two lyves, and the longest of theym leveing, yet wyll I be agreable to depart with the seyd CCC. mark, payable ayen in forme above seyd [*and to geve theym ther boord for a yer or two*].[1]

And if thes or eny of the conclusyons may be takyn, I am agreable to make the bargayn swer, or ellys no more to be spokyn of.

906

JOHN PYMPE TO SIR JOHN PASTON[2]

To Master Sir John Paston, be this letter delyverid in Calis.

[MARCH] HONWRE and joye be to yow, my ryght gode master, and most assured brother ; letyng yow know that al yowre welwillers and servaunts, in these partyes, that I know, fare well, and better wold, if they mowht here of

[1] These words are crossed out with the pen.
[2] [From Fenn, ii. 226.] This letter, Fenn tells us, was endorsed under the address in a handwriting of the time which he believed to be Sir John Paston's—'Jon Pympe, xvj. die Mar'., anno E. 4, 17,' showing the date at which it was received.

yowre wellbeyng, and forthwith sum of yowre Frenche and 1477 Borgoyne tidyngs ; ffor we in these partyes be in grete drede [MARCH lest the French Kyng with sum assaults shuld in eny wise distourbe yow of yowr soft, sote [*sweet*], and sewre slepys, but as yet we no thyng can here that he so disposeth hym.

Mary, we have herd sey, that the frowys[1] of Broggys, with there hye cappes, have gyven sum of yow grete clappys, and that the fete of her armys doyng is such, that they smyte al at the mowthe, and at the grete ende of the thyeh ; but in faith we care not for yow, for we know well that ye be gode ynowh at defence. But we here sey, that they be of such corage, that they gyve yow moo strokys than ye do to them, and that they strike sorer than ye also. But I thynk that the English ladyes and jentylwomen, and the pore also, can do as well as they, and lyst not to lerne of them no thyng ; and therefor we drede lest ther hye corages shuld meve them to make yow warre also. But God defend, for by my trowth than have ye much to do ; for hit were better and more ese for to labor iij. or fowre dayes with mattokks and pykeisys to over turne yowr sande hills, as we here saye ye do ryht wurshipfully, than only one day to endure theyre fers encountrys ; so as ye myht owther gete or save yowr wurshippys by ; and loke that ye trust to have no rescow of us, for, so God me helpe, we have y nowh to do in these partyes with the same werrs. But in one thyng we preyse yowre sadnessys and discrecionys ryht much, that is, in kepyng of yowr trewse and pese with the Kyng of Fraunce, as the Kyng hath commaundid ; and a grete reson why, for hit were to much for yow to have werre with all the world at onys ; ffor the werre a fore seid kepith yow blameles ; ffor every resonable man wetyth well, that hit is to much for eny pepyll levyng to do bothe at onys.

Syr, as for the more parts off my thowht, I praye yow recomaunde me un to yowr self, prayyng yow that y may contynew in such case as yowr godenes hath taken me of old, and if ye lyst to send eny tydyngs, or other thyng to the

[1] *Frau's, i.e.* women. The writer's pleasantry in this passage is certainly rather coarse.

1477 partyes that were wont to warme theym by yowr fyre, in feith [MARCH] I shall do yowr erand.

And as for barley, hit is of the same pryce that hit was wont to be of, and is the most sure corne, and best enduryng that may be. And, syr, where that sumtyme was a lytyll hole in a wall, is now a dore large ynowh and esy passage, whereof ye were the deviser, and have thank for yowr labor of sum partyes, but no thyng lastyth evyr. Y mene that y trow, my passage shall hastyly faile me, and the dore shalbe shet up agayne, lesse than Fortun be agreable to have my counseile kept ; for not long ago, makyng my entre at that passage, I saw a sparow that useth those ewrys [*eireys*], and I saw her sytt so stille that y cowde not endure, but y must neds shote her, and so, God me help, I smote her, I trow evyn to the hert ; and so I drede me lest owther the barley wyll ete the sparow, or ells the sparow wyll ete the barley, but as yet all is well, but reson shewt me that hit must neds fayle by contynewauns, lesse than I forsake bothe the sparow and the barley also.[1]

Syr, I have thank for the shew that I onys made of yow and daily gramercy, and ye theire prayer.

Syr, forthemore I beseche yow, as ye wyll do eny thyng for me, that ye se o day for my sake, and for yowr own plesure, all the gode hors in Caleys, and if ther be among theym eny pric[2] horse of deds, that is to sell, in especiall that he be well trottyng of his owne corage, with owte fors[3] of sporis, and also a steryng [*stirring*] hors if he be, he is the better ; I pray yow send me word of his color, deds, and corage, and also of his price, feynyng as ye wold by hym yowrself, and also I wold have hym sumwhat large, not with the largest ; but no smalle hors, as more than a dowble hors ; prayyng yow above all thyngs to have this in remembrauns, and that hastily as may be, for ther is late promysed me help to such an entent,

[1] Perhaps this enigmatical passage may have reference to the Mrs. Barly mentioned in No. 903.
[2] In the modern version, Fenn reads here, 'any prized horse of deeds,' a reading which seems to me questionable.
[3] 'Fort' in Fenn, which is probably a misprint, as the word is spelled 'force' on the opposite page.

and I wote not how long hit shall endure ; and therfor I be- 1477 seche yow send me word by tyme. [MARCH

I trow the Frenshe men have taken up al the gode hors in Pycardye, and also they be wont to be hevy hors in labor, and that I love not, but a hevy hors of flesh, and lyht of corage y love well, for y love no hors that wyll al way be lene and slender like grehounds. God kepe yow.

Yowr, J. PYMPE.

Y pray yow to recomaund me to my cosyn Sir John Scot and all his, in especiall Mastres Benyngfeld.[1]

907

JOHN PYMPE TO SIR JOHN PASTON[2]

To Syr John Paston, Knyht, be this delyverid in Calice.

MASTER Paston, I recommaund me to yow ; and by [MARCH cause that I have wrytyn to yow iij. long letteres ; which as yet be answereles, I wote not whether that the length of mater acumbred yow, or elles the simpylnes of the effect displesid yow, or elles that ye have utterly refusid the proferes of my pore servyce and frendeship ; but which of these soo ever hit be, hit hevyeth me.

Syr, hit nedith not, I trow, to send yow the tidynges of these partyes, how be hit I have thryes send yow such as here were, in entent that ye shuld send us of yowres ; but as long as my lord and yowres is there, ye can not faile to have the certeynte of all owre English aventures, which is grete ese to yowr frendes and servauntes in this contre, for so much as they may make her letteres shorter by so much.

Syr, at the wrytyng of this letter, I was in Kent, where all thyng that I rejoisid, I wishid yow part of, or all ; and as for

[1] Margaret, daughter of Sir John Scot, and wife to Edmund Bedingfeld.—F.
[2] [From Paston MSS., B.M.] This letter was probably written about the end of March 1477, as the first of the three which preceded (No. 906) was received by Sir John in Calais on the 16th of the month.

THE PASTON LETTERS

myself, I am styll yowr servaunt and bedeman, and so am bownd to be so sore and sewrely, that I can not unbynde me.

Syr, this is the v. letter that I have sent yow, whereyn thys entent that folowyth was all wayes on, that is to say, that hit plesid yow sum on day to take so much labour for me for to se the jentyllest hors in Calice that is to be sold, and to lett me know of his colowre, dedes, and price, remembryng that he be also large as mesure wyll, for I love no small hors, nor hors that wyll evyr be lene and slendyr ; but I wold have hym hye truttyng, if hit wylbe, and if he be styryng with all, he shall plese me the better, for I wuld have hym all for the plesur, and for the werre, but if he myht be for bothe. Veryly ther is no tidynges on that side the se, safe only the welfare of yow and all other there, that I wuld so fayne here of as of a jentyll trottyng hors that were lyght and pleasaunt in dedes, if eny such be there. Flemysh hors I thenk ye have y nowh that wyll play for a myle or ij., but such we have here also ; how be hit I pray yow send me word of yowre store, and be sewre of the price, if ye like eny, or elles let sum man for yow.

No more, but God kepe yow, prayyng yow to recommaund me to my cosyn Syr John Scot, and to Syr Tyry Robsert. Let the letter be sent to the godewif of yowr loggyng. By yowr JOHN PYMPE.

908

JOHN PYMPE TO SIR JOHN PASTON [1]

*To Master Sir John Paston, Knight, be this
letter delyvered in Calis.*

FRESH amorouse sihts of cuntreys ferre and straunge
  Have all fordoone [2] your old affeccion ;
In plesurys new, your hert dooth score and raunge
So hye and ferre, that like as the fawcon

[1] [From Fenn, ii. 234.] We may as well place this letter—the only remaining one of the series that has been preserved—immediately after the other two. John Pympe seems to have been a very industrious correspondent, and the art of writing, in prose or verse, came to him very easily. [2] Destroyed.—F.

280

EDWARD IV

Which is alofte, tellith scorne to loke a down
On hym that wont was her feders to pyke and ympe ; [1]
Ryht so forgotyn ye have your pore Pympe,

That wrytith, sendith, and wisshith alday your wele
More than his owne ; but ye ne here, ne se,
Ne sey, ne send, and evyr I write and sele
In prose and ryme, as well as hit will be.
Sum evyll tong, I trow, myss sayeth of me
And ells your fast and feithfull frendelynes
Ye thenk mysspent on such as I, I gesse.

I wyll abate my customable concourse,
To yow so costuouse, [2] whan so evyr ye com agayn,
Which that I fele of reson, by the course
Of my proferid servyce, hath made yow so unfayne ;
For veryly the water of the fowntayne
With brede only forthwith yowre presens
Me shuld content much more than your expense.

But ay deme I thus that Fortun hath hyryd yow,
For she but late of sorowys moo than many
Hath rakyd un to myn hert an hepe more than a moowe,
And wuld that ye shuld ley thereon on hye
Your hevy unkyndenes to make hit fast to lye,
And God knowth well hit cannot long lye there
But hit wyll bryng me to the chirch bere.

Take hit away therefore, y praye yow fayre,
For hardyly my hert beryth hevy y nowh,
For there is Sorow at rest as in hys chayre,
Fixid so fast with hys prikks rowh,
That in gode feith I wote not whan I lowh, [3]
For, Master Paston, the thyng whereon my blisse
Was holly sette, is all fordoone, I wysse.

By your JOHN PYMPE,
thes beyng the vj. letter that I have send yow.

[1] A term in Falconry, signifying the adding a piece to a feather in a hawk's wing.—F. [2] Expensive.
[3] Laughed ? Fenn in his modern version reads 'when I love.'

281

THE PASTON LETTERS

Alway prayyng yow to remembre the hors that I have in every letter wryten for ; as thus, that hit wuld plese yow to undrestond who hath the gentyllest hors in trottyng and steryng that is in Calis, and if he be to sell, to send me word of hys pris, largenesse, and colour. Hytt is told me, that the Master Porter hath a coragiouse ronyd hors, and that he wuld putt hym away by cause he is daungerous in companye ; and of that I force [care] not, so that he be nott chorlissh at a spore, as plungyng ; and also I sett not by hym, but if he trotte hye and gentilly. No more, but God kepe yow.

JOHN PYMPE.

909

SIR JOHN PASTON TO JOHN PASTON [1]

To hys weell belovyd brother, John Paston, Esquyer.

I RECOMANDE me to yow, letyng yow weete that I receyvyd a letter of yowres by Edward Hensted ij. dayes aftre that Whetley was departyd from me, whyche he hadde forgetyn in hys caskett, as he seyde, wheroff I sholde have sent yow answer by Whetley, iff I had hadde it tofore he wente, notwithstandyng I am ryght lothe to wryghte in that mater offte ; for for a conclusion I wrote to my moodre by Peerse Moody alle that I myght and wolde doo ther in. Ye have also nowe wretyn ageyn. Yow neede nott to praye me to doo that myght be to yowr profyght and worship, that I myght doo ofter than ones, or to late me weete theroff ; for to my power I wolde do for yow, and take as moche peyne for yowr weell, and remembre itt when per case ye sholde nott thynke on it yowr selffe. I wolde be as gladde that one gaffe yow a maner of xx*li.* by yeer, as iff he gave it to my selff by my trowthe.

Item, wher ye thynke that I may with concience recompence it ageyn on to owr stokke off other londys that I have

[1] [From Paston MSS., B.M.] This letter is clearly written in answer to an application by John Paston to his brother to aid him in making arrangements with Sir Thomas Brews in the spring of 1477. Although the signature is lost, the handwriting is that of Sir John Paston.
282

EDWARD IV

off that valywe in fee symple, it is so that Snaylwell, by my grauntefadres will ones, and by my fadris will sceconderely, is entaylyd to the issyw of my fadres body.

Item, as for Sporle xx*li.* by yeer, I hadde ther off butt xx. marke by yere, whyche xx. marke by yeer and the x. marke ovyr, I have endangeryd, as ye weell knowe off that bargayne, whyche, iff itt be nott redemyd, I most recompence some other maner off myne to one off my bretheryn for the seyde x. marke, ovyr xx. marke that longyth to me ; wherffor I kepe the maner off Runham. Than have I fe symple londe the maner of Wynterton with Bastwyk and Billys, whyche in alle is nott xx. marke by yeer, whyche is nott to the valywe off the maner off Sparham. And as for Castre, it weer noo convenyent londe to exchange for suche a thyng, nor it weer not polesy for me to sett that maner in suche case for alle maner of happis. I nede nott to make thys excuse to yowe, but that yowr mynde is troblyd. I praye yow rejoyse nott yowr sylffe to moche in hope to opteyne thynge that alle yowr freendys may nott ease yow off ; for if my moodre were dysposyd to gyve me and any woman in Ingelande the best maner that she hathe, to have it to me and my wyffe, and to the heyres off our too bodyes begotyn, I wolde nott take it off hyr, by God.

Stablysshe your selffe upon a goode grownde, and grace shall folowe. Yowr mater is ferre spoken off, and blowyn wyde, and iff it preve noo better, I wolde that it had never be spoken off. Also that mater noysyth me that I am so onkynde that I lett alle togedre. I thynke notte a mater happy, nor weell handelyd, nor poletykly dalte with, when it can never be fynysshyd with owte an inconvenyence ; and to any suche bargayne I kepe never to be condescentyng, ner of cowncell. Iffe I weer att the begynnyng of suche a mater, I wolde have hopyd to have made a better conclusyon, if they mokke yow notte. Thys mater is drevyn thus ferforthe with owte my cowncell, I praye yow make an ende with owte my cowncell. Iffe it be weell, I wolde be glad ; iff it be oderwyse, it is pite. I praye yow troble me no moore in thys mater. . . . [1]

[1] The lower part of this letter seems to have been cut off, and how much is lost does not appear.

283

910

JOHN PASTON AND MARGERY BREWS[1]

1477 MEMORANDUM.—To kepe secret fro my moder that the bargayn is full concludyd.

Item, to let hyr have fyrst knowlage that in the chapell, wher as ye wold had ben no book nye by x. myle, that whyn Mastyr Brews seyd that he wold shortly have eyther more lond in joyntour then Sweynsthorp and x. mark ought of Sparham, or ellys that some frend of myne shold paye the vj^{xx}li., so that it shold not be payed of the maryage money, that then I sware on a book to hym that I wold never of my mocyon endanger moder nor broder ferther then I had done ; for I thought that my modyr had done myche for me to geve me the maner of Sparham in syche forme as she had done. But Mastyr Breus wyll not agre, with ought that my mastress hys doughter and I be mad swer of it now in hand, and that we may take the hole profytes, what so ever fortune.

Item, to enforme my moder that if so be that we may be pute in possessyon of all the hole maner duryng oure two lyves, and the lengest of leveing, that then Mastyr Brews wyll geve me in maryage with my mastresse hys doughter CCCC. markes, payable in hand l$li.$, and so yerly l$li.$ tyll the some of CCCC. mark bew full payed.

Item, that wher as he had leyd up C$li.$ for the maryage of a yonger doughter of hys, he wylle lend me the same C$li.$ and xx$li.$ more, to pledge ought my lond, and he to be payed ayen hys C$li.$ and xx$li.$ by x$li.$ by yer.

Item, to avyse my modyr that she brek not for the yerly valew of Sparham above the x. mark dwryng hyr lyve.

[1] [From Paston MSS., B.M.] This paper, which is in John Paston's hand, was evidently written about the same time as the letter immediately following, in which it is mentioned that Margaret Paston had given up the manor of Sparham to her son. The paper is endorsed in a more modern hand : ' Notes touching the mariage betwene Jo. Paston, Ar', and Margery Brews.'

911

SIR JOHN PASTON TO MARGARET PASTON[1]

To my ryght worshypfull moodre, Margret Paston.

PLEASE it yow to weete, that I have receyvyd yowr letter, **1477** wherein is remembryd the gret hurte, that by liklihod **MARCH 2** myght ffalle to my brother, iff so be that thys matter betwyn hym and Sir Thomas Brewses doghtre take nott effecte ; wheroff I wolde be as sory as hym selffe reasonably ; and also the welthy and convenyent marriage that scholde be iff it take effecte ; wheroff I wolde be as gladde as any man ; and ame better content nowe, that he scholde have hyr, than any other, that evyr he was hertoffoor abowte to have hadde, consyderyd hyr persone, her yowthe, and the stok that she is comyn offe, the love on bothe sydes, the tendre ffavor that she is in with hyr ffader and mooder, the kyndenesse off hyr ffadr and moodr to hyr in departyng with hyr, the ffavor also, and goode conceyte that they have in my brother, the worshypfull and vertuous dysposicion off hyr ffadr and moodr, whyche pronostikyth that, of lyklihod, the mayde sholde be vertuous and goode ; all which concyderyd, and the necessary relyffe that my brother most have, I mervayle the lesse, that ye have departyd, and gevyn hym the maner off Sperham, in such fforme as I have knowleche off by W. Gornay, Lomner, and Skypwyth ; and I ame ryght gladde to se in yow suche kyndenesse on to my brother as ye have doon to hym ; and wolde by my trowthe lever than C$li.$ that it weer ffee symple londe, as it is entaylyd, whyche by liklyhood scholde prosper with hym and hys blode the better in tyme to come, and sholde also never cause debate in owr bloode in tyme to come, whyche Godde dyffende, ffor that weer onnaturell.

Item, another inconvenyence is, wher as I undrestande that the maner is gevyn to my brother, and to hys wyff, and to the issywe bytwen them bygoten ; iff the case weer soo, that he

[1] [From Fenn, ii. 238.]

1477 and she hadde yssywe togedr a dowtr or moo, and hys wyffe
MARCH 28 dyed, and he maried afftr another, and hadde issywe a sone, that sone sholde have noon londe, and he beyng hys ffadres heyr, and ffor th'enconvenyence that I have knowe let in ur[1] in case lyke, and yit enduryth in Kente, by tweyn a jentylman and his suster, I wolde ye toke the advyce off yowr concell in thys poynt, and that that is past yow by wryghtyng or by promise, I deme verrely in yow, that ye dyd it off kyndenesse, and in eschwyyng off a moor yll that myght befall.

Item, wher as it pleasyth yow that I sholde ratefye, grawnt, or conferme the seyd gyfte on to my brother, it is so, that with myn honeste I may nott, and ffor other cawses. The Pope will suffre a thyng to be usyd, but he will nott lycence nor grant it to be usyd nor don, and soo I. My brother John knowyth myn entent weel i now heer to ffoor in this mater ; I will be ffownde to hym as kynde a brother as I may be.

Item, iff it be soo that Sir T. Brews and hys wyff thynke that I wolde troble my brother and hys wyff in the seid maner, I can ffynde no meene to putte them in sywerte ther off, but iff it neede, to be bownde in an obligacion with a condicion that I shalle nott trowble ner infefe them therin.

Item, I thynke that she is made sywer i now in astate in the londe, and that off ryght I deme they shall make noone obstacles at my wryghtyng, ffor I hadde never none astate in the londe, ner I wolde nott that I had hadde.

No mor to yow at thys tyme, but Allmyghty God have yow in kepyng.

Wretyn at Caleys, the xxviij. daye of Marche, anno E. iiij. xvij°.

By yowr sone,   J. PASTON K.

[1] In ure, *i.e.* in practice.

912

SIR JOHN PASTON TO JOHN PASTON[1]

To John Paston, Esquyer.

RYGHT worshypfull and hertely belovyd brother, I **1477** recomaunde me to yow, letyng yow weete, that as **APRIL 1** by Pyrse Moody, when he was heer, I hadde no leyser to sende answer in wryghtyng to yow, and to my cosyne Gurnaye, off yowr letteris ; butt ffor a conclusion ye shalle ffynde me to yow as kynde as I maye be, my concience and worshyp savyd, whiche, when I speke with yow and them, ye bothe shall weell undrestande. And I praye God sende yow as goode speede in that mater as I wolde ye hadde, and as I hope ye shall have er thys letter come to yow ; and I praye God sende yow yssywe betwyne yow, that maye be as honorable as ever was any off your ancestris and theris, wheroff I wolde be as gladde in maner as off myn owne. Wherffor I praye yow sende me worde how ye doo, and iff Godde ffortune me to doo weell, and be off any power, I woll be to Sir Thomas Brewse, and my lady hys wyffe, a verry sone in lawe ffor yowr sake, and take them as ye doo, and doo ffor them as iff I weer in case like with them as ye bee. No moor, but Jesus have yow in kepyng.

Wretyn at Caleys, the xiiij. daye off Aprill, anno E. iiij. xvij°.

As ffor tydyngs her, the Frenshe Kynge hathe gothen many off the towns off the Duk of Burgoyne, as Seynt Quyntyns, Abevyle, Motrell ; and now off late he hathe goten Betoyne and Hedynge with the castell ther, whyche is one off the ryallest castells off the worlde ; and on Sonday at evyn the Ameralle off Fraunce leyde seege at Boloyne ; and thys daye it is seyde, that the Frenshe Kynge shalle come thyddr ; and thys nyght it is seyde, that ther was a vysion seyne abowte the walls of Boloyne, as it hadde ben a woman

[1] [From Fenn, ii. 244.]

77
- 14

with a mervylowse lyght ; men deme that Owr Lady ther will shewe hyrselff a lover to that towne. God fforfende that it weer Frenshe, it weer worthe xl.m^{l}.li. [£40,000] that it wer Englyshe.   J. PASTON, K.

913

MARGARET PASTON TO DAME ELIZABETH BREWS[1]

To the ryght wurchypfull and my verry good [*lady and cosyn, Dame Elyzabeth*][2] *Brews.*

E 11

RYGHT wurcheful and my cheff lady and cosyn, as hertly as I can, I recomaunde me to yow. Madam, lyeketh yow to undyrstand that the cheff cause of my wrytyng to yow at thys season ys thys : I wot well yt ys not unremembred with yow the large comunycacyon that dyvers tymes hathe ben had towchyng the maryage of my cosyn Margery, yowyr dowghter, and my son John ; of whyche I have ben as glad, and now late wardes as sory, as evyr I was for eny maryage in myn lyve. And wher or in whom the defawte of the breche ys, I can have no perfyte knowlage ; but, madam, yf yt be in me or eny of myn, I prey yow assygne a day when my cosyn yowyr husbond and ye thynk to be at Norwych to wardes Salle, and I wyll com theder to yow ; and I thynk or ye and I departe, that the defawte schall be knowe where yt ys, and also that, with yowyr advyse and helpe and myn to gedyrs, we schall take some wey that yt schal not breke ; for yf yt dyd, yt wer non honoure to neyther partyes, and in cheff to them in whom the defawte ys, consyderyng that it ys so ferre spokun.

And, madam, I prey yow that I may have perfyte knowlage be my son Yelverton,[3] berar here of, when thys metyng schall be, yf ye thynk it expedyent, and the soner the better,

¹ [From Paston mss., B.M.] This is another letter relative to the negotiations for the marriage of John Paston and Margery Brews, which took place in 1477.
² The words bracketed are indistinct, but we follow Fenn's reading.
³ William Yelverton, grandson of Judge Yelverton, now married to Anne Paston, one of Margaret's daughters.

288

in eschewyng of worsse ; for, madam, I know well, yf yt be not concludyd in ryght schort tyme, that as for my son he entendyth to doo ryght well by my cosyn Margery, and not so well by hym sylf, and that schuld be to me, nor I trust to yow no gret plesur, yf yt so fortunyd, as God deffend, Whom I beseche to send yow your levest desyers.   1477 JUNE 11

Madam, I besech yow that I may be recomawndyd by this bylle to my cosyn yowr husbond, and to my cosyn Margery, to whom I supposyd to have gevyn an othyr name or thys tyme.

Wretyn at Mawteby, on Seynt Barnaby is Day.

      By your,   MARGARET PASTON.

914

SIR JOHN PASTON TO JOHN PASTON[1]

To John Paston, Esquyer.

I RECOMAND me to yow, letyng yow weete that I have spoken to Herry Colett,[2] and entretyd hym in my best wyse ffor yow, soo that at the last he is agreyd to a resonable respyght ffor the xv*li.* that ye sholde have payd hym at Mydsomer, as he seyth, and is gladde to do yow ease or plesyr in all that he maye ; and I tolde hym that ye wolde, as I supposyd, be heer at London, herr nott long to, and than he lokyth afftr that ye sholde come see hym, ffor he is sheryff, and hathe a goodely hows.   JUNE 23

Item, my Lady off Oxennfforth[3] lokyth afftr yow and Arblaster bothe.

My Lord off Oxennfford[4] is nott comen in to Inglonde that I can perceyve, and so the goode lady hathe nede off helpe and cowncell howe that she shall doo.

¹ [From Fenn, ii. 248.]
² Sir Henry Colet was Lord Mayor of London in 1486.—F.
³ Margaret, daughter of Richard Neville, Earl of Salisbury ; she was, during the imprisonment of her lord, in great distress.—F.
⁴ John de Vere, Earl of Oxford, was at this time a prisoner in the Castle of Hammes, in Picardy ; what expectation there was of his coming into England at this time I know not.—F.

VOL. V.—T   289

-77
E 23

No moor at thys tyme, butt God have yow in kepyng.

Wretyn att London on Seynt Awdryes Daye, anno E. iiij^{d} xvij°.

Tydyngs butt that yisterdaye my Lady Marqueys off Dorset,[1] whych is my Lady Hastyngs dowtr, hadyd chylde a sone.

Item, my Lord Chamberleyn is comyn hyddr ffro Caleys, and redyn with the Kynge to Wyndeshor, and the Kyng will be here ageyn on Mondaye.   J. P., K.

915

JOHN PASTON TO MARGARET PASTON[2]

E 29

RYGHT worchepfull and my most good and kynd moder. Moder, in as humbyll wyse as I can or may, I recomand me to yow, and beseche yow of your dayly blyssyng. Moder, please it yow to undyrstond that tyll thys day Dame Elyzabeth Brews hathe ben so syke that she myght nevyr, sythe she cam to Salle, have leyser to comon of my mater with Master Brews tyll thys day ; and thys day with gret peyn, I thynk the rather because Heydon[3] was ther, the mater was comond, but other answer than she hathe sent yow in hyr lettre closed her in can she not have of hyr husbond. Wherfor, modyr, if it please yow, myn advyse is to send hyr answer ayen in thys forme folowing, of some other manys hand.

[*Margaret Paston to Dame Elyzabeth Brews.*]

'RYGHT worchepfull and my verry good lady and cosyn,

¹ Cecily, wife of Thomas Grey, Marquis of Dorset, was great grand-daughter and heir of William Bonvile, Lord Bonvile, who was beheaded by order of Margaret of Anjou, after the second battle of St. Albans in 1461.
² [From Paston mss., B.M.] This letter, with the two subjoined, are drafts written on the same paper in John Paston's hand. They must belong to the year 1477, being on the same subject, already so often referred to, of the negotiations for John Paston's marriage. Fenn had added addresses to all these letters, and a signature to the first, which are not in the original ms.
³ John Heydon of Baconsthorpe, who died on the 27th September 1479.—Inquisition p.m., 19 Edw. IV., No. 72.

290

as hertly as I can, I recomand me to yow. And, madam, I am ryght sory, if it myght be otherwyse, of the dysease, as I undyrstand by the berer herof, that my cosyn your husband and ye also have had a season, whyche I prey God soone to redresse to your bothe easeis. And, madam, I thank yow hertly that ye have remembred the mater to my cosyn your husband, that I spak with you of at syche tyme as I was last with you at Norwyche, to my gret comfort. And I wyse, madam, I am ryght sory that John Paston is no more fortunate then he is in that mater ; for, as I undyrstand by your lettyr, my cosyn your husbond wyll geve but an Cli., whyche is no money lyek for syche a joyntore as is desyred of my son, thow hys possybylyte wer ryght easy. But, madam, when I mad that large grant in the maner of Sperham that I have mad to hym and my cosyn your doughter, he told me of an other some that he shold have with hyr then of an Cli. He hathe befor thys be wont to tell me none untrowthe ; and what I shall deme in thys mater, I can not sey, for me thynkyth if more then an Cli. wer promysyd on to hym by my cosyn your husbond and yow, that ye wold not lett to geve it hym, with ought so wer that I or he abryggyd eny thyng of our promess, whyche I wot well neyther I or he intend to do, if I may undyrstand that hys seying to me was trowthe, and that it may be performyd ; but wyst I that he told me otherwyse then my cosyn yowr husbond and ye promysed hym, to deseyve me of Sparham, by my trowthe, thow he have it, he shall lese as myche for it, iff I leve, and that shall he well undyrstand the next tyme I se hym.   1477 JUNE 29

'And, madam, I pray God send us good of thys mater, for as for hys broder Sir John also, I sent ones to hym for it to have mad good the same graunt that I grauntyd yow with hys assent, to them and to ther issu of ther ij. bodyes lawfully comyng, and he dyd not ther in as I desyred hym. And ther for I prey yow pardon me for sendyng on to hym eny more ; for, madam, he is my sone, and I can not fynd in my hert to becom a dayly petycyoner of hys, sythe he hathe denyed me onys myn axing. Peraventure he had ben better to have performyd my desyer ; and what hys answer was on to me,

291

THE PASTON LETTERS

1477 JUNE 29

John Paston can tell yow as well as I. But, madam, ye ar a moder as well as I, wher I prey tak it non other wyse bot well, that I may not do by John Paston, as ye wyll have me to do; for, madam, thow I wold he dyd well, I have to purvey for more of my chylder then hym, of whyche some be of that age, that they can tell me well inow that I dele not evenly with theym to geve John Paston so large, and theym so lytyll; and, madam, for syche grwgys and other causys, I am ryght sory that the graunte is knowyn that I have mad, with ought it myght take effect. And therfor, madam, fro hensforthe I remyght all thyng to yowr dyscressyon, besechyng yow, the rather for my sake, to be my son Johnis good lady; and I prey God preserve yow to Hys plesure, send yow hastyly yowr hele ayen, and my cosyn yowr husbond also, to whom I prey yow that I may hertly be recomandyd, and to my cosyns Margery and Margaret Byllyngforthe.

'Wretyn at Mawtby, on Seynt Petrys Day.
'Yowr, MARGARET PASTON.'

'An other lettyr to me that I may shewe.

'I gret yow well, and send you Godes blessyng and myn, letyng yow wet that I undyrstand well by my cosyn, Dame Elyzabeth Brewsys lettyr, whyche I sende yow her with, wherby ye may undyrstand the same, that they intend not to performe thos proferys that ye told me they promysyd yow, trustyng that ye told me none other wyse then was promysed yow. Wherfor I charge yow on my blyssyng that ye be well ware how ye bestow your mynd with ought ye have a substance wher upon to leve; for I wold be sory to wet yow myscary; for if ye do, in your defawt looke never aftyr helpe of me. And also I wold be as sory for hyr as for eny gentywoman leveing, in good feythe; wherfor I warne yow, be ware in eny wyse; and look ye be at Mawtby with me as hastyly as ye can, and then I shall tell yow more. And God kepe yow.
'Wretyn at Mawtby, on Seynt Petrys Day.
'Your modyr, M. P.'

292

EDWARD IV

916

SIR JOHN PASTON TO MARGARET PASTON [1]

To the ryght worshypfull Mestresse Margret Paston.

1477 AUG.

PLEASE it yow to weete that I have receyvyd yowr letter, wretyn the Tywesdaye nexte afftre Seynt James Daye, wherin ye desyre me to remembre Kokett, and also to be helpyng to my brother Johnes mariage. As for Kokett, as God helpe me, I knowe nott yitt the meanes possible that I myght paye hym by thatt daye, ffor thoos materis that be off grettest wyght and charge, and that stonde nerrest my weell, that is to seye, the sywerte off the maner off Castre, and the mater betwen Anne Hault and me shall, with Goddes grace, thys terme be at a perffyght ende, whyche will charge me fferther than I have mony as yitt, or lyke to have byffor that tyme, off myne owne, and, as God helpe me, I wote nott where to borow.

Item, I most paye with in thys iij. yeer iiijᶜ [400] marke to Towneshende, or ellis fforffett the maner off Sporle, and thus my charges be gretter than I maye a weye with, concidryd suche helpe as I have; and iff it ffortunyd that I fforffetyd the maner off Sporle, ye weer never lyke to se me myry afftre, so God helpe me. Ye gave me ones xxli. to it wardes, and ye promyttyd as moche, whyche I receyvyd, and synnys off my mony off seide maner growyng that come to yowr handys was receyvyd by yow ageyn the seyd xlli., whyche, when Kokett scholde be payed, was nott yowr ease to departe wyth. Neverthelesse ye may yitt, when yow lyketh, perfforme yowr sayde gyffte and promyse, and thys somme owyng to Kokett is nott so moche; neverthelesse I suppose that ye be nott so weell purveyed. Wherffor, iff it please yow at yowr ease her afftre to performe yowr seyde gyffte and promyse, so that I may have it with in a yer or ij. or yitt iij., I sholde per case gete yowr obligacion to yow ageyn ffrom Kokett, and he pleasyd.

[1] [From Paston MSS., B.M.]

293

THE PASTON LETTERS

1477 AUG. 7

Wherffor I beseche yow that I maye have an assyngnement of suche dettes as been owyng yow, payeable at leyser off suche mony as is owyng ffor the woode at Basyngham or ellys wher; ffor, so God helpe me, I sholde ellys wylfully ondoo myselffe, wherin I beseche yow to sende me an answer in hast.

Item, as towchyng the mariage off my brother John, I have sente hym myn advyce, and tolde hym wherto he shall truste, and I have grauntyd hym as moche as I maye. I wolde that I weer at on communycacion atwyen them for hys sake, whyche I sholde if I myght. As for my comyng home, I ame nott yitt sertayn therof; I shalle hast me as faste as I canne, with the grace of God, Who have yow in Hys kepyng.

I beseche yow to remembre the premyssis, and to helpe me, and with Goddes grace, thes ij. materis above wretyn, bothe of Castre and Mestresse Anne Hault, shall be endyd to my profyth and rest, and moor ovyr, er awghte longe to, with Goddes grace, the maner of Sporle to be owte of danger; promyttyng yow that I shall doo in Kokettes mater as moche as is possible for me to doo to yower plesyr. It shall never neede to prykk nor threte a free horse. I shall do whatt I can.

Wretyn the Thorysdaye next byffore Seynt Lawrence, anno E. iiijᵗⁱ xvij.

By yowre sone,
JOHN PASTON, K.

917

MARGARET PASTON TO SIR JOHN PASTON [1]

AUG. 11

YT ys soo that I undyrstonde be yowyr letter wretyn the Thyrsday nexte be fore Seynt Lauerons, that ze wulde have knowlage how that I wuld be demenyd in Cokettes mater; qweche I send you here undyr wretyn. I

[1] [From Paston MSS., B.M.] This letter is not addressed, the original being a corrected draft, but there is no doubt it was written to Sir John Paston in reply to the last. It is endorsed in a more modern hand: 'Copia literæ Jo. Paston, mil., a matre sua.'

294

EDWARD IV

1477 AUG.

putte yow in certeyn that I wull nevyr pay him peny of that duty that ys owyng to hym, thow he sue me for yt, not of myn owyn pursse; for I wul nat be compellyd to pay yowyr dettes azens my well, and thow I wuld, I may nat. Where fore I a wyse yow to see me savyd harmelesse azens hym for yowyr owyn a wauntage in tyme cumyng, for yf I pay yt, at longe wey ze xall bere the losse.

And where as ze wryte to me that I gave yow xxli., and promysyd odyr xxli., that ys nat soo, for I wutte wele yf I had soo doon, ze wuld nat assynyd me be yowyr letterys of yowyr owyn hande wrytyng, the whech I have to schew, that I schuld resseyve a zen the same summe of Wylliam Pecok, and of yowyr fermores, and byars of yowyr wood of Sporle; and take this for a full conclusyon in thys mater, for yt xall be noon othyr wyse for me than I wryte here to yow.

I mervel meche that ze have delte azen soo symply wyth Sporle, consyderyng that ze and yowyr frendys had so meche to doo for to geetyt yow azen onys; and ye havyng noo gretter materes of charge than ze have had sythyn yt was laste pleggyt owte, yt causyth me to be in gret dowte of yow what yowyr dysposycion wul be here aftyr for swheche lyfelood as I have be dysposyd before this tyme to leve yow after my decesse. For I thynke veryly that ye wulde be dysposyd here aftyr to selle or sette to morgage the lond that ye xulde have after me yowyr modyr as gladdly and rathyr than that lyfe lood that ye have after yowyr fadyr. Yt grevyth me to thynke upon yowyr gydeyng after the greet good that ze have had in yowyr rewle sythyn yowyr fadyr deyyd, whom God assoyle, and soo symply spendyt as yt hath ben. God geve yow grace to be of sadde and good dysposyn here after to Hys plesans, and comforte to me, and to all yowyr frendys, and to yowyr wurchyp and profyte here after.

And as for yowyr brothyr Wylliam, I wuld ye xulde purvey for hys fyndyng, for as I told yow the laste tyme that ye ware at home, I wuld no lenger fynde hym at my cost and charge; hys boord and hys scole hyer ys owyng sythyn Seynt Thomas Day afore Cristmesse, and he hathe greet nede of gownys and odyr gere that whare necessary for hym to have

295

1477
G. 11 in haste. I wulde ze xulde remembyrt and purvey them, for as for me, I wul nat. I thynke ze sette butte lytyl be myn blessyng, and yf ye dede, ye wulde a desyyrd yt in yowyr wrytyng to me. God make yow a good man to Hys plesans.

Wretyn at Mawteby, the day after Seynt Laucrons, the yere and the renge of Kyng E. the iiij[te] the xvij. zere.

Be yowyr Modyr.

918

EDMUND BEDYNGFELD TO SIR JOHN PASTON[1]

Un to the ryght wurschepful Sir John Paston, Knyght.

G. 17 MASTER PASTON, after all dew recomandacion, and herty dissire to here of your good hele, plese yt you to wete I have spoken with Sir John of Medilton as wel as I cowde, and yt had ben for myself, for his hoby that ye dissired, and tolde hym he myght wel forbere hym nowe in as moche as Mastres Jane was ded, and that yt is a great cost for hym to kepe moo hors than he nedyth ; and he answered me, that he wold selle hym with good will, but ther shuld no man bie hym under x*li.* Flemesch ;[2] and I offered hym in your name, x. marke, for he wold not here of none other ambelyng horse, that ye myght geve hym therfore. And also my lord dissired to have bowte hym for the Lord Schauntrell that is cheff capteyn of Seynt Omers ; and he wold no lesse lete my lord have hym than x*li.* and so my lord bowte another, and gave hym the seide lord, for he thoughte this to dere ; neverthelesse he wol not selle hym to no man under that mony, that he sette hym on, and so ye may bye your plesur in hym and ye lest ; for otherwyse he wol not doo for you, as I conseve.

[1] [From Fenn, ii. 250.] The events referred to in this letter prove that it was written in the year 1477.
[2] Between £5 and £6 English, and equal in value to upwards of £20 at this present time, apparently a great price for a hobby.—F.

296

And as for tydyngs in theyse partyes, the Frenche Keng 1477 leyzth at sege at Seynt Omers, on the one side of the town a AUG. 17 myle of, but he hath no gret ordenaunce ther ; and they of the town skyrmysh with them every day, and kepe a passage halff a myle with oute the town ; and the French Keng hath brenned all the townys, and fayre abbeys, that were that way aboute Seynt Omers, and also the cornes weche ar there. And also, as yt ys seide for serteyn, the French Keng hath brenned Cassell, that ys myn hoold Lady of Burgeynys[1] joynttor, and all the countre there aboute, whereby she hath lost a gret part of her lyvelod ; and that is a sherewed tokyn that he menyth wel to the Keng, howur suffereygn Lord, when he intendyth to distroye her.

Morover Sir Phylep de Crevekere hath takyn them that were in Fynys with inne this iiij. dayes to the noumbre of xiiij. personys, and the remnaunt where fled, and he had them to the French Keng, that he intendyth to brenge his armye thorwe theyse marchys into Flaundres ; wherefore my lord hath do brokyn all the passages excep Newham bryge, weche is wached, and the turne pyke shette every nyght. And the seide French Keng with inne these iij. dayes rayled gretely of my lord to Tygyr Pursevaunt, opynly byfore ij. hundred of his folks ; wherefore yt ys thaught here that he wold feynde a quarell to sett upon thys town, yf he myght gete avantage. And as I understonde, the Emperorys sone[2] ys maryed at Gaunte as this day ; and ther cam with hym but iiij. hundred horse, and I can here of no moo that be comyng in serteyn ; and in mony he brengyth with hym an hundred thowsand dokets, wheche is but a smalle thyng in regard for that he hath to doo. Wherefore, I fere me sore, that Flaundres will be lost ; and yf Seynt Omers be whonnyn, all is gon, in my conceyt. Never the lesse they say there shuld come gret powere after the Em-

[1] Margaret, sister to Edward IV., widow of Charles the Bold, Duke of Burgundy.
[2] Maximilian, son of the Emperor Frederick, married Mary, daughter and heir of Charles the Bold, Duke of Burgundy.—F.

297

1477
G. 17 perorys son ; but I be leve yt not, by cause they have ben so long of comyng.

And I pray you to recomaunde me unto Sir Tyrry Robsert, and that yt plese you to lete hym knowe of your tydyngs, and Hour Lord have you in His kepyng.

At Calais, the Sunday next after Hour Lady the Assumpsion.

Your,   E. BEDYNGFELD.[1]

919

AGNES AND WILLIAM PASTON[2]

G. 22 *The names of the maners of Agnes Pastons and William Paston, in Norffolk, how thai shuld be taken hede to this harvest, anno xvij°.*

And a copy of the same send to Richard Lynstede, the xxij. day of August, anno xvij°, per Bacheler Water.

Paston maner, ...	Se that the fermour in his corne on my moders fe. Seale dores and distrayne, and put in a newe fermour.
Wodemyl, ...	Distrayne.
Latymers, ...	Gadir the rente.
Sewardbys, ...	Gadir the rente.
Trunche, ...	Distrayne on the grounde after it is fellid, while it lieth on my moders fe.
Spriggeis, ...	Gader the rente.
Knapton fe, ...	
Crowmer, ...	Gadir the rente.
Owstoonde, ...	Distrayne.

[1] Edmund Bedyngfeld married Margaret, daughter of Sir John Scot, Comptroller of Calais, and was created a Knight of the Bath at the Coronation of Richard III. He was highly in favour with Henry VII., who paid him a royal visit at Oxburgh, in Norfolk, which fine seat he built. He died in 1496.—F.
[2] [From Paston MSS., B.M.] The heading of this document is taken from an endorsement on the original MS.

298

Rowton, ...	Distrayne, and arest the fermour. 1477
Riston, ...	Lete Lynstedes brother gader the AUG. 22 rente.
Oxned maner, ...	Se the fermour in his croppe, and after seale doris and distrayne, and lete hym not renne in dette as other fermours did.
Oxned mylle, ...	Se the fermour in his croppe, and after seall doris and distrayne, and lete hym not renne in dette as other fermours did.
Caster Cleres, ...	Aske the ferme.
Holkhams tenement, . .	Aske the ferme.
The mersh in Caster, . .	Aske the ferme.
Caster Bardolf, . . .	Aske the ferme a rent.
Caster Clere rentes, . . .	Distrayne tenauntes.
Holham rentes, ...	
Ormysby my fe, ...	
Somerton, ...	Se that he in his corn, and seall dores and distrayne, til he fynde suerty.
Thirn, ...	Aske the ferme.
Sowth Walsham, ...	
Halvyrzates, ...	
Todenham, ...	Aske the rente, and areste Smyth.
Cokfeldes, ...	Aske the rente.
Apawys, ...	Se he in his corn, and seall dores and distrayne.
Marlyngfor maner, . . .	Sele doris and distrayne.
Marlyngford mylle, . . .	Seale doris and distrayne.
Merlyngforde tenauntes, .	Distrayne.
Melton, ...	Se the croppe inned, and seale doris and distrayne.
Bonwell, ...	Aske rente.
Carleton, ...	Aske rente.
Thuxstons, ...	Aske rente.
Lynghall nuper Dokkynges,	Aske rente fro Mich. xvj. till xvij° and distrayne.

299

THE PASTON LETTERS

1477
AUG. 22

Bulmans nuper Dokkynges,	Aske rente fro Mich. xvjᵒ till xvijᵒ, and exorte Martyn to kepe the ferme still, and if he woll not, praye hym to gete a noder.
Yeaxham nuper Dokkynges,	Aske rente fro Mich. xvjᵒ till xvijᵒ, and gete a newe fermour, and incerse the rente, and make a newe terrar and rentall.
Styberd nuper Dokkynges,	Aske rent fro Mich. xvᵒ till Mich. xvijᵒ, and distrayne, and allowe no dewty of Dokkynges in abatyng my rente.
Thymbilthorp nuper Dok-kynges.	Aske rente fro Mich. xvᵒ till Mich. xvijᵒ, and distrayne, and allowe noe dewty of Dokkynges in abatyng my rente.

These maners that are trahid take gode hede that ye be in gode suertye of them this harvest tyme.

920

SIR JOHN PASTON'S WILL[1]

OCT. 31

[I, JOHN PASTON,] Knyght, in the last day of O[ctober, Anno] Domini m'cccclxxvjᵒ, will, graunte, and be queth my sowle to All myghty God, and to the . . . . . . Marye, Seint John Baptist, Seint Gorge, Seint Cristofur, and Seint Barbara ; and my body, yf I dyghe ny the Cyte of London, [to the chapel] of Owre Lady in the Whithe Frerys there, at the Northeest corner of the body of the chyrche, and there to be made an orator[y] . . . . . or muche leke as ys over Sir Thomas Browne in the Frere Prechours, to the valour

[1] [From Paston MSS., B.M.] The original of this document is mutilated. It is endorsed in a more modern hand, 'Testamentum Johannis Paston Senioris militis.'

300

of xxli., so that it may cause . . . . . . ther prayours
there, the rather to remembre my sowle, and to pray therefore ;
and that there be gevyn to the behoff . . . . . at plotte
of grounde be made suer unto me for ever the some of xx.
marc.

OCT. 31

. . . . dayly, be the space of an holl yere, by soumme well disposed brother of the same howse, and that the seyd brother . . . . . . [not]withstondyng yf I decesse in the counte of Norffolk, or there nye abouute, I wolde my bodye were buried at the prio[ry of Bromholm] . . . . . un to the Founders Toumbe, which arche is unto the North syde, and ryght agayn my fadyr toum[be] . . . . ith an awter and a toumbe for me, to the value of xxli., and that the howse there have a rewarde . . . . to the frerys of London, and that there be also a broder of that howse to synge for my sowle by one . . . . salarye.

a closette made at my cost over my faders body ther . . .
. . . . of xxli., so that owre cousyns . . .
. . . . have the more devocion to that place, and the rather reste there bodyes there the encresse of the . . . . encrese and profite of the howse, and reste on the religeus there of, lyke as owr auncetours have . . . . [a]nd to the entent that I disclosed but on to fewe persons concernyng the fee ferme that is payed . . . . Duke of Suffolk.

[Item, I will that my bro]ther, John, yf I dye with owth yssue leffull of my bodye, have the maner of Swaywell to hym and . . . . accordyng to the willez both of myn graunfader and of my fader, on whos sowles God have mercye, the . . . . esse.

[Item, I will that the] Bysshoppe of Wynchester, or his assygnes, woll and fynde suerte to do founde at the lyste iiij. prestys . . . . of John Fastolf and his frendys, &c., at Caster, and that there be bylded loggyng conveniant for those . . . . adjoynyng upon the bakhous over the gardeyn withouuth the

301

THE PASTON LETTERS

1477
OCT. 31

mote on the Weste syde of my . . . .
in the seid maner or maners yn Caster, graunt by chartour, grounde, space, and londe, convenyant for such . . . . .
. . . entre and yssue therunto, and to that entent, and byldyng or purchasyng of license of the kyng . . . . .
. . . profitez of the seid maners holly be expendid the terme of vij. yerez next after my dissece ; and, moreover, ... resorte theder in his owne persone to over see the werkys or byldyng or establyssyng of the seyd howse [he shall h]ave playn lyberte to dwell withinne my seid maner and fortresse the seid terme of vij. yerez, and that . . . . estys.

. . . . [cha]pell of Seint John Baptyst, withyn the seyd towne of Caster, with all the profitez yerly of that same begeny[ng] . . . .
. . ed to the seyd college or howse for evermore, with lycence therunto had of the Kyng and of the Pope, with . . .
. . . . . . in Caster before seyd, which londis, with the seyd chapell, schalbe of the yerly value of vijli. yerly . . .
. . ment of one prest above the charge that the Bysshope wyll do to pray for the sowles of my fader . . . .
. . . . Thomas Lyndys, clerk, and of Sir John Dawbeney. And that after this above wretyn be performed, yf that . . .
. . . es make astate by fyne reryd and enrolled in the Kynges courte of the seid maner and maners in Castre . . .
. . . . yssue of his bodye laufully comyeng, and for defaute of yssue of his body lawfully . . . . . .
[rem]ayne to the issue of my moders lawfully commynge. And for defaute of yssue of her body lawfully commyng . .
. . . . myn uncle, Edward Maudeby, and to the yssue of his body lawfully commynge. And that for defaute . . . . [comm]yng that the seyd maners remayn to my cousyn, Sir William Calthorp, and to the right eyrez . . . . defaute of issue of his body lawfully commynge, the seyd maners to reverte to the . . . .

[Item, I will that the priest of the chap]ell of the seyd collage be presented by the lordys of my seid maner . . .

302

. . . . ed by Syr John
Fastolff.

1477
OCT. 31

eryng de eadem villa vendatur per executores meos ad perimplendum et persolvendum.
em invenetit securitatem ad redimendum manerium de Sporle prædictum, quod si ipse . . . . x. acr' terræ de eisdem perquesit' de Johanne Kendall tempore debito dentur prædicto Johanni fratri [meo et hæredibus suis legiti]me procreatis ; et defectu exitus legitimi de prædicto Johanne fratre meo, tunc prædictæ terræ et tenementa remaneant . . . . triavi mei, legittime procreatis ; et pro defectu exitus legittimi prædicti triavi mei, tunc remaneant Willelmo . . . . [et hæredibus i]psius Willelmi legitime procreatis ; et pro defectu exitus legitimi prædicti Willelmi, tunc omnia prædicta terræ et tenementa [remaneant] . . . . assignatis imperpetuum ; proviso quod executores testamenti Willelmi Pekering habeant x. marcas pro . . . . . . et habeat xxxvij. acras terræ de prædictis terris sibi per voluntatem patris ejus assignatis sive legatis si tantæ . . . . terræ quæ idem Johannes vendidit sint de numero illarum acrarum sibi limitatarum per Nicholaum patrem prædicti Johannis ac . . . . recompensacionem ; eo quod idem Johannes forte credidit quod ipse juste potuit vendere, quæque terræ et tenementa in feofamento . . . . . [pat]ris, non obstante quod pater prædictus non declaravit quicquid faciendum de dictis terris suis ultra certas acras . . . . na ipsius patris.

303

921

WILLIAM PEKOC TO SIR JOHN PASTON[1]

To my ryth worschepffull master, Sir John Paston, Knyth, logyd at the Goorge, be Powll Warffe, in London, in hast.

1477
ov. 19

RYTH worcheful sir, I recomand me to yowr good masterchep. Plseyth you to wete that I have pur-weyid for for your heryng a non after your departyng, but I can yet no caryage, nowthir owte of Yermowth, ner in no oder place be twyn Wynterton and Leystoft, nowthir be lond nor be the se, not yet ; and specyally for your swanes. Hery Cook seyth he wolle no more come on the se with his good wylle. Ther is no man wyllyng to del with your swanes. Also, as for your hors, ye most ordayne a nothir keper than they have, or ellis ye chal not leke wel be them whan ye se hem ; they arn nowthir redyn nor corayd. Peris is meche owteward, and Whyte wol not a tende hem, nowdyr for Peris ner for me. They arn not watryd butt at the welle. Peris hath be ryth seke ; and yet, but for dyspleser of you, Peris had ben in hand with Whyte or this tyme. Ye muste be proveyd of a nothir hors keper, or elles it wol do you harm on your hors. Also, I have had iiij*li.* for to a sent you if I cowde have gete ony trosty man to youward. As for barly, I can non selle a bove xiiij*d.* the comb. As your leter that ye sent me, I have fownd a frere that hath promyssyd me to do'n his dever if it may be browte a bowte be ony mene in hast. Also there is a grete chyppe go to wrekke be for Wynterton, and there came up on your several grownd gret plente of bowe stawys and waynescotte, and clappalde[2] grete plente. I gate cartys and caryd to the towne that that was fownd on your fee. Mastras Clere hath sen down hyr men, and with

---

[1] [From Paston mss., B.M.] This letter is endorsed by Sir John Paston, 'Pekok, m. [*i.e.* mense] Decembris, anno E. iiij^ti xvij°.'
[2] Board cut to make casks.

304

THE PASTON LETTERS

1477
ov. 19

Wretyn at Mawteby on Sen Edmundis Evyn, the Kyng, in hast,

Be your man and servant,

WILLIAM PEKOC.

922

WILLIAM PEKOC TO SIR JOHN PASTON[1]

ov. 30

RYTH worchypfull ser, I recomand me to your good masterchep. Plesyth you, as for Pekrynges mater, I sent a frere in John Pekerynges name for the evydens ; and he had an answer that if he had a busschelful of evydenss, he chuld noon have of them, for he hath set the londe in trobill, nor he cowd have no seyte of none. Also remembir your ryth of your wreke at Wynterton. Thesse arn the menes namys of Wynterton, Robert Parker of West Somerton, John Longyard of Wynterton, Thomas Goodknape of the same, Will Wrantham and John Curteys of the same Wynterton, that caryid of your severel grownd xxij. carte ful of stuffe, viij^xx bowestavis, iij^xx and vij. waynescottes, xiiij^c clapalde,[2] v. barell ter, iiij. copil oris, and gret plante [*plenty*] of wreke of the schyppe that is worth meche mony, as ye chal understonde the trowth after this.

And as for your heryng that chuld in to Essexkes, they arn there, be the grace of God. As for your swanes, they chal be there be Our Ladys Day next comyng, I troste in God, Ho have your masterchyp in Is kepyng.

Wretyn at Mawteby, where as I am ryth werey, on Sen Andrews Day, Anno xvij° E.

Ser, if it plese your masterchep, I sold yet no barly, ner none can a bove xiiij*d.* the comb, as I sen word in a leter be John Russe ; and I toke iiij*li.* in mony to bryng to your materchep. The prysse of your heryng is iiij*li.* iijs. iiij*d.*,

---

[1] [From Paston mss., B.M.] There is no address on this letter, but it is endorsed, like the preceding, by Sir John Paston, 'Pekok, mense Decembris, anno E. iiij^ti xvij°.'
[2] *See* page 304, Note 2.

306

EDWARD IV

1477
NOV. 19

set alle the stuff and wrekke, and seyth that ye gete non there, for sche wol have it be the tytyl of the lete, and I have answerd there to, that che owte non to have be that tytil ; and so if ye wol comon with yor cownsel, I trow it to the lord of the soylle and not to the lete ; for the maner holdyth nothyng of hyr. Sche had never no wrekke nor growndage till withinne this xx. wynter. There is no maner in Wyynterton but your ; lesse your ryth now and lesse it for ever. I am threte to be trobelid there, for there ben v. men on lyve of the chyppe. The bordes had ben good for wyndownes and dores. Ye chuld have had thyme worthe the money, and sche had not lettyd it. Ther is com up ter [*tar*] at Caster v. or vj. barell. Men of Scrowby hath fet it awey. Ye must have a meen be sum wryte of trespas for them, or ellis it wol do yow meche harm here after. Rechard Kedman, John Pool, senior, and William Abbys, these arn summe of ther namys of Scrowby.

Item, I receyved a leter the Twis day befor Sen Edmunde the Kyng there as ye wryte to me for William Foster ; his sewirtesse ston chargyd for iiij*li.* vjs. viij*d.*, as John Seyve hath seyd to me or the tyme that I receyvyd your leter, but he hath ij. men of Norwech to sewirte to save hym and his felaw harmeless. Scharggar is on, and Vyncent the plomer is a nothir that chal bere the dawnger. And as for your swanes, I have gette a man that chal cary hem be lond, and that I chal send word with the swanes that the herynges chal com be water ; and if the chuld have ony heryng for your store, it wold be purveyd for, for heryng wol be dere or Lente.

Item, there arn wyndownes blow opyn in the place, and the wyndown of the gonne hows with inne the brege is revyn. I wot not whethir it was so or ye wente or not. My Lord of Norwech was at Caster Halle for to a cen the place as he cam to London ward. Ser, remembir your hors to have a better keper. Ser, to remembir thesse men of Scrowby, and comon with Master William Paston there in, for he partith with you both wrekke and growndage in Caster ; and he wold take the accyon in his lordes name that he delyth for, it ware a good wey, be my sympil wyth. God preserve you, and kepe yow, and bryng yow home a yen to your contre.

VOL. V.—U

305

EDWARD IV

1477
NOV. 30

besyd oder costes. Hery Cook wold goo with your swanes, for hys yefte chuld be vjs. viij*d.*, and there fore he wold yeffe you his labore, be so ye payd for his costes. Ipse dixit.

Be your servaunt,

WILL. PEKOC.

923

MARGERY PASTON TO JOHN PASTON[1]

To myryth reverent and worscheful husbond, Jon Paston.

DEC. 18

RYTH reverent and worscheful husbond, I recomaunde me to yow, desyryng hertyly to here of yowr wylfare, thankyng yow for the tokyn that ye sent me be Edmunde Perys, preyng yow to wete that my modyr sent to my fadyr to London for a goune cloth of mustyrddevyllers[2] to make of a goune for me ; and he tolde my modyr and me wanne he was comme home, that he cargeyt yow to beyit, aftyr that he were come oute of London.

I pre yow, yf it be not bowt, that ye wyl wechesaf to byit, and sendyt home as sone as ye may, for I have no goune to weyre this wyntyr but my blake and my grene a lyer,[3] and that is so comerus that I ham wery to weryt.

---

[1] [From Fenn, ii. 256.] It is curious that after so much negotiation for the marriage of John Paston and Margery Brews, we have no record in these letters when it actually took place ; but probably it was in August 1477, the last reference to it as an event not yet accomplished being on the 7th of that month (No. 916). In January 1478, John Paston talks of taking his wife to her father's house on account of her situation, and their first child was born in the course of the following summer. This letter seems to have been written in December. Fenn remarks that St. Thomas's Day might mean the Translation of St. Thomas à Becket, 7th July 1478, and 'Our Lady's Day' might be the Visitation of the Virgin, and July preceding. But this is simply impossible, because the letter is dated Thursday *before* St. Thomas's Day, which would in that case be the very same date as the Visitation of Our Lady, viz. the 2nd July 1478. Besides, if the first child of John Paston and Margery was not actually born before July, the latter was certainly much nearer to her confinement then than this letter would imply. *See* No. 936 in vol. vi.
A facsimile of this letter was published in the *European Magazine* for March 1787, and we have carefully compared the text with this facsimile.
[2] A kind of grey woollen cloth.
[3] Fenn suggests *Grenouilliere* or frog-colour, but I find no authority for such a word ; and I should suppose 'grene' to be a separate word, though what 'a lyer' is I cannot say.

307

THE PASTON LETTERS

As for the gyrdyl that my fadyr be hestyt me, I spake to hym ther of a lytyl before he zede to London last, and he seyde to me that the faute was in yow, that ze wolde not thynk ther uppe on to do makyt [*to get it made*]; but I sopose that ys not so; he seydyt but for a skwsacion. I pre yow, yf ye dor takyt uppe on yow, that ye wyl weche safe to do makyt a yens ye come home, for I hadde never more nede ther of than I have now, for I ham waxse so fetys[1] that I may not be gyrte in no barre of no gyrdyl that I have but of one. Elisabet Peverel hath leye sek xv. or xvj. wekys of the seye-tyka, but sche sent my modyr word be Kate, that sche xuld come hedyr wanne God sent tyme, thoow sche xuld be crod [*wheeled*] in a barwe.

Jon of Damm was here, and my modyr dyskevwyrd me to hym, and he seyed, be hys trouth that he was not gladder of no thyng that he harde thys towlmonyth, than he was ther of.

I may no lenger leve be my crafte, I am dysscevwyrd of alle men that se me.

Of alle odyr thyngys that ye deseyreyd that I xuld sende yow word of, I have sent yow word of in a letter that I dede wryte on Ouwyr Ladyis Day[2] laste was. The Holy Trenyte have yow in Hese kepyng.

Wretyn at Oxnede, in ryth gret hast, on the Thrusday next be fore Seynt Tomas Day.[3]

I pre yow that ye wyl were the reyng with the emage of Seynt Margrete, that I sent yow for a rememrraunse, tyl ye come home; ye have lefte me sweche a rememrraunse, that makyth me to thynke uppe on yow bothe day and nyth wanne I wold slepe.

Your ys,   M. P.

[1] This word commonly signifies neat or elegant, and seems to be used here ironically.
[2] Conception of Our Lady, 8th of December.—F.
[3] 21st December, the day of St. Thomas Apostle, or perhaps 29th December, the day of St. Thomas (à Becket) the Martyr.

EDWARD IV

924

ABSTRACT[1]

Bill in Parliament confirming the statute of Marlborough [52 Hen. iii.], with additions touching wardships, reliefs, etc., to take effect after Easter, 1480.

1478(?)

[The last Parliament before 1480 met on the 16th January 1478. This measure was probably introduced or intended for discussion at that period.]

925

JOHN PASTON TO SIR JOHN PASTON[2]

To my ryght worchepfull broder, Syr John Paston, Knyght.

SYR, aftyr all dutes of recomendacyon, lyeketh yow to undyrstand that I have comond with dyvers folkys of the Dwk of Suffolk now thys Crystmas and sythen, whyche let me in secret wyse have knowlage, lyek as I wrott on to yow, that he must mak a shefft for money, and that in all hast. Wherfor, syr, at the reverence of God, let it not be lachesyd, but with effect aplyed now, whyll he is in London, and my lady hys wyff also; for I assarteyn yow that C. mark wyll do more now in ther neede then ye shall peraventure do with CC. marks in tyme comyng, and thys season be not takyn. And alweys fynd the meane that my Lady of Suffolk and Syr R. Chamberleyn may be yowr gwydes in thys mater, for as for my lord, he nedyth not to be mevyd with it tyll it shold be as good as redy to the sealyng.

1478
JAN. 21

Syr, lyeketh yow also to remember that I told yow that Mastyr Yotton[3] had, as I cam last towardes London, desyred me, by a lettre of attorney wryttyn with hys owne hand, to se

[1] [From Paston mss., B.M.]
[2] [From Paston mss., B.M.]
[3] Dr. Yotton was the Queen's chaplain.—F.

THE PASTON LETTERS

th'enprowment of syche profytes as ar growing of hys chapell in Caster that ye gave hym; and at syche season as I told yow of it, ye sayd on to me that ye wold asay to make a bargayn with hym, so that ye myght have a prest to syng in Caster. Syr, me thynkes ye can not have so good a season to meve hym with it as now thys Parlement tyme, for now I thynk he shalbe awaytyng on the Quene; and also if ye myght compone with hym or he wyst what the valew wer, it wer the better, and I have promysed hym to send hym woord thys terme of the verry valew of it, and also syche mony as I cowd gader of it. Wherfor, syr, I prey yow that by the next messenger that ye can get to Pekok that ye wyll send hym woord to paye me for the lond in xxx. acres, as it hathe ben answerd before tym.

And as for tydynges here, we have none, but we wold fayne here of all your royalte at London, as of the maryage of my Lord of York,[1] and other Parlement mater; and so I prey yow that I may doo when ye have leyser.

Syr, I prey yow that Whetley may have knowlage that my broder Yelverton hathe promysed me to take hym xl*d*.; he owyth me by reason of his fermore at Caster more then that.

And, syr, as for my huswyff, I am fayne to carry hyr to se hyr fadyr and hyr frendes now thys wynter, for I trow she wyll be ought of facyon in somer. And so in my progresse fro my fadyr Brews on to Mawtby, I took Master Playter in my wey, at whoys hows I wrot thys bylle, the xxj. day of January, anno E. iiij*ti* xvij°. And I beseche God to preserve yow and yours.

Yowr,   J. PASTON.

Endorsed by Sir John Paston, 'J. P., anno xvij°.'

[1] Richard, Duke of York, second son to King Henry iv., married Ann, daughter and heir of John Mowbray, Duke of Norfolk, 15th January 1477-78.—F.

EDWARD IV

926

JOHN PASTON TO MARGARET PASTON[1]

To my ryght worchepfull modyr, Margaret Paston.

RYGHT worchepfull modyr, aftyr all dwtes of humble recomendacyon, in as humble wyse as I can, I beseche yow of your dayly blyssyng. Pleasyt yow to wett that at my being now at London, lyek as ye gave me in comandment, I mevyd to Mastyr Pykenham and to Jamys Hubart for ther being at Norwyche now thys Lent, that ye myght have ther avyses in syche maters as ye let me have understandyng of. And as for Mastyr Pykenham, he is now Juge of the Archys, and also he hathe an other offyce, whyche is callyd *Auditor Causarum*, and hys besynes is so gret in bothe thes offyces that he can not tell the season when that he shall have leyser to come in to Norffolk. But I left not tyll I had gotyn Jamys Hubbart and hym togedyrs, and then I told theym your intent; and then Mastyr Pykenham told Jamys and me hys intent, and he preyed Jamys that he shold in no wyse fayle to be with yow thys Lent. Not withstandyng it was no grete nede to prey hym myche; for he told Doctore Pykenham that there was no gentyl woman in Inglond of so lytyll aqueyntance as he had with yow, that he wold be glader to be servyse on to; and myche the glader, for he purposeth fro hensforthe duryng hys lyff to be a Norffolk man, and to lye with in ii. myle of Loddon, whyche is but viij. or x. myle at the most fro Mautby. And in conclusyon he hathe appoyntyd to awayte on yow at Norwyche the weke nexte aftyr Mydlent Sonday, all the hole weke, if nede be, all other maters leyd apart.

1478
FEB. 3

[1] [From Paston mss., B.M.] This letter appears from the contents to have been written after John Paston's marriage, at a time when his wife was staying at Swains-thorpe. He also apologises to his mother for his wife having detained two pounds out of a certain quantity of dates that he himself had sent to her from London by way of Swainsthorpe, as Margery thought them 'at this season right good meat,' apparently referring to her approaching confinement.

THE PASTON LETTERS

1478
FEB. 3

Also I comend with my brodyr Sir John at London of syche maters as ye wold have amendyd in the bylle that he sent on to yow, and he stake not gretly at it.

Also, modyr, I herd whyle I was in London wher was a goodly yong woman to mary, whyche was doughter to one Seff, a merser, and she shall have CC*li.* in money to hyr maryage, and xx. mark by yer of lond aftyr the dyssease of a steppe modyr of hyrs, whyche is upon l. yer of age; and or I departyd ought of London, I spak with some of the maydys frendys, and have gotyn ther good wyllys to have hyr maryd to my brodyr Edmund. Notwithstandyng, those frendys of the maydys that I comend with avysyd me to get the good wyll of one Sturmyn, whyche is in Mastyr Pykenhamys danger[1] so myche that he is glad to please hym; and so I mevyd thys mater to Mastyr Pykenham. And incontinent he sent for Sturmyn, and desyred hys good wyll for my brodyr Edmund, and he grantyd hym hys good wylle, so that he koud get the good wyll of the remenaunt that wer executours to Seff, as well as the seyd Sturmyn was; and thus-ferforthe is the mater. Wherfor modyr, we must beseche yow to helpe us forward with a lettyr .ro yow to Mastyr Pykenham to remembyr hym for to handyll well and dylygently thys mater now thys Lent; and for I am aqueyntyd with your condycyons of old that ye reke not who endytyth more lettres than ye, ther for I have drawyn a note to yowr secretarys hand, Freir Perse, whyche lettre we must prey yow to send us by the berer herof, and I trust it shall not be longe fro Mastyr Pykenham.

Your doughter of Sweynsthorpp and hyr sojornaunt E. Paston recomandyth hem to yow in ther most humble wyse, lowly besechyng yow of your blyssyng; and as for my brodyr, Edmund Sweynsthorpe, for none intrete that hys ostas your doughtyr, nor I koud intrete hym, myght not kepe hym, but that he wold have bene at home with yow at Mautby on Sonday last past at nyght; and as he was departyng fro hens, had we word fro Frenshes wyf that, God yeld yow, modyr, ye had govyn hym leve to dysporte hym her with us for a vij. or

[1] *i.e.* in his debt.

312

EDWARD IV

1478
FEB. 3

viij. dayes; and so the drevyll lost hys thank of us, and yet abode nevyr the lesse.

Your doughtyr sendyth yow part of syche poore stuff as I sent hyr fro London, besechyng yow to take it in gree, though it be lytyll plente that she sendyth yow. But as for datys, I wyll sey trowthe, ye have not so many by ij. pownd as wer ment on to yow, for she thynkys at thys season datys ryght good mete. What so ever it menyth, I prey God send us good tydynges, Whom I beseche to preserve yow and yours, and so send yow your myst desyred joye.

At Sweynsthorp, on Ashe Wednysday.

Your sone and humble servaunt,

J. PASTON.

Modyr, pleasit yow to remember that ye had need to be at Norwyche v. or vj. dayes befor that Jamys Hubbart and your consayll shall be ther with yow, for to look up your evydence and all other thynges redy. Also if ye thynk that thys bylle that I send yow herwith be good i now to send to Doctore Pykenham, ye may close up the same, and send it sealyd to me ayen, and I shall convey it forthe to hym.

927

WILLIAM BOTONER TO SIR JOHN PASTON[1]

To the Ryght worshypfull sir, Sir John Paston ch'l'r logged at the signe of the George next to Poulys Wharf; or to lefe thys letter at a barbourys house ovyr the seyd George to delyver it to Sir John Paston.

MARCH 1 PLESE yor gode masterschyp to wete that I herd thys day how a man wend that a jugement ys passed ayenst your entent yn the ende of the last terme (hyt was not of verray certeyn tolde me, but as a dreme) yn the kynges Chauncerye. I coude gefe none aunswer therto. I prai God

[1] [Add. MS. 34,889, f. 152.] This letter would seem to be of the year 1478. It will be seen by No. 925 that in the beginning of that year Sir John Paston wished to arrange with Dr. Yotton to get a priest to sing in Caister.

313

THE PASTON LETTERS

1478
MARCH 1

alle be well; hyt wold ease som of your frendes hertys yff they coude understand ony gode comfort. Sir, as for Robert,[1] I wold pray and requyre your maisterschep that he may for his lernyng be abydyng with your cousyn of Lincoln Inne, as yt was promysed, and to be occupyed under drede of displesir under subjecion, wyth erly rysyng accustomed, for slouth ys the moder and noryssher of all vices. He hath cost me moch goode and labour, and now he ys uppon hys makyng by vertues governance, or undoyng to the contrarye, and yn especyalle to be not conversant ne neere amongis women, as I was kept froo her [*their*] company xxx. yeres or ony suche were of my councelle, I thank God of yt. Sir, and ye write to me as ye lust, let no name be wythynne wryt whens yt com, and that yt be sent by sure comer to delyver yt me, for yt ys better brent then founde. Also your discrecion ought not loth (to take the cost and labour wolle not be gret, nether importune) for to send a man of purpose to my lord of [*sic*] Bysshop Waltham and to hys councell lerned, ye wete to whom, for redy serch to be made for the bill of half lefe of paper quantite of my hand I faythfully delyvered to Master T. Danvers for to ovyrsee, of the fyrst appoyntment ye wote off, that ye desyre so hertly to see as of othyr manyfolde wrytyngis belongyng to yow and to me. Yt ys seyd yne a vers: *Gutta cavat lapidem non vi set sepe cadendo,* &c.; to a slow man or a foryetefull or lothfull man must be importune callyng allway uppon hym tille he hafe hys entent, for now thys vacacion to spede or nevyr shall stand in yow no stede. I can no ferther then the walle.

Item, Sir, I comyned wyth Doctor Yotton at Camebrygge late, because there ys no dyvyne service seyd yn the free chapelle at C.,[2] that he wold hafe a grete concience yn yt, and to depart wyth an honest preste called Sir John Brykkys that ys now duellyng wyth a ryzt lovyng kynnesman of yowres; the seyd Doctor gevyng me to aunsuer he wold comyn wyth yow by Pasch,[3] and the rather wyth your gode wylle wold

[1] Is this Robert, son of Sir John's brother Edmund, who is mentioned in Margaret Paston's will? The will, dated 4th February 1482, will be found printed in the next volume. [2] Caister. [3] Easter.

314

EDWARD IV

1478
MARCH 1

depart to such one ye owe affeccion unto. Sir, I wold, as I dar tak uppon me to owen your affeccion to the seyd John Brickys, that he may wyth more help of your cellary hafe the better to lyve and serfe God there to abyde and do yow service also. I mene faythfullye, and soo I pray yow take yt; to remembre a thyng in seson ys gretely to commend, and of a spedy avantage. The blessed Trinite be wyth yow. Wret the fyrst day of Marche.—Your

W. BOTONERE.

To J. P. c.[1] at London.

Item, I had foryete to hafe remembred your maystershyp to hafe a bille to your baylly Pecok for to delyver my fermour of Tyrkbye C. or ii C. lawre and asshe, and than to plant yn my tenement at Thyrkbye, or foras many ye lust; for I lost the last waraunt that ye wrote me truly, and so I was not served.

Item, yff ye wryte to me, hyt hath nede to be by a sure comer, for I had levyr a letter be brent then lost *ne forte videant Romani* . . . and at reverence of Jhesu that my Robert lose no tyme, nether be idelle, for doubt of ymaginacions and temptacions. I trust wyth your principale help to be wyth the worshyppfull gentleman that made promysse to yow, &c.

928

CONSTANCE REYNFORTH TO SIR JOHN PASTON[2]

[*To Sir*] *John Paston, Chevalier, be this byll delyveryd in hast.*

MARCH 21 RYTH reverent and worcheful ser, I recomend me on to yowr masterschep, effectually desyryng to here of yowr welfare and contynual prosperite; and if it ples yow to here of my pour estat, I was in good hele at the

[1] John Paston, Chevalier. [2] [From Paston MSS., B.M.] The writer of this letter was Sir John Paston's mistress, by whom he left a natural daughter. The date is ascertained by an endorsement in Sir John's own hand, 'Custaunce Raynford, anno xviij°.'

315

THE PASTON LETTERS

1478
MARCH 21

makyng of this sympyll byll. Towchyng the cause of my wrytyng to yowr masterschep is, for as moche as I poyntyd with yow to a be with yow be the day that ye asynyd me of, the wheche, with outh yowr good supportacyon, I con not well have myn entent, withouth it ple yow to send oon of yowr men to me, and I psal provyd a letter in myn unkyll name, the wheche he psall delyver to my cosyn as he were myn unkyll masagear, and be this mene I wyll come at yowr request; for my cosyn wold I psuld not depart with hym, with outh it were to myn unkyll servyse; hoys and all others I refuse for yowres, yf my sympul servyse may be to yowr plesure. And of an answer herof I beseke yow be the brynger of my byll, and I wyll conforme me to yowr en tente, be the grace of Good, the Wheche mot preserve yow at all oures.

Wretyn at Cobham, the xxj. day of Marche.

By yowr woman and sevnt,

CONSTANS REYNFORTH.

929

SIR JOHN PASTON TO JOHN PASTON[1]

To John Paston, Esquier, ande to Osberne Berney, and to everyche off them, be thys letter delyveryd.

MAY 5

I RECOMAUNDE me to yowe, and thanke yow off yowr labor that ye hadde at Heylesdon and Drayton in seyng the woodys there. And it is soo heer that Ric. Ferore seyde, that he repentyd hym that evyr he dalte with any woode theer, and iff I hadde sente hym but the leest chylde that I hadde to have warnyd hym to leve he wolde notte have dalte therwyth; and he ffonde noe comfforte in the Chancery, but that he is lyke to contente me for the harmes and hurte that is doone, and moore ovyr he hathe an instrucyon that he shall ffelle noo moore.

Item, wheer as he desyryd me to be freendly to hym, I dalte so with hym, that I trowe he wylle reporte that I seyde

316

[1] [From Paston MSS., B.M.]

1478
MAY 5

and dalte moore cortesly with hym than he demyd that I wolde doo. Yitt for alle in convenyences that myght ffalle, I wolde be gladde to have a weell stomakyd felawe that wolde for my sake everye daye see the seyde woodes of Heylesdon and Drayton, and to knowe iff any weer fellyd heer afftre; and iffe there be any fellyd syns that Whetley was theer, and I can preve it by wytnesse, I sholde have better recompence for every tree than iiij. trees weer worthe.

Item, it is so that he hathe answeryd to my bille, wheryn he seythe that he never knywe byfor the subpena delyveryd hym that I hadde any clayme or entrest in the maner off Heylesdon, but that it was peasyble my Lordys off Suffolk. Wherffor I suppose that there be many men in Norwyche that comonyd with hym off the byenge off that woode ere evyr he made hys fulle bergayne, and per aventure some freendys off hys gave hym warnyng theroff, and off myn entrest. Iff any suche credyble mane that hadde hadde any suche langage to hym, or in hys companye, or than he bargayned, or any man that he laboryd to be halffe marchant or byer with hym, ar any man that refusyd to bye the seyd wood bycawse off myn entrest in the presence of Feror, any suche credyble man maye, iff he wyll, wytnesse ther in with me, or that dare avowe it, sholde be to me a remedy off alle that is fellyd. I praye yow, if ye can here any suche, that ye will in the presence off them make a bylle of remembraunce theroff, and off ther sayng, so that they maye her afftre wytnesse in the mater. Nevertthelesse, trowthe it is that he hadde knowleche ther off i nowe, and soo hadde every man off hys havore [*substance*] in Norwych, I dowt nott; and as for hym, I am sure he hadde knowleche, for so moche as he desyryd at hys bargayn to have a sywerte to be savyd harmeles ageyn me, whyche was grawntyd hym butt nott executyd. No mor, butt I hope with Goddys grace to have hastely goode remedy for the hole maner, and off Drayton therto, and alle the remenaunte.

Wretyn a London, the v. daye off Maye, anno E. iiijᵗⁱ xviijᵒ.

317

THE PASTON LETTERS

930

SIR JOHN PASTON TO MARGARET PASTON[1]

To my ryght worshypfull modre, Margret Paston, be thys delyvered.

1478
MAY 13

PLEASE it yow to weete, that wher as I entendyd to have ben at home thys Mydsomer, and purposyd with yowr goode helpe to have bygonne upon my ffadrys tombe, so that it myght have ben endyd thys somyr; it is soo, that ffor suche cawsys as ar nowe bygunne by twyen my Lorde off Suffolk and me, ffor the manerys off Heylesdon, Drayton, &c., for whyche materis I most nedys be heer thys nexte terme; therffor I deme it woll be afftr Mydsomer, er than I can see yow.

Please it yow also to weete that I comonyd with Master Pykenham to weete iff he wolde bye the clothe off golde, for soo moche as he desyryd ons to have bowte it, and he offryd me ons xx. marke therffor, nevertthelesse it coste me xxiiijli.; yit nowe, when that I spake to hym ther off, he refusyd to bye it, and seyde that he hadde nowe so many chargys that he maye nott. Butt it is soo that the Kynge dothe mak sertayne copys and vestymentys off like clothe, whyche he entendyth to gyve to the Coledge at Foodryngdre, wher my lorde hys ffadre is nowe buryed, and he byethe at a grete pryce.

I comonyd with the vestment maker ffor to helpe me fforthe with xij. yerds, and he hathe grauntyd me to doo, as Whetleye can telle yow; wherffor, iff it please yow that it be bystowyd ffor to make a towmbe ffor my ffadre at Bromholme, iff ye lyke to sende it hyddr, iffe it be solde I undretake or Mychel-messe, that ther shalle be a tombe, and somwhatt ellys oyvr my ffadris grave, on whoys sowle God have mersye, that ther shall noone be lyke it in Norffolk; and as ye shalle be gladde herafftr to see it; and God sende me leyser that I maye come home, and iff I doo not, yit the monye shall be putte to noon

318

[1] [From Fenn, ii. 260.]

1478
MAY 13

other use, butt kepyd by some that ye trust, tylle that it may be bystowyd acordyng as is above wretyn, and ellys I gyve yow cawse nevyr to truste me whylle ye and I lyve. When I was last with yow, ye grauntyd that the seyde clothe of golde sholde be bywaryd [*spent*] abowte thys werke, that is above wretyn, whyche iff ye wylle perfforme, I undretake that ther shalle be suche a towmbe as ye shalle be pleasyd at, thowgh it cost me xx. marke off myn owne purse besyde, iff I ons sette upon it.

No mor, but I beseche Goode have yow in Hys kepyng.

Wretyn at London, the Wednysdaye in Whyghtsonweke, anno E. iiijᵗⁱ xviijᵒ.

Please it yow to sende me worde by Whatley off yowr plesyr her in.

By your Sone,

JOHN PASTON, K.

931

WALTER PASTON TO MARGARET PASTON[1]

To his worchypfull moder, Margaret Paston, dwellyng in Mawtby, be this letter delyveryd in hast.

MAY 19

RYTGH reverent and worchypfull moder, I recomaund me on to yowr good moderchypp, besechyng yow to geve me yowr dayly benediccyon, desyeryng hartyly to heer of yowr prosperyte, whych God preserve to Hys plesure, and to yowr hartys desyyr, &c. I marvel soor that yow sent me noo word of the letter wych I sent to yow by Master Wylliam Brown at Ester. I sent yow word that tym that I xold send yow myn exspenses partyculerly; but as at thys tym the berar her of had a letter sodenly that he xold come home, and there fore I kowd have no leysur to send them yow on that wys; and there fore I xall wryt to yow in thys letter the hool som of my exspenses sythyns I was with

[1] [From Paston MSS., B.M.] This letter is printed in Fenn's fifth volume, and dated by him in 1478. I do not know on what evidence he assigns this particular year to it, except that, as he tells us elsewhere, Walter Paston took a degree at Oxford, and died in 1479.

319

1478
MAY 19

yow tyll Ester last paste, and also the reseytys, rekenyng the xx*s.* that I had of yow to Oxon wardys with the Buschopys fyndyng.

The hool some of reseytys ys v*li.* xvij*s.* vj*d.*, and the holl some of exspenses ys vj*li.* v*s.* v*d.* ob. qua., and that comth over the reseytys in my exspenses I have borowd of Master Edmund, and yt drawyth to viij*s.* And yet I recone none exspenses sythyns Ester. But as for them, they be non grete; and therfor I besech yow to send me mony by Syr Richard Cotman, brynger of thys letter, or ellys by the next masenger that yow kan have to me.

I besech yow that he that I sent by thys letter to yow may have good scher, yf he brynge yt hym selfe, as he telth me that he woll, for he ys a good lover of myn. Master Edmund Alyard recomaund hym specyaly to yow, and to all my brodyrn and systyrs, and to all yowr howshold; and I besech yow that I may be recomaundyd to all them also, and specyaly to my brodyr John the yonger. No more to yow at thys tym, but Allmythy Jhesus have yow in Hys kepyng. Amen.

Wretyn at Oxonforth, on Seynt Dunstonys Day and the xix. day of May.

By your sonn and scoler,

WALTER PASTON.

932

J. WHETLEY TO SIR JOHN PASTON[1]

To the ryght worsh[yp]full Sir John Paston, Knyght, loged at the sygne off the George at Powlys Wharff, in London, be thys delyverea in hast.

MAY 20

PLEAS it your meastershep to understond the dealyng of every thyng, the wych I was charged with at my departyng frome your measterchep.

Fyrst, your suppena to Denton was delyvered by me on Trenite Sondaye, in hys parych cherch, at Matens tyme, be

[1] [From Paston MSS., B.M.]

320

1478
MAY 20

ffor the substans of the parych ; and as for Drayton wod, it is not all down yet, but it drawes fast toward. I have the names of all the mynestres off and in that wod, and more schall know or I come, yf ther be any more dealyng, &c.

And as for Haylysdon, my Lord of Suffolk was ther on Wedensday in Whytson Weke, and ther dined, and drew a stew and toke gret plente of fych ; yet hath he left you a pyke or ij., agayn ye come, the wych wold be gret comford to all your frendes, and dyscomford to your enmys ; for at hys beyng ther that daye ther was never no man that playd Herrod in Corpus Crysty[1] play better and more agreable to hys pageaunt then he dud. But ye schall understond that it was after none, and the weder hot, and he so feble for sekenes that hys legges wold not bere hyme, but ther was ij. men had gret payn to kepe hym on hys fete ; and ther ye were juged. Som sayd ' Sley ;' some sayd ' Put hym in preson.' And forth com my lord, and he wold met you with a spere, and have none other mendes for the troble at ye have put hym to but your hart blod, and that will be gayt with hys owen handes ; for and ye have Haylesdon and Dreton, ye schall have hys lyff with it. And so he comford your enmys with that word that thay have dealed and dealeth with the wod, and most pryncepall nowe is Nycolesse Ovye. For as for Ferrer,[2] the Meare, he delys not with owt it be under covert ; for it is sayd that he be soght my lord that he myght have other sygnementes for hys money that he had payd, for playnly he wold deall no mor with the wod. And so my lord hath set in the Bayly of Cossay, and all is doon in hys name ; and as for hys servauntes, thay dayly thret my measter your brother and me to slay for comyng of ther lordes ground, and thay say that we made an entre ; and thay beth answerd as ye comaunded me, for many a gret chalaunge make thay to Mester John, both Measter Wodhowse, Wysman, with other dyveres that I know not ther names ; but he holdeth hys own that thay gayt no grownd of hym. And thys he lettes thaym knowe

[1] Corpus Christi Day, the Thursday after the Octave of Whitsuntide, was famous for the acting of Mysteries , particularly at Chester.—F.

[2] Richard Farrer, Farrour, or Ferriour, was five times Mayor of Norwich, namely, in 1473, 1478, 1483, 1493, and 1498.—F.

VOL. V.—X

321

1478
MAY 20

that if thay bete hym or any of hys, thay schall aby vj. for on, and so thay deall not but with ther tonges ; and as yet, syth Ferrer was at London, there passes not iij. acres of wod down but thay cary fast for fere of rayn, &c.

Also, sir, I trust to bryng or send hastely the cloth off gold, for it hath ben largely tempted ; but as yet I have none playn answer, but put in hope. Also I have spoken with Popy for your money, and delyvered hym your letter, the wych, as he sayth, is a straunge thyng to hym, for, as I understond, he that owght thys deute was uncle to thys yong man, and he sayth that hys fader was never exsecutor to hym, nor never mynestred ; and I told hym howe that hys fader was bound for the same deute, in so mech and my measter wold have forgevyn part of the same deute, he wold have payed it ; and so he will be at London thys terme, and speke with you, and thys is hys answer.

Morover Wyllyam Worsestre, mevyd unto me of onne Sir Wylliam Bokkyng, exsecutor and brother to John Bokkyng, the whych was one of Sir John Fastolf hys clerkes, the whych mater I knewe not, nor had no comaundement be you to deall therin, and so I told hym. Never the lesse he sayd that ye promysed hym to have sent your will to have bene done in that mater by me, and so he troweth that it was owt of your mynd at my departyng. Yff so be that ye will any thyng to be doon by me or I come to yow in that mater, let me have knowlege shortly, for I thynk to be with yow in the weke folowyng aftyr thys wryten, with owt I may have more comford of money then I have yet.

And as for my meastres, your moder hath ben gretly deseased and so seke that she wened to have dyed, and hath made her wyll,[1] the wyche ye shall understond more when I come, for ther is every man for hym selff. I know not the sercomstance of every thyng as yet, and therfor I writ no more to you therin, but I am promysed to know or I depart from thens.

[1] The will now made by Margaret Paston was afterwards cancelled, as that which was proved after her death in 1484 was dated on the 4th of February 1482, 21 E. IV.

322

Also I spake with William Barker, and he sayth that I shall have the stuff or I depart, or els the monye agayn that he hade of Wylliam Pecoke.

1478
MAY 20

Also, sir, as for your lond be syd Bromholm that ye had of Bakton, it hath layn un ocupyed syth ye were ther.

Moreover, my Lord of Suffolk[1] is remevyd in to Suffolk the morow after that he had bene at Hayleson, and my lady purposed to remeff after on thys day, Corpus Crysty Evyn, by the grace of Jesu, Who preserve yow ever in worchep.

Wryten at Norwych, on Wedensday Corpus Crysty Evyn, anno E. iiij[d] xviij°.

Item, as for the knowleg that Ferror denyed by hys othe that he knew never no tytle nor entrest that ye had in and to Haylsdon and Dreton, as yet we can not know ; but thys thay will record all that were at the delyveraunce of the wryt that he sayd my lord had promysed to save hym harmles, in so mech that Wysman was bownd to Ferrour to save hym harme-les, and he had for bryngyng that mater about, that Ferrour shuld have the wod, xx*s.*

Your servaunt, J. WHETLEY.

933

MARGARET PASTON TO SIR JOHN PASTON[2]

To the ryght worshypfull Sir John Paston, Knyght.

MAY 27

I GREET yow well and send yow Goddys blyssyng and myn, latyng yow wete that I have sent yow be Whetele the clothe of golde, chargyng yow that yt be not solde to none other use than to the performyng of yowyr fadyrs toombe, as ye send me worde in wrytyng ; yf ye sell yt to any othyr use, by my trowthe, I shall never trost yow wyll I leve.

[1] John de la Pole, Duke of Suffolk, etc., married Elizabeth, third daughter of Richard Plantagenet, Duke of York, and sister of Edward IV. They both lie buried at Wingfield, in Suffolk.—F.

[2] [From Fenn, ii. 264.]

323

THE PASTON LETTERS

Remembyr that yt coste me xx^ti marke the pleggyng owte of yt, and yf I wher not glad to se that made, I wolde not departe from it. Remembyr yow what charge I have had with yow of late, whyche wyl not be for my ease this ij. yer ; whan ye may better, I trost ye whyll remembyr yt.

My cosyn Clere dothe as meche coste at Bromhom as whylle drawe an *Cli.* upon the deskys in the quere, and in othyr places, and Heydon in lyke whyse, and yf ther shulde no thyng be don for yowyr fadyr, yt wolde be to gret a schame for us alle, and in cheffe to se hym lye as he dothe.

Also as I understond that my cosyn Robert Clere thynkyth gret on kyndenesse in delyng wyth hym of Pecoke, for certeyn pasture that ye[1] grawntyd hym to have, and Pecoke hath letyn it to othyr, suche as he lyste to lete yt to, not withstondyng my cosyn hath leyd the pastur with hys catell, and Pecok hathe strenyd them.

I thynk thys delyng is not as yt shulde be. I wolde that iche of yow shulde do for other, and leve as kynnysmen and frendys ; for suche servawnts my make trobyll by twyxe yow, wheche wher a ageynste cortesy, so nyhe newbors as ye be, he is a man of substance and worchyp, and so wylle be takyn in thys schyr ; and I wer lothe that ye shulde lese the good wylle of suche as may do for yow.

Item, wher as ye have begonne your cleyme in Heylysdon and Drayton, I pray God send yow good spede and foderance in yit. Ye have as good a season as ye wulde wysche, consyderyng that yowyr adversary standys not in best favyr with the Kynge.

Also ye have the voyse in this contre, that ye may do as meche with the Kyng, as any knygth that ys longyng to the corte. Yf yt be so, I pray God contynu yt ; and also that ye shuld mary rygth nygth of the Qwenys blood ; qwat sche ys we are not as certeyn, but yf yt be so, that yowyr lond schuld come agayne by the reason of yowyr maryage, and to be sett in rest, at the reverence of God for sake yt nowt, yf ye can fynde in yowyr harte to love hyr, so that sche be suche one as ye can

[1] Fenn's literal text reads 'that be grawntyd,' which seems to be an error. In the modern transcript it is 'that ye granted.'

EDWARD IV

thynke to have issu by, or ellys, by my trowthe, I had rather that ye never maryd in yowyr lyffe.

Also, yf yowyr mater take not now to good effecte, ye and all yowyr frendys may repent them that ye began yowyr cleyme, with owte that ye have take suche a suyr wey, as may be to yowyr intent, for many inconvenyens that may falle ther of. God send yow good spede in all yowyr maters.

Wretyn at Mawteby, the day after Seynt Austyn in May, the xviij. yer of Kyng Edward the iiij^te.

Be yowyr Modyr.

934

OXNEAD PARSONAGE[1]

The comodytys off the parsonage and the valew off the benyfyce off Oxned.

MY new parson off Oxned, whan he is instute and inducte, at the first entre in to the chyrch and benefyce off Oxned, must off awncyent custom long contynued with in the dyosesse off Norwyche, pay to the byschopp off Norwych, for the first frutes off the seyd benefyce, xiiij. marke ; for wyche xiiij. marke, iff the new parson be wytty and have favour a bowt the Byschops offycers, he schall have days off paiment to pay the seid xiiij. marke in xiiij. yere, that is, a marke a yere, till it be payd ; so that he can fynd suffycyent mene to be bownd to the Bischopp be obligacion to kepe his days off payment.

And the chyrch is but litill, and is resonable plesaunt, and reparyd. [And the] dwellyng place of the parsonage is a yoynyng to the . . . . d well howsyd and reparyd, hall, chamberes, barn, doffhowse, and all howsys off offyce.

[1] [From Paston MSS., B.M.] The date of this document is shown by the following mutilated endorsement : '. . . . . parsonage of Oxnede made xxxj. Julii, A° xviij° E. iiij^ti.' The first words were doubtless 'The value of,' or something to that effect ; but the paper is mutilated.

THE PASTON LETTERS

And it hath a doffhowse worth a yere, xiiijs. iiijd.

And it hath ij. large gardens with frute, and is yonynge to the place and chyrch yard, wher off the frute is worth yerly, xxvjs. viijd.

And ther longith to the seid parsonage in fre lond, arable, pasture and medowe ayonyng to the seid parsonage, xxij^ti acre or more, wher off every acre is worth ijs. ; to latyn [*to let*], iijli. iiijd.

And William Paston, Justice, qwan he[1] cam fyrst to dwell in the maner of Oxned, paid to the parson that was than for the corne growyng on the parsonage londys and for the tythynges, ondely but in corne whan it was inned in to the barn, xxiiijli.

And the same yere the parson had all the awterage and oder profytes be syde the seyd xxiiijli.

It is yerly worth, as the world goth now, xli.

And it is butt an esy cure to kepe, ffor ther ar natt past xx^ti persons to be yerly howselyd.[2]

The parsonage stant be a fresh ryver syde.

And ther is a good markett town callyd Alysham, within ij. myle off the parsonage.

And the cyte of Norwych is within vj. myle off the parsonage.

And the see is within x. myle off the parsonage.

And if a parson cam · now, and warr presentyd, institute, and inducte, he shuld have by the lawe all the cropp that is now growyng, that was eryd and sowyn off the old parsons cost, growyng on the parsonage landes now, as his own good, and all the tyth off all maner graynys off the maner, londes, and tenantes londes,[3] towardes his charges off the fyrst frutes. And if it ware innyd it war (the crop now growyng)[4] worth his first frutes.

[1] 'William Paston, Justice, qwan he.' These words are a correction, interlined, in the hand of William Paston, the uncle of Sir John. The text stood originally, 'And my hosbond and I whan we.'
[2] *i.e.* to receive the sacrament.
[3] *Off the maner londes and tenantes londes.* These words are interlined by William Paston.
[4] This parenthesis is an interlineation by William Paston.

EDWARD IV

[1] He that hath this benefice, and he were a pore man, myght have lycens to have service be side.

The Beshop ought not to have the valew of this cropp for the arrerages of the fyrst fruttes that Sir Thomas Everard, last parson of Oxned, oght to the Bysshop whan he died, for the said Sir Thomas Everard was bond to the Bisshop in an obligacion for the said frutes, and the said Sir Thomas Everard, for to defraude the Bysshop and oder men that he owid mony to, gaff a way his gooddes to serten persons, qwech persons toke a way the said goodes, and also durres and wyndow of the said parsonage ; and it is though that both the Bysshop and the patron myght take accions a gayns the said persons.

935

ABSTRACT[2]

Presentation by Agnes Paston of Richard Lyncoln, S.T.P., to the parish church of Oxened, *vice* Thomas Everard, deceased.

London, 5 Aug. 1478.

[1] What follows is in William Paston's hand.
[2] [From Paston MSS., B.M.]

END OF VOLUME V

Printed by T. and A. Constable, Printers to His Majesty
at the Edinburgh University Press

**The
Paston Letters**
Volume 6

THE PASTON LETTERS

Edward IV

936

SIR JOHN PASTON TO JOHN PASTON [1]

To John Paston, Esquyer, be thys lettre delyveryd, or to my mestresse, hys wyffe, at Norwych, to delyver to hym.

BROTHER John, I recomaund me to yow, and I thanke   1478
God, my sustr yowr wyffe, and yow, off my ffayr   AUG. 25
nevywe Crystofore, whyche I undrestande ye have,
wher off I ame ryght gladde, and I praye God sende yow
manye, if it be Hys plesyr ; nevertheless ye be nott kynde,
that ye sende me no wetyng ther off ; I hadde knowlege by
ffootemen, or ever ye kowde ffynde any messenger on horsbak
to brynge me worde theroff.

Sir, it is soo, that the Duke off Bokyngham shall come on
pilgrymage to Walsyngham, and so to Bokenham Castell to
my lady hys sustr ;[2] and then it is supposyd that he shalle to
my Lady off Norffolk.[3]   And myn oncle William comythe
with hym ; and he tellyth me, that ther is like to be troble in
the maner off Oxenhed ; wherffor I praye yow take hedde lesse
that the Duke off Suffolk councell pley therwith now at the
vacacion [4] off the beneffyse, as they ded with the beneffice off

[1] [From Fenn, ii. 270.]
[2] Joan, sister to Henry, Duke of Buckingham, was the second wife of Sir William Knevet, Knight, of Bokenham Castle, in Norfolk.—F.
[3] Elizabeth, widow of John Mowbray, Duke of Norfolk.—F.
[4] Agnes Paston, grandmother to Sir John, presented Thomas Everard to the Rectory of Oxnead in 1475, and in 1479, she again presented William Barthulmew, so that the Duke of Suffolk either did not attempt to disturb her right ; or at least did not succeed, if he endeavoured to do it.—F.   It will be seen by No. 935 that before presenting William Barthulmew she presented Dr. Richard Lyncoln.

VOL. VI.—A   I

THE PASTON LETTERS

1478   Drayton, whyche by the helpe off Mr. John Salett and Donne
UG. 25   hys man, ther was a qweste made by the seyde Donne, that
ffownde that the Duke off Suffolk was verrye patrone, whyche
was ffalse, yitt they ded it ffor an evydence ; but nowe iff any
suche pratte scholde be laboryd, it is I hope in bettr case, ffor
suche a thynge most needs be ffownde byffor Master John
Smyth, whyche is owr olde ffreende ; wherffor I praye yow
labor hym, that, iff neede bee, he maye doo use a ffreends torne
therin.

Item, bothe ye and I most neds take thys mater as owr
owne, and it weer ffor noon other cawse butt ffor owr goode
grawnt dames sake ; neverthelesse ye woote well, thatt ther is
an other entresse longyng to usse afftr her dyscease ; iffe ther
be any suche thynge begune ther by suche a fryer or prest, as
it is seyde, I mervayle that ye sente me no worde ther off ;
butt ye have nowe wyffe and chyld, and so moche to kar ffor,
thatt ye fforgete me.

As for tydyngs her, I her telle that my cosyn Sir Robert
Chamberleyn hathe entyrd the maner of Scolton uppon yowr
bedffelawe [1] Conyerse, wheroff ye sende me no worde.

Item, yonge William Brandon is in warde and arestyd ffor
thatt he scholde have by fforce ravysshyd and swyvyd an olde
jentylwoman, and yitt was nott therwith easyd, but swyvyd
hyr oldest dowtr, and than wolde have swyvyd the other sustr
bothe ; wherffor men sey ffowle off hym, and that he wolde
ete the henne and alle hyr chekynnys ; and som seye that the
Kynge entendyth to sitte uppon hym, and men seye he is lyke
to be hangyd, ffor he hathe weddyd a wedowe.

Item, as ffor the pagent that men sey that the Erle off
Oxenforde [2] hathe pleyid atte Hammys, I suppose ye have
herde theroff ; itt is so longe agoo, I was nott in thys contre
when the tydyngs come, therfor I sent yow no worde theroff.

But ffor conclusion, as I her seye, he lyepe the wallys, and
wente to the dyke, and in to the dyke to the chynne ; to

[1] A word at this time, implying a friend, or intimate acquaintance, who really slept in the same bed.   *See* Steevens' Shakspeare, *Henry V.* Act ii. Sc. 2.—F.
[2] John de Vere, Earl of Oxford, had been for several years a prisoner in the Castle of Hammes, in Picardy.   He became a favourite of Henry VII. and died in the reign of Henry VIII.—F.

2

EDWARD IV

whatt entent I can nott telle ; some sey, to stele awey, and   1478
some thynke he wolde have drownyd hymselffe, and so it is   AUG. 25
demyd.

No mor, but I ame nott sertayne whether I shall come
home in haste or nott.

Wretyn at London, the daye nexte Seynt Bartelmewe,[1]
anno E. iiij^d xviij°.   JOHN PASTON, K.

937

ABSTRACT [2]

WILLIAM PASTON TO NICHOLAS GOLDEWELL

Spoke to him on Sunday about a clerk presented by William Paston's   OCT. 9
mother to the Church of Oxnead, and not admitted, though the presentation
was delivered to Master John Bulman, my lord's deputy, within the time
limited by law.   Requests him to get the Bishop to do him justice.   The
living is of small value, and the delay can be of little benefit to my lord.
Desires an answer by the bearer, Sir William Upgate, Vicar of Castre.
Norwich, 9 Oct.

[The MS. is a corrected draft partly in William Paston's own hand, endorsed
'The copy of a lettre to Mr. Nicholas Goldewell, broder to   Busshopp of Norwich, ix° Octobris, anno xviij° E. iiij^d, by Sir William Ubgate, Vicar of Castre.']

938

ABSTRACT [3]

WILLIAM PASTON TO WILLIAM POPE OF BACTON

Cannot be at the Court at Paston on Monday next.   Bids him warn the   OCT. 17
tenants to keep the Court on Friday instead, and to bring their rents, for he will
be there himself.   He is also to warn the tenants of Bakton to-morrow openly

[1] St. Bartholomew's Day is the 24th August.   'The day *next* St. Bartholomew' should be the 25th, unless the writer meant to say 'next before.'
[2] [From Paston mss., B.M.]
[3] *Ibid.*

3

THE PASTON LETTERS

1478
OCT. 17
in the church of the said Court to be kept on Friday next; also the tenants of Swaffeld, Mundesley,[1] Edyngthorpe, and Wytton.

Norwich, Saturday after St. Edward,[2] the —— October.

[The MS. is a draft with corrections in the handwriting of William Paston, endorsed—'The copy of a lettre to William Pope of Bacton, the xvij. day of Octobre, anno xviij° E. iiij[ti], by William Dam of Rughton.']

939

WILLIAM PASTON, JUNIOR, TO JOHN PASTON[3]

To hys worchepful brodyr, John Paston, be thys delyvered in hast.

NOV. 7
RYGHT reverent and worchepful brodyr, I recomaunde me on to yow, desyrynge to here of yowre welfare and prosperite; letynge yow wete that I have resevyd of Alwedyr a lettyr and a nobyll in gowlde therin. Ferthermor my creansyr [*creditor*], Mayster Thomas,[4] hertely recomandyd hym to yow, and he praythe yow to sende hym sum mony for my comons; for he seythe ye be xx[tij]s. in hys dette, for a monthe was to pay for when he had mony laste.

Also I beseche yow to sende me a hose clothe, one for the halydays of sum colore, and a nothyr for the workyng days, how corse so ever it be it makyth no matyr; and a stomechere, and ij. schyrtes, and a peyer of sclyppers. And if it lyke yow that I may come with Alwedyr be watyr, and sporte me with yow at London a day or ij. thys terme tyme, than ye may let all thys be tyl the tyme that I come, and than I wol telle you

¹ This name is very ill written, and looks more like 'Maxsley'; but Mundesley is the only place in the neighbourhood that seems at all probable.
² Translation of St. Edward the Confessor, 13th October. The Saturday after it in 1478, was the 17th, but the writer has left only a blank for the day.
³ [From Paston MSS., B.M.] William Paston, the writer of this letter, was a younger son of old John Paston, and brother of the John Paston to whom the letter is addressed. He was born, as Fenn tells us, in 1459, and it will be seen by what is said of him in Letter 842 that he could not possibly be older. He was now at Eton finishing his education, and we have a letter from him written there on the 23rd of February 1479, which gives good reason for attributing this to the November immediately before.
⁴ Thomas Stevenson. *See* Letter 942 *post*.

4

when I schall be redy to come from Eton, by the grace of God, Whom have yow in Hys kepyng.

147
NOV.

Wretyn the Saturday next aftyr All Halown Day, with the hand of your brodyr,

WYLLIAM PASTON.

940

ERRANDS TO MARLINGFORD[1]

DO[2] Gerald of Marlingford come to me, and know were he ys become; in qw[at] place he hydyth hym, he dothe but distroyh hym self.

147
JAN.

Do on Steward [of] Colton, a tenaunte of Marlingford, come to me.

Do[2] Sir John Chapman,[3] parson of Oure Ladies Chyrche, send hider the bill of rekenyng of Richard Hervy, shewyng what stokke was delivered be Richard Hervy to Harry Hervy, and also a bille what costes that Richard H[ervy] . . . . of at that tyme.[4]

Do[2] John Brigg come to me and bryng me suyrte for hys dette, and know qwat wey the parson off Melton takyth with hym.

. . de the par[sone] off Melton come to me to Norwych, for tell [him that] and he come nat hastely he schall nat fynd me here.

Item, pray the parson off Melton to call up on the parteculer tenauntes off Melton that have had parteculer fermys fro Michaelmas xvij. til Michaelmas xviij. to pay ther fermys.

¹ [From Paston MSS. B.M.] This is a paper of memoranda by William Paston, partly in his own handwriting, endorsed—'Erandes to Marlyngford, the xvij. day of Januar, anno xviij°, wer off a copy was delyvered at Sent Edmundes the same d[ay].'
² 'Do,' *i.e.* cause.   ³ He was rector of St. Mary's Church, Melton.
⁴ This paragraph is crossed out in the MS.

5

THE PASTON LETTERS

941

WILLIAM PYKENHAM TO MARGARET PASTON[1]

To my Mastresse M[argaret Paston], att Norwiche.

1479
FEB. 2
MY worschypfull mastresse, I recomende me un to yow, and thanke yow of yowr approvyd ensewryd gyudenesse evermore shewde, and so I pray yow to contenew. I have resyvyd yowr letter, and undrestonde yowr desyre, wyche ys ageyns the lawe for three causys. Oon ys, for yowr son Watre ys nott tonsewryd, in modre tunge callyd Benett; a nodre cause, he ys not xxiiij. yeer of aghe, wyche ys requiryd complete; the thyrde, ye owte [*he ought*] of ryzte to be preyst within dwelmothe after that he ys parson, wyth owte so were he hadd a dyspensacion fro Rome be owre Holy Fadre the Pope, wyche I am certen can not be hadde. Therfor I present not yowr desyre un to my lorde,[2] lest ye [*he*] wolde have takyn yt ta a dysplesur, or else to take a grete sympylnesse in yowr desyre, wyche shulde cause hym, in suche matres as xall fortune yow to spede with hym a nodre tyme, to shew un to yow the rigur of the lawe, wyche I wolde be lothe; therfor present a nodre man abyll. Haske consell of Mr. John Smythe, and sease of yowr desyre in thysse partey, for yt ys not goodely nether Goddely; and lete not yowr desyre be knowyn, aftyr my avyse. Be not wrothe, thowe I sende un to yow thusse playnyly in the matre; for I wolde ye dede as wele as any woman in Norfolke, [that ys, wyth rygth],[3] to yowr honor, prosperite, an to the plesur of

¹ [From Paston MSS., B.M.] Walter Paston, to whom this letter refers, died in August 1479. This letter was probably written in the beginning of the same year. The date certainly cannot be 1478, if No. 926 has been assigned to the right year, for it will be seen that the writer was then in London, and so much occupied that he had little prospect of visiting Norfolk for some time.
² James Goldwell was consecrated by Pope Sextus IV. Bishop of Norwich in 1472. He resided much at his manor of Hoxne, where he died in 1498.—F.
³ These words are struck through with the pen.

6

Godde, with yowre and all yowres, Ho have yow in Hyse blessyd kepyng.

147
FEB.

From Hoxne on Candylmasse Day.

WILLIAM PYKYNHAM.[1]

I sende yow yowr presente agen in the boxe.

942

WILLIAM PASTON, JUNIOR, TO JOHN PASTON[2]

To his worchepfull broder, John Paston, be thys delyvered in hast.

RYGHT reverent and worchepfull broder, after all dewtes of recomendacion, I recomaunde me to yow, desyryng to here of your prosperite and welfare, whych I pray God long to contynew to Hys plesore, and to your herts desyr; letyng yow wete that I receyved a letter from yow, in the whyche letter was viijd. with the whyche I schuld bye a peyer of slyppers.

FEB.

Ferthermor certyfying yow, as for the xiijs. iiijd. whyche ye sende by a jentylmannys man, of my borde, cawlyd Thomas Newton, was delyvered to myn hostes, and soo to my creancer [*creditor*], Mr. Thomas Stevenson; and he hertely recomended hym to yow.

Also ye sende me worde in the letter of xijli. fyggs and viijli. reysons. I have them not delyvered, but I dowte not I shal have, for Alwedyr tolde me of them, and he seyde that they came aftyr in an other barge.

And as for the yong jentylwoman, I wol certyfye yow how I fryste felle in qweyntaince with hyr. Hir ffader is dede; ther be ij. systers of them; the elder is just weddyd; at the whych weddyng I was with myn hostes, and also desyryd by

¹ William de Pykenham became Chancellor of Norwich and Archdeacon of Suffolk in 1471, and was also some time Rector of Hadleigh in Suffolk, where he built the grand gate or tower before the parsonage. He died in 1497.—F.
² [From Fenn, i. 296.] This letter was written on the 23rd of February, and the Monday following the date was the first Monday of Lent. These particulars prove the letter to have been written in 1479, when William Paston was between nineteen and twenty years of age.

7

THE PASTON LETTERS

479
B. 23 the jentylman hym selfe, cawlyd Wylliam Swanne, whos dwyll-
ynge is in Eton.

So it fortuned that myne hostes reportyd on me odyrwyse
than I was wordy; so that hyr moder comaundyd hyr to
make me good chere, and soo in good feythe sche ded. Sche
is not a bydynge ther sche is now; hyr dwellyng is in London;
but hyr moder and sch come to a place of hyrs v. myle from
Eton, were the weddyng was, for because it was nye to the
jentylman whych weddyd hyr dowtyr. And on Monday next
comynge, that is to sey, the fyrst Monday of Clene Lente,
hyr moder and sche wyl goo to the pardon at Schene, and soo
forthe to London, and ther to abyde in a place of hyrs in Bowe
Chyrche Yerde; and if it plese yow to inquere of hyr, hyr
modyrs name is Mestres Alborow, the name of the dowtyr is
Margarete Alborow, the age of hyr is be all lykelyod xviij. or
xix. yere at the fertheste. And as for the mony and plate,
it is redy when soo ever sche were weddyd; but as for the
lyvelod, I trow not tyll after hyr modyrs desese, but I can not
telle yow, for very certeyn, but yow may know by inqueryng.
And as for hyr bewte, juge yow that when ye see hyr, yf so
be that ye take the laubore, and specialy beolde hyr handys,
for and if it be as it is tolde me, sche is dysposyd to be thyke.

And as for my comynge from Eton, I lake no thynge
but wersyfyynge, whyche I troste to have with a lytyll contynuance.

Quæritur, Quomodo non valet hora, valet mora? Unde
dicitur?

> Arbore jam videas exemplum. Non die possunt,
> Omnia suppleri; sed tamen illa mora.

And thes too verse afore seyde be of myn own makyng.

No more to yow at thys tyme, but God have yow in Hys
kepyng.

Wretyn at Eton the Even of Seynt Matthy the Apostyll
in haste, with the hande of your broder.

WYLL'M PASTON, Jun'.

¹ I am favoured by Lady Beatrice Pretyman with a facsimile of this Latin theme
and distich from the original MS. My reading of the contracted words differs from
that printed originally by Fenn.

8

943

PARSONAGE OF OXNEAD¹

MEMORANDUM.—The day that the lapse went out, 1479
which is such day vj. monethes as the seid parson
died, was on Tewesday, Our Lady Day, the Nativite,
the viijᵗᵉ day of Septembre last past, anno xviijᵒ.

The day of vj. monethes affter Our seide Lady Day, the
Nativite was on Seint Mathes Day² the Apostell, last past,
whiche was the xxiiij. day of Februare, and so I deme eyther
the Bisshoppe of Norwiche hath presented or els it is in the
gifft of my Lord Cardinall³ nowe. Inquere this mater, for the
Bisshoppe of Norwich lythe in London, and shall doo till Our
Ladys Day this Lenton, as it is said here.

My moder delivered Sir William Holle his presentacion
the xiij. day of August, anno xviijᵒ, which was nere a monethe
or the day of the vj. monethes went out and past. Wherfore
the Bisshoppe ought to present my moders clarke. Neverthelesse the Bisshoppys officeres aunsware this sayng, that if
sondry persones deliver ij. sondrye presentacions for to diverse
clarkes to the Bisshoppes officers for one benefice, that then
the seid partyes shuld sue to the Bisshop at ther cost to have
out an inquerre to inquere de vero patrono, sayng forther more,
that if they sue nat out this inquerre with affect, and that the
lapse fall, than it is lefull for the Bisshop to present, and it
is told me that the lawe is this, that the Bisshoppe, be his
office with out any sute of the parties, shall call an inquerre
afore hym to inquere de vero patrono, and he shall assign them
a day to bryng in a verdett, and he shall warne bothe partyes
to be ther at, and he shall amytte his clarke that is founde
patron.

¹ [Add. Charter 17,251, B.M.] It is sufficiently evident that the date of this
paper must be later than the 24th February, 1479. It appears to be a set of
memoranda or instructions by William Paston, addressed to his servant Richard
Lee. The MS. is a small roll of paper very mutilated and partly illegible from the
effect of damp.
² St. Matthias' Day (not St. Matthew's) is meant.
³ Thomas Bourchier, Archbishop of Canterbury.

9

THE PASTON LETTERS

479 Yet the Bisshopp useth nat to do this, but there as bothe
partyes that present are myghty [and wher as he thynketh it
were a jopardy to hym]¹ to sue the Bisshoppe if he did them
any wrong, and wher as ther is a doubtable mater; but in this
case the prest that troubleth my moder is but a simple felowe,
and he is appostata, for he was somtyme a White Frere, and of
simple repetacyon, and of litill substans, as my moder can tell,
wherfore Bisshoppys use nat in suche litill casys to take so
streyte an inquerre, and specyally wher as one hath contynued
patron with out interupcion so long as my moder hath done,
for she hath contynued more than l. wynter; wherfore I pray
yow shewe my cousyn Lovell this bill, and fynde some meanes
to intrete the Bisshopp by the meane of James Hobard,² which
is grete with the Bisshopp, and is nowe Reder of Lyncoln Inne
this Lent. And late my lady speke to James Hobard in the
mater. If it please my moder ther is a prest callde Sir ———³
which is thought by the tenauntes of Oxned a metely man to
be parson ther; the most thyng that I dowte, bicause Sir
William Holle, whom my moder presented, is ronne away,
and if the Bisshop will nat present my moders clarke in her
title, than I wold that the labour myght be made to the
Bisshopp, that he myght present my moders clarke, suche on
as shoe will name, in his one title.

Ric. Lee, like as ze may understand be this writing, where
as I understod that the Bisshopp myght have kept the benefice
but vj. monethes after the patrons vj. monethes war worn out,
now I understand the contrary, for I understand he may kepe
it a twelmo[nethe] and a day . . . . [several lines lost]
. . . .

Also, if ze knew any yong preste in London that setteth
billis upon Powlys dorr per aventure wold be glad to have it,
and woll be glad also to serve my lady and my moder for it
for a season, I can no more say but purvay a mean to the
Bisshopp, that som mon may be put in by my moders title.

. . . . . of the consistore in Norwich, and he hath

¹ Crossed out in MS.
² Afterwards Attorney-General to Henry VII. He was Reader of Lincoln's Inn
in Lent, 18 Edward IV.
³ Blank in MS.

10

a broder in the Tower, is master of the Mynt under Brice, 1479
called Bartilmew Rede, and a nother broder is a goold smyth
dwelling in the Chepe Side called ———¹ Reede. And he is
eyther loged with on of these, his breder, or els at the Jorge
in Lumbard Strete, or els at the Cok and the Bell at Billinges
gate, a brue hous, for the sei[d] gold smyth hath maried a
bruewyf, and kepeth the brue hous, (?) and he can good skylle
to helpe in this mater of the benefice of Oxned.

Also, Ric. Lee, who so ever shalbe [presented to the]
benefice of Oxned, he muste tell hym, I must pay xiiij. marc
to the frutes, and ther for shall he have [da]yes of payment to
pay a marc azey[n] if he d[o] gete hym frendschip. And also,
Richard, at the makyng of this letter I mend (?) to have ben
sure (?) . . . . . . and now I in na . . . . .
for if it please my moder, me thynke it was well done, Sir
William Storor had . . . .

[The rest unintelligible.]

944

EDMUND ALYARD TO MARGARET PASTON²

To his worshepful mastres, Mastres Margaret Paston.

RIGHT worshepful mastres, I recommande me unto yow MARCH 4
as lowly as I kan, thankyng yow for your goodnes at
all tymis; God graunt me to deserve it, and do that
may plese yow.

As for your son Water, his labor and lernyng hathe be,
and is, yn the Faculte of Art, and is well sped there yn, and
may be Bacheler at soche tyme as shall lyke yow, and then to
go to lawe. I kan thynk it to his preferryng, but it is not

¹ Blank in original.
² [From Paston MSS., B.M.] It appears by subsequent letters that Walter Paston
actually took a degree at Oxford at Midsummer, and it will be seen by next letter,
which is dated by its endorsement, that he must have done so in 1479—the year of
his death.

11

THE PASTON LETTERS

1479
MARCH 4   good he know it on to the tyme he shal chaunge ; and as I conceyve ther shal non have that exibeshyon to the Faculte of Lawe. Therfore meve ze the executores that at soche tyme as he shal leve it, ye may put a nother yn his place, soche as shal lyke you to prefer. If he shal go to law, and be made Bacheler of Art be fore, and ye wolle have hym hom this yere, then may he be Bacheler at Mydsomor, and be with yow yn the vacacion, and go to lawe at Mihelmas. Qwhat it shal lyke yow to commande me yn this or eny odir, ye shal have myn service redy.

I pray yow be the next masenger to send me your entent, that swech as shal be necessary may be purveyid yn seson. And Jesu preserve yow.

At Oxinforth, the iiij. day of March.

> Your scoler,
>   EDMUND ALYARD.

945

WALTER PASTON TO SIR JOHN PASTON[1]

To hys ryth reverend broder, Sir John Paston, at Caster Hall, in Norfolk.

MAY 22   AFTER all dw reverens and recomendacions, likyth yt yow to understond that I reseyvyd a letter fro my broder John, where by I understod that my moder and yow wold know what the costes of my procedyng schold be. I sent a letter to my broder John, certyfyyng my costes, and the causys why that I wold procede ; but as I have sent word to my moder, I purpose to tary now tyll yt be Mychylmas, for yf I tary tyll than, sum of my costys schall be payyd ; for I supposed, whan that I sent the letter to my broder John, that the Qwenys broder[2] schold have procedyd at Mydsomer, but he woll tary now tyll Michylmas ; but as I send word to

---

[1] [From Paston MSS., B.M.] This letter is endorsed in a contemporary hand, apparently Sir John Paston's own, 'anno xix°,' showing that it was written in the nineteenth year of Edward IV.

[2] Lionel Woodville, afterwards Bishop of Salisbury.

12

THE PASTON LETTERS

1479
JUNE 30   yf yow come to Oxon, ye schal see the letter, and all the leterys that yow sent me sythynnys I came to Oxon.

And also Master Brown had that same tyme mysch mony in a bage, so that he durst nat bryng yt with hym, and that same letter was in that same bage, and he had for gete to take owt the letter, and he sent all to geder by London, so that yt was the next day after that I was maad Bachyler or than the letter cam, and so the fawt was not in me.

And yf ye wyl know what day I was maad Baschyler, I was maad on Fryday was sevynyth, and I mad my fest on the Munday after. I was promysyd venyson a geyn my fest of my Lady Harcort, and of a noder man to, but I was deseyvyd of both ; but my gestes hewld them plesyd with such mete as they had, blyssyd be God, Hoo have yow in Hys kepyng. Amen.

Wretyn at Oxon, on the Wedenys day next after Seynt Peter.

> W. PASTON.

947

ABSTRACT[1]

JULY 7   Bill witnessing the delivery of plate by Geoffrey Hunt on behalf of William Paston to John Davy and Alice, his wife, late wife of John Gygges of Burnham, 7 July, 19 Edw. IV. The parcels are :—'A round salt covered, parcel gilt at the borders, weighing 19 oz. 1½ qr., and also 6 silver spoons, square sharp knoppys, weighing 5 oz. 3 qr. 1 dwt.'; which Davy and his wife engage to keep safely, and redeliver to William Paston or Geoffrey Hunt before the feast of St. Faith next coming.

[*Two seals.*]

948

ABSTRACT[2]

WILLIAM PASTON TO THOMAS LYNSTED

JULY 11   Hears that he has felled wood and firs, etc. 'Also Jullis hath do made saw (?) zattes.' Desires him to 'find the means that the young spring may be

---

[1] [From Paston MSS., B.M.]   [2] *Ibid.*

14

EDWARD IV

my moder, I wold be Inceptor be fore Mydsomer, and there fore I besechyd her to send me sum mony, for yt woll be sum cost to me, but not mych.   1479
MAY 2

And, syr, I besech yow to send me word what answer ye have of the Buschopp of Wynchester for that mater whych ye spak to hym of for me whan I was with yow at London. I thowth for to have had word there of or thys tyme. I wold yt wold come, for owr fyndyng of the Buschopp of Norwych begynnyth to be slake in payment. And yf ye know not whath thys term menyth, 'Inceptor,' Master Edmund, that was my rewler at Oxforth, berar here of, kan tell yow, or ellys any oder gradwat.

Also I pray yow send me word what ys do with the hors I left at Totnam, and whyder the man be content that I had yt of, or nat. Jesu preserve yow to Hys pleswre and to yowr most hartys desyyr.

Wretyn at Oxforth, the Saturday next after Ascensyon of Yowr Lord.

> WALTER PASTON.

946

WALTER PASTON TO JOHN PASTON[1]

To hys ryth trusty and hartyly belovyd broder, John Paston, abydyng at the Georg, at Powlys Qwharfe, in London, be this letter delyveryd.

RYGTH worchypfull and hartyly belovyd broder, I recomaund me on to yow, desyeryng feythfoly to here of yowr prosperyte, qwhych God preserve, thankyng yow of dyverse letterys that yow sent me. In the last letter that yow sent to me, ye wryt that yow schold have wryt in the letter that yow sent by Master Brown, how that I schold send yow word what tyme that I schold procede, but ther was non such wrytyng in that letter. The letter is yet to schew, and   JUNE 3

---

[1] [From Paston MSS., B.M.] *See* preliminary note to Letter 944, p. 11, note 2.

13

EDWARD IV

saved, and the wood fenced. . . . . And also let me be answered both for the old payment and the new of wood sale.'   1479
JULY 1
11 July.

P.S.—'If Jullis have made a gate, it is the better for the spring,' etc.

[The MS. is a very illegible note in William Paston's hand, written on a small scrap of paper, and endorsed 'A letter to Thomas Linsti[d], the —— (*blank*) day of Julii, anno xix. E. iiij[t].']

949

WILLIAM PASTON TO HENRY WARYNS[1]

HARRY WARYNS, I grete you well, and I thanke you for youre labour. And as for the tenauntez of Knapton, I understand by youre writing that they take non oder consideration to my sendyng but that I call so fast on my fee, for cause they thynke that I am aferd lest I shuld have it no longer ; and as for that, I pray yow tell them for ther ungentilnes I woll have my fee of them, and in that maner and in non oder place ; and ferthermor I shall fynd the mene that they shall paye it more hastely here after. And as for the money that they offyr to pay at the fest of Advincula Sancti Petri, receyve ye it off them and I shall assign one to receyve it azen of yow. As for the delivere of the catell, I fele be zowr wrytyng they will non sounar pay it thow ther catell shuld dye ffor ffawte off mete. Wer for, affor the money be paid I putt that in zour discresseon wheder ze will deliver them or nay ; as ze do I hold me content.

Also as for Thomas Child, I understande be zour wrytyng he will not seale the indenture be cawse ther is no some of mony sertayne ne days of payment sett in the indentur ; and as for that, I will neyther sett some nor days after his will ; and if he will nat seale that, he shall never seale none for me ; and at last I am sure he shall sell. I send zow azen the same indenture that ze sent me, that ze may kepe it still as long as   JULY 1

---

[1] [Add. MS. 34,889, f. 133.] The year of this letter appears by the endorsement. The MS. is a draft, partly in a clerk's hand, corrected and continued in that of William Paston himself.

15

THE PASTON LETTERS

1479
Y 19
Thomas Chyld abyde now at Paston, in aventure the casse may hap that he will sell yt herafter ; and yff he be on departid, than send me both the indenture[s] to London be some massenger. As for Waryn Kynge, wer I understand be zour wrytyn that he seyth he delyver me all evydens, I understand not that ; and as for rentall I am sure he deliver me none, and yff so be that he can make the rentall be hart, I wold he did make on [one], for it war necessare for me ; for I understande be zow that ther was no rent gaderid this xv. ar xvj. zer for defallte off a rentall ; and therfor yt is I had a call on the prior of Bromholm for the xxx. comb malt that ze toke hym. Wrytyn at Norton the xix. day of Jull'

By   W. PASTON.

Endorsed by the writer :—

‘A letter to Harry Waryns the xix day of Jule, A° xix E. iiijᵗ by John Ancell off Paston.’

950

WILL OF WALTER PASTON [1]

s. 18
IN Dei nomine, Amen. Ego, Walterus Paston, clericus, in bona et sana memoria existens, condo testamentum meum apud Norwicum xviiij° die mensis Augusti in hunc modum. Inprimis lego animam meam Deo Omnipotenti, Beatæ Mariæ et omnibus Sanctis, et corpus meum ad sepeliendum in ecclesia Sancti Petri de Hundegate, coram ymagine Sancti Johannis Baptistæ. Item, lego summo altari præfatæ ecclesiæ, ijs. iiijd. Item, lego reparacioni ecclesiæ supradictæ, ijs. vjd. Item, Fratri Johanni Somerton, bachalaureo, vs. Item, lego Magistro Edmundo unam togam penulatam cum manicis de mynkys. Item, lego Roberto Wulff unam togam viridem ——² cum chamelet. Item, lego Roberto Holand, filio spirituali, togam meam curtam. Item, lego

[1] [From Paston MSS., B.M.] It will be seen by the next letter that Walter Paston was dead before the 21st August 1479. This will was probably drawn up on the very day he died, or just before.
² Blank in MS.

16

THE PASTON LETTERS

1479
3. 19
First, a bason and an ewer with iij. combis in a skochyn.
Item, a silver potte.
A layer of silver, parte gilte with an acorne on the knoppe.
A gilte stonding couppe ponsid with a cover.
A chasid pece with a cover aparte gilte.
ij. playne pecys.
ij. deppe disshis.
x. sponys.
A white playne coppe with a starre in the botom with a cover.
A standing coppe gilte with a cover.
A candellstik of silver with a sokette.
A trevett of silver.
A salt of silver with a brokyn cover.
A cover for a playn pece, the knoppe gravid with armys.

RICHARD LEE.

Endorsed—‘Plate of William Paston left with John Russhe, the xiij. day of Sept., a° xix°.’

952

[EDMUND PASTON TO JOHN PASTON [1]]

. 21
SUER dydynges arn com to Norwyche that my grandam is dyssessyd, whom God assoyle. Myn uncle had a messenger zesterday that she shuld not escape, and this day cam a nother at suche tyme as we were at masse for my brother Water, whom God assoyle ! Myn uncle was comyng to have offered, but the last messenger retornyd hym hastely, so that he toke hys hors incontynent to enforme more of owr hevynes. My syster ys delyverd, and the chyld passyd to God, Who send us Hys grace.

Dokkyng told me sekretly that for any hast myn uncle shuld ryde by my Lady of Norffolk to have a iij. skore persons, whyther it is to convey my grandham hyder or

[1] [From Paston MSS., B.M.] This letter is neither signed nor addressed, but is in the handwriting of Edmund Paston, and is endorsed by John Paston the younger, ‘Dies mortis A. P.’

18

EDWARD IV

Magistro Roberto Hollar unam togam penulatam cum gray. 1479
Item, lego Johanni Parker mantellum meum rubeum. Item, AUG. 18
lego Magistro Roberto Hollere unum pulvinar vocatum le bolstar. Item, lego Magistro Edmundo Alyard unum pulvinar. Item, lego Ricardo Richardson unam togam penulatam ad manus cum menyver. Item, volo quod residuum bonorum meorum in Oxonia sit ad usum Magistri Edmundi Alyard, sic quod solvat . . . .¹ Johanni Skelton et Thomæ Coco. Item, volo quod oves meæ, quas habet Willelmus Bataly senior in villa de Mawteby, dividantur equaliter inter fratrem meum Edmundum Paston, et sororem meam Annam Yelverton, et sororem meam Margeriam Paston, uxorem fratris mei Johannis Paston. Item, lego terras et tenementa manerij mei de Cressyngham, si possum dare, fratri meo Johanni Paston armigero, sibi et hæredibus suis, sub condicione ista, quod si contingat fratrem meum prædictum, Johannem Paston, esse hæredem patris mei, quod nullo modo habeat terras et tenementa prædicta, sed quod frater meus Edmundus Paston habeat terras et tenementa prædicta sibi et suis hæredibus. Residuum vero bonorum non legatorum lego et do disposicioni executorum meorum, ut et ipsi fideliter disponant pro anima mea.

Hujus autem testamenti mei executores condo per præsentes, fratrem meum Johannem Paston, armigerum, pro ista patria, et Magistrum Edmundum Alyard pro bonis meis remanentibus Oxoniæ.

951

WILLIAM PASTON'S PLATE [2]

THIS indenture made the xix. day of August, anno xix° AUG. 19
[witnesseth]³ that I, Richard Lee, have delivered to Mr. John Russhe thes parcellis folowyng of plate [and]⁴ of silver :—

¹ Here occurs a short word, which is to me unintelligible. It seems to be written ‘puli.’
² [Add. MS. 27,451, f. 2, B.M.]
³ Omitted in MS.   ⁴ Erased.

VOL. VI.—B   17

EDWARD IV

1479
AUG. 21
nowght he cowde not sey ; I deme it is rather to put them in possessyon of some of her londes.

Wretyn the Saterdaye the xxi. daye of August, anno E. iiijᵗⁱ xix°.

953

ABSTRACT [1]

MANOR OF MARLINGFORD

Declaration by Robert Mill, John Hobbes, John Claryngton, Thomas AUG. 26
Davy, John Brygge, John Watyr, and William Parson, tenants of the manor of Marlyngford, before the Abbot of St. Benet's, John [R]adclyf Fywater,² Mr. John Smyth, Robert Ippeswell, William Lomnor, John Paston, Esq., William Yelverton, senior, John Coke, alderman, William Bastard, gentleman, and William Fuller, that they have always held of the manor in the name of Agnes Paston, daughter, and one of the heirs of Edmund Bery, Knt., and in her name only, till Saturday [21 Aug.] before St. Bartholomew Apostle, 19 Edw. IV., when her son, William Paston, desired them to attorn to him without showing writing or evidence.

Done in the parlour of John Cooke, 26 Aug., 19 Edw. IV.   Signed: ‘Thomas, Abbot of Seynt Benettes of Hulme.’—‘J. Radclyff Fytzwauter.’— ‘John Smyth, clerk.’—‘Robert Ipeswell.’—‘Will. Lomnor.’—‘W. Yelverton.’ —‘John Cook.’—‘Will'm Bastard.’—‘Will. Fuller.’

954

MEMORANDA [3]

AUG.
MEMORANDUM, uppon the presse at the ferther ende is a box with ij. or iij. bondellis with evydence off Oxenhed and Hawteyn.

Memorandum, that ther is rollis tytelyd uppon them ‘Contra Willelmum Pas[ton],’ and they be owther uppon the

¹ [From Paston MSS., B.M.]
² John Radcliff, son and heir of Sir John Radcliff, called Lord Fitzwalter in No. 450 (vol. iii.). He was summoned to Parliament as Lord Fitzwalter in the first year of Henry VII.
³ [From Paston MSS., B.M.] These memoranda are in the handwriting of Sir John Paston. From the inquiry whether Agnes Paston was yet buried the date is evidently in August 1479.

19

1479
AUG.
presse, or on the cowntre, or on the shelffe by the cowntre, or ellys in the cowntre on . . . that syde next the shelffe.

To enquire, off myn, oncle William, off Jane, off my grauntd[ames] wylle, and whoo wrot itt, and whether she be buried or noo, and who were present at hyr wylle makyng, and iff she spoke . . . . . owte off her londes.

Inquire—

    Off the Kynge,
    The Chaunceler,
    Milorde Chamberleyn,
    Sir Thomas Mongomere,
    Mi Lorde Cardynall,
    Master Bele, and hys clerke, ffor my faderes wille.

955

RICHARD CALLE TO MARGARET PASTON [1]

1479,
or
earlier
Plesith it your mastrership to witte, that I sende you a boxe with evidence of Baktons londes, weche plesith it you to delyver to my master, Sir John, so that I may have my money that is behynde. And as for Sporle, I sende you an endenture of the bercars [2] and iij. obligacions eche of v. marke. And as for any endenture of the wode sale I made non, but a noote breefely of the effecte, wech I sende you, as I tolde my mastre at Cristemas, and that tyme he seide to me he was the better plesid, and so I ded no more therto; and an obligacion of Cli. weche they be bounde to hym to performe ther ther covinauntes; weche remayneth in the handes of the veker of Sporle. And I send you also ij. billes of the parcell of the wode sale, bothe the wynter sale and the somer sale, wherof the veker of Sporle and William Halman have the other parties of them, as he comaunded hym selfe at the begynnyng. And lete my countrelle doo what hym liste. I fynd hym a trewe man; he dothe as he hath reported that he shuld go on my harond, and so I undrestond from the[m] he hath do; but thow I have lost a frende of hym in that quarter, I have mo frendes in that contre the[n] hee, etc. Mastres, it were goode to remembre

---

[1] [From Paston MSS., B.M.] This letter is not addressed, but seems to have been intended for Margaret Paston. The date is not very material, but as it mentions Sir John Paston, it cannot be later than 1479, the year in which he died. Perhaps it is about the year 1472. *See* Nos. 819, 820.

[2] Barkers, or tanners to whom the bark of the woods had been sold.

20

1479
OCT. 29
supose that he hathe gaddryd at Paston and other places, by thys tyme; ffor with owte I have thys *xli.*, as God helpe me, I ffer I shalle doo butt litell goode in noo mater, nor yitt I woote nott howe to come home, but iff I have it.

This geer hathe troblyd me so, that itt hathe made me moor than halffe seke, as God helpe me.

Item, I understande that myn oncle William hathe made labor to th' Exchetor, and that he hathe bothe a wrytte off *essend.* clowsyth extr.; and also a *supercedeas.* I have wretyn to the Exchetor ther in off myn entent, iff myn oncle hadde hys wyll in that, yitt sholde he be never the nerre the londe, butt in effecte he shold have thys advantage, whyche is behovefull ffor a weyke mater to have a colour, or a clooke, or a botrase.

But on Tywesdaye I was with the Bysshop off Hely,[1] whyche shewyth hymselffe goode and worshypfull; and he seyde that he sholde sende to myn oncle William, that he sholde nott procede in no suche mater, till that he speke with hym; and moor ovyr that he sholde cawse hym to be heer hastelye; in whyche mater is no remedy as nowe, but iff it wer soo, that the Exchetor, iff he be entretyd to sytte by myn oncle William, whyche percase he shall nott, that iff my brother John and Lomnor have knowleche off the daye, and they myght be ther; Lomnor can geve evydence i now in that mater with owte the boke; and mor ovyr that they see bothe the letter and the other noote, that I sente to the Exchetor, and with helpe off the Exchetor all myght be as beste is; and iff my brother and Lomnor take labor her in, I shal recompence ther costs.

Wretyn in haste with schort advisement on the Frydaye next Seynt Symonds and Jude, anno E. iiij[ti] xix°.

Late my brother John se thys bille, for he knoweth mor off thys mater.

JOHN PASTON, K.

---

[1] John Morton, afterwards Archbishop of Canterbury, and Cardinal.

22

1479
or
earlier
your stuffe of heryng nough this fisshyng tyme. I have goten me a frende in Lestoftot to helpe to purvey me of an vij. or viij. barell, and shal not stonde me upon above vj*r*. viij*d*. a barell, so that he may have money nough in the begynnyng, ye shal do more nough with xl*s*. then ye shal do at Cristemes with v. marke. The fisshyng at Yermouth wol not be so goode as it wolbe at Leystoft, for the haven wol not prove yette, etc. Almyghty God kepe you. Wrete this daye.

Be your servaunt, R.C.

956

SIR JOHN PASTON TO MARGARET PASTON [1]

To the ryght worshypfull mestresse, Margret Paston, be thys delyveryd.

1479
OCT. 2
PLEASE it yow to weet, that I have ben heer at London a xiiij. nyght, wheroff the ffyrst iiij. dayes I was in suche ffeer off the syknesse, and also ffownde my chambr and stuffe nott so clene as I demyd, whyche troblyd me soor; and as I tolde yow at my departyng, I was nott weell monyed, ffor I hadde nott paste x. marke, wheroff I departyd xl*s*. to be delyveryd off my olde bedfelawe; and then I rode be yonde Donstaple, and ther spake with on off my cheffe witnessis, whyche promysed me to take labor, and to gete me wryghtyngs towchyng thys mater bytwyen me and the Duke of Suffolk,[2] and I rewardyd hym xx*s*.; and then, as I informyd yow, I payed v. marke incontynent uppon my comyng hyddr to replegge owte my gowne off velwett and other geer.

And then I hopyd to have borowyd some off Townesend, and he hath ffoodyd me[3] fforthe evyrsynys, and in effecte I cowde have at the most, and at the sonest yisterdaye xx*s*. wherffor I beseche yow to purveye me C*s*. and also to wryght to Pekok, that he purveye me as moche, C*s*. whyche I

---

[1] [From Fenn, ii. 276.]   [2] John de la Pole, Duke of Suffolk.—F.

[3] Fenn reads 'ffoodyd ne,' and in the modern copy 'fooded not forth,' of which some fanciful explanations are suggested in a footnote. The true reading ought certainly to be ' me ' and not ' ne,' the meaning evidently being ' he has put me off ever since.' ' To fode out with words ' is an expression which, as Halliwell informs us, occurs in Skelton, Harrington, etc.

21

957

JOHN PASTON TO SIR JOHN PASTON [1]

To Syr John Paston, Knyght.

1479
NOV. 6
SYR, aftyr all dwtes of recomendacyon, pleasyt to undyrstand, that, acordyng to your lettre sent me by Wyllson, Lomnore and I mett at Norwyche and drew ought a formable bylle ought of your, and send it ayen to th'Exchetore Palmer by my brodyr Edmund, whyche had an other erand in to that contre to spek with H. Spylman, to get hys good wyll towardes the bargayn lyek to be fynyshed hastyly betwyx Mastres Clyppysby and hym. And, syr, at the delyvere of the bylle of inquisicyon to th'Exchetour, my brodyr Edmund told hym that accordyng to your wryghtyng to me, I spak with myn oncle William, and told hym that I undyrstood by yow that my Lord of Elye had aswell desyred hym in wryghtyng as you by mouthe, that non of you shold swe to have the inquisycion fond aftyr your intentys tyll other weyes of pese wer takyn betwyx you; wherfor my brodyr Edmund desyred hym that with ought myn oncle labord to have it fond for hym, ellys that he shold not procede for yow; but th'Exchetour answerd hym that he wold fynd it for you, aftyr your byll, of hys owne autorite; and so it was fond. But, syr, ye must remembre that my Lord of Ely desyred myn oncle as well as you to surcease, as I put myn oncle in knowlage, and myn oncle at the fyrst agreid that he wold make no more sute a bought it, in trust that ye wold do the same, acordyng to my Lord of Elys desyer; wherfor ye had ned to be ware that th'Exchetor skyppe not from you, when he comyth to London, and sertyfye it, or ye spek with hym. Th'Exchetor shalbe at London by Twysdaye or Wednysday next comyng, at John

---

[1] [From Paston MSS., B.M.] It will be seen from the contents that this letter must have been written after the receipt of the last, or of one to the same effect addressed to John Paston.

23

479
ov. 6 Leeis house, for he shall ryd forwardys as on Monday next comyng be tymys, &c.

Syr, your tenauntes at Crowmer sey that they know not who shalbe ther lord ; they marvayll that ye nor no man for yow hathe not yet ben there. Also, when I was with myn oncle, I had a longe pystyll of hym, that ye had sent Pekok to Paston, and comandyd the tenauntes ther that they shold pay non arersgys to hym, but if [unless] they wer bond to hym by obligacyon for the same ; myn oncle seythe it was other wyse apoyntyd be for the arbytrorys ; they thought, he seythe, as well my Mastyr Fytzwalter as other, that he shold receyve that as it myght be gadryd ; but now he seythe, that he wottyth well some shall renne away, and some shall wast it, so that it is nevyr lyek to be gadryd, but lost, and so I trow it is lyek to be of some of the dettors, what for casuelte of dethe and thes other causes befor rehersyd ; wherfor me thynkyth if it were apoyntyd befor the arbytrors that he shold receyve theym, as he seythe, it wer not for you to brek it, or ellys if he be pleyn executor to my grauntdam, then also he ought to have it. I spek lyek a blynd man, do ye as ye thynk, for I was at no syche apoyntment befor th'arbytrors, nor I know not whethyr he is executor to my grauntdam or not, but by hys seying.

Also, syr, ye must of ryght, consyderyng my brodyr Edmundys diligence in your maters, sythe your departyng, helpe hym forwardys to myn oncle Syr George Brown, as my brodyr Edmund preyid yow in hys lettyr that he sent on to yow by Mondys sone of Norwyche, dwellyng with Thomas Jenney, that myn oncle Syr George may gett to my brodyr Edmund of the Kyng the wardshepp of John Clyppysby, son and heyer to John Clyppysby,[1] late of Owby, in the conte of Norffolk, Sqwyr, dwryng the nonnage of my Lord and Lady of York,[2] thow it cost iiij. or v. mark the swte. Let myn oncle

[1] The writer probably intended to say 'son and heir to William Clippesby,' who died about this time. His widow Catherine, the daughter of John Spelman, Esq., of Stow Bekerton, soon afterwards married Edmund Paston.

[2] Richard, Duke of York, son of Edward iv., at this time a child of seven years old, and Anne Mowbray, daughter of the late Duke of Norfolk, to whom he was married in 1478.

24

958

WILLIAM PASTON TO ROBERT WALSH[1]

479
NV. 22 YET wold I tary, all be yt I have taryd your comyg this halff yer, for I deme her suche men as schall well undyrstond myn titill good ; yff any man have good tytyll I am suyr that myn is gode. I dar well juperde to take a dystres, wedyr they come or nat, and so I wyll ze know. Wer for, in so much as I left myn distress for iowr dysyr, so that I be answerid off myn mony acordyng to myn ryth, ar else send me answer, one ar oder [one or other], and lett me take the avantage that the Kynge lawys will zeff me be dystress qweche I have delayed, me thynk to long, for any thank that I have.

Wretyn at Norwich, the xxij. Novembre.

959

JULLYE TO HIS FATHER[2]

NOV.
Well beloved fader, my master prayed you that ye will sende knowlach be my broder as sone as these men be come to Knapton, and that ye may laye a weche to knowe ho sone they be come, and sende me be your sone ar else be some other trusty man ; and I have take your son a grote for his laubour. And do this in hast ; for wheder they com or nat I wille take a distresse ther, and thatt will abide[3] till I knowe the dealing of them this ij. ar iij. dayes for to know wheder they wille come or nat, and ther after shall I be demaned.

Endorsed in William Paston's hand—A letter fro ——[4] Jullye, clark of Sent Edmundes, to his fadyr, to North Walsham, the ——[4] day Novembr', anno xix.

[1] [From Paston MSS., B.M.] This letter or fragment of a letter is a corrected draft in William Paston's hand, and is endorsed by him :—'A letter to Roberd Walsche of Colby, the —— day off Novembre, anno xix.'

[2] [From Paston MSS., B.M.]

[3] ' Wer I lothe ' has been crossed through, and ' thatt will abide ' written over.

[4] Blanks in MSS.

26

Syr George be clerk of the haniper, and kepe the patent, if it 1479 be grantyd, tyll he have hys mone, and that shall not be NOV. 6 longe to.

Myn oncle Syr George may enforme the Kyng for trowthe, that the chyld shall have no lond duryng hys yong modyrs lyff, and ther is no man her that wyll mary with hym withought they have some lond with hym, and so the gyft shall not be gret that the Kyng shold geve hym ; and yet I trow he shold get the modyr by that meane, and in my conseyt the Kyng dothe but ryght if he graunt my brodyr Edmund Clyppysbys son in recompense for takyng my brodyr Edmundes son, otherwyse callyd Dyxsons, the chyldys fadyr being alyve. Dyxson is ded, God have hys sowle, Whom I beseche to send you your most desyred joye.

Wretyn at Norwyche, on Seynt Leonardes Day.

J. PASTON.

Syr, it is told me that Nycolas Barlee, the Scyuer, hathe takyn an axion of dett ayenst me thys terme. I prey yow let Whetley or some body spek with hym, and lete hym wet that if he swe me softly thys terme, that he shall be payed or the nexte terme be at an end. It is a bought vj*li.*, and in feythe he shold have had it or thys tyme, and our threshers of Sweynsthorp had not dyed upp ; and if I myght have payed it hym a yer ago, as well as I trust I shall sone aftyr Crystmass, I wold not for xij*li.* have brokyn hym so many promessys as I have.

Also, syr, I prey yow send me by the next man that comyth fro London ij. pottys of tryacle of Jenne,—they shall cost xvj*d.*,—for I have spent ought that I had with my yong wyf, and my yong folkys, and my sylff, and I shall pay hym that shall bryng hem to me, and for hys caryage. I pray you lett it be sped.

The pepyll dyeth sore in Norwyche, and specyally abought my house, but my wyff and my women come not ought, and fle ferther we can not ; for at Sweynsthorpe, sythe my departyng thens, they have dyed, and ben syke nye in every house of the towne.

25

960

MANOR OF KNAPTON[1]

Mr. Thomas Pasche of Wynsowr toke the astate and retorne to the Dean and Colage of Wynsowr *infra Castrum.*

And one ——[2] Holme, atornay off corte, is recognis (?) and was at stat takyn.

Robert Walsch off Colby j. myl. et di' fro Blyklyng is steward.

Here folow revys of Knapton :—

Fro M. xvij. till xviij°, Martyn Smyth.

F[ro] M. xviij. till xix°, Roberd Fraunk (?), his place bonde.

Fro M. xix. till xx°, Thomas Frank, his place fre.

961

CRESSINGHAM MANOR[3]

RECEYVED at Cressingham, the Thirsday nex aftyr 1479 Seynt Edmund[4] at the corte ther v*li.* x*s.* by the NOV. 25 handes of me, John Paston, Sqwyer.

Wherof payed to my modyr for costys don up on the beryng of Walter Paston, and whyll he lay sek, and for the hyer of a man comyng with the seyd Water fro Oxenford xx*d.* . . . . xxix*s.* xj*d.*

Item, payed to William Gybson for j. horse sadyll and brydyll lent to Water Paston by the seyd William, ... xvj*s.*

Item, gevyn the seyd man comyng fro Oxenford with the seyd Water by the handys of J. Paston, ... xx*d.*

[1] [From Paston MSS., B.M.] This is a paper of memoranda in the handwriting of William Paston, endorsed ' A mater tochyng Knapton for my fee.'

[2] Blank in MS.

[3] [From Paston MSS., B.M.] This paper is in the handwriting of John Paston the younger. The reference to the burial of Walter Paston proves it to be of the year 1479.

[4] St. Edmund's Day is the 20th November. The Thursday after it in 1479 was the 25th.

27

THE PASTON LETTERS

1479
NOV. 25

Item, payed for dyvers thynges whyll Water
    Paston lay sek, ...   iiij*d*.
Item, for the costes of John Paston rydyng
    to kepe the coort at Cressingham, *anno*
    supradicto, whych was iiij. dayes in doing,
    for the styward mygh not be ther at the
    day prefyxid, ...   iij*s*. iiij*d*.

962

JOHN PASTON TO MARGARET PASTON[1]

*To my ryght worchepfull modyr, Margaret Paston, at Seynt
Peter of Hundgate.*

NOV.

RYGHT worchefull modyr, aftyr all dwtes of humble
    recomendacyon, as lowly as I can, I beseche yow of
    your dayly blyssyng and preyeres. And, moder,
John Clement, berer heroff, can tell yow, the mor pite is, if
it pleasyd God, that my brodyr is beryed in the Whyghte
Fryers at London ; whych I thought shold not have ben, for I
supposyd that he wold have ben beryed at Bromholme, and
that causyd me so sone to ryd to London to have purveyd
hys brynging hom, and if it had ben hys wylle to have leyn at
Bromholm, I had purposyd all the wey as I have redyn to
have brought hom my grauntdame[2] and hym to gedyrs ; but
that purpose is voyd as now. But thys I thynke to do when
I com to London to spek with my Lord Chamberleyn,[3] and to
wynne by hys meanys my Lord of Ely,[4] if I can ; and if I
may by eny of ther meanys cause the Kyng to take my
servyse and my quarrell to gedyrs, I wyll, and I thynk that

---

[1] [From Fenn, ii. 280.] Sir John Paston died in London on the 15th November
1479, as Fenn informs us. I presume he had some authority for the precise date,
which I have not seen. The inquisition *post mortem* is not now to be found ; but the
writ to the Escheator still exists, and is dated 30 Nov., 19 Edw. IV. This letter refers
not only to the burial of Sir John Paston, but also to the death of his grandmother
Agnes. The year was one of great mortality.
[2] Agnes, widow of William Paston the Judge.
[3] William, Lord Hastings.
[4] John Morton, afterwards Archbishop of Canterbury, and Cardinal, etc.

28

Sir George Brown, Sir Jamys Radclyff, and other of myn
aqueyntance, whyche wayte most upon the Kyng, and lye
nyghtly in hys chamber, wyll put to ther good wyllys. Thys
is my wey as yet. And, modyr, I besech yow, as ye may
get or send eny messengers, to send me yowr avyse and my
cosyn Lomeners to John Leeis hows, taylere, with in Ludgate. I have myche more to wryght, but myn empty hed
wyll not let me remembre it.

    Also, modyr, I prey that my brodyr Edmond may ryd to
Marlyngforthe, Oxenhed, Paston, Crowmer, and Caster, and
all thes maners to entre in my name, and to lete the tenants of
Oxenhed and Marlyngfor know that I sent no word to hym
to take no mony of theym but ther attornement ; wherfor he
wyll not, tyll he her fro me ayen, axe hem non, but lete hym
comand theym to pay to servaunts of myn oncles, nor to hym-
sylff, nor to non othyr to hys use, in peyne of payment ayen
to me. I thynk if ther shold be eny money axid in my name,
peraventure it wold make my Lady of Norfolk ayenst me, and
cause hyr to thynk I dellt more contrary to hyr plesure than
dyd my brodyr, whom God pardon of Hys gret mercy. I
have sent to entre at Stansted and at Orwellbery, and I have
wretyn a bylle to Anne Montgomery and Jane Rodon to
make my Lady of Norffolk, if it wyll be.

    Your sone and humble servaunt,

        J. PASTON.

1479
NOV.

963

WILLIAM LOMNOR TO JOHN PASTON[1]

To the ryght worchypfull John Paston, Squyer, yn haste.

MY Master Paston, I recomaunde me to yow, preyyng
    God to have mercy on my master your brother
    sowle, to whom ye ar heyre, and also to my mastras
your grauntdam. Wherfore be th'avyse of my mastras your

NOV. 28

---

[1] [From Paston MSS., B.M.] It is apparent from the contents that this letter was
written shortly after the decease of Sir John Paston in November 1479.

29

THE PASTON LETTERS

1479
NOV. 28

carful moder, your brothere Edmund, on Sunday next before
Sent Andrew, rod to Marlyngforth, and before alle the
tenauntez, examynid on James, kepere ther for Will. Paston,
where he was the weke next before Sent Andrew, and there
he seyd that he was not at Marlingforth from the Monday
unto the Thorday at evyn, and soo there was no man there
but your brothers man at the tyme of his decese ; so be that
your brothere dyyd sesid, and your brothere E. bad your man
kepe possession to your behoffe, and warned the tenauntez to
pay noo man, til ye hadde spoke them. So mesemyth that
ys a remyttir to your old taylyd titell ; comon with your concell. Forther, at afternoon he was at Oxned to understande
how they had doo, and Peris kepyd your brotheres possession
at that tyme ; and your oncle his man was not there, but he
assyned anothere pore man to be ther. Whethere that con-
tynuid the possession of W. Paston or not be remembrid, &c.

    And after the decese, &c., W. Paston sent the man that
kepyd possession to fore to entre and kepe possession, wheche
was noo warent be tha poyntment, for ye stande at your liberte
as for ony apoyntment or comunycacion hadde before, and
soo men seme it wer good for yow to stande at large til ye
here more ; yf ye myght have my Lord Chamberleyns good
faver and lordship, it were ryght expedyent. As for my
Lord of Ely, dele not wyth hym be owr avyse, for he woll
move for trete, and elles be displesid. Your brother Edmund
sent to John Wymond, and he sent word he wolle be a mene
of trete, but wold take noo parte, and as I sopose that was be
Heydons avyse ; for your uncle sent to me to be with hym,
and also the same man rodd to Heydon and Wymondham,
&c. The brenger of this letter can tell, for he was with
your brothere E. at these placez.

    Forther, my mastras your moder gretyth yow well, and
sendyth yow her blessyng, requiryng yow to come oute of
that here [*air*] alone as ye may ; and your brothere E.
comaundid hym to yow, and he doth hys dylygens, and parte
for yow full well and saddely yn many behalvys, and hath
brought my maistras your wyfe to Topcrofte on Friday last,
and they fare all well there ; and he yntendith to see my

30

Master Fitz Water, whech lythe at Freton, ner Long
Stratton. And God be your gide yn all your maters, and
brenge yow sone home.

    Wretyn at Norwyche, on Sonday at nyght next before
Sent Andrew, and delyverd on Monday next be the morwyn.

    Be your,   W. LOMNOUR.

1479
NOV. 28

964

ABSTRACT[1]

[WILLIAM PASTON TO ROBERT WALSH]

Thinks his dealing not very commendable, seeing that the writer is not paid
his fee, according to the promise made by him and Fouke of Knapton, when
they were with him at Norton. I had a distress and left it for your sake, but
you show no consideration for me, etc.

[This is a draft in the handwriting of William Paston. To it is attached a small
slip with these words, 'A letter fro William Paston to Robert Walsch and Robert
Fouk of Knapton.']

965

JOHN PASTON TO MARGARET PASTON[2]

*To my ryght worchepfull and most kynd modyr,
Margarett Paston.*

RYGHT werchepfull modyr, aftyr all dutes of humble
    recomendacyon, as lowly as I can, I beseche yow of
    your dayly blessyng and preyer. Pleasyt yow to
undyrstand that wher as ye wyllyd me by Poiness to hast me
ought of the heyer that I am in, it is so that I must pwt me
in God, for her must I be for a season, and in good feyth I

DEC.

---

[1] [From Paston MSS., B.M.]
[2] [From Paston MSS., B.M.] It is evident from the contents that this letter was
written shortly after the death of Sir John Paston. The year 1479 was a year of great
mortality, in which the Paston family lost three of its members. The letter is not
signed, but is in John Paston's hand.

31

1479
EC.

shall never, whyll God sendyth me lyff, dred mor dethe than shame; and thankyd be God, the sykness is well seasyd here, and also my besyness puttyth awey my fere. I am drevyn to labore in lettyng of th'execucyon of myn unkynd onclys entent, wher in I have as yet non other dyscorage, but that I trust in God he shall fayle of it.

I have spokyn with my Lord of Ely[1] dyvers tymys, whyche hathe put me in serteynte by hys woord, that he wyll be with me ayenst myn oncle in iche mater that I can shewe that he entendyth to wrong me in; and he wold fayne have a resonable end betwyx us, wher to he wyll helpe, as he seythe. And it is serteyn my brodyr, God have hys soule, had promysyd to a byde the reule of my Lord Chamberleyn[2] and of my Lord Ely; but I am not yett so far forthe, nor not wyll be, tyll I know my Lord Chamberleyns intent, and that I purpose to do to morow, for then I thynk to bewith hym, with Godes leve. And sythe it is so that God hathe purveyd me to be the solysytore of thys mater, I thank Hym of Hys grace for the good lordes, mastrys, and frendys that He hathe sent me, whyche have perfytely promysyd me to take my cause as ther owne, and those frendes be not a fewe.

And, modyr, as I best can and may, I thank yow and my cosyn Lomenore of the good avyse that ye have sent me, and I shall aplye me to do ther aftyr. Also, modyr, I beseche you on my behalf to thank myn cosyn Lomnorre for the kindness that he hathe shewyd on to me in gevyng of hys answer to myn onclys servaunt, whyche was with hym.

Modyr, I wryght not so largely to yow as I wold do, for I have not most leyser; and also when I have ben with my Lord Chamberleyn, I purpose not to tery longe aftyr in London, but to dresse me to yow wardes; at whyche tyme I trust I shall brynge yow more serteynte of all the fordell [advantage] that I have in my besyness then I can as yett wryght.

I am put in serteynte by my most specyall good mastyr, my Mastyr of the Rollys,[3] that my Lord of Ely is, and shal be

1 John Morton, Bishop of Ely.   2 Lord Hastings.
3 Robert Morton.

32

bettyr lord to me then he hathe shewyd as yet, and yet hathe he delt with me ryght well and honourably.

1479
DEC.

Modyr, I beseche yow that Pekok may be sent to purvey me as myche money as is possybyll for hym to make ayenst my comyng home, for I have myche to pay her in London, what for the funerall costes, dettes, and legattes that must be content in gretter hast then shalbe myn ease. Also I wold the ferme barly in Flegge, as well as at Paston, if ther be eny, wer gadryd, and iff it may be resonably sold, then to be sold or putt to the maltyng; but I wold at Caster that it were ought of the tenauntes handys for thynges that I here (kepe ye consell thys fro Pekok and all folkys), whyche mater I shall appese, if God wyll geve me leve.

966

JOHN PASTON AND HIS UNCLE WILLIAM[1]

THES be th'enjuryes and wrongys done by William Paston to John Paston, hys nevew.

After
1479

Fyrst, the maners of Marlyngforthe, Stansted, and Horwellbery wes gev[en to] William Paston, Justyce, and to Agnes, hys wyff, and to th'eyers of ther tw . . . . to whom the seyd John Paston is cosyn and heyer, that is to sey, son to John, son and heyer to the seyd William and Agnes.

Item, wher the [seyd William Paston was seasyd of the maner of ——], Ed. Clere with other infeofyd to the use of the seyd Will[iam][2] and of hys heyres, the whyche William made hys wyll that th[e said Agnes], hys [wife], shold have the seyd maner for terme of hyr lyff. And aftyr th[at he] dyed, and the seyd Agnes occupyed for terme of hyr seyd lyff . . . . of the seyd feoffes the seyd maner; and aftyrwardes the seyd

1 [From Paston mss., B.M.] It is evident that this paper was drawn up some time after the death of Sir John Paston in 1479. It is in his brother John's handwriting.
2 'Ed. Clere—Will[iam].'—These words are interlined in place of the words in italics within brackets, which are struck through.

VOL. VI.—C   33

After
1479

fter . . . . . . Afftyr whoys dethe Sir John Paston, Knyght, as cosyn and heyer to t[he said William], in to the seyd maner entred, and dyed with ought issue of hys bodye. . . . . . John as brodyr and heyer to the seyd Sir John, [and cosyn and heyer is lett . .],[1] . . seyd maner entred, and is lettyd to take the profytys of the same by . . . . of the maners of Marlyngforthe, Stansted, and Horwelbery befor r . . . . by the meanys of the seyd Wylliam.

967

JOHN PASTON TO ——[2]

1479-
80

SIR, I pray yow that ye will send sum chyld to my Lord of Bukingham place, and to the Crown, wich as I conseive is called Gerardes Hall, in Bred Stret, to inquere whedir I have any answer of my letter sent to Caleys, whech ye know off; and that ye will remembre my brotheris ston, so that it myth be mad er I cumm ageyn, and that it be klenly wrowgth. It is told me that the man at Sent Bridis is no klenly portrayer; [the]rfor I wold fayn it myth be portrayed be sum odir man, and he to grave it up.

Sir, it is informyd sum personis in this cuntre that ye know that the frere will sew a nodir delegaci fro Rome, direkt to sum byschop of Ingland, to amend his mater, &c.; and how be it that it may not gretly hurt, yet the seyd persones, &c., wold not he shuld have his entent, in asmoch as his suggestion is untrew, but rather they wold spend mony to lette it. I suppose the Abbot of Bery shuld labor for him rather than anodir, becawse the sey Abbot is a perteynor to the lord that is the freris mayntener, &c.; wherefor, ser, my moder and I pray yow enquere after a man callid Clederro,

1 These words are struck through.
2 [From Paston mss., B.M.] As this letter refers to the making of a tombstone for Sir John Paston, it may be presumed to have been written either at the end of the year 1479, or in the course of the year 1480. The ms. is a rough draft, apparently in the hand of Edmund Paston. It has been slightly mutilated, and apparently since the letter was printed in Fenn's fifth volume.

34

whych is solisitor and attorne with Master Will. Grey, that late was the Kingges proktor at Rome, and the seyd Clederro sendith matiers and letters owth of Ingelond to his seyd master ever[y] monith, &c. He is well knowe in London, and among the Lumbardes, and with the Bischop of Winchesteris men, but I wot not wher he dwellit in London, and I suppos if ye speke with him, he knowith me. Plese yow to comone with him of this mater, but let him not wete of the mater atwix my modir and him; but desir him to wryth to his master to lett this, if it may be, or elles to se the best wey that he have not his intent, and to comon with the proktor of the Whith Freris at Rome to hep forth, for the freris here have laborid to my moder, and praid her to lette his ontrewe intent, and have wrete to her proketor befor this. And I suppose if ye speke to the prior of the freris at London, he will wrrth to her seyd proktor, &c., but tell the prior no word that I know [ther]of, but let him wete if he will wryth to his proktor, odir men shall help forth.

1479-
80

More over, that ye will tell Cledero that I am not seker that the frere laborith thus, but be talis of freris and odir; nevertheles let him wrrth to his master that [for] whatsomevyr he do herin, he shall be truly content for his labor and costes. And if ye think that Cledro will writh effectually herin, geff hym j. noble, [bid] hym let his master know that my Lord of Wynchester[1] and Danyell ow godwill to the part that he shall labor for. And if thar be fown no sech sewth be the seyd [fre]re, yet wold I have sum thing fro Rome to anull the old bull, &c., or to apeyr [impair] it [if] it myth be do esily, &c., and tyding wheder ther be any sech sute, &c.

Your own, &c.

[For] how beit that it may nowthir avayl ner hurt, yet my moder will this be do. [I] send yow the copi of the bull, and how execucion was do, and informacion of the mater imparte, &c. And, sir, I sha content your noble, &c. And I pray yow red it over, and spede yow homeward, and bring this letter home with yow, &c.

1 William Waynflete, Bishop of Winchester.

35

THE PASTON LETTERS

968

AN INVENTORY OF PLATE[1]

1479 In primis, a sallt with j. cover,	xx. unces di. & di. quart.
j. stumpe of a salte,	ij. unces & di.
j. flat salt with a squyrell,	j. unce iij. quarters.
iiij. Parys cuppis with a cover, with a rose in the botom, weyeng	lvj. unces j. quarter.
ij. holowe disshes,	xxix. unces iiij. quarter di.
j. chafre of silver,	ix. unces j. quarter.
xij. sylver spones, whereof my lady hath one.	
j. lytil spone of Rippyngales,	j. quarter & di. quarter, j. d. ob. qᵗ. di.
j. lityll spone for egges,	j. quarter & di. quarter ob.
j. prikettes nuper Howis,	ix. unces ij. d. weight,
j. preket nuper Howis,	viij. unces iij. quarters & di.
j. long sokett.	
j. nother long soket.	
vj. sokettes, with branches to remeve.	
iiij. wherwilles to the same.	
j. playne pees for potage, per estima- cionem,	xj. unces j. quarter.
j. playn pees nuper Frere Water,	iiij. unces j. quarter.
j. nother playn peece nuper Frere Walter,	iiij. unces di. quarter.
j. chaleis,	xv. unces & di. quarter.
ij. cruettes,	vij. unces iij. quarters.
a paxbred,[2]	ij. unces di. quarter j. d.
j. holowe barbore bason, bought of Colet.	
j. standing pece couvered, bought of Elingham.	xv. unces & j. quarter.
iij. gilt spones.	
j. spone for grene gynger, gilt,	j. unce j. quarter j. qᵗ. & di.
j. gilte cup covered, wel shapen with trayle, with j. knop with a kroune enamelid,	xxxiij. unces & di. & di. quarter.
j. nothir cupp standing covered, gilt, bell shapen with trailles, with a playn knopp not enamelid,	xxiij. unces & j. quarter.

[1] [From Paston MSS., B.M.] This inventory was certainly drawn up after the death of Agnes Paston, but how many years later it is impossible to say.
[2] A silver plate with a figure of the Crucifixion upon it given to be kissed at Mass.

j. maser Sipton.	
ij. masers.	
iij. gilt spones.	
j. gynger spone.	
j. bag whiteleder, wherin is all this stuff folowyng this lyne :—	
iij. girdels Staunton.	
j. girdel upholdester.	
Fawcon Skern coppe.	
Hans Eborlyn girdel.	
Purs gold with Jane Aske harnes.	
ij. lynen bagges lityll with broke silver and j. old harneis gilt.	
Furst, a standing cuppe with a cover therto plommed, weyeng	xxiiij. unces di.
Item, a standing coppe curid gilt, weyeng	xxxvj. unces.
Item, a nother standing cupp cuerid gilt, weying	xv. unces iij. qᵗ. & di.
Item, a goblette of silver and gilt covered	xiiij. unces j. quarter & di.
Item, a nother goblett gilt, weyeng	xij. unc' & j. d. weight.
Item, a nothir goblet gilt, weyeng .	vij. unc'.
Item, a standing white pees with a cover withoute a knoppe, weyeng	xxij. unces.
Item, a salt with a pale covered,	xiiij. unc' j. quarter.
Item, a rounde salt covered,	xix. unc' j. quarter di.
Item, a rounde salt uncovered,	viij. unces.
Item, a basonne of	xxxv. unc' j. quarter.
Item, an ewer to the same of	xv. unc' & di. quarter.
Item, an ewer,	xiiij. unc' di. quarter.
Item, vj. silver sponys with square sharp knoppes of	v. unces iij. quarter j. d. wight.
Item, spone for grene gynger of	iij. quarters & ij. d. wight.
Item, a grete gilt chalis with a patent longing to the same, weying	xlij. unces j. quarter.
Item, a litil standing pece chacid plumtes, with a kover to the same,	x. unces j. quarter.
Item, a blak notte standing of silver and gilt, with a kover to the same, weying	xviij. unc'.
Item, a grete maser with a prend in the botom, and the armes of Seint Jorge, weying	xv. unc' j. quarter & di.
Item, a nother maser sownde in the botom and a sengilbonde,	viij. unc' & j. quarter.
Item, a lytil maser with a foote, weying .	viij. unc'.
Item, a nother maser with a lytill foote, weing	viij. unc'.

THE PASTON LETTERS

1479 Item, a nothir litill maser with an higher foote, weying	x. unces & j. quarter.
Item, xxⁱⁱ spones on a bundell, weying .	xvj. unc. j. quarter.
Item, vj. spones with acorns, weying	v. unc' & di. quarter.
Item, a peyre bedes of corall with pater- nostris of silver and gilt, and a knopp of smale perle, weying	vj. unc' j. quarter.
In primis, j. standing cuppe covered playne with a rounde knoppe, weyeng	xxv. unces.
j. nodir cuppe of golde covered playne with a chacid knoppe, weying	xxiij. unces iij. quarters.
j. layer of gold with a crokid spoute, weyeng	xiij. unces iiij. quarters.
j. nothir layer of golde, weyeng	xiij. unces j. quarter j. d.
j. chaleis of fyne golde in pecis broken,	xxiij. unces.
j. coppe of golde covered, chacid with a perle,	xxj. unces.
j. salte covered with a berall gairneshid,	v. unces j. quarter.
j. nothir salt covered, garnyshed with stones,	v. unces iij. quarter.
j. par of gilt basouns covered, weyeng	viijˣˣ. xix. unces & di.
j. salte gilte, weyeng,	xxviij. unces di. quarter.
j. cover to the same, weyeng,	viij. unces j. quarter.
j. nothir salte gilte withoute a cover,	xxvij. unces iij. quarters.
j. standing pees gilte, with a cover Skern	xxxvij. unces j. quarter.
j. nothir standing pees gilte with a cover, A. P.	xxj. unces di. & di. quarter.
j. flatte pees covered, gilt, A. P.	xviij. unces & di.
j. potte for grene gynger gilte,	x. unces & di. iiij. d. ob.
j. cover to the same, weyeng	j. unce j. quarter.
j. stonding cuppe covered parcell gilt, Sir Buk,	xvj. unces & j. quarter.
j. salt covered parcell gilt, Sir Ric',	xij. unces & di.
j. paxe parcell gilte, Staunton,	xij. unces.
j. standing cuppe with a kever, parcell gilt, Staunton,	xix. unces & di.
j. goblett for Rynesh wyne covered,	xj. unces & di.
j. powder boxe,	vj. unces j. quarter di. quarter.
j. noder powder boxe,	viij. unces j. quarter.
j. candilstykke with a lous [loose] sokett and j. preket, P,	xvij. unces di. quarter.
ij. candilstikkes with ij. lous preketes, Skern,	xxxj. unces di. quarter.
di. doss. [half a dozen] sylver spones, Shipton,	vj. unces di. & di. quarter.
di. doss. spones, Stanton,	vij. unces.
j. bason, P.	xlv. unces di.

j. bason, Sparke,	lx. unces.
j. bason, Sturmer, with a spoute,	xxxiiij. unces. j. quarter j. d. q.
j. bason, Sturmer, withoute a spoute,	xxxij. unces j. quarter di. quarter j. d. qᵗ.
j. bason, Rous,	l. unces iiij. quarters.
j. ewer, P.	xvj. unces & di. & di. quarter.
j. ewer, Sparke,	xx. unces.
j. ewer, Sturmer,	xiiij. unces j. quarter and di. quar- ter qᵗ.
j. ewer, Sturmer,	xiiij. unces di. di. quarter j. d. ob. qᵗ.
j. ewer, Rous,	xviij. unces.
j. pott, Hous,	lvij. unces.
j. pott, P.	xxviij. unces iiij. quarter di. ij.
j. pott, S. . . lett,	xv. unces.
j. pott, Rous,	xxxv. unces.
j. pott, Spark,	xxvij. unces j. quarter.
j. flagon,	xxxix. unces.
j. layer,	ix. unces a quarter & di.
j. layer,	ix. unces j. quarter & ij. di.
vj. Parys cuppis with a cover, Skerne,	lxx. unces iiij. quarters di.
j. grete boll pees, with a cover, Noris,	xl. unces j. quarter.
xxiij. disshis of sylver, Skerne,	xvijˣᵗ vj. unces di.
iiij. chargeours,	vˣˣx. unces.
xxvij. dishes,	xxˣˣxj. unces di. & di. quarter.
xxiij. sawcers,	vjˣˣxv. unces.
[1] xij. flatt cuppis of silver, P. and Staunton,	vˣˣv. unces iij. quarters.
[1] iiij. coveres to the same, P. and Staunton,	xl. unces.
j. chargeour priour (?) water,	xlvj. unces j. quarter di.

969

ABSTRACT[2]

WILLIAM PASTON TO HIS BROTHER EDMUND PASTON

Encloses the will of his father, 'such as my brother hath'; who says he had it out of the register. My business is no further advanced since I left you, except that my brother has got a pardon of the alienation made by the Bishop of Winchester. Can get no estate in it except according to his father's will, viz. to himself and his heirs-male. My brother's will is that I should have

After 1479

[1] These two entries are bracketed together in the MS., and 'Shend bi Ley' (?) written in the margin. [2] [From Paston MSS., B.M.]

fter
479
Runham, which is £8 a year at least, in recompense of the 10 marks out of Sporle, if he would release all his right in that manor. There is nothing touching you in my brother's[1] will, for I read it over and will write it also; ' so that I woll have the same for my copy that he wrote with his own hand.'

Recommend me heartily to my sister your wife.

London, 22 Feb.

[The writer of this was William, the son of the eldest John Paston, not that uncle William with whom the two younger John Pastons had so many disputes. I see nothing to fix the date beyond the fact that the letter was written after Sir John Paston's death.]

970

WILLIAM PASTON TO JOHN KYNG[2]

To John Kynge, Fermour of my Maner of Hartwelbury, in Kelsall, besides Royston, be this delyverd.

480
s. 24
JOHN KYNG, I grete yow hartely well; and I understond as well by my frende, Syr William Storar, as by Ric. Browne, that as well my kynnesman Syr John Paston that dede is, as my kynnesman John Paston that now leveth, have ben with yow, and yovyn yow many grete thretis, for that ye acordyng to the trowth, tolde unto them that ye ocupyed my maner of Harwelbury be my leese, and be my ryght. And further more I understond, notwithstondyng the seyde grete thretis, that ye, lyke a full trewe, harty frende, have delyd and fastely abedyn in my tytill, and wolde not retorne to none of them. Wherfor I hartely thank yow; and furthar more to corage yow in yowr fast dealyng, I schew onto yow that I have ryght bothe in law and in concience, wherby I promyse yow on my feythe to defende yow and save yow harmeles for the occupacion of the londe, or any thynge that ye schall doo in my titill a gaynst hym, and it schulde cost me as moche as the maner is worth, and also another tyme to doo as moche for yow, and it ly in my powre, yf ye have ony mater to doo ther as I may doo for yow.

[1] Sir John Paston, who died in 1479.
[2] [From Paston mss., B.M.] It is scarcely necessary to point out that this letter was probably written within a year after Sir John Paston's death.

40

And, also, I here say, by my seid frende, Syr William Storar, and by Ric. Brown, that ye ar of suche substaunce, and of suche trust, and suche favor in the contre ther, that it lithe in yowr powre to do a goode turne for yowr frende.

Wretyn at London, the xxiiij[ti] day of Februari.

Be WILLIAM PASTON.

1480
FEB. 24

971

GEORGE, SERVANT TO WILLIAM PASTON, TO JOHN KYNG[1]

To John Kyng of Therfeld, in Herdfordshire.

Right trusty and welbeloved frende, I comaunde me to you. And, Ser, I tolde my maister that ye wolde have ben with him or this; for which cause he mervaileth ye kepe nat your promyse. Wherfore I avise you to come and bryng my maister his money afore this fest of Cristmasse.

And, also, ye ar yerly behynde of a boore or els ten shillinges after the price of oon bore. And where ye be owyng your boore for ij. yerys, I wolde avyse you to delyver unto Ser William Storer the seid dute, or els I counceile you to send my maister a resonable somme of money with thies boores afore Cristmasse for your thanke, consideryng his kynde dealyng, as well in sufferaunce of your money as in youre owne matier.

Writen at London, the xvj[th] day of Decembre.

Be your frende, GEORGE, servaunte to Mr. W. PASTON.[2]

Date uncertain

972

JOHN, PRIOR OF BROMHOLM, TO JOHN PASTON[3]

To my right worchipful maister, John Paston, Sqwyer.

RIGHT worchipful maister, I recomaunde me un to yow, desiryng to knowe of youre welfare and prosperyte, wheche Jesu maynteyne and encrease to His pleser after youre hertys desyre, thankyng yow ever of youre good

1480-7

[1] We place this letter after the last for convenience. Its date is unimportant.
[2] The subscription is in a different hand from the letter itself, which is in a clerk's hand, very well written.
[3] [From Fenn, iii. 400.] On the date of this letter Fenn remarks as follows:—
' John Titleshale was prior of Bromholm from 1460 for about twenty years. This

41

480-7
maistership to me shewed at alle tymes withoute deserte on my behalve, prayng yow, and hirtely besechyng of youre goode contynuance. Please it yowre maistership, for as moche as it [is] moved on to the my good maisters, the counsell of the Duche of Lancastr, that they be weelwillyng to make laboure on to my Sovereyn Lady the Qween at youre good instaunce for certeyn tymber toward my dortour at Bromholm, in wheche myn specyall desyre is to have viij. principall beemys, everych on in length xj. zerds. I am not expeert in makyng of any supplicacion, besechyng youre maistership to take it uppon you to do it make after your avyce, alegged all poverte, as youre worchipfull discrecion can moche better than I can enforme; and I remitte all to youre wysdam, ever besechyng you to calle this matyer to youre remembraunce. No more at this tyme, but the Holy Trinite mote have yow in His governaunce, and sende you longe lyf to endure to His pleser.

Wreten the xiiij[e] day of Octobr.

Youre preest and chapeleyn, JOHN, Priour of Bromholm.

letter must have been written therefore either on the 14th October 1460, or on the same day in 1465, as Edward IV. married in that year, and J. Paston died in May 1466. If it was written in the former, the request [for timber] must have been to Queen Margaret; if in the latter, to Elizabeth, the Queen of Edward IV.' In these observations Fenn overlooks the possibility of the letter having been addressed to any other John Paston than the first of that name; and neither of the two years, which alone suit that supposition, has much internal probability. It is inconceivable that the letter could have been written in 1460, when Queen Margaret had retired into Wales after the battle of Northampton, and it is almost equally improbable that the date could have been 1465, when John Paston, the father, was in prison. We have very little doubt that the letter was addressed to John Paston the youngest, called of Gelston, long after his father's death, and after that of his brother Sir John also. John Tytleshale, who was Prior of Bromholm in 1460, was succeeded, at what date we are not informed, by John Macham; and after him John Underwood, Bishop of Chalcedon, suffragan of the Bishop of Norwich, was prior in 1509. The date of this letter, however, must lie between 1480 and 1487, in which latter year John Paston the youngest was created a knight for his services at the battle of Stoke.

42

973

ABSTRACT[1]

Appointment touching ' Ayeseldys wyff.' Her friends to labour for her acquittal of the felony, without letting of Wremmegey's wife, etc. £20 to be deposited ' in mene hand ' by the friends of A's wife, to be delivered on her acquittal to Darby and other frends of W.'s wife. Also Master Yelverton shall have his £3 due to him from Ayseldys wife paid by both parties.

Signed—John Yelverton.

Not after 1481

[I can find no other reference to the matter referred to in this paper, and cannot tell the date; but as John Yelverton, the son of the judge, died on the 9th July 1481 (Blomefield, x. 31), it cannot be later than that year.]

974

EDMUND PASTON TO WILLIAM PASTON[2]

To my brother, Wylliam Paston, be this delyverd.

I HARTELY recomawnd me to zow. Here is lately fallyn a wydow in Woorstede, whyche was wyff to one Bolt, a worstede marchaunt, and worth a m[l].li., and gaff to hys wyff a C. marke in mony, stuffe of howsold, and plate to the valew of an C. marke, and xli. be zere in land. She is callyd a fayer jantylwoman. I wyll for zour sake se her. She is ryght systyr, of fader and modyr, to Herry Ynglows. I purpose to speke with hym to gett hys good wyll. Thes jantylwoman is abowght xxx. zeres, and has but ij. chyldern, whyche shalbe at the dedes charge; she was hys wyff but v. zere. Yf she be eny better than I wryght for, take it in woothe I shew the leeste. Thus lete me have knowlache of

About 1481(?)

[1] [From Paston mss., B.M.]
[2] [From Paston mss., B.M.] There is nothing to show the date of this letter, except the fact that William Paston did not come of age before the year 1481, so that it is not likely to be earlier. Perhaps it may be a few years later, in which case the widow would not have been very much his senior; but that circumstance was not likely, in those days, to have been greatly regarded in the matter.

43

THE PASTON LETTERS

About zowr mynde as shortly as ze can, and whan ze shall moun be 1481(?) in this cuntre. And thus God send zow good helth and good aventure.

From Norwyche, the Saterday after xij[the] day.

Your,   E. PASTON.

975

EDMUND PASTON TO MARGARET PASTON[1]

*To my ryght wurchypfull and especiall good mother,
Margaret Paston.*

Between
1481-4

R YGHT worchypfull and moste especialle good modyr, in my moste umble wyse, with alle my dute and ser-vyse, I recomawnd me to yow, besechynge zow of zour blyssyng, whyche is to me moste joy of erthely thynge; and it plese zow to be so good and kynd modyr to me to for-geve me, and also my wyffe, of owr leude offence that we have not don ower dute, whyche was to have seyn and ave waytyd up on zow or now. My huswyffe trustythe to ley to zow her huswyferey for her excuse, wyche I muste beseche zow not to accepte, for in good faythe I deme her mynde hathe ben other weys ocapyed than as to huswyfery, whyche semyth welle by the latchesnes of the tylthe of her landdes. I beseche God for the forderawnce of them as now rewarde zow and the good parson of Mautby, and also Mastyer Baley, who I wende woold not have balkyd this pore loggeyng to Norwyche wardes.

I undyrstand by the brynggger here of that ze entende to ryde to Walsyngham; yf it please zow that I may wete the seayson, as my dute is, I shalle be redy to awayte up on zow.

[1] [From Paston mss., B.M.] Fenn dates this letter 1479-80, suggesting that it must have been written very soon after Edmund Paston's marriage with the widow of William Clippesby, as it seems to imply that he had not yet carried his bride to pay her duty to his mother. I do not, for my part, know the date of this marriage, and I suspect Fenn had no other clue to it than the fact that William Clippesby, the lady's first husband, died on the 24th September 1479; but I presume his widow was still unmarried when she proved his will on the 18th May 1480 (see Blomefield, xi. 144). I consider, therefore, that the letter must have been written between the years 1481 and 1484, as Margaret Paston died in November of the latter year.

44

EDWARD IV

Plese it zow that the brynggar here of cam to me for xs. Betw[een] viijd. whyche I shuld ow hys fadyr; trew it was at my laste 148[?] departyng from hym, I owte hym somych, but sertaynly or I cam at Thetfford homewardes, I thowt of concyence he owte to have restoryd me as myche. I had my horsse with hym at lyvery, and amonge alle one of them was putte to gresse and to labur, so that he dyed of a laxe by the wey. I payed for hard mete ever to hym.

Plese it zow to delyver Kateryn vs., wyche I send zow in this bylle. I am not assartaynd how she is purveyde of mony towardes her jornay. Yf her fadyr cowde not acleymed jd. of me, I woold not se her dysporveyd, yf I myght, nor the poreste chyld that is belonggyng to hys loggeyng.

Modyr, my wyffe is boold to send zow a tokyn. I beseche zow pardon alle thyngges not done acordyng to dute. I beseche God send zow the accomplyshment of zour moste and woorchypfull desyers.

At Owby, the Saterday next before Candylmes.

Zour umble son and servant,
EDMOND PASTON.

976

MONASTERY OF ST. FAITH[1]

Robertus filius domini Walteri de Mauteby militis insp[ex]sit cartas 14[?] an[tiquas] . . . . concessas Deo et monasterio Sanctæ Fidis quinque AU quarteria salis annualis redditus . . e olim . . . . quinque *wayes* percipienda de salinis ma[r]issi de Mauteby secundum mensuram ejusdem [mari]ssi. Quam quidem concessionem prædictus Robertus ratificat . . . . suum sub sigillo suo quid est[2]. And this deed sawe John Paston at the seid Seynt Feythes, mense Augusti Anno xxjº Regis E. [Q]uarti. And for this rent a . . the prior and the monkys there shewyd [to th]e seyd John, the same moneth and tyme, thes obitis foloyng tightled in the . . . . they s[ay]d that they . . . . . whiche wold be knowyn and wachid. So the sayd . . . . the obbites . . . . bi Maltby xij. die mensis Aprilis. Et d'ns d'nii (?)

JOHANNES DE MALTE[Y].

[1] [Add. Charter 17,252, B.M.]
[2] Here occurs a representation of a shield in the middle of the text of the ms.

45

THE PASTON LETTERS

977

ABSTRACT[1]

ANONYMOUS TO MRS. [MARGARET PASTON?]

There is no tachment made in the land unless it be done privily. The sheriff has been thrice, in our town in these three weeks. As for the panel of Frances' matter, there is none of the sheriff's deputies but Francis to inquire of.

[I am quite unable to attach a date to this letter, or to conjecture by whom it was written. Even the person to whom it is addressed is very uncertain, though I have suggested Margaret Paston.]

978

MARGARET PASTON'S WILL.[2]

1482
FEB. 4

I N the name of God, amen. I, Margaret Paston, widowe, late the wiff of John Paston, Squier, doughter and heire to John Mauteby, Squier, hole of spirit and mynde, with perfite avisement and good deliberacion, the iiij[te] day of Febru-ary, in the yer of Our Lord God a m[l]cccclxxxj. make my testa-ment and last wille in this fourme folowyng. First, I betake my sowle to God Almyghty and to Our Lady His blissid Moder, Seint Michael, Seint John Baptist, and to Alle Seintes, and my body to be beried in the ele of the cherch of Mautby, byfore the ymage of Our Lady there. In which ele reste the bodies of divers of myn aunceteres, whos sowles God assoile.

Item, I bequethe to the high awter of the seid cherch of Mautby xxs.

Item, I wulle that the seid ele in which my body shalbe beried be newe robed, leded, and glased, and the walles therof heyned [*heightened*] convenyently and werkmanly.

Item, I wulle that myn executours purveye a stoon of marble to be leyde alofte upon my grave within a yer next after my decesse; and upon that stoon I wulle have iiij. scochens sett at the iiij. corners, wherof I wulle that the first

[1] [From Paston mss., B.M.]   [2] [Add. Charter, 17,253, B.M.]
46

EDWARD IV

scochen shalbe of my husbondes armes and myn departed, the 14[?] ij[de] of Mawtebysarmes and Berneys of Redham departed, the FEB. iij[de] of Mawtebysarmes and the Lord Loveyn departed, the iiij[te] of Mawtebysarmes and Sir Roger Beauchamp departed. And in myddys of the seid stoon I wull have a scochen sett of Mawtebysarmes allone, and under the same thise wordes wretyn, 'In God is my trust,' with a scripture wretyn in the verges therof rehersyng thise wordes, 'Here lieth Margret Paston, late the wif of John Paston, doughter and heire of John Mawteby, Squier,' and so forth, in the same scripture rehersed the day of the moneth and the yer that I shall decesse: 'on whos sowle God have mercy.'

Item, I wulle that myn executours shall purveye xij. pore meen of my tenauntes, or other if they suffice not, the whiche I wulle shalbe apparailled in white gownes with hodes accord-ing, to holde xij. torches abowte myn herse or bere at such tyme as I shalbe beried, during the exequies and masse of my beryng; which xij. torches I wille remayne in the seid cherch of Mawteby whil they may last for my yerday.

Which yerday I wull myn heire kepe in the same cherch for me my seid husbond and myn aunceteres yerly during the terme of xij. yeres next after my decesse;[1] and I wulle that ich of the seid xij. pore meen the day of my beriing have iiijd. Also, I wulle that iche preste being at my berying and masse have viijd., and ich clerk in surplys iijd. Also, I wull that the preste which shall berie me have vjs. viijd., so that he seye over me at the tyme of my berying all the whole service that to the berying belongeth.

Also, I wulle that from the day and tyme that I am beried unto the ende of vij. yeres than next folowyng be ordeyned a taper of wexe of ali. to brenne upon my grave ich Sonday and haliday at alle divine service to be seid or sunge in the seid cherch and dailly at the masse of that preest that shalle singe there in the seid ele for my sowle.

Item, I wulle that vj. tapers, ich of iiijli., brenne abowte myn herse the day of my beryng, of which I wull that iiij.

[1] In the margin is written in John Paston's hand, 'Memorandum, v. yer to come to kepe the yerday.'

47

482
EB. 4

yerly be kept to brenne abowte myn herse whan my yerday shalbe kept aslong as they may honestly serve.

Item, I wulle have an honest seculer prest to synge and pray in the seid ele for my sowle, the sowles of my father and mother, the sowle of the seid John Paston, late my husband, and for the sowlys of his aunceteres and myn during the terme of vij. yeres next after my decesse.

Item, I wulle that myn executours purveye a compleet legende in oon book, and an antiphoner in an other book, which bookes I wull be yeven to abide ther in the seid cherch to the wurschip of God aslonge as they may endure.[1]

Item, I wulle that every houshold in Mauteby as hastily as it may be convenyently doo after my decesse have xij*d*.

Item, to the emendyng of the cherch of Freton in Suffolk I bequethe a chesiple and an awbe.[2]

And I wulle that ich houshold being my tenaunt there have vj*d*.

And I bequethe to the emendement of the cherch of Basyngham a chesiple and an awbe.[3]

And I wulle that every houshold there have viij*d*.

Item, I bequeth to the emendyng of the cherch of Matelask a chesiple and an awbe.[4]

And I wull that every pore houshold that are my tenauntes there have viij*d*.

Item, I bequethe to the emendyng of the cherch of Gresham a chesiple and an awbe.[5]

And I wulle that ich pore houshold that be my tenauntes there have vj*d*.

Item, I wulle that ich pore houshold late my tenauntes at Sparham have vj*d*.

Item, to the reparacion of the cherch of Redham there as I was borne I bequeth v. marc and a chesiple of silk with an awbe with myn armes therupon to the emendement of the same cherche.[6]

[1] In margin, 'v*li*. v*js*. viij*d*.' This and the marginal notes which follow are all in John Paston's hand.   [2] In margin, 'xv*js*. viij*d*.'   [3] *Ibid.*   [4] *Ibid.*   [5] *Ibid.*

[6] In margin, 'v*li*.'

Item, to iche of the iiij. houshes of Freres in Norwich, xx*s*.

1482
FEB. 4

Item, to iche of the iiij. houshes of Freres of Yermouth and at the South toun to pray for my sowle I bequeth xx*s*.

Item, to the ankeres at the Frere Prechours in Norwich I bequeth iij*s*. iiij*d*.

And to the ankeres in Conesford I bequeth iij*s*. iiij*d*.

Item, to the anker at the White Freres in Norwich I bequethe iij*s*. iiij*d*.

Item, to iche hole and half susters at Normans in Norwich, iiij*d*.

Item, to the Deen and his bretheren of the Chepell of Feld, to the use of the same place to seye a *dirige* and a masse for my sowle, xx*s*.

Item, to the hospitalle of Seint Gile in Norwich, also for a *dirige* and a masse for my sowle, xx*s*.

Item, to iche of the iiij. pore meen, and to either of the susters of the seid hospitall, ij*d*.

Item, to the mother cherche of Norwiche for a *dirige* and masse, xx*s*.

Item, to iche lepre man and woman at the v. Yates in Norwich, iij*d*.

And to iche forgoer at every of the seid yates, ij*d*.

Item, to iche lepre without the North gates at Yermouth, iij*d*. ; and to the forgoer ther, ij*d*.

Item, to iche houshold of the parish of Seint Peter of Hungate in Norwich that wull receyve almes, have iiij*d*.

Item, I wull have a *dirige* and a masse for my sowle at the parisshe cherche of Seint Michael of Coslany in Norwich, and that every preste ther havyng his stipend being therat have iiij*d*., and iche clerk in surplys of the same parissh than ther being have ij*d*., and the parissh clerk vj*d*., and the curat that shall seye high masse have xx*d*., and I bequeth to the reparacion of the bellys of the same cherche vj*s*. viij*d*., and to the sexteyn there to rynge at the seid *dirige* and masse, xx*d*.

Item, I wull that myn executours shall geve to the sustentacion of the parson or preste that shall for the tyme mynystre

482
EB. 4

the sacramentez and divine service in the cherch of Seint Petre of Hungate in Norwich, xx*li*. of lawfull money ;[1] whiche xx*li*. I will it be putt in the rule and disposicion of the cherch reves of the same cherche for the tyme being by the oversight of the substancialle persones of the seid parissh, to this intent, that the seid cherch reves, by the oversight as is before-seid, shall yerly yeve, if it so be that the profites of the seid cherch suffice not to fynde a prest after ther discrecions, part of the seid xx*li*. to the seid parson or preste, unto the seid xx*li*. be expended.

Item, I bequeth to Edmund Paston, my sone, a standing pece white covered, with a white garleek heed upon the knoppe, and a gilt pece covered with an unicorne, a fetherbedde and a traumsom at Norwich, and the costers[2] of worsted that he hath of me.

Item, I bequeth to Katerine his wiff a purpill girdill harneisid with silver and gilt and my bygge bras chafour, a brasen morter with an iren pestell, and a stoon morter of cragge.

Item, I yeve and graunte to Robert, sone of the seid Edmund, alle my swannes morken with the merke called Dawbeneys merk, and with the merk late Robert Cutler, clerk, to have hold and enjoye the seid swannes with the seid merkes to the seid Robert and his heirs for evermore.

Item, I bequeth to Anne, my doughter, wiff of William Yelverton, my grene hangyng in my parlour at Mauteby, a standing cuppe with a cover gilt with a flatte knoppe and a flatte pece with a cover gilt withoute, xij. silver spones, a powder boxe with a foot and a knoppe enamelled blewe, my best corse girdill blewe herneised with silver and gilt, my primer, my bedes of silver enamelled.

Item, I bequeth to the seid Anne, my fetherbedde with sillour,[3] curteyns and tester[4] in my parlour at Mauteby, with a white covering, a peire blankettes, ij. peire of my fynest shetes iche of iij. webbes, a fyne hedshete of ij. webbes, my

[1] In margin, 'xx*li*.'   [2] Pieces of tapestry used on the sides of tables, beds, etc.—*Halliwell.*   [3] Canopy of tapestry.   [4] Head of the bedstead.

best garnyssh of pewter vessell, ij. basyns with ij. ewres, iij. candelstekes of oon sorte, ij. bras pottes, ij. bras pannes, a bras chafour to sett by the fyre, and a chafour for colys.

1482
FEB. 4

Item, I require myn executours to paie to the seid William Yelverton and Anne the money that I shall owe them of ther mariage money the day of my decesse of such money as shalbe receyved of such londes as I have putte in feffement to accomplissh my wille.

Item, I bequeth to William Paston, my sone my standing cuppe chased parcell gilt with a cover with myn armes in the botom and a flatte pece with a traill upon the cover, xij. silver spones, ij. silver saltes wherof oon is covered the hole bedde of borde alisaundre as it hangeth on the gret chaumber at Mauteby, with the fetherbedde, bolster, blankettes, and coveryng to the same, ij. peire shetes, ij. pilwes, and my best palet, a basyn, an ewre, and a litel white bedde that hangeth over the gresyngges in the litell chaumber at Mauteby for a trussyng bedde.

Item, I bequeth an C. marc in money to be paied and bestowed to the use and byhoff of the seid William Paston after this forme folowyng ; that is to sey, in purchasyng of as moche lond to him and to his heires as may be had with the same money, or ellys to bye a warde to be maried to him if eny suche may be goten, or ellys to be paied to him assone as it may be convenyently gadered and receyved of sucche londes as by me are put in feffement as is beforseid after the ele in Mauteby cherche be fynsshed and performed as is beforseid, and after the stipend of the preste lymyted to singe for me be yerly levied, as well as the money be dispended upon the keping of my yerly obite. And if the seid William dye or he come to the age of xxj. yer, than the seid C. marc to be disposed for the wele of my sowle by myn executours.

Item, I bequeth to John Paston my sone a gilt cuppe standyng with a cover and a knoppe liche a garkeek heed, vj. gobelettes of silver with oon cover.

Item, I bequeth to Margery Paston, the wif of the seid John, my pixt of silver with ij. silver cruettes and my massebook with all myn awterclothes.

THE PASTON LETTERS

1482
FEB. 4

Item,[1] I bequeth to William Paston, sone of the seid John Paston, and Elizabeth his suster, C. marc whan they come to laufull age, to be take and receyved of the londes beforseid; and if either of them die or they come to the seid age, than I wull that the part of him or hir so deying remayne to the survyver of them at laufull age, and if they bothe dye or they come to the seid age, than I wull that the seid C. marc be disposed for the helth of my sowle by th'avise of myn executours.

Item, I bequeth to Custaunce, bastard doughter of John Paston, Knyght, whan she is xx. yer of age, x. marc, and if she die bifore the seid age, than I wull that the seid x. marc be disposed by myn executours.

Item, I bequeth to John Calle, sone of Margery my doughter, xx*li.* whan he cometh to the age of xxiiij. yer, and if the seid John dye or he cometh to the seid age, than I wull that the seid xx*li.* evenly be divided attwen William and Richard, sones of the seid Margery, whan they come to the age of xxiiij. yer; and if either of the seid William and Richard dye or he come to the seid age, than I wull that the part of him so dying remayne to the survyver; and if bothe the seid William and Richard dye or the come to the seid age, than I wull that the seid xx*li.* be disposed by the good advys of myne executours for me and my frendes.

Item, I bequethe to Marie Tendalle, my goddoughter, my peir bedys of calcidenys gaudied[2] with silver and gilt.

Item, I wull that iche of myn other godchilder be rewarded by th'avyse of John Paston, my sone.

Item, I bequeth to Agnes Swan my servaunt, my muster-develys gown furred with blak, and a girdell of blak harneised with silver gilt and enamelled, and xxs. in money.

Item, to Simon Gerard my silver gobelet cured and a flatt pece with verges gilt, and myn hole litel white bedde in my chapell chaumber at Mauteby with the fetherbedde liche as it is nowe

---

[1] Opposite this paragraph is written in the margin in John Paston's hand: 'C. marke. Solut' E. P. *l.* marke.'

[2] Halliwell explains 'gaudees' as 'the larger beads in a roll for prayer.' According to Palsgrave they represented the *Paternoster.*

52

in the seid chapell, with a peire blankettes, a peire shetes, and a pilwe of doune.

148
FEB.

Item, to John Heyth a materas with a traunsom, a peire shetes, a peire blankettes, and a coverlight.

Item, I wull that myn housholt be kept after my decesse by half a yer, and that my servauntes wages be truly paied at ther departing, and also that every persone being my servaunt the day of my decesse have a quarter wages beside that they at her departing have do service fore.

Item, I wull that alle suche maners, londes, and tenementes, rentes and services whiche are descended unto me by weye of inheritaunce immediatly after my decesse remayne unto myn heires accordyng to the last wille of Robert Mauteby, Squier, my grauntfader, except suche londes as I have putte in feffement to accomplissh therof my last wille, and except v. marc of annuyte which I have graunted out of the maner of Freton in Suffolk to Edmund Paston, my sone, Katherine his wiff, and Robert, ther sone, for terme of ther lyves.

Item, I bequeth to Anne, my doughter, x*li.* to hir propre use.

And to Osbern Berney x. marc of the money comyng of the londes by me put in feffement as is beforseid.

Item, I wull that the residewe of the stuffe of myn houshold unbiquothen be divided equally betwen Edmund and William, my sones, and Anne, my doughter.

The residewe of all my godes and catalle and dettes to me owing I yeve and comitte to the good disposicion of myn executours to performe this my testament and last wille, and in other dedes of mercye for my sowle, myn aunceterez sowlez, and alle Cristen sowles, to the most pleaser of God and profit to my sowle.

Of this my testament, I make and ordeyne the seid John Paston, Squier, my sone, Thomas Drentall, clerk, Simon Gerard and Walter Lymyngton myn executours.

And I bequeth to the seid John Paston for his labour x*li.*

And to iche of myn other executours for their labour v. marc.

In witnesse wherof to this my present testament I have putto my seal. Yevyn day and yer biforseid.

53

THE PASTON LETTERS

979

JOHN PASTON TO MARGARET PASTON[1]

To my ryght worchepfull modyr, Margaret Paston.

1482(?)

RYGHT worchepfull modyr, in my most humble wyse I recomand me to yow, besechyng yow of your dayly blyssyng. And when I may, I wyll with as good wyll be redy to recompence yow for the cost that my huswyff and I have put yow to, as I am now bond to thank yow for it, whyche I do in the best wyse I can. And, modyr, it pleasyd yow to have serteyn woordys to my wyff at hyr depertyng, towchyng your remembrance of the shortnesse that ye thynk your dayes of, and also of the mynd that ye have towardes my brethryn and systyr your chyldyr, and also of your servauntes, wher in ye wyllyd hyr to be a meane to me, that I wold tendyr and favore the same. Modyr, savyng your plesure, ther nedyth non enbasatours nor meanys betwyx yow and me; for ther is neyther wyff nor other frend shall make me to do that that your comandment shall make me to do, if I may have knowlage of it; and if I have no knowlage, in good feyth I am excuseabyll bothe to God and yow. And, well remembryd, I wot well ye ought not to have me in jelusye for one thyng nor other that ye wold have me to accomplyshe, if I overleve yow; for I wot well non oo man a lyve hathe callyd so oft upon yow as I, to make your wylle and put iche thyng in serteynte, that ye wold have done for your sylff, and to your chyldre and servauntes. Also at the makyng of your wylle, and at every comunycacyon that I have ben at with yow towchyng the same, I nevyr contraryed thyng that ye wold have doon and performyd, but alweyso ffyrd my sylff to be bownde to the same. But, modyr, I am ryght glad that my wyff is eny thyng your favore or trust; but I am ryght sory that my wyff, or eny other chyld or servaunt of your shold be in bettyr favore or

---

[1] [From Paston mss., B.M.] This letter, which was undoubtedly written during the later years of Margaret Paston, may be conveniently placed after her will.

54

trist with yow then my sylff; for I wyll and must forbere and put fro me that, that all your other chyldre, servauntes, prestys, werkmen, and frendys of your that ye wyll ought bequethe to, shall take to theym. And thys have I, and evyr wylbe redy on to, whyll I leve, on my feyth, and nevyr thought other, so God be my helpe, Whom I beseche to preserve yow and send yow so good lyff and longe, that ye may do for youre sylff and me aftyr my dyssease; and I beshrewe ther hertys that wold other or shall cause yow to mystrust, or to be unkynd to me or my frendys.

1482(?)

At Norwyche, thys Monday, with the hand of your sone and trwest servaunt,

JOHN PASTON.

980

T. CRYNE TO JOHN PASTON[1]

To my wurshepfull and tendrest maister, John Paston, Esquyer.

RIGH wurshepfulle, one of my most kyndest and tenderest, and undeserved most contynuell maister, I recomaunde me to you. And where your trusty maistershep willeth me to come to Norwich, pleas it you I may not; for ever, as in long tyme passed, on Thursday in Esterne Weke, begynne Maister Heydons courtes and letes, the vieu of the halfyere of the houshold accompte, the closyng up fynally of th'accomptes of alle bailievs, so that the resceyvour may make his fynall accompte, which wille extende in alle to xiiij. dayes and more; and to this season is my duete, and elles I shulde not faill your pleasure.

1482
APRIL 1

Moreover, pleas it you, my Lord Riviers in his owne persone hath bene atte Hikelyng, and his counseill lerned, and serched his fees for his homages, among which ye be for Begvyles pasture in Somerton, and, I suppose, Wynterton, late Sir John Fastolfes; my maistres your modre for Mawtebyes in Waxham; wherein I beseche you previde, for I have done therein hertofore, asfer as I myght, &c. What it

---

[1] [From Paston mss., B.M.]

55

meneth, my lord is sette sore to approwement and husbondry. His counseill hath tolde him he may sette his fynes for respite of homage at his pleasure, &c.

I besech you my maistresse may have worde of this. And oure blessed Lord ever mutte preserve you, and be your governour and defender.

Wreten at Thorplond, this Wednesday in Esterne Weke, fallyng the x. day of Aprill, anno E. iiij^d xxij.

Your servaunt,   T. CRYNE.

(margin: 1482 IL 10)

981

ABSTRACT[1]

Grant by Margaret Paston to her son Edmund and his wife Catherine and to Robert their son, of an annuity of five marks out of the manor of Freton, Suffolk, with power to distrain for payment.

9 Oct. 22 Edw. IV.

(margin: T. 9)

982

MARGERY PASTON TO JOHN PASTON[2]

To my right worshipfull master, John Paston, in haste.

RIGHT reverent and worshipfull sir, in my moste umble vice, I recomaunde me unto yow, as lowly as I can, &c. Plese you to wete, John Howes, Alexander Qwharteyn, John Fille, with the parson and the newe myller of Marlyngforthe, have goten Thom' At Welles carte of Estetodenham,

(margin: 82(?) DV. I)

[1] [From Paston MSS., B.M.]
[2] *Ibid.* This letter, it will be seen, must have been written before the death of Margaret Paston in 1484, and from what is stated in No. 953, it is certainly not earlier than 1479. The date, moreover, must be between 1480 and 1482, for it is stated that the outrages here complained of occurred on the Monday and Tuesday before the letter was written; and in the next letter we find that there was a new outrage of the same description on Friday. If Hallowmas Day, the date of this letter, was a Wednesday in 1484, the year must be 1480, if a Thursday 1481, and if Friday 1482. We are rather inclined to think it was the latter.

56

fermour to myn uncle William Paston, Herry Hervy of Meelton Magna, fermour and baly to my seide uncle, Ric. Barkers carte of the seide towne of Meelton, late fermour, and yette is in daunger to[1] my seide uncle, and William Smythes carte of Brandon juxta Bernham Broom, late fermour and baly, and also in daunger to[1] my seide uncle, on Monday and Twesday last past, caryed a wey from Merlyngforth in to the place at Seint Edmondes in Norwich, xij. of yowr greete plankes, of the weche they made vj. loodes, beryng a bowte the seide cartes, bowes and gleves, for feere of takyng a wey. Sir, as for yowr servauntes of Marlyngforth, they withholde her catell and hem selfe bothe from the coorte, and come not within the lordship, nor make noon attornment, exept Thom' Davy and John Water, weche absentyng of the tenauntes is to them a greet hurt and los, for lak of sedyng ther londes with ther wynter corn; besechyng you for Godes sake to remembre som remedy for them.

My Lady Caltorp hath ben at Geppeswich on pilgry mache, and came homward be my Lady of Norffolk, and ther was moche communicacion of yowr mater be twix you and myn uncle, seyng to my Lady Caltorp, ye nede not a gonne to London, ye myght have an ende at home; rememberyng to my seid Lady Caltorp of the mocion that he made towchyng the maner of Sporle, promyttyng to my lady to abyde that, and to write and seale as largely as any man wol desire hym. And at his departyng from my lady he was not mery, what the cauce was I wot not [but he was not mery of your departyng].[2] My Lady Calthorp desireth me to write yow to have ende, for he intendes largely to have a peace with yow, as he seth; but truste hym not to moche, for he is not goode.

My mother in lawe thynketh longe she here no word from you. She is in goode heele, blissed be God, and al yowr babees also. I mervel I here no word from you, weche greveth me ful evele; I sent you a letter be Brasiour sone of Norwiche, wher of I here no word. No more to you

(margin: 1482(?) NOV. I)

[1] 'In danger to' signifies either in debt or otherwise responsible to another person.
[2] These words are crossed out in the MS.

57

THE PASTON LETTERS   EDWARD IV

at this tyme, but Almghty Jesu have you in Hes blissed kepyng.

Wreten at Norwich, on Allowmes Day at nyght.

Be yowr servaunt and bedewoman,
     MARGERY PASTON.

Sir, I prey yow, if ye tary longe at London, that it wil plese to sende for me, for I thynke longe sen I lay in yowr armes.

(margin: 82(?) DV. I)

983

MARGERY PASTON TO JOHN PASTON[1]

To my ryght wurchupfull mayster, John Paston, Esquyer, be this letter delyverd in hast.

MYNE owyn swete hert, in my most humylwyse, I recomaund me on to you, desyryng hertly to here of your welfar, the wheche I beseche Alle myghty God preserve and kepe to His plesur, and your hertes desyer.

Ser, the cause of my wrytyng to you at this tyme : on Friday att nyght last past come Alexander Wharton, John Hous, and John Fille, with ij. good carts well mannyd and horsyd with hem to Marlyngford, and there at the maner of Malyngford and at the mille lodyn bothe cartes with mestlyon[2] and whete, and betymys on Saturday, in the mornyng, they departyd fro Marlyngford towardes Bongey, as it is seyd ; for the seyd cartes come fro Bongey, as I soppose, by the sendynge of Bryon ; for he goth hastyly over the se, as it is seyd. And as I suppose he wyll have the mestlyon over with hym, for the most part of the cart loodes was mestlyon, &c.

Item, ser, on Saturday last past, I spacke with my cosyn Gornay, and he seyd, if I wold goo to my Lady of Norffolk,

(margin: V. [3])

[1] [From Paston MSS., B.M.] For evidence of date, see preliminary note to last letter.
[2] Mixed corn, commonly rye and wheat, which were most in demand to make bread of.

58

and beseche hyr good grace to be your good and gracyous lady, she wold so be, for he seyd that one word of a woman should do more than the wordes of xx. men, yiffe I coude rewyll my tonge, and speke non harme of myn unkyll. And if ye comaund me so for to do, I trist I shuld sey nothynge to my ladys displesure, but to your profyt ; for me thynkyth bi the wordes of them and of your good fermore of Oxned, that thei wyll sone drawe to an ende. For he cursyth the tyme that ever he come in the ferme of Oxned, for he seyth that he wotyth well that he shall have a grette losse, and yet he wyll not be a knowyn wheder he hathe payd or nought ; but whan he sethe his tyme, he wyll sey trowth.

I understood by my seyd cosyn Gornay that my lady is nere wery of hyr parte, and he seyth my lady shal come on pylgremage in to this towne, but he knowth not wheder afore Cristmes or aftyr ; and if I wold thanne gete my Lady Calthorpe, my moder in lawe, and my moder, and myselfe, and come before my lady, besechyng hyr to be your good and gracyous lady, he thynkyth ye shull have an ende ; for fayne she wold be redde of it with hyr onowr savyd, but yette money she wold have.

No more to you at this tyme, butte I mervell sore that I have no letter from you, but I prey God preserve you, and send me good tydynges from you, and spede you well in your materes. And as for me, I have gotyn me anothyr logyn felawe, the ferst letter of hyr name is Mastras Byschoppe. She recomaundyth hyr to you by the same tokyn that ye wold have had a tokyn to my Mayster Bryon.

Att Norwych, the Sonday next after the Fest of All Seyntes.

Be yowr servaunt and bedewoman,
     MARGERY PASTON.

(margin: 1482(?) NOV. [3])

59

THE PASTON LETTERS

984

B. R. TO JOHN PASTON[1]

To the right worshipfull John Paston, squier, with my lord Chamburlayn.

1479-
83

RIGHT worshipfull sir, y recommaunde me to you, as hartily as y can, desiring to undrestand zour welefare, and also to knowe somwhat certainly hou your matier dothe with your uncle, and hou fer ye be, for in thes parties y assertayne you, moche mater is shewed and proclaimed in worshipful presence, fer fro th'entent of your welewillers, of the discorage and reprofe in maner of you, and by such as men supposed you to have ben right wele favoured with, and the contrary shewed in the presence of right worshipfull, and right many, and as it is said, iij. scor in nombre, with such termes and under such forme, as it is reported, as is full hevy to diverse here for to here. Hou it is ye knowe beste, and hou it is I pray you lete your frendis in this cuntre undirstand; for right a worshipfull persone told me of this, to the which y coude not answer, I se al day the world so unsure. But, Sir, ye did of policy some thingis that peradventure, and it were to do, ye wold take anothir avise, &c. I can nomore but *sapienti pauca*, &c. And I biseche you, Sir, send me some tidingis of the parties beyonde the se, for owr wyves here speke of many thingis, &c. Moreovir, Sir, Margarete Ronhale told me late that my maistres your wif fareth wele, blissed be Almighti God, and all your other frendis here, blissed be God. Sir, it is so that, as y am enformed, there is a soudiour of Caleis called John Jacob, of olde tyme duelling in Lynne.[2] I pray you to inquir secretly what maner man he ys, and in

[1] [Add. MS. 34,889, f. 220.] This letter is probably late in the reign of Edward IV. John Paston would seem to have entered the service of Hastings, the Lord Chamberlain, some time after the death of his brother Sir John in 1479. See No. 993.

[2] Against this passage in the margin is written in another hand:—'Mᵈ. pro Barnard.'

60

EDWARD IV

what condicion there, for I know a man hath to do with him; but be ye beknowen of no thinge, but that ye list wisely to enquere what he is and of what condicion, &c. And if there be any thing in thies parties that y can do you service yn, I pray you commaunde you, and I shalbe as redy to the accomplishment therof to my power, as any man lyvyng; and that knowith God, Who I bieche to send me good tidingis for you, and you your noble desires. From Weston.—By yours, B. R.

147·
83

985

WILLIAM PASTON AND SIR JOHN FASTOLF[1]

TO alle maner of pepill to whome this present wrytyng shall come unto, se, or here, we, William Barker, late of Blofeld, in the cownte of Norffolk, clark, and Margret Wyssetour, wedow, late the wyf of William Wyssetyr, late of Pokethorp, be Norwich, gentylman, dyssesid, send gretyng in our Lord God Everlastyng.

For as meche as it is merytory to wytnesse and testyfy the treuth in materes dowtabill or beyng in varyaunce, whan ony persons is lefully ther to requyred, It is so that I, the seid William Barker, was late howshold servaunte be the space of xxj. yere with Sir John Fastolf, Knyght, dyssesid, and had wedded Annes, late dyssesid, that was the hoole syster, bothe on to Sir Thomas Howes, clerk, dyssesid, and also hoole syster to Isabell, modyr to the seid Margret Wyssetyr, which forseid Thomas Howys and William Wyssetyr were bothe howshold

[1] [Add. Charter 17,256, B.M.] This declaration was drawn up after the death of William Worcester, and perhaps after that of William Paston also. The exact date of Worcester's death is uncertain. We only know that he was alive as late as 1480, when he visited Oxford on his travels and measured some of the churches there (*see* his *Itinerarium*, 296), and that he was dead in Richard III.'s time. The document, however, may be conveniently placed at the end of the reign of Edward IV. The original MS. is a sheet of paper mutilated on the right-hand side towards the end. The seals of William Barker and Margaret Worcester are attached by tails of parchment to a parchment binding at the bottom. On the back is written in a more modern hand:—' A Testymonyall that William Paston, Gent., was kinsman to Sir Jo. Fastolf, and other matters within concernyng the landes somtyme Holhams in Caster, afterwardes the sayd William Paston.'

61

THE PASTON LETTERS

servauntes many yerys to the seid Sir John Fastolf, and were with hym in such syngler trust that he made them bothe his feoffes in alle his landes with in the reame of Ynglond, and also his exsecutores: Be it knowen to alle maner persons that we, the seid William Barker and Margret Wyssetyr, testyfy, depose, and wytnesse for trouthe that we have full serteyn prof and knowlache that William Paston, of the seid counte of Norffolk, jentylman, was kynnysman unto the seid Sir John Fastolf, and was with hym in ryght syngler gode favour and trust; wherupon the seid Sir John Fastolf made the seid William Paston one of his seid feoffes in all his seyd maneres, londes, and tenementes, rentes, and servyces with in this seid reame of Ynglond, and made this seid William prevy to many of his materys of gret charge, and putt the seid William Paston to many lawbores in his lyf, which the seid William Paston ded of gode love and kynd dysposycion, for he never had of the seid Sir John Fastolf fee ne reward in hys lyf; notwithstondyng he had for the seid Syr John Fastolf and for his materes many grete lawboures, costes, jornays, and besynesse in the lyf of the seid Sir John Fastolf, and ded for hym many kynd dedes at his owne charge, for the which the seid Sir John, and he had contenuyd lyff, wold have largely have recompensed. And also the seid William Paston had, aftir the desesse of the seid Sir John Fastolf, at the desyr and instans of the exsecutores of the seid Syr John, had many gret lawboures, costes, and jurnays to his gret peyne, as well in rydyng to London many and sundry tymes, contenuyng many yeres to help suche materes as were devysyd ayens the seid exsecutors, and also to answer to suche accions and sutys and byll putt into the Kynges Chauncery, wherupon wryttes of *subpena* dyvers and many tymes made upon gret peynys were delyvered to the seid William to appere in the Kynges Chauncery, which were taken be gret astates and be suche myghty persons as wold have recoveryd the lond wrongfully, and thus trobelyd the seid William Paston, be cause he was a feffee, and taryd hym there and his councell· to his gret inportunabill charges. Wherupon we, the seid William Barker and Margret Wyssetyr depose, wytnesse, and be this present

62

EDWARD IV

sertyfye for trouthe that we war present whan the seid Sir Thomas Howys and William Wyssetyr, in parcell of recompens of suche forseid lawbours and costes as the seid William Paston had had, as wele in the lyfe of the seid Sir John as after his dyssese, graunted and yaf to the seid William Paston a peyer of basons coveryd of sylver of Parysh towche and over gylt, powncyd and imbossyd with rooses, and with grete large amellys [*enamels*] in the botome of bothe basons, with serteyn bestys inbossyd stondyng with inn an hegge of sylver and gylt upon the seid amellys, which bothe basons ded way of Troy weyt ixˣˣ· unces, and also a gredeyren of sylver of Parysse towche, not gylt, weying of Troy weyth ——[1] unces, and also a gret chargeour of sylver of Parysse towche, not gylt, weying of Troy weyth ——[1] unces, to have and to hold to the seid William, his eyres, exceckutores, and assignes, as his own godes for ever. And also we wytnesse that we ware also present whan, for a serteyn som of mony to be payd be the seid William Paston, whereof a parte be comenawnt was payd be the seid amellys, which bothe basons ded say the seid William Paston to the seid Sir Thomas Howys, and a parte to on Edmond Holkham, and the remenaunt was payd to one Margret Holkham, syster to the seid Edmond; and so the seid William Paston had clerly payed all the seid mony. The seid Thomas Howse and William Wyssetyr bargayned, sold, and graunted to the seid William Paston, his eyres, exsecutores, and assignes, in fee sympille for ever, a tenement called Methis, otherwyse called Holkham, with alle the londes and tenementes, rentes and servyces, free or bond, and with all the apportenaunces ther to belongyng, in the town of Cayster ond oder townnys adjoynyng with inne the seid cownte of Norffolk, and delyvered to the seid [William] Paston and to his assignes a state of all the seid tenementes, londes, rentes, and servyces, with all the seid aportenaunces . . .
. . . . sold and bargayned to the seid William Paston alle suche londes, rente, and servyces as the seid Sir John Fastolf . . . . or be the ryght of ony manere that he or ony man to his use had in possession, or that the seid Thoma[s] . . . . ony other be

[1] Blank in original.

63

THE PASTON LETTERS

the reson that they were feffes of trust of the seid John Fastolf had or claymed to have . . . . or claymed to have to be yssant or chargeabill oute or upon the seid tenement called Methe[s] . . . . londes, tenementes, rentes, servyces at ony tyme afore or than longyng to the seid tenement or owt . . . . . a manere called Hornynghall, with the apportenaunces, late Clerys, in the seid toun of Castyr, to have [and to hold to the said William] Paston, his eyres and assygnes, the seid lond, rent, and servyce for ever mor. And utterly be ther dede and . . . . and dyscharged the seid William Paston, his eyres and his assygnes for yeldyng of payment of ony . . . . servyce; and also dyscharged all the seid tenement and the seid manere, and alle oder the premysses, with alle the . . . . as now have or shalle here aftir be possessoneres of the seid tenement or manere with the aportenaunces . . . . more. Alle whiche mater afore rehersid, and every parte therof, we, the seid William Barker and Margre[t Wyssetyr . . . .] trew, and we, and iche one of us, will at alle tyme be redy to wytnesse and depose the same be ony suche . . . . persones outh to do or may do afore ony Juge Spyrytualle or Temperall as we will answer a fore God [at the dreadful] day of Dome. In wytnesse wherof we, the seid William Barker and Margret Wyssetyr, to this present have sett to our [sealles].

Wretyn the ———[1] day of the ———[1] yer of the reyn of Kyng.

(L. S.)   (L. S.)

[1] Blanks in MS.   [2] So in MS.

64

986

ABSTRACT [1]

W. BARKER TO [MARGARET PASTON?]

Begs her 'maystrasshipp' to inform his rightworshipful master of the conduct of Master Keche at Wetyng, who on Monday means to be there with a great fellowship.

[This letter is unimportant, but as being written by William Barker it may conveniently be placed after the last No., although probably addressed to Margaret Paston, and if so, most likely during the life of her husband. It appears by inquisition post-mortem, 1 Edw. IV., No. 46, that Elizabeth, Countess of Oxford, held the manor of Weting in Feltwell of the Duke of Norfolk.]

987

JOHN PASTON'S BOOKS [2]

The Inventory off Englysshe Boks off John . . . . . made the v. daye of Novembre, anno regni Regis E. iiij. . . . . .

1. A boke had off myn ostesse at the George off *the Dethe off Arthr begynyng at Cassa&[elaun, Guy Earl of] Warwyk, Kyng Ri. Cur de Lyon, a Cronic[le] to Edwarde the iiij.*, prec. . . . .

2. Item, a Boke of Troylus whyche William Bra . . . . . . hath hadde neer x. yer, and lent it to Dame . . . . Wyngfelde, and *ibi ego vidi*; valet . . . . . .

3. Item, a blak Boke with *the Legende off Lad[ies, la Belle Dame] saunce Mercye, the Parlement off Byrd[es, the Temple of]*

[1] [From Paston MSS., B.M.]

[2] [From Fenn, ii. 300.] This is a catalogue of the books either of John Paston the younger or of John Paston, Knight, most probably the former, drawn up in the reign of Edward IV., but owing to the decay of the original MS. we cannot tell in what year. It certainly could not have been earlier than 1475, when *The Game and Play of the Chess* was first printed by Caxton. It is in itself a remarkable thing that the expression 'in print' should have got into use even during the reign of Edward IV.; but one may suppose that such an expression could hardly have been current for at least a year or two after the first printed book appeared. We therefore, without deciding the year, place the paper at the end of King Edward's reign.

VOL. VI.—E

65

THE PASTON LETTERS

Glasse, Palatyse and Scitacus, the Me[ditations of . . . .] the Greene Knyght; valet,—

4. Item, a Boke in preente off the Pleye off the [Chess].

5. Item, a Boke lent Midelton, and therin is *Bele Da[me sans] Mercy the Parlement of Byrds, Balade . . . . off Guy and Colbronde, off the Goos th . . . . . . , the Dysputson bytwyen Hope and Dyspeyr, ... Marehaunts, the Lyffe of Seynt Cry[stofer].*

6. A reede Boke that Percyvall Robsart gaff m[e] . . . . off the medis off the Masse, the Lamentacion . . . . off Chylde Ypotis, a Preyer to the Vernyclr . . . . callyd the Abbeye off the Holy Goost,*

7. Item, in quayers :—*Tully de Senectute* in . . . . wheroff ther is no mor cleer wretyn . . . .

. . . .

8. Item, in quayers :—*Tully, or Cypio,*[1] *de Ami[citia]*[2] leffte with William Worcester ; valet . . . .

9. Item, in qwayers, a Boke of the Polecye of In . . .

10. Item, in qwayers, a Boke *de Sapiencia* . . . . wherin the ij. parson is liknyd to Sapi[ence] . . . . .

11. Item, a Boke *de Othea*,[3] text and glose, valet . . . . in quayers.

Memorandum,[4] myn olde Boke off Blasonyngs off a[rms].

Item, the nywe Boke portrayed and blasoned.

Item, a copy off Blasonyngs off armys and th . . . . names to be fownde by letter.

Item, a Boke with armys portrayed in paper . . . . .

Memorandum, my Boke of Knyghthod and the man[er]

[1] *Quere*, if Cypio is not a mistake from 'Somnium Scipionis,' a piece which is usually printed with the 'de Amicitia,' and probably accompanied it in this manuscript.—F.

[2] It is a curious circumstance that this book should be here mentioned as left with William Worcester, who with the assistance of John Tiptoft, Earl of Worcester, and John Phrea or Free, a monk of Bristol, translated it.—F.

[3] *See* vol. v. p. 3, Note 1.

[4] These further memoranda seem to have been added at a later period, probably in the reign of Henry VII., as the last entry is of 'a book of new statutes from Edward IV.'

66

off makyng off Knyghts, off Justs, off Tor[neaments] ffyghtyng in lystys, paces holden by so[ldiers] . . . . . and chalenges, statuts off weer, and de Regim[ine Principum], valet

Item, a Boke off nyw Statuts ffrom Edward the iiij.

988

VERSES BY A LADY [1]

Verses written by a Lady in the reign of Henry VI. or Edward IV. to an absent Lord with whom she was in love.

MY ryght good lord, most knyghtly gentyll knyght,
On to your grace in my most humbyll wyse,
I me comand, as it is dew and ryght,
Besechyng yow at leyser to advise
Upon thys byll, and pardon myn empryse,
Grownaye on foly, for lak of provydence,
On to your lordshep to wryght with owght lycence.

But wher a man is with a fevyr shake,
Now hot, now cold, as fallyth by aventure,
He in hys mynd conjecte wyll, and take
The nyghest meane to worche hys cuyre,
More pacyently hys peynys to endure ;
And ryght so I, so it yow not dysplease,
Wryght in thys wyse my peynys to apease.

For when I cownt and mak a reknyng
Betwyx my lyfe, my dethe, and my desyer,
My lyfe, alas ! it servyth of no thyng
Sythe with your partyng, depertyd my plesyer.

[1] [From Fenn, ii. 304.] It is not apparent by whom these verses were written, or to what lord they were addressed. They may have been from the Countess of Oxford to her husband after he escaped abroad in 1471 (*see* vol. v., No. 775). Or they may have been the production of Lydgate writing in the name of a lady parted from her lord. We place them, as Fenn did, for convenience, at the end of the letters of Edward's time.

67

THE PASTON LETTERS

Wyshyng your presence setyth me on fyer ;
But then your absence dothe my hert so cold,
That for the peyne I not [1] me wher to hold.

O owght on absence, ther foolys have no grace,
I mene mysylf, nor yet no wytt to gwye
Theym owt of peyne to com on to that place,
Wher as presence may shape a remedye ;
For al dysease, now fye on my folye,
For I dyspeyryd am of your soone metyng,
That God I prey me to your presence bryng.

Farwell, my lord, for I may wryght no more,
So trowblyd is my hert with hevynesse ;
Envye also, it grewyth me most sore,
That thys rude byll shall put hym sylf in presse [2]
To se your lordshepe of hys presumptuousnesse
Er I my sylf ; but yett ye shall not mysse
To have my hert to for my byll, I wys.

Whyche I comytt and all my hole servyse
Into your hands, demeane it as you lyst ;
Of it I kepe [3] to have no more franchyse
Then I hertlesse swyrly me wyst,
Savyng only that it be as tryst, [4]
And to yow trew as evyr was hert, and pleyn
Tyll cruell dethe depart yt up on tweyn.

Adew dysport, farwell good companye,
In all thys world ther is no joye I weene ;
For ther as whyleom I sye with myn iee,
A lusty lord leepyng upon a grene,
The soyle is soole, no knyghts ther be seen,
No ladyse walk ther they wer wont to doone ;
Alas, some folk depertyd hense to soone.

[1] 'I not' stands for 'I ne wot,' or 'I wot not,' that is, *I know not.*
[2] Readiness.—F.   [3] I care.—F.
[4] *Quere,* whether this means *sorrowful* or *trusty.*—F.
68

THE PASTON LETTERS

991.

John Downyng to Edmund Paston

Is a simple servant of his mother and miller of Wood Mill.   Complains of Will. Sybbeson, whom Edmund Paston well knows to have been ' defawtyf in many other thyngs,' and who embezzles wheat and rye, and prevents him getting any good of a close he holds of Paston's mother.
North Walsham, Thursday before St. Brice.[1]

[Some memoranda of receipts are written across the back.]

[1] St. Brice's Day is 13th November.

70

EDWARD IV

Some tyme also men myght a wageor make,
And with ther bowys a ffeld have it tryed,
Or at the Paame ther, ther plesure for to take,
Then wer they loose, that now stand as tyed,
I not [1] wher to thys world may be aplyed ;
For all good cher on evyn and on morow,
Whyche then was made, now tornyth me to sorow.

989–991
ABSTRACTS [2]

The letters following are all probably of the reign of Edward IV., but their dates are quite uncertain.

989.

J. Paston [of Gelston] to Richard Croft

Will not venture to ride in this weather, not being well at ease.   Sends three bills of John Calle and Robert Salle's receipts and payments brought by the former.   Cannot find the new fermall of Caster here, so he has given the bearer the key of his coffer at Yarmouth.   If you would ride with him, I think you will find it there.   Agrees to John Wynne's bills, desiring to be allowed £5 for Byshoppis of Yarmouth, and for herring delivered to my cousin Loveday ; but John Wynne must not sell my farm barley to pay them, as I wish all the barley in his charge malted for my Lord Mountjoy.   I send a warrant for the sheriff to warn the persons in Flegge and Yarmouth impanelled between the King and me to be at Thetford assizes on Wednesday next.   Give it to Simon Garrard.
Norwich, Wednesday.

990.

Sir Thomas Hert to his worshipful Mistress, [Margaret Paston ?]

Giving her an account of the numbers of her sheep and lambs at Sparham from Drayton and Taverham, and those with the shepherd at Heylesdon.
Heylisdon, Thursday before Lady Day the Nativity.[3]

[Under this letter is written in a modern hand—'37 Hen. 6,' but this date is certainly too early.   Thomas Hert was Vicar of Stalham in 1482.]

[1] See Note 1 on last page.   [2] [From Paston mss., B.M.]
[3] The Nativity of St. Mary the Virgin, 8th September.

69

THE PASTON LETTERS

Edward V.

992

RICHARD, DUKE OF GLOUCESTER, TO LORD NEVILL [1]

To my Lorde Nevyll, in hast.

MY Lorde Nevyll, I recommaunde me to you as hartely   148
as I can ; and as ever ye love me, and your awne   JUNE
weale and securty, and this Realme, that ye come to
me with that ye may make, defensably arrayde, in all the hast
that ys possyble, and that ye wyll yef credence to . . . . .

[1] [From Fenn, v. 302.]   This letter was not a part of the Paston correspondence, but was printed by Fenn in the series as a letter of much historical interest from a copy given him by the Rev. John Brand, secretary to the Society of Antiquaries.   The following memoranda accompanied the copy :—
  'Extract from an ancient ms. of pedigrees, etc., in quarto, late in the possession of Sir Walter Blackett, Bart., and now the property of John Erasmus Blackett, Esq., Alderman of Newcastle-upon-Tyne ; p. 333, under title of " *A Coppie of some Letters which were found in Rabie Castle after the Rebellion, to shew the fashion . . . . of those times.*"   The above ms. is of the date of James I., though there are several continuations in a more modern hand.
  'This copy has doubtless been a transcript of an original letter of the Duke of Gloucester, afterwards King Richard III., and written just before his seizure of the crown.
  'Raby Castle is in the county of Durham.'
  Fenn adds that it does not appear clearly who this Lord Nevill was.   But as the letter was found in Raby Castle after the great rebellion of the Earls of Northumberland and Westmoreland, in 1569, it was evidently addressed to one of that family of Nevills, the heads of which were Earls of Westmoreland.   In 1483 the Earl of Westmoreland's name was Ralph Nevill, but he died in the year following, and was succeeded in the title by Ralph, son and heir of his brother, John, Lord Nevill, who was slain at Towton.   It was this Ralph, then heir-presumptive to the earldom, who is here called Lord Nevill.   He had got his father's attainder reversed in 1472, and his title of Lord Nevill was recognised.   *See* G. Ele's *Peerage,* viii. 112.

71

THE PASTON LETTERS

1483
JUNE 11
Richarde Ratclyff, thys beerrer, whom I nowe do sende to you, enstructed with all my mynde and entent.

And, my lord, do me nowe gode servyce, as ye have always befor don, and I trust nowe so to remember you as shalbe the makyng of you and yours. And God sende you goode fortunes.

Wrytten att London, xj. day of Jun, with the hande of your hertely lovyng cousyn and master,

R. GLOUCESTER.

993

ELIZABETH, DUCHESS OF SUFFOLK, TO JOHN PASTON[1]

On to Jan Paston, in haste.

Not
after
1483
MASTYR PASTON, I pray yow that it may plese yow to leve yowr logeyng for iij. or foro days tyl I may be porved of anodyr, and I schal do as musche to yowr plesyr. For Godys sake, say me not nay ; and I pray yow rekomaund me to my Lord Chambyrleyn.

Yowr frend, ELIZABETH.

[1] [From Fenn, ii. 292.] This is a holograph letter of Elizabeth, Duchess of Suffolk, the sister of Edward IV. There can be little doubt that the Lord Chamberlain referred to is the Lord Hastings who has been very frequently mentioned in this correspondence ; and if so, the letter cannot be later than 1483, as he was beheaded in that year on the 13th June, by order of the Protector Richard, Duke of Gloucester. We may therefore place it for convenience among the letters of Edward V.'s time, though undoubtedly it may be a few years earlier. Facsimiles of the original, both back and front, are given by Fenn. It is endorsed in the hand of John Paston, the younger (certainly not in that of his brother Sir John, as Fenn supposed)—' Littra Ducisse Suff.'

THE PASTON LETTERS

Richard III.

994

JOHN, DUKE OF NORFOLK, TO JOHN PASTON[1]

To my right welbeloved frynde, John Paston, be this delivred in hast.

RIGHT welbeloved frynde, I comaunde me to you. It is soo that the Kentysshmen be up in the weld, and sey that they wol come and robbe the cite, which I shall lett yf I may.

1483
OCT. 10

Therefore I pray you that with alle diligence ye make you redy and com hidder, and bring with you six talle felaws in harnesse, and ye shall not lyse yowr labour, that knoweth God, Whoo have you in His keping.

Written at London, the xth day of October.

Yowr frend, J. NORFFOLK.

[1] [From Fenn, ii. 314.] Sir John Howard was created Duke of Norfolk on the 28th June 1483, and was killed in the battle of Bosworth on the 22nd August 1485. This letter seems to have been written in October 1483, when it first became known that a series of insurrections were about to take place in different counties, of which the Duke of Buckingham was the principal leader. It was on the 12th October, just two days after this letter was written, that King Richard himself at Lincoln heard of Buckingham's intended treason.

THE PASTON LETTERS

995

ABSTRACT[1]

1484
Proviso to be inserted in an Act of Parliament in favour of Margaret, widow of John Paston, touching her right to the manor of Castre.

Below is written—' Guy Fayrefax, Knyght, [Ric. Pygot, one of the King's Serjeants of the Law,][2] and Roger Townesend, [another of][2] the King's Serjeants of the Law.

[This proviso must have been drawn up in connection with some measure that was to have come before the Parliament of January 1484. Earlier it cannot be, as Roger Townesend was not appointed King's Serjeant till June 1483 ; and as Margaret Paston died in November 1484, it could not possibly be later.]

996

ABSTRACT[3]

FEB. 8
Release by John, Duke of Norfolk, and William, Earl of Nottingham, kinsman and heir of John, late Duke of Norfolk, to John Paston, Esq., brother and heir of Sir John Paston, Knight, of all right and title in the manor of Caister called Redehams, Vawx, and Bosouns by Great Yarmouth, of which Sir John Paston was disseised unjustly by the said late Duke.

997

THE DUKE OF SUFFOLK TO THOMAS JEFFREYS[4]

The Duc of Suffolk.

To Thomas Jeffreys our ffermour of Maundevills, greting.

MAY 1
WE wole and streitly charge you that ye content and paie unto the bringer herof for money imployed in our houshold thre pound thretennne shillings and foure pens for such stuff as we our owne person have promysed,

[1] [From a MS. in the Bodleian Library.]   [2] Scored out.
[3] From a Document transcribed by Sandford in his Genealogy of the Paston Family, and printed by Mr. Worship in the *Norfolk Archæology.*
[4] [From Fenn, ii. 316.]

RICHARD III

and not to be failed upon our worship. Of the which some of lxxiijs. iiijd. so by you contented and paied, we wole and also stretly charge our auditors for the tyme being, by virtu of this our writing, signed with our hand, to make you dew and pleyn allowaunce at your next accompt.

1484
MAY 1

At Wingfeld, the first day of May in the first yer of Kyng Richard the iii^{de}.

SUFFOLK.

And ffayle not on peyn [of] losyng off yor fferme.

998

COMPLAINTS OF JOHN PASTON AGAINST HIS UNCLE WILLIAM[1]

All so the seyde John Paston, now compleynaunt, seyth that John Paston, fadyr off the same John, was seased off the maner callyd Hollwellhawe, wyth th'appurtenaunces in Estodenham, joyntly wyth all the londis, tenementes, rentes, and services, whyche sume tyme were John Jerham, Ewstase Rows, John Davy,[2] vikere off the chyrche off Estodenham, ande Water Danyell, or any off thers, lyeng in the townys off Estodenham, Mateshalle, Mateshalebergh, and othir townys adjoynyng, ande off all the londis and tenementes, rentes, services, and lybertes wyth ther appurtenaunces callyd Toleys, lyeng in the townys off Wymondham and Carleton and othir townys adyoynyng, whyche sume tyme were William Thuxston ; and off the scite off on mese [*messuage*] wyth a pece londe lyenge in a croffte to the same mese adyoynyng, wyche is accomptyde xiiij. acres off londe wyth th'appurtenaunces, callyd Colneys, othyr wys callyd Whynnes in Carleton ——[3] in hys demeane as off ffee ; ande so beyng seased ther off, up on trust enffeffede William Yelverton, Justys, John Fastolff, Knyght, Myles Stapelton, Knyght, and othir, to be hadde to them and theyr heyrs for ever, be the fores wher off they were ther off seased in theyr demeane as off ffee, ande afftyr the seyd ffeffment in forme afforseyd mad, the seyd John Paston the fadyr disseassed. The ryght off the whyche maner, londis, tenementes, and othir the premysses, afftyr the desses of the seyd John

1484

[1] [From Add. Charter 17,257, B.M.] It appears from the contents that this paper must have been drawn up nearly five years after Sir John Paston's death. It is a corrected draft, apparently of a Bill in Chancery, and some of the corrections are in Sir John Paston's hand.
[2] He was vicar of East Tuddenham from 1398 to 1434.
[4] Blank in MS.

THE PASTON LETTERS

1484 the fadyr, owith to come to the seyd John, now compleynaunt, as sone and heyr off the seyd John Paston, ffor as myche as the seyd John the fadyr made no wylle nor mencyon of the aforeseyd maner, londis, tenementes, nor off othir the premysses, whyche maner, londis, and tenementes, and othir the premysses the seyd William Paston hath, and agenst the cours of the lawe ocupyeth.

Item, the seid John requerith an astate to be takyn in those londys lymyted to William the sone for deffaut off issu off Clement Paston by the will of there fadir accordyng to the seid will, as well as in those londis that ar or shuld be purchased with the m^l [1000] mark accordyng to th'endentur mad by twyn th'executors of William Paston, Justice, that is to sey, to the seid William the son, and to the eyres of his body, and for defaute of yssue of his bodye, to remayn to th'eyers of William Paston, Justice, which the seid John is.

All so the seyd John Paston, now compleynaunt, seyth that ther be decayed at Marlyngfford and Oxenhed be meane off th'enterupsion off the seyd William tweyn water melles, wher off iche was letyn ffor x. marke be yer. And all so othir howsyng be the same ockasion at Oxenhed, Marlyngfford, Stansted, and Orwelbury decayed to the hurt off the seyd John Paston off v. C. [500] mark whech the seyd John Paston desyreth to be recompensede.

Item, the seid John axith of the seid William for wast don in the maner of Paston for lak of reparacion, xlli.

Item, the seid William hath takyn awey owth of the maners of John Paston, that is to sey, of hes maners of Paston, Oxened, Marlyngford, Stansted, and Horwelburye, siche stoff and greynys, catell and hotilementis of the seid maners as were agreyd be the executors of the seyd William Paston, Justyse, to be left and latyn with the seid maners to the value of xlli.

Item, the seid John axith to be restored to all the evydence longyng to the maners aforesaid and other the premysses which the seid William wrongfully withholdith.

Item, the seid John axith to hys possession which he hath of [and] in the maner of Caster and other maners adyongnyng, the relesse of all such title and interest as the seid William hath be wey of feffement in the foresaid maner and maners, in like forme as other his cofeffes have in tyme past relassed to Sir John Paston, whoos eyre the seid John is.

Also, the seid John Paston desireth the performance of diverse comenauntis and articles conteyned in diverse indentures and writynges mad be the avise of the reverend fadir in God, William, Bisschoppe of Lyncolne,[1] supervisour of the testement of the seid William Paston, Justice, bytwix th'executors of the same William Paston for kepyng of the trewe intent and will of the seid William Paston, Justice, as by the same indentures and writynges redye to be schewed more pleynlye shall appere, the entent and performance of whiche writyng is interupted and brokyn be the seid William Paston and his meanys to the hurt and damage off the seyd John Paston, now compleynaunt off ———.[2]

Item, the seid William hath, contrary to trouuth and conscience, vexed and trouubled and put to cost and charge the seid John nowe be the space of v. yer saffe a quarter,[3] and hath distorbede the same John to take and perceyve th'issus

[1] William Alnwick, Bishop of Lincoln, who died in 1449.   [2] Blank in MS.
[3] Originally written 'a yere and more,' and corrected.

76

RICHARD III

and profetes off the same maners, to the hurt and damage off the seyd John in   1484 defendyng of his right off and in the maners afforeseyd of ij. m^l mark, besyde greffe, gret labour and disseace that the seid John hath dayly be putt onto by th'okcasion afforseyd.[1]

Item, accordyng to the will of William Paston, Justice, the seid John axith to be restored to parth of such goodis as hath ben dispendid by John Paston the fader, Sir John Paston, and the seid John nowe compleynaunt, in defence, kepyng, and recoveryng of such londis as were William Paston, Justice, which draweth above the summa of mli.

Item, where on ———[2] Lomnor had a cofur in kepyng and and D.m^l mark in the same be extymasion to the use of John Paston, fadir of the forsayed Sir John and John, the seid William Paston fraudelently atteyned the seid cofur wyth the seyd sume of money after the dissece of the seid John the fadir, and had it in his kepyng serteyn dayes, and did wit t his pleasur unknowyn to the seid Sir John Paston and John Paston, his brother; and after at Herry Colettes[3] house the seid William brought the seid cofur to the seid John Paston, Knyght, and there openyd the seid cofur, where was then lefte but CC. old noblis which wer be extymacion in value Cli. And the seid William toke ther the seid gold awey with hym, ageyn the will of seid Sir John, and witholdith the same, whereof the seyd John preyeth to be restored.

Item, the seid William atteynyd and gate a payer of basons of silver and parte or all gilt from the seid Sir John Paston and John Paston, now compleynaunt, abouuth such season as he toke the cofur and coyne aforerehersed, which basons were in value C. mark; and the seid William yet witholdith the seid basons, to the whyche the seyd John preyeth also to be restored.

Item, the seid William gate in to his possession a charger of silver in value x. marke, and iij. bollys of silver that were in kepyng of Bacheler Water, a Frier Carmelit of Norwich, to th'entent that a certeyn coost shuld have ben doon upon the liberarye of the Friers Carmelites aforesaid for the sowlis of William Paston, Justice, and Augnes, his wiff; which charger and bollys the seid William yet witholdith and kepith to his owne use, and therfore the seid charges ar not fulfylled.

Item, the seid John axith restitucion of suche inportable charges as the seid William hathe put the forsaid Sir John onto by the space of many yeres, as in plesures doyng and rewardis, which apperith by writyng of the hande of the seid Sir John; which pleasures and charges the seid Sir John was constreyned to doo in defence of the seid William; wher of the seid John axeth to have amendys of Cli mark.

Item, by the occacion and meanys of the seid William, the seid Sir John was constreyned to lende onto the Reverende Fadere in God, George, late Archebsschop of York 4 m^l mark, which was nát payed ageyn by the summa of Cli. The seid John axith to be restorid ther of.

Item, the seid William hath fellyd tymbre and wodys in the maners of the

[1] This paragraph is very much corrected.   [2] Blank in MS.
[3] Father of the celebrated Dean Colet.
[4] George Nevill, Archbishop of York, died on the 8th June 1476.

77

THE PASTON LETTERS

1484 seid John, that is to sey, the maners of Oxened and Marlyngford, to the hurth of the seid John of xxli.

Item, the seyd John Paston, compleynaunt, axith to be restoryd to alle syche money as hathe be takyn and dyspendyd by alle siche persones as have ben assigned by meanes of the seyd Wyllam to distorbe and interupt the seyd John, compleynaunt, of hys ryght, tyghtyll, possessyon, entrest, of and in the maners, londis, and tenementes, and other the premysses dwryng the seyd v. yer sauff a quarter, as well as to all syche money as hathe ben dyspendyd dwryng the seyd v. yer sauff a quarter by the servauntys of the seyd compleynaunt by hym assigned to tery and abyd up on the seyd maners, londes, and tenementes, and other the premysses ther, to kepe the possessyon of the seyd compleynaunt, whyche extendith to the some of xlli. and above.

Item, the seyd John, compleynaunt, axith to be restoryd to all syche money as hathe bene receyved by meanys of the seyd William, dwryng the seyd v. yer sauff a quarter, of syche as ar or have ben fermors or tenauntes of the maners, londis, and tenementis aforeseyd duryng the seyd season, as well as to all syche money as is not levyable of dyvers of the seyd fermors and tenauntes fallyn in poverte sythe the trowblows season of the v. yer sauff a quarter befor rehersed, whyche extendeth to the some of CCli. or above.

999

MARGERY PASTON TO JOHN PASTON[1]

To my ryght worschipful husbond, John Paston.

1484(?)   R YGHT worschipful husbond, I recomaund me onto you.
DEC. 24   Plese it you to wete that I sent your eldest sunne to my Lady Morlee[2] to have knolage wat sports wer husyd in her hows in Kyrstemesse next folloyng aftyr the decysse of my lord, her husbond; and sche seyd that ther wer non dysgysyngs, ner harpyng, ner lutyng, ner syngyn, ner non

[1] [From Fenn, ii. 330.] Fenn supposes with great probability that this letter was written in 1484, the year of Margaret Paston's death. No earlier date is possible, seeing that even in 1484 John Paston's eldest son was only in his seventh year, and he had at the date of this letter two sons capable of being sent on messages; so that, if anything, we should be inclined to put it later. But we know of no later death in the family that could have occasioned the writing of such a letter, and the time of Margaret Paston's death and of the proving of her will agree very well with Fenn's hypothesis. From the calendar prefixed to an old MS. missal in the possession of the late Mr. C. W. Reynell, I found that she died on the 4th November 1484. Her will was proved at Norwich on the 18th December following.
[2] Widow of William Lovel, Lord Morley, who died the 26th July 1476.—F.

78

RICHARD III

lowde dysports, but pleyng at the tabyllys, and schesse, and   1484(?)
cards. Sweche dysports sche gave her folkys leve to play and   DEC. 2?
non odyr.

Your sunne dede hese heyrne [*errand*] ryght wele as ye shal her aftyr this. I sent your yonger sunne to the Lady Stabylton,[1] and sche seyd acordyng to my Lady Morlees seyng in that, and as sche hadde seyn husyd in places of worship[2] ther as sche hathe beyn.

I pray you that ye woll asur to your some man at Caster to kepe your botry, for the mane that ye lefte with me woll not take upon hym to breve[3] dayly as ye commandyt. He seyth he hath not usyd to geve a rekenyng nothyr of bred nor alle [*ale*] tyll at the wekys end; and he seyth he wot well that he shuld not condenyth [*give satisfaction*] and therfor I soposse he shall not abyd, and I trow ye shall be fayne to purveye another man for Symond, for ye har never the nerer a wysse man for hym.

I ham sory that ye shall not [be] at hom be for Crystemes. I pray you that ye woll come as sone as ye may. I shall thynke myself halfe a wedow, because ye shal not be at home, &c. God have you in Hys kepyng.

Wretyn on Crestemes Evyn.   By yor,   M. P.

1000

ABSTRACT[4]

STANSTED AND HARWELLBURY

The manor of Stansted is in the county of Suffolk. The estate of this   1484(?)

[1] Sir Miles Stapleton died in 1466. His widow Catherine seems to have married in the following year Sir Richard Harcourt of Ellenhale (Blomefield, ix. 321), but, according to a practice not uncommon at that time, she may have retained the name of Lady Stapleton.
[2] 'Places of worship'; *i.e.*, in families of distinction.
[3] To make up accounts.
[4] [From Paston MSS., B.M.] This is a paper of notes relating to the manors of Stansted in Suffolk and Harwellbury in Herts, addressed to a lady who is styled 'Madam' and 'your Grace,' and who, though not named, was undoubtedly the

79

THE PASTON LETTERS

484(?) manor passed not by the deed that the estate was taken by at Huntingfeld, in Norf.,[1] but I claim this manor by my mother's gift. 'This manor is but a mile from Clopton's and not far from Smalbrigge, where your Grace is now.' John Barell is farmer of this manor, who, when I came to your Grace just after my mother's death, confessed before your servants, Piers Rumbold and William Smyth, that he was privy of mine estate in my mother's days, and took the farm of me at that time. 'Madam, this is the man ye sent your servant W. Smyth to, for to keep the possession there; and after he had tarried there awhile he took a promise of the farmer that he should pay no money to nobody without commandment from your Grace; contrary to which promise, by the favour of some folks that your Grace can deem, he hath paid my nephew a £10 or £20.' I think, Madam, you need send no man to keep possession there; but your Grace might send a servant thither to show the tenants your displeasure, inasmuch as he hath broken his promise with your Grace, and threaten to distrain.

The manor of Harwellbury is in Hertfordshire, four miles from your manor of Weston Baldok[2] and two from Roiston. This manor also passed not by the estate taken in Norfolk, not being in the same shire. Of this manor 'he'[3] received no money, for the farmers are true and fear not his threats. The manor is worth £8.

Duchess of Norfolk. Compare No. 962. The writer is perhaps John Paston of Gelston; in which case the date must be after 1484, as he speaks of his mother as being dead. More probably it was his uncle William, and John Paston is the nephew referred to in the paper itself. But even in that case the document cannot be five years earlier, as Agnes Paston died in 1479.

[1] Should be Suffolk.
[2] The Dukes of Norfolk of the family of Mowbray owned this manor.
[3] The writer's nephew?

RICHARD III

1001

PROCLAMATION AGAINST HENRY TUDOR[1]

R. R.

Ricardus, etc. salutem. Precipimus tibi, etc.

FORASMOCHE as the Kyng our sovereign Lord hath 1485 certeyn knowlege that Piers, Bisshop of Exeter,[2] Jasper JUNE 23 Tydder,[3] son of Owen Tydder, callyng hymself Erle of Pembroke, John, late Erle of Oxon,[4] and Sir Edward Wodevyle,[5] with other dyvers his rebelles and traytours, disabled and atteynted by the auctorite of the High Court of Parlement, of whom many be knowen for open murdrers, advoutrers [*adulterers*], and extorcioners, contrary to the pleasure of God, and a yenst all truth, honour, and nature, have forsakyn there naturall contrey, takyng them first to be under th'obeisaunce of the Duke of Bretayn,[6] and to hym

---

[1] [From Fenn, ii. 318.] The MS., as Fenn tells us, was endorsed in an ancient hand, 'Kent Cherfys [*Sheriffs*].—Copia literæ Regis R. III. persuadentis subditos suos ad resistendum Henr' Tydder, postea Regem Angliæ ac declarantis a quo idem Henricus descendebat.' Another but imperfect copy of this proclamation will be found in the Harleian MS., No. 433, f. 220 b. A similar proclamation had been issued on the 7th December 1484, of which a copy will also be found in the same Harleian volume at folio 273 b. Sir Henry Ellis has also printed in his *Original Letters* (2 Ser. i. 162) a copy of this proclamation as set forth in the original warrant for issuing it, which the King addressed to the Bishop of Lincoln as Chancellor. The MS. followed by Ellis was a transcript from one of the records formerly in the Tower. I have compared these different texts throughout with that printed by Fenn, and noted all variations that are of any consequence. The two Harleian texts I have called A. and B., the former being that of the proclamation issued on the 7th December preceding. The text printed by Ellis I have called E.
[2] Peter Courtney, Bishop of Exeter, after the miscarriage of the Duke of Buckingham's conspiracy, fled into Bretagne to the Earl of Richmond, who, after he became Henry VII., promoted this Prelate to the See of Winchester in 1486, in which he died in 1492.—F.
[3] Jasper Tudor of Hatfield, half-brother to Henry VI. He was created Duke of Bedford in 1485.
[4] John de Vere, Earl of Oxford, who had escaped from the Castle of Hammes.—F.
[5] Sir Edward Wodevile, brother to the Queen of Edward IV.—F. The names given in text A. are 'Piers, Bisshop of Excestre, Thomas Grey, late Marques Dorset, Jasper, late Erle of Pembroche, John, late Erle of Oxenford, and Sir Edward Wideville.'
[6] Francis II., the last Duke of Bretagne, was overthrown by Charles VIII., King of France, and died in 1488.—F.

THE PASTON LETTERS

1485 promysed certeyn thyngs whiche by him and his counsell were JUNE 23 thought thynggs to gretly unnaturall and abominable for them to graunt, observe, kepe, and perfourme, and therfore the same utterly refused.

The seid traytours,[1] seyng[2] the seid Duke and his counsell wolde not aide nor socour theym ner follow there wayes, privily departed oute of his contrey in to Fraunce, and[3] there takyng theym to be under the obeisaunce of the Kynggs auncient enemy, Charlys,[4] callyng hymself Kyng of Fraunce, and to abuse and blynde the comons of this seid Realme, the seid rebelles and traitours have chosyn to be there capteyn one Henry Tydder,[5] son of Edmond Tydder, son of Owen Tydder,[6] whiche of his ambicioness and insociable[7] covetise[8] encrocheth[9] and usurpid[10] upon hym the name and title of royall astate of this Realme of Englond, where unto he hath no maner interest, right, title, or colour, as every man wole knowyth;[11] for he is discended of bastard blood bothe of ffather side and of mother side, for the seid Owen the graunfader was bastard borne, and his moder was doughter unto John, Duke of Somerset, son unto John, Erle of Somerset, sone unto Dame Kateryne Swynford, and of ther[12] indouble[13] avoutry [*adultery*] gotyn, wherby it evidently apperith that no title can nor may [be][14] in hym, which fully entendeth to entre this Reame, purposyng a conquest. And if he shulde atcheve his fals entent and purpose,

---

[1] 'The said traytours.' They. A.   [2] that. A. B. E.
[3] 'and' omitted in A. B. and E.
[4] Charles VIII. ascended the throne in 1483, and died in 1498.—F.
[5] Henry Tudor, Earl of Richmond, who in 1483 became King of England, by the title of Henry VII.—F.
[6] 'one Herry . . . . Owen Tydder' oon Herry late calling himself Erle of Richemond. A.   [7] 'ambicious and insaciable.' A. B. E.
[8] 'stirred and excited by the confederacie of the Kinges said rebelles and traytours,' added in A.   [9] Here text B. comes to an end.   [10] 'usurpeth.' E.
[11] From here to the end of the paragraph is omitted in A.
[12] 'ther' her. A.
[13] This either means double adultery, that is adultery on both sides; or indubitable, undoubted adultery.—F. I suspect the true reading to be 'and of her in double avowtry gotyn.' It is a great question whether John, Earl of Somerset, John of Gaunt's eldest son by Catherine Swynford, was not born during the life of her lawful husband as well as during that of John of Gaunt's lawful wife.—See *Excerpta Historica*, 155-6.
[14] Supplied from E.

RICHARD III

every man is lif, livelod, and goddes shulde be in his hands, 1485 liberte, and disposicion, wherby sholde ensue the disheretyng JUNE 23 and distruccion of all the noble and worshipfull blode of this Reame for ever, and to the resistence and withstondyng wherof every true and naturall Englishman born must ley to his hands for his owen suerte and wele.

And to th'entent that the seid Henry Tydder myght the rather atcheve his fals intent and purpose by the aide, supporte, and assistence of the Kynggs seid auncient enemy of Fraunce,[1] hath covenaunted and bargayned with hym and all the counsell of Fraunce to geve up and relese inperpetuite all the right, title, and cleyme that the Kyng[es] of Englond have, had, and ought to have, to the Crowne and Reame of Fraunce, to gether with the Duchies of Normandy, Anjoy, and Maygne, Gascoyn and Guyne, castell[es] and townys of Caleys, Guysnes, Hammes, with the marches apperteynyng to the same,[2] and discevir and exclude the armes of Fraunce oute of the armes of Englond for ever.

And in more prove and shewing of his seid purpose of conquest, the seid Henry Tidder hath goven as well to dyvers of the seid Kynggs enemys as to his seid rebelles and traitours, archebisshoprikes, bisshoprikes, and other dignitees spirituels, and also the ducheez, erledomez, baronyes, and other possessions and inheritances of knyghts, squyres, gentilmen, and other the Kynggs true subjetts withynne the Reame, and entendith also to chaunge and subverte the lawes of the same, and to enduce and establisse newe lawes and ordenaunces amongez the Kynggs seid subjetts.[2] And over this, and beside the alienacions of all the premyssez into the possession of the Kynggs seid auncient enemys to the grettest anyntisshment,[3] shame, and rebuke that ever myght falle to this seid land, the seid Henry Tydder and others, the Kynggs rebelles and traitours aforeseid, have extended [*intended*] at there comyng,

---

[1] The beginning of this sentence in A. is as follows:—'And to th'entent to accheve the same by th'aide, support, and assistence of the Kinges seid auncyent ennemyes and of this his royaume.'
[2] From the words 'and discevir' to the sentence beginning 'And over this,' all is omitted in A.
[3] Aneantisement—anientised is used by Chaucer in his Tale of Melibeus, for reducing to nothing.—F.

THE PASTON LETTERS

1485
JUNE 23 if they may be of power,[1] to do the most cruell murdrers, slaughterys, and roberys, and disherisons that ever were seen in eny Cristen reame.

For the wich, and other inestymable daungers to be escheuved, and to th'entent that the Kynggs seid rebelles, traitours, and enemys[2] may be utterly put from there seid malicious and fals purpose[3] and sone discomforted,[4] if they enforce to land,[5] the Kyng our sovereign Lord[6] willith, chargeth, and comaundith all and everyche of the naturall and true subgetts of this his Reame to call the premyssez to there mynds, and like gode and true Englishmen to endover themselfs with all there powers for the defence of them, there wifs, chylderyn, and godes, and heriditaments ayenst the seid malicious purposes and conspiracions which the seid auncient enemes[7] have made with the Kynggs seid rebelles and traitours[8] for the fynall distruccion of this lande as is aforesaid. And our said sovereign Lord, as a wele willed, diligent, and coragious Prynce, wel put his moost roiall persone to all labour and payne necessary in this behalve for the resistence and subduyng of his seid enemys, rebells, and traitours[9] to the moost comforte, wele, and suerte of all[10] his true and feithfull liege men and subgetts.

And over this, our seid sovereign Lord willith and comaundith all his seid subgetts to be redy in there most defensible arraye to do his Highnes servyce of werre, when thy be opyn proclamacion, or otherwise shall be comaunded so to do, for the resistence of the Kynggs seid rebelles, traitours, and enemyes. Et hoc sub periculo, &c.—T. me ipso apud Westmonasterium, xxiij. die Junij, Anno regni nostri secundo.

[1] 'if they may be of power,' omitted in A.
[2] rebelles and traytours. A.   [3] malicious purposes. A.
[4] discomfited. A. E.
[5] Or rather, made good their landing by force.—F.
[6] desireth. A. E.   [7] the auncyentes ennemyes of this lande. A.
[8] 'and traitours,' omitted in A.
[9] rebelles, traitours, and enemyes. A. In which text the proclamation ends with these words, and is followed by the usual words addressed to the Chancellor as his authority for making out the proclamation: 'And thise oure lettres shall be your sufficient warrant in that behalve.' This warrant to the Chancellor is dated 'at oure Castell of Notyngham, the xxj. day of Juyn, the secund yere of our reigne,' two days before the proclamation was issued.   [10] and singlier. A.

84

1002

THE DUKE OF NORFOLK TO JOHN PASTON[1]

To my welbelovyd frend, John Paston, be thys byll delyveryd in hast.

WELBELOVYD frend, I cummaunde me to yow, letyng yow to undyrstond that the Kyngs enmysse be a land, and that the Kyng wold hafe set forthe as uppon Monday but only for Howre Lady Day ;[2] but for serten he gothe forward as uppon Tewsday, for a servant of myne browt to me the sertente.

1485
AUG.

Wherfor, I pray yow that ye met with me at Bery,[3] for, be the grace of God, I purposse to lye at Bery as uppon Tewsday nyght, and that ye brynge with yow seche company of tall men as ye may goodly make at my cost and charge, be seyd that ye have promysyd the Kyng ; and I pray yow ordeyne them jakets of my levery, and I shall contente yow at your metyng with me.

Yower lover,   J. NORFFOLK.

[1] [From Fenn, ii. 334.] This letter must have been written in August 1485, some days after the landing of the Earl of Richmond, afterwards Henry VII., at Milford Haven.   [2] The Assumption of Our Lady, 15th of August.
[3] Bury St. Edmund's in Suffolk.

85

THE PASTON LETTERS

Henry VII.

bothe were my fadyrs clerkys at that tyme. And I remembre and wot well that Jamys Gressham was with my fadyr at Seynt Brydys duryng all hys siknesse and at hys disseasse, and thys wyll I wyttnesse whyle I leve for a trowthe, as knowith God, Whom I beseche to preserve you and yours.

1485
SEPT. 2

And, nevew, I prey yow recomand to my neese your wyff, whom I wold be glad to se onys a yen in London, wher thys bylle was wretyn, signed with myn hand, and sealed with my seale [the Thursday next befor Whyghtsonday, the second yer of Kyng Richard the Thred],[1] the xxiij. daye of September the first yer of the reyngne of Kyng Herry the vijth.

Your loveing awnte,   EL[IZA]BETH BROWNE.

[1] This date is scratched through with the pen.

1003

DAME ELIZABETH BROWNE TO JOHN PASTON[1]

To my ryght worchepfull and hertly beloved nevew, John Paston, Sqwyer.

1485
SEPT. 23

RIGHT worchepfull, and my ryght hertly beloved nevew, I recomand me to yow. And wher as ye desier me to send yow woord whether my brodyr John Paston, your fadyr, was with my fadyr and hys, whom God assoyle, duryng hys last syknesse and at the tyme of hys disseasse at Seynt Brydis, or nowght.

Nevew, I assarteyn yow upon my feythe and poore honore that I was xiiij., xv. yer or xvj. yer old, and[2] at Seynt Brydis with my fadyr and my modyr when my fadyrs last syknesse took hym, and tyll he was disseassid ; and I dare depose befor ony persone honorable that when my fadyrs last siknesse tooke hym, my brodyr your fadyr was in Norffolk, and he came not to London tyll aftyr that my fadyr was disseassid, and that can Sir William Cootyng[3] and Jamys Gressham record, for they

[1] [From Paston MSS., B.M.] The MS. from which this letter is printed is not in the handwriting of Dame Eliz. Browne. It is a corrected draft in the handwriting of John Paston, with the address at the head.
[2] The words 'xiiij. —— old, and' are an interlineation, J. P. apparently did not know his sister's exact age at the time and wished her to supply it.
[3] Rector of Swainsthorpe from 1444 to 1450, and of Titchwell from 1450 to 1457. He was presented to the former living by Judge Paston and John Dam.

86

1004

ELIZABETH, COUNTESS OF SURREY, TO JOHN PASTON[2]

To myn ryght worshefull cosyn, John Paston, Esquyer.

MYN ryght worshipfull cosyn, I recomawnde me hertly to you, thankyng you of your greet kyndnes and lovyng disposicion towardys myn lord and me at all tymes, which I pray God I may leve to see the acquytell ther of to your plesure, prayeng you of your good continuans.

OCT.

Cosyn, I shewyd you myn mynde that I wolde have myn shildern to Thorpe,[3] wher in, God yelde you, it pleasyd you to sey that I shulde have hors of you to help to conveye them thyder ; but now I undirstonde myn Lord Fitz Walter[4] hath dischargyd myn lordys servauntes thens, affermyng up on

[2] [From Paston MSS., B.M.] This letter must have been written either in 1485 or in 1486. Thomas Howard, Earl of Surrey, was taken prisoner at the battle of Bosworth on the 22nd August 1485, and was not released from confinement till 1487, in which latter year also John Paston, to whom this letter is addressed, was knighted at the battle of Stoke on the 16th June. Most likely the letter is of the year 1485, at the beginning of the Earl's imprisonment, and when Henry VII. had been just six weeks upon the throne.   [3] In Norfolk.—F.
[4] John Ratcliff, Lord Fitzwalter, who was summoned to Parliament in September 1485.

87

THE PASTON LETTERS

485
CT. 3

them that they shulde have had unfittyng langage of the Kynges Grace. Cosyn, I trust that ye and all the jentilmen of the shire, which have had knowleche of myn lordes servauntes, kan sey that her to for they have not ben of that disposicion to be lavas of theyr tungys, whan they had moore cause of booldnes than they have nowe. I wolde not have thowght myn Lord Fitzwalter wolde have takyn so forforth displeasure for the keepyng of x. or xij. men at Thorpe ; I woot weell ther exceded not iij. mees[1] meet, good and bad. I truste, all thow I weer a soel woman, to mayntene so many at the leeste, what so evyr I dyde moore.

I trustyd to have fowndyn myn Lord Fitzwalter better lord to me, seyng whan I was wyth myn Lord of Oxenforth, up on myn desyre and request at that tyme made un to hym, he promysed me to be good lord to myn lord and me, wher of I praye you to put hym in remembrauns, trustyng yit be the meene of you to fynde hym better lord to me her aftyr.

I have fownde myn Lord of Oxenforth singuler very good and kynde lord to myn lord and me, and stedefaste in hys promys, wher by he hath wonne myn lordys service as longe as he leevyth, and me to be hys frewe beedwoman terme of myn lyve ; for hym I drede mooste, and yit as hyther to I fynde hym beste. I pray you good cosyn, the rather by your meane, that I may have the continuauns of hys good lordship, and to myn poore power I truste to deserve it. I pray you, cosyn, that thys byll may recomawnde [me][2] to myn Lady Brews and to myn cosyn, your wyf.

From Mynster, in the Yle of Shepey, the iijde day of Octobre. I pray you yeve credens to the berer of thys, and to Thomas Jenney, whan he comyth to you.

[3] Your faythefoull cosyene,   E. SURREY.

[1] A mess was a party of four at dinner.
[2] Omitted in MS.
[3] These last words were written by the Countess, the letter by her secretary.—F.

88

HENRY VII

1005

ELIZABETH, COUNTESS OF SURREY, TO WILLIAM HARWARD[1]

WYLLIAM HARWARD, I woll that ze delyver to Robert Thorppe of Norwych v. marc off the next money that ze gadyr ; for he hath lent it me, and I have sygned hym to be payed of yow as sone he comyth hom.

1485, or later

E. SURREY.

1006

THE DUKE OF SUFFOLK TO JOHN PASTON[2]

To our trusty and welbeloved John Paston, Sheriff of Suffolk and Norffolk.

THE DUC OF SUFFOLK.

RIGHT welbeloved, we grete you well. And for asmuche as the King our sovereigne Lord hath late addressed his letters of comission undre his seale unto us, reciting by the same that his highness undrestondith certayn his rebells associate to his old enmys of Scotland, entending not only to trowble his peax, the nobles and subjects of this Realme to destroy, their goods and possessions to spoill, and reward at thair liberties, but also the lawes of this lond and holy Chirche to subvert.

1485
OCT. 20

Our said moost drad soverayn Lord, as a Cristen Prince, ... his said enmys and rebels to resist, hath assigned and comaunded us to do all maner . . . . and others defensible able to labour, as well archers as hob-

[1] [Add. MS. 34,889, f. 228.] This brief note, like No. 1004, was probably written during the imprisonment of the writer's husband. The text is entirely crossed through, doubtless to show that the transaction was closed.
[2] [From Fenn, ii. 326.] John Paston was Sheriff of Norfolk in the first year of Henry VII., and entered on his duties at Michaelmas 1485. This letter therefore is of that year.

89

THE PASTON LETTERS

485
T. 20

byllers,[1] to come before us and charge them . . . . . armed and arayed, every man aftre his degre and power, to attend uppon his person, and uppon us, to do him service in defence as well of the Chirche as of the said nobles and subjects of this Realm, against his said enmys and rebels.

We therfore wull, and in our said sovereigne Lords name straitly charge and comaunde you, that in all possible hast ye do this to be proclamed :—And that all maner men able to do the King service, as well knights, esquiers, and gentlemen, as townships and hundreds, as well within franchesse and libertes as without, within the counties of Suffolk and Norffolk, and that they be charged to be redy at all tymes uppon an howre warnyng, and ordered according to the last comission afore this, to attend uppon his Grace and uppon us to do him service, whatsoever they shalbe comaunded, not failing herof, as ye wull answer at your perile. Goven at Long Stratton, the xx. day of October.

And forthermore, that ye yeve credence unto our servaunt this bringer, as this same day we receyved the Kings commission at iiij. aftre none.

SUFFOLK, yor frende.

1007

MARGERY PASTON TO JOHN PASTON[2]

To my mastyr, John Paston, be this delyvird.

486
AN. 21

RYGHT reverent and wortshepfull syre, in my most umbill weysse I recomaunde me to you, desyryng to here of your welfare, the wytche I beseche God to preserve to His plesur and so your hartes desyir. Syr, I thank you for the venyson that ye sent me ; and youre schepe is seylyd owt of the havene as this daye.

Syr, I send you be my brodyr Wyllem your stomachere of damaske. As for youre teppet of velvet, it is not here ; An seythe that ye put yt in your casket at London.

[1] Light horsemen.
[2] [From Paston MSS., B.M.]

90

HENRY VII

Syr, your chyldryn be in goode helle, bellsside be God.

1486
JAN. 21

Syr, I prey you sende me the gowild, that I spak to you of be the nexst man that comythe to Norwytche.

Syr, your mast that laye at Yermowyth is letyn to a scheppe of Hull for xiijs. iiijd., and if ther fawyll ony hurt ther to, ye schall have a newe mast ther for.

No mor to you at this time, but Almyty God have you in His kepyng. Wretyn at Castyr Hawill, the xxj. daye of Janever, in the furst yere of Kyng Harry the vijth.

Be your servaunt,   MARGERY PASTON.

I prey God no ladyis no more ovyr com you, that ye geve no lenggar respyt in your materys.

1008

ALICE, LADY FITZHUGH, TO JOHN PASTON[1]

To my right trusty and welbeloved son,[2] Sir John Paston, be this delyvered.

JON PASTON, I recommaunde me to you in my moste hertely maner. And wher I understande be my doghter Lovell, ye desyre to know whedir I woll have the bargane ye made for me in Norwich or nay, and if I wol, I moste content therfor now in mercs ; Son, in good faith it is so, I shal receyve no mony of the revenowse of my lyvelod afore Mydsommer ; and also I have payd accordyng to my promise to Sir William Cabell a great payment, the which ye knowe wel was due to be payde, so that I can not be of power to

FEB. 24

[1] [From Fenn, ii. 336.] There is a difficulty in dating this letter only from the address being to Sir John Paston. It has every appearance of having been written in the year 1486, when Francis, Viscount Lovel, lay concealed shortly before his outbreak with Humphrey and Thomas Stafford. But in that case the prefix 'Sir' before John Paston's name must not be taken as indicating that he was then a knight ; for he was not knighted till the battle of Stoke in June 1487.
The writer of this letter was the widow of Henry, Lord Fitzhugh, who died on the 12th June 1472. She was the daughter of Richard Nevill, Earl of Salisbury, and sister of Warwick the Kingmaker.
[2] I find no evidence of any real relationship between Paston and Lady Fitzhugh.

91

THE PASTON LETTERS

1486
FEB. 24

content therfore, for the which I am right sory, for I know well I shall never have such a bargane.

Also my doghtyr Lovell[1] makith great sute and labour for my sone hir husbande. Sir Edwarde Franke hath bene in the North to inquire for hym; he is comyn agayne, and cane nogth understonde wher he is. Wherfore her benevolers willith hir to continue hir sute and labour; and so I can not departe nor leve hir as ye know well; and if I might be there, I wold be full glad, as knowith our Lorde God, Whoo have you in His blissid kepynge.

From London, the xxiiij[th] day of February.
　　　　　Your loving moder,
　　　　　　　ALISE, LADY FITZHUGH.

1009

MARGARET, COUNTESS OF OXFORD, TO JOHN PASTON[2]

To my right trusti and welbiloved John Paston, Shrieve of Norffolk and Suffolk.

MAY 19

RIGHT trusti and welbiloved, I recomaund me unto you. And for as moche as I am credebly enfourmed that Fr.aunceis, late Lorde Lovell, is now of late resorted into the Yle of Ely, to the entente by alle lykelyhod, to finde the waies and meanes to gete him shipping and passage in your costes, or ellis to resorte ageyn to seintuary, if he can or maie;

I therfor hertily desire praie you, and neverthelesse, in the Kinges name, streitly chargie you that ye in all goodly haste

[1] Francis, Viscount Lovel, married Anne, daughter of Alice, Lady Fitzhugh.
[2] [From Fenn, ii. 338.] The date of this is quite certain from the subject to which it refers, as well as from the fact of John Paston being at the time Sheriff of Norfolk and Suffolk. Francis, Viscount Lovel, was one of the principal adherents of Richard III., and was attainted after the accession of Henry VII. in 1485. For some time he lay concealed, but in the spring of 1486 he attempted to raise an insurrection along with Humphrey and Thomas Stafford, who had broken out of their sanctuary at Colchester. He is said to have been drowned in the Trent in 1487, in endeavouring to escape after the battle of Stoke. But according to another story he lived in concealment for some time after.

92

HENRY VII

1486
MAY 19

endevore your self that suche wetche or other meanes be used and hadde in the poorts, and creks, and othre places wher ye thinke necessary by your discrecion, to the letting of his seid purpose; and that ye also use all the waies ye can or maie by your wisdom, to the taking of the same late Lorde Lovell. And what pleasur ye maie do to the Kings Grace in this matier, I am sure, is not to you unknowen. And God kepe you.

Wretyn at Lavenham, the xix. day of May.
　　　　　　MARGARET OXYNFORD.[1]

1010

HENRY VII. TO JOHN PASTON[2]

To our trusty and welbeloved John Paston, one of our Esquiers for our Body, Shreife of our countys of Norffolk and Suffolk.

BY THE KING.

AUG.

TRUSTY and welbeloved, we greet you well. And whereas we send at this time our trusty and welbeloved clerke and counseilor, Mr. Edmunde Chaderton, to do and execute certein things by our commandement in those parties, like as he can shew to you more at large; We desire and pray you that ye not only yeve unto him therein credence, but also, for the effectuall and speedy performance of the same, ye will be unto him from time to time in every-thinge, as the case shall require, adviseinge, aidinge, and assistinge, as we singularly trust you, and as ye desire to do us pleasure.

Yeven under our Signet at our mannor of Shene, the xij[th] day of August.

[1] Margaret, daughter of Richard Neville, Earl of Salisbury, and sister of Richard, the great Earl of Warwick, was the first wife of John de Vere, Earl of Oxford.—F.
[2] [From Sandford's Genealogy of the Paston Family.] This letter is derived from Mr. Worship's article in the *Norfolk Archeology* on a MS. Genealogy of the Paston family. The date must be 1486, during John Paston's shrievalty. The transcript is of the seventeenth century.

93

THE PASTON LETTERS

1011

JOHN, LORD FITZWALTER, TO JOHN PASTON[1]

To my right wurshipfull cosyn, John Paston, esquyer.

1486
SEPT. 19

RIGHT wurshipfull cosyn, I recomaunde me to you, certifeyng you that, where as I understond ye have distreyned Richard Caus of Byngham[2] for issuez ronne uppon hym in th'escheker to the summe of iiij[li]. and odde sylver, I pray you that ye wull, the rather for my sake, showe hym the favour that ye may doo, savyng youre sylfe, and that ye wulle not be harde uppon hym; but if ye kan by th'advys of councell this next terme fynde the meanes for youre discharge uppon youre acompte in th'escheker, that than ye wull lete hym be so in reste and peas withoute more paymentz for that cause; the which I prey you to tendre the rather because I fynde the seid Richard Cans at all tymez my trewe servaunt, and I shall be as redy to the acomplyshment of all youre resonable desirez with Goddis grace, Who kepe you. At Attelburgh, this Tuesday next before Seint Mathuz Day.—Zowr Cosyn and frend,
　　　　　　J. SIEUR FYTZWAUTER.

[1] [Add. MS. 34,889, f. 176.] This letter is probably of the year 1486, when John Paston was sheriff. Its contents, as will be seen, are somewhat similar in character to those of No. 1024, written a year or two later, after John Paston had been knighted.
[2] Binham in Norfolk.

94

HENRY VII

1012

THE EARL OF OXFORD TO JOHN PASTON[1]

To my right trusty and right welbelovyd Councellor, John Paston, Esquier.

1486
JAN. 24

JOHN PASTON, I comaund me to you. And as for such tithynge as ye have sent hider, the Kyng had knowlech therof more than a sevyn-nyght passed. And as for such names as ye have sent, supposyng theym to be gone with the Lord Lovell, they be yitt in England, for he is departyng with xiiij. personys and no moe. At the Kynges comyng to London I wold advise you to see his Highnes. And Almyghty God kepe you.

Writen at Wyndesore, the xxiiij[th] day of January.
　　　　　　OXYNFORD.

Endorsed: The Countis of Oxfordes lettre.

1013

JOHN, PRIOR OF NORWICH, TO ——[2]

148

RIGHT worchupfull serys, we recomaunde us all unto you in oure most herty wyse. And it is so that longe and many yerys ther hath ben hangyng a grete variaunce and a growge bitwix Annes Paston deceassed, late the wyff of William Paston, Justice, and William Paston now lyvyng, and Clement Paston deceassid, ther sones, one the

[1] [From Douce MS. 393, f. 78.] Francis, Viscount Lovel, after trying to raise a rebellion in England in 1486, escaped abroad to Flanders, and joined the Earl of Lincoln in the following spring in an invasion of England in behalf of Lambert Simnel. This letter appears therefore to have been written in the beginning of the year 1487.
[2] [From Paston MSS., B.M.] The writer of this letter was John Bonwell, who was made Prior of Norwich in 1480, and died in 1488. As it is actually dated in the second year of Henry VII., it must have been written either after the 22nd August in 1486 or before that date in 1487. Most probably it is of the latter year. It is endorsed in a contemporaneous hand—'Billa Prioris Norwic' pro missa perpetue fundanda.' One or two words are now lost by the decay of the paper, which seem to have been visible in the text when Fenn copied the MS. for his fifth volume.

95

THE PASTON LETTERS

1487 oone parte, and John Paston, the sone of the seide William Paston, Justice, and of the seide Annes his wiff, also deceassid, and Ser John Paston, Knyght, deceassed, and John Paston yet lyvyng, sones to the seide John deceassid, on the othir parte. And now the seide variaunce contynueth betwixe the seide William and John that now is lyvyng of and upon the right, title, and possessioun of the maners of Sporle, Woodhall, Pagrave, Cressyngham, Swaynesthorpe, and Est Bekham, all [in] this cuntre of Norffolk.

Likith it you to wete that the seide William Paston, Justice, in his lyve was a speciall lover and frende to our monastery, and for synguler love and trust that he hadde to be remembred amonge us after hys deceasse, not with stondyng h[e de]lyed at London, yet he bequest his body to be beryed, and is beryed in the chapell of Our Lady with inne oure monastery. [And] the seide William Paston, Justice, oftyn and many tymes in his pleyn lyfe, the seide Annes beyng present, he shewed unto the Priour of our monastery that was than, called Dawn John Heverlonde,[1] and to Dawn John Molett,[2] that was Priour after, to Dawn John Fornsett, Doctour of Devynyte, Dawn Richard Walsham, our sexten, and to Dawn John Wechyngham, and to many dyverse other that were of his acqueyntaunce, and that he had trust unto to breke his mynde for the wele of his soule, that were thanne olde fadirs of our monastery, and arn now decessed, that it was his verry last will that ought of the seide maners schuld be perpetually immortaysed a serteyn londe, or annuyte of suche valewe, that every suche monke that syngith the last messe in the seide chapell, wher the body of the seide William Paston light beryed, schuld have that day that he songe messe ther iiij*d.* to pray for the soules of the seide William, and of Annes his wif, and for ther auncetrys, kynred, consanguynyte, affynyte, and frendes, and for all Cristen soules ; and over that, a serteyn summe of money yerly to be payed to have the obytt of the seide William and Annes zerly kept with *dirige* and masse in the seide chapell.

¹ John Haverland was Prior of Norwich from 1436 to 1453.
² Prior from 1453 to 1471.

96

And it is so that many yeres aftir the decesse of the 1487 seide William, Justice, ther were many men lyvyng bothe of olde brethern of oures afore rehersyd, and of other that cowde aborne witnesse in this mater, and that knewe the mynde of the seide William Paston, Justice, that it was his last will, of whiche men many now be deceassed ; and no merveill, for it is upon a xliij. yere past sithen the seide William, Justice, deyed. And also the seide Annes that was hys wif lyved more thanne xxx. wynter aftir hir husbonde, and was in singuler trust with her husbonde, and one of his executours, and wele knowen in this cuntre, a woman of vertuos lyvyng and disposicion, and of goode discrecioun and conscience, and knewe hir husbondes mynde and last will as wele as ony lyvyng creature ; she witnessed alway that it was hire husbondes last will to have this perpetuall messe, and called on it all the dayes of hir lyfe, and also atte her decesse ; and sche seide that [it] was the will of her husbonde that the annuyte schulde go oute of the seide maner of Swaynesthorpe. The seide John Paston decessed wolde have hadde it graunted owte of the seide maner of Cressyngham ; and summe of the executours wolde have hadde the seide messe to a contynued but for the terme of iiij** yere, and wolde have made writyng accordyng ; but the seide Annes wolde not ther of, but seide alway that it was the last will of hir husbonde to have the messe made perpetuall, and the executours schewid to us that they wolde se the wyll perfourmed ; and ther upon the executours, be ther comon assent, lefte a cofre with a grete substaunce of money of the goodes of the seide William, Justice, to be kepte with inne our monastery, and tolde and schewed to us that the seide gode schuld never be departid nor hadde oute of our place till we wer made sure of the seide annuyte. And duryng all that season that the seide cofer with the goodes was with ynne our monastery, it was alway schewid to us that the seide annuyte schulde be mortaysed in perpetuyte, and duryng all that season that the seid cofer was in our place, we hadde money yerly yoven us to pray for his soule to kepe [his obytt]¹ ; and be menys devysed with oute the knowleche of

¹ The writing is here blurred and indistinct, being written on an erasure.

VOL. VI.—G 97

THE PASTON LETTERS

1487 the seide Annes, or of ony of our brethern, all the goode that was in the seide cofre was conveyed oute of our monastery, and after that dede done, ther was no more money yoven us, nowther to kepe the seide obit, ner to pray for the soull of the seide William, as be the seide executours, savyng that the seide Annes, duryng hir lyve, yaff us of hir owne cost yerly to remembre the soule, and that that hath be done sythen, hath be don of our owne devocion, and this many zerys ther hath no thing be yoven us, notwithstondyng of our own devocion we have rehersid his name in oure bede rolle every Sonday.

And now it is informed us that as wele the seide William as the seide John hath putt all ther title and interest, as wele in and of all the seide maners, londes, and tenementys as of the seide goodes in the awarde and jugement of the Right Reverend Fader in God, my Lord of Ely,¹ Chaunceler of Inglond, Ser Reynold Bray, Knyght, and in you tweyne. And in asmoche as ze be of our cuntre and speciall frendes to our monastery, and longest acqueyntyd with you, that makith me and all my brethren the more bolde to schewe this our mater and interest unto you, beseching yow bothe to tendre the mater, and to schewe it bothe to my Lorde of Ely and to Ser Reynolde Bray, that atte suche tyme as ze have the examynacion of the title of theise seide maners, that ze will vouche saff of your charite to schewe this mater and our interest in this behalf, and of the seide annuyte, and how that we aught of right to have a graunt of it oute of the seide maners.

And in this mater we hertily pray yow to take remembraunce and speciall labour, so that we may trust that it schall not askape your handes, nowe that the mater is putte in yowe ; and all our monastery schall pray for you, and also rewarde you to your plesur, and over that, ze schall do her in suche a goode dede that God schall rewarde you.

Wretyn in our monastery, the —² day of ——,² the secunde yer of the regne of Kyng Herry the vijᵗʰ.

By JOHN, Prior off Northwich
and the Covent.

¹ John Alcock. ² Blanks in MS.

98

HENRY VII

1014

SIR EDMUND BEDINGFIELD TO JOHN PASTON¹

*Un to my ryght wurshypfull cosyn, John Paston, Esquyer,
for the Body.*

RYGHT wurshypfull cosyn, I recomawnd me un to you 1487 as hertly as I can, letyng you wytte I was with my MAY 16 Lorde Stuarde² as on Munday laste paste, by the desyir of them that I myght not sey ney to. I herde all that was seyd there, but they gaate non avawntage, wurde, nor promyse off me ; but they thought in asmoche as they ware the beste in the shere, that every man owghte to wayte and go with them. Wherto yt was answerd that oure master,³ nexte the Kynge, havynge hys commysshon, muste nedys have the jentylmen and the contre to a wayte up on hym by the vertu of the same ; but yt was thought I owght not to obeye no copy of the commisshon, withoute I had the same under wexe, where in hathe ben gret argument, whyche I understoode by reporte a fortnyte paste, and that causyd me to sende unto my lorde to have the very commysshon, whyche he sente me, and a letter, where off I sende you the copy here in closyd.

As for you, ye be sore takyn in sum place, seyng that ye intende swyche thynges as ys lyke to folow gret myscheffe. I seyd I undyrstood non swyche, nor thynges lyke it ; and yt ys thoughte ye intende nat to go forthe thys jorneye, nor no jentylman in that quarter but Robert Brandon that hath promysyd to go with them, as they seye.

I understonde Sir Wylliam Bolen⁴ and Sir Harry Heydon⁵

¹ [From Paston MSS., B.M.] This letter and that which follows were written during the period of Lambert Simnel's rebellion. The rebels were at this time in Ireland, but they soon after invaded England, and were defeated at the battle of Stoke on the 16th June 1487. Francis, Viscount Lovel, took part in the movement, and is supposed to have perished in the battle, or shortly after it.
² John Ratcliff, Lord Fitzwalter.—See Campbell's *Materials for a History of Henry VII.*, i. 92, 241.
³ Probably the Earl of Oxford.—See next letter.
⁴ Sir William Boleyn, of Blickling, had been made a Knight of the Bath at the Coronation of Richard III. He died in 1505.—F.
⁵ Sir Henry Heydon, of Baconsthorp, Knight, had been steward of the household to Cecilia, Duchess of York, and died in 1503.—F.

99

THE PASTON LETTERS

1487
MAY 16

ware at Thetforde in to Kente ward, but they returnyd in to Norffolk a geyne ; I thynke they wull not goo thys jorney, yff the Kynge nede. Ser Harry was at Attylborow on Saterday. I wene he had a vyce there to turne a zen ; wher for, cosyn, yt ys good to understonde the sertente what jentylmen intende to goo, and be assuryd to go together, that I may have wurde ; my cosyn Hoptun hathe promysyd that he wull be oon. As fore Wysman, he seythe he wull be off the same, but I can have no holde.

Furthermore, cosyn, yt ys seyd that after my lordys departyng to the Kynge ye ware mette at Barkwey, whyche ys construid that ye had ben with the Lady Lovell, but wrathe seyd never well ; and in asmoche as we understonde my lordys plesur, yt ys well doon we dele wysly therafter. And, nexte to the Kynge, I answerd pleynly I was bownde to do him service, and to fullfylle hys comaundment to the uttermest off my powere, by the grace off God, Who ever preserve you to Hys plesur.

Wretyn at Oxburgh, the xvj. day of Maye.

Your cosyn,   E. BEDYNGFELD.[1]

1015

[THE EARL OF OXFORD?] TO SIR EDMUND BEDINGFIELD[2]

MAY (?)

WHERE AS I understonde by your late wrytyng un to me, that ye have ryght well endevyrd you to th'execucion of the Kynges comission and comawnd-ment, in preparyng your selffe with the jentylmen and other of

[1] Sir Edmund Bedingfield was made a Knight of the Bath at the Coronation of Richard III. He was likewise in high favour with Henry VII, who paid him a royal visit at Oxburgh, in Norfolk. He died in 1496.—F.

[2] [From Paston MSS., B.M.] The MS. from which this letter was printed was evidently the copy of a letter, which was enclosed in the preceding. Fenn supposes with great probability that the writer was the Earl of Oxford, but the MS. being only a copy, there is no signature attached. Commissions of array were issued on the 7th April 1487 for the counties of Suffolk, Norfolk, and Essex, with special instructions for repairing and guarding the beacons for fear of an invasion. The Commissioners for the County of Norfolk were John, Duke of Suffolk, John, Earl of Oxford, John Radcliff, Lord Fitzwalter, and fifteen others, among whom was John Paston.—See Patent Roll, 2 Hen. VII., p. 2, m. 6, in dorso.

100

THE PASTON LETTERS

Knyghtes made at the same Batayll.

1487
JUNE 16

The sone and heyr of the Lord Audeley.[1]

Sir Edward Noreys.	Sir Gregory . . . .
Sir Robert Clyfford.	Sir Thomas Bl[ount].
Sir George Hopton.	Sir Robert Cheyny.
Sir John Paston.	Sir William Car[ew].
Sir Thomas Lovell.	Sir John Wy[ndham].
Sir Humfrey Savage.	Sir Simond . . .
Sir Herry Willoughby.	Sir Roger Be[llingham].
Sir John Sapcotes.	Sir John . . . . .
Sir William Vampage.	Sir George Nevil . .
Sir Antony Brone.	Sir Robert Radcly[ff].
. . . . .	Sir Jamys Par[ker].
. . . . .	Sir Edward Dar[ell].
. . . . .	Sir Edward Pekeryn[g].
. . . . .	Sir Thomas of W[olton].
	Sir William Sand[es].

A mutilated endorsement in Sir John Paston's hand reads, '. . . . . prisoners . . . . . fownd.'

1017

DAME ELIZABETH BREWS TO SIR JOHN PASTON[2]

To my rytth worchupfull son, Sir Jon Paston, be thys byll delyvyrd in hast.

1487,
or later

RYTH worchupfull son, I recommend me on to zow and to my lady zowyr wyf, and thankyng zow harttyly for the grett labyr thatt ze had on Thorys day for me, and for zowyr kyndnes ; for and odyr had don asse ze ded, I

[1] Sir James Audeley, as his name is given in Leland's list. This was Sir James Touchet, who succeeded his father as Lord Audeley in 1491, and was beheaded and attainted in 1497.

[2] [From Paston MSS., B.M.] Fenn dates this letter 'about 1487.' It cannot be earlier than June of that year, and may be a few years later. But the date is unimportant. This letter appears to be a holograph. The next is written by a scribe.

102

HENRY VII

the contre, to be redy to do the Kyng servyce, whyche I have shewid un to the Kynges Hyghnes, so that hys Grace ys ryght well content and ryght thankfully acceptyth the same, under-stondynge the ryght good myndys and dysposyschon off you and off other jentylmen there towardes hys Grace. How be yt, hys Hyghnes wull not as zytte put you to ony further labur or charge, for somoche as hys rebellys and enemyes be in to Irlande ; neverthelesse hys Grace wull that the contre be redy at all tymis to do hys Hyghnes servyce up on resonabull warnyng ; for so moche as the Kynges Grace intendythe to make provysyon to sende an armi in to Irlonde in haaste, nat knowyng as zytte whether that ye, and other aboute you shall be desyird to bere ony charge there to or no. And where as yt ys mervellyd that ye had not the Kynges comysshon, under hys gret seall, I send yt to you with thys my wrytyng, wyll-ynge you nat to procede further to eny execushon theroff tyll swyche tyme as ye have other wise in comawndment, alwey thankyng hertyly the jentylmen, and all other for ther good wyllys towardes me.

1487
MAY (?

1016

KNIGHTS MADE AT THE BATTLE OF STOKE[1]

Sir Edmond Benyngfeld.	[Sir Richard De]levere.
Sir Jamys Blount.	Sir J[ohn] Mortumer.
Sir Richard Croft.	Sir William Troutbeke.
Sir [Humfrey] Stanley.	

JUNE 1

[1] [Add. MS. 34,889, f. 135.] This is only a fragment, the first part of which is lost. The seven names at the beginning are the end of a list of knights bannerets made upon the field. Then follow the names of those who were merely dubbed knights ; but this list, too, is imperfect, not merely by the mutilation of some names, but because another leaf would certainly have been required to give them all. Compare another copy of these lists in Leland's *Collectanea*, iv. 214-15, where the names in the second list stand in a different order. Several of the mutilated names here have been filled in from Leland ; but, curiously enough, that list gives no Sir Gregory and no Sir Simon. Since this was in type the Editor has found a complete list, more accurate than Leland's, which will be printed at the end of these letters.

101

HENRY VII

had had my purpos ; qwerfor I prey God do be them asse they do be me.

1487,
or late

Son, I must prey zow to have a dosseyn men in harnes, with bowys and wepyn convenyent for them, that I may feche my stres ageyn. The schrevys man wasse here wythe me, and [j. of] yowyres, he seyth he ys, and he hatth mad me feythful promes that he wol be wyth me ageyn on Monday, qwerfor I prey zow harttyly, son, and reqwere zow that zowyr men may be wyth me on Monday, as my werry tros ys in zow, qwo sknowyth blyssyd Jesu, Hom haff zow and zowyr in Yss keppyng.

Be zowyr trew modyr,

DAM ELYSABETHE BREWYSSE.

1018

DAME ELIZABETH BREWS TO SIR JOHN PASTON[1]

To my right worshipfull son, Sir John Paston, Knyght, be this delyverd.

RIGHT worshipfull son, I recommaund me unto you and to my lady my doughter your wyfe, and I send you both Cristes blyssyng and myne. And, son, I thank you hertely for my son, William Brews ; and I moste pray you for the reverens of Jesu to help hym for your tenauntes and myne, or els John Dynne will owver rewle them. And, son, God thank you, ye helpyd ons Whyte of Metfeld, and so I must beseche you nowe to do, and that it wold pleas you to gyffe credans unto the Priour of the Wyhte Freres, for I have shewed unto hym my mynd ; and as ye do, I hold me content. And, son, we ladys and jentil women in this contrey that is

1488(?

[1] [From Paston MSS., B.M.] The date of this letter is nearly as indefinite as that of the last, but it certainly lies between the year 1487, when Sir John Paston was knighted, and 1489, when William Brews died. If the latter part of the letter refers to the levying of a subsidy, in which the Bishop of Chester may have been one of the King's agents, the date is probably about the end of the year 1488. Sir Thomas Brews, the writer's husband, died in 1482.

103

488 (?) wedows, be sore trobyld with the Bysshop of Chester,[1] and haskith of us more than we may pay, and that knowith All myghty Jesu, Who have you in His blyssed kepyng.

Be your moder,

DAME ELIZABETH BREWS.

1019

SIR JOHN PASTON TO DAME MARGERY PASTON [2]

To Dame Margery Paston, at Oxenhed.

1486-95 MASTRESS MARGERY, I recomand me to yow. And I prey yow in all hast possybyll to send me, by the next swer messenger that ye can gete, a large playster of your *flose ungwentorum* for Kynges Attorney, Jamys Hobart, for all hys dysease is but an ache in hys knee. He is the man that brought yow and me togedyrs, and I had lever then xl*li*. ye koud with your playster depart hym and hys peyne. But when ye send me the playster, ye must send me wryghtyng hough it shold be leyd to and takyn fro hys knee, and hough longe it shold abyd on hys kne unremevyd, and hough longe the playster wyll laste good, and whethyr he must lape eny more clothys aboute the playster to kepe it warme or nought. And God be with yow.

Your, JOHN PASTON.

[1] The Bishops of Coventry and Lichfield were often called Bishops of Chester before the foundation of the modern Bishopric of Chester by Henry VIII. John Hales or Halse was Bishop of Coventry from 1459 to 1490.
[2] [From Paston MSS., B.M.] James Hobart was the King's Attorney-General from 1486 to 1509, and Dame Margery Paston died in 1495. There is nothing to fix the date of this letter more precisely.

1020

THE QUEEN TO THE EARL OF OXFORD [1]

To oure right trusty and enterly beloved cosyn, Th'Erll of Oxon.

BY THE QUENE.

RYGHT trusty and enterly beloved cosyn, we grete you well, lattyng you wete hou it is commen un to oure knowlege that where as ze newly entred upon oure welbeloved Symon Blyant, gentilman, in to the maner of Hemnals in Cotton, descended and belongyng unto hym by right of enheritaunce, as it is seid, ze ther upon desired the same Symon to be agreable for hys part to put all maters of variance thenne dependyng atwene hym and oon Sir John Paston, Knyght, pretendyng a title unto the seid maner into th'award and jugement of two lenerd men, by you named and chosen as arbitrours atwene them ; and in case that the same arbitrours of and upon the premisses neither yave oute nor made suche awarde be for the brekyng up of Pasche [*Easter*] terme nowe last passed, ze of your owne offre graunted and promysid unto the seid Symon, as we be enformed, to restore hym forwyth there upon unto hys possession of the seid maner. And how it be that the same Symon, at youre mocion and for the pleasir of youre lordshyp, as he seith, aggreed un to the seid compromyse, and ther upon brought and shewed hys evydence concernyng, and sufficiently provyng hys ryght in the seid maner un to the seid arbitrours, and that they have not made nor yolden out betwene the said parties any suche awarde ; yet have not ze restored the same Symon unto hys possession of the seid maner, but contynuelly kepe hym owt of the same, wich, yf it so be, is not only to hys right grete hurt and hinderaunce, but also oure mervaile. Wher-

1487-1502

[1] [From Paston MSS., B.M.] This letter and that which follows, relating to the manor of Cotton, are both quite uncertain in point of date, except that they cannot be earlier than 1487, when Sir John Paston was knighted, nor later than 1502, as the Queen and Sir John Paston himself both died in the year following.

1487-1502 fore we desire and pray you ryght affectuesly that ze woll the rather at the contemplacion of thees oure lettres, shew unto the said Symon, in hys rightfull interesse and title in the seid maner all the favorable lordshyp that ze goodely may, doyng hym to be restored and put in to hys lawfull and peasible possession of the same, as fer as reason, equite, and good conscience shall require, and youre seid promise, in suche wyse that he may undyrstond hym selfe herynne to fare the better for oure sake, as oure verray trust is in you.

Yeven under oure signet at my Lordes Palois of Westmynstre, the xxv. day of Juyn.

[ELEZEBETH.][1]

Subskrybyd with the Quenys hand.

1021

THE EARL OF OXFORD TO SIR JOHN PASTON [2]

To our hertly welbilovyd John Paston, Knyght.

1487-1502 RIGHT hertly welbilovyd, I grete you wele. And where Sir John Howard, Knyght, Sir Gilberde Debenham, Knyght, gederith grete feloship of men, purposyng on Monday next comyng to take stresses of the Lady Roos ; and I deme that they undre the colour of the same entende to set on Coton, and to gete it if they may ; I therfor councelle you to sende downe a certeine of your men or elles come your silfe for the save garde of the said Coton. Also that ye yeve credence un to the brynger herof. And our Lorde kepe you.

Wrytyn at the lodge in Lavenham the last day of Juylle.

OXYNFORD.

[1] This name is written in a different character, intended as a representation of the Queen's signature which it somewhat resembles. The writing, however, is crossed out. It is probably the work of the same pen that wrote the words below, though these are in a smaller hand.
[2] [From Douce MS. 393, f. 84.] *See* preliminary note to the last letter.

1022

JOHN DAUBENEY TO [SIR JOHN PASTON] [1]

PLEASE your masterchep to have knowlage that my Lord Archebyschop of Yorke [2] is in god helle, blyssyd be God. And I came to hym as on Monday last past, and toke hym your letter. And whan I had takyn hym and he had over sey it, he merveylle sor of hyr dysposicion, a bad me not care, ye shuld do welle i nowe. And than he told me that he had spokyn to Master William Paston for a note of a letter, hewghe it is best to write to hyr. And so on Tewysday Master William and I, and Skerne of my Lord of Oxenfordis hows, and mad (*sic*) toke hym on Wednysday o [*i.e.* one] not of a letter the wyche I send you ; and whan he sey it he thowght it to long, and mad one after his ownne entent, the wiche I send yow a copy of. Also I send yow a copy of the letter that the quene sent to my Lord of Oxenford for the maner of Cotton for Blyaunt ; but my Lord of Yorke told to Skerne that he wold in any wysse that my Lord of Oxenford shuld help yow to kepe possession. And so Skerne purposythe to be with in thys v. deyes at home, for to enforme my Lord of Oxenford of my Lord of Yorke is entent, and that he se in no wysse that no man do yow no wrong as moche as my Lord of Oxenford powyr may help yow ; for Skerne came from my Lord of Oxenford to my Lord of Yorke for the same mater, for that my Lord of Yorke shuld informe the quene of the mater, and be cause the quene hathe take hyr chambre my Lord of Yorke toke Skerne a rynge for a tokyn to my Lord Tresorer [3] that he shuld excuse my Lord of Oxenford to the quene, for as moche as ye hathe (*sic*) infeffid my Lord of Oxenford in a trost in the maner of Cotton he may

[1487-1502] AUG.

[1] [Add. MS. 34,889, f. 48.] The letter here referred to from the Queen to the Earl of Oxford seems undoubtedly to be No. 1020 ; and the date must accordingly be between 1487 and 1502. The reference to the Queen's confinement does not help us to much greater precision, for the time of year does not agree with any known occasion. But some years are distinctly excluded, and the only possible ones are 1487, 1488, 1490, or from 1493 to 1497 inclusive, or 1500, or 1501.
[2] Archbishop Rotherham. [3] John, Lord Dynham.

THE PASTON LETTERS

[1487-
1502]
AUG.

no lesse doo but helpe yow. Item, thys day is the messenger gone to my Lady of Suffolk with my Lordis letter. I shall have a answer at the morn on Monday, I trost to God, ryght god, &c., it cowd non ere be sped. My Lord hath be all this weke at the Cowncell at Chelchyche and j. day at Chenne.[1] Item, I send yow iij. writtis for feleneys and trespace and ij. for Mariete mater. Also your flowyr; Also a letter of Cablys; Also a write for Playter, a letter to Mestres Clere. Item, my Lord wylle in any wyse that ye kepe welle all the lyvelod that ye have of Sir John Fastolff, and that ye suffyr no man to entre no lond nor place, lord nor other personys, what sum ever they be. Ye may veryly thynke he ys your speciall god lord, and that ye shall knowe in tyme comyng. I understand that Calle dothe passyngly welle in your maters in the spirituall lawe, as his letter makyth mencion, &c. Wretyn at London the Satyrday before Seynt Lawrens day.

Your servaunt,   JOHN DAUBENEY.

1023

ABSTRACT[2]

R[OBERT] CLERE TO SIR JOHN PASTON, KNIGHT

Not
before
1487

Your farmer of Mauteby has not given surety and paid poundage for his cattle, as he pretends. I hope you will not encourage him, when he tells you he owes me no duty, and that he took not my 'merch' for twenty years, but only so long as he continued in Heryngby farm. I denied him the replevin, because the ground of my farm is parcel of ancient demesne. Your tenants complain of me without cause. I hope you will not be displeased if I ask them simply for what is due to me. I never said 'that ye shuld hang upon many bushes.' I have always been glad to say or do my best for you, as any poor gentleman in Norfolk. I pray you bring forth my accuser that I may come to my answer, and know who would make variance between us.

Ormesby, 24 Oct.

[The writer of this letter was Robert Clere of Ormesby, who was knighted in 1494, and was sheriff of Norfolk and Suffolk in 1501. The expression 'your' farmer of Mauteby, shows that it was written after the death of Margaret Paston, and that the Sir John addressed must have been her second son, to whom the manor of Mauteby descended. The date is, therefore, not earlier than 1487 when this Sir John was knighted, and may be many years later.]

---

[1] Sheen.   [2] [From Paston MSS., B.M.]

108

1024

JOHN, LORD FITZWALTER, TO SIR JOHN PASTON[1]

*To my right worshipfull cosyn, Syr John Paston, Knight,
be thys lettre delyvered.*

RIGHT worshipfull cosyn, in my most herty wise I [comme]nd me to yow. And where I am enformed that ye have takyn a disthresse within the [Du]chy of Lankastir for suche money as was commyng toward you of ryght for the tyme that ye were shiryef, me seme, cosyn, ye aught not to take it within the said Duchy of noon auncyen demene holdyn upon the King; for there be places inow to gadir it upon without the said auncyen demene, and so ye cannot lose it. And also, cosyn, I am enformed that it is paied alredy to oon John Burnam, which is of sufficiency inow. For whiche cause mesemythe it werne resone to levey it upon hym than ther where as is noon auctorite to levey it upon. Wherfore, cosyn, I pray you to be good mastir for my sake to thies pore men, whiche be the Kingz tenauntz, and to shew them the favour that ye may. And I shall be as glad to doo you as gret plesure in tyme commyng, by Goddz grace, Who preserve you.

Wretyn at Attylborow, the vij. daie of Apryll.

Zowir cosyn and frend,
[J.] SIR FYTZ WAUTER.

1488(?)
APRIL 7

[1] [From Paston MSS., B.M.] Sir John Paston had been sheriff in the year 1485-6, but he did not receive his knighthood till June 1487 at the battle of Stoke, so that this letter cannot be earlier than 1488. It is, however, not unlikely to have been written in that year, or one or two years later. The writer, Lord Fitzwalter, was beheaded and attainted in 1495 as an adherent of Perkin Warbeck.

109

THE PASTON LETTERS

1025

LORD FITZWALTER TO SIR JOHN PASTON[1]

*To my right wourschippfull and hertely welbeloved cousyn,
Sir John Paston, Knyght, this be delyvered.*

1488-
94

RIGHT wourschippfull cousyn, in as hertely wyse as I cane, I recommaund me to you. And forasmoche as ther was appoynted a day that ye and my cousyn Heydon, Sir Robert Brandon, the Kynges Attorney, and other of the worschippfull of this schyr, should have mett here before this tyme of Estren, it was so longe or the Kynges Attorney was commen in to the contre, and the tyme so shorte, that it hathe bene thowght there myght be non convenable tyme affor this. Wherfor they be agreed that they and ye should mete here on Thursday next commyng. Prayinge you, therfor, that ye wolbe here at that tyme, trustynge to Godes mercy that a right good wey shalbe hadde betyx yow that all grugges and rancores shalbe layd a parte. And therfor, cousyn, I praye yow that ye wol not fayle for to be here, and what I canne do for yow, ye shall fynde it redy with Godes grace, Who have yow in His most blessed and assured kepyng.

Wreten on Good Fryday last passed.

Zowir lofyng cosyn,
J. SIR FITZ WAUTER.

[1] [From Paston MSS., B.M.] The date of this letter, as of the last, must be between the years 1488 and 1494.

110

1026

WILLIAM PASTON TO SIR JOHN PASTON[1]

To Sir John Paston, be thys lettyr delyvered.

AFTYR all dewe recomendacion, pleasyt yow to undyr-stonde that my lorde[2] hathe ben with the Kynge in Wyndesour at Seynt Georgys Feste, and ther at the same feste were bothe the inbaceours of Breten and of Flaundyrs, as well fro the Kynge of Romayns[3] as fro the yonge Duke.[4] But I can not schew yow the certeyn whedyr we schall have with them warre or pease; but I undyrstonde for certeyn that all suche capeteyns as wente to the see in Lente, that is to sey, Sir Charlys Somersett, Sir Richard Hawte, and Syr Wylliam Vampage, makythe them redy to goo to the see ageyn as schortely as they can, to what intente I can not sey.

Also, where as it was seyde that my Lord Woddevyle and other schulde have gone over in to Breten, to have eyded the Duke of Breten,[5] I can not tell of non suche eyd. Butt upon that seynge ther came many men to Sowthehamton, where it was seyd that he schulde have takyn schyppyng, to have waytyd upon hym over; and soo whan he was countyr-maundyd, thos that resortyd thedyr, to have gone over with hym taryde there styll in hope that they schuld have ben lycensyd to have gone over; and whan they sey [saw] no lykeleod that they schuld have lycens, there was ij.C. of them that gete them in to a Breten schyppe, the whyche was late come over with salte, and bad the mayster sett them a lond in

1488
MAY 13

[1] [From Paston MSS., B.M.] There can be no doubt this letter was written in the year 1488, after Sir Edward Woodville (called Lord Woodville) had gone over to aid the Duke of Brittany against the French, and at the beginning of the rebellion of the young Prince of Scotland (afterwards James IV.) against his father, James III., who was defeated in battle, and afterwards murdered in June of that year.
[2] The Earl of Oxford.
[3] Maximilian, Archduke of Austria, was elected King of the Romans in 1486.
[4] Philip, Duke of Burgundy, son of Maximilian.
[5] Francis II., Duke of Brittany.

111

THE PASTON LETTERS

1488
MAY 13

Breten. And they had nott seylyd not paste vj. leges butt they aspied a Frencheman, and the Frencheman mad over to them ; and they ferde as thow they wolde not have medylde with them, and all the Englysche men went undyr the hetchys, soo that they schewyd no more but those that came to Sowthehamton with the schype, to cawse the Frenchemen to be the more gladder to medyll with them ; and soo the Frencheman burdyd them, and then they that were undyr the hetches came up, and soo toke the Frencheman, and caryed the men, schyppe, and all in to Breaten.

Also, ther was ther an inbaceatour fro the Kynge of Schottes,[1] who is now put in grete trobyll be hys son and other of the lordes of hys londe.

Syr, as I came homewerde be London, I spake there with Emonde Dormand, and he seyd that he had wretyn onto yow, but he had none aunswere ; wherfor he prayd me that if I knew ony man comynge towerdes Norwhyche, and I wold wrythe on to yow that he ferythe, if ye see none other dyreccion, that he schall be comittyd to the Flete.

Also, he schewyd me that Herry Wyott wholde fynde the mene to have yow condemnyd, and recover the obligacion of xl*li.* ageyns yow, and soo he seythe he whote nott how to doo, for he is halfe dysmayd ; he ferythe lesse that he schall never come home. But he intendythe to plede the obligacion fulfylyd at Norwyche, for he seythe ther is non other remedy to save yow fro the condemnacion, tyl that he herythe otherwyse from yow, whyche he thynketh longe aftyr.

Wretyn at Henyngham, the xiij[te] day of May, with the hand of your brodyr,

WYLLIAM PASTON.

---

[1] James III.—*See preliminary note.*

HENRY VII

1027

THOMAS ANDREW TO WILLIAM PASTON[1]

To the ryght . . . . William Paston Squyer
. . . . . my Lord of Ox[ford].

RYGHT worchipfull sir, in my best maner I recommend me unto you as he that is and shalbe at your commandment. Sir, I beseche you to showe my good lord and yours that a cordyng to his commandment I have sesed the good of the parson of Testerton[2] and of Henry Fox, exsepe thos goodis of the sayd Fox that whare formerly sesed be the servantis of my Lord of Surrey ; and, Sir, all thos goodis that I have sesed of them both are nat worthe lytyll mony lytyll past xl*s.* or iij*li.* at the m[os]t, exsepe the parsons corne ; and if that may betakyn a way thane the Chyrche may not be served, and that whar pety. I besech yow that I may knowe my Lordis plesur in that be halfe, for els I thynke the baly of the franches will have all, for Testyrton is in the Dowchy. And so I am leek to have lytyll or nowt for all my lawbour and costis withowt my Lord be my good lord in that be halff be your mene.

Sir,[3] I pray you tell my Lord that the fryer of Lynne that . . . ak . . . . cheff, for he served a cherche in Norfolk callyd Hornyngtoft and ther . . . . . . rd a p . . . . s callyd Master Thomas Mertyn, and as I wene he had felows privy to that robery (?) an[d ot]her that be nat yet knowyn, and if he whare well a posed he wold tel[1], &c.

Also[4] Henry Fox and the parson of Testerton whar gretely (?) acuequyentyd and conversand with one Sir William, a

1488(?)
DEC. 1 (?)

---

[1] [Add. MS. 34,889, f. 139.] This letter is manifestly of the same year as No. 1028, which apparently was written about A.D. 1488-1490. Most probably the exact year is 1488, when the 'Monday next St. Andrew' was the very day following, *i.e.* 1st December—unless it was 1494, when the same thing occurred.
[2] Richard Fenwyk.
[3] Opposite this and the next paragraph the word 'No[ta]' occurs in the margin, in the same hand, apparently, as the text.
[4] See footnote 3 *supra.*

THE PASTON LETTERS

1488(?)
DEC. 1 (?)

chanon of Hempton Abbay, cause my Lord to inquere if he whar owt privy of the mony makyng or eny other of that Abbay of Hempton. I know nothyng but that they whar gret to gether, &c. Sir, I besech you, be good master to Fox wyff if ye may ; how be it he is nowght, but peraventure he may amend, but she is ryght a good woman be my troughe, and it whar gret pety but she and her chyld myght have somwat. And, my Lord, or ye send me eny letter ye may send it me be John a More, this brynger, if he cum agayne, or els be Fox wyff if her husband be not gone to London. And ever Jhesu preserve you to your most gentyll hertis desyer. At Ryburgh this Monday next Sent Andrew.—Your servant,

THOMAS ANDREW.

1028

THOMAS ANDREW TO WILLIAM PASTON[1]

To the ryght worchipfull mayster, William Paston, Squyer,
with my Lord of Oxynford, [be t]his bill delyverd in hast.

DEC. 16

RYGHT worchipfull sir, I recomaund me un to you in my best maner, acordyng to my deute. Sir, I sent you a letter by Henre Fox wyff, and I had non answer from you of it. On of the gretest thynges that I wrot to you of, was that the fryer shuld be aposed, howo was prevy with hym, whan he robbed Master Martyn, the prest, at Hornyngtoft in Norffolk ; also that Fox and the parson of Testerton,[2] shuld be aposed if eny of Hempton Abbay whar out [were aught] prevy to the mony makyng.

Sir, now I beseche you to send me a copy of thes mony makers confeschon, and ther namys, for I ame bothe sworne on the quest of the *oyer determiner,* and also on the quest at large, and of that we most make our verdyte at the sessyons

---

[1] [From Paston MSS., B.M.] Thomas Andrew, the writer of this letter, was a servant of William Paston, the uncle of Sir John, but the William Paston to whom this letter is addressed seems to have been Sir John's brother, whom we find to have been in service with the Earl of Oxford during the years 1488-90.
[2] Richard Fenwyk was rector of Testerton from 1482-1504.

HENRY VII

after Crystmes for the quest at large ; for we toke day over at the last sessyons tyll the sessyons after Crestmes for the quest at large. Lytefot, of your hows, is sworne on the *oyer determiner.*

I beseche you to speke with my lord, to know of his good lordchepe how we shall demene ourselff in that be half ; and I beseche you send me word as sone as ye can.

I thynk that Yelvertons servant, that is with you in preson, shall com a gayne hether, and he may bryng your letter to me. He[1] bryngythe you this letter, and if it may be nat a fendyng, I pray you be good master to Yelverton for my sake. I have fownd hym a good persone.

Sir, I shall not be with my lady is grace[2] this Crystmes, far her grace shalbe with the Kynges Grace after Crystmes ; and thane I shall awayt on her grace, wher ye shall have my servyce be the grace of Jesu, He preserve you.

At Ryburgh, the xvj. day of December.

And ye hepe [help] nat, I am leke to losse moche mony of my costes for thes mony makers. I pray helpe, &c.

Your servant,
THOMAS ANDREW.

1488(?)
DEC. 16

1029

T. GRIGGS TO SIR JOHN PASTON[3]

To the Right Honorable Sir John Paston, Knyght, be
this delyverid.

RIGHT reverent and honorable, after the ordre of all diew recommendacion had, I recomaunde me un to your maistership. Sir, it is so that John Talyour of Brytcham, debite [*deputy*] in your office of Th'admirallite, was

1489
FEB. 2

---

[1] Apparently this 'he' means Yelverton himself, his servant being at the time a prisoner in the Earl of Oxford's custody. Fenn erroneously reads 'in person' instead of 'in preson' in the previous sentence.
[2] Fenn supposes 'my lady's grace' to be the Countess of Richmond, the King's mother. I should think, however, it was more probably the Lady Anne Beaufort, wife of William Paston the uncle, the writer being in their service.
[3] [From Paston MSS., B.M.] This letter is evidently of the same year as that which follows it, to which we refer the reader.

THE PASTON LETTERS

1489
FEB. 2

with me this mornyng to have myn advyce in this mater folowyng, the whiche is this.

There was taken ageyns Thornham, in the Kynges streeme, leyng ij. fadam and an halff depe upon the see, a whalle fyssh, by Thornham men labouryng all nyght on Sunday nyght last was, and so have slayn it, and brought to lande ; upon the whiche your said debite hath ben ther as yister day, and seysed my lordes part therof ; wherof the puple was glad it shuld so be. Than John a Lowe was there, and he seyd to your debite that he wold have the Kynges part in this wise, that the Kyng and my lord shuld part the halff. Sir, the lawe cyvylle seyth thus, 'If any fyssh ryall be founde on the see, that is to say, whalle, bales, sturgion, porpeys, or gra[m]peys, that my Lord Admyrall shall have the halvendele,' &c.

I thynke my lord[1] hath the Kynges prerogatyff upon the see, the whiche I remytte to your discrecion, &c.

Sir, by lyklyhode, without ye take hede and send thedir som of youres, my lordes part shall be litill. It is a greet fissh and a ryall ; your debite sheweth me it is xj. fadam and more of length, and ij. fadam of bygnes and depnes in the mydde fyssh.

Sir, remember what ye have to do ; there came not suche a casualte in your tyme of your office, &c. Wherfore this, by th'enfourmacion of your sayd debite, cause me to wryte un to you this sympill bille, praying you to pardone me of the writyng, for it was don in hast ; and this bille I sent to Willyam Brykkes your servant, to Matelask, by masse tyme, to brynke it to you. And this day they purpose to breke it. Do hereyn now as it please you, and Allmighti God have you and all youres in Hese kepyng; besechyng you that this symple bille may recomaunde my pouer wiff un to your maistershipp.

Wretyn on Candilmas Day, in hast, at Welles.

Your,   T. GRIGGES.

[1] The Earl of Oxford was Lord Admiral.

1030

MARGERY PASTON TO SIR JOHN PASTON[1]

To my rygth wurchypfull mastyr, Syr John Paston, Knyth, this lettyr be delyvered in hast.

RYGTH reverent and worchypfull sir, in the most owmble wyse I recomand me un to yow, desyryng to here of yowre welfare, the qwech God long contynew.

Sir, myn brodyr Wyllyam recomawnd hym on to yow. And as for the lettyr that ze sent on to hym, he hath schewyd my lord the entent ther off, and he thynkyth hym self, that it is no part of hys dute to have any part of the fysch, or any mony that schuld grow ther of. Never the lasse, my lord, acordyng as yowr desyre was in the letter, had qwestyond John a Lowe of thys fych, afor the comyng of John Danyel, what he had doon with all ; and he answerd, as for the nedyr chavyll [*jaw*] therof, he had put it in sewrte, and leyd it in a howse, be cawse youre debyte [*deputy*] seasyd it to myn lords use, tyll it myth be undyrstond wedyr the propyrte ware in the Kyng or in my lord ; and so my lord held hym well content it schud be so, in so moche as the Kyng and my lord have comawndyd John a Lowe that thys forsayd chavyll schuld be browth up to the Kyng in all goodly hast.

Fardermore, my brodyr Wyllyam perseyvyd be yowre

1489
FEB. 10

[1] [From Paston MSS., B.M.] This letter is erroneously dated by Fenn 1487-8. Although Lord Woodville made an unauthorised expedition into Brittany in the spring of 1488, which is alluded to in No. 1026, no succours were sent by Henry for the relief of the Duchy till after the crushing defeat of Duke Francis at the battle of St. Aubin (July 28, 1488). The Duke died on the 9th September following, and his daughter Anne became Duchess of Brittany. Commissions to raise archers for the relief of Brittany were issued in December, and musters were commanded to be taken in February 1489.

THE PASTON LETTERS

1489
FEB. 10

wrytyng that ye cowd make the remnawnth of the fych worth a iiij*li.* to my lord. My lord wold ze schuld not trobyll yowre self no more with all, becawse he thynkyth that the propyrte is not in hym. And also anodyr, my brodyr Wyllyam heryth sey in the corte, that the Kyng and my lord be content that the remenaunt of the fych be to the use of them of the cuntre, the wech ze schall here the more serteyn therof here after.

Also my broder Wyllyam seyth, that my lord wyllyd yow that ze schuld send the retorne of the comyscion as hastyly as ze can, and mervell that ze hath not sent it up or thys.

As touards the brekyng up of the Parlement,[1] many lykelywoodes ther be, that it schuld contynew no wyle, and these be they. My Lord the Archebyschop of Yorke departyd as zysterday, and my Lord of Northethomyrlond schall goo as on Fryday ; and also all schuch folkys as schall goo in to Breten schall be at Portysmowth on Satyrday cum forthnyth, and the Munday after on see bord, at wech seassun the Kyng intentyd to be ther to take the mustyrs.

And as for thos jantylmen that toke schyppyng to a gon over in to Breten up on a fortnyth a goo, that is to sey, Syr Richard Egecum, the cowntroller,[2] Sir Roberd Clyfford, Syr John Trobylvyll, and John Motton, sarjant porter, be a ryvyd ageyn up on the cost of Yngland, save all only Syr Richard Egecum, wech londyd in Breten, and ther was in a towne callyd Morleys, wech a non up on hys comyng was besegyd with the Frenchmen, and so skapyd hardly with hys lyff, the wech towne the Frenchemen have gotyn, and also the town callyd Breest ; how be it the castell holdyth, as we here say.

And ther be apoyntyd serteyn captens at thys seasun, wech be Lord Bruke, Sir John Cheney, Sir John of Arundell, Sir John Becham, Sir John Gray, myn broder Awdley, myn unkyll Syr Gylberd Debnam,[3] and Thomas Stafford, and many odyr knytys and esqwyrys.

[1] Parliament was dissolved on the 27th February 1489.
[2] Sir Richard Edgecombe was Controller of the King's Household.
[3] Sir Thomas Brews, Margery Paston's father, took for his second wife Elizabeth, daughter of Sir Giles, and sister of Sir Gilbert Debenham.

HENRY VII

And, sir, I thanke yow for the lettyr that ze sent me. Also, syr, I have fulfyllyd myn pylgremage, thanke it be God.

1489
FEB. 10

Also, sir, we undyrstond that it is anactyd of every x. marke of mevable goodes xx*d.* to the Kyng, besyd the tennyth of every mannys londys.

And, sir, my brodyr Heydon schall send yow the serteyn of all odyr thyngys grawntyd at thys Parlement, for he hath cawsed John Danyell to tery all thys day for hys letter, be cawse he was with the Kyng at Westmestre, that he myth not entend to wryth it tyl nyth.

Also, sir, Master Calthorp hath payd j.C. marke to the Kyng. Also, sir, I have delyverd the x*li.* to Master Hawes, and reseywed of hym the oblygacion. Also, I have delyverd the xx*ti* marke to Edmund Dorman, be my brodyr Heydons comawndment.

No more to yow at thys tyme, but God and the Holy Trinyte have yow in Her kepyng. And myn syster Anne, with all the company, recomawnd hem on to yow.

Wretyn at London, the x. day of Februar.

Be yowr servaunt,   MARGERY PASTON.

THE PASTON LETTERS

1031

WILLIAM PASTON TO SIR JOHN PASTON[1]

To hys broder, Sir John Paston, be thys letter aelyvered.

SIR, I recomaunde me to yow, letynge yow wete that . .
. . . .[2]

As for my Lord Treserer,[3] he was not with the
Kynge of all the counsell tyme, the whyche was endyd on the
iij^de day of Marche. And theder come my Lorde of Northe-
thombyrland the fyrste day of Marche, and departyd the even
afore the makyng of thys letter, and hath endentyd with the
Kynge for the kepynge owt of the Schottys and warrynge on
them, and schall have large money, I can not telle the some
for certeyn.

Also ther is an rover takyn at Brystowe, on [*one*] Cowper,

[1] [From Fenn, ii. 158.] This letter was unquestionably written in the reign of
Henry VII., and not in that of Edward IV., to which Fenn assigned it. The
writer, William Paston, was only born in the year 1459, and was still pursuing his
studies at Eton so late in Edward's reign as the year 1479, in the end of which year
his eldest brother, Sir John Paston, died. The Sir John Paston to whom this is
addressed must therefore be the second son of John Paston, Esquire, who was knighted
at the battle of Stoke in 1487, and died in 1503. The year in which the letter was
written is, however, still doubtful. I do not find by the Privy Seal dates of Henry VII.
that such a progress as is here spoken of was ever carried out. Apparently it was
intended that, beginning on Monday fortnight after the date of the letter, the King
should occupy a fortnight on the way from London to Norwich, and arrive there on
Palm Sunday Eve. The year must therefore have been one in which Palm Sunday
Eve fell between the 5th and the 11th of April, and Easter Day between the 13th and
19th April. The earliest year that will suit these conditions is 1489, when Easter fell
on the 19th April; and that this was the true date of the letter is made probable by
several other circumstances. In 1489 the King was staying at Sheen during March.
A great council had certainly met in the end of the year 1488 about the affairs of
Brittany, and is very likely to have prolonged its meetings or renewed them from
time to time to the 3rd March following. Moreover, if our date be correct, it supplies
an interesting and highly probable fact with regard to Henry, Earl of Northumberland, the fourth of the line of Percy, who was slain in an insurrection in the north in
April following, showing that he was with the King at Sheen in the beginning of
March, and had undertaken by indenture to protect the Borders against the Scots,
not long before he found himself called upon to put down the King's rebellious subjects in Yorkshire.
[2] Here follows some account relative to a grant from the Crown, etc.—F.
[3] John, Lord Dynham.

120

THE PASTON LETTERS

Syr, my lorde hathe sente on to the most parte of the
gentyl men of Essex to wayte upon hym at Chelmnysford,
where as he entendythe to mete with the Kynge, and that
they be well apoyntyd, that the Lankeschere men may see
that ther be gentylmen of as grete sobestaunce that thei be
able to bye alle Lankeschere. Men thynke that ye amonge
yow wol doo the same. Your contre is gretely bostyd of, and
also the inabytors of the same. I beseche you to remembr
my hors that ye promisyd me. God kepe yow.

Wretyn at Schene in haste, the vij. day of Marche, with
the hande of your brodyr,

WYLLIAM PASTON.

1032

THE EARL OF OXFORD TO SIR JOHN PASTON[1]

*To the righte worshipfull and my righte intierly belovyd
Sir John Paston, Knyghte.*

RIGHTE worshipfull and righte intierly belovyd, I
commaunde me to you. And acording to the Kyng
our soverayne Lordis commaundemente late to me
addressid, I desire and pray you that ye woll in all godely
haste, upon the sighte hereof, prepare youre selfe to be in a
redinesse with as many personnes as ye herbyfore grauntid to
do the Kyng servyce in my company diffensibely arayed and
therupon so to resorte unto me in all godely haste possyble
upon a day warnyng, horsid and harnessid, to be at the
Kynges wayges. And God kepe yow.

Writen at my castelle of Hedingham, the xij. day of
Marche.   OXYNFORD.

[1] [Douce MS. 393, f. 79.] The date at which this letter was written is uncertain,
but it may very probably have reference, like some later letters in this year, to the
King's proposed journey northwards, as it will be seen by the last No. that he intended to have visited the Earl at Hedingham.

122

HENRY VII

as I wene, and he is lyke to be hanged, and he confessythe
more of hys felawis. Also Edward Heestowe of Dovere is
apechyd of treson of many straunge poynts; and hys accuser
and he were bothe afore the Kynge, and then they were takyn
apert. And he hymselfe confessyd it that hys accusere accusyd
hym of, and many other thyngs more than he was accusyd of.
And he had many lords and gentylmen to aunswere for hys
trowthe and his demenynge afore tyme, for, as I hard sey,
bothe the Kynge in a maner, nor non of the tother lords nor
gentylmen belevyd not hys accuser, tyl that he confessyd it
hym selfe; and so he is in the Towre and lyke to be dede.

As for the Kynges comynge into the contre. On Monday
come fortenyght he well lye at the Abbey of Stratteforde and
so to Chelmnsford, than to Syr Thomas Mongehombrey, than
to Hevenyngham,[1] than to Colchestyr, than to Ipswyche, than
to Bery, than to Dame Anne Wyngfelds, and so to Norwych;
and there woll he be on Palme Sunday Evyn,[2] and so tary
there all Ester, and than to Walsyngham. Wherefore ye had
nede to warne Wylliam Gogyne and hys felaws to purvey them
of wyne i now, for every man berythe me on hande[3] that the
towne schalbe dronkyn drye as Yorke was when the Kynge
was there.

Syr, Mayster Sampson recomaunde hym on to yow, and
he hathe sende yow a rynge be Edmonde Dorman, and besydys
that he requeryd me to wryte on to yow that it were best for
yow to purvey yow of some gentyl meny thynges ageyns the
Kyngs comyng, for suere he well brynge yow gests i now, and
therfore purvey yow theraftyr. Also he sendythe yow worde
that it is my lords mende that my syster with all other godely
folkys there abowt scholde acompeny with Dame Elsebethe
Calthrop[4] because there is noo grete lady ther abowte ageyns
the Kyngs comyng, for my lorde hathe made grete boste of
the fayre and goode gentylwomen of the contre, and so the
Kynge seyd he wolde see them sure.

[1] Not Haveningham in Suffolk, but Heveningham, Hevingham, or, as it is now
commonly written, Hedingham, in Essex, the seat of the Earl of Oxford.
[2] 11th April.   [3] *See* vol. ii. p. 110, Note 1.
[4] Elizabeth, wife of Sir William Calthorpe, was daughter and coheir of Sir Miles
Stapleton.

121

HENRY VII

1033

WILLIAM PASTON TO THE BAILIFF OF MAUTBY[1]

To the Baly of Mawlteby.

MAYSTER Baly, I recomaunde me on to yow, praynge
yow that ye woll sende me be Wylliam Kokkys[2]
berer her of, iiij. nobylles in golde, putt in to the
same boxe that thys byll is in, as thow it wer evydens; for I
have tolde the masengere that he schulde brynge me nothyng
but evydens, for he is in a manere departyng owt of my
servyse, wherfore I wold nott he knew so myche of my
counsell. And as for the remenaunte, I wellde ze schulde
kepe it tyll I come my selfe.

And if Bayard be onsolde, I pray yow late hym be made
fatte ageyns the Kynge come in to the contre, what so ever I
pay for the kepyng of hym, and I schall wete how goode a
corser I schall be my selfe, at my comyng in to the contre, be
the grace of God, Who have yow in kepyng.

Wretyn at Henyngham.

Be your,   WYLLIAM PASTON.

[1] [From Fenn, iv. 310.] This letter is dated from Heningham, or Hedingham,
one of the places which, as we have seen in No. 1031, the King was to have visited on
his intended journey northwards in 1489. I have little doubt, therefore, that it was
written in that year. The writer, according to Fenn, was William Paston, Sir
John's uncle; but it is remarkable that in this same year William Paston, Sir John's
brother, writes to him from Heningham, and as the signatures of the two Williams
were not very unlike each other, one may fairly suspect that Fenn has here made an
error. This suspicion is, moreover, confirmed by the fact that Mautby was the property of Margaret Paston, who died in 1484, and that it could not possibly have
descended to her brother-in-law William, though her son William may have had an
interest in it.
[2] Fenn prints the name 'Hokkys,' but as the reading in the modernised version is
Cocks, I presume this is a printer's error.

123

THE PASTON LETTERS

1034

THE EARL OF OXFORD TO EDMUND PASTON[1]

To my right welbiloved Edmond Paston, Esquier.

Between
1486-9

RIGHT welbiloved, I grete you wele. And where as certein landes which late were the Lord Scales by title of enheritaunce, be discendid to me, and to my welbiloved cousin William Tyndale, it is accordid bitwixt me and my said cousin that the profites of the said landes, shalle neither be taken by my resceivoire nor his, but that an indifferent persone shalle take and resceive the same profittes to the use of us bothe till suche tyme as a resonable particion may laufully be made in that behalf. Wherfore as wele as I my said cousin, havyng speciall confidence and trust in you, desire and hertly pray you to take the laboure and peyn atte oure costes and charges, to take and resceive the profites of alle the said landes, to oure use and behofe, deliveryng alwey the oon moyte of your receites to my resceivoure, and the other moitee to my said cousin Tyndale, whan so ever the said profites by you so shalle be taken and resceived. Yevyng you full auctorite and power by this my writyng to execute the same.
Written atte Newe Market the vij[th] day of Aprill.
OXYNFORD.

[1] [Douce MS. 393, f. 81.] A portion of the lands of Thomas, Lord Scales, whose widow, Elizabeth, married Anthony Woodville, Earl of Rivers,—and among others the manor called Scales's Manor in Hockwold,—descended after the death of this Elizabeth to William Tyndale, who was knighted at the coronation of Arthur, Prince of Wales, on the 30th November 1489. (See Blomefield, ii. 180, and Leland's *Collectanea*, iv. 250-2.) As this letter must have been written after the accession of Henry VII., when the Earl of Oxford returned from banishment, and before William Tyndale was made a knight, the date is between 1486 and 1489.

HENRY VII

1035

THE SCALES LANDS[1]

EDMUND PASTON, receyvor of the Scalys landes, askyth to be allowed of xij*li*. xijs. viij*d*. whiche hangith over his hede in his accompte made bifore Robert Sharp at the Feste of the Purificacion of our Lady laste paste, for his costes and expenses for two yeres, as hyt apperith in the sayde accomptes.

Item, the sayde Edmund askyth to be allowed for his costes and expenses of this yere, Cxviij*li*. iiij*d*., beside his costes commynge and goynge to this accompte.

Item, for his rewarde of the saide iij. yeres *ad placitum dominorum*. Whereof ys allowed for his costes by the comaundement of my lorde,   x*li*.

Item, allowed by the [2]

Endorsed in same hand as the MS., Billa Edmundi Paston.

1036

HENRY VII. TO THE EARL OF OXFORD[3]

RIGHT trusty and entierly beloved cousin, we grete 1489 you well. Inasmuch as it hath liked God to sende APRIL 22 us good tidinges oute of Bretayn, such as we dought not but that ye be desirous to undrestonde, we wryte unto you of them as thay be comen to our knowlage, and as foloueth.

The Lord Malpertuis, now late with us in ambassade from our dere cousine, the Duchesse of Bretayne, shippid at our

[1] [Douce MS. 393, f. 80.] It is evident that this document is at least three years later than the preceding, but it is placed here for convenience.
[2] Here the MS. breaks off abruptly.
[3] [From Paston MSS., B.M.] This letter was evidently written in the same year as No. 1030, in which it is mentioned that Sir Richard Edgecombe and others had gone over to Brittany.

THE PASTON LETTERS

1489
APRIL 22

porte of Dortmouth, and arrived at Saynt Powle de Lyon, in Bretayn, on Palme Sonday,[1] at iiij. after noone, from whens he wrote us the disposicion and the state of the countre there, and of the landyng and the demeanyng of oure armee. We received his wrytyng on Monday last, at evynsong tyme; and be cause he was of Bretayn borne, and favorable to that partie, we ne gave such trust to his tidinges, as was thought to us surete to wryte to you theruppon.

This daye, aftre High Masse, comyth unto us from oute of Bretayne forsaid, and with a new ambassade from our said cousine, Fawcon, oon of our pursivantes, that ratifieth the newes of the seid Lord Malpertuis, which ben these.

After the garysson of Frenshmen in the towne of Gyngham[2] had certeinte of the landyng of our armee, thei drewe downe the fabours[3] of Gyngham, and made thayme mete to defende a siege; but assone as thei undirstode that our said armee jornayned towardes theim, they left the same Gyngham, where our said armee arrived the Thursday next before Palme Sonday, and was received with procession, logged and received, refreshed in the town iiij. dayes. And goyng towardes the said Duchesse, thei must passe to the castell and borugh of Monconter. In that castell was also a garnisson of Frenshemen, which incontinently, upon worde that our said armee drwe towardes theym, the Frenshmen did cast downe gret parte of the walles, and fled from thens; in that castell and borugh our seid armee kept thair Estre. The castell of Chawson, adjoyning nere to the towne of Saynt Bryak, was also garnisond with Frenshmen; that castell they set on fire, and soo fled in the townes of Henebone and Vannes[4] were garnisond with Frenshmen, which breke downe the walles of the townes, and putte them selff to fligth. Th'inhabitantes a bought Brest have layd siege therunto, and goten the Base Courte of the Frenshmen or the departyng of our said pursivaunt. The garnson of the towne of Concarnewe, which is oon of the grettest strenghes of all Bretayn, was besieged in

[1] 12th April.   [2] Guingamp.
[3] Fauxbourgs, which Fenn supposes here to mean portcullises, but I know not if the word was ever used in such a sense. Perhaps what is meant is, that they destroyed the suburbs to fortify their position.   [4] The word 'which' appears to be omitted.

HENRY VII

like wyse, and drevyn to that necessite that thei with in 1489 offerid, ar his said departyng, to avoyde the towne with staffe APRIL 22 in hande; how that is takyn, or what is more done sithens, he cannot telle.

Oure said cousine, the Duchesse, is in her citee of Raynes; and our right trusti knyght and counsellour, Sir Richard Eggecombe, there also, havyng cheeff rule abowte her; and the Marchall of Bretayn arredieth hym to joyne with them in alle haste with a gode band of men. Mony noble men of that countree repair to our said armee to take their partie.

These premisses in substaunce we have be wrytyng, aswell from the cheff capytaynes of our said armee, as from our comptrollour[1] forsaid. And that our said armee, blessid be God, hath among theyme selfe kepte such love and accorde, that no maner of fray or debate hath bene bitwene theym sithens the tyme of thair departing out this our Reame. Yoven under our signed, at our castell at Hartford, the xxij. day of Aprill.

Syr, thys is the copye of the lettyr that the Kynge sente my Lorde of Oxynford of tydyynges owte of Breten.
Be yowre brodyr,   WYLLIAM PASTON.

1037

THE EARL OF OXFORD TO SIR JOHN PASTON[2]

To the right worshipfull and my right welbeloved Sir John Paston, Knyght.

RIGHT worshipfull and right welbeloved, I comaunde APRIL 30 me to you. And for as moche as it is certeinly unto the Kynges Grace shewed that my Lord of Northumberland havyng the auctorite to se the Kynges

[1] Sir Richard Edgecombe.
[2] [Douce MS. 393, f. 83.] The Earl of Northumberland was slain in the North on the 28th April 1489, while endeavouring to put down a revolt against payment of the subsidy.

1489
RIL 30 money levied in the North parties, had knowleche that certeyne persones of combnes wer assembled at Topclif, and at
a nother lordship of his nygh to the same, saying that they
wolde pay no money; my seid Lord of Northumberland heryng therof, and that they wer but naked men, addressed hym
self towardes theym withoute eny harneys in pesible maner,
trustyng to have appeased theym. Howe be it, as hit is seid,
that he is distressed and that they have taken hym or slayne
hym; whiche the Kyng entendeth to punysshe. I therfore
desire and hertely pray you in all godely haste to be with me
at Hedyngham, there for to knowe more clierly the Kynges
plesir in this behalve. Writen at Hertford the last day of
Aprile.

Also I send to you a comyssion of licence to shepp corne,
which I pray you to do to be proclaymed in alle haste.

OXYNFORD.

1038

THE EARL OF OXFORD TO SIR JOHN PASTON [1]

*To the right worshipfull and my right welbeloved
counceilour, Sir John Paston, Knyght.*

MAY 6
RIGHT worshipfull and right welbeloved counceilour, I
comaunde me to you. And where as I understand
by your wrytyng that a grete shippe is perisshed with
you in thoo parties, and that ye have ben gretely occupied
aboute the savyng of the goodes of the same; and that the
merchauntes therof ben disposed to put their wynes to sale, of
the whiche ye maye by a ton for Cs. and litel more; I may by
in this cuntrey for iiijli., wherfore if ye may by there eny
better chepe, I pray you to purveye for me, such as ye seme
necessary.

And forsomoche as ye may nat be here with me at this
tyme, I desire and pray you to prepare and ordeyne your self

[1] [From Paston mss., B.M.] For the date of this letter, see preliminary note
to the next.

128

with as many men in harneys as ye godely may, to do the 1489
Kyng service in my company, at the Kynges charge and MAY 6
costes, so as ye and they may be with me at Cambrige, upon
Tewesday[1] next comyng; and that ye faile nat herof, as my
right especial trust is in you.

Writen at my castell of Hedyngham, the vj. daye of May.

OXYNFORD.

1039

WILLIAM PASTON TO SIR JOHN PASTON [2]

To hys brodyr, Syr John Paston.

SYR, I recomaunde me on to yow. And where as ye MAY
desyre that I schulde sende yow worde of suche tydyng
as Phylyp Lewes and Wyndesor bryngythe fro the
corte, they be come thens bothe, but we here of no tydynges
that they brynge, but that yondyr folkys abyde stylle abowte
the place where as thys onhappy dede was done, and not with
no grete nowmbyr, they sey not paste with v. or vj. C., where
they were moste. Howbeyt they have made proclamacions
in the cuntrey to mete with oder of ther affynyte as on Tuesday last past, as it aperythe in the copy of ther proclamacion
heraftyr folowyng. Also they schewe the Kynge intendythe
to holde on hys jurney. And Phylyp Lewes is redyn ageyn
to the Kyng, and schall brynge with hym money for all ther
wages that schall be in my lordys retynew, as yow and vj. of
Syr Wylliam Bolens servauntes and od[yrs].

Syr, Mr. Clopton sye [*saw*] yowre lettyr, and a seythe he
knew my lordes mende suche, that he durste not meve hym
with it. Ther was Syr Wylliam Say, but Clopton wolde not

[1] 12th May.
[2] [From Paston mss., B.M.] It is evident that this letter was written shortly
after the preceding, which is dated the 6th May. In that letter Paston is desired to
be at Cambridge on the Tuesday following to do the King service, and here we find
that it was intended by the King himself to have been there, leading an army against
some Northern rebels in person. The expressions in the beginning of this letter leave
very little doubt that the insurrection referred to was that in which the Earl of
Northumberland was slain on the 28th April 1489.—*See* Leland's *Collectanea,* iv.
246.

129

1489 it schulde be knowen of non other but your selfe. He sent
MAY my lorde be a servaunt of hys xli. to have excusyid hym, and
it wolde not be takyn, and that I mervell of. Howbeyt he
brake thus fer to my lorde; he asched hym how many he
apoyntyd yow to brynge with yow, and he answerde hym
xxti, and than he schewyd hym yowr charges that ye have had.
My lorde seyd ye myght have men a nowe, and ther wages
schal be payd for. Clopton aunswerde how that it wolde
coste yow large money, besyde ther wages, to hors them and
hernes them; and how that, to sey the trowthe, ye were not
well at ese.

Not withstandynge all thys, my lorde wyllyd that ye
schulde come to hym to Cambryge on Tuesday at nyght, with
as many as ye myght, and ye and he schulde do well i now.
Soo Clopton thyngyth that and ye brynge a dosen with yow,
it is suffycyent; howbeyt that Syr Emonde Bedvngfeld, Syr
Thomas Tyrell, and Syr Ryc. Lewes have ben with my lorde,
and yche of them have offyrde to mete with my lorde at
Cambryge with xxx. men a pese of them. So I wolde not ye
schulde be to ferre undyr them; wherfor I thynke best that
ye purvey yow so as and ye schulde goo forthe yor selfe, for I
can perseve non othyr wyse.

My bedfelawe Cornwaleys is maryed in the Northe, and
he came as yesternyght to my lorde streyt owt of the contre,
and he scheythe [*showeth*] non othyr wyse but as I have wretyn
here afore in thys lettyr.

Ye schall have for yor self and for yche of your servauntes
horsyd and hernessyd xxs. in hande at Cambryge for a monthe,
and I truste we schal have done or xx. days to an ende, with
the grace of God, Who have yow in kepynge.

At Henyngham.

Be your brodyr,
WYLLIAM PASTON.

[*The Rebels' Proclamacion.*]

To be knowyn to all the northe partes of England, to
every lorde, knyght, esquyer, gentylman, and yeman that they

130

schalbe redy in ther defensable aray, in the est parte, on 1489
Tuysday next comyng, on Aldyrton More, and in the west MAY
parte on Gateley More, the same day, upon peyne of losyng
of ther goodes and bodyes, for to geynstonde suche persons as
is abowtward for to dystroy oure suffereyn Lorde the Kynge
and the Comowns of Engelond, for suche unlawfull poyntes as
Seynt Thomas of Cauntyrbery dyed for; and thys to be fulfyllyd and kept by every ylke comenere upon peyn of dethe.

And thys is in the name of Mayster Hobbe Hyrste, Robyn
Godfelaws brodyr he is, as I trow.

1040

THE BISHOP OF DURHAM TO SIR JOHN PASTON [1]

*To the right worshypful sire, and my right trusty and right entierly
wel beloffyd freynde, Sire John Paston, Knyght.*

IHΣ. Xρς.

RYGHT wortchipful sire, and myne especial and of long 1490
tyme apprevyd, trusty and feythful frende, I in JAN. 27
myne hertyeste wyse recommaunde me un to you.
And for as myche as I hafe coles and odyr thynges in thise
parties, and also ye hafe in those parties cornes, wyne, and
wax, and as I am enfourmyd ye be noght evyl wyllyd to
dele with me, no more than I am to dele with you in utter-
yng, and also in receyvyng of suche thynges, the whiche
myght be to the profete of us bothe, I ther fore send un to
you at thys tyme thys berer, William Walkere, gentylman
usshere of my chamber, to commune with you herein, so that
by delyberation suche a wey may be takyn in thys byhalfe as
may be to the profete of either of us, and wher by our
familiarite and frendeship may be encrescyd in tyme to cum.
Where un to for our old acquayntance to gedyr, ye shal fynde
me ful redy after my powere, by the grace of our Lorde,

[1] [From Paston mss., B.M.]

131

THE PASTON LETTERS

1490
JAN. 27

Who ever kepe you, and send you myche worship and long prosperite.

Scribyllyd in the moste haste, at my castel or manoir of Aucland, the xxvij. day of January 1489.[1]

Your own trewe luffer and frende,
JOHN DURESME.[2]

1041

LUMEN HARYSON TO [SIR JOHN PASTON][3]

About 1490(?)

ONERABYLL and well be lovyd knythe, I commend me on to zour masterchepe and to my lady zowyr wyffe. I thanke zowyr mastyrchepe that ze have don for me. I sen my lady a lytyll pes of Renysch wyne of the best, of x. gallons, and halfe a hondyrd orrygys. I schall send hyr mor a geyns Pencost that sche may have fresche. And Renold have not gyve me the to nobyls and xljd., that ze told me off for the wyne. And my servys be nyzt and be day to zowr commawndment. Zyff zowyr mastyrchep wyll ony thyng wyth me, I xall be at Cley. No more than God be wyth zow.

Wrytyn up on the Tuysday aftyr Palme Sonday.
LUMEN HARYSON.
At zowyr comawndment.

[1] 1490 according to the modern computation, beginning the year in January instead of on the 25th March.

[2] John Sherwood, Bishop of Durham. He was appointed to that see by the Pope in 1485 at the solicitation of King Richard III. He was a man of high character and learning, and one of the earliest Greek scholars in England.

[3] [From Paston MSS., B.M.] This letter was printed in volume v. of the original edition, p. 380. I do not know Sir John Fenn's reason for considering it to have been written 'about 1490,' but as I see nothing to the contrary, I keep it under his date. The writer was probably one of the German merchants of the Hanse, and the name with which he signs the letter seems to have been a little Anglicised. It is endorsed by Sir John, 'Lumen Henrikson.'

HENRY VII

1042

SIR JOHN PASTON TO [LORD FITZWALTER][1]

HUMBLY besecheth your good lordshepe, your dayly servaunt and beedman, John Paston, more kayteff than knyght, that it may please you of your specyall grace to dyrect ought your lettres, sygned with your hand and sealid with your seall, to the dreedfull man, Jamys Radcliff of Byllingforth, Sqwyer, fermour of your wareyn ther, ought of wheys wareyn no maner of man nor vermyn dare take on hym, for dought of your seyd dredfull [man], to take or carye awey eny of your game ther, for fere [of being] hangyd up among other mysdoers and forfaytours, as wesellis, lobsters [stoats], polkattys, bosartys [hawks], and mayne currys,—that the seyd Jamys shall, upon the syght of your seyd wryghtyng, delyver, or cause to be delyverd, to your seyd besecher or to hys depute, delyverer of your seyd lettres, at hys fyrst syght of the same, vj. coupyll blake conyes or rennyng rabbettys, or some blake and some whyght to the seyd nombre, to store with a newe grownd of your seyd besechers at Oxenhed, more lyeke a pynnefold than a parke. And your seyd besecher shall daylye prey to God for the preservacyon of your noble estate longe t'endure.

[1] [From Paston MSS., B.M.] This humorous petition, though it bears no address, was certainly drawn up for presentation to Sir John Radcliff, Lord Fitzwalter, the writer of Letters 1024 and 1025, for he was lord of the manor of Billingford in Norfolk, and James Radcliff, the farmer of his warren, was evidently his kinsman. The date is probably, as Fenn suggests, 'about 1490,' certainly before 1495, when Lord Fitzwalter was beheaded. The MS. is a rough draft in Paston's hand.

1490
Abo

1490

THE PASTON LETTERS

1043

THE EARL OF SURREY TO SIR JOHN PASTON[1]

To my right worshipfull cousine, Sir John Paston, Knyght.

1490,
or later

RIGHT worshipfull cousine, in right harty wyse I commaunde me unto you. And where I understand by Thomas Hartforde, a bower of Norwiche, berer herof, hath been putt to grete vexacion and trouble by oon Thomas Hogan, scomaker, of Norwiche, and that I perceyve ye have harde the matier depending in travers bitwixt the saide parties; I therfore desire you that, in the right of the forsayd Thomas Hartford, ye wolbe unto hym gode maistir, and the bettir for this myn instaunce, as my singler trust is in you.

And where I conceyve also that the same Thomas is noysed in Norffolk for a Scotesman borne, ye shall understande that I perceyve wele, by suche honest folkes as I have hard speke within the citie of York, that the saide Thomas was borne their, and his fathir there inhabityng, and his god fathirs and mothers, the which bee right honest persones; and for that this is true, and not feyned, ye shall understand the Maiour of the citie of York and his brethren hath made grete instaunce unto me to writ for the saide Thomas, for whom I must nedes do, because thaye arre my nye neighbours, as our Lord knoweth, Who have you in His blissid saufegard.

Written in the castell of Shirehoton, the xxiiij[th] day of April.

Your lovyng cousin, THOMAS SURREY.

[1] [From Paston MSS., B.M.] Thomas Howard, Earl of Surrey, the writer of this letter, fought for Richard III. at the battle of Bosworth, and was taken prisoner. He was, however, after some years' confinement, liberated from the Tower, and taken into favour. In 1489 the King sent him into the North to put down the rebellion in which the Earl of Northumberland was slain, and afterwards made him his lieutenant-general north of Trent; and for ten years he resided continually in those parts. The date of this letter, therefore, cannot be earlier than 1490, though it may be several years later.

HENRY VII

1044

THE EARL OF SURREY TO SIR JOHN PASTON[1]

To my right worshipfull Cousin, Sir John Paston.

COUSIN Paston, in my most herty wyse I recomaund me unto you, and thank you for many kyndnesses of late tyme past, and also for that ye have bene so good maister unto my sarvaunt William May, and now at his comyng to me ye have at your greate coste sent him to me dressed in suche wise as is veray necessary for me to have men appareled; for the whiche your kindnesse I think myselfe right muche beholden to do you pleasure and it moght lye in my power, which I wuld right gladly do, as knoweth our Lord, whom I beseche to send you moche harte pleasure. Wreten at Sherifhoton, the vj[th] day of July, with the hand of

Your lovyng Cousin, THOMAS SU[RREY].[2]

1490
or late

1045

THE EARL OF OXFORD TO SIR JOHN PASTON[3]

To the right worshipfull and my right intierly welbelovyd counsellour, Sir John Paston, Knyght.

RIGHT worshipfull and right intierly welbelovyd counsellour, I commaund me hertely to you. And forasmoche as for certayne especiall causes moving, there be sessions appoynted to be holden at Gyppiswiche, the

1491
MARCH

[1] [MS. in Pembroke College, Cambridge.] This letter may well follow the last as being probably of the same year. At all events it lies within much the same range of date.

[2] Mutilated. Below is written in a later hand, and also mutilated: 'Thomas Howard, Earl of Surrey, the . . . . of Scots at Flodden.' The letter is indorsed 'Litt. Com. Surrey.'

[3] [From Paston MSS., B.M.] As 'Friday se'nnight after Easter' was the 15th April, Easter Day must have fallen on the 3rd in the year in which this letter was written. This would suit either 1491 or 1496.

THE PASTON LETTERS

91 (?) Friday sevenyght aftre Estre, which shall be the xv. day of
RCH 27 Aprile, where I purpose then certaynly to be, and to have
aswell the matere by twene Sir Edmounde Benyngfeld[1] and
Yelverton[2] there to be harde and commenyd, as diverse othre
grete maters in that contrey necessary to be had in comynycacion; I therfor desire and pray you that ye fayle nat to be
there the same day, bryngyng with you the forseide Yelverton,
trusting that then suche direccion shall be takyn in that matere
as can be thought resonable, and to the weale of the parties;
nat doubting but that Sir Edmound Benyngfeld shall be there
in like wise. And Almyghty God kepe you.

Wretin at my castell of Hedingham, the xxvij. day of
Marche.

OXYNFORD.

1046

HENRY VII. TO THE EARL OF OXFORD[3]

1491
PRIL 6 RYGHT trusty and ryght welbelovyd cousyn, we grete
yow well, &c. In that ye desyer all the dogers
[*fishing smacks*] of thos partes schuld have our licens
to departe in the viage towardes Islond, as they have ben
accustommyd to do yerly in tyme passyd, and that ye woll
undertak they shall have with them no more quantites of
graynes then woll only suffice for ther vitallyng and expensis;
we late yow witte that owr fully interly belovyd cousyn the
Kyng of Demarke hath showyd and compleynyd un to us by
dyverse his letters, that when our subjectes come to the seid
Islelond, beyng in hys obeissaunce, they stelle, robbe, and
exstorte his subjectes ther ageynse ryght and conciens. Wherfore, the seyd doggeres fyndyng sufficient surte be forne yow,
such as ye will answer unto us, that they shall not have with
them no graynes mo then shall only suffice for ther vitallyng,

---

[1] Bedingfield.
[2] William Yelverton, Sir John Paston's brother-in-law, grandson of the Judge.
[3] [From Paston MSS., B.M.]

136

nor odyr thyng woth them that ys for bedyn, and that also **1491**
they shall not in goyng, comyng, nor in ther beyng at the seyd **APRIL 6**
Islond, take noo thyng but that they treuly pay or agre for,
and frendly entrete our seyd cousyns subjectes withowth eny
robbyng or exstartyng them in there bodyes ner goodys; we
be content the seyd doggeres make ther viages thedyr at ther
libertes, eny our wrytyng or comandment mad in to the contrary nat withstandyng; and ellys we woll that our restraynte
of ther thedyr goyng stond styll in his strenthe and vertu.

Yovyn ondir our signet, at our maner of Shene, the vj[th]
day of Aprile.

JOHN VER, Erle of Oxynford, Gret Chambyrleyn and
Admirall of Ynglond, Viscount Bulbek, and Lord Skalys, to
all them that this present wrytyng shall see or here, gretyng.
And for asmuch as I late have recevyd the Kyng our Sovereyn
Lords letters, beryng date the vj[th] day of this monyth of
Aprile, accordyng to a copy of the same, signyd with myn
hand, wiche my ritht trusty servant, John Rowe, Marchall of
my Admyralite, hath for to showe;

Know ye that I, the seyd Erle and Admirall, have assygned
and deputyd my seyd servant to see our seyd Sovereyn Lordes
lettyrs pleynly executyd acordyng to the tenure of the same,
and by thys present wrytyng have yevyn to hym full autoryte
and pouer to put undyr arest all such doggeres as be dysposyd
to mak the viage towardes Islond, to such tyme as they have
fownd surte afor me, accordyng to owr seyd Sovereyn Lordys
comandment, for ther demenyng in the seyd viagys.

Yovyn under myn signett and signee manuell, the xth day
of Aprile the vj. yere of the reygne of our seyd Sovereyn Lord
Kyng Hery the vij[th]

137

THE PASTON LETTERS

1047

THE EARL OF OXFORD TO SIR JOHN PASTON[1]

To the right worshipfull and my right welbeloved
Sir John Paston, Knyght.

491(?)
ULY 31 RIGHT worshipfull and right welbeloved, I comaunde me
to you. And where as I late receyved your wrytyng,
beryng date the xxvj. day of this present monthe, by
the whiche I understand that one Richard Calle toke certeyne
men of werre robbyng upon the coste there; and in somoche
as I understand that they be under the obeissaunce of the
Kyng of Denmarke, I wolle and desyre you that ye delyver
theym unto the seid Richard Calle to take his avauntage of
theym as prisoners, seyng my dutee reserved in every thyng,
as my trust is in you. And Almyghty God kepe you.

Writen at my castell of Hedyngham, the last day of Jule.
OXYNFORD.

1048

THE OLD AND NEW BAILIFFS OF YARMOUTH
TO SIR JOHN PASTON[2]

To oure right reverent and worshipfull and special good
maister, Maister Paston.

1491
[SEPT.] RIGHT reverent and worshipfull sir, and oure veray
lovyng and curteys good mayster, we recomaund us
on to you in as feythefull wyse as on oure part aper-
teynith; and hertely we thanke you for your labour and letter,

---

[1] [From Paston MSS., B.M.] The date of this letter is uncertain, but, as Fenn
suggests, it is not unlikely to have been written in the year 1491, when it may be
supposed that Danish sailors endeavoured to requite the injuries inflicted by the
English in Iceland, of which mention is made in the last letter.
[2] [From Paston MSS., B.M.] 'Several ordinances,' says Fenn, 'respecting corporation business, made by the men of Yarmouth, through Sir John Paston and Lord
Oxford's attention to them, received the King's assent by his Attorney-General in
1491. It was for their activity in those matters, I presume, that this letter of thanks,
etc. was addressed to Sir John.' The time of year appears by the letter itself to be
about Michaelmas.

138

whiche ye sent to us be your servaunt, be the whiche we wer **1491**
asserteynid of the Kynges pleasure, and to acomplyshe the **[SEPT.]**
same, we with the assistens of youre maistirship wyll put us in
oure devoir.

We were at your manoir of Castir to have sen your
maistirshyp, but ye were departyd as well from Yermouth
yistirday, as this day from Castre. We wold have ben joyous
to have seen your maistirshyp, if our fortune so had ben.

Sir, we be enfourmyd that ore old special good Lord of
Oxford, in whom we founde as gret favour be the mediacion
of your maystirship, as ever we had of any creature, as we have
wrytyng to shewe, in recumpens of whiche at all tymes sethyn
hise lordshyp hathe had our preyeris; and now we wold have
waytid upon hise lordshyp, but your maystirship knowith well
we may not be absent on Mychilmesse Day for dyverse con-
sederacions. Wherfore we beseke your good maystirshyp, ye
lyke of your jentilnesse, to recomaund us unto our seyd good
lord, and to make our exkuse to hym, and to do hyse lordshyp [to be] presentyd with a porpeyse, whiche we send yow
be the brynger of thys; and if we had any othyr deyntes to
do hym a pleasure, we wold, that knowyth God, Whom we
beseke of Hyse infenit mercy to preserve the Kyng our
Soverayn Lord, and oure seyd good lord, and you, and all the
frutys of you from all adversite.

Youre loveres and bedmen, the old
Baliffes of Yermouth, and the newe
Balyffes that now shalbe.

139

THE PASTON LETTERS

1049

THE EARL OF OXFORD TO SIR JOHN PASTON[1]

To the right worshipfull and my right intierly welbelovyd counceillor, Sir John Paston, Knyght.

About 1491(?)
OCT. 20

RIGHT worshipfull and right intierly welbelovyd coun-ceillor, I comaund me to you. And where as I late have receyved your writing, wherby I . . . . . . the demeanyng of Richard Barkeley and his shipp as other, I have ta . . . . . of hym to be redy at all tymes to answer to all suche thynges as can be l . . . . he demeanyng. I woll therfor that ye suffre hym, his men and shippys, ... d as for a last of hering and an half, whiche I undirstond by hy . . . . . . of his, I woll that ye delyver hit to the controller of my howshold. A . . . . . o put undyr suertie all suche hering so takyn or revid by the carveyll of . . . . any other. And God kepe you.

Wretin at Melford, the xx. day of Octobre.

And where as I am enformyd that ye take hym nat for my servaunt, and so he ys noysed in the contrey ther, I woll that hit be knowin that I take hym as my servaunt, and so will do as long as I know no cause of the contrary.

OXYNFORD.

[1] [From a MS. in the Bodleian Library.] The MS. of this letter is mutilated, but it is perfectly intelligible, as it is the first of three relating to the same subject, of which Fenn has printed the second in his fifth volume. The date of the matter referred to is, however, uncertain, and I follow the example of Fenn in assigning the correspondence conjecturally to the year 1491, in which we have other letters from the Earl, as Admiral, to Sir John, as his Vice-Admiral.

140

THE PASTON LETTERS

1051

THE EARL OF OXFORD TO SIR JOHN PASTON[1]

To the right worshipfull and my right welbeloved counceilour, Sir John Paston, Knyght.

About 1491(?)
OCT. 28

RIGHT worshipfull and right welbeloved counceilour, I comaunde me to you. Certifieint you that I wolde have be right glad to have had you, the iij. persones that enformed you of Berkeleys demenyng, and Berkeley to-geder, to th'entent that I myght have had ripe knowleche of their demenyng, to have shewed the Kynge at my comyng unto His Grace. Nevertheles, sith I understand by your late wrytyng, to me brought by the seid Berkeley the xxviij. day of this present monthe, beryng date the Monday next before Seynt Symond Day and Jude, that ther is nat so grete defaute in the same Berkeley as ye by your former writinges to me sent wend [*thought*] ther had be, and that the defaute, if eny be, is in one Spenser, maister of the shippe belongyng to the seid Berkeley, and that ye thynke also that such suretee as I have take of the same Berkeley is sufficient inogh, better or more than nedeth for that cause, and that in your mynde ye thynke he woll be of gode guydyng and demenyng in tyme comyng ; I woll and desire you that ye delyver hym his shippes, men, and goodes, accordyng to my first wrytyng to you sent in that behalve. And Almyghty God kepe you.

Writen at my castell of Hedingham, the xxviij. day of Octobre.

OXYNFORD.

[1] [Douce MS. 393, f. 90.] See preliminary note to Letter 1049.

142

HENRY VII

1050

THE EARL OF OXFORD TO SIR JOHN PASTON[1]

To the right worshipfull and my right intierly welbelovyd councellour, Sir John Paston, Knyght.

RIGHT worshipfull and right intierly welbeloved coun-cellour, I comaund me to you. And where as I undirstond, by your writing to me delyverid by this berar, the roborye and dispoyling of certayn Corvers of Holond and Selond, done by the shipp callyd *the Foole*, wherof Robert Spenser was maister, aswell in herryng, vitayle, and takelyng, as ye be enfourmyd by iij. personnys of the same shippe, and of th'entent and disposicion of the master and feleshyp of the same, whiche shewe, as ye write, that Barkeley, aswell with that shipp as with a prise that he hathe bought, late takyn of the Frenchemen, were disposid and determenyd to do myche harme, wherupon ye have indevorid you to breke the same ; how be hit that the seid Barkeley hath be late with me, and found suertie in a *Cli.* to answer to all suche demean-yng, when he shall be callyd ; and therupon I wrote to you to suffre hym, his men, and shippis to departe at libertie ; yet nevyrtheless, conciidering your large writing, I can nat be content in my mynde to suche tyme as I may here bothe you and Barkeley to geder ; willing therf[or that ye do] kepe the shippys and goodes in suertie, and to be with me your selfe . . . . well may, bringyng with you suche iij. personnys as have . . . . certaynte of this mater ; and so I have wretin to Barkeley . . . . . se to answer to the same. And God kepe you.

Wretin \ . . . . of Octobre.

Also yf the be eny of the Duchemen . . . . any sute for ther gode, that ye then cause one of . . . . . . to shewe and clayme ther owne.

OXYNFORD.

[1] [From Paston MSS., B.M.] See preliminary note to last letter.

Abov
1491
OCT.

141

HENRY VII

1052

THE EARL OF OXFORD TO SIR JOHN PASTON[1]

To my righte trusty and righte welbelovyd counceillours, Sir Rauff Shelton and Sir John Paston, Knyghtes.

RIGHTE trusty and righte welbelovyd counceillours, I comaunde me to you. And ffor as moche as one Thomas Charlys of Norwiche late hathe presentid unto me a bille of complaynte agaynste Symonde White, gentylman, dwellyng in Shotesham, shewing by the same suche wrongis as the saide Symonde hathe done and daily dothe to the saide Thomas, as by the saide bille, whiche I sende you with this, more playnely apperith ; I therfor desire and pray you that ye woll do calle the saide parties byfore you, and upon due examinacion had upon the mater conteyned in the saide bille, ye take suche direction as may acorde with righte and gode consciens, so as the saide Thomas Charlis heraftur have no cause to resorte to me complaynyng. And Almightie God kepe you.

Writen at my castelle of Hedingham, the xv. daye of Septembre.

OXYNFORD.

1053

WILLIAM PASTON TO SIR JOHN PASTON[2]

To the ryght worchepfull Sir John Paston, Knyght.

AFTYR all dew recomendacion, lyke it yow to undyr-stond that Syr Herry Heydon schewyd me that it is agreyd be Syr Edmond Bedyngfeld, that the mater betwyx hym and my brodyr Yelverton[3] schalbe comynd at

[1] [Douce MS. 393, f. 89.] This letter is quite uncertain in point of date, except that it must have been written between 1487 and 1503. We place it, therefore, for convenience, after other letters of the Earl of Oxford.
[2] [From Paston MSS., B.M.] This letter refers to Henry VII.'s proposed invasion of France, which, after long preparation, actually took place in October 1492.
[3] William Yelverton, the grandson of the Judge, who married Anne Paston, the writer's sister.

Year
uncer
tain

149
FEB.

143

492
B. 18

Norwyche, and there a dyreccion to be takyn in the same mater, mete for them bothe.

Syr, the Kyng sendythe ordynaunce dayly to the see syde, and hys tentes and alys [*pavilions*] be a makyng faste, and many of them be made ; and there is also grete provysyon made be gentylmen that scholde goo wythe Hys Grace or hors, harnese, tents, halys, gardyvyans [*knapsacks*], cartes, and othyr thynges that scholde serve them for thys journey that the Kynge entendythe to take on hand, soo that belykelyod Hys Grace wolbe goyng sone upon Ester. And so I entende, aftyr that I here heaftyr, to goo to Caleys to purvey me of harneys, and suche thynges as I schall nede besydes hors, undyr that forme that my costes schalbe payd fore.

Syr, I am as yet no bettyr horsyd than I was whan I was wythe yow, nor I wote not where to have none, for hors flesche is of suche a price here that my purce is schante [*scarce*] able to bye one hors ; wherfor I beseche yow to herkyn [*hearken*] for some in yowre contre. Syr, my cosyn, John Heydon, tolde me that the Prior of Waburnes horse was rially amendyd, and that the Abott of Seynt Benetes schewed hym there was a bay hors of a persons nyght onto Seynt Benetis, and that the abot wolde gete hym for my cosyn Heydon at a resonable price. Syr, my cosyn, John Heydon, woll geve me hys entrest in that hors, if the abot have bowght hym, and so ye may lete the abot have knowlege ; and if he have not bowght hym, I beseche yow sende to see hym, for I wote not how to do with-owt yowre helpe aswell in horsyng of me as in other thynges.

At the makyng of thys lettyr, I cannot acerteyn yow what person it is that owythe thys hors. If I can know, I wolle send yow worde in a bylle I sende to Thomas Jullys be the berer herof.

Syr, as towardes my jurney to Caleys, the whyche I entende [*intended*] to have tane at my laste beyng with yow, it was so, I was dysapoyntyd of Thomas Dey and an other man I scholde have had be hys menys, as ye have had knowlege of or now ; and also I had went [*thought*] to have had folkys a mette with me at Hedyngham, whyche ded nott. My lorde,[1] seyng was

[1] The Earl of Oxford.

144

dysesyd, and also none otherwyse purveyd, wyllyd me in ony wyse to tary on tyl hys comyng to London, and sent myn excuse to my Lorde Dawbeney undyr thys forme how that I was sore disesyd ; notwythestondyng I was welewyllyd to have come to fulfyll my promesse, but he cowde not sofyr me, seyng me soo dysesyd ; and so my Lord Dawbeney was sory of my dysese and content that I taryd.

1492
FEB. 18

Syr, I beseche yow to holde me excusyd for kepyng of Thomas Lynsted, yowr servaunt, and hym bothe. It is soo that he and I bothe have ben in hand with my unkyll[1] for hys mater, and yett wee have hym at noo good poynt ; but I troste we schall have. Syr, if I take thys jurney to Caleys, I moste beseche yow to forbere hym lenger, and if I goo not to Caleys, thow I be lothe to forbere hym, yet I schall brynge hym with me schortly in to Norfolke, ye to have hym, if ye lyste, with the grace of God, Who have yow in kepyng.

Wretyn at London, the xviij. day of February, with the hande of yowre pore brodyr,

WYLLIAM PASTON.

1054

ROGER L'ESTRANGE TO SIR JOHN PASTON[2]

To the ryth worchypfull Syr John Paston, Knyth,
be thys delyveryd.

MASTYR PASTON, I recomawnd me to yow. Syr, so it is that I am not yet purveyd of men to my nowmbyr of archers, suych as chold go hovyr see with me ; wer for, syr, I be ceche yow that it wold plese yow at thys tyme to do so mych for me as to a purveyd me of ij. or iij., such as ye thynk chold be for me.

APRIL 16

Syr, I undyrstond Syr Tery Robstertt lyth but lyttyll

[1] William Paston the elder.
[2] [From Paston MSS., B.M.] This letter is probably of the year 1492, when the King was going over to France. But there are other occasions, both earlier and later, on one of which it might have been written.

145

492
IL 16

from yow, were, as I trow, he myde help me of j. by yowyr menys, and as for ther wages, they xall have the Kynges wages and some what elles, so that I trost that they xall be plessyd. Syr, I be cech yow to tak the peyne for me at thys tyme, and I xall do yow that servys that lyth in me, by the grace of Jesu, Ho preserve you.

On Monday next aftyr Palme Sonday, by yowyr howne to hys pouyr, ROGER LESTRAUNGE.

Syr, I be sech yow that thys byll may recomawnd me on to my lady,[1] and I trost I xall a wayt on you sone on Estyr.

1055

WILLIAM BARNARD TO WILLIAM PASTON[2]

To his right wurchipfull master, William Paston, and Mr. Deryk
dwellyng with my Lord of Oxinford, this lettir be delyvered
in hast.

About
492

RIGHT wurchipfull Maister William Paston, with myn good Lord of Oxinford, and myn welbelovyd Mr. Deryk, I recomaund me on to you. And it is soo that I kepe a prisoner of my lordis to answer to William Greve, maryner of Gret Yermouth, the wiche he brought hym to me by my lordis auctorite of a warand from Bell Key ; and the seid William Greve chargid me with hys prisoner, named Phillyp Barbour, and chargid me with hym for x*li.*, and so I kepe hym, and have kept hym this ij. yer and an half. And I have aftyr and many tymes askyd and requryed of the seid William Greve of mony for his bord, for he promysid and appoyntid with me for every weke ij*s.*, and I to take charge for to answer hym of hys prysoner aforeseid ;

[1] Probably Margaret, first wife of the Earl of Oxford.
[2] [From Paston MSS., B.M.] The date of this letter is very uncertain, but it is probably about the year 1492, as William Paston does not seem to have been in the Earl of Oxford's service many years before or after that date.

146

and so I have be chargith with hym ij. yeris and an half to my gret cost and charge, and nowh the seid William Greve intendith to pay me noon mony, butt he is a bowght to remeve the prysoner by a pryvy seall to abarre me from myn mony. Wher I am enformyd that noon prysoner of my lordis shuld nat be remevyd out of my lordis pryson, nor crafftid so out of pryson till he had answerd ther to seche causes as he lyth fore, and specially for alle suche costis and chargis as his kepar is charged for hym for his costis of exspensis ; and that doon, I woll be redy to delyver hym to the seid William Greve [to] pay me for his costis as it shalbe demyd with reason. Be-sechynd and prayeng you bothen too to be so good ma[istris unto] me that ye woll shewe this mater on to my lord, and to knowe my lordis meend whedyr it shall please hym that I shall delyver hym by a pryvy seall in this causis or nay, for the bryngar herof is the prysoner. And if it be my lordis mend that the prysoner shall appere to that pryvy seall, that it woll plese my lord to be so good and gracyous lord on to the prysoner to send hym to his councell to London, to tendyr this mater for the pore prysoner, and to consydre the gret losse that the seid William Greve intendith to putto his servaunt William Barnard, marchall and kepar of [my] lordis gayle in Yermouth, and servaunt [to?] Robert Crowmer, depute for my lord in the partyes of Norffolk and Suffolk. I shuld a browte up my sylf, but we be now in gret besynes in kepyng of my lordis honorabyll courtis in Norffolk and Suffolk.

About
1492

Wretyn the last day of Aprill.

By your, WILLIAM BARNARD,
that I can or may.

147

1056

EDMUND PASTON TO SIR JOHN PASTON[1]

To the ryght wurshupfull Sir John Paston, Knyght,
be this delyvered.

Before
1493

RYGHT wurshypfull Sir, I recomawnd me to zow. As zesterday I was with my cosyn Clere ;[2] he lythe at Borow, and my mastres hys wyveffe,[3] be cause the plage reygnyth at Ormysby. And so of hys own mocyon he mevyd to me of the maryage of my nevew zour soon, and as glad foolkes woold be to bargayn as ever ze wyste, and soo hathe shewyd me that ze shuld have as myche as Sir E. Bedyngfelld, whyche was v. C. marke. Moore over he shewyd that he woold depart with it to Sir Roger T.[4] or to Harry Colett, whyche he shewyd ze woold not of, but to have the mony at zour dysposyssyon ; and me semys be hys report that he knowyth well that yf ze delle with Sir H. H.,[5] he wyll be in a suerte that the mony that he shuld depart wit shuld goo to the redemyng of zour landes, and other zowr dawngeres. Moore over he shewyd me that the mony whyche ze skyftyd of H. Colett was th[oug]ht be Sir Harry H. that Sir R. Townesend shuld have ben contentte with it, whyche is knowyn the contrary, and causyd hym to geve delay in that be halffe to zow. I know well this jantylman berythe zow as good mynde as any man alyve, my mastres hys mother,[7] and allso my mastres hys wyve in lyeke wyesse ; and me semys he

[1] [From Paston MSS., B.M.] This letter cannot be later than the year 1493, as Sir Roger Townsend died on the 9th December in that year (Inq. p. m. 10 Hen. VII., No. 170). Moreover the will of Elizabeth Clere of Ormesby was proved, according to Blomefield, on the 6th March 1492-3. But as Sir John Paston's eldest son was only born in 1478, the date is not likely to be many years earlier.
[2] Sir Robert Clere of Ormesby.
[3] Probably his first wife Anne, daughter of Sir William Hopton. His second was Alice, daughter of Sir William Boleyn.
[4] Townsend. [5] Sir Henry Heydon.
[7] Elizabeth, widow of Robert Clere of Ormesby, the father of Sir Robert. She was the daughter of Thomas Owydale, Uvedale, or Dovedale, of Tacolneston, in Norfolk.

148

1057

SIR HENRY HEYDON TO SIR JOHN PASTON[1]

To myn ryght worchypfull cosyn, Sir John Paston, knyght.

1488-
1492
MARCH 4

COSYN Paston, I recommend me to you and wn to myne good ladie your wiff. As for your mater betwyx you and your wncle,[2] I have shewid it soe to my ladie of Norffolk and to hym, that it is agreed yee to entre in to Marlyngford and all other maners in debate in your name, and to kepe your courtes, sell your wodis, and to doo therwith as with your own. Wherupon I avise you, as soone as ye may, send som discrete man to kepe your courtis and to lette your fermys and selle your wodis to your most avayll. Your presens theer shall bee costly, and what is bee heende in the fermourz or tenauntz handez sethyn the reken-yng last be ffor myne ladiez servauntz and yourz, that thei bee warnyd kurtesly to paie it by a day, except in ony wise I avyse you nat to make ony thretis to ony fermour or tenaunt, for ony dealing affor this tyme, but to gett in fayernesse till I speke with you ; and in ony wyse that yee nor ony your ser-vauntz have noon wordis in this mater, but that it is agreed bee myne ladie you to have your peasebill possession. And as for Huntingffeldis, as yee have before ocupyed, ocupie still without noyse. I pray you folowe myne avise in this. I have hadde laubour, I trust thorowe your cause it shall nat be in vain *laboraverunt*, and suffyr this bill hyddyr too to speke to your sellf in privite, and to noon other. How yee and myne ladie, and in what sylk or clooth yee will have these tweyn yong innocentis[3] maried inne, iff it shuld bee pur-

[1] [Add. MS. 33,597, f. 9.] This letter must be addressed to the later Sir John. The manor of Marlingford belonged to Agnes Paston, who died about the same time as her grandson the first Sir John, and her right accordingly descended to his brother John, who was knighted at the battle of Stoke, 16th June 1487. His claim was dis-puted for a time by his uncle, but some arrangement was come to, apparently before the year 1493. (*See* No. 1056.)
[2] William Paston, son of the judge.
[3] Probably Sir John Paston's eldest son and a daughter of Sir Robert Clere. (*See* No. 1056.)

150

makys not the dowghttes to delyver zow hys mony that other men do of the delyverye of thers. Foor trowthe, he shewythe me hys mynde, whyche is thus : yf ze wyll putt lande in feffe-ment for zeres, to the full contentacyon of Townesend, Colett, and of my uncle, whyche he and all men thynke ze muste be charged to, or ever ze goo thorow, and that zour next frendes have the receyte of it tyll it be full contente and payed, thus, or suche a suer weye to be had for the well of all parteys, I darre say he is not alyve wyll indevour hym with better wyll to deele with zow, and, as my mynde servys me, streytte hym-sylffe, as it may be booryn, be syde my mastes hys modyrs v. C. My mastres hys wyffe, on my feythe I darr say, the moste harty body to zow wordes in this be halffe that is alyve, and the fayneeste body woold be to have it accomplyshyd.

Syr, I thenke ze be to wardes London, and well I woot zowre mynde is to ease zour sylffe as hastely as ze may ; I pray God ze do to zour honur, and to zour moste well to gederys.

Marchandes or new jantylmen I deme wyll proferr large ; noon other dyspreysed, ze know the contynewance of this man, and how he is alyed. Well I woott yf ze depart to London, ze shall have proferes large ; yf zour jornay be not but to ease yow in that be halfe, be my poor avyce slake for iij. or iiij. days, for ever me semys I shuld not have ben brokyn to so largely, but that they entende it hastely to say to zow. Sythe I was ther, I undyr stande yf it had not happyd me to have seyne them as zester day, she wold this day have made her cowntenance to have seyn her nes, Bothas (?) dowter, wyche is at Pallynges for fere of the plage, and have comyn seyne [*come and seen*] my wyffve, and specyally to have de syrid us to meve zow towardes them, and in trowthe so she hasse.

I pray God ze do as well to zour honur as I woold do my sylfe. Yf ze wyll tery thys lytell season be foor rehersyd, yf ze lyste, I woott well ze may have the mater moor largely comyned ; and yf ze tary tyll Monday, I wyll awayte on zow to Hynengham, with Godes grace, Who ever preserve zow and zours.

Your,

E. PASTON.
149

veyed at London to send me word, or ellys at Norwich, as it shall please you and myne ladie, ther after I shall applie me. For it must bee ordyrd be you in the yong husbondis name. Your penauns off your wncles mater shall yee knowe whan I kom hoome. Ther is non other meane but to sell your wodis and tymber in all your manors to your most avayll, except theere as it kan nat bee forborn for diverse causys. And iff you list to command mee ony thyng in these partyez, send me word be myn servaunt, berer heerof.

Wretin the iiij[th] day off March.—Your own to his powr,

H. HEYDON.

1058

SIR T. LYNG TO SIR JOHN PASTON[1]

To my rigth wurchypful master, Sir John Paston, Knyth, in hast.

MEMORANDUM, that thes be the namys that war mad Knytes of the Bath, the Thwrsday be for Alhalow Day.

Fyrst, My Lord Herry, Duke of Yorke.
My Lord Haryngton, Lord Marcas sun.[2]
My Lord Clyfford.
My Lord Fyvaren.
My Lord Dakyr of the Sowth.
My Lord Strange. Lord Stranges sun.
Sir John Arundell of the West.
Sir Water Grefyth of Lonkaschyre.
Sir Jarveys a Clyffton of Yorkechyre.
Sir Roberd Harcorth of the West.
Sir Edmund Trayford.
Sir Herry Marney of Esexe.

[1] [From Paston MSS., B.M.] This letter gives the list of the Knights of the Bath made on the occasion of Henry the King's second son being created Duke of York in 1494.
[2] Thomas Grey, son of Thomas Grey, first Marquis of Dorset, who succeeded his father in 1501.

151

THE PASTON LETTERS

Sir Roger Newborow.
Sir Raff Rither of Yorkechyre.
Sir Thomas Bawd of Harforth chyre.
Sir John Speke.
Sir Houmfrey Fulford.
Sir Roberd Lytton.
Sir Pers Egecome.
Sir Roberd Clere.
Sir Thomas Fayrefaxe.
Sir Richard Knythley.
Sir Wyllem Cheke.

Also Master Robert Southwell is Hey Schreve of Nor-ffolke.
Memorandum, that saforn is at xvjs. jli. the lowest price.
Also, the Kynge and the Qwene went crowned on Halow-messe Day last ; and my Lord of Schrewsbery bare my Lord Harry, Duke of Yorke, in hys harmys ; and x. byschopis, with myters on ther hedes, goyng be for the Kyng that day rownd a bowt Westmynster Hawle, with many odyr gret astates.
Sir, ther hath be so gret cownsell for the Kynges maters, that my Lord Chawnsler kept not the Ster Chawmber thys viij. days, but one day at London, on Sent Lenardes Day.
Be yowre pore prest and servaund,

SIR T. LYNG.

The lowest pryse of saforn is xvjs.
Item, the Knytes of the Bath.
Item, the Knytes of the Schyre.
Item, of recordes a yenst me.
Syr, ther hath record a yenst me, Syr John Seyve, Vecry of Barton, John Anond, Richard Elwyn of Wytton, John Bowlond of Totyngton, sumnor, whech arne all forsworyn on the Crwsifyxe a yenst me.

152

HENRY VII

1059

THE CORPORATION OF YARMOUTH TO SIR JOHN PASTON[1]

To our right honorable and especyall good maister, Ser John Paston, Knyght, this letter be delyvered in hast.

RIGHT wurchipfull ser, we recomaund us onto your good maistership, sertefyeng you that Robart Albon of Yermouth with many more of our neybors, this Sater-day arn comen hom from Caunterbury. And Robart Albon hath spokyn with the English captayns of the Kynges rebellys ther, part of theym that arn takyn ; and Robart Albon and his company seith that ther wer takyn and slayn to the noumbre of vij^{xx}, wherof were v. captayns, iiij. of them he named, oon Mounford, Whyght, Belt, and Corbett : he coude nott telle the fyfft capteyns name. And they told hym that they have apoynted to have a town of strength, for they wold an had Sandwich, and the countre had nott a resistid them. And so Belt seid on to Robart Albon he wyst weell that he was but a deed man, and for asmoche as he wist that he was of Yermouth, he shewid hym that they woll have Yermouth or they xall dye for it, as Robart seyth to us.
And this is a mater of trewth, and therfore we desyre and pray your good maistership, that we may have your myghty help of ayde and socowr, and that it woll please you to comon with Maister Mayer of Norwiche, to meve hym of hys sokour, but in especyall that we may have your maistership amongs us, with suche strength of your good councell, as your maistership shall thynk most best for the Kynges pleasur, and for the sewyrtye of us alle ; for we putt us in devyr to furnysh the town with all that we can doo, for we know noon oder but that they may be here by possybylyte this nyght or to morow

[1] [From Paston MSS., B.M.] This letter refers to the attempt of Perkin Warbeck at Deal, where a number of his followers landed on the 3rd July 1495, and were all either killed or taken prisoners by the people.

153

THE PASTON LETTERS

att nyght at the ferdest. No more to you, but Jesu preserve you.
Wretyn at Yermouth, in hast, this Saterday, the xj. day of July.

Be your owyn, the Balyffes of Yer-mouth, with our Brethern and Comons of the same Town.

1060

ROBERT CROWMER TO SIR JOHN PASTON[1]

To my right especyall and syngler good maister, Ser John Paston, Knyght, this letter be delyvered.

WURCHIPFUL ser, I recomaund me on to you. Maister Balyffes, with alle myn Maisteris of the town of Yermouth, thankith you hartilly, and trustyng feythfully of your ayde and comford at neede ; and if any suche cause happith with us, they woll feythfully send you word in all the hast possyble, up on the syght of the shippis.
Ser, ferdermor, ther is a ship of our town come hom from Seint John of Amyas, and he seyth that on Seint Thomas Day[2] ther came to Seint Wallrens,[3] in Normandie, an hoye of Dor-deryght, with viij. horsis, with many saddilles and brydilles ; ther in wer viij. or ix. Englysh men, the wiche toke the shippes boot, and went on lond at Staplis,[4] and arn renne a wey up in to the cuntre. And the Admiralles Depewty sesonyd the ship and hors, and all that they found ther in, to the Kyng our soverayn Lordes behooff ; and the Duche men were leyde in pryson. This is a mater of trowth, for

[1] [From Paston MSS., B.M.] This letter refers to the dispersion of Warbeck's fleet after the attempt at Deal. It would appear, as Fenn remarks, that on receipt of the preceding letter Sir John had promised aid to the town of Yarmouth, for which promise they here return thanks. The handwriting of this letter is the same as that of the last.
[2] The Feast of the Translation of St. Thomas Apostle, 3rd July.
[3] *Qu.* St. Vallery ? [4] Etaples.

154

HENRY VII

William Carre of our town, maryner, and oder of our town, see this doon in deed. And as for the shippes with the Kynges rebellars, they be furth out of Cambyr[1] westwards ; whyder they be, thei can not sey, but the Duche men seid to William Carre that they trustid on one man shuld help them with many men. Thes is suche tydynges as the Amyas men brout hom.
Ser, if it woll please your maistership that ye myght have leyser, I desyre and pray you to come sporte you, and to see how weell we have appareld and furnyshid our town, I wold be right gladd, and I trust to Almyghty God that it wold please your maistership right weell, and with your betyr advyce we woll doo more to our power, that knowith God, the wiche Lord preserve you.
Wretyn at Yermouth, on Relyk Sonday.[2]

By your servaunt, ROBART CROWMER.

1061

ELIZABETH, DUCHESS OF NORFOLK, TO SIR WILLIAM KNIVET AND OTHERS[3]

To my ryght entyerly and welbelovid frendes, Sire William Knevette, Sire John Paston, Sire Robert Clere, Knyghtes, the Kynges Attorney, Phelippe Calthorpe, Richard Suthwell, Squyers, and to yche of theym.

ELIZABETH, DUCHESSE OF NORFFOLK.

RIGHT entyerly welbelovyd frendys, I comaunde me to you. And for as moche as I understande that Sire Harry Grey, that is the verry owner and possessioner of the maner of Ketryngham, is nowe in gret age, and as it is

[1] The point called the Camber, near Rye.
[2] Relic Sunday is the third Sunday after Midsummer Day, and fell on the 12th July in 1495.
[3] [From Paston MSS., B.M.] The writer of this letter was the widow of John Mowbray, the last Duke of Norfolk of that name, who died in 1475. She survived her husband many years, and Fenn says, though I know not on what authority, that she was alive in 1496. Sir Harry Grey, it appears, made his will on the 28th Sep-

155

THE PASTON LETTERS

1495
SEPT. 14
seide, of right seekely disposicion, and that after his deceasse the right and title therof shall of right belonge to my right welbelovid servaunt Thomas Martyn, and his nevewe and heyre of blood, and his eyre therof by reason of entaylys :— What the seid Sire Harry entendith to do therin, I knowe not, but it rennyth in reporte, that he is in purpose to dis-herite the seid Thomas Martyn therof, contrary to all right and good conscience. In eschuenge wherof, I desire and pray you as hertely as I can, that it wull leeke you to be so good maistyrs to the seid Thomas as, by your wisdams and dis-crecion, the seid Sire Harry, by you or some of you, may be moved of conscience and of kyndenesse to his blood to have regard to the seid right, and not to do eny thyng that shuld be disheryson to his seid nevewe, and to have the more tender consideracion to your mocion, for that the seid Thomas is to dyverse of you of kynne and aliaunce, and to many other gentilmen within the shere in leeke cas. And for the con-sideracion that I have, that the seid Sire Harry and Thomas his nevewe, were of my lordes nere blode, whoes soule Jesu pardon and assoyle, it were to gret a pete to see hym by dis-heryson to falle to penury and poverte, wher by your good exortacion in consideracion of the premissis, and mo odir by your wisdamys to be remembred, in the lif of the seid Sire Harry suche inconveniences may be better remadyed ; wherin ye shall not only do an almas dede, and a gret pleasir to God, but also to me for that blodes sake a singuler pleasir, and cause me heraftir therather to considir thynge that shall con-cerne your resonabill pleasir, with Goddes grace, Who ever kepe you.

At Erle Soham, this xiiij^{ne} day of Septembyr.

tember 1492 (Blomefield, v. 93), and one might imagine this letter was written in the same month and year. The inquisition upon his death, however, was only taken on the 26th October, 12 Hen. VII. (1496), and it does not state the day on which he died. The jurors found Thomas Martyn, who was then thirty years old and over, to be his kinsman and next heir, but that Ketteringham Hall was devised to the use of his wife Jane and of others after her death. It is certain, moreover, that this letter could not have been written before the year 1495 when Sir Robert Clere was knighted ; and that is probably the very year, as Sir Harry Grey was dead at least in October 1496, and most likely a month or two earlier.

1062

WILLIAM PASTON TO SIR JOHN PASTON[1]

To my most special good father, Ser John Paston, Knyght.

1495

AFTER most humbyl wyse of recommandacion, in my Abo most lovyngly wyse, I beseche yow of your dayly blyssyng, showyng yow that I am at Ser John Fortescu place, be cause they swet so sor at Cambryge. Also I shew yow that Mr. Thomas Clark ys desessyd, hows sowle God have mercy.

Also, I beseche yow that ye wol se a remedy for the comun of Snaylwel, for the Bayly of Snaylwel and on of your fermors war with my tutor and me, and sheuyd me that all the comun shuld a be takyn away butt for Mr. Cotton and the Vecur of Fordan,[2] hom I beseche yow to thank. Fro Pamsborow.[3]

Be your most humbyl servaunt,

WILLIAM PASTON.

[1] [From Paston MSS., B.M.] Fenn says, I cannot tell on what grounds, that this letter must have been written between 1491 and 1495. At the earlier of these dates the writer could not have been more than twelve years old, but as lads were sent to the university at a much earlier age in those days than in ours, even the earlier of these dates is not impossible. The style of the letter, however, is not boyish, and I should have been inclined to place it a year or two later even than Fenn's latest date, but that there is no clear evidence to go by. The sweating sickness was prevalent in England at different times during the reign of Henry VII.; and there is no particular record of its visiting Cambridge.
[2] Fordham in Cambridgeshire, north of Newmarket. Snailwell lies between.
[3] Punsborne, near Hatfield, in Hertfordshire.

THE PASTON LETTERS

1063

MARGARET, COUNTESS OF RICHMOND, TO ———[1]

BY THE KYNGES MODER.

Between
1497
and
1503

TRUSTY and right welbeloved, we greet you well. And wher by the meanes of our trusty and right wel-beloved Sir Reynold Bray, Sir Thomas Lovell, and Sir Henry Heydon, Knights, there was a full agreement made and concluded, and also put in writinge, betwen our trusty and right welbeloved Sir John Savile, Knight, and Gilbert Talbot, Esquier, on th'one partie, and yow on th'other, for divers lands which they ought to have in the right of their wives, daughters and heyers to William Paston, Esquier, their late fader deceassed, which lands ye by mighty power kepe and withholde from them without any just title, as they afferme ; and albeit the said agrement was made by your minde and consent, yet ye ne doe performe the same, to our merveile, if it be so. Wherefore we desier and also counsell yow without delay upon the sight hereof now shortly to ride to the court to the said arbitrators, now ther being, with whom ye shall finde your adverse partie, or other in their names fully authorized, to abide such final ende and conclusion in the premisses as shall be consonant with the said agrement, without further troubles or busines therin hereafter to be had ; and that ye will thus do in any wise, so as we be not driven (through your defalte) to put to our hands for further remedye to be had in the premisses.

Yeven under our signet at our mannor of Colly Weston, the xth day of February.

[1] [From Sandford's *Paston Genealogy.*] William Paston, the uncle of the two Sir Johns, died in 1496, and this letter must have been written either in the year following or between that date and 1503, when Sir Reginald Bray died. William Paston's will, which will be found in the Appendix, was dated 7th September 1496, and proved on the 28th November following. He married Anne Beaufort, daughter of Edmond, Duke of Somerset, and was therefore uncle to the writer of this letter, Margaret, Countess of Richmond, the mother of King Henry VII. The person to whom the letter is addressed is not named, but it is not unlikely to have been Sir John Paston the second.

1064

ELIZABETH, DUCHESS OF NORFOLK, TO SIR JOHN PASTON[1]

To my right welbeloved frende, Sire John Paston, Knyght.

ELIZABETH, DUCHES OF NORFOLK.

1497
FEB.

I COMMAUNDE me to you, thankyng you as hartely as I can for your labour and substancyall serching owte of Thomas Martynz matyr, preing you of contenuance, and of your best advyse therin, how he shall breke the mater so as, by your helpe and wysdam, a frendely comunycacion may be hadde, so as the mater may be had in examynacion by suche gentylmen as shalbe named by th'assent of bothe parties, suche as tendyr and love the wele of bothe parties, and also the pees and tranquyllyte of the cuntre, and love to eschewe variaunce and parties in the cuntre, wherin ye shall not only do a greete pleasure to me, but a grete dede of charyte for the profight and ease of both parties, and also a pleasure to God, Who have you in keping.

At Erle Soham lodge, this xxviij. day of February.

N. E. N.

[1] [From Paston MSS., B.M.] It seems probable that this letter was written in the February following Sir Harry Grey's death. (*See* No. 1061.)

1065

THE EARL OF OXFORD TO SIR JOHN PASTON AND ANOTHER[1]

To my right trusty and right welbel[oved Sir] John Paston, Knyght, and Sir . . . . . Knyght, ... of them.

1499
AUG. 20

RIGHT trusty and welbeloved councellours, I comaunde me to you. And where the Kinges Grace is lately acerteinyed that Th'Erl of Suffolk is departid owt of this his Realme, Hys Grace hath commaundid me to wryte unto you that ye incontynent uppon the sight of this my writing endeavour you to enquyre aswell of such persones as be departid over with the seid Erle as of theim that accompanyed hym in his repayre to the see, and retornyd ageyn, or in any wyse were prevy to the same, and theruppon, in as goodly hast as ye kan, to put them and every of them in suertie savely to be kept, and therof t'acerteyn me, to th'entent ye maye knowe his ffurther pleasure in the same. And if ye shall at any tyme herafter perceyve any suspect person nyghe unto the see costes which shall seme unto you to be of the same affynyte, than His Grace will that ye put them in lyke suertie. And Almighti God have you in His keping.

Written at Gaddishill, in the Ile of Wight, the xxᵗⁱ daye of August.　　　　　　　　　　　　　　OXYNFORD.

[1] [Douce MS. 393, f. 87.] Edmund de la Pole, Earl of Suffolk, escaped abroad on the 1st July 1499, and proclamations were issued on the 20th August following (the day on which this letter was written) against persons leaving the kingdom without a license. (See my *Letters and Papers Illustrative of the Reigns of Richard III. and Henry VII.*, vol. i. preface p. xl., vol. ii. p. 377.) It appears that the King was at this time staying at Godshill, in the Isle of Wight, the place from which this letter is dated (see *Excerpta Historica*, p. 122).

1066

HENRY VII. TO SIR JOHN PASTON[1]

To our trusty and welbeloved knight, Sir John Paston.

BY THE KINGE.

1500
MARCH 20

TRUSTY and welbeloved, we grete yow well, letting yow wete that our derest cousins, the Kinge and Queene of Spaine, have signified unto us by their sundry letters that the right excellent Princesse, the Lady Katherine, ther daughter, shal be transported from the parties of Spaine aforesaid to this our Realme, about the moneth of Maye next comeinge, for the solempnization of matrimony betweene our deerest sonne the Prince and the said Princesse. Wherfore we, considering that it is right fitting and necessarye, as well for the honor of us as for the lawde and praise of our said Realme, to have the said Princesse honourably received at her arriveall, have appointed yow to be one amonge others to yeve attendance for the receivinge of the said Princesse; willinge and desiringe yow to prepare yourselfe for that intent, and so to continue in redynesse upon an houres warninge, till that by our other letters we shall advertise yow of the day and time of her arrivall, and where ye shall yeve your said attendance; and not to fayle therin, as ye tender our pleasure, the honor of yourselfe, and of this our foresaid Realme.

Yeven under our signet at our mannor of Richmount, the xxᵗʸ day of Marche.

[1] [From the *Paston Genealogy*, compiled by Sandford, and printed by Mr. Worship, in the *Norfolk Archæology*.] Catherine of Arragon was expected in England in the spring of the year 1500, although she did not actually arrive till October 1501, owing to some alteration of plans.

THE PASTON LETTERS

1067

RICHARD CALLE TO SIR JOHN PASTON[1]

To the right reverent and honurable, my master, Sir John Paston, Knyght.

Before
1503

PLESITHT it your mastership to remembre, I shewyd onto you in Lente that I had bought Baktons place. Sir, it is so that John Bakton grauntid to John Trovy hes sone in lawe, hes mese with all the londes and tenements, &c., takyng of the seide John Trovy viij. marke of annuyte yerly, terme of hes lyf; wherupon endenture were made and a state delyverd. Upon the weche I bargeyned with Trovy, payng to hym for hes parte c. marke and x., wherof he hadde in hande iiij*li*. vj*s*. viij*d*. and xv*li*. xiij*s*. iiij*d*. shulde be payd at such tyme as I had a lawfull astate, weche was apoynted before Michelmes last past; weche is not yet done. Wherfore he hath forfeted an obligacion of xl*li*. that he was bounde in to me for the same astate; ther was no defaute in me, for my money was there redy. And, sir, in the same weke yter your mastership departed out of this contre, Bakton and the seide Trovy come to Bakton, and sent for me, and there were we appoynted for the same bargeyn and accorded, wenynge to me and to all tho that were there it had ben fully concl[uded] . . . . . my suertes and for all other thynges. And sodenly Bakton departed hem be the avice of [the Prior of Bro]mholme, and John Bowle and other, weche meved Bakton that I shulde not have my bargein; and so they entende to putte me from my bergain. And master Fitzlawes, Kn[i]ght, of Esex, hath sent me a letter, weche I sende you closed herin; and at hes enstaunce I have grauntid Trovy an

[1] [From Paston MSS., B.M.] From the mention of 'Master Fitzlewes, Knight of Essex,' I am inclined to think this letter must be of the reign of Henry VII., and addressed to the later Sir John. Sir Lewis Fitzlewes of West Horndon, in Essex, was attainted as a Lancastrian in 1471, but the manor was restored to his son, Sir Richard, by Henry VII., who presented to the living from 1494 to 1519. The letter, however, must of course be earlier than 1503, the year in which Sir John Paston died.

HENRY VII

ende for vj*li*. and my iiij*li*. vj*s*. viij*d*., and my costes that I have done on the place, weche with these mony and costes drawith xij*li*. If I may have all these money payd onto me within xiiij. dayes after Cristemas, I wol take non avauntage of the obligacion, weche Trovy is bounde to me. I suppose Mr. Lawes woll speke to you of thes mater. I beseche you that ye wol be goode master to me herin, for I am lothe to be putte from my bergain. I am in suerte there is no man wol geve so moche for it as I wolde, and they nede not to fere them of ther payment, for I ofer them iiij. suertes, the worste of them is worthe all the lande; yet Bakton mystrustes me, and nede not. If I had it, I wolde truste to make it a goode thynge, for ther is moche thynge ther by that myght be had in to it, weche causeth me to be the more desirous to it. I shewe your mastership the previte of my mynde, trustynge ye wolbe good mastre to me, and I shal pray to God for you and for all youres.

Wreten at Felmyngham, the Saterday next before Sein Marteyn.

Be your servaunt,
R. CALLE.

Before
1503

1068

ABSTRACT[1]

[RICHARD CALLE] TO [SIR JOHN PASTON?]

Reminds him that four or five years ago he received from the writer 'certain wainscoat' and certain fish for his household, a hogshead of wine, spars, 'clapholt,' etc. in full discharge of all former debts. Will always be ready to repay what his correspondent has paid for him to the King. Received of him a millstone, price £3, for which Calle gave a ryall in earnest, and delivered 1 quarter cod to Philip Loveday. I am grateful for the pains taken by 'your mastership' on my account, etc.

Year
uncertain

[The handwriting of this letter seems to be that of Richard Calle, but much older looking than that of most of his letters. As there is no distinct evidence of date, we place it after another letter of his, which seems to be late.]

[1] [From Paston MSS., B.M.]

1069

SIR JOHN KENDAL TO SIR JOHN PASTON[1]

*To the right worshipful and my right entierly welbeloved
cosin and frende, Sir John Paston, Knight.*

Before
1503

RIGHT worshipfull sir, I recommaunde me unto you. I
wryte this onely unto you, to advise you that I was
mynded that my cousin Clippesby,[2] berer herof, shuld
wele have maryed here in thies partes, wherin your nyce[3]
toke hevy conceyte, thinking in hir mynde, that I was not
willing that my said cousin shulde marye with hir.

At that tyme I knewe not what love was bitwix them, but
now I undrestand that bothe there myndes is to mary to
geders; wherunto on my parte, I am agreble and wel content,
desiring and praying you to be the same, and to be the better
frende unto them at this my prayer and instaunce. And what
pleasir as I may doo unto you in thies partes shal be redye, in
that I may, at your desires. And I pray you to recommaunde
me to my cousin your nyce. And Jesu preserve you.
Writen at London, the first day of Juyn.
Your own, the Priour of Saint Johns,
SIR JOHN KENDAL.

[1] [From Paston MSS., B.M.] Sir John Kendal was Prior of St. John's from 1491
to 1501, and probably later, so that there is nothing clearly to fix the date of this
letter, except that it was written before the death of Sir John Paston in 1503.
[2] John Clippesby, Esq. of Oby.
[3] Constance, daughter of William Paston, Sir John's brother.

1070

MARGARET, COUNTESS OF OXFORD, TO SIR JOHN PASTON[1]

*To my right trusty and hertely wilbilovede sone, Sir John
Paston, Knyght.*

RIGHT trusty and hertely wilbiloved sone, I recom-   Year
mennde me to you, and send you Godes blyssynge   uncer-
and myn. And where oon John Malpas my olde   tain
servaunt, brynger herof, hath purchacede a writt directede to
you and othre Justices of Peace in the shires of Norffolk and
Suffolk, and also to the Sheryff of the same, for to put hym in
pessible possescion in such certayn landes of his, accordynge
to the Kynges writt; I pray you therfor hertely, and of my
blyssynge charche you that at this my pour request and desir
ye wole pute you in your faythfull devoir with othere Justaces
associete with you, to see the execuscion doon and performyede
accordynge to the saide writt. And Almyghty God evere
more preserve you, my nown dere sone.
Writene in my lordes castell of Hethyngham, the xv. day
of January.

MARGRET OXYNFORD.

[1] [From Paston MSS., B.M.] I see nothing certain about the date of this letter,
except that it must have been addressed to the later Sir John Paston (for in his
brother's time the Earl of Oxford was an exile, and his Countess Margaret in needy
circumstances), so that the date must lie between 1488 and 1503. For what reason
the Countess calls Sir John her son I cannot explain.

1071

SIR JOHN PASTON TO WILLIAM PASTON AND RICHARD LIGHTFOOTE[1]

*To my brother William Paston and my cosyn Richard Lightfoote,
and to iche of theym.*

1503

MASTYRS bothe, I recomand me to yow, and send yow
closid herin a booke of the seying of dyvers folkis,
which testyfiee ayenst Thomas Rutty and other. I
prey yow shewe it to my lordys[2] good lordshepe, and that I
may know hys plesur ferther in as hasty wyse as may be, that
I may ordre me ther aftyr. I had gret labore to come by the
woman that was in servyse with Rutty, whiche sie [saw] all
ther conversacyons many yeris. She is now in servyse with
Richard Calle. And I have Thomas Bange in prison at Norwyche with the Shrevys of Norwych. The woman seythe he
is as bold a theffe as eny is in Ingland; but he wyll nowghte
confesse, nor I handelyd hym not sore to cause hym to confesse. But and Ruty knewe that he and the woman be in hold,
and hathe told talis, I thynke it wyll cause Rutty to shewe the
pleynesse.
Clerk and Roger Heron are endightid at this sessyons at
Norwyche, last holdyn on Twysday last past, for robbing of

[1] [From Paston MSS., B.M.] This letter is anonymous, but is in the handwriting of Sir John Paston, the younger of that name. From the mention of his wife
and 'the widow, her daughter Leghe,' it was evidently written not during the life of
Margery Brews, his first wife, who must have died about the year 1495, but after his
marriage to another. This second wife was Agnes, daughter of Nicholas Morley,
Esq., of the well-known family at Glynd, in Sussex, and had already been twice
married before her marriage with Sir John. Her first husband was John Hervey, Esq.
of Thurleigh, Beds, Usher of the Chamber to King Edward IV. Her second was
John Isley of Sundridge, Kent. By the former she had a daughter, Isabel, married
to John Leghe or Alyghe, Esq. of Addington, Surrey, who proved his father-in-law's
will in 1494. She herself survived her own third husband, Sir John Paston, and
died in 1510. Her will, in which she calls herself 'Dame Agnes Paston,' is at the
principal registry at Somerset House, dated the 31st May in that year, and proved on
the 19th June following. For these particulars I was indebted to the genealogical
researches of the late Colonel Chester, and *Notes and Queries*, 5th S. ix. 326, 370,
414, 512.
[2] The Earl of Oxford.

the pardoner; and so is Rotty and all his felawshepe that the   1503
woman hathe apechid. According to hir apechement, Raff
Taylour is over the see; Robert Fenne is dede; John Baker
and William Taylour ar yett untakyn. If my lord send for
T. Bange or the woman, some of my lordis servauntes had
need to come for theym; for I can not do in the cause for
lake of men and horse, for my wyff ridith this next week in to
Kente, to the wydow, hir doughtir Leghe.
And as for Ramesey, liek a prowde, lewde, obstynat foole,
he wyll not come befor my brothe[r] Sir R. Clere, nor me,
but he seythe he wyll be with my lord hastyly, and shewe hys
mynde to his lordshepe, whiche I beleve not. The substancyall marchantys of Norwyche hathe shewid ther myndys to
my brother Sir R. Clere and me that he entendith to William
Bayly gret wronge in his reknynges.

1072

THE EARL OF OXFORD TO SIR JOHN PASTON[1]

*To the right worshipfull and my right entierly welbelovyd
Sir John Paston, Knyght.*

RIGHT worshipfull and right intierly belovyd, I com-   After
maund me hartely to you. And where as your broder   1503?
William, my servaunte, ys so troubelid with sekenes
and crasid in his mynde, that I may not kepe hym aboute me,
wherfor I am right sory, and at this tyme sende hym to you,
prayng especially that he may be kepte surely and tendirly
with you, to suche tyme as God fortune hym to be bettyr
assurid of hym selfe and his myndes more sadly disposid,
whiche I pray God may be in shorte tyme, and preserve you
longe in gode prosperite.
Writen at my place in London, the xxvj. day of Juyn.

OXYNFORD.

[1] [From Douce MS. 393, f. 86.] This letter is probably later in date than the
last, as it would appear that when the last was written, William Paston was still in
the Earl of Oxford's service.

THE PASTON LETTERS

1073

THE EARL OF OXFORD'S STEWARD TO THE 'BLACK KNIGHT'[1]

Sinescallus Comitis Oxoniæ Nigro Militi.

NON decet Sinescallo tam magni Comitis
    Ut Comes Oxoniæ verbis in Anglicis
    Scrittere epistolas, vel suis in nuncijs
    Aliquid proponere si non in Latinis.

Igitur ille pauperculus prædicti Comitis
Magnus Sinescallus magni Comitatis
Nuncupatur Norff. Latinis in verbis
    Apud Knapton in curia in forma Judicis.

Tibi nigro militi salutem, et omnibus
    Notifico, quod Langdon ille homunculus
Nullam pecuniam liberare vult gentibus,
    Quod est magnum impedimentum nostris operibus.

Idcirco tibi mando sub pœna contemptus,
    Quod tu indilate proprijs manubus
Scribas tuas lettras, quod ille homunculus
    Copiam pecuniæ deliberet gentibus.

Sin autem per littras has nostras patentes
Ego et operarij, qui sunt consentientes
Omnes una voce promemus suos dentes
    Nisi liberet pecuniam, cum simus egentes.

Teste meipso apud Knapton prædicta,
    Est et michi testis Maria Benedicta,
Quod vicesimo die Julij non inde relicta
    Erat summa solidi, res hæc non est ficta.

[1] [From Fenn, iv. 458.] The 'Black Knight,' to whom this facetious doggrel was addressed, seems to me to have been most probably the later Sir John Paston, whose services the Earl of Oxford, as the reader is aware, continually made use of. The manor of Knapton came to John, 12th Earl of Oxford, who died in 1462, by his marriage with Elizabeth, grand-daughter of Sir John Howard.

168

HENRY VII

1074

EAST BECKHAM[1]

WHERE Sir John Paston and Roger Townesende have agreed and promysed to obey as we, Jamys Hobart and John Yaxley will devyse for the varians of the maner of Estbekham : We devyse and a warde that Sir John Paston shall have the seid maner to hym, and to his heires ; and he therfor shall paye to the seid Rogyr xl*li.* at Pentecoste nexte, and at Halowmesse nexte aftyr that xl*li.*, and at Pentecoste next aftyr that xx*li.* ; and the same Syr John shall have the arrerages of the seid maner. And if the seid Sir John refuse to have the maner, then the seid Rogyr to have the same maner, with the arrerages as is a forseid, payeng to the seid Sir John the seid C*li.* at the dayes aforseid ; and the seid Syr John to geve answer which he will chose the viij. daye of this moneth.

1503
FEB. 6

Yevyn the vj. daye of Februarii, anno R. R. H. vij. xviij°.

And all this to be perfurmyd and put in surte after our avise. And we devise that he that shall have the land, shall paie to th' other at Halwemes come twelvemonyth, ten mark, besides the seid C*li.*, because th'arrerages have ben long in the tenauntes handes.

          JOHN YAXLEE.
          JAMYS HOBART.

[1] [From Paston MSS., B.M.]

169

THE PASTON LETTERS

1075

ARCHBISHOP WARHAM TO WILLIAM PASTON[1]

To my cousyn Master William Paston.

1503
PT. 6

COUSYN PASTON, I recommaunde me unto you, and have received your letter, by the which I have undrestand of the deth of my cousyn your fadre, whose soule Jesu assoile. I wol counsaile and exhorte you to take it as wel and as paciently as ye can, seeyng that we al be mortal and borne to dey. And where as ye desire to have a letter *ad colligendum*, after myne advise ye shal doo wel to be here with me at Michaelmas next commyng, and at your then commyng I shalbe glad to doo you the best confort and helpe that I can ; counsailing that ye in the meane tyme doo not entremedyll in any wise with th'admynystring of any parte of your faders goodes, nor with the receiving of his debtes, for divers causes, as at your comyng hudre ye shal knowe more.

The meane season, loke that ye be of as confortable chere as ye can, exhorting my lady, your modre in lawe,[2] to be in like wise, to whom I pray you to have me recommendyd. Thus fare ye hertily wel.

From London, the vj[th] day of Septembre.

        Your,   WILLIAM, ELECTE OF LONDON.

[1] [From Paston MSS., B.M.] The writer of this letter was William Warham, who was first Bishop of London, and afterwards Archbishop of Canterbury. According to the signature, he was Bishop-elect of London at the time it was written, but we are persuaded that it is a slip of the pen. He was elected Bishop of London in 1502, and was consecrated on the 5th October ; but it is clear from the preceding No. that Sir John Paston was alive as late as the beginning of February 1503. In the year 1503, however, Warham was translated to Canterbury. The bull for his translation was issued on the 29th November 1503, but doubtless he was elected some time before ; and it is quite intelligible how, being actually Bishop of London, he should have written 'Elect of London' in place of 'Elect of Canterbury.' Moreover, the allusion to the business of the administration agrees entirely with this supposition.

[2] Agnes, widow of John Hervey, Esq. of Thurley, Beds. *See* p. 166, Note 1.

170

HENRY VII

1076

JOHN KENDAL TO [WILLIAM PASTON ?][1]

1503,
or
later (?)

YOUR pore servaunt and bedeman, John Kendale, besecheth your good and gracious masterschepp, at the reverence of God and in the wey of charyte, to remembre that my maister your fader, on whos soule God have mercy, had fro me x. acres of free londe that I bout of the executours of Nicholas Pekeryng of Filby for xx. marc paid on j. day, to pay to executours of Edmonde Norman for purchase of ij. partes of Holm Halle, somtyme Edmonde Norman.

Also my seide maister, your fader, had fro John Kendale the croppe of the seide x. acres londe, sowen with barly and peson, wherof v. acres were weel somerlayde[2] to the seid barly, the whiche croppe the seide John Kendale schulde a made worth to hym iiij*li.* xiij*s.* iiij*d.*, althow ther had be but xx. quarteres barly growyng on viij. acres and half of londe, that is to seyn up on an acre ij. quarter, iiij. busshelz, and the half acre in avayle, besyde j. acre and an half of peson, for the seide John Kendale solde his malt at Ormesby mad of the barly growyng the same yer that the foreseid croppe was taken fro hym, for iiij*s.* viij*d.* a quartere ; and so he myght a solde the same and meche more if he had had it.

Also my seid maister, your fader, hath caused the foreseid John Kendale to a foreborne the ferme of the seide x. acres

[1] [From Paston MSS., B.M.] If this petition was addressed to any member of the Paston family, I should think it must have been William Paston, the son of the later Sir John. That would make the date at least as late as the year 1503, when his father died. If it was either of the two Sir Johns, 'my master your father' would be John Paston, Esquire, who died in 1466. But Nicholas Pickering of Filby is said to have been buried in the steeple of Filby church in the year 1466, and it is evident that 'my master your father' survived him more than nine years.

Edmund Norman, whose executors are here spoken of, died as far back as 1444. Blomefield says he was seised of two parts of the manor of Filby, but does not mention him as being also owner of two parts of Holm Hale. The two parts of Filby were afterwards held in trust by Sir John Fastolf ; but William Pickering and Cecily, his wife, were lords of the whole manor and settled it on John Paston, who released it to Nicholas Pickering in 1450.—Blomefield, xi. 218, 221.

[2] Kept fallow for some time previous to sowing.

171

THE PASTON LETTERS

1503, of londe be the space of ix. yer, be the yer xvj*s*. & viij*d*., that
or   is, the ferme of j. acre xx*d*., wherof the somme conteyneth
later (?) vij*li*. x*s*. beside j. yer receyved of Hagh.[1]

1077

ABSTRACT[2]

1504
DEC. 10 Receipt given by Thomas Bradbury, alderman of London, to William
Paston, Esq. of Norfolk, 10th Dec. 1504, for £5 in full payment of half a
year's rent.

1078

WILLIAM MAKEFYRR TO DARCY AND ALYNGTON[3]

*To the ryght worschypfull Master Roger Darsy and Master Gylys
Alyngton, beyng at the Jeorge, in Lumberd Strett, be thys
delyveryd in hast.*

1506
JAN. 17 RYGHT worschypfull masters, I recomend me un to you,
certifying you that the Kynges Grace and the Kyng
of Castyle mett this day at thre of the cloke, apon
Cleworth Greyn, ij. mylle owt of Wyndesower, and ther the
Kyng reseyvyd hym in the goodlyest maner that ever I sawe,
and ech of them enbracyd oder in armys.

To schew you the Kynges aparell of Yngland, thus it was :
—hys hors of bay, trappyd with nedyll warke ; a gown of purpuyr velvyt, a cheyn with a joerge of dyamondes, and a hood
of purpuyr velvyt, whych he put not of at the mettyng of the

[1] Here the MS. ends abruptly.
[2] [From Paston MSS., B.M.]
[3] [From Paston MSS., B.M.] This letter gives an account of the meeting of
Henry VII. and Philip, King of Castile, near Windsor, during the time when the
latter was detained in England in the beginning of the year 1506. It is well known
how after setting out from the Low Countries to take possession of his kingdom of
Castile, Philip met with a storm, and was driven to land on our coast, and how, on
hearing of it, Henry invited him to visit him at his Court, where he staid for some
time while the damage done to his fleet was being repaired.

172

HENRY VII

seyd Kyng of Castylle ; hys hatt and hys bonett he avalyd, 1506
and the Kyng of Castylle in cas lyke. And the Kyng of JAN.
Castyll rod apon [a] sorellyd hoby, whych the Kyng gave un
to hym ; hys apparell was all blak, a gown of blak velvytt, a
blak hood, a blak hatt, and hys hors harnes of blake velvytt.

To schew you of the Kynges company, my Lord Harry of
Stafforth[1] rod in a gown of cloth of tuyssew, tukkyd, furryd
with sabulles, a hatt of goldsmyth worke, and full of stons,
dyamondes, and rubys, rydyng apon a sorellyd courser bardyd
with a bayrd of goldsmythes wark, with rosys and draguns
red.

And my Lord Markas[2] rydyng apon a bald sorelyd hors,
with a deyp trapper full of long tassels of gold of Venys, and
apon the crowper of hys hors a whytt fedyr, with a cott apon
hys bak, the body goldsmyths wark, the slevys of cremysyne
velvyt, with letters of gold.

My Lord of Kent[3] apon a sorelyd hors, bald, the harnes of
Venys gold, with a deyp frynges of half zerd of lengh. My
Lord of Kent cott was on barr of cloth of gold, an oder of
cremysyn velvyt, pyrlyd with a demy manche cut of by the
elbowe. Thyes be the lords that bare the bruyt.

Sir Hew Waghan apon a bay hors trappyd with cremysyn
velvyt full of gylt bels, a gown of blak velvyt, and a cheyn of
gold, bawdryk wys, worth v. hondreth pownd.

Thys be the sperys : Master Sant John apon a blak hors,
withh arnes of cloth of gold with tasselles of plunkytt and
whytt, a cott of plunkytt and whytt, the body of goldsmyths
werk, the s[l]evys full of spanguls.

John Carr and William Parr cotts lyke, the horsys gray,
of Parr trappyd with cremysyn velvyt with tasselles of gold,
and bels gylt. Carr hors bay with an Almayn harnes of sylver,

[1] Henry, Earl of Stafford, eldest son and heir of Edward Stafford, Duke of
Buckingham, who was attainted and beheaded in 1521.
[2] Thomas Grey, Marquis of Dorset, was the son of Thomas, the late Marquis,
who was the son of Elizabeth, Queen of Edward IV. by her first husband, Sir John
Grey of Groby. This nobleman in the next reign became Lord of the Marches
between England and Scotland, which he stoutly kept and boldly maintained. He
died in 1530, 22 Hen. VIII.—F.
[3] George Gray, Earl of Kent, was a true soldier to, and a favourite of Henry, and
survived this pageant a very short time, dying within the year.—F.

173

THE PASTON LETTERS

1506 an ynch brod of betyn sylver, both the cottes of goldsmythes
JAN. 17 wark the bodys, the slevys on stryp of syllver, the oder gylt.
Edward Nevell apon a gray hors trappyd with blak velveyt
full of small belles, hys cott the on half of greyn velvyt, the
oder of whytt cloth of gold ; thyse to the rutters of the spers,
with oder dyvers well appontyd.

On the Kyng of Castylles party, the Lord Chamberlayn
cheyff, I can not tell hys name as yett ; hys apparell was sad,
and so was all the resydeu of hys company with clokes of sad
tawnye blake, gardyd, sum with velvyt and sum with sarsnyt,
not passyng a dosyn in nowmber. It is sayd ther is many by
hynd, wych cums with the Queyn of Castyll, wych schall cum
apon Teyusday.

When the Kyng rod forth to Wyndesouer Castyle, the
Kyng rode apon the ryght hand the Kynges of Castylle, how
be it the Kynges Grace offeryd hym to take hym apon the
ryght hand, the whych he refussyd. And at the lyghtyng the
Kyng of Castyle was of hys hors a good space or owr Kyng
was a lyght ; and then the Kynges Grace offeryd to take hym
by the arm, the whych he wold not, bot toke the Kyng by the
arme, and so went to the Kynges of Castylle chamber, whych
is the rychestly hangyd that ever I sawe ; vij. chambers to
geder hangyd with cloth of arras wroght with gold as thyk as
cowd be ; and as for iij. beds of astate, no kyng Crystyned can
schew sych iij.

Thys is as fer as I can schew you of this day, and when I
can know mor, ye schall have knowiege.

From Wyndesouer this Saterday, at v. of the cloke.

By yours,   WILLIAM MAKEFYRR.

174

HENRY VII

1079

AN INVENTORY[1]

James Gloys, j. dongge,[2]	.	.	.	iij*s*.
Item, a coverlete,	.	.	.	v*s*.
Item, ij. blankettes,	.	.	.	vj*s*. viij*d*.
Item, ij. pare of shettes,	.	.	.	x*s*.
Item, a sellore,[3]	.	.	.	xij*d*.
Item, a rosour, .	.	.	.	viij*d*.
Item, v. shertes,	.	.	.	viij*s*.
Item, j. roset cape,	.	.	.	iiij*d*.
Item, iiij. gownes,	.	.	.	xxvj*s*. viij*d*.
Item, a curt baron,	.	.	.	xl*d*.
Item, iij. gyrdylles,	.	.	.	vj*d*.
Item, ij. payre of hossen,	.	.	.	vj*s*.
Item, j. song boke, pris	.	.	.	xx*d*.
Item, j. dowbelet of fustian,	.	.	iij*s*.	iiij*d*.
Item, j. grene cotte,	.	.	.	ij*s*.
Item, ij. payre schone,	.	.	.	xiiij*d*.
Item, j. box with j. porse of cloth of gold,	.	.	xl*d*.
Item, j. crosse silver,	.	.	.	xl*d*.
Item, j. sawtere,	.	.	.	vj*s*. viij*d*.
Item, j. premere,	.	.	.	ij*s*.
Item, j. boke of statutis,	.	.	.	xl*d*.
Item, j. boke of *vitas Patrum*,	.	.	ij*s*.
Item, j. purs in the bedstraw with	.	.	xx*s*.
Item, j. boke of xij. chapetyrs of Lynccoln, and a boke of safistre,[4]	.	.	x*s*.
Item, vj. steyned paperis,	.	.	.	xij*d*.
Item, ij. schochenes,	.	.	.	viij*d*.

[1] [From Add. Charter 17,255, B.M.] This inventory might perhaps have been
inserted in the year 1474, after the death of James Gloys, with whose name it begins.
(*See* No. 857.) The year in which it was drawn up is, however, by no means certain,
as the articles seem to have belonged to many different owners ; and it may be conveniently referred to here at the end of our collection.
[2] A mattress.
[3] A bed canopy.
[4] Sophistry, *i.e.* dialectics.

THE PASTON LETTERS

Item, a swerd, pris,	vjs. viijd.
Item, a towayle,	xd.
Item, a *supersedyas* of Gloys, Osborn and Snallewell.	
Item, a bleu gown of William Tavernerys,	xs.
Item, a blake cloke,	vjs.
Item, a bottell for wine of a potell,	xijd.
Item, a peyre of tabille of horne and box,	xvjd.
Item, a confessionall,	ijs.
Herre Boll, a dongge,	xld.
Item, a traunsom,	ijs.
Item, a paire of schettis,	iiijs.
Item, a blanket,	iijs.
Item, a coverlet,	ijs.
Item, a pillow of down,	xijd.
Item, ij. curteynes,	ijs.
Item, gownes,	xs.
Item, a dowblet of fostian,	xld.
Item, iij. schertes,	vs.
Item, a towayle,	viijd.
Item, a blake hod,	ijs.
Item, ij. cofforys stuffet,	ijs.
Unde, j. was sprwys chyst with,	xxs.
Item, j. clasp of sylver,	xijd.
Item, of payse money,	xijd.
Item, ix. ferthynges,	ijd. ob.
Item, a lytyll chyst,	vjd.
Item, ij. pors with,	ijs. vjd. ob.
Item, iiij. rynges,	iijs.
Item, a box with bedys, qwere of ij. payre of jett, with Paternosterys of corall,	xld.
Item, a poyre of jett, pris,	xijd.
Item, v. payre of box,	xd.
Item, a payre of ambre,	xviijd.
Item, a purs of welwet,	viijd.
Item, iij. payre of knyffes,	xd.
Item, a payr of hernishede knyffes,	xijd.

HENRY VII

Item, v. napettes,	vd.
Item, iij. hedkercheffes, pris	xijd.
Item, a box with sylke and perryll,	iijs.
Item, a powche of rosset damaske,	xxd.
Item, a payre of gold weghtes in a case,	ijs.
Item, a broch of sylver with a crown,	xvjd.
Item, a payre of beddes of segamore,	iiijd.
Item, a box of tene with sylver wire.	
Item, iij. new gyrdyll, pris	ixd.
Item, in the second coffer was bokes, pris	xvjd.
Item, a boke of Seynt Thomas de *Veritatibus*, pris	xs.
Item, a red boke with Hugucio and Papie,	xxs.
Item, iij. bokes of soffistre,	xxd.
Item, maney other smale bokes,	xs.
Item, iij. cappis,	xd.
Item, a surplice,	xld.
Item, iij. letterys of pardon,	xs.
Item, a stevynyd[1] clothe, a crucifix,	xxd.
Item, a payre of dowbyll glovys, furredde with lambe,	vjd.
Item, ij. payr of hosson,	vs.
Item, a combe of veveri,[2]	vjd.
John Osborn, a cott of rosset, pris	iijs. iiijd.
Item, a stomaucher of a zerd of gode new hollond clothe,	xd.
Item, iiij. payre of sokkes, pris	viijd.
Item, ij. payre of lyncloys,	viijd.
Item, ij. payre of hosson,	iiijs.
Item, a payre of schone,	vjd.
Item, a payre schettes,	iiijs.
Item, iij. gyrdyll,	ixd.
Jamus Halmon, iiij. schettes,	xs.
Item, ij. schertis and a quarter of lynclothe,	ijs. vjd.

[1] Parti-coloured.   [2] Ivory.

THE PASTON LETTERS

Item, a pelow bere,	vja.
Item, ij. payre of sockes,	iijd.
Item, a gown furret with blake lom,	xs.
Item, a payre of cremessen hossen,	iijs.
Item, a payre spores, a pare of glovis,	xvjd.
Item, iij. gyrdyll,	ixd.
Item, a stomaker of lenclothe,	viijd.
Item, a payre of shone,	vjd.
Item, staffe, pris	iiijd.
Item, a sakke,	viijd.
Syngleton, a payr of bottes and a parre of sporis,	iijs. iiijd.
Item, a sadyll, a paytrell and a brydoll and ij. gerthis,	xs.
Item, a payre of dowbelet slevys of blake, }	
Item, a payre of slevys of rosset, }	iijs.
Item, a payr of stokes of fustian,	[viijd.][1]
Item, a pare of schone,	vjd.
Item, a schyrt,	xxd.
Item, a purs with	ijs.
Item, a gyrdyll, a payre of patanys,	iiijd.
Item, a dagar knyffe, pris	iiijd.
Katryn Wilton, a donge,	iijs. iiijd.
Item, a coverlet,	iijs. iiijd.
Item, a blanket,	iijs.
Item, a payr of shettes,	iiijs.
Item, a pelow of doun,	xijd.
Item, a payre of new hosson,	viijd.
Item, a gown and a kertyll,	vjs.
Item, a cors harnesshet with blake, pris	xxd.
Item, a hod,	iijs. iiijd.
Item, a kercher of lawn, pris	xxd.
Item, ij. kercher of therd,	xijd.
Item, a payre off bedys of ambre,	xxd.
Item, a new canvasse.	

[1] Struck through with the pen.

HENRY VII

Jane Belton, a blanket,	iijs. iiijd.
Item, a shette,	ijs.
Item, a kerchey therd, and ther in was vjs. viijd. of gold.	
Item, a payre of beydys of jette with Patter nosteris of corall, pris	xxd.
Item, a payre of turnerys of lawn,	xxd.
Item, a yerd of lynclothe,	viijd.
Item, a payre of hossen,	viijd.
Item, a smoke,	xxd.
Item, a kercher of thred,	viijd.
Symond Houston, a payre of bottes, a payre of sporis,	iiijs.
Purrey, a blw gown,	viijs.
Item, a bridull and a feterloke,	xvjd.
Item, a payr of hossen, a payr of schon,	ijs. vjd.
Item, a pare of furred glovys.	
Frere John Alderiche, ij. quaris of prayeris. Item, a powtenere with a payre of bedys of jette. Item, a scapelerey with an hodde,	vjs. viijd.
John Keduray, a payre of lynclothys, j. gown of blw,	vjs. viijd.
Item, a payre of hossen,	xxd.
Item, a payre of schone,	vijd.
Item, a payre of glovys and a hatt,	xijd.
Simond Sadiller, a payre of sporis,	xijd.
Item, a knyff hernyshid with sylver,	xijd.
Robert Fen, a gown,	vjs.
Item, a cappe,	iiijd.
Item, a peyre of hossen,	xvjd.
Item, a chart (?), pris	xvjd.

THE PASTON LETTERS

Richard Charlys, a peyr of hossen,	. .	xvj*d.*
Item, a dager, .	. . .	xvj*d.*
Item, a gyrdyll, .	. . .	ij*d.*
Item, a cappe of rosset,	. .	iiij*d.*
Jhon Faster, a horne,	. .	viij*d.*
John Judde, a chert, pris	. .	xvj*d.*
Item, a peyr of bedys of jett,	. .	viij*d.*
William Bemond, a custell, pris .	.	xvj*d.*
Item, a perre of bottes, pris	. ij*s.*	
Item, a peyre of glovys of otter.		
Water Wynter, a shert,	. .	xij*d.*
A dager, .	. . .	xij*d.*
A purs with	. . .	x*d.*
Sander Koke, a mourey gown,	. vj*s.*	
Item, a cotte of moster develers,[1]	.	xl*d.*
Item, a blanket, .	. iij*s.*	
Item, a peyre of shettes,	. iiij*s.*	
Item, iij. peyr of shoys,	. .	xx*d.*
Item, a peyr of sokkes,	. .	ij*d.*
Item, a hatt,	. .	xij*d.*
Item, a peyr of patanys, a cappe of violet, ⎫		
Item, iij. gyrdyll, and a cerchey [*kerchief*], ⎬		xij*d.*
Item, ij. of[2] of hossen, pris	. iij*s.*	
Snallewell, a schet, pris	. .	xx*d.*
Item, ij. shurtes, a peyr ofe lynclothis,	.	xx*d.*
Item, ij. dowbelettes, pris	. .	xl*d.*
Item, iij. gyrdyll, ij. cappes,	. .	xv*d.*
Item, ij. peyr of hossen,	. .	xl*d.*
Item, a lyneng to a gown, .	.	xx*d.*
Item, an hodde, .	. .	xl*d.*

[1] Grey woollen cloth. [2] So in MS.

180

THE PASTON LETTERS

Hadlegh

Item for horsmete there, .	. .	j*d.*
Item for brede and drynke there,	. .	j*d.*

Taderston

Item for horsmete there, .	. .	ij*d. ob.*
Item for Williamis dyner there, .	.	ij*d.*

Coylchestere

Item for horsmete there, .	. .	ix*d.*
Item for the sadelere, .	. .	iiij*d.*
Item payd to the smyth, .	. .	vij*d.*
Item for brede and drynke there,	.	ij*d.*

Wytham

Item for horsmete there, .	. .	j*d.*
Item for brede and drynke there,	.	j*d. ob.*

Chelmesford

Item for oure dyner there, .	. .	iiij*d*
Item for horsmete there,	. .	j*a.*

Brentwoae

Item for horsmete there,	. .	j*a.*
Item for brede and drynke there,	.	j*d. ob.*
Item for a dosyn poyntis, .	.	ij*d.*
Summa expens,	. . vs.	

Endorsed: Wykes.

182

HENRY VII

John Bube (?), ane hatt, pris	. .	x*d.*
Item, a bowe, pris	. . .	vj*d.*
Item, a peyr of bottes,	. .	*xvj*d.*
Item, a purs with	. . .	iiij*d.*
Item, a cappe, .	. .	iiij*d.*
Herry Gunnold, tablys and stolys, pris	. vs.	

1080

WYKES'S BILL[1]

Towardis my Lord of Oxford.

In primis at Brentwode for horsmete, .	.	ij*d.*

Chelmesford

Item for our dyner there, .	. .	iiij*d. ob.*
Item for horsmete there, .	. .	ij*d.*

Brambtre

Item for horsmete there, .	. .	j*d.*
Item for drynke there, .	. .	*ob.*

Hydyngham

Item for oure soper there, .	. .	iiij*d.*
Item for horsmete there, .	. .	iiij*d.*
Item for wayshyng of my shert and botes, .		j*d. ob.*

Laneham

Item for horsmete there, .	. .	j*d.*

[1] [Add. MS. 34,889, f. 231.] This bill of travelling expenses cannot be assigned to any particular year; but it would seem to be of the reign of Henry VII.

181

HENRY VII

1081

T. BALKEY TO JOHN PASTON[1]

To his ryght wurshipfull maister, John Paston, Esquier, this byll be delyverid in hast.

RYGHT wurshipfull and myne especyall good maister, I Da comaund me vonto your good maistership. Sir, it is unc so that there hath ben a gret rumour and mervelous ta noyse of yower departyng ffro Yermoth ; for summe seid that ye were departed in a Duch ship and some seid in aspaynessh ship and some seid in yower ship, and some seid ayein your wyll ye were departed ; of wych departyng my lord Steward hadde knowleche and comaunded a noon after your old servaunt Rychard Fitzwater to ryde to Norwich, and so to Yermoth, to knowe the trowth. And at Norwich I spoke with your seid servaunt, and ther he shewed vonto me that my lord hadde send another of his servauntis vonto my Lord of Oxynford to shew vonto his lordship of your departyng, &c., and fferthermore he shewed vonto me prevyly that my Lord hath imagyned and purposed many grevous thyngis ayens your Maistership ; for wych cawse he shewed wnto me that in any wyse your mastership shuld not come that wey, and I shall shewe your maistership moch more at your comyng, with the grace of God, whoo ever preserve your good maistership. At Norwich the Sonday next after Sent Marke.—Your servaunt, T. BALKEY.

[1] [Add. MS. 33,597, f. 10.] There is nothing in the rest of the Paston correspondence to throw any light upon this letter, either as to the date at which it was written, or as to the person addressed, whether it be John Paston the eldest or the younger of the two Johns, his sons.

183

THE PASTON LETTERS

1082

ANONYMOUS TO MASTER PASTON[1]

MAISTER PASTON, it is so that my Lord desireth to have his lyverey as for this yere to be of the colour that he hadde him self a demye gowne of, and his childern hadde of the same ayenst Cristmasse laste was; I wot never whether ye remembre it or nay. Yt was a medelled tawney, som what rede, and it was bought at Watkyn Stalworthes. I pray you assaye among the clothe makers in your countre howe a man may bye a cloth of them. Ye muste remembre the gentilmen muste have better than the yomen, and the yomen better than the gromes. And ye knowe well that ye and I the laste yere pourvoied my lord of the gentilmenes lyverey and the yomens for iijs. a yerde, one with a nother, and the gromes for ijs. viijd., and boughte all at the drapers in London. Wherfore my Lord woll thinke to be served of better clothe and lesse price at the clothe makers. I wolde have sente you an example but I can not gette it.

1083

ROBERT KYLLYGREWE TO RICHARD WASSE[2]

Thys letter be delyvyrde on to my fadyrynlav Rychard Wasse dewelly yn the parris of Morton.

WELLE belovyd fadyr, y recommende me on to you, and y thonke you of your gode cherre to me beyng vyt you laste, &c. Fadyr, hyt ysso asfor the promysse that ys by twyxt you and me, y hope to God to

[1] [Add. MS. 34,889, f. 148.] This letter contains a great many uncertainties. The writer is anonymous, the person addressed is by no means clear, and the lord referred to cannot be determined. Neither is there any means of arriving at an approximate date.
[2] [Add. MS. 34,889, f. 181.] It is difficult to connect this letter with the rest of the Paston correspondence, or to give any idea as to its date.

184

THE PASTON LETTERS

1084

MEMORANDUM[1]

Memorandum to speke with William Byrde be the same tokne, I came home from London to Norwich on Mydsomer evyn last past, and the same even I cam home to his howse, and brought hym xs. for a gyrdyll off myn that he had in his kepyng for a plegge off myn; and if so be that he wilnat ley out thes money, let hym send me the bill indentyd off my jowellys closyd in a letter with a signet off myn that my wiff hath in her keping.
Endorsed—Vyall.

1085-8

ABSTRACTS[2]

The following letters are probably all of the time of Henry VII. They are all addressed to a Mr. William Paston, but perhaps not all to the same person. The first two are apparently to William Paston, the brother of the two Sir Johns. The third is doubtful. The last may be to the son of the second Sir John.

1085.—John Wryght to Master William Paston at Hynnyngham.—Has received from him a bill with 3s. 6d., part payment of the cotton russet. 'The rest we shall drink when ye come to London.' Does not understand Paston's order for other 9 yards. Does he wish frieze, cotton or plain blanket?—London, St. Catherine's Even.

1086.—John Breton of Hadley to Master William Paston.—Desires him to be good master to the bearer, 'a poor kinsman of mine,' to whom my lord[3] has written sharply, that he may come before my lord for his answer.

1087.—Petyr Marham to his master, William Pastun.—Desires his advice, as Robert Gaunley, sometime his 'prentice, has taken an action against him at the common law.

1088.—William Ocley to Master William Paston.—Has spoken with young Wyndam in Master Digby's presence. He was grateful to Paston for his loving mind towards him, and said he would receive 'the two riall' himself, and buy no new gear till he knew the King's pleasure touching his pardon.—London, 3 Sept.

[1] [From Paston MSS., B.M.] I cannot tell by whom this memorandum was drawn up, nor do I know to what it refers. But as the MS. appears to belong to the Paston collection, and is of the period, I have not thought it right to omit it. The name 'Vyall' which is written on the back of the paper occurs in No. 756.
[2] [From Paston MSS., B.M.]   [3] The Earl of Oxford.

186

HENRY VII

contayne you of my promysse. So by that y am so lenge on y payde on to you, Fadyr, hyt ysso ye have y lefte me yn so grete a danger wyt the reparasyon of Wolston ande wythe Benet Barnarde that y am so lenge byhynde vyt you of my promys; nere the les y have sende you by Herry Penennec iiij. mark a fore Crystmas, ande the wederyng fyl so fowle a konnot go on to you. Fadyr, hyt yesso y have payde Benet Barnarde viij. marke for the fe that ye made on to hym, and more y moste pay hym for you, for he axyt of you yn holle xijli. wyt the fe, ande hys labor that a dyde for you yn London. For he sayt that ye nevyr payde hym of no fyne, nodyr for no odyr coste that a dyde for you wylle ye werre yn thys contray. Therfore y pray you to sende on to me a dyscharge for the sayde xijli., or ellys a wolle dystrayne me and put me to scharge an coste as a hath strayne my tenenttes byfore for thys mater and costys. For dermore Boryng hath take an accion yn the comyn law ayenst us bothe, entendyng to dryve us to a new particion, for a shewyth owre to tenentes to tempe ande meve them to cry fore a noder particion, ande to have suche as plesyth hym to hys reteyne; and therfore, but we have the better consayle hyt woll cost moch mony wyth owt dowt. Ther fore send me suche evydens as may dyscharge and save bothe you and me, wyche byth yn your hon dysposal; hyt hath coste me xls. for the accion that he hath take ayenst Tomas Snel and Wyllyam Snell, for bycause that T. Snell forbede[1] Bouryng ys tenents fro my wode yn Boter towne, which bythe alders. Your doctor [*daughter*] recommende hyr on to you and prayyt of your dayly blessyng, and sche hat a son, bleste by God. Namore to you at thys tymme. God have you yn Hys kepyng.—By your Son,
ROBERTE KYLLY GREWE.

[1] 'forbede' repeated in MS.

185

HENRY VII

NOTE TO NO. 1016.

As stated in the footnote at p. 101, since the above document was in type the Editor came upon a complete copy of this list of knights made at the battle of Stoke, which, being also more accurate than that in Leland's *Collectanea*, is here printed in full. It is apparently the original MS. of which No. 1016 is a mutilated copy, and is written on two flyleaves of the copy of Caxton's *Game and Play of Chess* in the King's Library in the British Museum.

The names of the banerettes made at the batell of Stoke by syde Newerke apon Trent, the xvj. day of June the ijde yer of Harry the vij.

Sir Gilbert Talbott.	Sir John Cheny.	Sir William Stoner.

Thes iij. wer made by fore the bataile, and after the bataile wer made the same day:—

Sir John of Arundell.	Sir James Blount.	Sir John Mortymer.
Sir Thomas Cookesay.	Sir Ric' of Croffte.	Sir William Troutbeke.'
Sir John Forteskew.	Sir Humfrey Stanley.	
Sir Edmond Benyngfeld.	Sir Ric' Delaber.	

Knyghtys made at the same bataile:—

Sir ——[1] Audeley, son and heyre of the Lord Audeley.	Sir William Tyrwytt.	Sir Edward Darell.
	Sir Ameas Paullett.	Sir Edward Pykeryng.
Sir Edward Norys.	Sir William Troutebeke.	Sir Thomas of Wolton.
Sir Robert Clyfford.	Sir Raff Langforthe.	Sir William Sandys.
Sir George Hopton.	Sir James Haryngton.	Sir Robert Brandon.
Sir Robert of Broughton.	Sir Harry Boulde.	Sir Thomas a Poole.
Sir John Paston.	Sir ——[2] Devenyshe.	Sir Morys Barkeley.
Sir Thomas Lovell.	Sir William Redmyll.	Sir Rauffe Shyrley.
Sir Humfrey Savage.	Sir Gregory Lovell.	Sir John Longvyll.
Sir Harry Wyloughby.	Sir Thomas Blount.	Sir William Lityiton.
Sir John Sabacotys.	Sir Robert Cheyny.	Sir William Norys of Lancas ...
Sir William Vampage.	Sir William Carew.	
Sir Antony Browne.	Sir John Wyndam.	Sir John Dygby.
Sir Ric' Poole.	Sir Roger Belyngam.	Sir Thomas Hansard.
Sir Thomas Terell.	Sir John a Mosgrave.	Sir Christoffre Wroughton.
Sir Ric' Lews.	Sir George Nevyll the bas[tard] of the Tour.[3]	Sir Thomas Lyne.
Sir Thomas Grey.		Sir Morys a Barow.
Sir Nycholas Vaux.	Sir Robert Ratcleff.	
Sir Edwarde of Borough.	Sir James Parker.	

[1] Blank in MS. Leland supplies the name as Sir James.
[2] Blank in MS. 'John' in Leland.
[3] 'The bastard of the Tour' looks as if it had been added by the same hand at a later date.

187

Witnesses—'Nich'o Priori de Bromholm, Rich. Jernemuth Monacho, Rich. Vicario Ecclesiæ de Paston prædicta, Johanne Kyng, capellano, Roberto Gynne, et aliis.'

Proved at Norwich, '2 Oct. An. Dom. supradicto.'

14[.]
JUN[.]

APPENDIX

WILLS

FROM the Principal Registry of the Court of Probate at Somerset House, and from the Diocesan Registers at Norwich. For the Memoranda of the latter I am indebted to the kindness of Dr. Jessopp.

I

CLEMENT PASTON[1]

WILL OF 'CLEMENS PASTON DE PASTON, sanæ mentis,' etc. (no style of Armiger or any other designation), A.D. 1419, June.

1419
JUNE

Leaves his soul to God, St. Margaret, and All Saints; his body to be buried in the parish church of St. Margaret at Paston, between the north door and the tomb of his wife Beatrix.

Legacies—(1) To the High Altar (sum not named); (2) To the Vicar of Paston for tithes, etc., 3s. 4d.; (3) For the lights 'Beatæ Margaretæ in cancella . . . coram ymagine Beatæ Margaretæ, vj li. cer.'; (4) 'Item, luminibus super le Rodelofte ejusdem ecclesiæ, xij d.'; (5) For the reparation, etc. of the church, 3s. 4d.; (6) To the Vicar of Bakton (as above), 2s.; (7) For the repair, etc. of the Trunch church, 8d.; (8) For the repair of Monslee church, 6d.; (9) 'Item, Priori et Conventui de Bromholm, vjs. viijd.

The residue to Martha, 'quæ fuit uxor Johannis Bakton, sorori meæ, et Willelmo Paston, filio meo,' that they may pay his debts, make restitution for any wrongs done, and expend the rest in works of charity and piety for the good of his own soul, that of Beatrix, his wife, the souls of his deceased parents and benefactors, 'et animabus fidelium defunctorum.'

[1] [Reg. Dioces. Norvic., Hyrning, f. 51, b.]

188

2

WILLIAM PASTON, THE JUDGE[1]

I.—[*Testament.*]

In Dei nomine Amen. Ego, Willelmus Paston de Paston, sanæ mentis et memoriæ, condo testamentum meum in hunc modum. In primis, lego animam meam Omnipotenti Deo, Beatæ Mariæ, et omnibus Sanctis, et corpus meum sepeliendum ad finem Australem altaris in Capella Beatæ Mariæ in fine Orientali ecclesiæ Cathedralis Sanctæ Trinitatis, Norwici. Et si contingat corpus meum ibidem sepeliri, lego cuilibet monacho sacerdoti ecclesiæ prædictæ qui singulis diebus aliqua septimana per septem annos proximo sequentes post mortem meam missam de Spiritu Sancto in capella prædicta tempore celebrationis summæ missæ in eadem ecclesia decantaverit, ad exorandum in eadem missa de Spiritu Sancto, et in aliis divinis per ipsum diebus illis factis, pro anima mea et animabus uxoris meæ, patrum, matrum et omnium consanguineorum et benefactorum nostrorum, et omnium quorum debitores sumus, et omnium per nos injuriam patientium, et eorum omnium pro quibus Deo est deprecandum et omnium fidelium defunctorum septem de nac' (?). Item, lego Roberto nunc priori ecclesiæ Sancti Andreæ de Bromholm quadraginta solidos; et cuilibet monacho ejusdem ecclesiæ conventus de Bromholm sex solidos et octo denarios; et executoribus testamenti Ricardi Causton, nuper vicarii ecclesiæ de Paston, viginti solidos; et executoribus testamenti Adæ, nuper vicarii ecclesiæ de Bakton, sex solidos et octo denarios; ita quod remittant et relaxent in conscientiis suis animabus prædictis si quæ per earum aliquam sibi debita fuerint. Et si hoc remittere et relaxare recusaverint, de prædictis legatis nihil habeant, sed in omnibus quæ sibi per animas prædictas vel earum aliquam deberi rationabiliter aut evidenter, in conscientia vel aliter, juxta discretionem executorum meorum, aut majoris partis eorundem, probaverint aut verificaverint, sibi satisfaciant executores mei. Residuum vero bonorum meorum omnium non legatorum do et lego Agneti uxori meæ, Johanni filio meo, Willelmo Bakton et Johanni Damme de Sustede, quos ordino et constituo executores hujus testamenti mei, ut ipsi inde disponant pro[ut] in justis conscientiis suis magis viderint Deo placere et animabus prædictis prodesse. In cujus rei testimonium præsentibus sigillum meum apposui. Datum decimo die Januarii anno regni Regis Henrici Sexti post Conquestum vicesimo secundo. Hujus autem testa-

144[.]
JAN[.]

[1] [Register Luffenam, 29.]

189

APPENDIX

1444
JAN. 10

menti mei venerabilem in Christo patrem et dominum, dominum Willelmum Lincolniensem Episcopum[1] ordino et constituo supervisorem.

II.—[*Last Will, 31 Jan. 1444.*][2]

Universis et singulis ad quos præsens scriptum indentatum pervenerit. Ego Willelmus Paston de Paston gratias, reverencias et honores. Cum diversæ personæ ad usum, proficuum et denominationem mea feoffatæ sive seisitæ existant sibi et hæredibus suis in feodo simplici in et de uno mesuagio, uno molendino, et certis terris, tenementis redditibus et serviciis cum pertinentiis in Paston, Bakton, Edithorp, Witton, et Moneslee, ac in aliis villis adjacentibus in comitatu Norffolk, quæ nuper fuerunt Clementis Paston, patris mei jam defuncti, cujus animæ propitietur Deus; ac de certis terris et tenementis, parcellis manerii vocati Latymers, remanentibus ultra et præter alia terras et tenementa parcellas dicti manerii nomine meo adiu[3] est dat' Priori et conventui ecclesiæ Sancti Andreæ de Bromholm et successoribus suis; quam perquisitionem prædicti prioris dominus Rex nunc per literas suas perdonavit; et uno tofto et uno columbari et aliis terris et tenementis cum pertinentiis in Bakton, Paston, Edithorp, Witton, et Casewik quæ nuper fuerunt Hugonis atte Fen de Jernemouthe; et de aliis terris et tenementis in Paston et Bakton per prædictos priorem et conventum mihi et aliis ad usum meum et hæredibus meis datis et concessis; et de et in uno mesuagio et certis terris, tenementis, redditibus, et serviciis cum pertinentiis in Estsomerton, Westsomerton, He[nnesby?], Martham, Wynterton in Flegge, ac in aliis villis adjacentibus, et in Heigham Porter, Veteri Bokenham et Bokenham Castell, in eodem comitatu, tam illa quæ . . . . . . [quam] illa quæ nuper fuerunt Galfridi Somerton, avunculi mei, videlicet fratris Beatricis, matris meæ carissimæ jam defunctæ, quæ . . . . Et in et de manerio de Oxenede, ac certis terris, tenementis et serviciis in Oxenede, Burgh, Skeyton, Marsham . . . . [et in] aliis villis adjacentibus cum pertinentiis in eodem comitatu, quæ nuper fuerunt Roberti Salle militis, et Willelmi Clopton militis, firmarii (?) . . . . . sive aliquorum vel alicujus eorum in eodem comitatu: Et in et de maneriis de Marlyngford, Riston, Vaux, et Shipd[am] . . . . medietate quatuor marcatarum, sive medietate unius marisci nuper Thomæ Ocam (?) [cum pertinentiis] in eodem comitatu . . . . mesuagiis, ac certis terris, tenementis, redditibus et serviciis cum pertinentiis in Estodenham et aliis v[illis] . . . . in eodem comitatu . . . . . . Honyngham: Et in et de uno mesuagio ac certis terris et tenementis, redditibus et serviciis . . . . . . in Wy . . . . in comitatu prædicto quæ nuper

[1] William Alnwick, Bishop of Lincoln from 1436 to 1449. He had been Bishop of Norwich before he was presented to Lincoln.

[2] [The ink in some parts of this document is so very much faded that about half of each line is almost or quite illegible.]

[3] So in MS.

190

THE PASTON LETTERS

fuerunt Willelmi Thuxton, Armigeri, vocata Tolyes: Et . . . . . .

Ricardi Doket in Carleton et aliis villis adjacentibus: Et in et de duobus . . . . . villis adjacentibus: Et in et de una pecia terræ in Carleton vocata W . . . .

manerio de Snaylwell et aliis terris et tenementis quæ quondam fuerunt Johannis . . . . de Ac in et de manerio de Stanstede cum pertinentiis in comitatu Suffolk, et de Horwelbury continue absque aliqua conditione collusione seu covina, istis tamen . . . . mesuagiis, terris, tenementis, redditibus et serviciis prædictis ultimo . . . . conscientia mea, lege Dei et Angliæ illæsa, fieri et exequi et adimpleri . . . . Sciatis me, præfatum Willelmum Paston, ultimam voluntatem de præmissis . . . . . ligenti deliberacione declarasse, fecisse et limitasse juxta effectum verborum sequentium . . . . seu seisitæ et omnes aliæ personæ quas in prædictis maneriis, terris et tenementis vel aliqua parcella eorum ad . . . . imposterum feoffari contigerit, hæredes et assignati sui, quandocumque post mortem meam . . . . ejus sufficiens warantum in hac parte habentibus racionabiliter requisitæ fuerint per cartas . . . . dum . . . . . . præfatæ Agneti prædicta maneria de Oxenede, Marlyngforde, Stanstede, Horwelbury, et Sh . . . . dictas pa . . . . . . de Latymers dictis priori et conventui minime datas, et prædicta mesuagia, molendinum, terras et tenementa, quæ fuerunt prædicti prioris et conventus, Roberti Salle, Willelmi Clopton, Francisæ, Clementis Paston, Hugonis atte Fen, seu alicujus eorum, ac medietatem prædictorum marisci et quatuor marcatorum redditus, in toto, per communem æstimationem, ad valenciam centum librarum per annum; habenda et tenenda eidem Agneti et assignatis suis ad totam vitam ejusdem Agnetis: Ita quod eadem maneria de Oxenede, Marlyngforde, Stanstede et Horwelbury, et terræ et tenementa quæ fuerunt Roberti Salle, Willelmi Clopton et Francisæ, seu alicujus eorum, cum pertinentiis, post mortem præfatæ Agnetis remaneant hæredibus de corpore meo et corpore prædictæ Agnetis exeuntibus. Et prædicta manerium de Shipdene et parcella manerii de Latymers, ac dicta mesuagia, molendinum, terræ et tenementa nuper Clementis Paston et Hugonis atte Fen, seu alicujus eorum, cum pertinentiis, post mortem prædictæ Agnetis, feoffandas, hæredes et assignatos suos revertantur, ad perficiendum inde hanc ultimam voluntatem meam? Et si nullus extiterit hæres de corpore meo et corpore prædictæ Agnetis exiens, quod tunc post mortem ejusdem Agnetis prædictum manerium de Oxenede et dictæ terræ et tenementa nuper prædictorum Roberti Salle, Willelmi Clopton et Francisæ, seu unius eorum, cum pertinentiis, ad prædictos feoffatos et hæredes suos similiter revertantur, ad

144[.]
JAN[.]

191

VOL 6

APPENDIX

444 perficiendam inde hanc ultimam voluntatem meam. Et quod prædicta maneria
N. 10 de Marlyngford, Stanstede et Horwelbury, cum pertinentiis, remaneant rectis hæredibus Edmundi Barry militis, patris prædictæ Agnetis, imperpetuum. Item, volo quod prædictæ personæ, ut prædicitur, feoffatæ seu feoffandæ, hæredes seu assignati sui, paciantur et permittant Robertum Clere, armigerum, Edmundum Clere, armigerum, Johannem Pagrave, armigerum, Willelmum Bakton de Bakton, et Johannem Damme de Sustede, vel duos eorum, per communem assensum eorum quinque, prædictum manerium de Snaylwell et prædicta alia terras et tenementa in Snaylwell, in toto, per communen estimacionem, ad valenciam quadraginta marcarum per annum, occupare, et exitus et proficua inde percipere et habere, a festo Sancti Michaelis proximo sequenti post mortem meam usque Edmundus filius meus jam ætatis xviij. annorum pervenerit ad ætatem xxj. annorum. Et quod iidem Robertus Clere, Edmundus Clere, Johannes Pagrave, Willelmus Bakton et Johannes Damme, seu dicti duo eorum, viginti marcas annuatim provenientes de eisdem exitibus et proficuis, inter prædictum festum Sancti Michaelis et dictam ætatem prædicti Edmundi, filii mei, per commune avisamentum et assensum suum et prædictæ Agnetis, annuatim distribuant in elemosinis inter notos, pauperes et debiles, tam hospicia tenentes quam alios qui non vadunt mendicatum, et pro missis, sacerdotum oracionibus, et suffragiis devotorum pauperum utriusque sexus, tam religiosorum quam aliorum, celebrandis et fiendis, pro anima mea et prædictæ Agnetis, et animabus patrum et matrum nostrorum, et omnium consanguineorum et benefactorum nostrorum, et omnium quorum debitores sumus, et omnium per nos injuriam patientium, et eorum omnium pro quibus Deo est deprecandum, et omnium fidelium defunctorum; et de eisdem exitibus et proficuis prædicto Edmundo, filio meo quousque ad dictam ætatem xxj. annorum pervenerit, rationabiles victum, vestitum, apparatum et sustentationem, juxta gradus sui exigenciam, sic quod non superbiat, inveniant, et eum tam ad artis dialecticæ per dimidium annum, juris civilis per unum annum, ac juris regni Angliæ postea ad sufficienciam, si fieri poterit, sub sana tutela providenter ponant, et ipsum in eisdem continuare et residere faciant, prout eisdem melius visum fuerit ipsum Edmundum in hac parte sapere et intelligere et sibi in futurum prodesse; et domos, muros, ædificia, et clausuras in eodem manerio nostro existentia rationabiliter reparari faciant, et redditus et servicia et alia onera inde debita solvant, et hoc quod de eisdem exitibus et proficuis ad dictum ætatem dicti Edmundi remanserit juxta sanas conscientias suas eidem Edmundo satisfaciant tempore quo ipse juxta hanc voluntatem meam statum de eodem manerio receperit et habuerit. Item, volo quod prædictæ personæ, prout prædicitur, feoffatæ seu f[eoffandæ], hæredes seu assignati sui, paciantur et permittant prædictos Robertum Clere, Edmundum Clere, Johannem Pagrave, Willelmum Bakton et Johannem Damme, vel duos eorum per communem assensum eorum quinque, prædictum manerium de Beauchamp et Hollewelhalle et dicta alia mesuagia, terras, tenementa, tofta, clausuras, redditus et servicia, quondam Ricardi Doket, Willelmi Thuxton, Johannis Patgris senioris, Johannis Whynne et Eustachii Rows, seu aliquorum vel alicujus eorum, in Wymondham, Carleton, Bonnewell, Estodenham, et aliis villis adjacentibus, per communem estimacionem ad valenciam xxv. marcarum per annum occupare, et exitus et proficua inde percipere

192

THE PASTON LETTERS

et habere, a prædicto festo Sancti Michaelis usque Willelmus filius meus, jam ætatis vij. annorum, pervenerit ad ætatem xviij. annorum; et quod iidem Robertus Clere, Edmundus Clere, Johannes Pagrave, Willelmus Bakton et Johannes Damme, vel dicti duo eorum, quinque marcas annuatim provenientes de eisdem exitibus per octo annos proximo sequentes prædictum festum Sancti Michaelis, per discretionem et avisamentum sua et prædictæ Agnetis, annuatim distribuant inter pauperes et debiles prædictos et [pro][1] missis, orationibus et suffragiis celebrandis et . . . . in forma prædicta, et de eisdem exitibus et proficuis prædicto Willelmo filio meo usque ad dictam ætatem xviij. annorum pervenerit . . . . statum et sustentacionem juxta gradus sui exigenciam, sic quod non superbiat, inveniant et tribuant, et . . . . . . ad scholas ponant et ibidem continuare et residere faciant prout prædicitur de prædicto filio meo Edmundo, et domos, muros et clausuras et ædificia in dict. . . . . et tenementis . . . repararent, et redditus et servicia et alia onera inde solvant, et de residuo dictorum exituum et proficuorum dicto Willelmo filio meo satisfaciant . . . . statum de eisdem manerio, terris et tenementis juxta hanc voluntatem meam . . . . hæredes seu assignati sui paciantur et permittant prædictam Agnetem . . . . prædicta mesuagia, terras [et] tenementa in Est Somerton, West Somerton, Hennesby, Martham, et Wynterton, tam illa quæ fuerunt . . . . quam illa quæ . . . . de Reston in toto per communem æstimacionem ad valenciam xxv. marcarum . . . . occupare, et exitus et [proficua ?] inde percipere et gaudere a prædicto festo Sancti Michaelis usque Clemens filius meus . . . . xviij. annorum; et quod eadem Agnes de eisdem exitibus et proficuis prædicto Clementi Paston . . . . ad dictam ætatem xviij. annorum, et Elizabeth filiæ meæ quousque maritetur, racionabiles victum, vestitum, ... exigenciam, sic quod non superbiant, et de eisdem exitibus et proficuis nutriatur honeste . . . . filiam, prædictam Elizabetham, prout statui suo convenit, ac inveniat et ponat prædictum Clementem, filium meum, tam ad scholas grammaticales quam alias et cæteras erudiciones, prout prædicitur de prædictis fratribus suis; et domos, muros, clausuras, et ædificia in eisdem mesuagio, terris et tenementis existentia, racionabiliter reparari faciat, et redditus et servicia et alia onera inde debita solvat, ac annuatim quousque dictus Clemens, filius meus, ad dictam ætatem xviij. annorum [pervenerit ?][1] distribuat manu propria in elemosinis, juxta discretionem suam, inter magis pauperes et debiles creaturas, in honore Quinque principalium Vulnerum et Passionis Domini nostri Jesu Christi, et Quinque Gaudiorum Beatæ Mariæ Virginis et Matris ejus, pro animabus prædictis, quinque marcas; et de hoc quod de eisdem exitibus et proficuis ad dictam ætatem prædicti Clementis, filii mei, remanserit, satisfaciat eadem Agnes juxta 1444
JAN. 10

[1] Omitted in MS.

VOL. VI.—N 193

THE PASTON LETTERS

444 sanam conscienciam suam eidem Clementi tempore quo ipse juxta hanc volun-
N. 10 tatem meam statum de eisdem manerio, mesuagiis, terris, et tenementis, de prædictis personis feoffatis sive feoffandis receperit; et quod dictæ personæ feoffatæ seu feoffandæ, hæredes, seu assignati sui, infra xl. dies proximo sequentes postquam ipsi post festum Sancti Michaelis proximo post mortem meam per Johannem Paston, filium meum primogenitum, racionabiliter fuerint requisiti, per facta sua tripartita et indentata, dimittent, liberent et assignent prædicto Johanni Paston, jam ætatis xx. annorum et amplius, prædictum manerium de Gresham cum pertinentiis, habendum eidem Johanni ad totam vitam suam; Ita quod si contingat prædictum Johannem Paston aliquem exitum vel hæredem de corpore Margaretæ nunc uxoris suæ procreare, quod tunc idem manerium cum pertinentiis post mortem ejusdem Johannis remaneat dictæ uxori suæ, tenendum sibi ad terminum vitæ ejusdem uxoris. Et si prædictus Johannes Paston nullum exitum vel hæredem de corpore dictæ uxoris suæ procreaverit, tunc immediate post mortem ejusdem Johannis idem manerium cum pertinentiis hæredibus masculis de corpore meo exeuntibus integre remaneat. Et si nullus fuerit hæres masculus de corpore meo exiens, quod tunc idem manerium cum pertinentiis integre remaneat prædictæ Agneti, uxori meæ, habendum et tenendum eidem Agneti ad totam vitam ejusdem Agnetis; Ita quod tunc post ejusdem Agnetis mortem idem manerium cum pertinentiis ad prædictos donatores et hæredes suos revertatur, ad exequendum et perficiendum inde hanc voluntatem meam. Et quod eædem personæ feoffatæ seu feoffandæ, hæredes seu assignati sui, infra xl. dies proximo sequentes postquam ipsi, post festum Sancti Michaelis proximo post mortem meam, et postquam prædictus Edmundus, filius meus, fuerit ætatis xxj. annorum plenarie completorum, racionabiliter fuerint requisitæ, per consimilia facta dimittant, liberent et assignent prædicto Edmundo, filio meo, prædictum manerium de Snaylwell, et prædicta terras et tenementa nuper Johannis Langham de Snaylwell, in Snaylwell, ac dictam reversionem manerii de Shipdene et prædictarum parcellarum manerii de Latymers, dictis priori et conventui minime data,[1] ac dictorum mesuag', molendini, terrarum et tenementorum quæ fuerunt prædictorum prioris et conventus, ac Clementis, patris mei, et Hugonis atte Fen, aut unius eorum, post mortem prædictæ Agnetis, habenda et tenenda eidem Edmundo et hæredibus masculis de corpore ipsius Edmundi exeuntibus. Et si contingat ipsum Edmundum sine hærede masculo de corpore suo exeunte obire, quod tunc eadem manerium, terræ, tenementa et reversio cum pertinentiis hæredibus de corpore ejusdem Edmundi exeuntibus remaneant. Et si nullus fuerit hæres de corpore prædicti Edmundi exiens, quod tunc eadem manerium, terræ, tenementa et reversio remaneant hæredibus de corpore meo exeuntibus. Et si nullus fuerit hæres de corpore meo exiens, quod tunc prædicta reversio ad predictos donatores et hæredes suos revertatur, et prædictum manerium de Snaylwell, terræ et tenementa, cum pertinentiis, remaneant prædictæ Agneti ad totam vitam suam. Ita quod, post ejus mortem, idem manerium cum pertinentiis ad prædictos donatores et hæredes suos similiter revertatur, ad perficiendum et perimplendum hanc voluntatem meam. Et quod eædem personæ feoffatæ seu feoffandæ, hæredes seu assignati sui, infra xl. dies proximo sequentes post festum Sancti

[1] Sic in origine.

194

APPENDIX

Michaelis proximo post mortem meam, et postquam prædictus Willelmus filius meus fuerit ætatis xviij. annorum plenarie completorum, racionabiliter fuerint requisitæ, per consimilia facta dimittant, et liberent et assignent prædicto Willelmo filio meo, prædicta maneria de Hollewelhalle et Beauchamp, et dicta mesuagia, terras et tenementa, redditus et servicia nuper Willelmi Thuxston Armigeri, Ricardi Doket, Eustachii Rows et Johannis Patgrys, seu unius eorum, in Estodenham, Wymondeham, Carleton, Bonewell, et aliis villis adjacentibus, habenda et tenenda eidem Willelmo et hæredibus de corpore suo exeuntibus. Et si contingat ipsum Willelmum sine hærede de corpore suo exeunte obire, quod tunc eadem maneria, terræ, tenementa, redditus et servicia, cum pertinentiis, remaneant Clementi Paston, filio meo, et hæredibus de corpore suo exeuntibus. Et si idem Clemens obierit sine hærede de corpore suo exeunte, eadem maneria, terræ, tenementa, redditus et servicia cum pertinentiis remaneant dictæ Agneti ad totam vitam suam. Ita quod post ejus mortem eadem maneria, terræ et tenementa cum pertinentiis ad præfatos donatores et hæredes suos revertantur, ad implendum et perficiendum inde hanc voluntatem meam. Et quod prædictæ personæ [feoffatæ] seu feoffandæ infra quadraginta dies proximo sequentes post festum Sancti Michaelis postquam prædictus Clemens filius meus post mortem meam fuerit ætatis xviij. annorum plenarie completorum racionabiliter fuerint requisitæ per consimilia facta dimittant, liberant et assignent prædicto Clementi filio meo prædictum manerium de Ryston, et prædicto mesuagia, terras, tenementa, redditus et servicia cum pertinentiis in Est Somerton, West Somerton, et aliis villis adjacentibus et in Heigham Potter, Bokenham et Bokenham Castell, habenda et tenenda eidem Clementi filio meo et hæredibus de corpore suo exeuntibus. Et si contingat ipsum Clementum filium meum obire sine hærede de corpore suo exeunte, quod tunc eadem manerium, mesuagia, terræ, tenementa, redditus et servicia remaneant prædicto Willelmo, filio meo et hæredibus de corpore suo exeuntibus. Et si contingat ipsum Willelmum sine hærede de corpore suo exeunte obire, quod tunc eadem manerium, mesuagia, terræ, tenementa, redditus et servicia cum pertinentiis remaneant hæredibus de corpore meo exeuntibus. Et si nullus fuerit de corpore meo exiens, quod tunc eadem manerium, mesuagia terræ et tenementa cum pertinentiis remaneant prædictæ Agneti, tenenda sibi ad totam vitam suam. Ita quod eadem manerium, mesuagia, terræ et tenementa, cum pertinentiis, post mortem prædictæ Agnetis, ad prædictos donatores et hæredes suos revertantur ad perficiendum inde hanc voluntatem meam. Item ad amorem et favorem inter prædictos Johannem, Edmundum, Willelmum, et Clementem filios meos et prædictam Elizabeth et præfatos hæredes suos, eorumque mutuam caritatem hinc inde nutriendum (?) et amplificandum, volo et ordino per præsentes quod si aliqua terræ seu tenementa, sibi aut eorum alicui, per prædictas personas feoffatas seu feoffandas vel eorum hæredes vel assignatos in forma prædicta per dona et concessiones, immediate, in feodo talliato seu alio statu, per remanere aut alio quovis modo, danda seu concedenda, versus prædictos Johannem, Edmundum, Willelmum et Clementem, filios meos, et prædictam Elizabeth aut hæredes suos prædictos absque culpa recuperentur, vel aliqua inde parcella recuperetur, vel status eorum inde adnihiletur, quod infra unum annum proximo tunc sequentem residui eorum de porcionibus suis terrarum et tenementorum prædictorum, ut prædicitur, sibi dandorum et 1444
JAN. 10

195

1444 JAN. 10 concessorum, juxta ratam annui valoris earundem portionum suarum, debitam faciant recompensacionem cæteris eorum de quorum porcionibus dictas recuperaciones vel status adnihilaciones fieri contigerit. Ita quod onus perdicionis in hac parte, si quod evenerit inter ipsos juxta ratam annui valoris portionum suarum uniformis sit et æqualis. Item, ad finem quod iste articulus præsentis voluntatis meæ proximo præcedens per prædictos Johannem, Edmundum, Willelmum et Clementem, filios meos, ac prædictam Elizabetham et hæredes suos prædictos sufficiencius et plenius exequatur, et quod dicta dona et concessiones immediate vel per remanere in feodo talliato vel alio statu, ut prædicitur, sibi faciendo per eorum facta, feoffamenta, cartas, scripta, vel alio modo non discontinuarentur, volo et ordino quod prædictæ personæ feoffatæ seu feoffandæ eorum hæredes et assignati, antequam ipsi aliquem statum de prædictis terris et tenementis aut parcella inde prædictis Johanni, Edmundo, Willelmo et Clementi, filiis meis, et prædictæ Elizabeth et hæredibus suis prædictis, seu eorum alicui, faciant, per scriptum suum indentatum dent et concedant prædicto Edmundo, filio meo, unum annuum redditum triginta librarum legalis monetæ, habendum et percipiendum eidem Edmundo et hæredibus suis masculis de corpore suo exeuntibus de prædicto manerio de Gresham ad festa Paschæ et Sancti Michaelis æquis portionibus, una cum sufficienti clausula districtionis in dicto manerio fiendæ pro non solucione ejusdem annui redditus sub forma et condicionibus subsequentibus: videlicet, quod prædictus annuus redditus sit et remaneat in suspenso et non levetur, solvatur, nec percipiatur quovismodo, quousque dictus Johannes Paston vel aliquis hæres suus masculus de corpore suo exiens aliquod donum sive concessionem, immediate vel per remanere, in feodo talliato vel alio statu, de manerio prædicto cum pertinentiis eidem Johanni fiendum, per factum, feoffamentum, cartam vel scriptum, seu alio modo, in parte vel toto, discontinuaverit seu discontinuari fecerit, vel quousque prædictus Johannes Paston, vel aliquis hæres suus masculus de corpore suo exiens, prædictum articulum præsentis voluntatis meæ sic incipiendum 'Item ad amorem et favorem,' &c. in aliqua ex parte sua perimplendo infregerit, non perfecerit, vel non observaverit, vel sic tam omnibus et singulis quibus aliquod donum sive concessio, immediate vel per remanere, in feodo talliato vel in aliquo alio statu, de prædicto manerio cum pertinentiis dicto Johanni Paston vel alicui hæredum de corpore suo exeuntium per prædictas personas feoffatas seu feoffandas, hæredes seu assignatos suos, in forma prædicta fiendum per prædictum Johannem Paston vel aliquem hæredum suorum prædictorum discontinuatum fuerit non legitime recontinuatum, quam omnibus et singulis annis quibus articulus prædictus præsentis voluntatis meæ sic incipiens 'Item ad amorem et favorem,' &c. per prædictum Johannem Paston vel aliquem hæredum suorum prædictorum in aliquo ex parte sua perimplendo confractus, non tentus, aut non impletus, fuerit non debite reformatus. Et per consimile factum suum indentatum dent et concedant prædicto Willelmo filio meo unum annuum redditum triginta librarum consimilis monetæ habendum et percipiendum annuatim prædicto Willelmo et hæredibus suis de corpore suo exeuntibus a tempore quo prædictus Johannes filius meus mortuus fuerit sine hærede masculo de tempore [1] suo exeunte de prædicto manerio de Gresham cum pertinentiis ad

[1] So in MS.

festa prædicta æquis portionibus, una cum sufficienti clausula districtionis in eodem manerio fiendæ pro non solutione ejusdem annui redditus sub forma et conditionibus sequentibus, videlicet, quod idem annuus redditus sit et remaneat in suspenso et non levetur nec solvatur, aut percipiatur quovismodo quousque prædictus Johannes Paston, vel Edmundus Paston, vel aliquis hæres masculus de corpore alicujus eorum exiens, aliquod donum sive concessionem, immediate vel per remanere, in feodo talliato vel in alio statu, de eodem manerio cum pertinentiis, aut parcella inde, eidem Johanni vel Edmundo fiendum, per factum, feoffamentum, cartam, vel scriptum, seu alio modo, in parte aut toto, discontinuaverit seu discontinuari fecerit, vel quousque aliquis eorum prædictum articulum præsentis voluntatis meæ sic incipientum 'Item ad amorem et favorem,' &c. in aliquo ex parte sua perimplendo infregerit, non perfecerit, vel non observaverit. Et per consimile factum suum indentatum dent et concedant prædicto Clementi, filio meo, unum annuum redditum triginta librarum consimilis monetæ, habendum et annuatim percipiendum prædicto Clementi, filio meo, et hæredibus de corpore suo exeuntibus a tempore quo uterque prædictorum Johannis Paston et Edmundus (*sic*) Paston mortuus fuerit sine hærede masculo de corpore suo exeunte de prædicto manerio [1] de Gresham ad festa prædicta æquis porcionibus, una cum clausula districtionis in forma prædicta, sub forma et condicionibus subsequentibus, videlicet, quod idem annuus redditus sit et remaneat in suspenso, et non levetur, solvatur nec percipiatur quovismodo, quousque prædictus Johannes Paston, vel prædictus Edmundus Paston, vel aliquis masculus de corpore alicujus eorum exiens, vel prædictus Willelmus Paston, filius meus, vel aliquis hæres de corpore suo exiens, aliquod donum sive concessionem, immediate vel per remanere, [2] in feodo talliato vel alio statu, dicto Johanni Paston, Edmundo Paston, vel Willelmo Paston, filiis meis, vel eorum alicui fiendum per feoffamentum, cartam vel scriptum, seu alio modo, in parte aut toto discontinuaverit, seu discontinuari fecerit, vel quousque aliquis eorum prædictum articulum præsentis voluntatis meæ sic incipientem 'Item ad amorem,' &c. in aliquo ex parte sua perimplendo infregerit, non fecerit, vel non observaverit. Et per consimile factum suum indentatum dent et concedant prædictæ Elizabeth unum annuum redditum triginta librarum consimilis monetæ, habendum et percipiendum eidem Elizabeth et hæredibus de corpore suo exeuntibus a tempore quo uterque prædictorum Johannis et Edmundi filiorum meorum mortuus erit sine hærede masculo de corpore suo exeunte, et uterque prædictorum Willelmi et Clementis, filiorum meorum, mortuus fuerit sine hærede de corpore suo exeunte de prædicto manerio de Gresham ad festa prædicta æquis porcionibus, una cum clausula districtionis in forma prædicta, forma et condicionibus subsequentibus, videlicet, quod idem annuus redditus sit et remaneat in suspenso et non levetur, solvatur, nec percipiatur quovismodo, quousque prædictus Johannes Paston aut prædictus Edmundus Paston, vel aliquis hæres masculus de corpore alicujus eorum exiens, vel quousque prædictus Willelmus Paston seu prædictus Clemens, filii mei, vel aliquis hæres de corpore alicujus eorum exiens . . . . . . sive concessionem, immediate vel per remanere, in feodo talliato vel

[1] *de prædicto manerio.* These words are repeated in the MS.
[2] *vel per remanere*, repeated in MS.

1444 JAN. 10 alio statu, dictis Johanni Paston, Edmundo Paston, Willelmo Paston, et (?) Clementi Paston, vel alicui eorum, fiendum, per factum, feoffamentum, cartam vel scriptum, seu alio modo, in parte aut toto . . . . manerio . . . . . discontinuari fecerit, vel quousque aliquis eorum prædictum articulum præsentis voluntatis meæ sic incipientem 'Item ad amorem,' &c. in aliquo ex parte sua perimplendo infregerit, non perfecerit, vel non observaverit. Item, volo quod [si ?] aliquis prædictorum Johannis, Edmundi, Willelmi, et Clementis, filiorum meorum, ante dictam ætatem suam xviij. annorum obierit, quod tunc prædictæ personæ feoffatæ seu feoffandæ, eorum hæredes et assignati, patiantur et permittant prædictos Robertum Clere, Edmundum Clere, Johannem [Pagrave], Willelmum Bakton, et Johannem Damme, vel duos eorum per communem assensum eorum quinque, prædictam porcionem terrarum et tenementorum prædicto sic obeunti, ut prædictum est, dandam et concedendam occupare et exitus et proficua inde percipere et habere quousque illi qui proxime post mortem dicti sic obeuntis juxta effectum præsentis voluntatis dictam portionem haberet et teneret fuerit ætatis xviij. annorum plene completorum, et tunc infra quadraginta dies proximo tunc sequentes postquam racionabiliter fuerint requisiti, per scripta sua indentata dimittant, liberent, et assignent eandem porcionem cum pertinentiis ipsi qui, ut prædicitur, tunc juxta hanc voluntatem meam porcionem illam haberet et teneret, habendam et tenendam sibi in forma prædicta. Et si prædicti Robertus Clere, Edmundus Clere, Johannes Pagrave, Willelmus Bakton, et Johannes Damme, vel dicti duo eorum eadem exitus et proficua disponant et distribuant in solucione debitorum quæ me debere contingat, et reformacione et satisfactione mesprisionum et extortionum, si quas fecerim, et pro animabus prædictis in forma prædicta per discretionem prædictæ Agnetis et executorum meorum. Item, volo quod prædicta Elizabeth filia mea habeat ducentas libras legalis monetæ ad maritagium suum si ipsa per avisamentum prædictæ Agnetis et executorum meorum maritetur. Proviso semper quod eadem Elizabeth pari sexu et ætate in bona et competenti consanguinitatis linea maritata sit, et per maritagium illud habeat statum sufficientem et securum in lege sibi et viro suo et hæredibus de corporibus suis exeuntibus, si fieri potent, seu saltem ad totam vitam suam, in terris et tenementis valoris quadraginta librarum per annum ad minus. Et si eadem Elizabeth antequam maritata fuerit, obierit, quod tunc dictæ pecuniæ summa pro maritagio ejus limitata in solucione debitorum quæ me debere contingat, et in reformacione et satisfactione mesprisionum et extorcionum, si quas fecerim, et pro animabus prædictis fideliter distribuatur, per discretionem prædictæ Agnetis et executorum meorum. In cujus rei testimonium ego præfatus Willelmus Paston præsentibus sigillum meum apposui. Datum tricesimo primo die Januarii anno regni Regis Henrici Sexti post Conquestum vicesimo secundo.

Probata fuerunt prædicta testamentum et ultima voluntas coram nobis, Alexandro Prowet, decretorum inceptore, ac reverendissimi in Christo patris et domini, domini Johannis, permissione Divina Cantuariensis archiepiscopi commissario generali, &c., vicesimo quarto die mensis Novembris anno Domini millesimo CCCC^mo^ xliiij^to^ et legitime pronunciatum pro eisdem, administratioque omnium bonorum &c. honestæ mulieri, Agneti, relictæ dicti defuncti, primitus

protestanti (et protestata fuit palam, publice et expresse, judicialiter coram nobis quod voluit agere et petere partem sibi de jure et consuetudine in hac parte debitam, in casu quo præfatus defunctus in testamento sive ultima voluntate quoad æquivalenciam partis hujusmodi minime ordinavit et disposuit), ac discretis viris Johanni, filio dicti defuncti dum vixit, Willelmo Bakton et Johanni Damme, executoribus in eodem testamento nominatis, sub forma protestationis dictæ Agnetis commissa extitit in debita juris forma; ac præfati executores habent crastinum Purificationis Beatæ Mariæ Virginis proximo futurum ad exhibendum inventarium &c. ex præfixione nostra. 1444 JAN.

3

JOHN PYRKE [1]

WILL OF JOHN PYRKE, RECTOR OF ST. MICHAEL AND ST. PETER'S, LONG STRATTON

Leaves to John Paston, Esquire, 'unam cistam rubram de sp . . . . ,' and some other articles. 1479

Executors, John Paston, Esquire, and William Martin of Long Stratton, each to have for his trouble vj*s*. viij*d*.

Date of will, 8 Sept. 1479. Proved 13 Nov. 1479 by John Paston alone.

4

ROBERT PASTON OF WIVETON [2]

In Dei nomine, Amen. Quarto die Septembris Anno Domini Millesimo CCCC^mo^lxxxij^o^, Ego Robertus Paston de Wyveton, compos mentis et sanæ memoriæ meæ existens, condo testamentum meum sive ultimam meam voluntatem in hunc modum: In primis, lego animam meam Deo Omnipotenti et Beatæ Mariæ Virgini et Omnibus Sanctis, corpusque meum sepeliendum ubicunque Deus disposuerit. Item, lego summo altari de Weveton prædicto pro decimis meis oblitis et male compensatis, xx*d*. Item, Gildæ Beatæ Mariæ ibidem, xij*d*. Item, Gildæ Sancti Johannis Baptistæ ibidem, xij*d*. Item, lumini super pelvem coram Crucifixo ibidem, viij*d*. Item, lego lumini de *le Torchys* ibidem, vj*d*. Item, reparacioni capellæ Beatæ Mariæ in cimiterio 1482 SEPT.

[1] [Norwich Episcop. Reg., 16.]
[2] [Norwich Archdeaconry Reg., vol. i. f. 29, b.] [I do not know whether this Robert Paston was at all nearly related to the family, whose correspondence is contained in these volumes; but this will and the will of his wife Margaret, which follows, are interesting in themselves, and deserve a place, even on account of the testator's surname.]

1482 SEPT. 4 ibidem, vj*d*. Item, campanis in campanili ibidem, viij*d*. Item, reparacioni capellæ Sanctæ Trinitatis super Pontem, vj*d*. Item, volo quod Margaretta uxor mea habeat sibi et assignatis suis meam partem cujusdam navis vocatæ *le Gylys*, cum omni apparatu prædictæ parti navis pertinenti et prædictam partem navis prædicta Margareta sumptibus suis reparabit. Item, volo quod prædicta Margareta uxor mea habeat ad terminam vitæ suæ messuagium meum cum omnibus pertinentiis, commoditatibus, utensilibus, et necessariis prædicto messuagio concernentibus; et post decessum prædictæ Margaretæ volo ut prædictum messuagium meum vendetur, et de pecunia inde proveniente volo quod Alicia filia mea ad conjugium semen habeat v. marcas: Et si contingat quod prædicta Alicia obiret antequam conjuncta fuerit, tunc volo quod prædictas marcas executores disponant in operibus caritatis in ecclesia Wyveton prædicto . . . . Item, volo cum residua pecuniæ de prædicto messuagio provenientis . . . . ad celebrandum in ecclesia de Weveton prædicta pro anima mea et anima dictæ Margaretæ [&c.] . . . . Et requiro in nomine Jesu feoffatos meos ut ipsi faciant legitimum statum ei vel eis qui messuagium prædictum adquirere voluerit aut voluerint sine contradictione sive impedimento aliquibus. Item, lego Willelmo Wynterton, iij*s*. iiij*d*. Item, lego negoti meo [*no name*] unam togam, unam deploidam, unum par caligarum ad disposicionem Margaretæ uxoris meæ.—The rest of his goods to be disposed of by his executors at their discretion for the good of his soul.

Executors—his wife Margaret and Edmund Shotery, clerk.

Proved at Cley, 9 Oct. 1482.

5

MARGARET PASTON[1]

1484 In Dei nomine, Amen. Ego, Margareta Paston de Weveton, vidua, bonæ memoriæ existens die Lune xx. post Dominicam in Albis[2] anno Domini nostri 1484to, condo testamentum meum ac ultimam voluntatem in hunc modum. In primis, lego et commendo animam meam Deo Omnipotenti, Redemptori meo, Beatæ Mariæ Virgini, et Omnibus Sanctis celestis curiæ, corpus quemeum sepeliendum in cimiterio ecclesiæ Beatæ [*no name*] de Weveton prædicta, cujus summo altari lego pro decimis meis non solutis, xx*d*. Item, lego fraternitati Gildæ Sancti Joannis Baptistæ unum pannum le drapre. Item, lego pictuis (*sic*) porticæ ejusdem ecclesiæ, xiij*s*. iv*d*., quæ summa remanet in manibus Johannis Andrews. Item, lego emendacioni ecclesiæ prædictæ, iij*s*. iv*d*. Item, reparacioni campanarum ibidem, vj*d*. Item, lego lumini Altaris, iiij*d*.

[1] [Norwich Archdeaconry Reg., vol. i. f. 76, a.]

[2] So in MS., but the date would be more intelligible without the numeral 'xx.' *Dominica in Albis* means sometimes Whitsunday, sometimes the Sunday after Easter. The Monday following would in the one case be 7 June, in the other 19 April, in 1484.

Item, lumini *le Torchys*, vj*d*. Item, lego reparacioni capellæ Beatæ Mariæ ibidem, vj*d*. Item, lego fraternitati Beatæ Mariæ de Salthous, xx*d*., et Summo Altari ibidem, xij*d*. Item, reparacioni campanarum ibidem, iiij*d*. Item, lumini Aratrub'm (?), iv*d*. Item, volo quod messuagium meum cum omnibus terris dicto messuagio pertinentibus vendatur per meos executores, et summa pecuniæ inde (*sic*) dispensatur per eosdem in celebratione missarum per bonum presbyterum scolarem celebratorem in ecclesia Beatæ Mariæ de Weveton prædicta pro anima mea et animabus omnium parentum et benefactorum meorum. Item, lego Aliciæ Bastard quinque marcas de dicto messuagio receptas. Et si contigerit ipsum Aliciam discedere ab hac luce, tunc volo quod Alicia filia mea habeat inde 33*s*. 4*d*., et residuum remaneat executoribus meis. Item, volo quod feoffati mei deliberent totam seisinam et possessionem de et in messuagio prædicto, cum omnibus suis pertinentiis [*blot*] qui requisiti fuerint per executores meos. Residuum omnium bonorum meorum non legatorum do et lego et concedo meis executoribus ut ipsi ordinent et disponant pro salute animæ meæ et animabus benefactorum meorum, prout melius Deo Omnipotenti placeat, quos ordino et constituo Edmundum Shortere, clericum et Johannem Say meos executores et legitimos attornatos. In cujus rei testimonium præsentibus sigillum apposui. 1484

Proved at Cley, 14 June, anno prædicto.

6

DAME ELIZABETH BROWNE[1]

In Dei nomine, Amen. The xviijth' day of the moneth of May in the yere of Our Lord God m^{l}cccclxxxvij. and in the secund yere of the reign of King Henry the vij. I, Dame Elisabeth late wife of Sir George Brown, Knyght, being of hoole mynde and in good memorye, thanked be Allmyghty God, make and ordeign this my present testament and last will yn maner and forme folowing, that is to say:— 1487 MAY 18

First, I bequeith my soul to Allmyghty God, Our Lady Saint Mary and to all the Holy Company of Hevon; and my body to be buried withyn the churche of the Blak Freris within Ludgate with my forsaid housband Sir George; to the whiche place I bequeith xxj*li*. for my said housbandes soul and myne, our fadres and modres soules and for all Cristen soules to be praid for. And for xiij. trentalles of Saint Gregory to be said and songyn for us and thaym by the freris of the said place, as in diriges and masses with all other observaunces belonging to the same, in maner and forme folowing; That is to wete, in the day or morow after my discesse vij. trentallis; and every weke folowing unto my monthes mynde oon trentall, and iij. trentalles at my monthes mynde biside the solempne dirige and masse that is to be requyred for me at that tyme. And I charge myne executours to see that the premisses be

[1] [Register Milles, 12.]

1487 MAY 18 done and performed, and also the said freris to feche me from the place where I die unto thair said place where I have lymyted afore to be buried. Also, I wull that as sone as my body is buryed and th'expenses therof done and paid that myn executours provide and see that my dettes be contented and paid. Also, I bequeith to the vicar of the church of Dorking in the county of Surrey for my forsaid housbandes soul and myne, our faders and modres, and for all the soules that we be bound unto, to be praid for within the yer after my discesse, as in diriges and masses to be said or song by hym or his deputie and to have us specially in remembraunce in thayr memento by oon hole yer, xx*s*. Also, I bequeith to the reparacion of the forsaid churche of Dorking xx*s*. Also, I bequeith to the parson of Saint Albans in Wodstrete within London for diriges and masses to be said or song by hym or his deputie, in like wise as the vicar of Dorking is charged, as is afore rehersed, xx*s*. Also, I bequeith to the reparacion of the stepull of the said churche of Saint Albane xx. solidos. Also, I bequeith to the prisoners of Newgate and Ludgate, Kinges Bench and Marshallsee, to every of those places to be praid for, xx*d*. Also, I bequeith to bedred folkes and other pour householders, aswell men as women, dwelling within London and without in the suburbis of the same, and moste specially souche as have knowen me and I thaym, xl*s*., as by the discrecions and advises of myne executours it shall be thought best to be done. Moreover I geve and biqueith to my doughter Mary, to the promocion of her mariage, all my plate and other juelles, with all myne hole apparell, and all my stuff of houshold being within my dwelling place or any other within the citee of London or suburbes of the same, that is to say:—First, a standing cupp of silver gilt, chaced with plompes, weyeng with the cover, knoppe and devise xlij. unces *et dimidium*. Item, a standing cupp of silver and gilt, chaced with flowres, weying with the cover, the knopp and devise, xxvij. unces *et dimidium*. A playn standing cupp of silver gilt, weing with the cover, the knopp and the devise xxx. unces. A standing cupp of silver and gilt, chaced with half plompes, weying with the cover, knopp and devise xx. unces and *dimidium*. A playn standing cupp of silver gilt weying with cover and the knoppe and the devyse xxvij. unces and an half. A standyng cuppe of silver and gilt, weyng with the cover, the knoppe and the devyse xxvj. unces. A saltseler of sylver and gilte, weyng with the cover, the knoppe and the devyse xxiij. unces. A saltseler of sylver and gilt, without a cover, weying xxij. unces and an halfe. A litill saltseler of sylver and gilt, weying with the cover and the knoppe and the devyse xv. unces and an half. A litell saltseler of sylver and gilt, without the cover, weying viij. unces and an halfe. And vj. bolles of sylver, parcelles gilt, weying iiij.$^{xx.}$ xviij. unces. And ij. peces of sylver with a cover weying xlviij. unces. A dosen and a half of silver sponys weying xxiij. unces, and iij. sponys of silver and gilt weying iij. unces and iij. quartrons, and a long spone of sylver and gilt for ginger, weying j. unce and iij. quartrons. Item, a chafing disshe of sylver weying xxvj. unces. And ij. litell crewettes of sylver, weying viij. unces. A chalese of sylver and gilt with the paten, weying xj. unces. An haly water stok of silver with the lid, handill, and spryngill, weying xij. unces. An Agnus with a baleys iij. saphires, iij. perlys with an image of Saint Antony apon it. And a tablet with the Salutacion of Our Lady, and the iij. Kingis of

Collayn. A bee with a grete pearl. A dyamond, an emerawde, iij. grete perlys hanging apon the same. A nother bee with a grete perle, with an emerawde and a saphire, weying ij. unces iij. quarters. A pece of the Holy Crosse, crossewise made, bordured with silver aboute; iij. brode girdilles, oone of tawny silke with bokill a pendaunt, another of purpill with bokyll and pendaunt, and the iij$^{de.}$ of purpill damaske with bokell and pendaunt. And vj. barres of silver and gilt, and iij. brode harnysed girdilles, oone white tisshew, another red tysshew gold, and the iij^{de} a playne grene coorse. A muskeball of gold weying halfe an unce, and ij. bokilles and ij. pendauntes of gold, oone playne and the other pounsyd, weying an unce and a quarter. And a harnysed girdill enameled with rowsclare, weying halfe an unce. A dymysoynt[1] with a rubye and an amatyste weying j. unce and an halfe. An harnysed girdill of golde of damaske with a long pendaunt, and a bokill of golde chekkyd, weying j. unce. A grete bed of a state of verdure, and a counterpoynt to the same. And iiij. curteyns of grene tartron. A grete federbed, a bolster, and vj. fetherbeddys over woren, vj. bolsters. And iiij. mattarasses, lytyll over woren, xij. pellowes of downe, v. newe carpettys of ij. ellys in lengeth and yarde and halfe brode. iij. fyne pelow beres, and a grete counterpoynt of tapstery werk of v. yardes and a quarter longe and iiij. yardes brode. A hanging for a chamber of grene say borduryd with acrons of xxxv. yerdes longe; a whyte spervyour; ij. counterpoyntes, an hanging bed, with a lyon thereupon; and the valence white, grene, and red, and iiij. blew courtens to the same. And two coverlettes with lyons; a blak testour for a bed, with iiij. blak curtens, and vj. pecys of blak hanging to the same; ij. cusshens of blak velvet; a cusshyn of blak damask; a cusshen of grene worstede; a long cusshen of blewe saten figure. A blak coveryng for a bed of borde alisaunder. And xj. peces of grene saye, borduryd with acorns, to hang with a chambre. A vestment of blak velwet with orfrayes, browderyd with my saide husbondys armes and myne; an awbe; j. chesyppill, with a stole, and all that belongeth therto; ij. corporas casys of cloth of gold; j. olde vestment; an awbe; an awter clothe wyth the image of Our Lorde; a corporas case of blewe cloth of golde. A nother of blewe saten and russet. An awter clothe of staynyd werke. And iij. stenyd clothes with imagis in them to hang a chapell. ij. awter clothes of white sylke with red crosses, and ij. curtens with white frengis and red. And iiij. curtens, ij. of rayed sarsenet, and two of grene. An awter clothe; a litell pece of grene tartron; a payer of fustyans of iiij. breddys iij. yerdys iij. quarters long. A paire of fyne shetys overworne of iiij. yerdes brede. An hede shete and iij. payer of newe shetys of iij. levis, of ij. ellys and an half long. And two payer of shetys of ij. levis and an half long. And iij. hed shetys of ij. bredys, and vj. paier of shetys over worne of ij. levis. And vj. paier of houshold shetis. And two paier of wollen blankettes. And a violet gowne, furryd with martrons. A blak gowne furryd with gray. A blak gowne furryd with white. A blak gowne furryd with martrons. And a nyght gowne of blak furryd with martrons. A kirtill of tawny chamlet. A purfill of ermyns of ij. skynne depeth, and iij. yardys and an half long. A purfill of martrons of j. skynne 1487 MAY 18

[1] A metal facing for a girdle.

VOL 6

THE PASTON LETTERS

1487 MAY 18 depeth, and iiij. yardis long. A purfill of shankes of ij. skynne deppeth, and iiij. yardis long. A bonet of poudrid ermyns. And a pece of cloth of golde with dropis, which was of a duplade. And a dosen of diaper napkyns of flour de lyce werke and crownes. And a dosen and a half of naptkyns of playne clothe with blew pelowers, and a pece of clothe of diaper werke to make with a dosen naptkyns. A bordecloth of floure de lice werk and crownes of x. yardis and an half long, and iij. yardis brode. And a nother bordecloth of flour de lyce werk and crownes, viij. yardes and a half long, ij. yardes and a quarter brode; a towell of diaper of flower delice werke and crownys of xx^ti yardys long, and iij. quarters brode. Another towell of flower delice werke and crownys of iij. quarters brode and xviij. yardes long. A nother of latise werke and diaper of iij. quarter brede xiiij. yerdes di' long. Another towell of iiij. greynys, and a fret of viij. yerdes di' long. A nother towell of latise werk and crownys vj. yerdes and di' long and iij. quarters brede. And two towellis of great diaper werke, iij. yerdes and a quarter long and iij. quarter brode. And a pece of new creste clothe conteygnyng xxiij. ellys. And two towellys of great diaper werkes of xiij. yerdes long and iij. quarter in brede. And vij. grete cofers, v. chestis, ij. almaryes like a chayer, and a blak cofer bounden with iron. vj. yoyned stoles, iiij. kaskettys, v. litell joynyd stoles. A litill table, ij. yerdes long. A rounde table, ij. trestelles, ij. garnysshe and di' of pewter vessell counterfete, wherof j. garnysshe and di' is newe; and vj. great kandelstikkis newe of laton, and iiij. newe bellyd kandelstikkis, ij. litill kandelstikkis, vij. basens of pewater, and v. brasse pannys, of the which oon is xvj. galons, and two of them of viij. galons a pece, and the other ij. more lesse. A grete standing chafer of laton with a lyon apon the lydde, ij. chafers of brasse, and ij. litill brasse pottys, ij. grete cobardys, and ij. other cobardys more and lesse, ij. fyer pannys, a lityll skelet. A ladill and a scomer of laton, ij. colondyrs, ij. spyttys, ij. dreping pannes of iron, iij. dressing knyfys, ij. lechyng knyfys, ij. choppyng knyfys. A tryvet. A brasen morter with a pestell of iron, ij. stone morters, ij. gredyrons, j. payer of potte hokys, a flesshe hoke, and a kolerake. Provydid alwey that myn executours by the advyse of myn overseers ordeigne and put in safegarde to be kept after my discease in to som religious place unto the day of my said doughters mariage, and to the behofe and promocyon of the same, all and every part of the forsaid plate and juelx with all other stuffe of houshold by me to her, as is abovewritten, yoven and bequethed, except souche stuffe as canne not be kept from mowghtes, which I will she have the rule and governaunce of for the safegarde of the same and for her wele. And if my saide doughter Mary dye unmaryed, then I yeve and bequethe all the forsaid plate with all other stuffe of housholde to my soon Mathewe her brother. And if it fortune that he dye unmaryed, as God forfende, then I yeve and bequeth all and every part of my forsaid plate, juelx, and stuffe of housholde unto my soon Sir Edward Ponyngis. And yef it fortune the said Edward to dye, as God defende, that then all the forsaid juelx and other stuffe above written, except a playne standing cuppe of sylver and gilt, with the cover, the knoppe, and the devyse of the same with gryffons hede in the botom wrought apon blewe asure, weying xxvj. uncis, which I geve to my doughter in lawe, Dame Isabell Ponyngis, to be dyvydyd by th'advice of

APPENDIX

the overseers of this my present testament and last wille, and evynly to be departed unto Antony Browne and Robert Browne, my brethern in lawe, they to do with it thair fre wille. And as touching myne Agnus, tablettes with dyamondys, saphires, perlys, grete and small crosses, gurdillis, dymyseyntes, gownys, with all other thingis longing to myne apparayle, as is above written, yef it fortune my said doughter Mary decease, I geve and bequethe all and every part of it to my kynnyswoman Margaret Hasslake. And if the said Margaret dye, that then all the said apparell particularly written before remaigne to my said doughter-in-lawe Dame Isabell Ponyngys. Also xx. marc which I lent unto my son Sir Edward Ponynges, I woll that it be distributyd by the discrecion of myn executours and overseers among souche as been knowen my servauntys at the day of my discease. The residue of all my singuler goodes, catallys, and juellys after my dettys payde, and my bequestes performyd and fulfyllyd, and burying done, I geve and fully bequeth to my sonnys, Ser Edward Ponyngis and Mathew Browne, and theym to dispose and do theire fre wille, to pray and to do for my soule as they wolde I sholde do for them, as they will aunswer afore God. And of this my testament and last wille I make and ordeigne myn executours my forsaid sonnes, Ser Edward Ponyngys and Mathew Browne, and theire supervysours Humphrey Conyngesby and Richard Tuke. And I bequeth to every of myne executours for thair labour lx*s.*, and to every of myne overseers for thair labours xl*s.* In Wittenesse hereof, I the said Dame Elizabeth to this my present testment and last wille have put my seale. Yoven at London, the day and yere abovesaide. 148 MAY

Probatum fuit suprascriptum testamentum coram domino apud Lamehith xxvj^to die mensis Junii, anno Domini supradicto, ac approbatum &c. Et commissa fuit administratio &c., Matheo Browne, filio ejusdem et executori &c. de bene &c. Ac de pleno inventario &c., citra festum Sancti Petri quod dicitur *ad Vincula*, reservata potestate committendi &c., Edwardo Ponynges militi, executori &c.

7

WILLIAM PASTON [1]

In Dei nomine, Amen. The vij^th day of the moneth of Septembre in the yere of Our Lord God m^l.CCCClxxxxvj., I, William Paston of London, gentilman, being of hooll mynde and in good memory, laud and praysing be unto Almighti God, make and ordeigne this my present testament and last wille in maner and fourme folowing, that is to sey :—Furst, I geve and bequeith my soule unto my saide Lorde God, to our blessed Lady Sainte Marye Virgyne, and to all the holy companye of Heven. And I will that my body be buried in the church of Blak Frerez, in London, at the north ende of the high altar 149 SEPT.

[1] [Register Horne, 12.]

THE PASTON LETTERS

1496 SEPT. 7 there by my Lady Anne, late my wife. Also, I will that there be yeven unto the saide church of Blak Friers, where my saide body shall lye, to be praide for, and for the place of my saide burying to have a large stone upon the saide Lady Anne and me, a convenient rewarde by th'advise and discrecion of myne executours underwriten. Also, I will that all my dettes be wele and truely contente and paide. Also, I wille that xx*li.* in money be geven and disposed for my soule and all Christen soules in dedes of pitee and charitee the day of my saide burying, that is to sey :—emonges pouer people and prisoners within the citee of London and withoute. Also I will that I have a preste of honest conversacion to synge bothe for me, and for suche as I am chargid to do syng for at Cambrige, as my servant, Thomas Andrewe, can shew by the space of viij. yeres. Also, I will that for every wronge by me done in my life tyme a dewe recompence be made there fore by th'enformacion of my saide servante, Thomas Andrew, in that behalf. Also, I will that all my landes and tenementes with th'appurtenances be devyded bytwene my ij. doughters, Agnes and Elizabeth, by the discresion of my executours underwritten, and after th'enformacion of my saide servaunte, Thomas Andrew, to whome I have shewid my entent and mynde in the same manye tymes, and often to have to theym and to the heires of theire ij. bodies lawfully begoten. Also, I wille that all the revennuyes of my fee symple landes, over and a bove the reparacions and charges of the same that shalbe due at Mychelmas next after my deceasse be takyn of my tenauntes and fermours there by favoure, and that the same revenues go to the contentacion and payment of my saide dettes assone as it can be convenyently gadred and levied, &c. Also, I will that none of my tenantes nor fermers, suche as be of grete age and fallith in poverte, be in any wise vexid or t[r]oublid after my deceasse by my executours underwritten for no maner of olde dettes due unto me before the day of my deces. Also, I will that nether my heires, executours, nor non other person for theim, nor in theire names, in any wise vex, sue, or trouble the saide Thomas Andrew, my servaunte, after my deceasse of or for any maner of rekenynges or other maters bitwene hym and me in all my life tyme, but utterly thereof I discharge hym and will, and will that he be therof acquyte and discharged in that behalve as I have shewid and declared in my life unto my doughter Elizabeth, Mastres Hide, Master Ursewik, Archedecon of Richemonde, Master Doctor Myddelton, Master Thomas Madies, chapeleyn to my Lorde Cardinall,[1] Master John Shaa, Alderman of London, Master Reede, Master Christofer Mildelton, proctours of the courte of Canterbury, and many other honorable folkis, and to my servauntes in my life tyme, consideryng that he hathe ben my trewe and feithfull servant these xix. yeres or more, in which seasone he hath had dyvers grete paynfull besynes and labours in my causis, by whose gode policie and meanes I have purchased moche of my saide fe symple landes, which also canne geve best enformacion how all suche landes as I have purchased stonden, and what consciens is there in, and howe every thyng shalbe ordred. Also, I will that the churche of Saynte Petre, in Wodenorton have a hole vestyment of the price of v. marc. Also, I will that Elizabeth Crane be wele maried at my

[1] Cardinal Morton.

APPENDIX

costis, or ellis by the menes of my doughters, unto suche a personne as may dispende by yere xx. marc, or ellis to a gode marchaunt or other craftisman. Item, I will that Christofer Talbot be treuly contentid and paied of his yerely annuyte of v. merke by yere duryng his life. Item, I will that Thomas Dokkyng have surely his annuyte of xl*s.* by yere duryng his life. Item, I wille that the bargayne of Adam Sowter be recompensid after th'enformacion had of my saide servaunte, Thomas Andrew. Also, I will that every of my servauntes be rewarded for theire good and diligent laboure and attendance had a bowte me after the discresion of my executours underwritten. Also, I will that all suche of my godes moveable in Warwikes Inne, and in my place callid Castre Clere, in Norffolk, and in my place in Norwiche, be solde by the discresion of my executours, tawarde and for the contentacion and payment of my saide dettes and performance of this my present will. Also, I will that the vicar of Fyncham be recompensid of his bargayne betwene hym and me after th'enformacion of the saide Thomas Andrewe. Item, I will that all my servauntes, suche as be behynde of their wages and dueties, be trewly content and paied. Also, I will that all other my godes not bequethid, this my will fulfilled, my dettes paied, and all my wronges recompensed by th'enformacion of the saide Thomas Andrew, be departid bytwixte my ij. doughter beforesaide after the discresion of my saide executours. And also, for as moche as I have not sufficient redy money, and that my dettis cannot be redely levied, therfore I will that money be made of all suche plate as I have for the haste of contentacion of my dettes that I owe of my buriallis. And of this my present testament and laste will I make and ordeyne and constitute my executours the moste reverend fadre in God my Lorde Cardinall, the right high and myghty Prynces, my lady the Kynges modre, my Lord Dawbeney, and Sir Edwarde Poynynges, Knyght, my nevew, whome I hartely beseche in executyng and performyng this my laste will to do and dispose concernyng the same in every thyng as they shall thynke best to the pleasure of Almyghty God, and for the helthe of my sowle and all Cristen sowles. 149 SEPT.

Probatum fuit suprascriptum testamentum coram domino apud Lamehith, xxviij^o die mensis Novembris, Anno Domini Millesimo CCCC^o nonagesimo sexto, juramento Thomæ Andrew et Laurencii Canwike, testium, quibus Thomæ et Lawrencio commissa fuit administracio per viam intestati, pro eo et ex eo quod executores in suo testamento nominati ex certis causis legitimis refutarunt, de bene et fideliter administrand' eadem juxta et secundum vires ipsius defuncti testamentum sive ultimam voluntatem, ac primo de solvend' æs alienum in quo idem defunctus hujusmodi mortis suæ tempore extitit obligatus, deinde legata in hujusmodi suo testamento contenta, quatenus bona et debita &c., ad sancta &c.

THE PASTON LETTERS

8

MARGARET PASTON[1]

I, Margaret Paston, widow, 'late wife of Edmond Paston, Squier. . . . . 24° Nov. MCCCCCIV. . . . . . my sinful bodie to be buried in the chyrche of Our Lady in Iteryngham.'

'Item, to the Hey Awter of the chirche of Sharington, vjs. viijd.
'Item, to the reparacion of the said churche, xxs.
'Item, to the reparacion of the chirch of Manington, xs.
'Item, to the reparacion of the chirch of Itteringham, iijs. ivd.
'Item, to the Hey Awter of Itteringham, iijs. ivd.
'Item, to the Gilde of Oure blessid Ladi there, iijs. ivd.
'Item, to the Heigh Awter of Saxthorpe, ijs.
'Item, to the Heigh Awter of the chirche of Little Baningham, iijs. iiijd.
'Item, to the Heigh Awter of the chirche of Woolterton, ijs.
'Item, to the Heigh Awter of the chirche of Wood Dalling, iijs. iiijd.
'Item, to the reparacion of heigh way in Woolterton, vs.

'Item, I will that my son William Lumnor have c. sheep. xxiij. nete, x. quarters wheat, xx. quarters barley, x. quarters oats, and as many horse, cartes, plowghes, and harowghes, with alle her apparell, as shall extende to the valu of viii. xiijs. iiijd., beside alle the foreseide shepe, &c.' . . . . in recompense of all goods . . . . that Thomas Brigge, late my husbande, by his testament and last will bequeathed or gave to the said William Lumnor . . . . He to have all the hangings in the grey chamber over the parlour within the manor place of Manington, and the great bed with the covering and hangings, 'which is of tapestrie worke;' . . . . also all the hangings of the halle and parlour, 'with the falte table in the parlure, and all the tables and stooles in the haule, and all the rede hangings of the rede chaumber over the pantry and botry, and a bede of red saye' . . . . . viz., its belongings, pillows, coverlets, &c., &c.

'Item, to the said William Lumner, my son, ij. grete rosting aundernes, iij. spetes, ij. brass pots with all the brewing vessells.

Item, to my daughter, Margaret Browne, 'my fruntelet of purpill velvet, my girdill whereof the herneys is silver and gilt, and the corse is of damaske gold, and also my fruntelet of crymsyn velvet.'

Item, to my daughter Elizabeth Whymbergh my dymysent silver and gilt, and my corse of crymsyn velvet pirled with gold, and also a fruntlet of crymsyn velvet.

Item, to Margaret Lomnor, my daughter-in-lawe, my prymer clad with grene velvet.

Item, to my daughter, Anne Lomnor, my russet gown pervild with menks, and my best coral bedes conteyning once fifty, and my best bonnett.

Item, to Elizabeth Gayne, xiijs. iiijd., to the bying of a gowne for her.

¹ [Reg. Norvic. 'Rix' f. 107.]

208

APPENDIX

Item, to my son, John Lomnor, a brass pott, a basin, with an ewer of pewter with a roose of lateyn in the bottom of the said basin, and four platters, and four dishes, and iiij. sawcers of pewter.

Item, to my son, Henry Lomnor, xls.
Item, to my nephew, Thomas Lomnor . . . . a feather bed, &c., &c.
Item, to my nephew, James Lomnor . . . . . a feather bed, &c.

'And all the residue of alle my goodes and catallis, sylver plate, and all my detts to me owing, above not bequeathed nor assigned, I give and bequeath to my son, William Lomnor, whom I ordeine and make my executor,' first to pay debts, and distribute the remainder 'to the most plesure to God and helthe to my sowle.'

Proved at Norwich, 19 May 1505, by William Lumnor.

9

DAME AGNES PASTON[1]

'Dame Agnes Paston, widow, late the wife of Sir John Paston, Knight, deceased,' makes her will 31 May, A.D. 1510, 2 Hen. VIII. To be buried, if she die in London, in the church of the Black Friars, by her husband John Harvy; or, if she die in Kent, in the parish church in Sondryche. Goods in three chests to be divided among her three sons, George, Thomas, and Edward. Bequeaths to her son George Hervy a pair of large sheets of her own spinning, and all her bedding at Sondryche to her son Thomas Isley. Other bequests to John Palmer of Otteford, to the parson of Brasted, to her daughter Isabel Isley, her cousin Alys Petham, to Margaret Palmer, to Mrs. Bygote 'with my Lady Marqueys.'² To her son-in-law William Hatteclyff a basin and ewer, parcel gilt, for 20 marks, if he will give so much for it; otherwise it is to go to her sons George Harvy and Edw. Isley. To her son George a silver salt with a cover, at Leuesham. To her chaplain Sir Robert 'the complete bedde within my little draught chambre att Sonderiche,' and 10 marks a year for 5 years, to pray for her soul and the souls of John Hervy, Sir John Paston, and John Isley, her husbands. To her son Thomas Isley's children, and her own and her daughter Isabel Hatteclyff's children, 5 marks each. To her son George Hervy, 'a standing cupp with a kever, silver and gilt with sekylles,' and a gold cross. To her daughter Isley a ring with a rebewe. To her son Thomas Isley her gelding. Other bequests to her cousins Margaret Palmer and Thos. Waserer's wife; also to young Potter, the man of law, to Agnes Waserer, and to Eliz. mother to Thomas Waserer's wife, to Joan Julles, William Tidman, to her servant Kyllingworth, to Vincent her housekeeper, to Sir Robert, parish priest of Sonderyche, to Sir William of Nokold. Mr. Robert Scalys parson of Braysted to be overseer of her will; her sons George Harvy and Thos. Isley to be her executors.

Proved at Lambeth, 19 June 1510.

¹ [Register Benet, 29.]   ² Cecily, widow of Thomas, first Marquis of Dorset.

209

CHRONOLOGICAL TABLE OF PUBLIC AND PRIVATE OCCURRENCES

[This Table is intended partly to serve the purpose of a Table of Contents to the more important Letters, partly to enable the reader to see at a glance the bearing of particular transactions on the general history of the times. The Nos. quoted are those of the Letters.]

210

CHRONOLOGICAL TABLE

211

THE PASTON LETTERS

1435

Aug. *Peace Conferences at Arras—broken off by England.*
14 Sept. *Death of the Duke of Bedford at Rouen. The Duke of York made Regent.*
21 Sept. *The Duke of Burgundy deserts England, and makes a separate peace with France.*

1436

Recovery of Paris by the French.
The Duke of York lands in Normandy, and recovers several places from the French.
Calais besieged by the Duke of Burgundy, but relieved by the Duke of Gloucester.

1437

19 Feb. *James I. of Scotland murdered.*
16 July. *The Duke of York recalled from France, and the Earl of Warwick sent in his place.*

1439

Death of Warwick at Rouen. York made Regent again.
Peace Conferences at Calais—ineffectual.

About 1440

John Paston's introduction to Margaret Mauteby, 34. His marriage to her, 35.

1440

Release of the Duke of Orleans, 36.

1443

John Paston ill in London, 47.

1444

Feb. William Paston and Chief-Justice Fortescue both too ill to go on circuit, 51.
14 Aug. Death of William Paston, 56.

CHRONOLOGICAL TABLE

1445

Disputes of Agnes Paston with the Vicar of Paston, 62.
22 April. *Marriage of Henry VI. with Margaret of Anjou, 62.*

1447

Parliament of Bury.—Arrest and death of Gloucester. Death of Cardinal Beaufort.

1448

17 Feb. John Paston dispossessed of Gresham by Lord Molynes, 102.
A relief claimed by Lady Morley, 75.
Daniel said to be out of favour, 75.
22 May. Affray at Coventry between the retainers of Sir Robert Harcourt and Sir Humphrey Stafford, 78.

1449

Mar. Death of Edmund Paston—his nuncupative will dated 21 March, 85.
May. *Robert Wenyngton captures a fleet of 100 ships, 90.* Friar Hauteyn's claim to Oxnead, 63, 87.
6 Oct. John Paston again occupies Gresham, 88, 102.
The King in the Marches of Wales, 96.
Capture of Rouen by the French.
Stephen Scrope a suitor of Elizabeth Paston, 93, 94.

1450

28 Jan. John Paston's wife driven out of Gresham, 102, 103.
7 Feb. *Impeachment of the Duke of Suffolk, 101.*
John Paston presents a petition to the King in Parliament against Lord Molynes, 102.
Mar. Foreigners light on the coast of Norfolk, and take people prisoners, 105, 106.
15 April. Battle of Fourmigni—Sir Thomas Kiriel taken prisoner, 120.
30 April. The Duke of Suffolk's letter to his son, 117.
April or May. Daniel enters the manor of Brayston, 108, 119.
2 May. *The Duke of Suffolk murdered at sea, 120, 121.*
May. New appointments to offices of state, 123.
Jack Cade's rebellion, 126.
12 Aug. *Loss of Cherbourg, the last place held by the English in Normandy, 131.*
Aug. Disturbances in Norfolk, 132, 133.
Thomas Denyes and the Earl of Oxford, 123, 124, 132.
J. Paston's dispute with Lord Molynes, 131, 135, 136, 139, 145.

THE PASTON LETTERS

1450

Sept. *The Duke of York comes over from Ireland, and causes a change of administration, 142, 143.*
Molynes and his men indicted of felony, 147.
Oct. Election of two knights of the shire for Norfolk, 148, 149.
Nov. *Meeting of Parliament—Oldhall chosen Speaker, 151.*
Tuddenham and Heydon unpopular in Norfolk, 154, 170.
Dec. Oyer and terminer in Suffolk, at Beccles, 160, 161.
Oyer and terminer going into Norfolk, 162.

1451

Jan. An oyer and terminer for Kent, 169.
Oyer and terminer to be held at Norwich at Easter, 174, 175.
John Paston re-enters Gresham, 178.
25 Feb. Bettes arrested at a court held by Gonnor at Routon, 178.
1 Mar. Heydon's horse brought through Aylesham into Norwich, 179, 180.
1 Mar. Tuddenham and Heydon expected to regain their ascendency, 184.
Petition to Parliament against Sir Thomas Tuddenham, 185.
April. Tuddenham and Heydon to be indicted at Norwich, 186.
May. Lord Molynes and his men indicted at Walsingham, 189, 190; acquitted by favour of the King, 189, 193.
1 July. Death of Sir Harry Inglos, 201.
Aug. *Surrender of Bayonne:—entire loss of Gascony and Guienne by the English.*
Dec. Daniel hoping to re-enter Brayston, 206: which he did soon after, 119.

1452

7 April. Good Friday. *A general pardon granted by the King.*
April. The Duke of Norfolk coming to Norfolk to redress disorders, 210, 211, 212.
The King also coming into Norfolk, 210, 211.
Outrages of Charles Nowell and others, 212, 213, 215, 217, 241.
Roger Church, being taken prisoner by his own consent, accuses many gentlemen of sedition, 214, 216, 217, 218, 219, 241.
An army sent under Shrewsbury to recover Guienne.
18 Dec. The Duke of York pawns jewels to Sir J. Fastolf, 184.

1453

Building operations [at Caister?], 224, 225.
April. Visit of Margaret of Anjou to Norwich, 226.
July. Deaths of Philip Berney and Sir John Heveningham, 227, 228.
July. *The Earl of Shrewsbury defeated and slain at Castillon. Final loss of Guienne.*
Aug. *The King falls ill at Clarendon.*
Dec. ? The Duke of Norfolk's petition against Somerset, 230.

CHRONOLOGICAL TABLE

1454

Jan. *The King's imbecility, 235.*
York and other Lords coming up to London, 235.
12 Jan. Walter Ingham waylaid and beaten by procurement of Thomas Denyes, 238.
Thomas Denyes and his wife put in prison, 239, 240, 244, 245.
22 Mar. *Death of Cardinal Kemp, 239.*
3 April. *The Duke of York made Protector.*

1454 ?

Marriage proposed between John Clopton and Elizabeth Paston, 242, 243.

1454

May or June. *Defeat of the French in an attack on Jersey and Guernsey, 247.*
6 June. Wardship of Thomas Fastolf of Cowhaw, granted to John Paston and Thomas Howys, 248.—Paid for by Sir J. Fastolf, 271.—Disputed by Sir Philip Wentworth, 248, 263, 266, 267, 277, 278, 289, 292, 307.
9 June. *Edward the King's son created Prince of Wales, 247.*
5 July. *The Duke of York and other Lords coming up from the North—Lords appointed to keep the sea, 249.*
11 July. Marriage proposed for Elizabeth Paston by Lord Grey of Hastings, 250, 252.
July. *The Duke of York is commissioned to convey the Duke of Exeter to the North, and commit him to Pomfret Castle, 254.*
Aug. ? Sir John Fastolf goes to reside at Caister, 254, 260.
Sept. *Pestilence in London, 260.*
Nov. Fastolf proposes to sue an attaint, 267, 268.
25 Dec. *The King recovers from his illness, 270.*

1455

5 Feb. *Somerset released from the Tower.*
7 Feb. Sir J. Fastolf resents words spoken at a dinner at Norwich, 272.
4 Mar. *The questions between Somerset and York referred to arbitrators.*
17 Mar. Presentation to Stokesby church, 273, 274.
29 Mar. Sir Thomas Howes vexed by Andrews and others, 276, 297.
22 May. *The first battle of St. Albans, 283-5, 287.*
June. Election of Howard and Chamberlain for Norfolk, 288, 291, 294, 295.
[June or July]. *Attempt of the Scots on Berwick.*
7 July. Poynings acquitted of treason, etc., 297.
19 July. Dispute between Warwick and Lord Cromwell before the King, 299.

THE PASTON LETTERS

CHRONOLOGICAL TABLE

THE PASTON LETTERS

CHRONOLOGICAL TABLE

THE PASTON LETTERS

1463

1464

CHRONOLOGICAL TABLE

1465

1466

THE PASTON LETTERS

1466

1467

1468

CHRONOLOGICAL TABLE

1468

1469

THE PASTON LETTERS

1469

Sept. Sir John Paston attempts to negotiate with the Duke of Norfolk through the medium of the King's Council, 722, 723, 726-9.
12 Sept. Margaret Paston warns Sir John of the distress of the garrison at Caister, 724.
15 Sept. Sir John Paston disbelieves his mother's warning, 725.
20 Sept. *Rivers and his son, Sir J. Woodville, put to death by the insurgents.*
26 Sept. Caister surrendered, 730-4.
5 Oct. John Paston desires instructions about the discharged garrison of Caister, 735.
Oct. *The King, having recovered his liberty, returns to London,* 736.
[Oct.] Richard Calle and Margery Paston at Blackborough Nunnery, 737.
6 Nov. Sale of Beckham by Sir John Paston to Roger Townsende, 738.
Dec. Two widows sue an appeal against John Paston, 740, 751.

1470

Mar. *Insurrection of Sir Robert Welles*—the King goes into Lincolnshire to put it down, 742, 743.
Mar. *Battle of Losecoatfield (Stamford),* 760.
May. Letters of W. Worcester about Titchwell, 744, 745.
22 June. John Paston and others charged with felony in killing men at the siege of Caister, 746, 747.
22 June. The Duchess of Norfolk promises to intercede for John Paston with her husband, 746.
14 July. Agreement of Bishop Waynflete and Sir J. Paston for the termination of disputes about Fastolf's will, 750.
15 July. Margaret Paston complains of her sons, 752.
July, Aug. Sir J. Paston pledges plate, 748, 749, 754.
5 Aug. *Rebellion in the North.—Clarence and Warwick expected to land in England,* 753.
10 Aug. Endowment of Magdalen College, Oxford, with Fastolf's lands, 755.
7 Sept. Edward anticipates an invasion of Kent, 758.

HENRY VI. RESTORED

1470

12 Oct. *Queen Elizabeth Woodville in Sanctuary,* 759.
12 Oct. The Earl of Oxford befriends John Paston, 759.
Dec. The Duke of Norfolk evacuates Caister and releases it to Bishop Waynflete, 763-5.
28 Dec. Calthorpe, wishing to reduce his household, advises Margaret Paston to provide a marriage for her daughter Anne, 766.

CHRONOLOGICAL TABLE

1471

14 Feb. Lord Beauchamp releases his interest in Caister, etc. to John Paston, 768.
14 Mar. *Edward IV. lands at Ravenspur.—His landing anticipated by the Earl of Oxford,* 769.
19 Mar. Oxford orders the lieges of Norfolk to meet him at Lynn to resist King Edward, 770.
[Mar.] *Clarence goes over to Edward IV.,* 771.
Register of writs against Sir J. Paston and others, 772.

EDWARD IV. RESTORED

1471

14 April. *Battle of Barnet.—John Paston wounded,* 774, 776.
18 April. *News of Queen Margaret's landing,* 774.
Escape of the Earl of Oxford, 775.
4 May. *Battle of Tewkesbury,* 777.
12 May. *Attempt of the Bastard Falconbridge on London.*
21 May. *Death of Henry VI.*
23 June. Caister again taken by a servant of the Duke of Norfolk (W. Worc. Itin. 368), 778.
5 July. Lord Scales (Rivers) offers to befriend John Paston, 778.
17 July. The King signs a bill of pardon to John Paston, 780.
15 Sept. *The Bastard Falconbridge beheaded,* 781, 782.
Sir J. Paston desires his brother to watch Caister, 781.
Great mortality in England, 781.
28 Sept. Sir J. Paston wishes to have the measure of his father's tomb, and some measurements at Gresham, 782.
Sept. The King and Queen on pilgrimage to Canterbury, 782.
One of the two widows married, 783.
28 Oct. A general pardon proposed, 784.
Inventory of Sir J. Paston's deeds, 785.
5 Nov. Death of J. Berney of Witchingham, 787.
29 Nov. Margaret Paston is annoyed at Sir John's extravagance, 791.
Valuation of Sporle Wood, 793, 819.

1472

8 Jan. Sir John Paston receives his pardon, 795.
Queen Margaret is removed to Wallingford, 795.
23 Jan. John Paston urges his brother to obtain probate of his father's will, 796.
John Paston interrupts a court which Gurney attempts to hold at Saxthorpe, 796.

THE PASTON LETTERS

1472

5 Feb. The one widow comes up to London to sue the appeal, 797.
17 Feb. Sir John Paston and Anne Haulte, 798.
The King intercedes with Clarence for Gloucester, 798.
Purchasers offer for Sporle Wood, 798.
30 April. The Earl of Northumberland gone home into the North, 800.
Sickness prevalent, 800.
Archbishop Nevill committed to the Tower, and then sent to sea, 800.
The Countess of Oxford still in St. Martin's, 800.
A daughter born to the Queen at Windsor, 800.
14 May. Arrangement with Gurney about Saxthorpe, 801.
25 May. Sir John Paston's lands will not pay his debts under present management—his mother will disinherit him if he sell any land, 802.
5 June. Margaret Paston likely to be troubled about Sir J. Fastolf's goods, 803, 805.
Henry Heydon has bought Saxthorpe and Titchwell, 803, 804.
Sir T. Lynde's goods, 804, 805.
The Earl of Arran in London, 804, 805.
8 July. Altercations with Sir James Gloys, 805, 810.
20 Sept. Sir John Paston proposed for the borough of Maldon, 808, 809.
21 Sept. Conferences with the Duchess of Norfolk about Caister, 809.
29 Sept. John Paston desires a goshawk, 810, 812, 817.
4 Nov. Sir J. Paston jests with the Duchess of Norfolk on her condition, 812.
Rivers coming home from Brittany, 812.
The Duchess of Norfolk wishes to have Margaret Paston with her at her confinement, 878. [This letter has been accidently misplaced in the year 1475.]
8 Nov. Approaching confinement of the Duchess, 813.
John Paston going to Framlingham, 813-5, 817.
19 Nov. Dr. Alen's wife, 814, 816.
22 Nov. John Paston going to Calais, 815.
24 Nov. John Paston delivers a ring to a lady for his brother, 817.
27 Nov. Sale of Sporle Wood, 829.
Nov. or Dec. Margaret Paston desires a license to have the sacrament in her chapel, 821.
Sir John Paston should come home to be at the christening of the Duchess of Norfolk's child, 821.
7 Dec. Agreement of Bishop Waynflete and William Worcester, 822.
18 Dec. Bishop Waynflete intercedes with the Duchess of Norfolk about Caister, 823.
Christening of the Duke of Norfolk's child, 823.
John Paston is 'not the man he was,' 823.
John Paston's petition to the Duke, 824.

CHRONOLOGICAL TABLE

1473

18 Jan. Margaret Paston wishes her son Walter not to be too hasty in taking orders, 825.
Illness of John Berney of Reedham, 825.
3 Feb. Sir J. Paston writes from Calais of a visit he had paid to the Duke of Burgundy's court at Ghent, 826.
8 Mar. J. Paston urges his mother to borrow £100 for Sir John, 828, 831, 842.
8 Mar. 'Frenchmen whirling on the coasts,' 828, 829.
26 Mar. John Blennerhasset chosen collector in Norfolk, 829, 830.
'Rather the Devil, we say, than more taxes,' 829.
2 April. *The Queen and Prince coming out of Wales to Leicester,* 830.
Murder of the Count of Armagnac, 830.
Lewis XI. on the Somme, 830.
12 April. *The King to be after Easter at Leicester,* 831.
John Paston's tomb, 831, 843.
Sir John Paston and Anne Haulte, 831.
Sir John Paston's instructions touching Sporle, 831, 842.
16 April. Truce between Burgundy, France, and England, 832.
The Earl of Oxford at Dieppe, meaning to sail to Scotland, 832.
Sir John Paston troubled about his servants, 832, 834.
18 May. *Landing of the Earl of Oxford in Essex,* 833.
John Paston going to Compostella, 833, 836.
5 July. Edmund Paston at Calais, 836.
28 Aug. Armour for Sir John Paston, 838.
16 Sept. Hastings to Sir J. Middleton and Sir J. Paston, 839.
30 Sept. *The Earl of Oxford takes St. Michael's Mount by surprise, but is afterwards besieged there.*
6 Nov. *The dispute between Clarence and Gloucester,* 841, 842.
The King has sent for the Great Seal, 841.
22 Nov. Death of Sir James Gloys, 842.
A dispensation may be had at Rome as to Anne Haulte, 842, 843.
Anne Paston and Yelverton, 842.
Citations touching John Paston's will, 842, 843.
25 Nov. *The Earl of Oxford still besieged at St. Michael's Mount,* 843.
Will Margaret Paston dwell at Caister, if it be recovered ? 843.
Tenants of Sporle troubled, 844.

1474

Feb. *Lewis XI. at Amiens,* 846.
20 Feb. *The Earl of Oxford surrenders, and is compelled to sue for his life,* 846.
Sir J. Paston expects to have Caister again, 846.

THE PASTON LETTERS

1474

26 April. Hastings to John Paston at Guisnes, 847.
25 July. John Paston, Elizabeth Eberton, and another lady, 850, 858.
24 Oct. Will. Paston pledges plate to Eliz. Clere, 851.
3 Nov. The Vicar of Paston to Margaret Paston, complaining of Henry Warns who intimidates the tenants at Paston, 852, 853. [These two letters should have been placed in the year 1479.]
[Nov.] Sir John Paston recovered from illness, 856.
   Money matters between Sir J. Paston, and Townsend, and his uncle William, 856, 857, 861, 863, 864.
   Edmund Paston well amended, 856.
   Sir James Gloys' books, 856, 857, 863, 865.
20 Nov. Sir J. Paston redeems Sporle, 857.
   Agnes Paston recovered from illness, 857.
   Margaret, daughter of William Paston, dead, 857.
   John Paston and Lady Walgrave, 858, 860.
   John Paston and Stockton's daughter, 858.
   A French embassy in London, 858.
[About 8 Dec.] Edward IV. visits Norwich, 863.
11 Dec. Lady Walgrave rejects John Paston's ring—her muskball, 860.

1475

17 Jan. Sir J. Paston going to Flanders, 861.
   Siege of Neuss by Charles the Bold, 861.
29 Jan. William Paston endeavouring to get possession of Oxnead, 862.
   Sporle Wood cannot be sold in whole to advantage, 863, 865.
   Sir J. Paston ill in his eye and leg, 863, 865.
5 Feb. Efforts for the recovery of Caister, 864.
   Sir J. Paston detained at Calais, 864.
5 Mar. Margaret Paston will apply to the Archbishop of Canterbury for the license to have sacrament in her chapel, 866.
29 Mar. The Duchess of Norfolk going to Walsingham, 868.
23 May. Margaret Paston writes of money difficulties—'the King goeth so near us in this country,' 871.
   Pecock has paid two taxes for Sir J. Paston, 871.
   Sir J. Paston's brothers going over sea, 871.
13 June. Edmund Paston going over to Calais, 873.
10 Aug. The Duchess of York at St. Bennet's, 874.
29 Aug. *Peace of Pecquigny*, 875.
11 Sept. *The King's army returned to Calais*, 875.
   The King had spoken to the Duke of Norfolk about Caister, 875, 877.
   Sir John Paston the worse for Calais air, 875.

228

CHRONOLOGICAL TABLE

1475

10 Oct. How to get Caister again, 876.
   The King going to Walsingham, 876.
23 Oct. John Paston sick, 877.
   Petition of Sir J. Paston to the King for recovery of Caister, 879.

1476

17 Jan. Death of the Duke of Norfolk, 881.
21 Jan. Sir John Paston gone up to London to petition the King about Caister, 882.
23 Jan. Sir John Paston's 'sending to Caister' is ill taken, 883, 884, 885.
2 Mar. John Paston recommends Richard Stratton to Lord Hastings, 886.
   John Paston to [Margery Brews]—a love-letter, 887.
12 Mar. Sir John Paston crosses with Hastings to Calais, 888.
21 Mar. Lord Rivers at Rome, 889.
   Conquest of Lorraine by Charles the Bold, 889.
6 May. John Paston welcomes his brother Sir John again to England, 890.
   John Paston thinks of Mr. Fitzwalter's sister, 890.
27 May. The King has promised that Sir J. Paston shall have Caister, 891.

1477

5 Jan. *Defeat and death of Charles the Bold at Nanci*, 900.
   Letters about John Paston and Margery Brews, 894-9.
14 Feb. Great council begun yesterday, 900.
8 Mar. Dame Eliz. Brews desires to meet Margaret Paston at Norwich, and not at Langley, 901.
8 Mar. Terms offered by Sir Thomas Brews, 902, 904, 905.
9 Mar. The 'matter of Mrs. Barly,' 903.
   Letters of John Pympe to Sir J. Paston, 906-8.
   Sir J. Paston refuses to help his brother's marriage, 909, 916.
   The match between John Paston and Margery Brews, 910, 911, 913, 915.
14 April. Lewis XI. has gained many of the Duke of Burgundy's towns, 912.
23 June. Debt of Sir J. Paston to Henry Colet, 914.
7 Aug. Manor of Sporle mortgaged to Townsend, 916, 917.
11 Aug. Margaret Paston will not pay Sir John Paston's debt to Cocket, 917.
   Sir J. Paston to pay his brother William's board and school-hire, 917.
17 Aug. *Lewis XI. besieges St. Omer's, and burns Cassel*, 918.
22 Aug. Manors of Agnes and William Paston, 919.

229

THE PASTON LETTERS

1477

31 Oct. Sir John Paston's will, 920.
19 Nov. Wreck at Winterton—Sir J. Paston's claims as lord of the manor, 921, 922.
18 Dec. Margery Paston with child, 923.

1478

21 Jan. Dr. Yotton and the chapel at Caister, 925.
   Marriage of Richard, Duke of York, and Anne Mowbray, 925.
   John Paston going to take his wife Margery to see her father, 925.
3 Feb. Dr. Pykenham now Judge of the Arches, 926.
   A match for Edmund Paston, 926.
   A present of dates from Margery Paston to her mother-in-law Margaret, 926.
18 Feb. *Execution of the Duke of Clarence*.
21 Mar. Constance Reynforth to Sir John Paston, 928.
5 May. Woods at Hellesdon and Drayton, 929.
   The Duke of Suffolk's claim there, 929, 930.
13 May. Tomb of John Paston the father not begun, 930.
   The King buying cloth of gold, 930.
19 May. Walter Paston at Oxford, 931.
20 May. The Duke of Suffolk at Hellesdon, 932.
   William Worcester and Sir William Bocking, 932.
   Margaret Paston very ill, 932.
27 May. Margaret Paston sends cloth of gold for her husband's tomb, 933.
   Sir J. Paston's claim in Hellesdon and Drayton, 933.
   Sir J. Paston going to marry a kinswoman of the Queen, 933.
31 July. Oxnead Parsonage, 934-7, 943.
25 Aug. Birth of John Paston's son Christopher, 936.
   The Duke of Buckingham going on pilgrimage to Walsingham, 936.
   William Brandon a ravisher, 936.
   The Earl of Oxford at Hammes, 936.
7 Nov. William Paston, junior, at Eton, 939, 942.

1479

18 Jan. Errands to Marlingford, 940.
2 Feb. Dr. Pykenham informs Margaret Paston that her son Walter is not yet qualified to hold a benefice, 941.
4 Mar. Walter Paston ready to take his B.A. and proceed in law, 944.
22 May. He would be inceptor before Midsummer, 945.
30 June. He takes his degree, 946.

230

CHRONOLOGICAL TABLE

1479

7 July. Plate of William Paston, 947, 951.
18 Aug. Will of Walter Paston, 950.
21 Aug. Deaths of Agnes Paston and Walter, 952.
26 Aug. William Paston claims the manor of Marlingford, 953.
   Sir J. Paston inquires about his grandmother's will, 954.
29 Oct. Sir J. Paston's dispute with Suffolk, etc., 956.
   He is very ill, 956.
   Bishop Morton offers to mediate between him and his uncle William, 956, 957.
6 Nov. The tenants of Crowmer know not who shall be their lord, 957.
25 Nov. Money received and spent at the manor court at Cressingham, 961.
Nov. Death and burial of Sir John Paston, 962.
   John Paston wishes his brother Edmund to enter Marlingford, etc. in his name, 962.
   Proceedings of Edmund Paston at Marlingford and Oxnead, 963.
Dec. The great mortality abated, 965.
   Bishop Morton promises to favour John Paston against his uncle, 965.
   Injuries done to John Paston by his uncle William, 966.

1479-80

Touching a tombstone for Sir John Paston, 967.
Inventory of plate, 968.

1480

24 Feb. William Paston to John King, farmer of Harwelbury, 970.
   John, Prior of Bromholm, to John Paston, desiring him to procure of the Queen timber for his 'dortour,' 972.

About 1481?

Edmund Paston will see a widow in Worsted for his brother William, 974.
Edmund Paston desires his mother's forgiveness that he and his wife have not waited on her, 975.

1482

4 Feb. Margaret Paston's will, 978.
   John Paston to his mother about her will, 979.
1 Nov. Tenants of Marlingford molested by William Paston's officers, 982, 983.
   Declaration of William Barker and Margaret, widow of William Worcester, in behalf of William Paston, 985.
   Inventory of John Paston's books, 987.
   Verses by a lady to an absent lord, 988.

231

THE PASTON LETTERS

EDWARD V

1483

11 June. Richard, Duke of Gloucester, to Lord Nevill, desiring him to come up to London with a body of men, 992.
Elizabeth, Duchess of Suffolk, to John Paston, requesting him to leave his lodging for a few days, 993.

RICHARD III

1483

10 Oct. The Duke of Norfolk to John Paston on an insurrection in the Weald of Kent, 994.
Oct. *The Duke of Buckingham's rebellion.*

1484

1 May. An order by the Duke of Suffolk to a farmer to pay money, 997.
Complaints of John Paston against his uncle William, 998.
4 Nov. Death of Margaret Paston, 999.
Manors of Stansted and Harwelbury, 1000.

1485

23 June. *Proclamation of Richard III. against Henry Tudor,* 1001.
1 Aug. *The Earl of Richmond lands at Milford Haven,* 1002.
22 Aug. *The Battle of Bosworth.*

HENRY VII

1485

23 Sept. Dame Elizabeth Browne to John Paston about the circumstances of her father's death, 1003.
3 Oct. The Countess of Surrey complains to J. Paston that her husband's servants have been discharged by Lord Fitzwalter, 1004.
20 Oct. Proclamations ordered against rebels confederated with the Scots, 1006.

1486

24 Feb. Alice, Lady Fitzhugh, to John Paston about her 'daughter Lovel's' suit for her husband, 1008.
19 May *Viscount Lovel escaped into the Isle of Ely,* 1009.

232

CHRONOLOGICAL TABLE

1487

24 Jan. Lord Lovel's adherents, 1012.
The Prior of Norwich touching a bequest of Judge Paston to his monastery, 1013.
May. *Rebellion of Lambert Simnel,* 1014, 1015.
16 June. *Battle of Stoke,* 1016.
Dame Elizabeth Brews to Sir J. Paston for twelve men in harness to recover a distress, 1017.

1488?

The Bishop of Chester asks of widows more than they can pay, 1018.

1486-95

Sir J. Paston to Dame Margery, his wife, for a plaster for the King's attorney, James Hobart, 1019.

1488

Sir Edward Woodville goes over unauthorised to aid the Duke of Brittany, 1026.
Rebellion against James III. in Scotland, 1026.

1489

2 Feb. A whale taken off Thornham, 1029, 1030.
7 Mar. The Earl of Northumberland agrees with the King about keeping out the Scots, 1031.
Intended progress of the King to Norfolk, 1031, 1033.

1486-9

Edmund Paston appointed receiver of lands of Lord Scales, 1034, 1035.

1489

22 April. Henry VII. to the Earl of Oxford—*favourable news of the war in Brittany,* 1036.
28 April. *Insurrection in Yorkshire—the Earl of Northumberland killed,* 1037, 1039.
6 May. Sir J. Paston ordered to meet the King at Cambridge with a body of men, 1038, 1039.

233

THE PASTON LETTERS

1490

27 Jan. Sherwood, Bishop of Durham, to Sir John Paston, 1040.
Humorous petition of Sir J. Paston to Lord Fitzwalter, 1042.
The Earl of Surrey certifies that Thomas Hartford is not a Scotchman, 1043.

1491

6 April. Complaints of the King of Denmark against English ships resorting to Iceland, 1046.
[Sept.] The old and new Bailiffs of Yarmouth ask Sir J. Paston's mediation with the Earl of Oxford, 1048.
Oct. The Earl of Oxford to Sir J. Paston about Richard Barkeley and his ship, 1049-51.

1492

18 Feb. Preparations for the invasion of France, 1053, 1054.
30 April. William Barnard to William Paston complaining that he has been obliged to keep a prisoner at his own cost, 1055.

1492-3

Letters of Elizabeth, Duchess of Norfolk, in behalf of Thomas Martin, 1061, 1064.

1493

Proposal of Sir R. Clere for the marriage of Sir J. Paston's son, 1064.

1494

Nov. *Creation of the King's second son as Duke of York*—Knights of the Bath made on the occasion, 1058.

1495

3 July. *Attempt of Perkin Warbeck to land at Deal,* 1059, 1060.
Young William Paston, at Sir J. Fortescue's place on account of the plague at Cambridge, 1062.

1497-1503

Margaret, Countess of Richmond, to [Sir J. Paston?] touching the inheritance of the daughters of William Paston, 1063.

234

CHRONOLOGICAL TABLE

1499

20 Aug. Sir J. Paston to inquire who were privy to the Earl of Suffolk's flight beyond sea, 1065.

1500

20 Mar. Sir J. Paston to be ready to attend on the Princess Catherine of Spain on her arrival in England, 1066.

Before 1503

Proposed marriage of Clippesby with a niece of Sir J. Paston, 1069

After 1503

William Paston, Sir John's brother, 'crased in mind,' 1072.
The Earl of Oxford's steward to the 'Black Knight,' in Latin verse, 1073.

1503

6 Feb. Award touching East Beckham between Sir John Paston and Roger Townsend, 1074.
6 Sept. Archbishop Warham to William Paston on the death of his father, Sir John, 1075.
John Kendal to [William Paston?] touching lands bought of the executors of Nich. Pickering of Filby, 1076.

1506

31 Jan. *Account of the Visit of Philip, King of Castile, to Henry VII. at Windsor,* 1078.

235

INDEX

LETTERS AND TITLES

[In this Index will be found the names of the writers of the different letters, and of the persons written to, with the titles of other papers. The numbers referred to here are those of the letters, while the General Index refers to the volume and page, in which each name will be found. For the convenience, however, of persons using this Index, the Nos. contained in each volume are indicated at the head of every page.]

VOL. II., Nos. 1 to 259.—VOL. III., 260 to 487.—VOL. IV., 488 to 694.—
VOL. V. 695 to 935.—VOL. VI. 936 to 1088.

237

THE PASTON LETTERS

VOL. II., Nos. 1 to 259.—VOL. III., 260 to 487.—VOL. IV., 488 to 694.—

238

INDEX OF LETTERS AND TITLES

VOL. V., 695 to 935.—VOL. VI., 936 to 1088.

239

THE PASTON LETTERS

Vol. II., Nos. 1 to 259.—Vol. III., 260 to 487.—Vol. IV., 488 to 694.—

240

INDEX OF LETTERS AND TITLES

Vol. V., 695 to 935.—Vol. VI., 936 to 1088.

VOL. VI.—Q

241

THE PASTON LETTERS

Vol. II., Nos. 1 to 259.—Vol. III., 260 to 487.—Vol. IV., 488 to 694.—

242

INDEX OF LETTERS AND TITLES

Vol. V., 695 to 935.—Vol. VI., 936 to 1088.

243

THE PASTON LETTERS

INDEX OF LETTERS AND TITLES

THE PASTON LETTERS

INDEX OF LETTERS AND TITLES

THE PASTON LETTERS

252

INDEX OF LETTERS AND TITLES

253

THE PASTON LETTERS

GENERAL INDEX

OF

NAMES, PLACES, SUBJECTS, AND

OBSOLETE WORDS

[Entries are ordinarily made under the form of spelling most in conformity with modern usage, but in the case of puzzling variants cross references are given.]

255

THE PASTON LETTERS

GENERAL INDEX

THE PASTON LETTERS

GENERAL INDEX

THE PASTON LETTERS — GENERAL INDEX

THE PASTON LETTERS — GENERAL INDEX

THE PASTON LETTERS — GENERAL INDEX

THE PASTON LETTERS

GENERAL INDEX

THE PASTON LETTERS

GENERAL INDEX

THE PASTON LETTERS

GENERAL INDEX

THE PASTON LETTERS

GENERAL INDEX

THE PASTON LETTERS

300

GENERAL INDEX

301

THE PASTON LETTERS

302

GENERAL INDEX

303

THE END

ERRATA

VOL. I.

Page 122, line 15, for 'Bourges' read 'Bourg.'

VOL. II.

Page 30, line 7 from bottom of No. 15, for 'No. 8,' read 'No. 13.'
   „ 154, add to footnote 3, 'He was slain at the second battle of St. Albans on the 17th Feb. 1461.'

VOL. III.

Page 135, footnote 1, strike out the words after 'Elizabeth Paston,' on third line from the bottom, and add, 'was no longer the wife of Robert Poynings, but his widow, for he was killed at the second battle of St. Albans on the 17th Feb. 1461.'

VOL. V.

Page 310, note 1, for 'Henry IV.' read 'Edward IV.'
   „ 314, note 1. This suggestion is quite a mistake. See 'my Robert' in the PS., p. 315.

Printed by T. and A. Constable, Printers to His Majesty
at the Edinburgh University Press